The World Encyclopedia of the Film

Associate editors: John M. Smith and Tim Cawkwell

GALAHAD BOOKS • NEW YORK CITY

Published by arrangement with
Literary Services & Productions, Ltd.,
London, England

Copyright © by November Books Limited 1972
All rights reserved
ISBN 0-88365-133-5
Library of Congress catalog card number: 73-90832
Printed in the United States of America

GALAHAD BOOKS · NEW YORK CITY

Stills by courtesy of Afterimage, Allied Artists, American International, Bob Clampett, Columbia, Dave Curtis, Walt Disney, Fox, Joel Finler, Metro-Goldwyn-Mayer, Monogram, National Film Archive, Paramount, Rank, Republic, RKO, Tony Rayns, United Artists, Universal, Mike Wallington, Warner Brothers.

Contents

Introduction

This book is the most comprehensive film encyclopedia available in any language. It combines breadth of selection with careful, detailed research and an unparalleled degree of completeness within individual entries. Every attempt has been made to ensure a balanced selection of entries and to respect the enormously different kinds of cinema which they represent. From Hollywood and the great national cinemas to documentary and the 'Underground' every aspect of the cinema is covered through its creators – the directors, actors, writers, cameramen, set designers and many others are all represented.

The preparation of this volume has lasted continuously since 1964. Although the original concept remains essentially unaltered, there have been numerous changes in the book's general shape and comprehensiveness. A comparatively small book was once intended; the present is several times larger than earliest estimates supposed – and several times more useful.

The number of people who have worked on the book is extraordinarily large, and on page x an attempt is made at least to acknowledge many of them. Their number and the very size of the book necessitated a checking job of inhuman proportions. We have had to rely on existing research, and there may be errors, but work goes on for future editions. The associate editors will be grateful to receive suggestions about the quality of the information offered. New editions will incorporate additional entries.

It is not possible to say how grateful we are to the British Film Institute's Information Department, upon whose resources, patience and co-operation the entire work depended. For the irritation, inconvenience, difficulties and boredom we have caused amongst its staff, we apologise. The apology, like the thanks, can only be inadequate.

It was felt appropriate to present a single large volume, rather than resort to the easier method of producing many small volumes. The interaction between the cinema's parts is better conveyed in this way. The method of providing a biographical entry, as detailed as seemed feasible or relevant, as well as a list of film credits, as complete (or suitable) as possible, was felt to give the feel of a career better than would any other.

The silent period is somewhat less well covered than is the sound period, but we are sure it will not be felt to have been unfairly treated, in view of the book's proportions and intentions. The cinema's technical and artistic pioneers have, we hope, been treated with the respect they deserve. The imbalance in favour of the American cinema reflects the medium's historical development much better than does the snobbery of traditional highbrow accounts. The prominence given to actors, choreographers and others is not out of place; it may be that not enough attention has been given to animators. Some 'Underground' film-makers are included, as well as some who worked in abstract, or concrete, film: they are better represented for the period before World War II than since. A choice had to be made. The case of Third World cinema is a similar one. In every field the new work found valuable most recently could not be well covered: the areas for expansion and improvement are evident to us. Entries were updated to the end of 1971.

The principles of selection within the chosen areas perhaps needs explanation, though the material should, we hope, be found simple to use. Apart from pioneering technical work, the book's centre is in its choice of directors. The film lists accompanying the biographical entries for directors are, as often as was found possible or justifiable, complete. Where they are not complete, the heading says so. Entries for people other than directors usually have lists which include only those films whose director has an entry to himself. Exceptions are self-explanatory.

The dating of films is according to the American copyright system, where that is appropriate, and dates generally are release dates. Where the date of production differed considerably from the release date, both are given. Alternative titles are given as often as possible: they are included in directors' lists and in the Index, where they are cross-referenced. Translations of foreign titles are, usually, provided alongside the original if the language is one in which English readers might otherwise find it hard to get their bearings; where the language is likely to be fairly accessible to English readers, original and alternative release titles for the country of origin, the UK and USA are given. Where a foreign-language film has more than one foreign title, the explanation is usually that the film is an international co-production.

The Index constitutes a massive reference work in itself. Each film mentioned in the rest of the book is included there with date, main credits (i.e., on the whole, those which are mentioned in individual personal entries in the main body of the book), certain technical specifications, releasing organisations (in most cases), and alternative titles. Personal credits in the Index are usually by surname only. Where there is more than one person with an entry in the book with a particular surname, an initial is given, or if that too is insufficient, then the name is given in full. When a personal credit is given – for reasons of celebrity – to a person who has no entry in the main body of the book, the name is italicised. At the end of the list of abbreviations there is a list of recurring surnames with an explanatory note. Film titles in the Index are listed alphabetically, but definite and indefinite articles are ignored for this purpose. Re-makes are noted as such only when it seems a particularly interesting fact.

List of abbreviations

A note on lengths of films

The length of silent films is given in the Index in metres (m) or feet (ft), that of sound films in minutes (min). The abbreviation si (silent) is used in the case of silent films projected at 24 frames per second. In certain cases the length is given in reels, thus: 1rl (1 reel) and 2rs (2 reels). The abbreviation sh is used for short films where no length is given.

Recurring surnames

The following lists contain only those names which are used in the Index with either an initial or a christian name in order to avoid confusion with their namesakes in the encyclopedia. Thus we distinguish B Hecht and H Hecht, and Ingmar and Ingrid Bergman. However, where the namesake is not included in the encyclopedia, the name does not bear an initial, e.g. although there is a Wallace and a Noah Beery, only Wallace is among the entries and therefore does not carry an initial.

List of contributors

Joy Bedford
Richard Bedford
Paul Botham
Sue Craig
Lorraine Creech
George Davis
Lindsay Doran
Phil Drummond
Judy Ferguson
Simon Field
George Folsey
Jill Forbes
Marjorie Grieveson
Phil Hardy
Peggy Imeg
Allen Kent
Elizabeth Kingsley-Rowe
Christine Kirby
Neil Kirk
Angela Kirtland
Phil Knowles
John Kobal
Larry Lucas
Tom Milne
Maxine Molyneux
Bob Mundy
Elias Noujain
Maurice Prior
Linda Redford
Valerie Robbins
Tony Russell
Peter Sainsbury
Elizabeth Sussex
Mike Wallington

Biographical entries

A

ABBAS, Khwaga Ahmad

Writer and director. Panipat, Punjab, India 1914–
Alighar University, then journalist on Bombay Chronicle and part-time publicity work at Bombay Talkies. From 1938: film critic for Bombay Chronicle: promoted to editorship of Sunday edition. Scripted *Naya Sansar* (1941), produced in Hindi by Bombay Talkies. Founded Indian People's Theatre Association to produce 'socially significant' plays which included his own 'Dharti Ke Lal', filmed in 1946. 1952: founded own company, Naya Sansar Productions, for which wrote and directed *Munna* (1954), in Hindi, the first Indian feature without songs and dances. Wrote 2 song-and-dance films with proletarian themes for actor Raj Kapoor (who also produced and directed): *Awara* (1951) and *Shri 420* (1955). 1957: *Pardesi* was Mosfilm and Naya Sansar co-production, shot partly in jrussia. 1962: as journalist launched attack on attitude of Mark Robson and Indian government agencies involved in production of *Nine Hours to Rama*, then on location in Delhi.

Films as director include: 1946: Dharti Ke Lal (+s). 1954: Munna (+s). 1957: Pardesi – Khazdeni Za Tri Morya (+co-p/co-s; co-d V. M. Pronin).

ABBOTT, Bud

Actor. Asbury Park, New Jersey 1895–
Mother was rider with Barnum's Circus. 1916: started in theatre, in menial jobs, becoming manager and, eventually, actor. Produced own shows. Straight man to Lou Costello in vaudeville and radio. 1940: their first film as supporting comedians, *One Night in the Tropics*. 1941: starred in *Buck Privates*. Worked mainly for Universal until split with Costello after *Dance With Me, Henry* (1956) ended film career. Tried a solo comeback in Las Vegas. Retired.

Films as actor with Lou Costello include: 1941: Hold That Ghost. 1942: Rio Rita. 1945: Bud Abbott and Lou Costello in Hollywood. 1948: The Noose Hangs High. 1949: Abbott and Costello Meet the Killer: Boris Karloff. 1952: Jack and the Beanstalk.

ABBOTT, George

Stage producer and director. Forestville, New York 1887–
Responsible for some 500 Broadway productions. 1929–31: worked in films as writer-director for Paramount: also wrote scenario of *All Quiet on the Western Front* (1930). Later films (from 1940) are adaptations of his Broadway productions.

Films as director: 1929: Why Bring That Up? (+co-s); Half Way to Heaven (+s). 1930: Manslaughter (+s); The Sea God (+s). 1931: Stolen Heaven (+s); Secrets of a Secretary (+co-s); My Sin (+co-s); The Cheat. 1940: Too Many Girls (+p). 1957: The Pajama Game (+co-p/co-s; co-d Stanley Donen). 1959: Damn Yankees – What Lola Wants (+co-p/s; co-d Stanley Donen).

ACHARD, Marcel

Director and writer. Sainte-Foy-lès-Lyon 1899–
Prompter at Vieux-Colombier Theatre, Paris. Journalist and playwright. 1931: first film as writer Jean Choux's *Jean de la Lune*. 1934–35: wrote 2 films in USA. 1949: first film as director a remake of *Jean de la Lune*.

Films as writer include: 1934: The Merry Widow. 1935: Folies Bergère. 1936: Mayerling. 1937: Gribouille; Le Messager. 1938: Orage; L'Etrange Monsieur Victor (co-di). 1940: Untel Père et Fils (co). 1941: Parade en Sept Nuits (+st). 1942: L'Arlesienne; Felicie Nanteuil. 1943: Les Petites du Quai aux Fleurs. 1944: Lunegard; La Belle Aventure. 1946: Petrus (st/di). 1956: Le Pays d'où je viens.

Films as director and writer: 1949: Jean de la Lune (+st/di). 1950: La Valse de Paris (+st/di).

ADAM, Ken

Designer. Berlin 1921–
1934: arrived in England: Bartlett School of Architecture. War service in Pioneer Corps and RAF. 1947–48: draughtsman on films including *The Queen of Spades*. 1948–55: assistant or associate art director, e.g. on *Captain Horatio Hornblower, RN*, *The Crimson Pirate*, *Helen of Troy*. Art director for European scenes of *Around the World in 80 Days* (1956). 1956–62: art director. From 1963: production designer. Also research work for *Ben-Hur* (1959), ships for *John Paul Jones* (1959) and initial designs for *The Long Ships* (1963), etc.

Films as art director include: 1957: Night of the Demon. 1958: Gideon's Day. 1959: Ten Seconds to Hell; The Angry Hills; The Rough and the Smooth. 1960: The Trials of Oscar Wilde (co). 1961: Sodom and Gomorrah. 1962: Dr No.

Films as production designer include: 1963: Dr Strangelove. 1964: Goldfinger. 1965: The Ipcress File. 1966: Thunderball. 1967: You only Live Twice. 1970: The Owl and the Pussycat. 1971: Diamonds are Forever.

ADLER, Buddy, *or*
Maurice E.

Producer. New York 1909–1960 Los Angeles
Columbia and Pennsylvania Universities. Wrote many magazine fiction stories. From 1936: writer of short subjects for MGM regular series. World War II: US Signal Corps, becoming Lieutenant-Colonel. Went back to MGM as producer for a year. 1946–53: Producer at Columbia, then joined Fox. 1956: succeeded Darryl Zanuck as executive head of production at Fox. Married actress Anita Louise. Oscar for best film (1953), *From Here to Eternity*.

Films as producer include: 1949: The Dark Past. 1950: No Sad Songs for Me. 1953: From Here to Eternity; Salome. 1955: Violent Saturday; Soldier of Fortune; House of Bamboo; Love Is a Many-Splendored Thing; The Left Hand of God; The Lieutenant Wore Skirts. 1956: The Bottom of the Bottle; The Revolt of Mamie Stover: Bus Stop: Anastasia. 1957: Heaven Knows,

Bud Abbott (left), Boris Karloff and Lou Costello in Abbott and Costello Meet the Killer.
Ken Adam's set for Goldfinger, *directed by Guy Hamilton.*
Anouk Aimée in Lola, *directed by Jacques Demy.*

Mr Allison; A Hatful of Rain. 1958: South Pacific; The Inn of the Sixth Happiness.

ADORÉE, Renée

(Jeanne de la Fonte) Actress. Lille, France 1898–1933 Sunland, California
Started as circus dancer with her father's troupe. Danced with Folies Bergère and toured Europe. 1920: Hollywood. No films after 1930 because of illness.

Films as actress include: 1920: The Strongest. 1926: La Bohème; Tin Gods; The Exquisite Sinner; The Black Bird. 1927: The Big Parade. 1928: The Cossacks. 1929: The Pagan; Tide of Empire. 1930: Call of the Flesh.

AGEE, James

Writer. Knoxville, Tennessee 1909–1955 New York
Harvard Poetry Prize; edited Harvard Advocate; graduated in 1932. 1934: volume of verse, 'Permit Me Voyage'. Joined staff of Fortune magazine; one assignment resulted in book 'Let Us Now Praise Famous Men' (1941) with photographs by Walker Evans. 1939–43: worked for Time magazine. 1943–48: film critic for The Nation. 1948: worked on In the Street with Helen Levitt and Janice Loeb. 1951: novel, 'The Morning Watch'. 1953: wrote TV series on the life of Abraham Lincoln. Posthumous publications include novel, 'A Death in the Family' (1958, awarded Pulitzer Prize), 'Letters to Father Flye' (1962).

Films as writer: 1949: The Quiet One (cy/di). 1951: The African Queen (co-s). 1952: Face to Face ep The Bride Comes to Yellow Sky. 1955: The Night of the Hunter.

AGOSTINI, Philippe

Director and cinematographer. Paris 1910–
Italian family. Ecole de Photographie in Paris. Started as assistant cinematographer on documentary by Jean Benoit-Levy, with whom he continued to work for a year and a half. Then assistant cinematographer to Georges Perinal, Armand Thirard, Curt Courant on Le Jour se lève (1939), and others. Assistant director to Pierre Chenal. From 1943: worked regularly as cinematographer. From 1957: directed features. Married actress Odette Joyeux.

Films as cinematographer include: 1943: Itto. 1941: Jeunes Timides. 1942: Le Mariage de Chiffon; Lettres d'amour. 1943: Les Anges du péche; Douce. 1945: Les Dames du Bois de Boulogne; Sylvie et le fantôme. 1946: Les Portes de la nuit. 1948: Les Dernieres Vacances. 1952: Le Plaisir (co). 1954: Du Rififi chez les hommes. 1956: Si Paris nous etait conte; Le Pays d'où je viens; Paris Palace-Hôtel.

Films as director: 1954: Ordinations. 1957: Le Naïf aux quarante enfants (+co-s). 1958: Tu es Pierre. 1959: Le Dialogue des Carmelites (co-d R. Bruckberger). 1961: Rencontres. 1963: La Soupe aux poulets.

AIMÉE, Anouk or
ANOUK

(Françoise Sorya) Actress. Paris 1932–
Father an actor. Studied dancing at Marseilles Opera and, at 14, acting in Paris. 1947: spotted by Henri Calef for La Maison sous la mer; then in Marcel Carne's unfinished La Fleur de l'âge. 1948: first starred in Les Amants de Vérone. 1949–50: films in UK and Spain. 1952: 'Sud' on Paris stage. Husbands include Nicos Papatakis, singer Pierre Barouh and (1970) Albert Finney.

Films as actress include: 1950: The Golden Salamander. 1952: Le Rideau Cramoisi. 1955: Les Mauvaises Rencontres. 1957: Pot-bouille. 1958: Montparnasse 19; La Tête contre les murs. 1959: Les Dragueurs; La Dolce Vita. 1960: Le Farceur. 1961: Lola; L'Imprevisto; Il Giudizio Universale. 1962: Sodom and Gomorrah. 1963: Otto e mezzo. 1966: Un Homme et une femme. 1969: The Appointment; Model Shop. 1968: Un Soir . . . Un Train.

ALAZRAKI, Benito

Director and producer. Mexico 1923–
At 24 produced and co-wrote Enamorada (1946), first work in cinema. 1955: first film as director Raices with technical supervision by Carlos Velo and written in collaboration with him. 1962: in USA made The Time and the Touch under pseudonym Carlos J. Arconti.

Films as director: 1955: Raices – The Roots (+co-s). 1958: Inferno de Almas; La Tijera d'oro. 1962: The Time and the Touch (+co-s).

ALCORIZA, Luis

Writer and director. Madrid 1920–
Now naturalised Mexican. Parents actors. Nomadic education in Europe. 1937: acting debut with parents; collaborated with Luis Buñuel on scenario Los Naufragios de la calle providencia, the basis of El Angel Exterminador (1962). 1939: to Mexico as actor with Blanch Sisters Company; started acting in Mexican films. 1948: abandoned acting for writing; has written books, worked on scripts with his wife, Raquel Rojas, and with Buñuel and Norman Foster. 1961: started directing. Juego Peligroso was Brazilian-Mexican co-production.

Films as writer in collaboration include: 1949: El Gran Calavera. 1950: Los Olvidados. 1951: La Hija del engaño. 1952: El Bruto; El. 1954: El Rio y la muerte. 1956: La Mort en ce jardin. 1959: La Fièvre monte à El Pao. 1962: El Angel Exterminador.

Films as director: 1961: Los Jovenes – The Young Ones (+st/s/ad). 1962: Tlayucan – The Pearls of Saint Lucia (+s); Tiberoneros – A morte espreita no mar. 1964: Safo; El Gangster. 1965: Tarahumara – Always Further On (+s). 1966: Juego Peligroso – Jôgo Peligroso (co-d Arturo Ripstein).

ALDO, G. R.

(Aldo Graziati) Cinematographer. Treviso, Italy 1905–1953 Albara di Painiga, Italy
From 1923: in France. From 1948: films mainly Italian. 1953: accidental death during making of Senso.

Films as cinematographer include: 1947: La Certosa di Parma; La Terra trema. 1949: Cielo sulla palude. 1951: Miracolo a Milano. 1952: Othello (co); Umberto D; Tre Storie Proibite. 1953: Stazione Termini; La Provinciale. 1954: Senso (co).

ALDRICH, Robert

Director. Cranston, Rhode Island 1918–
University of Virginia. At RKO for 3 years as production clerk, then second assistant director. 1945–52: first assistant to Jean Renoir (The Southerner), William Wellman (The Story of GI Joe), Fred Zinnemann, Albert Lewin (The Private Affairs of Bel-Ami), Robert Rossen (Body and Soul), Lewis Milestone (Arch of Triumph, The Red Pony), Richard Fleischer (So This Is New York), Abraham Polonsky (Force of Evil), Ted Tetzlaff (The White Tower), Joseph Losey (M, The Prowler), Charles Chaplin (Limelight); brief appearance in Losey's The Big Night. 1946–48: under contract to Enterprise Studios as assistant director, unit production manager, studio manager and writer. 1951: associate producer with Harold Hecht on Ten Tall Men. 1952: switched to TV after working as assistant to Charles Lamont on Abbott and Costello Meet Captain Kidd; directed 17 of NBC TV series 'The Doctor', also scripting 3; directed 4 of 'China Smith' series starring Dan Duryea, who played same character in World for Ransom. 1953: first feature as director. 1957: shot most of Garment Center; replaced by Vincent Sherman who was credited. 1959: 2 films made in UK heavily cut before release. From The Big Knife, his production company, the Associates and Aldrich, produced many of his films, plus The Ride Back (1957) and Whatever Happened to Aunt Alice? (1969).

Films as director: 1953: The Big Leaguer. 1954: World for Ransom (+co-p); Apache; Vera Cruz. 1955: Kiss Me Deadly (+p); The Big Knife (+p). 1956: Autumn Leaves; Attack (+p). 1957: The Garment Center – The Garment Jungle (uc; co-d Vincent Sherman). 1959: The Angry Hills; Ten Seconds to Hell (+co-s). 1961: The Last Sunset. 1962: Sodom and Gomorrah (co-d Sergio Leone); What Ever Happened to Baby Jane? (+p). 1963: 4 for Texas (+p/co-s). 1964: Hush, Hush, Sweet Charlotte (+p). 1965: The Flight of the Phoenix (+p). 1967: The Dirty Dozen. 1968: The Legend of Lylah Clare (+p); The Killing of Sister George (+p). 1970: Too Late the Hero (+p/co-st/co-s). 1971: The Grissom Gang (+p).

ALEKAN, Henri

Cinematographer. Paris 1909–
Parents Bulgarian immigrants. Conservatoire des Arts et Metiers. 1928: after trying for 3 years, obtained work as assistant cameraman. Between film jobs set up and ran a successful puppet theatre. 1931: camera operator. During 1930s worked for Georges Perinal, Michel Kelber and for Eugen Schüftan on Drôle de drame (1937), Quai des brumes (1938). 1941: first feature as cinematographer Tobie est un ange (destroyed in a fire and never shown). 1944: with Andre Michel founded Service Cinematographique du Comite d'Action de la Resistance.

Films as cinematographer include: 1946: La Bataille du Rail; La Belle et la bête. 1947: Les Maudits. 1948: Une Si Jolie Petite Plage. 1951: Juliette ou la cle des songes. 1952: Stranger on the Prowl; Quand tu liras cette lettre. 1953: Roman Holiday (co). 1960: Austerlitz (co). 1962: Le Couteau dans la plaie (co). 1964: Topkapi. 1966: Triple Cross. 1969: Mayerling. 1970: Figures in a Landscape. 1971: Soleil Rouge.

ALEXANDROV, Grigori

(Grigori Mormonenko) Director. Yekaterinburg, Russia 1903–

Doorman at cinema in Yekaterinburg. Worked in front-line theatre on Eastern Front; went to Moscow. 1923: at Proletkult Theatre acted in *Kinodnevnik Glumova*, Sergei Eisenstein's short film interlude in his production of Alexander Ostrovsky's 'Enough Simplicity in Every Wise Man'; also assistant director to Eisenstein at Proletkult. 1924–25: acted in *Stachka (1924)* and collaborated on its script, and *Bronenosets 'Potyomkin'* (1925). 1926: with rest of Eisenstein group began work on *Staroie i novoie*; work interrupted for making of *Oktyabre*. Co-writer and co-director on this and, after work resumed, on *Staroie i novoie*. Work as scriptwriter included the Vasilievs' first fiction film as directors: *Spyaschaya krasavika* (1930). 1929–30: in Europe with Eisenstein and Tisse. 1930: all 3 under contract to Paramount, to Hollywood (*see* Eisenstein). Made 2 shorts: *Romance Sentimentale* (made in France, his first solo work, though Eisenstein credited as co-director) and *Internationale*. Last collaboration with Eisenstein, on *Que Viva Mexico!* 1934: first musical comedy *Vesyolye Rebyata* from script turned down by Eisenstein. 1938: supervised filming in colour of May Day Parade. 1944: member of new Artistic Council with Eisenstein, Vsevolod Pudovkin, Mikhail Romm and others to plan all film production. 1947: *Vesna* made partly in Prague. *Kaspichy* (1944) and *Russkii Suvenir* (1960) are documentaries.

Films as co-director and script collaborator to Eisenstein: 1927: Oktyabre – October – Ten Days That Shook the World. 1929: Staroie i novoie – The Old and The New – Generalnaia Linnia – The General Line. 1931: Que Viva Mexico! (*uf*).

Films as director: 1930: Romance Sentimentale. 1933: Internationale. 1934: Vesyolye Rebyata – Jazz Comedy – Moscow Laughs – The Jolly Fellows (*+s*). 1936: Cirk – Circus. 1938: Volga-Volga (*+s*). 1940: Svetlyi Put – Tanya – The Bright Path. 1943: Odna Semia – One Family. 1944: Kaspichy – Men of the Caspian. 1947: Vesna – Spring. 1949: Vstrecha na Elbe – Meeting on the Elbe. 1952: Kompozitor Glinka – Glinka – Glinka-Man of Music (*+co-s*). 1958: Chelovek cheloveku – Man to Man. 1960: Russkii Suvenir – Russian Souvenir. 1961: Lenin in Polsce – Lenin in Poland. 1965: Pered Oktyabre – Before October.

ALEXEÏEFF, Alexander

Animator. Kazan, Russia 1901–

Childhood near Istanbul. Studied painting in Paris. Worked at Chauve-Souris Theatre under Sergei Soudekine, decorator for Ballets Russes. Designed sets for Ballets Russes and Ballets Suedois. Decor, e.g. for Theodore Komisarjevsky, Georges Pitoeff, Louis Jouvet and Gaston Baty; also costumes. Book illustrator using wood engravings, e.g. on French editions of 'The Brothers Karamazov', 'The Fall of the House of Usher'. Married Claire Parker who worked on many of his films. 1935: used puppets in *La Belle au Bois Dormant*. Most work in France apart from e.g. some German films in 1930s and *En passant* (1943) made in USA for National Film Board of Canada. Many advertising shorts. Techniques used include Totalisation (composite image produced by swinging pendulum), Pin Screen (image produced by raising or lowering headless pins on board).

Films (and names of sponsors for commercials) as animator include: 1932: Parade Sools. 1933: Une Nuit sur le Mont Chauve—A Night on a Bare Mountain. 1935: La Belle au bois dormant; Lingner Werke; Opta Empfangt. 1936: Parade chapeaux; Le Trône de France. 1937: Franck Aroma; La Crème Simon (*3 films*); Les Vêtements Sigrand; Huilor; L'Eau d'Evian. 1938: Balatum; Les Fonderies Martin; Les Oranges de Jaffa. 1939: Les Gaines Roussel; Cenpa; Le Gaz (*uf*) 1943: En passant. 1951: Fumees (*co-d Georges Violet*). 1952: Masques. 1954: Nocturne (*co-d Georges Violet*); Rimes (*co-d Georges Violet*); Pure Beaute. 1955: Le Buisson Ardent; Sève de la terre—The Earth's Cap. 1956: Osram (*4 films*). 1957: Cent pour Cent; Constance (*cr*); Quatre Temps. 1958: Cocinor (*distributor's credit sequence*); Anonyme; Automation. 1960: Divertissement; A propos de Jivago. 1963: The Trial (*animated preface*). 1963: Le Nez—The Nose. 1966: L'Eau.

ALLÉGRET, Marc

Director. Basel, Switzerland 1900–

Law at Ecole des Sciences Politiques, Paris. Secretary to his uncle Andre Gide; accompanied him to Congo, making first film. Returned to Paris; made shorts, worked in theatre. Assistant to Robert Florey. Became artistic director on Robert Florey's *L'Amour chante* (1930), co-directed with Augusto Genina *Les Amants de minuit* (1930). 1931: completed Florey's *Le Blanc et le noir* when Florey left for Hollywood; wrote *L'Amour à l'américaine*; first solo feature as director *Mam'zelle Nitouche*. 1947–51: made 3 films in UK, one in Canada. 1951: returned to France. Besides features, later work includes shorts on magic and occultism. Brother is Yves Allégret.

Films as director: 1927: Voyage au Congo. 1929: Papoul. 1930: La Meilleur Bobonne; J'ai quelque chose à vous dire; Le Blanc et le noir (*co-d Robert Florey*). 1931: Les Amants de minuit (*co-d Augusto Genina*); Mam'zelle Nitouche; Attaque Nocturne. 1932: Fanny; La Petite Chocolatière. 1934: Le Lac-aux-Dames; L'Hôtel du Libre Echange; Sands famille; Zou-Zou. 1935: Les Beaux Jours. 1936: Sous les yeux d'occident; Aventure à Paris; Les Amants Terribles. 1937: Gribouille. 1938: La Dame de Malacca; Entree des artistes; Orage. 1939: Le Corsaire. 1941: Parade en sept nuits. 1942: L'Arlesienne; Felicie Nanteuil. 1943: Les Petites du Quai aux Fleurs. 1944: Lunegarde; La Belle Aventure. 1946: Petrus. 1947: Blanche Fury. 1949: The Naked Heart – Maria Chapdelaine (*+s*). 1951: Blackmailed; Avec Andre Gide – Andre Gide; La Demoiselle et son revenant. 1952: Jean Coton (*+s*). 1953: Julietta (*+co-s*). 1954: L'Amante di Paridi – The Face That Launched a Thousand Ships – Helen of Troy; Femmina; Futures Vedettes (*+co-s*). 1955: l'Amant de Lady Chatterley (*+s*). 1956: En Effeuillant la marguerite – Mamzelle Striptease (*+co-s*). 1957: L'amour est en jeu – Ma Femme, ma gosse et moi. 1958: Sois belle et tais-toi (*+co-st/co-s*). 1959: Un drôle de dimanche; Les Affreux. 1961: Les Parisiennes *ep* Sophie (*+co-st*). 1962: Le Démon de minuit. 1963: L'Abominable Homme des douanes. 1970: Le Bal du Comte d'Orgel (*+co-s*).

La Terra trema. *directed by Luchino Visconti, photographed by G. R. Aldo.*

Frank Sinatra and Anita Ekberg in Robert Aldrich's 4 For Texas.

Lenin w Polsce. *directed by Grigori Alexandrov.*

ALLÉGRET, Yves

Director. Paris 1907–

Sound engineer and editor at Braunberger-Richebe. Assistant to his brother Marc Allégret (1931: *Mam'zelle Nitouche*, 1934: *Le Lac-aux-Dames*) and to Augusto Genina (1931: *Les Amants de minuit*), Paul Fejos (1931: *L'Amour à l'américaine*; *Fantômas*), Jean Renoir (1932: *La Chienne*). Directed shorts including *Ténériffe, Prix et profit* (1932), *Le Gagnant* (1935), *Jeune Fille de France* (1938). 1935–40: art director e.g. on *Forfaiture* (1937). 1941: began directing features in Nice under pseudonym Yves Champlain. Negative φ *Tobie est un ange* was destroyed in a fire. 1957: directed 'La Guerre du sucre' on stage. Was married to Simone Signoret; their daughter is actress Cathérine Allégret.

Features as director: 1936: Vous n'avez rien à declarer? (*co-d Léo Joannon*). 1941: Jeunes Timides – Les Deux Timides; Tobie est un ange (*ur*). 1942: La Roue tourne (*uf*). 1943: La Boîte aux rêves (*+co-s*). 1945: Les Démons de l'aube. 1948: Dédée d'Anvers (*+co-s*) – Dédée; Une Si Jolie Petite Plage – Such a Pretty Little Beach. 1949: Manèges. 1950: Les Miracles n'ont lieu qu'une fois. 1951: Nez de cuir (*+s*); Les Sept Péchés Capitaux *ep* La Luxure. 1952: La Jeune Folle 1953: Mam'zelle Nitouche (*+co-s*); Les Orgueilleux – The Proud Ones (*+co-s*). 1954: Oasis. 1955: La Meilleure part (*+co-s*). 1957: Méfiez-vous, fillettes – Young Girls Beware; Quand la femme s'en mêle. 1958: La Fille de Hambourg – The Girl from Hamburg; L'Ambitieuse. 1960: Le Chien de pique (*+co-s*). 1962: Konga Yo (*+co-s*). 1963: Germinal. 1967: Johnny Banco (*+co-s*). 1970: Invasion.

ALLIO, René

Director. Marseille, France 1924–

Family of Italian origin. Studied painting. Paris exhibitions of paintings from 1957. 1951–62: theatrical work as designer and director. 1951–57: sets for Arras Festival. From 1957: collaboration with Roger Planchon at Théâtre de la Cité in Villeurbanne. Worked on several Brecht plays, e.g. 'The Caucasian Chalk Circle'. Also designs for Comédie Française, Théâtre National Populaire, Strasbourg Opera, Royal Shakespeare Company and National Theatre, London. 1960: directed first film, animated short shown during production of Arthur Adamovr's adaptation of Nikolai Gogol's novel 'Dead Souls'. 1962: set designer on Jacques Baratier's *La Poupée*. 1964: first feature as director.

Films as director: 1960: Les Ames Mortes. 1962: La Meule – The Haystack (*+s*). 1964: La Vieille Dame Indigne – The Shameless Old Lady (*+s*). 1967: L'Une et l'autre – The Other One; Skin Deep (*+s*). 1968: Pierre et Paul (*+s*). 1970: Les Carnisards (*+st/co-s/di*).

ALLYSON, June

(Ella Gaisman). Actress, Lucerne. New York 1917–

Broadway immediately after leaving school, in chorus of 'Sing Out the News' and other musicals. Speciality numbers and understudy to Betty Hutton in 'Panama Hattie'. 1943: spotted by MGM for *Girl Crazy*. 1944: first starred in *Two Girls and a Sailor*. 1945: married Dick Powell. Own TV series. 1970: took over part in 'Forty Carats' on Broadway.

Films as actress include: 1943: Thousands Cheer. 1948: Words and Music. 1953: Battle Circus; Remains To Be Seen; The Glenn Miller Story]. 1954: Executive Suite; Woman's World. 1955: The Shrike; Strategic Air Command. 1956: You Can't Run Away From It; The Opposite Sex. 1957: Interlude. 1958: A Stranger In My Arms.

ALTON, John

Cinematographer. Hungary 1901–

1924: laboratory technician for MGM. 1928: cameraman for Paramount. 1931: to Paris, in charge of Paramount camera department. Installed studios in South America; wrote, directed and photographed many Spanish language movies. 1937: returned to Hollywood. World War II: US Signal Corps. Then cinematographer on low budget films. Author of textbook on cinematography, 'Painting With Light'. Oscar for colour photography, for ballet sequence of *An American in Paris* (1951), his first Hollywood work in colour.

Films as cinematographer include: 1947: Driftwood; T-Men. 1948: Raw Deal; He Walked by Night. 1949: Border Incident; Reign of Terror. 1950: Devil's Doorway; Mystery Street; Father of the Bride. 1951: Father's Little Dividend; An American in Paris (*co*). 1953: Battle Circus; Take the High Ground; Count the Hours. 1954: Cattle Queen of Montana; The Big Combo; Silver Lode; Passion. 1955: Escape to Burma; Pearl of the South Pacific; Tennessee's Partner. 1956: Slightly Scarlet; The Catered Affair; Tea and Sympathy; Tea House of the August Moon. 1957: Designing Woman; The Brothers Karamazov. 1960: Elmer Gantry.

ALTON, Robert

(Alton Hart) Choreographer. Bennington, Vermont 1906–1957 Hollywood

Dancer with the Mordkin Ballet Troupe. Staged water ballet at Fort Worth World Fair and Aquacade at New York World Fair. Directed Broadway productions including 'Ziegfeld Follies' and 'Anything Goes'. 1936: started in films directing musical sequences in *Strike Me Pink*. Choreographer mainly for MGM while continuing to direct musicals on Broadway.

Films as choreographer include: 1945: The Harvey Girls. 1946: Ziegfeld Follies. 1948: The Pirate (*co*); Easter Parade; Words and Music. 1949: The Barkleys of Broadway. 1950: Annie Get Your Gun. 1951: Show Boat. 1952: The Belle of New York. 1953: Call Me Madam; I Love Melvin. 1954: White Christmas; There's No Business Like Show Business.

Films as director: 1947: Merton of the Movies. 1950: Pagan Love Song.

ALWYN, William

Composer. Northampton, England 1905–

Royal Academy of Music; diploma in composition. 1936: music for documentary *The Future's in the Air*. Many film scores since, notably for Carol Reed.

Films as composer include: 1943: Desert Victory (*co, uc*). 1944: Tunisian Victory (*co, uc*). 1945: The True Glory; The Rake's Progress. 1946: Green for Danger; 1947: Odd Man Out. 1948: The Fallen Idol. 1950: The Golden Salamander. 1952: The Crimson Pirate. 1953: The Million Pound Note. 1957: Manuela. 1960: Swiss Family Robinson. 1963: The Running Man.

AMFITHEATROF, Daniele

Composer. St Petersburg, Russia 1901–

Royal Conservatory of Music in Rome. Guest conductor of leading European and American symphony orchestras before going to Hollywood to compose film scores.

Films as composer include: 1934: La Signora di tutti. 1943: Lassie Come Home. 1948: An Act of Murder; Letter From an Unknown Woman; Another Part of the Forest. 1949: House of Strangers; The Fan. 1951: Storm Warning; The Desert Fox. 1954: The Naked Jungle; Human Desire. 1955: Trial. 1956: The Last Hunt. 1957: Spanish Affair. 1958: From Hell to Texas. 1959: Edge of Eternity; That Kind of Woman. 1960: Heller in Pink Tights.

ANDERSON, Gilbert M. (Broncho Billy)

(Max Aaronson). Director, producer and actor. Pine Bluff, Arkansas 1883–1971 Hollywood

1900: stage actor; also in vaudeville. Acted in many Edwin S. Porter films starting with *The Great Train Robbery* (1903). 1907: with George K. Spoor founded Essanay Film Manufacturing Company. Acted and usually directed and wrote almost 400 one-reelers. 'Broncho Billy' series began with *Broncho Billy and the Baby* (1908) based on 'Three Godfathers'. Some early films directed by Reginald Barker. 1915: with Charles Chaplin in *The Champion*. 1916: sold Essanay shares and retired. Brief come-back in series of 2-reelers with Stan Laurel at Metro; retired from acting after disagreements with studio (1920). Ran Progressive Pictures under own name (still operating in 1950). Honorary Oscar (1951) as 'motion picture pioneer, for his contributions to the development of motion pictures as entertainment'. 1965: acted in *The Bounty Killer*.

ANDERSON, Lindsay

Director. Bangalore, South India 1923–

Father a Scottish Major-General. Cheltenham College and Wadham College, Oxford. World War II: officer in 60th Rifles and Intelligence Corps. 1946: returned to Oxford; co-founder, editor and regular contributor to film magazine Sequence which continued from London (1948–52); then wrote for Sight and Sound and various journals. From 1948 made industrial films, sponsored films and documentaries until 1957. 1952: book, 'Making a Film' on Thorold Dickinson and *Secret People*; producer and actor in James Broughton's *The Pleasure Garden*. 1955–56: directed 5 episodes of 'The Adventures of Robin Hood' for TV. 1956–59: one of the originators of Free Cinema programmes at London National Film Theatre, which included his documentaries *Wakefield Express* (extract), *O Dreamland, Every Day Except Christmas*. From 1957: theatre director: many plays at Royal Court Theatre and 'Billy Liar' at Cambridge Theatre, 'Andorra' at National Theatre, London, 'The Cherry Orchard' at Chichester Festival Theatre. 1963: first feature as director *This Sporting Life*. Directed 'Inadmissible Evidence' in Warsaw.

where he also made *Raz Dwa Trzy*. Directed TV commercials. Occasional appearances as an actor. One of associate artistic directors at Royal Court Theatre. Oscar for documentary short subject *Thursday's Children* (1954).

Films as director: 1948: Meet the Pioneers. 1949: Idlers that Work. 1952: Three Installations; Wakefield Express. 1953: Thursday's Children (*co-d Guy Brenton*); O Dreamland. 1954: Trunk Conveyor. 1955: Green and Pleasant Land; Henry; The Children Upstairs; A Hundred Thousand Children; £20 a Ton; Energy First; Foot and Mouth. 1957: Every Day Except Christmas. 1963: This Sporting Life. 1966: The White Bus. 1967: Raz Dwa Trzy – The Singing Lesson. 1968: If . . . (+*co-p*).

ANDERSON, Maxwell

Playwright. Atlantic, Pennsylvania 1888–1959 Stamford, Connecticut
Son of a Baptist minister. 1911: graduated from University of North Dakota. Later took an MA in English at Stanford University California. 1911–1918: various jobs including teaching and editorial work on San Francisco newspapers. 1918–24: newspaperman in New York. 1923: wrote first play 'The White Desert'; play 'What Price Glory?' written with Lawrence Stallings, filmed in 1926. 1933: won Pulitzer Prize. 1938: co-founded The Playwright's Company which produced many of his subsequent plays. Wrote librettos for operas by Kurt Weill, 'Knickerbocker Holiday' (1938) and 'Lost in the Stars' (1949). Also poetry. Married three times.

Films as writer include: 1930: All Quiet on the Western Front (*ad*). 1932: Rain (*ad*). 1948: Joan of Arc (*fpl*). 1957: The Wrong Man (*co*)

ANDERSON, Michael

Director. London 1920–
Son of actor Lawrence Anderson. At 15 started at Elstree Studios as messenger boy; then assistant director and unit manager. 1938: small part as actor in *The Housemaster*; also in *Stolen Life*. Assistant, notably to Anthony Asquith (*Pygmalion*), Noel Coward and David Lean (*In Which We Serve*), Carol Reed. World War II: Royal Signal Corps. Some Hollywood films in early 1960s. Son, Michael Anderson Jr, is actor in American films and TV.

Films as director: 1949: Private Angelo (*co-d Peter Ustinov*). 1950: Waterfront. 1951: Hell is Sold Out. 1952: Night Was Our Friend. 1953: Dial 17; Will Any Gentleman?; The House of the Arrow. 1954: The Dambusters. 1956: 1984; Around the World in 80 Days. 1957: Yangtse Incident. 1958: Chase a Crooked Shadow. 1959: Shake Hands with the Devil (+*p*); The Wreck of the Mary Deare. 1960: All the Fine Young Cannibals. 1961: The Naked Edge. 1963: Wild and Wonderful. 1964: Flight from Ashiya; Operation Crossbow. 1966: The Quiller Memorandum. 1968: The Shoes of the Fisherman (*ur*).

ANDERSSON, Bibi

Actress. Stockholm 1935–
Studied drama at Terserus. 1953: first film *Dumbom*. 1954–56: student at Royal Dramatic Theatre; re-

turned there in 1959–62 and again in 1965. 1956–59 Malmö City Theatre. 1961: in *Nasilje na trgu* in Yugoslavia. 1962: Uppsala City Theatre. 1965: first American film, *Duel at Diablo*. Married director and writer Kjell Grede.

Films as actress include: 1954: Herr Arnes Pengar. 1955: Sommarnattens Leende. 1956: Sista paret ut. 1957: Det Sjunde Inseglet; Smultronstället. 1958: Nära livet; Ansiktet. 1960: Djävulens Øga. 1961: Lustgården. 1962: Älskarinnan. 1964: För att inte tala om alla dessa kvinnor; Ön (*r* 1966). 1966: Persona; Syskonbädd 1782. 1967: Le Viol. 1968: Flickorna. 1970: En Passion. 1971: Beroringen.

ANDERSSON, Harriet

Actress. Stockholm 1932–
Drama school. Chorus work on stage. Revue entertainer. Theatrical work: Malmö City Theatre (1953–55); Intiman (1956); Hälsingborg City Theatre (1961). Advertising films. Features from 1950 notably for Ingmar Bergman and husband Jörn Donner. Drama on Swedish TV, e.g. as Eliza in 'Pygmalion'.

Films as actress include: 1950: Medan staden sover. 1952: Trots; Sommaren med Monika. 1954: En Lektion i kärlek. 1955: Kvinnodröm; Sommarnattens Leende. 1956: Sista paret ut. 1961: Såsom i en spegel; Barbara. 1963: En Söndag i september. 1964: För att inte tala om alla dessa kvinnor; Att älska: Älskande Par. 1965: Här börjar äventyret. 1966: Tvärbalk. 1967: Stimulantia *ep* Han-Hon. 1968: Flickorna. 1970: Anna.

ANDRESS, Ursula

Actress. Berne, Switzerland 1936–
German parents. Spotted at 16 on vacation in Rome; in some Italian films from 1953. 1957–66: married to John Derek; directed by him in *Once Before I Die* (1967). First major film part: *Dr No* (1962).

Films as actress include: 1963: 4 for Texas. 1965: She; What's New, Pussycat?; Les Tribulations d'un chinois en Chine. 1966: The Blue Max. 1967: Casino Royale. 1970: Perfect Friday. 1971: Soleil Rouge.

ANDREWS, Dana

Actor. Collins, Mississippi 1912–
Sam Houston College, Huntsville. Certified Public Accountant. 1931: moved to Los Angeles. Trained as singer and studied acting at Pasadena Playhouse where he was spotted by a Goldwyn talent scout. 1939: MGM contract. 1940: Fox arranged to share contract. First film: *The Westerner* (1940). TV. Younger brother is actor Steve Forrest.

Films as actor include: 1940: Sailor's Lady. 1941: Tobacco Road; Ball of Fire. 1942: The Ox-Bow Incident. 1943: The North Star. 1944: Laura. 1945: State Fair; Fallen Angel. 1946: Canyon Passage; A Walk in the Sun; The Best Years of Our Lives. 1947: Boomerang!; Daisy Kenyon; Night Song. 1948: The Iron Curtain. 1949: My Foolish Heart. 1950: Where the Sidewalk Ends. 1952: Assignment Paris. 1955: Strange Lady in Town. 1956: While the City Sleeps; Beyond a Reasonable Doubt. 1957: Night of the Demon. 1958: The Fearmakers. 1962: Madison

June Allyson with James Stewart (right) in The Glenn Miller Story *directed by Anthony Mann.*
The Big Combo, *directed by Joseph H. Lewis, and photographed by John Alton.*
O Dreamland. *directed by Lindsay Anderson.*

Avenue. 1964: The Satan Bug; In Harm's Way. 1967: Hot Rods to Hell. 1968: The Devil's Brigade.

ANDREWS, Julie

Actress. London 1935–

1947: London stage debut in 'Starlight Roof'. Subsequently in many West End shows. 1954: Broadway debut in 'The Boy Friend', then 'My Fair Lady' with which returned to London (1958). TV in UK and USA includes 'Saturday Spectacular', 'Sunday Night at the London Palladium' and 'The Julie Andrews Show'. From 1961: on Broadway in 'Camelot'. Married to designer Tony Walton and then (1969) to Blake Edwards. 1964: first films; Oscar as best actress, *Mary Poppins*.

Films as actress: 1964: Mary Poppins; The Americanization of Emily; The Sound of Music. 1966: Hawaii; Torn Curtain. 1967: Thoroughly Modern Millie. 1968: Star! 1970; Darling Lili.

ANDRIOT, Lucien

Cinematographer. Paris 1897–

1916: assistant cinematographer and then cinematographer with World Film Corporation in Hollwood for directors Albert Capellani and Léonce Perret. Worked for various companies including many independents. Also TV.

Films as cinematographer include: 1917: The Silent Master. 1918: Lafayette! We Come! 1920: The Connecticut Yankee at King Arthur's Court. 1927: Loves of Carmen (*co*). 1931: Daddy Long Legs. 1932: Prestige. 1936: The Gay Desperado. 1940: The Lady in Question. 1941: Dance Hall. 1943: Jitterbugs. 1945: The Southerner; And Then There Were None. 1946: A Scandal in Paris; The Diary of a Chambermaid; The Strange Woman. 1949: Outpost in Morocco.

ANGER, Kenneth

Director. Santa Monica, California 1932–

Grew up in Hollywood where he appeared in several films including *A Midsummer Night's Dream* (1935). Made his first film at 7. 1946: first film to be exhibited, *Escape Episode* (sound version). 1948: began a feature on Hollywood in the 1920s, *Puce Women,* of which only a short fragment, *Puce Moment,* is exhibited. From 1950, in France. 1951–52: project to film Lautréamont's 'Chants de Maldoror'. 1953: shot *Eaux d'artifice* in Italy. 1954: returned to Los Angeles, made first version of *Inauguration of the Pleasure Dome* for projection on a single screen; second version (1958) was for sychronised projection on triple screen; final 'Sacred Mushroom' version (1966) was re-edited for single screen. 1955: made *Thelema Abbey* in Sicily for BBC (copy lost). 1959–61: worked on almost completed project *Histoire d'O.* 1964: received Ford grant for a long work of which only the sequence, *Kustom Kar Kommandos,* was completed. 1966: began colour feature, *Lucifer Rising,* which he abandoned after theft of rough-cut following a benefit screening. 1969: began shooting second version of this in Europe. 1971: renewed *La Lune des lapins* (1950, unfinished), using material discovered in Paris Cinemathèque. Book: 'Hollywood Babylon.'

Films which have been exhibited: 1946: Escape Episode (*sound version*). 1947: Fireworks. 1949: Puce Moment. 1953: Le Jeune Homme et la mort; Eaux d'artifice. 1954: Inauguration of the Pleasure Dome (*first version*). 1955: Thelema Abbey. 1958: Inauguration of the Pleasure Dome (*second version*). 1964: Scorpio Rising. 1965: Kinstom Kar Kommandos. 1966: Inauguration of the Pleasure Dome (*third version*). 1969: Invocation of my Demon Brother. 1971: La Lune des lapins – Rabbit's Moon; Lucifer Rising, Chapter One.

ANNABELLA

(Suzanne Charpentier) Actress. Paris 1909–

After leaving school did odd jobs and played minor parts in film studios at Joinville. First large part: *Napoléon vu par Abel Gance* (1926). First starred in *Le Million* (1931). English-speaking debut: *Wings of the Morning* (1937). On Broadway in Elia Kazan's production of 'Jacobowsky and the Colonel' (1944). Married actors Jean Murat, Tyrone Power.

Films as actress include: 1933: Quatorze Juillet. 1936: La Bandera. 1937: Under the Red Robe. 1938: Hôtel du Nord; Suez. 1947: 13 Rue Madeleine. 1948: Dernier Amour.

ANNAKIN, Ken

Director. Beverley, Yorkshire 1914–

From 1930 worked as income-tax clerk, then tax inspector. Emigrated to New Zealand, then Australia and America. Returned to England; worked in car sales, journalism, experimental theatre; some work as film extra. Amnesia ended war service in RAF. 1941: producer Sydney Box got him job as camera assistant with Verity Films. Camera operator, assistant director, scriptwriter and co-director on documentaries before first feature as director in 1947.

Films as director include: 1947: Holiday Camp. 1948: Miranda; Quartet *ep* The Colonel's Lady. 1949: Landfall. 1950: Trio *eps* The Verger, Mr Know-all. 1951: Hotel Sahara. 1952: The Story of Robin Hood – The Story of Robin Hood and His Merrie Men; The Planter's Wife – Outpost in Malaya. 1956: Loser Takes All; Three Men in a Boat. 1957: Across the Bridge. 1958: Nor the Moon by Night. 1960: Swiss Family Robinson. 1961: Very Important Person. 1962: The Fast Lady; The Longest Day (*co-d 3 others*). 1963: The Hellions. 1965: Those Magnificent Men in Their Flying Machines or How I Flew from London to Paris in 25 hours and 11 minutes (*+co-s*). 1966: Battle of the Bulge. 1967: The Long Duel (*+p*). 1968: Those Daring Young Men in their Jaunty Jalopies – Monte Carlo or Bust (*+p/co-s*); The Biggest Bundle of Them All.

ANOUILH, Jean

Writer and director. Bordeaux, France 1910–

Worked in publicity agency, then secretary to Louis Jouvet. 1936: first film as writer in collaboration *Les Dégourdis de la onzième.* Wrote several films in collaboration with Jean Aurenche. 1943: first film as director, from own play. Films adapted by others from his plays include *Monsoon* (1952) from 'Romeo and Jeanette', *Waltz of the Toreadors* (1962), *Becket* (1964).

Films as writer in collaboration include: 1936: Les Degourdis le la onzième; Vous n'avez rien à declarer? (*co-di*) 1947: Monsieur Vincent. 1948: Pattes Blanches (*+ di*); Anna Karenine (*+ co-di*). 1965: La Ronde (*alone*).

Films as director: 1943: Le Voyageur sans baggages (*+co-ad/di/fpl*). 1951: Deux Sous de violettes.

ANSTEY, Edgar

Producer and director. Watford, Hertfordshire 1907–

1930–34: with John Grierson at Empire Marketing Board Film Unit. 1933: first film as director. 1934–35: organised Shell Film Unit. 1935: independent producer of documentaries. 1936–38: director of production on March of Time in London then foreign editor of the series in New York. 1940: joined board of directors of Film Centre, London and editorial board of Documentary Newsletter. 1941–48: acted through Film Centre as producer in charge of Shell Film Unit; film consultant to British Commercial Gas Association; associate producer on Ministry of Agriculture film programme. Regular productions for Ministry of Agriculture. 1946–49: film critic for The Spectator. BBC film critic. 1949: married Canadian producer Daphne Lilly. From 1949: Films Officer, British Transport Commission. 1956: chairman, British Film Academy. 1963–67: led British Council delegations to USSR. 1964 and 1966: governor, British Film Institute. 1967: chairman, Society of Film and TV Arts. Senior Fellow and member of Council of Royal Academy of Arts. Governor of West Surrey College of Art and Design.

Films as director: 1933: Uncharted Waters. 1934: Eskimo Village; Granton Trawler. 1935: Housing Problems (*co-d Arthur Elton*); Dinner Hour.

ANTHEIL, George

Composer. Trenton, New Jersey 1900–1959 New York

Studied composition under Ernest Bloch at Curtis Institute, Philadelphia. 1922: debut as pianist in recital at Wigmore Hall, London. 1924: wrote score for *Ballet Mécanique*. 1930: assistant musical director at Berlin Municipal Theatre. 1935: first feature scores for Ben Hecht and Charles MacArthur. Film scores mainly for Columbia and Paramount; continued writing concert music and operas.

Films as composer include: 1935: Once in a Blue Moon; The Scoundrel. 1937: The Plainsman; Make Way for Tomorrow. 1938: The Buccaneer. 1939: Union Pacific (*co*). 1940: Angels Over Broadway. 1946: Specter of the Rose. 1949: Knock On Any Door; We Were Strangers. 1950: In a Lonely Place; House by the River. 1952: The Sniper. 1953: The Juggler. 1955: Not as a Stranger. 1957: The Pride and the Passion.

ANTHONY, Joseph

(Joseph Deuster) Director. Milwaukee, Wisconsin 1912–

University of Wisconsin. Pasadena Playhouse School. 1934: first film as actor; others include *Shadow of the Thin Man* (1941). Collaborated on scripts including *Crime and Punishment* (1935) and *Meet Nero Wolfe*

(1936). 1935: actor in repertory at Rice Playhouse (Martha's Vineyard, Massachusetts). 1937: Broadway debut in 'Professor Mamlock'. 1940–41: Agnes De Mille's partner in series of dance concerts. 1937–42: co-founder, director and actor, American Actors' Company which ran off-Broadway studio and summer theatre at Branford, Connecticut. World War II: US Army Signal Corps, Intelligence. 1947: directed his own play 'Returned Night'. Stage actor, e.g. in 'Peer Gynt' with ANTA (1951). Directed Broadway productions including 'The Rainmaker' (1954), 'The Most Happy Fella' (1956), 'Under the Yum Yum Tree' (1960), 'Mary Mary' (1961), '110 in the Shade', 'The Rainmaker' (1963).

Films as director: 1956: The Rainmaker. 1958: The Matchmaker. 1959: Career. 1961: All in a Night's Work. 1963: La Città Prigionera – Conquered City – The Captive City.

ANTONIONI, Michelangelo

Director. Ferrara, Italy 1912–
Economics at University of Bologna. During studies was journalist on Ferrara newspaper. Started abortive 16mm documentary. Worked in bank. 1939: moved to Rome. Contributor to film magazines including Cinema (1940, continuing occasionally until 1949). 1940–41: student of direction at Centro Sperimentale; left after a few months. 1942: assistant to Marcel Carne on *Les Visiteurs du soir* and Enrico Fulchignoni on *I Due Foscari*; worked on script of latter and Roberto Rossellini's *Un Pilota ritorna*. 1943: filmed first short, *Gente del Po,* edited from surviving half of footage in 1947. 1947: collaborated on script of *Caccia Tragica*. 1948–50: made shorts. 1950: first feature as director, *Cronaca di un amore*. 1952: worked on script of *Lo Sceicco Bianco. I Vinti* was shot in 3 countries (Italy, France and UK) and 3 languages. 1955: producer for Intergovernmental Committee on European Migration of short, *Uomini in più* (directed by Nicolo Ferrari). 1957: in theatre directed Monica Vitti in 'I Am a Camera'; wrote with Elio Bartolini and directed comedy, 'Scandali Segreti'. 1958: uncredited, director in collaboration on *Nel segno di Roma. Blow Up* was shot in UK; *Zabriskie Point* in USA, both for Carlo Ponti and MGM.

Films as writer and director: 1943 Gente del Po (r 1947). 1948: N.U. – Nettezza Urbana. 1949: L'Amorosa Menzogna; Superstizione. 1950: Sette; Canne un vestito; La Villa dei mostri; La Funivia del Faloria; Cronaca di un amore (+ st; co-s). 1953: I Vinti (co-s); La Signora senza camelie (+ st; co-s); L'Amore in città ep Tentato Suicidio (co-s). 1955: Le Amiche – The Girl Friends (co-s). 1957: Il Grido – The Cry (+ st/co-s). 1958: Nel Segno di Roma – La Regina del deserto (uc; co-d Riccardo Freda). 1960 L'Avventura (+ st; co-s). 1961: La Notte – The Night (+ st; co-s). 1962: L'Eclisse – The Eclipse (co-s). 1964: Deserto Rosso – The Red Desert (co-s). 1965: I Tre Volti ep Prefazione (d only). 1966: Blow-Up (co-s). 1970: Zabriskie Point.

ARBUCKLE, Roscoe (Fatty)

Actor and director. Smith Center, Arkansas 1887–1933 New York
From 1904: vaudeville, fairgrounds, then musical comedy. Formed touring group with Walter Reed.

1909: extra at Keystone. 1913: leading parts in Mack Sennett Keystone comedies, becoming actor-director (1914). Many shorts with Mabel Normand, several with Charles Chaplin as actor or director. 1917: formed partnership with Joseph M. Schenck, the Comicque or Comique Film Corporation. 1917–19: 2-reelers with Buster Keaton as supporting actor. 1920–21: on manslaughter charge over death of model Virginia Rappe at Labor Day party. 1922: acquitted at second trial but campaign against him led by Hearst press ruined career. Directed pseudonymously. As William Goodrich directed shorts for Educational and (1927) a few features. 1932: attempted comeback at Warners, but died after release of a few films.

Films as actor include: Passions-He Had Three; The Tell-Tale Light; Mabel's Dramatic Career; The Gypsy Queen; When Dreams Come True; The Speed Kings; Fatty's Flirtation. 1914: In the Clutches of the Gang; A Film Johnnie; The Knockout; The Masquerader; The Rounders. 1915; The Little Teacher. 1921: The Dollar-a-year Man.

Films as actor and director include: 1914: The Alarm; Fatty and the Heiress; Fatty's Finish; The Sky Pirate – A Sky Pirate; Those Happy Days; That Minstrel Man; Those Country Kids; Fatty's Gift; A Brand New Hero; Fatty's Debut; Fatty Again; Zipp, the Dodger; An Incompetent Hero; Fatty's Jonah Day; Fatty's Wine Party; The Sea Nymphs; Leading Lizzie Astray; Shotguns that Kick; Fatty's Magic Pants; Fatty and Minnie-He-Haw. 1915: Mabel and Fatty's Wash Day; Fatty and Mabel's Simple Life – Mabel and Fatty's Simple Life; Fatty and Mabel at the San Diego Exposition; Mabel, Fatty and the Law; Fatty's New Role; Mabel and Fatty's Married Life; Fatty's Reckless Fling; Fatty's Chance Acquaintance; That Little Band of Gold; Fatty's Faithful Fido; When Love Took Wings; Mabel and Fatty Viewing the World's Fair at San Francisco, Cal.; Miss Fatty's Seaside Lovers; Fatty's Plucky Pup – Foiled by Fido; Fatty's Tintype Tangle – Fido's Tin-Type Tangle; Fickle Fatty's Fall; The Village Scandal; Fatty and the Broadway Stars. 1916: Fatty and Mabel Adrift; He Did and He Didn't – Love and Lobsters; The Bright Lights – The Lure of Broadway; His Wife's Mistake; The Other Man; The Waiters' Ball; His Alibi; A Cream Puff Romance – A Reckless Romeo. 1917: The Butcher Boy; The Rough House; His Wedding Night; Oh, Doctor!; Coney Island – Fatty at Coney Island. 1918: Out West – The Sheriff; The Bell Boy; Moonshine; Goodnight Nurse; The Cook. 1919: A Desert Hero; Backstage; The Hayseed; The Garage. 1920: A Country Hero.

Films as director include: 1916: The Moonshiners. *Under pseudonym William Goodrich*: 1926: Cleaning Up (+ s). 1927: The Red Mill; Special Delivery. 1931: Smart Work; Windy Riley Goes to Hollywood. 1932: Keep Laughing; Moonlight and Cactus; Anybody's Goat; Bridge Wives; Hollywood Luck; Mother's Holiday; It's a Cinch.

ARDREY, Robert

Writer. Chicago 1908–
University of Chicago. 1930: studied writing with Thornton Wilder; then 5 years of various jobs including statistician, piano player, bank clerk, to earn living while writing. 1936: first play, 'Star Spangled', produced; Guggenheim fellowship. 1938: 'Casey

Kenneth Anger.
Cronaca di un amore *directed by Michelangelo Antonioni.*
Mabel Normand and Fatty Arbuckle in *Fatty and Mabel Adrift.*

Jones' (directed by Elia Kazan for Group Theater) and 'How to Get Tough About It' both on Broadway; went to Hollywood for job with Sam Goldwyn. 1939: 'Thunder Rock' (directed by Kazan for Group Theater) failed in New York but became successful (1940) in London and on British tour; filmed (1944) in Britain. World War II: at Office of War Information in New York. 1963: 10-year grant from Wilkie Brothers Foundation for anthropological research. Novels: 'Worlds Beginning' (1944); 'Brotherhood of Fear' (1952). Anthropological works published: 'African Genesis' (1961); 'The Territorial Imperative' (1966); 'The Social Contract' (1970).

Films as writer include: 1940: They Knew What They Wanted. 1946: The Green Years (co). 1948: The Three Musketeers. 1949: The Secret Garden; Madame Bovary. 1955: Quentin Durward. 1959: The Wonderful Country. 1962: The Four Horsemen of the Apocalypse (co). 1966: Khartoum.

ARKOFF, Samuel Z.

Producer. Fort Dodge, Iowa 1918–
University of Colorado, University of Iowa, Loyola University Law School. World War II: USAAF cryptographer. 1950: attorney in entertainment law, involved in first filmed network TV programme in USA. 1954: co-founder of American Releasing, began collaboration with James H. Nicholson. 1955: co-founder of American International, became producer. In 1958 made 22 films.

Films as producer in collaboration include: 1963: The Comedy of Terrors. 1965: City in the Sea; Sergeant Deadhead, the Astronut; Dr Goldfoot and the Bikini Machine. 1966: The Ghost in the Invisible Bikini. 1969: De Sade.

Films as executive producer in collaboration include: 1961: The Pit and the Pendulum. 1962: Tales of Terror; Panic in the Year Zero. 1963: The Raven; The Haunted Palace; X-the Man with X-Ray Eyes. 1965: Die Monster, Die. 1967: Devil's Angels. 1970: Bloody Mama.

ARLETTY

(Arlette-Léonie Bathiat) Actress. Courbevoie, France 1898–
Worked in munitions factory and as secretary, mannequin and artist's model. Started in cinema as singer and dancer after starring in operetta 'Yes' at the Théâtre des Capucines. First film: Un Chien qui rapporte (1930). Operetta at Bouffes-Parisien, and other stage parts in Paris including 'Un Tramway nommé Desir' (1950).

Films as actress include: 1935: Pension Mimosas. 1937: Les Perles de la couronne. 1938: Désiré; Hôtel du Nord. 1939: Le Jour se lève; Fric Frac. 1941: Madame Sans-gêne. 1942: Les Visiteurs du soir. 1945: Les Enfants du paradis. 1947: La Fleur de l'âge (uf). 1953: Le Grand Jeu. 1954: L'Air de Paris; Huis Clos.

ARLING, Arthur E.

Cinematographer. Missouri 1906–
New York Institute of Photography. 1927: joined Fox as camera assistant. 1939: camera operator for Gone With The Wind. After World War II as officer in US Navy became cinematographer. Oscar for colour cinematography on The Yearling (1946, with Charles Rosher and Leonard Smith).

Films as cinematographer include: 1947: Captain from Castile (co). 1949: You're my Everything. 1950: Wabash Avenue. 1952: Belles on Their Toes. 1954: Red Garters. 1955: The Glass Slipper. 1956: Love Me or Leave Me; I'll Cry Tomorrow. 1958: This Happy Feeling. 1959: Pillow Talk; Take a Giant Step. 1962: Boys' Night Out; The Notorious Landlady. 1963: My Six Loves; Strait-jacket. 1964: The Secret Invasion.

ARLISS, George

(Augustus George Andrews) Actor. London 1868–1946 London
Harrow School. Stage debut at 18. 1899: married Florence Montgomery who appeared with him in 'Disraeli'. 1901: on tour to USA with Mrs Patrick Campbell's company, and stayed there for over 20 years. Broadway debut, 'The Devil' (1908). Screen debut in silent film of his stage success, Disraeli (1921). Appeared in several other silent films of his stage plays and repeated some as talkies. Autobiography published 1927. Under contract to Warners from 1930. Retired from screen in 1937 because wife was going blind. Son is director Leslie Arliss. Oscar as Best Actor for Disraeli (sound version, 1929).

Films as actor include: 1922: The Man Who Played God. 1932: The Man Who Played God (rm). 1933: Voltaire. 1934: The House of Rothschild; The Iron Duke. 1935: Cardinal Richelieu. 1937: Dr Syn.

ARLISS, Leslie

(Leslie Andrews) Director. London 1901–
Son of actor and actress George and Florence Arliss. London journalist and critic (films and theatre for Johannesburg Star) before entering films as writer (1932), notably on Rhodes of Africa (1936) and The Foreman Went to France (1942). From 1941: directed a number of shorts as well as features. Since 1953: directing film series for TV.

Features as director: 1941: The Farmer's Wife (co-d Norman Lee). 1942: The Night Has Eyes. 1943: The Man in Grey (+co-s). 1944: Love Story (+co-s). 1945: The Wicked Lady. 1947: A Man about the House (+co-s). 1948: Idol of Paris. 1949: Saints and Sinners (+p/co-s). 1952: The Woman's Angle (+co-s). 1955: See How They Run (+co-s); Miss Tulip Stays the Night.

ARMENDARIZ, Pedro

Actor. Churubusco, Mexico 1912–1963 Los Angeles
From 7, lived in USA and was completely bilingual. 1935–44 acted in over 40 Mexican films. First became known elsewhere with Maria Candelaria (1943). 1947: first English language film, The Fugitive, for John Ford; then in 2 more Ford films. From 1953: also in French and Italian films. Committed suicide on learning he had cancer. Many of his Mexican films were directed by Emilio Fernandez.

Films as actor include: 1941: La Isla de la pasión. 1942: Soy Puro Mexicano. 1943: Flor Silvestre. 1944: Las Abandonadas; Bugambilia. 1945: La Perla; Enamorada. 1948: Maclovia; Three Godfathers; Fort Apache. 1949: La Malquerida; Tulsa; We Were Strangers. 1950: The Torch. 1952: El Bruto; Lucrezia Borgia. 1955: The Littlest Outlaw; La Rebellion de los Colgados; Diane. 1955: The Conquerer. 1956: Uomini e lupi. 1957: The Big Boodle; Manuela. 1959: The Little Savage; The Wonderful Country. 1961: Francis of Assisi. 1963: Captain Sinbad; From Russia With Love.

ARNOLD, Jack

Director. Newhaven, Connecticut 1916–
Ohio State University and American Academy of Dramatic Arts. Acted on Broadway, in British and American films. 1942–45: US Air Force; produced 25 documentaries for State Department, Army and industry. Feature director (1952–59) at Universal.

Films as director: 1953: Girls in the Night; It Came from Outer Space; The Glass Web. 1954: Creature from the Black Lagoon. 1955: Revenge of the Creature; Tarantula (+co-st); The Man from Bitter Ridge; Red Sundown. 1955: Outside the Law. 1957: The Tattered Dress; The Incredible Shrinking Man; Man in the Shadow – Pay the Devil; The Lady Takes a Flyer. 1958: The Space Children; High School Confidential; Monster on the Campus. 1959: No Name on the Bullet (+co-p); The Mouse that Roared. 1961: Bachelor in Paradise. 1964: The Lively Set; A Global Affair. 1968: Hullo Down There.

ARNOLD, Malcolm

Composer. Northampton, England 1921–
Studied trumpet, piano and composition at Royal College of Music. 1940: joined London Philharmonic as trumpeter; on demobilisation returned as first trumpet (1948). Awarded Mendelssohn scholarship by Royal College of Music. First film score, The Sound Barrier (1952). Oscar for score, Bridge on the River Kwai (1958).

Films as composer include: 1955: I Am a Camera. 1956: 1984; Trapeze. 1957: Island in the Sun. 1958: The Key; Roots of Heaven; The Inn of the Sixth Happiness. 1960: The Angry Silence. 1961: The Inspector; Whistle Down the Wind. 1962: The Lion. 1963: Nine Hours to Rama; The Chalk Garden. 1964: The Thin Red Line. 1965: The Heroes of Telemark.

ARNOUL, Françoise

(Françoise Annette Gautsch) Actress. Constantine, Algeria 1931–
Father a general in French artillery. Studied at Bauer-Theron Institute. First film, L'Epave (1949). Also TV.

Films as actress include: 1950: Quai de Grenelle. 1952: Les Amants de Tolède. 1955: French Cancan. 1956: Si Paris nous était conté; Le Pays d'où je viens. 1957: Sait-on jamais? 1958: La Chatte. 1961: La Morte-saison des amours. 1963: Le Diable et les dix commandements. 1971: Le Petit Théâtre de Jean Renoir ep Le Roi d'Yvetat.

ARTAUD, Antonin

Actor, writer and theatrical director. Marseille, France 1896–1948 Ivry-sur-Seine

With Charles Dullin at Théâtre de l'Atelier. 1917: first film as actor. 1923: letters to Jacques Rivière, later published, describing mental breakdown. First published prose poem 'L'Ombilic des limbes' (1925) and 'Le Pèse-nerfs'. 1926: helped found Théâtre Alfred Jarry; little success in later ventures as theatrical producer. 1928: scripted *La Coquille et le clergyman;* disowned the film. 1938: published series of articles on theatrical doctrine, 'Le Théâtre et son double'. Several film projects.

Films as actor include: 1917: Mater Dolorosa. 1923: Fait Divers. 1926: Napoléon Vu par Abel Gance. 1928: La Passion de Jeanne d'Arc; Tarakanova; L'Argent. 1931: L'Opéra de quat'sous. 1933: Mater Dolorosa (*sound version*).

ARTHUR, Jean

(Gladys Green) Actress. New York 1908–
A Christy model and appeared on New York stage before starting screen career in 2-reelers; first film as actress *Cameo Kirby* (1923). Later in features; first starred in *The Poor Nut* (1927). 1932–34: left Hollywood for stage, returning to films as Broadway star. Retired from films after *Shane* (1952). Occasional TV appearances since. Head of Drama Department at Vassar College.

Films as actress include: 1924 Bringin' Home the Bacon; Fast and Fearless. 1925: Seven Chances; Tearin' Loose. 1926: Double Daring; The Fighting Cheat. 1927: Horse Shoes. 1928: Warming Up. 1929: The Canary Murder Case; The Greene Murder Case; Halfway to Heaven; Mysterious Dr Fu Manchu. 1930: Danger Lights; Street of Chance; Paramount on Parade; Young Eagles. 1935: The Whole Town's Talking; Diamond Jim. 1936: Mr Deeds Goes to Town. 1937: The Plainsman; History Is Made at Night; Easy Living. 1938: You Can't Take It With You. 1939: Only Angels Have Wings; Mr Smith Goes to Washington. 1940: Too Many Husbands; Arizona. 1941: The Devil and Miss Jones. 1942: The Talk of the Town. 1943: The More the Merrier. 1948: A Foreign Affair.

ASQUITH, Anthony

Director. London 1902–1968 London
Youngest son of 1st Earl of Oxford and Asquith (Liberal Prime Minister, 1908) by his second marriage, to Margot Tennant. Scholarship from Winchester College to Balliol College, Oxford. Wanted to be a musician; played piano excellently. 1925: founder member of the Film Society with Bernard Shaw, H. G. Wells, Julian Huxley and others. 1926: visited Hollywood for 6 months and observed Mary Pickford, Douglas Fairbanks and Charles Chaplin at work. From 1927: employed by British Instructional Films at Surbiton Studios; assistant and double for star on *Boadicea*. Scriptwriter, editor and associate director on *Shooting Stars* (1927). First British director to join newly formed Association of Cinematograph and Allied Technicians (1933); president from 1937 until his death. 1946: formed International Screenplays Ltd with Terence Rattigan and Anatole de Grunwald. 1953: produced 'Carmen' at Covent Garden, first opera there since World War II, with Nell Rankin in title role. 1961: injured in car crash. Frequent lecturer; wrote many articles on cinema. Vice-president (1957)

of National Liberal Party with his half-sister, Lady Violet Bonham Carter (later Lady Asquith). At death, preparing to direct *The Shoes of the Fisherman.*

Films as director: 1928: Underground. 1929: The Runaway Princess – Princess Priscilla's Fortnight. 1930: A Cottage on Dartmoor. 1931: Tell England – Battle of Gallipoli; Dance, Pretty Lady. 1932: Marry Me; The Window Cleaner. 1933: The Lucky Number. 1934: Unfinished Symphony (+*ad*). 1935: Forever England; Moscow Nights – I Stand Condemned. 1938: Pygmalion (*co-d Leslie Howard*). 1939: French Without Tears. 1940: Quiet Wedding; Channel Incident. 1941: Freedom Radio – The Voice in the Night; Cottage to Let; Bombsight Stolen; Rush Hour. 1942: Uncensored. 1943: We Dive at Dawn; The Demi-Paradise – Adventure for Two; Welcome to Britain (*co-d Burgess Meredith*). 1944: Fanny by Gaslight; Man of Evil; Two Fathers (+*s*). 1945: The Way to the Stars; Johnny in the Clouds. 1947: While the Sun Shines. 1948: The Winslow Boy. 1950: The Woman in Question – Five Angles on Murder. 1951: The Browning Version. 1952: The Importance of Being Earnest (+*s*); The Net – Project M7; The Final Test. 1954: The Young Lovers – Chance Meeting. 1955: On Such a Night. 1956: Carrington VC – Court Martial. 1958: Orders to Kill. 1959: The Doctor's Dilemma; Libel. 1960: The Millionairess; Two Living, One Dead. 1962: Guns of Darkness. 1963: The V.I.P.'s; An Evening with the Royal Ballet (*co-d Anthony Havelock Allan*). 1964: The Yellow Rolls-Royce.

ASTAIRE, Fred

(Frederick Austerlitz) Actor. and choreographer. Omaha, Nebraska 1899–
Studied dancing from 1904. 1906: first appeared in vaudeville act with sister, Adele. 1915: with her in *Fanchon the Cricket*. From 1916: on Broadway with Adele until her marriage (1932). 1931: made a Vitaphone short with her in New York. Appeared alone in 'The Gay Divorce' (New York and London). 1933: first feature, *Dancing Lady* for MGM led to 7-year contract with RKO. Second film *Flying Down to Rio* (1933), started series with Ginger Rogers (until 1939, plus *The Barkleys of Broadway,* 1949). World War II: entertained troops in Europe. 1947: opened own Ballroom Dancing Studios in New York. TV, e.g. 'An Evening with Fred Astaire'. 1949: Special Oscar, 'for his unique artistry and his contribution to the techniques of musical pictures'.

Films as actor include: 1934: The Gay Divorcee. 1935: Roberta; Top Hat. 1936: Follow the Fleet; Swing Time. 1937: Shall We Dance. 1938: Carefree. 1939: The Story of Vernon and Irene Castle. 1942: Holiday Inn. 1946: Ziegfeld Follies; Yolanda and the Thief. 1948: Easter Parade. 1950: Royal Wedding. 1952: The Belle of New York. 1953: The Band Wagon. 1955: Daddy Long Legs (+ *co-chor*). 1957: Funny Face; Silk Stockings. 1959: On the Beach. 1961: The Pleasure of his Company. 1962: The Notorious Landlady. 1968: Finian's Rainbow. 1969: The Midas Run.

Films as choreographer include: 1943: The Sky's the Limit. 1956: Funny Face (*co*).

ASTOR, Mary

(Lucille Langhanke) Actress. Quincey, Illinois 1906–·
Ambitious father pushed her into films after she won

It Came From Outer Space *directed by Jack Arnold.*
Freedom Radio, *directed by Anthony Asquith.*
Cyd Charisse and Fred Astaire in The Band Wagon *directed by Vincente Minnelli.*

beauty contest sponsored by film magazine. Hollywood from 1920; first film, *The Beggar Maid* (1921). Established as star by *Don Juan* (1926). Married 4 times; first husband director Kenneth Hawks (brother of Howard Hawks) died in air crash in 1930. 1936: sensational diary produced in court in custody case over daughter; alleged that 'lurid' sections concering George S. Kaufman were forged. Stage appearances from 1929 (in Los Angeles). 1945: first Broadway appearance. Autobiography 'My Story' and several novels. Oscar as best supporting actress, *The Great Lie* (1941).

Films as actress include: 1925: Don Q, Son of Zorro. 1927: Rough Riders. 1932: Red Dust. 1933: Easy to Love. 1936: Dodsworth. 1937: The Prisoner of Zenda. 1938: The Hurricane. 1940: Brigham Young. 1941: The Maltese Falcon. 1944: Meet Me in St Louis. 1947: Cass Timberlane. 1948: Act of Violence. 1949: Little Women; Any Number Can Play. 1956: A Kiss Before Dying. 1958: A Stranger in My Arms. 1961: Return to Peyton Place. 1964: Youngblood Hawke; Hush, Hush Sweet Charlotte.

ASTRUC, Alexandre

Director. Paris 1923–
Parents journalists; mother editor of Jardin des Modes. Studied law and literature. Novel, 'Les Vacances', published (1945). Assistant, e.g. to Marc Allegret on *Blanche Fury* (1947, in UK) and Marcel Achard on *Jean de la lune* (1949). Worked on adaptation of *La P . . . Respectueuse* (1952). Literary critic; then film critic, e.g. for Combat, La Gazette du Cinema, La Nef, Cine-Digest, Cahiers du Cinema. 1948: article 'La Camera-stylo' appeared in Ecran Français; directed two 16mm shorts. 1949: founder (with Jean Cocteau, André Bazin, Roger Leenhardt, etc) of Cine-Club Objectif 49, and of Festival du Film Maudit, Biarritz. 1955: first feature as director. TV work includes *Le Puits et le pendule* (1963) and *Evariste Gallois*.

Films as director: 1948: Aller-retour; Ulysse et les mauvaises rencontres. 1952: Le Rideau Cramoisi. 1955: Les Mauvaises Rencontres. 1958: Une Vie (+co-s). 1960: La Proie pour l'ombre. 1962: Education Sentimentale 61. 1966: La Longue Marche. 1968: Flammes sur l'Adriatique.

ATTENBOROUGH, Richard

Actor and director. Cambridge, England 1923–
Royal Academy of Dramatic Art. 1942: screen debut (*In Which We Serve*) and London stage debut ('Ah, Wilderness!'); many subsequent stage appearances. 1943–46: RAF. 1959: formed Beaver Films with Bryan Forbes and co-produced *The Angry Silence* (1960). Produced *Whistle Down the Wind* (1961) and *The L-Shaped Room* (1961); first Hollywood appearance: *The Flight of the Phoenix* (1965). 1969: first film as director, *Oh! What a Lovely War*; also co-produced it. Married to actress Sheila Sim. Brother is British TV producer David Attenborough.

Films as actor include: 1946: A Matter of Life and Death. 1947: Brighton Rock; London Belongs to Me. 1948: The Guinea Pig. 1950: Morning Departure. 1951: The Magic Box. 1956: Private's Progress. 1957: Brothers-in-Law. 1959: I'm All Right, Jack. 1960: The

Angry Silence (+co-p); The League of Gentlemen (+ co-p). 1963: The Great Escape. 1964: Seance on a Wet Afternoon (+ co-p); Guns at Batasi. 1968: Only When I Larf. 1971: 10 Rillington Place.

AUDIARD, Michel

Writer and director. Paris 1920–
After brief schooling, tried making career as racing cyclist, arc-welder, then optician, delivered papers on bicycle, wrote for Etoile du Soir, wrote novels, worked on Cinevie. First film script, *Mission à Tangiers* (1949). Dialogue and scenarios for more than 50 films. Directed short *La Marche* (1951) and features *Faut pas prendre les enfants du bon Dieu pour des canards sauvages*, *Une Veuve en or* (1969), *Elle boit pas, elle fume pas, elle drague pas . . . mois elle cause!* (1970), *Le Paumé* (1971), *Le Drapeau Noir flotte sur le marmite* (1971).

Films as writer include: 1953: Les Trois Mousquetaires. 1955: Gas-Oil. 1956: Mort en fraude (co-s). 1957: Retour de Manivelle (di); Les Miserables (di). 1958: Maigret tend un piège (co-s). 1959: Les Grandes Familles (co-ad/di); Archimède, le clochard (co-ad/di); Babette s'en va-t-en guerre (di). 1960: La Française et l'amour ep L'Adultère (co-s). 1961: Un Taxi pour Tobrouk (co-s); Le Bâteau d'Emile. 1962: Melodie en sous sol.

AUGUST, Joseph H.

Cinematographer. 1890–1947 Hollywood
1911: began working in cinema. 1917– 22: worked on W. S. Hart westerns for Ince Productions. 1919: a founder and a charter member of American Society of Cinematographers. 1925: returned to Hart for *Tumbleweeds*. Other work mainly for Fox and RKO.

Films as cinematographer include: 1915: The Despoiler. 1916: Civilisation (co); The Aryan (co). 1917: The Silent Man. 1918: He Comes Up Smiling; Riddle Gawne; Branding Broadway; The Narrow Trail; Wolves of the Rail; Blue Blazes Rawden; Tiger Man; Selfish Yates; Shark Monroe; The Border Wireless. 1919: Breed of Men; The Poppy Girl's Husband; Money Corral; Square Deal Sanderson; Wagon Tracks; Sand! 1920: The Toll Gate; The Cradle of Courage. 1921: Three Word Brand; White Oak. 1923: Big Dan; The Man Who Won; Cupid's Fireman. 1924: The Vagabond Trail; Not a Drum Was Heard. 1925: Tumbleweeds; Lightnin'; The Fighting Heart; The Folly of Vanity. 1926: The Road to Glory; Fig Leaves. 1927: The Beloved Rogue; Two Arabian Knights (co). 1928: The Farmer's Daughter; Napoleon's Barber. 1929: Strong Boy; The Black Watch; Salute. 1930: Men Without Women (co); Born Reckless; Up the River; The Seas Beneath; The Brat. 1932: No More Orchids. 1933: Man's Castle; The Cocktail Hour. 1934: No Greater Glory; Twentieth Century; The Captain Hates the Sea. 1935: The Whole Town's Talking; The Informer. 1936: Sylvia Scarlett; Mary of Scotland. 1937: The Plough and the Stars; A Damsel in Distress; Fifty Roads to Town. 1939: The Hunchback of Notre Dame; Gunga Din. 1940: Primrose Path. 1941: All That Money Can Buy. 1945: They Were Expendable. 1949: Portrait of Jennie.

AUREL, Jean

Director. Paris 1925–
Studied architecture. Course at IDHEC; critic on Arts;

assistant to Augusto Genina. 1948: directed first short, *Joan Miró*. Many shorts including *Fêtes Galantes* (1950), *L'Affaire Manet* (1951), *Coeur d'amour épris* (1951), *Les Aventures Extraordinaires de Jules Verne* (1952), *L'Embarquement pour le ciel* (1953). Worked on scripts including *Porte des lilas* (1957) and *Le Trou* (1960). Features as director with Cecil Saint-Laurent as writer.

Films as director: 1962: 14–18. 1963: La Bataille de France (+co-s); De l'amour (+co-st). 1967: Lamiel (+co-s). 1968: Manon 70 (+ co-s/co-s co-di). 1969: Les Femmes (+co-ad). 1970: Etes-vous fiancée à un marin Grec ou à une pilote de ligne (+ co-s).

AURENCHE, Jean

Writer. Pierrelatte, France 1904–
Started work in a publicity agency with Jean Anouilh and Simone Signoret's father. Began in the cinema writing scripts for advertising shorts; worked on these with Marcel Carne as director (1930–32). 1936: first features as writer in collaboration with Jean Anouilh. 1945: wrote story for short *Le Voleur de paratonnerre*. Since 1943 has worked almost invariably with Pierre Bost (*q.v.* for list of collaborations); most of work has been literary adaptation.

Films as writer include: 1936: Vous n'avez rien a declarer? (co-di). 1942: Le Mariage de chiffon (co-s/di); Lettres d'amour (co-s/di). 1945: Sylvie et le fantôme (+di). 1957: Notre Dame de Paris (co-ad/co-di). 1961: Vive Henri IV . . . vive l'amour! (co-s). 1965: Le Journal d'une femme en blanc (co-s/co-di). 1966: Nouveau Journal d'une femme en blanc.

AURIC, Georges

Composer. Lodève, France 1899–
Pupil of Caussade at Paris Conservatoire and of d'Indy at the Scuola Cantorum. The youngest member of the Groupe des Six. 1930: first film score, for Jean Cocteau. Appeared in *Entr'acte* (1924).

Films as composer include: 1930: Le Sang d'un poète. 1932: A nous la liberte. 1937: Gribouille. 1938: Orage; Entree des artistes. 1939: Macao, l'enfer du jeu. 1943: L'Eternel Retour. 1945: Dead of Night; Caesar and Cleopatra. 1946: La Belle et la bête; La Symphonie Pastorale. 1947: Les Jeux sont faits. 1948: L'Aigle à deux têtes; It Always Rains on Sunday; Les Parents Terribles. 1949: Passport to Pimlico; Queen of Spades. 1950: Orphee. 1952: La P . . . Respectueuse. 1953: Roman Holiday; Moulin Rouge; Le Salaire de la peur. 1955: Lola Montès. 1956: Le Mystère Picasso. 1957: Celui qui doit mourir; Heaven Knows, Mr Allison. 1958: Bonjour Tristesse; Les Bijoutiers du clair de lune. 1961: Aimez-vous Brahms?; The Innocents. 1962: Le Rendez-vous de minuit. 1965: Thomas l'Imposteur. 1969: The Christmas Tree.

AURTHUR, Robert Alan

Writer. New York 1922–
University of Pennsylvania 1942–46: US .Marine Corps. Author of 'History of the 3rd Marine Division' (1946). 1946–50: short stories in New Yorker, Harpers, Esquire, Saturday Evening Post. 1951: novel, 'The Glorification of Al Toolum'. 1947–50: partner in Circle Records. 1951–58: freelance TV dramatist.

1961: vice-president Talent Associates – Paramount Ltd; president Edgwater Productions. 1956: first film as writer. 1969: first film as director.

Films as writer include: 1956: Edge of the City – A Man Is Ten Feet Tall (+ co-p). 1959: Warlock. 1963: Lilith (co-s). 1966: Grand Prix. 1969: The Lost Man (+ d).

AUTANT-LARA, Claude

Director. Luzarches, France 1903–
Schooling in Paris and London. Ecole des Beaux Arts, Paris. 1919: entered films as set designer on *Le Carnaval des vérités*. 1923: second assistant director on *Paris qui dort* and assistant director on *Le Voyage Imaginaire*; directed first film. 1923–27: directed, worked as art director, e.g. for Marcel L'Herbier, Jean Renoir, René Clair, and as assistant to Clair. 1930–32: in Hollywood directing French language versions of films for MGM, including 2 with Buster Keaton. 1936: directed *My Partner Mr Davis* in London. Short *Construire un feu* (1927) was first film made in Henri Chrétien's Hypergonar system, forerunner of CinemaScope.

Films as designer include: 1919: Le Carnaval des verités. 1920: L'Homme du large. 1921: Villa Destin. 1922: Don Juan et Faust. 1926: Nana. 1928: Le Diable au coeur.

Films as director: 1923: Fait Divers. 1926: Vittel. 1927: Construire un feu (r 1930). 1930: Buster se marie (*French version of* Spite Marriage). 1932: Le Plombier Amoureux (*French version of* The Passionate Plumber); L'Athlète Incomplet (*French version of* Love is a Racket); Le Gendarme est sans pitie; Un Client Sérieux; Monsieur Le Duc; La Peur des coups; Invite Monsieur à diner. 1933: Ciboulette (+ co-s). 1936: My Partner Mr Davis – The Mysterious Mr Davis. 1937: Le Ruisseau. 1939: Fric-Frac. 1942: Le Mariage de chiffon; Lettres d'amour. 1943: Douce. 1945: Sylvie et le fantôme. 1947: Le Diable au corps – Devil in the Flesh. 1949: Occupe-toi d'Amélie – Keep an Eye on Amelia. 1951: L'Auberge Rouge – The Red Inn; Les Sept Pechés Capitaux – The 7 Deadly Sins *ep* L'Orgueil. 1953: Le Bon Dieu sans confession (+ co-s); Le Rouge et le noir – Scarlet and Black; Le Ble en herbe – Ripening Seed (+ co-s). 1955: Marguérite de la nuit. 1956: La Traversee de Paris – Pig Across Paris. 1958: En Cas de malheur – Love is My Profession; Le Joueur. 1959: La Jument Verte – The Green Mare's Nest; Les Régates de San Francisco. 1960: Le Bois des amants – Between Love and Duty. 1961: Non uccidere (+ co-ad); Tu ne tueras point; Vive Henri IV . . . vive l'amour!; Le Comte de Monte-Cristo – The Story of the Count of Monte Cristo. 1962: Le Meurtrier – Enough Rope. 1963: Le Magot de Josefa. 1965: Le Journal d'une femme en blanc – A Woman in White. 1966: Nouveau Journal d'une femme en blanc. 1967: Le Plus Vieux Metier du monde *ep* Aujourd'hui. 1968: Le Franciscain de Bourges. 1969: Les Patates.

AUTRY, Gene

Actor and singer. Tioga, Texas 1907–
From 1930: wrote many songs starting with 'That Silver Haired Daddy of Mine', written in collaboration, and including 'Rudolph the Red-Nosed Reindeer' which won platinum record for sales of 2½ million. Radio performer from 1940 with 'Melody Ranch'. First film: *In Old Sante Fe* (1934), then 2 serials (1935). 1935–47: in almost 60 singing westerns produced by Republic, always playing himself and with horse Champion. 1942–45: pilot, then Flight Officer with Air Transport Command. 1946: formed own company, Gene Autry Productions, releasing over 30 films through Columbia (last in 1953). From 1950: TV films for own company, Flying A Pictures.

AVERY, Tex *or* Fred

Animator. Texas 1907–
1930–36: animator, then (1936) director for Walter Lantz at Universal. 1936–42: director for Leon Schlesinger at Warner. 1942–55: director for Fred Quimby at MGM. 1955–56: worked on 'Chilly Willy' series for Lantz at Universal. From 1956: commercials for Cascade of California.

Animated films as director (or supervisor†) include: 1936: I'd Love to Take Orders From You†; Porky the Rain Maker†; Porky the Wrestler†. 1937: Porky's Duck Hunt†; Daffy Duck and Egghead†. 1938: The Isle of Pingo Pongo; The Mice Will Play†. 1939: Dangerous Dan McGoo†; Detouring America†. 1940: A Wild Hare†. 1943: Dumb-hounded; Red Hot Riding Hood. 1944: Screwball Squirrel; Happy-Go-Nutty. 1945: The Screwy Truant; Swing Shift Cinderella; The Shooting of Dan McGoo. 1946: Hen Pecked Hoboes. 1947: Slap Happy Lion; King-Size Canary. 1948: Little Tinker; Half-Pint Pygmy; Lucky Ducky; The Cat That Hated People. 1949: Bad Luck Blackie; Little Rural Red Riding Hood; The Counterfeit Cat. 1950: Garden Gopher; The Cuckoo Clock. 1951: Symphony in Slang; Droopy's Good Deed; Droopy's Double Trouble. 1954: The Three Little Pups; Homesteader Droopy; Dixieland Droopy; Billy Boy; The Flea Circus; Drag-Along-Droopy. 1955: Deputy Droopy; I'm Cold; Chilly Willy in the Legend of Rockabye Point. 1956: Millionaire Droopy. 1957: Cat's Meow. 1958: Polar Pests.

AXELROD, George

Writer and director. New York 1922–
Began as assistant stage manager on production of 'Kind Lady' in New York. Some acting in summer stock. World War II: US Army Signal Corps. Then scriptwriter for radio and TV: over 400 scripts including hillbilly show 'Grand Ole Opry'. Novel, 'Beggar's Choice' (1947); sketches for theatre revue 'Small Wonder' (1948). First play 'The Seven Year Itch' (1952) ran for 1,141 performances in New York before going successfully on tour. 1954: went to Hollywood, scripted first film *Phffft* from own story. For next few years commuted between Hollywood and New York; directed several plays on Broadway including his own 'Will Success Spoil Rock Hunter?' (1955) and 'Goodbye Charlie' (1959), both filmed without his participation. Book, 'Where am I now – when I need me?' (1971).

Films as writer: 1954: Phffft. 1955: The Seven Year Itch (co-s). 1956: Bus Stop. 1961: Breakfast at Tiffany's. 1962: The Manchurian Candidate (+ co-p). 1963: Paris When It Sizzles (+ co-p). 1964: How to Murder Your Wife (+ p).

Films as director: 1966: Lord Love a Duck (+ p/co-s). 1968: The Secret Life of an American Wife (+ p/s).

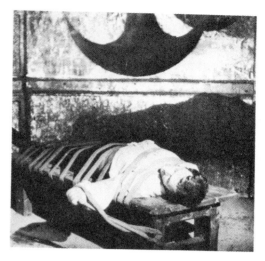

Le Puits et La Pendule. *directed by Alexandre Astruc.*
They Were Expendable. *directed by John Ford, photographed by Joseph H. August.*
Virgil Ross, Sid Sutherland, Tex Avery, Chuck Jones and Bob Clampett, at the door of "Termite Terrace.... in 1935".

AYRES, Lew

(Lewis Ayer) Actor. Minneapolis, Minnesota 1908–
University of Arizona. Played in college orchestra. Later toured with jazz band. 1929: first film, *The Sophomore*, for Pathé. 1936: directed *Hearts of Bondage*. Dr Kildare in MGM series, from *Young Dr Kildare* (1938) to *Dr Kildare's Victory* (1941). 1942: conscientious objector; volunteered for non-combatant medical service in World War II; served under fire in front lines in Pacific. 1947: narrated Frank Tashlin's *The Way of Peace*, made for the Lutheran Church. 1955: wrote, produced, narrated and financed religious film documentary, *Altars of the East*, also published as book (1956). 1957–60: on US National Committee for UNESCO. 1958: host on CBS-TV 'Frontier Justice'. Own TV show, 'Religions of the World'. Wives include (1933–40) Ginger Rogers.

Films as actor include: 1929: The Kiss. 1930: All Quiet on the Western Front; Common Clay. 1931: The Iron Man. 1933: State Fair. 1938: Holiday. 1948: Johnny Belinda. 1950: The Capture. 1962: Advise and Consent. 1964: The Carpetbaggers.

AZNAVOUR, Charles

(Aznavourian) Singer and actor. Paris 1924–
Armenian family came to Paris from Turkey and Russia in 1923. Stage debut reciting Oriental poems at 3. Left school at 11 to act and sing. 1942–50: worked with actor Pierre Roche; wrote songs for Edith Piaf and Maurice Chevalier. From 1950, solo singer. 1959: star billing at Alhambra, Paris, and first successful disc. 1956: first film.

Films as actor include: 1958: La Tête contre les murs. 1959: Les Dragueurs. 1960: Le Passage du Rhin; Le Testament d'Orphée; Tirez sur le pianiste. 1961: Un Taxi pour Tobrouk. 1963: Les Vierges. 1969: The Adventurers.

B

BACALL, Lauren

(Betty Joan Perske) Actress. New York 1924–
1941: American Academy of Dramatic Art. 1942: model and radio work; first New York stage appearance in walk-on part in 'Johnny 2 × 4'. Subsequent stage parts include Charlie in 'Goodbye Charlie' (1959). 1945: first film, *To Have and Have Not*. Some TV in 1955–56 and 1963. 1970: on Broadway in 'Applause', as Margo Channing (musical version of *All About Eve*, 1950). Husbands include (1945–57) Humphrey Bogart and (1961–69) Jason Robards Jr.

Films as actress include: 1945: Confidential Agent. 1946: The Big Sleep. 1947: Dark Passage. 1948: Key Largo. 1950: Young Man with a Horn; Bright Leaf. 1953: How to Marry a Millionaire. 1955: Blood Alley; The Cobweb. 1956: Written on the Wind. 1957: Designing Woman. 1963: Shock Treatment. 1964: Sex and the Single Girl. 1966: Harper.

BACHELET, Jean

Cinematographer. Azans, France 1894–
From 1912: newsreel photographer in Russia. 1924–39: cinematographer on many Jean Renoir films.

Films as cinematographer include: 1924: Une Vie sans joie (*co*); La Fille de l'eau (*co*). 1926: Nana (*co*). 1927: Charleston; Marquitta (*co*). 1928: La Petite Marchande d'allumettes; Tire-au-flanc. 1930: La Petite Lise. 1934: Madame Bovary. 1936: Le Crime de Monsieur Lange; Les Bas-fonds. 1938: Remontons les Champs Elysées. 1939: La Règle du jeu (*co*). 1941: Nous les gosses. 1952: La Vie d'un honnête homme.

BACON, Lloyd

Director. San Jose, California 1889–1955 Burbank, California
Son of stage actor Frank Bacon; commenced stage career at 2. After college worked in vaudeville, appeared on Broadway. Entered cinema as gagman and actor. Acted in several Chaplin films, e.g. *In the Park, The Jitney Elopement* (1915), *The Floorwalker, The Vagabond, The Fireman* (1916). War service in US Navy as officer. Acted in Triangle comedies. From 1921: directed 2-reelers for Mack Sennett; with Sennett until 1926. 1926–43: almost all films for Warners. 1928: directed the first dialogue film *The Singing Fool*. Directed several musicals with choreography by Busby Berkeley beginning with *42nd Street* (1933). 1944–54: worked mainly for Fox, including *Call Me Mister* (1951) with choreography by Busby Berkeley, only collaboration after 1936. Last 3 films for RKO.

Films as director since 1926: 1926: Finger Prints; Private Izzy Murphy; Broken Hearts of Hollywood. 1927: The Heart of Maryland; White Flannels; A Sailor's Sweetheart; Brass Knuckles. 1928: Pay as You Enter; The Lion and the Mouse; Women They Talk About; The Singing Fool. 1929: Stark Mad; No Defence; Honky Tonk; Say It With Songs; So Long Letty. 1930: She Couldn't Say No; The Other Tomorrow; A Notorious Affair; Moby Dick; Office Wife. 1931: Sit Tight; Kept Husbands; Fifty Milliion Frenchmen; Gold Dust Gertie; Honor of the Family. 1932: Fireman, Save My Child; Manhattan Parade; Famous Ferguson Case; Miss Pinkerton; You Said a Mouthful; Crooner. 1933: Picture Snatcher; Mary Stevens, M.D.; 42nd Street; Footlight Parade; Son of a Sailor. 1934: Wonder Bar; A Very Honorable Guy; 6 Day Bike Rider; He Was Her Man; Here Comes the Navy. 1935: Devil Dogs of the Air; In Caliente; Frisco Kid; The Irish in Us; Broadway Gondolier. 1936: Cain and Mabel; Gold Diggers of 1937; Sons O'Guns. 1937: Marked Woman; San Quentin; Submarine D-1; Ever Since Eve. 1938: A Slight Case of Murder; Cowboy from Brooklyn; Boy Meets Girl; Racket Busters. 1939: Wings of the Navy; Indianapolis Speedway; Espionage Agent; Invisible Stripes; A Child is Born; The Oklahoma Kid. 1940: Three Cheers for the Irish; Brother Orchid; Knute Rockne—All American. 1941: Honeymoon for Three; Footsteps in the Dark; Affectionately Yours; Navy Blues. 1942: Larceny, Inc; Wings for the Eagle; Silver Queen. 1943: Action in the North Atlantic. 1944: Sunday Dinner for a Soldier; The Sullivans. 1945: Captain Eddie. 1946: Wake Up and Dream; Home, Sweet Homicide. 1947: I Wonder Who's Kissing Her Now? 1948: You Were Meant for Me; Give My Regards to Broadway; An Innocent Affair – Don't Trust Your Husband. 1949: Mother is a Freshman – Mother Knows Best; It Happens Every Spring; Miss Grant Takes Richmond – Innocence is Bliss. 1950: The Good Humor Man; The Fuller Brush Girl – Affairs of Sally; Kill the Umpire. 1951: Call Me Mister; The Frogmen; Golden Girl. 1953: She Had to Say Yes – Beautiful but Dangerous; Walking My Baby Back Home; The French Line; The I Don't Care Girl. 1954: She Couldn't Say No.

BADAL, Jean *or* Janos

Cinematographer. Budapest 1927–
4 years at school of photography. Assistant cinematographer, cinematographer on shorts, then on some Hungarian features. Left Hungary during 1956 revolution; to France. Worked on dubbing and for French newsreels; did lighting for 'La Reine Verte' (made by Maurice Bejart for Belgian TV). 1960: first French feature as cinematographer, *Les Mauvais Coups*.

Films as cinematographer include: 1957: Bakaruhaban. 1962: Le Rendez-vous de minuit; Education Sentimentale 61. 1963: Un Roi sans divertissement. 1965: What's New, Pussycat? 1967: Playtime (*co*). 1970: La Promesse de l'aube. 1971: Les Assassins de l'ordre.

BADGER, Clarence G.

Director. San Francisco 1880–1964 Sydney, Australia
Actor, typographer and journalist before joining Mack Sennett studio as continuity writer (1915); directed Sennett's first 3-reeler. Worked for First National, Goldwyn, Metro, Famous Players, Paramount, Columbia. 1940: emigrated to Australia to direct a Zane Grey production which was abandoned before completion on Grey's death. Settled in Australia for retirement.

Films as director include: 1916: Haystacks and Steeples. 1918: The Floor Below. 1919: Jubilo; Sis Hopkins; Almost a Husband. 1921: An Unwilling Hero (+*p*); Boys Will Be Boys; Doubling for Romeo. 1922: Quincy Adams Sawyer. 1923: Potash and Perlmutter. 1926: Miss Brewster's Millions; The Rainmaker. 1927: A Kiss in a Taxi; It (+*co-p*); Señorita; Manpower. 1928: Red Hair; Three Weekends; Hot News. 1929: Paris (+*p*). 1930: No, No, Nanette; The Bad Man; Woman Hungry; Sweethearts and Wives; Murder Will Out. 1931: The Hot Heiress. 1933: When Strangers Marry. 1937: Rangle River

BAKER, Carroll

Actress. Johnstown, Pennsylvania 1931–
Ballerina in California at 16. 1953: New York stage debut in walk-on part. Some stage work – New York and summer stock. Studied at Actors' Studio. 1955: married Jack Garfein. First major film part: *Giant* (1956). 1962: on New York stage in 'Come on Strong'.

Films as actress include: 1953: Easy to Love. 1956: Baby Doll. 1958: The Big Country. 1961: Something Wild. 1962: How the West Was Won *ep* The Civil War. 1964: Station Six—Sahara; The Carpetbaggers; Cheyenne Autumn. 1965: The Greatest Story Ever

Told; Sylvia; Harlow. 1967: L'Harem. 1971: Captain Apache.

BAKER, Roy Ward

Director. London 1916–
1934: on leaving school joined Gainsborough Studios and within 4 years had moved from 3rd to 1st assistant director. 1st assistant on *The Lady Vanishes* (1938) and 3 Carol Reed pictures. 1940–43: infantry officer, then transferred to Army Kinematograph Service. 6 months as production manager then directed films for forces. 1947: first feature as director, for Two Cities. 1951–53: 4 films in Hollywood for Fox. Also directed for TV series, including many episodes of 'The Saint' and 'The Avengers'.

Features as director: 1947: The October Man. 1948: The Weaker Sex. 1949: Paper Orchid. 1950: Morning Departure – Operation Disaster; Highly Dangerous. 1951: The House in the Square – I'll Never Forget You. 1952: Don't Bother to Knock; Night Without Sleep. 1953: Inferno. 1955: Passage Home. 1956: Jacqueline; Tiger in the Smoke. 1957: The One That Got Away. 1958: A Night to Remember. 1961: The Singer Not the Song; Flame in the Streets. 1962: The Valiant. 1963: Two Left Feet (+ p). 1967: The Anniversary; Quatermass and the Pit – Five Million Miles to Earth. 1969: Moon Zero Two. 1970: The Vampire Lovers; The Scars of Dracula. 1971: Dr Jekyll and Sister Hyde.

BAKER, Stanley

Actor. Glamorgan, South Wales, 1928–
Spotted in school play for first film, *Undercover* (1943). Appeared on London stage and with Birmingham Repertory Company. 1946: National Service with Royal Army Service Corps. TV plays. Subsequent stage work included 'A Sleep of Prisoners', London (1951), New York and American tour. Formed Diamond Productions with Cy Endfield; co-produced and appeared in *Zulu* (1964) and *Sands of the Kalahari* (1965). Director of Harlech Television. Production company formed with Michael Deeley started with *Robbery* (1967).

Films as actor include: 1951: Captain Horatio Hornblower, RN. 1953: The Cruel Sea; Knights of the Round Table. 1955: Richard III. 1956: Helen of Troy; Alexander the Great. 1959: The Angry Hills; Blind Date. 1960: The Criminal. 1961: The Guns of Navarone. 1962: Sodom and Gomorrah; Eve. 1963: In the French Style. 1967: Accident. 1968: Where's Jack? (+ p). 1970: Perfect Friday.

BALABAN, Barney

Studio head. Chicago, Illinois 1887–1971 Byram, Connecticut
Western Union messenger, then chief clerk with the Western Cold Storage Company. 1908: entered film industry as part-owner of Kedzic Theatre, Chicago. Built up cinema chain; merger with that of Sam Katz resulted in one of the largest chains in Mid-West. 1925: Balaban and Katz joined Paramount. 1935: replaced Adolph Zukor as president of Paramount in reorganisation after 2 years of bankruptcy; president until 1962, then chairman of the board. Son was Burt Balaban, producer and writer (died 1965).

BALÁSZ, Béla

(Béla Balogh) Director. Szeged, Hungary 1885–1949 Prague, Czechoslovakia.
Poet and novelist. Librettist for Béla Bartok. 1915: began as director. After Hungarian Revolution in 1919, went to Austria then Germany. 1931: in collaboration with (both uncredited) Bertolt Brecht and Slatan Dudow, scripted *Die Dreigroschenoper*. 1932: scripted Leni Riefenstahl's *Das blaue Licht*. 1933–45: in Russia. Much work as writer and actor. Books include: 'Der sichtbare Mensch oder die Kultur des Films' (1924), 'Der Geist des Film' (1925), 'Film: Werden und Wesen einer neue Kunst' (1948).

Films as director include: 1915: Agyu es harang. 1916: Maki allast vallal; Elnémut harangok. 1917: Az elitélt; Lotti esredesi; Vengerkák; Obsitos; A Koldusgrof; A Pál-utcai fiuk. 1918: Itivatalnok urak; Rang és mód; Voios kérdojel; Halálos csönd; Sphynx; Aszonyfaló; Egyenloség; Csaszar katonai; Udvari levego. 1921: A Megfagyottgyermek. 1922: Fehér galambok Fekete varosban. 1924: Pal-utcai fiuk. 1932: Das blaue Licht. 1935: Edes mostoha. 1936: Havi 200 Fix. 1937: Urilany szobát keves. 1938: Azurexpress. 1939: Karoszék. 1940: Mária két ejsza kája. 1941: Ne kerdezd ki voltam. 1943: Opiumkeringo.

BALCON, Sir Michael

Producer. Birmingham, Warwickshire 1896–
Left school at 17. Apprentice in diamond-buying department of manufacturing jeweller. World War I: volunteered for service, but rejected because of eye defect. With Dunlop Rubber Company in Birmingham; after 2 years personal assistant to managing director. With Victor Saville set up distribution company, Victory Motion Pictures, in the Midlands. 1922: went into independent production in London with Saville and John Freedman; first film, *Woman to Woman* (directed by Graham Cutts). Formed Gainsborough Pictures with Cutts. Bought Islington Studios from Paramount. Produced series of films starring Ivor Novello, including Alfred Hitchcock's *The Lodger* (1926). From 1932: director of production at Shepherd's Bush and Islington Studios, making about 18 films a year for distribution through Gaumont British. Financed Robert Flaherty's *Man of Aran* (1934). 1937–38: in charge of British production for MGM, but made only one film, *A Yank at Oxford* (1938). From 1938: in charge of production at Ealing Studios. World War II: documentaries for the Ministry of Information as well as features. 1944–55: contract for distribution of Ealing Films through Rank; films included *Dead of Night* (1945), *The Overlanders* (1946) and Ealing comedies from *Hue and Cry* (1947) to *The Ladykillers* (1955). Ealing Studios sold to BBC TV. 1955–58: Ealing Films at MGM's British studios. 1959: formed independent company, Michael Balcon Productions. Subsequently chairman of Bryanston Films, and then of British Lion until 1965. Director of Border Television. Wrote autobiography, 'Michael Balcon Presents . . . A Lifetime of Films' (1969).

Films as producer include: 1923: The White Shadow. 1924: The Passionate Adventure. 1925: The Blackguard; The Prude's Fall (co); The Pleasure Garden. 1926: The Mountain Eagle. 1927: Downhill; Easy Virtue. 1933: The Good Companions; I Was a Spy.

Lauren Bacall in Douglas Sirk's Written on the Wind, *with Rock Hudson and Robert Stack.*
Education Sentimentale, *directed by Alexandre Astruc, photographed by Jean Badal.*
Quatermass and The Pit, *directed by Roy Baker.*

1934: The Man Who Knew Too Much; Little Friend. 1935: The Thirty-Nine Steps. 1936: Secret Agent; Sabotage; Tudor Rose. 1939: The Ware Case. 1941: The Big Blockade. 1942: Went the Day Well?; Next of Kin. 1943: Nine Men; San Demetrio, London; The Bells Go Down. 1944: Champagne Charlie. 1945: Painted Boats. 1946: The Captive Heart; The Overlanders. 1947: Frieda. 1948: It Always Rains on Sunday; Against the Wind; Scott of the Antarctic. 1949: Kind Hearts and Coronets; Passport to Pimlico; Whisky Galore; Eureka Stockade. 1950: The Blue Lamp. 1951: The Man in the White Suit; The Lavender Hill Mob; Where No Vultures Fly. 1952: Secret People; Mandy. 1953: The Cruel Sea. 1955: The Ladykillers. 1956: The Long Arm; Man in the Sky. 1958: Nowhere to Go. 1959: The Scapegoat.

BALDI, Gian Vittorio

Director. Bologna, Italy 1930–
Critic. Taught editing in film course at Rome University. 1949–61: producer of historical films for Italian TV; secretary of TV directors' association. 1957: acted in Renato Castellani's *I Sogni nel Cassetto*. From 1958: directed shorts. 1960: short *Luciano*, (*via dei capellari*), early version of material which became first feature *Luciano* (1962). 1961: supervised by Cesare Zavattini directed an episode of *Le Italiane e l'amore*. Production company IDI Cinematografica co-produced *Chronik der Anna Magdalena Bach* (1967), *Trio* (1967), *Porcile* (1969) and own *Fuoco!* (1968). Also producer on films for RAI-TV.

Films as director: 1958: Il Pianto delle zitelle. 1959: La Vigilia di mezza estate; Via dei cessati spiriti. 1960: Luciano (*via dei capellari*); La Casa delle vedove – The Widow's Home Ritratto di pina. 1961: Il Bar di Gigi; Il Corredo di sposa; Le Italiane e l'amore – Latin Lovers *ep* La Prova d'amore – Proof of Love. 1962: Luciano (+*co-s*). 1965: La Fleur de l'age ou les Adolescentes *ep* Fiametta (+*s*). 1968: Fuoco! – Fire (+*co-p/s*).

BALL, Lucille

Actress. Jamestown, New York 1911–
Drama school. Chorus of road show, 'Rio Rita'. Career in modelling, interrupted for 4 years after skating accident. Columbia contract for 6 months, but first film for Goldwyn: in chorus of *Roman Scandals* (1933). 1935: RKO contract. 1937: some stage work; first radio performance. 1942–47: MGM contract. 1940–60: married to Desi Arnaz; together formed Desilu Productions (1950), which became one of the largest producers of TV series; co-starred in TV series 'I Love Lucy' (1951–57). 1962: Bought Arnaz out of Desilu. Subsequent TV includes 'Lucille Ball Comedy Hour' (1964) and 'The Lucy Show' with her 2 children. 1968: sold Desilu to Gulf and Western for $17 million. Occasional Broadway plays.

Films as actress include: 1934: Broadway Bill. 1935: Top Hat. 1936: Winterset. 1937: Stage Door. 1942: The Big Street. 1943: Thousands Cheer. 1946: Ziegfeld Follies; The Dark Corner. 1947: Lured. 1949: Miss Grant Takes Richmond; Easy Living. 1950: The Fuller Brush Girl. 1954: The Long, Long Trailer. 1960: The Facts of Life. 1963: Critic's Choice.

BALLARD, Lucien

Cinematographer. Miami, Florida 1908–
Universities of Oklahoma and Pennsylvania. 5 years at Paramount as assistant on camera, cutting and direction, then camera operator. 1935: associate cinematographer to Josef Von Sternberg on *The Devil Is a Woman*; to Columbia with him as cinematographer on *Crime and Punishment*. Married Merle Oberon (1945–49).

Films as cinematographer include: 1936: The King Steps Out. 1939: Let Us Live. 1941: Wild Geese Calling. 1942: The Undying Monster. 1943: Tonight We Raid Calais; Holy Matrimony. 1944: The Lodger. 1945: This Love of Ours. 1947: Night Song. 1948: Berlin Express. 1951: Fixed Bayonets. 1952: Diplomatic Courier. 1954: Prince Valiant; The Raid. 1955: The Magnificent Matador. 1956: A Kiss Before Dying; The King and Four Queens; The Killing. 1957: Band of Angels. 1958: Buchanan Rides Alone; Murder by Contract. 1959: Al Capone; City of Fear. 1960: The Rise and Fall of Legs Diamond; Pay or Die. 1961: Marines Let's Go. 1962: Ride the High Country. 1963: Wall of Noise. 1965: The Sons of Katie Elder. 1966: Nevada Smith. 1967: Hour of the Gun. 1968: The Party. 1969: The Wild Bunch. 1970: That's the Way It Is; The Ballad of Cable Hogue. 1971: Arruza.

BANCROFT, Anne

(Anna Maria Luisa Italiano) Actress. New York 1931–
American Academy of Dramatic Art and Actors' Studio (member since 1958). From 1950, appeared in TV plays and serial. Contract with Fox. First film, *Don't Bother to Knock* (1952). On Broadway in 'Two for the See-Saw' (1958) and 'The Miracle Worker' (1959). Oscar as Best Actress for *The Miracle Worker* (1962). Played Mother Courage on Broadway (1963).

Films as actress include: 1954: Demetrius and the Gladiators. 1956: The Last Frontier; Nightfall. 1957: The Restless Breed. 1962: The Miracle Worker. 1964: The Pumpkin Eater. 1966: Seven Women. 1967: The Graduate.

BANCROFT, George

Actor. Philadelphia, Pennsylvania 1882–1956 Hollywood
US Naval Academy. Successful actor on New York stage before first film (1922). 1923: married stage actress Octavia Brooke. 1925–33: contract actor at Paramount. 1933: *Blood Money* for 20th Century Fox (released by United Artists); then some stage parts. Retired in 1940s.

Films as actor include: 1925: The Pony Express. 1926: Sea Horses. 1927: Underworld. 1928: The Docks of New York; The Dragnet. 1929: Thunderbolt. 1930: Paramount on Parade. 1931: Scandal Sheet. 1932: The World and the Flesh. 1936: Mr Deeds Goes to Town. 1938: Angels With Dirty Faces; Submarine Patrol. 1939: Each Dawn I Die; Stagecoach; Green Hell. 1940: Young Tom Edison; Northwest Mounted Police. 1941: Texas. 1942: Syncopation.

BANKHEAD, Tallulah

Stage actress. Huntsville, Alabama 1903–1968 New York

Family was in Alabama politics. Convent school. Won beauty contest; began acting on stage; occasional films from 1918. 1923–30: in UK. 1930: to Hollywood on contract to Paramount and MGM until 1932. No more films until 1944. Own TV show.

Films as actress include: 1918: When Men Betray; Thirty a Week. 1928: His House in Order. 1931: The Cheat; Tarnished Lady. 1932: The Devil and the Deep; Thunder Below; Faithless. 1944: Lifeboat. 1945: A Royal Scandal. 1953: Main Street to Broadway. 1964: Fanatic.

BANKY, Vilma

(Vilma Loncit) Actress. Budapest 1903–
Appeared in European silent films including *Quo Vadis?* (1925). Brought to Hollywood by Samuel Goldwyn. First American film: *The Dark Angel* (1925). With Valentino in *The Eagle* (1925) and *The Son of the Sheik* (1926); a number of films with Ronald Colman. Few sound films. Hungarian accent ended career in early 1930s. 1927: married actor Rod LaRocque.

Films as actress include: 1926: The Winning of Barbara Worth. 1927: The Night of Love; The Magic Flame. 1928: Two Lovers; The Awakening. 1930: A Lady to Love.

BARA, Theda

(Theodosia Goodman) Actress. Cincinnati, Ohio 1890–1955 Los Angeles
Began in films as an extra. Became famous with first major part, as a 'vampire' in *A Fool There Was* (1915). Fox contract. 1919: left Hollywood for New York stage. 1926: screen come-back in *Madame Mystery* followed by other Hal Roach comedies, burlesquing former 'vamp' image. Retired soon afterwards. Married director Charles Brabin.

Films as actress include: 1915: Carmen. 1916: Romeo and Juliet; Under Two Flags. 1917: Camille. 1918: Salome. 1919: The Siren's Song.

BARATIER, Jacques

Director. Montpellier, France 1918–
Studied law. Journalist, theatre critic. Worked in radio. Started in films as assistant director. 1948–55: directed shorts; *Pablo Casals* for US TV.

Films as director: 1949: Les Filles du soleil; Désordre. 1951: La Cité du midi – Flying Trapeze. 1952: La Vie du vide. 1953: Métier de danseur. 1954: Chevalier de Menilmontant; Histoire du palais idéal. 1955: Pablo Casals. 1956: Paris la nuit (*co-d Jean Valère*). 1958: Goha. 1962: La Poupee – He, She or It? (+*p*). 1963: Dragées au poivre – Sweet and Sour (+*co-st*). 1964: Eves Futures. 1965: L'Or du Duc (+*co-st*). 1967: Desordre à vingt ans – Eden Miseria – Disorder is Twenty Years Old (*incorporates* Desordre, *1949*). 1970: Piège.

BARBARO, Umberto

Critic and director. Acireale, Sicily 1902–1959 Rome
Founder and editor of magazine Bianco e Nero; first three volumes contain his critical debate with Luigi

Chiarini. 1943: used term 'neo-realism' for first time in Neo-Realist Manifesto published in Cinema. Taught at Centro Sperimentale di Cinematografica for 7 years (1936–43); became its director in 1946. Also taught at Lodz Film School and Warsaw Institute of Film. Translated Pudovkin, Eisenstein and Béla Balász into Italian. Books include 'Film: Soggetto e sceneggiatura' (1939), 'Il Film e il risarcimento marxista dell'arte' (1960), 'Servitù e grandezza del cinema' (1962). From 1934 collaborated on some scripts, including Giuseppe De Santis's *Caccia Tragica* (1947). Director or co-director of 3 shorts; directed feature *L'Ultima Nemica* (1937).

Films as director: 1933: I Cantieri dell'Adriatico. 1937: L'Ultima Nemica. 1947: Carpaccio (*co-d R. Longhi*). 1948: Caravaggio (*co-d R. Longhi*).

BARBERA, Joseph

Animator and producer. New York 1911–
American Institute of Banking. Magazine cartoonist. Sketch artist for Van Beuren Associates. 1932: writer on 'Tom and Jerry' series for Van Beuren Studio. From 1937: animator and writer at MGM. 1940: first film for Fred Quimby at MGM, *Gallopin' Gals,* in collaboration with William Hanna (*q.v.*).

BARDEM, Juan Antonio

Director. Madrid 1922–
Parents are actors who have appeared in some of his films. Unsuccessful actor, then agricultural student. Studied cinema at the Instituto de Investigaciones Cinematograficas, met Luis Garcia Berlanga there. 1949–50: made 2 16mm shorts, one with Berlanga. With Berlanga wrote scripts, some filmed by other directors, before co-directing first film (1951). 1952: writer in collaboration and 2nd-unit director on Berlanga's *Bienvenido, Mister Marshall.* Founded film magazine Objectivo (1953), banned by government after 9 issues (1955). President of ASDREC, Spanish directors' syndicate.

Films as director and writer: 1949: Paseo sobre una guerra antigua (*co-s; co-d Luis Garcia Berlanga*). 1950: Barajas, Aeropuerto Internacional – Aeropuerto. 1951: Esa pareja feliz (*r 1953; +co-s; co-d Luis Garcia Berlanga*). 1953: Novio a la vista (*co-d only; co-d Luis Garcia Berlanga*). 1954: Cómicos; Felices Pascuas (*co-s*). 1955: Muerte de un ciclista – Death of a Cyclist. 1956: Calle Mayor – Grand Rue (*co-s*). 1957: La Muerte de Pio Baroja (*ur; d only*). 1958: La Venganza – Vengeance. 1959: Sonatas (*d only*). 1960: A las cinco de la tarde – At Five O'Clock in the Afternoon (*co-s*). 1962: Los Inocentes (*co-s*). 1963: Nunca pasa nada – Nothing Ever Happens (*co-s*). 1965: Les Pianos Mecaniques – The Uninhibited.

BARDOT, Brigitte

(Camille Javal) Actress. Paris 1934–
Father industrialist. In early teens modelled girls' clothes for family friends. 1952: first film, *Le Trou Normand*; married Roger Vadim, then on Paris Match. Later husbands: actor Jacques Charrier and German industrialist Gunther Sachs. Records and TV.

Films as actress include: 1955: Les Grandes Manœuvres; La Lumière d'en face; Cette Sacree Gamine.

1956: Helen of Troy; En effeuillant la marguerite; Et Dieu . . . créa la femme. 1958: Les Bijoutiers du clair de lune; En cas de malheur. 1960: La Vérite. 1962: Vie Privee; Le Repos du guerrier. 1963: Le Mépris; Une Ravissante Idiote. 1965: Viva Maria! 1967: A coeur joie; Histoires Extraordinaires *ep* William Wilson. 1968: Shalako. 1969: Les Femmes; L'Ours et la poupée. 1971: Boulevard du Rhum; Les Petroleuses.

BARNES, George

Cinematographer. 1893–1953
Began in films with Thomas H. Ince Productions (until 1921). Then with various companies, notably Goldwyn and other independents in late 1920s and early 1930s. 1933–38: with Warners and First National. Last films were for Cecil B. De Mille and Paramount. Married 7 times; wives included Joan Blondell (1932–35).

Films as cinematographer include: 1919: The Haunted Bedroom. 1922: Conquering the Woman; Woman, Wake Up; The Real Adventure; Dusk to Dawn. 1923: Alice Adams; Peg O' My Heart. 1925: The Eagle (*co*). 1928: The Awakening; Sadie Thompson (*co*). 1931: Street Scene. 1935: Gold Diggers of 1935. 1937: Hollywood Hotel (*co*). 1939: Jesse James. 1940: The Return of Frank James (*co*); Rebecca. 1941: Meet John Doe; That Uncertain Feeling. 1944: Frenchman's Creek; None But the Lonely Heart. 1945: The Bells of St Mary's; The Spanish Main; Spellbound. 1946: Sister Kenny. 1948: Good Sam; Force of Evil. 1949: Samson and Delilah. 1952: The Greatest Show on Earth (*co*). 1953: War of the Worlds.

BARNET, Boris

Director. Moscow 1902–1965
Moscow School of Art and Architecture. 1919: volunteered for Red Army. Boxer, then member of Lev Kuleshov's workshop. 1924: along with almost all members of workshop took part in making of *Neobychainiye Priklucheniya Mistera Vesta v stranye Bolshevikov*; acted in it and in *Shakhmatnaya Goryachka.* 1926: collaborated with Fedor Otsep on direction and script of serial *Miss Mend*; also acted in it. 1927: directed Anna Sten in *Devushka s korobkoi*; made *Moskva v Oktyabre* for anniversary of Revolution with co-operation of surviving leaders and designs by Alexander Rodchenko. 1928: acted in *Potomok Chingis-Khan.* 1929: acted in Otsep's *Zhivoi Trup.* 1929–30: 3 shorts on popular science subjects. To 1936: worked mainly for Mezhrabpom-Russ, then for several studios. 1941–42: shorts in 'Fighting Film Albums'. 1965: committed suicide.

Films as director: 1926: Miss Mend (*+ co-s/w; co-d Fedor Otsep*). 1927: Devushka s korobkoi – The Girl With the Hat Box; Moskva v Oktyabre – Moscow in October (*+w*). 1928: Dom na Trubnoi – The House on Trubnaya Square. 1931: Ledolom – Thaw. 1933: Okraina – Patriots (*+co-s*). 1936: U samova sinevo morya – By the Bluest of Seas (*co-d S. Mardonov*). 1939: Noch v Sentyabre – A Night in September (*+ w*). 1940: Staryi Nayezhdnik – The Old Jockey (*r 1959*). 1945: Odnazhdi Noch – One Night (*+w*). 1947: Podvig razvedchika – The Scout's Exploits (*+ w*). 1948: Stranitsy zhizn – Pages of Life (*co-d A. Macheret*). 1951: Schedroye Leto – Bountiful Summer. 1952: Kontsert masterov Ukrainskovo iskusstva – Concert of the Masters of Ukrainian Art (*+s*). 1955:

Crime and Punishment, *directed by Josef Von Sternberg, photographed by Lucien Ballard.*
Tallulah Bankhead and John Hodiak in Hitchcock's Lifeboat.
Brigitte Bardot in Le Repos du guerrier *directed by Roger Vadim.*

Liana (+*co-s*). 1957: Poet; Borets i kloun – The Wrestler and the Clown (*co-d K. Yudin*). 1959: Annushka. 1961: Alenka. 1963: Polustanok – Whistle Stop (+ *co-s*).

BARRAULT, Jean-Louis

Actor-manager. Vésinet, France 1910–
From 1930: assistant teacher at Collège Chaptal; studied history of art at Louvre school. Worked for 4 years with Charles Dullin at Théâtre de L'Atelier, starting to direct (1935) with 'Autour d'une mère', his adaptation of William Faulkner's 'As I Lay Dying'. Developed own interpretation of traditional mime (*mimodrame*). 1940: joined Comédie Française as actor and director. 1946: to Theatre Marigny as co-director with wife, Madeleine Renaud; formed company with her. 1959–68: director of Théâtre de l'Odéon. First film as actor *Les Beaux Jours* (1935). 1970: adapted writings of Alfred Jarry for stage show 'Jarry sur la butte': staged it, acted in it.

Films as actor include: 1936: Mademoiselle Docteur; Un Grand Amour de Beethoven. 1937: Drôle de drame; Les Perles de la couronne; Orage. 1941: Parade en sept nuits; Le Destin Fabuleux de Désirée Clary. 1942: La Symphonie Fantastique. 1945: Les Enfants du paradis. 1950: La Ronde. 1954: Si Versailles m'était conté. 1960: Le Dialogue des Carmélites. 1961: Le Testament du Docteur Cordelier. 1962: The Longest Day.

BARRETO, Victor Lima

Director. Sao Paulo, Brazil 1905–
Expelled from seminary. Mackenzie College, Araraquara. Actor, writer, photographer, journalist. 1936: first short film as director *Carnaval Paulista*. 1953: wrote and directed first feature. Member of board of Vera Cruz production company. 1969: wrote story and co-scripted Anselmo Duarte's *Quelé do Pajeú*.

Short films as director include: 1951: Painel. 1952: Santuário. 1954: O Sertanejo; Sao Paulo en Festa (*uf*); Arte Coboda; O Livro.

Features as director: 1953: O Cangaceiro – The Bandit (+*st/s/w*). 1961: A Primeira Missa – The First Mass (+*st/s/w*).

BARRY, John

Composer. York, England 1933–
In teens worked as a projectionist in cinema chain owned by father. At 19, played trumpet with regimental army band stationed at Cyprus. Studied music under Dr Francis Jackson of York Minster; correspondence course with Bill Russo. 1958: formed John Barry Seven, backing group to Adam Faith for 5 years; it also recorded separately. First film score *Beat Girl* (1959). Also music for stage, e.g. music for 'Lolita My Love' (1971), TV and commercials. Oscar for best original score *The Lion in Winter* (1968). Was married to actress Jane Birkin.

Films as composer include: 1960: Never Let Go. 1962: The L-Shaped Room. 1963: From Russia With Love; Zulu. 1964: Goldfinger; Séance on a Wet Afternoon. 1965: The Knack – and How to Get It; Thunderball; The Ipcress File; 4 in the Morning. 1966: The Whisperers; The Chase; The Quiller Memorandum. 1967: You Only Live Twice. 1968: Petulia; Boom. 1969: The Appointment; Midnight Cowboy. 1970: Monte Walsh. 1971: The Last Valley; Walkabout; Diamonds are Forever; Murphy's War.

BARRYMORE, Ethel

(Ethel Blythe) Actress. Philadelphia, Pennsylvania 1879–1959 Beverly Hills, California
Sister of John and Lionel Barrymore. Convent education in Philadelphia. Stage debut at 15. 1914: first film. Only one film between 1919 and 1944. Oscar as supporting actress for *None But the Lonely Heart* (1944). Autobiography 'Memories' (1953).

Films as actress: 1914: The Nightingale. 1917: The White Raven. 1919: The Divorcee. 1933: Rasputin and the Empress. 1944: None But the Lonely Heart. 1945: The Spiral Staircase. 1947: The Farmer's Daughter; Moss Rose; Night Song. 1948: The Paradine Case; Moonrise. 1949: Portrait of Jennie; The Great Sinner; That Midnight Kiss; Pinky; The Red Danube. 1951: Kind Lady; The Secret of Convict Lake; It's a Big Country. 1952: Just For You; Deadline–USA. 1953: The Story of Three Loves *ep* Mademoiselle; Main Street to Broadway. 1954: Young at Heart. 1957: Johnny Trouble.

BARRYMORE, John

(John Blythe) Actor. Philadelphia, Pennsylvania 1882–1942 Hollywood
Brother of Ethel and Lionel Barrymore. Studied art in London and New York. 1903: began as stage actor. 1913: first film, *An American Citizen*. 1933: Technicolor tests of 'Hamlet' soliloquies (preserved incomplete in Museum of Modern Art). Married 4 times; third wife (1928–35) was actress Dolores Costello. Children: actress Diana Barrymore (1922–60), actor John Drew Barrymore (born 1932).

Films as actor include: 1920: Dr Jekyll and Mr Hyde. 1924: Beau Brummel. 1926: Don Juan. 1927: The Beloved Rogue; Tempest. 1929: Eternal Love. 1930: Moby Dick. 1931: Svengali; The Mad Genius. 1932: Arsène Lupin; Grand Hotel; A Bill of Divorcement. 1933: Rasputin and the Empress; Dinner at Eight. 1934: Long Lost Father; Twentieth Century. 1936: Romeo and Juliet. 1937: Maytime. 1939: The Great Man Votes; Midnight.

BARRYMORE, Lionel

(Lionel Blythe) Actor. Philadelphia, Pennsylvania 1878–1954 Chatsworth, California
Brother of Ethel and John Barrymore. Educated in New York, then joined touring stock company as actor. Studied painting in Paris for 3 years. 1909: began in films with D. W. Griffith for whom he also wrote scripts, e.g. *The Tender-Hearted Boy* (1913). Gave up stage in late 1920s. 1929–31: directed films. 1938–45: Dr Gillespie in MGM series, from *Young Dr Kildare* (1938) and continuing after departure of Lew Ayres with *Calling Dr Gillespie* (1942), *Dr Gillespie's New Assistant* (1942) and *Dr Gillespie's Criminal Case* (1943). From early 1940s, continued acting although confined to wheelchair. Also pianist, composer, etcher. Wrote autobiography 'We Barrymores' and novel 'Mr Cantomwine'. Oscar (1930–31) as Best Actor for *A Free Soul*.

Films as actor include: 1912: Friends. 1924: Decameron Nights; America. 1925: Die Frau mit dem schlechten Ruf. 1927: Body and Soul. 1928: Drums of Love; Sadie Thompson. 1932: Mata Hari; Arsène Lupin; Grand Hotel; Rasputin and the Empress. 1933: Dinner at Eight. 1934: Treasure Island. 1935: The Personal History, Adventures, Experience and Observations of David Copperfield, the Younger; The Return of Peter Grimm. 1936: The Road to Glory; Camille. 1937: Captains Courageous. 1938: A Yank at Oxford; Young Dr Kildare. 1939: On Borrowed Time. 1944: A Guy Named Joe. 1946: Duel in the Sun. 1947: It's a Wonderful Life. 1948: Key Largo. 1951: Bannerline; Lone Star. 1953: Main Street to Broadway.

Films as director: 1929: Madame X; The Unholy Night; The Green Ghost. 1930: His Glorious Night (+*p/m*); The Rogue Song (+*p*). 1931: Ten Cents a Dance.

BARTHELMESS, Richard

Actor. New York 1895–1963 New York
Mother was actress. Began as film extra. First part in *War Brides* (1916). Notably in D. W. Griffith films including *Broken Blossoms* (1919), *Way Down East* (1920). Bought rights to *Tol'able David* and made it for own production company, Inspiration Pictures, which continued for some years. Retired in 1941 after appearing in 76 films. Last was *The Spoilers* (1942).

Films as actor include: 1921: Tol'able David. 1928: Wheel of Chance. 1930: The Dawn Patrol. 1931: The Last Flight. 1932: The Cabin in the Cotton. 1934: Massacre; A Modern Hero. 1939: Only Angels Have Wings.

BARTHOLOMEW, Freddie

Actor. London 1924–
Brought up in UK. 1935: on holiday in New York spotted by MGM for first film *The Personal History, Adventures, Experience and Observations of David Copperfield, The Younger*. MGM contract. Became US citizen. Vaudeville and summer stock; nightclubs in Australia. 1949: returned to USA. Last film: *St Benny the Dip* (1951). TV: stage manager, director, executive.

Films as actor include: 1935: Anna Karenina. 1936: Little Lord Fauntleroy; Lloyd's of London; The Devil is a Sissy. 1937: Captains Courageous. 1938: Lord Jeff. 1940: Tom Brown's Schooldays. 1942: A Yank at Eton.

BARTOSCH, Berthold

Painter and architect. Bohemia 1883–1968 Paris
1929: moved to Paris and lodged in attic of Vieux Colombier Theatre until death. 1931: made only film, *L'Idée* entirely by himself. Arthur Honegger composed score. Film was banned in UK for anti-clerical and communist tendencies.

BARZMAN, Ben

Writer. Toronto, Canada 1911–
Reed College (graduated 1932) until 1939. Journalist in British Columbia. Wrote novels e.g. 'Twinkle, Twinkle Little Star' and musical revues: 'Labor

Pains', 'Horrorscope', 'Meet the People', 'Laugh at Troubles'. 1942: writer in Hollywood. 1949: to UK, blacklisted; thereafter worked in Europe, at first pseudonymously.

Films as writer include: 1942: True to Life. 1948: The Boy With Green Hair (*co*). 1949: Give Us This Day. 1952: Stranger on the Prowl (*ps Andrea Forzano*). 1956: Celui qui doit mourir. 1957: Time Without Pity. 1959: Blind Date (*co*). 1961: The Damned (*co*). 1963: The Visit; The Fall of the Roman Empire (*co*). 1965: The Heroes of Telemark (*co*). 1966: The Blue Max.

BASS, Saul

Graphic designer. New York 1920–
1936–40: studied at Art Students League, then Brooklyn College. From 1932, worked as designer and commercial artist, on posters and other publicity work. 1955: first film title design, for Otto Preminger; pioneered use of over-all graphic style for credits, posters, letter-headings, publicity material, etc. Many commercials and sponsored shorts for TV; also animated sequence for TV. Own films are sponsored documentaries.

Films as director include: 1963: The Searching Eye. 1964: From Here to There. 1968: Why Man Creates.

Films as designer of credits: 1954: Carmen Jones. 1955: The Man With the Golden Arm; The Shrike; The Big Knife; The Seven Year Itch; The Racers. 1956: Storm Center; Edge of the City; Around the World in 80 Days. 1957: Saint Joan; The Pride and the Passion. 1958: Bonjour Tristesse; Cowboy; The Big Country; Vertigo. 1959: Anatomy of a Murder; North by North West. 1960: Exodus; Psycho (+ *visual consultant*); Spartacus (+ *visual consultant*); Ocean's 11; The Facts of Life. 1961: West Side Story (+ *visual consultant*); Something Wild. 1962: Advise and Consent; Walk on the Wild Side; The Victors (+ *prologue*). 1963: Nine Hours to Rama; The Cardinal; It's a Mad, Mad, Mad, Mad World. 1964: In Harm's Way. 1965: Bunny Lake is Missing. 1966: Seconds; Not With My Wife, You Don't (+ *animation sequences*); Grand Prix (+ *visual consultant/editor of racing sequences*).

BATALOV, Alexei

Director and actor. Russia 1928–
Nephew of actor Nikolai Batalov. Theatrical family; brought up in a flat in Moscow Arts Theatre, both parents members of company. During World War II, painter and decorator at theatre. 1944: first film as actor *Zoya*. 1950: graduated from Moscow Arts Theatre Studio. 1950–53: Soviet Army Theatre. 1954: second film as actor *Bolchaya Semya*. Moscow Arts Theatre. 1956: played part in Marc Donskoy's *Mat* which uncle played in Vsovolod Pudovkin's version (1926). 1959: first film as director, short for Lenfilm.

Films as director: 1959: Shinel – The Overcoat. 1966: Tri Tolstyaka – The Three Fat Men (+ *co-s/w*; *co-d Iosif Shapiro*).

Films as actor include: 1954: Bolshaya Semya. 1956: Mat. 1957: Letyat zhuravli. 1958: Dorogoi Moi Chelovek. 1960: Dama s sobachkoi. 1961: Devyat Dni odnogo goda. 1964: Den schastya.

BATCHELOR, Joy

Animator. London 1914–
From 1940: co-producer and director with Halas and Batchelor Cartoon Films. *See* John Halas.

BAVA, Mario

Director and cinematographer. San Remo, Italy 1914–
Father sculptor. Entered films as camera assistant, became operator, then cinematographer. 1946–50: directed and photographed shorts. 1959: first work as director in features, uncredited collaboration on *La Battaglia di Maratona*. 1960: first solo feature as director *La Maschera del demonio*. 1961: directed 2nd-unit on *Le Meraviglie di Aladino*. Photographed several of his early features as director. Pseudonyms: John Foam, Marie Foam, John M. Old.

Films as cinematographer include: 1939: Il Tacchino Prepotente. 1943: Uomini e cieli. 1949: Quel Bandito sono io. 1950: E'arrivato il cavaliere; Vita da cani. 1951: Guardie e ladri. 1953: Gli Eroi della domenica; Viale della speranza. 1954: Terza liceo; Cose da pazzi (*co*). 1955: La Donna Più Bella del mondo. 1956: Mio Figlio Nerone; I Vampiri. 1958: Agi Murad il diavolo bianco; Caltiki il mostro immortale. 1960: Esther and the King.

Films as director and cinematographer: 1946: L'Orrechio. 1947: Santa Notte; Legenda Sinfonica (*co-d M. Melani*). 1949: Variazioni Sinfoniche. 1950: L'Amore nell'arte (*d* only). 1959: La Battaglia di Maratona (*uc, co-d Jacques Tourneur, Bruno Vailati, uc*). 1960: La Maschera del demonio – Black Sunday; Mask of the Demon – Revenge of the Vampire (+ *co-s*). 1961: Ercole al centro della terra – Hercules in the Centre of the Earth (+ *co-s*). 1961: Gli Invasori – Erik the Conqueror – Fury of the Vikings (+ *co-s*). 1962: La Ragazza che sapeva troppo – The Evil Eye (+ *co-s; co-c*).

Films as director: 1963: I Tre Volti della paura – Black Sabbath (+ *co-s*). La Frusta e il corpo – Night is the Phantom; Seddok, Son of Satan – Atom Age Vampire (+ *p*). 1964: Sei Donne per l'assassino – Blood and Black Lace (+ *co-s*); La Strada per Fort Alamo. 1965: Terrore nello spazio – Planet of Blood – Planet of Vampires; Raffica di cotelli. 1966: Dr Goldfoot and the Girl Bombs; Dr G and the Love Bombs – I Due Mafiosi dell FBI – Le Spie vengone dal semifreddo; Operazione paura – Curse of the Dead (+ *co-s*). 1967: Diabolik – Danger: Diabolik (+ *co-s*). 1970: Cinque Bambole per la luna di Agosto – Five Dolls for an jaugust Moon; Roy Colt and Winchester Jack; Un Hacha para la luna de miel.

BAXTER, Anne

Actress. Michigan City, Indiana 1923–
Drama schools in New York from 11. 1937–40: studied under Maria Ouspenskaya. 1936: New York stage debut. Until 1939: on Broadway and in summer stock. 1940: first film; Fox studio school; Fox contract until 1952. Considerable TV work. 1971: in Moss Hart's 'Light Up the Sky' in Hollywood. 1946–53: married to actor John Hodiak. Oscar as supporting actress for *The Razor's Edge* (1946).

Richard Barthelmess and Douglas Fairbanks in The Dawn Patrol *directed by Howard Hawks.*
The Fall of the Roman Empire, *directed by Anthony Mann, co-scripted by Ben Barzman.*
The Beatles in Help! *directed by Richard Lester.*

Films as actress include: 1941: Charley's Aunt; Swamp Water. 1942: The Magnificent Ambersons. 1943: Five Graves to Cairo; The North Star. 1945: A Royal Scandal. 1948: The Walls of Jericho; Yellow Sky. 1950: All About Eve. 1952: The Outcasts of Poker Flat; O. Henry's Full House *ep* The Last Leaf. 1953: I Confess; The Blue Gardenia. 1956: The Ten Commandments. 1957: Three Violent People. 1960: Cimarron. 1962: Walk on the Wild Side. 1965: The Family Jewels. 1971: Fool's Parade.

BAXTER, Warner

Actor. Columbus, Ohio 1893–1951 Beverly Hills, California
First job with Underwood Typewriter Company in San Francisco. Juvenile then adult leads with Tulsa stock company. 1914: to Hollywood. Contract with stock company in Los Angeles. In 'Lombardi, Ltd' in New York and on 2 year tour. 1918: first film for Goldwyn. Married actress Winifred Bryson (1917). 1929–40: worked mainly for Fox. 1943–49: 'Crime Doctor' series for Columbia. Oscar as Best Actor (1928–29) for *In Old Arizona*, in which replaced Raoul Walsh who had lost eye in motor accident.

Films as actor include: 1922: If I Were Queen. 1926: Mannequin; Aloma of the South Seas; The Great Gatsby; Miss Brewster's Millions. 1928: Ramona; West of Zanzibar. 1931: Daddy Long Legs. 1933: 42nd Street. 1934: Broadway Bill. 1936: The Prisoner of Shark Island; The Road to Glory. 1937: Slave Ship. 1941: Adam had Four Sons. 1943: Crime Doctor. 1944: Lady in the Dark.

BAZIN, André

Critic. Angers, France 1918–58 Paris
Ecole Normale de Saint-Cloud. Studied literature; wanted to teach but refused job because of stutter. Worked with Travail et Culture to encourage cultural activities among workers. 1944: worked at IDHEC. 1947: founded La Revue du Cinema, which became Les Cahiers du Cinema, founded by Bazin and Jacques Doniol-Valcoze in 1950. 1945–50: wrote on cinema for L'Ecran Français, Esprit, Le Parisien Libere. Books include: 'Orson Welles' (1950), 'Vittorio De Sica' (1951), 'Qu'est-ce que le cinema?' (1958–61). At death left book on Renoir unfinished; François Truffaut assembled material for publication. Numerous articles in Cahiers du Cinema. Adopted rigorous distinction between 'reality' and 'the image'. Championed naturalism, neo-realism. Attacked his protege François Truffaut and other Cahiers writers for rigid adherence to '*la politique des auteurs*'.

BEATLES, The

Composers, actors, singers. John Lennon: Liverpool, Lancashire 1940– . Paul MacCartney Liverpool 1942– . George Harrison: Liverpool 1943– . Ringo Starr (Richard Starkey): Liverpool 1940–
John's father a waiter at sea. 1956: formed and led pop group The Quarrymen. Paul's father cotton salesman and inspector for Corporation Cleansing Department; 14 when mother died of cancer; joined The Quarrymen. George's father bus driver. George joined The Quarrymen in 1958. Ringo's parents separated when he was 3: mother became barmaid; apprentice fitter then drummer in groups. John to art college. group became The Rainbows. George apprentice electrician. Group appeared on 'Carrol Levis Discoveries' TV show as Johnny and the Moondogs. Then known briefly as The Silver Beatles: worked in Hamburg clubs. Ringo joined John's group in 1962. Some recording work in Germany, then (1962) first British record 'Love Me Do'. 1964: American visit; John's first book 'In His Own Write'; first film as actors and composers. 1964–66: tours. 1965: each awarded MBE; George Dunning's TV company made animated series based on the group; John's book 'A Spaniard in the Works'. 1966: final American tour; last British live concert; began to work separately for films; George married model Patti Boyd and visited India, studied music with Ravi Shankar; group made hour-long TV film *Magical Mystery Tour*. 1968: to India; George Dunning made animated feature *Yellow Submarine* based on their songs; Old Vic production based on 'In His Own Write'; publication of Hunter Davies' authorised biography 'The Beatles'. 1969: John married Yoko Ono, with whom he had performed and recorded and they made their first film as directors in collaboration; John returned his MBE. 1970: last film appearance as a group *Let It Be*, documentary record of recording session; the film won Oscar for best original song score. Own company, Apple, with many subsidiaries.

Films as Beatles: 1964: A Hard Day's Night (*songs* John and Paul; *w* all); Yeah Yeah Yeah New York Meets the Beatles (*w* all). 1965: Help! (*songs* John, Paul and George; *w* all). 1966: The Family Way (*m* Paul). 1967: Magical Mystery Tour (*d/p/s/e/w* all); How I Won the War (*w* John). 1968: Candy (*w* Ringo); Wonderwall (*m* George); Yellow Submarine (*songs*, all). 1970: Let It Be (*w* all; (*+ex-p*) co-songs).

Films directed by John Lennon and Yoko Ono: 1969: Rape; Two Virgins; Number 5. 1970: Apotheosis; Legs – Up Your Legs Forever (*+ wv*). 1971: The Fly.

BEATON, Cecil

(Walter Hardy) Photographer and designer. London 1904–
Published several volumes of portraits, memoirs and photographic souvenirs. During World War II, documentary photographer for Ministry of Information and (from 1942) loaned to Air Ministry as official RAF photographer. 1935: designed scenery and costumes for ballets in C. B. Cochran's production of 'Follow the Sun'. 1946: acted in San Francisco and, later, New York production of 'Lady Windermere's Fan'; also designed it. Other stage design work includes 'Return of the Prodigal' (1948), 'Charley's Aunt' (1949) and 'Aren't We All' (1953) in London; 'Cry of the Peacock' (1950), 'Quadrille' (1954) and 'My Fair Lady' (1957) in New York; 'School for Scandal' (1962) for Comedie Française. Designed costumes for films from 1941, e.g. *Beware of Pity* (1946), *An Ideal Husband* (1948), *Anna Karenina* (1948), *The Doctor's Dilemma* (1959), *On a Clear Day You Can See For Ever* (1970, in collaboration). Oscar for costume design: *Gigi* (1958).

Films as production designer include: 1958: Gigi (*+ cos*). 1964: My Fair Lady (*+ cos*; *co-des*).

BEATTY, Warren

(Warren Beaty) Actor. Richmond, Virginia 1937–
Younger brother of Shirley MacLaine. A year at Northwestern University School of Speech, then Stella Adler's acting school, New York. Small TV parts. Broadway debut in 'A Loss of Roses'. 1961: first film as actor. 1967: produced and acted in *Bonnie and Clyde*.

Films as actor: 1961: Splendor in the Grass; The Roman Spring of Mrs Stone. 1962: All Fall Down. 1963: Lilith. 1965: Mickey One; Promise Her Anything. 1966: Kaleidoscope. 1967: Bonnie and Clyde (*+ p*). 1968: The Only Game in Town. 1971: Dollars.

BECKER, Jacques

Director. Paris 1906–1960 Paris
Mother ran fashion house for some years; father director of the Societe d'Accumulateurs Fulmen; they were friends of the Cezanne and Renoir families. At about 13, first met Jean Renoir. 1923: worked for a short time in father's firm. 1925: joined Compagnie Generale Translantique; as purser on ship from Le Havre to New York, met King Vidor who offered him a small part in *The Crowd* (1928), but parents forbade him to go to Hollywood. 1926: service in 4 Regiment de Hussards at Rambouillet. 1929: small part in Jean Renoir's Le Bled. 1932: first film as assistant to Renoir, *La Nuit de carrefour*; assistant also on *Bouda Sauvé des eaux* (1932), *Chotard et Compagnie* (1933), *Madame Bov ary* (1934), *Partie de campagnie*, *Les Bas-fonds* (1936), *La Grande Illusion* (1937), *La Marseillaise* (1938), frequently appearing in small parts. 1933: started to direct for production company set up by his friend, Halley des Fontaines, making medium length films for Warners, the first supervised by Pierre Prevert. 1939: started feature *L'Or du Cristobal*; shooting interrupted by lack of money; film bought and finished quickly by another company, disowned by Becker. 1940: French army; over a year as prisoner of war; repatriated after simulating epilepsy. 1957: took over direction and re-wrote script of *Montparnasse 19* after death of Max Ophüls. Son is director Jean Becker (born 1933). At time of death, married to actress Françoise Fabian.

Films as director: 1934: Le Commissaire est bon enfant (*+ co-s/w*; *co-d Pierre Prévert*); Le Gendarme est sans pitie (*+ co-s/w*; *co-d Pierre Prévert*). 1935: Tête de turc – Une Tête qui rapporte – Le Bourreau (*+ co-s*). 1939: L'Or du Cristobal (*uc*). 1942: Dernier atout (*+ co-p/co-s*). 1943: Goupi Mains-Rouges – It Happened at the Inn (*+ co-s*). 1945: Falbalas (*+ co-s*). 1947: Antoine et Antoinette (*+ co-s*). 1949: Rendez-vous de Juillet (*+ s/co-st*). 1951: Edouard et Caroline (*+ co-s*). 1952: Casque d'or (*+ co-s/di*). 1953: Rue de l'estrapade – Françoise Steps Out (*+ co-s*). 1954: Touchez-pas au grisbi – Honour Among Thieves (*+ co-s*). 1955: Ali-Baba et les quarante voleurs – Ali-Baba (*+ co-s*). 1957: Les Aventures d'Arsene Lupin (*+ co-s*). 1958: Montparnasse 19 – The Lovers of Montparnasse (*+ s*). 1960: Le Trou – The Hole (*+ co-s*).

BEERY, Wallace

Actor. Kansas City, Kansas 1885–1949 Beverly Hills, California
Son of police sergeant; younger brother of actor Noah Beery. Joined Ringling Circus at 16; everything from stable boy to comic actor. 1904: in New York sang in musical shows with Henry Savage company. 1912: walk-on parts in films. 1914–15: contracted to

Essanay; 1-reel comedies included series as Swedish housemaid Sweedie, many scripted by Louella Parsons. 1915: also studio manager and second-string director to new Essanay studios. 1916: with Universal as actor and director (also wrote and produced – parts included housemaid, now Swedey, in 1-reelers; series of 10 2-reelers, *Timothy Dobbs, That's Me*). Eloped with Gloria Swanson, divorced 1918. Acted in features from 1917, but continued making 1-reel comedies for Nestor, released by Universal until 1919. Late 1920s at Paramount; then MGM. Special Academy Award (1931–32) for *The Champ*.

Films as actor include: 1917: The Little American. 1919: The Love Burglar; Soldiers of Fortune; Behind the Door; Victory. 1920: The Mollycoddle. 1921: The Four Horsemen of the Apocalypse. 1922: Robin Hood. 1925: The Pony Express; So Big. 1928: Old Ironsides; Beggars of Life. 1929: Chinatown Nights. 1930: The Big House; Billy the Kid; Min and Bill. 1932: Grand Hotel; Flesh. 1933: Dinner at Eight; Tugboat Annie; The Bowery. 1934: Viva Villa!; Treasure Island. 1935: China Seas; Ah, Wilderness! 1938: Port of Seven Seas. 1939: Sergeant Madden. 1941: The Bad Man; Barnacle Bill.

BELLOCCHIO, Marco

Director. Piacenza, Italy 1939–
Son of a lawyer and a teacher. Catholic schools. Philosophy at the University of the Sacred Heart, Milan; simultaneously attended Accademia dei Filo-drammatici. 2 years studying acting and direction at Centro Sperimentale, Rome, graduating 1962. Scholarship to Slade School of Art, London. Directed short, *La Colpa e la pena* and 2 documentaries, *Abbasso il zio* and *Ginepro fatto uomo* before making first feature (1966). On stage, directed 'Timon of Athens'. TV direction.

Films as director: 1966: I Pugni in tasca – Fists in the Pocket (*+ s/st*). 1967: La Cina è vicina – China is Near (*+ co-s/st*); Amore e rabbia *ep* Discutiamo, Discutiamo – Vangelo 70 (*r* 1969). 1971: In Nome del padre (*+ s*).

BELMONDO, Jean Paul

Actor. Neuilly-sur-Seine, France 1933–
Father sculptor. Conservatoire National d'Art Dramatique (1953–56). From 1956: stage parts including 'Oscar' (1958). 1958: first film as actor *Sois belle et tais-toi*.

Films as actor include: 1958: Les Tricheurs. 1959: Charlotte et son Jules; A bout de souffle; A Double Tour; Classe tous risques. 1961: La Viaccia; Leon Morin, Prêtre; Une Femme est une femme. 1962: Un Singe en hiver; Cartouche; Le Doulos. 1963: L'Homme de Rio. 1964: La Chasse à L'Homme; Week-end a Zuydcoote; Par un beau matin d'ete. 1965: Les Tribulations d'un chinois en Chine; Pierrot le fou. 1966: Paris brûle-t-il? 1967: Le Voleur. 1968: Ho! 1969: La Sirène du Mississippi. 1971: Les Maries de l'an II; Le Casse.

BENCHLEY, Robert

Actor and humourist. Worcester, Massachusetts 1889–1945 New York

Philosophy degree at Harvard, then publicity work. Began in the cinema writing and acting in 1-reelers, e.g. *Robert Benchley in the Treasurer's Report, Robert Benchley in the Sex Life of the Polyp, Robert Benchley in the Spellbinder* (1928). 1-reeler *How to Sleep* won Oscar for short subject (1935). 1938–42: series of comedy shorts for MGM and Paramount.

Features as actor include: 1933: Dancing Lady. 1935: China Seas. 1940: Foreign Correspondent (*+ co-s, uc*). 1941: The Reluctant Dragon. 1942: I Married a Witch; The Major and the Minor. 1944: Song of Russia; Practically Yours. 1946: The Bride Wore Boots; Road to Utopia.

BENDIX, William

Actor. New York 1906–1964 Los Angeles
Son of Max Bendix, violinist and conductor of Metropolitan Opera Orchestra. 1911: first film appearance at Vitagraph. Minor league baseball player. 1928–33: grocery manager in Newark. After cabaret work, joined New York Federal Theatre project. 1935: small parts in 6 Theatre Guild plays, then in summer stock. First big part as Policeman Krupp in Theatre Guild's 'The Time of Your Life'. 2 years later joined Hal Roach. In features from 1942. 1944–53: 'Life of Riley' on radio and TV and other TV parts, and (from 1960) more stage work.

Films as actor include: 1942: Woman of the Year; Wake Island. 1944: Lifeboat; The Hairy Ape. 1945: A Bell for Adano. 1946: The Dark Corner. 1947: The Web. 1949: The Big Steal. 1951: Detective Story. 1952: Macao; Blackbeard the Pirate. 1958: The Deep Six. 1959: The Rough and the Smooth. 1962: Boys' Night Out. 1963: For Love or Money.

BENEDEK, Laslo

Director. Budapest 1907–
Studied psychiatry at University of Vienna. Also story writer and magazine photographer. Vacation work as camera assistant in films. Assistant cinematographer, then cinematographer for Ufa and Terra in Germany. Period in cutting rooms, for both companies. In early 1930s worked as editor, then assistant producer on 15 films under Joe Pasternak in Berlin and (from 1933) Vienna, for Universal. Editor and dialogue director on one film in Paris, then 2 years in UK as scriptwriter. 1937: to Hollywood, as montage director with Slavko Vorkapich at MGM, then associate producer to Pasternak. 1948: first film as director, for Pasternak. Much TV work. 1951: co-produced *Storm over Tibet*.

Films as director: 1948: The Kissing Bandit. 1949: Port of New York. 1951: Death of a Salesman. 1953: The Wild One. 1954: Bengal Brigade. 1955: Kinder, Mütter und ein General. 1957: Affair in Havana. 1959: Moment of Danger – Malaga. 1960: Recours en grâce. 1966: Namu the Killer Whale (*+ p*). 1971: The Night Visitor.

BENNETT, Charles

Scriptwriter. Shoreham-by-Sea, Sussex 1899–
Actor. First script: *The Return* (1927). From 1929: scripts for Alfred Hitchcock, in UK and after going to USA (1938). 3 scripts for Cecil B. De Mille. Directed

Montparnasse 19, *directed by Jacques Becker.*
Jean-Paul Belmondo in Jean-Pierre Melville's Le Doulos.
Laslo Benedek's The Wild One, *with Marlon Brando.*

and scripted *Madness of the Heart* (1949) in UK, and *No Escape* (1953) in USA.

Films as writer in collaboration include: 1929: Blackmail (+*fpl*). 1934: The Man Who Knew Too Much (*co-st*). 1935: The Thirty-Nine Steps (*co-ad*). 1936: Sabotage; Secret Agent. 1937: King Solomon's Mines. 1938: Young and Innocent. 1940: Foreign Correspondent. 1942: Reap the Wild Wind. 1943: Forever and a Day. 1944: The Story of Doctor Wassell. 1947: Ivy (*alone*); The Unconquered. 1952: The Green Glove (+ *st*; *alone*). 1955: The Man Who Knew Too Much. 1959: The Big Circus. 1960: The Lost World. 1965: City in the Sea.

BENNETT, Compton

Director. Tunbridge Wells, Kent 1900–
Left school at 15; odd jobs with furnishing company; worked as interior decorator. Signaller in World War I. Then art school course with money earned by organising dance band. Layout work in advertising for 5 years. Bought 16mm camera and made amateur films. Job in cutting rooms at Baldwin Studios. 1932: editing assistant for Alexander Korda. Made advertising shorts at Denham. Directed documentaries, *Find, Fix and Strike* (1942), *Men of Rochdale* (1946). 1948–50: in Hollywood on MGM contract.

Features as director: 1945: The Seventh Veil. 1946: The Years Between. 1947: Daybreak. 1949: My Own True Love; That Forsyte Woman – The Forsyte Saga. 1950: King Solomon's Mines (*co-d Andrew Marton*). 1951: So Little Time. 1952: The Gift Horse – Glory at Sea; It Started in Paradise – Fanfare for Figleaves. 1953: Desperate Moment. 1957: That Woman Opposite; After the Ball; The Flying Scot – Mailbag Robbery. 1960: Beyond the Curtain. 1965: How to Undress in Public Without Undue Embarrassment.

BENNETT, Constance

Actress. New York 1905–1965 Fort Dix, New Jersey
Daughter of actor Richard Bennett; sister of actresses Joan and Barbara Bennett. 1922: first film. 1926–29: retired from screen, returning in sound films. Married 5 times; 4th husband (1941–45) was Gilbert Roland.

Films as actress include: 1930: Common Clay. 1932: What Price Hollywood? 1933: Our Betters. 1934: The Affairs of Cellini. 1937: Topper. 1938: Merrily We Live. 1940: Escape to Glory. 1941: Two-Faced Woman; Wild Bill Hickok Rides. 1946: Centennial Summer. 1947: The Unsuspected. 1954: It Should Happen To You. 1965: Madame X.

BENNETT, Joan

Actress. Palisades, New Jersey 1910–
Sister of Constance Bennett. 1928: first New York stage appearance. 1929: first film, *Bulldog Drummond*. 1945: with Walter Wanger (third husband, married 1940), Fritz Lang and Dudley Nichols, formed independent company, Diana Productions, responsible for *Scarlet Street* (1945) and *Secret Beyond the Door* (1948). 1951: Wanger convicted of shooting her agent, Jennings Lang, in the groin allegedly 'because he broke up my home'. 1962: divorce from Wanger. Stage appearances include national tours of 'BB and C' (1951–53) and 'Janus' (1956–57); 'Love Me Little' in

New York (1958). Succeeded Cornelia Otis Skinner in 'The Pleasure of his Company'. 1963: 'Never Too Late' in London.

Films as actress include: 1929: Disraeli. 1930: Moby Dick. 1933: Little Women. 1938: Trade Winds. 1939: The Man in the Iron Mask. 1941: Man Hunt. 1943: Margin for Error. 1944: The Woman in the Window. 1945: Scarlet Street. 1947: The Macomber Affair; The Woman on the Beach. 1949: The Reckless Moment. 1950: Father of the Bride. 1955: We're No Angels. 1956: There's Always Tomorrow.

BENNY, Jack

(Benjamin Kubelsky) Actor. Chicago, Illinois 1894–
Jewish immigrant parents. At 15, job as violinist in orchestra of Barrison Theatre in home town, Waukegan, left home to form touring vaudeville act with leader of this orchestra. 1913: vaudeville act with pianist Lyman Woods, on Orpheum Circuit. Enlisted in US Navy; revue 'Maritime Frolics' at Great Lakes Naval Training Station (1918). After discharge returned to vaudeville as comedian; first stage name Ben K. Benny; New York and touring in 1920s. 1927: married; wife joined act as Mary Livingstone. 1929: first film *The Hollywood Revue*. 1931: lead comic in Earl Carroll's 'Vanities' on Broadway. From 1932: much radio work beginning with Ed Sullivan programme. TV from 1950. 1955: dropped own radio programme to concentrate on TV show. From 1956: gave many fund-raising concerts. 1963: own variety show on Broadway. Also cabaret.

Films as actor include: 1935: Broadway Melody of 1936. 1936: College Holiday; The Big Broadcast of 1938. 1937: Artists and Models. 1938: Artists and Models Abroad. 1939: Man About Town. 1940: Love Thy Neighbor; Buck Benny Rides Again. 1941: Charley's Aunt. 1942: To Be Or Not To Be; George Washington Slept Here. 1945: Hollywood Canteen; The Horn Blows at Midnight. 1954: Susan Slept Here (*uc*). 1962: Gypsy (*uc*). 1967: A Guide for the Married Man.

BENOÎT-LÉVY, Jean

Director. Paris 1888–1959 Paris
Son of Edmond Benoît-Levy, pioneer of French cinema. Period as assistant director. From 1920: director of shorts. 1922: co-directed first feature with Jean Epstein. From 1926: co-directed several films with Marie Epstein. 1920–40: made 400 shorts. 1939: last feature *Feu de paille*. To USA; professorship at New School for Social Research, New York (1941–46). From 1946: made documentaries and shorts for UNESCO. Made films for French TV and supervised French educational films. Almost all his films are educational. Organiser and executive of most French film guilds and unions. Books: 'Visual Instruction in the United States' (1936), 'The Art of the Motion Picture' (1946).

Features as director: 1922: Pasteur (*co-d Jean Epstein*); Ames d'enfants. 1926: Peau de pêche (*co-d Marie Epstein*). 1929: Maternite. 1930: Le Petit Jimmy. 1931: Le Chant de la mine et du feu. 1933: La Maternelle – Nursery School (+ *s*; *co-d Marie Epstein*); Le Coeur de Paris. 1934: Itto (*co-d Marie Epstein*). 1936: Helène. 1937: La Mort du Cygne; Altitude

3,200 (*co-d Marie Epstein*). 1939: Feu de paille; Ballerina.

BÉRARD, Christian

Designer. Paris 1902–1949 Paris
Painter, pupil of Vuillard. First work in theatre was decor for Jean Cocteau's 'La Voix Humaine' (1930). Then 10 years designing stage decors for Louis Jouvet. Also worked for Roland Petit's ballet company. Designed decor for 3 Cocteau films.

Films as designer: 1946: La Belle et la bête (+ *co-s*). 1948: L'Aigle à deux têtes (+ *co-s*). 1949: Les Parents Terribles (*co-dec*).

BERGMAN, Ingmar

Director. Uppsala, Sweden 1918–
Son of Protestant minister. Stockholm University. 1938: started directing amateur productions at Mäster Olofsgården Theatre, Stockholm. 1941–42: at Saga Theatre in the Medborgarhus; produced own play, 'Kaspers död' (Death of Punch). 1943–44: at Dramatikerstudion and Student Theatre. 1944: writer and assistant director of Alf Sjöberg's *Hets*. From 1944: director on professional stage, notably: 1944–46: Hälsingborg City Theatre; Malmö City Theatre, where productions included own play 'Rakel och Biografvaktmästaren' (basis of the first episode of *Kvinnors väntan*). 1946–50: Göteborg City Theatre, directing his own 'Dagen slutar tidigt' (The Day Ends Early) and 'Mig till skräck' (To My Terror), etc. 1952–58: Malmö City Theatre; productions included his own 'Mordet in Barjärna' (1952), 'Skymlingslekar', a ballet written in collaboration with Carl Gustav Kruuse (1954), his own 'Trämålning' (1955). 1959: staged 'Sagan' in Paris and 'Faust' in London; became director at Royal Dramatic Theatre, Stockholm; produced Stravinsky's 'The Rake's Progress' at the Royal Opera, Stockholm. 1963–66: Head of Royal Dramatic Theatre. Has also directed plays on radio and TV. 1969: *Riten*, film made for TV showing in Sweden. Staged 'Hedda Gabler' in UK, 'The Dream' in Venice. Wrote 'The Lie' commissioned by European Broadcasting Union, shown on BBC TV (1970). Married 6 times.

Films as director and writer: 1945: Kris – Crisis. 1946: Det regnar på vår kärlek – It Rains on Our Love (*co-s*). 1947: Skepp till Indialand – A Ship to India – The Land of Desire; Musik i mörker – Night is My Future (*d only*). 1948: Hamnstad – Port of Call. 1949: Fängelse – Prison – The Devil's Wanton; Törst – Thirst – Three Strange Loves (*d only*); Till Glädje – To Joy. 1950: Sånt händer inte här – This Can't Happen Here – High Tension (*d only*); Sommarlek – Summer Interlude – Illicit Interlude (*st/co-s*). 1952: Kvinnors väntan – Waiting Women – Secrets of Women; Sommaren med Monika – Summer with Monika – Monika (*co-s*). 1953: Gycklarnas afton – Sawdust and Tinsel – The Naked Night. 1954: En Lektion i kärlek. 1955: Kvinnodröm – Journey into Autumn – Dreams; Sommarnattens Leende – Smiles of a Summer Night. 1957: Det Sjunde Inseglet – The Seventh Seal; Smultronstället – Wild Strawberries. 1958: Nära livet – So Close to Life – Brink of Life (*co-s*); Ansiktet – The Face – The Magician. 1959: Jungfrukällan – The Virgin Spring (*d only*). 1960: Djävulens öga – The Devil's Eye. 1961: Såsom i en spegel – Through a

Glass Darkly. 1963: Nattvardsgästerna – Winter Light – The Communicants; Tystnaden – The Silence. 1964: För att inte tala om alla dessa kvinnor – Now About These Women (co-s with Erland Josephson; joint pseudonym Buntel Ericsson). 1966: Persona. 1967: Stimulantia ep Daniel (+ c). 1968: Vargtimmen – Hour of the Wolf; Skammen – Shame – The Shame. 1969: Riten – The Rite. 1970: En Pasion – Passion – The Passion of Anna. 1971: Beröringen – The Touch.

Films as writer: 1944: Hets. 1947: Kvinna utan ansikte. 1948: Eva (co-s/st). 1950: Medan standen sover (st only). 1951: Frånskild (co-s/st). 1956: Sista paret ut (co-s/st). 1961: Lustgården (co-s).

BERGMAN, Ingrid

Actress. Stockholm 1915–

Spotted in play she wrote, staged and acted in for the Royal Dramatic Theatre School. 1935: first film part. About 11 films including 1 for Ufa and 6 directed by Gustav Molander, notably *Intermezzo* (1936), before Hollywood contract with David Selznick and American version of *Intermezzo* (1939). Married Roberto Rossellini (1949), impresario Lars Schmidt (1958). Stage and TV appearances, e.g. Rossellini's stage production of 'Jeanne au bûcher' (1954) which toured Europe and was filmed by him as *Giovanna d'Arco al rogo*; 'Hedda Gabler' on British TV and Paris stage (1962); 'Captain Brassbound's Conversion' in London and on Broadway (1971). Oscars as Best Actress for *Gaslight* (1944), *Anastasia* (1956).

Films as actress include: 1941: Dr Jekyll and Mr Hyde. 1943: Casablanca; For Whom the Bell Tolls. 1944: Gaslight. 1945: The Bells of St Mary's; Spellbound. 1946: Saratoga Trunk; Notorious. 1948: The Arch of Triumph; Joan of Arc. 1949: Under Capricorn; Stromboli, Terra di Dio. 1952: Europa '51. 1953: Siamo donne ep Ingrid Bergman; Viaggio in Italia. 1954: Angst. 1956: Eléna et les hommes. 1958: The Inn of the Sixth Happiness; Indiscreet. 1961: *Aimez-vous Brahms?* 1964: The Visit; The Yellow Rolls-Royce. 1967: Stimulantia ep Smycket. 1969: Cactus Flower.

BERGNER, Elisabeth

Actress. Vienna 1900–

Apprentice under Lia Rosen of Volksbühne in Vienna; acted there for Max Reinhardt, e.g. in 'Peer Gynt' and Shaw's 'Saint Joan'. 1923: first film. 1924: in *Nju*, first of her many films directed by Paul Czinner. 1933: married him. Since 1933 has lived mainly in Britain; single films in USA (1942) and Germany (1962). Theatrical work includes 'L'Aide-Mémoir' in Hamburg (1970).

Films as actress include: 1926: Der Geiger von Florenz. 1927: Donna Juana. 1928: Liebe. 1929: Fräulein Else. 1931: Ariane. 1932: Der Träumende Mund. 1934: Catherine the Great. 1935: Escape Me Never. 1936: As You Like It. 1937: Dreaming Lips. 1939: Stolen Life. 1942: Paris Calling. 1962: Die Glücklichen Jahre der Thorwalds.

BERKELEY, Busby

(William Berkeley Enos) Director and choreographer. Los Angeles 1895–

After graduation started mail-order shoe business. During World War I Entertainment Officer for 3rd Army of Occupation in Germany. After war, actor and director for various stock companies. Producer, director, actor and choreographer on Broadway before joining Warners as choreographer (1930). 1933: also director. Worked mainly for Warners and First National (1930–39), then MGM (1939–53) as director and/or choreographer. Since 1953 has only worked as 2nd-unit director on *Easy to Love* (1953), *Rose Marie* (1954) and *Billy Rose's Jumbo* (1962) – some uncredited choreography on latter two.

Films as choreographer include: 1932: Bird of Paradise. 1933: The Kid from Spain; 42nd Street; Gold Diggers of 1933; Footlight Parade. 1934: Fashion of 1934; Dames. 1936: Gold Diggers of 1937. 1941: Ziegfeld Girl; Lady Be Good. 1942: Born to Sing. 1943: Girl Crazy (co). 1951: Call Me Mister. 1952: Million Dollar Mermaid.

Films as director: 1933: She Had to Say Yes (co-d George Amy). 1935: Gold Diggers of 1935; Bright Lights; I Live for Love. 1936: Stage Struck. 1937: The Go Getter; Hollywood Hotel. 1938: Men Are Such Fools; Garden of the Moon; Comet Over Broadway. 1939: They Made Me a Criminal; Babes in Arms; Fast and Furious. 1940: Forty Little Mothers; Strike Up The Band. 1941: Blonde Inspiration; Babes on Broadway. 1942: For Me and My Gal. 1943: The Gang's All Here. 1946: Cinderella Jones. 1949: Take Me Out to the Ball Game.

BERLANGA, Luis Garcia

Director. Valencia, Spain 1921–

Philosophy and humanities at Valencia University; wrote film criticism for various papers. Volunteered for Azul division; 1 year fighting on Russian front. From 1943, wrote film scripts usually in collaboration; one of these written with José Luis Colina won first prize in national contest for film scripts (1950). From 1947: studied at Instituto de Investigaciónes Cinematograficas; there made experimental and documentary films: *Paseo sobre una guerra antigua* (co-directed and co-scripted by Juan Antonio Bardem, 1949), *Tres Cautos* (1949), *Circo* (1950).

Features as director: 1951: Esa pareja feliz (r 1953; + co-s; co-d Juan Antonio Bardem). 1952: Bienvenido, Mr Marshall! – Welcome, Mr Marshall (+ co-s). 1953: Novio a la vista (co-d Juan Antonio Bardem). 1956: Los Gancheros; Calabuch. 1957: Los Jueves Milagro ep Arriverderci Dimas (+ st/co-s). 1961: Plácido (+ co-s). 1962: Les Quatres Vérités ep El Leñador y la muerte. 1963: El Verdugo – The Executioner – Not On Your Life (+ co-s). 1967: Las Pirañas (+ co-s). 1970: ¡Vivan los novios!.

BERMAN, Pandro S.

Producer, Pittsburgh, Pennsylvania 1905–

Son of Harry M. Berman, general manager of Universal. Worked way up to head of cutting department at RKO. Assistant to David O. Selznick; then producer for RKO. 1940: signed long-term contract as producer at MGM for which has made over 80 films. Announced *Move* (1970) as his last feature.

Films as producer include: 1934: The Gay Divorcee;

Det Sjunde Inseglet, *directed by Ingmar Bergman.*
Ingrid Bergman in Giovanna D'Arco al rogo. *directed by Roberto Rossellini.*
Dames, *choreographed by Busby Berkeley.*

Of Human Bondage. 1935: Alice Adams; Top Hat. 1936: Sylvia Scarlett; Mary of Scotland; Winterset; Swing Time. 1937: Quality Street; Stage Door; A Damsel in Distress. 1938: Carefree. 1939: The Hunchback of Notre Dame. 1944: The Seventh Cross. 1946: Undercurrent; The Sea of Grass. 1949: Madame Bovary. 1950: Father of the Bride. 1953: Battle Circus. 1955: Blackboard Jungle. 1956: Bhowani Junction. 1957: The Brothers Karamazov. 1960: Butterfield 8. 1962: Sweet Bird of Youth. 1963: The Prize.

BERNARD-AUBERT, Claude

Director. Durtal, France 1930–
Press and TV correspondent in Indochina war. 1956: first film as director based on this experience. 1958: export ban placed on *Les Tripes au Soleil*.

Films as director: 1956: Patrouille de choc (+ *st/s*). 1958: Les Tripes au soleil (+ *co-st*). 1959: Match contre la mort. 1960: Les Lâches vivent d'espoir (+ *co-st*). 1961: A fleur de peau (+ *st/co-s*). 1962: Polyorchia – Les Moutons de Praxos – A l'aube de troisième jour (+ *co-st*). 1966: Le Facteur s'en va-t-en guerre. 1969: L'Ardoise (+ *co-s/di*).

BERNHARDT, Curtis (Kurt)

Director. Worms, Germany 1899–
State School for Dramatic Art, Frankfurt-am-Main. Actor and producer on Berlin stage. Film director from 1926. From 1930: films in France and (1936–38) UK. 1940: to USA, directing for Warners, then from 1947 mainly for MGM, until 1956.

Films as director: 1926: Qualen der Nacht (+ *co-s*). 1927: Das letzte Fort. 1928: Schinderhannes (+ *co-s*); Das grosse Los. 1929: Der Frau nach der Man sich sehnt – Enigma. 1930: Die letzte Kompanie – The Last Company; L'Homme qui assassina. 1931: Die Mann der den Mord Beging. 1932: Der Rebell (*co-d Luis Trenker*); Der grosse Rausch. 1933: Der Tunnel (*and French version*, Le Tunnel). 1934: L'Or dans la rue. 1936: The Beloved Vagabond. 1938: Carrefour. 1939: Nuit de decembre. 1940: My Love Came Back; The Lady with Red Hair. 1941: Million Dollar Baby. 1942: Juke Girl. 1943: Happy Go Lucky. 1945: Conflict. 1946: Devotion; My Reputation; A Stolen Life. 1947: Possessed. 1949: The High Wall; The Doctor and the Girl. 1951: Payment on Demand (+ *co-s*); Sirocco; The Blue Veil. 1952: The Merry Widow. 1953: Miss Sadie Thompson. 1954: Beau Brummel. 1955: Interrupted Melody. 1956: Gaby. 1960: Stefanie in Rio. 1961: Damon and Pythias. 1964: Kisses For My President (+ *p*).

BERNHARDT, Sarah

(Henriette-Rosine Bernard) Actress. Paris 1844–1923 Paris
Dutch mother. 1862: entered Comedie Francaise. 1872: broke contract with L'Odeon to accept contract with Comedie Française. 1879: British stage debut. American, South American, European and Russian tours. Victorien Sardou wrote series of plays for her. 1893: bought Théâtre de la Renaissance; acted there in e.g. Gabriele D'Annunzio's 'La Città Morta'. 1899: bought second theatre, named it Théâtre Sarah Bernhardt; acted there e.g. in title role of 'Hamlet'. 1900: first film as actress. 1912: *La Reine Elisabeth* made in England: acquired by Adolph Zukor for American release, one of the earliest features. 1914: leg amputated; continued to act with artificial leg. 1922: acted for last time in Paris: Italian tour; last performance in Turin; at death left *La Voyante* unfinished. Films mainly directed by Louis Mercanton. Wrote 3 plays: 'L'Aveu' (1888), 'Adrienne Lecouvreur' (1908), 'Un Coeur d'Homme' (1911). Author of books 'Ma Double Vie, Mémoires' (1907), 'L'Art du Théâtre, la voix, le geste, la pronunciation' (1923). Also novelist, sculptress, painter.

Films as actress: 1900: Le Duel d'Hamlet. 1908: Tosca(*ur*). 1911: La Dame aux camelias. 1912: La Reine Elisabeth – Elisabeth, Reine d'Angleterre – Queen Elizabeth. 1913: Adrienne Lecouvreur(+ *s*). 1916: Jeanne Dore. 1917: Mères Francaises. 1923: La Voyante (*uf*).

BERNSTEIN, Elmer

Composer. New York 1922–
1934: won private scholarship from teacher at Juillard School, who guided career as pianist. Also studied on personal scholarships under Aaron Copland, Roger Sessions and Stefan Wolpe. World War II in US Air Force radio unit. Then for 3 years wrote musical shows for United Nations radio department and gave concerts. Apart from feature scores, has written vocal and chamber music and scores for short films of Ray and Charles Eames. Scores for several TV series. 1970: vice-president of AMPAS. Oscar for original score, *Thoroughly Modern Millie* (1967).

Films as composer include: 1952: Sudden Fear. 1955: The Man With The Golden Arm. 1956: The Ten Commandments. 1957: Men in War; Fear Strikes Out; The Tin Star; Sweet Smell of Success. 1958: God's Little Acre; Desire Under the Elms; Some Came Running. 1959: The Story on Page One. 1960: The Magnificent Seven; The Rat Race. 1961: The Comancheros. 1962: Walk on the Wild Side; Bird Man of Alcatraz; To Kill a Mockingbird. 1963: Hud; Love with the Proper Stranger. 1964: The Carpetbaggers; The World of Henry Orient. 1965: Baby, the Rain Must Fall; The Hallelujah Trail; The Sons of Katie Elder; The Reward. 1966: Seven Women; The Silencers; Hawaii. 1968: The Scalphunters. 1969: The Midas Run (*co-song*). 1970: The Liberation of L. B. Jones; Cannon for Cordoba. 1971: Blind Terror.

BERNSTEIN, Leonard

Composer. Lawrence, Massachusetts 1918–
Studied music at Harvard and the Curtis Institute of Music, Philadelphia. 1943: debut as conductor of New York Philharmonic Orchestra. 1944: wrote music for ballet 'Fancy Free', the basis of his stage musical 'On the Town' (1944). Composed Broadway musicals 'Wonderful Town' (1953), 'Candide' (1956), 'West Side Story' (1957). For CBS TV wrote and appeared in 'A Copland Celebration' (1970) and 'Beethoven's Birthday: a Celebration in Vienna with Leonard Bernstein' (*co-wrote*, 1971). Own production company.

Films as composer: 1949: On the Town. 1954: On the Waterfront. 1961: West Side Story.

BERRY, John

Director. New York 1917–
Toured in vaudeville at 10; expelled from 3 schools. At 17 began acting and directing in New York State. Joined Shakespearean company, then repertory at Greenhaven, Connecticut. In New York, directed and acted in a number of plays. 1936: with Orson Welles's production of 'Julius Caesar' then assistant stage manager and assistant to Welles at Mercury Theatre; acted there in e.g. 'Native Son' (1941). Production of 'Cry Havoc' seen in Chicago by talent scout, went to Hollywood on Paramount contract (1943). 1946: first film as director. Made documentary *Dix de Hollywood* (1951). Left Hollywood for political reasons. 1952: settled in France.

Features as director: 1946: Miss Susie Slagle's; From This Day Forward. 1947: Cross My Heart. 1948: Casbah. 1949: Tension. 1951: He Ran All the Way. 1952: C'est arrive à Paris. 1954: Ça va barder (+ *co-s*). 1955: Je suis un sentimental (+ *co-s*); Don Juan (+ *co-s*). 1957: Tamango (+ *co-s*). 1958: Oh, que mambo. 1964: Maya. 1967: A tout casser (+ *co-s*).

BERRY, Jules

(Jules Paufichet) Actor. Paris 1889–1951 Paris
Interrupted university studies to go on stage; 12 years at Théâtre des Galéries Saint-Ubert in Brussels. First film: *Cromwell* (1911). Regularly in films from 1928 until his death.

Films as actor include: 1928: L'Argent. 1936: Le Crime de Monsieur Lange. 1939: Le Jour se lève. 1942: Les Visiteurs du soir; La Symphonie Fantastique.

BERTOLUCCI, Bernardo

Director. Parma, Italy 1940–
Son of poet, Attilio Bertolucci. Between 12 and 15 started to make 16mm amateur films; wrote poetry. Moved with family to Rome; met Pier Paolo Pasolini and worked as an assistant director on *Accattone* (1961). 1962: volume of poems published, 'In cerca del mistero'. 1965–66: wrote and directed *La Via del petrolio*, film in 3 episodes for TV, sponsored by AGIP. 1966: in Suez, started *Il Canale*, while shooting part II of *La Via del petrolio*; did not complete it, though credited with direction. Collaborated on story of *C'era una volta il west* (1969). 1971: made *1900* for Italian TV.

Films as director and writer: 1962: La Commare Secca (*co-s*). 1964: Prima della rivoluzione. 1966: La Via del petrolio; Il Canale. 1967: Amore e rabbia – Love and Anger – Vangelo 70 *ep* Agonia – Agony (*r* 1969;+*s*). 1968: Partner (*co-s*). 1970: Il Conformista; Strategia del ragno – The Spider's Strategy (*co-s*).

BIBERMAN, Herbert J.

Writer and director. Philadelphia, Pennsylvania 1900–71
After graduation, 4 years in family textile business. Left to study drama for 2 years at Yale, then a year in Europe. At Theatre Guild of New York for 3 years as actor, stage manager and director. 1930: married actress Gale Sondergaard then a member of the

Theatre Guild. 1935: to Hollywood on Columbia contract. As well as writing, e.g. story for *Together Again* (1944), and directing, worked as associate producer for United Artists (1946). One of first board of directors of Screen Directors' Guild, founder-member of Hollywood Anti-Nazi League and of Motion Picture Artists' Committee, which organised aid to Republicans in Spanish Civil War. One of the 'Hollywood Ten'; 6 months jail sentence and $1,00 fine after 1947 hearings of House Committee on Un-American Activities. Wrote book 'Salt of the Earth' on making of film under aegis of International Union of Mill, Mine and Smelter Workers.

Films as director include: 1935: One Way Ticket. 1936: Meet Nero Wolfe. 1944: The Master Race (+ *st/co-s*). 1953: Salt of the Earth. 1969: Slaves (+ *co-s*).

BICKFORD, Charles

Actor. Cambridge, Massachusetts 1891–1967 Los Angeles
Massachusetts Institute of Technology. Civil engineer, labourer and sailor. 1913: in burlesque on Columbia circuit. 1914: in stock company, Boston. US Army Engineering Corps during World War I. From 1919: on New York stage. Spotted for films playing tramp in 'Outside Looking In'; in films from 1929. Co-author of play, 'The Cyclone Lover', performed 1928. Autobiography 'Bulls, Balls, Bicycles and Actors' published 1965.

Films as actor include: 1929: Dynamite. 1930: Anna Christie. 1932: Thunder Below; Vanity Street. 1933: This Day and Age. 1937: The Plainsman; High, Wide and Handsome. 1940: Of Mice and Men. 1942: Reap the Wild Wind. 1943: The Song of Bernadette. 1944: Wing and a Prayer. 1945: Fallen Angel. 1946: Duel in the Sun. 1947: The Woman on the Beach; Brute Force. 1948: Johnny Belinda. 1949: Whirlpool. 1950: Riding High; Branded. 1954: A Star Is Born. 1955: Not as a Stranger; The Court Martial of Billy Mitchell. 1957: Mister Cory. 1958: The Big Country. 1960: The Unforgiven. 1963: Days of Wine and Roses. 1966: A Big Hand for the Little Lady.

BIRO, Lajos

Writer. Vienna 1880–1948 London
First contact with cinema when Ernst Lubitsch, looking for a subject suitable for Pola Negri, chose comedy 'A Carnö' – 'The Czarina' (1912), Biro's first work, written in collaboration with Melchior Lengyel, which became *Forbidden Paradise* (1924), remade as *A Royal Scandal* (1945). Mauritz Stiller's *Hotel Imperial* (1927), Robert Florey's *Hotel Imperial* (1939), and Billy Wilder's *Five Graves to Cairo* (1943) all adapted from Biro's play 'Hotel Imperial'. 1924–32: to Hollywood. 1932: moved to England as executive director and screenplay writer for Alexander Korda's newly founded London Films.

Films as writer include: 1927: The Last Command; The Way of All Flesh (*co*). 1928: The Yellow Lily (*st/ad*); The Haunted House (*co*). 1933: The Private Life of Henry VIII (*co-st*). 1934: Catherine the Great (*co-st*); The Private Life of Don Juan. 1935: The Scarlet Pimpernel (*co*); Sanders of the River (*co*). 1937: Knight without Armour. 1939: The Four Feathers

(*co-di*); The Thief of Bagdad (*st*). 1948: An Ideal Husband.

BIROC, Joseph

Cinematographer.
Studio office boy. Assistant to George Folsey at RKO. Worked for numerous studios. Much TV work.

Films as cinematographer include: 1947: It's a Wonderful Life; Magic Town. 1948: A Miracle Can Happen (*co*); My Dear Secretary. 1949: Roughshod; Johnny Allegro. 1951: Cry Danger. 1952: Red Planet Mars. 1953: The Twonky; Appointment in Honduras. 1954: World for Ransom. 1955: Bengazi. 1956: Tension at Table Rock. 1957: The Garment Center; China Gate; Run of the Arrow; Unknown Terror; Forty Guns. 1958: Underwater Warrior; Home Before Dark; Verboten. 1959: Born Reckless; The FBI Story. 1960: Ice Palace; 13 Ghosts. 1961: Gold of the Seven Saints; Operation Eichmann; The Devil at 4 O'Clock. 1962: Hitler; Confessions of an Opium Eater. 1963: Bye Bye Birdie; Toys in the Attic; Under the Yum Yum Tree. 1964: Viva Las Vegas; Hush . . . Hush, Sweet Charlotte. 1965: I Saw What You Did; The Flight of the Phoenix. 1966: The Russians Are Coming, the Russians Are Coming; The Swinger. 1967: Warning Shot; Tony Rome; Fitzwilly. 1968: The Detective; The Legend of Lylah Clare; Lady in Cement; The Killing of Sister George. 1970: Too Late the Hero. 1971: The Grissom Gang.

BITZER, Billy

(Gottfried Wilhelm Bitzer) Cinematographer. Boston, Massachusetts 1870–1944 Hollywood
Newsreel cameraman, e.g. covering notification of William McKinley that he was presidential candidate, and the Spanish-American War. Mechanic and electrician with Edison. 1896: joined Biograph as electrician and rose to head cameraman. 1908: began working with D. W. Griffith and continued with him for 16 years, on more than 1,000 films. 1913: left Biograph with Griffith to shoot features at Mutual. 3-year personal contract with him. 1915: sole cameraman for *The Birth of the Nation*; invested $7,000 in the film and recovered $240,000. 1916: for *Intolerance* had 3 other cameramen working with him. 1924: left Griffith after quarrel. 1928: returned to photograph Griffith's films, collaborating with Karl Struss. In late 1930s worked in small New York photographic studio and as repair man in the Museum of Modern Art Film Library.

Films as cinematographer include: 1913: Judith of Bethulia. 1914: The Battle of the Sexes. 1915: The Birth of a Nation. 1916: Intolerance (*co*). 1918: Hearts of the World. 1919: Broken Blossoms (*co*). 1920: Way Down East (*co*). 1924: America (*co*). 1928: The Battle of the Sexes (*co*); Drums of Love (*co*). 1929: Lady of the Pavements (*co*).

BJÖRK, Anita

Actress. Tällberg, Sweden 1923–
Royal Dramatic Theatre Drama School, Stockholm. 1942: first film, *Himlaspelet*. From 1945 acted at Royal Dramatic Theatre. Regularly in films from 1946. From 1952 made some films outside Sweden. Hitchcock's original choice for female lead in *I Confess*

Salt of the Earth, *directed by Herbert Biberman.*
Hearts of the World, *directed by D. W. Griffith, photographed by G. W. Bitzer.*
Gunnar Björnstrand in Nattvardsgästerna, *directed by Ingmar Bergman.*

(1953); replaced by Anne Baxter at insistence of studio. TV plays from 1962.

Films as actress include: 1947: Kvinna utan ansikte. 1950: Kvartetten som sprängdes; Fröken Julie. 1952: Kvinnors väntan. 1954: Night People. 1956: Sången om den eldröda blomman. 1961: Nasilje na trgu. 1964: Älskande Par. 1969: Adalen 31.

BJÖRNSTRAND, Gunnar

Actor. Stockholm 1909–
Royal Dramatic Theatre Drama School. Much theatrical work. 1931: first film part in French version of a Swedish picture. Regularly in films from 1942.

Films as actor include: 1944: Hets. 1952: Kvinnors väntan. 1953: Gycklarnas afton. 1954: En Lektion i kärlek. 1955: Kvinnodröm; Sommarnattens leende. 1957: Det Sjunde Inseglet; Smultronstället. 1958: Ansiktet. 1960: Djävulens Öga. 1961: Såsom i en spegel. 1963: Nattvardsgästerna. 1964: Älskande Par. 1966: Persona; Syskonbädel 1782. 1967: Stimulantia ep Smycket. 1968: Skammen.

BLACKTON, J. Stewart

Director. Sheffield, Bedfordshire, 1875–1941 Hollywood
To USA at 10. Performed in variety. Freelance journalist for 'New York World'; sent to interview Thomas A. Edison, who filmed his variety act as *Blackton, the Evening World Cartoonist*. 1896: with theatre colleague Albert A. Smith bought an Edison Projecting Kinetiscope, exhibited Edison films in New England; with Smith founded Vitagraph. 1898: their first film *The Burglar on the Roof* written, designed, acted by Blackton, photographed by Smith; *The Battle of Santiago Bay* used models. 1900: Vitagraph incorporated by Blackton, Smith, William T. Rock (respectively: director, cinematographer, producer). 1900–17: directed and supervised films for Vitagraph, including (from 1906) animation and at least 10 films of Shakespeare's plays; became Vice President and Secretary. 1906: *Humorous Phases of Funny Faces* was the first film to animate drawings with the single frame method, a technique also used with real objects in *The Haunted Hotel* (1908). 1918: withdrew, company under control of Guarantee Trust Company. 1918–21: worked for Sales Corporation and Pathé. 1922–23: directed *The Glorious Adventure* and 2 other films in England. 1926: last films, for Warners. 1930: ruined, introduced shows of his films dressed in 1900 costume.

Films as director include: 1898: The Burglar on the Roof (+ s/des/w); Tearing Down the Spanish Flag; The Battle of Santiago Bay. 1900: Happy Hooligan (+ w). 1903: A Gentleman of France. 1905: Raffles, the Amateur Cracksman; The Adventures of Sherlock Holmes. 1906: Humorous Phases of Funny Faces. 1907: The Haunted Hotel. 1908: Making Moving Pictures. 1909: The Magic Fountain Pen; Shakespeare's Tragedy, King Lear; The Life Drama of Napoleon Bonaparte and Empress Josephine of France. 1911: Vanity Fair. 1913: Hamlet. 1915: The Battle Cry of Peace (+ s/e). 1916: Whom the Gods Destroy (+ ad). 1917: Scenes from Country Life (in 6 parts). 1919: Life's Greatest Problem (+ p). 1922: The Glorious Adventure (+ p/s). 1924: The Beloved Brute. 1925: Tides of Passion; The Redeeming Sin.

1926: Bride of the Storm (+ p); The Passionate Quest (+ p).

BLANCHE, Francis

Actor. Paris 1921–
Father actor, Louis Blanche. Wrote and produced for radio. Writer of songs, plays, revue sketches, operetta libretto and ballet story. 1948: first film as actor, *L'Assassin est à l'écoute*; also worked on script. 1962: directed, co-wrote and acted in *Tartarin de Tarascon*.

Films as actor include: 1959: Babette s'en va-t-en guerre; La Jument Verte. 1960: Un Couple. 1961: Les Snobs. 1962: The Happy Thieves. 1963: Un Drôle de paroissien; Les Tontons Flingueurs. 1964: Le Repas des fauves. 1966: Les Compagnons de la marguérite. 1967: Belle de jour. 1968: La Grande Lessive.

BLANKE, Henry

Producer. Berlin 1901–
Son of a painter. 1919–20: with Ufa. 1920–22: with Lubitsch still at Ufa. 1922–26: personal assistant to Lubitsch on his first American pictures. 1926–27: returned to Ufa where he was production manager on *Metropolis*. Joined Warners as head of German operation (1928–30); head of foreign production at Warners in Hollywood (1930–31), then producer. 1937–41: associate producer on many big Warners films. Remained with Warners until 1961. *Hell Is For Heroes* (1962) was for Paramount.

Films as producer include: 1936: Anthony Adverse. 1937: The Life of Emile Zola (as-p). 1938: Jezebel (as-p). 1939: Juarez (as-p). 1940: The Sea Hawk (as-p). 1941: The Maltese Falcon (as-p). 1943: Edge of Darkness. 1948: The Treasure of the Sierra Madre. 1949: The Fountainhead; Beyond the Forest. 1951: Lightning Strikes Twice. 1953: So Big. 1956: Serenade. 1959: Westbound; The Nun's Story. 1961: Rachel Cade.

BLASETTI, Alessandro

Director. Rome 1900–
Studied law. 1924–25: film critic for L'Impero. Founded 2 film magazines, Il Mondo dello Schermo (which became Lo Schermo, then Cinematografo) and Lo Spettacolo d'Italia. 1929: first film, *Sole*, produced by Cooperativa Augustus, formed by him and several others, including Goffredo Alessandrini. 1930–31: films for Cines. 1932–34: director of the first film school, attached to the Accademia Musicale di S. Cecilia. From 1932: short films, including first Italian colour film *La Caccia alla volpe nella campagna Romana* (1938). Acted in some of his films and (playing himself) in *Bellissima* (1951). Also TV films.

Features as director and writer in collaboration: 1929: Sole (+ e). 1930: Nerone (d/co-e only). 1931: Resurrectio (+ st/s/co-e); Terra Madre (+ co-e). 1932: Palio (+ co-e); La Tavola dei poveri (+ co-e). 1933: Il Caso Haller (d/co-e only). 1934: 1860 (+ co-e); L' Impiegata di Papà (d/co-e only); Vecchia Guardia (+ co-e). 1935: Aldebaran (+ w). 1937: La Contessa di Parma (+ co-e). 1939: Ettore Fieramosca (+ co-e); Retroscena (+ co-st/co-e). 1940: Un'Avventura di Salvator Rosa (+ co-e). 1941: *La Corona di ferro – The Iron Crown* (+ co-st); La Cena delle beffe. 1942: Quattro Passi fra

le nuvole – Four Steps in the Clouds (+ w). 1943: Nessuno torna indietro. 1946: Un Giorno nella vita (+ co-st); Il Testimone (supervision + co-s only). 1949: Fabiola. 1950: Prima Comunione – His Majesty Mr Jones – First Communion – Father's Dilemma (d only; + co-p). 1952: Altri Tempi – Infidelity (+ co-st). 1953: La Fiammata – Pride, Love and Suspicion. 1954: Tempi Nostri – Slice of Life. 1955: Peccato che sia una canaglia – Too Bad She's Bad. 1956: La Fortuna di essere donna – Lucky to Be a Woman. 1957: Amore e chiacchiere. 1958–59: Europa di notte – European Nights. 1960: Io amo, tu ami – I Love, You Love (d only). 1963: Liola – A Very Handy Man. 1965: Io, Io, Io . . . e gli altri – Me, Me, Me . . . and the Others. 1969: Simon Bolivar.

BLAUSTEIN, Julian C.

Producer. New York 1913–
Harvard. 1935: entered films as reader for Universal and rose to story editor (1936–38). 1938–39: in charge of story department at MCA. 1939–40: story editor at Paramount. 1941–46: US Signal Corps Photo Center. 1946–48: supervised story editing for Selznick. 1949: producer at Fox, then Columbia (1956) and MGM (1959).

Films as producer include: 1950: Broken Arrow. 1951: The Day the Earth Stood Still; The Guy Who Came Back. 1952: The Outcasts of Poker Flat. 1954: Désirée. 1955: The Racers. 1956: Storm Center. 1958: Cowboy; Bell, Book and Candle. 1961: Two Loves. 1962: The Four Horsemen of the Apocalypse. 1966: Khartoum. 1971: The Beguiled.

BLOM, August

Director. Copenhagen, Denmark 1869–1942 Copenhagen
Acted in theatre. Entered films as writer for Nordisk. Acted in films, including *Monoclen* (1906) and *Revolutions Bryllup* (1909); directed remake of latter in 1914. 1910: became principal director for Nordisk. 1910–11: discovered Asta Nielsen, directed her in 3 films. 1913: made *Atlantis* from play by Gerhardt Hauptman.

Films as director include: 1910: Robinson Crusoe (+ s); Livets storme; Hamlet (+ s); Den Doddet Halsband (+ s); Ved faengslets port. 1911: Livets storme (+ s); Madame Putiphar (+ s/w); Ballet Danserinden (co-d Urban Gad); Flyveren og journaliste – Ens Hustru; Dodens brud (+ s); Fader og son. 1912: Guvernorens Datter (+ s); Den Sorte kansler (+ s); Hjerternes kamp. 1913: Den Farlige Adler (+ s); Pressens magt (+ s); Af elskovs naade (+ s/w); Atlantis (+ s); Höjt spil (+ s); Vasens hemmelighed (+ s); 1914: Arbejdet adler (+ s); Revolutions Bryllup (+ s); Pro patria (+ w-s); Truel lykke; Den Störste kaerughed. 1915: Syndens datter (+ s); For sit lands aere; Kaerlighedslaengel; Giftpilen (+ s). 1916: Verdens undergang (+ s); Gillekop (+ s). 1918: Maharajaens undlingshustru; Grevindens aëre; Dentelles; Via Crucis. 1920: Prometheus (12 eps); Hans Gode Genius (+ s). 1924: Det Store Hjerte (+ s); Den Store Magt (+ s). 1925: Hendes Naade dragonem (+ s); Praesten i vejlby (+ s).

BLONDELL, Joan

Actress. New York 1909–
Parents professional actors; appeared on stage a few

months old. Stage role with James Cagney in 'Penny Arcade' (1929) led to both being brought to Hollywood for film version, *Sinner's Holiday* (1930). Then second leads in musicals (mainly for Warners), moving to straight comedies. Title role in *Stand In* (1937). Appeared in several TV series. Married (1932–35) George Barnes, (1936–44) Dick Powell, (1947–50) Mike Todd.

Films as actress include: 1931: The Public Enemy; Night Nurse. 1932: The Greeks Had a Word for Them. 1933: Gold Diggers of 1933; Footlight Parade. 1945: A Tree Grows in Brooklyn. 1946: Adventure. 1947: Nightmare Alley. 1957: Will Success Spoil Rock Hunter? 1961: Angel Baby. 1965: The Cincinnati Kid. 1971: Support Your Local Gunfighter.

BLOOM, Claire

Actress. London 1931–
1940–42: war evacuee to USA. From 1943: drama training in UK. Guildhall School of Music and Drama (1946–47); Central School of Speech and Drama (1947–48). 1946: debut with Oxford Repertory Company; bit part in 'The White Devil' (1947) at Shakespeare Memorial Theatre, Stratford-on-Avon. 1948: Stratford-on-Avon. 1949–50: 'The Damask Cheek', 'The Lady's Not for Burning', 'Ring Round the Moon' in London. Joined Old Vic Company (1952–54) and on American tour (1956–57). First film, *The Blind Goddess* (1948), under Rank contract. First important part: *Limelight* (1951). Subsequent stage appearances in London and on Broadway, e.g. 'Hedda Gabler' (1971). Married (1959–69) to Rod Steiger, then (1969) to producer Hillard Elkins.

Films as actress include: 1955: Richard III. 1956: Alexander the Great. 1957: The Brothers Karamazov. 1958: The Buccaneer. 1959: Look Back in Anger. 1960: Schachnovelle. 1962: The Chapman Report. 1963: The Haunting. 1964: The Outrage. 1965: The Spy Who Came in From The Cold. 1968: Charly; Three into Two Won't Go. 1969: The Illustrated Man.

BLUE, James

Director. Tulsa, Oklahoma 1930–
Oregon University. Army service, then returned to Oregon for Master's degree. 1956–58: IDHEC. With New York advertising agency, Benton and Bowles, making TV commercials. 1959: travelled to Algeria; began to make documentaries. In Algeria made feature *Les Oliviers de la Justice* (1962). 1963: US Information Service Film Department. 1966: supervised prologue of *Hawaii*. 1969: Filmmaker in Residence at American Film Institute's Center for Advanced Film Studies in Los Angeles. Lecturer in Film at UCLA.

Films as director: 1959: Amal, le voleur. 1960: La Princesse Muette; L'Avare (co-d R. Hermeantier). 1962: Les Oliviers de la Justice – The Olive Trees of Justice (+ s/w). 1963: The March – The March to Washington; Letter from Colombia; School at Rincon Santo. 1968: A Few Notes on Our Food Problem.

BLYTH, Ann

Actress. Mount Kisco, New York 1928–
Drama school. Began on New York radio at 5. 3 years with San Carlo Opera Company. Broadway debut at 13, playing Paul Lukas's daughter in 'Watch on the Rhine'. 1944: first films for Universal; most films there until 1952. 1953–57: with MGM. Since 1958: mainly TV guest spots.

Films as actress include: 1945: Mildred Pierce. 1946: Swell Guy. 1947: Brute Force. 1948: A Woman's Vengeance; Another Part of the Forest. 1949: Top o' the Morning; Our Very Own. 1951: The Great Caruso; Thunder on the Hill. 1952: The World in His Arms; Sally and Saint Anne. 1953: All the Brothers Were Valiant. 1954: The Student Prince; Rose Marie. 1955: Kismet. 1957: The Helen Morgan Story.

BOEHM, Sydney

Writer. Philadelphia, Pennsylvania 1908–
Lehigh University. 1930–45: reporter, e.g. for New York Journal-American and an agency. 1944: collaborated on original story for *A Guy Named Joe*. Producer as well as writer on some of later 1950s films for Fox.

Films as writer include: 1944: Knickerbocker Holiday (*co*). 1950: Mystery Street (*co*); Branded (*co*); Union Station. 1951: When Worlds Collide. 1953: The Big Heat; Second Chance (*co*). 1954: The Raid; Black Tuesday. 1955: Violent Saturday; The Tall Men (*co-s*). 1956: The Revolt of Mamie Stover. 1958: Harry Black and the Tiger. 1959: Woman Obssessed (+ *p*). 1960: Seven Thieves (+ *p*). 1965: Sylvia.

BOETTICHER, Jr, Budd *or*

Oscar

Director. Chicago 1916–
Ohio State University; football and basketball player. Became interested in bullfighting while resting in Mexico after football season; became pupil of matador Lorenzo Garcia. Consultant on bullfighting for *Blood and Sand* (1941); credited with conceiving dance number 'El Torero'. Messenger at Hal Roach Studio. 1943–44: assistant director, e.g. on *The More the Merrier* (1943) and *Cover Girl* (1944). 1944: co-director on B-features, then director at Columbia. B-features at Columbia (1944–45), Eagle Lion (1948) and Monogram (1949–50), all as Oscar Boetticher Jr. 1946: directed several propaganda films for US services; one, *The Fleet that Came to Stay,* distributed commercially. From 1951 credited as Budd Boetticher, first on *The Bullfighter and the Lady* for Batjac, released by Republic. 1951–53: at Universal. 1956–59: *Seven Men from Now* for Batjac started series of westerns starring Randolph Scott; others mostly produced by Scott and Harry Joe Brown for Columbia. Directed TV pilot for 'Maverick'; other work for TV includes *The Sword of D'Artagnan* (1951), series pilot later given theatrical release, and 4 episodes of 'The Dick Powell Show'. 1962–68: in Mexico shooting bullfighting documentary *Arruza;* wrote book based on problems shooting it, 'When In Disgrace'. Also wrote novel, 'The Long Hard Year of the White Rolls-Royce' and original screenplay for *Two Mules for Sister Sara* (1970).

Films as director: 1944: One Mysterious Night; The Missing Juror. 1945: A Guy, A Gal and A Pal; Escape in the Fog; Youth on Trial. 1946: The Fleet That Came to Stay. 1948: Assigned to Danger; Behind Locked

Metropolis. *directed by Fritz Lang, produced by Henry Blanke and Erich Pommer.*
The Rise and Fall of Legs Diamond, *directed by Budd Boetticher.*
Dirk Bogarde and James Fox in Joseph Losey's The Servant.

Doors. 1949: The Wolf Hunters; Black Midnight. 1950: Killer Shark. 1951: The Bullfighter and the Lady; The Sword of D'Artagnan; The Cimarron Kid. 1952: Red Ball Express; Bronco Buster; Horizons West. 1953: City Beneath the Sea; Seminole; The Man from The Alamo; Wings of the Hawk; East of Sumatra. 1955: The Magnificent Matador – The Brave and the Beautiful. 1956: The Killer is Loose; Seven Men from Now. 1957: The Tall T; Decision at Sundown. 1958: Buchanan Rides Alone. 1959: Ride Lonesome (+ p); Westbound. 1960: Comanche Station (+ p); The Rise and Fall of Legs Diamond. 1959–68: Arruza (r 1971; + p/s). 1969; A Time for Dying (+ s).

BOGARDE, Dirk

(Derek Van Den Bogaerd) Actor. London 1920–
Father art editor of The Times. 1936: scholarship to Royal Academy of Art. Stage manager at Q Theatre. 1939: began as actor with Amersham Repertory Company. 1940: Army Intelligence, Photographic Interpretation Unit. Spotted in 'Power Without Glory' (1947) on London stage; Rank contract. Continued stage appearances after first film (1948).

Films as actor include: 1948 Quartet ep Alien Corn. 1949: The Blue Lamp. 1951: Blackmailed. 1954: The Sleeping Tiger. 1956: Ill Met by Moonlight. 1960: Song Without End. 1961: The Singer not the Song; Victim. 1962: The Password is Courage. 1963: The Servant. 1964: King and Country. 1965: Darling. 1966: Modesty Blaise. 1967: Accident; Sebastian. 1968: The Fixer. 1969: Justine. 1971: Morte a Venezia.

BOGART, Humphrey

Actor. New York 1899–1957 Los Angeles
In US Navy, then worked on Wall Street. At 19, manager of touring theatrical company. Small parts as actor; second lead in 'Swifty' on Broadway (1920), then leading parts during 1920s. First films under contract to Fox, starting with A Devil with Women (1930). On Broadway played Duke Mantee in 'The Petrified Forest' (1935); repeated part as first major screen role (1936). From 1936: Warners contract. Fourth wife was Lauren Bacall (married 1945). From 1949: some films for own company, Santana Pictures. Oscar as Best Actor for The African Queen (1951).

Films as actor: 1930: A Devil with Women; Up the River. 1931: Body and Soul; Bad Sister; Women of All Nations; A Holy Terror. 1932: Love Affair; Three on a Match; Big City Blues. 1934: Midnight. 1936: The Petrified Forest; Two Against the World; Bullets or Ballots; China Clipper; Isle of Fury; The Great O'Malley; Black Legion. 1937: San Quentin; Marked Woman; Kid Galahad; Dead End; Stand-In; Swing Your Lady. 1938: Men Are Such Fools; The Amazing Dr Clitterhouse; Racket Busters; Angels with Dirty Faces. 1939: King of the Underworld; The Oklahoma Kid; Dark Victory; You Can't Get Away with Murder; The Roaring Twenties; The Return of Dr X; Invisible Stripes. 1940: Virginia City; It All Came True; Brother Orchid; They Drive by Night. 1941: High Sierra; The Wagons Roll at Night; The Maltese Falcon. 1942: All Through the Night; The Big Shot; In This Our Life (uc); Across the Pacific. 1943: Casablanca; Action in the North Atlantic; Thank Your Lucky Stars; Sahara. 1944: Passage to Marseille. 1945: To Have and Have

Not; Conflict. 1946: The Big Sleep; Two Guys from Milwaukee (uc). 1947: The Two Mrs Carrolls; Dead Reckoning; Dark Passage. 1948: The Treasure of the Sierra Madre; Key Largo. 1949: It's a Great Feeling; Knock on Any Door; Tokyo Joe. 1950: Chain Lightning; In a Lonely Place. 1951: The Enforcer; Sirocco; The African Queen. 1952: Deadline—USA. 1953: Battle Circus. 1954: Beat the Devil; The Caine Mutiny; Sabrina; The Barefoot Contessa; Love Lottery (uc). 1955: We're No Angels; The Left Hand of God; The Desperate Hours. 1956: The Harder They Fall.

BOGEAUS, Benedict E.

Producer. Chicago 1904–1968 Hollywood
Married film actress Dolores Moran (divorced 1962). Worked in real estate in Chicago; moved to Hollywood in 1940. 1941: became owner of General Service Studios. First film as producer: The Bridge of San Luis Rey (1944) for own company. Always worked as independent. Productions include series of films directed by Allan Dwan (1954–61). Died of heart attack.

Films as producer include: 1944: Dark Waters. 1946: The Diary of a Chambermaid (co). 1947: The Macomber Affair (co). 1948: A Miracle Can Happen (co). 1950: Johnny One Eye. 1951: My Outlaw Brother. 1953: Count the Hours; Appointment in Honduras. 1954: Silver Lode; Passion; Cattle Queen of Montana. 1955: Escape to Burma; Pearl of the South Pacific; Tennessee's Partner. 1956: Slightly Scarlet. 1957: The River's Edge. 1958: Enchanted Island; From the Earth to the Moon; The Most Dangerous Man Alive (r 1961). 1959: Jet Over the Atlantic.

BOLESLAVSKY or
BOLESLAWSKI, Richard

(Ryszard Srzednicki Boleslavsky) Director. Warsaw 1889–1937 Hollywood
University of Odessa, technical schools in Odessa. 1906–15: actor at Moscow Art Theatre under Stanislavsky. Acted in films from 1914; directed from 1915. 1918: co-directed and acted in agit-film Khleb. In Civil War joined Polish regiment of lancers. Also served as cameraman and organised filming of Polish version of the war. 1919: theatre in Warsaw. 1922: in Germany acted in Carl Dreyer's Die Gezeichneten; went to New York to work on Broadway. Directed for New York stage; 'The Vagabond King', 'Mr Moneypenny', 'The Three Musketeers', 'The Miracle', 'Macbeth'. 1929: to Hollywood as dialogue director. 1930: directed first American film Treasure Girl, a Pathe short. 1933–34: with MGM. 1934: co-directed Hollywood Party with Allan Dwan and Roy Rowland. 1935: with Fox. Returned to MGM for last 2 films. 1937: The Last of Mrs Cheyney completed after his death. Author of books on Stanislavsky's method of acting.

Films as director include: (complete from 1930) 1918: Khleb – Bread (co-d Boris Sushkevich; + w). 1919: Bohaterstwo Polskiego Skavto. 1921: Cud Nad Wisla. 1930: Treasure Girl; The Last of the Lone Wolf. 1931: The Gay Diplomat; Woman Pursued. 1933: Rasputin and the Empress; Storm at Daybreak; Beauty for Sale. 1934: Men in White; Fugitive Lovers; Operator 13; The Painted Veil; Hollywood Party (co-d, uc).

1935: Clive of India; Les Miserables; Metropolitan; O'Shaughnessy's Boy. 1936: The Garden of Allah; Theodora Goes Wild; Three Godfathers. 1937: The Last of Mrs Cheyney.

BOLOGNINI, Mauro

Director. Pistoia, Italy 1923–
Architecture at Florence University. Design and direction at Centro Sperimentale di Roma. Assistant to Luigi Zampa, Mario Zampi, Yves Allegret, Jean Delannoy. 1953: first film as director. Directed several scripts by Pasquale Festa Campanile, several by Pier Paolo Pasolini e.g. La Giornaya Balorda (1959), written in collaboration with Alberto Moravia. 1969: co-wrote Antonio. 1970: staged 'La Traviata' in Verona.

Films as director: 1953: Ci troviamo in galleria. 1954: I Cavalieri della regina (+ co-s). 1955: Gli Inamorati – Wild Love (+ co-s); La Vena d'oro (+ co-s). 1956: Guardia, guardia scelta, brigadiere e maresciallo. 1957: Marisa la civetta (+ co-s). 1958: Giovani Mariti – Young Husbands (+ co-s). 1959: Arrangiatevi; La Notte Brava – Night Heat (+ co-s). 1960: I Bell'- Antonio; La Giornata Balorda – From a Roman Balcony – A Day of Sin. 1961: La Viaccia – The Love Makers. 1962: Senilità; Agostino (+ w). 1963: La Corruzione. 1964: Le Bambole – Four Kinds of Love ep Monsignor Cupido; I Tre Volti; La Mia Signora eps I Mieri Cari; Luciana; La Donna e una cosa meravigliosa. 1965: Madamigella di Maupin – Le Chevalier de Maupin. 1966: Le Streghe ep Senso Civico – The Civic Sense; Le Fate – Sex Quartet – The Fairies – The Queens ep Fata Elena. 1967: Le Plus Vieux Metier du monde ep Nuits Romaines. 1968: Un Bellissimo Novembre. 1970: Metello (+ co-s).

BOLT, Robert

Playwright. Sale, Cheshire 1924–
First play produced on London stage: 'Flowering Cherry' (1957). A Man for All Seasons based on his play, produced on London stage in 1960. Married to Sarah Miles.

Films as writer: 1962: Lawrence of Arabia (co). 1965: Dr Zhivago. 1966: A Man for All Seasons (+ fpl). 1970: Ryan's Daughter (+ st).

BONDARCHUK, Sergei

Actor and director. Bilozeka, Ukraine, Russia 1920–
As child moved to Tanganrog with parents. Amateur dramatics. Rostov Theatrical College. State debut in front-line army ensemble. 1946: Institute of Cinema Art. 1947–48: first film as actor, Sergei Gerasimov's Molodaya Gvardiya in which all parts were played by Gerasimov's students. 1951: took leading part in Taras Shevchenko. 1956: took lead in Otello. 1960: acted in Era notte a Roma, first Soviet actor to act outside Iron Curtain countries. 1959: first film as director, in which he also acted. 1964–67: directed Voina i mir, played Pierre Bezhukov; made in 4 parts, condensed to 2 for American release.

Films as actor include: 1953: Admiral Ushakov. 1955: Poprigunya; Neokonchennaya Povest.

Films as director and actor: 1959: Sudba cheloveka – Destiny of a Man. 1964–67: Voina i mir – War and

Peace (+ *co-s*; part I: Andrei Bolkonsky, 1964; part II: Natasha Rostova, 1966; part III: Borodino–1812, 1967; part IV: Pierre Bezukhov, 1967). 1970: Waterloo (*d* only; + *co-s*).

BOORMAN, John

Director. London 1933–

Father a publican. At 16 started dry-cleaning business in partnership; left it after 2 years. National service as sergeant. From 21: assistant editor for Independant TV News; started ITN programme 'Day By Day'. To Southern TV, worked in documentary for 2 years. Took over BBC documentary unit at Bristol. 1965: on leave of absence, first film as director *Catch Us If You Can*; returned to BBC. 1967: first American film *Point Blank*.

Films as director: 1965: Catch Us If You Can. 1967: Point Blank. 1968: Hell in the Pacific. 1970: Leo the Last (+ *co-s*).

BOOTH, Shirley

(Thelma Booth Ford) Actress. New York 1907–

First stage appearance at 12 under name Thelma Booth in 'Mother Carey's Chickens'. Much work in stock companies before first Broadway success, 'Three Men on a Horse' (1935). 1929–41: married to Ed Gardner, radio comedian; both in radio series 'Duffy's Tavern' (1940–42). On Broadway, e.g. in 'Come Back, Little Sheba' (1950); repeated role in film and won Oscar as Best Actress (1952). 4 films for Paramount; 3 for Hal Wallis. Title role in TV series 'Hazel'.

Films as actress: 1953: Come Back, Little Sheba; Main Street to Broadway. 1954: About Mrs Leslie. 1958: Hot Spell; The Matchmaker.

BORGNINE, Ernest

Actor. Hamden, Connecticut 1918–

First acted in school in Newhaven. Truck driver. World War II: gunner's mate in US Navy. After war enrolled at Randall School of Dramatic Art in Hartford, Connecticut. 4½ years with Barter Theater in Virginia. TV plays in New York. Films from 1951. On Broadway in 'Mrs McThing' with Helen Hayes (1952). Oscar as best actor for *Marty* (1955). TV series: 'McHale's Navy'. Acted in Fielder Cook's TV film for NBC *Sam Hill: Who Killed the Mysterious Mr Foster?*

Films as actor include: 1951: The Mob; From Here to Eternity. 1954: Johnny Guitar; Vera Cruz; Bad Day at Black Rock. 1955: Violent Saturday. 1956: The Catered Affair; The Best Things in Life Are Free. 1958: The Vikings. 1960: Pay or Die. 1961: Il Giudizio Universale. 1962: Barabbas. 1965: The Flight of the Phoenix. 1967: Chuka; The Dirty Dozen. 1968: The Legend of Lylah Clare; Ice Station Zebra. 1971: Hannie Caulder; Willard.

BOROWCZYK, Walerian

Animator and director. Kwilicz, Poland 1923–

1946–51: Academy of Art in Cracow, painting and lithography. While student made amateur documentary shorts. Continued to make experimental shorts, e.g. in 1952 by drawing and painting directly on film. 1954: to Warsaw as lithographic artist and poster designer.

mainly using photo-montage. Visited Paris; made 2 shorts there: *Photographies Vivantes* and *Atelier de Fernand Léger*. On return to Warsaw met Jan Lenica; began collaboration. 1958: animation consultant on Stanislaw Jedryka's *Stadion*; moved to Paris. 1959: on *Terra Incognita* used pinscreen developed by Alexandre Alexeïeff. 1960: joined Cineastes Associes. Many cinema and TV commercials e.g. *Holy Smoke* (1963) for Wills' Tobacco. Scripts many of his films. Animated credit sequences for *Les Félins* (1964) and *La Vie de château* (1965). *Le Théâtre de Monsieur et Madame Kabal* (1967), *Goto, l'île d'amour* (1968) and *Blanche* (1971) are feature length.

Live-action films as director include: 1953: Glowa. 1954: Photographies Vivantes; Atelier de Fernand Leger. 1956: Jesien. 1966: Rosalie. 1967: Gavotte (+ *s*); Diptyque – Diptych (+ *st/c*). 1968: Goto, l'île d'amour – Goto, Island of Love (+ *s/di*). 1971: Blanche (+ *s*).

Animated films as director include: 1957: Byl sobie raz – Once Upon a Time (+ *co-s/co-dec*; co-d Jan Lenica); Striptease (*co-d Jan Lenica*). 1958: Dom – House (+ *co-s/co-dec*; co-d Jan Lenica); Nagrodzone Uczvcte – Love Rewarded (+ *co-s*; co-d Jan Lenica); Szkola – School (+ *s/c*). 1959: Terra Incognita (+ *c*); Le Magicien (+ *p/c/w*); Les Astronautes (*co-d/co-s Chris Marker*). 1960: Le Dernier Voyage de Gulliver (+ *s*; *uf*). 1961: Boite a musique (*co-d Jan Lenica*); Solitude (*co-d Jan Lenica*). 1962: Le Concert de Monsieur et Madame Kabal – The Concert of Mr and Mrs Kabal (+ *s*). 1963: L'Encyclopedie de grand'maman en 13 volumes; Holy Smoke (+ *s/dec*); Renaissance (+ *s/dec*). 1964: Les Jeux des anges. 1965: Le Dictionnaire de Joachim – Joachim's Dictionary. 1967: Le Théâtre de Monsieur et Madame Kabal (+ *st/s/dec*). 1969: Le Phonographe.

BORZAGE, Frank

Director. Salt Lake City, Utah 1893–1962

1906: stage debut. 1913: actor in Hollywood. 1916: joined Thomas H. Ince as actor; moved from bit parts to leading roles in Ince films; also started directing. 1916: actor/director on 9 films. 1917–19: some films for Triangle. 1920: first major film as director, *Humoresque*. 1925–32: with Fox. *Seventh Heaven* won first Oscar (1927–28) for direction; also won Janet Gaynor first Oscar as actress. Oscar (1931–32) for direction of *Bad Girl*. 1937–42: mainly with MGM.

Films as director: 1916: Life's Harmony; The Silken Spider; The Code of Honor; Nell Dale's Men Folks; That Gal of Burke's; The Forgotten Prayer; The Courtin' of Calliope Clew; Nugget Jim's Pardner; The Demon of Fear (*all + w*). 1917: Flying Colors. 1918: The Ghost Flower; The Curse of Iku. 1919: Whom the Gods Would Destroy; Toton; Prudence on Broadway; Shoes that Danced; Ashes of Desire. 1920: Humoresque. 1921: The Duke of Chimney Butte; Get Rich Quick Wallingford. 1922: Back Pay; Silent Shelby (+ *w*); Billy Jim; The Good Provider; The Valley of Silent Men; The Pride of Palomar. 1923: Children of Dust (+ *p*); The Nth Commandment; Song of Love; The Age of Desire (+ *p*). 1924: Secrets. 1925: The Lady – Lady (+ *p*); Daddy's Gone A'Hunting (+ *p*); Wages for Wives; The Circle; Lazybones. 1926: Marriage License?; The First Year; The Dixie Mer-

Humphrey Bogart in Edward Dmytryk's The Left Hand of God.
Ernest Borgnine in Nicholas Ray's Run for Cover.
Gary Cooper and Helen Hayes in Frank Borzage's A Farewell to Arms.

chant; Early to Wed. 1927: Seventh Heaven. 1928: Street Angel. 1929: The River; Lucky Star; They Had to See Paris. 1930: Song o' My Heart; Liliom. 1931: Doctors' Wives; Bad Girl; Young as You Feel. 1932: Young America; After Tomorrow. 1933: A Farewell to Arms; Secrets; Man's Castle. 1934: No Greater Glory; Little Man What Now?; Flirtation Walk (+p). 1935: Living on Velvet; Stranded; Shipmates Forever. 1936: Desire; Hearts Divided. 1937: Green Light; History is Made at Night; Big City. 1938: Mannequin; Three Comrades; Shining Hour. 1939: Disputed Passage. 1940: Strange Cargo; The Mortal Storm; Flight Command. 1941: Smilin' Through; The Vanishing Virginian. 1942: Seven Sweethearts. 1943: Stage Door Canteen; His Butler's Sister. 1944; Till We Meet Again. 1945: The Spanish Main. 1946: I've Always Loved You; Magnificent Doll. 1947: That's My Man. 1948: Moonrise. 1958: China Doll. 1959: The Big Fisherman. 1961: Antinea—l'amante della città sepolta – Atlantis, the Lost Continent – The Lost Kingdom (uc, co-d Edgar G. Ulmer, Giuseppe Masini).

BOSÈ, Lucia

Actress. Milan, Italy 1931–
Worked in *pasticceria* in Milan. 1947: Miss Italy. 1950: first film *Non c'è pace tra gli ulivì*. 1956: married matador Luis Miguel Domingúin and retired from films; returned for guest appearance with him in *Le Testament d'Orphée* (1960). After separation from Domingúin, returned to films.

Films as actress include: 1950: Cronaca di un amore. 1952: Le Ragazze di Piazza di Spagna – Girls of the Spanish Steps; Roma ore undici. 1953: La Signora senza camelie. 1954: Muerte de un Ciclista – Death of a Cyclist. 1955: Gli Sbandati. 1956: Cela s'appelle l'aurore. 1969: Fellini—Satyricon; Sotto il segno dello scorpione. 1970: Metello.

BOST, Pierre

Writer. Lasalle, France 1901–
Playwright and novelist during 1920s and '30s. Plays include adaptation of Graham Greene's 'The Power and the Glory'. Script writer from 1942, in collaboration with Jean Aurenche from 1943.

Films as writer in collaboration with Jean Aurenche include: 1943: Douce. 1945: La Symphonie Pastorale (di). 1947: Le Diable au Corps. 1949: Au—delà des grilles (ad/di); Occupe-toi d'Amélie. 1951: L'Auberge Rouge. 1952: Jeux Interdits (co-s). 1954: Le Rouge et le Noir; Le Blé en herbe (co-s/di). 1956: Gervaise (ad/di); La Traversèe de Paris. 1958: En cas de malheur. 1959: Les Régates de San Francisco. 1961: Non uccidere (co-ad). 1962: Le Meurtrier. 1963: Le Magot de Josefa.

BOSUSTOW, Stephen

Producer. Victoria, British Columbia, Canada 1912–
Drummer with various well-known bands. Began as commercial artist with small company. 1932: worked with Ub Iwerks on *Flip the Frog*. 1934: worked with Walter Lantz at Universal. 1934–41: writer and sketcher for Walt Disney, e.g. on first animations for *Snow White*, stories for *Bambi* and *Fantasia*. 1942: production illustrator for Hughes Aircraft; then formed own industrial film company and advertising service.

1944: made his name with *Hell Bent for Election*, President Roosevelt's election campaign film. 1945: with David Hilberman, Zachary Schwartz and Ed Gershman, formed UPA (United Productions of America) which made commercials, animated shorts and eventually some features; acted as producer (from 1947) and president. 1961: sold interest in UPA to make travel and educational films. Oscars for best cartoon won by 3 UPA productions, *Gerald McBoing Boing* (1950), *When Magoo Flew* (1954), *Mr Magoo's Puddle Jumper* (1956). His production company received Oscar for 'short subject-animated' *Is It Always Right to be Wrong?* produced by Nick Bosustow.

BOULTING, John *and* Roy

Directors. Bray, Berkshire 1913–
Twin brothers. Together founded film society at school in Reading. From 1930, John worked in London film distributor's office; Roy went to Canada; wrote dialogue at Trenton Studios, Ontario; returned to work as film salesman, then assistant director at Marylebone Studios, London; joined there by John (1935). 1937: John went to Spain as ambulance driver in Civil War; brothers formed Charter Film Productions. Began with featurettes and documentaries, Roy directing, John producing. World War II: John in RAF, rose to Flight Lieutenant; Roy in Royal Artillery Corps, reaching Captain. 1941: Roy was cameraman for Army film unit on Vaagno commando raid. 1945: John's first film as director, *Journey Together,* for RAF film unit. From 1945: films together, alternating as producer and director. 1951: contract with MGM to make 5 films. 1958: joined British Lion Films. 1962: High Court action with cinematograph technician's union (ACTT) over membership of union; action lost; compromise arranged. 1967–69: John was managing director of British Lion. Roy married Hayley Mills.

Films directed by Roy Boulting (produced by John Boulting except during 1943–45): 1938: The Landlady; Ripe Earth; Seeing Stars; Consider Your Verdict. 1939: Trunk Crime. 1940: Inquest; Pastor Hall; Dawn Guard. 1942: Thunder Rock; They Serve Abroad. 1943: Desert Victory (uc). 1944: Tunisian Victory (uc, co-d Frank Capra, uc). 1945: Burma Victory (+cy). 1947: Fame Is The Spur. 1948: The Guinea Pig (+co-s). 1951: Single-handed – Sailor of the King – Able Seaman Brown – Brown on Resolution; High Treason (+co-s). 1954: Seagulls Over Sorrento (+co-s) – Crest of the Wave. 1955: Josephine and Men. 1956: Run for the Sun (+co-s). 1957: Happy is the Bride; Brothers in Law. 1959: I'm All Right Jack (+co-p); Carlton-Browne of the F.O. 1960: Suspect (+co-p); A French Mistress (+co-p). 1966: The Family Way. 1968: Twisted Nerve (+co-p). 1970: There's A Girl in My Soup.

Films directed by John Boulting (produced by Roy Boulting unless otherwise stated): 1945: Journey Together (+s; p RAF Film Unit). 1947: Brighton Rock – Young Scarface. 1950: Seven Days to Noon (p/co-s Roy Boulting). 1951: The Magic Box (p Ronald Neame). 1956: Private's Progress (+co-s). 1957: Lucky Jim (+co-p). 1963: Heavens Above! (+co-s). 1965: Rotten to the Core (p/co-s Roy Boulting).

BOURGOIN, Jean *or* Yves

Cinematographer. Paris 1913–
Photographic school. Began as assistant to cinemato-

graphers including Curt Courant and Christian Matras. First films as cinematographer during early 1940s. 1943–50: called himself Yves Bourgoin.

Films as cinematographer include: 1943: Goupi mains-rouges (co). 1946: Voyage—surprise. 1948: Dédee d'Anvers. 1949: Manèges. 1950: Justice est faite. 1952: Nous sommes tous des assassins. 1954: Avant le déluge. 1955: Confidential Report. 1958: Mon Oncle; Orfeu Negro. 1961:' The Counterfeit Traitor. 1962: The Longest Day. 1964: Pas question le samedi. 1970: Qui?

BOURGUIGNON, Serge

Director. Maignelay, France 1929–
Father aviator. Art school and IDHEC. Assistant to Jean-Pierre Melville on *Les Enfants Terribles* (1950) and to André Zwobada, with whom directed first short. 1954: film-making in Borneo. 1955–56: led party making films in India; *Sikkim, Terre Secrète* was feature length. Other expeditions, e.g. to Tibet, China, Malaya and Burma. 1958: 9 months in Mexico writing screenplay for abortive project, *Marie Lumière*. 1962: Oscar for *Cybèle, ou les dimanches de Ville d'Avray* as best foreign language film.

Films as director: 1952: Le Rhin, Fleuve International (co-d André Zwobada). 1953: Médecin des sols. 1954: Démons et Merveilles de Bali; Bornéo. 1956: Sikkim, Terre Secrète – Le Langage du sourire. 1957: Jeune Patriarche. 1959: Escale; L'Etoile de mer; Le Montreur d'ombres. 1960: Le Sourire. 1962: Cybèle, ou les dimanches de ville d'Avray – Sundays and Cybele (+s/w). 1964: La Chevauchée. 1965: The Reward (+s). 1967: A coeur joie – Two Weeks in September (+co-s); The Picasso Summer (ur).

BOURVIL

(André Raimbourg) Actor and singer. Petrot-Vicquemare, France 1917–70 Paris
Spent childhood at Bourville, hence professional name. Worked as baker at Rouen for 5 years. During military service ran musical and comedy companies. Then provincial theatre companies; contracted to operetta company in Paris until start of World War II. 1945: first film. Song writer.

Films as actor include: 1949: Miquette et sa mère. 1954: Si Versailles m'était conté. 1956: La Traversee de Paris. 1958: Le Miroir à deux faces. 1959: La Jument Verte. 1961: Tout l'or du monde. 1962: The Longest Day. 1963: Un Drôle de paroissien; Le Magot de Josefa. 1965: Les Grandes Gueules. 1969: L'Etalon. 1970: Le Mur de l'Atlantique; Le Cercle Rouge.

BOW, Clara

Actress. New York 1905–1965 Hollywood
Typist. 1922: won screentest as beauty contest prize; led to bit part in *Beyond the Rainbow*, edited out of finished film; first appearance in *Down to the Sea in Ships* for Whaling Film Corporation. To 1935; worked for several companies including First National, Warners, Fox and Universal. 1926–31: with Famous Players-Lasky and Paramount. 1931: released from contract because of ill-health; married actor Rex Bell (later Lieutenant-Governor of Nevada). 1932–33: made comeback in 2 films for Fox, *Call Her Savage*

and *Hoop-la*: no further work in cinema. 1947: appeared on TV in 'Mrs Hush'.

Films as actress include: 1923: The Enemies of Women; Black Oxen. 1924: Grit. 1925: Eve's Lover; Kiss Me Again; The Plastic Age. 1926: Dancing Mothers; Mantrap; Kid Boots. 1927: It; Children of Divorce; Hula. 1928: Red Hair; Ladies of the Mob; The Fleet's In; Three Weekends. 1929: Wings. 1930: Paramount on Parade; True to the Navy; Love Among the Millionaires; Her Wedding Night. 1931: No Limit.

BOYD, Stephen

(William Miller) Actor. Belfast, Northern Ireland 1928–

Canadian father. At 16 joined Ulster Group Theatre. 1946: to Canada; acted on radio and in summer stock. From 1952: appeared with Windsor Repertory Company and Midland Theatre Company in England. 1954: small parts on London stage. 1955: first film, *An Alligator Named Daisy*.

Films as actor include: 1956: The Man Who Never Was. 1957: Island in the Sun; Seven Thunders; Les Bijoutiers du clair de lune. 1958: The Bravados. 1959: The Best of Everything; Woman Obsessed; Ben-Hur. 1961: The Big Gamble; The Inspector. 1962: Billy Rose's Jumbo; Vénus Impériale. 1964: The Fall of the Roman Empire. 1966: La Bibbia. 1968: Shalako. 1969: Slaves. 1971: Kill.

BOYER, Charles

Actor. Figeac, France 1897–

University of Toulouse; Sorbonne. 1917–21: studied acting at Conservatoire de Paris. 1920: first film: *L'Homme du Large*. Leading parts on Paris stage and several French silent films. Some sound films also in Germany; French versions of American films in Hollywood until 1931. English-speaking films in Hollywood since 1932: has also appeared in many European plays and films (only American films 1938–52). 1955: partner in TV company, 4 Star Productions; starred in its series 'The Rogues'; has also directed. 1934: married actress Pat Patterson.

Films as actor include: 1934: Liliom. 1935: Private Worlds. 1936: Mayerling; The Garden of Allah. 1937: Orage; Tovarich; Conquest; History Is Made at Night. 1938: Algiers. 1939: Love Affair; When Tomorrow Comes. 1940: All This and Heaven Too. 1941: Hold Back the Dawn; Back Street. 1942: Tales of Manhattan. 1943: Flesh and Fantasy (+ co-p). 1944: Gaslight. 1945: Confidential Agent. 1946: Cluny Brown; The Arch of Triumph. 1948: A Woman's Vengeance. 1951: The 13th Letter. 1953: Madame de . . . 1955: The Cobweb. 1957: La Parisienne. 1958: The Buccaneer. 1961: Fanny. 1962: The Four Horsemen of the Apocalypse. 1963: Love Is a Ball.

BOYLE, Robert

Art director

Began career with RKO. 1942: first film as art director *Saboteur*. Moved to Universal in late 1940s.

Films as art director include: 1958: Buchanan Rides Alone. 1959: The Crimson Kimono (co). 1961: Cape Fear. 1963: The Birds (co). 1964: Marnie (co). 1965:

The Reward (co); Do Not Disturb (co). 1966: The Russians Are Coming, the Russians Are Coming. 1967: How To Succeed in Business Without Really Trying; Fitzwilly; In Cold Blood. 1968: The Thomas Crown Affair. 1969: Gaily, Gaily (des). 1970: The Landlord (des). 1971: Fiddler on the Roof (des).

BRACKETT, Charles

Producer. Saratoga Springs, New York 1892–1969
Father partner in law firm and represented district in New York State Legislature. 1915: graduated from Williams College; Harvard Law School – course interrupted by World War I. Liaison service in France; Médaillon d'honneur en argent. 1920: first novel 'The Counsel of the Ungodly' published; graduated from Harvard Law School. 6 years in father's law firm. Regular contributor to Saturday Evening Post, Collier's, Vanity Fair, etc. 1925: novel, 'Weekend'. 1926–29: drama critic of The New Yorker. Other novels include 'That Last Infirmity' (1926), 'American Colony' (1929), 'Entirely Surrounded' (1934). 1932: to Hollywood on 6-week Paramount contract; remained at Paramount until 1950, but *Piccadilly Jim* (1936) was for MGM. 1938–50: collaborated with Billy Wilder as co-scenarist and (from 1943) producer. From 1950: producer at Fox. 1938–39: president of Screen Writers' Guild. 1949–50: twice president of Academy of Motion Picture Arts and Sciences. Senior partner in family law firm. President of Trust Company owning business concerns in Saratoga Springs. Oscars for *The Lost Weekend* (screenplay, with Wilder, 1945), *Sunset Boulevard* (story and screenplay with Wilder and D. M. Marshman Jr, 1950); *Titanic* (story and screenplay with Walter Reisch and Richard Breen, 1953); honorary award for outstanding services to the Academy (1957).

Films as writer (those with Billy Wilder marked†) include: 1931: Secrets of a Secretary (st). 1935: College Scandal (co); The Crusades (co). 1936: Piccadilly Jim (co). 1938: Bluebeard's Eighth Wife (co†). 1939: Midnight (co†); Ninotchka (co†). 1940: Arise, My Love (co†). 1941: Hold Back the Dawn (co†); Ball of Fire (co†). 1942: The Major and the Minor (co†).

Films as writer and producer: 1943: Five Graves to Cairo (co†). 1945: The Lost Weekend (co†). 1946: To Each His Own (st/co-s). 1948: The Emperor Waltz (co†); A Foreign Affair (co†); Miss Tatlock's Millions (co). 1950: Sunset Boulevard (co†). 1951: The Mating Season (co); The Model and the Marriage Broker (co). 1953: Niagara (co); Titanic (co). 1955: The Girl in the Red Velvet Swing (co). 1956: Teenage Rebel (co). 1959: Journey to the Centre of the Earth (co).

Films as producer: 1944: The Uninvited. 1954: Garden of Evil; Woman's World. 1955: The Virgin Queen. 1956: The King and I; D-Day, the 6th of June. 1957: The Wayward Bus. 1958: The Gift of Love; Ten North Frederick. 1959: The Remarkable Mr Pennypacker; Blue Denim. 1960: High Time. 1962: State Fair.

BRADBURY, Ray

Writer. Waukegan, Illinois 1922–
Author of many science fiction novels and short stories. Films adapted by others from his work include *Fahrenheit 451* (1966) and *The Illustrated Man*

Desert Victory *directed by Roy Boulting.*
Clara Bow.
Mothlight, *by Stan Brakhage.*

(1969). Film projects for which he wrote scripts: *Mañana* (1957), *The Martian Chronicles* (1961)..

Films as writer: 1953: It Came From Outer Space. 1956: Moby Dick (*co*).

BRADLEY, David

Director and producer. Winnetka, Illinois 1920–
1935: entered Todd School, Woodstock. After leaving made shorts including *Treasure Island, Dr X, A Christmas Carol, Emperor Jones*. 1940: first feature-length film. In Hollywood worked with Maria Ouspenskaya. 1940–42: studied at School of Speech, Northwestern University. 1941: directed Charlton Heston and Thomas Blair in *Peer Gynt* (1942). 1942: made short *Sredni Vashtar*. Served in US Army Signal Corps. Worked on army films in London, Paris, Munich, Brussels. Studied at MGM photographic school and later at photographic centre, Astoria, Long Island. Became member of Cinamathèque Française; worked at studio where Nuremberg films were handled. 1946: produced, wrote, photographed, edited and acted in Thomas Blair's *Macbeth*. 1951: worked for MGM as assistant. 1952: for MGM directed *Talk about a Stranger*. Worked for other studios on features only occasionally. From 1969: full-time teaching at UCLA in motion picture history.

Features as director and producer: 1940: Oliver Twist (+*ad/co-c/e/m/w*). 1941: Peer Gynt (+*co-ad/co-c/e/w*). 1949: Julius Caesar (*r* 1952: +*ad/w*).

Features as director: 1952: Talk about a Stranger. 1958: Dragstrip Riot. 1960: Twelve to the Moon.

BRAGAGLIA, Carlo Ludovico

Director. Frosinone, Italy 1894–
Son of Francesco Bragaglia, director-general of Cines. 1918: began in minor capacities at Cines. With brother Anton, director, designer, critic, founded Casa d'Arte Bragaglia (1918) and Teatro degli Indipendenti (1922). Became cinematographer, editor, writer. Directed shorts. 1932: first feature as director *O la borsa O la vita!*. Directed Vittorio de Sica several times, from *Un Cattivo Soggetto* (1933). Directed brother Arturo in several films. 1939: first film with Totò *Animali Pazzi* (1939).

Films as director: 1933: O la borsa O la vita! (+*co-s*); Non son gelosa; Un Cattivo Soggetto. 1934: Quella Vecchia Canaglia; Frutto Acerbo. 1936: Amore. 1937: La Fossa degli angeli – The Angel's Pit (+*co-s*). 1939: Animali Pazzi; Belle o brutte si sposan tutte; L'Amore si fa cosi. 1940: Pazza di gioia (+*st/s*); Un Mare di guai (+*co-s/co-st/co-di*; *co-d Luigi Zampa*); Una Famiglia Impossibile; Il Prigioniero di Santa Cruz. 1941: La Forza Bruta; Allessandro, sei grande!; Barbablù (+*s*); Due Cuori sotto sequestro (+*s*); L'Allegro Fantasma (+*st*; *uc*; *co-d Amleto Palermi*). 1942: La Scuola dei timidi; Violette nei capelli (+*s*); Se io fossi onesto (+*co-s*); La Guardia del corpo (+*s*); Non ti pago!; Casanova farebbe cosi (+*s/st*). 1943: Fuga a due voci (+*s/st*); Il Fidanzato di mia moglie (+*s/st*). 1944: Non sono superstizioso, ma . . . ; 'Tutta la vita in Ventiquattr'ore; La Vita è bella (+*s*). 1945: Lo Sbaglio di essere vivo. 1946: Torna a Sorrento; Pronto, chi parla? 1947: L'Altra; Albergo luna-camera Trentaquattro; La Primula Bianca. 1949: Totò le Mokò.

1950: Il Falco Rosso; Figaro qua, Figaro la; Totò cerca moglie; Le Sei Moglie di Barbablù. 1951: 47, morto che parla (+*co-s*); Una Bruna Indiavolata. 1952: L'Eroe sono Io – I'm the Hero; A Fil di spada – At Sword's Point; Il Segreto delle tre punte – The Secret of the Three Sword Points. 1953: Don Lorenzo. 1955: Orient Express; La Cortigiana di Babilonia – The Slave Woman – The Queen of Babylon (+*s*). 1956: Il Falco d'oro. 1957: Gerusalemme Liberata – Jerusalem Set Free – The Mighty Crusaders; Lazzarella. 1958: Caporale di giornata – Soldier on Duty: Io, mammeta e tu – Me, Mother and You; E' permesso maresciallo?; La Spada e la croce – The Sword and the Cross; Le Cameriere (+*co-d Sergio Grieco*). 1959: Annibale – Hannibal (*co-d Edgar G. Ulmer, uc*). 1960: Gli Amori di Ercole – The Loves of Hercules; Le Vergini di Roma – The Virgins of Rome – The Amazons of Rome – The Warrior Women (*co-d Vittorio Cottafavi, uc*). 1961: Pastasciutta nel deserto – Spaghetti in the Desert; Ursus nella Valle dei Leoni – Ursus in the Valley of the Lions. 1962: I Quattro Monaci – The Four Monks. 1963: I Quattro Moschettieri – The Four Musketeers.

BRAHM, John

(Hans Brahm) Director. Hamburg, Germany 1893–
Father stage actor Ludwig Brahm; uncle theatre impresario Otto Brahm. 1918: became one of first-string directors at the Burgtheater, Vienna. 1930: leading director at Deutsches Kunstlertheater, Berlin. 1933: directing at Lessing Theater, Berlin (sometimes billed Hans Brehm); left for Paris. 1935–36: in London, production supervisor and editor on *Scrooge* (1936); first film as director, also in London, a re-make of *Broken Blossoms* (1919); brought to Hollywood by Myron Selznick. From 1955: gave up cinema for TV; about 150 TV films during next 10 years, in series including 'Thriller', 'Alfred Hitchcock Hour', 'Twilight Zone'. Married German actress Dolly Haas.

Films as director: 1936: Broken Blossoms. 1937: Counsel for Crime. 1938: Penitentiary; Girls' School. 1939: Let Us Live; Rio. 1940: Escape to Glory – Submarine Zone. 1941: Wild Geese Calling. 1942: The Undying Monster. 1943: Tonight We Raid Calais; Wintertime. 1944: The Lodger; Guest in the House. 1945: Hangover Square. 1946: The Locket. 1947: The Brasher Doubloon – The High Window; Singapore. 1951: Il Ladro di Venezia – The Thief of Venice. 1952: The Miracle of Our Lady of Fatima; Face to Face *ep* The Secret Sharer. 1953: The Diamond Queen. 1954: The Mad Magician; Die goldene Pest. 1955: Vom Himmel gefallen – Special Delivery; Bengazi. 1967: Hot Rods to Hell.

BRAKHAGE, Stan

Director. Kansas City, Missouri 1933–
Adopted out of Kansas at 2 weeks, settled in Denver. 1950: Dartmouth College, left after nervous breakdown in first term. 1953: first film as director; cinematography at San Francisco Institute of Fine Arts; returned to Denver. 1954–55: San Francisco. 1955: New York, co-directed with Joseph Cornell, and photographed, *Tower House*. 1956: worked in Raymond Rohauer's cinema, commissioned by him to make *Flesh of Morning*. All films in 16mm except *Songs* (1964–70) and *Sexual Meditations No. 1: Motel* (1970), in 8 mm.

Films as director: 1953: Interim; Unglassed Windows Cast a Terrible Reflection. 1954: Desistfilm; The Extraordinary Child (*co-d Larry Jordan*). 1955: In Between; The Way to Shadow Garden; Reflections on Black; The Wonder Ring; Tower House (+*c*; *co-d Joseph Cornell*). 1956: Zone Moment; Flesh of Morning; Nightcats; Loving. 1957: Daybreak & Whiteye. 1958: Anticipation of the Night. 1959: Wedlock House: an Intercourse; Window Water Baby Moving; Cat's Cradle; Sirius Remembered. 1960: The Dead. 1961: Thigh Line Lyre Triangular; Prelude; Dog Star Man; Films by Stan Brakhage: an Avant-Garde Home Movie. 1962: Blue Moses; Dog Star Man: Part I; Silent Sound Sense Stars Subotnick & Sender. 1963: Oh Life—A Woe Story—the A Test News; Mothlight; Dog Star Man: Part II. 1964: Dog Star Man: Part III; Dog Star Man: Part IV. 1965: The Art of Vision (*version of* Dog Star Man); Two: Creeley/McClure; Pasht; Three Films: Blue White, Blood Tone, Vein; Fire of Waters; Black Vision. 1964–70: Songs (1–31). 1967–70: Scenes from Under Childhood. 1968: Love Making. 1969: The Weir-Falcon Saga. 1970: The Machine of Eden; The Animals of Eden and After; Eyes; Deus Ex; Sexual Meditations No 1: Motel. 1971: Fox Fire Child Watch.

BRANDO, Marlon

Actor. Omaha, Nebraska 1924–
Military Academy, then studied at Dramatic Workshop of New School for Social Research, New York. Actor in summer stock. 1944: Broadway debut in 'I Remember Mama'; other Broadway parts before 2-year run in lead of 'A Streetcar Named Desire' (from 1947). 1950: first film. 1959: formed own company, Pennebaker Productions, for which he directed *One-Eyed Jacks,* replacing Stanley Kubrick after disagreement prior to start of shooting in 1958; company's other productions include *Paris Blues* (1961). Sister is actress Jocelyn Brando. Married actresses Anna Kashfi (1957–59) and Movita. Oscar as best actor for *On the Waterfront* (1954).

Films as actor: 1950: The Men. 1951: A Streetcar Named Desire. 1952: Viva Zapata. 1953: Julius Caesar; The Wild One. 1954: On the Waterfront; Desirée. 1955: Guys and Dolls. 1956: The Teahouse of the August Moon. 1957: Sayonara. 1958: The Young Lions. 1959: The Fugitive Kind. 1961: One-Eyed Jacks (+*d*). 1962: Mutiny on the Bounty; The Ugly American. 1964: Bedtime Story. 1965: The Saboteur – Code Name Morituri. 1966: The Chase; The Appaloosa. 1967: A Countess from Hong Kong; Reflections in a Golden Eye. 1968: Night of the Following Day; Candy; I Queimada!. 1971: The Nightcomers.

BRASS, Tinto

Director. Milan, Italy 1933–
Lived in Venice until completion of law studies. 2 years working in Cinemathèque Française; at same time worked as assistant editor to Joris Ivens. Assistant director to Alberto Cavalcanti on *Les Noces Vénitiennes* (1958) and Roberto Rossellini on *India* (1958) and *Il Generale della Rovere* (1959).

Films as director: 1963: In capo al mondo – Chi lavora è perduto (+*s/e*). 1964: Ça ira – Il Fiume della rivolta; La Mia Signora *eps* I Miei Cari, L'Uccellino.

1965: Il Disco Volante. 1966: Yankee. 1967: Col cuore in gola (+ *st/co-s/e*). 1969: Nero su bianco – Black on White. 1970: L'Urlo; Dropout. 1971: La Vacanza (+ *st/co-s/e*).

BRASSEUR, Pierre

(Pierre Espinasse) Actor. Paris 1903–
Mother actress Germaine Brasseur. By 15, stage actor. 1925: first films. Frequent films from 1930. Wrote poems; wrote, produced and acted in plays in Paris and Brussels. Toured in 'Tchao' (1971). 1968: book of reminiscences 'Ma Vie en vrac'. Father of actor Claude Brasseur.

Films as actor include: 1925: La Fille de l'eau: Madame Sans-Gêne. 1932: Quick. 1934: Le Sexe Faible. 1936: Vous n'avez rien à déclarer? 1938: Quai des brumes. 1941: Jeunes Timides. 1942: Lumière d'ete. 1943: Adieu Leonard. 1945: Les Enfants du paradis. 1946: Les Portes de la nuit. 1948: Les Amants de Vérone. 1952: Le Plaisir. 1954: La Tour de Nesle; Oasis. 1955: Napoléon. 1957: Porte des Lilas. 1958: La Loi; La Tête contre les murs. 1959: Les Yeux sans visage. 1960: Il Bell 'Antonio; Candide; Le Dialogue des Carmelites. 1961: Pleins Feux sur l'assassin. 1963: Les Bonnes Causes; Le Magot de Josefa. 1965: La Vie de château; Un Mondo Nuovo. 1966: Le Roi de coeur. 1968: Les Oiseaux vont mourir au Perou. 1971: Les Mariés de l'an II.

BRAULT, Michel

Cinematographer and director. Montreal, Canada 1928–
Studied philosophy at University of Montreal. Amateur films with Claude Jutra. Assistant camera-man at National Film Board of Canada during summer vacation (1950). Commercial photographer. Worked on TV series. 1956: joined NFBC as cinematographer. Worked on 'Candid Eye' series. 1960: in France as cinematographer for Jean Rouch and Mario Ruspoli. 1963: co-directed with Jutra *Les Enfants de silence* for TV; artistic and technical adviser, also cinemato-grapher, on *Seul ou avec des autres,* made by students at University of Montreal. 1964: directed *Le Temps Perdu,* half-hour documentary for TV.

Films as director: 1947: Le Dement du Lac Jean Jaune (*co-d Claude Jutra*). 1949: Mouvement Perpetuel (*co-d Claude Jutra*). 1958: Les Raquetteurs – De gais Lurons en congrès – The Snowshoers (+ *c*; *co-d Gilles Groulx*). 1961: La Lutte – The Fight (+ *co-c/co-e*; *co-d Claude Jutra, Marcel Carrière, Claude Fournier*). 1962: Québec–USA – L'Invasion Pacifique (+ *c*; *co-d Claude Jutra*); Pour la suite du monde – The Moontrap (+ *co-c*; *co-d Pierre Perrault*). 1963: *Les Enfants du silence* (+ *c*; *co-d Claude Jutra*). 1964: La Fleur de l'age ou les Adolescantes *ep* Geneviève; Le Temps Perdue. 1966: Entre la mer et l'eau douce – Geneviève (+ *co-s/co-c*). 1967: Les Enfants de neant (+ *c*; *co-d Annie Tresgot*). 1970: Moncton (+ *c*; *co-d Pierre Perrault*). 1971: L'Acadie, L'Acadie (+ *c*: *co-d Pierre Perrault*).

Films as cinematographer include: 1956: Pierrot des Bois. 1958: Les Mains Nettes (*co*). 1959: Felix Le Clerc, Troubadour; Normétal. 1961: Chronique d'un ete (*co*). 1962: La Punition (*co*). 1963: A tout prendre – Take it All (*co*). 1965: Poussière sur la ville (*co*). 1966:

Rouli-roulant. 1968: Ce soir-là, Gilles Vigneault (*co*). 1969: Le Beau Plaisir. 1970: Eloge du Chiak (*co-c; + st/e*); Marie-Christine. 1971: Mon Oncle Antoine.

BRAY, John Randolph

Animator
Cartoons for Life Magazine, Judge, Puck and Brooklyn Eagle. 1910: made *The Artist's Dream (or) The Dachshund and the Sausage,* released 1913. Worked on animation with Max Fleischer, by super-imposition with reference to corners and cross lines. Started 'Colonel Heeza Liar' series and set up John Randolph Bray Studios, where helped in industrial development of animation by means of cels, translucent sheets, a peg system and serial production, with division of labour. 1915: studio produced scientific films (Bray Pictograph series) and US Army training films. 1916: produced first commercial animated cartoon in colour; made *Colonel Heeza Liar Wins the Pennant.* 1917: formed Bray-Hurd Process company with Earl Hurd. 1919: Magazine of the Screen (Bray Pictograph), *How We Breathe.* 1920: company be-came Goldwyn-Bray Company; produced Goldwyn Bray Comics, e.g. *Happy Hooldini (and) Lampoons, All for the Love of a Girl and Lampoons;* produced *Elements of the Automobile* series for US Army. 1922–23: produced series of 'Colonel Heeza Liar' for Bray Productions Inc. 1925–27: produced series in-cluding 'Dinkey Doodle', 'Unnatural History' and 'Hot Dog Cartoons'. 1927: documentary on the Colorado River Expedition, *Bride of the Colorado.* 1931: produced *Father Nile* for Bray Products Corporation. During 1930s: several existing companies produced documentaries. 1941–45: documentaries on aircraft maintenance for Bray Studios Inc. Specialised in films for educational and training purposes, including health and safety films, some with French or Spanish narrat-ion, some for TV.

BRDECKA, Jiri

Director and writer. Hranice, Czechoslovakia 1917–
From 1936: art history at Prague University, until closed by Germans. World War II: journalist, film critic. 1940: published book 'Limonádovy Joe', later turned into play. 1943: began at Prague Cartoon Film Studio. From 1947: writing and other collaborations with Jiri Trnka. 1949: to Barrandov studio. 1964: his play basis of Oldrich Lipsky's *Limonádovy Joe.* Writings include short stories..

Films as writer in collaboration include: 1948: Cisařuv slavik. 1949: Arit prérie. 1953: Stare povesti české; O skleničku vic. 1958: Slava; Bombománie. 1959: Sen noci svatojanské; Taková láska.

Films as director include: 1946: Perak a SS – Perak Against the SS (*co-d/co-s Jiri Trnka*). 1947: Vzducholod a láska – The Zeppelin and Love. 1958: Než nám narost a křidla – How Man Learned to Fly (+ *s*); Jak se člověk naučil létat – A Comic History of Aviation. 1959: Pozor! – Look Out! (+ *s*). 1960: Naše karkulka – Our Little Red Riding Hood (+ *s*). 1961: Závada není na vašem přijimači (+ *s*); Člověk podvodon – Man Underwater (*co-d Ladislav Capek*; + *s*). 1962: Rozum a cit – Reason and Emotion (+ *s*). 1963: Špatně namalovaná slepice – The Grotesque Chicken (+ *s*); Slowce M – The Letter M; – The Minstrel's Song. 1964: A Song of Love. 1965:

Angie Dickinson and Marlon Brando in The Chase, *directed by Arthur Penn.*
Vanessa Redgrave in La Vacanza, *directed by Tinto Brass.*
Gidget Goes to Rome, *directed by Paul Wendkos, produced by Jerry Bresler.*

Dezerter – The Deserter; Felicity of Love. 1966: Why is the Mona Lisa Smiling?; On Watch in the Forest – Forester's Song. 1968: Power of Destiny; Pomsta – Revenge (*ep*); Pražske noci – Prague Nights (*ep*); The Hand (*+ s*). 1971: Aristotele (*co-d Max Massimino Garnier*).

BRECHT, Bertolt

Playwright. Augsburg, Germany 1898–1956 East Berlin.
1930: book 'Sur le cinéma' (reprinted 1970). 1931: collaborated with G. W. Pabst on script of *Die Dreigroschenoper* from his own play. 1932: co-scripted Slatan Dudow's *Kühle Wampe* and wrote the lyrics. 1933: emigrated to USA. 1943: with Fritz Lang wrote story for *Hangmen Also Die!*; screenplay credited to John Wexley. 1947: play 'Galileo' directed by Joseph Losey, with John Hubley as designer, on Los Angeles and New York stage; left America the day after being 'unfriendly' witness at hearing of House Committee on Un-American Activities. From 1948: in East Berlin; founded theatrical company, the Berliner Ensemble. His songs sung by Paul Robeson in *Das Lied der Ströme* (1954).

Films as writer in collaboration: 1931: Die Dreigroschenoper (*+fpl; co-s, uc*). 1932: Kühle Wampe (*st/co-s/lyr*). 1943: Hangmen Also Die! (*+ co-st*). 1956: Herr Puntila und sein Knecht Matti (*+fpl; co-ad*).

BREEN, Richard L.

Writer. Chicago 1919–
1940–42: freelance radio writer. 1942–46: US Navy. After war, worked as screen writer. 1957: wrote and directed *Stopover Tokyo*. Has been President of the Screenwriters' Guild and the Writers' Guild of America. Oscar for story and screenplay *Titanic* (with Charles Brackett and Walter Reisch, 1953).

Films as writer include: 1948: A Foreign Affair (*co*); Miss Tatlock's Millions (*co*). 1951: The Model and the Marriage Broker (*co*). 1952: O. Henry's Full House (*co*). 1953: Niagara (*co*); Titanic (*co*). 1955: Pete Kelly's Blues (*+ as-p*). 1959: The FBI Story (*co*). 1960: Wake Me When It's Over. 1962: State Fair. 1963: Mary, Mary.

BREER, Robert

Director. Detroit, Michigan 1926–
1943–46: art at Stanford. From 1949: participated in group and one-man shows in Europe, USA and Cuba. 1952: first film as director *Form Phases I*. All films are shorts; makes use of Mutascopes; cinematographer on all his films.

Films as director: 1952: Form Phases I. 1953: Form Phases II and III. 1954: Form Phases IV; Image by Images I; Un Miracle (*co-d Pontus Hulten*). 1955: Image by Images II and III; Image by Images IV; Motion Pictures; Cats. 1956–57: Recreation I; Recreation II. 1957: Jamestown Baloos; Par Avion; A Man and his Dog out for Air. 1958–59: Eyewash. 1960: Homage to Jean Tinguely's Homage to New York; Inner and Outer Space. 1961: Blazes. 1962: Horse over Tea Kettle; Pat's Birthday (*co-d Claes Oldenburg*). 1963: Breathing. 1964: Fist Fight. 1966: 66. 1968: 69; PBL; PBL II. 1971: '70.

BRENNAN, Walter

Actor. Swampscott, Massachusetts 1894–
Served as a private in World War I. Drifted to Hollywood; began there as stuntman (1923). Started playing old men at 32 after teeth knocked out in mob scene. Established as character actor by *Barbary Coast* (1935). Oscars as supporting actor: *Come and Get It* (1936). *Kentucky* (1938), *The Westerner* (1940). Also TV including series 'The Real McCoys' (from 1957), 'The Guns of Will Sonnett'.

Films as actor include: 1935: Man on the Flying Trapeze; The Wedding Night. 1936: Three Godfathers; These Three; Fury. 1938: The Buccaneer. 1939: Stanley and Livingstone. 1940: Northwest Passage. 1941: Meet John Doe; Sergeant York; Swamp Water. 1942: Pride of the Yankees. 1943: Hangmen Also Die; The North Star. 1944: Home in Indiana. 1945: To Have and Have Not. 1946: Centennial Summer; My Darling Clementine. 1947: Driftwood. 1948: Red River. 1950: Surrender. 1951: Along the Great Divide. 1954: Bad Day at Black Rock; The Far Country. 1959: Rio Bravo. 1962: How the West Was Won. 1966: The Oscar. 1969: Support Your Local Sheriff!

BRENON, Herbert

Director. Dublin 1880–1958 Los Angeles
Father London editor and critic. Educated in Dublin and at London University. 1896: went to New York. From 1897, call boy at Daly's Theater; toured as theatrical and vaudeville stage manager and actor. Settled in Johnston, Pennsylvania; directed vaudeville and theatre; ran nickelodeon. 1906: contract with Universal as editor and writer. 1910: first film as director (also wrote and acted), *All For Her*; directed, wrote own screenplays and occasionally acted, started with a film a week, then 2 films a month. 1913–19: some films in UK including *Ivanhoe* (1913), *The Secret of the Air* (1914), *Victory and Peace* (1918), *Twelve-Ten* (1919). From 1914: contract with Fox; directed Theda Bara in several films including *The Clemenceau Case* and *The Two Orphans* (1915). 1916: contract for 6 pictures with Unione Cinematografica Italiana. 1918: became naturalised American citizen. 1920–21: Fox contract. 1922–27: Paramount contract. By 1928, had directed over 300 films; publicly opposed talkies. Sound films in Hollywood (until 1932) and UK. 1940: retired.

Films as director include (complete from 1925): 1910: All For Her (*+ s/w*). 1912: The Nurse. 1913: Ivanhoe; Absinthe; Kathleen Mavourneen. 1914: Leah, the Forsaken; The Secret of the Air; Neptune's Daughter. 1915: Across the Atlantic; The Clemenceau Case (*+ s*); Kreutzer Sonata (*+ s*); Sin (*+ s*); Whom the Gods Destroy; The Soul of Broadway (*+ s*); Two Orphans (*+ s*). 1916: A Daughter of the Gods (*+ st/s*); War Brides; Marble Heart (*+ s*); Ruling Passion. 1917: The Fall of the Romanoffs; Eternal Sin; Lone Wolf; Empty Pockets. 1918: Victory and Peace. 1919: Principessa Misteriosa; A Sinless Sinner; Twelve-Ten (*+ p*). 1921: The Passion Flower; The Sign on the Door (*+ co-s*); Beatrice. 1922: A Stage Romance; Any Wife; The Wonderful Thing (*+ co-s*); Shackles of Gold; Moonshine Valley; The Stronger Passion. 1923: The Custard Cup; The Rustle of Silk (*+ p*); The Woman with 4 Faces; The Spanish Dancer. 1924: The Side Show of

Life (*+ p*); The Alaskan; Shadows of Paris (*+ p*); The Breaking Point; Peter Pan. 1925: The Little French Girl; The Street of Forgotten Men; A Kiss for Cinderella. 1926: Dancing Mothers; The Song and Dance Man; The Great Gatsby; Beau Geste (*+ co-ad*); God Gave Me 20 Cents. 1927: The Telephone Girl; Sorrell and Son (*+ s*). 1928: Laugh Clown Laugh (*+ p*). 1929: The Rescue. 1930: Lummox; The Case of Sergeant Grischa. 1931: Beau Ideal; Transgression. 1932: Wine, Women and Song; The Girl of the Rio. 1935: Honour's Easy; Royal Cavalcade. 1936: Living Dangerously; Someone at the Door. 1937: The Dominant Sex; Spring Handicap; The Live Wire. 1938: Yellow Sands; The Housemaster. 1940: The Flying Squad.

BRESLER, Jerry

Producer. Denver, Colorado 1912–
Worked for an investment company before becoming production manager and producer for Supreme Pictures Corporation. Own company, Tower Productions, which made an early 16mm sound feature. Then unit production manager at MGM. 1942: associate producer of shorts at MGM, then producer. At MGM produced training films for services and morale films for US consumption. Producer of features at MGM. 1945: moved to Universal, then to Columbia. 1953: produced Ray Bolger TV series at MGM. 1960: producer, releasing through Columbia.

Films as producer include: 1948: Another Part of the Forest. 1951: The Mob. 1958: The Vikings (*co*). 1960: Because They're Young. 1961: Gidget Goes Hawaiian. 1963: Gidget Goes to Rome. 1965: Major Dundee; Love has Many Faces. 1967: Casino Royale (*co*).

BRESSON, Robert

Director. Bromont-Lamothe, France 1907–
Classics and philosophy at university; then painter in Paris. Collaborated on a few scripts in 1930s and directed a single film (1934). 1939: worked on René Clair's *Air Pur* until shooting stopped by outbreak of World War II. One year in a German prisoner-of-war camp. Writer-director from 1943. Dialogue for *Les Anges du péché* by Jean Giraudoux, for *Les Dames du Bois de Boulogne* by Jean Cocteau; thereafter responsible for own dialogue. Abortive projects include *Ignace de Loyola, Lancelot du lac* and 'Garden of Eden' section of *La Bibbia* for Dino De Laurentiis.

Films as director and writer: 1934: Les Affaires Publiques (*d/co-e only*). 1943: Les Anges du péché. 1945: Les Dames du Bois de Boulogne. 1950: Le Journal d'un curé de campagne – Diary of a Country Priest. 1956: Un Condamné à mort s'est échappé – A Man Escaped. 1959: Pickpocket. 1961: Le Procès de Jeanne d'Arc – The Trial of Joan of Arc. 1966: Au hasard, Balthazar – Balthazar. 1967: Mouchette. 1969: Une Femme Douce – A Gentle Creature. 1971: Quatre Nuits d'un rêveur.

BRIALY, Claude

Actor. Aumale, Algeria 1933–
Son of high-ranking French army officer. Studied philosophy at Strasbourg University, acting at Paris Conservatoire. Provincial repertory before army ser-

vice. 1956: began acting in films; first feature part, *Eléna et les hommes*.

Films as actor include: 1956: La Sonate à Kreutzer; Le Coup du berger. 1957: Un Amour de poche; Tous les garçons s'appellent Patrick. 1958: Le Beau Serge; Les Cousins. 1959: Les Quatre Cent Coups. 1960: Le Bel Age; Les Godelureaux. 1961: Une Femme est une femme. 1962: L'Education Sentimentale 61. 1963: Chateau en Suède. 1964: La Ronde; Tonio Kroeger. 1966: Le Roi de coeur. 1967: La Mariée était en noir. 1970: Le Bal du Comte d'Orgel; Le Genou de Claire.

BRIDIE, James

(Osborne Henry Mavorne) Writer. Glasgow, Lanarkshire 1888–1951
Medicine at Glasgow University. Practised in Glasgow. World War I: served in Royal Army Medical Corps. 1928: Scottish National Players produced his play 'Sunlight Sonata' written under pseudonym Mary Henderson. Practising physician until 1938. 1937: first film credit: his adaptation of Bruno Frank's play was basis of *Storm in a Teacup*. Mainly theatrical career. World War II: served in RAMC. 1947–50: writer on films directed by Alfred Hitchcock. Plays include; 'The Anatomist' (1931), 'Jonah and the Whale' (1932), 'Marriage is No Joke' (1934), 'Colonel Wotherspoon' (1934), 'Moral Plays' (1936), 'The King of Nowhere' (1938), 'Mr Bolfry' (1943), 'Dr Angelus' (1947).

Films as writer include: 1937: Storm in a Teacup (*fpl*). 1947: The Paradine Case (*co-ad*). 1949: Under Capricorn (*s*). 1950: Stage Fright (*additional di*).

BRODINE, Norbert

(Norbert Brodin) Cinematographer. St Joseph, Missouri 1897–
Columbia University. Worked in Los Angeles camera shop. World War I: US Army photographer. 1919: entered films. 1919–23: worked mainly for Goldwyn, youngest cinematographer in the industry. 1924–28: worked mainly for First National and Warners; under contract to Frank Lloyd. 1929–31: mainly Pathe and RKO-Pathe. From 1930: Known as Brodine. 1932–33: frequently at MGM. 1934–36: at Universal. 1937–41: for Hal Roach at MGM and United Artists. From 1943: almost all films for Fox. 1952: last film; became photographer for Hal Roach TV Productions. TV work includes The Loretta Young Show.

Films as cinematographer include: 1919: Almost a Husband. 1921: A Tale of Two Worlds; The Invisible Power; The Man from Lost River; The Grim Comedian. 1923: Dulcy; Brass; Within the Law; Black Oxen. 1924: The Silent Watcher. 1925: Her Husband's Secret; Winds of Chance. 1926: The Wise Guy; The Splendid Road. 1927: The Romantic Age; Brass Knuckles. 1928: Pay as You Enter; Five and Ten Cent Annie; The Lion and the Mouse; Beware of Bachelors (*co*). 1930: The Divorcee; Let Us Be Gay. 1931: The Guardsman. 1932: Night Court; Wild Girl; Uptown New York. 1933: Whistling in the Dark; Counsellor at Law. 1934: Little Man What Now?; Cheating Cheaters. 1935: The Good Fairy. 1936: Libeled Lady. 1937: Topper. 1938: Merrily We Live; There Goes My Heart. 1939: Topper Takes a Trip; Captain Fury; The Housekeeper's Daughter. 1940: Of Mice and Men; One Million BC; Turnabout. 1941: Road Show. 1943:

Dr Gillespie's Criminal Case; The Dancing Masters. 1945: The Bullfighters; Don Juan Quilligan; The House on 92nd Street. 1946: Sentimental Journey; Somewhere in the Night. 1947: 13 Rue Madeleine; Kiss of Death; Boomerang! 1948: Sitting Pretty. 1949: I Was a Male War Bride (*co*); Thieves' Highway. 1951: The Frogmen; The Desert Fox. 1952: Five Fingers.

BRONNER, Robert

Cinematographer
Worked in MGM matte-painting department. Cinematographer from 1955. Most films for MGM.

Films as cinematographer include: 1955: It's Always Fair Weather. 1956: Meet Me in Las Vegas; The Opposite Sex. 1957: Ten Thousand Bedrooms; Silk Stockings; Jailhouse Rock; Don't Go Near the Water. 1958: The Sheepman; The Tunnel of Love; Party Girl. 1959: The Mating Game; Ask Any Girl; It Started With a Kiss. 1960: Please Don't Eat the Daisies; Where the Boys Are. 1961: Gidget Goes Hawaiian; Pocketful of Miracles. 1962: The Horizontal Lieutenant. 1963: Gidget Goes to Rome (*co*). 1964: The 7 Faces of Dr Lao.

BRONSTON, Samuel

Producer. Bessarabia, Russia 1909–
Educated at Sorbonne. Salesman for MGM in France. 1942: executive producer on 2 films for Columbia in Hollywood. 1943: founded Samuel Bronston Pictures, releasing through Columbia; made only *Jack London* (1943). 1957: travelling through Spain, learned that many US corporations had blocked funds which could only be reinvested there. Obtained backing for $4,000,000 from several American corporations to film *John Paul Jones* (1959). Although this was unsuccessful he found backers for *King of Kings* (1961), eventually including MGM for whom modified film and added initial battle. Great success of third Spanish film, *El Cid* (1961), encouraged him to build vast studios near Madrid and make two more almost simultaneously, thus over-extending financial resources. Main backer, Pierre S. Dupont, withdrew leaving him insolvent. Suit filed by Dupont concerning a further $2½ million finally settled against Bronston in 1971; perjury indictments dating from 1966 led to judgement against him on one count – fined $2,000.

Films as producer (from 1959): 1959: John Paul Jones. 1961: King of Kings; El Cid. 1963: 55 Days at Peking. 1964: The Fall of the Roman Empire; Circus World.

BROOK, Clive

(Clifford Brook) Actor. London 1887–
Mother was opera singer Charlotte May Brook. British Army. 1918: first stage appearance. 1920: first film, *Trent's Last Case*, and London stage debut. 1921–44: no theatrical work. 1924: first American film, *Christine of the Hungry Heart*. 1945: directed and acted in *On Approval*. 1946: toured in and directed 'The Play's the Thing'. 1950: US stage debut in 'Second Threshold'. Repeated role in New York and London, and on American and British TV. Also on TV: 'The Play's the Thing'. Children are actors Faith and Lyndon Brook.

Films as actor include: 1923: Woman to Woman. 1925: Seven Sinners. 1926: Three Faces East. 1927:

Dominique Sanda in Robert Bresson's Une Femme Douce.

The Home on 92nd Street, *directed by Henry Hathaway, photographed by Norbert Brodine.*

Louise Brooks and Fritz Kortner in Die Buchse der Pandora, *directed by G. W. Pabst.*

Hula Underworld. 1928: Forgotten Faces. 1929: The Four Feathers. 1931: East Lynne; Tarnished Lady. 1932: Shanghai Express; Sherlock Holmes. 1933: Cavalcade. 1935: The Dictator. 1937: Action for Slander. 1939: The Ware Case. 1941: Freedom Radio. 1963: The List of Adrian Messenger.

BROOK, Peter

Director. London 1925–

At Oxford University made short *A Sentimental Journey* from Laurence Sterne, produced by Instructional Screen Corporation. 1944: shorts for Gaumont British Instructional. Worked with Sir Barry Jackson at Birmingham Repertory Theatre; at 20 directed Paul Scofield in 'King John' there. 1946: followed Jackson to Stratford-upon-Avon; also started directing on London stage. 1949–58: director of productions at Covent Garden Opera House. 1955: his production of 'Hamlet' with Paul Scofield was first British company to appear in Moscow since 1917. Also directed in New York, e.g. 'Eugen Onegin' at Metropolitan Opera, and Paris, e.g. 'Le Balcon' and 'Cat on a Hot Tin Roof'. 1962: appointed co-director of Royal Shakespeare Theatre, Stratford-upon-Avon. Stage productions with Royal Shakespeare Company include 'Marat/Sade' in London (1964) and New York (1965) and 'US' (1968). Wrote TV plays 'The Birthday Present', 'Box for One' (both 1955). 1953: TV production of 'King Lear' in New York.

Features as director: 1953: The Beggar's Opera. 1960: Moderato Cantabile – Seven Days ... Seven Nights (+ co-s). 1962: Lord of the Flies (+ s). 1966: The Persecution and Assassination of Jean-Paul Marat, as performed by the inmates of the Asylum of Charenton, under the direction of the Marquis de Sade. 1967: Red, White and Zero *ep* The Ride of the Valkyries (*ur*). 1968: Tell Me Lies (+ *ad*). 1969: King Lear (*r* 1971).

BROOKS, Louise

Actress. Wichita, Kansas 1900–

Dancer with Ziegfeld Follies. 1925: first film: *The Street of Forgotten Men*. Early films mainly for Paramount. 1928–29: in Germany for G. W. Pabst. One film in France, then in US mainly minor films until retirement after *Overland Stage Raiders* (1938). Wrote memoirs 'Naked on my Goat' but destroyed manuscript before publication; also unpublished book '13 Women in Films'; numerous articles. Was married to director Eddie Sutherland.

Films as actress include: 1926: The American Venus; A Social Celebrity; Love 'Em and Leave 'Em; It's the Old Army Game; The Show-Off; Just Another Blonde. 1927: The City Gone Wild. 1928: A Girl in Every Port; Beggars of Life. 1929: The Canary Murder Case; Die Büchse der Pandora; Das Tagebuch einer Verlorenen. 1930: Prix de beauté. 1931: God's Gift to Women; It Pays to Advertise. 1937: When You're in Love; King of Gamblers.

BROOKS, Richard

Director and writer. Philadelphia, Pennsylvania 1912–
1934: sports reporter on Philadelphia Record. From 1936: radio work at WNEW and NBC. 1940: theatre direction in New York. 1941: to Los Angeles

to write short stories for radio (NBC); first film work, writing dialogue for Universal. World War II: US Marine Corps. 1945: first novel, 'The Brick Foxhole', filmed as Crossfire (1947). Later novels: 'Boiling Point' (1948), 'The Producer' (1951). 1946–49: scriptwriter, first for Mark Hellinger. 1950: writer/director contract with MGM. 1960: married Jean Simmons. From *Lord Jim*, independent producer/director/writer releasing through Columbia or United Artists.

Films as writer include: 1944: My Best Gal (*st*). 1946: Swell Guy. 1947: Brute Force. 1948: To the Victor; Key Largo (*co*). 1949: Any Number Can Play. 1950: Mystery Street (*co*). 1951: Storm Warning (+ *co-st*; *co-s*).

Films as director: 1950: Crisis (+ *s*). 1951: The Light Touch (+ *s*). 1952: Deadline–USA – Deadline (+ *s*). 1953: Battle Circus (+ *s*); Take the High Ground. 1954: The Flame and the Flesh; The Last Time I Saw Paris (+ *co-s*). 1955: Blackboard Jungle (+ *s*). 1956: The Last Hunt (+ *s*); The Catered Affair – Wedding Breakfast. 1957: Something of Value (+ *s*); The Brothers Karamazov (+ *s*). 1958: Cat on a Hot Tin Roof (+ *co-s*). 1960 Elmer Gantry (+ *s*). 1961: Sweet Bird of Youth (+ *s*). 1965: Lord Jim (+ *p/s*). 1966: The Professionals (+ *p/st/s*). 1967: In Cold Blood (+ *p/s*). 1969: The Happy Ending (+ *p/s*). 1971: Dollars (+ *st/s*).

BROUGHTON, James

Director

Earlier films made in San Francisco. 1947: first film *Potted Psalm*. Films all shorts, usually 16mm. 1954: *The Pleasure Garden* made in England, produced by Lindsay Anderson and shot in 35mm. Poetry published in a number of anthologies; *Four in the Afternoon* (1951) based on own book of poems 'Musical Chairs'. Also playwright, e.g. 'Summer Fury' (1957), 'Burning Questions' (1958), 'The Last Word' (1959), 'How Pleasant it is to Have Money' (1964). Assisted on most of his films by Kermit Sheets, who acted in *Loony Tom, the Happy Lover* (1954).

Films as director: 1947: The Potted Psalm (*co-d Sidney Peterson*). 1948: Mother's Day (+ *p/s*). 1951: Four in the Afternoon (+ *s/c/wv*); The Adventures of Jimmy (+ *s/w/n*). 1954: The Pleasure Garden (+ *s*); Loony Tom, the Happy Lover – Loony Tom (+ *s/c*). 1967: The Bed. 1970: The Golden Positions. 1971: This Is It.

BROWN, Clarence L.

Director. Clinton, Massachusetts 1890–
Electrical and mechanical engineering at University of Tennessee. World War I as flying cadet, then instructor; life-long interest in flying. 1915–23: with World Films; assistant, with John Gilbert, to Maurice Tourneur. Editor, then wrote titles, then 2nd-unit director. Co-directed *The Last of the Mohicans* (1920), taking over when Tourneur fell ill. *Robin Hood Jr* (1923) was credited to Clarence Bricker. 1923–25: Universal contract. 1926–52: director at MGM; films included 7 with Greta Garbo. 1949: produced *The Secret Garden*. 1953: produced *Never Let Me Go*, then retired. University of Tennessee built

Clarence Brown Theater for the Performing Arts and Cinema.

Films as director: 1920: The Last of the Mohicans (*co-d Maurice Tourneur*); The Great Redeemer. 1921: The Foolish Matrons (*co-d Maurice Tourneur*). 1922: The Light in the Dark (+ *co-s*). 1923: Robin Hood Jr (*uc*); Don't Marry for Money; The Acquittal. 1924: The Signal Tower; Butterfly; Smouldering Fires. 1925: The Goose Woman; The Eagle 1926: Kiki. 1927: Flesh and the Devil. 1928: Trail of '98; A Woman of Affairs. 1929: Wonder of Women. 1930: Navy Blues; Anna Christie; Romance. 1931: Inspiration; A Free Soul; Possessed. 1932: Emma; Letty Lynton; The Son-Daughter. 1933: Looking Forward; Night Flight. 1934: Sadie McKee; Chained. 1935: Anna Karenina; Ah, Wilderness! 1936: Wife vs Secretary; The Gorgeous Hussy. 1937: Conquest; Marie Walewska. 1938: Of Human Hearts. 1939: Idiot's Delight; The Rains Came. 1940: Edison, the Man. 1941: Come Live with Me (+ *p*); They Met in Bombay. 1943: The Human Comedy (+ *p*). 1944: The White Cliffs of Dover; National Velvet. 1946: The Yearling (+ *p*). 1947: Song of Love (+ *p*). 1949: Intruder in the Dust (+ *p*). 1950: To Please a Lady (*ep*); It's a Big Country (*co-d 5 others*). 1951: Angels in the Outfield – Angels and Pirates (+ *p*). 1952: When in Rome (+ *p*); Plymouth Adventure (+ *p*).

BROWN, Harry Joe

Director and producer. Pittsburgh, Pennsylvania 1893–
Universities of Michigan and Syracuse. Directed college plays during vacations. Stage work as actor, prop man and director, partly in vaudeville, before entering films (1920). Various film jobs, some with own unit. Associate producer, director or supervisor often on shorts, then feature producer. 1927: first film as director. 1938–41: with Fox, associate producer to Zanuck, and producer. Worked with Randolph Scott from early 1940s. From 1947: many films with Scott, some for their own companies (Producers-Actors Corporation and Ranown Pictures); films as independent producer without Scott also released through Columbia. Independent TV producer through own Federal Telefilm Corporation.

Films as director: 1927: The Land Beyond the Law; Gun Gospel; The Wagon Show. 1928: The Cloud Patrol (+ *co-p*); Code of the Scarlet; The Sky Ranger; The Skywayman. 1929: The Air Derby (+ *co-p*); The Lawless Legion; The Royal Rider. 1931: A Woman of Experience. 1932: Madison Square Garden. 1944: Knickerbocker Holiday (+ *p*).

Films as producer include: 1935: Captain Blood; The Florentine Dagger; I Found Stella Parish. 1936: Ceiling Zero; Hearts Divided; The Great O'Malley. 1938: Alexander's Rag Time Band (*as-p*). 1939: The Gorilla (*as-p*). 1941: Western Union (*as-p*). 1943: The Desperadoes. 1948: Coroner Creek. 1949: The Doolins of Oklahoma. 1950: The Nevadan. 1951: Santa Fe; Man in the Saddle. 1953: The Stranger Wore a Gun. 1955: Lawless Street. 1956: 7th Cavalry. 1957: The Guns of Fort Petticoat; The Tall T (+ *co-pc*); Decision at Sundown (+ *co-pc*). 1958: Buchanan Rides Alone (+ *co-pc*); Screaming Mimi. 1959: Ride Lonesome (*ex-p/co-pc*). 1960: Comanche Station (*ex-p/co-pc*). 1964: Son of Captain Blood.

BROWNING, Tod

Director. Louisville, Kentucky 1882–1962 Santa Monica, California

Ran away from school to join a circus. Later became a clown with Mutt and Jeff; toured world with partner as 'The Lizard and the Coon'. Comedian in 'World of Mirth' troupe. 1914: went to Hollywood; work at Biograph and Reliance Majestic. Acted in *The Mother and the Law* for D. W. Griffith, who used him on *Intolerance* as assistant director and writer. 1917: first films as director; reputation made by *The Virgin of Stamboul* (1920). Remade the successful *Outside the Law* (1921) as a talkie (1930). 1942: retired.

Films as director: 1917: Jim Bludso; Peggy, the Will o' the Wisp; The Jury of Fate. 1918: Which Woman; The Eyes of Mystery; The Legion of Death; Revenge; The Deciding Kiss; The Brazen Beauty; Set Free. 1919: The Wicked Darling; The Exquisite Thief; The Unpainted Woman; A Petal in the Current; Bonnie Bonnie Lassie (*+co-s*). 1920: The Virgin of Stamboul (*+co-s*). 1921: Outside the Law (*+p/s*); No Woman Knows. 1922: Wise Kid; The Man Under Cover; Under Two Flags (*+ad*). 1923: Drifting (*+co-s*); The White Tiger (*+co-s*); The Day of Faith. 1924: The Dangerous Flirt; Silk Stocking Sal. 1925: The Unholy Three; The Mystic; Dollar Down. 1926: The Black Bird; The Road to Mandalay (*+co-st*). 1927: The Show; The Unknown; London After Midnight (*+p/st*). 1928: West of Zanzibar; The Big City. 1929: Where East is East (*+p/st*); The Thirteenth Chair. 1930: Outside the Law (*+st*). 1931: Dracula; The Iron Man. 1932: Freaks. 1933: Fast Workers. 1935: Mark of the Vampire. 1936: The Devil Doll (*+st*). 1939: Miracles for Sale.

BRUCKMAN, Clyde

Director and writer. San Bernardino, California 1894–1955 Santa Monica, California

Journalist. Writer at Warners. 1921: joined Buster Keaton's company as writer. 1926: first film as director, in collaboration with Keaton *The General*; wrote it with him. 1926–28: director for Hal Roach at MGM and for Pathe. 1927: supervised by Leo McCarey, directed Stan Laurel and Oliver Hardy (not as a team) in *Call of the Cuckoo*, then (1927–28) under McCarey's supervision directed them as a team in 4 films. 1929–32: films for Harold Lloyd's company. 1931: made *Everything's Rosie* for RKO. 1932–33: directed Paramount films for Mack Sennett. 1935: *Spring Tonic* for Fox based on play co-written by Ben Hecht 'Man Eating Tiger'. 1935: last film as director *Man on the Flying Trapeze* for Paramount. 1939–41: wrote several films in which Keaton acted. 1955: suicide.

Films as writer in collaboration include: 1923: Our Hospitality; Three Ages. 1924: The Navigator; Sherlock Jr. 1925: Seven Chances. 1938: Professor Beware (*co-ad*)

Films as director: 1926: The General (*+co-ad/co-st*). 1927: Call of the Cuckoo; Putting Pants on Philip; Speedy Smith; The Battle of the Century; Horse Shoes; A Perfect Gentleman; Love 'em and Feed 'em. 1928: The Finishing Touch; Leave 'em Laughing. 1929: Welcome Danger (*+co-s*). 1930: Feet First. 1931: Everything's Rosie. 1932: Movie Crazy. 1933:

Too Many Highballs; The Human Fish; The Fatal Glass of Beer. 1935: Spring Tonic; Man on the Flying Trapeze.

BRUN, Joseph

Cinematographer.

Entered films at Paramount in Joinville, France. Cinematographer at 30. Worked freelance.

Films as cinematographer include: 1951: The Whistle at Eaton Falls. 1952: Walk East on Beacon. 1953: Martin Luther. 1955: Vom Himmel gefallen. 1956: Edge of the City. 1958: Windjammer (*co*); Wind Across the Everglades. 1959: The Last Mile; Middle of the Night; Odds Against Tomorrow. 1960: Thunder in Carolina; Girl of the Night. 1962: Hatari! (*co, uc*). 1969: Slaves; Trilogy (*co*).

BRYNNER, Yul

Actor. Sakhalin, Russia 1915–

Parents Swiss and Mongolian. Worked as singer with gypsy groups in Paris, then acrobat and aerialist at Cirque d'Hiver until serious fall at 17. Stagehand at Théâtre des Mathurins. Philosophy degree at Sorbonne. From 1941: toured USA in Shakespearean company; broadcast news and propaganda for Voice of America; TV series with first wife Virginia Gilmore (married 1944–60). 1946: Broadway debut in 'Lute Song'. TV director with CBS. 1949: first film, *Port of New York*. 1950: on Broadway in 'The King and I' with Gertrude Lawrence. Oscar as Best Actor for *The King and I* (1956). Has made documentaries about refugee children for United Nations; wrote book about this, 'Bring Forth the Children' (1961).

Films as actor include: 1956: The Ten Commandments; Anastasia. 1957: The Brothers Karamazov. 1958: The Buccaneer; The Journey. 1959: The Sound and the Fury; Solomon and Sheba; Once More with Feeling. 1960: The Magnificent Seven; Le Testament d'Orphée; Surprise Package. 1964: Invitation to a Gunfighter. 1966: The Return of the Seven. 1967: The Double Man. 1968: Villa Rides. 1971: Romance of a Horse Thief.

BUCHHOLZ (*or* BUCHOLZ), Horst

(Also in English-dubbed versions of German films as Henry Brookholt) Actor. Berlin 1933–

Escaped from childrens' camp in Bohemian forest after collapse of Third Reich. 1948: started on stage, first as an extra. 1949: worked at dubbing foreign films into German. 1953–54: studied acting. In plays including Anouilh's 'School for Fathers', Bruckner's 'Elizabeth of England', Shakespeare's 'Richard III', Schiller's 'Rauber', J. M. Barrie's 'Peter Pan'. 1954: first film.

Films as actor include: 1954: Marianne de ma jeunesse. 1956: Die Halbstarken. 1957: Felix Krull; Monpti. 1959: Tiger Bay. 1961: Fanny; One, Two, Three. 1963: Nine Hours to Rama; La Noia. 1964: La Fabuleuse Aventure de Marco Polo. 1967: Le Avventure e gli amori di Miguel Cervantes.

Anne Francis and Glenn Ford (right) in Richard Brook's Blackboard Jungle.
Clarence Brown and Karl Freund during the shooting of Madame Walewska.
Los Olvidados, *directed by Luis Buñuel.*

BUCHMAN, Sidney

Writer and producer. Duluth, Minnesota 1902–
Columbia and Oxford Universities. Assistant stage director to Robert Atkins at the Old Vic Theatre, London, for a year. Wrote plays in New York: 'This One Man', 'Storm Song', 'Acute Triangle'. 1931: writing contract with Paramount for 3 years. 1934: screenplay, *Whom the Gods Destroy* for Columbia led to contract, starting with some rewrite work, uncredited, on *Broadway Bill*; later also produced for Columbia. Established reputation with screenplay of *Theodora Goes Wild* (from original story by Mary McCarthy, 1936). Producer only on *To the Ends of the Earth* (1948). 1951: refused to co-operate with Congressional Committee on Un-American Activities; cited for contempt of Congress; fined $150 and given 1-year suspended sentence. Thereafter lived in Cannes, without credited work until early 1960s. Oscar for screenplay: *Here Comes Mr Jordan* with Seton I. Miller (1941).

Films as writer include: 1932: If I Had a Million (*co*); The Sign of the Cross (*co*). 1935: She Married Her Boss. 1936: The King Steps Out. 1938: Holiday (*co*). 1939: Mr Smith Goes to Washington. 1942: Talk of the Town (*co*). 1944: A Song to Remember. 1945: Over 21 (+ *p*). 1951: Saturday's Hero; Boots Malone. 1961: The Mark (+ *co-pc*). 1963: Cleopatra (*co*). 1965: The Group (+ *p*).

BUÑUEL, Luis

Director. Calanda, Spain 1900–
Jesuit College in Saragossa. 1917–18: agriculture, then philosophy and letters at Madrid University; became friendly there with García Lorca and Salvador Dali. 1920: founded first Spanish film society. In Paris became associated with the Surrealists; assistant to Jean Epstein on 2 films. In collaboration with Dali directed and wrote *Le Chien Andalou* (1928); *L'Age d'Or* (1930, also with Dali) brought offers from MGM for Buñuel and the star, Lya Lys. Few months in Hollywood, then returned to Spain. Dubbing controller for Paramount; producer on Spanish-American co-productions for Warners. 1935–36: executive producer on 4 Spanish features. 1937: contributed to documentary *España leal en armas* (or *Madrid 36*). In France, supervised *Espagne 39*, directed by Jean-Paul Le Chanois. In USA worked for Museum of Modern Art, New York. 1944–46: dubbing work for Warners. 1947: resumed directing on low budget films in Mexico for producer Oscar Dancigers; international success with *Los Olvidados* (1950). From 1955, worked in France as well as Mexico. *Viridiana* (1961) shot in Spain, but censorship prevented showing there; *Tristana* (1970) also shot in Spain.

Films as director: 1928: Un Chien Andalou (+ *co-p/co-s/e/w*; *co-d Salvador Dali*). 1930: L'Age d'or (+ *co-s*; *co-d Salvador Dali*). 1932: Las Hurdes – Terre sans pain – Land Without Bread (+ *e*). 1947: Gran Casino. 1949: El Gran Calavera. 1950: Los Olvidados – The Young and the Damned (+ *co-s*). 1951: Susana; La Hija del engano; Una Mujer sin amor; Subida al cielo. 1952: El Bruto – The Brute (+ *co-s*); Robinson Crusoe – The Adventures of Robinson Crusoe (+ *co-s*); El (+ *co-s*). 1953: Cumbres Borrascosas – Abismos de pasión (+ *s*); La Ilusion viaja en tranvia. 1954: El Rio y la muerte (+ *co-s*). 1955: Ensayo de un crimen – The Criminal Life of Archibaldo de la Cruz (+ *co-s*). 1956: Cela s'appelle l'aurore (+ *co-s*); La Mort en ce jardin – Evil Eden (+ *co-s*). 1958: Nazarin (+ *co-s*). 1959: La Fièvre monte à El Pao – Los Ambiciosos – Republic of Sin (+ *co-s*). 1960: The Young One – La Joven – Island of Shame (+ *co-s*). 1961: Viridiana (+ *co-s*). 1962: El Angel Exterminador – The Exterminating Angel (+ *s*). 1964: Le Journal d'une femme de chambre – Diary of a Chambermaid (+ *co-s*). 1965: Simón del desierto – Simon of the Desert (+ *s*). 1967: Belle de jour (+ *co-s*). 1968: La Voie Lactée – The Milky Way (+ *co-s*). 1970: Tristana (+ *ad/co-s/di*).

BUREL, Léonce-Henri

Cinematographer and director. Indret, France 1892–
From 1915: cinematographer with Films d'Art; worked frequently with Abel Gance. Cinematographer on 4 films by Robert Bresson. Has also directed.

Films as cinematographer include: 1915: La Folie du Docteur Tube. 1916: Les Gaz Mortels; Le Droit à la vie; La Zone de la mort. 1917: Mater Dolorosa. 1918: La Dixième Symphonie: J'Accuse! (*co*). 1922: La Roue (*co*). 1923: Crainquebille (*co*). 1925: Visages d'enfants (*co*); L'Image (*co*). 1926: Napoléon vu par Abel Gance (*co*). 1927: L'Equipage. 1930: Nuits de prince. 1932: Baroud (*co*). 1938: La Mort du cygne. 1940: La Venus Aveugle (*co*). 1951: Le Journal d'un curé de campagne. 1956: Un Condamné à mort s'est échappé. 1959: Pickpocket. 1961: Le Procès de Jeanne d'Arc. 1963: Un Drôle de paroissien.

Films as director: 1922: La Conquête des Gaules (*co-d*). 1929: L'Evadée (*co-d*). 1932: La Fada.

BURKS, Robert

Cinematographer. 1910–1968
To 1954: worked for Warners. 1954–61: with Paramount.

Films as cinematographer include: 1948: A Kiss in the Dark. 1949: The Fountainhead; Task Force (*co*); Beyond the Forest. 1950: The Glass Menagerie. 1951: The Enforcer; Strangers on a Train; Come Fill the Cup; Close to My Heart. 1952: Mara Maru; Room For One More. 1953: I Confess; So This is Love; Hondo (*co*); The Boy From Oklahoma. 1954: Dial M for Murder; Rear Window. 1955: To Catch a Thief; The Trouble With Harry. 1956: The Man Who Knew Too Much; The Vagabond King. 1957: The Wrong Man; The Spirit of St Louis. 1958: Vertigo; The Black Orchid. 1959: North By Northwest; But Not For Me. 1960: The Rat Race; The Great Imposter. 1961: The Pleasure of His Company. 1962: The Music Man. 1963: The Birds. 1964: Marnie. 1965: Once a Thief; A Patch of Blue.

BURNETT, W. R. *or* William R.

Writer. Springfield, Ohio 1899–
Miami Military Institute and Ohio State University. Began as novelist; became screenwriter after filming of his novel *Little Caesar* (1930). Later films adapted by others from his novels include *Dark Hazard* (1934), *Dark Command* (1940), *The Asphalt Jungle* (1950). *Yellow Sky* (1948) based on his story. *Iron Man* (1951) is remake of *The Iron Man* (1931).

Films as writer include: 1931: The Iron Man (*st*). 1932: Scarface, Shame of the Nation (*co-ad/co-di*). 1935: The Whole Town's Talking (*st*). 1941: High Sierra (+ *fn*; *co-s*). 1942: Wake Island (+ *co-st*; *co-s*); This Gun for Hire (*co*). 1946: San Antonio (+ *co-st*; *co-s*); Nobody Lives Forever (+ *st*). 1951: The Racket. 1955: Captain Lightfoot (+ *fst*; *co-s*); I Died a Thousand Times. 1957: Short Cut to Hell. 1961: Sergeants Three (+ *st*). 1963: The Great Escape (*co*).

BURR, Raymond

Actor. New Westminster, British Columbia, Canada 1917–
Stanford University. Worked as sheep herder in New Mexico. Began acting career on stage; also directed at Pasadena Playhouse. 1946: first film, *San Quentin*. 1957–65: played Perry Mason on TV. Has own production company; is involved in art galleries in Arizona and New Mexico. Proxy parent to 17 orphans in various parts of the world. TV series: 'A Man Called Ironside', 'The Boss'. Owns an island in the Fiji chain.

Films as actor include: 1946: San Quentin. 1947: Desperate. 1948: Ruthless; Sleep My Love; Raw Deal; Walk a Crooked Mile. 1949: Bride of Vengeance; Abandoned. 1951: M; New Mexico; A Place in the Sun. 1952: Mara Maru; Horizons West. 1953: The Blue Gardenia. 1954: Rear Window; Passion. 1956: Great Day in the Morning; The Brass Legend. 1957: Ride the High Iron; Crime of Passion; Affair in Havana. 1968: P. J.

BURTON, Richard

(Richard Jenkins) Actor. Pontrhdyfen, South Wales 1925–
Gained place at Oxford under tuition of teacher Philip Burton, whose name he took. 1943: stage debut in 'Druid's Rest' at Royal Court, Liverpool, then London (1944). 1947: stage contract with Tennent; appeared in plays by Christopher Fry including 'The Lady's Not For Burning' in London (1949) and New York (1950). 1953–56: Old Vic, roles included Hamlet. First film as actor *The Last Days of Dolwyn* (1949). First Hollywood film, *My Cousin Rachel* (1952). 1966: formed production company Taybur, with second wife Elizabeth Taylor (married 1964). 1968: co-produced and co-directed with Nevill Coghill *Dr Faustus*. 1970: awarded CBE. Theatre, TV and records.

Films as actor include: 1953: The Robe; The Desert Rats. 1955: Prince of Players. 1956: Alexander the Great. 1958: Bitter Victory. 1959: Look Back in Anger. 1963: Cleopatra; The V.I.P.'s. 1964: Night of the Iguana; Beckett. 1966: Who's Afraid of Virginia Woolf? 1967: The Taming of the Shrew; The Comedians. 1968: Boom; Dr Faustus; Candy. 1969: Staircase. 1971: Raid on Rommel.

BUSCH, Niven

Writer. New York 1903–
Father former vice-president of Lewis J. Selznick Enterprises. Contributed articles and verse to national magazines while at school. 1926: went to Princeton University but left to pay off accumulated debts; worked on Time magazine in books, sport, miscellany and cinema departments. 1927–31: associate editor of Time; staff editor and contributor to New Yorker,

covering boxing, football, hockey; wrote profiles, collected material for first book 'Twenty-one Americans'; turned down Time contract and went to Hollywood. First film work as collaborator on script of *The Crowd Roars* (1932). Films adapted by others from his original stories or novels include *In Old Chicago* (1938), *Duel in the Sun* (1946), *The Furies* (1950). Own production company, Hemisphere Films, made *Pursued* (1947). 1942–52: married to Teresa Wright.

Films as writer include: 1933: College Coach (*co*). 1934: Babbitt (*co-ad*). 1940: The Westerner (*co*). 1946: The Postman Always Rings Twice (*co*). 1947: Moss Rose (*ad*); Pursued. 1951: Distant Drums (*fst/co-s*).

BUTLER, David

Director. San Francisco, California 1894–
Father a stage director. Theatrical childhood, including work as actor. 1918–19: actor for D. W. Griffith. From 1920: worked in production house, continuing as actor. 1927: first film as director *High School Hero*; co-wrote story. 1927–38: worked almost entirely for Fox; then RKO, Paramount, Warners. 1944–55: all films for Warners. 1955–57: worked for Fox, RKO, Paramount, Warners. Specialised in musical comedies. To 1940: worked on many of his scripts and stories. Produced 3 of his films.

Films as actor include: 1918: The Greatest Thing in Life. 1919: The Girl Who Stayed at Home; The Other Half. 1921: The Sky Pilot. 1922: The Village Blacksmith. 1923: Hoodman Blind. 1926: The Blue Eagle. 1927: Seventh Heaven. 1929: Salute.

Films as director: 1927: High School Hero (*+ co-st*); Win That Girl; Masked Emotions (*co-d Kenneth Hawks*). 1928: The News Parade (*+ co-st*); Prep and Pep. 1929: William Fox Movietone Follies of 1929 (*+ st*); Chasing Through Europe (*co-d Alfred E. Werker*); Sunnyside Up (*+ s*). 1930: Just Imagine (*+ s*); High Society Blues. 1931: Delicious; A Connecticut Yankee; Business and Pleasure; Down to Earth; Handle With Care; Hold Me Tight. 1933: My Weakness (*+ co-s*). 1934: Bottoms Up (*+ co-st/co-s*). 1934: Handy Andy; Have a Heart (*+ co-s*); Bright Eyes (*+ co-st*). 1935: The Little Colonel; The Littlest Rebel; Doubting Thomas. 1936: Captain January; White Fang; Pigskin Parade – Harmony Parade. 1937: You're a Sweetheart; Ali Baba Goes to Town. 1938: Kentucky; Kentucky Moonshine – Three Men and a Girl; Straight, Place and Show – They're Off. 1939: East Side of Heaven (*+ co-st*); That's Right You're Wrong. 1940: If I Had My Way (*+ p/co-st*); You'll Find Out (*+ p/co-st*). 1941: Caught in the Draft; Playmates. 1942: The Road to Morocco; They Got Me Covered. 1943: Thank Your Lucky Stars. 1944: Shine on Harvest Moon; The Princess and the Pirate. 1946: San Antonio (*co-d Raoul Walsh, uc*); The Time, the Place and the Girl; Two Guys From Milwaukee. 1947: My Wild Irish Rose. 1948: Two Guys from Texas – Two Texas Knights. 1949: Look for the Silver Lining; It's a Great Feeling; John Loves Mary. 1950: Tea for Two; The Daughter of Rosie O'Grady. 1951: Painting the Clouds With Sunshine; Lullaby of Broadway. 1952: Where's Charley?; April in Paris. 1953: By the Light of the Silvery Moon; Calamity Jane. 1954: The Command – Rear Guard; King Richard and the Crusaders. 1955: Jump into

Hell; Glory (*+ p*); The Right Approach. 1956: The Girl He Left Behind. 1967: C'mon Let's Live a Little.

BUTLER, Hugo

Writer. Calgary, Alberta, Canada 1914–68
Washington University, Seattle. Journalist, playwright. 1937: first film as writer *Big City* in collaboration with Dore Schary. 1937–43: worked for MGM. From 1945: worked for numerous studios. 1958: co-wrote *Cowboy* uncredited. 1960: wrote *The Young One* in collaboration under pseudonym H. B. Addis.

Films as writer include: 1937: Big City (*co*). 1939: The Adventures of Huckleberry Finn. 1940: Young Tom Edison (*co-st/co-s*); Edison, the Man (*co-st*); Wyoming (*co*). 1941: Barnacle Bill (*co*). 1942: A Yank on the Burma Road (*co-st/co-s*). 1943: Lassie Come Home. 1945: The Southerner (*ad*). 1946: From This Day Forward; Miss Susie Slagle's. 1949: Roughshod (*co*). 1950: Eye Witness (*co-st/co-s*). 1951: The Prowler (*co*). 1952: The First Time (*co-st/co-s*). 1962: Eve (*co*). 1963: Sodom and Gomorrah; A Face in the Rain (*co-ad*). 1968: The Legend of Lylah Clare (*co*).

C

CACOYANNIS, Michael

Director. Cyprus 1922–
Father Athenian lawyer. Studied classics in Greece, law in UK. World War II: unable to return home, became producer of BBC broadcasts to Greece. Studied at Central School of Speech and Drama. Joined Old Vic Company; acting debut as Herod in Oscar Wilde's 'Salomé'. Other parts in 'Captain Brassbound's Conversion', 'The Purple Fig Tree' and 'Caligula'. 1951: tried unsuccessfully for work as director, then returned to Greece to direct film for which 3 actor friends had found producer.

Films as director and writer: 1953: Kyriakatiko xypnima – Windfall in Athens. 1955: Stella; To Koritsi me ta mavra – The Girl in Black. 1957: To Telefteo psemma – A Matter of Dignity (*+ co-e*). 1960: Eroica – Our Last Spring (*+ p; co-s*); Il Relitto – The Wastrel. 1961: Electra (*+ p*). 1965: Zorba the Greek (*+ p*). 1967: The Day the Fish Came Out (*+ p; co-s*). 1971: The Trojan Women (*+ co-p*).

CAGNEY, James

Actor. New York 1899–
Columbia University. 1920: chorus of 'Pitter Patter' on Broadway. 1921–25: vaudeville with wife Frances. 1925–30: Broadway plays and revue, including 'Penny Arcade' (1929). Film debut in adaptation of this, *Sinner's Holiday* (1930). 1930–42: almost exclusively with Warners. 1942: formed production company with brother William Cagney, which made 3 features (released through United Artists); returned to Warners with *White Heat* (1949). From 1952: films for various companies. 1957: directed *Short Cut to Hell*. Occasional TV. Retired after *One Two Three* (1961). Sister is actress Jeanne Cagney. Oscar as Best Actor for *Yankee Doodle Dandy* (1942).

North by Northwest, *directed by Alfred Hitchcock, photographed by Robert Burks.*
Raymond Burr in Great Day In The Morning, *directed by Jacques Tourneur.*
James Cagney in Billy Wilder's One, Two, Three.

Films as actor include: 1930: The Doorway to Hell. 1931: Public Enemy; Other Men's Women. 1932: The Crowd Roars. 1933: Hard to Handle; Picture Snatcher; Mayor of Hell; Footlight Parade. 1934: Jimmy the Gent; He Was Her Man; Here Comes the Navy. 1935: Devil Dogs of the Air; G Men; The Irish in Us; A Midsummer Night's Dream; Frisco Kid. 1936: Ceiling Zero. 1938: Boy Meets Girl; Angels With Dirty Faces. 1939: The Oklahoma Kid; Each Dawn I Die; The Roaring Twenties. 1940: The Fighting 69th; Torrid Zone; City for Conquest. 1941: The Strawberry Blonde; The Bride Came C.O.D. 1942: Captains of the Clouds. 1943: Johnny Come Lately. 1945: Blood on the Sun. 1947: 13 Rue Madeleine. 1948: The Time of Your Life. 1949: White Heat. 1950: Kiss Tomorrow Goodbye. 1951: Come Fill the Cup. 1952: What Price Glory. 1953: A Lion is in the Streets. 1955: Run for Cover; Love Me or Leave Me; Mister Roberts. 1956: Tribute to a Bad Man. 1958: Never Steal Anything Small. 1960: The Gallant Hours.

CAINE, Michael

(Maurice Micklewhite) Actor. London 1933–
1949: left school; office boy in film producer's office. 1950: labourer; evening drama classes at youth club. 1951: National Service, including action in Korea with Royal Fusiliers. 1953: worked in Smithfield meat market; assistant stage manager with a repertory company at Horsham. 1954: repertory at Lowestoft; 3 months with Joan Littlewood's Theatre Workshop. 1956: first film, A Hill in Korea, and walk-on parts in other films. 1959: understudy to Peter O'Toole in 'The Long and the Short and the Tall'. Acted in 'Next Time I'll Sing to You'. 1963: first major film part, Zulu. 1964: TV appearances in 'The Other Man' and 'Hobson's Choice'. 1965: signed 5-year 11-film contract with Harry Saltzman. Was married to actress Patricia Haines.

Films as actor include: 1965: The Ipcress File. 1966: Alfie; The Wrong Box. 1967: Hurry Sundown; Billion Dollar Brain. 1968: Play Dirty; The Magus. 1970: Too Late the Hero. 1971: The Last Valley; Kidnapped.

CAMERINI, Mario

Director. Rome 1895–
Studied law. Military service in World War I; prisoner of war. 1919: entered cinema, working for cousin, Augusto Genina. 1920–23: co-writer and assistant to Genina on 3 films: Tre meno due (1920), Moglie, marito e ... (1920), and Cirano di Bergerac. Co-wrote most of his films, several with Renate Castellani and Cesare Zavattini. 1956: co-scripted King Vidor's War and Peace.

Features as director: 1923: Jolly, clown da circo (+ co-s). 1924: La Casa dei pulcini (+ st). 1925: Voglio tradire mio marito; Maciste contro lo sceicco (+ st); Saetta, principe per un giorno. 1927: Kiff Tebbi. 1929: Rotaie. 1930: La Riva dei bruti. 1931: Figaro e la sua gran giornata; L'Ultima Avventura (+ co-s). 1932: Gli Uomini, che mascalzoni! (+ co-st/co-s); T'amerò sempre (+ st). 1933: Cento di questi giorni (+ st; co-d Augusto Camerini); Giallo. 1934: Il Cappello a tre punte; Come le foglie (+ co-s). 1935: Darò un milione (+ co-s). 1936: Il Grande Appello (+ st/co-s); Ma non è una cosa seria. 1937: Der Mann, der Nicht nein sagen

kann (German version of Ma non è una cosa seria); Il Signor Max (+ co-s). 1938: Batticuore (+ co-s). 1939: I Grandi Magazzini (+ co-st/co-s); Il Documento (+ co-s/e). 1940: Centomila Dollari (+ co-s); Una Romantica Avventura (+ co-s). 1941: I Promessi Sposi (+ co-s). 1942: Una Storia d'amore (+ co-st/co-s). 1943: T'amerò sempre (rm 1932; + st/co-s). 1945: Due Lettere Anonime (+ co-s). 1946: L'Angelo e il diavolo (+ co-s). 1947: La Figlia del capitano – The Captain's Daughter (+ co-s). 1948: Molti Sogni per le strade (+ co-s). 1950: Il Brigante Musolino – The Fugitive (+ co-s); Due Moglie sono troppe (+ co-s). 1952: Moglie per una notte. 1953: Gli Eroi della domenica (+ co-st/co-s). 1955: Ulisse – Ulysses; La Bella Mugnaia – The Miller's Wife (+ co-s; rm Il Cappello a tre punte, 1934). 1956: Suor Letizia – Last Temptation – When Angels Don't Fly (+ co-s). 1957: Vacanze a Ischia (+ co-s). 1958: Primo Amore (+ co-st/co-s). 1959: Via Margutta – Run with the Devil (+ st/co-s). 1960: Crimen – Killing at Monte Carlo. 1961: I Briganti Italiani – Seduction of the South (+ co-s). 1963: Kali-Yug, la dea della vendetta – Kali-Yug, Goddess of Vengeance; Il Mistero del tempio indiano.

CAMUS, Marcel

Director. Chappes, France 1912–
Studied to become art teacher. World War II: 4 years as prisoner of war; directed plays in prison camps and designed sets. After Liberation became assistant to Henri Decoin and Jacques Feyder on Macadam (1946). First assistant to Jacques Becker starting with Antoine et Antoinette (1946). Directed short, Renaissance du Havre (1950). Technical adviser to Daniel Gelin for Les Dents Longues (1952) and to other directors before making first feature (1956). Collaborated on scripts of all his features.

Features as director and writer in collaboration: 1956: Mort en fraude – Fugitive in Saigon. 1958: Orfeu Negro – Black Orpheus. 1960: Os Bandeirantes. 1962: L'Oiseau de paradis. 1965: Le Chant du monde (s alone). 1967: L'Homme de New York. 1968: Vivre la nuit (+ ad). 1970: Le Mur de l'Atlantique; Un Ete sauvage.

CANNON, Robert

Animator. 1910–64 Northridge, California
1934: started in Warners cartoon department; animator on e.g. Porky's Duck Hunt (1937), Porky's Naughty Nephew (1938), Porky and Daffy (1938), Porky's Picnic (1939), Porky's Midnight Matinée (1941). Also worked for Disney. 1944: helped found United Productions of America; vice-president (1945). Animator on e.g. Robin Hoodlum (1948). 1950: creator of Gerald McBoing Boing, character based on story by Dr Seuss; rights later sold to CBS TV (1955). 1952: created Christopher Crumpet character. 1963: teacher, San Fernando College. Oscar for best cartoon to Gerald McBoing Boing (1950).

Animated films as director include: 1947: Brotherhood of Man. 1951: Gerald McBoing Boing; The Oomphas. 1952: Madeline; Willie the Kid. 1953: Christopher Crumpet; Gerald McBoing Boing's Symphony; The Little Boy with a Big Horn. 1954: Fudget's Budget; How Now Boing Boing; Ballet-oop. 1955: Christopher Crumpet's Playmate. 1956: Gerald McBoing Boing on Planet Moo; The Jay Walker.

CANTOR, Eddie

(Edward Itzkowitz) Actor and singer. New York 1893–1964 Hollywood
Orphaned as baby; brought up by Russian grandmother. Debut at 14 at Clinton Music Hall. Joined Gus Edward's 'Kid Kabaret'. Later worked as a singing waiter in Coney Island restaurant. 1914–15: toured with Lola Lee as 'Cantor and Lee'; married Ida Tobias of 'Ida, Sweet as Apple Cider'. 1916: musical comedy with the Canary Cottage Company on West Coast; met Irving Berlin; established by singing Berlin's songs. 1917–19: appeared in 'Ziegfeld Follies'. 1920: first star in parts in 'The Midnight Rounders', 'Make it Snappy'. 1923: in 'Kid Boots'; made film debut in adaptation, Kid Boots (1926). 1931: 5-year, 5-film, contract with Samuel Goldwyn. Radio personality. 1937: elected president of American Federation of Radio Artistes. 1941: on Broadway in 'Banjo Eyes'. 1957: autobiography 'Take My Life'. TV appearances.

Films as actor include: 1930: Whoopee. 1933: The Kid from Spain; Roman Scandals. 1937: Ali Baba Goes to Town. 1940: 40 Little Mothers. 1943: Thank Your Lucky Stars. 1948: If You Knew Susie (+ p).

CANUTT, Yakima

(Enos Edward Canutt) Director and stuntman. Colfax, Washington 1895–
German-Dutch father and Scottish-Irish mother. Nicknamed 'Yakima' when 1914 newspaper photograph of him riding in rodeo mistakenly captioned 'Cowboy from Yakima takes flight'. 1914–22: champion rodeo cowboy; 5 world title belts as 'all-round' cowboy. 1925–44: stuntman and actor; began in westerns at Universal. Invented many standard tricks including rigging wagon with wire to disintegrate on cue and tripping horse to fall as if shot. Films as stuntman include Stagecoach (1939). From 1944: second unit director, also making B-features for Republic. 1967: special Academy Award for 'creating the profession of stuntman as it exists today and for the development of many safety devices used by stuntmen everywhere'. 2 sons, both stuntmen, one named Yakima.

Films as director: 1945: Sheriff of Cimarron. 1948: Oklahoma Badlands; Carson City Raiders; Sons of Adventure. 1947: G-Men Never Forget (serial in 12 eps; co-d Fred Brannon).

Films as second unit director include: 1951: The Great Missouri Raid. 1952: Ivanhoe. 1956: Zarak. 1959: Ben-Hur (co). 1961: El Cid. 1964: The Fall of the Roman Empire. 1966: Khartoum. 1967: The Flim Flam Man. 1970: Song of Norway: Rio Lobo.

CAPRA, Frank

Director. Palermo, Sicily 1897–
1903: family emigrated to Los Angeles. Trained as engineer at the California Institute of Technology; edited school paper there. Left college to enlist in artillery. 1918: joined 'scenario' school run to finance film which was never completed. Worked for independent comedy companies and film laboratory before directing some Screen Snap Shots for Columbia (1921). Assistant and gagman for Hal Roach and Mack Sennett. 1926: first feature as director for Harry

Langdon at First National. 1928: first film for Columbia; remained there until 1939. From 1936: also produced. Started World War II as Major in US Signal Corps; made combat documentaries for Orientation Branch of US War Department and Army Pictorial Service. President of Liberty Films Inc, formed with William Wyler, George Stevens and Samuel Briskin (1945); company taken over by Paramount. For William Wellman wrote story of *Westward the Women* (1951). 1951: left Paramount; out of films for 8 years. Has directed films for TV. Autobiography, 'Frank Capra, the Name Above the Title' (1971). Oscar as director for *Mr Deeds Goes to Town* (1936).

Films as director (from 1923): 1923: Fultah Fisher's jboarding House. 1926: The Strong Man. 1927: Long Pants; For the Love of Mike. 1928: That Certain Thing; So This is Love; The Matinee Idol; The Way of the Strong; Say it with Sables (+ *co-st*); Submarine; The Power of the Press. 1929: The Younger Generation; The Donovan Affair; Flight (+ *di*). 1930: Ladies of Leisure; Rain or Shine. 1931: Dirigible; The Miracle Woman; Platinum Blonde. 1932: Forbidden (+ *st*); American Madness; The Bitter Tea of General Yen. 1933: Lady for a Day. 1934: It Happened One Night; Broadway Bill. 1936: Mr Deeds Goes to Town (+ *p*). 1937: Lost Horizon (+ *p*). 1938: You Can't Take It With You (+ *p*). 1939: Mr Smith Goes to Washington (+ *p*). 1941: Meet John Doe – John Doe, Dynamite (+ *p*). 1942: Prelude to War; The Nazis Strike (*co-d Anatole Litvak*). 1943: The Battle of Britain; Divide and Conquer (*co-d Anatole Litvak*); The Battle of China (*co-d Anatole Litvak*). 1944: Arsenic and Old Lace. 1945: Know Your Enemy: Japan (*co-d Joris Ivens*); Tunisian Victory (*uc, co-d Roy Boulting, uc*); Two Down and One to Go. 1947: It's a Wonderful Life (+ *p/co-s*). 1948: State of the Union – The World and His Wife (+ *co-p*). 1950: Riding High (+ *p*). 1951: Here Comes the Groom (+ *p*). 1959: A Hole in the Head (+ *p*). 1961: A Pocketful of Miracles (+ *co-p*; *rm* Lady for a Day, *1933*).

CAPRIOLI, Vittorio

Director and actor. Naples, Italy 1921–
National Academy of Dramatic Art until 1942. Acted in Carli-Rocca-De Sica Company, and that of Besozzi and Gioi. Cabaret with Jacques Fabbri, Mouloudji, Marcel Marceau and Marcello Pagliero at the Rose Rouge in Paris; appeared with Django Reinhardt. Worked at Piccolo Teatro, Milan. 1951: with Franca Valeri and Alberto Bonucci, founded Teatro dei Gobbi (The Hunchbacks' Theatre); co-wrote and acted in 'Carnet de notes' in Paris, UK and North America. 1957–58: co-wrote, co-produced and acted in musical comedy 'Lina e il cavaliere' with wife Franca Valeri.

Films as director: 1961: Leoni al sole (+ *co-s/w*). 1962: Parigi o cara (+ *st/co-s/w*). 1963: Cuori infranti *ep* La Manina de Fatma (+ *co-s/w*); I Maniaci. 1968: Scusi, facciamo l'amore – Listen, Let's Make Love (+ *co-s*). 1970: Splendorie e miserie di Madame Royale (+ *st/co-s*).

Films as actor include: 1950: Luci del varietà. 1952: Altri Tempi. 1954: Tempi Nostri. 1959: Arrangiatevi; Il Generale della Rovere. 1960: Zazie dans le métro; A porte chiuse. 1962: I Giòrni Contati; Adieu Philippine. 1964: La Donna è una cosa meravigliosa.

CARDIFF, Jack

Cinematographer and director. Yarmouth, Norfolk 1914–
1918: started in films as child actor. 1927: camera assistant. 1936: camera operator for London Films. Worked as operator on *The Ghost Goes West* and *Knight Without Armour*. 1937: joined Technicolor; colour operator on the first British Technicolor picture, *Wings of the Morning*. Then photographed travelogues for Technicolor. 1940: cinematographer on features; specialised in colour. Took over direction of *Young Cassidy* (1965) after John Ford fell ill. 1958: began directing. Oscar for best colour cinematography: *Black Narcissus* (1947).

Films as cinematographer include: 1945: Caesar and Cleopatra (*co*). 1946: A Matter of Life and Death. 1947: Black Narcissus. 1948: The Red Shoes. 1949: Under Capricorn. 1950: The Black Rose. 1951: Pandora and the Flying Dutchman; The African Queen. 1954: The Barefoot Contessa. 1956: War and Peace (*co*); The Brave One. 1957: The Prince and the Showgirl; Legend of the Lost. 1958: The Vikings. 1961: Fanny.

Films as director: 1958: Intent to Kill. 1959: Beyond This Place. 1960: Sons and Lovers; Scent of Mystery; Holiday in Spain. 1962: My Geisha; The Lion. 1964: The Long Ships. 1965: Young Cassidy (*co-d John Ford*); The Liquidator. 1967: The Mercenaries. 1968: Girl on a Motorcycle (+ *co-s*).

CARDINALE, Claudia

Actress. Tunis, Tunisia 1939–
Italian parents. In Tunisia, brief appearance in *Goha*. 1957: as winner of beauty contest, invited by Unitalia Film for 5-day trip to Venice Film Festival; publicity there led to films, starting with *I Soliti Ignoti* (1958). Has since appeared in French, British and American films. 1967: announced marriage to producer Franco Cristaldi, previously kept secret.

Films as actress include: 1959: La Prima Notte; Un Maledetto Imbroglio. 1960: Rocco e i suoi fratelli; Il Bell'Antonio; I Delfini; La Ragazza con la valigia. 1961: La Viaccia. 1962: Senilità; Cartouche. 1963: Il Gattopardo; Otto et mezzo; La Ragazza di bube. 1964: Gli Indifferenti; Circus World; The Pink Panther. 1965: Blindfold; Vaghe Stelle dell'Orsa; Una Rosa per tutti. 1966: Lost Command. 1967: Don't Make Waves. 1971: Les Petroleuses; Bello Onesto Emigrata Australia sposerebbe compaesan illibata; Krasnaya Palatka.

CARETTE, Julien

Actor. Paris 1897–1966
Studied at Conservatoire de Paris; failed drama examinations. Stage debut in Molière's 'Dépit Amoureux', followed by appearances in revue and at Théâtre du Vieux-Colombier under Jacques Copeau. 1932: film debut in Jacques Prévert's *L'Affaire est dans le sac*. 1937: first film for Jean Renoir, *La Grande Illusion*. Actor in over 100 films. Died of burns received in accident.

Films as actor include: 1937: Gribouille. 1938: La Bête Humaine; La Marseillaise. 1939: La Règle du jeu.

L'Uccello del Paradiso, *directed by Marcel Camus.*
Peter Falk, Glenn Ford and Hope Lange in Pocketful of Miracles, *directed by Frank Capra.*
Harry Carey in John Ford's The Outcasts of Poker Flat.

1943: Adieu Léonard. 1945: Sylvie et le fantôme. 1946: Les Portes de la nuit. 1948: Une Si Jolie Petite Plage. 1949: Occupe-toi d'Amélie. 1951: L'Auberge Rouge. 1953: La Fête à Henriette. 1956: Si Paris nous était conté. 1958: Le Joueur.

CAREY, Harry

Actor. New York 1878–1947 Balboa Beach, California

1917–19: star of mainly western series directed by John Ford at Universal; 2 shorts, then features. Further features in 1921. Occasionally collaborated with Ford on story, script, or direction, or produced. Acted in 26 Ford films. Wrote and acted in plays, 'Montana' and 'The Heat of Alaska'. 1948: Ford's *Three Godfathers*, a remake of *Marked Men* (1919), was dedicated to his memory, with son, Harry Carey Jr, in a leading part.

Films as actor include: 1917: The Soul Herder; Cheyenne's Pal; Straight Shooting; The Secret Man; A Marked Man; Bucking Broadway (+ *p*). 1918: The Phantom Raiders (+ *p*); Wild Women; Thieves' Gold; The Scarlet Drop; Hell Bent (+ *co-s*); A Woman's Fool; Three Mounted Men. 1919: Roped; A Fight for Love; Bare Fists; Riders of Vengeance (+ *co-s*); The Outcasts of Poker Flat; The Ace of the Saddle; The Rider of the Law; A Gun Fightin' Gentleman (+ *co-st*); Marked Men. 1921: The Freeze Out; The Wallop; Desperate Trails. 1929: The Trail of '98. 1931: Trader Horn; Bad Company. 1933: Sunset Pass; Man of the Forest; The Thundering Herd. 1935: Barbary Coast. 1936: The Prisoner of Shark Island; Sutter's Gold; Valiant is the Word for Carrie. 1937: Souls at Sea. 1938: You and Me. 1939: Mr Smith Goes to Washington. 1940: They Knew What They Wanted. 1941: The Shepherd of the Hills; Among the Living; Sundown. 1942: The Spoilers. 1943: Air Force. 1944: The Great Moment. 1946: Duel in the Sun; The Sea of Grass. 1948: Red River.

CARLSEN, Henning

Director. Aalborg, Denmark 1927–

From 1947: worked as writer and director of shorts; made over 30 documentaries including *Limfjorden, De Gamle*. 1962: first feature, *Dilemma* shot in English in South Africa. 1966: *Sult* was the first Danish/Swedish co-production.

Features as director: 1962: Dilemma – A World of Strangers (+ *s/e*). 1964: Hvad med os? – How About Us? 1965: Kattorna – The Cats (+ *co-s*). 1966: Sult – Hunger (+ *p/co-s*). 1968: Mennesker mødes og sød musik opstaar i hjertet – Människor möts och ljuu musik uppstär i hjertat – People Meet (+ *co-p/co-s/e*). 1969: Klabautermanden – We Are All Demons! (+ *p/co-s*). 1971: Er i bange (+ *p/co-s*).

CARMICHAEL, Hoagey

(Hoagland Howard C. Carmichael) Song writer, singer and actor. Bloomington, Indiana 1899–

1926: law degree; played and composed while a student; met Bix Beiderbecke, for whom wrote 'Stardust'. Tried to set up law practice in Florida. Bandleader; arranger for music publishing house. 1937: first film work, small part and song in *Topper*. 1938–42: no film work. 1943: began collaboration with Johnny Mercer. 1951: Oscar for song 'In the Cool, Cool, Cool

of the Evening' from *Here Comes the Groom*. Own radio and TV shows. Acted in films only occasionally; sang own songs in *To Have and Have Not* (1945) and *Canyon Passage* (1946). Autobiography, 'The Stardust Road'.

Films as actor include: 1946: The Best Years of Our Lives. 1950: Johnny Holiday. 1952: The Las Vegas Story; Belles on their Toes.

Films as song writer include: 1938: College Swing (*song*); Sing You Sinners (*song*); Men with Wings (*song*); Say it in French (*song*). 1943: True to Life (*co-songs*). 1944: To Have and Have Not (*co-songs;* + *w*). 1946: Canyon Passage (*songs;* + *w*). 1953: Gentlemen Prefer Blondes (*co-songs*). 1962: Hatari! (*co-song*).

CARNÉ, Marcel

Director. Paris 1909–

Son of cabinet-maker, for whom started as apprentice. Worked for insurance company while studying cinematography at night school. 1928: camera assistant to Georges Périnal on Jacques Feyder's *Les Nouveaux Messieurs*. 1929: started writing articles for *Cinémagazine*; camera assistant on Richard Oswald's *Cagliostro*; helped by friend shot amateur documentary, *Nogent, Eldorado du dimanche*. 1930–32: directed publicity shorts (around 2 minutes each) with scripts by Jean Aurenche, décor and costumes by Paul Grimault. Assistant director to René Clair on *Sous les toits de Paris* (1930) and to Feyder on *Le Grand Jeu* (1933), *Pension Mimosas* (1934) and *La Kermesse Héroique* (1935). 1936–47: films all with Jacques Prévert as writer, except for *Hôtel du Nord*. Last film together, *La Fleur de l'age*, abandoned because of financial disagreements among producers.

Films as director: 1929: Nogent, Eldorado du dimanche (+ *co-s; co-d Michel Sanvoisin*). 1936: Jenny. 1937: Drôle de drame – Bizarre Bizarre. 1938: Quai des brumes; Hôtel du Nord. 1939: Le Jour se lève – Daybreak. 1942: Les Visiteurs du soir – The Devil's Envoys. 1945: Les Enfants du paradis – Children of Paradise. 1946: Les Portes de la nuit. 1947: La Fleur de l'âge (*uf*). 1950: La Marie du port. 1951: Juliette ou la clé des songes (+ *co-s*). 1953: Thérèse Raquin (+ *co-s*). 1954: L'Air de Paris (+ *co-s*). 1956: Le Pays d'où je viens (+ *co-ad*). 1958: Les Tricheurs – Youthful Sinners. 1960: Terrain Vague (+ *co-s*). 1962: Du Mouron pour les petits oiseaux (+ *co-s*). 1965: Trois Chambres à Manhattan (+ *co-s*). 1968: Les Jeunes Loups – The Young Wolves. 1971: Les Assassins de l'ordre (+ *co-ad*).

CAROL, Martine

(Maryse Mourer) Actress. Biarritz, France 1922–67 London

Studied acting with Roland Manuel and later René Simon. 1942: discovered by Gaston Baty; acted in 'Phèdre', 'Les Caprices de Marianne', 'La Mégère Apprivoisée' and went on provincial tour. 1943: first film, *La Ferme aux loups* (under stage name, Maryse Arley). Second husband was Christian-Jaque, who directed a number of her films.

Films as actress include: 1948: Les Amants de Verone. 1950: Caroline Chérie. 1952: Les Belles de nuit;

Adorables Créatures; Lucrèzia Borgia. 1955: Nana; Lola Montès; Les Carnets du Major Thompson. 1959: La Prima Notte; Ten Seconds to Hell; Nathalie, Agent Secret. 1961: Vanina Vanini.

CARON, Leslie

Actress and dancer. Boulogne-Billancourt, France 1931–

Mother was dancer. From 1944: trained as balletdancer at Conservatoire de Paris. From 1946: dancing small solos for Roland Petit at Ballets des Champs-Elysées. Starred in 'La Rencontre' (1949) in Paris and on tour of Europe and Middle East; spotted by Gene Kelly. 1951: film debut, *An American in Paris*. Long term MGM contract. 1954–55: tour with Ballets de Paris under direction of Roland Petit. 1955: debut as stage actress in 'Orvet', written and directed by Jean Renoir. Second husband Peter Hall (married 1956–66) directed London stage debut as 'Gigi'. 1961: played 'Ondine' with Royal Shakespeare Company.

Films as actress include: 1952: Glory Alley. 1953: The Story of Three Loves *ep* Mademoiselle; Lili. 1955: Daddy Long Legs; The Glass Slipper. 1959: The Doctor's Dilemma. 1961: Fanny; Guns of Darkness. 1962: The L-Shaped Room. 1964: Father Goose. 1966: Paris brûle-t-il? 1967: Il Padre di famiglia.

CARRADINE, John

(Richmond Reed Carradine) Actor. New York 1906–

Grandfather founded the Holy Rollers. Father newspaperman, mother physician. Began as scene painter and quick-sketch artist. 1925: debut as stage actor in 'Camille' in New Orleans. 1927: in 'Window Panes' in New York; walked to Hollywood supporting himself en route by doing quick sketches. Appeared in films from *Tol'able David* (1930) until 1934 as John Peter Richmond. 1941: 'The Vagabond King' in Los Angeles and San Francisco. 1943: producer/director of own repertory company at Geary Theatre, San Francisco and on tour; acted in 'The Merchant of Venice', 'Hamlet', 'Othello'. 1946: Broadway debut, 'The Duchess of Malfi'. Many subsequent New York stage appearances including 'Volpone' (1948). 'The Madwoman of Chaillot' (1948) also on tour, 'The Time of Your Life' (1955), 'A Funny Thing Happened on the Way to the Forum' (1962). Some TV from 1949. Son is actor David Carradine.

Films as actor include: 1932: The Sign of the Cross. 1933: The Invisible Man. 1934: Cleopatra; The Black Cat. 1935: Bride of Frankenstein; Les Misérables; The Crusades. 1936: The Prisoner of Shark Island; Ramona; Mary of Scotland; Winterset; The Garden of Allah. 1937: Captains Courageous. 1938: The Hurricane; Four Men and a Prayer; Alexander's Ragtime Band; Submarine Patrol. 1939: Jesse James; The Three Musketeers; Drums Along the Mohawk; Stagecoach. 1940: Chad Hanna; The Return of Frank James; Brigham Young; The Grapes of Wrath. 1941: Western Union; Blood and Sand; Man Hunt; Swamp Water; Son of Fury. 1942: Reunion in France; The Black Swan. 1944: Hitler's Madman. 1944: Bluebeard. 1945: Fallen Angel. 1947: The Private Affairs of Bel Ami. 1954: Johnny Guitar; The Egyptian. 1955: Stranger on Horseback; The Kentuckian. 1956: Around the World in 80 Days; The Ten Commandments. 1957: The True Story of Jesse James. 1958: The Last Hurrah. 1960: The

Adventures of Huckleberry Finn; Sex Kittens Go to College. 1962: The Man who Shot Liberty Valance. 1964: The Patsy; Cheyenne Autumn. 1969: The Good Guys and the Bad Guys. 1970: The McMasters.

CARROLL, Madeleine

(Marie-Madeleine Bernadette O'Carroll) Actress. West Bromwich, Staffordshire 1906–
Birmingham University. Taught French before first stage appearance in 'The Lash' (1927) in New Brighton. Many stage appearances during next 5 years. First film, *The Guns of Loos* (1928). Hollywood debut, *The World Moves On* (1934). Naturalised American citizen (1943). World War II: active in Allied Relief Fund, United Seamen's Service, American Red Cross; gave up career at its peak to return to London where sister was killed in blitz. Resumed film acting after the war until 1950; appeared on New York stage in 'Goodbye My Fancy' (1948). 1964: Pre-Broadway tour of 'Beckman Place'. Radio work from 1937, notably Orson Welles's production of 'Jane Eyre' (1940). TV in 1950s and '60s. Second of 3 husbands (1942–46) was Sterling Hayden.

Films as actress include: 1929: Atlantic. 1933: I Was a Spy. 1934: The Dictator. 1935: The Thirty-Nine Steps. 1936: Secret Agent; Lloyd's of London; The General Died at Dawn. 1937: The Prisoner of Zenda. 1938: It's All Yours; Blockade. 1940: North-west Mounted Police; My Son, My Son. 1949: The Fan.

CARTIER-BRESSON, Henri

Photographer. Chanteloup, France 1908–
Studied painting under André Lhôte; a year at Cambridge University. As photographer went to Ivory Coast with miniature camera. 1934: with Jean Renoir in Mexico. Assistant to Renoir on *La Vie est à nous, Une Partie de campagne* (1936), and *La Règle du jeu* (1939). 1938: co-directed *Return to Life*, a Frontier Films documentary on medical services in Spain. 1947: technical advisor on documentary short *Le Retour* for Les Services Américains de l'Information. 1962: Shot linking photographs in *L'Amour à vingt ans*. 1969: his work used in Wolf Koenig and Rex Tasker's *Quebec as Seen by Cartier-Bresson*. 1970: photographed *Cartier-Bresson's California* for CBS TV. 1971: directed *Southern Exposures by Henri Cartier-Bresson* for CBS TV.

CASARES, Maria

Actress, Corunna, Spain 1922–
Hospital nurse during Spanish Civil War. Father diplomat; at end of war took refuge in France. Studied acting at Conservatoire de Paris. 1942: appeared at Théâtre des Mathurins. 1944: first film, *Les Enfants du paradis*. Mainly stage actress; occasional film appearances.

Films as actress include: 1945: Les Dames du Bois de Boulogne. 1947: La Certosa di Parma. 1950: Orphée. 1956: Le Théâtre National Populaire. 1960: Le Testament d'Orphée.

CASPARY, Vera

Writer. Chicago 1904–
Educated in Chicago. 1926–28: editor of magazine Dance. First novels published 1929. Co-author of occasional plays. *Laura* (1944) is based on her novel.

Films as writer include: 1937: Easy Living (*st*). 1949: A Letter to Three Wives (*ad*). 1951: I Can Get It For You Wholesale (*ad*). 1953: The Blue Gardenia (*st*); Give a Girl a Break (*st*). 1958: Les Girls (*st*). 1961: Bachelor in Paradise (*st*).

CASSAVETES, John

Actor, director. New York 1929–
Studied at American Academy of Dramatic Art. Stock companies, then TV in Hollywood and New York; programmes include 'Omnibus', Kraft TV Theatre and (1959–60) 'Johnny Staccato' series. 1953: first film as actor, 1956: taught at Burt Lane's actors' workshop; developed *Shadows* from exercise with class of actors including those in film; financed it himself and with contributions given after TV discussion of project. Paramount contract as director, producer, writer resulted only in *Too Late Blues* (1962). Disowned *A Child is Waiting* (1962) after re-editing by Stanley Kramer. Worked briefly for Screen Gems, making TV shows and, in Canada, acting at CBC. 1954: married actress Gena Rowlands.

Films as director: 1961: Shadows. 1962: Too Late Blues (+*p/co-s*); A Child is Waiting. 1968: Faces (+*s*). 1970: Husbands (+*s/w*). 1971: Minnie and Moscowitz (+*s/w*).

Films as actor include: 1955: The Night Holds Terror. 1956: Crime in the Streets; Edge of the City. 1957: Affair in Havana. 1958: Saddle the Wind. 1964: The Killers. 1967: The Dirty Dozen. 1968: Rosemary's Baby.

CASSEL, Jean-Pierre

(Jean-Pierre Crochon) Actor. Paris 1932–
Dramatic Training at the Cours René Simon. 1953: discovered by Gene Kelly for *The Happy Road* (1956). 1954–59: small parts in films; stage and TV. Established by *Les Jeux de l'amour* (1959) and 2 other Philippe de Broca films.

Films as actor include: 1960: Le Farceur; Candide. 1961: L'Amant de cinq jours. 1962: Le Caporal Epinglé. 1963: Cyrano et d'Artagnan; Les Plus Belles Escroqueries du monde *ep* L'Homme qui vendit la Tour Eiffel; Nunca pasa nada. 1965: Those Magnificent Men in their Flying Machines or How I Flew from London to Paris in 25 hours and 11 minutes; Les Fêtes Galantes. 1966: Paris brûle-t-il? 1967: Jeu de massacre. 1969: Oh! What a Lovely War.

CASTELLANI, Renato

Director. Finale Ligure, Italy 1913–
Until 1925 lived in Argentina where father worked for Kodak. School in Geneva, then studied architecture in Milan. 1934: jointly scripted and directed radio programme 'In Linea'. 1936: began in films as assistant to Mario Camerini on *Il Grande Appello*. 1937: practising architect in Milan. 1938–41: films in Rome, worked on scripts and as assistant to Augusto Genina, Mario Camerini, and Alessandro Blasetti. 1941: first film as director. 1958: *Venere Imperiale* abandoned after disputes between Gina Lollobrigida and produc-

Per Oscarssen in Henning Carlsen's Svalt.
Jack Palance and Martine Carol in Ten Seconds To Hell, *directed by Robert Aldrich.*
Madeleine Carroll and Henry Fonda in William Dieterle's Blockade.

41

tion company, eventually directed by Jean Delannoy (1962). Spent 3 years making 5 programmes on Leonardo da Vinci for Italian TV (also wrote, 1971).

Films as director: 1941: Un Colpo di pistola – A Pistol Shot (*+co-s*). 1942: Zazà (*+co-s*). 1943: La Donna della montagna – The Woman from the Mountain (*+co-s*). 1946: Mio Figlio Professore – My Son, the Professor (*+co-s*). 1948: Sotto il sole di Roma (*+co-s/co-st*). 1950: E primavera – Springtime in Italy (*+co-s/co-st*). 1951: Due Soldi di speranza – Two Pennyworth of Hope (*+co-s/co-st*). 1954: Giulietta e Romeo – Romeo and Juliet (*+co-s/co-st*). 1957: I Sogni nel cassetto (*+s/st*). 1959: Nella città l'inferno – Caged (*+co-s*). 1961: Il Brigante – Italian Brigands (*+co-s*). 1963: Mare Matto (*+co-s/co-st*). 1964: Tre Notte d'amore *ep* La Vedova; Controsesso *ep* Una Donna d'affari (*+co-s/co-st*). 1967: Questi Fantasmi – Ghosts, Italian Style (*+co-s*). 1969: A Brief Season.

CASTLE, William

Director and producer. New York 1914–
Broadway acting debut at 15. Stage manager. 1932: directed 'Dracula' on stage. 1932–39: Broadway director and actor on Broadway and in summer stock; wrote and directed radio series, including 'Lights Out', 'The Romance of Helen Trent'. 1939: brought to Hollywood by Harry Cohn. 1943: first film as director. 1943–63: almost all films for Columbia. 1958: first film as director and producer. TV producer, including series 'Meet McGraw'. 1955: formed own production company. 1964–66: worked for Universal. From 1966: with Paramount. 1968: produced *Rosemary's Baby* and *The Riot*.

Films as director: 1943: The Chance of a Lifetime. 1944: The Whistler; She's a Soldier Too; When Strangers Marry; Mark of the Whistler. 1945: Voice of the Whistler (*+co-s*); The Crime Doctor's Warning. 1946: Just Before Dawn; Mysterious Intruder; The Crime Doctor's Manhunt; The Return of Rusty. 1947: The Crime Doctor's Gamble. 1948: Texas, Brooklyn and Heaven – The Girl from Texas; The Gentleman from Nowhere. 1949: Johnny Stool Pigeon; Undertow. 1950: It's a Small World (*+co-s*). 1951: Hollywood Story; The Fat Man; Cave of Outlaws. 1953: Serpent of the Nile; Fort Ti; Drums of Tahiti; Conquest of Cochise; Slaves of Babylon; Charge of the Lancers; Jesse James vs the Daltons. 1954: Masterson of Kansas; The Saracen Blade; Battle of Rogue River; The Iron Glove; The Law vs Billy the Kid; The Americano. 1955: Duel on the Mississippi; The Gun That Won the West; New Orleans Uncensored – Riot on Pier Six. 1956: The Houston Story; Uranium Boom.

Films as director and producer: 1958: Macabre; The House on Haunted Hill. 1959: The Tingler. 1960: 13 Ghosts. 1961: Homicidal (*+n*); Mr Sardonicus. 1962: Zotz!; The Old Dark House. 1963: Thirteen Frightened Girls – The Candy Web; Straitjacket. 1964: The Night Walker. 1965: I Saw What You Did. 1966: Let's Kill Uncle; The Busy Body. 1967: The Spirit is Willing; Project X.

CAVALCANTI, Alberto

(Alberto de Almeida-Cavalcanti) Director, producer, set decorator, and writer. Rio de Janeiro, Brazil 1897–

Son of mathematician of Italian extraction. Studied law. 1913: to Switzerland, studied architecture. To Paris as interior decorator, then set decorator for Marcel L'Herbier, and writer. 1926: first film as director. 1929: directed Jean Renoir in *La P'tite Lilie* and *Le Petit Chaperon Rouge*. 1933: wrote *Tire-au-Flanc*. Directed Renée Falconetti on Paris stage. Invited to Britain by John Grierson. 1936: sound recordist on *Night Mail*. 1939–40: worked for GPO Film Unit, Crown Film Unit, as producer and director. 1941–47: worked for Ealing. 1942: made compilation *Film and Reality* for British Film Institute. To Brazil. 1949–52: worked for Vera Cruz, became head of production, sacked as communist through American intervention. 1953: joined Kino Film. Returned to Europe. Worked with Bertolt Brecht on script of *Herr Puntilla und sein Knecht Matti* (1956); directed it in Austria under Brecht's supervision for DEFA. With Joris Ivens supervised the 5 episodes of *Die Vind Rose* (1956). 1960–61: TV work in Britain, and a film for Children's Film Foundation. 1962: wrote script of *Yerma*; production abandoned, turned into play, produced in Spain. Returned to stage direction for first time since 1920s. 1968: taught at UCLA. Worked for French TV. Book 'Film e Realidad' published in Brazil.

Films as set decorator include: 1924: L'Inhumaine (*co*). 1924: Feu Mathias Pascal (*co*).

Films as producer include: 1936: Big Money. 1937: The Savings of Bill Blewitt. 1938: North Sea; Happy in the Morning; Men in Danger. 1939: The First Days – A City Prepares; Speaking from America; Squadron 992; Spare Time. 1940: Spring Offensive – An Unrecorded Victory. 1941: The Big Blockade. 1942: The Foreman went to France; Find, Fix and Strike. 1944: The Halfway House (*as-p*). 1951: Painel. 1952: Santuario.

Films as director: 1926: Rien que les heures (*+p/co-s*). 1928: En rade (*+co-s/e*); Yvette (*+s/e*); Le Train sans yeux (*+e*). 1929: La P'tite Lilie – La Petite Lili; La Jalousie de Barbouille (*+s/e/dec*); Le Capitaine Fracasse (*+co-s/e*); Le Petit Chaperon Rouge (*+co-ad/co-di/e/dec*); Vous verrez la semaine prochaine. 1930: Toute sa vie; A Cançao do berco (*Portuguese version of* Toute sa vie). 1931: Dans une île perdue (*+s*); A mi-chemin du ciel; Les Vacances du diable. 1932: Tour de chant (*+s*); En lisant le journal; Le Jour du frotteur (*+s/e*); Revue Montmartroise; Nous ne ferons jamais du cinéma. 1933: Le Mari Divorce – Le Garçon Divorce. 1934: Coralie et Cie (*+s*); Le Tour de chant (*+s*); Pett and Pott (*+s/e*); New Rates. 1935: Coal Face (*+s*); SOS Radio Service. 1936: Message from Geneva (*+s*). 1937: We Live in Two Worlds; The Line to Tcherva Hut; Who Writes to Switzerland (*+s*). 1938: Four Barriers (*+s*). 1939: Men of the Alps; A Midsummer Day's Work (*+s/dec*). 1941: The Yellow Caesar. 1942: Film and Reality; Went the Day Well?; Alice in Switzerland; Greek Testament. 1943: Watertight (*+s*). 1944: Champagne Charlie. 1945: Dead of Night (*ep*). 1947: Nicholas Nickleby; They Made Me a Fugitive – I Became a Criminal; The First Gentleman. 1949: For Them that Trespass. 1952: Simão, o caolho (*+p*); O Canto do mar (*+p/co-st*). 1954: Mulher de Verdade (*+p*). 1955: Herr Puntila und sein Knecht Matti (*+co-ad*). 1958: La Prima Notte; Les Noces Venitiennes. 1960: The Monster of Highgate Ponds. 1967: Story of Israel: Thus Spake Theodor Herzl (*+s*).

CAVALIER, Alain

(Alain Fraissé) Director. Vendôme, France 1931–
Faculté des Lettres, Paris, then IDHEC. Assistant to Edouard Molinaro (1956) on some shorts, to Louis Malle on *Ascenseur pour l'échafaud* (1957) and *Les Amants* (1957). 1958: directed short, *Un Américain*. 1965: worked on script of Jean-Paul Rappeneau's *La Vie de château*. Second wife is actress Irène Tunc.

Features as director: 1962: Le Combat dans l'île (*+co-st*). 1964: L'Insoumis (*+s/co-ad*). 1967: Mise à sac (*+co-st/co-s*). 1968: La Chamade (*+co-s/co-di*).

CAYATTE, André

Director and writer. Carcassonne, France 1909–
Degrees in Arts and Law. Then novelist (1930–39), lawyer at the Paris bar; journalist on L'Oeuvre and L'Intransigeant. From 1938, worked as writer for films: e.g. on scenario of *Entrée des artistes* (1938), adaptation of *Remorques* (1941), collaborated on story and dialogue for *Caprices* (1941), dialogue for *Le Camion Blanc* (1942). 1942: first film as director. 1951: technical consultant on Henri Storck's *Banquet des fraudeurs*. *La Vie Conjugale* (1963) consists of 2 films, *Jean-Marc* and *Françoise*, designed to be distributed separately but simultaneously.

Films as director: 1942: La Fausse Maîtresse. 1943: Au Bonheur des dames (*+co-s*). 1944: Pierre et Jean (*+s*); Le Dernier Sou (*+st*). 1945: Roger-la-Honte (*+s*); Sérénade aux nuages (*+co-s*). 1946: Le Revanche de Roger-la-Honte (*+s*); Le Chanteur Inconnu. 1947: Les Dessous des cartes (*+co-s*). 1948: Les Amants de Verone (*+st*). 1949: Retour à la vie *ep* Tante Emma. 1950: Justice est faite – Justice Has Been Done (*+co-s*). 1952: Nous sommes tous des assassins – Are We All Murderers? (*+co-s*). 1954: Avant le deluge (*+co-s*). 1955: Le Dossier Noir (*+co-s*). 1956: Oeil pour oeil – An Eye for an Eye (*+co-s*). 1958: Le Miroir à deux faces (*+co-st*). 1960: Le Passage du Rhin – The Crossing of the Rhine (*+co-st/co-s*). 1962: Le Glaive et la balance – Two are Guilty (*+st*). 1963: La Vie Conjugale (*+co-st/co-s*). 1965: Piège pour Cendrillon – A Trap for Cinderella (*+co-s*). 1967: Les Risques du métier (*+st/co-s*). 1969: Les Chemins de Khatmandou – The Road to Katmandu (*+st/co-s*). 1970: Mourir d'aimer (*+co-s*).

CAYROL, Jean

Writer. Bordeaux 1911–
Studied law in Bordeaux. 1927: set up and edited magazine Les Cahiers du fleuve. 1936–42: librarian at Bordeaux Chamber of Commerce. World War II: in espionage; prisoner of war (1943). Published poems and essays; novels include: 'Je vivrai l'amour des autres'; 'On vous parle' (1947); 'Le Vent de la memoire' (1952); 'Le Deménagement' (1956); 'Corps Etrangers' (1959); 'Le Froid du soleil' (1963); 'Midiminuit' (1966); 'J'entends encore' (1968). From 1956: editor of magazine Ecrire. Director of publishing house, Les Editions du Seuil. For Alain Resnais wrote commentary for *Nuit et brouillard* (1955) and script for *Muriel* (1963). Films as director in collaboration with Claude Durand, except for *La Déesse* (1966); all shorts except for *Le Coup de grâce* (1965).

Films as director, in collaboration with Claude

Durand: 1960: On vous parle (+ *co-s/co-cy*). 1961: La Frontière (*alone*; + *co-s/co-c*); Madame se meurt (+ *co-s/co-cy*). 1962: De tout pour faire un monde (*alone*). 1965: Le Coup de grâce (+ *s*). 1966: La Deesse (*alone*; + *s*).

CECCHI D'AMICO, Suso

Writer. Rome 1914–
Daughter of producer and writer Emilio Cecchi. Studied classics in Rome and English at Cambridge. Worked as translator from English and French into Italian (e.g. 'The Merry Wives of Windsor', 'Othello'). Began as scriptwriter working in collaboration with novelist Ennio Flaiano on scenario for Renato Castellani's *Mio Figlio Professore* (1946).

Films as writer in collaboration include: 1946: Vivere in pace; L'Onorevole Angelina. 1947: Il Delitto di Giovanni Episcopo. 1948: Ladri di biciclette (*co-ad*). 1949: Fabiola; Au-delà des grilles. 1950: E Primavera. 1951: Miracolo a Milano (*co-ad*); Bellissima. 1952: Altri tempi; Processo alla città. 1953: I Vinti; Siamo donne *ep* Anna Magnani; La Signora senza camelie. 1954: Tempi Nostri; Senso. 1955: Proibito; Le Amiche. 1957: Kean; Le Notti Bianche. 1958: La Sfida; I Soliti Ignoti. 1959: Nella città d'inferno; I Magliari. 1960: Risate di gioia; Rocco e i suoi fratelli. 1962: Boccaccio 70 *ep* Il Lavoro; Salvatore Giuliano. 1963: Il Gattopardo. 1964: Gli Indifferenti (*s alone*). 1965: Vaghe Stelle dell'Orsa. 1967: Lo Straniero; The Taming of the Shrew. 1970: Metello. 1971: La Mortadella.

CHABROL, Claude

Director. Paris 1930–
Father and grandfather pharmacists. Studied pharmacy in Paris. Wrote for Cahiers du Cinema for 4 years, also for Arts. With Eric Rohmer wrote 'Hitchcock' (1957). Worked as press attache in Paris for Fox. Inheritance by first wife enabled making of *Le Beau Serge* (1958). His production company (AJYM) produced Jacques Rivette's *Le Coup du berger* (1956), Eric Rohmer's *Le Signe du lion* (1959), Philippe de Broca's *Les Jeux de l'amour* (1959) and *Le Farceur* (1960). With François Truffaut's company, AJYM produced Rivette's *Paris nous appartient* (1961). Small parts as actor in some of these and some of his films as director; also in Jacques Doniol-Valcroze's *L'Eau à la bouche* (1959) and Marcel Moussy's *Saint-Tropez Blues* (1960). Officially technical adviser to Jean-Luc Godard on *A bout de souffle* (1959). 1964: directed 'Macbeth' at Théâtre Recamier; married actress Stephane Audran.

Films as director: 1958: Le Beau Serge (+ *p/st*); Les Cousins (+ *p/s*). 1959: A Double Tour – Web of Passion – Leda. 1960: Les Bonnes Femmes; Les Godelureaux (+ *co-s*). 1961: Les Sept Péchés Capitaux *ep* L'Avarice. 1962: L'Oeil du malin – The Third Lover (+ *s*); Ophelia; Landru – Bluebeard. 1963: Les Plus Belles Escroqueries du monde *ep* L'Homme qui vendit la Tour Eiffel. 1964: Le Tigre aime la chair fraîche – The Tiger Likes Fresh Blood; Paris vu par . . . *ep* La Muette (+ *s/w*). 1965: Marie-Chantal contre le docteur Kha (+ *co-s*); Le Tigre se parfume à la dynamite – An Orchid for the Tiger (+ *w*). 1966: La Ligne de demarcation (+ *co-s*); Le Scandale – The Champagne Murders. 1967: La Route de Corinthe (+ *w*).

1968: Les Biches – The Does – The Girlfriends (+ *co-s*); La Femme Infidèle (+ *s*). 1969: Que la bête meure – Killer! – This Man Must Die; Le Boucher (+ *s*). 1970: La Rupture (+ *s*). 1971: Juste avant la nuit.

CHALLIS, Christopher

Cinematographer. London 1919–
Started as assistant cameraman with Gaumont-British News; later Technicolor technician on *The Drum* (1938) and on several 'World Window' travelogues. 1940–46: RAF Film Unit cameraman. 1946: 2nd-unit cinematographer on *A Matter of Life and Death*, first of 6 films with Michael Powell and Emeric Pressburger; camera operator to Jack Cardiff on *Black Narcissus* and *The Red Shoes*. Frequent collaborator with American directors on films made in UK.

Films as cinematographer include: 1948: The Small Back Room. 1950: The Elusive Pimpernel. 1951: Gone to Earth; The Tales of Hoffman. 1953: Genevieve; Saadia. 1954: The Flame and the Flesh; Fire Over Africa (*co*). 1955: Oh Rosalinda!; Footsteps in the Fog; Quentin Durward. 1956: The Battle of the River Plate; The Spanish Gardener; Ill Met by Moonlight. 1959: Blind Date. 1960: Surprise Package; Sink the Bismark; The Grass is Greener; Never Let Go. 1962: HMS Defiant. 1963: The Victors. 1964: The Long Ships; A Shot in the Dark. 1965: Those Magnificent Men in their Flying Machines or How I Flew from London to Paris in 25 hours and 11 minutes; Return from the Ashes. 1966: Arabesque. 1967: Two for the Road. 1968: A Dandy in Aspic; Chitty Chitty Bang Bang. 1969: Staircase. 1970: The Private Life of Sherlock Holmes.

CHAMPION, Gower

Choreographer. Geneva, Illinois 1921–
At 2 moved with family to Los Angeles. 1936–41: after winning dancing contest with partner Jean Tyler, toured night clubs and appeared on Broadway in 'Streets of Paris' (1939), 'The Lady Comes Across' and 'Count Me In' (1940). World War II: served in Coast Guard. 1943–44: toured in 'Tars and Spars'; assigned to troop transport. 1946: formed dancing team with Marjorie Belcher (under name 'Gower and Bell' until marriage in 1947) and toured in cabaret. Choreographed musicals, 'Lend an Ear', 'Small Wonder' (1948) and 'Make a Wish' (1951) on Broadway. 1955: staged and appeared in 'Three for Tonight' with Harry Belafonte; directed and choreographed: 'Bye, Bye Birdie' (1960); 'Carnival!' (1961); 'My Father and Me' (1963); 'Hello Dolly!' (1964). Staged 'Prettybelle' in Boston (1971). Dance direction and guest appearances on TV; directs TV spectaculars; series 'Marge and Gower Champion Show' (1957). First film appearance in *Till the Clouds Roll By* (1946). 1951: first film with Marge, *Show Boat*, then MGM contract. 1963: directed *My Six Loves*. Staged 1969 Oscar ceremonies.

Films as dancer or actor include: 1951: Mr Music; Show Boat. 1952: Lovely to Look At. 1953: Give a Girl a Break (+ *chor*). 1955: Three for the Show; Jupiter's Darling.

CHANDLER, Jeff

Drama school, stagehand, then actor in stock com-

The Tingler, *directed by William Castle.*
Yellow Caesar, *directed by Alberto Cavalcanti.*
Jeff Chandler and Joseph Cotten in Robert Wise's Two Flags West.

pany. 1941: attempted to launch small stock company in Elgin, Illinois. 1942–45: US Army service. 1945: radio work in Hollywood; spotted by Dick Powell. First film, *Johnny O'Clock* (1947). 1949: 10-year contract with Universal. With agent Meyer Mishkin formed Earlmar Productions; made *Drango* (1957) for United Artists release. Recording contract with Decca (1954). 1955: wrote lyric for title song of *Six Bridges to Cross*. 1957: debut as nightclub singer in Las Vegas.

Films as actor include: 1949: Abandoned. 1950: Deported; Broken Arrow; Two Flags West. 1951: Bird of Paradise. 1952: Red Ball Express. 1953: East of Sumatra. 1954: Sign of the Pagan. 1957: Man in the Shadow; Jeanne Eagels. 1958: A Stranger in My Arms. 1959: Ten Seconds to Hell. 1960: The Plunderers (+ *co-ex-p*). 1961: Return to Peyton Place; Merrill's Marauders.

CHANDLER, Raymond

Novelist and screenwriter. Chicago 1888–1959 La Jolla, California
Dulwich College, London; private tutors in France and Germany. From 1909: journalist in London. World War I: Canadian Expeditionary Force and RAF. Business career in USA. 1933: first magazine fiction published. Films adapted by others from his novels include *The Falcon Takes Over* (1942) and *Murder My Sweet* (1944) both based on 'Farewell My Lovely', *The Big Sleep* (1946), *The Lady in the Lake* (1946), *The Brasher Doubloon* (1947) based on 'The High Window'. Also wrote some screenplays. Adapted none of own novels for films.

Films as writer in collaboration: 1944: Double Indemnity; And Now Tomorrow. 1945: The Unseen. 1946: The Blue Dahlia (*alone*). 1951: Strangers on a Train.

CHANEY, Lon

Actor. Colorado Springs, Colorado 1883–1930 Los Angeles
Learned pantomime through childhood need to communicate with deaf mute parents. Touring shows, then small film parts in early slapstick comedies; over 50 films for Universal by 1915. Also directed 6 shorts for Universal (1915). First large part *Riddle Gawne* (1918), then played cripple in *The Miracle Man* (1919). Established by *The Hunchback of Notre Dame* (1923). 1925–29: series of films directed by Tom Browning at MGM starting with *The Unholy Three* (1925). Died just after completing first sound film, remake of *The Unholy Three*. Played by James Cagney in *Man of a Thousand Faces* (1957). His son Creighton Chaney became actor as Lon Chaney Jr, later Lon Chaney.

Films as actor include: 1914: Richelieu. 1919: Victory. 1920: Treasure Island. 1921: Outside the Law. 1922: The Light in the Dark; Oliver Twist. 1924: He Who Gets Slapped. 1925: The Tower of Lies; The Phantom of the Opera. 1926: The Road to Mandalay. 1927: London After Midnight; Mockery. 1928: The Big City; Laugh Clown Laugh; West of Zanzibar; While the City Sleeps. 1929: Where East is West.

Shorts as director: 1915: The Stool Pigeon; For Cash; The Oyster Dredger (+ *s*); The Violin Maker (+ *w*); The Trust (+ *w*); The Chimney's Secret (+ *s/w*).

CHAPLIN, Charles

Director, writer and actor. London 1889–
1894: first music-hall appearance with father, who died shortly after from alcoholism. 1896: mother in hospital; with half-brother Sydney sent to orphanage. 1898: joined music-hall team, Eight Lancashire Lads; sent to boarding school; Sydney joined ship bound for Africa as cabin boy. 1901: on return, Sydney became 'manager' of 2 brothers who toured halls in provinces for some years. 1907: with Fred Karno, travelling with company to France (1909), USA and Canada (1910–12). 1912: on second trip with Karno to USA, spotted by vice-president of Keystone; declined offer of film contract. 1913: accepted new offer of $150 per week; on expiration of Karno contract went to work for Mack Sennett at Keystone. 1914–15: 35 films for Keystone, mainly 1-reel, some 2-reel and 1 6-reel, *Tillie's Punctured Romance* (1915); after 6 months and 20 films was director and writer of all his shorts. 1915: with Essanay at $1250 per week made 14 films, 1-reelers (2), 2-reelers (11) and a 4-reeler, *Charlie Chaplin's Burlesque on Carmen*, extended from planned 2 reels after Chaplin's departure. *Triple Trouble* (1918), assembled by Essanay, includes part of *Police* (1916) and *Life* (1915), an uncompleted dramatic film. 1916: contract for 12 2-reelers in a year with Mutual at $10,000 per week plus $150,000 on signature. 1917: contract with First National to pay him $1,075,000 for 8 films in 18 months and guarantee the costs of production; made 9 films (1917–23) – 2-reelers (3), 3-reelers (3), a 4-reeler and a 6-reeler plus *The Bond*, ½-reel propaganda film for Liberty Bonds. All films at Essanay, Mutual and First National photographed by Roland Totheroh; almost all had Edna Purviance as leading actress. Founded own production company (1917) and opened own studio (1918). 1919: one of the founders of United Artists. 1923: first film for United Artists, *A Woman of Paris*, only one until *The Countess from Hong Kong* (1967) in which not star. 1928: shooting of *City Lights* interrupted by success of sound; continued with sound and completed for 1931 première. From 1947 political convictions provoked various public expressions of hostility towards him. 1952: left USA permanently after selling most of interests in United Artists. Since 1953 has lived in Switzerland; 2 films made in London. 1964: publication of 'My Autobiography'. Composed musical themes for all his sound films. 3rd of 4 wives was Paulette Goddard (1933–42), 4th (married 1943) Oona O'Neill, daughter of Eugene O'Neill. Son by 2nd wife is actor Sydney Chaplin.

Films as actor: 1914: Making a Living; Kid Auto Races at Venice; Mabel's Strange Predicament; Between Showers; A Film Johnnie; Tango Tangles; His Favorite Pastime; Cruel, Cruel Love; The Star Boarder; Mabel at the Wheel; Twenty Minutes of Love; The Knock-Out. 1915: Tillie's Punctured Romance.

Films as director, writer and actor: 1914: Caught in a Cabaret – The Waiter – Jazz Waiter – Faking with Society (*co-d Mabel Normand*); Caught in the Rain – At It Again; A Busy Day – Militant Suffragette; The Fatal Mallet – Pile Driver (*co-d Mack Sennett*); Her Friend the Bandit (*co-d Mabel Normand*); Mabel's Busy Day – Love and Lunch – Charlie and the Sausages (*co-d Mabel Normand*); Mabel's Married Life – When You're Married – The Squarehead (*co-d Mabel Normand*);

Laughing Gas – Tuning His Ivories – Down and Out – The Dentist; The Property Man – Getting His Goat – The Roustabout; The Face on the Bar Room Floor – The Ham Artist; Recreation; The Maquerader – Putting One Over – The Female Impersonator; His New Profession – The Good For Nothing – Helping Himself; The Rounders – Oh, What a Night – Two of a Kind – Revelry; The New Janitor – The Porter – The Blundering Boob; Those Love Pangs; Dough and Dynamite – The Doughnut Designer; Gentlemen of Nerve – Some Nerve; His Musical Career – The Piano Movers – Musical Tramps; His Trysting Place; Getting Acquainted – A Fair Exchange; His Prehistoric Past. 1915: His New Job; A Night Out; The Champion – Champion Charlie; In the Park; The Jitney Elopement; The Tramp; By the Sea; Work – The Paperhanger; A Woman – A Perfect Lady – Charlie and the Perfect Lady; The Bank – Charlie at the Bank; Shanghaied; Life (*uf*); A Night in the Show – Charlie at the Show. 1916: Charlie Chaplin's Burlesque on Carmen – Carmen; Police; The Floorwalker; The Fireman; The Vagabond; One A.M.; The Count; The Pawnshop; Behind the Screen; The Rink. 1917: Easy Street; The Cure; The Immigrant; The Adventurer. 1918: A Dog's Life; Shoulder Arms; The Bond – Charles Chaplin in a Liberty Loan Appeal. 1919: Sunnyside; A Day's Pleasure. 1921: The Idle Class; The Kid. 1922: Pay Day. 1923: The Pilgrim; A Woman of Paris (+*p*). 1925: The Gold Rush (+*p*). 1928: The Circus (+*p/m*). 1931: City Lights (+*p/m*). 1936: Modern Times (+*p/m*). 1940: The Great Dictator (+*p/m*). 1947: Monsieur Verdoux (+*p/m*). 1952: Limelight (+*p/m/chor/songs*). 1957: A King in New York (+*p/m*). 1967: A Countess from Hong Kong (+*p/di/m*).

Early compilation films include: 1916: The Essanay – Chaplin Revue of 1916 (*composed of* The Tramp + His New Job + A Night Out). 1918: Chase Me, Charlie (*British compilation of Essanay shorts*); Triple Trouble (*Essanay compilation including parts of* Work, Police *and* Life, plus non-Chaplin material).

CHARISSE, Cyd

(Tula Ellice Finkles) Actress. Amarillo, Texas 1922–
Started ballet lessons at 8. At 12 sent to Hollywood Professional School. 1935: joined de Basil's Ballet Russe and toured USA. 1939: married ballet instructor Nico Charisse during European tour which was curtailed by outbreak of war. As Lily Norwood small parts in films and first appearance dancing in *Something to Shout About* (1942). 1945: went to MGM as Cyd Charisse for ballet sequence of Ziegfeld Follies; MGM contract. 1948: married singer Tony Martin. TV and nightclub appearances.

Films as actress include: 1943: Mission to Moscow (*ps Lily Norwood*). 1945: The Harvey Girls. 1949: Tension; East Side, West Side. 1951: Mark of the Renegade. 1951: The Wild North; Singin' in the Rain. 1953: The Band Wagon. 1954: Deep in My Heart; Brigadoon. 1955: It's Always Fair Weather. 1957: Silk Stockings. 1962: Two Weeks in Another Town. 1966: The Silencers.

CHARRELL, Erik

Director. Breslau, Germany 1895–
Theatre producer, and choreographer of spectacular

musicals and ballet. First theatrical production, 'An Alle' (1934), at the Grosses Schauspielhaus, Berlin; others include 'White Horse Inn' (1931) at London Coliseum. First film as director, *Der Kongress tanzt* (1931), later banned in Germany (1937), also made French- and English-language versions. 1934: directed *Caravan* in America for Fox in English and French versions. Only other film work, script of *Im weissen Rössl* (1952), script and choreography for *Feuerwerk* (1954).

CHASE, Borden

(Frank Fowler) Writer. New York 1900–1971 Los Angeles

A year in US Navy. Boxer, Taxi driver. In bootlegging and protection rackets. Worked on Holland Tunnel, basis of first film as writer in collaboration *Under Pressure* (1935) for Fox, based on own co-story. Wrote for many magazines, including Saturday Evening Post, Argosy. 1938: *The Devil's Party* based on his novel 'Hell's Kitchen has a Pantry'. 1944: with Howard Hawks founded Motion Picture Alliance for the Preservation of American Ideals. 1942–50: worked for several studios including Republic, Warners, United Artists. 1947: based *Red River* on own story 'The Chisholm Trail.' From 1950: mainly with Universal, wrote several films produced by Aaron Rosenberg. 1965: scripted *Gunfighters of the Casa Grande* from own novel 'Viva Gringo'.

Films as story writer include: 1942: Dr Broadway. 1948: The Man from Colorado. 1954: Vera Cruz.

Films as writer include: 1935: Under Pressure (*co-st/co-s*). 1942: The Fighting Seabees (*st/co-s*). 1945: This Man's Navy (*+ st*). 1946: I've Always Loved You (*+ fst*). 1947: Red River (*fst/co-s*). 1950: Montana (*co-s*). 1950: Winchester '73 (*co-s*). 1951: The Iron Man (*co-s*); Lone Star (*+ fst*). 1952: Bend of the River; The World in His Arms. 1953: Sea Devils. 1954: The Far Country. 1955: Man Without a Star. 1956: Backlash. 1957: Night Passage. 1965: Gunfighters of the Casa Grande (*co-s*). 1969: Backtrack.

CHASE, Charley

(Charles Parrott) Director and actor. Baltimore, Maryland 1893–1940 Hollywood

Started in vaudeville with Irish monologues, songs, dancing. At 21 became film actor: briefly at Universal then (1914) to Keystone, in several films directed by Chaplin. 1915: first film as director, in collaboration with Ford Sterling for Sennett. 1916: to Fox. 1917: first film as sole director and actor. Moved to Roach. Directed several times by brother James Parrott; frequently directed himself. 1936: first feature as actor Gus Meins' *Kelly the Second*; *Neighborhood House*, originally a feature, was cut to 2 reels. Moved to Columbia, returning to 2-reelers. 1940: died of heart attack. Usually directed under name Charles Parrott; also known as Paul Parrott, Poll Parrott.

Films as actor include: 1914: His New Profession; Dough and Dynamite; Gentlemen of Nerve. 1915: Tillie's Punctured Romance.

Films as director and actor: 1915: The Hunt (*co-d only; co-d Ford Sterling*). 1917: Chased into Love (*+ s*). 1918: Hello Trouble. 1919: Ship Ahoy (*+ s*).

1920: Kids is Kids. 1933: The Bargain of a Century; Luncheon at Twelve; Midsummer Mush; Sherman Said It. 1934: You Said a Hatful!; Fate's Fathead; Something Simple (*co-d Walter Weems*). 1935: The Chases of Pimple Street. 1937: Oh, What a Knight! 1938: The Old Raid Mule; Tassels in the Air; Ankles Away (*+ s*); Halfway to Hollywood; Violent is the Word for Curly; Mutts to You; A Nag in the Bag; Flat Foot Stooges. 1939: Mutiny on the Body!; Boom Goes the Groom; Saved by the Belle; Static in the Attic.

Films as director in collaboration with Eddie Dunn and actor: 1933: The Cracked Ice Man. 1934: I'll Take Vanilla; Another Wild Idea; Four Parts; It Happened One Day.

Films as director in collaboration with Harold Law and actor: 1935: Manhattan Monkey Business; Life Hesitates at 40. 1936: The Count Takes the Count; Vamp Till Ready; Neighborhood House.

CHAYEFSKY, Paddy

Writer. New York 1923–

First play, musical comedy, written in army hospital in UK while recovering from war wound. Worked on Garson Kanin–Carol Reed film *The True Glory* (1945). Returned to New York to work in uncle's print shop; left after 6 months to write short stories and documentary films. TV plays include 'Marty' and 'The Catered Affair'. Has also written for Broadway and radio. Oscar for screenplay of *Marty* (1955).

Films as writer include: 1955: Marty (*+ fpl*). 1957: The Bachelor Party (*+ fpl*). 1958: The Goddess. 1959: Middle of the Night (*+ fpl*). 1964: The Americanization of Emily. 1969: Paint Your Wagon (*ad*).

CHERKASOV, Nikolai

Actor. Leningrad 1903–1966

From 1918: stage actor. 1926: title role in Leningrad production of 'Don Quixote'. Stage work also includes 'Boris Godunov'. 1937–39: acted in the 2 parts of *Piotr Pervyi*. 1938: played title role in *Aleksandr Nevskii*; in elections for Supreme Soviet became deputy from Kuibyshev district of Leningrad. 1939: played Maxim Gorky in *Lenin v 1918 godu*. 1944–45: title role in the 2 parts of *Ivan Groznyi*.

Films as actor include: 1937: Deputat Baltiki. 1938: Chelovek s ruzhyom. 1942: Yevo zovut Sukhe-Bator. 1947: Vesna; Pirogov; Vo imya zhizni. 1957: Don Quixote.

CHEVALIER, Maurice

Actor and singer. Paris 1888–1972 Paris

Electrician and apprentice engraver before debut as singer and entertainer in Café des Trois Lions, Paris (1900). 1906–14: toured music-halls; at Folies Bergère as dancing partner with Mistinguett (1910). 1911–14: appeared in short films by Max Linder. World War I: in French infantry; prisoner of war (1915–18). 1919: first London appearance in revue, 'Hello America'. 1929: New York debut in Ziegfeld's last midnight revue; Hollywood debut in *Innocents of Paris*. 1929–33: all films for Paramount. 1936–56: only in British and French films. Stage appearances in London, New York, Paris and extensive tours, notably

Charles Chaplin in The Gold Rush.
Cyd Charisse in Party Girl, *by Nicholas Ray.*
Nicolai Cherkasov in Eisenstein's Alexander Nevsky.

1947–50. TV includes 'Maurice Chevalier Show' for NBC, French series 'Maurice de Paris'. Autobiography 'Mome à cheveux blancs' (1970).

Films as actor include: 1930: The Love Parade; Paramount on Parade. 1931: The Smiling Lieutenant. 1932: One Hour with You; Love Me Tonight. 1934: The Merry Widow. 1936: The Beloved Vagabond. 1937: L'Homme du jour. 1938: Break the News. 1939: Pièges. 1947: Le Silence est d'or. 1957: Love in the Afternoon. 1958: Gigi. 1959: Count Your Blessings. 1960: A Breath of Scandal; Can-Can; Pepe. 1961: Fanny. 1963: A New Kind of Love. 1964: I'd Rather Be Rich.

CHIARI, Mario

Designer. Florence, Italy 1909–
Graduated in architecture. Entered cinema as writer and assistant director to Alessandro Blasetti (1940–49). Designed theatrical sets and costumes, including work for Luchino Visconti. 1951: collaborated on script of *Miracolo a Milano*. First 3 films are documentaries.

Films as art director or production designer include: 1950: Vulcano. 1953: La Carrozza d'oro; I Vitelloni. 1956: War and Peace. 1958: La Tempestà. 1960: Jovanka e l'altri; La Battaglia di Maratona (co-dec). 1962: Barabbas. 1966: La Bibbia. 1967: Doctor Dolittle. 1971: La Spina Dorsale del diavolo.

Films as director: 1942: Monte Sant'Angelo; Boschi sul mare. 1943: I Trulli di Alberobello. 1948: Fabiola (co-d *Alessandro Blasetti*). 1954: Amori di mezzo secolo (ep).

CHRETIEN, Henri

Inventor. Paris 1879–1956 Washington, DC
In mid-1920s did research on anamorphic lens process, patented as Hypergonar. Occasional uses before 1939, notably for Claude Autant-Lara's *Construire un feu* (1927 r 1930). 1952: sold patent to Twentieth Century-Fox, who launched it as CinemaScope with *The Robe* (1953).

CHRISTENSEN, Benjamin

Director. Viborg, Denmark 1879–1959 Copenhagen
1902: opera singer in Aarhus. Became actor then director at Aarhus Theatre. Opera producer. 1908: wrote scripts for August Blom. 1913: directed, wrote and acted in first film. 1921: played Satan in *Häxan*. 1923: *Unter Juden* was a German production made in Sweden. 1924: to Dekla Bioskop in Germany to act in Carl Drover's *Mikaël*; remained to direct 2 films. 1926–30: to Hollywood; 2 films for MGM, 5 for First National. Additional direction on *The Mysterious Island* (1929). Returned to Denmark, made 3 more films there. From 1942: in retirement.

Films as director: 1913: Det Hemmelighedsfulde X – The Mysterious X (+ s/w). 1915: Haevnens nat – The Night of Revenge (+ s/w). 1921: Häxan – Witchcraft Through the Ages (+ s/w). 1923: Unter Juden – Among Jews; Seine Frau die Unbekannte – His Mysterious Adventure (+ s). 1925: Die Frau mit dem schlechten Ruf – The Woman Who Did. 1926: The Devil's Circus (+ s/st). 1927: Mockery (+ st). 1928:

The Hawk's Nest; The Haunted House. 1929: The House of Horror; The Mysterious Island (co-d Lucien Hubbard; *Maurice Tourneur*); Seven Footprints to Satan. 1939: Skilsmissens børn – The Children of Divorce (+ s). 1940: Barnet – The Child (+ co-s). 1941: Gaa med mig hjem – Return With Me. 1942: Damen med de lyser handsker – The Lady with the Coloured Gloves.

CHRISTIAN-JAQUE

(Christian Maudet) Director. Paris 1904–
Architecture at Ecole des Beaux-Arts and Ecole des Arts Decoratifs; also studied music. 1927–30: film critic for Cinégraf. 1927–32: designed posters; assistant and art director to Julien Duvivier, etc; also wrote screenplays. 1932: directed 4 shorts. 1933: started directing features with *Adémar Lampiot* (co-directed with Paul Mesnier) and *Le Tendron d'Achille*. 1933–37: prolific director of comedies. 1962: started *La Fabuleuse Aventure de Marco Polo* as *L'Echiquier de Dieu*, but project abandoned; finished by others in 1964. 5 wives include actresses Simone Renant (married 1938), René Faure (married 1945) and Martine Carol (married 1952); latter 2 starred in his films.

Films as director include: 1936: Francois Ier. 1937: Les Perles de la couronne – Pearls of the Crown (co-d *Sacha Guitry*). 1938: Les Disparus de Saint-Agil. 1941: L'Assassinat du Père Noël – The Murder of Father Christmas. 1942: La Symphonie Fantastique; Carmen. 1944: Sortilèges – The Sorcerer; Voyage sans espoir. 1945: Boule de Suif. 1946: Revenant. 1947: La Certosa di Parma – La Chartreuse de Parme. 1948: D'homme à hommes (+ co-s). 1949: Souvenirs Perdus. 1951: Fanfan la Tulipe (+ co-s). 1952: Adorables Creatures (+ s); Lucrezia Borgia – Lucrèce Borgia (+ co-st/co-s). 1954: Madame Du Barry – La Du Barry (+ co-s). 1955: Si tous les gars du monde . . . – Race for Life (+ co-s); Nana (+ co-s). 1957: La Loi c'est la loi (+ co-ad). 1959: Babette s'en va-t-en guerre – Babette Goes to War. 1960: La Française et l'amour – Love and the Frenchwoman ep Le Divorce. 1961: Madame Sans-Gêne – Madame. 1963: Les Bonnes Causes; La Tulipe Noire – The Black Tulip. 1964: La Fabuleuse Aventure de Marco Polo – L'Echiquier de Dieu – The Fabulous Adventures of Marco Polo (co-d Denys de la Patellière, *Noel Haoward*); Le Repas des fauves. 1965: La Guerra Segreta – The Dirty Game (co-d *Terence Young, Carlo Lizzani*). 1968: Lady Hamilton Zwischen Schmach und Liebe – Emma Hamilton. 1969: Qui veut tuer Carlos? – Dead Run (+ co-s). 1971: Les Petroleuses.

CHRISTIE, Julie

Actress. Assam, India 1941–
Daughter of tea planter. English boarding schools; studied art in France and at Brighton Technical College. Central School of Speech and Drama. 1957–60: actress in repertory theatres. 1961: title role in TV serial 'A for Andromeda'. 1962: first film, *The Fast Lady*. 1963: established by part in *Billy Liar*; 'Comedy of Errors' with Royal Shakespeare Company, London and American tour. Oscar as Best Actress for *Darling* (1965).

Films as actress include: 1965: Young Cassidy; Dr Zhivago. 1966: Fahrenheit 451. 1967: Far from the Madding Crowd. 1968: Petulia. 1971: The Go-Between.

CHUKHRAI, Grigori

Director. Melitopol, Ukraine 1921–
1939: to State film school (VGIK); the school was mobilised soon after. World War II service in Soviet Air Force parachute corps including Battle of Stalingrad, and as infantry officer commissioned from the ranks; wounded 5 times, twice seriously. After war, returned to VGIK: studied under Sergei Yutkevitch and Mikhail Romm; graduated 1951. 2½ years as assistant, e.g. to Romm on *Admiral Ushakov* (1953). To Mosfilm in Moscow. 1956: first film as director. 1964: produced *Zhili-byli starik so starukhoi*.

Films as director: 1956: Sorok Pervyi – The Forty-first. 1959: Ballada o soldatye – Ballad of a Soldier (+ co-s). 1961: Chistoye Nebo – Clear Skies. 1966: Lyudi – People. 1970: Stalingradskaya Bitva – The Battle of Stalingrad.

CHYTILOVA, Vera

Director. Ostrava, Czechoslovakia 1929–
Worked as model. Barrandov studios: script-girl, assistant director. Prague Film School, to 1953. 1962: first film as director.

Films as director: 1962: Strop – Ceiling; Pytel blech – A Bag of Fleas. 1963: O Něčem Jinem – Something Different – About Something Else (+ s). 1965: Perlicki na dne – Pearls of the Deep ep Automatu svet (+ co-s). 1966: Sedmikrásky – Daisies (+ co-s/co-st). 1970: Ovoce rajských stromů jíme – We May Eat of the Fruit of the Trees of the Garden (+ co-s).

CIAMPI, Yves

Director. Paris 1921–
Musical family. 1938: amateur shorts. 1940–45: member of the Resistance; awarded Légion d'Honneur. 1945: made amateur short dedicated to LeClerc Division *Les Compagnoms de la gloire*. 1946: qualified as doctor. 1947: assistant to Jean Dreville on 2 films. 1948: technical advisor to André Hunebelle on *Métier de fous*; directed first feature. 1949: technical advisor to Hunebelle on *Mission à Tangiers* and *Millionaires d'un Jour*. 1955–58: President of Syndicat des Techniciens de la Production Cinématographique. From 1959: President of Association National des Médecins-Cineastes et des Cineastes Scientifiques de France. TV director; member of ORTF programme committee. Wife is Keiko Kishi who acted in his *Typhon sur Nagasaki* (1957) and *Qui êtes-vous, M. Sorge?* (1960).

Films as director: 1938: Evocation. 1940: Le Cancer. 1941: Mort Interdite. 1945: Les Compagnons de la gloire. 1946: Les Cadets du Conservatoire. 1948: Suzanne et les brigands. 1949: Pilote de guerre . . . pilote de ligne. 1950: Un Certain Monsieur. 1951: Un Grand Patron. 1952: Le Plus Heureux des hommes. 1953: Le Guérisseur; L'Esclave. 1955: Les Heros sont fatigués – Heroes and Sinners. 1957: Typhon sur Nagasaki. 1958: Le Vent se leve (+ co-st). 1960: Qui êtes-vous, M. Sorge? (+ co-st). 1962: Liberte (+ co-st). 1964: Le Ciel sur la tête. 1968: A quelques jours près (+ co-st).

CLAIR, René

(René Chomette) Director. Paris 1898–

1917: volunteer in ambulance corps at front; invalided out. 1919: journalist on L'Intransigeant. Actor, e.g. for Jacob Protazanov in *Pour une nuit d'amour* (1921), *Le Sens de la mort* (1922) and under pseudonym René Clair in Louis Feuillade's *Les Deux Gamines* (1920), *Parisette* and *L'Orpheline* (1921). Critic on Paris-Journal. 1922: assistant to Jacques de Baroncelli in Belgium. 1922–24: film editor of Le Théâtre et Comœdia Illustré. 1924: first film as director. 1930: with Augusto Genina wrote script for *Prix de beauté*. 1935–38: in UK, made *The Ghost Goes West* for Alexander Korda; formed production company with Jack Buchanan to make *Break the News*. 1939: began *Air Pur* in France, interrupted by war. 1940–45: made 4 films in Hollywood, then returned to France. Scripted all his French films except *Entr'acte*, written by Francis Picabia and shown between acts of ballet 'Relâche', produced by Rolf de Maré's Ballets Suédois. Books 'Reflexion Faite' (1951), 'Cinéma d'hier et d'aujourd'hui' (1970), and novels 'Adams' (1926), 'De Fil en Aiguille' (1941, first published 1947) and 'La Princesse de Chine' (1951). 1951: adapted and produced Theophile Gautier's 'Une Larme du Diable' for radio. Translated Garson Kanin's 'Born Yesterday' for Paris stage as 'Voyage à Washington'.

Films as director and writer: 1924: Paris qui dort – Le Rayon Invisible – The Crazy Ray; Entr'acte (*d/e only*). 1925: Le Fantôme du Moulin Rouge; Le Voyage Imaginaire. 1926: La Proie du vent. 1927: Un Chapeau de paille d'Italie – The Italian Straw Hat. 1928: Les Deux Timides; La Tour. 1930: Sous les toits de Paris. 1931: Le Million. 1932: A nous la liberté – Liberté chérie. 1933: Quatorze Juillet. 1934: Le Dernier Milliardaire. 1935: The Ghost Goes West (*co-s*). 1938: Break the News – Fausses Nouvelles (*+ co-p; co-s*). 1939: Air Pur (*co-s; uf*). 1941: The Flame of New Orleans (*co-s*). 1942: I Married a Witch (*d only + co-p*). 1943: Forever and a Day (*+ co-p; co-d 10 others*). 1944: It Happened Tomorrow (*co-s*). 1945: And Then There Were None – Ten Little Niggers (*+ p; co-s*). 1947: Le Silence est d'or (*+ co-p*). 1950: La beauté du diable (*co-s*). 1952: Les Belles de nuit – Night Beauties. 1955: Les Grandes Manoeuvres – Summer Manoeuvres. 1957: Porte des lilas (*co-s*). 1960: La Française et l'amour – Love and the French-woman *ep* Mariage. 1961: Tout l'or du monde (*co-s*). 1962: Les Quatre Vérites – The Three Fables of Love *ep* Les Deux Pigeons. 1965: Les Fêtes Galantes.

CLARKE, Charles G.

Cinematographer. Potter Valley, California 1899–

1919: Film laboratory work for D. W. Griffith. By 1920 was second cameraman. From 1922: cinematographer. 1927–33: with Fox. 1933: to MGM, then returned to Fox in 1938, where he stayed for the rest of his career. Last film in 1962.

Films as cinematographer include: 1927: Ham and Eggs at the Front; Upstream. 1928: Four Sons; The Red Dance; Riley the Cop. 1934: Tarzan and his Mate; The Cat and the Fiddle (*co*); Viva Villa! (*co*); Evelyn Prentice. 1935: The Winning Ticket; Shadow of Doubt; Woman Wanted. 1937: Under Cover of Night; The Thirteenth Chair; Stand-In. 1938: Safety in Numbers. 1939: Frontier Marshal; Mr Moto Takes a Vaca-

tion. 1940: Young As You Feel; Viva Cisco Kid. 1942: Moontide. 1943: Guadalcanal Diary; Wintertime (*co*). 1945: Junior Miss. 1946: Margie. 1947: Captain from Castile (*co*); Miracle on 34th Street. 1948: The Iron Curtain. 1949: Slattery's Hurricane. 1950: The Big Lift. 1951: Golden Girl. 1952: Red Skies of Montana; Kangaroo; Stars and Stripes Forever. 1953: Destination Gobi. 1954: Night People; The Bridges at Toko-Ri; Black Widow. 1955: Prince of Players; Violent Saturday; The Virgin Queen. 1956: Carousel; The Man in the Gray Flannel Suit; Three Brave Men. 1957: Oh Men! Oh Women!; Stopover Tokyo. 1958: The Hunters; The Barbarian and the Geisha; These Thousand Hills. 1959: The Sound and the Fury; A Private's Affair; Hound Dog Man. 1960: Flaming Star. 1961: Return to Peyton Place. 1962: Madison Avenue.

CLARKE, Shirley

Director. New York 1925–

After dancing school and university, studied modern dance with Martha Graham Dancers. 1942: first work as choreographer performed at 92nd Street YMCA. 1946: president of National Dance Association which sent ballet companies and films abroad. 1953: abandoned dancing for the cinema. 1960: first feature, *The Connection*. 1962: with Jonas Mekas founded Film Maker's Co-op, New York. Worked on 11-screen film, *Man and Polar Regions* for Expo 67, Montreal. Acted in Agnès Varda's *Lions Love* (1969). Subject of French TV programme by André S. Labarthe, Noel Burch.

Films as director: 1953: Dance in the Sun (*+ p/c/e*). 1954: In Paris Parks (*+ p/c/e*). 1955: Bullfight (*+ p/c/e*). 1957: A Moment in Love (*+ p/c/e*). 1958: Loops (*+ p/c/e*); Bridges-Go-Round (*+ p/c/e*); The Skyscraper (*+ e; co-d Willard Van Dyke*). 1960: A Scary Time (*+ co-s/c*); The Connection (*+ co-p*). 1963: The Cool World (*+ co-s/e*). 1967: Portrait of Jason (*+ e*).

CLARKE, T. E. B.

Writer. Watford, Hertfordshire 1907–

Charterhouse School; Cambridge University. Began as journalist; on editorial staff of Daily Sketch (1936). 1944: first film as scriptwriter, the documentary *For Those in Peril*. 1971: wrote series 'From a Bird's Eye View' for NBC TV.

Films as writer include: 1944: Champagne Charlie (*co-lyr*). 1945: Johnny Frenchman (*+ st*); Dead of Night (*additional di*). 1947: Hue and Cry (*+ st*). 1948: Passport to Pimlico (*+ st*); The Blue Lamp. 1951: The Lavender Hill Mob (*+ st*); Encore *ep* The Ant and the Grasshopper. 1953: The Titfield Thunderbolt (*+ st*). 1958: A Tale of Two Cities; Gideon's Day. 1960: Sons and Lovers (*co*).

CLAVELL, James

Writer and director. Sydney, Australia 1924–

World War II: Captain in Royal Artillery. 1942: captured by Japanese on Java, held in Changi prison, Singapore. 1946–47: Birmingham University. Then salesman in London. Made pilot episodes for TV series. 1953: went to USA. Naturalised American citizen. From 1958: wrote scripts. 1959: first film as

Julie Christie.
Chapeau De Paille D'Italie, *directed by René Clair.*
Simone Signoret and Laurence Harvey, in Room At The Top, *directed by Jack Clayton.*

director, producer and writer. Has written poetry, plays, e.g. 'Countdown at Armageddon', 'E=MC²'; also novels, e.g. 'King Rat', filmed by Bryan Forbes (1962), 'Tai-Pan' (1966) filmed by Michael Anderson.

Films as writer: 1958: The Fly; Watusi. 1963: The Great Escape (co); 633 Squadron (co). 1964: The Satan Bug (co).

Films as director and producer: 1959: Fives Gates to Hell (+ s). 1960: Walk Like a Dragon (+ co-st/co-s). 1962: The Sweet and the Bitter (+ s). 1968: Where's Jack? (d only); To Sir with Love (+ s). 1971: The Last Valley (+ s).

CLAYTON, Jack

Director. Brighton, Sussex 1921–
1935: became assistant at London Films. Assistant director, then editor for Warners and Fox in London. World War II: served in RAF cinematography unit, directed many documentaries, e.g. *Naples is a Battlefield* (1944–46). 1948: director of production on *An Ideal Husband*. From 1949: associate producer on e.g. own short *The Bespoke Overcoat* (1955). 1958: first feature as director.

Films as associate producer include: 1949: The Queen of Spades (co). 1953: Moulin Rouge. 1954: Beat the Devil; The Good Die Young. 1955: I am a Camera. 1956: Dry Rot (p). 1957: The Story of Esther Costello (ex-p).

Features as director: 1958: Room at the Top. 1961: The Innocents (+ p). 1964: The Pumpkin Eater. 1967: Our Mother's House.

CLÉMENT, René

Director. Bordeaux, France 1913–
Architectural student at Ecole des Beaux Arts. At 18 made first short, 16mm animated, *César chez les Gauloises*. Forced to abandon studies at 20 by death of father. 1933: gag writer with Jacques Tati. From 1934, also cinematographer on short documentaries. 1936: first professional short as director, *Soigne ton gauche*, also first appearance of Tati in his comic characterisation. 1939–40: military service in cinematographic section of French Army. At CATJC (precursor of IDHEC) at same time as Henri Alekan. 1943: assistant director to Yves Allégret for *La Boîte aux rêves*. 1946: technical adviser to Jean Cocteau on *La Belle et la bête* before completion of own first feature, *La Bataille du rail*.

Films as director: 1936: Soigne ton gauche. 1937: L'Arabie Interdite – Arabie Inconnue (+ s/c). 1938: La Grande Chartreuse. 1939: La Bièvre. 1940: Le Triage. 1942: Ceux du rail. 1943: La Grande Pastorale. 1944: Chefs de demain. 1946: La Bataille du rail (+ s); Le Père Tranquille. 1947: Les Maudits (+ co-ad). 1949: Au-delà des grilles – La Mura di Malapaga. 1950: Le Château de verre (+ co-s). 1952: Jeux Interdits – Forbidden Games (+ co-s). 1954: Knave of Hearts – Monsieur Ripois – Lovers, Happy Lovers (+ co-s). 1956: Gervaise. 1958: La Diga sul pacifico – The Sea Wall. 1959: Plein Soleil – Purple Noon. 1961: Che gioia vivere – Quelle Joie de vivre. 1963: Le Jour et l'heure (+ co-ad). 1964: Les Félins – The Love Cage – The Joy House (+ co-s). 1966: Paris brûle-t-il? – Is

Paris Burning? 1969: Passager de la pluie – Rider on the Rain. 1971: La Maison sous les arbres (+ co-ad/co-s).

CLIFT, Montgomery

Actor. Omaha, Nebraska 1920–1966 New York
No formal theatrical training. 1933: appeared in summer stock. 1935: on Broadway in 'Fly Away Home', then 'Jubilee'. Subsequent New York appearances included 'There Shall Be No Night' (1940), 'The Skin of our Teeth' (1942), 'The Searching Wind' (1944), 'You Touched Me' (1945), 'The Seagull' (1954). 1948: first films.

Films as actor: 1948: The Search; Red River. 1949: The Heiress. 1950: The Big Lift. 1951: A Place in the Sun. 1953: Stazione Termini; I Confess; From Here to Eternity. 1957: Raintree County. 1958: The Young Lions. 1959: Lonelyhearts; Suddenly Last Summer. 1960: Wild River. 1961: The Misfits; Judgement at Nuremberg. 1962: Freud, the Secret Passion. 1966: L'Espion.

CLINE, Eddie

Director. Kenosha, Wisconsin 1892–1948 Hollywood
To 1913: theatrical work. Assistant at Keystone. 1915: directed Fox Sunshine Comedies. 1916: became director for Sennett at Triangle-Keystone, films usually scripted by Sennett. 1920–23: collaboration with Buster Keaton at Comique. 1925: returned to Sennett. Collaboration with W. C. Fields began with *Million Dollar Legs* (1932) but mainly 1940–41. Worked frequently for Fox, First National and Universal. 1946–48: last films, for Monogram.

Films as director include (complete from 1923): 1916: Sunshine; His Bread and Butter; Her First Beau. 1917: Her Nature Dance; The Dog Catcher's Love; The Pawnbroker's Heart; A Bedroom Blunder – Room 23; That Night. 1918: The Kitchen Lady; Those Athletic Girls; His Smothered Love; The Summer Girls; Whose Little Wife are You; Hide and Seek, Detectives; A School House Scandal; Training for Husbands. 1919: Cupid's Day Off; East Lynne with Variations; When Love is Blind; Hearts and Flowers. 1920: Training for Husbands. 1923: Circus Days (+ co-ad). 1924: Off His Trolley (+ co-s); Galloping Bungalows (+ co-s); The Plumber (+ s); Little Robinson Crusoe; When a Man's a Man; The Good Bad Boy; Captain January; Along Came Ruth. 1925: Tee for Two (+ s); The Beloved Bozo; Bashful Jim; A Sweet Pickle (+ s); The Soapsuds Lady; Hotsy—Totsy (+ s); Cold Turkey; Love and Kisses; The Rag Man; Old Clothes. 1926: A Love Sundae; That Gosh-Darn Mortgage (+ s); Gooseland (+ s); Spanking Breezes; The Ghost of Folly; Puppy Lovetime; Smith's Baby; Alice Be Good (+ co-s); When a Man's a Prince; Smith's Vacation (+ co-s); The Prodigal Bridegroom; A Harem Knight (+ co-s); A Blonde's Revenge (+ co-s); Flirty Four Flushers. 1927: The Girl from Everywhere; Let it Rain; Soft Cushions; The Jolly Jilter; The Bull Fighter. 1928: Ladies' Night in a Turkish Bath; Vamping Venus; The Head Man; Love at First Flight; The Crash. 1929: Broadway Fever; His Lucky Day; The Forward Pass. 1930: Don't Bite Your Dentist; In the Next Room; Take Your Medicine; Sweet Mama. 1931: In Conference; The Girl Habit; The Naughty Flirt. 1932: Million Dollar Legs. 1933: So This is Africa. 1934: Peck's Bad

Boy; The Dude Ranger. 1935: The Cowboy Millionaire; When a Man's a Man; It's a Great Life! 1936: F-Man. 1937: On Again – Off Again; Forty Naughty Girls; High Flyers. 1938: Hawaii Calls; Breaking the Ice; Peck's Bad Boy with the Circus; Go Chase Yourself. 1940: The Villain Still Pursued Her; The Bank Dick; My Little Chickadee. 1941: Never Give a Sucker an Even Break; Meet the Chump; Hello Sucker. 1942: What's Cookin'?; Give Out, Sisters; Snuff Smith, Yard Bird; Behind the Eight Ball; Private Buckaroo. 1943: Crazy House; He's My Guy; Ghost Catchers. 1944: Night Club Girl; Slightly Terrific; Swingtime Johnny. 1945: Penthouse Rhythm; See My Lawyer. 1946: Bringing Up Father (+ co-st). 1948: Jiggs and Maggie in Society (+ co-st/co-s); Jiggs and Maggie in Court (co-d William Beaudine; + co-st/co-s).

Films as director and writer in collaboration with Buster Keaton: 1920: One Week; Convict 13; The Scarecrow. 1921: Neighbors; The Haunted House; Hard Luck; The High Sign; The Playhouse; The Boat; The Paleface. 1922: Cops; The Electric House; My Wife's Relations; The Frozen North; Day Dreams. 1923: The Balloonatic; The Love Nest.

CLOQUET, Ghislain

Cinematographer. Anvers, Belgium 1924–
Photographic school and IDHEC, From 1947: assistant cameraman, e.g. to Edmond Séchan. From 1949: cinematographer, first on shorts, then features, some in collaboration with Sacha Vierny. Taught at IDHEC (1954–62) and (from 1962) at Institut National Supérieur des Arts du Spectacle, Brussels. Has worked for French TV.

Films as cinematographer include: 1950–53: Les Statues meurent aussi. 1955: Nuit et brouillard (co). 1956: Toute la mémoire du monde. 1957: Le Mystère de l'atelier 15 (co); Un Amour de poche. 1959: Classe Tous Risques. 1960: Le Bel Age (co); Le Trou; Description d'un combat. 1963: Le Feu Follet. 1965: Mickey One; De Man de zijn haar kort liet knippen. 1966: Au hasard, Balthazar. 1967: Les Demoiselles de Rochefort; Mouchette; Benjamin. 1969: Une Femme Douce; Un Soir, un train. 1970: La Maison des bories; Peau d'ane. 1971: Rendezvous à Bray.

CLOTHIER, William H.

Cinematographer. Decator, Illinois 1903–
1923: arrived in California; assistant cameraman at Paramount. 1934: became cinematographer. Out of work after a strike, went to Mexico, cinematographer there. To Spain, worked for 4 years on Spanish films. 1938: returned to USA as second cameraman, e.g. on *Fort Apache* (1948). From 1947: returned to cinematography. Warners contract.

Films as cinematographer include: 1952: Confidence Girl. 1954: Track of the Cat. 1955: The Sea Chase; Blood Alley; Sincerely Yours; Man in the Vault. 1956: Goodbye My Lady; Seven Men from Now; Gun the Man Down. 1957: Bombers B-52. 1958: Darby's Rangers; Fort Dobbs; Lafayette Escadrille; China Doll. 1959: The Horse Soldiers. 1960: The Alamo. 1961: Ring of Fire; The Deadly Companions; The Comancheros. 1962: The Man Who Shot Liberty Valance; Merrill's Marauders. 1963: Donovan's Reef; McLintock!. 1964: A Distant Trumpet; Cheyenne

Autumn. 1965: Shenandoah; The Rare Breed; Stagecoach; Way . . . Way Out. 1967: The Way West; The War Wagon. 1969: The Undefeated. 1970: Chisum; The Cheyenne Social Club.

CLOUZOT, Henri-Georges

Director and writer. Niort, France 1907–
Studied mathematics, political science; to naval school at Brest. Abandoned preparation for diplomatic career. 1927–30: journalist on Paris-Midi. Assistant director to Anatole Litvak, E. A. Dupont. 1931: made short. 1932–33: to Berlin to direct and write French versions of German films. 1934: wrote libretto to Maurice Yvain's opera 'La Belle Histoire'. 1931–41: scriptwriter. 1932: co-scripted Carmine Gallone's *Ma Cousine de Varsovie* and *Un Soire de rafle*. 1934–38: in Swiss sanitorium. 1939: wrote *Le Duel*. 1940: wrote 1-act play 'On prend les mêmes'. 1941: wrote *Les Inconnus dans la maison*. 1942: wrote play 'Comedie en trois actes'; first film as director and writer in collaboration. 1950: in Brazil; film *Brazil* not made; material used as basis for book 'Le Cheval des dieux'. His wife Vera Clouzot acted in several of his films, e.g. *Le Salaire de la peur* (1953), *Les Diaboliques* (1955), and co-wrote with him *La Verité* (1960). 1955: prevented by illness from directing his script for *Si tous les gars du monde*, made by Christian-Jacque. 1964: abandoned *L'Enfer* after several days' shooting. Wrote almost all own films in collaboration often with Jean Ferry or Jérôme Geronimi. 3 unpublished plays. Filmed concerts conducted by Herbert Von Karajan, for TV.

Films as director and writer in collaboration: 1942: L'Assassin habite au 21. 1943: Le Corbeau. 1947: Quai des orfèvres. 1949: Manon; Retour à la vie *ep* Le Retour de Jean. 1950: Miquette at sa mère. 1953: Le Salaire de la peur. 1955: Les Diaboliques. 1956: Le Mystère Picasso (+ s). 1957: Les Espions. 1960: La Verité. 1964: L'Enfer (*d only; uf*). 1968: La Prisonnière – Woman in Chains.

CLURMAN, Harold

Theatrical director. New York 1901–
1926: studied acting and direction under Richard Boleslavsky and Maria Ouspenskaya at American Laboratory Theatre. Drama critic. 1931: with Lee Strasberg founded Group Theatre. Pupils at his drama course included Elia Kazan. 1937: sole director of Group Theatre after departure of Strasberg because of disagreement. 1941: end of Group Theatre. Director on New York stage. 1946: brief stay in Hollywood; directed *Deadline at Dawn* with screenplay by Clifford Odets for RKO; then returned to theatre. Married actress and drama coach Stella Adler (1943).

COBB, Lee J.

Actor. New York 1911–
Studied to be violinist, but broke wrist. 1929: tried unsuccessfully for work in Hollywood. 1931–33: actor and director at Pasadena Playhouse. Freelance actor on tour and in New York. From 1935 with Group Theatre, e.g. in Clifford Odet's 'Waiting for Lefty' (1935), 'Thunder Rock' directed by Elia Kazan (1939). 1937: first films; in Odet's 'Golden Boy' directed by Harold Clurman for Group Theatre; in London production (1938) and film (1939). 1940: with Theatre

Guild, then California Radio Production Unit of US Army Air Corps. 1949: in Arthur Miller's 'Death of a Salesman' directed by Kazan on Broadway. Occasional TV from 1960.

Films as actor include: 1937: Ali Baba Goes to Town. 1939: Golden Boy. 1943: Tonight We Raid Calais; The Moon Is Down; The Song of Bernadette. 1944: Winged Victory. 1946: Anna and the King of Siam. 1947: Boomerang!; Johnny O'Clock; Captain from Castile. 1948: Call Northside 777; The Miracle of the Bells; The Dark Past. 1949: Thieves' Highway. 1951: Sirocco. 1954: On the Waterfront. 1955: The Racers; The Left Hand of God. 1956: The Man in the Gray Flannel Suit. 1957: Twelve Angry Men; The Garment Center; The Three Faces of Eve. 1958: The Brothers Karamazov; Man of the West; Party Girl; The Trap. 1959: Green Mansions. 1960: Exodus. 1962: The Four Horsemen of the Apocalypse; How the West Was Won. 1965: Our Man Flint. 1967: In Like Flint. 1970: The Liberation of L. B. Jones. 1971: Lawman.

COBURN, Charles

Actor. Macon, Georgia 1877–1961 New York
Began as programme seller in theatre in Savannah, Georgia; at 17 manager of the theatre. Acted in stock company in Chicago, then touring USA. 1901: first appeared on New York stage. 1903: established as stage actor by performance in 'The Christian'. 1906: married actress Ivah Wills and formed Coburn Shakespearean Players with actress wife, and toured USA. 1935: first film, *The People's Enemy*. Oscar as best supporting actor: *The More the Merrier* (1943). Last film: *Pepe* (1960).

Films as actor include: 1938: Of Human Hearts; Vivacious Lady; Lord Jeff. 1939: Bachelor Mother; Idiot's Delight; Made for Each Other; Stanley and Livingstone; In Name Only. 1940: Road to Singapore; Edison the Man. 1941: The Lady Eve; The Devil and Miss Jones; Our Wife; H.M. Pulham Esq. 1942: King's Row; In This Our Life; George Washington Slept Here. 1943: The Constant Nymph; Heaven Can Wait; Princess O'Rourke. 1944: Wilson. 1945: A Royal Scandal; Rhapsody in Blue; Over 21; Colonel Effingham's Raid. 1946: The Green Years. 1947: Lured; The Paradine Case. 1948: B.F.'s Daughter. 1949: Everybody Does It. 1951: Mr Music. 1952: Monkey Business; Has Anybody Seen My Gal? 1953: Gentlemen Prefer Blondes; Trouble Along the Way. 1954: The Long Wait. 1955: How to be Very, Very Popular. 1956: Around the World in 80 Days. 1957: Town on Trial. 1959: John Paul Jones.

COBURN, James

Actor. Laurel, Nebraska 1928–
Studied acting at Los Angeles City College and Stella Adler's school in New York. Stage debut in West Coast production of 'Billy Budd'; TV commercials and TV plays in New York. First film as actor: *Ride Lonesome* (1959). Own production company.

Films as actor include: 1959: Face of a Fugitive. 1960: The Magnificent Seven. 1962: Hell is for Heroes. 1963: The Great Escape; Charade. 1965: A High Wind in Jamaica; Major Dundee; Our Man Flint. 1966: What Did You Do in the War, Daddy? 1967: In Like Flint; The President's Analyst. 1968: Duffy.

Robert Bresson's Mouchette *photographed by Ghislain Cloquet.*
Cheyenne Autumn, *directed by John Ford, photographed by William H. Clothier.*
Lee J. Cobb in Vincente Minnelli's The Four Horsemen Of The Apocalypse.

COCHRAN, Steve

(Robert Alexander Cochran) Actor. Eureka, California 1917–1965 at sea, off the Guatemala coast
University of Wyoming. Actor in stock and touring companies. Season at Carmel Shakespeare Festival, California. With Mae West in 'Diamond Lil' on Broadway and on tour. World War II: organised and directed shows for West Coast army camps. 1945: film debut. 1949–53: with Warners. 1953: formed own company, Robert Alexander Productions – involved in 2 films, *Come Next Spring* (1955) and *Il Grido* (1957). 1967: directed, produced, photographed and acted in *Tell Me in the Sunlight*. Much TV work.

Films as actor include: 1946: The Kid From Brooklyn; The Best Years of Our Lives. 1947: A Song is Born. 1949: White Heat. 1950: The Damned Don't Cry; Dallas; Storm Warning; Highway 301. 1951: Jim Thorpe, All American. 1953: She's Back on Broadway; Back to God's Country. 1954: Private Hell 36. 1955: Come Next Spring. 1956: Slander. 1957: Il Grido. 1958: I, Mobster. 1959: The Big Operator; The Beat Generation. 1961: The Deadly Companions.

COCTEAU, Jean

Director and writer. Maisons Lafitte, France 1889–1963 Milly La Forêt, France
Studied at Lycee Condorcet. 1917: wrote outline for ballet 'Parade' by Erik Satie; set out aesthetic principles for Satie's followers in the Groupe des Six. Libretti include Arthur Honegger's opera 'Antigone' and Igor Stravinsky's opera-oratorio 'Oedipus Rex' (1927). Also playwright from 1920s, e.g. 'Antigone' (1922), 'Orphée' (1924), 'La Machine Infernale' (1934), 'Les Chevaliers de la table ronde' (1937), 'Les Parents Terribles' (1938). Wrote poetry, aphorisms ('Le Rappel à l'ordre', 1926), novels (e.g. 'Thomas l'Imposteur', 1923; 'Les Enfants Terribles', 1930). 1930: first film as director backed by the Vicomte de Noailles, who also produced Luis Buñuel's *L'Age d'Or*. Wrote all own films. Scripted many films by others. Played Alfred de Musset in *La Malibran* (1943). Films by others based on his works include Roberto Rossellini's *Una Voce Umana* (episode in *L'Amore*, 1947), Jacques Demy's *Le Bel Indifférent* (1957). Painter, including church murals. Member of Académie Française. Protégés included Jean Marais and novelist Raymond Radiguet.

Films as writer and director: 1930: Le Sang d'un poéte – The Blood of a Poet (+e/n). 1946: La Belle et la bête – Beauty and the Beast. 1948: L'Aigle à deux têtes – The Eagle with Two Heads (+fpl); Les Parents Terribles (+fpl). 1950: Orphée – Orpheus; Coriolan. 1952: La Villa Santo-Sospir (+p/c/w). 1960: Le Testament d'Orphée – The Testament of Orpheus (+w).

Films as writer: 1940: La Comédie du bonheur (di). 1943: Le Baron Fantôme (+wv; di); L'Eternel Retour (st/s/di). 1945: Les Dames du Bois de Boulogne (di). 1947: Ruy Blas (ad/di). 1948: Les Noces de sable (s/cy+wv); La Leggenda di Sant' Orsola (+wv; cy). 1950: Les Enfants Terribles (co-s/di/fn). 1951: Vénus et ses amants (cy); Le Rossignol de l'Empereur de Chine (+wv; cy; French version of Cisařův slavik, 1949). 1952: La Corona Negra (s); A l'aube du monde (cy/n). 1960: La Princesse de Clèves (ad/di). 1965: Thomas l'Imposteur (co-s/co-di/fn).

COHL, Emile

(Emile Courtet) Animator. Paris 1857–1938 Paris
1878: Pupil of caricaturist André Gill. Caricaturist and photographer. 1906: complained to Léon Gaumont about plagiarism of illustrations, given job as writer. 1907: became director using live action and animation. 1910: moved to Pathe. 1912: to Eclipse, then Eclair. 1912–14: to USA for Eclair, with George MacManus animated series 'Snookums'. Returned to France. Ruined by World War I; attempted come-backs in 1923 and 1935. Died in a fire.

Films as animator include: 1907: Course aux potirons; La Vie à rebours. 1908: Fantasmagorie; La Cauchemar de Fantoche; Les Allumettes Animées; Une Drame chez les Fantoches; Le Journal Anime; Le Petit Soldat qui devient Dieu; Les Frères Boutdebois. 1909: Les Transfigurations; La Lampe qui file; Les Joyeux Microbes; Génération Spontanee; Don Quichotte; Les Lunettes Féeriques; Aventures Extraordinaires d'un bout de papier; Le Linge Turbulent; Les Locataires d'à côté. 1910: Le Binettoscope; Le Petit Chanteclair; Le Tout Petit Faust; L'Enfance de l'art; Le Retapeur de cervelle; Rien n'est impossible a l'homme; Le Peintre Neo-impressioniste. 1911: Poudre de vitesse; Les Melons Baladeurs. 1912: Les Jouets Animés; Aventures d'un bout de papier; L'Homme sans tête; Cuisine Express. 1913: Le Baron de Crac; Aventures de Maltracé; Monsieur Stop. 1917: Les Aventures de pieds-nickelés (co-d Benjamin Rabier). 1923: L'Oreille. 1935: La Conquête d'Angleterre.

COHN, Harry

Studio head. New York 1891–1958 Phoenix, Arizona
Started work before leaving school; at 14 sang in chorus of a play. Sang in vaudeville, then joined cavalry. Singer at film shows. Older brother Jack became assistant to production manager of Carl Laemmle's IMP company. 1913: Jack Cohn produced feature *Traffic in Souls* (recovered 79 times its $5700 cost); Harry Cohn was one of the film's travelling exhibitors. Continued working with his brother for Laemmle on production. 1919: with Joe Brandt the brothers formed CBC (from their initials). 1924: because initials produced unfortunate nicknames, changed CBC's title to Columbia. Their staple product was 2-reel comedies and other short subject series, including one for film fans called *Screen Snapshots* (1922–23). 1929: the Cohns bought out Brandt; Harry became President, in charge of West Coast production. Nicknamed The White Fang. For his funeral, a sound stage at Columbia was converted into a 1400 seat chapel.

COLBERT, Claudette

(Lily Cauchoin) Actress. Paris 1905–
Family moved to New York when she was 5. 1923: New York stage debut as actress, 'The Wild Westcotts'; first starred in 'The Marionette Man' (1925) in Washington. 1927: first film, *For the Love of Mike*. Then Paramount contract, beginning with Paramount's first talkie *The Hole in the Wall* (1929). 1952–55: worked in Europe in films and theatre. Broadway appearances. First husband (1928–35) was Norman Foster. Oscar as Best Actress, *It Happened One Night* (1934).

Films as actress include: 1929: The Hole in the Wall. 1930: Manslaughter. 1931: The Smiling Lieutenant; Secrets of a Secretary. 1932: The Sign of the Cross. 1933: I Cover the Waterfront; Three Cornered Moon. 1934: Four Frightened People; It Happened One Night; Cleopatra; Imitation of Life. 1935: The Gilded Lily; Private Worlds; She Married Her Boss. 1936: The Bride Comes Home; Under Two Flags. 1937: Maid of Salem; I Met Him in Paris; Tovarich. 1938: Bluebeard's Eighth Wife. 1939: Zaza; Midnight; Drums Along the Mohawk. 1940: Boom Town; Arise My Love. 1941: Skylark; Remember the Day. 1942: The Palm Beach Story. 1943: So Proudly We Hail; No Time for Love. 1944: Since You Went Away; Practically Yours. 1945: Guest Wife; Tomorrow Is Forever. 1946: Without Reservations. 1948: Sleep, My Love. 1950: Three Came Home. 1951: Thunder on the Hill. 1952: The Planter's Wife. 1954: Si Versailles m'était conté. 1961: Parrish.

COLE, Jack

Choreographer and dancer. New Brunswick, New Jersey 1914–
Studied with Ted Shawn, Ruth St Denis, Charles Weidman and others. 1931: debut as dancer in 'Job' in New York. 1930–33: toured with Shawn, Humphrey-Weidman groups. 1933: Broadway debut in 'The School for Husbands'. Danced with own group. 1943: danced with Ziegfeld Follies. Choreography for stage includes: 'Something for the Boys' (1943), 'Alive and Kicking' (1950), 'Kismet' (1953), 'Candide' (1959), 'Kean' (1961), 'A Funny Thing Happened to Me on the Way to the Forum' (1962), 'Foxy' (1964). Choreographer mainly for Columbia and Fox, dancer for Fox and MGM. Work in TV includes 'The Perry Como Show', 'The Bob Hope Show', 'The Sid Caesar Show'. Cabaret work.

Films as choreographer and dancer include: 1941: Moon over Miami. 1944: Kismet. 1952: Lydia Bailey. 1957: Designing Woman.

Films as choreographer include: 1951: On the Riviera; David and Bathsheba. 1952: The Merry Widow. 1953: Gentlemen Prefer Blondes; The Farmer Takes a Wife. 1957: Les Girls. 1960: Let's Make Love.

COLMAN, Ronald

Actor. Richmond, Surrey 1891–1958 Santa Barbara, California
World War I: in London Scottish; wounded at Messines. Stage debut in sketch of Rabindranath Tagore, toured in variety. 1916: London stage. 1917: acted in a 2-reeler, unreleased. 1919–20: 2 films for Cecil Hepworth. 1920: New York. Acting in 'La Tendresse' was spotted by Henry King, who gave him lead in *The White Sister* (1924) and other films. Second wife (married 1938) was Benita Hume. Acted in radio with her in 'The Jack Benny Show'. 1950–52: own radio show; then (1954) on TV. Oscar as Best Actor for *A Double Life* (1947).

Films as actor include: 1919: Sheba. 1920: Anna the Adventuress. 1925: Romola; Lady Windermere's Fan; Stella Dallas. 1926: The Winning of Barbara Worth. 1927: The Magic Flame. 1929: Condemned. 1930: Raffles. 1932: Arrowsmith; Cynara. 1934: Bulldog Drummond Strikes Back. 1935: Clive of India; A Tale of Two Cities. 1936: Under Two Flags. 1937: Lost Horizon; The Prisoner of Zenda. 1938: If I Were King. 1939: The Light That Failed. 1940: Lucky Partners. 1941: My Life With Caroline. 1942: The Talk of the Town; Random Harvest. 1944: Kismet. 1947: The Late George Apley; A Double Life. 1956: Around the World in 80 Days.

COLPI, Henri

Editor and director. Brigue, Switzerland 1921–
University at Montpellier. 1945: IDHEC. Edited magazine Ciné-Digest. From 1950: film editor. Made shorts before first feature (1960). Wrote radio play with A. Rivemale: 'L'Eléphant dans la maison'. Books: 'Le Cinéma et ses hommes' (1947), 'Défense et illustration de la musique dans le film' (1963).

Films as editor include: 1954: La Pointe Courte. 1955: Nuit et brouillard (co). 1956: Le Mystère Picasso. 1957: A King in New York. 1958: Du côté de la côte. 1959: Hiroshima Mon Amour (co). 1961: L'Année Dernière à Marienbad (co).

Films as director: 1951: Des Rails sous les Palmiers (+ e; co-d M.-A. Colson-Malleville). 1953: Barrage du Chatelot; Architecture et lumière (co-d J.-P. Ganancia). 1956: Materiaux Nouveaux, demeures nouvelles. 1961: Une Aussi Longue Absence. 1962: Codine (+ co-st/e/co-m). 1966: Mona, l'etoile sans nom. 1967: Symphonie nr 3 in es-dur, Opus . 55 'Eroica' von Ludwig van Beethoven – Beethoven 3rd Symphony-Eroica. 1970: Heureux qui comme Ulysse . . . (+ co-s).

COMDEN, Betty

Writer. New York 1916–
University of New York. 1939–44: she and Adolph Green appeared in nightclubs with group, The Revuers. All writing in collaboration with Green. Many Broadway musicals. 1947: first film. 1949: with Green and Roger Edens wrote lyrics for *Take Me Out to the Ball Game*.

Films as writer in collaboration with Adolph Green: 1947: Good News (+ co-lyr). 1949: The Barkleys of Broadway (+ st); On the Town (+ st/fco-mpl/lyr). 1952: Singin' in the Rain (+ co-lyr). 1953: The Band Wagon. 1955: It's Always Fair Weather (+ st/s/ly). 1958: Auntie Mame. 1960: Bells Are Ringing (+ s/fco-mpl/lyr). 1964: What a Way to Go (+ lyr).

COMENCINI, Luigi

Director. Salò, Italy 1916–
Studied architecture. 1937: first short film as director *La Novelletta*. 1938: film critic with Alberto Lattuada for Corrente. Work in film conservation with Lattuada resulted in setting up Cineteca Italiana and Mostra del cinema at Milan Triennale. After World War II, film critic for L'Avanti! and Tempo; also photographer. 1946: short *Bambini in città*. 1947: co-scripted Mario Soldati's *Daniele Cortis*. 1949: scripted Lattuada's *Il Mulino del Po*; first feature as director and writer in collaboration. 1951: co-wrote Pietro Germi's *La Città si difende*. 1955: co-wrote story, and co-scripted Dino Risi's *Il Segno di Venere*. Also TV.

Films as director from 1949: 1949: Il Museo dei sogni.

1950: L'Imperatore di Capri; L'Ospedale del delitto. 1951: Persiane chiuse – Behind Closed Shutters. 1952: La Tratta delle bianche – White Slave Trade – Girls Marked Danger. 1953: Son tornata per te – Heidi. 1954: La Valigia dei sogni. 1964: Tre Notte d'amore *ep* La Vedova; Le Bambole – Four Kinds of Love *ep* Il Trattato di Eugenetica – A Treatise on Eugenics. 1965: Il Compagno Don Camillo; La Bugiarda. 1966: Incompreso – Misunderstood. 1967: Italian Secret Service.

Films as director and writer in collaboration from 1948: 1948: Proibito rubare. 1953: Pane, amore e fantasia. 1954: Pane, amore e gelosia. 1955: La Bella di Roma – Roman Signorina. 1956: La Finestra sul Luna Park. 1957: Mariti in città. 1958: Mogli pericolose. 1960: Tutti a casa – Everybody Go Home. 1961: A cavallo della tigre – Jail-Break – On the Tiger's Back. 1962: Il Commissario. 1963: La Ragazza di bube – Bebo's Girl. 1964: La Mia Signorina *ep* Eritrea. 1965: La Bugiarda. 1969: Infanzia, vocazione e prima esperienze di Giacomo Casanova, veneziano – Casanova; Senza sapere niente di lei.

CONNERY, Sean

Actor. Edinburgh, Midlothian 1930–
Royal Navy, as able seaman. Labourer and lifeguard. Studied art and modelled in art school. 1953: in London, stage debut in chorus of 'South Pacific'; also on tour. Repertory in London. 1956: first film as actor *No Road Back*. 1959: first American film *Darby O'Gill and the Little People*. With Claire Bloom in BBC TV production 'Anna Karenina'. 1962: first portrayal of James Bond, chosen for role by readers of Daily Express; married actress Diane Cilento. Own production company.

Films as actor include: 1957: Action of the Tiger; Hell Drivers. 1959: Tarzan's Greatest Adventure; Darby O'Gill and the Little People. 1962: The Longest Day; Dr No. 1963: From Russia with Love; Woman of Straw. 1964: Goldfinger; Marnie. 1965: The Hill; Thunderball. 1966: A Fine Madness. 1967: You Only Live Twice. 1968: Shalako. 1971: Diamonds Are Forever; The Anderson Tapes; Krasnaya Palatka.

CONSTANTINE, Eddie

Actor. Los Angeles 1917–
Began as singer, with operatic training. Debut on American radio. Moved to Paris (1947) when wife Hélène Mussel got contract with the Ballets des Champs-Elysées. Sang in nightclubs, theatre, on radio. Spotted by Edith Piaf to co-star in Marcel Achard's operetta 'La Petite Lili' (1949). Records. 1952: first film. Also TV, cabaret.

Films as actor include: 1954: Avanzi di galera; Ça va barder. 1955: Je suis un sentimental. 1956: Folies-Bergère. 1959: SOS Pacific. 1960: Le Chien de pique. 1961: Les Sept Péchés Capitaux *ep* La Paresse; Cleo de 5 à 7. 1962: Une Grosse Tête; Bonne Chance, Charlie. 1965: Alphaville, une étrange aventure de Lemmy Caution.

CONTE, Richard

Actor. Jersey City, New Jersey 1914–
Father Italian barber. Wall Street messenger, truck

Jean Cocteau's Le Testament D'Orphée.
Claudette Colbert (bottom right) in Irving Pichel's Tomorrow And Forever.
Singin' In The Rain. *directed by Gene Kelly and Stanley Donen, co-scripted by Betty Comden (and Adolph Green).*

driver, dance-band pianist, waiter at Connecticut summer camp where members of Group Theatre saw him in staff show (1935). Persuaded to take up scholarship at Neighborhood Playhouse, New York, after seeing performance of 'Waiting for Lefty'. Minor Broadway parts; lead in road show of 'Golden Boy'. Broadway success in 'Jason' (1942). World War II: medical discharge from army after 9 months. 1943: first film as actor, *Guadalcanal Diary*; Fox contract. TV work.

Films as actor include: 1944: The Purple Heart. 1945: A Bell for Adano. 1946: A Walk in the Sun; Somewhere in the Night. 1947: 13 Rue Madeleine; The Other Love. 1948: Call Northside 777; Cry of the City. 1949: Thieves' Highway; Whirlpool. 1953: The Blue Gardenia. 1954: The Big Combo. 1956: I'll Cry Tomorrow. 1957: Full of Life; The Brothers Rico. 1958: La Diga sul Pacifico. 1959: They Came to Cordura. 1960: Ocean's 11. 1963: Who's Been Sleeping in My Bed? 1964: Circus World. 1965: The Greatest Story Ever Told; Synanon. 1967: Hotel; Tony Rome. 1968: Lady in Cement.

CONWAY, Jack

Director. Graceville, Minnesota 1887–1952 Los Angeles
Left school in Tacoma, Washington, to work on railroad. 1907: joined small stock company in Santa Barbara, California. 1909: joined Nestor Motion Picture Company as actor. Starred in many films including *Her Indian Hero* and *The Valley of the Moon*. 1913: first film as director, *The Old Armchair*. 1915–17: personal assistant to D. W. Griffith. 1920: MGM contract, which continued for rest of career. Married daughter of actor Francis X. Bushman (1926).

Films as director include (complete from 1924): 1912: Snowball and his Pal (+ *w*). 1913: The Old Armchair. 1914: Captain McLean. 1915: The Penitentes. 1916: The Beckoning Trail; Judgement of the Guilty; Bitter Sweet; The Social Buccaneer; The Silent Battle; The Measure of a Man; The Mainspring. 1917: Jewel in Pawn; Polly Redhead; Her Soul's Inspiration; The Little Orphan; Come Through; The Charmer. 1918: Desert of Wheat; You Can't Believe Everything; Bond of Fear; Because of a Woman; Little Red Decides; Her Decision. 1919: Restless Souls (+ *w*); Diplomatic Mission; Desert Law. 1920: The Servant in the House; Lombardi, Ltd. 1921: Dwelling Place of Light; Money Changers; The Spenders; The U.P. Trail; The Kiss; A Daughter of the Law; The Killer (+ *w*); The Lure of the Orient (+ *w*); The Rage of Paris. 1922: The Millionaire; Step On It; A Parisian Scandal; Across the Deadline; Another Man's Shoes; Don't Shoot; The Long Chance. 1923: The Prisoner; Sawdust; Quicksands; What Wives Want; Trimmed in Scarlet; Lucretia Lombard. 1924: The Trouble Shooter; The Heart Buster. 1925: The Roughneck; The Hunted Woman; The Only Thing. 1926: Brown of Harvard; Soul Mates. 1927: The Understanding Heart; 12 Miles Out. 1928: Smart Set; Bringing Up Father; While the City Sleeps; Alias Jimmy Valentine. 1929: Our Modern Maidens. 1930: Untamed; They Learned About Women (*co-d Sam Wood*); The Unholy Three; New Moon. 1931: The Easiest Way; Just a Gigolo. 1932: Arsène Lupin; But the Flesh is Weak; Red Headed Woman. 1933: Hell Below; The Nuisance; Solitaire Man. 1934: Viva Villa!; The Girl from Missouri; The Gay Bride. 1935: One New York Night; A Tale of Two Cities. 1936: Libeled Lady. 1937: Saratoga. 1938: A Yank at Oxford; Too Hot to Handle. 1939: Let Freedom Ring; Lady of the Tropics. 1940: Boom Town. 1941: Love Crazy; Honky Tonk. 1942: Crossroads. 1943: Assignment in Brittany. 1944: Dragon Seed (*co-d Harold S. Bucquet*). 1947: High Barbaree; The Hucksters. 1948: Julia Misbehaves.

COOK, Elisha, Jr

Actor. San Francisco 1906–
Chicago Academy of Dramatic Art. In vaudeville from 14; stage actor. In Theatre Guild production of 'Ah, Wilderness!'. In films from 1936. Occasional TV parts. 1963: on stage played Giuseppe Girola in Bertolt Brecht's 'Arturo Ui'.

Films as actor include: 1936: Pigskin Parade. 1937: They Won't Forget. 1940: Public Deb No 1. 1941: The Maltese Falcon; I Wake Up Screaming. 1944: Phantom Lady; Up in Arms; Dark Waters. 1946: Cinderella Jones; Two Smart People; The Big Sleep. 1947: Born to Kill; The Long Night. 1949: The Great Gatsby. 1952: Don't Bother to Knock. 1953: Shane; Thunder Over the Plains. 1954: Drum Beat. 1955: The Indian Fighter. 1956: The Killing. 1957: The Lonely Man; Baby Face Nelson; Plunder Road. 1959: Day of the Outlaw. 1960: Platinum High School. 1961: One-Eyed Jacks. 1963: Papa's Delicate Condition; The Haunted Palace; Johnny Cool. 1967: Welcome to Hard Times. 1968: Rosemary's Baby. 1970: El Condor.

COOPER, Gary

Actor. Helena, Montana 1901–1961 Holmby Hills, California
Father British barrister, then judge in Montana Supreme Court. Brought up on father's ranch; tried unsuccessfully to become cartoonist. Occasional stunt work in films; acted in 2-reeler, *Poverty Row* (1925). Spotted by Samuel Goldwyn for first feature film as actor, *The Winning of Barbara Worth* (1926). From *It* (1927) under contract to Paramount; most 1930s films for Paramount. Produced *Along Came Jones* (1945). In 1950s formed own company, Baroda Productions. Oscars as Best Actor for *Sergeant York* (1941), *High Noon* (1952). Honorary Oscar (1960).

Films as actor include (complete from 1934): 1927: Children of Divorce. 1928: The Legion of the Condemned; Half a Bride; The Patriot. 1929: Wings; Wolf Song; Betrayal; The Virginian. 1930: Paramount on Parade; The Texan; Morocco. 1931: City Streets. 1933: A Farewell to Arms; Today We Live; Design for Living; Alice in Wonderland. 1934: Operator 13: Now and Forever. 1935: The Wedding Night; The Lives of a Bengal Lancer; Peter Ibbetson. 1936: Desire; Mr Deeds Goes to Town; The General Died at Dawn; Hollywood Boulevard. 1937: The Plainsman; Souls at Sea. 1938: The Adventures of Marco Polo; Bluebeard's Eighth Wife; The Cowboy and the Lady. 1939: Beau Geste; The Real Glory. 1940: The Westerner; Northwest Mounted Police. 1941: Meet John Doe; Sergeant York; Ball of Fire. 1942: The Pride of the Yankees. 1943: For Whom the Bell Tolls. 1944: The Story of Dr Wassell; Casanova Brown. 1945: Along Came Jones (+ *p*). 1946: Saratoga Trunk; Cloak and Dagger. 1947: Unconquered; Variety Girl. 1948: Good Sam. 1949: The Fountainhead; It's a Great Feeling; Task Force. 1950: Bright Leaf; Dallas. 1951: You're in the Navy Now; Starlift; It's a Big Country; Distant Drums. 1952: High Noon; Springfield Rifle. 1953: Return to Paradise; Blowing Wild. 1954: Garden of Evil; Vera Cruz. 1955: The Court-Martial of Billy Mitchell. 1956: Friendly Persuasion. 1957: Love in the Afternoon. 1958: Ten North Frederick; Man of the West. 1959: The Hanging Tree; They Came to Cordura; The Wreck of the Mary Deare; Alias Jesse James (*uc*). 1961: The Naked Edge.

COOPER, Merian C.

Producer. Jacksonville, Florida 1893–
US Naval Academy, Annapolis; left Navy before graduating to become merchant seaman on sailing ships. Then newspaperman. 1916: enlisted in infantry. World War I: Lieutenant in Aviation Corps, then Captain. From 1918: Lieutenant-Colonel in Polish army; for 2 years piloted combat plane against Bolsheviks. Widely travelled as news correspondent. 1926: began association with Ernest B. Schoedsack, at first producing and directing in collaboration. Left films temporarily to work in aviation; director of several aviation companies. From 1932: with RKO; producer on several Schoedsack films, executive producer on many others including John Ford's *The Lost Patrol* (1934). World War II: colonel in US Army Air Corps, retired as Brigadier-General. 1947: formed Argosy Pictures with John Ford, co-producing a number of Ford films released through RKO, then Republic. 1952: director of Cinerama Inc. Author of several books including 'Grass', 'The Sea Gypsy', 'Things Men Die For'. 1952: honorary Oscar for 'his many innovations and contributions to the art of motion pictures'.

Films as producer include: 1926: Grass (*co-p*; + *co-c*; *co-d Ernest B. Schoedsack, Marguerite Harrison*). 1927: Chang (*co-p*; *co-d Ernest B. Schoedsack*). 1929: The Four Feathers (*co-p*; *co-d Ernest B. Schoedsack, Lothar Mendes*). 1933: King Kong (*co-p*; + *co-st*; *co-d Ernest B. Schoedsack*). 1935: She; The Last Days of Pompeii. 1938: The Toy Wife. 1947: The Fugitive (*co-p*). 1948: Fort Apache (*co-p*); Three Godfathers (*co-p*). 1949: She Wore a Yellow Ribbon (*co-p*); Mighty Joe Young (+ *st*; *co-p*). 1950: Wagonmaster (*co-p*); Rio Grande (*co-p*). 1952: The Quiet Man (*co-p*). 1953: This is Cinerama (*co-p*); The Sun Shines Bright (*co-p*). 1956: The Searchers (*co-p*).

COPLAND, Aaron

Composer. New York 1900–
Studied under Rubin Goldmark and Nadia Boulanger. 1928–31: organised series of concerts in US. Works include ballets 'Billy the Kid' (1938), 'Rodeo' (1942), 'Appalachian Spring' (1944), opera 'The Tender Land' (1954), 3 symphonies, a piano concerto, an orchestral suite, chamber music. Author of books including 'Our New Music' (1941), 'What to Listen For in Music' (1939, revised 1957). Oscar for music score, *The Heiress* (1949).

Films as composer: 1939: The City. 1940: Of Mice and Men; Our Town. 1943: North Star. 1949: The Red Pony. 1961: Something Wild.

COPPOLA, Francis Ford

Director and writer. Detroit, Michigan 1939–
Father conducted orchestras of touring shows. Brought up in California and New York. Wrote and directed plays at college, e.g. wrote books and lyrics for musical 'The Delicate Touch'. Studied film at UCLA; wrote screenplay 'Pilma, Pilma'. Worked on nudist movies, then for Roger Corman in various capacities including writer. 1962: first film as director, made in Eire and produced by Corman. Subsequently also scripted films by others e.g. uncredited work on early version of script for *Reflections in a Golden Eye* (1967). Married Eleanour Neil, set decorator on his first film as director. Production company, American Zoetrope. Shared Oscar for original screenplay, *Patton* (1970).

Films as writer include: 1965: Paris brûle-t-il? (*co*). 1966: This Property is Condemned (*co*). 1970: Patton (*+co-st; co-s*).

Films as director: 1962: Dementia 13 – The Haunted and the Hunted (*+s*). 1967: You're a Big Boy Now (*+s*). 1968: Finian's Rainbow. 1969: The Rain People.

COREY, Wendell

Actor. Dracut, Massachusetts 1914–1968 Hollywood
Began as electrical salesman. From 1935: actor in summer stock. Broadway debut as actor in 'Comes the Revelation' (1942), followed by 'Strip for Action' (1942), 'The First Million' (1943). Produced season of summer stock in Providence, Rhode Island (1943). 1945: in 'Dream Girl' on Broadway. 1946: directed, produced and acted in stock in repertory of 10 plays. 1947: first film, *Desert Fury*; appeared in 'The Voice of the Turtle' on London stage; in radio series 'McGarry and his Mouse'. Further theatre and TV (series include 'Harbor Command', 'Peck's Bad Girl', 'Eleventh Hour'). President of the Academy of Motion Picture Arts and Sciences.

Films as actor include: 1947: I Walk Alone. 1948: The Search; Man-Eater of Kumaon; Sorry, Wrong Number. 1949: The Accused; Any Number Can Play; The File on Thelma Jordan. 1950: No Sad Songs for Me; The Furies. 1951: The Great Missouri Raid; The Wild Blue Yonder. 1952: The Wild North; My Man and I. 1954: Rear Window. 1955: The Big Knife. 1956: The Killer is Loose; The Rainmaker. 1957: Loving You. 1965: Agent for H.A.R.M.

CORMAN, Roger

Director and producer. Los Angeles 1926–
Engineering at Stanford University. US Navy for 3 years. Started at Fox as messenger boy, became story analyst. Modern English Literature at Oxford University for one term. Returned to Hollywood. Literary agent; wrote scripts. 1954: first script to be produced *Highway Dragnet*; co-produced it. Formed own company. From 1954: all films released by American International, except *The Intruder* (1961) made independently. 1954: first film as director and producer. 1962: executive producer on *Dementia 13*. 1967: executive producer on *Targets*; began *A Time for Killing* (1968), completed by Phil Karlson. 1968: began *De Sade* (1969), completed by Cy Endfield. Brother is Gene Corman who produced, e.g. *The Secret Invasion* (1964).

Films as director: 1956: Swamp Women. 1957: She-Gods of Shark Reef – Shark Reef. 1962: Tower of London. 1964: The Secret Invasion.

Films as director and producer: 1954: Five Guns West. 1955: Apache Woman; The Day the World Ended. 1956: It Conquered the World; Naked Paradise – Thunder over Hawaii; Gunslinger; Oklahoma Woman. 1957: Rock All Night; Teenage Doll; Attack of the Crab Monsters; Not of This Earth; Viking Women vs the Sea Serpent – Viking Women; The Undead; Carnival Rock. 1958: Sorority Girl – The Bad One; Machine Gun Kelly; I, Mobster – The Mobster (*co-p*); Teenage Caveman – Out of the Darkness; War of the Satellites (*+w*). 1959: A Bucket of Blood; The Wasp Woman. 1960: Ski Troop Attack (*+w*); The Last Woman on Earth; The Little Shop of Horrors; Creature from the Haunted Sea; The Fall of the House of Usher – The House of Usher. 1961: Atlas; The Pit and the Pendulum; The Intruder – The Stranger. 1962: The Premature Burial; Tales of Terror – Poe's Tales of Terror. 1963: The Young Racers (*+w*); The Terror; The Raven; The Haunted Palace; X – The Man with X-Ray Eyes – The Man with the X-Ray Eyes. 1964: The Masque of the Red Death; The Tomb of Ligeia – Ligeia. 1966: The Wild Angels. 1967: The St Valentine's Day Massacre; The Trip. 1968: How to Make It – What's in it for Harry? (*ur*); A Time for Killing – The Long Ride Home (*uc*; *co-d Phil Karlson*). 1970: Bloody Mama; GAS-S-S – G-A-S-S-S or it Became Necessary to Destroy the World in Order to Save It. 1971: Von Richthofen and Brown – The Red Baron.

CORNELIUS, O. Henry

Director. South Africa 1913–1958 London
From 1931: student at Max Reinhardt Academy of Dramatic Art, Berlin. 1933: stage director at Schiller Theatre, Berlin; went to study at Sorbonne; freelance journalist in Paris. 1934: assistant film editor at Studios de Montrouge. 1935: to UK; assistant editor on Rene Clair's *The Ghost Goes West*. 1935–40: editor for London Films. 1940–43: deputy director of the film division (Union Unity). South Africa; wrote, directed and produced 14 documentaries. 1943–49: with Ealing Films; associate producer of *Painted Boats, Hue and Cry* and *It Always Rains on Sunday* (also co-wrote it). 1949: directed first feature, *Passport to Pimlico*. 1951: formed production company, Sirius Films. *Law and Disorder*, unfinished at death, completed by Charles Crichton.

Features as director: 1949: Passport to Pimlico. 1951: The Galloping Major (*+co-s*). 1953: Genevieve. 1955: I Am a Camera. 1958: Next to No Time (*+s*); Law and Disorder (*co-d Charles Crichton*).

CORNELL, Jonas

Director. 1938–
1959–64: university; wrote 2 novels in early 1960s. Critic for literary magazine BLM; editor of theatre magazine Dialog. 1964–65: Swedish Film School. First film, a short, *Hej* (1965), shown on TV. 1967: first feature. 1968: directed Alexei Arbuzov's 'The Promise' at City Theatre of Luleå. Married Agneta Ekmanner, who appears in his first features.

Films as director: 1965: Hej (*+s*). 1967: Puss och

Elisha Cook Jnr. being disposed of in Sidney Salkow's Chicago Confidential.
Charles Bronson in Machine Gun Kelly, *directed by Roger Corman.*
Edmund O'Brien and Julie London in Hubert Cornfield's The Third Voice.

kram – Hugs and Kisses (+ s). 1969: Som natt och dag – Like Night and Day (+ s).

CORNFIELD, Hubert

Director. Istanbul, Turkey 1929–
Father head of European production for Fox. Childhood in Paris and Lisbon. School of Fine Arts and Music, New York; University of Pennsylvania. 1950–52: worked for Fox Publicity Department in Paris, e.g. poster design. Worked with Actors' Studio, New York. Directed 16mm film, The Color is Red. TV work, e.g. on 'Operation Cicero' series. 1961: began Angel Baby, replaced by Paul Wendkos after a week of shooting. 1962: Pressure Point heavily re-edited by producer Stanley Kramer.

Features as director: 1955: Sudden Danger. 1957: Lure of the Swamp; Plunder Road. 1959: The Third Voice (+ co-s). 1962: Pressure Point (+ co-s). 1968: The Night of the Following Day (+ co-s).

CORTESE, Valentina

(In USA, Valentina Cortesa) Actress. Milan, Italy 1925–
1941: first films; star parts after 3 films (1942). Stage appearances during World War II. Performance in Italian-British co-production, The Glass Mountain (1948) led to first Hollywood film, Thieves' Highway (1949). On Milan stage, acted in 'St Joan of the Stockyards' (1970). Married actor Richard Basehart.

Films as actress include: 1941: La Cena delle beffe. 1944: Nessuno torna indietro. 1946: Un Americano in vacanza; Roma, Città Libera. 1947: I Miserabili. 1949: Black Magic. 1951: The House on Telegraph Hill. 1952: Secret People. 1954: The Barefoot Contessa; Avanzi di galera. 1955: Magic Fire; Le Amiche. 1956: Calabuch. 1962: Barabbas; La Ragazza che sapeva troppo. 1965: Giuletta degli spiriti. 1968: The Legend of Lylah Clare. 1970: Erste Liebe.

CORTEZ, Stanley

(Stanley Krantz) Cinematographer. New York 1908–
Mother Hungarian. Father Austrian, designer of men's clothes. New York University. Worked with portrait photographers in New York. Assistant on Pathe serial. 1926: to Paramount as camera assistant. Second cameraman for several studios. 1932: directed, wrote and photographed short, Sherzo. 1936: first film as cinematographer Four Days' Wonder. To 1948: worked mainly for Universal, exceptions including collaboration on The Magnificent Ambersons (1942) for RKO. World War II: US Signals Corps. 1950–56: films mainly released by United Artists. Then several studios, including Warners, Paramount, Fox, Universal. Brother is actor Riccardo Cortez.

Films as cinematographer include: 1940: Alias the Deacon. 1942: The Magnificent Ambersons (co); The Powers Girl. 1943: Flesh and Fantasy (co). 1944: Since You Went Away (co). 1947: Smash Up. 1948: Secret Beyond the Door. 1949: The Man on the Eiffel Tower. 1950: The Underworld Story. 1953: The Diamond Queen. 1954: Black Tuesday. 1955: The Night of the Hunter. 1956: Man from Del Rio. 1957: Top Secret Affair; The Three Faces of Eve. 1958: Thunder in the Sun. 1960: Dinosaurus! 1961: Back

Street. 1963: Shock Corridor; The Naked Kiss. 1966: The Ghost in the Invisible Bikini. 1969: The Bridge at Remagen. 1970: Tell Me That You Love Me, Junie Moon (co-cr).

COSTA-GAVRAS, Costi

Director. Athens 1933–
Russian father, Greek mother. To France at 18; began course in literature at Sorbonne, then IDHEC. Became assistant to Yves Allegret, René Clair, Henri Verneuil. To Greenland to shoot stock material for a film later abandoned. Assistant director on La Baie des anges (1962), Le Jour et l'Heure (1962) and Les Félins (1964). 1965: first film as director.

Films as director: 1965: Compartiment Tueurs – The Sleeping Car Murders. 1966: Un Homme de trop – Shock Troops. 1968: Z (+ co-ad). 1970: L'Aveu – The Confession.

COSTELLO, Lou

(Louis Francis Cristillo) Actor. Paterson, New Jersey 1906–1959 Hollywood
Prize-fighter and shop assistant, then labourer at Warners and MGM. Stuntman until injured doubling for Dolores del Rio in The Trail of '98 (1929). Burlesque comedian in stage musicals and on radio, in which joined up with straight man Bud Abbott. 1939: appeared at Atlantic City Steel Pier; some radio work, notably 'The Kate Smith Show'; Broadway musical 'Streets of Paris'. Then Universal contract and first film with Bud Abbott, One Night in the Tropics (1940). After splitting with Bud Abbott in 1957, made one more film, The 30-Foot Bride of Candy Rock (1959). For film list see ABBOTT, Bud.

COTTAFAVI, Vittorio

Director. Modena, Italy 1914–
1935–38: studied direction at the Centro Sperimentale di Cinematografia, Rome. 1938: entered film industry as clapperboy. From 1939: collaborated on scripts: Goffredo Alessandrini's Abuna Messias (1939) and Nozze di sangue (1940), A. Vergano's Quelli della montagna (1942); assistant director to, e.g. Vittorio de Sica, Alessandro Blasetti, Augusto Genina; also 2nd-unit director. 1943: first film as director. 1944–45: ran own publishing house. Supervised Gianparlo Callegari's I Piombi di venezia (1952). 1957: directed 'L'Avaro' (from Molière), first of many TV films, from works by, e.g. Ibsen, Dostoyevsky, Sophocles, Dürrenmatt, Tennessee Williams, Lorca, Victor Hugo, Pirandello, Tolstoy. Directed a few shots only of Le Vergine di Roma; uncredited (1960).

Films as director: 1943: I Nostri Sogni. 1948: Lo Sconosciuto di San Marino (co-d M. Waszinsky); La Grande Strada (co-d M. Waszinsky). 1949: La Fiamma che non si spegre. 1951: Una Donna La ucciso (+ co-s). 1952: Il Boia di Lilla – La Vita Avventurosa di Milady. 1953: Il Cavaliere di Maison Rouge; Traviata '53; In amore si pecca in due. 1954: Avanzi di galera; Nel gorgo del peccato; Una Donna Libera. 1956: Fiesta Brava (uf; + co-s). 1958: La Rivolta dei gladiatori – The Warrior and the Slave Girl. 1959: Le Legioni di Cleopatra; Messalina – Messalina, Venere Imperatrice. 1960: La Vendetta di Ercole – Goliath and the Dragon. 1961: Ercole alla

conquista di Atlantide – Hercules Conquers Atlantis. 1965: Los Cien Caballeros – The Hundred Horsemen (+ co-s).

COTTEN, Joseph

Actor. Petersburg, Virginia 1905–
Hickman School of Expression, Washington. Various jobs before joining little theatre group in Miami, Florida. 1930: New York; assistant stage manager and understudy in 'Dancing Partner'. 1931: leading man at Copley Theatre, Boston; on Broadway in 'Absent Father', 'Accent on Youth', 'The Postman Always Rings Twice'. Joined Federal Theatre; in 'Horse Eats Hat', Orson Welles's adaptation of 'Un Chapeau de paille d'Italie' (1936). Played leads at Welles's Mercury Theatre, e.g. 'Julius Caesar' (1937). On Broadway opposite Katherine Hepburn in 'Philadelphia Story' (1939). Series of radio performances. 1941: first film, Citizen Kane. During World War II appeared in Welles's 'Mercury Wonder Show' for troops. 1946–49: contract with David O. Selznick. 1950–56: some films on Fox contract. Also TV from 1954. 1956: formed Fordyce Productions to do TV series, 'The Joseph Cotten Show'. 1958: 'Once More With Feeling' on Broadway. 1960: married second wife, actress Patricia Medina, with whom he has appeared in several plays on tour and in New York.

Films as actor include: 1941: Lydia. 1942: The Magnificent Ambersons. 1943: Journey into Fear; Shadow of a Doubt. 1944: Gaslight; Since You Went Away. 1945: I'll Be Seeing You; Love Letters. 1946: Duel in the Sun. 1947: The Farmer's Daughter. 1949: Portrait of Jennie; Under Capricorn; Beyond the Forest. 1950: Two Flags West; The Third Man. 1951: September Affair; Peking Express. 1952: Untamed Frontier; The Steel Trap. 1953: Niagara; Blueprint for Murder. 1955: Vom Himmel gefallen. 1956: The Bottom of the Bottle; The Killer is Loose. 1957: The Halliday Brand. 1958: Touch of Evil (uc); From the Earth to the Moon. 1960: La Sposa Bella. 1961: The Last Sunset. 1964: Hush, Hush, Sweet Charlotte. 1966: The Money Trap. 1968: Petulia. 1969: Tora! Tora! Tora!

COURANT, Curtis (or Curt)

Cinematographer.
Jewish parents. Cinematographer in Germany during 1920s. 1933: left Germany for France, then also UK (1933–36). 1937–40: in France. In USA collaborated with Rollie Totheroh and Wallace Chewing on Monsieur Verdoux (1947).

Films as cinematographer include: 1920: Hamlet. 1925: Quo Vadis? 1929: Frau im Mond (co). 1933: Ciboulette. 1934: The Man Who Knew Too Much; The Iron Duke. 1936: Spy of Napoleon; The Man in the Mirror. 1938: La Bête Humaine. 1939: Le Jour se lève; Louise. 1940: De Mayerling a Sarajevo (co). 1947: Monsieur Verdoux (co). 1962: It Happened in Athens.

COURTENAY, Tom

Actor. Hull, Yorkshire 1937–
Read English at London University; failed finals. 1958: scholarship to Royal Academy of Dramatic Art. 1960–61: member of Old Vic Company with which stage debut in Chekhov's The Seagull at the Edin-

burgh Festival. 1962: first film. Title role in 'Private Potter' on TV; then in film (1963). 1964: in 'Andorra' at the National Theatre. 1966: 'The Cherry Orchard' and 'Macbeth' at the Chichester Festival Theatre. 1967: Ibsen's 'Ghosts' on TV. 1968: acting at University Theatre, Manchester. 1970: in 'Peer Gynt' in Manchester. 1971: acted in and provided 50% backing for 'Charley's Aunt' in London.

Films as actor include: 1962: The Loneliness of the Long Distance Runner. 1963: Private Potter; Billy Liar. 1964: King and Country; Operation Crossbow. 1965: Dr Zhivago. 1966: King Rat. 1967: The Night of the Generals; The Day the Fish Came Out. 1968: A Dandy in Aspic. 1969: Otley.

COUSTEAU, Jacques-Yves

Director. Saint-Andre, France 1910–
1943: first documentary. Has since made oceanographic films, from specially constructed boat 'Calypso', developing own equipment. Also TV series and TV films. Oscar (1964) for *Le Monde sans soleil* as best documentary feature.

Films as director and producer: 1943: Par dix-huit mètres de fond. 1945: Epaves. 1947: Paysages du silence. 1948–49: Au large des côtes Tunisiennes (*d only*); Autour d'un récif; Les Phoques du Rio d'Oro – Les Phoques du Sahara; Dauphins et Cetaces (*d only*). 1950: Une Sortie du 'Rubis' – Une Plongée du 'Rubis'; Carnet de plongee. 1952: La Mer Rouge. 1953: Un Musee dans la mer. 1956: Le Monde du silence – The Silent World (*co-d Louis Malle*). 1964: Le Monde sans soleil – World Without Sun (*co-d*).

COUTARD, Raoul

Cinematographer and director. Paris 1924–
Intended to be chemist; worked in photographic labs. At 20 joined French army; sent to Indochina. 5 years as photographer and reporter for Indochine Sud-Est Asiatique, Radar, Life, Paris-Match. Formed own company with Jean Garcenot; worked with Luciano Emmer on ethnographic work for Musee de l'Homme. 1957–58: photographed 4 films directed by Pierre Schoendoerffer, produced by Georges de Beauregard. 1959: first feature as cinematographer *A bout de souffle,* for Beauregard, beginning of collaboration with Jean-Luc Godard. 1967: first film as director *Tu es danse et vertige.* 1970: directed documentary on Vietnam war *Hoa Binh.*

Films as cinematographer include: 1957: Than, le pêcheur; La Passe du diable. 1958: Ramuntcho. 1959: Pêcheur d'islande; A bout de souffle. 1960: Tirez sur le pianiste; Les Grandes Personnes; Le Petit Soldat (*r 1963*). 1961: Une Femme est une femme; Lola; Chronique d'un ete (*co*); Tire au flanc; Jules et Jim. 1962: La Poupee; L'Amour à vingt ans *ep* Le Premier Amour. 1962: Vivre sa vie. 1963: Les Vacances Portuguaises; Le Mepris; Les Carabiniers. 1964: Bande à part; La Peau Douce; Un Monsieur de compagnie; Une Femme Mariee. 1965: La 317e Section; Alphaville, une etrange aventure de Lemmy Caution; Pierrot le Fou. 1966: Made in USA; L'Espion; Deux ou Trois Choses que je sais d'elle. 1967: The Sailor from Gibraltar; La Chinoise; La Mariee etait en noir; Weekend; Z. 1970: L'Aveu; Etes-vous fiancee à un marin grec ou à une pilote de ligne; La Liberte en croupe; Les Aveux les Plus Doux.

COWARD, Sir Noël

Writer and actor. Teddington, Middlesex 1899–
Stage debut at 12 in 'The Goldfish'. Stage in London; in repertory in Birmingham and Liverpool and on tour until 1919. 1918: film debut in *Hearts of the World.* 1920: wrote and appeared in first play 'I'll Leave it to You' in London. 1925: first appearance on Broadway co-directing his own play 'The Vortex'. Stage producer, playwright, director, actor, composer, lyricist. Plays as writer include 'Hay Fever' (1925), 'Private Lives' (1930), 'Cavalcade' (1931), 'Design for Living' (1933), 'Blithe Spirit' (1941), 'This Happy Breed' (1943). 1942–46: 4 films with David Lean as co-director or director. Numerous books include autobiographical 'Present Indicative' and 'Future Indefinite'. Also TV, radio, cabaret.

Films include: 1935: The Scoundrel (*w*). 1942: In Which We Serve (*co-d David Lean/p/s/m/w*). 1944: This Happy Breed (*p/fpl*). 1945: Blithe Spirit (*co-p/fpl/s*); Brief Encounter (*co-p/ad/fpl*). 1950: The Astonished Heart (*s/fpl/m/w*). 1952: Meet Me Tonight (*s/w*). 1956: Around the World in 80 Days (*w*). 1960: Our Man in Havana (*w*); Surprise Package (*w*). 1963: Paris When It Sizzles (*w*). 1965: Bunny Lake is Missing (*w*). 1968: Boom! (*w*).

CRAIN, Jeanne

Actress. Barstow, California 1925–
Model ('Miss Long Beach' and other titles) before first film, *The Gang's All Here* (1943). All films for Fox until 1953. First film, *Home in Indiana* (1944). Infrequent appearances in 1960s.

Films as actress include: 1944: In the Meantime; Darling; Winged Victory. 1945: State Fair. 1946: Leave Her to Heaven; Centennial Summer; Margie. 1949: A Letter to Three Wives; The Fan; Pinky. 1951: People Will Talk; Take Care of My Little Girl. 1952: The Model and the Marriage Broker; O. Henry's Full House *ep* The Gift of the Magi. 1953: Dangerous Crossing; Vicki. 1954: Duel in the Jungle. 1955: Man Without a Star; The Second Greatest Sex. 1956: The Fastest Gun Alive. 1957: The Joker is Wild. 1961: Twenty Plus Two. 1962: Madison Avenue. 1967: Hot Rods to Hell.

CRAWFORD, Broderick

Actor. Philadelphia, Pennsylvania 1911–
Parents were actors Lester and Helen Broderick. Vaudeville, radio and summer stock. Acted on Broadway, e.g. with the Lunts in 'Point Valaine' (1935) directed by Noël Coward. Contract with Samuel Goldwyn; first film, *Woman Chases Man* (1937). In play, 'Of Mice and Men' (1937). 1942–45: sergeant in USAAF. TV series: 'Highway Patrol'. From mid-1950s also in European films. Oscar as Best Actor for *All the King's Men* (1950).

Films as actor include: 1939: Beau Geste; Eternally Yours; The Real Glory. 1940: Slightly Honorable; When the Daltons Rode; Seven Sinners; Trail of the Vigilantes. 1942: Larceny Inc. 1947: Night Unto Night. 1948: The Time of Your Life. 1949: A Kiss in

Vittorio Cottafavi.
Teresa Wright and Joseph Cotten in Andrew L. Stone's The Steel Trap.
Hoa-Binh, directed by Raoul Coutard.

the Dark; Anna Lucasta. 1951: Born Yesterday; The Mob. 1952; Scandal Sheet; Last of the Comanches. 1954: Night People; Human Desire. 1955: New York Confidential; Big House, USA; Not As a Stranger; Il Bidone. 1956: The Fastest Gun Alive; Between Heaven and Hell. 1958: The Decks Ran Red. 1960: La Vendetta di Ercole. 1961: Nasilje na trgu. 1964: A House Is Not a Home. 1965: Up From the Beach. 1966: The Oscar.

CRAWFORD, Joan

(Lucille Le Sueur) Actress. San Antonio, Texas 1904–
Worked in cafe to pay for dancing lessons in Kansas City. At 13 won dancing contest. Started in chorus of road show. Chorus work on Broadway. MGM test; extra in *Pretty Ladies* (1925); featured as dancer in *Sally, Irene and Mary* (1925). First star part, *Our Dancing Daughters* (1928). Long-term contract with MGM, for which all films until 1943, except *Rain* (1932) and *They All Kissed the Bride* (1942). Husbands include (1929–33) Douglas Fairbanks Jr, (1935–39) Franchot Tone, and Alfred Steele (married 1956). Took over latter's place on board of Pepsi Cola on his death (1959). Oscar as Best Actress for *Mildred Pierce* (1945).

Films as actress include: 1926: Tramp, Tramp, Tramp. 1927: The Unknown. 1930: Untamed; Montana Moon; Paid. 1931: This Modern Age; Possessed. 1932: Grand Hotel; Rain; Letty Lynton. 1933: Today We Live; Dancing Lady. 1934: Sadie McKee; Chained; Forsaking All Others. 1935: I Live My Life. 1936: The Gorgeous Hussy; Love on the Run. 1937: The Last of Mrs Cheyney. 1938: Mannequin; The Shining Hour. 1939: The Women. 1940: Strange Cargo; Susan and God. 1941: A Woman's Face; When Ladies Meet. 1942: Reunion in France. 1945: Hollywood Canteen. 1947: Humoresque; Possessed; Daisy Kenyon. 1949: Flamingo Road. 1952: Sudden Fear. 1953: Torch Song. 1954: Johnny Guitar. 1956: Autumn Leaves. 1959: The Best of Everything. 1962: What Ever Happened to Baby Jane? 1963: Straight-jacket.

CRICHTON, Charles

Director. Wallasey, Cheshire 1910–
History at New College, Oxford. Started in cutting rooms at Denham Studios (1931). Edited documentaries for Alberto Cavalcanti, and many features for London Films including *Sanders of the River* (1935), *Elephant Boy* (1936) and *The Thief of Bagdad* (1940). 1940–56: at Ealing. 1941: first short as director, *The Young Veterans*. 1942: associate producer on *Nine Men*. 1944: first feature as director. Took over *Law and Disorder* (1958) on death of Henry Cornelius. 1962: started *Bird Man of Alcatraz* in Hollywood; replaced by John Frankenheimer. TV work includes episodes of 'The Avengers', 'Danger Man' also Ibsen's 'The Wild Duck'.

Features as director: 1944: For Those in Peril. 1945: Painted Boats; Dead of Night *ep* The Golfing Story. 1947: Hue and Cry. 1948: Against the Wind; Another Shore. 1949: Train of Events (*co-d Basil Dearden, Sidney Cole*). 1950: Dance Hall; The Lavender Hill Mob. 1952: Hunted – Stranger in Between. 1953: The Titfield Thunderbolt. 1954: The Love Lottery; The Divided Heart. 1956: Man in the Sky. 1958: Law and Disorder (*co-d Henry Cornelius*); Floods of Fear (*+ s*). 1960: The Battle of the Sexes; The Boy Who Stole a Million (*+ co-s*). 1964: The Third Secret. 1965: He Who Rides a Tiger.

CRISP, Donald

Actor and director. Aberfeldy, Perthshire 1880–
Educated at Eton and Oxford. Boer War: served in 10th Hussars; fought at Kimberley, Ladysmith; wounded at Tugela Heights. 1906: to New York; appeared in opera; acted and directed in theatre. Began in films with Biograph; assistant director to D. W. Griffith; acted in Griffith films. From 1914: also director (until 1930).

Films as actor include: 1911: The Adventures of Billy. 1914: Battle of the Sexes; The Escape; Home Sweet Home; The Mountain Rat. 1915: The Birth of a Nation. 1916: Intolerance. 1919: Broken Blossoms. 1926: The Black Pirate. 1929: The Pagan; Trent's Last Case. 1931: Svengali. 1932: A Passport to Hell; Red Dust. 1934: What Every Woman Knows. 1935: Laddie; Oil for the Lamps of China; Mutiny on the Bounty. 1936: Mary of Scotland; The Charge of the Light Brigade; The Great O'Malley. 1937: Parnell; The Life of Emile Zola. 1938: Jezebel; The Amazing Dr Clitterhouse. 1939: Wuthering Heights; The Private Lives of Elizabeth and Essex; Juarez. 1940: The Story of Dr Ehrlich's Magic Bullet; The Sea Hawk. 1941: Dr Jekyll and Mr Hyde; How Green Was My Valley. 1943: Lassie Come Home. 1944: National Velvet. 1950: Bright Leaf. 1954: Prince Valiant. 1955: The Long Gray Line; The Man from Laramie. 1958: Saddle the Wind; The Last Hurrah. 1963: Spencer's Mountain.

Films as director include: 1914: The Dawn. 1916: Ramona. 1917: The Countess Charming. 1918: Under the Top; The Goat. 1919: It Pays to Advertise; Why Smith Left Home; Too Much Johnson; Poor Boob; Love Insurance. 1920: Miss Hobbs; The Six Best Cellars; Held by the Enemy. 1921: Appearances; The Princess of New York; The Bonnie Briar Bush (*+ w*). 1923: Ponjola. 1924: The Navigator (*co-d Buster Keaton*). 1925: Don Q, Son of Zorro (*+ w*). 1926: Man Bait; Young April, Sunnyside Up. 1927: Nobody's Widow; Vanity (*+ p*); The Fighting Eagle (*+ p*); Dress Parade (*+ p*); Stand and Deliver (*+ p*); The Cop (*+ p*). 1930: Runaway Bride.

CROMWELL, John

Director. Toledo, Ohio 1888–
1907: began as actor with stock company in Cleveland. 1908: to New York; toured with minor companies, becoming associated with William A. Brady's company as actor and stage manager. 1911: began to direct for Brady. 1912: appeared in 'Little Women' on Broadway. 1923: independently produced 'Tarnish' and other plays. 1929: first film as actor, *The Dummy*; co-directed first film. Until 1932 worked for Paramount; 1933–35 for RKO; then mainly for United Artists and RKO. 1942: returned to stage as actor in 'Yankee Point'. 1944–45: president of the Screen Directors' Guild. On Broadway acted in 'Point of No Return' (1952), 'Sabrina Fair' (1953), 'Mary, Mary' (1961) and directed 'Sabrina' (1954). *De sista stegen* (1960) was made in Sweden.

Films as director: 1929: Close Harmony (*co-d A. Edward Sutherland*); The Dance of Life (*co-d A. Edward Sutherland*); The Mighty. 1930: Street of Chance (*+ w*); Tom Sawyer; The Texan; For the Defense. 1931: Scandal Sheet; Rich Man's Folly; The Vice Squad; Unfaithful. 1932: The World and the Flesh. 1933: Sweepings; The Silver Cord; Double Harness; Ann Vickers. 1934: Spitfire; This Man is Mine; Of Human Bondage; The Fountain. 1935: Jalna; Village Tale; I Dream Too Much. 1936: Little Lord Fauntleroy; To Mary—With Love; Banjo on my Knee. 1937: The Prisoner of Zenda. 1938: Algiers. 1939: Made for Each Other; In Name Only. 1940: Abe Lincoln in Illinois; Victory. 1941: So Ends Our Night. 1942: Son of Fury. 1944: Since You Went Away. 1945: The Enchanted Cottage. 1946: Anna and the King of Siam. 1947: Dead Reckoning; Night Song – Memory of Love. 1950: Caged; The Company She Keeps. 1951: The Racket. 1958: The Goddess. 1959: The Scavengers. 1960: De sista stegen – A Matter of Morals.

CRONJAGER, Edward

Cinematographer. 1904-1960
Began as assistant cameraman. From 1926: cinematographer for Famous Players–Lasky then Paramount. 1930-36: with RKO. 1936-46: almost all films for Fox. 1946-51: with several studios, including RKO. 1952-54: returned to Fox. Last film in 1954. Married actress Kay Sutton; divorced.

Films as cinematographer include: 1925: Woman-handled. 1926: Let's Get Married; Say it Again; The Quarterback; Paradise for Two. 1927: Knockout Reilly; Manpower; The Gay Defender. 1928: Sporting Goods; Easy Come, Easy Go; Warming Up. 1929: Redskin (*co*); Nothing But the Truth; The Wheel of Life; Fashions in Love. 1931: Cimarron; Young Donovan's Kid. 1932: Roar of the Dragon; The Conquerors. 1933: Sweepings; If I Were Free. 1934: Spitfire; Strictly Dynamite; Kentucky Kernels. 1935: The Nitwits; Jalna. 1936: The Texas Rangers. 1937: Wife, Doctor and Nurse. 1940: I Was an Adventuress; Young People. 1941: Western Union (*co*); Rise and Shine. 1942: Friendly Enemies; The Pied Piper; Life Begins at 8.30. 1943: Heaven Can Wait; The Gang's All Here; Margin for Error. 1944: Home in Indiana. 1945: Nob Hill; Colonel Effingham's Raid. 1946: Do You Love Me?; Canyon Passage. 1947: Honeymoon. 1948: A Miracle Can Happen (*co*); An Innocent Affair. 1950: House by the River. 1951: I'd Climb the Highest Mountain. 1952: Lure of the Wilderness. 1953: Treasure of the Golden Condor. 1954: The Siege at Red River.

CROSBY, Bing

(Harry Lillis Crosby) Actor and singer. Tacoma, Washington 1904–
Gonzaga University; sang with University Glee Club. Drummer with the Juicy Seven; singer with Paul Whiteman's band in late 1920s. 1930: first film, *King of Jazz*. Nightclub singer at Coconut Grove. 1930-31: 8 short films as singer, for Mack Sennett. Radio work. From *The Big Broadcast* (1932) most films for Paramount until 1956. Throughout career also extremely successful on records. Formed Crosby Enterprises to handle numerous business interests including co-production deal with Paramount and later Fox. His

company financed *Willard* (1971). Own TV company and TV show; also does TV spectaculars. Married actresses Dixie Lee (1930–52; sons include actor Gary Crosby) and Kathryn Grant (married 1957). Oscar as Best Actor for *Going My Way* (1944).

Films as actor include: 1933: Going Hollywood. 1936: Anything Goes. 1937: Waikiki Wedding. 1938: Dr Rhythm; Sing You Sinners. 1939: Paris Honeymoon; East Side of Heaven. 1940: Road to Singapore; If I Had My Way; Rhythm on the River. 1941: Road to Zanzibar; Birth of the Blues. 1942: Holiday Inn; The Road to Morocco; Star Spangled Rhythm. 1944: The Princess and the Pirate. 1945: The Bells of St Mary's. 1946: Blue Skies. 1947: Variety Girl; Road to Rio. 1948: The Emperor Waltz. 1949: A Connecticut Yankee in King Arthur's Court. 1950: Riding High. 1951: Here Comes the Groom; Mr Music. 1953: Scared Stiff (*uc*). 1954: The Country Girl; White Christmas. 1956: High Society. 1959: Say One for Me. 1960: High Time. 1962: The Road to Hongkong. 1964: Robin and the Seven Hoods. 1966: Stagecoach.

CROSBY, Floyd

Cinematographer. New York 1899–
1919: worked in cotton industry and stock brokerage. Photographer on William Beebe's expedition to Haiti. 1931: Oscar for first feature as cinematographer *Tabu*. Worked on documentaries of Robert Flaherty, Joris Ivens, Pare Lorentz, as operator and cinematographer. 1942: collaborated with Irving Lerner on Flaherty's *The Land*. 2 collaborations with James Wong Howe: *The Brave Bulls* (1951), *The Old Man and the Sea* (1958). Never under contract. Son is rock musician David Crosby.

Films as cinematographer include: 1931: Tabu (*co*). 1937: The River (*co*). 1940: The Fight for Life; Power and the Land. 1947: My Father's House. 1950: Of Men and Music (*co*). 1951: The Brave Bulls (*co*). 1952: High Noon. 1954: Five Guns West. 1956: Naked Paradise; Attack of the Crab Monsters; Rock All Night. 1957: She-Gods of Shark Reef. 1958: The Old Man and the Sea (*co*); War of the Satellites; Machine Gun Kelly; I, Mobster; The Cry Baby Killer. 1959: The Wonderful Country (*co*); Crime and Punishment, USA. 1960: Freckles; The Fall of the House of Usher; The Explosive Generation. 1961: The Pit and the Pendulum; A Cold Wind in August. 1962: The Premature Burial; Tales of Terror; Hand of Death. 1963: The Young Racers; The Raven; The Yellow Canary; X – The Man with X-Ray Eyes; The Haunted Palace. 1964: Comedy of Terrors; Pajama Party. 1966: Fireball 500.

CROSLAND, Alan

Director. New York 1894–1936 Los Angeles
Began as journalist and theatre critic. From 1909, actor and stage manager. 1912: joined Edison, working on e.g. publicity. 1914–19: directed shorts. 1917: first feature as director, *Kidnapped*, followed by other features for Edison. From 1919: with other companies including Selznick, Cosmopolitan and Paramount. From 1925: mainly with Warners for whom directed *Don Juan* (1926), the first feature with synchronised music score, included in first Vitaphone programme, and *The Jazz Singer* (1927), first feature including synchronised dialogue. Died in car crash.

Films as director include (complete from 1924): 1920: The Flapper. 1923: The Enemies of Women. 1924: Under the Red Robe; Unguarded Women; Miami; Sinners in Heaven (+*p*); Three Weeks. 1925: Compromise; Contraband; Bobbed Hair. 1926: Don Juan; When a Man Loves. 1927: The Beloved Rogue; Old San Francisco; The Jazz Singer. 1928: Glorious Betsy. 1929: On with the Show; General Crack. 1930: Song of the Flame; Big Boy; Viennese Nights; Captain Thunder. 1931: Children of Dreams. 1932: The Silver Lining – Thirty Days (+*p*); Week Ends Only. 1934: The Personality Kid; Massacre; Midnight Alibi; The Case of the Howling Dog. 1935: It Happened in New York; Mr Dynamite; King Solomon of Broadway; The White Cockatoo. 1936: The Great Impersonation.

CRUZE, James

(Jens Cruz Bosen) Director. Ogden, Utah 1884–1942 Hollywood
Danish immigrant parents. Until 1900, worked as farm boy, then went to San Francisco; various labouring jobs before joining medicine show, and then travelling theatre group. 1903: organised own troupe of players; associates included film actor Luke Cosgrove and director George Melford. 1906–11: acted in repertory in New York. 1911: first film as actor, *A Boy of Revolution*, and first leading role in *She*. 1913–23: married to Marguerite Snow, actress from *She*. 1914: established popularity as actor in Thanhouser serial *The Million Dollar Mystery* and sequel *Zudora* (1914–15). 1915: broke leg doing stunt work for Thanhouser; reappeared as character actor (1917). 1918: first film as director. Gave up acting after 1919. 1921: directed 5 films starring Roscoe Arbuckle. 1923–27: contract as director with Famous Players-Lasky. 1924–30: married to Betty Compson, who appeared in many of his films. 1925: in collaboration wrote story for *Waking Up the Town*. 1927: 3 films with the De Mille Producing Corporation, then freelanced. 1930–32: formed own production company, and supervised Walter Lang's *Hello Sister*. Production company went bankrupt. 1932: directed 3 episodes in *If I Had a Million*, one dropped in favour of Ernst Lubitsch's. 1936: directed financially disastrous *Sutter's Gold* for Universal from subject earlier worked on by Sergei Eisenstein for Paramount. Then 4 films for Republic before retiring after heart attack (1938).

Films as director (possibly incomplete before 1923): 1918: Too Many Millions; The Dub. 1919: Alias Mike Moran; The Roaring Road; You're Fired; The Love Burglar; The Valley of the Giants; The Lottery Man; An Adventure in Hearts; Hawthorne of the USA. 1920: Terror Island; Mrs Temple's Telegram; The Sins of St Antony; What Happened to Jones; A Full House; Food for Scandal; Always Audacious; The Charm School. 1921: The Dollar-a-year Man; Crazy to Marry; Gasoline Gus (*ur*); Skirt Shy (*ur*); Via Fast Freight (*ur*). 1922: One Glorious Day; Is Matrimony a Failure?; The Dictator; The Old Homestead; Thirty Days. 1923: The Covered Wagon; Hollywood; Ruggles of Red Gap (+*p*); To the Ladies (+*p*). 1924: The Fighting Coward (+*p*); The Enemy Sex; Merton of the Movies (+*p*); The City That Never Sleeps (+*p*); The Garden of Weeds (+*p*). 1925: The Goose Hangs High (+*p*); Welcome Home (+*p*); Marry Me (+*p*); Beggar on Horseback (+*p*); The Pony Express (+*p*); Waking Up the Town (+*co-st*). 1926: Mannequin

Donald Crisp in Mutiny On The Bounty, *directed by Frank Lloyd.*
Bing Crosby in Frank Tashlin's Say One For Me.
Born Yesterday, directed by George Cukor, with Howard St. John and Broderick Crawford.

(+p). 1927: We're All Gamblers (+p); The City Gone Wild (+p); On to Reno. 1928: Old Ironsides (+p); The Red Mark; The Mating Call; Excess Baggage (+p). 1929: A Man's Man (+p); The Duke Steps Out (+p). 1930: Once a Gentleman; The Great Gabbo; She Got What She Wanted (+co-p/pc). 1931: Salvation Nell (+co-p/pc). 1932: Washington Merry-go-round (+pc); If I Had a Million eps The Streetwalker; The Old Ladies' Home. 1933: Sailor be Good; Racetrack (+pc); I Cover the Waterfront; Mr Skitch. 1934: David Harum; Their Big Moment; Helldorado. 1935: Two Fisted. 1936: Sutter's Gold. 1937: The Wrong Road. 1938: Prison Nurse; The Gangs of New York; Come on Leathernecks.

CUKOR, George

Director. New York 1899–
Parents of Hungarian Jewish descent, in legal profession. After military training, started as assistant stage manager in Chicago (1918). 1919: stage manager for Edgar Selwyn and the Schubert Brothers on Broadway. 1920–28: some acting; directed summer stock company at Rochester, New York, in which Bette Davis, Miriam Hopkins and Robert Montgomery started acting. 1926–29: directed Broadway plays, starting with 'The Great Gatsby'. Recommended by Rouben Mamoulian to Jesse Lasky, went to Hollywood as dialogue director at Paramount. Then at Universal, dialogue director on All Quiet on the Western Front before returning to Paramount as director (1930). 1932: directed most of One Hour With You for Ernst Lubitsch but received inadequate credit. Went to RKO, working mainly with David Selznick. With Selznick to MGM; made majority of films there until 1950. Replaced by Victor Fleming on Gone With the Wind (1939) at insistence of Clark Gable for paying too much attention to female roles. Completed direction of Song Without End (1960) after death of Charles Vidor. Something's Got to Give (1962) abandoned after dismissal of Marilyn Monroe; portions appear in compilation, Marilyn (1963); entirely re-shot by Michael Gordon as Move Over, Darling (1963). Took over Justine (1969) after dismissal of Joseph Strick.

Films as director: 1930: Grumpy (co-d Cyril Gardner); The Virtuous Sin – Cast Iron (co-d Louis Gasnier). 1931: The Royal Family of Broadway (co-d Cyril Gardner); Tarnished Lady; Girls About Town. 1932: One Hour With You (uc; co-d Ernst Lubitsch); What Price Hollywood?; A Bill of Divorcement; Rockabye; Our Betters. 1933: Dinner at Eight; Little Women. 1934: The Personal History, Adventures, Experience and Observations of David Copperfield, the Younger – David Copperfield. 1935: Sylvia Scarlett. 1936: Romeo and Juliet; Camille. 1938: Holiday – Free to Live; Zaza. 1939: Gone With the Wind (uc; co-d Victor Fleming, Sam Wood, uc); The Women; Susan and God – The Gay Mrs Treval. 1940: The Philadelphia Story. 1941: A Woman's Face; Two-Faced Woman; Her Cardboard Lover; Keeper of the Flame. 1943: Resistance and Ohm's Law. 1944: Gaslight – The Murder in Thornton Square; Winged Victory. 1947: Desire Me (uc; co-d Jack Conway). 1948: A Double Life. 1949: Edward, My Son; Adam's Rib. 1950: A Life of Her Own. 1951: Born Yesterday; The Model and the Marriage Broker. 1952: The Marrying Kind; Pat and Mike. 1953: The Actress. 1954: It Should Happen to You; A Star Is Born. 1955: Bhowani Junction. 1957: Les Girls; Wild Is the Wind.

1959: Heller in Pink Tights; Song Without End (uc, co-d Charles Vidor). 1960: Let's Make Love. 1962: The Chapman Report; Something's Got to Give (uf). 1964: My Fair Lady. 1969: Justine (co-d Joseph Strick, uc).

CUMMINGS, Jack

Producer. New Brunswick, Canada 1906–
Nephew of Louis B. Mayer. In mid-1920s, started as office boy at MGM. Then successively script boy, assistant director, director and producer of shorts. Co-producer of features with Charles Reisner, then producer (1934) at MGM. 1959: moved to Fox. 1964: back at MGM.

Films as producer include: 1943: I Dood It. 1944: Bathing Beauty. 1950: Three Little Words. 1953: Give a Girl a Break; Kiss Me Kate. 1954: Seven Brides for Seven Brothers; The Last Time I Saw Paris. 1956: The Teahouse of the August Moon. 1959: The Blue Angel. 1960: Can-Can. 1961: Bachelor Flat. 1964: Viva Las Vegas (co-p).

CUMMINGS, Robert or Bob

Actor. Joplin, Missouri 1910–
Training as aeronautical engineer ended by Depression. American Academy of Dramatic Art. 1931: appeared in 'The Roof' on Broadway, also 'Earl Carroll's Vanities', 'Ziegfeld Follies'. 1935: to Hollywood with 'Follies' road company; first films. Some credits as Brice Hutchens. 1935–38: with Paramount. 1939–41: mainly with Universal. World War II: aviation instructor; honorary colonel in Air National Guard. 1948: co-produced and acted in Let's Live a Little. 1954: in 'Twelve Angry Men' on TV; own TV programme, The Bob Cummings Show (from 1955).

Films as actor include: 1935: So Red the Rose. 1936: Hollywood Boulevard. 1937: Souls at Sea; Wells Fargo. 1938: College Swing; You and Me. 1939: Rio. 1941: Free and Easy; The Devil and Miss Jones. 1942: Kings Row; Saboteur. 1943: Forever and a Day; Flesh and Fantasy; Princess O'Rourke. 1945: You Came Along. 1948: Sleep, My Love. 1949: The Accused; Reign of Terror. 1950: Paid in Full. 1952: The First Time. 1953: Marry Me Again. 1954: Dial M For Murder. 1955: How to be Very, Very Popular. 1962: My Geisha. 1964: The Carpetbaggers; What a Way to Go. 1966: Stagecoach.

CURTIS, Tony

(Bernard Schwartz) Actor. New York 1925–
World War II: US Navy, in submarines; medical discharge. Drama workshop; toured in stock. Spotted in Cherry Lane Theatre production, 'Golden Boy'. 1948: first film part, dancing with Yvonne de Carlo in Criss Cross; Universal contract. Most films there until 1957, then frequent Universal films until 1963. UK TV series 'The Persuaders'. Was married to Janet Leigh (1951–62), Christine Kaufman (1963–67).

Films as actor include: 1949: The Lady Gambles. 1950: Winchester '73. 1951: The Prince Who Was a Thief. 1952: Flesh and Fury; No Room for the Groom. 1953: Houdini; Forbidden. 1954: Beachhead; The Black Shield of Falworth; So This is Paris. 1955: Six Bridges to Cross. 1956: Trapeze; The Rawhide Years. 1957:

Mister Cory; Sweet Smell of Success. 1958: The Vikings; Kings Go Forth; The Defiant Ones; The Perfect Furlough. 1959: Operation Petticoat; Some Like it Hot. 1960: Who Was That Lady?; Spartacus; The Rat Race; The Great Imposter. 1961: The Outsider. 1962: Forty Pounds of Trouble; Taras Bulba. 1963: The List of Adrian Messenger; Captain Newman M.D.; Paris When it Sizzles. 1964: Goodbye Charlie; Sex and the Single Girl. 1965: The Great Race. 1966: Not With My Wife You Don't; Drop Dead Darling. 1967: Don't Make Waves. 1968: The Boston Strangler.

CURTIZ, Michael or
COURTICE, Michael

(Mihaly Kertesz) Director. Budapest, Hungary 1888–1962 Hollywood
Royal Academy of Theatre and Art. Actor and stage manager in Hungary; formed own theatrical company. Worked as actor throughout Europe, e.g. in Sweden, where met Mauritz Stiller. Entered films as assistant to Victor Sjöström; thereafter directed in Hungary (to 1919). From 1914: served in Austro-Hungarian army, twice wounded on Eastern Front; finished war as newsreel cameraman in Constantinople. Directed in Europe until 1926, including Hungary, Austria, Germany (from 1921), Italy (1921). 1926: first Hollywood film, Third Degree, for Warners. Worked for Warners until 1953. From 1954: mainly with Fox and Paramount. Married to actress Lucy Doraine (until 1923), star of some of his early films. Oscar for direction of Casablanca (1943) which also received Oscar as Best Film.

Films as director (from 1919): 1919: Die Dame mit den schwarzen Handschuhen; Der Stern von Damaskus; Gottesgeissel; Die Dame mit Sonnenblumen. 1920: Herzogin Satanella; Miss Dorothy's Bekenntnis; Labyrinth des Grauens. 1921: Miss Tutti Frutti; Wege des Schrecken. 1922: Sodom und Gomorrha – The Queen of Sin (+co-s). 1923: Samson und Dalila. 1924: Die Sklavenkönigin – Moon of Israel. 1925: Der Junge Medardus; Der Spielzeug von Paris. 1926: Fiaker N.13; Der Goldene Schmetterling; Red Heels; The Road to Happiness; The Third Degree. 1927: A Million Bid; Good Time Charley; The Desired Woman. 1928: Tenderloin. 1929: The Glad Rag Doll; Madonna of Avenue A; The Gamblers; Hearts in Exile; Noah's Ark. 1930: Mammy; Under a Texas Moon; The Matrimonial Bed; Dämon des Meeres (German version of Moby Dick, 1930); A Soldier's Plaything – A Soldier's Pay; Bright Lights; River's End. 1931: God's Gift to Women – Too Many Women; The Mad Genius. 1932: The Woman from Monte Carlo; The Strange Love of Molly Louvain; Alias the Doctor; The Cabin in the Cotton; Doctor X; Twenty Thousand Years in Sing-Sing. 1933: The Mystery of the Wax Museum; The Keyhole; Private Detective 62; Goodbye Again; The Kennel Murder Case; Female. 1934: Mandalay; Jimmy the Gent; The Key; British Agent. 1935: Black Fury; The Case of the Curious Bride; Captain Blood; Little Big Shot; Front Page Woman. 1936: The Walking Dead; The Charge of the Light Brigade; Mountain Justice. 1937: Stolen Holiday; Kid Galahad; The Perfect Specimen. 1938: Gold is Where You Find It; The Adventures of Robin Hood; Four's a Crowd; Four Daughters; Angels with Dirty Faces. 1939: Sons of Liberty; Dodge City; Daughters Courageous; The Private Lives of Elizabeth and Essex – Elizabeth the Queen. 1940: Four Wives; Virginia City; The Sea Hawk; Santa Fe Trail. 1941: The Sea Wolf; Dive Bomber. 1942: Captains of the Clouds. 1943: Yankee Doodle Dandy; Casablanca; Mission to Moscow; This is the Army. 1944: Passage to Marseille; Janie. 1945: Roughly Speaking; Mildred Pierce. 1946: Night and Day. 1947: Life with Father; The Unsuspected. 1948: Romance on the High Seas – It's Magic (+ co-p); My Dream Is Yours (+ p). 1949: Flamingo Road; The Lady Takes a Sailor. 1950: The Breaking Point; Bright Leaf; Young Man with a Horn – Young Man of Music. 1951: Force of Arms; Jim Thorpe, All American – Man of Bronze; I'll See You in my Dreams. 1952: The Story of Will Rogers; The Jazz Singer. 1953: Trouble Along the Way; The Boy from Oklahoma. 1954: The Egyptian; White Christmas. 1955: We're No Angels. 1956: The Scarlet Hour (+ p); The Vagabond King; The Best Things in Life are Free. 1957: The Helen Morgan Story – Both Ends of the Candle. 1958: King Creole; The Proud Rebel. 1959: The Hangman; The Man in the Net; A Breath of Scandal. 1960: The Adventures of Huckleberry Finn. 1961: Francis of Assisi; The Comancheros.

CYBULSKI, Zbygniew

Actor. Knigze, Ukraine 1928–1967 Wroclaw, Poland Academy of Commerce; journalism at Cracow Jagiellonian University; acted while a student. Cracow Drama School. With Bogumil Kobiela founded students' theatre (Bim Bom), at Gdansk. Artistic manager, director, writer in collaboration and actor. Directed on stage by Andrzej Wajda. 1954: first film as actor Pokolenie. 1956: further stage collaboration with Kobiela. From 1958: acted regularly in films. 1960: co-wrote and acted in Janusz Morgenstern's Do Widzenia do Jutra. 1962: In France. 1964: in Switzerland. 1967: about to direct film from own script, killed in railway accident.

Films as actor include: 1958: Popióli i diament; Osmy Dzień tygodnia. 1959: Pociąg; Niewinni Czarodzieje. 1962: La Poupee; L'Amour a vingt ans ep Warsaw; Jak Być Kochana. 1963: Rozstanie. 1964: Rekopis znaleziony w Saragossie; Att älska. 1966: Szyfry.

CZINNER, Paul

Director. Budapest 1890–
Child prodigy violinist. 1904: to Vienna. 1916: became journalist. Wrote play, 'Satan's Mask' (1919). Earliest films as director in Berlin. 1924: directed and wrote Nju, starring Elizabeth Bergner. Married her and directed her later films. 1930: followed her to UK. Became British citizen, directing only 2 more German films: Ariane and Der traumende Mund (re-made as Dreaming Lips, 1937). 1940: to USA as theatrical producer, directing his wife, e.g. in 'Miss Julie'. 1949: after tour of Australia, returned to UK. In 1950s started to specialise in multiple–camera film of stage productions, particularly ballet.

Films as director from 1926: 1926: Der Geiger von Florenz (+ s). 1927: Donna Juana (+ co-s). 1928: Liebe. 1929: Fräulein Else. 1930: The Way of Lost Souls. 1931: Ariane. 1932: Der Träumende Mund (+ co-s). 1934: Catherine the Great. 1935: Escape Me Never. 1936: As You Like It. 1937: Dreaming Lips. 1939: Stolen Life. 1955: Don Giovanni. 1956: Kings and Queens; Salzburg Pilgrimage. 1957: The Bolshoi

Ballet. 1959: The Royal Ballet. 1961: Der Rosen-kavalier. 1965: Romeo and Juliet.

D

DA COSTA, Morton

(Morton Tecosky) Director. Philadelphia, Pennsylvania 1914–
Temple University, where acted, directed and designed theatrical productions. Toured as actor, then (1937) co-founded Civic Repertory Theater, Dayton, Ohio, where directed about 60 plays. Broadway debut as actor: 'The Skin of Our Teeth' (1942). 1948: directed 'The Alchemist' at New York City Center; Maurice Evans's assistant on national tour of 'Man and Superman'; directed at New York City Center until 1951. 1952–53: director at St Louis Municipal Opera; wrote book and lyrics for 'Rip Van Winkle'. From 1952: directed on Broadway, e.g. 'No Time for Sergeants' (1955), 'Auntie Mame' (1956), 'The Music Man' (1957), 'Saratoga' (1959).

Films as director: 1958: Auntie Mame. 1962: The Music Man (+ p). 1963: Island of Love (+ p).

DAGOVER, Lil

(Martha Maria Lilitts) Actress. Madiven, Java 1897–
1919: first film Das Kabinett des Dr Caligari. 1932: only American film The Woman from Monte Carlo. German stage and TV. Married playwright Fritz Daghofer.

Films as actress include: 1919: Hara-Kiri. 1920: Die Spinnen. 1921: Der müde Tod. 1922: Dr Mabuse, der Spieler. 1923: Seine Frau, die Unbekannte. 1925: Zur Chronik von Grieshuus; Tartüff. 1931: Der Kongress tanzt. 1936: Schlussakkord. 1937: Die Kreutzersonate.

DAHLBECK, Eva

Actress. Stockholm, Sweden 1920-
Drama school of Royal Dramatic Theatre, Stockholm; acted at Royal Dramatic Theatre. First film as actress Rid i natt (1942). Also writer; scripted Yngsjomordet (1966).

Films as actress include: 1948: Eva. 1949: Bar a en mor. 1951: Fästmö uthyres. 1952: Trots; Kvinnors väntan. 1953: Barabbas. 1954: En Lektion i kärlek. 1955: Kvinnodröm; Sommarnattens Leende. 1956: Sista paret ut. 1958: Nära livet. 1960: De sista stegen. 1961: The Counterfeit Traitor. 1964: För att inte tala om alla dessa kvinnor; Älskande Par. 1965: Kattorna; Morianerna. 1966: Les Creatures.

DAILEY, Dan

Actor. New York 1917–
Dancing school, then vaudeville on Long Island; in chorus at Roxy, New York; worked for Minsky. Broadway debut in 'Babes in Arms' (1939). 1940: MGM contract (until 1942); first film, The Mortal Storm (1940). 1942–46: US Army Signal Corps, then Cavalry Lieutenant in Italy. 1947–57: mainly with Fox, starting with Mother Wore Tights (1947). Stage

Zbygniew Cybulski in Andrzej Wajda's Popol i Diament.
Lil Dagover in Tartüff.
L' Age d'Or. written and directed by Luis Buñuel and Salvador Dali.

59

(e.g. 'The Odd Couple'), TV (e.g. 'Four Just Men', 'The Governor and J.J.') and nightclubs (e.g. in Las Vegas on 5-year contract, 4 weeks per year). Few films since 1957.

Films as actor include: 1940: Susan and God. 1941: Ziegfeld Girl; Lady Be Good. 1942: Sunday Punch; Panama Hattie; Give Out, Sisters. 1948: Give My Regards to Broadway; You Were Meant for Me. 1950: When Willie Comes Marching Home. 1951: I Can Get it For You Wholesale. 1952: What Price Glory; Meet Me at the Fair. 1954: There's No Business Like Show Business. 1955: It's Always Fair Weather. 1956: The Best Things in Life Are Free. 1957: The Wings of Eagles; Oh, Men! Oh, Women! 1960: Pepe. 1962: Hemingway's Adventures of a Young Man.

DALI, Salvador

Writer and director. Figueras, Spain 1904–
Studied art in Paris and Madrid. Painter. Designer and costume designer for opera and ballet. 1928: in collaboration with Luis Buñuel directed, wrote and produced *Le Chien Andalou* and acted in it. 1930: in collaboration with Buñuel wrote and directed *L'Age d'or*. 1935: lectured at Museum of Modern Art, New York. 1940: settled in USA. Converted to Catholicism, many religious paintings. 1945: scripted dream sequence in *Spellbound*. Some amateur shorts. Returned permanently to Spain. 1960: exhibition of jewels, London. Books include 'The Secret Life of Salvador Dali', 'Dali on Modern Art', 'The World of Salvador Dali', 'Diary of a Genius', 'Abrégé d'une Histoire Critique du Cinéma'.

DALIO, Marcel

Actor. Paris 1900–
In theatre at 13. After demobilisation (1919), revue and acted in little theatres in Montmartre. 1933: first film as actor *Le Chapeau*. 1940: some theatre work in Canada, then Hollywood films. After Liberation, also worked in Europe.

Films as actor include: 1937: Pépé-le-moko; Les Perles de la couronne; La Grande Illusion; Cargaisons Blanches. 1938: Entrée des artistes; Mollenard. 1939: La Règle du jeu. 1941: Unholy Partners; The Shanghai Gesture. 1943: The Constant Nymph; The Song of Bernadette. 1944: Wilson. 1945: To Have And Have Not; A Bell for Adano. 1948: Dédée d'Anvers; Les Amants de Vérone. 1952: The Snows of Kilimanjaro. 1954: Sabrina. 1955: Les Amants du tage. 1956: Miracle in the Rain. 1959: Pillow Talk; The Man Who Understood Women; Classe tous risques. 1960: Can–Can. 1962: Cartouche. 1963: Donovan's Reef. 1969: Justine. 1970: Catch-22; The Great White Hope. 1971: Aussi loin que l'amour.

DAMIANI, Damiano

Director. Pasiano, Italy 1922–
Studied fine arts in Milan. 1946–47: designed sets for 2 films. 1946–56: directed about 30 shorts; scripted others; worked as assistant director. Shorts brought him to attention of Cesare Zavattini, who co-scripted first features.

Features as director: 1960: Il Rossetto – Red Lips (+co-s). 1961: Il Sicario (+co-s). 1962: L'Isola di Arturo – Arturo's Island (+co-s). 1963: La Rimpatriata – The Reunion (+co-s); La Noia – The Empty Canvas (+co-s). 1966: La Strega in amore – The Witch in Love – The Strange Obsession. 1968: Il Giorno della civetta – Mafia (+co-s); Quien sabe? – A Bullet for the General. 1971: Confessione di un commissario di polizia al procurature della reppubblica (+co-s).

DANIELS, William H.

Cinematographer. Cleveland, Ohio 1895–1970 Los Angeles
University of Southern California. 1917: assistant cameraman at Triangle. 1918: cinematographer at Universal. Assisted Ben Reynolds on *Foolish Wives* (1921), and later worked with him on 3 other films directed by Erich von Stroheim. 1922–23: with Samuel Goldwyn. 1924: freelance. 1924–46: under contract to MGM; then with various studios. 1961–63: president, American Society of Cinematographers. 1965: producer and cinematographer on *Marriage on the Rocks*. Oscar for black and white cinematography on *The Naked City* (1948).

Films as cinematographer include: 1923: Merry-Go-Round (co). 1925: Greed (co); The Merry Widow (co). 1926: The Boob. 1927: Flesh and the Devil. 1928: The Mysterious Lady; A Woman of Affairs. 1929: Wild Orchids; The Last of Mrs Cheyney; The Kiss. 1930: Anna Christie; Romance. 1931: A Free Soul; Inspiration; Susan Lenox. 1932: Grand Hotel. 1933: Rasputin and the Empress; The White Sister; Dinner at Eight; The Stranger's Return. 1934: Queen Christina; The Barretts of Wimpole Street. 1935: Anna Karenina; Naughty Marietta. 1936: Romeo and Juliet; Camille; Rose Marie. 1937: Personal Property. 1938: Marie Antoinette. 1939: Ninotchka; Another Thin Man (co). 1940: The Shop Around the Corner; The Mortal Storm. 1941: Back Street; So Ends Our Night; Shadow of the Thin Man; Dr Kildare's Victory. 1942: Keeper of the Flame; For Me and My Gal. 1947: Lured; Brute Force. 1949: Woman in Hiding. 1950: Winchester '73; Deported. 1951: The Lady Pays Off; Bright Victory; Thunder on the Hill. 1952: Pat and Mike; Glory Alley; Plymouth Adventure. 1953: Thunder Bay; Forbidden; The Glenn Miller Story. 1954: The Far Country. 1955: Strategic Air Command; The Shrike. 1956: The Unguarded Moment. 1957: Night Passage; Interlude. 1958: Some Came Running; Cat on a Hot Tin Roof; A Stranger in My Arms. 1959: A Hole in the Head. 1960: Ocean's 11; Can–Can. 1961: Come September. 1962: How the West Was Won (co); Billy Rose's Jumbo. 1964: Robin and the Seven Hoods (+as-p). 1965: Von Ryan's Express. 1967: Valley of the Dolls. 1970: Move.

D'ANNUNZIO, Gabriele

Writer. Pescara, Italy 1863–1938 Gardone Riviera, Italy
Rome University; first book of poems 'Primo Vere' while a student. From 1896: playwright. 1889–90: volunteered for year in cavalry. 1897–1900: deputy in Italian parliament. 1901: dedicated play 'Francesca da Rimini' to Eleanora Duse. 1908–15: lived in France. 1911: first film adaptation of his work. 1914: only original dramatic work for cinema *Cabiria,* for which contributed only basic material including character names. Urged war against Austria; served in army, navy and air force: wounded. 1919: judging peace treaty unsatisfactory, seized Fiume. 1920: abandoned Fiume; scripted documentary *Il Paradiso nell'ombra delle spade (Fiume d'Italia durante l'occupazione dei legionari)*. 1924: became Prince of Monte Nevoso. 1927: Italian government undertook publication of his works. Poetry includes 'Odi Navali' (1893), 'Gli Inni Sacri della guerra giusta' (1914). Plays include 'La Gioconda' (1898), 'La Figlia di Jorio' (1904), 'La Nave' (1908). Novels include 'Giovani Episcopo' (1891), 'Il Fuoco' (1900), 'Notturno' (1921). Many political and patriotic addresses and writings.

Films based on his writings include: 1911: La Fiaccola sotto il moggio; La Gioconda; La Nave; La Figlia di Jorio. 1916: La Crociata degli innocenti; La Fiaccola sotto il moggio (rm); La Gioconda (rm); La Figlia di Jorio (rm); Forse che si forse che no; Giovanni Episcopo. 1917: Il Ferro. 1920: La Nave (rm +co-d). 1947: Il Delitto di Giovanni Episcopo (rm Giovanni Episcopo *1916*).

Films as writer: 1914: Cabiria (co). 1920: Il Paradiso nell'ombra delle spade (Fiume d'Italia durante l'occupazione dei legionari).

DANTON, Ray

Actor. New York 1931–
Carnegie Institute of Technology. Radio and summer stock. In London production of 'Mr Roberts'. 1951–53: US Army. 1955: first films. Much TV work. Since 1964 in Italian films and US TV. Married to Julie Adams.

Films as actor include: 1956: I'll Cry Tomorrow; Outside the Law. 1958: Too Much, Too Soon; Tarawa Beachhead. 1959: The Big Operator; Yellowstone Kelly; The Beat Generation. 1960: The Rise and Fall of Legs Diamond; Ice Palace; A Fever in the Blood. 1961: A Majority of One; The George Raft Story. 1962: The Chapman Report; The Longest Day.

DAQUIN, Louis

Director. Calais, France 1908–
Studied law and business. Worked in advertising. From 1932: assistant director to, e.g. Julien Duvivier (*Pépé-le-Moko*, 1936), Abel Gance (*Un Grand Amour de Beethoven,* 1936), Jean Grémillon (*Remorques,* 1941); also worked as production manager. 1941: first film as director. 1954: *Bel Ami,* banned by French censor; release held up for 3 years. Subsequent films made abroad. Worked in Rumania and Germany.

Films as director: 1941: Nous les gosses. 1942: Madame et le mort; Le Voyageur de la Toussaint. 1943: Premier de cordée. 1945: Patrie. 1946: Nous continuons la France. 1947: Les Frères Bouquinquant (+co-s). 1949: Le Parfum de la dame en noir; Le Point du jour. 1950: Maître après Dieu; La Bataille de la vie. 1954: Bel Ami (r 1957). 1957: Les Chardons du Baragan. 1959: La Rabouilleuse – Les Arrivistes.

DARC, Mireille

Actress. Toulon, France 1939–
Drama training at Toulon Conservatoire and in Paris. Model. Discovered by producer Claude Barma who gave her small part in TV production. Films from

1960. 1964: on Paris stage in French adaptation of 'Barefoot in the Park'. 1970: acted in *Madly*, scripted from her original treatment (under pseudonym Mireille Aigroz).

Films as actress include: 1961: La Bride sur le cou. 1964: Monsieur; La Chasse à l'homme. 1965: Les Bons Vivants (*ep*); Les Barbouzes; Galia. ·1966: Du Rififi à Paname; Ne nous fâchons pas; La Grande Sauterelle. 1967: Fleur d'oseille. 1968: Weekend; Those Daring Young Men in their Jaunty Jalopies. 1970: Elle boit pas, elle fume pas, elle drague pas, mais· . . . elle cause!; Madly (+ *st*).

DARNELL, Linda

Actress. Dallas, Texas 1923–1965 Chicago
Father a postal clerk. Amateur theatricals. Discovered through talent contest at 16. 1939: first films. 1939–50: Fox contract. First of 3 husbands was J. Peverell Marley (1943–52). On Broadway in 'Harbor Lights'. Fewer films after 1951; summer stock, cabaret and much TV including 'Wagon Train' and 'Burke's Law'. Died in fire.

Films as actress include: 1939: Hotel for Women; Day-Time Wife. 1940: Brigham Young; The Mark of Zorro; Chad Hanna. 1941: Blood and Sand; Rise and Shine. 1944: It Happened Tomorrow; Buffalo Bill; Summer Storm. 1945: Hangover Square; Fallen Angel. 1946: Centennial Summer; Anna and the King of Siam; My Darling Clementine. 1947: Forever Amber. 1948: The Walls of Jericho; Unfaithfully Yours; A Letter to Three Wives. 1949: Slattery's Hurricane; Everybody Does It. 1950: No Way Out; Two Flags West. 1951: The Guy Who Came Back; The 13th Letter; The Lady Pays Off; Saturday Island. 1952: Night Without Sleep; Blackbeard the Pirate. 1953: Second Chance. 1954: This Is My Love. 1965: Black Spurs.

D'ARRAST, Harry d'Abbadie

Director. Argentine 1893–1968 Monte Carlo
Family minor aristocracy. Educated in Paris and Switzerland. In Hollywood from 1922; French technical adviser (with Jean de Limur) on Charles Chaplin's *A Woman of Paris* (1923). Assistant director to Chaplin on *The Gold Rush* (1925); later disagreement with him led to removal of own credit on sound re-issue. Introduced by Chaplin to Marion Davies and William Randolph Hearst. 1926: contract with their company, but no assignment. 1927: began as director on Adolphe Menjou films starting with *Service for Ladies,* under name H. d'Abbadie. Uncredited on *Raffles* (1930) due to disagreement with Samuel Goldwyn during making. After *Laughter* (1930) no work for 3 years. 1933: *Topaze* for David O. Selznick, who re-cut it after disagreement. Directed wife, Eleanor Boardman, in his last film, *The Three Cornered Hat* (1935). From 1934, lived in Europe except 1940–46 in Hollywood without work. Retired to family home, small ruined castle in Basses-Pyrénées.

Films as director: 1927: Service for Ladies; A Gentleman of Paris; Serenade. 1928: The Magnificent Flirt (+ *co-s*); Dry Martini. 1930: Raffles (*uc*); Laughter (+ *co-st*). 1933: Topaze. 1935: The Three Cornered Hat.

DARRIEUX, Danielle

Actress. Bordeaux, France 1917–
University and Conservatoire in Paris. 1931: first film *Le Bal*. 1937: stage debut. Also singer. Chevalier de la Légion d'Honneur. 1935–41: married to Henri Decoin who directed her in *Abus de confiance* (1937), *Battements de Coeur* (1939), *Premier Rendez-vous* (1941) and *La Verité Sur le Bébé Donge* (1951). 1970: took over lead in Broadway musical 'Coco' from Katharine Hepburn. 1971: on stage in musical, 'Ambassador'.

Films as actress include: 1934: Mauvaise Graine; L'Or dans la rue. 1936: Mayerling. 1938: Katia; The Rage of Paris. 1942: La Fausse Maîtresse. 1947: Ruy Blas. 1949: Jean de la lune; Occupe-toi d'Amélie. 1950: La Ronde. 1952: Le Plaisir; Rich, Young and Pretty; Five Fingers; Adorables Créatures. 1953: Madame de . . . 1954: Le Rouge et le noir. 1955: Napoléon; L'Amant de Lady Chatterley. 1956: Si Paris nous était conté; Alexander the Great; Pot-Bouille. 1958: Marie-Octobre. 1961: Vive Henri IV . . . vive l'amour!; The Greengage Summer. 1962: Landru. 1963: Le Diable et les dix commandements. 1965: Le Coup de grâce. 1966: L'Homme à la Buick. 1967: Les Demoiselles de Rochefort. 1968: Les Oiseaux vont mourir au Pérou.

DARWELL, Jane

(Patti Woodward) Actress. Palmyra, Missouri 1880–1967 Woodland Hills, California
Theatrical work from 1906: stock company in Chicago, on Broadway and at Providence, Rhode Island. 1914: Hollywood; under contract to Jesse L. Lasky Feature Play Company (1914–16); first film, *The Capture of Aguinaldo* (1914). 1916–30: occasional films, also stage. From 1930: frequent films. Some TV. Oscar as supporting actress for *The Grapes of Wrath* (1940).

Films as actress include: 1914: Rose of the Rancho. 1930: Tom Sawyer. 1931: Huckleberry Finn. 1932: Back Street. 1933: Bondage; Before Dawn; Only Yesterday; Roman Scandals; Design for Living. 1934: Happiness Ahead; Wonder Bar; Fashion of 1934; Desirable; The Firebird; David Harum; Heat Lightning; The Scarlet Empress; One Night of Love; Bright Eyes; Journal of a Crime. 1935: One More Spring; Life Begins at Forty; Metropolitan; Navy Wife. 1936: The Country Doctor; Captain January; Private Number; White Fang; Ramona. 1937: Nancy Steele is Missing; Love is News; Slave Ship; The Singing Marine; Dangerously Yours. 1938: Battle of Broadway. 1939: Jesse James; The Rains Came; Gone With the Wind. 1940: Chad Hanna; Brigham Young. 1941: All that Money Can Buy. 1942: The Great Gildersleeve; The Ox-Bow Incident. 1943: Gildersleeve's Bad Day; Government Girl; Stage Door Canteen; Tender Comrade. 1944: Sunday Dinner for a Soldier. 1946: My Darling Clementine. 1947: Keeper of the Bees. 1948: Three Godfathers. 1950: Wagonmaster; Caged; The Daughter of Rosie O'Grady; Surrender; Three Husbands. 1951: The Lemon Drop Kid; Journey into Light. 1952: We're Not Married. 1953: It Happens Every Thursday; The Sun Shines Bright. 1956: There's Always Tomorrow. 1958: The Last Hurrah. 1959: Hound Dog Man. 1964: Mary Poppins.

Ray Danton in The Rise and Fall of Legs Diamond, *directed by Bud Boetticher.*
Charles Bickford and Linda Darnell in The Fallen Angel, *directed by Otto Preminger.*
Troy Donahue and Claudette Colbert in Parrish, *directed by Delmer Daves.*

DASSIN, Jules

Director. Middletown, Connecticut 1911–
1934–36: studied drama in Europe. 1936–40: actor at Yiddish Art Theatre, New York; radio writer. Directed 'Medicine Show' (1940) on Broadway; occasional theatre work thereafter. 1940: at RKO, assistant on *They Knew What They Wanted* and *Mr and Mrs Smith*; joined MGM; directed shorts mainly on famous musicians, also 2-reeler, *The Tell-Tale Heart* (1941). 1942: first feature as director, *Nazi Agent*. 'Suspected' witness at 1947 hearings of House Committee on Un-American Activities. 1950: left USA; worked in Europe, mainly France and Greece. 1968: made *Up-tight* in USA. 1970: defendant *in absentia* in Greek sedition trial.

Features as director: 1942: Nazi Agent; The Affairs of Martha – Once Upon a Thursday; Reunion – Reunion in France – Mademoiselle France. 1943: Young Ideas. 1944: The Canterville Ghost. 1945: A Letter for Evie. 1946: Two Smart People. 1947: Brute Force. 1948: The Naked City. 1949: Thieves' Highway (+ *w*). 1950: Night and the City. 1954: Du Rififi chez les hommes – Rififi (Means Trouble) (+ *co-s/w*). 1957: Celui qui doit mourir (+ *co-s*). 1958: La Loi – Where the Hot Wind Blows (+ *co-s*). 1959: Pote tin kyriaki – Never on Sunday (+ *p/s/w*); Phaedra (+ *p/co-s/w*). 1963: Topkapi (+ *p*). 1966: 10:30 P.M. Summer (+ *p/co-s*). 1968: Survival! (+ *co-p*); Uptight (+ *co-s*). 1970: La Promesse de l'aube – Promise at Dawn (+ *s*).

DAVES, Delmer

Director and writer. San Francisco 1904–
Law at Stanford University. 1927: assistant prop man at Metropolitan for James Cruze. 1928: to MGM as prop assistant to Cruze. 1929: first film as actor, Cruze's *The Duke Steps Out*. 1931: first film as writer in collaboration *Shipmates*. 1932: to Warners as writer. 1936–42: freelance writer. 1943: first film as director. 1943–49: almost all films for Warners. 1950–54: with Fox. 1954–59: with several companies, including Columbia, Warners, Fox. 1959–65: with Warners, usually director, producer and writer.

Films as director: 1948: To the Victor. 1949: A Kiss in the Dark. 1950: Broken Arrow. 1952: Return of the Texan. 1953: Never Let Me Go. 1954: Demetrius and the Gladiators. 1956: Jubal. 1957: 3.10 to Yuma. 1958: Cowboy; Kings Go Forth; The Badlanders. 1959: The Hanging Tree.

Films as director and writer: 1944: Destination Tokyo (*co-s*); The Very Thought of You (*co-s*). 1945: Hollywood Canteen; Pride of the Marines (*co-s*). 1947: The Red House; Dark Passage. 1949: Task Force. 1951: Bird of Paradise. 1953: Treasure of the Golden Condor. 1954: Drum Beat. 1956: The Last Wagon (*co-s*). 1964: Youngblood Hawke.

Films as director, producer and writer: 1960: A Summer Place. 1961: Parrish; Susan Slade. 1962: Rome Adventure – Lovers Must Learn. 1963: Spencer's Mountain (*d/p only*). 1965: The Battle of the Villa Fiorita.

DAVIES, Marion

(Marion Cecilia Douras) Actress. New York 1897–1961 Los Angeles

Convent education, then mannequin in Fifth Avenue shop. From 1914: dancer in 'Chu Chin Chow' in Philadelphia and later on Broadway. 1916: joined Ziegfeld Follies, where met William Randolph Hearst. 1918: first film, *Runaway Romany* for which also wrote story and screenplay; Hearst formed production company, Marion Davies Film Company (later Cosmopolitan Pictures), to make her a star. Until 1922, alternated between stage and screen appearances as light comedienne. From 1922: films only. 1925–34: films released through MGM. 1934–37: films released through Warners. From 1937: in virtual retirement at Beverley Hills and Palm Springs. 1951: on death of Hearst married Captain Horace Brown.

Films as actress include: 1919: Getting Mary Married; The Dark Star. 1920: The Restless Sex. 1926: Beverly of Graustark; Quality Street (+ *p*); The Fair Co-ed. 1928: The Patsy; The Cardboard Lover; Show People (+ *co-p*). 1929: Marianne; The Hollywood Revue. 1930: Not So Dumb. 1931: The Bachelor Father (+ *co-p*); It's a Wise Child (+ *co-p*); Five and Ten (+ *co-p*). 1932: Polly of the Circus; Blondie of the Follies (+ *p*). 1933: Going Hollywood; Peg o' my Heart. 1934: Operator 13. 1935: Page Miss Glory. 1936: Cain and Mabel; Hearts Divided. 1937: Ever Since Eve.

DAVIS, Bette

Actress. Lowell, Massachusetts 1908–
From 1925: Mariarden School of Dancing and John Murray Anderson Dramatic School, New York. Acted in George Cukor's stock company at Rochester, and with Provincetown Players. 1929: Broadway debut in 'Broken Dishes'. 1931: contract with Universal; first film, *Bad Sister*. 1932: at Warners starred with George Arliss in *The Man Who Played God*; under Warners contract until *Beyond the Forest* (1949). 1936: tried to break contract by making film in UK. Studio issued injunction preventing this and won subsequent court case, but waived share of costs and welcomed her back. President of the Academy of Motion Picture Arts and Sciences (1941). Produced and starred in *A Stolen Life* (1946). Co-founder and president of Hollywood Canteen. 1930–52: Broadway appearances; has since appeared in, e.g. 'The Night of the Iguana' (1961). Wrote autobiography, 'The Lonely Life' (1963). Fourth husband (1950–60) was actor Gary Merrill. Oscars as Best Actress for *Dangerous* (1935) and *Jezebel* (1938).

Films as actress include: 1931: Seed; Waterloo Bridge. 1932: So Big; Cabin in the Cotton; Three on a Match. 1933: Twenty Thousand Years in Sing-Sing; Ex-Lady; Bureau of Missing Persons. 1934: Fashion of 1934; Jimmy the Gent; Fog Over Frisco; Of Human Bondage. 1935: Front Page Woman; Special Agent; Bordertown. 1936: The Petrified Forest; Satan Met A Lady. 1937: Marked Woman; That Certain Woman; It's Love I'm After; Kid Galahad. 1938: The Sisters. 1939: Dark Victory; Juarez; The Private Lives of Elizabeth and Essex; The Old Maid. 1940: All This and Heaven Too; The Letter. 1941: The Great Lie; The Bride Came C.O.D.; The Little Foxes. 1942: The Man Who Came To Dinner; In This Our Life; Now, Voyager. 1943: Thank Your Lucky Stars; Old Acquaintance; Watch on the Rhine. 1944: Mr Skeffington; Hollywood Canteen. 1945: The Corn is Green. 1946: Deception. 1948: Winter Meeting; June Bride. 1949: Beyond the Forest. 1950: All About Eve. 1951: Payment on Demand. 1952: Phone Call from a Stranger; Another Man's Poison. 1953: The Star. 1955: The Virgin Queen. 1956: The Catered Affair; Storm Center. 1959: The Scapegoat; John Paul Jones. 1961: Pocketful of Miracles. 1962: What Ever Happened to Baby Jane? 1963: La Noia. 1964: Hush, Hush, Sweet Charlotte; Dead Ringer; Where Love Has Gone. 1965: The Nanny. 1967: The Anniversary.

DAVIS, Desmond

Director. London, 1928–
Clapper boy at 16. Photography at Regent Street Polytechnic, London. World War II: served in Army Film Unit. Returned to industry, worked through ranks of camera team. 1950: directed shorts. 2nd-unit cinematographer then joined Woodfall as camera operator. 1963: Tony Richardson enabled him to make first feature as director, scripted by Edna O'Brien. 1964: formed own company; directed *The Uncle*, released only in USA, in producer's version. 1965: *I Was Happy Here* was first film selected for 100% financial backing under National Film Finance Corporation/Rank scheme to encourage independent production in UK; co-scripted by Edna O'Brien. 1967: *Smashing Time* first film financed by ABC TV (US) through Carlo Ponti. 1970: formed production company with Rita Tushingham.

Films as director: 1963: The Girl with Green Eyes. 1964: The Uncle (+ *co-s*). 1965: I Was Happy Here – Time Lost and Time Remembered (+ *co-s*). 1967: Smashing Time. 1969: A Nice Girl Like Me (+ *co-s*).

DAY, Doris

(Doris Kappelhoff) Actress and singer. Cincinnati, Ohio 1924–
Began as dancer; by 12 in Fanchon and Marco stage show. After car accident, studied singing; appearance on Cincinnati radio show led to job in local nightclub. Then 3 years with Les Brown's Band. 1948: spotted by Michael Curtiz; Warners contract (until 1954); first film. 1951: married Martin Melcher who became her manager and co-produced most films until death (1968). Recording star. Own TV series and shows.

Films as actress: 1948: Romance on the High Seas. 1949: My Dream is Yours; It's a Great Feeling. 1950: Young Man With a Horn; Tea for Two; The West Point Story. 1951: Storm Warning; Lullaby of Broadway; On Moonlight Bay; Starlift; I'll See You in my Dreams. 1952: April in Paris; The Winning Team. 1953: By the Light of the Silvery Moon; Calamity Jane. 1955: Lucky Me; Young at Heart; Love Me or Leave Me. 1956: The Man Who Knew Too Much; Julie. 1957: The Pajama Game. 1958: Teacher's Pet; The Tunnel of Love. 1959: It Happened to Jane; Pillow Talk. 1960: Please Don't Eat the Daisies; Midnight Lace. 1961: Lover Come Back. 1962: That Touch of Mink; Billy Rose's Jumbo. 1963: The Thrill of It All; Move Over, Darling. 1964: Send Me No Flowers. 1965: Do Not Disturb. 1966: The Glass-Bottom Boat. 1967: Caprice. 1968: The Ballad of Josie; Where Were You When the Lights Went Out?; With Six You Get Eggroll.

DAY, Richard

Designer. Victoria, British Columbia 1896–
1918–19: set designer at Universal on films directed by Erich von Stroheim. 1921: became art director. 1921–28: shared art director credit and sometimes costume credit with Von Stroheim, moving with him to MGM, Paramount and United Artists. 1928–38: worked on films released by United Artists. 1939–47: with Fox. From 1948: mainly with RKO and United Artists. Oscars as art director for *The Dark Angel* (1935), *Dodsworth* (1936), *How Green was My Valley* (1941, with Nathan Juran), *This Above All* (1942, with Joseph Wright), *My Gal Sal* (1942, with Joseph Wright), *A Streetcar Named Desire* (1951), *On the Waterfront* (1954).

Films as designer include: 1921: Foolish Wives (*co;* + *co-cost*). 1922: Merry-Go-Round (*co;* + *co-cost*). 1923: Greed (*co*). 1925: The Merry Widow (*co;* + *co-cost*). 1928: The Wedding March (*co;* + *co-cost*); Queen Kelly (*co*). 1932: Arrowsmith. 1933: The Bowery; Roman Scandals. 1934: The House of Rothschild; Looking for Trouble. 1935: The Wedding Night; Barbary Coast; The Dark Angel; Les Miserables; The Call of the Wild (*co*); Clive of India. 1936: Come and Get It!; These Three; The Gay Desperado; Dodsworth. 1937: Stella Dallas; Dead End. 1938: The Hurricane (*co*); The Goldwyn Follies; The Cowboy and the Lady. 1939: Young Mr Lincoln (*co*); Charlie Chan at Treasure Island (*co*); Drums Along the Mohawk (*co*). 1940: Charlie Chan in Panama (*co*); Viva Cisco Kid (*co*); Young People (*co*); The Return of Frank James (*co*). 1941: Tobacco Road (*co*); How Green was My Valley (*co*); Blood and Sand (*co*). 1942: This Above All (*co*); My Gal Sal (*co*); Ten Gentlemen from West Point (*co*); The Ox-Bow Incident (*co*). 1946: The Razor's Edge (*co*). 1947: Boomerang! (*co*); The Ghost and Mrs Muir (*co*); Captain from Castile (*co*); I Wonder Who's Kissing Her Now (*co*). 1948: Joan of Arc; Force of Evil (*co*). 1949: My Foolish Heart; Our Very Own. 1950: Edge of Doom. 1951: Cry Danger; A Streetcar Named Desire. 1952: Hans Christian Andersen (*co*). 1954: On the Waterfront. 1959: Solomon and Sheba. 1960: Exodus. 1961: Something Wild. 1964: Cheyenne Autumn; Goodbye Charlie. 1965: The Greatest Story Ever Told. 1970: Tora, Tora, Tora (*co*).

DEAN, James

Actor. Fairmont, Indiana 1931–1955 Paso Robles, California
Theatre arts at University of California, Los Angeles. 1950: extra on TV; appeared on Broadway; to Hollywood after appearance in Andre Gide's 'The Immoralist'. 1951: first film, *Sailor Beware*. 1955: first major part in *East of Eden*. TV work as actor. *The James Dean Story* compiled after death in car crash.

Films as actor: 1951: Sailor Beware; Fixed Bayonets. 1952: Has Anybody Seen My Gal? 1955: East of Eden; Rebel Without a Cause. 1956: Giant. 1957: The James Dean Story.

DEARDEN, Basil

Director.   Westcliffe-on-Sea,   Essex   1911–1971 London
Theatrical family. Assistant stage manager. Grand

Theatre, Fulham, London. Production manager to Basil Dean. 1931: with Dean to Ealing, worked in many capacities on, e.g. George Formby comedies. 1938–41: variously writer, assistant director, associate producer at Ealing. 1941: co-directed first feature, *The Black Sheep of Whitehall* with Will Hay. 1943: first solo feature, *The Bells Go Down*. With *Saraband for Dead Lovers* (1948) began association with Michael Relph as producer or sharing producer/director credit. 1959: Dearden and Relph established Allied Film Makers. Produced e.g. Relph's *Rockets Galore* (1958) and co-produced with him e.g. *Desert Mice* (1959). Worked on TV series 'The Persuaders'. Died in road accident.

Films as director (credits shared with Michael Relph marked †): 1941: The Black Sheep of Whitehall (*co-d Will Hay*). 1942: The Goose Steps Out (*co-d Will Hay*). 1943: My Learned Friend (*co-d Will Hay*); The Bells Go Down. 1944: Halfway House; They Came to a City (+ *co-s*). 1945: Dead of Night *ep* The Hearse Driver. 1946: The Captive Heart. 1947: Frieda. 1948: Saraband for Dead Lovers (*co-d* †). 1949: Train of Events (*co-d Sidney Cole, Charles Crichton*); The Blue Lamp. 1950: Cage of Gold. 1951: Pool of London; I Believe in You (+ *co-p/co-st* †; *co-d* †). 1952: The Gentle Gunman. 1953: The Square Ring (+ *co-p* †; *co-d* †). 1954: The Rainbow Jacket. 1955: Out of the Clouds (+ *co-p* †; *co-d* †); The Ship That Died of Shame (+ *co-p/s*); Who Done It? (+ *co-p* †; *co-d* †). 1957: The Smallest Show on Earth. 1958: Violent Playground. 1959: Sapphire. 1960: The League of Gentlemen; Man in the Moon (+ *co-s* †). 1961: The Secret Partner; Victim. 1962: All Night Long (+ *co-p* †; *co-d* †); Life For Ruth. 1963: The Mindbenders; A Place to Go; Woman of Straw. 1964: Masquerade. 1966: Khartoum. 1968: Only When I Larf; The Assassination Bureau. 1970: The Man Who Haunted Himself (+ *co-s* †).

D'EAUBONNE, Jean

Designer. Talence, France 1903–1971
Pupil of sculptor Antoine Bourdelle. Began by painting posters, then assistant designer in films, e.g. to Lazare Meerson. Sets for many films in late 1930s. During German occupation of France, went to Switzerland, where worked on Jacques Feyder's *Une Femme disparaît* (1942); returned to France after Liberation.

Films as set designer include: 1930: Le Sang d'un poète. 1932: Pour un sou d'amour. 1940: De Mayerling à Sarajevo. 1946: Macadam. 1947: La Certosa di Parma. 1949: Black Magic. 1950: Orphee; La Ronde. 1952: Le Plaisir (*co*); Casque d'or. 1953: La Fête à Henriette; Rue de l'Estrapade; Madame de ... 1954: Touchez-pas au grisbi. 1955: Marianne de ma jeunesse; Lola Montès (*co*). 1958: Bitter Victory; The Reluctant Debutante; Montparnasse 19. 1960: Crack in the Mirror. 1961: The Big Gamble; Madame Sans-Gêne. 1963: Love is a Ball; Charade; Paris When It Sizzles. 1970: Elle boit pas, elle fume pas, elle drague pas, mais ... elle cause; Sur la route de Salina. 1971: Le Cri du cormoran le soir au-dessus des jonques; Le Drapeau Noir flotte sur la marmite.

DE BARONCELLI, Jacques

Director. Avignon, France 1881–1951 Paris
Father Marquis de Baroncelli-Javon. Began as journal-

Bette Davis and Victor Buono in Whatever Happened to Baby Jane?, *directed by Robert Aldrich.*
James Dean.
Life For Ruth, *directed by Basil Dearden.*

ist on L'Eclair, L'Opinion, Le Monde Illustré. 1915: entered films, forming own company, Lumina; first film, *La Maison de l'espoir* (1915). By 1918 had produced, written and directed about 30 films. After World War I: concentrated on literary adaptations. Son is Jean de Baroncelli, film critic of Le Monde.

Films as director include: 1918: Le Roi de la mer. 1919: Ramuntcho. 1920: La Rafale; Le Secret du Lonestar. 1921: Champi–Tortu; Le Rêve. 1922: Le Père Goriot. 1923: Nêne. 1924: Pêcheurs d'islande; Gitanes. 1925: Nitchevo. 1926: Le Passager. 1927: Duel. 1929: La Femme et le pantin. 1931: L'Arlésienne. 1934: Crainquebille; Mystère de Paris. 1937: Nitchevo (*rm 1925*); Michael Strogoff; Feu! 1938: Belle Etoile. 1941: Le Pavillon brûle. 1942: La Duchesse de Langeais; Haut de vent. 1943: Les Mystères de Paris. 1945: Marie La misère. 1946: La Rose de la mer. 1947: Rocambole.

DE BOSIO, Gianfranco

Director. Verona, Italy 1924–
Resistance activities during World War II. 1949: founded University Theatre at Padua; directed it until 1953. A year in Paris working with Marcel Marceau and Jean-Louis Barrault. Directed plays for various companies before becoming director at Turin Teatro Stabile. Wrote first screenplay with another theatrical director, Luigi Squarzina, and directed it for 22 dicembre, production company formed by Ermanno Olmi and critic Tullio Kezich. 1969: staged early Renaissance play 'La Betia' (filmed it in 1971).

Films as director: 1963: Il Terrorista (+ *co-st/co-s*). 1971: La Betia (+ *co-s*).

DE BROCA, Philippe

Director. Paris 1933–
Began studying photography at school, then at École Vaugirard. Went as cameraman on expedition shooting Berliet advertising documentary in Sahara; worked on documentaries for a year in North Africa. National Service in army film unit in Algeria. Worked as *stagiaire* with Henri Decoin and Georges Lacombe. 1958–59: assistant director to Pierre Schoendoerffer on *Ramuntcho,* to Claude Chabrol on *Le Beau Serge, Les Cousins, A Double Tour,* to François Truffaut on *Les 400 Coups.* First film as director, and *Le Farceur* (1960) both for Chabrol's company. 1965: formed own production company to make *Le Roi de coeur.*

Feature films as director: 1959: Les Jeux de l'amour – Playing at Love (+ *co-s*). 1960: Le Farceur – The Joker (+ *co-s*). 1961: L'Amant de cinq jours – Infidelity (+ *co-s*); Les Sept Péchés Capitaux *ep* La Gourmandise. 1962: Cartouche – Swords of Blood (+ *co-s*); Les Veinards – People in Luck *ep* La Vedette (+ *s*). 1963: L'Homme de Rio – That Man from Rio. 1964: Un Monsieur de compagnie. 1965: Les Tribulations d'un chinois en Chine – Up to His Ears. 1966: Le Roi de coeur – King of Hearts (+ *p*). 1967: Le Plus Vieux Métier du monde *ep* Mademoiselle Mimi. 1968: Le Diable par la queue – The Devil by the Tail. 1969: Les Figurants du Nouveau Monde – Les Caprices de Marie – Give Her the Moon. 1971: La Poudre d'escampette.

DECAË, Henri

Cinematographer. Saint Denis, France 1915–
Made amateur films before studying at École Vaugirard. Started in cinema on sound recording and sound editing for Poste Parisien sound studios. Military service as cameraman for French Air Force. 1941: made short with brother, *Eaux Vives.* Worked on publicity and scientific films, directing as well as photographing. 1947: met Jean-Pierre Melville and shot *Le Silence de la Mer* (1948) with hand-held technique; later used this in new wave films (from 1957). Has directed a number of shorts including *Glaciers* (1942), *Au delà du visible* (1943), *A tous les vents* (1944), *Trois Hommes en Corse* (1949), *Carnaval Sacré* (1950).

Films as cinematographer include: 1950: Les Enfants Terribles. 1955: Bob le flambeur. 1956: S.O.S. Noronha. 1957: Ascenseur pour l'échafaud. 1958: Le Beau Serge; Les Amants; Les Cousins. 1959: Les Quatre Cents Coups; A Double Tour; Plein Soleil. 1960: Les Bonnes Femmes. 1961: Che gioia vivere; Léon Morin, prêtre; Les Sept Péchés Capitaux (*3 eps*). 1962: Vie Privée; Cybèle ou les Dimanches de Ville d'Avray. 1963: L'Aîné des Ferchaux; Le Jour et l'heure; Dragées au poivre. 1964: La Ronde; Weekend à Zuydcoote. 1965: Viva Maria! 1967: Night of the Generals; Le Voleur; Le Samouraï; The Comedians; Diaboliquement Vôtre. 1970: Hello-Goodbye; Le Cercle Rouge.

DE CARLO, Yvonne

(Peggy Middleton) Actress. Vancouver, British Columbia, Canada 1922–
Started to learn dancing at 6. Amateur theatricals. Dancer in Vancouver, then Hollywood nightclubs. 1942: Paramount contract, at first playing opposite men being screen-tested; first bit parts in films. Picked by Walter Wanger to play lead in *Salome, Where She Danced* (1945) for Universal; with Universal until 1950. Married to stuntman Robert Morgan, who lost leg, crushed under logs in train battle of *How The West Was Won.* TV work, e.g. series 'The Munsters'. Broadway debut in 'Enter Laughing' and on tour. 1971: on Boston stage in 'Follies'.

Films as actress include: 1942: This Gun for Hire; The Road to Morocco. 1943: For Whom the Bell Tolls; True to Life; So Proudly We Hail. 1944: Practically Yours; The Story of Dr Wassell; Here Come the Waves; Kismet. 1947: Brute Force. 1948: Casbah; Criss Cross. 1951: Hotel Sahara; Silver City. 1952: The San Francisco Story. 1953: Sea Devils; Cruisin' Down the River. 1954: Passion. 1955: Magic Fire. 1956: The Ten Commandments. 1957: Band of Angels. 1958: Timbuktu. 1963: McLintock! 1964: A Global Affair. 1968: The Power. 1970: The Delta Factor.

DECOIN, Henri

Director. Paris 1896–1969 Paris
Pilot in World War I. Sports journalist for L'Auto, L'Intransigeant, Paris Soir. 1926: wrote novel 'Quinze Rounds'. From 1929: scriptwriter. 1932: writer and assistant director on *Un Soir de rafle.* 1934: scripted *L'Or dans la rue* and co-scripted *Poliche.* 1933: first film as director. Playwright, e.g. 'Hector', 'Jeux

Dangereux', 'Le Téméraire', 'Normandie'. First two wives, actresses Blanche Montel (1917–34) and Danielle Darrieux (1935–41).

Films as director: 1933: Je vous aimerai toujours. 1935: Toboggan (+ *s/di*); Le Domino Vert. 1936: Les Bleus du ciel. 1937: Mademoiselle ma mère; Abus de confiance (+ *ad*). 1938: Retour à l'aube (+ *ad*). 1939: Battements de coeur. 1941: Premier Rendez-vous. 1942: Les Inconnus dans la maison – Strangers in the House; Mariage d'amour (+ *co-ad/co-di*); Le Bienfaiteur (+ *ad*). 1943: L'Homme de Londres (+ *ad*); Je suis avec toi. 1946: La Fille du diable (+ *ad*). 1947: Non coupable (+ *ad*); Les Amants du pont Saint-Jean; Les Amoureux sont seuls au monde. 1948: Entre onze heures et minuit (+ *co-ad*). 1949: Au grand balcon. 1950: Trois Télégrammes – Three Telegrams – Paris Incident (+ *co-ad/di*). 1951: Clara de Montargis (+ *s/ad/di*); Le Désir et l'amour (+ *di*); La Verité sur le Bébé Donge – Truth about our Marriage. 1952: Les Amants de Tolède. 1953: Dortoir des Grandes – Girls' Dormitory (+ *co-ad*). 1954: Bonnes à tuer (+ *co-ad/co-di*); Razzia sur la chnouf – Chnouf (+ *co-ad*); Les Intrigantes; Le Billet de logement *ep* Secrets d'alcóve – The Bed (+ *co-s/co-ad/co-di*). 1955: L'Affaire des poissons (+ *co-ad*). 1956: Folies Bergères; Le Feu aux poudres (+ *ad*). 1957: Tous peuvent me tuer – Anyone Can Kill Me (+ *co-s*); Charmants Garçons. 1958: La Chatte – The Face of the Cat (+ *co-s*). 1959: Pourquoi viens-tu si tard? (+ *co-s*); Nathalie, agent secrèt. 1960: La Chatte sort ses griffes – The Cat shows her claws (+ *co-ad*); Tendre et Violente Elisabeth – Passionate Affair (+ *co-ad*); La Française et l'amour – Love and the Frenchwoman *ep* L'Enfance; Le Pavé de Paris (+ *co-ad*). 1961: Maléfices – Where the Truth Lies (+ *co-s*). 1962: Le Masque de fer. 1963: Parias de la gloire; Casablanca, nid d'espions. 1964: Nick Carter va tout casser.

DE FILIPPO, Eduardo

(Eduardo Passarelli) Director. Naples, Italy 1900–
Theatrical family. With brother Peppino de Filippo, joined Eduardo Scarpetta's theatre company, as actor. 1930: began to write sketches and 1-act plays. 1932: formed theatre company with Peppino and sister, Titina de Filippo, performing in Neapolitan dialect, until separation after World War II. Then ran own theatre in Naples to revive local masque tradition, e.g. in plays by Scarpetta. 1940: first film as director, *In campagna è caduta una stella,* in which he also acted. Acted in films from 1952, e.g. in *Le Ragazze di piazza di spagna* (1952), *Traviata '53* (1953), *L'Oro di Napoli* (1954). Writer in collaboration on Vittorio de Sica's *Ieri, oggi, domani* (1963) and *Matrimonio all'Italiana* (1964), from own play 'Filumena Marturano' (which he filmed, 1951). 1971: revived 'Questi Fantasmi' in Rome.

Films as director: 1940: In campagna è caduta una stella (+ *st/co-s/w*). 1943: Ti conosco, Mascherina! (+ *st/s/w*). 1950: Napoli milionaria (+ *co-p/co-s/fpl/w*). 1951: Filumena Marturano (+ *co-s/fpl/w*); Les Sept Péchés Capitaux – I Sette Peccati Capitali – The Seven Deadly Sins *ep* L'Avarice et la colère (+ *co-s/w*). 1952: Marito e moglie – Husband and Wife (+ *co-s/fpl/w*); Ragazze da marito (+ *co-s/w*). 1953: Napoletani a Milano (+ *co-s/w*). 1954: Questi Fantasmi (+ *co-s/fpl*). 1958: Fortunella (+ *w*). 1959: Il Sogno di una notte di mezza sbornia (+ *w*).

DE FOREST, Dr Lee

Inventor. Council Bluffs, Iowa 1873–1961 Hollywood
To 1899: Yale. 1906: invented audion, an amplifying
valve which could be used as generator, amplifier and
detector of radio waves. 1919–24: worked on Phonofilm, an experiment in synchronised sound: modulation
of sound waves to electrical fluctuations, used to
fluctuate intensity of light source photographed on edge
of film. 1923: first demonstration of Phonofilm at Rivoli
Theatre, New York. Not taken up by the industry.

DE FUNÈS, Louis

Actor. Courbevoie, France 1914–
Secondary education, then window-dresser at Prisunic
until World War II. 2 months studying acting under
René Simon. Sundry jobs, then stage actor; small parts
for 10 years before success in 'Oscar'. In films from
1945.

Films as actor include: 1947: Antoine et Antoinette.
1952: La Vie d'un honnête homme. 1954: Le Blé en
herbe; Le Mouton à cinq pattes. 1956: Courte-tête; La
Traversée de Paris. 1960: Candide. 1962: Les Veinards
ep La Vedette. 1963: Le Diable et les dix commandements. 1967: Oscar. 1968: Le Tatoué. 1969: Hibernatus.

DE GIVRAY, Claude

Director. Nice, France 1933–
1939: moved to Paris. Studied at the Sorbonne. Wrote
for Cahiers du Cinéma and Arts. Assistant on e.g. *Les
Mistons* (1957) and *Le Beau Serge* (1958). 1958–60:
military service. 1961: first film as director. Collaborated on script of Pierre Kast's *Le Grain de sable*
(1965). 1965: directed for TV *Le Système de law* and
Sacha Guitry. 1970: co-wrote *Domicile Conjugal* with
François Truffaut.

Films as director: 1961: Tire-au-flanc 62 (+ *co-st*).
1962: Une Grosse Tête (+ *co-s*). 1963: Un Mari à prix
fixe. 1964: L'Amour à la chaine (+ *co-st*).

DE GRUNWALD, Anatole

Producer and writer. St Petersburg. Russia 1910–1967
London
Son of Tsarist diplomat; emigrated to UK during
Russian Revolution. Caius College, Cambridge, and
Sorbonne. Journalist. Assistant to Anthony Asquith.
1939–41: scriptwriter, e.g. for Asquith and Leslie
Howard. From 1943: producer and writer, e.g. for
Asquith; worked for Two Cities, becoming director of
company. 1946: formed own production company.
1949: first film as producer only, Thorold Dickinson's
The Queen of Spades; continued also to write until
1959. From 1959: producer for MGM, including 3
Asquith films. Playwright; 'Gentlemen's Relish' and
'Bridge of Sighs' produced in West End. Younger
brother, producer Dimitri de Grunwald, worked with
him in 1950s.

Films as writer: 1939: French Without Tears (*co*).
1940: Freedom Radio (*co*); Quiet Wedding (*co*). 1941:
Cottage to Let (*co*); Pimpernel Smith. 1942: The First
of the Few.

Films as producer and writer: 1943: The Demi-
Paradise. 1945: The Way to the Stars (*co-s*). 1947:

While the Sun Shines (*co-s*). 1948: The Winslow Boy
(*co-s*). 1951: Home at Seven. 1959: The Doctor's
Dilemma; Libel (*co-s*).

Films as producer: 1949: Queen of Spades; The Last
Days of Dolwyn. 1963: Come Fly With Me; The
V.I.P.'s. 1964: The Yellow Rolls-Royce.

DE HAVILLAND, Olivia

Actress. Tokyo 1916–
English parents. Younger sister is Joan Fontaine. Convent education, and tutored by mother, former actress
Lillian Ruse. Lived in USA from age of 3. Stage debut
with Saratoga Community Players (1933). Turned down
scholarship to play Hermia in Max Reinhardt's Hollywood Bowl production of 'A Midsummer Night's Dream'
(1934); screen debut in film version (1935). 1935–42:
contract with Warners. 1943: contested Warners' right to
hold her to extra contract time, equal to length of previous
suspension by studio; carried case through courts at own
expense for 2 year period during which no work with
other studios; won decision which acted as legal pre-
cedent. 1949–53: touring USA as stage actress. Author
of 2 books on experiences with the French (second
husband French). Oscars as Best Actress for *To Each His
Own* (1946). *The Heiress* (1949).

Films as actress: 1935: A Midsummer Night's Dream;
Alibi Ike; The Irish in Us; Captain Blood. 1936:
Anthony Adverse; The Charge of the Light Brigade.
1937: Call It a Day; The Great Garrick; It's Love I'm
After. 1938: Gold is Where You Find It; Hard to Get;
The Adventures of Robin Hood; Four's a Crowd.
1939: Wings of the Navy; Dodge City; The Private
Lives of Elizabeth and Essex; Gone With the Wind.
1940: Raffles; My Love Came Back; Santa Fe Trail.
1941: The Strawberry Blonde; Hold Back the Dawn;
They Died With Their Boots On. 1942: The Male
Animal; In This Our Life. 1943: Princess O'Rourke;
Government Girl; Thank Your Lucky Stars. 1946:
Devotion; The Well Groomed Bride; To Each His
Own; The Dark Mirror. 1948: The Snake Pit. 1949:
The Heiress. 1952: My Cousin Rachel. 1955: That
Lady; Not as a Stranger. 1956: The Ambassador's
Daughter. 1958: The Proud Rebel. 1959: Libel. 1962:
Light in the Piazza. 1964: Hush, Hush, Sweet
Charlotte; Lady in a Cage. 1969: The Adventurers.

DELANNOY, Jean

Director. Noisy-le-Sec, France 1908–
Lille University. 1927: entered films as actor.
1930–35: film editor. 1933: first short film as director.
1936–38: assistant director to Jacques Deval and Félix
Gandéra; directed first feature. *Ne tirez pas Dolly!*
(1937).

Films as director: 1933: Franche Lippée. 1934: Une
Vocation Irrésistible. 1935: Paris-Deauville. 1937: Ne
tirez pas Dolly! 1938: La Vénus de l'or (+ *co-s*). 1939:
Macao, l'enfer du jeu. 1940: Le Diamant Noir. 1941:
Fièvres. 1942: L'Assassin a peur de la nuit; Pontcarral,
Colonel d'Empire. 1943: L'Éternel Retour. 1944: Le
Bossu. 1945: Le Part de l'ombre. 1946: La Symphonie
Pastorale. 1947: Les Jeux sont faits (+ *co-s*). 1948:
Aux yeux du souvenir (+ *co-s*). 1949: Le Secret de
Mayerling (+ *co-s*). 1950: Dieu a besoin des hommes.
1951: Le Garçon Sauvage. 1952: La Minute de vérité.
1953: Destinées – Love, Soldiers and Women *ep*

Yvonne De Carlo in Raoul Walsh's Band of Angels.
Anna Magnani (left) *in Renato Castellani's* Nella
Città L'Inferno.
Barabbas, *directed by Richard Fleischer and produced
by Dino De Laurentiis.*

Jeanne; La Route Napoléon. 1954: Obsession (+ *co-s*); Secrets d'alcôve – Il Letto – The Bed *ep* Le Lit de La Pompadour. 1955: Chiens Perdus sans collier (+ *co-s*). 1956: Marie-Antoinette – Shadow of the Guillotine. 1957: Notre-Dame de Paris – The Hunchback of Notre Dame. 1958: Maigret tend un piège – Maigret Sets a Trap (+ *co-s*); Guinguette (+ *co-s*). 1959: Maigret et l'affaire Saint-Fiacre (+ *co-s*); Le Baron de l'Écluse (+ *co-s*). 1960: La Française et l'amour – Love and the Frenchwoman *ep* L'Adolescence; La Princesse de Clèves. 1961: Le Rendez-vous (+ *co-s*). 1962: Vénus Impériale. 1964: Les Amitiés Particulières – This Special Friendship. 1965: Le Majordôme; Le Lit à deux places – The Double Bed (+ *co-d François Dupont-Midy, Gianni Puccini*). 1966: Les Sultans (+ *co-s*). 1967: Le Soleil des Voyous – Action Man. 1970: La Peau de torpédo (+ *co-s*).

DE LA PATELLIÈRE, Denys

Director. Nantes, France 1921–
Nephew of painter, A. de la Patellière. University, then École de St-Cyr military academy. World War II: in French Army. 1945–47: worked in film laboratory. 1947–49: editor on Actualités Françaises newsreel. Directed some shorts. Assistant director to Maurice Labro, Georges Lacombe, Richard Pottier, Léo Joannon, Georges Lampin. 1953: assistant director and co-scriptwriter on Joannon's *Le Défroqué*. 1955: directed first feature. 1964: finished *La Fabuleuse Aventure de Marco Polo*, begun in 1962 by Christian-Jacque. Work on commercials.

Features as director: 1955: Les Aristocrates (+ *co-s*). 1956: Le Salaire du péché (+ *co-s*). 1957: Les Oeufs de l'autruche – The Ostrich Has Two Legs; Retour de manivelle – There's Always a Price Tag (+ *s*); Thérèse Etienne (+ *co-s*). 1959: Les Grandes Familles (+ *co-ad*); Rue des prairies (+ *co-s*). 1960: Les Yeux de l'amour (+ *co-s*). 1961: Un taxi pour Tobrouk – Taxi to Tobruk (+ *co-s*). 1962: Le Bateau d'Emile; Pourquoi Paris (+ *co-s*). 1963: Tempo di Roma. 1964: La Fabuleuse Aventure de Marco Polo – L'Echiquier de Dieu – The Fabulous Adventures of Marco Polo (+ *co-s/co-ad*; *co-d Denys de la Patellière, Noel Howard*). 1965: Le Tonnerre de Dieu – God's Thunder (+ *co-s*). 1966: Du Rififi à Paname – Rififi in Paris – The Upper Hand; Le Voyage du père; Soleil Noir – Black Sun – Dark Sunlight. 1967: Caroline Chérie. 1968: Le Tatoué. 1970: Sabra.

DE LAURENTIIS, Dino

Producer. Torre Annunziata, Italy 1919–
At 15 began travelling for father's spaghetti business. 1937: studied at Centro Sperimentale di Cinematografia, working as film extra to support himself. Worked as actor, handyman, property man, cashier, assistant director, unit production manager. 1940: began as producer in Turin. 1941: founded Real Cine, Turin. 1942: executive producer of Lux Film. 1949: married Silvana Mangano. 1950–54: associated with Carlo Ponti in production company Ponti-De Laurentiis. 1971: sold Dinocittà studios to Italian government. Business interests include electronic hardware. Oscars for 'foreign language films' *La Strada* (1956) and *Le Notti di Cabiria* (1957)..

Films as producer (i.e. head of production company) include: 1949: Riso Amaro. 1950: Il Brigante Musolino (*co*). 1951: Anna (*co*). 1952: Europa '51 (*co*). 1953: Dov è la libertà? (*co*); La Lupa (*co*). 1954: Mambo (*co*); La Strada (*co*); La Romana (*co*); L'Oro di Napoli (*co*). 1955: Ulisse (*co*); La Bella Mugnaia (*co*); La Donna del fiume (*co*). 1956: War and Peace (*co*). 1957: Le Notti di Cabiria. 1958: La Diga sul Pacifico; La Tempestà. 1960: Jovanka e l'altri; La Grande Guerra. 1962: I Due Nemici; Barabbas. 1966: La Bibbia. 1967: Lo Straniero. 1968: Barbarella. 1969: A Brief Season; Bandits in Sicily. 1970: Waterloo; The Valachi Papers. 1971: La Spina Dorsale del diavolo (*co*).

DELERUE, Georges

Composer. Roubaix, France 1925–
Conservatoire: pupil of Darius Milhaud. Music for theatre, first for Jean Vilar's Théâtre National Populaire, for Jean-Louis Barrault and Comédie Française. Composed ballet based on Alexandre Dumas' 'Les Trois Mousquetaires'. Conductor of symphonic programmes on French radio and TV. Composed music for commercials; conducted film scores composed by others e.g. for Alain Resnais shorts and some features. From 1953: composer for shorts. 1959: composed waltz tune only for *Hiroshima mon Amour*. From 1960: very prolific: up to 14 film scores a year. By end of 1970 had written 90 film scores, 80 TV scores. Music for 'Son et Lumière' at Hôtel des Invalides.

Films as composer include: 1957: Les Marines. 1958: La Première Nuit; L'Opéra-Mouffe. 1960: Le Bel Age (*co*); Merci, Natercia; Le Farceur. 1961: La Morte-Saison des amours; L'Amant de cinq jours; Une Aussi Longue Absence; Jules et Jim. 1962: Cartouche; Rififi à Tokyo; L'Immortelle (*co*). 1963: Vacances Portugaises; L'Aîné des Ferchaux; Nunca pasa nada; French Dressing. 1964: The Pumpkin Eater; La Peau Douce. 1966: A Man for All Seasons; Le Roi de coeur. 1967: Our Mother's House. 1968: Le Diable par la queue. 1969: A Walk with Love and Death. 1970: Il Conformista; Heureux qui comme Ulysse...; La Promesse de l'aube. 1971: Mira; Les Deux Anglaises et le Continent; The Horsemen.

DEL GIUDICE, Filippo

Producer. Trani, Italy 1892–
Lawyer in Italy. 1933: to UK. 1939–40: interned in Isle of Man. Joined Two Cities as legal advisor. From 1939: worked in production on films directed by Anthony Asquith, David Lean, Carol Reed, Laurence Olivier. From 1946: 'in charge of production' on several films; became managing director of Two Cities. 1948–49: administration for Pilgrim Pictures on *The Guinea Pig* (1948) and *Private Angelo* (1949). 1958: retired to monastery.

Films as producer in collaboration include: 1946: School for Secrets; Men of Two Worlds. 1947: Odd Man Out; Vice Versa; Fame is the Spur. 1948: Hamlet.

DELLUC, Louis

Director and critic. Cadouin, France 1890–1924 Paris
Journalist and playwright. 1917–19: with Henri Diamant-Berger ran magazine Le Film. 1918–23: film critic for Paris-Midi under title Cinéma at Cie. 1919: wrote Germaine Dulac's *La Fête Espagnole*. 1920: founded Journal du Ciné-Club; first film as director, in collaboration. Wrote all own films. Central figure in French avant-garde cinema. Posthumous story for Alberto Cavalcanti's *Le Train sans yeux* (1926). Books of film criticism include: 'Cinéma et Cie' (1919), 'Photogénie' (1920), 'Charlot' (1921), 'Drames de Cinéma' (1923). 1921: founded magazine, Cinéa; ran it until ended by financial problems (1923). Pioneer of film society movement. Died of tuberculosis.

Films as director and writer: 1920: Fumée Noire (*co-d René Coiffart*); L'Américain ou le chemin d'Ernoa; Le Silence. 1921: Le Tonnerre – Evangeline et le Tonnerre; Fièvre. 1922: La Femme de nulle part. 1924: L'Inondation.

DELON, Alain

Actor. Sceaux, France 1935–
At 17 served in French Army in Indo-China. 1957: first film as actor Yves Allégret's *Quand la femme s'en mêle*. 1961: in Luchino Visconti's Paris production of 'Tis Pity She's a Whore'. From 1964, involved in own production companies. Produced *Borsalino* (1970).

Films as actor include: 1958: Sois belle et tais-toi. 1959: Plein Soleil. 1960: Rocco e i suoi fratelli. 1961: Che gioia vivere. 1962: L'Eclisse; Mélodie en sous-sol. 1963: Il Gattopardo. 1964: Les Félins; L'Insoumis; The Yellow Rolls-Royce. 1965: Once a Thief. 1966: Lost Command; Paris brûle-t-il?; Texas Across the River. 1967: Les Aventuriers; Histoires Extra-ordinaires *ep* William Wilson; Le Samouraï; Dia-boliquement Vôtre. 1968: La Piscine. 1969: Le Clan des Siciliens. 1970: Borsalino (+ *p*); Madly (+ *p*); Le Cercle Rouge; Doucement les basses! 1971: Soleil Rouge.

DEL RIO, Dolores

(Lolita Dolores Asunsolo de Martinez) Actress. Durango, Mexico 1905–
Father bank president of Spanish-Basque extraction, mother descended from the Toltecs. At 4 fled with family from Pancho Villa. Convent in Mexico City; married at 15. To Hollywood. 1925: first film as actress *Joanna*. On move to United Artists, sued; settled out of court. 1930: married Cedric Gibbons. Broke contract because of illness. Moved to RKO, who bought *The Dove* and re-titled it *The Girl of the Rio* (1932). Moved to Warners; made *Accused* (1936) in UK. Began to study stage acting. 1941: divorced Gibbons. Returned to Mexico, acted in Mexican and (from 1944) Spanish films. 1943: MGM released *Maria Candelaria* as *Portrait of Maria*. 1947: first American film since return to Mexico *The Fugitive*, mainly made in Mexico. 1948: in Argentina made *Historia de una mala mujer* based on 'Lady Windermere's Fan'. Offered role in *Broken Lance* (1954) but visa delayed on grounds of Communist sympathies and granted too late; replaced by Katy Jurado. 1959: married stage producer Lewis A. Riley, Jr; first starred for him in 'The Road to Rome' in Buenos Aires. Much stage work in Latin America, including 'Ghosts', 'The Little Foxes', 'Dear Liar'. Acted in summer stock in USA, 'Anastasia'. 1960: returned to Hollywood to make *Flaming Star*. TV work includes 'I Spy' series, 'The Public Prosecutor' for US Steel Hour, 'Hotel Paradiso' for CBS and (with Cesar Romero) 'The Actress and the Bullfighter'.

Films as actress include: 1926: What Price Glory? 1927: Loves of Carmen. 1928: The Red Dance. 1929: The Trail of '98. 1932: The Girl of the Rio; Bird of Paradise. 1934: Wonder Bar; Madame Du Barry. 1935: In Caliente; I Live for Love. 1937: The Lancer Spy. 1943: Journey into Fear; Flor Silvestre; Maria Candelaria. 1947: The Fugitive. 1948: Historia di una mala mujer. 1949: La Malquerida. 1960: Flaming Star. 1964: Cheyenne Autumn. 1967: C'era una Volta.

DEL RUTH, Roy

Director. Philadelphia, Pennsylvania 1895–1961 Los Angeles
Brother of writer and gagman, Hampton del Ruth. Lived in London. Returned to Philadelphia; reporter on Philadelphia North American and Philadelphia Enquirer. 1916: joined Mack Sennett as scenarist; first film as writer *She Loved a Sailor*. 1917: began directing 2-reelers, including films with Billy Bevan, Ben Turpin, Harry Langdon. 1925: first feature film as director. 1955–61: directed for TV, including 'Warner Brothers Hour', '4 Star Theatre', 'Adventure in Paradise'.

Features as director: 1925: Eve's Lover; Hogan's Alley. 1926: Three Weeks in Paris; The Man Upstairs; The Little Irish Girl; Footloose Windows; Across the Pacific. 1927: Wolf's Clothing; The First Auto; If I Were Single; Ham and Eggs at the Front – Ham and Eggs. 1928: Five and Ten Cent Annie; Powder My Back; The Terror; Beware of Bachelors. 1929: Conquest; Desert Song; The Hottentot; Gold Diggers of Broadway; The Aviator. 1930: Hold Everything; Second Floor Mystery; Three Faces East; Divorce Among Friends; The Life of the Party. 1931: My Past; The Maltese Falcon; Blonde Crazy – Larceny Lane; Side Show. 1932: Taxi; Beauty and the Boss; Winner Take All; Blessed Event. 1933: Employees' Entrance; The Mind Reader; The Little Giant; Bureau of Missing Persons; Captured!; Lady Killer. 1934: Bulldog Drummond Strikes Back; Upperworld; Kid Millions. 1935: Folies Bergere – Folies Bergere; Broadway Melody of 1936; Thanks a Million. 1936: It Had to Happen; Private Number; Born to Dance. 1937: On the Avenue; Broadway Melody of 1938. 1938: Happy Landing; My Lucky Star. 1939: Tail Spin; The Star Maker; Here I am a Stranger. 1940: He Married His Wife. 1941: Topper Returns; The Chocolate Soldier. 1942: Maisie Gets Her Man. 1943: Du Barry Was a Lady. 1944: Broadway Rhythm; Barbary Coast Gent. 1947: It Happened on Fifth Avenue (+ p). 1948: The Babe Ruth Story (+ p). 1949: Red Light (+ p); Always Leave Them Laughing. 1950: The West Point Story. 1951: On Moonlight Bay; Starlift. 1952: About Face; Stop. You're Killing Me. 1953: Three Sailors and a Girl. 1954: Phantom of the Rue Morgue. 1959: The Alligator People. 1960: Why Must I Die?

DELVAUX, André

Director. Louvain, Belgium 1926–
Studied music. Taught Dutch literature, German philosophy. Played piano accompaniment to silent films at Belgian Cinemathèque. Made TV films on Jean Rouch, Federico Fellini, Polish directors. Then studied at film school. 1966: first feature as director co-produced by Flemish TV and Ministry of Education.

Features as director: 1966: De Man de zijn haar kort liet knippen – The Man Who Had His Hair Cut Short (+ co-s). 1969: Un Soir, un train (+ ad/di/co-song). 1971: Rendezvous à Bray (+ s).

DE MILLE, Cecil B.

Director. Ashfield, Massachusetts 1881–1959 Hollywood
Father actor and playwright Henry Churchill De Mille. Mother an actress. Moved to New Jersey. Father became preacher, mother ran girls' school. To 1898: Pennsylvania Military College. Ran away to join Spanish-American war, rejected as under age. Academy of Dramatic Arts, New York. 1900: stage debut in 'Hearts are Trumps', then toured. 1902: married actress Constance Adams, toured together. 1906–13: wrote several plays in collaboration with brother William De Mille. Worked in opera as director and singer, director of orchestra. 1907–11: writing collaboration with David Belasco. In collaboration with Jesse L. Lasky wrote several operettas. Mother became theatrical agent: worked as her office administrator at Astor Theatre; company sold. 1913: with Jesse Lasky, Samuel Goldfish and Arthur Freed founded Lasky Feature Play Company; first film as director, in collaboration *The Squaw Man* (1914); began to release through Paramount. Also worked as writer and supervising director on films of others. 1914–15: filmed several of David Belasco's plays; wrote almost all own scripts; collaborated with brother on script of *The Wild Goose Chase* (1915); several scripts by brother. 1917: mother co-wrote story of *The Devil Stone*; his first use of colour (mechanical tinting; De Mille–Wyckoff process) for *Joan the Woman*. To 1930: many scripts by Jeanie MacPherson, sometimes in collaboration with him. World War I: captain of Home Guard in Hollywood. 1919: founded first commercial air service in America. 1919–21: 6 films with Gloria Swanson. 1920: own production company. 1922: bank president. 1925: from Thomas Ince's widow bought Producers' Distributing Corporation, amalgamated with own company as Cinema Corporation of America; acquired cinemas. 1927: MGM contract. From 1929: produced most of own films. 1931: with Frank Borzage, Lewis Milestone and King Vidor formed Director's Guild. 1932: Paramount contract. 1936: started Lux Radio Theatre, adaptations of films, usually using different stars. 1937: chosen as senatorial candidate by Los Angeles convention of Republican party: declined the offer. 1940: produced, narrated and edited documentary *Land of Liberty*. 1945: forced to give up radio work when refused to subscribe to campaign to prevent California citizens working unless they were union members; because of this, never allowed to work in TV. Publicly denounced unions; founded De Mille Corporation for Political Liberty. 1946: worked during Paramount strike. Cameo acting appearances in about 20 Paramount films. Filmed many special prologues and trailers in which he appeared. Died of heart attack.

Films as director and writer: 1914: The Squaw Man (co-d Oscar Apfel); The Call of the North; The Rose of the Rancho. 1915: The Arab; The Girl of the Golden West; The Unafraid; The Captive (co-s); The Wild Goose Chase (co-s); Chimmie Fadden; Kindling; Temptation; Chimmie Fadden Out West (co-s). 1916: The Trail of the Lonesome Pine. 1917: A Romance of the Redwoods (co-s). 1927: The King of Kings (co-s).

Jean Gabin and Alain Delon in Le Clan des Siciliens. *directed by Henri Verneuil.*
Cecil B. De Mille directing The Call of the North.
Catherine Deneuve in Jacques Demy's Les Parapluies de Cherbourg.

67

Films as director: 1914: The Virginian; What's His Name. 1915: The Warrens of Virginia; The Arab; Maria Rosa; Carmen; The Cheat. 1916: The Golden Chance; The Dream Girl; The Heart of Nora Flynn. 1917: The Little American; The Woman God Forgot; The Devil Stone. 1918: The Whispering Chorus; Old Wives for New; We Can't Have Everything; Till I Come Back to You; The Squaw Man (*rm 1914*); Don't Change Your Husband. 1919: For Better for Worse; Male and Female. 1920: Why Change Your Wife; Something to Think About. 1921: Forbidden Fruit; The Affairs of Anatol. 1922: Fool's Paradise; Saturday Night; Manslaughter. 1923: Adam's Rib; The Ten Commandments. 1924: Feet of Clay. 1925: The Golden Bed; The Road to Yesterday. 1926: The Volga Boatman. 1928: The Godless Girl. 1934: Four Frightened People. 1935: The Crusades.

Films as director and producer: 1914: The Man from Home (+ *s*). 1917: Joan the Woman. 1924: Triumph. 1929: Dynamite. 1930: Madam Satan. 1931: The Squaw Man (*rm 1914*). 1932: The Sign of the Cross. 1933: This Day and Age. 1934: Cleopatra. 1937: The Plainsman. 1938: The Buccaneer. 1939: Union Pacific. 1940: Northwest Mounted Police. 1942: Reap the Wild Wind. 1944: The Story of Dr Wassell. 1947: Unconquered. 1949: Samson and Delilah. 1952: The Greatest Show on Earth (+ *cy*). 1956: The Ten Commandments.

DEMY, Jacques

Director. Pont-Château, France 1931–
Collège Technique and École des Beaux Arts, Nantes, École Nationale Photographie et Cinématographie. Assistant to, e.g. Pierre Grimault and Georges Rouquier. From 1955: made shorts, 2 in collaboration with J. Masson. 1960: first feature as director, *Lola*. 1962: married Agnès Varda. 1969: *Model Shop* made in USA. Michel Legrand wrote music for French features.

Films as director: 1955: Le Sabotier du Val-de-Loire (+ *cy*). 1957: Le Bel Indifférent. 1958: Musée Grévin (*co-d J. Masson*). 1959: La Mère et l'enfant (*co-d J. Masson*); Ars (+ *s/cy*). 1961: Lola (+ *s*); Les Sept Péchés Capitaux *ep* La Luxure (+ *s*). 1962: La Baie des anges (+ *s*). 1964: Les Parapluies de Cherbourg (+ *s*). 1967: Les Demoiselles de Rochefort (+ *s*). 1969: Model Shop (+ *p/s/co-di*). 1970: Peau d'âne (+ *s*).

DENEUVE, Cathérine

Actress. Paris 1943–
Daughter of actor Maurice Dorléac, and younger sister of actress Françoise Dorléac. 1960: offered first film part in *Les Portes claquent*, while still at school. 1962: directed by Roger Vadim (by whom later had child) in *Le Vice et la vertu*. 1965: married photographer David Bailey. 1966: appeared with sister in *Les Demoiselles de Rochefort*. Sister killed in car accident while on vacation with her.

Films as actress include: 1961: Les Parisiennes *ep* Sophie. 1963: Les Vacances Portugaises. 1964: Les Parapluies de Cherbourg; La Chasse à l'homme; Un Monsieur de compagnie. 1965: Repulsion; Le Chant du monde; La Vie de château. 1966: Les Créatures. 1967: Belle de jour; Benjamin. 1968: Manon 70; La Chamade. 1969: Mayerling; The April Fools; La Sirène du Mississippi. 1970: Tristana; Peau d'âne.

DERAY, Jacques

Director. Lyon, France 1929–
Studied drama under René Simon. Small parts as actor in films and plays. From 1952: assistant director to, e.g. Henri Verneuil, Norbert Carbonnaux, Luis Buñuel, Jules Dassin, Marcel Camus, and most frequently Gilles Grangier. 1960: first film as director.

Films as director: 1960: Le Gigolo (+ *co-s*). 1962: Rififi à Tokyo – Rififi in Tokyo. 1963: Symphonie pour un massacre – The Corrupt (+ *co-st/co-s*). 1964: Par un beau matin d'été (+ *co-st*). 1965: L'Homme de Marrakech – Gold Fever (+ *co-s*); Les Pillards – La Route aux diamants – That Man George! 1966: Avec la Peau des autres. 1968: La Piscine – The Sinner. 1970: Borsalino (+ *co-s*). 1971: Doucement les basses! (+ *co-di*); Un Peu de soleil dans l'eau froide.

DEREK, John

(Derek Harris) Director and actor. Hollywood 1926–
Son of director, writer and producer Lawson Harris, mother an actress. Parents divorced when he was 5. Spotted by Fox talent scout; under contract for a year without making films, then drafted into US Army. Service in Philippines and Japan. Returned to Hollywood: Columbia contract. 1948: married actress Pati Behrs. 1949: first film as actor *Knock on any Door*. To 1954: most films for Columbia, several for Republic. From 1954: mainly Fox and Paramount. 1957–66: married to Ursula Andress. 1967: acted with her in own first film as director *Once Before I Die*; also produced it. TV work as actor includes series 'Frontier Circus'.

Films as actor include: 1949: Knock on any Door. 1950: All the King's Men; Rogues of Sherwood Forest. 1951: Saturday's Hero; Mask of the Avenger. 1952: Scandal Sheet. 1954: The Adventures of Hajji Baba. 1955: Prince of Players; Run for Cover; Annapolis Story. 1956: The Ten Commandments. 1957: Omar Khayyam. 1960: Exodus.

DEREN, Maya

Director. Russia 1908–1961 New York
Father psychiatrist, emigrated to USA in 1927. Educated in Switzerland, New York University, Smith College. Dancer, and secretary to Katherine Dunham Dancers. Recorded Haitian music, wrote book 'The Divine Horseman: the Living God of Haiti'. 1943: first film as director, in collaboration with husband Alexander Hammid (Hackenschmied) *Meshes of the Afternoon*. Unable to obtain sufficient distribution, hired Provincetown Playhouse, Greenwich Village for showings. Established Creative Film Foundation to provide cash awards: supported e.g. Stan Brakhage, Robert Breer, Stan Vanderbeek. Book: 'An Anagram of Ideas on Art, Form and Film' (1946).

Films as director: 1943: Meshes of the Afternoon (+ *w*; *co-d Alexander Hammid*). 1944: The Witch's Cradle (*uf*); At Land (+ *w*). 1945: Choreography for Camera; Pas de deux. 1946: Ritual in Transfigured Time. 1948: Meditation on Violence. 1959: Very Eye of Night.

DE ROBERTIS, Francesco

Director. San Marco in Lamis, Italy 1903–1959 Rome
Naval Academy, then naval career. Amateur play-wright from 1932. 1940: first film, a naval documentary. Head of Italian Navy Cinematography Section. 1941: directed *Uomini sul fondo*, shot entirely aboard a submarine. Commissioned, supervised and co-wrote Roberto Rossellini's *La Nave Bianca*, which started as documentary about hospital ship and became feature. From 1945: wrote and directed commercial features; also scripted 2 features.

Films as director and writer: 1940: Mine in vista. 1941: Uomini sul fondo – SOS Submarine (+ *p/co-m*). 1942: Alfa Tau. 1943: Marina senza stella; Uomini e cieli (+ *m*). 1945: La Vite Semplice. 1947: La Voce di Paganini (+ *co-s*). 1948: Fantasmi del mare (*d only*). 1949: Il Murato. 1950: Gli Amanti di Ravello. 1952: Carica Eroica – Heroic Charge. 1954: Mizar – Frogman Spy. 1955: Uomini-ombra. 1956: La Donna che venne dal mare (+ *st/co-s*). 1958: Ragazzi della marina (*d only*).

DE ROCHEMONT, Louis

Producer. Chelsea, Massachusetts 1899–
1917–23: officer in US Navy. 1923–27: associate editor of William Randolph Hearst's International Newsreel, released by Universal. 1927–28: European director of Pathe News. 1928–34: directed shorts for Movietone; also started 2 series of Movietone shorts (1934). 1933–34: 'March of the Years' series for Columbia. 1935–42: produced 'March of Time' series, backed by Time Magazine; series continued until 1949 (from 1946 in 16 mm 'Forum Edition'). 1943: became feature producer at Fox. 1948–52: produced documentary series, 'The Earth and Its Peoples'. Produced *Cinerama Holiday* (1955), second film in Cinerama 3-camera/projector process, and *Windjammer* (1958), only film in similar Cinemiracle process. Then independent producer.

Features as producer include: 1945: The House on 92nd Street. 1947: 13 Rue Madeleine; Boomerang! 1951: The Whistle at Eaton Falls. 1960: Man on a String. 1961: The Roman Spring of Mrs Stone.

DESAILLY, Jean

Actor. Paris 1920–
1942: left Paris Conservatoire with first prize for acting; first film part, in Louis Daquin's *Le Voyageur de la Toussaint*. 1942–46: acted at Comédie Française; then joined Jean-Louis Barrault–Madeleine Renaud company, also appearing in many films. Films as script collaborator include *Point de chute* (1970).

Films as actor include: 1945: Sylvie et le fantôme. 1946: La Symphonie Pastorale; La Revanche de Roger-la-honte. 1949: Occupe-toi d'Amélie; Le Point de Jour. 1954: Si Versailles m'était conté. 1955: Les Grandes Manoeuvres. 1958: Maigret tend un piège. 1961: Les Sept Péchés Capitaux *ep* La Luxure. 1962: Le Doulos. 1964: La Peau Douce. 1967: The 25th Hour.

DE SANTIS, Giuseppe

Director. Fondi, Italy 1917–
Abandoned university studies to become journalist. As film critic, wrote (1940–44) for magazine Cinema. Scriptwriter on *Ossessione* (1942), *Desiderio* (1946) and *Il Sole sorge ancora* (1947) before becoming director.

Films as director: 1947: Caccia Tragica – The Tragic Pursuit (+ *co-st/co-s*). 1949: Riso Amaro – Bitter Rice (+ *co-st/co-s*). 1950: Non c'è pace tra gli ulivi – Blood on Easter Sunday – No Peace Among the Olives (+ *co-st/co-s*). 1952: Roma ore undici (+ *co-s*). 1953: Un Marito per Anna Zaccheo – A Husband for Anna (+ *s*). 1954: Giorni d'amore (+ *co-s*). 1956: Uomini e lupi (+ *co-st*). 1957: Cesta duga godina dana – The Road a Year Long (+ *co-s*). 1964: Italiano, brava gente – Oni shli na Vostock – They Went to Vostok (+ *co-s*).

DE SETA, Vittorio

Director. Palermo, Sicily 1923–
Architecture at Rome University. 1954: co-writer, uncredited and assistant on Jean-Paul le Chanois' *Le Village Magique*, made in Sicily. 1954: first short film as director. 1957: in collaboration scripted Mario Camerini's *Vacanze a Ischia*, uncredited. 1961: first feature as director. Wife, actress Vera Gherarducchi, collaborated with him on scripts of first 2 features. 1969: made a feature in France. Also TV work.

Short films as director, cinematographer and editor: 1954: Lu Tempu di li pisci spata; Isole di fuoco. 1955: Sulfatara; Pasqua in Sicilia – Easter in Sicily; Contadini del mare – Bluefin Fury; Parabolo d'oro. 1957: Pescherecci – Fishermen. 1958: Pastori di Orgosolo; Un Giorno in barbagia. 1959: I Dimenticati.

Features as director: 1961: Banditi a Orgosolo (+ *p/cos/c*). 1966: Un Uomo a meta – Almost a Man (+ *p/st/co-s*). 1969: L'Invitata – L'Invitée.

DE SICA, Vittorio

Director and actor. Sora, Italy 1902–
Successful stage actor before starting to act regularly in films (1932); 3 earlier films in 1922, 1926 and 1928. 1935: met Cesare Zavattini, scenarist for *Daró un milione*. 1940: began directing and/or co-scripting some films as actor. 1942: *I Bambini ci guardano*, first film as director but not star, with Zavattini as co-scenarist, as on almost all later films as director. Acting career continued alongside directorial work. Films as director up to *Il Tetto* (1956) were mainly small scale neo-realist works. 1961: success of *La Ciociara* made him director of films for international market. TV work includes series on great lyric tenors.

Films as director: 1940: Rose Scarlatte (+ *w*); Maddalena zero in condotta (+ *co-s/w*). 1941: Teresa Venerdì (+ *co-s/w*); Un Garibaldino al convento (+ *co-ad/w*). 1942: I Bambini ci guardano – The Children Are Watching Us (+ *co-s*). 1946: La Porta del cielo (+ *co-ad*); Sciuscia – Shoeshine (+ *co-s*). 1948: Ladri di biciclette – Bicycle Thieves (+ *p/co-ad*). 1950: Miracolo a Milano – Miracle in Milan (+ *p/co-ad*). 1952: Stazione Termini – Indiscretion of an American Wife (+ *co-p*). 1953: Umberto D (+ *co-p/co-ad*). 1954: L'Oro di Napoli – Gold of Naples (+ *co-s/w*). 1956: Il Tetto – The Roof. 1961: La Ciociara – Two Women (+ *co-s*); Il Giudizio Universale (+ *w*). 1962: Boccaccio 70 *ep* La Riffa. 1963: I Sequestrati di Altona – The Condemned of Altona; Il Boom; Ieri, oggi, domani – Yesterday, Today and Tomorrow. 1964: Matrimonio all'Italiana – Marriage, Italian Style. 1965: Un Mondo Nuovo – Un Monde Nouveau. 1966: Caccia alla volpe – After the Fox; Le Streghe *ep* Una Sera come le altre. 1967: Sept fois femme – Woman Times 7. 1968: Gli Amanti – A Place for Lovers. 1970: I Girasoli – Sunflower; Il Giardino dei Finzi-contini. 1971: Le Coppie *ep* Il Leone.

Films as actor include: 1932: Gli Uomini . . . che mascalzoni! 1935: Darò un milione. 1936: Ma non è una cosa seria! 1937: Il Signor Max. 1939: Castelli in aria; I Grandi Magazzini. 1943: I Nostri Sogni (+ *cos*). 1944: Nessuno torna indietro. 1946: Roma Città Libera. 1947: Lo Sconosciuto di San Marino. 1952: Altri Tempi. 1953: Madame de . . .; Pane, amore e fantasia. 1954: Tempi nostri; Pane, amore e gelosia. 1955: Peccato che sia una canaglia; La Bella Mugnaia; Il Segno di Venere; Pane, amore e . . . 1956: Il Bigamo; La Donna che venne dal mare. 1957: Padri e figli; Souvenir d'Italie; Vacanze a Ischia; Amore e chiacchiere; Il Medico e lo stregone; A Farewell to Arms. 1958: Kanonenserenade; Les Noces Vénitiennes. 1959: La Prima Notte; Il Generale della Rovere. 1960: Austerlitz; Il Vigile; Le Pillole d'Ercole; The Millionairess; It Started in Naples. 1961: Vive Henri IV . . . vive l'amour! 1965: The Amorous Adventures of Moll Flanders. 1968: The Shoes of the Fisherman (*ur*); The Biggest Bundle of Them All.

DE TOTH, André

(Andreas Toth) Makò, Hungary 1910–
Educated in Budapest. 1928: first play produced in Hungary. Theatrical career interrupted by law studies at Hungarian Royal University. Films as actor, editor, writer and 2nd-unit director in Hungary and then Germany. 1938: first films as director, in Hungary. 1939: filmed German invasion of Poland; worked for Alexander Korda's London Films as 2nd-unit director on *The Thief of Bagdad* (1940). 1941: to Hollywood; worked as truck driver, cowboy, until hired by Korda as 2nd unit director on *Rudyard Kipling's Jungle Book* (1942). 1943: first American film as director, *Passport to Suez*, for Columbia. 1944–51: with various companies, mainly independents. Co-author of story for Henry King's *The Gunfighter* (1950). 1951: contract with Warners. In spite of having only one eye, directed *House of Wax* (1953), first feature in 3-D produced by a major studio. From 1959: worked in Europe, especially Italy. 1961–62: 2 films co-directed with Riccardo Freda. 1966: seriously injured in skiing accident. In semi-retirement until Harry Saltzman invited him to be executive producer on *Billion Dollar Brain* (1967). Replaced René Clément as director of *Play Dirty* (1968). Produced John Guillermin's *El Condor* (1970). First wife (1944–52) was Veronica Lake.

Films as director (since 1943): 1943: Passport to Suez. 1944: None Shall Escape; Dark Waters. 1947: Ramrod; The Other Love. 1948: Pitfall. 1949: Slattery's Hurricane. 1951: Man in the Saddle. 1952: Carson City; Springfield Rifle; Last of the Comanches – Sabre and the Arrow. 1953: House of Wax; The Stranger Wore a Gun; Thunder Over the Plains. 1954: Riding Shotgun; The City is Dark – Crime Wave; The Bounty Hunter; Tanganyika. 1955: The Indian Fighter. 1957: Monkey on My Back; Hidden Fear (+ *co-s*). 1959: The Two-Headed Spy; Day of the Outlaw. 1960: Man on a String – Confessions of a Counterspy; Morgan Il Pirata – Morgan the Pirate (+ *s*). 1961: I Mongoli – The Mongols (*co-d Riccardo Freda*). 1962: Oro per i Cesari – Gold for the Caesars (*co-d Riccardo Freda*). 1968: Play Dirty.

Vittorio de Seta's Banditi A Orgosolo, *with Michèle Cossu.*
Vittorio De Sica in Mario Moncelli's Padri e Figli . . . .
Catherine Deneuve and Pierre Clementi in Benjamin, *directed by Michel Deville.*

DEVILLE, Michel

Director. Boulogne-sur-Mer, France 1931–
Started as amateur with 8mm short made while
student. Worked for Henri Decoin on 13 films as
stagiaire, then assistant director. 1958: first film as
director, *Une Balle dans le canon*, in collaboration with
Charles Gérard. Technical adviser to Jean Meyer on 2
films with Comédie Française, *Le Bourgeois
Gentilhomme* (1958) and *Le Mariage de Figaro* (1959).
1960: directed *Ce Soir ou jamais*, beginning partnership with Nina Companeez who co-wrote script and
edited. Directed TV short, *Les Petites Demoiselles*
(1964).

Features as director: 1958: Une Balle dans le canon –
A Slug in the Heater (*co-d Charles Gérard*). 1960: Ce
Soir ou jamais – Tonight or Never (*+ p/co-s*). 1961:
Adorable Menteuse (*+ p/co-s*). 1962: A cause, à cause
d'une femme (*+ p/co-s*). 1963: L'Appartement des
filles (*+ co-s*). 1964: Lucky Jo (*+ co-st*). 1965: On a
volé la Joconde (*+ co-st*). 1966: Martin Soldat – Kiss
Me General (*+ co-st*). 1967: Benjamin (*+ co-st*). 1968:
Bye Bye Barbara (*+ co-s*). 1970: L'Ours et la poupée
– The Bear and the Doll. 1971: Raphael, ou le
débauche.

DEWEVER, Jean

Director. Paris 1927–
Studied law, then IDHEC. Assistant on 26 features
directed by e.g. Jacques Becker, Marcel L'Herbier,
Yves Ciampi, Roger Vadim, Peter Glenville.
1954–59: directed 8 shorts. 1961: first feature as
director.

Short films as director: 1954: Opération La Fontaine.
1955: La Crise du logement; L'Agriculture. 1956: Au
Bois Piget; Tante Esther. 1958: La Vie des autres; Des
Logis et des hommes. 1959: Contrastes (*co-d Robert
Menegoz*).

Features as director: 1961: Les Honneurs de la guerre.
1970: César Grandblaise (*+ co-ad*).

DIAMOND, I. A. L.

(Itek Dommnici) Ungeny, Rumania 1920–
1929: to USA. Christian name changed to Isadore
at school. (initials A. L., added later, stand for
nothing). Engineering at Columbia University; edited
Spectator, collaborated on one Columbia Variety
Show, wrote next three. To MGM as junior writer.
1944: first film as writer *Murder in the Blue Room* for
Universal. Moved to Warners, Paramount, Fox. 1957:
first film in collaboration with Billy Wilder *Love in the
Afternoon*, as co-writer. Later collaboration with
Wilder as associate producer and co-writer; released
by United Artists. 1960: shared Oscar with him for
The Apartment. Only films without Wilder since 1956:
Michael Kidd's *Merry Andrew* (1958), Gene Saks'
Cactus Flower (1969).

Films as writer in collaboration include: 1946: Two
Guys from Milwaukee (*+ co-st*). 1948: Romance on the
High Seas (*ad only*); Two Guys from Texas. 1949: It's
a Great Feeling (*st only*). 1951: Love Nest (*alone*).
1952: Monkey Business; Something for the Birds.
1956: That Certain Feeling. 1957: Love in the Afternoon.

**Films as writer and associate producer, both in
collaboration:** 1959: Some Like it Hot. 1960: The
Apartment. 1961: One, Two, Three. 1963: Irma la
Douce. 1964: Kiss Me, Stupid. 1966: The Fortune
Cookie. 1970: The Private Life of Sherlock Holmes
(*as-p/co-s*).

DICKINSON, Angie

Actress. Kulm, North Dakota 1931–
Glendale College. Beauty contest win led to TV debut
and first film, *Lucky Me* (1955) for Warners. 1959–62:
with Warners. 1963–65: with Universal. 1965:
married composer Burt Bacharach. TV work includes
TV feature and commercial.

Films as actress include: 1955: Man with the Gun;
Tennessee's Partner. 1956: Gun the Man Down;
Tension at Table Rock. 1958: Cry Terror. 1959: Rio
Bravo. 1960: Ocean's 11; A Fever in the Blood. 1961:
Rachel Cade. 1962: Rome Adventure; Jessica. 1963:
Captain Newman M.D. 1964: The Killers. 1965: The
Art of Love. 1966: The Chase; Cast a Giant Shadow.
1967: Point Blank; The Last Challenge. 1969: Young
Billy Young; Some Kind of a Nut. 1971: Pretty Maids
All in a Row.

DICKINSON, Thorold

Director. Bristol, England 1903–
1922: Keble College, Oxford; produced college plays.
1925: worked with director George Pearson in France,
collaborating on film scripts. 1926: stage director with
Lena Ashwell's repertory company in Notting Hill
Gate, London. 1927: editor for Welsh–Pearson. 1929:
visited USA to study sound techniques; then sound
editor for British and Dominion, Gainsborough and
Stoll Films. 1933: edited Cyril Gardner's *Perfect
Understanding*. At Ealing Studios, edited and produced Carol Reed's first feature (1935). 1937: first
feature as director. 1937: Association of Cine Technicians' delegate to USSR; on return campaigned for
national film quota. 1938: with Ivor Montagu's unit in
Spain to make documentaries for Republicans in Civil
War; directed short, *Spanish ABC* (1938). Other shorts
include *Yesterday is Over Your Shoulder* (1940). 2nd-
unit director on Victor Schertzinger's *The Mikado*
(1939). 1939–41: Ministry of Information shorts.
1941–43: head of production, Army Kinematograph
Service; produced 17 training films. 1949–50: script-
writer at Associated British. 1952–53: Chairman of
British Film Academy. 1953–55: made *Hill 24
Doesn't Answer* in Israel. 1956–61: in charge of
United Nations Film Services in New York, producing
documentaries; supervised and wrote feature-length
Power Among Men (1959) directed by Gian Luigi
Polidoro and Alexander Hammid. 1961: Senior
Lecturer in Film, Slade School of Fine Art, University
College, London. 1967: Professor of Film at Slade.
Co-author with Catherine de la Roche of 'The Soviet
Cinema', author of pamphlet 'The Role of the Direc-
tor', and numerous articles, and book 'A Discovery of
Cinema'.

Features as director: 1937: The High Command. 1939:
The Arsenal Stadium Mystery. 1940: Gaslight. 1942:
Next of Kin; The Prime Minister. 1946: Men of Two
Worlds – Kisenga, Man of Africa (*+ co-s*). 1949:
Queen of Spades. 1951: Secret Police (*+ co-s*). 1955:
Hill 24 Doesn't Answer (*+ co-p*).

DICKSON, William Kennedy Laurie

Inventor and director. Minihic-sur-Rance, France
1860–1935 Twickenham, Middlesex
In USA from 1879. 1883: employed by Thomas
Edison. 1884: head of testing and experimental department of Edison's Goerck Street Works, New York. By
1885, Edison's official photographer; also worked on
Edison Electric Tube Company's project to lay electrical conduits under the streets of New York and Brooklyn. 1887: worked on Edison ore-milling project at
Lamp Works, Harrison, New Jersey; also astronomical
research and photography; began microphotograph
research and Kinetoscope work in Edison laboratories.
1888: co-inventor with Edison of ore-milling process;
became head of ore-milling department- started microphotograph experiments. 1889: experiments with
cylinders covered with microphotographs. 1890:
bought or built an Anschütz tachyscope, and demonstrated motion picture projection; with Edison took out
patent for Magnetic Ore Separator. By 1891, had
produced motion picture camera. 1891: shot *Monkeyshines*, microphotograph cylinder motion picture; also
produced prototype Kinetoscope 'peepshow' machine
for viewing it; received samples of George Eastman's
50ft strips of celluloid film, 35mm wide. Modified
Kinetoscope prototype for viewing continuous loop of
film strip; first showed him raising hat. 1892: marketing of Kinetoscope planned. Produced 'Black Maria'
camera to take strip film, working at about 39
frames/second (1892). On Edison's property at West
Orange, New Jersey, designed film studio for it, with
camera on rails for tracking shots. 1893: shot and
copyrighted several films. 1894: publication of his
book 'The Life and Times of Thomas Alva Edison'
written with his sister Antonia; *Fred Ott's Sneeze*
filmed and copyrighted as *Edison Kinetoscopic Record
of a Sneeze, January 7, 1894*. Worked on several 1-
minute films of prize-fight bouts in studio, experi-
menting with artificial lighting; shot first outdoor film;
experimented with combination of Kinetoscope and
phonograph; with Herman Casler designed the
Mutoscope which used cinematographic images in
book form, flicked through mechanically or by hand.
1895: Mutograph camera supplying material for
Mutoscope ready for testing; with sister wrote book
'History of the Kinetograph, Kinetoscope and Kineto-
Phonograph'; resigned from Edison's employ; with
Elias B. Koopman, Harry Norton Marvin and Casler
formed American Mutoscope Company in Jersey City.
1896: patented Mutograph camera and Mutopticon
projector; studio erected on roof of 841 Broadway,
New York; also shot films at Atlantic City, Philadelphia, Buzzard's Bay, West Point, Niagara Falls.
Mutopticon renamed Biograph and introduced at Alvin
Theatre, Pittsburg (14 September 1896), then in Philadelphia and New York (openings: Columbia Theatre,
Brooklyn, 28 September; Grand Opera House, Manhattan, 5 October; Koster and Bial's Music Hall, 26
October; Keith's in Union Square, 18 July 1897,
staying until 15 July 1905). With Billy Bitzer, who was
also Biograph's projectionist, shot *Wm. McKinley
Receiving Telegram Announcing His Election* (1896).
1897: left USA; for several years supplied American
Biograph with films, e.g. of Boer War, before leaving
film business to set up own experimental laboratory in
London. 1911: returned to USA to testify in Motion
Picture Patents Company litigation. 1928–33: invol-

ved in patent claims for 'Geneva intermittent' movement in movie cameras.

DIETERLE, William

Director and actor. Ludwigshafen, Germany 1893–
At 16 apprenticed to group of touring players: took small parts, shifted scenery, worked as handyman. 1911: first film as actor *Fiesco* while on tour in Heidelberg. Spent World War I in Switzerland; major roles on Zurich stage. Returned to Germany, joined Max Reinhardt's company as actor. 1921: second film *Der Geier-wally* and 4 others. 1923: first film as director and actor *Menschen am Wege* (Marlene Dietrich's first film); also wrote it. 1924: opened own theatre, Das Dramische Theater in Berlin. 1928: formed own production unit at Deutsche First National, made 2 films. 1929: made 4 films for Deutsche Universal. 1930: to Hollywood to make German versions of American films. 1931: directed first English language film *The Last Flight*. 1930–39: with Warners, except for *The Hunchback of Notre Dame* (1939) for RKO. 1940: left Warners, formed own company. 1942–47: worked for MGM, Paramount, Universal and Selznick. 1950: made *Vulcano* in Italy. 1949–57: worked for Paramount and Columbia. From 1958: in Europe. From 1960: director of Bad Herstelder Festival and stage director, living in Liechtenstein, then Austria.

Films as actor include: 1921: Der Geierwally; Hintertreppe. 1922: Lucrezia Borgia. 1923: Die gruene Manuela; Die Austreibung. 1924: Carlos und Elisabeth; Das Wachsfigurenkabinett. 1926: Qualen der Nacht; Faust. 1930: Dämon des Meeres.

Films as director and actor: 1923: Menschen am Wege (+ s) – Men at the Crossroads. 1927: Das Geheimnis des Abbe X – Der Mann der nicht Lieben darf (+ s) – Secret of Abee X (+ s). 1928: Geshlecht in Fesseln – Sex in Chains; Die Heilige und ihr Nahrr – The Saint and her Fool. 1929: Eine Stunde Gluecke – One Hour of Happiness; Frühlingsrauschen; Ich Lebe für Dich; Das Schweigen im Walde – The Silence of the Forest; Ludwig der Zweite, König von Bayern. 1930: Eine Stunde Glück – One Hour of Happiness; Der Tanz geht weiter (*German version of* Those Who Dance). 1959: Il Vendicatore – Revolt on the Volga – Dubrowsky.

Films as director: 1930: Die Maske fallt (*German version of* The Way of All Men). 1931: The Last Flight; Her Majesty, Love. 1932: Jewel Robbery; Man Wanted; Lawyer Man; Six Hours to Live; The Crash; Scarlet Dawn. 1933: From Headquarters; Grand Slam; The Devil's in Love; Adorable. 1934: Fashion of 1934; Fog Over Frisco; Madame Dubarry; The Secret Bride. 1935: A Midsummer Night's Dream (*co-d Max Reinhardt*); Dr Socrates; The Story of Louis Pasteur; Concealment. 1936: The White Angel; Satan Met a Lady. 1937: Another Dawn; The Life of Emile Zola; The Great O'Malley. 1938: Blockade. 1939: Juarez; The Hunchback of Notre Dame. 1940: The Story of Dr Ehrlich's Magic Bullet – Dr Ehrlich's Magic Bullet; A Dispatch from Reuter's – This Man Reuter. 1941: All That Money Can Buy (+ p). 1942: Syncopation (+ p); Tennessee Johnson. 1944: Kismet. 1945: I'll Be Seeing You; This Love of Ours; Love Letters. 1946: The Searching Wind. 1949: The Portrait of Jennie; The Accused: Rope of Sand. 1950: Paid in Full – Bitter Victory; Vulcano – Volcano (+ p); Dark City. 1951: September Affair; Red Mountain; Peking Express; Boots Malone. 1952: The Turning Point. 1953: Salome. 1954: Elephant Walk. 1955: Magic Fire (+ p). 1957: Omar Khayyam. 1960: Die Fastnachtsbeichte – Ash Wednesday Confession; Herrin der Welt.

DIETRICH, Marlene

(Maria Magdalena Dietrich von Losch) Actress. Berlin 1901–
Father in Royal Prussian Police, stepfather in Regiment of Grenadiers. Studied violin at Hochschule fur Musik; abandoned studies, on medical advice. Failed first attempt to enter Max Reinhardt's Deutsche Theaterschule. Began to use name Marlene Dietrich. Chorus girl in touring company, then successfully auditioned for Deutsche Theaterschule. First major role, in 'Der grosse Bariton' with Albert Basserman. 1923: first film as actress *Der kleine Napoleon* for Ufa; spotted by production assistant Rudolf Sieber for *Tragödie der Liebe*. 1924: married him; briefly retired, but appeared in husband's home movies released in Germany as short, *Die glückliche Mutter*. 1926: returned to films as extra in *Die freudlose Gasse* and to theatre. Stage work included 'Duell am Lido', then 'Broadway' in Vienna; acted in Reinhardt's Josefstadter Theatre in 'Die Schule von Uznach' and in his productions of 'Es Ligt in der Luft' and 'Zwei Kravatten'. In latter, spotted by Joseph Von Sternberg for *Der blaue Angel* (1930), the first German sound film. 1930: to USA; first American film *Morocco*. 1931: *The Blue Angel* distributed in USA by Paramount. 1930–36: all films for Paramount, 7 directed by Von Sternberg. 1936: opened Cecil B. De Mille's Lux Radio Theatre with Clark Gable in 'The Legionnaire and the Lady'. Worked for Selznick and Alexander Korda; rejected Hitler's offer to return to German cinema. 1939: American citizen. 1939–44: mainly with Universal. World War II: in Europe for USO; broadcasts in German and French for Office of War Information. From 1944: with several studios including Paramount and (1956–61) United Artists. Made films in France and Britain. Wrote some scripts for radio series 'Cafe Istanbul' and acted in it; acted on CBS radio in 'Time for Love'. 1953: ringmaster of circus in Madison Square Garden; began cabaret appearances. 1960: returned to Germany, as entertainer. Tours in own show. 1963: narrated feature documentary on Hitler, *The Black Fox*. Many recordings. Book: 'Marlene Dietrich's ABC'. Chevalier de la Légion d'Honneur.

Films as actress include: 1923: Der kleine Napoleon; Tragödie der Liebe; Mensch en am Wege. 1926: Die freudlose Gasse. 1928: Eine DuBarry von Heute. 1929: Die Frau, nach der man sich Sehnt; Das Schiff der Verlorenen Menschen. 1930: Der Blaue Angel; Morocco. 1931: Dishonored. 1932: Shanghai Express; Blonde Venus. 1933: The Song of Songs. 1934: The Scarlet Empress. 1935: The Devil is a Woman. 1936: Desire; I Loved a Soldier (*uf*); The Garden of Allah. 1937: Knight without Armour; Angel. 1939: Destry Rides Again. 1940: Seven Sinners. 1941: The Flame of New Orleans; Manpower. 1942: The Lady is Willing; The Spoilers. 1944: Kismet. 1947: Golden Earrings. 1948: A Foreign Affair. 1950: Stage Fright. 1951: No Highway in the Sky. 1952: Rancho Notorious. 1956: Around the World in 80 Days. 1957: Witness for the Prosecution. 1958: Touch of Evil. 1961: Judgment at Nuremburg. 1963: Paris When it Sizzles.

I. A. L. Diamond (right) *and Billy Wilder, relaxing during the shooting of* The Private Life of Sherlock Holmes.
Marlene Dietrich.
Mickey Mouse and Pluto in Mickey's Garden, *directed by Walt Disney and Ub Iwerks.*

DI PALMA, Carlo

Cinematographer. Rome 1925–
Began as assistant camera operator on Renato Castellani's *Un Colpo di pistola* (1942), then on *Ossessione* (1943) and *Roma, Città Aperta* (1945); camera operator on *Domani è troppo tarde* (1950). Cinematographer from 1954. Some credits as Charles Brown.

Films as cinematographer include: 1960: La Lunga Notte del '43. 1961: L'Assassino; Leoni al sole. 1962: Parigi o cara. 1963: Omicron. 1964: Deserto Rosso. 1965: I Tre Volti *ep* Prefazione; L'Armata Brancaleone. 1966: Blow-Up. 1969: The Appointment. 1971: La Pacifista.

DISNEY, Walt

Producer. Chicago, Illinois 1901–1966 Burbank, California
Newsboy on father's paper in Kansas City, Missouri. Moved to Chicago; mailman. At 16 joined Red Cross Ambulance Corps; to France immediately after World War I. Returned to Kansas. 1919–22: commercial artist, with Ub Iwerks; work included animated shorts. Made shorts for Newman Theatre in Kansas City; formed own company. Bankrupt; to Hollywood then New York to find buyers for *Alice in Cartoonland* (1926–27) series combining live action and animation; released through Universal. Brought in Iwerks. 1927: began 'Oswald the Rabbit' series. 1928: created Mickey Mouse who appeared in 2 silents, the first being *Plane Crazy* and first sound cartoon *Steamboat Willie* (1928), drawn by Iwerks; national distribution for series. 1929: first of 'Silly Symphonies', *The Skeleton Dance* at Columbia. Pluto first appeared in *The Chain Gang* (1930), not named till 1931: Goofy first appeared 1932; Donald Duck in 1934. 1931: partial conversion to colour. 1932–37: with United Artists. To 1935: given exclusive rights by Technicolor for use of 3-colour process for cartoons; to 1934 used colour only in 'Silly Symphonies'. 1937: made *Snow White and the Seven Dwarves*, first animation feature, in colour; his studios developed multiplane camera; moved to RKO. 1940: *Pinocchio* shot entirely on multiplane camera; lacking bank credit, sold stock to public for first time. 1948: first nature film, short *Seal Island*. 1950: first completely live-action feature *Treasure Island*. 1954: first TV series 'Disneyland'. 1955: opened Disneyland Park, California. 1967: last personally supervised film *The Jungle Book*. 1971: Walt Disney World opened, in Florida. Won 29 Oscars.

Features as producer include: 1937: Snow White and the Seven Dwarves. 1940: Pinocchio; Fantasia. 1941: The Reluctant Dragon; Dumbo. 1942: Bambi; Saludos amigos. 1944: The Three Caballeros. 1946: Make Mine Music!; Song of the South. 1949: The Adventures of Ichabod and Mr Toad; Cinderella. 1951: Alice in Wonderland. 1952: The Story of Robin Hood (*pc*). 1953: Peter Pan; The Living Desert. 1954: 20,000 Leagues under the Sea; The Vanishing Prairie. 1955: Lady and the Tramp. 1958: The Sleeping Beauty. 1963: The Sword in the Stone. 1965: Mary Poppins. 1967: The Jungle Book.

DI VENANZO, Gianni

Cinematographer. Teramo, Italy 1920–1966
Assistant to Otello Martelli and Aldo Tonti. 1941: first feature as assistant *Un Colpo di Pistola*. From 1952: cinematographer on features. Died while making *The Honey Pot*; film completed by his regular operator Pasquale di Santis, without credit.

Films as cinematographer include: 1951: Achtung, banditi! 1953: Ai margini della metropoli; Amore in città. 1954: Cronache di poveri amanti; Le Ragazze di Sanfrediano. 1955: Le Amiche; Lo Scapolo; Gli Sbandati. 1956: Suor Letizia. 1957: Kean; Il Grido; La Loi c'est la loi. 1958: La Sfida; I Soliti Ignoti. 1959: La Prima Notte. 1960: I Delfini; Crimen. 1961: Il Carabiniere a cavallo; La Notte. 1962: L'Eclisse; Salvatore Giuliano; Eve. 1963: Otto e mezzo; I Basilischi; Le Mani sulla città; La Ragazza di Bube. 1965: Il Momento della verità; Giulietta degli spiriti. 1967: The Honey Pot (*co*).

DMYTRYK, Edward

Director. Grand Forks, British Columbia, Canada 1908–
Parents Ukrainian emigrés. 1919: to Los Angeles. 1923: messenger boy at Paramount, then part-time projectionist. 1 year at California Institute of Technology; returned to Paramount as full-time projectionist. Edited Spanish versions of films; edited *The Royal Family of Broadway* (1930), shot in Paramount's Long Island Studio. Editor at Paramount until 1939. 1935: first feature as director. 1939: edited and took over direction (uncredited) of *Million Dollar Legs*; subsequently director only. 1941: Columbia. 1942: moved to RKO; after *Hitler's Children* (1943), signed 7-year contract. 1947: among 10 names given to Committee on Un-American Activities by Sam Wood, cited for contempt of Congress and fired by RKO. 1947–49: 3 films in UK. 1950: ordered to return to USA for renewal of passport; on return sentenced to $1000 fine and 6 months in jail for contempt of Congress. 1951: went before Committee again, recanted; signed to make *Mutiny* for the King Brothers and 4 films for Stanley Kramer. Married actress Jean Porter.

Films as editor include: 1934: Belle of the Nineties (*co*). 1935: Ruggles of Red Gap. 1939: Zaza; Love Affair (*co*).

Films as director: 1935: The Hawk. 1939: Million Dollar Legs (*+ e*; *uc*, *co-d* Nick Grinde); Television Spy. 1940: Emergency Squad; Mystery Sea Raider; Golden Gloves; Her First Romance. 1941: The Devil Commands; Under Age; Sweetheart of the Campus; The Blonde From Singapore; Confessions of Boston Blackie; Secrets of the Lone Wolf. 1942: Counter Espionage; Seven Miles from Alcatraz. 1943: The Falcon Strikes Back; Hitler's Children; Captive Wild Woman; Behind the Rising Sun; Tender Comrade. 1945: Murder My Sweet – Farewell My Lovely; Back to Bataan; Cornered; Till the End of Time. 1947: Crossfire; So Well Remembered. 1949: Give Us This Day; Obsession – The Hidden Room. 1952: Mutiny; The Sniper; Eight Iron Men. 1953: The Juggler. 1954: The Caine Mutiny; Broken Lance; The End of the Affair. 1955: Soldier of Fortune; The Left Hand of God. 1956: The Mountain (*+ p*). 1957: Raintree County. 1958: The Young Lions. 1959: Warlock (*+ p*); The Blue Angel. 1962: Walk on the Wild Side; The Reluctant Saint (*+ p*). 1963: The Carpetbaggers. 1964: Where Love Has Gone. 1965: Mirage. 1966: Alvarez Kelly. 1968: Lo Sbarco di Anzio – The Battle for Anzio; Shalako.

DONAT, Robert

Actor. Manchester, Lancashire 1905–1958 London
Studied acting under James Bernard in Manchester. 1921: first appearance as actor in 'Julius Caesar' with Birmingham Repertory Company; then with various repertory companies. 1931–34: West End stage. 1932: first film, *Men of Tomorrow*. Second film, *That Night in London* (1932) directed by Rowland V. Lee who directed his first Hollywood film, *The Count of Monte Cristo* (1934). 1939: acted in season with Old Vic Company, London. 1943: managed Westminster Theatre, London, but did not act there. 1949: directed, produced, wrote and acted in *The Cure for Love*. Lifelong sufferer from chronic asthma. TV appearances in UK. Married actress Renée Asherson. Oscar as Best Actor for *Goodbye, Mr Chips* (1939).

Films as actor include: 1933: Cash; The Private Life of Henry VIII. 1935: The Thirty-Nine Steps; The Ghost Goes West. 1937: Knight Without Armour. 1938: The Citadel. 1942: The Young Mr Pitt. 1945: Perfect Strangers. 1947: Captain Boycott. 1948: The Winslow Boy. 1951: The Magic Box. 1958: The Inn of the Sixth Happiness.

DONEN, Stanley

Director. Columbia, South Carolina 1924–
Studied dancing and worked in local theatre before going to University of South Carolina. Left for New York and theatre. In chorus of 'Pal Joey' (1940) and 'Best Foot Forward' (1941), both starring Gene Kelly. Solo dancer in 'Beat the Band', directed by George Abbott. Went to Hollywood for *Best Foot Forward* (1943), becoming assistant choreographer to Charles Walters. Then assistant choreographer at MGM, e.g. to Kelly on *Cover Girl* (1944), *Anchors Aweigh* (1945) and *Take Me Out to the Ball Game* (1949); wrote story for latter with Kelly and directed a sequence. Partnership with Kelly continued intermittently as directors until *It's Always Fair Weather* (1955), his last film for MGM. *Indiscreet* (1958) was made in UK, where he settled, forming own companies. No American films since *Damn Yankees* (1959).

Films as director: 1949: On the Town (*co-d Gene Kelly*). 1951: Royal Wedding – Wedding Bells (*+ co-chor*); Love is Better than Ever – The Light Fantastic. 1952: Singin' in the Rain (*+ co-d/co-chor Gene Kelly*); Fearless Fagan. 1953: Give a Girl a Break (*+ co-chor*). 1954: Deep in My Heart (*+ co-chor*); Seven Brides for Seven Brothers. 1955: It's Always Fair Weather (*co-d Gene Kelly*). 1957: Funny Face (*+ co-chor*); Kiss Them for Me; The Pajama Game (*+ co-d/co-p George Abbott*). 1958: Indiscreet (*+ co-p*). 1959: Damn Yankees – What Lola Wants (*+ co-d/co-p George Abbott*); Once More With Feeling (*+ co-p*). 1960: Surprise Package (*+ p*); The Grass Is Greener (*+ co-p*). 1963: Charade (*+ p*). 1966: Arabesque (*+ p/pc*). 1967: Two for the Road (*+ p/pc*); Bedazzled (*+ p/pc*). 1969: Staircase (*+ p/pc*).

DONIOL-VALCROZE, Jacques

Director and actor. Paris 1920–
Studied in law faculty, Paris; arts faculty, Montpellier. 1946–47: worked on Cinémonde. 1946–49: joint editor of Revue du Cinéma. Founder member and secretary of Club Objectif 49; helped in organisation of

Festival du Film Maudit (Biarritz, 1950) and Rendez-vous de Biarritz (1951). 1952: founder with André Bazin, Léonide Keigel and Lo Duca, and joint editor of Cahiers du Cinéma. 1952–59: film critic on France-Observateur. 1956–58: directed shorts. 1959: first feature as director. Worked on scripts, including Pierre Kast's *Le Bel Age* (1960). *Jean-Luc Godard* (1964) and *La Bien-Aimée* (1966) made for TV. Novel: 'Les Portes du Baptistère'.

Films as actor include: 1956: Le Coup du berger. 1960: Le Bel Age. 1962: L'Immortelle. 1963: Les Vacances Portugaises. 1970: Le Voyou.

Films as director: 1956: Bonjour, Monsieur La Bruyère. 1957: L'Oeil du maître. 1958: Les Surmenés. 1959: L'Eau à la bouche – The Game of Love (+ *st/s*). 1960: Le Coeur Battant (+ *st*). 1962: La Dénonciation (+ *st*). 1964: Jean-Luc Godard. 1966: La Bien Aimée. 1967: Le Viol (+ *st/s*). 1970: La Maison des Bories.

DONNER, Clive

Director. London 1926–
1942: started in Rank cutting rooms; assistant editor, e.g. on *On Approval* (1942), *The Way Ahead* (1944), *The Passionate Friends* (1948), *Madeleine* (1949), and *Pandora and the Flying Dutchman* (1950). From 1951: editor, e.g. on *The Card* (1952), *The Million Pound Note* (1953), *Genevieve* (1953), *I Am a Camera* (1955), *The Purple Plain* (1954). 1956: first film as director. First 2 films for Rank, then freelance. 1960–61: directed 2 Merton Park productions for Anglo Amalgamated and 2 16mm shorts, *Weekend in Paris* and *The Purple Stream*. Since 1965: has also worked in Europe and USA. TV work as director includes documentaries for Granada TV and BBC, episodes in 'Danger Man' series and commercials. Directed Frank Marcus's 'The Formation Dancers' in West End.

Features as director: 1956: The Secret Place. 1958: Heart of a Child. 1960: Marriage of Convenience. 1961: The Sinister Man. 1962: Some People. 1963: The Caretaker. 1964: Nothing but the Best. 1965: What's New Pussycat? 1967: Luv; Here We Go Round the Mulberry Bush (+ *p*). 1969: Alfred the Great.

DONNER, Jörn

Director and writer. Helsinki, Finland 1933–
Studied in Italy and France. From 1951: film critic for newspaper Dagens Nyheter in Stockholm. From 1955: directed shorts, e.g. *Aamu Kaupungissa* (1955), *Näinä Päivinä* (1955), *Porkala* (1956), *Vettä* (1956), *Vittnesbörd om Henne* (1961). Author of books including fiction, reportage, essays (including 'Våra filmproblem', 1953), poetry and critical study of Bergman 'Djävulens ansikte: Ingmar Bergmans filmer' (1962). Wrote for various European magazines. 1963: first feature as director and writer, in Sweden. Worked in Swedish TV. Films from 1968 made in Finland. Has produced several Finnish films by other directors and directed for theatre. Wife, Harriet Andersson, appears in some of his films. With Aito Makinen founded Suomen Elokuva Arkisto, the Finnish film archive.

Features as director and writer: 1963: En Söndag i september – A Sunday in September. 1964: Att älska – To Love. 1965: Här börjar äventyret. 1966: Tvärbalk –

Rooftree (+ *e*). 1967: Stimulantia *ep* Han–Hon – He-She. 1968: Mustaa Valkoisella – Black on White (+ *p/e/w*). 1969: 69 (+ *p/w*). 1970: Naisenkuvia – Portraits of Women (+ *p/co-e/w*); Anna (+ *co-pc*).

DONSKOI, Marc

Director. Odessa 1901–
To 1925: studied medicine, piano and musical composition in Odessa; performed 3 years military service; play 'Zaria Svobody' produced. 1925: to Moscow. 1926: studied with Sergei Eisenstein; became assistant director, assistant editor, scriptwriter, and took small parts as actor. 1927: to Bielgoskino studios, Leningrad; made first film as director in collaboration. 1934: in collaboration made first talkie, supervised by Sergei Yutkevich at Vostokkino, *Pesnya o schastye*; entered Soyouzdietfilm studios, Moscow, remained there till World War II. 1935: made Russian version of James Whale's *The Invisible Man*. Met Gorky. 1938–40: 'Gorky' trilogy based on Gorky's writings. 1940: art director on Y. Vasilchikov's *Brat geroya*. 1942: short in 'Fighting Film Album'. 1944: Kiev studio restored; joined them. 1945: joined Communist Party. 1946: returned to Soyuzdietfilm, now renamed Gorky Studio. 1949: Stalin had *Alitet ukhodit v gori* banned; much of it destroyed. 1954–56: returned to Kiev Studio. *Mat* (1954) and *Foma Gordeyev* (1959) based on writings of Gorky. 1957: returned to Gorky Studio. His wife scripted *Dorogoi Tsenoi* (1958) and *Zdravstvuitye, deti!* (1962), *Serdtse materi* (1967), *Vernost materi* (1967)—the latter 2 comprise biography of Lenin's mother.

Films as director: 1927: V bolshom gorodye – In the Big City (+ *co-s*; *co-d Mikhail Averback*). 1928: Tsena Cheloveka – Man's Value (*co-d Mikhail Averback*). 1929: Pizhon – The Fop. 1930: Chuzhoi Berez – The Other Shore; Ogon – The Fire. 1934: Pesnya o schastye – Song About Happiness (*co-d Vladimir Legoshin*). 1938: Detstvo Gorkovo – The Childhood of Gorky (+ *co-s*). 1939: V lyudyakh – My Apprenticeship. 1940: Moi Universiteti – My Universities (+ *co-s*). 1941: Romantiki – Children of the Soviet Arctic (+ *co-s*). 1942: Kak zakalyalas Stal – How the Steel was Tempered (+ *s*). 1944: Raduga – Rainbow (+ *co-s*). 1945: Nepokorenniye Semia Tarassa – Unconquered (+ *co-s*). 1947: Selskaya Uchitelnitsa – Varvara – The Village Teacher. 1949: Alitet ukhodit v gori – Zakonye bolshoi zemli – Alitet Leaves for the Hills (+ *co-s*). 1950: Nachi Chempiony – Our Champions – Sportivnaya Slava – Sporting Fame. 1956: Mat – Mother (+ *co-s*). 1958: Dorogoi Tsenoi – At a High Cost. 1959: Foma Gordeyev – Thomas Gordeyev (+ *co-s*). 1962: Zdravstuitye deti! – Hello Children! 1967: Serdtsye materi – Heart of a Mother – Sons and Mothers (+ *p*); Vernost materi – A Mother's Devotion (+ *p*).

DOUGLAS, Gordon M.

Director. New York 1909–
First appearance as film actor at 3 or 4. After college worked in MGM offices. Small part in *Glorifying the American Girl* (1929) expanded to major role. Contract as actor with Paramount but no films; then actor for Hal Roach in series of films, and remained as assistant editor, gagman, assistant director. Became director on 'Our Gang' series of comic shorts. 1936: co-directed first feature, *General Spanky*, a Hal Roach

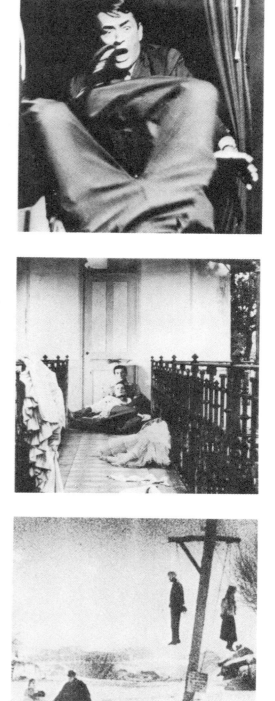

Gregory Peck in Mirage, *directed by Edward Dmytryk.*
L'Eau à la Bouche, *directed by Jacques Doniol-Valcroze.*
Marc Donskoi's Rainbow.

Feature Comedy. 1937–8: directed comedy shorts for Roach. First solo feature: *Zenobia* (1939). Scriptwriter, e.g. on *Topper Returns* (1941). 1971: directed 2 weeks' shooting on *The Skin Game* during illness of Paul Bogart.

Films as director include (complete from 1940): 1936: General Spanky (*co-d Fred Newmayer*); Pay as You Exit; Spooky Hooky; Reunion in Rhythm; Glove Taps. 1937: Three Smart Boys; Hearts Are Thumps; Rushin' Ballet; Bored of Education; Roamin' Holiday; Night n' Gales; Fishy Tales; Our Gang Follies of 1938: Framing Youth; The Pigskin Palooka; Mail and Female. 1938: Bear Facts; Canned Fishing; Came the Brawn; Feed 'em and Weep; Hide and Shriek; The Little Ranger; Aladdin's Lantern. 1939: Zenobia – Elephants Never Forget. 1940: Saps at Sea. 1941: Niagara Falls; Broadway Limited. 1943: The Great Gildersleeve; Gildersleeve's Bad Day; Gildersleeve on Broadway. 1944: A Night of Adventure; Gildersleeve's Ghost; Girl Rush; The Devil with Hitler; The Falcon in Hollywood. 1945: First Yank into Tokyo; Zombies on Broadway. 1946: San Quentin; Dick Tracy vs Cueball. 1948: The Black Arrow; If You Knew Susie; Walk a Crooked Mile. 1949: The Doolins of Oklahoma – The Great Manhunt; Mr Soft Touch (*co-d Henry Levin*). 1950: The Nevadan – Man from Nevada; The Fortunes of Captain Blood; Rogues of Sherwood Forest; Between Midnight and Dawn; Kiss Tomorrow Goodbye. 1951: The Great Missouri Raid; Only the Valiant; Come Fill the Cup. 1952: I Was a Communist for the FBI; Mara Maru; The Iron Mistress. 1953: She's Back on Broadway; The Charge at Feather River; So This Is Love – The Grace Moore Story; 1955: Them; Young at Heart; The McConnell Story – Tiger in the Sky; Sincerely Yours. 1956: Santiago – The Gunrunner. 1957: The Big Land – Stampeded; Bombers B-52 – No Sleep Till Dawn. 1958: Fort Dobbs; The Fiend Who Walked the West; Up Periscope. 1959: Yellowstone Kelly. 1961: Rachel Cade – The Sins of Rachel Cade; Gold of the Seven Saints; Claudelle Inglish – Young and Eager – Jilted. 1962: Follow That Dream. 1963: Call Me Bwana. 1964: Rio Conchos; Robin and the Seven Hoods. 1965: Sylvia; Harlow. 1966: Way . . . Way Out; Stagecoach. 1967: Chuka; In Like Flint; Tony Rome. 1968: The Detective; Lady in Cement. 1969: Barquero. 1971: They Call Me *Mister* Tibbs; The Skin Game (*co-d Paul Bogart*).

DOUGLAS, Kirk

(Issur Danielovitch Demsky) Actor. Amsterdam, New York 1916–
St Lawrence University; American Academy of Dramatic Art. 1941: New York stage debut in 'Spring Again'. 1942: 'Three Sisters' on Broadway, under name George Spelvin Jr. World War II: naval service as lieutenant. Stage until 1945, succeeding Richard Widmark in 'Kiss and Tell' (1943) and in 'Trio' (1944). Later in stock (1951) and on New York stage (1963). First film, *The Strange Love of Martha Ivers* (1946). 1955: formed own company, Bryna Productions, for which made many later films, occasionally taking production credit. Also TV from 1957. 1970: produced Anthony Newley's *Summertime*. Son is actor Joel Douglas.

Films as actor: 1947: Mourning Becomes Electra; Out of the Past; I Walk Alone. 1948: The Walls of Jericho;

My Dear Secretary. 1949: A Letter to Three Wives; Champion. 1950: Young Man With A Horn; The Glass Menagerie. 1951: Ace in the Hole; Along the Great Divide; Detective Story. 1952: The Big Trees; The Big Sky; The Bad and the Beautiful. 1953: The Story of Three Loves *ep* Equilibrium; The Juggler; Act of Love. 1954: 20,000 Leagues Under the Sea. 1955: The Racers; Man without a Star; Ulisse; The Indian Fighter. 1956: Lust for Life. 1957: Top Secret Affair; Gu..fight at the OK Corral; Paths of Glory. 1958: The Vikings (*+ co-p*); Last Train from Gun Hill. 1959: The Devil's Disciple. 1960: Strangers When We Meet; Spartacus (*+ ex-p*). 1961: The Last Sunset; Town Without Pity. 1962: Lonely Are the Brave; Two Weeks in Another Town; The Hook. 1963: The List of Adrian Messenger; For Love or Money. 1964: Seven Days in May; In Harm's Way. 1965: The Heroes of Telemark. 1966: Paris brûle-t-il?; Cast a Giant Shadow. 1967: The War Wagon; The Way West. 1968: The Brotherhood; A Lovely Way to Die. 1969: The Arrangement. 1970: There Was a Crooked Man. 1971: A Gunfight.

DOUGLAS, Melvyn

(Melvyn Hesselberg) Actor. Macon, Georgia, 1901–
Began in Shakespearean repertory. 1928: Broadway debut in 'A Free Soul'. 1931: first film, *Tonight or Never*, in part played on Broadway; married co-star Helen Gahagan during run of play (1931), David Belasco's last production. 1941: head of Arts Division of the Offices of Civil Defense, Washington. 1942–45: enlisted in US Army, rising from private to Major. After war, co-produced 'Call Me Mister' on Broadway. Acted on Broadway, e.g. in 'Inherit the Wind', Jean Anouilh's 'Waltz of the Toreadors' and Gore Vidal's 'The Best Man'. Toured in USA and Australia. Also on TV. Directed first production of Sean O'Casey's 'Within the Gates'. 1952–61: no films. Oscar as supporting actor for *Hud* (1963).

Films as actor include: 1932: Prestige; The Old Dark House. 1933: Counsellor at Law. 1935: She Married Her Boss; Annie Oakley. 1936: And So They Were Married; The Gorgeous Hussy; Theodora Goes Wild. 1937: Captains Courageous; I Met Him in Paris; Angel. 1938: The Toy Wife; The Shining Hour. 1939: Ninotchka. 1940: Too Many Husbands; Third Finger, Left Hand. 1941: That Uncertain Feeling; Two-Faced Woman; A Woman's Face. 1943: Three Hearts for Julia. 1946: The Sea of Grass. 1947: The Guilt of Janet Ames. 1948: Mr Blandings Builds His Dream House. 1949: My Own True Love; A Woman's Secret; The Great Sinner. 1950: My Forbidden Past. 1962: Billy Budd. 1964: Advance to the Rear. 1965: Rapture. 1967: Hotel.

DOUGLAS, Paul

Actor. Philadelphia, Pennsylvania 1907–1959 Hollywood
Yale University for a year, then radio announcer. Started in films as sports commentator and writer; continued in this for 11 years. 1935: stage debut in 'Double Dummy'. From 1946: 1024 performances on Broadway in 'Born Yesterday', then left stage for Hollywood. 1949: first film, *A Letter to Three Wives*; at Fox until 1951. Married 5 times; last 2 wives were actresses Virginia Field (divorced 1946) and Jan Sterling (married 1950).

Films as actor include: 1949: It Happens Every Spring; Everybody Does It. 1950: Panic in the Streets; 14 Hours; The Guy Who Came Back; Angels in the Outfield. 1952: When in Rome; Clash by Night; We're Not Married. 1953: Forever Female. 1954: Executive Suite; The Maggie; Green Fire. 1956: Joe Macbeth; The Solid Gold Cadillac. 1957: This Could Be the Night; Beau James. 1958: Fortunella. 1959: The Mating Game.

DOVZHENKO, Alexander

Director. Sosnitsa, Ukraine 1894–1956 Moscow
Son of middle-class farmers. At Teacher's Institute for 4 years studied physics, natural science, athletics; at University studied biology; at Commerical Institute studied economics and technology. World War I: service on Polish front. In Kiev worked in administration of education. 1921: transferred to People's Commissariat for renovation of Kharkov. Worked for ambassador in Poland and as secretary at Berlin consulate. Studied painting. 1923: returned to Kharkov; worked on newspapers and magazines as artist. Some portraits reproduced in monthly magazine of VUFKU studio 'Kino'. 1926: left Kharkov for Odessa, joined the studio, directed first film in collaboration. 1927: first feature as director. 1930: after release of *Zemlya* visited Berlin and Paris; returned to make *Ivan*, his first sound film. 1935: *Aerograd* his first film made outside Ukraine; Tissé part-photographed it, leaving to work on *Bezhin Lug*. Mosfilm objected to the film, Dovzhenko appealed to Stalin directly, who also suggested subject of next film *Shchors*. As every decision had to be submitted to officials, scripting took 11 months, shooting 20 months. Appointed head of Kiev Studio. Period with army: edited front-line paper, wrote leaflets, wrote a play. To Moscow, published stories, novel, sequel to play. Only wartime work in films was in newsreels and as supervisor and scriptwriter. Wrote play about Ivan Michurin, turned it into script, filmed it in 1947 as *Michurin*; revised and released in 1948. 1956: about to commence shooting *Poema o morye*, died of heart attack. His wife Yulia Solntseva, collaborator since *Zemlya*, realised several of his projects. Kiev studio renamed Dovzhenko Studio. *See* SOLNTSEVA, Yulia.

Films as director: 1926: Vasya Reformator – Vasya the Reformer (*+ s; co-d F. Lokatinsky, Iosif Rona*); Yagodka lyubvi – Love's Berries (*+ s*). 1927: Sumka Dipkurera – The Diplomatic Pouch (*+ ad/w*). 1928: Zvenigora. 1929: Arsenal (*+ s*). 1930: Zemlya – Earth (*+ s*). 1932: Ivan (*+ s*). 1935: Aerograd – Frontier (*+ s*). 1939: Shchors (*+ s; co-d Yulia Solntseva*). 1940: Osvobozhdenie – Liberation (*+ e; co-d Yulia Solntseva*). 1945: Pobeda na pravoberezhnoi Ukrainye i izgnanie Nemetsikh zakhvatchikov za predeli Ukrainskikh Sovetskikh zemel – Victory in the Ukraine and the Expulsion of the Germans from the Boundaries of the Ukrainian Soviet Earth (*+ cy/n; co-d Yulia Solntseva*). 1948: Michurin (*+ s/fpl*).

DREIER, Hans

Designer. Bremen, Germany 1885–
Engineering and architecture at Munich University. West Africa as supervising architect for German government. 1919: became designer for Ufa in Berlin, e.g. on *Danton* (1921). 1923: to Hollywood; first American film as designer *The Hunchback of Notre*

Dame for Universal. 1924: made *Forbidden Paradise* for Famous Players–Lasky. 1924–28: 11 films with Ernst Lubitsch. 1933–49: 11 films with Cecil B. De Mille, 8 in collaboration with Roland Anderson. 1928–51: with Paramount, then retired. Oscar for colour art direction on *Frenchman's Creek* (1945).

Films as designer (from 1927, most in collaboration) include: 1928: The Patriot. 1930: The Love Parade; Monte Carlo. 1931: The Smiling Lieutenant. 1932: Dr Jekyll and Mr Hyde; The Man I Killed; One Hour with You; Trouble in Paradise. 1933: Design for Living; This Day and Age. 1934: Cleopatra. 1935: The Crusades; The Devil is a Woman. 1936: Desire; The Texas Rangers. 1937: The Plainsman; Angel; Make Way for Tomorrow; Wells Fargo. 1938: Bluebeard's Eighth Wife; You and Me; The Buccaneer. 1939: Union Pacific. 1940: Northwest Mounted Police; Dr Cyclops. 1941: Hold Back the Dawn. 1942: Reap the Wild Wind; The Glass Key. 1943: For Whom the Bell Tolls. 1944: The Story of Dr Wassell; Lady in the Dark; Frenchman's Creek. 1945: Salty O'Rourke; Incendiary Blonde. 1946: O.S.S. 1947: Unconquered; The Perils of Pauline. 1948: Emperor Waltz; Sorry, Wrong Number. 1949: Samson and Delilah. 1950: Sunset Boulevard. 1951: A Place in The Sun.

DRESSLER, Marie

(Leila Koerber) Actress. Coburg, Ontario, Canada 1869–1934 Beverley Hills, California
Circus, vaudeville, Broadway and opera. 1915: first film as actress *Tillie's Punctured Romance*. Most films for MGM. Oscar as Best Actress for *Min and Bill* (1930). Autobiography: 'Life Story of an Ugly Duckling'.

Films as actress include: 1927: Breakfast at Sunrise; The Joy Girl. 1928: Bringing Up Father; The Patsy. 1929: The Hollywood Revue; The Divine Lady; The Vagabond Lover. 1930: The Girl Said No; Anna Christie; Let Us Be Gay. 1932: Emma; Prosperity. 1933: Tugboat Annie; Christopher Bean.

DREYER, Carl Theodor

Director. Copenhagen 1889–1968 Copenhagen
Adopted after mother's death. Took office jobs and worked for a telegraph company. Joined the 'Emancipated Youth' organisation and (1910) began writing theatre notices for radical provincial papers. Air Sports reporter for the Berlingske Tidende newspaper in Copenhagen; trained himself as balloon pilot. 1912: while working for another paper, Extrabladet, started writing titles for Nordisk Film Company. Then adapted novels, wrote scripts including *Grevindens aëre* (1918) and *Via Crucis* (1918) and worked as film editor. 1919: first film as director. Scripted or co-scripted all his films. 1942–54: directed and/or wrote shorts, some for Danish Government. From 1965: managed cinema Dagmar Teatret in Copenhagen under government auspices.

Features as director and writer: 1919: Praesidenten – The President (+ *a*); Blade af Satans bog – Leaves from Satan's Book (+ *co-a*). 1920: Prästänkan – The Parson's Widow. 1922: Die Gezeichneten – Love One Another; Der var engang – Once Upon a Time (*co-s*). 1924: Mikaël (*co-s*). 1925: Du skal aere din hustru – Thou Shalt Honour Thy Wife (+ *a*; *co-s*); Glomsdals-

bruden – Bride of Glomdal (+ *a*). 1928: La Passion de Jeanne d'Arc – The Passion of Joan of Arc – Jeanne d'Arc. 1932: Vampyr, ou L'Étrange Aventure de David Gray (*co-s*; + *co-p*). 1943: Vredens dag – Day of Wrath – Dies Irae. 1945: Två Människor – Two People (+ *co-e*). 1954: Ordet – The Word. 1964: Gertrud.

Shorts as director and writer: 1942: Mødrehjaelpen – Good Mothers. 1946: Vandet på landet (*co-s*). 1947: Landsbykirken – The Danish Village Church. (*co-s*); Kampen mod kraeften (*co-s*). 1948: De naaede faergen – They Caught the Ferry (*co-d Jorgen Roos*). 1949: Thorvaldsen. 1950: Storstrømsbroen. 1954: Et slot i et slot – Krogen og kronberg – Castle Within a Castle (*co-d Jorgen Roos*).

DRU, Joanne

(Joanne Letitia La Cock) Actress. Logan, West Virginia 1923–
Model under name Joanne Marshall before first film, *Abie's Irish Rose* (1946). Also TV. First 2 husbands were (1941–49) singer Dick Haymes and (1949–56) actor John Ireland.

Films as actress include: 1948: Red River. 1949: She Wore a Yellow Ribbon. 1950: All the King's Men; Wagonmaster; 711 Ocean Drive. 1951: Vengeance Valley; Mr Belvedere Rings the Bell. 1952: Return of the Texan; My Pal Gus. 1953: Thunder Bay; Forbidden. 1954: The Siege at Red River; Three Ring Circus; Day of Triumph. 1955: Sincerely Yours. 1956: Hell on Frisco Bay. 1959: The Light in the Forest. 1960: September Storm. 1965: Sylvia.

DUARTE, Anselmo

(Anselmo Duarte Bento) Director and writer. São Paulo, Brazil 1920–
Evening studies in economics; edited magazine O Observador Econômico e Financeiro. Studied dancing. 1942: acted in Orson Welles' unfinished film *It's All True*. Brief military service. Became extra. From 1947: acted regularly in Brazil, Argentina, Portugal, Spain, Italy including Riccardo Freda's *O Caçoulha do Barulho* (1949). 1957: first film as director and writer.

Films as director and writer: 1957: Absolutamente Certo! (+ *w*). 1962: O Pagador de promessas. 1965: Veredo do Salvaçao (+ *p*). 1969: Quelé do Pajeú (*co-s*); O Impossivel Acontece *ep* O Reimplante (+ *st*).

DUDOW, Slatan

Director. Sofia, Bulgaria 1903–1963 East Berlin
Son of railway worker. Directed plays at school. 1922: went to Berlin to study as architect; attended Institute of Theatrical Science at Berlin University. Director of workers' theatre group. Assistant to stage director Leopold Jessner. 1929: went to Moscow to collect material for thesis on Moscow theatre; directed short, *Seifenblasen.* 1932: directed *Kühle Wampe*, which Bertolt Brecht co-scripted. Member of German Communist Party; left Germany (1933); emigré in France, Italy and Switzerland. 1946: returned to East Germany. Resumed directing films for DEFA; also worked in theatre.

Films as director: 1929: Seifenblasen. 1930: Wie lebt

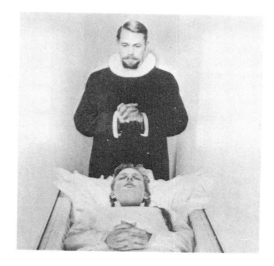

Kirk Douglas in Vincente Minnelli's Two Weeks in Another Town.
Zemlya, *directed by Alexander Dovzhenko*.
Ordet, *by Carl Dreyer*.

der Berliner Arbeiter (uf). 1932: Kühle Wampe. 1949: Unser täglich Brot (+ co-s). 1950: Familie Benthin (+ co-s; co-d Kurt Matzig). 1952: Frauenschicksale (+ co-s). 1954: Starker als die Nacht. 1956: Der Hauptmann von Köln (+ co-s). 1959: Verwirrung der Liebe (+ s).

DULAC, Germaine

(née Germaine Saisset-Schneider) Director. Amiens, France 1882–1942 Paris
Studied journalism; then theatre critic and playwright, e.g. 'L'Emprise' (1908). 1916: first film as director; usually also produced. 1919: *La Fête Espagnole* written by Louis Delluc. 1928: *La Coquille et le Clergyman* written by Antonin Artaud. Last films were shorts based on pieces of music. 1929: gave up directing own films to make newsreels for Pathé-Journal, France Actualités-Gaumont and Le Cinéma au Service de l'Histoire. From 1920: critical and historical writings on cinema.

Films as director: 1916: Géo le Mystérieux. 1917: Vénus Victrix; Les Soeurs Ennemies; Ames de fous (+ s). 1918: Dans l'ouragan de la vie. 1919: La Cigarette; La Fête Espagnole. 1920: Malencontre. 1921: La Mort du soleil; La Belle Dame sans merci. 1922: Gossette. 1923: La Souriante Madame Beudet (+ s). 1924: Le Diable dans la ville. 1925: Ame d'artiste. 1926: La Folie des vaillants. 1927: Antoinette Sabrier; Oublié – La Princesse Maudane; L'Invitation au voyage. 1928: La Coquille et le clergyman; Étude Cinématographique sur une arabesque; Thème et variations. 1929: Disque 927.

DUMONT, Margaret

Actress. 1889–1965 Hollywood, California
Singer. Appeared on stage with George M. Cohan, toured Europe. 1917: extra in *A Tale of Two Cities*. 1925: on Broadway in 'The Cocoanuts' (1925) and 'Animal Crackers' (1928) with the Marx Brothers. Acted in film versions of these shows and other Marx Brothers films. Episode with W. C. Fields in *Tales of Manhattan* (1942) dropped before film publicly shown. TV.

Films as actress include: 1929: The Cocoanuts. 1930: Animal Crackers. 1931: The Girl Habit. 1933: Duck Soup. 1934: Kentucky Kernels. 1935: A Night at the Opera. 1936: Song and Dance Man; Anything Goes. 1937: A Day at the Races; High Flyers. 1942: Never Give a Sucker an Even Break; Born to Sing. 1943: The Dancing Masters. 1944: Up in Arms; Seven Days Ashore; Bathing Beauty. 1945: The Horn Blows at Midnight; Billy Rose's Diamond Horseshoe. 1946: Little Giant. 1952: Stop, You're Killing Me. 1958: Auntie Mame. 1964: What a Way to Go!

DUNAWAY, Faye

Actress. Bascom, Florida 1941–
University of Florida; Boston University School of Fine and Applied Arts. Turned down Fulbright Scholarship. Instead worked under Elia Kazan in Lincoln Center Repertory Company for 3 years. 1966: first film; signed 6-picture deal with Otto Preminger, starting with *Hurry Sundown*. 1968: Preminger filed suit in New York alleging breach of contract; settled out of court. Also TV work.

Films as actress: 1967: The Happening; Hurry Sundown; Bonnie and Clyde; The Extraordinary Seaman (r 1969). 1968: The Thomas Crown Affair; Gli Amanti. 1969: The Arrangement. 1970: Little Big Man; Puzzle of a Downfall Child. 1971: La Maison sous les arbres; Doc.

DUNING, George

Composer. Richmond, Indiana 1908–
Cincinnati Conservatory of Music; University of Cincinnati. Musical director; film scores from 1947. Until 1962 composed mainly for Columbia; then for various companies.

Films as composer include: 1947: The Corpse Came C.O.D.; The Guilt of Janet Ames. 1949: The Dark Past. 1955: Five Against the House; The Man from Laramie; The Long Gray Line (m ad). 1956: Picnic; Storm Center. 1957: Full of Life; 3.10 to Yuma. 1958: Cowboy; Bell, Book and Candle; Me and the Colonel. 1959: It Happened to Jane; The Last Angry Man. 1960: Man On a String; Strangers When We Meet; The World of Suzie Wong. 1961: Gidget Goes Hawaiian; Two Rode Together; The Devil at 4 o'Clock. 1962: The Notorious Landlady. 1963: Critic's Choice; Island of Love; Toys in the Attic. 1964: Ensign Pulver. 1966: Any Wednesday.

DUNNE, Irene

Actress. Louisville, Kentucky 1904–
Chicago College of Music. 1920: stage debut, 'Irene' in Chicago. 1922: Broadway debut, 'The Clinging Vine'; subsequent Broadway appearances during the 1920s; toured in 'Show Boat' (1929). 1930: first film, *Leathernecking*. Films mostly for RKO until 1935. No films since *It Grows on Trees* (1952). TV and work for United Nations.

Films as actress include: 1931: Cimarron. 1932: Symphony of Six Million; Back Street. 1933: The Silver Cord; Ann Vickers; If I Were Free. 1934: This Man is Mine; Stingaree. 1935: Sweet Adeline; Magnificent Obsession. 1936: Show Boat; Theodora Goes Wild. 1937: High Wide and Handsome; The Awful Truth. 1938: Joy of Living. 1939: Love Affair; When Tomorrow Comes. 1940: My Favourite Wife. 1941: Penny Serenade; Unfinished Business. 1942: Lady in a Jam. 1944: A Guy Named Joe; The White Cliffs of Dover; Together Again. 1945: Over 21. 1946: Anna and the King of Siam. 1947: Life with Father. 1948: I Remember Mama. 1950: The Mudlark.

DUNNE, Philip

Director and writer. New York 1908–
After Harvard University, worked in banking and commerce. Started as writer by selling short story to New Yorker magazine. Moved to Hollywood after selling a story; scriptwriter from 1934. World War II: chief of overseas branch of film production for Office of War Information. From 1939: writer at Fox. 1955–61: director and writer and/or producer at Fox. Wrote and spoke for John F. Kennedy during 1960 presidential campaign.

Films as writer include: 1934: The Count of Monte Cristo (+ co-s/co-di). 1936: The Last of the Mohicans. 1938: Suez (co). 1939: The Rains Came (co); Stanley

and Livingstone (co). 1940: Johnny Apollo (co). 1941: How Green Was My Valley. 1947: The Late George Apley; The Ghost and Mrs Muir; Forever Amber (co). 1948: Escape. 1949: Pinky (co). 1951: Anne of the Indies (co). 1952: Way of a Gaucho (+ p). 1953: The Robe. 1954: The Egyptian (co); Demetrius and the Gladiators. 1965: The Agony and the Ecstasy.

Films as director: 1955: Prince of Players (+ p); The View from Pompey's Head – Secret Interlude (+ p/s). 1956: Hilda Crane (+ s). 1957: Three Brave Men (+ s). 1958: Ten North Frederick (+ s); In Love and War. 1959: Blue Denim – Blue Jeans (+ co-s). 1961: Wild in the Country; The Inspector – Lisa. 1965: Blindfold (+ co-s).

DUNNING, George

Animator. Toronto, Canada 1920–
Ontario College of Art. Book illustrator. 1943–48: with animation group of National Film Board of Canada, under Norman McLaren. 1946–47: animated films in collaboration with Colin Low – *Cadet Rousselle* (1946), *Up, Right and Wrong* (1947) and *The Adventures of Baron Münchausen* (1947, unfinished). 1948: to France. From 1956: worked in London for e.g., UPA. 1962–65: produced series 'The Beatles' animated for American TV by Jack Stokes. Also produced films, e.g. Toru Murakamis' *Power Train* (1962). 1966: directed in collaboration and produced *Canada is My Piano*, using triple screen, for Expo 67 in Montreal.

Films as animator include: 1943: Grim Pastures. 1944: J'ai tant dansé; Auprès de ma blonde. 1945: Three Blind Mice; Keep Your Mouth Shut (co-d Norman McLaren). 1947: Arbre Généalogique. 1959: The Wardrobe (+ p). 1962: The Ever Changing Motor Car (+ p; co-d Alan Ball); The Flying Man (+ d/p); The Apple (d/p/co-anim). 1962–65: The Adventures of Thud and Blunder. 1966: Canada is My Piano (+ p; co-d Bill Sewell). 1967: The Ladder (+ d/p). 1968: Yellow Submarine. 1970: Hands, Knees and Boomps-a-Daisy.

DUPONT, Ewald-André

Director. Leitz, Germany 1891–1956 Los Angeles
University of Berlin. Journalist and first film critic for BZ am Mittag. Wrote scripts, including Richard Oswald's *Renn Fieber* (1916). Story editor for Oswald. 1917: became director. Scripted Oswald's *Es werde Licht* (1918). Worked with Joe May, and in production in Germany and Italy. 1927: first American film *Love Me and the World is Mine* for Universal; wrote Herbert Wilcox's *Madame de Pompadour*. Returned to Germany. 1928–30: films in UK for British-International as own producer. 1929: made *Atlantic*, first entirely sound film made in Europe. From 1933: in USA; worked for, e.g. Universal, MGM, Paramount. After *Hell's Kitchen* (1939) left cinema; published magazine Hollywood Tribune; founded own actor's agency (1941); became press attaché. 1951: returned to films with *The Scarf*. Last films mainly released by United Artists. 1955: in collaboration scripted William Dieterle's *Magic Fire* for Republic. Also TV. Died of cancer.

Films as director include (complete from 1920): 1918: Das Geheimnis der Amerika-Docks (+ s); Europa – Postlagernd (+ s). 1919: Die Apachen; Das Grand

Hotel Babylon. 1920: Mord ohne Täter (+ co-s); Der weisse Pfau (+ co-s). 1921: Der Geier-wally – Ein Roman aus den Bergen – Geyerwally (+ s); Kinder der Finsternis (in 2 parts; + co-s). 1922: Sie und die Drei. 1923: Das alte Gesetz – Baruch; Die grüne Manuela – Ein Film aus dem Sueden. 1925: Der Demütige und die Sängerin (+ co-s); Variété – Vaudeville – Variety (+ s). 1927: Love Me and the World is Mine (+ co-s). 1928: Moulin-Rouge (+ s); Piccadilly. 1929: Atlantic – Atlantik (+ p/s). 1930: Cape Forlorn – Love Storm – Menschen im Käfig – Le Cap Perdu (+ co-s); Two Worlds (+ p). 1931: Salto Mortale. 1932: Peter Voss, der Millionendieb (+ co-s). 1933: Der Läufer von Marathon; Ladies Must Love. 1935: The Bishop Misbehaves – The Bishop's Misadventures. 1936: A Son Comes Home; Forgotten Faces; A Night of Mystery. 1937: On Such a Night; Love on Toast. 1939: Hell's Kitchen (co-d Lewis Seiler). 1951: The Scarf (+ s). 1953: Problem Girls; The Neanderthal Man; The Steel Lady – Secret of the Sahara – Treasure of Kalifa. 1954: Return to Treasure Island – Bandit Island of Karabei.

DURAS, Marguerite

Writer and director. French Indo-China 1914–
Lived in Indo-China until age of 17; studied law and physical science. Novelist from 1949. Playwright from 1955. Works adapted by others from her novels include René Clément's La Diga sul Pacifico (1958), Tony Richardson's The Sailor from Gibraltar (1967). Films as scriptwriter from 1959; as director from 1966. Moderato Cantabile, Une Aussi Longue Absence and Détruire, dit-elle are based on her novels, La Musica on her play. Play 'L'Amante Anglaise' produced in New York as 'A Place Without Doors'.

Films as writer include: 1959: Hiroshima mon amour. 1960: Moderato Cantabile. 1961: Une Aussi Longue Absence (co). 1966: 10.30 pm Summer (co); Les Rideaux Blancs.

Films as director and writer: 1966: La Musica (+ co-d Paul Seban). 1969: Détruire, dit-elle – Destroy, She Said. 1971: Jaune le soleil (+ co-e).

DURBIN, Deanna

(Edna Mae Durbin) Actress. Winnipeg, Manitoba, Canada 1921–
Radio. 1936: first film MGM short, Every Sunday Afternoon. All features made under Universal contract, starting with Three Smart Girls (1936). On radio with Eddie Cantor. 1948: retired from films. Married Universal official Vaughn Paul (1941–43, divorced), Felix Jackson, who produced some other films (1945–48, divorced), film executive Charles David (1950), her director on Lady on a Train (1945).

Films as actress include: 1937: One Hundred Men and a Girl. 1938: Mad About Music; That Certain Age. 1939: Three Smart Girls Grow Up; First Love. 1940: Spring Parade. 1941: It Started with Eve. 1944: His Butler's Sister; Christmas Holiday. 1947: Something in the Wind.

DURYEA, Dan

Actor. White Plains, New York 1907–1968 Hollywood
Cornell University, then 6 years in advertising. Broad-

way debut as a G-man in 'Dead End'. Success in 'The Little Foxes' led to appearance in film (1941). 1945–50: mainly with Universal. Frequent appearances on TV; own series, 'China Smith', and regular part in 'Peyton Place'.

Films as actor include: 1941: The Little Foxes; Ball of Fire. 1942: The Pride of the Yankees. 1943: Sahara. 1944: Man from Frisco; Mrs Parkington; None But the Lonely Heart; The Ministry of Fear; The Woman in the Window. 1945: The Valley of Decision; The Great Flamarion; Along Came Jones; Scarlet Street. 1948: Another Part of the Forest; Criss Cross. 1949: Too Late for Tears. 1950: One Way Street; Winchester '73. 1953: Thunder Bay. 1954: World for Ransom; This is My Love; Silver Lode. 1956: Storm Fear. 1957: Battle Hymn; The Burglar; Night Passage. 1960: Platinum High School. 1962: Six Black Horses. 1965: The Flight of the Phoenix.

DUSE, Eleanora

Actress. Vigevano, Italy 1858–1924 Pittsburgh, Pennsylvania
Daughter of comic actors Alessandro Vincenzo Duse and Angelica Cappolletto; infancy spent on tour with parents. 1887: formed own company. 1889: Many European tours. 1893: first American tour. 1897: Gabriele D'Annunzio wrote for her 'Il Sogno di un Mattino di Primavera'. From 1909: no foreign tours for 13 years. 1916: made only film as actress Cenere; collaborated on script, and on direction with Arturo Ambrosio. Offers for films included one from D. W. Griffith. 1922–23: toured Europe and USA. 1924: further American tour; last played in 'La Porta Chiusa'.

DUVIVIER, Julien

Director. Lille, France 1896–1967 Paris
Studied in Paris. Small parts as stage actor. Became assistant, then writer at Gaumont; worked with directors Marcel L'Herbier, Louis Feuillade and Bernard Deschamps. 1919: directed and wrote Haceldama, probably first film as director. 1922: made Der unheimliche Gast in Germany. 1924: made La Machine à refaire la vie, documentary compilation on cinematography; re-made it as sound film (1933). 1934: Maria Chapdelaine made on location in Canada. 1936: made Le Golem in Czechoslovakia. 1938: to USA to make The Great Waltz; returned to France. 1941: made Lydia in Britain; then to USA; 3 films there. 1943: made The Imposter in Algeria. After World War II, returned to France. 1948: made Anna Karenina in Britain. Black Jack (1949) and Le Retour de Don Camillo (1953) made in Spain. Scripted or co-scripted almost all his films, several in collaboration with Charles Spaak.

Films as director include: 1919: Haceldama – Le Prix de sang (+ s) 1920: La Réincarnation de Serge Renaudier (+ s) 1921: L'Agonie des aigles (co-d Bernard Deschamps) 1922: Les Roquevillard (+ s); L'Ouragan sur la montagne (+ st/s); Der unheimliche Gast. 1923: Le Reflet de Claude Mercoeur (+ s); Credo – La Tragédie de Lourdes (+ s); L'Oeuvre Immortelle. 1924: La Nuit de la revanche (+ st/s); Coeurs Farouches (+ s); La Machine à refaire la vie (co-d H. Lepage). 1925: L'Abbé Constantin (+ st); Poil de carotte (+ co-s). 1926: Le Mariage de Mlle. Beulemans

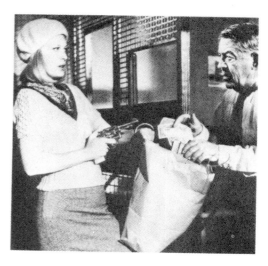

Faye Dunaway in Bonnie and Clyde, directed by Arthur Penn.
Rock Hudson in Blindfold, directed by Philip Dunne.
Dan Duryea and Joan Bennett in Fritz Lang's Scarlet Street.

(+s). 1927: L'Agonie de Jérusalem (+s); Le Mystère de la Tour Eiffel – Tramel s'en fiche; L'Homme à l'Hispano. 1928: Le Tourbillon de Paris; La Divine Croisière (+s). 1929: La Vie Miraculeuse de Thérèse Martin (+s); Maman Colibri (+co-s); Au Bonheur des dames (+co-s). 1930: David Golder. 1931: Cinq Gentlemen Maudits (+s); Die fünf verfluchten Gentlemen (+s; *German version of* Cinq Gentilshommes Maudits). 1932: Allô Berlin! Ici Paris! (+s); Poil de carotte (+s; *rm 1925*); La Vénus du collège. 1933: La Tête d'un homme (+co-s); La Machine à refaire la vie (*rm 1924*); Le Petit Roi (+s). 1934: Le Paquebot Tenacity (+co-s); Maria Chapdelaine – The Naked Heart (+s). 1935: Golgotha (+s); L'Homme du jour (+co-s). 1936: La Bandéra (+co-s); La Belle Équipe (+st/co-s); Le Golem – The Legend of Prague (+co-s). 1937: Pépé le Moko (+co-s); Un Carnet de bal – Christine (+co-ad/s). 1938: The Great Waltz. 1939: La Fin du jour (+co-ad/s); La Charrette Fantôme (+s). 1940: Untel Père et Fils – Heart of a Nation (+st/co-s). 1941: Lydia (+co-st). 1942: Tales of Manhattan (+st/co-s). 1943: Flesh and Fantasy – Obsessions (+p). 1944: The Imposter (+st/s). 1946: Panique (+co-s). 1948: Anna Karenina (+co-s). 1949: Au Royaume des cieux – Woman Hunt (+ad/s); Black Jack (+co-s). 1950: Sous le ciel de Paris coule la Seine – Under the Paris Sky (+co-ad/s). 1951: Le Petit Monde de Don Camillo – Il Piccolo Mondo di Don Camillo – Don Camillo – The Little World of Don Camillo (+co-s). 1953: La Fête à Henriette – Henriette (+st/co-s); Le Retour de Don Camillo – Il Ritorno di Don Camillo – The Return of Don Camillo (+co-ad/co-s). 1954: L'Affaire Maurizius – On Trial (+s); Marianne de ma jeunesse (+s). 1956: Voici le temps des assassins – Murder à la carte (+co-s). 1957: L'Homme à l'imperméable (+co-s/co-di); Pot-Bouille – The House of Lovers (+ad/co-s). 1958: Marie-Octobre (+co-ad); La Femme et le pantin – A Woman Like Satan (+co-ad). 1960: Boulevard (+co-ad); La Grande Vie. 1961: La Chambre Ardente – The Burning Court – The Curse and the Coffin (+co-ad). 1963: Le Diable et les dix commandements – The Devil and the Ten Commandments (+co-s). 1964: Chair de poule – Highway Pickup (+co-ad). 1967: Diaboliquement Vôtre – Diabolically Yours (+co-ad).

DWAN, Allan

Director. Toronto 1885–

Father was merchant and later politician. 1893: family settled in Chicago. Studied electrical engineering at Notre Dame University; appeared in college dramatics; football star. 1907: after graduation, stayed on to teach mathematics and physics and coach football. 1908: joined Peter Cooper Hewitt Company as illuminating engineer. 1909: went to Essanay studios to work on use of mercury vapour lamps. Sold some stories there; hired as scenario editor. 1910: scenario editor with American Film Co, founded by executives from Essanay. Went to Tucson, Arizona as unit manager for AFC with director Frank Beal. Company moved to California. 1911: replaced Beal as director. 1911–13: directed over 250 films, mainly 1-reelers, and supervised over 250 more. Company employed Marshall Neilan as actor and Victor Fleming as assistant cameraman. From 1912: Neilan and Wallace Reid alternated as directors on second company under Dwan's supervision. 1913: broke with his star, J. Warren Karrigan; moved with Neilan and Reid to Universal, again directing and supervising shorts; also

directed first feature, *Richelieu* (1914). 1914: features at Famous Players. 1915: joined the Triangle–Fine Arts unit headed by D. W. Griffith, films included 4 with Douglas Fairbanks as star and sometimes writer. 1917–18: writer and director for Fairbanks with whom he later made *Robin Hood* (1922) and *The Iron Mask* (1929). 1919: 2 films for William Randolph Hearst and Marion Davies. From 1920 also producer on some films. 1923–26: at Famous Players–Lasky; films included 8 with Gloria Swanson. 1926–32: mainly with Fox and First National for which also produced, e.g. Mervyn LeRoy's *Harold Teen* (1928). 1932: in Europe to take a cure in Germany, made 3 films in UK. 1934: co-directed *Hollywood Party* with Richard Boleslavsky and Roy Rowland. 1935–40: under contract to Fox; films include 6 with Claire Trevor and 3 with Shirley Temple. 1946–53: at Republic. 1954: met independant producer Benedict Bogeaus with whom he made almost all remaining films. 1956: 2 films for TV. Last film shot in 1958.

Features as director: 1914: Richelieu (+s); Wildflower (+co-s); The County Chairman (+s); The Straight Road; The Conspiracy; The Unwelcome Mrs Hatch. 1915: The Dancing Girl; David Harum; The Love Route; The Commanding Officer; May Blossom; The Pretty Sister of José; A Girl of Yesterday; The Foundling (ur); Jordan is a Hard Road (+s). 1916: Betty of Greystone; The Habit of Happiness – Laugh and the World Laughs (+st/co-s); The Good Bad Man – Passing Through; An Innocent Magdalene; The Half-Breed – The Carquenez Woods; Manhattan Madness; Fifty-Fifty (+st). 1917: Panthea (+s); The Fighting Odds; A Modern Musketeer (+s). 1918: Mr Fix-It (+s); Bound in Morocco (+s); He Comes Up Smiling 1919: Cheating Cheaters; Getting Mary Married; The Dark Star; Soldiers of Fortune; The Luck of the Irish. 1920: The Forbidden Thing (+p/co-s). 1921: A Perfect Crime (+p/s); A Broken Doll (+p/s); The Scoffer (+p); The Sin of Martha Queed (+p/s); In the Heart of a Fool (+p); A Perfect Crime (+p/s); The Broken Doll (+p). 1922: The Hidden Woman; Superstition (+p); Robin Hood. 1923: The Glimpses of the Moon (+p); Lawful Larceny; Zaza (+p); Big Brother (+p). 1924: A Society Scandal (+p); Manhandled (+p); Her Love Story (+p); Wages of Virtue (+p); Argentine Love (+p). 1925: Night Life of New York (+p); Coast of Folly (+p); Stage Struck (+p). 1926: Sea Horses (+p); Padlocked (+p); Tin Gods (+p); Summer Bachelors (+p). 1927: The Music Master (+p); The Joy Girl (+p); East Side West Side (+s); French Dressing (+p). 1928: The Big Noise (+p). 1929: The Iron Mask; Tide of Empire; The Far Call; Frozen Justice; South Sea Rose. 1930: What a Widow! (+p); Man to Man. 1931: Chances; Wicked. 1932: While Paris Sleeps. 1933: Her First Affaire; Counsel's Opinion. 1934: I Spy; Hollywood Party (co-d, uc). 1935: Black Sheep – Star for a Night (+st); Navy Wife – Beauty's Daughter. 1936: The Song and Dance Man; Human Cargo; High Tension – Trouble Makers; 15 Maiden Lane. 1937: Woman-Wise; That I May Live One Mile From Heaven; Heidi. 1938: Rebecca of Sunnybrook Farm; Josette; Suez. 1939: The Three Musketeers; The Gorilla; Frontier Marshal. 1940: Sailor's Lady; Young People; Trail of the Vigilantes. 1941: Look Who's Laughing (+p); Rise and Shine. 1942: Friendly Enemies; Here We Go Again (+p). 1943: Around the World (+p). 1944: Up In Mabel's Room; Abroad with Two Yanks. 1945:

Brewster's Millions; Getting Gertie's Garter (+co-s). 1946: Rendezvous with Annie – Corporal Dolan AWOL (+as-p). 1947: Calendar Girl (+as-p); Northwest Outpost (+as-p); Driftwood. 1948: The Inside Story (+p); Angel in Exile (co-d Philip Ford). 1949: Sands of Iwo-Jima. 1950: Surrender (+as-p). 1951: Belle le Grand; 1951 The Wild Blue Yonder – Thunder Across the Pacific – Bombs Over Japan. 1952: I Dream of Jeanie; Montana Belle. 1953: The Woman They Almost Lynched; Sweethearts on Parade (+as-p); Flight Nurse (+co-lyr). 1954: Silver Lode; Passion; Cattle Queen of Montana. 1955: Escape to Burma; Pearl of the South Pacific; Tennessee's Partner (+co-s). 1956: Slightly Scarlet; Hold Back the Night. 1957: The River's Edge; The Restless Breed. 1958: Enchanted Island; The Most Dangerous Man Alive (r 1961).

E

EAMES, Charles *and* Ray

Designers and short film-makers. Charles: St Louis, Missouri 1907– . Ray (Kaiser): details unknown

Charles studied architecture at Washington University. 1930: set up own practice. Worked with Eliel and Eero Saarinen. 1940: with Eero Saarinen designed chairs for Museum of Modern Art's Organic Furniture Competition. 'Eames Chairs' among first successful moulded plywood and moulded plastic chairs to be mass-produced in USA. 1940: married Ray, a painter: shared all subsequent credits. 1941: perfected inexpensive lamination process for wood veneers; Charles worked in MGM art department. World War II: designed equipment for US Navy. Designed toys and furniture which became subjects of some of their films. 1949: designed Santa Monica House shown in *House* (1955). 1950: first film. Worked in TV design. From 1953: multi-media demonstrations in information presentation, using e.g. printed and other visual material, and smells. 1957: worked on aerial sequences in Billy Wilder's *The Spirit of St Louis*. 1959: in collaboration with John Whitney made film for multi-screen presentation at American Exhibition in Moscow, commissioned by State Department, *Glimpses of USA*. 1960: directed sequences in CBS TV film *Fabulous Fifties*. 1962: made government-commissioned multi-screen introduction for Science Exhibition at Seattle; directed sequences in CBS TV film *The Good Years*. 1964: for New York World's Fair made *Think*, using 22 screens. 1967: as part of report to Department of Interior on proposed National Aquarium made *National Aquarium Presentation*. 1970: Charles occupied Chair of Poetry at Harvard. All films are shorts directed and written by both, photographed by Charles. Elmer Bernstein scored several; Glen Fleck assistant on many. Some films for schools, some for companies e.g. IBM and ALCOA. Adviser on design and environment to West German, Indian and US governments. Consultant teacher in various universities. Awarded almost every outstanding design award. Designer of packaging, and other consumer and industrial products.

Films as directors and writers, photographed by Charles: 1950: Traveling Boy. 1952: Parade – Here

They Come Down the Street; Blacktop. 1953: Bread; Calligraphy; Communications Primer. 1954: Sofa Compact. 1955: 2 Baroque Churches in Germany; House; Textiles and Ornamental Arts of India. 1956: Eames Lounge Chair. 1957: Day of the Dead; Toccata for Toy Trains; The Information Machine. 1958: The Expanding Airport; Herman Miller at the Brussels Fair. 1959: De Gaulle Sketch; Glimpses of USA (co-d John Whitney). 1960: Jazz Chair; Introduction to Feedback. 1961: IBM Mathematics Peep Show; Kaleidoscope; Kaleidoscope Shop. 1962: ECS; House of Science; Before the Fair. 1962-63: IBM Fair Presentation Film, parts I and II. 1964-65: Think - View from the People Wall (single screen version). 1965: IBM Puppet Shows; IBM at the Fair; Westinghouse ABC; The Smithsonian Institution; The Smithsonian Newsreel. 1966: Boeing the Leading Edge. 1967: IBM Museum; A Computer Glossary; National Aquarium Presentation; Schuetz Machine 1968: Lick Observatory; Babbage; Powers of 10. 1969: Photography and the City; Tops.

EASTMAN, George

Industrialist. Waterville, New York 1854-1932 Rochester, New York

Worked in bank. Compounded workable formula for dry plates, constructed machine to coat them automatically. To UK: patented the machine, released on royalty basis, then sold UK rights for £500. 1884: founded photographic factory, specialising in roll film; patented 'stripping paper', replacing heavy glass as backing material for emulsion. Later set emulsion on a grainless transparent base, celluloid, made in 200-foot lengths: basis of his fortune. 1888: put first popular camera on market, No 1 Kodak. 1889: patented later-alled perforated film. 1889-92: manufactured 35mm film for Thomas Edison. World-wide monopoly in photographic products until 1909. 1920-23: manufactured film for amateurs on 16 mm and 8 mm. 1924: bought Pathé factories in Europe and UK. Lost lawsuit to Ansco company over patents rivalry: paid $5 million; lost lawsuit to US Government under Sherman monopoly laws, settled by arbitration. Large donations to Rochester University, Massachusetts Institute of Technology, and charities. Opened dental clinics in, e.g. London and Rome. Gave his workers stock valued at $10 million.

EASTWOOD, Clint

Actor. San Francisco 1930-

High School basketball star. Lumberjack, then army service. Studying at Los Angeles College when offered Universal contract. 1955: first film, Francis in the Navy. Small parts at Universal and RKO. From 1956: in CBS TV series 'Rawhide'; 7 years in TV. First starring film part in Italian western Per un pugno di dollari (1964). First film as director and actor Play Misty for Me (1971), in which Donald Siegel acted.

Films as actor (complete from 1964): 1964: Per un pugno di dollari. 1965: Per qualche dollari in più. 1966: Le Streghe ep Una sera come le altre. 1967: Il Buono, il brutto, il cattivo. 1968: Hang 'em High; Coogan's Bluff. 1969: Where Eagles Dare; Paint Your Wagon. 1970: Two Mules for Sister Sara; Kelly's Heroes. 1971: The Beguiled; Play Misty for Me (+ d); Dirty Harry.

EDENS, Roger

Producer. Hillsboro, Texas 1905-1970 Hollywood
Began as pianist in pit orchestra in New York. Accompanist and vocal arranger for Ethel Merman; continued association after joining MGM as musical supervisor (1933). 1940: associate to Arthur Freed at MGM. 1954: producer at MGM and Paramount. 1962: associate producer at MGM. Contributed music and/or lyrics to Ziegfeld Follies (1946), Good News (1947), Take Me Out to the Ball Game (1949), Funny Face (1957). Oscars for scoring musicals: Easter Parade (with Johnny Green, 1948), On the Town (with Lennie Hayton, 1949), Annie Get Your Gun (with Adolph Deutsch, 1950).

Films as producer include: 1946: The Harvey Girls (as-p). 1947: Good News (as-p). 1953: The Band Wagon (as-p). 1954: Deep In My Heart. 1957: Funny Face. 1962: Billy Rose's Jumbo (as-p). 1964: The Unsinkable Molly Brown (as-p). 1969: Hello, Dolly! (as-p).

EDESON, Arthur

Cinematographer. New York 1891-1970
Began as portrait photographer; entered cinema as assistant cameraman during World War I, becoming cinematographer in 1917 with Douglas Fairbanks's company, Artcraft. On many Douglas Fairbanks films until mid-'20s. 1936-47: worked mainly for Warners. Last film before retirement, The O'Flynn (1948), produced by Douglas Fairbanks Jnr. 1953: President of American Society of Cinematographers.

Films as cinematographer include: 1917: In Again, Out Again; Wild and Woolly; Reaching for the Moon. 1919: Cheating Cheaters. 1921: The Three Musketeers. 1922: Robin Hood (+ co-special effects) 1924: The Thief of Bagdad. 1926: Stella Dallas. 1927: The Patent Leather Kid (co). 1929: In Old Arizona (co). 1930: All Quiet on the Western Front; The Big Trail (co). 1931: Frankenstein. 1932: The Old Dark House. 1933: The Invisible Man. 1935: Mutiny on the Bounty. 1936: China Clipper; Ceiling Zero. 1937: They Won't Forget. 1939: Each Dawn I Die. 1941: Sergeant York (co); The Maltese Falcon, 1943: Casablanca. 1944: The Conspirators; The Mask of Dimitrios. 1946: Two Guys from Milwaukee.

EDISON, Thomas Alva

Inventor. Milan, Ohio 1847-1931 Orange, New Jersey Dutch Father, Scottish mother. 3 months schooling. 1859: railroad newsboy. 1862: telegraph operator in various cities; studied and experimented in spare time. 1868: took out first patent for electrical vote recorder. 1874: invented stock tickers, telegraph systems, and electric pen from which mimeograph was developed. 1877: applied for patent for phonograph. 1879: made incandescent lamp in which loop of carbonised cotton thread glowed in vacuum for more than 40 hours. For next 10 years invented and exploited methods of generating and distributing electricity. 1883: hired W. K. L. Dickson; patented 'Edison Effect' – thermionic emission – basis of diode valve. 1885: patented method of transmitting telegraphic signals from moving trains or between ships, by induction. From 1887: manufactured and sold motor-driven phonograph with cylindrical wax records; later developed disc form of record with diamond point for music, then Ediphone

Unidentified female and Jimmy Durante in Hollywood Party, *partly directed by Allan Dwan.*
Clint Eastwood in Per Un Pugno Di Dollari, *directed by Sergio Leone.*
Howard Hawks's Sergeant York, *co-photographed by Arthur Edeson.*

for office dictation. 1888: appointed Dickson head of his ore-milling department; Eadweard Muybridge lecture in Orange attended by Edison and Dickson; Edison announced work to combine reproduction of image and sound; set Dickson working on preliminary development of recording moving images with drum covered in micro photographs; filed his first motion picture Caveat, i.e. description of proposed invention that operates as 6 months bar to other patent applications for same invention. During lifetime, filed 120 Caveats, each for a number of patentable items. 1889: filed 3 more motion picture Caveats in order to 'keep alive' original filing, supporting claim with descriptions of fictitious apparatus. Dickson began motion picture experiments, subsidiary to company's work with iron ore; Edison met Étienne-Jules Marey in Paris. 1890: first Edison-sponsored motion picture demonstration with Anschütz tachyscope; with Dickson patented magnetic ore separator; collaborated with George Parsons Lathrop on science fiction novel. 1891: applied for 3 patents (for a Kinetoscope camera, a Kinetoscope 'peepshow' viewer and a machine to project motion pictures at a rate of 46 frames per second), which were never fully accepted; litigation continued until 1916. 1892: planned marketing of Kinetoscope; 'Black Maria' film studio designed by Dickson built on Edison's West Orange Property (completed 1893). 1894: opened first Kinetoscope parlour in New York, followed by others, e.g. in Chicago, San Francisco, Ashbury Park, Atlantic City, Philadelphia, Washington D.C. 1895: abandoned synchronised sound experiments; manufactured and sold 45 Kinetophones, with non-synchronised music via earphones to accompany Kinetoscope images; Dickson left Edison's company. Kinetoscope business began to decline on invention and introduction of first successful motion picture projector, the Vitascope, by C. Francis Jenkins and Thomas Armat (1895); Edison laboratory continued making films for others' projectors. From 1896: many lawsuits instigated by Edison for infringement of alleged motion picture patents; used Horizontal Feed camera (dated by him and his lawyers as in use since 1889, but probably built 1895–96) and another spurious camera built 1903–05 as evidence during litigation. 1906: court ruling against Edison. 1908: conceived sound synchronisation by rigid rod along cinema connecting projector to phonograph behind screen. 1909: co-founder of Motion Picture Patents Company. 1910: William Friese-Greene travelled to USA to testify in re-opened motion picture patents case; US Supreme Court ruled that Friese-Greene held master patent as of 1889. 1911: Dickson testified in Patent Company's litigation. 1913: public demonstration of rigid shaft synchronisation at Edison laboratory. 1916: litigation ended when Motion Picture Patents Company overthrown by US Supreme Court. World War I: Edison laboratory worked on naval problems, also production of phenol and other chemicals for US Government. 1926: Edison wrote to Royal Photographic Society of Great Britain confessing some claims false. 1927: admitted same to US National Academy of Sciences. 1928: presented spurious camera built between 1903 and 1905 to Henry Ford. By 1928 had taken out 1,033 patents.

EDWARDS, Blake

Director, writer and producer. Tulsa, Oklahoma 1922–
From a theatrical family. Served in US Coast Guard.

Acted in films from 1942, e.g. *Ten Gentlemen from West Point* (1942), *In the Meantime, Darling* (1944). 1948: played second lead in Richard Quine's first film as director *Leather Gloves*. 1948–49: produced in collaboration and co-wrote *Panhandle* (also acted) and *Stampede*, both directed by Lesley Selander for Allied Artists. Wrote many radio shows, originated 'Richard Diamond' for Dick Powell. 1952: returned to film work; began writing collaboration with Richard Quine. They wrote 7 films, including 4 specially written for Mickey Rooney. For TV, directed own scripts, e.g. on 'Four Star Playhouse'. 1955: first film as director. Wrote story of his own *He Laughed Last* (1956) in collaboration with Quine. 1962: his script, written 4 years previously, re-written for Quine's *The Notorious Landlady*. TV work, including series 'Peter Gunn' and 'Mister Lucky'. 1964: took over direction of *A Shot in the Dark* from Anatole Litvak. 1967: based *Gunn* on TV series 'Peter Gunn'. 1968: directed Julie Andrews in *Darling Lili*. 1969: married her. Produced most of own films since 1964. 1970: formed production company with Harold Robbins and Alden Schwimmer.

Films as writer in collaboration include: 1952: Sound Off; Rainbow 'Round my Shoulder. 1953: Cruisin' Down the River; All Ashore. 1954: Drive a Crooked Road (*alone*). 1955: My Sister Eileen. 1957: Operation Mad Ball. 1962: The Notorious Landlady.

Films as director and writer: 1955: Bring Your Smile Along (+ *co-st*). 1956: He Laughed Last (+ *co-st*). 1957: Mister Cory. 1958: This Happy Feeling. 1964: The Pink Panther (*co-s*). 1965: The Great Race (*co-st*).

Films as director and producer: 1964: A Shot in the Dark (+ *co-s*). 1966: What Did You Do in the War, Daddy? (+ *co-st*); Gunn (+ *st/co-s*). 1968: The Party (+ *st/co-s*). 1970: Darling Lili (+ *co-s*). 1971: Wild Rovers (+ *s*; *co-p*).

EGGELING, Viking

Director. Lund, Sweden 1880–1925 Berlin
1897: to Paris. 1917: to Zurich. Worked on scroll drawings. From 1918: collaborated with Hans Richter. 1921: to Berlin. 1923–24: with assistance of Erna Niemayer filmed one of his scrolls as animated short *Symphonie Diagonale* (included in *30 Years of Experiment*, compiled by Richter in 1951); financial help from Ufa. Remade it 3 times; publicly shown only once, in Berlin accompanied by music of Beethoven. Died of septic angina.

EISENSTEIN, Sergei

Director. Riga, Russia 1898–1948 Moscow
Son of an architect. 1914–17: architectural–engineering studies at School of Public Works, Petrograd. 1918: enlisted in Red Army: poster-painter, theatrical designer. 1920: to Moscow. 1921–22: theatrical set and costume designer; collaborated with Sergei Yutkevitch on 'Macbeth'; worked on 'Heartbreak House' for Vsevolod Meyerhold and on Jack London's 'The Mexican' for Proletkult theatre. 1923: directed 'The Mexican' for Proletkult; directed Grigori Alexandrov as actor; directed by Alexander Ostrovsky in 'Enough Simplicity for Every Wise Man'; first film as director used in the production and in Dziga Vertov's *Kino-Pravda*. 1924: *Stachka* produced by Goskino and Proletkult; assisted by Alexandrov.

Before its release left Proletkult to work for Sevzapkino. With Esther Shub re-edited *Dr Mabuse, der Spieler* (1922) for Soviet showing. 1925: *Bronenosets 'Potyomkin'* for Goskino; Alexandrov assistant and actor. 1926: to Berlin to introduce the film. 1927–29: worked for Sovkino. He and Alexandrov began *Staroie i novoie*, interrupted work to make *Oktyabre*, then returned to it. 1929: with Alexandrov and Edouard Tissé travelled to Berlin, Switzerland, Paris, London; attended congress of independent films at La Sarraz; collaborated on an unfinished film; began to teach film. 1930: threat of deportation averted by protests of writers and artists; credited as co-director of Alexandrov's *Romance Sentimentale* though had little hand in it. Put under Paramount contract by Jesse Lasky: to USA. Scenario for *An American Tragedy* rejected by Paramount who broke contract. Upton Sinclair agreed to finance a film in Mexico. 1931: from Mexico sent 60,000 metres of film to Hollywood laboratories for development. Break with Sinclair, refused visa to return to USA. When visa granted, not allowed to spend time in Hollywood. Sinclair agreed to send negative to Moscow; shipped it, ordered it returned, agreement with Sol Lesser to have material edited in USA. 1933: Lesser's film *Thunder Over Mexico* released. Taught at Moscow Film Institute. 1935: began shooting of *Bezhin Lug*; work halted. 1936: second version half-completed then stopped. 1937: denounced by Boris Shumyatsky, general director of Soviet cinema; Eisenstein publicly criticised himself, began work on *Aleksandr Nevskii* for Mosfilm. Other projects halted by war. 1939: artistic head of Mosfilm; Marie Seton made *Time in the Sun* from Eisenstein's Mexican material from footage not used in *Thunder in Mexico*; other portions used in *Death Day* (1933), edited by Upton Sinclair; in Pathé Shorts; and in features, e.g. *Viva Villa!* (1934). 1940: directed and designed 'Die Walküre' at Bolshoi Theatre. 1941: Mosfilm moved to Alma-Ata, where *Ivan Groznyi* shot. 1941–45: shooting and editing *Ivan Groznyi*, parts I and II, using some colour in part II, for Central Cinema Studio, Alma-Ata. 1946: coronary; part II condemned by Central Committee on Cinema and Theatre; placed in archives. 1947: prepared part III to be in colour; saw American-edited versions of Mexican footage. 1948: died of heart attack. 1958: part II released; Jay Leyda assembled *Eisenstein's Mexican Project* from unused material. 1966: Yutkevitch and Naum Kleimann assembled montage of stills from *Bezhin Lug*, music by Sergei Prokofiev, who wrote music for *Aleksandr Nevskii* and *Ivan Groznyi*. Tissé photographed all his films, often in collaboration. Eisenstein's writings on cinema include 'Film Form', 'Film Sense', essays and lectures.

Films as director: 1923: Kinodnevik Glumova – Glumov's Film-Diary. 1924: Stachka – Strike (+ *co-s*). 1925: Bronenosets 'Potyomkin' – Battleship Potemkin. 1927: Oktyabre – October – Ten Days That Shook the World (+ *co-s*; *co-d Grigori Alexandrov*). 1929: Staroie i novoie – The Old and the New – Generalnaya Linnia – The General Line (+ *co-s*; *co-d Grigori Alexandrov*); Sturm über la Sarraz – Kampf des unabhängigen gegen den kommerziellen Film (+ *w*; *co-d Hans Richter, Ivor Montagu*). 1931: Que Viva Mexico (*uf*; *co-d Grigori Alexandrov*). 1935: Bezhin Lug – Bezhin Meadow (*uf*). 1938: Aleksandr Nevskii – Alexander Nevsky (+ *co-s*; *co-d Dmitri Vasiliev*). 1944: Ivan Groznyi (I) – Ivan the Terrible, part I (+ *s*). 1945: Ivan Groznyi: Boyarskii

zagovor – Ivan the Terrible, part II: the Boyars' Plot
(r 1958; +s).

EISLER, Hanns

Composer. Leipzig, Germany 1898–1962 East Berlin
Studied under Arnold Schoenberg in Vienna. First film
score for Walter Ruttmann's short *Opus III* (1925).
From 1927: worked with Bertolt Brecht and Kurt
Weill; composed incidental music for Brecht's 'Galileo
Galilei'. From 1929: wrote music for European films
including Joris Ivens documentaries. Left Germany
because of Nazi regime to live in USA. Music for some
American films and incidental music for Clifford Odets
and George Bernard Shaw plays. 1947: unfriendly
witness before House Un-American Activities
Committee; deportation ordered by the United States
Immigration Service. In East Germany organised and
composed music for workers' choirs. Composed East
German National Anthem and much concert music.
Book, 'Composing for the Film'.

Films as composer include: 1932: Kühle Wampe (co);
Komsomol. 1934: Le Grand Jeu; Nieuwe Gronden—
New Earth. 1939: The Four Hundred Million; Pete
Roleum and his Cousins (co). 1941: A Child Went
Forth. 1943: Hangmen Also Die! 1944: None But the
Lonely Heart. 1945: Jealousy; The Spanish Main.
1946: Deadline at Dawn; A Scandal in Paris. 1947:
The Woman on the Beach; So Well Remembered.
1949: Unser täglich Brot. 1952: Frauenschicksale.
1955: Bel Ami; Nuit et Brouillard. 1956: Herr Puntila
und sein Knecht Matti.

EKBERG, Anita

Actress. Malmö, Sweden 1931–
Began as photographer's model. 1951: 'Miss Sweden'.
Hollywood from 1953. Attracted attention on Bob
Hope's Christmas Tour (1954). Husbands included
actor Anthony Steel. 1953–62: worked mainly in Italy.

Films as actress include: 1955: Blood Alley; Artists
and Models; Man in the Vault. 1956: War and Peace;
Back from Eternity; Hollywood or Bust; Zarak. 1957:
Valerie. 1958: Paris Holiday; Screaming Mimi. 1959:
La Dolce Vita. 1960: I Mongoli. 1962: Boccaccio '70
ep Le Tentazioni del Dottor Antonio. 1963: 4 for
Texas; Call Me Bwana. 1966: The Alphabet Murders;
Way . . . Way Out. 1967: Woman Times Seven. 1970:
Clowns.

EKK, Nikolai

Director. Moscow 1898–
Son of railway worker. Acting and direction at State
Theatre School under Vsevolod Meyerhold. Acted
in theatre, became stage manager. State Cinema
School. Wrote for theatre and films. Technician at
Mezhrabpom Studio. 1928–39: worked on documentaries. 1931: made *Putyovka v zhizn*, first Soviet film to
be conceived and written as sound film; used professional and non-actors. 1936: made *Grunya
Kornakova*, first Soviet fiction colour film. Unrealised
projects include *Hamlet*. To Kiev studio.

Films as director include: 1931: Putyovka v zhizn –
The Road to Life (+ co-s). 1936: Grunya Kornakova –
Nightingale, Little Nightingale (+ co-s). 1939:
Sorochinskaya Yamarka – Sorochinsky Fair (+ s).

EKMAN, Hasse

Director, writer and actor. Stockholm 1915–
Son of actor Gosta Ekman. Educated in Stockholm.
1932: stage debut in Goteborg. 1933: first film as actor
Hemslavinnor. 1935: studied in Hollywood. 1936–39:
worked for Svensk Filmindustri. 1938: wrote biography of father 'Gosta Ekman'; first film as writer
Blixt och dunder (and acted). 1940–45: worked for
Terra Film. From 1940: scripted many films directed
by Schamyl Bauman, acted in several. 1940: first film
as director. 1946–47: worked at Europa Film.
1948–52: returned to Terra Film. 1949–53: acted in 3
films directed by Ingmar Bergman. 1953–64: returned
to Svensk Filmindustri. Number of script collaborations with Stig Olin and acted in his *Gula Divisionen*
(1954). 1955: autobiography 'Den Vackra Aukungen'.
1956: novel 'Kurre Korint och Drömfabriken'. Also
stage director.

Films as director and actor: 1941: Första Divisionen –
First Division. 1942: Lågor i dunklet – Flames in the
Dark. 1943: Ombyte av tåg – Changing Trains –
Unexpected Meeting. 1944: En Dag skall gry – A Day
Shall Dawn. 1945: Kungliga Patrasket – The Royal
Rabble; Vandring med månen – Wandering with the
Moon; Fram för Lilla Märta – Three Cheers for Little
Marta. 1946: I Dödens väntrum – In Death's Waiting
Room; Möte i natten – Nightly Encounter; Medan
porten var stängd – When the Door was Closed. 1947:
En fluga gör ingen sommar – One Swallow Doesn't
Make a Summer. 1948: Var sin väg – Each Goes His
Own Way; Lilla Märta kommer tillbaka – Little Marta
Returns; Banketten – The Banquet. 1949: Flickan från
tredje raden – The Girl from the Gallery. 1950: Hjärter
Knekt – Jack of Hearts. 1956: Sjunde Himlen – The
Seventh Heaven (+ m/lyr); Ratataa. 1957: Med glorian
på sned – With the Halo Askew; Jazzgossen – The
Jazz Boy (+ lyr). 1958: Den Stora Amatören – The
Great Amateur. 1959: Fröken Chic – Miss Chic;
Himmel och pannkaka – Good Heavens. 1960:
Kärlekens decimaler – The Decimals of Love; På en
bänk i en park – On a Bench in a Park.

Films as director: 1940: Med dej i mina armor – With
you in My Arms. 1942: Lyckan kommer – Luck
Arrives. 1943: Sjätte skottet. 1944: Excellensen – His
Excellency; Som folk är mest – Like Most People.
1950: Flicka och hyacinter – Girl with Hyacinths –
The Suicide; Den Vita Katten – The White Cat.
1952: Eldfågeln – The Fire Bird. 1953: Vi tre debutera
– We Three are Making our Debut. 1954: Gabrielle.
1956: Egen Ingång – Private Entrance. 1957:
Sommarnöje sokes – A Summer Place is Wanted.
1961: Stöten – The Job. 1963: Min Kära är en ros – My
Love is a Rose. 1964: Aktenskapsbrottaren.

Films as writer include: 1956: Kyssen på kryssen (co).
1953: Glasberget (+ w). 1959: Det Svänger på slottet
(co).

Films as actor include: 1933: Kära Släkten. 1936:
Intermezzo. 1949: Fängelse; Törst. 1953: Gycklarnas
Afton.

ELTON, Sir Arthur

Producer and director. London 1906–
Marlborough College and Jesus College, Cambridge.
1927: joined script department of Gainsborough

The Great Race, *directed by Blake Edwards.*
Battleship Potemkin, *directed by Sergei Eisenstein.*
Eisenstein's Bezhin Meadow.

Pictures. 1929: repertory in Germany. 1931: joined Empire Marketing Board Film Unit. 1934–37: GPO Film Unit. 1938: founded Film Centre, London. 1937–45: with Ministry of Information, from 1941 supervisor of films. 1952–54: produced 5 films directed by Bert Haanstra for Shell.

Films as director: 1931: Shadow on the Mountain; Upstream. 1932: Voice of the World. 1933: Aero Engine (+ s/e). 1935: Housing Problems (co-d Edgar Anstey); Workers and Jobs (+ p). 1940: Men Behind the Meters.

ELVEY, Maurice

(William Seward Folkard) Director. Darlington, Yorkshire 1887–1967 Brighton, Sussex
No education. At 9: streetseller; later hotel pageboy. Became stage actor and director. 1911: founded Adelphi Play Society. 1913: first films as director, shorts; first feature The Great Gold Robbery. Worked for Motograph, British and Colonial, Hepworth, Butcher's, Ideal. 1918: moved to Stoll, where made 100 films. 1924: to Hollywood, made e.g. Curly Top and My Husband's Wives, both for Fox. 1926: in Germany directed Tragödie einer Ehe for Ufa; joined Gaumont–British. Later worked for e.g. Gainsborough, British Lion, Fox–British etc. 1956: collaborated on script of Terence Fisher's The Last Man to Hang. 1961: retired after losing an eye. Made over 300 films. Married actress Isobel Elsom.

Films as director include: 1913: Maria Marten (+ p). 1914: The Suicide Club (+ p). 1915: Florence Nightingale (+ p). 1916: When Knights were Bold (+ p). 1917: Smith (+ p). 1918: Dombey and Son; Hindle Wakes (+ p); Adam Bede; Nelson (+ p). 1919: Comradeship – Comrades in Arms. 1921: The Hound of the Baskervilles; The Fruitful Vine. 1922: The Passionate Friends. 1923: The Sign of Four; Sally Bishop; Don Quixote. 1924: Curly Top; My Husband's Wives. 1925: The Flag Lieutenant. 1927: Hindle Wakes; Roses of Picardy (+ co-p). 1929: High Treason. 1930: School for Scandal; Balaclava (co-d Milton Rosmer). 1931: Sally in our Alley; The Water Gipsies; The Lodger. 1933: The Wandering Jew. 1935: The Tunnel – Transatlantic Tunnel. 1936: Spy of Napoleon; The Man in the Mirror. 1937: A Romance in Flanders. 1938: The Return of the Frog. 1939: Sons of the Sea. 1940: Under Your Hat. 1943: Salute John Citizen; The Lamp Still Burns. 1944: Medal for the General. 1946: Beware of Pity. 1951: The Late Edwina Black. 1953: House of Blackmail; Is Your Honeymoon Really Necessary. 1954: What Every Woman Wants; The Happiness of Three Women. 1955: You Lucky People. 1956: Fun at St Fanny's; Stars in Your Eyes; Dry Rot. 1957: Second Fiddle.

EMERSON, John

Director and writer. Sandusky, Ohio 1874–1956 Pasadena, California
Chicago and Heidelberg Universities. Father Episcopalian minister. Began training for ministry. 1904: on stage in New York; actor on Broadway until 1911. 1908–11: stage manager for the Schuberts. 1911–15: general stage manager for Charles Frohman. 1914–22: directed over 25 plays on Broadway. From 1915: in films as director and writer (occasionally at first as actor); began with Triangle, directing early Douglas Fairbanks films. 1917: with Fairbanks's company, Artcraft. 1919: married Anita Loos, with whom wrote plays (directing them on stage), film adaptations, screenplays and stories. 1922: gave up directing in favour of writing. With Anita Loos adapted Gentlemen Prefer Blondes (1928) from their play and her story. Films written by others from their plays include The Social Register (1934). From 1931: with MGM; co-producer on San Francisco (1936) and producer on Mama Steps Out (1937), both with screenplays by Anita Loos. Wrote 2 books with her: 'How to Write Photoplays' (1918) and 'Breaking Into the Movies' (1921). Retired 1937.

Films as director include: 1915: Ghosts; Old Heidelburg (+ ad). 1916: His Picture in the Papers (+ co-s). 1917: Wild and Woolly; Down to Earth (+ co-s); In Again, Out Again; Reaching for the Moon (+ co-s). 1918: Come On In (+ co-p/co-s); Goodbye, Bill (+ co-p/co-st). 1919: Oh, You Women! (+ co-st/co-s). 1922: Polly of the Follies (+ co-s).

Films as writer in collaboration with Anita Loos include: 1925: Learning to Love (st/ad). 1931: The Struggle (st only). 1934: The Girl from Missouri.

EMMER, Luciano

Director. Milan, Italy 1918–
1940: interrupted university law studies to make short documentaries on painters. Until 1949: made only shorts, all co-directed and co-written with Enrico Gras and (to 1943) Tatiana Grauding. 1950: first feature Domenica d'agosto – Sunday in August. Continued to make occasional shorts. 1954: artistic supervision on Gli Eroi d'Artide. 1956: A chacun son paradis in collaboration with Robert Enrico, feature-length documentary. Scripted all own films, often in collaboration. Then moved to TV.

Films as director and writer (to 1949 in collaboration with Enrico Gras and Tatiana Grauding; 1944–49 with Gras only): 1940: Racconto da una affresco – Giotto; Il Paradiso Terrestre (r 1946). 1941: Romanzo di un'epoca. 1942: Guerrieri (+ n); Il Cantico delle creature (+ n). 1943: Destino d'amore (ur); Il Paese del nascita Mussolini; Il Conte di Luna. 1947: Bianchi Pascoli (+ n); Sulla via di Damasco (+ n); San Gennaro; La Terra del melodramma. 1948: Isole della laguna – Islands on the Lagoon; Romantici a Venezia – Romantics in Venice; Il Paradiso Perduto – Bosch; Il Dramma di Cristo (+ n); La Leggenda di Sant'Orsola – The Legend of St Ursula; Luoghi Verdiani – Sulle Rome di Verdi. 1949: I Fratelli Miracolosi – The Miraculous Brothers (+ n); Allegoria di primavera – The Story of Spring – Botticelli (+ n); L'Invenzione della Croce – La Leggenda della Croce – Legend of the True Cross (+ n); La Colonna Traiana (+ n). 1950: Domenica d'agosto – Sunday in August (co-s); Goya – Festa di S Isadoro. 1951: Matrimonio alla modo (+ n); Parigi è sempre Parigi – Paris is Always Paris (co-s). 1952: Le Ragazze di Piazza di Spagna – Girls of the Piazza di Spagna – Three Girls from Rome. 1953: Leonardo da Vinci. 1954: Terza Liceo – High School (co-s); Camilia (co-s); Picasso. 1956: Il Bigamo – The Bigamist – A Plea for Passion; A chacun son paradis – Il Paradiso Terrestre – Ritual of Love (+ co-s; co-d Robert Enrico). 1957: Il Momento più bello – The Most Wonderful Moment. 1960: La Ragazza in vetrina – Woman in the Window (+ co-ad/co-s).

ENDFIELD, Cy (or C. Raker)

Director and writer. 1914–
Yale University and New Theatre School, New York. Taught dramatic technique; directed Summer Theatre, Upper New York State and Community Theatre, Montreal. World War II: US Army Signal Corps. Writer of shorts, e.g. John Nesbitt's 'Passing Parade' series, and radio scripts. Writer, then director on 'Joe Palooka' series and other features for Monogram. Moved to UK in early 1950s because of McCarthyism. Uncredited script work, e.g. on Night of the Demon (1957). Co-directed 3 films uncredited with Charles de Lautour. Formed production company with Stanley Baker; made Zulu (1964) and Sands of the Kalahari (1965) for it.

Films as director: 1946: Gentleman Joe Palooka (+ s). 1947: Stork Bites Man. 1948: The Argyll Secrets. 1949: Joe Palooka in the Big Fight. 1950: Underworld Story – The Whipped; The Sound of Fury. 1952: Tarzan's Savage Fury. 1953: Limping Man (uc; co-d Charles de Lautour). 1954: The Master Plan (ps Hugh Baker; + s). 1955: Impulse (uc; co-d Charles de Lautour); The Secret (+ s). 1956: Child in the House (uc; + s; co-d Charles de Lautour). 1957: Hell Drivers (+ s). 1958: Sea Fury (+ co-s). 1959: Jet Storm (+ co-s). 1961: Mysterious Island. 1964: Hide and Seek; Zulu (+ co-p/co-s). 1965: Sands of the Kalahari (+ co-p/s). 1969: De Sade (co-d Roger Corman, uc).

ENGEL, Morris

Director. New York 1918–
Educated New York public schools. 1953–55: wife Ruth Orkin collaborated on first 2 independently made features. Pioneer in shooting with direct sound on location using lightweight, portable apparatus including 35mm camera of own design. Also professional still photographer.

Films as director: 1953: The Little Fugitive (+ co-p/co-s/c; co-d Ruth Orkin). 1955: Lovers and Lollipops (+ p/co-s/c; co-d Ruth Orkin). 1958: Weddings and Babies (+ p/s).

ENRICO, Robert

Director. Liévin, France 1931–
Italian parents. Father international motor-cycle champion and had cycle shop in Toulon. Theatrical work with Les Théophiliens, a medieval group, at Sorbonne. IDHEC. 1952–53: directed and photographed TV films Le Brésil des Théophiliens and Jeanne à Rouen. 1954–56: editor and/or assistant director on numerous documentaries. 1956: co-directed feature-length documentary A chacun son paradis with Luciano Emmer. 1957–59: wrote and directed documentaries for French Army during National Service. TV films since 1964 include: Daphné, Le Rempailleur de Saint-Sulpice, Le Redevance du fantôme. First feature, Au coeur de la vie (1962) included La Rivière du Hibou (1961) and 2 other adaptations of Ambrose Bierce stories. 1963: La Rivière du Hibou won Oscar as best live action short subject.

Theatrical films as director: 1956: Jehanne; A chacun son paradis – Il Paradiso Terrestre – Ritual of Love (+ co-e; co-d Luciano Emmer). 1959: Villes-Lumière (co-d Paul de Roubaix). 1960: Le Métier des autres (+ cy); Thaumatopoea. 1961: La Rivière du Hibou – Incident at Owl Creek – An Occurence at Owl Creek Bridge. 1962: Au Coeur de la vie including 3 eps La Rivière du Hibou, Chikamauga, L'Oiseau Moquerr (+ s); Montagnes Magiques – Magic Mountains. 1963: La Belle Vie (+ s). 1964: Contrepoint. 1965: Les Grandes Gueules – The Wise Guys – The Big Shots (+ co-s). 1967: Les Aventuriers (+ co-s); Tante Zita – Aunt Zita – Zita. 1968: Ho! (+ co-s) – Ho! Criminal Face. 1971: Un Peu, beaucoup, passionnément (+ co-s); Boulevard du Rhum (+ co-ad/co-di).

ENRIGHT, Raymond

Director. Anderson, Indiana 1896–1965 Hollywood
Gagman and editor for Sennett; left to serve in World War I. To Warners. 1927: first film as director. 1927–41: with Warners and First National. 1942–51: mainly with Universal, Columbia, RKO.

Films as director: 1927: Girl from Chicago; Jaws of Steel; Tracked by the Police. 1928: Domestic Troubles; Land of the Silver Fox; Little Wildcat. 1929: Stolen Kisses; Skin Deep; Kid Gloves. 1930: Dancing Sweeties; Scarlet Pages; Golden Dawn; Song of the West. 1932: Play Girl; The Tenderfoot. 1933: Blondie Johnson; Silk Express; Tomorrow at 7; Havana Widows. 1934: I've Got Your Number; 20 Million Sweethearts; Circus Clown; Dames; St Louis Kid. 1935: Traveling Saleslady; While the Patient Slept; Alibi Ike; We're in the Money; Miss Pacific Fleet. 1936: Snowed Under; Earthworm Tractors; China Clipper; Sing Me a Love Song. 1937: Ready, Willing and Able; Slim; Back in Circulation; The Singing Marine; Swing Your Lady; Gold Diggers in Paris. 1938: Hard to Get; Going Places. 1939: Naughty But Nice; On Your Toes; Angels Wash Their Faces. 1940: An Angel from Texas; Brother Rat and a Baby; River's End. 1941: The Wagons Roll at Night; Thieves Fall Out; Bad Men of Missouri; Law of the Tropics; Wild Bill Hickock Rides. 1942: The Spoilers; Men of Texas; Sin Town. 1943: The Iron Major; Gung Ho!; Good Luck, Mr Yates. 1945: China Sky; Man Alive; One Way to Love. 1947: Trail Street; Albuquerque; Return of the Bad Men; Coroner Creek; South of St Louis. 1950: Montana (co-d Raoul Walsh, uc); Kansas Raiders. 1951: Flaming Feather. 1953: The Man from Cairo – Avventura ad Algeri.

EPSTEIN, Jean

Director. Warsaw 1897–1953 Paris
French father, Polish mother. 1907–14: studied at Fribourg, Switzerland. 1914–20: medicine at Lyon. Met Auguste Lumière; collaborated with him on bibliographical research. 1920: first manuscript accepted by publisher; worked as secretary; assisted Louis Delluc on La Tonnerre. 1922: co-directed Pasteur with Jean Benoît-Lévy. 1923: become director for Pathé. 1925: made Photogénies but destroyed it. 1926: formed own company. Luis Buñuel was assistant on Mauprat (1926) and La Chute de la Maison Usher (1928). 1935: Marius et Olive à Paris not shown; removed name from credits. Often assisted by sister, Marie Epstein. Books on cinema include 'Bonjour Cinéma' (1921), 'Le Cinéma vu de l'Etna' (1925), 'L'Intélligence d'une machine' (1946), 'Le Cinéma en diable' (1947), 'Esprit du cinéma' (1955).

Films as director (documentaries marked†): 1922: Pasteur (co-d Jean Benoît-Lévy); Les Vendanges†. 1923: L'Auberge Rouge; Coeur Fidèle (+ st); La Belle Nivernaise; La Montagne Infidèle†. 1924: La Goutte de sang; Le Lion des Mogols (+ e). 1925: L'Affiche; Photogénies (ur); Le Double Amour; Les Aventures de Robert Macaire. 1926: Mauprat; Au pays de Georges Sand† (+ p). 1927: La Glace à trois faces (+ p); Six et demi-onze (+ p). 1928: La Chute de la Maison Usher (+ p). 1929: Finis terrae; Sa Tête (+ st/s). 1930: Mor'Vran – La Mer des corbeaux†; Le Pas de la mule†. 1931: Notre-Dame de Paris†; La Chanson des peupliers; Le Cor. 1932: L'Or des mers; Les Berceaux; La Villanelle des berceaux; Le Vieux Chaland; L'Homme à l'Hispano. 1933: La Châtelaine du Liban. 1934: Chanson d'Armor (+ co-s); La Vie d'un grand journal† (uc). 1935: Marius et Olive à Paris (uc, ur). 1936: Coeur de gueux; La Bretagne†; La Bourgogne†. 1937: Vive la vie†; La Femme du bout du monde. 1938: Les Bâtisseurs†; La Relève†; Eau Vive† (+ s). 1939: Artères de France†. 1947: Le Tempestaire. 1948: Les Feux de la mer†.

EPSTEIN, Julius J.

Writer. New York 1909–
Father proprietor of livery stable. Brother of Philip G. Epstein. Penn State College. Wrote number of 1-act plays; radio publicist. 1935: first film as writer. 1935–48: most films for First National and Warners. 1939–36: several scripts in collaboration with Jerry Wald. 1939–54: all films in collaboration with brother beginning with Daughters Courageous. 1954–58: films include 3 without brother. 1957: their last collaboration The Brothers Karamazov. From 1959: with several studios. Plays written in collaboration with brother: 'And Stars Remain' (1936), 'Rufus and his Wife' (1941), 'Chicken Every Sunday' (1944; filmed by George Seaton, 1949), 'That's the Ticket' (1948). Shared Oscar with brother and Howard Koch for Casablanca (1943). Married actress Frances Sage (1936–45).

Films as writer in collaboration include: 1935: Living on Velvet (+ co-st); Stars over Broadway; I Live for Love (+ co-st); In Caliente; Little Big Shot. 1936: Sons O' Guns. 1937: Confession (co-ad). 1938: Four Daughters. 1954: Young at Heart. 1959: Take a Giant Step.

Films as writer include: 1955: The Tender Trap. 1957: Kiss Them For Me. 1960: Tall Story. 1961: Fanny. 1962: Light in the Piazza. 1964. Send Me No Flowers. 1965: Return from the Ashes.

Films as writer in collaboration with Philip G. Epstein include: 1939: Daughters Courageous (+ co-st). 1940: No Time for Comedy; Saturday's Children; Four Wives. 1941: Honeymoon for Three; The Strawberry Blonde; The Bride Came C.O.D. 1942: The Man Who Came to Dinner; The Male Animal; Yankee Doodle Dandy. 1943: Casablanca. 1944: Arsenic and Old Lace; Mr Skeffington (+ co-p). 1948: Romance on the High Seas. 1949: My Foolish Heart. 1951: Take Care of My Little Girl. 1953: Forever Female. 1954: The Last Time I Saw Paris. 1957: The Brothers Karamazov (+ co-ad).

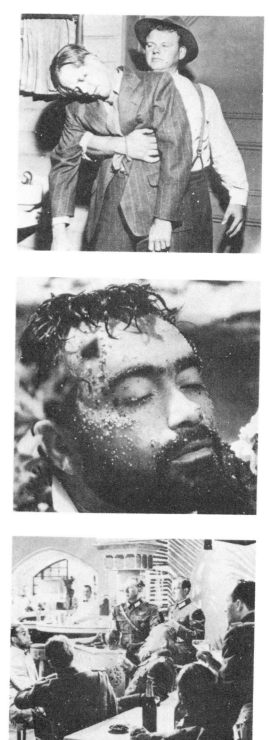

Underworld Story, *directed by Cy Endfield.*
La Rivière du Hibou (Incident at Owl Creek), *directed by Robert Enrico.*
Michael Curtiz' Casablanca, *written by Julius J. and Philip G. Epstein.*

ERMLER, Friedrich

Director. Lettonie, Russia 1898–1967 Leningrad
1919: joined Communist Party. In Civil War fought in Red Army on northern front; captured by White troops, tortured. Leningrad Institute of Screen Arts, Leningrad Photo-Cinema Techicum, studied acting. Organised KEM (Experimental Film Workshop) in opposition to FEX, planned and staged films; unable to shoot because stock not available. 1924: first film, a short documentary. 1926: first feature as director, in collaboration. 1932: co-directed *Vstrechnyi* with Sergei Yutkevich; they also collaborated on script; music by Dmitri Shostakovich. 1935: made *Krestyanye* after preparing by living for a year on collective farm; went on Shumyatsky delegation to Europe and USA. 1938–39: *Velikii Grazhdanin* dealt with recent Moscow trials; Lenfilm administration very obstructive; largely on evidence of their interference with this film, most of them were later removed. Appointed head of Lenfilm. 1943: *Ona za shchishchayet rodinu* one of few Soviet films dubbed for release in English. Was one of first to return to Lenfilm in Leningrad. Busy with directing own films replaced as head of Lenfilm by Sergei Vasiliev (1943). 1946: *Velikii Perelom* had been a project since 1942, had spent periods at front to check on its realism; battle-scenes shot in ruins of Leningrad. 1961–62: films for TV. From 1935 almost all films for Lenfilm.

Films as director: 1924: Skarlatina. 1926: Katkabumazhnyi ranet – Katka's Reinette Apples (*co-d Edward Johanson*). 1927: Deti buri – Children of the Storm (*co-d Edward Johanson*). 1928: Parizhskii Sapozhnik – Parisian Cobbler; Dom v sugribakh – The House in the Snow-drifts. 1929: Oblomok imperii – Fragment of an Empire (*+ co-s*). 1932: Vstrechnyi – Counterplan (*+ co-s*; *co-d Sergei Yutkevich*). 1935: Krestyanye – Peasants (*+ co-s*). 1938–39: Velikii Grazhdanin – A Great Citizen (*+ co-s*; in 2 parts). 1940: Osen – Autumn (*co-d I. Menakev*). 1943: Ona za shchishchayet rodinu – She Defends Her Country. 1946: Velikii Perelom – The Great Turning Point. 1950: Velikaya Sila – Great Strength (*+ s*). 1955: Neokonchennaya Povest – Unfinished Story. 1958: Pervyi Den – The First Day.

ETAIX, Pierre

Director and actor. Roanne, France 1928–
Apprenticed to T. C. Hanssen, maker of stained-glass windows; intended to be painter. 1949–55: assistant producer on various films; much amateur acting. Acted in Robert Bresson's *Pickpocket* (1959) and Claude de Givray's *Une Grosse Tête* (1962). Gagman to Jacques Tati on *Mon Oncle* (1958). 1959–60: partner to clown Nino; appeared in cabaret, music-hall and TV. 1960: appeared at Paris Olympia in Tati's show 'Jour de fête'. First shorts, *Rupture* (1961) and *Heureux Anniversaire* (1962) co-directed with Jean-Claude Carrière who also co-wrote scripts for later films. First feature as director, *Le Soupirant* (1963). Actor and co-writer on all his films. Wife is actress Annie Fratellini who acted with him in *Le Grand Amour*. Both appear in Federico Fellini's *I Clowns* (1970).

Films as director, co-writer and actor: 1961: Rupture – The Break (*co-d Jean-Claude Carrière*). 1962: Heureux Anniversaire – Happy Anniversary (*co-d Jean-Claude Carrière*). 1963: Le Soupirant – The

Suitor. 1964: Nous n'irons plus au bois. 1965: Yoyo; Insomnie – Insomnia; Tant qu'on a la santé – As Long as You're Happy. 1968: Le Grand Amour – The Great Love. 1971: Pays de Cocagne (*+ idea*).

EVANS, Dame Edith

Stage actress. London 1888–
1912: first stage appearance as amateur. Then toured with Ellen Terry. 1915–16: in 2 films directed by Henry Edwards. Then no films until *Queen of Spades* (1949). Established as stage actress by performance in 'The Way of the World' (1924).

Films as actress: 1915: A Welsh Singer. 1916: East is East. 1949: Queen of Spades; The Last Days of Dolwyn. 1952: The Importance of Being Earnest. 1959: Look Back in Anger; The Nun's Story. 1963: Tom Jones; The Chalk Garden. 1965: Young Cassidy. 1967: Fitzwilly; The Whisperers. 1968: Prudence and the Pill. 1969: Crooks and Coronets; The Madwoman of Chaillot. 1970: David Copperfield; Scrooge; Upon This Rock.

EVEIN, Bernard

Designer. Saint-Nazaire, France 1929–
Fine Arts at Nantes (where met Jacques Démy). Decoration at IDHEC. 1949: began in films as assistant decorator. Decorator on Démy's short *Le Bel Indifférent* (1957). 1958–60: decorator in collaboration with Jacques Saulnier. Designed 2 of Delphine Seyrig's dresses for *L'Année Dernière à Marienbad* (1961). 1962–63: worked at Théâtre de France.

Films as art director include: 1958: Les Amants (*co*); Les Cousins (*co*). 1959: La Sentence (*co*); A Double Tour (*co*); Les Quatre Cents Coups; Le Farceur; Les Jeux de l'amour (*co*); A View from the Bridge. 1960: Une Femme est une femme; Zazie dans le métro; Les Scélérats (*co*); 1961: Lola; L'Amant de cinq jours; Cléo de 5 à 7. 1962: Le Combat dans L'île; A View from the Bridge; Cybèle, ou Les Dimanches de Ville d'Avray; Le Rendez-vous de minuit; Vie Privée. 1963: Le Feu Follet. 1964: Les Parapluies de Cherbourg; L'Insoumis. 1966: Qui êtes-vous, Polly Magoo? 1967: Les Demoiselles de Rochefort; Woman Times Seven. 1970: L'Aveu.

EWELL, Tom

(Yewell Tompkins) Actor. Owensboro, Kentucky 1909–
Won Kentucky State Declamation Contest. University of Wisconsin. Professional stage debut with Al Jackson stock company while still student. Salesman at Macy's. 1934: Broadway debut in 'They Shall Not Die'; then in 28 successive flops on Broadway. 1940: film debut, *They Knew What They Wanted*. 1943–46: Lieutenant in US Navy. 1947: stage success in 'John Loves Mary'. 1946–49: toured in 'Stage Door', 'Tobacco Road', 'Key Largo'. 1952: 'The Seven Year Itch' on Broadway. Subsequent Broadway appearances include 'Tunnel of Love' (1957), 'Patate' (1958), 'A Thurber Carnival' (1960). Radio from 1935. Much TV including 'Tom Ewell Show' (1960).

Films as actor include: 1949: Adam's Rib. 1950: A Life of Her Own; Mr Music; American Guerilla in the Philippines. 1955: The Seven Year Itch; The Lieu-

tenant Wore Skirts; The Girl Can't Help It. 1961: Tender is the Night. 1962: State Fair.

F

FÁBRI, Zoltán

Director. Budapest 1917–
Trained as painter at Academy of Fine Arts, Budapest, then transferred to Academy of Dramatic Art. Contract with National Theatre in Budapest; directed Shakespeare and Giraudoux plays, designed sets and acted until World War II. Prisoner of war until 1945; then theatre work in Budapest. 1950: appointed art director of the Budapest Film Studio; designed film sets. 1952: first film as director. Also scripted and designed sets some of own films. 1965: made TV film *Vízivárosi nyár*.

Films as director: 1952: Vihar – The Storm. 1954: Életjel – Fourteen Lives Saved. 1955: Körhinta – Merry-Go-Round – Little Fairground Swing (*+ co-s/dec*). 1956: Hannibál tanár úr – Professor Hannibal (*+ co-s*). 1957: Bolond Április – Summer Clouds – April Fools (*+ dec*). 1958: Édes Anna – Anna (*+ co-s/dec*). 1959: Dúvad – The Brute – The Beast (*+ s/dec*). 1961: Két félidö a pokolban – The Last Goal – Eleven Men – Two Half-times in Hell (*+ dec*). 1963: Nappali sötétség – Darkness in Daytime (*+ s/dec*). 1964: Húsz óra – Twenty Hours. 1967: Utószezon – Late Season. 1969: A Pal utcai fiuk – The Boys of Paul Street.

FAIRBANKS, Douglas

(Douglas Elton Ulman) Actor. Denver, Colorado 1883–1939 Beverly Hills, California
Educated at Denver and Boulder, Colorado. 1900: first stage appearance at the Academy of Music, Richmond. 1902: Broadway debut. Theatre until 1914. 1915: first film, *The Lamb*. Contract with D. W. Griffith. 1917: formed own company Artcraft, which bscame Douglas Fairbanks Picture Corporation (1918) then Elton Corporation. Wrote occasional scripts sometimes under pseudonym Elton Thomas. 1919: with Mary Pickford, Charles Chaplin and D. W. Griffith formed distribution company United Artists. Retired 1935. Second of 3 wives was Mary Pickford (1920–36, divorced). Commemorative Oscar (1939) 'recognising the unique and outstanding contribution of Douglas Fairbanks, first President of the Academy, to the international development of the motion picture'.

Films as actor (for own production company 1917–32) include—credits as Elton Thomas marked[†]: 1916: The Habit of Happiness (*+ co-s*); The Good Bad Men (*+ s*); The Half Breed; Manhattan Madness. 1917: In Again, Out Again; Wild and Woolly; Down to Earth (*+ st*); Reaching for the Moon; A Modern Musketeer. 1918: Headin' South; Mr Fix-It; Bound in Morocco; He Comes Up Smiling. 1919: When the Clouds Roll By (*+ co-st/co-s*). 1920: The Mollycoddle. 1921: The Three Musketeers. 1922: Robin Hood (*+ st*). 1924: The Thief of Bagdad (*+ st[†]*). 1926: The Black Pirate (*+ st[†]*). 1928: The Gaucho (*+ st[†]*); Show People (*w only*). 1929: The Iron Mask (*+ co-s[†]*); The Taming of the Shrew. 1931: Reaching for the Moon; Around the World in 80 Minutes with Douglas Fairbanks (*+ co-d*

Victor Fleming). 1932: Mr Robinson Crusoe (+ *st*†). 1934: The Private Life of Don Juan.

FAIRBANKS, Jr, Douglas

(Douglas Elton Ulman Jr) Actor. New York 1909–
Son of Douglas Fairbanks by first wife. Harvard Military School, Los Angeles; Pasadena Polytechnic; also studied in London, Paris and Germany. 1922: contract with Jesse L. Lasky; first film, *Stephen Steps Out* (1923). 1927: appeared in John Van Druten's 'Young Woodley' in Los Angeles. 1928–33: married to Joan Crawford. First film in UK *Catherine the Great* (1934). 1935: formed Criterion company to produce films in Britain. Returned to Hollywood for *The Prisoner of Zenda* (1937). World War II in US Navy as officer commanding flotilla of raiding craft for commandos; awarded D.S.C. 1946: formed production company, Fairbanks Corporation; films mostly in Hollywood until 1949. Awarded K.B.E. (1949). No films as actor since 1951. 1951: formed Douglas Fairbanks Ltd in Britain and Dougfair Corporation in USA. From 1952: much TV as producer including 'Douglas Fairbanks Presents' series. Also produced films in UK, e.g. *Chase a Crooked Shadow* (1958). 1970: acted in 'Pleasure of his Company' in Chicago.

Films as actor include: 1928: The Power of the Press; A Woman of Affairs. 1929: Our Modern Maidens. 1930: The Dawn Patrol; Little Caesar. 1931: Chances. 1932: Love is a Racket; Scarlet Dawn. 1933: Morning Glory; Captured! 1937: Jump for Glory; The Prisoner of Zenda. 1938: Joy of Living; The Rage of Paris. 1939: Gunga Din; Rulers of the Sea. 1940: Green Hell; Angels Over Broadway. 1941: The Corsican Brothers. 1948: The Exile (+ *p/co-s*); That Lady in Ermine.

FALCONETTI, Renée

Stage actress. Sermano, Corsica 1893–1946 Buenos Aires, Argentina
From 18: stage actress. Paris Conservatoire. Directed on stage by Alberto Cavalcanti. From 1929: stage producer. Acted with Comédie Française. During World War II in Switzerland, then South America, acting in classical roles. Only film appearance was in *La Passion de Jeanne d'Arc* (1928). Often known as Maria or Marie Falconetti.

FANCK, Arnold

Director. Frankenthal, Germany 1889–
Doctor of Geology. Founder of Freiberg school of cameramen. From 1920: directed number of short documentaries in collaboration. 1926: responsible for Peni Riefenstahl's entry into films. 1926–33: directed her in 6 films. Partly responsible for her becoming a director. *Die Tochter des Samurai* (1937) was made in Japan, *Ein Robinson* (1940) in Chile.

Features as director: 1920: Das Wunder des Schneeschuhs (+ *co-s/co-c/w*; *co-d* Dr Tavern). 1921: Im Kampf mit dem Berge (+ *s/co-c*). 1922: Das Wunder des Schneeschuhs, *Part 2*; Eine Fuchsjagd auf Skiern durchs Engadin (+ *s/co-c*). 1924: Der Berg des Schicksals (+ *s/co-c*). 1926: Der heilige Berg (+ *s*). 1927: Der grosse Sprung (+ *s*). 1929: Die weisse Hölle von Piz Palü (+ *co-s*; *co-d* G. W. Pabst). 1930: Sturme über dem Montblanc (+ *s*). 1931: Der weisse Rausch. 1933: SOS Eisberg (+ *co-s*; *co-d* Tay Garnett). 1934:

Der ewige Traum – Der Konig des Mont-Blanc (+ *s*); Balmat. 1937: Die Tochter des Samurai – Die Liebe der Mitsu (+ *s*). 1940: Ein Robinson – Das Tagebuch eines Matrosen (+ *co-s*).

FAPP, Daniel

Cinematographer
Attended college in Kansas. Entered film industry through Standard Labs. About 1920, became assistant at Paramount. Cinematographer from 1941. Worked mainly for Paramount.

Films as cinematographer include: 1941: World Premier. 1942: My Heart Belongs to Daddy. 1944: And Now Tomorrow. 1945: Kitty; Hold That Blonde. 1946: To Each His Own. 1947: Easy Come, Easy Go; Suddenly It's Spring; Golden Earrings. 1948: Hazard; Dream Girl. 1949: Bride of Vengeance; Red, Hot and Blue; Song of Surrender. 1950: No Man of Her Own; Union Station. 1951: The Lemon Drop Kid; Darling, How Could You! 1953: The Caddy; Money From Home. 1954: Knock on Wood; Living It Up. 1955: Run For Cover; The Far Horizon; Artists and Models. 1956: The Birds and the Bees; Hollywood or Bust. 1957: The Joker is Wild; The Devil's Hairpin. 1958: Desire Under the Elms; Kings Go Forth; The Trap. 1959: The Five Pennies; L'il Abner. 1960: Let's Make Love. 1961: West Side Story; Bachelor Flat; One, Two, Three. 1962: The Pigeon That Took Rome. 1963: The Great Escape; A New Kind of Love; Fun in Acapulco; Move Over, Darling. 1964: The Unsinkable Molly Brown; Send Me No Flowers; The Pleasure Seekers. 1965: Our Man Flint. 1966: Lord Love a Duck; Spinout. 1968: Five Card Stud; Ice Station Zebra. 1969: Marooned.

FARROW, John Villiers

Director. Sydney, Australia 1904–1963 Hollywood
Educated privately in Australia, UK and in Europe for naval career. Merchant Navy, then 2 years in US Marine Corps. Published first short stories while still sailor. Member of scientific expeditions. Wrote screenplays, e.g. for *The Woman from Moscow* (1928). In Tahiti; compiled French-English Tahitian dictionary (1932). As writer contracted to Charles R. Rogers starting with *A Woman of Experience* (1931), scripted from own play 'The Registered Woman', then to MGM. 1936: co-wrote *Tarzan Escapes*; married Maureen O'Sullivan. 1937–39: writer-director at First National and Warners. 1939–40: at RKO; left to join Royal Canadian Navy Information Department; then at sea, with Royal Navy in Atlantic. Invalided out, went to Hollywood (1942), but returned to active duty. Worked on biography of Thomas More and (1942) wrote 'Pageant of the Popes'. Novels: 'Laughter Ends' (1934) and 'Damien the Leper' (1937). 1942–49: worked mainly for Paramount; then with various companies. Some second unit work in *Hondo* (1953) is by John Ford. Oscar for best written screenplay (adapted), *Around the World in 80 Days* (with James Poe and S. J. Perelman, 1956).

Films as director: 1937: Men in Exile; West of Shanghai; War Lord. 1938: The Invisible Menace; She Loved a Fireman; Little Miss Thoroughbred; My Bill; Broadway Musketeers. 1939: Women in the Wind; Sorority House; The Saint Strikes Back; Five Came Back; Full Confession; Reno. 1940: Married and in Love; A Bill

Dame Edith Evans.
Tom Ewell and Jayne Mansfield in The Girl Can't Help It, *directed by Frank Tashlin.*
Howard Hawks's To Have and Have Not, *co-scripted by William Faulkner from the novel by Ernest Hemingway.*

of Divorcement. 1942: Wake Island. 1943: Commandos Strike at Dawn; China. 1944: The Hitler Gang. 1945: You Came Along. 1946: Two Years Before the Mast. 1947: California; Easy Come, Easy Go; Blaze of Noon; Calcutta. 1948: The Big Clock; Beyond Glory; The Night Has a Thousand Eyes. 1949: Alias Nick Beal; Red Hot and Blue (+ co-s). 1950: Where Danger Lives; Copper Canyon. 1951: His Kind of Woman (co-d Richard Fleischer, uc); Submarine Command. 1953: Ride, Vaquero!; Plunder of the Sun; Hondo; Botany Bay. 1954: A Bullet is Waiting. 1955: The Sea Chase (+ p). 1956: Back From Eternity (+ p). 1957: The Unholy Wife. 1959: John Paul Jones (+ co-s).

FARROW, Mia

Actress. Hollywood 1945–
Daughter of Maureen O'Sullivan and director John Farrow. Educated in Beverly Hills, then convent and finishing school in UK. Contracted polio at 9; 4 months in iron lung. 1962: won National Forensic League Drama Award for South California for dramatic monologues. 1963: appearances on Broadway. 1964: film debut; started in TV series 'Peyton Place'. 1966–68: married to Frank Sinatra. 1970: married André Previn. Sang in title rôle in Honegger's 'Joan of Arc at the Stake'. TV feature work in USA.

Films as actress: 1964: Guns at Batasi. 1968: A Dandy in Aspic. 1968: Rosemary's Baby; Secret Ceremony. 1969: John and Mary. 1971: Blind Terror.

FAULKNER, William

Novelist. New Albany, Mississippi 1897–1962 Charlottesville, Virginia
Films adapted by others from his novels include Intruder in the Dust (1949), The Tarnished Angels (1957, from 'Pylon'), The Long, Hot Summer (1958, from 'The Hamlet'), The Sound and the Fury (1959), Sanctuary (1961, from 'Sanctuary, and 'Requiem for a Nun'), The Reivers (1969). Wrote dialogue for Howard Hawks's Today We Live (1933), based on his Saturday Evening Post story 'Turnabout'. Further film work mainly for Hawks.

Films as writer: 1933: Today We Live (di/fst). 1936: The Road to Glory (co-s). 1937: Slave Ship (ad). 1945: To Have and Have Not (co-s); The Big Sleep (co-s). 1955: Land of the Pharaohs (co-st/co-s).

FAURE, Elie

Critic. Sainte-Foy-la-Grande, France 1873–1937 Paris
Lycée Henri IV; pupil of Henri Bergson. To 1899: medical studies. Practised medicine. 1902: art critic for L'Aurore. 1905–09: lectures on history of art at popular university, La Fraternelle. 1909–21: 4-volume history of art. World War I: military doctor. Writings on cinema collected in 'Fonction du Cinéma'.

FAYE, Alice

(Alice Leppert) Actress. New York 1912–
Began as professional dancer at 14. 1931: Broadway appearance in 'George White's Scandals' with Rudy Vallee; singer with his orchestra. 1934: film debut in George White's Scandals. Films all for Fox except Every Night at Eight (1935) and You're a Sweeetheart

(1937). Retired from films 1945, apart from State Fair (1962). Married singer Tony Martin (1937–40), actor and bandleader Phil Harris (1941) with whom co-starred in 'The Bandwagon' on radio. Also TV appearances.

Films as actress include: 1934: She Learned About Sailors; 365 Days in Hollywood. 1935: Music is Magic. 1937: On the Avenue; You Can't Have Everything. 1938: In Old Chicago; Alexander's Ragtime Band. 1939: Tail Spin; Rose of Washington Square; Barricade. 1940: Little Old New York. 1941: The Great American Broadcast. 1943: The Gang's All Here. 1945: Fallen Angel.

FAZENDA, Louise

Actress. Lafayette, Indiana 1895–1962 Beverly Hills
Stuntwork at Universal. 1915: first featured role in 2-reeler, A Game Old Knight, for Mack Sennett. Almost all films for Sennett until 1921, mainly 2-reelers. Also with Warners, then freelance work at Paramount, First National and MGM. 1921: vaudeville. 1927: married Hal Wallis. Last film, The Old Maid (1939).

Films as actress include: 1918: The Kitchen Lady; Those Athletic Girls; The Summer Girls. 1919: Rip and Stitch Tailors; Hearts and Flowers; A House Divided. 1921: Wedding Bells out of Tune. 1922: The Beautiful and the Damned. 1923: The Spider and the Rose; The Gold Diggers. 1925: The Night Club. 1926: The Bat; The Lady of the Harem. 1928: Tillie's Punctured Romance. 1929: The House of Horrors. 1930: Rain or Shine. 1931: Cuban Love Song. 1933: Alice in Wonderland. 1935: Broadway Gondolier. 1936: Colleen. 1937: Ever Since Eve; Swing Your Lady.

FEHER, Imre

Director. Hungary 1926–
1946: philosophy in Budapest. 1947–50: Budapest Film and Theatre School. Entered films e.g. as assistant producer. 1957: first film as director. Teacher at Budapest Film School. Also playwright.

Films as director: 1957: Bakaruhában – A Sunday Romance; Egi madár – A Bird of Heaven. 1959: Gyalog a mennyországba – Walking to Heaven; Kard és kocka – Sword and Dice. 1962: Húsz evre egymástól – The Truth Cannot be Hidden; Asszony a telepen – Woman at the Helm. 1966: Harlekin és szerelmese – Harlequin and her Love.

FEJOS, Paul

Director. Budapest 1897–1963 New York
Studied medicine. Served on Italian front in World War I, organised theatrical productions. Returned to Hungary, designed theatre and film sets. 1920: first film as director. 1923: to USA. 1928: first American film financed by Edward Spitz The Last Moment. 1928–30: directed for Universal, MGM. 1931: to France. 1932: Hungary. Refused to comply with MGM's demand that he return to Hollywood. 1933–35: worked in Austria, Denmark. 1935–36: travelled in Madagascar, made 'Svarta Horizonter' series of documentaries for Svensk Filmindustri. 1937–38: travelled in East Indies. New Guinea. Siam.

made further series of documentaries. 1939: returned to USA. 1939–45: documentaries in Sweden. 1941: became Director of Research, Wenner-Gren Foundation for Anthropological Research. 1955: became its President.

Films as director: 1920: Pán; Lidécnyomás; Ujraélok. 1921: Fekete kapitány; Arsen Lupin utolso kalandja. 1922: Szenzacio. 1923: Egri csillagok (uf). 1928: The Last Moment (+ st/s/e); Lonesome. 1929: Broadway; The Last Performance – Erik the Great – Erik, the Great Illusionist. 1930: Captain of the Guard (uc, co-d John S. Robertson); Menschen hinter Gittern (German version of Big House). 1931: L'Amour à l'américaine (co-d Claude Heymann); Fantômas. 1932: Tavaszi zapor – Marie, légende hongroise; Itel a balston. 1933: Sonnenstrahl (+ co-st). 1934: Frühlingsstimmen; Flugten fra millionerne (+ s); Menschen im Sturm. 1935: Fange Nr 1 (+ st); Fredlös; Det Gyldne Smil (+ s). 1936: Svarta Horisonter (series: Danstavlingen i esira; Skonhetssalongen i djungeln; Varldens mest anvandbara trad; Djungeldansen; Havets djavul; Vera faders gravar). 1938: Stammen lever an; Bambualdern pa mantaivei; Houdingens son ar dod; Draken pa komodo; Byn vid den trivsamma brunnen; Tambora; Attsegla an noduaandigt; Saggakh – En handfull ris – Man och kvinna. 1941: Yagua.

FELDMAN, Charles K.

(Charles Gould) Producer. New York 1904–68 Beverley Hills, California
Orphaned; adopted in New Jersey. University of Michigan; University of Southern California. Worked as camera assistant while a student. 1928: set up law practice in Los Angeles with Hollywood clientele. Into partnership as agent; business sold in 1963. As agent represented e.g. Darryl F. Zanuck, David O. Selznick, Sol C. Siegel, Walter Wanger, Otto Preminger, Henry King, Henry Hathaway, many actors. Became producer; not credited on many early films; often only company credit. 1968: died of cancer.

Films as producer include: 1948: Red River (ex-p). 1950: The Glass Menagerie (co). 1951: A Streetcar Named Desire. 1955: The Seven Year Itch (co). 1962: A Walk on the Wild Side. 1965: What's New Pussycat? (co). 1966: The Honey Pot (co). 1967: Casino Royale (co).

FELLINI, Federico

Director. Rimini, Italy 1920–
Cartoonist in Rome, then wrote radio sketches for Giulietta Masina. Also wrote sketches for travelling comedians; became writer for comedian Macario. 1939–40: gagman on films directed by Mario Mattoli. From 1941: worked on scripts, including short that grew into Roma, Città Aperta. Assistant director to Roberto Rossellini on this, Paisà and L'Amore in which also acted. 1943: married Giulietta Masina, who later starred in some of his films. 1950: co-directed Luci del varietà with Alberto Lattuada. 1952: first solo work as director. I Clowns (1970) made for RAI-TV. Played himself in Alex in Wonderland (1970). Honorary doctorate in humane letters at Columbia University (1970). Subject of Gideon Bachmann's Ciao, Federico! (1970).

Films as writer in collaboration include: 1945: Tutta la città canta; Roma, Città Aperta. 1946: Paisà 1947: Il Delitto di Giovanni Episcopo. 1948: Senza pietà; L'Amore *ep* Il Miracolo (*+ w*). 1949: In nome della legge; Il Mulino del Po. 1950: Francesco, giullare di Dio; Il Cammino della speranza (*+ co-st*). 1951: La Città si difende. 1953: Il Brigante di Tacca del Lupo (*co-st only*). 1958: Fortunella.

Films as director and script collaborator include: 1950: Luci del varietà – Lights of Variety – Variety Lights (*co-d Alberto Lattuada*). 1952: Lo Sciecco Bianco – The White Sheik. 1953: I Vitelloni – The Young and Passionate – The Loafers; Amore in città *ep* Una Agenzia Matrimoniale. 1954: La Strada. 1955: Il Bidone – The Swindle. 1956: Le Notti di Cabiria – Nights of Cabiria. 1959: La Dolce Vita. 1962: Boccaccio '70 *ep* Le Tentazioni del dottor Antonio. 1963: Otto e mezzo – Eight and a Half. 1965: Giulietta degli spiriti – Juliet of the Spirits. 1967: Histoires Extraordinaires *ep* Toby Dammit (*+ co-s*). 1969: Fellini Satyricon (*+ co-dec*). 1970: I Clowns.

FERNANDEL

(Fernand Joseph Désiré Contandin) Actor. Marseilles, France 1903–1971 Paris
Stage debut at 5; in music-hall while still at school. From 1922 appeared on vaudeville circuits in France and North Africa. 1930: first film as actor. Over 20 films before Marcel Pagnol signed him for *Angèle* (1934). Continued stage appearances in plays and operettas. Service in 15th Division of Supply, also theatre in French Army; demobilised 1940. Music-hall appearances during Occupation. Toured USA and Canada. Stage parts repeated in films, e.g. *La Fille du puisatier* (1940) and *Tu m'as sauvé la vie* (1950). Directed some of own films, e.g. *Simplet* (1942), *Adrien* (1943), *Adhémar ou le jouet de la fatalité* (under supervision of Sacha Guitry, 1951). Later also produced, including some films for joint company with Jean Gabin, Gafer. 1970: attack of pleurisy held up a further 'Don Camillo' film, to be directed by Christian-Jacque, then film cancelled. Chevalier de la Légion d'Honneur. Son is actor Frank Fernandel.

Films as actor include: 1931: On purge bébé. 1932: Le Rosier de Madame Husson. 1936: François Ier 1937: Regain; Un Carnet de bal. 1938: Le Schpountz. 1939: Fric Frac. 1946: Naïs; Escale au soleil. 1951: Topaze; L'Auberge Rouge; La Table aux crevés; Le Fruit Défendu. 1952: Le Petit Monde de Don Camillo. 1953: Le Retour de Don Camillo; Ennemi Public No 1; Mam'zelle Nitouche. 1954: Le Mouton à cinq pattes. 1955: Ali-Baba et les quarante voleurs. 1956: Around the World in 80 Days. 1957: L'Homme à l'imperméable. 1958: Paris Holiday; La Vie à deux. 1959: La Vache et le prisonnier. 1960: Crésus. 1963: Le Diable et les dix commandements; La Cuisine au beurre. 1964: L'Age Ingrat. 1965: Don Camillo à Moscou. 1966: L'Homme à la Buick. 1970: Heureux qui comme Ulysse . . .

FERNANDEZ, Emilio

Director. Hondo, Coahuila, Mexico 1904–
Attended military college. 1924: first film appearance, in Mexico. 1924–33: in USA. Worked as actor from 1938. 1941: first film as director. 1943–50: almost all films photographed by Gabriel Figueroa. Re-made his 1946 film *Enamorada* in Hollywood as *The Torch*

(1950). Worked also in Cuba (1954), Spain (1954) and Argentina (1955). 1960: some exteriors on *The Unforgiven*. Married Columba Dominguez, actress in several of his films. From mid-1960s acted in Mexican-made films for US companies.

Films as actor include: 1928: The Gaucho. 1965: The Reward. 1966: The Appaloosa; The Return of the Seven. 1969: The Wild Bunch.

Films as director: 1941: La Isla de la pasión (*+ st/s*). 1942: Soy puro mexicano (*+ st/s*). 1943: Flor Silvestre (*+ co-s/w*); Maria Candelaria – Portrait of Maria (*+ st/co-s*). 1944: Las Abandonadas (*+ st/co-s/co-di*); Bugambilla (*+ st/co-s*). 1945: Pepita Jimenez (*+ co-s*). 1946: La Perla (*+ co-s*); Enamorada. 1947: Rio Escondido (*+ st*). 1948: Maclovia (*+ co-s*); Pueblerina (*+ st*); Salón México (*+ st/s*). 1949: La Malquerida (*+ co-s*); Duelo en las montañas. 1950: The Torch – The Bandit General; Victimas del pecado (*+ co-st/co-s*); Un Dia de vida (*+ st*); Islas Marias. 1951: Siempre Tuya (*+ co-st/co-s*); La Bien Amada (*+ st*); El Mar y tu (*+ st*); Acapulco (*+ co-st/co-s*). 1952: Cuando levanta la niebla. 1953: La Red (*+ co-st/co-s*); El Rapto (*+ co-st/co-s*); Reportaje (*+ co-st/co-s*). 1954: La Rosa Blanca (*+ co-st/co-s*); Nosotros Dos (*+ co-st/co-s*); Le Rebelion de los Colgados (*co-d Alfredo B. Crevenna*). 1955: La Tierra del Fuego se apaga (*+ co-s*). 1956: Una Cita de amor. 1957: El Impostor (*+ co-s*). 1962: Pueblito (*+ co-st/co-s*).

FERRER, José

(José Vicente Ferrer y Cintron) Director and actor. Santruce, Puerto Rico 1909–
Princeton University. Began as stage actor. 1935: New York debut, 'A Slight Case of Murder'. 1940: in Broadway revival of 'Charley's Aunt'. 1942: played Iago to Paul Robeson's Othello; first wife, Uta Hagen (married 1938–48), played Desdemona. Later directed on Broadway. 1948: first film as actor. 1955: first film as director and actor. On Broadway in 'Man of La Mancha'. TV and cabaret in USA. 1953: married third wife, singer Rosemary Clooney. Oscar as Best Actor for *Cyrano de Bergerac* (1950).

Films as director and actor: 1955: The Shrike. 1956: Cockleshell Heroes; The Great Man (*+ co-s*). 1958: The High Cost of Loving. 1961: Return to Peyton Place (*d only*). 1962: State Fair (*d only*).

Films as actor include: 1948: Joan of Arc. 1949: Whirlpool. 1950: Crisis; Cyrano de Bergerac. 1952: Anything Can Happen. 1953: Moulin Rouge; Miss Sadie Thompson. 1954: The Caine Mutiny; Deep in My Heart. 1962: Lawrence of Arabia. 1963: Nine Hours to Rama. 1964: Stop Train 349. 1965: Ship of Fools; The Greatest Story Ever Told. 1967: Enter Laughing; Le Avventura e gli amori di Miguel Cervantes.

FERRER, Mel

(Melchor Gaston Ferrer) Director, producer and actor. Elberon, New Jersey 1917–
Son of physician. Princeton University, where won Playwright's Award. Wrote children's book 'Tito's Hat'; editor with publishing house in Brattleboro, Vermont; acted in summer stock at Cape Cod Playhouse, Dennis, Massachusetts. First Broadway appear-

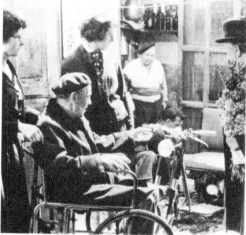

$8\frac{1}{2}$, *by Federico Fellini.*
Fernandel in Gerd Oswald's Paris Holiday.
Marco Ferreri's El Cochecito.

ances as dancer, e.g. in Cole Porter's 'You Never Know'; on Broadway as actor in 'Cue for Passion' and 'Kind Lady'. Radio work in Texas and Arkansas; then director-producer for NBC Radio. 1945: entered films as dialogue director; first films as director and as actor. 1947: signed as actor-producer-director by David O. Selznick; directorial assistant to John Ford on *The Fugitive*; with Gregory Peck, Dorothy McGuire, Joseph Cotten founded La Jolla Playhouse, California, for which directed. Broadway work as actor in 'Strange Fruit' and director of 'Cyrano de Bergerac' and 'Heart Song'. 1954: married Audrey Hepburn (divorced 1968). Produced *El Greco* (1964) and *Wait Until Dark* (1967). From 1964: worked mainly in Spain. Also producer.

Films as actor include: 1951: The Brave Bulls. 1952: Scaramouche; Rancho Notorious. 1953: Lili; Knights of the Round Table. 1954: Saadia. 1955: Oh, Rosalinda. 1956: War and Peace; Eléna et les hommes. 1957: The Sun Also Rises. 1958: The World, the Flesh and the Devil. 1960: Et mourir de plaisir. 1962: The Longest Day. 1964: The Fall of the Roman Empire; Sex and the Single Girl; El Greco (+ *p*).

Films as director: 1945: The Girl of the Limberlost. 1946: Vendetta (*r 1950; co-d, uc Howard Hughes, Preston Sturges, Stuart Heisler, Max Ophüls*). 1950: The Secret Fury. 1959: Green Mansions. 1967: Cabriola – Every Day Is a Holiday (+ *p/st/co-s/w*).

FERRERI, Marco

Director. Milan, Italy 1928–
Worked as vet and journalist. 1951: co-founder of filmed magazine series 'Documenti Mensile', consisting of sections by e.g. Michelangelo Antonioni, Vittorio De Sica, Cesare Zavattini, Luchino Visconti, Alberto Moravia. Worked with Zavattini on production of *L'Amore in città* (1953). 1956: went to Spain selling Totalscope anamorphic lenses. First 3 films as director in Spain. From 1961: director in Italy. *L'Uomo dai cinque palloni*, made as feature, cut by producer, Carlo Ponti, and included as episode in *Oggi, domani e dopodomani* (1964). Complete version re-dubbed and re-edited with 3 new sequences by Ferreri released as *L'Uomo dai palloncini* (1968). Acted in Pier Paolo Pasolini's *Porcile* (1969). One of heads of a production company, then left to form own company (1971). Work for TV.

Films as director: 1957: El Pisito. 1959: Los Chicos – The Boys (+ *co-s*). 1960: El Cochecito. 1961: Le Italiene e l'amore – Latin Lovers *ep* L'Infideltà Coniugale. 1963: Una Storia Moderna: L'Ape Regina – The Conjugal Bed (+ *co-s*). 1964: La Donna Scimmia; Controsesso *ep* Il Professore (+ *co-s*); Oggi, domani e dopo-domani *ep* L'Uomo dai cinque palloni (+ *co-s*). 1965: Marcia Nuziale (+ *co-s*). 1967: L'Harem. 1968: L'Uomo dai palloncini (+ *co-s*). 1969: Dillinger è morto – Dillinger is Dead; Il Seme dell'uomo (+ *co-s*).

FERZETTI, Gabriele

(Pasquale Ferzetti) Actor. Rome 1925–
1942: first film part. After World War II: Accademia d'Arte Drammatica; expelled after 2 years for taking screen test; regularly in films from 1947. Stage debut with Morelli-Stoppa company at Piccolo Teatro, Rome

(1948). 1950–51: acted with Teatro Nazionale Popolare. 1951: with Gioi-Cimara-Ferzetti company. 1951–55: worked mainly in films. 1955: theatre with Pagnani-Villi-Foà company.

Films as actor include: 1947: I Miserabili. 1948: Fabiola. 1950: I Falsari. 1953: La Provinciale; Il Sole negli occhi. 1955: Le Amiche. 1956: Donatella. 1957: Souvenir d'Italie. 1960: L'Avventura. 1962: Jessica; Vénus Impériale. 1966: La Bibbia; A ciascuno il suo. 1968: Un Bellissimo Novembre. 1969: C'era una volta il west. 1970: L'Aveu.

FESTA CAMPANILE, Pasquale

Director and scriptwriter. Melfi, Italy 1927–
Law at university. Wrote short stories for newspapers and literary journals. Edited magazine La Fiera Letteraria. Worked in radio. Several literary prizes, e.g. for novel 'La Nonna Sabella'. 1949: first script work. Most scripts in collaboration with Massimo Franciosa. 1963: co-directed first film with Franciosa.

Films as writer (all in collaboration with Massimo Franciosa and, usually, others) include: 1956: Poveri ma belli. 1957: La Nonna Sabella; Belle ma povere. 1958: Giovani Mariti. 1960: Rocco e i suoi fratelli. 1961: La Viaccia; L'Assassino. 1962: Le Quattro Giornate di Napoli; Smog. 1963: Il Gattopardo; Una Storia Moderna; L'Ape Regina.

Films as director and writer: 1963: Un Tentativo Sentimentale (+ *co-ad/co-s; co-d Massimo Franciosa*); Le Voci Bianche – White Voices (+ *co-s; co-d Massimo Franciosa*). 1964: La Costanza della regione (*co-s*). 1965: Una Vergine per il principe – A Maiden for a Prince – A Virgin for the Prince (*co-s*). 1966: Adulterio all' Italiana – Adultery Italian Style (*st/co-s*); La Ragazza e il Generale – The Girl and the General (*co-st/co-s*). 1967: La Cintura di castità – The Chastity Belt – On My Way to the Crusades, I Met a Girl Who...; Il Marito è Mio e ... l'amazzo quando mi pare – Drop Dead, My Love (+ *s*). 1968: La Matriarca – The Libertine. 1969: Con quale amore, con quanto amore (*co-s*). 1970: Quando le donne quevano la coda (*co-s*).

FEUILLADE, Louis

Director. Lunel, France 1873–1925 Paris
Father wine commissionaire. Catholic seminary. 1891: joined cavalry. 4 years' service, reaching sergeant. Worked in wine business. To Paris, journalist. Period in Catholic publishing house; resigned. Own magazine La Tomate for 3 months. 1905: a friend sent scripts by Feuillade to Léon Gaumont. Alice Guy (artistic director at Gaumont) offered him work as director, which he turned down. 1906: first film as writer *Attrapez mon chapeau*; supplied 3 scripts a week to Gaumont; became director. 1907: when Alice Guy became head of Gaumont in New York, replaced her as artistic director. Made many series including 63 films of the child Bébé (1910–13). Began to make serials, beginning with *Fantômas* (1913–14). Many historical films, comedies. 1915: 4 months in French army, invalided out. 1915–16: serial *Les Vampires* temporarily banned for ridiculing police. Made over 700 films, wrote almost all. Financially assisted René Clair.

Films as director and writer include: 1906: C'est papa

qui prend le plunge; Le Billet de banque. 1907: Un Facteur trop ferré; Vive le sabotage; La Course des belles mères; L'Homme Aimanté. 1908: Le Roman de soeur Louise; Un Tic. 1909: Les Heures. 1910–13: Bébé (*series of 63*). 1911: Aux Lions les chrétiens. 1911–13: La Vie telle qu'elle est (*series of 15*). 1912: Le Proscrit. 1912–16: Bout-de-Zan (*series of 45*). 1913: L'Intruse; Erreur Tragique; Un Drame au pays Basque; Fantômas (*serial, 5 eps*); Juve contre Fantômas – Fantômas II (*4 eps*); La Mort qui tue – Fantômas III (*6 eps*). 1914: Fantômas contre Fantômas – Fantômas IV (*4 eps*); Le Faux Magistrat – Fantômas V. 1915–16: Les Vampires (*10 eps*). 1916: Judex – Le Plus Grand Succés de René Cresté (*12 eps*). 1917: La Nouvelle Mission de Judex (*12 eps*). 1918: Vendémiaire (*4 parts*); Tih Minh (*12 eps*). 1919: Le Nocturne; L'Homme sans visage; Énigme – Le Mot de l'énigme; Barabas (*12 eps*). 1920: Les Deux Gamines (*12 eps*). 1921: L'Orpheline (*12 eps*); Parisette (*12 eps*); Saturnin ou le bon allumeur. 1922: Le Fils du filibustier (*12 eps*). 1923: Vindicta (*5 parts*); Le Gamin de Paris. 1924: La Fille bien gardée; Lucette; Le Stigmate (*6 eps*).

FEUILLÈRE, Edwige

(Edwige Cunati) Actress. Vésoul, France 1907–
1928: entered Paris Conservatoire. 1929: married Pierre Fresnay. From 1930: stage actress. Used pseudonym Cora Lynn both on stage and for small parts in films. 1931–33: Comédie Française. Other stage work, e.g. for Compagnie Barrault-Renaud; acted in e.g. Alexandre Dumas's 'La Dame aux camélias' (1940–42 and 1952–53), Jean Cocteau's 'L'Aigle à deux têtes' (1946), Jean Giraudoux's 'La Folle de Chaillot' (1965–66), Racine's 'Phèdre'. Also actor-director on stage. Later theatre work with own company. Chevalier de la Légion d'Honneur.

Films as actress include: 1931: Mam'zelle Nitouche. 1933: Topaze. 1935: Golgotha; Lucrèce Borgia. 1936: Mister Flow. 1937: Marthe Richard au service de la France. 1938: J'étais une aventurière; La Dame de Malacca. 1939: Sans lendemain. 1940: De Mayerling à Sarajevo. 1942: L'Honorable Cathérine; La Duchesse de Langeais. 1946: L'Idiot. 1948: Woman Hater; L'Aigle à deux têtes. 1949: Souvenirs Perdus. 1952: Adorables Créatures. 1954: Le Blé en herbe. 1957: Quand la femme s'en mêle. 1958: En cas de malheur; La Vie à deux.

FEYDER, Jacques

(Jacques Frédérix) Director and writer. Ixelles, Belgium 1887–1948 Rive de Praugins, Switzerland
Military school in Belgium. 1910: stage actor in Paris. Entered films as actor and assistant. 1913–15: acted in films of e.g. Louis Feuillade. 1915: first film as director in collaboration. 1916: directed shorts for Gaumont. 1917: in Belgian Army, wounded; married actress Françoise Rosay with whom he had acted. Returned to direction. 1923: made *Visages d'enfants* in Switzerland. 1925: writer in collaboration on Julien Duvivier's *Poil de carotte*. 1926: in Austria. 1927: French citizen. 1928: in Germany. 1929: to Hollywood with his wife; first American film *The Kiss* for MGM. 1931: 2 further films for MGM. Also made French and German versions of Hollywood films. 1931: returned to Paris. 1937: in UK directed *Knight Without Armour*. 1937: to Germany. 1941: to Switzerland with his wife. 1942:

directed there, and in collaboration with his wife produced, *Une Femme disparaît.* 1943: supervised *Matura Reise.* With his wife toured Switzerland, Algeria and Tunisia; she acted in sketches which he wrote and directed. After World War II, returned to France. 1945: theatrical producer. 1946: last work in films, writing and supervision of Marcel Blistène's *Macadam.* Scripted many of own films; writing collaboration with Charles Spaak (1928–35). His wife acted in several of his films including *Gribiche* (1925), *Le Grand Jeu* (1934), *La Kermesse Héroïque* (1935), *Fahrendes Volk* (1937), *Une Femme disparaît* (1942).

Films as director: 1915: M Pinson, policier (*co-d Gaston Ravel*). 1916: Têtes de femmes, femmes de tête; L'Homme de compagnie; Tiens, vous êtes à Poitiers; L'Instinct est maître. 1917: Le Pardessus de demi-saison; Les Vieilles Dames de l'hospice; Le Ravin sans fond (*co-d Raymond Bernard*). 1930: Anna Christie (*German version*); Le Spectre Vert (*French version of* The Unholy Night); Si l'empereur savait ça – Olympia. 1931: Son of India; Daybreak. 1937: Knight Without Armour. 1939: La Loi du nord.

Films as director and writer: 1916: Le Pied qui étreint; Le Bluff; Un Conseil d'ami; Le Frère de lait; Le Billard Cassé; Abrégeons les formalités; Le Trouvaille de bouchu. 1919: La Faute d'orthographie. 1921: L'Atlantide. 1923: Crainquebille (*+ des*); Visages d'enfants (*+ des; co-d Françoise Rosay*). 1925: L'Image (*+ co-st*); Gribiche. 1926: Carmen (*+ co-e; co-d Françoise Rosay*). 1927: Au Pays du roi lépreux. 1928: Thérèse Raquin – Du sollst nicht Ehe brechen. 1929: The Kiss. 1942: Une Femme disparaît (*+ co-p*).

Films as director, and writer in collaboration: 1929: Les Nouveaux Messieurs. 1934: Le Grand Jeu. 1935: Pension Mimosas; La Kermesse Héroïque. 1937: Fahrendes Volk – Les Gens du voyage.

FIELDS, W. C.

(William Claude Dukinfield) Actor. Philadelphia, Pennsylvania 1879–1946 Pasadena, California
Father emigrated from UK. Toured USA as comedy juggler for over 18 years before joining Ziegfeld (1915), for whom appeared in 'The Ziegfeld Follies' and 'Midnight Frolic' until 1921. 1915: first short as comedy juggler, *Pool Sharks.* From 1922: actor as well as comic in George White's 'Scandals', 'Comic Supplement' and a musical, 'Poppy'. From 1925, regularly in films. 1926–28: with Paramount, mainly at Long Island studios. Returned to stage in 'Earl Carroll's Vanities' on Broadway. Wrote many of his later films, often under pseudonyms, e.g. Mahatma Kane Jeeves, Otis Criblecoblis, Charles Bogle. 1932–38: with Paramount except for 4 shorts for Mack Sennett (1932–34) and *The Personal History, Adventures, Experience and Observations of David Copperfield, the Younger* (1935) for MGM. 1939–41: at Universal. Guest parts only in last 4 films; episode in *Tales of Manhattan* (1942) dropped before film publicly shown.

Films as actor: 1915: Pool Sharks; His Lordship's Dilemma. 1925: Janice Meredith; Sally of the Sawdust. 1926: It's the Old Army Game; That Royle Girl; So's Your Old Man. 1927: Running Wild; Two Flaming Youths; The Potters. 1928: Tillie's Punctured Romance; Fools for Luck. 1930: The Golf Specialist;

Her Majesty Love. 1932: The Dentist; If I Had a Million *ep* The Auto; Million Dollar Legs; International House. 1933: The Barber Shop (*+ st*); The Fatal Glass of Beer; The Pharmacist (*+ st*); Alice in Wonderland; Tillie and Gus. 1934: Six of a Kind; You're Telling Me; Mrs Wiggs of the Cabbage Patch; It's a Gift (*+ st; ps Charles Bogle*); The Old-Fashioned Way (*+ st; ps Charles Bogle*). 1935: Mississippi; Man on the Flying Trapeze (*+ co-st; ps Charles Bogle*); The Personal History, Adventures, Experience and Observations of David Copperfield, the Younger. 1936: Poppy. 1938: The Big Broadcast of 1938. 1939: You Can't Cheat an Honest Man (*+ st; ps Charles Bogle*). 1940: The Bank Dick (*+ s; ps Mahatma Kane Jeeves*); My Little Chickadee (*+ co-s*). 1941: Never Give a Sucker an Even Break (*+ st; ps Otis Criblecoblis*). 1942: Tales of Manhattan (*not in released version*). 1944: Follow the Boys; Song of the Open Road. 1945: Sensations of 1945.

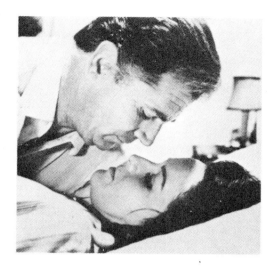

FIGUEROA, Gabriel

Cinematographer. Mexico City 1907–
Studied design and violin. Intended to become painter. Worked in photographic studio. 1932: entered films as assistant to Alex Phillips. 1935: attended advanced photographic course in Hollywood. Cinematographer from 1936. 1950: *The Torch* is American re-make, made in Mexico, of *Enamorada* (1946).

Films as cinematographer include: 1943: Flor Silvestre; Maria Candelaria. 1944: Las Abandonadas; Bugambilla. 1946: La Perla; Enamorada. 1947: Rio Escondido (*co*); The Fugitive. 1948: Tarzan and the Mermaids (*co*); Maclovia; Salón México. 1949: La Malquerida; Duelo en las montañas. 1950: The Torch; Victimas del pecado; Un Día de vida. 1952: El Mar y tu; Cuando levanta la niebla. 1953: El. 1958: Nazarin. 1959: La Fièvre monte à El-Pao. 1960: The Young One. 1962: El Angel Exterminador. 1964: Night of the Iguana. 1965: Simón del desierto. 1970: Kelly's Heroes.

FINCH, Peter

(William Mitchell) Actor. London 1916–
Australian father, English mother. From 10 educated in Australia. Various jobs during Australian depression; straight man to a vaudeville comedian; some theatre and (from 1938) occasional films in Australia. World War II: gunner; organised troop shows. 1948: in British film made in Australia *Eureka Stockade* (1949). Spotted by Laurence Olivier on Australian tour. 1949: under contract to Olivier, West End debut with Edith Evans in 'Daphne Laureola'; first film in UK *Train of Events* (1949). 1961: directed, wrote and produced short *The Day*. Project as director and writer *The Hero* to be made in Italy failed for lack of Italian finance.

Films as actor include: 1950: The Wooden Horse; The Miniver Story. 1952: The Story of Robin Hood. 1953: The Story of Gilbert and Sullivan. 1954: Father Brown; Elephant Walk. 1955: Passage Home; Dark Avenger; Josephine and Men. 1956: A Town Like Alice; The Battle of the River Plate. 1957: Robbery Under Arms. 1958: Windom's Way. 1959: The Nun's Story. 1960: The Trials of Oscar Wilde; Kidnapped. 1961: Rachel Cade; No Love for Johnnie. 1963: The Girl with Green Eyes. 1964: The Pumpkin Eater.

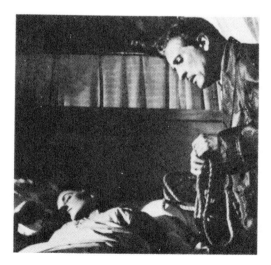

Gabriele Ferzetti and Lisa Gastoni in Salvatore Samperi's Grazie Zia.
Tih Minh. *directed by Louis Feuillade.*
El. *directed by Luis Buñuel and photographed by Gabriel Figueroa.*

1965: Judith; The Flight of the Phoenix. 1966: 10.30 pm Summer. 1967: Far from the Madding Crowd. 1968: The Legend of Lylah Clare. 1971: Sunday, Bloody Sunday; Krasnaya Palatka.

FINNEY, Albert

Actor and director. Salford, Lancashire 1936–
Son of bookmaker. Salford Grammar School and Royal Academy of Dramatic Art. 1956–58: acted with Birmingham Repertory Company, where seen by Charles Laughton. 1958: London West End stage debut in Laughton's production of 'The Party'. 1959: season with Royal Shakespeare Company; as Laurence Olivier's understudy, took over title role of 'Coriolanus'. 1960: directed by Lindsay Anderson in 'The Lily White Boys' at the Royal Court Theatre, and 'Billy Liar' on the West End stage; first film part, The Entertainer; first starring role, Saturday Night and Sunday Morning. From 1961: played John Osborne's 'Luther' in London, Edinburgh, Paris, Holland and (2 years later) New York. 1963: actor-director at Glasgow Citizen's Theatre. From 1965: acted at National Theatre, London for 15 months, e.g. in John Arden's 'Armstrong's Last Goodnight'; formed own production company (with actor Michael Medwin) Memorial Enterprises, which made e.g. Lindsay Anderson's If... (1968); his own first film as director, Charlie Bubbles (1967) and Gumshoe (1971). 1968: acted in 'A Day in the Death of Joe Egg' on Broadway. 1970: married Anouk Aimée. 1971: in 'Alpha Beta' at Royal Court Theatre, London.

Films as actor: 1960: The Entertainer; Saturday Night and Sunday Morning. 1963: Tom Jones; The Victors; Night Must Fall (+ co-p). 1967: Two for the Road; Charlie Bubbles (+ d); Picasso Summer. 1970: Scrooge. 1971: Gumshoe.

FISCHER, Gunnar

Cinematographer. Ljungby, Sweden 1910–
Studied in Copenhagen. 1935: began in Svensk Filmindustri as assistant to cinematographer Julius Jaenzon. Cinematographer from 1939. 1948–60: cinematographer on most of Ingmar Bergman's films. Also director of shorts: Mamsell Josabeth (1963), Djävulens instrument (also photographed, 1965), Drottningholmsteatern (photographed and co-directed, 1965).

Films as cinematographer include: 1942: Jacobs stege. 1945: Två manniskor. 1948: Hamnstad. 1949: Törst; Till glädje. 1950: Sånt händer inte här; Sommarlek. 1952: Kvinnors väntan; Sommaren med Monika. 1955: Sommarnattens leende. 1957: Möten i skymningen; Det Sjunde Inseglet; Smultronstället. 1958: Ansiktet. 1959: Det Svänger på slottet. 1960: Djävulens Öga. 1961: Pojken i trädet; Lustgården; Een blandt mange; Vittnesbörd om henne. 1962: Siska (co); Kort är sommaren. 1964: 491. 1965: Stimulantia ep Han-Hon. 1971: Beröringen (cr).

FISCHINGER, Oskar

Animator. Gelnhausen, Germany 1900–1967 Hollywood
Trained as engineer. 1920: first films made with wax-cutting machine patented by him. 1922: to Munich. Cartoon-work. 1925: to Berlin. 1926: first public light-show. 1927: completion of first 4 Studien shorts; work in advertising. 1928: special effects and cinematography in collaboration on Frau im Mond. 1932: first experiments with synthetic sound. To 1936: work in Studien shorts, numbers 6–12 animated to musical pieces. 1936: to USA; made Allegretto, animated to jazz theme, for MGM; special effects on The Big Broadcast of 1937. Animated episode Bach Toccata and Fugue for Walt Disney's Fantasia (1940) based on his designs, but rejected by him. 1942: worked on Orson Welles' unfinished It's All True; Radio Dynamics was result of projected colour film to accompany Louis Armstrong's music, but final version is silent. Continued to make animated shorts set to music. 1951: invented Lumigraph light-producing device. Work in advertising at most stages of career, e.g. Kreise (1933), Muratti greift Ein (1934), Muratti Privat (1934), Quadrate (1934), Muntz TV (1953), Oklahoma (1954).

Films as animator include: 1920–24: Wax Experiments. 1921–27: Studien nr 1–4. c1925: Spirals. 1925–29: Silhouettes. 1927: Regenbogen–1, ein Formspiel; Munchen-Berlin Wanderung. 1928–29: Studie nr 5. c1929: Seelische Konstruktionen – Spiritual Constructions. 1929: Studie nr 6; Studie nr 7. 1930: Studie nr 8. 1931: Studie nr 9; Studie nr 10; Liebesspiel; Coloratura. 1932–36: Studien nr 11–12. 1933: Kreise – Circles. 1934: Muratti Privat; Muratti greift Ein; Komposition in Blau – Composition in Blue; Quadrate – Squares. 1936: Allegretto. 1938: An Optical Poem. 1941: An American March. 1942: Radio Dynamics. 1948: Motion Painting. 1951: Lumigraph Test Reel. 1953: Muntz TV. 1954: Oklahoma.

FISHER, Terence

Director. London 1904–
Naval School, HMS Conway. Served in Merchant Navy. Entered films in 1933, became assistant editor to Ian Dalrymple; worked in Gaumont–British cutting rooms. 1936–47: editor on e.g. Tudor Rose (1936) and The Wicked Lady (1945). Director at Rank from 1948. 1952: joined Hammer Films. TV work as director e.g. on 'Robin Hood' and 'Dial 999' series.

Films as director: 1948: Colonel Bogey; To the Public Danger; Portrait from Life; Song for Tomorrow. 1949: Marry Me. 1950: The Astonished Heart (co-d Anthony Darnborough); So Long at the Fair (co-d Anthony Darnborough). 1951: Home to Danger. 1952: The Last Page; Stolen Face; Wings of Danger. 1953: Four-Sided Triangle; Mantrap; Spaceways; Blood Orange. 1954: Final Appointment; Mask of Dust; Face the Music; Children Galore; The Stranger Came Home – The Unholy Tour. 1955: Murder by Proxy; Stolen Assignment; The Flaw. 1956: The Last Man to Hang. 1957: The Curse of Frankenstein; Kill Me Tomorrow. 1958: Dracula; The Revenge of Frankenstein. 1959: The Mummy; The Hound of the Baskervilles; The Stranglers of Bombay; The Man Who Could Cheat Death. 1960: The Brides of Dracula; Sword of Sherwood Forest; The Two Faces of Dr Jekyll – House of Fright. 1961: The Curse of the Werewolf. 1962: The Phantom of the Opera. 1963: Sherlock Holmes. 1964: The Earth Dies Screaming; The Horror of it All; The Gorgon. 1965: Dracula, Prince of Darkness. 1966: Island of Terror; Frankenstein Created Woman. 1967: Night of the Big Heat. 1968: The Devil Rides Out. 1969: Frankenstein Must Be Destroyed.

FITZGERALD, Francis Scott Key

Writer. St Paul, Minnesota 1896–1940
1913–17: Princeton University. Left college to join army. 1917: 2nd Lieutenant. 1918: 1st Lieutenant. 1918–19: aide-de-camp to Brigadier-General. 1922: first film based on his work The Beautiful and Damned. 1926: The Great Gatsby based on his novel via play by Owen Davis; remade in 1949. Uncredited script work on e.g. Raffles (1930), The Women (1939), Gone with the Wind (1939), Madame Curie (1943). 1954: story 'Babylon Revisited' filmed as The Last Time I Saw Paris. Played by Gregory Peck in Beloved Infidel (1959); 'Tender is the Night' filmed in 1962. Latter 2 films directed by Henry King.

FLAHERTY, Robert

Director. Iron Mountain, Michigan 1884–1951 Vermont
Son of mining engineer; at 12 began to accompany father on expeditions to Canadian goldfields. Educated in Toronto and at Michigan College of Mines. Several years prospecting for iron in Northern Canada. Explored and mapped Canadian sub-arctic areas (1910–16) for William Mackenzie, builder of Canadian Northern Railway. Made first film (17½ hours long, fire destroyed all but one print) of Eskimos on expedition to Baffin Island. Revillon Frères Fur Company financed Nanook of the North (1922) and secured Pathé distribution. Moana (1926) commissioned by Jesse Lasky. Lived for year with family in Samoa before starting 10 months' shooting. Moana was first feature to use panchromatic film throughout as orthochromatic film would not render colour of Samoans' skin. Story of a Potter (1925) shot in New York for Metropolitan Museum of Art. Parts of film shot for uncompleted The 24 Dollar Island (1926) worked into montage for backdrop of New York Roxy. Withdrew from directing White Shadows in the South Seas because of disagreement with MGM over cast and story. Made Acoma, the Sky City (1928) on Pueblo Indians for Fox, but print destroyed in fire. Tabu (1931) made independently with F. W. Murnau as producer and co-director. 1931: went to UK to work with John Grierson. Returned to USA and made The Land (1942) for Pare Lorentz's US Film Unit. Louisiana Story (1948) was financed by Standard Oil with a budget of $250,000. Re-edited Curt Oertel documentary (originally 1940) as The Titan – The Story of Michelangelo.

Films as director: 1922: Nanook of the North (+ s/co-titles/c). 1925: Story of a Potter – Pottery Maker (+ s/e). 1926: Moana (+ s/c/e); The 24 Dollar Island (+ s/e; uf). 1928: White Shadows in the South Seas (co-st only); Acoma, the Sky City (+ s; ur). 1931: Tabu (+ st/co-s/co-c; co-d F. W. Murnau); Industrial Britain (+ c). 1934: Man of Aran (+ s/c). 1936: Elephant Boy (co-d Zoltan Korda). 1942: The Land (+ co-c/s/co-cy/n). 1948: Louisiana Story (+ s).

FLEISCHER, Max and Dave

Animators. Max: Vienna 1889– . Dave: New York 1894–
Max studied at Art Students' League and Mechanic's and Tradesman's School, New York. Became errand

boy for paper on which John Randolph Bray worked as cartoonist; worked with him. Became cartoonist on small newspaper. 1914: worked on educational films. 1920: Max and Dave, with brother Joe as equipment repairer, began 'Out of the Inkwell' series combining animation and live action. 1923: Max did animation for *The Einstein Theory of Relativity,* produced and supervised by Einstein's associates; also worked on 2 live-action films, *Evolution* and *Adventures in the Far North.* 1931–38: 'Betty Boop' series. 1933–43: 'Popeye' series. 1938: first animated feature *Gulliver's Travels.* By 1940: had taken out over 75 patents. 1941: second feature *Mr Bug Goes to Town.* To 1942: distributed by Paramount. 1942: split up. Dave owned studio in Florida, became head of animation at Columbia. Max moved to TV. Son of Max is Richard Fleischer.

FLEISCHER, Richard O.

Director. New York 1916–

Son of Max Fleischer. Abandoned medical studies at Brown University to enrol at Yale School of Drama. Formed theatrical group, the Arena Players. 1940–43: started in films on newsreels and shorts for RKO in New York. 1945: shorts in 'This is America' series and 'Flickers Flashbacks' compilations. Features from 1946. Mainly with RKO until 1951. 1955–70: mainly with Fox, except 2 films for United Artists and period with Dino De Laurentiis in Italy which produced only *Barabbas* (1962). 1971: worked in UK; took over direction of *The Last Run* from John Huston. Oscar (1947) for documentary feature, *Design for Death* (copyrighted 1948).

Films as director: 1946: Child of Divorce. 1947: Banjo. 1948: Design for Death; So This Is New York; Bodyguard. 1949: The Clay Pigeon; Follow Me Quietly (*co-d Anthony Mann, uc*); Make Mine Laughs; Trapped. 1950: Armored Car Robbery. 1951: The Narrow Margin. 1952: The Happy Time. 1953: Arena. 1954: 20,000 Leagues Under the Sea. 1955: Violent Saturday; The Girl in the Red Velvet Swing. 1956: Bandido; Between Heaven and Hell. 1958: The Vikings; These Thousand Hills. 1959: Compulsion. 1960: Crack in the Mirror. 1961: The Big Gamble. 1962: Barabbas. 1966: Fantastic Voyage. 1967: Doctor Dolittle. 1968: The Boston Strangler. 1969: Che! 1970: Tora! Tora! Tora! (*co-d Toshio Masuda, Kinji Fukasaki*). 1971: 10 Rillington Place; Blind Terror – See No Evil; The Last Run.

FLEMING, Rhonda

(Marilyn Louis) Actress. Los Angeles 1923–
Mother musical comedy actress. Educated in Beverly Hills; studied singing, dancing, acting. Reached semifinals of radio talent contest; appeared in Hollywood show 'Blackouts'. Signed by Fox; inactive for 6 months. 1943: appeared (freelance) in *In Old Oklahoma*; signed by Selznick. Fewer films in 1960s, some in Italy; TV and records. Third husband (1960–62) actor Lang Jeffreys; fourth husband director Hall Bartlett (married 1966).

Films as actress include: 1944: Since You Went Away; When Strangers Marry. 1945: The Spiral Staircase. 1947: Out of the Past. 1949: A Connecticut Yankee in King Arthur's Court. 1951: Cry Danger. 1953: Serpent of the Nile; Inferno. 1954: Yankee Pasha.

1955: Tennessee's Partner; La Cortigiana di Babilonia. 1956: The Killer is Loose; Slightly Scarlet; While the City Sleeps. 1957: Gunfight at the OK Corral; Gun Glory. 1958: Home Before Dark. 1959: Alias Jesse James; The Big Circus. 1960: The Crowded Sky. 1964: The Patsy (*uc*).

FLEMING, Victor

Director. Pasadena 1883–1949 Cottonwood, Arizona
1910: hired as assistant cameraman by Allan Dwan at American Film Co. From 1915: at Triangle, cinematographer e.g. on Dwan's *The Good Bad Man* (1916) and *A Modern Musketeer* (1917). World War I: service in photographic section of US Army Signal Corps and on President Wilson's staff during peace conferences. 1919: first film as director, for Douglas Fairbanks. 1922–29: with Famous Players/Paramount. From 1932: at MGM for all remaining films except *The Farmer Takes a Wife* (1935) and *Joan of Arc* (1948). Took over direction of *The Good Earth* (1937) after suicide of George Hill during shooting but fell ill; replaced by Sidney Franklin. Oscar for direction of *Gone With the Wind* (which also won Oscar as Best Picture, 1939); took entire direction credit for 9 weeks' shooting, after preparation and 3 weeks' shooting by George Cukor and before 10 weeks' shooting by Sam Wood.

Films as director: 1919: When the Clouds Roll By (*co-d Ted Reed*). 1920: The Molly Coddle. 1921: Woman's Place. 1922: Anna Ascends; The Lane that had no Turning; Red Hot Romance. 1923: Dark Secrets; The Law of the Lawless; To the Last Man; The Call of the Canyon. 1924: Empty Hands (*+p*); The Code of the Sea. 1925: Adventure; The Devil's Cargo; A Son of his Father; Lord Jim. 1926: Mantrap; The Blind Goddess. 1927: The Rough Riders; The Way of All Flesh; Hula. 1928: Abie's Irish Rose (*+p*); The Awakening. 1929: Wolf Song; The Virginian. 1930: Common Clay; Renegades. 1931: Around the World in Eighty Minutes with Douglas Fairbanks (*co-d Douglas Fairbanks*). 1932: The Wet Parade; Red Dust. 1933: Bombshell – The Blonde Bombshell; The White Sister. 1934: Treasure Island. 1935: Reckless; The Farmer Takes a Wife. 1937: The Good Earth (*uc; co-d George Hill, Gustav Machaty, Sidney Franklin*); Captains Courageous. 1938: Test Pilot. 1939: The Wizard of Oz; Gone With the Wind (*co-d, uc, George Cukor, Sam Wood*). 1941: Dr Jekyll and Mr Hyde (*+p*). 1942: Tortilla Flat. 1944: A Guy Named Joe. 1945: Adventure. 1948: Joan of Arc.

FLICKER, Theodore J.

Director. Freehold, New Jersey 1930–
RADA. Then actor in repertory. Director on Broadway. Founded own theatre in St Louis, Missouri. Directed jazz musical 'The Nervous Set' on Broadway. Founded New York theatre, The Premise; worked with company, The Living Premise, as producer, director, writer, actor. 1964: first film as director. Assistant director on Alexander Mackendrick's *Don't Make Waves* (1967). TV work as director includes espisodes of 'The Man from Uncle', 'The Dick Van Dyke Show', 'The Rogues', 'The Andy Griffith Show'.

Films as director: 1964: The Troublemaker (*+co-st/co-s/w*). 1967: The President's Analyst (*+st/s*).

The Narrow Margin, *directed by Richard Fleischer.*
Rhonda Fleming *at the time of* Alias Jesse James, *directed by Norman McLeod.*
Victor Fleming's Gone With the Wind.

FLOREY, Robert

Director. Paris 1900–

During childhood watched Georges Méliès at work. Private schools in France and Switzerland. At 17, sports journalist in Geneva. Then writer, actor and assistant director on Swiss 1-reelers. Wrote for Cinémagazine. Assistant to Louis Feuillade at Gaumont, acted with René Clair in Feuillade's serial *L'Orpheline* (1921). Went to Hollywood as film journalist. 1922: technical director to Emmett J. Flynn on *Monte Cristo* for Fox. Gagman at Fox, also wrote comedies and occasionally acted. Director of foreign publicity for Mary Pickford and Douglas Fairbanks, then on Rudolph Valentino's American and European tour. 1923: first film as director. At MGM, assistant director to John M. Stahl, Edmund Goulding, Robert Z. Leonard, King Vidor; also directed screen tests and 2nd-units. 1926: after director fell ill, completed Louis J. Gasnier's *That Model from Paris*. Assistant to Frank Borzage on *Seventh Heaven* (1927), to Henry King on *The Magic Flame* (1927) and *The Woman Disputed* (1928). 1927–28: directed 4 experimental shorts. At Paramount, directed features, also tests, numerous musical shorts, sound interview film with Admiral Byrd and 1-reeler with Elinor Glyn. 1930: directed French language films for Pierre Braunberger in Britain, (*La Route est belle*), Germany (*L'Amour chante*, also in German and Spanish versions), and France (*Le Blanc et le noir*, co-directed by Marc Allégret). 1933–35: with Warners and First National. 1935–40: with Paramount. Then with various companies. 1947: among assistant directors on *Monsieur Verdoux*. 1950: awarded Légion d'Honneur; made last film for cinema, *The Vicious Years*. 1952–63: directed many films for TV. Author of 8 books on cinema.

Films as director include (features complete): 1923: 50–50. 1927: One Hour of Love; The Romantic Age; Face Value. 1927–28: The Life and Death of 9413—A Hollywood Extra – A Hollywood Extra – Hollywood Rhapsody (+ *st/s*); The Loves of Zero (+ *st*); Johann the Coffinmaker (+ *st*); Skyscraper Symphony (+ *st*). 1928: Night Club. 1929: Pusher-in-the-Face; The Hole in the Wall; The Cocoanuts (co-d *Joseph Santley*); Battle of Paris – The Gay Lady. 1930: La Route est belle; L'Amour chante; Komm' zu mir zum Rendezvous (*German version of* L'Amour chante); El Professor de mi señora (*Spanish version of* L'Amour chante); Le Blanc et le noir (co-d *Marc Allégret*). 1932: Murders in the Rue Morgue; Man Called Back; Those We Love. 1933: Girl Missing; Ex-Lady; House on 56th Street. 1934: Bedside; Smarty; Registered Nurse; I Sell Anything. 1935: I Am a Thief; The Woman in Red; The Florentine Dagger; Going Highbrow; Don't Bet on Blondes; The Pay-Off; Ship Cafe. 1936: The Preview Murder Mystery; 'Til We Meet Again; Hollywood Boulevard. 1937: Outcast; King of Gamblers; Mountain Music; This Way Please; Daughter of Shanghai. 1938: Dangerous to Know; King of Alcatraz. 1939: Disbarred; Hotel Imperial; The Magnificent Fraud; Death of a Champion. 1940: Women Without Names; Parole Fixer. 1941: The Face Behind the Mask; Meet Boston Blackie; Two in a Taxi; Dangerously They Live. 1942: Lady Gangster (*ps Florian Roberts*). 1943: The Desert Song; Roger Touhy, Gangster – The Last Gangster. 1944: Man from Frisco. 1945: God is My Co-Pilot; Danger Signal. 1947: The Beast with Five Fingers. 1948: Tarzan and the Mermaids; Rogue's Regiment; Outpost in Morocco. 1949: The Crooked Way; Johnny One-Eye. 1950: The Vicious Years – The Gangster We Made.

FLYNN, Errol

Actor. Hobart, Tasmania 1909–1959 Vancouver

Father was Theodor-Thomson Flynn, oceanographer and biologist. Educated in Australia, London and Paris, then returned to Australia. Many jobs there, including distributing Labour Party leaflets. For 7 years travelled in Polynesia, New Guinea, Tahiti, Hong Kong, India, Marrakesh, Marseille. 1929: guide to Herman F. Erben during making of a documentary in New Guinea. 1933: played Fletcher Christian in Erben's *In the Wake of the Bounty* (released only in Australia; bought by Irving Thalberg during preparation of *Mutiny on the Bounty* in 1935). 1933: reached London. Abandoned dramatic studies, played in repertory, including Northampton for 18 months. Took Shakespearean leads. Wrote play 'Cold Rice' produced in Midlands. Acting in 'A Man's House' in Stratford spotted by Warners talent scout. 1935: British film as actor *Murder at Monte Carlo*: to Hollywood before its release; played corpse in *The Case of the Curious Bride*; took lead in *Captain Blood*, first of several films in which he was directed by Michael Curtiz. 1935–41: acted with Olivia de Havilland in 8 films. 1950–52: directed shorts *Whaling in the Pacific* and *The Cruise of the Zaca*. 1952: broke Warners contract to become independent producer. Bankrupted by his abandoned project *William Tell* which he was to produce and direct. Worked for several studios including Universal, Warners, United Artists, British Lion. 1958: played John Barrymore in *Too Much, Too Soon*. 1958: acted in stage production of 'The Master of Thornfield'. Joined Fidel Castro; last film, *Cuban Rebel Girls* banned in USA. Books: 'Beam Ends' (1937), 'Showdown' (1946), 'My Wicked, Wicked Ways' (1959). Married actresses Lily Damita (1935–42), Nora Eddington (1943–49), Patrice Wymore (1950 until his death). Son is actor Sean Flynn.

Films as actor include: 1935: Don't Bet on Blondes; Captain Blood. 1936: The Charge of the Light Brigade. 1937: Green Light; The Prince and the Pauper; Another Dawn; The Perfect Specimen. 1938: The Adventures of Robin Hood; Four's a Crowd; The Sisters; The Dawn Patrol. 1939: Dodge City; The Private Lives of Elizabeth and Essex. 1940: Virginia City; The Sea Hawk; Santa Fe Trail. 1941: Footsteps in the Dark; Dive Bomber; They Died with Their Boots On. 1942: Desperate Journey; Gentleman Jim. 1943: Edge of Darkness; Thank Your Lucky Stars; Northern Pursuit. 1944: Uncertain Glory. 1945: Objective Burma. 1946: San Antonio. 1948: Silver River. 1949: The Adventures of Don Juan. 1949: It's a Great Feeling; That Forsyte Woman. 1950: Montana; Kim; Rocky Mountain; 1952: Mara Maru. 1953: The Master of Ballantrae. 1954: Lilacs in the Spring. 1955: Dark Avenger; King's Rhapsody. 1956: Istanbul. 1957: The Big Boodle; The Sun Also Rises. 1958: Too Much, Too Soon; Roots of Heaven.

FOLSEY, George

Cinematographer.

At 14, office boy to Adolph Zukor at Famous Players. In several capacities, then became one of earliest camera assistants, and cinematographer (from 1919). 1921: to California; worked for Paramount, to 1932. From 1934: worked for MGM.

Films as cinematographer include: 1923: The Bright Shawl. 1926: The Savage. 1927: Her Wild Oat; No Place to Go. 1929: Applause; The Cocoanuts; The Hole in the Wall. 1930: Animal Crackers; Laughter. 1931: Stolen Heaven; The Smiling Lieutenant; Secrets of a Secretary; My Sin; The Cheat. 1932: The Big Broadcast. 1934: Men in White; Operator 13; Chained; Forsaking All Others (*co*). 1935: Reckless; Page Miss Glory; I Live My Life; Kind Lady. 1936: Hearts Divided; The Gorgeous Hussy. 1937: The Last of Mrs Cheyney. 1938: Mannequin; The Shining Hour. 1939: Lady of the Tropics; Remember? 1940: Third Finger, Left Hand. 1941: Come Live With Me; Free and Easy; The Trial of Mary Dugan; Lady Be Good. 1942: Panama Hattie; Seven Sweethearts; Dr Gillespie's New Assistant; Andy Hardy's Double Life (*co*). 1943: Three Hearts for Julia; Thousands Cheer. 1944: A Guy Named Joe (*co*); The White Cliffs of Dover; Meet Me in St Louis (*co*). 1945: The Clock; The Harvey Girls. 1946: Ziegfeld Follies (*co*); The Green Years; Till the Clouds Roll By; The Secret Heart. 1947: Green Dolphin Street; If Winter Comes. 1948: State of the Union. 1949: Take Me Out to the Ball Game; The Great Sinner; Adam's Rib; Malaya. 1950: A Life of Her Own. 1951: Vengeance Valley; Shadow in the Sky. 1952: Lovely to Look At; Million Dollar Mermaid. 1953: All the Brothers Were Valiant. 1954: Executive Suite; Seven Brides for Seven Brothers; Tennessee Champ; Deep in My Heart. 1955: Hit the Deck; The Cobweb. 1956: Forbidden Planet; The Fastest Gun Alive. 1957: House of Numbers; Tip on a Dead Jockey. 1958: Saddle the Wind; The High Cost of Loving; Imitation General; Torpedo Run.

FONDA, Henry

Actor. Grand Island, Nebraska 1905–

University of Minnesota. 1925: stage debut at Omaha Community Playhouse. Many appearances in stock, e.g. in Dennis, Massachusetts, then Falmouth, Washington, Baltimore, Maine, Westchester. Also worked occasionally as director and set designer. Broadway debut in walk-on part, 'The Game of Love and Death' (1929). Subsequent Broadway appearances, 'I Love You Wednesday' (1932), 'Forsaking All Others' (1933), 'New Faces' (1934), 'The Farmer Takes a Wife' (1934); screen debut in film version of latter (1935). World War II: Air Combat Intelligence Officer; Bronze Star and Presidential Citation. Postwar Broadway appearances include 'Mr Roberts' (1948, also on tour, 1951), 'Two for the Seesaw' (1958), 'Critic's Choice' (1960), 'A Gift of Time' (1962). 1957: formed own production company for *Twelve Angry Men*. 1959: star and co-producer of TV series 'The Deputy'. Also TV series 'The Smith Family'. Staged 'The Caine Mutiny Court-Marshal' in Los Angeles (1971). Appeared in *Directed by John Ford* (1971). First of 5 wives was actress Margaret Sullavan (1931–33); children by second marriage are Jane Fonda and actor Peter Fonda.

Films as actor include: 1935: The Farmer Takes a Wife; Way Down East; I Dream Too Much. 1936: The Trail of the Lonesome Pine; Spendthrift. 1937: You Only Live Once; That Certain Woman. 1938: I Met My Love Again; Jezebel; Blockade; Spawn of the North. 1939: Jesse James; Let us Live; Young Mr

Lincoln; Drums Along the Mohawk. 1940: The Grapes of Wrath; The Return of Frank James; Chad Hanna. 1941: The Lady Eve; Wild Geese Calling. 1942: Rings on her Fingers; Tales of Manhattan; The Big Street; The Male Animal; The Magnificent Dope; The Immortal Sergeant; The Ox-Bow Incident. 1946: My Darling Clementine. 1947: The Long Night; The Fugitive; Daisy Kenyon. 1948: A Miracle Can Happen; Fort Apache. 1955: Mister Roberts. 1956: War and Peace. 1957: Twelve Angry Men (+ co-p); The Wrong Man; The Tin Star. 1958: Stage Struck. 1959: Warlock. 1962: Advise and Consent; How the West was Won; The Longest Day. 1963: Spencer's Mountain; Fail Safe. 1964: The Best Man; Sex and the Single Girl; In Harm's Way. 1965: The Rounders. 1966: Battle of the Bulge. 1967: Welcome to Hard Times. 1968: Madigan; Yours, Mine and Ours; The Boston Strangler. 1969: C'era una volta il West. 1970: There Was a Crooked Man; The Cheyenne Social Club; Too Late the Hero. 1971: Sometimes a Great Notion.

FONDA, Jane

Actress. New York 1937–
Daughter of Henry Fonda. Vassar College. Studied at Actor's Studio (member from 1960). 1954: stage debut in 'The Country Girl' at Omaha. Appearances in stock. 1960: New York Stage debut, 'There Was a Little Girl'; first film as actress *Tall Story*. On Broadway in 'Invitation to a March' (1960), 'The Fun Couple' (1962), 'Strange Interlude' (1963). *Jane* (1963) a Robert Drew/Richard Leacock film about her, covers unsuccessful Broadway opening of 'The Fun Couple'. 1965: married Roger Vadim. 1970: bound over to a Federal Grand Jury on charges of drugs smuggling and assaulting customs officer.

Films as actress include: 1962: Walk on the Wild Side; The Chapman Report; Period of Adjustment. 1963: Sunday in New York. 1964: Les Félins; La Ronde. 1965: Cat Ballou. 1966: La Curée; The Chase. 1967: Hurry Sundown. 1968: Barbarella. 1969: They Shoot Horses, Don't They?

FONTAINE, Joan

(Joan de Havilland) Actress. Tokyo 1917–
Sister of Olivia de Havilland. Took name of mother's second husband. Educated in California. Studied with Max Reinhardt. 1935: stage debut in touring production of 'Kind Lady'; first film as actress. Theatre work includes 'Tea and Sympathy' (1953), succeeding Deborah Kerr on Broadway; 'Hilary' (1959). 'Susan and God' (1960) on tour. Married 4 times; first husband actor Brian Aherne (1939–45, divorced). Acted in over 40 radio plays including 'Pride and Prejudice' (1945). TV from 1956. Oscar for best actress *Suspicion* (1941).

Films as actress include: 1937: Quality Street; A Damsel in Distress. 1939: Gunga Din; The Women. 1940: Rebecca. 1942: This Above All. 1943: The Constant Nymph. 1944: Jane Eyre; Frenchman's Creek. 1947: Ivy. 1948: The Emperor Waltz; Kiss the Blood off my Hands; Letter from an Unknown Woman; You Gotta Stay Happy. 1950: Born to be Bad. 1951: September Affair; Darling, How Could You! 1952: Something to Live For; Ivanhoe; Decameron Nights. 1953: The Bigamist. 1954: Casanova's Big

Night. 1956: Serenade; Beyond a Reasonable Doubt. 1957: Island in the Sun; Until They Sail. 1958: A Certain Smile. 1962: Tender is the Night.

FORBES, Bryan

Director, writer, actor, head of production. London 1926–
Scholarship to RADA; novel published while a student. 1942: stage debut 'The Corn is Green' in London. 1945–48: Army Intelligence. 1948: first film as actor *The Small Back Room*. 1954: first film as writer, uncredited additional dialogue on *The Black Knight*. 1958: with Richard Attenborough founded own company. 1959: in collaboration with him produced *The Angry Silence* and wrote it. 1961: first film as director. 1969–71: head of production at EMI, Elstree; supervised programme of 11 films at total budget of 4 million pounds including own *The Raging Moon* (1971). When 'limited budget' policy abandoned, remained in non-executive capacity. Theatrical work as actor includes 'The Heiress'; TV work as actor includes 'The Breadwinner', 'French Without Tears', 'Johnnie was a Hero', 'The Gift,' 'The Road'. Wife is Nanette Newman who acted in many of his films, beginning with *The L-Shaped Room* (1962).

Films as actor include: 1950: The Wooden Horse. 1952: The World in his Arms. 1953: Appointment in London; Sea Devils; The Million Pound Note. 1954: An Inspector Calls. 1955: The Colditz Story; Passage Home. 1956: The Last Man to Hang. 1958: The Key. 1961: The Guns of Navarone. 1964: A Shot in the Dark.

Films as writer include: 1956: Cockleshell Heroes (co); House of Secrets (co). 1958: I Was Monty's Double (+ w). 1959: The Captain's Table (co). 1960: The Angry Silence (+ co-p); The League of Gentlemen (+ w); Man in the Moon (co). 1961: Only Two Can Play. 1964: Station 6—Sahara (co). 1964: Of Human Bondage.

Films as director: 1961: Whistle Down the Wind. 1962: The L-Shaped Room (+ s). 1964: Seance on a Wet Afternoon (+ s/co-p). 1966: King Rat; The Wrong Box (+ p). 1967: The Whisperers (+ s). 1968: Deadfall (+ s). 1969: The Madwoman of Chaillot. 1971: The Raging Moon (+ s).

FORD, Aleksander

Director. Lodz, Poland 1908–
1928: two short documentaries on his native city, *Nad ranem* and *Tetno Polskiego Manchesteru*. 1930: first feature as director *Mascotte*. 1930–39: features and documentaries; semi-documentary on poverty of lower-class Poles and Jews, banned in Poland but seen in France under title *Nous arrivons*. 1934: made *Sabra* in Palestine with actors of Habima Theatre. Belonged to group of radical film-makers known as 'Start'. World War II: military training films. 1943: with many members of 'Start' founded Cinematography Section in Polish Army, and made 2 Army documentaries; made documentary *Bitwa pod Lenino* in Russia. 1944: made documentary on concentration camps *Majdanek, oboz smierci*. 1945: after Liberation became head of Polish film industry. 1947: head of Film Polski. From 1947: producer and director. 1954: decor and supervision as Andrzej Wajda's *Pokolenie*. 1968: deposed as head of

Henry Fonda in The Best Man.
Krzyzacy, *directed by Aleksander Ford.*
Glenn Ford in Vincente Minnelli's The Four Horsemen of the Apocalypse.

studio film unit in Lodz film school; rejected criticism; removed from the Party. Now lives in Israel.

Features as director include: 1930: Mascotte. 1932: Legion Ulicy – The Legion of the Street. 1934: Przebudzenie – The Awakening; Sabra. 1936: Droga Mlodych – Youth's Journey. 1937: Ludzie Wisley (co-d). 1948: Ulica Graniczna – Border Street – That Others May Live (+ co-s). 1952: Mlodosc Szopin – The Young Chopin (+ s). 1954: Piatka z Ulicy Barskiej – Five Boys from Barska Street (+ co-s). 1957: Osmy Dzien Tygodnia – The Eighth Day of the Week (+ s). 1960: Krzyzacy – Knights of the Teutonic Order (+ co-s). 1964: Pierwszy Dien Wolnosci – The First Day of Freedom. 1966: Der Arzt stellt fast – The Doctor Speaks – Angeklagt nach paragraph 218.

FORD, Glenn

(Gwyllin Ford) Actor. Quebec, Canada 1916–
Acting debut at 4 in 'Tom Thumb's Wedding'. Stage manager, Wilshire Theatre, Santa Monica. Acted in 'The Children's Hour', 'The Golden Boy'. 1938: toured with 'Soliloquy'. 1939: first film as actor *Heaven with a Barbed Wire Fence*. 1942–45: US Marine Corps. To 1949: films mainly for Columbia. Worked for several studios, then freelance. TV series 'Cade's County'. Own company. Married dancer Eleanor Powell (1943–59). Son is actor Peter Ford.

Films as actor include: 1940: The Lady in Question. 1941: So Ends Our Night; Texas. 1943: The Desperadoes; Destroyer. 1946: Gilda; A Stolen Life. 1947: Framed. 1948: The Loves of Carmen; The Return of October. 1949: Undercover Man; Mr Soft Touch. 1950: The White Tower. 1951: The Secret of Convict Lake. 1952: The Green Glove; Young Man with Ideas. 1953: The Man from the Alamo; Terror on a Train; Plunder of the Sun; The Big Heat; Appointment in Honduras. 1954: Human Desire; The Americano. 1955: The Violent Men; The Blackboard Jungle; Interrupted Melody; Trial; Ransom! 1956: The Fastest Gun Alive; Jubal; The Teahouse of the August Moon. 1957: Don't Go Near the Water; 3.10 to Yuma. 1958: Cowboy; The Sheepman; Torpedo Run; Imitation General. 1960: The Gazebo; Cimarron. 1961: Pocketful of Miracles (+ co-as-p). 1962: The Four Horsemen of the Apocalypse; Experiment in Terror. 1963: The Courtship of Eddie's Father; Love is a Ball. 1964: Advance to the Rear; Fate is the Hunter. 1965: The Rounders. 1966: The Money Trap; Paris brûle-t-il? 1967: The Last Challenge; A Time for Killing.

FORD, John

(Sean Aloysius O'Feeny, or O'Fearna) Director. Cape Elizabeth, Maine 1895–
Thirteenth and youngest child of Irish emigrants. Father owned a saloon in Portland, Maine. 1913: after graduation from High School, directly to Hollywood; joined his brother, Francis Ford, a contract director/ writer/actor at Universal. Labourer and third assistant prop man; used name Jack Ford until *Cameo Kirby* (1923). 1914: prop man, bit parts, stunt man, assistant on serials and 2-reelers directed by brother; then larger parts. Extra (a Klansman) in *The Birth of a Nation* (1915). 1917: first films (2-reelers) as director, writer and star; third film first of 26 with Harry Carey; first feature, *Straight Shooting*. Except for 2 Buck Jones

features at Fox (1920–21), continued at Universal until late 1921. Then at Fox until 1931. 1930: first film with Dudley Nichols as writer *Men Without Women*. Then worked for various studios, occasionally producing own films. 1941: joined US Navy, Chief of Field Photographic Branch of Office of Strategic Services; team included Gregg Toland, Joseph Walker, Budd Schulberg, Garson Kanin, Robert Parrish. After war, started to prepare film of evidence for Nuremberg Trials; project dropped. 1950–53: some films co-produced with Merian C. Cooper for their company, Argosy Films. As Rear-Admiral, USNR, made 2 documentaries on Korea for services (1951, 1959). 1968–71: made documentary *Vietnam, Vietnam* for US Information Agency; unreleased. Subject of and appears in *Directed by John Ford* (1971). Directed films for TV: *The Bamboo Cross* (with Jane Wyman, 1955), *Rookie of the Year* (with Vera Miles and John Wayne, 1955), *The Colter Craven Story* (1960), *Flashing Spikes* (with James Stewart, 1962). Oscars for direction: *The Informer* (1935), *The Grapes of Wrath* (1940), *How Green Was My Valley* (1941), *The Quiet Man* (1952). Oscars for documentaries: *The Battle of Midway* (1942), *December 7th* (1943).

Films as director: 1917: The Tornado (+ s/w); The Scrapper (+ s/w); The Soul Herder; Cheyenne's Pal (+ st); Straight Shooting; The Secret Man; A Marked Man (+ st); Bucking Broadway. 1918: The Phantom Riders; Wild Women; Thieves' Gold; The Scarlet Drop (+ st); Hell Bent (+ co-s); A Woman's Fool; Three Mounted Men. 1919: Roped; The Fighting Brothers; A Fight for Love; By Indian Post; The Rustlers; Bare Fists; Gun Law; The Gun Packer (+ co-st); Riders of Vengeance (+ co-s); The Last Outlaw; The Outcasts of Poker Flat; The Ace of the Saddle; The Rider of the Law; A Gun Fightin' Gentleman (+ co-st); Marked Men. 1920: The Prince of Avenue A; The Girl in No 29; Hitchin' Posts; Just Pals. 1921: The Big Punch (+ co-s); The Freeze Out; The Wallop; Desperate Trails; Action; Sure Fire; Jackie. 1922: Little Miss Smiles; The Village Blacksmith. 1923: The Face on the Barroom Floor; Three Jumps Ahead (+ s); Cameo Kirby; North of Hudson Bay; Hoodman Blind. 1924: The Iron Horse; Hearts of Oak. 1925: Lightnin'; Kentucky Pride; The Fighting Heart; Thank You. 1926: The Shamrock Handicap; The Blue Eagle; Three Bad Men (+ co-s). 1927: Upstream. 1928: Mother Machree; Four Sons; Hangman's House; Napoleon's Barber; Riley the Cop. 1929: Strong Boy; The Black Watch (co-d Lumsden Hare); Salute. 1930: Men Without Women (+ co-st); Born Reckless (co-d Andrew Bennison); Up the River (+ co-s, uc). 1931: Seas Beneath; The Brat. 1932: Arrowsmith; Air Mail; Flesh. 1933: Pilgrimage; Dr Bull. 1934: The Lost Patrol; The World Moves On; Judge Priest. 1935: The Whole Town's Talking; The Informer; Steamboat Round the Bend. 1936: The Prisoner of Shark Island; Mary of Scotland. 1937: The Plough and the Stars; Wee Willie Winkie. 1938: The Hurricane (co-d Stuart Heisler, uc); The Adventures of Marco Polo (2nd, uc); Four Men and a Prayer; Submarine Patrol. 1939: Stagecoach (+ p); Young Mr Lincoln; Drums along the Mohawk. 1940: The Grapes of Wrath; The Long Voyage Home. 1941: Tobacco Road; Sex Hygiene; How Green Was My Valley. 1942: The Battle of Midway (+ c/co-e/co-cy); Torpedo Squadron. 1943: December 7th (co-d Gregg Toland); We Sail at Midnight. 1945: They Were Expendable (+ p). 1946: My Darling Clementine. 1947: The Fugitive (+ co-p).

1948: Fort Apache (+ co-p); Three Godfathers (rm Marked Men 1919; + co-p). 1949: She Wore a Yellow Ribbon (+ co-p). 1950: When Willie Comes Marching Home; Wagonmaster (+ co-p); Rio Grande (+ co-p). 1951: This Is Korea! 1952: What Price Glory; The Quiet Man (+ co-p). 1953: The Sun Shines Bright (+ co-p); Mogambo; Hondo (2nd, uc). 1955: The Long Gray Line; Mister Roberts (co-d Mervyn LeRoy). 1956: The Searchers. 1957: The Wings of Eagles; The Rising of the Moon. 1958: So Alone; The Last Hurrah (+ p); Gideon's Day – Gideon of Scotland Yard. 1959: Korea; The Horse Soldiers. 1960: Sergeant Rutledge. 1961: Two Rode Together. 1962: The Man Who Shot Liberty Valance; How the West Was Won ep The Civil War. 1963: Donovan's Reef (+ p). 1964: Cheyenne Autumn. 1965: Young Cassidy (co-d Jack Cardiff). 1966: 7 Women. 1968–71: Vietnam, Vietnam (ur).

FOREMAN, Carl

Writer. Chicago 1914–
1910: parents to USA from Russia. University and law school; reporter in Chicago. Publicist for stage personalities; wrote and directed plays. To Hollywood: reader, story analyst then laboratory assistant at major studios. First script, a medical documentary. Worked on features. World War II: joined group (including John Huston and Anatole Litvak) producing army orientation films. Formed independent company (with Stanley Kramer and George Glass), wrote scripts. After trouble with the Un-American Activities Committee, repudiated by Kramer and blacklisted. To UK, worked anonymously at first, notably on *The Bridge on the River Kwai* (1957), then Columbia backed him as writer-producer for his own company. 1963: first film as director. 1965: first film as producer. 1968: became President of Writers' Guild of Great Britain. 1970: awarded CBE. Governor of British Film Institute (resigned 1971).

Films as writer include: 1948: So This is New York (co). 1949: Champion; Home of the Brave. 1950: Young Man With a horn (co); The Men (+ st); Cyrano De Bergerac. 1952: High Noon. 1954: The Sleeping Tiger (co; ps Derek Frye). 1957: Bridge on the River Kwai (co, uc). 1958: The Key (+ ex-p). 1961: The Guns of Navarone (+ ex-p). 1963: The Victors (+ d/p). 1969: MacKenna's Gold (+ co-p).

Films as producer include: 1965: Born Free. 1969: The Virgin Soldiers (ex-p).

FORMAN, Milos

Director. Kaslov, Czechoslovakia 1932–
Parents died in concentration camp. 1955–57: graduated from Prague Film School. 1956: wrote scripts, including Alfred Radok's *Dĕdeček Automobil* (1956) on which he was also assistant. Followed Radok to Lanterna Magica Theatre as director. 1963: made 16mm short on Semafor Theatre in Prague, *Konkurs*; it retained this title when his next short *Kdyby Ty Muziky Nebyly* was added to make it feature-length. 1964: first dramatic feature *Cerny Petr*. Collaboration with cinematographer Miroslav Ondricek; assistants included Ivan Passer, Jaroslav Papousek. Married actresses Jana Brejchova and Vera Kresadlova. 1969: to USA; formed production company there (1971).

Films as director and writer in collaboration: 1963: Konkurs - Talent Competition; Kdyby Ty Muziky Nebyly – If There was No Music. 1964: Cerny Petr – Peter and Pavla. 1965: Lasky Jedne Plavovlasky – A Blonde in Love - Loves of a Blonde (+ st). 1967: Hori ma Penenko - The Fireman's Ball - Like a House on Fire. 1971: Taking Off.

FOSSE, Bob

Actor, choreographer and director. Chicago, Illinois 1925–

With father on vaudeville tours; achieved full professional status by 13. Broadway chorus, season in burlesque. World War II: US Navy. Variety shows on Pacific Islands and Japan. In cast of 'Call Me Mister', studied acting. When show closed formed team with dancing partner Mary Ann Niles. Spotted for first film as actor while in 'Pal Joey'. 1952: married musical comedy star Joan McCracken. 4 films as actor, returned to Broadway. 1955–58: choreographed films. Directed 'The Pajama Game'; married its star Gwen Verdon; they formed partnership. Stage work also includes 'Damn Yankees', 'Sweet Charity', 'Little Me', 'How to Succeed in Business Without Really Trying'.

Films as actor: 1953: Give a Girl a Break; The Affairs of Dobie Gillis; Kiss Me Kate.

Films as choreographer: 1955: My Sister Eileen (+ w). 1957: The Pajama Game. 1959: Damn Yankees (+ w).

Films as director: 1969: Sweet Charity (+ chor).

FOSTER, Norman

(Norman Hoeffer) Director and actor. Richmond, Indiana 1900–

Acted in touring companies. First major stage role in 'The Barkers'. 1929: first film as actor Gentlemen of the Press. To 1936: actor, mainly for Paramount, Warners, MGM, Fox. 1936: first film as director was also last film as actor. 1936–41: with Fox. 1943: for RKO directed Journey into Fear in collaboration with Orson Welles, from script by Joseph Cotten. 1943–45: 2 Mexican Films. 1948–53: with several studios, including Universal, Columbia, MGM. 1952: made Navajo with all-Indian cast: From 1955: several films for Walt Disney. 1960: The Sign of Zorro re-edited from Disney TV series. TV work includes 'Disneyland'.

Films as actor include: 1931: It Pays to Advertise; No Limit. 1932: Alias the Doctor; Under Eighteen; Steady Company; Play Girl; Strange Justice. 1933: State Fair; Pilgrimage. 1934: Strictly Dynamite. 1935: The Bishop Misbehaves. 1936: Fatal Lady; High Tension.

Films as director: 1936: I Cover Chinatown (+ w). 1937: Fair Warning (+ s); Think Fast, Mr Moto (+ co-s); Thank You, Mr Moto (+ co-s). 1938: Walking Down Broadway; Mr Moto Takes a Chance (+ co-st); Mysterious Mr Moto (+ co-s). 1939: Charlie Chan in Reno; Mr Moto Takes a Vacation (+ co-s); Charlie Chan at Treasure Island. 1940: Charlie Chan in Panama; Viva Cisco Kid. 1941: Ride Kelly Ride; Scotland Yard. 1943: Journey into Fear (co-d Orson Welles, uc); Santa. 1945: Hora de la verdad. 1948: Rachel and the Stranger; Kiss the Blood Off My Hands. 1949: Tell It to the Judge. 1950: Father is a Bachelor (co-d Abby Berlin); Woman on the Run (+ co-s). 1951: Navajo (+ s). 1952: Sky Full of Moon (+ s). 1953: Sombrero (+ s). 1955: Davy Crockett, King of the Wild Frontier (+ co-s). 1956: Davy Crockett and the River Pirates (+ co-s). 1959: The Nine Lives of Elfego Baca (+ s/co-songs). 1960: The Sign of Zorro (+ co-s). 1966: Indian Paint (+ s). 1967: Brighty of the Grand Canyon (+ s).

FOX, William

Studio Head. Tulchva, Hungary 1879–1952 New York German parents; to USA as infant. After working for a tailor, bought penny arcade peepshow; after 20 years owned 1000 cinemas in America, 1912: went into production; Fox Film Corporation founded in 1915. Acquired Gaumont–British and 300 cinemas in Britain. Attempted to buy control of Loew's Inc., but prevented by Wall Street Crash, government intervention and a serious accident. 1930: Fox Films sold. Salvaged money from interests in sound. 1933: subject of book, 'Upton Sinclair Presents William Fox'. 1936: voluntarily in bankruptcy court. 1942: charged with conspiracy to defraud the government and obstruct justice; served half of a year's sentence.

FRADETAL, Marcel

Cinematographer. Villefranche-sur-Saône, France 1908–

Assistant to Rudolf Maté and Harry Stradling during their pre-war French period. Prisoner during World War II. From 1946: collaboration with Georges Rouquier, including Le Chaudronnier (1949), Le Sel de la terre (1950). From 1948: collaboration with Georges Franju on shorts from 1948 and features from 1960, including TV episode Les Rideaux Blancs (1966). Almost all films are shorts. Directed short L'Homme d'aujourd'hui (1952).

Films as cinematographer include: 1946: Le Charcutier de Machonville; Jeux des enfants. 1948: La Sang des bêtes; Ceux du ballon rond. 1950: Faits Divers à Paris; Renaissance du Havre; En passant par la Lorraine. 1952: Le Fleuve; L'Homme en marche; Hôtel des Invalides; Le Rhin, fleuve internationale. 1956: Le Théâtre National Populaire ; Sur le pont d'Avignon. 1957: Notre Dame, cathédrale de Paris; Le Bel Indifférent. 1959: Le Huitième Jour. 1960: Vacances en enfer. 1961: Pleins Feux sur l'assassin. 1963: Judex. 1965: Thomas l'Imposteur. 1966: Les Rideaux Blancs. 1970: La Faute de l'Abbé Mouret.

FRAKER, William A.

Director and cinematographer.

Studied film at University of Southern California. Stills photographer on films. Editing assistant, work in commercials. Camera assistant, then operator e.g. on The Professionals (1966). Cinematographer on commercials. 1966: photographed TV series 'Daktari'. 1967: first feature as cinematographer, Games. 1970: after Paint Your Wagon asked by Lee Marvin to direct him: first film as director.

Films as cinematographer include: 1967: The President's Analyst. 1968: Rosemary's Baby; Bullitt. 1969: Paint Your Wagon.

Films as director: 1970: Monte Walsh.

(left to right) James Stewart, Woody Strode, Vera Miles, John Wayne, John Qualen in John Ford's The Man Who Shot Liberty Valance.

Milos Forman, at the camera, on location for Taking Off.

Judex, directed by Georges Franju and photographed by Marcel Fradetal.

FRANCIS, Anne

Actress. Ossining, New York 1934–
Calendar photographs at 6 months; model for children's clothing, toy and food advertisements. Star of a Saturday morning radio show. On Broadway in 'Lady in the Dark', playing Gertrude Lawrence at 12. 1946: MGM contract; first film, *Summer Holiday* (1947). Returned to New York, modelling and TV. 1951: Fox contract. Since worked for various companies. TV includes series 'Honey West', and TV features.

Films as actress include: 1949: Portrait of Jennie. 1951: The Whistle at Eaton Falls; Elopement. 1952: Lydia Bailey. 1953: A Lion is in the Streets. 1954: Susan Slept Here; Bad Day at Black Rock. 1955: Battle Cry; Blackboard Jungle; The Scarlet Coat. 1956: Forbidden Planet. 1957: Don't Go Near the Water. 1960: The Crowded Sky. 1964: The Satan Bug. 1968: Funny Girl.

FRANCIS, Freddie

Director and cinematographer. London 1918–
Apprenticed to a stills man on leaving school. Worked for Gaumont–British, then clapper boy at British International; to British and Dominion, then camera assistant at Pinewood. World War II: in Army Kinematographic Service. Operator for London Films. Worked for several studios and freelanced as cinematographer. 1961: first film as director: returned to cinematography to work on *Night Must Fall*. Oscar for black and white photography on *Sons and Lovers* (1960).

Films as cinematographer include: 1956: Moby Dick (*2nd*). 1957: Time Without Pity. 1958: Next to No Time; Virgin Island; Room at the Top. 1960: The Battle of the Sexes; Sons and Lovers; Saturday Night and Sunday Morning. 1961: The Innocents. 1964: Night Must Fall.

Films as director: 1961: 2 and 2 Make 6. 1962: Vengeance. 1963: Paranoiac; Nightmare; The Evil of Frankenstein. 1964: Traitor's Gate. 1965: Dr Terror's House of Horrors; The Skull. 1966: Hysteria; Psychopath; The Deadly Bees; They Came From Beyond Space. 1967: Torture Garden. 1968: Dracula Has Risen from the Grave; The Intrepid Mr Twigg (*r* 1971). 1969: Mumsy, Nanny, Sonny, and Girly. 1971: Trog; Gebissen wird nur Nachts – Happening der Vampire.

FRANCIS, Kay

(Katherine Gibbs) Actress. Oklahoma City, Oklahoma 1903–
Mother was stage actress Katherine Clinton. 1925: Broadway debut in 'Hamlet'. 1929: first film as actress, *Gentlemen of the Press*. 1929–32: mainly with Paramount. 1932–39: mainly Warners. Then worked for several studios. 1945–46: actress-producer for Monogram. 1946: retired from films after 67 features in 17 years. 1952: retired from stage after 'Theatre' in stock.

Films as actress include: 1929: The Cocoanuts. 1930: The Street of Chance; Paramount on Parade; A Notorious Affair; Raffles; For the Defense; Let's Go Native; The Virtuous Sin. 1931: Ladies' Man; Scandal Sheet; The Vice Squad; Transgression; Guilty Hands;

Girls About Town. 1932: Man Wanted; Jewel Robbery; One Way Passage; Trouble in Paradise; Cynara. 1933: The Keyhole; Storm at Daybreak; Mary Stevens, M.D.; House on 56th Street. 1934: Wonder Bar; Mandalay; Dr Monica; British Agent. 1935: Stranded; I Found Stella Parish. 1936: The White Angel; Give Me Your heart. 1937: Stolen Holiday; Another Dawn. 1938: My Bill; The Secrets of an Actress; Comet over Broadway. 1939: Women in the Wind; In Name Only. 1940: It's a Date; When the Daltons Rode; Little Men. 1941: Charley's Aunt; The Feminine Touch. 1945: Divorce (*+ co-p*). 1946: Wife Wanted (*+ co-p*).

FRANJU, George

Director. Fougères, France 1912–
Trained as theatrical designer. With Henri Langlois founded film society Le Cercle du Cinéma and made short *Le Métro*. 1937: they helped found the Cinémathèque Française and started film magazine CINEMAtographe (two issues only). 1938: became executive secretary of Fédération Internationale des Archives du Film. 1944–54: general secretary of Institut de Cinématographie Scientifique. Artistic supervisor of Ado Kyrou's short, *La Déroute* (1958). 1958: first feature as director *La Tête contre les murs*. Innocently involved in the Ben Barka affair: a meeting with him used to lure Ben Barka to his kidnapping. 1966: 2 TV films: *Les Rideaux Blancs* in Germany (script by Marguérite Duras) and *Marcel Allain*.

Films as director: 1934: Le Métro (*co-d Henri Langlois*). 1949: Le Sang des bêtes (*+ s*). 1950: En passant par la Lorraine (*+ s*). 1952: Hôtel des Invalides (*+ s*); Le Grand Méliès (*+ s*). 1953: Monsieur et Madame Curie (*+ s*). 1954: Les Poussières (*+ s*); Navigation Marchande (*+ cy*). 1955: A propos d'une rivière – Au fil de la rivière – La Salmon Atlantique (*+ s*). 1956: Mon Chien (*+ s*); Le Théâtre National Populaire (*+ s*); Sur le pont d'Avignon (*+ s*). 1957: Notre-Dame, cathédrale de Paris (*+ s*). 1958: La Première Nuit (*+ ad*); La Tête contre les murs – The Keepers. 1959: Les Yeux sans visage – Eyes without a Face – The Horror Chamber of Dr Faustus (*+ co-ad*). 1961: Pleins Feux sur l'assassin – Spotlight on Murder. 1962: Thérèse Desqueyroux – Thérèse (*+ co-s*). 1963: Judex. 1965: Thomas l'Imposteur – Thomas, the Imposter (*+ co-s*). 1970: La Faute de l'Abbé Mouret (*+ co-s*).

FRANK, Melvin

Director, writer and producer. Chicago 1913–
University of Chicago; while a student wrote play in collaboration with Norman Panama. 1938: to Hollywood with him; worked as radio writer for three years e.g. on 'The Bob Hope Show'. 1942: radio consultant to War Department; first film as writer (story only) *My Favorite Blonde* in collaboration with Panama. From 1950: directed, wrote and produced films with Panama; shared same credit until 1956. From 1962: own production company in Britain, directed its first production *Road to Hong Kong*. 1942–45 and 1954–60: mainly with Paramount; also MGM and others.

Films as writer in collaboration with Norman Panama: 1943: Happy Go Lucky (*co*); Thank Your Lucky Stars. 1944: And the Angels Sing. 1946: Monsieur

Beaucaire. 1947: It Had to be You. 1948: Mr Blandings Builds His Dream House; The Return of October. 1954: White Christmas (*co*).

Films as director, writer and producer in collaboration with Norman Panama: 1950: The Reformer and the Redhead. 1951: Strictly Dishonorable; Callaway Went Thataway. 1952: Above and Beyond (*co-s*). 1954: Knock on Wood. 1956: The Court Jester (*+ st*); That Certain Feeling (*co-s*).

Films as director and co-producer with Norman Panama: 1959: The Jayhawkers (*+ co-s*). 1960: The Facts of Life (*+ co-s, with Panama*); Li'l Abner (*+ co-s, with Panama*).

Films as producer and co-writer: 1958: The Trap (*co-p only, with Panama*). 1962: Road to Hong Kong. 1966: A Funny Thing Happened to Me on the Way to the Forum.

Films as director, producer and co-writer: 1965: Strange Bedfellows (*+ co-st*). 1968: Buona Sera, Mrs Campbell.

FRANK, Robert

Director. Zurich, Switzerland 1924–
Professional photographer; books of photographs include 'The Americans'. 1958: Became American citizen; directed first film in collaboration, based on third act of Jack Kerouac's unpublished play 'The Beat Generation' and narrated by Kerouac. 1966: cinematographer on *Chappaqua*.

Films as director: 1958: Pull My Daisy (*co-d Alfred Leslie*). 1961: Sin of Jesus. 1963: O.K. End Here. 1968: Me and My Brother (*+ s/c*). 1971: Conversations in Vermont.

FRANKENHEIMER, John

Director. New York 1930–
1947: La Salle Military Academy. Art at Williams College, Massachusetts; military service; Reserve Officer's Training Corps, then photographic squadron. 1953: discharged; acted on radio and TV; directed for radio in Washington. Assistant to Sidney Lumet on TV, then first direction, for CBS, 'The Plot against King Solomon'. Much TV, e.g. 'The Snows of Kilimanjaro'. Director in summer stock. 1957: first film as director. Replaced Charles Crichton on *Bird Man of Alcatraz* (1962) and Arthur Penn on *The Train* (1965). Own production company. Married actress Evans Evans, who appears in several of his films.

Films as director: 1957: The Young Stranger. 1961: The Young Savages. 1962: All Fall Down; Bird Man of Alcatraz; The Manchurian Candidate (*+ co-p*). 1964: Seven Days in May. 1965: The Train. 1966: Seconds; Grand Prix. 1967: The Extraordinary Seaman (*r* 1969). 1968: The Fixer. 1969: The Gypsy Moths. 1971: I Walk the Line (*+ co-pc*); The Horsemen (*+ co-pc*).

FRANKLIN, Sidney

Director and producer. San Francisco, California 1893–
1915: assistant operator for Bosworth Company.

1916–18: with brother Chester directed for Triangle and Talmadge Corporation. Often directed Talmadge sisters, especially Constance. 1920–26: almost all films for First National and Warners. From 1924: all films for MGM, except *The Dark Angel* (1935) for United Artists. 1937: abandoned direction for production: all films as producer for MGM, including 4 of Mervyn Leroy's. 1957: directed and produced last film, a remake of own *The Barretts of Wimpole Street* (1934).

Films as director: 1916: Martha's Vindication (+ *co-d*). 1918: The Safety Curtain; The Forbidden City. 1919: The Hoodlum; Heart O' The Hills; The Probation Wife. 1920: Two Weeks. 1922: Smiling Through (+ *co-s*); The Primitive Lover; East is West. 1923: Brass; Dulcy; Tiger Rose (+ *p*). 1924: Her Night of Romance. 1925: Learning to Love; Her Sister from Paris. 1926: Beverley of Graustark; Duchess of Buffalo; Quality Street. 1928: The Actress. 1929: Wild Orchids; The Last of Mrs Cheyney. 1930: Devil May Care; A Lady's Morals – Jenny Lind; The Lady of Scandal – The High Road. 1931: Private Lives; The Guardsman. 1932: Smilin' Through. 1933: Reunion in Vienna (+ *p*). 1934: The Barretts of Wimpole Street. 1935: The Dark Angel. 1937: The Good Earth (+ *co-d, uc, George Hill, Gustav Machaty, Victor Fleming*). 1957: The Barretts of Wimpole Street (*rm* 1934; + *p*).

FRANKOVICH, Mike *or* M. J.

Writer and producer. Bisbee, Arizona 1910–
Adopted son of comedian Joe E. Brown. UCLA. 1934: radio producer and commentator. 1938: dialogue director and editor at Universal. 1940: to Republic as editor and assistant director. World War II: US Army. 1949: left Republic. 1952: to UK as independent producer. 1955: appointed UK head of Columbia. 1963: returned to USA as head of Columbia's world production, and vice-president. 1967: resigned to become independent producer, releasing through Columbia. Married Binnie Barnes, who acted in e.g. *Decameron Nights* (1952).

Films as producer include: 1951: Fugitive Lady. 1952: Decameron Nights. 1954: Fire Over Africa. 1955: Footsteps in the Fog (*co*). 1956: Joe Macbeth. 1969: Bob and Carol and Ted and Alice; Marooned; Cactus Flower. 1970: There's a Girl in My Soup (+ *co*). 1971: Dollars.

FREDA, Riccardo

Director. Alexandria, Egypt 1909–
1918: to Milan. Gave up University to study sculpture. At 24 attended Centro Sperimentale di Cinematografia. Wrote scripts e.g. for Eduardo de Filippo (*In campagna e caduta una stella*, 1940) and Luigi Zampa (*L'Abito nero da sposa*, 1943). 1938: wrote in collaboration, edited and acted in *Piccoli Naufraghi*. 1942: first film as director. 1948: directed shorts under pseudonym Renato Dery. Two early features shot in Brazil. 1958: 2nd-unit director on film directed without credit by Michelangelo Antonioni *Nel segno di Roma*. From 1959: occasionally used pseudonym Robert Hampton. Directed action sequences in e.g. *I Mongoli* (1961), *Oro per i Cesari* (1962). 1962: *Le Sette Spade del vendicatore* is remake of his first film as director.

Features as director and writer in collaboration: 1942: Don Cesare di Bazan – Là Lama del Giustiziere. 1943:

Non canto più. 1945: Tutta la città canta – Sei per otto, quarantotto (+ *e*). 1946: Aquila Nera – The Black Eagle. 1947: I Miserabili (*in 2 parts*). 1948: Il Cavaliere Misterioso – Le Cento Donne di Casanova. 1949: Il Conte Ugolino – Il Cavaliere di ferro. 1951: Il Tradimento; Le Vendetta di aquila nero. 1952: La Leggenda del piave (+ *st*); Spartaco – Spartacus the Gladiator – Sins of Rome. 1953: Teodora, Imperatrice di Bisanzio – Theodora Slave Empress (+ *co-ad*). 1955: Da qui all'eredite. 1956: Beatrice Cenci – I Maledetti (+ *co-e*); I Vampiri – Lust of the Vampire (+ *w*). 1957: Agguato a Tangeri – Trapped in Tangiers. 1960: I Giganti della Tessaglia – Gli Argonauti – The Giant of Thessaly. 1962: Sette Spade del vendicatore – Sette Spade per il re – The Seventh Sword.

Films as director and writer: 1948: Guarany. 1949: O Cacoulha do Barulho (+ *e*); Il Figlio di d'Artagnan. 1964: Giulietta e Romeo – Romeo and Juliet.

Films as director: 1951: Vedi Napoli e poi muori – Perfido Ricatto (+ *co-songs*). 1958: Agi Murad, il diavolo bianco – The White Warrior. 1959: Caltiki, il mostro immortale – Caltiki, the Immortal Monster. 1961: I Mongoli – The Mongols (*co-d Andre de Toth*); Caccia all'uomo – Le Avventure di Dox – Dox, caccia all'uomo; Maciste alla corte del Gran Khan – Samson and the Seven Miracles of the World. 1962: Maciste all'inferno; L'Orribile Segreto del Dottor Hitchcock – Raptus – The Secret of Dr Hitchcock; Lo Spectro – The Ghost; Solo contro Roma – Vengeance of the Gladiators – The Fall of Rome (+ *co-d N. Vicario*); Oro per i Cesari – Gold for the Caesars (+ *co-d Andre de Toth*). 1963: Il Magnifico Avventuriero – Magnificent Adventurer.

FREED, Arthur

Producer. Charleston, South Carolina 1894–
Worked for music publisher in Chicago on stage with Marx Brothers in Chicago; vaudeville acts. In US Army 1917–19, then more vaudeville. From 1929: wrote songs for films. 1939: first film as producer. 1940: to MGM; remained there. Produced 4 Academy Award Shows. 1964: president of Academy of Motion Picture Arts & Sciences. Oscars for Best Picture: *An American in Paris* (1951), *Gigi* (1958). Discovered Judy Garland, Gene Kelly, June Allyson.

Films as producer include: 1939: Babes in Arms. 1940: Strike Up the Band. 1941: Babes on Broadway. 1942: For Me and My Gal. 1943: Cabin in the Sky; Girl Crazy. 1945: The Clock; Yolanda and the Thief; The Harvey Girls. 1946: Ziegfeld Follies. 1947: Summer Holiday. 1948: Easter Parade; Words and Music; The Pirate. 1949: Take Me Out to the Ball Game; The Barkleys of Broadway; On the Town. 1950: Annie Get Your Gun; Crisis. 1951: Royal Wedding; Show Boat; An American in Paris. 1952: The Belle of New York; Singin' in the Rain. 1953: The Band Wagon. 1954: Brigadoon. 1955: Kismet; It's Always Fair Weather. 1956: Invitation to the Dance. 1957: Silk Stockings. 1960: The Subterraneans; Bells are Ringing. 1962: Light in the Piazza.

FREGONESE, Hugo

Director. Buenos Aires, Argentina 1908–
Medical school in Buenos Aires, then journalist. 1935: to USA; Columbia University. 1938: returned to

Judex, directed by Georges Franju.
Burt Lancaster in Bird Man of Alcatraz, *directed by John Frankenheimer.*
Edward G. Robinson (right) in Black Tuesday, *by Hugo Fregonese.*

Argentina, made shorts. Became editor, assistant director, then director. 1949: scriptwriter in Hollywood, then director. From 1956: also worked in Europe. Married actress Faith Domergue.

Films as director: 1943: Pampa Barbara (*co-d*). 1946: Donde mueren las palabras – When Words Fail. 1947: Apenas un delincuente. 1950: Saddle Tramp; One Way Street. 1951: Apache Drums; Mark of the Renegade. 1952: My Six Convicts; Untamed Frontier; Decameron Nights. 1953: Blowing Wild; Man in the Attic (*uc, co-d R. L. Jacks*). 1954: The Raid; Black Tuesday. 1956: I Girovaghi. 1957: Seven Thunders. 1958: Live in Fear (*+p/co-s*); Harry Black and the Tiger – Harry Black. 1961: Marco Polo. 1964: Apache's Last Battle – Old Shatterhand – Les Cavaliers Rouges. 1966: Pampa Salvaje – Savage Pampas (*+ co-s*).

FRELENG, Friz (Isadore)

Animator. Kansas City, Missouri
1924: first work in animation. 1927: to Walt Disney in California. 1 year in New York on 'Krazy Kat' series. 1930: return to Hollywood. At Warners worked in Looney Tunes, Merrie Melodies. 1949: under name Isadore Freleng directed in collaboration with Chuck Jones *So Much for So Little,* Warners government health cartoon. At Warners until 1969, except for 2 years at MGM. 1963: with David de Patie founded De Patie–Freleng Enterprises. Took over animated production from Warners and associated with Mirisch and United Artists to make series 'The Pink Panther' and 'The Inspector'; made other TV series and commercials. TV work includes titles and other sequences for 'My World—and Welcome to It' based on James Thurber drawings. Much title work for films.

Films as animator include: 1944: Bugs Bunny and the Three Bears. 1947: Tweetie Pie; Bugs Bunny Rides Again. 1951: Canary Row. 1953: Bugs and Thugs. 1954: Dog Pounded; Captain Hareblower; I Gopher You. 1955: By Word of Mouse; Speedy Gonzales; Pizzicato Pussycat; From A to Z-Z-Z; Sahara Hare; Tweety's Circus; Red Riding Hoodwinked. 1956: Rabbitson Crusoe; Tugboat Granny; Tweet and Sour. 1957: Birds Anonymous; Greedy for Tweety; Show Biz Bugs; Tweet Zoo. 1958: A Pizza Tweety-Pie; A Bird in a Bonnet.

FREND, Charles

Director and editor. Pulborough, England 1909–
Trinity College, Oxford. 1931: became editor with British International Pictures. 1933–37: editor with Gaumont–British, including 3 films directed by Alfred Hitchcock. 1937–39: editor with MGM in UK. 1941: first film as director, an Ealing semi-documentary. 1942: made *The Foreman Went to France,* produced by Alberto Cavalcanti. 1962: made *Finche dura la tempestà* in Italy. Lecturer, London School of Film Technique. Also TV director. 1967: made *The Sky Bike* for Children's Film Foundation. 1970: collaborated on 2nd-unit direction of *Ryan's Daughter.*

Films as editor include: 1933: Waltzes from Vienna. 1936: The Secret Agent; Sabotage. 1937: Young and Innocent – A Girl was Young. 1938: A Yank at Oxford; The Citadel. 1939: Goodbye, Mr Chips. 1940: Major Barbara.

Films as director: 1941: The Big Blockade (*+ w, uc*). 1942: The Foreman Went to France. 1943: San Demetrio, London. 1945: Johnny Frenchman; Return of the Vikings.). 1947: The Loves of Joanna Godden. 1948: Scott of the Antarctic. 1949: A Run for Your Money; The Magnet. 1953: The Cruel Sea. 1955: Lease of Life. 1956: The Long Arm. 1957: Barnacle Bill. 1960: Cone of Silence. 1962: Girl on Approval; Finche dura la tempestà – Beta Som – Torpedo Bay. 1967: The Sky Bike.

FRESNAY, Pierre

Actor. Paris 1897–
Conservatoire National d'Art Dramatique. 1915: stage debut at Comédie Française then film debut. 1916–19: French Army, reaching 2nd Lieutenant. 1920: on London stage in 'Le Misanthrope'. 1921: second film. 1924–26: toured UK in French classics. Went to New York with 'Conversation Piece'. 1937: actor-manager at Théâtre de la Michodière, Paris. Married actress Yvonne Printemps; directed her in *Le Duel* (1939).

Films as actor include: 1931: Marius. 1932: Fanny. 1934: The Man Who Knew Too Much. 1935: Le Roman d'un jeune homme pauvre; César. 1936: Koenigsmark; Sous les yeux d'Occident. 1937: La Grande Illusion. 1942: L'Assassin habite au 21; La Main du diable. 1943: Le Corbeau; Le voyageur sans bagages. 1945: La Fille du diable. 1947: Monsieur Vincent. 1949: La Valse de Paris. 1951: Un Grand Patron. 1953: La Route Napoléon; Le Défroqué. 1954: Les Evadés. 1955: Les Aristocrates. 1957: Les Oeufs de l'autruche.

FREUND, Karl

Cinematographer. Koenigshof, Bohemia 1890–
1905: assistant projectionist after apprenticeship to Berlin rubber-stamp manufacturer. 1906: first projectionist to be granted license by Berlin Fire Department. 1908: newsreel cameraman for Pathé in Berlin. Austrian Army for three months of World War I; released as overweight. 1916: cinematographer on Robert Wiene's *Frau Eva.* 1919: Started own laboratory for processing film on which he had been either cinematographer or operator. During 1920s worked on many films directed by F. W. Murnau. 1926: Production head of Fox–Europa. 1929: to Hollywood. 1937: Oscar for cinematography, *The Good Earth.* During 1950s; cinematographer on various TV shows (e.g. 'I Love Lucy').

Films as cinematographer include: 1920: Satanas; Der Golem, wie er in die Welt kam. 1922: Der brennende Acker; Lucrezia Borgia (*co*). 1923: Die Austreibung; Die Finanzen des Grossherzogs. 1924: Mikäel (*co*); Der letzte Mann. 1925: Tartüff; Variété. 1926: Faust. 1927: Metropolis. 1929: Fraulein Else (*co*). 1931: Dracula; Strictly Dishonorable (*co*). 1932: Back Street; Air Mail. 1937: The Good Earth; Parnell; Conquest. 1938: Letter of Introduction. 1939: Golden Boy (*co*). 1940: Pride and Prejudice. 1942: Tortilla Flat. 1944: A Guy Named Joe (*co*); The Seventh Cross. 1946: Undercurrent. 1948: Key Largo.

Films as director: 1932: The Mummy. 1933: Moonlight and Pretzels – Moonlight and Melody. 1934: Madame Spy; The Countess of Monte Cristo; Uncer-

tain Lady; Gift of Gab; I Give My Love. 1935: Mad Love – The Hands of Orlac.

FRIČ, Martin

Director and writer. Prague 1902–1968
Father railway engineer. 1920: worked in cabaret and theatre. Commentator for silent films. Wrote film stories, acted in secondary roles; lab assistant then cameraman. Assistant to Josef Rovensky and Karel Lamac writing scripts in collaboration with them. 1929: first film as director, with Lamac as actor; later directed Lamac several times. 1931: directed 2 films in collaboration with Lamac. 1932: acted in 2 films directed by Lamac. 1933–37: several script collaborations with Hugo Haas; directed him several times.

Films as director: 1929: Páter Vojtech – Father Voitech (*+ s*). 1931: Dobrý voják Svejk – Good Soldier Schweik; On a jeho sestra – He and His Sister (*co-d Karel Lamac*); To neznáte Hadimrsku – Hadimrsku Doesn't Know (*co-d Karel Lamac*). 1932: Anton Spelec, ostrostrelec – Anton Spelec, the Thrower; Chuda Holka; Kantor Ideál – Conduct Unsatisfactory; Sestra Angelika – Sister Angelica. 1933: Popbocnik Jeho Výsosti – Assistant to His Highness; Revisor – Accountant; S Vyloucenim Verejnosti – Closed Doors; U Snedeného Krámu – The Ransacked Shop. 1934: Poslední Muz – The Last Man. 1935: Hrdja jednó noci – Hero for a Night; Jedenácté Prikázáni – The Eleventh Commandment. 1936: Páter Vojtech – Father Voitech (*rm* 1929); Svádlenka – The Seamstress; Ulicka v ráji – Paradise Road. 1937: Advokátka Vera – Vera the Lawyer; Hordubalové – The Hordubal Brothers; Lidé na kre – Lost on the Ice; Tri Vejce do skla – Three Eggs in a Glass. 1938: Krok do tmy – Madman in the Dark; Skola základ zivota – School, the Beginning of Life. 1939: Eva tropí hlouposti – Eva Plays the Fool; Jiny Vzduch – Fresh Air; Muz z Neznáma – Reluctant Millionaire. 1940: Baron Prášil; Druhá Smena – Second Lawyer; Katakomby – Catacombs; Muzikantská Liduska – The Musician's Girl. 1941: Roztomilý Clovek; Tezky zivot dobrodruha – Adventure is a Hard Life. 1943: Barbora Hlavsová; Experiment. 1944: Počestné Paní Pardubické – The Respectable Ladies of Pardubické. 1945: Prstynek – The Wedding Ring. 1946: 13 Revir – Beat 13. 1948: Návrat domu – Return Home. 1949: Petistovka – Motor Cycles; Pytlákova Schovanka – The Poacher's God-daughter. 1950: Zocelemi – The Steel Town; Past – The Trap. 1951: Císařův Pekař – The Emperor and his Baker; Bylo to v Máji – May Events (*co-d Vaclar Berdych*). 1963: Král králů – King of Kings. 1964: Hvězda zvaná pelyněk – A Star Named Wormwood. 1966: Lidé na kolekach – People on Wheels. 1967: Nejlepši ženská mého živote – The Best Girl in My Life.

Films as director and writer in collaboration: 1929: Varhanik n Svateho Vita – The Organist of St Vita. 1930: Vse pro laska – All for Love. 1933: Zivot je pes – Dog's Life (*+ co-st*). 1934: Hej rup! (*+ co-st*); Mazlicek – The Effeminate One (*+ co-st*). 1935: At zije neboztik – Long Live Kindness (*+ co-st*). 1936: Jánosik. 1937: Mavrost nade vse – Morality Above All; Svet patri nám – The World Belongs to Them (*+ co-st*). 1939: Cesta do hubin studákovy duse – Searching the Hearts of Students; Kristián – Christian (*co-st only*). 1941: Hotel Modráhvezda; Teticka – Auntie's Fantasies. 1942: Valentin Dobrotivŷ. 1947:

Varuj! – Warning; Capkovy Povidky – Tales by Capek. 1948: Polibek ze stadionu – A Kiss from the Stadium (+ co-st). 1953: Tajemstvi Krve – The Mystery of Blood. 1954: Psohlarci – Dog's Heads. 1955: Mistvi Zimnich sporti – Master of Winter Sports; Nechte to na mně! – Leave it to Me. 1956: Zaostrit, prosim – Watch the Birdie. 1958: Povoden – The Flood; Theodor Pistek; Dnes naposled. 1959: Princezna se zlatov hvezdor – The Princess with the Golden Star. 1960: Ruzena naskova. 1961: Tereza Brzková (co-st only); Eman Fiala (co-st only).

FRIEDHOFER, Hugo W.

Composer. San Francisco 1902–
Father a cellist. Left school at 16; office boy. Design department of lithography firm; studied painting at night. At 18 began musical training; by 1923, professional musician. 1923–25: with People's Symphony Orchestra, San Francisco. 1925: with Granada Theatre Orchestra. 1929: to Hollywood; arranger for Fox. 1934: to Warners, orchestrator for Leo Forbstein. 11 years in orchestration at Warners, then freelanced. From 1937: also composer for films. Late 1950s: worked mainly for Fox. Oscar for score, *The Best Years of Our Lives* (1946).

Films as composer include: 1944: Lifeboat; Home in Indiana; Wing and a Prayer. 1947: Wild Harvest; Body and Soul. 1948: Joan of Arc. 1950: Broken Arrow. 1951: Ace in the Hole. 1952: The Outcasts of Poker Flat; The Marrying Kind. 1953: Hondo (co); Island in the Sky. 1954: Vera Cruz. 1955: Violent Saturday; The Girl in the Red Velvet Swing. 1956: The Revolt of Mamie Stover; The Harder They Fall. 1957: An Affair to Remember. 1958: The Young Lions; The Barbarian and The Geisha. 1959: Woman Obsessed. 1961: One-Eyed Jacks. 1964: Secret Invasion. 1971: Von Richtofen and Brown.

FRIESE-GREENE, William

(William Edward Green) Inventor. Bristol, England 1855–1921 London
1869: apprenticed briefly to a photographer. 1874: married, combining wife's surname with his own; opened first studio, in Bath. 1884: built his first motion picture camera, using glass plates; made *The Birth of a Smile* consisting of 4 slides of himself. 1885: exhibited and published material on his camera. 1887: finished work on projector for his glass plates; started work on camera to use strips of sensitised paper. 1888: completed camera to use 50-foot strips of paper with perforated edges; paper not strong enough to exceed projection at 7 or 8 f.p.s. and not sufficiently transparent; with assistant Alfred Parker began work on celluloid strips. 1889: using camera built by himself, and celluloid film with frame size of 3 inches square, moving at 10 f.p.s., shot moving pictures in Hyde Park; built another camera, using smaller gauge of film running at 12 f.p.s.; patented the camera; worked on projector; work published. 1890: public projection in Chester; bankrupt, briefly imprisoned, then employed by wife. 1893: experimented with colour film. 1910: to USA for American Supreme Court's inquiry into motion picture patents; Edison's claims set aside in favour of Friese-Green's 1889 patent. Patented 64 inventions in all. 1917: ruined by World War I; parted from second wife through poverty, took factory job. Collapsed and died after making speech at meeting of cinema businessmen. 1951: played by Robert Donat in *The Magic Box*.

FRY, Christopher

Playwright. Bristol, England 1907–
Wrote plays while a schoolmaster. 1949–50: 'The Lady's Not for Burning', with Richard Burton, produced in London and New York. Occasional film work from 1952. Uncredited collaboration on *Ben-Hur* (1959), a major rewrite during shooting.

Films as writer: 1952: The Beggars' Opera (*additional di/lyr*). 1953: The Queen is Crowned (*cy*). 1959: Ben-Hur (*co-s, uc*). 1962: Barabbas. 1966: La Bibbia.

FULLER, Samuel

Director, producer, writer. Worcester, Massachusetts 1911–
Newspaper seller, copy boy for New York Journal at 15. At 17: crime reporter for New York Graphic, San Diego Sun. Short stories; novels: 'Burn, Baby, Burn' (1935), 'Test Tube Baby' (1936), 'Make Up and Kiss' (1938) and 'The Dark Page' (1944, filmed as *Scandal Sheet*, 1952), 'Crown of India' (1966), 'The Rifle' (1969). Started in films as a scriptwriter (1936) e.g. on *Gangs of New York* (1938). Co-author of story for *Confirm or Deny* (1941). World War II: war correspondent; US Army, decorated for bravery. Later films as writer include *Shockproof* (1949), *The Command* (1953). Produced some, wrote almost all his films. 1967: removed name from credits of *Caine*, edited against his wishes. Also TV. Appeared as himself in *Pierrot le Fou* (1965) and *Brigitte et Brigitte* (1966).

Films as director and writer: 1948: I Shot Jesse James. 1949: The Baron of Arizona. 1950: The Steel Helmet (+ co-p). 1951: Fixed Bayonets. 1952: Park Row (+ co-p); Pickup on South Street. 1953: Hell and High Water (co-s). 1955: House of Bamboo (di). 1956: Run of the Arrow (+p). 1957: China Gate (+p); Forty Guns (+p). 1958: Verboten! (+p). 1959: The Crimson Kimono (+p). 1961: Underworld U.S.A. (+p); Merrill's Marauders (co-s). 1963: Shock Corridor (+p). 1964: The Naked Kiss (+ co-p). 1968: Caine – Shark.

FURIE, Sidney J.

Director. Toronto, Ontario, Canada 1933–
Film school. 1954: TV producer, e.g. 'Hudson Bay' (1959–60). 1957–59: first two features as director, in Canada. 1960: to London; executive director for Gala World Film Productions. From 1965: Hollywood.

Films as director: 1957: A Dangerous Age (+ s). 1959: A Cool Sound from Hell (+s). 1960: Dr Blood's Coffin; The Snake Woman. 1961: The Young Ones; During One Night (+p/s). 1962: The Boys. 1963: The Leather Boys. 1964: Wonderful Life – Singer's Paradise. 1965: The Ipcress File. 1966: The Appaloosa – Southwest to Sonora. 1967: The Naked Runner. 1968: The Lawyer (+ co-s). 1970: Little Fauss and Big Halsy.

FURSE, Roger

Designer and painter. Ightham, Kent 1903–
Educated at Eton, Slade School of Fine Art, and in Paris. 5 years in New York as commercial artist, portrait painter. 1934: first design for London stage,

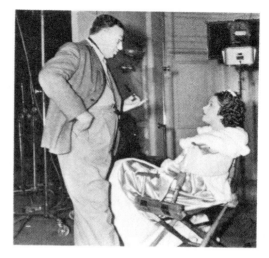

Der Golem, directed by Paul Wegener and Carl Boese, photographed by Karl Freund.
Karl Freund with Myrna Loy on location for John M. Stahl's Parnell.
Shock Corridor, directed by Samuel Fuller.

'The Tidings brought to Mary'. 1938: established as designer by 'Othello' at Old Vic. Much subsequent work for plays and ballet. World War II: Royal Navy, temporarily released for first film work, costumes and armour for *Henry V*. From 1948: film production designer. 1949: costumes and designs for *Under Capricorn*. Costume work also includes *Knights of the Round Table* (1953).

Films as designer include: 1947: Odd Man Out (*dec*). 1948: Hamlet. 1952: Ivanhoe (*co-a*). 1956: Richard III. 1957: The Prince and the Showgirl; Saint Joan. 1958: Bonjour Tristesse. 1962: The Road to Hong Kong.

FURTHMAN, Jules

(Jules Grinnel Furthmann) Writer and director. Chicago, Illinois 1888–1966 Oxford, England
Literature at Northwestern University. Worked on newspapers, magazines. 1916: writer for Universal. 1920: moved to Fox; wrote first film as director. To 1932: mainly with Fox, Paramount. 1933–41: mainly MGM, United Artists. From 1944: mainly Warners, Fox, Paramount. 1945–46: 2 collaborations with William Faulkner. Brother of writer Charles Furthman; they co-wrote story of *The City Gone Wild* (1927) and wrote *Thunderbolt* (1929) together.

Films as director and writer: 1920: The Land of Jazz (*co-st/d*). 1921: The Blushing Bride (+ /*st*); Colorado Pluck (*ad*). 1951: Jet Pilot (*r 1957*; + *p*; *co-d, uc*; *co-d Josef Von Sternberg*).

Films as writer include: 1920: The White Circle (*co*). 1921: The Big Punch (*co*). 1923: North of Hudson Bay (+ *st*). 1925: Any Woman (*co*); Sackcloth and Scarlet (*co*). 1926: The Wise Guy. 1927: The City Gone Wild (+ *co-st*); Barbed Wire (*co-s/ad*); The Way of All Flesh (+ *co-st*); Hotel Imperial (*co*). 1928: The Dragnet (*co*); The Docks of New York. 1929: Thunderbolt (*co-s/co-st*); Broadway (*co-s/co-ad*); Abie's Irish Rose; The Case of Lena Smith. 1930: Morocco; Common Clay; Renegades. 1931: Over the Hill (*co*); The Yellow Ticket (+ *co-di*); Merely Mary Ann. 1932: Shanghai Express; Blonde Venus (*co*). 1933: Bombshell (*co*). 1935: China Seas (*co*); Mutiny on the Bounty (*co*). 1936: Come and Get It (*co*). 1938: Spawn of the North. 1939: Only Angels Have Wings. 1940: The Outlaw (*r 1946*). 1941: The Shanghai Gesture (*co*). 1945: To Have and Have Not (*co*). 1946: The Big Sleep. 1947: Moss Rose (*co*); Nightmare Alley. 1950: Pretty Baby (*co-st*). 1951: Peking Express (*ad; rm Shanghai Express 1932*). 1959: Rio Bravo (*co*).

FUSCO, Giovanni

Composer. Sant'Agata dei Goti, Italy 1906–
Younger brother of musician Tarcisco Fusco. Studied piano, composition, conducted at the Accademia di Santa Cecilia, Rome; sang in choir of St Peter's. Composed 2 operas, 'La Scala di seta' and 'L'Ultimo Venuto', symphony 'Balletto' and numerous songs. From 1936: music for films. 1942–45: Italian army. Scores for 4 Antonioni shorts, most of his features.

Films as composer include: 1946: Martin Roumagnac. 1950: Cronaca di un amore. 1953: La Signora senza camelie; I Vinti. 1955: Le Amiche. 1957: Il Grido. 1959: Hiroshima mon amour (*co*). 1960: Il Rossetto;

L'Avventura; I Delfini. 1962: Il Mare; L'Eclisse. 1963: I Fuorilegi del matrimonio. 1964: Gli Indifferenti; Deserto Rosso. 1966: La Guerre est finie. 1967: Sovverivi.

G

GABIN, Jean

(Alexis Moncorgé). Actor. Meriel, France 1904–
Parents in musical comedy, cabaret. Left school at 13; labourer, shop assistant. 1923: in crowd scene at Folies-Bergère. 1925: returned from Navy service; stand-in at Bouffes Parisiens. 1926–27: toured France in musicals, operetta. 1927: engaged by Mistinguette at Moulin Rouge. 1928: contract with Bouffes Parisiens. 1930: entered films. 1939: joined French navy; special leave (1940) to finish *Remorques* (1941). 1941: to USA on German occupation of France; appeared in *Moontide* (1942), *The Imposter* (1944). 1943: joined Free French in Algeria. After demobilisation awarded Military Medal, Croix de Guerre and (later) Légion d'Honneur. 1950: returned to stage in 'La Soif' after 20 years' absence. 1958: contributed original idea for *Archimède, le clochard*. With Fernandel, formed production company, Gafer: first production *L'Age Ingrat* (1964).

Films as actor include: 1934: Maria Chapdelaine. 1936: La Belle Équipe; La Bandéra; Les Bas-fonds. 1937: Pépé le Moko; La Grande Illusion; Gueule d'amour. 1938: Quai des brumes; La Bête Humaine. 1939: Le Jour se lève. 1946: Martin Roumagnac. 1949: Au-delà des grilles. 1950: La Marie du port. 1952: Le Plaisir. 1954: Touchez-pas au Grisbi; L'Air de Paris. 1955: Napoléon; French Cancan. 1956: La Traversée de Paris. 1958: Maigret tend un piège; En cas de malheur. 1959: Les Grandes Familles. 1962: Un Singe en hiver; Mélodie en sous-sol. 1964: Monsieur; L'Age Ingrat (+ *co-pc*). 1965: Du Rififi à Paname. 1967: Le Pacha. 1969: Le Clan des Siciliens. 1971: Le Drapeau Noir flotte sur la marmite.

GABLE, Clark

Actor. Cadiz, Ohio 1901–1960 Hollywood
Studied medicine in night-class at University of Akron. Began in theatre as call boy, then toured as actor with several stock companies including the Jewell Players (1921–22). During 1920s worked mainly in theatre, including Broadway. Extra, bit parts in films e.g. *Forbidden Paradise* (1924), *The Merry Widow* (1925). From 1930: mainly with MGM. 1942–43: US Air Force. 1956: own production company, made *The King and Four Queens*. 5 wives included Carole Lombard (1939–42). Oscar as Best Actor for *It Happened One Night* (1934).

Films as actor include: 1931: The Easiest Way; A Free Soul; Night Nurse; Susan Lenox; Possessed. 1932: Red Dust; Polly of the Circus; Strange Interlude. 1933: The White Sister; Night Flight; Dancing Lady. 1934: Men in White; Manhattan Melodrama; Forsaking All Others; Chained. 1935: Call of the Wild; China Seas; Mutiny on the Bounty; After Office Hours. 1936: Wife vs. Secretary; San Francisco; Cain and Mabel; Love on the Run. 1937: Parnell; Saratoga. 1938: Test Pilot;

Too Hot to Handle. 1939: Idiot's Delight; Gone with the Wind. 1940: Strange Cargo; Comrade X; Boom Town. 1941: Honky Tonk; They Met in Bombay. 1942: Somewhere I'll Find You. 1946: Adventure. 1947: The Hucksters. 1948: Homecoming. 1949: Command Decision; Any Number Can Play. 1950: Key to the City; To Please a Lady. 1951: Across the Wide Missouri; Lone Star. 1953: Never Let Me Go; Mogambo. 1955: Soldier of Fortune; The Tall Men. 1957: Band of Angels. 1958: Run Silent, Run Deep; Teacher's Pet. 1960: It Started in Naples. 1961: The Misfits.

GALEEN, Henrik

Director. 1882–
Actor and director in theatre; worked with Max Reinhardt for a year. Theatre in Switzerland. 1910: entered cinema as actor. 1922: wrote *Nosferatu-eine Symphonie des Grauens*. 1924: wrote *Das Wachsfigurenkabinett*. 1929: made *After the Verdict* in UK, silent. 1933: to USA.

Films as director: 1914: Der Golem (+ *co-sw*). 1920: Judith Trachtenberg. 1923: Stadt in Sicht (+ *s*). 1924: Liebesbriefe der Baronin von S . . . (+ *co-s*). 1926: Der Student von Prag (+ *co-s*). 1928: Alraune – Daughter of Destiny – Mandragore (+ *s*). 1929: After the Verdict. 1933: Salon Dora Green.

GALLONE, Carmine

Director, Taggia, Italy 1886–
French mother, Neapolitan father. At 15 wrote first play. 1911: won national contest for verse tragedy 'Britannico'. 1928: made *Inferno di amore* in Russia and Poland. Made *Terra senza donne* (1929) and *Eine Nacht in Venedig* (1933) in Germany. 1931: made *The City of Song* in UK. 1931–32: in France to make *Un Soir de rafle* and *Un Fils d'Amérique*. Many musical and operatic films in 1940s and 1950s. 1955: *Madama Butterfly* made in Japan for Toho with Japanese cast. 1956: made *Michel Strogoff* in France. 1958: made *Polikushka* in Germany. Wife Soava Gallone acted in 12 of his films.

Films as director include: 1913: Il Bacio di Cirano. 1914: Turbine d'odio; La Donna Nuda. 1915: Avator; Fior di male; Marzia Nuziale; Redenzione; Maria di Magadala; Senza colpa. 1916: La Falena; Malombra. 1917: La Storia di un peccato; Storia dei tredici. 1919: Maman Poupée. 1920: Amleto e i suo clown – On With the Motley. 1921: Nemesis; Il Mare di Napoli. 1922: Marcella. 1923: I Volti dell'amore; La Cavalcata Ardente. 1924: Il Corsaro (*co-d Augusto Genina*). 1926: Gli Ultimi Giorni di Pompei – The Last Days of Pompeii. 1927: Celle qui domine (*co-d*). 1928: S.O.S.; Inferno di amore. 1929: Terra senza donne – Das Land ohne Frauen. 1931: The City of Song – La Città Canora. 1932: Un Soir de rafle; Un Fils d'Amérique; Le Roi des palaces; Le Chant du marin; Ma Cousine de Varsovie. 1933: Eine Nacht in Venedig – Una Notte a Venezia; Going Gay. 1934: For Love of You; Two Hearts in Waltz Time. 1935: E lucean le stelle; Casta Diva; Wenn die Musik nicht war – Liszt Rhapsody. 1936: Mon Coeur t'appelle; Opernina. 1937: Scipio l'Africano; Cristoforo Colombo. 1938: Solo per te; Manège; Marionette; Giuseppe Verdi. 1939: Il Sogno di Butterfly; Manon Lescaut. 1940: Oltre l'amore; Melodie Eterne; Amami Alfredo. 1941: L'Amante

Segreta – Troppo bella; Primo Amore; La Regina di Navarra. 1942: Le Due Orfanelle – The Two Orphans; Odessa in fiamme. 1943: Harlem – Knock Out; Tristi Amori. 1945: Il Canto della vita. 1946: Biraghin; Davanti a lui tremava tutta Roma; Rigoletto. 1947: La Signora dalle camelie. 1949: La Traviata – The Lost One; La Forza del destino – The Force of Destiny; La Leggenda di Faust – Faust and the Devil. 1950: Il Trovatore – The Troubadour; Addio Mimi; Taxi di Notte – Bambino. 1951: Messalina – The Affairs of Messalina. 1952: Puccini – His Two Loves; Vissi d'arte, vissi d'amore; Senza veli (+co-s). 1953: La Cavalleria Rusticana – Fatal Desire. 1954: Casa Ricordi – House of Ricordi; Casta Diva (rm). 1955: Madama Butterfly – Madame Butterfly; Don Camillo e l'onorevole Peppone – Don Camillo's Last Round. 1956: Michel Strogoff – Michael Strogoff; Tosca. 1958: Polikushka. 1959: Cartagine in fiamme – Carthage in Flames.

GANCE, Abel

Director. Paris 1889–
Chaptal College. 1906: articled clerk in solicitor's office. 1907: wrote first screenplay, *Mireille*; joined Théâtre du Parc, Brussels, as actor. Later screenplays include *Napoléon auf St Helena* (1929), *La Reine Margot* (1953), *La Roue* (1956). 1909: first film as actor, *Molière*. 1911: first film as director; also scripted most of own films. 1917–18: Army Cinematograph Unit. 1926: introduced triple screen (Polyvision) with *Napoléon vu par Abel Gance*. 1929: patented Perspective Sonore; first to use stereophonic sound, for *Napoléon Bonaparte* (1934). *Magirama* (1956) is compilation of previous films, including *J'accuse!*, *Quatorze Juillet 1953*. 1971: added and reworked scenes for new version of *Napoleon* called *Bonaparte et la Révolution*, backed by Claude Letouch.

Films as writer and director: 1911: La Digue – Pour sauver la Hollande; Le Nègre Blanc (co-s; +w; co-d Jean Joulout); Il y a des pieds au plafond. 1912: Le Masque d'horreur; Un Drame au Château d'Acre – Les Morts reviennent-ils?; L'Enigme de dix heures. 1915: La Folie du Docteur Tube; Fioritures – La Source de beauté; Le Fou de la falaise; Le Périscope; Ce que les flots racontent. 1916: Barbereuse; L'Héroïsme de Paddy; Stass et Compagnie; Les Gaz Mortels – Brouillard sur la ville; La Fleur des ruines; Le droit à la vie – The Right to Live; La Zone de la mort. 1917: Mater Dolorosa – The Call of Motherhood – The Sorrowing Mother. 1918: La Dixième Symphonie; J'accuse! 1922: La Roue. 1923: Au secours! – The Haunted House (co-s). 1926: Napoléon vu par Abel Gance (+e/w). 1928: Marines et cristaux. 1931: La Fin du monde (+c/w). 1933: Mater Dolorosa (rm 1917); Le Maître des forges; La Dame aux camélias; Napoléon Bonaparte (rm 1926). 1935: Le Roman d'un jeune homme pauvre; Lucrèce Borgia. 1936: Le Voleur de femmes; Un Grand Amour de Beethoven – Beethoven; Jerome Perreau, héros des Barricades (d only). 1937: J'accuse! – That They May Live (rm). 1939: Louise (co-s); Paradis Perdu (co-s). 1940: La Vénus Aveugle. 1941: Une Femme dans la nuit (+s; co-d Edmond Gréville). 1942: Le Capitaine Fracasse (co-s). 1944: Manolete (uf). 1953: Quatorze Juillet 1953. 1954: Latour de Nesle. 1956: Magirama (co-d). 1960: Austerlitz – The Battle of Austerlitz (+s/di; co-d Roger Richebé). 1963: Cyrano et

d'Artagnan. 1971: Bonaparte et la Révolution (+cop/co-e).

GARBO, Greta

(Greta Louisa Gustafsson) Actress. Stockholm 1905–
From 14, barber's assistant, shopgirl. 1921–22: appeared in 2 short advertising films; spotted in street for part of bathing belle in comedy short *Luffar-Peter* (1922). 1922–24: scholarship to Royal Dramatic Theatre Drama School, Stockholm. 1924: became protégée of Mauritz Stiller, who named her Garbo; first feature, *Gösta Berlings Saga*. 1925: made *Die freudlose Gasse* in Germany; went to Hollywood, thereafter with MGM until retirement (1941). Frequently rumoured to be making comeback; Technicolor test (1950) for Walter Wanger for unrealised project to have been directed by Max Ophüls. Never married.

Features as actress: 1924: Gösta Berlings Saga. 1925: Die freudlose Gasse. 1926: Ibarez' Torrent; The Temptress. 1927: Flesh and the Devil. 1928: Love; The Divine Woman; The Mysterious Lady; A Woman of Affairs. 1929: Wild Orchids; The Single Standard; The Kiss. 1930: Anna Christie; Romance. 1931: Inspiration; Susan Lenox. 1932: Mata Hari; Grand Hotel; As You Desire Me. 1934: Queen Christina; The Painted Veil. 1935: Anna Karenina. 1936: Camille. 1938: Conquest. 1939: Ninotchka. 1941: Two-Faced Woman.

GARDNER, Ava

Actress. Smithfield, North Carolina 1922–
Trained as secretary. At 18 visited New York; brother-in-law took photographs of her that led to MGM screen test. 1941: MGM contract. Married Mickey Rooney (1942–43), Artie Shaw (1945–47), Frank Sinatra (1951–57), all divorced. 1954: settled in Spain. 1958: MGM contract expired.

Films as actress include: 1943: Hitler's Madman; Young Ideas. 1946: The Killers. 1947: Singapore. 1949: The Great Sinner; The Bribe; East Side, West Side. 1950: My Forbidden Past. 1951: Pandora and the Flying Dutchman; Show Boat. 1952: The Snows of Kilimanjaro. 1953: Ride, Vaquero!; Mogambo; Knights of the Round Table. 1954: The Barefoot Contessa. 1956: Bhowani Junction. 1957: The Sun Also Rises. 1959: The Naked Maja; On the Beach; La Sposa Bella. 1963: Fifty-five Days at Peking. 1964: Seven Days in May; Night of the Iguana. 1966: La Bibbia. 1969: Mayerling.

GARFEIN, Jack

Director. Mukacevo, Czechoslovakia 1930–
Survivor of Auschwitz concentration camp. To USA. 1947–49: New School for Social Research. 1948: acted in 'The Burning Bush'. 1950: American Theatre Wing. From 1954: member of Actor's Studio. 1955: married Carroll Baker; directed her in *Something Wild* (1961). On stage directed 'End as a Man' (1953), 'Girls of Summer' (1956), 'The Sin of Pat Muldoon' (1957), 'Shadow of a Gunman' (1958), 'Arms and the Man' (stock production). Also stage and TV producer. Directed for TV: dramatic segment of 'The Kate Smith Show'. Scripted for TV: 'A Man Dies'. Assistant to Elia Kazan on *Baby Doll* and to George Stevens on *Giant*. 1956: first feature as director, for Columbia.

Clark Gable and Hedy Lamarr in Comrade X. *by King Vidor.*
Nosferatu, *directed by F. W. Murnau and scripted by Henrik Galeen, from Bram Stoker's novel* Dracula.
Lana Turner and John Garfield in Tay Garnett's The Postman Always Rings Twice.

1961: *Something Wild* made entirely in New York, involving many people from Actor's Studio.

Films as director: 1957: The Strange One – End as a Man. 1961: Something Wild.

GARFIELD, John

(Julius Garfinkle) Actor. New York 1913–1952 New York.

Father a coat-presser. Mother died when he was 7. member of various street gangs in the Bronx until Angelo Patri School fostered interest in drama. Trained at Heckster Foundation Drama Workshop and American Laboratory Theatre; small parts with Eva la Galliene's Civic Repertory Company in New York; recommended by Clifford Odets to the Group Theatre. 1933: small part in first film *Footlight Parade*. 1935–37: appeared in Group Theatre productions including 'Awake and Sing'. 1938: contract with Warners, star part in *4 Daughters*; thereafter worked almost entirely in films. 1947: left Warners to form own company, Enterprise Productions. 'Unfriendly' witness at the 1951 hearings of the House Committee on Un-American Activities.

Films as actor include: 1939: They Made Me a Criminal; Juarez; Daughters Courageous. 1940: Castle on the Hudson. 1941: The Sea Wolf; Out of the Fog. 1942: Dangerously They Live; Tortilla Flat. 1943: Air Force; Thank Your Lucky Stars. 1944: Destination Tokyo. 1945: Hollywood Canteen; Pride of the Marines. 1946: The Postman Always Rings Twice; Nobody Lives Forever. 1947: Humoresque; Body and Soul; Gentleman's Agreement. 1948: Force of Evil. 1949: We Were Strangers. 1950: Under my Skin; The Breaking Point. 1951: He Ran All the Way.

GARLAND, Judy

(Frances Gumm) Actress. Grand Rapids, Minnesota 1922–1969 London

Song and dance team with her two sisters. 1935: with Deanna Durbin in 1-reel MGM musical *Every Sunday*. 1936: *Pigskin Parade* on loan to Fox. 1937–50: all films for MGM. 1939: special Oscar. 1945–50: married to Vincente Minnelli. 1949: nervous collapse during production of *Annie Get Your Gun*; replaced by Betty Hutton. Assigned to replace June Allyson on *Royal Wedding* but repeatedly tried to injure herself; contract with MGM dissolved. MGM period includes 4 films directed by Busby Berkeley, 4 by Minnelli. 1954–63: worked for Warners, Columbia, United Artists, Also cabaret singer. Daughter is actress Liza Minnelli.

Films as actress: 1936: Pigskin Parade. 1937: Broadway Melody of 1938; Thoroughbreds Don't Cry. 1938: Everybody Sing; Listen Darling; Love Finds Andy Hardy. 1939: The Wizard of Oz; Babes in Arms. 1940: Strike Up the Band; Little Nellie Kelly; Andy Hardy Meets Debutante. 1941: Ziegfeld Girl; Life Begins for Andy Hardy; Babes on Broadway. 1942: For Me and My Gal. 1943: Presenting Lily Mars; Girl Crazy; Thousands Cheer. 1944: Meet Me in St Louis. 1945: The Clock; The Harvey Girls. 1946: Ziegfeld Follies; Till the Clouds Roll By. 1948: The Pirate; Easter Parade; Words and Music. 1949: In the Good Old Summertime. 1950: Summer Stock. 1954: A Star is Born. 1960: Pepe (*wv*). 1961: Judgment at Nurem-

berg. 1962: Gay Purr-ee (*wv*); A Child is Waiting; I Could Go On Singing.

GARMES, Lee

Cinematographer and director. Peoria, Illinois 1898– Father horticulturist. Parents divorced when child. Entered films in New York as camera assistant. 1916: moved to Hollywood. Worked for Thomas Ince as painter's assistant and prop man; assistant to e.g. D. W. Griffith, Malcolm St Clair. 1924: first film as cinematographer *Find Your Man*. 1934–40: collaborated with Ben Hecht and Charles MacArthur on direction of 4 films. 1937–41: producer; e.g. co-produced (and technical supervisor on) *Dreaming Lips* (1937). 1946: associate producer of Hecht's *Specter of the Rose*. 1952: last film with Hecht *Actors and Sin*. Worked mainly for Paramount and Fox.

Films as cinematographer and director in collaboration with Ben Hecht and Charles MacArthur: 1934: Crime Without Passion. 1935: Once in a Blue Moon; The Scoundrel. 1940: Angels over Broadway (*co-d Hecht only*). 1952: Actors and Son (*co-d Hecht only*).

Films as cinematographer include: 1924: Find Your Man. 1926: The Grand Duchess and the Waiter; A Social Celebrity; The Show Off; The Popular Sin. 1927: The Garden of Allah; The Private Life of Helen of Troy. 1928: The Little Shepherd of Kingdom Come; The Yellow Lily. 1929: Love and the Devil; Say it With Songs. 1930: Lilies of the Field; Song of West; The Other Tomorrow; Morocco- Bright Lights. 1931: Dishonored; City Streets; An American Tragedy. 1932: Shanghai Express; Scarface, Shame of the Nation (*co*); Strange Interlude; Smilin' Through. 1939: Gone with the Wind (*co, uc*). 1941: Lydia (*+ as-p*). 1942: Rudyard Kipling's Jungle Book (*co*); Footlight Serenade; China Girl. 1943: Forever and a Day (*co*). 1944: Since You Went Away (*co*); Guest in the House; None Shall Escape. 1945: Love Letters; Paris Underground. 1946: The Searching Wind; Duel in the Sun (*co*). 1947: The Secret Life of Walter Mitty; Nightmare Alley; The Paradine Case. 1949: Caught; My Foolish Heart; Roseanna McCoy. 1950: Our Very Own. 1951: Saturday's Hero; Detective Story. 1952: The Captive City; The Lusty Men. 1953: Thunder in the East. 1955: Land of the Pharaohs (*co*); The Desperate Hours; Man with the Gun. 1956: The Bottom of the Bottle; Abdullah's Harem; D-Day the Sixth of June. 1957: The Big Boodle. 1959: The Big Fisherman; Happy Anniversary. 1962: Hemingway's Adventures of a Young Man. 1966: A Big Hand for the Little Lady. 1968: The Shoes of the Fisherman (*ur*).

GARNER, James

Actor. Norman, Oklahoma 1928–

Joined Merchant Marine on leaving school. Awarded Purple Heart for service in US Army during Korean War. Studied drama at Berghof School, New York; toured with road companies. 1954: on Broadway in 'The Caine Mutiny Court Martial'. TV, e.g. lead in 'Maverick' series. 1956: Warners contract. Own production company.

Films as actor include: 1956: Towards the Unknown; The Girl He Left Behind. 1957: Sayonara. 1958: Darby's Rangers. 1960: Cash McCall. 1961: The Child-

ren's Hour. 1963: The Great Escape; The Thrill of It All; Move Over, Darling. 1964: 36 Hours. 1965: The Art of Love; Mister Buddwing. 1966: Grand Prix; Duel at Diablo; A Man Could Get Killed. 1967: Hour of the Gun. 1968: The Pink Jungle. 1969: Support Your Local Sheriff! 1971: Support Your Local Gunfighter (*+ co-pc*).

GARNETT, Tay

Director. Los Angeles 1905–

Aviator, engineer. 1920: entered films, various jobs. 1924: in collaboration wrote *Off His Trolley* and *Honeymoon Hardships* at Sennett–Pathé. 1926–28: wrote scripts. 1928: first film as director. 1935: novel, 'Man Laughs Back'. 1939: acted in *Eternally Yours*. Produced own *Slightly Honourable* (1940), *Unexpected Uncle, Weekend for Three* (both 1941). Director on TV series 'Wagon Train', 'The Untouchables', 'Jesse James', and others.

Films as director: 1928: Celebrity (*+ co-s*); The Spieler (*+ co-s*). 1929: The Flying Fool (*+ co-s*); Oh Yeah! (*+ ad*). 1930: Officer O'Brien; Her Man. 1931: Bad Company (*+ co-s*). 1932: One Way Passage; Okay America; Prestige (*+ co-ad*). 1933: Destination Unknown; S.O.S. Eisberg – S.O.S. Iceberg (*co-d Arnold Fanck*). 1935: China Seas; She Couldn't Take It; Professional Soldier. 1937: Slave Ship; Love Is News; Stand-In. 1938: Joy of Living; Trade Winds (*+ st*). 1939: Eternally Yours (*+ w*). 1940: Slightly Honorable (*+ p*); Seven Sinners. 1941: Cheers for Miss Bishop. 1942: My Favorite Spy. 1943: Bataan; The Cross of Lorraine. 1944: Mrs Parkington. 1945: Valley of Decision. 1946: The Postman Always Rings Twice. 1947: Wild Harvest. 1949: A Connecticut Yankee in King Arthur's Court – A Yankee in King Arthur's Court. 1950: The Fireball (*+ co-s*). 1951: Soldiers Three; Cause for Alarm! 1952: One Minute to Zero. 1953: Main Street to Broadway. 1954: The Black Knight. 1956: Seven Wonders of the World (*co-d 4 others*). 1960: A Terrible Beauty – The Night Fighter. 1963: Cattle King – Guns of Wyoming. 1970: The Delta Factor (*+ p*).

GARSON, Greer

Actress. County Down, Ireland 1908–

London University. Repertory in Birmingham. 1933: London stage debut in 'Golden Arrow', with Laurence Olivier. 1935–38: West End stage, including 'Mademoiselle' directed by Noël Coward. 1938: Hollywood; first film, *Remember?* (1939). Films for MGM until *Strange Lady in Town* (1955) for Warners. 1958: replaced Rosalind Russell on Broadway in 'Auntie Mame'.

Films as actress include: 1939: Goodbye, Mr Chips. 1940: Pride and Prejudice. 1941: Blossoms in the Dust; When Ladies Meet. 1942: Random Harvest; Mrs Miniver. 1943: Madame Curie. 1944: Mrs Parkington. 1945: Valley of Decision. 1946: Adventure. 1947: Desire Me. 1948: Julia Misbehaves. 1949: That Forsyte Woman. 1950: The Miniver Story. 1953: Julius Caesar; Scandal at Scourie. 1954: Her Twelve Men. 1955: Strange Lady in Town. 1960: Pepe. 1965: The Singing Nun.

GARY, Romain

Director and writer. Vilno, Russia 1914–

Educated in Nice: studied law at Aix-en-Provence and

Paris; Slav languages at Varsovie. 1945: diplomatic secretary in Sofia; first novel 'L'Education Européenne'. 1949: diplomatic service in Berne. 1952: secretary to French delegation at United Nations in New York. 1955: diplomatic service in London. 1956–60: Consul-General in Los Angeles. 1958: first film as writer *The Roots of Heaven* adapted from own novel 'Les Racines du Ciel' (1956). 1959:-novel 'Les Couleurs du Jour' (1952) filmed as *The Man Who Understood Women*. 1963: married Jean Seberg. 1965: novel 'Lady L' (1959) filmed. 1967–68: *chargé de mission* to Georges Gorse, Minister of Information. 1968: directed and wrote *Les Oiseaux vont mourir au Perou*, in which his wife acted. 1970: *La Promesse de l'autre* made by Jules Dassin from Gary's autobiographical novel. 1971: directed and wrote *Kill*. Chevalier de la Légion d'Honneur.

GASSMAN, Vittorio

Actor. Genoa, Italy 1922–
Accademia d'Arte Drammatica, Rome. 1943: stage debut. From 1946: acted in films. Also directed in Italian theatre. 1953: MGM contract. 1957: in collaboration with Francesco Rosi directed and wrote *Kean*. From 1959: TV, e.g. wrote, produced, acted in series 'The Matador'. 1960: formed own theatre company, Teatro Popolare Italiano, Rome. Second wife Shelley Winters (1952–54).

Films as actor include: 1947: La Figlia del capitano. 1949: Riso Amaro. 1954: Mambo. 1955: La Donna Più Bella del mondo. 1956: War and Peace; Kean (+ co-d/co-s). 1957: La Tempestà; I Soliti Ignoti. 1960: La Grande Guerra. 1961: Il Giudizio Universale. 1962: Barabbas; Il Sorpasso. 1963: I Mostri. 1965: L'Armata Brancaleone. 1967: Il Tigre. 1970: Contestazione Generale. 1971: In Nome del popolo Italiano; Brancaleone alle crociate.

GATTI, Armand

Director and writer. Monaco 1924–
Reporter, novelist, poet and playwright. Books include 'Chine', 'Sibérie moins zéro plus l'infinie', 'Bas-relief pour un décapité'. Plays include 'Le Poisson Noir', 'Le Voyage du Grand Tchou', 'L'Enfant-rat', 'Le Crapaud-Buffle', 'Le Quetzal', 'La Deuxième Existence du camp de Tatenberg', 'Chronique d'une planète provisoire'. 1958: scripted Jean-Claude Bonnardot's *Moranbong*, made at invitation of North Korean government, banned in France for 5 years. 1960: first film as director made in Yugoslavia. 1961: photographed Marco Ferreri's episode of *Le Italiane e l'amore*. 1962: made *El Otro Cristobal* in Cuba. In Germany put on his play 'La Passion du General Franco' (retitled 'Passion en Violet, Jaune et Rouge') and made *Der Ubergang uber den Ebro* for German TV. Unmade scripts include *Clara* (meant to be directed in collaboration with Jan Kadar) and *La Commune* for French TV. 1966: commentary for Joris Ivens' *Le Mistral*. 1968: play 'Passion en Violet, Jaune et Rouge' banned in France.

Films as director and writer: 1960: L'Enclos – The Enclosure (co-s). 1962: El Otro Cristobal.

GAUDIO, Tony

(Antonio G. Gaetano) Cinematographer. Rome 1885–1951 Burlingame. California

Father a photographer. Emigrated to USA as a child. Lab technician in photographic studio. 1907: joined Independent Motion Picture Company. Cinematographer from 1910. Worked mainly for First National and Warners; under contract for most of career. Oscar for best cinematography, *Anthony Adverse* (1936).

Films as cinematographer include: 1920: The Mark of Zorro. 1922: The Eternal Flame. 1923: Ashes of Vengeance. 1925: The Lady. 1926: The Temptress. 1927: Two Arabian Knights (co). 1929: She Goes to War (co); General Crack. 1930: Hell's Angels (co); Little Caesar. 1933: The World Changes; Ladies Must Love. 1934: Mandalay; Fog Over Frisco. 1935: Oil for the Lamps of China; Front Page Woman; Dr Socrates; The Story of Louis Pasteur. 1936: The White Angel. 1937: The King and the Chorus Girl; Another Dawn; The Life of Emile Zola. 1938: The Adventures of Robin Hood (co). 1939: Juarez; The Old Maid. 1940: Till We Meet Again; The Letter. 1941: High Sierra. 1943: The Constant Nymph. 1944: Days of Glory; A Song to Remember (co). 1949: The Red Pony.

GAUMONT, Léon

Entrepreneur and producer. Paris 1863–1946 Saint-Maxine, France
Collège de Sainte-Barbe. After military service managed small incandescent lamp factory. Moved to Comptoir Général de Photographie; became director. 1895: reorganised company, found backers, including Gustave Eiffel; Demeny Chronophotographe (or Bioscope) on market. From 1896: produced *actualités*, at first secondary to sale of apparatus. 1898: his secretary Alice Guy directed their first narrative film with sets, *Les Mésaventures d'une tête de veau*; she followed it with others. 1902: marketed apparatus synchronising gramophone and cinematograph. 1905: Société Gaumont built at Buttes-Chaumont, the biggest film studio then in existence; sound financial backing, but strict economy; marketed films in Europe and USA. 1906: Alice Guy left for USA; Louis Feuillade replaced her as artistic director at Gaumont. Also exhibitor. 1910: brought out improvement to synchronising apparatus with loud-speakers distributed through auditorium.

GAYNOR, Janet

(Laura Gainor) Actress. Philadelphia, Pennsylvania 1906–
1924: extra at Hal Roach studios. 1925: played female lead in westerns at Universal; changed name to Janet Gaynor. 1927: *Sunrise* made her a star. She and Charles Farrell worked as a team, starting with *Seventh Heaven* (1927); 12 films together. 1938: married Gilbert Adrian, MGM dress designer; retired. Occasional TV and stage; small role in *Bernardine* (1957). 1927–28: Oscar as actress (first to be awarded) for *Sunrise, Street Angel* and *Seventh Heaven*.

Films as actress include: 1926: The Shamrock Handicap; The Blue Eagle. 1927: Sunrise; Seventh Heaven. 1928: Street Angel; Four Devils. 1929: Lucky Star; Sunny Side Up. 1930: The Man Who Came Back; High Society Blues. 1931: Daddy Long Legs; Merely Mary Ann; Delicious. 1932: Tess of the Storm Country. 1933: State Fair; Adorable. 1934: Carolina;

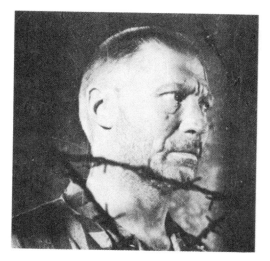

Richard Devon in Tay Garnett's Guns of Wyoming.
Vittorio Gassman and Virna Lisi in Una Vergine Per Il Principe. *directed by Pasquale Festa Campanile.*
L'Enclos. *directed by Armand Gatti.*

Servant's Entrance. 1935: The Farmer Takes a Wife; One More Spring. 1936: Small Town Girl. 1937: A Star Is Born. 1938: Three Loves Has Nancy.

GAYNOR, Mitzi

(Francesca Mitzi Marlene de Charney von Gerber) Actress. Chicago 1930–
Hungarian descent. At 12: in Hollywood shows. At 14: corps de ballet of Los Angeles Civic Light Opera. Stage musicals. 1950: first film *My Blue Heaven*. Fox then Paramount contracts. From 1961: also cabaret.

Films as actress include: 1951: Golden Girl; Take Care of My Little Girl. 1952: We're Not Married; Down Among the Sheltering Palms. 1953: The I Don't Care Girl. 1954: There's No Business Like Show Business. 1956: The Birds and the Bees. 1957: The Joker is Wild; Les Girls. 1958: South Pacific. 1959: Happy Anniversary. 1960: Surprise Package. 1963: For Love or Money.

GÉLIN, Daniel

Actor. Angers, France 1921–
Childhood in St Malo. Studied drama at Conservatoire de Paris and under René Simon. From 1939: small film parts. 1941: stage debut in 'Les Tourbières de Scapin'. 3 years at Théâtre des Maturins; many subsequent stage appearances. 1952: directed and acted in *Les Dents Longues*. 2 volumes of poems. Also TV. 1945–52: married actress Danièle Delorme.

Films as actor include: 1946: Martin Roumagnac. 1949: Rendezvous de juillet. 1950: La Ronde. 1951: Edouard et Caroline. 1952: Le Plaisir. 1953: Rue de l'Estrapade; Sang et lumières. 1954: La Romana; Si Versailles m'était conté. 1955: Les Amants du Tage; Napoléon. 1956: En effeuillant la marguerite. 1957: The Man Who Knew Too Much; Mort en fraude. 1958: La Fille de Hambourg. 1959: Le Testament d'Orphée; La Proie pour l'ombre. 1961: La Morte-saison des amours. 1963: Les Vacances Portugaises. 1965: Compartiment tueurs. 1966: Paris brûle-t-il?; La Ligne de démarcation. 1971: Le Souffle au coeur.

GENINA, Augusto

Director. Rome 1892–1957 Rome
1913: began as story writer, including 3 films directed by Baldassare Negroni; first film as director in Spain. 1923: wrote story for Mario Camerini's *Jolly, clown da circo*. 1925–26: films for own company. 1927–30: films in France and Germany. 1930: first sound film made in France *Prix de beauté*, co-written with René Clair from G. W. Pabst's story. 1930–35: films in France. Worked in Austria and Germany, returned to Italy. 1955: made last film *Frou Frou* in France.

Films as director: 1913: La Moglie di sua eccellenza. 1914: Il Segreto del Castello di Monroe; La Parole che uccide; Il Piccolo Cerinaio; La Fuga degli amanti; Dopo il veglione; L'Anello di Siva. 1915: Mezzanotte (+s/st); La Gelosia; La Doppia Ferita (+s/st); Lulù. 1916: Cento HP; Le Conquista dei diamanti; L'Ultimo Travestimento; Il Dramma della corona; Il Sogno di un giorno (+st); Il Sopravvissuto; La Signora Ciclone (+co-s); La Menzogna (+st/s); Il Presagio (+st/s).

1917: Il Siluramento dell'oceania (+st/s); Lucciola (+co-st); Maschiaccio (+st). 1918: Il Principe dell'impossibile (+s); Femmina – Femina (+st); L'Onestà del peccato (+co-st/s); Kalidaa – La Storia di una mummia; Il Trono e la seggiola; Addio giovinezza (+ad/s); I Due Crocifissi (+s); L'Emigrata. 1919: La Maschera e il volto; Lucrezia Borgia; Noris (+st); Lo Scaldino (+s); Bel Ami; Debito d'odio; La Donna e il cadavere (+s); Le Avventure di Bijou (+st). 1920: La Douloureuse; I Tre Sentimentale (+s); Tre Meno Due; I Diabolici; Il Castello della malinconia; L'Avventura di Dio; La Ruota del vizio (+s); Moglie, marito e ... (+st). 1921: L'Incatenata; Crisi; L'Innamorata. 1922: Lucie de Trécoeur; Una Donna passó; Un Punto Nero; La Peccatrice senza peccato. 1923: Cirano di Bergerac; Germaine. 1924: Il Corsaro (co-d Carmine Gallone); La Moglie Bella. 1925: Il Focolare Spento – Il Più Grande Amore (+pc). 1926: L'Ultimo Lord (+s/pc). 1927: Addio giovenezza (rm 1918: +co-ad/co-s); Die weisse Sklavin; Die Geschichte einer kleine Pariserin – Sprung ins Glück – Totte et sa chance; Die Gefangene von Shanghai (+st; co-d Geza Ven Bolvary). 1928: Scampolo; Liebeskarnaval (+s). 1929: Un Dramma a 16 anni; Quartier Latin. 1930: Prix de beauté (+co-s). 1931: Les Amants de minuit (co-d Marc Allégret); Paris-béguin; La Femme en homme. 1932: Ne Sois pas jalouse (+st/co-s). 1934: Nous ne sommes plus des enfants. 1935: Vergiss mein Nicht. 1936: Blumen aus Nizza; La Gondole aux chimères; Squadrone Bianco (+co-s). 1937: Frauenliebe – Frauenleid (+st/s); Naples au baiser de feu. 1939: Castelli in aria – Ins blaue Leben (+co-s). 1940: L'Assedio dell'Alcazar (+co-st/co-s). 1942: Bengasi (+co-st/co-s). 1949: Cielo sulla palude (+ad/co-s). 1950: L'Edera – Devotion (+co-s). 1952: Tre Storie Proibite – 3 Forbidden Stories (+co-st/co-s). 1953: Maddalena (+co-s). 1955: Frou Frou (+co-ad/co-s).

GERASIMOV, Sergei

Director. Urals 1906–
FEX actor: worked in films of Grigori Kozintsev and Leonid Trauberg; also their assistant e.g. on *Novyi Vavilon* (1929). From 1930: director. Films co-directed until *Lyubliyu li tebya* (1934). 1933: acted in Vsevolod Pudovkin's *Desertir*. 1936: Yutkevich co-wrote *Semero smelykh*. 1939: revised script of *Uchitel* in accordance with views expressed by 1,000 teachers, attacked educational system. 1941: scripted *Maskarad* from Lermontov and acted in it; directed first of 'Fighting Film Album' shorts. 1944: joined Communist Party. Became head of documentary film studio; gave assignments to directors new to documentary features: Yuli Raizman, Alexander Zarkhi, Joseph Heifitz and Yutkevich. 1947: *Molodaya Gvardiya* made in two parts: part I had been completed when original novel found to be ideologically suspect; part I revised and part II made with greater attention to official requirements; released in 1948; later condensed into single shorter film. 1949: attended Cultural and Scientific Conference for World Peace in New York; denounced self-assertion and violence of Hollywood films.

Films as director: 1930: Dvadtsat Dva neschastya – Twenty-Two Misfortunes (co-d C. Bartenev). 1932: Serdtsye Solomona – The Heart of Solomon (+s; co-d M. Kressin). 1934: Lyubliyu li tebya – Do I Love You? (+s). 1936: Semero smelykh – The Bold Seven. 1938: Komsomolsk (+co-s). 1939: Uchitel – The

Teacher (+s). 1941: Maskarad – Masquerade (+s/w). 1943: Nepobedimye – The Invincibles (co-d Mikhail Kalatozov). 1944: Bolshaya Zemlya – The Big Land (+s). 1948: Molodaya Gvardiya – The Young Guard (+s; in 2 parts). 1952: Osvobozhdennyi Kitai – China Liberated; Selskii Vrach – The Country Doctor. 1955: Nadezhda. 1958: Tikhii Don – Quiet Flows the Don (+s; in 2 parts). 1962: Lyudi i zveri – Men and Beasts (+s; in 2 parts). 1967: Zhurnalist – The Journalist (+s/w; in 2 parts). 1970: U ozera – By the Lake (+s).

GERMI, Pietro

Director and actor. Genoa, Italy 1914–
Acting and direction at the Centro Sperimentale di Cinematografia. Assistant to Alessandro Blasetti; scenarist. 1945: first film as director, supervised by Blasetti. Acted in several of own films and in *Jovanka e l'altri* (1960), *Il Rossetto* (1960).

Films as director: 1945: Il Testimone (+st/co-s). 1948: Gioventù Perduta – Lost Youth (+st/co-s). 1949: In nome della legge – In the Name of the Law (+co-s). 1950: Il Cammino della speranza – The Road to Hope (+co-st/co-s). 1951: La Città si difende – Four Ways Out – Passport to Hell (+co-s). 1953: La Presidentessa – The Lady President; Il Brigante di Tacca del Lupo (+co-st/co-s). 1954: Amori di mezzo secolo ep Guerra 1915–18; Gelosia (+co-s). 1956: Il Ferroviere – Man of Iron – The Railroad Man (+co-s/w). 1957: L'Uomo di paglia – The Seducer – Man of Straw – A Sordid Affair (co-st/co-s/w). 1959: Un Maledetto Imbroglio (+co-s/w). 1962: Divorzio all'italiana – Divorce, Italian Style (+co-st/co-s). 1963: Sedotta e abbandonata – Seduced and Abandoned (+co-st/co-s). 1966: Signori e Signore – The Birds, the Bees and the Italians (+co-s). 1967: L'Immorale. 1971: Le Castagne sone buone (+co-s).

GHERARDI, Piero

Designer. Arezzo, Italy 1909–71
Self-taught artist. From 1946: designer in films, e.g. for Mario Soldati, Mario Monicelli, Federico Fellini. Designs for stage include 'The White Devil' (1969) and 'Antony and Cleopatra' (1971) at National Theatre, London.

Films as designer include: 1947: Senza pietà. 1952: Camicie Rosse. 1954: Proibito. 1956: Padri e figli. 1957: Le Notti di Cabiria. 1959: La Dolce Vita; Kapò. 1960: Il Gobbo. 1963: Otto e mezzo. 1965: L'Armata Brancaleone; Giulietta degli spiriti. 1968: Queimada! 1969: The Appointment.

GHIONE, Emilio

Director, actor and writer. Turin, Italy 1879–1930 Rome
Father a painter. Service in cavalry. 1909: engaged as horseman for first film as actor. Small roles for Aquila and Itala in Turin, then to Rome. Cines contract, under pseudonym. 1911: played lead in *San Francesco, il poverello d'Assisi*. 1912: moved to Celio. 1913: first film as director. 1914: Caesar contract as leading actor and artistic supervisor. Moved to Tiber and Italia. Became independent producer. 1923–24: several films in Germany. 1925: Il Mondo published his memoirs. Work in theatre. Novel 'L'Ombra di Za la Mort' based on character he played in films, beginning with

Danzatrice della taverna nera (1914). 1927: hospitalised; Milanese newspaper Il Torchio raised fund to help him. 1928–29: theatre; acted in 'Broadway'. To Paris, wrote book 'Le Cinéma en Italie'. Told he had not long to live, returned to Rome.

Films as actor include: 1911: La Gerusalemme Liberata; San Francesco, il poverello d'Assisi. 1912: Idillio Tragico; Lacrime e sorrisi. 1913: L'Anima del demi-monde; La Maestrina; Tramonto; L'Arma dei Vigliacchi; In faccia al destino; Terra Promessa; La Gloria; L'Arrivista; L'Ultima Carta. 1914: Histoire d'un pierrot. 1925: La Cavalcata Ardente.

Films as director and actor include: 1913: La Cricca Dorata (+ s). 1914: Danzatrice della taverna nera. 1915: Anime Buie (+ s); La Banda delle Cifre (*in 3 parts*; + s); Guglielmo Oberdan, il martire di Trieste (+ s); Il Naufragatore (+ s); Tresa (+ s). 1916: Don Pietro Caruso; La Grande Vergogna (+ s); Tormento Gentile; Un Dramma Ignorato (+ s). 1917: Il Numero 121 (+ s); L'Ultima Impresa (+ s); Il Triangolo Giallo (*in 4 parts*; + s). 1918: I Topi Grigi (*in 8 parts*; + s); Nel Gorgo (+ s). 1919: Dollari e Fraks (+ p/s). 1920: L'Ultima Livrea (+ p/s); I Quattri Tramonti (+ p/s); Il Quadrante d'oro (+ p/s). 1921: Za la Mort contro Za la Mort (+ p/s). 1923: Ultimissime della notte (+ p/s); Il Sogno di Za la Vie (+ p/s). 1924: Za la Mort e Za la Vie (+ p/s).

Films as director: 1913: Idolo Infranto (+ s). 1914: L'Amazzone Mascherata (+ w). 1915: Cicernacchio (+ s); La Sposa della morte. 1916: La Rosa di Granada (+ s).

GIBBONS, Cedric

Art director. New York 1893–1960 Westwood, California
Private education. 1916: first film as designer. 1916–17: US Navy. 1917–18: worked for Edison. 1918–23: with Goldwyn. 1924: became head of MGM art department. 1928: assistant director on *A Woman of Affairs*. 1934: only film as director *Tarzan and his Mate*. 1955: retired. Oscars for art direction: *The Bridge of San Luis Rey* (1928–29), *The Merry Widow* (1934), *Pride and Prejudice* (1940), *Blossoms in the Dust* (1941), *The Yearling* (1946), *Little Women* (1949), *An American in Paris* (1951), *The Bad and the Beautiful* (1952), *Julius Caesar* (1953) – last 5 shared. Married Dolores del Rio (1930–41).

Films as art director include: 1919: The World and its Woman. 1923: The Christian. 1927: Mockery (*co*); The Big Parade (*co*); Ben-Hur (*co*). 1928: The Student Prince in Old Heidelberg. 1931: Possessed; Private Lives. 1932: Grand Hotel. 1933: Dinner at Eight. 1934: The Merry Widow; Men in White; Tarzan and his Mate (+ d). 1935: The Personal History, Adventures, Experience and Observations of David Copperfield, the Younger (*co*); A Night at the Opera; Mutiny on the Bounty. 1936: Romeo and Juliet (*co*); San Francisco. 1937: A Day at the Races; Maytime; Captains Courageous; The Good Earth; Conquest. 1938: Marie Antoinette; The Girl of the Golden West. 1939: The Wizard of Oz (*co*). 1940: Pride and Prejudice (*co*). 1941: Blossoms in the Dust (*co*). 1943: Bataan. 1944: Gaslight; National Velvet (*co*). 1945: The Picture of Dorian Gray (*co*). 1946: The Yearling (*co*). 1949: Little Women (*co*). 1951: Showboat (*co*);

An American in Paris (*co*). 1952: The Bad and the Beautiful (*co*). 1953: Julius Caesar (*co*). 1954: Executive Suite (*co*); Brigadoon (*co*). 1955: Blackboard Jungle (*co*). 1956: I'll Cry Tomorrow (*co*).

GIELGUD, Sir John

Actor. London 1904–
Westminster School. Lady Benson's School and RADA. 1921: debut. 1924: Romeo in 'Romeo and Juliet' then repertory work in Oxford; first film *Who is the Man?* 1928: first appearance in USA. 1970: Directed by Lindsay Anderson in 'Home' at Royal Court Theatre, London. Mainly stage actor.

Films as actor include: 1933: The Good Companions. 1936: Secret Agent. 1942: The Prime Minister. 1953: Julius Caesar. 1956: Richard III. 1957: The Barretts of Wimpole Street; Saint Joan. 1964: Becket. 1967: Sebastian. 1968: The Charge of the Light Brigade; The Shoes of the Fisherman (*ur*). 1969: Oh! What a Lovely War.

GILBERT, John

Actor. Logan, Utah 1897–1936 Hollywood
Parents were touring players. Hitchcock Military Academy, then jobs included stage manager in Washington (1914). 1915: to Hollywood, extra; contract with Thomas H. Ince's Triangle Films; leading parts by 1917. 1920: appeared in 3 films directed by Maurice Tourneur, collaborating on the scripts of 2. 1921: directed *Love's Penalty*. 1921–24: contract with Fox, acted usually in films written by Jules Furthman. Then with MGM until last film, for Columbia. Appeared opposite Greta Garbo 3 times including *Queen Christina* (1934). High-pitched voice prevented career in sound films. 4 wives included actresses Leatrice Joy, Ina Claire, Virginia Bruce.

Films as actor include: 1919: The White Heather; Heart o' the Hills. 1920: The Servant in the House; The Great Redeemer (+ *co-s*); The White Circle (+ *co-s*); Deep Waters. 1923: Cameo Kirby. 1924: His Hour; He Who Gets Slapped; Wife of the Centaur. 1925: The Merry Widow. 1926: La Boheme; Bardelys the Magnificent. 1927: The Big Parade; Flesh and the Devil; The Show; 12 Miles Out. 1928: Love; Masks of the Devil; A Woman of Affairs. 1930: His Glorious Night; Redemption; Way for a Sailor. 1932: Downstairs (+ *st*). 1933: Fast Workers. 1934: The Captain Hates the Sea.

GILBERT, Lewis

Director. London 1920–
From 1932: child actor on stage. Acted in films e.g. *Over the Moon* (1939). Assistant director with London Films, Associated British, Mayflower Films, RKO. World War II: Royal Air Force, transferred to US Air Corps Film Unit. 1944: joined Gaumont Instructional and later Realist; director and writer in collaboration on documentaries e.g. *Sailors Do Care* (1944), *The Ten Year Plan* (1945), *Arctic Harvest* (1946). 1947: directed first feature, a children's film. Then director for various British companies including Gainsborough (1948-49), also feature producer and writer.

Features as director: 1947: The Little Ballerina (+ s). 1949: Under One Roof. 1950: Once a Sinner; There is

Stefania Sandrelli in Pietro Germi's Sedotta e Abbandonata.

L'Armata Brancaleone, *directed by Mario Monicelli, décor by Piero Gherardi.*

Ziegfeld Follies, *directed by Vincente Minnelli, art direction by Cedric Gibbons and others.*

Another Sun – Wall of Death. 1951: Scarlet Thread. 1952: Emergency Call – Hundred Hour Hunt; Time, Gentlemen, Please; Cosh Boy – The Slasher (+ co-s). 1953: Johnny on the Run (+ p); Albert R.N. – Spare Man – Break to Freedom. 1954: The Good Die Young (+ co-s); The Sea Shall not Have Them (+ co-s). 1955: Cast a Dark Shadow. 1956: Reach for the Sky (+ s). 1957: The Admirable Crichton (+ s). 1958: Carve Her Name with Pride (+ p/s); A Cry from the Streets (+ p). 1959: Ferry to Hong Kong (+ s). 1960: Sink the Bismarck; Light up the Sky (+ p). 1961: The Greengage Summer – Loss of Innocence; The Mutineers. 1962: H.M.S. Defiant – Damn the Defiant. 1963: The Seventh Dawn. 1966: Alfie (+ p). 1967: You Only Live Twice. 1969: The Adventurers (+ p/co-s). 1971: Friends (+ p/st).

GILLIAT, Sidney

Director, producer, writer. Edgeley, Cheshire 1908–
Father edited London Evening Standard. Reader for British International; wrote titles for Harry Lachman's *Under the Greenwood Tree* (1929), adaptation from novel made by Frank Launder. Gagman for Walter Forde. 1930: to Gainsborough, reader and scriptwriter. Scripts for Walter Forde, also Carmine Gallone's *My Heart is Calling* (1934). To Gaumont–British. 1936: co-wrote play with Launder, 'The Body was Well Nourished'. 1938: with Alma Reville they wrote Alfred Hitchcock's *The Lady Vanishes*. 1940–42: with Launder wrote scripts for Carol Reed. 1943: first film as director, in collaboration with Launder, *Millions Like Us*. 1944: they formed company to make *The Rake's Progress* (1945). Subsequently divided direction, writing and producing between them in varying permutations. 1948: worked in association with London Films. 1956: Columbia contract. Founder-member of Screenwriters' Association. 1961: became Chairman of Shepperton studios. Librettist for Malcolm Williamson's opera, 'Our Man in Havana'.

Films as writer include: 1933: Falling For You; Friday the 13th. 1934: My Heart is Calling. 1936: The Man Who Changed His Mind. 1938: A Yank at Oxford (co-st); The Lady Vanishes (co). 1939: Jamaica Inn (co); Ask a Policeman. 1940: Night Train to Munich (co); The Girl in the News. 1941: Kipps. 1942: The Young Mr Pitt (co). 1944: 2,000 Women (co). 1946: I See a Dark Stranger (co; + p). 1947: Captain Boycott (p only). 1948: The Blue Lagoon (co; + p). 1955: Geordie (co; + co-p). 1958: Bridal Path (co-p only). 1960: The Pure Hell of St Trinian's (+ co-p).

Films as director: 1943: Millions Like Us (+ co-s; co-d Frank Launder). 1944: Waterloo Road (+ s). 1945: The Rake's Progress – Notorious Gentleman (+ co-p/co-s). 1946: Green for Danger (+ co-s). 1948: London Belongs to Me (+ co-s). 1950: State Secret (+ co-p/s). 1953: The Story of Gilbert and Sullivan (+ co-p/co-s). 1955: The Constant Husband (+ co-p/co-s). 1956: Fortune is a Woman – She Played With Fire (+ co-p/co-s). 1958: Left, Right and Centre (+ co-p/co-s); Only 2 Can Play (+ co-ex-p). 1966: The Great St Trinian's Train Robbery (+ p; co-d Frank Launder).

GIOVANNI, José

Writer and director. Corsica 1923–
Education interrupted by World War II: active in French Resistance. Many years in prison where started

to write novels. 1957: published first novel, 'Le Trou' which he co-scripted for film (1960). Scripted all films of his novels except *Ho!* (1968). From 1966: director; first film based on an episode in his novel 'Les Aventuriers', which he previously adapted for Robert Enrico's film (1967).

Films as scriptwriter include: 1959: Classe tous risques (co-s/fn). 1960: Le Trou (co-s/co-di/fn). 1965: Le Deuxième Souffle (co-di/fn). 1967: Les Aventuriers (co-di/fn).

Films as director: 1966: La Loi du survivant – The Law of Survival (+ s/fn). 1968: La Rapace – Birds of Prey (+ s). 1971: Un Aller Simple (+ ad/di); Ou est passé Tom? (+ ad/di).

GIRARDOT, Annie

Actress. Paris 1931–
Studied drama at Conservatoire de Paris. Joined Comédie Française; acclaimed for performance in Jean Cocteau's 'La Machine à écrire' (1956). 1956: first film as actress *L'Homme aux clefs d'or*. 1957: left Comédie Française to act in Luchino Visconti's production of 'Two for the See-Saw'. 1960: established by *Rocco e i suoi fratelli*. Married actor Renato Salvatori.

Films as actress include: 1958: Maigret tend un piège. 1960: Recours en grâce; La Proie pour l'ombre. 1962: Smog; La Vice et la vertue. 1963: La Donna Scimmia. 1964: Trois Chambres à Manhattan. 1967: Vivre pour vivre. 1969: Dillinger è morto. 1970: Mourir d'aimer; Il Seme dell'uomo; Elle boit pas, elle fume pas, elle drague pas, mais . . . elle cause.

GIROTTI, Massimo

Actor. Mogliano, Italy 1918–
Studied engineering. From 1939: acted in films. From 1945: also stage actor; directed in the theatre by Alessandro Blasetti, Luchino Visconti; played Shakespearean roles at the Teatro Nazionale. Also TV from 1956.

Films as actor include: 1940: La Tosca. 1942: Un Pilota ritorna; Ossessione. 1943: Desiderio (r 1946). 1946: La Porta del cielo; Un Giorno nella vita. 1947: Caccia Tragica. 1948: Gioventù Perduta; Anni Difficili. 1949: Fabiola. 1950: Cronaca di un amore. 1951: Nez de cuir. 1952: Roma ore undice; Spartaco. 1953: Ai margini della metropoli. 1954: Senso. 1956: Marguérite de la nuit. 1962: Vénus Impériale. 1964: La Fabuleuse Aventure de Marco Polo. 1968: Teorema. 1971: Krasnaya Palatka.

GISH, Dorothy

(Dorothy De Guiche) Actress. Massillon, Ohio 1898–1968 Rapallo, Italy
Younger sister of Lillian Gish. 1902: stage debut in 'East Lynne'. 1903: to New York in the play. Toured with sister in 'The Little Red Schoolhouse'. Association with Mary Pickford, who introduced the sister to D. W. Griffith. 1912: at Biograph; extra, then first film as actress *An Unseen Enemy*. 1920: opposite James Rennie and directed by her sister in *Remodeling Her Husband*. Married James Rennie. 1925–30: in British films. 1928–44: left films for Broadway and London stage; acted in e.g. 'Life With Father', 'The Inspector General'.

Films as actress include: 1912: The New York Hat. 1918: Hearts of the World. 1921: Orphans of the Storm. 1923: The Bright Shawl. 1925: Romola; Clothes Make the Pirate. 1926: Nell Gwynn. 1927: Madame de Pompadour; Tip Toes. 1930: Wolves. 1944: Our Hearts Were Young and Gay. 1946: Centennial Summer. 1963: The Cardinal.

GISH, Lillian

(Lillian De Guiche) Actress. Springfield, Ohio 1896–
Elder sister of Dorothy Gish. 1902: stage debut in 'Convict Stripes'. New York: small part with Sarah Bernhardt. On tour with sister in 'The Little Red Schoolhouse'. With Mary Pickford in 'The Good Little Devil'; introduced by her to D. W. Griffith. 1912: extra, then actress in *An Unseen Enemy*. 1920: directed her sister in *Remodeling Her Husband*. 1930–41: stage, including 'Uncle Vanya', 'Camille', 'Hamlet', 'Life with Father'. 1942: return to films. 1969: autobiography 'Lillian Gish: The Movies, Mr Griffith and Me'. Also TV.

Films as actress include: 1912: Two Daughters of Eve; The Musketeers of Pig Alley; The New York Hat. 1913: The Mothering Heart; The Battle at Elderbush Gulch; Judith of Bethulia. 1914: The Hunchback; The Tear that Burned. 1915: Enoch Arden; The Birth of a Nation. 1916: Intolerance; Daphne and the Pirate; Diane of the Follies. 1917: The House Built Upon Sand. 1918: Hearts of the World. 1919: Broken Blossoms; True Heart Susie. 1920: Way Down East. 1921: Orphans of the Storm. 1924: The White Sister. 1925: Romola. 1926: La Boheme; The Scarlet Letter. 1927: Annie Laurie. 1928: The Enemy; The Wind. 1930: One Romantic Night. 1933: His Double Life. 1943: The Commandos Strike at Dawn. 1946: Miss Susie Slagles'; Duel in the Sun. 1948: Portrait of Jennie. 1955: The Cobweb; The Night of the Hunter. 1958: Orders to Kill. 1960: The Unforgiven. 1966: Follow Me, Boys. 1967: Warning Shot; The Comedians.

GLASSBERG, Irving

Cinematographer
1947: first film. 1947–58: worked for Universal. 1958–59: last two films for Canon Productions.

Films as cinematographer include: 1947: The Web. 1948: Casbah. 1949: Undertow. 1950: Shakedown; Kansas Raiders. 1951: The Fat Man; The Prince Who Was a Thief; Cave of Outlaws; The Strange Door. 1952: Bend of the River; Flesh and Fury; Sally and Saint Anne; Duel at Silver Creek; The Lawless Breed. 1953: The Mississippi Gambler; Walking My Baby Back Home. 1954: The Black Shield of Falworth. 1955: Captain Lightfoot; Backlash. 1956: Outside the Law; The Rawhide Years. 1957: The Tarnished Angels; The Lady Takes a Flyer. 1958: Day of the Badman; Twilight for the Gods; The Rabbit Trap. 1959: Cry Tough.

GLENNON, Bert

Director and cinematographer. Anaconda, Montana 1895–
Stanford University. 1912: entered films at Keystone. 1920: became cinematographer. 1923–28: with Famous Players – Lasky and Paramount. 1928–32:

films as director. 1930: wrote script in collaboration for *Second Wife*. Worked for several studios; with Warner Brothers from 1941–46 and 1951–54. 1964: last film as cinematographer.

Films as director include: 1928: The Perfect Crime; Gang War. 1929: The Air Legion; Syncopation. 1930: Around the Corner; Girl of the Port; Paradise Island. 1931: In Line of Duty. 1932: South of Santa Fe.

Films as cinematographer include: 1921: A Daughter of the Law; The Kiss. 1923: The Ten Commandments (*co*). 1924: Changing Husbands; Triumph. 1925: Are Parents People?; Wild Horse Mesa; A Woman of the World. 1926: Good and Naughty. 1927: Barbed Wire; The City Gone Wild; Hotel Imperial; Underworld; We're All Gamblers; The Woman on Trial. 1928: The Last Command; The Patriot; Street of Sin. 1932: Blonde Venus; The Half-Naked Truth. 1933: Gabriel over The White House; Melody Cruise; Morning Glory; Alice in Wonderland. 1934: The Scarlet Empress. 1935: Show Them No Mercy. 1936: The Prisoner of Shark Island; Lloyd's of London; Can This be Dixie? (*co*). 1938: The Hurricane. 1939: Stagecoach; Young Mr Lincoln; Drums Along the Mohawk (*co*). 1940: Our Town; The Howards of Virginia. 1941: Dive Bomber (*co*); They Died with Their Boots On. 1942: Juke Girl; Desperate Journey. 1943: Mission to Moscow; This is the Army (*co*); The Desert Song. 1944: Destination Tokyo; The Very Thought of You. 1945: Hollywood Canteen. 1946: San Antonio. 1947: The Red House. 1948: Ruthless. 1949: Red Light. 1950: Wagon Master; Rio Grande. 1953: The Moonlighter; Thunder over the Plains; House of Wax (*co*). 1954: Riding Shotgun; The Mad Magician. 1956: Davy Crockett and the River Pirates. 1960: Sergeant Rutledge.

GLENVILLE, Peter

Director. London 1913–
Parents were actors Shaun Glenville and Dorothy Ward. Abandoned law studies at Oxford to act. From 1930: with Stratford repertory for 1 year; then Old Vic, Manchester repertory. From 1939: acted in films e.g. *Uncensored* (1942). 1944–45: theatre director with Old Vic. Then directed plays in London and New York e.g. 'Separate Tables', 'Dylan' on Broadway. 1955: first film as director. From 1958: director in Hollywood and UK. 1970: directed Terence Rattigan's 'Bequest to the Nation' on stage.

Films as director: 1955: The Prisoner. 1958: Me and the Colonel. 1961: Summer and Smoke. 1962: Term of Trial (+*s*). 1964: Becket. 1966: Hotel Paradiso (+*p/s/n*). 1967: The Comedians (+*p*).

GODARD, Jean-Luc

Director. Paris 1930–
Studied at Nyon (Switzerland) and Paris. 1949: ethnology at Sorbonne. 1950: first article (on Joseph Mankiewicz) in Gazette du Cinéma. Early writing, e.g. first articles for Cahiers du Cinéma, under pseudonym Hans Lucas. 1951: financed Jacques Rivette's *Quadrille*. 1954: worked on construction of a Swiss dam, subject of first short. 1956: reviewer for Arts; started writing regularly for Cahiers; financed Eric Rohmer's *Le Sonate à Kreutzer*. Wrote less frequently for Cahiers after first feature as director. Small parts in some of own films. e.g. as assistant director to Fritz

Lang in *Le Mépris*; also in e.g. *Le Signe du Lion* (1959) and *Cléo de 5 à 7* (1961). Own company, Anouchka Films, participated in production of most of his films since *Bande à part*; it also produced Jean Eustache's *Le Père Noël a les yeux bleus* (1965). From 1968: member of Dziga Vertov film group. Making of *One Plus One* (1969) is subject of Richard Mordaunt's *Voices* (1968). *One A.M.* left unfinished in 1968, incorporated in D. A. Pennebaker's *One P.M.* (1970). Married actresses Anna Karina, Anne Wiazemsky, who acted in his films.

Films as director and writer: 1954: Operation Beton (+*n*). 1955: Une Femme Coquette (*ps* Hans Lucas; +*c*). 1957: Tous les garçons s'appelle Patrick – Charlotte et Véronique (*d only*). 1958: Une Histoire d'eau (*co-d only*; *co-d* François Truffaut). 1959: Charlotte et son Jules (+*wv*); A bout de souffle – Breathless (+*w*). 1960: Le Petit Soldat – The Little Soldier (*r* 1963; +*w*). 1961: Une Femme est une femme; Les Sept Pechés Capitaux – The Seven Deadly Sins *ep* La Paresse. 1962: Vivre sa vie – It's My Life – My Life to Live; Rogopag – Laviamoci il cervello *ep* Le Nouveau Monde. 1963: Les Carabiniers – The Soldiers (*co-s*); Le Mépris – Il Disprezzo – Contempt – A Ghost at Noon (+*w*); Les Plus Belles Escroqueries du monde *ep* Le Grand Escroc. 1964: Bande à part – The Outsiders – Band of Outsiders; Une Femme Mariée – La Femme Mariée – The Married Woman; Paris vu par ... – Six in Paris *ep* Montparnasse et Levallois (*organisation/s*). 1965: Alphaville – Une Etrange Aventure de Lemmy Caution; Pierrot le fou – Crazy Pete. 1966: Masculin-Féminin; Made in U.S.A.; Deux ou Trois Choses que je sais d'elle. 1967: Le Plus Vieux Metier du monde *ep* Anticipation; Loin du Vietnam – Far from Vietnam (*co-d 4 others*); La Chinoise; Amore e rabbia – Love and Anger *ep* L'aller et retour andante e ritorno des enfants prodigues dei figli prodighi – Love – Vangelo 70 (*r* 1969). 1968: Weekend. 1969: Le Gai Savoir; One Plus One – Sympathy for the Devil.

Films in collaboration with Jean-Pierre Gorin: 1968: Un Film comme les autres; British Sounds – See You at Mao. 1969: Vent d'est; Lotte in Italia; Pravda. 1971: Vladimir and Rosa.

GODDARD, Paulette

(Paulette Levy) Actress. Whitestone, New York 1911– Model. Spotted by Florenz Ziegfeld. 1927: New York stage in 'Rio Rita'. Theatrical work includes 'The Waltz of the Toreadors' (with Melvyn Douglas), 'Caesar and Cleopatra'. Married Charles Chaplin (1933–42): acted in *Modern Times* (1936) and *The Great Dictator* (1940). Also radio, TV. Married Burgess Meredith (1944–50) and (from 1958) Erich Maria Remarque.

Films as actress include: 1933: The Kid from Spain. 1938: The Young in Heart; Dramatic School. 1939: The Women; The Cat and Canary. 1940: The Ghost Breakers; Northwest Mounted Police. 1941: Pot o' Gold; Second Chorus; Hold Back the Dawn. 1942: Reap the Wild Wind; The Forest Rangers; Star Spangled Rhythm. 1943: So Proudly We Hail. 1944: I Love a Soldier. 1945: Kitty. 1946: The Diary of a Chambermaid. 1947: Suddenly it's Spring; Variety Girl; Unconquered. 1948: An Ideal Husband; A Miracle Can Happen; Hazard. 1949: Anna Lucasta;

Lillian Gish in D. W. Griffith's Hearts of the World. Destination Tokyo, *directed by Delmer Daves and photographed by Bert Glennon.*
Jean-Luc Godard.

Bride of Vengeance. 1952: Babes in Bagdad. 1953: Charge of the Lancers. 1964: Gli Indifferenti.

GOETZ, William

Producer. New York 1903–

Adopted son of comedian Joe E. Brown. Pennsylvania College. Sports commentator, radio announcer. Boy actor with Mary Pickford in some of her later films. Scripted westerns, became assistant director, editor. In 1920s producer at Paramount, MGM. 1930: became associate producer at Fox. Vice-president of 20th Century-Fox on merger. 1942: member of board of directors. 1942–43: when Zanuck did war service, took charge of production. 1943: formed International Pictures Inc., merged with Universal (1946). To 1953: production executive for Universal-International. 1954–64: president of William Goetz Productions, releasing through Columbia. Became First Vice-President of Columbia. 1964–67: Vice-President, Production of Seven Arts Associates Corporation. First to give top stars percentage of profits (James Stewart on *Winchester '73*). Married English actress Binnie Barnes, and Edith Mayer, eldest daughter of Louis B. Mayer. Brother is Ben Goetz, head of MGM production in Britain.

Films as associate producer include: 1933: The Bowery (*co*). 1934: The House of Rothschild (*co*). 1935: Les Miserables (*co*); Folies Bergere; Cardinal Richelieu; The Call of the Wild; Clive of India.

Films as producer include: 1944: Jane Eyre. 1955: The Man from Laramie. 1956: Autumn Leaves. 1957: Sayonara. 1958: Me and the Colonel. 1959: They Came to Cordura. 1960: The Mountain Road; Song Without End. 1961: Cry for Happy. 1966: Assault on a Queen.

GOFF, Ivan

Writer. Perth, Australia 1910–

1926–30: journalist in Australia. 1933–36: journalist in London. 1936: to Hollywood as Daily Mirror correspondent. From 1940: scripts in collaboration for Warners and Republic; first film as writer *My Love Came Back*. World War II: military service. Hollywood as journalist and scriptwriter for Warners, then various companies including Fox (1952–53), Ross Hunter/Universal International (1960). From 1949: collaboration with Ben Roberts, with whom he wrote play 'Portrait in Black' (filmed 1960). Wrote TV series 'The Rogues', novel 'No Longer Innocent'. Produced TV series 'Mannix' with Roberts. For film list, *see* ROBERTS, Ben.

GOLD, Ernest

Composer. Vienna 1921–

Grandson of a concert pianist, son of a composer and concert violinist. Began composing at 5. Vienna State Academy. 1938: When Germans took over Austria, to New York. Studied there with Otto Cesana; worked as accompanist and pop song writer. 1945: piano concerto. To Hollywood, studied under George Antheil, began writing for films. Oscar for score of *Exodus* (1960).

Films as composer include: 1952: Willie The Kid. 1956: Gerald McBoing Boing on Planet Moo. 1958:

Too Much Too Soon; The Defiant Ones. 1959: On The Beach; Battle of the Coral Sea. 1960: Inherit The Wind; Exodus. 1961: The Last Sunset; Judgment at Nuremberg. 1962: Pressure Point. 1963: It's a Mad, Mad, Mad, Mad World. 1965: Ship of Fools. 1969: The Secret of Santa Vittoria.

GOLDBECK, Willis

Writer, director, producer. New York, 1900–

Collegiate School and Worcester Academy. Journalist, reporter, essayist, publicist. Scriptwriter for several companies, wrote films of e.g. Rex Ingram, Herbert Brenon, George Fitzmaurice, Tod Browning. 1942: first film as director. Directed several films scripted by Harry Ruskin, based on characters of Max Brand. All films as director for MGM up to *Dark Delusion* (1947), then to United Artists and Columbia. 1951: last film as director *Ten Tall Men* (also produced and co-wrote). 1955–56: produced 2 films directed by Stuart Heisler for Warners. 1948: wrote story of *Colossus of New York* for Paramount. 1960–62: with James Warner Bellah wrote two John Ford films and produced them, one in collaboration.

Films as writer include: 1923: Scaramouche. 1924: Peter Pan; The Alaskan; The Side Show of Life (*co*). 1928: Lilac Time (*ad*). 1932: Freaks (*co*). 1955: Tiger by the Tail.

Films as director: 1942: Dr Gillespie's New Assistant (+ *co-s*). 1943: Dr Gillespie's Criminal Case. 1944: Rationing; Three Men in White; Between Two Women. 1945: She Went to the Races. 1946: Love Laughs at Andy Hardy. 1947: Dark Delusion. 1950: Johnny Holiday. 1951: Ten Tall Men (+ *co-st*).

Films as producer: 1955: I Died a Thousand Times. 1956: The Lone Ranger. 1960: Sergeant Rutledge (*co*; + *co-s*). 1962: The Man Who Shot Liberty Valance (+ *co-s*).

GOLDSMITH, Jerry

Composer. Los Angeles

Studied piano; also composition with Mario Castelnuovo Tedesco. Studied composition for films under Miklos Rosza at USC. Composed for radio, then TV, e.g. 'Dr Kildare', 'The Man from Uncle'. From 1957, composer for films. Also compositions for concert hall.

Films as composer include: 1959: City of Fear. 1960: Studs Lonigan. 1962: Freud, the Secret Passion. 1963: The List of Adrian Messenger; Lilies of the Field. 1964: Seven Days in May; In Harm's Way. 1966: Seconds. 1967: Warning Shot; The Hour of the Gun. 1968: Planet of the Apes; The Detective; Bandolero! 1969: The Illustrated Man; Justine. 1970: Tora! Tora! Tora!; The Traveling Executioner; Rio Lobo; The Ballad of Cable Hogue. 1971: The Mephisto Waltz; Wild Rovers.

GOLDWYN, Samuel

(Samuel Goldfish) Producer. Warsaw 1884–

Office boy in Poland before running away from home at 11. To relatives in England; blacksmith's assistant. To USA at 15; apprenticed in glove factory then set up own glove business. 1913: formed Lasky Feature

Plays with brother-in-law Jesse L. Lasky and Cecil B. De Mille. 1916: merger with Adolph Zukor's Famous Players to form Famous Players-Lasky; left shortly after to set up Goldwyn Picture Corporation with Selwyn brothers. 1918: changed name to Goldwyn. 1919: broke with Selwyns for 18 months, finally splitting up in 1922. 1924: sold interest in Goldwyn Picture Corp. to Metro Productions, which became Metro-Goldwyn-Mayer. Independent producer from then until virtual retirement in 1959. Released through United Artists from 1927 and mainly RKO from 1940. Noted for the large salaries he paid his stars e.g. $20,000 to Geraldine Farrar for 8 weeks' work in 1915, also for hiring famous writers e.g. Maurice Maeterlinck. Memoir 'Behind the Screen' (1923). Married Blanche Lasky, actress Frances Howard. Irving G. Thalberg Memorial Award (1946).

Films as producer include: 1919: Jubilo. 1921: Doubling for Romeo. 1926: Stella Dallas; The Winning of Barbara Worth. 1932: Arrowsmith; Cynara. 1933: The Kid from Spain. 1935: The Dark Angel; The Wedding Night. 1936: Dodsworth. 1937: Beloved Enemy; Dead End. 1938: The Goldwyn Follies; The Cowboy and the Lady; The Hurricane. 1939: Wuthering Heights. 1940: The Westerner. 1941: The Little Foxes. 1942: The Pride of the Yankees. 1943: The North Star. 1944: The Princess and the Pirate. 1946: The Best Years of Our Lives; The Kid from Brooklyn. 1947: The Secret Life of Walter Mitty. 1948: A Song is Born. 1949: My Foolish Heart; Roseanna McCoy. 1952: Hans Christian Andersen. 1955: Guys and Dolls. 1959: Porgy and Bess.

GOLITZEN, Alexander

Designer, Moscow 1907–

Emigrated to USA. From 1935: designer, beginning at United Artists. Early credits as Alexander Golizen. From 1942: freelance. 1943: Oscar in collaboration for *The Phantom of the Opera*. From 1944: almost all work for Universal. From 1960: supervising art director at Universal. 1960: Oscar in collaboration for *Spartacus*. Art director on most films produced by Ross Hunter.

Films as designer include (most in collaboration): 1935: The Call of the Wild. 1938: The Hurricane. 1941: That Uncertain Feeling. 1945: Scarlet Street. 1946: Magnificent Doll. 1947: Smash-up. 1948: Letter from an Unknown Woman. 1952: The World in His Arms. 1953: City Beneath the Sea; The Mississippi Gambler; Seminole; Take Me to Town; All I Desire; The Man From The Alamo; Thunder Bay; The Glenn Miller Story. 1954: The Black Shield of Falworth; Sign of the Pagan; So This is Paris; The Far Country. 1955: Captain Lightfoot; Man Without a Star; This Island Earth; All That Heaven Allows; Tarantula; Red Sundown. 1956: Away All Boats; The Rawhide Years; Written on the Wind. 1957: Battle Hymn; Mister Cory; The Incredible Shrinking Man; The Tattered Dress; Interlude. 1958: This Happy Feeling; A Time to Love and a Time to Die; Touch of Evil; Live Fast, Die Young; Raw Wind in Eden; The Perfect Furlough; The Wonderful Years; A Stranger in My Arms; Never Steal Anything Small. 1959: Imitation of Life; Pillow Talk; Operation Petticoat. 1960: The Great Imposter; College Confidential. 1961: The Last Sunset; Tammy Tell Me True; Back Street; Flower Drum Song. 1962:

To Kill a Mockingbird. 1963: The Thrill of it All. 1964: Man's Favorite Sport. 1965: Shenandoah; The Art of Love; Mirage; Moment to Moment. 1967: Thoroughly Modern Millie; The King's Pirate. 1968: P.J.; Madigan; Coogan's Bluff. 1969: Hellfighters. 1971: Raid on Rommel; The Beguiled; One More Train to Rob; Shoot Out.

GOODRICH, Frances

Writer. Belleville, New Jersey 1891–
Actress; first Broadway appearance in 1931; by then also writing plays. 1930: first success as playwright in collaboration with Albert Hackett, 'Up Pops Dad'. 1931: married him, her third husband; they collaborated on scripts from 1933.

Films as writer in collaboration with Albert Hackett include: 1933: Penthouse. 1934: Fugitive Lovers (co); Hide Out; The Thin Man. 1935: Ah, Wilderness!; Naughty Marietta (co); Rose-Marie (co). 1936: After the Thin Man; Small Town Girl (co). 1944: Lady in the Dark; The Hitler Gang. 1947: It's A Wonderful Life (co). 1948: The Pirate. 1950: Father of the Bride. 1951: Father's Little Dividend. 1953: Give a Girl a Break. 1954: Seven Brides for Seven Brothers (co); The Long, Long Trailer. 1959: The Diary of Anne Frank (+fpl). 1962: Five Finger Exercise.

GORDON, Michael

Director, Baltimore, Maryland 1909–
John Hopkins University, postgraduate studies in Dramatic Art at Yale. Worked in theatre as technician, stage manager, actor and director. Joined Columbia's editing department, also dialogue director. 1943: first film as director, for Columbia. From 1947: worked mainly for Universal. Blacklisted. 1953: *Wherever She Goes* produced in Australia.

Films as director: 1943: Crime Doctor; One Dangerous Night. 1947: The Web. 1948: Another Part of the Forest; An Act of Murder. 1949: The Lady Gambles; Woman in Hiding. 1950: Cyrano de Bergerac. 1951: I Can Get it For You Wholesale; The Secret of Convict Lake. 1953: Wherever She Goes (+s). 1959: Pillow Talk. 1960: Portrait in Black. 1962: Boys' Night Out. 1963: For Love Or Money; Move Over, Darling. 1965: A Very Special Favour. 1966: Texas Across The River. 1968: The Impossible Years. 1970: How Do I Love Thee?

GORDON, Ruth

Writer and actress. Wollaston, Massachusetts 1896–
American Academy of Dramatic Art. 1915: stage debut in New York in 'Peter Pan'; in many Broadway productions. Married to Garson Kanin; with him wrote 4 scripts for George Cukor. Wrote and acted in 'Over Twenty-One' produced in New York (1944). Oscar as supporting actress for *Rosemary's Baby* (1968). 1970: published autobiography 'Myself and Others'.

Films as actress include: 1940: Abe Lincoln in Illinois; The Story of Dr Ehrlich's Magic Bullet. 1941: Two-Faced Woman. 1943: Edge of Darkness; Action in the North Atlantic. 1966: Inside Daisy Clover.

Films as writer include: 1948: A Double Life (co).

1949: Adam's Rib (co). 1952: The Marrying Kind (co); Pat and Mike (co). 1953: The Actress (+fpl).

GOSHO, Heinosuke

Director. Tokyo 1902–
Son of a geisha, but became father's heir on death of legitimate half-brother. Tokyo University. 1923: entered Shochiku. Assistant for 2 years to Yasujiro Shimazu. 1925: first film as director. 1931: made the first Japanese sound film *Madamu to Nyobo*. After World War II moved to Toho; left after labour dispute. 1949–54: independent. TV work as story writer: first major Japanese director to work in TV. Has TB.

Films as director and writer: 1925: Nanto no Haru – Spring in Southern Islands; Otoko Gokoro – Man's Heart; Seishun – Youth. 1926: Hatsukoi – First Love; Musume – Daughter; Itoshino Wagako – My Beloved Child; Kanojo – Girlfriend. 1927: Karakuri Musume – Tricky Girl; Shojo no Shi – Death of a Maiden; Okama – Moon-faced. 1928: Suki Nareba Koso – If You Like It; Doraku Goshinan – Debauchery is Wrong. 1929: Jonetsu no Ichiya – One Night of Passion; Ukiyo Buro – The Bath Harem. 1930: Dokushin-sha Goyojin – Bachelors Beware; Dai-Tokyo no Ikkaku – A Corner of Great Tokyo. 1931: Shima no Ratai Jiken – Island of Naked Scandal; Yoru Hiraku; Gutei Kenkei. 1936: Oboroyo no Onna – Woman of a Pale Night; Shindo – The New Road (in 2 parts). 1937: Hanakogo no Uta – Song of a Flower Basket. 1948: Omokage – Image. 1951: Wakare-gumo – Dispersing Clouds – Drifting Clouds. 1954: Osaka no Yado – An Inn at Osaka – Hotel at Osaka. 1956: Aru yo Futatabi – Twice on a Certain Night. 1962: Kaachan Kekkon Shiroyo – Get Married Mother. 1963: Hyakuman-nin no Musumetachi – A Million Girls. 1965: Osorezan no Onna – An Innocent Witch.

Films as director: 1925: Sora wa Haretari – No Clouds in the Sky – The Sky is Clear; Tosei Tamatebako – A Casket for Living. 1926: Machi no Hitobito – Town People; Honryu – A Rapid Stream; Haha-yo Koishi – Mother's Love; Kaeranu Sasabue. 1927: Sabishii Ranbomono – The Lonely Roughneck; Hazukashii Yume – Intimate Dream; Mura no Hanayome – The Village Bride. 1928: Kami Eno Michi – Road to God; Hito no Yo No Sugata; Gaito no Kishi; Yoru no Meneko; Shin Joseikan – A New Kind of Woman. 1929: Oyaji to Sonoko. 1930: Hohoemu Hinsei – A Smiling Character; Shojo Nyuys – The Girl Nyuyo; Onna-yo Kimi no Na o Kegasu Nakare – Woman, Don't Make Your Name Dirty; Dai Shinrin – Big Forest; Kinuyo Monogatari – Story of Kinuyo; Aiyoko no Yoru – Desire of Night; Jokyu Aishi – Sad Story of a Barmaid. 1931: Madamu to Nyobo – The Neighbour's Wife and Mine – Madame and Wife; Wakaki Hi no Kangeki – Memories of Young Days. 1932: Niisan no Baka – My Stupid Brother; Ginza no Yanagi – Willows of Ginza; Satsueiji Romansu-Renai Annai – A Studio Romance; Hototogisu – Cuckoo; Koi no Tokyo – Love in Tokyo. 1933: Hanayome no Negoto – The Bride Talks in her Sleep; Izu no Odoriko – Dancing Girls of Izu; Tengoku ni Musube Koi – Heaven Linked with Love; Juku no Haru – The Nineteenth Spring; Shojo-yo Sayonara – Goodbye My Girl; Aibu – Caress. 1934: Onna to Umareta Karanya – Now That I was Born a Woman; Sakuru Ondo; Ikitoshi Ikerumono – Everything that Lives; Hanamuko no Negoto – The Bridegroom Talks in his

Danny Kaye in Elliot Nugent's Up in Arms. *produced by Sam Goldwyn.*
Douglas Sirk's A Time to Love and a Time to Die. *co-designed by Alexander Golitzen.*
Waga Ai. *directed by Heinosuke Gosho.*

Sleep. 1935: Hidari Uchiwa; Akogare – Yearning; Fukeyo Koikaze; Jinsei no Onimotsu – Burden of Life. 1936: Okusama Shakuyosho – A Married Lady Borrows Money. 1940: Mokuseki – Wooden Head. 1942: Shinsetsu – New Snow. 1944: Goju no To – The Five-Storied Pagoda. 1945: Izu no Musumetachi – The Girls of Izu. 1947: Ima Hitotabi no – Once More. 1952: Asa no Hamon – Morning Conflicts 1953: Entotsu no Mieru Basho – Where Chimneys are Seen – Four Chimneys. 1954: Ai to Shi no Tanima – The Valley Between Love and Death; Niwatori wa Futatabi Naku – The Cock Crows Twice. 1955: Takekurabe – Growing Up – Daughters of Yoshiwara. 1957: Kiiroi Karasu – Behold Thy Son – Yellow Crow; Banka – Elegy of the North. 1958: Hotarubi – Firefly Light; Yoku – Avarice; Ari no Machi no Maria – Maria of the Ant Village; Hibari no Takekurabe. 1959: Karatachi Nikki – Journal of the Orange Flower. 1960: Waga Ai – When a Woman Loves; Shiroi Kiba – White Fangs. 1961: Ryoju – Hunting Rifle; Kumo ga Chigireru Toki – As the Clouds Scatter; Aijo no Keifu. 1966: Kaachan to Juichi-nin no Kodomo – Our Wonderful Years. 1967: Utage – Rebellion in Japan. 1968: Onna to Misoshiru – Woman and Bean Soup; Meiji Haru Aki.

GOULDING, Edmund

Director. London 1891–1959 Los Angeles
1912–14: stage actor in London. From 1914: British army in France. 1919: to USA; play written in collaboration with Edgar Selwyn, 'Dancing Mothers', produced on Broadway; began to write for Selznick Pictures. Then writer with Inspiration, Tiffany, Fox. 1922: first film as director, based on own novel. From 1925: director with Fox and MGM, also producing and writing. 1929–31: director and writer with various companies including Paramount. 1932–35: director and writer with MGM. Director only from 1938. From 1937, mainly with Warners. From 1946: with Fox. Also composer and songwriter e.g. 'Your Magic Spell is Everywhere', 'Mam'selle', title song for *Teenage Rebel*.

Films as scriptwriter include: 1921: Tol'able David. 1922: Peacock Alley; Fascination (*st/ad*); Broadway Rose (*st/s*). 1932: Flesh (*st only*).

Films as director: 1922: Fury (*+st/fn*). 1925: Sun Up (*+p/s*); Sally, Irene and Mary (*+p/s*). 1926: Paris (*+s*). 1927: Women Love Diamonds (*+p/st*). 1928: Love (*+p*). 1929: The Trespasser (*+p/s*). 1930: The Devil's Holiday (*+st/s/m*); Paramount on Parade (*co-d 10 others*). 1931: Reaching for the Moon (*+co-s*); The Night Angel (*+s*). 1932: Blondie of the Follies; Grand Hotel. 1934: Riptide (*+s*). 1935: The Flame Within (*+s*). 1937: That Certain Woman (*+s*). 1938: The Dawn Patrol; White Banners. 1939: Dark Victory; The Old Maid; We Are Not Alone. 1940: 'Til We Meet Again. 1941: The Great Lie. 1943: The Constant Nymph; Claudia; Forever and a Day (*+co-p; co-d 6 others*). 1946: Of Human Bondage; The Razor's Edge. 1947: Nightmare Alley. 1949: Everybody Does It. 1950: Mister 880. 1952: We're Not Married; Down Among the Sheltering Palms. 1956: Teenage Rebel (*+song*). 1958: Mardi Gras.

GRABLE, Betty

(Elizabeth Grasle) Actress. St Louis, Missouri 1916–
From 14: dancer. Band singer. 1929: first film Let's

Go Places. 1935: toured with Wheeler and Wolsey. 1937: vaudeville with Jackie Coogan. 1940: New York stage 'Dubarry was a Lady'. 1940–55: Fox contract. 1967: on Broadway in 'Hello, Dolly'. Nightclubs, TV. Married actor Jackie Coogan (1937–40 divorced), bandleader Harry James (1943–65, divorced).

Films as actress include: 1930: Whoopee. 1931: Kiki. 1932: Hold 'em Jail; The Greeks had a Word for Them; Probation. 1933: The Kid from Spain; Cavalcade. 1934: The Gay Divorcee. 1935: The Nitwits. 1936: Follow the Fleet; Pigskin Parade. 1937: This Way Please. 1938: College Swing; Give Me a Sailor. 1939: Man About Town; Million Dollar Legs. 1940: Tin Pan Alley; Down Argentine Way. 1941: I Wake up Screaming; Moon Over Miami; A Yank in the RAF; Hot Spot. 1942: Footlight Serenade. 1943: Sweet Rosie O'Grady. 1945: Billy Rose's Diamond Horseshoe. 1946 The Shocking Miss Pilgrim. 1947: Mother Wore Tights. 1948: That Lady in Ermine; When My Baby Smiles at Me. 1949: The Beautiful Blonde from Bashful Bend. 1950: My Blue Heaven; Wabash Avenue. 1951: Call Me Mister. 1953: How to Marry a Millionaire; The Farmer Takes a Wife. 1955: Three for the Show; How to be Very, Very Popular.

GRAETZ, Paul

Producer. Leipzig, Germany 1899–1966 Neuilly, France.
Head of German production company Terra Film. 1933: to France, set up Transcontinental Film and Paris Export Film (both pre-war) and Transcontinental Television. From 1933: worked entirely in France and USA. American citizen. Died during completion of *Paris brûle-t-il?* Chevalier de la Légion d'Honneur.

Films as producer: 1937: Altitude 3,200. 1939: La Charrette Fantôme. 1940: Untel Père et fils. 1947: Le Diable au corps. 1950: Dieu a besoin des hommes. 1952: Roma ora undice – It Happened in Rome. 1954: Knave of Hearts. 1955: Les Hommes en blanc. 1957: Bitter Victory. 1958: Faibles Femmes. 1961: Vu du pont. 1965: Paris brûle-t-il?

GRAHAME, Gloria

(Gloria Grahame Hallward) Actress. Pasadena, California 1925–
Father industrial designer; mother British actress. Understudied Miriam Hopkins in 'The Skin of our Teeth' on Broadway; noticed by Louis B. Mayer in 'A Highland Fling'; MGM contract. 1944: first film, *Blonde Fever*. Married actor Stanley Clements (1945–48, divorced), Nicholas Ray (1948–52, divorced), producer Cy Howard (1954–57, divorced). From 1959: TV. Oscar as supporting actress, *The Bad and the Beautiful* (1952).

Films as actress include: 1947: It's a Wonderful Life; Merton of the Movies; Crossfire. 1949: A Woman's Secret; Roughshod. 1950: In a Lonely Place. 1952: Macao; The Greatest Show on Earth; Sudden Fear. 1953: Man on a Tightrope; The Big Heat. 1954: Human Desire; The Good Die Young. 1955: The Cobweb; Oklahoma!; Not as a Stranger. 1956: The Man Who Never Was. 1959: Odds Against Tomorrow.

GRANGER, Farley

Actor. San Jose, California 1925–
Studied acting with Sanford Meisner, Stella Adler, Lee Strasberg. At 17 spotted by Sam Goldwyn and put under contract. 1943: first film *The North Star*. 1944–46: US Navy Special Services, reaching Major. To 1951: films mainly for RKO. Stage work includes 'The King and I', 'Brigadoon', 'Advise and Consent', 'The Crucible', 'Hedda Gabler', 'Liliom'. Also Italian films. TV: 'Arrowsmith', 'Freud', 'The Prisoner of Zenda', 'Caesar and Cleopatra'. 1955: professional stage debut in 'John Loves Mary'.

Films as actor include: 1944: The Purple Heart. 1948: They Live By Night; Rope; Enchantment. 1949: Side Street; Our Very Own. 1950: Edge of Doom; 1951: Strangers on a Train; I Want You. 1952: O'Henry's Full House *ep* The Gift of the Magi; Hans Christian Andersen. 1953: The Story of Three Loves *ep* Mademoiselle; Small Town Girl. 1954: Senso. 1955: The Girl in the Red Velvet Swing.

GRANGER, Stewart

(James LaBlache Stewart) Actor. London 1913–
Webber-Douglas School of Dramatic Art. Repertory in Hull and Birmingham. 1936: London stage debut. Acted in London with Vivien Leigh in 'Serena Blandish'. 1939: first film as actor *So This is London*. World War II: in Black Watch, invalided out. Returned to British films. 1951–63: worked mainly for MGM. 1956: became American citizen. Italian and West German films. Also TV. Married actresses Elspeth March (divorced 1950) and Jean Simmons (1950–60, divorced).

Films as actor include: 1943: The Man in Grey. 1944: Love Story; Fanny by Gaslight; Waterloo Road. 1945: Caesar and Cleopatra. 1947: Captain Boycott; Blanche Fury. 1948: Saraband for Dead Lovers; Woman Hater. 1949: Adam and Evelyne. 1950: King Solomon's Mines. 1951: Soldiers Three; The Light Touch. 1952: The Wild North; The Prisoner of Zenda; Scaramouche. 1953: Salome; Young Bess; All the Brothers were Valiant. 1954: Beau Brummel; Green Fire. 1955: Moonfleet. 1956: Bhowani Junction; The Last Hunt. 1957: Gun Glory. 1958: Harry Black and the Tiger. 1960: North to Alaska. 1961: The Secret Partner. 1962: Sodom and Gomorrah; Marcia o crepa. 1964: The Secret Invasion. 1967: The Last Safari.

GRANGIER, Gilles

Director. Paris 1911–
In commerce until his business collapsed during the Depression. 1933: joined Paramount at Joinville Studios as actor. Became assistant director e.g. to Sacha Guitry on *Désirée* (1938). 1939–42: army service; escaped as prisoner of war. 1943: directed first film, *Ademai, Bandit d'honneur*. Also TV.

Films as director include (complete from 1953): 1945: L'Aventure de Cabassou. 1951: L'Amour, Madame. 1953: La Vièrge du Rhin; Fâites-moi confiance. 1954: Le Printemps, l'automne et l'amour; Poisson d'avril. 1955: Gas-Oil. 1956: Le Sang à la tête; Le Rouge est mis; Reproduction Interdite; Trois jours à vivre (*+s*). 1957: Échec au porteur (*+co-s*). 1958: Le Désordre et la nuit. 1959: Archimède, le clochard; 125, rue Montmartre (+*co-s*). 1960: Les Vieux de la vieille. 1961: Le Cave se rebiffe (+*co-s*). 1962: Le Voyage à Biarritz; Gentleman d'Epsom (+*co-s*). 1963: Maigret voit rouge; La Cuisine au beurre. 1964: L'Âge Ingrat. 1965: Les Bons Vivants *eps* La Fermeture *and* Le Procès – How to Keep the Red Lamp Burning; Train d'enfer. 1966: L'Homme à la Buick (+*s*). 1967: Une Cigarette pour une ingénue (*uf*). 1968: Fin de journée.

GRANT, Cary

(Alexander Archibald Leach) Actor. Bristol, England 1904–
At 15 joined Pender troupe of acrobatic comedians; music-hall tours of England. 1920: toured USA. Fairgrounds and vaudeville. 5 years in musical comedy, including understudy for Paul Gregory in 'Golden Dawn'; with Jeanette Macdonald in 'Boom, Boom' (1929); with Fay Wray in 'Nikki'. 1932: to Hollywood; spotted by B. P. Schulberg; first film as actor *This is the Night*. Director of Fabergé Inc. Among marriages: actresses Virginia Cherrill (1933–35, divorced), Betsy Drake (1949, divorced) and Dyan Cannon (1965–68, divorced).

Films as actor include: 1932: This is the Night; Blonde Venus; Merrily We Go To Hell; The Devil and the Deep. 1933: She Done Him Wrong; I'm No Angel; Alice in Wonderland. 1934: Born to be Bad. 1936: Big Brown Eyes; Sylvia Scarlett. 1937: When You're in Love; Topper; The Awful Truth. 1938: Bringing up Baby; Holiday. 1939: Only Angels Have Wings; Gunga Din; In Name only; His Girl Friday. 1940: My Favorite Wife; The Howards of Virginia; The Philadelphia Story. 1941: Suspicion; Penny Serenade. 1942: Talk of the Town; Once Upon a Honeymoon. 1943: Mr Lucky. 1944: None But the Lonely Heart; Destination Tokyo; Arsenic and Old Lace. 1946: Night and Day; Notorious. 1947: The Bishop's Wife; The Bachelor and the Bobby-Soxer. 1948: Mr Blandings Builds his Dream House. 1949: I was A Male War Bride. 1950: Crisis. 1951: People Will Talk. 1952: Monkey Business; Room for One More. 1953: Dream Wife. 1955: To Catch a Thief. 1957: The Pride and the Passion; Kiss Them for Me; An Affair to Remember. 1958: Indiscreet; Houseboat. 1959: North by Northwest; Operation Petticoat. 1960: The Grass is Greener. 1962: That Touch of Mink. 1963: Charade. 1964: Father Goose. 1966: Walk Don't Run.

GRANT, James Edward

Writer. Chicago 1904–66 Burbank, California
Left university to become reporter on Chicago Herald; syndicated column 'It's a Racket'. Novelist wrote for films from 1935. Also directed 2 films. 1971: his screenplay used in *Support Your Local Gunfighter*. Wrote play 'Plan M', brief run on Broadway in 1942.

Films as writer include: 1935: Whipsaw (*st*). 1937: Danger—Love at Work (*st/co-s*). 1938: Josette. 1939: Miracles for Sale (*co*). 1941: They Dare Not Love (*st*); Johnny Eager (*st/co-s*). 1942: The Lady Is Willing (*st/co-s*). 1945: The Great John L (+*co-p*). 1949: Sands of Iwo-Jima (*co*); Johnny Allegro (*st*). 1950: Surrender (*st/co-s*). 1951: Flying Leathernecks; Two of a Kind (*fn*); The Bullfighter and the Lady. 1952: Big Jim McLain (*co*). 1953: Hondo. 1956: The Last Wagon (*co*). 1957: Three Violent People. 1958: The Sheepman (*st/co-s*); The Proud Rebel (*fst*). 1960: The Alamo. 1963: McLintock!; Donovan's Reef (*co*).

Films as director: 1946: The Angel and the Badman (+*s*). 1954: Ring of Fear.

GRAU, Jorge

Director. Barcelona, Spain 1930–
Instituto de Teatro, Barcelona. Worked in theatre, e.g. actor and writer. To Madrid. Wrote for Documentos; wrote scripts. 1957: first short film as director. To Italy: Centro Sperimentale di Cinematografia, Rome. Returned to Spain, made several shorts, wrote book on acting and articles. Assisted Riccardo Freda, Mauro Bolognini. 1962: first feature as director, from script he wrote in 1957.

Short films as director: 1957: El Don del mar. 1959: Costa Brava '59. 1960: Sobre Madrid; Medio siglo en un pincel. 1961: Barcelona, vieja amiga; Laredo, costa de esmeralda; Ocharcoaga; Niños.

Features as director: 1962: Noche de verano (+*st/co-s*). 1963: El Espontaneo (+*co-st/co-s*). 1964: Acteón (+*st/s*). 1967: Una Historia de amor (+*co-s*). 1969: Historia de una chica sola (+*co-s*). 1970: Cantico.

GREDE, Kjell

Director. 1936–
MA degree. Teacher, writer, painter. Short film; *Sotaren*. 1968: first feature, children's film, based on novels of Maria Gripe. Awarded Chaplin Prize, shown at London and Berlin Festivals. Wife is Bibi Andersson.

Films as director: 1968: Hugo och Josefin – Hugo and Josefin (+*co-s*). 1970: Harry Munter (+*s*).

GREEN, Adolph

Writer. New York 1915–
1939–44: cabaret with Betty Comden, Judy Holliday in group The Revuers. 1944: with Comden wrote book and lyrics for 'On the Town'; they acted in it on Broadway. Together, wrote for Broadway 'Billion Dollar Baby', 'Two on the Aisle', 'Wonderful Town', 'Peter Pan', 'Do Re Mi', 'Bells are Ringing', 'Subways are for Sleeping'. 1947–48: acted in 'Bonanza Bound' in Philadelphia. 1947: first film *Good News*. 1949: with Comden and Roger Edens wrote lyrics for *Take Me Out to the Ball Game*. 1958: with Comden appeared in 'A Party', expanded as 'A Party with Betty Comden and Adolph Green'. 1960: married singer and actress Phyllis Newman. For list, *see* COMDEN, Betty.

GREEN, Guy

Cinematographer. Somerset, England 1913–
1929: entered films. 1935: camera assistant at Elstree. Operator on *One of our Aircraft is Missing* (1942), *In Which We Serve* (1942), *This Happy Breed* (1944). From 1944: cinematographer. 1954: first film as director. 1955: last film as cinematographer. Oscar for black and white cinematography: *Great Expectations* (1947).

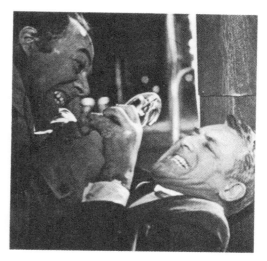

Betty Grable.
Gloria Grahame in Vincente Minnelli's The Cobweb.
Cary Grant (right) and George Kennedy in Stanley Donen's Charade.

Films as cinematographer include: 1944: The Way Ahead. 1946: Great Expectations. 1947: Blanche Fury (co). 1948: Oliver Twist. 1949: The Passionate Friends. 1950: Madeleine. 1951: Captain Horatio Hornblower, R.N. 1953: The Beggar's Opera. 1955: I Am a Camera.

Films as director: 1954: River Beat. 1955: Portrait of Alison (co). 1956: Lost; House of Secrets. 1957: The Snorkel. 1958: Sea of Sand. 1959: SOS Pacific. 1960: The Angry Silence. 1961: The Mark. 1962: Light in the Piazza. 1963: Diamond Head; A Patch of Blue (+ s). 1967: Pretty Polly. 1968: The Magus. 1970: A Walk in the Spring Rain.

GREENE, Graham

Writer. Berkhampstead, Hertfordshire 1904–
Mainly novelist, also playwright. Roman Catholic from 1927. Newspaper correspondent, editor, co-director; film critic of The Spectator (1935–40). From 1937: occasional scripts, usually adaptations of own work. 1937: *The Green Cockatoo* based on his screen-story. 1957: adopted G. B. Shaw's play for *St Joan*. Many works adapted by others, including *This Gun for Hire* (1942), *Went the Day Well?* (1942), *The Ministry of Fear* (1944), *Confidential Agent* (1945), *The Fugitive* (1947), *The End of the Affair* (1954), *Short Cut to Hell* (1957), *Across the Bridge* (1957), *The Quiet American* (1958).

Films as writer based on own works: 1947: Brighton Rock (co). 1948: The Fallen Idol. 1949: The Third Man. 1954: La Mano dello straniero (+ as-p). 1956: Loser Takes All. 1960: Our Man in Havana. 1967: The Comedians.

GREENSTREET, Sydney

Actor. Sandwich, Kent 1879–1954 Hollywood
1902: Ben Greet Academy of Acting. Tea-planter in Ceylon. 1905: Broadway debut in 'Everyman'. Stage actor for 41 years; at 61, spotted by John Huston for first film *The Maltese Falcon* while touring with the Lunts. Almost all films for Warners. 1949: retired (through illness) after *Malaya*.

Films as actor include: 1941: The Maltese Falcon; They Died With Their Boots On. 1942: Across the Pacific. 1943: Casablanca; Background to Danger. 1944: Passage to Marseille; The Mask of Dimitrios; The Conspirators. 1945: Hollywood Canteen; Conflict; Pillow to Post. 1946: Three Strangers; Devotion; The Verdict. 1947: The Hucksters. 1948: Ruthless. 1949: Flamingo Road; Malaya.

GREENWOOD, Joan

Actress. London 1921–
Father was artist Sydney Earnshaw Greenwood. Studied ballet. RADA. 1938: stage debut in 'The Robust Invalid'. 1941: first film as actress, *John Smith Wakes Up*. London stage; Worthing repertory. 1944: 'Hamlet', with Donald Wolfit's company. 1954: Broadway debut in 'The Confidential Clerk'.

Films as actress include: 1943: The Gentle Sex. 1947: The Man Within; The October Man. 1948: The White Unicorn; Saraband for Dead Lovers. 1949: Whisky Galore; Kind Hearts and Coronets. 1950: The Man in

the White Suit. 1952: The Importance of Being Earnest. 1954: Father Brown; Knave of Hearts. 1955: Moonfleet. 1958: Stage Struck. 1961: Mysterious Island. 1963: Tom Jones. 1964: The Moon-spinners.

GREGORETTI, Ugo

Director. Rome, Italy 1930–
Journalist. Work in TV, became director, especially of social documentaries. 1961: first film as director for cinema. After *Le Belle Famiglie* (1964), returned to TV. TV work includes *Controfagotto* (1961), *I.R.A.S.* (1966) and *Il Circolo Pickwick* (6-episode adaptation of 'Pickwick Papers', 1967).

Films as director and writer: 1961: I Nuovi Angeli – The New Angels (+ s). 1962: Rogopag – Laviamoci il cervello *ep* Il Pollo Ruspante (+ s). 1963: Les Plus Belles Escroqueries du monde – The Beautiful Swindlers *ep* Naples; Omicron (+ s). 1964: Le Belle Famiglie (+ s).

GRÉMILLON, Jean

Director. Bayeux, France 1901–59 Paris
Studied at Brest and Dinan; musical studies took him to Paris: pupil of Vincent d'Indy. Played violin accompaniment for silent films. Military service. Title writer, then editor. 1924–26: directed industrial shorts. 1926: wrote musical accompaniment for *Tour au large*. Scored several of his sound films. Also edited some of his early films. 1936: Luis Buñuel was executive producer on *Centinela! Alerta!* 1943–58: President of Cinémathèque Française. 1948: Jean Anouilh co-scripted *Pattes Blanches*. Directed 2 films in collaboration with Pierre Kast: *Les Charmes de l'existence* (1949), *Goya ou les désastres de la guerre* (1951).

Films as director from 1926: 1926: Tour au large (+ s/e). 1927: Maldone; Gratuites (+ e). 1928: Bobs (+ e). 1929: Gardiens de Phare (+ e). 1930: La Peyite Lise. 1931: Dainah la métisse. 1932: Pour un sou d'Amour (+ e); Le Petit Babouin (+ e/m). 1933: Gonzague – L'Accordeur (+ ad/s). 1934: La Dolorosa. 1935: Valse Royale. 1936: Pattes de mouches (+ co-s); Centinela! Alerta!. 1937: Gueule d'amour. 1938: L'Etrange Monsieur Victor. 1941: Remorques. 1942: Lumière d'été. 1943: Le Ciel est à vous. 1945: Le Six juin à l'aube (+ s/m/cy). 1945: Pattes Blanches. 1949: L'Apocalypse de Saint-Sèvres; Les Charmes de l'existence (+ co-s/cy; co-d Pierre Kast); Printemps de la liberté (uf; + s/di/m). 1950: L'Etrange Madame X. 1951: Caf' Conc' (uf); Goya ou les désastres de la guerre (+ m/cy; co-d Kast); Alchimie (+ s); Astrologie – Miroir de la vie (+ co-m). 1953: Au coeur de l'Ile de France (+ co-m); L'Amour d'une femme (+ st/co-s). 1955: La Maison aux images (+ s). 1956: Haute Lisse (+ m). 1958: André Masson et les quatre éléments (+ m/cy).

GRÉVILLE, Edmond T.

Director, Paris 1906–
Writer, journalist, worked in avant-garde theatre. Assistant director to e.g. E.-A. Dupont on *Piccadilly* (1929), Abel Gance and Jacques de Baroncelli. First films as director were in silent period – publicity films, shorts, an avant-garde work *La Naissance des heures*. Acted occasionally e.g. *Sous les toits de Paris* (1930).

1934: returned to directing. Worked in France, Holland, UK, USA. British films include *Mademoiselle Docteur* (English version of G. W. Pabst's *Salonique, nid d'espions*). 1941: finished *Une Femme dans la nuit*, begun by Abel Gance. 1951: assistant to Raoul Walsh on *Captain Horatio Hornblower, R.N.* Directed Erich von Stroheim in 3 films. 1964: TV film *Péril au paradis*.

Films as director include: 1933: Remous. 1937: Brief Ecstasy; Mademoiselle Docteur. 1938: Secret Lives. 1939: L'Ile du péché; Ménaces. 1941: Une Femme dans la nuit (co-d Abel Gance). 1948: The Romantic Age; Noose. 1953: L'Envers du paradis (+ s). 1954: Le Port du désir. 1957: Quand sonnera midi. 1959: L'Ile du bout du monde (+ co-s); Les Mains d'Orlac – The Hands of Orlac (+ co-s); Beat Girl. 1962: L'Accident (+ co-s).

GRIERSON, John

Producer and director. Kilmadock, Stirlingshire 1898–1972 Bath, Somerset
World War I: Royal Navy. 1923: Philosophy at Glasgow University. Lecturer at Durham University. 3 years in USA on Rockefeller Foundation research fellowship in social science. 1928: joined Empire Marketing Board. 1929: only film as director, first film as producer; supervised Basil Wright's *Conquest*. 1930: set up Empire Marketing Board Film Unit, which was taken over by General Post Office. From 1933: head of GPO Film Unit. 1937: left GPO to set up Film Centre, advisory body to government. 1937–39: advisor to Imperial Relations Trust. Drafted Bill, setting up National Film Board of Canada. 1939: to Canada as Film Commissioner, in charge of National Film Board of Canada. 1941: produced *Churchill's Island* which won Oscar for NFBC. 1942–43: General Manager, Canadian Wartime Information Board, produced 'World in Action' series. 1945: set up International Film Associates, in New York, but could not arrange distribution. 1947–48: to Europe; Director of Mass Communications for UNESCO. 1948–50: controller of films for Central Office of Information, London. 1950–55: head of government-sponsored Group 3. 1952: produced Philip Leacock's feature *The Brave Don't Cry*. From 1957: with Scottish TV; TV programme *This Wonderful World*. At 70, 3 months as Professor of Mass Communications at McGill University, Canada. Published articles collected in 'Grierson on Documentary' (1946, 1966).

Films as producer include: 1929: Drifters (+ d/s/e). 1931: Industrial Britain (+ e); O'er Hill and Dale. 1933: Windmill in Barbados; Uncharted Waters; Industrial Britain (co); Cargo from Jamaica. 1934: Granton Trawler; Pett and Pott; The Song of Ceylon. 1936: 6.30 Collection; Coal Face; Night Mail (co). 1937: We Live in Two Worlds; Children at School. 1938: The Face of Scotland.

GRIFFITH, David Wark

Director. Crestwood, Kentucky 1875–1948 Hollywood
Family of Irish origin. Father a doctor, captain in Mexican War, and colonel of a Southern cavalry regiment in American Civil War. Family ruined by the civil war. Theatre critic on Louisville Courier, owned by one of his relatives. Wrote plays. Became actor (c

1899) in Louisville. 1904: acted in New York in 'Trilby', 'East Lynne'. 1905: played Lincoln in 'The Ensign'; on tour in 'Fedora', 'The Financier', 'Ramona'. Met actress Linda Arvidson Johnson, married her in 1906. Wrote poetry, stories, plays. Some early writings later used in films, e.g. his play 'War' (1907) was part-basis of *America* (1924). 1907: Poetry, stories published in Collier's, Cosmopolitan, Leslie's Weekly; his play 'A Fool and a Girl' produced in Washington, then Baltimore. Script *Tosca* turned down by Edwin S. Porter, but given acting job. Directed by Porter in *Rescued from an Eagle's Nest* (1907). 1908: in films directed by Wallace Mc-Cutcheon: *The Music Master, When Knights Were Bold, The Stage Rustler*. Continued to act on stage: 'Elizabeth, Queen of England', 'Magda', 'Rosmersholm'. Wrote scripts for Biograph and acted in them: *Old Isaac, The Pawnbroker, Ostler Joe, At the Crossroads of Life*. Biograph contract as writer and director; first film as director; directed Mack Sennett's first film as actor which was Griffith's first comedy *Balked at the Altar*. 1909: directed 144 films, including the earliest of Mary Pickford. 1910: directed 104 films; supervised films of Thomas Ince, Sennett and others. 1911: directed 68 films, averaging 300 to 600 metres. *Enoch Arden* made in two parts shown separately. 1912: directed 31 films, mainly 3-reelers. Among new actors: Mae Marsh, Lionel Barrymore, the Gish Sisters. 1913: directed 24 films mainly 3-reelers, but also *Judith of Bethulia* (4 reels) the longest American film to date. Moved to Reliance-Majestic, a subsidiary of Mutual. New company, Epoch, formed to produce *The Birth of a Nation*. Among assistants on the film: Erich von Stroheim, W. S. van Dyke. Immense financial success, but denounced by churches and press as inciting racial hatred; film used as a pretext for race-riots. Defended himself in pamphlet 'The Rise and Fall of Free Speech in America'. 1916: *Intolerance* cost $2 million; financial disaster, creditors repaid over 10 years; modern episode released separately, *The Mother and the Law*; assistants again included von Stroheim and van Dyke. In 1915 had founded Triangle Company: main directors Griffith, Ince, Sennett; now supervised work of many new directors, including Christy Cabanne, Jack Conway, John Emerson, Allan Dwan, Sidney Franklin, W. S. van Dyke. From March 1915 to June 1917: supervised 77 films. At invitation of David Lloyd George, to England and France to make *Hearts of the World* to help Allied war effort. Some scenes shot in front line; excess war-footage used in later films. Moved to Paramount and First National. 1919: with Charles Chaplin, Mary Pickford and Douglas Fairbanks founded United Artists. 1921: last financial success, *Orphans of the Storm*. 1931: retired from films. Was intended to have producer credit on *One Million B.C.* (1940) but left the film and most of his ideas not used. G. W. Bitzer was his cinematographer from *After Many Years* (1908) to *The Struggle* (1931), except for period 1924–28.

Films as director include (complete from 1914): 1908: The Adventures of Dollie; Balked at the Altar; A Smoked Husband; The Call of the Wild; After Many Years; The Taming of the Shrew; The Song of the Shirt; Mr Jones at the Ball; For Love of Meat. 1909: Edgar Allan Poe; The Curtain Pole; The Politician's Love Story; A Fool's Revenge; A Drunkard's Reformation; Resurrection; Two Memories; The Cricket on the Hearth; The Violin Maker of Cremona; Lonely Villa; Her First Biscuits; The Way of Man; Richelieu,

or the Cardinal's Conspiracy; Sweet and Twenty; They Would Elope; The Better Way; '1776' or the Hessian Renegades; Getting Even; In Old Kentucky; The Awakening; Pippa Passes, or the Song of Conscience; The Little Teacher; Lines of White on a Sullen Sea; Nursing a Viper; A Corner in Wheat; To Save Her Soul. 1910: The Call; The Cloister's Touch; The Englishman and the Girl; The Thread of Destiny; In Old California; Gold is Not All; The Way of the World; The Unchanging Sea; Ramona; The Face at the Window; What the Daisy Said; An Arcadian Maid; Wilful Peggy; The Iconoclast; Simple Charity; The Golden Supper; White Roses. 1911: Crossing the American Prairies in the Early Fifties; The Italian Barber; His Trust Fulfilled; The Lily of the Tenements; A Decree of Destiny; The Lonedale Operator; The Spanish Gypsy; How She Triumphed; Enoch Arden, parts I and II; Fighting Blood; The Last Drop of Water; A Change of Spirit; Her Awakening; The Battle. 1912: Lena and the Geese; Man's Genesis; Granny; Home Folks; The Mender of Nets; A Siren of Impulse; The Female of the Species; The Old Actor; A Lodging for the Night; A Pueblo Legend; An Unseen Enemy; Friends (+ s); A Feud in the Kentucky Hills; In the Aisles of the Wild; The One She Loved; The Painted Lady; The Musketeers of Pig Alley; The Massacre; Gold and Glitter; My Baby; The Informer; Brutality; The New York Hat; My Hero; A Cry for Help. 1913: Primitive Man or the Wars of the Primal Tribes; Oil and Water; Fate; The Perfidy of Mary; The Little Tease; The Lady and the Mouse; The Wanderer; The House of Darkness; Just Gold; The Mothering Heart; Her Mother's Oath; The Mistake; The Coming of Angelo; The Tender-Hearted Boy; Two Men of the Desert; In Prehistoric Days; The Battle at Elderbush Gulch; Judith of Bethulia. 1914: Battle of the Sexes; The Escape; Home Sweet Home; The Avenging Conscience. 1915: The Birth of a Nation (+ co-s); 1916: Intolerance (+ co-s); The Mother and the Law (*modern ep of* Intolerance). 1917: Hearts of the World (+p/s); The Great Love (+p/s); The Greatest Thing in Life (+p/s). 1919: A Romance of Happy Valley (+p); The Girl Who Stayed at Home (+p); Broken Blossoms (+p/s); True Heart Susie (+p); Scarlet Days (+p); The Greatest Question (+p). 1920: The Idol Dancer (+p); The Love Flower (+p); Way Down East (+p). 1921: Dream Street (+p); Orphans of the Storm (+s). 1922: One Exciting Night (+s). 1923: The White Rose. 1924: America (+fpl); Isn't Life Wonderful. 1925: Sally of the Sawdust. 1926: That Royle Girl; The Sorrows of Satan. 1927: Drums of Love; The Battle of the Sexes (*rm* 1914). 1929: Lady of the Pavements. 1930: Abraham Lincoln. 1931: The Struggle.

GRIGGS, Loyal

Cinematographer

Straight from high school to Paramount as camera assistant. Worked in special effects. 1951: became cinematographer. Most films for Paramount.

Films as cinematographer include: 1953: Shane. 1954: Elephant Walk; White Christmas. 1955: The Bridges at Toko-ri (*co*); We're No Angels. 1956: That Certain Feeling; The Ten Commandments (*co*); Three Violent People. 1957: The Buster Keaton Story; The Tin Star; The Sad Sack. 1958: Hot Spell; The Buccaneer. 1959: The Handman; The Jayhawkers. 1960: Visit to a Small Planet; Walk Like A Dragon; G. I. Blues. 1961: Mantrap. 1963: Papa's Delicate Condition. 1964: In

Omicron. *directed by Ugo Gregoretti.*
Lillian Gish in Broken Blossoms. *directed by D. W. Griffith.*
In Harm's Way. *directed by Otto Preminger, photographed by Loyal Griggs.*

Harm's Way. 1965: Tickle Me; The Slender Thread; The Greatest Story Ever Told (co). 1966: The Night of the Grizzly (co). 1967: Hurry Sundown (co). 1968: In Enemy Country.

GRIMAULT, Paul

Animator. Neuilly-sur-Seine, France 1905–
Father an archaeologist. École des Arts Appliqués, Germain-Pilon. Advertising designer, then publicity films. 1936: formed own company with André Sarrat, 'Les Gémeaux'. 1937: used triple screen for Électricité. 1945: wrote Le Voleur de Paratonnerre from story by Jean Aurenche. 1946: co-wrote La Flute Magique with Roger Leenhardt. 2 films co-written with Jacques Prévert, Le Petit Soldat (1947) and La Bergère et le ramoneur (1952), latter a feature; La Faim du Monde (1958) was written by Prévert alone. 1964: producer only on La Demoiselle et le violoncelliste. President of l'Association des Artistes et Amis du Cinéma d'Animation. To 1963: short publicity films. Also films for TV.

Short films as animator include: 1936: Monsieur Pipe (uf). 1937: Électricité. 1937–39: Gô chez les oiseaux. 1941: Les Passagers de la Grande Oure. 1942: Le Marchand de notes. 1943: L'Épouvantail (+ co-s). 1945: Le Voleur de Paratonnerre (+ s). 1946: La Flute Magique (+ co-s). 1947: Le Petit Soldat (+ co-s). 1958: La Faim du monde (+ p).

Features animator: 1952: La Bergère et le ramoneur (+ co-s). 1967: Le Roi et l'oiseau.

GROSS, Anthony

Painter and etcher. London 1905–
Book illustrator. Official war artist. Teacher of etching and engraving at Slade School of Fine Art, London. Made a few animated films in collaboration with Hector Hoppin. 1936: started but abandoned animated sequence for Alexander Korda's The Shape of Things to Come. 1937: Foxhunt made for Korda.

Animated films made in collaboration with Hector Hoppin: 1934: Joie de Vivre. 1937: Foxhunt. 1938: Indian Fantasy.

GROULX, Gilles

Director. Montreal, Canada 1931–
One of 14 children. Commercial course; office work. Painting at art school. Film assignments for TV; editor in Radio-Canada News Service. 1955–58: directed 3 shorts in collaboration with Alain Stanké. 1958: joined National Film Board of Canada as director, editor, cameraman. 1961: edited Jacques Giraldeau's Vieil Age. 1962: photographed Hubert Auquin's Le 5 Septembre à Saint-Henri, edited Seul ou avec d'autres, made by Montreal students.

Films as director include (complete from 1959): 1955: Les Héritiers. 1958: Les Raquetteurs – De Gais Lurons en congrès (+ e; co-d Michel Brault). 1959: Normetal (uc; + e; co-d Claude Fournier). 1960: La France sur un caillou (+ e; co-d Claude Fournier). 1961: Golden Gloves (+ e/c). 1962: Voir Miami (+ e). 1964: Un Jeu si simple (+ e). 1964: Le Chat dans le sac (+ s/e). 1969: Ou êtes-vous donc? (+ s). 1969: Entre tu et vous (+ s/e).

GRUEL, Henri

Animator. Mâcon, France 1923–
1946: entered films with Arcady. From 1949: worked as cinematographer, designer, editor, recordist. 1953: first film as animator Martin et Gaston: co-wrote music, for English release (1954), score by Temple Abady substituted. First 3 films based on stories and drawings by children; first 2 produced by Nikos Papatakis. 1959: collaborated with Jan Lenica on Monsieur Tête. 1964: first feature as animator Le Roi du Village.

Films as animator include: 1953: Martin et Gaston (+ co-m). 1954: Gitanos et papillons. 1955: Le Voyage de Badabou (+ m); La Rose et le radis (+ m). 1956: Le Voyageur. 1957: La Joconde – Mona Lisa; The Story of an Obsession (+ m); Coeur de cristal. 1958: Métropolitain (co-d Laure Garcin). 1959: Une Atome qui vous veut du bien (+ m); Douze Mois; Monsieur Tête (co-d Jan Lenica). 1960: La Lutte contre le froid. 1961: Notre Paris (co-d André Fontaine). 1962: Étroits sont les vaisseaux (co-d Laure Garcin). 1963: Mose. 1964: Le Roi du village. 1966: Les Contes Zaghaura (co-d André Fontaine).

GUAZZONI, Enrico

Director. Rome 1876–1949 Rome
Painting at Istituto di Belli Arti, Rome. 1907: interior decorator of Moderno cinema in Rome; Technical advisor on Eduardo Bencivenga's Raffaello Sanzio e la fornarina; first film as director. 1911: directed Emilio Ghione in San Francesco, il poverello d'Assisi. From 1916: writer at Cines. 1942: last film; retired.

Films as director and writer: 1907: Un Invito a pranzo. 1909: La Nuova Mammina. 1910: Andreuccio da Perugia (+ dec); Agrippina (+ dec); Bruto (+ dec); Adriana di Berteaux. 1911: La Gerusalemme Liberata (+ dec); I Maccabei (+ dec); Gradenico e Tiepolo ovvero amori e congiure a Venezia; San Francesco, il poverello d'Assisi. 1912: Quo Vadis? (+ co-dec). 1913: Il Lettino Vuoto; Marc Antonio e Cleopatra (+ dec); Scuola d'eroi. 1914: Caius Giulio Cesare (+ co-dec); Immolazione (+ dec); L'Istruttoria. 1915: L'Amica (co-s); Alma Mater. 1916: Marc Antonio e Cleopatra; Madame Tallien (+ dec/co-s). 1918: Fabiola (+ co-st). 1920: Il Sacco di Roma e Clemento VII (co-s). 1923: Messalina (co-s). 1928: La Sperduta di Allah (co-s). 1929: Myriam (co-s). 1932: Il Domo del mattino. 1934: Signora Paradiso. 1935: Il Re Burlone. 1936: Ho perduto mio marito. 1938: Il Suo Destino (co-s); Il Dottor Antonio. 1939: Ho visto brillare le stelle. 1940: Antonio Meucci (co-s).

Films as director: 1915: Ivan il Terribile. 1918: Fabiola; Lady Macbeth. 1936: Re di denari; I Due Sergenti. 1940: La Figlia del Corsaro Verde. 1941: I Pirati della Malesia; Oro Nero. 1942: La Fornarina.

GUERRA, Ruy

Director. Lourenço Marques, Mozambique, 1931–
Educated in Mozambique and Portugal. 1952–54: IDHEC; also worked with Jean Delannoy and on SOS Noronha (1956). 1958: in Brazil, started two films, Oros (1960) and O Cavalo de Oxumare (1961), both unfinished. 1969: played lead in Benito Cereno.

Films as director: 1962: Os Cafajestes – The Unscru-pulous Ones (+ co-s). 1964: Os Fuzis – The Guns (+ st/co-s/e). 1969: Sweet Hunters (+ co-s/lyr). 1970: Os Deuses e os mortos – The Gods and The Dead (+ co-s/co-e).

GUFFEY, Burnett

Cinematographer. Del Rio, Tennessee 1905–
1923–27: assistant cameraman at Fox. 1928–44: camera operator, e.g. on The Informer (1935), Foreign Correspondent (1940), Cover Girl (1944). 1944: first film as cinematographer Sailor's Holiday. 1944–66: all films for Columbia. From 1967: for several studios including Columbia, Warners, Fox. Oscar for black and white cinematography on From Here to Eternity (1953).

Films as cinematographer include: 1945: The Girl of the Limberlost; My Name is Julia Ross. 1946: Gallant Journey (co); So Dark the Night. 1947: Johnny O' Clock. 1948: The Sign of the Ram; To the Ends of the Earth. 1949: Undercover Man; Knock on Any Door; The Reckless Moment. 1950: All the King's Men; In a Lonely Place. 1951: Sirocco. 1952: Scandal Sheet; Assignment Paris (co); The Sniper. 1953: From Here to Eternity. 1954: Human Desire; Private Hell 36. 1955: The Violent Men; Tight Spot; Three Stripes in the Sun. 1956: The Harder They Fall; Nightfall; Storm Center. 1957: The Brothers Rico; The Strange One; Decision at Sundown. 1958: Screaming Mimi; Me and the Colonel. 1959: Edge of Eternity; They Came to Cordura; Gidget; Let No Man Write My Epitaph. 1960: The Mountain Road; Hell to Eternity. 1961: Cry for Happy; Homicidal; Mr Sardonicus. 1962: Kid Galahad; Bird Man of Alcatraz. 1964: Flight from Ashiya (co); Good Neighbour Sam. 1966: King Rat; The Silencers. 1967: How to Succeed in Business Without Really Trying; Bonnie and Clyde; The Ambushers (co). 1969: Where It's At; The Madwoman of Chaillot (co); Some Kind of a Nut (co). 1970: The Great White Hope.

GUILLERMIN, John

Director. London 1925–
French parents. City of London School. Served in RAF. 1947: directed documentaries and shorts in France. 1949: scripts in UK; directed and scripted first feature. Director in UK for companies including Columbia, Rank, MGM. From 1964: Fox contract; some work in USA.

Films as director: 1949: Torment (+ co-p/s). 1951: Smart Alec; Two on the Tiles; Four Days. 1952: Song of Paris; Miss Robin Hood. 1953: Operation Diplomat (+ co-s). 1954: Adventure in the Hopfields; The Crowded Day. 1955: Dust and Gold; Thunderstorm. 1957: Town on Trial. 1958: The Whole Truth; I Was Monty's Double. 1959: Tarzan's Greatest Adventure (+ co-s). 1960: The Day They Robbed the Bank of England; Never Let Go (+ co-st). 1962: Waltz of the Toreadors; Tarzan Goes to India (+ co-s). 1964: Guns at Batasi. 1965: Rapture. 1966: The Blue Max. 1968: P. J. – New Face in Hell. 1969: The Bridge at Remagen; House of Cards. 1970: El Condor.

GUINNESS, Sir Alec

Actor. London 1914–
1934: Fay Compton Studio of Dramatic Art and studied with Martita Hunt. 1936: Old Vic. 1937–38:

member of the John Gielgud Company, adapted and acted in 'Great Expectations', also 'Thunder Rock'. 1942: New York 'Flare Path'. Royal Navy reaching Lieutenant. Stage work since 1946 includes: 'The Brothers Karamazov', 'King Lear', 'St Joan', 'The Government Inspector', 'The Prisoner', 'Hotel Paradiso', 'Ross'. 1946: first film *Great Expectations*. 1955: awarded CBE. 1957: Oscar as Best Actor *The Bridge on the River Kwai*. 1959: Knighted. Married actress Merula Salaman.

Films as actor include: 1948: Oliver Twist. 1949: Kind Hearts and Coronets; A Run for Your Money. 1950: Last Holiday; The Mudlark. 1951: The Lavender Hill Mob; The Man in the White Suit. 1952: The Card. 1954: Father Brown. 1955: To Paris with Love; The Prisoner; The Ladykillers. 1957: Barnacle Bill. 1959: The Horse's Mouth (+ *s*); The Scapegoat. 1960: Our Man in Havana; Tunes of Glory. 1961: A Majority of One. 1962: H.M.S. Defiant; Lawrence of Arabia. 1964: The Fall of the Roman Empire. 1966: Hotel Paradiso; The Quiller Memorandum. 1967: The Comedians. 1970: Scrooge; Cromwell.

GUITRY, Sacha

Director, writer and actor. St Petersburg, Russia 1885–1957 Paris
Son of actor Lucien Guitry. Actor under stage name Lorcey. 1905: debut as playwright, 'Nono'; wrote over 100 plays, also stage producer and continued to act. 1915: directed documentary *Ceux de chez nous*, showing many artists, writers and others including his father. From 1935: directed features all of which he wrote (often from own stage plays) and acted in most. Films made by others from his plays include *Le Blanc et le noir* (1930), *Les Deux Couverts* (1935), *Lucky Partners* (from 'Bonne Chance', 1940). *Adhémar ou le jouet de la fatalité* (1951) directed in collaboration with Fernandel; also wrote script and lyrics. Last film script, *La Vie à deux* directed by Clément Duhour (1958).

Films as writer, director and actor: 1935: Pasteur (*fpl*); Bonne Chance (*fpl*). 1936: Le Nouveau Testament (*fpl*; *co-d Alexandre Ryder*); Le Roman d'un tricheur (*fn*); Mon Père avait raison (*fpl*); Faisons un rêve (*fpl*); Le Mot de Cambronne (*fpl*). 1937: Les Perles de la couronne (+ *st/s/co-d Christian Jacque*); Quadrille (*fpl*; + *p*). 1938: Désirée; Remontons les Champs-Elysées. 1939: Ils étaient neuf célibataires. 1941: Le Destin Fabuleux de Désirée Clary. 1942: La Nuit du cinéma (*d* only). 1943: Donne-moi tes yeux; La Malibran. 1947: Le Comédien (*fpl*). 1948: Le Diable Boiteux (*fpl*). 1949: Aux deux colombes (*fpl*); Toa (*fpl*). 1950: Le Trésor de Cantenac; Tu m'as sauvé la vie (*fpl*); Debureau (*fpl*). 1951: La Poison. 1952: La Vie d'un honnête homme (*d/s/lyr* only); Je l'ai été trois fois. 1953: Si Versailles m'était conté. 1955: Napoléon. 1956: Si Paris nous était conté; Assassins et voleurs (*d/s* only). 1957: Les trois font la paire (*co-d/s* only; *co-d Clément Duhour*)..

H

HAANSTRA, Bert

Director. Holten, Holland 1916–
As a boy made amateur films in 9.5 mm. During 1930's: press photographer. 1948: cinematographer.

1949: first short as director. 1952: made *Dijkbouw* for Sir Arthur Elton. To 1954: documentaries for Elton at Royal Dutch-Shell. 1958: first feature as director *Fanfare*. Producer for Petroleum Films Bureau.

Short films as director, writer and editor: 1949: Die Muiderkring herleeft – The Muiden Circle Lives Again. 1950: Spiegel van Holland – Mirror of Holland (+ *c*). 1951: Nederlandse beeldhouwkunst tijdens de late middeleeuwenen – Medieval Dutch Sculpture (*d/e* only); Panta Rhei (+ *c*). 1952: Dijkbouw – The Dike Builders (+ *co-c*). 1954: Strijd zonder einden – The Rival World. 1955: God Shiva. 1956: En der zee was niet meer – And There was no More Sea (+ *pc*); Rembrandt schilder van de mens – Rembrandt, Painter of Man. 1957: Over glas gesproken. 1960: De Zaak MP – The MP Case (*co-s/co-e*).

Short films as director and writer: 1953: Aardolie – The Changing Earth; The Search for Oil; The Wildcat. 1954: The Oilfield. 1958: Glas – Glass (+ *pc*). 1962: Delta-Phase One (+ *pc*); Zoo (*d* only).

Features as director and writer: 1958: Fanfare (*co-s/co-e*). 1964: Alleman – The Human Dutch – Twelve Millions (+ *n/pc*). 1966: The Voice of the Water (+ *pc*).

HAAS, Charles F.

Director. Chicago 1913–
English at Harvard College. 1935: extra, assistant director at Universal. Outside reader for RKO, writer at Republic. Directed, wrote and produced documentaries; worked on industrial films in New York. 1941: US Signal Corps; training films, Air Force films and newsreels. 1946: Producer at Universal. 1948: wrote and produced *Moonrise*. Uncredited script work. 1950: directed films for Telephone Company. TV director. 1955: first feature as director. Then mainly with MGM and Universal. Wrote an early, unused version of script for *Joe Macbeth* (1956). Much work as TV director.

Films as director: 1955: Star in the Dust; Showdown at Abilene; Screaming Eagles. 1957: Summer Love. 1958: Wild Heritage. 1959: The Beat Generation; The Big Operator; Girl's Town. 1960: Platinum High School.

HACKETT, Albert

Writer. New York 1900–
Theatrical family. Child actor, then into vaudeville. Appeared in a few silent films, e.g. *Anne of Green Gables* (1919). From 1933: scripts in collaboration with his wife Frances Goodrich. For list *see* GOODRICH, Frances.

HADJIDAKIS, Manos

Composer. Athens 1925–
Studied music at Athens Odeon. From 1946: composed over 150 film scores. 1960: Oscar for song 'Never on Sunday'.

Films as composer include: 1955: I Mayiki Polis; Stella; To Koritsi me ta mavra. 1956: Drakos. 1957: To Telefteo psema; I Paranomi. 1959: Pote tin Kyriaki. 1960: To Potami. 1962: The Zoo Spartans. 1970: The Invincible Six.

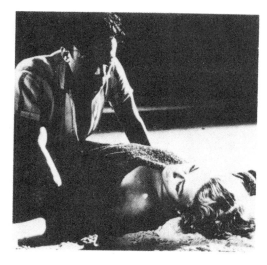

Os Cafajestes, *directed by Ruy Guerra.*
(*left to right*) *Madlyn Rhue, Ray Danton, Rosalind Russell and Alec Guinness in* A Majority of One, *produced and directed by Mervyn LeRoy.*
John Forsythe and Jean Simmons in The Happy Ending, *directed by Richard Brooks and photographed by Conrad Hall.*

HALAS, John

Animator. Budapest 1912–

Educated Hungary and Paris. 1928–31: assistant to George Pal. From 1934: produced his own cartoon films; to England in 1936. 1940: formed Halas and Batchelor Cartoon Films with Joy Batchelor, whom he married in 1941. Produced and directed many cartoons for cinema and TV. Also commercials; animated promotional, scientific and instructional films. By 1962, company had produced over 700 educational films. Most of output is for USA, including several cartoon series. They were art directors in *Cinerama Holiday* (1955) and animated drawings for *Private's Progress* (1955).

Films produced and directed in collaboration with Joy Batchelor include: 1941: Pocket Cartoon (*co-d Alexander McKendrick*). 1946: Magic Canvas (*d alone*). 1949: Heave Away My Johnny (*+ s*). 1953: The Owl and the Pussycat (*co-p*); The Figurehead. 1954: Animal Farm (*co-p*). 1956: The History of the Cinema. 1958: The Christmas Visitor (*d alone*). 1961: For Better, For Worse. 1964: Automania 2000 (*d/p alone*). 1967: Ruddigore (*d Batchelor alone*). 1970: Children and Cars (*d/p Halas alone*).

HALL, Conrad

Cinematographer, Papeete, Tahiti 1926–

University of Southern California Film Department, studied under Slavko Vorkapich. Formed production company with friends, drew lots to decide who was to photograph their films, and won. Made *Running Target* over period of 18 months. Shot footage for Disney nature features *The Living Desert* (1953) and *Islands of the Sea* (1959). Operator for Robert Surtees, Ernest Haller, Floyd Crosby, Hal Mohr, Ted McCord. 1969: Oscar for *Butch Cassidy and the Sundance Kid*. TV work includes 'Stoney Burke' and 'Outer Limits'.

Films as cinematographer include: 1958: Edge of Fury (*co*). 1965: Wild Seed; Incubus; The Saboteur – Code Name Morituri. 1966: Harper; The Professionals. 1967: Divorce American Style; Cool Hand Luke; In Cold Blood. 1968: Hell in the Pacific. 1969: Butch Cassidy and the Sundance Kid; The Happy Ending; Tell Them Willie Boy is Here.

HALL, Peter

Director. Bury St Edmunds, Suffolk 1930–

Perse School and St Catherine's College Cambridge. Directed over 20 productions while at Cambridge. 1953: professional debut as director, Theatre Royal, Windsor. Assistant director (from 1954), director (from 1955) of Arts Theatre, London. 1957: formed own producing company, the International Playwright's Theatre. Directed London, Broadway, Stratford-on-Avon. 1960–68: managing director of Royal Shakespeare Company; thereafter co-director. 1966: first film work directing members of Royal Shakespeare Company in fragments of 'Edward II' for *The Deadly Affair*. Married Leslie Caron (1956–66, divorced).

Films as director: 1968: Work is a 4-Letter Word; A Midsummer Night's Dream. 1969: 3 into 2 Won't Go. 1970: Perfect Friday.

HALLDOFF, Jan

Director. Söder, Sweden 1940–

1964: Stills photographer on *491* and *Att Alska*. First short *Haltimme – Time Out* produced by Bengt Forslund. Two further shorts. 1966: first feature as director. Stig Claesson collaborated with him on scripts of all his shorts and first 3 features; *Ola och Julia* (1968) produced by Bengt Forslund.

Features as director and writer in collaboration: 1966: Myten – The Myth. 1967: Livet är Stenkull – Life's Just Great; Ola och Julia – Ola and Julia. 1968: Korridoren – The Corridor. 1970: En Dröm om frihet. 1971: Rötmånad.

HALLER, Daniel

Designer and director. Los Angeles 1929–

UCLA: designed college theatre productions. Designer at La Jolla Community Theatre. 4 years study at Chouinard Art institute. 1954: designed television commercials. 1955: work in Hollywood. Art director for American International, notably on films directed by Roger Corman. 1965: first film as director.

Films as art director include: 1958: I, Mobster. 1959: A Bucket of Blood. 1960: The Fall of the House of Usher. 1961: The Pit and the Pendulum. 1962: Panic in Year Zero; The Premature Burial. 1963: Diary of a Madman; X-The Man with X-Ray Eyes. 1964: The Comedy of Terrors; Pajama Party.

Films as director: 1965: Monster of Terror – Die, Monster, Die – The House at the End of the World. 1967: Devil's Angels. 1968: The Wild Racers. 1970: Paddy; Pieces of Dreams.

HALLER, Ernest

Cinematographer. Los Angeles 1896–1970 Maria del Rey, California

Bank clerk. 1914: entered films as actor with Biograph. Camera operator on serial *The Hazards of Helen* (1915) and *Wolves of the Rail* (1918). 1920: first feature as cinematographer *Yes or No*. 1921–24: worked mainly for Famous Players–Lasky. 1925–32: mainly with First National. Worked in New York. 1932–36: mainly Paramount, MGM, Warners. 1936–51: almost all films for Warners. 1953–64: several studios, including Fox, Allied Artists, Warners. Oscar for colour cinematography *Gone with the Wind* (with Ray Rennahan, 1939).

Films as cinematographer include: 1921: The Gilded Lily. 1924: Rough Ridin'; Empty Hearts. 1925: Parisian Nights; Any Woman (*co*); Bluebeard's Seven Wives. 1926: The Dancer of Paris. 1927: For the Love of Mike; French Dressing. 1928: Harold Teen; Wheel of Chance; Naughty Baby. 1929: Weary River; House of Horror (*co*); Drag; Young Nowheres. 1930: Son of the Gods; A Notorious Affair; The Dawn Patrol; The Lash. 1931: Ten Cents a Dance; Chances; Honor of the Family; Girls About Town. 1932: The Woman from Monte Carlo; Night after Night; The Crash; Scarlet Dawn. 1933: House on 56th Street; Easy to Love. 1934: Journal of a Crime; The Key; Desirable; British Agent; The Firebird. 1935: Mary Jane's Pa; Escapade. 1936: The Voice of Bugle Ann; Mountain Justice; The Great O'Malley.

1937: Call it a Day; That Certain Woman; The Great Garrick. 1938: Jezebel; Four's a Crowd; Four Daughters; Brother Rat. 1939: Dark Victory; The Roaring Twenties; Invisible Stripes; Gone with the Wind (*co*). 1940: All This, and Heaven Too; No Time for Comedy. 1941: Honeymoon for Three; Footsteps in the Dark; The Bride Came C.O.D.; Manpower; Blues in the Night. 1942: In This Our Life; George Washington Slept Here. 1944: Mr Skeffington. 1945: Mildred Pierce. 1946: Saratoga Trunk; Devotion; A Stolen Life (*co*); Deception; The Verdict. 1947: Humoresque; The Unfaithful. 1948: My Girl Tisa; Winter Meeting. 1949: My Dream is Yours; Always Leave Them Laughing. 1951: Jim Thorpe—All American; On Moonlight Bay. 1955: Magic Fire; Rebel Without a Cause. 1956: Strange Intruder. 1957: Men in War; Back from the Dead; Plunder Road. 1958: God's Little Acre; Man of the West. 1959: The Miracle; The Third Voice. 1961: Armored Command. 1962: Pressure Point; What Ever Happened to Baby Jane? 1963: Lilies of the Field. 1964: Dead Ringer.

HAMER, Robert

Director. Kidderminster, Worcestershire 1911–63 London

Corpus Christi College, Cambridge. 1934: clapper boy at Gaumont British. 1935: to London Films, becoming editor and writer. Edited *Vessel of Wrath* (1938), *Jamaica Inn* (1939); co-edited *St Martin's Lane* (1938). To Ealing, edited *Ships with Wings* (1941), *The Foreman Went to France* (1942). From 1943: associate producer at Ealing Studios, e.g. *San Demetrio, London* (also co-wrote; 1943), *Fiddlers Three* (1944). 1945: first work as director. Occasional script work, e.g. *A Jolly Bad Fellow* (1963), *Fifty-five Days at Peking* (additional dialogue; 1963). TV work includes 'A Month in the Country'.

Films as director: 1945: Dead of Night *ep* The Haunted Mirror (*+ s*); Pink String and Sealing Wax. 1948: It Always Rains on Sunday (*+ co-s*). 1949: Kind Hearts and Coronets (*+ co-s*); The Spider and the Fly. 1952: His Excellency (*+ s*); The Long Memory (*+ s*). 1954: Father Brown (*+ s*). 1955: To Paris With Love. 1959: The Scapegoat (*+ s*). 1960: School for Scoundrels.

HAMILTON, Guy

Director. Paris 1922–

Educated in Paris and Haileybury, Canada. 1939: apprentice at Victorine Studios, Nice. 1940: joined British Paramount News. 1941–46: Royal Navy. 1946–52: assistant director, e.g. on *They Made Me a Fugitive* (1947), *Anna Karenina* (1948), *The Fallen Idol* (1948), *The Third Man* (1949), *The Outcast of the Islands* (1951), *The African Queen* (1951). 1952: first film as director. 1963: removed name from credits of *The Party's Over* after censor's cuts.

Films as director: 1952: The Ringer. 1953: The Intruder. 1954: An Inspector Calls. 1955: The Colditz Story (*+ co-s*). 1956: Charley Moon. 1957: Manuela. 1959: The Devil's Disciple (*co-d Alexander McKendrick, uc*); A Touch of Larceny. 1962: I Due Nemici – The Best of Enemies. 1963: The Man in the Middle; The Party's Over (*uc*). 1964: Goldfinger. 1966: Funeral in Berlin. 1969: The Battle of Britain. 1971: Diamonds are Forever.

HAMMETT, Dashiell

Writer. St Mary's Country, Maryland 1894–1961 New York.

Pinkerton Detective on Fatty Arbuckle case. Novels adapted by others include *The Maltese Falcon* (1931, 1941), *The Thin Man* (1934), *The Glass Key* (1936, 1942). *City Streets* (1931) based on his story; wrote screenplay for *Watch on the Rhine* (1943) from Lillian Hellman's play. 1951: before the House Committee on Un-American Activities; 6 months jail for contempt of court; on release sued by tax authorities for large arrears; stopped writing.

HANI, Susumu

Director. Tokyo 1929–

Father historian Hani Goro. Educated at his grandmother's private school. 1948: joined Japanese news service agency; then film department of publishing firm. Stills photographer for 5 years. From 1954: directed documentaries. 1960: directed first feature; married actress Sachiko Hidari; directed her in *Kanojo to Kare* (1963). Made *Buwana Toshi no Uta* in East Africa and *Andesu no Hanayome* in Peru. Writings include collection of essays on film (1962), reports on film-making in Africa (1965), the Andes (1966) and by Navajo Indians (1968). Also scripts for radio and TV.

Documentary films as director include: 1954: Kyoshitsu no kodomotachi – Children in the Classroom. 1955: Eo kaku kodomotachi – Children Who Draw. 1957: Dobutsu-en nikki – Zoo Diary. 1958: Horyu-ji – The Horyu-ji Temple.

Feature films as director: 1960: Furyo Shonen – Bad Boys. 1962: Mitasareta Seikatsu – A Full Life (+ co-s). 1963: Te wo Tsunagu Kora – Children Hand in Hand; Kanojo to Kare – She and He (+ s). 1965: Buwana Toshi no Uta – Song of Bwana Toshi (+ co-s). 1966: Andesu no Hanayome – Bride of the Andes (+ co-p/s). 1968: Hatsukoi jigokuhen – Nanini – Inferno of First Love (+ co-p/co-s). 1969: Aido – Aido—Slave of Life.

HANNA, William

Producer and writer. Melrose, New Mexico 1920–

Studied engineering and journalism. Joined Leon Schlesinger's Cartoon company. 1938: became writer and director of MGM cartoons, 1940: began collaboration with Joseph Barbera on *Gallopin' Gals*. To 1957: they made over 200 films in 'Tom and Jerry' series. 1957–69: worked for Screen Gems, TV subsidiary of Columbia; series worked on include 'Huckleberry Hound', 'Quick Draw McGraw', 'The Flintstones', 'Yogi Bear', 'Tales of Tin-Tin', 'Top Cat', 'The Jetsons', 'Shazzan!' TV cartoons by computer. 1966: animated feature *The Man Called Flintstone*. Animated sequences for features, including *Anchors Aweigh* (1945) and *Invitation to the Dance* (1956). Oscars for work at MGM: *The Yankee Doodle Mouse* (1943), *Mouse Trouble* (1944), *Quiet Please!* (1945), *The Cat Concerto* (1946), *The Little Orphan* (1948), *The Two Mouseketeers* (1951), *Johann Mouse* (1952).

HANOUN, Marcel

Director. Tunis 1929–

1951–53: worked as photographer and journalist. 1953–54: director and cinematographer on industrial and educational films. 1955: directed short, *Gérard de la Nuit*. 1956: director and cinematographer on shorts for TV, *Croquis de l'islande* and *Des hommes qui ont perdu Racine*. 1958: first feature, for TV. 1960–63: in Spain, director and cinematographer on TV films including *Le Christ dans la cité*; cinematographer on Spanish production, *Operacion H*; reporter/cameraman for French TV.

Features as director and writer: 1958: Une Simple Histoire (d/c only). 1959: Le Huitième Jour (st/co-s). 1965: Octobre à Madrid (+p/st/c). 1967: L'Authentique Procès de Carl Emmanuel Jung (+p/st). 1968: Le Printemps (co-s/co-ad/co-di). 1969: L'Hiver.

HARDY, Oliver

(Norvell Hardy) Actor. Harlem, Georgia 1892–1957

Trained as singer. Ran own cinema. 1913: first film as actor *Outwitting Dad*. Worked for e.g. Lubin, Vitagraph, Gaumont; early credits under real name, or as Babe Hardy. 1920: with Buck Jones in several films directed by W. S. Van Dyke for Fox. From 1921: worked with Larry Semon, then for Roach. 1926: began partnership with Stan Laurel. From 1939: some work in features without Laurel. For main list, see LAUREL, Stan.

Films as actor include: 1920: The Fly Cop. 1921: The Sawmill. 1923: The Three Ages. 1924: The Girl in the Limousine; Kid Speed. 1939: Zenobia. 1949: The Fighting Kentuckian. 1950: Riding High.

HARLAN, Russell

Cinematographer. Los Angeles 1903–

Entered films as double and stunt man. Camera assistant then camera operator. 1929: additional photography on *Wings*. 1937: became cinematographer. Worked on training films during World War II; shot Hopalong Cassidy films and many small westerns up to 1943. 1948–64: photographed most Howard Hawks films (except Fox comedies).

Films as cinematographer include: 1942: Silver Queen; Hoppy Serves a Writ. 1943: Tarzan's Desert Mystery (co). 1945: A Walk in the Sun. 1947: Ramrod. 1948: Red River. 1951: The Thing. 1952: The Big Sky; Ruby Gentry. 1954: Riot in Cell Block 11. 1955: The Blackboard Jungle; Land of the Pharaohs (co). 1956: The Last Hunt; Lust for Life (co). 1957: Witness for The Prosecution; Something of Value; This Could be the Night. 1958: Run Silent, Run Deep; King Creole. 1959: Rio Bravo; Day of the Outlaw; Operation Petticoat. 1960: Pollyanna. 1962: Hatari! (co); The Spiral Road; To Kill a Mockingbird. 1963: A Gathering of Eagles. 1964: Man's Favorite Sport?; Dear Heart. 1965: The Great Race. 1966: Hawaii. 1970: Darling Lili.

HARLAN, Veidt

Actor and director. Berlin, 1899–1964 Capri

Stage actor and director. Trained as actor by Max Reinhardt and first wife Dora Gerson. With G. W. Pabst worked uncredited on *Tiefland* (1922). Acted e.g. in *Polizeiakte 909* (1934). 1937: Hilda Korber, his second wife, acted in *Der Herrscher*. Third wife Kristina Soederbaum leading lady in almost all his films after 1937. Acted on stage in 'Jugend': filmed it in

Whatever Happened to Baby Jane?, *directed by Robert Aldrich and photographed by Ernest Haller.*
Oliver Hardy in Putting Pants on Philip. *directed by Clyde Bruckman.*
Kolberg. *directed by Veidt Harlan.*

1938. *Maria der Magd* (1936) and *Das unsterbliche Herz* (1939) based on plays by his father. Tobis contract as director and writer. 1939: *Die Reise nach Tilsit* was a remake of F. W. Murnau's *Sunrise*. Goebbels commissioned him to direct *Jud Süss* (1940). 1942: worked with technicians for 6 months to improve Agfacolor process for *Die goldene Stadt*. After World War II, blacklisted until after 1950 trial. 1950–51: tried by two courts for crimes against humanity for his part in making *Jud Süss*; acquitted. 1954: burned all available copies to prevent use as anti-Semitic propaganda by Arab League. Own film company. Autobiography, 'Im Schatten meiner Filme'.

Films as director: 1935: Die Pompadour (+ *co-s*; *co-d Willy Schmidt-Gentner, Heinz Helbig*); Krach im Interhaus. 1936: Katerlampe; Der müde Theodore; Maria der Magd (+ *co-s*); Alles für Veronica. 1937: Die Kreutzersonate; Der Herrscher; Mein Sohn, der Herr Minister. 1938: Jugend; Verwehte Spuren (+ *co-s*). 1939: Das unsterbliche Herz (+ *co-s*); Die Reise nach Tilsit (+ *co-s*). 1940: Jud Süss (+ *s*). 1941: Pedro soll hangen. 1942: Der Grosse König (+ *s*); Die goldene Stadt (+ *co-s*). 1943: Immensee (+ *co-s*). 1944: Opfergang (+ *co-s*). 1945: Kolberg (+ *co-s*). 1950: Unsterbliche Geliebte. 1951: Hanna Amon. 1952: Die blaue Stunde. 1953: Sterne über Colombo; Die Gefangene des Maharadscha. 1954: Verrat an Deutschland (+ *co-s*). 1957: Das dritte Geschlecht – Anders als Du und Ich – The Third Sex. 1958: Liebe kann wie Gift sein; Ich werde Dich auf Händen tragen. 1962: Die blonde Frau des Maharadscha.

HARLINE, Leigh

Composer. Salt Lake City, Utah 1907–69 Los Angeles
University of Utah. Joined Utah Radio Orchestra. Worked in radio in Los Angeles. 1937: invited by Walt Disney to write first film music, *Snow White and the 7 Dwarfs* in collaboration. From 1941: freelance, for e.g. Disney. Also conductor and arranger. Oscar for music, *Pinocchio* (1940, in collaboration), and song 'When You Wish Upon a Star' from *Pinocchio*.

Films as composer include: 1942: The Pride of the Yankees. 1945: The More the Merrier. 1946: Crack Up. 1947: The Bachelor and the Bobby-Soxer. 1948: Mr Blandings Builds his Dream House. 1949: The Big Steal. 1950: The Company She Keeps. 1952: Monkey Business. 1953: The Desert Rats. 1954: Susan Slept Here; Broken Lance. 1955: House of Bamboo. 1956: The Bottom of the Bottle; 23 Paces to Baker Street; Teenage Rebel. 1957: No Down Payment. 1958: 10 North Frederick; Man of the West; These Thousand Hills. 1959: Warlock. 1962: The Wonderful World of the Brothers Grimm.

HARLOW, Jean

(Harlean Carpenter) Actress. Kansas City, Missouri 1911–37 Hollywood
Parents separated when she was a child; took mother's maiden name. 1927: eloped at 16 (divorced 1931). From 1927: appeared in films as extra, e.g. *New York Nights* (1929)), *The Love Parade* (1930), also in 2-reelers e.g. Laurel and Hardy comedies for Hal Roach. 1930: established as star by *Hell's Angels*. From 1931: most films for MGM. 1932: married MGM producer Paul Bern who died 2 months later. 1933–35: married to cinematographer Harold Rosson. 1965: Fictional-

ised biography by Irving Shulman filmed as *Harlow*, played by Carroll Baker; played by Carol Lynley in rival Electronovision film biography, *Harlow*.

Films as actress include: 1929: Double Whoopee; Bacon Grabbers. 1931: The Public Enemy; Platinum Blonde; The Iron Man. 1932: Red Dust; Red-Headed Woman. 1933: Bombshell; Dinner at Eight; Hold Your Man. 1934: The Girl from Missouri. 1935: Reckless; China Seas. 1936: Wife vs Secretary; Libeled Lady. 1937: Saratoga.

HARRIS, Richard

Actor. Limerick, Eire 1933–
Father owner of flour mill. 1952: career delayed by tuberculosis. From 1954: London Academy of Music and Dramatic Art. 1956: London West End stage debut, 'The Quare Fellow'. 1957: joined Joan Little-wood's Theatre Workshop. Much theatre work followed, notably West End production, 'The Ginger Man' (1959). In films from 1958. 1963: solo performance in Lindsay Anderson's Royal Court Theatre production, 'The Diary of a Madman', which he adapted from Nikolai Gogol in collaboration with Anderson. Since *Camelot* (1967) also singer; records include hit 'MacArthur Park'. TV, including series 'The Iron Harp'. 1970: first work as director: took over *Bloomfield* from Uri Zohar; made in Israel.

Films as actor include: 1959: Shake Hands with the Devil. 1960: A Terrible Beauty. 1961: The Guns of Navarone. 1962: Mutiny on the Bounty. 1963: This Sporting Life. 1964: Deserto Rosso. 1965; Major Dundee; The Heroes of Telemark. 1966: La Bibbia; Hawaii. 1967: Caprice. 1968: The Molly Maguires. 1970: A Man Called Horse; Cromwell. 1971: Bloomfield (+ *co-d*; *co-d Uri Zohar*).

HARRISON, Rex

Actor. Huyton, Lancashire 1908–
Stage debut while a student. Repertory in Liverpool. 1930: London stage debut in 'Getting George Married'. 1932: understudy to Herbert Marshall in 'Another Language'. 1936: New York debut 'Sweet Aloes'. Acted in 'French Without Tears', 'Design for Living'. 1940–44: in RAF, reaching Flight Lieutenant. 1946: first American film, *Anna and the King of Siam*. Acted in 'Anne of the Thousand Days', 'Bell, Book and Candle'. 1953–54: stage actor-director 'The Love of Four Colonels' and 'Bell, Book and Candle'. 1955: directed 'Nina'. 1956: 'My Fair Lady' in London. 1958: with the musical to New York. Married Lilli Palmer (1943–47, divorced) who appeared with him in 'No Time for Comedy' (1941) and *The Rake's Progress* (1945) and 2 subsequent films; also married Kay Kendall (1957–59, widowed) and Rachel Roberts (1962).

Films as actor include: 1930: School for Scandal. 1937: Storm in a Teacup; School for Husbands. 1938: The Citadel; St Martin's Lane. 1941: Major Barbara. 1945: Blithe Spirit. 1947: The Ghost and Mrs Muir; The Foxes of Harrow. 1948: Unfaithfully Yours; Escape. 1952: The Four Poster. 1953: Main Street to Broadway. 1954: King Richard and the Crusaders. 1955: The Constant Husband. 1958: The Reluctant Debutante. 1960: Midnight Lace. 1962: The Happy Thieves. 1963: Cleopatra. 1964: My Fair Lady; The

Yellow Rolls-Royce. 1965: The Agony and the Ecstasy. 1967: The Honey Pot; Doctor Dolittle. 1969: Staircase.

HART, Moss

Writer. New York 1904–61 Palm Springs, Florida
Educated in New York. 1925: first play 'The Hold-Up Man'. 1932: collaborated with Irving Berlin on musical comedy 'Face the Music'. Collaboration as playwright with George S. Kaufman e.g. on 'I'd Rather Be Right' (1937). 1937: they received Pulitzer Prize for 'You Can't Take It With You'. 3 plays co-written with Kaufman filmed; *You Can't Take It With You* (1938), *The Man Who Came To Dinner* (1942), *George Washington Slept Here* (1942). 1944: Albert Hackett and Frances Goodrich adapted his play for *Lady in the Dark*; first film as writer, *Winged Victory*, from own play. 1948: Ranald MacDougall wrote and produced *The Decision of Christopher Blake* based on Hart's play 'Christopher Blake'. 1959: wrote autobiography 'Act One'. Directed 'My Fair Lady' on stage. 1960: produced and directed 'Camelot' on stage. 1964: *Act One* based on play taken from his autobiography.

Films as writer: 1944: Winged Victory. 1947: Gentleman's Agreement. 1952: Hans Christian Andersen. 1954: A Star is Born. 1955: Prince of Players.

HART, William S.

Actor, writer and director. Newburgh, New York 1870–1946 Saugus, California
As a boy worked as trail hand. New York stage debut at 19; theatre actor for 20 years before entering films. Made his name in stage production of 'Ben Hur' (1900). 1913: began as film actor through friendship with Thomas H. Ince. Directing and acting for Triangle by 1915. Ince credited as producer or supervisor on many of his later films particularly until 1918. From 1917 until last film *Tumbleweeds* (1925) had own production company except for *Pinto Ben*; directed, produced and scripted many of his films. Author of books including autobiography 'My Life, East and West' (1929). Retired for 2 years after marrying actress Winifred Westover (1921).

Films as actor include: 1915: The Disciple (+ *d/p*). 1916: The Aryan; Hells Hinges; The Return of Draw Egan. 1917: The Silent Man (+ *d*); The Narrow Trail (+ *d/p/pc/st*). 1918: The Tiger Man (+ *d/pc*); Riddle Gawne (+ *st*); Branding Broadway (+ *d/co-pc*); Wolves of the Rail (+ *d/pc*); Blue Blazes Rawden (+ *d/pc*); Selfish Yates (+ *d/pc*); Shark Monroe (+ *d/pc*); The Border Wireless (+ *pc*). 1919: Breed of Men (+ *pc*); The Poppy Girl's Husband (+ *pc*); The Money Corral (+ *pc*); Square Deal Sanderson (+ *pc*); Wagon Tracks (+ *pc*); Sand! (+ *pc*). 1920: The Cradle of Courage (+ *pc*); The Toll Gate (+ *p/co-pc/co-st*). 1921: White Oak (+ *pc/st*); Three Word Brand (+ *pc*). 1923: Wild Bill Hickok (+ *p/pc/st*). 1924: Singer Jim McKee (+ *p/pc/st*); Pinto Ben (+ *d/fpm*). 1925: Tumbleweeds (+ *pc*).

HARVEY, Laurence

(Larushka Mischa Skikne) Actor and director. Janiskis, Lithuania 1928–
1934: to South Africa. 1943–46: service in South African Army, including entertainment. 1946: RADA

for 3 months. 1946–47: repertory in Manchester. 1948: first film as actor *House of Darkness*. Became British subject. Stage actor in London and on Broadway. 1958–59: Old Vic American tour, title role in 'Henry V'. Directed 'Simply Heavenly' on stage. TV in UK and USA. 1963: first film as director *The Ceremony*, also wrote and acted in it. 1967: on death of Anthony Mann, completed direction of *A Dandy in Aspic*, uncredited. Produced and acted in *L'Assoluto Naturale*. Married Margaret Leighton (1957–61, divorced).

Films as director and actor: 1963: The Ceremony (+ *p/s/di*). 1968: A Dandy in Aspic (*uc, co-d Anthony Mann*).

Films as actor include: 1949: Landfall. 1950: There Is Another Sun; The Black Rose. 1951: Scarlet Thread; I Believe in You. 1954: Giuletta e Romeo; King Richard and the Crusaders; The Good Die Young. 1955: I am a Camera; Storm over the Nile. 1956: Three Men in a Boat. 1957: After the Ball; Room at the Top. 1960: Butterfield 8; The Alamo. 1961: Summer and Smoke; Two Loves. 1962: A Walk on the Wild Side; The Manchurian Candidate; The Wonderful World of the Brothers Grimm. 1963: The Running Man; A Girl Named Tamiko. 1964: The Outrage; Of Human Bondage. 1965: Darling. 1969: L'Assoluto Naturale. 1970: WUSA. 1971: Ein Kampf um Rom.

HARVEY, Lillian

Actress. London 1907–68 Antibes
German father, English mother. World War I: in Germany; educated there, became naturalised. Studied ballet. Danced in Budapest, Berlin, Vienna. 1925: first film as actress *Der Fluch*. In Berlin revue, spotted by producer Richard Eichberg who gave her lead in *Leidenschaft* which he also directed. Several early films with him. Films in Germany, England, France. 1933: first American film *My Lips Betray*. Fox contract. Several films in 1930s with Paul Martin. World War II: in England. 1948: to Denmark. Married Danish impressario Valeur Larsen. 1953: retired to French Riviera.

Films as actress include: 1927: A Night in London. 1930: Nie wieder Liebe. 1931: Der Kongress tanzt. 1932: Quick; Happy Ever After. 1933: Ich und die Kaiserin; My Weakness. 1935: Let's Live Tonight. 1939: Castelli in aria.

HAS, Wojciech J.

Director. Cracow, Poland 1925–
Studied art. 1946: graduated from Film Institute in Cracow. Assistant director at Lodz Film Studios. Moved to documentary studio. 1947–51: documentary shorts. 1951–56: educational shorts. 1957: first feature.

Features as director: 1957: Petla – The Noose (+ *co-s*). 1958: Pozegnania – Farewells (+ *co-s*). 1960: Wspolny Pokoj – One Room Tenants (+ *s*). 1961: Rozstanie – Partings. 1962: Zloto – Gold. 1963: Jak byc Kochana – How to be Loved. 1964: Rekopis Znaleziony w Saragossie – The Saragossa Manuscript. 1966: Szyfry – The Code. 1968: Lalka – The Doll (+ *s*).

HASKIN, Byron

Director and cinematographer. Portland, Oregon 1899–
University of California, Berkeley. Cartoonist for San Francisco Daily News; worked in advertising and industrial photography. Entered films as cameraman for Pathé. 1920: assistant director for Selznick, then camera assistant. From 1923: cinematographer. 1927: at Warners and Columbia directed 2 films; then cinematographer only until returning to direction in 1947. Worked for numerous companies.

Films as director: 1927: Ginsberg the Great; The Siren. 1947: I Walk Alone. 1948: Man-Eater of Kumaon. 1949: Too Late for Tears. 1950: Treasure Island. 1951: Tarzan's Peril – Tarzan and the Jungle Queen; Warpath; Silver City – High Vermilion. 1952: Denver & Rio Grande. 1953: War of the Worlds; His Majesty O'Keefe. 1954: The Naked Jungle. 1955: Long John Silver; Conquest of Space. 1956: The First Texan; The Boss. 1958: From the Earth to the Moon. 1959: The Little Savage; Jet Over the Atlantic. 1960: September Storm. 1961: Armored Command. 1963: Captain Sinbad. 1964: Robinson Crusoe on Mars. 1968: The Power (*co-d George Pal*).

HATHAWAY, Henry

Sacramento, California, 1898–
1908: child actor with American Film Company. 1914–17: messenger-boy at Universal; then juvenile roles. 1918: gunnery instructor, US Army. 1921: prop man for Frank Lloyd. Assistant director for Paul Bern. Started directing short westerns, then features for Paramount; under contract until 1941. Produced some of his later films. 1963: replaced by Phil Karlson on *Rampage*. 1964: additional direction on *Of Human Bondage*.

Films as director: 1932: Wild Horse Mesa. 1933: Heritage of the Desert; Under the Tonto Rim; Sunset Pass; Man of the Forest; To the Last Man; The Thundering Herd. 1934: Come on Marines!; The Last Round-up; The Witching Hour; Now and Forever. 1935: The Lives of a Bengal Lancer; Peter Ibbetson. 1936: The Trail of the Lonesome Pine; Go West, Young Man; I Loved a Soldier (*u/f*). 1937: Souls at Sea. 1938: Spawn of the North. 1939: The Real Glory. 1940: Johnny Apollo; Brigham Young – Brigham Young, Frontiersman. 1941: The Shepherd of the Hills; Sundown. 1942: Ten Gentlemen from West Point; China Girl. 1944: Home in Indiana; Wing and a Prayer. 1945: Nob Hill; The House on 92nd Street. 1946: The Dark Corner. 1947: 13 rue Madeleine; Kiss of Death. 1948: Call Northside 777. 1949: Down to the Sea in Ships. 1950: The Black Rose. 1951: Rawhide; Fourteen Hours; The Desert Fox – Rommel—Desert Fox; You're in the Navy Now. 1952: Diplomatic Courier; O'Henry's Full House *ep* The Clarion Call. 1953: Niagara; White Witch Doctor. 1954: Prince Valiant; Garden of Evil. 1955: The Racers – Such Men are Dangerous. 1956: The Bottom of the Bottle – Beyond the River; 23 Paces to Baker Street. 1957: Legend of the Lost (+ *p*). 1958: From Hell to Texas – Manhunt. 1959: Woman Obsessed. 1960: Seven Thieves; North to Alaska (+ *p*). 1962: How the West Was Won *ep* The Rivers, the Plains, the Outlaws. 1963: Rampage (*uc, co-d Phil Karlson*). 1964: Of Human Bondage (*co-d Ken Hughes*); Circus

Jean Harlow, Edward Woods and James Cagney in William Wellman's Public Enemy.
W. S. Hart in Tumbleweeds.
Clifton Webb (left) and William Bendix in The Dark Corner, *directed by Henry Hathaway.*

World – The Magnificent Showman. 1965: The Sons of Katie Elder (+ p). 1966: Nevada Smith (+ p). 1967: The Last Safari (+ p). 1968: Five Card Stud. 1969: True Grit. 1971: Raid on Rommel; Shoot Out.

HAWKINS, Jack

Actor. London 1910–
Italia Conti Stage School. London stage debut at 14 in 'Saint Joan'. Actor with Sybil Thorndike's travelling company. Supporting roles on stage and screen in the 1930s. World War II: military service. Then appeared in London and toured Europe in plays by Shaw and Shakespeare. TV includes NBC productions of 'Caesar and Cleopatra' and 'The Fallen Idol'. 1966: operation for cancer of the throat, subsequent performances dubbed. Director of Peter O'Toole's production company, Keep Films.

Films as actor include: 1931: The Lodger. 1933: The Good Companions. 1935: Peg of Old Drury. 1942: Next of Kin. 1948: The Fallen Idol; The Small Back Room. 1950: The Elusive Pimpernel; The Black Rose. 1951: No Highway in the Sky. 1952: Mandy. 1953: The Cruel Sea. 1955: Land of the Pharaohs; The Prisoner. 1957: The Bridge on the River Kwai. 1958: Gideon's Day. 1959: Ben-Hur. 1961: Two Loves. 1962: Lawrence of Arabia. 1963: Rampage. 1964: Guns at Batasi. 1965: Lord Jim; Judith. 1968: Shalako. 1970: Waterloo. 1971: Jane Eyre.

HAWKS, Howard Winchester

Director. Goshen, Indiana 1896–
Cornell University. Props department of the Famous Players–Lasky Studio during vacations. World War I: Second Lieutenant in Army Air Corps. Drove racing cars professionally; built a few cars and aeroplanes. 1922–4: set up and produced films independently with e.g. Marshall Neilan and Allan Dwan. Also involved in making 2-reel comedies. 1924–6: in charge of story department at Paramount; wrote or conceived over 40 films. Signed by Fox in 1925. 1926: first film as director. His brothers Kenneth and William also worked in films: Kenneth died in an air crash after co-directing *Masked Emotions* (1927) and directing *Big Time* (1929); William produced, among others, *The Tall Men* (1955) and *Cowboy* (1958). Under contract to Fox until 1929, not since under contract. Began association with William Faulkner when he bought story for *Today We Live* (1933) when the writer was working in book store at Macy's. 1944: with Borden Chase founded Motion Picture Alliance for the Preservation of American Ideals. Produced *Corvette K-225* (1943), directed by his assistant Richard Rosson, and *The Thing* (1951), directed under his supervision by his editor Christian Nyby; produced several of own films. 'Discovered' or brought to prominence Ella Raines, Lauren Bacall and Angie Dickinson. Worked, often uncredited, on the scripts of all his films.

Films as director: 1926: The Road to Glory (+ st); Fig Leaves (+ st). 1927: The Cradle Snatchers; Paid to Love. 1928: A Girl in Every Port (+ st)- Fazil; The Air Circus (co-d Lewis Seiler). 1929: Trent's Last Case. 1930: The Dawn Patrol – The Flight Commander (+ co-s). 1931: The Criminal Code. 1932: The Crowd Roars (+ st); Scarface, Shame of the Nation – Scarface (+ co-p); Tiger Shark. 1933: Today We Live (+ p).

1934: Viva Villa! (uc; co-d Jack Conway); Twentieth Century (+ p). 1935: Barbary Coast – Port of Wickedness. 1936: Ceiling Zero; The Road to Glory; Come and Get It! – Roaring Timber (co-d William Wyler). 1938: Bringing Up Baby (+ p). 1939: Only Angels Have Wings (+ p/st); His Girl Friday (+ p). 1940: The Outlaw (r 1946; uc, co-d Howard Hughes). 1941: Sergeant York; Ball of Fire. 1943: Air Force. 1945: To Have and Have Not (+ p). 1946: The Big Sleep (+ p). 1947: A Song Is Born. 1948: Red River. 1949: I Was A Male War Bride – You Can't Sleep Here. 1952: The Big Sky (+ p); O. Henry's Full House ep The Ransom of Red Chief; Monkey Business. 1953: Gentlemen Prefer Blondes. 1955: Land of the Pharaohs (+ p). 1959: Rio Bravo (+ p). 1962: Hatari! (+ p). 1964: Man's Favorite Sport (+ p). 1966: Red Line 7000 (+ p/co-s). 1967: El Dorado (+ p). 1970: Rio Lobo (+ p).

HAY, Will

Actor and director. Aberdeen, Scotland 1888–1949 London
Amateur then professional music-hall. World tour; engagements in USA, South Africa. 1934: first film as actor *Those Were the Days*. To 1939: Gainsborough, then Ealing. 1941–43: writer and co-director of several of his films. 1943: retired from films owing to ill-health. Worked in radio. Book on astronomy, 'Through My Telescope'. Son and daughter, Will and Gladys Hay are music-hall artistes.

Films as actor include: 1934: Radio Parade of 1935. 1935: Boys Will Be Boys (+ s); Dandy Dick 1936: Windbag the Sailor; Where There's A Will. 1937: Oh, Mr Porter!. 1938: Convict 99; Hey, Hey U.S.A. 1939: Old Bones of the River; Ask a Policeman; Where's That Fire. 1941: The Ghost of St Michael's; The Big Blockade.

Films as director in collaboration with Basil Dearden, and actor: 1941: The Black Sheep of Whitehall. 1942: The Goose Steps Out. 1943: My Learned Friend.

HAYDEN, Sterling

(John Hamilton) Actor. Montclair, New Jersey 1916–
1941: first film as actor *Virginia* for Paramount; Madeleine Carroll, his wife since 1937, acted in it. 1941: US Marine Corps. 1946: divorced. 1947: returned to Paramount. From 1950: worked for several studios. 1954–58: worked frequently for United Artists. Autobiography, 'The Wanderer'.

Films as actor include: 1941: Bahama Passage. 1947: Variety Girl; Blaze of Noon. 1950: The Asphalt Jungle. 1951: Journey into Light; Flaming Feather. 1952: Denver & Rio Grande. 1953: The Star; Take Me to Town; So Big. 1954: The City is Dark; Prince Valiant; Johnny Guitar. 1955: The Last Command. 1956: The Killing. 1957: Crime of Passion; Valerie. 1958: Terror in a Texas Town. 1963: Dr Strangelove, or How I Learned to Stop Worrying and Love the Bomb. 1969: Sweet Hunters. 1970: Loving.

HAYDN, Richard

Actor and director. London 1905–
Box-office clerk, chorus boy on London stage. Small

role in 'This Year of Grace'. In repertory tour to West Indies. London revue 'Members Only'. Radio. Broadway revue 'Set to Music' with Beatrice Lillie, remained in America. 1940: to Hollywood. 1941: first film *Charley's Aunt*. 1948–51: director. Book 'The Journal of Edwin Carp' based on his stage and film character.

Films as actor include: 1941: Ball of Fire. 1945: And Then There Were None. 1946: Cluny Brown. 1947: Forever Amber; The Late George Apley. 1948: The Emperor Waltz. 1952: The Merry Widow. 1953: Money from Home. 1954: Her Twelve Men. 1955: Jupiter's Darling. 1960: Please Don't Eat the Daisies. 1962: Mutiny on the Bounty. 1965: The Sound of Music.

Films as director: 1948: Miss Tatlock's Millions (+ w). 1950: Dear Wife. 1951: Mr Music.

HAYER, Nicholas

Cinematographer. Paris 1898–
Brazilian mother. Army cameraman. 1923: worked in Siberia. 1924–28: worked in Indo-China. 1928–34: MGM newsreels. From 1934: worked on features. 1958: directed short *Problème Berlin*. 1960: joined ORTF.

Films as cinematographer include: 1934: Le Paquebot Tenacity (co). 1939: Macao, l'enfer du jeu (co); L'Or du Cristobal. 1942: Dernier Atout; Le Capitaine Fracasse. 1943: Le Corbeau. 1945: Falbalas. 1946: Panique. 1950: Orphée; Trois Télégrammes. 1951: Sous le ciel de Paris coule la Seine. 1952: Le Petit Monde de Don Camillo. 1954: Bel Ami (r1957). 1958: Deux Hommes dans Manhattan (co). 1959: Le Signe du lion.

HAYES, Helen

(Helen Brown) Actress. Washington 1900–
Stage debut at 5. Became a leading actress in American theatre. Appeared occasionally in films from the 1920s. Married Charles MacArthur (1928–56, widowed), son is actor James MacArthur. Oscar as Best Actress, *The Sin of Madelon Claudet* (1931). Oscar as supporting actress for *Airport* (1970).

Films as actress include: 1932: Arrowsmith; The Son-Daughter. 1933: The White Sister; A Farewell to Arms; Night Flight. 1934: What Every Woman Knows. 1943: Stagedoor Canteen. 1952: My Son John. 1956: Anastasia. 1970: Airport.

HAYES, John Michael

Writer. Worcester, Massachusetts 1919–
1948–51: radio writer on various series. 1952: became writer in films.

Films as writer include: 1952: Red Ball Express. 1953: Thunder Bay (st/co-s); Torch Song (co). 1954: Rear Window. 1955: The Trouble with Harry; To Catch a Thief. 1956: The Man Who Knew Too Much (co). 1957: Peyton Place. 1958: The Matchmaker. 1960: Butterfield 8 (co). 1962: The Children's Hour. 1963: The Chalk Garden. 1964: The Carpetbaggers; Where Love Has Gone. 1965: Harlow; Judith (co). 1966: Nevada Smith (+ st).

HAYS, Will H.

Administrator. Sullivan, Indiana 1879–1954 Sullivan, Indiana

Father Presbyterian elder. Wabash College, Crawfordsville, Indiana. Lawyer in father's firm. Local and national political career. 1918: Chairman of Republican National Committee. 1920: organised presidential and congressional campaigns resulting in Warren Harding's victory. 1921: appointed Postmaster General. 1922: resigned to become first president of Motion Picture Producers and Distributors of America, which became known as Hays Office, to provide self-censorship for the industry. Defeated movement for state censorship of films, convinced bankers to grant credit to studios. 1929–30: drew up 'Hays Code' for moral standards of Hollywood films and behaviour of actors. Attempted to withdraw ban on Fatty Arbuckle to allow him to write and direct, prevented by national outcry. Morality clause subsequently written into every contract; books, stories and scripts submitted to Hays Office before purchase. 1945: retired, to resume law career; acted as advisor to the Office until 1950. Presbyterian elder. 1955: posthumously published autobiography 'The Memoirs of Will H. Hays'. Hays Code in operation until 1966.

HAYWARD, Louis

Actor. Johannesburg, South Africa 1909–
Stage work in England and on Broadway. 1932: first film *Self Made Lady*. Much work for RKO, United Artists. Owner of Associated Film Artists. Also TV work. Married Ida Lupino (1939–45, divorced).

Films as actor include: 1935: The Flame Within. 1936: Anthony Adverse. 1937: The Woman I Love. 1938: The Rage of Paris. 1939: Duke of West Point; The Man in the Iron Mask. 1940: My Son, My Son; Dance, Girl, Dance; The Son of Monte Cristo. 1941: Ladies in Retirement. 1945: And Then There Were None. 1946: The Strange Woman. 1948: Ruthless; The Black Arrow; Walk a Crooked Mile. 1949: I Pirati di Capri. 1950: House by the River; The Fortunes of Captain Blood. 1951: The Lady and the Bandit. 1953: The Royal African Rifles. 1956: The Search for Bridey Murphy. 1967: Chuka.

HAYWARD, Susan

(Edythe Marriner) Actress. Brooklyn, New York 1918–
Fashion and photographer's model; Hollywood screen test (1938). 1939: first films. To 1942: mainly Warners and Paramount. To 1955: mainly Fox. First husband was actor Jess Barker (1944–53, divorced). Oscar as Best Actress, *I Want to Live* (1958).

Films as actress include: 1939: Beau Geste. 1941: Adam Had Four Sons; Among the Living. 1942: Reap the Wild Wind; I Married a Witch. 1944: The Hairy Ape. 1946: Canyon Passage; Deadline at Dawn. 1947: Smash-Up. 1948: Tap Roots. 1949: My Foolish Heart; Tulsa. 1951: I Can Get It For You Wholesale; Rawhide; David and Bathsheba. 1952: The Lusty Men; The Snows of Kilimanjaro. 1953: White Witch Doctor. 1954: Demetrius and the Gladiators; Garden of Evil; Untamed. 1955: The Conqueror. 1956: I'll Cry Tomorrow. 1959: Woman Obsessed. 1961: Ada; Back

Street. 1964: Where Love Has Gone. 1967: The Honey Pot; Valley of the Dolls.

HAYWORTH, Rita

(Margarita Carmen Cansino) Actress. New York 1918–
Father's family were dancers in Spain. Mother, from theatrical family, had been a Ziegfeld girl. 1927: family settled in Los Angeles. 1932: professional stage debut at Carthay Circle Theatre, Los Angeles. Dancing act with father at resort night clubs. 1935–37: first films as actress, under name Rita Cansino; 1 year contract with Fox; 14 low budget pictures on Columbia contract; then unemployed for 8 months. Cut and bleached hair, had hair line on forehead raised by electrolysis, studied acting, dancing and singing, changed name. Under contract to Columbia until 1957 and their leading actress in 1940s. First film as freelance, *Separate Tables* (1958). Retired during marriage to Aly Khan (1949–51, divorced) and during marriage to singer Dick Haymes (1953–55, divorced). 3 other husbands including Orson Welles (1943–47, divorced), producer James Hill (1958–61, divorced).

Films as actress include: 1936: A Marriage to Garcia; Meet Nero Wolfe; Human Cargo. 1939: Only Angels Have Wings. 1940: The Lady in Question; Angels over Broadway; Susan and God. 1941: Affectionately Yours; The Strawberry Blonde; Blood and Sand. 1942: Tales of Manhattan. 1944: Cover Girl. 1945: Tonight and Every Night. 1946: Gilda. 1948: The Loves of Carmen; The Lady from Shanghai. 1953: Salome; Miss Sadie Thompson. 1957: Fire Down Below; Pal Joey. 1959: They Came to Cordura; The Story on Page One. 1962: The Happy Thieves. 1964: Circus World. 1966: The Money Trap. 1967: L'Aventuriero. 1968: I Bastardi. 1970: Sur la Route de Salina.

HEARST, William Randolph

Producer. San Francisco 1863–1951 Beverley Hills
Son of a US Senator. Harvard. Founded Hearst group of newspapers and magazines. In films for more than 30 years, starting with a newsreel, the Hearst Selig Weekly, ending when his International Newsreel (Metrotone News) became MGM's News of the Day near the end of his life. 1918: formed Marion Davies Film Company (later Cosmopolitan Productions) to support the career of his mistress Marion Davies. His two dozen newspapers syndicated the column of Louella Parsons. Refused to accept advertising for *Citizen Kane* (1941) which was thought to be based on his life – invested $30 million on antiques and $40 million on real estate.

HÉBERT, Pierre

Animator. Montreal, Canada 1944–
Anthropology at University of Montreal. Films from 1962. From 1965: with the National Film Board of Canada. Animated films range from 14 minutes to 20 seconds in length; also a number of 8 mm cassettes for teaching French. 1968: some animation work for *Jusqu'au coeur*.

Films as animator include: 1962: Histoire Grise; Histoire d'une pépite. 1964: Opus 1. 1965: Op Hop. 1967: Opus 3; Explosion de la population; Une Souris la semaine prochaine.

Sterling Hayden in Johnny Guitar, *directed by Nicholas Ray.*
Susan Hayward advertizing Lux toilet soap.
Neville Brand and Dana Andrews in Where the Sidewalk Ends, *written by Ben Hecht and directed by Otto Preminger.*

HECHT, Ben

Writer and director. New York 1894–1964
Family of Russian Jewish emigrés. 1910–23: journalist for e.g. Chicago Journal, Chicago Daily News. 1919: Correspondent in Germany and Russia for 75 newspapers. Founder of Chicago Literary Times. Early novels include 'The Florentine Dagger'. 1927: Oscar for first screen credit, story of *Underworld*. 1934: first script collaboration with Charles MacArthur, *Twentieth Century*, based on their play; they founded production company in New York; made first film as directors in collaboration. 1935: jointly awarded Oscar for story of *The Scoundrel*. 1940: *His Girl Friday* remake of Lewis Milestone's film of their play *The Front Page* (1931). Their association ended about 1947. 1954: autobiography 'A Child of the Century'. 1956: scripted *Miracle in the Rain* from own novel. 1958: his co-script for *Kiss of Death* (1947) used as basis for *The Fiend Who Walked the West*. Completed musical play 'Chicago' shortly before his death. 1969: *Gaily, Gaily* based on his autobiographical novel. Novels include 'I Hate Actors'; numerous plays and stories. TV work includes 'Lights Diamond Jubilee' (1954) for Selznick, and 'Hello Charlie' (1960) based on early life of Charles MacArthur.

Films as director, producer and writer (to 1936 in collaboration with Charles MacArthur): 1934: Crime Without Passion (+ *co-st*). 1935: The Scoundrel (+ *co-st*); Once in a Blue Moon. 1936: Soak the Rich (+ *co-st*). 1940: Until I Die. 1941: Angels over Broadway (+ *st*; *co-d* Lee Garmes). 1946: Specter of the Rose (+ *st*). 1952: Actors and Sin (+ *fst*; *co-d* Lee Garmes).

Films as writer in collaboration with Charles MacArthur include: 1931: The Front Page (*fpl*). 1934: Twentieth Century (+ *fpl*). 1935: Barbary Coast (+ *st*). 1939: Gunga Din (*st*); Wuthering Heights. 1940: His Girl Friday (*fpl*). 1950: Perfect Strangers (*fpl*). 1962: Billy Rose's Jumbo (*fn*).

Films as writer include: 1927: Underworld (*st*). 1930: The Great Gabbo (*st*). 1932: Scarface, Shame of the Nation (*st*). 1933: Hallelujah, I'm a Bum! (*st*); Design for Living; Viva Villa! 1935: The Florentine Dagger (*fn*). 1937: Nothing Sacred. 1938: The Goldwyn Follies (+ *st*). 1939: It's a Wonderful World (+ *co-st*); Lady of the Tropics (+ *st*). 1940: Comrade X (*co*). 1941: Lydia (*co*). 1942: Tales of Manhattan (*co-st/co-s*); The Black Swan (*co*); China Girl (+ *p*). 1945: Spellbound. 1946: Notorious. 1947: Ride the Pink Horse (*co*); Kiss of Death (*co*). 1948: The Miracle of the Bells (*co*). 1950: Whirlpool (*co*); Where the Sidewalk Ends. 1952: Monkey Business (*co*). 1954: Ulysses (*co*). 1955: The Indian Fighter (*co*). 1956: Miracle in the Rain (+ *fn*); The Iron Petticoat (+ *st*). 1957: Legend of the Lost (*co-st/co-s*); A Farewell to Arms. 1964: Circus World (*co*).

HECHT, Harold

Producer. New York 1907–
At 16 joined American Laboratory Theatre, New York; studied for 5 years under e.g. Richard Boleslawsky, Maria Ouspenskaya. Danced e.g. at Metropolitan Opera House and with Martha Graham. To Hollywood as dancer and dance director for Boleslawsky. Dance director on many films including

Horse Feathers (1932), *She Done Him Wrong* (1933). Broadway actor. 1934: joined the Federal Theater Project. When this ended, returned to Hollywood. Established a literary department for agent Nat Goldstone, later became his partner. World War II: US Army for 4 years. Returned to Hollywood: formed own agency for actors and directors. Spotted Burt Lancaster on New York stage in 'A Sound of Hunting' and signed him. 1947: Hecht and Lancaster formed Norma Productions, which developed, with James Hill, into the Hecht–Hill–Lancaster Company.

Films as producer include: 1950: The Flame and the Arrow. 1951: Ten Tall Men. 1952: The First Time; The Crimson Pirate. 1953: His Majesty O'Keefe. 1954: Apache. 1955: Marty; The Kentuckian. 1957: The Bachelor Party; Sweet Smell of Success (*ex-p*). 1958: Run Silent, Run Deep; Separate Tables. 1959: The Devil's Disciple. 1961: The Young Savages (*ex-p*). 1962: Bird Man of Alcatraz. 1963: Wild and Wonderful. 1964: Flight from Ashiya. 1965: Cat Ballou. 1967: The Way West.

HEFLIN, Van

Actor. Walters, Oklahoma 1910–71 Hollywood
New York stage debut in 'Mr Moneypenny'. Joined Hedgerow Theater. Yale Dramatic School. Denver stock company. Broadway understudy in 'Sailor Beware'. 1936: Spotted by Katherine Hepburn for his first film *A Woman Rebels*. 1936–39: Worked for RKO. Stage: 'The Philadelphia Story' with Katherine Hepburn. Radio. 1941–49: Worked for MGM. 1942: Oscar as supporting actor for *Johnny Eager*. World War II: US Army reaching Second Lieutenant. From 1951: worked for many companies. Also Italian films. Married actress Frances Neal (1942–68, divorced).

Films as actor include: 1937: The Outcasts of Poker Flat. 1940: Santa Fe Trail. 1941: The Feminine Touch; Johnny Eager; H. M. Pulham, Esq. 1942: Kid Glove Killer; Seven Sweethearts. 1943: Presenting Lily Mars. 1946: The Strange Love of Martha Ivers. 1947: Green Dolphin Street; Possessed. 1948: B. F.'s Daughter; Tap Roots; The Three Musketeers; Act of Violence. 1949: Madame Bovary; East Side, West Side. 1951: Weekend with Father; The Prowler. 1952: My Son John. 1953: Shane; Wings of the Hawk. 1954: Woman's World; Black Widow; Tanganyika; The Raid. 1955: Battle Cry. 1956: Patterns. 1957: 3.10 to Yuma. 1958: Gunman's Walk; La Tempestà. 1959: They Came to Cordura. 1960: Jovanka e l'altri. 1963: To Be A Man. 1965: The Greatest Story Ever Told; Once a Thief. 1966: Stagecoach.

HEIFITZ, Joseph

Director. Minsk, Russia 1905–
With Alexander Zarkhi, graduated from Leningrad Technicum of Screen Arts; they went to Sovkino in Leningrad, became scriptwriters in collaboration, ending with *Transport ognya* (1930). 1928: made their first film as directors in collaboration. Moved to Lenfilm. They co-directed several films in which Nikolai Cherkasov acted. 1945: assigned by Sergei Gerasimov to make *Razgrom Japonii*, documentary compilation on defeat of Japan. 1950: last film together *Ogni Baku*, unreleased for 8 years. Each subsequently directed films alone.

Films as director in collaboration with Alexander Zarkhi: 1928: Pesn o metallye – Song of Steel (+ *co-s/co-e*; *co-d* M. Schapiro, V. Granatman). 1930: Veter v Litso – Facing the Wind. 1931: Polden – Noon (+ *co-s*). 1933: Moia Rodina – My Fatherland (+ *co-s*); Goryachie Denecki – Hectic Days (+ *s*). 1937: Deputat Baltiki – Baltic Deputy (+ *co-s*); Chlen pravitelstva – The Great Beginning 1942: Yevo zovut Sukhe-Bator – His Name is Sukhe-Bator. 1944: Malachev Kirgan (+ *s*). 1947: Vo imya zhizni – In the Name of Life (+ *co-s*). 1948: Dragotsennye zerna – The Precious Seeds 1950: Ogni Baku – Flames over Baku (*r* 1958).

Films as solo director: 1954: Bolshaya Semya – The Big Family. 1956: Delo Rumyantseva – The Rumiantsev Case (+ *co-s*). 1958: Dorogoi Moi Chelovek – My Dear Fellow (+ *co-s*). 1960: Dama s sobachkoi – The Lady with a Little Dog (+ *s*). 1962: Gorizont – Horizon. 1963: Den schastya – A Day of Happiness (+ *co-s*). 1966: V gorodye S – In the Town of S (+ *s*).

HEISLER, Stuart

Director. Los Angeles 1894–
1913: started as editor with Famous Players–Lasky. 1914: moved to Sennett. Later, editor for Goldwyn at United Artists and for Adolf Zukor at Paramount. 1924: wrote story for The Silent Stranger. 1936: first film as director. 1937: directed some exteriors on John Ford's *The Hurricane*. To 1946: worked mainly for Paramount, later for many companies, notably Warners. 1951: *Storm Warning* co-written by Richard Brooks. 1955: remade Raoul Walsh's *High Sierra* (1941) as *I Died a Thousand Times*; this and *The Lone Ranger* (1956) produced by Willis Goldbeck for Warners. Also TV work.

Films as editor include: 1933: Roman Scandals. 1935: The Wedding Night; Men Without Names; Peter Ibbetson; Dark Angel. 1936: Klondike Annie; The Big Broadcast of 1937.

Films as director: 1936: Straight from the Shoulder; Poppy. 1937: The Hurricane (*uc, co-d* John Ford). 1940: The Biscuit Eater; God Gave Him a Dog. 1941: The Monster and the Girl; Among the Living. 1942: The Remarkable Andrew; The Glass Key. 1944: The Negro Soldier. 1945: Along Came Jones. 1946: Blue Skies; Vendetta (*r* 1950; *uc, co-d* Mel Ferrer, Howard Hughes, Preston Sturges, Max Ophüls). 1947: Smash Up – The Story of a Woman. 1949: Tulsa; Tokyo Joe. 1950: Chain Lightning; Dallas. 1951: Storm Warning; Journey into Light; Saturday Island – Island of Desire. 1953: The Star. 1954: Beachhead; This is My Love. 1955: I Died a Thousand Times. 1956: The Lone Ranger; The Burning Hills. 1962: Hitler.

HELLER, Otto

Cinematographer. Prague 1896–1970
Projectionist in Prague. 1928: first film as cinematographer *Der erste Küss*. Worked on large number of Czech films, many directed by Carl Lamac, a few by Martin Frič. 1937: to London.

Films as cinematographer include: 1926: Kreutzerova Sonata. 1929: Pater Vojtech. 1931: On a jeho sestra; To neznate Madimrsku. 1932: Anton Spelec, ostrostrelec; Kantor Idéal. 1933; Pobocnik jeho vysosti. 1934: Hej rup! 1935: Jedenacte Prikazani. 1936: Ulicka v raji. 1937: Svet patri nam; Filosofska Historie; The High Command (co). 1938: Krok do tmy. 1945: I Live in Grosvenor Square. 1949: Queen of Spades. 1950: The Woman With No Name. 1952: The Crimson Pirate. 1953: His Majesty O'Keefe. 1954: The Divided Heart. 1955: The Ladykillers. 1956: Richard III. 1957: Manuela. 1958: The Sheriff of Fractured Jaw. 1959: Ferry to Hong Kong. 1961: Victim. 1962: The Light in the Piazza. 1963: Woman of Straw. 1964: Masquerade. 1965: The Ipcress File. 1966: Alfie; Funeral in Berlin. 1968: Duffy. 1971: Bloomfield.

HELLINGER, Mark

Producer. New York 1903–47 Hollywood
1921: work in advertising. 1923–30: wrote for New York Daily News and Chicago Tribune syndicate. 1930–38: daily columnist for New York Daily Mirror and King Features Syndicate, wrote Sunday page for 'March Of Events' section in Hearst newspapers. 1932: Night Court for MGM based on his play in collaboration. Wrote last Ziegfeld Follies to be produced. 1934: wrote story of Broadway Bill for Columbia. 1939: story writer on The Roaring Twenties for Warners. 1940–41: associate producer, under Hal Wallis at Warners. 1941: first film as producer Rise and Shine for Fox. 1943: returned to Warners. 1944: war correspondent in South Pacific and India for Hearst newspapers. 1945–47: Warners. From 1946: Universal. Own company. Writings include 'Moon Over Broadway', 'The Ten Million', 'Hot Cha'. A New York theatre named after him.

Films as associate producer include: 1940: Torrid Zone; Brother Orchid (supervisor); They Drive By Night. 1941: The Strawberry Blonde; High Sierra; Manpower.

Films as producer include: 1941: Rise and Shine. 1942: Moontide. 1943: Thank Your Lucky Stars. 1945: The Horn Blows at Midnight. 1946: The Killers; Swell Guy. 1947: Brute Force. 1948: The Naked City.

HELLMAN, Lillian

Writer. New Orleans 1905–
1934: established as playwright by a successful production of 'The Children's Hour'; she adapted it as These Three (1936) and as The Children's Hour (1962). From 1935: writer for films, several based on own plays. Adaptations of her work by others include Watch on The Rhine (1943), Another Part of the Forest (1948), Toys in the Attic (1963). Autobiography 'An Unfinished Woman' (1969) describes her relationship with Dashiell Hammett.

Films as writer include: 1935: The Dark Angel (co). 1937: Dead End (+fco-pl). 1941: The Little Foxes (+fpl). 1943: The North Star (+st). 1946: The Searching Wind (+fpl). 1966: The Chase.

HELM, Brigitte

(Gisele Eve Schittenheim) Actress. Berlin 1907–
1927: without prior experience, chosen by Fritz Lang, who saw her in student production, for a leading role in her first film as actress Metropolis. 1927–32: directed

in 3 films by G. W. Pabst. 1931–32: made The City of Song and The Blue Danube in England. 1935: last film Ein idealer Gatte.

Films as actress include: 1927: Die Liebe der Jeanne Ney. 1928: Begierde; L'Argent. 1930: Alraune. 1931: The City of Song. 1932: Die Herrin von Atlantis; The Blue Danube. 1933: Der Läufer von Marathon.

HEMINGWAY, Ernest

Novelist. Oak Park, Illinois 1899–1961 San Francisco de Paula, Cuba
World War I: volunteer in American ambulance unit serving with French army; later with Italian arditi. Became European correspondent for Toronto Star; later Paris correspondent for William Randolph Hearst's Syndicated News Service. 1937–38: covered Spanish Civil War for paper Alliance; collaborated in making of Spanish Earth (1937), wrote and spoke American commentary. 1941: war correspondent in China. 1943: first film adaptation of his work. 1944–45: war correspondent in Europe. 1953: Honorary game warden, Kenya; Pulitzer Prize for 'The Old Man and the Sea'. 1954: Nobel Prize in Literature. 1961: suicide. 1964: publication of autobiographical 'A Moveable Feast'. Adapters include Dudley Nichols, William Faulkner, Casey Robinson (on 3 films) and Ben Hecht. To Have and Have Not (1945) remade as The Breaking Point (1950) and The Gun Runners (1958); The Killers (1946) remade 1964.

Films based on writings: 1943: For Whom the Bell Tolls. 1945: To Have and Have Not. 1946: The Killers. 1947: The Macomber Affair. 1950: Under My Skin; The Breaking Point. 1952: The Snows of Kilimanjaro. 1957: A Farewell to Arms; The Sun Also Rises. 1958: The Old Man and the Sea; The Gun Runners. 1962: Hemingway's Adventures of a Young Man. 1964: The Killers.

HEMMINGS, David

Actor. Guildford, Surrey 1941–
At 9, sang soprano in English Opera Group's production, 'The Turn of the Screw'. 1950–55: toured with the Group until his voice broke. Briefly at Epsom School of Art. 1956: first film as actor, for Children's Film Foundation. Some TV, including 'Out of the Unknown' series; sang in night club. 1961: acted in 'The Skyvers' at Royal Court Theatre. Other stage work. Second wife, actress Gayle Hunnicutt.

Films as actor include: 1957: Saint Joan. 1962: Some People. 1966: Blow-Up. 1967: Barbarella. 1968: The Charge of the Light Brigade; Only When I Larf. 1969: Alfred the Great.

HENNING JENSEN,
Astrid and Bjarne

Directors. Astrid: Copenhagen 1914–. Bjarne: Copenhagen 1908–
Bjarne studied in Germany, UK and Denmark; wrote for theatre. 1935–38: Astrid stage actress, in Copenhagen. 1940–45: Bjarne made films alone. 1940–60: most films in collaboration. Several films by Astrid alone, including 2 features. Most films are documentaries. Their son Lars Henning Jensen appeared in

Van Heflin (right) in Phil Karlson's Gunman's Walk. Storm Warning, *directed by Stuart Heisler.* *Rudolph Klein-Rogge and Brigitte Helm in* Metropolis.

several of their films. 1956: Astrid scripted Jorgen Storm–Peterson's *Nye venner*.

Bjarne: films as director and writer alone: 1940: Cykledrengene i Torvegraven. 1941: Hesten på kongens nytoru; Brunkul; Arbejdet kalder. 1942: Sukker – Sugar. 1943: Korn – Corn; Heste – Horses (co-s); Follet (co-s); Papir – Paper. 1945: Brigaden i Sverige; Frihedsfonden. 1946: Ditte Menneskebarn – Ditte—Child of Man. 1955: En Saefangst i Nordgronland (d only); Hvor Bjergene sejler – Where Mountains Float.

Bjarne: films as director with Astrid as co-writer and assistant: 1941: Christian IV som bygherre – Christian IV—Master Builder. 1943: Nar man kun er ung. 1944: De Danske Sydhavsoer. 1962: Kort är sommaren – Pan.

Films as directors and writers in collaboration: 1943: SOS kindtand – SOS Molars. 1945: Flyktinger Finner en hamn. 1947: Stemning i April; De Pokkers Ungers – Those Blasted Kids (co-s). 1948: Kristinus Bergman. 1950: Vesterhavsdrenge – Boys from the West Coast. 1953: Solstik (d only). 1954: Tivoligarden Spiller. 1960: Paw – Paw-Boy of Two Worlds.

Astrid: films as director alone: 1945: Danske Politi i Sverige (+ s). 1947: Denmark Grows Up (co-d Hagen Hasselbalch, Søren Melson). 1949: Palle Alene i verden – Palle Alone in the World (+ co-s). 1951: Kranes Konditori (+ s). 1952: Ukjent Mann (+ s). 1954: Balletens Born – Ballet Girl. 1955: Kaerlighed på kredit (+ s). 1966: Utro – Unfaithful. 1968: Mej och dej – Me and You.

HENREID, Paul

(Paul Julius von Hernfeid) Director and actor. Trieste 1908–
Acted on Vienna stage in Max Reinhardt's company. Acted in Austrian films. London stage, then (1939–40) British films, as Paul von Henreid. 1940: to USA. 1941: became American citizen, 1942: first American film *Joan of Paris* for RKO. To 1946: worked mainly for Warners. 1947–53: several studios, including United Artists and Columbia. 1952: first film as director, also produced and acted in it. From 1954: worked mainly for MGM. Also TV director.

Films as director: 1952: For Men Only (+ p/w). 1956: A Woman's Devotion (+ w). 1958: Live Fast, Die Young; Girls on the Loose. 1964: Dead Ringer – Dead Image. 1966: Blues for Lovers (+ co-s).

Films as actor include: 1937: Victoria the Great. 1939: Goodbye Mr Chips. 1940: Night Train to Munich. 1942: Joan of Paris; Now, Voyager. 1943: Casablanca. 1944: The Conspirators; In Our Time. 1945: The Spanish Main; Hollywood Canteen. 1946: Deception; Of Human Bondage; Devotion. 1947: Song of Love. 1949: Rope of Sand. 1953: Siren of Bagdad. 1954: Deep in My Heart. 1956: Meet Me in Las Vegas. 1957: Ten Thousand Bedrooms. 1959: Never So Few. 1962: The Four Horsemen of the Apocalypse. 1964: Operation Crossbow. 1969: The Madwoman of Chaillot.

HEPBURN, Audrey

Actress. Brussels 1929–
Educated in UK. World War II: in Occupied Holland: took part in shows to raise money for the Resistance. Studied ballet in Amsterdam. 1948: to UK, studied ballet at Marie Rambert's School. Musicals, revues. 1951: first film as actress, *Laughter in Paradise*. 1951: spotted by Ray Ventura for Broadway 'Gigi'; long run, also toured. 1953: Oscar as Best Actress for first American film *Roman Holiday*. 1954: on Broadway in 'Ondine' with Mel Ferrer, whom she married (divorced 1968).

Films as actress include: 1951: The Lavender Hill Mob. 1952: Secret People. 1954: Sabrina. 1956: War and Peace. 1957: Funny Face; Love in the Afternoon. 1959: The Nun's Story; Green Mansions. 1960: The Unforgiven. 1961: Breakfast at Tiffany's. 1962: The Children's Hour. 1963: Charade; Paris When It Sizzles. 1964: My Fair Lady. 1966: How to Steal a Million. 1967: Two for the Road; Wait Until Dark.

HEPBURN, Katherine

Actress. Hartford, Connecticut 1909–
1928: Bryn Mawr College. Studied acting with Frances Robinson-Duff, and dancing with Michael Mordkin. 1928: professional debut in 'The Czarina' in Baltimore and acted in 'Holiday'. 1932: first film *A Bill of Divorcement*. 1933: Oscar as Best Actress for *Morning Glory*. 1939: acted in 'The Philadelphia Story! 1952: London debut in 'The Millionairess'. 1955: Australian tour with Old Vic in 'The Taming of the Shrew'. 1970: on Broadway in 'Coco'. Acted in 8 films directed by George Cukor.

Films as actress include: 1933: Little Women. 1934: Spitfire. 1935: Alice Adams. 1936: Sylvia Scarlett; Mary of Scotland; A Woman Rebels. 1937: Quality Street; Stage Door. 1938: Bringing Up Baby; Holiday. 1940: The Philadelphia Story. 1942: Woman of the Year; Keeper of the Flame. 1944: Stage Door Canteen; Dragon Seed. 1946: Undercurrent; The Sea of Grass. 1947: Song of Love. 1948: State of the Union. 1949: Adam's Rib. 1951: The African Queen. 1952: Pat and Mike. 1955: Summer Madness. 1956: The Iron Petticoat; The Rainmaker. 1957: Desk Set. 1959: Suddenly Last Summer. 1962: Long Day's Journey into Night. 1967: Guess Who's Coming to Dinner. 1969: The Madwoman of Chaillot. 1971: The Trojan Woman.

HEPWORTH, Cecil Milton

Director and producer. Lambeth, London 1874–1953 Greenford, Middlesex
Assisted his father T. C. Hepworth, magic lantern lecturer. 1895: designed and patented hand-feed lamp for lanterns which was sold to R. W. Paul. 1896: assisted Birt Acres at first Royal Film Show; researched ignition of celluloid and published findings in Amateur Photographer. 1897: author of book 'Animated Photography'; adapted American Bioscope; joined Charles Urban's Warwick Trading Company. 1898: patented method of continuous developing, printing and drying; began as director, cinematographer, occasionally actor on short films. 1899: set up film processing laboratory at Walton-on-Thames. 1904: formed Hepworth Manufacturing company; with cousin Monty Wicks established Hepwix film studio. 1905–13: worked mainly as producer. 1910: patented the Vivaphone, gramophone synchronised to film; productions using it included *Speech by Bonar Law, Speech by F. E. Smith*. 1911: with W. G. Barker and A. C. Bromhead started British Board of Film Censors through Kinematograph Manufacturers Association. From 1914: directed features. 1916: Royal Show for *Comin' thro' the Rye*. 1919: formed Hepworth Picture Plays; capitalised in new studios and equipment. 1923: forced out of business by slump that affected whole British film industry. Lectured throughout UK with compilation of his early documentaries and comedies under title 'The Story of the Film'. 1924–52: employed by National Screen Services, making trailers and shorts. 1939–45: made advertising shorts for National Savings campaign, also Food Facts series. 1951: author of autobiography 'Came the Dawn'. Retired in 1952.

Short films as producer include: 1898: Express Trains (in a Railway Cutting); Ladies' "Tortoise" Race; Donkey Race; Procession of Prize Cattle; Driving Past of Four in Hands; Henley Regatta (6 parts); The Quarrelsome Anglers; Two Fools in a Canoe. 1899: Boat Race; English Soldier Tearing Down the Boer Flag; The Stolen Drink; Two Cockneys in a Canoe. 1900: Queen Victoria's Visit to Dublin; The Kiss; The Eccentric Dancer; City Imperial Volunteers Leaving for South Africa; Wiping Something Off the Slate; The Explosion of a Motor Car; How it Feels to be Run Over. 1901: Queen Victoria's Funeral (3 parts); The Coronation of King Edward VII; How the Burglar Tricked the Bobby; The Glutton's Nightmare. 1902: The "Call to Arms"; That Eternal Ping-Pong; "Peace with Honour". 1903: Alice in Wonderland; Firemen to the Rescue. 1904: A Den of Thieves. 1905: Rescued by Rover. 1914: Blind Fate (+ d). 1918: The Refugee (+ d); Tares (+ d/c).

Features as director and producer include: 1914: The Basilisk (+ s/c). 1915: Barnaby Rudge (+ ad); The Canker of Jealousy; Courtmartialled; The Man Who Stayed at Home (+ c); The Outrage; Sweet Lavender (+ c); The Baby on the Barge. 1916: Iris (+ c); Trelawney of the Wells; Annie Laurie; Sowing the Wind (p only); Comin' Thro' the Rye; The Marriage of William Ashe (+ c); Molly Bawn. 1917: The Cobweb; The American Heiress. 1918: Nearer My God to Thee; The Blindness of Fortune (p only); The Touch of the Child (+ ad); Boundary House (+ c). 1919: The Forest on the Hill; The Nature of the Beast (+ c); Sunken Rocks; Sheba. 1920: Anna the Adventuress; Alf's Button; Helen of Four Gates; Mrs Erricker's Reputation. 1921: Tinted Venus; Narrow Valley; Wild Heather; Tansy. 1923: Mist in the Valley; Strangling Threads; Comin' Thro' the Rye (rm 1916). 1927: The House of Marney (d only).

HERRMANN, Bernard

Composer. New York 1911–
New York University and Juilliard School. 1931–32: founded and conducted the New Chamber Orchestra. 1936: music for Orson Welles' Mercury Playhouse Theater. Conducted orchestras including the New York Philharmonic. Film scores, opera and ballet music. 1955–64: worked on all Alfred Hitchcock's films; played conductor in Albert Hall sequence of *The Man Who Knew Too Much* (1956); sound consultant on *The Birds* (1963). Also TV, including 'Alfred Hitchcock Presents' and 'The Virginian'. Oscar for score of *All That Money Can Buy* (1941).

Films as composer include: 1941: Citizen Kane. 1942:

The Magnificent Ambersons. 1945: Hangover Square. 1946: Anna and the King of Siam. 1947: The Ghost and Mrs Muir. 1951: The Day the Earth Stood Still; On Dangerous Ground. 1952: The Snows of Kilimanjaro; Five Fingers. 1953: King of the Khyber Rifles; White Witch Doctor. 1954: Garden of Evil; The Egyptian (co). 1955: Prince of Players; The Trouble With Harry; The Kentuckian. 1956: The Man Who Knew Too Much; The Man in the Gray Flannel Suit. 1957: The Wrong Man; A Hatful of Rain. 1958: Vertigo; The Naked and the Dead. 1959: North by Northwest; Blue Denim; Journey to the Centre of the Earth. 1960: Psycho. 1961: Mysterious Island; Cape Fear. 1962: Tender is the Night. 1964: Marnie. 1966: Fahrenheit 451. 1967: La Mariée était en noir. 1968: Twisted Nerve.

HERSHOLT, Jean

Actor. Copenhagen 1886–1956 Beverley Hills
Parents were Henry and Claire Hersholt of Danish Folk Theatre. Stage training at Dagmar Theatre, Copenhagen. Toured Scandinavia in repertory. 1906: appeared in the first Danish film, for Great Northern Film Company. 1912: in Canada and USA. 1914–15: under contract to Thomas Ince. 1916: first American film as actor Bullets and Brown Eyes. Prolific in silent period, when also director. Also radio work. Production executive.

Films as actor include: 1922: Tess of the Storm Country. 1923: Greed. 1925: Don Q, Son of Zorro. 1926: Stella Dallas; Don Q; The Old Soak. 1927: Alias the Deacon. 1928: The Student Prince in Old Heidelberg. 1929: Abie's Irish Rose. 1930: The Case of Sergeant Grischa; The Hell Harbor; Viennese Nights. 1931: Daybreak; Susan Lenox; Private Lives. 1932: Grand Hotel; Emma; Night Court; The Mask of Fu Manchu; Flesh. 1933: Christopher Bean; Dinner at Eight. 1934: Men in White; The Fountain. 1935: Mark of the Vampire. 1936: His Brother's Wife; Reunion; The Country Doctor; The Painted Veil; Sins of Man. 1937: Seventh Heaven; Heidi. 1938: Happy Landing; Alexander's Ragtime Band. 1943: Stage Door Canteen. 1949: Dancing in the Dark. 1955: Run for Cover.

HESTON, Charlton

Actor. Evanston, Illinois 1924–
Father a mill-operator. Drama training at Northwestern University. While a student, worked in daytime radio shows in Chicago. 1942: first film as actor David Bradley's Peer Gynt. 1944: married Lydia Clarke, later actress. 3 years in USAAF in Aleutians, mainly as radio operator in B-29s. Moved to New York. 1946: costume designer for Thomas Blair's Macbeth. With wife worked as director and actor at Thomas Wolfe Memorial Theater, Asheville, North Carolina. 1948: Broadway debut in 'Antony and Cleopatra'; summer stock in Pennsylvania. 1950: first Hollywood film Dark City. To 1958: films mainly for Paramount and Fox. Theatrical work includes 'State of the Union', 'The Glass Menagerie', 'Macbeth', 'Mister Roberts', 'Detective Story', 'A Man for All Seasons'. TV work includes 'Julius Caesar', 'Jane Eyre', 'Wuthering Heights', 'The Taming of the Shrew'. Oscar as Best Actor for Ben-Hur (1959).

Films as actor include: 1949: Julius Caesar. 1952: The Greatest Show on Earth; The Savage; Ruby Gentry. 1953: Arrowhead; Bad for Each Other; The President's Lady. 1954: The Naked Jungle. 1955: The Far Horizon; Lucy Gallant. 1956: The Ten Commandments. 1957: Three Violent People. 1958: Touch of Evil; The Buccaneer; The Big Country. 1959: Ben-Hur; The Wreck of the Mary Deare. 1961: El Cid. 1962: The Pigeon that Took Rome. 1963: Fifty-Five Days at Peking; Diamond Head. 1965: The Greatest Story Ever Told; Major Dundee; The War Lord; The Agony and the Ecstasy. 1966: Khartoum. 1967: Counterpoint. 1968: Planet of the Apes. 1970: Julius Caesar.

HICKOX, Sidney

Cinematographer. New York 1895–
1915: entered films as assistant cameraman at Biograph. 1916: cinematographer in New York. 1917: US Navy Air Service, chief photographer. 1925: to First National. Remained there when company taken over by Warners.

Films as cinematographer include: 1930: Top Speed. 1931: Too Young to Marry; The Last Flight. 1932: The Crowd Roars; A Bill of Divorcement; The Hatchet Man; Purchase Price; So Big. 1933: Frisco Jenny; Grand Slam; Central Airport; Lilly Turner; Mary Stevens, M.D.; Female; Sensation Hunters. 1934: Dames (co); Twenty Million Sweethearts; Heat Lightning; Circus Clown. 1935: The Right to Live; Bright Lights; Special Agent; I Found Stella Parish; Stranded; Living in Velvet. 1937: Stolen Holiday; Slim; San Quentin. 1938: A Slight Case of Murder; Men are Such Fools; My Bill. 1939: Women in the Wind; Indianapolis Speedway. 1941: The Wagons Roll At Night; Thieves Fall Out; Law of the Tropics. 1942: Gentleman Jim. 1943: Edge of Darkness; Northern Pursuit. 1944: Uncertain Glory. 1945: To Have and Have Not; The Horn Blows at Midnight. 1946: The Big Sleep; The Man I Love. 1947: Dark Passage; Cheyenne. 1948: Fighter Squadron (co); Silver River. 1949: One Sunday Afternoon (co). 1949: White Heat. 1950: Three Secrets. 1951: Distant Drums; Along the Great Divide; Lightning Strikes Twice. 1953: Blowing Wild. 1955: Them; Battle Cry.

HILDYARD, Jack

Cinematographer. London 1915–
1932: began as clapper-boy at Elstree. From 1946: cinematographer. 1963: worked on the British stage in Cleopatra. 1957: Oscar for The Bridge on the River Kwai.

Films as cinematographer include: 1946: School for Secrets; While the Sun Shines. 1947: Vice Versa. 1952: The Sound Barrier. 1954: Hobson's Choice. 1955: Summer Madness; The Deep, Blue Sea. 1956: Anastasia; The Living Idol. 1957: The Bridge on the River Kwai. 1958: The Gypsy and the Gentleman; The Journey. 1959: Suddenly Last Summer; The Devil's Disciple. 1960: The Sundowners; The Millionairess. 1962: The Road to Hong Kong. 1963: Cleopatra (co); Fifty-Five Days at Peking; The VIP's. 1964: Circus World; The Yellow Rolls-Royce. 1965: El Valle de los caidos. 1966: Battle of the Bulge; Modesty Blaise. 1967: Casino Royale; The Long Duel. 1968: Villa Rides.

Modesty Blaise, directed by Joseph Losey, photographed by Jack Hildyard.
Rod Taylor in Alfred Hitchcock's The Birds.
Alfred J. Hitchcock in his own film, Topaz.

HILL, George Roy

Director. Minneapolis, Minnesota 1922–
Music at Yale and Trinity College, Dublin. Acted in Cyril Cusack's repertory company. Returned to USA, toured with Margaret Webster's Shakespearian company. World War II: military service in Pacific. Korean War: 2 years service, reaching Major. 1954: acted in own TV play 'My Brother's Keeper' about Korean War. For a year adapted scripts and novels for TV; became assistant director. 1956: directed, wrote, produced 'A Night to Remember' for TV. TV work includes 'The Helen Morgan Story', 'A Child of Our Time', 'Judgment at Nuremberg'. 1957: first Broadway play as director 'Look Homeward Angel'. Theatrical work as director includes 'The Gang's All Here', 'Green Willow', 'Moon on a Rainbow Shawl' and 'Period of Adjustment'. 1962: first film as director.

Films as director: 1962: Period of Adjustment. 1963: Toys in the Attic. 1964: The World of Henry Orient. 1966: Hawaii. 1967: Thoroughly Modern Millie. 1969: Butch Cassidy and the Sundance Kid.

HITCHCOCK, Alfred J.

Director. London 1899–
St Ignatius' College. Then trained as engineer specialising in mechanical drawing. Technical senior clerk, then in advertising department of W. T. Henley Telegraph Company. 1920: joined Famous Players–Lasky at their newly-opened British studio in Islington, writing and designing titles. 1922: completed the direction of *Always Tell Your Wife* in collaboration with Seymour Hicks, when the director was taken ill; retained at Islington when Famous Players–Lasky stopped production and Michael Balcon formed independent company there. 1922: began production and direction on *Number Thirteen*, not completed. Assistant director and designer to Graham Cutts on *Woman to Woman* (1922), *The White Shadow* (1923), *The Passionate Adventure* (1924), *The Blackguard* (1925), *The Prude's Fall* (1925); also scriptwriter (in collaboration on first 2). 1925: first completed film as director, *The Pleasure Garden*. Next 4 films produced by Michael Balcon at Islington. 1927: to Elstree Studios; John Maxwell produced his next films until 1932. *Blackmail* (1929) started as silent, but released also in sound version. 1932: produced *Lord Camber's Ladies*. 1934–39: directing at Lime Grove and Elstree Studios. 1940: to Hollywood to work for David O. Selznick. 1948–54: with Warners; co-produced *Rope* and *Under Capricorn* with Sidney Bernstein. 1954–60: films released through Paramount, except *The Wrong Man* (Warners), *North by Northwest* (MGM). Since 1963: released through Universal. 1971: made Chevalier de Légion d'Honneur. 1955: began series of half-hour filmed TV shows, 'Alfred Hitchcock Presents', as executive producer and host; directed some episodes. Formed company, Shamley Productions, which made 2 series of 1-hour programmes, 'Suspicion' (1957) and series for 'Ford Star Time' (1960); Hitchcock directed 1 programme in each. 1962: expanded his half-hour series as 'The Alfred Hitchcock Hour'. Married to Alma Reville (1926), assistant or writer on many of his films.

Films as director: 1922: Always Tell Your Wife (co-d Seymour Hicks). 1925: The Pleasure Garden. 1926: The Mountain Eagle; The Lodger (+ co-s). 1927: Downhill; Easy Virtue; The Ring (+ co-s). 1928: The Farmer's Wife (+ ad); Champagne (+ ad). 1929: The Manxman; Blackmail (+ co-s). 1930: Elstree Calling (co-d Adrian Brunel); Juno and the Paycock (+ co-s); Murder. 1931: The Skin Game (+ s). 1932: Rich and Strange; Number Seventeen (+ s). 1933: Waltzes from Vienna. 1934: The Man Who Knew Too Much. 1935: The Thirty-Nine Steps. 1936: The Secret Agent; Sabotage – A Woman Alone. 1937: Young and Innocent – A Girl Was Young. 1938: The Lady Vanishes. 1939: Jamaica Inn. 1940: Rebecca; Foreign Correspondent. 1941: Mr and Mrs Smith; Suspicion. 1942: Saboteur (+ story). 1943: Shadow of a Doubt. 1944: Lifeboat; Bon Voyage; Aventure Malgache (ur). 1945: Spellbound. 1947: The Paradine Case.

Films as director and producer: 1921: Number Thirteen (+ e; uf). 1946: Notorious (+ st). 1948: Rope (co-p). 1949: Under Capricorn (co-p). 1950: Stage Fright. 1951: Strangers on a Train. 1953: I Confess. 1954: Dial M for Murder; Rear Window. 1955: To Catch a Thief. 1956: The Trouble with Harry; The Man Who Knew Too Much. 1957: The Wrong Man. 1958: Vertigo. 1959: North by Northwest. 1960: Psycho. 1963: The Birds. 1964: Marnie. 1966: Torn Curtain. 1969: Topaz.

HOCH, Winton C.

Cinematographer
Studied at California Institute of Technology and (1931); worked as research physicist. Lens technician at Technicolor; helped research and design 3-colour system. 1941: first film as cinematographer. Worked freelance. Oscars for colour cinematography: *Joan of Arc* (1948, with Joseph Valentine and William V. Skall), *She Wore a Yellow Ribbon* (1949) and *The Quiet Man* (1952, with Archie Stout).

Films as cinematographer include: 1941: Dive Bomber (co). 1942: Captains of the Clouds (co). 1948: Tap Roots (co); Three Godfathers; Joan of Arc (co). 1949: Tulsa; She Wore a Yellow Ribbon. 1950: Halls of Montezuma (co). 1951: Bird of Paradise; Jet Pilot (r 1957). 1952: The Quiet Man (co). 1953: Return to Paradise. 1955: Mister Roberts. 1956: The Searchers. 1957: The Young Land (co). 1959: This Earth is Mine (co); The Big Circus. 1960: The Lost World. 1962: Sergeants 3. 1964: Robinson Crusoe on Mars. 1968: The Green Berets.

HOLDEN, William

(William Franklin Beedle, Jr.) Actor. O'Fallon, Illinois 1918–
Studied radio drama, then worked in radio. 1937: stage debut in 'Manya' in Pasadena; offered Paramount contract. 1939: starred in first film as actor *Golden Boy*. 1943–45: US Air Force, reaching Lieutenant. Worked mainly for Paramount and Columbia. Formed own company. Vice President, Screen Actors' Guild. Married to actress Brenda Marshall since 1941. 1953: Oscar as Best Actor for *Stalag 17*.

Films as actor include: 1939: Invisible Stripes. 1940: Our Town; Arizona. 1941: I Wanted Wings; Texas. 1942: The Fleet's In; The Remarkable Andrew. 1947: Variety Girl; Blaze of Noon. 1948: The Man from Colorado; Apartment for Peggy; Rachel and the Stranger. 1949: The Dark Past; Miss Grant Takes Richmond. 1950: Dear Wife; Sunset Boulevard; Union Station. 1951: Born Yesterday; Submarine Command; Force of Arms; Boots Malone. 1952: The Turning Point. 1953: Forever Female; Stalag 17; The Moon is Blue; Escape from Fort Bravo. 1954: The Country Girl; Executive Suite; Sabrina. 1955: The Bridges at Toko-Ri; Love is a Many-Splendored Thing. 1956: Picnic; The Proud and the Profane; Toward the Unknown. 1957: The Bridge on the River Kwai. 1958: The Key. 1959: The Horse Soldiers. 1960: The World of Suzie Wong. 1961: The Counterfeit Traitor. 1962: Satan Never Sleeps; The Longest Day; The Lion. 1963: Paris When It Sizzles; The Seventh Dawn. 1966: Alvarez Kelly. 1967: Casino Royale. 1968: The Devil's Brigade. 1969: The Wild Bunch; The Christmas Tree. 1971: Wild Rovers.

HOLLAENDER, Frederich

(Frederick Hollander in USA) Composer. London 1896–
German parents. Academy of Music, Berlin. Then composer for Max Reinhardt stage productions, also revues e.g. 'Tingel Tangel'; songwriter. From 1930: music for films. 1933: directed, and wrote music for *Ich und die Kaiserin* to USA; became composer for Paramount.

Films as composer include: 1930: Der blaue Engel (songs); Der Andere (co). 1931: Der Mann der seinen Mörder sucht (co). 1932: Stürme der Leidenschaft (co). 1933: Ich und die Kaiserin (+ d). 1936: Desire. 1937: Angel (song); One Hundred Men and a Girl (co-songs). 1941: Footsteps in the Dark. 1945: Conflict. 1948: A Foreign Affair. 1949: Caught. 1951: Born Yesterday. 1954: It Should Happen to You. 1955: We're No Angels.

HOLLIDAY, Judy

(Judith Tuvim) Actress. New York 1921–65
1939–44: originated and appeared in cabaret group The Revuers, with Adolph Green and Betty Comden. 1944: first film as actress *Greenwich Village*. 1945: New York stage debut in 'Kiss Them for Me'. Stage work includes 'Born Yesterday' (1946 and 1951), 'Dream Girl', 'Bells are Ringing', 'Hot Spot'. 1950–56: worked for Columbia. Married musician David Oppenheim (1948–58, divorced). 1950: Oscar as Best Actress for *Born Yesterday*.

Films as actress include: 1944: Something for the Boys; Winged Victory. 1949: Adam's Rib. 1950: Born Yesterday. 1952: The Marrying Kind. 1954: It Should Happen to You; Phffft. 1956: The Solid Gold Cadillac. 1957: Full of Life. 1960: Bells are Ringing.

HOLT, Seth

Director. Palestine 1923–71 London
Actor in repertory at Liverpool, then Bideford, Devon. 1942: to Strand Films as assistant editor on documentaries. To Ealing as first assistant editor at invitation of brother-in-law Robert Hamer. Cut Antarctic sequence in *Scott of the Antarctic* (1948), worked on Hamer's *Kind Hearts and Coronets* (1949). Edited Hammer's *The Spider and the Fly* (1949), 4 films directed by Charles Crichton including *The Titfield Thunderbolt* (1953, also 2nd-unit director), and Alexander MacKendrick's *Mandy* (1952). From 1955: associate producer on films

scripted by William Rose e.g. *The Ladykillers* (1955), *The Man in the Sky* (1957). 1958: first film as director, scripted in collaboration with Kenneth Tynan. 1960: When Ealing closed, returned to editing e.g. *The Battle of the Sexes, Saturday Night and Sunday Morning*, and at Tony Richardson's request re-edited *The Entertainer*. Director and editor on TV series; also commercials. 1961: made *Taste of Fear* for Hammer. 1965: bought original script of *If...*; worked on it before offering it to Lindsay Anderson. 1968: shot two-thirds of *Monsieur Lecoq* for Columbia who abandoned it. Began independent Italian production *Diabolique*, also abandoned. Own production company Holtmallinson; executive producer on documentary *Barbed Water*.

Films as director: 1958: Nowhere to Go (+ *co-s*). 1961: Taste of Fear. 1964: Station 6—Sahara – Endstation 13 Sahara. 1965: The Nanny. 1967: Escape Route – Danger Route. 1971: Blood From The Mummy's Tomb (*co-d* Michael Carreras, *uc*).

HONEGGER, Arthur

Composer. Le Havre, France 1892–1955 Paris
Swiss parentage. Member of Groupe des Six. From 1922: composed for cinema, at first accompaniment for silents. His oratorio 'Jeanne au bûcher' based on Paul Claudel's play, filmed by Roberto Rossellini as *Giovanna d'Arco al rogo* (1954). Played role of composer in *Un Revenant*. (1946). Documentary *Arthur Honegger* (1955) directed by Georges Rouquier.

Films as composer include: 1922: La Roue. 1923: Fait Divers. 1926: Napoléon vu par Abel Gance. 1931: L'Idée. 1935: L'Équipage. 1936: Mayerling. 1937: Mademoiselle Docteur; La Citadelle du silence (*co*). 1938: Pygmalion. 1945: Les Démons de l'aube (*co*).

HOPE, Bob

(Leslie Townes Hope) Actor. London 1903 –
Vaudeville double-act with George Byrne; tours. 1927: Broadway debut in 'The Sidewalks of New York'. Solo, cabaret and toured in vaudeville. 1934: acted in 'Roberta'. From 1934: radio. 1935–36: on Broadway in 'Ziegfeld Follies' and with Jimmy Durante and Ethel Merman in 'Red, Hot and Blue'. Short films, then first feature as actor *The Big Broadcast of 1938* (1938). Wartime tours. To 1956: all films for Paramount except *The Road to Morocco* (1942). 1958: acted in 'Roberta'. Books: 'They Got Me Covered' (1941), 'I Never Left Home' (1944), 'So This is Peace' (1946), 'Have Tux, Will Travel' (1955), 'I Owe Russia $1200' (1963).

Films as actor include: 1938: College Swing; Give Me a Sailor. 1939: Never Say Die; the Cat and the Canary. 1940: The Ghost Breakers; Road to Singapore. 1941: Road to Zanzibar; Caught in the Draft. 1942: Road to Morocco; Star Spangled Rhythm; They Got Me Covered. 1943: Let's Face It. 1946: Monsieur Beaucaire. 1947: My Favorite Brunette; Road to Rio. 1948: The Paleface. 1950: Fancy Pants. 1951: The Lemon Drop Kid; My Favorite Spy. 1952: Son of Paleface. 1953: Off Limits; Here Come the Girls. 1954: Casanova's Big Night. 1955: The Seven Little Foys. 1956: That Certain Feeling; The Iron Petticoat. 1957: Beau James. 1958: Paris Holiday. 1959: Alias Jesse James. 1960: The Facts of Life. 1961: Bachelor in Paradise. 1962: The Road to Hong Kong. 1963:

Critic's Choice; Call Me Bwana. 1964: A Global Affair. 1966: Boy, Did I Get a Wrong Number! 1967: 8 on the Lam. 1968: The Private Navy of Sergeant O'Farrell. 1969: How to Commit Marriage.

HOPKINS, Kenyon

Composer. Coffeeville, Kansas
Son of a minister. Oberlin College, Temple University and Contemporary School of Music in New York. US Navy for 3 years. Composed works for concert hall while working as arranger for several orchestras in New York. 1951–61: chief composer-arranger for Radio City Music Hall; worked on several TV series. More than 20 record albums of jazz arrangements and original orchestral suites. Became head of music department for CBS TV; resigned in 1964 to return to films.

Films as composer include: 1957: Twelve Angry Men; The Strange One. 1959: The Fugitive Kind. 1960: Wild River. 1961: Wild in the Country; The Hustler. 1963: The Yellow Canary; Lilith. 1967: Doctor, You've Got to be Kidding. 1968: The First Time.

HOPKINS, Miriam

Actress. Bainbridge, Georgia 1902 –
Syracuse University. Chorus dancer, vaudeville. From 1923: stage actress: 'An American Tragedy', 'Flight', 'Lysistrata'. 1929: London debut in 'The Bachelor Father'. 1930: first film as actress *Fast and Loose*. 1933: acted in 'Jezebel'. 1934: returned to vaudeville. 1942: replaced Tallulah Bankhead in 'The Skin of Our Teeth'. Also acted in 'The Perfect Marriage', 'Laura', 'The Heiress', 'Hay Fever'. 1957–60: 'Look Homeward, Angel'. Married Anatole Litvak (1937–39, divorced).

Films as actress include: 1931: The Smiling Lieutenant. 1932: Dr Jekyll and Mr Hyde; Two Kinds of Women; The World and the Flesh; Trouble in Paradise. 1933: Design for Living; The Strangler's Return. 1934: The Richest Girl in the World. 1935: Becky Sharp; Splendor; Barbary Coast. 1936: These Three. 1937: The Woman I Love. 1939: The Old Maid. 1940: Virginia City; The Lady with Red Hair. 1942: A Gentleman After Dark. 1943: Old Acquaintance. 1949: The Heiress. 1951: The Mating Season. 1952: The Outcasts of Poker Flat; Carrie. 1962: The Children's Hour. 1966: The Chase.

HOPPER, Hedda

(Elda Furry) Journalist. Hollidaysburg, Pennsylvania 1890–1966 Los Angeles
Quaker family; father a butcher. Chorus girl then acted in 6 plays on Broadway. Married DeWolf Hopper who named her Hedda; to Hollywood with him in 1916. Occasional appearances in films. 1935: worked for Elizabeth Arden salon; acted in 'Dinner at Eight' in Los Angeles. From 1936: wrote Hollywood column syndicated by 'Chicago Tribune', 'New York Daily News' and others. Monthly appearances in Art Linklater TV Show. World War II: toured as entertainer to servicemen. 1960: when Nikita Krushchev visited Hollywood, she wrote that she would not attend a luncheon honouring a communist; only columnist to stay away. 2 autobiographies, 'From Under My Hat' (1952), 'The Whole Truth and Nothing But' (1963). Son is actor William Hopper.

Judy Holliday (centre) does a take-off of Marlon Brando in Vincente Minnelli's Bells are Ringing.
Carroll Baker in Seth Holt's Station 6 – Sahara.
Lionel Jeffries, Anita Ekberg and Bob Hope in Call Me Bwana, *directed by Gordon Douglas.*

Films as actress include: 1926: Don Juan. 1927: Adam and Evil. 1933: Pilgrimage. 1935: Alice Adams. 1939: The Women. 1941: I Wanted Wings. 1942: Reap the Wild Wind. 1950: Sunset Boulevard. 1964: The Patsy.

HORNER, Harry

Art director. Czechoslovakia 1910–
Architecture at Vienna University. While architect in Vienna, met Max Reinhardt, became actor for him. 1935: to US as his assistant on pageant, 'The Eternal Road'. Stage designer in New York. 1940: first film credit on *Our Town* with William Cameron Menzies. 1942–45: US Army. 1949: Oscar for best black and white art direction (with John Meehan) for *The Heiress*. Directed several low-budget films. Now in Canada.

Films as art director include: 1950: Born Yesterday (co-des). 1959: The Wonderful Country. 1961: The Hustler (des). 1964: The Luck of Ginger Coffey.

Films as director: 1952 Beware, My Lovely; Red Planet Mars. 1953: Vicki. 1954: New Faces. 1955: A Life in the Balance 1956: Man from Del Rio; The Wild Party.

HORTON, Edward Everett

Actor. New York 1888–1971 Encino, California
1908–09: Polytechnic Institute, Brooklyn; Columbia College. Actor-manager in theatre. Actor-producer with brother W. D. Horton on Hollywood stage. Stage work includes 'Springtime for Henry', 'The Reluctant Debutante', 'Roberta'. In films from 1918. Sound films mainly for Paramount, Warners, RKO, MGM.

Films as actor include: 1923: Ruggles of Red Gap; To the Ladies. 1925: Marry Me; Beggar on Horseback. 1926: La Bohème. 1928: The Terror. 1930: Wide Open; Once a Gentleman. 1931: Reaching For the Moon; The Front Page; Smart Woman. 1932: Trouble in Paradise; Roar of the Dragon. 1933: Alice in Wonderland; Design for Living. 1934: The Merry Widow; The Gay Divorcee. 1935: The Devil is a Woman; In Caliente; Little Big Shot; Top Hat. 1936: Heart's Dividend; The Man in the Mirror. 1937: The King and the Chorus Girl; The Perfect Specimen; Danger—Love at Work; Lost Horizon; Angel; The Great Garrick; Hitting a New High. 1938: Bluebeard's Eighth Wife; College Swing; Holiday. 1939: That's Right You're Wrong. 1941: Ziegfeld Girl. 1942: I Married an Angel; The Magnificent Dope; Thank Your Lucky Stars. 1943: Forever and a Day; The Gang's All Here. 1944: Summer Storm; Arsenic and Old Lace. 1946: Cinderella Jones. 1948: All My Sons. 1957: The Story of Mankind. 1961: Pocketful of Miracles. 1963: It's a Mad, Mad, Mad, Mad World. 1964: Sex and the Single Girl.

HOSSEIN, Robert

Actor and director. Paris 1927–
René Simon's Drama School, then stage actor. 2 years as stage director at Théâtre Grand Guignol where productions included 'Les Salauds vont en enfer'. Wrote 2 plays, 'Les Voyous', 'Responsabilité Limitée'. 1954: first film as actor, *Du Rififi chez les hommes*. 1955: began as director, also writing his own scripts.

Was married to Marina Vlady. Father a composer, wrote music for *Les Salauds vont en enfer* (1955).

Films as actor include: 1957: Sait-on jamais; Méfiez-vous, fillettes. 1961: Madame Sans-Gêne. 1962: Le Repos du guerrier. 1966: La Musica. 1971: Le Casse.

Films as director, writer and actor: 1955: Les Salauds vont en enfer. 1956: Pardonnez nos offenses. 1958: Toi . . . le venin. 1959: La Nuit des espions; Les Scélérats. 1960: Le Goût de la violence. 1961: Le Jeu de la verité. 1963: La Mort d'un tueur. 1964: Les Yeux Cernés; Le Vampire de Düsseldorf. 1967: J'ai tué Raspoutine. 1968: Une Corde . . . un colt. 1970: Point de Chute (co-s).

HOUSEMAN, John

Producer. Bucharest, Rumania c. 1903–
Father a French grain merchant, mother British. Educated in France and UK. Before becoming writer, worked as farm hand and bank clerk in Argentina and then in grain business in London and various parts of USA. 1934: directed his first Broadway show, collaborating with Virgil Thompson on Gertrude Stein's 'Four Saints in Three Acts'. Then directed Ibsen's 'Lady From the Sea' and the Theatre Guild production of 'Valley Forge'. 1935: produced 'Panic' with Orson Welles in lead, and 'Dr Faustus' directed by Welles. 1937: Houseman and Welles founded Mercury Theater. Also Mercury Theater radio programmes for CBS including Welles's version of 'War of the Worlds'. 1941: to Hollywood as vice-president of David O. Selznick Productions. Resigned 10 days after Pearl Harbour to join OWI as chief of Overseas Radio Programmes. 1943: producer for Paramount, later for RKO. On Broadway directed 'Lute Song' and produced 1950 'King Lear' revival. Produced and directed one of the first experimental TV programmes for CBS: 'Sorry, Wrong Number'. 1937–38: associate professor of English at Vassar. 1951: lecturer in drama at Barnard College. Co-author of Broadway play 'In Time To Come' (filmed as *Wilson*, 1944). Produced TV series 'The Seven Lively Arts' and 'Playhouse 90'.

Films as producer include: 1948: They Live By Night; Letter From an Unknown Woman. 1951: On Dangerous Ground. 1952: The Bad and the Beautiful. 1953: Julius Caesar. 1954: Executive Suite. 1955: Moonfleet; The Cobweb. 1956: Lust for Life. 1962: All Fall Down; Two Weeks in Another Town.

HOWARD, Leslie

(Leslie Howard Stainer) Actor and director. London 1893–1943 Bay of Biscay
Dulwich College. Started in theatre in touring company of 'Peg o' my Heart'. 1917: first film as actor *The Happy Warrior*. 1918–19: own company produced 3 unsuccessful shorts. Stage work in UK and USA includes 'Charley's Aunt', 'The Green Hat', 'The Animal Kingdom'. 1930: first American film as actor *Outward Bound* for Warners. 1932: first British film since 1920, *Service for Ladies*. 1933: turned down part opposite Garbo in *Queen Christina*. American films mainly for MGM; also worked for Pickford, Fox, RKO, First National, United Artists. 1938: directed *Pygmalion* in collaboration with Anthony Asquith. From *Intermezzo* (1939) which he associate produced, all films British. Plane shot down as returning to London.

Films as actor include: 1931: Never the Twain Shall Meet; A Free Soul; Five and Ten. 1932: Service for Ladies; Smilin' Through. 1933: Secrets; Berkeley Square. 1934: Of Human Bondage; British Agent. 1936: The Petrified Forest; Romeo and Juliet. 1937: It's Love I'm After; Stand-In. 1939: Gone With the Wind; Intermezzo (+ as-p). 1941: 49th Parallel.

Films as director and actor: 1938: Pygmalion (co-d Anthony Asquith). 1941: Pimpernel Smith – Mister V (+ p). 1942: The first of the Few – Spitfire. 1943: The Gentle Sex (co-d only; co-d Maurice Elvey).

HOWARD, Trevor

Actor. Margate, England 1916–
Early years in Ceylon, USA, Canada. Educated in USA and England. RADA. 1934: stage debut 'Revolt in a Reformatory'. World War II service: 6th Airborne Division, invalided out (1943). 1945: first film *The Way Ahead*. Theatrical work includes 'The Rivals', 'Crime and Punishment', 'French Without Tears', 'The Devil's General', 'The Cherry Orchard'. Married actress Helen Cherry.

Films as actor include: 1945: Brief Encounter. 1946: I See a Dark Stranger; Green for Danger. 1947: So Well Remembered; They Made Me a Fugitive. 1949: The Passionate Friends; The Third Man. 1950: Odette; The Golden Salamander; The Clouded Yellow. 1951: Outcast of the Islands. 1952: The Gift Horse. 1953: La Mano dello straniero. 1956: Cockleshell Heroes; Around the World in 80 Days. 1957: Manuela. 1958: The Key; Roots of Heaven. 1959: Moment of Danger. 1960: Sons and Lovers. 1962: Mutiny on the Bounty; The Lion. 1963: The Man in the Middle. 1964: Father Goose; Operation Crossbow. 1965: Von Ryans Express; The Liquidator. 1966: Triple Cross. 1967: The Long Duel; Pretty Polly. 1968: The Charge of The Light Brigade. 1969: The Battle of Britain. 1970: Ryan's Daughter. 1971: The Night Visitor; Kidnapped.

HOWARD, William K.

Director. St Mary's, Ohio 1899–1954 Hollywood
Engineering and law at Ohio State University. Worked as exhibitor with film distributor in Cincinnati, then sales manager for Vitagraph in Minnesota. World War I: in American Expeditionary Force. 1919: to Hollywood after failing to find film work in New York; sales adviser for Universal. 1920: worked as assistant director for Universal. 1921: first film as director for Fox. Later contracts with De Mille's Producers Distributing Corporation (1926–27), Fox (1928–33), MGM (1935–36). In early 1930s used a regular team of cinematographer, editor, art director; also frequently worked with James Wong Howe. 1937: films in UK. 1945: offered a series of subjects by Republic: directed only one, his last film.

Films as director: 1921: What Love Will Do. 1922: Extra! Extra!; Deserted at the Altar (co-d Al Kelley); Lucky Dan. 1923: Danger Ahead; The Fourth Musketeer; Captain Fly-by-Night; Let's Go. 1924: The Border Legion; East of Broadway. 1925: Code of the West; The Light of Western Stars; The Thundering Herd. 1926: Volcano; Red Dice; Bachelor Brides; Gigolo. 1927: White Gold; The Main Event. 1928: A Ship Comes In; The River Pirate. 1929: Christina; The

Valiant; Love, Live and Laugh. 1930: Good Intentions; Scotland Yard. 1931: Don't Bet on Women; Transatlantic; Surrender. 1932: The Trial of Vivienne Ware; The First Year; Sherlock Holmes. 1933: The Power and the Glory. 1934: The Cat and the Fiddle; This Side of Heaven; Evelyn Prentice. 1935: Vanessa; Rendezvous; Mary Burns, Fugitive. 1936: The Princess Comes Across. 1937: Fire Over England; The Squeaker – Murder on Diamond Row. 1939: Back Door to Heaven (+ p/s). 1940: Money and the Woman. 1941: Bullets for O'Hara. 1942: Klondike Fury. 1943: Johnny Come Lately – Johnny Vagabond. 1944: When the Lights Go on Again. 1945: A Guy Could Change (+ as-p).

HOWE, James Wong

(Wong Tung Jim) Cinematographer. Kwantung, China 1899–
1904: father brought family to USA. 1914: father died; sent to live with foster parents, ran away. Unsuccessful boxer, then briefly delivery boy and bell-hop at Beverly Hills hotel before hired by Lasky Studio: in cutting rooms, then slateboy. 3rd camera assistant for 3 years, camera operator for 3 years. 1922: first film as cinematographer *Drums of Fate*. 1929: visited China; on return found work difficult to obtain. 1930: produced, directed and photographed a film in spare time. 1936: shot 3 films in England. 1938: his first colour film, *The Adventures of Tom Sawyer*, caused him to be banned by Technicolor from using process for 3 years, because used only a fourth of the recommended lighting in cave scenes. 1938–47: Warner's contract. 1948: freelance; to China to shoot background material for *Rickshaw Boy*, which he planned to produce, direct and photograph. Communist advance led him to abandon project and return to US. Directed *Go Man Go* (1954), co-directed *The Invisible Avenger* (1957) with John Sledge; produced, directed and photographed 16mm short about Chinese–American painter *The World of Dong Kingman*. Oscar for black and white cinematography on *The Rose Tattoo* (1955).

Films as cinematographer include: 1927: The Rough Riders. 1931: The Criminal Code; The Yellow Ticket. 1933: Walking Down Broadway (ur). 1934: Viva Villa! (co). 1935: Mark of The Vampire. 1937: Under the Red Robe (co). 1938: The Adventures of Tom Sawyer. 1941: Strawberry Blonde. 1943: Hangmen Also Die!; Air Force; The North Star. 1945: Counter-attack; Objective Burma. 1947: Pursued; Body and Soul. 1950: The Baron of Arizona. 1951: The Brave Bulls (co). 1953: Come Back, Little Sheba; Main Street to Broadway. 1955: The Rose Tattoo. 1956: Picnic. 1957: Sweet Smell of Success. 1958: The Old Man and the Sea (co); Bell, Book and Candle. 1960: Song Without End. 1963: Hud. 1964: The Outrage. 1966: Seconds. 1967: Hombre. 1968: The Molly Maguires.

HOYNINGEN-HUENE, George

Colour consultant.   –1968 Hollywood
Successful photographer in Paris in 1930s and '40s. To Hollywood on photographic project: book of photographs on film-making not published. 1954–61: employed as colour consultant, on films of George Cukor. Also work in interior decoration.

Films as colour consultant: 1954: A Star is Born.

1955: Bhowani Junction. 1957: Les Girls. 1959: Heller in Pink Tights (co). 1960: Let's Make Love. 1961: The Chapman Report.

HUBLEY, John *and* Faith

Animators. John: Marinette, Wisconsin 1914–
John: Art Center School, Los Angeles. To 1941: worked for Disney. 1941–45: made training films for US Air Force. 1945–55: at UPA e.g. created 'Mr Magoo' series. 1947: collaborated on story of *Brotherhood of Man*. 1952: animation sequence for *The Fourposter*. Faith: film editor, music editor, script supervisor, e.g. to James Wong Howe on *Go Man Go* (1954) and to Sidney Lumet on *Twelve Angry Men* (1957) and *That Kind of Woman* (1959). 1955: they formed own production company. John became visual consultant to Channel 13 in New York. 1961: *Of Stars and Men* is part of full-length film. 1966: John became president of ASIFA (International Association of Animated Film-Makers). Also work as designers on features, titling, commercials. Oscars for *Moonbird* (1959), *The Hole* (1962).

Films as director (John): 1948: Robin Hoodlum. 1949: The Magic Flute; The Ragtime Bear. 1950: Trouble Indemnity. 1951: Gerald McBoing Boing (co). 1952: Rooty Toot Toot. 1958: A Date with Dizzy. 1961: Children of the Sun. 1962: The Hole. 1971: Eggs.

Films in collaboration (John and Faith): 1956: Adventures of an Asterisk. 1957: Harlem Wednesday. 1958: Tender Game. 1959: Moonbird. 1961: Of Stars and Men. 1964: The Hat. 1966: Herb Alpert and the Tiajuana Brass Double Feature. 1968: Windy Day. 1969: Of Men and Demons.

HUDSON, Rock

(Roy Scherer Fitzgerald, Jr) Actor. Winnetka, Illinois 1925–
1944–46: US Navy. 1948: under contract to Raoul Walsh; first film as actor *Fighter Squadron*. 1949: Universal contract. Studied acting under Sophie Rosenstein. Own company. Most films for Universal. TV series 'McMillan and Wife'.

Films as actor include: 1949: Undertow. 1950: One Way Street; Winchester '73. 1951: Iron Man; The Fat Man; Air Cadet. 1952: Bend of the River; The Lawless Breed; Has Anybody Seen My Gal?; Horizons West. 1953: Seminole; Sea Devils; Back to God's Country; Gun Fury. 1954: Taza, Son of Cochise; Magnificent Obsession; Bengal Brigade. 1955: Captain Lightfoot; All That Heaven Allows; Never Say Goodbye; Written on the Wind. 1956: Giant; Never Say Goodbye; Written on the Wind. 1957: Something of Value; Battle Hymn; A Farewell to Arms; The Tarnished Angels. 1958: Twilight for the Gods. 1959: This Earth is Mine; Pillow Talk. 1961: The Last Sunset; Come September; Lover Come Back. 1962: The Spiral Road. 1963: A Gathering of Eagles. 1964: Send Me No Flowers; Man's Favorite Sport? 1965: A Very Special Favor; Blindfold. 1966: Seconds. 1968: Ice Station Zebra. 1969: The Undefeated. 1970: Darling Lily; Hornet's Nest. 1971: Pretty Maids All in a Row.

HUFFAKER, Clair

Writer. Magna, Utah 1927–
World War II: US Navy from age 16. Princeton and

Robert Hossein (left) and Brigitte Bardot in Le Repos du Guerrier. *directed by Roger Vadim.*
The Molly Maguires. *directed by Martin Ritt, and photographed by James Wong Howe.*
Rock Hudson and Dorothy Malone in The Last Sunset. *directed by Robert Aldrich.*

Columbia Universities. Sub-editor for Time magazine, worked there 5 years. To France: Sorbonne, and University in Nice. To Hollywood; writer for films from 1957. More than a dozen novels, almost all filmed. Also short stories, TV plays, magazine articles. 1969: formed own company, became executive-producer and co-producer of own material.

Films as writer include: 1960: Seven Ways from Sundown (st/s); Flaming Star (co-s/fn). 1961: The Commancheros (co-s). 1964: Rio Conchos (co-s/fn). 1967: The War Wagon (s/fn). 1970: Flap (s/fn).

HUGHES, Howard

Producer and studio head. Houston, Texas 1905–
At 18 took over management of father's business, the Hughes Tool Company. From 1927: producer. Launched as stars Jean Harlow with Hell's Angels (1930) and Jane Russell with The Outlaw (1940, released 1946). As aviator, broke world's airspeed record (1937) and record time for flight round the world (1938). Owner of 74% of Trans World Airlines, in addition to his aircraft company and oil interests. 1948: owned a third of RKO stock. 1952: sold out to a syndicate after loaning them the money for the purchase. 1954: bought whole of RKO and became first man to be sole owner of major studio. 1955: sold RKO; until then chairman of the board. 1957: married Jean Peters, who retired from films. Has virtually disappeared from public life. 1971: divorced; US Court of Appeals ordered him to pay over $14½ million in damages to TWA.

Films as producer include: 1930: Hell's Angels (+ d). 1931: The Front Page. 1932: Scarface, Shame of the Nation (co-p). 1933: Bombshell. 1940: The Outlaw (r 1946; +co-d; co-d Howard Hawks, uc). 1946: Vendetta (r 1950 +co-d, uc; co-d 4 others).

HUGHES, Ken

Director. Liverpool, Lancashire 1922–
Won national amateur film contest at 14. From 1937: rewind boy at local cinema, then 3 years with BBC. 1934: made documentary, Soho, which he directed, produced, wrote, and photographed; joined World Wide Pictures as writer and director of documentaries including training films for Admiralty and War Office. From 1945: directed fiction shorts including a number of the 'Scotland Yard' series in early 1950s. From 1952: director of features, also scriptwriter. 2 novels, 'High Wray' (on which he based The House Across the Lake, 1954) and 'The Long Echo'. The Small World of Sammy Lee (1963) based on his TV and stage play, 'Sammy'. Wrote TV serial 'Solo for a Canary'.

Features as director and writer: 1952: Wide Boy. 1953: The Brain Machine; Little Red Monkey (co-s); Confession; Timeslip; Black Thirteen (d only). 1954: The House Across the Lake (+fn). 1956: Joe Macbeth (d only); Wicked as they Come (co-s). 1957: The Long Haul. 1960: Jazzboat (co-s); In the Nick; The Trials of Oscar Wilde. 1963: The Small World of Sammy Lee (+p/fpl). 1964: Of Human Bondage (co-d only; co-d Henry Hathaway). 1966: Drop Dead Darling – Arrivederci Baby (+p/co-st). 1967: Casino Royale (co-d only; co-d 4 others). 1968: Chitty Chitty Bang Bang (co-s). 1970: Cromwell.

HUNTER, Evan

Writer. New York 1926–
1944–46: US Naval Reserve. 1950: completed studies. 1955: first film adaptation of his work Blackboard Jungle. 1960: first film as writer Strangers When We Meet, from own novel. Films adapted by others from his novels: The Young Savages (1961) based on 'A Matter of Conviction'; Mister Buddwing (1965) based on 'Buddwing'; Last Summer (1969); Le Cri du cormoran le soir au-dessus des jonques (1971). Large number of mystery novels written under pseudonym Ed McBain became basis of TV series '87th Precinct'.

Films as writer: 1960: Strangers When We Meet (+fn). 1963: The Birds.

HUNTER, Jeffrey

(Henry H. McKinnies) Actor. New Orleans, Louisiana 1927–69 Van Nuys, California
New York summer stock. US Navy. Studied radio at Northwestern University (1947–49) and UCLA. While a student acted in 'Years Ago', 'The Rivals'. 1950: while in 'All My Sons', spotted for Fox contract. 1951: first film Fourteen Hours. Also Italian films. Documentary producer. Own record company. Married actress Barbara Rush (1950–55, divorced).

Films as actor include: 1951: Call Me Mister; The Frogmen; Take Care of My Little Girl; Single Handed. 1952: Red Skies of Montana; Lure of the Wilderness. 1955: Seven Angry Men. 1956: A Kiss Before Dying; The Searchers. 1957: The True Story of Jesse James; No Down Payment. 1958: In Love and War; Mardi Gras; The Last Hurrah. 1960: Sergeant Rutledge; Hell to Eternity; Key Witness. 1961: King of Kings. 1962: The Longest Day. 1967: A Guide for the Married Man. 1968: Custer of the West; The Private Navy of Sergeant O'Farrell.

HUNTER, Ross

(Martin Fuss) Producer. Cleveland, Ohio 1921–
Taught English in high school, then speech and theatre at Western Reserve University. 1944–49: starred in 29 B features. Unsuccessful as actor, returned to teaching. 1952: associate producer at Universal. From 1953: producer at Universal.

Films as producer include: 1953: Take Me To Town (co); All I Desire. 1954: Taza, Son of Cochise; Magnificent Obsession. 1955: Captain Lightfoot; All That Heaven Allows. 1956: There's Always Tomorrow. 1957: Battle Hymn; Tammy and the Bachelor; Interlude. 1958: This Happy Feeling; The Wonderful Years; A Stranger in my Arms. 1959: Imitation of Life; Pillow Talk (co). 1960: Portrait in Black; Midnight Lace (co). 1961: Back Street; Tammy Tell Me True; Flower Drum Song. 1963: The Thrill of It All. 1964: The Chalk Garden; I'd Rather Be Richer. 1965: The Art of Love. 1967: Thoroughly Modern Millie. 1970: Airport.

HURWITZ, Leo

Director
Helped to found and worked with Film and Photo League. Worked with Pare Lorentz, Paul Strand and others on documentaries in 1930s; collaborated on cinematography for The Plow that Broke the Plains (1936). 1937: a co-founder of Frontier Films. Collaborated on editing of Heart of Spain (1948); also worked on 'The World Today' newsreels; World War II: documentaries for Office of War Information. Became chief of news and special events for CBS TV News and a director of film productions for UN. TV documentaries and commercials; industrial and theatrical shorts. 1967: contributed to For Life, Against the War. 1969: appointed chairman of graduate programme of Institute of Film and Television at New York University's School of Arts.

Films as director include: 1938: Pay Day (co-d Paul Strand). 1942: Native Land (+co-st/co-s/e; co-d Strand). 1948: Strange Victory (+ e).

HUSTON, John

Director and writer. Nevada, Missouri 1906–
Son of Walter Huston. At 3 appeared in act with his mother on one-night stands across Texas. Random education. As youth keen amateur boxer; some professional boxing under pseudonym. 1925: appeared as actor in 2 off-Broadway productions. From 1926: honorary commission as Lieutenant in Mexican Cavalry; trained as horseman; short stories published by American Mercury. Painter in Paris; lived in England; reporter on New York Graphic. 1928–30: acted in 3 films directed by William Wyler, The Shakedown (1928), Hell's Heroes (1929), The Storm (1930). 1931: began as scriptwriter for Wyler. Then Warners contract as writer; also scripts for other companies using pseudonyms. 1941: first film as director for Warners; remained there until 1948. World War II: commission in US Army, reaching Major; made 3 war documentaries. 1949: formed company, Horizon, with S. P. Eagle (Sam Spiegel), which produced 2 of his films, and The Prowler (1951). Uncredited for work as producer and writer on Spiegel's production The Stranger (1946). From 1949: films released through various companies. Wrote 'Frankie and Johnny', marionette play produced in 1929; also 3 act play 'In Time to Come' in collaboration with Howard Koch, directed by Otto Preminger in New York (1941). Directed 'A Passenger to Bali' (1940) and 'No Exit' (1946) on New York stage. Acted in several of his films, also The Cardinal (1963), Casino Royale (1967), Candy (1968), and La Spina Dorsale del diavolo (1971). Married 4 times; third wife actress Evelyn Keyes; daughter of fourth marriage Anjelica Huston is actress. Oscars for best director and screenplay, The Treasure of the Sierra Madre (1948).

Films as writer include: 1931: A House Divided (di). 1932: Murders in the Rue Morgue (di). 1938: The Amazing Dr Clitterhouse (co); Jezebel (co). 1939: Juarez (co). 1940: The Story of Dr Ehrlich's Magic Bullet (co). 1941: High Sierra (co); Sergeant York (co). 1946: Three Strangers (co-st/co-s).

Films as director: 1941: The Maltese Falcon (+ s). 1942: In This Our Life (+ co-s); Across the Pacific. 1943: Report from the Aleutians (+ s). 1944: The Battle of San Pietro (+ s/co-c/n). 1945: Let There Be Light (ur; + co-s/co-c). 1948: The Treasure of the Sierra Madre (+ co-s/w); Key Largo (+ co-s). 1949: We Were Strangers (+ co-s/w). 1950: The Asphalt Jungle (+ co-s). 1951: The Red Badge of Courage (+ s); The African Queen (+ co-s). 1953: Moulin Rouge (+ p/co-s). 1954:

Beat the Devil (+ *co-s*). 1956: Moby Dick (+ *co-p/co-s*). 1957: Heaven Knows, Mr Allison (+ *co-s*). 1958: The Barbarian and the Geisha; Roots of Heaven. 1960: The Unforgiven. 1961: The Misfits. 1962: Freud, The Secret Passion (+ *co-s*). 1963: The List of Adrian Messenger (+ *w*). 1964: Night of the Iguana (+ *co-p/co-s*). 1966: La Bibbia – The Bible ... in the Beginning (+ *n/w*). 1967: Casino Royale (*co-d 4 others*); Reflections in a Golden Eye. 1969: Sinful Davey; A Walk with Love and Death (+ *co-p*). 1970: The Kremlin Letter (+ *co-s*).

HUSTON, Walter

(Walter Houghston) Actor. Toronto, Canada 1884–1950 Hollywood
Vaudeville team with Bayonne Whipple, whom he married in 1914. 1924: Broadway debut 'Mr Pitt'; also 'Desire under the Elms', 'Kongo', 'Dodsworth', 'Othello', 'Knickerbocker Holiday'. 1929: first film as actor *Gentlemen of the Press*. 1940: directed on stage by his son John Huston, in 'A Passenger to Bali'. Appeared in many of his son's films. Also radio.

Films as actor include: 1929: The Virginian. 1930: Abraham Lincoln; The Bad Man; The Virtuous Sin. 1931: The Criminal Code; The Star Witness; A House Divided. 1932: The Woman from Monte Carlo; The Wet Parade; Night Court; American Madness; Rain. 1933: Gabriel Over The White House; Hell Below; The Prizefighter and the Lady; Ann Vickers; Storm at Daybreak. 1936: Rhodes of Africa; Dodsworth. 1938: Of Human Hearts. 1939: The Light that Failed. 1940: The Outlaw (*r* 1946). 1941: All that Money Can Buy; Swamp Water; The Shanghai Gesture. 1942: In This Our Life. 1943: Yankee Doodle Dandy; Mission to Moscow; Edge of Darkness; The North Star. 1944: Dragon Seed. 1945: And Then There Were None. 1946: Dragonwyck; Duel in the Sun. 1947: Summer Holiday. 1948: The Treasure of The Sierra Madre. 1949: The Great Sinner. 1950: The Furies.

I

IBERT, Jacques

Composer. Paris 1890–1962
Trained at Conservatoire. 1919: Won Prix de Rome. From 1931: composer for films. 1937–55: director of French Academy in Rome. 1955–56: director of Paris Opéra. His ballet 'Le Cirque' was one of 3 comprising *Invitation to the Dance* (1956).

Films as composer include: 1931: Les Cinq Gentlemen Maudits. 1933: Don Quichotte. 1935: Golgotha. 1936: Koenigsmark. 1939: La Charrette Fantôme. 1946: Panique. 1948: Macbeth. 1955: Marianne de ma jeunesse.

ICHAC, Marcel

Director. Rueil, France 1906–
Studied painting. Journalist, publicist and photographer before began making films. From 1933: directed over 50 shorts on exploration and mountaineering. 1936: accompanied first French expedition to the Himalayas. 1939: made *Missions de France* for

French Commissariat in New York. 1943: for *Sondeurs d'abîmes*, was first film-maker to accompany a potholing expedition. 1949: accompanied French polar expedition. 1952: the resulting film *Groënland* was then his longest (about 50 minutes). 1959: *Les Étoiles de Midi*, shot on Mont Blanc, was his first feature. Book: 'A l'assaut des Aiguilles du Diable'.

Films as director include: 1936: Karokoram (+ *c/e*). 1942: A l'assaut des Aiguilles du Diable (+ *p/c*). 1943: Sondeurs d'abîmes (+ *co-c*). 1952: Groënland – Groënland, Terre des Glaces (+ *p*; *co-d Jean-Jacques Languepin*). 1953: Nouveaux Horizons (+ *p/cy/c*); Victoire sur l'Annapurna (+ *p/e/co-n*). 1959: Les Étoiles de Midi (+ *co-s/co-di*).

ICHIKAWA, Kon

Director. Ujiyamada, Japan 1915–
Ichioka Commercial School, Osaka. 1933: began in animation at J. O. Studio Kyoto, which became Toho; stayed, became assistant to e.g. Yutaka Abe, Tomizo Ishida. 1946: made puppet film not shown because scenario not submitted to US occupation authorities. 1947: shot footage for feature *Toho Sen-Ichiya*. From 1948: directed features. 1953: returned to animation with *Pusan*. 1966: directed and with Sumie Tanaka co-scripted TV production in 26 episodes 'Gengi monogatari'. 1967: further return to animation with *Topo Gigio e i sei ladri*. 1970: Directed 8 screen film for Osaka festival. Married scriptwriter Natto Wada, collaborator on many of his films from 1949.

Films as director: 1946: Musume Dojoji – A Girl at Dojo Temple (*ur*). 1947: Toho Sen-Ichiya – A Thousand and One Nights with Toho (*uf*; *co-d*). 1948: Hana Hiraku – A Flower Blooms; Sanbyaku Rokujugo-ya – 365 Nights (*in 2 parts*). 1949: Ningen Moyo – Design of a Human Being; Hateshinaki Jonetsu – Passion Without Limit. 1950: Ginza Sanshiro – Sanshiro at Ginza; Netsudei-chi – The Hot Marshland (+ *co-s*); Akatsuki no Tsuiseki – Pursuit at Dawn. 1951: Ye-Rai-Shang – Nightshade Flower (+ *co-s*); Koibito – The Lover (+ *co-s*); Mukokuseki-Mono – The Man Without A Nationality; Nusumareta Koi – Stolen Love (+ *co-s*); Bungawan Solo – River Solo Flows (+ *co-s*); Kekkon Koshin-kyoku – Wedding March (+ *co-s*). 1952: Lucky San – Mr. Lucky (+ *co-s*); Wakai Hito – Young Generation (+ *co-s*); Ashi ni Sawatta Onna – The Woman Who Touched the Legs (+ *co-s*); Ano te kono te – This Way, That Way (+ *co-s*). 1953: Pusan – Poo-san – Mr. Poo (+ *co-s*); Aoiro Kakumei – The Blue Revolution; Seishun Zenigata Heiji – Youth of Heiji Zenigata (+ *co-s*); Aijin – The Lovers. 1954: Watashi no Subete O – All of Myself (+ *co-s*); Okuman Choja – A Billionaire (+ *co-s*); Josei ni Kansuru Junisho – Twelve Chapters about Women. 1955: Seishun Kaidan – Ghost Story of Youth; Kokoro – The Heart. 1956: Biruma no Tategoto – The Burmese Harp; Shokei no Heya – Punishment Room; Nihonbashi – Bridge of Japan. 1957: Manin Densha – The Crowded Train (+ *co-s*); Ana – The Hole; Tohoku no Zunmutachi – The Men of Tohoku. 1958: Gennma to Bijo to San-Akunin – Money and Three Bad Men; Enjo – Conflagration – Flame of Torment. 1959: Sayonara Konnichiwa – Goodbye, Good Day; Kagi – The Key – Odd Obsessions (+ *co-s*); Nobi – Fires on the Plain; Keisatsukan to Boroyuku-dan – Police and Small

Imitation of Life, *directed by Douglas Sirk and produced by Ross Hunter.*
Freud: The Secret Passion, *directed by John Huston.*
Kon Ichikawa's *Ototo.*

Gangsters. 1960: Ginza no Mosa – A Ginza Veteran; Bonchi (+ co-s); Jokyo – A Woman's Testament – Code of Women (ep); Ototo – Her Brother. 1961: Kuroi Junin no Onna – Ten Black Women. 1962: Hakai – The Sin; Watashi wa Nisai – Being Two Isn't Easy. 1963: Yukinojo Henge – The Revenge of Yukinojo – An Actor's Revenge; Taiheiyo Hitoribotchi – Alone on the Pacific – My Enemy the Sea. 1964: Dokonji Monogotari – Zeni no Odori – Money Talks. 1965: Tokyo Orinpukku – Tokyo Olympiad (+ co-s). 1967: Topo Gigio e i sei ladri – Topo Gigio: La Guerra del Missile – Toppo Jijo no Botan Senso. 1968: Tournament; Kyoto. 1971: Ai Futatabi – To Love Again.

IMAI, Tadashi

Director, Tokyo 1912–

Son of priest. Imperial University, Tokyo; while student arrested twice as communist. 1934: abandoned studies for continuity job with J. O. Studios in Kyoto (forerunner of Toho). Became scriptwriter. From 1939: director. During World War II, obliged to make propaganda films e.g. *Boro no Kesshitai* (1942). After war became communist. 1948: founded own production company.

Films as director: 1939: Numazu Heigakko – Numazu Military Academy; Wararega Kyokan – Our Instructor. 1940: Tajinko Mura – Village of Tajinko; Onna no Machi – Women's Town; Kakka – The General. 1941: Kekkon no Seitai – Married Life. 1942: Boro no Kesshitai – Suicide Troops of the Watch Tower. 1944: Ikari no Umi – The Angry Sea. 1946: Minshu no Teki – Enemy of the People; Jinsei Tombogaeri – Life is Like a Somersault. 1947: Chikagai Nijuyojikan – Twenty-Four Hours of a Secret Life (co-d Hideo Sekigawa, Kiyoshi Kusuda). 1949: Aoi-Sanmyaku – Blue Mountains; Onna no Kao – Woman's Face. 1950: Mata Au Hi Made – Until the Day We Meet Again – Until Our Next Meeting; Dikkoi Ikiteru – And Yet We Live – We Are Living. 1951: Gembako no Zu – Pictures of the Atom Bomb. 1952: Yamabiko Gekko – Echo School. 1953: Nigorie – Muddy Waters – Troubled Waters; Himeyuri no To – Tower of Lilies – The Girls of Okinawa. 1955: Aisurebakoso – Because I Love (ep); Koko ni Izumi Ari – Here is a Spring; Yukiko. 1956: Mahiru no Ankoku – Darkness at Noon – Shadows in Sunlight. 1957: Jun-ai Monogatari – Story of Pure Love; Kome – Rice. 1958: Yoru no Tsuzumi – Night Drum – Adulteress. 1959: Kiku to Isamu – Kiku and Isamu. 1961: Shiroi Gake – The Cliff; Are ga Minato no Hi da – Pan Chopali. 1962: Nippon no Obochan – Old Women of Japan. 1963: Bushido Zankoku Monogatari – Bushido-Samurai Saga – Oath of Obedience. 1964: Echigo Tsutsuishi Oyashirazu – Story from Echigo. 1965: Adauchi – Revenge. 1967: Satashi ga Kowareru Toki – When The Cookie Crumbles. 1968: Fushin no Toki – Time of Reckoning – When You Can't Believe Anyone. 1969: Hashi no Nai Kawa – Bridge Across No River – River Without a Bridge.

IMAMURA, Shohei

Director. Japan 1926–

Waseda University. Entered films at Shochiku. 1954: moved to Nikkatsu. 1958: first film as director. Also wrote scripts for others. Worked frequently with cinematographer Masahisa Himeda.

Films as director: 1958: Nusumareta Yokujo – The Stolen Desire; Nishiginza Ekimae – Lights of Night; Hateshinaki Yokubo – Endless Desire. 1959: Nianchan – My Second Brother – The Diary of Sueko. 1961: Buta to Gunkan – Hogs and Warships. 1963: Nippon Konchuki – The Insect Woman. 1964: Akai Satsui – Unholy Desire. 1966: Jinruigaku Nyumon – The Pornographer – An Introduction to Anthropology (+ co-s). 1967: Ningen Johatsu – A Man Vanishes. 1968: Kamigami no Fukaki Yokubo – Kuragejima: Legends from a Southern Island – A Profound Longing of the Gods.

INCE, Thomas H.

Producer and director. Newport, Rhode Island 1882–1924 Hollywood

Parents earned precarious living on stage. Stage actor at 6. Acted with stock companies; on Broadway at 15; song-and-dance man in vaudeville. From 1902: lifeguard at Atlantic Highlands, New Jersey; staged vaudeville acts; returned to Broadway in drama and musical comedy. From 1905: promoted own stock company for short time; feature part in musical comedy 'For Love's Sweet Sake' for 2 years. 1910: began in films as actor with Independent; moved to Biograph for a few weeks, returning to Independent to direct; contract director for Carl Laemmle after making 1 film. In Cuba, out of reach of Patents Trust agents, to direct series of films; few were made. 1911: joined Adam Kessel and Charles O. Bauman's New York Motion Picture company to take charge of their West Coast studio; hired Miller Brothers' '101 Ranch Wild West Show' and 18,000 acres of land to make Westerns; employed John Ford's brother Francis as director of a second production unit. 1912: Independent and NYMP merged to form anti-Patent company, Universal. Ince issued his productions (totalling over 150 in 1913) under various trade names e.g. Broncho, Domino, Kay-Bee; produced Civil War subjects and westerns. 1914: first feature as director, *The Battle of Gettysburg*; then made larger films and abandoned directing for producing. Directors who worked under him included Fred Niblo, Henry King, Frank Borzage. 1915: with D. W. Griffith and Mack Sennett formed Triangle production company to rival growing monopoly of Adolph Zukor; produced and supervised *The Iron Strain* for opening programme at Knickerbocker Theater on Broadway; built big new studios at Culver City. Ince's productions starring William S. Hart brought in most revenue for Triangle. Towards the end of World War I, broke with Triangle, contracted with Zukor to produce films for Paramount/Artcraft for which he constructed another studio at Culver City. Meanwhile William Hart westerns directed by Lambert Hillyer were still being made under Ince's name as producer. 1919: contract with Hart ran out; Zukor broke with Ince who was forced out of Paramount/Artcraft and formed distributing company Associated Producers with Mack Sennett, Allan Dwan, Maurice Tourneur, Marshall Neilan and others. 1922: Associated Producers merged with First National; became independent producer releasing through First National. 1924: died suddenly following party cruise on William Randolph Hearst's yacht. Brothers John and Ralph both film actors and directors. Married (1907) actress Eleanor Kershaw.

Films as director in collaboration include: 1911: Little Nell's Tobacco; Their First Misunderstanding; The

House That Jack Built; A Dream; Sisters; The Aggressor; In The Sultan's Garden; A Dog's Tale; Artful Kate; A Manly Man; The Fisher Maid; In Old Madrid; For Her Brother's Sake; The Message in the Bottle. 1914: The Wrath of the Gods; The Typhoon. 1915: The Coward. 1916: The Deserter; The Dividend; Home; Peggy; Civilisation.

Films as director: 1911: The New Cook (+ s/w); Across the Plains – War on the Plains (+ s); The Hidden Trail; The Prospector's Daughter; His Message. 1912: On the Firing Line; Custer's Last Raid; The Colonel's Ward; The Law of the West; A Double Reward; The Colonel's Peril; The Colonel's Son; The Clod; The Mosaic Law; With Lee in Virginia; The Winning of Wonega; His Nemesis; The Battle of the Red Men; Blazing the Trail; The Indian Massacre; A Mexican Tragedy; A Tale of the Foothills; The Invaders; For Freedom of Cuba; The Lieutenant's Last Fight – Custer's Last Fight; When Lee Surrenders. 1913: For the Cause; The Paymaster's Son; The Boomerang; The Seal of Silence; The Soldier's Honor; The Deserter; A Call to Arms; The Brand; The Hateful God; The Ambassador's Envoy; The Yellow Flame; The Favorite Son; A Romance of the Sea; The Shadow of the Past; The Drummer of the 8th; The Pride of the South; Days of '49. 1914: The Battle of Gettysburg; The Last of the Line; The Hour of Reckoning; A Relic of Old Japan. 1915: The Despoiler.

INGE, William

Writer. Independence, Kansas 1913–

To 1935: University of Kansas. Acted in college plays, summer stock. 1937: graduated from Iowa State College. 1937–43: College teacher. 1943–46: drama, music and film critic for St Louis Star-Times. 1946–49: taught English at Washington University. 1947: first play 'Farther Off from Heaven'. 1953: first film based on his work *Come Back, Little Sheba*; Pulitzer Prize for play 'Picnic'. 1956: 'Picnic' adapted for film by Daniel Taradash. 1956: play 'Bus Stop' (1955) adapted for film by George Axelrod. 1960: 'Farther Off from Heaven' adapted as *The Dark at the Top of the Stairs* by Harriet Frank, Jr and Irving Ravetch. 1961: first film as writer *Splendor in the Grass* from own story, received Oscar for original story and screenplay. 1961: Splendor in the Grass. 1962: writer on *All Fall Down*. 1963: *The Stripper* based on his play 'A Loss of Roses' (1959). 1964: refused co-writer credit on Harvey Hart's *Bus Riley's Back in Town*. Plays not filmed: 'Natural Affection' (1963), 'Where's Daddy?' (1966).

INGRAM, Rex

(Reginald Ingram Montgomery Hitchcock) Director. Dublin 1892–1950 Hollywood

At 19, to America, leaving law course at Trinity College, Dublin. 1911–13: various jobs, then studied sculpture at Yale School of Fine Arts. Became actor for Vitagraph and Edison; wrote scripts for Fox including some Theda Bara films. From 1916: director usually with Universal; scripted most. 1920: joined Metro; June Mathis, head of script department, wrote scripts for him e.g. *The Four Horsemen of the Apocalypse* (1921); began long collaboration with John Seitz as cinematographer; married Alice Terry who was to star in many of his films. 1923: cut 24-reel version of *Greed* to 18 reels for Erich von Stroheim. From 1925: settled in Nice; directed 5 films for American market including *Baroud* (1933), his last film as director and only sound picture. Acted in *The Thief of Bagdad* (1940) and *The Talk of the Town* (1942).

Films as director: 1916: The Great Problem (+*p/s*); Broken Fetters (+*p/s*); The Chalice of Sorrows (+*ad*); Black Orchids (+*s*). 1917: The Reward of the Faithless (+*p/s*); The Pulse of Life (+*s*); The Flower of Doom (+*s*); The Little Terror (+*s*). 1918: His Robe of Honor; Humdrum Brown. 1919: The Day She Paid. 1920: Under Crimson Skies; Shore Acres; Hearts Are Trumps. 1921: The Four Horsemen of the Apocalypse; The Conquering Power (+*p*). 1922: Turn to the Right; The Prisoner of Zenda (+*p*); Trifling Women (+*p/st*). 1923: Where the Pavement Ends (+*p/ad*); Scaramouche (+*p*). 1924: The Arab. 1926: Mare Nostrum; The Magician (+*ad*). 1927: The Garden of Allah (+*p*). 1929: The Three Passions (+*p/s*). 1933: Baroud (+*p/co-st/co-s/w*).

IVENS, Joris

Director. Nijmegen, Holland 1898–

1911: Made film of his family *Brandende Straal*. 1917–22: commercial, economic studies in Rotterdam. World War I: served in artillery unit. 1923: to Berlin to study photochemistry. Studies as photographic technician at factories in Dresden and Jena. 1926: returned to Holland, became director φ father's camera and photographic goods company. 1927: made scientific shorts for University of Leyden. 1929: became committee member of Film-Liga, first Dutch film society. With brother started film-making department in father's company. 1930: travelled to Russia and England. 1932: invited to Russia to make *Komsomol*. 1933–34: made films in Holland and Belgium. 1935–36: to Russia and USA. 1937: with Ernest Hemingway, Louise Rainer, Frederic March, Lillian Hellman, John Dos Passos and Archibald MacLeish, formed production company, whose profits were to be used to send medical supplies to Spanish Republic; made *Spanish Earth* in Spain. 1939: made *The Four Hundred Million* in China; footage used in Frank Capra's *The Battle of China* (1944). 1940: commissioned by American government to make *Power and the Land*. 1941: became lecturer at UCLA. 1942–44: worked in USA and Canada; appointed High Commissioner of Film for Dutch East Indies, then held by Japanese. 1945: resigned post when Holland failed to recognize Indonesian Republic. 1946–55: worked in Czechoslovakia, Poland, Bulgaria, Russia. 1956: with Alberto Cavalcanti co-ordinated the 5 episodes of *Die Vind Rose*; produced Gérard Philipe's *Les Aventures de Till l'Espiègle* for DEFA. From 1957: worked in Europe, China, Africa, South America, Viet-Nam. 1970: film for Italian television.

Films as director: 1928: De Brug – The Bridge (+*p/s/c/e*); Étude de mouvements (+*s/c/e*); La Bar de Juffrouw Heyens (+*s/c/e*); Branding (+*c/e*; *co-d Mannus Franken*). 1929: Regen – Rain (+*c/e*; *co-d Mannus Franken*); Schaatsenrijden (+*s/c/e*); IK-Film (+*co-s/co-c/co-e*; *co-d Hans van Meerten*). 1930: Zuiderzee (+*s/co-c/e*); Wij bouwen – We are Building (+*s/c/e*; in 4 parts: 1. Nieuwe Architectuur; 2. Heien; 3. Caissonbouw Rotterdam; 4. Zuid Limburg – Spoor-

wegbouw in Limbourg); Congtres der vakvereenigingen (+*s/co-c/e*); Timmerfabriek (+*s/co-c/co-e*). 1931: Philips-Radio – Symphonie van den arbeid – Industrial Symphony (+*s/co-c/e*); Creosoot (+*e*). 1932: Komsomol – Pem o gerojach – Youth Speaks (+*co-s/e*). 1933: Borinage – Misère au borinage (+*co-s/co-c*; *co-d Henri Storck*); Hein. 1934: Nieuwe Gronden – New Earth (+*s/co-c/e/cy/u*). 1937: Spanish Earth (+*s/co-c*). 1939: The Four Hundred Million (+*s*). 1940: Power and the Land. 1941: Our Russian Front – Notre Front Russe (+*co-s*; *co-d Lewis Milestone*); New Frontiers (*uf*). 1942: Action Stations (+*s/e*); Alone. 1945: Know Your Enemy: Japan (*co-d Frank Capra*). 1946: Indonesia Calling (+*s/e*). 1947: Pierwsze Lata – The First Years. 1950: Pokoj zwyeciezy swiata (+*co-s*; *co-d Jerzy Bossak*). 1951: My za mir – Freundschaft siegt (*co-d Ivan Pyriev*). 1952: Wyscig pokoju Warszawa-Berlina-Praga. 1954: Das Lied der Strome (+*co-s*). 1957: La Seine a rencontré Paris (+*s*); Lettres de Chine (*in 3 eps*;+*s*). 1958: Six Cents Million avec vous (+*s*). 1959: L'Italia non e' un paese povero (+*co-s/co-e*). 1960: Demain à Nanguila (+*s*). 1961: Carnet de viaje (+*s*); Pueblo en armas (+*s*). 1962: ... A Valparaiso (+*s*); El Circo màs pequeño del mundo (+*s*). 1964: Le Train de la victoire. 1965: Viet-Nam! 1966: Le Mistral (+*co-s*); Le Ciel, la terre – The Threatening Sky; Rotterdam-Europoort. 1967: Loin du Viet-Nam – Far from Vietnam (+*co-p*; *co-d 4 others*). 1968: Dix-septième parallèle (*co-d Marceline Loridan*); Le Peuple et ses fusils: La Guerre Populaire au Laos (*co-d 7 others*); Rencontre avec le Président Ho Chi Minh (*co-d Marceline Loridan*).

IVES, Burl

(Burl Icle Ivanhoe Ives) Actor. Jasper County, Illinois 1909–

Itinerant in USA, Canada, Mexico. Studied with vocal coach Ekka Toedt. 1937–38: New York University. 1938: on stage, e.g. in 'Ah, Wilderness!' 1938: Broadway debut in 'The Boys from Syracuse'. Studied acting with Benny Schneider. Toured in 'I Married an Angel'. 1942–43: US Army; medical discharge. Stage debut as singer in 'This is the Army'. Entertained troops, made recordings for Office of War Information. Broadway: 'Sing Out Sweet Land.' 1945: first film as actor *Smoky*. Broadway; 'Showboat', 'Cat on a Hot Tin Roof'. Published collections of folk ballads and tales. Oscar as supporting actor in *The Big Country* (1958). Also cabaret, radio, recordings, concerts. Autobiography 'Wayfaring Stranger'.

Films as actor include: 1948: Green Grass of Wyoming; Station West; So Dear to My Heart. 1950: Sierra. 1955: East of Eden. 1956: The Power and the Prize. 1958: Wind Across the Everglades; Desire Under the Elms; Cat on a Hot Tin Roof; The Big Country. 1960: Our Man in Havana. 1964: The Brass Bottle. 1970: The McMasters.

IVORY, James

Director. Berkeley, California 1930–

University of Oregon, film department of University of Southern California; wrote, produced, directed and photographed documentary *Venice: Theme and Variations* while a student. Two further documentaries *The Sword and the Flute* and *The Delhi Way*, on India, latter for Asia Society of New York. Partnership with

Civilization, *directed by Thomas Ince.*
Spanish Earth, *directed by Joris Ivens.*
Western Approaches, *directed by Pat Jackson.*

Ismail Merchant. 1963: first feature *The Householder* in English and Pakistani versions. First 2 features written in collaboration with novelist R. Prawer Jhabvala, photographed by Subrata Mitra. Satyajit Ray wrote music for *Shakespeare Wallah* (1965). 1970: formed his own production and distribution company.

Features as director: 1963: The Householder. 1965: Shakespeare Wallah. 1968: The Guru. 1970: Bombay Talkie (+ *co-s*).

IWERKS, Ub

Animator, Kansas City, Kansas 1901–1971
Worked in commercial art studio with Walt Disney and Rudolph Ising. 1926–27: Chief animator on series 'Alice in Cartoonland'. 1927–28: animated 'Oswald the Rabbit' series with Disney at Universal. Received 'drawn by' credits on early Mickey Mouse cartoons, the first of which was *Plane Crazy* (1928). 1931–33: created own series 'Flip the Frog' for MGM. 1933–34: 'Willie Whopper' series for MGM. 1937–38: worked on Color Rhapsody series with Scrappy character for Screen Gems. Returned to Disney. Supervised special effects e.g. on *20,000 Leagues Under the Sea* (1954). 1963: special photographic advisor on *The Birds*. 1964: shared in an Academy Award for his work on Color Travelling Matte Composite Cinematography, used in *Mary Poppins*.

Films as animator include: 1928: Steamboat Willie. 1929: Barnyard Battle; The Gallopin' Gaucho; The Jazz Fool; Jungle Rhythm; The Karnival Kid; Mickey's Choo Choo; The Opry House; When the Cat's Away; Hell's Bells. 1934: Don Quixote. 1937: The Foxy Pup; Merry Mannequins; Skeleton Frolic. 1938: The Frog Pond, Midnight Frolics; Snowtime. 1939: Crop Chasers: Gorilla Hunt: Nell's Yells.

J

JACKSON, Pat

Director. London 1916–
1934: went straight from school into GPO Film Unit. 1936: co-directed short *Big Money* with Harry Watt. 1937: assistant to Norman McLaren on *Book Bargain*. 1938: first short as solo director. Remained as documentary director when Crown Film Unit replaced GPO Film Unit. 1944: first feature as director, for Crown. 1945–50: in Hollywood on MGM contract; made one film. From 1950: directed features in UK. TV including some episodes of 'Man in a Suitcase' and 'The Prisoner' series; many commercials.

Short films as director: 1936: Big Money (*co-d Harry Watt*). 1938: Men in Danger; Happy in the Morning. 1939: The First Days – A City Prepares (*co-d Humphrey Jennings, Harry Watt*). 1940: Health in War. 1941: Ferry Pilot. 1942: Builders.

Features as director: 1944: Western Approaches (+ *s*). 1949: Shadow on the Wall. 1951: White Corridors (+ *co-s*); Encore. 1952: Something Money Can't Buy (+ *co-s*). 1956: The Feminine Touch. 1957: The Birthday Present. 1958: Virgin Island. 1960: Snowball.

1961: What a Carve Up! 1962: Seven Keys; Don't Talk to Strange Men. 1964: Seventy Deadly Pills (+ *s*); Dead End Creek (+ *co-s*).

JACOBSSON, Ulla

Actress. Gothenburg, Sweden 1929–
Studied acting at Gothenburg City Theatre. 1949: professional stage debut. Acted at Karlstad City Theatre and Intiman in Stockholm. Films from 1951: worked in Germany, France, Britain.

Films as actress include: 1951: Bärande Hav; Hon dansade en sommar. 1954: Karin Månsdotter; Herr Arnes Pengar. 1955: Sommarnattens leende. 1956: Sången om den eldröda blomman. 1958: Det kom två män. 1963: Love is a Ball. 1964: Zulu. 1965: The Heroes of Telemark; Nattmara. 1968: Bainse.

JACOPETTI, Gualtiero

Director. Florence, Italy 1922–
Father a banker. University of Florence. Journalist. 1961: first film as director with Franco Prosperi and Paolo Cavara as 'associate' directors. Subsequent films directed in collaboration with Franco Prosperi.

Films as director in collaboration with Franco Prosperi: 1961: Mondo Cane No 1 – A Dog's Life (+ *e/cy*). 1962: La Donna del mondo – Eva Sconosciuta – Women of the World (+ *cy/e*). 1963: Mondo Cane No 2 (+ *co-p/co-s/cy*). 1965: Africa Addio – Africa Blood and Guts (+ *co-s*).

JAKUBOWSKA, Wanda

Director. Warsaw 1907–
History of Art at Warsaw University. 1929: co-founder of 'Start', organisation to back experimental films. 1932: first films as director, in collaboration with Eugeniesz Cekalski and Jerzy Zarpycki (communist documentary shorts). 1935: collaborated with Cekalski on *Na Start*; worked with Alexander Ford. 1937: co-founder of cooperative production company. 1939: first feature, in collaboration, *Nad Niemnem* (lost during World War II). 1942–45: in Nazi concentration camps. 1948: made *Ostatni Etap*, about concentration camps.

Films as director: 1932: Reportaz Nr 1 – Reportage Nr 1 (*co-d Eugeniesz Cekalski, Jerzy Zarpycki*); Reportaz Nr 2 – Reportage Nr 2 (*co-d Cekalski, Zarpycki*). 1935: Na Start (*co-d Cekalski*). 1939: Nad Niemnem – On the Banks of the Niemen (*co-d Karol Szolowski*). 1946: Buhujem nowe wsie. 1948: Ostatni Etap – The Last Stage (+ *co-s*). 1953: Zolnierz zwyciestwa – Soldiers of Victory (+ *s*). 1955: Opowiesc Atlantycka – An Atlantic Story. 1957: Pogegnanie z diablem – Farewell to the Devil (+ *co-s*). 1958: Krol Macius Pierwszy – King Matthew I (+ *co-s*). 1960: Spotkania w mroku – Encounters in the Dark (+ *co-s*); Historia wspolczesna – A Contemporary Story – It Happened Yesterday. 1964: Konec naseho casu – The End of Our World. 1965: Goraca Linia – The Hot Line.

JANCSÓ, Miklós

Director. Vác, Hungary 1921–
Simultaneously studied law, ethnography and the history of art. 1944: doctor of law. 1950: graduated

from drama and film school in Budapest. Began as film-maker with news films. Made documentaries from 1954 and fiction shorts from 1956 to 1963, 16 in all. 1958: first feature film as director. Several international co-productions.

Features as director, and (from 1967) writer in collaboration: 1958: A Harangok Rómába mentek – The Bells Have Gone to Rome. 1960: Három csillag – Three Stars (*co-d Károly Wiedemann, Zoltán Várkonyi*). 1963: Oldás és kötés – Cantata (+ *s*). 1964: Így jöttem – My Way Home. 1965: Szegénylegények – The Round-Up. 1967: Csillagosok, katonák – The Red and the White. 1968: Csend és kiáltas – Silence and Cry. 1969: Fényes szelek – The Confrontation; Sirocco d'Hiver – Sirokko – Winter Wind. 1971: Egi barany – Agnus Dei (+ *co-s*); La Pacifista – The Pacifist (+ *co-s*); Il Giovane Attila (+ *co-s*).

JANNINGS, Emil

Actor. Rorschach, Switzerland 1884–1950 Stroblhof, Austria
In repertory and with strolling players. 1914: with Max Reinhardt's company at Deutsches Theater, Berlin. Encouraged to enter film career by Ernst Lubitsch; directed by him in German films. 1925–29: Hollywood films. Oscar (1927–28) as Best Actor for *Way of All Flesh* (1927) and *The Last Command* (1928). All his sound films made in Germany. Acted in Nazi propaganda films. Married actresses Gussi Holl and Lucie Hoflich. From 1945: in retirement.

Films as actor include: 1914: Arme Eva. 1916: Frau Eva. 1917: Wenn vier dasselbe tun; Ein fidele Gefangnis; Die Seeschlacht. 1918: Fuhrmann Henschel; Die Augen der Mumie Ma. 1919: Madame DuBarry. 1920: Kohlchiesels Tochter; Anna Boleyn; Vendetta. 1921: Die Bergkatze. 1922: Weib des Pharao. 1923: Tragödie der Liebe. 1924: Nju; Das Wachsfigurenkabinett; Der letzte Mann. 1925: Variété; Quo Vadis; Tartuff. 1926: Faust. 1928: The Street of Sin; The Patriot. 1929: Betrayal. 1930: Der blaue Engel. 1932: Sturme der Leidenschaft. 1935: Der alte und der junge Konig. 1937: Der Herrscher. 1939: Robert Koch, der Bekämpfer des Todes. 1941: Ohm Kruger.

JARRE, Maurice

Composer. Lyon, France 1924–
After Paris Conservatoire, played in orchestra of Jean-Louis Barrault Theatre Company, with Pierre Boulez. 1951: first theatre score for Jean Vilar's Avignon Festival production, 'Le Prince de Hambourg'; when Vilar became director of Théâtre National Populaire, he made Jarre resident composer and conductor. His work for TNP includes a musical comedy. Also composed for *son et lumière* before music for short films (from 1951) and features (from 1958). Oscar for 'Substantially Original Music Score', *Lawrence of Arabia* (1962).

Films as composer include: 1952: Hôtel des Invalides. 1956: Théâtre National Populaire; Sur le pont d'Avignon. 1957: Le Bel Indifférent. 1958: La Tête contre les murs. 1959: Les Yeux sans visage; Les Dragueurs. 1960: Crack in the Mirror; The Big Gamble. 1961: Pleins Feux sur l'assassin; Le Temps du ghetto; La Bride sur le cou. 1962: Lawrence of Arabia;

The Longest Day (co); Cybèle, ou les Dimanches de ville d'Avray; Les Oliviers de la justice; Thérèse Desqueyroux. 1963: Mourir à Madrid; Judex. 1964: Behold a Pale Horse; The Collector. 1966: Doctor Zhivago. 1967: The Night of the Generals; The Extraordinary Seaman (r 1969). 1968: Isadora; Villa Rides; Five Card Stud; The Fixer. 1969: Topaz. 1970: La Caduta degli dei; El Condor; Ryan's Daughter. 1971: Soleil Rouge.

JARVA, Risto

Director. Helsinki, Finland 1934–
Engineering chemist. Photographic work. From 1959: directed shorts. 1962: founded own production company; first feature as director, in collaboration with Jaakko Pakkasvirta; they also wrote, produced, photographed, and edited it. 1964: collaborated with him on the direction of X-Paroni. 1965: directed Pakkasvirta in Onnenpoli. 1967: they scripted Työmiehen päiväkirja. 1968: produced Pakkasvirta's Vihreä leski. Continued to direct shorts as well as features.

Features as director, producer, writer, cinematographer and editor in collaboration: 1962: Yö vai päivä – Night or Day (co-c; co-d Jaakko Pakkasvirta). 1964: X-Paroni – Baron X (p/s/c/e alone; co-d Pakkasvirta, Spede Pasasen). 1965: Onnenpoli – Game of Luck (d/p/s/c/e alone). 1967: Työmiehen päiväkirja – A Worker's Diary (d/p/c/e alone; co-s). 1969: Ruusujen aika – Time of Roses (p/s/c/e alone; co-d Titta Karakorpi). 1971: Bensaa Svonissa – Rally (d/s only).

JASNY, Vojtěch

Director. Kelc, Czechoslovakia 1925–
World War II: in forced labour camp. Studied philosophy, 1947–51: cinematography at Academy of Arts, Prague; while there made first film as director, in collaboration with Karel Kachyňa. Není Stále zamračeno – The Clouds Will Roll Away, from own script. 1950–55: series of documentaries in collaboration with Kachyňa, including one in China. 1955: first feature was last film in collaboration with him. 1957: collaborated with poets Pavel Kohout and Frantisek Daniel on script of Zarijove noci. Several scripts for others.

Features as director: 1955: Dnes večer vsechno skončí – Everything Ends Tonight (co-d Karel Kachyna). 1956: Bez Obav. 1957: Zářijové noci – September Nights (+ co-s). 1958: Touha – Desire (+ co-s). 1960: Přežil jsem svou smrt – I Survived Certain Death. 1961: Procesí k panence – Pilgrimage to the Virgin Mary. 1963: Az přijde kocour – That Cat (+ co-s). 1965: Dumky – Pipes. 1968: Všichni dobři rodáci – All Good Citizens.

JASSET, Victorin

Director. Fumay, France 1862–1913 Paris
Began as painter and designer. 1900: directed pantomimes at the Hippodrome, Paris. 1905: began to direct films at new Gaumont studios at Buttes-Chaumont. 1906: collaborated with Alice Guy on La Vie du Christ. 1907: after disagreement with Léon Gaumont, worked with Georges Hatot in Marseille. From 1908: at Eclair company; directed serials e.g. Nick Carter, made outdoors with improvised scripts; American actor André Liabel got fan mail as Nick Carter. Also

made realistic dramas. Most of his films are lost. 1912: wrote essay on film direction. Died while directing episode in serial Protéa.

Films as director include: 1908: Âme Corse (+s); Meskal le contrebandier (+s); Nick Carter (+s). 1909: Riffle Bill (+s); Le Vautour de la sierra (+s); Les Dragonnades sous Louis XIV (+s); Morgan le pirate (+s); Nouveaux Exploits de Nick Carter (+s). 1910: Zigomar (+s). 1911: La Fin de Don Juan (+s); Rédemption; Nick Carter contre Paulin Broquet (+s); Zigomar, Roi des Voleurs (+s); 1912: Zigomar Contre Nick Carter (+s); Zigomar peau d'Anguille (+s); 1913: Balao, ou des pas au Plafond (+s); Protea (+s).

JAUBERT, Maurice

Composer. Nice 1900–40 Azerailles, France
Nice Conservatory. Worked as lawyer. 1930–35: director of music for Pathé. Also worked for GPO Film Unit in London. Died in action.

Films as composer include: 1929: Le Petit Chaperon Rouge. 1932: L'Affaire est dans le sac. 1933: La Vie d'un fleuve; Zéro de conduite; Quatorze Juillet. 1934: Le Dernier Milliardaire; L'Atalante; L'Ile de Pâques (+n). 1937: Drôle de drame; Un Carnet de bal; Les Maisons de la misère; Altitude 3,200; We Live in Two Worlds. 1938: Quai des brumes; Hôtel du Nord. 1939: La Fin du jour; Le Jour se lève; Air Pur (uf).

JEANSON, Henri

Writer. Paris 1900–70 Honfleur, France
Father taught political economy. Educated in Paris. Some work as actor. 1924: reporter for Paris-Soir. Contributor to e.g. Crapouillot, La Flèche, Le Canard Enchaîné, L'Intransigeant, Combat. Playwright. Worked in films frequently as dialoguist. 1949: directed, produced and co-wrote Lady Paname. 1957: worked with Max Ophüls on Montparnasse 19; on latter's death Jacques Becker completely rewrote script. Plays include 'Marie-Octobre' (filmed 1958). 1964: Paris When it Sizzles based on La Fête à Henriette (1953) which he co-wrote. 1967: TV critic for L'Aurore. Book, 'Mots, Propos, Aphorismes' (1971).

Films as writer include: 1936: Mister Flow. 1937: Un Carnet de Bal (co-ad); Pépé le Moko (co-s/di). 1938: Hôtel du Nord (ad/di); Entrée des Artistes (co-s/ad/di). 1942: La Nuit Fantastique; Carmen. 1947: Boule de suif. 1947: Les Maudits (di); Les Amoureux sont seuls au monde. 1948: Aux Yeux du souvenir (co-st/co-s/di). 1949: Au Royaume des cieux (di); Lady Paname (d/p/co-s). 1951: Fanfan la Tulipe; Le Garçon Sauvage (ad/di). 1952: La Minute de la verité (co-s/di). 1953: La Fête à Henriette (co-s/di). 1954: Madame DuBarry. 1955: Nana; Marguérite de la nuit. 1957: Pot-Bouille (di); Montparnasse 19 (ad). 1958: Guinguette (co-s/co-st/di); Marie-Octobre (di). 1959: La Vache et le prisonnier. 1960: L'Affaire d'une nuit. 1961: Vive Henri IV . . . Vive l'Amour! (co-s/di); Madame Sans-Gêne. 1962: Le Glaive et la balance (di). 1963: Les Bonnes Causes (ad/di); Paris When it Sizzles (co-st). 1964: Le Repas des fauves. 1965: Le Majordôme (co-s).

Emil Jannings in Der Letzte Mann.
Eija Pokkinen and Jaakko Pakkasvirta in Risto Jarva's Onnenpoli.
Listen to Britain, directed by Humphrey Jennings.

JENNINGS, Humphrey

Director. Walberswick, Suffolk 1907–50 Poros, Greece

Father an architect. Perse School and Pembroke College, Cambridge. 1929: graduated with starred first in English tripos; research at Pembroke in Elizabethan art and literature. Acted and designed sets for theatre; wrote a few articles for magazine Experiment; published revised text of 'Venus and Adonis' (1930). Also painter and poet; poems published only in limited edition in New York the year after his death. Belonged to Cambridge group including I. A. Richards, Jacob Bronowski, William Empson, Malcom Lowry, Kathleen Raine. 1934: joined GPO Film Unit under John Grierson; acted in *The Glorious Eighth of June*; designed sets and appeared in *Pett and Pott*; first film as director. 1936: colour direction (Gasparcolour) on Len Lye's *The Birth of the Robot*; acted in Stuart Legg's *The Voice of Britain* for BBC; organiser and exhibitor in first international exhibition of surrealist paintings in London. 1937: co-edited (with Charles Madge) 'May the 12th', a Mass Observation Day-Survey. 1938: exhibited his paintings at London Gallery. 1939–47: directed documentaries with GPO Film Unit for the Ministry of Information, which became Crown Film Unit from 1941: produced *V.I.* (1944). 1944–47: travelled to France, Sicily, Burma, Egypt. 1947: joined Wessex Films for which he made last 2 documentaries. Uncompleted book, 'Pandaemonium', a collection of quotations from English literature (1660–1880) to show the changing relationship between man and the machine that culminated in the industrial revolution. Killed in fall from cliff, inspecting Greek locations for film, *The Good Life*, completed after his death.

Films as director: 1934: Poste Haste (+e); Locomotives. 1939: Spare Time (+s); Speaking from America; The First Days – A City Prepares (*co-d Harry Watt, Pat Jackson*); SS Ionian – Her Last Trip. 1940: Spring Offensive – An Unrecorded Victory; Welfare of the Workers; London Can Take It (*co-d Harry Watt*); Britain Can Take It (*shortened UK version of*) London Can Take It. 1941: Heart of Britain – This is England (*extended US version*); Words for Battle (+s). 1942: Listen to Britain (+*co-e; co-d Stewart McAllister*). 1943: Fires Were Started – I Was a Fireman (+s). 1944: The True Story of Lilli Marlene (+s/w); The 80 Days (+p). 1945: A Diary for Timothy (+s); A Defeated People (+s). 1947: The Cumberland Story (+s). 1949: Dim Little Island (+p). 1950: Family Portrait (+s).

JESSUA, Alain

Director. Paris 1923–

Into films on leaving school. Studied under Jacques Becker on *Casque d'or* (1952). 1952–53: assisted Jacques Baratier on shorts. Then assistant to Max Ophüls on *Madame de . . .* (1953); *Lola Montès* (1955), also to Yves Allégret, Marcel Carné. 1957: produced and directed first short. 1964: produced, directed and scripted first feature. Married actress Anna Gaylor (1961).

Films as director: 1957: Léo la Lune – Leo the Moon (+p; *co-d Robert Giraud*). 1964: La Vie à l'envers – Life Upside Down (+p/s). 1967: Jeu de massacre – Comic Strip Hero (+s).

JEWISON, Norman

Director. Toronto, Canada 1926–

University of Toronto; studied under Marshall McLuhan. Writer and actor for BBC in London, then producer and director for CBC in Canada. From 1958: producer and director for CBS in New York e.g. 'The Broadway of Lerner and Loewe', 'The Judy Garland Show', 'The Harry Belafonte Show'. TV work took him to West Coast; first film as director (1962). 1965: replaced Sam Peckinpah on *The Cincinnati Kid*. 1970: produced Hal Ashby's *The Landlord*. 5-film contract with Mirisch for United Artists replaced before expiry with 6-film contract. 1969: first film under new contract.

Films as director: 1962: 40 Pounds of Trouble. 1963: The Thrill of it All. 1964: Send Me No Flowers. 1965: The Art of Love; The Cincinnati Kid. 1966: The Russians are Coming, the Russians are Coming (+p). 1967: In the Heat of the Night. 1968: The Thomas Crown Affair (+p). 1969: Gaily, Gaily – Chicago, Chicago (+p). 1971: Fiddler on the Roof (+p).

JOANNON, Léo

Director. Aix-en-Provence, France 1904–69 Paris

Studied law. 1922–25: assistant at Gaumont. 1925–26: assistant at Ciné-Romans. Assisted e.g. Augusto Genina, G. W. Pabst, Carmine Gallone. Became writer then cinematographer. From 1930: director. 1943: produced Bernard Roland's *La Collection Ménard*. From 1947: own studios, for which he produced and directed. 1950: directed Laurel and Hardy in *Atoll K*, their last film. 1957: co-wrote with Julien Duvivier the latter's *Pot-Bouille*. Acted in some of own films, also in e.g. *Les Aristocrates* (1955). Several novels e.g. 'Nostalgie' (1929). Chevalier du Légion d'Honneur. Died of heart attack.

Films as director: 1930: Adieu les copains (+s). 1932: Suzanne (*co-d Raymond Rouleau*). 1933: Six Cent Mille Francs par mois. 1934: Bibi la Purée. 1935: Train de plaisir; Quelle Drôle de gosse. 1936: Mais n'te promène donc pas toute nue; Le Chanteur de minuit; Le Traverseur d'Atlantique; Vous n'avez rien à declarer? (*co-d Yves Allégret*). 1937: L'Homme sans coeur. 1938: Alerte en Mediterranée – Hell's Cargo (+st/s); Escape: L'Emigrante. 1940: Documents Secrets. 1941: Caprice (+st). 1942: Le Camion Blanc (+co-st/co-s). 1943: Lucrèce; Le Carrefour des enfants perdus. 1949: Le Quatre-vingt-quatre prend des vacances (+co-ad). 1950: Atoll K – Robinson Crusoeland – Utopia (+st). 1951: Drôle de noce (+co-p/co-st/co-s). 1953: Le Défroqué (+st/co-ad/w). 1955: Le Secret de Soeur Angèle (+st/ad/co-di). 1956: L'Homme aux clefs d'or (+st/co-ad). 1958: Le Désert de Pigalle (+co-s/w); Tant d'amour perdu (+st/co-ad). 1961: L'Assassin est dans l'annuaire (+co-ad). 1962: Fort du fou (+co-ad). 1966: Trois Enfants dans le désordre (+co-s). 1967: Les Arnaud – The Arnauds (+co-s).

JOHNSON, Nunnally

Writer. Columbus, Georgia 1897–

Reporter and columnist for e.g. New York Herald Tribune. Magazine fiction and articles. 1930: published volume of short stories, 'There Ought To Be A Law'. From 1933: wrote for films. 1935: associate producer then producer, as well as writer. 1943: founded International Pictures, later amalgamated with Universal. From 1948: with Fox, writing, producing and (from 1954) directing.

Films include: 1935: Baby Face Harrington (*co-s*). 1936: The Prisoner of Shark Island (*as-p/s*). 1939: Jesse James (*as-p/st/s*). 1940: The Grapes of Wrath (*as-p/s*). 1941: Tobacco Road (s). 1942: Roxie Hart (p/s). 1943: Holy Matrimony (p/s). 1944: The Keys of the Kingdom (*co-s*); The Woman in the Window (p/s). 1945: Along Came Jones (s). 1946: The Dark Mirror (p/s). 1950: Three Came Home (p/s); The Mudlark (p/s). 1951: The Desert Fox (p/s). 1952: My Cousin Rachel (p/s). 1953: How to Marry a Millionaire (p/s). 1954: Night People (*d/p/s*); Black Widow (*d/p/s*). 1955: How to be Very, Very Popular (*d/p/s*). 1956: The Man in the Gray Flannel Suit (*d/s*). 1957: The Three Faces of Eve (*d/p/s*); Oh, Men! Oh, Women! (*d/p/s*). 1959: The Man Who Understood Women (*d/p/s*). 1960: Flaming Star (*co-s*); La Sposa Bella – The Angel Wore Red (*d/s*). 1962: Mr Hobbs Takes A Vacation (s). 1964: The World of Henry Orient (*co-s*). 1967: The Dirty Dozen (*co-s*).

JOHNSON, Van

(Charles Van Johnson) Actor. Newport, Rhode Island 1916–

1935: New York stage debut, as dancer. 1936: Broadway debut, Vaudeville tours, cabaret. 1940: Understudy for Eddie Bracken, Desi Arnaz, and Richard Kollmar in 'Too Many Girls', also appeared in 'Pal Joey'. 1940: first film as actor *Too Many Girls*. Also stage and films in UK and Spain.

Films as actor include: 1942: Somewhere I'll Find You; Dr Gillespie's New Assistant. 1943: Pilot No 5; Dr Gillespie's Criminal Case; The Human Comedy; Madame Curie. 1944: A Guy Named Joe; The White Cliffs of Dover; Two Girls and a Sailor; Thirty Seconds Over Tokyo; Weekend at the Waldorf. 1945: Thrill of a Romance. 1948: State of the Union. 1949: Command Decision; Grounds for Marriage; In the Good Old Summertime; Battleground. 1951: Three Guys Named Mike; It's A Big Country. 1952: Invitation; When In Rome; Plymouth Adventure. 1953: Remains To Be Seen; Easy to Love. 1954: The Caine Mutiny; Brigadoon; The Last Time I Saw Paris; The Siege at Red River; The End of the Affair. 1956: The Bottom of the Bottle; 23 Paces to Baker Street; Miracle In the Rain. 1957: Kelly and Me; Action of the Tiger. 1959: Web of Evidence. 1967: Divorce American Style. 1968: Where Angels Go, Trouble Follows; Yours, Mine and Ours.

JOLSON, Al

(Asa Yoelson) Singer and actor. St Petersburg, Russia 1886–1950 San Francisco

Father a Rabbi; mother died in Russia. To USA as a boy. Began as vaudeville entertainer. Broadway success as singer in the 1920s. 1926: persuaded by Warners to accept shares in their nearly-bankrupt company in lieu of salary for appearing in film of recent stage hit, *The Jazz Singer*; outstanding success (1927) as first part-talking feature film (musical accompaniment and 4 talking or singing sequences). Then made films as well as appearances as nightclub and revue entertainer. Film biographies: *The Jolson Story*

(1946) and *Jolson Sings Again* (1949) with Larry Parks in title role and Jolson singing on soundtrack. 4 wives include singer and dancer Ruby Keeler.

Films as actor: 1927: The Jazz Singer. 1928: The Singing Fool. 1929: Say it with Songs; Sonny Boy. 1930: The Big Boy; Mammy. 1933: Hallelujah I'm a Bum. 1934: Wonder Bar. 1935: Go Into Your Dance. 1936: The Singing Kid. 1939: Rose of Washington Square; Hollywood Cavalcade; Swanee River. 1945: Rhapsody in Blue.

JONES, Chuck
(Charles M.)

Animator. Spokane, Washington 1912–
Art studies. Seaman, then variety of jobs including portrait painting. 1931–33: worked for Ub Iwerks, then Walter Lantz. 1933: became assistant at Warners under Leon Schlesinger. 1938: first cartoon as director, *The Night Watchman*. While at Warners worked on many cartoons including Porky the Pig, Daffy Duck, Bugs Bunny, Private Snafu, and Inki; directed all the Roadrunner and Pepe Le Pew cartoons made at Warners. World War II: training films for Army. 1949: with Friz Freleng made government health cartoon *So Much for So Little*. 1953: with Disney from July to November; worked on *Sleeping Beauty*. Worked with Freleng on Bugs Bunny TV show. 1962: Warners Cartoon Department closed down. 1963: produced Tom and Jerry series for MGM. 1970: Executive Producer and co-director on animated feature *The Phantom Tollbooth*; became director of children's programmes for ABC Television. Also science films. Oscars for *So Much for So Little* (1949) as a documentary short, *For Scent-imental Reasons* (1949) as a cartoon, *The Dot and The Line* (1965).

Films as animator include: 1939: Little Brother Rat. 1940: Elmer's Candid Camera; Elmer's Pet Rabbit. 1944: Hell Bent for Election. 1945: Fresh Airedale; Hare Conditioned; Hair Raising Hare. 1947: What's Brewin' Bruin? 1949: Bear Feat; Long-Haired Hare. 1951: Bunny Hugged, The Rabbit of Seville. 1952: Feed the Kitty. 1953: Duck Amuck. 1955: One Froggy Evening. 1957: What's Opera Doc? 1970: The Phantom Tollbooth (*co-d Abe Levitow*).

JONES, Jennifer

(Phylis Isley). Actress. Tulsa, Oklahoma 1919–
Parents toured in vaudeville tent shows. First professional stage appearance in tent shows and stock companies touring South- and Mid-West. 1936–37: at American Academy of Dramatic Art, studied under Constance Collier, Michael Chekhov, Uta Hagen, Lee Strasberg. After graduation worked on radio, in summer stock and as a model. First film (1939), then return to New York. Contract after discovery by David Selznick, who sent her to act in a William Saroyan play in Santa Barbara (1941) as training. 1954: Broadway in 'Portrait of a Lady'. Married Robert Walker (1939–45), then David Selznick (1949–65, widowed). Oscar as Best Actress (1943) for *The Song of Bernadette*.

Films as actress include: 1944: Since You Went Away. 1945: Love Letters. 1946: Cluny Brown; Duel in the Sun. 1949: Portrait of Jennie; We Were Strangers;

Madame Bovary. 1951: Gone to Earth. 1952: Carrie; Wild Heart – Gone to Earth; Ruby Gentry. 1954: Stazione Termini; Beat the Devil. 1955: Love is a Many-Splendored Thing; Good Morning, Miss Dove. 1956: The Man in the Gray Flannel Suit. 1957: A Farewell to Arms; The Barretts of Wimpole Street. 1962: Tender is the Night.

JONES, Shirley

Actress. Smithton, Pennsylvania 1934–
Started singing lessons at 6. In school plays; winner of State singing contest, and Miss Pittsburgh. Studied acting at Pittsburgh Playhouse. 1953: auditioned for Richard Rodgers and Oscar Hammerstein II who immediately began training her for *Oklahoma!* by giving her a small part in 'Me and Juliet' on Broadway and the lead on tour. 1958: nightclub tour with husband, Jack Cassidy; acted in summer stock; plays and musicals on TV; industrial variety shows. Oscar as supporting actress for *Elmer Gantry* (1960).

Films as actress include: 1955: Oklahoma! 1956: Carousel. 1957: April Love. 1958: Never Steal Anything Small. 1960: Elmer Gantry; Pepe. 1961: Two Rode Together. 1962: The Music Man. 1963: The Courtship of Eddie's Father; A Ticklish Affair. 1964: Dark Purpose. 1965: The Secret of My Success. 1970: The Cheyenne Social Club.

JOUVET, Louis

Actor. Crozon, France 1887–1951 Paris
Founded the Théâtre d'action d'art. 1913: first film as actor *Shylock*. 1914–18: military service. 1919: repertory in New York. 1922: stage manager at Comédie des Champs Elysées. From 1924: stage director, including 'Knock', 'La Machine Infernale'. Long collaboration with Jean Giraudoux; staged his plays. 1934: taught at Paris Conservatoire. 1941: produced 'Knock' in Switzerland. To South and Central America. 1945: returned to France. Own stage production company, producing plays of e.g. Jean Genet, Giraudoux.

Films as actor include: 1933: Topaze. 1935: La Kermesse Héroïque. 1936: Les Bas-fonds; Mister Flow. 1937: L'Alibi; Drôle de drame; Un Carnet de bal. 1938: Hôtel du Nord. 1939–41: Volpone. 1939: La Fin du jour. 1946: Les Chouans. 1947: Quai des Orfèvres. 1948: Entre onze heures et minuit. 1949: Retour à la vie; Lady Paname. 1950: Miquette et sa mère. 1951: Knock.

JULIAN, Rupert

Director. Auckland, New Zealand 1889–
From 1905: acted in repertory in Australia, South Africa, Europe and USA. Various casual jobs in USA. Began to act in films in the late 1910s. Directed for several companies e.g. Bluebird, Renowned. 1919–25: worked for Universal. 1923: replaced Erich von Stroheim on *Merry-Go-Round*. 1925–27: worked for Cecil B. de Mille's Producers Distributing Corporation. 1930: made *Love Comes Along* for RKO, *The Cat Creeps* for Universal.

Films as director include (complete from 1922): 1916: Bettina Loved a Soldier; The Evil Woman Do; The Right to be Happy; The Bugler of Algiers. 1917: Mother of Mine (+ *co-s*); A Kentucky Cinderella.

Tony Curtis, Stubby Kaye and Tom Reese in 40 Pounds of Trouble, *directed by Norman Jewison.*
Night People, *directed by Nunnally Johnson, with Gregory Peck.*
Lon Chaney in The Phantom of the Opera, *directed by Rupert Julian.*

1918: The Kaiser – The Kaiser, the Beast of Berlin (+ w). 1919: The Fire Flingers (+ w). 1922: The Girl who Ran Wild (+ s). 1923: Merry-Go-Round (co-d Erich von Stroheim). 1924: Love and Glory (+ co-s). 1925: The Phantom of the Opera; Hell's Highroad. 1926: Three Faces East; Silence. 1927: The Country Doctor; The Yankee Clipper. 1928: Leopard Lady; Walking Back. 1930: Love Comes Along; The Cat Creeps.

JUNE, Ray

Cinematographer. Ithaca, New York c. 1898–1958 Hollywood

Cornell University. World War I: photographer in US Signal Corps. In 1920s, taught motion picture photography at Columbia University. Cinematographer by 1924. 1936–54: under contract to MGM. 1954: freelance.

Films as cinematographer include: 1928: So This is Love. 1929: New York Nights. 1931: Indiscreet (co); Reaching for the Moon; Bought. 1932: Arrowsmith; Cynara; Horse Feathers. 1933: Secrets; I Cover the Waterfront. 1934: The Girl from Missouri; The Gay Bride; Treasure Island (+ co). 1935: China Seas; Barbary Coast. 1936: Wife vs Secretary. 1937: Night Must Fall; Saratoga. 1938: Test Pilot. 1939: Babes in Arms. 1940: Strike Up the Band. 1941: H.M. Pulham, Esq; Love Crazy; Ziegfeld Girl. 1943: I Dood It. 1948: Three Daring Daughters; The Sun Comes Up. 1949: The Secret Garden; Shadow on the Wall. 1950: Crisis; The Reformer and the Redhead. 1951: It's a Big Country (co); Strictly Dishonorable; Callaway Went Thataway. 1952: Just This Once; Invitation; Above and Beyond. 1953: Code Two; Easy to Love; A Slight Case of Larceny; Sombrero. 1954: Hot Blood; The Court Jester; Day of Triumph. 1957: Funny Face. 1958: Houseboat.

JÜRGENS, Curd

Actor and director. Munich 1912–

Educated in Vienna and Berlin. 1935: first film as actor Der Königswaltzer, from 1950: occasionally also director. 1957: first American film as actor The Enemy Below. Also theatrical work. Married model Simone Boucheron and actress Eva Bartok.

Films as actor include: 1936: Die Unbekannte. 1937: Zu neuen Ufern. 1940: Operette. 1943: Frauen sind Keine Engel. 1945: Wiener Mädeln. 1948: Das singende Haus. 1951: Das Geheimnis einer Ehe. 1952: 1 April 2000. 1953: Praterherzen. 1954: Das Bekenntnis der Ima Kahr. 1955: Die Ratten; Des Teufels General; Les Héros sont fatigués. 1956: Michel Strogoff; Et Dieu créa la femme; Teufel in Seide; Orient-Express. 1958: Bitter Victory; Les Espions; Tamango; Schinderhannes; This Happy Feeling; Me and the Colonel; The Inn of the Sixth Happiness; The Blue Angel. 1959: Ferry to Hong Kong; I Aim at the Stars. 1960: Schachnovelle. 1963: Die Dreigroschenoper. 1964: Lord Jim; DM-Killer. 1966: Jardinier d'Argenteuil. 1967: Der Lügner und die Nonne. 1969: Ohrfeigen. 1970: Hello-Goodbye. 1971: The Mephisto Waltz; Kill; Nicholas and Alexandra.

Films as director and actor: 1950: Prämien auf den Tod (+ co-s). 1951: Gangster premiere (+ co-s). 1956: Ohne Dich wird es Nacht. 1961: Bankraub in der rue Latour.

JUTRA, Claude

Director. Montreal, 1930–

1946–52: University of Montreal, then medical studies. 1947–49: directed 2 amateur shorts in collaboration with Michel Brault. Studied at Théâtre de Nouveau Monde school then in Paris with René Simon; studied film direction on Canadian Arts Council in France. Worked on TV series, 'Images en boites', 'Cinéma Canadien', 'Profils'; wrote TV play 'l'Ecole de la peur'; with Michel Brault directed 'Les Enfants du silence' for TV. From 1954: worked chiefly with National Film Board of Canada. 1957: worked with Norman McLaren; acted in A Chairy Tale; published a diary of shooting. 1959: made Anna la Bonne in France. 1960: collaborated with Jean Rouch on Le Niger-Jeune République; diary of shooting published in Cahiers du Cinéma. 1962: wrote commentary for and edited Petit discours de la méthode. Many of his films photographed by Michel Brault.

Films as director: 1947: Le Dément du Lac Jean Jaune (+ co-d Michel Brault). 1949: Mouvement Perpetuel (+ s; co-d Michel Brault). 1956: Pierrot des bois (+ s/e/w); Les Jeunesses Musicales (+ s). 1957: A Chairy Tale – Il était une chaise (+ w; co-d Norman McLaren). 1958: Les Mains Nettes. 1959: Anna la bonne; Felix Leclerc, Troubadour; Fred Barry, Comédien (+ s). 1961: Le Niger-Jeune République (+ e); La Lutte (+ co-c/co-e; co-d Michel Brault, Claude Fournier, Marcel Carrière). 1962: Quebec-USA (+ c; co-d Michel Brault). 1963: Les Enfants du silence (+ cy/e; co-d Michel Brault); A tout prendre (+ s/e/w). 1966: Comment Savoir; Rouli-Roulant (+ co-c/cy/e). 1969: Wow (+ s co-e). 1970: Marie-Christine (co-d Geneviève Bujold). 1971: Mon Oncle Antoine.

JUTZI, Piel (Phil)

Director. Rheinpfalz 1894–

1919: first film as director Die Rache des Banditen. In 1920s worked frequently as cinematographer, e.g. in collaboration photographed Fedor Otsep's Der lebende Leichnam and most of own films. 1928: Hunger in Waldenburg banned. Worked as cinematographer at least to 1942.

Films as director include: 1919: Die Rache des Banditen; Der maskierte Schrecken (+ s); Das blinkende Fenster (+ s). 1920: Das Licht scheuen . . .; Red Bull, der letzte Apache. 1926: Klass und Datsch, die Pechvögel (+ s/c/dec). 1927: Die Machnower Schleusen (+ s/c); Kindertragödie. 1928: Hunger in Waldenburg (+ c). 1929: Mutter Krausens Fahrt ins Glück (+ c); Berlin-Alexanderplatz. 1935: Kosak und die Nachtigall; Lockspitzel Asew.

K

KALATOZOV, Mikhail

(Mikhail Kalatozishvili) Director. Tiflis, Russia 1903– Business school. Entered films as cinematographer. 1930: first 2 films as director, made in Georgia. 1932: next film Gvozd v sapogye unreleased because of pressure

from army; it was defended in 'Proletarskoye Kino'. Withdrew from direction for 7 years, became administrator in Tiflis studio. Presented script on Shamil, Caucasus hero; denounced for distortion of history; unmade. 1939: returned to direction with Muzhestvo. 1941–45: consul in Los Angeles. 1964: made O Soy Cuba in Cuba, scripted by Yevtushenko.

Films as director: 1930: Slepaya – Blind; Sol Svanetii – Salt for Svanetia (+ s). 1932: Gvozd v sapogye – Nail in the Boot (ur). 1939: Muzhestvo – Manhood. 1941: Valerii Chkalov – Wings of Victory. 1943: Nepobedimye – The Invincibles (+ co-s; co-d Sergei Gerasimov). 1950: Zagovor obrechyonnikh – Conspiracy of the Doomed. 1954: Vernye Druzya – True Friends. 1956: Pervyi Eshelon – The First Echelon; Vikhri Vrazhdebyne – The Hostile Wind. 1957: Felix Dzerzhinsky; Letyat Zhuravli – The Cranes are Flying. 1960: Neotpravlennoe Pismo – The Letter That was not Sent. 1964: O Soy Cuba – Ja-Kuba – I am Cuba. 1971: Krasnaya Palatka – The Red Tent.

KALMUS, Herbert Thomas

Colour technician and producer. Chelsea, Massachusetts 1881–1963

1904: Physics graduate of MIT. 1906: PhD at Zurich. Taught at MIT; specialised in chemistry and metallurgy. 1914: partnership with engineers Daniel Comstock and W. B. Westcott. 1915: set up Technicolor Corporation. 1918: directed and produced The Gulf Between using additive process, largely as demonstration film. 1922: set up Technicolor Inc, produced The Toll of the Sea using subtractive system. Many films in next few years used some colour largely because Technicolor was patented and Kalmus' company processed the films e.g. Ben-Hur (1926). 1926–28: supervised promotional demonstration shorts. By early 1930s perfected 3-colour subtractive system which became standard. 1950: Technicolor Inc dissolved. 1902–21: married to Natalie Dunfee with whom he collaborated.

KANIN, Garson

Producer, director, scriptwriter. Rochester, New York 1912–

American Academy of Dramatic Arts. 1937–39: assistant to George Abbott on series of stage comedies: 'Boy Meets Girl', 'Brother Rat', 'Room Service', 'What a Life'. 1938: assistant to Samuel Goldwyn; first film as director. 1941: began military service. 1942: directed army morale film Ring of Steel for Office of Emergency Management. 1948: scripted George Cukor's A Double Life; association continued through several films, often starring Judy Holliday. 1969: directed first solo feature since 1941. Book, 'Tracy and Hepburn' (1971).

Films as writer include: 1948: A Double Life (co). 1949: Adam's Rib (co). 1951: Born Yesterday (fpl). 1952: The Marrying Kind (co); Pat and Mike (co). 1954: It Should Happen To You. 1956: The Girl Can't Help It (fst). 1959: High Time (st). 1960: The Rat Race (+ fpl).

Films as director: 1938: A Man to Remember; Next Time I Marry. 1939: The Great Man Votes; Bachelor Mother. 1940: My Favorite Wife; They Knew What They Wanted. 1941: Tom, Dick and Harry. 1942:

Ring of Steel. 1945: The True Glory (co-d Carol Reed). 1969: Where It's At (+ s); Some Kind of a Nut.

KANTER, Hal

Writer and director. Savannah, Georgia 1918–
Writer for TV comedy including 'Amos 'n' Andy' and the Danny Kaye, Bing Crosby, Ed Wynn and George Gobel shows. 1949: for stage, produced 'The George Gobel Show'. 1951–54: writer for Paramount. From 1956: director and writer at RKO, starting with a film starring George Gobel.

Films as writer include: 1951: My Favorite Spy (di). 1953: Off Limits (+ st); Money from Home; Casanova's Big Night (co). 1954: About Mrs Leslie (co). 1955: Artists and Models (co); The Rose Tattoo. 1958: Mardi Gras (co). 1960: Let's Make Love (additional di). 1961: Bachelor in Paradise (co); Blue Hawaii; Pocketful of Miracles (co). 1963: Move Over, Darling (co). 1965: Dear Brigitte.

Films as director: 1956: I Married a Woman. 1957: Loving You (+ co-s). 1958: Once Upon a Horse (+ st/s).

KAPER, Bronislau

Composer. Warsaw, Poland 1902–
Warsaw Conservatory. 1903–33: composed scores for German films, usually in collaboration. After working in Vienna, London and Paris, began working in Hollywood in 1940. 1953: Oscar for Best Score of a Dramatic or Comedy Picture, Lili. Also TV.

Films as composer include: 1930: Alraune. 1940: Comrade X. 1941: Two-Faced Woman; Johnny Eager; H.M. Pulham, Esq. 1942: Keeper of the Flame. 1943: Bataan; The Cross of Lorraine. 1944: Gaslight. 1946: The Stranger; The Courage of Lassie. 1947: Green Dolphin Street. 1948: Act of Violence. 1949: The Great Sinner; The Secret Garden. 1950: A Life of her Own; Key to the City. 1951: Shadow in the Sky; The Red Badge of Courage; Three Guys named Mike; Jet Pilot (r 1957). 1953: The Actress; Ride, Vaquero!; The Naked Spur. 1955: Them!; The Glass Slipper. 1956: Somebody Up There Likes Me. 1957: Don't Go Near the Water; The Barretts of Wimpole Street; The Brothers Karamazov. 1958: Auntie Mame. 1959: Green Mansions. 1960: Butterfield 8; Home from the Hill. 1961: Two Loves. 1962: Mutiny on the Bounty. 1964: Kisses for my President.

KARINA, Anna

Actress. Copenhagen 1941–
Left school at 16, studied painting; worked as photographic model. 1957: first film, Pigin och skoene, short made in Denmark. 1958: went to Paris; in fashion features for magazines Jours de France and Jardin des modes; engaged by Pierre Cardin as model. Made advertising films in Paris and London. Rejected part in A bout de souffle offered by Jean-Luc Godard; first film Le Petit Soldat (1960). Married Godard after making Une Femme est une femme (1961). 1967: Last film with Godard.

Films as actress include: 1960: Ce Soir ou jamais. 1961: Une Femme est une femme. 1962: Vivre sa vie. 1963: Dragees au poivre. 1964: Bande à part; La

Ronde; De l'amour. 1965: Alphaville; Pierrot le fou. 1966: Made in USA. 1967: Lo Straniero; Le Plus Vieux Métier du monde ep Anticipation. 1969: Justine. 1971: Rendez-vous à Bray.

KARLOFF, Boris

(William Henry Pratt) Actor. London 1887–1969 Midhurst, Sussex
Diplomatic training. 1910–16: acted in stock. 1941: New York stage debut in 'Arsenic and Old Lace'. Other work in theatre includes: 'On Borrowed Time', 'The Linden Tree', 'The Shop at Sly Corner', 'Peter Pan', 'The Lark'.

Films as actor include: 1916: The Dumb Girl of Portici. 1920: The Last of the Mohicans; The Deadlier Sex. 1925: Forbidden Cargo. 1926: The Bells. 1927: Two Arabian Knights. 1928: Old Ironsides; Burning the Wind; The Fatal Warning. 1929: King of the Kongo; The Unholy Night; Burning the Wind. 1930: The Utah Kid. 1931: The Criminal Code; Five Star Final; Frankenstein; Young Donovan's Kid; The Mad Genius; The Yellow Ticket; Tonight or Never. 1932: Business and Pleasure; Alias the Doctor; The Miracle Man; The Mummy; Scarface, Shame of the Nation; The Old Dark House; The Mask of Fu Manchu. 1934: The Black Cat; The Lost Patrol. 1935: Bride of Frankenstein. 1936: The Man Who Changed His Mind; The Walking Dead. 1937: West of Shanghai. 1938: The Invisible Menace. 1941: You'll Find Out; The Devil Commands. 1945: Isle of the Dead; The Body Snatcher. 1946: Bedlam. 1947: The Secret Life of Walter Mitty; Unconquered; Lured. 1948: Tap Roots. 1949: Abbott and Costello Meet the Killer: Boris Karloff. 1951: The Strange Door. 1959: Frankenstein–1970. 1963: The Raven; The Terror. 1964: The Comedy of Terrors. 1966: The Ghost in the Invisible Bikini. 1968: The Sorcerers; Targets.

KARLSON, Phil

(Phil Karlstein) Director. Chicago 1908–
Educated at Loyola Schools in Chicago and Los Angeles. Art Institute of Chicago; while student became gagman at Buster Keaton studios. 1927–29: props department at Universal. Became editor, studio manager, production manager, assistant director. Assisted e.g. Stuart Walker, also on films of Tom Mix. Managed Byron Foy for a year. 1940–43: US Air Corps as civilian flight instructor. 1942: associate producer on Between us Girls. From 1944: director. 1949: Down Memory Lane was compilation film on American silent films. 1959: made The Scarface Mob as pilot for TV series 'The Untouchables'. 1961: Richard Widmark, only credited as producer and actor, completed The Secret Ways. 1963: replaced Henry Hathaway on Rampage. 1968: replaced Roger Corman on A Time for Killing.

Films as director: 1944: A Wave, a Wac and a Marine. 1945: There Goes Kelly; GI Honeymoon; The Shanghai Cobra. 1946: Live Wires; Swing Parade of 1946: Dark Alibi; Behind the Mask; Bowery Bombshell; The Missing Lady; Wife Wanted. 1947: Black Gold; Louisiana; Kilroy was Here. 1948: Rocky; Adventures in Silverado; Thunderhoof. 1949: The Big Cat; Ladies of the Chorus; Down Memory Lane. 1950: The Iroquois Trail. 1951: Lorna Doone; The

Bing Crosby in drag; from Blake Edwards' High Time, based on a story by Garson Kanin.
Boris Karloff in Daniel Haller's Monster of Terror.
Robert Stack in The Scarface Mob, directed by Phil Karlson.

Texas Rangers; Mask of the Avenger. 1952: Scandal Sheet – Dark Page; The Brigand; Kansas City Confidential – The Secret 4. 1953: 99 River Street. 1954: They Rode West; Hell's Island. 1955: Tight Spot; Five Against the House; The Phenix City Story. 1957: The Brothers Rico. 1958: Gunman's Walk. 1959: The Scarface Mob. 1960: Hell to Eternity- Key Witness. 1961: The Secret Ways (co-d Richard Widmark, uc); The Young Doctors. 1962: Kid Galahad. 1963: Rampage (co-d Henry Hathaway, uc). 1966: The Silencers. 1968: A Time for Killing – The Long Ride Home (co-d Roger Corman, uc); The Wrecking Crew. 1970: Hornet's Nest.

KARMEN, Roman

Newsreel operator and director. Odessa, Russia 1906– With Tissé on Kara-Kum expedition, filmed drive from Moscow to desert and back. To Spain to film Civil War; in bombardment ꝍ Madrid; 2 films made from his Spanish material, including Ispaniya edited by Esther Shub in 1939. 1938–39: to China; in bombing of Shanghai. 1940: for Sedovchy lived in polar regions for 4 months. 1942: in Leningrad under siege; spoke at Conference on American and British cinema organised by VOKS. 1945: one of over 40 photographers on Berlin. Areas worked in include Albania, Turkmenistan, Kazakhstan, Georgia, Caspian, India, Vietnam, Cuba.

Films as director and cinematographer include: 1932: Moskva – Moscow. 1940: Sedovchy – The Sedovites; Den novogo mira – A Day in the New World. 1941: V Kitai – In China. 1942: Leningrad v borbye – Leningrad in Combat (co-c; co-d 3 others). 1945: Albaniya. 1953: Povest o neftyanikakh Kaspiya – Story of the Caspian Oil Men. 1954: Vietnam. 1959: Utro India – Indian Morning; Pokoriteli Morya – Conquered Seas. 1960: Cuba Segodnya – Cuba Today. 1963: Gost o ostrova svobody – Guest on Freedom Island. 1965: Velikaya Otechestvennaya – The Great Patriotic War.

KAST, Pierre

Director. Paris 1920–
Sorbonne University. World War II: worked in Resistance. After Liberation, journalist on Action. From 1945: worked with Henri Langlois at Cinématheque Française. From 1948–49: assistant to Jean Grémillon (Le Printemps de la liberté, Pattes Blanches). 1949: collaborated with Grémillon on first short film as director. 1951–55: assistant to René Clément on Jeux Interdits (1952), Jean Renoir on French Can-Can (1955), Preston Sturges on Les Carnets du Major Thompson (1955). 1952: with Boris Vian and J. P. Vitet directed play 'Cinémassacre'. 1957: first feature as director. Also TV films including Le Grain de sable (1965), La Naissance de l'empire romain' (1965), Carnets Brésiliens (1967). Writings in Cahiers du Cinéma, Positif, Revue du Cinéma, Cinéma 54–58, L'Ecran, 'L'Encyclopédie de la Pléiade'.

Short films as director: 1949: Les Charmes de l'existence (+ s; co-d Jean Grémillon). 1951: Les Femmes du Louvre (+ co-s); Les Désastres de la guerre (+ co-s; co-d Jean Grémillon); Encyclopédie Filmée, arithmétique. 1952: La Guerre en dentelles – Jacques Callot, correspondant du guerre (+ s/m); Je sème a tout vent (+ co-s). 1953: A nous deux, Paris!; La Chasse à l'homme (+ s). 1954: L'Architecte Maudit.

Claude-Nicolas Ledoux; Monsieur Robida, prophète et explorateur du temps. 1955: Nos ancêtres les explorateurs. 1956: Le Corbusier, l'architecte du bonheur. 1958: Des ruines et des hommes (co-d); Images pour Baudelaire. 1959: Une Question d'assurance; Japon, d'hiver et d'aujourdhui (co-d). 1965: La Brûlure de mille soleils – The Radiance of a Thousand Suns – The Fire of a Thousand Suns (+ s).

Features as director: 1957: Un Amour de poche. 1960: Merci, Natercia; Le Bel Âge – Love is When You Make it (+ co-s). 1961: La Morte—saison des amours – Les Liaisons Amoureuses – The Season for Love (+ co/s). 1963: Les Vacances Portugaises. 1967: Drôle de jeu – The Most Dangerous Game.

KATZMAN, Sam

Producer. New York, 1901
1924–31: with Fox, First National and Cosmopolitan, from prop boy to production manager and assistant producer. 1931: started producing low-budget pictures, a field in which he has since specialised including 'Bowery Boys' and 'Jungle Jim' series. His big successes were Rock Around the Clock (1956) and Don't Knock the Rock (1957). The plot of the former reappeared almost unchanged in Don't Knock the Twist (1962). Moved from Columbia to MGM.

KAUFMAN, Boris

Cinematographer. Biatystok, Poland 1906–
Brother of Dziga Vertov and cinematographer Mikhaïl Kaufman. Sorbonne University. Involved in brother's group of documentary film-makers. From 1928: work as cinematographer in Paris included La Marche des machines and Jean Vigo's 4 films. From 1931: cinematographer with Paramount in Paris. 1935: cinematographer in collaboration on Lucrèce Borgia. 1940–41: served in French army. 1942: to USA; worked for National Film Board of Canada (1942–43) and on American war documentaries (1943–45). Then freelance cinematographer in New York, working for various companies. Oscar for best black and white cinematography, On the Waterfront (1954).

Short films as cinematographer: 1929: A propos de Nice, point de vue documentée. 1931: Taris ou la natation. 1946: Journey into Medicine. 1948: Terribly Talented. 1950: The Tanglewood Story.

Features as cinematographer include: 1933: Zéro de conduite. 1934: L'Atalante. 1956: Baby Doll. 1957: Twelve Angry Men. 1959: That Kind of Woman; The Fugitive Kind. 1961: Splendor in the Grass. 1962: Long Day's Journey into Night. 1964: The World of Henry Orient (co). 1965: The Pawnbroker; The Group. 1968: Bye, Bye Braverman; The Brotherhood. 1970: Tell Me That You Love Me, Junie Moon.

KAUFMAN, George S.

Writer. Pittsburgh, Pennsylvania 1889–1961 New York
Mainly playwright, almost always with collaborators. Also novelist. The Cocoanuts (1929) taken from his play, with music by Irving Berlin. Films adapted by others from work with Edna Ferber include The Royal Family of Broadway (1931), Dinner at Eight (1933), Stage Door (1937). Films adapted by others

from plays written with Moss Hart include You Can't Take it with You (1938), The Man Who Came to Dinner (1942), George Washington Slept Here (1942). 1948: directed The Senator was Indiscreet. Also wrote in collaboration the plays on which The Solid Gold Cadillac (1956) and Silk Stockings (1957) were based.

Films as writer in collaboration include: 1933: Roman Scandals (co-st). 1935: A Night at the Opera (co-st/co-s).

KÄUTNER, Helmut

Director. Dusseldorf, Germany 1908–
Art, philology and drama at Munich University. Cabaret as actor and writer. 1939: began in films as scriptwriter; wrote and directed his first film. Scripts include many of own films. 1957: to Hollywood to make 2 films for Universal. Also stage and TV direction. Married actress Erika Balqué.

Films as director: 1939: Kitty und die Weltkonferenz (+ s); Die acht Entfesselten. 1940: Frau nach Mass (+ s); Kleider machen Leute (+ s). 1941: Auf Wiedersehn, Franziska. 1942: Anuschka (+ co-s); Wir maken Musik (+ s). 1943: Romanze in Moll (+ co-s). 1944: Grosse Freiheit Nr 7 – La Paloma (+ co-s). 1945: Unter den Brücken (+ co-s). 1947: In jenen Tagen (+ co-s). 1948: Film ohne Fitel (+ co-s); Der Apfel ist ab (+ co-d/co-s/co-lyr/fpl). 1949: Königskinder (+ co-s). 1950: Epilog (+ co-s). 1951: Weisse Schatten (+ co-s). 1952: Käpt'n Bay-Bay (+ co-s). 1953: Die letzte Brücke (+ co-s). 1954: Bildnis einer Unbekannten (+ co-s); Ludwig II. 1955: Des Teufels General (+ co-s); Ludwig II; Griff nach den Sternen; Himmel ohne Sterne (+ co-s/fpl). 1956: Ein Mädchen aus Flandern (+ co-s); Der Hauptmann von Köpenick (+ co-s). 1957: Die Zürcher Verlobung (+ co-s); Auf Wiedersehen, Franziska Monpti (+ co-s). 1958: The Wonderful Years – The Reckless Years – The Restless Years; A Stranger in my Arms; Der Schinderhannes. 1959: Der Rest ist Schweigen (+ s); Die Gans von Sedan (+ co-s). 1960: Das glas Wasser (+ s). 1961: Schwarzer Kies (+ co-s); Des Traum von Lieschen Müller. 1962: Die Rote – The Redhead. 1964: Das Haus in Montevideo; Lausbubengeschichten. 1970: Die Feuerzangenbowle.

KAWALEROWICZ, Jerzy

Director. Gwodziec, Poland 1922–
1946: graduated from Cracow Film Institute; also studied fine arts. 1948–51: assistant to e.g. Wanda Jakubowska; also writer. 1952: first film as director, in collaboration. 1954: Pamiatka z celulozy and Pod gwiazda Frygijska are 2 parts of one film. 1955: became artistic director of KADR film unit.

Films as director and writer in collaboration: 1952: Gromada – The Village Mill (co-d only; co-d Kazimierz Sumerski). 1954: Pamiatka z celulozy – A Night of Remembrance; Pod gwiazda Frygijska – Under the Phrygian Star. 1956: Cień – The Shadow (d only). 1957: Prawdziwy koniec wielkiej wojny – The Real End of the Great War. 1959: Pociąg – Night Train. 1961: Matka Joanna od Aniolow – The Devil and the Nun – Mother Joan of the Angels. 1965: Faraon – Pharaoh. 1969: Gra – The Game (d only). 1971: Maddalena (+ co-s).

KAYE, Danny

(David Daniel Kaminski) Actor. New York 1913–
Radio and vaudeville work. Dancing act, toured US and the Far East. Cabaret. 1939: Broadway debut in own show, 'The Straw Hat Revue' with Sylvia Fine and Imogene Coca. 1940: 'Lady in the Dark', with Gertrude Lawrence; married Sylvia Fine. 1941: in 'Let's Face It'. World War II: entertainment, USO tours. 1944: first film as actor *Up in Arms*. On stage acted in 'The Inspector General', on which Sylvia Fine was associate producer. Tours of US, Canada, UK. To 1952: films mainly for RKO. Later films usually for Paramount or Columbia. Radio, TV, cabaret.

Features as actor include: 1945: Wonder Man. 1946: The Kid from Brooklyn. 1947: The Secret Life of Walter Mitty; A Song is Born. 1949: It's a Great Feeling; The Inspector General. 1951: On the Riviera. 1952: Hans Christian Andersen. 1954: Knock on Wood; White Christmas. 1956: The Court Jester. 1958: Me and the Colonel; Merry Andrew. 1959: The Five Pennies. 1961: On the Double. 1963: The Man from the Diner's Club. 1969: The Madwoman of Chaillot.

KAZAN, Elia

(Elia Kazanjoglou). Director. Istanbul 1909–
Parents (of Greek origin) tried unsuccessfully to settle in Berlin (1911), returned home and (1913) emigrated to New York. 1930: degree from Williams College. 2 years at Yale University Drama School. 1931: first stage work as director, S. N. Behrman's 'The Second Man' for the Toy Theatre, Atlantic City. 1932: joined Group Theatre as apprentice, then stage manager. Also acted on stage until 1941, including parts in 5 plays by Clifford Odets. 1934: first film appearance in Ralph Steiner's short *Pie in the Sky*; co-author and co-director of 'Dimitroff' presented by the League of Workers' Theatre. 1937: directed and wrote a short, photographed by Ralph Steiner. 1938: director for Group Theatre. Directed many plays by e.g. Thornton Wilder, Tennessee Williams, Robert Anderson, Archibald Macleish, William Inge; they include (1947 to 1964): 'All My Sons', 'Death of a Salesman', 'After the Fall', 'A Streetcar Named Desire', 'Camino Real', 'Cat on a Hot Tin Roof', 'Sweet Bird of Youth', 'Tea and Sympathy', 'The Dark at the Top of the Stairs', 'J.B.'. 1940–41: small parts in 2 films directed by Anatole Litvak. 1941: directed feature for US Department of Agriculture. 1945: directed his first Hollywood film. Novels: 'America America' (1962), 'The Arrangement' (1967), 'The Assassins' (1971). Oscars for direction: *Gentleman's Agreement* (1947), which also won Oscar as Best Film, and *On the Waterfront* (1954). From 1955: also producer. Made *Baby Doll* (1956), *A Face in the Crowd* (1957) and *Wild River* (1960) for his own company.

Films as director: 1937: The People of the Cumberlands (+ s). 1941: It's Up to You. 1945: A Tree Grows in Brooklyn. 1946: The Sea of Grass. 1947: Boomerang!; Gentleman's Agreement. 1949: Pinky (co-d John Ford, u). 1950: Panic in the Streets. 1951: A Streetcar Named Desire. 1952: Viva Zapata! 1953: Man on a Tightrope. 1954: On the Waterfront. 1955: East of Eden (+ p). 1956: Baby Doll (+ p). 1957: A Face in the Crowd (+ p). 1960: Wild River (+ p). 1961: Splendor in the Grass (+ p). 1963: America, America – The Anatolian Smile (+ p/s/fn). 1969: The Arrangement (+ p/s/fn).

KEATON, Buster

(Joseph Francis Keaton) Actor and director. Pickway, Kansas 1895–1966 Hollywood
At 3 began to appear in parents' vaudeville act. 1917: left the act: to New York. Turned down place in Schubert revue to make series of shorts directed by Fatty Arbuckle for Paramount-Famous Players Lasky. 1918: to France in US Army. Returned to 2-reelers, for Metro then First National. 1920: first feature as actor *The Saphead* written by June Mathis; first film as director and actor 2-reeler *One Week* in collaboration with Eddie Cline. 1921: made *The Goat*, first film for own company. 1923: began series of features for Metro; married Natalie Talmadge (divorced 1933). 1924: broke his neck making *Sherlock, Jr*. 1926: To United Artists. Made last 4 silents there, and first sound film *Spite Marriage*. 1929–33: features for MGM. 1930–32: French versions of *Spite Marriage* and *The Passionate Plumber* directed by Claude Autant-Lara: *Buster se Marie* and *Le Plombier Amoureux*. 1934: to Europe, acted in *Le Roi des Champs-Elysées* in France, and *The Invaders* in UK. 1934–37: shorts for First National, Sennett and Educational. 1937: in psychiatric clinic. 1938: returned to MGM as uncredited gagman (e.g. for Red Skelton), writer and assistant director, director and actor on 3 1-reelers. 1939–45: small roles. 1946: in Mexico acted in *El Moderno Barba Azul*. Occasional film roles; appeared in European circuses. 1948: acted in *Un Duel à mort*, short based on sketch used at Cirque Médrano. TV in Britain. 1957: supervised *The Buster Keaton Story* for Paramount; played by Donald O'Connor. 1965: solo performance in *Film*, written for him by Samuel Beckett, intended to be first of a trilogy.

Films as director and writer in collaboration with Eddie Cline, and actor: 1920: One Week; Convict 13; The Scarecrow. 1921: Neighbors; The Haunted House; Hard Luck; The High Sign; The Playhouse; The Boat; The Paleface. 1922: Cops; The Electric House (+ pc); My Wife's Relations (+ co-pc); The Frozen North (+ co-pc); Day Dreams (+ pc). 1923: The Balloonatic (+ pc); The Three Ages (+ p; co-d only, with Cline).

Films as director and actor: 1921: The Goat (+ pc/cos; co-d Malcolm St Clair). 1922: The Blacksmith (+ co-s; co-d Malcolm St Clair). 1923: The Love Nest (+ pc); Our Hospitality (+ p; co-d Jack Blystone). 1924: Sherlock, Jr (+ p); The Navigator (+ p; co-d Donald Crisp). 1925: Seven Chances (+ p); Go West (+ p/st). 1926: Battling Butler (+ p); The General (+ p/co-st). 1938: Life in Sometown, USA; Hollywood Handicap; Streamlined Swing.

Films as actor include: 1917: The Butcher Boy; The Rough House; His Wedding Night; Oh, Doctor!; Coney Island. 1918: Out West; The Bell Boy; Moonshine; Goodnight Nurse; The Cook. 1919: Back Stage; The Garage. 1920: A Country Hero; The Saphead. 1927: College (+ p). 1928: Steamboat Bill, Jr; The Cameraman (+ p). 1929: Spite Marriage; The Hollywood Revue. 1930: Free and Easy; Doughboys. 1931: Parlor, Bedroom and Bath (+ p); Sidewalks of New York (+ p). 1932: Speak Easily; The Passionate Plumber (+ pc). 1933: What! No Beer? 1934: Le Roi des Champs-Elysees; The Invaders; The Gold Ghost,

Matka Joanna Od Aniolow, *directed by Jerzy Kawalerowicz.*
Buster Keaton in The General.
Richard Widmark and company in Street with No Name, *by William Keighley.*

141

Allez Oop. 1935: Palooka from Paducah; Hayseed Romance; Tars and Stripes; The E-Flat Man; One Run Elmer. 1936: The Timid Young Man; Three on a Limb; Grand Slam Opera (+ co-s); Blue Blazes; Mixed Magic; The Chemist. 1937: Jail Bait; Love Nest on Wheels. 1939: Mooching through Georgia; Pest from the West; Nothing but Pleasure. 1940: The Villain Still Pursued Her; Pardon My Berth Marks; The Spook Speaks; The Taming of the Snood; L'il Abner. 1941: His Ex Marks the Spot; General Nuisance; She's Oil Mine; So You Won't Squawk. 1943: Forever and a Day. 1949: You're My Everything; In the Good Old Summertime; The Lovable Cheat. 1950: Sunset Boulevard. 1952: Limelight; Paradise for Buster (ur). 1956: Around the World in 80 Days. 1960: The Adventures of Huckleberry Finn. 1963: It's a Mad, Mad, Mad, Mad World. 1964: The Railrodder. 1965: Film. 1966: A Funny Thing Happened on the Way to the Forum.

Films as gagman include: 1944: Bathing Beauty (uc). 1949: Neptune's Daughter (uc); A Southern Yankee.

Films as story writer in collaboration: 1939: The Jones Family in Hollywood; The Jones Family in Quick Millions.

KEEL, Howard

Actor. Gillespie, Illinois 1919–
1945: stage debut in 'Carousel'. 1947: first film as actor The Small Voice, in UK. Appeared in 'Oklahoma' in London and New York. Also in 'Saratoga'. To 1955: most films for MGM. 1957: replaced Richard Kiley in 'No Strings'. Work in stock includes: 'Kismet', 'Mr Roberts', 'Sunrise at Campobello', 'Kiss Me, Kate', 'The Rainmaker', 'South Pacific', 'The Crossing'. TV and radio in USA and UK.

Films as actor include: 1949: Hideout. 1950: Annie Get Your Gun; Pagan Love Song. 1951: Showboat; Texas Carnival; Three Guys Named Mike; Callaway Went Thataway. 1952: Desperate Search; Lovely to Look At. 1953: Ride, Vaquero!; Fast Company; Calamity Jane; Kiss Me, Kate. 1954: Rose Marie; Deep in My Heart; Seven Brides for Seven Brothers. 1955: Kismet; Jupiter's Darling. 1958: Floods of Fear. 1959: The Big Fisherman. 1961: Armored Command. 1966: Waco. 1967: The War Wagon.

KEIGHLEY, William

Director. Philadelphia, Pennsylvania 1893–
Educated in US and at Alliance Française, Paris. 1914–32: acted in, then directed stage plays in New York. 1932: assistant director on Jewel Robbery, Scarlet Dawn and The Cabin in the Cotton. 1933: wrote dialogue for House on 56th Street. Director from 1932; all his films for Warners except for 2 (1947–48). Married actress Genevieve Tobin (1938), directed her in Easy to Love (1934), No Time for Comedy (1940).

Features as director: 1932: The Match King (co-d Howard Bretherton). 1933: Ladies They Talk About (co-d Howard Bretherton). 1934: Easy to Love; Journal of a Crime; Dr Monica; Big-Hearted Herbert; The Kansas City Princess; Babbitt. 1935: The Right to Live; The G Men; Mary Jane's PA; Special Agent; Stars over Broadway. 1936: The Singing Kid; The Green Pastures (co-d Marc Connelly); Bullets or Ballots; God's Country and the Woman. 1937: The Prince and the Pauper;

Varsity Show. 1938: The Adventures of Robin Hood (co-d Michael Curtiz); Valley of the Giants; The Secrets of an Actress; Brother Rat. 1939: Yes, My Darling Daughter; Each Dawn I Die. 1940: The Fighting 69th; Torrid Zone; No Time for Comedy. 1941: Four Brothers; The Bride Came C.O.D. 1942: The Man Who Came to Dinner; George Washington Slept Here. 1947: Honeymoon. 1948: The Street with No Name. 1950: Rocky Mountain. 1951: Close to my Heart (+ s). 1953: The Master of Ballantrae.

KEITH, Brian

(Robert Keith, Jr) Actor. Bayonne, New Jersey 1921–
Son of actor Robert Keith. In one film as a child (1924). 1942–45: US Marine Corps. Acted in stock and radio, then TV. First important Broadway part in 'Mr Roberts'; other parts include 'The Moon is Blue' and 'Darkness of Noon'. 1960: TV in 'The Westerner' and (from 1966) 'Family Affair'. 1960–64: films mainly for Disney.

Films as actor include: 1955: The Violent Men; Tight Spot. 1956: Nightfall. 1957: Run of the Arrow. 1958: Fort Dobbs. 1961: The Parent Trap; The Deadly Companions. 1965: The Hallelujah Trail; The Rare Breed. 1966: The Russians are Coming, the Russians are Coming; Nevada Smith. 1967: Reflections in a Golden Eye. 1971: Something Big.

KELBER, Michel

Cinematographer. Kiev, Russia 1908–
French nationality. Architecture at the Ecole des Beaux-Arts. 1928: worked on avant-garde films. Assistant cinematographer at Gaumont, then at Paramount's studio at Saint-Maurice. Worked under Harry Stradling. 1932: cinematographer on shorts, notably by Claude Autant-Lara. 1933: first feature as cinematographer. 1940: refugee in Switzerland. 1943: in Madrid; photographed several Spanish films. Returned to France after World War II.

Films as cinematographer include: 1937: Gribouille (co); Carnet de bal (co). 1939: Jeunes Filles en détresse; Pièges; Air Pur. 1943: Une Femme disparaît. 1947: Le Diable au corps; Ruy Blas. 1948: Les Parents Terribles. 1949: Jean de la lune. 1950: Le Beauté du diable. 1954: Le Grand Jeu; Le Rouge et le noir. 1955: French Cancan. 1956: Calle Mayor. 1957: Pot-Bouille; Bitter Victory. 1959: John Paul Jones. 1962: A View from the Bridge. 1963: In the French Style. 1965: Mata Hari, Agent M21.

KELLER, Harry

Director and producer. Los Angeles 1913–
Entered films as editor for National Screen Service. 1936–50: in charge of editing at Universal, then Republic; edited e.g. R. G. Springsteen's The Arizona Cowboy (1950), Allan Dwan's Belle Le Grand (1951). 1949: first film as director. 1951: first film as producer. 1950–53: mainly director at Republic, occasionally producing. From 1956: director at Universal. From 1964: producer only, except for In Enemy Country (1968).

Films as producer include: 1964: Send Me No Flowers. 1965: Mirage; That Funny Feeling. 1966: Texas Across the River. 1971: The Skin Game.

Films as director and producer: 1951: Fort Dodge Stampede (as-p); Desert of Lost Men (as-p). 1952: Leadville Gunslinger (as-p); Black Hills (as-p). 1968: In Enemy Country.

Films as director: 1949: The Blonde Bandit. 1950: Tarnished. 1952: Rose of Cimarron; Thundering Caravans. 1953: Marshal of Cedar Rock; Bandits of the West; Savage Frontier; El Paso Stampede; Red River Shore. 1956: The Unguarded Moment. 1957: Man Afraid; Quantez. 1958: Day of the Bad Man; The Female Animal; Voice in the Mirror; Step Down to Terror. 1960: Seven Ways from Sundown. 1961: Tammy, Tell Me True. 1962: Six Black Horses. 1963: Tammy and the Doctor. 1964: The Brass Bottle.

KELLY, Gene

(Eugene Curran Kelly) Director, choreographer, actor. Pittsburgh, Pennsylvania 1912–
Dancing lessons from early childhood. Education interrupted by Depression. Graduated from University of Pittsburgh (1933). Formed double act, working in beer halls, with brother Fred Kelly. Opened dancing schools directed by his mother; worked in nightclubs. 1937: to New York. 1938: first Broadway chorus job. Acted in summer stock; singing and acting part in a Theatre Guild production; dance director at Diamond Horseshoe. Chosen by Rodgers and Hart to play title part in 'Pal Joey'. Film contract (1940) with Selznick sold to MGM. Worked for MGM and on loan to Columbia. 1945–47: US Navy. 1947: returned to MGM. 1949: wrote Take Me Out to the Ball Game with Stanley Donen, who had worked as his assistant on choreography; they directed On the Town together. 1951: won the first Oscar for screen choreography, for An American in Paris. Choreographed many of the films in which he danced. 1959: directed and choreographed ballet 'Pas de dieux' at Paris Opera. Married actress Betsy Blair (1940–57, divorced).

Films as actor include: 1942: For Me and My Gal. 1943: Pilot No 5; Du Barry Was a Lady; Thousands Cheer; The Cross of Lorraine. 1944: Cover Girl (+ chor); Christmas Holiday. 1945: Anchors Aweigh (+ chor). 1946: Ziegfeld Follies. 1948: The Pirate (+ co-chor); The Three Musketeers; Words and Music. 1949: Take Me Out to the Ball Game (+ co-st/co-chor). 1950: Summer Stock (+ chor). 1951: An American in Paris (+ chor). 1954: Brigadoon (+ chor); Deep in my Heart. 1957: Les Girls. 1960: Inherit the Wind. 1964: What a Way to Go. 1967: Les Demoiselles de Rochefort.

Films as director (and until 1956, actor): 1949: On the Town (+ chor/w; co-d Stanley Donen). 1951: Singin' in the Rain (+ co-chor/w; co-d Stanley Donen). 1955: It's Always Fair Weather (+ chor/w; co-d Stanley Donen). 1956: Invitation to the Dance (+ s/chor/w); The Happy Road (+ p/w). 1958: The Tunnel of Love. 1962: Gigot. 1967: A Guide for the Married Man. 1970: The Cheyenne Social Club (+ p).

KELLY, Grace

Actress. Philadelphia, Pennsylvania 1929–
Uncles were playwright George Kelly and vaudeville artist Walter C. Kelly. American Academy of Dramatic Arts. 1949: Broadway debut in 'The Father' with Raymond Massey. TV. MGM contract: also

worked for United Artists, Warners, Paramount, Fox. Oscar as Best Actress for *The Country Girl* (1954). The film was her last; married Prince Rainier of Monaco (1956) and retired from films.

Films as actress: 1951: Fourteen Hours. 1952: High Noon. 1953: Mogambo. 1954: Dial M for Murder; Rear Window; The Country Girl; Green Fire. 1955: The Bridges at Toko-Ri; To Catch a Thief. 1956: The Swan; High Society.

KENDALL, Kay

Actress. Hull, Yorkshire 1927–59 London
Parents were dance team Terry and Pat Kendall. At 12, in London Palladium chorus. Toured in revues. Variety act with sister Kim who appeared with her in several wartime films. 1944: first film as actress *Fiddlers Three*. 1946–49: stage. TV drama 'Sweethearts and Wives' led to leading role in *Lady Godiva Rides Again* (1951). TV, in 'The River'. 1952: Rank contract. 1955: with Rex Harrison in *The Constant Husband*; married him in 1957. From 1957: American films. London stage in 'The Bright One' produced by her husband. 1959: last film *Once More With Feeling*. Died of leukaemia.

Films as actress include: 1944: Champagne Charlie. 1946: London Town. 1950: Dance Hall. 1952: Wings of Danger; It Started in Paradise. 1953: Man Trap; The Square Ring; Genevieve. 1954: Doctor in the House. 1955: Quentin Durward. 1956: Abdullah's Harem. 1957: Les Girls. 1958: The Reluctant Debutante.

KENNEDY, Arthur

Actor. Worcester, Massachusetts 1914–
Carnegie Technical Institute (1936). Group Theatre; road companies; on Broadway from 1934. 1940: Warners contract. World War II: USAF Motion Picture Unit. Stage appearances include 'All My Sons' (1947) and 'Death of a Salesman' (1948). Some TV parts. Worked mainly for Warners (1940–47), Universal and MGM.

Films as actor include: 1941: High Sierra; They Died With Their Boots On. 1942: Desperate Journey. 1943: Air Force. 1947: Boomerang!; Cheyenne. 1949: Champion. 1950: The Glass Menagerie. 1952: Rancho Notorious; The Bend of the River; The Lusty Men. 1955: The Man from Laramie; Trial; Naked Dawn; The Desperate Hours. 1956: The Rawhide Years. 1957: Peyton Place. 1958: Some Came Running. 1960: A Summer Place; Elmer Gantry. 1962: Barabbas; Lawrence of Arabia. 1964: Italiano, Brava Gente; Cheyenne Autumn. 1966: Nevada Smith; Monday's Child. 1968: Caine.

KENNEDY, Burt

Director and writer. Muskegon, Michigan 1923–
World War II: service in cavalry, using horses to 1943. 1947–50: radio writer. From 1950: writer for John Wayne's TV production company for 6 years. 1955–66: scripted e.g. 4 films for Budd Boetticher. 1961: first film as director. Returned to TV as director, writer and producer on 'Combat' series. From 1963: returned to films, writing most of his own scripts. Own production company.

Films as writer: 1955: Man in the Vault. 1956: Seven Men from Now (+ *st*); Gun the Man Down. 1957: The Tall T. 1958: Fort Dobbs (*co-st/co-s*). 1959: Ride Lonesome; Yellowstone Kelly. 1960: Comanche Station. 1962: Six Black Horses. 1966: Return of the Gunfighter (*co-st only*).

Films as director: 1961: The Canadians (+ *s*). 1963: Mail Order Bride – West of Montana (+ *s*). 1965: The Rounders (+ *s*). 1966: The Money Trap; Return of the Seven. 1967: Welcome to Hard Times – Killer on a Horse (+ *s*); The War Wagon. 1969: Support Your Local Sheriff!; Young Billy Young (+ *s*); The Good Guys and the Bad Guys. 1970: Dirty Dingus Magee. 1971: Support Your Local Gunfighter (+ *ex-p*); Hannie Caulder (+ *co-s under ps Z. X. Jones*); La Spina Dorsale del diavolo – The Deserter.

KENNEDY, George

Actor. New York 1925–
Son of a professional musician and a ballerina. At 2, in touring company of 'Bringing Up Father'. At 7, had own children's radio show in New York; continued in radio work to 17. World War II: active service in US Army, work in shows; severe back injury. Technical advisor on 'Sergeant Bilko' TV series and acted in some episodes. Acted in later series, e.g. 'Peter Gunn'. 1961: first film as actor *The Little Shepherd of Kingdom Come*. Leading role in 'Gunsmoke' TV series. Oscar as supporting actor for *Cool Hand Luke* (1967).

Films as actor include: 1962: Lonely are the Brave. 1963: The Man from the Diner's Club. 1964: Charade; Strait-jacket; McHale's Navy. 1965: Hush, Hush Sweet Charlotte; In Harm's Way; Shenandoah; Mirage; The Sons of Katie Elder. 1966: The Flight of the Phoenix. 1967: Hurry Sundown; The Dirty Dozen; Cool Hand Luke; The Ballad of Josie. 1968: Bandolero!; The Pink Jungle. 1969: The Boston Strangler; Guns of the Magnificent Seven; The Good Guys and the Bad Guys; Gaily Gaily. 1970: Airport; Tick . . . Tick . . . Tick; Hostile Witness; Dirty Dingus Magee. 1971: Fool's Parade.

KENNEDY, Joseph P.

Financier, production supervisor. Boston, Massachusetts 1888–1969 Hyannis Port, Massachusetts
Son of saloon-keeper. 1912: graduated from Harvard. State banking examiner. At 25 America's youngest bank president. 1914: married daughter of mayor of Boston. After World War I acquired New England cinema chain. Advisor to banks on loans to film industry. 1926: bought Film Booking Office of America, moved to New York, then Hollywood. Supervised production specialising in second features. Arranged mergers leading to foundation of RKO-Radio. Multi-millionaire after 32 months in film industry; briefly continued as consultant and financier to Gloria Swanson when she produced own films, instrumental in suppressing von Stroheim's *Queen Kelly* (1928). Left films for banking and politics. Occasionally advisor to the industry. 1937: author of unreleased report on mismanagement of Paramount. 1938–40: Ambassador to Court of St James. Sons include John Fitzgerald Kennedy, Robert F. Kennedy and Edward H. Kennedy.

Gene Kelly and Judy Garland in Vincente Minnelli's The Pirate.
Gary Cooper and Grace Kelly in Fred Zinnemann's High Noon.
George Kennedy and Gregory Peck in Mirage, *directed by Edward Dmytryk.*

KERR, Deborah

(Deborah Jane Kerr-Trimmer) Actress. Helensburgh, Scotland 1921–

1930–38: Sadler's Wells Ballet School. 1938: London debut in corps de ballet in 'Prometheus'. 1939: first film as actress *Contraband*. Work in repertory and for ENSA. Stage work includes 'Dear Brutus', 'Heartbreak House', 'Angel Street'. 1953: New York debut in 'Tea and Sympathy'. American films mainly for MGM, Columbia, Paramount, Fox. 1960: married screenwriter Peter Viertel.

Films as actress include: 1941: Major Barbara; Love on the Dole. 1942: Hatter's Castle. 1943: The Life and Death of Colonel Blimp. 1945: Perfect Strangers. 1946: I See a Dark Stranger. 1947: Black Narcissus; The Hucksters; If Winter Comes. 1949: Edward, My Son. 1950: King Solomon's Mines; Please Believe Me. 1951: Quo Vadis. 1952: The Prisoner of Zenda. 1953: Julius Caesar; Thunder in the East; Young Bess; From Here To Eternity. 1954: The End of the Affair. 1956: Tea and Sympathy; The Proud and the Profane; The King and I. 1957: Heaven Knows, Mr Allison; An Affair to Remember. 1958: Bonjour Tristesse; Separate Tables; The Journey. 1959: Count Your Blessings; Beloved Infidel. 1960: The Sundowners; The Grass is Greener. 1961: The Naked Edge; The Innocents. 1963: The Chalk Garden. 1964: The Night of the Iguana. 1967: Casino Royale. 1969: The Gypsy Moths; The Arrangement.

KERSHNER, Irvin

(Irvin Kerschner) Director. Philadelphia, Pennsylvania 1923–

Tyler School of Fine Arts, Philadelphia, design at UCLA, film at USC. Worked in advertising. 1950–52: made 4 documentaries for United States Information Service in Middle East: *Malaria, Childbirth, Locust Plague, Road of 100 Days*. 1953–55: directed and photographed documentaries for West Coast TV in 'Confidential File' series. Directed TV series 'The Rebel'. 1958: first feature, an independent Roger Corman production. 1964: made *The Luck of Ginger Coffey* in Canada.

Features as director: 1958: Stake Out on Dope Street (+ *co-s*). 1959: The Young Captives. 1961: The Hoodlum Priest. 1963: A Face in the Rain. 1964: The Luck of Ginger Coffey. 1966: A Fine Madness. 1967: The Flim Flam Man – One Born Every Minute. 1970: Loving.

KIDD, Michael

Choreographer. New York 1919–

1937: professional debut in musical 'The Eternal Road'. Member of American Ballet at the Metropolitan Opera. 1937–40: 'Ballet Caravan', working up to soloist. Danced title role in 'Billy the Kid' to music by Aaron Copland. 1941–42: soloist and assistant director of 'Dance Players'. 1942–47: soloist of Ballet Theatre. 1945: choreographed and danced in 'On Stage!'. 1947: dance director and choreographer on Broadway musicals including 'Finian's Rainbow' and 'Can-Can'. 1955: first film as actor *It's Always Fair Weather*. Directed *Merry Andrew* (1958).

Films as choreographer include: 1952: Where's Charley? 1953: The Band Wagon. 1954: Knock on Wood; Seven Brides for Seven Brothers. 1955: Guys and Dolls. 1958: Merry Andrew (+ *d*).

KIEGEL, Leonard

Director. London 1929–

Parents of Russian origin. Father Leonard Kiegel was director of Cinéphone. Aesthetics at Sorbonne. 1947–49: worked in 16mm. 1949: founded Objectif 49, revolutionary film society. Helped to arrange Festival du Film Maudit, Biarritz. 1951: his father helped to found and manage Cahiers du Cinéma of which son was co-administrator. 1950–57: assistant to René Clément. 1960: made short *Duke Ellington in Paris* for American TV. 1961: first feature *Leviathan*.

Short films as director include: 1950: Les Déchaînés. 1958: André Malraux. 1960: La Paysanne Pervertie.

Features as director: 1961: Leviathan – The Footbridge (+ *co-s*). 1965: La Dame de pique – The Queen of Spades. 1970: Qui?.

KING, Allan

Director. Vancouver, Canada 1930–

Philosophy at University of British Columbia. Cab-driver. 1953–54: travelled in Europe, worked in England. 1954: joined CBC Vancouver film unit, worked there for 7 years. 1956: first film as director *Skid Row* for TV. Returned to London. Consultant to Rediffusion TV in reorganisation of film unit. Formed Allan King Associates, making sponsored films, usually for TV. 1966: made *Warrendale*, documentary on home for mentally subnormal children; material also used for *Children in Conflict* (1967) an 18-part series. 1967: established Toronto office; subsequently produced on both sides of Atlantic.

Films as director include: 1956: Skid Row; The Yukoners. 1957: Portrait of a Harbour; Gyppo Loggers; The Pemberton Valley. 1958: Morocco; Where Will They Go? 1959: Bull Fight; Saigon (*p/c only*). 1960: Rickshaw; Josef Drenters. 1961: A Matter of Pride; Dreams; 3 Yugoslavian Portraits. 1962: The Pursuit of Happiness; Joshua, a Nigerian Portrait. 1963: The Peacemakers; The Field Day. 1964: Lynn Seymour; Bjorn's Inferno; Christopher Plummer (*co-d William Brayne*); Running Away Backwards – Coming of Age in Ibiza. 1965: The Most Unlikely Millionaire. 1966: Warrendale (+ *p*). 1967: Children in Conflict (*series*); The Creative Person (*13-part series*; *exec p all eps, d ep* Who is James Jones?). 1968: The New Woman. 1969: A Married Couple (+ *p*).

KING, Henry

Director. Christianburg, Virginia 1892–

Grandson of officer on Robert E. Lee's staff, son of plantation owner. 1909: worked in trainmaster's office of Norfolk and Western Railroad. At 21 in vaudeville, then leading parts in Shakespeare. 1912: entered films as actor for Lubin company and acted in films for Balboa, Pathé and in Ince westerns. 1916: first film as director *Who Pays*, Pathé serial in 8 episodes. Early credits as Harry King. 1917–20: directed numerous western shorts starring William Russell, acted in several. Made shorts for General, then Mutual. 1917: New York stage in 'Top O' the Morning'. 1918–19:

made films written by Stephen Fox for American. From 1919: actor and writer for Lubin, director for Pathé and Inspiration. 1921: acted for last time in *Help Wanted—Male*. 1920–21: series of films with Anna Q. Nilsson and H. B. Warner. 1921: only film for First National *Tol'able David*. 1924–29: worked for Paramount, Goldwyn, United Artists. 1929: returned to Inspiration to make *She Goes to War*. From 1930: all films for Fox, except *This Earth is Mine* (1959) for Universal. Leon Shamroy photographed many of his films; Barbara McLean edited 25. 2 late films adapted from Hemingway: *The Snows of Kilimanjaro* (1952), *The Sun Also Rises* (1957); also directed part of *The Old Man and the Sea* (1958). Several films written by Lamar Trotti.

Films as director (complete from 1921): 1916: Who Pays. 1917: Southern Pride; A Game of Wits; The Mate of the Sally Ann. 1918: Beauty and the Rogue; Powers That Pray; Hearts or Diamonds; The Locked Heart; When a Man Rides Alone; Hobbs in a Hurry; All the World to Nothing. 1919: Brass Buttons; Some Liar; Where the West Begins; Sporting Chance; This Hero Stuff; Six Feet Four; A Fugitive from Matrimony; $23\frac{1}{2}$ Hours Leave; Haunting Shadows. 1920: One Hour Before Dawn; Dice of Destiny; When We Were 21; Help Wanted—Male (+ *w*). 1921: Mistress of Shenstone; Salvage; The Sting of the Lash; Tol'able David. 1922: The 7th Day; Sonny; The Bondboy. 1924: The White Sister. 1925: Romola; Any Woman (+ *p*); Sackcloth and Scarlet (+ *p*). 1926: Stella Dallas; Partners Again (+ *p*); The Winning of Barbara Worth. 1927: The Magic Flame (+ *p*). 1928: The Woman Disputed (+ *p*; *co-d Sam Taylor*). 1929: She Goes to War (+ *p*); Hell Harbor (+ *p*). 1930: Lightnin'; The Eyes of the World (+ *p*). 1931: Merely Mary Ann; Over the Hill. 1932: The Woman in Room 13. 1933: State Fair; I Loved You Wednesday (*co-d William Cameron Menzies*). 1934: Carolina; Marie Galante. 1935: One More Spring; Way Down East. 1936: The Country Doctor; Lloyds of London; Ramona. 1937: Seventh Heaven. 1938: In Old Chicago; Alexander's Ragtime Band. 1939: Jesse James; Stanley and Livingstone. 1940: Little Old New York; Maryland; Chad Hanna. 1941: A Yank in the RAF; Remember the Day. 1942: The Black Swan. 1943: The Song of Bernadette. 1944: Wilson. 1945: A Bell for Adano. 1946: Margie. 1947: Captain from Castile. 1948: Deep Waters. 1949: Twelve O'Clock High; Prince of Foxes. 1950: The Gunfighter. 1951: I'd Climb the Highest Mountain; David and Bathsheba. 1952: Wait Till the Sun Shines, Nellie; O. Henry's Full House – Full House *ep* The Gift of the Magi; The Snows of Kilimanjaro. 1953: King of the Khyber Rifles. 1955: Untamed; Love is a Many-Splendored Thing. 1956: Carousel. 1957: The Sun Also Rises. 1958: The Bravados; The Old Man and the Sea (*uc, co-d Fred Zinneman, uc, John Sturges*). 1959: This Earth is Mine; Beloved Infidel. 1962: Tender is the Night.

KINOSHITA, Keisuke

Director. Hamamatsu, Japan 1912–

Ran away from home when permission refused to enter films. Studied photography. 1933: began work in labs of Shochiku. Assistant cameraman. 1936: assistant to Yasujiro Shimazu. 1939: first film as writer *Gonin no Kyodai*. 1943: first film as director. 1951: made first Japanese colour film *Karumen Kokyo ni Kaeru*. 1965: moved to Toho. Frequent work on own scripts.

Films as director include: 1943: Hana Saku Minato – The Blossoming Port; Ikiteiru Magoroku – Magoroku is Still Alive. 1944: Rikugun – Army; Kanko no Machi – Jubilation Street. 1946: Osone-ke no Asa – A Morning with the Osone Family; Waga Koiseshi Otome – The Girl I Loved. 1947: Kekkon – Marriage; Fujicho – Phoenix. 1948: Onna – Woman; Shozo – A Portrait; Hakai – Apostasy. 1949: Ojosan Kampai – Here's to the Girls; Yotsuya Kaidan – The Yotsuya Ghost Story – Illusion of Blood (2 parts); Yabure-Daiko – The Broken Drum. 1950: Konyaku Yubiwa – Engagement Ring. 1951: Karumen Kokyo ni Kaeru – Carmen Comes Home (+ s/st); Zenma – The Good Fairy; Shonen-ki – Youth; Umi no Hanabi – Sea of Fireworks. 1952: Karumen Junjosu – Carmen's Pure Love. 1953: Nihon no Higeki – A Japanese Tragedy. 1954: Onna no Sono – The Eternal Generation – The Garden of Women; Nijushi no Hitomi – Twenty-four Eyes (+ s). 1955: Toi Kumo – Distant Clouds; Nogiku no Gotoki Kimi Nariki – She was Like a Daisy – She Was Like a Wild Chrysanthemum – My First Love Affair (+ s). 1956: Yuyake-Kumo – Clouds at Twilight – Farewell to Dreams; Taiyo to Bara – The Rose on his Arm. 1957: Yorokubi mo Kanashimi mo Ikutoshitsuki – The Lighthouse – Times of Joy and Sorrow; Fuzen no Tomoshibi – Candle in the Wind – Danger Stalks Near (+ s). 1958: Norayama Bushi-ko – The Ballad of the Narayama; Kono Ten no Niji – The Eternal Rainbow (+ s). 1959: Kazahana – Snow Flurry; Sekishun-cho; Kyo mo Mata Kakute Arinan – Thus Another Day. 1960: Haru no Yume – Spring Dreams (+ s); Fuefuki-gawa – The River Fuefuki. 1961: Eien no Hito – The Bitter Spirit – Immortal Love (+ s). 1962: Kotoshi no Koi – New Year's Love; Futari de Aruita Ikushunju – Ballad of a Workman. 1963: Utae Wakodotachi – Sing Young People; Shito no Densetsu – A Legend or Was It? 1964: Koge – The Scent of Incense. 1967: Natsukashiki Fueya Taiko – Eyes, the Sea and a Ball.

KINUGASA, Teinosuke

Director. Mie, Japan 1896–

Sasayama private school. 1914: stage debut. Female impersonator on stage. 1917: entered films as actor with Nikkatsu; worked as female impersonator; continued as actor until 1932. 1922: took part in strike when Nikkatsu began to hire actresses; moved to Makino; first film as director. 1926: formed own company, with Shochiku distribution contract; first production *Kurutta Ippeiji*; actors had also to perform other functions; film almost seized by creditors but financially successful. 1928–31: began studies in Russia under Sergei Eisenstein; ran out of money, left for Berlin; showed *Jujiro* to UFA; film also shown in Paris. 1950: to Daiei. Managing director of Japan Film Director's Guild. On board of directors of Daiei.

Films as director and writer: 1922: Niwa no Kotori – Two Little Birds; Hibana – Spark. 1923: Hanasake Jijii; Jinsei o Mitsumete; Onna-yo Ayamaru Nakare; Konjiki Yasha – The Golden Demon; Ma no Ike – The Spirit of the Pond. 1924: Choraku no Kanata – Beyond Decay; Kanojo to Unmei – She Has Lived Her Destiny (in 2 parts); Kiri no Ame – Fog and Rain (+ w); Kishin Yuri Keiji; Kyoren no Buto – Dance Training; Mirsu – Love; Shohin – Shuto; Shohin – Shusoku; Jashumon no Onna – A Woman's Heresy. 1925: Koi to Bushi – Love and a Warrior. 1928: Jujiro – Crossways – Crossroads – Shadows over Yoshiwara

(+ w). 1931: Reimei Izen – Before Dawn (+ w). 1932: Ikonokotta Shinsengumi – The Surviving Shinsengumi; Chushingura – The Loyal 47 Ronin – The Vengeance of the 47 Ronin (+ w). 1933: Tenichibo to Iganosuke; Futatsu Doro – Two Stone Lanterns; Koina no Ginpei – Gimpei from Koina. 1934: Kutsukate Tokijiro; Fuyaki Shinju; Ippon Gatana Dohyoiri – A Sword and the Sumo Ring; Nagurareta Kochiyama. 1935: Kurayami no Ushimatsu; Yukinojo Henge – Yukinojo's Disguise – Yukinojo's Revenge (co-s; parts 1 and 2). 1936: Yukinojo Henge (co-s; part 3). 1937: Osaka Natsu no Jin – The Summer Battle of Osaka. 1938: Kuroda Seichuroku. 1940: Hebihimesama – Miss Snake Princess (2 parts). 1941: Kawanakajima Kasen – The Battle of Kawanakajima. 1947: Joyu – Actress. 1949: Kobanzame (part 2); Koga Yashiki – Koga Mansion. 1951: Beni Komori; Tsuki no Watari-dori – Migratory Birds under the Moon; Meigatsu Somato – Lantern under a Full Moon. 1952: Shurajo Hibun (in 2 parts); Daibutsu Kaigen – Saga of the Great Buddha. 1953: Jigokumon – Gate of Hell. 1954: Yuki no Yo no Ketto – The Duel of a Snowy Night; Hana no Nagadosu – End of a Prolonged Journey; Tekka Bugyo. 1955: Kawa no Aru Shitamachi no Hanshi – It Happened in Tokyo; Bara Ikutabi – A Girl isn't Allowed to Love; Yushima no Shiraume – The Romance of Yushima. 1956: Yoshinaka o Meguru Sannin no Onna – Three Women around Yoshinaka; Hibana – Spark; Tsukigata Hanpeita (2 parts). 1957: Ukifune – Floating Vessel; Naruto Hicho – A Fantastic Tale of Naruto. 1958: Haru Koro no Hana no En – A Spring Banquet; Osaka no Onna – A Woman of Osaka. 1959: Shirasagi – The Snowy Heron – The White Heron; Joen – Tormented Flame; Kagero Ezu – Stop the Old Fox. 1960: Uta Andon – The Lantern. 1961: Midare-gami – Dishevelled Hair; Okoto to Sasuke – Okoto and Sasuke. 1963: Yoso – The Sorcerer.

Films as director: 1924: Tsuma no Himitsu – Secret of a Wife; Koi – Love (+ w); Sabishiki Mura – Lonely Village; Koi to wa Narinu. 1925: Shinju Yoimachigusa; Tsukigata Hanpeita; Wakaki Hi no Chuji; Nichirin – The Sun. 1926: Tenichibo to Iganosuke; Kurutta Ippeiji – A Crazy Page (+ w); Kirinji; Teru Hi Kumoru Hi – Shining Sun Becomes Clouded; Hikui-dori – Cassowary; Ojo Kichiza; Oni Azami; Kinno Jidai – Epoch of Loyalty; Meoto Boshi – Star of Married Couples (+ w); Goyosen; Dochu Sugoruku Bune; Dochu Sugoruku Kago – The Palanquin; Akatsuki no Yushi – A Brave Soldier at Dawn; Gekka no Kyojin – Moonlight Madness. 1928: Benten Kozo – Gay Masquerade; Keiraku Hichu; Kaikokuki – Tales from a Country by the Sea (+ w); Chokon Yasha – Female Demon. 1931: Tojin Okichi. 1943: Susume Dokuritsuki – Forward Flag of Independence. 1945: Umi no Bara – Rose of the Sea. 1946: Aru Yo no Tonosama – Lord for a Night. 1947: Yottsu no Koi no Monogatari – Four Love Stories – Circus of Love (ep). 1950: Satsujinsha no Kao – The Face of a Murderer. 1963: Uso – When Women Lie – Lies (ep). 1967: Chiisana Tobosha – The Little Runaway (co-d Nkandrovich).

KIRSANOV, Dimitri

Director. Dorpat, Russia 1889–1957 Paris

1923: with parents to France. École Normale de Musique, Paris. Directed first wife Nadia Sirbirskaya in several early films, e.g. *Ménilmontant* (1924),

Irvin Kershner's The Hoodlum Priest.
Warrendale. *directed by Allan King.*
Gregory Peck (left) and Richard Jaeckel (right) in Henry King's The Gunfighter.

145

Brumes d'automne (1929). 1933: *Rapt* made in Switzerland, music by Arthur Honegger. 1953: produced *Mécanisation et remembrement* for French Ministry of Agriculture. Second wife Monique Kirsanoff, editor. Died of heart attack.

Films as director: 1923: L'Ironie du destin – The Irony of Fate (+ *s/w*). 1924: Ménilmontant (+ *p/s/co-c*). 1926: Sylvie Destin (+ *s*). 1927: Sables. 1929: Brumes d'automne (+ *s*). 1931: Les Nuits de Port Said (*co-d*). 1933: Rapt – La Separation des races. 1935: Les Berceaux. 1936: Visages de France; La Fontaine d'Aréthuse; La Jeune Fille au jardin. 1937: Franco de Port (+ *s/di*). 1938: La Plus Belle Fille du monde ne peut donner que ce qu'elle a (+ *s/di/e*); L'Avion de minuit (+ *co-di; co-ad*). 1939: Quartier sans soleil (+ *s/di; r* 1945). 1946: Deux Amis. 1949: Faits Divers à Paris (+ *p*). 1950: Arrière Saison (+ *st/p*). 1951: La Mort du cerf – Chasse à Courre à Villiers-Cotterets. 1952: Le Témoin de minuit. 1955: Le Craneur. 1956: Ce Soir les jupons volent. 1957: Miss Catastrophe.

KJAERULFF-SCHMIDT, Palle

Director. Copenhagen 1931–
Son of actor Helge Kjaerulff-Schmidt. Studied English, French. Student theatre director of plays by e.g. William Saroyan, Tennessee Williams, Aristophanes. TV director e.g. 'Britannicus', 'Waiting for Godot'. 1957: wrote first film as director. 1959: first film with Klaus Rifbjerg as writer *De Sjove Ar*. Theatre direction in Copenhagen includes Harold Pinter's 'The Homecoming'. 1969: in collaboration, scripted *Skal vi lege skjul*.

Films as director: 1957: Bundfald – Dregs (+ *s*). 1959: De Sjove År. 1962: Weekend. 1964: To – Two People. 1965: Sommerkrig – Summer War. 1966: Der var engang en krig – Once There was a War – Once Upon a War. 1967: Historien om Barbara – Story of Barbara. 1968: I den gronne skov – In the Green of the Woods; Taenk påa et tal – Think of a Number (+ *s*).

KJELLIN, Alf
or KENT, Christopher

Actor and director. Lund, Sweden 1920–
Brief period at drama school in Stockholm. From 1937: actor in Swedish films and radio. 1947: to Hollywood under contract to David Selznick; appeared in American films under name of Christopher Kent. From 1955: directed Swedish films. In 1960s acted in films in various countries. TV direction for Alfred Hitchcock and others in USA, e.g. on 'I Spy' series. 1969: first American film as director.

Films as actor include: 1940: Den ljusnande framfid. 1944: Hets. 1946: Iris och löjtnantshjärta. 1947: Kvinna utan ansikte. 1949: Madame Bovary. 1950: Sant händer inte här. 1951: Sommarlek. 1952: My Six Convicts; The Iron Mistress; The Juggler. 1962: The Victors. 1965: Ship of Fools. 1968: Ice Station Zebra.

Films as director: 1955: Flickan i regnet – Girl in the Rain (+ *co-s/w*). 1957: Sjutton ar – Seventeen Years Old (+ *co-s*). Möten i skymningen – Encounters at Dusk. 1959: Det Svänger på slottet – Swinging at the

Castle. 1960: Bara en kypare – Only a Waiter. 1961: Lustgården – Pleasure Garden. 1962: Siska. 1969: The Midas Run. 1970: The McMasters – The McMasters . . . Tougher than the West Itself!

KLEIN, William

Director. New York 1926–
Service in US Army: demobilised in Paris and remained there. Studied painting with Fernand Léger. 1951–54: exhibitions in Brussels, Milan, Paris; painted murals for Italian architects. 1955: visit to New York. 1957: published book of photographs of New York and similar book on Rome; fashion photographer for Vogue. 1958: first film as director *Broadway by Light*. 1960: made short *Comment tuer une cadillac*; technical advisor and visual con *Zazie dans le métro*. 1961–62: published books of photographs on Tokyo and Moscow. 1962–63: several TV films in documentary series 'Cinq Colonnes a l'une' including one with participation of Simone Signoret. 1964–65: further TV documentaries, including *Cassius le Grand* (1964) made up from 3 of own shorts. 1966: first feature as director.

Features as director: 1966: Qui êtes-vous, Polly Maggoo? – Who Are You, Polly Maggoo? (+ *s*). 1967: Loin du Vietnam – Far From Vietnam (+ *co-p; co-d 4 others*). 1968: Mr Freedom (+ *s*). 1969: Festival Pana fricain (+ *s*). 1970: Eldridge Cleaver, Black Panther (+ *c/e*).

KLUGE, Alexander

Director. Halberstadt, Germany 1932–
Studied law, history, clerical science. Law practice. 1958: first book published 'Die Universitätsverwaltung'. 1958–59: assistant to Fritz Lang. 1960: first short film as director, in collaboration. From 1963: several films as writer. 1966: first feature as director. Books include 'Kulturpolitik und Ausgabenkontrolle' (1961), 'Lebensläufe' (1962), 'Schlachtbeschreibung' (1964).

Short films as director: 1960: Brutalität in Stein (+ *co-s; co-d Peter Schamoni*). 1961: Thema Amore; Rennen (*co-d Paul Kruntorad*); Rennfahrer. 1963: Lehrer im Wandel. 1965: Portrait einer Bewährung. 1967: Frau Blackburn wird gefilmt. 1970: Feuerlöscher E. A. Winterstein.

Features as director: 1966: Abschied von Gestern – Yesterday Girl (+ *p/s*). 1968: Die Artisten in der Zirkuskuppel: ratlos – Artists at the Top of the Big Top: Disorientated (*p/s*). 1969: Ein Arzt aus Halberstadt; Die unbezähmbare Leni Peickert. 1971: Der grosse Verhau (+ *p/s*); Das Krankheitsbild des schlachtener-problem Unteroffiziers in der Endsehlacht (*co-d O. Mai and E. Zemann*); Willy Tobler und der Untergang der 6 Flotte.

KOBAYASHI, Masaki

Director. Otaru, Japan 1915–
Philosophy at Waseda University. 1941: began at Shochiku Ofuna studios as assistant director. From 1942: military service, prisoner in Sino-Japanese War. 1946: returned to Shochiku Ofuna, became assistant to Keisake Kinoshita; several scripts for him. 1952: first film as director.

Films as director: 1952: Musuko no Seishun – My Son's Youth. 1953: Magakoro – Sincere Heart; Kabe Atsuki Heya – Room with Thick Walls. 1954: Mittsu no Ai – Three Loves; Kono Hiroi Sora no Dokokani – Somewhere Beneath the Wide Sky. 1955: Uruwashiki Saigetzu – Beautiful Days. 1956: Anata Kaimasu – I'll Buy You; Izumi – The Fountainhead. 1957: Kuroi Kawa – Black River; Ningen no Joken – The Human Condition Part 1; No Greater Love (+ *co-s*). 1960: Ningen no Joken – The Human Condition Part 2; Road to Eternity (+ *co-s*). 1961: Ningen no Joken – The Human Condition Part 3; A Soldier's Prayer (+ *co-s*). 1962: Karami-ai – The Inheritance. 1963: Seppuku – Harakiri. 1964: Kaidan – Kwaidan – The Woman of the Snow. 1967: Joi-uchi – Rebellion. 1968: Nippon no Seishun – Hymn to a Tired Man – Diary of a Tired Man. 1971: Inochi Bonifuro – Inn of Evil.

KOCH, Howard

Writer. New York 1902–
Columbia Law School, graduated 1925. Playwright, including 'Give Us This Day' and 'In Time to Come'. 1928: scripted Orson Welles' radio broadcast 'War of the Worlds'. 1940: first work in films, contribution to treatment of *Virginia City*. Blacklisted; no work in Hollywood after 1951. Under own name scripted British films from 1961. Oscar for screenplay, *Casablanca* shared with Julius J. and Philip G. Epstein.

Films as writer: 1940: The Letter. 1943: Mission to Moscow. 1950: No Bad Songs for Me. 1951: The 13th Letter. 1961: The Greengage Summer. 1962: The War Lover.

Films as writer in collaboration include: 1940: The Sea Hawk. 1941: Shining Victory; Sergeant York. 1943: Casablanca. 1944: In Our Time. 1945: Rhapsody in Blue. 1946: Three Strangers (+ *co-st*). 1948: Letter from an Unknown Woman.

KOCH, Howard W.

Producer and director. New York 1916–
Runner on Wall Street, then assistant editor at Fox. Assistant director at Fox, Eagle Lion and MGM. Freelance 2nd-unit director and producer for Aubrey Schenck Productions. 1954: directed *Shield for Murder* in collaboration with Edmond O'Brien. Then directed low-budget movies and continued producing others. Also TV producer and directed episodes of e.g. 'The Untouchables', 'Maverick'. Vice-president of Sinatra Enterprises and executive producer on many Frank Sinatra films. 1964: production and studio head at Paramount.

Films as executive producer include: 1961: Sergeants 3. 1962: The Manchurian Candidate. 1963: 4 for Texas. 1964: Robin and the 7 Hoods. 1965: None But the Brave. 1967: The President's Analyst.

Films as director: 1954: Shield for Murder (*co-d Edmond O'Brien*). 1955: Big House USA. 1957: Untamed Youth; Bop Girl; Jungle Heat; The Girl in Black Stockings. 1958: Fort Bowie; Violent Road – Hell's Highway; Frankenstein–1970; Andy Hardy Comes Home. 1959: The Last Mile; Born Reckless.

KOENIG, Wolf

Director and animator. Dresden, Germany 1927–
1937: to Canada: with family to farm at Galt, Ontario.
1948: to National Film Board as splicer. Became
assistant editor, caricaturist for animation, camera
operator, writer. Photographed puppet films then
Neighbours (1952). 1952: directed in collaboration
with Colin Low and Robert Verrall and animated *The
Romance of Transportation in Canada*. From 1954:
collaboration with Colin Low: photographed *Corral*
(1954), photographed and edited and wrote commentary for *Gold* (1955); directed in collaboration with
him and photographed in collaboration *City of Gold*
(1957). 1957–60: with Roman Kroitor worked on TV
series 'Candid Eye' (for which he had original idea) as
photographer, writer and editor. 1960: in collaboration
photographed Low's *Universe*. 1960–65: director in
collaboration with Kroitor. 1961: was director of
production with Kroitor on Low's *Days of Whisky
Gap*; and on *The*. 1969: in collaboration produced
Bretislav Pojar's *To See or Not to See*.

Films as director include: 1952: The Romance of
Transportation in Canada (+ *anim*; *co-d Colin Low*,
Robert Verrall). 1957: City of Gold (+ *co-c*; *co-d Colin
Low*); It's a Crime.

Films as director in collaboration with Roman Kroitor:
1960: Glenn Gould—on the Record (+ *co-p/c*); Glenn
Gould—off the Record (+ *co-p/c*). 1961: Festival in
Puerto Rico (+ *co-e*). 1962: Lonely Boy. 1963: The
Canadian Businessman. 1965: Stravinsky (+ *c/e*).

KOHLMAR, Fred

Producer. New York 1905–69 Hollywood
Son of a Broadway actor. Office boy for a stage
producer. Rose to become manager of touring company. Broadway publicist for some years before joining
William Morris Agency and move to Hollywood.
Executive assistant to Samuel Goldwyn for 7 years.
1939: made 5 films in his first year as an independent
producer. To Fox, and in 1950s to Columbia.

Films as producer include: 1947: The Ghost and Mrs
Muir; The Late George Apley; Kiss of Death. 1950:
When Willie Comes Marching Home. 1951: You're in
the Navy Now. 1954: Phffft; It Should Happen to You.
1955: My Sister Eileen. 1956: Picnic; The Solid Gold
Cadillac. 1957: Full of Life; Pal Joey. 1958: Gunman's
Walk. 1961: The Devil at Four O'Clock. 1962: The
Notorious Landlady. 1963: Bye Bye Birdie. 1966:
How to Steal a Million.

KOMEDA K. T.

(Krxystof Komeda-Trzcinski, Christopher Komeda)
Composer. Poland 1932–69 Warsaw
Medical school, qualified as doctor. Jazz pianist. 1958:
first collaboration with Roman Polanski on *Ewag
ludzie z szafa*. Scored most of Polanski's shorts and
all his features to 1968. Work in Poland includes
Niewinne Czarodzieje (1960). 1961: with Polanski to
France to score *Le Gros et le maigre*. 1965–66: with
him in England to work on *Repulsion* and *Cul-de-Sac*.
1966: in Denmark wrote music for *Sult*; in France
composed scores for 2 films directed by Jerzy
Skolimowski. 1967: in England with Polanski, worked
on *Dance of the Vampires*. 1968: with him to USA to

write music for *Rosemary's Baby*; its producer
William Castle invited him also to write music for
Riot, Komeda's last film; in car accident in Los
Angeles, did not recover consciousness; taken to
Warsaw. 1969: Henning Carlsen's *Klabautermanden*
dedicated to him.

Films as composer include: 1958: Ewag ludzie z szafa;
Anioly spadaja. 1960: Niewinne Czarodzieje. 1961: Le
Gros et le maigre. 1962: Ssaki; Noz w wodzie. 1963:
Les Plus Belles Escroqueries du monde *ep* Amsterdam.
1965: Repulsion; Kattorna. 1966: Cul-de-Sac; Sult;
Bariera; Le Départ. 1967: Klatki; Dance of the
Vampires. 1968: Rosemary's Baby; Riot.

KORDA, Sir Alexander

Producer and director. Turkeye, Hungary 1893–1956
London
Brother of Vincent and Zoltan Korda. Teacher and
journalist. Royal University of Budapest. 1916–19:
directed, wrote, photographed and edited numerous
films. To Vienna, then Berlin; directed wife Maria
Korda in several films. 1926: to Hollywood. Worked
there for First National and Fox. 1930: divorced; to
France, made 2 films for Paramount. 1931: to England.
1932: first British film as director and producer *Service
for Ladies*; founded London Film Productions. 1939:
founded Alexander Korda Film Productions; married
Merle Oberon, actress in several of his films; 4 days
after war declared, began first British wartime propaganda film *The Lion Has Wings*. 1943: became chief of
MGM production in Britain. Knighted. 1946: resigned
from MGM to form London Film Productions. 1947:
founded British Film Academy. 1948: last film as
director and producer *An Ideal Husband*, and last film
as producer only. From 1949: executive producer. To
1954: on Board of commercial TV company. Controlling share in British Lion.

Films as director include (complete from 1920):
1916–19: Fehér Ejszakák (+ *s*); Mesek az Ivógéprol
(+ *s*); 1917: Mágnás Miska; Mágia; Fáun; Harrison és
Barrison. 1919: Ave Caesar; Yamata. 1920: Seine
Majestät das Bettlekind. 1922: Herrin der Meere.
1925: Der Tänzer meine Frau. 1926: Eine Dubarry
von Heute; Madame Wünscht Keine Kinder. 1927:
The Stolen Bride; The Private Life of Helen of Troy.
1928: The Yellow Lily; The Night Watch. 1929: Love
and the Devil; The Squall; Her Private Life. 1930:
Women Everywhere; Lilies of the Field; The Princess
and the Plumber. 1931: Rive Ğauche; Marius.

Films as producer and director: 1923: Das unbekannte
Morgen (+ *s*). 1924: Tragödie in Hause Hapsburg.
1932: Service for Ladies – Reserved for Ladies;
Wedding Rehearsal. 1933: The Private Life of Henry
VIII; The Girl from Maxim's. 1934: The Private Life
of Don Juan. 1936: Rembrandt. 1941: That Hamilton
Woman – Lady Hamilton. 1945: Perfect Strangers –
Vacation from Marriage (*co-p*). 1948: An Ideal
Husband.

Films as producer: 1933: Men of Tomorrow; That
Night in London; Counsel's Opinion; Cash. 1934:
Catherine the Great. 1935: Sanders of the River; The
Ghost Goes West; Moscow Nights. 1936: Forget Me
Not; Things to Come; Knight Without Armour. 1936:
Elephant Boy; Claudius (*uf*). 1938: The Drum. 1939:
The Four Feathers; The Lion Has Wings. 1940: The

William Klein's Cassius Le Grand.
Seppuku. *directed by Masaki Kobayashi.*
Mickey Rooney (right) in The Last Mile. *directed by
Howard W. Koch.*

Thief of Bagdad; Lydia. 1942: Rudyard Kipling's Jungle Book. 1948: Anna Karenina; The Fallen Idol.

Films as executive producer include: 1937: Dark Journey; Storm in a Teacup; Action for Slander. 1938: South Riding. 1939: The Spy in Black. 1948: The Winslow Boy. 1949: The Small Back Room; That Dangerous Age; The Third Man; The Cure for Love. 1950: My Daughter Joy; Gone to Earth; Seven Days to Noon; The Happiest Days of Your Life; The Wooden Horse. 1952: Cry, the Beloved Country; The Tales of Hoffman; Outcast of the Islands. 1952: The Sound Barrier; Home at Seven; The Ringer. 1953: The Story of Gilbert and Sullivan; The Heart of the Matter; Hobson's Choice; The Man Between. 1954: The Constant Husband. 1955: A Kid for Two Farthings; The Deep Blue Sea; Storm over the Nile; Richard III.

KORDA, Vincent

Designer. Turkeye, Hungary 1897–
Younger brother of Sir Alexander and Zoltan Korda. Studied painting in Hungary under Béla Grünwald then at Academies of Vienna, Florence and Paris. 1916–17: served in Hungarian Army. 1931: to Paris. Almost all films produced by Alexander Korda. From 1939: worked for London Films. From 1946: production designer for British Lion. Became British citizen.

Films as designer include: 1932: Marius. 1933: The Private Life of Henry VIII. 1934: Catherine the Great; The Private Life of Don Juan. 1935: Sanders of the River. 1936: The Ghost Goes West; Things to Come; Rembrandt. 1937: Claudius (uf). 1938: The Drum. 1939: The Four Feathers; The Lion Has Wings. 1940: The Thief of Bagdad. 1941: That Hamilton Woman – Lady Hamilton. 1942: To Be or Not to Be; Rudyard Kipling's Jungle Book. 1945: Perfect Strangers. 1948: An Ideal Husband. 1948: The Fallen Idol. 1955: The Deep Blue Sea; Summertime.

KORDA, Zoltan

Director. Turkeye, Hungary 1895–1961 Los Angeles
Brother of Sir Alexander and Vincent Korda. 1914–18: infantry officer in Austro-Hungarian Army. 1923: entered films as cameraman in Austria. 1924: editor with Ufa in Germany and for Alexander Korda in Hungary. 1926: first film as director made in Germany. 1930: joined Alexander in USA; co-wrote original story of Alexander's *Women Everywhere*. 1936: married actress Joan Gardner. 1937: became British citizen. 1940–48: in Hollywood. 1956–61: returned to Hollywood.

Films as director: 1927: Die Elf Teufel. 1933: Cash. 1935: Sanders of the River; Conquest of the Air. 1936: Elephant Boy (co-d Robert Flaherty); Forget Me Not. 1937: Revolt in the Jungle. 1938: The Drum – Drums. 1939: The Four Feathers. 1942: Rudyard Kipling's Jungle Book – The Jungle Book. 1943: Sahara (+ co-s). 1945: Counter-Attack – One Against Seven. 1947: The Macomber Affair. 1948: A Woman's Vengeance (+ p). 1952: Cry the Beloved Country – African Fury (+ co-p). 1955: Storm over the Nile (+ p; co-d Terence Young).

KORNGOLD, Erich Wolfgang

Composer. Brno, Czechoslovakia 1897–1957 Hollywood
Child prodigy; composed pantomime performed when he was 13, successful opera 'Die tote Stadt' at 23. Also conductor. From 1935: music for Warners. American citizen from 1943. 1955: Small role in *Magic Fire*. Oscars for music, *Anthony Adverse* (1936, Best Score), *The Adventures of Robin Hood* (1938, Best original Score).

Films as composer include: 1935: A Midsummer Night's Dream (arranger); Captain Blood; The Green Pastures. 1939: Juarez; The Private Lives of Elizabeth and Essex. 1940: The Sea Hawk. 1943: The Constant Nymph. 1946: Of Human Bondage. 1956: Magic Fire (+ w; arranger).

KOSMA, Joseph

Composer. Budapest 1905–69
Studied composition and direction at Budapest Conservatory; worked in Hungarian films. 1933: settled in Paris. Naturalised French. First film work for Jean Renoir. Also composer for ballet and pantomimes and settings for poems e.g. wrote ballet 'Rendez-vous' (1945) with Jacques Prévert, and collaborated with him on lyric poem 'Encore une fois sur le fleuve' (1947).

Films as composer include: 1936: Le Crime de Monsieur Lange (co); Jenny (co); Une Partie de campagne. 1937: La Grande Illusion. 1938: La Bête Humaine; La Marseillaise (co). 1943: Adieu Léonard (as Georges Mourqué). 1945: Les Enfants du paradis (co). 1946: Les Portes de la nuit. 1947: Voyage-surprise. 1949: Le Sang des bêtes. 1950: En passant par la Lorraine. 1956: Cela s'appelle l'aurore; Eléna et les hommes; Calle Mayor. 1959: Dejeuner sur l'herbe; Le Huitième Jour. 1960: La Francoise et l'amour. 1961: Le Testament du Docteur Cordelier; Snobs. 1963: Le Caporal Epinglé; La Poupée; In the French Style.

KOSTER, Henry

(Hermann Kösterlitz) Director. Berlin 1905–
Academy of Fine Arts, Berlin. From 1921: cartoonist, commercial artist, film critic; ran agony column in a Berlin weekly. 1926: produced, wrote and directed publicity films. From 1927: writer with UFA, Terra, Aafa. Then at Universal Studios, Berlin, where he directed and scripted first film, *Das Abenteuer einer schönen Frau* (1932). Directed films in Budapest, Berlin, Vienna, Amsterdam. 1936: to Hollywood; changed name. To 1942: worked for Universal; then with various companies. 1950–56: with Fox, including first CinemaScope film, *The Robe* (1953). Then with various companies e.g. Universal, Fox.

Films as director include: 1936: Three Smart Girls. 1937: One Hundred Men and a Girl. 1938: The Rage of Paris. 1939: First Love; Three Smart Girls Grow Up. 1940: Spring Parade. 1942: Between Us Girls (+ p). 1944: Music for Millions. 1947: The Unfinished Dance. 1949: The Inspector General; Come to the Stable. 1950: Harvey; Wabash Avenue. 1951: Mr Belvedere Rings the Bell; No Highway – No Highway in the Sky; O. Henry's Full House – Full House ep The Cop and the Anthem. 1952: My Cousin Rachel. 1954: Desiree. 1955: Good Morning Miss Dove; The Virgin Queen; A Man Called Peter. 1956: D-Day the Sixth of June; The Power and The Prize. 1957: My Man Godfrey. 1959: La Maja Desnude – The Naked Maja. 1961: Flower Drum Song. 1962: Mr Hobbs Takes a Vacation. 1963: Take Her, She's Mine. 1965: Dear Brigitte; The Singing Nun.

KOUNDOUROS, Nikos

Director. Athens 1929–
Sculpture and painting at École des Beaux Arts, Paris. Directed several shorts. 1954: first feature as director.

Features as director: 1954: I Maijiki Polis – The Magic City. 1956: Dracos – The Ogre of Athens. 1958: I Paranomi – The Outlaws – The Hunted (+ s). 1960: To Potami – The River (+ co-p/co-s) 1963: Mikres Afrodites – Young Aphrodites (+ co-p/co-s). 1967: To Prosopo tes Medousas – Face of the Medusa (+ co-s).

KOZINTSEV, Grigori

Director. Kiev, Russia 1905–
Collaboration with Leonid Trauberg while engaged in theatrical work in Kiev. They organised ambulant studio theatre: Sergei Yutkevich took part. 1921: in Petrograd the three founded FEX (Factory of the Eccentric Actor) and issued manifestos. 1923: group's last stage production. 1924: invited by Sevzapkino to make short comedy film: his first film as director in collaboration with Leonid Trauberg. 1926: they made 2 films for Leningradkino; Ivan Moskvin became their usual photographer. 1927–29: worked for Sovkino and Soyuzkino; all subsequent films for Lenfilm. 1929: visit to Paris before making *Novyi Vavilon – The New Babylon* in which Vsevolod Pudovkin acted. 1931: made *Odna* as silent, sound added: their first film to have music by Dmitri Shostakovich. 1935–39: 'Maxim' trilogy about a party worker. Working alone contributed to 'Fighting Film Album'. 1945: they made first Lenfilm post-war production *Prostiye Lyudi*. 1946: this film banned by resolution of Central Committee; not released till 1956. 1947: end of collaboration with Trauberg; alone made *Pirogov*. 1948–52: theatrical work in Leningrad. From 1957: series of films adapted from Western literature; *Gamlet* and *Korol Lir* scripted from translations by Boris Pasternak.

Films directed in collaboration with Leonid Trauberg: 1924: Pokhozhdeniya Oktyabriny – The Adventures of Oktyabrina (+ s). 1925: Mishki protiv Yudenicha – Mishka Against Yudenich (+ co-s). 1926: Chortovo Koleso – The Devil's Wheel; Shinel – The Cloak. 1927: Bratishka (+ s); SVD – The Club of the Big Deed. 1929: Novyi Vavilon – The New Babylon (+ s). 1931: Odna – Alone (+ s). 1935: Yunost Maksima – The Youth of Maxim (+ s). 1937: Vozvrashchenie Maksima – The Return of Maxim (+ co-s). 1939: Vyborgskaya Storona – The Vyborg Side (+ s). 1945: Prostye Lyudi – Plain People (+ s; r 1956).

Features as solo director: 1947: Pirogov. 1953: Bielinsky (+ co-s). 1957: Don Quixote (+ co-s). 1964: Gamlet – Hamlet (+ s). 1971: Korol Lir – King Lear.

KRAMER, Stanley

Producer and director. New York 1913–
Family worked in film distribution. New York Univer-

sity. 1933–34: worked on Hollywood backlots. 1934–35: MGM research department. 1935–38: film editor. Writer for Columbia (1939) and Republic (1940). 1941: returned to MGM, assistant to producer David L. Loew e.g. on *So Ends Our Night* (1941), *The Moon and Sixpence* (1942). Also wrote for radio (1939–41) including 'The Rudy Vallee Show' and some scripts for Edward G. Robinson. 1942–45: US Signal Corps, worked on training films. 1947: formed Screen Plays Inc; first independent production in 1948; company called Stanley Kramer Productions from 1949. Released through United Artists, except for 3-year release arrangement with Columbia (1951–54). 1955: first film as director. 1961: Academy of Motion Picture Arts and Sciences' Irving Thalberg Award for consistently high quality in film-making.

Films as producer: 1948: So This is New York. 1949: Champion; Home of the Brave. 1950: The Men; Cyrano de Bergerac. 1951: Death of a Salesman. 1952: My Six Convicts; High Noon; The Happy Time; The Four Poster; The Sniper; Eight Iron Men; The 5,000 Fingers of Dr T. 1953: The Juggler; The Member of the Wedding; The Wild One. 1954: The Caine Mutiny. 1962: Pressure Point (+ *e*); A Child is Waiting (+ *e*). 1964: Invitation to a Gunfighter.

Films as director and producer: 1955: Not as a Stranger. 1957: The Pride and the Passion. 1958: The Defiant Ones. 1959: On the Beach. 1960: Inherit the Wind. 1961: Judgment at Nuremberg. 1963: It's a Mad, Mad, Mad, Mad World. 1965: Ship of Fools. 1967: Guess Who's Coming to Dinner. 1969: The Secret of Santa Vittoria. 1970: R.P.M. 1971: Bless the Beasts and Children.

KRAMPF, Gunther

Cinematographer. Vienna 1899–
Educated in Berlin and Vienna. 1920s: worked mainly in Germany, then to Paris. 1931: With director Karl Grune to UK. 1931–36: worked for Gaumont-British. Then for Associated British and other companies.

Films as cinematographer include: 1922: Der Verlorene Schuh. 1924: Orlacs Hande. 1926: Der Student von Prag (*co*). 1928: Die Buchse der Pandora; Schinderhannes. 1930: Alraune; Die Letzte Kompagnie. 1933: Der Tunnel. 1947: Fame is the Spur.

KRASKER, Robert

Cinematographer. Perth, Australia 1913–
Studied at art schools in Paris before coming to London (1930). Entered films with Alexander Korda Productions. Cinematographer for RKO British and Two Cities. Then worked for independents. Oscar for black and white cinematography on *The Third Man* (1950).

Films as cinematographer include: 1945: Henry V; Caesar and Cleopatra (*co*); Brief Encounter. 1947: Odd Man Out. 1949: The Third Man. 1952: Cry the Beloved Country. 1953: Never Let Me Go. 1954: Giuletta e Romeo. 1956: Alexander The Great; Trapeze. 1957: The Rising of the Moon; The Story of Esther Costello. 1958: The Quiet American. 1959: The Doctor's Dilemma. 1960: The Criminal. 1961: El Cid; Romanoff and Juliet. 1962: Guns of Darkness; Billy Budd. 1963: The Running Man. 1964: The Fall of the Roman Empire; The Collector (*co*). 1965: The Heroes of Telemark.

KRASNA, Norman

Writer. Corona, Long Island 1909–
After university and law school became assistant drama editor for New York Morning World. Drama editor for New York Graphic. Assistant publicity director at Warners. 1932: started writing scripts. Many of his stage plays filmed, often adapted by him. 1937: started producing some of his films as writer. Directed 3 films from own scripts. 1950: formed Wald-Krasna Productions, releasing through RKO. 1952: sold interest to Jerry Wald. 1956: own production company. Oscar for original screenplay of film he directed *Princess O'Rourke* (1943).

Films as writer include: 1936: Fury (*st*). 1937: Big City (+ *p*; *st*). 1938: You and Me (*st*). 1941: Mr and Mrs Smith (+ *st*); The Devil and Miss Jones (+ *co-p*; *st*); The Flame of New Orleans (*st/co-s*). 1954: White Christmas (*co*). 1956: Bundle of Joy (*co*). 1958: Indiscreet (+ *fpl*). 1960: Who Was That Lady? (+ *p*); Let's Make Love (+ *st*). 1963: Sunday in New York.

Films as writer and director: 1943: Princess O'Rourke. 1950: The Big Hangover(+ *p/st*). 1956: The Ambassador's Daughter(+ *f*).

KRASNER, Milton

Cinematographer
1933: became cinematographer. Worked for numerous companies. 1950: to Fox, specialised in 'Scope and De Luxe Color.

Films as cinematographer include: 1941: The Lady from Cheyenne. 1943: Gung Ho! 1944: The Woman in the Window. 1946: Without Reservations. 1950: All About Eve; No Way Out. 1951: Rawhide; I Can Get it for You Wholesale. 1952: Monkey Business; The Model and the Marriage Broker. 1954: Three Coins in the Fountain; Garden of Evil (*co*); Demetrius and the Gladiators; Desiree. 1955: The Seven Year Itch; The Rains of Ranchipur; 23 Paces to Baker Street. 1957: Kiss Them for Me; An Affair to Remember; Boy on a Dolphin. 1959: The Remarkable Mr Pennypacker; Count Your Blessings (*co*); The Man Who Understood Women. 1960: Home from the Hill; Bells are Ringing. 1961: Go Naked in the World; King of Kings (*co*). 1962: The Four Horsemen of the Apocalypse; Sweet Bird of Youth; Two Weeks in Another Town; How the West was Won (*co*). 1963: The Courtship of Eddie's Father; A Ticklish Affair; Love with The Proper Stranger. 1964: Advance to the Rear; Looking for Love; Fate is the Hunter; Goodbye Charlie. 1965: The Sandpiper; The Singing Nun. 1966: Red Line 7000. 1967: Hurry Sundown (*co*); The St Valentine Day's Massacre. 1968: The Ballad of Josie.

KRAUSS, Werner

Actor. Gestungshausen, Germany 1884–1959 Vienna Provincial theatre, then e.g. in Berlin with Max Reinhardt. 1916: began career in films with help of Richard Oswald; directed by him in several films. 1933: London stage. Acted in Nazi films. 1948: became Austrian national. Married actress Marie Bard.

Charles Laughton (right) *in* The Cop and the Anthem, *an episode from* O. Henry's Full House, *directed by Henry Koster.*
Novyi Vavilon *by Grigori Kozintsev and Leonid Trauberg, assisted by Sergei Gerasimov.*
Werner Krauss in Robert Wiene's Das Kabinett des Doktor Caligari.

Films as actor include: 1916: Hoffmanns Erzahlungen; Zirkusblut. 1917: Die Rache dér Toten; Seeschlacht. 1918: Es werde Licht; Das Tagebuch einer Verlorenen. 1919: Die Prostitution. 1920: Das Kabinett des Doktor Caligari. 1921: Die Bruder Karamazoff; Lady Hamilton; Scherben. 1923: Das Alte Gesetz; I.N.R.I.; Der Puppenmacher von Kiangning; Der Schatz; Das unbekannte Morgan. 1924: Decameron Nights; Das Wachsfigurenkabinett. 1925: Die freudlose Gasse; Tartuff. 1926: Geheimnisse einer Seele; Der Student von Prag; Nana. 1927: Funkzauber. 1940: Jud Süss. 1943: Paracelsus. 1950: Prämien auf den Tod.

KROITOR, Roman

Director. Yorkton, Saskatchewan, Canada 1927–
Philosophy at University of Manitoba. 1949: to National Film Board of Canada as assistant producer. 1951: edited and wrote commentary for Colin Low's *The Age of the Beaver*. 1954: first film as director. 1957–60: with Wolf Koenig worked on TV series 'Candid Eye' as producer, director, editor. 1957: wrote Low's *City of Gold*. 1960: in collaboration with Low directed *Universe*; also wrote it. 1961: director of production with Wolf Koenig on Low's *Days of Whisky Gap*. From 1961: directed several films in collaboration with Wolf Koenig. 1964: producer in collaboration of Don Owen's *Nobody Waved Good-bye* (1964) and Low's TV film *The Hutterites* (1965). Worked on Canadian multi-screen film for Osaka Expo 70.

Films as director: 1954: Paul Tomkowitz, Railway Switchman (+*co-s*). 1955: Farm Calendar (+*s/cy*). 1957: The Great Plains. 1961: The Living Machine (+*p*). 1966: Above the Horizon (*co-d Hugh O'Connor*; +*co-p*).

Films as director in collaboration with Wolf Koenig: 1960: Glenn Gould—on the Record (+*co-p*); Glenn gould—off the Record (+*co-p*). 1961: Festival in Puerto Rico (+*p/co-e*). 1962: Lonely Boy (+*p*). 1963: The Canadian Businessman. 1965: Stravinsky.

KUBRICK, Stanley

Director. New York 1928–
Father a doctor. Photographer on magazine Look for 4 years. 1951: directed, scripted, photographed and edited 2 16 mm documentaries *Day of the Fight* and *Flying Padre* both released by RKO. 1952–54: 2nd unit TV director on series of 'Omnibus' about Abraham Lincoln. 1953: financed by friends and relatives, directed, produced, photographed and edited first feature, turned down by major distributors, released by Joseph Burstyn. 1955: *Killer's Kiss* released by United Artists. No salary from first 2 features. 1957–59: MGM contract, unused. Formed production company with James B. Harris, who produced *The Killing* (1956), *Paths of Glory* (1957), *Lolita* (1962). Partnership ended, became own producer. 1960: replaced Anthony Mann on *Spartacus*. From 1961: resident in England, films released by Rank/Universal–International, Columbia, MGM. Production of *2001: A Space Odyssey* lasted almost 4 years, final cost about $12 million.

Features as director: 1953: Fear and Desire (+*p/c/e*). 1955: Killer's Kiss (+*co-p/st/s/c/e*). 1956: The Killing (+*s*). 1957: Paths of Glory (+*co-s*). 1960: Spartacus.

1962: Lolita. 1963: Dr Strangelove, or How I Learned to Stop Worrying and Love the Bomb (+*p/co-s*). 1968: 2001: A Space Odyssey (+*p/co-s*). 1971: Clockwork Orange (+*p/s*).

KULESHOV, Lev

Director. Tambov, Russia 1899–1970 Moscow
1916–1917: designer Khanzhonkov studio. 1917: first theoretical writings published in 'Vestnik Kinematografiya'. 1918: first film as director *Proekt inzhenera Praita*; assigned by Vladimir Gardin to head 're-editing section' of Moscow Film Committee. Then head of Newsreel Section (where Dziga Vertov was at that time) and carried out first editing experiments including 'Kuleshov Effect' with old footage. Directed newsreels, including *Ural* with Edouard Tissé as cameraman. To Eastern front, supervised group of cameramen. 1919: invited to teach in State Film School. 1920: to Western front with own group, made *Na krasnom frontye*, shot on washed, recoated positive film as no negative available. 1921: took work in commercial films to support his mistress Alexandra Khokhlova and her son. She became his assistant on all his films and acted in several (married officially in 1956). Returned to film school, worked on training of actors. No stock, so staged plays in cinematic style. Boris Barnet, Vsevolod Pudovkin joined the group. 1923: after setting up independent experimental laboratory, continued editing experiments on film; Goskino invited group to work for them. 1924: he directed their first film *Neobychainye Priklucheniya mistera Vesta v stranye Bolshevikov*. After group's 2nd film, 1½ years without work, then for Goskino made *Po zakonu* based on Jack London's story 'The Unexpected'. 1927: opened workshop in Georgia; set up educational programme; production of *Parovoz No B-100* stopped; newsreel and advertising shorts. 1933: *Gorizont* and *Velikii Uteshitel* made with many of his old stock company. 1935: denounced at Congress of Film Workers for a 1934 film on which he was artistic supervisor. 1940: invited by Sergei Yutkevich to Children's Film Studio. 1944: through efforts of Sergei Eisenstein became head of Moscow Film Institute, where he taught until his death. Writings include 'The Practice of Film Direction' (1935) and 'Fundamentals of Film Direction' (1941).

Films as director: 1918: Proekt inzhenera Praita – Engineer Prite's Project (+*dec*). 1919: Pesn lyubvi Nedopetaya – The Unfinished Love Song (+*dec; co-d Vitold Polonsky*). 1920: Na krasnom frontye – On the Red Front (+*s/e/w*). 1924: Neobychainye Priklucheniya mistera Vesta v stranye Bolshevikov – The Extraordinary Adventures of Mr West in the Land of the Bolsheviks (+*co-s/e*). 1925: Luch smerti – The Death Ray (+*w*). 1926: Po zakonu – By the Law – Dura Lex (+*co-s/e*). 1927: Vasha Znakomaya – Zhurnalista – The Journalist – Your Acquaintance (+*co-s/e*); Parovoz No B-100 – Locomotive No B-100 (*uf*). 1929: Veselaya Kanareika – The Gay Canary (+*e*); Dva-buldi-dva – Two-Buldi-Two (*co-d Nina Agadzhanova-Shutko*). 1931: Sorok Serdets – Forty Hearts (+*e*). 1933: Gorizont – Horizon (+*co-s/e*); Velikii Uteshitel – The Great Consoler (+*co-s/dec/e*). 1940: Sibiryaki – The Siberians. 1941: Sluchai v vulkanye – Incident in a Volcano (*co-d 3 others*). 1942: Klyatva Timura – The Oath of Timur. 1944: My s Urala – We of the Urals.

KULIK, Buzz

(Seymour Kulik) Director. New York 1922–
1941–45: US Army. From 1946: producer/director with J. Walter Thompson advertising agency, worked for Lux-Video and Kraft on TV. 1956–64: producer/director with CBS TV e.g. 'The Defenders', 'Dr. Kildare', the 'Dick Powell Playhouse'. 1961: directed first film. 1964: vice-president in charge of West Coast productions for CBS. 1965: joined Bob Banner Associates. 1967: to Paramount as producer/director. 1971: television advisor to Senator Edward Muskie on his presidential campaign.

Films as director: 1961: The Explosive Generation. 1963: The Yellow Canary. 1964: Ready for the People. 1967: Warning Shot (+*p*); Sergeant Ryker – The Court Martial of Sergeant Ryker – The Case Against Paul Ryker. 1968: Villa Rides; Riot.

KULLE, Jarl

Actor. Angelholm, Sweden 1927–
Royal Dramatic Theatre drama school, Stockholm. From 1949: actor at Royal Dramatic Theatre, also (from 1959) at the Oscars theatre. Appeared in classic roles and musicals e.g. 'My Fair Lady', 'How to Succeed in Business without Really Trying'. In films from 1947. 1968: wrote, directed and acted in *Bokhandlaren som slutade bada – The Bookseller who Gave up Bathing*. 1970: wrote, directed and acted in *Ministern*.

Films as actor include: 1950: Kvartetten som sprängdes. 1951: Kvinnors väntan. 1952: Trots. 1953: Barabbas. 1954: Karin. Månsdotter. 1955: Sommarnattens leende. 1956: Sista paret ut; Sången om den eldröda blommau. 1957: En drömmares vandring; Ingen morgandag. 1960: Djävulens öga; Änglar, finns dom . . . 1962: Kort är Sommaren. 1963: För att inte tala om alla dessa kvinnor. 1964: Käre John. 1965: Syskonbädd 1782.

KURI, Yoji

Animator. Fukui, Japan 1928–
1950: Bunka Gakuin Art School, Tokyo. Became cartoonist. 1958: first cartoon album published. 1959: first film as animator. Own studio in Tokyo. Also advertising and TV work.

Films as animator: 1959: Nihiki-no Sama – Two Sauries; Kitte-no Genso – Stamp Fantasia. 1960: Warai-no Ningen – People; Fasshon – Fashion. 1961: Ningen Dōbutsuen – Human Zoo – Clap Vocalism. 1962: Ai – Love; Isu – The Chair; Atchi wa Kotchi – Here and There. 1963: Kiseki – Locus; Zero no Hakken – The Discovery of Zero; Botan – The Button. 1964: Otoko to Onna to Inu – Man, Woman and Dog; Ring-Ring Bōi – Ring Ring Boy; Aos; Chiisana Kūkan – Small Space. 1965: Kao – The Face; Tonari-no Yarō – The Man Next Door; Mado – The Window; Samurai. 1966: Chiisana Sasayaki – Little Murmur; Sado-no Tamago – The Eggs; Satsujinkyō Shidai – Au Fou! (+*p/c/dec*). 1967: Heya – The Room (+*p*); Hana – The Flower (+*p/st*); Anata wa Nani o Kangaete Iru Ka? – What Do You Think? (+*p*). 1968: Futatsu-no Yakizakana – Two Grilled Fish (+*p/st*).

KURNITZ, Harry *or* Marco Page

Writer. New York 1908–68 Hollywood
Began as journalist; on editorial staff of newspapers and magazines in New York and Philadelphia. 1938: joined MGM as writer when they purchased his novel 'Fast Company'. Wrote novels under own name and detective stories under name of Marco Page. With MGM until 1945. Thereafter worked for various companies. Broadway plays filmed include 'Once More with Feeling' (filmed 1959), 'A Shot in the Dark' (filmed 1964).

Films as writer include: 1939: Fast and Furious. 1941: Shadow of the Thin Man (+ *st*; *co-s*). 1942: They Got Me Covered; Pacific Rendezvous (*co*). 1944: See Here, Private Hargrove; The Thin Man Goes Home (*co-st*). 1945: What Next, Corporal Hargrove? (+ *st*). 1947: The Web (*st*); Something in the Wind (*co*). 1948: A Kiss in the Dark (+ *p*). 1949: The Adventures of Don Juan (*co*); The Inspector General (*co*); My Dream is Yours (*co*). 1950: Pretty Baby (+ *p*; *co-s*); Of Men and Music (*co*). 1953: Tonight We Sing (*co*); Melba (+ *st*); The Man Between. 1954: Love Lottery. 1955: Land of the Pharaohs (*co-st/co-s*). 1956: The Happy Road (*co*). 1957: Witness for the Prosecution (*co*). 1959: Once More with Feeling (+ *fpl*). 1960: Surprise Package. 1962: Hatari! 1964: Goodbye Charlie. 1966: How to Steal a Million.

KUROSAWA, Akira

Director. Tokyo 1910–
The youngest of 7 children of a sports teacher. 1927: enrolled in a school of Western painting. Some pictures were exhibited; tried to make a living as an illustrator. Joined the Japan Proletariat Artists' Group. 1936: answered a newspaper advertisement for assistant directors at PCL studios. Assisted Kajiro Yamamoto and wrote scripts. 2 scripts published, one received prize from Education Minister; some scripts were not considered suitable for filming until after World War II. Of 3 filmed before Kurosawa started directing, 2 were made by Satsuo Yamamoto including *Uma* (1941) on which Kurosawa was 2nd-unit director. 1943: first film as director. 1948: scripted *Shozo*. Since 1957, has also been involved in producing and financing his films. Since 1960 made for own company. Most films released through Toho. 1971: Attempted suicide.

Films as director and co-writer: 1943: Sugata Sanshiro – Judo Saga (*in 2 parts*; *s*; + *co/e*). 1944: Ichiban Utsukushiku – Most Beautiful (*s*). 1945: Zoku Sugata Sanshiro (*s*); Tora no O o Fumu Otokotachi – Tora No-o – They Who Tread on the Tiger's Tail (*s*). 1946: Asu o Tsukuru Hitobito – Those who Make Tomorrow (*co-d only*; *co-d Kajiro Yamamoto, Hideo Segikawa*); Woga Seishun ni Kuinashi – No Regrets for Our Youth. 1947: Subarashiki Nichiyobi – One Wonderful Sunday. 1948: Yoidore Tenshi – Drunken Angel. 1949: Shizukanaru Ketto – Quiet Duel; Nora Inu – Stray Dog. 1950: Shubun – Scandal; Rashomon. 1951: Hakuchi – The Idiot. 1952: Ikiru – Doomed – Living. 1954: Shichinin no Samurai – The Seven Samurai, The Magnificent Seven. 1955: Ikimono no Kiroku – Record of a Living Being – I Live in Fear. 1957: Kumonosu-jo – Throne of Blood (+ *co-p*); Donzoko – The Lower Depths (+ *co-p*). 1958: Kakushi Toride no San-Akunin – The Hidden Fortress (+ *co-p*). 1960: Warui Yatsu Hodo Yoku Nemuru – The Bad

Sleep Well (+ *co-p/pc*). 1961: Yojimbo (+ *pc*). 1962: Tsubaki Sanjuro – Sanjuro (+ *pc*). 1963: Tengoku to Jigoku – High and Low – Heaven and Hell (+ *pc*). 1965: Akahige – Red Beard (+ *pc*). 1970: Dodeskaden (+ *co-s*).

KYO, Machiko

Actress. Osaka 1924–
1936: ballet school; worked as dancer until discovery for Daiei (1949).

Films as actress include: 1950: Rashomon. 1951: Genji monogatari. 1953: Ani Imoto; Ugetsu Monogatari; Jigokumon. 1955: Yokihi. 1956: Akasen chitai; The Teahouse of the August Moon. 1957: Yoru no Cho. 1959: Sayonara konnichiwa; Kagi. 1960: Jokyo; Bonchi.

L

LA CAVA, Gregory

Director. Towanda, Pennsylvania 1892–1952 Malibu Beach, California
Calabrian origin. Chicago Institute of Art, New York Art Students' League. 1911–16: magazine caricaturist. From 1918: collaborated with Walter Lantz designing cartoons for comics including 'Katzenjammer'. From 1923: directed feature films. Until 1928: with Famous Players–Lasky releasing through Paramount. Then worked for various companies, notably RKO.

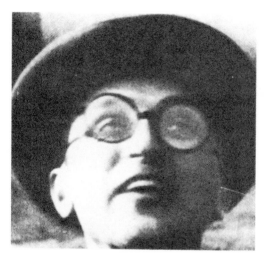

Films as director: 1923: The New School Teacher; Restless Wives. 1925: Womanhandled. 1926: Let's Get Married; So's Your Old Man; Say it Again. 1927: Paradise for Two (+ *p*); Running Wild; Tell it to Sweeney (+ *p*); The Gay Defender (+ *p*). 1928: Feel my Pulse (+ *p*); Half a Bride. 1929: Saturday's Children; Big News. 1930: His First Command. 1931: Laugh and Get Rich (+ *s*); Smart Woman. 1932: Symphony of Six Million – Melody of Life; The Age of Consent; The Half Naked Truth (+ *co-s*). 1933: Gabriel Over the White House; Bed of Roses (+ *co-di*). 1934: Gallant Lady; The Affairs of Cellini; What Every Woman Knows. 1935: Private Worlds (+ *co-s*); She Married Her Boss. 1936: My Man Godfrey (+ *p*). 1937: Stage Door. 1939: 5th Avenue Girl (+ *p*). 1940: Primrose Path (+ *p/co-s*). 1941: Unfinished Business (+ *p*). 1942: Lady in a Jam (+ *p*). 1947: Living in a Big Way (+ *st/co-s*).

LADD, Alan

Actor. Hot Springs, Arkansas 1913–64 Palm Springs, Florida
Radio drama. Joined Universal training unit for young actors. 1932: bit part in *Once in a Lifetime* for Universal. 1932–39: many bit parts. 1942: married Sue Carol, an ex-actress who became his manager. 1942–54: mainly Paramount. 1954–57: Warners. 1954: formed own company. 1964: last film *The Carpetbaggers*.

Films as actor include: 1936: Pigskin Parade. 1937: Souls at Sea. 1938: The Goldwyn Follies; Come On Leathernecks. 1939: Rulers of the Sea. 1940: The

The Killing, *by Stanley Kubrick.*
Neobychainye Priklucheniya Mistera Vesta v Stranye Bolshevikov, *directed by Lev Kuleshov.*
Akahige, *with Toshiro Mifune, directed by Akira Kurosawa.*

Howerds of Virginia. 1942: Joan of Paris; This Gun for Hire; The Glass Key; Lucky Jordan; Star Spangled Rhythm. 1943: China. 1944: And Now Tomorrow. 1945: Salty O'Rourke. 1946: The Blue Dahlia; OSS; Two Years Before the Mast. 1947: Calcutta; Variety Girl; Wild Harvest. 1948: Beyond Glory. 1949: The Great Gatsby. 1950: Captain Carey, USA; Branded. 1951: Red Mountain; The Iron Mistress. 1953: Shane; Thunder in the East; Desert Legion; Botany Bay; The Red Beret. 1954: Saskatchewan; Drum Beat; Hell Below Zero. 1955: The McConnell Story. 1956: Santiago; Hell on Frisco Bay. 1957: Boy on a Dolphin. 1958: The Deep Six; The Proud Rebel; The Badlanders. 1959: The Man in the Net. 1964: The Carpetbaggers.

LAEMMLE, Carl

Studio head. Laupheim, Germany 1867–1939 Hollywood
1884: emigrated to USA. 1906: opened his first cinema in Chicago. 1909: formed International Motion Pictures. 1912: with associates, formed Universal. With William Fox, was one of independents who fought against the attempted monopoly of production and distribution by General Film Company under Thomas Edison who held patents and were trying to block all other film production. Laemmle campaign against General and its subsidiary, The Motion Picture Patents Company, included series of cartoons using the character of General Flimco to contrast General's wealth and greed with the plight of small exhibitors. 1915: court decision abolished General Film. Under Laemmle, Universal became one of the major Hollywood studios. 1936: retired. His biggest success was *All Quiet on the Western Front* (1930). His son, Carl Laemmle Jr, became a producer.

LAKE, Veronica

(Constance Frances Marie Okelman) Actress. New York 1919–
McGill University. Stage work, then MGM screen test seen by Arthur Hornblow. Paramount contract. 1940: first film *All Women Have Secrets,* under pseudonym Constance Keane. Series of films with Alan Ladd. Theatrical work includes Broadway (1963), and London (1969) in 'A Streetcar Named Desire' with Ty Hardin. Married art director John Detlie (divorced 1943), Andre de Toth (1944–52, divorced), music publisher and composer Joseph McCarthy (1955–59, divorced). Autobiography, 'Veronica'.

Films as actress include: 1941: I Wanted Wings; Sullivan's Travels. 1942: This Gun for Hire; The Glass Key; Star Spangled Rhythm; I Married a Witch. 1943: So Proudly We Hail. 1944: The Hour Before the Dawn. 1946: Miss Susie Slagle's; The Blue Dahlia. 1947: Ramrod; Variety Girl. 1948: Saigon; Isn't it Romantic. 1949: Slattery's Hurricane.

LAMARR, Hedy

(Hedwig Kiesler) Actress. Vienna 1915–
At 16: discovered by Max Reinhardt. Austrian films. 1938: first American film *Algiers*. MGM contract. 6 husbands include actor John Loder (1943–47, divorced).

Films as actress include: 1933: Extase. 1939: Lady of the Tropics. 1940: I Take This Woman; Boom Town; Comrade X. 1941: Come Live With Me; Ziegfeld Girl; H. M. Pulham Esq. 1942: Tortilla Flat; Crossroads; White Cargo. 1944: The Conspirators; Experiment Perilous. 1945: Her Highness and the Bellboy. 1946: The Strange Woman. 1947: Dishonored Lady. 1949: Samson and Delilah. 1950: A Lady Without Passport; Copper Canyon. 1951: My Favorite Spy. 1954: L'Amante de Paride; Femmina. 1958: The Female Animal.

LAMBERT, Gavin

Writer. London 1924–
Cheltenham College and Magdalen College, Oxford. 1948–49: writer for Gaumont-British Screen Services; with Lindsay Anderson and others, an editor of Sequence. 1949: appointed director of British Film Institute publications, editor of Sight and Sound. 1955: wrote and directed short film *Another Sky,* made in Morocco. 1958: collaborated with Nicholas Ray on script for *Bitter Victory.* 1959: published novel 'The Slide Area – Scenes of Hollywood Life'. Remained in Hollywood as scriptwriter. Also novelist.

Films as writer include: 1960: Sons and Lovers (co). 1961: The Roman Spring of Mrs Stone. 1966: Inside Daisy Clover (+fn).

LAMORISSE, Albert

Director. Paris 1922–70 near Teheran, Persia
École des Roches and IDHEC. 1946: in Tunisia assistant director on short *Kairouan.* 1947: directed first film there. 1950: *Bim, le petit Ane* had commentary by Jacques Prévert. Photographed several documentaries including *Guatemala* (1955). 1958: started to use Mélievisien, perfected by him. 1960: first feature *Le Voyage en ballon.* Injured in avalanche making film in the Alps; 1 year in hospital. Killed in helicopter crash while making documentary in Persia. Books include 'Versailles' (1967), 'Le Vent des amoureux' (1967), 'Paris jamais vu' (1968).

Films as director: 1947: Djerba (sh, +cy). 1950: Bim, le petit Ane. 1953: Crin Blanc, le cheval sauvage – The White Stallion. 1956: Le Ballon Rouge – The Red Balloon (+s). 1960: Le Voyage en ballon. 1965: Fifi la Plume (+s).

LAMOTHE, Arthur

Director. Saint-Mont, France 1928–
Studied agriculture in Toulouse. Viticulture then woodcutter. Union secretary in Saint-Mont cooperative. 1953: to Canada. 1954: Political Economy at University of Montreal. 1955–56: co-founder of magazine Images. Wrote for Cité Libre. 1958: to Radio-Canada. For TV prepared programmes on foreign policy and worked on series 'Tribune-Libre', 'L'Evènement', 'Ciné-Club'. 1960–61: taught film in Montreal. Handled publicity for Montreal Festival. 1962: to National Film Board of Canada as writer, researcher; first film as director. 1965: left NFBC to found La Société Genéral Cinématographique.

Films as director include: 1965: Poussière sur la ville (+c/co-e). 1968: Ce Soir-là, Gilles Vigneault (+co-e); Actualités Québecoises (series of 6; co-d 6 others). 1970: Un Homme et son boss (co-d Guy Borremans).

Films as director and writer include: 1962: Bûcherons de la Manouane (+co-e). 1963: De Montréal a Manicouagan. 1965: La Neige a fondu sur la Manicouagan (+e). 1967: Le Train de Labrador. 1968: Au-delà des murs (+e). 1969: Pour une éducation de qualité (series of 6; +co-e). 1970: Le Mépris n'aura qu'un temps; Le Monde de l'enfance (uf; +co-cy); Révolution Industrielle; Techniques Minières.

LAMOUR, Dorothy

(Dorothy Kaumeyer) Actress. New Orleans, Louisiana 1914–
1931: winner of beauty contest, Miss New Orleans. 1936: starred in first film *The Jungle Princess.* From 1940: appeared in each of the 'Road' series. Most films for Paramount. TV, recordings, and cabaret.

Films as actress include: 1937: High, Wide and Handsome; Swing High, Swing Low. 1938: The Hurricane; The Big Broadcast of 1938: Spawn of the North. 1939: Man About Town; St Louis Blues; Disputed Passage. 1940: Chad Hanna; Johnny Apollo; Road to Singapore. 1941: Aloma of the South Seas; Caught in the Draft; The Road to Zanzibar. 1942: The Road to Morocco; The Fleet's In; Beyond the Blue Horizon; They Got Me Covered. 1943: Riding High. 1944: And The Angels Sing. 1945: A Medal for Benny; Masquerade in Mexico. 1947: My Favourite Brunette; Road to Rio; Wild Harvest. 1948: A Miracle Can Happen. 1949: Slightly French. 1952: The Greatest Show on Earth. 1953: The Road to Bali. 1962: The Road to Hong Kong. 1963: Donovan's Reef. 1964: Pajama Party.

LANCASTER, Burt

Actor and producer. New York 1913–
Studied physical education at New York University. Vaudeville and circus acrobatics ended by injury. US Army; USO. Spotted by stage producer Irving Jacobs for 'A Sound of Hunting'. 1946: Signed by Mark Hellinger for first film *The Killers.* Formed production company with Harold Hecht; first production *Kiss the Blood Off My Hands* (1948). Warner contract arranged to include release of his own independent productions. Brief return to circus acrobatics. 1955: directed *The Kentuckian.* 1960: Oscar as Best Actor for *Elmer Gantry.* To 1949: worked for Paramount and Warners. Later for several companies, especially Warners and United Artists. 1971: On Stage in San Francisco in 'Knickerbocker Holiday'.

Films as actor include: 1947: Desert Fury; Brute Force; I Walk Alone. 1948: Sorry, Wrong Number; All My Sons; Criss-Cross. 1949: Rope of Sand. 1950: The Flame and the Arrow; Mister 880. 1951: Ten Tall Men; Vengeance Valley; Jim Thorpe—All American. 1952: The Crimson Pirate. 1953: Come Back, Little Sheba; His Majesty O'Keefe; From Here to Eternity. 1954: Apache; Vera Cruz. 1955: The Rose Tattoo. 1956: Trapeze; The Rainmaker. 1957: Gunfight at the OK Corral; Sweet Smell of Success. 1958: Separate Tables. 1959: The Devil's Disciple. 1960: The Unforgiven. 1961: The Young Savages; Judgement at Nuremburg. 1962: Bird Man of Alcatraz; A Child is Waiting. 1963: Il Gattopardo. 1964: Seven Days in May. 1965: The Hallelujah Trail; The Train. 1966: The Professionals. 1968: The Scalphunters; Castle Keep; The Swimmer. 1969: The Gypsy Moths.

LANDAU, Ely A.

Producer. New York 1920–
World War II: in US Air Force. Then to TV, working for a producer then as director. 1951: Founded Ely Landau Inc. 1957: President of National Telefilm Associates Inc. 1961: resigned to produce films. As TV producer, specialised in telefilms of plays e.g. 'Juno and The Paycock', 'Waltz of the Toreadors', 'The Cherry Orchard', 'The Iceman Cometh'. Owns two art house cinemas in New York.

Films as producer include: 1962: Long Day's Journey Into Night. 1965: The Pawnbroker. 1969: The Madwoman of Chaillot. 1970: King; A Filmed Record . . . Montgomery to Memphis.

LANG, Charles B., Jr

Cinematographer. Bluff, Utah 1902–
Started in films at Paramount Film Laboratory; became camera assistant. 1926: first feature as cinematographer, but studio disappointed with results and he returned to work as assistant. 1929–52: cinematographer at Paramount. Then freelance. Oscar for cinematography on *A Farewell to Arms* (1933).

Films as cinematographer include: 1930: Tom Sawyer. 1931: The Vice Squad; Unfaithful. 1933: She Done Him Wrong. 1935: Peter Ibbetson (*co*); The Lives of a Bengal Lancer. 1936: Desire (*co*). 1937: Angel; Souls at Sea. 1938: You and Me; Spawn of the North. 1939: Zaza; The Cat and the Canary. 1941: Sundown; The Shepherd of the Hills (*co*). 1947: The Ghost and Mrs Muir. 1948: Miss Tatlock's Millions; A Foreign Affair. 1949: Rope of Sand. 1951: September Affair; Red Mountain. 1952: Sudden Fear. 1953: The Big Heat; Salome. 1954: It Should Happen to You; Sabrina. 1955: Queen Bee; The Man From Laramie. 1956: Autumn Leaves; The Solid Gold Cadillac; The Rainmaker. 1957: Gunfight at the OK Corral; Wild is the Wind. 1958: The Matchmaker; Separate Tables; Last Train from Gun Hill. 1959: Some Like it Hot. 1960: Strangers When We Meet; The Magnificent Seven. 1961: One Eyed Jacks. 1962: How the West Was Won (*co*). 1963: Critic's Choice; Charade; Paris When It Sizzles. 1964: Sex and the Single Girl. 1967: Hotel; The Flim Flam Man; Wait Until Dark. 1969: The Stalking Moon; How to Commit Marriage; Cactus Flower.

LANG, Fritz

Director. Vienna 1890–
Father a leading Viennese architect. 1905: entered the Realschule to study architecture. 1908: studied painting at Vienna Academy of Graphic Arts. Continued studies in Munich and Paris. World tour, living by painting postcards and drawing for newspapers. World War I: wounded 3 times, 4 decorations. During periods in hospital wrote scripts; sold them to Berlin film companies, at first receiving no credit. 1917: scripted 2 films for Joe May, *Die Hochzeitim Excentricclub* and *Hilde Warren und der Tod*. 1919: collaborated with Thea Von Harbou on an adaptation of her novel 'Das Indische Grabmal', filmed by Joe May (1921) and in a new adaptation by Lang (1959). 1919: first film as director. Collaborated with Thea Von Harbou on scripts of all his German films from *Das wandernde Bild* (1920). 1933: offered job of Third Reich's official

film director by Josef Goebbels but, having had trouble with Nazis over 2 previous films and being of Jewish ancestry, left for Paris, where he made *Liliom* before leaving for US. 1945–48: *Scarlet Street* and *Secret Beyond the Door* made for Diana Productions of which he was founder and president; the other members were Walter Wanger and Joan Bennett. 1958: returned to Germany to make *Das Indische Grabmal,* which was released in two parts, the first known as *Der Tiger von Eschnapur*; the English language version, *Tiger of Bengal,* (UK) or *Journey to the Lost City* (US) included both sections edited down to less than half their combined original length.

Films as director: 1919: Halbblut (*+ s*); Der Herr der Liebe (*+ w*); Die Spinnen, Part I: Der goldene See (*+ s*); Hara-Kiri. 1920: Die Spinnen, Part II: Das brillanten Schiff (*+ s*); Das wandernde Bild (*+ co-s*); Vier um die frau (*+ co-s*). 1921: Der Müde Tod – Destiny – Between Two Worlds (*+ co-s*). 1922: Dr Mabuse, der Spieler, Part I: Dr Mabuse der Spieler – Ein Bild der Zeit; Part II: Inferno – Menschen der Zeit (*+ co-s*). 1924: Die Nibelungen, Part I: Siegfried – Siegrid's Tod; (*sound version*); Part II: Kriemhilds Rache – Kriemhild's Revenge (*+ co-s*). 1927: Metropolis (*+ co-s*). 1928: Spione (*+ p/co-s*); 1929: Frau im Mond – By Rocket to the Moon – The Girl in the Moon (*+ p/co-s*). 1931: M – Mörder unter Uns (*+ co-s*). 1932: Das Testament des Dr Mabuse – The Last Will of Dr Mabuse (*+ p/co-s*). 1933: Liliom (*+ co-s*). 1936: Fury (*+ co-s*). 1937: You Only Live Once. 1938: You and Me (*+ p*). 1940: The Return of Frank James. 1941: Western Union; Man Hunt; Confirm or Deny (*uc, co-d Archie Mayo*). 1942: Hangmen Also Die! – Lest We Forget (*+ co-p/co-st/co-s*). 1944: The Ministry of Fear; The Woman in the Window. 1945: Scarlet Street (*+ p*). 1946: Cloak and Dagger. 1948: Secret Beyond the Door (*+ p*). 1950: House by the River; American Guerilla in the Philippines – I Shall Return. 1952: Rancho Notorious; Clash by Night. 1953: The Blue Gardenia; The Big Heat. 1954: Human Desire. 1955: Moonfleet. 1956: While the City Sleeps; Beyond A Reasonable Doubt. 1959: Der Tiger von Eschnapur (*+ co-s*); Das Indische Grabmal (*+ co-s*). 1960: Die tausend Augen des Dr Mabuse – The Thousand Eyes of Dr Mabuse (*+ p/co-s*).

LANG, Walter

Director. Memphis, Tennessee 1898–1972 California University of Tennessee. From 1916: commercial artist; first stage appearance in walk-on part with Sarah Bernhardt company. 1918: produced, directed and acted in army show, touring Europe; studied at Art Student's League; worked as illustrator; acted with David Belasco's company. 1921: acted in films; assistant director, set and costume designer on Pearl White features in New York. 1924: in California with Marion Davies' company. 1926: first film as director *The Earth Woman.* Worked with various companies notably Columbia. From 1937: with Fox.

Films as director: 1925: Red Kimono. 1926: The Earth Woman; Golden Web; Money to Burn. 1927: The Satin Woman (*+ st/s*); Ladybird; Sally in Our Alley; The College Hero; By Whose Hand? 1928: The Desert Bride; Shadows of the Past; The Night Flyer. 1929: The Spirit of Youth. 1930: Brothers; Hello Sister. 1931: Hellbound. 1932: No More Orchids. 1933: The Warrior's Husband. 1934: The

Albert Lamorisse's Fifi La Plume.
Burt Lancaster, co-producer and actor in Richard Brook's Elmer Gantry.
Harry Langdon.

Mighty Barnum. 1935: Carnival. 1936: Love Before Breakfast. 1937: Wife, Doctor and Nurse; Second Honeymoon. 1938: The Baroness and the Butler; I'll Give a Million. 1939: The Little Princess. 1940: The Blue Bird; Star Dust; Tin Pan Alley; The Great Profile. 1941: Moon over Miami; Weekend in Havana. 1942: Song of the Islands; The Magnificent Dope. 1943: Coney Island. 1944: Greenwich Village. 1945: State Fair. 1946: Sentimental Journey; Claudia and David. 1947: Mother Wore Tights. 1948: Sitting Pretty; When My Baby Smiles at Me. 1949: You're My Everything. 1950: Cheaper By the Dozen; The Jackpot. 1951: On the Riviera. 1952: With a Song in My Heart. 1953: Call Me Madam. 1954: There's No Business Like Show Business. 1956: The King and I. 1957: The Desk Set. 1959: But Not for Me. 1960: Can-Can; The Marriage-Go-Round. 1961: Snow White and the Three Stooges – Snow White and the Three Clowns.

LANGDON, Harry

Actor, producer and director. Council Bluffs, Iowa 1884–1944 Hollywood
Cartoonist, barber, prop boy, travelling medicine show. Minstrel company. Vaudeville for 20 years. Short films for almost all major studios. 1923: joined Sennett. 1924–27: 2-reelers, then films written and directed by Frank Capra. 1926–28: own production company; director on three of his own films. To Hal Roach and MGM. 1940: collaborated on script of *A Chump at Oxford*. 1941: collaborated on stage version of 'Road Show', and co-wrote *Road Show*.

Films as actor include: 1924: Picking Peaches; Smile Please; Shanghaied Lovers; Flickering Youth; The Cat's Meow; His New Mamma; The First 100 Years; The Luck of the Foolish; The Hansom Cabman – Be Careful. 1925: The Sea Squaw; His Marriage Wow; Plain Clothes; Remember When?; Lucky Stars; There He Goes. 1926: Saturday Afternoon; Ella Cinders; The Strong Man (*pc*); Tramp, Tramp, Tramp (*pc*). 1927: His First Flame; Long Pants (*pc*); Three's a Crowd (*d/pc*). 1928: The Chaser (*d/pc*); Heart Trouble (*d/pc*). 1930: See America Thirst; A Soldier's Plaything. 1933: Hallelujah I'm a Bum. 1939: Zenobia. 1943: Spotlight Scandals. 1944: Block Busters. 1945: Swingin' on a Rainbow.

LANGLOIS, Henri

Smyrna, Turkey 1914–
Journalist. 1934: with Georges Franju founded Cinémathèque Francaise. 1935: founded Cercle du Cinéma. Became secretary-general and director of Cinémathèque: collection of films goes back to 1896, includes scripts, books, magazines, costumes, models, cameras etc. Hid 50,000 films to prevent their being destroyed by Nazis. 1968: became Visiting Professor at Sir George Williams University, Montreal; dismissed from Cinémathèque, with staff of 60. Demonstrations led by François Truffaut, Jacques Demy and Claude Chabrol led to reinstatement, though official subsidies withdrawn. 1970: subject of *Langlois*.

LANTZ, Walter

Animator. New York 1900–
Studied at Art Student's League. Newspaper cartoonist. From 1922: worked for Bray Studios, collaborating with Isadore Klein on series including 'The Katzenjammer Kids', 'Happy Hooligan', 'Mutt and Jeff', 'Colonel Heeza Liar'. Created and worked on Pete the Pup and Dinky Doodle. 1927: to California; gagman for Sennett and Hal Roach. 1928–38: 'Oswald the Rabbit' series at Universal. 1938: joined Disney, in charge of 100 men producing 10 cartoons per year. Returned to Universal: created Woody Woodpecker, dubbed by voice of his wife, actress Grace Stafford. World War II: worked on large number of training films. Series subsequently worked on include 'Chilly Willy', 'Hickory, Dickory and Doc' and 'Oswald the Rabbit'.

LANZA, Mario

(Alfred Arnold Cocozza) Singer and actor. New York 1921–59 Rome
Berkshire School of Music. 1942–45: military service, then appeared in Columbia Concerts. 1945–46: programme and contract with Victor Records. 1947: soloist with Boston and Philadelphia symphony orchestras; contract with MGM following Hollywood Bowl concert. 1949: first film, *That Midnight Kiss*. 1952: Left Hollywood after contract dispute with MGM. 1956: returned to work for Warners and Columbia before making last 2 films for MGM. Constant over-weight problem; died of heart attack.

Films as actor include: 1951: The Great Caruso. 1952: Because You're Mine. 1954: The Student Prince (*wv only*). 1956: Serenade. 1959: For the First Time.

LASHELLE, Joseph

Cinematographer. Los Angeles 1905–
Worked in Paramount laboratory, became assistant cameraman. Operator for Fox, including *How Green was My Valley* (1941), *The Song of Bernadette* (1943). 1944: replaced Lucien Ballard on *Laura* when Otto Preminger replaced Rouben Mamoulian; reshot Ballard's footage. 12 Oscar nominations, Oscar for black and white cinematography, *Laura*.

Films as cinematographer include: 1944: Laura; The Eve of St Mark. 1945: Hangover Square; A Bell for Adano; Fallen Angel. 1946: Cluny Brown. 1947: The Foxes of Harrow; The Late George Apley. 1948: Deep Waters. 1949: The Fan. 1950: Where the Sidewalk Ends. 1951: The Guy Who Came Back; The 13th Letter. 1952: The Outcasts of Poker Flat; Les Miserables; My Cousin Rachel. 1953: Dangerous Crossing. 1954: River of No Return. 1955: Marty; The Conqueror (*co*). 1956: Run for the Sun. 1957: Bachelor Party; Crime of Passion; Fury at Showdown; The Abductors; No Down Payment. 1958: The Long Hot Summer; The Naked and The Dead. 1959: Career. 1960: The Apartment. 1962: How the West was Won *ep* The Civil War; A Child is Waiting. 1963: Irma la Douce. 1964: Kiss Me Stupid; Wild and Wonderful. 1965: Seven Women. 1966: The Chase; The Fortune Cookie. 1969: Eighty Steps to Jonah.

LASKY, Jesse L.

Producer. San Francisco 1880–1958 Beverley Hills, California
Reporter in San Francisco. Cornet player with travelling medicine show; played with orchestra in Hawaii. Duo cornet act with sister Blanche. 1902: began partnership with R. A. Rolfe, produced short plays, went into vaudeville management and production. 1912: lost $100,000 trying to launch restaurant in New York. 1913: with Samuel Goldwyn, Arthur S. Friend and Cecil B. De Mille founded Jesse Lasky Feature Plays. 1916: merged with Adolph Zukor's Famous Players, became vice-president in charge of production. 1932: forced out of company (by now Paramount) due to fall in stock. To Fox, producer for 5 years. 1935: became president of Pickford-Lasky Corporation. 1938–40: radio producer. From 1941: producer at Warners, then RKO. 1950: to MGM. 1957: returned to Paramount; published autobiography 'I Blow My Horn'. Son is writer Jesse Lasky, Jr.

Films as producer include: 1933: Berkeley Square. 1934: I am Suzanne; Springtime for Henry. 1935: Helldorado; Redheads on Parade; The Gay Deception. 1936: The Gay Desperado (*co*); One Rainy Afternoon. 1937: Hitting a New High. 1941: Sergeant York (*co*). 1944: The Adventures of Mark Twain. 1945: Rhapsody in Blue. 1946: Without Reservations. 1948: The Miracle of the Bells (*co*).

LASSALLY, Walter

Cinematographer. Berlin 1926–
1939: emigrated to UK. 1945: entered films as clapper boy. 1950: cinematographer for Basic Films; shot many shorts before his first feature (1956). Has worked in Pakistan and for Michael Cacoyannis in Greece.

Films as cinematographer include: 1953: Thursday's Children. 1954: Pleasure Garden. 1955: To Konitsi me ta maura. 1959: We Are the Lambeth Boys; Beat Girl. 1961: A Taste of Honey; Electra. 1962: The Loneliness of the Long Distance Runner. 1963: Tom Jones. 1964: Psyche 59. 1965: Zorba the Greek. 1969: 3 into 2 Won't Go.

LASZLO, Ernest

Cinematographer. Hungary 1906–
1926: to USA. 1927: began as camera assistant for Christie. Moved to Paramount. 1930: became operator, e.g. on *Hold Back the Dawn* (1941), *The Major and The Minor* (1942). 1943: first film as cinematographer *The Hitler Gang*. 1943–49: Paramount contract, frequently loaned out. 1953: last Paramount film *Stalag 17*, then freelance. Oscar for black and white cinematography, *Ship of Fools* (1965).

Films as cinematographer include: 1946: Two Years Before the Mast. 1947: Road to Rio. 1949: D.O.A. 1950: Riding High (*co*). 1951: M. 1952: The First Time; The Steel Trap. 1953: Stalag 17; The Moon is Blue. 1954: The Naked Jungle; Vera Cruz; Apache; About Mrs Leslie. 1955: Kiss Me Deadly; The Kentuckian; The Big Knife. 1956: Bandido; While the City Sleeps. 1957: Valerie. 1960: Inherit the Wind. 1961: The Last Sunset; Judgment at Nuremberg. 1963: 4 for Texas; It's a Mad, Mad, Mad, Mad World. 1964: One Man's Way. 1965: Baby, the Rain Must Fall; Ship of Fools. 1966: Fantastic Voyage. 1967: Luv. 1968: Star!; The First Time. 1969: Daddy's Gone a-Hunting.

LATHROP, Philip H.

Cinematographer
1934: camera loader. 1938: assistant to Joseph

Valentine. War service, then assistant and operator to e.g. Russell Metty on *Touch of Evil* (1958). 1957: first film as cinematographer *Monster of the Piedras Blancas*. Worked mainly for Universal-International, Warners and MGM.

Films as cinematographer include: 1958: Girls on the Loose; Wild Heritage; The Saga of Hemp Brown; Monster of The Piedras Blancas; The Perfect Furlough; Money, Women and Guns. 1962: Experiment in Terror; Lonely are the Brave. 1963: Days of Wine and Roses. 1964: The Pink Panther; The Americanisation of Emily; In Harm's Way (*2nd-unit*). 1965: 36 Hours; The Cincinnatti Kid; Never Too Late. 1966: What Did You Do in the War, Daddy?. 1967: The Happening; Don't Make Waves; Gunn; Point Blank. 1968: Finian's Rainbow; I Love You Alice B. Toklas. 1969: The Gypsy Moths; The Illustrated Man; They Shoot Horses, Don't They? 1970: The Traveling Executioner; Rabbit, Run. 1971: Wild Rovers.

LATTUADA, Alberto

Director. Milan 1914–

Son of the composer Felice Lattuada who was to compose most of the scores for son's films. Studied architecture. Wrote articles on the cinema and was involved with Luigi Comencini and others in the antecedents of the Italian Film Archive. Started in cinema as set decorator (1933), as assistant in charge of colour (1935) and as assistant director and writer on 2 films (1940–41), including *Piccolo Mondo Antico*. Wrote a 'Photographic Atlas' published in 1941. President of Italian Cinemathèque.

Films as director: 1942: Giacomo l'idealista (+ *co-s*). 1944: La Freccia nel fianco – La Freccia – The Arrow (+ *co-s*): La Nostra Guerra. 1946: Il Bandito (+ *st/co-s*). 1947: Il Delitto di Giovanni Episcopo Giovanni Episcopo – Flesh Will Surrender (+ *co-s*); Senza Pietà – Without Pity (+ *co-s*). 1949: Il Mulino del Po (+ *co-ad*). 1950: Luci del varieta – Lights of Variety (*co-d Federico Fellini*). 1951: Il Cappotto – The Overcoat (+ *co-s*). 1953: La Lupa; Amore in città – The Vixen – The She Wolf (+ *ad/co-s*) *ep* Gli Italiani si voltano (+ *co-st/co-s*); La Spiaggia – The Beach (+ *st/co-s*). 1954: Scuola Elementare (+ *st/co-s*). 1957: Guendalina (+ *co-s*). 1958: La Tempestà – Tempest. 1960: I Dolci Inganni (+ *st/co-s*); Lettere di una novizia (+ *co-s*). 1961: L'Imprevisto – The Unexpected. 1962: La Steppa – The Steppe (+ *co-s*); Mafioso. 1965: La Mandragola – The Mandrake. 1966: Matchless (+ *co-s*). 1967: Don Giovanni in Sicilia. 1968: Fraulein Doktor – The Betrayal (+ *co-s*). 1970: Venga a prendero il caffe da noi.

LAUGHTON, Charles

Actor and director. Scarborough, Yorkshire 1899–1962 Hollywood

RADA. From 1926: stage actor, including 'The Government Inspector', 'The Pillars of Society', 'The Cherry Orchard', 'Liliom', 'Alibi', 'Payment Deferred'. 1928: first film as actor short *Bluebottles*. 1929: married Elsa Lanchester. To 1931: British films. 1931: on Broadway in 'Payment Deferred'; resulted in Paramount contract. 1932: first American film *The Old Dark House*. From 1933: worked for many companies, notably MGM. RKO. 1933: Oscar for *The Private Life*

of Henry VIII. 1933-34: Old Vic. 1935: Comédie Française. 1937: in partnership with Eric Pommer and John Maxwell formed own company, Mayflower, and produced 3 films with himself as star: *Vessel of Wrath* (1938), *St Martin's Lane* (1938), *Jamaica Inn* (1939). 1940: acted in *They Knew What They Wanted*, produced by Pommer; became American citizen. 1949: with Agnes Moorehead, Charles Boyer, Cedric Hardwicke founded first Drama Quartet; they acted on Broadway and at Carnegie Hall, 1954: made *Hobson's Choice*, his first British film since 1939. 1955: only film as director *The Night of the Hunter*, did not act in it. 1959: played King Lear at Stratford. 1962: last film *Advise and Consent*. Theatrical work includes Joseph Losey's production of 'Galileo' in Los Angeles and New York; also stage director.

Films as actor include: 1929: Piccadilly. 1932: The Old Dark House; If I Had a Million *ep* The Clerk; The Sign of the Cross. 1933: The Island of Lost Souls; The Private Life of Henry VIII. 1934: The Barretts of Wimpole Street. 1935: Ruggles of Red Gap; Les Miserables; Mutiny on the Bounty. 1936: Rembrandt. 1937: Claudius (*uf*). 1938: The Vessel of Wrath; St Martin's Lane. 1939: Jamaica Inn; The Hunchback of Notre Dame. 1940: They Knew What They Wanted. 1942: The Tuttles of Tahiti; Tales of Manhattan. 1943: Forever and a Day; This Land is Mine. 1944: The Canterville Ghost; The Suspect. 1947: The Paradine Case. 1948: The Arch of Triumph; The Big Clock; The Man on the Eiffel Tower (*p*). 1949: The Bribe. 1951: The Blue Veil. 1952: O. Henry's Full House *ep* The Cop and Anthem. 1953: Young Bess; Salome. 1954: Hobson's Choice. 1957: Witness for the Prosecution. 1960: Spartacus. 1962: Advise and Consent.

LAUNDER, Frank

Director, writer and producer. Hitchin, Hertfordshire 1907–

Civil Servant in Official Receiver's Office in Brighton. Acted in Brighton repertory. Wrote play 'There Was No Signpost'. Title writer for British International. 1929: scripted first British dialogue film, *Under the Greenwood Tree* which Sidney Gilliat had previously worked on as a silent; first collaborated. 1935: alone, freelanced for Warners. 1936: to Gainsborough as writer and script editor; with Gilliat and Alma Reville wrote *The Lady Vanishes*. 1939–42: with Gilliat scripted several films directed by Carol Reed. 1940: their play 'The Body was Well Nourished' (1936) produced in London. 1943: first film as director, in collaboration with Gilliat, *Millions Like Us*. 1944: they formed own company to make *The Rake's Progress* which Gilliat directed. Subsequently divided direction, writing and producing between them in various permutations, e.g. produced Gilliat's *London Belongs to Me* (1948) and co-produced Gilliat's *Left, Right and Centre* (1958). 1948: worked for London Films. 1956: Columbia contract. Honorary secretary and founder member of Screenwriters Association. Married actress Bernadette O'Farrell.

Films as writer include: 1935: I Give My Heart. 1937: Oh Mr Porter! 1938: The Lady Vanishes (*co*). 1939: A Girl Must Live. 1940: Night Train to Munich (*co*). 1941: Kipps (*co*). 1942: The Young Mr Pitt (*co*).

Films as director, and writer in collaboration with Sidney Gilliat: 1943: Millions Like Us. 1944: 2,000

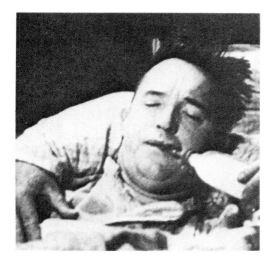

Akim Tamiroff (left front), Orson Welles (with cigar) and Philip Lathrop (right) shooting Touch of Evil.
Charles Laughton (right) in Jean Renoir's This Land is Mine.
Stanley Laurel in Their First Mistake. *directed by George Marshall.*

Women. 1946: I See a Dark Stranger – The Adventuress. 1947: Captain Boycott. 1948: The Blue Lagoon. 1950: The Happiest Days of Your Life (+p). 1951: Lady Godiva Rides Again (+co-p). 1952: Folly to Be Wise (+co-p). 1954: Belles of St Trinian's (+co-p). 1955: Geordie (+co-p). 1957: Blue Murder at St Trinian's (+co-p). 1958: Bridal Path (s alone +co-p). 1960: The Pure Hell of St Trinians (d only). 1966: The Great St Trinian's Train Robbery.

LAUREL, Stan

(Arthur Stanley Jefferson) Ulverston, Lancashire 1890–1965 Santa Monica, California
Music hall performer. 1907: appeared with Fred Karno troupe. 1910: American tour with Chaplin. 1913: second American tour; remained in USA, retaining British citizenship. Changed name during American vaudeville career. 1917: first film as actor Nuts in May; associated by chance with Oliver Hardy in Lucky Dog. Worked for Larry Semon, Hal Roach and in series 'Stan Laurel Comedies'; studios include Vitagraph, Universal. 1926: Roach contract as gagman and director; co-directed Get 'em Young and replaced Oliver Hardy as actor. 1927: their first film as a team Putting Pants on Philip. Directed or supervised by Leo McCarey until late 1930; then fewer shorts. 1931: first feature Pardon Us began as 2-reeler, expanded because of expense of sets. 1936–37: produced 2 features. After 1945 only one film together, made in France. They continued to make stage appearances. Most films for MGM. Compilation films include Laurel and Hardy's Laughing 20s (1965), The Crazy World of Laurel and Hardy (1966), Further Perils of Laurel and Hardy (1967).

Short films as actor with Oliver Hardy: 1917: Lucky Dog. 1926: 45 Minutes from Hollywood. 1927: Duck Soup; Slipping Wives; Love 'em and Weep; Why Girls Love Sailors; With Love and Hisses; Sailors, Beware!; Do Detectives Think?; Flying Elephants; Sugar Daddies; Call of the Cuckoo; The Second Hundred Years; Hats Off. 1928: Putting Pants on Philip; The Battle of the Century; Leave 'em Laughing; The Finishing Touch; From Soup to Nuts; You're Darn Tootin' – The Music Blasters; Their Purple Moment; Should Married Men Go Home; Early to Bed; Two Tars; Habeas Corpus; We Faw Down – We Slip Up. 1929: Liberty; Wrong Again; That's My Wife; Big Business; Double Whoopee; Berth Marks; Bacon Grabbers; Angora Love; Unaccustomed As We Are; Men o' War; Perfect Day; They Go Boom; The Hoosegow. 1930: Night Owls; Blotto; Be Big; Brats; The Laurel-Hardy Murder Case; Below Zero; Hog Wild – Aerial Antics; Another Fine Mess. 1931: Chickens Come Home; Laughing Gravy; Our Wife; Come Clean; One Good Turn; Beau Hunks – Beau Chumps; Helpmates. 1932: Any Old Port; The Music Box; The Chimp; County Hospital; Scram; Their First Mistake. 1933: Towed in a Hole; Twice Two; Me and My Pal; The Midnight Patrol; Busy Bodies; Dirty Work. 1934: The Private Life of Oliver VIII; Going Bye Bye; Them Thar Hills; The Live Ghost. 1935: Tit for Tat; The Fixer Uppers; Thicker Than Water.

Features as actor with Oliver Hardy: 1929: Hollywood Revue of 1929. 1930: Rogue Song. 1931: Pardon Us – Jailbirds. 1932: Pack Up Your Troubles. 1933: The Devil's Brother – Fra Diavolo; Sons of the Desert – Sons of the Legion – Fraternally Yours – Convention City. 1934: Babes in Toyland – Wooden Soldiers; Hollywood Party. 1935: Bonnie Scotland. 1936: The Bohemian Girl; Our Relations (+p). 1937: Way Out West (+p); Pick a Star. 1938: Swiss Miss; Block Heads. 1939: The Flying Deuces. 1940: A Chump at Oxford; Saps at Sea. 1941: Great Guns. 1942: A Haunting We Will Go. 1943: Air Raid Wardens; Jitterbugs; The Dancing Masters. 1944: The Big Noise; Nothing But Trouble. 1945: The Bullfighters. 1950: Atoll K – Robinson Crusoeland – Utopia.

LAURIE, Piper

(Rosetta Jacobs) Detroit, Michigan 1932–
Screentested while a schoolgirl. 1950: first film Louisa. Almost all films for Universal; broke contract in order to freelance. Broadway and TV. Married critic Joseph Morgenstern (1962).

Films as actress include: 1951: The Prince Who Was a Thief. 1952: Son of Ali Baba; No Room for the Groom; Has Anybody Seen My Gal? 1953: The Mississippi Gambler; The Golden Blade. 1955: Ain't Misbehavin'. 1957: Until They Sail; Kelly and Me. 1961: The Hustler.

LAUTNER, Georges

Director. Nice 1926–
Son of a jeweller; mother actress Renée Saint-Cyr. Educated in Paris. Ecole Libre de Sciences Politiques then law at University of Paris. Various jobs, including architectural planning and stage design. Entered films as camera assistant. 1952–57: assistant director. 1953: first film as director, short Plus Belle que la nature. 1958: first feature as director.

Features as director and writer in collaboration: 1962: L'Oeil du monocle. 1963: Les Tontons Flingueurs. 1964: Des Pissenlits par la racine. 1965: Galia. 1966: La Grande Sauterelle. 1967: Fleur d'oseille.

Features as director: 1958: La Mome aux boutons. 1959: Marche ou crève. 1961: Arrêtez les tambours; Le Monocle Noir; En plein cirage; Le Septieme Jure. 1964: Le Monocle rit jaune. 1965: Les Barbouzes; Ne nous fachons pas; Les Bons Vivants – How to Keep the Red Lamp Burning (title ep). 1967: Le Pacha (+st/s). 1968: Michel Strogoff. 1970: Sur la route de Salina (+co-s).

LAWFORD, Peter

Actor. London 1923–
1931: first film as actor Poor Old Bill. 1938: first American film Lord Jeff. To 1959: worked mainly for MGM. Own production company. 1969–70: owned nightclub in Los Angeles. Married Patricia Kennedy (1954–66, divorced).

Films as actor (from 1946) include: 1946: Cluny Brown; My Brother Talks to Horses. 1947: Good News. 1948: Easter Parade; Julia Misbehaves; On an Island With You. 1949: Little Women; The Red Danube. 1950: Please Believe Me. 1951: Royal Wedding. 1952: Kangaroo; Just This One; You For Me. 1954: It Should Happen To You. 1959: Never So Few. 1960: Exodus; Ocean's 11; Pepe. 1961: Sergeants Three. 1962: Advise and Consent; The Longest Day.

1964: Dead Ringer. 1965: Sylvia; Harlow. 1966: The Oscar. 1969: The April Fools; Hook, Line and Sinker. 1970: One More Time.

LAWRENCE, Gertrude

(Alexandra Dagmar Lawrence-Klasen) Actress. London 1898–1952 New York
Mainly stage actress, notably in revue and in musical comedies by Noël Coward. Occasional films from 1929. Autobiography, 'A Star Danced' (1959). Played by Julie Andrews in biography Star! (1968).

Films as actress include: 1932: Lord Camber's Ladies. 1936: Rembrandt. 1943: Stage Door Canteen. 1950: The Glass Menagerie.

LAWSON, John Howard

Writer. New York 1894–
Son of journalist. 1914–15: cable editor for Reuters Press in New York. 1917–19: served in ambulance unit in France and Italy. Journalist in Rome. 1934: to Hollywood as writer for MGM; co-wrote Success at Any Price, based on own play 'Success Story' (1932); freelanced. 1943: script for Sahara based on an incident in Mikhail Romm's Triniadstat (1937). 1945: script for Counter-Attack from play based on 'Pobyeda' by Ilya Vershinin and Mikhail Ruderman. 1948: found guilty of contempt of Congress during Un-American Activities hearings, served 1-year gaol term. Plays include: 'Roger Bloomer' (1923), 'Processional' (1925), 'The International' (1928), 'The Pure in Heart' (1934), 'Gentlewoman' (1934), 'Marching Song' (1937). Books include: 'Theory and Technique of Playwriting' (1936), 'Theory and Technique of Playwriting and Screenwriting' (1949), 'The Hidden Heritage' (1950), 'Film in the Battle of Ideas' (1953), 'Film: the Creative Process' (1964). Teacher at Stanford and at Loyola University, Los Angeles; Visiting Professor in theatre history at University of Judaism, Los Angeles.

Films as writer include: 1938: Blockade; Algiers. 1939: They Shall Have Music (co). 1940: Four Sons; Earthbound (co). 1943: Action in the North Atlantic; Sahara (co). 1945: Counter-Attack. 1947: Smash-up.

LAWTON, Charles, Jr

Cinematographer. Los Angeles 1904–65
1926: assistant to George Folsey at First National. Became operator. 1932: operator for Folsey at MGM. 1937: became cinematographer. Worked mainly for MGM and Columbia.

Films as cinematographer include: 1937: My Dear Miss Aldrich. 1939: Miracles for Sale; Nick Carter, Master Detective. 1941: Free and Easy (co); The Vanishing Virginian. 1942: Fingers at the Window (co). 1943: Young Ideas. 1944: Up in Mabel's Room; Abroad with Two Yanks. 1945: Brewster's Millions; Getting Gertie's Garters; One Way to Love; The Return of Monte Cristo. 1948: The Lady From Shanghai; The Black Arrow. 1949: Shockproof; Slightly French; The Doolins of Oklahoma; Mr Soft Touch (co). 1950: The Nevadan; Rogues of Sherwood Forest. 1951: Man in the Saddle; Mask of the Avenger. 1952: The Happy Time; Paula; Last of the Comanches. 1953: Cruisin'

Down the River; All Ashore. 1954: Drive a Crooked Road; They Rode West. 1955: The Long Gray Line; My Sister Eileen; Bring Your Smile Along. 1956: Jubal. 1957: Full of Life; The Tall T; 3.10 to Yuma; Operation Mad Ball. 1958: Cowboy; Gunman's Walk; The Last Hurrah. 1959: The Gene Krupa Story; It Happened to Jane; Ride Lonesome. 1960: Comanche Station; Man on a String (co). 1961: Two Rode Together. 1963: Spencer's Mountain. 1964: Youngblood Hawke.

LEACOCK, Philip

Director and producer. London 1917–
1935: entered films, working in various capacities on documentaries. 1938: British Army, reaching Captain. Directed training films for Royal Army Ordnance Corps and top-secret film for presentation by Churchill at Quebec Conference. Made short documentaries. 1946: directed first feature, a semi-documentary. From 1948: Crown Film Unit. 7-year Rank contract ended in 1958; then USA for Hecht-Lancaster and Columbia. TV director: pilot and 6 episodes of 'Route 66'; also 'The Great Adventure', 'The Defenders', 'The Alfred Hitchcock Hour', 'Rawhide'. Executive producer and producer of TV series 'Gunsmoke'. 1968: produced Firecreek. Brother is director Richard Leacock.

Short films as director include: 1940: Island People (co-d Paul Rotha); The Story of Wool. 1951: Out of True; Life in Her Hands; Festival in London.

Features as director: 1946: Riders of the New Forest. 1952: The Brave Don't Cry. 1953: Appointment in London; The Kidnappers – Little Kidnappers. 1955: Escapade. 1956: The Spanish Gardener. 1957: High Tide at Noon. 1958: Innocent Sinners; The Rabbit Trap. 1959: Take a Giant Step; Let No Man Write My Epitaph. 1960: Hand in Hand. 1961: 13, West Street; Reach for Glory. 1962: The War Lover. 1963: Tamahine.

LEACOCK, Richard

Director and cinematographer. London 1921–
1938: to America. 1940–55: cinematographer, e.g. on several films directed by Willard Van Dyke. World War II: army cinematographer. 1955: first film as director, produced by Van Dyke; met Robert Drew, journalist on Life magazine; got sponsoring by Time Inc. 1959–62: with Drew produced films for Time-Life Broadcasting. Member of Drew Associates with Robert Drew, Greg Shuker and D. A. Pennebaker. Several films photographed by Pennebaker. Brother of Philip Leacock.

Films as cinematographer include: 1941: To Hear Your Banjo Play (co). 1948: Louisiana Story. 1949: Mount Vernon. 1950: Years Of Change. 1952: New York University (co). 1969: One PM (co; +w). 1970: Maidstone (co); Original Cast Album: Company (co). 1971: Sweet Toronto (co).

Films as director: 1955: Toby and the Tall Corn. 1956: F100. 1960: Yankee No!; Balloon (co-d Don Pennebaker); Primary (co-d Pennebaker, Robert Drew); On the Pole (+co-c/co-e; co-d Pennebaker). 1961: Eddie Sachs at Indianapolis – Eddie (co-d Drew); Pete and Johnny; Kenya 61; Football – Mooney v Fowle (co-d Drew); X-15 Pilot (+c; co-d

Robert Andrew). 1962: Susan Starr (co-d Pennebaker); David (co-d Pennebaker); Nehru – The Living Camera (+c; co-d Gregory Shuker). 1963: The Chair (+co-e; co-d Pennebaker, Shuker); Jane (co-d Drew); Happy Birthday, Blackie; Aga Khan; Quint City USA – Happy Mother's Day, Mrs Fisher. 1964: Republicans–the New Breed. 1966: Igor Stravinsky: a Portrait.

LEAN, David

Director. Croydon, Surrey 1908–
Began as clapper-boy at Lime Grove Studios. From 1928: camera assistant, cutting room assistant, assistant director. From 1930: editor with Gaumont Sound News, British Movietonews. 1935–42: editor at Elstree e.g. on Escape Me Never, French Without Tears, 49th Parallel. 1942: first film as director, in collaboration with Noël Coward. 1943: with Ronald Neame and Anthony Havelock-Allan founded production company Cineguild. 1952–53: producer/director on 2 films for Alexander Korda's London Films. 1955: first used foreign location, for Summer Madness. Oscars for direction, The Bridge on the River Kwai (1957), Lawrence of Arabia (1962). Was married to actresses Kay Walsh and Ann Todd.

Films as director: 1942: In Which We Serve (co-d Noël Coward). 1944: This Happy Breed. 1945: Blithe Spirit; Brief Encounter (+co-s). 1946: Great Expectations (+co-s). 1948: Oliver Twist (+co-s). 1949: The Passionate Friends – One Woman's Story. 1950: Madeleine. 1952: The Sound Barrier – Breaking the Sound Barrier (+p). 1954: Hobson's Choice (+p/co-s). 1955: Summer Madness – Summertime (+co-s). 1957: The Bridge on the River Kwai. 1962: Lawrence of Arabia. 1965: Doctor Zhivago. 1970: Ryan's Daughter.

LÉAUD, Jean-Pierre

Actor. Paris 1944–
Mother an actress, father an assistant director. A bit part, then answered advertisement in France-Soir and got leading part in Les Quatre Cent Coups at 14. 1964: assistant on La Peau Douce and Mata Hari. 1965: assistant director on Alphaville and Pierrot le Fou. 1967: stage debut at Avignon Festival.

Films as actor include: 1959: Le Testament d'Orphée. 1962: L'Amour à vingt ans ep Le Premier Amour. 1965: Le Père Noël a les yeux blancs; Masculin-Féminin. 1966: Made in USA. 1967: Le Départ; La Chinoise; Week-end. 1968: Baisers Volés; Le Gai Savoir. 1970: Domicile Conjugal; Der Leone Have Sept Cabecas. 1971: Les Deux Anglaises et le continent.

LEAVITT, Sam

Cinematographer
About 1925, began work at Paramount's Long Island Studio. Became assistant in late 1920s, operator then in 1952, cinematographer. Worked freelance.

Films as cinematographer include: 1952: The Thief. 1953: Mission Over Korea; China Venture. 1954: A Star Is Born; Carmen Jones (co). 1955: Annapolis Story; The Court Martial of Billy Mitchell; The Man

Commanche Station, directed by Budd Boetticher and photographed by Charles Lawton, Jr.
In Which We Serve, co-directed by David Lean and Noel Coward.
Major Dundee, directed by Sam Peckinpah and photographed by Sam Leavitt.

with the Golden Arm. 1956: The Right Approach; Crime In the Streets; The Wild Party. 1957: Hell Ship Mutiny (co); Spanish Affair. 1958: The Defiant Ones; The Fearmakers. 1959: Pork Chop Hill; Anatomy of a Murder; The Crimson Kimono; Five Gates to Hell. 1960: Seven Thieves; Exodus. 1961: Cape Fear. 1962: Advise and Consent. 1963: Diamond Head. 1964: Shock Treatment. 1965: Major Dundee; Dr Goldfoot and the Bikini Machine. 1967: Guess Who's Coming to Dinner; Where Angels Go, Trouble Follows. 1968: The Wrecking Crew.

LE CHANOIS, Jean-Paul

(Jean-Paul Dreyfus) Director. Paris 1909–
Father a doctor. Studied law, philosophy, psychiatry. Journalist. Member of 'Octobre' theatre group as actor, director. 1930: secretary on La Révue du Cinéma. 1932: acted in *L'Affaire est dans le sac*; assistant director and editor on 3 films directed by Julien Duvivier. 1933–39: assistant director on films directed by e.g. Maurice Tourneur, Jean Renoir, Max Ophüls. 1938: first film as director, a documentary; directed newsreels in Spain, Czechoslovakia. Films as writer include: *La Main du Diable* (1942) and *L'Impasse des Deux Anges* (1948). Scripted many of his own films, often in collaboration. Also song-writer. Wife is editor Emma Le Chanois. Book, 'Mademoiselle, êtes-vous libre?' taken from TV serial he wrote.

Films as director: 1938: La Vie d'un homme; Le Temps des cérises. 1939: Une Idée à l'eau – L'Irrésistible Rebelle. 1946: Messieurs Ludovic (+ad/di). 1947: Au coeur de l'orage (+c/cy). 1949: L'Ecole Buissonière (+st/co-s). 1950: La Belle que voilà (+di); Sans laisser d'adresse (+co-ad/di). 1953: Agence Matrimoniale (+ad/di). 1954: Le Village Magique (+st/di); Papa, maman, la bonne et moi (+co-st/co-ad/di); Les Evadés (+co-ad/co-di). 1955: Papa, maman, ma femme et moi (+co-st/ad-di). 1956: Le Cas du Docteur Laurent (+co-st). 1957: Les Misérables (+co-s). 1959: Pardessus le mur (+st). 1960: La Française et l'amour – Love and the Frenchwoman *ep* La Femme Seule (+ad/di). 1962: Mandrin – Mandrin, bandit gentilhomme (+co-s/di). 1964: Monsieur. 1966: Jardin d'Argenteuil – Blüten, Gauner und die Nacht von Nizza.

LEDERER, Charles

Writer and director. New York 1911–
Father stage producer. University of California. 1931: first film as writer, additional dialogue for *The Front Page*. 1942: first film as director. World War II: military service. 1940–52: 5 films in collaboration with Ben Hecht. With Luther Davis wrote book for musical play 'Kismet' (produced New York, 1953); they scripted film adaptation *Kismet* (1955). 1958: directed, wrote story and scripted *Never Steal Anything Small* based on unpublished and unproduced play 'Devil's Hornpipe' by Maxwell Anderson and Rouben Mamoulian. Most films for MGM; also worked for United Artists, Paramount, Warners, Columbia, Fox, RKO.

Films as director: 1942: Fingers at the Window. 1951: On the Loose. 1958: Never Steal Anything Small (+st/s).

Films as writer in collaboration include: 1931: The Front Page (co-di). 1933: Topaze. 1935: Baby Face Harrington (co-di). 1937: Mountain Music. 1939: Within the Law. 1940: Comrade X; I Love You Again. 1941: Love Crazy. 1943: Slightly Dangerous. 1947: Kiss of Death; Ride the Pink Horse. 1949: I Was a Male War Bride. 1950: Wabash Avenue (+co-st). 1952: Monkey Business. 1955: Kismet (+fco-mpl). 1956: Gaby. 1957: The Spirit of St Louis (ad). 1958: The Friend Who Walked the West (rm Kiss of Death 1947; +co-s). 1960: Can-Can; Ocean's 11.

Films as writer include: 1939: Broadway Serenade; His Girl Friday. 1949: Red, Hot and Blue (st). 1951: The Thing. 1952: Fearless Fagan. 1953: Gentlemen Prefer Blondes. 1957: Tip on a Dead Jockey. 1959: It Started with a Kiss. 1962: Mutiny on the Bounty; Follow That Dream.

LEE, Gypsy Rose

(Rose Louise Hovick) Actress. Seattle, Washington 1914–70 Los Angeles
On stage from age 6. 1937–38: Fox contract as Louise Hovick, then worked for numerous companies. Stage performances include vaudeville, burlesque, cabaret and as actress: 'Ziegfeld Follies' (1936), 'Du Barry Was a Lady' (1939), 'Gypsy Rose Lee and Her American Beauties' (1949), 'The Women' (1953), 'Auntie Mame' (1960), 'The Threepenny Opera' (1961). Author of 3 books, including 'The G-String Murders' filmed as *Lady of Burlesque* (1943). *Gypsy* (1962) is based on her autobiographical writings *via* a Broadway musical.

Films as actress include: 1937: Ali Baba Goes to Town. 1938: Sally, Irene and Mary; My Lucky Star. 1943: Stage Door Canteen. 1946: Doll Face (+fpl as Louise Hovick). 1958: Wind Across the Everglades; Screaming Mimi. 1963: The Stripper.

LEE, Jack

Director. Stroud, Gloucestershire 1913–
1938: joined GPO Film Unit as a junior producer. Edited a number of documentaries including *London Can Take It* (1940). 1941–46; director with GPO Film Unit and then Crown Film Unit; feature documentaries from 1943. 1947–48: directed 2 features for Wessex. Then feature director for various companies e.g. Rank. 1961: to Australia, formed own production company.

Films as director: 1941: The Pilot is Safe. 1942: Ordinary People (co-d J. B. Holmes). 1943: Close Quarters (+s). 1944: By Sea and Land. 1945: The Eighth Plague. 1946: Children on Trial (+co-s). 1947: The Woman in the Hall (+co-s). 1948: Once a Jolly Swagman (+co-s). 1950: The Wooden Horse (+co-s). 1952: South of Algiers – The Golden Mark. 1953: Turn the Key Softly (+co-s). 1956: A Town Like Alice (+s). 1957: Robbery Under Arms. 1958: The Captain's Table. 1960: Circle of Deception.

LEENHARDT, Roger

Director. Paris 1903–
Journalist, radio commentator, literary critic. From 1933: director of shorts. From 1935: film critic on e.g. Fontaine. Ecran Francais. 1936–39: wrote for Esprit.

1944–46: wrote for Lettres Francaises; later for Cahiers du Cinéma. Co-founder of Objectif 49. Formed own production company. Scripts for other directors include *L'Amour autour de la maison* (1946), Jean Lods' *Aubusson* (1946). Scripted most of own films. Several films about writers and artists. 1947: first feature *Les Dernières Vacances*. 1962: only other feature *Le Rendez-vous de minuit*. 1964: made for TV *La Fille de la montagne*; acted in *Une Femme Mariée*.

Short films as director: 1933: Lettre de Paris. 1934: Le Vrai Jeu; L'Orient qui vient (co-d René Zuber); RN 37; Revêtements Routiers; Pavage Moderne; Le Rezzou (co-d René Zuber). 1940: Fêtes de France (co-d René Zuber). 1943: A la poursuite du vent; Le Chant des ondes. 1945: Le Chantier en ruines; Lettre de Paris (+s). 1946: Le Barrage de l'aigle; Naissance du cinéma. 1948: La Côte d'Azur (+s); Le Pain de barbarie (+s); Entrez dans la danse (+s). 1950: Métro; La Fugue de Mahmoud (+s). 1951: Victor Hugo – Le Père Hugo (+s; co-d Yvonne Berber). 1953: Du Charbon et des hommes; La France est un jardin – France is a Garden (+p). 1954: François Mauriac; Louis Capet – Louis XVI (co-d Jean-Paul Vivet). 1955: La Conquête de l'Angleterre; Notre Sang; Les Transmissions Hydrauliques; Le Bruit. 1957: Paris est le désert francais (+p). 1958: Jean-Jacques Rousseau (co-d Jean-Paul Vivet); Bâtir à notre age (+p); En Plein Midi (+p). 1959: Daumier (+p). 1960: Paul Valéry (+p/s); Le Maître de Montpellier (+p); Entre Seine et mer (+p). 1962: L'Homme à la pipe. 1963: Des Femmes et les fleurs; Monsieur de Voltaire; George 1964: 1989. 1965: Corot; Naissance de la photo. 1966: Le Coeur de la France; Le Beatnik et le minet.

Features as director: 1947: Les Dernières Vacances (+s). 1962: Le Rendez-vous de minuit – Rendezvous at Midnight (+ co-p/co-s).

LEFÈBVRE, Jean-Pierre

Director. Montreal, Canada 1941–
Ran film society at college. 1960–62: University of Montreal; film reviews for student paper. From 1960: contributor to Objectif. After a year spent travelling in Europe, became teacher at Loyola College, Montreal (1963–65). Published collection of poems 'Le Temps que dure l'avenir', and several magazine articles. Own production company, Les Productions Jean-Pierre Lefebvre, which became Cinak Inc in 1969.

Films as director: 1964: L'Homoman (+p/s/c). 1965: Le Revolutionnaire (+p/s). 1966: Patricia et Jean-Baptiste (+p/s/w); Mon Oeil (+s, uf). 1967: Il ne faut pas mourir pour ça (+p/co-s); Mon Amie Pierette (+s). 1968: Jusqu'au coeur (+s). 1969: La Chambre Blanche – The House of Light (+s/pc). 1970: Un Succès Commercial – Q-bec My Love (+s/pc). 1971: Les Maudits Sauvages (+s).

LÉGER, Fernand

Painter. Argentan, France 1881–1955 Paris
Cubist painter. After World War I, did designs for projected cartoon *Charlot Cubiste* which was never completed. 1924: designed laboratory sequence for *L'Inhumaine*; in collaboration with Dudley Murphy made experimental film, *Le Ballet Mécanique*. 1936: worked on costume designs for *Things to Come*. 1944–46: wrote sketch 'The Girl with the Prefabri-

cated Heart' for Hans Richter's *Dreams that Money Can Buy*.

LEGRAND, Michel

Composer. Paris 1932–
Conservatoire de Paris e.g. under Nadia Boulanger. At 16 worked as jazz accompanist. 1954: issued first long-playing record, 'I Love Paris'. Wrote and conducted suite of ballets for Roland Petit; worked with Maurice Chevalier. TV in France and USA. Composed for films from 1953.

Films as composer include: 1959: Terrain Vague (co). 1960: L'Amérique Insolite; Une Femme est une femme; Le Coeur Battant. 1961: Lola; Cléo de 5 à 7; Les Sept Péchés Capitaux (co); Un Coeur gros comme ça. 1962: Vivre sa vie; Eve; La Baie des anges. 1963: Le Joli Mai; Les Parapluies de Cherbourg. 1964: Bande à part. 1965: La Vie de château. 1967: Les Demoiselles de Rochefort; Qui êtes-vous Polly Maggoo? 1968: The Thomas Crown Affair; La Piscine; Ice Station Zebra; Play Dirty. 1969: The Happy Ending. 1970: Peau d'ane. 1971: Summer of '42; Les Mariés de l'an II; The Go-Between.

LEHMAN, Ernest

Writer. New York 1920–
Brought up on Long Island. Studied writing at City College, New York. Journalist; copy editor on Wall Street. Wrote articles, e.g. for Collier's Magazine, short stories in spare time. 1948: co-wrote story of *The Inside Story*. From 1954: scripts, mainly for MGM, Fox, United Artists, including 4 for Robert Wise. 1957: from own story, co-wrote, with Clifford Odets, *Sweet Smell of Success*. Scripted several musicals, beginning with *The King and I* (1956). From 1966: also producer of films he scripted. 1970: was to have written, produced and directed *Portnoy's Complaint*, abandoned as censorship grading likely to be too low.

Films as writer: 1948: The Inside Story (co-st). 1954: Executive Suite; Sabrina (co). 1956: Somebody Up There Likes Me; The King and I. 1957: The Sweet Smell of Success (fst/co-s). 1959: North by Northwest. 1960: From the Terrace. 1961: West Side Story. 1963: The Prize. 1965: The Sound of Music.

Films as writer and producer: 1966: Who's Afraid of Virginia Woolf? 1969: Hello, Dolly!

LEIGH, Janet

(Jeanette Helen Morrison) Actress. Merced, California 1927–
Studied music at College of the Pacific. Model. Discovered by Norma Shearer. 1947: first film *The Romance of Rosy Ridge*; MGM contract to 1953. 1949: first starring role, on loan to RKO, in *Holiday Affair*. 1951: married Tony Curtis, acted with him in e.g. *Houdini* (1953); divorced in 1962. From 1953: worked for several companies, notably Universal, Columbia.

Films as actress include: 1947: If Winter Comes. 1948: Hills of Home; Act of Violence; Words and Music. 1949: Little Women; The Doctor and the Girl; The Red Danube; That Forsyte Woman. 1951: Strictly Dishonorable; Angels in the Outfield; It's a Big Country; Jet Pilot (r 1957). 1952: Just This Once; Scaramouche; Fearless Fagan. 1953: The Naked Spur; Houdini; Walking My Baby Back Home. 1954: Prince Valiant; Living It Up; Rogue Cop; The Black Shield of Falworth. 1955: Pete Kelly's Blues; My Sister Eileen. 1956: Safari. 1958: Touch of Evil; The Vikings; The Perfect Furlough. 1960: Who Was That Lady?; Psycho; Pepe. 1962: The Manchurian Candidate. 1963: Bye Bye Birdie. 1966: Harper; Three on a Couch. 1968: Hello Down There.

LEIGH, Vivien

(Vivian Mary Hartley) Actress. Darjeeling, India 1913–
Educated in England, Italy, Germany, France. Studied at Comédie Française and RADA. 1934: first film as actress *Things Are Looking Up*. 1935: stage debut in 'The Green Sash'. Theatrical work includes 'Doctor's Dilemma', 'The Skin of Our Teeth', 'School for Scandal', 'Antigone' and in 1949 'A Streetcar Named Desire'. 1951: acted in Laurence Olivier's productions of 'Ceasar and Cleopatra' and 'Antony and Cleopatra', in London and New York. Toured Australia, New Zealand, Mexico and South America. 1959: in 'The Skin of Our Teeth' for American TV. Oscars for *Gone With the Wind* (1939) and *A Streetcar Named Desire* (1951). Knight's Cross of the Legion of Honour. Married Laurence Olivier (1940–60, divorced).

Films as actress include: 1934: Gentlemen's Agreement. 1937: Dark Journey; Storm in a Teacup; Fire Over England. 1938: St Martin's Lane; A Yank at Oxford. 1940: Waterloo Bridge. 1941: That Hamilton Woman. 1945: Caesar and Cleopatra. 1948: Anna Karenina. 1955: The Deep, Blue Sea. 1961: The Roman Spring of Mrs Stone. 1965: Ship of Fools.

LEISEN, Mitchell

Director. Menominee, Michigan 1898–
Studied architecture; draughtsman for architectural firm. Entered films in 1919. Costume designer for Cecil B. De Mille on Babylonian sequence of *Male and Female* (1919), art director in collaboration on *The Ten Commandments* (1923) and art director on all De Mille's films from *The Road to Yesterday* (1925) until *This Day and Age* (1933). Also designed costumes for *Robin Hood* (1922) and *Thief of Bagdad* (1924). Assistant director before starting to direct (1933). Played small parts in *Hold Back the Dawn* (1941), *Variety Girl* (1947) and *Miss Tatlock's Millions* (1948). 1963: *Here's Las Vegas* was a tour of night-clubs, produced by Equity. Directed for TV, including episodes of 'Shirley Temple Storybook' and 'Wagon Train', and *The Incredible Jewel Robbery* (1960), TV film with the Marx Brothers. Runs a dance studio and night club in Hollywood.

Films as director: 1933: Cradle Song. 1934: Death Takes a Holiday; Murder at the Vanities. 1935: Behold My Wife; Four Hours to Kill; Hands Across the Table. 1936: 13 Hours by Air; The Big Broadcast of 1937. 1937: Swing High, Swing Low; Easy Living. 1938: The Big Broadcast of 1938; Artists and Models Abroad. 1939: Midnight. 1940: Remember the Night (+p); Arise My Love. 1941: I Wanted Wings; Hold Back the Dawn (+w). 1942: The Lady Is Willing (+p); Take A Letter, Darling. 1943: No Time for Love (+p). 1944: Lady in the Dark; Frenchman's Creek; Practi-

Gypsy Rose Lee.
Robert Wise's West Side Story, *written by Ernest Lehman.*
Mein Kampf, *by Erwin Leiser.*

cally Yours. 1945: Kitty; Masquerade in Mexico. 1946: To Each His Own. 1947: Suddenly It's Spring; Golden Earrings. 1948: Dream Girl. 1949: Bride of Vengeance; Song of Surrender. 1950: Captain Carey – After Midnight; No Man of her Own. 1951: The Mating Season; Darling, How Could You! 1952: Young Man with Ideas. 1953: Tonight We Sing. 1955: Bedevilled. 1957: The Girl Most Likely. 1963: Here's Las Vegas. 1967: Spree!

LEISER, Erwin

Director. Berlin 1923–

1938: fled to Sweden after November Pogrom. 1946: graduated from University of Lund. Literary and dramatic critic for Swedish trade union paper. 1950–58: cultural editor of Morgan Tidningen, newspaper supporting social democratic government. Produced radio features, published international theatre almanac, translated several volumes of poetry. 1958: TV work. From 1959: made documentary films. Author of book on documentary,

Films as director: 1959: Den Blodiga Tiden – Mein Kampf (+ s/e). 1961: Eichmann und das Dritte Reich – Eichmann and the Third Reich – Murder by Signature (+ s). 1962: Wähle das Leben – Choose Life (+ s/co-p). 1966: Deutschland, Erwache (+ p).

LELOUCH, Claude

Director. Paris 1937–

Making films from 13; prizewinner in amateur festival at Cannes for first film, La Mal du siècle. Professional film-maker from 1956; at first made shorts for TV; shot mid-length Quand le rideau se lève (1957) in Moscow. 1957–60: military service; made 10 shorts for Army Film Unit including SOS hélicoptère. 1960: first feature made with his family's financial help. 1961–62: more than 200 commissioned shorts. Then directed mainly features, which he also photographed. Own production company; backed Abel Gance's Bonaparte et la révolution. Oscar for best foreign language film, Un Homme et une femme (1966).

Short films as director and cinematographer include: 1956: USA en vrac; Une Ville comme les autres. 1964: Vingt-quatre Heures d'amants. 1965: Pour un maillot jaune.

Features as director and cinematographer: 1960: Le Propre de l'homme. 1963: L'Amour avec des si. 1964: La Femme Spectacle; Une Fille et des fusils – The Decadent Influence. 1965: Les Grands Moments. 1966: Un Homme et une femme – A Man and a Woman (+ st/co-ad/co-di). 1967: Vivre pour vivre (+ co-s). 1968: Treize Jours en France – Challenge in the Snow (co-d/co-s only; co-d François Reichenbach). 1969: La Vie, l'amour, la mort (+ co-s); Un Homme qui me plaît (+ co-st). 1970: Le Voyou (+ co-s/c). 1971: Iran; Smic, Smac, Smoc (+ s).

LEMMON, Jack

(John Uhler Lemmon III) Actor. Boston, Massachusetts 1925–

Acting debut, aged 4 in 'Gold in Them Thar Hills'. Harvard (BA, BSc). US Naval Reserve, communications officer. Radio. Produced and acted in TV series with Cynthia Stone. New England stock company.

1953: Broadway in 'Room Service'. 1954: first film as actor It Should Happen To You. Formed own company. 1957: wrote harmonica theme for Fire Down Below. Acted in 'Face of a Hero' on TV (1958) and on Broadway (1960). Married actresses Cynthia Stone (1950–56, divorced) and Felicia Farr (1962). 1971: directed Kotch. Oscar as supporting actor for Mister Roberts (1955).

Films as actor include: 1954: Phffft. 1955: My Sister Eileen; Three for the Show. 1956: You Can't Run Away From It. 1957: Fire Down Below; Operation Mad Ball. 1958: Cowboy; Bell, Book and Candle. 1959: It Happened to Jane; Some Like it Hot. 1960: The Apartment; Pepe. 1962: The Notorious Landlady. 1963: Under the Yum Yum Tree; Irma la Douce; Days of Wine and Roses. 1964: Good Neighbour Sam. 1965: How to Murder Your Wife. 1965: The Great Race. 1966: The Fortune Cookie. 1967: Luv. 1969: The April Fools.

LENI, Paul

Director and designer. Stuttgart, Germany 1885–1929 Hollywood

Art Metalwork College and Academy of Fine Arts, Berlin. Costume and set designer with Max Reinhardt; then designed film posters and sets. Art director on silent films from 1914; director from 1916. 1921–23: directed expressionist cabaret 'Die Gondel' in Berlin. 1923–24: produced pantomime 'Prologe'. 1927: went to Hollywood, made last films there.

Films as designer include: 1914: Das Panzergewölbe. 1921: Die Geierwally; Kinder der Finsternis (both parts). 1923: Tragödie der Liebe. 1925: Der Tänzer meiner Frau. 1926: Fiaker N 13; Der goldene Schmetterling.

Films as director: 1916: Das Tagebuch des Dr Hart. 1917: Dornröschen (+ s/c/dec/cos); Das Rätsel von Bangalor (+ dec; co-d Alexander Antalffy). 1919: Platonische Ehe; Prinz Kuckuck (+ co-dec). 1920: Fiesko (+ co-dec); Patience (+ dec). 1921: Die Verschwörung zu Genua (+ co-dec); Hintertreppe (+ dec; co-d Leopold Jebner). 1924: Das Wachsfigurenkabinett – Waxworks – 3 Wax Men (+ dec). 1927: The Cat and the Canary; The Chinese Parrot. 1928: The Man Who Laughs. 1929: The Last Warning.

LENICA, Jan

Animator. Poznan, Poland 1928–

Music and architecture at Warsaw Polytechnic. 1945–50: cartoonist. 1950–57: poster designer, specialising in collage film posters; also exhibition designer, book illustrator; wrote scripts. 1957–58: collaborated on several films with Walerian Borowczyk in Poland. From 1959: several visits to France and Germany. 1961: again collaborated with Borowczyk on two films. From 1963: lived in West Germany; Die Nashorner (1963) adapted from Ionesco.

Films as animator in collaboration with Borowczyk: 1957: Byl Sobie Raz – Once Upon a Time (+ s/dec); Striptease; Nagrodzone Uczucte – Love Rewarded (+ s). 1958: Dom – House (+ s/dec). 1961: Solitude; Italia 61; Boîte à musique.

Films as animator: 1959: Le Langage des fleurs;

Monsieur Tête (co-d Henri Gruel). 1960: Nowego Janka Muzykanta. 1961: Italia 61. 1962: Labirynt – Labyrinth (+ s/dec). 1963: Die Nashorner – The Rhinoceros. 1964: A (+ s). 1965: La Femme Fleur – Woman is a Flower. 1967: Quadratonien – Quadratonia. 1968: Adam II.

LENYA, Lotte

(Karoline Blamauer) Actress. Vienna 1900–

1914–20: studied ballet and drama in Vienna. 1926: married Kurt Weill. Theatrical work in Germany includes work of Bertolt Brecht and Kurt Weill e.g. 'Die Dreigroschenoper', 'Aufstieg und Fall der Stadt Mahagonny', 'Die Sieben Todsündens'. 1933: to USA. Stage work there includes 'The Eternal Road', 'The Threepenny Opera', 'The Seven Deadly Sins', 'Brecht on Brecht'. 1955: visited Brecht and the Berliner Ensemble in East Germany. Many concerts in Europe and USA and recordings.

Films as actress include: 1931: Die Dreigroschenoper. 1961: The Roman Spring of Mrs Stone. 1963: From Russia with Love.

LEONARD, Robert Z.

Director. Chicago 1889–1968 Beverly Hills, California

Studied law at University of Colorado, then moved to Hollywood. Worked in light opera company. From 1907: contract as actor with Selig Polyscope company. From 1916: director with various companies notably Universal and Paramount. 1922–24: films for his own company, Tiffany. 1925–55: producer and director with MGM. Made La Donna più bella del mondo in Italy, Kelly and Me for Universal, then retired. Was married to actresses Mae Murray and Gertrude Olmstead, both of whom appeared in his films.

Films as director: 1916: The Plow Girl. 1917: A Mormon Maid; Princess Virtue; Face Value (+ co-st). 1918: Her Body in Bond; The Bride's Awakening; Danger, Go Slow (+ co-s); Modern Love (+ co-st). 1919: The Delicious Little Devil; The Big Little Person; The Scarlet Shadow; What Am I Bid?; The Way of a Woman; April Folly; The Miracle of Love. 1920: The Restless Sex. 1921: The Gilded Lily (+ p); Heedless Moths. 1922: Fascination (+ pc); Peacock Alley (+ pc); Broadway Rose (+ pc). 1923: The French Doll (+ pc); Jazzmania (+ pc); Fashion Row (+ p/pc). 1924: Love's Wilderness; Circe, the Enchantress (+ pc); Madamoiselle Midnight (+ pc). 1925: Cheaper to Marry; Bright Lights (+ p); Time, the Comedian. 1926: Dance Madness; The Waning Sex; Mademoiselle Modiste. 1927: The Demi-Bride (+ p); A Little Journey (+ p); Adam and Evil; Tea for Three (+ p). 1928: Baby Mine (+ p); The Cardboard Lover. 1929: A Lady of Chance (+ p); Marianne (+ p). 1930: In Gay Madrid (+ p); The Divorcée (+ p); Let Us Be Gay (+ p). 1931: The Bachelor Father (+ co-p); It's a Wise Child (+ co-p); Five and Ten (+ co-p); Susan Lenox – The Rise of Helga (+ p). 1932: Lovers Courageous (+ p); Strange Interlude (+ p). 1933: Peg O' My Heart (+ p); Dancing Lady. 1934: Outcast Lady (+ p). 1935: After Office Hours (+ co-p); Escapade (+ co-p). 1936: The Great Ziegfeld (+ co-p); Piccadilly Jim (+ co-p). 1937: Maytime (+ co-p); The Firefly (+ co-p). 1938: The Girl of the Golden West. 1939: Broadway Serenade (+ p). 1940: New Moon

(+*p*); Pride and Prejudice; Third Finger, Left Hand. 1941: Ziegfeld Girl; When Ladies Meet (+*co-p*). 1942: We Were Dancing (+*co-p*); Stand By for Action (+*co-p*). 1943: The Man from Down Under (+*co-p*). 1944: Marriage is a Private Affair. 1945: Week-end at the Waldorf (+*co-p*). 1946: The Secret Heart. 1947: Cynthia. 1948: BF's Daughter. 1949: The Bribe; In The Good Old Summertime. 1950: Nancy Goes to Rio; Duchess of Idaho; Grounds for Marriage. 1951: Too Young to Kiss. 1952: Everything I Have is Yours. 1953: The Clown; The Great Diamond Robbery. 1954: Her Twelve Men. 1955: The King's Thief; La Donna più bella del mondo – Beautiful but Dangerous – La Bella des belles. 1956: Kelly and Me.

LERNER, Alan Jay

Writer and lyricist. New York 1918–
1940: graduated from Harvard. Wrote plays in collaboration with Arthur Pearson; Frederick Loewe wrote music to his lyrics. Stage plays co-written include 'What's Up' (1943), 'The Day Before Spring' (1945), 'Brigadoon' (1947), 'Love Life' (1948), 'Paint Your Wagon' (1951), 'My Fair Lady' (1956), 'Camelot' (1960), 'On a Clear Day You Can See Forever' (1965) 'Lolita, My Love' (1971). Scripted 3 films for Vincente Minnelli (one adapted from own musical play); Joshua Logan directed 2 films adapted from his musical plays, *Camelot* (1967) and *Paint Your Wagon* (1969), the latter produced by Lerner but adapted by Paddy Chayefsky. Also produced 'Camelot' on New York stage. 'Gigi', for which he wrote lyrics, received Oscar for best song (1958). 1960: became President of Dramatists' Guild of America.

Films as writer: 1951: An American in Paris (+*st*); Royal Wedding (+*st*). 1954: Brigadoon (+*fco-mpl*). 1958: Gigi (+*lyr*). 1964: My Fair Lady (+*fco-mpl*). 1967: Camelot (+*fco-mpl*). 1970: On a Clear Day You Can See Forever (+*lyr*).

LERNER, Irving

Editor, director, producer. New York 1909–
Columbia University. Research editor for 'Encyclopaedia of the Social Sciences' (Columbia). Commercial stills photographer. Produced films for Department of Anthropology, Columbia. 1939: 2nd-unit director on Dudley Murphy's *One Third of a Nation*. Edited documentary shorts for Paramount. Re-edited many Mayer and Burstyn releases, also directed shorts for them. 1944: produced *Toscanini: Hymn of the Nations* for Office of War Information; produced and supervised short *A Place to Live*. Head of Production, Educational Film Institute of New York University. 1958: *Murder By Contract* made in 8 days. 1959: *City of Fear* made in 7½ days. 1961: technical consultant on *The Savage Eye*. 1968: produced *Custer of the West* and directed 2nd unit. 1971: associate producer on *Captain Apache*.

Films as editor include: 1940: Valley Town. 1941: The Children Must Learn. 1960: Spartacus (*co-e*; +*2nd d*).

Films as director include: 1948: Muscle Beach (*co-d Joseph Strick*). 1949: C-Man (+*p*). 1953: Man Crazy. 1958: Edge of Fury (*co-d Robert Gurney, Jr*); Murder By Contract. 1959: City of Fear. 1960: Studs Lonigan. 1963: To Be a Man – Cry of Battle. 1968: Royal Hunt of the Sun.

LEROY, Mervyn

Director. San Francisco 1900–
Newsboy at 10. Won stage contest for best imitation of Charlie Chaplin. Solo act in season at Exposition, then played vaudeville double-act. Wardrobe assistant in Hollywood, then worked with William De Mille. Another year in vaudeville before returning to Hollywood as actor in silent films. 1927: first film as director. Until 1938: worked mainly with First National and Warners. 1939–53: mainly with MGM. From 1954: returned to Warners. Short as director and co-producer, *The House I Live In* won special Academy Award (1945).

Films as director: 1927: No Place to Go. 1928: Harold Teen; Flying Romeos; Oh Kay!; Naughty Baby. 1929: Hot Stuff; Little Johnny Jones; Broadway Babies. 1930: Playing Around; Numbered Men; Little Caesar; Showgirl in Hollywood; Top Speed. 1931: Gentleman's Fate; Too Young to Marry; Tonight or Never; Local Boy Makes Good; Five Star Final; Broad Minded. 1932: I Am a Fugitive from a Chain Gang; Heart of New York; Elmer the Great; Three on a Match; The World Changes; High Pressure; Big City Blues; Two Seconds. 1933: Hard to Handle; Gold Diggers of 1933; Tugboat Annie. 1934: Hi! Nellie; Heat Lightning; Happiness Ahead. 1935: Oil for the Lamps of China; Sweet Adeline; Page Miss Glory; I Found Stella Parish. 1936: Three Men on a Horse. 1937: They Won't Forget; The King and the Chorus Girl. 1938: Fools for Scandal. 1940: Waterloo Bridge; Escape. 1941: Blossoms in the Dust; Johnny Eager; Unholy Partners. 1942: Random Harvest. 1943: Madame Curie. 1945: Thirty Seconds over Tokyo; The House I Live in (+*co-p*). 1946: Without Reservations. 1948: Homecoming. 1949: Little Women (+*p*); Any Number Can Play; East Side, West Side. 1951: Quo Vadis? (*co-d, uc, Anthony Mann*); Lovely to Look at. 1952: Million Dollar Mermaid; Latin Lovers. 1954: Rose Marie (+*p*). 1955: Mister Roberts (*co-d John Ford*); Strange Lady in Town (+*p*). 1956: The Bad Seed (+*p*); Toward the Unknown – Brink of Hell (+*p*). 1957: No Time for Sergeants (+*p*). 1958: Home Before Dark (+*p*). 1959: The FBI Story (+*p*). 1960: Wake Me When It's Over (+*p*). 1961: The Devil at Four O'Clock (+*co-p*); A Majority of One (+*p*). 1962: Gypsy (+*p*). 1963: Mary, Mary (+*p*). 1965: Moment to Moment (+*p*).

Films as producer include: 1937: The Great Garrick. 1939: At the Circus; Stand Up and Fight; The Wizard of Oz.

LESSER, Sol

Producer. Spokane, Washington 1890–
At 17, set up as local film distributor in San Francisco. 1916: became partner in cinema chain. For 10 years managed theatre chain and produced films starring Jackie Coogan. 1926: sold theatre interests to Fox; after a year in Europe and organising another theatre chain, returned to production. 1941: joined RKO as executive in charge of feature production. 1945: resigned to become independent. Made his first Tarzan film in 1938. 1942–58: produced, on average, one Tarzan film per year. Supervised editing of two compilations from Sergei Eisenstein's *Que Viva Mexico!* material: *Thunder Over Mexico!* (1933) and *Death Day* (1934).

Jack Lemmon in Blake Edwards' Days of Wine and Roses.
Das Wachsfigurenkabinett, *directed and designed by Paul Leni.*
The Great Ziegfeld, *directed by Robert Z. Leonard.*

Films as producer include: 1934: Peck's Bad Boy; The Dude Ranger. 1940: Our Town. 1942: The Tuttles of Tahiti. 1943: Stage Door Canteen. 1947: The Red House. 1948: Tarzan and the Mermaids. 1951: Tarzan's Peril. 1952: Tarzan's Savage Fury.

LESTER, Richard

Director. Philadelphia, Pennsylvania 1932–
While studying clinical psychology at Philadelphia University sang in group with spot on TV. Remained in Philadelphia TV as stage hand, foreman, assistant director and (for 2 years) director. 1954: travelled to North Africa, Spain, France; café pianist and guitarist. From 1955: in England. TV work as director including comedy series with Peter Sellers and Spike Milligan, episodes in 'Mark Sabre' series (1957), split with Joseph Losey. Has made many TV commercials. 1959: directed first film which he photographed and edited in collaboration with Peter Sellers. Directed first 2 Beatles films.

Films as director: 1959: The Running, Jumping and Standing Still Film (+ co-c/co-e/m). 1962: It's Trad, Dad! – Ring-a-Ding Rhythm. 1963: The Mouse on the Moon. 1964: A Hard Day's Night. 1965: The Knack, and How to Get It; Help!. 1966: A Funny Thing Happened on the Way to the Forum. 1967: How I Won the War (+ p). 1968: Petulia. 1969: The Bed-sitting Room (+ co-p).

LEVIN, Henry

Director. Trenton, New Jersey 1909–
University of Pennsylvania. Actor, stage manager and director in theatre before going to Hollywood as dialogue director with Columbia in 1943. 1944–51: director with Columbia. 1952–59: mainly with Fox. 1960–64: with MGM. Then returned to Columbia.

Films as director include: 1945: I Love a Mystery. 1946: The Return of Monte Cristo. 1947: The Guilt of Janet Ames; The Corpse Came C.O.D. 1948: The Mating of Millie. 1949: Mr Soft Touch (co-d Gordon Douglas); Jolson Sings Again. 1950: The Flying Missile. 1951: Two of a Kind. 1952: Belles on their Toes. 1953: The President's Lady (+ ass-p); The Farmer Takes a Wife. 1955: Dark Avenger. 1957: The Lonely Man; April Love; Bernardine. 1959: The Remarkable Mr Pennypacker; Journey to the Centre of the Earth. 1960: Where the Boys Are. 1961: Le Meraviglie di Aladine – The Warders of Aladdin. 1962: The Wonderful World of the Brothers Grimm (co-d George Pal). 1963: Come Fly With Me. 1966: Murderer's Row. 1967: Kiss the Girls and Make Them Die; The Ambushers.

LEVINE, Joseph E.

Entrepreneur and producer. Boston, Massachusetts 1905–
Father a tailor. With brother owned chain of dress stores. Bought a cinema. 1938–59: promoted and distributed films, including French, Italian, and Japanese; national distribution from 1943. In late 1950s ran cinema chain around Boston. 1959: bought Pietro Francisci's *Ercole e la Regina di Lidia* for $120,000, launched it with $1·5 million publicity campaign, as *Hercules Unchained*; saturation booking in USA.

1963: subject of Maysles Brothers' *Showman*. Credited on few of the films he 'presented'; produced some.

Films as producer include: 1964: The Carpetbaggers; Where Love has Gone. 1965: Harlow.

Films as executive producer include: 1964: Matrimonio all'Italiano – Marriage Italian Style. 1965: The Tenth Victim; Sands of the Kalahari. 1966: The Oscar; Nevada Smith. 1967: The Caper of the Golden Bulls; Sept Fois Femme; Il Tigre; Robbery. 1968: The Lion In Winter. 1970: Sunflower; Soldier Blue; La Promesse de l'autre. 1971: Carnal Knowledge.

LEWIN, Albert

Director, producer and writer. New York 1894–1968 New York
Brought up in Newark, New Jersey. New York and Harvard Universities. 1916–18: taught English at Missouri University. Drafted; armed forces; at end of World War I, worked for American Jewish Relief Committee, becoming assistant national director; also drama and film critic for Jewish Tribune. Began in films as reader for Samuel Goldwyn. Script clerk for King Vidor, Victor Sjöström; then assistant editor. 1924–28: scenarist with Metro, becoming head of MGM's story department, then personal assistant to Irving Thalberg. From 1929: associate producer e.g. of *The Kiss* (1929), *The Cuban Love Song* (1931), *Red-Headed Woman* (1932), *What Every Woman Knows* (1934), *Mutiny on the Bounty* (1935), *China Seas* (1935), *Devil May Care* (1930), *The Guardsman* (1931), *The Good Earth* (1937). 1937: on death of Irving Thalberg, joined Paramount as producer. 1940: formed independent company with David L. Loew, releasing through United Artists, for which he made his first film as director in 1942. 1943: returned to MGM as producer, director and writer. Made *Saadia* in Morocco and *The Living Idol* in Mexico. Also wrote occasional scripts for other companies. 1966: published novel 'The Unaltered Cat'.

Films as writer include: 1926: Quality Street (co-ad/co-s). 1927: A Little Journey. 1928: The Actress (co). 1951: Call Me Mister (co). 1952: Down Among the Sheltering Palms (co). 1966: Boy, Did I Get a Wrong Number! 1967: Eight on the Lam (co-s).

Films as producer include: 1937: True Confession. 1938: Spawn of the North. 1939: Zaza. 1941: So Ends Our Night (co-p).

Films as writer and director: 1942: The Moon and Sixpence (+ co-pc). 1945: The Picture of Dorian Gray. 1947: The Private Affairs of Bel Ami (+ co-pc). 1951: Pandora and the Flying Dutchman (+ co-p). 1953: Saadia (+ p). 1957: The Living Idol (+ co-p/st).

LEWIS, Jerry

Director and actor. Newark, New Jersey 1926–
1949: first film as actor *My Friend Irma* based on CBS radio programme. To 1956: series of Paramount comedies with Dean Martin; Frank Tashlin directed 2 of the later ones. After ending partnership with Martin, continued in Paramount comedies, often directed by Tashlin. 1956: formed own company whose first film was *The Delicate Delinquent* (1957). 1958: *Rock-a-Bye Baby* based on story by Preston Sturges. 1960: first

film as director *The Bellboy*. From 1966: films as director released by Columbia. Also continues to appear in films as actor only. Married singer Patti Palmer (1944). Book, 'The Total Film-Maker' (1971).

Films as actor include: 1949: My Friend Irma. 1953: Scared Stiff; The Caddy; Money from Home. 1954: Living It Up; Three Ring Circus. 1955: Artists and Models. 1956: Pardners; Hollywood or Bust. 1957: The Sad Sack. 1958: Rock-a-bye Baby (+ p); The Geisha Boy (+ p). 1959: Don't Give Up The Ship. 1960: Visit to a Small Planet; Cinderfella (+ p). 1962: It's Only Money. 1963: Who's Minding the Store. 1964: The Disorderly Orderly. 1966: Way . . . Way Out. 1969: Hook, Line and Sinker (+ p).

Films as actor and director: 1960: The Bellboy (+ p/s). 1961: The Ladies' Man (+ p/co-s); The Errand Boy (+ co-s). 1963: The Nutty Professor (+ co-s). 1964: The Patsy (+ co-s). 1965: The Family Jewels (+ p/co-s). 1966: Three on a Couch (+ p). 1967: The Big Mouth (+ p/co-s). 1970: One More Time; Which Way to the Front? – Ja, Ja, mein General! But Which Way to the Front?

LEWIS, Joseph H.

Director. New York 1900–
Began as camera boy at MGM, then editor. 1935: film editor at Mascot Pictures. 2nd-unit director at Republic and later Universal. 1937–38: directed features at Universal. World War II: served in US Signal Corps. 1939–49: worked mainly with Columbia and Monogram. 1946: directed musical numbers for *The Jolson Story*. Thereafter director with various companies, including MGM. TV work includes episodes of 'The Rifleman', 'Gunsmoke', 'Big Valley'.

Films as director: 1937: Navy Spy (co-d Crane Wilbur); Courage of the West; Singing Outlaw. 1938: The Spy Ring – International Spy; Border Wolves; The Last Stand. 1939: Two-Fisted Rangers. 1940: Blazing Six Shooters; Texas Stagecoach; The Man from Tumbleweeds; Boys of the City; The Return of Wild Bill; That Gang of Mine; Pride of the Bowery. 1941: Criminals Within; Invisible Ghost; The Mad Doctor of Market Street. 1942: Bombs Over Burma (+ co-s); The Silver Bullet; The Boss of Hangtown Mesa. 1943: Secrets of a Co-Ed – Silent Witness. 1944: Minstrel Man. 1945: The Falcon in San Francisco; My Name is Julia Ross. 1946: So Dark the Night; The Jolson Story (co-d Alfred E. Green). 1947: The Swordsman. 1948: The Return of October. 1949: Undercover Man; Deadly Is the Female – Gun Crazy. 1950: A Lady Without Passport. 1952: Retreat – Hell!; Desperate Search. 1953: Cry of the Hunted. 1954: The Big Combo. 1955: Lawless Street. 1956: 7th Cavalry. 1957: The Halliday Brand. 1958: Terror in a Texas Town.

LEWTON, Val

(Vladimir Ivan Lewton). Producer. Yalta, Russia 1904–1951 Hollywood
Mother (sister of Alla Nazimova) took him to New York when he was 7. Columbia University. Wrote journalism, stories and poetry while mother worked as writer and translator for MGM. Wrote novel 'No Bed of Her Own' and a history of the Cossacks which was noticed by David Selznick. Story editor for Selznick

for 9 years. 1935: with Jacques Tourneur directed action sequences in *A Tale of Two Cities*. Producer at RKO where some of his films were directed by Tourneur: specialised in low-budget horror films. Moved to MGM then Universal, where he made only 1 film. Died shortly after signing contract as producer with Stanley Kramer.

Films as producer: 1943: Cat People (+ *co-st, nc*); I Walked with a Zombie; The Leopard Man; The Seventh Victim; The Ghost Ship. 1944: The Curse of the Cat People; Youth Runs Wild; Mademoiselle Fifi. 1945: The Body Snatcher; Isle of the Dead. 1946: Bedlam 1949: My Own True Love. 1950: Please Believe Me. 1951: Apache Drums.

L'HERBIER, Marcel

Director. Paris 1890–

Studied law and literature; diploma from Ecole des Hautes Etudes Sociales. Lecturer and literary critic. Journalist: wrote for Paris Midi, Comoedia, Opéra, Le Monde. 1914–18: served in army film unit. From 1917: wrote scripts. 1917: first film as director. From 1918: also artistic supervisor. 1932: became technical advisor to Comité Internationale du Cinéma d'Enseignement et de la Culture. 1939–45: President of Association des Auteurs de Films and of Centre Internationale des Ecoles du Cinéma. 1943: founded IDHEC. President of Cinémathèque Francaise. From 1952: worked in TV as director and producer. 1953: last film for cinema. TV productions include: 'La Cinémathèque Imaginaire', 'Le Jeu de l'amour et du hasard', 'Le Criterium du film francais', 'Cinéma en liberté', 'Le Criterium du film fantastique', 'Télé-ciné-club'. Author, poet and playwright; publications include: 'Aux Jardins des jeux secrets', 'L'Enfantement du mort', 'Intelligence du cinématographe'.

Films as director: 1917: Phantasmes. 1918: Rose France. 1919: Le Berçail; Le Carnaval des vérités. 1920: L'Homme du large. 1921: Prométhée banquier; Eldorado; Villa Destin. 1922: Don Juan et Faust. 1924: L'Inhumaine – Futurismo (+ *co-s*). 1925: Feu Mathias Pascal – The Late Matthew Pascal. 1927: Le Vertige; Le Diable au coeur. 1928: L'Argent. 1930: Nuits de prince. 1931: L'Enfant d'amour; Le Mystère de la chambre jaune; Le Parfum de la dame en noir. 1933: L'Epervier – Bird of Prey. 1934: L'Aventurier; Le Bonheur. 1935: Veillées d'armes; La Route Imperiale; Children's Corner. 1936: Le Scandale; Les Hommes Nouveaux; La Porte du large – Door to the Open Sea (+ *co-s*); Nuits de feu (+ *co-s*). 1937: La Citadelle du silence; Forfaiture. 1938: La Tragédie Impériale; Adrienne Lecouvreur; Terre de feu (+ *co-p*); Entente Cordiale. 1939: La Brigade Sauvage; La Mode Rêvée. 1940: La Comédie du bonheur. 1941: Histoire de rire; La Vie de bohème. 1942: La Nuit Fantastique – Fantastic Night; L'Honorable Cathérine. 1945: Au Petit Bonheur. 1946: L'Affaire du collier de la reine. 1947: La Revoltée (+ *ad*). 1948: Les Derniers Jours de Pompéï – Gli Ultimi Giorni di Pompei (+ *co-ad/di*). 1953: Le Père de Mademoiselle (+ *co-ad*; *co-d Robert Paul Dagan*).

LINDBLOM, Gunnel

Actress. Göteborg, Sweden 1931–
Göteborg City Theatre drama school. In films from 1952. 1954–59: at Malmö City Theatre; played lead-

ing parts in classics directed by Ingmar Bergman. 1968: contract with Royal Dramatic Theatre, Stockholm; appearances included Alf Sjoberg's production of 'The Father'. Played lead in 'Miss Julie' for BBC.

Films as actress include: 1952: Kärlek. 1957: Det Sjunde Inseglet; Smultronstället. 1959: Jungfrukällan. 1963: Nattvardsgästerna; Tystnaden. 1964: Älskande Par. 1965: Rapture. 1966: Svält. 1968: Flickorna. 1969: Fadern.

LINDER, Max

(Gabriel Leuvielle) Actor and director. Saint-Loubès 1883–1925 Paris

Family turned from theatre to viticulture. Conservatoire of Bordeaux for 2 years; small roles in classics and modern plays at Théâtre des Arts, Bordeaux, under pseudonym Lacerda. 1904: to Paris. 1904–06: failed entrance examination for Conservatoire 3 times; entered once under name Linder. 1905: first films as actor. Acted in Paris theatres, beginning with 'Le Tour du monde d'un gamin de paris'. Made between 5 and 10 films a week for 2 years at Pathé, directed by e.g. Louis Gasnier, Ferdinand Zecca. 2 years at Théâtre de l'Ambigu: used name Linder. 1906–07: under contract at Théâtre des Variétés. From 1908: worked almost exclusively in films. 1907–14: acted in more than 350 films at Pathé. 1910: became artistic director on own films. 1911: became own director with technical assistance from René Leprince up to 1914; Spanish tour. 1912: toured Central Europe and Russia. In Paris combined film and sketches in stage act; used this formula on European tour; sketches included 'Pédicure pour amour', basis for film *Max Pédicure* (1914); accompanied on stage by pianist Dmitri Tiomkin. 1914: made patriotic *Le 2 Août 1914*; prevented by ill-health from joining army, volunteered as driver of own car. Pneumonia; long convalescence. 1915: to Italy to persuade Italy to join war on side of Allies; returned to France. Ill health; to Lausanne, organised shows there, worked for Deuxième Bureau, made several films. Admitted to military hospital. 1916: visited by Charles K. Spoor, who wanted him to replace Chaplin (who was now at Mutual); to America for Essanay. 1917: first American film *Max Comes Across*, made in Chicago; moved to California, made 2 more films. Returned to France; performed in shows for French and American soldiers. Built own cinema, Ciné Max Linder. 1919: acted in and co-wrote *Le Petit Café*. 1920: acted in and wrote *Le Feu Sacré*; returned to Hollywood; became own producer at Universal. To New York: made unsuccessful attempt to obtain Goldwyn distribution contract; now made features; after making 3, returned to Paris; no new film until 1923. 1923: acted in and co-wrote Abel Gance's *Au Secours!*; Allied Artists prevented its distribution in France and USA. 1925: made *Roi du Cirque* in Vienna; attempted suicide; became President of Societé des Auteurs de Films for three months; prepared *Le Chasseur de Chez Maxim's*; he and his wife committed suicide. 1963: his daughter Maud Max Linder compiled anthology *En compagnie de Max Linder*.

Films as director, writer and actor: 1911: Max dans sa famille; Max en convalescence; Voisin-voisine; Max veut faire du théâtre; Max Cuisinier par amour – Max et Jane font des crêpes; Max et Jane en voyage de noces; Max lance la mode; Max reprend sa liberté;

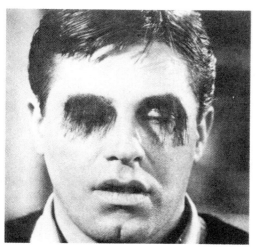

Joseph E. Levine.
Jerry Lewis in The Patsy.
Gunnel Lindblom in Mai Zetterling's Älskande Par.

163

Max et son chien Dick; Max Amoureux de la teinturière. 1912: Le Succès de la prestidigitation – Max Escamoteur; Une Nuit Agitée; La Malle au mariage; Max Cocher de fiacre; Matche de boxe entre patineurs à roulettes; Max Professeur de tango; Max et les femmes – Oh! Les femmes!; Une Idylle à la ferme; Un Pari Original; Max Peintre par amour; Le Mal de mer; La Vengeance du domestique; Voyages de noces en Espagne; Max et l'Entente Cordiale; Max veut grandir; Un Mariage au téléphone; Le Roman de Max; Max pratique tous les sports (co-s only). 1913: Comment Max fait le tour du monde; Max fait des conquêtes; Max n'aime pas les chats; Max et le billet doux; Max part en vacances – Les Vacances de Max; Max à Monaco; Max a peur de l'eau; Max Asthmatique; Un Enlèvement en hydroplane; Le Rendezvous de Max; Le Rivalité de Max; Un Mariage Imprévu; Le Hasard et l'amour; Les Escarpins de Max; Le Chapeau de Max; Max Virtuose. 1914: Max Pédicure; Max Illusioniste; N'embrassez pas votre bonne (d/s only); L'Anglais Tel que Max le parle; Max et le mari jaloux; Max et la doctoresse; Max Mâitre d'hôtel; Max Médecin malgré lui; Max dans les airs. 1915: Max devrait porter des bretelles; Max et l'espion; Max et le sac. 1916: Max et la main qui etreint; Max entre deux feux – Max entre deux femmes. 1917: Max Comes Across; Max Wants a Divorce; Max in a Taxi. 1921: Seven Years Bad Luck (+p); Be My Wife (+p). 1922: The Three Must-Get-Theres (+pc). 1924: Le Roi du cirque (co-d E.-E. Violet).

Films as director and actor: 1911: Max est charitable; Max est distrait; Max et son âne; Max a un duel; Max Victime du quinquina. 1912: Max contre Nick Winter; Max Bandit par amour; Que peut-il avoir?; La Fuite de gaz; Max Boxeur par amour; Max Collectionneur de chaussures; Max Jockey par amour; Max Toréador; Max Emule de Tartarin; Amour Tenace. 1913: Le Duel de Max; Qui a tué Max? – Max Assassiné; Max au couvent. 1914: Max Sauveteur; La Médaille de sauvetage – Max Décoré; Max et le commissaire; Max et le baton de rouge; Le 2 Août 1914.

LINDFORS, Viveca

(Elsa Viveca Torstens-dotter) Actress. Uppsala, Sweden 1920–
Father a publisher. 1938–41: at Royal Dramatic Theatre, Stockholm. 1940: first film as actress *Snurriga Familjen*. 1941–42: acted at Royal Dramatic Theatre in e.g. 'The Corn is Green', 'Key Largo', 'French Without Tears'. 1943–46 films in Sweden, Italy, Austria, Switzerland. 1945: returned to Royal Dramatic Theatre. 1947: to Hollywood; first American film *Night Unto Night* directed by Donald Siegel whom she married in 1949. 1952: on Broadway with Edward O'Brien in 'I've Got Sixpence'. 1953: acted in Siegel's *No Time for Flowers* and divorced him. 1954: married playwright George Tabori; later acted in plays adapted and staged by him: 'Miss Julie', 'The Stronger', 'Brecht on Brecht'. 1954–55: acted in 'Anastasia' on Broadway. 1956: with Orson Welles in 'King Lear' in New York. 1961: toured with Actor's Studio in South America in 'Sweet Bird of Youth', 'I am a Camera', 'Miss Julie', 'The Zoo Story', 'Suddenly last Summer'. TV work includes 'Letter from an Unknown Woman' (1952), 'The Bridge of San Luis Rey' (1958), 'The Paradine Case' (1962) and many series. Co-founder of Berkshire Theatre Festival; appeared there in 'The

Threepenny Opera'. 1967: acted in 2 1-act plays by husband under title 'The Niggerlovers' in New York.

Films as actress include: 1945: Maria på Kavarngården. 1946: I dödens väntrum. 1947: Night unto Night. 1948: To the Victors. 1949: The Adventures of Don Juan. 1950: Backfire; Singoalla; No Sad Songs for Me; Dark City; The Flying Missile; Journey into Light. 1952: The Raiders; No Time for Flowers. 1955: Run For Cover; Moonfleet; The Halliday Brand. 1957: I Accuse. 1958: Weddings and Babies; La Tempestà. 1960: The Story of Ruth; The Temple of the Swinging Doll. 1961: King of Kings; The Damned. 1964: An Affair of the Skin. 1965: Sylvia. 1967: The Witnesses (n); Dark Dreams of August.

LINDGREN, Lars-Magnus

Director. Västerås, Sweden 1922–
Worked as civil engineer before joining Sandrews, in advertising film department; made about 300 advertising films and 20 shorts including *Pyret söker plats – Pyret Applies for a Job, En slant är en slant, inte sant? – A Coin is a Coin, Kärlek och statistik – Love and Statistics*. From 1957: directed features.

Features as director: 1957: En Drömmares Vandring – A Dreamer's Walk. 1960: Änglar, finns dom . . . – Do You Believe in Angels? – Love-Mates (+s). 1963: Kurragömma – Hide and Seek (+p). 1964: Käre John – Dear John (+s). 1966: Träfracken – The Sadist – The Coffin (+s). 1967: Svarta Palmkronor – The Black Palm Trees (+s).

LINDON, Lionel

Cinematographer. San Francisco 1905–
1920: worked in Paramount laboratory. Became foreign negative cameraman. 1923: first camera assistant on *The Ten Commandments*. 1930: became operator. 1943: first film as cinematographer *Let's Face It*. Paramount contract, frequently loaned out, then freelance, including TV, e.g. 'Ironside'.

Films as cinematographer include: 1944: Going My Way. 1945: A Medal for Benny; Masquerade in Mexico. 1946: The Blue Dahlia; Monsieur Beaucaire; OSS. 1948: Tap Roots (co); Isn't it Romantic. 1949: Alias Nick Beal; Top o' the Morning; Without Honor. 1950: Quicksand; The Great Rupert; Destination Moon. 1951: Only the Valiant; Submarine Command; Drums in the Deep South. 1952: Japanese War Bride; The Turning Point. 1954: Hell's Island; Casanova's Big Night. 1955: Conquest of Space; A Man Alone; Lucy Gallant. 1956: The Scarlet Hour; Around the World in 80 Days (co). 1958: I Want to Live. 1959: Alias Jesse James. 1961: The Young Savages. 1962: Too Late Blues; The Manchurian Candidate. 1965: McHale's Navy Joins the Air Force. 1966: The Trouble with Angels; Boy, Did I Get a Wrong Number!; Grand Prix. 1967: The Extraordinary Seaman (r 1969).

LINDSTRÖM, Rune

Writer and actor. Vastanfors, Sweden 1916–
Studied in Uppsala; while student wrote play 'Himlaspelet'. 1942: first film as writer *Himlaspelet* in collaboration with Alf Sjoberg, also first film as actor,

in leading part. 1946: only film as director and writer *Tant Grön, Tant Brun och Tant Gredelin*. 1949: wrote songs for *Smeder på luffen*. Many scripts for Gustav Molander and Arne Mattsson; most scripts in collaboration. 3 other plays; art director for ballet; book illustrator; radio and TV work.

Films as writer in collaboration include: 1942: Himlaspelet (+fco-pl/w). 1947: Rallare. 1948: Nu borjar livet. 1949: Kvinna i vit. 1952: For min heta ungdoms skull; Kärlek. 1955: Männen i mörker.

Films as writer include: 1943: Ordet (+w). 1945: Kejsaren av Portugallien. 1946: Tant Grön, Tant Brun och Tant Gredelin – Aunt Green, Aunt Brown and Aunt Lilac (+d); Det är min modell. 1948: Farlig vår. 1954: Fortrollod vandring. 1955: Hemsöborna. 1956: Sången om den eldröda blomman. 1958: Körkarlen.

Films as actor include: 1965: Nattlek; Yngsjömordet. 1966: Syskonbädd 1782. 1968: Skammen. 1969: Bamse.

LIPSTEIN, Harold

Cinematographer
Entered films in process department at MGM, then assistant cameraman. 1949: first film as cinematographer *Ambush*. To 1953: worked for MGM. From 1954: freelance.

Films as cinematographer include: 1950: The Skipper Surprised His Wife. 1951: Bannerline. 1952: Fearless Fagan. 1953: Cry of the Hunted. 1954: The Adventures of Hajji Baba. 1955: Wichita. 1956: Pillars of the Sky; The Great Man. 1957: The River's Edge; Pal Joey. 1958: Never Steal Anything Small. 1959: Damn Yankees; No Name on the Bullet. 1960: Heller in Pink Tights. 1962: Hell is for Heroes; The Chapman Report. 1963: Rampage; Palm Springs Weekend. 1965: None But the Brave. 1966: The Night of the Grizzly (co); Let's Kill Uncle.

LITVAK, Anatole
(Anatol Lutwak in Germany)

Director. Kiev, Russia 1902–
Philosophy at University of St Petersburg. From 1922: joined Leningrad dramatic group; attended State School of Theatre. From 1923: worked at Nordkino film studios as assistant director, set decorator. 1924: wrote scripts in collaboration; first film as director. 1925: left Russia for Berlin and Paris; assistant editor on G. W. Pabst's *Die freudlose Gasse*; assistant director on several films. 1930–32: director with Ufa in Berlin. 1933: made *Sleeping Car* for Gaumont British in London, then joined Pathé in Paris, where films included *Mademoiselle Docteur* completed by G. W. Pabst in 1936. 1936: to Hollywood; first American film *The Woman I Love* for RKO, a remake of his *L'Equipage* (1935); then Warners until 1941. Then worked for various companies notably Fox. World War II: became Lieutenant Colonel in 8th Air Force; worked with Frank Capra on *Why We Fight* series, directing or co-directing 5 episodes; in charge of combat photography and motion picture operations in Normandy; awards on demobilisation included Légion d'honneur, Croix de guerre. From 1947: co-produced or produced many of his films, working internationally.

1962: injured in fall in Paris while shooting *The Third Dimension* which became Blake Edward's *A Shot in the Dark*. 1966: co-produced Jules Dassin's *10.30 pm Summer*. Married Miriam Hopkins (1937–39, divorced).

Films as director: 1924: Tatiana – Hearts and Dollars. 1930: Dolly macht Karriere. 1931: Nie wieder Liebe – Calais Douvres (+*s*). 1932: Coeur de lilas; Das Lied einer Nacht – Be Mine Tonight – Tell Me Tonight. 1933: Sleeping Car; Cette Vieille Canaille (+*co-s*). 1935: L'Equipage (+*co-s*). 1936: Mayerling. 1937: The Woman I Love; Tovarich. 1938: The Amazing Dr Clitterhouse (+*co-p*); The Sisters. 1939: Confessions of a Nazi Spy. 1940: Castle on the Hudson; City for Conquest; All This, and Heaven Too. 1941: Out of the Fog, Blues in the Night. 1942: This Above All; The Nazis Strike (*co-d Frank Capra*); Divide and Conquer (*co-d Frank Capra*). 1943: The Battle of Russia. 1944: The Battle of China (*co-d Frank Capra*). 1945: War Comes to America (+*co-s*). 1947: The Long Night (+*co-p*). 1948: Sorry, Wrong Number (+*co-p*); The Snake Pit (+*co-p*). 1951: Decision Before Dawn (+*p*). 1953: Un Acte d'amour – Act of Love (+*p/co-s*). 1955: The Deep, Blue Sea (+*p*). 1956: Anastasia. 1957: Mayerling. 1958: The Journey – Some of Us May Die (+*p*). 1961: Aimez-vous Brahms? – Goodbye Again (+*p*). 1962: Le Couteau dans la plaie – 5 Miles to Midnight. 1967: The Night of the Generals. 1969: La Dame dans l'auto avec des lunettes et un fusil – The Lady in the Car with Glasses and a Gun (+*co-p*).

LIZZANI, Carlo

Director. Rome 1917–
Wrote for Italian magazine Cinema and in first issue of Bianco e Nero; theoretician of neo-realism. Early films are documentaries. Assistant to Giuseppe De Santis, Alberto Lattuada, Roberto Rossellini. 1951: first feature as director. Many censorship difficulties. 1967: produced all episodes of *Amore e rabbia*, directed one.

Films as writer in collaboration: 1946: Il Sole Sorge Ancora (+*w*). 1947: Caccia Tragica (+*w*). 1948: Germania anno zero; Riso Amaro. 1949: Non c'e pace tra gli ulivi. 1954: Siluri Umani.

Films as director include (complete from 1951): 1949: Viaggio al sud; Via Emilia Km 147. 1950: Nel mezzogiorno qualcosa e cambiato; Modena, Città del Emilia Rossa. 1951: Achtung, banditi (+*co-s*). 1953: Ai margini della metropoli (+*co-s*); Amore in Citta *ep* L'Amore che si paga. 1954: Cronache di poveri amanti (+*co-s*). 1956: Lo Svitato (+*co-s*). 1958: La Muraglia Cinese – Il Fiume Giallo – Behind the Great Wall. 1959: Esterina – L'Herbe Folle. 1960: Il Gobbo – The Hunchback of Rome (+*co-s*). 1961: Il Carabiniere a cavallo; L'Ora di Roma (+*co-s*). 1962: Il Processo di Verona. 1964: La Celestina (+*co-s*); Amori Pericolosi (+*co-d*); La Vita Agra. 1965: Thrilling *ep* L'Autostrada del sole; La Guerra Segreta – The Dirty Game (*co-d Terence Young*; *Christian-Jacque*). 1966: Lutring – Svegliati e uccidi – Wake Up and Kill – Too Soon to Die (+*co-st*). 1967: Amore e rabbia – Vangelo 70 – Love and Anger *ep* L'Indifferenza – Indifference (*r* 1969; +*p/s*); Requiescant; Banditi a Milano. 1968: Assassino a Sarajevo. 1969: Barbagia; L'Amante di Gramigna – The Bandit.

LLOYD, Frank

Director. Glasgow, Lanarkshire 1889–1960 Santa Monica, California
Son of musical comedy actor. From 1903: stage actor in UK. 1910: went to USA; actor at Universal. 1916: began as director. 1917–19: director for Fox, also wrote most of own scripts. 1919–21: with Goldwyn, also occasionally supervising productions. 1921: became American citizen. 1922–30: films released mainly through First National, made for e.g. Joseph M. Schenck and (from 1923) own production company. 1929: president of Academy of Motion Picture Arts and Sciences. 1931–34: director at Fox. From 1935: worked for various companies usually as producer and director. 1942: produced *The Spoilers*; co-produced *Saboteur*. 1947: made short for USAAF, *The Last Bomb*. Oscars as director, *The Divine Lady* (1928–29), *Cavalcade* (1932–33), for Best Picture, *Mutiny on the Bounty* (1935).

Features as director: 1916: The Code of Marcia Gray; Sins of her Parent (+*s*). 1917: The Price of Silence (+*s*); A Tale of Two Cities (+*s*); American Methods (+*s*); When a Man Sees Red (+*s*); The Heart of a Lion (+*s*); The Kingdom of Love (+*s*). 1918: Les Miserables (+*co-s*); Blindness of Divorce (+*s*); True Blue (+*s*); For Freedom; The Rainbow Trail (+*co-s*); The Riders of the Purple Sage (+*s*). 1919: The Man Hunter (+*s/st*); Pitfalls of a Big City; The Loves of Letty. 1920: The Silver Horde; The Woman in Room 13; Madame X (+*co-s*); The Great Lover; A Voice in the Dark; The World and its Woman. 1921: Roads of Destiny; A Tale of Two Worlds; The Invisible Power (+*p*); The Sin Flood; The Man from Lost River; The Grim Comedian. 1922: The Eternal Flame; Oliver Twist (+*co-s*). 1923: Within the Law; Ashes of Vengeance (+*s*); The Voice from the Minaret; Black Oxen (+*pc*). 1924: The Silent Watcher; The Sea Hawk. 1925: Winds of Chance (+*pc*); Her Husband's Secret (+*pc*); The Splendid Road (+*pc*). 1926: The Wise Guy (+*pc*); The Eagle of the Sea. 1927: Children of Divorce (+*p*). 1928: Adoration (+*p*). 1929: The Divine Lady (+*p*); Weary River; Drag; Dark Streets (+*p*); Young Nowheres (+*p*). 1930: Son of the Gods (+*p*); The Way of All Men (+*p*); The Lash (+*p*). 1931: Right of Way (+*p*); The Age for Love; East Lynne. 1932: A Passport to Hell. 1933: Cavalcade; Berkeley Square; Hoop-La. 1934: Servants' Entrance. 1935: Mutiny on the Bounty (+*p*). 1936: Under Two Flags. 1937: Maid of Salem (+*p*); Wells Fargo (+*p*). 1938: If I Were King (+*p*). 1939: Rulers of the Sea (+*p*). 1940: The Howards of Virginia (+*p*). 1941: The Lady from Cheyenne; This Woman is Mine (+*p*). 1943: Forever and a Day (+*co-p*; *co-d 6 others*). 1945: Blood on the Sun. 1954: The Shanghai Story. 1955: The Last Command.

LLOYD, Harold

Actor. Burchard, Nebraska 1894–1971 Hollywood
1907: first important stage role 'Tess of the D'Urbevilles'. Stock company. 1912: toured in 'Trilby', 'Oliver Twist'. Film extra then 'Willie Work' series for Hal Roach. Pathe contract. 1916: 'Lonesome Luke' series started. 1924: founded the Harold Lloyd Corporation. 1936: *The Milky Way* for Paramount. 1941–42: producer only on *A Girl, A Guy and A Gob* and *My Favourite Spy* (both for RKO). 1946: returned to film acting in *The Sin of Harold Diddlebock*.

Max Von Sydow in Svarta Palmkronor. *directed by Lars-Magnus Lindgren.*
The Nazis Strike. *directed by Frank Capra and Anatole Litvak.*
Harold Lloyd.

Daughter is acctress Gloria Lloyd. Married actress Mildred Davis who often acted with him. 1952: special Oscar as master comedian and good citizen.

Films as actor include: 1917: Over the Fence. 1919: His Royal Slyness. 1920: Bumping into Broadway; Captain Kidd's Kids; From Hand to Mouth; Haunted Spooks; An Eastern Westerner; High and Dizzy; Get Out and Get Under; Number, Please. 1921: Now or Never; Among Those Present; I Do; Never Weaken; A Sailor-made Man. 1922: Grandma's Boy; Doctor Jack. 1923: Safety Last; Why Worry?. 1924: Girl Shy (+ pc); Hot Water (+ pc). 1925: The Frenchman (+ pc). 1926: For Heaven's Sake (+ pc). 1927: The Kid Brother (+ pc). 1928: Speedy (+ pc). 1929: Welcome Danger (+ pc). 1930: Feet First (+ pc). 1932: Movie Crazy (+ pc). 1934: The Cat's Paw (+ pc). 1936: The Milky Way. 1938: Professor Beware (+ p). 1946: The Sin of Harold Diddlebock.

LOCKWOOD, Margaret

(Margaret Day) Actress. Karachi, India 1916–
Educated in England. Stage training under Italia Conti. 1928: stage debut 'A Midsummer Night's Dream'. RADA. 1934: first film as actress *Lorna Doone*. 1935–40: in 7 films directed by Carol Reed, from *Midshipman Easy* to *The Girl in the News*. 1949: returned to the stage: 'Private Lives', 'Pygmalion', 'Subway in the Sky', 'An Ideal Husband'. 1955: retired from films. Also TV.

Films as actress include: 1935: Some Day; Midshipman Easy. 1936: The Beloved Vagabond. 1937: Who's Your Lady Friend? 1938: The Lady Vanishes; Bank Holiday. 1939: Rulers of the Sea; A Girl Must Live. 1940: The Stars Look Down; Night Train to Munich; The Girl in the News; Quiet Wedding. 1943: The Man in Grey. 1944: Love Story. 1945: The Wicked Lady. 1949: Madness of the Heart. 1950: Highly Dangerous. 1952: Trent's Last Case. 1955: Cast a Dark Shadow.

LODS, Jean

Director. Vesoul, France 1903–
1926–28: with Léon Moussinac and Francis Jourdain founded 'Les Amis de Spartacus', the first organisation of film societies. 1930: medical films. 1934–35: made *Histoire d'Odessa* in Russia; lived there in later 1930s. Co-founder of IDHEC; director of studies 1943–52. 1951: book published by UNESCO, 'La Formation Professionelle des Techniciens du Film'.

Short films as director include: 1928: Vingt-Quatre Heures en trente minutes. 1929: Champs-Elysées. 1932: Le Mile avec Jules Ladoumègue. 1933: La Vie d'une fleuve. 1934–35: Histoire d'Odessa. 1943: Aristide Maillol, Sculpteur. 1946: Aubusson et Jean Lurçat – Aubusson. 1955: Hommage à Albert Einstein. 1960: Mallarmé.

LOEW, Marcus

Studio head. New York 1870–1927 New York
Father Austrian immigrant waiter. Left school at 9; map colourer, salesman of advertising sheets, then worked in fur factory. 1888: independent fur broker. 1899: went into theatrical real estate. From 1904: in arcade and nickelodeon business: with Joe and Nicholas Schenck and Adolph Zukor built up vaudeville and legitimate theatre interests, merging as Loew's Consolidated Enterprises (1910). 1919: company controlled some 150 cinemas, became Loew's Inc. 1920: bought Metro Company. 1924: merged with Goldwyn and Mayer companies to become MGM. Son Arthur Loew superintended overseas expansion in 1920s. Left personal fortune of over $30 million.

LOGAN, Joshua

Director. Texarkana, Texas 1908–
Culver Military Academy and Princeton University. 1931: 8 months studying under Constantin Stanislavsky at the Moscow Art Theatre. From 1933: stage director, mainly of Broadway musicals including 'Annie Get Your Gun' (1946), 'The World of Suzie Wong' (1958), 'Mr President' (1962). Also wrote plays in collaboration e.g. with Gladys Hurlbut 'Higher and Higher' (1940), with Thomas Heggen 'Mr Roberts' (1948), with Richard Rodgers and Oscar Hammerstein 'South Pacific' (1949), with S. N. Behrman 'Fanny' (1949). 1936–38: contract with United Artists; first film work as dialogue director on Richard Boleslavsky's *The Garden of Allah*; co-directed *I Met My Love Again*. 1942–45: Captain in USAAF. 1956: made *Picnic* (which he directed on Broadway in 1953) and *Bus Stop*, both from plays by William Inge. 1956–58: worked for several studios. From 1960: Warners, Paramount.

Films as director: 1938: I Met My Love Again (co-d Arthur Ripley). 1956: Picnic; Bus Stop. 1957: Sayonara. 1958: South Pacific (+ fco-pl). 1960: Tall Story (+ p). 1961: Fanny (+ p/fco-pl). 1964: Ensign Pulver (+ p/co-s). 1967: Camelot. 1969: Paint Your Wagon.

LOLLOBRIGIDA, Gina

Actress. Subiaco, Italy 1927–
Studied sculpture and painting. Model. 1946: first film as actress *Aquila Nera*. 1949: first important role in *Miss Italy*. Films in Italy then France. 1954: first American film, *Beat the Devil*. 1957: actor-producer with Vittorio de Sica on *Anna Di Brooklyn*.

Films as actress include: 1951: Fanfan la Tulipe. 1952: Les Belles de nuit; La Provinciale. 1953: Le Grand Jeu. 1954: Beat the Devil; La Romana. 1955: Dangerous; La Donna Più Bella del mondo; Trapeze. 1957: Notre Dame de Paris. 1958: La Loi. 1959: Never So Few; Solomon and Sheba. 1961: Go Naked in the World; Come September. 1963: Woman of Straw. 1964: Le Bambole *ep* Monsignor Cupido. 1966: Hotel Paradiso. 1971: Un Bellissima Novembre.

LOMBARD, Carole

(Jane Alice Peters) Actress. Fort Wayne, Indiana 1908–1942 Table Rock Mountain, nr. Las Vegas, Nevada
At 12, discovered by Allan Dwan. First film as actress *A Perfect Crime* (1921). Fired from second film by Mary Pickford, who found out her age. Hired by Chaplin, for a film never made. 1925: second film appearance as female lead in Buck Jones western, *Hearts and Spurs*. Fox contract. Mack Sennett bathing beauty; changed name. 1930: Paramount contract; made 22 Paramount films. 1931–33: married William Powell (divorced 1933). 1939: married Clark Gable. Died in a plane crash while on bond drive for Hollywood Victory Committee.

Films as actress include: 1929: Big News. 1930: Fast and Loose. 1931: It Pays to Advertise. 1934: Twentieth Century; We're Not Dressing; Now and Forever; The Gay Bride. 1935: Hands Across the Table. 1936: My Man Godfrey. 1937: Nothing Sacred; Swing High, Swing Low; True Confession. 1938: Fools for Scandal. 1939: Made for Each Other; In Name Only. 1940: Vigil in the Night; They Knew What They Wanted. 1941: Mr and Mrs Smith. 1942: To Be or Not To Be.

LOOS, Anita

Writer. Sisson, California 1893–
Daughter of Richard Beers Loos; actress in his theatre company (1898). 1905: wrote first script *The New York Hat*. 1906–15: scripts for more than 400 short subjects. Married John Emerson; they collaborated for several years, often with Douglas Fairbanks, before forming company. Scripted many of her husband's films often in collaboration with him. They wrote play 'The Social Register' (1931) and directed it on stage; filmed by Marshal Neilan in 1934. Co-author with husband of book 'Breaking into the Movies'. 1925: wrote story 'Gentlemen Prefer Blondes' for Harper's Bazaar: filmed in 1928: turned into play in 1926, and book in 1928; filmed again in 1953, from musical version which she wrote with Joseph Fields. Other plays: 'Information Please' (1919: filmed as *A Temperamental Wife* same year), 'The Whole Town's Talking' (1923), 'The Fall of Eve' (1915), 'Happy Birthday' (1946). Books: 'But Gentlemen Marry Brunettes' (1928), 'A Mouse is Born' (1951), 'No Mother to Guide Her' (1962). 1963–64: stage actress. Main contracts as writer: 1916–17: Fine Arts Triangle; 1917: Artcraft; 1920–25: First National; 1932–42: MGM.

Films as writer include: 1912: The New York Hat (rm 1905). 1917: In Again – Out Again (st); Reaching for the Moon (co); Wild and Woolly; Down to Earth. 1918: Goodbye, Bill (+ co-p; co-st); Come On In (+ co-p; co-s). 1919: A Temperamental Wife (+ co-supervised; co-s/fpl); Oh, You Women! (co-st/co-s); Getting Mary Married (co). 1921: Woman's Place (co-p only); Red Hot Romance (co-p only). 1922: Polly of the Follies (co). 1925: Learning to Love (co-st/co-ad). 1928: Gentlemen Prefer Blondes (fco-pl/fst/co-ad). 1931: The Struggle (co-st). 1932: Red Headed Woman; Blondie of the Follies (di); The Barbarian (co-di/co-s). 1933: Lady of the Night (st); Hold Your Man (+ st/co-s). 1934: The Girl from Missouri (st). 1937: San Francisco (co). Saratoga (co-st/co-s); Mama Steps Out (st/s). 1939: The Women (co). 1940: Susan and God. 1941: They Met in Bombay (co); Blossoms in the Dust. 1942: I Married an Angel.

LOREN, Sophia

(Sophia Villani Scicolone) Actress. Rome 1934–
Trained as a teacher. Model. Extra, then met Carlo Ponti who guided her career; married him in 1957. First film as actress, semi-documentary *Africa Sotto il mare*. Made 20 films in 3 years. Italian films, American films in Europe, then in 1957, to Hollywood. 1961: Oscar for *Two Women*.

Films as actress include: 1951: Quo Vadis; Il Sogno di Zorro. 1954: Tempi Nostri; L'Oro di Napoli. 1955: La Donna del fiume; Too Bad She's Bad; The Miller's Beautiful Wife; Pane, amore e... 1957: Boy on a Dolphin; The Pride and the Passion; Legend of the Lost. 1958: Desire Under the Elms; The Key; Houseboat: The Black Orchid. 1959: That Kind of Woman. 1960: Heller in Pink Tights; It Started in Naples; A Breath of Scandal; The Millionairess. 1961: El Cid; Madame Sans-Gêne. 1962: Boccaccio 70. 1963: I Sequestrati di Altona; Ieri, oggi, domani; The Fall of the Roman Empire; Matrimoni o all'Italiana. 1965: Operation Crossbow; Lady L; Judith; Arabesque. 1967: A Countess from Hong Kong; C'era una volta; Questi Fantasmi. 1970: I Girasoli; La Moglie del prete. 1971: La Mortadella.

LORENTZ, Pare

Director. Clarksburg, West Virginia 1905–

1924–27: Clarksburg University. 1927–38: film critic on Clarksburg newspaper. Belonged to Paul Strand's Frontier Film group. 1936: first film as director. 1938–41: Chief of US Film Services. 1942: invited Robert Flaherty to make *The Land* for Department of Agriculture. 1942–45: Commanding Officer, Overseas Technical Unit, USAAF. 1946–47: Chief of Films, Theatre and Music Department, Civil Division, War Department, for Occupied Countries. Several books e.g. 'Censored – The Private Life of the Movies', 'The Roosevelt Years', 'The River'.

Films as director: 1936: The Plow That Broke the Plains (+ s). 1937: The River (+ s). 1940: The Fight for Life (+ s). 1941: Ecce Homo – Name, Age and Occupation (uf).

LORRE, Peter

Actor. Rosenberg, Hungary 1904–64

First professional stage appearance at 17; also worked as bank clerk. 1922–31: acted in Vienna, Zurich and Berlin (stage debut in 1928). First film *Frühlings Erwachen* (1929); then starred in *M* (1931). On rise of Hitler, to France, acted in *Du haut en bas* (1933); in UK, *The Man Who Knew Too Much* (1934), *Secret Agent* (1936); in USA, *Mad Love, Crime and Punishment* (1935). 1937–39: starred in 'Mr Moto' series for Fox. Returned to Germany to direct and star in *Die Verlorene* (1951).

Films as actor include: 1936: Crack-up. 1937: The Lancer Spy. 1940: Strange Cargo. 1941: The Face Behind the Mask; They Met in Bombay; The Maltese Falcon. 1943: Casablanca; Background to Danger; The Constant Nymph; The Cross of Lorraine. 1944: Passage to Marseille; The Mask of Dimitrios; Arsenic and Old Lace; Hollywood Canteen. 1946: Three Strangers; The Verdict. 1947: The Beast with Five Fingers. 1949: Rope of Sand. 1954: Beat the Devil; 20,000 Leagues under the Sea. 1955: Congo Crossing. 1957: Silk Stockings; The Sad Sack. 1959: The Big Circus. 1962: Tales of Terror. 1963: The Raven. 1964: The Comedy of Terrors; The Patsy.

LOSEY, Joseph

Director. La Crosse, Wisconsin 1909–

1925–29: medicine at Dartmouth College; theatre with Dartmouth Players. 1929–30: literature at Harvard Graduate School. 1930: began writing on theatre for leading US magazines and papers; stage manager on Broadway and in London. From 1933: stage direction including experimental productions, and Moscow production in English of 'Waiting for Lefty' (1935), plays and Living Newspaper programmes for the Federal Theatre, Bertold Brecht's 'Galileo' in Hollywood and New York (1947) and 2 plays in London (1954–55). 1938: supervised production of 60 educational films for Rockefeller Foundation Human Relations Commission. 1939: directed first short film, in colour and 3D for New York World's Fair. 1940–43: staged War Relief Shows and (1942) worked in radio. 1943: in US Army Signals Corps, made 2 shorts. 1945: staged Roosevelt Memorial Show at Hollywood Bowl. Staged Academy Show (1946) and 'The Lunch Hour Follies' (professional variety shows, part educational, part entertainment, presented to factory workers in lunch breaks). 1948: first feature. 1951: worked on screenplay of *The Tall Target*. 1952: shot *Stranger on the Prowl* in Italy; Hollywood blacklist prevented his return to US; film released with direction (and script by Ben Barzman) credited to Andrea Forzano. Made 2 features in UK under pseudonyms. 1958: started directing TV commercials and (1960) made a sponsored short.

Films as director: 1939: Pete Roleum and his Cousins (+ p/s). 1941: A Child Went Forth (+ co-p/s; co-d John Ferno); Youth Gets A Break (+ s). 1945: A Gun in his Hand. 1948: The Boy with Green Hair. 1950: The Lawless – The Dividing Line. 1951: The Prowler; M (rm 1931); The Big Night (+ co-s). 1952: Stranger on the Prowl – Imbarco a mezznotte – Encounter (ps Andrea Forzano). 1954: The Sleeping Tiger (ps Victor Hanbury; + p). 1956: The Intimate Stranger – Finger of Guilt (ps Joseph Walton). 1955: A Man on the Beach. 1957: Time Without Pity. 1958: The Gypsy and the Gentleman. 1959: Blind Date – Chance Meeting. 1960: The Criminal – The Concrete Jungle; First on the Road. 1962: The Damned – These Are the Damned; Eve. 1963: The Servant (+ co-p). 1964: King and Country. 1966: Modesty Blaise. 1967: Accident. 1968: Boom; Secret Ceremony. 1970: Figures in a Landscape. 1971: The Go-Between.

LOURIÉ, Eugène

Designer and director. Russia c. 1905–

1921: to Paris, studied painting and design. 1928: costumes for *Cagliostro*. From 1934: designer for films. From 1936: frequently designed for Jean Renoir. 1942: to USA. Also Hollywood films from 1943. To 1948: some stage work. 1953: first film as director, in Hollywood. 1955: returned briefly to France as technical consultant on Sacha Guitry's *Napoléon*. Some films as 2nd-unit director. 1958: wrote in collaboration *Revolt in the Big House*. Also TV director, e.g. series 'Foreign Intrigue'.

Films as designer include: 1936: Sous les yeux de l'occident; Le Grand Refrain; Aventure à Paris; Les Bas-fonds (co). 1937: La Grande Illusion; Le Messager. 1938: La Tragédie Impériale. 1939: La Règle du jeu (co); Sans Lendemain; L'Or du Cristobal. 1943: This Land is Mine (des). 1944: The Imposter (co). 1945: The Southerner. 1946: The Diary of a Chambermaid. 1947: The Long Night. 1948: A Woman's Vengeance. 1951: The River (co). 1952: Limelight. 1953: The Diamond Queen. 1954: So This is Paris

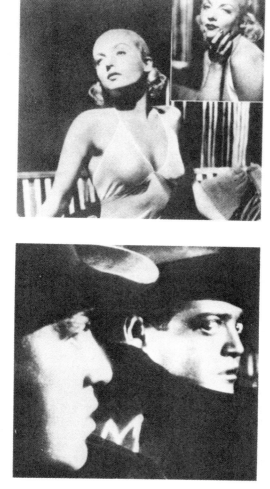

Carole Lombard in a 1933 publicity pose.
Peter Lorre in M.
John Barrymore, Jr. in Joseph Losey's The Big Night.

(co). 1962: Confessions of an Opium Eater. 1963: Shock Corridor (co); The Flight from Ashiya (des); The Naked Kiss (co). 1965: Crack in the World. 1966: Battle of the Bulge. 1968: Custer of the West; The Royal Hunt of the Sun.

Films as director: 1953: The Beast from 20,000 Fathoms. 1958: The Colossus of New York. 1959: Behemoth the Sea Monster – The Giant Behemoth (+ s; co-d Douglas Hickox). 1961: Gorgo (+ co-st).

LOW, Colin

Director and animator. Cardston, Alberta 1926–
6 months at art school in Calgary. 1945: recruited by Norman McLaren for National Film Board of Canada as graphic artist. 1946–47: animation in collaboration with George Dunning. 1948: to Stockholm to study commercial design. 1950: became head of animation at NFBC. 1951–61: collaborated with Wolf Koenig and Roman Kroitor. 1959: made City Out of Time, documentary on Venice commissioned by National Gallery, Ottawa. 1961: Koenig and Kroitor were directors of production on his Days of Whisky Gap. 1963: produced in collaboration Arthur Lipsett's 21–87. 1965: made The Hutterites for TV, produced in collaboration by Roman Kroitor. Continued to supervise NFBC animation unit.

Films as animator in collaboration with George Dunning: 1946: Cadet Rousselle. 1947: Up, Right and Wrong; The Adventures of Baron Munchausen (uf).

Films as director: 1947: Time and Terrain. 1948: Science Against Cancer. 1951: The Age of the Beaver. 1952: The Romance of Transportation in Canada (co-d Wolf Koenig, Robert Verrall). 1954: Corral (+ s). 1955: Jolifou Inn; Gold. 1957: City of Gold (+ co-c; co-d Wolf Koenig). 1959: City Out of Time. 1960: Universe (co-d Roman Kroitor; + co-dec); Circle of the Sun (+ s). 1961: Days of Whisky Gap. 1963: Pot-Pourri (co-d Victor Jobin). 1965: The Hutterites. 1970: The Winds of Fogo.

LOY, Myrna

(Myrna Williams) Actress. Helena, Montana 1905–
Discovered by Rudolph Valentino. 1925: first film Monta Bell's Pretty Ladies. To 1930: worked mainly for Warners and Fox. From 1932: mainly MGM. 1950: film advisor for UNESCO. Co-chairman of National Committee against Discrimination in Housing. Broadway: 'There Must Be a Lady'. TV: 'Meet Me in St Louis'. Also stage. Husbands include producer Arthur Hornblow Jr (1936–42, divorced).

Films as actress include: 1927: Ben-Hur; The Jazz Singer. 1928: Crimson City; Noah's Ark. 1929: The Desert Song; The Black Watch. 1930: Under a Texas Moon; Renegades. 1931: The Naughty Flirt; Body and Soul; A Connecticut Yankee in King Arthur's Court. 1932: The Wet Parade; The Woman in Room 13; Arrowsmith; Emma; Love Me Tonight; The Mask of Fu Manchu. 1933: The Prizefighter and the Lady; Penthouse; Topaze; Night Flight. 1934: Men in White; Stamboul Quest; Manhattan Melodrama; Broadway Bill; The Thin Man. 1935: Whipsaw. 1936: To Mary – with Love; Libeled Lady; Wife vs Secretary; The Great Ziegfeld; After the Thin Man. 1937: Parnell: Double Wedding: Man-Proof. 1938:

Too Hot to Handle; Test Pilot. 1939: The Rains Came; Another Thin Man. 1940: I Love You Again; Third Finger, Left Hand. 1941: Love Crazy; Shadow of the Thin Man. 1944: The Thin Man Goes Home. 1946: The Best Years of Our Lives. 1947: The Bachelor and ·the Bobby Soxer. 1948: The Senator was Indiscreet; Mr Blandings Builds His Dream House. 1949: The Red Pony. 1950: Cheaper By the Dozen. 1956: The Ambassador's Daughter. 1958: Lonelyhearts. 1960: From the Terrace; Midnight Lace. 1969: The April Fools.

LOY, Nanni

Director. Cagliari, Sardinia 1925–
Studied at Centro Sperimentale di Cinematografica, Rome. Made 2 documentaries before his professional films. 1950–55: assistant director e.g. to Luigi Zampa, Augusto Genina. 1956: first feature as director in collaboration with Gianni Puccini. Devised, directed and appeared in TV programme 'Specchio Segreto' in which he interviewed people throughout Italy. 1964: actor in Ugo Gregoretti's Le Belle Famiglie.

Features as director: 1956: Parola di ladro (+ co-st/co-s; co-d Gianni Puccini). 1957: Il Marito (+ co-s; co-d Gianni Puccini). 1959: Audace Colpo dei soliti ignoti – Fiasco in Milan (+ co-s). 1961: Un Giorno da leoni (+ co-st/co-s). 1962: Le Quattro Giornate di Napoli – The Four Days of Naples (+ co-st/co-s). 1965: Made in Italy (+ co-s). 1967: Il Padre di famiglia – Head of the Family (+ co-st/s). 1971: Detenuto in attesa di guidizio.

LUBITSCH, Ernst

Director. Berlin 1892–1947 Hollywood
Family of Russian-Jewish origin. At 19, acting for Max Reinhardt; with him until 1918. From 1913: also acted in short comedies, usually as a Jewish tailor. Began directing films in 1915, and wrote some. 1916: first big success, Schuhpalast Pinkus, his first film with Hans Kräly who scripted most of his films up to 1929, and with Ossi Oswalda who appeared in a dozen more of his films in the next 3 years, after which Pola Negri became his usual leading actress. Abandoned theatre in 1918. 1923: to USA to make Rosita for Mary Pickford. 1932: his episode in If I Had a Million replaced deleted James Cruze episode. During mid-1930s was Director of Production at Paramount. 1936: supervised Frank Borzage's Desire. Died during shooting of That Lady In Ermine (1948), finished by Otto Preminger (who under his supervision had directed A Royal Scandal in 1945). Produced Dragonwyck (1946) but because of illness left direction to its writer, Joseph L. Mankiewicz.

Films as director: 1914: Fraulein Seifenschaum – Miss Soapsuds (+ s/w). 1915: Blinde Kuh – Blind Man's Buff (+ w); Auf Eis geführt – A Trip on the Ice (+ w); Zucker und Zimt – Sugar and Spice (co-d; + co-s/w); Leutenant auf Befehl – Lieutenant by Command (+ w); Wo is mein Schatz? – Where is my Treasure? (+ w); Als ich tot war – When I Was Dead (+ s/w); Schwarze Moritz – Black Moritz (+ w); Schuhpalast Pinkus – Schuh-Salon Pinkus – Shoestore Pinkus (+ w); Der gemischte Frauenchor – The Mixed Ladies Chorus (+ w); Der G.M.B.H. Tenor – The Tenor Inc. (+ w). 1917: Ossis Tagebuch – Ossi's Diary (+ co-s); Der Busenkönig – The Blouse King (+ w): Wenn Vier

dasselbe tun – When Four do the Same (+ co-s); Fidele Gefängnis – The Merry Jail (+ w). 1918: Prinz Sami (+ w); Der Rodelcavalier – The Toboggan Cavalier (+ w); Der Fall Rosentopf – The Rosentopf Case (+ w); Die Augen der Mummie Ma – The Eyes of the Mummy Ma; Das Mädel vom Ballet – The Ballet Girl; Carmen – Gypsy Blood; Führmann Henschel; Marionetten. 1919: Meier Aus Berlin – Meyer from Berlin (+ w); Meine Frau, die Filmschauspielerin – My Wife, the Film Star (+ co-s); Schwabenmädle – The Schwab Maiden – The Girl from Swabia; Die Austernprizessin – The Oyster Princess (+ co-s); Rausch – Intoxication; Der lustige Ehemann – The Merry Husband (+ s); Madame du Barry – Passion; Die Puppe – The Doll (+ co-s); Ich nöchte kein Mann sein – I Don't Want to be a Man (+ co-s). 1920: Kohlhiesels Töchter – Kohlhiesel's Daughters (+ co-s); Romeo und Julia im Schnee – Romeo and Juliet in the Snow (+ co-s); Sumurun – One Arabian Knight (+ co-ad); Anna Boleyn – Deception. 1921: Die Bergkatze – The Mountain Cat – The Wild Cat (+ co-s). 1922: Das Weib des Pharao – The Lovers of Pharaoh; Die Flamme – Montmartre. 1923: Rosita. 1924: The Marriage Circle; Three Women (+ co-st); Forbidden Paradise. 1925: Kiss Me Again; Lady Windermere's Fan. 1926: So This Is Paris. 1927: The Student Prince – In Old Heidelberg. 1928: The Patriot. 1929: Eternal Love; The Love Parade. 1930: Paramount on Parade (co-d 10 others); Monte Carlo. 1931: The Smiling Lieutenant (+ co-s). 1932: The Man I Killed – Broken Lullaby; One Hour With You (co-d George Cukor, uc); Trouble in Paradise (+ p); If I Had A Million ep The Clerk (+ s). 1933: Design for Living. 1934: The Merry Widow; Angel (+ p). 1938: Bluebeard's Eighth Wife. 1939: Ninotchka; The Shop Around the Corner. 1941: That Uncertain Feeling. 1942: To Be or Not To Be (+ co-p/co-st). 1943: Heaven Can Wait. 1946: Cluny Brown. 1948: That Lady In Ermine (co-d Otto Preminger, uc).

LUGOSI, Bela

(Bela Blasko) Actor. Lugos, Hungary 1882–1956 Hollywood
Educated in Budapest. 1901: began as stage actor; classic roles in Budapest and throughout Europe. 1912–19: member of Hungarian National Theatre, Budapest; appeared in a number of Hungarian films as Arisztid Olt. 1919: to Berlin when Hungarian Socialist régime was overthrown. Appeared in Der Januskopf (1920), then went to USA. American citizen from 1931. 1955: admitted to state institution at own request after public confession of drug addiction.

Films as actor include: 1929: The Thirteenth Chair. 1930: Renegades; Wild Company. 1931: Murders in the Rue Morgue; Women of All Nations; Dracula; Broad Minded. 1932: Chandu, the Magician; The White Zombie. 1934: The Black Cat; Gift of Gab. 1935: Mark of the Vampire. 1939: Ninotchka. 1941: Invisible Ghost. 1945: Zombies on Broadway; The Body Snatcher. 1946: Devil Bat's Daughter.

LUKAS, Paul

(Pal Lukacs) Actor. Budapest 1895–1971 Tangier
1914–15: service in Hungarian army; wounded. Studied at National Theatre, Budapest. Acted in 'Watch on the Rhine'. Hungarian films. Spotted by Jesse Lasky and Adolph Zukor. 1928: first American

film. To 1932: worked mainly for Paramount; later for numerous companies. New York stage: 'The Doll's House', 'Watch on the Rhine'. 1943: Oscar for *Watch on the Rhine*.

Films as actor include: 1928: The Wolf of Wall Street; Two Lovers; The Woman from Moscow. 1929: Halfway to Heaven. 1930: Young Eagles; The Devil's Holiday; Grumpy. 1931: The Vice Squad; City Streets; Unfaithful; Strictly Dishonorable. 1932: A Passport to Hell; Rockabye. 1933: Little Women; Grand Slam; The Kiss Before the Mirror; Captured!; By Candlelight. 1934: Glamour; The Fountain. 1935: I Found Stella Parish. 1936: Dodsworth. 1938: The Lady Vanishes. 1939: Captain Fury; Confessions of a Nazi Spy. 1940: The Ghost Breakers; Strange Cargo. 1941: The Monster and the Girl; They Dare Not Love. 1943: Hostages. 1944: Experiment Perilous; Uncertain Glory; Address Unknown. 1946: Temptation; Deadline at Dawn. 1948: Berlin Express. 1950: Kim. 1954: 20,000 Leagues under the Sea. 1958: Roots of Heaven. 1960: Scent of Mystery. 1962: Tender is the Night; The Four Horsemen of the Apocalypse. 1963: Fifty-Five Days at Peking; Fun in Acapulco. 1965: Lord Jim.

LUMET, Sidney

Director. Philadelphia, Pennsylvania 1924–
Father Yiddish actor Baruch Lumet, with whom he made stage debut at 4. Educated at stage school and Columbia University. Child actor in theatre and films including 'Sun Up to Sun Down' (1937) directed by Joseph Losey. 1942–46: US Army. Then resumed acting career. 1947: formed off-Broadway stage group. From 1950: TV director, including series 'Danger' (1951–53), 'You Were There' (1953–55), plays 'This Property is Condemned' (1958), 'The Iceman Cometh' (1960). From 1955: also stage director. 1957: directed first film, an adaptation of a TV play.

Films as director: 1957: Twelve Angry Men. 1958: Stage Struck. 1959: That Kind of Woman; The Fugitive Kind. 1962: A View From The Bridge; Long Day's Journey into Night. 1963: Fail Safe. 1965: The Pawnbroker; The Hill; The Group. 1966: The Deadly Affair (+ *p*). 1968: Bye Bye Braverman (+ *p*); The Sea Gull (+ *p/pc*). 1969: The Appointment. 1971: The Anderson Tapes.

LUMIÈRE, Louis
and Auguste

Louis: Besançon, France 1864–1948 Bandol, France; Auguste: Besançon, France 1862–1954 Lyons, France
Father, Antoine Lumière, had photographic business in Besançon; moved to Lyons in 1871, opened factory for manufacture of dry plates. 1878–80: Louis studied Physics. After piano course helped father to perfect gelatino-bromide dry plate. 1881: factory moved to Lyon-Montplaisir. 1882: on point of bankruptcy Louis invented formula 'Etiquette Bleue'. 1885: Louis took photographs at 1/300th of a second. 1892: Louis and Auguste announced procedure of colour photography developed from processes of du Hauron and Lippman. 1893: 'Société Antoine Lumière et ses fils' founded; Louis and Auguste managed it after father's retirement. 1894: Auguste worked on a motion picture camera using non-perforated strip film: Louis abandoned a

camera which perforated strip film just before exposure, and constructed film perforator; contract with New York Celluloid Company; Louis invented the *cinématographe* which moved film by use of claws. 1895: manufacture of 35mm strip film on American celluloid. Patent taken out for apparatus to take and view chronophotographic pictures using triangular cam for claw-bearing frame, named Cinématographe. Louis made first version of *La Sortie des usines*. Additional patent for receiving reel. More films made; Cinématographe Lumière opened in Paris by Antoine, showing films to paying public. 1896: presentation of Cinématographe in several European countries, USA and India; world tour. Patent taken out for 'simultaneous representation of movements and sound in the projection of moving pictures. 1900: Paris Universal Exhibition: projection of Cinématographe Lumiere on screen 16×21 metres. Patent for 'photorame': circular photographic panorama (not moving) exploited in Paris in 1902. 1903: patent for 'Autochrome' colour plates; production and sale of films abandoned. 1914–18: diversification of production. 1920: Louis abandoned direction of the factories. 1934: Louis made his first 3D films, premiered in Paris in 1936. Auguste conducted considerable medical research, author of many scientific works.

LUPINO, Ida

Director and actress. London 1918–
Theatrical background. Father was comedian Stanley Lupino, cousin was comedian Lupino Lane. RADA. 1932: met Allan Dwan in England, he gave her a leading role in her first film *Her First Affair*. English films; to Hollywood. From 1934: worked for Paramount. From 1940: Warners. Married actor Louis Hayward (1938–45, divorced) who appeared with her in *Ladies in Retirement* (1941). 1949: produced and co-wrote *Not Wanted*. From 1950: film and TV director. Also producer of films as director, and composer.

Films as actress include: 1934: Search for Beauty; Come on Marines! 1935: Paris in Spring; Peter Ibbetson. 1936: Anything Goes; The Gay Desperado. 1937: Artists and Models. 1939: The Light That Failed. 1940: They Drive by Night. 1941: High Sierra; The Sea Wolf; Out of the Fog. 1942: Moontide. 1943: Forever and a Day; Thank Your Lucky Stars. 1944: In Our Time. 1945: Hollywood Canteen; Pillow to Post. 1946: Devotion; The Man I Love. 1947: Deep Valley. 1948: Road House. 1949: Women in Hiding. 1951: On Dangerous Ground. 1952: Beware, My Lovely. 1954: Private Hell 36. 1955: The Big Knife. 1956: While the City Sleeps; Strange Intruder.

Films as director and producer: 1950: Outrage (+ *co-s*); Never Fear (+ *p/co-s*). 1951: Hard, Fast, and Beautiful. 1953: The Bigamist (+ *w*); The Hitch-hiker (+ *co-s*). 1966: The Trouble with Angels (*d only*).

LUPU-PICK

Director. Jassy, Romania 1886–1931 Berlin
1914: entered films as actor. 1916: went to Germany; subsequent films as actor included *Es werde Licht* (1918), *Spione* (1928). 1916–19: also stage work in Berlin and Hamburg under Max Reinhardt. 1917: formed own film production company. 1918: first film as director. 1927: in UK made *A Night in London* for British International. 1929: to Paris to direct epilogue

Tom Dugan in Ernst Lubitsch's To Be or Not to Be.
Sean Connery in Sidney Lumet's The Hill.
Ida Lupino.

to Abel Gance's *Napoléon*; made *Les Quatre Vagabonds* there. President of an actors' union.

Films as director include: 1918: Die Weltspiegel (+ co-s); Die Liebe des Van Royk (+ co-s); Die Rothenburger (+ co-s/w). 1919: Die Tolle heirat von Laló (+ co-s); Der Seelen Käufer; Herr über Leben und Tod (+ co-s); Kitsch; Marionetten der Leidenschaft (+ co-s); Mein Wille ist gesetz. 1920: Niemand weiss es (+ co-s/w); Misericordia – Tötet nicht mehr; Grausige Nächte. 1921: Der Dummkopf (+ w); Scherben (+ co-s). 1922: Aus den Erinnerungen eines Frauenarztes (*Part 2*; + w); Zum Paradies der Damen (+ co-s/w). 1923: Weltspiegel. 1924: Sylvester. 1925: Die Panzergewölbe (+ co-s); Haus der Lüge (+ co-s). 1927: A Night in London. 1929: Napoléon auf St Helena. 1931: Les Quatre Vagabonds; Gassenhauer.

LYE, Len

Animator. New Zealand 1901–
Wellington Technical College, Canterbury College of Fine Arts, Christchurch. 1921: experiments in Sydney; possibly first to draw directly on to film. 1925: to London. Joined GPO Film Unit under John Grierson. 1928: first film as director, *Tusalava,* produced by London Film Society. 1935–37: *Colour Box, Rainbow Dance, Trade Tattoo* produced by GPO Film Unit, *The Birth of the Robot* by Shell-Mex. 1940–45: films for Realist. 1946–49: series of animated documentaries for Realist and others. 1944–51: 7 films for 'March of Time' series. 1949: left England for Canada and USA. 1969: lectured at Cambridge Animation Festival. American citizen. Last 3 films produced by Ann Zeiss. Worked on moving sculptures.

Films as director: 1928: Tusalava. 1935: Colour Box; Kaleidoscope. 1936: The Birth of the Robot; Rainbow Dance. 1937: In Time With Industry; Trade Tattoo; North or Northwest. 1939: Swinging the Lambeth Walk; When the Pie Was Opened; Colour Flight. 1940: Musical Poster No. 1. 1941: Newspaper Train. 1942: Work Party; Kill or be Killed. 1943: Cameramen at War; Planned Crops. 1952: Colour Cry; The Fox Chase. 1956: Rhythm. 1958: Free Radicals.

LYNLEY, Carol

Actress. New York 1942–
From age 7, ballet training. From 10, modelling. TV extra. At 14, with Sybil Thorndike in 'The Potting Shed'. In 'Blue Denim' on stage and in film version (1959). 1958: first film as actress *The Light in the Forest*. Also TV.

Films as actress include: 1959: Hound Dog Man. 1961: The Last Sunset; Return to Peyton Place. 1963: Under the Yum Yum Tree; The Cardinal; The Stripper. 1964: The Pleasure Seekers. 1965: Bunny Lake is Missing; Harlow. 1967: Escape Route. 1969: The Maltese Bippy.

M

MacARTHUR, Charles

Writer and director. Scranton, Pennsylvania 1895–1956 New York

Reporter for Chicago Herald and Examiner, Chicago Tribune, New York American. 1931: *The Front Page* based on play written in collaboration with Ben Hecht; joined MGM as writer. 1934: first script collaboration with Hecht *Twentieth Century,* based on their play; they founded production company in New York. 1934: their first film as directors in collaboration. 1935: jointly awarded Oscar for story of *The Scoundrel*. 1939: *The Front Page* remade as *His Girl Friday*. World War II: Major in US Army. Association with Hecht ended about 1947. Film adaptations of his plays include *Lulu Belle* (1948). 1960: Ben Hecht's TV play 'Hello Charlie' based on MacArthur's early life. Married actress Helen Hayes (1928); adoptive father of actor James MacArthur.

Films as director, producer, script and story writer in collaboration with Ben Hecht: 1934: Crime Without Passion. 1935: The Scoundrel; Once in a Blue Moon (*d/p/s only*). 1936: Soak the Rich.

Films as writer in collaboration with Ben Hecht include: 1931: The Front Page (*fpl*). 1934: Twentieth Century (+ *fpl*). 1935: Barbary Coast (+ *st*). 1939: Gunga Din (*st*); Wuthering Heights; His Girl Friday (*fpl*). 1950: Perfect Strangers (*fpl*). 1962: Billy Rose's Jumbo (*fn*).

Films as writer include: 1930: Paid (*co-ad/di*); Way for a Sailor (*co-s/di*). 1931: New Adventures of Get Rich Quick Wallingford (*s/di*). 1933: Rasputin and the Empress (+ *st*). 1940: I Take This Woman (*st*). 1948: The Senator was Indiscreet.

MACDONALD, Jeanette

Actress. Philadelphia, Pennsylvania 1907–65 Houston, Texas
Studied singing and dancing from infancy. First professional stage appearance at 9. Chorus girl then leading roles in musicals, e.g. George Gershwin's 'Tip Toes' (1925). 1930: first film as actress, with Maurice Chevalier, her co-star in several films. Also appeared opposite Clark Gable and Ramon Novarro. To 1932: worked mainly for Paramount, except for 3 films for Fox (1930–31). Then at MGM. 1935: began partnership with Nelson Eddy. 1937: married actor Gene Raymond; acted with him in *Smilin' Through* (1941). 1949: retired from films; then some stage and TV work.

Films as actress: 1930: The Love Parade; The Vagabond King; Let's Go Native; Monte Carlo; The Lottery Bride; Oh, for a Man. 1931: Don't Bet on Women; Annabelle's Affairs. 1932: One Hour with You; Love Me Tonight. 1934: The Cat and the Fiddle; The Merry Widow. 1935: Naughty Marietta. 1936: Rose-Marie; San Francisco. 1937: Maytime; The Firefly. 1938: The Girl of the Golden West; Sweethearts. 1939: Broadway Serenade. 1940: New Moon; Bitter Sweet. 1941: Smilin' Through. 1942: I Married an Angel; Cairo. 1944: Follow the Boys. 1948: Three Daring Daughters; The Sun Comes Up.

MACDONALD, Joseph

Cinematographer. Mexico City 1906–
Degree in mining engineering, University of Southern California. Started in films washing plates in stills

library. Then assistant cameraman at First National (1921). After studio bought by Warners, freelanced, then (1929) to Fox. 1943: to Fox as cinematographer. 1960: freelance.

Films as cinematographer include: 1944: The Big Noise; In the Meantime Darling. 1945: Captain Eddie. 1946: My Darling Clementine; The Dark Corner. 1948: Call Northside 777; Yellow Sky. 1949: Down to the Sea in Ships; Pinky. 1950: Panic in the Streets. 1951: Fourteen Hours; You're in the Navy Now. 1952: Viva Zapata!; What Price Glory. 1953: Niagara; Pickup on South Street; How to Marry a Millionaire. 1954: Hell and High Water. 1955: House of Bamboo; The Racers. 1956: Bigger than Life. 1957: Will Success Spoil Rock Hunter?; A Hatful of Rain; The True Story of Jesse James. 1958: Ten North Frederick; The Fiend Who Walked the West. 1960: Pepe. 1962: Walk on the Wild Side. 1963: The List of Adrian Messenger. 1964: Rio Conchos; The Carpetbaggers; Invitation to a Gunfighter; Where Love Has Gone; Flight from Ashiya. 1965: Mirage.

MACDONALD, Richard

Designer. Banffshire, Scotland
1939: began studies at Royal College of Art, London; studies interrupted by war service in Royal Navy, became commissioned officer. 1946: completed studies. Taught painting at Camberwell School of Arts and Crafts, London. Worked on titles of *Summer Madness* (1955). Began collaboration with Joseph Losey, as design consultant, on *The Sleeping Tiger* (1954). 1971: designed credits for *The Go-Between*.

Films as design consultant: 1954: The Sleeping Tiger. 1955: A Man on the Beach. 1956: The Intimate Stranger. 1957: Time Without Pity. 1958: The Gypsy and the Gentleman. 1959: Blind Date. 1960: The Criminal. 1962: The Damned. 1964: King and Country.

Films as production designer: 1963: The Servant. 1966: Modesty Blaise. 1967: Far From the Madding Crowd. 1968: Boom; Secret Ceremony.

Film as art director: 1962: Eve (*co*).

MACDOUGALL, Ranald

Director and writer. Schenectady, New York 1915–
Odd jobs, including usher at Radio City Music Hall before becoming successful as a writer of radio shows and one-act plays. 1945: entered films. 1955: started directing, mainly for MGM.

Films as writer include: 1945: Objective Burma (*co*); Mildred Pierce (*co*). 1954: The Naked Jungle (*co*). 1955: We're No Angels. 1956: The Mountain. 1963: Cleopatra (*co*).

Films as director and writer: 1955: Queen Bee. 1957: Man on Fire. 1958: The World, the Flesh and the Devil. 1960: The Subterraneans (*d only*). 1961: Go Naked in the World.

MACGOWAN, Kenneth

Producer. Winthrop, Massachusetts 1888–1963 Los Angeles
Harvard University. Then journalist: dramatic critic-

ism for New York Globe and Theatre Arts Magazine. 1924–25: director at the Provincetown Playhouse at invitation of Eugene O'Neill. 1926–29: writer, lecturer, independent theatre producer. Joined RKO as writer; associate producer from 1932. First short as producer *La Cucaracha* (1934); first feature as producer, in collaboration with Rouben Mamoulian, *Becky Sharp* (1935) in 3-colour Technicolor. 1935: left RKO for Fox; remained there as producer to 1944. 1947: last film, for Paramount. Then ran Theatre Arts department at UCLA.

Films as associate producer include: 1933: Topaze; Double Harness; Little Women. 1934: If I Were Free; Long Lost Father. 1936: To Mary – with Love; Lloyds of London. 1938: Four Men and A Prayer; Kentucky Moonshine; In Old Chicago. 1939: Stanley and Livingstone. 1940: The Return of Frank James; Brigham Young. 1941: Man Hunt.

Films as producer include: 1935: Jalna. 1939: Young Mr Lincoln. 1944: Lifeboat. 1947: Easy Come, Easy Go.

MACHATY, Gustav

Director. Prague 1901–1963 Munich
From 1918: actor in Czech films, some of which he scripted. 1919: first film as director; acted in and co-wrote *Dama s malou nozkou* and *Vztekly zenich*. 1920–24: in USA; assisted D. W. Griffith, and, uncredited, Erich von Stroheim on *Foolish Wives* (1921). Returned to Czechoslovakia. 1933: his last Czech film *Extase*. 1934: made *Nocturno* in Austria. 1936: made *Ballerine* in Italy. 1936–45: in USA. 1937: directed parts of *The Good Earth,* uncredited. Made 2 features and a 'Crime Does Not Pay' short; assisted Sam Wood and Clarence Brown. To Germany. No further work in cinema until co-wrote G. W. Pabst's *Es Gescha am 20 Juli* (1955). 1956: wrote and directed last film.

Films as director: 1919: Teddy by kovril (+ *co-s/w*). 1926: Kreutzerova Sonata – The Kreutzer Sonata (+ *s*). 1927: Svejk v civilu. 1929: Erotikon (+ *s*). 1931: Načeradec, kral kibicu (+ *co-s*); Ze Soboty na Nedeli – From Saturday to Sunday. 1933: Extase – Ecstasy (+ *co-s*). 1934: Nocturno. 1936: Ballerine. 1937: The Good Earth (*uc*; *co-d 3 others*). 1938: The Wrong Way Out. 1939: Within the Law. 1945: Jealousy (+ *p/co-s*). 1956: Suchkind 312 (+ *s*).

MACHIN, Alfred

Director. Blenlecques, France 1877–1930 Paris
1900–11: worked as cameraman with Charles Pathé. 1911: began directing Babylas comedies for Pathé. 1912: director with Belge Cinéma, a Pathé subsidiary. 1914: returned to France, joined French Army Film Unit. 1917: worked as cameraman on French sequences of *Hearts of the World*. 1920–27: worked in collaboration with Henri Wulschleiger.

Films as director include: 1912: La Fleur Sanglante; Les Moulins chantent et pleurent – L'Ame des Moulins; L'Or qui brûle; La Révolte des gueux. 1913: Saïda a enlevé Manneken-pis; Au ravissement des dames. 1914: Maudite soit la guerre – Le Moulin Maudit. 1920: On attend Polochon.

Films as director and writer in collaboration with Henri

Wulschleiger include: 1921: Pervenche. 1923: Bête comme des hommes. 1924: L'Enigme du Mont Agel; Les Millions de l'oncle James – Les Héritiers de l'oncle James. 1925: Le Coeur des gueux. 1927: Le Manoir de la peur – L'Homme Noir.

MACISTE

(Bartolomeo Pagano) San Ilario, Italy 1878–1947 Italy
Docker in Genoa. 1913: won audition held by Giovanne Pastrone for part of Maciste in *Cabiria*, made 1914. From 1915: under name Maciste starred in own series in Italy, some films directed by Pastrone. 1920: intended to retire, but signed up for German films. 1922–23: own series in Germany e.g. Carl Boese's *Maciste und die Chinesische Truhe*. 1924: returned to Italy, resumed series there, including Mario Camerini's *Maciste contro lo sceicco* (1925). Series continued to 1928, last films directed by Baldassare Negroni. Character played by other actors in later films.

MACKENDRICK, Alexander

Director. Boston, Massachusetts 1912–
Born while parents on trip to USA. School of Art, Glasgow. Then worked as commercial artist. e.g. cartoons for advertising films. 1937: in collaboration with his cousin, wrote film script which was immediately sold; engaged as scriptwriter at Pinewood. 1938–39: wrote and directed shorts. From 1939: with the Ministry of Information Film Unit. 1943–45: in charge of documentary and newsreel production for Psychological Warfare branch in Rome. 1946: joined Ealing as writer and (from 1948) director. Collaborated on scrips of e.g. *Saraband for Dead Lovers* (1948), *The Blue Lamp* (1949), *Dance Hall* (1950). 1956–61: to Hollywood, directed 2 films for Hecht-Hill-Lancaster for United Artists release and began *The Guns of Navarone* (completed by J. Lee Thompson when Mackendrick fell ill). Then, worked for various companies, based in UK.

Short films as director include: 1941: The Pocket Cartoon (+ *co-p/co-s*; *co-d John Halas, Joy Batchelor*). 1942: Carnival in the Clothes Cupboard; Fable of the Fabrics. 1943: Abu series (*4 eps*).

Features as director: 1948: Whisky Galore – Tight Little Island (+ *co-s*). 1951: The Man in the White Suit (+ *co-s*). 1952: Mandy – The Crash of Silence. 1954: The Maggie – High and Dry. 1955: The Ladykillers. 1957: Sweet Smell of Success. 1959: The Devil's Disciple (*uc*; *co-d Guy Hamilton*). 1963: Sammy Going South – A Boy Ten Feet Tall. 1965: A High Wind in Jamaica. 1967: Don't Make Waves.

MACLAINE, Shirley

Actress. Richmond, Virginia 1934–
Father an orchestra leader, mother a dancer. Brother is Warren Beatty. Professional debut as dancer at 4, in Richmond. Acted while at College. 1950: to New York. Chorus of 'Oklahoma!', corps de ballet of 'Kiss Me Kate'. TV commercials, publicity work, then major role in 'Me and Juliet'. Replaced Carol Haney in 'The Pajama Game'. Under contract to Hal Wallis at Paramount. 1954: married stage director and impresario Steve Parker. 1955: first film as actress, *The Trouble With Harry*. 1962: acted in *My Geisha* produced by

My Darling Clementine. directed by John Ford and photographed by Joseph MacDonald.
Harry Belfonte in Ranald MacDougall's The World, the Flesh, and the Devil.
Clifton Webb and William Holden in Leo McCarey's Satan Never Sleeps.

husband. Autobiography, 'Don't Fall off the Mountain' (1970).

Films as actress include: 1955: Artists and Models. 1956: Around the World in 80 Days. 1958: Hot Spell; The Matchmaker; The Sheepman; Some Came Running. 1959: Ask Any Girl; Career. 1960: Can-Can; Ocean's 11; The Apartment. 1961: All in a Night's Work; Two Loves. 1962: My Geisha; The Children's Hour; Two for the Seesaw. 1963: Irma la Douce. 1964: What a Way to Go; John Goldfarb Please Come Home; The Yellow Rolls Royce. 1966: Gambit. 1967: Sept Fois femme. 1969: Sweet Charity. 1970: Two Mules for Sister Sara.

MACMURRAY, Fred

Actor. Kankakee, Illinois 1908–
Chicago Art Institute. Dance band singer. Extra in films. 1930: on Broadway in 'Three's a Crowd, with Clifton Webb. Understudy to Bob Hope on 'Roberta'. 1934: first film as actor *Friends of Mr Sweeney*. To 1945: most films for Paramount. Then freelanced. Own company. Also in TV. Married dancer Lillian Lamont (1936–53, widowed) and actress June Haver (in 1954).

Films as actor include: 1935: The Gilded Lily; Alice Adams; Hands Across the Table. 1936: The Bride Comes Home; 13 Hours By Air; The Texas Rangers; The Trail of the Lonesome Pine. 1937: True Confession; Maid of Salem; Swing High, Swing Low. 1938: Sing You Sinners; Men With Wings. 1939: Invitation to Happiness. 1940: Little Old New York; Remember the Night; Too Many Husbands. 1941: New York Nights; Dive Bomber. 1942: The Lady is Willing; Take a Letter, Darling; The Forest Rangers; Star Spangled Rhythm. 1943: Above Suspicion; No Time for Love. 1944: Double Indemnity; And the Angels Sing; Practically Yours. 1945: Murder He Says; Where Do We Go from Here; Captain Eddie. 1947: Singapore; Suddenly It's Spring. 1948: The Miracle of the Bells; A Miracle Can Happen; An Innocent Affair. 1950: Never a Dull Moment. 1951: A Millionaire for Christy; Callaway Went Thataway. 1954: The Caine Mutiny; Pushover; Woman's World. 1955: The Rains of Ranchipur; The Far Horizon. 1956: There's Always Tomorrow. 1957: Quantez. 1958: Day of the Badman. 1959: Face of a Fugitive. 1960: The Apartment. 1961: The Absent-Minded Professor. 1962: Bon Voyage! 1963: Son of Flubber. 1964: Kisses for My President. 1966: Follow Me, Boys.

McCAREY, Leo

Director. Los Angeles 1898–
Law at University of Southern California. Became lawyer and songwriter. 3rd assistant on Tod Browning's *The Virgin of Stamboul* (1920); assisted Browning at Universal until 1923, also made first film as director, *Society Secrets* (1921). 1923–29: directed and supervised many films for Hal Roach. 1926: Roach made him production vice-president. Brought Laurel and Hardy together for their early films as a team, scripting some, and supervised them in 9 films (1927–28). 1928–29: directed then in *We Faw Down* (1928), *Liberty* (1929), and *Wrong Again* (1929). 1930–32: Paramount. Fox. United Artists. 1933–37: Paramount only. 1937–52: Columbia. RKO. Paramount. 1938: co-wrote story of *The Cowboy and the*

Lady. 1940: produced, co-wrote story of, and supervised *My Favorite Wife*. 1944: Oscar for story of *Going My Way*, which received 2 other Oscars (Best Picture, Best Screenplay). 1955–56: TV director. 1957: *An Affair to Remember* was re-make of own *Love Affair* (1939). 1958: took over Frank Tashlin's project *Rally Round the Flag, Boys!* Last 3 films for Fox.

Films as director (complete from 1926): 1926: Be Your Age; Tell 'em Nothing. 1928: We Faw Down – We Slip Up. 1929: Liberty; Wrong Again; The Sophomore; Red Hot Rhythm (+ *co-s*). 1930: Let's Go Native; Wild Company; Part-Time Wife (+ *co-s*). 1931: Indiscreet (+ *co-s*). 1933: The Kid From Spain (+ *st*); Duck Soup. 1934: Six of a Kind; Belle of the Nineties. 1935: Ruggles of Red Gap. 1936: The Milky Way. 1937: Make Way for Tomorrow (+ *p*); The Awful Truth (+ *p*). 1939: Love Affair (+ *co-st*). 1942: Once Upon a Honeymoon (+ *p/co-st*). 1944: Going My Way (+ *p/st*). 1945: The Bells of St Mary's (+ *p/st*). 1947: Good Sam (+ *p/co-st*). 1952: My Son John (+ *p/st/co-s*). 1957: An Affair to Remember (+ *st/co-s*). 1958: Rally 'Round the Flag, Boys! (+ *p/co-s*). 1961: Satan Never Sleeps – The Devil Never Sleeps (+ *p/co-s*).

McCAY, Winsor

Animator
From 1905: comic strip for New York Herald, 'Little Nemo in Slumberland'. 1909: first film as animator *Little Nemo*. 1910: made *Gertie the Trained Dinosaur* to accompany his vaudeville act. Many others of his films used in this way. 1967: Expo 67, Montreal undertook preservation work, saving 44 cans out of 60.

Films as animator include: 1909: Little Nemo. 1910: Gertie the Trained Dinosaur; How a Mosquito Operates. 1914: Gertie. 1916: Bug Vaudeville; The Pet; Winsor McCay and his Jersey Skeeters. 1917: Gertie on Tour; Adventures of a Rarebit Eater (*series*). 1918: The Sinking of the Lusitania. 1920: The Flying House.

McCLEOD, Norman Z.

Director. Grayling, Michigan 1898–1964 Hollywood
Son of clergyman. Natural Science at University of Washington. World War I: combat pilot in Royal Canadian Air Force. 1919–27: gagman, writer for Christie Comedies. 1928: to Fox; first film as director, for Fox. 1930–36: almost all films for Paramount. 1930–31: directed Marx Brothers in 2 films. 1931: wrote *Skippy* with Joseph Mankiewicz. Directed 2 films which he wrote with Mankiewicz. 1937–46: worked mainly for MGM, United Artists, RKO. 1938–39: several films for Hal Roach. 1946–47: 2 films with Danny Kaye. From 1947: several films with Bob Hope; worked mainly for Paramount and RKO.

Films as director: 1928: Taking a Chance. 1930: Along Came Youth (*co-d Lloyd Corrigan*). 1931: Monkey Business; Finn and Hattie (+ *co-s*; + *co-d Norman Taurog*); Touchdown; Skippy (+ *co-s*). 1932: The Miracle Man; Horse Feathers; If I Had a Million *ep* The Forger. 1933: Mama Loves Papa; Alice in Wonderland (+ *co-s*); A Lady's Profession. 1934: Many Happy Returns; A Melody in Spring. 1935: Here Comes Cookie; Redheads on Parade. 1936: Pennies from Heaven; Early to Bed; Mind Your Own

Business. 1937: Topper. 1938: Merrily We Live; There Goes My Heart. 1939: Topper Takes a Trip; Remember? (+ *co-st/co-s*). 1940: Little Men. 1941: The Trial of Mary Dugan; Lady Be Good; Jackass Mail. 1942: Panama Hattie; The Powers Girl – Hello Beautiful. 1943: Swing Shift Maisie – The Girl in Overalls. 1946: The Kid from Brooklyn. 1947: The Secret Life of Walter Mitty; Road to Rio. 1948: The Paleface; Isn't it Romantic. 1950: Let's Dance. 1951: My Favorite Spy. 1953: Never Wave at a WAC – The Private Wore Skirts – The Newest Profession. 1954: Casanova's Big Night. 1957: Public Pigeon No 1. 1959: Alias Jesse James.

McCORD, Ted

Cinematographer. Sullivan County, Indiana
Entered films at 19. 1921: shot part of feature at Paramount. 1924: first film as full cinematographer for First National. Worked mainly for First National and Warners.

Films as cinematographer include: 1928: Code of the Scarlet; The Crash. 1929: The Royal Rider. 1932: False Faces. 1941: Singapore Woman; Bullets for O'Hara; Wild Bill Hickok Rides. 1943: Action in the North Atlantic. 1947: Deep Valley. 1948: The Treasure of the Sierra Madre; Johnny Belinda; June Bride. 1949: Flamingo Road; The Lady Takes a Sailor. 1950: Young Man With a Horn; The Damned Don't Cry; The Breaking Point; Rocky Mountain. 1951: Goodbye My Fancy; Force of Arms; Starlift; I'll See You in My Dreams. 1952: Stop, You're Killing Me. 1955: East of Eden; I Died a Thousand Times. 1956: The Burning Hills; The Girl He Left Behind. 1957: The Helen Morgan Story. 1958: The Proud Rebel. 1959: The Hanging Tree. 1960: Private Property; The Adventures of Huckleberry Finn. 1961: War Hunt. 1962: Hero's Island; Two For the Seesaw. 1965: The Sound of Music. 1966: A Fine Madness.

McCREA, Joel

Actor. Los Angeles 1905–
To 1934: worked frequently for RKO. Also for e.g. Paramount, MGM, Warners. 1952: British film *Rough Shoot*. Married actress Frances Dee. Son is actor Jody McCrea.

Films as actor include: 1929: So This is College; Dynamite; The Single Standard. 1930: Lightnin'. 1931: Kept Husbands; Girls About Town. 1932: Business and Pleasure; Bird of Paradise; The Most Dangerous Game; Rockabye. 1933: The Silver Cord; Bed of Roses. 1934: Gambling Lady. 1935: Private Worlds; Barbary Coast. 1936: Come and Get It!; Banjo on My Knee; These Three. 1937: Dead End; Wells Fargo. 1938: Youth Takes a Fling. 1939: Union Pacific; They Shall Have Music; Espionage Agent. 1940: He Married His Wife; Foreign Correspondent; Primrose Path. 1941: Reaching for the Sun; Sullivan's Travels. 1942: The Great Man's Lady; The Palm Beach Story. 1943: The More the Merrier. 1944: Buffalo Bill; The Great Moment. 1947: Ramrod. 1949: South of St Louis; Colorado Territory. 1950: Stars in My Crown; Saddle Tramp. 1952: The San Francisco Story. 1955: Stranger on Horseback; Wichita. 1956: The First Texan. 1957: Trooper Hook. 1958: Fort Massacre; Cattle Empire. 1959: The Gunfight at Dodge City. 1962: Ride the High Country.

McGUIRE, Dorothy

Actress. Omaha, Nebraska 1918–

Radio. 1938: understudy to Martha Scott in 'Our Town', then took over from her. Acted in stock. Toured with John Barrymore in 'My Dear Children'. 1940: understudy to Julie Haydon on tour in 'The Time Of Your Life'. 1941: playwright Rose Franken spotted her for 'Claudia' on Broadway. 1943: first film as actress *Claudia*. To 1950: worked for Fox and RKO. Then several companies.

Films as actress include: 1945: A Tree Grows in Brooklyn; The Enchanted Cottage; The Spiral Staircase. 1946: Till the End of Time. 1947: Gentleman's Agreement. 1950: Mister 880. 1951: I Want You; Callaway Went Thataway. 1952: Invitation. 1954: Three Coins in the Fountain. 1955: Trial. 1956: Friendly Persuasion. 1957: Old Yeller. 1959: This Earth is Mine; The Remarkable Mr Pennypacker. 1960: A Summer Place; The Dark at the Top of the Stairs; Swiss Family Robinson. 1961: Susan Slade. 1962: Summer Magic. 1965: The Greatest Story Ever Told. 1971: Flight of the Doves.

McINTIRE, John

Actor. Spokane, Washington 1907–

Radio announcer. Acted with partner Jeanette Nolan, whom he married in 1936. In films from 1949. 1961: took over from Ward Bond in TV series 'Wagon Train'; since then rarely in films. Much other TV work.

Films as actor include: 1949: Down to the Sea in Ships; Ambush. 1950: The Asphalt Jungle; No Sad Songs for Me; Winchester '73. 1951: Westward the Women. 1952: The World in his Arms; Horizons West; The Lawless Breed. 1953: A Lion is in the Streets. 1954: The Far Country. 1955: Stranger on Horseback; The Kentuckian; The Phenix City Story. 1956: Backlash. 1957: The Tin Star. 1959: The Gunfight at Dodge City. 1960: Psycho; Elmer Gantry; Flaming Star. 1961: Two Rode Together.

McLAGLEN, Andrew V.

Director. London 1920–

Son of Victor McLaglen. University of Virginia. From 1940: worked for aircraft company. Appeared in Gregory Ratoff's *Paris Underground* (1945) because his size (6′ 7″) was needed. From 1951: worked as assistant director e.g. on *The Bullfighter and the Lady* (1951), *The Quiet Man* (1952), *Blood Alley* (1955). 1952: directed his first 2 films for Monogram; since with various companies. 1953: production manager on *Hondo*. 1956: produced *Seven Men from Now*. Much TV as director; 6½ year contract with CBS including over 250 episodes in series e.g. 'Have Gun, Will Travel', 'Gunsmoke', 'Perry Mason', 'Gunslinger', 'The Virginian'. From 1968: Universal contract.

Films as director: 1952: Here Come the Marines; Wild Stallion. 1955: Man in the Vault. 1956: Gun the Man Down. 1957: The Abductors. 1960: Freckles. 1961: The Little Shepherd of Kingdom Come. 1963: McLintock! 1965: Shenandoah; The Rare Breed. 1966: Monkeys, Go Home! 1967: The Way West. 1968: The Ballad of Josie; The Devil's Brigade; Bandolero! 1969: Hellfighters; The Undefeated. 1970:

Chisum. 1971: Fool's Parade; Something Big; One More Train to Rob.

McLAGLEN, Victor

Actor. Tunbridge Wells, Kent 1886–1959 Newport Beach, California

Life Guards for 3 years, dismissed as under age. Boxer, wrestler in Britain. Boxing champion of Eastern Canada. Travels included USA, India, South Africa. 1914–18: Irish Fusiliers serving in Mesopotamia, reaching Captain. Provost-Marshal of Bagdhad. Toured USA, Australia in vaudeville. 1920–24: British films. 1925: spotted by J. Stuart Blackton for first American film as actor *The Beloved Brute*. 1933: became American citizen. Many films for Fox. Over 100 films. 1958: last film *Sea Fury* in Britain. Son is Andrew V. McLaglen, who directed him in *The Abductors* (1957). Oscar as best actor for *The Informer* (1935).

Films as actor include: 1920: The Call of the Road. 1922: The Glorious Adventure. 1924: The Passionate Adventure. 1925: Winds of Chance. 1926: What Price Glory? 1927: Loves of Carmen. 1928: A Girl in Every Port. 1929: The Cock-Eyed World; The Black Watch; Hot for Paris. 1931: Women of All Nations; Dishonored; Wicked. 1932: While Paris Sleeps. 1934: The Lost Patrol; The Wharf Angel; Murder at the Varieties; The Captain Hates the Sea. 1935: Under Pressure; Professional Soldier. 1936: Klondike Annie; Under Two Flags. 1937: Wee Willie Winkie. 1939: Let Freedom Ring; Gunga Din; Captain Fury; Full Confession; Rio. 1941: Broadway Limited. 1942: China Girl. 1943: Forever and a Day. 1944: Roger Tuohy, Gangster; The Princess and the Pirate. 1947: Calendar Girl; The Foxes of Harrow. 1948: Fort Apache. 1949: She Wore a Yellow Ribbon. 1950: Rio Grande. 1954: Prince Valiant. 1955: Bengazi. 1956: Around the World in 80 Days.

McLAREN, Norman

Director. Stirling, Scotland 1914–

Glasgow School of Art, specialising in interior design. Made first film by washing begged print of a 35mm commercial film and painting directly on to it with brush and coloured ink. 16mm documentary *Seven Till Five* on a day in art school led to financial backing from the school for *Camera Makes Whoopee*. This and *Colour Cocktail* seen by John Grierson who invited him to join GPO Film Unit; worked there 1937–39. Camera work on Ivor Montague's *Defence of Madrid*. 1939: to New York. 1941: joined National Film Board of Canada. 1949–50: in China for UNESCO, teaching audio-visual aids. 1950: The subject of *Pen Point Percussion*. Techniques include sequential photography of alterations of pastel drawing, 3D, and synthetic sound.

Films as director include: 1934: Hand-Painted Abstractions. 1934–35: Seven Till Five; Camera Makes Whoopee; Colour Cocktail. 1936–37: Hell Unlimited (*co-d Helen Biggar*). 1937–39: Book Bargain; News for the Navy; Many a Pickle; Love on the Wing. 1939: The Obedient Flame; Allegro (*co-d Mary Ellen Bute*); Scherzo. 1939–41: Dots; Spook Sport (*co-d Ellen Bute*); Loops; Rumba; Stars and Stripes; Boogie Doodle. 1941–43: Mail Early; V for Victory; Five for Four; Hen Hop; Dollar Dance (*+cr*). 1944: Alouette. 1945: C'est l'aviron; Keep Your Mouth Shut (*co-d*

Ben Johnson and John Wayne in Chisum, *directed by Andrew V. McLaglen.*
Le Merle. *directed by Norman McLaren.*
Steve McQueen as Bullitt, *by Peter Yates.*

George Dunning). 1946: Là haut sur les montagnes; A Little Phantasy on a Nineteenth Century Painting; Hoppity Hop. 1947: Fiddle de Dee; La Poulette Grise. 1948: A Phantasy. 1949: Begone, Dull Care (_co-d Evelyn Lambert_). 1950: Around is Around (_co-d Lambert_); Chalk River Ballet (_co-d René Jodoin_). 1951: Now is the Time. 1952: Twirligig; Neighbours; Two Bagatelles. 1955: Blinkity Blank. 1956: One, Two, Three (_uf_); Rhythmetic (_co-d Lambert_). 1957: A Chairy Tale (_co-d Claude Jutra_). 1958: Le Merle (_co-d Lambert_). 1959: Short and Suite (_co-d Lambert_); Serenal; Mail Early for Christmas; The Wonderful World of Jack Paar (_cr_). 1960: Lines Vertical (_co-d Lambert_); Lines Horizontal (_co-d Lambert_). 1961: New York Lightboard; New York Light Record. 1962: Opening Speech. 1963: Dance Squared. 1964: Christmas Cracker (_co-d 3 others_); Canon (_co-d Grant Munro_). 1965: Mosaic (_co-d Mosaic_). 1968: Pas de deux. 1969: Spheres. 1970: Striations.

McQUEEN, Steve

Actor. Slater, Missouri 1930 –
1950: discharged from US Marine Corps, minor stage work in New York. 1952: graduated from Neighborhood Playhouse; won scholarship to Uta Hagen-Herbert Berghof Dramatic School, studied there 2 years. Summer stock in 'Peg O' My Heart' with Margaret O'Brien; Rochester Stock Company with Ethel Waters in 'Member of the Wedding'; with Melvyn Douglas in 'Time Out for Ginger'. Joined Actor's Studio. On Broadway in 'The Gap', replaced Ben Gazzara in 'Hatful of Rain'. 1956: first film as actor. Played lead in CBS TV series 'Wanted—Dead or Alive' until 1961. MGM contract, non-exclusive. First MGM film under contract: _The Honeymoon Machine_. Worked for several other companies. Formed own company; production deal with Warners-7 Arts for 6 films, 3 as actor-producer, 3 as producer only; _Bullitt_ (1968) was first film under this arrangement.

Films as actor: 1956: Somebody Up There Likes Me. 1957: Never Love a Stranger. 1958: The Great St Louis Bank Robbery; The Blob. 1959: Never So Few. 1960: The Magnificent Seven. 1961: The Honeymoon Machine. 1962: Hell is for Heroes; The War Lover. 1963: The Great Escape; Love With the Proper Stranger; Soldiers in the Rain. 1965: Baby, the Rain Must Fall (_+ co-pc_); The Cincinnatti Kid (_+ co-pc_). 1966: The Sand Pebbles (_+ co-pc_); Nevada Smith (_+ pc_). 1968: The Thomas Crown Affair (_+ co-pc_); Bullitt (_+ pc_).

MADDOW, Ben

Writer and director. New Jersey
Columbia University. 1947: first film as writer _Framed_. 1950: wrote _The Asphalt Jungle_ in collaboration with John Huston. 1951: first film as writer and director. To 1952: worked mainly for Columbia and MGM, then no credited work in films for 7 years. 1953: published first novel '44, Gravel Street'. 1959: with Joseph Strick and Sidney Myers wrote, produced, directed and edited _The Savage Eye_. 1960: returned to Hollywood films with _The Unforgiven_ for United Artists. 1963: wrote and co-produced Joseph Strick's _The Balcony_. Directed and wrote _The Stairs_ for National Mental Health Association. Author of novel 'Omega', one-act plays 'In a Cold Room' and 'Ram's Horn', also poetry and stories.

Films as director and writer include: 1951: The Steps of Age. 1959: The Savage Eye (_+ co-p/co-e; co-s; co-d Joseph Strick, Sidney Myers_). 1964: An Affair of the Skin (_+ co-p/st_). 1969: Storm of Strangers.

Films as writer include: 1948: The Man from Colorado (_co_); Kiss the Blood off my Hands (_co-ad_). 1949: Intruder in the Dust. 1950: The Asphalt Jungle (_co_). 1952: Shadow in the Sky. 1956: The Last Frontier (_co, uc_). 1957: Men in War (_co, uc_). 1960: The Unforgiven. 1961: Two Loves. 1963: The Balcony (_+ p_). 1967: The Way West (_co_). 1969: The Chairman – The Most Dangerous Man in the World; The Secret of Santa Vittoria (_co_). 1971: The Mephisto Waltz.

MADSEN, Forrest Holger

Director and writer. Copenhagen 1878–1943 Copenhagen.
1896: stage debut as actor. Much theatre work. 1909: first film as director and writer. 1909–16: worked for Nordisk. 1914–16: directed 4 scripts written by Carl Dreyer. 1916: they wrote _Pax Aeterna_ in collaboration. 1917: to Dansk-film. 1918–20: Nordisk. 1924: Dansk-film. 1925: Union-Ufa. 1926–29: Dansk-film. 1930: Ufa. 1934–36: last films as director, for Dansk-film. 1937–43: to Enghave Bio as actor. Acted occasionally in own films.

Films as director and writer: 1909: Sherlock Holmes (_+ w_). 1912: Gögleren. 1913: Mens pesten raser; Ballettens datter; Princesse Elena; Den Hvide Dame; Fra fyrste til knejpevaert; Et vanskeligt valg; Elskovleg. 1914: Opiumsdrömmen; Endelig Alene; Unden freadreland; Trold kan taemmes; Evangeliemandensliv; Spiritisten (_co-s_). 1915: Cigaretpigen; Kornspekulantens datter; Danserindens haevn (_co-s_). 1916: Lykken; Den Aerelose; For sin faders skyld (_co-s_); Manden uden smil; Hendes moders lofte; Nattens mysterium; Livets Goglrspil; Fange No 113; Natt evandreren; Hans rigtige kone; Pax Aeterna (_co-s_); Praestens datter. 1917: Retten sejrer; Hendes Helt; Skovens born. 1918: Mod lyset; Folkets van; Manden der sejrede. 1919: Har jeg ret til at tage mit eget liv?; Det storste i verden. 1920: Gudernes yndling. 1924: Midnatsgaesten. 1925: Hellige Lögne; Der evangelimann (_+ w_). 1926: Kniplinger; Skaebnenatten; Tobias Buntschuh (_+ w_). 1927: Midnatsjaegernen; Kunsten at leve livet. 1929: Laengslernes nat. 1936: Sol over Danmark.

Films as director: 1912: Guldet og vort hjerte. 1913: Under mindernes trae; Elskovs Magt; Staalkongens Vilje; Under skaebnens hjul; Lykken Dräber; Millionärdrengen. 1914: Den Mystiske fremmede; Et Huskors; Barnets magt; Et Harems eventyr; Tempeldanserindens elskov; Barnevennerne; Testamentets hemmelighed; En Opstandelse; Ned med vaabnene (_r 1916_); Krig og kaerlighed. 1915: Ansigtet; En Aeresoprejsning; Hvem er gentlemantyven?; Manden uden fremtid; Krigens fjende; Kaerlighedens triumph; I Livets branding; Notitsen i morgenbladet; Sjäeletyven; Acostates forste offer; Den Frelsende film; Den Omstridte jord; Hvor sorgene glemmes; Grevinde hjertelös; Hittabarnet; Guldets Gift; En Kunstners genembrud; Hvo som elsker sin fader. 1916: Maaneprinsessen; Lydia; Bornenes Synd. 1918: Himmelskibet. 1930: Nein, nein, Nanette. 1934: Kobenhavn-Kalundborg.

MAGNANI, Anna

Actress. Rome 1908 –
Academy of Dramatic Art, Rome. Cabaret, vaudeville. First film as actress _La Cieca di Sorrento_ (1934). Directed by Goffredo Alessandri in _Cavalleria_ (1936); after marrying him she temporarily retired. World War II: during the Liberation appeared in revues for American troops. Rossellini engaged her for _Roma Città Aperta_. 1953: US tour. 1955: at request of Tennessee Williams, acted in _The Rose Tattoo_: Oscar as Best Actress. 1970: debut for Italian television.

Films as actress include: 1941: Teresa Venerdi. 1943: Campo dei fiori. 1946: Il Bandito. 1947: L'Onorevole Angelina. 1948: Amore; Molti Sogni per le strade. 1949: Vulcano. 1951: Bellissima. 1952: La Carrozza d'oro. 1953: Siamo donne _ep_ Anna Magnani. 1957: Wild is the Wind. 1960: The Fugitive Kind. 1962: Mamma Roma.

MAHIN, John Lee

Writer. Evanston, Illinois 1902 –
From 1932: writer at MGM; collaborated on adaptation and dialogue of _Scarface, Shame of the Nation_. 1933: acted in and co-wrote dialogue for _Hell Below_. 1953: scripted _Mogambo_, a remake of _Red Dust_ (1932) which he wrote. To 1954: worked mainly for MGM. Then for various companies. 1959: with Martin Rackin formed company to make _The Horse Soldiers_ and wrote it with him. 1960: with Rackin produced _Revak, lo schiavo di Cartagine_.

Films as writer include: 1932: The Wet Parade (_ad_). 1934: Treasure Island; Eskimo; Chained. 1936: Love on the Run. 1940: Boom Town. 1941: Dr Jekyll and Mr Hyde. 1951: Show Boat. 1952: My Son John (_ad_). 1954: Elephant Walk. 1956: The Bad Seed. 1958: No Time for Sergeants.

Films as writer in collaboration include: 1933: Bombshell. 1934: Laughing Boy. 1935: Naughty Marietta. 1936: Wife vs Secretary; Small Town Girl; The Devil is a Sissy. 1937: Captains Courageous. 1938: Too Hot to Handle. 1941: Johnny Eager. 1942: Tortilla Flat; Down to the Sea in Ships. 1951: Quo Vadis. 1955: Lucy Gallant. 1957: Heaven Knows, Mr Allison. 1960: North to Alaska. 1962: The Spiral Road. 1965: Moment to Moment.

MAIBAUM, Richard

Writer. New York 1909 –
Universities of New York and Iowa. Producer on Broadway. Acted with New York Shakespearean Repertory Company. 1935: to Hollywood. Scripts for MGM, Columbia, Paramount, Fox. Theatrical producer. World War II: US Army, Combat Film Division. From 1946: occasionally produced. Also TV work.

Films as writer include: 1936: Gold Diggers of 1937 (_+ fco-pl_). 1942: Ten Gentlemen from West Point. 1945: See My Lawyer (_+ fco-pl_). 1946: O.S.S. (_+ p_). 1949: Song of Surrender (_+ p_). 1954: Hell Below Zero (_ad_). 1956: Zarak. 1963: From Russia with Love. 1968: Chitty Chitty Bang Bang.

Films as writer in collaboration include: 1937: They Gave Him a Gun. 1940: 20 Mule Team. 1941: I

Wanted Wings. 1949: The Great Gatsby (+p). 1953: The Red Beret. 1956: Bigger Than Life (+co-st); Cockleshell Heroes. 1957: No Time to Die (+co-st). 1960: The Day They Robbed the Bank of England (co-ad); Killers of Kilimanjaro (co-st). 1962: Doctor No. 1964: Goldfinger. 1965: Thunderball. 1971: Diamonds are Forever (co).

MAILER, Norman

Director. Long Branch, New Jersey 1925–
Brought up in Brooklyn. To Harvard at 16, majored in aeronautical engineering, won college award for writing; graduated in 1943. War service in Armoured Cavalry Regiment, active service in Pacific, basis of novel 'The Naked and the Dead' (1948) which was adapted by Denis and Terry Sanders for Raoul Walsh's film (1958). Wrote novels, poetry, journalism. 1952–63: edited Dissent. 1955: co-founder of The Village Voice. Married 4 times, wives include actress Beverly Bentley; divorced second wife after attacking her with dagger, basis of novel 'An American Dream' (1964): film adaptation, An American Dream (1966). 1968: first film as director Beyond the Law, premiered at Notre Dame University. 1969: ran as reform candidate in New York mayoral election.

Films as director and writer: 1968: Beyond the Law (+co-p/co-e/w); Wild 90 (+co-p/w). 1970: Maidstone (+p/st/co-e/w).

MAINWARING, Daniel

Writer
Father was an English immigrant farmer in the Sierra Nevada. Teacher and journalist before working as a publicist for major studios. 1930: first novel 'One Against the Earth', then wrote detective stories. 1942: first film as writer, in collaboration, Secrets of the Underground. Until 1955 worked under pseudonym Geoffrey Homes.

Films as writer include: 1947: Out of the Past (+fu). 1949: The Big Steal (co). 1950: The Lawless (+fn). 1951: The Tall Target (co-st). 1955: Annapolis Story (co); The Phenix City Story (co). 1956: Invasion of the Body Snatchers. 1957: Baby Face Nelson (co). 1958: The Gun Runners (co). 1961: Antinea, l'amante della città sepolta.

MAKAVEJEV, Dušan

Director. Belgrade, 1932–
1955: diploma in psychology from Faculty of Philosophy, Belgrade. 1955–59: studied in directorial department of Academy for Theatre, Radio, Film and Television. Film critic on student magazine. Co-directed Vladimir Mayakovsky's 'The Bath-house' at Belgrade student theatre. 1955–58: experimental films at Kino-Club; first worked as professional director, 13 documentaries for Zagreb film. 1965: book of essays 'A Kiss for Comradess Slogan' published.

Features as director and writer: 1966: Covek nije tijka – Man is not a Bird. 1967: Ljubavni slucaj, tragedija sluzbenice P.T.T. – Switchboard Operator – Love Dossier or the Tragedy of a Switchboard Operator. 1968: Nevinost bez zastite – Innocence Unprotected (+dec). 1971: WR-Misterije organizma – WR-Mysteries of the Organism.

MALDEN, Karl

(Mladen Sukilovich) Actor and director. Gary, Indiana 1914–
Father was Serbian actor. Goodman Theatre Dramatic School, Chicago. Broadway: 'Golden Boy', 'Key Largo'. US Army, reaching corporal. On Broadway, directed by Elia Kazan in 'Truckline Cafe', 'All My Sons', 'A Streetcar Named Desire'. Also acted in 'Desire Under the Elms', 'The Desperate Hours'. Oscar as supporting actor for A Streetcar Named Desire (1951). 1957: Warners contract, directed Time Limit.

Films as actor: 1940: They Knew What They Wanted. 1944: Winged Victory. 1947: 13 rue Madeleine; Boomerang! 1950: The Gunfighter; Where the Sidewalk Ends. 1951: Halls of Montezuma; A Streetcar Named Desire; Decision Before Dawn. 1952: Diplomatic Courier; Operation Secret; Ruby Gentry. 1953: I Confess; Take the High Ground. 1954: Phantom of the Rue Morgue; On the Waterfront. 1956: Baby Doll. 1957: Fear Strikes Out; Bombers B–52. 1959: The Hanging Tree. 1960: Pollyanna; The Great Imposter. 1961: Parrish; One-Eyed Jacks. 1962: Bird Man of Alcatraz; All Fall Down; Gypsy; How the West was Won. 1963: Come Fly With Me. 1964: Dead Ringer; Cheyenne Autumn. 1965: The Cincinnatti Kid. 1966: Nevada Smith; The Silencers; Murderers' Row. 1967: Hotel; The Adventures of Bullwhip Griffin; Billion Dollar Brain. 1968: Blue. 1971: Wild Rovers.

MALLE, Louis

Director. Thumeries, France 1932–
Educated by Jesuits at Fontainebleau; studies interrupted by war. 1950: political science at Sorbonne. 1951–53: IDHEC. From 1953: made shorts. Sailed on Jacques-Yves Cousteau's ship 'Calypso', worked with underwater team photographing wreck of 'Andrea Doria' off coast of Massachusetts. Stage and TV assistant. 1956: directed in collaboration with Cousteau Le Monde du silence; assistant director to Robert Bresson on Un Condamné à mort s'est échappé. 1957: first feature as director. 1962: produced and supervised Le Combat dans l'île. TV work includes Bons Baisers de Bangkok (1964) and series Inde 68 (1969); when latter shown by BBC (1970), Indian government closed BBC's Delhi office in protest at the film's concentration on poverty. From 1968: Vice-president of Société des réalisateurs de films.

Films as director: 1953: Fontaine de Vaucluse. 1955: Station 307. 1956: Le Monde du silence – The Silent World (+co-c; co-d Jacques-Yves Cousteau). 1957: L'Ascenseur pour l'échafaud – Lift to the Scaffold (+co-s). 1958: Les Amants (+co-s). 1960: Zazie dans le Métro (+co-s). 1962: Vie Privée – A Very Private Affair (+co-s). 1963: Le Feu Follet – Will of the Wisp (+co-s); Touriste Encore. 1965: Viva Maria! (+co-s). 1967: Le Voleur (+co-s); Histoires Extraordinaires ep William Wilson. 1969: Inde 68 – Louis Malle's India; Calcutta (+cy). 1971: Le Souffle au coeur (+s).

MALONE, Dorothy

(Dorothy Maloney) Actress. Chicago 1925–
Dancing classes from age 3. Winner of local high school acting competitions. Prizes for singing and writing at Southern Methodist University. Spotted by

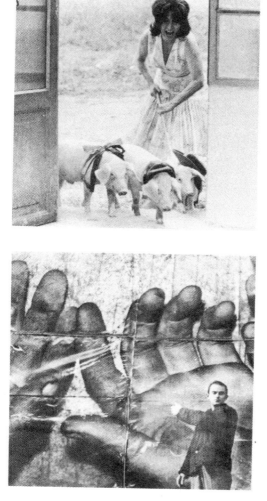

Anna Magnani in Pasolini's Mamma Roma.
Čovek nije tica, *directed by Dušan Makavejev.*
Dorothy Malone and Rock Hudson in Robert Aldrich's The Last Sunset.

RKO scout in college production of 'Starbound'; year's training in Hollywood. Appearance in 'Ladies Unmasked' (Studio Club) led to Warners screen test and contract. 1943: first film as actress *Falcon and the Co-Eds*. 1943–44: films under real name, including *One Mysterious Night* (1944). TV appearances include 'Peyton Place'. Oscar as supporting actress for *Written on the Wind* (1956).

Films as actress include: 1944: One Mysterious Night. 1945: Hollywood Canteen. 1946: The Big Sleep; Night and Day. 1948: Two Guys from Texas; To the Victor. 1949: One Sunday Afternoon, South of St Louis; Colorado Territory. 1950: The Nevadan. 1953: Scared Stiff. 1954: Pushover; Five Guns West; Private Hell 36. 1955: Young at Heart; Battle Cry; Sincerely Yours; Artists and Models. 1956: Pillars of the Sky; Written on the Wind; Tension at Table Rock. 1957: Quantez; The Tarnished Angels; Man of a Thousand Faces; Tip on a Dead Jockey. 1958: Too Much, Too Soon. 1959: Warlock. 1960: The Last Voyage. 1961: The Last Sunset.

MALRAUX, André

Director. Paris 1901–
Archaeologist in Far East; Communist activity in China. Fought for Republicans in Spanish Civil War. 1939: in Barcelona, in last months of Republic, made only film as director, documentary *L'Espoir* (released 1945). Novels include 'La Condition Humaine' (1933), 'L'Espoir' (1937), 'Les Noyers de l'Altenburg' (1940). Critical work includes 'Esquisse d'une psychologie du cinéma' (1940) and 'Essais de la psychologie de l'art'. Gaullist Minister of Culture.

MAMOULIAN, Rouben

Director. Tiflis, Russia 1896–
Armenian family. At 7, moved to Paris with them; at 12 returned to Tiflis; then to Moscow to study law. Studied at Moscow Art Theatre studio. 1918: organised own theatre studio in Tiflis; worked as theatre critic on a local paper. 1920: to London with Russian Repertory Company and studied theatre at King's College, London. 1923: directed a play at St James's Theatre in Moscow Art Theatre style. 1923–26: directed operas at Eastman Theatre, Rochester, New York. 1926: taught at Theatre Guild school. 1927: directed at Guild Theatre, starting with 'Porgy'. Other plays as director include Eugene O'Neill's 'Marco Millions' (1928), Karel Capek's 'R.U.R.' (1929) and his own adaptation of Ivan Turgenev's 'A Month in the Country'. 1931: directed Arnold Schoenberg's 'Die glückliche Hand' at Metropolitan Opera, New York. 1930: first film as director, made in New York, to Hollywood, abandoned theatre. 1935: *Becky Sharp* (1935) was the first feature film in 3-colour Technicolor; returned to direct 'Porgy and Bess' (adapted from 'Porgy'). 1943: directed first production of 'Oklahoma' for Theatre Guild. Directed other musicals including 'Carousel' (1945), 'St Louis Woman' (1946), 'Lost in the Stars' (1949) and 'Arms and the Girl' (1951) of which he was co-author. Also wrote with Maxwell Anderson 'The Devil's Hornpipe', filmed as *Never Steal Anything Small* (1958). Left *Porgy and Bess* (1959) after disagreement with Sam Goldwyn; film completed by Otto Preminger. Directed first attempt at shooting *Cleopatra,* abandoned because of Elizabeth Taylor's illness.

Films as director: 1930: Applause. 1931: City Streets. 1932: Dr Jekyll and Mr Hyde (+*p*); Love Me Tonight (+*p*). 1933: The Song of Songs (+*p*). 1934: Queen Christina; We Live Again (+*p*). 1935: Becky Sharp (+*co-p*). 1936: The Gay Desperado. 1937: High, Wide and Handsome. 1939: Golden Boy. 1940: The Mark of Zorro. 1941: Blood and Sand. 1942: Rings on Her Fingers. 1947: Summer Holiday. 1957: Silk Stockings.

MAN, Ray

Painter and photographer. Philadelphia, Pennsylvania 1890–
One of the founders of the Dada movement and long associated with surrealism. During 1920s and '30s worked in Paris, mainly as photographer; experimented with photography without a camera, exposing objects placed directly on photographic printing paper. Made a few films from 1923. 1924: appeared as actor in René Clair's *Entr'acte*. 1925: assistant director to Marcel Duchamp on *Anémic Cinéma*. 1944–46: wrote and directed one of the episodes on Hans Richter's *Dreams that Money Can Buy*. 1963: wrote autobiography 'Self Portrait'.

Films as director: 1923: Le Retour à la raison (+*c*). 1926: Emak Bakia (+*p/c*). 1928: L'Etoile de mer (+*p/c*). 1929: Les Mystères du Château du Dé (+*c*). 1935: Essai de simulation de délire cinématographique (*co-d André Breton, Paul Éluard*). 1944–46: Dreams that Money Can Buy *ep* Ruth Roses and Revolvers (+*s*).

MANCINI, Henry

Composer. Cleveland, Ohio 1924–
Julliard School of Music; studies interrupted by war service. 1943–45: US Army and Air Force. Pianist-arranger with Glenn Miller/Tex Beneke Orchestra. 1947: married singer Ginny O'Conner. Studied with Ernst Krenek, Mario Castelnuoveo-Tedesco, Dr Alfred Sendry. 1952: joined Universal-International. 1953: arranged Miller's music for *The Glenn Miller Story*. 1955: music for song in *Six Bridges to Cross*. Became composer at Universal, then TV work: 'Peter Gunn', 'Mr Lucky'. 1960: returned to cinema. Subsequently worked for numerous studios including Universal, Paramount, United Artists, Fox. Oscars for score *Breakfast at Tiffany's* (1961) and song 'Moon River' from same film. Book on orchestration 'Sounds and Scores: A Practical Guide to Professional Orchestration'.

Films as composer include: 1958: Touch of Evil. 1960: High Time; The Great Imposter. 1961: Breakfast at Tiffany's; Bachelor in Paradise. 1962: Hatari!; Mr Hobbs Takes a Vacation. 1964: The Pink Panther; Charade; Man's Favorite Sport?; A Shot in the Dark; Dear Heart. 1966: What Did You Do in the War, Daddy?; Arabesque. 1967: Two for the Road; Gunn; Wait Until Dark. 1968: The Party. 1969: Gaily, Gaily. 1970: Sunflower; Darling Lili. 1971: The Night Visitor; Sometimes a Great Notion.

MANFREDI, Nino

Actor. Castro dei Volsci, Italy 1921–
University studies in jurisprudence, then drama school. Dubbed films, worked in radio drama and revue. 1947:

acted in 'L'Uomo e il fucile' at Prague Youth Festival. Stage work includes 'All My Sons', 'Anthony', 'The Tempest', 'Oedipus Rex', 'Six Characters in Search of an Author', 'Liliom', 'Intermezzo', 'Encounter in the Night'. 1951: film dubbing. 1953: film career proper began, though a few earlier appearances. 1962: acted in stage musical comedy 'Rugantino'; first film as director, episode (which he also co-wrote and acted in) of *L'Amore Difficile*. 1971: first full-length film as director *Per Grazie Ricevuta*.

Films as actor include: 1956: Totò, Peppino e la ... mala femmina; Guardia, guardia scelta briagadiere a maresciallo. 1957: Camping. 1958: Caporale di Giomata; Venezia, la luna e tu. 1959: Audace colpo dei soliti ignoti. 1960: Le Pillole d'Ercole. 1961: Il Giudizio Universale; A cavallo della tigre. 1962: Anni Rugenti. 1963: El Verdugo; La Parmigiana. 1964: Le Bambole *ep* Le Telefonata. 1965: Io la conoscevo bene; Made in Italy; Una Rosa per tutti; Operazione San Gennaro. 1966: Adulterio all'Italiana. 1967: Il Padre di Famiglia. 1970: Contestazione Generale. 1971: La Betia.

MANGANO, Silvana

Actress. Rome 1930–
Italian father, English mother. Trained as dancer. Spotted by director Mario Costa. 1948: first film as actress *Elisir d'amore*; after *Riso Amaro* turned down offer of Hollywood contract in favour of 3-year contract with Lux in Italy; married Dino de Laurentiis who produced many of her films.

Films as actress include: 1949: Black Magic; Riso Amaro. 1950: Il Brigante Musolino. 1951: Anna. 1954: Mambo; L'Oro di Napoli. 1955: Ulisse. 1956: Uomini e lupi. 1958: La Tempestà; La Diga sul Pacifico. 1960: Jovanka e l'altri; La Grande Guerra; Crimen. 1961: Il Giudizio Universale. 1962: Barabbas; Il Processo di Verona. 1964: La Mia Signora. 1965: Il Disco Volante. 1966: Le Streghe. 1967: Edipo Re. 1968: Teorema. 1971: Morte a Venezia; Il Decamerone.

MANKIEWICZ, Herman J.

Writer. New York 1897–1953 Hollywood
Elder brother of Joseph L. Mankiewicz. University education, then journalist; foreign correspondent and drama critic; first drama editor of the New Yorker. From 1926: also wrote for Hollywood films; collaborated with Tod Browning on story for *The Road to Mandalay* (1926) for MGM. From 1928: worked on films directed by Josef Von Sternberg at Paramount e.g. titles for *The Last Command* (1928), *The Dragnet* (1928), dialogue for *Thunderbolt* (1929). Executive producer on *Monkey Business* (1931), *Horse Feathers* (1932), *Duck Soup* (1933). Later with various companies including MGM and RKO. Oscar for original screenplay, *Citizen Kane* (1941, in collaboration with Orson Welles).

Films as writer include: 1931: The Royal Family of Broadway (*co*). 1933: Dinner at Eight (*co*). 1935: After Office Hours. 1937: My Dear Miss Aldrich (*st/s*; +*p*). 1939: It's a Wonderful World (*co-st*). 1941: Rise and Shine. 1942: Stand by for Action (*co*); Pride of the Yankees (*co*). 1944: Christmas Holiday. 1945: The Spanish Main (*co*); The Enchanted Cottage (*co*). 1949: A Woman's Secret (+*p*).

MANKIEWICZ, Joseph L. (Leo)

Director, producer and writer. Wilkes Barre, Pennsylvania 1909–

Son of a schoolmaster and younger brother of Herman J. Mankiewicz. Columbia University. To Berlin as reporter for Chicago Tribune. Translated titles of Ufa films into English. Returned to Hollywood and worked as a writer with his brother, first writing titles for silent versions of sound films (1929). 1934: left Paramount for MGM. 1936: producer at MGM. 1943: producer at Fox. 1946: replaced Ernst Lubitsch as director of *Dragonwyck*. Own company, Figaro Inc, produced *The Barefoot Contessa* (1954), *The Quiet American* (1958), and *I Want to Live* (1958) which was produced by Walter Wanger and had the youngest of the Mankiewicz brothers, Don, as co-author of script. 1961: took over direction of *Cleopatra* from Rouben Mamoulian after first abortive attempt at shooting in Britain. Directed 'La Boheme' for Metropolitan Opera in New York. *Carol for Another Christmas* (1964) made for United Nations and intended for television. 1950: Oscars as director and writer of screenplay for *All About Eve*, which also received Oscar as Best Picture.

Films as writer include: 1929: Close Harmony; The Man I Love; Thunderbolt. 1930: Slightly Scarlet (*co*). 1931: Finn and Hattie (*co*); Skippy (*co*). 1932: Million Dollar Legs (*co*); This Reckless Age (*+ di*). 1933: Alice in Wonderland (*co*). 1934: Manhattan Melodrama (*co*); Our Daily Bread (*di*); Forsaking All Others. 1935: I Live My Life.

Films as producer include: 1936: Three Godfathers; Fury. 1938: Mannequin; Three Comrades; The Shining Hour. 1940: Strange Cargo; The Philadelphia Story. 1942: Woman of the Year; Reunion in France. 1944: Keys of the Kingdom (*+ co-s*). 1958: I Want to Live (*pc*).

Films as director: 1946: Dragonwyck (*+ s*); Somewhere in the Night (*+ co-s*). 1947: The Late George Apley; The Ghost and Mrs Muir. 1948: Escape. 1949: A Letter to Three Wives (*+ s*); House of Strangers. 1950: No Way Out (*+ co-s*); All About Eve (*+ s*). 1951: People Will Talk (*+ s*). 1952: Five Fingers. 1953: Julius Caesar (*+ s*). 1954: The Barefoot Contessa (*+ p/s*). 1955: Guys and Dolls (*+ s*). 1958: The Quiet American (*+ p/s*). 1959: Suddenly Last Summer (*+ p*). 1963: Cleopatra (*+ co-s*). 1967: The Honey Pot (*+ co-p/s*). 1970: There Was a Crooked Man (*+ p*).

MANN, Anthony

(Emil or Anton Bundsmann; Anton Mann) Director. San Diego, California 1906–67 Berlin.

Minor capacities in theatre then actor at Triangle Theatre, Greenwich Village, New York. 1925–26: acted in 'The Dybbuk', 'The Little Clay Cart'. New York stage director: 'Thunder on the Left', 'Cherokee Night', 'The Big Blow', 'So Proudly We Hail'. Worked with David Belasco, Rouben Mamoulian, Chester Erskine, James Stewart. 1938: signed by Selznick as casting director and talent scout. Supervised screen tests for e.g. *The Adventures of Tom Sawyer, Intermezzo, Gone With the Wind, Rebecca*. 1939: to Paramount; assistant to e.g. Preston Sturges on *Sullivan's Travels*. 1942: directed first feature. 1942–47: films

mainly for RKO, Republic. 1947–50: 6 films photographed by John Alton. 1948: uncredited completion of *He Walked by Night*. 1949: co-wrote Richard Fleischer's *Follow Me Quietly* and completed it, uncredited. 1950: took over Fritz Lang's project *Winchester '73*. 1949–52: mainly MGM. 1951: uncredited, directed 'Fire of Rome' sequence in *Quo Vadis*. 1952–53: Universal. 1950–53: 5 films produced by Aaron Rosenberg; 1950–55: 8 films with James Stewart; 5 films photographed by William Daniels. 1957: began *Night Passage*, replaced by James Neilson. 1960: began *Spartacus*, replaced by Stanley Kubrick. Directed 3 films written or co-written by Borden Chase, 6 by Philip Yordan. From 1961: in Europe. Last 2 films British, released by Columbia. 1967: died of heart attack while shooting Berlin stage of *A Dandy in Aspic*; completed by Laurence Harvey, uncredited. Married Sarita Montiel, directed her in *Serenade* (1956).

Films as director: 1942: Dr Broadway; Moonlight in Havana. 1943: Nobody's Darling. 1944: My Best Gal; Strangers in the Night. 1945: The Great Flamarion; Two O'Clock Courage; Sing Your Way Home. 1946: Strange Impersonation; The Bamboo Blonde. 1947: Desperate (*+ co-st*); Railroaded; T-Men (*+ co-s, uc*). 1948: Raw Deal; He Walked by Night (*co-d, uc; co-d Alfred Werker*). 1949: Reign of Terror; Follow Me Quietly (*+ w-st; co-d, uc; co-d Richard Fleischer*); Border Incident; Side Street. 1950: Devil's Doorway; The Furies; Winchester '73. 1951: The Tall Target. 1952: Bend of the River – Where the River Bends. 1953: The Naked Spur; Thunder Bay; The Glenn Miller Story. 1954: The Far Country. 1955: Strategic Air Command; The Man from Laramie. 1956: The Last Frontier; Serenade. 1957: Men in War; Night Passage (*co-d, uc; co-d James Neilson*); The Tin Star. 1958: God's Little Acre (*+ co-p*); Man of the West. 1960: Spartacus (*uc; co-d Stanley Kubrick*); Cimarron. 1961: El Cid. 1964: The Fall of the Roman Empire. 1965: The Heroes of Telemark. 1967: A Dandy in Aspic (*+ p; co-d Laurence Harvey, uc*).

MANN, Daniel

Director. New York 1912–

Started as musician in resort hotels, then on tour in Canada as actor. Studied stage direction. World War II: in US Army, reaching sergeant; served in India and Burma. Directed stage and TV and taught drama. On Broadway directed 'Come Back Little Sheba', 'The Rose Tattoo', 'Paint Your Wagon'. Hired by Hal Wallis to direct first film.

Films as director: 1953: Come Back Little Sheba. 1954: About Mrs Leslie. 1955: The Rose Tattoo. 1956: I'll Cry Tomorrow; The Teahouse of the August Moon. 1958: Hot Spell. 1959: The Last Angry Man. 1960: The Mountain Road; Butterfield 8. 1961: Ada. 1962: Five Finger Exercise; Who's Got the Action? 1963: Who's Been Sleeping in My Bed? 1965: Judith; Our Man Flint. 1968: For Love of Ivy. 1969: A Dream of Kings. 1971: Willard.

MANN, Delbert

Director. Lawrence, Kansas 1920–

Vanderbilt and Yale Universities, then US Air Force (1942–45). 1947–49: directed Town Theatre of Columbia. South Carolina. 1949: assistant director on

Cyd Charisse in Silk Stockings. *directed by Rouben Mamoulian.*
El Cid. directed by Anthony Mann.
Jayne Mansfield in Will Success Spoil Rock Hunter?. *by Frank Tashlin.*

NBC-TV. 1949–55: directed for ABC-TV, working on drama programmes. Films mainly for United Artists and Universal. 1955: first film received Oscar for best direction.

Films as director: 1955: Marty. 1957: The Bachelor Party. 1958: Desire Under the Elms; Separate Tables. 1959: Middle of the Night. 1960: The Dark at the Top of the Stairs. 1961: Lover Come Back; The Outsider. 1962: That Touch of Mink. 1963: A Gathering of Eagles. 1964: Dear Heart; Quick Before It Melts (+ co-p). 1965: Mister Buddwing. 1967: Fitzwilly – Fitzwilly Strikes Back. 1968: The Pink Jungle. 1971: Jane Eyre: Kidnapped.

MANSFIELD, Jayne

Actress. Bryn Mawr, Pennsylvania 1934–67 near New Orleans, Louisiana.
Married at 16. Miss Photoflash 1952 and many other beauty titles. Pin-up photographs. Spotted during publicity junket for *Underwater*. 1955: first film as actress *Pete Kelly's Blues*. On Broadway in 'Will Success Spoil Rock Hunter?'. Nightclub performer. Husbands include muscleman Mickey Hargitay and Matt Cimber, who had directed them in 'Bus Stop' (1964). Killed in motor accident on the way to a TV engagement.

Films as actress include: 1956: The Girl Can't Help It. 1957: The Burglar; The Wayward Bus; Will Success Spoil Rock Hunter?; Kiss Them for Me. 1958: The Sheriff of Fractured Jaw. 1960: Too Hot to Handle. 1961: The George Raft Story. 1962: It Happened in Athens. 1967: Spree!.

MARAIS, Jean

(Jean Villain-Marais) Actor. Cherbourg, France 1913–
Brought into films by Marcel l'Herbier. 1937: on Paris stage in chorus of Jean Cocteau's 'Oedipe Roi' and 'Les Chevaliers de la Table Ronde'. Cocteau wrote 'Les Parents Terribles' for him and for Yvonne Bray; acted in it (1938). 1939–40: in French army. 1941: first major film role, in *Le Pavillon brûle*. During the Occupation, acted in *La Machine à écrire* and French classics. 1944: in LeClerc Division of US 3rd Army. Croix de Guerre. Later theatrical work includes: 'Les Parents Terribles', 'La Machine Infernale', 'Deux sur un balançoire', 'L'Aigle à deux têtes'. Comédie Française.

Films as actor include: 1942: Le Lit à colonne. 1943: L'Eternal Retour. 1944: Le Voyage sans espoir. 1946: La Belle et la bête; Les Chouans. 1947: Ruy Blas. 1948: L'Aigle à deux têtes; Les Parents Terribles. 1950: Orphee; Le Château de verre. 1952: La Voce del silenzio. 1956: Eléna et les hommes. 1957: Le Notti Bianchi. 1960: Austerlitz; Le Testament d'Orphée. 1961: Pontius Pilate. 1970: Peau d'âne.

MARCEAU, Marcel

Actor. Strasbourg, France 1923–
Mime artist. 1946: first appeared on Paris stage. 1947: formed Compagnie de Mime Marcel Marceau. Extensive tours and TV appearances. Short films show him and his company at work.

Films as actor: 1950: Mic-Mac. 1952: Il Cappotto –

The Overcoat. 1954: Pantomimes. 1955: Un Jardin Public. 1967: Barbarella.

MARCH, Fredric

(Fredric McIntyre Bickel) Actor. Racine, Wisconsin 1897–
University of Wisconsin. Banking, modelling, extra. Stage debut in 'Deburau'; to New York with it; acted there in Al Jolson's production 'Lei Aloha'. Stock in Dayton, Ohio. 1924: took lead in 'Melody Man'. European tour, then returned to stock, with Florence Eldridge: he married her in 1927. 1929: first film as actor *The Dummy*. To 1934: almost all films for Paramount. Then worked for numerous studios. Acted with his wife in *The Studio Murder Mystery* (1929), *Les Miserables* (1935), *Mary of Scotland* (1936). Returned to stage with her in 'Your Obedient Husband' (1939), 'Hope for a Harvest' (1941), 'The Skin of Our Teeth' (1943). USO. 1949: in England acted in *Christopher Columbus*. Also TV. Oscars as Best Actor for *Dr Jekyll and Mr Hyde* (1932) and *The Best Years of Our Lives* (1946).

Films as actor include: 1930: Paramount on Parade; Manslaughter; Laughter. 1931: The Night Angel; My Sin; The Royal Family of Broadway. 1932: Smilin' Through; The Sign of the Cross. 1933: Design for Living. 1934: Death Takes a Holiday; The Barretts of Wimpole Street; The Affairs of Cellini; We Live Again. 1935: Anna Karenina; The Dark Angel. 1936: Mary of Scotland; Anthony Adverse; The Road to Glory. 1937: A Star is Born; Nothing Sacred. 1938: The Buccaneer; There Goes My Heart; Trade Winds. 1940: Susan and God; Victory. 1941: So Ends Our Night; One Foot in Heaven. 1942: I Married a Witch. 1944: The Adventures of Mark Twain. 1948: Another Part of the Forest. 1951: It's a Big Country; Death of a Salesman. 1953: Man on a Tightrope. 1954: Executive Suite. 1955: The Desperate Hours; The Bridges at Toko-Ri. 1956: Alexander the Great; The Man in the Gray Flannel Suit. 1959: Middle of the Night. 1960: Inherit the Wind. 1963: I Sequestrati di Altona. 1964: Seven Days in May. 1967: Hombre.

MAREY, Étienne-Jules

Beaune, France 1830–1904 Paris, France
1864: director of a physiology laboratory. 1867: Professor of Natural History at Collège de France. Studied horse-gallop prior to the publication of Eadweard Muybridge's work in 1878. 1881: Muybridge's visit to France, together with invention of gold bromide-gelatinous plate, led him to use photography in his studies of movement. 1882: constructed fixed-plate chronophotograph camera to produce successive images of motion on one fixed plate; constructed *'fusil photographique'* using circular revolving photographic plate to obtain separate consecutive pictures, at rate of up to 12 per second. 1887: began experiments with paper film after arrival in France of Kodak rolls. 1888: presentation of camera using paper film moved by electric motor and regularly halted by electro-magnetic apparatus 15 times per second. 1889: with Georges Demeny developed celluloid film perforated to fit own camera gate. 1890: experimented with use of camera as projector; patented camera using celluloid film. By 1892: achieved up to 110 pictures per second; constructed his first projector, developed from camera.

Because of slowness in taking out patent for projector was beaten by others and his reputation ruined.

MARKER, Chris

Director and writer. Belleville, near Paris 1921–
Author of novel and a book on Jean Giraudoux. Editor of a series of books 'Petit Planète'. Also wrote and photographed a book on North Korea, 'Coréennes' (1959). 1957: wrote commentary for Alain Resnais' *Le Mystère de l'atelier 15*. Author of original commentary (much changed by director) for *L'Amerique Insolite* (1960) and commentaries for *A Valparaiso* (1963) and *Le Volcan Interdit* (1966). Contributed to and undertook final editing of *Loin du Vietnam* (1967). Writer of all his films and cinematographer on many. From 1968: all his films produced and distributed by SLON film collective. 1969: helped found Medvedkine group at Besançon; made *A bientôt j'espère* with them.

Films as director and writer: 1952: Olympia '52. 1953: Les Statues meurent aussi (ur; co-s; co-d Alain Resnais). 1955: Dimanche à Pékin. 1958: Lettre de Sibérie. 1956: Le Mystère de l'atelier 15 (co-d Alain Resnais). 1959: Les Astronautes (co-s; co-d Walerian Borowczyk). 1960: Description d'un combat. 1961: Cuba Si! 1963: Le Joli Mai; La Jetée. 1965: Le Mystère Koumiko. 1966: Si c'était quatre dromadaires. 1968: La Sixième Face du Pentagon. 1969: A bientôt j'espère. 1970: La Bataille des dix millions (co-d Valerie Magoux); Les Mots ont un sens.

MARKOPOULOS, Gregory J.

Director. Toledo, Ohio 1928–
1940: first 8 mm film. 1945–47: University of Southern California. 1947: first 16mm film *De Sang, de la volupté et de la mort*. 1950–51: in Paris. 1951–54: military service. 1954–58: in Greece; shooting of *Serenity* abandoned. 1966: appointed Visiting Associate Professor of Art at Institute of Chicago, with special reference to film; resigned in 1967. 1968: TV opera for Bavarian television. Writes, edits and photographs all his films. Books, 'Quest for Serenity' and 'Chaos Phaos I–IV'.

Films as director: 1940: A Christmas Carol. 1947: Du Sang, de la volupté et de la mort (in 3 parts). 1948: The Dead Ones (35 mm). 1950: Swain (+ w). 1951: Flowers of Asphalt; Arbres aux champignons (uf). 1952: Eldora. 1954–61: Serenity (uf). 1963: Twice a Man. 1965: The Death of Hemingway (35 mm). 1966: Galaxie; Through a Lens Brightly; Mark Turbyfill; Ming Green. 1967: Himself as Herself; Eros, O Basileus; The Illiac Passion (+ w); Bliss; Gammelion. 1968: The Mysteries. 1969: Political Portraits; Sorrows, Moment. 1970: The Olympian; Alph.

Films finished but not yet shown: 1967: The Divine Damnation. 1969: Index-Hans Richter. 1970: Genius. 1971: Doldertal 7; Hagiographia; 35 Boulevard General Koenig.

MARLEY, J. Peverell

Cinematographer. San Jose, California 1901–
Hollywood High School. Cinematographer with Famous Players-Lasky by early 1920s. From 1927: worked mainly for Pathé. From 1929: a number of films for MGM. 1934–43: mainly Fox. Then worked

mainly for Warners. 1956: additional photography for *The Ten Commandments*. Married Linda Darnell (1943–52, divorced).

Films as cinematographer include: 1923: The Ten Commandments (*co*). 1924: Feet of Clay. 1925: The Golden Bed; The Road to Yesterday. 1926: The Volga Boatman. 1927: The King of Kings. 1928: The Godless Girl. 1929: Dynamite. 1931: Wicked. 1933: Fast Workers; This Day and Age. 1934: The Mighty Barnum. 1935: Clive of India. 1936: Winterset. 1938: Alexander's Ragtime Band; In Old Chicago; Suez. 1939: The Three Musketeers. 1941: Swamp Water; Charley's Aunt; The Great American Broadcast (*co*). 1945: Pride of the Marines. 1946: Of Human Bondage; Night and Day (*co*). 1947: Life with Father; Night unto Night. 1950: Kiss Tomorrow Goodbye. 1952: The Greatest Show on Earth (*co*). 1953: The Charge at Feather River. 1954: Phantom of the Rue Morgue; Drum Beat. 1956: Serenade. 1957: The Spirit of St Louis (*co*). 1958: The Left Handed Gun. 1959: Westbound. 1961: Rachel Cade.

MARQUAND, Christian

Actor and director. Marseille 1927–

Arab-Spanish parentage. Began as stage actor at 17. Appeared in Paris and London. 1946: first film as actor *La Belle et la bête*. Continued to act for stage as well as films. 1962: began as director, supervised by Roger Vadim. 1967: convicted on drugs charge in London. Married Tina (née Aumont) daughter of Maria Montez and Jean-Pierre Aumont.

Films as actor include: 1947: Quai des orfèvres. 1952: Lucrezia Borgia. 1956: Et Dieu créa la femme. 1957: Sait-on jamais? 1958: Une Vie. 1961: The Longest Day.

Films as director: 1962: Les Grands Chemins – Of Flesh and Blood (+ *co-s*). 1968: Candy.

MARSH, Mae

Actress. Madrid, New Mexico 1895–68 Hermosa Beach, California

1912: extra in *The Old Actor*; Griffith contract. 1917: moved to Goldwyn. Also films in UK, Germany. 1925: retired to marry. 1931: returned in *Over the Hill*. 1960: directed by John Ford in TV series 'Wagon Train'. Book of verse, 'When They Ask My Name'.

Films as actress include: 1912: A Siren of Impulse; The Lesser Evil; Lena and the Geese; The New York Hat; Man's Genesis. 1913: Fate; The Battle at Elderbush Gulch; Judith of Bethulia. 1914: The Escape; Home Sweet Home; The Avenging Conscience. 1915: The Birth of a Nation. 1916: Intolerance *ep* The Mother and the Law. 1923: Paddy's the Next Best Thing; The White Rose. 1940: The Grapes of Wrath. 1945: A Tree Grows in Brooklyn. 1948: The Snake Pit. 1950: The Gunfighter. 1953: The Robe. 1956: While the City Sleeps; The Searchers. 1957: The Wings of Eagles; Julie. 1960: Sergeant Rutledge. 1963: Donovan's Reef.

MARSHALL, George

Director. Chicago 1891–

St John's Military Academy. Deerfield. Wisconsin and Chicago University. 1914: entered films as extra with Universal; later cameraman. 1917: military service in World War I. 1919: began as director with Pathé e.g. *The Adventures of Ruth* (1919–20) series; worked with Mack Sennett. 1920–22: features for Fox including *Prairie Trails* (1920) with Tom Mix, then Universal (1923). 1924: shorts for Fox. 1925: supervizing director of all Fox shorts units. From 1928: shorts for Pathé, Van Beuren, Warner. From 1932: directed sound features; also 2 Laurel and Hardy shorts, *Their First Mistake* (1932), *Towed in a Hole* (1933). Wrote story for Malcolm St Clair's *Olsen's Big Moment* (1933).

Sound features as director: 1932: Pack up your Troubles (*co-d Raymond McCarey*). 1934: Ever Since Eve; Wild Gold; She Learned about Sailors; 365 Days in Hollywood. 1935: Life Begins at Forty; $10 Raise; In Old Kentucky; Show Them No Mercy; Music is Magic. 1936: A Message to Garcia; The Crime of Doctor Forbes; Can This be Dixie? (+ *co-st*). 1937: Nancy Steele is Missing; Love under Fire. 1938: The Goldwyn Follies; Battle of Broadway; Hold that Co-Ed. 1939: You Can't Cheat an Honest Man; Destry Rides Again. 1940: The Ghost Breakers; When the Daltons Rode. 1941: Pot O' Gold; Texas. 1942: Valley of the Sun; The Forest Rangers; Star Spangled Rhythm. 1943: True to Life; Riding High. 1944: And the Angels Sing. 1945: Murder He Says; Incendiary Blonde. 1946: The Blue Dahlia; Monsieur Beaucaire. 1947: The Perils of Pauline; Variety Girl. 1948: Hazard; Tap Roots. 1949: My Friend Irma. 1950: Fancy Pants; Never a Dull Moment. 1951: A Millionaire for Christy. 1952: The Savage. 1953: Off Limits; Scared Stiff; Houdini; Money from Home. 1954: Red Garters; Duel in the Jungle; Destry. 1955: The Second Greatest Sex. 1956: Pillars of the Sky. 1957: The Guns of Fort Petticoat; Beyond Mombasa; The Sad Sack. 1958: The Sheepman; Imitation General. 1959: The Mating Game; It Started with a Kiss; The Gazebo. 1961: Cry for Happy. 1962: The Happy Thieves; How the West was Won *ep* The Railroad. 1963: Papa's Delicate Condition. 1964: Dark Purpose – L'Intrigo (*co-d Vittorio Sala*); Advance to the Rear – Company of Cowards? 1966: Boy, Did I Get a Wrong Number! 1967: Eight on the Lam.

MARSHALL, Herbert

Actor. London 1890–1966

1911: stage debut in 'The Adventures of Lady Ursula'. American and Canadian tours; acted on Broadway. Service in British Army. 1921: American and Canadian tours. 1927: first film as actor *Mumsie*. Theatrical work continued to 1939. To 1949: worked mainly for Paramount, MGM, RKO. Then for several companies including United Artists and Universal. Married actresses Edna Best (1928–40, divorced) and Boots Mallory (1958, widowed).

Films as actor include: 1930: Murder. 1931: Michael and Mary; Secrets of a Secretary. 1932: Trouble in Paradise; The Faithful Heart; Blonde Venus. 1933: Solitaire Man; I Was a Spy. 1934: Riptide; Four Frightened People; The Painted Veil; Outcast Lady. 1935: The Dark Angel; The Good Fairy; The Flame Within; Accent on Youth. 1936: A Woman Rebels; 'Til We Meet Again. 1937: Angel. 1938: Mad About Music. 1939: Zaza. 1940: Foreign Correspondent; A Bill of Divorcement; The Letter. 1941: The Little Foxes; When Ladies Meet. 1942: The Moon

Cuba Si!, *directed by Chris Marker.*
Gregory Markopoulos.

Francesco. Giullare Di Dio. *directed by Roberto Rossellini and photographed by Otello Martelli.*

and Sixpence. 1943: Young Ideas. 1944: Andy Hardy's Blonde Trouble. 1945: The Enchanted Cottage. 1946: Duel in the Sun; The Razor's Edge; Crack-Up. 1947: Ivy. 1948: The High Wall. 1949: The Secret Garden. 1950: The Underworld Story. 1951: Anne of the Indies. 1952: Angel Face. 1954: The Black Shield of Falworth. 1955: The Virgin Queen. 1958: Wicked As They Come; Stage Struck. 1960: A Fever in the Blood; Midnight Lace. 1963: The List of Adrian Messenger. 1965: The Third Day.

MARTELLI, Otello

Cinematographer. Rome 1902–
From 1918: camera assistant; cinematographer from 1921. 1950: began collaboration with Federico Fellini.

Films as cinematographer include: 1934: Vecchia Guardia. 1946: Paisà. 1947: Caccia Tragica. 1948: Amore; Riso Amaro. 1949: Stromboli. 1950: Luci di varietà; Francesco, Giullare di Dio. 1951: Anna. 1952: Roma ore undici. 1953: Un Marito per Anna Zaccheo; I Vitelloni (co). 1954: La Strada. 1955: La Donna del fiume; Il Bidone. 1956: La Fortuna di essere donna. 1957: Guendalina. 1958: La Diga sul Pacifico; La Loi. 1959: La Dolce Vita; La Ragazza in vetrina. 1962: Boccaccio '70 ep Le Tentazioni del Dottor Antioni. 1963: Il Maestro di Vigevano; Cyrano et d'Artagnan.

MARTIN, Dean

(Dino Crocetti) Actor. Steubenville, Ohio 1917–
Boxer, croupier, singer. Radio, TV, cabaret with Jerry Lewis. 16 films with him, beginning with My Friend Irma (1949). 1957: first solo film as actor Ten Thousand Bedrooms. Also own TV series and cabaret. Married former model Jeanne Biegger (1949).

Films as actor with Jerry Lewis include: 1953: Scared Stiff; The Caddy; Money From Home. 1954: Living It Up; Three Ring Circus. 1955: Artists and Models. 1956: Pardners; Hollywood or Bust.

Films as actor include: 1958: The Young Lions; Some Came Running. 1959: Rio Bravo; Career; Who Was That Lady?; Bells are Ringing; Ocean's 11. 1961: Ada; All in a Night's Work; Sergeants 3. 1962: Who's Got the Action? 1963: Toys in the Attic; Who's Been Sleeping in My Bed?; 4 for Texas. 1964: What a Way to Go; Kiss Me, Stupid; Robin and the Seven Hoods. 1965: The Sons of Katie Elder. 1966: The Silencers; Texas Across the River. 1967: The Ambushers. 1968: Bandolero!; The Wrecking Crew. 1971: Something Big.

MARTINELLI, Elsa

Actress. Trastavere, Italy 1935–
Daughter of poor government employee. At age of 16 started work in bar; spotted and became model. Film work, then launched by Kirk Douglas in The Indian Fighter (1955).

Films as actress include: 1956: Donatella. 1957: Manuela. 1959: Costa Azzura; La Notte Brava. 1960: Un Amore a Roma; Et Mourir de plaisir. 1963: Hatari!; Rampage; Le Procès. 1964: La Fabuleuse Aventure de Marco Polo. 1965: La Decima Vittima. 1967: Le Plus Vieux Metier du monde ep Nuits Romaines; Sept Fois Femme. 1969: Les Chemins de Khatmandou.

MARTOGLIO, Nino

Director. Catania, Sicily 1870–1921 Catania, Sicily
To 1913: theatrical work using 19th-century Sicilian dialect. 1913: began as scriptwriter with Cines de Roma; first film as director. 1915: with Roberto Damesi founded company Morgana Film; abandoned films for playwriting and comedy; company collapsed.

Films as director: 1913: Il Romanza. 1914: Capitan Blanco; Sperduti nel buio, 1915: Teresa Raquin.

MARTON, Andrew

Director. Budapest, Hungary 1904–
1922: editor with Sascha Films and Vita Films in Vienna. 1923: to Hollywood with Ernst Lubitsch. 1926: returned to Europe as chief editor to Tobis Films, Berlin. 1928: edited Lubitsch's The Student Prince in Old Heidelberg. 1931: first film as director, in collaboration, in Germany; to Budapest. 1936–37: 3 films in Britain. 1938: to Hollywood. 1944–60: worked mainly for MGM. Then for various companies. Often 2nd-unit director. TV work includes 'Daktari', 'Man and the Challenge', 'Cowboy in Africa'.

Films as director: 1931: Die Nacht ohne pause (co-d Fritz Wenzler); Hirsekorn. 1933: Nordpol-ahoi! 1935: Miss Provident. 1936: The Spy in White – The Secret of Stamboul; Wolf's Clothing. 1937: School for Husbands. 1940: A Little Bit of Heaven. 1944: Gentle Annie. 1946: Gallant Bess. 1950: King Solomon's Mines (co-d Compton Bennett). 1951: Storm Over Tibet. 1952: The Wild North; The Devil Makes Three. 1954: Gypsy Colt; Prisoner of War; Men of the Fighting Lady. 1955: Green Fire. 1956: Seven Wonders of the World (co-d 4 others). 1958: Underwater Warrior. 1962: It Happened in Athens; The Longest Day (co-d 3 others). 1964: The Thin Red Line. 1965: Clarence the Cross-Eyed Lion; Crack in the World; Birds Do It!; El Valle de los caidos. 1966: Around the World Under the Sea (+p). 1967: Africa-Texas Style (+p).

Films as 2nd-unit director include: 1951: The Red Badge of Courage. 1957: A Farewell to Arms. 1959: Ben-Hur (co). 1963: Fifty-Five Days at Peking; Cleopatra (co). 1964: The Fall of the Roman Empire (co). 1970: Catch-22 (co).

MARVIN, Lee

Actor. New York 1924–
Expelled from several schools; enlisted in US Marine Corps while still a student (1943). Seriously wounded on service in South Pacific. Started to act while recovering. First professional appearance, off Broadway. With American Theater Wing on GI Bill of Rights. On Broadway in 'Billy Budd' and in touring companies e.g. of 'A Streetcar Named Desire'. In films from 1951. Many TV shows (over 250) including 'M Squad' and 'Lee Marvin Presents'. Oscar as Best Actor for Cat Ballou (1965).

Films as actor include: 1951: You're in the Navy Now. 1952: The Duel at Silver Creek; Diplomatic Courier; Eight Iron Men; Down Among the Sheltering Palms. 1953: The Big Heat; Seminole; The Stranger Wore a Gun; Gun Fury; The Wild One. 1954: The Caine Mutiny: The Raid: Bad Day at Black Rock. 1955:

Violent Saturday; A Life in the Balance; I Died a Thousand Times; Not as a Stranger; Pete Kelly's Blues. 1956: Seven Men from Now; Attack!; Pillars of the Sky. 1957: Raintree County. 1961: The Comancheros. 1962: The Man Who Shot Liberty Valance. 1963: Donovan's Reef. 1964: The Killers. 1965: Ship of Fools; Cat Ballou. 1966: The Professionals. 1967: The Dirty Dozen; Point Blank; Sergeant Ryker. 1969: Paint Your Wagon. 1970: Monte Walsh.

MARX Brothers

Actors. Harpo (Adolph Arthur) New York 1888–1964 Hollywood; Groucho (Julius Henry) New York 1890– ; Chico (Leonard) New York 1887–1961 Hollywood; Zeppo (Herbert) New York 1900–
Groucho singer on stage at 14; lead in touring show 'The Man of Our Choice'. Brother Gummo (Milton) joined the act, then Harpo and an extra member, as 'The 4 Nightingales'. Chico worked for music publisher, then joined the act, followed by mother and sister. Vaudeville in Brooklyn, Newark, Chicago, San Francisco. Act managed by grandmother, then father joined act and managed it till after MGM contract. 1924: act turned into Broadway play 'I'll Say She Is'. 1926: first film Humorisk unfinished. 1929: The Cocoanuts followed stage routines almost exactly, based on stage show of same name. 1929–33: worked for Paramount; after Animal Crackers (1930) contract for 5 films. 1935–41: all films for MGM except for Room Service (1938) for RKO. 1950: Love Happy, from a story by Harpo. Groucho and Harpo appeared alone in several films. Later films for United Artists. Groucho co-scripted The King and the Chorus-Girl (1937) with Norman Krasna; did TV quiz show 'You Bet Your Life' for 14 years; wrote several books: 'The Groucho Letters', 'You Bet Your Life', 'Memoirs of a Mangy Lover'. Harpo wrote book 'Harpo Speaks'. 1960: Harpo, Chico, Groucho directed by Mitchell Leisen in The Incredible Jewel Robbery, on TV.

Harpo, Groucho, Chico, Zeppo: films as actors: 1929: The Cocoanuts. 1930: Animal Crackers. 1931: Monkey Business. 1932: Horse Feathers. 1933: Duck Soup.

Harpo, Groucho, Chico: films as actors: 1935: A Night at the Opera. 1937: A Day at the Races. 1938: Room Service. 1939: At the Circus. 1940: Go West. 1941: The Big Store. 1946: A Night in Casablanca. 1950: Love Happy. 1957: The Story of Mankind.

Harpo alone: films as actor: 1925: Too Many Kisses. 1943: Stage Door Canteen.

Groucho alone: films as actor: 1947: Copacabana. 1951: Mr Music; Double Dynamite. 1952: A Girl in Every Port. 1957; Will Success Spoil Rock Hunter? 1968: Skidoo.

MASELLI, Francesco

Director. Rome 1930–
Entered Centro Sperimentale di Cinematografia at 16. 1949: assistant director to Luigi Chiarini (Patto col diavolo), Michelangelo Antonioni (L'Amorosa Menzogna); began as documentary director. Also assistant to Antonioni, and writer in collaboration, on Cronaca di un amore (1950), La Signora senza camelie (1953). Assistant to Roberto Rossellini on

Anna Magnani episode of *Siamo donne* (1953). 1955: first feature as director. 1961: directed 'Il Trovatore' at the Teatro al Fenice, Venice.

Films as director include: 1949: Bagnaia paese italico; Tibet Proibito. 1950: Finestre. 1951: Sport Minore; Bambini; Zona Pericolosa; Stracciaroli. 1952: Ombrellai; Stracciaroli; I Fiori. 1953: Città che dorme; Amore in città *ep* La Storia di Caterina; Festa dei morti in Sicilia; Uno Spettacolo di pupi. 1954: Cantamaggio a Cervarezza. 1955: Gli Sbandati (+ *co-st/co-s*). 1956: La Donna del giorno (+ *co-s*); Bambini al cinema. 1959: Adolescenza. 1960: I Delfini (+ *co-st/co-s*); La Suola Romana. 1961: Le Italiane e l'amore – Latin Lovers *ep* Le Adolescenti – Adolescents. 1963: Gli Indifferenti – Time of Indifference. 1966: Fai in fretta ad uccidermi . . . ho freddo! – Kill Me Quick, I'm Cold (+ *co-s*). 1968: Una Coppia Tranquilla – A Fine Pair (+ *co-s*).

MASINA, Giulietta

Actress. Bologna, Italy 1920–
University of Rome. Studied acting in Rome. 1943: married Federico Fellini. Radio drama. 1946: first film. Directed by her husband in several films. Also TV.

Films as actress include: 1950: Luci del varietà. 1952: Lo Sceicco Bianco. 1954: La Strada. 1955: Il Bidone. 1957: Le Notti di Cabiria. 1958: Fortunella. 1960: Das kunstseiderne Mädchen. 1965: Giulietta degli spiriti. 1966: Scusi, lei e' favorevole o contrario? 1969: The Madwoman of Chaillot.

MASON, James

Actor. Huddersfield, Yorkshire 1909–
Cambridge University. 1931: toured in 'The Rascal'. 1932–33: touring and repertory; Old Vic, with Charles Laughton, Flora Robson, Roger Livesey. 1935: first film as actor *Late Extra*. 1936: with Pamela Kellino in *Troubled Waters*. Returned to stage in 'Pride and Prejudice'. With Pamela Kellino wrote play 'Flying Blind'; acted on stage with her. 1941: married her; they wrote and acted in 'I Met a Murderer'. ENSA. Directed and acted in 'Jupiter Laughs'. 1947: in 'Bathsheba' with wife in title role. Own company. 1956: produced and acted in *Bigger Than Life*. 1964: divorced. Duaghter is actress Portland Mason.

Films as actor include: 1936: The Spy in White. 1937: The High Command; Fire Over England. 1942: Thunder Rock; Hatter's Castle. 1943: The Bells Go Down; The Man in Grey. 1944: Fanny By Gaslight. 1945: The Seventh Veil; The Wicked Lady. 1947: Odd Man Out. 1949: East Side, West Side; Madame Bovary; The Reckless Moment. 1950: One Way Street. 1951: Pandora and the Flying Dutchman; The Desert Fox. 1952: Face to Face; Five Fingers; The Prisoner of Zenda. 1953: The Story of Three Loves *ep* The Jealous Lover; Botany Bay; The Desert Rats; Julius Caesar; The Man Between. 1954: Prince Valiant; 20,000 Leagues Under the Sea; A Star is Born. 1957: Island in the Sun. 1958: Cry Terror; The Decks Ran Red. 1959: North By Northwest; Journey to the Centre of the Earth. 1960: The Trials of Oscar Wilde. 1961: Escape from Zahrain. 1962: Hero's Island; Finche dura la tempestà; Lolita. 1964: The Fall of the Roman Empire: The Pumpkin Eater. 1965: Lord Jim. 1966:

The Deadly Affair; The Blue Max. 1968: Duffy. 1969: Mayerling. 1971: De la part des copains; Kill.

MASTROIANNI, Marcello

Actor. Frosinone, Italy 1924–
Studied acting at Centro Teatro, Rome University. From 1948: many stage appearances under direction of Luchino Visconti, including plays by Shakespeare, Tennessee Williams, Arthur Miller, Chekhov. In films from 1947. From early 1950s worked mainly in films. 1959: established international reputation in *La Dolce Vita*. Also TV.

Films as actor include: 1947: I Miserabili. 1950: Domenica d'agosto. 1951: Parigi è sempre Parigi. 1952: Le Ragazze di piazza di Spagna. 1954: Tempi Nostri; Cronache di poveri amanti; Giorni d'amore. 1956: Il Bigamo. 1957: Padre e figli; Le Notti Bianche. 1958: La Loi; I Soliti Ignoti; Racconti d'estate. 1959: La Dolce Vita. 1960: Adua e le compagne; Il Bel-l'Antonio. 1961: La Notte; L'Assassino; Divorzio al-l'Italiana. 1962: Vie privée; Cronaca Familiare. 1963: Otto e mezzo; I Compagni; Ieri, oggi, domani; Matrimonio all'Italiano; Casanova 70. 1965: La Decima Vittima. 1967: Lo Straniero. 1969: Gli Amanti. 1970: Leo the Last; I Girasoli. 1971: La Moglie del prete.

MATÉ, Rudolph

Cinematographer and director. Cracow, Poland 1898–1964 Hollywood
Studied art at Budapest University. 1919: on graduation joined Alexander Korda as camera assistant; after 3 months was first cameraman. Moved from Budapest to Vienna then to Berlin. 2nd-unit work for Erich Pommer. 1923: photographed material to lengthen *Mikäel* (produced by Pommer). 1928: established in Paris, photographed *La Passion de Jeanne d'Arc*. 1931: after shooting *Vampyr* in France, worked in England, Italy, Spain, Yugoslavia and Poland. 1934: Hollywood. 1947: began directing. 1948: produced *The Return of October*.

Films as cinematographer include: 1928: La Passion de Jeanne d'Arc. 1932: Vampyr ou l'Etrange Aventure de Allan Grey. 1933: Liliom (*co*). 1934: Le Dernier Milliardaire (*co*). 1936: Professional Soldier; Dodsworth; Come and Get It! (*co*); Our Relations. 1937: Stella Dallas. 1938: Trade Winds. 1939: Love Affair. 1940: Foreign Correspondent; My Favorite Wife. 1942: To Be or Not To Be; The Pride of the Yankees. 1943: Sahara. 1944: Cover Girl (*co*). 1946: Gilda.

Films as director include: 1947: It Had to Be You (+ *co-c*; *co-d Don Hartman*). 1949: The Dark Past; D.O.A. 1950: No Sad Songs For Me; Branded; Union Station. 1951: When Worlds Collide; The Prince Who Was a Thief. 1952: The Green Glove; Paula; Sally and Saint Anne. 1953: The Mississippi Gambler; Second Chance; Forbidden. 1954: The Siege at Red River; The Black Shield of Falworth. 1955: The Violent Men – Rough Company; The Far Horizon. 1956: The Rawhide Years; Miracle in the Rain; Port Afrique. 1957: Three Violent People. 1958: The Deep Six. 1959: For the First Time. 1960: The Immaculate Road; Revak, lo schiavo di Cartagine – Revak the Rebel – The Barbarians. 1962: The 300 Spartans (+ *co-p*). 1963: Seven Seas to Calais – Il Re dei sette mari: Aliki (+ *co-p*).

Lee Marvin in The Dirty Dozen, *directed by Robert Aldrich.*
Claudia Cardinale in I Delfini, *directed by Francesco Maselli.*
Barbara Stanwyck and Edward G. Robinson in The Violent Men, *directed by Rudolph Maté.*

MATHESON, Richard

Writer. 1926–
At 7 was Aunt Jean's Column in Sunday edition of Brooklyn Eagle. World War II: US Army. After war moved to Los Angeles. Author of many novels, including 'Someone is Bleeding', 'Fury on Sunday', 'The Incredible Shrinking Man', 'I am Legend', 'A Stir of Echoes'. 1957: first film as writer *The Incredible Shrinking Man*. TV work includes 'Twilight Zone'.

Films as writer include: 1957: The Incredible Shrinking Man. 1959: The Beat Generation (*co*). 1960: The Fall of the House of Usher. 1961: The Pit and the Pendulum. 1962: Tales of Terror; The Raven. 1963: Comedy of Terrors (+ *as-p*). 1968: The Devil Rides Out. 1969: De Sade.

MATHIS, June

Writer. Leadville, Colorado 1892–1927 New York
Theatrical family. Began in theatre and music hall. 1918: engaged by Edwin Carewe as writer at Metro. 1919: promoted to head of script department. Adapted novel for film, *The Four Horsemen of the Apocalypse* (1921) and negotiated for Rex Ingram as its director and Rudolph Valentino as its star. 1922: to Famous Players–Lasky with Valentino to work on *Blood and Sand*. 1923: Metro gave her job of reducing and rearranging 18 reel version of *Greed* to 10 reel version finally released. Collaborated as writer for MGM on uncompleted version of *Ben-Hur* begun in Italy, as well as final version. From 1926: also scripted and occasionally produced for First National.

Films as writer include: 1918: Eye for Eye (*co-ad*). 1919: The Brat. 1920: Hearts are Trumps. 1921: Camille (+ *ad*); The Conquering Power (*ad*). 1922: Turn to the Right (*co*); Wild Oranges (*co*). 1927: The Magic Flame (*co*).

MATRAS, Christian

Cinematographer. Valence, France 1903–
Started in films as newsreel cameraman after World War I; later on documentaries. 1926: directed and photographed short *De Babord à Tribord* shot during a voyage on cruiser 'Jeanne d'Arc'. Then features.

Films as cinematographer include: 1937: La Grande Illusion. 1938: Paradis Perdu; Entrée des artistes. 1939: Le Duel; La Fin du jour. 1942: Pontcarral, Colonel d'empire. 1944: Le Voyageur sans bagage. 1945: Boule de suif. 1947: Les Jeux sont faits. 1948: L'Aigle à deux têtes. 1949: Souvenirs Perdus. 1950: La Ronde; La Valse de Paris. 1952: Fanfan La Tulipe. 1953: Madame De . . . 1955: Lola Montès; Les Carnets du Major Thompson (*co*). 1956: Les Aventures de Till Espiègle; Oeil pour oeil. 1957: Les Espions. 1958: Montparnasse 19. 1961: Paris Blues. 1962: Thérèse Desqueyroux. 1964: Cartouche. 1967: Sept Fois Femme. 1968: Les Oiseaux vont mourir au Pérou. 1970: Le Bal du comte d'Orgel. 1971: Variétés.

MATTHAU, Walter

Actor. New York 1923–
On stage at 4 in religious play at a New York City settlement. Filing clerk: boxing instructor: basketball coach; radio operator. 1942–45: with USAAF in Europe; 6 battle stars. 1946–47: studied with Erwin Piscator at Dramatic Workshop of New School for Social Research. On Broadway from 1948. Plays include 'Once More with Feeling' (1958) and 'The Odd Couple' (1965). First film 1955. Directed and acted in *Gangster Story* (1961).

Films as actor include: 1955: The Kentuckian; The Indian Fighter. 1956: Bigger Than Life. 1957: A Face in the Crowd. 1958: King Creole. 1960: Strangers When We Meet. 1962: Lonely Are the Brave; Who's Got the Action?. 1963: Charade; Island of Love; Fail Safe; Goodbye Charlie. 1964: Ensign Pulver. 1965: Mirage. 1966: The Fortune Cookie. 1967: Guide for the Married Man. 1968: Candy. 1969: Hello, Dolly!; Cactus Flower. 1971: Kotch.

MATTSSON, Arne

Director. Uppsala, Sweden 1919–
1941: assistant to Per Lindberg. 1942: first short as director while in Swedish army. 1943–44: script writer. 1944–47: became director for Lux. 1947–50: worked for Svensk Filmindustri. 1950–56: Nordisk Tonefilm. 1956–61: Sandrews. From 1961: freelance. Also worked in Argentina, Ireland, Spain.

Films as director from 1944: 1944: Och alla dessa kvinnor – And All These Women. 1945: Maria på kvarngården – Marie in the Windmill; Sussie; I som här inträdden – You Who Are About to Enter. 1946: Rötägg – Bad Eggs; Peggy på vift – Peggy on a Spree. 1947: Pappa sökes – Father Wanted; Det kom en gäst – A Guest Came (+ *co-s*); Rallare – The Railway Workers (+ *co-s*); Farlig Vår – Dangerous Spring. 1949: Kvinna i vitt – Woman in White. 1950: Nar kärleken kom till byn – When Love Comes to the Village (+ *s*); Kastrull resan – Saucepan Journey; Kyssen på kryssen – The Kiss on the Cruise (+ *co-s*). 1951: Bärande Hav – Rolling Sea; Hon dansade en somnar – One Summer of Happiness. 1952: Hård Klang – Dull Clang; For min heta ungdoms skull – Because of My Hot Youth. 1953: Kärlekens Bröd – The Bread of Love. 1954: Storm över Tjurö (+ *s*); Förtrollad Vandring – Enchanted Walk; Salka Valka. 1955: Männen i morker – Men in Darkness; Hemsöborna – The People of Hensö. 1956: Litet bo – A Little Place of One's Own; Flickan i frack – Girl in a Dress-coat. 1957: Livets Vår – Spring of Life; Ingen morgandag – No Tomorrow. 1958: Damen i svart – Woman in Black; Körkarlen – Phantom Carriage; Det kom tva män – There Came Two Men; Mannekäng i Rött – Mannequin in Red. 1959: Ryttare i blått – Rider in Blue; Får jag låna din fru – May I Borrow Your Wife? 1960: När mörkret faller – When Darkness Falls; Sommar och syndare – Summer and Sinners. 1961: Ljuvlig är sommernatten – The Summer Night is Sweet. 1962: Biljett till paradiset – Ticket to Paradise; Vita frun – Lady in White; Vaxdockan – The Doll. 1963: Den Gula Bilen – The Yellow Car; Det ar hos mig han har varit – Yes, He's Been With Me. 1964: Blåjackor – Boys in Blue. 1965: Här kommer bärsärkarna – Two Vikings; Morianerna – Morianna (+ *co-s*). 1966: Nattmara – Nightmare (+ *co-s*); Yngsjömordet – Woman of Darkness. 1967: Mordaren – En Helt vanlig person – The Murderer – An Ordinary Person. 1969: Bamse – The Teddy Bear; Anna och Eva – Ann and Eve.

MATURE, Victor

Actor. Louisville, Kentucky 1916–
Drama training at Pasadena Playhouse. 1936: stage debut in 'The Paths of Glory'. First leading part in 'Autumn Crocus'. 1939: first film as actor *The Housekeeper's Daughter* for United Artists. Hal Roach contract, shared with RKO, then Paramount. To 1954: films mainly for RKO and Fox. 1941: on Broadway in 'Lady in the Dark' with Gertrude Lawrence. World War II: service in US Coast Guard. Later films mainly for Columbia and United Artists. 4 wives include actress Frances Evans (divorced 1940).

Films as actor include: 1940: One Million BC; No, No, Nanette. 1941: Shanghai Gesture. 1942: Footlight Serenade. 1946: My Darling Clementine. 1947: Moss Rose; Kiss of Death. 1948: Cry of the City. 1949: Easy Living; Red, Hot and Blue; Samson and Delilah. 1950: Wabash Avenue. 1951: Gambling House. 1952: Something for the Birds; The Las Vegas Story; Million Dollar Mermaid. 1953: Affair with a Stranger; The Robe. 1954: Demetrius and the Gladiators; The Egyptian; Betrayed. 1955: Violent Saturday. 1956: The Last Frontier; Safari; Zarak. 1957: The Long Haul; No Time to Die. 1958: China Doll; Timbuktu. 1959: The Big Circus (+ *co-pc*); Annibale. 1965: Caccia alla volpe.

MAY, Joe

(Joseph Mandel) Director and writer. Vienna 1880–1954 Hollywood
University of Berlin. Owner of textile firm; car salesman. Directed operettas in Hamburg. Entered films in 1911, for Continental. Collaboration with Ernst Reicher resulted in 'Stuart Webbs' detective series (1914). Several films written by Fritz Lang, including *Die Hochzeit im Excentricclub* (1917) and *Das Indische Grabmal* (1921). Several films with Paul Leni as art director. Directed his wife Mia in several films including *Veritas vincit* (1919), *Das Indische Grabmal* (1921), *Tragödie der Liebe* (1923). Own production company. 1919: produced and co-wrote Leni's *Platonische Ehe*. 1921: cost of *Das Indische Grabmal* was 20 million marks. 1931–33: in France. 1934: returned to Germany. From 1934: in USA. Scripted e.g. *The Invisible Woman* (1940), in collaboration, and co-wrote story of *Uncertain Glory* (1944). American films mainly for Universal.

Films as director: 1912: In der Tiefe des Schachtes (+ *s*); Vorgluten des Balkanbrandes (+ *s*). 1913: Ein Ausgestossener (*in 2 parts*); Heimat und Fremde (+ *s*); Verschleierte Bild von gross Kleindorf; Die Unheilbringende Perle (+ *s*); Entsagungen. 1914: Die geheimnisse Villa; Der Mann im Keller; Der Spuk im Hause des Professors; Das Panzergewölbe. 1915: Das Gesetz der Mine (+ *p/s*); Charly, der Wunderaffe (+ *s*); Sein schwierigster Fall (+ *p/co-s*); Der Geheimskretär (+ *p/co-s*). 1916: Die Gespensteruhr (+ *p/co-s*); Die Sünde der Helga Arndt (+ *p/co-s*); Nebel und Sonne (+ *p/s*); Ein blatt Papier (+ *p/co--s*); Die Tat der Gräfin Worms – Ein einsam Grab (+ *p/s*; *co-d Karl Gerhardt*); Wie Ich Detektiv wurde (+ *p/s*); Das rätselhafte Inserat (+ *p/s*; *co-d Karl Gerhardt*). 1917: Das Geheimnis der leeren Wasserflasche (+ *p*); Des Vaters letzter Wille (+ *p*); Die Silhouette des Teufels (+ *p*); Der Onyxknopf (+ *p*); Hilde Warren und der Tod (+ *p*); Der shwarze Chauffeur (+ *p/s*); Krähen Fliegen um den Turm (+ *p/co-s*): Die Hochzeit im Excentricclub (+p); Die Liebe der Hetty Raymond (+p); Ein Lichstrahl im Dunkel (+p); Das Klima von Vancourt (+p). 1918: Sein bester Freund (+p); Wogen des Schicksals (+p/s); Opfer (+p/s); Die Kaukasierin (+p/s; co-d Jens W. Krafft); Die Bettelgräfin (+p/co-s; co-d Bruno Ziener); Ihr grosses Geheimnis (+p/s). 1919: Veritas vincit (in 3 parts; +p/co-st); Fraulein Zahnarzt (+p/co-s). 1919–20: Die Herrin der Welt (in 8 parts; +p/co-s). 1920: Die Schuld der Lavinia Morland (+p/co-s); Legende von der heiligen Simplicia (+p). 1921: Das Indische Grabmal – Above All Law (in 2 parts; +p). 1923: Tragödie der Liebe (in 4 parts; +p). 1925: Der Farmer aus Texas (+p/co-s). 1926: Dagfin (+p/co-s). 1928: Heimkehr – Homecoming (+p). 1929: Asphalt (+p). 1931: Ihre Majestät, die Liebe (+p); . . . Und Das ist die Hauptsache (+p); Paris-Mediterranée – Into the Blue. 1932: Le Chemin de bonheur. 1933: Voyages de noces; Tout pour l'amour; Le Dactylo se marie; Ein Lied für Dich (+p). 1934: Music in the Air. 1937: Confession. 1939: Society Smugglers; The House of Fear. 1940: The Invisible Man Returns (+ co-st); The House of the Seven Gables; You're Not So Tough. 1941: Hit the Road. 1944: Johnny Doesn't Live Here.

MAYER, Carl

Writer. Graz, Austria 1894–1944 London
Son of speculator who committed suicide; supported family from childhood, working in theatre and as painter, travelling extensively. From 1919: collaborated on scripts, e.g. Das Kabinett des Dr Caligari (1919). 1927: refusing offers to go to Hollywood, wrote script in Europe for F. W. Murnau's first American film, Sunrise; supplied Walter Ruttman with idea for Berlin, die Sinfonie der gross Stadt. 1932: to London; occasionally consultant, on e.g. Pygmalion (1935) and World of Plenty (1943). In last years adviser for Two Cities and Gabriel Pascal, and consultant on films produced by Paul Rotha for Ministry of Information. Wrote scripts in UK, unfilmed.

Films as writer include: 1919: Das Kabinett des Dr Caligari (co). 1920: Genuine; Der Gang in die Nacht. 1921: Der Bucklige und die Tanzerin; Schloss Vogelod; Hintertreppe. 1924: Der letzte Mann. 1925: Tartuffe. 1927: Sunrise. 1928: Four Devils (co). 1931: Ariane.

MAYER, Louis B.

Studio head. Minsk, Russia 1885–1957 Hollywood
Emigrated to Canada with parents and began working in father's scrap metal business as child, then set up own junk business. 1907: bought cinema in Haverill, Massachusetts, thereafter building up chain of cinemas and theatres. 1914: bought distribution rights of D. W. Griffith's The Birth of a Nation. By 1916: had gone into film production. 1918: set up film studio in Brooklyn then Los Angeles. 1924: merger with Marcus Loew's Metro company and Samuel Goldwyn's company; became MGM's production chief with Irving Thalberg as his assistant. 1927: founded Academy of Motion Picture Arts and Sciences of which he was president (1931–36). 1951: clashed with heads of MGM parent company, Loew's Inc; resigned from board. 1951–54: adviser to Cinerama Corporation. Twice married; 2 daughters by first marriage; married William Goetz and David O. Selznick. Academy Award for distinguished service to the motion picture industry (1950).

MAYES, Wendell

Writer. Carruthersville, Missouri 1918–
Several colleges, but never graduated. 1957: first screenplay in collaboration.

Films as writer include: 1957: The Spirit of St Louis (co); The Enemy Below. 1958: From Hell to Texas (co); The Hunters. 1959: The Hanging Tree (co); Anatomy of a Murder. 1962: Advise and Consent. 1964: In Harm's Way. 1965: Van Ryan's Express (co). 1967: Hotel (+p). 1969: The Stalking Moon (ad).

MAYO, Archie L.

Director. New York 1891–1968 Guadalajara, Mexico
Theatrical work, then to Hollywood. 1917–26: began as gagman, then wrote and directed short comedies, including Christie Comedies. 1926–27: worked for MGM and some smaller companies. 1927–37: all films for Warners, except Vengeance (1930) for Columbia and Night After Night (1932) for Paramount. 1938–40: films released by Goldwyn, United Artists, Universal. 1940–44: all films for Fox. 1941–42: replaced Fritz Lang on Confirm or Deny and Moontide. 1946: last 2 films released by United Artists; after Angel on My Shoulder retired.

Features as director: 1926: Money Talks; Unknown Treasures; Christine of the Big Tops. 1927: Johnny Get Your Hair Cut (co-d B. Reaves Eason); Quarantined Rivals; Dearie; Slightly Used; The College Widow. 1928: Beware of Married Men; Crimson City; State Street Sadie; On Trial. 1929: My Man; Sonny Boy; The Sap; Is Everybody Happy?; The Sacred Flame. 1930: Vengeance; Wide Open; Courage; Oh Sailor Behave; The Doorway to Hell. 1931: Illicit; Svengali; Bought. 1932: Under 18; The Expert; Two Against the World; Night After Night. 1933: The Life of Jimmy Dolan; Mayor of Hell; Ever in My Heart; Convention City. 1934: Gambling Lady; Desirable; The Man With Two Faces. 1935: Go Into Your Dance – Casino de Paris; Bordertown; The Case of Lucky Legs. 1936: The Petrified Forest; I Married a Doctor; Give Me Your Heart; Black Legion. 1937: Call it a Day; It's Love I'm After. 1938: The Adventures of Marco Polo; Youth Takes a Fling. 1939: They Shall Have Music. 1940: The House Across the Bay; Four Sons. 1941: The Great American Broadcast; Charley's Aunt; Confirm or Deny (co-d Fritz Lang, uc). 1942: Moontide (co-d Fritz Lang, uc); Orchestra Wives. 1943: Crash Dive. 1944: Sweet and Low Down. 1946: A Night in Casablanca; Angel on My Shoulder.

MAYO, Virginia

(Virginia Jones) Actress. St Louis, Missouri 1920–
Studied at aunt's drama school in St Louis. Dancer in vaudeville. On Broadway in 'Banjo Eyes' with Eddie Cantor, with the show to Billy Rose's Diamond Horseshoe. Spotted by Sam Goldwyn. 1944: first major film role The Princess and the Pirate. 1945–48: 4 films with Danny Kaye. 1948: Warners contract. Married actor Michael O'Shea (1947).

Films as actress include: 1944: Up In Arms. 1945: Wonder Man. 1946: The Kid from Brooklyn; The Best Years of Our Lives. 1947: The Secret Life of Walter Mitty; A Song is Born. 1949: Colorado Territory;

Hintertreppe, directed by Leopold Jessner, assisted by Paul Leni and scripted by Carl Mayer.
Black Legion, directed by Archie Mayo.
The Rolling Stones in Gimme Shelter, directed by Albert and David Maysles.

White Heat; Always Leave Them Laughing; Red Light. 1950: The Flame and the Arrow; The West Point Story. 1951: Along the Great Divide; Painting the Clouds with Sunshine; Captain Horatio Hornblower, RN; Starlift. 1952: The Iron Mistress. 1953: She's Back on Broadway. 1954: King Richard and the Crusaders. 1955: Pearl of the South Pacific; The Silver Chalice. 1956: Great Day in the Morning; Congo Crossing. 1957: The Big Land; The Story of Mankind. 1958: Fort Dobbs. 1959: Westbound; Jet Over the Atlantic.

MAYSLES, Albert *and* David

Directors and photographer. Albert: Brookline, Massachusetts 1926– ; David: Brookline, Massachusetts 1932–

Albert taught psychology at Boston University until 1955; to Russia to make *Psychiatry in Russia*. David worked as assistant to producer on *Bus Stop* (1956) and *The Prince and the Showgirl* (1957), the latter for Marilyn Monroe's production company. 1957: first film together as directors *The Youth of Poland* made on motorbike tour of Poland, parts shown on NBC TV. 1959–62: Albert photographed films of D. A. Pennebaker and Richard Leacock. 1960–62: both members of Drew Associates with Robert Drew, Pennebaker, Leacock and Greg Shuker. Made together number of films exclusively for TV, e.g. *Truman Capote* (1966) for National Educational Television. 1963: Joe E. Levine, subject of *Showman* refused permission for it to be shown in theatres, but allowed TV transmission. 1964: covered Beatles' visit to New York for Granada TV; Albert photographed *Montparnasse-Levallois*, Jean-Luc Godard's episode in *Paris vu par …* Albert usually photographer, David soundman and editor.

Films photographed by Albert include: 1955: Psychiatry in Russia (+ *d*). 1959: Opening in Moscow. 1960: Primary (*co*). 1961: Yankee No. 1964: Paris vu par … *ep* Montparnasse-Levallois. 1968: A Journey to Jerusalem (*co*). 1969: Monterey Pop (*co*).

Films in collaboration include: 1957: The Youth of Poland. 1961: Kenya; Safari ya Gari. 1963: Showman. 1964: What's Happening – Yeah Yeah Yeah: New York Meets the Beatles. 1965: Meet Marlon Brando. 1966: Truman Capote. 1969: Salesman. 1971: Gimme Shelter (*co-c*; + *w*; *co-d Charlotte Zwerin*).

MEEKER, Ralph

Actor. Minneapolis, Minnesota 1920–

1938–42: Northwestern University. First professional acting appearance in 1943, then in USO production 'Ten Little Indians'. 1944: with US Navy in Mediterranean. 1945: assistant stage manager and actor in 'Strange Fruit'; then in 'Cyrano de Bergerac' (1946). Took over from Marlon Brando in 'A Streetcar Named Desire'. 1947: In 'Mister Roberts'. Films from 1951. Some TV work.

Films as actor include: 1951: Teresa; Shadow in the Sky. 1952: Glory Alley. 1953: The Naked Spur; Code Two. 1955: Kiss Me Deadly. 1957: Run of the Arrow; Paths of Glory. 1961: Something Wild. 1963: Wall of Noise. 1967: The Dirty Dozen; The St Valentine's Day Massacre. 1968: The Detective. 1971: I Walk the Line; The Anderson Tapes.

MEERSON, Lazare

Designer. Russia 1900–38 London

Emigrated from Russia after Revolution to Germany. From 1924: worked in French films. Painted frescoes of Casino, Monte Carlo. From 1936: worked in London.

Films as designer include: 1925: Feu Mathias Pascal (*co*); Gribiche. 1926: Carmen; La Proie du vent. 1927: Un Chapeau de paille d'Italie. 1928: Les Nouveaux Messieurs. 1930: Sous les toits de Paris. 1931: Jean de la lune. 1932: A nous la liberté. 1933: Quatorze Juillet. 1934: Le Grand Jeu. 1935: Pension Mimosas; La Kermesse Heroïque. 1936: As You Like It. 1937: Knight Without Armour. 1938: Break the News; The Citadel (*co*).

MEHBOOB

Director. Kashipura, near Bombay 1909–

1927: began as extra with Imperial Film Company, Bombay. Playing larger parts by 1931. 1932: wrote and sold story to newly formed Sagar Movietone, Bombay; began as director with this subject. For 10 years one of Sagar's leading directors. 1942: formed own company Mehboob Productions; thereafter producer and director on all his films, not usually employing writers but allowing plots to develop as shooting proceeded. 1943: introduced actress Nargis to the screen in *Taqdeer*. *Aan* and *Bharat Mata* (starring Nargis) were shown widely in the East and reached English-speaking countries.

Films as director include: 1932: Al Hilal (+ *st*). 1937: Jagirdar. 1939: Aurat – Woman. 1942: Roti (+ *p*). 1943: Taqdeer – Fate (+ *p*). 1952: Aan – Savage Princess (+ *p*). 1957: Bharat Mata – Mother India (+ *p/st*).

MEKAS, Adolfas

Director. Semeniskai, Lithuania 1922–

Cowherd until Nazi invasion. World War II: on underground resistance newspapers; prisoner in Nazi concentration camps. 1945–50: in displaced persons camps. 1950: to New York with brother Jonas. From 1955: one of editors of magazine Film Culture, founded by Jonas Mekas. 1961: leading part in brother's first feature, *Guns of the Trees*. 1963: directed first film. 1964: directed, in collaboration with brother, *The Brig*. 1970: *Companeras and Companeros* made in Cuba. Has written several short stories.

Films as director: 1963: Hallelujah the Hills (+ *s/e*). 1964: The Brig (*co-d Jonas Mekas* + *e*). 1965: Doublebarrelled Detective Story. 1967: Windflowers (+ *m*). 1968: Victory Lane. 1970: Companeras and Companeros (*co-d David and Barbara Stone*).

MEKAS, Jonas

Director

Brother of Adolfas Mekas. Worked on resistance newspapers, imprisoned in concentration camps during World War II. 1945–50: in displaced persons camps. Then to New York. 1953: made first documentary, *Grand Street*. 1955: founded magazine Film Culture; editor-in-chief since. Began reviewing films for The Village Voice. From 1957: a central figure in promoting underground films. 1959–61: shot footage on

Salvador Dali, still to be definitively edited. 1961: made first feature. 1962: formed the Film Makers Co-operative, based on the ideas of Maya Deren. 1963: assistant director on Adolfas Mekas' *Hallelujah the Hills*. 1967: contributed to *For Life, Against the War*. 1969: released first draft of *Diaries, Notes and Sketches (also known as 'Walden')*, covering years 1964–69; it includes *Report Millbrook, Hare Krishna* and *Circus Notebook* (all 1966). Bit parts in several independent films including Adolfas Mekas' *Doublebarrelled Detective Story* (1965), Gregory Markopoulos' *Galaxie* (1966); also in Stan Brakhage's *Song XV*, which is dedicated to him.

Films as director: 1953: Grand Street. 1955: Silent Journey. 1961: Guns of the Trees. 1963: Moirès; Film Magazine of the Arts (+ *co-c/co-e*). 1964: The Brig (+ *c*; *co-d Adolfas Mekas*); Award Presentation to Andy Warhol (+ *w*). 1964–69: Diaries, Notes and Sketches (also known as 'Walden') (+ *c/w*).

MÉLIÈS, Georges

Director. Paris 1861–1938 Paris

Father a shoemaker then owned luxury footwear factory: wealthy. 1881–82: military service in French Infantry, reaching corporal. 1882–83: Ecole des Beaux-Arts; opposed by father who made him work in his factory; worked mainly on machines as mechanic. 1884: to London, worked in large store; became amateur conjuror. 1886: father retired; took over business with brother Gaston; appearances as conjuror. 1888: left business to Gaston, became manager and proprietor of Théâtre Robert-Houdin. 1889–90: cartoonist on La Griffe under pseudonym Géo Smile. Writer, designer and machine maker at his theatre (productions fewer after 1896). Made automatons from Robert Houdin's designs and his own. Magic lantern shows part of programmes. 1896: bought an English bioscope and films of William Paul and Edison; included in theatre shows; had camera constructed based on bioscope projector; had Eastman stock perforated; first film as director *Une Partie de čartes* and acted in it copying a film of that subject by the Lumière brothers; first films mainly in open air, a few with conjuring tricks; took out patent under name Kinetograph; 78 films that year. 1897: 54 films, including 3 with singer Paulus as actor, for inclusion in act at Robert-Houdin; use of artificial light; some 'reconstructed newsreels'; built studio at Montreuil; theatre used as cinema every evening, rest of time for conjuring. 1898: 31 films, also publicity films to be shown in open air. 1899: 33 films. 1900: 31 films, including 17 made at Exposition Universelle. 1901: 27 films. 1902: 22 films totalling 1320 metres, including *Couronnement du roi Edouard VII* financed by American producer Charles Urban: preceeded event depicted then presented as newsreel; took copyright action to protect his films in USA. 1903: 29 films; opened American office; brother Gaston began to produce films in USA. 1904: 45 films. 1905: 12 films totalling 2360 metres. 1906: 18 films. 1907: 19 films. 1908: 45 films totalling 9000 metres. 1909: few films; President at Congrès Internationale des Fabricants des Films: decision to standardise film perforation. 1910–13: few films. 1913: last film, *Le Voyage de la Famille Bourrichon*. World War I: ran theatre for convalescents at military hospital. 1915–23: transformed Montreuil studio into Theatre of Varieties. 1923: Théâtre Robert-Houdin demolished. 1931:

presented with Croix de la Légion d'Honneur by Louis Lumière. 1925: second marriage, to Charlotte Faes, former member of Robert-Houdin troupe, owner of a Paris shop, which they both now ran. Acted in publicity shorts. 1937: participated in radio programme.

Films as director include: 1896: Un Petit Diable; Sauvetage en rivière (*in 2 parts*); Le Régiment; Une Nuit Terrible; Effet de mer sur les rochers; Danse Serpentine; Le Papier Protée; Grandes Manoeuvres; Escamotage d'une dame chez Robert Houdin; Le Fakir, mystère indien. 1897: Chicot, dentiste américaine; Le Cauchemar; Hallucination de l'alchimiste; Le Chateau Hanté; Exécution d'un espion; La Cigale et la fourmi; Le Cabinet de Méphistophélès; Le Chirurgien Américain; Après le bal, le tub ou le bain de la Parisienne; Le Magnétiseur. 1898: Faust et Marguerite; Combat Naval devant Manille; Pygmalion et Galathée; La Damnation de Faust; Rêve d'artiste; La Tentation de Saint-Antoine. 1899: Cléopatre; Le Diable au couvent; Force doit rester à la loi; Automaboulisme et autorité; Le Christ marchant sur les eaux ou le miracle des flots; L'Affaire Dreyfus (*in 12 parts*); Cendrillon; L'Homme Protée. 1900: Fatale Méprise; Le Miracle du brahmine; L'Homme-orchestre (*+ w*); Jeanne d'Arc (*+ w*; *in 12 parts*); Les Sept Péchés Capitaux; Remerciement au Public; Coppélia ou la poupée animée; La Malade Hydrophobe ou l'homme qui a des roues dans la tête. 1901: Congrès des nations en Chine; Mésaventures d'un aéronaute; Le Brahmine et le papillon; Le Petit Chaperon Rouge (*in 12 parts*); Excelsior!; L'Omnibus des toqués ou les échappés de Charenton; La Vengeance de Bouddha ou la fontaine sacrée; Barbe-Bleu; Phrénologie Burlesque. 1902: Le Rêve du Paria; Nain et géant; Eruption Volcanique à la Martinique; Le Voyage dans la lune (*+ p/s/dec/cos/w*; *in 30 parts*); Les Trésors de Satan; L'Homme-mouche; Voyages de Gulliver; Robinson Crusoe en vingt-cinq tableaux. 1903: La Corbeille Enchantée; Cake-Walk Infernal; Les Mousquetaires de la reine; Le Mélomane (*+ w*); Le Royaume des fées (*in 30 parts*); Le Parapluie Fantastique ou dix femmes sous une ombrelle; Faust aux enfers ou la damnation de Faust (*in 15 parts*). 1904: Les Apaches; Un Peu de feu S.V.P.; Siva l'Invisible; Sorcellerie Culinaire; Le Barbier de Séville; Le Juif Errant. 1905: La Grotte aux surprises; L'Ange de Noël (*in 7 parts*); Menuet Lilliputien; Le Miroir de Venise ou les mésaventures de Shylock; Les Chevaliers du chlorophorme; La Tour de Londres et les derniers moments d'Anne de Boleyn (*in 5 parts*); L'Ile de Calypso: Ulysse et Polyphème; Rip Van Winkle (*in 10 parts*). 1906: Le Dirigeable Fantastique ou le cauchemar d'un inventeur; Jack le Ramoneur (*in 25 parts*); L'Honneur est satisfait; L'Anarchie chez Guignol; Les Quatre Cents Farces du diable (*+ s/dec*; *in 35 parts*). 1907: Deux Cent Mille Lieues sous les mers ou le cauchemar d'un pêcheur (*in 30 parts*); Le Tunnel sous la Manche ou le cauchemar franco-anglais (*in 30 parts*); Hamlet, Prince de Danemark; Satan en prison. 1908: La Cuisine de l'ogre; La Civilisation à travers les âges (*in 11 parts*); Les Torches Humaines de Justinien; Le Rêve d'un fumeur d'opium; La Prophétesse de Thebes; Lulli ou le violon brisé (*in 4 parts*); Rivalité d'amour; Pour l'étoile, S.V.P. 1909: La Gigue Merveilleuse; Le Papillon Fantastique. 1910: Si j'étais roi. 1911: Les Aventures du Baron Munchausen; A la conquête du pole; Cendrillon ou la pantoufle mystérieuse (*in 45 parts*). 1913: Le Chevalier des neiges.

MELLOR, William C.

Cinematographer.   –1963 Hollywood
Began in film laboratory at Paramount. Assistant to Victor Milner. Cinematographer by 1936. Remained with Paramount until 1943. After World War II: worked for various companies. 1950–54: mainly with MGM. From 1957: mainly with Fox. Oscars for black and white cinematography, *A Place in the Sun* (1951), *The Diary of Anne Frank* (1959).

Films as cinematographer include: 1937: Make Way for Tomorrow. 1938: Stolen Heaven. 1939: Hotel Imperial; The Magnificent Fraud; Disputed Passage. 1940: Road to Singapore; The Great McGinty. 1941: Reaching for the Sun. 1947: Blaze of Noon. 1948: The Senator was Indiscreet. 1949: Too Late for Tears. 1950: Love Happy; The Next Voice You Hear. 1951: Soldiers Three; It's a Big Country (*co*); Across the Wide Missouri. 1952: My Man and I; Carbine Williams. 1953: The Naked Spur; The Affairs of Dobie Gillis. 1956: The Last Frontier; Giant. 1957: Peyton Place; Love in the Afternoon. 1960: Crack in the Mirror. 1961: Wild in the Country; The Big Gamble. 1962: State Fair; Mr Hobbs Takes a Vacation. 1965: The Greatest Story Ever Told (*co*).

MELVILLE, Jean-Pierre

(J.-P. Grumbach) Director. Paris 1917–
Changed name after reading 'Moby Dick'. Amateur films on 8mm, 9·5mm, 16mm before founding own company, Melville Productions. With *Le Silence de la mer* (1947), began working with small crew entirely on location. Acted in *A bout de souffle* (1959), and in own *Deux Hommes à Manhattan* (1958); narrator of *Bob le flambeur* (1955). Scripted and produced most of own films.

Films as director (complete from 1948): 1946: Vingt-quatre heures de la vie d'un clown (*+ p/s*). 1947: Le Silence de la mer (*+ p/s/co-e*). 1950: Les Enfants Terribles (*+ pc/co-s/des/cy*). 1952: Quand tu liras cette lettre. 1955: Bob le Flambeur (*+ st/co-s/des/cy*). 1958: Deux Hommes à Manhattan (*+ s/co-c/w*). 1961: Léon Morin, Prêtre (*+ s*). 1962: Le Doulos (*+ p/s*). 1963: L'Aîné des ferchaux – Un Jeune Homme – Magnet of Doom (*+ st/s*). 1965: Le Deuxième Souffle – Second Wind – The Second Breath (*+ s*). 1967: Le Samourai – The Samurai (*+ s*). 1969: L'Armée des ombres – Shadow Army (*+ s*). 1970: Le Cercle Rouge (*+ s*).

MENJOU, Adolphe

Actor. Pittsburgh, Pennsylvania 1890–1963 Los Angeles
Culver Military Acadamy. Cornell University: acted with Cornell Theatrical Group. 1912: joined stock company in Cleveland, Ohio; made first films for Vitagraph. Vaudeville and other stage work in New York. 1914: military service in France and Italy, reaching Captain. To California, to act in films. A major witness for House Committee on Un-American Activities. Autobiography, 'It Took 9 Tailors'.

Films as actor include: 1917: The Amazons. 1921: The Three Musketeers. 1923: Woman of Paris. 1924: The Marriage Circle. 1925: Are Parents People? 1926: The Sorrows of Satan. 1930: Morocco; New Moon. 1931: The Easiest Way; The Front Page. 1932: Prestige; Forbidden. 1933: Morning Glory; A Farewell to Arms:

James Dean in George Stevens' Giant, *photographed by William C. Mellor.*
Le Doulos, *by Jean-Pierre Melville.*
Jiri Menzel's Rozmarné Léto.

Convention City; Easy to Love. 1934: Journal of a Crime; The Mighty Barnum. 1935: Gold Diggers of 1935; Broadway Gondolier. 1936: The Milky Way. 1937: One Hundred Men and a Girl; Stage Door; A Star is Born. 1938: The Goldwyn Follies; Letter of Introduction. 1939: That's Right, You're Wrong; The Housekeeper's Daughter; Golden Boy. 1940: A Bill of Divorcement. 1941: Road Show. 1942: Syncopation; Roxie Hart. 1943: Hi Diddle Diddle. 1945: Man Alive. 1946: Heartbeat; The Bachelor's Daughters. 1947: The Hucksters. 1948: State of the Union. 1949: My Dream is Yours; Dancing in the Dark. 1950: To Please a Lady. 1951: The Tall Target; Across the Wide Missouri. 1952: The Sniper. 1953: Man on a Tightrope. 1956: Bundle of Joy; Ambassador's Daughter. 1957: The Fuzzy Pink Nightgown; Paths of Glory. 1960: Pollyanna.

MENZEL, Jiri

Director. Czechoslovakia 1938–
1962–64: assistant to Vera Chytilova. 1963: graduated from Prague Film School. Director and actor at Prague Theatre Club. Several films as actor. 1965: first film as director.

Films as actor include: 1962: Strop. 1964: Každý den odvahu. 1966: Návrat ztraceného syna.

Films as director: 1965: Perličky na dne – Pearls from the Deep ep Mr Baltazar's Death; Zločin v dívčí skole – Crime at the Girls' School (title ep). 1966: Ostře sledované vlaky – Closely Observed Trains (+ co-s/w). 1968: Rozmarné Léto – Indian Summer – Capricious Summer (+ co-s). 1969: Skrivánci na nitich – Larks on a Thread.

MENZIES, William Cameron

Designer and director. New Haven, Connecticut 1896–1957 Hollywood
Educated in Scotland and at Yale. Began career in England with Famous Players-Lasky in special effects and design. 1923: in collaboration designed Douglas Fairbanks' independent production The Thief of Bagdad. 1927–28: received the first Oscar for art direction for The Tempest and The Dove. From 1931: director; occasionally designer on own films. 1933: co-wrote Norman Z. McLeod's Alice in Wonderland. 1936: in England directed and designed Alexander Korda's production Things to Come. 1939–43: designed 2 films of John Cromwell, 4 of Sam Wood. 1940: associate producer on The Thief of Bagdad. 1944: directed and produced Address Unknown. 1947: producer only on Ivy and co-producer only on Reign of Terror. 1953: directed and designed The Maze in 3D. 1956: last film as associate producer and designer, Around the World in 80 Days.

Films as designer include: 1925: The Eagle. 1926: Fig Leaves (co). 1927: The Tempest. 1927–28: The Loves of Zero. 1928: The Dove. 1939: Gone With the Wind. 1940: Our Town; Foreign Correspondent. 1941: So Ends Our Night. 1943: For Whom the Bell Tolls. 1948: The Arch of Triumph.

Films as director: 1931: The Spider (co-d Kenneth McKenna); Always Goodbye (+ a; co-d Kenneth McKenna). 1932: Chandu, the Magician (co-d Marcel Varnel). 1933: I Loved You Wednesday (co-d Henry King). 1934: The Wharf Angel (co-d George Somnes).

1936: Things to Come (+ a). 1940: The Green Cockatoo. 1944: Address Unknown (+ p). 1951: Drums in the Deep South (+ a); The Whip Hand (+ a). 1953: Invaders from Mars (+ des); The Maze (+ a).

MERCOURI, Melina

Actress. Athens 1925–
Father Greek Minister of Home Affairs and Mayor of Athens. Drama school of Greek National Theatre, followed by successful stage career in Athens. 1952: lead parts in comedies on Paris stage. Campaigned against Greek military regime, and deprived of Greek passport; exile since 1967. Also singing. Married Jules Dassin.

Films as actress include: 1955: Stella. 1957: Celui qui doit mourir; The Gypsy and the Gentleman. 1958: La Loi. 1960: Pote tin kyriaki. 1961: Il Guidizio Universale; Phaedra; Vive Henri IV, Vive l'amour. 1963: The Victors. 1964: Topkapi. 1965: Les Pianos Mécaniques. 1966: 10.30 pm Summer. 1969: Gaily, Gaily. 1970: La Promesse de l'aube.

MEREDITH, Burgess

Actor. Cleveland, Ohio 1907–
Acted in repertory and in stock company. From 1933: on Broadway in 'Little Ol' Boy', 'She Loves Me Not', 'The Barretts of Wimpole Street', 'Flowers of the Forest', 'Winterset', 'High Tor'. 1940: 'Liliom'. 1936: first film as actor Winterset. Service in US Air Force. 1949: directed and acted in The Man on the Eiffel Tower. Also TV. Married Paulette Goddard (1944–49, divorced).

Films as actor include: 1939: Idiot's Delight; Of Mice and Men. 1940: Castle on the Hudson. 1941: That Uncertain Feeling; Second Chorus; Tom, Dick and Harry. 1945: The Story of GI Joe. 1946: The Diary of a Chambermaid (+ co-p/co-s); Magnificent Doll. 1948: A Miracle Can Happen. 1961: Advise and Consent. 1963: The Cardinal. 1964: In Harm's Way. 1967: Hurry Sundown; Torture Garden. 1968: Stay Away Joe. 1969: Mackenna's Gold. 1970: There was a Crooked Man.

MESSEL, Oliver

Costume designer. London 1904–
Eton and Slade School of Art. Theatrical work. 1934: first film as costume designer The Private Life of Don Juan. 1934–36: worked for London Films. 1936: to Hollywood to work on Romeo and Juliet. Returned to London. 1949: last film The Queen of Spades. Subsequently worked only in theatre.

Films as costume designer include: 1936: Romeo and Juliet (co). 1940: The Thief of Bagdad (co). 1945: Caesar and Cleopatra. 1948: The Winslow Boy.

METTY, Russell L.

Cinematographer. Los Angeles 1906–
Worked in Standard Film Laboratory. Moved to Paramount, became assistant cameraman. 1929–44: worked for RKO. 1935: first film as cinematographer in collaboration, West of the Pecos. Freelanced, then to International. 1953–59: 10 films directed by Douglas Sirk. 1960: Oscar for colour cinematography on Spartacus.

Films as cinematographer include: 1938: Bringing Up Baby; Next Time I Marry. 1939: The Great Man Votes. 1940: Irene; No, No, Nanette; Sunny. 1941: Weekend for Three. 1942: The Big Street. 1943: Forever and a Day (co); Around the World; Hitler's Children. 1944: The Master Race. 1945: The Story of GI Joe. 1946: The Stranger. 1948: The Arch of Triumph; All My Sons; Kiss the Blood Off My Hands. 1949: The Lady Gambles; We Were Strangers. 1952: The World in his Arms. 1953: Seminole; The Man from the Alamo; Take Me to Town. 1954: Taza, Son of Cochise; Sign of the Pagan; Magnificent Obsession. 1955: Man Without a Star; All that Heaven Allows. 1956: Written on the Wind; Miracle in the Rain; There's Always Tomorrow. 1957: Mister Cory; Battle Hymn. 1958: A Time to Love and a Time to Die; Touch of Evil. 1959: Imitation of Life. 1960: Portrait in Black; Spartacus (co); Midnight Lace. 1961: The Misfits. 1962: That Touch of Mink. 1964: I'd Rather Be Rich. 1965: The Art of Love; The War Lord. 1966: The Appaloosa; Texas Across the River. 1967: Thoroughly Modern Millie; Rough Night in Jericho; Counterpoint. 1968: The Secret War of Harry Frigg; Madigan; The Pink Jungle. 1970: How Do I Love Thee?

MEYERS, Sidney

Director. 1894–
Violinist in symphony orchestras. 1934: film critic for New Theatre Magazine as Robert Stebbins. 1936: co-founder with Paul Strand of Frontier Films. 1937: wrote and produced China Strikes Back. 1938–42: sound editor on Strand's and Leo Hurwitz's Native Land. 1942–46: American editor for British Information Services; Chief Film Editor for OWI. 1946: with Janice Loeb and Helen Leavitt founded Film Documents Inc. 1948: directed 16mm feature The Quiet One. 1956: edited Edge of the City for MGM. 1969: in collaboration edited Tropic of Cancer.

Films as director: 1940: White Flood (co-d). 1941: The History and Romance of Transportation (co-d). 1949: The Quiet One (+ co-s/co-e). 1959: The Savage Eye (+ co-p/co-s/co-e; co-d Joseph Strick, Ben Maddow).

MICHEL, André

Director. Paris 1910–
Studied law. Film critic. Assistant to e.g. G. W. Pabst, Curtis Bernhardt. 1938: with Marcel l'Herbier co-produced Terre du Feu. 1944: with Henri Alekan founded and ran Service Cinématographique du Comité d'Action de la Résistance; first film as director, short for this group. 1948: first feature-length documentary Combat sans haine. 1951: first feature Trois Femmes, trois âmes.

Films as director: 1944: Dix Minutes sur le FFI. 1945: La Rose et le réséda – Rose and the Mignonette. 1947: Sport et Parapluie. 1948: Combat sans haine. 1949: Edgar et sa bonne; Maroc d'aujourd'hui. 1951: Trois Femmes, trois âmes (in 3 parts). 1953: Aventures au Radio-Circus. 1954: Geständnis unter vier Angen. 1955: La Sorcière. 1958: Sans famille. 1961: Ton Ombre est la mienne. 1962: Comme un poisson dans l'eau. 1964: Tous les enfants du monde.

MIFUNE, Toshiro

Actor. Tsingtao, China 1920–
Japanese parents: to Japan as child. Began as photo-

186

grapher. World War II: 5 years in Japanese Army. Film actor from 1946. 1963: formed own production company, and directed and acted in *Gojuman-nin no Isan – Legacy of the Five Hundred Thousand*. Also TV.

Films as actor include: 1948: Yoidore tenshi. 1949: Shizukanaru Ketto; Nora Inu. 1950: Shubun; Konyaka Yubiwa; Ishinaka Sensei Gyojoki; Rashomon. 1951: Hakuchi. 1952: Saikaku Ichidai Onna. 1954: Shichinin no Samurai. 1955: Ikimono no Kiroku. 1956: Tsuma no Kokoro. 1957: Kumonosu-jo; Donzoko. 1958: Kakushi toride no San-Akunin; Sengoku Guntoden. 1960: Warui Yatsu Hodo Yoku Nemura. 1961: Yojimbo. 1962: Sanjuro. 1963: Tengoku to Jigoku. 1965: Akahige. 1966: Grand Prix. 1967: Joi-uchi. 1968: Hell in the Pacific. 1971: Soleil Rouge.

MILES, Vera

(Vera Ralston) Actress. Boise City, Oklahoma 1930– 1948: beauty contest winner. TV plays, including a pilot 'The Lawbreakers' directed by Joseph M. Newman, released theatrically outside America. 1951–59: worked mainly for RKO, Warners, Allied Artists. 1960–62: almost all films for Paramount. 1964–66: worked for Buena Vista; subsequently for Warners and Paramount. Under personal contract to Alfred Hitchcock. Married actor Gordon Scott (1956, divorced).

Films as actress include: 1952: For Men Only. 1953: The Charge at Feather River. 1955: Wichita. 1956: The Searchers; Autumn Leaves; 23 Paces to Baker Street. 1957: The Wrong Man; Beau James. 1959: The FBI Story; Web of Evidence. 1960: Jovanka e le altre; A Touch of Larceny; Psycho. 1961: Back Street. 1962: The Man who Shot Liberty Valance. 1964: The Hanged Man. 1967: The Spirit is Willing; Gentle Giant. 1969: Sergeant Ryker.

MILESTONE, Lewis

Director. Odessa, Ukraine 1895–
Educated in Russia, Germany, Belgium. 1913: to USA. 1917: US Signal Corps. 1920: entered film industry as editor. 1921: assistant and editor to Henry King. 1923–24: worked with Ince, Sennett, William A. Seiter. 1933–47: directed numerous Broadway plays. From 1933: stage producer. 1962: began *PT 109*, replaced by Leslie H. Martinson. TV producer.

Films as director: 1925: Seven Sinners (+ *co-st/co-ad*); The Caveman. 1926: The New Klondike. 1927: Two Arabian Nights. 1928: The Garden of Eden (+ *p*); The Racket. 1929: Betrayal; New York Nights. 1930: All Quiet on the Western Front. 1931: The Front Page. 1932: Rain (+ *p*). 1933: Hallelujah, I'm a Bum – Hallelujah, I'm a Tramp. 1934: The Captain Hates the Sea. 1935: Paris in Spring. 1936: Anything Goes; The General Died at Dawn. 1939: The Night of Nights. 1940: Of Mice and Men (+ *p*); Lucky Partners. 1941: Our Russian Front – Notre Front Russe (+ *co-s*; *co-d Joris Ivens*); My Life With Caroline (+ *p*). 1943: Edge of Darkness; The North Star. 1944: The Purple Heart. 1945: A Walk in the Sun (+ *p*). 1946: The Strange Love of Martha Ivers. 1948: The Arch of Triumph (+ *co-s*); No Minor Vices (+ *p*). 1949: The Red Pony (+ *p*). 1951: Halls of Montezuma. 1952: Kangaroo;

Les Miserables. 1953: Melba. 1954: They Who Dare. 1955: La Vedova – The Widow (+ *ad*). 1959: Pork Chop Hill. 1960: Ocean's 11 (+ *p*). 1962: Mutiny on the Bounty. 1963: PT 109 (*uc, co-d Leslie H. Martinson*).

MILHAUD, Darius

Composer. Aix-en-Provence, France 1892–
Studied music at Conservatoire de Paris. One of Groupe des Six. Marcel L'Herbier asked him to conduct music during screening of *L'Inhumaine* (1923). 1929: wrote music for Alberto Cavalcanti's *La P'tite Lili*. From 1934: frequent film scores. 1937: collaborated with Arthur Honegger on *La Citadelle du silence*. Extracted piano suite 'L'Album de Madame Bovary' from his score for *Madame Bovary* (1934), 'Cortège Funèbre' from his score for *L'Espoir* (1945), a divertissement for wind quintet from his score for *Gauguin* (1950). 1944–46: composed music for and appeared in Man Ray episode of Hans Richter's *Dreams that Money Can Buy*.

Films as composer include: 1933: L'Hippocampe. 1938: Mollenard; La Tragédie Impériale. 1947: The Private Affairs of Bel-Ami. 1950: La Vie commence demain.

MILLAND, Ray

(Reginald Truscott-Jones) Actor and director. Neath, Wales 1907–
Household Cavalry. Stage name Jack Milland. Toured in 'The Woman in Room 13'. 1929: first film as actor *Plaything*. 1931: first American film *The Bachelor Father*. London revues. 1932: married Hollywood show-girl Muriel Weber. British and American films. 1934: Paramount contract. USO. Radio work. To 1949: most films for Paramount. Subsequent work for several studios, including Warners, Fox, MGM. 1955: first film as director and actor *A Man Alone*. 1970: on Broadway in 'Front Page'. Oscar as Best Actor for *The Lost Weekend* (1945).

Films as actor include: 1931: Bought; Just a Gigolo; Blonde Crazy. 1932: Polly of the Circus. 1934: Bolero; We're Not Dressing; Many Happy Returns. 1935: Four Hours to Kill!; The Glass Key; The Gilded Lily. 1936: Next Time We Love; Three Smart Girls; The Big Broadcast of 1937. 1937: Wings over Honolulu; Easy Living. 1938: Men With Wings; Say it in French. 1939: Beau Geste; French Without Tears; Hotel Imperial. 1940: Arise My Love; Irene. 1941: I Wanted Wings; Skylark. 1942: Reap the Wild Wind; The Major and the Minor; Star Spangled Rhythm. 1943: Forever and a Day. 1944: Till We Meet Again; The Ministry of Fear; The Uninvited; Lady in the Dark. 1945: Kitty. 1947: Golden Earrings; Variety Girl; California. 1948: The Big Clock. 1949: Alias Nick Beal; It Happens Every Spring. 1950: A Life of Her Own; Copper Canyon. 1951: Circle of Danger; Close to My Heart. 1952: Something to Live For; The Thief. 1954: Dial M for Murder. 1955: The Girl in the Red Velvet Swing. 1957: The River's Edge. 1962: The Premature Burial. 1963: X — the Man with the X-Ray Eyes.

Films as director and actor: 1955: A Man Alone. 1956: Lisbon (+ *as-p*). 1957: The Safecracker. 1962: Panic in Year Zero. 1967: Hostile Witness (*r 1970*).

Orson Welles in his own film, Touch of Evil, *photographed by Russell Metty, assisted by Philip Lathrop. Toshiro Mifune in Akira Kurosawa's* Rashomon. *Ray Milland (right) in his own film,* Panic in Year Zero.

MILLER, Ann

(Lucille Ann Collier) Actress. Chireno, Texas 1919–
Professional dancer from 12. Vaudeville. 1937: first
film as actress *New Faces of 1937*. To 1940: most films
for RKO. 1940–46: mainly Columbia, Paramount.
From 1948: almost all films for MGM. 1957: retired
from films.

Films as actress include: 1937: Stage Door. 1938:
Room Service; Having Wonderful Time; You Can't
Take It With You. 1940: Too Many Girls. 1943:
Reveille with Beverley. 1945: Eadie Was a Lady. 1948:
Easter Parade; The Kissing Bandit. 1949: On the
Town. 1951: Texas Carnival. 1952: Lovely to Look
At. 1953: Small Town Girl; Kiss Me, Kate. 1954:
Deep in My Heart. 1956: The Opposite Sex.

MILLER, Arthur

Writer. New York 1915–
Worked $2\frac{1}{2}$ years in New York, then University of
Michigan. 1938: returned to New York. Connected
briefly with Federal Theater Project. Wrote radio
scripts for several network programmes. 1944: Broadway production of 'The Man Who had All the Luck';
published book of reportage on the Army 'Situation
Normal' and novel 'Focus'. 1948: first film adapted
from his work. 1949: Pulitzer Prize for 'The Death of a
Salesman'. 1950: adapted Ibsen's 'An Enemy of the
People'. 1956: married Marilyn Monroe. 1961:
scripted *The Misfits* from own story and turned it into
novel; Marilyn Monroe acted in the film; he divorced
her. 1967: book of short stories 'I Don't Need You
Any More'. Work published in e.g. Colliers, Harpers,
Esquire, Nation, Holiday, The Atlantic.

Films adapted from his plays: 1948: All My Sons.
1951: Death of a Salesman. 1957: Les Sorcières de
Salem. 1962: Vu du pont.

Film as writer: 1961: The Misfits (+ *st*).

MILLER, Arthur C.

Cinematographer. New York 1895–1970
Father an engineer. Several jobs. Small parts in
westerns in New York State. Assistant cameraman.
1918: moved to California; first feature as cinematographer *A Japanese Nightingale*. 1918–19: worked for
Pathe and Famous Players-Lasky in New York and
California. 1923–25: with First National. To 1925:
almost all films directed by George Fitzmaurice.
1925–27: worked for Producers' Distributing Corporation. 1927–30: all films for Pathe, except *Bellamy
Trial* for MGM. 1931–32: with several companies.
1932–50: all films for Fox, except *The Men in Her Life*
(1941) for Columbia. 1951: last film *The Prowler* for
United Artists. Intended to work on *The African Queen*
but found had tuberculosis; recovered and retired.
1954: president of American Society of Cinematographers. Oscars for black and white cinematography:
How Green was My Valley (1941), *The Song of
Bernadette* (1943), *Anna and the King of Siam* (1946).

Films as cinematographer include: 1927: Nobody's
Widow; Vanity; The Fighting Eagle. 1928: The Cop;
Annapolis; The Spieler. 1929: The Flying Fool;
Sailor's Holiday; Big News; Oh, Yeah! 1930: Officer
O'Brien: His First Command (*co*); The Lady of

Scandal (*co*). 1931: Bad Company. 1932: Okay
America; Me and My Gal; Hold Me Tight. 1933:
Sailor's Luck; My Weakness; Bright Eyes. 1935: The
Little Colonel; Black Sheep. 1936: White Fang. 1937:
Pigskin Parade; Wee Willie Winkie; Heidi. 1938: The
Baroness and the Butler; Rebecca of Sunnybrook
Farm; Submarine Patrol. 1939: The Little Princess
(*co*); The Rains Came; Here I am a Stranger. 1940:
The Blue Bird; Johnny Apollo; The Mark of Zorro.
1941: Tobacco Road; Man Hunt; The Men in Her Life
(*co*); How Green was My Valley. 1942: This Above
All; The Ox-Bow Incident; Immortal Sergeant (*co*).
1943: The Moon is Down; The Song of Bernadette.
1944: The Purple Heart; The Keys of the Kingdom.
1945: A Royal Scandal. 1946: Dragonwyck; Anna
and the King of Siam; The Razor's Edge. 1947:
Gentlemen's Agreement. 1948: The Walls of Jericho.
1949: A Letter to Three Wives. 1950: Whirlpool; The
Gunfighter. 1951: The Prowler.

MILLER, David

Director. Paterson, New Jersey 1909–
In New York wrote copy for film trailers. 1929: to
Hollywood, edited documentary shorts including
travelogues. 1930: editor at Columbia. Also writer for
American Cavalcade. 1933: to Metro as editor of
shorts. Became director of Metro shorts. 1937: Oscar
for short subject in colour *Penny Wisdom*. 1941: made
first feature as director, for MGM. World War II:
service in US Army: worked with Frank Capra on
'Why We Fight' series. 1946: made documentary
Seeds of Wisdom. 1956: *The Opposite Sex* a remake of
George Cukor's *The Women* (1939).

Features as director: 1941: Billy the Kid. 1942:
Sunday Punch; Flying Tigers. 1949: Top O' the Morn-
ing; Our Very Own. 1950: Love Happy. 1951:
Saturday's Hero. 1952: Sudden Fear. 1954: The
Beautiful Stranger – Twist of Fate (+ *st*). 1955: Diane.
1956: The Opposite Sex. 1957: The Story of Esther
Costello – The Golden Virgin. 1959: Happy Anniver-
sary. 1960: Midnight Lace. 1961: Back Street. 1962:
Lonely are the Brave. 1963: Captain Newman, M.D.
1968: Hammerhead.

MILLER, Seton I.

Writer and producer. Chehalis, Washington 1902–
Yale University. 1926: began in films as technical
advisor and actor in *Brown of Harvard* for MGM.
1927: joined Fox as writer; collaborated on several
scripts for Howard Hawks at Fox, then other
companies until 1932. 1930–40: mainly with Warners.
1944–47: mainly with Paramount as producer and
writer; frequently worked with John Farrow, produced
his *California* (1947). 1949: joined Robert Stillman
Productions as associate producer and writer. Then
worked for e.g. United Artists, Universal. Wrote and
produced TV series 'Rogue for Hire'. Oscar for screenplay, in collaboration with Sidney Buchman, *Here
Comes Mr Jordan* (1941).

Films as writer include: 1927: Paid to Love (*co*). 1928:
A Girl in Every Port; Fazil (*co*); The Air Circus (*co*).
1930: The Dawn Patrol (*co*). 1931: The Criminal Code
(*co-ad/co-di*). 1932: Scarface, Shame of the Nation
(*co-ad/co-di*); The Crowd Roars (*co*); If I Had a Million
(*co*). 1935: G Men (+ *st*); Frisco Kid (*co-st/co-s*). 1937:
Kid Galahad. 1938: The Adventures of Robin Hood

(*co-st/co-s*); The Dawn Patrol (*co*); Penitentiary (*co*).
1940: The Sea Hawk (*co*); Castle on the Hudson (*co*).
1942: The Black Swan (*ad/co-s*). 1944: The Ministry of
Fear (+ *p*). 1946: Two Years before the Mast (+ *p*; *co-s*).
1947: Calcutta (+ *p/st*). 1948: Fighter Squadron
(+ *p/st*). 1953: The Mississippi Gambler (+ *st*). 1954:
Bengal Brigade (*ad*). 1959: The Last Mile.

MILLS, Hayley

Actress. London 1946–
Daughter of John Mills and writer Mary Hayley Bell.
1959: film debut with father in *Tiger Bay;* then Disney
contract. 1965: directed by father in *Sky West and
Crooked*. Honorary Oscar for most outstanding
juvenile performance of 1960, in *Pollyanna*. 1970: in
'The Wild Duck'. Married Roy Boulting.

Films as actress include: 1961: In Search of the
Castaways; The Parent Trap; Whistle Down the Wind.
1963: The Chalk Garden. 1964: The Moonspinners.
1965: Sky West and Crooked. 1966: The Trouble with
Angels; The Family Way. 1968: Twisted Nerve. 1971:
Mr Forbush and the Penguins.

MILLS, John

Actor. North Elmham, Norfolk 1908–
Clerk in corn merchant's office in Ipswich. Travelling
salesman in London; attended Celia Raye School of
Dancing there. From 1928: chorus boy on London
stage. 1930: played Puck in 'A Midsummer Night's
Dream' at Old Vic. Toured Far East in repertory.
1931: juvenile lead in C. B. Cochrane revue. 1932:
first film as actor, *The Midshipmaid*. World War II:
Royal Engineers as private, then commission with
Royal Monmouthshire Rifles; invalided out (1942).
1948: Rank contract 1961: appeared in Broadway
production of 'Ross'. 1965: directed, produced, and
acted in *Sky West and Crooked*. Married writer Mary
Hayley Bell; daughters actresses Juliet and Hayley
Mills. Oscar as supporting actor for *Ryan's Daughter*
(1971).

Films as actor include: 1936: Tudor Rose. 1937:
O.H.M.S. 1939: Goodbye Mr Chips. 1940: The Green
Cockatoo. 1941: Cottage to Let. 1942: The Young Mr
Pitt; In Which We Serve. 1943: We Dive at Dawn.
1944: This Happy Breed; Waterloo Road. 1945: The
Way to the Stars. 1946: Great Expectations. 1947: So
Well Remembered; The October Man. 1948: Scott of
the Antarctic. 1950: Morning Departure. 1952: The
Long Memory; The Gentle Gunman. 1954: Hobson's
Choice; The End of the Affair. 1955: The Colditz
Story; Escapade. 1956: War and Peace. 1957: Town
on Trial. 1958: Ice Cold in Alex; I Was Monty's
Double. 1959: Tiger Bay. 1960: The Swiss Family
Robinson; Tunes of Glory. 1961: The Singer not the
Song; Flame in the Streets. 1963: The Chalk Garden.
1965: King Rat. 1966: The Wrong Box; The Family
Way. 1967: Africa-Texas Style. 1969: Oh! What a
Lovely War.

MILNER, Victor

Cinematographer. New York City 1893–
1912–15: worked at Balboa Studio, Long Beach,
California. Later with Universal. Cinematographer by
1918. 1924: worked for MGM. 1925–52: with
Famous Players-Lasky then Paramount.

Films as cinematographer include: 1924: The Red Lily; Thy Name is Woman. 1925: East of Suez. 1926: The Wanderer; The Cat's Pajamas. 1927: Children of Divorce; The Way of All Flesh. 1928: The Woman from Moscow. 1930: The Love Parade; Let's Go Native; Monte Carlo; Paramount on Parade (co); The Texan. 1932: The Man I Killed; One Hour with You; Love Me Tonight; Trouble in Paradise. 1933: The Song of Songs; Design for Living. 1934: Cleopatra. 1935: The Crusades; So Red the Rose. 1936: Desire (co); The General Died at Dawn. 1938: The Buccaneer. 1939: Union Pacific; The Great Victor Herbert. 1940: Northwest Mounted Police (co); Christmas in July. 1941: The Lady Eve; The Monster and the Girl. 1942: Reap the Wild Wind (co). 1944: The Story of Dr Wassell (co); The Great Moment; The Princess and the Pirate. 1946: The Strange Love of Martha Ivers. 1950: The Furies. 1952: Carrie. 1953: Jeopardy.

MIMICA, Vatroslav

Director and animator. Omis, Yugoslavia 1923–
World War II: in Resistance. Literary critic and editor of youth review Izvor. Studied medicine in Zagreb. 1949: entered cinema as manager and art director of Jadran Film. 1952: first film as director. Features then animated films; subsequently returned to features. Some work in Italian films.

Short films as animator and writer include: 1959: Kod fotografa – At the Photographer's; Inspektor se vraca kuci – The Inspector Returns Home; Jaje – The Egg. 1962: Mala Kronika – Everyday Chronicle. 1963: Tifusari – Typhoid.

Features as director: 1952: U oluji – In the Storm. 1955: Jubilej G. Ikla – Mr Ikle's Jubilee. 1961: Solimane il Conquistare – Suleiman the Conquerer (+ co-s; co-d Mario Tota). 1965: Prometej sa Otaka Viševice – Prometheus from the Island of Visevice. 1966: Pondeljak ili Utorak – Monday or Tuesday (+ co-s). 1967: Kaja, ubit cú te – Kaya, I'll Kill You (+ co-s). 1969: Dogadaj – The Event (+ co-s). 1970: Hranjenik.

MINGOZZI, Gian Franco

Director. Ferrara, Italy 1932–
1956: diploma in Law. Centro Sperimentale di Roma. Assisted Federico Fellini on La Dolce Vita, Boccaccio 70, and Otto e mezzo. 1959: first films as director, shorts in Spain. 1964: worked briefly at Office National du Film, Montreal. 1967: first feature as director. Also films for TV.

Short films as director: 1959: Gli Uomini e i tori; Festa a Pamplona. 1961: Via dei Piopp001; Le Italiane e l'amore ep La Vedova Bianca. 1962: La Taranta; Il Finestre. 1963: Il Putto; Il Mali Mestieri. 1964: Notte su una minoranza. 1965: Al nostro sonno inquieto; La Violenza (uf). 1966: Con il cuore fermo Sicilia; Michelangelo Antonioni, storia di un autore.

Features as director: 1967: Trio (+ st). 1968: Sequestro di personna – Ransom in Sardinia (+ co-s). 1970: La Sensitiva.

MINNELLI, Vincente

Director. Chicago 1913–
On stage at 3 in Minnelli Brothers tent show. Toured Middle East with show in which his Italian father was violinist and leader of orchestra, and mother (of French extraction) was leading lady. Competition from cinema reduced success of company; family settled in Delaware. Left school at 16; to Chicago, worked for photographer, then stage manager and costume designer on the Balaban and Katz theatre circuit. Designer of costumes and sets at Paramount Theatre, New York. Designed production of 'Du Barry' for Grace Moore; art director at Radio City Music Hall. Directed ballets, including 'El Amor Brujo', and Broadway musicals. 1937: briefly under contract to Paramount in Hollywood. 1940: offered MGM contract by Arthur Freed; worked in various departments before first film as director (1943). Then under contract to MGM for about 25 years. Only film on loan elsewhere was Goodbye Charlie, for Fox. Collector of paintings; helped finance experimental films e.g. by Man Ray and Hans Richter.

Films as director: 1943: Cabin in the Sky; I Dood It – By Hook or by Crook. 1944: Meet Me in St Louis. 1945: The Clock; Yolanda and the Thief. 1946: Ziegfeld Follies; Undercurrent. 1948: The Pirate. 1949: Madame Bovary. 1950: Father of the Bride. 1951: An American in Paris; Father's Little Dividend. 1952: The Bad and the Beautiful. 1953: The Band Wagon; The Story of Three Loves ep Mademoiselle. 1954: The Long, Long Trailer; Brigadoon. 1955: The Cobweb; Kismet, 1956: Lust for Life; Tea and Sympathy. 1957: Designing Woman; The Seventh Sin (uc, co-d Ronald Neame). 1958: Gigi; The Reluctant Debutante; Some Came Running. 1960: Home from the Hill; Bells Are Ringing. 1961: The Four Horsemen of the Apocalypse; Two Weeks in Another Town. 1963: The Courtship of Eddie's Father. 1964: Goodbye Charlie. 1965: The Sandpiper. 1970: On a Clear Day You Can See Forever.

MIRANDA, Carmen

(Maria do Carmo Miranda da Cunha) Actress. Lisbon 1913–55 Los Angeles
Brought up in Brazil. Radio, recordings, films in South America. 1939: on Broadway in 'The Streets of Paris'. Worked in cabaret. 1940: first film as actress Down Argentine Way. Also TV work.

Films as actress include: 1941: That Night in Rio; Week-end in Havana. 1942: Springtime in the Rockies. 1943: The Gang's All Here. 1944: Greenwich Village; Something for the Boys. 1946: Doll Face. 1947: Copacabana. 1948: A Date with Judy. 1950: Nancy Goes to Rio. 1953: Scared Stiff.

MIRANDA, Isa

Actress. Milan 1912–
Model. Milan Academy of Dramatic Art, 1934: first major film role La Signora di tutti. Theatrical work in Italy, France, UK, USA. London stage in 'Orpheus Descending'. Films in France, Germany, Italy, USA. Also TV work. Poet, novelist, painter. Married producer Alfredo Guarini.

Films as actress include: 1933: Il Caso Haller. 1934:

Gene Tierney in Whirlpool *directed by Otto Preminger and photographed by Arthur C. Miller.*
Two Weeks in Another Town, *directed by Vincente Minnelli.*
The Mirisch Brothers, *(left to right)* Walter, Marvin *and* Harold.

Come le foglie. 1937: Scipione L'Africano. 1939: Hotel Imperial. 1942: Malombra. 1943: Zaza. 1945: Lo Sbaglio di essere vivo. 1949: Au-delà des grilles. 1950: La Ronde. 1953: Siamo Donne *ep* Isa Miranda. 1954: Avant le déluge. 1955: Summer Madness; Gli Sbandati. 1957: Une Manche et la Belle. 1964: The Yellow Rolls-Royce.

MIRISCH BROTHERS

Harold J.: Executive. New York 1907–
Film buyer for Warners theatres in Wisconsin. 1930–37: zone manager. 1937–41: exhibitor in Milwaukee. 1941–46: film buyer for RKO. 1947: vice-president of Monogram and Allied Artists. 1957: became president of Mirisch Company.
Walter M.: Producer. New York 1921–
University of Wisconsin. 1943: business administration at Harvard Graduate School. 1938–40: worked for Skouras Theatres Corporation. 1940–42: Oriental Theatre Corporation. From 1945: Monogram and Allied Artists. 1951: became executive producer for Allied Artists; first film as producer *Cavalry Scout*. From 1957: vice-president in charge of production for Mirisch Company. 1960–61: president, Screen Producer's Guild. Member of Board of Governors of Academy of Motion Picture Arts and Sciences, and (from 1969) vice-president.

Walter: films as producer include: 1953: The Maze. 1955: An Annapolis Story; Dark Avenger. 1958: Fort Massacre; Man of the West. 1959: The Gunfight at Dodge City; The Man in the Net. 1961: By Love Possessed. 1962: Two for the Seesaw. 1963: Toys in the Attic. 1966: Hawaii. 1967: In the Heat of the Night; Fitzwilly. 1969: Sinful Davey; Some Kind of a Nut.

MISRAKI, Paul

Composer. Constantinople 1908–
Studied music in Paris. 1929–39: with Ray Ventura Orchestra for which composed many songs. To South America during World War II. Converted to Roman Catholicism, composed some sacred music. 1945: returned to Paris. Many popular songs; number of operettas. Acted in *Tourbillon de Paris* (1939).

Films as composer include: 1949: Manon. 1950: Le Rosier de Madame Husson. 1951: Atoll K. 1953: Les Orgueilleux; L'Envers du paradis. 1955: Confidential Report; Ali Baba et les quarante voleurs; Chiens Perdus sans collier. 1956: Et Dieu créa la femme; En effeuillant la marguérite; La Mort en ce jardin. 1959: Les Cousins; Les Bonnes Femmes (*co*). 1965: Alphaville, une étrange aventure de Lemmy Caution.

MITCHELL, Thomas

Actor. Elizabeth, New Jersey 1892–1962 Beverley Hills, California
Actor, writer, director on Broadway. 1935: to Hollywood. Worked for Columbia, then several studios. 1946–47: MGM, then several studios. Oscar as supporting actor for *Stagecoach* (1939).

Films as actor include: 1936: Craig's Wife; Theodora Goes Wild. 1937: Make Way for Tomorrow; Lost Horizon; When You're in Love. 1938: The Hurricane; Trade Winds. 1939: The Hunchback of Notre Dame;

Only Angels Have Wings; Mr Smith Goes to Washington; Gone With the Wind. 1940: The Long Voyage Home; The Outlaw (*r* 1946); Three Cheers for the Irish; Our Town; Angels Over Broadway. 1941: Out of the Fog. 1942: Joan of Paris; Moontide; This Above All; Tales of Manhattan; The Immortal Sergeant; The Black Swan. 1943: Flesh and Fantasy; Bataan. 1944: The Sullivans; Wilson; Dark Waters; Buffalo Bill. 1945: The Keys of the Kingdom; Captain Eddie. 1946: Adventure; The Dark Mirror. 1947: The Romance of Rosy Ridge; High Barbaree. 1948: Silver River. 1949: Alias Nick Beal. 1951: Journey into Light. 1952: High Noon. 1954: Destry. 1956: While the City Sleeps. 1961: By Love Possessed; Pocketful of Miracles.

MITCHUM, Robert

Actor. Bridgeport, Connecticut 1917–
Sister, nightclub performer Julie Mitchum, responsible for his entering Long Beach Theater Guild. Wrote children's plays, and comedy material for his sister. 1942: extra in films e.g. *Hoppy Serves a Writ*. 1944–54: acted mainly in RKO films. Then worked for several companies, including United Artists. 1948: arrested on narcotics charge while making *The Big Steal* (1949). 1958: wrote story and acted in *Thunder Road* with his son, Jim Mitchum. Briefly associated in production with Raymond Stross: *The Angry Hills* (1959), *A Terrible Beauty* (1960).

Films as actor include: 1943: The Human Comedy; Corvette K-225; The Dancing Masters; Gung Ho! 1944: Cry Havoc; When Strangers Marry; Girl Rush; Thirty Seconds Over Tokyo. 1945: The Story of GI Joe. 1946: Undercurrent; The Locket; Till the End of Time. 1947: Pursued; Crossfire; Desire Me; Out of the Past. 1948: Rachel and the Stranger; Blood on the Moon. 1949: The Red Pony; The Big Steal. 1950: Where Danger Lives; My Forbidden Past. 1951: His Kind of Woman; The Racket. 1952: Macao; The Lusty Men; Angel Face; One Minute to Zero. 1953: Second Chance; White Witch Doctor. 1954: River of No Return; Track of the Cat; She Couldn't Say No. 1955: Not As a Stranger; The Night of the Hunter; Man With the Gun. 1956: Foreign Intrigue; Bandido. 1957: Heaven Knows Mr Allison; Fire Down Below; The Enemy Below. 1958: The Hunters. 1959: The Angry Hills; The Wonderful Country. 1960: A Terrible Beauty; The Grass is Greener; Home from the Hill; The Sundowners. 1961: The Last Time I Saw Archie; Cape Fear. 1962: The Longest Day; Two for the Seesaw. 1963: The List of Adrian Messenger; Rampage; The Man in the Middle. 1964: What a Way to Go; Mister Moses. 1967: El Dorado. 1968: Lo Sbarco di Anzio; Villa Rides. 1969: Young Billy Young; The Good Guys and the Bad Guys. 1970: Ryan's Daughter.

MITRA, Subrata

Cinematographer. 1931–
Stills photographer. 1951: tried unsuccessfully to become camera assistant on *The River,* being shot in Calcutta, observed shooting; began collaboration with Satyajit Ray on *Pather Panchali* (1954), his first film as cinematographer. Worked briefly in Hindi film industry. From 1963: photographed James Ivory's films.

Films as cinematographer include: 1957: Aparajito. 1958: Paras Pather; Jalsaghar. 1959: Apur Sansar. 1960: Devi. 1962: Kanchenjunga. 1963: Mahanagar; The Householder. 1964: Charulata. 1965: Shakespeare Wallah. 1966: Nayak. 1968: The Guru. 1970: Bombay Talkie.

MITRY, Jean

(Jean René Pierre Goetgheluck Le Rouge Taillard des Acres de Presfontaines) Director and critic. Soissons, France 1907–
Theoretical physics and epistemology at Sorbonne University. From 1924: technical assistant and assistant editor on films directed by e.g. Marcel L'Herbier, Abel Gance. 1925–35: journalist and film reviewer on e.g. Ciné pour Tous, Cinémonde, Photo Ciné. 1929: directed first film in collaboration. 1932–35: dubbing editor. 1936: with Henri Langlois and Georges Franju founded Cinémathèque Française; director of its archive until 1940 and during 1943–47. Also edited several films (1936–40). From 1944: Professor in history and aesthetics of cinema at IDHEC. 1952: edited *Le Rideau Cramoisi*. 1959: first feature as director. From 1963: editor of IDHEC's Filmographie Universelle research series. Also editor of Classiques du Cinéma series for Editions Universitaires. Many books and pamphlets e.g. 'Esthétique et psychologie du cinéma', a dictionary of the cinema and monographs on directors, e.g. John Ford. 1969: Professor of Film, Montreal University, Canada.

Films as director: 1929: Paris-cinéma (*co-d* Pierre Chenal). 1949: Pacific 231. 1950: Le Paquebot Liberté – Liberté. 1951: Rêverie pour Claude Débussy; En bateau; Images pour Débussy. 1952: Hauteterre; Le Fleuve; Au pays des grandes causses. 1955: Symphonie Mécanique. 1956: Le Miracle des ailes; Ecoles de pilotage; La Machine et l'homme. 1957: Ecrire en images (*+ s/e*); Chopin (*+ e*). 1959: Enigme aux Folies-Bergères. 1960: Rencontres (*+ e*); La Grande Foire – The Big Fair.

MIX, Tom

Actor. Mix Run, Pennsylvania 1880–1940 Florence Cowboy, Texas Ranger, deputy marshal in Oklahoma, trick rider in rodeos. 1911: in US cavalry in Mexican civil war. From 1913: appeared as actor in 1-reelers and 2-reelers for Selig Polyscope; also directed or produced, and wrote, most of them. 1917: joined Fox as actor, occasionally directing and writing features until 1920. Remained with Fox until 1928. Popularity waned after coming of sound. 1932–33: last films, for Universal. Died in car crash.

Films as actor include: 1913: The Escape of Jim Dolan (*+ s*). 1914: The Way of the Redman (*+ p/s*); The Man from the East (*+ d/s*); A Child of the Prairie (*+ d/s*); The Heart of the Sheriff (*+ p/s*). 1916: The Raiders (*+ p/s*); A Western Masquerade (*+ p/s*); The Sheriff's Blunder (*+ d/s*); The Pony Express Rider (*+ d/s*). 1917: Tom and Jerry Mix (*+ d/s*); Six Cylinder Love (*+ d/s*). 1918: Western Blood (*+ st*). 1920: Desert Love (*+ st*); The Daredevil (*+ d/s/st*); The Terror (*+ st*); Prairie Trails. 1923: Three Jumps Ahead; North of Hudson Bay. 1924: The Heart Buster. 1925: Riders of the Purple Sage; The Rainbow Trail; Dick Turpin. 1926: My Own Pal. 1927: The Last Trail. 1928: A Horseman of the Plains; Painted Post. 1929: The

Drifter. 1932: Destry Rides Again. 1933: Terror Trail; The Rustlers Roundup.

MIYAGAWA, Kazuo

Cinematographer. Kyoto, Japan 1908–
Kyoto Commercial School. 1935: cinematographer at Nikkatsu Studios. From 1942: worked mainly at Daei. 1965: in collaboration supervised cameras on *Tokyo Orinpikku.*

Films as cinematographer include: 1950: Rashomon. 1951: Oyusama; Genji Monogatari. 1952: Nishijin no Shimai. 1953: Senbazuru; Ugetsu Monogatari; Gion-bayashi; Yokubo; Uwasa no Onna. 1954: Sansho Dayu; Chikamatsu Monogatari. 1955: Shin Heike Monogatari. 1956: Yoru no Kawa; Akasen chitai. 1957: Yoru no Cho. 1958: Enjo; Ukigusa. 1960: Jokyo (*Yoshimura ep*); Bonchi; Ototo. 1961: Konki; Yojimbo. 1962: Hakai. 1963: Echizen Takeningyo. 1964: Dokonjo Monogatari – Zeni no Odori.

MIZOGUCHI, Kenji

Director. Tokyo 1898–1956 Kyoto
Because of parents' poverty left school at 13. 1913: apprenticed to kimono designer. 1916: studied painting, specialising in Occidental-style art, at Aoibashi Art Institute. 1917: layout man on newspaper in Kobe. 1918: returned to Tokyo. 1920: became assistant director at Nikkatsu, although wanting to act. 1922: walk-out of Nikkatsu staff because women to be allowed to take female parts in films led to staff shortage, gave him chance to direct. 1932: left Nikkatsu for Shinko. 1934: joined Nikkatsu Tokyo, for one film; then in Kyoto founded Dai-ichi company with Masaichi Nagata; it broke up in 1936. 1937–38: at Shinko. 1939: appointed advisor on films to Japanese government; started working for Shochiku. After World War II: worked mainly for Shin Toho and Daei. 1950: freelance. 1954: studied colour techniques in USA before making *Yokihi* (1955) (co-production with Hongkong). 1955: made a director of Daei. 1957: died during making of *Osaka Monogatari;* film finished by Kimisaburo Yoshimura.

Films as director: 1922: Ai ni Yomigaeru Hi – The Day When Love Returns; Furusato – Hometown (+ s); Seishun no Yumeji – Dreams of Youth (+ s); Joen no Chimata – Town of Fire; Haizan no Uta wa Kanashi – Sad Song of the Defeated (+ s); 8l3 – Rupimono; Chi to Rei – Blood and Soul (+ s). 1923: Kiri no Minato – Foggy Harbour; Yoru – Night (+ s); Haikyo no Naka – Among the Ruins (+ s); Toge no Uta – Song of the Mountain Pass (+ s). 1924: Kanashiki Hakuchi – Sad Idiot (+ co-s); Gendai no Jowo – Queen of Modern Times; Josei wat Suyoshi – Women are Strong; Shichimencho no Yukue – Turkeys in a Row; Samidare Soshi – May Rain and Silk Paper; Jin Kyo – The World Down Here. 1925: Musen Fusen – No Fight Without Money; Kanraku no Onna – Woman of Pleasure (+ co-s); Akatsuki no Shi – Death at Dawn; Kyokubadan no Jowo – Queen of Circus; Gakuso o Idete – After Years of Study (+ co-s); Shiragiku wa Nageku; Daichi Wa Hohoemu – Smile of our Earth (*ep*); Akai Yuhi Ni Terasarete – In the Red Rays of the Sleeping Sun; Furusato no Uta – Song of the Native Country; Ningen – Man; Gaijo no Sukechi – Street Sketches; Shirayuri wa Nageku – Lament of a White

Lily. 1926: Nogi Shogun to Kuma San – General Nogi and Kuma San; Doka-o – King of a Penny (+ s); Kami-ningyo Haru no Sassayaki – Paper Doll's Whisper of Spring; Shin Ono Ga Tsumi – My Fault Continued; Kyoren no Onna Shisho – Passion of a Woman Teacher; Kane – Money (+ co-s); Kaikoku Danji – Children of the Sea; Kin ou Kane (+ co-s). 1927: Ko-on – Gratitude to the Emperor; Jihi Shincho – Like the Changing Heart of a Bird. 1928: Hito no Issho – Life of a Man (*in 3 parts*). 1929: Nihonbashi – The Nihon Bridge (+ s); Tokyo Koshin-Kyoku – Tokyo March; Asahi Wa Kagayaku – The Rising Sun is Shining; Tokai Kokyogaku – Metropolitan Symphony. 1930: Furusato – Hometown; Tojin Okichi – Okichi the Stranger. 1931: Shikamo Karera wa Yuku – And Yet They Go On. 1932: Toki no Ujigami – Timely Mediator; Manmo Kengoku no Reimei – The Dawn of the Founding of Manchukuo and Mongolia. 1933: Takino Shiraito – White Threads of the Cascades (*co*); Gion Matsuri – Gion Festival (+ s); Kamikaze Ren – Group Kamikaze; Shimpu Ren. 1934: Aizo Toge – The Gorge Between Love and Hate; Orizuru Osen – Paper Cranes from Osen. 1935: Maria no Oyuki – Virgin from Oyuki; Gubijinso – Poppies. 1936: Naniwa Ereji – Naniwa Hika – Naniwa Elegy (+ co-s); Gion no Shimai – Sisters of Gion. 1937: Aien-Kyo – The Gorge Between Love and Hate. 1938: Ah Furusato – Ah Kokyo – Ah, My Hometown; Roei no Uta – Song of the Camp. 1939: Zangiku Monogatari – The Story of the Lasty Chrysanthemums. 1940: Naniwa Onna – Woman of Osaka (+ co-s); Geido Ichidai Otoko – The Life of an Artist. 1942: Musashi Miyamoto; Genroku Chushingura – Loyal 47 Ronin (*in 2 parts*). 1944: Danjuro Sandei – Three Generations of Danjuro. 1945: Hissyo Ka – Song of Victory (*co*); Meito Bijomaru – Bijomaru Sword. 1946: Josei no Shori – Women's Victory; Utamaro o Meguru Gonin no Onna – Utamaro and his Five Women. 1947: Joyu Sumako no Koi – Love of Actress Sumako. 1948: Yoru no Onna Tachi – Women of the Night; Waga Koi wa Moenu – Flame of my Love. 1950: Yuki Fujin Ezu – Sketch of Madame Yuki. 1951: Oyusama – Miss Oyu; Musashino Fujin – Women of Musashino. 1952: Saikaku Ichidai Onna – The Life of O-Haru. 1953: Ugetsu Monogateri (+ co-s); Gion Bayashi – Gion Music. 1954: Sansho Dayu – Sansho the Bailiff; Chikamatsu Monogatari – Story from Chikamatsu; Uwasa no Onna – Woman in the Rumour. 1955: Yokihi – Princess Yang Kwei Fei; Shin Heike Monogatari – New Tales of the Taira Clan. 1956: Akasen Chitai – Street of Shame. 1957: Osaka Monogatari – An Osaka Story (*co-d Kimisiburo Yoshimura*).

MOCKRIDGE, Cyril J.

Composer. London 1896–
Royal Academy of Music, London. 1922: to USA; worked as arranger and composer. 1931: began in films as orchestral arranger, then musical director. Composer from early 1940s. Worked mainly for Fox. Also music for TV series.

Films as composer include: 1946: The Dark Corner; Cluny Brown; My Darling Clementine. 1947: The Late George Apley; Nightmare Alley. 1948: The Walls of Jericho; Road House. 1952: Deadline USA. 1953: River of No Return. 1955: The Lieutenant Wore Skirts. 1956: Bus Stop (*co*); The Solid Gold Cadillac. 1957: Will Success Spoil Rock Hunter. 1958: Rally

Robert Mitchum in Cape Fear, *directed by J. Lee Thompson.*
Pather Panchali, *directed by Satyajit Ray and photographed by Subrata Mitra.*
Shin Heike Monogatari, *directed by Kenji Mizoguchi and photographed by Kazuo Miyagawa.*

191

'Round the Flag, Boys! 1960: Flaming Star. 1962: The Man Who Shot Liberty Valance. 1963: Donovan's Reef.

MOCKY, Jean-Pierre

(Mokiejeswki) Director and actor. Nice, France 1929– Polish descent. Acted on Paris stage at 18, opposite Maria Cesares. University of Strasbourg. Studied law and drama. Photographic retouching; produced plays in South of France. Actor in films since 1944. 1956: made own adaptation of 'Les Têtes contre les murs'; later asked Georges Franju to direct. 1958: wrote and acted in the film. 1959: first film as director. Scripts all his own films. Own production company.

Films as actor include: 1946: L'Affaire du collier de la reine. 1950: Orphée; Dieu a besoin des hommes. 1953: I Vinti. 1955: Gli Sbandati. 1956: Le Rouge est mis. 1958: La Tête contre les murs (+ s).

Films as director and writer: 1959: Les Dragueurs – The Young Have No Morals. 1960: Un Couple – The Love Trap (co-s). 1961: Les Snobs. 1962: Les Vierges (co-s). 1963: Un Drôle de parroisien – Heaven Sent. 1964: La Grande Frousse – The Big Scare. 1965: La Bourse et la vie – Your Money or Your Life. 1966: Les Compagnons de la marguerite – Order of the Daisy (co-s). 1968: Lat Grande Lessive – The Big Wash! (co-s). 1969: L'Etalon – The Stud (+ w; co-s); Solo (+ w; co-s). 1971: L'Albatross (+ w; co-s).

MODOT, Gaston

Actor. Paris 1887–1970
Trained as architect. 1905–07: worked as artist in Montmartre. Appeared in films from 1908.

Films as actor include: 1917: Mater Dolorosa. 1919: La Fête Espagnole. 1921: Fièvre. 1930: Sous les toits de Paris; L'Age d'or. 1931: L'Opéra de quat'sous; Fantômas. 1933: Quatorze juillet. 1936: Le Bandéra; La Vie est à nous. 1937: Pépé le Moko; Mademoiselle Docteur; La Grande Illusion. 1938: La Marseillaise. 1939: La Règle du jeu; La Fin du jour. 1942: Dernier atout. 1944: Les Enfants du Paradis. 1947: Antoine et Antoinette; Le Silence est d'or. 1949: La Beauté du diable; Rendez-vous de juillet; Le Point de jour. 1952: Casque d'or. 1955: French Can Can. 1956: Cela s'appelle l'aurore; Eléna et les hommes. 1958: Les Amants. 1961: Le Testament du Dr Cordelier.

MOHR, Hal

Cinematographer. San Francisco 1893–
Father ran wholesale woollens firm. Father Jewish, mother Catholic. 2 years of high school. Built own camera, shot and sold own newsreels in violation of patents monopoly. Film inspector at Sol Lesser's Film Exchange, ran Lesser's newsreel company. Made 1-reel record of last open night of San Francisco's Pacific Street, *Last Night of the Barbary Coast*. Worked for portrait photographers, then publicity for Thomas Ince. An unfinished film as director. 1915: editor at Universal. To Hal Roach; directed Harold Lloyd in *The Big Idea* (1918). Army service, including period in photographic section of Signal Corps. Photographed 1-reel westerns, then to Ralph Ince. Assistant to Charles Rosher. From 1922: worked for several companies. 1927–29: mainly Warners. Then Universal, Pathe, RKO-Pathe. 1932–35: Most work for Fox. 1935–39: mainly Warners. 1939–48: mainly Universal. Then to e.g. Columbia, United Artists. Oscars as cinematographer for *A Midsummers Night's Dream* (1935) and *The Phantom of the Opera* (1943, in collaboration).

Films as cinematographer include: 1926: The Third Degree. 1927: A Million Bid; Old San Francisco; The Heart of Maryland; Slightly Used; The Jazz Singer. 1928: Tenderloin; Glorious Betsy; The Wedding March (co). 1929: Noah's Ark (co); Broadway; The Last Performance. 1930: Big Boy; The Cat Creeps (co). 1931: A Woman of Experience; The Big Gamble. 1932: Week Ends Only; Tess of the Storm Country. 1933: State Fair; The Warrior's Husband; I Loved You Wednesday; The Devil's in Love. 1934: Carolina; David Harum; Servant's Entrance. 1935: Under Pressure; Captain Blood. 1936: The Walking Dead; Bullets or Ballots; The Green Pastures. 1938: I Met My Love Again. 1939: Back Door to Heaven (co); Rio. 1940: When the Daltons Rode. 1941: Cheers for Miss Bishop; Pot O' Gold. 1943: Watch on the Rhine (co). 1945: Salome, Where She Danced (co). 1948: Another Part of the Forest. 1951: The Big Night. 1952: Rancho Notorious; The Four Poster. 1953: The Member of the Wedding; The Wild One. 1956: The Boss. 1957: Baby Face Nelson. 1958: The Lineup; The Gun Runners. 1960: The Last Voyage. 1961: Underworld USA. 1963: The Man from the Diners' Club.

MOLANDER, Gustav

Director. Helsinki, Finland 1888–
Father a writer. Drama school of Royal Dramatic Theatre, Stockholm. 1909–11: actor at Swedish theatre in Helsinki. 1911–13: at Intiman. 1913–26: at Royal Dramatic Theatre, Stockholm, where he was principal and teacher at the drama school from 1921. From 1916: wrote scripts e.g. *Terje Vigen* (1916), *Thomas Graals bästa film* (1917), *Sången om den eldröda blomman* (1919), *Herr Arnes pengar* (1919). 1920: first film as director. From 1923: director with Svensk Filmindustri. Also TV director.

Films as director: 1920: Bodakungen – King of Boda (+ s). 1921: En Ungdomsaventry (+ s). 1922: Thomas Graals – Thomas Graals Myndling – Thomas Graals Ward (+ s); Parlorna (+ s); Amatorfilmen – The Amateur Film. 1923: Malarpirater – Pirates on Lake Malar (+ s). 1924: 33.333 (+ s); Polis Paulus Påskasmall – Constable Paulus's Easter Bomb (+ s). 1925: Ingmarsarvet – The Ingmar Inheritance; Till Osterland – To the Orient. 1926: Hon, den Enda – She, the Only One (+ co-s); Hans Engelska Fru – His English Wife. 1927: Förseglade Läppar – Sealed Lips; Parisiskor – Women of Paris. 1928: Synd – Sin. 1929: Hjärtats triumf – Triumph of the Heart. 1930: Fridas Visor – Frida's Songs (+ co-s). 1931: Charlotte Löwensköld; Från yttersta skären; En Natt – One Night. 1932: Svarta Rosor – Black Roses; Karlek och kassabrist – Love and Deficit (+ s); Vi som gar koksvagen – We Go Through the Kitchen (+ s). 1933: Kara Släkten – Dear Relatives (+ s). 1934: En Stilla Flirt – A Quiet Affair; Fasters Miljoner – My Aunt's Millions; Ungkarlspappan – Bachelor Father. 1935: Swedenhielms; Under falsk flagg – Under False Colours; Brollopsresan – The Honeymoon Trip. 1936: På solsidan – On the Sunny Side; Intermezzo (+ co-s); Familjens Hemlighet – The Family Secret. 1937: Sara lär sig folkvett – Sara Learns Manners; Der Kan man kalla kärlek; Dollar. 1938: En Kvinnas Ansikte – A Woman's Face; En Enda Natt – One Single Night; Ombyte förnöjer – Vanity is the Spice of Life. 1939: Emilie Högqvist (+ co-s). 1940: En, men ett lejon – One, but a Lion; Den Ljusnande Framtid – Bright Prospects (+ co-s). 1941: I natt eller aldrig – Tonight or Never; Striden går vidare – The Fight Goes On. 1942: Jacobs stege – Jacob's Ladder; Rid i natt – Ride Tonight (+ s). 1943: Alskling, jag ger mig – Darling, I Surrender; Ordet – The Word; Det Brinner en eld – There Burned a Flame. 1944: Den Osynliga Muren – The Invisible Wall. 1945: Kejsaren av Portugallien – The Emperor of Portugal (+ co-s); Galgmannen – Mandragora. 1946: Det Är min modell – It's My Model. 1947: Kvinna utan ansikte – The Woman Without a Face. 1948: Nu börjar livet – Life Begins Now; Eva (+ co-s). 1949: Kärleken segrar – Love Will Conquer. 1950: Kvartetten som sprängdes – The Quartet that Split Up. 1951: Fastmo uthyres – Fiancée for Hire; Frånskild – Divorced. 1952: Trots – Defiance; Karlek – Love. 1953: Glasberget – Unmarried. 1954: Herr Arnes Pengar – Sir Arne's Treasure (+ co-s). 1955: Enhörningen – The Unicorn. 1956: Sången om den eldröda blomman – The Song of the Scarlet Flower. 1967: Stimulantia ep Smycket – The Necklace (+ s).

MOLINARO, Édouard

Director. Bordeaux, France 1928–
University education. A number of amateur films by 1949. Then assistant director to Maurice de Canonge, Pierre Billon, Andre Barthomieu. 1949–53: made about 20 technical and industrial shorts. 1953–57: directed a number of short films. 1957: first feature as director.

Features as director include: 1957: Le Dos au mur. 1958: Des femmes disparaissent. 1960: Une Fille pour l'été (+ co-s). 1961: Les Sept Péchés Capitaux – The Seven Deadly Sins ep L'Envie. 1962: Arsène Lupin contre Arsène Lupin (+ co-s). 1963: Une Ravissante Idiote – A Ravishing Idiot. 1964: La Chasse à l'homme. 1966: Peau d'espion – To Commit a Murder (+ co-s). 1967: Oscar (+ co-s). 1969: Hibernatus; Mon Oncle Benjamin. 1970: La Liberté en croupe (+ co-s). 1971: Les Aveux les plus doux (+ co-ad/co-di).

MONICELLI, Mario

Director and writer. Rome 1915–
Literature and philosophy at Pisa and Milan Universities. 1935: amateur film *I Ragazzi della Via Paal* in Venice Film Festival; entered industry as clapper-boy. 1936–39: assistant director to e.g. Augusto Genina. 1940: wrote first script *La Granduchessa si diverti*. 1940–49: wrote series of scripts with S. V. Steno. 1949: they directed their first film *Totò cerca casa*. Made 7 comedies in collaboration with Steno, then first solo feature.

Solo films as director: 1954: Totò e Carolina (+ co-s). 1955: Proibito (+ co-s); Un Eroe di nostri tempi (+ co-st). 1956: Donatella. 1957: Padri e figli – Like Father Like Son (+ co-s); Il Medico e lo stregone. 1958: I Soliti Ignoti – Person Unknown (+ co-s). 1960: La Grande Guerra – The Great War (+ co-s); Risate di gioia – The Passionate Thief (+ co-s). 1962: Boccaccio '70 ep Renzo e Luciana (+ co-s). 1963: I

Compagni – The Strikers – The Organizer (+ *co-s*). 1964: Casanova 70. 1965: L'Armata Brancaleone (+ *co-s*). 1966: Le Fate – The Fairies – The Queens – Sex Quartet *ep* Fata Armenia. 1967: La Ragazza con la pistola – The Girl with a Pistol. 1969: To, è morta la nonna! (+ *co-s*). 1970: Le Coppie *ep* Il Frigorifero. 1971: Mortadella (+ *co-s*); Brancaleone alle crociate.

MONROE, Marilyn

(Norma Jean Baker or Mortenson) Actress. Los Angeles 1926–1962 Los Angeles
Brought up in orphanages, numerous foster homes. Photographer's model; first screen test for Fox in 1946. 1947: debut in small part for Fox. Occasional films for other companies but Fox contract from 1952. 1962: studio stopped shooting on her last film *Something's Got To Give* and commenced lawsuit against her; film started again as *Move Over, Darling* (1963) starring Doris Day. Died of an overdose of barbiturates. 3 husbands include baseball player Joe Di Maggio (1954, divorced) and Arthur Miller (1956–61, divorced).

Films as actress: 1947: Dangerous Years. 1949: Ladies of the Chorus. 1950: Love Happy; A Ticket to Tomahawk; The Asphalt Jungle; All About Eve; The Fireball; Right Cross. 1951: Home Town Story; As Young as You Feel; Love Nest; Let's Make It Legal. 1952: Clash by Night; We're Not Married; Don't Bother to Knock; Monkey Business; O. Henry's Full House *ep* The Cop and The Anthem. 1953: Niagara; Gentlemen Prefer Blondes; How to Marry a Millionaire. 1954: River of No Return; There's No Business like Show Business. 1955: The Seven Year Itch. 1956: Bus Stop. 1957: The Prince and the Showgirl (+ *pc*). 1959: Some Like it Hot. 1960: Let's Make Love. 1961: The Misfits.

MONTALBAN, Ricardo

Actor. Mexico City 1920–
Education in Mexico and Los Angeles. 1936: to New York; small parts on stage. 1939: first major stage role in 'Her Cardboard Lover'. Summer stock. 1942: returned to Mexico. 5 years as actor in Mexican films. 1947: MGM contract; first American film as actor *Fiesta*. 1944: married Georgiana Young, sister of Loretta Young. To 1953: almost all films for MGM. Then worked for several studios. Also TV, e.g. 'Gunsmoke'.

Films as actor include: 1945: Pepita Jimenez. 1947: Fiesta. 1948: The Kissing Bandit; On an Island with You. 1949: Border Incident; Battleground. 1950: Right Cross; Mystery Street. 1951: Across the Wide Missouri; Mark of the Renegade. 1952: My Man and I. 1953: Latin Lovers; Sombrero. 1954: The Saracen Blade. 1955: A Life in the Balance. 1957: Sayonara. 1962: The Reluctant Saint; Hemingway's Adventures of a Young Man. 1963: Love is a Ball. 1964: Cheyenne Autumn. 1965: The Singing Nun. 1966: The Money Trap. 1969: Sweet Charity. 1971: La Spina Dorsale del diavolo.

MONTAND, Yves

(Ivo Livi) Actor. Monsummano Alto, Italy 1921–
1923: with family to France on rise of Mussolini. Various jobs after leaving school in Marseilles. Produced and appeared in amateur vaudeville shows: joined local music-hall troupe. 1943–45: played in music-hall in Paris. In films from 1946. Also stage actor e.g. French production of Arthur Miller's 'The Crucible'. From 1965: mainly film actor. 1951: married Simone Signoret. 1965–70: 3 films directed by Costa-Gavras.

Films as actor include: 1946: Les Portes de la nuit. 1949: Souvenirs Perdus. 1953: Le Salaire de la peur. 1955: Napoléon; Marguerite de la nuit. 1957: Les Sorcières de Salem. 1958: La Loi. 1960: Let's Make Love. 1961: Sanctuary; Aimez-vous Brahms? 1965: Compartiment-tueurs. 1966: La Guerre est finie; Paris brûle-t-il? 1967: Vivre pour vivre. 1968: Z. 1969: Un Soir, un train; Le Diable par la queue. 1970: L'Aveu; On a Clear Day You Can See Forever; Le Cercle Rouge.

MONTEZ, Maria

(Maria Vidal Silas y Gracia) Actress. Barahona, Dominican Republic 1920–51 Paris
Father a Spanish scholar. Ran away from convent school. 1936: acted on Belfast stage. To USA. Model. Universal contract. To 1947: almost all films for Universal. 1943: married actor Jean-Pierre Aumont. 1948: financed and acted in Siren of Atlantis, released by United Artists. Settled in France. 1951: last film *Il Ladro di Venezia*.

Films as actress include: 1940: Boss of Bullion City; The Invisible Woman. 1941: That Night in Rio; South of Tahiti. 1942: Mystery of Marie Roget; Arabian Knights. 1943: White Savage. 1944: Follow the Boys; Cobra Woman. 1945: Sudan. 1946: Tangier. 1948: The Exile.

MONTGOMERY, Robert

Director and actor. Beacon, New York 1904–
Father president of New York Rubber Company. Began as stage actor. 72 weeks with Rochester stock company under direction of George Cukor. In films from 1926. 1929: MGM contract as actor. 1935: president of Screen Actors Guild. World War II: in Field Ambulance Service, then naval officer in London and South Pacific. 1944: put on inactive list as Lieutenant-Commander; returned to MGM for *They Were Expendable* (1945), acting and directing shots for back-projection plates. 1946: first film as director for MGM. Thereafter independent director. From 1950: left films for TV including producer/director of series 'Robert Montgomery Presents . . .' 'Friendly' witness at 1947 hearings of House Committee on Un-American Activities. 1952: Gold Medal for 'courageous American citizenship in fighting against Communist infiltration of the Motion Picture and Radio fields'. 1954: for 17 months, director of New York store, Macey's; senior executive on NBC; President Eisenhower's advisor on TV and public relations e.g. directed speech on H-bomb and Communist threat. 1960: formed production company with James Cagney to produce and direct *The Gallant Hours*.

Films as actor include: 1930: Untamed; The Divorcee; The Richest Man in the World. 1931: The Easiest Way; Inspiration; Private Lives. 1932: But the Flesh is Weak; Letty Lynton; Lovers Courageous; Blondie of the Follies. 1933: Hell Below; Night Flight. 1934: Riptide; Hide-out; Fugitive Lovers; Forsaking All Others. 1935: Vanessa. 1936: Piccadilly Jim. 1937:

Barbara Steele in Mario Moncelli's L'Armata Brancaleone.
Marilyn Monroe in River of No Return, *directed by Otto Preminger.*
Robert Montgomery (left), Joan Crawford and William Powell in The Last of Mrs Cheyney, *directed by Richard Boleslawski.*

The Last of Mrs Cheyney; Night Must Fall; Ever Since Eve. 1938: The First Hundred Years; Three Loves Has Nancy. 1940: The Earl of Chicago. 1941: Rage in Heaven; Mr and Mrs Smith; Here Comes Mr Jordan; Unfinished Business. 1948: June Bride.

Films as director and actor: 1946: Lady in the Lake. 1947: Ride the Pink Horse. 1949: Once More, My Darling. 1950: Eye Witness. 1960: The Gallant Hours (d/p only).

MONTIEL, Sara or Sarita

Actress, Criptana, Spain 1929–
Convent school. Spotted by producer Vincente Casanova. 1944: first film as actress *Te quiero para mi*. 1944–48: acted in Spanish films e.g. *Don Quijote de la Mancha*. From 1950: Mexican films. 1954: first American film *Vera Cruz*. 1956: directed by Anthony Mann in *Serenade* and married him. Continued to act in Mexican films; last American film *She-Gods of Shark Reef* (1957).

Films as actress include: 1954: Vera Cruz. 1956: Serenade. 1957: Run of the Arrow; She-Gods of Shark Reef.

MOORE, Ted

Cinematographer. South Africa 1914–
1930: to England. World War II: RAF pilot; member of RAF Film Unit; awarded DFC and Croix de Guerre for daylight sorties on U-boat pens and Gestapo headquarters. Camera operator on *Outcast of the Islands* (1951), *The African Queen* (1951), *Genevieve* (1952). Cinematographer from 1953; worked on 6 films directed by Terence Young. Oscar for cinematography in colour, *A Man for All Seasons* (1966).

Films as cinematographer include: 1956: Cockleshell Heroes (co); Zarak (co). 1962: Dr No. 1963: From Russia with Love. 1964: Goldfinger. 1965: Thunderball; The Amorous Adventures of Moll Flanders. 1966: A Man for All Seasons. 1967: The Last Safari. 1968: Shalako; The Prime of Miss Jean Brodie. 1969: Country Dance (r 1971). 1971: Diamonds are Forever.

MOOREHEAD, Agnes

Actress. Clinton, Massachusetts 1906–
University of Wisconsin, Bradley University (MA, PhD). American Academy of Dramatic Art, New York. Studied pantomime with Marcel Marceau in Paris. Taught speech, drama, English. 1919: stage debut in chorus of St Louis Municipal Opera; continued for 4 seasons. 1923: began in radio as singer. Theatrical work in New York and St Louis, then AADA Stock Company (1929). Joined Orson Welles' Mercury Theatre of the Air. 1941: first film as actress *Citizen Kane*. With Charles Laughton in First Drama Quartet's staged reading of 'Don Juan in Hell'; stage work in San Francisco, Boston and on tour. 1930–52: married actor Jack Lee. 1953–58: married director Robert Gist. Also TV, e.g. 'Bewitched'.

Films as actress include: 1942: The Magnificent Ambersons; The Big Street. 1943: Journey into Fear; Government Girl. 1944: Jane Eyre; Since You Went Away; The Seventh Cross; Dragon Seed; Mrs Parkington. 1945: Her Highness and the Bellboy; Our Vines Have Tender Grapes. 1947: Dark Passage; Summer

Holiday. 1948: Johnny Belinda. 1949: The Stratton Story; The Great Sinner; Without Honor. 1950: Caged. 1951: Fourteen Hours; Show Boat; The Blue Veil. 1952: The Blazing Forest. 1953: Main Street to Broadway; Scandal at Scourie. 1954: Magnificent Obsession. 1955: Untamed; The Left Hand of God; All That Heaven Allows; The Conqueror. 1956: Meet Me in Las Vegas; The Swan; The Revolt of Mamie Stover; Pardners; The Opposite Sex. 1957: The True Story of Jesse James; Jeanne Eagles; Raintree County; The Story of Mankind. 1958: La Tempestà. 1960: Pollyanna. 1961: Bachelor in Paradise; Twenty Plus Two. 1962: Jessica; How the West was Won. 1963: Who's Minding the Store? 1964: Hush, Hush, Sweet Charlotte. 1965: The Singing Nun.

MOORSE, George

Director. Bellmore, New York 1936–
Mother born in Latvia, father in London. Hofstra College and Washington Square College, New York. Wrote about jazz, painting; worked for Grove Press, New York; contributed to magazines e.g. Harper's Bazaar, New York Writing. 1957: travelled to Greece, Holland, Germany. 1959: settled in Munich. 1963: published novel 'Skin-Coty'. 1964: made first 2 shorts in Berlin and London. 1965: directed first feature in Holland.

Films as director include: 1964: Inside Out; London Pop. 1965: Zero in the Universe (+ co-s/e/w). 1967: Der Findling – The Foundling – The Orphan (+ co-s); Kuckucksjahre (+ co-s). 1968: Liebe und so weiter; Der Griller; Robinson. 1971: Lenz (+ s).

MOREAU, Jeanne

Actress. Paris 1928–
Mother a Tiller Girl. Studied acting at Conservatoire de Paris. 1948: professional stage début with Comédie Française. 1952: joined Théâtre National Populaire. In films from 1948. 1957: established screen reputation in *Ascenseur pour l'échafaud*. 1949–50: married Jean-Louis Richard. Also singing.

Films as actress include: 1954: Touchez pas au Grisbi. 1957: Le Dos au mur; Les Amants. 1959: Les Liaisons Dangereuses. 1960: Jovanka e l'altri; Moderato Cantabile; La Notte. 1961: Jules et Jim. 1962: Eve; La Baie des anges. 1963: Le Procès; Le Feu Follet. 1964: Le Journal d'une femme de chambre; Mata-Hari, agent H.21. 1965: The Train; Viva Maria. 1966: Campanadas a medianoche; Mademoiselle. 1967: The Sailor from Gibraltar; La Mariée était en noir; Une Histoire Immortelle. 1968: Le Corps de Diane. 1970: Monte Walsh. 1971: Le Petit Théâtre de Jean Renoir ep La Belle Epoque.

MORGAN, Michèle

(Simone Roussel) Actress. Neuilly-sur-Seine, France 1920–
Educated in Dieppe and drama school in Paris. Small parts in films from 1935. 1937: first large part in *Gribouille*. 1940: to Hollywood. Some American films for various companies. 1948: returned to Europe for *The Fallen Idol* and *Fabiola*. Then mainly in European films. 1953: appeared in New York TV production of 'La Dame aux camélias'. Married (1942–49) William Marshall; his company made *Symphonie Pastorale*

(1948) in which she starred. Divorced Marshall to marry actor Henri Vidal, who died in 1959.

Films as actress include: 1938: Orage; Quai des brumes. 1939: La Loi du nord. 1940: Untel père et fils. 1941: Remorques. 1942: Joan of Paris. 1944: Passage to Marseille. 1950: Le Château de verre. 1950: L'Etrange Madame X. 1951: Les Sept Péchés Capitaux ep L'orgeuil. 1953: Les Orgueilleux. 1954: Oasis. 1955: Les Grands Manoeuvres. 1956: Si Paris nous était conté. 1958: Le Miroir à deux faces. 1960: Les Scélérats. 1962: Landru. 1967: Benjamin.

MORI, Masayuki

Actor. Tokyo 1911–
Father novelist Takeo Arishima. Kyoto University, then stage debut; worked with various theatrical companies. 1942: first films for Toho.

Films as actor include: 1945: Tora no O o Fumo Otokotachi. 1948: Anjo-ke no Butokai. 1949: Yabure-Daiko. 1950: Rashomon. 1951: Hakuchi; Musashino Fujin; Nusumarete Koi. 1953: Ugetsu Monogatari; Ani Imoto; Senbazuru. 1955: Yokihi; Ukigumo; Kokoro. 1957: Banka; Arakure. 1958: Yoru no Tsuzumi. 1959: Kotan no Kuchibue. 1960: Ototo; Onna ga Kaidan o Agaru Toki; Musume Tsuma Haha; Warui Yatsu Hodo Yoku Nemuru. 1961: Onna no Kunsho. 1963: Bushido Zankoku Monogatari; Taiheiyo Hitoribotchi.

MOROSS, Jerome

Composer. New York 1913–
1931–32: Juillard Graduate School, studied music education at New York University. 1947: became Guggenheim Fellow. Compositions include: 'Symphony' (1942), 'Willie the Weeper' (1945), 'The Eccentricities of Davy Crocket' (1945), 'Riding Hood Revisited' (1946), 'The Golden Apple' (1950), 'The Last Judgment' (1953), 'Gentlemen, Be Seated!' (1955).

Films as composer include: 1958: The Proud Rebel; The Big Country. 1959: The Jayhawkers. 1960: The Mountain Road; The Adventures of Huckleberry Finn. 1962: Five Finger Exercise. 1963: The Cardinal.

MORRIS, Oswald

Cinematographer. Ruislip, Middlesex 1915–
1932: entered industry as clapper boy. After World War II, demobilised, and became camera operator, e.g. on *Green For Danger* (1946), *Oliver Twist* (1948). 1952–58: photographed 5 films directed by John Huston; devised process for combining colour and monochrome for *Moby Dick* (1956).

Films as cinematographer include: 1952: Moulin Rouge. 1954: Beat the Devil (co); Knave of Hearts. 1956: Moby Dick. 1957: Heaven Knows, Mr Allison (co); A Farewell to Arms (co). 1958: Roots of Heaven; The Key. 1959: Look Back in Anger. 1960: Our Man in Havana; The Entertainer. 1961: The Guns of Navarone. 1962: Lolita; Satan Never Sleeps. 1965: The Hill. 1967: The Taming of the Shrew. 1968: Oliver! 1969: Goodbye, Mr Chips. 1970: Scrooge. 1971: Fiddler on the Roof.

MOSJOUKINE see
MOZHUKHIN, Ivan

MOSKVIN, Andrei

Cinematographer. St Petersburg, Russia 1901-61 Leningrad

Photographed films for FEX. 1926: began collaboration with Grigori Kozintsev and Leonid Trauberg with *Chortovo Koleso*. Worked with them at Sovkino, Leningradkino and Lenfilm. 1944: shot interiors on *Ivan Groznyi* (I). 1946: shot the whole of part II. Photographed films directed by Kosintzev alone.

Films as cinematographer include: 1926: Katka-bumazhnyi ranet (*co*); Chortovo Koleso; Shinel (*co*). 1927: SVD; Bratishka. 1929: Novyi Vavilon. 1931: Odna. 1935: Yunost Maksima. 1937: Vozvrashchenie Maksima. 1939: Vyborgskaya Storona (*co*). 1943: Aktrisa. 1944-45: Ivan Groznyi (*co*; *in 2 parts*). 1945: Prostye Lyudi (*r* 1956). 1947; Pirogov (*co*). 1953: Bielinsky (*co*). 1957: Don Quixote (*co*). 1958: Rass-Kazi o Leninye (*co*). 1960: Dama s sobachkoi.

MOUSSINAC, Léon

Critic. Laroche-Migennes, France 1890-1964 Paris

1920-28: film critic for Le Mercure de France. 1921-37: critic for L'Humanité. Also from 1921 wrote for La Gazette des 7 Arts, Le Monde. 1925: author of 'Naissance du cinéma'. Personal friend of Sergei Eisenstein. 1926: organised screening of *Bronenosets 'Potyomkin'* in Paris. 1927: founded workers' cine-club Les Amis de Spartacus (dissolved by police in 1928). 1928: author of 'Le Cinéma Soviétique'. 1929: author of 'Panoramique du cinéma'. Was secretary-general of the Librairie Centrale des Beaux-Arts and director of Editions Sociales Internationales. 1946: author of 'L'Age Ingrat du cinéma'. 1947-49: director of l'IDHEC. 1963: author of 'Serge Eisenstein'.

MOUSSY, Marcel

Writer and director. Alger, Algeria 1924-

Universities of Paris, Harvard. Studied philosophy and English. To 1951: taught English at Etampes. Wrote plays, 'Le Dernier Métro pour Cythère' (1948), 'Mississippi' (1955), and novels, 'Le Sang Chaud' (1950), 'Babylonia' (1950), 'Arcole à la terre promise' (1954), 'Les Mauvais Sentiments' (1957). Several scripts for radio, and for TV series *Si c'était vous!* 2 script collaborations with François Truffaut. 1966: directed and wrote 2 features for TV.

Films as writer: 1959: Les Quatre Cents Coups (*ad/di*); La Sentence (*co*). 1960: Tirez sur le pianiste (*co-ad/co-di*). 1966: Paris, brûle-t-il? (*French di*).

Films as director and writer: 1960: Saint-Tropez Blues. 1961: Les Grandes Pelouses – The Great Fields. 1966: 22 rue de la Victoire (*TV*); Quand la liberté du ciel (*TV*).

MOZHUKHIN, Ivan
(or Mosjoukine)

Actor. Penza, Russia 1889-1939 Paris

Parents of aristocratic origin. Studied law in Moscow.

then actor with touring company in Kiev and at Moscow Dramatic Theatre. 1911: first films. 1915-19: twenty-six films with Yakov Protazanov. 1920: to Paris, where he worked as director and scriptwriter in collaboration on several films. 1927: to USA to appear in *Surrender*; then signed with Ufa to act in 4 films in Berlin. Career declined after the coming of sound. Last appearance in 1936. First wife was actress Nathalie Lissenko who played opposite him in Russian films.

Films as actor include: 1915: Nikolai Stavrogin. 1916: Pikovaya Dama. 1917: Andrei Kozhukhov; Satana Likuyushchii. 1918: Otets Sergii. 1921: Justice d'abord; L'Enfant du carnaval (*+d/s*). 1922: Kean. 1923: L'Angoissante Aventure; Le Brasier Ardent (*+d/s*); Les Ombres qui passent (*+co-s*). 1924: Le Lion des Mogols (*+s*). 1925: Feu Mathias Pascal. 1927: Casanova. 1933: La Mille et Deuxième Nuit.

MULLIGAN, Robert

Director. New York 1925-

Father a policeman. World War II interrupted theological studies; served as radio operator in US Marine Corps. 6 months on copy desk of New York Times; to Fordham University as student in radio department. Joined CBS as messenger, becoming production assistant, then director e.g. 'Suspense' series and TV drama including 'Billy Budd', 'The Member of the Wedding', 'The Catered Affair'. 1957: first film. 1957-64: worked mainly for Universal and Paramount. From 1965: Warners. Also directed on Broadway.

Films as director: 1957: Fear Strikes Out. 1960: The Great Imposter; The Rat Race. 1961: Come September. 1962: The Spiral Road; To Kill a Mockingbird. 1963: Love with the Proper Stranger. 1965: Baby, the Rain Must Fall. 1966: Inside Daisy Clover. 1967: Up the Down Staircase. 1969: The Stalking Moon. 1971: The Pursuit of Happiness (*+ co-p*); Summer of '42.

MUNI, Paul
(Muni Weisenfreud)

Lwow, Poland 1895-1967 Santa Barbara, California

Parents were actors who emigrated to USA via London in 1902. First acting part at 12, playing man of 60. 1918: joined Yiddish Art Theatre in New York. Left to play an orthodox Jew in 'We Americans', which made him a leading Broadway actor. Went to Hollywood for Fox and changed name to Paul Muni. 1929: first film as actor *The Valiant*; only one more film before leaving Hollywood to re-establish himself on Broadway. Returned to Hollywood for *Scarface, Shame of the Nation* (1932). Because of its success, obtained Warners contract with script approval. Worked mainly for Warners in next 10 years. 1936: Oscar as Best Actor for *The Story of Louis Pasteur*. After 1945: concentrated on stage, only occasional films; last was The Last Angry Man (1959).

Films as actor include: 1932: Scarface, Shame of the Nation; I am a Fugitive from a Chain Gang. 1933: The World Changes. 1934: Hi, Nellie! 1935: Border Town; Dr Socrates; Black Fury; The Story of Louis Pasteur. 1937: The Good Earth; The Life of Emile Zola; The Woman I Love. 1939: Juarez; We are not Alone. 1941: Hudson's Bay. 1943: Commandos Strike at Dawn; Stage Door Canteen. 1944: A Song to

Jeanne Moreau as Catherine in Gordon Flemyng's Great Catherine.
Sue Lyon in Stanley Kubrick's Lolita, *photographed by Oswald Morris.*
Rock Hudson (centre) in Robert Mulligan's The Spiral Road.

Remember. 1945: Counter-attack. 1946: Angel on My Shoulder. 1952: Stranger on the Prowl.

MUNK, Andrzej

Director. Cracow, Poland 1921–61 near Warsaw
Gave up studying architecture to study as cinematographer and director at Lodz film school. Directed shorts and co-directed *Gwiazdy musza plonac* (1954) with Witold Lesiewicz before made first feature in 1955. 1960–61: directed 3 plays for TV. Making *Pasazerka*, was killed in a car accident; version with scenes shot by Munk linked by stills and edited by Witold Lesiewicz was released in 1963.

Films as director: 1949: Sztuka Mlodych (+ *s*). 1950: Zaczelo sie w Hiszpanii (+ *e*). 1951: Nauka blizej zycia (+ *co-c*); Kierunek nowa huta. 1952: Poemat Symfoniczny 'Bajka' St Moniuszki; Pamietniki chlopow (+ *s*). 1953: Kolejarskie slowo (+ *s*). 1954: Gwiazdy musza plonac (+ *s*, co-d *Witold Lesiewicz*). 1955: Niedzielny Poranek – One Sunday Morning (+ *s*); Blekitny Krzyz – Men of the Blue Cross (+ *s*). 1956: Czlowiek na torze – Man on the Track (+ *co-s*). 1957: Eroica. 1958: Spacerek Staromiejski – A Walk in the Old City of Warsaw (+ *s*). 1959: Zezowate szczescie – Bad Luck – Cross-Eyed Fortune; Polska Kronika Filmowa Nr 52 A-B. 1961: Pasazerka – Passenger (+ *co-s*).

MURNAU, Friedrich Wilhelm

(F. W. Plumpe) Director. Bielefeld, Westphalia 1889–1931 Santa Barbara, California
Higher degree from Heidelberg University, then joined Max Reinhardt's theatre company. Airman during World War I. Theatre director in Zurich and Berne. Directed propaganda films in Switzerland for German Embassy. 1919: first feature as director. 1926: to Hollywood to make 3 films for Fox. 1929: *Tabu* was produced independently with Robert Flaherty, released by Paramount (1931); died after car crash, a week before its premiere.

Features as director: 1919: Der Knabe in blau – The Child in Blue; Satanas. 1920: Sehnsucht – Longing; Der Januskopf – Janus Faced; Abend . . . Nacht . . . Morgen; Der Gang in die Nacht; Love's Mockery – The Walk in the Night; Der Bucklige und die Tanzerin – The Hunchback and the Dancer. 1921: Marizza, gennant die Schmuggler – Madonna – Marizza, Called the Smuggler – Madonna; Schloss Vogelod – The Haunted Castle. 1922: Nosferatu, eine Symphonie des Gravens; Der brennende Acker – The Burning Acre; Phantom. 1923: Die Austreibung – Driven from Home – Expulsion; Die Finanzen des Grossherzogs – Finances of the Grand Duke. 1924: Der letzte Mann – The Last Laugh. 1925: Tartüff. 1926: Faust. 1927: Sunrise. 1928: Four Devils. 1930: Our Daily Bread – City Girl; Die zwolfte Stunde – Eine Nacht des Grauens (*sound version of* Nosferatu, eine Symphonie des Grauens). 1931: Tabu (+ *co-p/co-s*; co-d *Robert Flaherty*).

MURPHY, Audie

Actor. Kingston, Texas 1924–71 Roanoke, Virginia
World War II: US Infantry, reaching Lieutenant; received 24 decorations. Spotted by James Cagney. 1948: first film as actor *Beyond Glory*. 1955: acted in *To Hell and Back* based on his autobiographical book dealing with war experiences. 1957: acted in and part-financed *The Guns of Fort Petticoat*. Most films for Universal. Married actress Wanda Hendrix (1949–50, divorced). Killed in plane crash.

Films as actor include: 1948: Texas, Brooklyn and Heaven. 1950: Sierra; Kansas Raiders. 1951: The Red Badge of Courage; The Cimarron Kid. 1952: Duel at Silver Creek. 1954: Destry. 1957: Night Passage; The Guns of Fort Petticoat (+ *co-pc*). 1958: The Gun Runners; The Quiet American. 1959: No Name on the Bullet. 1960: The Unforgiven; 7 Ways from Sundown. 1962: 6 Black Horses.

MURPHY, George

Actor. New Haven, Connecticut 1902–
Yale. Dancing partnership with Juliette Henkel, married her in 1926. Cabaret. 1927: Broadway debut in 'Good News' then 'Hold Everything!' and 'Of Thee I Sing'. To London. 1934: return to Broadway in 'Roberta' and first film as actor *Kid Millions*. 1940: vice-president of Screen Actors Guild; was its president in 1944 (2 terms). Most films for MGM and RKO. 1950: Special Oscar for 'interpreting the motion picture industry to the country at large'. 1952: last film *Walk East on Beacon*. 1957: directed Jamboree. 1961: directed rally in Hollywood Bowl 'America's Answer to Communism'. US Senator. To 1970: board member of Technicolor. Autobiography 'Say – Didn't You Used to be George Murphy?' (1970).

Films as actor include: 1937: Broadway Melody of 1938; You're a Sweetheart; Letter of Introduction; Hold That Co-Ed; Little Miss Broadway. 1940: Little Nellie Kelly; Broadway Melody of 1940; Public Deb No 1. 1941: Rise and Shine; Tom, Dick and Harry; A Girl, A Guy and a Gob. 1942: For Me and My Gal; The Powers Girl. 1943: Bataan; This is the Army. 1944: Broadway Rhythm. 1947: Cynthia; The Arnelo Affair. 1948: The Big City. 1949: Battleground; Border Incident. 1951: It's a Big Country.

MURPHY, Richard

Director and writer. Boston, Massachusetts 1912–
Editor and feature writer for Literary Digest before entering film industry (1937). 1942–45: Captain in US Signal Corps. 1945–54: contract writer for Fox. Directed 2 films.

Films as writer include: 1947: Boomerang. 1948: Cry of the City; Deep Waters. 1949: Slattery's Hurricane (*co*). 1951: You're in the Navy Now (+ *st*). 1953: The Desert Rats (+ *st*). 1954: Broken Lance. 1959: Compulsion.

Films as writer and director: 1955: Three Stripes In The Sun – The Gentle Sergeant. 1960: The Wackiest Ship in the Army.

MURRAY, Don

Actor. Hollywood 1929–
Father was dance director and stage manager Dennis Murray, mother was a Ziegfeld girl. 1946–48: American Academy of Dramatic Arts. 1950: first major role, in 'The Rose Tattoo' in Chicago. 1951: with the play to Broadway, and on tour. During Korean War was conscientious objector. 1952–55; worked with Italian refugees. 1955: return to stage in 'The Skin of Our Teeth' in Paris, Washington, Chicago and New York and repeated the role on TV. 1956: first film *Bus Stop* with Hope Lange whom he married (1956–61, divorced). To 1961: films for Fox and United Artists. Then worked for several companies. TV 'The Hasty Heart', 'Billy Budd'. Own production company. 1970: directed and co-wrote first feature, *The Cross and the Switchblade*.

Films as actor include: 1957: The Bachelor Party; A Hatful of Rain. 1958: From Hell to Texas; These Thousand Hills. 1959; Shake Hands with the Devil. 1961: The Hoodlum Priest. 1962: Escape from East Berlin; Advise and Consent. 1964: One Man's Way. 1965: Baby, the Rain Must Fall. 1969: Childish Things (+ *p/s*).

MUSURACA, Nicholas

Cinematographer
1908: began as driver for J. Stuart Blackton. Various odd jobs at Vitagraph, becoming camera assistant there. 1919: became cinematographer at Vitagraph then at RKO up till 1954. 1957–58: freelance.

Films as cinematographer include: 1926: Bride of the Storm; The Passionate Quest. 1929: Side Street (*co*). 1931: Cracked Nuts; Smart Woman. 1934: Long Lost Father. 1939: Sorority House; Five Came Back; Golden Boy. 1940: Tom Brown's Schooldays; Little Men. 1941: The Gay Falcon. 1942: The Tuttles of Tahiti. 1943: Cat People; Forever and a Day (*co*); The Seventh Victim; The Ghost Ship. 1944: The Curse of the Cat People; Girl Rush. 1945: China Sky; Back to Bataan; The Spiral Staircase. 1946: Deadline at Dawn; Bedlam; The Locket. 1947: Out of the Past. 1948: Blood on the Moon; I Remember Mama. 1949: I Married a Communist. 1950: Where Danger Lives. 1951: The Whip Hand. 1952: A Girl in Every Port; Clash by Night. 1953: The Hitch-hiker; Split Second. 1954: Susan Slept Here. 1957: Man on the Prowl. 1958: Too Much, Too Soon (*co*).

MUYBRIDGE, Eadweard

(Edward James Muggeridge) Photographer. Kingston-on-Thames, Middlesex 1830–1904 Kingston-on-Thames, Middlesex
1852: to USA. Among first to use spring-activated shutter, introduced many refinements to still photography. 1872–77: photographed horse's gallop using 12, 18 and 24 still cameras aligned and operated by trip-wires, proving that at times a galloping horse had all 4 feet off ground. At suggestion of Etienne-Jules Marey and Scientific American worked on projecting his work using zoetrope; patented his apparatus. 1880: using zoogyroscope projected his work – first motion picture presentation. 1881: visited France with zoogyroscope (later renamed zoopraxiscope) stimulating Marey to use motion picture photography in his studies of animal movement, and Emile Reynaud to perfect his 'praxinoscope à projections'. From 1885: carried on work with grant from University of Pennsylvania. 1887: published 'Animal Locomotion; an Electro-Photographic Investigation of Consecutive Phases of Animal Movements 1872–1885'. 1893: lectured at Chicago World Fair, presenting zoopraxiscope. 1900: retired to Kingston-on-Thames.

N

NAGATA, Masaichi

Studio Head. Kyoto, Japan 1906–
Okura Commercial School. 1924: entered films, becoming a producer at Nikkatsu. With Mizoguchi and Daisuke set up production company, Dai-ichi. 1936: dissolved Dai-ichi; entered Shinko. 1942: formed production company Daiei. 1947: became its president. To 1971: owned Lotto Orions, professional baseball team. Producer of many Japanese films shown internationally including *Rashomon* (1950).

NAKADAI, Tatsuya

Actor. Japan 1930–
Drama school and some stage experience. In films from 1953: frequently directed by Kobayashi.

Films as actor include: 1953: Kabe Atuski Heya. 1957: Kuroi Kawa; Ningen no Joken (Part 1). 1959: Kagi. 1960: Enjo; Ningen no Joken (Part 2). 1961: Ningen no Joken (Part 3); Yojimbo; Eien no Hito. 1962: Sanjuro; Karami-ai. 1963: Seppuku; Tengoku to Jogoku; Gojuman-nin no Isan. 1964: Kaidan *ep* Yuki-Onna. 1965: Tanin nokao. 1971: Inochi Bonifuro.

NAPOLEON, Art

Director. 1923–
1942–45: US Navy combat pilot. 1946–56: worked for TV; directed many TV films. Wrote film scripts for e.g. Jerry Hopper. 1957: first film as director, for United Artists. Wrote asl own films in collaboration with wife Josephine, also produced *Man on the Prowl* (1957) and *The Activist* (1969) with her.

Films as director and writer in collaboration: 1957: Man on the Prowl (+ *co-p*). 1958: Too Much, Too Soon. 1964: Ride the Wisd Surf (*uc, co-d Don Taylor*). 1969: The Activist (+ *co-p*).

NARUSE, Mikio

Director. Tokyo 1905–1969
Orphaned when very young. Left school early. 1926: became assistant at Shochiku. Assistant to Yasujiro Shimazu and Yoshimobu Ikeda. 1930: first film as director. 1934: moved to PCL Studios; stayed as employee of Toho when in 1936 it was formed to distribute PCL's films. To 1950: often wrote own scripts.

Films as director and writer: 1930: Chanbara Fufu – Mr and Mrs Swordplay; Oshikiri Shinkon Ki – Record of Newly-Weds; Fukeiki Jidai – Depression Period. 1931: Koshiben Ganbare – Hardworking Clerk; Nikai no Himei; Uwaki wa Kisha ni Notte – Fickleness Gets on the Train; Hige no Chikara – Beard of Strength; Onna wa Tamoto o Goyojin. 1932: Eraku Naru – Erroneous Practice; Kimi to Wakarete – Apart from You. 1933: Yogoto no Yume – Everynight Dreams. 1935: Otome-gokoro Sannin Shimai – Three Sisters with Maiden Hearts; Tsuma yo Bara no Yoni – Wife, Be Like a Rose. 1936: Tochuken Kumoemon – On the Way to Spider Gate: Kimi to Yuku Michi: Asa no

Namiki-michi – Dawn in the Boulevard. 1937: Nyonin Aishu – New Grief; Nadare – Avalanche. 1938: Tsuruhachi Tsurujiro – Tsuruhachi and Tsurujiro. 1939: Hataraku Ikka – The Whole Family Works; Magokoro – Sincerity. 1940: Tabiyakusha – An Itinerant Actor. 1941: Natsukashi no Kao – A Dearly Loved Face; Hideko no Shasho-San. 1944: Tanoshikikana Jinsei. 1946: Ore mo Omae mo. 1947: Haru no Mezame – Spring Awakening. 1949: Furyo Shojo – The Bad Girl. 1950: Shiroi Yaju – White Beast. 1958: Anzukko.

Films as director: 1930: Junjo – Pure Love; Ai wa Chikara da – Strength of Love. 1931: Ne Kofun Shicha Iyayo – Now Don't Get Excited; Tonari no Yane no Shita; Aozora ni Naku – Weeping Blue Sky. 1932: Mushibameru Haru – Lost Spring; Nasanu Naka – Stepchild. 1933: Boku no Marumage; Soho – Careless. 1934: Kagirinaki Hodo. 1935: Joyu to Shinij – The Actress and the Poet; Saakas Goningumi; Uwasa no Musume – The Girl in the Rumour. 1937: Kafuku (*in 2 parts*). 1941: Shanhai no Tsuki – The Moon over Shanghai. 1942: Haha wa Shinazu. 1943: Uta Andon – Song of a Lantern. 1944: Shibaido – Theatre. 1945: Shori no Hi Made – Victory in the Sun; Sanju-Sangendo Toshiya Monogatari. 1946: Urashima Taro ni Koei – The Descendants of Taro Urashima. 1950: Yottsu no Koi no Monogatari – Four Love Stories – Circus of Love (*ep*); Ishinaka Sensei Gyojoki – Conduct Report on Professor Ishinaka; Ikari no Machi – Town of Anger; Bara-gassen. 1951: Ginza-gesho; Maihime – Dancing Princess; Meshi – Repast – A Married Life. 1952: Okuni to Gohei; Okasan – Mother; Inazuma – Lightning. 1953: Fufu – Husband and Wife; Tsuma – A Wife; Ani Imoto – Older Brother, Younger Sister. 1954: Yama no Oto – Sounds from the Mountains – The Echo; Bangiku – Late Chrysanthemums, 1955: Ukigumo – Floating Clouds; Kuchizuke – The First Kiss (*ep*). 1956: Shuu – Sudden Rain; Tsuma no Kokoro – Wife's Heart; Nagareru – Flowing. 1957: Arakure – Untamed Woman. 1958: Iwashigumo – The Summer Clouds. 1959: Kotan no Kuchibue – A Whistle in My Heart. 1960: Onna ga Kaidan o Agaru Toki – When a Woman Ascends the Stairs; Musume Tsuma Haha – Daughters, Wives and a Mother; Yoru no Nagare – Flowing Night – The Lovelorn Geisha (*co-d Yuzo Kawashima*); Aki Tachinu – The Approach of Autumn. 1961: Tsuma Toshite Onna Toshite – As a Wife, As a Woman. 1962: Onna no Za – A Woman's Place; Horoki – Lonely Lane. 1963: Onna no Rekishi – A Woman's Life. 1964: Midareru – Yearning. 1966: Onna no Naka ni Iru Tanin – The Thin Line; Hikinige – Moment of Terror – Hit-and-Run. 1967: Midare-gumo – Two in the Shadow – Scattered Clouds.

NAZIMOVA, Alla

Actress. Yalta, Russia 1879–1945
Theatrical work includes 'Hedda Gabler', 'Zaza'. American stage debut in 'The Chosen People'. 1916: first film *War Brides*. Also toured in the stage version. 1922: with husband actor-director Charles Bryant produced and herself acted in *A Doll's House* and *Salome*. 1939: period advisor on *Zaza*. Produced several of her films as actress.

Films as actress include: 1918: The Revelation; Eye for an Eye (+ *p*). 1919: The Brat. 1920: The Heart of a Child. 1921: Camille (+ *p*). 1924: Madonna of the Streets. 1925: The Redeeming Sin. 1940: Escape.

Der letzte Mann by F. W. Murnau.
Ugetsu Monogatari, directed by Kenji Mizoguchi and produced by Masaichi Nagata.
Tatsuya Nakadai in Kobayashi's Seppuku.

1941: Blood and Sand. 1944: The Bridge of San Luis Rey; In Our Time.

NEAGLE, Anna

(Marjorie Robertson) Actress. London, 1904–
Daughter of actress Florence Neagle. Chorus girl in London musicals. 1925: in revue with Jack Buchanan, Jessie Matthews, Tillie Losch, and with the show to Broadway. Small parts in British films. 1931: invited by Jack Buchanan to join 'Stand Up and Sing', and Herbert Wilcox gave her a part in *Goodnight Vienna*. She married him (in 1943) and made over 30 films with him. RKO contract. 1951–54: stage. Discovered Frankie Vaughan. From 1957: actor-producer. 1965: 'Charly Girl'.

Films as actress include: 1933: Bitter Sweet. 1934: Nell Gwynn. 1937: Victoria the Great. 1938: Sixty Glorious Years. 1939: Nurse Edith Cavell. 1940: Irene; No, No, Nanette. 1941: Sunny. 1942: Wings and the Woman. 1943: The Yellow Canary; Forever and a Day. 1945: A Yank in London. 1950: Odette. 1951: The Lady with the Lamp. 1954: Lilacs in the Spring. 1955: King's Rhapsody. 1957: These Dangerous Years (+ *p*). 1959: The Lady is a Square.

NEAL, Patricia

(Patsy Louise Neal) Actress. Packard, Kentucky 1926–
Drama at Northwestern University. Understudy to Vivian Vance in 'The Voice of the Turtle' and took the role on Broadway. Eugene O'Neill was responsible for her being hired by Theatre Guild for 'The Devil Take a Whittler'. Lillian Hellman gave her part in 'Another Part of the Forest'. 1949: first film *John Loves Mary*. Warners contract. 1964: Oscar for *Hud*. 1967: series of strokes, causing severe paralysis. Broadway and London stage: 'The Children's Hour', 'The School for Scandal', 'A Roomful of Roses', 'Cat on a Hot Tin Roof', 'Suddenly Last Summer', 'The Miracle Worker'. Radio, TV. Married writer Roald Dahl.

Films as actress include: 1949: The Fountainhead; It's a Great Feeling; The Hasty Heart. 1950: Bright Leaf; Three Secrets; The Breaking Point. 1951: Operation Pacific; The Day the Earth Stood Still; Weekend with Father. 1952: Diplomatic Courier; Something for the Birds. 1954: Immediate Disaster. 1957: A Face in the Crowd. 1961: Breakfast at Tiffany's. 1964: Psyche 59; In Harm's Way.

NEAME, Ronald

Director. London 1911–
Son of photographer and director Elwin Neame and actress Ivy Close. 1927: entered films as messenger and call boy at Elstree Studios. 1928: assistant cameraman on *Blackmail*. 1928–29: freelance stills photographer. 1929–34: camera operator. 1934–46: cinematographer. 1943: with Anthony Havelock-Allan and David Lean formed production company Cineguild. From 1947: worked as director; also producer in late '40s and early '50s. From 1957: directed occasional films in USA, but worked mainly in Britain.

Films as cinematographer include: 1938: Pygmalion. 1941: Major Barbara. 1942: One of Our Aircraft is Missing; In Which We Serve. 1944: This Happy Breed. 1945: Blithe Spirit.

Films as producer include: 1946: Brief Encounter (*co-p*; + *co-s*); Great Expectations (*co-p*; + *co-s*). 1947: Oliver Twist. 1949: The Passionate Friends. 1951: The Magic Box.

Films as director: 1947: Take My Life. 1950: The Golden Salamander (+ *co-s*). 1952: The Card (+ *p*). 1953: The Million Pound Note. 1956: The Man who Never Was. 1957: The Seventh Sin (*co-d Vincente Minnelli, uc*). 1958: Windom's Way. 1959: The Horse's Mouth. 1960: Tunes of Glory. 1961: Escape from Zahrain (+ *p*). 1962: I Could Go on Singing. 1963: The Chalk Garden. 1964: Mister Moses. 1966: Gambit; A Man Could Get Killed (*co-d Cliff Owen*). 1968: The Prime of Miss Jean Brodie. 1970: Scrooge.

NEFF, Hildegard

(Hildegarde Knef) Actress. Ulm, Germany 1925–
1942: joined Ufa training school as actress. 1944: first film *Traumerei* but her scenes cut. 1945: joined Deutsches Theatre; worked to revive post-war Berlin stage. Broadcasting and films in Germany. 1949–50: under contract to David O. Selznick, brought to Hollywood; contract unused. Returned to Germany. Spotted by Anatole Litvak, made first American film *Decision Before Dawn* (1951). Later worked both in USA and Germany. Acted on Broadway. Also singing. Book, 'The Gift Horse' (1970).

Films as actress include: 1945: Unter den Brucken. 1946: Die Mörder sind unter Uns. 1948: Film ohne Titel. 1952: Diplomatic Courier; The Snows of Kilimanjaro. 1953: La Fete à Henriette; The Man Between. 1954: Geständnis unter vier Augen. 1958: Madeleine und der Legionar. 1962: Lulu; Landru. 1963: Die Driegroschenoper.

NEGRI, Pola

(Barbara Apollonia Chapulek) Actress. Janova, Poland 1897–
Father a gypsy. Imperial Ballet School, St Petersburg. Then stage training at Warsaw Konservatorium. 1913: stage début in Warsaw; changed her name. Polish films then to Berlin in 1917 at invitation of Max Reinhardt. 1923: first film in USA *Bella Donna* 1929–30: in UK, then back to Hollywood. 1935: to Austria and Germany. 1940: returned to Hollywood.

Films as actress include: 1918: Die Augen der Mumie Ma. 1919: Madame Dubarry; Carmen. 1920: Sumurun. 1923: Die Flamme; Hollywood; The Spanish Dancer. 1924: Shadows of Paris; Forbidden Paradise. 1925: East of Suez; A Woman of the World. 1926: Good and Naughty. 1927: Hotel Imperial; Woman on Trial; Barbed Wire. 1928: The Woman from Moscow. 1934: Madame Bovary; 1936: Moskau-Shanghai. 1943: Hi, Diddle Diddle. 1964: The Moonspinners.

NEGULESCO, Jean

Director. Craiova, Rumania 1900–
Ran away to Vienna at 15. From 1919: painter in Bucharest; then art director, costume designer and painter in Paris. 1927: art exhibition in New York; remained in USA. From 1934: assistant director to Harlan Thompson, Benjamin Glazer; then wrote for films e.g. stories for *Swiss Miss* (1938, in collaboratiorfi, *Rio* (1939). 1940–44: directed Warners shorts with mainly musical subjects; *Woman at War* in co-operation with US Army. 1941–48: directed features for Warners. 1949–50: 2 films for Fox in UK. 1948–68: almost all films for Fox. Married (1946) Dusty Anderson who plays minor roles in most of his films.

Features as director: 1941: Singapore Woman. 1944: The Mask of Dimitrios; The Conspirators. 1946: Nobody Lives Forever; Three Strangers. 1947: Humoresque; Deep Valley. 1948: Road House; Johnny Belinda. 1949: Britannia Mews – The Forbidden Street. 1950: The Mudlark; Under My Skin; Three Came Home. 1951: Take Care of My Little Girl. 1952: Phone Call for a Stranger; Lydia Bailey; Lure of the Wilderness; O. Henry's Full House *ep* The Last Leaf. 1953: Scandal at Scourie; Titanic; How to Marry a Millionaire. 1954: Three Coins in the Fountain; Woman's World. 1955: Daddy Long Legs; The Rains of Ranchipur. 1957: Boy on a Dolphin. 1958: The Gift of Love; A Certain Smile. 1959: Count your Blessings; The Best of Everything. 1962: Jessica. 1964: The Pleasure Seekers. 1969: The Heroes. 1970: Hello-Goodbye; The Invincible Six.

NEILAN, Marshall A.

Director. San Bernardino, California 1891–1958 Woodland Hills, California
Left school at 11 to work for Fruit Growers' Express; office boy in claims department of Sante Fe railroad; played juvenile parts with Belasco stock company. 1905: returned to school for 2 years, then studied mechanical engineering for 3 years. Began in films as actor with Kalem Company; also wrote scripts and worked as assistant director. Actor with American Film Company, Universal, Biograph. 1911: returned to Kalem as general manager and head director. 1916: began directing features for Selig Polyscope; also wrote scripts. From 1917: with Famous Players-Lasky and Artcraft, directing Mary Pickford in several films; producer to Cecil B. De Mille as director-general on *Those Without Sin*. 1919–22: associated mainly with First National as producer and director; films (1921–22) usually for own production company. 1923–26: directed for MGM, also occasionally producing. From 1926: directed for Famous Players-Lasky, First National and (from 1928) various other companies. Made last film in 1937.

Films as director include (omitting many shorts): 1916: The Cycle of Fate (+ *s*); the Prince Chap; The Country That God Forgot (+ *s*). 1917: Those Without Sin; The Bottle Imp; The Tides of Barnegat; The Girl at Home; The Silent Partner; Freckles; The Jaguar's Claws; Rebecca of Sunnybrook Farm; A Little Princess. 1918: Stella Maris; Amarilly of Clothes-Line Alley; M'liss; Hit-the-Trail Holliday; Heart of the Wilds. 1919: Three Men and Girl; Daddy Long Legs. 1920: In Old Kentucky; Her Kingdom of Dreams; Go and Get It (+ *pc*; *co-d John Symonds*). 1921: Don't Ever Marry (+ *pc*; *co-d Victor Heerman*); Dinty (+ *st/pc*; *co-d John MacDermott*); Bob Hampton of Placer; Bits of Life (+ *pc*). 1922: Penrod (+ *p/pc*); Fools First (+ *p/pc*); Minnie (+ *s/pc*; *co-d Frank Urson*); Stranger's Banquet (+ *pc*). 1923: The

Eternal Three (+ *st*; *co-d Frank Urson*); The Rendez-vous. 1924: Dorothy Vernon of Haddon Hall; Tess of the d'Urbervilles. 1925: Sporting Venus; The Great Love. 1926: Mike (+ *st*); The Skyrocket; Wild Oats Lane (+ *pc*); Diplomacy; Everybody's Acting (+ *st*). 1927: Venus of Venice; Her Wild Oat. 1928: Three-Ring Marriage; Take Me Home; Taxi 13; His Last Haul. 1929: Black Waters; The Awful Truth; Tanned Legs; The Vagabond Lover. 1930: Sweethearts on Parade. 1931: Catch as Catch Can. 1934: Chloe, Love is Calling You; Social Register; The Lemon Drop Kid. 1935: This is the Life. 1937: Sing While You're Able; Swing It, Professor.

NEILSON, James

Director. 1918–
War photographer in US Marine Corps. TV producer, e.g. 'Wagon Train', 'Alfred Hitchcock Presents'. From 1957: directed films; began by replacing Anthony Mann on *Night Passage*. From 1961: frequently directed Walt Disney productions.

Films as director: 1957: Night Passage (*co-d Anthony Mann, uc*). 1958: The Country Husband. 1961: Moon Pilot. 1962: Hand of Death; Bon Voyage!; Geronimo's Revenge; Summer Magic. 1963: Dr Syn, Alias The Scarecrow. 1964: The Moon-Spinners. 1965: The Legend of Young Dick Turpin. 1966: Return of the Gunfighter. 1967: The Adventures of Bullwhip Griffin; Gentle Giant. 1968: Where Angels Go, Trouble Follows; The First Time – You Don't Need Pyjamas at Rosie's. 1969: Flareup.

NELLI, Piero

Director. Pisa, Italy 1926–
Interrupted University studies to become assistant to Giuseppe de Santis on *Riso Amaro* (1949) and *Non c'e pace tra gli ulivi* (1950). 1950: first short film as director. 1954: first feature as director. Returned to shorts. 1961: returned to features. Subsequently, made further shorts and worked in TV.

Short films as director include: 1950: Cavatori di Marmo. 1951: Patto d'amicizia. 1952: Salviamo, la montagna muore. 1953: Crepuscolo di un mondo,

Features as director: 1954: La Pattuglia Perduto (+ *co-s*). 1961: Le Italiane e l'amore – Latin Lovers *ep* Le Sfregiata – The Slasher.

NELSON, Ralph

Director. New York 1916–
1933–41: stage actor, including Broadway with Leslie Howard. 1936–41: stage manager with the Lunts. World War II: served in USAAF. 1944: his play 'Mail Call' produced on Broadway. 1945: Broadway production of his play 'The Wind is Ninety'. 1945–48: writer for films, actor on TV. 1948–49: director for NBC TV. 1949–52: director and producer for CBS TV. From 1952: freelance director. TV work includes 'Television Theatre', 'Studio One', 'ABC Album', 'Playhouse 90', 'Dupont Show of the Month'. Also directed Old Vic cast in 'Hamlet' on TV. Work in theatre includes direction of 'Cinderella', 'Aladdin', 'This Happy Breed' and on Broadway 'The Man in the Dog Suit'; also directed and produced his own play 'The Man in the Funny Suit'. 1962: first film as director *Requiem for a*

Heavyweight for Columbia. 1963: directed *Soldier in the Rain*, written and produced by Blake Edwards. Worked for several studios including Fox, MGM, Universal, United Artists.

Films as director: 1962: Requiem for a Heavyweight. 1963: Lilies of the Field; Soldier in the Rain. 1964: Fate is the Hunter; Father Goose; Once a Thief. 1966: Duel at Diablo (+ *co-p*). 1967: Counterpoint. 1968: Charly. 1969: Tick ... Tick ... Tick (+ *co-p*); Soldier Blue. 1971: Flight of the Doves (+ *p/co-s*).

NEMEC, Jan

Director. Prague 1936–
1960: graduated from Prague film school. 1963: edited compilation documentary *Pamet naseho*; began to make shorts. 1964: first feature as director. Continued to make shorts.

Features as director: 1964: Démanty noci – Diamonds of the Night (+ *co-s*). 1965: Perlicki na dne – Pearls of the Deep *ep* Podveniki – The Imposter (+ *co-s*). 1966: O slavnosti a Hostech – The Party and the Guests – Report on the Party and the Guests (+ *co-s/w*); Mučedníci lásky – Martyrs of Love (+ *co-s*; *in 3 parts*).

NEWMAN, Alfred

Composer. New Haven, Connecticut 1901–70 Hollywood
Eldest of 10 children; first public concert as pianist in 1908. At 9 sent to New York to study piano, then composition. At 12, supported self and family; one of his piano recitals sponsored by Ignace Paderewski; 5 shows a day in vaudeville at Harlem Opera House. 1917: début as conductor, 'George White's Scandals'. Then conducted e.g. 'Funny Face', starring Fred Astaire. 1930: to Hollywood to arrange and orchestrate score for *Reaching for the Moon* (1931), lent to Sam Goldwyn, worked for him until 1939 as composer and conductor. 1940: musical director of Fox. Brothers, Lionel and Emil, under him there. Studied under Arnold Schoenberg, who had settled in Los Angeles. Oscars for scores of *Alexander's Ragtime Band* (1938), *Tin Pan Alley* (1940), *The Song of Bernadette* (1943), *Love is a Many-Splendored Thing* (1955). Oscars for scoring musical picture: *Mother Wore Tights* (1947), *With a Song in my Heart* (1952), *Call Me Madam* (1953), *The King and I* (with Ken Darby, 1956), all directed by Walter Lang, and *Camelot* (1967, with Ken Darby).

Films as composer include: 1931: Street Scene; Indiscreet. 1932: Rain; Arrowsmith; Cynara. 1933: I Cover the Waterfront; The Bowery. 1934: The House of Rothschild; One Night of Love; Our Daily Bread; We Live Again. 1935: Barbary Coast; The Wedding Night; The Call of the Wild; Clive of India. 1936: Dodsworth; Come and Get It! 1937: Stella Dallas; Dead End; You Only Live Once; The Prisoner of Zenda; Wee Willie Winkie; Slave Ship. 1938: The Hurricane; Alexander's Ragtime Band. 1939: Wuthering Heights; Gunga Din; Young Mr Lincoln; Beau Geste; Drums Along the Mohawk; The Hunchback of Notre Dame; The Rains Came; The Real Glory. 1940: Vigil in the Night; The Grapes of Wrath; The Mark of Zorro; Foreign Correspondent; They Knew What They Wanted; Tin Pan Alley; Brigham Young. 1941: Man Hunt; How Green Was My Valley (*song*); Ball of

Pola Negri at the time of Malcolm St. Clair's A Woman of the World.
Jessica. *directed and produced by Jean Negulesco.*
Mickey Rooney, Anthony Quinn and Jackie Gleason in Requiem for a Heavyweight. *directed by Ralph Nelson.*

Fire; Blood and Sand. 1942: The Battle of Midway; Roxie Hart; The Black Swan. 1943: Heaven Can Wait; December 7th; The Song of Bernadette. 1944: Wilson; The Purple Heart. 1945: A Tree Grows in Brooklyn; A Royal Scandal; A Bell for Adano. 1946: Dragonwyck; The Razor's Edge. 1947: Gentleman's Agreement; Captain from Castile; The Kiss of Death; Mother Wore Tights. 1948: The Snake Pit; Call Northside 777; Yellow Sky; Cry of the City. 1949: A Letter to Three Wives; Pinky; Twelve O'Clock High; The Prince of Foxes. 1950: When Willie Comes Marching Home; The Gunfighter; Panic in the Streets; All About Eve; No Way Out. 1951: David and Bathsheba; Fourteen Hours; Wait Till the Sun Shines Nellie. 1952: What Price Glory; O. Henry's Full House (co); The Snows of Kilimanjaro (co); With a Song in my Heart. 1953: The Robe; Call Me Madam. 1954: Hell and High Water; The Egyptian (co). 1955: The Seven Year Itch; Love is a Many-Splendored Thing. 1956: Bus Stop (co); Anastasia; The King and I. 1958: The Bravados (co). 1959: The Diary of Anne Frank. 1962: How the West Was Won. 1970: Airport.

NEWMAN, Joseph M. *or* Joe

Director. Logan, Utah 1909–
Started work as office boy at MGM (1925). 1931–37: assistant director to e.g. George Hill, Ernst Lubitsch. 1937: sent to MGM British studios as assistant in organisation. 1938: returned to Hollywood, started directing with a short in 'Crime Does Not Pay' series. Directed MGM shorts, e.g. *Vendetta* (1942), until first feature (1942). Major in US Army Signals; made 32 shorts for Army including *Diary of a Sergeant* (1945). 1946: on demobilisation returned to features. 1953: directed *Smoke Jumpers*, short on forest fires, which were subject of *Red Skies of Montana* (1952). 1960: *The Lawbreakers* was a TV pilot released theatrically outside US.

Features as director: 1942: Northwest Rangers. 1948: Jungle Patrol. 1949: The Great Dan Patch – Ride a Reckless Mile; Abandoned. 1950: 711 Ocean Drive. 1951: Lucky Nick Cain – I'll Get You For This; The Guy Who Came Back; Love Nest. 1952: Red Skies of Montana; The Outcasts of Poker Flat; Pony Soldier – Macdonald of the Canadian Mounties. 1953: Dangerous Crossing; The Human Jungle. 1955: Kiss of Fire; This Island Earth. 1956: Flight to Hong Kong (+p/cos). 1957: Death in Small Doses. 1958: Fort Massacre. 1959: The Gunfight at Dodge City; The Big Circus; Tarzan, the Ape Man. 1960: The Lawbreakers. 1961: King of the Roaring Twenties, The Story of Arnold Rothstein – The Big Bankroll; A Thunder of Drums; The George Raft Story – Spin of a Coin; Twenty Plus Two – It Started in Tokyo.

NEWMAN, Paul

Director and actor. Shaker Heights, Ohio 1925–
Studied drama at Kenyon College. World War II: 3 years as radio operator in naval torpedo planes in the Pacific. From 1949: summer stock in Williams Bay, Wisconsin, then with Woodstock Players, Illinois. On the death of father managed family's sporting-goods store for 2 years, then enrolled at Yale School of Drama. To New York; TV parts included 'The Web', 'The Mask'; on Broadway in 'Picnic', 'The Desperate Hours'. Warners contract. 1955: first film as actor. 1956–57: actor with MGM. Then with various com-

panies. Directed Martin Ritt in 5 films. Second wife (from 1958) Joanne Woodward. 1968: directed her in (and produced) *Rachel, Rachel*. 1970: took over direction of *Sometimes a Great Notion* (1971).

Films as actor: 1955: The Silver Chalice. 1956: Somebody Up There Likes Me; The Rack. 1957: Until They Sail; The Helen Morgan Story. 1958: The Long Hot Summer; Cat on a Hot Tin Roof; Rally 'Round the Flag, Boys!; The Left-Handed Gun. 1959: The Young Philadelphians. 1960: From the Terrace; Exodus. 1961: The Hustler; Paris Blues. 1962: Sweet Bird of Youth; Hemingway's Adventures of a Young Man. 1963: Hud; A New Kind of Love; The Prize. 1964: What a Way to Go!; The Outrage. 1965: Lady L. 1966: Torn Curtain; Harper. 1967: Hombre; Cool Hand Luke. 1968: The Secret War of Harry Frigg. 1969: Winning (+ co-pc); Butch Cassidy and the Sundance Kid (+ co-pc). 1970: WUSA (+ co-p). 1971: Sometimes a Great Notion – Never Give an Inch (+ co-d; co-d Richard Colla, uc).

NEWMEYER, Fred

Director. Central City, Colorado 1888–
Sacred Heart College, Denver. 3 years as professional baseball player. 1913: utility man at Universal; subsequently assistant director. From 1921: directed features for Sam Taylor, Hal Roach and other producers, releasing through Associated Exhibitors until 1922, and Pathe Exchange until 1925. 1925–31: worked for various companies notably Famous Players-Lasky, First National, Universal, Pathe. From 1932: freelance director with several independent companies. 1936: last film *General Spanky* was a Hal Roach Feature Comedy.

Films as director: 1921: Never Weaken; A Sailor-Made Man; Grandma's Boy. 1922: Doctor Jack. 1923: Safety Last; Why Worry. 1924: Girl Shy (co-d Sam Taylor); Hot Water (co-d Sam Taylor). 1925: The Freshman; Seven Keys to Baldpate; The Perfect Clown. 1926: The Savage; The Quarterback; The Lunatic at Large. 1927: The Potters; Too Many Crooks; On Your Toes; That's My Daddy. 1928: Warming Up; The Night Bird. 1929: It Can Be Done; The Rainbow Man; Sailor's Holiday. 1930: The Grand Parade; Queen High; Fast and Loose. 1931: Subway Express; 1932: Discarded Lovers; They Never Came Back; The Fighting Gentleman; The Gambling Sex. 1933: Easy Millions; The Big Race. 1934: The Moth; No Ransom; Secrets of Chinatown. 1936: General Spanky (co-d Gordon Douglas).

NEWTON, Robert

Actor. Shaftesbury, Dorset 1905–56 Beverly Hills, California
1920: stage début in 'Henry IV'. Actor-manager in Birmingham repertory. Toured South Africa. 1924: London stage début in 'London Life'. 1931: in New York, succeeded Laurence Olivier in 'Private Lives'. 1932: first film as actor *Reunion*. 1937: first major film part, in *Fire Over England*. Theatrical work includes 'Bitter Sweet', 'No Orchids for Miss Blandish', 'Once Upon a Time', 'The Greeks Had a Word For It', 'Whiteoaks'. Daughter is actress Sally Newton.

Films as actor include: 1937: Dark Journey; Claudius (uf). 1938: Vessel of Wrath. 1939: Jamaica Inn. 1940:

The Green Cockatoo; Channel Incident; Gaslight. 1941: Major Barbara. 1942: Hatter's Castle; They Flew Alone. 1944: This Happy Breed. 1945: Henry V. 1947: Odd Man Out. 1948: Oliver Twist. 1949: Obsession. 1950: Treasure Island; Waterfront. 1951: Soldiers Three; Tom Brown's Schooldays. 1952: Les Miserables; Blackbeard the Pirate. 1953: The Desert Rats. 1954: The High and the Mighty. 1955: Long John Silver. 1956: Around the World in 80 Days.

NIBLO, Fred

Director. York, Nebraska 1874–1948 New Orleans, Louisiana
1890–1902: vaudeville entertainer and actor. 1902–04: toured with The Four Cohans. 1905–07: travelled in Africa, then toured USA, giving lantern lectures on travels. 1904–17: actor in vaudeville and on Broadway. 1917: married Enid Bennett, actress with Thomas H. Ince's film company which he joined as a 'producing director'. 1918–20: directed films for Ince; wife played star roles. 1920–21: 2 films for Douglas Fairbanks' company. 1922–30: films mainly for Louis B. Mayer and then MGM; producer on some. Last films for RKO. After retiring from films, returned to the stage in his 70s.

Films as director: 1918: The Marriage Ring; Fuss and Feathers; Happy Though Married; When Do We Eat? 1919: The Haunted Bedroom; The Law of Men; Partners Three; The Virtuous Thief; Dangerous Hours; What Every Woman Learns; Stepping Out. 1920: Sex; The Woman in the Suitcase; The False Road; Hairpins; Her Husband's Friend; Silk Hosiery; The Mark of Zorro. 1921: The Three Musketeers; Mother O' Mine; Greater than Love. 1922: The Woman He Married; Rose O' the Sea; Blood and Sand. 1923: The Famous Mrs Fair; Strangers of the Night (+ co-p). 1924: Thy Name is Woman; The Red Lily (+ st). 1926: The Temptress. 1927: Ben-Hur; Camille (+p); The Devil Dancer (+p). 1928: The Enemy (+p); Two Lovers (+p); The Mysterious Lady; Dream of Love. 1930: Redemption (+p); Way Out West. 1931: Young Donovan's Kid; The Big Gamble. 1932: Diamond, Cut Diamond (co-d Maurice Elvey).

NICHOLS, Dudley

Writer and director. Wapakoneta, Ohio 1895–1960 Hollywood
Started as journalist. Foreign correspondent and star reporter for the New York World, as well as writing fiction. 1929: to Hollywood to write dialogue for sound films. To 1947: wrote many films directed by John Ford. 1944: wrote prologue for re-issue of *The Sign of the Cross* (1932). Also director and producer. Oscar for screenplay of *The Informer* (1935).

Films as writer include: 1931: Seas Beneath. 1933: Pilgrimage (di). 1934: The Lost Patrol (co); Judge Priest (co). 1935: Steamboat 'Round the Bend (co); The Informer; The Crusades (co). 1936: Mary of Scotland. 1937: The Plough and the Stars. 1938: The Hurricane; Bringing up Baby (co). 1939: Stagecoach. 1940: The Long Voyage Home. 1941: Swamp Water; Man Hunt. 1943: Air Force; For Whom the Bell Tolls; This Land is Mine (+ co-p; co-s/di). 1944: It Happened Tomorrow (co-s/co-di); And Then There Were None (co). 1945: Scarlet Street; The Bells of St Mary's. 1947: The Fugitive. 1949: Pinky (co). 1951: Rawhide (+ st).

1952: Return of the Texan; The Big Sky. 1954: Prince Valiant. 1956: Run for the Sun (co). 1957: The Tin Star. 1959: The Hangman. 1960: Heller in Pink Tights (co).

Films as director and writer: 1943: Government Girl (+p). 1946: Sister Kenny (+p; co-s). 1947: Mourning Becomes Electra (d/co-p only).

NICHOLS, Mike

(Michael Igor Peschowsky) Director. Berlin 1931– Father a Russian Jewish emigré. Psychiatry at University of Chicago. Member of Compass Players Theatre Company. 1950–53: studied with Lee Strasberg. Worked in cabaret in New York. 1960: teamed with Elaine May for Broadway production 'An Evening With Mike Nichols and Elaine May', directed by Arthur Penn. 1962: stage actor in Philadelphia in 'A Matter of Position'. Stage director in New York, including 'Barefoot in the Park', 'The Knack', 'Luv', 'The Odd Couple', 'The Apple Tree', 'The Little Foxes', 'Plaza Suite'. 1966: first film as director. 1970: directed Maggie Smith and Robert Stephens in Los Angeles stage production of Noël Coward's 'Design for Living'.

Films as director: 1966: Who's Afraid of Virginia Woolf? 1967: The Graduate. 1970: Catch 22. 1971: Carnal Knowledge (+p).

NIELSEN, Asta

Actress. Vesterbro, Denmark 1883– Royal Theatre School and Copenhagen stage. 1910: first film as actress *Afgrunden*. 1911–36: Germany. 1920: formed own company and made one film for it, *Hamlet*. 1932: her only sound film *Unmoegliche Liebe*. 1939: on Copenhagen stage in 'Toni Draws a Horse'. Married Peter Urban Gad who directed her in 30 films.

Films as actress include: 1910: Ved faengslets port. 1911: Livets Storme; Ballet Danserinden. 1919: Kurfürstendamm; Rausch. 1920: Reigen. 1923: I.N.R.I. 1924: Lebende Buddhas. 1925: Die freudlose Gasse. 1927: Gehetzte Frauen.

NILSSON, Leopoldo Torre *see* TORRE NILSSON, Leopoldo

NIVEN, David

Actor. Kirriemuir, Scotland 1910– 1927: Sandhurst Military College. 1929–32: Highland Light Infantry. To Canada, then USA. Extra, walk-on in 27 westerns, then small parts. 1935: first major part in *Splendor*. World War II: service in Rifle Brigade and commandos, reaching major; Allied Forces Network, reaching Lieutenant-Colonel. American Legion of Merit. Many British films. 1951: on Broadway in 'Nina'. On Hollywood stage in 'The Moon is Blue'. Books: 'Round the Rugged Rocks' (novel), 'Once Over Lightly' (1951), 'The Moon is Blue' (autobiography). 1958: Oscar as Best Actor for *Separate Tables*.

Films as actor include: 1936: Rose-Marie; Dodsworth; The Charge of the Light Brigade. 1937: The Prisoner of Zenda; Four Men and a Prayer; Beloved Enemy.

1938: The Dawn Patrol; Bluebeard's Eighth Wife. 1939: Wuthering Heights; Bachelor Mother; The Real Glory; Eternally Yours. 1940: Raffles. 1942: The First of the Few. 1944: The Way Ahead. 1946: Magnificent Doll; A Matter of Life and Death. 1947: The Other Love; The Bishop's Wife. 1948: Enchantment; A Kiss in the Dark. 1950: The Elusive Pimpernel. 1951: Soldiers Three. 1953: The Moon is Blue. 1954: Love Lottery. 1955: The King's Thief. 1956: Carrington VC; Around the World in 80 Days; The Birds and the Bees. 1957: The Little Hut; Oh, Men! Oh, Women!; My Man Godfrey. 1958: Bonjour Tristesse. 1959: Ask Any Girl; Happy Anniversary. 1960: Please Don't Eat the Daisies. 1961: The Guns of Navarone. 1962: Guns of Darkness; I Due Nemici. 1963: Fifty-Five Days at Peking; La Città Prigionera. 1964: The Pink Panther; Bedtime Story. 1965: Lady L. 1967: Casino Royale; The Extraordinary Seaman (r 1969). 1968: The Impossible Years; Before Winter Comes.

NOIRET, Philippe

Actor. Lille, France 1931– 1950–51: studied drama under Roger Blin, then joined the Centre Dramatique de l'Ouest, producing 3 plays. 1953: joined Théâtre National Populaire in Paris, acted in many plays; also radio, TV and cabaret work in nightclubs. 1956: acted in *La Pointe Courte*. 1960: established as film actor in *Zazie dans le métro*.

Films as actor include: 1961: Tout l'or du monde. 1963: Cyrano et d'Artagnan; Thérèse Desqueyroux. 1965: Lady L; La Vie de château; Qui êtes-vous, Polly Magoo? 1966: Les Sultans. 1967: L'Une et l'autre. 1968: Mr Freedom; The Assassination Bureau. 1969: Justine; Topaz; Les Figurants du nouveau monde. 1971: Murphy's War; Les Aveux Les Plus Doux.

NOLAN, Lloyd

Actor. San Francisco 1902– Stanford University. Pasadena Playhouse. Toured in 'The Front Page'. From 1929: on Broadway in 'Cape Cod Follies', 'Sweet Stranger', 'Reunion in Vienna', 'One Sunday Afternoon' and others. 1935: first film as actor *Stolen Harmony*. To 1939: worked mainly for Paramount. Then worked frequently for Fox, also MGM, Warners and others. 1950–51: returned to stage. Directed on stage by Charles Laughton in 'The Caine Mutiny' and took the part on TV.

Films as actor include: 1935: G-Men; She Couldn't Take It; One Way Ticket. 1936: 15 Maiden Lane; Big Brown Eyes; The Texas Rangers. 1937: Wells Fargo; King of Gamblers. 1938: King of Alcatraz. 1939: St Louis Blues; The Magnificent Fraud. 1940: The House Across the Bay; Johnny Apollo; The Man I Married. 1941: Blues in the Night. 1942: Apache Trail. 1943: Bataan; Guadalcanal Diary. 1945: A Tree Grows in Brooklyn; The House on 92nd Street; Captain Eddie. 1946: Lady in the Lake; Somewhere in the Night; Two Smart People. 1947: Wild Harvest. 1948: Street With No Name; The Sun Comes Up. 1949: Easy Living. 1951: The Lemon Drop Kid. 1953: Island in the Sky. 1956: Toward the Unknown; The Last Hunt; Santiago. 1957: A Hatful of Rain; Peyton Place. 1960: Portrait in Black. 1961: Susan Slade. 1963: The Girl Hunters. 1964: Circus World. 1965: Never Too Late. 1967: The Double Man. 1968: Ice Station Zebra.

A Thunder of Drums, *directed by Joseph M. Newman.*
Paul Newman in Martin Ritt's The Outrage.
Martin Balsam and Jon Voight in Mike Nichols' Catch-22.

NORMAND, Mabel

Actress. Boston, Massachusetts 1894–1930 Monrovia, California

Artist's model, fashion and publicity model then Biograph extra. With Sennett at Biograph, Keystone, Keystone–Triangle, and several other companies. Left Sennett for brief period making 15 films for Goldwyn. Acted often with Fatty Arbuckle, Chaplin and Ford Sterling, and directed by each of them. Most of her films directed by Sennett; she co-directed *Tomboy Bessie* (1912) and *Mabel at the Wheel* (1914) with him. Co-directed several with Chaplin, directed several alone. 1918: first feature as actress *Mickey*. From 1919: directed several times by Victor Schertzinger. 1922: involved in circumstances connected with murder of director William Desmond Taylor, but exonerated. Press campaign ruined career. Twice attempted come-back: with Sennett in 1923, with Hal Roach in 1926, without success.

Films as actress include: 1911: The Diving Girl; A Victim of Circumstances; Why He Gave Up. 1912: The Fatal Chocolate; A Spanish Dilemma; Oh, Those Eyes!; The Fickle Spaniard; A Dash Through the Clouds; An Interrupted Elopement; The Water Nymph; The New Neighbour; Pedro's Dilemma; Stolen Glory; The Ambitious Butler; The Flirting Husband; The Grocery Clerk's Romance; At Coney Island; Mabel's Lovers; At It Again; The Deacon's Troubles; A Temperamental Husband; The Rivals; Mr Fix It; A Desperate Lover; A Bear Escape; A Family Mixup; A Midnight Elopement; Mabel's Adventures; The Duel; Mabel's Stratagem. 1913: Saving Mabel's Dad; The Cure That Failed; For Lizzie's Sake; The Mistaken Masher; Just Brown's Luck; The Battle of Who Run; Mabel's Heroes; Heinze's Resurrection; The Professor's Daughter; A Tangled Affair; A Red Hot Romance; A Doctored Affair- The Sleuths at the Floral Parade; A Rural Third Degree; A Strong Revenge; Foiling Fickle Father (+ d); Love and Pain; The Rube and The Baron; At Twelve O'Clock; Her New Beau; On His Wedding Day; Father's Choice; That Ragtime Band; A Little Hero; Mabel's Awful Mistake; The Foreman of the Jury; Barney Oldfield's Race for a Life; Passions—He Had Three; The Hansom Driver; The Speed Queen; The Waiter's Picnic; For Love of Mabel; The Telltale Light; A Noise from the Deep; Love and Courage; Professor Bean's Removal; Baby Day; Mabel's New Hero; Mabel's Dramatic Career; The Gypsy Queen; When Dreams Come True; The Bowling Match; The Speed Kings; Lovesickness at Sea; A Muddy Romance; Cohen Saves the Flag; Zuzu the Band Leader; The Gusher; Fatty's Flirtation. 1914: A Misplaced Foot; Mabel's Stormy Love Affair; In the Clutches of the Gang; Won in a Closet (+ d?); Mabel's Bare Escape; Mabel's Strange Predicament; Mack at it Again; Caught in a Cabaret – The Waiter – Jazz Waiter – Faking with Society (+ co-d Charles Chaplin); Mabel's Nerve (+ d); The Fatal Mallet; Her Friend the Bandit (+ co-d Charles Chaplin); Mabel's Busy Day – Love and Lunch – Charlie and the Sausages (+ co-d Charles Chaplin); Mabel's Married Life – When You're Married – The Square head (+ co-d Charles Chaplin); Mabel's New Job (+ d); Those Country Kids; Mabel's Latest Prank (+ d?); Mabel's Blunder (+ d?); Hello Mabel (+ d?); Gentlemen of Nerve; His Trysting Place; Fatty's Jonah Day; Fatty's Wine Party; The Sea Nimphs; Getting Acquainted. 1915: Tillie's Punctured Romance; Mabel and Fatty's Wash Day; Fatty and Mabel's Simple Life – Mabel and Fatty's Simple Life; Fatty and Mabel at the San Diego Exposition; Mabel, Fatty and the Law; Mabel and Fatty's Married Life; That Little Band of Gold; Mabel and Fatty Viewing the World's Fair at San Francisco; Mabel's Wilful Way; Mabel Lost and Won; The Little Teacher; Fatty's Tintype Tangle – Fido's Tintype Tangle; My Valet; Stolen Magic. 1916: Fatty and Mabel Adrift; He Did and He Didn't– Love and Lobsters; Bright Lights – The Lure of Broadway. 1918: Mickey; The Floor Below. 1919: Sis Hopkins; The Pest; When Doctors Disagree; Pinto; Jinx. 1920: The Slim Princess; What Happened to Rosa. 1921: Molly O'; Oh, Mabel Behave. 1922: Head Over Heels. 1923: Suzanna; The Extra Girl. 1926: Raggedy Rose; One Hour Married; The Nickel Hopper.

NORTH, Alex

Composer. Chester, Pennsylvania 1910–

Curtis Institute (1928–29) and Juilliard School of Music (1932–34). Composed for ballet, radio, TV and theatre. 1937–50: composed scores for 40 documentaries. 1942–46: US Army. 1947–48: Guggenheim Fellowship. 1951: first feature as composer *A Streetcar Named Desire*.

Films as composer include: 1951: Death of a Salesman. 1952: Pony Soldier; Les Miserables; Viva Zapata! 1954: Go Man Go; Désirée. 1955: The Racers; The Rose Tattoo. 1956: I'll Cry Tomorrow; The King and Four Queens; The Rainmaker; The Bad Seed. 1958: Hot Spell; The Long Hot Summer. 1959: The Sound of Fury. 1960: Spartacus. 1961: The Misfits; Sanctuary. 1962: The Children's Hour. 1963: Cleopatra. 1964: Cheyenne Autumn. 1968: The Devil's Brigade; The Shoes of the Fisherman (*ur*). 1969: A Dream of Kings. 1971: Willard.

NOVAK, Kim

Actress. Chicago, Illinois 1933–

Los Angeles City College. Model while still at school. Toured as 'Miss Deep Freeze'. 1953: chosen through model agency as chorus girl for *The French Line*; did not appear but was spotted at work. Columbia contract. 1954: first film as actress *Pushover*. To 1962: worked mainly for Columbia. 1965–66: married to actor Richard Johnson. 1966: road accident; awarded $49,000 damages.

Films as actress: 1954: Pushover; Phffft. 1955: Five Against the House; The Man with the Golden Arm. 1956: Picnic; The Eddy Duchin Story. 1957: Jeanne Eagels; Pal Joey. 1958: Vertigo; Bell, Book and Candle. 1959: Middle of the Night. 1960: Pepe; Strangers When We Meet. 1962: Boys' Night Out; The Notorious Landlady. 1964: Of Human Bondage; Kiss Me, Stupid. 1965: The Amorous Adventures of Moll Flanders. 1968: The Legend of Lylah Clare. 1969: The Great Bank Robbery.

NOVARRO, Ramon

(Ramon Samaniegos) Actor. Durango, Mexico 1899–1968 Los Angeles

Vaudeville and other stage appearances. Extra, then small film parts. 1922: spotted by Rex Ingram for *The Prisoner of Zenda*. Worked frequently for MGM. Directed Spanish versions of many of his American films. 1930: directed *La Sevillana*. Also TV.

Films as actor include: 1917: The Little American. 1918: The Goat. 1922: The Rubaiyat of Omar Khayyam; Trifling Woman. 1923: Where the Pavement Ends; Scaramouche. 1924: The Red Lily; Thy Name is Woman; The Arab. 1925: The Midshipman. 1927: Ben-Hur; Lovers?; The Road to Romance. 1928: The Student Prince in Old Heidelberg; A Certain Young Man. 1929: The Pagan. 1930: Devil May Care; In Gay Madrid. 1931: Daybreak; Son of India. 1932: Mata Hari; The Son-Daughter. 1933: The Barbarian. 1934: The Cat and the Fiddle; Laughing Boy. 1937: The Sheik Steps Out. 1938: A Desperate Adventure. 1949: We Were Strangers; The Big Steal. 1960: Heller in Pink Tights.

NUGENT, Elliott

Director. Dover, Ohio 1900–

Father actor and writer J. C. Nugent. Stage début at 4 in vaudeville with parents. Ohio State University. 1921: Broadway début as actor; leading part by 1922. From 1922: wrote plays in collaboration with his father e.g. 'The Poor Nut' in which they both appeared in 1925, which was filmed in 1927, and (in 1931) as *Local Boy Makes Good*. 1929: actor/writer/director contract with MGM; in collaboration with father adapted and stage directed *Wise Girls* from their play 'Kempy' and acted in it. Other scripts in collaboration with father include *The Unholy Three* (1930), also acted in it. 1930: for Sam Wood, collaborated on story and dialogue and acted in *The Richest Man in the World*. 1932: with James Flood co-directed 2 films for Warners and First National. Then worked for various companies including RKO (1933–34). 1934–41: mainly with Paramount. 1940–47: also stage actor and in collaboration wrote plays, including 'The Male Animal' (with James Thurber). 1952: left films for theatre; co-presented 'The Seven Year Itch' (1952), 'The Wayward Saint' (1955); co-produced and directed 'The Greatest Man Alive' (1957). 1965: autobiography 'Events Leading up to the Comedy'.

Films as director: 1932: The Mouthpiece (*co-d James Flood*); Life Begins (*co-d James Flood*). 1933: Whistling in the Dark (+ s); Three Cornered Moon; If I Were Free. 1934: She Loves Me Not; Strictly Dynamite; Two Alone. 1935: Love in Bloom; Enter the Madam: College Scandal; Splendor. 1936: And So They Were Married; Wives Never Know. 1937: It's All Yours. 1938: Professor Beware; Give Me a Sailor. 1939: Never Say Die; The Cat and the Canary. 1941: Nothing But the Truth. 1942: The Male Animal. (+ *fco-pl*). 1943: The Crystal Ball. 1944: Up in Arms. 1947: My Favorite Brunette; Welcome Stranger. 1948: My Girl Tisa. 1949: Mr Belvedere Goes to College; The Great Gatsby. 1950: The Skipper Surprised His Wife. 1951: My Outlaw Brother – My Brother, The Outlaw. 1952: Just for You.

NUGENT, Frank S.

Writer. New York 1908–66 Los Angeles

Journalism at Columbia University. Police and general reporter on New York Times e.g. on Lindbergh kidnapping, then assistant in film department. 1936: editor and film critic. 1940: brought to Hollywood by Darryl F. Zanuck as script critic for Fox. 1944: left Fox.

Wrote for several magazines. 1947: married John Ford's daughter Barbara; first film as writer, Ford's *Fort Apache*. 1956–59: screen branch president for Writers Guild of America.

Films as writer include: 1948: Fort Apache; Three Godfathers (*co*). 1949: She Wore a Yellow Ribbon (*co*); Tulsa (*co*). 1950: Wagonmaster (*co*); Two Flags West (+ *st*; *co-s*). 1952: The Quiet Man; Angel Face (*co*). 1953: The Red Beret (*co*). 1954: They Rode West (*co*). 1955: Mister Roberts (*co*); The Tall Men. 1956: The Searchers. 1957: The Rising of the Moon. 1958: Gunman's Walk; The Last Hurrah. 1959: North West Frontier (*st*). 1961: Two Rode Together. 1963: Donovan's Reef (*co*).

NYKVIST, Sven

Cinematographer. Moheda, Sweden 1922–
School in Germany. 1941: camera assistant with Sandrews in Stockholm. 1945: first film as cinematographer. 1952: made 2 documentaries. 1959: wrote *Resan till Lambarene,* an African travelogue. 1965: directed and photographed *Lianbron – The Vine Bridge.*

Films as cinematographer include: 1953: Barabbas; Gycklarnas afton (*co*); Salka Valka. 1954: Karin Månsdotter; Storm över Tjurö. 1956: Flickani frack. 1957: En drommares vandring. 1958: Damen i svart. 1959: Jungfrukällan; Får jag låna din fru?; Domaren; De sista stegen. 1961: Såsom i en spegel. 1962: Nattvardsgästerna. 1963: Tystnaden. 1964: För att inte tala om alla dessa kvinnor; Klänningen; Älskande par; Att älska. 1966: Persona. 1968: Vargtimmen; Skammen. 1969: Riten. 1970: En Passion; Erste Liebe. 1971: Beroringen; The Last Run.

O

OBERON, Merle

(Estelle Merle O'Brien Thompson) Actress. Tasmania 1911–
At 7 moved with family to India. La Martinière College, Calcutta. To London, failed audition for HMV Film Company, became dance hostess, worked at Café de Paris. 1930: first film *Alf's Button*; for 2 years played bit parts. Spotted by Alexander Korda, 7-year contract, given lead in *Wedding Rehearsal* (1932), acted in Korda's first 3 films as director. 1935: first American film *The Dark Angel.* 1935–40: worked for United Artists, Korda having shared her contract with Goldwyn. 1937: returned to UK to make *Claudius*: her car accident led to abandonment of film and first major insurance claim collection for an uncompleted film. 1939–45: married to Korda. From 1940: worked for several companies, including Columbia, RKO, United Artists. 1945–49: married Lucien Ballard. 1952: returned to UK to make *24 Hours of a Woman's Life.* 1956–63: no films. TV series 'Assignment Foreign Legion'.

Films as actress include: 1932: Service for Ladies; Wedding Rehearsal; Men of Tomorrow. 1933: The Private Life of Henry VIII. 1934: The Private Life of Don Juan. 1935: The Scarlet Pimpernel; The Dark Angel; Folies Bergere. 1936: These Three. 1937: Claudius (*uf*); The Beloved Enemy. 1938: The Cowboy and the Lady. 1939: Wuthering Heights; The Lion Has Wings. 1940: 'Til We Meet Again. 1941: Affectionately Yours; Lydia; That Uncertain Feeling. 1943: Forever and a Day; Stage Door Canteen. 1944: The Lodger; Dark Waters; A Song to Remember. 1945: This Love of Ours. 1946: Temptation. 1947: Night Song. 1948: Berlin Express. 1952: 24 Hours of a Woman's Life. 1954: Désirée; Deep in My Heart. 1965: The Oscar. 1967: Hotel.

OBOLER, Arch

Director, producer and writer. Chicago, Illinois 1909–
Father engineer. University of Chicago. 1938–45: director and writer for NBC radio on series 'Lights Out' and 'Arch Oboler's Plays'. 1940: for MGM scripted in collaboration *Escape.* 1945: first film as director and writer *Strange Holiday.* 1948: wrote story for *A Miracle Can Happen.* Own production company. Radio plays published: 'Ivory Tower' (1940), 'This Freedom' (1941), 'Plays for Americans' (1942), 'Free Word Theatre' (1944), 'Oboler Omnibus' (1945). Much TV work.

Films as director and writer: 1945: Strange Holiday (+ *st*); Bewitched. 1947: The Arnelo Affair.

Films as director, producer and writer: 1951: Five. 1952: Bwana Devil. 1953: The Twonky. 1961: 1+1: Exploring the Kinsey Reports. 1967: The Bubble.

O'BRIEN, Edmond

Actor. New York 1915–
A year at Fordham University, then scholarship to Neighborhood Playhouse School. Joined Orson Welles' Mercury Theatre of the Air. On Broadway from 1947. In films from 1939. Also in some radio and TV. Co-directed *Shield for Murder* (1954) with Howard W. Koch; co-produced and directed *Mantrap* (1961). Oscar as supporting actor (1954) for *The Barefoot Contessa.*

Films as actor include: 1939: The Hunchback of Notre Dame. 1944: Winged Victory. 1946: The Killers. 1947: The Web. 1948: A Double Life; Fighter Squadron. 1949: White Heat. 1952: The Turning Point. 1953: Julius Caesar. 1954: The Barefoot Contessa. 1955: Pete Kelly's Blues. 1956: The Girl Can't Help It. 1959: Up Periscope. 1960: The Last Voyage; The Great Imposter. 1962: The Man Who Shot Liberty Valance; Bird Man of Alcatraz; The Longest Day. 1964: Seven Days in May; Rio Conchos; The Hanged Man. 1965: Synanon; Sylvia. 1966: Fantastic Voyage; Peau d'espion.

O'BRIEN, George

Actor. San Francisco 1900–
Camera assistant, extra, stuntman. 1922: first film *White Sands.* 1924: first leading part, in *The Iron Horse.* Many films for Fox. From 1936: mainly RKO.

Films as actor include: 1924: The Man Who Came Back. 1925: The Fighting Heart; Thank You. 1926: Fig Leaves; Three Bad Men; The Blue Eagle. 1927: Paid to Love; Sunrise; East Side, West Side. 1929: Noah's Ark; Salute. 1931: Seas Beneath; A Holy

Ramon Novarro in Fred Niblo's Ben-Hur.
Såsóm i en spegel (Through a Glass Darkly), directed by Ingmar Bergman and photographed by Sven Nykvist.
Edmond O'Brien (centre), Jayne Mansfield and Tom Ewell in The Girl Can't Help It. *directed by Frank Tashlin.*

Terror. 1934: Ever Since Eve; The Dude Ranger. 1935: When a Man's a Man. 1947: My Wild Irish Rose. 1948: Fort Apache. 1949: She Wore a Yellow Ribbon. 1964: Cheyenne Autumn.

O'BRIEN, Margaret

Actress. Los Angeles 1937–
Mother and sister, dancers. Child model: cover picture led to first film, a government short with James Cagney, then into features. To 1951: all films for MGM. After Columbia's Her First Romance (1951) retired from regular work in films, worked in repertory, radio and TV.

Films as actress include: 1941: Babes on Broadway. 1942: Journey for Margaret. 1943: Dr Gillespie's Criminal Case; Thousands Cheer; Lost Angel; Madame Curie. 1944: Jane Eyre; The Canterville Ghost; Meet Me in St Louis; Music for Millions. 1945: Our Vines Have Tender Grapes. 1947: The Unfinished Dance. 1948: Big City. 1949: Little Women; The Secret Garden. 1951: Her First Romance. 1955: Glory. 1960: Heller in Pink Tights.

O'CONNELL, L. William

Cinematographer. Chicago 1890–
Working in films by 1919. Cinematographer from 1920. Worked for various companies mainly Fox (1927–35), Warners (1935–40), Columbia (1941–45) then Monogram and Pathe until his last film as cinematographer in 1949. 1950: became light-direction engineer for ABC TV centre in Hollywood.

Films as cinematographer include: 1921: The Sky Pilot; A Broken Doll (co). 1923: The Woman of Bronze; The Fourth Musketeer. 1925: The Beloved Brute; The Redeeming Sin. 1927: The Cradle Snatchers; The Monkey Talks; Paid to Love. 1928: A Girl in Every Port; Fazil; Four Devils (co). 1930: Wild Company; Renegades; The Princess and the Plumber. 1932: Scarface, Shame of the Nation (co). 1935: In Old Kentucky. 1937: West of Shanghai. 1942: Klondike Fury. 1944: One Mysterious Night; The Missing Juror. 1946: Bringing up Father. 1948: Assigned to Danger; Jiggs and Maggie in Society,

O'CONNOR, Donald

Actor. Chicago 1925–
Son of acrobat John E. O'Connor. Joined family act while an infant; later sang and danced. 1938: spotted for Sing You Sinners. Paramount contract, made 11 films in 1 year. 1940–41: toured in vaudeville with family. 1944: joined US Air Corps, married Gwen Carter who appeared on stage with him. 1942–51: worked for Universal. 1951: in London and on tour in UK with wife. From 1952: worked mainly for Fox, Universal, Paramount.

Films as actor include: 1938: Sing You Sinners; Men With Wings. 1939: Death of a Champion; Million Dollar Legs; On Your Toes; Beau Geste. 1942: Private Buckaroo; Give Out, Sisters. 1947: Something in the Wind. 1952: Singin' in the Rain. 1953: Call Me Madam; Walking My Baby Back Home; I Love Melvin. 1954: There's No Business Like Show Business. 1957: The Buster Keaton Story. 1961: Cry for Happy. 1965: That Funny Feeling.

ODETS, Clifford

Writer. Philadelphia 1906–63 Hollywood
Left high school after 2 years to work as actor, gag writer and sound effects man for radio. Playwright with Group Theatre, New York, for which he wrote 'Waiting for Lefty' and 'Till the Day I Die' (both 1935). 1936: to Hollywood. Films adapted from his plays include Golden Boy (1939), Clash By Night (1952), The Country Girl (1954) and The Big Knife (1955). Directed and wrote 2 films. His first wife was Luise Rainer.

Films as writer include: 1936: The General Died at Dawn. 1946: Deadline at Dawn. 1947: Humoresque. 1957: Sweet Smell of Success (co). 1961: Wild in the Country.

Films as director and writer: 1944: None But the Lonely Heart. 1959: The Story on Page One.

O'HARA, John

Writer. Pottsville, Pennsylvania 1905–70
Father a doctor. Educated New York. Worked on newspapers, magazines in New York and Pennsylvania as reporter, copy reader, columnist, war correspondent, drama and film critic. Many short stories including 'Pal Joey' (1940) which he adapted as musical comedy for Rodgers and Hart (also 1940): filmed 1957. 1940: first film as writer, in collaboration. All films as writer for Fox; none in period 1943–55. From 1957: all film adaptations of his work made by others.

Films as writer: 1940: He Married His Wife (co); I Was an Adventuress (co). 1942: Moontide. 1956: The Best Things in Life are Free (st).

Films adapted from his work by others include: 1957: Pal Joey. 1958: Ten North Frederick. 1960: Butterfield 8; From the Terrace.

O'HARA, Maureen

(Maureen Fitzsimmons) Actress. Dublin 1920–
Mother was Abbey Theatre singer and actress Marguerite Fitzsimmons. Abbey Theatre School London College of Music. 1939: first film as actress Jamaica Inn. To US. 1946: became American citizen. Formed production company with L. B. Merman, Will Price and John Payne. To 1949: worked mainly for RKO and Fox. 1949–56: mainly Universal. Then several companies. Married directors George Hanley Brown (1938–41, annulled) and Will Price (1941–53, divorced).

Films as actress include: 1939: The Hunchback of Notre Dame. 1940: A Bill of Divorcement. 1941: How Green Was My Valley. 1942: The Black Swan; Ten Gentlemen from West Point; Immortal Sergeant. 1943: This Land Is Mine. 1944: Buffalo Bill. 1945: The Spanish Main. 1946: Do You Love Me?; Sentimental Journey. 1947: The Foxes of Harrow; Miracle on 34th Street. 1948: Sitting Pretty. 1949: Britannia Mews; A Woman's Secret; Father was a Fullback. 1950: Rio Grande. 1952: Kangaroo; The Quiet Man. 1955: The Magnificent Matador; The Long Gray Line. 1956: Lisbon. 1957: The Wings of Eagles. 1960: Our Man in Havana. 1961: Deadly Companions; The Parent Trap. 1962: Mr Hobbs Takes a Vacation. 1963: McLintock!;

Spencer's Mountain. 1964: The Battle of the Villa Fiorita. 1965: The Rare Breed. 1970: How Do I Love Thee? 1971: Big Jake.

OLIVIER, Sir Laurence

Actor and director. Dorking, Surrey 1907–
1918: stage debut in 'Julius Caesar'. On stage in Stratford; repertory in Birmingham. 1930: Married actress Jill Esmond; first film as actor. 1937: Old Vic 'Hamlet', 'Henry V'. 1940: married Vivien Leigh. War service in Fleet Air Arm, reaching Lieutenant. Became co-director of Old Vic. 1945: first film as director and actor. Directed 'King Lear' in London and toured Australia and New Zealand with Old Vic in e.g. 'Richard III'. 1948: directed and produced Hamlet and received Oscar as Best Actor. 1949: directed and acted in 'School for Scandal', 'Antigone'. 1949: produced 'A Streetcar Named Desire'. 1951: produced and acted with Vivien Leigh in 'Caesar and Cleopatra' and 'Antony and Cleopatra' in London and New York. Toured Eastern Europe in 'The Entertainer'. 1960: title role in 'Becket' in New York. 1961: married Joan Plowright. Director of Chichester Festival Theatre where he directed and acted in 'Uncle Vanya'. 1963: director of National Theatre of Great Britain; directed e.g. 'Hamlet' 'Othello'. 1970: Made life peer.

Films as actor include: 1930: The Temporary Widow. 1931: Friends and Lovers; The Yellow Ticket. 1935: Moscow Nights. 1936: As You Like It. 1937: Fire Over England. 1939: Wuthering Heights. 1940: Rebecca; Pride and Prejudice. 1941: 49th Parallel; That Hamilton Woman. 1943: The Demi-Paradise. 1951: The Magic Box. 1952: Carrie. 1953: The Beggar's Opera. 1959: The Devil's Disciple. 1960: Spartacus; The Entertainer. 1962: Term of Trial. 1965: Bunny Lake Is Missing. 1966: Othello; Khartoum. 1968: The Shoes of the Fisherman (ur).

Films as director and actor: 1944: Henry V. 1948: Hamlet (+ co-p). 1955: Richard III (+ p). 1957: The Prince and the Showgirl (+ p). 1970: Three Sisters.

OLIVER, Edna May

(Edna May Nutter) Actress. Malden, Massachusetts 1883–1942 Hollywood
From 1904: acted in stock. From 1916: on Broadway. 1924: recreated stage role in first film as actress Icebound for Famous Players-Lasky. Worked mainly for RKO and MGM. 1941: last film Lydia.

Films as actress include: 1925: Lucky Devil. 1926: The American Venus; Let's Get Married. 1929: The Saturday Night Kid. 1931: Cimarron; Laugh and Get Rich. 1932: Ladies of the Jury; Hold 'Em Jail; The Conquerors. 1933: Only Yesterday; Little Women; Alice in Wonderland; Ann Vickers. 1935: The Personal History, Adventures, Experience and Observations of David Copperfield, the Younger; A Tale of Two Cities. 1936: Romeo and Juliet. 1937: Parnell; Rosalie. 1939: Nurse Edith Cavell; Drums Along the Mohawk; The Story of Vernon and Irene Castle. 1940: Pride and Prejudice.

OLMI, Ermanno

Director. Bergamo, Italy 1931–
Studied acting, became stage producer. 1954–61:

made over 30 documentaries for Edison Volta. 1961–65: worked for own production company based in Milan. Films as producer include his own *I Fidanzati* (1962), Gianfranco De Bosio's *Il Terrorista* (1963). TV producer and director of documentaries. Films for TV include *Storie di Giovani* (1967), *I Recuperanti* (1969), *Durante l'estate* (1971).

Features as director: 1959: Il Tempo si è fermato – Time Stood Still (+ s). 1961: Il Posto – The Job – Sound of Trumpets (+ st/s/e). 1962: I Fidanzati – The Engagement (+ p/s). 1964: E venne un uomo – A Man Named John – And There Came a Man (+ co-s). 1969: Un Certo Giorno – One Fine Day (+ s/e).

OLSEN and JOHNSON

(John Sigvard Ole Olsen) Peru, Indiana 1892–1963 Mexico; (Harold 'Chic' Johnson) Chicago 1891–1962 Las Vegas
Acting team. Played double act in comedy–vaudeville from 1915. 1930–45: a few films together. Olsen also made 2 film appearances without Johnson.

Films as acting team: 1930: Oh Sailor Behave. 1931: Fifty Million Frenchmen; Gold Dust Gertie. 1941: Hellzapoppin. 1943: Crazy House. 1944: Ghost Catchers. 1945: See My Lawyer.

ONDŘÍČEK, Miroslav

Cinematographer. Prague 1933–
Training at Documentary Film Studios, Prague. From 1963: association with Milos Forman on documentaries and features. 1966 and 1967: invited to England by Lindsay Anderson to photograph 2 films.

Films as cinematographer include: 1963: Konkurs; Kydyby ty muziky nebly. 1965: Lasky jedne plavovlasky. 1966: Intimni Osvetleni; Mucednini lasky; The White Bus. 1967: Hori ma Panenko. 1968: If... 1971: Taking Off.

OPHÜLS, Max

(Max Oppenheimer). Director. Sarrebruck 1902–57 Hamburg
Family were in men's clothing business. Hamburg University. 1918: after trying journalism studied acting. 1919: first part, in Sarrebruck. 1920–22: actor in Stuttgart and Aix-la-Chapelle. 1923: debut as theatre director in Dortmund. 1924–25: directed mainly operettas at Elberfeld-Barmen. 1926: directed at the Vienna Burgtheater. 1927: directed about 30 plays in Frankfurt. 1928: directed important productions (Shakespeare, Molière, Kleist) in Breslau; wrote and directed a comedy for children; some work for radio. 1930: started in films in Berlin as actor and assistant to Anatole Litvak on *Nie wieder Liebe,* and directed own first film. *Une Histoire d'amour* is a French version of *Liebelei,* partly reshot and partly dubbed. In 1934, with Saar plebiscite, opted for French nationality. 1934–40: worked in France, apart from *La Signora di tutti* in Italy and *Komedie om geld* in Holland. 1940: moved to Switzerland where he directed 2 plays (including 'Romeo and Juliet') and began a film which was unfinished. 1941: went to USA where many film projects aborted; did not complete a film there until 1947. 1950: returned to France. 1954: worked as a director for radio in

Baden-Baden and took one small part in a radio play. 1957: died during his first production since 1933 at Schauspiel Theater in Hamburg, 'Der tolle Tag' (from 'Le Mariage de Figaro'). 1959: memoirs published posthumously as 'Spiel im Dasein' (French translation 'Max Ophüls par Max Ophüls' 1963). His project on Modigliani was filmed by Jacques Becker as *Montparnasse 19* and dedicated to his memory. Son is director, Marcel Ophüls.

Films as director: 1930: Dann schon lieber Lebertran (+ co-s). 1931: Die verliebte Firma (+ co-s). 1932: Die verkaufte Braut – The Bartered Bride (+ co-s); Die lachenden Erben (+ co-s); Liebelei (+ co-s). 1933: Une Histoire d'amour (+ co-s); On a volé un homme; La Signora di tutti (+ co-s). 1935: Divine (+ co-s). 1936: Valse Brillante de Chopin; Ave Maria de Schubert; Komedie om geld (+ co-s); La Tendre Ennemie (+ co-s). 1937: Yoshiwara – Kohana (+ co-s). 1938: Werther – Le Roman de Werther (+ co-s); Sans lendemain (+ co-s). 1940: De Mayerling à Sarajevo (+ co-s); L'Ecole des femmes. 1947: The Exile (+ co-s); Letter from an Unknown Woman (+ co-s); Caught. 1949: The Reckless Moment. 1950: Vendetta (*uc, co-d Preston Sturges, Stuart Heisler, Howard Hughes, Mel Ferrer*); La Ronde (+ co-s). 1952: Le Plaisir (+ co-s). 1953: Madame de ... (+ co-s). 1955: Lola Montès – Lola Montez – The Sins of Lola Montes (+ co-s).

ORSINI, Valentino

Director. Pisa, Italy 1926–
Critic and organiser of film societies. From 1948: long collaboration with Taviano Brothers with whom he ran Teatro della Cronaco for workers at Leghorn. 1954: co-wrote their first film *San Miniato Luglio 44.* 1959: collaborated with them in assisting Joris Ivens on TV film *L'Italia non è un paese povero.* 1962: first film as director in collaboration with them. 1963: collaboration. 1968: first solo film as director.

Films as director in collaboration with Taviano Brothers: 1962: Un Uomo da bruciare – A Man for Burning (+ s). 1963: I Fuorilegge del matrimonio (+ co-st/co-s).

Films as director: 1968: I Dannati della terra. 1970: Corbari.

OSBORN, Paul

Writer. Evansville, Louisiana 1901–
University of Michigan. Taught English at Michigan and Yale. Playwright: 'The Vinegar Tree', 'The Ledge', 'Mornings at Seven'. 1939: *On Borrowed Time* (produced by Sidney Franklin) based on his play. Scripted 3 MGM films produced by Sidney Franklin, then worked for e.g. Warners, Fox. 2 of his scripts directed by Mervyn Leroy, 2 by Joshua Logan, 2 by Elia Kazan. 1960: *The World of Suzie Wong* based on his play.

Films as writer include: 1943: Madame Curie (co). 1944: Cry Havoc. 1946: The Yearling. 1948: Homecoming. 1949: Portrait of Jennie (co). 1952: Invitation. 1955: East of Eden. 1957: Sayonara. 1958: South Pacific. 1959: Wild River.

Maureen O'Hara in McLintock!, *directed by Andrew V. McLaglen.*
Lawrence Olivier in Tony Richardson's The Entertainer.
Anton Walbrook and Simone Signoret in Max Ophüls' La Ronde.

OSBORNE, John

Writer. London 1929–

Father Welsh commercial artist, mother barmaid. State schools and private education to 16. Copywriter, journalist. 1948: became actor. 1948–49: toured in 'No Room at the Inn'. 1949: became stage producer in Huddersfield, Lancashire. 1951: stage actor–manager in Ilfracombe. Acted in provincial repertory and in London. 1956: 'Look Back in Anger', his fourth play. 1959: first film as writer *Look Back in Anger*. Founder–director of Woodfall production company and own company. Plays include 'The Entertainer' (1957), 'Luther' (1961), 'Plays for England' (1962), 'Inadmissible Evidence' (1964), 'A Patriot for Me' (1964), 'A Bond Honoured' (1966), 'The Hotel in Amsterdam' (1968), 'Time Present' (1968), 'The Right Prospectus' (1970), 'Very Like a Whale' (1970). 1970: In *Erste Liebe*. Married actress Pamela Elizabeth Lane (1951–57), actress Mary Ure (1957–63), critic and novelist Penelope Gilliatt (from 1963). Oscar for 'screenplay based on another medium' *Tom Jones* (1963).

Films as writer: 1959: Look Back in Anger (*additional di/fpl*). 1960: The Entertainer (*co-s/fpl*). 1963: Tom Jones. 1968: Inadmissible Evidence (*s/fpl*).

OSHIMA, Nagisa

Director. Kyoto, Japan 1932–

1954: joined Shochiku after graduation from Department of Law, Kyoto University. Worked as assistant for 5 years before directing his first film (1959). Left Shochiku to form own production company, Sozosha (1961). 1962–64: director and writer of some documentaries for Nihon TV; directed TV series, 'Asia no akebono' (The Dawn of Asia) (1964–65) and documentaries *Daitoa senso – The Pacific War* (1968), *Mo taku-to to bunkadaikakumei – Mao Tse-Tung and the Cultural Revolution* (1969). From 1965: Own production company. Married to actress Akiko Koyama.

Films as director: 1959: Ai to Kibo no Machi – A Town of Love and Hope (+ *s*). 1960: Seishun Zankoku Monogatari – Naked Youth, a Story of Cruelty (+ *s*); Taiyo no Hakaba – The Sun's Burial (+ *co-s*); Nihon no Yoru to Kiri – Night and Fog in Japan (+ *co-s*). 1961: Shiiku – The Catch. 1962: Amakusa Shiro Tokisada – The Rebel (+ *co-s*). 1965: Etsuraku – The Pleasures of the Flesh (+ *s*); Yunbogi no Nikki – The Diary of Yunbogi (+ *s/c*). 1966: Hakuchu no Torima – Violence at Noon. 1967: Ninja Bugeicho – Band of Ninja (+ *co-s*); Nihon Shunka-ko – A Treatise on Japanese Bawdy Song (+ *pc/co-s*); Muri Shinja Nihon no Natsu – Japanese Summer; Double Suicide (+ *pc/co-s*). 1968: Koshikei – Death by Hanging (+ *co-p/co-s*); Kaeyyekita Yopparai – Three Resurrected Drunkards (+ *co-s*); Shinjuku Dorobo Nikki – Diary of a Shinjuku Thief (+ *co-s/e*). 1969: Shonen – Boy. 1971: Tokyo; Senso Sengo Hiwa – He Died After the War; Gishiki – The Ceremony.

O'SULLIVAN, Maureen

Actress. County Roscommon, Ireland 1911–

Convents in Ireland, England, France. 1930: first film as actress. 1930–31: all films for Fox. 1932–42: mainly MGM. 1934–42: played Jane to Johnny Weissmuller's Tarzan in 6 films. On Chicago stage in 'A Roomful of Roses'. 1962: Broadway debut in 'Never Too Late'; acted in film adaptation (1965). Also stage. Married John Farrow (1936–63, widowed). Daughter is Mia Farrow.

Films as actress include: 1930: So This Is London; Just Imagine; The Princess and the Plumber. 1931: A Connecticut Yankee in King Arthur's Court. 1932: Tarzan the Ape Man; The Silver Lining; Strange Interlude; Okay America. 1933: Cohens and Kellys in Trouble; Tugboat Annie. 1934: The Thin Man; Hide-Out; Tarzan and His Mate; The Barretts of Wimpole Street. 1935: The Flame Within; Anna Karenina; The Personal History, Adventures, Experience and Observations of David Copperfield, the Younger. 1936: The Voice of Bugle Ann; Tarzan Escapes; The Devil Doll. 1937: A Day at the Races. 1938: The Crowd Roars; A Yank at Oxford; Port of Seven Seas. 1939: Tarzan Finds a Son!; Let Us Live. 1941: Tarzan's Secret Treasure. 1942: Tarzan's New York Adventure. 1948: The Big Clock. 1950: Where Danger Lives. 1953: All I Desire; Mission Over Korea. 1957: The Tall T. 1965: Never Too Late.

OSWALD, Gerd

Director. Berlin 1919–

Son of Richard Oswald. Vienna stage as a child. 1933: with father to England; worked in several capacities on films, including his father's. To USA: acted in several little theatres. For 15 years, assistant director and production manager with independents, Paramount and Fox. 1952–54: associate producer or co-producer on 3 films in Europe for Fox: *Man on a Tightrope, Night People* and *Oasis*. 1956: first film as director. 1956–59: worked for United Artists. 1959: to West Germany. From 1955: TV work includes 'Twentieth Century Fox Hour', 'George Sanders Mystery Theatre', 'Playhouse 90', 'Perry Mason', 'Outer Limits', 'Star Trek'.

Films as director: 1956: A Kiss Before Dying; The Brass Legend. 1957: Crime of Passion; Fury at Showdown; Valerie. 1958: Paris Holiday; Screaming Mimi. 1959: Am Tag als der Regen kam – The Day the Rains Came. 1960: Schachnovelle – Three Moves to Freedom (+ *co-s*). 1961: Brainwashed. 1962: The Longest Day (*uc, co-d 3 others*). 1963: Tempestà su Ceylon. 1965: Agent for H.A.R.M. 1969: 80 Steps to Jonah. 1970: Bunny O'Hare (+ *p/co-s*).

OSWALD, Richard

(Richard W. Ornstein). Director. Vienna 1880–1963 Düsseldorf, West Germany

1893–1907: in repertory and at Vienna Academy of Dramatic Art. 1907–1913: leading stage roles in Germany and Austria; began writing and directing plays. 1913: entered films as story editor with Vitaskop in Berlin. 1914: first film banned by government for its pacifist sentiments, never released. 1915: first released film *Die Geschichte der Stillen Mühle*. 1919: head of production at Bioscop. 1921: formed own company. 1925: bankrupt. Producer–director with Westi, then freelance director. 1933: to Austria. 1938: to Paris, where directed *Tempête sur l'Asie*, then to USA. From 1956: TV. Son is Gerd Oswald.

Films as director include: 1916: Hoffmanns Erzählungen (+ *p/co-s*); Renn Fieber (+ *p*); Zirkusblut (+ *p/s*). 1917: Die Rache der Toten (+ *s*); Die Seeschlacht. 1917–18: Es Werde Licht (*in 3 parts*; + *p/co parts 1 & 2*). 1918: Das Tagebuch einer Verlorenen (+ *p/s*). 1919: Anders als die Andern (+ *p/co-s*); Die Prostitution (+ *p/s*); Die Reise um die Erde in 80 Tagen (+ *p/s*); Unheimliche Geschichten (+ *p/s*). 1920: Der Reigen (+ *p/s*); Kurfürstendamm (+ *p/s*); Manolescus Memoiren (+ *p*). 1921: Lady Hamilton (+ *p*). 1922: Lucrezia Borgia (+ *p/s*). 1924: Don Carlos und Elisabeth (+ *p/s*). 1926: Dürfen wir schweigen? (+ *s*). 1927: Funkzauber (+ *p*); Gehetzte Frauen (+ *p*). 1928: Cagliostro. 1929: Frühlings Erwachen (+ *p*). 1930: Dreyfus (+ *p*); Alraune. 1931: Der Hauptmann von Koepenick. 1932: Unheimliche Geschichten (*rm* 1919). 1938: Tempête sur l'Asie. 1942: Isle of Missing Men; The Captain of Koepenick – I Was a Criminal (*rm* 1931). 1949: The Lovable Cheat.

O'TOOLE, Peter

Actor. Connemara, Ireland 1933–

Moved to Leeds as child. Journalist. Acted in repertory. Service in Royal Navy. 1954: scholarship to RADA, in class of Albert Finney, Richard Harris, Alan Bates. Stage work in Bristol. On London stage in 'Oh! My Papa!' 1959: acted in 'The Long and the Short and the Tall'. 1960: first film as actor. Stratford repertory. Acted in 'Ride a Cock Horse', 'Baal', 'Juno and the Paycock'. 1968: on American TV in 'Present Laughter'. Own company, Keep Films. Married actress Sian Phillips.

Films as actor: 1960: Kidnapped; The Day They Robbed the Bank of England; The Savage Innocents (*uc*). 1962: Lawrence of Arabia. 1964: Becket (+ *pc*). 1965: Lord Jim; What's New, Pussycat? 1966: How to Steal a Million; La Bibbia. 1967: The Night of the Generals; Casino Royale (*uc*). 1968: Great Catherine (+ *pc*); The Lion in Winter. 1969: Goodbye, Mr Chips; Country Dance (*r* 1971). 1971: Murphy's War.

OUSPENSKAYA, Maria

Actress. Tula, Russia 1876–1949 Hollywood

1911: actress at Moscow Art Theatre. 1924: remained in USA after tour. Worked in Richard Boleslavsky's experimental theatre group. 1936: first film as actress *Dodsworth*. Studios include MGM, Warners, Fox, RKO.

Films as actress include: 1937: Conquest. 1939: Love Affair; The Rains Came; Judge Hardy and Son. 1940: The Mortal Storm; The Story of Dr Ehrlich's Magic Bullet; Waterloo Bridge; The Man I Married; Dance, Girl, Dance. 1941: The Shanghai Gesture. 1942: Kings Row; Mystery of Marie Roget. 1946: I've Always Loved You. 1949: A Kiss in the Dark.

OWEN, Don

Director. Toronto 1934–

Training at National Film Board of Canada, worked on documentaries. 1960: joined Office National du Film. 1962: first film as director. 1964: first feature *Nobody Waved Goodbye* was also first feature of NFBC. TV films include: *Toronto Jazz* (1962), *You Don't Back Down* (1965), *Ladies and Gentlemen: Mr Leonard Cohen*.

Films as director: 1962: The Runner (+s). 1964: Nobody Waved Goodbye (+s). 1966: High Steel; Notes for a Film About Donna and Gail (+co-s). 1967: The Ernie Game (+s).

OZU, Yasujiro

Director. Tokyo 1903–63

Waseda University. 1923: entered film industry as assistant to Tadamoto Okuba at Shochiku. 1927: directed first film *Zange no Yaiba*. Originated tatami-level camera-work. 1958: first colour film *Higanbana*. Made 54 films.

Films as director: 1927: Zange no Yaiba – Sword of Penitence (+st). 1928: Wakado no Yume – Dreams of Youth (+s); Nyobo Funshitsu – Wife Lost (+co-s); Kabocha – Pumpkin (+st); Hikkoshi Fufu – A Couple on the Move; Nikutaibi – Body Beautiful. 1929: Takara no Yama – The Treasure Mountain (+st); Wakakihi – Days of Youth (+co-s). Wasei Kenka Tomodachi – Fighting Friends; Daigaku wa Deta Keredo – I Graduated, But . . .; Kaishain Seikatsu – The Life of an Office Worker; Tokkan Kozo – A Straightforward Boy. 1930: Kekkon-gaku Nyumon – Introduction to Marriage; Hogaraka ni Ayume – Walk Cheerfully; Rakudai wa Shita-Keredo – I Flunked, But . . . (+st); Sono yo no Tsuma – That Night's Wife; Erogami no Onryo – The Revengeful Spirit of Eros; Ashi ni Sawatta Koun – Luck Touched my Legs; Ojosan – Young Miss; Shukujo to Hige – The Lady and her Favourites. 1931: Bijin Aishu – Beauty's Sorrows; Tokyo no Gassho – Chorus of Tokyo (+co-s). 1932: Haru wa Gofujin Kara – Spring Comes with the Ladies (+st). Umarete wa Mita Keredo – I was Born, But . . . (+st); Seishun no Yume ima Izuko – Where are the Dreams of Youth?; Mata au hi Made – Until the Day we Meet Again. 1933: Tokyo no Onna – Woman of Tokyo; Hijosen no Onna – Women on the Firing Line (+st); Dekigokoro – Passing Fancy (+fn). 1934: Haha o Kowazuya – Mother Ought to be Loved; Ukigusa Monogatari – A Story of Floating Weeds. 1935: Hakoiri Musume – Young Virgin; Tokyo Yoitoko – Tokyo is a Nice Place (+s); Tokyo no Yado – An Inn in Tokyo. 1936: Daigaku yoi Toko – College is a Nice Place (+st); Hitori Musuko – The Only Son (+st). 1937: Shukujo wa Nani o Wasuretaka – What did the Lady Forget? (+co-s). 1941: Toda-ke no Kyodai – The Toda Brothers and the Sisters (+co-s). 1942: Chichi Ariki – There was a Father (+co-s). 1947: Nagaya Shinshi-roku – Record of a Tenement Gentleman (+co-s). 1948: Kaze no Naka no Mendori – A Hen in the Wind (+co-s). 1949: Banshun – Late Spring (+co-s). 1950: Munakata Shimai – The Munakata Sisters (+co-s). 1951: Bakushu – Early Summer (+co-s). 1952: Ochazuke no Aji – The Flavour of Green Tea over Rice (+co-s). 1953: Tokyo Monogatari – Tokyo Story – Their First Trip to Tokyo (+co-s). 1956: Soshun – Early Spring (+co-s). 1957: Tokyo Boshoku – Twilight in Tokyo (+co-s). 1958: Higanbana – Equinox Flower (+co-s). 1959: Ohayo – Too Much Talk – Good Morning (+co-s); Ukigusa – Tales of the Floating Weeds; Parting at Dusk (+co-s). 1960: Akibiyori – Late Autumn (+co-s). 1961: Kohayagawa-ke no Aki – Early Autumn (+co-s). 1962: Samma no Aji – An Autumn Afternoon – The Widower – The Taste of Mackerel (+co-s).

P

PABST, George Wilhelm

Director. Raudnitz, Czechoslovakia 1885–1967 Vienna

1905: became actor in Switzerland, then in Salzburg, Berlin and New York. 1914: in France; interned as an enemy national. 1919: actor with Elisabeth Bergner in Vienna. 1920: Berlin, started in films with producer-director Carl Froelich, as actor in *Im Banne der Kralle* (1921) and as writer and assistant director on *Der Taugenichts* and *Luise Millerin* (both 1922). 1923: directed *Der Schatz* for Froelich's company. 1931: *Die Dreigroschenoper* was a German–American co-production also shot in a French version, *L'Opéra de quat'sous*, while *Kameradschaft* was a German–French co-production. 1932: *Die Herrin von Atlantis* was also shot in a French version as *L'Atlantide*. 1933: in France apart from one film in Hollywood until he returned to Austria in 1939: *Don Quichotte* (1933) was also shot in an English version with George Robey as Sancho Panza. 1937: sound version of *Die freudlose Gasse* released in USA as *Streets of Sorrow*. Supervised two films directed by Mark Sorkin. *Der Fall Molander* (1943) shot in Prague but interrupted during editing by the Russian advance and completed under Russian control and released in 1949. 1949: producer in Vienna of 3 films by other directors. 1952–53: Italy. 1954: West Germany.

Films as director: 1923: Der Schatz (+s). 1924: Gräfin Donelli. 1925: Die freudlose Gasse. 1926: Geheimnisse einer Seele; Man Spielt nicht mit der Liebe. 1927: Der Liebe der Jeanne Ney. 1928: Begierde; Die Buchse der Pandora. 1929: Die weisse Hölle von Piz Palü (co-d Arnold Fanck); Das Tagebuch einer Verlorenen. 1930: Westfront 1918 – Vier von der Infanterie; Skandal um Eva. 1931: Die Dreigroschenoper – L'Opéra de quat'sous – The Threepenny Opera; Kameradschaft. 1932: Die Herrin von Atlantis – L'Atlantide. 1933: Don Quichotte – Don Quixote; Du haut en bas. 1934: A Modern Hero. 1936: Mademoiselle Docteur. 1938: Le Drame de Shanghai. 1939: Jeunes Filles en détresse. 1941: Komödianten (+co-s). 1943: Paracelsus; Der Fall Molander (uc). 1947: Der Prozess. 1949: Geheimnisvolle Tiefe. 1952: La Voce del silenzio – The House of Silence (+co-s). 1954: Cose da pazzi; Das Bekenntnis der Ina Kahr. 1955: Der letzte Akt; Es geschah am 20 Juli. 1956: Rosen für Bettina – Licht in der Finsternis – Ballerina; Durch die Wälder, durch die Auen (+s).

PAGE, Geraldine

Actress. Kirksville, Missouri 1924–

Chicago Academy of Fine Arts; studied under Uta Hagen. Stage appearances from 1940. 1955: Actors' Studio. Films from 1947. Broadway parts, including 'Summer and Smoke', 'Sweet Bird of Youth', 'The Immoralist'. Second husband actor Rip Torn (from 1963).

Films as actress include: 1953: Hondo; Taxi. 1961: Summer and Smoke. 1962: Sweet Bird of Youth. 1963: Toys in the Attic. 1964: Dear Heart. 1966: Monday's Child. 1967: You're a Big Boy Now. 1969: Trilogy. 1971: The Beguiled; J. W. Coop.

The final scene in Koshikei, *directed by Nagisa Oshima.*
Keiji Sada (right) and Mariko Okada in Samma No Aji, *directed by Yasujiro Ozu.*
G. W. Pabst's Es geschah am 20 Juli.

PAGLIERO, Marcello

Director. London 1907–
Genoese father, French mother. In Italy from 1914. Degree in law. From 1941: writer in collaboration on e.g. *Paisà* (1947). 1943: first film as director. Acted in e.g. *Roma città aperta* (1945), *Les Jeux sont faits* (1947), *Dedée d'Anvers* (1947). From 1949: mainly director. 1953: collaborated on stage production of 'La Mandragola' at the Teatro delle Arti in Rome. 1956: made *L'Odyssée du capitaine Steve* in Australia. 1958: acted in Pierre Kast's *Le Bel Age*. 1960: made *20,000 Lieues sur la terre* in Russia.

Films as director: 1943: 07, Taxi (+ *s*). 1946: Desiderio (+ *co-s*; *co-d Roberto Rossellini*); Roma, città libera. 1950: Un Homme marche dans la ville; La Rose Rouge. 1951: Les Amants de Bras-Mort; Azur. 1952: La Putain Respectueuse (*co-d Brabant*). 1953: Destinées *ep* Due Donne. 1954: Vestire gli ignudi; Le Vergine moderne (+ *w*). 1955: Chéri-Bibi. 1956: L'Odyssée du capitaine Steve. 1960: 20,000 Lieues sur la terre (+ *s*).

PAGNOL, Marcel

Director, producer and writer. Aubagne, France 1895–
Son of a school-teacher. After obtaining degree, taught English in a college at Tarascon (1915). Continued teaching in schools in Aix-en-Provence (1918), Marseille (1920) and at the Lycée Condorcet in Paris (1922). Became a successful playwright and founded film magazine, Les Cahiers du film. 1931: Scripted and produced *Marius* from his own play. Set up studio in Marseille. There produced and from 1933 sometimes directed films which he wrote. Jean Renoir's *Toni* made there. 1932: *Fanny* from his story. Films adapted from his plays include *Topaze* (Louis Gasnier, 1933), *Port of Seven Seas* (1938, written by Preston Sturges after 'Fanny' and 'Marius'), *Fanny* (1961 based on the 'Marius' trilogy) and *Mr Topaze* (1961).

Films as director and producer: 1933: Le Gendre de Monsieur Poirier. 1934: Angèle (+ *s*); Jofroi (+ *s/di*); L'Article 330. 1935: Cigalon; Merlusse (+ *di*). 1936: César (+ *s/fpl*); Topaze (*d/s/st only*). 1937: Regain – Harvest (+ *s/di*). 1938: Le Schpountz (+ *s/st*); La Femme du boulanger (+ *s/di*). 1940: La Fille du puisatier (+ *s/di*). 1941: La Prière aux étoiles (*uf*). 1948: La Belle Meunière (*co-d*). 1951: Topaze (+ *s/st*). 1952: Manon des sources. 1954: Les Lettres de mon moulin (*d/s only*).

PAINLEVÉ, Jean

Director. Paris 1902–
Son of mathematician Paul Painlevé. Medical studies. 1925: first film as director. 1930: founded l'Institut du Cinéma Scientifique. 1933: co-founder of l'Association pour la Documentation Photographique et Cinématographique dans les Sciences. Resistance during World War II. 1945: appointed Directeur du cinéma français. 1947: remade his 1939 film *Solutions Françaises*. 1958: remade his 1928 film *Les Oursins*.

Films as director include: 1925: Évolution de l'oeuf d'épinoche (gastroteus Aculeatus) de la fécondation à l'éclosion (+ *c*); La Daphnie; Le Sérum du Docteur Normet. 1926: La Pieuvre. 1927: Bernard-l'Ermite. 1928: Les Oursins. 1929: Les Crabes; Les Crevettes; Mouvements Protoplasmiques dans les cellules d'Elodea Canadensis en milieux isotonique, hypertonique, hypotonique. 1930: Hyas et Stenorinque. 1931: Caprelles; Pantapodes. 1933: L'Hippocampe; Evolution d'un grain d'argent dans une émulsion photographique. 1935: La Culture des tissus et formation de macrocytes; Electrolyse du nitrate d'argent. 1936: Barbe-Bleue (*co-d René Bertrand*); Voyage dans le ciel; Images mathématiques de la quatrième dimension; Images Mathématiques de la lutte pour la vie; L'Evolution Géologique de la chaîne des Alpes; Similitudes de longueurs et des vitesses. 1939: Solutions Françaises; La Chirurgie Correctrise et Réparatrice. 1945: Le Vampire (+ *c*). 1946: Jeux d'enfants. 1947: Notre Planète la Terre; Assassins d'eau douce (+ *c*); L'Oeuvre Scientifique de Pasteur (+ *s/co-c/cy*); Solutions Françaises (*rm* 1939); Ecriture du mouvement. 1955: Albinisme. 1956: Réactions Nutritives d'haliotis: réactions d'haliotis, de clamys et de différents échinodermes à la présence de certains stellerides. 1957: Influence de la lumière sur les mouvements de l'oeuf de truite. 1958: Les Oursins (*rm* 1929); Eleutheria en culture. 1959: Embrogynèse d'Orizias Latipes. 1960: Danseuses de la mer. 1964: Destructeurs marins des bois. 1965: Méthode de gymnastique penchant; Arénicole. 1967: Amours de la pieuvre; Dynamique de l'évolution de l'oeuf de pieuvre.

PAL, George

Producer and director. Cegled, Hungary 1908–
Draughtsman, worked in a Hungarian film studio. To Berlin: designer for Ufa. Set up own studio to make advertising films in Eindhoven, Holland. Horlicks contract led to his going to USA. 1940: began making Paramount cartoons, using puppetoons. 1946: work in educational film. 1947: began work in feature-length cartoons. Pioneered combination of live-action and cartoon, used in *Tom Thumb* (1958). From 1950: produced live-action films. 1950: produced 2 films for Eagle Lion, both directed by Irving Pichel. 1951–55: produced for Paramount, including 3 films directed by Byron Haskin. From 1958: producer–director for MGM.

Features as producer include: 1950: The Great Rupert; Destination Moon. 1951: When Worlds Collide. 1953: Houdini; The War of the Worlds. 1954: The Naked Jungle. 1955: Conquest of Space.

Features as producer and director. 1958: Tom Thumb. 1960: The Time Machine; Atlantis, the Lost Continent. 1962: The Wonderful World of the Brothers Grimm (*co-d Henry Levin*). 1964: The 7 Faces of Dr Lao. 1967: The Power (*co-d Byron Haskin*).

PALANCE, Jack *or*
Walter Jack

(Walter Palanuik). Actor. Lattimer, Pennsylvania. 1921–
University of North Carolina, and Stanford University. Professional boxer. World War II: 3 years in US Air Corps. Plane went down in flames, and his severe facial burns required major plastic surgery. 1948: in 'The Seagull' in Stanford and on Broadway. From 1949: on Broadway; replaced Brando in 'A Streetcar Named Desire'. 1950: first film as actor. 1955: played Cassius in 'Julius Caesar' at opening of Shakespeare Festival Theatre at Stratford, Connecticut. Also in cabaret and TV, e.g. 'Requiem for a Heavyweight'. From 1958: many films outside USA especially in Italy. 1965: toured in 'Heaven can Wait' as actor and director. Formed production company with Robert Aldrich.

Films as actor include: 1950: Panic in the Streets. 1952: Sudden Fear. 1953: Shane; Second Chance; Man in the Attic. 1954: Sign of the Pagan. 1955: Kiss of Fire; The Big Knife; I Died a Thousand Times. 1956: Attack! 1959: Ten Seconds to Hell. 1960: Austerlitz; I Mongoli. 1961: Il Giudizio Universale. 1962: Barabbas. 1963: Le Mépris. 1967: The Professionals. 1968: Torture Garden. 1969: Che! 1970: The McMasters; Monte Walsh. 1971: The Horsemen.

PALMER, Lilli

(Maria Lilli Peiser) Actress. Posen, Germany 1914–
Mother an actress. Ilka Grüning School of Acting, Berlin. Acted in repertory, worked in cabaret. Stage debut in 'Die eiserne Jungfrau'. 1934: to London. 1935: first film as actress *Crime Unlimited*. 1938: return to stage. 1941: acted on stage with Rex Harrison. 1943: married him. 1945: acted with him in *The Rakes's Progress*. 1946: first American film as actress *Cloak and Dagger*. Subsequent films for numerous companies including Warners, Paramount, MGM. New York stage in 'Caesar and Cleopatra'. Acted with her husband in 'Bell, Book and Candle'. 1953: returned to Germany. 1958: divorced. 1965: on TV in *Le Grain de Sable*.

Films as actress include: 1936: Secret Agent. 1939: A Girl Must Live. 1942: Thunder Rock. 1943: The Gentle Sex. 1946: Beware of Pity. 1947: Body and Soul. 1948: My Girl Tisa; No Minor Vices. 1952: The Four Poster. 1953: Main Street to Broadway. 1959: But Not For Me. 1960: Conspiracy of Hearts. 1961: The Pleasure of His Company; The Counterfeit Traitor. 1962: Finche dura la tempestà; La Rendez-vous de minuit. 1964: Operation Crossbow; The Amorous Adventures of Moll Flanders. 1965: Le Tonnerre de Dieu. 1968: Nobody Runs Forever. 1969: De Sade. 1970: La Peau de sable.

PANAMA, Norman

Director, writer and producer. Chicago 1914–
University of Chicago; while a student wrote play in collaboration with Melvin Frank. 1938: to Hollywood with him; worked as radio writer for 3 years, writing for e.g. Groucho Marx, Rudy Vallee. Wrote sketches for New York stage, including Schubert revue 'Keep Off the Grass' (1939). 1942: first film as writer in collaboration with Frank. From 1950: directed, wrote and produced films with Frank; shared same credit until 1956. From 1962: own production company in Britain, first production *The Road to Hong Kong*. 1942–45 and 1954–60: worked mainly for Paramount; worked also for MGM and others.

Films as writer in collaboration with Melvin Frank: 1942: My Favorite Blonde (*st*). 1943: Happy Go Lucky (*co*); Thank Your Lucky Stars (*co*). 1944: And the Angels Sing. 1946: Monsieur Beaucaire. 1947: It Had to be You. 1948: Mr Blandings Builds His Dream House; The Return of October. 1954: White Christmas (*co*).

Films as director, writer and producer in collaboration with Melvin Frank: 1950: The Reformer and the Redhead. 1951: Strictly Dishonorable; Callaway Went Thataway. 1952: Above and Beyond (+ *co-s*). 1954: Knock on Wood. 1956: The Court Jester (+ *st*); That Certain Feeling (*co-s*).

Films as producer in collaboration with Melvin Frank: 1959: The Jayhawkers. 1960: The Facts of Life (+ *s*); Li'l Abner (+ *s*).

Films as director: 1958: The Trap – The Baited Trap (+ *co-p/co-s*). 1966: Not With My Wife You Don't (*p/co-st/co-s*). 1969: How to Commit Marriage; The Maltese Bippy.

PAPATAKIS, Niko

Director and producer. Addis Ababa, Ethiopia 1918– Greek father, Ethiopian mother. Studies in Greece. At 19: emigrated to Paris. 1951: opened 'Rose Rouge' nightclub; married Anouk Aimée. 1952–54: producer for Jean Genet and Henri Gruel. 1961: co-produced *Shadows*. 1962: first film as director *Les Abysses*, adapted from Genet's play 'Les Bonnes'. Returned to Greece for a year, planning *Pâtres du désordre*. 1966: to Greece, began shooting. 1967: shooting made impossible by political situation; unfinished film returned to France.

Films as producer: 1952: Un Chant d'amour. 1953: Martin et Gaston. 1954: Gitanos et papillons. 1961: Shadows (*co*).

Films as director: 1962: Les Abysses. 1967: Pâtres du désordre (*uf*). 1968: Thanos & Despina.

PARKER, Eleanor

Actress. Cedarville, Ohio 1922–
Apprentice at Cleveland Playhouse, then Martha's Vineyard. 1940–41: Pasadena Community Playhouse, spotted by talent scout. Warners contract. 1941: first film as actress *They Died With Their Boots On,* but her scene cut from finished film. 1942: first film appearance in short *Soldiers in White*. To 1950: worked for Warners. 1952–60: worked for MGM.

Films as actress include: 1943: Mission to Moscow. 1944: The Very Thought of You. 1945: Hollywood Canteen; Pride of the Marines. 1946: Of Human Bondage. 1947: The Voice of the Turtle. 1950: Chain Lightning; Caged; Three Secrets. 1951: A Millionaire for Christ; Detective Story. 1952: Scaramouche; Above and Beyond. 1953: Escape from Fort Bravo. 1954: The Naked Jungle. 1955: Many Rivers to Cross; Interrupted Melody. 1956: The Man with the Golden Arm; The King and Four Queens. 1957: The Seventh Sin. 1959: A Hole in the Head. 1960: Home from the Hill. 1961: Return to Peyton Place. 1965: The Sound of Music. 1966: The Oscar. 1967: Warning Shot; Il Tigre.

PARLO, Dita

(Grethe Gerda Kornstadt) Actress. Stettin, Germany 1906–1972 Paris
Ballet training. Stage training at Ufa acting school. From 1928: German films. 1932–33: American films. From 1934: almost all her films French. 1940: arrested as a German, returned to Germany. From 1950: very occasional films. 1965 last film.

Films as actress include: 1928: Heimkehr; Die Dame mit der Maske. 1931: Menschen hinter Gittern. 1932: The Honor of the Family. 1933: Mr Broadway. 1934: L'Atalante; Rapt. 1937: Mademoiselle Docteur; La Grande Illusion. 1938: Paix sur le Rhin; Le Courier de Lyon; La Rue sans joie; Ultimatum. 1939: L'Inconnue de Monte Carlo. 1940: L'Or du 'Cristobal'. 1950: Justice est faite. 1957: Quand le soleil montera. 1965: La Dame de Pique.

PARRISH, Robert

Director, editor, actor. Columbus, Georgia 1916– 1928–32: actor in small parts. 1933: became assistant director at RKO, then editor. Edited documentaries, including 2 directed by John Ford. Editor for MGM, Universal, Fox and on films released by United Artists. 1951: first film as director. Worked for many studios as director; made several films in UK including *The Purple Plain* (1954).

Films as editor include: 1942: The Battle of Midway (*co*). 1943: December 7th. 1947: Body and Soul. 1948: A Double Life; No Minor Vices. 1949: Caught. 1950: All the King's Men (*co*); Of Men and Music (*co*).

Films as director: 1951: The Mob; Cry Danger. 1952: The San Francisco Story; Assignment Paris; My Pal Gus; Rough Shoot – Shoot First. 1954: The Purple Plain. 1955: Lucy Gallant. 1957: Fire Down Below. 1958: Saddle the Wind. 1959: The Wonderful Country. 1963: In the French Style. 1965: Up From the Beach. 1967: Casino Royale (*co-d 4 others*); The Bobo. 1968: Duffy. 1969: Doppelganger. 1971: A Town Called Bastard.

PARSONS, Louella

Journalist. Freeport, Illinois 1893–
Began on theatre column of Dixon Morning Star, then Chicago Tribune. 1912: wrote screenplay for Essanay; contract as writer of 2-reelers. Wrote film column for Chicago Record Herald, New York Morning Telegraph. From 1934: radio column 'Hollywood Hotel' led to film of the same name in which she appeared. As Hollywood gossip columnist, famous rival of Hedda Hopper. Articles syndicated on newspaper chain owned by William Randolph Hearst. Author of autobiography 'The Gay Illiterate' (1944) also 'Tell it to Louella' (1961).

Films as actress include: 1937: Hollywood Hotel. 1946: Without Reservations. 1951: Starlift.

PASCAL, Gabriel

Director and producer. Arad, Hungary 1894–1954 New York
1914: as actor, directed by Urban Gad, and worked with Gad's wife, Asta Nielson. World War I: Lieutenant in Hungarian Hussar regiment. Studied agriculture at Hungarian National Economy College, then acting at Hofburg Theatre, Vienna. Actor at Vienna Volkstheater; formed own theatre company in Rome. From 1921: in films as producer and actor in Italy, then France, Germany. Travelled widely during 1930s. 1935: contract with George Bernard Shaw to produce

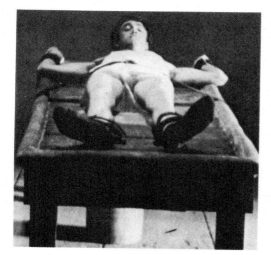

Lilli Palmer in Roger Leenhardt's Le Rendez-vous de Minuit.
Broderick Crawford in Robert Parrish's Up From the Beach.
Mamma Roma, *directed by Pier-Paolo Pasolini.*

Pygmalion and beginning of long partnership as exclusive screen interpreter of Shaw's plays. 1938: produced *Pygmalion* directed by Anthony Asquith and Leslie Howard. 1941: produced and directed *Major Barbara*. 1944–45: produced and directed *Caesar and Cleopatra*, stretching budget from £250,000 to £1,300,000; newspaper attacks and questions in the House of Commons about this extravagance during wartime. 1946: film described as 'a disastrous loss' by J. Arthur Rank who terminated contract with Pascal to make another picture; Pascal censured by general council of Association of Cine-Technicians and forbidden to function again, except under severe restrictions, on the floor of any British studio; left England for Hollywood. 1952: produced *Androcles and the Lion* for RKO after Shaw's death. Thereafter turned to the stage, and before his death interested Alan Jay Lerner and Frederick Loewe in the idea of a musical version of 'Pygmalion' for Broadway.

PASOLINI, Pier Paolo

Director and writer. Bologna, Italy 1922–
Father belonged to noble family in Bologna. Mother Susanna Pasolini, descended from Friulan peasant stock, appeared as Christ's mother in *Il Vangelo secondo Matteo*. Childhood in various parts of Northern Italy. Wrote poems from age of 7. Began university studies at Bologna. From 1950: lived in Rome. From 1954: collaborated on scripts. From 1952: author of many books including poems, criticism, novels e.g. 'Ragazza di vita' (1955), 'Una Vita Violenta' (1959). 1956: with friends in Bologna founded the review 'Officina'. 1961: first film as director; writer on all his films. Has published film scripts and literary versions of films e.g. 'Mamma Roma', 'Teorema' as a novel; also many articles on cinema. 1963: given a 4-month suspended prison sentence for offending the Roman Catholic religion in *La Ricotta*, his episode of *Rogopag*. Occasional appearances as actor e.g. in *Il Gobbo* (1960), *Requiescant* (1967).

Films as writer in collaboration include: 1954: La Donna del fiume. 1956: Le Notti di Cabiria. 1957: Marisa la civetta. 1958: Giovani Mariti. 1959: La Notte Brava. 1960: Morte di un amico: Il Bel Antonio; La Giornata Balorda; La Lunga Notte del '43. 1970: Ostia.

Films as director and writer: 1961: Accattone. 1962: Mamma Roma; Rogopag *ep* La Ricotta (*+ st*). 1963: La Rabbia *first ep*. 1964: Sopraluoghi in Palestina per 'Il vangelo secondo Matteo' (*+ cy/co-n*); Comizi d'amore (*+ cy/co-n/w*); Il Vangelo secondo Matteo – The Gospel According to St Matthew. 1966: Uccellacci e uccellini – The Hawks and the Sparrows; Le Streghe *ep* Le Terra vista dalla luna. 1967: Edipo Re – Oedipus Rex (*+ s/w*); Amore e rabbia – Vangelo 70 – Love and Anger *ep* La Sequènza del fiore di carta – The Sequence of the Paper Flower. 1968: Teorema – Theorem (*+fn*); Appunti per un film Indiano; Capriccio all 'Italiana *ep* Che cosa sono le nuvole? 1969: Porcile – Pigsty (*in 2 parts*); Medea. 1971: Il Decamerone – The Decameron (*+ w*); I Muri di sana (*d only*).

PASSER, Ivan

Director. Prague 1933–
Attended Prague film school without graduating. 1964–67: with Jaroslav Papousek was assistant director on 3 features directed by Milos Forman, and earlier short *Konkurs* (1963). 1965: first film as director, short intended as episode of *Perlicky na dne* but shown separately. His wife Vera Kresadlova acted in *Intimi Osvetleni* (1966). 1971: *Born to Win* made in USA.

Films as director: 1965: Fadni Odpoledne – A Boring Afternoon (*+ co-s*). 1966: Intimi Osvetleni – Intimate Lighting (*+ co-s*). 1968: Legenda o krasne Julice – The Legend of Beautiful Julia. 1971: Born to Win (*+ co-s*).

PASTERNAK, Joe

Producer. Hungary 1901–
1921: in Philadelphia. Moved to New York, worked in cafeteria and took short course at drama school. Dishwasher at Paramount, Long Island for 6 months, then waiter. Noticed by Allan Dwan and given small acting part. 1923: 4th assistant director to Dwan. 1925: 1st assistant director. 1926: wrote and directed 2-reel comedy, seen by Wesley Ruggles who hired him as assistant director at Universal. 1928: to Europe as associate producer for Universal. 1929: producer. Worked in Berlin, Vienna and Budapest. 1936: Returned to Hollywood; associate producer on *Three Smart Girls*, which launched Deanna Durbin; produced others of her films. 1941: Producer at MGM where he has remained. Autobiography 'Easy The Hard Way' (1956). Most of his films are musicals and light comedy.

Films as producer include: 1929: Das Schweigen im Walde. 1939: Destry Rides Again. 1940: Seven Sinners. 1941: The Flame of New Orleans. 1942: Seven Sweethearts. 1943: Thousands Cheer. 1944: Song of Russia. 1945: Anchors Aweigh. 1950: Summer Stock. 1953: Latin Lovers; Easy to Love. 1954: The Flame and the Flesh. 1955: Love Me or Leave Me. 1956: The Opposite Sex; Meet Me in Las Vegas. 1957: This Could Be the Night. 1958: Party Girl. 1959: Ask Any Girl. 1960: Please Don't Eat The Daisies. 1962: Billy Rose's Jumbo (*co*). 1963: The Courtship of Eddie's Father. 1964: Looking For Love.

PASTRONE, Giovanni

Director. Montechioro d'Asti, Italy 1883–1959 Turin
1905: joined Rossi & Co., first film company in Turin. Became artistic director, then administrative director; company became Itala. 1908: first film as director. 1914: wrote own *Cabiria* though Gabriele D'Annunzio took main credit. Became supervisor of all Itala productions. 1920: retired after Itala ceased to be independant. 1921: returned to help re-construct Itala. 1923: retired and devoted himself to medical studies. Directed certain films under pseudonym Piero Fusco.

Films as director: 1908: Giordano Bruno, Eroe di Valmy. 1910: Agnese Visconti; La Caduta di Troia. 1912: Padre (*co-d Dante Testa*). 1914: Cabiria (*+ co-s*). 1915: Il Fuoco (*co-d Zacconi*); Maciste. 1916: Maciste Alpino (*co-d Romano Borgnetto, Luigi Maggi*); Tigre Reale. 1919: Heliogabale; Hedda Gabler. 1923: Povere Bimbe.

PATHÉ, Charles

Industrialist. Chevry-Cossigny, France 1863–1957 Monaco
Worked as waiter and on fairgrounds. 1894: at Versailles Fair first saw Edison's phonograph. Set up business in phonograph industry, until saw Lumière films. 1904: Pathé Frères began to produce films. 1908: Pathé-Journal Newsreel began. Set up own studios, laboratories, owned world-wide chain of cinemas e.g. in Australia, Japan, Brazil, India. Financed much of Méliès' work. 1909: sold in USA more than twice as many films as all US companies. By 1914: employed 5000 people. After 1918: on advice of financiers, business broken up. 1929: retired. 1934: business collapsed. Wrote number of books on film industry in retirement.

PATRONI GRIFFI, Giuseppe

Director. Naples 1924–
Worked in Neapolitan radio until success of first play 'D'Amore si muore'. After World War II: to Rome. Theatrical writer in collaboration with Franca Valeri, Vittorio Caproli and Enrico Medioli. 1962: second play 'Anima Nera' filmed by Roberto Rossellini from own adaptation; first film as director and writer. 1967: co-wrote *C'era una volta*. 1969: made *Metti una sera a cena*, adaptation of own play. Book of short stories 'Ragazzo di Trastevere' (1955).

Films as director and writer: 1962: Il Mare. 1969: Metti una sera a cena – The Love Circle (*+fpl*).

PAUL, Robert William

Inventor and producer. London 1869–1943 London
City of London School and Finsbury Technical College. Learnt instrument-making. Worked in Bell Telephone Company factory, Antwerp. 1891: opened own business in London for manufacture of electrical and other scientific instruments. 1894: began to manufacture copies of Thomas Edison's Kinetoscope. By 1895 had constructed 60 Kinetoscopes; made films of the Derby and Boat Race to be shown on them; wrote to Edison suggesting exchange of films; Edison declined. Signed up Birt Acres as cameraman. 1896: published details of his projector, the Animatograph for sale at £5, first demonstrated at Finsbury Technical College; Animatograph renamed Theatrograph and later patented as the Bioscope, installed in small hall at Olympia and then moved to the Alhambra for 2 years. 1896 Derby screened on evening of Derby Day. 1897: redesigned his projector to safeguard against fire; bought field at Muswell Hill, London, for erection of studio, Paul's Animatograph Works, with C. Howard Cricks as manager. Constructive and inventive work on projectors and other motion picture equipment gradually became subsidiary to film production e.g. topical actualities, trick films or comedies running a few minutes mostly directed by Walter Booth. 1910: retired from film-making. 1920: fellow and later vice-president of Physical Society of London. Also developed 'unipivot' moving coil voltmeter and ammeter; with Sir William Bragg invented the Bragg-Paul pulsator for treating respiratory paralysis. His business was later absorbed by the Cambridge Instrument Company.

Films as producer include: 1895: The Shoe Black; Rough Sea at Dover. 1896: Persimmon's Derby; The Soldier's Courtship; An Engineer's Workshop; The Terrible Railway Accident; Kiddies' Cake Walk; The Human Fly – Upside Down; Barnet Horse Fair; Mr Pecksniff Fetches the Doctor: An Accident Victim

Revives; A Chess Dispute; London Express at Wood Green. 1897: Devant's Hand-Shadows; Chirgwin, The 'White-Eyed Kaffir'; The Deonzo Bros. in their Wonderful Tub-Jumping Act; Mr. Maskelyne (of the Egyptian Hall) Spinning Plates and Basins; Mel B. Spurr Gives "The Village Blacksmith"; Jubilee; Andalusian Dance; Last Days of Pompeii. 1898: Nursery; Glasgow Fire Brigade; Cory; Whitewash and Miller; Twin's Tea Party – Children at Table; A Railway Collision; Monorail; Disaster, Launching of H.M.S. Albion; Britannia; Stocks; Courtship; Come Along, Do!; Deserter; Queen Victoria in Dublin. 1899: Battlefield; Bombardment of Mafeking; The Haunted Curiosity Shop; The Artist and the Flower Girl. 1900: The Royal Engineer's Balloon; Cronje's Surrender to Lord Roberts. 1901: Plucked from Burning; The Gambler's Fate, or the Road to Ruin; The Funeral of Queen Victoria; Undressing Extraordinary – The Troubles of a Tired Traveller. 1902: Cheese Mites, or Lilliputians in a London Restaurant; 'Ora Pro Nobis' or the Poor Orphan's Last Prayer; Tramp and Turpentine Bottle – Greediness Punished; Facial Expressions; The Magic Sword. 1903: Pie Eating Contest; Return of T.R.H. The Prince and Princess of Wales; Voyage of the 'Arctic' or How Captain Kettle discovered the North Pole; Delhi Durbar; The Troublesome Collar; Hammerfest; The Sun – Picture of the Midnight Sun at Scarl. 1904: A Collier's Life. 1905: A Victim of Misfortune; From Paddington to Penzance (Tour of the West of England by G.W.R.) (*in 11 parts*); Launching of Japan's New Warship 'Katori'. 1906: The ? Motorist – P.A.K.; The Curate's Dilemma, or The Story of an Ant Hill; He Cannot Get a Word in Edgeways; Jam-making; The Dancer's Dream; The Royal Review of Scottish Volunteers. 1910: The Butterfly (*ur*).

PAXINOU, Katina

(Katina Konstantopoulou) Actress. Piraeus, Greece 1900–

Studied music for 3 years at a Geneva conservatory. Trained as opera singer in Berlin and Vienna. Athens Opera company under Dimitri Mitropoulos. 1924: first appearance as actress, in Greece. 1930: first appearance on Broadway. During 1930s translated and produced English and American plays in Athens. 1934–40: annually played in own production of 'Ghosts' in Athens. 1939: appeared on London stage. 1943: first film *For Whom the Bell Tolls*. English-language films mainly for Paramount and Warners. 1950–55: National Theatre in Athens. 1959: acted on BBC TV in 'Blood Wedding'. 1960–61: Italian films.

Films as actress include: 1945: Confidential Agent. 1947: California; Mourning Becomes Electra. 1949: Prince of Foxes. 1955: Confidential Report – Mr Arkadin. 1959: The Miracle. 1960: Rocco e i suoi fratelli – Rocco and his Brothers. 1962: Le Procès. 1970: Un Eté Sauvage.

PAXTON, John

Writer. Kansas 1911–

Began in journalism. 1935–36: press agent. 1937–38: associate editor, Stage magazine. From 1939: freelanced. 1941: publicity work for New York Theatre Guild. 1942: went to Hollywood; scriptwriter with RKO notably on films directed by Edward Dmytryk (1945–47). In the 1950s wrote scripts for various

companies including 3 for Warwick Films in London and 2 Stanley Kramer productions.

Films as writer include: 1945: Murder my Sweet; Cornered. 1946: Crack Up (*co*). 1947: Crossfire; So Well Remembered. 1949: Rope of Sand (*co*). 1950: Of Men and Music (*co*). 1951: Fourteen Hours. 1953: The Wild One. 1955: A Prize of Gold; The Cobweb. 1959: On the Beach.

PAYNE, John

Actor. Roanoake, Virginia 1912–

Metropolitan Opera: minor roles. University of Virginia. Drama at Columbia University. Acted in stock. Supported Beatrice Lillie in 'At Home Abroad'. MGM contract: first film as actor *Dodsworth* (1936), only film under this contract. Subsequently worked for many studios including MGM, United Artists, Warners, Paramount, Fox. Service in US Army Air Corps. Own company, with Maureen O'Hara. Also TV work. Songwriter, nightclub singer, cinema owner. Married Gloria De Haven (1944–1950, divorced).

Films as actor include: 1937: Fair Warning. 1938: College Swing; Garden of the Moon. 1939: Wings of the Navy; Indianapolis Speedway. 1940: Maryland; Star Dust; Tin Pan Alley. 1941: The Great American Broadcast; Weekend in Havana; Remember the Day. 1946: Sentimental Journey; The Razor's Edge; Wake Up and Dream. 1947: Miracle on 34th Street. 1949: The Crooked Way. 1950: 99 River Street. 1952: Kansas City Confidential; Caribbean. 1953: The Vanquished. 1954: Hell's Island; Silver Lode. 1955: Tennessee's Partner. 1956: The Boss; Slightly Scarlet; Hold Back the Night. 1957: Hidden Fear.

PECK, Gregory

Actor. La Jolla, California 1916–

University of California, played in 'Moby Dick' while a student. Acted in stock; toured in 'The Doctor's Dilemma'. On Broadway in 'Morning Star', 'The Willow and I', 'Sons and Soldiers'. 1943: spotted by writer and producer Casey Robinson for first film as actor, *Days of Glory* (1944). Contracts with Fox, MGM, RKO, with Robinson and David O. Selznick. 1946: on stage in 'The Playboy of the Western World'. 1947: operated a stock company with Joseph Cotten, Dorothy McGuire, Jennifer Jones, Mel Ferrer. 1959: own production company for *Pork Chop Hill*. Producer and executive. 1962: Oscar as Best Actor for *To Kill A Mocking Bird*.

Films as actor include: 1944: The Keys of the Kingdom. 1945: The Valley of Decision; Spellbound. 1946: Duel in the Sun; The Yearling. 1947: The Macomber Affair; The Paradine Case; Gentleman's Agreement. 1948: Yellow Sky. 1949: The Great Sinner; Twelve O'Clock High. 1950: The Gunfighter; 1951: Captain Horatio Hornblower, RN; Only the Valiant; David and Bathsheba. 1952: The Snows of Kilimanjaro. 1953: Roman Holiday. 1954: Night People; The Purple Plain. 1956: Moby Dick; The Man in the Gray Flannel Suit. 1957: Designing Woman. 1958: The Big Country (+ *co-p*); The Bravados. 1959: Pork Chop Hill (+ *pc*); On the Beach. 1961: The Guns of Navarone; Cape Fear. 1962: How the West was Won. 1963: Captain Newman, MD. 1964: Behold a Pale Horse. 1965: Mirage. 1966: Arabesque. 1969:

Party Girl, *produced by Joe Pasternak, directed by Nicholas Ray, with Lee J. Cobb* (right).
Gregory Peck in Stanley Donen's *Arabesque.*
Richard Harris (centre) in Major Dundee. *directed by Sam Peckinpah.*

211

Mackenna's Gold; The Stalking Moon; The Chairman; Marooned. 1971: I Walk the Line; Shoot Out.

PECKINPAH, Sam

Director. Peckinpah Mountain, Madera, California 1926–

Grandfather, father and brother were Superior Court judges. Grandfather bought mountain, gave his name to it in 1868. World War II: US Marine Corps; 38 months in China. Studied drama at the University of Southern California. Worked in TV as stage-hand, then scriptwriter e.g. 'Gunsmoke' series, director e.g. 'The Westerner' series. 1956: dialogue director on and small part in *Invasion of the Body Snatchers*; worked on other films for Allied Artists. 1961: first films as director; directed 2 episodes of 'Dick Powell Show' on TV. 1966: scripted *The Glory Guys*. 1968: co-scripted *Villa Rides*.

Films as director: 1961: The Deadly Companions. 1962: Ride the High Country – Guns in the Afternoon. 1965: Major Dundee (+ *co-s*). 1969: The Wild Bunch (+ *co-s*). 1970: The Ballad of Cable Hogue. 1971: Straw Dogs (+ *co-s*).

PENN, Arthur

Director. Philadelphia 1922–

Son of a watchmaker. 1943: enlisted US Infantry. Towards end of war joined Joshua Logan's theatre company. 1946: demobilised; to Black Mountain College, North Carolina then Universities of Perugia and Florence. Studied at Actor's Studio and with Michael Chekhov in Los Angeles. 1951: floor manager at NBC. 1953: wrote 3 TV plays; began as director on 'First Person'. 1953–55: directed 'Philco Playhouse' 1954: directed 'Blue Denim' on stage. 1956: for TV directed 'The Miracle Worker', 'Portrait of a Murderer' for 'Playhouse 90', and 'Private Property'. 1958: first film as director. 1957–58: on Broadway directed 'Two for the Seesaw'. .1958: directed 'Charley's Aunt' on 'Playhouse 90'; wrote stage version of 'Fiorello'. 1959–62: on Broadway directed 'The Miracle Worker', 'Toys in the Attic', 'All the Way Home', 'An Evening with Nichols and May', and 'In the Counting House'. First 2 films produced by Fred Coe, with whom he had worked in TV. 1963: after one week's shooting on *The Train* replaced by John Frankenheimer at Burt Lancaster's request; directed 'Lorenzo' on Broadway. 1964: directed Broadway musical 'Golden Boy'. 1965: directed and produced *Micky One* with Warren Beatty as actor. 1966: directed 'Flesh and Blood'; offered *Bonnie and Clyde* when project turned down by Jean-Luc Godard and François Truffaut: produced by Warren Beatty who played lead.

Films as director: 1958: The Left Handed Gun. 1962: The Miracle Worker. 1965: Mickey One (+ *p*). 1966: The Chase. 1967: Bonnie and Clyde. 1969: Alice's Restaurant (+ *co-s*); Little Big Man.

PENNEBAKER, D.A.

Director and cinematographer. Evanston, Illinois 1930–

Mechanical engineering at M.I.T. and Yale. Own electronics research company. Worked in advertising in New York. 1955: directed industrial film for New York stock exchange. 1958: made loops for American pavilion at Brussels World's Fair. 1959: made documentary on American exhibition in Moscow. 1959–63: worked as director, co-director and cinematographer on TV series 'Living Camera' including *Adventures of the New Frontier* made in office of John F. Kennedy. Member of Drew Associates with Robert Drew, Richard Leacock, and Gregory Shuker with all of whom he collaborated. Photographed several films for Leacock and with him founded (1963) New York production and distribution company. 1966: made *Herr Strauss* for Bavarian TV. Photographed several films for Norman Mailer. 1970: *One P.M.* includes footage from Jean-Luc Godard's unfinished *One American Movie* (1968).

Films as cinematographer include: 1963: Mr Pearson. 1968: Beyond the Law (*co*); Wild 90 (+ *w*); One American Movie – One A.M. 1970: Maidstone (*co*).

Films as director include: 1953: Daybreak Express (+ *p*). 1959: Opening in Moscow. 1960: Primary (*co-d Richard Leacock, Robert Drew*); Breaking it up at the Museum; Balloon (*co-d Richard Leacock*); On the Pole (+ *co-c/co-e*; *co-d Richard Leacock*). 1962: David (*co-d Richard Leacock*). 1963: The Chair (*co-d Richard Leacock, Gregory Shuker*); Crisis (+ *c*). 1964: Elizabeth and Mary (+ *co-c/co-e*); Casals at 88; Lambert & Co. 1965: RFK—Two Days (*uf*). 1967: Don't Look Back (+ *co-p/s/co-c/e*). 1969: Monterey Pop (+ *s/co-c*); Godard on Godard – Two American Audiences (*co-d Mark Woodcock*); You're Nobody Till Somebody Loves You – Timothy Leary's Wedding (+ *co-p*); Moscow—Ten Years After; Awake at Generation (*uf*). 1970: One P.M. (+ *s/co-c/e*); Original Cast Album: 'Company' (+ *co-c*). 1971: Sweet Toronto (+ *p/co-c*).

PEPPARD, George

Actor. Detroit, Michigan 1933–

Mother on music faculty of University of California. US Marine Corps for 18 months on leaving school. Civil engineering, then drama at Purdue University; fine arts at Carnegie Institute of Technology. Simultaneously worked on small radio station; taught fencing. From 1949: appearances as actor at Pittsburgh Playhouse, then Oregon Shakespeare Festival. Studied at Actors' Studio, New York. 1957: first film as actor, small part in *The Strange One*. Worked in TV.

Films as actor include: 1959: Pork Chop Hill. 1960: Home from the Hill; The Subterraneans. 1961: Breakfast at Tiffany's. 1962: How the West was Won *ep* The Civil War. 1963: The Victors. 1964: The Carpetbaggers; Operation Crossbow. 1965: The Third Day. 1966: The Blue Max. 1968: P. J. 1969: House of Cards. 1970: Cannon for Cordoba. 1971: One More Train to Rob.

PEREIRA, Hal

Designer

1933–40: theatrical designer. 1942–46: unit art director, Paramount. 1947–50: on Paramount Home Office executive staff for domestic and international companies. 1950: appointed supervising art director, Paramount. Almost all films for Paramount, a few for United Artists, Allied Artists. 1955: Oscar in collaboration for *The Rose Tattoo*.

Films as art director include (from 1951, in collaboration): 1944: Double Indemnity (*co*). 1951: Ace in the Hole; The Lemon Drop Kid; Peking Express; Here Comes the Groom; When Worlds Collide; Detective Story (*a alone*); Red Mountain. 1952: My Son John; The Greatest Show on Earth; Carrie; Caribbean; Son of Paleface (*a alone*); The Turning Point. 1953: Come Back, Little Sheba; The War of the Worlds (*a alone*); Shane; Stalag 17; Houdini; Sangaree; Roman Holiday; Botany Bay. 1954: Knock on Wood; The Naked Jungle; Elephant Walk; Jivaro; Rear Window; Sabrina; White Christmas. 1955: Conquest of Space; Run for Cover; Strategic Air Command; The Far Horizons; The 7 Little Foys; To Catch a Thief; The Desperate Hours; The Trouble with Harry; The Rose Tattoo; Artists and Models. 1956: The Court Jester; The Man Who Knew Too Much; The Proud and the Profane; That Certain Feeling; The Vagabond King; The Mountain; The Ten Commandments. 1957: Three Violent People; Fear Strikes Out; Funny Face; Lonely Man; The Gunfight at the OK Corral; The Tin Star (*a alone*); Wild is the Wind. 1958: Teacher's Pet; Vertigo; Hot Spell; The Space Children; Houseboat; The Buccaneer. 1959: The Five Pennies; That Kind of Woman; L'il Abner. 1960: The Bellboy. 1961: One-Eyed Jacks; The Ladies' Man; Breakfast at Tiffany's; Pocketful of Miracles; The Errand Boy. 1962: Hell is for Heroes; Hatari! 1963: Hud; The Nutty Professor; Come Blow Your Horn; Donovan's Reef; McLintock!; Who's Minding the Store; Love With the Proper Stranger. 1964: Robinson Crusoe on Mars; The Patsy; The Disorderly Orderly. 1965: Sylvia; The Family Jewels; Harlow; The Sons of Katie Elder. 1966: Red Line 7000; The Night of the Grizzly; Nevada Smith; This Property is Condemned; Waco; The Swinger. 1967: Warning Shot; Chuka; The Caper of the Golden Bulls; El Dorado; The Spirit is Willing; The President's Analyst. 1968: No Way to Treat a Lady.

PERIES, Lester James

Director. Ceylon 1921–

From 1939: journalist in London, including 7 years as London correspondent of The Times of Ceylon; made 2 amateur shorts. 1949: returned to Ceylon as assistant to British documentarist Ralph Keene. 1954: directed first professional film for Ceylon Government Film Unit, of which Keene was head. 1957: first feature as director.

Films as director: 1950: Farewell to Childhood (*co-d Hereward Jansz*); A Sinhalese Dance. 1951: Soliloquy. 1954: Conquest of the Dry Zone. 1955: Be Safe or Be Sorry. 1956: Rekava – The Line of Destiny. 1960: Sandesaya – The Message. 1961: Too Many, Too Soon. 1962: Home from the Sea. 1964: Gamperaliya – The Changing Countryside; Forward into the Future. 1966: Delovak Athara – Between Two Worlds (+ *co-s*). 1967: Ransalu – The Yellow Robe. 1968: Golu Hadawatha – The Silence of the Heart. 1969: Akkara Paha – Five Acres of Land. 1970: Steel; Forty Leagues from Paradise; A Dream of Kings.

PÉRINAL, Georges

Cinematographer. Paris 1897–1965 London

1913: entered films as projectionist then cameraman on shorts for Pathé. Demobilised after after World War I. freelance work shooting industrial and advertising films, and as projectionist. Made documentaries with Jean Grémillon. Photographed René Clair's first sound films. 1933: Alexander Korda arrived in Paris; Périnal signed contract which ended only on Korda's death. Worked in England with Korda and would have gone with him to Hollywood but refused permission to work by ASC. Oscar for colour cinematography for *The Thief of Bagdad* (1940).

Films as cinematographer include: 1927: Six et demionze. 1928: La Tour (*co*). 1929: Les Nouveaux Messieurs (*co*). 1930: Sous les toits de Paris; Le Sang d'un poète. 1932: A Nous la liberté; Le Million. 1933: Quatorze juillet; The Girl from Maxim's; The Private Life of Henry VIII. 1934: Catherine the Great; The Private Life of Don Juan. 1935: Sanders of the River (*co*). 1936: Things to Come; Rembrandt; Claudius (*uf*). 1938: The Drum. 1939: The Four Feathers. 1940: The Thief of Bagdad. 1942: The First of the Few. 1943: The Life and Death of Colonel Blimp. 1948: An Ideal Husband; The Fallen Idol. 1955: L'Amant de Lady Chatterley. 1957: A King in New York; Saint Joan. 1958: Bonjour Tristesse. 1959: Once More With Feeling.

PERKINS, Anthony

Actor. New York 1932–
Son of actor Osgood Perkins. Columbia University. 1946: first professional engagement. 1953: first film as actor *The Actress*. 1954: on Broadway in 'Tea and Sympathy'. 1957: in 'Look Homeward, Angel'. 1960: musical debut in 'Greenwillow'. Several films for Paramount. Also European films. Recordings, TV.

Films as actor include: 1956: Friendly Persuasion. 1957: Fear Strikes Out; The Lonely Man; The Tin Star. 1958: Desire under the Elms; The Matchmaker; La Diga sul Pacifico. 1959: Green Mansions; On the Beach. 1960: Tall Story; Psycho. 1961: Aimez-vous Brahms? 1962: Phaedra; Le Couteau dans la plaie. 1963: Une Ravissante Idiote; Le Procès. 1965: The Fool Killer. 1966: Paris, brûle-t-il?; Le Scandale. 1970: WUSA; Catch-22. 1971: La Décade Prodigieuse.

PERLBERG, William

Producer. New York 1899–
Cornell University. World War I: service in US Navy. General assistant at William Morris Agency; organised its West Coast branch (1928–33). Helped Harry Cohn re-organise casting department at Columbia. Associate producer then producer at Paramount. Moved to Fox, returned to Paramount, then to MGM. From 1946: long collaboration with George Seaton. For their films together *see* SEATON.

Films as producer include: 1936: The King Steps Out. 1939: Golden Boy. 1941: Charley's Aunt. 1942: Ten Gentlemen from West Point. 1943: The Song of Bernadette. 1945: State Fair. 1947: Forever Amber. 1948: Escape. 1949: Slattery's Hurricane; Britannia Mews; It Happens Every Spring. 1950: Wabash Avenue. 1952: Anything Can Happen (*co*). 1954: The Country Girl (*co*). 1955: The Bridges at Toko-Ri (*co*). 1957: The Tin Star (*co*). 1960: The Rat Race. 1967: Half a Sixpence (*co-ex-p*).

PERRAULT, Pierre

Director. Montreal 1927–
Classics. 1948: began law studies at Montreal University. History of law at Paris University; international law at Toronto University. 1954–56: practised law in Montreal. 1956: became writer for Société Radio-Canada; radio series include 'Le Chant des hommes' (on international folklore), 'J'habite une ville' (on Montreal), 'Au pays de Neufve-France'. 1959–60: director of production on series of 13 TV films *Au pays de Neufve-France* for Radio-Canada and wrote commentary. Subsequent work for Office National du Film. 1962: from interview material collected for *Pour la suite du monde* also produced 39 radio episodes; wrote book from material gathered, 'Toutes Iles'. Wrote play 'Au Coeur de la rose'; also poet.

Films as director: 1963: Pour la suite du monde – The Moontrap (*co-d Michel Brault*). 1966: Le Règne du jour. 1969: Les Voitures d'eau; Le Beau Plaisir. 1970: Un Pays sans bon sens; Moncton (*co-d Michel Brault*). 1971: L'Acadie, L'Acadie (*co-d Michel Brault*).

PERRET, Léonce

Director and writer. Niort, Deux-Sèvres, France 1880–1935
Began as stage actor, played in repertory. 1907: directed *Mireille*. 1908: actor in series of shorts directed by Louis Feuillade at Gaumont Studios, Buttes-Chaumont; then in series produced by Berlin Gaumont. 1910–16: in France, directed and acted e.g. in Léonce series. 1917–21: in Hollywood, directed and scripted films mainly for Pathé from 1919. From 1922 until his death, director in France.

Films as director and writer include: 1913: L'Enfant de Paris. 1917: The Silent Master. 1918: Lest We Forget; The Million Dollar Dollies; Lafayette! We Come! 1919: The Unknown Love (*d only*); The Thirteenth Chair; A Modern Salome. 1920: The ABC of Love; Tarnished Reputations; The Twin Pawns; Lifting Shadows; The Empire of Diamonds (*+ p*). 1921: The Money Maniac (*+ p*). 1923: Koenigsmark. 1925: Madame Sans-Gêne. 1926: La Femme Nue. 1933: Sappho. 1935: Les Précieuses Ridicules (*d only*).

PERRY, Frank

Director. New York 1933–
At 13 apprentice at Westport County Theatre, University of Miami, graduated 1951. 1952–54: US Army in South-East Asia. Worked in directors' unit of Actor's Studio. 1956: assistant to William Burke on 3 films. 1957: associate producer for Theater Guild in New York. 1: produced 'The Connection' in London. Co-produced TV documentary series 'Playwright at Work'. 1962: first film as director. 1967: some reshooting on *The Swimmer* directed without credit by Sidney Pollack. All films written or co-written by his wife, playwright Eleanor Perry. 1969: *Trilogy* consists of 3 TV films, released as feature.

Films as director: 1962: David and Lisa. 1963: Ladybug, Ladybug (*+ p*). 1967: The Swimmer (*+ co-p*; *co-d Sidney Pollack, uc*). 1969: Trilogy, – Truman Capote's Trilogy (*+ p*); Last Summer. 1970: Diary of a Mad Housewife (*+ p*). 1971: Doc (*+ p*).

Warren Beatty and Faye Dunaway in Bonnie and Clyde, *directed by Arthur Penn.*
The set, co-designed by Hal Pereira, for Alfred Hitchcock's Rear Window.
Marcello Mastroianni in L'Assassino, *directed by Elio Petri.*

PETERS, Jean

Actress. Canton, Ohio 1926–
University of Michigan; won campus popularity contest and trip to Hollywood. Fox contract. 1947: first film as actress *Captain from Castile*. All films for Fox except *Apache* (1954) for United Artists. 1956: retired from films on marriage to Howard Hughes. 1971: divorced Hughes, married film executive Stanley Hough, who was assistant director on her first film.

Films as actress include: 1948: Deep Waters. 1949: It Happens Every Spring. 1951: Take Care of My Little Girl; Anne of the Indies. 1952: Wait Till the Sun Shines, Nellie; Viva Zapata!; Lure of the Wilderness; O. Henry's Full House *ep* The Last Leaf. 1953: Niagara; Pickup on South Street; A Blueprint for Murder; Vicki. 1954: Apache; Three Coins in the Fountain; Broken Lance. 1955: A Man Called Peter.

PETRI, Elio

Director. Rome 1929–
Literature at Rome University. 1949–50: film critic for L'Unità. Directed several documentaries including *I Sette Contadini* (1949). 1952–60: scripted about 20 films, including, in collaboration with Giuseppe de Santis and Cesare Zavattini *Roma ore undice* (1952), and *Il Gobbo* (1960). 1961: first feature as director. Collaborated on scripts of own films.

Features as director and co-writer: 1961: L'Assassino – The Assassin. 1962: I Giorni Contati – Days are Numbered. 1963: Il Maestro di Vigevano. 1964: Alta Infideltà – High Infidelity – Sex in the Afternoon *ep* Peccato nel pomeriggio. 1965: La Decima Vittima – The 10th Victim. 1966: A ciascuno il suo – To Each His Own. 1968: Un Tranquillo Posto di campagna – A Quiet Place in the Country (+ *co-st*). 1970: Indagine su un cittadino ad di sopra di ogni sospetto – Investigation of a Citizen Above Suspicion.

PETROV, Vladimir

Director and writer. St Petersburg, Russia 1896–1965
Theatrical training in St Petersburg, and under Gordon Craig in London. 1917: stage debut as actor in St Petersburg and provinces. 1925–27: work in films as assistant director. 1928: first film as director in collaboration. One of first Soviet directors to make children's films. 1931: collaborated on script of N. I. Lebedyev's *Tovarnyi No 717*.

Films as director and writer: 1928: Dzhoi i druzhok – Dzhoi and his Friends (+ *co-s*; *co-d* M. Khukhunashvili). 1930: Fritz Bauer; Ledyanaya Sudba – The Cold Feast (*co-s*). 1932: Plotina – The Carpenter; Beglets – The Fugitive (*co-s*). 1934: Groza – Thunderstorm. 1937: Piotr Pervyi – Peter the Great (*part I*; *co-s*). 1939: Piotr Pervyi (*Part II*; *co-s*; *co-d* C. Bartenev). 1944: Yubilei – Jubilee. 1945: Bez viny vinovatye – Guilty though Guiltless. 1952: Revizor. 1957: Poedinok – The Duel.

Films as director: 1928: Zolotoi Med – Golden Honey (*co-d* N. Bersenev). 1929: Adres Lenina – Lenin's Address. 1941: Chapayev s nami – Chapayev is With Us. 1943: Neulovimyi Yan – The Elusive Jan (*co-d* I. Annenskii*). 1944: Kutuzov. 1949: Stalingradskaya Bitva – Battle of Stalingrad (*2 parts*). 1951: Sportiv-

naya Chest – Sporting Honour. 1956: Trista let tomu – 300 Years Ago.

PEVNEY, Joseph

Director. New York City 1913–
Began vaudeville career at 13 as junior member of a song and dance team. 1933: university in New York. Stage actor, e.g. in 'Home of the Brave', 'Counsellor at Law', 'Key Largo'. World War II in US Army in Europe. On demobilisation, film actor. Films as actor include *Body and Soul* (1947), *Street with No Name* (1948), *Thieves' Highway* (1949). 1950: gave up acting; became director for Universal. TV, including 'Star Trek'.

Films as director: 1950: Shakedown; Undercover Girl. 1951: Iron Man; The Lady from Texas; Meet Danny Wilson; The Strange Door; Air Cadet. 1952: Flesh and Fury; Just Across the Street; Because of You. 1953: Desert Legion; It Happens Every Thursday; Back to God's Country. 1954: Yankee Pasha; Playgirl; Three Ring Circus. 1955: Six Bridges to Cross; Foxfire; Female on the Beach. 1956: Away All Boats; Congo Crossing; Istanbul. 1957: Man of a Thousand Faces; The Midnight Story; Tammy and the Bachelor. 1958: Torpedo Run; Twilight for the Gods. 1960: Cash McCall; The Crowded Sky; The Plunderers (+ *p*). 1961: Portrait of a Mobster. 1966: The Night of the Grizzly.

PHILIPE, Gérard

(Gérard Philip) Actor. Cannes 1922–1959 Paris
Studied drama with Jean Wall and Jean Huet in Cannes. Spotted by Claude Dauphin to tour in 'Une Grande Fille Tout Simple'. Studied with Denis d'Ines at Paris Conservatoire. Theatrical work includes 'Sodome et Gomorrhe', 'Federigo', 'Caligula', 'Ruy Blas', 'Le Cid'. 1943: first film *Les Petites du Quai aux Fleurs*. Films in UK, Mexico. Producer for Théâtre National Populaire. 1956: directed, co-wrote and acted in *Les Aventures de Till L'Espiègle*.

Films as actor include: 1946: L'Idiot. 1947: Le Diable aux corps; La Certosa di Parma. 1948: Une Si Jolie Petite Plage. 1949: Souvenirs Perdus. 1950: La Beauté du Diable; La Ronde; 1951: Juliette ou la clé des songes; Fan-Fan la Tulipe; Avec André Gide. 1952: Les Belles-de-Nuit. 1953: Les Orgueilleux. 1954: Si Versailles m'était conté; Knave of Hearts; Le Rouge et le Noir. 1955: Les Grandes Manoeuvres; La Meilleure Part; Si Paris Nous était conté. 1957: Pot-bouille. 1958: Montparnasse 19; Le Joueur; La Vie à deux. 1959: La Fièvre monte à El Pao; Les Liaisons Dangereuses.

PICAZO, Miguel

Director. Cazorla, Spain 1929–
Educated in Madrid and Guadalajara. Film critic. Abandoned electrical studies to work at library. Persuaded by poet Antonio Fernandez Molina to leave provinces. 1956: abandoned law studies in Madrid. Escola Oficial do Cinema. 1960: first film as director (graduation short) *Habitación de Alquilar*. 1961: unfinished film *Jimena*. 1964: first feature.

Films as director: 1960: Habitación de Alquilar. 1964: La Tria Tula (+ *co-s*). 1967: Oscuros Sueños de

Agosto – Dark Dreams of August. 1968: Homenaje para Adriana. 1969: La Tierra de los Alvargonzalez.

PICCIONI, Piero

Composer. Turin 1921–
Law studies. Radio work began while a student. Organised first jazz concerts in Italy. Became solicitor then barrister. 1944: conducted radio orchestra 013. 1950: began work in films, composing for documentaries. 1952: first feature as composer *Il Mondo le condannà*. 1957: score for re-issue of *The Kid* (1921). Musically self-taught. Some early credits under pseudonym Piero Morgan.

Films as composer include: 1953: La Spiaggia. 1956: La Donna che venne del mare; Guendalina; Nata di Marzo. 1958: La Tempestà. 1959: I Magliari; La Notte Brava; Via Margutta. 1960: La Giornata Balorda; Il Gobbo; Adua e le compagne; Il bell' Antonio. 1961: La Viaccia. 1962: Mafioso. 1963: Il Demonio; Le Mani sulla città; Un Tentativo Sentimentale; Il Boom. 1964: La Vita Agra; I Tre Volti; La Donna è una cosa meravigliosa (*co*). 1965: Il Disco Volante; Il Momento della verità; Io la conoscevo bene; La Decima Vittima; Fumo di Londra. 1966: Le Streghe. 1967: C'era una volta; Matchless (*co*). 1970: Uomini contro; Contestazione Generale. 1971: La Spina Dorsale del diavolo; Bello onesto emigrata Australia spostrebbe compaesan illibata.

PICCOLI, Michel

Actor. Paris 1925–
Italian parents. 1945–55: extensive stage appearances including many plays at the Théâtre Babylone; acted with the Renaud-Barrault company and Théâtre National Populaire. In films from late 1940s notably comedy shorts directed by Paul Paviot in early 1950s. 1966: married actress Juliette Greco.

Films as actor include: 1949: Le Point de jour. 1955: French Can-can; Les Mauvaises Rencontres. 1956: La Mort en ce jardin. 1962: Le Doulos. 1963: Le Mépris. 1964: Le Journal d'une femme de chambre; De l'amour. 1965: Le Coup de grâce; Lady L; Compartiment tueurs; Paris, brûle-t-il? 1966: Les Créatures. 1967: Belle de jour; Benjamin. 1968: Dillinger è morto; La Chamade; La Prisonnière. 1969: Topaz. 1970: L'Invasion; Max et les ferrailleurs. 1971: La Décade Prodigieuse; La Poudre d'escampette.

PICHEL, Irving

Director. Pittsburg, Pennsylvania 1891–1954 Hollywood
Harvard University. 1919: stage director with Schubert Company, New York. 1927: began in films as writer for MGM. 1930: Paramount contract as actor e.g. in *An American Tragedy* (1931), *The Miracle Man* (1932), *Cleopatra* (1934), *High Wide and Handsome* (1937); also, for other companies, *Wild Girl* (1932), *Special Agent* (1935), *Jezebel* (1938), *Juarez* (1939). 1932: began as director for RKO. 1936–37: director with Republic. Worked almost entirely as director in 1940s and 1950s. 1940–43: with Fox. 1941: produced Jean Renoir's *Swamp Water*. From 1944: director with various companies. Also lectured in dramatic art at Leland Stanford University and the University of

California. 1954: died before the completion of *Day of Triumph*.

Films as director: 1932: The Most Dangerous Game – The Hounds of Zaroff (+ *co-p*; *co-d* Ernest B. Schoedsack). 1933: Before Dawn. 1935: She (*co-d* Lansing C. Holden). 1936: The Gentleman from Louisiana; Beware of Ladies. 1937: Larceny on the Air; The Sheik Steps Out; The Duke Comes Back. 1939: The Great Commandment. 1940: Earthbound; The Man I Married. 1941: Hudson's Bay; Dance Hall. 1942: Secret Agent of Japan; The Pied Piper; Life Begins at Eight-Thirty. 1943: The Moon is Down; Happy Land. 1944: And Now Tomorrow. 1945: A Medal for Benny; Colonel Effingham's Raid; Tomorrow is Forever. 1946: The Bride Wore Boots; O.S.S.; Temptation. 1947: They Won't Believe Me; Something in the Wind. 1948: The Miracle of the Bells; Mr Peabody and the Mermaid. 1949: Without Honor. 1950: The Great Rupert; Quicksand; Destination Moon. 1951: Sante Fe (+ *w*). 1953: Martin Luther (+ *w*). 1954: Day of Triumph.

PICKFORD, Mary

(Gladys Mary Smith) Actress. Toronto 1893–
Mother was actress Gladys Smith. Stage debut at 5 in 'Bootle's Baby'. On tour with mother acted in 'The Fatal Wedding', 'Uncle Tom's Cabin', 'East Lynne', 'Edmund Burke'. New York: 'The Warrens of Virginia'. Biograph extra. First leading role *The Violin Maker of Cremona* (1909). Under contract to Adolph Zukor. Often acted with Owen Moore, whom she married. 1913: repeated stage role in film *A Good Little Devil*. 1915: President of Mary Pickford Famous Players Company. 1918: independent producer. 1919: with Charles Chaplin, Douglas Fairbanks, Sr, and D. W. Griffith was one of the founders of United Artists. 1920: married Fairbanks. 1923: brought Ernst Lubitsch to USA to direct her in *Rosita*. 1927: a sponsor of the Motion Picture Academy of Arts and Sciences. 1929: acted with her husband in *The Taming of the Shrew* and received Oscar as Best Actress for *Coquette*. 1934–35: published books 'Why Not Try God?', 'My Rendezvous with Life' and the novel 'The Demi-Widow'. 1935: Vice-President of United Artists. 1936: produced *One Rainy Afternoon* and *The Gay Desperado* (with Jesse L. Lasky). Radio. 1944: independent production company. Autobiography 'Sunshine and Shadow'. Also married Charles Buddy Rogers.

Films as actress include: 1914: Hearts Adrift; Tess of the Storm Country. 1917: Rebecca of Sunnybrook Farm; Poor Little Rich Girl; Pride of the Clan. 1918: Stella Maris. 1919: Daddy Long Legs; Heart o' the Hills. 1920: Pollyanna. 1921: Little Lord Fauntleroy. 1922: Tess of the Storm Country; Dorothy Vernon of Haddon Hall. 1931: Kiki. 1933: Secrets.

PIDGEON, Walter

Actor. East St John, New Brunswick, Canada 1897–
Toured in singing act with Elsie Janis. In New York musical 'Puzzles of 1925'. On London stage in 'At Home'. 1926: first film as actor *Mannequin*. Continued with stage work, e.g. in Hollywood acted in 'Androcles and the Lion'; on Broadway replaced Melvyn Douglas in 'No More Ladies'. 1935: with Tallulah Bankhead in 'Something Gay'. From 1936: concentrated on films. From 1937: films mainly for MGM.

Films as actor include: 1929: Her Private Life. 1930: Viennese Nights. 1931: The Hot Heiress. 1932: Rockabye. 1933: The Kiss Before the Mirror. 1934: Journal of a Crime. 1936: Big Brown Eyes; Fatal Lady. 1937: Saratoga; Man-Proof. 1938: Too Hot to Handle; The Shopworn Angel; The Girl of the Golden West. 1939: Nick Carter, Master Detective. 1940: Dark Command; Flight Command. 1941: Man Hunt; How Green Was My Valley; Blossoms in the Dust. 1942: Mrs Miniver; White Cargo. 1943: Madame Curie. 1944: Mrs Parkington. 1945: Weekend at the Waldorf. 1946: The Secret Heart; Holiday in Mexico. 1947: If Winter Comes. 1948: Julia Misbehaves. 1949: Command Decision; The Red Danube; That Forsyte Woman. 1951: Soldiers Three; Calling Bulldog Drummond; The Unknown Man. 1952: The Bad and the Beautiful; Million Dollar Mermaid. 1953: Scandal at Scourie. 1954: Executive Suite; The Last Time I Saw Paris; Deep in My Heart. 1955: Hit the Deck. 1956: Forbidden Planet. 1962: Advise and Consent. 1967: Warning Shot. 1968: Funny Girl.

PIETRANGELI, Antonio

Director. Rome 1919–68 Gaeta, Italy
Doctor of medicine, then became journalist. Wrote literary and film criticism in the early 1940s; worked on Bianco e Nero and Cinema. From 1942: collaborated on scripts e.g. *Ossessione* (1942), *Gioventù perduta* (1947), *Fabiola* (1948), *Europa 51* (1952), *Dov'è la libertà?* (1953), *La Lupa* (1953). 1953: first film as director.

Films as director: 1953: Il Sole negli occhi – Celestina (+ *s/st*); Amori di mezzo secolo *ep* 1910 (+ *co-st/co-s*). 1955: Lo scapolo – Alberto il Conquistatore (+ *co-s/st*). 1957: Souvenir d'Italie – It Happened in Rome (+ *co-s*); Nata di marzo (+ *co-s/st*). 1960: Adua e le compagne – Hungry for Love – Love à la carte (+ *co-s*). 1961: Fantasmi a Roma – Phantom Lovers – Ghosts in Rome (+ *co-s*). 1962: La Parmigiana (+ *co-s*). 1963: La Visita (+ *co-st/co-s*). 1964: Il Magnifico Cornuto – The Magnificent Cuckold. 1965: Io la conoscevo bene – I Knew Her Well (+ *co-st/co-s*). 1966: Le Fate – The Queens – The Fairies – Sex Quartet *ep* Fata Marta. 1968: Come, quando e con chi. 1969: L'Assoluto Naturale.

PINTER, Harold

Writer. London 1930–
Father a tailor of Portuguese-Jewish ancestry. 1948–58: stage actor under pseudonym David Baron, mainly in English and Irish provincial repertory. 1956: married Vivien Merchant, who later became actress. 1957: wrote first play 'The Room'. 1960: radio play 'The Dwarfs' (staged 1963). 1961: first TV play 'The Collection' (staged 1963). 1963: first film as writer was first collaboration with Joseph Losey. 1964: adapted own play for *The Caretaker*. 1967: on stage directed 'The Man in the Glass Booth'. 1969: directed 'Silence' on stage. Plays include 'The Birthday Party' (1957), 'A Slight Ache' (1958), 'The Homecoming' (1965). TV plays include 'The Lover' (1963), 'Tea Party' (1964), 'The Basement' (1967). Revue sketches include 'One to Another', 'Pieces of Eight'. Wife acted in *Accident* (1967). 1966: awarded CBE. 1969: appeared in *Pinter People*.

Films as writer: 1963: The Servant; The Caretaker.

Vladimir Petrov's Kutuzov.
Loretta Young and Alex Nicol in Joseph Pevney's Because of You.
Mary Pickford in The Little American, *directed by Cecil B. De Mille.*

215

1964: The Pumpkin Eater. 1966: The Quiller Memorandum. 1967: Accident. 1968: The Birthday Party. 1971: The Go-Between.

PINTOFF, Ernest

Director. Watertown, Connecticut 1931–
Lived in New York as a child. Syracuse University. 1945–53: jazz trumpeter. 1955: taught painting and design at Michigan State University. Worked at UPA studios in California while waiting for opening at University of Southern California. 1957: made *Flebus* for Terry Toons. 1958: formed own company. Work in TV advertising. Owns own studios where e.g. Leonard Glasser based. Two non-animated films: *The Shoes* and *Harvey Middleman, Fireman*; latter his first feature (1965).

Films as director: 1956: The Wounded Bird; Aquarium; Good Ole Country Music; Fight On for Old; Martians Come Back; Performing Painter; Blues Pattern. 1957: The Haunted Night; Flebus. 1960: The Violinist (+ *p*). 1961: The Interview (+ *p*); The Shoes (+ *p*). 1962: The Old Man and the Flower (+ *p*). 1963: The Critic (+ *p*). 1965: Harvey Middleman, Fireman (+ *p/s/m*). 1971: Dynamite Chicken; Who Killed Mary What's 'Er Name?.

PISCATOR, Erwin

Director. Ulm, Germany 1893–1966 Starnberg, Germany
1913: first stage appearance while student at Munich University. Organised and directed Constructivist theatre group. 1932–35: in Russia. 1954: only film as director *Vostanie Rybakov – Revolt of the Fisherman*. 1936: to Paris. Subsequently to USA. 1939: founded Drama Workshop at New School for Social Research, New York. To 1951: director of the Workshop. 1951: returned to Germany. Stage productions in West Germany, Holland, Sweden, Switzerland, Italy, France. Used film in many stage productions. Writings on theatre.

PITTS, Zasu

Actress. Parsons, Kansas 1898–1963 Hollywood
Extra. 1917: first film as actress *The Little Princess*. 1930: in European version only of *All Quiet on the Western Front*. During 1930s, series of comedy shorts with Thelma Todd. 1944–45: Broadway and on tour in 'Ramshackle Inn'. Often played in 'The Bat' and 'The Late Christopher Bean' on tour and in stock. Also radio and TV.

Films as actress include: 1918: How Could You Jean? 1919: Better Times. 1923: Three Wise Fools; Greed. 1924: Changing Husbands. 1925: Pretty Ladies; Lazybones. 1926: Mannequin; Monte Carlo. 1928: The Wedding March; Wife Savers. 1929: The Dummy; The Squall; Oh Yeah!; Her Private Life. 1930: No No Nanette; Monte Carlo; Honey; River's End; The Devil's Holiday. 1931: Bad Sister; Seed; The Guardsman; Finn and Hattie; Woman of Experience; The Big Gamble. 1932: Roar of the Dragon; Madison Square Garden; Walking Down Broadway (*ur*); The Man I Killed; Blondie of the Follies; Once in a Lifetime; Back Street. 1933: Mr Skitch; Her First Mate; Aggie Appleby Maker of Men. 1934: The Gay Bride; Their Big Moment: Dames: Mrs Wiggs of the Cabbage Patch.

1935: Ruggles of Red Gap; Spring Tonic; Going Highbrow. 1936: Sing Me a Love Song; Mad Holiday; 13 Hours By Air. 1939: Naughty But Nice; Nurse Edith Cavell; Eternally Yours. 1940: It All Came True; No No Nanette. 1941: Broadway Limited; Weekend for Three; Niagara Falls; The Bashful Bachelor. 1943: Let's Face It. 1947: Life With Father. 1952: Denver & Rio Grande. 1957: This Could Be the Night. 1959: The Gazebo. 1963: The Thrill of It All; It's a Mad, Mad, Mad, Mad World.

PIZZETTI, Ildebrando

Composer. Parma, Italy 1880–
Began as composer for theatre e.g. plays by Gabriele d'Annunzio. From 1905 composed operas; also wrote orchestral, choral and chamber music. Occasional film work from 1913 when he wrote music to be played by small orchestra during screenings of *Cabiria*.

Films as composer: 1913: Cabiria. 1937: Scipione l'Africano. 1941: I Promessi Sposi. 1948: Il Mulino del Po.

PLANER, Franz F.

Cinematographer. Karlsbad (Karlovy Vary), Czechoslovakia 1894–1963
Studied art with Professor Herman Wagner. Worked for a time as portrait photographer. 1923: assisted Karl Freund on Murnau's *Die Finanzen des Grossherzogs*. Then cinematographer for Erich Pommer. Worked in London before moving to Hollywood.

Films as cinematographer include: 1928: Alraune. 1932: Liebelei. 1935: The Dictator. 1938: Holiday. 1946: Her Sister's Secret. 1948: The Exile; Criss Cross; Letter From an Unknown Woman. 1949: Champion. 1950: 711 Ocean Drive; Cyrano De Bergerac. 1951: Death of a Salesman. 1953: Roman Holiday (*co*); 99 River Street. 1954: The Long Wait; A Bullet is Waiting; The Caine Mutiny; 20,000 Leagues Under the Sea (*co*). 1955: Not as a Stranger; The Left Hand of God. 1956: The Mountain. 1957: The Pride and the Passion. 1958: The Big Country. 1959: The Nun's Story. 1960: The Unforgiven. 1961: Breakfast at Tiffany's; King of Kings (*co*). 1962: The Children's Hour.

PLESHETTE, Suzanne

Actress. New York 1937–
Father managed cinemas for Paramount, then executive in radio and TV. Syracuse University. 1957: Broadway debut. 1958: first film. 1964: married and divorced Troy Donahue, and acted with him in *A Distant Trumpet*.

Films as actress include: 1958: The Geisha Boy. 1962: Rome Adventure; Forty Pounds of Trouble. 1963: The Birds; Wall of Noise. 1964: Youngblood Hawke; A Distant Trumpet; Fate is the Hunter. 1966: Mister Buddwing; Nevada Smith. 1967: The Adventures of Bullwhip Griffin. 1968: How to Make It. 1971: Support Your Local Gunfighter.

PLUMMER, Christopher

Actor. Toronto 1929–
From 1950: with Canadian Repertory Theatre.

Ottawa, Ontario. 1954: first appearance on New York stage. Much theatre work notably in Shakespeare e.g. played Henry V at Shakespeare Festival, Stratford, Ontario and Edinburgh Festival (1956). 1958: in Elia Kazan's production of 'J.B.' on Broadway. 1961: with Royal Shakespeare Company, Stratford-on-Avon; on London West End stage e.g. in 'Becket'. From 1951: much TV e.g. 'Hamlet' televised from Elsinore Castle. In films from 1957.

Films as actor include: 1958: Stage Struck. 1964: The Fall of the Roman Empire. 1965: The Sound of Music. 1966: Inside Daisy Clover. 1969: The Battle of Britain; The Royal Hunt of the Sun. 1970: Waterloo.

POE, James

Writer. Derry, New Hampshire 1923–
1941: Began on news desk of 'The March of Time' series for RKO. Subsequently wrote many scripts for documentary films, radio, TV. Oscar for best screen adaptation, in collaboration with John Farrow and S. J. Perelman, *Around the World in Eighty Days* (1956).

Films as writer: 1949: Without Honor. 1952: Scandal Sheet (*co*); Paula (*co*). 1953: A Slight Case of Larceny (*st*). 1955: The Big Knife. 1956: Attack! 1958: Hot Spell; Cat on a Hot Tin Roof (*co*); Last Train from Gun Hill. 1961: Sanctuary; Summer and Smoke (*co*). 1963: Toys in the Attic; Lilies of the Field. 1965: The Bedford Incident. 1968: The Riot. 1969: They Shoot Horses, Don't They?

POELZIG, Hans

Designer. Berlin 1869–1936
Academy of Breslau, then Technische Hochschule, Berlin. Before World War I: industrial architect, e.g. of chemical factory near Posen, Poland. 1918: invited by Paul Wegener to make sketches for decor of *Der Golem, wie er in die Welt kam* (1920); his wife sculptress Marlene Poelzig made detailed models; sets constructed by Kurt Richter. 1919: architect of Max Reinhardt's Grosses Schauspielhaus, columns sculpted by wife. Collaborated on decor of *Lebende Buddhas* (1924) and *Zur Chronik von Grieshuus* (1925). 1928–31: work on administrative buildings for I. G. Farben at Frankfurt-am-Main.

POGGIOLI, Ferdinando Maria

Director. Bologna, Italy 1897–1944 Rome
Higher School of Commerce, Bologna. Director of documentaries. Became editor, e.g. on *La Signora di tutti* (1934). 1936: returned to direction with *Arma Bianca*. 1942: in collaboration with Alberto Lattuada co-wrote own *Sissignora*.

Films as director: 1931: Impressioni Siciliani. 1932: Il Presepi; Paestum. 1936: Arma Bianca (+ *e*). 1939: Ricchezza senza domani (+ *co-s*). 1940: Addio Giovinezza! (+ *co-s*). 1941: L'Amore cantà. 1942: Sissignora (+ *co-s*); La Bisbetica Domata; La Morte Civile; Gelosia; L'Amico delle donne. 1943: Le Sorelle Materassi; Il Capello da prete.

POITIER, Sydney

Actor. Miami, Florida 1924–
1945: joined US Army and trained as physiotherapist

at a mental hospital. American Negro Theatre; alternated with Harry Belafonte in 'Days of Our Youth'. Also acted in 'You Can't Take It With You', 'Rain', 'Freight', 'The Fisherman', 'Riders to the Sea', 'Lysistrata'. 1944: appeared in US Army film *From Whence Cometh Help*. 1948: on Broadway in 'Anna Lucasta' and toured in the play. 1950: first Hollywood film *No Way Out*. 1959: Broadway 'A Raisin in the Sun'. Worked frequently for United Artists. Married dancer Juanita Hardy. 1963: Oscar as Best Actor for *Lilies of the Field*.

Films as actor include: 1952: Cry the Beloved Country; Red Ball Express. 1954: Go Man Go. 1955: Blackboard Jungle. 1956: Goodbye, My Lady; Edge of the City. 1957: Something of Value; Band of Angels. 1958: The Defiant Ones; All the Young Men. 1959: Porgy and Bess. 1961: Paris Blues. 1962: Pressure Point. 1963: Lilies of the Field. 1964: The Long Ships. 1965: A Patch of Blue; The Greatest Story Ever Told; The Slender Thread. 1966: To Sir With Love; Duel at Diablo. 1967: In the Heat of the Night; Guess Who's Coming to Dinner. 1968: For Love of Ivy (+ *st*). 1970: They Call Me *Mister* Tibbs.

POJAR, Bretislav

Animator. Susice, Czechoslovakia 1923–
Worked in animation in 1942 and immediately after World War II. Abandoned drawings for puppets, moved to Jiri Trnka's studio. Animated several of Trnka's films in collaboration. 1951: first film as solo animator, on which Trnka was art director, as he was on several of Pojar's early films. 1952: short documentary on painter *Joseph Mánes*. 1955: made live-action feature *Dobrodružství no Zlaté Zatoce*. 1958: on 2 films returned to use of animated drawings. 1959: in collaboration with Jiri Brdecka scripted his own *Bombománie*. Head of own studio. From 1966: work for National Film Board of Canada.

Films as director: 1952: Joseph Mánes (*in 2 parts*). 1955: Dobrodružství no Zlaté Zatoce – An Adventure in the Bay of Gold – The Big Fish.

Films as animator in collaboration with Jiri Trnka: 1945: Zasadil dedek repu. 1946: Darek; Zviratka a petrovsti. 1947: Spalicek. 1948: Císařův Slavik – The Emperor's Nightingale. 1949: Arie Prerie. 1950: Bajaja. 1951: Certuv Mlyn. 1953: Staré Pověsti Ceské – Old Czech Legends.

Films as animator and writer include: 1951: Perníkova Chaloupka – The Gingerbread Cottage. 1953: O Skleničku vic – A Little Drop Too Much (*co-s*). 1956: Špejbl na stopě – Spejbl on the Trail. 1957: Paraplíčko – The Little Umbrella. 1958: Slava – Fame; Bombománie – Bomb Mania (*co-s*). 1959: Lev a písnička – The Lion and the Ditty. 1960: Jak si zařídit byt – How to Furnish a Flat; Dobré Bydlení – A Good Place to Live; Půlnoční Dobrudružstvi – A Midnight Incident (+ *co-s*; *co-d* B. Sramek). 1963: Kočiči škola – School for Cats (*series of 3*). 1964: Uvodní Slovo pronese – A Few Words of Introduction – The Orator. 1965: Romance; Ideal. 1965–67: Come and Play, Sir (*series of 3*). 1966: It's Hard to Recognize a Princess. 1967: Hold onto Your Hats. 1969: To See or Not to See.

POLANSKI, Roman

Director. Paris 1933–
1954: first film as actor *Pokolenie*. 1955–59: made shorts at Lodz film school; acted in plays. 1959: acted in *Lotna* and *Niewinni Czarodzieje*. 1962: first professional work as director was also first feature *Nóž w wodzie*. 1963: to France, wrote *Aimez-vous les femmes?* 1964–68: in UK. 1968: to USA to make *Rosemary's Baby*.

Films as director: 1957: Rower – The Bicycle (*uf*); Morbectwo – The Crime; Rozbigimi zabawe – Breaking up the Party. 1958: Ewag Ludzie z szasa – Two Men and a Wardrobe (+ *s*). 1959: Anioly spadaja – When Angels Fall (+ *s*). 1962: Nóž w wodzie – Knife in the Water; Ssaki – Mammals (+ *co-s*). 1963: Le Gros et le maigre (+ *co-s/w*); Les Plus Belles Escroqueries du monde – The Beautiful Swindlers *ep* La Riviere de diamants – Amsterdam. 1965: Repulsion (+ *co-s*). 1966: Cul-de-Sac (+ *co-s*). 1967: Dance of the Vampires – The Fearless Vampire Killers or Pardon Me, But Your Teeth are in My Neck (+ *co-p/co-s/w*). 1968: Rosemary's Baby. 1971: Macbeth (+ *co-s*).

POLITO, Sol

Cinematographer. Hollywood, 1892–1960
Son of Italian immigrants. From 1918: cinematographer in Hollywood; under contract to Mutual, then worked for World Film Corporation and Mayflower. With Metro (1920), Fox (1921), Universal (1922), First National (1923), Hunt Stromberg (1924–25), Pathè (1926). Then almost all films for First National and Warners until 1947. Frequently cinematographer for Michael Curtiz (1936–43: 12 films), Mervyn LeRoy (1929–36: 7 films). 1949: last film.

Films as cinematographer include: 1919: Soldiers of Fortune. 1928: The Haunted House. 1929: Seven Footprints to Satan; Broadway Babies; The House of Horror (*co*). 1930: No No Nanette; Numbered Men; Woman Hungry. 1931: Five Star Final. 1932: I am a Fugitive from a Chain Gang. 1933: 42nd Street; Picture Snatcher; Gold Diggers of 1933. 1934: Hi, Nellie!; Wonder Bar; Flirtation Walk (*co*); Dr Monica; Madame Dubarry. 1935: The Woman in Red; G Men; In Caliente; Shipmates Forever; Frisco Kid. 1936: The Petrified Forest; Sons o' Guns; The Charge of the Light Brigade (*co*); Three Men on a Horse. 1937: The Prince and the Pauper; Varsity Show (*co*). 1938: Gold is Where You Find It; Valley of the Giants; Angels with Dirty Faces; The Adventures of Robin Hood (*co*). 1939: Dodge City; The Private Lives of Elizabeth and Essex. 1940: Four Wives; Virginia City; The Sea Hawk; City for Conquest (*co*); Santa Fe Trail. 1941: The Sea Wolf; Sergeant York (*co*). 1942: Captains of the Clouds (*co*). 1943: This is the Army (*co*). 1944: Arsenic and Old Lace. 1946: Cinderella Jones; Cloak and Dagger. 1947: The Long Night. 1948: Sorry Wrong Number.

POLLACK, Sidney

Director. 1934–
Studied acting in New York. Actor on TV and Broadway. 1960–64: directed episodes for TV series in Hollywood e.g. 'Ben Casey', the 'Bob Hope-Chrysler Theatre'. 1965: first film as director.

Zasu Pitts (left) in Erich Von Stroheim's Greed.
Christopher Plummer in Robert Wise's The Sound of Music.
Lionel Stander and Jack MacGowran in Cul-de-Sac, *directed by Roman Polanski.*

Films as director: 1965: The Slender Thread. 1966: This Property is Condemned. 1968: The Scalphunters; Castle Keep; The Swimmer (*uc, co-d Frank Perry*). 1969: They Shoot Horses, Don't They?

POLLET, Jean-Daniel

Director. Paris 1936–
Amateur 16mm films, then series of films for TV, and industrial shorts. 1964: Alexandre Astruc spoke commentary to *Basae*. 1959–60: worked on first feature *La Ligne de mire*, unfinished. 1965: first completed feature.

Short films as director include: 1957: Pourvu qu'on ait l'ivresse. 1961: Gala (*+p/s*). 1963: Méditerranée. 1964: Basae.

Features as director: 1959–60: La Ligne de mire (*uf*). 1964: Paris vu par *ep* Rue St Denis (*+ s*). 1965: Une Balle au coeur – A Shot in the Heart (*+ co-s*). 1967: Oniros; Le Horla (*+ s*). 1968: L'Amour c'est gai, l'amour c'est triste (*+ co-s*). 1969: Le Maître du temps (*+ co-s/co-di*).

POLONSKY, Abraham

Writer and director
Law at Columbia University. Taught at City College, New York from 1932 until the war. Worked in radio; wrote short stories and criticism; a novel accepted for publication, then withdrawn as unreadable. In OSS during World War II. Entered films at Paramount. Wrote a few scripts and directed one of them. Called before House Committee on Un-American Activities and blacklisted. To Europe. Returned to USA; wrote films pseudonymously. Writer on TV series 'You Are There'. 3 novels published, 'The World Above', 'The Season of Fear' (published in East Germany after he was blacklisted) and 'Mario and the Magician'.

Films as writer include: 1947: Body and Soul; Golden Earrings (*co*). 1951: I Can Get It For You Wholesale. 1968: Madigan (*co*).

Films as director: 1948: Force of Evil (*+ co-s*). 1969: Tell Them Willie Boy is Here (*+ s*). 1971: Romance of a Horse Thief.

POMMER, Erich

Producer. Hildesheim, Germany 1889–1966 Hollywood
Joined Gaumont in Paris; became general manager for Central Europe. 1913: same position at Eclair. 1914: returned to Germany to join Army; invalided out, seriously wounded. 1916: founded the German Eclair Company, DECLA, which merged (1919) with Bioscop. 1923: Ufa bought out Bioscop; joined Ufa board of directors as head of production and foreign department. 1926: joined Paramount, then MGM. 1927: returned to Ufa. 1933: being of Jewish descent, moved to Paris. 1934: USA as producer for Fox. 1936: came to UK. 1938–39: formed Mayflower Pictures with Charles Laughton and John Maxwell; made 3 films. In USA during World War II. 1946: returned to Germany to direct film production in American Zone. 1949: USA. 1951: resumed film production in

Germany.

Films as producer include: 1919: Das Kabinett des Dr Caligari; Halb Blut; Der Herr der Liebe. 1919–20: Die Spinnen. 1921: Schloss Vogelod; Der müde Tod. 1922: Doktor Mabuse, der Spieler; Phantom. 1923: Austreibung; Die Finanzen des Grossherzogs. 1924: Die Nibelungen; Der letzte Mann; Mikaël. 1925: Variété; Tartuff. 1926: Metropolis; Faust. 1927: Hotel Imperial (*+ co-s*). 1928: Spione. 1930: Der blaue Engel. 1931: Der Kongress tanzt. 1933: On a volé un homme. 1934: Liliom. 1938: Vessel of Wrath (*co-pc*); St Martin's Lane (*co-pc*). 1939: Jamaica Inn (*co-pc*). 1940: They Knew What They Wanted; Dance Girl Dance (*co*). 1955: Kinder, Mutter und ein General.

PONTECORVO, Gillo

Director. Pisa, Italy 1919–
Younger brother of Professor Bruno Pontecorvo. Studied chemistry, then correspondent for Italian journals in Paris. Worked as assistant director to Yves Allégret, Joris Ivens, Mario Monicelli, Giancarlo Menotti. 1953: began as documentary director in Italy. 1956: directed episode in film supervised by Joris Ivens and Alberto Cavalcanti. 1957: first complete feature as director.

Short films as director include: 1953: Missione Timiriazev. 1954: Uomini di Marmo; Porta Portese; Can dietro le sbarre; Festa a Castelluccio; Pane e zolfo.

Features as director: 1956: Die Wind Rose *ep* Giovanna. 1957: La Grande Strada Azzurra – Squarcia. 1959: Kapo (*+ co-s*). 1965: La Battaglia di Algeri – The Battle of Algiers (*+ co-st/co-m*). 1968: Queimada! – Burn! (*+ co-st*).

PONTI, Carlo

Producer. Milan 1910–
Studied law. 1940: first film as producer *Piccolo Mondo Antico*. After World War II settled in Rome, producing for Lux. 1950–54: produced in collaboration with Dino de Laurentiis, beginning with *Il Brigante Musolino* (1950). Then produced for own company (C. P. Cinematografica) and others including Exelsa and Enic. 1957: married Sophia Loren. 1958: to Hollywood as producer for Paramount; first American film *Black Orchid*. From 1961: several French-Italian co-productions. 1964: naturalised French. Continued to produce Italian films. 'Presented' in the West several Czechoslovak films including *Ostře Sledované Vlaky* (1966) and *Sedmikrásky* (1966).

Films as producer include: 1941: Sissignora. 1942: Giacomo l'idealista. 1945: La Freccia nel fianco; Un Americano in vacanza. 1946: La Primula bianca; Vivere in pace. 1947: I Miserabili; Gioventù Perduta; Senza pietà. 1948: Fuga in Francia. 1949: Quel Bandito son io!; Il Mulino del Po; L'Imperatore di Capri; Cuori senza frontiere; Totò cerca casa. 1950: Vita da cani; E arrivato il cavaliere. 1954: Un Americano a Roma. 1955: La Donna del fiume. 1956: Il Ferroviere; Guerra e pace; Ragazze d'oggi. 1957: Guendalina; Camping; Marisa la civetta; Nata di marzo. 1958: Black Orchid. 1959: That Kind of Woman. 1960: La Ciociara; Heller in Pink Tights. 1961: Une Femme est une femme (*co*); Madame Sans-Gêne. 1962: Cléo de 5 à 7; Boccaccio '70. 1963: I Sequestrati di Altona; Léon Morin, prêtre; L'Isola di

Arturo (*co*); Le Doulos (*co*); Landru (*co*); L'Oeil du malin (*co*); Ieri, oggi, domani; La Noia; La Donna Scimmia; Les Carabiniers (*co*); Le Mépris (*co*). 1964: Matrimonio all'Italiana; Controsesso; Le Vampire de Dusseldorf. 1965: Lady L; Oggi, domani, dopodomani; Doctor Zhivago. 1966: La Ragazza e il generale. 1967: C'era una volta; Questi Fantasmi; La 25me Heure. 1968: Colpo di Stato; L'Uomo dai palloncini; Smashing Time (*co*). 1969: Gli Amanti (*co*); I Girasoli (*co*). 1971: La Moglie del prete.

Films as producer in collaboration with Dino de Laurentiis include: 1950: Il Brigante Musolino. 1952: Europa '51; Guardie e ladri; Dov'è la libertà; Jolanda, la figlia del Corsaro Nero; La Lupa; Toto a colori; I Tre Corsari. 1953: Anni Facili; Ulisse. 1954: Mambo; L'Oro di Napoli; La Strada. 1956: War and Peace.

PONTING, Herbert

Cinematographer. Wiltshire 1870–1936
Banking. Travelled in USA and Far East. War correspondent. From 1900: devoted himself to photography. 1910–11: cameraman with Scott's Antarctic expedition. 1911: film first presented as *The Great White Silence*. 1930: final version *90 Degrees South*; wrote and recorded sound track.

PORTER, Edwin S.

Director. Pittsburgh, Pennsylvania 1869–1941 New York
Began as electrician. Then in US Navy. 1896: film salesman; went to Caribbean running film shows. 1897: organised outdoor shows of advertising films in New York; experimented with Edison projector; joined Thomas Edison as cinematographer. Shot newsreels consisting of 40 or 50 ft. strips of film joined together in sequences that ran for a few minutes, also short fiction series e.g. *Happy Hooligan* (1901–03). 1902–09: director for Thomas Edison, based in studio in the Bronx, New York. 1907: introduced D. W. Griffith to films as actor in *Rescued from an Eagle's Nest*. 1909: formed independent company Rex Pictures. 1912: joined Adolph Zukor when he formed Famous Players, acting as the creative partner in the business; in defiance of the Patent Company made a number of films in New York starring stage actors in their current successes; signed up Mary Pickford for productions in Hollywood. In 1914, Famous Players was producing a film a week. 1915: retired from films.

Films as director include: 1899: 'Columbia' Winning the Cup. 1901: President McKinley and Escort Going to the Capitol; President McKinley's Funeral Cortege at Buffalo, NY; President McKinley's Funeral Cortege at Washington, DC; The Old Maid Having Her Picture Taken; Happy Hooligan Surprised; Happy Hooligan April-Fooled; 'Columbia' and 'Shamrock II'; The Jeffreys and Ruhlin Sparring Contest at San Francisco; A Trip around the Pan-American Exposition. – A Trip Through the Columbia Exposition. 1902: Happy Hooligan Turns Burglar. 1903: The Life of an American Fireman; Happy Hooligan; Happy Hooligan's Interrupted Lunch; Happy Hooligan in a Trap; The Great Train Robbery; Uncle Tom's Cabin. 1904: The Ex-Convict; Old Maid and Fortune Teller; Capture of Yegg Bank Burglars. 1905: The Kleptomaniac; The Miller's Daughter; The Night Before Christmas – Hanging Stockings on a Christmas Tree;

The White Caps. 1906: Dream of a Rarebit Fiend; Life of a Cowboy. 1907: Rescued from an Eagle's Nest. 1910: Alice's Adventures in Wonderland. 1912: Count of Monte Cristo. 1914: Hearts Adrift. 1915: Sold.

POTTER, H. C.

Director. New York 1904–

Yale, graduated 1926. 1926–28: Yale School of Drama. 1928–35: stage director and actor; plays directed include 'Overture' and 'Wednesday's Child'. 1937: first films as director. 1939: wrote play 'What's a Fixer For?' 1943: made *Victory Through Air Power* in collaboration with Walt Disney who contributed animation sequences. 1943–44: served in US Army Air Transport Command. 1944–48: stage direction including 'Anne of a Thousand Days'. 1952–55: further return to stage. 1956–58: national secretary of Director's Guild of America.

Films as director: 1937: Beloved Enemy; Wings Over Honolulu. 1938: Romance in the Dark; The Shopworn Angel; The Cowboy and the Lady. 1939: The Story of Vernon and Irene Castle; Blackmail. 1940: Congo Maisie. 1941: Second Chorus; Hellzapoppin. 1943: Mr Lucky; Victory Through Air Power (*co-d Walt Disney*). 1947: The Farmer's Daughter; A Likely Story. 1948: Mr Blandings Builds His Dream House; The Time of Your Life; You Gotta Stay Happy. 1950: The Miniver Story. 1955: Three For the Show. 1957: Top Secret Affair – Their Secret Affair.

POWELL, Dick

Actor and director. Mountain View, Arkansas 1904–63 Hollywood

Educated in Little Rock. Worked in telephone company, then toured in vaudeville. Banjoist in Charles Davis' Band, Indianapolis. 1940: compere, singer and actor at Stanley Theatre, Pittsburgh. 1932: went to Hollywood; first films as singer and actor; worked mainly for Warners until 1939. From 1940: actor with various companies including Paramount, Universal, RKO, Columbia, MGM. 1953: first film as director for RKO. 1954: last film as actor. Producer/director with RKO, later with Columbia and Fox. Also TV: founded Four Star Television, produced many series including 'The Dick Powell Theatre'. Married 3 times including (1936–45) Joan Blondell, (1945–61) June Allyson.

Films as actor include: 1932: Blessed Event. 1933: Convention City; 42nd Street; Gold Diggers of 1933; Footlight Parade; College Coach. 1934: Wonder Bar; Dames; Happiness Ahead; Flirtation Walk; Twenty Million Sweethearts. 1935: Thanks a Million; Gold Diggers of 1935; Page Miss Glory; Broadway Gondolier; A Midsummer Night's Dream; Shipmates Forever. 1936: Hearts Divided; Stage Struck; Gold Diggers of 1937. 1937: On the Avenue; The Singing Marine; Varsity Show; Hollywood Hotel. 1938: Cowboy from Brooklyn; Hard to Get; Going Places. 1939: Naughty But Nice. 1940: Christmas in July. 1942: Star Spangled Rhythm. 1943: True to Life; Riding High; Happy Go Lucky. 1944: It Happened Tomorrow. 1945: Murder My Sweet; Cornered. 1947: Johnny O'Clock. 1948: To the Ends of the Earth; Pitfall; Rogue's Regiment. 1950: The Reformer and the Redhead; Right Cross. 1951: Cry Danger; The Tall Target; Callaway Went Thataway. 1952: The Bad and the Beautiful.

Films as director and producer: 1953: Split Second. 1955: The Conqueror. 1956: You Can't Run Away from It. 1957: The Enemy Below. 1958: The Hunters.

POWELL, Jane

(Suzanne Burce) Actress. Portland, Oregon 1929–
At 12 radio singer. To 1955: almost all films for MGM. 1959: TV in 'Meet Me in St Louis'. Nightclub singer, stage. Married ice-skating star Geary Steffen (1949–53, divorced).

Films as actress include: 1944: Song of the Open Road. 1946: Holiday in Mexico. 1948: Three Daring Daughters; A Date With Judy. 1950: Nancy Goes to Rio; Two Weeks With Love. 1951: Rich Young and Pretty; Royal Wedding. 1953: Small Town Girl; Three Sailors and a Girl. 1954: Athena; Seven Brides for Seven Brothers; Deep in My Heart. 1955: Hit the Deck. 1957: The Girl Most Likely. 1958: The Female Animal; Enchanted Island.

POWELL, Michael

Director. Canterbury, Kent 1905–
Began in banking. 1925–30: worked with Rex Ingram in Nice as stills photographer, cameraman, editor, actor, writer, assistant director. 1931: first film as director. 1943–57: with Emeric Pressburger formed production company Archer Films, directing, producing and scripting all their films in collaboration. 1944–52: occasionally directed in the theatre. 1964–65: directed some episodes in American TV series e.g. 'Espionage'. Many articles on films, also 2 novels '20,000 Feet on Foula' (1938), 'Graf Spee' (1956).

Features as director: 1931: Two Crowded Hours; Rynox; The Rasp; My Friend the King (*+ s*). 1932: The Star Reporter; Hotel Splendide; C.O.D.; Born Lucky; His Lordship. 1933: The Night of the Party; The Fire Raisers (*+ co-s*); Red Ensign (*+ co-s*). 1934: Crown v Stevens; Her Last Affaire; Something Always Happens; The Girl in the Crowd. 1935: Some Day; The Price of a Song; The Love Test; The Phantom Light; Lazy Bones. 1936: The Brown Wallet; The Man Behind the Mask. 1937: The Edge of the World (*+ s*). 1939: The Lion Has Wings (*co-d Brian Desmond Hurst, Adrian Brunel*); The Spy in Black – U-Boat 29. 1940: Contraband – Blackout (*+ co-s*); The Thief of Bagdad (*co-d Ludwig Berger, Tim Whelan*). 1941: 49th Parallel (*+ p*). 1958: Luna de Miel – Honeymoon (*+ co-p/co-s*). 1959: Peeping Tom (*+ p*). 1960: The Queen's Guards (*+ p*). 1964: Bluebeard's Castle. 1966: They're a Weird Mob (*+ p*). 1968: Age of Consent (*+ co-p*).

Films as director, producer and writer in collaboration with Emeric Pressburger: 1942: One of Our Aircraft is Missing. 1943: The Life and Death of Colonel Blimp; The Volunteer. 1944: A Canterbury Tale. 1945: I Know Where I'm Going. 1946: A Matter of Life and Death – Stairway to Heaven. 1947: Black Narcissus. 1948: The Red Shoes; The Small Back Room – Hour of Glory. 1950: The Elusive Pimpernel; Gone to Earth – The Wild Heart. 1951: The Tales of Hoffman. 1955: Oh Rosalinda! – Fledermaus 55 (*co-d Emeric Pressburger*). 1956: The Battle of the River Plate – Pursuit of the Graf Spee. 1957: Ill Met by Moonlight – Night Ambush.

Force of Evil, *directed by Abraham Polonsky.*
Production still from Carlo Ponti's production of Dr. Zhivago, *directed by David Lean.*
Anna Massey in Peeping Tom, *directed by Michael Powell.*

POWELL, William

Actor. Pittsburgh, Pennsylvania 1892–
American Academy of Dramatic Art. 1912: Broadway début in a bit part. 1922: first film as actor Albert Parker's *Sherlock Holmes*. Numerous films for Paramount. 1931–34: at Warners. 1934–47: mainly at MGM; 'Thin Man' series with Myrna Loy. Then worked for Warners, Universal, MGM, Fox and others. 1955: last film *Mister Roberts*. Married Carole Lombard (1931–33, divorced).

Films as actor include: 1926: Beau Geste; The Great Gatsby. 1927: Paid to Love. 1928: The Last Command; The Dragnet. 1932: One Way Passage. 1934: The Thin Man. 1935: Reckless. 1936: The Great Ziegfeld; My Man Godfrey; Libeled Lady. 1946: Ziegfeld Follies. 1947: Life with Father. 1951: It's a Big Country. 1953: How to Marry a Millionaire. 1955: Mister Roberts.

POWER, Tyrone

Actor. Cincinnati, Ohio 1914–58 Spain
Third generation of theatrical family. Studied under his father Shakespearean actor Tyrone Power. Stage appearances in summer stock and New York. 1932: first film as actor, bit part in *Tom Brown of Culver*. World War II: enlisted as private in US Marine Corps; Lieutenant from 1943. Subsequent stage appearances included 'Mr Roberts' in London (1950). Films mainly for Fox. 1956: with Ted Richmond formed independent production company, made *Seven Waves Away* in England. Died of heart attack on location in Spain for *Solomon and Sheba*; replaced by Yul Brynner.

Films as actor include: 1934: Flirtation Walk. 1936: Lloyd's of London. 1937: Love is News. 1938: In Old Chicago; Alexander's Ragtime Band; Marie Antoinette; Suez. 1939: Jesse James; Rose of Washington Square; The Rains Came. 1940: Johnny Apollo; Brigham Young; The Mark of Zorro. 1941: A Yank in the RAF; Blood and Sand; Son of Fury. 1942: This Above All; The Black Swan. 1943: Crash Dive. 1946: The Razor's Edge; Nightmare Alley; Captain from Castile. 1949: Prince of Foxes. 1950: The Black Rose; An American Guerrilla in the Philippines. 1951: Rawhide. 1952: Diplomatic Courier; Pony Soldier. 1953: The Mississippi Gambler. 1954: King of the Khyber Rifles. 1955: The Long Gray Line; Untamed. 1956: The Eddy Duchin Story. 1957: The Sun Also Rises; Witness for the Prosecution; The Rising of the Moon (+ n).

PRÉJEAN, Albert

Actor. Paris 1894–
Educated in France and Germany. From 1920: extra in films, then major roles. Theatrical work includes 'Le Petit Café', 'Sans Cérémonie'. Also Paris music-hall.

Films as actor include: 1924: Paris qui dort; Le Fantôme du Moulin Rouge; Le Miracle des loups. 1927: Un Chapeau de paille d'Italie. 1930: Sous les toits de Paris; Les Nouveaux Messieurs. 1934: Dédé. 1936: Jenny. 1937: L'Alibi. 1947: Les Frères Bouquinquant. 1951: Le Désir et l'amour.

PREMINGER, Otto

Director. Vienna 1906–
Father a lawyer. 1922: first stage role as Lysander in 'A Midsummer Night's Dream' in Vienna. 1923–25: assistant to Max Reinhardt in Josefstadt and Salzburg; took small roles. 1926: doctorate in law. 1926–27: artistic and financial director of Die Komodie Theatre, Vienna. 1928: director of Josefstadt theatre. 1929–31: work with company of actors including Elizabeth Bergner, William Dieterle, Oskar Homolka, Harry Horner, Hedy Lamarr, Peter Lorre, Luise Rainer. 1931: first film as director. 1933: head of Josefstadt theatre. 1933–34: supervised and directed productions. 1934–35: administrator and director. 1935: to USA; on stage directed 'Libel'. 1936: to Hollywood; first American film as director. 1936–50: all films for Fox. 1938: New York stage, directed 'Outward Bound'. 1938–41: taught stage direction and production at Yale. 1939–41: stage director. 1941: returned to Hollywood. 1942: acted in *The Pied Piper* and *They Got Me Covered*. 1943: became American citizen. First film under contract as producer and director *In the Meantime, Darling*. 1945: acted in *Where Do We Go From Here*; made *A Royal Scandal*, produced and supervised by Ernst Lubitsch; illegitimate son by Gypsy Rose Lee. 1948: on death of Lubitsch completed *That Lady in Ermine* without credit. 1951: stage direction on Broadway including 'The Moon is Blue'. 1952: *Angel Face* made for RKO. 1953: acted in *Stalag 17*; formed own company: first film *The Moon is Blue*, for United Artists, made simultaneously in American and German versions, acted in German version. 1954: return to Fox. Worked subsequently for Warners, United Artists, Columbia, Paramount. 1958: stage direction in Chicago. 1959: took over direction of *Porgy and Bess* after Rouben Mamoulian left. 1960: married Hope Bryce, costume advisor on many of his films; on stage directed 'Critic's Choice'. 1966: acted in 2 episodes of TV series 'Batman'. 1971: revealed that he is father of Gypsy Rose Lee's son, casting editor Eric Kirkland; adopted him.

Films as director: 1931: Die Grosse Liebe. 1936: Under Your Spell. 1937: Danger—Love at Work. 1943: Margin for Error (+ w). 1945: A Royal Scandal – Czarina. 1947: Forever Amber. 1948: That Lady in Ermine (uc, co-d Ernst Lubitsch). 1952: Angel Face. 1954: River of No Return. 1955: The Court-Martial of Billy Mitchell – One Man Mutiny. 1959: Porgy and Bess.

Films as director and producer: 1944: In the Meantime, Darling; Laura. 1945: Fallen Angel. 1946: Centennial Summer. 1947: Daisy Kenyon. 1949: The Fan – Lady Windermere's Fan; Whirlpool. 1950: Where the Sidewalk Ends. 1951: The 13th Letter. 1953: The Moon is Blue (co-p); Die Jungfrau auf dem Dach (+ w; German version of The Moon is Blue). 1954: Carmen Jones. 1955: The Man With The Golden Arm. 1957: Saint Joan. 1958: Bonjour Tristesse. 1959: Anatomy of a Murder. 1960: Exodus. 1962: Advise and Consent. 1963: The Cardinal. 1964: In Harm's Way. 1965: Bunny Lake is Missing. 1967: Hurry Sundown. 1968: Skidoo. 1970: Tell Me That You Love Me, Junie Moon. 1971: Such Good Friends.

PRESLE, Micheline

(Micheline Chassagne) Actress. Paris 1922–
Convent education. In films from 1938. 1939: leading role in *Jeunes Filles en détresse*. 1938: established as star in double role in *Paradis Perdu*. 1949: to Hollywood on Fox contract; appeared in 3 films. Also Italian films.

Films as actress include: 1945: Falbalas; Boule de suif. 1947: Le Diable au corps; Les Jeux sont faits. 1950: Under my Skin; An American Guerrilla in the Philippines. 1954: Si Versailles m'était conté. 1955: Napoléon. 1956: Beatrice Cenci. 1960: Une Fille pour l'été; Blind Date. 1961: L'Amant de cinq jours; Les Sept Péchés Capitaux ep La Luxure; L'Assassino. 1962: Le Diable et les dix commandements; Vénus Impériale. 1964: La Chasse à l'homme. 1965: La Religieuse. 1966: Le Roi de coeur. 1970: Le Bal du Comte d'orgel. 1971: Peau d'âne; Les Petroleuses.

PRESLEY, Elvis

Actor. Tupelo, Mississippi 1935–
Rockabilly then rock 'n' roll singer. 1954: first recordings. 1956: first film as actor *Love Me Tender*. From 1958: 2 years in US Army stationed in Germany. 1969: first non-singing film role in *Charro!*. 1970: the subject of *That's the Way it is*. Most films for MGM and Paramount. Also radio, TV.

Films as actor include: 1957: Loving You; Jailhouse Rock. 1958: King Creole. 1960: GI Blues; Flaming Star. 1961: Blue Hawaii; Wild in the Country. 1962: Follow That Dream; Kid Galahad. 1963: Fun in Acapulco. 1964: Viva Las Vegas; Roustabout. 1965: Tickle Me. 1966: Spinout. 1968: Stay Away Joe; Speedway. 1969: Charro!; The Trouble with Girls.

PRESSBURGER, Emeric

Director. Miskolc, Hungary 1902–
Prague and Stuttgart Universities. Journalist in Hungary and Germany. Worked in films as writer in Berlin and Paris. 1935: to UK. Association with Michael Powell began when Pressburger wrote screenplay for *The Spy in Black* (1939), story for *Contraband* (1940) and in collaboration with Powell produced and scripted *One of our Aircraft is Missing* (1942). 1943–47: joint production company with Powell; directed, produced and wrote all their films in collaboration. 1948: produced Thorold Dickinson's unreleased *Then and Now*. 1953: directed *Twice Upon a Time*. 1955: directed, produced and wrote *Oh, Rosalinda!* in collaboration with Michael Powell. 1957: produced and scripted Julian Amyes's *Miracle in Soho*. See POWELL, Michael.

PRESTON, Robert

(Robert Meservey) Actor, Newton Highlands, Massachusetts 1918–
Began in stock company, then acted at Pasadena Playhouse for 2 years. 1938: first film, *King of Alcatraz*. Paramount contract for 10 years. Then with various companies. World War II: worked in Intelligence. In 1950s also acted on Broadway e.g. in stage production then film, *The Music Man* (1962).

Films as actor include: 1939: Disbarred; Union Pacific; Beau Geste. 1940: Northwest Mounted Police. 1941: The Lady from Cheyenne; New York Town. 1942: Reap the Wild Wind; This Gun for Hire; Wake Island. 1947: The Macomber Affair; Wild Harvest; Variety Girl. 1948: Blood on the Moon; Big City ep

The Bride Comes to Yellow Sky. 1949: Tulsa; The Lady Gambles. 1951: My Outlaw Brother. 1952: Face to Face. 1956: The Last Frontier. 1960: The Dark at the Top of the Stairs; The Sundowners. 1962: How the West Was Won. 1963: Island of Love.

PRÉVERT, Jacques

Writer. Paris 1900–

Poet and song writer (e.g. 'Les Feuilles Mortes' with music by Joseph Kosma). 1932: wrote *L'Affaire est dans le sac* directed by his brother Pierre. Began collaboration with Marcel Carné with *Jenny* (1936). Acted in e.g. *La Vie commence demain* (1950) and collaborated on commentaries of several shorts e.g. *Aubervilliers* (1945) and *La Seine a rencontré Paris* (1957). *See* PRÉVERT, Pierre.

Films as writer include: 1932: L'Affaire est dans le sac (+ *di*). 1933: Ciboulette (*co-ad/di*). 1936: Le Crime de Monsieur Lange (*co-ad/di*); Jenny (*co-st/di*). 1937: Drôle de drame (+ *di*). 1938: Quai des brumes (+ *di*); Les Disparus de Saint-Agil (*co, uc*). 1939: Remorques (*co-ad*); Le Jour se lève (*di*). 1941: Les Visiteurs du soir (*co-s/co-di*). 1943: Lumière d'Été (*co-s/co-di*); Adieu Léonard (*co-s/di/co-lyr*). 1944: Les Enfants du paradis (+ *di*). 1945: Les Portes de la nuit (+ *di*); Le Petit Soldat (*co-ad*). 1946: Voyage-Surprise (*co-ad/di/lyr*). 1947: Le Petit Soldat (*co*). 1949: Lady Paname (*co*). 1950: La Marie du port (*co-di/co-s*). 1952: La Bergère et le ramoneur (*co-s/di*). 1957: Notre Dame de Paris (*co*).

PRÉVERT, Pierre

Director, writer and actor. Paris 1906–

Breton father. Publicist then projectionist for a Paris cinema. 1928: first film as actor *La Joie d'une heure*, first film as director in collaboration *Souvenirs de Paris*. 1929: assistant to Cavalcanti on *Le Petit Chaperon Rouge* and acted in it. Assistant director and assistant editor. 1930: acted in *L'Age d'or*. Assistant to Jean Renoir, Yves Allégret, Marc Allégret. 1932: first feature as director, and acted in it; written by brother Jacques. Assistant to Marc Allégret, Marcel Carné, Robert Siodmak. 1934: acted with brother in Yves Allégret's short *La Pomme de terre*. 1940–41: toured unoccupied North Africa, acting in Marcel Achard's 'Domino' with Pierre Brasseur, Maurice Duhamel. 1943: directed *Adieu Léonard* written in collaboration with brother. 1947: with brother co-wrote *Voyage-Surprise*. 1949: with brother co-wrote *Lady Paname*. 1951: became artistic director of cabaret-theatre La Fontaine des Quatre Saisons, Paris. 1958: artistic advisor on *Le Cerf Volant au bout du monde*. 1958–59: directed 2 shorts, one (*Paris la Belle*) with commentary by brother and including footage from *Souvenirs de Paris* (1928). From 1961: TV director; first TV film *Mon Frère Jacques* for Belgian TV and Belgian Cinemathèque. 1962: made *Chantons Francais* for American TV; on stage directed 'Lysistrata' and brother's 'Le Tableau des merveilles'. 1965: made *La Maison du passeur* in Brittany for French TV from own scenario adapted by brother. Other films for French TV include 'Reportage' (1964), on making of *Lady L* and *A la belle étoile* (1966).

Films as actor include: 1929: Le Petit Chaperon Rouge. 1930: L'Age d'or. 1934: La Pomme de terre. 1938: Mollenard. 1941: Jeunes Timides. 1942: Félicie Nanteuil.

Films as director and actor: 1928: Souvenirs de Paris – Paris Express (+ *st/w*; *co-d Marcel Duhamel*). 1932: L'Affaire est dans le sac (*d only*). 1933: Monsieur Cordon (*d only*). 1935: Le Commissaire est bon enfant – Le Gendarme est sans pitié (+ *co-s/w*; *co-d Jacques Becker*). 1943: Adieu Léonard (+ *st/co-d*). 1947: Voyage-Surprise (+ *st/co-s*). 1958: Paris mange son pain. 1959: Paris la Belle (+ *co-s*).

PREVIN, Andre

Composer. Berlin 1929–

Musical studies. 1939: to USA; studied under Joseph Achron in Los Angeles, then Castelnuovo-Tedesco. From 1949: film composer mainly for MGM. 1950–51: US Army service. 1968: appointed principal conductor of the London Symphony Orchestra. 1969: additional songs for *Paint Your Wagon*. 1970: married Mia Farrow. Oscars for scoring *Gigi* (1958) and *Porgy and Bess* (1959, with Ken Darby). Also scored *Kismet* (1955), *Silk Stockings* (1957), *Bells are Ringing* (1960), and *My Fair Lady* (1964).

Films as composer include: 1948: The Sun Comes Up. 1949: Tension; Border Incident; Shadow on the Wall; Scene of the Crime. 1950: Kim; The Outriders. 1953: The Girl who had Everything. 1954: Bad Day at Black Rock. 1956: The Fastest Gun Alive; Invitation to the Dance (*co*). 1957: House of Numbers; Designing Woman. 1960: Elmer Gantry; The Subterraneans; Who was that Lady? 1961: All in a Night's Work; One, Two, Three. 1962: The Four Horsemen of the Apocalypse; Long Day's Journey into Night; Two for the Seesaw. 1963: Irma la Douce. 1964: Kiss Me, Stupid; Dead Ringer; Goodbye Charlie. 1967: Valley of the Dolls.

PRICE, Vincent

Actor. St Louis, Missouri 1911–

Yale and London Universities. Intended to teach, but went into theatre. 1935: in London production of 'Chicago'; led to part of Albert in 'Victoria Regina' in London and on Broadway. 1938: first film as actor *Service DeLuxe*. Art collector; advisor on art buying to Sears Roebuck Co.; lecturer on art. Also TV series on cooking.

Films as actor include: 1939: The Private Lives of Elizabeth and Essex. 1940: Green Hell. 1941: Hudson's Bay. 1943: The Song of Bernadette. 1944: The Eve of St Mark; Buffalo Bill; Wilson; Laura; The Keys of the Kingdom. 1945: A Royal Scandal. 1946: Leave Her to Heaven; Dragonwyck. 1947: Moss Rose; The Long Night; The Web. 1948: The Three Musketeers; Rogue's Regiment. 1949: The Bribe. 1950: The Baron of Arizona. 1951: His Kind of Woman. 1952: The Las Vegas Story. 1953: House of Wax. 1954: Casanova's Big Night; The Mad Magician. 1955: The Son of Sinbad. 1956: Serenade; While the City Sleeps; The Ten Commandments. 1958: The Fly; The House on Haunted Hill. 1959: The Big Circus; The Tingler. 1960: The Fall of the House of Usher. 1961: The Pit and the Pendulum. 1962: Tower of London. 1963: The Haunted Palace; The Raven. 1964: The Masque of the Red Death; The Tomb of Ligeia; The Comedy of Terrors. 1965: City in the Sea; Dr Goldfoot and the Bikini Machine. 1969: The Trouble with Girls.

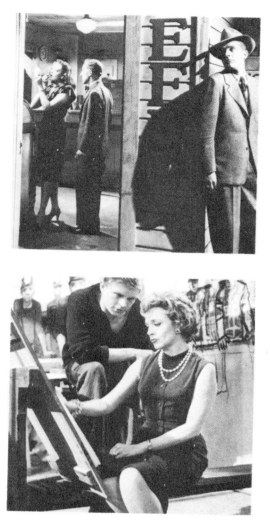

Linda Darnell, Percy Kilbright and Dana Andrews in Fallen Angel, *directed by Otto Preminger.*
Hardy Kruger and Micheline Presle in Joseph Losey's Blind Date.
Clifton Webb, Gene Tierney, Vincent Price and Judith Anderson in Laura, *directed and produced by Otto Preminger.*

PRIESTLEY, J. B.

Writer. Bradford, Yorkshire 1894–

Father a schoolmaster. Educated in Bradford, then Trinity Hall, Cambridge. 1914–19: military service, commissioned and wounded. From 1922: author. Journalist. 1931: in collaboration dramatised his novel 'The Good Companions' (filmed 1933 and 1957). 1932: first film adaptation of his work *The Old Dark House* based on his novel 'Benighted' (remade 1963). First of his plays to be filmed 'Dangerous Corner', in 1934. 1936–37: president of P.E.N. Club, London. Director of two London theatres; own production company for over 30 plays. 1939: first film as writer. Contributions to BBC radio include 'Postscripts 1940'. Chairman of 1941 Committee on War Aims. 1944: became president of Screenwriters Association. 1947–48: chairman of UNESCO International Theatre Institute Conference in Paris and Prague. 1948: chairman of British Theatre Conference. 1949: president of International Theatre Institute. 1954: *An Inspector Calls* adapted from his play by Desmond Davis. 1963: assisted in dramatisation of Iris Murdoch's 'A Severed Head'. 1965–67: member of National Theatre Board. Novels include 'Angel Pavement' (1930). Plays include 'Laburnum Grove' (1933). TV plays include 'Now Let Him Go', 'The Stone Faces', 'Doomsday for Dyson'. Wrote libretto 'The Olympians'. Other writings include 'The Art of the Dramatist' (1957), 'Literature and Western Man' (1960), 'Charles Dickens: A Pictorial Biography' (1964), 'Man and Time' (1964), 'Essays of Five Decades' (1969), 'The Prince of Pleasure' (1969). Wrote plays 'Dragon's Mouth' and 'The White Countess' in collaboration with archaeologist and writer Jacquetta Hawkes, whom he married in 1953.

Films as writer: 1939: Jamaica Inn (*co*). 1942: The Foreman Went to France. 1950: Last Holiday (+ *co-p*).

PRINZ, LeRoy

Choreographer and director. St Joseph, Missouri 1895–

Ran away from home at 15 to join French Foreign Legion. World War I: served in French aviation corps and 94th Aerial Squad. After war, directed dances at the Folies Bergère, Paris. 1920: to Mexico; trained student aviators. 1925: flew US Air Mail. From early 1930s worked as dance director in Hollywood. Choreographer with Paramount until 1941. From 1943: worked mainly for Warners. Directed 2 films in the 1940s, one of them a short. Production executive in films and theatre. 1967: president, Theatre of the Pacific, Honolulu. Oscar for short subject (2-reels), *A Boy and His Dog* (1946).

Films as choreographer include: 1932: The Sign of the Cross. 1934: Bolero; Come on Marines!; She Loves Me Not; Murder at the Vanities; Cleopatra. 1935: All the King's Horses; The Crusades. 1936: Anything Goes; Show Boat. 1937: Mountain Music; Artists and Models; High, Wide and Handsome; Waikiki Wedding. 1938: Artists and Models Abroad; Give Me a Sailor; Stolen Heaven. 1939: Zaza; The Great Victor Herbert; The Magnificent Fraud; Man About Town; Never Say Die; Union Pacific; Midnight. 1940: Buck Benny Rides Again; Road to Singapore. 1941: Aloma of the South Seas. 1943: Yankee Doodle Dandy;

Mission to Moscow; Thank Your Lucky Stars. 1944: Shine on Harvest Moon. 1945: The Horn Blows at Midnight; Rhapsody in Blue; Hollywood Canteen. 1946: The Time, the Place and the Girl; Night and Day; San Antonio. 1947: Cheyenne; Humoresque; My Wild Irish Rose; Pursued. 1956: The Ten Commandments (*co*). 1957: The Helen Morgan Story; Sayonara. 1958: South Pacific.

Films as director: 1941: All-American Co-Ed (+ *co-p/co-st*). 1946: A Boy and His Dog.

PROKOFIEV, Sergei

Composer. Ekaterinoslav, Russia 1891–1953 Moscow

1918: left Russia for concert tours in USA and Europe. 1920: settled in France, working with e.g. Sergei Diaghilev. 1930: in Paris wrote music for 4 shorts for Abram Room's Committee on sound films. 1932: returned to Russia. 1934: first feature as composer *Poruchik Kizhe*. 1938–45: collaboration with Sergei Eisenstein, including unmade projects. Music from his scores transposed for other films including *Make Mine Music* (1946), *The Iron Curtain* (1948). 1954 and 1961: ballets 'Romeo and Juliet' and 'Cinderella' filmed in Russia.

PROTAZONOV, Yakov

Director. Moscow 1881–1945 Moscow

Stage actor. 1909: first film as actor. From 1911: director. Worked in distribution offices of Thiemann and Reinhard. 1912: fiction film about Leo Tolstoy previewed for Tolstoy's relatives; Countess Alexandra Tolstoy objected to the film, so shown publicly only outside Russia. 1913: directed most of Thiemann and Reinhard's 'Golden Series' including *Klyuchi schastya* in collaboration with Vladimir Gardin; it was greatest bioscope success in pre-Revolutionary Russia. 1913–15: several films in collaboration with Gardin. 1915–19: directed Ivan Mozhukhin 26 times. Many literary adaptations. 1920: with Mozhukhin and technicians to Paris; joined 'La Société Russe Paul Thiemann'. For Thiemann studio directed e.g. *Le Sens de la mort* (1922) in which René Clair acted; also worked for Josef Yermoliev's company in Paris and for Ufa in Berlin. 1924: first film on return to Russia *Aelita*. 1928: Vsevolod Meyerhold acted in *Belyi Orel*, his only surviving film performance. 1929: made *Chiny i Lyudi*, first Soviet film adaptation of Anton Chekhov. Made over 80 films.

Films as director include (complete from 1921): 1911: Pesnya katorzhanina – The Prisoner's Song (+ *s*). 1912: Anfisa; Ukhod velikovo Startsa – Departure of a Grand Old Man. 1913: Kak khoroshi, kak svezhi byli rozy – How Fine, How Fresh the Roses Were (+ *s*); Razbitaya Vaza – The Broken Vase (+ *s*); Kak rydala dusha rebenka – How the Baby's Soul Sobs (+ *s*); Klyuchi Schastya – The Keys to Happiness (*co-d Vladimir Gardin*). 1914: Mimo zhizni – In the Presence of Life; Gnev Dionisa – The Wrath of Dionysus (+ *s*); Zhenshchina Zakhochet—Chorta obmorochit – The Lady Knows a Little of it—from the Devil. 1915: Peterburgskiye Trushchobi – Petersburg Slums (+ *co-s*; *co-d Vladimir Gardin*); Voina i mir – War and Peace (+ *co-s*; *co-d Vladimir Gardin*); Plebei – Plebeians (+ *s*); Nikolai Stavrogin (+ *co-s*). 1916: Grekh – Sin; Pikovaya Dama – The Queen of Spades; Zhenshchina s kinzhalom – Woman with a Dagger;

Plyaska smerti – The Dance of Death. 1917: Prokuror – Public Prosecutor; Andrei Kozhukhov (+ *s*); Satana Likuyushchii – Satan Triumphant (+ *s*); Proklyatye Milliony – Cursed Millions (+ *s*). 1918: Otets Sergii – Father Sergius. 1919: Tania korolevy – The Queen's Secret (+ *s*). 1921: Justice d'abord; Pour une nuit d'amour. 1922: Le Sens de la mort (+ *s*); L'Ombre du péché (+ *s*). 1923: L'Angoissante Aventure; Liebes Pilgerfahrt. 1924: Aelita. 1925: Yevo Prizyv – His Call – Broken Chains; Zakroishchik iz Torzhka – The Tailor from Torzhka. 1926: Protsess o Trokh Millionakh – The Trial of the Three Million (+ *co-s*). 1927: Chelovek iz restorana – The Restaurant Waiter; Sorok Pervyi – The Forty-First – The Isle of Death. 1928: Belyi Orel – The White Eagle (+ *co-s*); Don Diego i Pelageya – Don Diego and Pelagia. 1929: Chiny i Lyudi – Ranks and People (+ *co-s*; *co-d Mikhail Doller*). 1930: Prazdnik Svyatovo Yorgena – The Feast of Saint Jorgen (+ *s*). 1931: Tommi (+ *s*). 1934: Marionetki – Puppets (+ *s*). 1937: Bezpridannits – Without Dowry (+ *co-s*). 1938: Semiklassniki – Pupils of the Seventh Class (*co-d G. Levkoyer*). 1941: Salavat Yulayev. 1943: Nasreddin v Bukharye – Nasreddin in Bukhara.

PUDOVKIN, Vsevolod I.

Director. Penza, Russia 1893–1953 Riga, Russia

Physics and chemistry at University of Moscow. Russian artillery in World War I. 1915: wounded, taken prisoner. 3 years in prison camp. 1918: returned to Moscow. To 1929: chemist in laboratory of military plant. State Film School, pupil of Vladimir Gardin and Lev Kuleshov: assistant and actor for both. Followed Kuleshov to own studio, after disagreement with State School; pupils included Boris Barnet. 1921: last collaboration with Gardin, wrote *Golod . . . Golod . . . Golod* to create sympathy and funds for famine victims; with Kuleshov group acted in play based on Jack London's 'A Piece of Meat'. 1924: worked in many capacities on Kuleshov's *Neobychainiye Priklucheniya Mistera Vesta v Stranye Bolshevikov* and acted. 1925: worked similarly on *Luch smerti* then left Kuleshov to work for Mezhrabpom-Russ 1925–26: while making *Mekhanika golovnovo mozga* to popularise Ivan Pavlov's work in conditioned reflexes, also made short comedy *Shakhmatnaya Goryachka* using Kuxeshov's montage theories. Acted in own *Mat* (1926) and 5 of his subsequent films, and in films of other directors e.g. *Novyi Vavilon* (1929), *Zhivoi Trup* (1929). Began teaching at State Film School. European tour, including lectures in UK and Holland. 1933–34: wrote 'Film Acting'. 1940: with Esther Shub made *Kino za dvadtstat Let* documentary compilation. 1944: acted in *Ivan Grozny* (*I*). 1946: Central Committee condemned *Admiral Nakhimov*. 1947: own revised version released. Many of his films directed in collaboration. Many writings on film.

Films as director: 1921: Golod . . . Golod . . . Golod – Hunger . . . Hunger . . . Hunger (+ *co-s*; *co-d Vladimir Gardin*). 1925: Shakhmatnaya Goryachka – Chess Fever (*co-d Nikolai Shpikovsky*). 1926: Mekhanika golovnovo mozga – Mechanics of the Brain (+ *s*); Mat – Mother (+ *w*). 1927: Konets Sankt—Peterburga – The End of St Petersburg (+ *w*; *co-d Mikhail Doller*). 1928: Potomok Chingis Khan – Storm over Asia – The Heir to Genghis Khan (+ *w*). 1932: Prostoi Sluchai – Ochen Khorosho Zhivietsa – A Simple Case – Life is Good (*co-d Mikhail Doller*). 1933: Desertir –

Deserter (+w). 1938: Pobeda – Samyi Schastlivyi – Victory (co-d Mikhail Doller). 1939: Minin i Pozharskii – Minin and Pojarskü (co-d Mikhail Doller). 1940: Kino za dvadtsat let – Twenty Years of Soviet Cinema (+ co-d Esther Shub). 1941: Suvurov (co-d Mikhail Doller); Pir v Zhirmunka – Feast at Zhirmunka (co-d Mikhail Doller). 1942: Ubiitsy vykhodyat na dorogu – Murderers are at Large (+ co-s; co-d Yuri Tarich). 1943: Vo imya rodiny – In the Name of the Fatherland (+ co-s/w; co-d Dmitri Vasiliev). 1946: Admiral Nakhimov (r 1947; + w; co-d D. Vasiliev). 1948: Tri Vstrechi – Three Encounters (co-d Sergei Yutkevich, Alexander Ptushko). 1950: Zhukovsky (co-d D. Vasiliev). 1953: Vozvrashchenie Vasilya Bortnikova – The Return of Vassily Bortnikov.

PURVIANCE, Edna

Actress. Lovelock, Nevada 1894–1958 Hollywood
Spotted by Charles Chaplin. 1926: Chaplin produced *A Woman of the Sea*, but suppressed its release.

Films as actress include: 1915: A Night Out; The Champion; In the Park; The Jitney Elopement; The Tramp; By the Sea; A Woman; The Bank; Shanghaied; A Night in the Show. 1916: Charlie Chaplin's Burlesque on Carmen; Police; Triple Trouble; The Floorwalker; The Vagabond; The Count; Behind the Screen; The Rink. 1917: Easy Street; The Cure; The Immigrant. 1918: A Dog's Life; The Bond; Shoulder Arms. 1919: Sunnyside; A Day's Pleasure. 1921: The Kid; The Idle Class. 1922: Pay Day. 1923: The Pilgrim; A Woman of Paris. 1926: A Woman of the Sea (ur). 1952: Limelight.

Q

QUENEAU, Raymond

Writer. Le Havre, France 1903–
Father a businessman. University of Paris. 1927: emloyed at Comptoir National d'Escompte, Paris. 1936–38: journalist on L'Intransigeant. 1938: reader for Gallimard, publishers. 1941: Secretary General of Gallimard. 1950: first film as director *Le Lendemain*. 1954: first feature as writer. From 1955: director and editor of Encyclopédie de la Pléiade. 1959: novel 'Zazie dans le Métro' filmed. Also composer of songs.

Films as writer include: 1954: Knave of Hearts (co-di). 1956: La Mort en ce jardin (co). 1958: Le Chant du styrène. 1960: Un Couple (co).

QUILICI, Folco

Director. Ferrara, Italy 1930–
Son of journalist Nello Quilici. Law at Rome. Centro Sperimentale di Cinematografia. Expeditions to Africa, South America, Oceania, each producing film, book or article. Wrote for Epoca, Europeo, Life, Paris-Match. 1951: first short film as director. 1954: first feature documentary. 1954: assistant director and special location director on *Tam Tam Mayumba*. TV films include *Scoperta dell'Africa*. Books include 'I Viaggi del Capitano Cook' (1965), 'La Scoperta dell'Africa' (1966), 'Basilicata e Calabria viste del cielo' (1968).

Short films as director include: 1951: U-bu. 1952: Pinne e arpioni. 1954: Trofei d'Africa; Brazza; Storia di un elefante. 1957: Paul Gauguin.

Features as director: 1954: Sesto Continento – Blue Continent – Sixth Continent (+ co-c/w). 1956: L'Ultimo Paradiso – The Last Paradise (+ st/co-s). 1959: Dagli Appennini alle Ande (+ co-s). 1962: Ti-Koyo e il suo pescecane – Tiko and the Shark (+ co-s). 1963: Le Schiave esistono ancora – Slave Trade in the World Today (co-d Roberto Malenotti). 1971: Oceano (+ co-s).

QUIMBY, Fred

Producer. 1886–1965 Santa Monica, California
1918: designed, built and ran a cinema (The Iris Theater, Missoula, Montana). Worked in New York as general manager of Pathe distribution. 1921: Fred C. Quimby Inc produced *The World's Heavyweight Championship Contest Between Jack Dempsey and Georges Carpentier*. To Fox as manager of short subjects. 1926: to Metro in same capacity. 1931: started 'Tom and Jerry' series. 1937: supervised construction of MGM's cartoon studio. Headed short subject department and produced MGM cartoons until retirement in 1956. Series include Colonel Heeza Liar, Barney Bear, Droopy, Nibbles, Spike and Tyke. Directors he supervised include Tex Avery, William Hanna, Joseph Barbera. Oscars for *The Yankee Doodle Mouse* (1943), *Mouse Trouble* (1944), *Quiet Please* (1945), *The Cat Concerto* (1946), *The Little Orphan* (1948), *The Two Mouseketeers* (1951), *Johann Mouse* (1952).

QUINE, Richard

Director and actor. Detroit, Michigan 1920–
1931: on Broadway in 'Counsellor at Law'. 1933–35: film actor, then 6 years on stage: vaudeville, Broadway musicals, e.g. 'Very Warm for May' directed and designed by Vincente Minnelli, and 'My Sister Eileen'. Radio announcer. 1940–43: film actor. War service in US Coast Guard. 1948: co-produced his first film as director. 1948–50: film actor, dialogue director at Columbia, directed comedy shorts for Harry Cohn. From 1951: directed features only. 1952–62: Blake Edwards worked on scripts of 8 of his films, 5 in collaboration with him. 1955: they co-wrote story of Edwards' *Bring Your Smile Along*. 1956: they co-wrote story of Edwards' *He Laughed Last*. Films mainly for Columbia. Own production company.

Films as actor include: 1933: The World Changes; Counsellor at Law. 1934: Dames. 1941: Babes on Broadway. 1942: For Me and My Gal; Dr Gillespie's New Assistant; Stand By For Action. 1948: Words and Music. 1949: Command Decision; The Clay Pigeon. 1950: No Sad Songs For Me.

Features as director: 1948: Leather Gloves (+ co-p; co-d William Asher). 1951: Purple Heart Diary – No Time For Tears; Sunny Side of the Street. 1952: Sound Off (+ co-s); Rainbow 'Round My Shoulder (+ co-s). 1953: All Ashore (+ co-s); Cruisin' Down the River (+ co-st/co-s); Siren of Bagdad. 1954: Pushover; Drive a Crooked Road; So This is Paris. 1955: My Sister Eileen (+ co-s). 1956: The Solid Gold Cadillac. 1957: Full of Life; Operation Mad Ball. 1958: Bell, Book and Candle. 1959: It Happened to Jane – That Jane from Maine (+ p). 1960: Strangers When We Meet (+ co-p);

V. I. Pudovkin playing a merchant in Novyi Vavilon, *directed by Grigori Kozintsev and Leionid Trauberg. Kim Novak in Richard Quine's* Bell, Book and Candle. *Anthony Quinn in Nicholas Ray's* The Savage Innocents.

The World of Suzie Wong. 1962: The Notorious Landlady. 1962-63: Paris When It Sizzles (+ co-p). 1964: Sex and the Single Girl; How to Murder Your Wife. 1965: Synanon – Get Off My Back (+ p). 1966: Oh Dad, Poor Dad, Mamma's Hung You in the Closet and I'm Feelin' So Sad. 1967: Hotel. 1970: The Moonshine War.

QUINN, Anthony

Actor. Chihuahua, Mexico 1915–
Father cameraman for Selig. Appeared as child in a Selig film. Boxer, painter, labourer, acted in stock. 1936: first film as actor since childhood *Parole,* for Universal. 1937: married Katherine de Mille, adopted daughter of Cecil B. de Mille (separated 1965, then divorced). 1937–40: all films for Paramount. 1940–42: worked mainly for Warners. 1942–45: mainly for Fox. From 1945: with numerous companies. 1947: on stage in 'The Gentleman from Athens'. 1947–49: in Chicago company of 'A Streetcar Named Desire' for David O. Selznick. 1949–50: Southern tour of 'Born Yesterday'. 1958: took over direction of *The Buccaneer* on de Mille's illness. 1960: Broadway stage in 'Becket'. 1971: narration on *Arruza.* Creative head of 4 Star International. Oscars as supporting actor: *Viva Zapata!* (1952), *Lust for Life* (1956).

Films as actor include: 1937: Swing High, Swing Low; Waikiki Wedding; Daughter of Shanghai. 1938: The Buccaneer; Dangerous to Know; King of Alcatraz. 1939: Union Pacific; Television Spy. 1940: Emergency Squad; Road to Singapore; Parole Fixer; The Ghost Breakers; City for Conquest. 1941: Blood and Sand; Thieves Fall Out; They Died With Their Boots On. 1942: Larceny, Inc; The Road to Morocco; The Black Swan. 1943: The Ox-Bow Incident. 1944: Buffalo Bill; Roger Touhy, Gangster; Irish Eyes are Smiling. 1945: China Sky; Where Do We Go From Here; Back to Bataan. 1947: California; Black Gold. 1951: The Brave Bulls; Mask of the Avenger. 1952: Viva Zapata!; The World in His Arms; The Brigand. 1953: Seminole; City Beneath the Sea; Ride, Vaquero!; Blowing Wild. 1954: The Long Wait. 1955: Ulisse; The Magnificent Matador. 1956: Lust for Life; Man from Del Rio; The Wild Party. 1957: The River's Edge; Notre Dame de Paris; Wild is the Wind. 1958: Hot Spell; Last Train from Gun Hill. 1959: Warlock. 1960: Heller in Pink Tights; Portrait in Black; The Savage Innocents. 1961: The Guns of Navarone. 1962: Barabbas; Requiem for a Heavyweight; Lawrence of Arabia. 1964: Behold a Pale Horse; Der Besuch. 1965: Zorba the Greek; A High Wind in Jamaica. 1966: Lost Command. 1967: The Happening; L'Avventuriero – The Rover. 1968: The Shoes of the Fisherman (ur); La Bataille de San Sebastian. 1969: A Dream of Kings; The Secret of Santa Vittoria. 1970: R.P.M.; Flap.

R

RABIER, Jean

Cinematographer. 1927–
Industrial designer. After Liberation of France taught film at Conservatoire des Arts et Métiers. From 1948: camera operator. 1951–62: directed and photographed shorts and documentaries, including medical films made in Africa. Assistant and operator Henri Decaë. 1960: first film as cinematographer *Les Godelureaux.*

Films as cinematographer include: 1960: Les Godelureaux. 1961: Cléo de 5 à 7; Les Sept Péchés Capitaux *ep* L'Avarice, 1962: L'Oeil du malin; Ophélia; Landru; La Baie des anges; Rogopag *ep* Le Nouveau Monde. 1963: Les Plus Belles Escroqueries du monde *ep* L'Homme qui vendit la Tour Eiffel. 1964: Les Parapluies de Cherbourg; Le Tigre aime la chair fraîche; Le Bonheur (co); Paris vu par *ep* La Muette. 1965: Marie Chantal contre le docteur Kha; Le Tigre se parfume à la dynamite. 1966: La Ligne de Démarcation; Le Scandale. 1967: La Route de Corinthe. 1968: Les Biches; La Femme Infidèle. 1969: Que la bête meure; Le Boucher. 1970: La Rupture. 1971: Juste avant la nuit; La Décade Prodigieuse.

RACKIN, Martin

Writer. New York 1918–
Father operated silk mill in New Jersey, died when son was 11. Working weekends to augment family income, delivered hats; encouraged by a customer, Damon Runyon, continued studies while working evenings as copy boy at New York Mirror. After graduation worked for publicist, then returned to Mirror as assistant nightclub columnist. Then public relations director and story writer. Also wrote material for Red Skelton, and was co-author of a novel bought by Paramount. After 2 years with Ripley, went to RKO as writer. After 4 years in US Air Force, 3-year RKO contract. Then 2 years writing and directing 'The Red Skelton Show'. Producer at Warners. 1960: head of production at Paramount.

Films as producer include: 1957: The Helen Morgan Story. 1958: Darby's Rangers; Fort Dobbs; The Deep Six (+ co-s). 1959: The Horse Soldiers (+ co-p; + co-s).

Films as writer include: 1947: Desperate (ad). 1948: Fighter Squadron (ad). 1950: Three Secrets. 1951: The Enforcer (+ st); Distant Drums (co). 1955: Long John Silver (+ st). 1956: Lisbon (st); Hell on Frisco Bay (co); Santiago (co-s/fn). 1957: The Big Land (co). 1960: North to Alaska (co).

RADEMAKERS, Fons

Director. Rosendaal, Holland 1921–
Academy of Dramatic Art, Amsterdam. From 1940: worked as actor including appearance in Jacques Becker's Geneva production of 'Crime and Punishment'. After World War II, directed in theatre, e.g. 'Dantons Tod'. 1955–56: travelled in Europe working e.g. on *Eléna et les hommes, Il Tetto, Man in the Sky.* Further work as stage director. 1958: first film as director.

Films as director include: 1958: Dorp aan de riveir – Doctor in the Village. 1960: Makkers staakt uw wild geraas – That Joyous Eve. 1961: Het Mes – The Knife. 1963: Als twee druppels water – The Spitting Image – The Dark Room of Damocles. 1966: De Dans van de reiger – The Dance of the Heron. 1971: Mira (+ co-p/w).

RADOK, Alfred

Director. Kolodeje, Czechoslovakia 1914–
Philosophy at Prague University. Art critic and journalist. 1947: artistic advisor on *Parohy.* 1949: first film as director. Stage direction includes work in Pilsen and at Prague National Theatre. 1958: Magic Lantern programme at Expo 58; subsequently worked only in theatre. 1958 and 1960: artistic director of Laterna Magica experimental theatre. 1961: director at Prague municipal theatre.

Films as director: 1949: Daleká Cesta – Distant Journey (+ co-s). 1952: Divotvorny Klobouk – The Magic Hat (+ s). 1957: Dědeček Automobil – Old Man Motor Car (+ co-s).

RAFT, George

(George Ranft) Actor. New York 1903–
Boxer, dancer. Member of Capone gang, who financed his attempts to enter films; vaudeville then nightclubs. First film as actor *Hush Money* (1932). Also TV. To UK on retirement, but later banned by Immigration Authorities.

Films as actor include: 1931: Scarface, Shame of the Nation; Night After Night; If I Had a Million *ep* The Forger; Taxi. 1933: The Bowery. 1934: Bolero. 1935: Every Night at Eight; The Glass Key; She Couldn't Take It. 1936: It Had to Happen. 1937: Souls at Sea. 1938: Spawn of the North; You and Me. 1939: Each Dawn I Die; I Stole a Million; Invisible Stripes. 1940: The House Across the Bay; They Drive By Night. 1941: Manpower. 1943: Background to Danger. 1945: Nob Hill. 1949: Red Light; Johnny Allegro; Outpost in Morocco; A Dangerous Profession. 1951: Lucky Nick Cain. 1953: The Man from Cairo. 1954: Rogue Cop; Black Widow. 1956: Around the World in 80 Days. 1959: Some Like It Hot. 1961: The Ladies' Man. 1964: The Patsy.

RAIMU

(Jules Muraire) Actor. Toulon, France 1883–1946 Paris
Music-hall extra at Toulon Casino. Appeared in variety shows and café concerts. At Cigale and Folies Bergère. Appeared in some of the earliest French films. 1930: in revue with Sacha Guitry. Brief period with Comédie Française. 1931: directed by Guitry in *Le Blanc et le Noir.*

Films as actor include: 1910: L'Homme Nu. 1932: Fanny. 1943: Tartarin de Tarascon. 1936: César. 1937: Un Carnet de bal. 1938: La Femme du boulanger. 1940: La Fille du puisatier; Untel père et fils. 1942: Le Bienfaiteur; Les Inconnus dans la maison. 1943: Le Colonel Chabert. 1945: Les Greux au paradis. 1946: L'Homme au chapeau ronde.

RAINER, Luise

Actress. Vienna 1912–
1928: stage début in Düsseldorf. Member of Max Reinhardt's company in Berlin. 1930: first film *Ja, der Himmel uber Wien.* 1935: to USA made first American film *Escapade.* 1939: on London stage in 'Behold the Bride'. 1942: New York stage in 'A Kiss for Cinderella'. All American films for MGM, except last film *Hostages* (1943) for Paramount. Left Holly-

wood and continued on stage e.g. in 'Joan of Lorraine', 'The Circle of Chalk', 'The Lady from the Sea'. Also TV. Oscars for *The Great Ziegfeld* (1936), *The Good Earth* (1937). Married playwright and screenwriter Clifford Odets (1937–40, divorced).

Films as actress include: 1932: Sehnsucht 202. 1933: Heut' kommt's drauf an. 1937: Big City; The Emperor's Candlesticks. 1938: The Great Waltz; The Toy Wife.

RAINS, Claude

Actor. London 1889–1967 Sandwich, New Hampshire
First stage appearance at 11. Worked as call-boy, prompter, assistant stage manager, stage manager, actor in London West End theatres. 1911–12: toured Australia. 1913: London stage. 1914: stage manager with Harley Granville-Barker on tour of USA. World War I: served in London Scottish Regiment; Captain. 1922–26: professor and tutor at Royal Academy of Dramatic Art, London. 1933: film début in title role of *The Invisible Man*. 1938: naturalised American citizen. To 1944: most films for Warners. From 1945: with various companies. Much stage work; also radio. Married 6 times; first wife (from 1913) actress Isabel Jeans.

Films as actor include: 1934: Crime without Passion. 1936: Anthony Adverse; Hearts Divided. 1937: Stolen Holiday; The Prince and the Pauper; They Won't Forget. 1938: Gold is Where You Find It; The Adventures of Robin Hood; White Banners; Four Daughters. 1939: They Made Me a Criminal; Juarez; Daughters Courageous; Mr Smith Goes to Washington. 1940: Four Wives; The Sea Hawk. 1941: Four Mothers; King's Row. 1942: Now, Voyager. 1943: Casablanca; Forever and a Day. 1944: Passage to Marseille. 1945: This Love of Ours; Caesar and Cleopatra. 1946: Notorious. 1947: The Unsuspected. 1949: The Passionate Friends; Song of Surrender; Rope of Sand. 1950: Where Danger Lives. 1956: Lisbon. 1962: Lawrence of Arabia. 1965: The Greatest Story Ever Told.

RAKSIN, David

Composer. Philadelphia 1912–
Father ran a music store and conducted orchestra for silent films. Worked in dance bands and resident orchestra of CBS station at Philadelphia while at University of Pennsylvania. At 21 to New York; played in and arranged for dance bands, including Benny Goodman's. 1934: under contract to music publishers. 1936: first film work, 5 months' collaboration with Alfred Newman on Charles Chaplin's score for *Modern Times*. From 1936: wrote over 100 film scores. When Arnold Schoenberg moved to Los Angeles, Raksin studied with him.

Films as composer include: 1944: Laura. 1945: Fallen Angel. 1947: Daisy Kenyon; The Secret Life of Walter Mitty; Forever Amber. 1950: The Next Voice You Hear. 1951: Across the Wide Missouri. 1952: The Bad and the Beautiful; Pat and Mike. 1954: Apache; The Big Combo. 1956: Bigger than Life; Jubal (co). 1957: Until They Sail. 1958: Separate Tables. 1959: Al Capone. 1960: Pay or Die. 1962: Too Late Blues; Two Weeks in Another Town. 1964: Invitation to a Gunfighter; The Patsy. 1965: Sylvia.

RANDALL, Tony

Actor. Tulsa, Oklahoma 1924–
Northwestern University. Stage training under Sanford Meisner, Martha Graham and Henry Jacobi. Radio drama. 1941: stage début in 'Circle of Chalk'. 1942–46: US Army. On Broadway in 'Oh, Men! Oh, Women!' and repeated role in film (1957). On Broadway in 'Oh, Captain' and toured in 'Inherit the Wind'. Also TV e.g. a leading part in series 'The Odd Couple'.

Films as actor include: 1957: Will Success Spoil Rock Hunter?; No Down Payment. 1959: Pillow Talk; The Mating Game. 1960: The Adventures of Huckleberry Finn; Let's Make Love. 1962: Boys' Night Out; Lover Come Back. 1963: Island of Love. 1964: The 7 Faces of Dr Lao; Send Me No Flowers. 1966: The Alphabet Murders. 1968: Hello Down There.

RANK, J. Arthur (Lord)

Industrialist. Hull, Yorkshire 1888–1972 Costa Brava, Spain
School in Cambridge: left at 17. World War I: Ambulance Corps in France. Managed father's flour mills. From 1933: financed religious shorts. Founded Religious Film Society. Extended activities to commercial industry. 1935: founded British National Pictures. Acquired 25% interest in Universal. Formed General Film Distributors and General Finance Cinema Corporation. Acquired control of Gaumont-British and subsidiaries, then of Odeon Theatres. 1946: group of companies became Rank Organisation controlling the major part of British exhibition. In Canada acquired Odeon circuit. In USA formed Eagle-Lion Distributors. Controlled 70 companies, operated in 60 countries. 1952: biography 'Mr Rank' written by Alan Wood. 1953: transferred controlling interest in Rank Organisation to trustees to ensure control and organisation remain in British hands. Sold shares in Universal; films became lesser part of business interests; many British cinemas converted for other uses. 1957: raised to peerage.

RANODY, László

Director. South Hungary 1919–
Studied film at Academy for Dramatic Art, Budapest. 1942: diploma in law. Became artistic director of Hungarian Film Studios. Technical advisor on several films. 1950: first film as director.

Films as director: 1950: Csillagosok – Stars (+ *co-s, ur*). 1954: Hintónjáró szerelem – Love Travels by Coach. 1955: Szakadék – Discord. 1957: A Tettes Ismeretlen – Danse Macabre. 1959: Akiket a pacsirta elkísér – For Whom the Larks Sing. 1960: Légy jó mindhalálig – Be Good unto Death. 1964: Pacsirta – Skylark. 1966: Aranysárkány – The Golden Kite.

RAPEE, Erno

Composer. Budapest, Hungary 1891–
Conductor of orchestra in Rialto Movie Palace, New York when Hugo Reisenfeld its director. Composed scores to accompany films shown there and at Roxy Theatre. 1924: his compilation 'Moods and Motives for Motion Pictures' published, a guide for pianists, organists and leaders of small orchestras in cinemas. 1926: wrote 'Charmaine' for *What Price Glory?*,

George Raft (centre) in Billy Wilder's Some Like It Hot.
William Powell and Luise Rainer in The Emperor's Candlesticks.
Tony Randall in Frank Tashlin's Will Success Spoil Rock Hunter?

included it in score used. 1927: included his song 'Diane' in score for first-run engagement of *Seventh Heaven*; also included in score recorded for sound release. 1928: co-wrote theme of one of earliest sound films *Four Sons*. 1931: moved into work for radio.

Films as composer include: 1923: Robin Hood. 1924: The Iron Horse. 1926: What Price Glory? (*co*). 1927: Seventh Heaven (*co*).

RAPHAELSON, Samson

Writer. New York 1896–
University of Illinois. Taught English literature. Crime reporter on New York Times. Worked in advertising. Films scripted by others from his plays include *The Jazz Singer* (1927 and 1952), *Accent on Youth* (1935), *Mr Music* (1951) and *Hilda Crane* (1956). *Skylark* (1941) was adapted from his novel 'The Streamlined Heart' and play 'Skylark'; *Bannerline* (1951) was from his short story.

Films as writer include: 1931: The Smiling Lieutenant (*co*). 1932: One Hour with You; The Man I Killed (*co*); Trouble in Paradise. 1934: The Merry Widow (*co*); Caravan; Servants' Entrance. 1937: The Last of Mrs Cheyney (*co*); Angel. 1940: The Shop Around the Corner. 1941: Suspicion (*co*). 1943: Heaven Can Wait. 1945: The Harvey Girls (*co*). 1947: Green Dolphin Street. 1948: That Lady in Ermine. 1949: In the Good Old Summertime. 1953: Main Street to Broadway.

RAPPENEAU, Jean-Paul

Director and writer. Auxerre, France 1932–
Studied law. From 1952: worked as 2nd, then 1st assistant on features, directed by e.g. Jean Dréville. 1955–57: assistant director, later production director on shorts *Les biens de ce monde* and *Appelez le 17* (both directed by Edouard Molinaro), *Six Moins plus tard* and *Chemin de lumière*. 1957: first short film as writer *Entre la terre et le ciel*. 1958: wrote and directed short, *Chronique Provincial*. 1959: with Jacques Becker worked on script of *Trois Mousquetaires,* unfinished because of Becker's death. 1965: first feature as director.

Films as writer include: 1959: Signé Arsène Lupin; La Française et l'amour *ep* Le Mariage (*co*). 1960: Zazie dans le métro (*ad/di*). 1961: Vie Privée (*co*). 1962: Combat dans l'île (*di*); L'Homme de Rio (*co*). 1964: La Fabuleuse Aventure de Marco Polo (*co-ad*). 1965: La Vie de château – Château Life (*+ co-s*; *d*). 1971: Les Mariés de l'an II (*s/co-ad*; *+ d*).

RAPPER, Irving

Director. London 1898–
Went to New York at 8. While at New York University, stage director with Washington Square Players. Subsequent stage direction included 'The Late Christopher Bean' and 'Firebird' on Broadway. From 1936: dialogue director at Warners e.g. on *The Life of Emile Zola* (1937), Michael Curtiz's *Four Daughters* (1938). *Juarez* (1939), *The Story of Dr Ehrlich's Magic Bullet* (1940). 1941–47: directed features for Warners. Then director for various companies. 1960–61: made 2 films in Italy.

Films as director: 1941: Shining Victory; One Foot in Heaven (*+ co-p*). 1942: The Gay Sisters; Now, Voyager. 1944: The Adventures of Mark Twain. 1945: Rhapsody in Blue; The Corn is Green. 1946: Deception. 1947: The Voice of the Turtle. 1949: Anna Lucasta. 1950: The Glass Menagerie. 1952: Another Man's Poison. 1953: Forever Female; Bad for Each Other. 1956: Strange Intruder; The Brave One. 1958: Marjorie Morningstar. 1959: The Miracle. 1960: Giuseppe venduto dai fratelli – Sold into Egypt – Joseph and His Brethren (*co-d Luciano Ricci*). 1961: Ponzio Pilato – Pontius Pilate. 1970: The Christine Jorgensen Story.

RATHBONE, Sir Basil

Actor. Johannesburg, South Africa 1892–1967 New York
Repton school. Worked for Liverpool, London and Globe insurance companies. 1911: began stage career with Frank Benson's company at Ipswich. 1912: stage tour of USA, e.g. in Shakespeare. World War I: served with Liverpool Scottish Regiment; awarded Military Cross. In British films from early 1920s. 1925: first American film; star and co-author of 'Judas' on Broadway. With coming of sound alternated screen and Broadway appearances. Worked mainly in USA with occasional British films. From 1939: mainly films for Universal. From 1951: lecture and reading tours, e.g. on Elizabethan poetry and music at White House (1963). 1962: author of autobiography 'In and Out of Character'. 1962–67: several films for American International. Second wife (from 1962) screenwriter Ouida Bergère or Fitzmaurice.

Films as actor include: 1929: The Last of Mrs Cheyney. 1930: A Lady Surrenders; The Lady of Scandal. 1935: Captain Blood; The Personal History, Adventures, Experience, and Observations of David Copperfield, the Younger; Anna Karenina; The Last Days of Pompeii; A Tale of Two Cities. 1936: Romeo and Juliet; The Garden of Allah. 1937: Tovarich; Confession. 1938: The Adventures of Robin Hood; The Adventures of Marco Polo; If I Were King; The Dawn Patrol. 1939: Son of Frankenstein; Rio; Tower of London. 1940: Rhythm on the River; The Mark of Zorro. 1941: The Black Cat. 1942: Fingers at the Window; Crossroads. 1944: Bathing Beauty; Frenchman's Creek. 1946: Heartbeat. 1955: We're No Angels. 1956: The Court Jester. 1958: The Last Hurrah. 1962: Tales of Terror. 1964: The Comedy of Terrors. 1966: The Ghost in the Invisible Bikini.

RATOFF, Gregory

Director and actor. St Petersburg, Russia 1897–1960 Hollywood
Imperial School of Commerce, St Petersburg; University of St Petersburg Law School and Drama School. Began stage career as callboy at the Imperial Theatre, St Petersburg. World War I: served in Russian Army. 1918–22: left for Berlin, then toured Europe with stage company. 1922: to USA to appear on Broadway. 1929: film appearance in Vitaphone 1-reeler *Gregory Ratoff in For Sale*. From 1932: worked as film actor. From 1934: occasional screenwriting e.g. story for *You Can't Have Everything* (1937). 1936: first film as director. Most films for Fox but worked occasionally for e.g. Columbia, and various independents.

Films as actor include: 1932: Symphony of Six Million; What Price Hollywood? 1936: Under Two Flags; The Road to Glory. 1940: The Great Profile. 1950: All About Eve. 1957: The Sun Also Rises. 1959: Once More with Feeling. 1960: Exodus.

Films as director: 1936: Sins of Man (*co-d Otto Brower*). 1937: The Lancer Spy. 1939: Wife, Husband and Friend; Barricade; Rose of Washington Square; Hotel for Women; Day-Time Wife; Intermezzo. 1940: I was an Adventuress; Public Deb No 1. 1941: Adam Had Four Sons; The Men in Her Life (*+ p*); The Corsican Brothers. 1942: Two Yanks in Trinidad; Footlight Serenade. 1943: The Heat's On; Something to Shout About (*+ p*). 1944: Song of Russia; Irish Eyes are Smiling. 1945: Where do We Go from Here?; Paris Underground. 1946: Do You Love Me? 1947: Carnival in Costa Rica; Moss Rose. 1949: Black Magic. 1950: That Dangerous Age – If This Be Sin. 1951: Operation X – My Daughter Joy. 1953: Taxi. 1956: Abdullah's Harem (*+ p/w*). 1960: Oscar Wilde.

RATTIGAN, Terence

Writer. London 1911–
Harrow. Modern History at Trinity College, Oxford. 1934: wrote first play 'First Episode'. 1939: play 'French Without Tears' filmed. 1940: first film as writer in collaboration *Quiet Wedding*. A number of early script collaborations with Anatole de Grunwald. 1945: first production of his work in New York. 'O Mistress Mine'; wrote feature documentary on RAF *Journey Together*. 1947: in collaboration with Graham Greene wrote *Brighton Rock,* adapted from Greene's novel. 1960: wrote play 'Ross' based on life of T. E. Lawrence. Adapted several of own plays for films e.g. While the Sun Shines', 'The Winslow Boy', 'The Browning Version', 'The Deep Blue Sea', 'The Sleeping Prince' (as *The Prince and the Showgirl*), 'Separate Tables'. Several of his films directed by Anthony Asquith.

Films as writer include: 1942: Uncensored (*co*). 1945: The Way to the Stars (*+ co-st*). 1947: While the Sun Shines (*co*); Brighton Rock (*co*). 1948: The Winslow Boy (*co*, *+ co-st*). 1951: The Browning Version. 1952: The Sound Barrier (*+ st*). 1953: The Final Test (*+ st*). 1955: The Deep Blue Sea. 1957: The Prince and the Showgirl. 1958: Separate Tables (*co*). 1963: The VIP's (*+ st*). 1964: The Yellow Rolls-Royce (*+ st*). 1969: Goodbye, Mr Chips.

RAWSTHORNE, Alan

Composer. Haslingden, Lancashire 1905–71
Studied dentistry, then to Royal Manchester College of Music. 1932–34: taught at Dartington Hall. 1935: settled in London. 1937–39: composed for several Shell Film Unit documentaries. World War II: British Army. Work includes symphonies, concertos, choral and chamber works.

Films as composer include: 1939: The City. 1945: Burma Victory. 1946: The Captive Heart; School for Secrets. 1948: Saraband for Dead Lovers. 1951: Where No Vultures Fly. 1953: The Cruel Sea. 1954: West of Zanzibar; Lease of Life. 1956: The Man Who Never Was. 1958: Floods of Fear.

RAY, Aldo

(Aldo DaRe) Actor. Pen Argyl, Pennsylvania 1926–
Moved with family to Crockett, California at 2.
1942–46: US Navy. Resumed education; to
Berkeley, University of California. During election
campaign for sheriff of Crockett met David Miller
by chance, given role in *Saturday's Hero*. 8 months
as sheriff then Columbia contract. First films under
real name.

Films as actor include: 1951: Saturday's Hero; My
True Story. 1952: The Marrying Kind; Pat and
Mike. 1953: Miss Sadie Thompson. 1955: We're
No Angels; Three Stripes in the Sun. 1956: Night-
fall. 1957: Men in War. 1958: God's Little Acre;
The Naked and the Dead. 1959: The Siege of
Pinchgut. 1960: The Day They Robbed the Bank of
England. 1965: Sylvia. 1966: What Did You Do in
the War, Daddy? 1967: Welcome to Hard Times.
1968: The Green Berets.

RAY, Nicholas

(Raymond Nicholas Kienzle) Director. La Crosse,
Wisconsin 1911–
Won scholarship to Chicago University by writing
and directing series of radio programmes: studied
architecture under Frank Lloyd Wright. Toured as
stage actor and director in company with Elia Kazan,
acted in Kazan's first production as director.
Travelled widely in USA, then joined John Houseman's Phoenix Theatre company in New York. 1941:
when Houseman became chief of foreign service of
US Office of War Information's radio programmes,
took on Ray as director. 1943: wrote and directed
propaganda radio series 'Back Where I Come From'.
Stage producer and director, e.g. 'Lute Song' (1943).
1944–46: assistant on several films. including *A Tree
Grows in Brooklyn* (1945). 1946: directed Alfred
Drake on stage in 'Beggars' Holiday'. With
Houseman to CBS TV; adapted radio play 'Sorry,
Wrong Number' for TV. 1947: Houseman agreed to
produce *They Live By Night* only if Ray was writer
and director; first film as director. 1948–52: married
Gloria Grahame who acted in *A Woman's Secret*
(1949) and *In a Lonely Place* (1950). 1951: completed
Joseph von Sternberg's *Macao*. 1952: married
Elizabeth Utey who acted in *Party Girl* (1958). 1954:
associate producer on own *Johnny Guitar*. 1959: *The
Savage Innocents* partly made in Italy; remained in
Europe. Son is actor Anthony Ray who acted in *The
True Story of Jesse James*. 1947–52: worked mainly
for RKO; thereafter mainly for Paramount,
Columbia, Fox, Warners, MGM.

Films as director: 1948: They Live By Night – The
Twisted Road – Your Red Wagon (+ *ad*). 1949: A
Woman's Secret; Knock on any Door. 1950: In a
Lonely Place; Born to be Bad. 1951: On Dangerous
Ground; Flying Leathernecks. 1952: The Lusty Men;
Macao (*uc, co-d Joseph Von Sternberg*). 1954: Johnny
Guitar (+ *as-p*). 1955: Run for Cover; Rebel Without a
Cause (+ *st*). 1956: Hot Blood; Bigger Than Life.
1957: The True Story of Jesse James – The James
Brothers. 1958: Bitter Victory (+ *co-s*); Wind Across
the Everglades; Party Girl. 1960: The Savage Inno-
cents – Ombre Bianche (+ *s*). 1961: King of Kings.
1963: Fifty-Five Days at Peking.

RAY, Satyajit

Director. Calcutta, India 1921–
Son of Sukumar Ray, writer, painter, photographer. At
19 BA Hons (Econ), Calcutta University. 1940–42:
studied graphic art under Rabindranath Tagore. From
1943: employed in Calcutta branch of London advertising agency, became art director of the branch. Book
illustrator, designed book jackets, including Bibhuti
Banerji's novel 'Pather Panchali'. 1947: with
Chidananda Das Gupta founded Calcutta Film
Society. 1950: in London; on return met Jean Renoir
making *The River* (1951). Bought screen rights to
'Pather Panchali'; used own and wife's money until the
film taken over by West Bengal government in return
for producer's rights. Premiered at Museum of Modern
Art, New York. From 1961: composed music for his
films, also for James Ivory's *Shakespeare Wallah*
(1965).

Films as director: 1955: Pather Panchali – Song of the
Road (+ *s*). 1957: Aparajito – The Unvanquished (+ *s*).
1958: Paras Pathar – The Philosopher's Stone (+ *s*);
Jalsaghar – The Music Room (+ *s*). 1959: Apur Sansar
– The World of Apu (+ *s*). 1960: Devi – The Goddess
(+ *s*). 1961: Rabindranath Tagore (+ *s/n*); Teen Kanya
– Three Daughters – Two Daughters (+ *s/m*). 1962:
Kanchenjunga (+ *s/m*); Abhijan – Expedition (+ *s/m*).
1963: Mahanagar – The Big City (+ *m*). 1964:
Charulata – The Lonely Wife (+ *s/m*). 1965:
Kapurush-o-Mahapurush – The Coward and the Holy
Man (+ *s/m*). 1966: Nayak – The Hero (+ *s/m*). 1967:
Chiriakhana – The Menagerie – The Zoo (+ *s/m*). 1968:
Goupi Gyne, Bagha Byne – The Adventures of Goopy
and Bagha. 1970: Aranyer din Ratri – Days and Nights
in the Forest (+ *s/m*). 1971: Pratidwandi – Siddhartha
and the City – The Adversary (+ *s/m*).

REAGAN, Ronald

Actor. Tampico, Illinois 1912–
Radio sports announcer. 1937: first film *Love is on the
Air*. Acted in large number of films directed by Lewis
Seiler and Ray Enright. 1940–48: married to Jane
Wyman. All films for Warners until *Louisa* (1950) for
Universal; subsequently worked for numerous com-
panies. Films narrated include: *Beyond the Line of
Duty* (1942), *The Truth About Communism* (1963), *Let
the World Go Forth* (1965). From 1966: Republican
governor of California. Period as president of Screen
Actors' Guild.

Films as actor include: 1937: Hollywood Hotel; Swing
Your Lady. 1938: Boy Meets Girl; Cowboy from
Brooklyn; Brother Rat; Going Places. 1939: Dark
Victory; The Angels Wash Their Faces. 1940: Brother
Rat and a Baby; An Angel from Texas; Knute Rockne
– All American; Santa Fe Trail. 1941: The Bad Man;
Million Dollar Baby. 1942: King's Row; Juke Girl;
Desperate Journey. 1947: The Voice of the Turtle.
1948: Night Unto Night. 1949: John Loves Mary; It's
a Great Feeling; The Hasty Heart. 1951: Storm Warn-
ing. 1954: Prisoner of War; Cattle Queen of Montana.
1955: Tennessee's Partner. 1961: The Young Doctors
(*n only*). 1964: The Killers.

REDFORD, Robert

Actor. Santa Maria, California 1937–
University of Colorado and Prath Institute. Worked

Basil Rathbone and Greta Garbo in Anna Karenina.
directed by Clarence Brown.
Nicholas Ray directing The Savage Innocents.
Devi, *directed by Satyajit Ray.*

for IBM and Standard Oil. Studied acting at American Academy of Dramatic Art. 1958: stage debut in 'Tall Story'. 1962: first film. TV appearances include 'Alfred Hitchcock Presents', 'The Virginians'.

Films as actor: 1962: War Hunt. 1965: Situation Hopeless but not Serious; Inside Daisy Clover. 1966: The Chase; This Property is Condemned. 1967: Barefoot in the Park. 1969: Tell Them Willie Boy is Here; Butch Cassidy and the Sundance Kid; The Downhill Racer. 1970: Little Fauss and Big Halsy.

REDGRAVE, Sir Michael

Actor. Bristol, Gloucestershire 1908–

1931: Cambridge University. Actor-director in repertory. 1934: professional debut in 'Counsellor at Law'. 1936: at the Old Vic in 'Love's Labours Lost'. 1937: TV debut in 'Romeo and Juliet'. 1938: first film as actor *The Lady Vanishes*. 1941–42: Royal Navy. From 1942: stage actor and director. 1948: first Broadway appearance, in 'Macbeth'. 1950: in 'Hamlet' at Elsinore. Acted at Shakespeare Memorial Theatre. 1952: awarded CBE. 1954–57: governor of British Film Institute. 1956: directed 'A Month in the Country', was actor-director in 'The Sleeping Prince'. 1957: founded Michael Redgrave Productions. 1959: knighted. European and Russian tours. 1961: on Broadway in 'The Complaisant Lover'. Books: 'The Actor's Ways and Means' (1953), 'Mask or Face' (1958), 'The Mountebank's Tale' (1959). Married actress Rachel Kempson, Children are actor Corin Redgrave and actresses Vanessa and Lynn Redgrave.

Films as actor include: 1939: The Stars Look Down. 1941: Kipps; The Big Blockade. 1942: Thunder Rock. 1945: The Way to the Stars. 1946: Dead of Night. 1947: Mourning Becomes Electra; Fame is the Spur; 1948: The Man Within; Secret Beyond the Door. 1951: The Browning Version. 1952: The Importance of Being Earnest. 1954: The Sea Shall Not Have Them; The Dambusters. 1955: Oh, Rosalinda!; The Confidential Report. 1956: 1984. 1957: Time Without Pity. 1958: The Quiet American; Behind the Mask. 1959: Shake Hands with the Devil; The Wreck of the Mary Deare. 1960: Behind the Mask. 1961: No, My Darling Daughter; The Innocents. 1962: The Loneliness of the Long Distance Runner. 1965: Young Cassidy; The Hill; The Heroes of Telemark. 1969: Oh! What a Lovely War; Goodbye, Mr Chips. 1971: The Go-Between; The Trojan Women; Nicholas and Alexandra.

REDGRAVE, Vanessa

Actress. London 1937–

Daughter of Sir Michael Redgrave and Rachel Kempson. Central School of Speech and Drama. 1957: in repertory at Frinton-on-sea; toured in 'Come on Jeeves'. 1958: first film. Subsequent stage appearances included 'As You Like It' with Royal Shakespeare Company, 'The Prime of Miss Jean Brodie' in London. 1962–67: married to Tony Richardson.

Films as actress: 1958: Behind the Mask. 1966: Morgan, A Suitable Case for Treatment; Blow-up; A Man for all Seasons. 1967: Tonite Let's all Make Love in London; The Sailor from Gibraltar; Camelot. 1968: Red and Blue; Isadora; The Charge of the Light Brigade; The Sea Gull. 1969: Oh! What a Lovely War. 1970: Dropout. 1971: The Devils; La Vacanza.

REED, Sir Carol

Director. London 1906–

Actor from 1923. 1927: joined Edgar Wallace as stage manager and actor; became Wallace's representative at British Lion on the production of Wallace films. 1930: produced Wallace's play 'On the Spot' in New York. 1932: to Ealing as dialogue director to producer and director Basil Dean. 1935: first feature as director. 1938: wrote story for *No Parking*. World War II: with Army Kinematograph Unit; made documentary *The New Lot* (1943) on which he based feature *The Way Ahead* (1944). 1952: knighted. From 1956: occasional films in USA. 1961: began *Mutiny on the Bounty*, replaced by Lewis Milestone. Oscar as Best Director for *Oliver!* (1968), which also received Oscar as Best Picture.

Films as director: 1935: Midshipman Easy; It Happened in Paris (*co-d Robert Wyler*). 1936: Laburnam Grove; Talk of the Devil (*+ st*). 1937: Who's Your Lady Friend? 1938: Bank Holiday; Penny Paradise. 1939: Climbing High; A Girl Must Live; The Stars Look Down. 1940: Night Train to Munich – Gestapo; The Girl in the News. 1941: Kipps; A Letter from Home. 1942: The Young Mr Pitt. 1943: The New Lot. 1944: The Way Ahead. 1945: The True Glory (*co-d Garson Kanin*). 1947: Odd Man Out (*+ co-p*). 1948: The Fallen Idol. 1949: The Third Man. 1951: Outcast of the Islands (*+ pc*). 1953: The Man Between (*+ pc*). 1955: A Kid for Two Farthings. 1956: Trapeze. 1958: The Key. 1960: Our Man in Havana (*+ p*). 1963: The Running Man (*+ p*). 1965: The Agony and the Ecstasy (*+ p*). 1968: Oliver! 1970: Flap – The Last Warrior.

REED, Donna

(Donna Mullenger) Denison, Iowa 1921–

1941: first film as actress *Babes on Broadway*, At first known as Donna Adams. To 1946: all films for MGM. Then mainly for Paramount, Columbia, Universal, MGM. 1953: Oscar as supporting actress for *From Here to Eternity*. Also TV.

Films as actress include: 1941: Shadow of the Thin Man. 1942: The Courtship of Andy Hardy; Eyes in the Night; Apache Trail. 1943: The Human Comedy; Thousands Cheer; The Man from Down Under. 1944: See Here, Private Hargrove; Mrs Parkington. 1945: The Picture of Dorian Gray; They Were Expendable. 1947: It's a Wonderful Life; Green Dolphin Street. 1948: Beyond Glory. 1951: Saturday's Hero. 1952: Scandal Sheet. 1953: Trouble Along the Way; Gun Fury. 1954: The Last Time I Saw Paris; They Rode West. 1955: The Far Horizons; Ransom! 1956: Backlash. 1957: Beyond Mombasa. 1958: The Whole Truth. 1960: Pepe.

REEVES, Steve

Actor. Glasgow, Montana 1926–

Winner of muscle contests; Mr America (1947), Mr World, Mr Universe; French award 'Le Plus Bel Athlète du Monde'. Wordless stage parts. 1954: small part in *Athena*; spotted by Italian producer Pietro Francisci. 1957: first major role.

Films as actor include: 1957: Le Fatiche di Ercole. 1958: Agi Murad, il diavolo bianco. 1959: Ercole e la regina di Lidia; Gli Ultimi Giorni di Pompeii; La Battaglia di Maratona. 1960: Morgan il pirata, Il Ladro di Bagdad. 1962: Il Figlio di Spartacus.

REGGIANI, Serge

Actor. Reggio nell Emilia, Italy 1922–

From 1928: France, Paris Conservatoire. 1938: first film. 1940: stage debut in 'Le Loup-garou'. Theatrical work includes 'Les Parents Terribles', 'Un Homme comme les autres', 'Les Séquestrés d'Altona', 'Britannicus'. Married actress Janine Darcey. Also TV and singing.

Films as actor include: 1939: Nuit de Décembre. 1942: Le Voyageur de la Toussaint. 1943: Le Carrefour des enfants perdus. 1946: Les Portes de la nuit. 1947: La Fleur de l'age (*uf*); Le Dessous des cartes. 1948: Manon; Les Amants de Vérone. 1949: Au royaume des cieux; Le Parfum de la dame en noir. 1950: La Ronde. 1951: Casque d'or. 1952: Secret People. 1953: Act of Love. 1955: Napoléon; Les Salauds vont en enfer. 1957: Echec au porteur; Les Misérables. 1958: Marie-Octobre. 1960: Tutti a casa. 1961: Paris Blues. 1962: Le Doulos. 1963: Il Gattopardo. 1966: Le 25e Heure. 1967: Les Aventuriers. 1968: Il Giorno della civetta.

REICHENBACH, Francois

Director. Paris 1922–

Classical and musical education at Lyceé Janson-de-Sailly, Bachot. With Philippe Gerard wrote songs for e.g. Edith Piaf. 1947–52: European technical advisor to American museums seeking new acquisitions; art critic. 1953: first film 16 mm short on Longchamps horse race. Took amateur films to producer Pierre Braunberger, his cousin, who encouraged him to turn professional. 1955: first professional film *New York Ballade*. 1967: collaborated on cinematography of *Carmen*. 1968: cinematographer in collaboration on Chris Marker's *La Sixième Face du Pentagone*. TV films include *Bardot en Amérique* (1965), *Orson Welles* (1966). 1970: Oscar for *Arthur Rubinstein: L'amour de la vie* (1968).

Short films as director include: 1955: New York Ballade (*+ c*); Visages de Paris (*+ c*); Impressions de New York (*+ c*). 1956: Houston, Texas (*+ c*); Novembre à Paris; Le Grand Sud. 1957: Au Pays de Porgy and Bess; L'Américain se détend; Les Marines (*+ co-c*); Carnaval à la Nouvelle Orléans; L'Eté Indien. 1962: Weekend en mer; Retour à New York; A la mémoire du rock; Scènes de la vie de café; L'Amérique Lunaire (*+ c*); Le Paris des photographes; Le Paris des mannequins; Jeu I (*co-d Dirk Sanders*). 1963: Artifices; Histoire d'un petit garcon devenu grand; Illuminations (*+ c*). 1964: Anges Gardiens. 1965: Dunoyer de Segonzac (*co-d Monique Lepeuve*); Lapique; East African Safari; Lomelin (*+ c*). 1966: Aurora. 1967: Le Professeur de piano; Impressions de Paris.

Features as director: 1960: L'Amerique Insolite – America Through the Keyhole (*+ co-s*). 1961: Un Coeur Gros comme ça (*+ co-c*). 1962: Un Bol d'air a loué – La Douceur du village (*+ co-c*). 1963: Les Amoureux du 'France' (*+ co-s/co-c*; *co-d Pierre Grimblat*). 1968: Treize Jours en France – Challenge in the Snow (+*co-s*; *co-d Claude Lelouch*); Arthur Rubinstein: L'amour de la vie – Love of Life (+*co-p/co-s/c*; *co-d Gérard Patris*); Soy Mexico (+*c*). 1969: L'Indiscret. 1971: Yehudi Menuhin–Chemin de la lumière (+*c*; *co-d Bernard Gavoty*); The Great Medicine Ball Caravan (+*co-p*).

REINHARDT, Gottfried

Director and producer. Berlin 1914–

Father Max Reinhardt; brother producer Wolfgang Reinhardt. Educated in Berlin; followed his father to USA in early 1930s. 1933: assisted Ernest Lubitsch on *Design for Living*. Assistant to Walter Wanger, then assistant to producer Bernard H. Hyman e.g. worked on *Saratoga* and *San Francisco*. Also wrote e.g. story in collaboration for *I Live My Life* (1935), story for *The Great Waltz* (1938), story in collaboration for *Bridal Suite* (1939), and musicals 'Rosalinda' and 'Helen of Troy' for Broadway. 1940: producer for MGM. 1952: first film as director. World War II: served in Signal Corps. MGM until 1954: then with independents, sometimes in Europe.

Films as producer include: 1940: Comrade X. 1941: Rage in Heaven; Two-Faced Woman. 1949: The Great Sinner. 1951: The Red Badge of Courage (+*cy*).

Films as director: 1952: Invitation. 1953: The Story of Three Loves *eps* The Jealous Lover; Equilibrium. 1954: Betrayed. 1959: Abschied von den Wolken – Rebel Flight to Cuba. 1961: Town Without Pity (+*p*). 1965: Situation Hopeless But Not Serious (+*p*).

REINHARDT, Max

Director. Vienna 1873–1943 Hollywood
1903: began as theatre director in Berlin, and always worked mainly in the theatre. 1920: founded Salzburg Festival. 1933: left Germany for USA when Hitler came to power. Ran theatre school in Hollywood. Directed 3 films: 2 in Germany and one in Hollywood. Son is Gottfried Reinhardt.

Films as director: 1913: Eine Venezianische Nacht; Insel der Seeligen. 1935: A Midsummer Night's Dream (*co-d William Dieterle*).

REINIGER, Lotte

Animator. Berlin 1899–

Studied with Max Reinhardt. 1916: silhouettes for credits on *Rübezahls Mochgeit*. From 1919: made animated films using cut-paper silhouettes, photographed on illuminated glass table. 1926: her first feature, using this technique, photographed by husband Carl Koch. 1930: collaborated on script and animation of *Die Jagd nach dem Gluck*. 1936: left Germany for Paris, then England. 1938: did 'Théâtre d'ombres' for *La Marseillaise* which Koch scripted in collaboration. Joined GPO Film Unit, later Crown Film Unit. Made series of films for BBC TV including 'The Gallant Little Tailor'.

Films as director: 1919: Das Ornament des verliebten Herzens. 1920: Amor und das standhafte Ehepaar. 1921: Der fliegende Koffer; Der Stern Von Bethlehem. 1922: Aschenputtel – Cinderella; Dornroschen. 1926: Die Geschichte des Prinzen Ahmed – Das Abenteuer des Prinzen Ahmed – The Adventures of Prince Achmed. 1928: Doktor Dolittle und seiner Tiere – Das Abenteuer des Doktor Doolittle – The Adventures of Dr Doolittle. 1930: Zehn Minuten Mozart. 1931: Harlekin. 1932: Sissi. 1933: Carmen (+*p*). 1934: Das Rollende Rad (+*p*); Der Graf von Carabas (+*p*); Das gestohlene Herz – The Stolen Heart (+*p*). 1935: Der kleine Schornsteinfeger – The Little Chimney Sweep (+*p*); Galathea (+*p*); Papageno (+*p*). 1936: The King's Breakfast. 1937: Tocher. 1939: Dream Circus (*uf*). L'Elisir d'Amore. 1944: Die Goldene Gans (*uf*). 1951: Mary's Birthday. 1953: Aladdin; The Magic Horse; Snow White and Rose Red. 1954: The Three Wishes; The Grasshopper and the Ant; The Frog Prince; The Gallant Little Tailor; The Sleeping Beauty; Caliph Stork. 1955: Hansel and Gretel; Thumbelina; Jack and the Beanstalk – Jack the Giant Killer. 1956: The Star of Bethlehem. 1957: La Belle Hélène. 1958: The Seraglio. 1960: The Pied Piper of Hamelin. 1961: The Frog Prince. 1962: Wee Sandy. 1963: Cinderella.

REIS, Irving

Director. New York 1906–53 Woodland Hills, California
Columbia University. Worked in engineering department of Columbia Broadcasting System. Designed sound filter and wrote radio play 'Meridian Seven' to test it. 1934–37: founded and in charge of Columbia Workshop; director, producer and writer of radio drama; gave Orson Welles his start as director on radio. 1938: began in films as writer under contract to Paramount e.g. story and script for *King of Alcatraz*. From 1940: director with RKO. World War II: military service. From 1948: director with various companies.

Films as director: 1940: One Crowded Night; I'm Still Alive. 1941: Footlight Fever; The Gay Falcon; A Date with the Falcon; Weekend for Three. 1942: The Falcon Takes Over; The Big Street. 1946: Crack Up. 1947: The Bachelor and the Bobby Soxer. 1948: All My Sons; Enchantment. 1949: Roseanna McCoy; Dancing in the Dark. 1950: Three Husbands; Of Men and Music. 1951: New Mexico. 1952: The Four Poster.

REISENFELD, Hugo

Composer. Vienna 1883–

Vienna Conservatory. Violinist in Vienna Philharmonic. 1907: to USA. 1907–11: concert master, Manhattan Opera. 1911–15: with Century Opera. Director of orchestra at Rialto Movie Palace, New York when Erno Rapee its conductor. Took over management and musical direction of Rialto and Rivoli cinemas. Composed scores for numerous films: used in other Broadway cinemas and elsewhere in USA. Score for *Beau Geste* (1926) used for sound re-issue in 1931. Head of musical productions at United Artists. 1933: wrote music for British film *The Wandering Jew*. From 1936: worked for Republic. Compositions include symphonies, ballets, operettas.

Films as composer include: 1920: Humoresque. 1923: The Covered Wagon (*co*); The Ten Commandments. 1926: Beau Geste; The Volga Boatmen. 1927: King of Kings. 1931: Tabu. 1933: Thunder over Mexico; The Wandering Jew. 1936: Hearts of Bondage.

Night Train to Munich, *directed by Carol Reed*.
Castle of the Living Dead, *directed by Michael Reeves*.
The legs of Steve Reeves, clutched by Sylva Koscina in Hercules Unchained.

REISZ, Karel

Director. Ostava, Czechoslovakia 1926–
Came to England at 12. Quaker school in Reading. World War II: fighter pilot in Czech RAF squadron. 1945–47: chemistry at Emmanuel College, Cambridge. 1947–49: teacher at Marylebone Grammar School. 1949–52: freelance writer and film critic; contributed to magazine Sequence from 1950, with Lindsay Anderson co-edited final issue (1952); author of book 'The Technique of Film Editing' (1953). 1952–55: in charge of programme planning for National Film Theatre. 1955: made first short film in collaboration with Tony Richardson. From 1956: films officer with Ford Motor Company; directed *We Are the Lambeth Boys*, co-produced Anderson's *Every Day Except Christmas* (1957) for Ford 'Look at Britain' series. 1956–59: one of the originators of Free Cinema programmes at National Film Theatre, which included both his documentaries. 1960: first feature as director. 1963: produced Anderson's *This Sporting Life*. Many commercials. Second wife actress Betsy Blair.

Films as director: 1955: Momma Don't Allow (+ *co-s*; *co-d* Tony Richardson). 1959: We Are the Lambeth Boys. 1960: Saturday Night and Sunday Morning. 1964: Night Must Fall (+ *co-p*). 1966: Morgan, a Suitable Case for Treatment. 1968: Isadora – The Loves of Isadora.

REMICK, Lee

Actress. Boston, Massachusetts 1935–
Mother actress Patricia Remick. 1944–54: ballet lessons with Ruth Swoboda. From 1954: studied modern dance with Charles Weidman. 1952: stage debut, danced in summer stock. 1953: on Broadway in 'Be Your Age'. 1952–54: summer stock in 'Brigadoon', 'Show Boat', 'Oklahoma'. 1953–57: about 40 TV shows, including 'All Expenses Paid' in which spotted by Elia Kazan for first film as actress *A Face in the Crowd*. 1956: on tour in 'The Seven Year Itch'. Directed on stage by Arthur Penn in 'Wait Until Dark.' TV work includes 'A Diamond as Big as the Ritz' (1955), 'Damn Yankees' (1967). Worked mainly for Fox and Columbia.

Films as actress include: 1958: The Long, Hot Summer; These Thousand Hills. 1959: Anatomy of a Murder. 1960: Wild River. 1961: Sanctuary. 1962: Experiment in Terror. 1963: Days of Wine and Roses; The Running Man. 1965: Baby, the Rain Must Fall; The Hallelujah Trail. 1968: The Detective; No Way to Treat a Lady. 1971: Sometimes a Great Notion.

RENNAHAN, Raymond

Cinematographer. Las Vegas 1896–
Began in films about 1917. Worked with National Film Corporation. From 1921: research in colour processes. By 1933: cinematographer in colour. 1934: photographed *La Cucaracha*, the first live-action short in 3-colour Technicolor. 1935: for same production company, Pioneer, photographed *Becky Sharp*, the first feature in 3-colour Technicolor. Since worked as cinematographer with various companies. Now in TV.

Films as cinematographer include: 1933: The Mystery of the Wax Museum. 1939: Drums along the Mohawk (*co*): Gone with the Wind (*co*). 1940: Maryland (*co*);

Chad Hanna (*co*). 1941: Blood and Sand (*co*). 1943: For Whom the Bell Tolls. 1944: Lady in the Dark; Up in Arms. 1945: Incendiary Blonde. 1946: Duel in the Sun (*co*). 1947: California; The Perils of Pauline; Unconquered. 1948: The Paleface. 1949: A Connecticut Yankee in King Arthur's Court. 1950: The White Tower; The Great Missouri Raid. 1951: Silver City; Warpath. 1952: Denver & Rio Grande. 1955: Stranger on Horseback; Lawless Street. 1956: 7th Cavalry. 1957: The Halliday Brand; The Guns of Fort Petticoat.

RENOIR, Claude

Cinematographer. Paris 1913–
Grandson of painter Auguste Renoir, son of Pierre Renoir, nephew of Jean Renoir. 1932: assistant on *La Nuit du carrefour* and *Boudu Sauvé des eaux*. 1934: first film as cinematographer *Toni*. Camera operator on *La Grande Illusion* (1937) and *La Bête Humaine* (1938) on which he was also assistant. 1938: assistant director on *La Marseillaise*. 1939: director of production on *La Règle du jeu*. 1942: in collaboration directed *Opera-Musette*. 2nd-unit cinematographer on *Circus World* (1964).

Films as cinematographer include: 1936: Une Partie de campagne (*co*). 1942: Opera-Musette (+ *co-d* René Lefèvre). 1947: Monsieur Vincent. 1948: L'Impasse des deux anges. 1949: Rendezvous de juillet. 1951: Knock; The River. 1952: The Green Glove. 1953: Le Carrozza d'oro; Maddalena. 1955: Madame Butterfly. 1956: Eléna et les hommes; Le Mystère Picasso. 1957: Les Sorcières de Salem. 1958: Une Vie; Les Tricheurs. 1960: Et mourir de plaisir. 1963: Symphonie pour un massacre. 1964: L'Insoumis; L'Enfer (*co*). 1968: Barbarella. 1970: La Dame dans l'auto avec des lunettes et un fosil. 1971: Les Mariés de l'an II; Le Casse: The Horsemen.

RENOIR, Jean

Director. Paris 1894–
Son of painter Auguste Renoir. Studied philosophy and maths. 1913: joined cavalry. 1915: joined *chasseurs alpins*, reaching *sous-lieutenant*, wounded. 1916: observer in flying corps, reaching Lieutenant, wounded. After war, work in ceramics. 1920: married Catherine Hessling, his father's model. 1924: financed *Catherine* in which his wife acted; first film as director, also produced and designed it; his wife acted in his first 3 films as director. 9 films photographed by Jean Bachelet, mainly in period 1924–28. 1929: co-wrote Alberto Cavalcanti's *Le Petit Chaperon Rouge* and acted with wife in Cavalcanti's *La P'tite Lili*. 1936: directed in collaboration and supervised *Une Vie est à nous* for Popular Front; abandoned *Une Partie de campagne* because of bad weather; assisted by Yves Allégret, Jacques Becker, Jacques Brunius, Henri Cartier-Bresson, Luchino Visconti; Jacques Prévert wrote script to convert it into feature, not used. 1937: wrote and spoke French commentary for *Spanish Earth*. 1939: to Italy to make *La Tosca* at request of Italian government and to teach at Centro Sperimentale; on outbreak of World War II returned to Paris, joined cinematographic service of French Army. 1940: returned to Italy, made first sequence of *La Tosca*; abandoned film when Italy joined war; completed by Karl Koch; divorced. 1941: to USA; first American film *Swamp Water* for Fox. Other American

features for RKO, MGM, United Artists. In New York directed *Salut à la France* (1944) in collaboration; also made government and instructional films. 1944: married script-girl Dido Freire, Cavalcanti's niece. Formed and abandoned company for theatre. 1950: to India to make *The River*. 1951: returned to Europe. 1953: made *Le Carosse d'or* in Italy. Directed 'Julius Caesar' on stage in Arles. Wrote play 'Orvet' and in 1955 directed Leslie Caron in it. 1958: re-edited *La Grande Illusion* (1937) into definitive version. 1961: made *Le Testament du Dr Cordelier* for French TV. Books: novel 'Les Cahiers du capitaine Georges: Souvenirs d'amour et de guerre 1894–1945' (1966) and about his father 'Renoir' (1958). Also author of plays 'The Heirs' and 'Corola'; made adaptation of 'The Big Knife'. Nephew is cinematographer Claude Renoir who photographed 7 of his films in the periods 1935–37 and 1950–56. Brother is director of production Claude Renoir, assistant on 2 films in 1938 and director of production on *La Règle du jeu* (1939).

Films as director: 1924: La Fille de l'eau (+ *p/dec*). 1926: Nana (+ *p*). 1927: Charleston (+ *p*); Marquita. 1929: Le Bled. 1936: La Vie est à nous (*co-d* Jean-Paul le Chanois, Jacques Becker, André Zwoboda, Pierre Unik, Henri Cartier-Bresson). 1941: Swamp Water.

Films as director and writer: 1928: La Petite Marchande d'allumettes (*co-d* Jean Tedesco; *ad* + *co-p*); Tire-au-flanc (*co-ad*). 1929: Le Tournoi (*ad*). 1931: On purge bébé (*ad*); La Chienne (*co-s*). 1932: La Nuit du carrefour; Boudu Sauvé des eaux (*co-s*). 1933: Chotard et compagnie (*co-s*). 1934: Madame Bovary. 1935: Toni (*co-ad*). 1936: Le Crime de M Lange (*co-s*); Une Partie de campagne (+ *w*); Les Bas-fonds (*co-s*). 1937: La Grande Illusion (*co-s*). 1938: La Marseillaise (*co-s*); La Bête Humaine (+ *w*). 1939: La Règle du jeu (*co-s*). 1940: La Tosca (*co-s*; *co-d* Karl Koch). 1943: This Land is Mine (*co-s* + *co-p*). 1944: Salut à la France (*co-s*; *co-d* Garson Kanin, uc). 1945: The Southerner. 1946: The Diary of a Chambermaid (*co-ad*); The Woman on the Beach (*co-ad*). 1950: The River (*co-s*). 1952: La Carrozza d'oro (*co-ad*). 1955: French Can Can. 1956: Eléna et les hommes (+ *co-ad*). 1959: Le Déjeuner sur l'herbe (+ *pc*). 1961: Le Testament du Dr Cordelier (+ *pc*). 1962: Le Caporal Epinglé (*co-s*). 1971: Le Petit Théâtre de Jean Renoir.

RENOIR, Pierre

Actor. Paris 1885–1952 Paris
Son of painter Auguste Renoir, brother is Jean Renoir; father of Claude Renoir. 1905: Paris Conservatoire. In repertory at Théâtre de l'Odéon. 1910: in 'Chantecler' and 'Crainquebille' at Théâtre de la Porte Saint-Martin. 1911: first film La Digue. 1914–15: in French Army; Médaille Militaire, Croix de Guerre. 1916: returned to stage. 20-year partnership with Louis Jouvet. Director of Athenée Theatre, Paris.

Films as actor include: 1932: La Nuit du carrefour. 1934: Madame Bovary. 1935: Veille d'armes. 1936: Sous les yeux d'occident. 1937: La Citadelle du silence. 1938: La Marseillaise. 1939: Pièges. 1941: Histoire de rire. 1943: Le Voyageur sans bagages. 1944: Les Enfants du paradis. 1951: Knock.

RESNAIS, Alain

Vannes, France 1922–
Film course at IDHEC, left without completing it.

1945–50: on 16 mm made shorts and a feature not intended for public showing. They include a series on visits to painters, e.g. Hans Hartung. Remade his 16 mm *Van Gogh* in 35 mm for commercial showing. Editor of 5 films including *La Pointe Courte* (1954). Credited as artistic supervisor on William Klein's *Broadway by Light*.

Films as director (excluding 16 mm): 1948: Van Gogh (+ *e*). 1950: Gauguin (+ *e*); Guernica (+ *e*). 1953: Les Statues meurent aussi (*co-d Chris Marker*). 1955: Nuit et brouillard. 1956: Toute la mémoire du monde (+ *e*). 1957: Le Mystère de l'Atelier 15 (*co-d Chris Marker*). 1958: Le Chant du styrène (+ *e*). 1959: Hiroshima mon amour. 1961: L'Année Dernière à Marienbad – Last Year at Marienbad. 1963: Muriel. 1966: La Guerre est finie – The War is Over.

REVESZ, Gyorgy

Director. Budapest 1927–
To 1950: film school in Budapest. To Hunnia studios. 1954: first film as director.

Films as director: 1954: Ketszer ketto néha öt – 2 times 2 are Sometimes 5. 1956: Unnepi Vacsora – Gala Dinner. 1957: Ejfélkor – At Midnight. 1958: Micsoda Ejszaka – What a Night! (+ *co-s*). 1959: A Megfelelö Ember – The Right Man. 1961: Négyen az arban – Four Children in the Flood – Danger on the Danube. 1962: Angyaluk földje – The Land of Angels; Fagyosszenlek – Hail Days. 1963: Hogy Allunk, fiatalember? – Well, Young Man? 1964: Igen – Yes. 1965: Nem – No. 1966: Minden kezdet nehéz – All Beginnings are Hard. 1967: Egy Szerelem három ejszakája – Three Nights of Love. 1969: Az Oroszlán ugrani keszül - Isle of the Lion. 1970: Utazas a kopanyani korul – Journey Round My Skull.

REVILLE, Alma

Writer. 1900–
Began as editing secretary at Famous Players-Lasky's Islington studios, London. 1925: script-girl on Alfred Hitchcock's first completed film as director, *The Pleasure Garden*. 1926: assistant director on *The Lodger*; married Hitchcock. 1927–50: scriptwriter on many of Hitchcock's films, at first in collaboration with him and (from 1932) in collaboration with various other writers. Very infrequent work for other directors includes script collaboration on Richard Wallace's *It's in the Bag* (1945).

Films as writer in collaboration include: 1927: The Ring. 1930: Juno and the Paycock; Murder (*alone*). 1931: The Skin Game. 1932: Rich and Strange. 1933: Waltzes from Vienna. 1935: The Thirty-Nine Steps (*co-ad*). 1936: The Secret Agent; Sabotage. 1937: Young and Innocent. 1938: The Lady Vanishes. 1941: Suspicion. 1943: Shadow of a Doubt. 1947: The Paradine Case (*co-ad*). 1950: Stage Fright (*ad*).

REYNAUD, Emile

Inventor. Montreuil-sous-Bois, France 1844–1918 Ivry-sur-Seine, France
From 1857: mechanic's apprentice, photographer then physics teacher at school of arts and crafts, Puy-en-Velay. 1872: gave his first scientific conference. 1876: invented optical toy, the Praxinoscope, in which images on a revolving drum were reflected in a central ring of mirrors to give impression of moving pictures. 1877: presented Praxinoscope Théâtre (which had added scenery and a proscenium) at Paris Universal Exhibition. 1880: combined Praxinoscope with magic lantern to produce form of projection. 1888: took out patent on Théâtre Optique, for projection of animated drawings on perforated strip. 1889: presented Théâtre Optique at Paris Universal Exhibition. From 1890: made 15–20 minute paper strip 'films' for Théâtre Optique. 1892: first public performance of Théâtre Optique at the Musée Grevin, Boulevard Montmartre, Paris. From 1895: used photographs on celluloid instead of drawings on paper to make his pictures. 1900: closed Théâtre Optique owing to competition from motion picture industry; took job as architect's secretary; threw equipment and films into the Seine, saving only *Pauvre Pierrot* (1892) and *Autour d'une cabine* (1895).

Paper strip films as director include: 1891: Un Bon Bock. 1892: Clown et ses chiens; Pauvre Pierrot. 1895: Autour d'une cabine; Rêve au coin du feu.

Celluloid films as director include: 1896: Guillaume; Le Premier Cigare.

REYNOLDS, Ben

Cinematographer
Worked in various departments at Universal. 1917: first films as cinematographer, directed by John Ford. From 1918: shot a number of Erich von Stroheim's films for Universal, then MGM and Famous Players-Lasky. Otherwise with Universal until 1924. 1925–26: with MGM. Thereafter with various companies including Warners (1929). 1933–35: cinematographer with Paramount notably on several films by Henry Hathaway.

Films as cinematographer include: 1917: The Scrapper; The Soul Herder; The Secret Man. 1918: The Scarlet Drop; Hell Bent; A Woman's Fool; Blind Husbands. 1919: The Devil's Passkey. 1921: Foolish Wives (*co*). 1923: Merry-Go-Round (*co*); Greed (*co*). 1924: Butterfly; The Signal Tower. 1925: The Merry Widow (*co*). 1927: Silk Stockings. 1928: The Wedding March (*co*). 1929: Sonny Boy. 1930: Vengeance. 1933: Man of the Forest; To the Last Man; The Thundering Herd. 1934: Come on Marines! 1935: It's a Great Life!

REYNOLDS, Debbie

(Mary Frances Reynolds) Actress. El Paso, Texas 1932–
1948: won Miss Burbank contest, spotted by talent scout, put under contract. 1948: first film as actress *June Bride,* then continued in high school, specialising in dramatics, voice and dancing. 1950: graduated. 1955–59: married to Eddie Fisher. Films mainly for MGM. Also cabaret.

Films as actress include: 1950: Three Little Words. 1952: Singin' in the Rain. 1953: I Love Melvin; The Affairs of Dobie Gillis; Give a Girl a Break. 1954: Athena. 1955: Hit the Deck; The Tender Trap. 1956: The Catered Affair; Bundle of Joy; Meet Me in Las Vegas. 1957: Tammy and the Bachelor. 1958: This Happy Feeling. 1959: The Mating Game; Say One For

Jean Renoir's Toni.
Giorgio Albertazzi and Delphine Seyrig in L'Année Dernière à Marienbad. *directed by Alain Resnais.*
Robert Mitchum in Sheldon Reynolds' Foreign Intrigue.

Me; It Started With a Kiss; The Gazebo. 1960: The Rat Race; Pepe. 1961: The Pleasure of His Company; The Second Time Around. 1962: How the West Was Won. 1963: Mary, Mary. 1964: The Unsinkable Molly Brown; Goodbye Charlie. 1967: Divorce American Style.

REYNOLDS, Sheldon

Director. Philadelphia 1923–
University of New York. From 1945: worked in radio then TV as scriptwriter then director e.g. 'My Silent Partner', 'We the People', episodes for 'Danger' series. 1955: produced, wrote and directed for 'Foreign Intrigue' series which became subject of his first film as director (1956). Returned to TV until 1968; writer with Ronald Howard of 'Sherlock Holmes' series.

Films as director: 1956: Foreign Intrigue (+ p/s). 1968: Assignment to Kill (+ s).

RICE, Ron

Director. New York 1935–64 Acapulco, Mexico
Left school before leaving-age; into bicycle-racing. From 1958: filmed bicycle races on 8 mm. 1959: made untitled film combining painter's exhibition and nude girl running through sand dunes. 1960: shot undeveloped footage of Winter Olympics at Squaw Valley, California. 1960: met Vernon Zimmerman; they collaborated on The Flower Thief, made in 2 versions: longer version his first feature-length film. 1961: in New York began The Dancing Master, abandoned. 1962: to Mexico, shot most of Senseless: finished film contains footage from The Dancing Master. 1963: in New York making The Queen of Sheba Meets the Atom Man, abandoned. 1964: after making Chumlum returned to Mexico; ran out of money; admitted to hospital; died of bronchial pneumonia. His last material edited posthumously into The Mexican Footage.

Films as director: 1959: Untitled film. 1960: The Flower Thief (2 versions). 1962: Senseless. 1963: The Queen of Sheba Meets the Atom Man (wf). 1964: Chumlum; The Mexican Footage.

RICHARD, Jean-Louis

Director. Paris 1927–
Centre d'Art Dramatique and Conservatoire de Paris. From 1945: actor at Théâtre de l'Odéon, then assistant to Louis Jouvet on many productions. From 1951: directed in theatre. 1961: began in films as uncredited writer in collaboration on Pierre Grimblat's Me faire ça à moi. 1962: first film as director and co-writer. Work as writer included scripts in collaboration with François Truffaut for La Peau Douce (1964), Fahrenheit 451 (1966), La mariée était en noir (1967). 1949–50: married to Jeanne Moreau.

Films as director and writer in collaboration: 1962: Bonne Chance, Charlie. 1964: Mata-Hari, agent H21.

RICHARDSON, Sir Ralph

Actor. Cheltenham, Gloucestershire 1902–
Parents Quakers; father painter Arthur Richardson. Art school in Brighton. Painted theatre scenery. 1921: debut as actor in 'The Merchant of Venice' in Brighton.

4 years in provincial repertory. 1926: first London appearance in 'Yellow Sands'. 1929: toured South Africa in 'The Taming of the Shrew'. 1930–32: Old Vic, Malvern Summer Theatre. 1933: first film The Ghoul. 1935: toured USA in 'Romeo and Juliet'. World War II in Fleet Air Arm. 1944: released to become joint director of Old Vic with Laurence Olivier, John Burrell. 1947: knighted. 1951: directed and acted in Home at Seven. 1970: directed by Lindsay Anderson in 'Home' in London and New York.

Films as actor include: 1933: Friday the 13th. 1936: Things to Come. 1938: South Riding; The Citadel. 1939: The Four Feathers; The Lion Has Wings. 1943: The Volunteer. 1946: School for Secrets. 1948: Anna Karenina; The Fallen Idol. 1949: The Heiress. 1951: Outcast of the Islands; Home at Seven (+ d). 1952: The Sound Barrier. 1956: Richard III. 1959: Our Man in Havana. 1960: Oscar Wilde; Exodus. 1962: Long Day's Journey into Night. 1963: Woman of Straw. 1965: Dr Zhivago. 1966: The Wrong Box; Khartoum. 1969: Oh! What a Lovely War; The Bed Sitting Room; The Battle of Britain; The Midas Run. 1970: David Copperfield.

RICHARDSON, Tony

(Cecil Antonio Richardson) Director. Shipley, Yorkshire 1928–
Wadham College, Oxford; president of Oxford University Dramatic Society. Also ran amateur dramatic society in Bradford. 1951–56: producer for BBC TV e.g. series including 'The Makepeace Saga', plays including 'Othello', 'The Gambler'; directed in repertory theatre. 1954–57: contributed to Sight and Sound. 1956: one of the originators of Free Cinema programmes at National Film Theatre which included his first short directed and scripted in collaboration with Karel Reisz; directed 'Look Back in Anger' first of many plays for English Stage Company which he founded with George Devine at Royal Court Theatre. Since directed on Broadway, London West End stage, Shakespeare Memorial Theatre and elsewhere. 1958: with John Osborne formed production company, Woodfall. 1959: directed and produced first feature. 1960: with Harry Saltzman co-produced Karel Reisz's Saturday Night and Sunday Morning; directed first American film. 1963: executive producer on The Girl with Green Eyes. Also produced a number of his own films. 1962–67: married to Vanessa Redgrave. Oscar for direction of Tom Jones (1963), which also received Oscar as Best Picture.

Films as director: 1955: Momma Don't Allow (co-d Karel Reisz + co-s). 1959: Look Back in Anger. 1960: The Entertainer. 1961: Sanctuary; A Taste of Honey (+ p/co-s). 1962: The Loneliness of the Long Distance Runner (+ p). 1963: Tom Jones (+ p). 1964: The Loved One. 1966: Mademoiselle. 1967: The Sailor from Gibraltar (+ co-s). 1968: The Charge of the Light Brigade: Red and Blue. 1969: Laughter in the Dark; Hamlet. 1970: Ned Kelly (+ co-s).

RICHTER, Hans

Director. Berlin 1888–
Carpenter's apprentice. Berlin University and Hochschule für Bildende Kunst, Berlin. World War I: German Army, invalided out in 1916. 1919: Academy in Weimar. 1921: first film as director. 1925:

Rhythmus 25 based on scroll made in 1923. 1927: Inflation made as an introduction to a feature film. 1928–29: commercials. 1929: Rennsymphonie introduction to feature; book 'Filmgegner von Heute-Filmfreunde von Morgen'; with Sergei Eisenstein in Switzerland and London, directed him in Everyday. 1931–33: shot footage for Metall in Berlin, Moscow and Odessa; unfinished. 1933: in France and Holland. 1936–41: in Switzerland. 1939–41: commercials, documentaries. 1941: to USA. 1942: became director of Film Institute of City College, New York. 1944: first American film compilation The Movies Take a Holiday. 1944–46: produced film by expatriates in USA (including Fernand Léger and Man Ray), Dreams That Money Can Buy, and directed an episode. 1948: became Professor at Film Institute of City College, New York. 1963: made Alexander Calder: From the Earth to the Moon using footage from Dreams That Money Can Buy (1948) and 8 Mal 8 (1957). 1967: memoirs of years 1915–33 'Köpfe und Hinterköpfe'. Worked at various times with e.g. Darius Milhaud, Jean Cocteau, Max Ernst, Fernand Léger, Man Ray. Also painter. Book: 'Dada, Art and Anti-Art' (1965).

Films as director: 1921: Rhythmus 21 – Film is Rhythm (+ c/dec). 1923: Rhythmus 23 (+ dec). 1925: Rhythmus 25; Filmstudie 25 (+ co-c/dec). 1927: Inflation (+ s/dec). 1928: Vormittagsspuk – Ghosts Before Breakfast (+ dec/w). 1929: Rennsymphonie – Race Symphony (+ co-s); Zweigroschenzauber – Twopenny Magic; Nachmittag zu den Wettrennen; Alles dreht sich, alles bewegt sich! – 'Everything revolves, everything moves!' (+ co-s); Storm uber la Sarraz – Kampf des unabhangigen Gegen den kommerziellen Film (+ s/w; co-d Sergei Eisenstein, Ivor Montagu); Everyday. 1930: Neues Leben (+ s). 1931: Europa Radio. 1933: Hallo Everybody!; Metall (uf). 1936: Vom Blitz zum Fernsehbild – From Lightning to Television. 1938: Eine kleine Welt im Dunkelm (+ p); Die Enstehung der Farbe (+ p); Die Eroberung des Himmels (+ p); Hans im Glueck (+ p). 1939: Die Börse (+ p). 1944: The Movies Take a Holiday (+ e; co-d Herman Weinberg). 1944–46: Dreams That Money Can Buy ep Narcissus (+ p/s). 1951: 30 Years of Experiment. 1954: Minotaur. 1956: Dadascope, Part I. 1957: Passionate Pastime – Chesscetera (+ cy); 8 Mal 8 – 8 × 8 (+ p/s/dec). 1961: From Dada to Surrealism; 40 Years of Experiment. 1963: Alexander Calder: From the Earth to the Moon. 1967: Dadascope, Part II.

RIEFENSTAHL, Leni

Director, Berlin 1902–
Berlin School of Crafts. Ballet training under Mary Wigman, Jutta Klamt. Danced in Max Reinhardt's theatre company. 1923–24: danced and arranged dance programmes in Berlin, Dresden, Prague and Zurich. 1926: first film as actress Der heilige Berg. From 1931: own production company. 1932: first film as director, from screenplay by Belà Balàsz Das blaue Licht. 1936–38: documentaries, made at request of Hitler. 1941–54: intermittent work on Tiefland.

Films as actress: 1926: Der heilige Berg. 1927: Der grosse Sprung. 1929: Die weisse Hölle von Piz Palü. 1931: Der weisse Rausch. 1933: SOS Eisberg.

Films as director: 1932: Das blaue Licht (+ p/st/w). 1933: Sieg des Glaubens. 1935: Tag der Freiheit-

Unsere Wehrmacht. 1936: Triumph des Willens – Triumph of the Will. 1938: Olympiad: Fest der Schönhet (+s); Olympiad: Fest der Völker (+s). 1954: Tiefland (+s/p/c/w). 1956: Schwarze Fracht (uf).

RISI, Dino

Director. Milan 1917–
Father a doctor; brother poet, writer and film director Nelo Risi. Medicine, specialising in psychiatry, at University of Milan. 1940: assistant director to Alberto Lattuada and Mario Soldati. World War II: interned in Switzerland; followed Jacques Feyder's course in film direction at the Athénée de Genève. 1945: returned to Italy and began directing documentaries; also journalist. From 1951: in Rome as writer, then director of features. Wrote story and screenplay in collaboration for Lattuada's *Anna* (1951), screenplays in collaboration for *Totò e i re di Roma* (1951), *Gli Eroi della domenica* (1952).

Short films as director include: 1945: I Bersaglieri della signora. 1946: Barboni; Pescatorella; Strade di Napoli. 1947: Trigullio Minore; Cuore Rivelatore. 1948: Cortili il pittore della montagna; Verso la vita; Il Grido della città. 1949: Buio in sala; Il Sièro della verità.

Features as director: 1952: Vacanze col gangster – Vacation with a Gangster (+co-s/co-st). 1953: Il Viale della speranza (+co-p/co-st/co-s); Amore in città ep Paradiso per 4 ore. 1955: Il Segno di Venere – Sign of Venus; Pane, amore e ... – Scandal in Sorrento (+co-st/co-s). 1956: Poveri ma belli – Poor but Handsome – Girl in a Bikini (+co-s/co-st). 1957: La Nonna Sabella – Oh! Sabella (+co-s); Belle ma povere – Irresistible (+co-s). 1958: Venezia, la luna e tu – Venice, the Moon and You (+co-s); Poveri Milionàri (+co-s/co-st). 1959: Il Vedevo (+co-s/co-st); Il Mattatore – Love and Larceny. 1960: Un Amore a Roma; A porte chiuse – Behind Closed Doors (+co-st). 1961: Una Vita Difficile – A Difficult Life. 1962: Il Sorpasso – The Easy Life; Il Giovedì – Thursday (+co-s). 1963: La Marcia su Roma; I Mostri (+co-s). 1964: Le Bambole ep La Telefonata – Four Kinds of Love; Le Gaucho. 1965: L'Ombrellone – Weekend Italian Style (+co-s); I Complessi ep Una Giornata Decisiva – Complexes; Operazione San Gennaro – Treasure of San Gennaro – Operation San Gennaro (+co-st/co-s). 1966: I Nostri Mariti ep Nei secoli fedeli. 1967: Il Tigre – The Tiger and the Pussycat (+co-st); Il Profeta – Mr Kinky. 1968: Straziami, ma di baci saziami – Torture Me, But Kill me with Kisses (+co-st/co-s). 1969: Il Giovane Normale (+co-s). 1971: La Moglie del prete; In nome del popolo Italiano.

RISKIN, Robert

Writer. New York 1897–1955 Beverly Hills
Columbia University. From 17 wrote scripts. World War I: military service. Playwright; plays produced on Broadway. 1932: to Hollywood, Columbia contract. Long collaboration with Frank Capra. 1937: directed and wrote *When You're in Love*. His script for *Lady for a Day* (1933) used by Capra as basis for *Pocketful of Miracles* (1961). 1939: to Goldwyn as associate producer. 1942: married actress Fay Wray. 1943–45: chief of motion picture bureau of overseas branch of Office of War Information. Set up Robert Riskin Productions at RKO: first production *Magic Town*

(1947), also co-wrote its story. 1949: formed independent company, Equitable Pictures. From 1950: after surgery, bedridden until death. Oscar for adaptation, *It Happened One Night* (1934).

Films as writer for Frank Capra: 1931: The Miracle Woman (co-fpl); Platinum Blonde (di). 1932: American Madness. 1933: Lady for a Day. 1934: It Happened One Night; Broadway Bill (co). 1936: Mr Deeds Goes to Town. 1937: Lost Horizon. 1938: You Can't Take It with You. 1941: Meet John Doe. 1950: Riding High. 1951: Here Comes the Groom (co-st). 1961: Pocketful of Miracles (st).

Films as writer include: 1935: The Whole Town's Talking (di). 1944: The Thin Man Goes Home (+co-st). 1947: Magic Town (+p/co-st). 1950: Mister 880. 1956: You Can't Run Away from It (co).

RITT, Martin

Director. New York 1920–
Legal studies at St John's University, New York. 1937–42: professional stage actor. World War II: served in USAAF special forces. 1943–44: acted in Broadway production and then film, *Winged Victory*. 1946: directed first stage production, 'Mr Peebles and Mr Hooker'; subsequent theatre direction included 'The Men', 'Set My People Free', 'A View from the Bridge'. 1953: lectured at Actors' Studio, New York; began as TV actor and director including 'Danger' series. 1956: first film as director.

Films as director: 1956: Edge of the City – A Man is Ten Feet Tall. 1957: No Down Payment. 1958: The Long Hot Summer; Black Orchid. 1959: The Sound and the Fury. 1960: Jovanka e l'altri – Five Branded Women. 1961: Paris Blues. 1962: Hemingway's Adventures of a Young Man; Hud (+co-p). 1963: The Outrage. 1965: The Spy Who Came in from the Cold (+p). 1966: Hombre (+p). 1968: The Molly Maguires; The Brotherhood. 1970: The Great White Hope.

RITTAU, Günther

Director and cinematographer. Königshutte, Germany 1897–1971
Engineering at Berlin Polytechnic. Joined firm making optical instruments. Then worked on documentary films at Decla, becoming cinematographer. From 1924: cinematographer on feature films. 1939–48: worked as director. 1955–57: returned to cinematography.

Films as cinematographer include: 1924: Die Nibelungen (co). 1927: Metropolis (co). 1929: Asphalt. 1930: Der blaue Engel (co). 1932: Quick (co). 1955: Kinder, mutter und ein General.

Films as director: 1939: Brand im Ozean. 1941: U-Boote westwärts. 1942: Der Strom. 1943: Der ewige Klang – Der Geiger. 1944: Meine vier Jungens; Die Jahre vergehen – Der Senator. 1945: Eine alltägliche Geschichte. 1948: Vor uns liegt das Leben – Die fünf vom Titan.

RITTER, Thelma

Actress. New York 1905–69 New York
Father was singer Charles Ritter. American Academy of Dramatic Arts. From age 14: vaudeville, stock

Das Blaue Licht, *directed by Leni Riefenstahl.*
Richard Harris and Sean Connery in The Molly Maguires, *directed by Martin Ritt.*
Die Nibelungen, *directed by Fritz Lang, photographed by Carl Hoffmann and Günther Rittau.*

company. 1927: married actor Joseph Moran. Work in radio. 1947: spotted by George Seaton for her first film as actress *Miracle on 34th Street*. Paddy Chayevsky wrote 'The Catered Affair' for her.

Films as actress include: 1948: Call Northside 777. 1949: A Letter to Three Wives; Father Was a Full-back. 1950: All About Eve; Perfect Strangers. 1951: The Mating Season. 1952: The Model and the Marriage Broker; With a Song in my Heart. 1953: The Farmer Takes a Wife; Pickup on South Street; Titanic. 1954: Rear Window. 1955: Lucy Gallant; Daddy Long Legs. 1956: The Proud and the Profane. 1959: A Hole in the Head; Pillow Talk. 1961: The Misfits; The Second Time Around. 1962: Bird Man of Alcatraz; How the West was Won. 1963: For Love or Money; Move Over, Darling.

RIVA, Emmanuele

Actress. Cheniménil, France 1927–
1953: Centre d'Art Dramatique de la rue Blanche, Paris. From 1954: on stage in e.g. 'Espoir', 'L'Epouvantail', 'Les Enfants du soleil', 'Le Retour', 'La Journée d'une rêveuse'. Also TV, radio. 1959: first film as actress *Hiroshima mon amour*.

Films as actress include: 1959: Kapo; Le Huitième Jour. 1960: Recours en grâce; Adua e le campagne. 1961: Léon Morin, prêtre; Climats. 1962: Thérèse Desqueyroux. 1963: Le Ore dell'amore. 1965: Le Coup de grâce; Thomas l'Imposteur. 1966: Les Fruits Amers. 1967: Les Risques du métier.

RIVETTE, Jacques

Director. Rouen, France 1928–
University. 1949: first film, an untitled 16 mm short. 1950: with François Truffaut, Jean-Luc Godard and Eric Rohmer founded Gazette du Cinema. Assistant editor to Jean Mitry. 1952: began writing for Cahiers du Cinéma. 1954: interviewed Jacques Becker, Jean Renoir; junior assistant on Becker's *Ali Baba*, Renoir's *French Can-Can*; operator on e.g. Rohmer's short *Bérénice*. Wrote for Arts. 1955: With Truffaut, Godard, Charles Bitsch scripted *Les Quatre Jeudis*: not filmed. 1957–61: scripted, directed and edited first feature *Paris nous appartient*. 1963–65: editor-in-chief of Cahiers. 1966: made TV film *Jean Renoir: le patron*. Temporary government ban on release and export of *La Religieuse* (1965).

Films as director: 1949: Untitled short. 1951: Le Quadrille (*sh*). 1952: Le Divertissement. 1956: Le Coup du Berger. 1961: Paris Nous Appartient – Paris Belongs to Me (+ *co-s*). 1965: La Religieuse – The Nun (+ *co-s*). 1969: L'Amour Fou (+ *co-s*).

ROACH, Hal

Producer and director. Elmira, New York 1892–
At 17 to Alaska, prospected for gold. Ran business in Seattle. To Los Angeles. From 1912: occasional work as cowboy for Universal. 1914: with small legacy became producer, directing Harold Lloyd in numerous shorts as Willie Work. Formed company with Lloyd (Rolin) releasing through Pathe. Lloyd moved to Sennett after disagreement; returned for 'Lonesome Luke' series for 2 years (to 1917). From 1917: directed infrequently. 1919: moved to own studio in Culver City. 1923: engaged stage actor Will Rogers. Stan Laurel and Oliver Hardy acted in his films for several years: first teamed them in *Putting Pants on Philip* (1928). 1922–39: produced Our Gang series of shorts, actors included Mickey Rooney, directors included Frank Capra, George Sidney, George Stevens, Gordon Douglas. From 1927: released through MGM. 1940–42: released through United Artists. 1942: turned to production of features only. World War II: US Signal Corps and cinematography unit of USAAF. 1948: formed TV company. 1965: out of retirement to produce compilation *The Crazy World of Laurel and Hardy*. Oscars for *The Music Box* (1932) and *Bored of Education* (1936). Son is producer and director Hal Roach Jr.

Films as producer include: 1921: I Do (+ *co-st*; *co-d* *Sam Taylor*); Never Weaken; A Sailor Made Man (+ *co-st*). 1922: Grandma's Boy (+ *co-st*); Doctor Jack (+ *co-st*). 1927: Love 'em and Feed 'em. 1928: Leave 'em Laughing (+ *s*); The Finishing Touch; The Battle of the Century (+ *s*). 1931: Mama Loves Papa; Catch-as-Catch-Can. 1932: On the Loose (+ *p*); Pack Up Your Troubles; Their First Mistake. 1933: The Bargain of the Century. 1936: Pay as You Exit; Spooky Hookey; Bored of Education. 1937: Night n' Gales; Rushin' Ballet; Roamin' Holiday; Our Gang Follies of 1938; Fishy Tales; Framing Youth; Glove Taps; Mail and Female; Reunion in Rhythm; Hearts are Thumps; Topper; Three Smart Boys. 1938: Merrily We Live; There Goes My Heart; Came the Brawn; Hide and Shriek; Canned Fishing; Feed 'em and Weep. 1939: Captain Fury (+ *d*); The Housekeeper's Daughter (+ *d*); Topper Takes a Trip; Zenobia; Clown Princes. 1940: One Million B.C. (+ *co-d*; *co-d* *Hal Roach Jr*); Of Mice and Men; Turnabout (+ *d*); Saps at Sea. 1941: Roadshow; Broadway Limited; Niagara Falls; Topper Returns. 1944: The Devil with Hitler (*co*).

ROBBE-GRILLET, Alain

Director and writer. Brest, France 1922–
Agricultural scientist, then novelist. 1953: published first novel, 'Les Gommes', followed by 'Le Voyeur' (1955), 'La Jalousie' (1957), 'Dans le labyrinthe' (1959). 1961: wrote script and dialogue for Alain Resnais' *L'Année Dernière à Marienbad*. Thereafter both literary and film work. 1962: first film as director and writer; published collections of short stories ('Instantanes') and of critical essays ('Pour un nouveau roman'). 1965: novel 'La Maison de rendez-vous'. Also published scripts of *L'Année Dernière à Marienbad* and *L'Immortelle*. 1970: *L'Eden et après* banned. Literary adviser to publishing firm, Editions de Minuit.

Films as writer and director: 1962: L'Immortelle (+ *w*). 1966: Trans-Europ Express. 1969: L'Homme qui ment – Muž Který Lže – Shock Troops – The Man Who Lies. 1970: L'Eden et après.

ROBBINS, Jerome

Choreographer. New York 1918–
Studied chemistry at New York University before becoming dancer. 1941: soloist in American Ballet Theatre, for which he choreographed 4 ballets including 'Fancy Free' (1944) and 'Facsimile' (1947). 1949: associate artistic director of New York City Ballet; choreographed and danced leading role in many ballets; provided idea for *On the Town* (1949). Broadway choreographer (e.g. of 'West Side Story') and director. 1958: founded Ballets USA. 1961: special Oscar 'for his brilliant achievements in the art of choreography on film'.

Films as choreographer: 1956: The King and I. 1961: West Side Story (+ *co-d Robert Wise*).

ROBERTS, Ben

(Ben Eisenberg) Writer. New York 1916–
1932–35: New York University. 1938: freelance PR counsellor. Collaborated on Broadway shows: 'The Merry Widow', 'Jackpot', 'Dream with Music'. In collaboration with Ivan Goff wrote play 'Portrait in Black'. 1941: first film as writer *Borrowed Hero* for Monogram. 1943–48: no film work. From 1949: all credits in collaboration with Ivan Goff. 1949–54: mainly Warners. 1957–60: mainly Universal. 1960: adapted own play for *Portrait in Black*.

Films as writer in collaboration (from 1949, with Ivan Goff) include: 1942: Fly By Night (*co-st*). 1949: White Heat (*co*). 1950: Backfire (*co*). 1951: Goodbye My Fancy; Captain Horatio Hornblower, RN (*co*); Come Fill the Cup. 1952: The Gift Horse (*co*); O. Henry's Full House *ep* The Last Leap. 1953: White Witch Doctor; King of the Khyber Rifles. 1954: Green Fire. 1956: Serenade (*co*). 1957: Man of a Thousand Faces (*co*); Band of Angels (*co*). 1959: Shake Hands with the Devil. 1960: Portrait in Black (+ *fpl*); Midnight Lace.

ROBERTSON, Cliff

Actor. La Jolla, California 1925–
World War II: in US Naval Reserve, reaching Lieutenant. 1953: New York stage debut in 'Late Love'. Also acted in 'The Wisteria Trees', 'Orpheus Descending'. 1956: first film as actor *Picnic*. TV: 'Two Worlds of Charley Gordon', 'Days of Wine and Roses'. 1971: first film as director. Oscar as Best Actor for *Charly* (1968).

Films as actor include: 1956: Autumn Leaves. 1957: The Girl Most Likely. 1958: The Naked and the Dead. 1959: Battle of the Coral Sea; Gidget. 1961: Underworld USA; The Big Show; All in a Night's Work. 1962: The Interns. 1963: PT 109; Sunday in New York. 1964: The Best Man; My Six Loves; Masquerade. 1965: Up From the Beach; Love Has Many Faces. 1967: The Honey Pot. 1968: The Devil's Brigade; Charly. 1970: Too Late the Hero. 1971: J. W. Coop (+ *d/p/s*).

ROBINSON, Edward G.

(Emmanuel Goldenberg) Actor. Bucharest, Rumania 1893–
1903: to USA. 1910–12: Columbia University. 1912–13: American Academy of Dramatic Arts. Service in US Navy. 1913: professional stage debut in 'Paid in Full'. 1915: Broadway debut in 'Under Fire'. 1923: first film as actor *The Bright Shawl*. To 1930: continued to work in theatre. To 1942: films mainly for Warners. Then for numerous studios including RKO, United Artists, MGM, Columbia and others. 1951: returned to theatre. Acted in e.g. 'Darkness at Noon' (1951), 'Middle of the Night' (1956). Chevalier de la Légion d'Honneur.

Films as actor include: 1929: The Hole in the Wall. 1930: Little Caesar; A Lady to Love; Outside the Law. 1931: Five Star Final. 1932: The Hatchet Man; Tiger Shark; Two Seconds. 1933: The Little Giant. 1934: The Man with Two Faces. 1935: Barbary Coast; The Whole Town's Talking. 1936: Bullets or Ballots. 1937: Kid Galahad. 1938: A Slight Case of Murder; The Amazing Dr Clitterhouse. 1939: Confessions of a Nazi Spy; Blackmail. 1949: the Story of Dr Ehrlich's Magic Bullet; Brother Orchid; A Dispatch from Reuter's. 1941: Manpower; The Sea Wolf. 1942: Tales of Manhattan; Larceny Inc. 1943: Flesh and Fantasy. 1944: Double Indemnity; The Woman in the Window. 1945: Scarlet Street; Our Vines Have Tender Grapes. 1946: The Stranger. 1947: The Red House. 1948: The Night has a Thousand Eyes; All My Sons; Key Largo. 1949: House of Strangers; It's a Great Feeling. 1951: Operation X. 1953: The Big Leaguer; The Glass Web. 1954: Black Tuesday. 1955: The Violent Men; Tight Spot. 1956: Hell on Frisco Bay; The Ten Commandments; Screaming Eagles. 1959: A Hole in the Head. 1960: Seven Thieves; Pepe. 1962: My Geisha; Two Weeks in Another Town. 1963: The Prize; Sammy Going South. 1964: Good Neighbour Sam; Cheyenne Autumn; Robin and the Seven Hoods; The Outrage. 1965: The Cincinnatti Kid. 1968: The Biggest Bundle of Them All. 1969: MacKenna's Gold. 1970: Song of Norway.

ROBSON, Mark

Director. Montreal 1913–

San Diego Army and Navy Academy. Political science and economics at University of California, Los Angeles. 1932–35: worked in property department then assistant set dresser at Fox; studied law at Pacific Coast University in evenings. From 1935: with RKO in property department, film library, process department, then sound cutter, assistant film editor, editor e.g. in collaboration with Robert Wise on *Citizen Kane* (1941) and under Val Lewton e.g. on *Cat People* (1943) also on *Journey into Fear* (1943). 1943: began as director, with Lewton as producer on his first 5 films. From 1949: worked with Goldwyn and various other companies. 1954–55: made 2 films in UK. From 1956: also occasionally produced. 1960: formed own production company. 1961: produced Philip Dunne's *The Inspector* in Britain.

Films as director: 1943: The Seventh Victim; The Ghost Ship. 1944: Youth Runs Wild. 1945: Isle of the Dead. 1946: Bedlam (+ co-s). 1949: Champion; Home of the Brave; Roughshod; My Foolish Heart. 1950: Edge of Doom. 1951: Bright Victory; I Want You. 1953: Return to Paradise. 1954: Hell Below Zero; Phffft. 1955: The Bridges at Toko-Ri; A Prize of Gold; Trial. 1956: The Harder They Fall; The Little Hut (+ co-p). 1957: Peyton Place. 1958: The Inn of the Sixth Happiness. 1960: From the Terrace (+ p). 1962: Nine Hours to Rama (+ p); The Prize. 1965: Von Ryan's Express. 1966: Lost Command – The Centurians (+ p). 1967: Valley of the Dolls. 1969: Daddy's Gone A-Hunting (+ p). 1971: Happy Birthday Wanda June.

ROCHA, Glauber

Director. Bahia, Brazil 1938–

Journalist in Salvador and Rio de Janeiro. Director of production. 1959: first short film as director. 1959–61:

studied law, worked as film critic. Worked on Nelson Pereira dos Santos' *Vidas Secas*. 1960: 'Revisao Critica de cinema brasileira', essay published by Civilaçao Brasileira. 1962: film columnist for one year on Jurnal do Brasil. 1965–66: producer of films directed by Walter Lima Jr and Carlos Diegues. Declaration, 'Una Estetica da fame' published.

Films as director: 1959: O Patio. 1960: A cruz na praça. 1961: Barravento (+ co-s). 1964: Deus e o diabo na terra del sol (+ s/ad/lyrics). 1965: Amazonas. 1967: Terra em transe (+ co-p/s). 1969: Maranhoa '66; O Santo guerreiro contra o dragao da maldade – Antonio das Mortes (+ co-p/s/a). 1970: Der Leone have sept cabecas (+ co-s); Cabezas Cortadas.

ROEG, Nicholas

Cinematographer. London 1928–

World War II: served in army. Entered films in cutting rooms at MGM, then clapper-boy, assistant camera operator on e.g. *Ivanhoe* (1952), *Bhowani Junction* (1955). Films as camera operator include *Jazz Boat* (1959), *The Trials of Oscar Wilde* (1960), *The Sundowners* (1961). 1962: 2nd-unit cinematographer in collaboration on *Lawrence of Arabia*. Also wrote and directed musical and topical event shows for TV. Lighting cameraman for TV series e.g. 'Police Dog', 'Ghost Squad'. Cinematographer from 1962. Has also worked as film writer in collaboration e.g. on story for Cliff Owen's *A Prize of Arms* (1961). 1968: photographed his first film as director in collaboration, *Performance*.

Films as cinematographer include: 1963: The Caretaker. 1964: The Masque of the Red Death; Nothing but the Best. 1966: Fahrenheit 451; A Funny Thing Happened on the Way to the Forum. 1967: Far from the Madding Crowd. 1968: Petulia.

Films as director: 1968: Performance (r 1971; + c; co-d Donald Cammell). 1971: Walkabout (+ co-c).

ROGERS, Ginger

(Virginia Katherine McMath) Actress. Independence, Missouri 1911–

Mother writer Lela McMath, later Rogers. Was subject of custody wrangle after divorce of parents, twice kidnapped by father. 1924: stage debut at High School in play produced and written by mother. 1925: month's booking on Texas-Oklahoma vaudeville circuit as prize for winning Texas Charleston championship. 1926–28: vaudeville dancer in south and mid-west; married partner Jack Pepper. 1929: sang with Paul Ash orchestra; Broadway debut in 'Top Speed'; appeared in short films. 1930: first feature, *Young Man of Manhattan*; Paramount contract; starred in 'Girl Crazy' on Broadway. 1931: released from Paramount contract to freelance. From 1933: series of pictures co-starring Fred Astaire for RKO. World War II: in 10-minute training film, *Safeguarding Military Information*; appeared in trailer for war bonds. 1947: mother 'friendly' witness at hearings of House Committeee on Un-American Activities. Films for various companies in 1950s; also stage appearances including Broadway. 1965: on Broadway in 'Hello Dolly'. From 1954: much TV, including 'Tonight at 8.30' directed by Otto Preminger. Married 5 times; husbands include (1934–41) Lew Ayres, (1953–57) actor Jacques

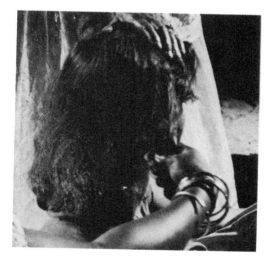

Alain Robbe-Grillet photographing a set for his L'Immortelle.
Edward G. Robinson in Vincente Minnelli's Two Weeks in Another Town.
Barravento. *directed by Glauber Rocha.*

Bergerac, (from 1961) actor and director William Marshall with whom she made *The Confession* (1964), not yet released. Is Christian Scientist. Oscar as Best Actress for *Kitty Foyle* (1940). 1965: replaced Carol Channing in 'Hello Dolly'.

Films as actress include: 1932: You Said a Mouthful. 1933: 42nd Street; Gold Diggers of 1933. 1934: Upperworld; Twenty Million Sweethearts; The Gay Divorcee. 1935: Roberta; Top Hat. 1936: Follow the Fleet; Swing Time. 1937: Stage Door; Shall We Dance. 1938: Vivacious Lady; Carefree. 1939: The Story of Vernon and Irene Castle; Bachelor Mother. 1940: Primrose Path. 1941: Tom, Dick and Harry. 1942: The Major and the Minor; Once Upon a Honeymoon. 1944: Lady in the Dark. 1946: Heartbeat; Magnificent Doll. 1949: The Barkleys of Broadway. 1950: Perfect Strangers. 1951: Storm Warning. 1952: We're Not Married; Monkey Business. 1953: Forever Female. 1954: Black Widow; The Beautiful Stranger. 1955: Tight Spot. 1956: Teenage Rebel. 1957: Oh, Men! Oh, Women!. 1965: Harlow.

ROGERS, Roy

(Leonard Slye) Actor. Cincinnati, Ohio 1912–
At 17 worked as cowhand in New Mexico. Formed singing group 'The Sons of the Pioneers'; sang on radio, made records e.g. 'The Last Roundup'. In films from 1935; starring roles from 1937. Until 1951 in over 90 westerns produced by Republic including *Dark Command* (1940). Usually with horse Trigger; when the first Trigger died in July 1965, withheld news for sake of horse's fans till April 1966; had him stuffed. Occasional appearances for other companies e.g. in *Rhythm on the Range* (1936), *Hollywood Canteen* (1945). TV in 1950s and '60s e.g. the 'Roy Rogers Show', 'Chevy Show'. 1947: married second wife actress Dale Evans who played opposite him in many films.

ROGERS, Will

Actor. Cologah, Oklahoma 1879–1935 Point Barrow, Alaska
Kemper Military Academy, Booneville, Missouri. Ranch hand and cow puncher. Worked on cattle boats (Buenos Aires to South Africa); returned to Oklahoma *via* New York. Appeared in Wild West show on tour, then in New York; vaudeville act. In films for Hal Roach. 1922–29: returned to Broadway. From 1929: acted in films for Fox. Mayor of Beverley Hills, California. Book 'The Cowboy Philosopher on the Peace Conference'. 1952: portrayed by his son Will Rogers Jr in *The Story of Will Rogers*.

Films as actor include: 1918: Laughing Bill Hyde. 1920: Scratch My Back. 1921: Boys Will be Boys. 1922: The Headless Horseman. 1926: Tip Toes. 1929: They Had to See Paris. 1930: Happy Days; So This is London. 1931: A Connecticut Yankee; Ambassador Bill; Down to Earth. 1932: Too Busy to Work; Business and Pleasure. 1933: State Fair; Doctor Bull; Mr Skitch; David Harum. 1934: Handy Andy; Judge Priest. 1935: The County Chairman; Life Begins at Forty; Steamboat Round the Bend; In Old Kentucky.

ROGOSIN, Lionel

Director. New York 1924–
Son of industrialist. Chemistry at Yale University.

Naval engineer. 1954: first film as documentary director. Formed own distribution company to show his films, also London distribution company in collaboration with Jimmy Vaughan. Bought Bleeker Cinema in Greenwich Village, New York. *On the Bowery* later shown in Free Cinema programmes at National Film Theatre, London. 1966: first feature-length film.

Films as director and producer: 1954: On the Bowery (+ e). 1958: Come Back Africa (+ e). 1963: Oysters are in Season. 1966: How Do You Like Them Bananas; Good Times, Wonderful Times. 1971: Black Roots (+ pc).

ROHMER, Eric

Director. Nancy, France 1920–
Professeur de Lettres. Wrote criticism for Revue de Cinema, Les Temps Modernes, La Parisienne, Arts. Editor-in-chief, La Gazette du Cinéma, Cahiers du Cinéma. 1949–50: first film as director, 16 mm short *Journal d'un scélérat*. 1951–61: second short *Présentation* in which Jean-Luc Godard acted. 1952: co-directed first feature (60 mins) *Les Petites Filles Modèles*, left unfinished. 1957: co-wrote book with Chabrol 'Hitchcock'. 1959: Chabrol's company financed *Le Signe du lion*. From 1962: all films (except TV) produced by Les Films du Losange of which he became director. 1964–66: films for educational TV, subjects include Edgar Allan Poe, La Bruyère, Pascal, Victor Hugo. 1965: made *Carl Dreyer* for TV, in series 'Cinéastes de notre temps'. Began series 'Six Contes Moraux' with short *La Boulangère de Monceau* (1962); all later films in series are features. Scripts all his films, edits most of them.

Short films as director and writer: 1950: Journal d'un scélérat (+ e). 1951–61: Présentation – Charlotte et son steak. 1954: Bérénice (+ e/w). 1956: La Sonate à Kreutzer (+ e/w). 1958: Véronique et son cancre (+ e). 1962: La Boulangère de Monceau (Six Contes Moraux No 1; +e). 1964: Nadja à Paris (+ e); Paris vu par ... ep Place de l'Etoile (+ e). 1966: Une Etudiante d'aujourd'hui (+ e). 1968: Fermière à Montfauçon.

Features as director and writer: 1952: Les Petites Filles Modèles (uf; + e; co-d P. Guilband). 1959: Le Signe du lion. 1963: La Carrière de Suzanne (Six Contes Moraux No 2; +e). 1966: La Collectionneuse (Six Contes Moraux No 4). 1968: Ma Nuit chez Maud – My Night at Maud's – My Night with Maud (Six Contes Moraux No 3; st/s/di/c). 1970: Le Genou de Claire – Claire's Knee (Six Contes Moraux No 5).

ROHRIG, Walter

Designer
Painter of theatre sets in Zurich. 1918: entered cinema. 1919: collaborated with Walter Reimann on e.g. *Das Kabinett des Dr Caligari*. 1920–36: collaboration with Robert Herlth. 1936: they designed, wrote and directed in collaboration *Hans im Glück*. 1942: last film *Rembrandt*.

Films as designer include: 1919: Das Kabinett des Dr Caligari (co). 1935: Valse Royale (co). 1942: Rembrandt.

Films as designer in collaboration with Robert Herlth include: 1921: Das Spiel mit dem Feuer; Der müde Tod. 1923: Der Schatz. 1924: Der letzte Mann. 1925: Zur Chronik von Grieshuus (co); Tartuff. 1926: Faust. 1930: Rosenmontag; Nie wieder Liebe. 1931: Der Mann, der seinen Mörder sucht. Der Kongress tanzt. 1933: Ich und der Kaiserin; Walzerkrieg. 1936: Hans im Glück (+ co-s; co-d Robert Herlth).

ROLAND, Gilbert

(Luis Antonio Damaso de Alonso) Actor, Chihuahua, Mexico 1905–
Grandfather and father were bullfighters. As child fled with family from Pancho Villa into Texas. 1927: spotted by Norma Talmadge for *Camille*. 1933: on stage in 'Camille' with Jane Cowl. Service in US Army Air Force Intelligence. Also Italian films. Book, 'Blood on the Horns'. Married Constance Bennett (1941–46, divorced). Brother is director Chico Alonso.

Films as actor include: 1926: The Blonde Saint. 1928: The Dove; The Woman Disputed. 1929: New York Nights. 1932: The Passionate Plumber; Call Her Savage. 1933: Gold Diggers of Paris; She Done Him Wrong; Our Betters. 1939: Juarez. 1940: The Sea Hawk. 1941: My Life with Caroline. 1942: Isle of Missing Men. 1949: We Were Strangers; Malaya. 1950: The Torch; Crisis; The Furies. 1951: The Bullfighter and the Lady; Ten Tall Men; Mark of the Renegade. 1952: Glory Alley; The Bad and the Beautiful; My Six Convicts; The Miracle of Our Lady of Fatima. 1953: Thunder Bay; The French Line. 1954: Underwater! 1955: The Racers; That Lady. 1956: Bandido; Around the World in 80 Days. 1957: Three Violent People; The Midnight Story. 1959: The Big Circus. 1964: Cheyenne Autumn. 1965: The Reward.

ROMAN, Ruth

Actress. Boston, Massachusetts 1925–
Theatrical work in Boston while at school; won drama scholarship. Little theatre groups, toured in stock. Broadway, then Hollywood. 1945: lead in Universal serial *Jungle Queen*, in 13 2-reel episodes. David O. Selznick put her under contract, though she first worked briefly at Paramount. To 1948: worked mainly for United Artists, Universal, Paramount. From 1948: worked mainly for RKO, Warners, Columbia. Also TV.

Films as actress include: 1943: Stage Door Canteen. 1944: Since You Went Away. 1945: You Came Along; Incendiary Blonde. 1946: A Night in Casablanca. 1948: The Big Clock; The Night Has a Thousand Eyes; Good Sam. 1949: The Window; Champion; Beyond the Forest; Always Leave Them Laughing. 1950: Three Secrets; Dallas. 1951: Lightning Strikes Twice; Strangers on a Train; Starlift. 1952: Invitation; Mara Maru; Young Man With Ideas. 1953: Blowing Wild. 1954: Tanganyika; The Shanghai Story; The Far Country. 1956: The Bottom of the Bottle; Joe Macbeth; Great Day in the Morning. 1958: Bitter Victory. 1965: Love Has Many Faces.

ROMANCE, Viviane

(Pauline Ronacher Ortmanns) Actress. Vienna 1912–
Appeared in 'L'Arlésienne' at Théâtre Sarah Bern-

hardt, Chorus-girl at Moulin Rouge. Model. 1931: small part in *La Chienne*. 1936: first starring role in *La Belle Equipe*. Producer with husband Clément Duhour.

Films as actress include: 1933: Ciboulette. 1934: Liliom. 1936: La Bandéra. 1937: Mademoiselle Docteur; Naples au baiser de feu. 1938: L'Etrange Monsieur Victor. 1940: La Vénus Aveugle. 1941: Une Femme dans la nuit. 1942: Carmen. 1943: La Boîte aux rêves. 1946: L'Affaire du collier de la reine; Panique. 1951: Les Sept Péchés Capitaux *ep* La Luxure. 1955: L'Affaire des poissons. 1962: Mélodie en sous-sol.

ROMERO, Cesar

Actor. New York 1907–

From 1926: dancer. 1927: on Broadway in 'Lady Do'. Acted in e.g. 'Social Register', 'Dinner at Eight'. Nightclubs. 1933: first film as actor *The Shadow Laughs*. 1937–49: worked mainly for Fox. 1939–40: title role in 'Cisco Kid' series. TV work includes 'The Cisco Kid', 'Zorro' and (with Dolores del Rio) 'The Actress and the Bullfighter'.

Films as actor include: 1934: The Thin Man; British Agent. 1935: Clive of India; Cardinal Richelieu; The Devil is a Woman; The Good Fairy; Diamond Jim; Show Them No Mercy. 1936: Love Before Breakfast; 15 Maiden Lane. 1937: Wee Willie Winkie; Dangerously Yours. 1938: My Lucky Star; Happy Landing. 1939: The Little Princess; Frontier Marshal. 1940: Viva Cisco Kid; He Married His Wife. 1941: The Great American Broadcast; Week-end in Havana. 1942: Tales of Manhattan; Orchestra Wives. 1943: Coney Island; Wintertime. 1947: Captain from Castile. 1948: That Lady in Ermine; Deep Waters; Julia Misbehaves. 1949: The Beautiful Blonde from Bashful Bend. 1954: Vera Cruz; The Americano. 1955: The Racers. 1956: Around the World in 80 Days. 1960: Ocean's 11. 1963: Donovan's Reef. 1964: A House is not a Home. 1965: Marriage on the Rocks. 1969: The Midas Run.

ROMM, Mikhail

Director. Irkutsk, Russia 1901–71

Moscow Film Academy. 1930–32: scriptwriter. Assistant at Soyuzkino. 1934: first film as director *Pushka* for Mosfilm, for whom made most of his films. 1937: made *Lenin v Oktyabre* which Stalin wanted, to commemorate Revolution: only 3 months elapsed from commencement of shooting to release. This and *Lenin v 1918 godu* (1939) written by Alexei Kapler. Tested for part of Elizabeth I of England for *Ivan Groznyi* Part III. 1948: made the first anti-American film of Cold War *Ruskii Vopros*; in collaboration compiled documentary *Zhivoi Lenin*. 1955: supervised Samson Samsonov's *Poprigunya*. Several films have scores by Aram Khatchaturian. Won 5 Stalin Prizes.

Films as director: 1934: Pushka – Boule de suif (*+ s*). 1937: Trinadtsat – The Thirteen (*+ co-s*); Lenin v Oktyabre – Lenin in October (*co-d Dimitri Vasiliev*). 1939: Lenin v 1918 godu – Lenin in 1918. 1943: Mechta – Dream (*+ co-s*). 1945: Chelovek No 217 – Man No 217 (*+ co-s*). 1948: Russkii Vopros – The Russian Question (*+ s*); Vladimir Ilyich Lenin (*co-d V. Belyaev*); Zhivoi Lenin (*co-d Marcia Slavinskaya*). 1950: Sekretnaya Missiya – Secret Mission. 1953: Admiral Ushakov; Korabli shturmuyut bastiony –

Ships attacking Forts (*part 2 of* Admiral Ushakov). 1956: Ubiistvo na ulitsye Dante – Murder on Dante Street (*+ co-s*). 1961: Devyat dni odnovo goda – Nine Days of One Year (*+ co-s*). 1965: Obyknovennie Fashizm – Ordinary Fascism (*+ co-s/e/n*).

RONDI, Brunello

Director. Tirano, Italy 1924–

1946: entered films as assistant director and writer in collaboration on *Ultimo Amore*. 1950: assistant to Roberto Rossellini on *Francesco, Giullare di Dio*. 1952: co-wrote Rossellini's *Europa 51* and Alessandro Blasetti's *Altri Tempi*. 1954: began collaboration with Federico Fellini. 1956: book published 'Neorealismo Italiano'. 1957: taught at Centro Sperimentale in Rome. 1958: wrote verse drama 'L'Assedio'. 1962: first film as director in collaboration. 1963: acted in *Le Ore dell'Amore*. Writings on contemporary music. 1969: his play the basis for Vittorio De Sica's *Gli Amanti*.

Films as director: 1962: Una Vita Violenta (*co-d Paolo Heusch*). 1963: Il Demonio (*+ st/co-s*). 1966: Domani non siamo piu qui. 1970: Le Tue Mani sul mio corpo – Shocking (*+ co-s*).

Films as writer in collaboration: 1962: Boccaccio '70 *ep* La Tentazioni del dottor Antonio. 1963: Otto e mezzo. 1965: Giulietta degli spiriti. 1969: Fellini-Satyricon; Scacco alla regina.

RONET, Maurice

Actor. Nice 1927–

Parents both actors. 1947: Conservatoire under René Alexandre. Numerous classic roles in Paris theatre, notably for Jean-Louis Barrault. 1949: first major film role in *Rendez-vous de juillet*. 1964: first film as director *Le Voleur de Tibidado*, also acted in it. From 1966: acted in several films directed by Claude Chabrol.

Films as actor include: 1949: Rendez-vous de juillet. 1951: Un Grand Patron; Les Sept Péchés Capitaux *ep* La Luxure. 1952: Lucrezia Borgia. 1955: Les Aristocrates. 1956: La Sorcière. 1957: Celui qui doit mourir; Ascenseur pour l'échafaud; Carve Her Name With Pride. 1959: Plein Soleil. 1961: Le Rendez-vous de minuit. 1962: Le Meurtrier. 1963: Tempestà su Ceylon; Le Feu Follet. 1965: Trois Chambres à Manhattan; Lost Command. 1966: La Longue Marche; La Ligne démarcation; Le Scandale. 1967: La Route de Corinthe; How Sweet it Is. 1968: Les Oiseaux vont mourir au Perou; La Piscine; La Femme Infidele. 1969: La Femme Ecarlate. 1970: Qui? 1971: Un Peu, beaucoup, passionnement; Raphael, ou le débauché.

ROOM, Abraham *or* Alexander

Director. Vilno, Russia 1894–

Dentist, journalist in Moscow. From 1914: amateur theatrical work. 1915–17: Leningrad Institute of Psycho-Neurology, directed student theatre. Worked in children's theatre. 1923: invited by Vsevolod Meyerhold to join Theatre of the Revolution, became director. State Film School, pupil of Lev Kuleshov; taught, had own studio. 1924: entered films as assistant; directed 2 films. 1925–26: made short on Jewish

Le Signe du Lion, *directed by Eric Rohmer.*
Der Müde Tod, *directed by Fritz Lang, with sets by Walter Röhrig, Robert Herlth and Hermann Warm.*
Lenin v Oktyabre, *directed by Mikhail Romm.*

agricultural project in South Russia, Mayakovsky collaborated on titles. 1926: assisted by Sergei Yutkevich on *Predatel*. 1927: Yutkevich designer on, and in collaboration directed *Tretya Meshchanskaya*. 1930: with Dziga Vertov, first to ask for sound at Sovkino, made the first Russian sound films on 5-Year Plan, using newsreel footage from film by Esther Shub and Vertov. Edouard Tissé photographed film about Tito *V gorakh Yugoslavii* (1946) and *Serebristaya pyl* (1953).

Features as director: 1924: Gonka za samogonkoi; Sto govorit MOC? – What says MOC? (+s). 1926: Bukhta smerti – Death Bay; Predatel Krasnaya Presnya – Red Presnya (co-d *L. Sheffer*).1927: Tretya Meshchanskaya – Three Meshchanskaya Street – Bed and Sofa (+co-s; *co-d Sergei Yutkevich*). 1928: Ukhaby zhizni – Hard Life (+co-s). 1930: Plan velikikh rabot – Plan for Great Works; Prividenie Kotoroye ne vozvrashchayetsya – The Ghost That Will not Return; Manometr No 1. 1931: Manometr No 2. 1936: Strogi Yunosha – The Stern Young Man. 1939: Eskadrilya N5 – Five Squadron. 1941: Veter s vostoka – Wind from the East. 1945: Nashestvie – The Invasion. 1946: V gorakh Yugoslavii – In the Mountains of Yugoslavia. 1948; Sud chesti ó The Tribunal of Honour. 1952: Shkola Zlosloviya ó School for Scandal. 1953: Serebristaya pyl ó Silver Dust. 1956: Serdtsye betsya vnov ó A New Heart.

ROONEY, Mickey

(Joe Yule Jr) Actor. New York 1922–
1927–34: as Mickey McGuire played comic strip character of same name in series of nearly 100 shorts. Changed name to Mickey Rooney in 1932. 1937–46: star of Andy Hardy series of features, starting with *A Family Affair* (1937). As adult played night club and variety dates, had own TV series and composed a number of songs. Autobiography published. First of 6 wives was Ava Gardner (1942–43). Most films for MGM. Co-directed with Albert Zugsmith *The Private Lives of Adam and Eve* (1960). 1970: on Broadway in 'W.C.' as W. C. Fields. Special Oscar (1940) for Andy Hardy characterisation.

Films as actor include: 1934: Manhattan Melodrama. 1935: Ah, Wilderness; A Midsummer Night's Dream. 1937: Captains Courageous; A Family Affair. 1938: Boy's Town. 1939: The Adventures of Huckleberry Finn; Babes in Arms. 1940: Strike Up the Band. 1943: The Human Comedy. 1944: National Velvet. 1946: Love Laughs at Andy Hardy. 1950: The Fireball. 1952: Sound Off. 1953: All Ashore; A Slight Case of Larceny. 1954: Drive a Crooked Road. 1955: The Bridges at Toko-Ri. 1957: Operation Mad Ball; Baby Face Nelson. 1958: Andy Hardy Comes Home. 1959: The Last Mile; The Big Operator. 1960: Platinum High School. 1961: King of the Roaring Twenties, the Story of Arnold Rothstein; Breakfast at Tiffany's. 1962: Requiem for a Heavyweight. 1963: It's a Mad, Mad, Mad, Mad World. 1964: The Secret Invasion. 1967: The Extraordinary Seaman (r 1969).

ROSAY, Francoise

(Francoise Bandy de Nalèche) Actress. Paris 1891–
Mother was actress Marie-Thérèse Sylviac. 1908–11: studied acting with Paul Mounet. 1913: first film as actress. 1914–17: studied singing at Conservatoire

National de Musique et de Déclamation. 1917: married Jacques Feyder. 1917–19: Paris Opera Company. 1922–28: French films. In collaboration with her husband directed *Visages d'enfants* (1925) and *Carmen* (1926). 1929–31: American films. 1932–38: German films. World War II to Switzerland where she and her husband produced *Une Femme disparait* (1942) while she taught at the Conservatoire de Genève. Toured Switzerland, Algeria, and Tunisia in sketches written and directed by her husband. 1944: London debut. After 1945: films in France, England, Belgium, Italy and Canada. Book: 'Le Cinéma, notre métier' (1956). 1961–62: New York stage.

Films as actress include: 1925: Gribiche. 1928: Les Deux Timides. 1930: Let Us Be Gay; Si L'empereur savait ça. 1934: Le Grand Jeu. 1935: Pension Mimosas; La Kermesse Heroïque. 1936: Jenny. 1937: Drôle de drame; Un Carnet de bal. 1938: Les Gens du voyage; Fahrendes Volk. 1942: Une Femme disparait (+co-p). 1944: The Halfway House. 1946: Macadam. 1949: Quartet *ep* Alien Corn; The Naked Heart. 1951: The September Affair; The 13th Letter; Les Sept Péchés Capitaux *ep* L'Orgueil; L'Auberge Rouge. 1954: La Reine Margot. 1955: That Lady. 1957: Interlude. 1959: The Sound and the Fury. 1960: Le Bois des amants.

ROSE, Reginald

Writer. New York 1921–
Worked as clerk, then publicist for Warner. Became advertising account executive and chief copywriter. World War II in US Air Force. 1951: first TV play; 'Bus to Nowhere'. Numerous TV plays before starting to write film scripts.

Films as writer include: 1956: Crime in the Streets (+st). 1957: Twelve Angry Men (+co-p/fpl). 1958: Man of the West. 1959: Man in the Net.

ROSENBERG, Aaron

Producer. New York 1912–
All-American university football player then (1934) started at Fox as assistant director. 1942–46: officer, US Marine Corps. On discharge joined Universal as assistant director, then associate producer and (1949) producer. In 1960s with MGM, then Fox.

Films as producer include: 1950: Winchester '73. 1952: Bend of the River; Red Ball Express; The World In His Arms. 1953: The Man from the Alamo; Thunder Bay; Wings of the Hawk; The Glenn Miller Story. 1954: Saskatchewan; The Far Country. 1955: Man Without A Star; The Shrike. 1956: The Great Man; Backlash. 1958: The Badlanders. 1961: Go Naked in the World. 1962: Mutiny on the Bounty. 1964: Shock Treatment. 1965: The Saboteur – Code Name Morituri; The Reward. 1967: Caprice. 1968: The Detective.

ROSENBERG, Stuart

Director. New York 1928–
Irish literature at New York University, where he continued as teacher. From 1959: directed many TV films for NBC, ABC and CBS. 1960: began first film as director, but left in sympathy with actors' strike; picture completed by Burt Balaban.

Films as director: 1960: Murder Incorporated (co-d *Burt Balaban*). 1967: Cool Hand Luke. 1969: The April Fools. 1970: Move; WUSA.

ROSENMAN, Leonard

Composer. New York 1924–
Began as painter. World War II; 3 years in US Air Force. From 1947: abandoned painting for music; studied theory and composition under Arnold Schoenberg and Roger Sessions. From 1952: studied nder Luigi Dallapiccola. 1953: commissioned to write one-act opera by Koussevitsky Foundation. Many chamber and choral compositions. Composed music for films from 1955.

Films as composer include: 1955: East of Eden; The Cobweb. 1956: Edge of the City. 1957: The Young Stranger. 1958: Lafayette Escadrille. 1959: Pork Chop Hill. 1960: The Plunderers; The Rise and Fall of Legs Diamond. 1961: The Outsider. 1962: Hell is for Heroes; The Chapman Report. 1966: Fantastic Voyage. 1969: Hellfighters. 1970: A Man Called Horse.

ROSI, Francesco

Director. Naples 1922–
Studied law in Naples, but during Allied campaign in Italy became an illustrator for children (drawings for 'Alice in Wonderland'). 1944: writer and director at Radio Naples. Assistant to stage director Ettore Giannini, writer of revue sketches (1947). 1948: with Franco Zeffirelli assisted Luchino Visconti on *La Terra Trema*. From 1950 collaborated on scripts including *Domenica d'Agosto* (1950), *Bellissima* (1951) and *I Vinti* (1953). 1952: completed *Camicie Rosse* which had been abandoned by its directors. 1955–56: dubbing director on Italian versions of foreign films. 1956: co-directed *Kean* with Vittorio Gassmann. 1958: first film as sole director.

Films as director: 1952: Camicie Rosse – Red Shirts (co-d *Goffredo Alessandrini, Franco Rossi*). 1957: Kean (+co-s). 1958: La Sfida. 1959: I Magliari. 1962: Salvatore Giuliano. 1963: Le Mani sulla città (+cost/co-s). 1965: Il Momento della verità (+co-p/st/s). 1967: C'era una volta – More than a Miracle – Cinderella, Italian Style (+co-s). 1970: Uomini contro (+co-p/co-s).

ROSS, Herbert

Choreographer and director. New York 1927–
Studied dancing under Doris Humphrey, Helene Platova, Laird Leslie in New York. 1943–50: studied acting under Herbert Berghof. Debut as actor in Shakespearean repertory in 1940s. Dancer and choreographer on stage and TV. 1969: first film as director.

Films as choreographer: 1954: Carmen Jones. 1961: The Young Ones. 1962: Summer Holiday. 1967: Doctor Dolittle. 1968: Funny Girl.

Films as director: 1969: Goodbye, Mr Chips (+chor). 1970: The Owl and the Pussycat. 1971: T. R. Baskin.

ROSSELLINI, Roberto

Director. Rome 1906–
Father architect. e.g. of cinemas. Worked in editing

and dubbing. From 1936: first film as director, first of series of amateur shorts made in own studio. 1938: *Prelude à l'après-midi d'un faune* banned as indecent; in collaboration with Goffredo Alessandrini directed and wrote *Luciano serra pilota*, first professional work. 1939: shorts photographed by Mario Bava. 1941: commissioned by Francesco De Robertis to make documentary *La Nave Bianca*; developed into first feature, first of 3 supervised by De Robertis, including *Un Pilota ritorna* written in collaboration with Michelangelo Antonioni and Ugo Betti. 1943: co-wrote and supervised *L'Invasore*; abandoned *Desiderio*, completed 3 years later by Marcello Pagliero. 1945–46: wrote *Roma, città aperta* and *Paisà* in collaboration with Federico Fellini. 1948: his episode in *L'Amore* adapted from Jean Cocteau's 'La Voix Humaine'. 1949: directed Ingrid Bergman for first time in *Stromboli, terra di Dio* for their production company; married her in 1950. 1950: made *Francesco, giullare di Dio* scripted in collaboration with Fellini. 1952: co-wrote and supervised *Medico Condotto*. 1953: in Naples, directed stage productions of 'Otello' and Paul Claudel's 'Jeanne au bûcher'. 1954: directed own adaptation of 'Jeanne au bûcher' as *Giovanna d'Arco al rogo*; supervised Carlo Ludovico Bragaglia's *Orient Express*; directed stage production of Gabriele D'Annunzio's 'La Figlia di Jorio'. 1956: first work for TV, short *Le Psychodrame*. 1958: divorced. 1961: supervised *Benito Mussolini*; on stage directed 'A View from the Bridge'. 1962: directed on stage Beniamino Joppolo's 'I Carabinieri'; in collaboration with Jean Gruault adapted it for Jean-Luc Godard's *Les Carabiniers*. 1964: supervised and wrote *L'Eta del ferro* directed by son Renzo Rossellini; includes excerpts from *Luciano serra pilota* and *Paisà*. From 1964: worked only for TV, including *Idea di un'isola* (1967) for American TV. 1967: wrote and supervised son's *La Lotta del'uomo per la sua sopravvivenza*. Music for his films often composed by son. Several technical inventions.

Films as director: 1936: Daphne. 1938: Prelude à l'aprés-midi d'un faune; Luciano serra pilota (+ *co-s*; *co-d Goffredo Alessandrini*). 1939: Fantasia Sottomarina; Il Tacchino Prepotente; La Vispa Teresa. 1941: Il Ruscello di Ripasottile; La Nave Bianca (+ *co-s*). 1942: Un Pilota ritorna. 1943: L'Uomo della croce (+ *co-s*); Desiderio (+ *co-s*; *co-d Marcello Pagliero*). 1945: Roma, città aperta – Open City (+ *co-s*). 1946: Paisà – Paisan (+ *p/co-st/co-s*). 1947: Germania, anno zero – Germany, Year Zero (+ *co-st/s*). 1948: L'Amore *ep* Una Voce Umana (+ *co-s*); La Macchina Ammazzacattivi (+ *co-st/s*). 1949: Stromboli, terra di Dio – Stromboli (+ *st/co-s/pc*). 1950: Francesco, giullare di Dio (+ *co-s*). 1951: Les Sept Péchés Capitaux – The Seven Deadly Sins *ep* L'Invidia (+ *st/co-s*); Europa '51 (+ *st*). 1953: Dov'è la libertà?; Viaggio in Italia – The Lonely Woman (+ *co-s*); Siamo donne *ep* Ingrid Bergman. 1954: Amori di mezzo secolo *ep* Napoli '43; Giovanna d'Arco al rogo (+ *s*); Die Angst – La Paura – Non credo più all'amore – Fear. 1956: Le Psychodrame. 1958: L'India Vista da Rossellini (+ *p*; *10 eps*). 1958: India (+ *st/co-s*). 1959: Il Generale della Rovere (+ *co-s*). 1960: Era notte a Roma (+ *co-s*); Viva l'Italia (+ *co-s*). 1961: Vanina Vanini – The Betrayer; Torino nei centi'anni. 1962: Anima Nera (+ *s*); Rogopag – Laviamoci il Cervello *ep* Illibatezza (+ *s*). 1966: La Prise de pouvoir par Louis XIV. 1967: Idea di un'isola. 1968: Atti degli Apostoli. 1970: Socrate (+ *co-s*).

ROSSEN, Robert

Director and writer. New York 1908–66
After amateur theatre at New York University, produced and wrote plays. His productions included 2 plays by Richard Maibaum and his own 'The Body Beautiful', which led to job as scenarist at Warners. An unperformed play 'Corner Pocket' was set (like *The Hustler*) in a pool hall. 1937–43: at Warners. 1947: first film as director. 1950: first film as producer and director. Wrote and produced most of his films. Also produced *The Undercover Man* (1949).

Films as writer: 1937: Marked Woman (*co-st/co-s*); They Won't Forget (*co*). 1938: Racket Busters (*co-st/co-s*). 1939: Dust Be My Destiny; The Roaring Twenties (*co*); A Child is Born. 1941: The Sea Wolf; Out of the Fog (*co*); Blues in the Night. 1943: Edge of Darkness. 1945: A Walk in the Sun. 1946: The Strange Love of Martha Ivers. 1947: Desert Fury. 1948: The Treasure of the Sierra Madre (*co, uc*).

Films as director: 1947: Johnny O'Clock (+ *s*); Body and Soul. 1950: All the King's Men (+ *p/s*). 1951: The Brave Bulls (+ *p*). 1954: Mambo (+ *co-s*). 1956: Alexander the Great (+ *p/s*). 1957: Island in the Sun. 1959: They Came to Cordura (+ *co-s*). 1961: The Hustler (+ *p/co-s*). 1963: Lilith (+ *p/s*).

ROSSI, Franco

Director. Florence 1919–
Abandoned law studies to become assistant to Mario Camerini: assistant to Renato Castellani (1947 and 1949), Aldo Vergano (1950), and Louis Trenker (1951). Directed radio programme 'Teatro del l' Usignuolo'. 1950: first film as director. 1952: worked on *Camicie Rossi*, completed by Francesco Rosi. From 1953: also occasionally writer in collaboration on films by others. 1959: supervised and co-wrote *Tutti Inamorati*. 1968: directed 8 episodes of 'The Odyssey' for TV. 1971: 'The Aeneid' for TV. On stage directed Giuseppe Patroni Griffi's play 'In Memoria di una signora amica'.

Films as director: 1950: I Falsari (+ *co-s*). 1952: Camicie Rossi – Red Shirts (*co-d Goffredo Alessandrini, Francesco Rosi*); Solo per te, Lucia. 1954: Il Seduttore (+ *co-s*). 1955: Amici per la pelle – Friends for Life (+ *co-s*). 1957: Amore a prima vista – Buenos Dias amor. 1958: Calypso (+ *co-st/co-s*; *co-d Leonardo Benvenuti, Golfiero Colonna*). 1960: Morte di un amico – Death of a Friend (+ *co-s*). 1961: Odissea Nuda – Nude Odyssey (+ *co-st/co-s*). 1962: Smog (+ *co-st/co-s*). 1964: Alta Infedeltà – Sex in the Afternoon – High Infidelity *ep* Scandaloso; Tre Notti d'amore *ep* La Moglie Bambina; Controsesso *ep* Cocaina de Domenica; Le Bambole – Four Kinds of Love *ep* La Minestra. 1965: Una Rosa per tutti – Rose for Everyone – Every Man's Woman; I Complessi – Complexes *ep* I Complesso della schiava nubiana. 1966: Le Streghe – The Witches *ep* La Siciliana (+ *s*); Non faccio la guerra, faccio l'amore – Don't Make War, Make Love. 1969: Giovinezza, Giovinezza.

ROSSI-DRAGO, Eleanora

(Palmina Omiccioli) Actress. Genoa 1925–
Italian father, Spanish mother. Model. Also stage and TV.

Salvatore Giuliano, *directed by Francesco Rosi.*
Robert Rossen at the time of Lilith.
Morte di un Amico, *directed by Franco Rossi.*

Films as actress include: 1951: Persiane Chiusi; Les Sept Péchés Capitaux ep L'Avarice et la colère; Tre Storie Proibite. 1952: La Tratta delle bianche. 1953: La Fiammata; L'Esclave; Destinées ep Due Donne. 1954: L'Affaire Maurizius; Vestire gli ignudi. 1955: Le Amiche. 1956: Suor Letizia; Donne Sole. 1957: Kean; Tous peuvent me tuer; Cesta Dugo Godina Dana. 1959: Dagli Appennini alle Ande; Un Maledetto Imbroglio; Estate Violenta. 1961: Caccia all' uomoo. 1966: La Bibbia.

ROSSIF, Frédéric

Director. Montenegro, Yugoslavia 1922–
1944: in French Foreign Legion. 1945–48: draughtsman at Renault, then at Citroën. 1948: 'bouncer' at Club St Germain-des-Prés. 1948–51: director and programmer at the Cinémathèque Française. From 1951: worked intermittently as producer and director for French TV. 1954: acted in Sacha Guitry's Si Versailles m'était conté. 1958: first short film as director. From 1960: director of cinema and TV department at Hachettes. 1961: first feature as director.

Films as director: 1958: Une Histoire d'éléphants. 1959: Vel d'Hiv. 1960: Le Monde Instantané. 1961: Imprévisibles Nouveautés – Unforeseeable Novelties; Le Temps du ghetto. 1962: De notre temps. 1963: Mourir à Madrid – To Die in Madrid; Les Animaux – The Animals. 1967: La Révolution d'Octobre – October Revolution (+co-p); The Witnesses. 1969: Pourquoi l'Amérique. 1971: Aussi loin que l'amour (+co-s).

ROSSON, Harold

Cinematographer
1908: small part actor at Vitagraph. Over next 6 years, various jobs including camera assistant at independent studios and on Allan Dwan productions at Famous Players while holding full-time job in stockbrokers office. From 1914: concentrated on film work, also selling cinema tickets and working as projectionist in Brooklyn. To Hollywood, where his family worked in films. Bit parts for Metro, dark-room work for stills man and other jobs as well as camera assistant. 1915: became operator. To New York, became cinematographer there. To 1929: with Famous Players-Lasky and Paramount. 1929: with Fox. 1930–53: with MGM. After 1953: a few films freelance.

Films as cinematographer include: 1923: Lawful Larceny; Dark Secrets; Zaza; Quicksands (co); The Glimpses of the Moon. 1924: Manhandled; A Society Scandal. 1925: The Little French Girl; The Street of Forgotten Men. 1927: A Gentleman of Paris; Jim the Conqueror; Service for Ladies. 1928: Gentlemen Prefer Blondes; The Docks of New York; The Dragnet; Three Weekends. 1929: Abie's Irish Rose; Frozen Justice; The Far Call; South Sea Rose; Trent's Last Case. 1930: Madam Satan. 1931: The Squaw Man; Son of India; The Cuban Love Song. 1932: Tarzan the Ape Man; Red-Headed Woman; Red Dust. 1933: Hell Below; Hold Your Man; Penthouse (co); Bombshell. 1934: This Side of Heaven; Treasure Island (co). 1935: The Ghost Goes West. 1936: The Garden of Allah; The Devil is a Sissy. 1937: Captains Courageous; They Gave Him a Gun. 1938: Too Hot to Handle. 1939: The Wizard of Oz. 1940: Take This Woman; Edison the Man; Flight Command. 1941:

Honky Tonk; Johnny Eager. 1942: Somewhere I'll Find You; Tennessee Johnson. 1944: An American Romance; Thirty Seconds Over Tokyo (co). 1946: My Brother Talks to Horses; Duel in the Sun (co). 1947: Living in a Big Way; The Hucksters. 1948: Homecoming. 1949: Command Decision; The Stratton Story; Any Number Can Play; On the Town. 1950: Key to the City; The Asphalt Jungle; To Please a Lady. 1951: The Red Badge of Courage; Lone Star; Love is Better than Ever. 1952: Singin' in the Rain. 1953: I Love Melvin; The Story of Three Loves (co); Dangerous when Wet; The Actress. 1954: Mambo. 1955: Strange Lady in Town; Ulisse (co); Pete Kelly's Blues. 1956: The Bad Seed; Toward the Unknown. 1957: The Enemy Below. 1958: No Time for Sergeants. 1967: El Dorado.

ROTA, Nino

Composer. Milan 1911–
Studied at Milan Conservatory, Santa Cecilia, Rome, and the Curtis Institute in Philadelphia. 1933: composed first film score.

Films as composer include: 1946: Vivere in pace. 1948: Senza pietà; Sotto il sole di Roma. 1950: E Primavera. 1951: Filumena Maturano; Anna; Lo Sceicco Bianco. 1953: I Vitelloni. 1954: La Strada. 1955: Il Bidone; Amici per la pelle. 1956: War and Peace. 1957: Le Notti Bianchi; Le Notti di Cabiria. 1958: La Diga sul Pacifico; Fortunella. 1959: La Dolce Vita; Plein Soleil; Rocco e i suoi fratelli. 1962: Boccaccio '70. 1963: Il Gattopardo. 1965: Giulietta degli spiriti. 1967: Histoires Extraordinaires ep Toby Dammit; The Taming of the Shrew. 1968: Romeo and Juliet. 1970: I Clowns; Waterloo.

ROTHA, Paul

Director, producer and writer. London 1907–
Slade School of Fine Art, London. Began as painter and designer. 1927–28: critic for The Connoisseur. Assistant in art department of British International Pictures at Elstree Studios; criticised lack of creative opportunities in studio and lost job. 1929: wrote history of the cinema, 'The Film Till Now' (first published 1930, revised with additional section by Richard Griffith 1948, enlarged 1960, revised with postscript by Rotha 1967). Joined Empire Marketing Board Film Unit under John Grierson. 1932: first film as director, shot in Asia and Africa for Imperial Airways. From 1935: also worked as producer of documentaries, e.g. Cover to Cover (1936), The Future's in the Air (1936), Today We Live (1937), World of Plenty (1943). 1936–37: director of production, Strand Films. 1937–38: in USA, researched at film library of Museum of Modern Art, lectured on documentary film under Rockefeller Foundation grant. 1939–45: Ministry of Information Film Unit. 1951: directed first feature. 1953–55: head of BBC documentary film unit. Books include 'Rotha on Film' (1958), 'Documentary Film' (first published 1936).

Films as director: 1932: Contact. 1933: The Rising Tide. 1934: Shipyard. 1935: The Face of Britain; Death on the Road. 1936: The Future's in the Air (+p). 1940: The Fourth Estate. 1945: Land of Promise. 1946: Total War in Britain. 1947: A City Speaks. 1948: The World is Rich. 1951: No Resting Place. 1952: World Without End (co-d Basil Wright). 1958: Cat and

Mouse (+p/s). 1959: Cradle of Genius. 1961: Das Leben von Adolf Hitler – The Life of Adolf Hitler (+cy/e). 1962: De Overval – The Silent Raid (+s).

ROTHAFEL, S. L. 'Roxy'

(S. L. Rothapfel) Cinema manager. Stillwater, Minnesota 1882–1931 Philadelphia
Son of immigrant German shoemaker, Polish mother. 1895: moved to New York with family. Many jobs, including callboy in Broadway theatres. 7 years in US Marine Corps. To Pennsylvania. Travelling book salesman. Barman; converted back-room into cinema. Worked on improvement of film presentations in vaudeville programmes. Converted Milwaukee Alhambra into cinema, handled presentation. 1913: to New York: took over Regent Theatre, assembled music library. Moved to Rialto and Rivoli, where directed orchestra, selected music to accompany films, supervised staging and lighting of musical numbers. During World War I, technical advisor on some government films; promoted to Major in US Marine Corps Reserve. Resigned from Rialto and Rivoli after disagreement over personal expenses. Moved to F. J. Godsol's theatres: started at California Theatre, Los Angeles (re-opened 1919), then to Capitol, New York (re-opened 1920); shortened his name to Rothafel. To Goldwyn-controlled theatres, which were to be enlarged and converted into circuit. 1922: first broadcast from stage: became regular network feature. 1925: ended shows and broadcasts to manage new theatre, the Roxy. 1927: Roxy opened. Accomodated 9,272 customers, orchestra of 100, ballet and chorus of 100, 300 further staff. Paid particular attention to design of screen, stage, acoustics, projection standards, lighting, executive communications, broadcasting room, rehearsal theatre, dressing rooms. Music library of 10,000 selections, 50,000 orchestrations. Also took over theatres in Rockefeller Centre. 1931: heart attack. After further illness found 'interim' management opposed to him and left. Briefly to Mastbaum Theatre, Philadelphia. Military honours at funeral. 1960: Roxy Theatre demolished.

ROTUNNO, Giuseppe

Cinematographer. Rome 1926–
1952: first film as cinematographer documentary Cristo non si è fermato a Eboli. From 1952: camera operator; worked on e.g. Senso and several films directed by Carmine Gallone including Madama Butterfly. 1955: first feature as cinematographer Pane, Amore e... 1959: to USA for On the Beach.

Films as cinematographer include: 1956: Tosca. 1957: Le Notti Bianche; La Ragazza del palio. 1958: Anna di Brooklyn; La Maja Desnuda. 1959: Policarpo, ufficiale di scrittura; On the Beach. 1960: La Grande Guerra (co); Jovanka e le altri; La Sposa Bella; Rocco e suoi fratelli. 1961: I Due Nemici; Fantasmi a Roma. 1962: Boccaccio '70 ep Il Lavoro. 1963: Ieri, Oggi, Domani; I Compagni; Il Gattopardo. 1964: La Bibbia. 1966: Le Streghe ep La Strega Bruciata Viva. 1967: Lo Straniero (co). 1969: Fellini-Satyricon. 1971: Carnal Knowledge.

ROUCH, Jean

Director. Paris 1917–
Doctorate in Literature. Civil engineer. Diploma of

l'Institut d'Ethnologie. 1941–45: ethnological field work in Nigeria, Senegal. 1947: first short film as director in collaboration with Jean Sauvy and Pierre Ponty. 1946–47: they made first exploration of whole length of the Niger. 1948–49: field-work alone in Nigeria. 1949–50: field-work with Roger Rosfelder in Nigeria and Gold Coast. All films in 16 mm except episode in *La Fleur de l'age oules adolescentes* (1964). 1955: made compilation of earlier shorts *Les Fils de l'eau*. 1958: first feature as director. 1960–61: co-directed *Chronique d'un eté* with Edgar Morin. Head of research at CNRS, Musée de l'Homme; Secretary-General of Comité du Film Ethnographique. Books include: 'L'Afrique Fantôme', 'Le Petit Dan', 'Migrations au Ghana'. TV work includes *La Punition* (1962).

Short films as director: 1947: Au pays des mages noirs (+ *s/c/e; co-d Jean Sauvy, Pierre Ponty*). 1949: Initiation à la danse des possédés (+ *p/c*); Hombori (+ *s*); Les Magiciens Noirs – Les Magiciens de Wanzerbe – Ouanzerbe, capitale de la magie (+ *p/c; co-d Marcel Griaule*); La Circoncision (+ *p/c*). 1951: Bataille sur le grand fleuve – Chasse a l'hippotame (+ *c*); Cimetière dans la falaise (+ *c*); Les Hommes qui font la pluie – Yenendi – Les Faiseurs de pluie – Rainmakers (+ *c*); Les Gens du Mil – La Culture du Mil (+ *c*). 1955: Les Maîtres Fous (+ *c/n*); Mamy Water – Pêche et le culte de la mer (+ *s/c*). 1957: Goumbe (+ *s*); Moro-Naba (+ *c*). 1960: Hampi (+ *s*). 1962: Abidjan, port de pêche (+ *s*); Urbanisme Africain (+ *s*); Le Mil; Pêcheurs du Niger (+ *s*); Monsieur Albert Prophète (+ *s/n*). 1963: Le Palmier à huile; Le Cocotier; Rose et Landry. 1964: L'Afrique et la recherche scientifique; Paris vu par . . . – Six in Paris *ep* Gare du Nord; La Fleur de l'âge ou les adolescentes *ep* Marie-France et Véronique (+ *s*); Les Veuves de quinze ans. 1966: Tambours de Pierre – Le Tambour des Dogons – Les Eléments pour une étude de rhythme. 1969: Le Signe (+ *s; co-d Germaine Dieterlen*).

Features as director: 1955: Les Fils de l'eau. 1958: Moi, un Noir – I, a Negro – Treichville (+ *s/c*). 1959: La Pyramide Humaine (+ *s/co-c*). 1961: Chronique d'un Eté – Chronicle of a Summer (+ *p/co-s/w; co-d Edgar Morin*). 1965: La Chasse au lion à l'arc – The Lion Hunters (+ *s/c/n*). 1966: La Goumbe des jeunes noceurs (+ *c*). 1967: Jaguar. 1970: Petit à petit (+ *st/c*).

ROULEAU, Raymond

Director. Brussels 1904–
Mother an actress. Studied music and painting. From 1924: worked in theatre as actor, director, set-designer. 1924–27: at the Théâtre de Marais, Brussels. 1927: left Brussels for Paris; first film as actor *L'Argent* (1928). Worked with Charles Dullin, the Pitoëffs, Artaud and at the Théâtre Daunou. 1932: first film as director. 1944–51: at the Théâtre de l'Oeuvre. Actor in films including some of his own.

Films as director: 1932: Suzanne (+ *w; co-d Leo Joannon*). 1933: Une Vie Perdue (+ *w*). 1936: Rose. 1937: Le Messager; Trois-six-neuf (+ *w*). 1945: Le Couple Idéal (+ *w; co-d Bernard-Roland*). 1957: Les Sorcières de Salem (+ *w*). 1961: Les Amants de Téruel (+ *s*).

ROUQUIER, Georges

Director. Lunel, France 1909–
Began as typographer and linotypist. 1929: made first

short film. 1929–42: artistic director of shorts section, International Films. From 1942: worked as documentary director. From 1946: films occasionally feature-length. Published 'L'Album de Farrebique' (1946).

Films as director: 1929: Vendanges (+ *p/s/c/e*). 1942: Le Tonnelier (+ *s*). 1943: Le Charron (+ *s*); L'Economie des métaux; La Part de l'enfant. 1946: Farrebique (+ *s*). 1949: Le Chaudronnier. 1950: Le Sel de la terre; Les Galeries de Malgovert. 1952: Le Lycée sur la colline; Un Jour comme les autres. 1953: Sang et lumière. 1954: Lourdes et ses miracles. 1955: Arthur Honegger. 1956: La Bête Noire; SOS Noronha (+ *co-s*).

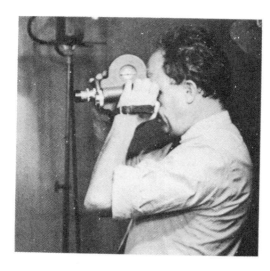

ROUSE, Russell

Director and writer. New York 1916–
Son of Edwin Russell, assistant director of early New York films. Labourer at Paramount, then property department. To MGM: script messenger. Formed writing collaboration with Clarence Greene; to 1942 worked freelance without credit. 1942–50: writers for Republic, MGM, United Artists on e.g. *D.O.A.* (1949). Own production company. 1951: first film as director, in collaboration with Leo Popkin. 1951–55 and 1964–66: writing collaboration with Greene continued. 1958–66: all his films produced by Greene. 1969: they wrote *Color Me Dead*.

Films as director and co-writer: 1951: The Well (*co-d Leo Popkin*). 1952: The Thief. 1953: Wicked Woman. 1955: New York Confidential. 1956: The Fastest Gun Alive. 1957: House of Numbers. 1958: Thunder in the Sun. 1964: A House is not a Home. 1965: The Oscar; The Caper of the Golden Bulls – Carnival of Thieves (*d only*).

ROWLAND, Roy

Director. New York *c*. 1910–
Educated in Los Angeles. Law at Manual Arts High School. University of Southern California. Script clerk then assistant at MGM. 1934: co-directed *Hollywood Party* with Richard Boleslewsky and Allan Dwan. 1936–41: directed shorts for MGM and US Army. 1943: first feature as director. At MGM 1943–51 and 1954–58. Son is actor Steve Rowland.

Features as director: 1934: Hollywood Party (*co-d, uc*). 1943: A Stranger in Town; Lost Angel. 1945: Our Vines Have Tender Grapes. 1946: Boys Ranch. 1947: Killer McCoy; The Romance of Rosy Ridge. 1948: Tenth Avenue Angel. 1949: Scene of the Crime. 1950: The Outriders; Two Weeks with Love. 1951: Excuse My Dust; Bugles in the Afternoon. 1952: The 5,000 Fingers of Dr T. 1953: Affair with a Stranger; The Moonlighter. 1954: Witness to Murder; Rogue Cop. 1955: Many Rivers to Cross; Hit the Deck. 1956: Meet Me in Las Vegas; These Wilder Years; Slander. 1957: Gun Glory. 1958: The Seven Hills of Rome. 1963: The Girl Hunters (+ *co-s*). 1965: Gunfighters of the Casa Grande. 1966: Sie Nannten ihn Gringo – La Ley del forastero – Man Called Gringo. 1967: The Sea Pirate.

ROY, Bimal

Director. Dacca, East Bengal 1909–66 Bombay
1932: began as assistant cameraman with New Theatres in Calcutta. Cinematographer to Pramathesh

Jean Rouch with his 16mm camera.
Rita Gam and Ray Milland in The Thief, *directed by Russell Rouse.*
Roy Rowland's The 5000 Fingers of Dr T.

Chandra Barua on a number of films including *Devdas* (1935), *Mukti* (1937). From 1942: worked as director for New Theatres, making Bengali and Hindi versions of his films. 1951: left Calcutta for Bombay where he made films in Hindi. 1952: formed own company, Bimal Roy Productions. 1963: last film.

Films as director: 1942: Udayer pathe. 1945: Humrahi. 1948: Anjangadh; Pehla admi. 1949: Mantra Mugdh. 1950: Tathapil. 1951: Maa. 1953: Do bigha zamin – Two Acres of Land (+ *p*). 1954: Parineta; Baap bete; Biraj Bahu; Naukari (+ *p*). 1955: Amanat (+ *p*; co-d *Arabind Sen*); Gotama the Buddha (+ *p*; co-d *Rajbans Khanna*). 1956: Devdas (+ *p*); Pariwar (+ *p*; co-d *Asit Sen*). 1958: Aparadhi kaun; Yahudi; Madhumati (+ *p*). 1959: Sujata. 1960: Parakh. 1961: Kabuliwala (+ *p*). 1962: Prem patra (+ *p*). 1963: Bandini.

ROZIER, Jacques

Director. Paris 1926–
Studied at IDHEC. Assistant on *French Can Can* (1955). TV assistant on drama programmes. From 1947: made shorts. Continued to do so after first feature as director *Adieu Philippine* (1961).

Films as director: 1947: Langage de l'écran. 1954: Une Epine au pied. 1955: La Rentrée des classes (+ *co-s/e*). 1958: Blue Jeans (+ *co-s/co-e*). 1962: Adieu Philippine (+ *co-s/co-e*). 1963: Dans le vent (+ *co-s/co-e*); Paparazzi (+ *s/e*). 1971: Du côté d'orouet (+ *s*).

ROZSA, Miklos

Composer. Budapest 1907–
Studied in Leipzig. 1931: on graduation, to Paris. 1933: to London to compose ballet music for Alicia Markova and Anton Dolin. 1936: musical director and composer for Alexander Korda's London Films. 1940: with Korda to Hollywood for *The Thief of Bagdad*. Remained in Hollywood. Subsequent work includes 4 films directed by Zoltàn Korda. To 1947: worked for several companies including United Artists, Paramount, Columbia. 1947–48: at Universal. From 1949: mainly for MGM.

Films as composer include: 1937: Knight Without Armour. 1939: The Four Feathers; The Spy in Black. 1941: Lydia; Sundown. 1942: Rudyard Kipling's Jungle Book. 1943: Five Graves to Cairo; Sahara. 1944: Double Indemnity; The Hour Before the Dawn; Dark Waters. 1945: Spellbound; Blood on the Sun. 1946: The Killers; The Strange Love of Martha Ivers. 1947: Brute Force; The Red House; The Macomber Affair; The Other Love. 1948: A Woman's Vengeance; Secret Beyond the Door; Kiss the Blood off My Hands; Criss Cross; The Naked City (*co*); A Double Life. 1949: Command Decision; The Bribe; The Red Danube; East Side, West Side; Madame Bovary; Adam's Rib. 1950: Crisis; The Asphalt Jungle. 1951: Quo Vadis. 1953: Julius Caesar; Young Bess. 1955: Moonfleet. 1956: Lust for Life; Tribute to a Bad Man; Bhowani Junction. 1957: Something of Value. 1958: A Time to Love and a Time to Die; The World, the Flesh and the Devil. 1959: Ben-Hur. 1961: King of Kings; El Cid. 1962: Sodom and Gomorrah. 1968: The Power; The Green Berets. 1970: The Private Life of Sherlock Holmes.

RUGGLES, Charles

Actor.   Los Angeles 1892–1970 Santa Monica, California
Brother of Wesley Ruggles. 1906: New York stage debut. 1914: married actress Adele Rowland. 1915: first film as actor *Peer Gynt*. 1950–61: stage work only.

Films as actor include: 1929: Gentlemen of the Press; Battle of Paris. 1930: Young Man of Manhattan. 1931: The Girl Habit; The Smiling Lieutenant. 1932: One Hour With You; Trouble in Paradise; Love Me Tonight; This Reckless Age; This is the Night. 1933: Alice in Wonderland; Mama Loves Papa; Melody Cruise. 1934: A Melody in Spring; Friends of Mr Sweeney; Six of a Kind. 1935: The Big Broadcast of 1936; Ruggles of Red Gap; People Will Talk; No More Ladies. 1936: Anything Goes; Early to Bed; Hearts Divided; The Preview Murder Mystery; Mind Your Own Business. 1938: Bringing Up Baby; Breaking the Ice. 1939: Yes, My Darling Daughter. 1940: Maryland; Public Deb No 1; No Time for Comedy. 1942: Friendly Enemies. 1944: Our Hearts Were Young and Gay. 1945: Incendiary Blonde; Bedside Manner. 1946: Gallant Journey; A Stolen Life; My Brother Talks to Horses. 1947: Ramrod; It Happened on Fifth Avenue. 1948: Give My Regards to Broadway. 1949: Look for the Silver Lining; The Loveable Cheat. 1961: All in a Night's Work; The Pleasure of His Company; The Parent Trap. 1966: Follow Me, Boys.

RUGGLES, Wesley

Director. Los Angeles 1889–1972 Santa Monica, California
Brother of Charles Ruggles. University of San Francisco. Then joined theatrical company. From 1914: actor in a number of Mack Sennett Keystone films including *Hushing the Scandal* (1915), also Triangle-Keystone films e.g. *A Submarine Pirate* and Charles Chaplin films for Essanay e.g. *Shanghaied* (1915), *Police* (1916). 1917: began as director with Vitagraph. 1918: war cameraman in Army Signal Corps. From 1919; director with various companies. Films mainly released through Universal in late 1920s, Paramount in 1930s when he also worked as producer. From 1940: with Columbia then MGM. 1944: contract with J. Arthur Rank. 1946: last film, *London Town* made in England, released in USA in 1953.

Films as director include: 1917: For France. 1922: If I were Queen. 1925: The Plastic Age. 1927: Silk Stockings. 1929: Condemned. 1930: Honey. 1931: Cimarron. 1932: Roar of the Dragon. 1933: College Humor; I'm No Angel. 1934: Bolero. 1935: The Gilded Lily; Accent on Youth. 1936: Valiant is the Word for Carrie (+ *p*); The Bride Comes Home (+ *p*). 1937: True Confession; I Met Him in Paris (+ *p*). 1938: Sing, You Sinners (+ *p*). 1940: Too Many Husbands; Arizona (+ *p*). 1941: You Belong to Me. 1942: Somewhere I'll Find You. 1943: Slightly Dangerous. 1944: See Here, Private Hargrove. 1946: London Town – My Heart Goes Crazy (+ *p/st*).

RUSH, Barbara

Actress. Denver, Colorado 1927–
Stage debut at 10 in Santa Barbara. University of California, Pasadena Playhouse Theatre Arts College.

In 'Antony and Cleopatra', spotted for Paramount. 1951: first film as actress *The First Legion*, first of 4 films directed by Douglas Sirk. Films mainly for Universal and Fox. Also TV, stage. Married Jeffrey Hunter (1950–55, divorced).

Films as actress include: 1951: Quebec; When Worlds Collide; Flaming Feather. 1953: Prince of Pirates; It Came from Outer Space. 1954: Magnificent Obsession; Taza, Son of Cochise; The Black Shield of Falworth. 1955: Captain Lightfoot; Kiss of Fire. 1956: Flight to Hong Kong; The World in My Corner; Bigger Than Life. 1957: Oh, Men! Oh, Women!; No Down Payment. 1958: Harry Black and the Tiger; The Young Lions. 1959: The Young Philadelphians. 1960: Strangers When We Meet. 1963: Come Blow Your Horn. 1964: Robin and the Seven Hoods. 1967: Hombre. 1969: Strategy of Terror.

RUSSELL, Jane

Actress. Bemidji, Minnesota 1921–
Daughter of actress Geraldina Jacobi. From 1937: model. From 1940: studied at Max Reinhardt's Musical Workshop and with Maria Ouspenskaya. Model pictures led to first film as actress *The Outlaw* (1940): 7-year contract with Howard Hughes otherwise unused. To 1955: worked mainly for RKO. 1955: 20-year contract with Howard Hughes. Married Robert Waterfield; with him formed company to make *The Fuzzy Pink Nightgown* (1957). TV commercials, summer stock, nightclubs.

Films as actress include: 1940: The Outlaw (*r* 1946). 1948: The Paleface. 1951: His Kind of Woman. 1952: The Las Vegas Story; Macao; Son of Paleface; Montana Belle. 1953: Gentlemen Prefer Blondes; The French Line. 1954: Underwater! 1955: Foxfire; The Tall Men. 1956: Hot Blood; The Revolt of Mamie Stover. 1957: The Fuzzy Pink Nightgown. 1964: Fate is the Hunter. 1966: Waco.

RUSSELL, John L.

Cinematographer
Electrical engineering at Pratt Institute. Assistant for Columbia. During 1940s, operator for Columbia and independents. Operator for e.g. Russell Metty. 1948: first film as cinematographer. Freelance.

Films as cinematographer include: 1948: Moonrise; Macbeth. 1951: The Man from Planet X. 1952: Park Row. 1953: Problem Girls. 1959: Girls Town. 1960: Psycho.

RUSSELL, Ken

Director. Southampton, Hampshire 1927–
World War II: served in Merchant Navy, then (from 1945) RAF. From 1947: studied photography at Southampton Technical College; freelance stills photographer; photographer for Picture Post. Made short amateur films e.g. *Amelia and the Angel* (1957), *Peep Show* (1958), *Lourdes* (1958). From 1959: with BBC TV as producer. TV films include *Poet's London* (1959), *Elgar* (1962), *A House in Bayswater* (1964), *Debussy* and *Douanier Rousseau* (1965), *Isadora Duncan* (1966), *Dante's Inferno* (1967), *Song of Summer* (1968), *Dance of the Seven Veils* (1970). 1963: first feature as director.

Features as director: 1963: French Dressing. 1967: Billion Dollar Brain. 1969: Women in Love. 1971: The Music Lovers (+p); The Devils (+co-p/s); The Boy Friend (+p/s).

RUSSELL, Rosalind

Actress. Waterbury, Connecticut 1911–
Educated in Catholic schools in Waterbury and New York. American Academy of Dramatic Art. 1930: in Theatre Guild's 'Garrick Gaieties' on Broadway. Cut-rate theatre circuit; spotted by Universal talent scout; contract. Left Universal for first film *Evelyn Prentice* (1934) at MGM. 1941: married Fred Brisson, son of Carl B. Brisson. Wartime USO shows. Campaigned for Republicans in Eisenhower election. Later theatrical work includes tour of 'Bell, Book and Candle', Broadway 'Wonderful Town'. Worked mainly for MGM to 1939, then mainly Columbia, RKO, Warners, MGM.

Films as actress include: 1934: Forsaking All Others. 1935: The President Vanishes; Reckless; China Seas. 1936: It Had to Happen; Under Two Flags. 1937: Night Must Fall; Man Proof. 1938: The Citadel; Four's a Crowd. 1939: The Women; His Girl Friday. 1940: No Time For Comedy. 1941: They Met in Bombay; The Feminine Touch. 1942: Take a Letter Darling. 1945: Roughly Speaking. 1946: Sister Kenny. 1947: The Guilt of Janet Ames; Mourning Becomes Electra. 1949: Tell it to the Judge. 1956: Picnic. 1958: Auntie Mame. 1961: A Majority of One. 1962: Five Finger Exercise; Gypsy. 1966: The Trouble with Angels; Oh Dad, Poor Dad, Mamma's Hung You in the Closet and I'm Feelin' So Sad. 1968: Where Angels Go, Trouble Follows.

RUTTENBERG, Joseph

Cinematographer. St Petersburg, Russia 1898–
Journalist and photographer in Boston. Produced own newsreel. 1915: started as first cameraman at Fox. 11 years at Fox, then moved to MGM. 1927–30: no films. 1962: left MGM after 36 years, moved to Paramount. Oscars for *The Great Waltz* (1938), *Mrs Miniver* (1942), *Somebody Up There Likes Me* (1956), *Gigi* (1958).

Films as cinematographer include: 1922: Silver Wings (co). 1926: Summer Bachelors. 1931: The Struggle. 1936: Fury; Three Godfathers. 1937: The Big City; A Day at the Races. 1938: Three Comrades; The Great Waltz. 1939: The Women (co). 1941: Dr Jekyll and Mr Hyde; Two-Faced Woman. 1942: Mrs Miniver; Woman of the Year; Random Harvest; Crossroads. 1943: Madame Curie. 1944: Gaslight; Mrs Parkington. 1945: The Valley of Decision. 1946: Adventure. 1948: Julia Misbehaves. 1949: Side Street. 1951: Cause for Alarm. 1953: Latin Lovers; Julius Caesar. 1954: Brigadoon; The Last Time I Saw Paris. 1955: Kismet. 1956: Somebody Up There Likes Me; The Swan; Invitation to the Dance. 1957: Until They Sail. 1958: Gigi; The Reluctant Debutante. 1959: Green Mansions; The Wreck of the Mary Deare (co). 1960: Butterfield 8 (co); The Subterraneans. 1961: Ada. 1962: Who's Got the Action? 1963: Who's Been Sleeping in My Bed? 1964: A Global Affair. 1965: Sylvia; Harlow; Love Has Many Faces. 1966: The Oscar. 1968: Speedway.

RUTTMANN, Walter

Director. Frankfurt, Germany 1887–1941 Berlin
To 1905: Goethe High School, Frankfurt. 1909: art school. 1910–14: painter. 1914–18: Lieutenant in German Army on Eastern Front. 1921: first film as director *Opus I*, first of series of abstract films. 1924: made 'Der Falkentraum' ('Dream of the Hawks') sequence in *Siegfried*; special effects sequences in *Lebende Buddhas*. 1926: ' magic and cloud effects' for *Die Geschichte des Prinzen Achmed*. 1927: with Erwin Piscator made *Hoppdà wir Leben*, sequence for stage production of a play by Toller. 1931: made *Feind im Blut* in Switzerland; in France 'artistic collaborator' on editing of *La Fin du monde*. 1932: in Italy made *Acciaio*, scripted by Luigi Pirandello. 1933: remade *Acciaio* in sound version as *Arbeit macht Glücklich*. From 1933: worked only in documentary. 1936: collaborated on editing of *Olympiad*. 1941: wounded mortally planning documentary on Eastern Front. Many articles; book published posthumously 'Der Deutsches Film'. *Opus IV* (1925) included in compilation *30 Years of Experiment* (1951).

Films as director: 1921: Opus I – Photodram; Opus II. 1923: Der Seiger; Das verlorene Paradies; Kantorowitz – Liköre; Gesolei. 1925: Opus III; Opus IV. 1926: Die Geschichte des Prinzen Achmed. 1927: Berlin, die Sinfonie der Grosstadt – Berlin, Symphony of a City. 1928: Wochenende – Weekend; Tönende Welle – Spiel der Wellen – Sounding Wave; Deutscher Rundfunk. 1929: Die Melodie der Welt – Die World Melody – The Melody of the World. 1931: In der Nacht; Feind im Blut. 1932: Acciaio – Steel (+co-s). 1933: Arbeit macht Glücklich – Stahl. 1934: Altgermanische Bauernkultur; Metall des Himmels. 1935: Stadt der Verheissung; Cannstatter Volksfest; Stuttgart. 1936: Dusseldorf (+co-s); Schiff in Not. 1937: Mannesmann. 1938: Henkel; Weltstrasse See – Hamburg; Im Dienste der Menschheit (+co-s); Im Zeichen des Vertrauens. 1939: Hinter den Zahlen (+co-s). 1940: Aberglaube; Deutsche Panzer; Volkskrankheit Krebs – Jeder Achte (+co-s).

RYAN, Robert

Actor. Chicago 1913–
Studied at Loyola Academy then at Dartmouth College; heavyweight boxing champion there for 4 years. Studied acting at Max Reinhardt's Workshop. In stock on East Coast. 1940: first film as actor *Golden Gloves*. 1941: first New York appearance in 'Clash by Night'. 1944–45: US Marine Corps. 1959: with John Houseman helped found UCLA Theatre Group; star of Irving Berlin musical 'Mr President' on Broadway. 1967: acted in 'Othello' and 'Long Day's Journey into Night' at Nottingham Playhouse. Also TV, e.g. in 'The Great Gatsby' (1958) and 'The Snows of Kilimanjaro' (1960).

Films as actor include: 1940: Northwest Mounted Police. 1943: Behind the Rising Sun; The Iron Major. 1947: The Woman on the Beach; Crossfire; Trail Street. 1948: Berlin Express; Act of Violence; The Boy With Green Hair; Return of the Bad Men. 1949: Caught; The Set-Up; I Married a Communist. 1950: The Secret Fury; Born to Be Bad. 1951: The Racket; On Dangerous Ground; Flying Leathernecks. 1952: Clash by Night; Horizons West; Beware, My Lovely. 1953: City Beneath the Sea; Inferno; The Naked Spur.

Richard Egan and Jane Russell in The Revolt of Mamie Stover, *directed by Raoul Walsh.*
Fury, *directed by Fritz Lang and photographed by Joseph Ruttenberg.*
Olympiad, *directed by Leni Riefenstahl and co-edited by Walter Ruttmann.*

1954: About Mrs Leslie; Her Twelve Men; Bad Day at Black Rock. 1955: Escape to Burma; House of Bamboo; The Tall Men. 1956: Back From Eternity. 1957: Men in War. 1958: God's Little Acre. 1959: Day of the Outlaw; Odds Against Tomorrow. 1961: Ice Palace; The Canadians; King of Kings. 1962: Billy Budd; The Longest Day. 1966: Battle of the Bulge; The Professionals; The Busy Body. 1967: The Dirty Dozen; Hour of the Gun. 1968: Lo Sbarco di Anzio. 1969: The Wild Bunch.

S

SABU

(Sabu Dastagir) Actor. Karapur, South India 1924–63 Hollywood

Trained as boy to handle elephants. Discovered by Robert Flaherty in elephant stable of the Maharajah of Mysore, and given part in *Elephant Boy* (1936). Schooling in England and contract with Alexander Korda. World War II: went to Hollywood to finish *Thief of Bagdad* (1940) and stayed in USA; service in US Air Force. Became US citizen. 1946–47: made 2 films in UK. 1948: married actress Marilyn Cooper. 1951: toured UK with circus act. To 1948: films mainly for United Artists and Universal.

Films as actor include: 1938: The Drum. 1942: Rudyard Kipling's Jungle Book. 1944: Cobra Woman. 1947: Black Narcissus. 1948: Man-Eater of Kumaon. 1963: Rampage.

SAGAN, Léontine

(Leontine Schlesinger) Director. Austria 1889–

Brought up in Vienna, then Johannesburg. 1910: went to Germany; studied under Max Reinhardt; worked in theatre in Dresden, Vienna, Frankfurt, Berlin. Left Germany after directing first film in 1931. 1932: directed film in UK. Thereafter worked exclusively in theatre. 1939–43: returned to South Africa. Co-founder of National Theatre, Johannesburg.

Films as director: 1931: Mädchen in uniform. 1932: Men of Tomorrow.

SAINT, Eva Marie

Actress. Newark, New Jersey 1924–

Bowling Green State University. TV, radio. Actor's Studio. On Broadway was understudy to Jocelyn Brando in 'Mr Roberts'. With Lillian Gish in 'The Trip to Bountiful' and with the play to Broadway. 1953: spotted by Sam Spiegel and Elia Kazan for her first film *On the Waterfront* (1954) for which she received an Oscar. Married director Jeffrey Hayden (1951). Several films for MGM.

Films as actress: 1954: On the Waterfront. 1956: That Certain Feeling. 1957: Raintree County; A Hatful of Rain. 1959: North by Northwest. 1960: Exodus. 1962: All Fall Down. 1964: 36 Hours. 1965: The Sandpiper. 1966: The Russians are Coming, The Russians are Coming; Grand Prix. 1969: The Stalking Moon. 1970: Loving.

ST CLAIR, Malcolm (Mal)

Director. Los Angeles 1897–1952

Son of an architect, worked briefly for him. 1916: sports cartoonist on Los Angeles Express. 1918: Keystone Cop extra then writer for Mack Sennett. 1919: first film as director in collaboration. Directed 2-reelers written by Sennett, then left him over disagreement about direction of *Bright Eyes* (1921). 1921–22: freelanced for Keaton's company. 1924: first feature, for Warners. 1925: contract with Famous Players-Lasky on condition that first film a success: *Are Parents People?*. Worked for Paramount, MGM, RKO. From 1933: most films for Fox. 1930–36: mainly in England on vacation. 1943–45: directed Stan Laurel and Oliver Hardy in 4 films. 1944: played small part as Kaiser in *Wilson*, cut from finished film.

Short films as director: 1919: Rip and Stitch Tailors (*co-d Mack Sennett*); The Little Widow (*co-d Mack Sennett*); No Mother to Guide Him (*co-d Erle C. Kenton*). 1920: Don't Weaken; Young Man's Fancy; He Loved Like he Lied. 1921: The Night Before; Sweetheart Days; Wedding Bells Out of Tune; Call a Cop; Bright Eyes; The Goat (*+co-s*; *co-d Buster Keaton*). 1922: The Blacksmith (*+co-s*; *co-d Buster Keaton*); Rice and Old Shoes; Christmas; Entertaining the Boss; Keep 'em Home; Their First Vacation; Twin Husbands. 1923: Fighting Blood (*serial, 12 1-reelers*). 1924: Telephone Girl (*serial, 12 2-reelers*; *co-d*).

Features as director: 1924: George Washington Jr; Find Your Man. 1925: The Lighthouse by the Sea; After Business Hours; A Woman of the World; On Thin Ice; The Trouble with Wives; Are Parents People?. 1926: A Social Celebrity (*+p*); The Show-Off; The Grand Duchess and the Waiter; The Popular Sin; Good and Naughty. 1927: Breakfast at Sunrise; Knockout Reilly (*+p*). 1928: Gentlemen Prefer Blondes; Sporting Goods; Beau Broadway; The Fleet's In. 1929: Side Street (*+co-s*); The Canary Murder Case; Night Parade. 1930: Montana Moon; Dangerous Nan McGrew; The Boudoir Diplomat; Remote Control. 1933: Goldie Gets Along; Olsen's Big Moment. 1936: Crack-Up. 1937: Time Out for Romance; Born Reckless; She Had to Eat; Dangerously Yours. 1938: A Trip to Paris; Safety in Numbers; Down on the Farm; Everybody's Baby. 1939: The Jones Family in Hollywood; The Jones Family in Quick Millions; Hollywood Cavalcade (*co-d*). 1940: Young as You Feel; Meet the Missus – The Higgins Family. 1941: The Bashful Bachelor. 1942: The Man in the Trunk; Over My Dead Body. 1943: 2 Weeks to Live; Jitterbugs; The Dancing Masters. 1944: Swing Out the Blues; The Big Noise. 1945: The Bullfighters. 1948: Arthur Takes Over; Fighting Back.

SALA, Vittorio

Director. Palermo, Sicily 1918–

Law studies. Centro Sperimentale di Cinematografia. 1938: first short as director *Palermo Normanna*. War service with Centro Cinematografico Militare. Worked in Sicilian radio. Film critic for Il Popolo. 1949: returned to film-making. 1950–56: about 50 shorts. 1956: first feature as director. Brother of Giuseppe Sala, director of Centro Sperimentale.

Short films as director include: 1938: Immagini e colore; Una Storia di pinturicchio; La Luce negli Impressionisti; Nebbia a Venezia; Ritmi di New York. 1949: Notturno. 1950: Il Piccolo Sceriffo. 1951: Venezia, la gondola. 1955: La Città del cinema.

Features as director: 1956: Donne Sole (*+ st/co-s*). 1959: Costa Azzura (*+co-st/co-s*). 1960: La Regina delle Amazzoni. 1962: I Dongiovanni della Costa Azzura (*uf*; *+co-st/co-s*). 1963: Double Purpose – L'Intrigo (*co-d George Marshall*); Canzoni nel mondo; Il Treno del sabato – The Saturday Train (*+co-s*). 1965: Berlino appuntamento per le spie – Spy in Your Eye. 1966: Ischia operazione amore (*+co-s*). 1967: Ray Master, l'inafferrabine. 1968: Il Signor Bruschino.

SALCE, Luciano

Director. Rome 1922–

To 1947: Accademia Nazionale d'Arte Drammatica, studied directing. Worked in theatre, cabaret, TV as actor, director, writer. 1950–54: in Brazil, first film as director. Returned to Italy, acted in several films, e.g. *Totò nella luna* (1958). 1960: returned to direction. 1968: *Kiss the Other Shiek* is an expansion of his episode in *Oggi, domani e dopodomani* (1964).

Films as director: 1953: Uma Pulga na balança; Floradas na serra. 1960: Le Pillole d'Ercole (*co-d Nino Manfredi*). 1961: Il Federale – The Fascist (*+co-s*). 1962: La Voglia Matta – This Crazy Urge – Crazy Desire (*+co-s/w*); La Cuccagna – The Land of Plenty (*+co-s/w*). 1963: Le Ore delli amore – The Hours of Love (*+co-s/w*); Le Monachine – The Little Nuns. 1964: Altà Infidelta *ep* La Sospirosa – Sex in the Afternoon – High Infidelity; El Greco (*+co-s*); Oggi, domani e dopodomani *ep* La Moglie Bionda (*+s/w*). 1965: Slaiom. 1966: Le Fate – The Fairies – The Queens – Sex Quartet *ep* Fata Sabina (*+co-s*). 1967: Ti ho sposato per allegria (*+co-s*). 1968: Colpo di stato (*+co-s*); Kiss the Other Shiek (*co-d Eduardo De Filippo*); La Pecosa Nera – The Black Sheep (*+co-s*). 1969: Il Prof Dr Guido Tersilli, primario della Clinica Villa Celeste, convenzionata con le mutue. 1971: Basta Guardala.

SALTZMAN, Harry

Producer. Sherbrooke, Quebec 1916–

At 2 moved to USA. 1932: to France. World War II: served in Royal Canadian Air Force. Manager in vaudeville and a travelling circus. Became TV producer, e.g. of 'Robert Montgomery Show'. In collaboration with Tony Richardson and John Osborne founded Woodfall Films. 1960: in collaboration with Richardson produced *Saturday Night and Sunday Morning*. From 1963: in collaboration with Albert R. Broccoli produced series of James Bond films, beginning with *Dr No*. 1965: produced *The Ipcress File*, first of several films with Michael Caine. Engaged Andre de Toth as executive director on *Billion Dollar Brain* (1967) and to replace René Clément on *Play Dirty* (1968). 1970: won control of Technicolor Inc.

Films as producer: 1959: Look Back in Anger. 1960: Saturday Night and Sunday Morning (*co*); The Entertainer. 1963: Doctor No (*co*); From Russia with Love (*co*). 1964: Goldfinger (*co*); E venne un uomo (*co-pc*). 1965: The Ipcress File; Thunderball (*co*); Un Mondo Nuovo (*co-pc*). 1966: Funeral in Berlin; Campanada a medianoche (*co-pc*). 1967: Billion Dollar Brain; You Only Live Twice (*co*). 1968: Play Dirty. 1969: L'Homme qui ment (*co-pc*); The Battle of Britain. 1971: Diamonds are Forever (*co*).

SAMSONOV, Samson

(Samson Iosifovich Edelstein) Novozybkov, Russia 1921–

At 1 moved to Moscow. 3 years at art school. Studied acting at studio of Chamber Theatre, Moscow. To Central Theatre of Transport, worked as actor, set designer; toured with company. At outbreak of World War II sent with company to Urals. 1943: returned to Moscow, enrolled in VGIK (State film school): pupil of Sergei Gerasimov. Training lasted 5½ years, included assistant-direction of *Molodaya gvardiya* (1948). To Studio Theatre of the Film Actor. With Gerasimov produced in Moscow 'The Grey-Haired Girl'. Produced stage version of 'Poprigunya'; became subject of first film as director (1955). 1957: made *Ognennye Versty*, based on Dudley Nichols' script for John Ford's *Stagecoach* (1939). Married actress Margaret Volodina who acted in several of his films. All films for Mosfilm. Became executive producer of one of Mosfilm's 6 sub-divisions.

Films as director: 1955: Poprigunya – The Gadfly – The Grasshopper (+ *s*). 1956: Za vitrinoi Univermaga – Behind the Shop Windows. 1957: Ognennye Versty – Fiery Miles. 1960: Rovesnik veka – Man of the Century. 1963: Optimisticheskaya Tragediya – Optimistic Tragedy (+ *co-s*). 1964: Tri Sestry – Three Sisters (+ *s*). 1967: Arena (+ *co-s*).

SANDERS, George

Actor. St Petersburg, Russia 1906–72, Barcelona
Mother horticulturist Margaret Kilbe, father rope manufacturer. Escaped Russian Revolution. Textile business. To South America in tobacco business, ended by Depression. Voice training; performed in revue 'Ballyhoo'. Member of piano act. Understudied Noël Coward in 'Conversation Piece'. 1936: first film as actor *Find the Lady*, and first American film *Lloyds of London*. Married actresses Zsa Zsa Gabor (1949–57), Benita Hume (1958–67). Brother of actor Tom Conway. 1950: Oscar as supporting actor for *All About Eve*.

Films as actor include: 1936: Things to Come. 1937: Love is News; Slave Ship; Lancer Spy. 1938: Four Men and a Prayer. 1939: The Saint Strikes Back; Confessions of a Nazi Spy; Nurse Edith Cavell. 1940: Green Hell; Rebecca; The House of the Seven Gables; Foreign Correspondent; Bitter Sweet. 1941: Rage in Heaven; Man Hunt; The Gay Falcon; A Date with the Falcon; Sundown; Son of Fury. 1942: The Falcon Takes Over; Her Cardboard Lover; Tales of Manhattan; The Moon and Sixpence; The Black Swan. 1943: This Land is Mine; They Came to Blow Up America. 1944: The Lodger; Summer Storm. 1945: The Picture of Dorian Gray; Hangover Square; The Strange Affair of Uncle Harry. 1946: A Scandal in Paris; The Strange Woman. 1947: The Private Affairs of Bel Ami; The Ghost and Mrs Muir; Lured; Forever Amber. 1948: Then and Now (*ur*). 1949: The Fan; Samson and Delilah. 1950: All About Eve. 1951: I Can Get it for You Wholesale; The Light Touch. 1952: Ivanhoe; Assignment Paris. 1953: Call Me Madam.

1954: King Richard and the Crusaders. 1955: Moonfleet; The Scarlet Coat; The King's Thief. 1956: While the City Sleeps; That Certain Feeling. 1957: The Seventh Sin. 1958: From the Earth to the Moon. 1959: That Kind of Woman; Solomon and Sheba; A Touch of Larceny. 1960: The Last Voyage; Cone of Silence. 1961: In Search of the Castaways. 1964: Dark Purpose; A Shot in the Dark. 1965: The Amorous Adventures of Moll Flanders. 1966: The Quiller Memorandum. 1967: Warning Shot; The Jungle Book (*wv*).

SANDERS, R. Denis

Director. New York 1929–
University of Yale and UCLA. From 1953: worked as documentary director; began with film on agriculture for the University of Nebraska. 1954: in collaboration with brother Terry Sanders scripted 'The Day Lincoln was Shot' for CBS TV. 1955: 2nd-unit director on *The Night of the Hunter*. 1955–58: directed for TV e.g. episodes of 'The Defenders', 'The Naked City'. 1958: with brother formed production company; directed first feature; in collaboration with brother wrote script for *The Naked and the Dead*. For TV made *The American West of John Ford*. Oscar for short subject (2-reel), *A Time Out of War* (1954).

Films as director include: 1953: Introduction to Jazz. 1954: A Time Out of War (+ *co-p/co-s*). 1959: Crime and Punishment USA. 1961: War Hunt (+ *co-p*). 1964: One Man's Way; Shock Treatment. 1968: Czechoslovakia 1918–1968. 1970: That's the Way It Is. 1971: Soul to Soul (+ *s/e*).

SANDERS, Terry

Producer. New York 1931–
Brother of Denis Sanders. UCLA. 1954: producer, writer in collaboration and cinematographer on *A Time Out of War*. Then producer on all brother's films except *Shock Treatment* (1964). 1955–58: directed for TV e.g. 'Hollywood and the Stars', 'The Legend of Marilyn Monroe'. 1958: with brother formed production company; they wrote occasional scripts in collaboration. *See* SANDERS, Denis.

SANDRICH, Mark

Director. New York 1900–45 Hollywood
Science and mathematics at Columbia University. 1923: began in films as property man at Fox. By 1927: was directing shorts for Educational/Lupino Lane and Fox. 1928: first feature as director, for Columbia. 1931–38: directed shorts and features, including Fred Astaire/Ginger Rogers musicals, for RKO. From 1939: feature director with Paramount; also produced from 1940. 1945: working on *Blue Skies* (completed by Stuart Heisler) when he died. Collaborated on stories for some of his shorts; also radio playwright. Oscar for short subject (comedy), *So This is Harris!* (1933).

Features as director: 1928: Runaway Girls. 1930: The Talk of Hollywood (+ *p*). 1933: Melody Cruise (+ *co-s*); Aggie Appleby Maker of Men. 1934: Hips, Hips, Hooray!; Cockeyed Cavaliers; The Gay Divorcee. 1935: Top Hat. 1936: Follow the Fleet; A Woman Rebels. 1937: Shall We Dance. 1938: Carefree. 1939: Man About Town. 1940: Buck Benny Rides Again

Mädchen in Uniform, *by Leontine Sagan.*
Eva Marie Saint and Warren Beatty in Frankenheimer's All Fall Down.
Samson Samsonov.

(+p); Love Thy Neighbour (+p). 1941: Skylark (+p). 1942: Holiday Inn (+p). 1943: So Proudly We Hail (+p). 1944: Here Come the Waves (+p); I Love a Soldier (+p).

SANTELL, Alfred or
Al Sautell

Director. San Francisco 1895–
Los Angeles University. Trained as architect. Began in films as scriptwriter for comedy shorts. Story writer with Lubin Manufacturing Company, also actor. From 1916: directed shorts for American Manufacturing Company. Then with Kalem Company and Mack Sennett. 1918–20: director and writer with Universal. From 1923: directed features. 1925–29: with First National. 1929–33: mainly Fox. 1933–42: mainly RKO and Paramount. From 1946: worked in TV.

Films as director include: 1924: Empty Hearts. 1925: Parisian Nights; Bluebeard's Seven Wives. 1926: The Dancer of Paris; Just Another Blonde. 1927: The Patent Leather Kid. 1928: The Little Shepherd of Kingdom Come (+p); Wheel of Chance. 1930: The Sea Wolf. 1931: Body and Soul; Daddy Long Legs. 1932: Polly of the Circus; Rebecca of Sunnybrook Farm; Tess of the Storm Country. 1933: Bondage. 1935: People Will Talk. 1936: Winterset. 1938: Having Wonderful Time; The Arkansas Traveler. 1939: Our Leading Citizen. 1941: Aloma of the South Seas. 1942: Beyond the Blue Horizon. 1943: Jack London. 1944: The Hairy Ape. 1945: Mexicana (+p). 1946: That Brennan Girl (+p).

SASLAVSKY, Luis

Director. Santa Fe, Argentina 1906–
Law studies. Wrote short stories, translations. Film critic. Film studies in USA. 1935: first film as director Crimen a las tres. 1946: produced, and wrote story of Daniel Tinayre's A sangre fria. 1948: story-writer on Tinayre's Pasaparto a Rio. From 1952: worked in France and Spain. 1963: story 'A sangre fria' basis of Manuel Mur-Oti's A hierro muere.

Films as director: 1935: Crimen a las tres. 1936: Escala en la ciudad. 1937: La Fuga. 1939: Puerta Cerrada; El Loro Serenata. 1940: La Casa del recuerdo. 1941: Historia de una noche. 1942: Cenizas al viento. 1943: Los Ojos mas lindas del mundo; Eclipse del sol. 1945: La Donna Duende. 1946: Cinco Besos. 1948: Historia di una male mujer. 1949: Vidalita. 1952: La Corona Negra. 1953: La Neige était sale. 1957: Les Louves – The She-Wolves. 1958: Premier Mai; Ce Corps tant désiré – Way of the Wicked. 1961: Historia de una noche. 1962: Tablao a la luna. 1963: Las Ratas; El Balcon de la luna. 1966: Las Mujeres los prefieren tantos.

SATIE, Erik

(Alfred Leslie) Composer. Honfleur, France 1866–1925 Paris
Only association with the cinema in 1924 when he commissioned Entr'acte from music he had written for ballet 'Relâche', subtitled 'un ballet instanéiste en deux actes, un entr'acte cinématographique et la queue du chien': he acted in it.

SAULNIER, Jacques

Designer. Paris 1928–
Son of a carpenter. Architecture at Ecole des Beaux Arts, then IDHEC. 1949–58: assistant designer. 1958: first film as designer in collaboration Les Amants. 1958–61: most films in collaboration with Bernard Evein, then solo.

Films as designer in collaboration with Bernard Evein include: 1958: Les Cousins. 1959: A double tour; Les Jeux de l'amour; Les Scélérats; La Sentence. 1961: L'Amant de cinq jours.

Films as designer include: 1960: Le Farceur; La Morte-Saison des amours; La Proie pour l'ombre; L'Année Dernière à Marienbad. 1961: Vu du pont; L'Education Sentimentale 61. 1963: Landru; Muriel; Du mouron pour les petits oiseaux. 1964: L'Echiquier de Dieu. 1965: What's New Pussycat?; La Vie de chateau; Mademoiselle. 1966: La Guerre est finie; Le Voleur. 1967: Tante Zita. 1968: Ho!; La Prisonnière.

SAURA, Carlos

Director. Huesca, Spain 1932–
Professional photographer from 18. Studied at the Instituto de Investigaciones y Experiencias Cinematográficas, now the Escuela Oficial de Cinematografia, where he was afterwards professor of direction until 1964. 1955: first film as director. 1957: graduation film was Una Tarde de domingo. 1957–63: taught in Official Film School; job not renewed. 1969: in collaboration wrote Antonio Saura's La Madrigueta.

Films as director: 1955: Antonio Saura. 1957: Una Tarde de domingo (+co-s/e). 1958: Cuenca (+s/c). 1959: Los Golfos – The Hooligans (+co-s). 1964: Llano por un bandido – Weeping for a Bandit (+co-s). 1965: La Caza – The Hunt (+co-s). 1967: Peppermint Frappé (+co-s). 1968: Stress es tres, tres (+co-s). 1970: El Jardin de los delices – The Garden of Delights (+co-s).

SAUTET, Claude

Director. Montrouge, France 1924–
Began as music critic, then ran re-education centre for juvenile delinquents. From 1946: studied at IDHEC. From 1948: assistant director e.g. on Les Yeux sans visage (1960) on whose script he collaborated. 1951: first short as director. 1955: first feature as director. Also writer in collaboration e.g. La Vie de château (1965), Les Mariés de l'an II (1971).

Films as director: 1951: Nous n'irons plus au bois. 1955: Bonjour sourire – Sourire aux lèvres. 1959: Classe tous risques. 1965: L'Arme à gauche – Guns for the Dictator; La Tête la Première. 1970: Les Choses de la vie (+co-s). 1971: Max et les ferrailleurs (+co-s).

SAVILLE, Victor

Producer and director. Birmingham, Warwickshire 1897–
World War I: London Irish Rifles, wounded. 1916: entered film industry as salesman. Became production manager. 1920: joined Gaumont-British: became scriptwriter. 1923: partnership with Michael Balcon. From 1927: director and producer. 1929: in USA to direct Woman to Woman. 1930: returned to UK. Worked for American companies and his own. 1936: joined Alexander Korda as associate producer. 1938: associate producer for MGM in Britain. 1939–60: with MGM in California; also made Tonight and Every Night (1945) for Columbia. 1961: to England to produce The Greengage Summer. Resumed association with Gaumont-British, formed a further company.

Films as producer: 1927: Hindle Wakes (+s); Roses of Picardy (co). 1937: Action for Slander. 1939: The Citadel; Goodbye, Mr Chips. 1940: The Earl of Chicago; Bitter Sweet; The Mortal Storm. 1941: A Woman's Face; Smilin' Through; The Chocolate Soldier. 1942: White Cargo; Keeper of the Flame. 1943: Above Suspicion. 1961: The Greengage Summer.

Films as director: 1927: The Arcadians (+p/s); The Glad Eye (+p/s; co-d Maurice Elvey); Tesha (+p/st/s). 1929: Kitty; Woman to Woman (+co-p); Me and the Boys (+p). 1930: The W Plan (+p/s); A Warm Corner (+p/s); The Sport of Kings (+p/s). 1931: Sunshine Susie – The Office Girl; Michael and Mary. 1932: Hindle Wakes (+s); The Faithful Heart; Love on Wheels. 1933: The Good Companions; I Was a Spy; Friday the Thirteenth. 1934: Evergreen; Evensong; The Iron Duke. 1935: Me and Marlborough; The Dictator – The Love Affair of the Dictator. 1936: First a Girl; It's Love Again. 1937: Storm in a Teacup (+p; co-d); Dark Journey – Anxious Years (+p). 1938: South Riding (+p). 1943: Forever and a Day (+co-p; co-d 6 others). 1945: Tonight and Every Night (+p). 1946: The Green Years. 1947: Green Dolphin Street; If Winter Comes. 1949: Conspirator. 1950: Kim. 1951: Calling Bulldog Drummond. 1952: 24 Hours of a Woman's Life – Affair in Monte Carlo. 1954: The Long Wait. 1955: The Silver Chalice.

SCHAFFNER, Franklin J.

Director. Tokyo 1936–
Lived in Tokyo till death of father in 1936: then to USA with mother. Actor. Assistant director on 'March of Time' series, then director for CBS TV including 'Studio One', 'Ford Theatre', 'Playhouse 90'. 1955: with George Roy Hill, Fielder Cook and Worthington Miner formed own company which produced TV show 'Kaiser Aluminium Hour'. From 1957: worked in Hollywood on TV series 'Playhouse 90' which included 'Twelve Angry Men', 'Caine Mutiny Court-Martial'; directed Mrs Kennedy's White House Tour for TV. 1961: on Broadway directed 'Advise and Consent', led to Fox contract; first feature unfinished. Returned to TV: worked on 'The Defenders' in New York. 1963: returned to features. Worked for Fox, United Artists, Warners. Oscar for Best Film, Patton (1970).

Films as director: 1961: A Summer World (uf). 1963: The Stripper – A Woman in July – Woman of Summer. 1964: The Best Man. 1965: The War Lord. 1967: The Double Man. 1968: Planet of the Apes. 1970: Patton. 1971: Nicholas and Alexandra (+co-pc).

SCHARY, Dore

Producer. Newark, New Jersey 1905–
Youngest of 4 children in immigrant family, which

built up a catering business. After working there, became actor in Cincinnati (1928), then on Broadway. Directed little theatre productions and wrote plays. 1932: hired as script-writer by Walter Wanger, who had read one of his plays; wrote e.g. *Big City* (1937, in collaboration). 1943: production executive at Vanguard Films. 1948: in charge of production at RKO. 1951: vice-president in charge of production at MGM. 1956: under pressure left MGM and has since been independent releasing through Warner. 1964: directed, wrote and produced *Act One* based on Moss Hart's autobiography. 1970: Commissioner for Cultural Affairs in New York. Oscar for original story of *Boy's Town* (with Eleanore Griffin, 1938).

Films as producer include: 1945: The Spiral Staircase. 1948: The Boy With Green Hair (*ex-p*). 1949: Battleground. 1950: The Next Voice You Hear. 1951: Westward the Women. 1953: Take the High Ground. 1954: Bad Day at Black Rock. 1956: The Last Hunt; The Swan. 1957: Designing Woman. 1958: Lonelyhearts.

SCHELL, Maria

Actress. Vienna 1926–
Father was Swiss playwright Hermann Ferdinand Schell, mother an actress: brothers are actors Karl and Maximilian Schell. Secretary. 1938: became a Swiss citizen. 1942: leading role in first film *Steibruch* in Switzerland. School of Theatre Arts, Zurich. Zurich stage, and State Theatre of Bern. 1945: acted at Josefstadt Theatre, Vienna. Under contract to Alexander Korda. Films in Switzerland, then (from 1948) Austria, France, Germany, Italy, UK. European tour with Albert Basserman in 'Faust'. 1957: first American film *The Brothers Karamazov*. TV work in USA includes 'For Whom the Bell Tolls' (1959), 'Ninotchka' (1960). Husband is film director Veit Relin.

Films as actress include: 1951: The Magic Box. 1954: Die letzte Brücke; The Heart of the Matter. 1955: Die Ratten. 1956: Gervaise. 1957: Rose Bernd; Le Notti Bianchi. 1958: Der Schinderhannes. 1959: The Hanging Tree. 1960: Cimarron. 1961: The Mark. 1968: Le Diable par la queue.

SCHELL, Maximilian

Actor. Vienna 1930–
Son of Swiss poet and dramatist Hermann Ferdinand Schell. Brother of Maria Schell. From 1938: lived in Switzerland. Studied in Zurich, Munich, Basle. Worked as actor, producer in theatre in Germany in 1950s; wrote and starred in 'The City Grows Dark' in Berlin. Also acted on Broadway and London e.g. Royal Court Theatre production of 'A Patriot for Me'. Played Hamlet on German TV. Appeared in John Frankenheimer's production of Hemingway's 'The Fifth Column' for US TV. In films from mid-1950s. 1969: produced and acted in *Das Schloss*. 1970: first film as director. Oscar as Best Actor for *Judgment at Nuremberg* (1961).

Films as actor include: 1955: Kinder, mütter und ein General. 1958: The Young Lions. 1962: Five Finger Exercise. 1963: I Sequestrati di Altona. 1964: Topkapi. 1966: The Deadly Affair. 1967: Counterpoint. 1969: Simon Bolivar. 1970: Erste Liebe (*+ d/co-p/co-s*).

SCHENCK, Nicolas

Studio head. Rybinsk, Russia 1881–1969 Miami Beach, Florida
Left Russia for USA at 9. Errand boy in drug store. With brother Joseph M. Schenck opened 2 drug stores, then amusement park in New York; bought interest in 2 theatres; joined Loew organisation. From 1910: secretary of Loew's Consolidated; Joseph ran the group's theatres until he left to work as producer in 1917. 1919: vice-president and general manager of Loew's Inc. 1927: on death of Marcus Loew, succeeded him as president of Loew's Inc. 1955: resigned as president in favour of Loew's son Arthur Loew, but stayed on as chairman of the board. 1956: became honorary chairman of Loew's Inc, then retired.

SCHERTZINGER, Victor

Director. Mahanoy City, Pennsylvania 1888–1941 Hollywood
Brown University and University of Brussels. Violinist with John Sousa and others. Several years as concert violinist in Europe. Orchestra leader on a number of musical comedies in New York theatres. Leader of Belasco theatre orchestra, Los Angeles. 1916: wrote music score for *Civilisation*. 1917: began as director with Thomas H. Ince. 1919–22: director with Goldwyn. 1923–25: worked for various companies including B. P. Schulberg's Preferred Pictures and Metro. Thereafter with Fox (1925–27), Paramount (1928–30), RKO and World Wide (1931–33), Columbia (1933–36), Paramount (from 1940). 1942: last film, released after his death.

Films as director include (complete from 1931): 1919: When Doctors Disagree; Pinto; Jinx; The Homebreaker. 1920: The Slim Princess; What Happened to Rosa. 1922: Head Over Heels. 1928: Forgotten Faces (*+p*). 1929: Redskin; The Wheel of Life (*+ song*); Fashions in Love (*+ co-songs*); Nothing but the Truth. 1930: Paramount on Parade (*co-d 10 others*). 1931: Friends and Lovers; The Woman Between. 1932: Uptown New York; Strange Justice. 1933: Cocktail Hour; The Constant Woman; My Woman. 1934: One Night of Love; Beloved. 1935: Love Me Forever (*+ st*); Let's Live Tonight. 1936: The Music Goes Round. 1937: Something to Sing About (*+ st/m*). 1939: The Mikado. 1940: Road to Singapore; Rhythm of the River. 1941: Road to Zanzibar; Kiss the Boys Goodbye; Birth of the Blues. 1942: The Fleet's In.

SCHIFRIN, Lalo

Composer. Buenos Aires, Argentina 1932–
Father Russian immigrant to Argentina. Studied under Olivier Messiaen at Conservatoire de Paris. Cantata 'Rise and Fall of the Third Reich' performed at Hollywood Bowl. Jazz pianist: member φ Dizzy Gillespie quintet. 1971: music for 'Jonathan the Great', staged by Joshua Logan. Also TV work.

Films as composer include: 1964: Les Félins. 1965: The Cincinnati Kid; Blindfold. 1967: Cool Hand Luke; The President's Analyst. 1968: Bullitt; Hell in the Pacific; Coogan's Bluff. 1969: Che! 1971: Pretty Maids All in a Row; Dirty Harry.

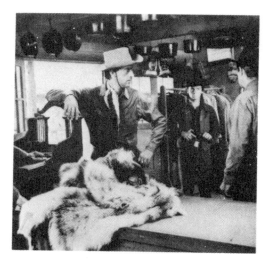

Geraldine Chaplin and José Luis Lopez Vazquez in Peppermint Frappé, *directed by Carlos Saura.*
Cliff Robertson in The Best Man, *directed by Franklin Schaffner.*
The Last Hunt, *directed by Richard Brooks and produced by Dore Schary.*

SCHLESINGER, John

Director. London 1926–
Oxford University. 1950: first short film as director. 1951: first film as actor *Singlehanded*. Acted in *Oh Rosalinda* (1955), *Battle of the River Plate* (1956), *Brothers in Law* (1957), *Seven Thunders* (1957) and in several TV plays. 1962: first feature as director. 1970: awarded OBE.

Films as director: 1950: The Starfish (*co-d Alan Cooke*). 1958: The Innocent Eye. 1960: Terminus. 1962: A Kind of Loving. 1963: Billy Liar. 1965: Darling. 1967: Far from the Madding Crowd. 1969: Midnight Cowboy. 1971: Sunday, Bloody Sunday.

SCHLESINGER, Leon

Producer. Philadelphia 1884–1949 Los Angeles
Porter, agent for opera libretti, theatre cashier, stage extra. About 1930 entered cinema. 1933–34: associate producer on first 2 of 'Looney Tunes' series at Warners, then became producer on *Buddy's Show Boat*, third in same series but for Vitaphone; initiated series 'Merrie Melodies' (1933). 1934–44: produced cartoons for Warners and Vitaphone. Animation team included Frank Tashlin, Bob Clampett, Tex Avery, Chuck Jones, Robert McKimson.

SCHNEE, Charles

Writer. Bridgeport, Connecticut 1918–62 Beverly Hills, California
1943: admitted to the bar after studying at Yale University and Law School. Elissa Landi starred in his play 'Apology' (1945); he then worked in minor production jobs at Universal and Paramount. Collaborated on script of *Red River* (1948) from own original script. Studio executive and producer at MGM. Oscar for screenplay of *The Bad and the Beautiful* (1952).

Films as writer include: 1948: Red River (*co*); They Live By Night. 1949: Easy Living. 1950: The Next Voice You Hear; The Furies; Born to be Bad (*co-ad*). 1951: Bannerline; Westward the Women. 1952: The Bad and the Beautiful. 1960: Butterfield 8 (*co*); The Crowded Sky. 1962: Two Weeks in Another Town.

SCHNEIDER, Romy

(Rosemarie Albach-Retty) Actress. Vienna 1938–
Mother actress Magda Schneider, father actor Wolf Albach-Retty. Brought into films by mother. 1953: first film. 1963: first American film *The Cardinal*. European theatrical work includes 'Tis Pity She's a Whore' and 'The Seagull'. Married German producer Harry Mayen.

Films as actress include: 1959: Die Halbzart. 1962: Boccaccio '70 *ep* Il Lavoro. 1963: The Cardinal; Le Procés; The Victors. 1964: Good Nieghbour Sam. 1965: What's New Pussycat? 1966: 10.30 pm Summer; Triple Cross. 1970: Qui? 1971: Max et les ferrailleurs; Bloomfield.

SCHOEDSACK, Ernest B.

Director. Council Bluffs. Iowa 1893–
1914: cameraman at Keystone studios. World War I: cameraman with US Signal Corps, shot documentary material at the front. Then news cameraman, widely-travelled. 1926: with Merian C. Cooper and Marguerite Harrison produced his first film as director (in collaboration) in Turkey. Cooper was director, producer, writer in collaboration on a number of later films. 1926–31: worked for Famous Players-Lasky and Paramount. 1932–35: with RKO. 1935: spent 6 months shooting location material in India for Henry Hathaway's *The Lives of a Bengal Lancer* but climate ruined film stock. 1937: with Columbia. 1926: married actress and explorer Ruth Rose who later wrote scripts for *Blind Adventure* (1933), *The Last Days of Pompeii* (1935), *Mighty Joe Young* (1949), story for *Son of Kong* (1934), script in collaboration for *King Kong* (1933); also directed in collaboration the Prologue of *This is Cinerama* (1953).

Films as director: 1926: Grass (*+ co-p/co-c; co-d Merian C. Cooper, Marguerite Harrison*). 1927: Chang (*+ co-p/c; co-d Merian C. Cooper*). 1929: The Four Feathers (*+ co-p; co-d Merian C. Cooper, Lothar Mendes*). 1931: Rango (*+ p*). 1932: The Most Dangerous Game – The Hounds of Zaroff (*+ co-p; co-d Irving Pichel*). 1933: King Kong (*+ co-p; co-d Merian C. Cooper*); Son of Kong; Blind Adventure. 1934: Long Lost Father. 1935: The Last Days of Pompeii. 1937: Trouble in Morocco; Outlaws of the Orient. 1940: Dr Cyclops. 1949: Mighty Joe Young. 1953: This is Cinerama (*uc, cu, co-d Ruth Rose*).

SCHOENDOERFFER, Pierre

Director. Chamaillières, France 1928–
Sailor, then war photographer in Indo-China; prisoner-of-war. Photographer/reporter for Paris Match, Paris-Presse, Candide. 1957: directed first film in collaboration in Afghanistan. Author of novel 'La 317e Section' which he filmed in 1965. 1966: directed 'Section Anderson' in series 'Cinq Colonnes à la une' for French TV.

Films as director: 1957: La Passe du diable (*co-d Jacques Dupont*); Thau le pêcheur. 1958: Ramuntcho (*+ co-s*). 1959: Pêcheur d'islande (*+ co-s*). 1962: Attention! Helicopteres. 1965: La 317e Section (*+ fn*). 1966: Objectif 500 millions.

SCHORM, Ewald

Director. Prague 1931–
1962: graduated from FAMU, Prague in same year as Vera Chytilova and Jiri Menzel. Worked on documentaries and newsreels in Documentary Film Studios. Made TV film *Gramo von ballet* using dance and animation. Work in theatre includes 'Crime and Punishment' at Prague Theatre Club. 1964: first feature as director. Continued to make shorts e.g. *Carmen* (1966). Acted in *O Slavnosti a hostech* (1966).

Features as director: 1964: Kazdy den odvahu – Everyday Courage (*+ co-s*). 1965: Perlicki na dne – Pearls of the Deep *ep* Domu radosti – The House of Joy (*+ co-s*). 1966: Návrat ztraceného syna – The Return of the Prodigal Son (*+ st/s*). 1967: Pet Holek na krku – Five Girls equals a Millstone Round One's Neck (*+ co-s*). 1968: Pražské Noci – Prague Nights *ep* O Chlebovich střevíčcich – Slipper of Bread (*+ s*). 1969: Fararuv konec – End of a Priest (*+ co-s*); Den Sedmy. osmà noc – Seventh Day. Eighth Night.

SCHÜFFTAN, Eugen

Cinematographer. Breslau, Germany 1893–
Studied painting, sculpture and architecture in Breslau before World War I. 1919: cartoonist. 1926–27: at Universal in Hollywood. 1928–39: cinematographer in Europe, first in Germany, then in France. 1931: in collaboration, directed and photographed *Das Ekel*. 1946: production supervisor on *A Scandal in Paris*. 1947: became a naturalised American and worked as technical consultant. Worked in USA and France and internationally. Invented the Schufftan Process (1923), first used in *Metropolis* (1927); it uses a partly silvered mirror to combine live action with photographic or model backgrounds e.g. in British Museum sequence of *Blackmail* (1929) and in *Things to Come* (1939). Oscar for black and white cinematography on *The Hustler* (1961).

Films as cinematographer include: 1929: Menschen Am Sonntag. 1931: Gassenhauer (*co*). 1932: Die Herrin von Atlantis (*co*). 1934: Du haut en bas. 1936: La Tendre Ennemie. 1937: Drôle de drame; Mademoiselle Docteur. 1938: Le Drame de Shanghai; Quai des brumes. 1939: Sans lendemain. 1952: Le Rideau Cramoisi. 1958: La Première Nuit; La Tête contre les Murs. 1959: Les Yeux sans visage. 1960: Un Couple. 1963: Lilith. 1965: Trois Chambres à Manhattan. 1966: Der Arzt stellt fast.

SCHULBERG, Ben P.

Studio head. Bridgeport, Connecticut 1892–1957
Began as reporter with New York Evening Mail. Then publicity director with Rex Pictures. From 1912: handled publicity for Adolph Zukor's Famous Players and (from 1916) Famous Players-Lasky. After World War I: left FPL to become independent producer releasing through United Artists; discovered Clara Bow. 1925–32: rejoined Zukor as general manager of Paramount's West Coast studio. Subsequently produced independently and for various companies including Columbia, Selznick International. After World War II: mainly unemployed. 1949: ran expensive campaign in trade press to advertise his availability. Father of Budd Schulberg.

SCHULBERG, Budd Wilson

Writer. New York 1914–
Son of B. P. Schulberg. 1931: publicist at Paramount. 1932: began writing for films. Novels include 'The Disenchanted', 'What Makes Sammy Run' (also as play), 'The Harder They Fall'. 1958: *Wind Across the Everglades* made for his company, Schulberg Productions, and produced by his brother Stuart Schulberg. Set up Writer's Workshop in Watts, California. Oscar for story and screen play of *On the Waterfront* (1954).

Films as writer include: 1941: Weekend for Three (*st*). 1943: Government Girl (*ad*). 1954: On the Waterfront (*+ st*). 1956: The Harder They Fall (*fn*). 1957: A Face in the Crowd (*+ fst*). 1958: Wind Across the Everglades.

SCHOFIELD, Paul

Actor. King's Norton Warwickshire 1922–
Mainly theatre actor. First major part in 'Adventure Story' directed by Peter Glenville. Stage work includes

'King Lear', 'The Power and the Glory', 'Expresso Bongo' and (in London and New York) 'A Man For All Seasons'. 1971: in Old Vic production of 'The Captain of Kopenick'. Married Joy Parker, with whom he often acted. Occasional films. Oscar as Best Actor, *A Man for All Seasons* (1966).

Films as actor: 1955: That Lady. 1958: Carve Her Name with Pride. 1964: The Train. 1966: A Man for All Seasons. 1969: King Lear (*r* 1971).

SCOTT, George C.

Actor. Wise, Virginia 1927–
Brought up in Detroit, Michigan. From 1945: 4 years in US Marine Corps. English and drama at University of Missouri. 1952–55: acted in various stock companies; worked in a number of unskilled jobs. 1956: played Richard III at New York Shakespeare Festival; then a succession of off-Broadway and Broadway roles. 1959: first films. TV includes 'The Power and the Glory', 'East Side, West Side'. Also director in theatre; formed Theatre of Michigan Company, Detroit. Third wife actress Colleen Dewhurst. Oscar as Best Actor for *Patton* (1970).

Films as actor: 1959: The Hanging Tree; Anatomy of a Murder. 1961: The Hustler. 1963: The List of Adrian Messenger; Dr Strangelove, or How I Learned to Stop Worrying and Love the Bomb. 1964: The Yellow Rolls Royce. 1966: Not with my Wife You Don't; La Bibbia. 1967: The Flim-Flam Man. 1968: Petulia. 1970: Patton. 1971: Jane Eyre; The Last Run.

SCOTT, Lizabeth

(Emma Matzo) Actress. Scranton, Pennsylvania 1922–
Drama school. First stage work as understudy to Tallulah Bankhead. 1945: spotted by Hal Wallis for first film as actress *You Came Along*. To 1947: worked mainly for Paramount, then mainly for Columbia, RKO, Paramount. 1952: made *Stolen Face* in UK.

Films as actress include: 1946: The Strange Love of Martha Ivers. 1947: Dead Reckoning; I Walk Alone. 1948: Pitfall. 1949: Too Late for Tears; Easy Living. 1950: Paid in Full; Dark City; The Company She Keeps. 1951: Two of a Kind; The Racket; Red Mountain. 1953: Scared Stiff; Bad for Each Other. 1954: Silver Lode. 1957: Loving You.

SCOTT, Randolph

Actor. Orange County, Virginia 1903–
University of North Carolina. Extra. 1931: first film as actor *Women Men Marry*. To 1935: almost all films for Paramount. Then worked for numerous companies. From late 1940s all films are westerns. From 1951: worked frequently for Warners. From 1955: also number of films for Columbia. In collaboration with Harry Joe Brown his company produced many of his late films.

Films as actor include: 1932: Wild Horse Mesa. 1933: Heritage of the Desert; Sunset Pass; Cocktail Hour; Man of the Forest; To the Last Man; Thundering Herd. 1934: The Last Round-Up. 1935: The Village; She; Roberta; So Red the Rose. 1936: Follow the Fleet; Go West, Young Man; The Last of the Mohicans. 1937:

High, Wide and Handsome. 1938: Rebecca of Sunnybrook Farm. 1939: Frontier Marshal; Jesse James. 1940: Virginia City; My Favourite Wife; When the Daltons Rode. 1941: Western Union. 1942: The Spoilers. 1943: Gung Ho!; The Desperadoes. 1945: China Sky. 1946: Home, Sweet Homicide. 1947: Albuquerque; Trail Street. 1948: The Return of the Bad Men; Coroner Creek. 1949: The Doolins of Oklahoma; The Walking Hills. 1950: The Nevadan. 1951: Santa Fe; Man in the Saddle; Starlift. 1952: Carson City. 1953: Thunder Over the Plains; The Stranger Wore a Gun. 1954: Riding Shotgun; The Bounty Hunter. 1955: Lawless Street (*+ as-p*). 1956: Seven Men from Now; 7th Cavalry (*+ as-p*). 1957: The Tall T (*+ co-pc*); Decision at Sundown (*+ co-pc*). 1958: Buchanan Rides Alone (*+ as-p/co-pc*). 1959: Ride Lonesome (*+ co-pc*); Westbound. 1960: Comanche Station (*+ co-pc*), 1962: Ride the High Country.

SEARS, Fred F.

Director. Boston, Massachusetts 1913–57 Hollywood
Boston College. Actor then impresario on Broadway. Opened The Little Theatre in Memphis, Tennessee. Taught dramatic art at Southwestern University. 1945: began in films; directed practically all his films for Columbia. Also TV e.g. 'Ford Theatre', 'Damon Runyon Theatre', 'Celebrity Playhouse'.

Films as director include: 1949: Horseman of the Sierra. 1950: Lightning Guns. 1951: Pecos River; Smoky Canyon. 1952: The Hawk of Wild River; The Kid from Broken Gun. 1953: Ambush at Tomahawk Gap; The Nebraskan; Mission Over Korea. 1954: Overland Pacific; The Miami Story; Massacre Canyon, The Outlaw Stallion – The White Stallion. 1955: Wyoming Renegade; Chicago Syndicate; Cell 2455, Death Row; Inside Detroit; Apache Ambush; Teenage Crime Wave. 1956: Fury at Gunsight Pass; Rock Around the Clock; Cha-Cha-Cha Boom!; The Werewolf; Earth vs. the Flying Saucers; Rumble on the Docks. 1957: Don't Knock the Rock; Utah Blaine; The Night the World Exploded; Calypso Heatwave; The Giant Claw; Escape from San Quentin. 1958: Going Steady; The World Was His Jury; Crash Landing; Ghost of the China Sea; Badman's Country.

SEATON, George

Director and writer. South Bend, Indiana 1911–
University of Mount St Vincent and Exeter Academy. From 1929: played The Lone Ranger on Detroit radio; director and actor with stock company in Detroit. 1933: began in films as writer with MGM e.g. wrote in collaboration story and script for *A Day at the Races* (1937). 1940–41: scriptwriter with Columbia. From 1942: with Fox e.g. script and story for *Coney Island* (1943), scripts for *The Song of Bernadette* (1943), *The Eve of St Mark* (1944). 1945: first film as director, for Fox. 1952: formed production company with William Perlberg. Subsequent films co-produced with him include *The Bridges at Toko-Ri* (1955), *The Tin Star* (1957), *The Rat Race* (1960). 1952–61: films released through Paramount. From 1962: films released through MGM. Author of play 'But Not Goodbye' (1943). President of the Academy of Motion Picture Arts and Sciences (1956). Oscars for best screenplays, *Miracle on 34th Street* (1947), *The Country Girl* (1954).

King Kong, *directed by Merian C. Cooper and Ernest B. Schoedsack.*
Metropolis, *directed by Fritz Lang, special lighting effects by Eugen Schüfftan.*
Randolph Scott in Comanche Station, *directed by Budd Boetticher.*

Films as director: 1945: Billy Rose's Diamond Horseshoe (+ s); Junior Miss (+ s). 1946: The Shocking Miss Pilgrim (+ s). 1947: Miracle on 34th Street (+ s); The Shocking Miss Pilgrim. 1948: Apartment for Peggy (+ s). 1949: Chicken Every Sunday (+ co-s). 1950: The Big Lift (+ s/st); For Heaven's Sake (+ s). 1952: Anything Can Happen (+ co-s). 1953: Little Boy Lost (+ s). 1954: The Country Girl (+ co-p/s). 1956: The Proud and the Profane (+ co-st/s). 1958: Teacher's Pet. 1961: The Pleasure of His Company; The Counterfeit Traitor. 1962: The Hook. 1964: 36 Hours (+ s). 1968: What's So Bad About Feeling Good? (+ p/co-st/co-s). 1970: Airport (+ s).

SEBERG, Jean

Actress. Marshalltown, Iowa 1938–
Father pharmacist, mother teacher. Drama at university, acted in 'Sabrina Fair' and 'Our Town'. Summer stock in Plymouth, Massachusetts and Cape May, New Jersey. 1957: discovered by Otto Preminger in contest for leading part in *Saint Joan,* her first film as actress. 1958: married Francois Moreuil. From 1959: acted also in French films. 1962: directed by Moreuil in *Playtime,* shortly before divorce. 1963: married novelist Romain Gary. 1968: directed by him in *Les Oiseaux vont mourir au Perou.*

Films as actress include: 1958: Bonjour Tristesse; A Certain Smile. 1959: The Mouse that Roared; Let No Man Write My Epitaph; A bout de souffle. 1961: L'Amant de cinq jours. 1963: Les Plus Belles Escroqueries du monde *ep* Le Grand Escroc; Lilith; In the French Style. 1965: Moment to Moment. 1966: La Ligne de démarcation; A Fine Madness. 1967: La Route de Corinth. 1969: Paint Your Wagon. 1970: Airport. 1971: Kill.

SÉCHAN, Edmond

Director and cinematographer. Montpellier, France 1919–
At first studied medicine, then attended Ecole Technique de Photographie et Cinématographie and IDHEC. Began as cameraman. From 1946: cinematographer on a number of shorts directed by Jacques Dupont. 1949: first short as director. 1960: first feature as director.

Films as cinematographer include: 1953: Crin Blanc, le cheval sauvage. 1956: Le Monde du silence (co); Le Ballon Rouge; Mort en fraude. 1957: Les Aventures d'Arsene Lupin; Tamango. 1959: Les Dragueurs. 1963: Love is a Ball. 1965: Les Tribulations d'un Chinois en Chine.

Films as director include: 1957: Niok (+ s). 1958: L'Histoire d'un poisson rouge (+ s). 1960: L'Ours (+ s/c). 1962: L'Haricot (+ s/c). 1968: Pour un amour lointain (+ co-s).

SEGAL, George

Actor. New York 1936–
Columbia University. 1956: worked briefly in New York theatre before being drafted. Military service. From 1959: stage and TV. 1961: first film as actor *The Young Doctors.* To 1964: combined stage and film careers, then concentrated on films.

Films as actor include: 1964: The New Interns; Invitation to a Gunfighter. 1965: Ship of Fools. 1966: King Rat; Lost Command; Who's Afraid of Virginia Woolf?; The Quiller Memorandum. 1967: The St Valentine's Day Massacre. 1968: No Way to Treat a Lady; Bye Bye Braverman. 1969: The Bridge at Remagen. 1970: The Owl and the Pussycat; Loving. 1971: Born to Win.

SEITZ, George B.

Director. Boston, Massachusetts 1880–1944 Hollywood
Brother of John B. Seitz. Eric Pape Art School. Actor, stage manager with John Craig's stock company. Wrote plays, stories. 1910: sold first play, 'The King's Game'. 1913: joined Pathe as writer; rewrote many of his stories as film scripts. 1914: actor and 'shooting script carpenter' on 20-episode Pearl White serial, *The Perils of Pauline.* From 1915: directed in collaboration and wrote Pearl White serials. 1916–21: had own production company Astra, making Pearl White serials for Pathe. Directed other serials, e.g. *Leather Stocking* (1924). 1925: left Pathe and serials. 1925–26: made 3 films for Paramount. Then worked for various companies notably Columbia. 1933–44: mainly with MGM.

Films as director: 1916–17: Pearl of the Army (*15 eps*). 1917: The Fatal Ring (*20 eps*). 1918: The House of Hate (*20 eps*); Getaway Kate; The Honest Thief. 1918–19: The Lightning Raider (+ co-s). 1919: The Black Secret (*15 eps*); Bound and Gagged (*10 eps*; +w). 1920: Pirate Gold (*10 eps*; +w); Rogues and Romance (+ p/st/s/w). 1920–21: Velvet Fingers (*15 eps*; +s/w). 1921: The Sky Ranger (*15 eps*; +w); Hurricane Hutch (*15 eps*). 1922: Go Get 'em Hutch (*15 eps*; +p). 1922–23: Plunder (+ co-s); Speed (*15 eps*). 1923–24: The Way of a Man (*10 eps*; +s). 1924: Leather Stocking (*10 eps*); The Fortieth Door (*10 eps*); Galloping Hoofs (*10 eps*); Into the Net (*10 eps*). 1925: Sunken Sailor (*10 eps*; +p); Wild Horse Mesa; The Vanishing American. 1926: Desert Gold (+ p); Pals in Paradise; The Last Frontier; The Ice Flood (+ co-s). 1927: Jim the Conqueror; Great Mail Robbery; The Blood Ship; Tigress; The Warning (+ s); Isle of Forgotten Women. 1928: After the Storm; Ransom (+ st); Beware of Blondes; The Circus Kid; Court-Martial; Hey Rube!; Blockade. 1929: Black Magic (+ p). 1930: Murder on the Roof; Guilty?; Midnight Mystery; Danger Lights. 1931: The Drums of Jeopardy; The Lion and the Lamb; Arizona; Shanghaied Love; Night Beat. 1932: Sally of the Subway (+ st/s/di); Docks of San Francisco; Sin's Pay Day; Widow in Scarlet; Passport to Paradise (+ st/s). 1933: Treason; The Thrill Hunter; The Woman in His Life. 1934: Lazy River. 1935: Desert Death; Shadow of Doubt; Only Eight Hours; Times Square Lady; Calm Yourself; Woman Wanted; Kind Lady. 1936: Exclusive Story; The Three Wise Guys; The Last of the Mohicans; Mad Holiday. 1937: Under Cover of Night; The Thirteenth Chair; A Family Affair; Mama Steps Out; Between Two Women; My Dear Miss Aldrich. 1938: You're Only Young Once; Judge Hardy's Children; Yellow Jack; Love Finds Andy Hardy; Out West With the Hardys. 1939: The Hardys Ride High; 6,000 Enemies; Thunder Afloat; Judge Hardy and Son. 1940: Kit Carson; Andy Hardy Meets Debutante; Sky Murder; Gallant Sons. 1941: Andy Hardy's Private Secretary; Life Begins for Andy Hardy.

1942: The Courtship of Andy Hardy; A Yank on the Burma Road; Pierre of the Plains; Andy Hardy's Double Life. 1944: Andy Hardy's Blonde Trouble.

SEITZ, John F.

Cinematographer. Boston, Massachusetts 1892–
1909: laboratory technician at St Louis Motion Picture Company. 1916: joined American Mutual. By 1919: worked as cinematographer. 1920–28: cinematographer for Metro notably on many Rex Ingram films. 1929–31: at First National. 1931–36: with Fox. 1937–40: with MGM. 1941–52: at Paramount where he worked with Preston Sturges, Billy Wilder. Then with various companies until retirement in 1960. Holder of a number of patents for photographic devices including 'matte' shot, 'changing screen'. Since retirement experimented in lavishly equipped laboratory.

Films as cinematographer include: 1920: Hearts are Trumps. 1921: The Four Horsemen of the Apocalypse; The Conquering Power. 1922: The Prisoner of Zenda; Turn to the Right; Trifling Women. 1923: Scaramouche; Where the Pavement Ends. 1924: The Arab. 1926: Mare Nostrum; The Magician. 1927: The Fair Co-ed. 1928: The Trail of '98; The Patsy; Adoration. 1929: The Divine Lady; The Squall; Her Private Life. 1930: Murder Will Out; In the Next Room; Sweethearts and Wives; The Bad Man. 1931: East Lynne; The Age for Love (co); Over the Hill. 1932: Woman in Room 13; A Passport to Hell; Six Hours to Live. 1933: Ladies They Talk About; Adorable; Mr Skitch. 1934: Marie Galante; Helldorado. 1935: One More Spring; Navy Wife (co). 1936: 15 Maiden Lane. 1937: Madame X. 1938: Lord Jeff. 1939: Sergeant Madden. 1941: Sullivan's Travels. 1942: Fly-By-Night; This Gun for Hire; The Moon and Sixpence; Five Graves to Cairo. 1944: Hail the Conquering Hero; Double Indemnity; The Miracle of Morgan's Creek. 1945: The Lost Weekend. 1947: Wild Harvest. 1948: The Big Clock; A Miracle Can Happen (co). 1949: The Great Gatsby. 1950: Sunset Boulevard. 1951: When Worlds Collide. 1952: The Iron Mistress. 1953: Botany Bay. 1954: Saskatchewan. 1955: The McConnell Story. 1956: Santiago. 1957: The Big Land. 1958: The Badlanders. 1959: The Man in the Net.

SELLERS, Peter

Actor. Southsea, Hampshire 1925–
World War II: served in RAF in India; he did camp concerts, then toured Middle East with Ralph Reader's 'Gang Show'. Began professional career at Windmill Theatre, London. 1949–56: acted in 'The Goon Show' for BBC radio. Many appearances at London Palladium including Royal Command Variety Performance (1954). Appeared in ITV comedy shows 'The Idiot Weekly', 'A Show Called Fred', 'Son of Fred', 'Yes, It's the Cathode Ray Tube Show'. In films from 1951. 1961: directed and acted in *Mr Topaze.* Also made records e.g. 'The Best of Sellers', 'Songs for Swingin' Sellers'. 1964: forced to give up leading part in Billy Wilder's *Kiss Me Stupid* because of serious heart condition. Was married to actresses Ann Hayes, Britt Ekland.

Films as actor include: 1955: The Ladykillers. 1959: Carlton-Browne of the F.O.; The Mouse that Roared; I'm All Right Jack. 1960: The Running, Jumping and

Standing Still Film (+ p/co-c/co-e); Never Let Go; The Millionairess. 1961: Only Two Can Play. 1962: Waltz of the Toreadors; Lolita. 1963: Heavens Above!; Dr Strangelove, or How I Learned to Stop Worrying and Love the Bomb. 1964: The Pink Panther; The World of Henry Orient; A Shot in the Dark. 1965: What's New Pussycat?; After the Fox. 1966: The Wrong Box; 1967: Casino Royale. 1968: The Party. 1970: There's a Girl in My Soup.

SELZNICK, David O.

Producer. Pittsburgh, Pennsylvania 1902–65 Hollywood

Son of a pioneer film producer, Lewis J. Selznick. Learned business under his father after whose retirement he promoted and produced speciality shorts and independent features. Then West Coast production representative for Associated Exhibitors. 1926: joined MGM rising from assistant story editor through assistant producer, story editor to be associate producer on Tim McCoy westerns. 1928: moved to Paramount as assistant to B. P. Schulberg, then head of production, and as associate producer. After being temporary production chief at Paramount during a lengthy absence by Schulberg, became vice-president in charge of production at RKO (1932). Then became vice-president at MGM (1933) where he headed own unit, 1936: founded own company, Selznick International Pictures. 1942: founded Vanguard Films Inc. 1949: president, Selznick Releasing Corporation; married Jennifer Jones. 1953: financed Stazione Termini. 1958: president, Selznick Company Inc.

Films as producer include: 1932: What Price Hollywood?; Bird of Paradise; A Bill of Divorcement. 1933: Topaze; Little Women; Dinner at Eight; Our Betters. 1934: Viva Villa! 1935: The Personal History, Adventures, Experience and Observations of David Copperfield, the Younger; Anna Karenina; A Tale of Two Cities. 1936: The Garden of Allah. 1937: A Star Is Born; Nothing Sacred; The Prisoner of Zenda. 1939: Gone With the Wind. 1940: Rebecca. 1944: Since You Went Away (+ s). 1945: Spellbound. 1946: Duel in the Sun (+ s). 1947: The Paradine Case (+ s). 1949: Portrait of Jennie (+ co-s). 1957: A Farewell to Arms.

SEMON, Larry

Director and actor. West Point Missouri 1889–1928 Victorville, California

1916: first film as director and actor The Man from Egypt; also, in collaboration, wrote it. Gagman and director for Vitagraph. Newspaper cartoonist. Directed most of own films as actor. Also directed by e.g. Fred Newmeyer. 1927: last film as actor, Underworld. Married actress Lucile Carlisle.

Films as director and actor include: 1917: Rough Toughs and Roof Tops (+ s); Plagues and Puppy Love. 1918: Bears and Bad Men (+ s). 1919: Passing the Buck (+ s); Between the Acts (+ s). 1921: The Fly Cop (+ s; co-d Mort Peebles). 1923: The Gown Shop (+ s); The Barnyard (+ s). 1924: Trouble Brewing (+ co-s; co-d James Davis); Kid Speed (+ co-s; co-d Noel Mason Smith); The Girl in the Limousine. 1925: The Wizard of Oz. 1927: Spuds (+ s).

Films as director in collaboration with Norman

Taurog, writer and actor, include: 1920: The Stage Hand; The Suitor; The Sportsman. 1921: The Sawmill; The Hick; The Bell Hop.

SENNETT, Mack

(Michael Sinnott) Director, producer and actor. Richmond, Ontario 1880–1960 Richmond, Ontario

Irish immigrant parents. At 17 to Connecticut with family; worked in American Iron Works. Then metal worker in Northampton, Massachusetts. Also trained as operatic bass. 1902: to New York; appeared in burlesque at Bowery Theatre and on tour with Frank Sheridan's company; singer and dancer in chorus of Broadway musicals; sang with the Cloverdale Boys and Happy Gondoliers groups. 1908: joined Biograph studios in New York; acted in shorts directed by D. W. Griffith, bit parts then leading roles in e.g. The Curtain Pole (1909). Wrote story for Griffith's Lonely Villa (1909). By 1911: directing Mabel Normand, Fred Mace and himself in comedy shorts for Biograph. By 1912: formed Keystone Film Company with Hollywood studio; made 2 ½-reel films a week. Introduced Sennett 'Bathing Beauties' and 'Keystone Kops'. Actors included Mabel Normand, Fred Mace, Ford Sterling, Sennett, then Fatty Arbuckle, Alice Davenport, Chester Conklin. By 1913: production stepped up to 4 films (i.e. 2 reels) a week; ran second production unit under Henry Lehrman; Mabel Normand also directed; began to make mainly one-reelers (2 a week); directed 2-reeler, Zuzu the Band Leader. During 1914: produced 3 1-reelers a week and a 2-reeler each month; employed Charles Chaplin as actor, then as director sometimes in collaboration with Mabel Normand; Fatty Arbuckle began to direct. 1915: directed feature, Tillie's Punctured Romance; with D. W. Griffith and Thomas Ince formed new production company Triangle; directed and acted in 3-reeler, My Valet for Triangle's opening programme at Knickerbocker Theatre, Broadway. From 1915 until end of career produced mainly 2-reelers (also occasionally directing and acting). 1915–18: actors who joined Keystone-Triangle included Wallace Beery, Gloria Swanson as a 'bathing beauty', Broadway stars Raymond Hitchcock, Eddie Foy; directors included Arbuckle, Clarence Badger, Eddie Cline. 1916: built studio for Mabel Normand on Sunset Boulevard and financed feature film, Mickey, which took a year to make and a further year to sell to a distributor before achieving financial success in 1918. 1917–21: produced series of 2-reelers for Paramount; directors included Cline and Mal St Clair, actors included Ben Turpin; also independently produced features e.g. Down on the Farm (1920), Married Life (1920), Love, Honor and Behave (1921), A Small Town Idol (1921) and Molly O' (1921) for which Mabel Normand, who had been working with Goldwyn, rejoined Sennett. Some of these made for Associated Producers, a consortium including Ince, Allan Dwan, Maurice Tourneur, releasing through First National. 1922: Associated Producers absorbed into First National, for which Sennett produced 2-reelers and a feature, The Crossroads of New York (1922). 1923: left First National and began long association with Pathe. Engaged actors Harry Langdon (first film Picking Peaches, 1924), Ralph Graves, Alice Day. Directors included Roy Del Ruth, Erle Kenton, Harry Edwards, Lloyd Bacon, Cline. Frank Capra joined writing team. 1926: began series 'Smith's Family' starring Raymond McKee, Ruth Hiatt. 1928: wrote and directed feature,

Jean Seberg in Les Oiseaux Vont Mourir au Perou, *directed by Romain Gary.*

Peter Sellers and Ursula Andress in What's New Pussycat?, *directed by Clive Donner.*

Mack Sennett.

The Good-Bye Kiss for First National; began 'Andy Hardy' series and 'Taxicab' series. 1929: production of comedy shorts began to decline on coming of sound; produced and directed comedy series for Educational Films. From 1932: produced 'Mack Sennett Comedies', 'Mack Sennett Featurettes', 'Andy Clyde Comedies' for Paramount which went bankrupt in 1935. Lost whole fortune and went back to Canada. 1939: returned to films as an associate producer with Fox. Special Academy Award for 'his lasting contribution to the comedy technique of the screen' (1937).

Films as director and actor (also producer from Pedro's Dilemma) include: 1911: Comrades; The Manicure Lady; A Dutch Gold Mine; The Village Hero; Trailing the Counterfeit; Their First Divorce Case; Caught with the Goods. 1912: The Fatal Chocolate; A Spanish Dilemma; Their First Kidnapping Case; The Would-Be Shriner; Pedro's Dilemma; Stolen Glory; The Ambitious Butler; At Coney Island; At It Again; The Rivals; Mr Fix It – Mr Fixer; A Bear Escape; Pat's Day Off; A Family Mixup; The Duel. 1913: The Mistaken Masher; The Battle of Who Run; The Stolen Purse; Mabel's Heroes; The Sleuth's Last Stand; The Sleuths at the Floral Parade; A Strong Revenge; The Rube and the Baron; Her New Beau; Mabel's Awful Mistake; Barney Oldfield's Race for a Life; The Hansom Driver; His Crooked Career; Mabel's Dramatic Career; Love Sickness at Sea – Lovesickness at Sea. 1914: Mack at it Again; Mabel at the Wheel (*co-d Mabel Normand*); The Fatal Mallet (*co-d Charles Chaplin*); His Talented Wife. 1915: Hearts and Planets; The Little Teacher; Stolen Magic; My Valet. 1921: Oh, Mabel Behave (*co-d Ford Sterling*).

SERLING, Rod

Writer. Syracuse, New York 1924–
World War II: US Army paratrooper. 1946–48: network radio writer. From 1948: network TV writer. 1950: graduated, Antioch College. Produced TV drama including 'Kraft Theatre', 'Studio 1', 'US Steel Hour', 'Playhouse 90', 'Suspense', 'Danger' and others. Executive producer and creator of 'The Twilight Zone'. TV plays 'The Rack' and 'Requiem for a Heavyweight' filmed; first film as writer *Patterns* (1956) from own story. 1965–66: national president, National Academy of TV Arts and Sciences. Host and writer on 'Rod Serling's Night Gallery' for NBC-TV.

Films as writer include: 1958: Saddle the Wind. 1962: Requiem, for a Heavyweight (*+fpl*). 1963: The Yellow Canary. 1964: Seven Days in May. 1968: Planet of the Apes (*co*).

SEYRIG, Delphine

Actress, Bayreuth, Germany 1932–
Spent childhood in Lebanon. 1952–55: studied drama. 1952: stage début in Paris. 1955–56: work on Paris stage included own productions. 1956: to USA. 1956–59: Actor's Studio and American TV. 1958: first film as actress *Pull My Daisy*. Acted on stage in Moscow. 1969: acted on TV in *Leys dans la vallée*.

Films as actress include: 1961: L'Année Dernière à Marienbad. 1963: Muriel, ou le temps d'un retour. 1966: La Musica. 1967: Accident. 1968: Baisers Volés; Mr Freedom. 1969: La Voie Lactée. 1970: Peau d'âne.

SHAMROY, Leon

Cinematographer. New York 1901–
Mechanics and engineering at Columbia University. To California, worked in photographic laboratory. Experimental films. 1928: photographed *The Last Moment* and, in Mexico, *Acoma, the Sky City*. 1930: toured Japan, China and the Dutch East Indies with a camera. 1932: signed up by B. P. Schulberg at Paramount, then films for Columbia, Walter Wanger and David Selznick as well (1935–39). 1940: contract with Fox. 1953: photographed *The Robe*, first Cinemascope film. Oscars for colour cinematography on *The Black Swan* (1942) and *Leave Her to Heaven* (1945).

Films as cinematographer include: 1933: Three Cornered Moon. 1935: Behold My Wife; Private Worlds; She Married her Boss; She Couldn't Take It; Mary Burns, Fugitive. 1936: Soak The Rich; Spendthrift. 1937: You Only Live Once; The Great Gambini. 1939: Made for Each Other. 1940: Little Old New York; I Was an Adventuress (*co*); Four Sons; Tin Pan Alley. 1941: The Great American Broadcast (*co*); Moon Over Miami (*co*); A Yank in the RAF; Confirm or Deny. 1942: Roxie Hart; Ten Gentlemen from West Point; The Black Swan. 1943: Crash Dive; Stormy Weather; Claudia. 1944: Buffalo Bill; Greenwich Village (*co*); Wilson. 1945: A Tree Grows in Brooklyn; Where Do We Go From Here; State Fair; The Shocking Miss Pilgrim. 1946: Leave Her to Heaven. 1947: Forever Amber; Daisy Kenyon. 1948: That Lady in Ermine. 1949: Prince of Foxes; Twelve O'Clock High. 1950: Cheaper By The Dozen; Two Flags West. 1951: On The Riviera; David and Bathsheba. 1952: With A Song In My Heart; Wait Till The Sun Shines, Nellie; Down Among The Sheltering Palms; The Snows of Kilimanjaro. 1953: Tonight We Sing; Call Me Madam; White Witch Doctor; The Robe; King of the Khyber Rifles. 1954: The Egyptian; There's No Business Like Show Business. 1955: Daddy Long Legs; Love is a Many-Splendored Thing; Good Morning, Miss Dove. 1956: The King and I; The Best Things in Life are Free; The Girl Can't Help It. 1957: The Desk Set. 1958: South Pacific; The Bravados; Rally 'Round the Flag, Boys!. 1959: Porgy and Bess; The Blue Angel; Beloved Infidel. 1960: Wake Me When It's Over; North to Alaska. 1961: Snow White and the Three Stooges. 1962: Tender is the Night. 1963: Cleopatra (*co*); The Cardinal. 1964: What a Way to Go; John Goldfarb, Please Come Home. 1965: The Agony and the Ecstasy. 1966: The Glass-Bottom Boat. 1967: Caprice. 1968: Planet of the Apes; The Secret Life of an American Wife; Skidoo. 1969: Justine.

SHANKAR, Ravi

Composer and musician. Benares, India 1920–
Father a Bengali Brahmin who went to London to practice law. 1930: when brother organised troupe of Indian musicians and dancers to go to Europe, whole family went. Catholic school in Paris then private tutors. 1936: first solo dance in brother's troupe. 1936: first lessons from Alladin Khan whose daughter he married in 1938. 1938: Brahmin initiation ceremony; returned to India. Radio broadcasts from Lucknow. 1944: to Bombay. 1944–46: with Indian People's Theatre Association. Began to compose for films e.g. *Dharta ke La*. (1946). 1946: with Indian National Theatre. 1947: with 2 brothers and colleagues formed India Renaissance Artists; soon disbanded. 1949: became director of music for External Services Division of All-India Radio. 1952: director of music for Home Services division. 1954: to Russia. 1956: to Europe and USA. Opened music schools in Bombay and Los Angeles. 1957: his music used in *A Chairy Tale*. In USA appeared at Newport Jazz Festival, Hollywood Bowl. George Harrison, Dave Brubeck studied with him. Recorded 2 albums with Yehudi Menuhin. 1971: the subject of *Raga*.

Films as composer include: 1955: Pather Panchali. 1957: Aparajito. 1958: Paras Pathar. 1959: Apur Sansar; The Sword and the Flute. 1966: Chappaqua (*co*). 1968: Charly.

SHARIF, Omar

(Michel Shalhoub) Actor. Alexandria, Egypt 1932–
At 4 moved to Cairo with family. Father a lumber importer. Victoria College, Cairo; worked with drama group. Salesman for father's firm. From 1954: acted in 24 Egyptian films and 2 French co-productions. Acted with Faten Hamama, married her in 1956. They formed production company in Cairo. 1962: first English-language film *Lawrence of Arabia*. Most subsequent work for Columbia.

Films as actor include: 1963: La Fabuleuse Aventure de Marco Polo. 1964: The Fall of the Roman Empire; Behold a Pale Horse; The Yellow Rolls-Royce. 1965: Genghis Khan; Dr Zhivago. 1967: The Night of the Generals; C'era una volta. 1968: Funny Girl. 1969: Mayerling; Mackenna's Gold; The Appointment; Che! 1971: The Last Valley; Le Casse; The Horsemen.

SHAVELSON, Melville

Director and writer. New York 1917–
Cornell University. Began in radio. 1938–43: directed 'The Bob Hope Show' on radio. 1944: entered films as writer in collaboration at RKO. Then scripts in collaboration for Paramount, Warners. 1955: first film as director. Until 1961 co-wrote all his films with Jack Rose, who was also his producer. Until 1963, with Paramount, then with independent companies, releasing through United Artists. Director for TV series 'My World and Welcome to It'. Book, 'How to Make a Jewish Movie' (1971) about making of *Cast a Giant Shadow* (1966).

Films as director and writer: 1955: The Seven Little Foys (*co-s*). 1957: Beau James (*co-s*). 1958: Houseboat (*co-s*). 1959: The Five Pennies (*co-s*). 1960: It Started in Naples (*co-s*). 1961: On the Double (*co-s*). 1962: The Pigeon that Took Rome (*+p*). 1963: A New Kind of Love (*+p*). 1966: Cast a Giant Shadow (*+ co-p*). 1968: Yours, Mine and Ours (*co-s*).

SHAW, Irwin

Writer. New York 1913–
Parents Russian immigrants. To 1934: Brooklyn College. Worked in radio. Drama critic for New Republic. 1936: wrote first play; first film as writer *The Big Game*. 1940: first book 'Bury the Dead'. Instructor in creative writing, New York University. 1941: play 'Gentle People' filmed as *Out of the Fog*. 1942–45: Private and Warrant Officer in US Signal Corps in Europe and Mediterranean. 1943–48: no film work.

1950: in collaboration with Robert Capa wrote 'Report on Israel'. Mentioned before House Committee on Un-American Activities for novel 'The Troubled Air'. 1957: novel 'The Young Lions' filmed. 1958: in collaboration with René Clément wrote *La Diga sul Pacifico*. 1962: his novel 'Two Weeks in Another Town' filmed. 1963: wrote and co-produced *In the French Style*. 1968: wrote and produced in collaboration with Jules Dassin *Survival*, documentary on Israeli-Egyptian War of 1967.

Films as writer include: 1942: The Talk of the Town (*co*); The Hard Way (*co*); Commandos Strike at Dawn. 1949: Easy Living (*st*). 1951: I Want You. 1953: Act of Love. 1955: Ulysses (*co*). 1957: Fire Down Below. 1958: Desire Under the Elms; Le Diga sul Pacifico (*co*). 1961: The Big Gamble. 1963: In the French Style (+ *co-p/st*). 1968: Survival (+ *co-p/st*).

SHEARER, Norma

Actress. Montreal 1904–
Extra for Universal then taken to MGM by Irving Thalberg. 1927: she married him. 1930: Oscar for *The Divorcee*. 1942: last film *Her Cardboard Lover*; retired.

Films as actress include: 1920: The Flapper; Way Down East. 1923: The Wanters. 1924: He Who Gets Slapped. 1925: Waking Up the Town; The Tower of Lies. 1926: The Devil's Circus; The Waning Sex. 1927: The Demi-Bride. 1928: The Student Prince in Old Heidelberg; The Actress. 1929: The Last of Mrs Cheyney. 1930: Let Us Be Gay. 1931: A Free Soul; Private Lives. 1932: Strange Interlude; Smilin' Through. 1934: The Barretts of Wimpole Street; Riptide. 1936: Romeo and Juliet. 1938: Marie Antoinette. 1939: Idiot's Delight; The Women. 1940: Escape. 1942: We Were Dancing.

SHERIDAN, Ann

(Clara Lou Sheridan) Actress. Denton, Texas 1915–
Beauty contests. 1933: first film *Search for Beauty*. Early credits under own name. To 1935: films mainly for Paramount. From 1935: known as Ann Sheridan. 1936–48: mainly for Warners. 1950–53: for Universal. Married actor George Brent (1932–43, divorced).

Films as actress include: 1934: Bolero; Come On, Marines!; Murder at the Vanities; Mrs Wiggs of the Cabbage Patch. 1935: Behold My Wife; The Glass Key; The Crusades. 1936: Sing Me a Love Song; Black Legion; The Great O'Malley. 1937: San Quentin. 1938: Angels with Dirty Faces; She Loved a Fireman; Cowboy From Brooklyn; Little Miss Thoroughbred; Letter of Introduction; Broadway Musketeers. 1939: Dodge City; They Made Me a Criminal; Naughty But Nice; Indianapolis Speedway; Angels Wash Their Faces. 1940: Torrid Zone; They Drive By Night; Castle on the Hudson; City for Conquest. 1941: Navy Blues. 1942: The Man Who Came to Dinner; Juke Girl; Wings for the Eagle; George Washington Slept Here. 1943: Edge of Darkness; Thank Your Lucky Stars. 1944: Shine on Harvest Moon. 1947: Nora Prentiss; The Unfaithful. 1948: Silver River; Good Sam. 1949: I Was a Male War Bride. 1952: Just Across the Street. 1953: Take Me to Town; Appointment in Honduras. 1955: Come Next Spring. 1956: The Opposite Sex.

SHERMAN, Lowell

Director and actor. San Francisco 1885–1934 Hollywood
1916–23: actor in New York. 1920: first film as actor, *Way Down East*. Then actor with various companies including Famous Players-Lasky, MGM, Warners. 1930: began as director, also actor, with RKO. From 1932: with various companies. From 1933: worked only as director. Formed production company to make last film released through Universal after his death.

Films as actor include: 1926: You Never Know Women. 1928: The Divine Woman; The Garden of Eden. 1929: A Lady of Chance; General Crack. 1930: Mammy; Ladies of Leisure. 1932: What Price Hollywood?

Films as director: 1930: Lawful Larceny (+ *w*); The Pay Off (+ *w*); The Royal Bed (+ *w*). 1931: Bachelor Apartment (+ *w*); High Stakes (+ *w*). 1932: The Greeks Had a Word for Them (+ *w*); False Faces (+ *p/w*); Ladies of the Jury. 1933: She Done Him Wrong; Morning Glory; Broadway Thru a Keyhole. 1934: Born to be Bad. 1935: Night Life of the Gods.

SHERMAN, Vincent

Director. Vienna, Georgia 1906–
Oglethorpe University, Atlanta. Stage actor. 1933: first film as actor *Counsellor at Law*. 1938–39: dialogue director or scriptwriter on a number of films for Warners. 1939: first film as director. Worked mainly for Warners. 1957: completed *The Garment Center* when Robert Aldrich abandoned it after argument with producers.

Films as director: 1939: The Return of Doctor X. 1940: Saturday's Children; The Man Who Talked Too Much. 1941: Underground; Flight from Destiny; All Through the Night. 1942: The Hard Way. 1943: Old Acquaintance. 1944: In Our Time. 1945: Mr Skeffington; Pillow to Post. 1947: Nora Prentiss; The Unfaithful. 1949: The Adventures of Don Juan; The Hasty Heart. 1950: Harriet Craig; Backfire; The Damned Don't Cry. 1951: The Lone Star; Goodbye My Fancy. 1952: Affair in Trinidad. 1957: The Garment Center – The Garment Jungle (*co-d Robert Aldrich*). 1958: The Naked Earth. 1959: The Young Philadelphians. 1960: Ice Palace; A Fever in the Blood. 1961: The Second Time Around. 1967: Le Avventuri e gli amori di Miguel Cervantes – Cervantes – The Young Rebel.

SHINDO, Kaneto

Director. Hiroshima 1912–
Father a farmer. 1934: began working in film laboratories. Scriptwriter from 1937. 1941: joined Shochiku as writer; collaborated with Kozaburo Yoshimura on several films, with Kenji Mizoguchi on *Waga koi wa Moenu* (1948), with Kon Ichikawa on *Akatsuki no Tsuiseki* (1950). 1950: with Yoshimura formed production company Kindai. 1951: first film as director. Has written some 200 scripts including some of Yoshimura's and own films.

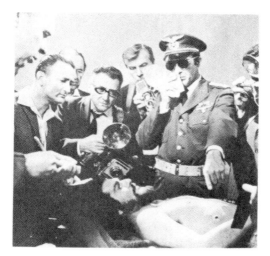

Jayne Mansfield in Frank Tashlin's The Girl Can't Help It, *photographed by Leon Shamroy.*
Omar Shariff as Che! (*foreground*), *directed by Richard Fleischer.*
Kuroneko, directed by Kaneto Shindo.

Films as director and writer: 1951: Aisai monogatari – The Story of a Beloved Wife. 1952: Nadare – Avalanche; Onna no Issho – A Woman's Life; Gembaku no Ko – Children of Hiroshima. 1953: Shukuzu – Epitome – Geisha Girl Ginko. 1954: Dobu – Gutter. 1955: Ookami – Wolves. 1956: Shirogane Shinju; Ryuri no Kishi. 1957: Umi no Yarodomo – Harbour Rats. 1958: Kanashimi wa Onna Dakeni – Only Woman Have Trouble; Daigo Fukuryu Maru – Lucky Dragon No 5. 1959: Hanayome san wa Seka Ichi – The Bride from Japan. 1960: Hadaka no Shima – The Island (+ co-p). 1962: Ningen – The Man. 1964: Haha – Mother. 1965: Onibaba – The Hole – The Demon. 1966: Akuto – The Conquest; Honno – Lost Sex – Instinct – Impotence. 1967: Sei no Kigen – The Origin of Sex-Libido. 1968: Yabu no Naka no Kuroneko – Kuroneko – Black Cat; Tsuyomushi Onna to Yowamushi Otoko – Strong Woman, Weak Man – Operation Négligé. 1969: Shokkaku – Odd Affinity; Kagero – Heat Wave Island.

SHOSTAKOVICH, Dmitri

Composer. St Petersburg, Russia 1906–
1924–25: played piano accompaniment for silent films. 1929: wrote score to accompany Grigori Kozintsev and Leonid Trauberg's silent *Novyi Vavilon*, rarely used in Russia, never abroad. 1931: wrote score for Kozintsev and Trauberg's *Odna* when soundtrack added; also Sergei Yutkevich's first sound film *Zlatye Gori*. 1935–39: wrote music for Kozintsev and Trauberg's 'Maxim' trilogy. 1935–47: worked mainly for Lenfilm. From 1947: worked mainly for Mosfilm. His theme from Yutkevich's *Vstrechnyi* adopted as United Nations hymn. From 1949: scored several films directed by Kozintsev alone.

Films as composer include: 1929: Novyi Vavilon. 1931: Odna; Zlatye Gory. 1932: Vstrechnyi. 1935: Yunost Maksima; Podrugi. 1937: Vozvrashchenie Maksima. 1938: Volochayevskie Dni; Velikii Grazhdanin (*Part I*); Chelovek s ruzhyom. 1939: Vyborgskaya Storona. 1944: Zoya. 1945: Prostye Lyudi (*r* 1956). 1947: Pirogov. 1948: Michurin; Molodaya Gvardiya. 1949: Vstrecha na Elbe; Padenie Berlina. 1956: Pervyi Eshelon. 1963: I sequestrati di Altona. 1964: Gamlet. 1971: Korol Lir.

SHUB, Esther

Director. Ukraine, Russia 1894–1959 Moscow
More than 5 years as editor: worked on 200 foreign fiction films and 10 Russian. 1927: for anniversary of February Revolution wrote and edited compilation film *Padenie dinasti Romanovikh* covering 1912–17, using footage from Tsar's own private films of his family; for anniversary of October Revolution wrote and edited *Velikii Put* compilation film covering 1917–27; both for Sovkino, involving much research and discovery of material, which was consulted by Sergei Eisenstein before making *Oktyabre* (1927). 1928: *Rossiya Nikolaya II i Lev Tolstoy* covered 1897–1912, including rare footage of Leo Tolstoy. 1939: edited Spanish war footage shot by Roman Karmen as *Ispaniya*. 1940: in collaboration with Vsevolod Pudovkin made *Kino za dvadtsat Let*, a compilation. Immediately after World War II worked in newsreel. Book of memoirs 'Kroupnym Planom'.

Films as director: 1927: Padenie dinasti Romanovikh

– Fall of the Romanov Dynasty (+s/e); Velikii Put – The Great Road (+s/e). 1928: Rossiya Nikolaya II i Lev Tolstoy – The Russia of Nicholas II and Leo Tolstoy (+s/e). 1930: Seyodnya – Today (+co-s/e). 1932: KSE – Komsomol—Patron of Electrification (+s/e). 1934: Moskva stroyit metro – Moscow Builds the Metro (+s/e). 1939: Ispaniya – Spain (+e). 1940: Kino za dvadtsat let – Twenty Years of Soviet Cinema (+co-e; co-d Vsevolod Pudovkin). 1947: Potu storonu Araksa – On the Banks of the Arax (+s).

SHUMLIN, Herman

Director. Atwood, Colorado 1896–
1924–25: reporter for theatrical weekly New York Clipper. Director in New York theatre from 1927. From 1931: assistant to Samuel Goldwyn. 1942–43: directed documentaries for Office of War Information. Directed 2 features for Warners.

Features as director: 1943: Watch on the Rhine. 1945: Confidential Agent.

SIDNEY, George

Director. New York 1911–
Parents both actors; father, L. K. Sidney also MGM executive. 1923: played small part in Tom Mix film shot at Denver. Musician in vaudeville bands. 1932: 2nd-unit director at MGM. Then directed shorts including some of the 'Our Gang' series e.g. *Clown Princes* (1939). 1941: first feature as director. With MGM until 1955. 1951–58: president of the Hanna and Barbera TV cartoon company. 1956–63: with Columbia. Then various companies including Paramount. Married to Lillian Burns, former drama coach and adviser to MGM stars, who became executive assistant to Harry Cohn at Columbia. 2 of his shorts received Oscars for 1-reelers, *Quicker 'n a Wink* (1940), *Of Pups and Puzzles* (1941).

Features as director: 1941: Free and Easy. 1942: Pacific Rendezvous. 1943: Pilot No 5; Thousands Cheer. 1944: Bathing Beauty. 1945: Anchors Aweigh; The Harvey Girls. 1946: Holiday in Mexico. 1947: Cass Timberlane. 1948: The Three Musketeers. 1949: The Red Danube (+st). 1950: Key to the City; Annie Get Your Gun. 1951: Show Boat. 1952: Scaramouche. 1953: Young Bess; Kiss Me, Kate. 1955: Jupiter's Darling. 1956: The Eddy Duchin Story. 1957: Jeanne Eagles (+p); Pal Joey. 1960: Who Was That Lady?; Pepe. 1963: Bye Bye Birdie; A Ticklish Affair. 1964: Viva Las Vegas – Love in Las Vegas (+co-p). 1966: The Swinger (+p). 1967: Half a Sixpence (+co-p).

SIDNEY, Sylvia

(Sophia Kosow) Actress. New York 1910–
1926: Theatre Guild School. Studied with Rouben Mamoulian, Alfred Lunt, Lynn Fontane and the Langners. 1926: stage début in 'The Challenge of Youth' and New York début in 'Prunella'. 1929: first film as actress *Thru Different Eyes*. 1932–36: films for Paramount. Then for several companies. 1943: toured in title role of 'Jane Eyre'. 1950: toured in 'The Innocents'. 1958–59: New York and on tour in 'Auntie Mame'. 3 husbands include actor Luther Adler (1938–47, divorced).

Films as actress include: 1931: City Streets; An American Tragedy; Street Scene. 1932: The Miracle Man; Merrily We Go to Hell. 1935: Behold My Wife; Accent on Youth. 1936: The Trail of the Lonesome Pine; Fury; Sabotage. 1937: You Only Live Once; Dead End. 1938: You and Me. 1941: The Wagons Roll at Night. 1945: Blood on the Sun. 1946: The Searching Wind; Mr Ace. 1952: Les Miserables. 1955: Violent Saturday.

SIEGEL, Donald

Director. Chicago 1912–
Jesus College, Cambridge, and RADA. Acted with the Contemporary Group in Hollywood before joining Warners (1935) as assistant film librarian. Became assistant editor then chief of Warners editing department. Did montage sequences for e.g. Michael Curtiz, Raoul Walsh, William Dieterle. 1945: directed shorts. 1946: first feature as director. Has worked in television as director, producer, and producer-director e.g. on series 'Johnny North'; produced 34 episodes of series 'The Legend of Jesse James'; *The Killers* and *The Hanged Man* both made (1964) for showing in parts on TV; former rejected for TV because of excessive violence; also made *Stranger on the Run* (1967) for TV. His short *Star in the Night* (1945) received Oscar.

Films as director: 1945: Star in the Night; Hitler Lives? 1946: The Verdict. 1947: Night unto Night. 1949: The Big Steal. 1952: Duel at Silver Creek; No Time for Flowers. 1953: Count the Hours – Every Minute Counts; China Venture. 1954: Riot in Cell Block 11; Private Hell 36. 1955: Annapolis Story – The Blue and the Gold. 1956: Invasion of the Body Snatchers; Crime in the Streets. 1957: Baby Face Nelson; Spanish Affair. 1958: The Lineup; The Gun Runners. 1959: Hound Dog Man; Edge of Eternity (+as-p). 1960: Flaming Star. 1962: Hell is for Heroes. 1964: The Killers; The Hanged Man. 1968: Madigan; Coogan's Bluff. 1970: Two Mules for Sister Sara. 1971: The Beguiled (+p); Dirty Harry (+p).

SIEGEL, Sol C.

Producer. New York 1903–
After university was reporter for New York Herald Tribune (1934), then executive producer on Gene Autry films at Republic. 1940: executive producer at Paramount. 1944: became independent producer. 1945: returned as producer to Paramount, then (1946) to Fox. 1955: independent producer releasing through MGM. 1958: vice-president in charge of production at MGM. 1962: independent producer again through MGM.

Films as producer include: 1946: Blue Skies. 1949: House of Strangers; Prince of Foxes; I Was A Male War Bride; A Letter to Three Wives. 1950: Panic in the Streets. 1951: I Can Get It For You Wholesale; Fourteen Hours. 1952: Deadline USA; Monkey Business; What Price Glory. 1953: Call Me Madam; Gentlemen Prefer Blondes. 1954: Broken Lance; Three Coins in the Fountain; There's No Business Like Show Business. 1956: High Society. 1957: Les Girls. 1958: Merry Andrew; Some Came Running. 1960: Home From the Hill. 1966: Walk Don't Run. 1968: No Way to Treat a Lady.

SIGNORET, Simone

(Simone-Henriette-Charlotte Kaminker) Actress. Wiesbaden, Germany 1921–

At first, extra. 1945: first major role in *Les Démons de l'aube*. 1947: married Yves Allégret who directed several of her early films. Also married Yves Montand; acted with him in 'Les Sorcières de Salem' on Paris stage. 1959: Oscar as Best Actress for *Room at the Top*.

Films as actress include: 1943: La Bôite aux rêves. 1946: Macadam. 1948: Dédée d'Anvers; Against the Wind. 1950: La Ronde; Le Traqué. 1951: Casque d'or. 1953: Thérèse Raquin. 1955: Les Diaboliques. 1956: Le Mort en ce jardin. 1957: Les Sorcières de Salem. 1960: Les Mauvais Coups; Adua e le campagne. 1962: Term of Trial. 1963: Le Jour et l'heure; Dragées au poivre. 1965: Ship of Fools; Les Compartiments Tueurs. 1966: Paris brûle-t-il?; The Deadly Affair. 1968: The Seagull. 1969: L'Armée des ombres. 1970: L'Aveu.

SILLIPHANT, Sterling

Writer. Detroit, Michigan 1918–

After university, joined publicity staff of Walt Disney (1938–41). 1941–42: on staff of publicity company working for Fox. 1942–43: assistant to Spyros Skouras, then in US Navy. 1946: with Fox. 1949: in charge of special events and promotions at Fox, then (1951) Eastern publicity manager. 1955: co-producer of *Five Against the House* for Columbia. 1958: his novel 'Maracaibo' filmed. Writer and producer for TV. Oscar for screenplay based on another medium, *In the Heat of the Night* (1967).

Films as writer include: 1955: Five Against the House (*co-s: +co-p*). 1956: Nightfall. 1958: The Lineup. 1965: The Slender Thread. 1967: In the Heat of the Night. 1968: Charly. 1970: A Walk in the Spring Rain (*+p*); The Liberation of L. B. Jones (*co*). 1971: Murphy's War.

SILVERSTEIN, Elliot

Director. Boston, Massachusetts 1927–

Drama at Yale University. Taught at Theatre Arts department of Brandeis University, where he staged Leonard Bernstein's one-act opera, 'Trouble in Tahiti'. Then worked for US TV arts programme 'Omnibus'; wrote TV adaptation of 'Antigone'. 1961: directed 'Portrait of a Man Running' for TV. 1962: first film as director.

Films as director: 1962: Belle Sommers. 1965: Cat Ballou. 1967: It's What's Happening – The Happening. 1970: A Man Called Horse.

SIMMONS, Anthony

Director

University of London, studies interrupted by World War II, then resumed. Barrister for 1 year. Worked on documentaries in Italy. 1950: wrote documentary scripts, made 16 mm films. 1953–54: films photographed by Walter Lassally. 1954: co-produced and co-wrote *The Passing Stranger*. 1957: co-produced Joseph Losey's *Time Without Pity*. 1959: first feature as director. Also worked in TV.

Films as director: 1953: Sunday by the Sea (*+ s*). 1954: Bow Bells (*+s*). 1956: The Gentle Corsican (*+s*). 1959: Your Money or Your Wife. 1965: 4 in the Morning (*+ s*).

SIMMONS, Jean

Actress. London 1929–

Dancing school. 1944: spotted for first film as actress *Give Us the Moon*. 1946: first major role, in *Great Expectations*. 1948: Laurence Olivier obtained her release from Rank for *Hamlet*. 1950: to USA, under contract to Howard Hughes for RKO. 1951: on stage in 'The Power of Darkness'. 1952: released from RKO. Married Stewart Granger (1950–60, divorced) and Richard Brooks (1960). Directed by Brooks in *Elmer Gantry* (1960) and *The Happy Ending* (1969).

Films as actress include: 1945: Caesar and Cleopatra. 1947: Woman in the Hall; Black Narcissus. 1948: The Blue Lagoon. 1949: Adam and Evelyne. 1950: So Long at the Fair; Cage of Gold; The Clouded Yellow. 1952: Androcles and the Lion; Angel Face. 1953: Young Bess; Affair with a Stranger; The Robe; The Actress. 1954: Desiree; The Egyptian; She Couldn't Say No; A Bullet is Waiting. 1955: Guys and Dolls. 1956: Hilda Crane. 1957: This Could Be the Night; Until They Sail. 1958: The Big Country. 1959: This Earth is Mine. 1960: Spartacus; The Grass is Greener. 1965: Mister Buddwing; Life at the Top. 1967: Divorce American Style.

SIMON, Michel

Actor. Geneva, Switzerland 1895–

From 1911: music-hall performer. 1922–25: on Paris stage. Theatrical work includes 'Hamlet', 'Les Basfonds', 'Siegfried', 'Six Personnages en quête d'auteur', 'Fric-Frac', 'Pygmalion'. From 1922: more than 60 films. On TV recreated stage role in 'Du vent dans les branches de Sassafras'.

Films as actor include: 1925: Feu Mathias Pascal. 1928: La Passion de Jeanne d'Arc; Tire-au-flanc. 1931: L'Enfant d'amour; Jean de la lune; On purge bébé; La Chienne. 1932: Boudu Sauvé des eaux. 1933: Du haut en bas. 1934: L'Atalante; Le Bonheur; Le Lac-aux-dames. 1936: Faisons un rêve; Sous les yeux d'occident. 1937: Naples au baiser de feu; Drôle de drame. 1938: Les Disparus de Saint-Agil; Quai des brumes; La Belle Etoile; Le Ruisseau. 1940: La Comédie du bonheur. 1943: Au bonheur des dames. 1946: Panique. 1947: Non coupable; Les Amants du pont Saint-Jean. 1949: Fabiola. 1950: La Beauté du Diable. 1951: La Poison. 1952: La Vie d'un honnête homme. 1953: Saadia. 1957: Les Trois font la paire. 1960: Austerlitz; Candide. 1962: Le Bâteau d'Emile; Le Diable et les dix commandments. 1963: Cyrano et d'Artagnan. 1965: The Train. 1970: Contestazione Generale. 1971: Blanche.

SIMON, Simone

Actress. Béthune, France 1911–

1930: worked for couturier in Paris. Studied singing. 1931: first films in very small roles. 1936: first film in Hollywood. 1956: last film. Stage work in France, New York and Canada.

Films as actress include: 1931: Mam'zelle Nitouche.

Riot in Cell Block 11, *directed by Don Siegel.*
Simone Signoret in Games, *directed by Curtis Harrington.*
Richard Harris in A Man Called Horse, *directed by Elliot Silverstein.*

1932: La Petite Chocolatière; Le Roi des palaces; Un Fils d'Amérique. 1934: Lac-aux-dames. 1935: Les Beaux Jours. 1937: Seventh Heaven. 1938: Josette; La Bête Humaine. 1941: All That Money Can Buy. 1943: Cat People. 1944: The Curre of the Cat People; Mademoiselle Fifi; Johnny Doesn't Live Here Any More. 1946: Petrus. 1950: La Ronde. 1952: Le Plaisir.

SINATRA, Frank

Actor. Hoboken, New Jersey 1915–
Band singer. 1941: first film *Las Vegas Nights*. To 1949: films mainly for MGM. 1951–62: worked for numerous companies including MGM. From 1963: number of films for Warners. 1965: directed and acted in *None But the Brave*. Cabaret; TV shows; recordings. 1971: announced retirement. Married Ava Gardner (1951–57, divorced) and actress Mia Farrow (1966–68, divorced). Oscar as supporting actor for *From Here to Eternity* (1953).

Films as actor include: 1945: Anchors Aweigh. 1948: The Kissing Bandit; The Miracle of the Bells. 1949: Take Me Out to the Ball Game: On the Town. 1951: Meet Danny Wilson. 1955: Young at Heart; Not as a Stranger; Guys and Dolls; The Man with the Golden Arm; The Tender Trap. 1956: Around the World in 80 Days; High Society. 1957: Pal Joey; The Pride and the Passion. 1958: Some Came Running. 1959: A Hole in the Head; Never So Few. 1960: Can-Can; Ocean's 11. 1961: The Devil at Four O'Clock; Sergeants 3. 1962: The Manchurian Candidate. 1963: Come Blow Your Horn; 4 For Texas; The List of Adrian Messenger. 1964: Robin and the Seven Hoods. 1965: Von Ryan's Express. 1966: Cast a Giant Shadow. 1967: The Naked Runner; Tony Rome. 1968: The Detective; Lady in Cement. 1970: Dirty Dingus Magee.

SINCLAIR, Upton Beall

Producer. Baltimore, Maryland 1878–
Son of a travelling salesman. 1897–1901: Columbia University. 1906: Socialist candidate for US House of Representatives for a New Jersey district; assisted government in Chicago stockyard investigation; attempted to found communistic colony at Englewood, New Jersey; moved to California. 1920: candidate for House of Representatives. 1922: candidate for US Senate. 1926: socialist Governor of California. 1930: second term; signed contract with Sergei Eisenstein to finance his Mexican project. 1932: forced an end to shooting; agreed to send negative to Russia for editing; had it shipped, then had it returned to Hamburg; made agreement with Sol Lesser, who was to edit it. Lesser made feature *Thunder in Mexico* (1933) from the footage and 2 shorts *Eisenstein in Mexico* and *Death Day*; controversy in world press. 1933: privately published book 'Upton Sinclair Presents William Fox'. 1934: received Democratic nomination for governor on 'old-age assistance' platform. Founder of American Civil Liberties Union in California. 1942: awarded Pulitzer Prize for 'Dragon's Teeth'. Books include 'The Goose-Step: a Study of American Education' (1923), 'Oil' (1927), 'World's End' (1940), 'Presidential Mission' (1942), 'My Lifetime in Letters' (1960), 'Autobiography of Upton Sinclair' (1962).

SINGER, Alexander

Director. New York 1932–
Office boy for March of Time. Photographer for magazines and New York Times. World War II: directed, photographed and edited reportage films for Armed Forces Film Unit. Returned to New York became assistant director and cameraman on features, worked in TV. 1956: assistant director on *The Killing*. 1960: worked in several capacities, including technical advisor on Leslie Stevens' *Private Property*. 1961: first feature as director led to Columbia contract.

Features as director: 1961: A Cold Wind in August. 1964: Psyche 59. 1965: Love Has Many Faces. 1971: Captain Apache.

SIODMAK, Robert

Director. Memphis, Tennessee 1900–
Born while parents travelling in America. Father a banker. Childhood in Liepzig and Berlin. 1917–20: University of Marburg. Actor, producer, director in repertory. 1921–23: successful in banking, then ruined by inflation. Started periodical Das Magazine, became salesman. 1925: returned to theatre. Wrote titles for imported American films. 1926: editor, combining shorts for feature release. 1929: first film as director in collaboration with Edgar G. Ulmer *Menschen am Sonntag,* also produced and co-wrote it. Worked for Ufa as scout for writers, editor, script assistant, assistant director, then director. 1933: Goebbels attacked *Brennendes Geheimnis*. To Paris. 1936: supervised *Le Grand Refrain*. 1940: to Hollywood. American films mainly for Universal. 1944: co-wrote story of *Conflict,* From 1952: worked in Europe, mainly West Germany. 1958: TV work on series 'O.S.S.', 'The Killers'.

Films as director: 1929: Menschen am Sonntag – People on Sunday (+*p/co-s*; +*p/co-d Edgar G. Ulmer); Abschied.* 1931: Voruntersuchung. 1932: Stürme der Leidenschaft – Storm of Passion – Tempest; Le Sexe Faible; Quick (*German and French versions*). 1933: Brennendes Geheimnis. 1934: La Crise est finie – Finie la crise – The Slump is Over. 1935: La Vie Parisienne; Mister Flow. 1937: Cargaison Blanches – Le Chemin de Rio – Traffic in Souls – French White Cargo. 1938: Mollenard – Capitaine Mollenard – Hatred; Ultimatum (*uc; co-d Robert Wiene*). 1939: Pièges – Snares – Personal Column. 1941: West Point Widow. 1942: Fly-by-Night; My Heart Belongs to Daddy; The Night Before the Divorce. 1943: Someone to Remember; Son of Dracula. 1944: Phantom Lady; Cobra Woman; Christmas Holiday. 1945: The Suspect; The Strange Affair of Uncle – Uncle Harry – The Zero Murder Case; The Spiral Staircase. 1946: The Killers; The Dark Mirror. 1947: Time out of Mind (+*p*). 1948: Cry of the City; Criss Cross. 1949: The Great Sinner; The File on Thelma Jordan – Thelma Jordan. 1950: Deported. 1951: The Whistle at Eaton Falls. 1952: The Crimson Pirate. 1953: Le Grand Jeu – Flesh and Woman. 1955: Die Ratten – The Rats. 1956: Mein Vater, der Schauspieler (+*p*). 1957: Nachts, wenn der Teufel kam – The Devil Strikes at Night (+*p*). 1959: Dorothea Angermann (+*p*); The Rough and the Smooth – Portrait of a Sinner; – Katja – The Magnificent Sinner; Bitter Sweet. 1960: Der Schulfreund – Mein Schulfreund (+*p*). 1961: L'Affaire Nina B – The

Nina B Affair (+*co-s*). 1962: Escape from East Berlin – Tunnel 28. 1964: Der Schut; Der Schatz der Azteken. 1965: Die Pyramide des Sonnengottes. 1968: Custer of the West. 1969: Der Kampf um Rom.

SIRK, Douglas *or* SIERCK, Dietlef

(Detclev Sierck) Director. Skagen, Jutland, Denmark 1900–
Universities of Hamburg, Copenhagen and Munich. Started working as producer and writer for Ufa, also acting, and writing articles for German magazines. 1935: first film as director for Ufa, where he remained as director, writer and actor until late 1930s. 1936: *La Chanson du souvenir* was a French version, made simultaneously, of *Das Hofkonzert*. Made films in various countries before going to Hollywood where he worked from 1943 to 1959; from *Thunder on the Hill* (1951) entirely for Universal, from 1953 mainly for Ross Hunter. After serious illness retired from films and returned to Germany. Has since directed in theatre in Germany and Switzerland. All his definitely established films as director i.e. those made in Germany and USA, are listed below.

Films as director include: 1935: April April; Das Madchen vom Moorhof; Stutzen der Gesellschaft. 1936: Das Hofkonzert (+ *co-s*); La Chanson du souvenir; Schlussakkord (+ *co-s*). 1937: La Habanera; Zu neuen Ufern – To New Shores (+ *co-s*). 1943: Hitler's Madman – Hitler's Hangman. 1944: Summer Storm (+ *co-s*). 1946: A Scandal in Paris. 1947: Lured. 1948: Sleep, My Love; Siren of Atlantis – Atlantis the Lost Continent (uc; *co-d 3 others*). 1949: Shockproof; Slightly French. 1950: Mystery Submarine. 1951: The First Legion (+ *co-p*); Thunder on the Hill; The Lady Pays Off; Weekend With Father. 1952: No Room for the Groom; Has Anybody Seen My Gal?; Meet Me At the Fair. 1953: Take Me To Town; All I Desire. 1954: Taza, Son of Cochise; Magnificent Obsession; Sign of the Pagan. 1955: Captain Lightfoot; All that Heaven Allows. 1956: There's Always Tomorrow; Never Say Goodbye (uc; *co-d Jerry Hopper*); Written on the Wind. 1957: Battle Hymn; Interlude; The Tarnished Angels – Pylon. 1958: A Time to Love and a Time to Die. 1959: Imitation of Life.

SÖBERG, Alf

Director. Stockholm 1903–
Studied at Royal Dramatic Theatre drama school, Stockholm. From 1925: actor at Royal Dramatic Theatre. 1929: first film as director; also directed for Swedish radio. From 1931: director at Royal Dramatic Theatre. Has since worked in films and theatre including productions of plays by Arthur Miller, Eugene O'Neill, Sartre, Strindberg.

Films as director: 1929: Den Starkaste – The Strongest (+ *st*). 1939: Med livet som insats – They Staked Their Lives (+ *co-s*); Den Blomstertid . . . – Flowering Time (+ *s*). 1941: Hem från Babylon – Home from Babylon (+ *co-s*). 1942: Himlaspelet – The Road to Heaven (+ *co-s*). 1944: Kungajakt – Royal Hunt (+ *st*); Hets – Frenzy – Torment. 1945: Resan bort – Journey Out (+ *s*). 1946: Iris och löjtnantshjärta – Iris and the Lieutenant (+ *s*). 1949: Bara en mor – Only a Mother (+ *co-s*). 1951: Fröken Julie – Miss Julie (+ *s*). 1952: Barabbas (+ *co-s*). 1953: Karin Månsdotter (+ *s*).

1954: Vildfåglar – Wild Birds (+ co-s). 1955: Sista Paret ut – Last Pair Out. 1960: Domaren – Jdge (+ co-s). 1964: Ön – The Island (r 1966; +co-s). 1969: Fadern – The Father (+ s).

SJOMAN, Vilgot

Director. Stockholm 1924–

Acted in school productions including 'A Midsummer Night's Dream' directed by Ingmar Bergman. Wrote first play at 17. Theatre critic in Vi. 1948: first novel 'Lektorn'. 1948–61: literary critic for Dagens Nyheter. 1949: 'Lektorn' filmed. 1952: scripted *Trots*. 1962: essay published 'I Hollywood'; co-wrote *Siska*; first film as director; assistant director on *Nattvardsgästerna* and published diary account of its making. 1968: acted in *Skammen*. Stage director at Royal Dramatic Theatre, Stockholm. Also TV director. Other writings include poetry.

Films as director and writer: 1962: Alskarinnan – The Mistress. 1964: 491 (*d only*); Klanningen – The Dress (*d only*). 1966: Syskonbädd 1782 – My Sister, My Love; Stimulantia *ep* Negressen iskäper (r 1967). 1967: Jag är nyfiken-gul – I am Curious-Yellow. 1968: Jag är nyfiken-blå – I am Curious-Blue. 1970: Ni ljuger – You're Lying; Lyckliga Skitar – Blushing Charlie (*co-s*).

SJÖSTRÖM, Victor David

Director and actor. Årjäng, Sweden 1879–1960 Stockholm

Mother an actress. Father emigrated to USA, later sent for family to join him. Brought up in New York, then sent by his father to school in Uppsala, Sweden. To Finland as actor; début in 1896. Acted in Russia and Sweden. 1898: stage manager of Swedish theatre in Helsinki. Much work in Swedish provinces. 1911: founded own company in collaboration. 1912: invited by Charles Magnusson to join Svenska Biografteatern; visited Vincennes studio in Paris to observe production; acted with Mauritz Stiller in *I Livets var*; first film as director, scripted and supervised by Stiller and banned; acted in Stiller's *De svarta Maskerna*. 1912–13: work in theatre. 1914: military service, though not continuously. Acted in numerous films directed by Stiller; frequently acted in own films to 1923. 1924: to USA, under contract to Samuel Goldwyn; first American film *He Who Gets Slapped*. Worked in America under name Victor Seastrom; produced most of his American films. Brought Hjalmar Bergman to USA: they collaborated on a script after Ibsen, turned down. 1930: returned to Sweden, directed one more film there. 1937: last film as director, in UK for Alexander Korda. Theatrical work continued. 1943–49: director of production at Svensk Filmindustri; responsible for e.g. Ingmar Bergman's début as director and making of *Hets* (1944). In theatre acted in 'Death of a Salesman'; continued to act in films. 1955: last film as actor *Smultronstället*. Married Lili Bech, who acted in his first film as director.

Films as director: 1912: Trädgårdsmästaren – Falskt Alarm – Varldens Grymhet – The Gardener (+ w); Ett Hemligt Giftermäl – Bekännelsen pä Dödsbädden – En Moder – A Secret Marriage; En Sommarsaga – A Summer Tale (ur); Lady Marions Sommarflirt – Lady Margon – Lady Marion's Summer Flirtation (+ w); Lojen och Tarar – Dragers Juveler – Smiles and Tears; Aktenskapsbyran – Pä detta numera vanliga satt – Har ni nagot att fortulla – The Marriage Bureau (+ s). 1913: Blodets Rost – The Voice of Blood (+ w); Ingeborg Holm (+ s); Halrblod-Halfbreed; Lirets Konflikter – Life's Conflicts (+ w); Prästen – The Clergyman; Kärlek starkare än Hat – Skogsdotterns Hemlighet – Tjuvskytten – Love Stronger than Hate; Miraklet – Underverket – The Miracle; Strejken – Arbetaren – The Strike (+ co-s/w). 1914: Dömen icke – Do Not Judge; Bra Flicka reder sig själv – A Good Girl Should Solve Her Own Problems (+ s); Sonad Skuld – Expiated Guilt (+ co-s); Det var i maj – It was in May (+ s); Hogfjällets Dotter – Lappflickan – Daughter of the High Mountain (+ s/w); Hjärtan som mötas – Chauf_foren – Hearts that Meet; Gatans Barn – Children of the Street. 1915: En av de mänga – One out of Many (+ s); Landshövdingens Döttrar – Tvillingsystrarna – The Governor's Daughters (+ s); Skomakare bliv vid bin läst – Keep to Your Trade (+ s); Judaspengar – Judaspengene – Judas Money; Skepp som mötas – Ships that Meet; I Prövningens Stund – At the Moment of Trial (+ s/w); Havsgamarna – Smugglarens Dotter – Sea Vultures; Hon segrade – Dödens besegrare – She was Victorious (+ s/w). 1916: Thérèse (+ co-s); Dödskyssen – The Kiss of Death (+ co-s/w); Terje vigen – A Man there Was (+ w). 1917: Berg-Ejvind och hans hustru – The Outlaw and his Wife (+ co-s/w); Tosen fran Stormyrtorpet – A Girl from the Marsh Croft (+ co-s). 1918: Ingmarssönerna – The Sons of Ingmar (*in 2 parts* + s/w). 1919: Klostret i Sendormir – The Monastery of Sendormir (+ s); Karin Ingmarsdotter – Karin, Daughter of Ingmar (+ co-s/w); Hans nads Testamente – His Grace's Will (+ co-s). 1920: Körkarlen – The Phantom Carriage – The Soul Shall Bear Witness (+ s/w); Mästerman – En Farlig Pant – The Executioner (+ w). 1921: Vem Dömer? – Love's Crucible (+ co-s). 1922: Det Omringade Huset – The Surrounded House (+ co-s/w). 1923: Eld Ombord – Fire on Board – The Hell Ship (+ w). 1924: He Who Gets Slapped (+ co-s); Name the Man. 1925: Confessions of a Queen; The Tower of Lies. 1926: The Scarlet Letter. 1928: The Wind; The Divine Woman; Masks of the Devil. 1930: A Lady to Love; Markurells i Wadköping – Väter und söhne – Father and Son (+ w). 1937: Under the Red Robe.

Films as actor include: 1912: De Svarta Maskerna; Vampyren; När kärleken dödar; Barnet. 1917: Thomas Graals Bästa Film. 1922: Thomas Graals Myndling. 1941: Striden går vidare. 1943: Det brinner en eld; Ordet. 1945: Kejsarn av Portugallien. 1947: Rallare. 1948: Farlig vår. 1950: Till glädje; Kvartetten som sprängdes. 1952: Hård Klang; Kärlek. 1955: Männen i mörker. 1957: Smultronstället.

SKLADÄNOVSKY, Max

Inventor. Berlin 1863–1939 Berlin

Father magic lantern lecturer Carl Skladänovsky. Apprenticed in photography, glass painting, theatre lighting equipment. 1879: made slides and dissolving view machine with 2 magic lanterns for his father's use at lectures; toured Germany and abroad with his father and brother Emil. 1889–92: constructed and toured with Mechanical Theatre, later Hamilton Theatre when Max and Emil took name Hamilton Brothers. 1890–97: designed and built camera, projector and other equipment e.g. for splitting, perforating, printing and processing film. 1892: shot 6-second film of brother walking across rooftop; made first 'flip-book'

Menschen am Sonntag, *co-directed by Robert Siodmak.* The Tarnished Angels, *directed by Douglas Sirk* Jeane-Pierre Léaud *in* Le Départ, *directed by Jerzy Skolimowski.*

from this. 1895: completed his first Bioskop projector; gave public showing of films at Wintergarten Theatre, Berlin. 1896–97: with improved camera and Bioskop made several films with which he toured Europe. Films consisted of actual or imagined scenes including a variety show, the Tivoli, Berlin streets, Napoleon on St Helena, the Maid of Orleans and brief comedy situations e.g. chasing a fly. From 1897: formed company PFA ('Projection For everyone') which manufactured and sold 'flip-books' and motion picture apparatus at Berliner Camera Works. 1935–38: gave honorary performances in Germany and Japan. Son Erich Skladánovsky is film historian.

SKOLIMOWSKI, Jerzy

Director. Warsaw, 1938–
1959: graduated from Warsaw University; collections of poetry, short stories published. Collaborated on script of *Niewinni czarodzieje* (1960) and wrote dialogue for e.g. *Noz w wodzie* (1962). 1960: State film school, Lodz; as student made medium length film *Boxing,* in which he acted. 1964: *Rysopis* constructed from his film school exercises. Since 1967: worked in Belgium, Czechoslovakia and UK. 1970: returned to Poland to re-edit *Rece do gory* suppressed in 1967.

Features as director: 1964: Rysopis – Identification Marks; None (+*p/s/a/e/w*). 1965: Walkover (+*s/e/w*). 1966: Bariera – Barrier (+ *s*). 1967: Le Départ (+ *co-s*); Rece do gory – Hands Up! (+ *s/a/w*). 1968: Dialog (*ep*; +*s*). 1970: The Adventures of Gerard (+ *co-s*); Deep End (+ *co-s*).

SKOUEN, Arne

Director. Oslo, Norway 1913–
1933: graduated, Oslo University, Seaman in Norwegian merchant fleet. 1935–36: sports editor for Oslo newspaper Dagbladet. 1936: journalism at Columbia. 1937: first novel published in Oslo. 1939: first play produced in Oslo. 1940–43: in press section of Norwegian Resistance. 1943: left Norway. Became Press Attaché, Norwegian diplomatic service in Stockholm, London, New York. 1946: Student Theatre Workshop, New York. Studied in Hollywood. 1947–57: literary critic for Oslo Verdens Gang. 1949: first film as director in collaboration, from own script based on own novel.

Films as director: 1949: Gategutter – Guttersnipes – Gods of the Street (+*s/fn*; co-d *Ulf Greber*). 1952: Nödlanding – Bad Luck. 1954: Sirkus Fandango – Circus Fandango; Det Brenner i natt! 1955: Barn av solen. 1957: Ni Liv – Nine Lives – We Die Alone. 1959: Herren oz hans tjenere – The Master and his Servants – A God and his Servants. 1960: Omringaal – Surrounded. 1969: An-Magritt.

SKOURAS, Spyros P.

Studio head. Skourohorion, Greece 1893–1971 New York
Son of a poor farmer. Educated at a theological seminary in Greece. 1910: to USA; commercial college in St Louis. Work as page-boy in St Louis hotel. 1914: with his brothers Charles and George, bought Olympia Theatre, St Louis. By 1926 owned 37 theatres. Sold own theatres to Warners-First National and (1929) became general manager of theatre circuit. 1931: president of Paramount's theatre subsidiary.

Appointed head of Fox Metropolitan Theatres; with brothers ran Wesco Corporation, which became National Theatres in 1942: resigned and became president of Fox. World War II: organised Greek War Relief Association. Bought patents to Cinemascope technique for Fox which made first Cinemascope film, *The Robe* (1953). 1962: chairman of board at Fox. Resigned under pressure from shareholders during financial crisis precipitated by making of *Cleopatra* (1963). His son, Plato Skouras, was producer at Fox.

SLOCOMBE, Douglas

Cinematographer. London 1913–
Educated in France. Began as newspaper photographer, contributed to Paris Match, Life. World War II: filmed invasion of Poland and Holland; material shot during war appeared in a number of films including *The Big Blockade* (1941) and *San Demetrio, London* (1943). After the war joined Ealing Studios as cinematographer at invitation of Alberto Cavalcanti; Ealing contract for 17 years.

Films as cinematographer include: 1945: Dead of Night. 1947: Hue and Cry. 1948: It Always Rains on Sunday; Saraband for Dead Lovers. 1949: Kind Hearts and Coronets. 1951: The Lavender Hill Mob; The Man in the White Suit. 1952: Mandy. 1954: Ludwig II. 1961: Taste of Fear. 1962: The L-Shaped Room; Freud, The Secret Passion. 1963: The Servant. 1964: Guns at Batasi. 1965: High Wind in Jamaica. 1966: The Blue Max. 1967: Dance of the Vampires. 1968: Boom; The Lion in Winter. 1971: The Music Lovers; Murphy's War.

SMIGHT, Jack

Director. Minneapolis, Minnesota 1926–
Catholic military school. Went into Army Air Corps at 17. World War II: served as First Lieutenant Navigator in South Pacific. Then theatre arts and psychology at University of Minnesota. Disc jockey in Minneapolis. Acted then directed at Plantation Playhouse, Minneapolis; also directed on Broadway. Much work as TV director including 250 daily segments for 'One Man's Family', episodes in 'US Steel Hour', 'Suspicion', 'Naked City', 'Alfred Hitchcock Presents', 'East Side West Side', 'Victor Borge Show', 'Dr Kildare'. 1964: first film as director.

Films as director: 1964: I'd Rather Be Rich. 1965: The Third Day (+*p*). 1966: Harper – The Moving Target; Kaleidoscope – The Bank Breaker (*re-issue*). 1968: No Way to Treat a Lady; The Secret War of Harry Frigg. 1969: Strategy of Terror; The Illustrated Man. 1970: The Traveling Executioner (+*p*); Rabbit, Run.

SMITH, Alexis

(Gladys Smith) Actress. Penticton, British Columbia 1921–
Ballet training as a child. Studied acting at Los Angeles City College. Discovered while a student. 1940: first film *The Lady with Red Hair*. To 1949: all films for Warners, then also e.g. Paramount, Universal. Also stage. Married actor Craig Stevens (1944).

Films as actress include: 1941: Affectionately Yours; Singapore Woman; Dive Bomber. 1942: Gentleman Jim. 1943: Thank Your Lucky Stars; The Constant

Nymph. 1944: Hollywood Canteen; The Adventures of Mark Twain. 1945: Rhapsody in Blue; Conflict; The Horn Blows at Midnight. 1946: San Antonio; Night and Day; One More Tomorrow; Of Human Bondage. 1947: Always Together. 1949: South of St Louis; Any Number Can Play. 1950: Montana; Undercover Girl. 1951: Here Comes the Groom; Cave of Outlaws. 1952: The Turning Point. 1953: Split Second. 1954: The Sleeping Tiger. 1957: Beau James. 1958: This Happy Feeling. 1959: The Young Philadelphians.

SMITH, George Albert

Inventor and director. Brighton, Sussex 1864–1959 Hove, Sussex
Professional portrait photographer in Brighton. Became interested in film as a way of illustrating his lectures on astronomy, hypnotism, psychic phenomena. 1896–98: built movie camera and began making his first films for the Warwick Trading Company run by American entrepreneur Charles Urban (naturalised British citizen from 1906). 1900: signed 2-year exclusive contract with Urban's company for the distribution of his films; built studio at St Ann's Well, Hove. 1901: directed film of Edward VII's coronation for Georges Méliès. 1902: financed by Urban to research into motion picture colour process. 1906: patented Kinemacolor. 1908: demonstrated Kinemacolor at inauguration of Urbanora House, new Wardour Street premises of Charles Urban Trading Company; lectured on subject at demonstration to Royal Society of Arts. 1909: first programmes including films in Kinemacolor at Palace Theatre, Shaftesbury Avenue; Urban set up the Natural Color Kinematograph Company for production and distribution of Kinemacolor films; Smith's interests in the process bought for £5,000, but services retained for further 5 years. 1911: first complete Kinemacolor programmes at the Scala; Urban's 2½ hour film of the Delhi Durbar of 1911 (shown in 1912) an outstanding commercial success. Patents for Kinemacolor sold to France, USA, Italy, Japan, Russia and Finland, Canada, Holland and Belgium, Brazil, Switzerland. Process began to decline at outbreak of World War I, and was defunct by 1916.

Films as director include: 1898: The Corsican Brothers; The Miller and the Sweep; Cinderella and the Fairy Godmother; Faust and Mephistopheles; Photographing a Ghost; Santa Claus; Hanging Out the Clothes or Master, Mistress and Maid; The Mesmerist; Woman Barber; Comic Faces; Waves and Spray; The Baker and the Sweep. 1900: Let Me Dream Again; Grandma's Reading Glass; As Seen Through a Telescope; Miss Ellen Terry at Home; Two Old Boys at the Music Hall. 1901: The House that Jack Built; The Little Doctor; The Mouse in the Art School; Mary Janes' Mishap. 1902: At Last! That Awful Tooth; Nursery Rhymes; Dorothy's Dream.

SOLDATI, Mario

Director and writer. Turin 1906–
Literature at Turin University, history of art at Rome. To USA: studied and taught at Columbia University; American correspondent of Il Lavoro. 1931: returned to Italy. From 1931: writer, assistant and editor especially on films of Mario Camerini. 1937: first film as director in collaboration with Fyodor Otsep. 1940: first film as solo director. 1946: acted in *Mio Figlio*

Professore. 1948: made 16 mm short *Chi è Dio?* 1955: co-writer and 2nd-unit director on *War and Peace*. 1957–58: TV film *Viaggio nella valle del Po, alla ricerca dei cibi genuini*. 1959: among 2nd-unit directors on *Ben-Hur*. 1960: TV film in collaboration with Cesare Zavattini *Chi Legge?*. Books include novels and reportage e.g. 'America, Prima Amore' (1935), 'La Verità sul caso Motta' (1941), 'Fuga in Italia' (1947), 'Lettere da Capri' (1954), 'Il ·Vero Sivestri' (1957).

Films as writer in collaboration include: 1932: Gli Uomini, che Mascalzoni!; La Tavola dei poveri. 1933: Cento di questi giorni (*s alone*); Giallo (*s alone*). 1936: Ma non e una cosa seria. 1937: Il Signor Max. 1941: Un Colpo di pistola. 1954: Questi Fantasmi.

Films as director and writer in collaboration: 1940: Dora Nelson (*+ co-st*); Tutto per la donna (*+ st*). 1941: Piccolo Mondo Antico – Little Old-Fashioned World; Tragica Notte. 1942: Malombria (*+ co-ad*). 1943: Quartieri Alti. 1945: Le Miserie del Signor Travet (*+ co-ad*). 1946: Eugenia Grandet. 1947: Daniele Cortis. 1948: Fuga in Francia – Flight into France (*+ co-st*). 1949: Quel Bandito sono io. 1950: Botta e risposta; Donne e briganti (*+ co-st*). 1951: E l'amor che mi rovina. 1952: Le Avventure di Mandrin – The Affair of Madame Pompadour – Mountain Brigand – Don Juan's Night of Love (*+ co-st*). 1953: La Mano dello straniero – The Strangler's Hand. 1954: Questa e la vita *ep* Il Ventaglino (*+ co-ad*). 1955: La Donna del fiume – Woman of the River. 1956: War and Peace (*2nd unit*). 1957: Era di venerdì 17; Italia Piccola.

Films as director: 1937: La Principessa Tarakanova (*+ co-st*; *co-d Fyodor Otsep*). 1939: Due Milioni per un sorriso (*co-d Carlo Borghesio*); La Signora de Monte Carlo (*+ co-st*; *co-d Andre Barthomieu*). 1948: Chi è Dio? 1951: Il Sogno di Zorro; OK Nerone – OK Nero. 1952: I Tre Corsari – The Three Pirates; Jolanda, la Figlia del Corsaro Nero; La Provinciale – Wayward Wife (*+ co-st*). 1959: Policarpo, ufficiale di scrittura – Policarpo – Policarpo de Tapetti, ufficiale di scrittura – Policarpo, Master Writer; Ben-Hur (*co-2nd unit*).

SOLNTSEVA, Yulia

Director. 1901–
At first actress e.g. in *Aelita* (1924). From 1930: assistant to her husband Alexander Dovzhenko, beginning with *Zemlya*. 1939: her first film as director in collaboration with him, *Schors*. 1943: co-directed *Bitva za nashu Sovetskayu Ukrainu,* documentary supervised and scripted by her husband. Worked on all stages of his planned trilogy on Ukrainian village; when he died of heart attack in 1956 she realised the projects (1958–65).

Films as solo director: 1943: Bitva za nashu Sovetskayu Ukrainu – The Fight for our Soviet Ukraine (*co-d I. Avdeyenko*). 1958: Poema o morye – Poem of the Sea. 1961: Povest plamennykh let – The Flaming Years. 1965: Zacharovanaya Desna – The Enchanted Desna.

SORDI, Alberto

Actor and director. Rome 1920–
1933: won competition organised by MGM to dub

Oliver Hardy's voice. Various jobs; then won amateur variety contest. 1938: first film. 1950: first major role.

Films as actor include: 1942: Casanova farebbe cosi. 1945: Le Miserie del Signor Travet. 1947: Il Delitto di Giovanni Episcopo. 1948: Sotto il sole di Roma. 1951: Toto e il re di Roma. 1952: Lo Sceicco Bianco. 1953: Ci troviamo in galleria; Un Giorno in pretura; I Vitelloni. 1954: Tempi Nostri; L'Arte di arrangiarsi. 1955: Un Eroe di nostri tempi. 1956: Mio Figlio Nerone. 1957: A Farewell to Arms. 1958: Fortunella; Ladro Lui, ladra lei. 1960: La Grande Guerra; Il Vigile; Crimen. 1961: Il Giudizio Universale. 1962: I Due Nemici; Mafioso. 1963: Il Boom; Il Maestro di Vigevano. 1965: Those Magnificent Men in their Flying Machines; Made in Italy. 1966: Le Fate *ep* Fata Marta; Le Streghe *ep* Senso Civico. 1970: Contestazione Generale. 1971: Detenuto in attesa di giudizio.

Films as director: 1965: Fumo di Londra. 1966: Scusi, lei è favorevole o contrario? 1967: Un Italiano in America. 1969: Amore Mio, aiutami (*+ co-s/w*). 1970: Le Coppie *eps* La Camera and *Il Leone*.

SOTHERN, Ann

(Harriette Lake) Actress. Valley City, North Dakota 1909–
Daughter of singer. Music at University of Washington. Voice training with mother in Hollywood. On Broadway in 'Smiles', 'America's Sweetheart', 'Everybody Welcome'; took over star part in 'Of Thee I Sing'. 1929: first film as actress *The Show of Shows*, credited as Harriet Lake. To 1949: worked mainly for RKO, then mainly Warners and MGM. TV work includes 'Lady with a Will', 'Variety', 'Private Secretary'. Daughter is actress Tish Sterling.

Films as actress include: 1934: A Melody in Spring. 1935: Folies Bergere. 1937: Danger—Love at Work. 1939: Fast and Furious; Hotel for Women. 1940: Congo Maisie; Brother Orchid. 1941: Lady Be Good. 1942: Maisie Gets Her Man; Panama Hattie. 1943: Three Hearts for Julia; Swing Shift Maisie; Thousands Cheer; Cry Havoc. 1948: Words and Music. 1949: A Letter to Three Wives. 1950: Nancy Goes to Rio. 1953: The Blue Gardenia. 1964: The Best Man. 1965: Sylvia.

SPAAK, Catherine

Actress. Paris 1945–
Father screenwriter Charles Spaak; uncle Belgian statesman Paul-Henri Spaak. Made first film appearance in documentary at 14. 1960: uncredited bit part in *Le Trou*; first major part in *I Dolci Inganni*. Wrote novel 'Larmes Chaudes'. Was married to actor Fabrizio Capucci.

Films as actress include: 1963: La Noia. 1964: La Calda Vita; La Ronde; Weekend à Zuydcoote. 1965: La Bugiarda; L'Armata Brancaleone. 1967: Hotel. 1968: L'Uomo dai palloncini. 1969: Con quale amore, con quanto amore.

SPAAK, Charles

Writer. Brussels 1903–
Brothers are poet and dramatist Paul Spaak, writer Claude Spaak, statesman Paul-Henri Spaak. From

Dance of the Vampires, *directed by Roman Polanski, photographed by Douglas Slocombe.*
Jack Smight's The Illustrated Man *with Rod Steiger.*
Alberto Sordi in Alberto Lattuada's Mafioso.

1928: scriptwriter, resident in France. About 100 scripts filmed, about 40 not. Many of his credits for dialogue only. 1949: only film as director *Le Mystère Barton*, also wrote it. Daughter is Catherine Spaak.

Films as writer include: 1929: Les Nouveaux Messieurs (*co*). 1933: Le Grand Jeu (*co-s/di*). 1934: Pension Mimosas (*co-s/di*). 1935: Les Beaux Jours; La Kermesse Héroïque (*fn/co-s*). 1936: La Bandéra (*co-di*); La Belle Equipe (*co*); Les Bas-fonds (*co-ad/co-dial*); L'Homme du Jour (*di*). 1937: La Grande Illusion (*co-di*); Gueule d'amour. 1938: L'Etrange M. Victor (*ad/co-s*); Mollenard (*co*). 1939: La Fin du jour (*co-ad/di*). 1940: Untel Père et fils (*+co-ad*). 1941: L'Assassinat du Père Noël (*di*). 1943: Le Ciel est à vous (*co*). 1946: L'Idiot; L'Homme au chapeau rond; La Revanche de Roger-la-Honte (*di*); Panique (*co-di*). 1948: D'hommes à hommes (*co*). 1949: Retour à la vie *ep* Tante Emma. 1950: Justice est faite (*co-di*). 1952: Nous sommes tous des assassins (*co-st/di*); Adorables Créatures (*di*). 1953: Thérèse Raquin (*co-di*); Le Grand Jeu (*co*). 1954: Avant le déluge (*+co-st*); Scuola Elementare; Le Dossier Noir (*co-di*). 1957: Quand la femme s'en mêle (*st*); Charmants Garçons. 1959: Katja. 1962: Cartouche (*co*).

SPARKUHL, Theodor

Cinematographer. Hanover, Germany 1894–1945
University of Hanover. 1911: started in projector department of Gaumont in Berlin. 1912: newsreel cameraman for Gaumont. 1913: first studio job for Eiko Film, Berlin. World War I as newsreel cameraman in Russia, Asia and Palestine for German government. Photographed many early films directed by Ernst Lubitsch (1918–23). 1923–28: cinematographer at Ufa. 1928–30: cinematographer at BIP, London, then at Baunberger Richebé in Paris. 1931: to USA.

Films as cinematographer include: 1918: Fuhrmann Henschel; Die Augen der Mumie Ma; Das Madel vom Ballet. 1919: Madame Dubarry; Die Austernprinzessin; Rausch; Die Puppe. 1920: Sumurun; Romeo und Julia im Schnee; Kohlhiesels Tochter; Anna Boleyn. 1921: Die Bergkatze. 1922: Das Weib des Pharao (*co*); Die Flamme (*co*). 1939: Beau Geste. 1942: Dr Broadway; Wake Island. 1944: Till We Meet Again. 1945: Salty O'Rourke.

SPERLING, Milton

Producer. New York 1912–
Shipping clerk, messenger boy at Paramount. 1931: secretary to Donald Ogden Stewart on European trip. 1932: script clerk at United Artists. Secretary for Zanuck, Warners, Hal Wallis. Associate producer, Edward Small Productions. Moved to Fox, became assistant to Winfield Sheeham then writer e.g. on *Happy Landing* (1938) and *Here I Am a Stranger* (1939). 1941–42: produced 3 films directed by Bruce Humberstone. 1942–45: served in US Marine Corps, reaching Captain. In charge of combat photographic unit films include *Tarawa* and *To the Shores of Iwo Jima*. 1945: organiser and president of United States Pictures, releasing through Warners. 1970: story for 'W.C.' on Broadway. Daughter is director, Karen Sperling.

Films as producer include: 1943: Crash Dive. 1946: Cloak and Dagger. 1947: Pursued. 1948: My Girl Tisa. 1949: South of St Louis. 1950: Three Secrets. 1951: The Enforcer; Distant Drums. 1952: Retreat—Hell! (*+st/s*). 1953: Blowing Wild. 1955: The Court-Martial of Billy Mitchell (*+co-st/co-s*). 1957: Top Secret Affair (*ex-p*). 1958: Marjorie Morningstar. 1960: The Rise and Fall of Legs Diamond. 1962: Merrill's Marauders (*+co-s*). 1966: The Battle of the Bulge (*+co-s*). 1971: Captain Apache (*+co-p*).

SPIEGEL, Sam

Producer. Jaroslau, Austria (now Poland) 1904–
University of Vienna before going to work as a Young Pioneer in Palestine. Became cotton broker and travelled to USA on business (1927). Gave series of lectures on European drama at University of California; one heard by MGM producer Paul Bern. To Hollywood for Bern as reader and adviser specialising in stories in foreign languages. Fired after 6 months. To Universal, which was producing films in Europe. 1928: to Europe and (1929) ran Universal European headquarters in Berlin. 1930: banning there of *All Quiet on the Western Front* after theatre bombed on opening night; managed to get ban lifted. 1933: when Hitler came to power, fled to Vienna, Paris and London. Unsuccessful project in Paris, to Mexico, prepared musical review, took it to New York. Returned to Hollywood and worked as S. P. Eagle until Elia Kazan persuaded him to put his own name to *On the Waterfront* (1954). 1947: formed Horizon Company with John Huston; first joint project, *We Were Strangers* (1949); Huston left the company amicably to make *Moulin Rouge* (1953).

Films as producer include: 1942: Tales of Manhattan (*co*). 1946: The Stranger (*co*). 1949: We Were Strangers. 1951: The Prowler; The African Queen. 1953: Melba. 1954: On the Waterfront. 1957: The Strange One; The Bridge on the River Kwai. 1959: Suddenly Last Summer. 1962: Lawrence of Arabia. 1966: The Chase. 1967: The Night of the Generals. 1971: Nicholas and Alexandra.

SPRINGSTEEN, R. G.

Director. Tacoma, Washington 1904–
University of Washington. Began in films as assistant director with Fox and Universal. Director from mid-1940s. 1945–57: worked with Republic. Then with various companies notably Allied Artists, Universal, then Paramount.

Films as director include: 1950: The Arizona Cowboy. 1955: I Cover the Underworld; Come Next Spring. 1958: Revolt in the Big House. 1959: King of the Wild Stallions. 1961: Operation Eichmann. 1965: Black Spurs. 1966: Apache Uprising; Waco.

STACK, Robert

Actor. Los Angeles 1919–
To Europe as child, returned to Los Angeles for high school. University of Southern California. 1938: Hollywood dramatic school. Declined Universal screen tests; on second offer, accepted. 1939: first film as actor *First Love*. To 1942: worked mainly for Universal. World War II: US Navy. From 1948: worked for numerous studios. 1956: married actress Rosemary Bowe. TV series 'The Untouchables'; same part in pilot for cinema release *The Scarface Mob*. Since 1969: co-star of TV series 'The Name of the Game'.

Films as actor include: 1940: The Mortal Storm; A Little Bit of Heaven. 1942: To Be or Not to Be; Men of Texas. 1948: A Date with Judy; Miss Tatlock's Millions; Fighter Squadron. 1950: Mr Music; My Outlaw Brother; The Bullfighter and the Lady. 1952: Bwana Devil. 1953: Conquest of Cochise. 1954: The High and the Mighty; The Iron Glove. 1955: House of Bamboo; Good Morning, Miss Dove. 1956: Great Day in the Morning; Written on the Wind. 1957: Tarnished Angels. 1958: The Gift of Love. 1959: John Paul Jones; The Scarface Mob. 1960: The Last Voyage. 1966: Paris brûle-t-il?; Le Soleil de voyous.

STAHL, John M.

Director. New York 1886–1950 Hollywood
Left school at 14 to go on stage with touring company. 1900–14: actor then stage director. From 1914: director with various independent film companies. 1920–26: director with First National. 1926–27: with MGM. 1928–30: with Tiffany Studios formed joint company Tiffany-Stahl Productions. During 1930s: director, mainly for Universal. In 1940s: all films for Fox.

Films as director (from 1918): 1918: Wives of Men (*+s/st*); Suspicion. 1919: Her Code of Honor; A Woman Under Oath. 1920: Women Men Forget; The Woman in his House. 1921: Sowing the Wind; The Child Thou Gavest Me (*+p*). 1922: The Song of Life (*+p*); The Dangerous Age (*+p*); One Clear Call (*+p*); Suspicious Wives. 1923: The Wanters (*+p*). 1924: Why Men Leave Home (*+p*); Husbands and Lovers (*+p*). 1925: Fine Clothes (*+p*). 1926: Memory Lane (*+p/co-st*); The Gay Deceiver. 1927: Lovers? (*+p*); In Old Kentucky (*+p*). 1930: A Lady Surrenders. 1931: Seed; Strictly Dishonorable. 1932: Back Street. 1933: Only Yesterday. 1934: Imitation of Life. 1935: Magnificent Obsession. 1937: Parnell. 1938: Letter of Introduction (*+p*). 1939: When Tomorrow Comes (*+p*). 1941: Our Wife. 1942: Immortal Sergeant. 1943 Holy Matrimony. 1944: The Eve of St Mark; The Keys of the Kingdom. 1946: Leave Her to Heaven. 1947: The Foxes of Harrow. 1948: The Walls of Jericho. 1949: Father was a Fullback; Oh, You Beautiful Doll.

STAMP, Terence

Actor. London 1940–
Drama school. Acted in provincial repertory. 1962: spotted by Peter Ustinov for first film as actor *Billy Budd*. On New York stage in 'Alfie'.

Films as actor include: 1962: Term of Trial. 1964: The Collector. 1966: Modesty Blaise. 1967: Far From the Madding Crowd; Histoires Extraordinaires *ep* Toby Dammit. 1969: Teorema.

STANWYCK, Barbara

(Ruby Stevens) Actress. New York 1907–
Orphan at 4. 1922: in chorus of Ziegfeld Follies. Appeared in revue, 'Keep Cool' (1924), 'Gay Paree' (1925). 1926: adopted stage name in 'The Noose' on

Broadway. 1927: first film as actress *Broadway Nights*, her only silent. 1930–39: acted in 34 films. 1933: with husband Frank Fay (divorced 1935) produced and appeared in 'Tattle Tales'. To 1935: worked mainly for Columbia and Warners. 1935–37: mainly RKO. 1937–48: mainly RKO, Fox, Warners, Paramount. 1948–53: mainly Paramount and MGM, From 1953: worked for numerous studios. TV work includes 'The Barbara Stanwyck Show' (1960–61), 'Wagon Train', 'Rawhide', 'The Untouchables', 'The Big Valley'. 1939–51: married to Robert Taylor.

Films as actress include: 1931: Ten Cents a Dance; Miracle Woman. 1932: Forbidden; So Big; The Bitter Tea of General Yen. 1934: The Secret Bride. 1935: The Woman in Red; Annie Oakley. 1936: His Brother's Wife. 1937: The Plough and the Stars; Stella Dallas. 1939: Union Pacific; Golden Boy. 1940: Remember the Night. 1941: The Lady Eve; Meet John Doe; You Belong to Me; Ball of Fire. 1942: The Great Man's Lady; The Gay Sisters. 1943: Lady of Burlesque; Flesh and Fantasy. 1944: Double Indemnity. 1945: Hollywood Canteen. 1946: My Reputation; The Bride wore Boots; The Strange Love of Martha Ivers. 1947: California; The Other Love. 1948: B. F.'s Daughter; Sorry, Wrong Number. 1949: The Lady Gambles; East Side, West Side; The File on Thelma Jordan. 1950: No Man of Her Own; The Furies; To Please a Lady. 1952: Clash by Night. 1953: Jeopardy; Titanic; All I Desire; The Moonlighter; Blowing Wild. 1954: Executive Suite; Witness to Murder; Cattle Queen of Montana. 1955: The Violent Men; Escape to Burma. 1956: There's Always Tomorrow; These Wilder Years. 1957: Crime of Passion; Trooper Hook; Forty Guns. 1962: Walk on the Wild Side. 1964: The Night Walker.

STARK, Ray

Producer

Flower-seller at Forest Lawns cemetery. Publicist then agent. 1961: with Elliot Hyman took over Seven Arts, buying up films for sale in groups to TV, financing theatrical productions and other entertainments. Company specialises in packaging films for major studios. In a single year, Seven Arts produced films for all the major studios and was involved in more productions than any one studio. Own production company.

Films as producer: 1960: The World of Suzie Wong. 1964: Night of the Iguana (*co*). 1966: Oh Dad, Poor Dad, Mamma's Hung You in the Closet and I'm Feeling So Sad. 1967: Reflections in a Golden Eye. 1968: Funny Girl (*+pc*). 1970: The Owl and the Pussycat (*+pc*).

STAUDTE, Wolfgang

Director and actor. Saarbrucken, Germany 1906–
Son of film and stage director Fritz Staudte. Stage training with Max Reinhardt and Erwin Piscator. To 1933: theatrical work. From 1931: films as actor. Directed and wrote commercials and shorts. 1943: first feature as director. Founded production company with Helmut Kautner and Harald Braun. 1943–45: worked for Tobis. 1946: to DEFA, made the first post-war German film *Die Mörder sind unter Uns*. In East Germany to 1953, then West Germany. 1955: co-wrote *Mutter Courage und ihre Kinder* with Brecht.

Films as actor include: 1931: Gassenhauer. 1939: Brand im Ozean. 1940: Jud Süss.

Films as director: 1943: Akrobet Scho-ö-ön (*+s*). 1944: Ich hab'von Dir geträumt. 1945: Frau uber Bord. 1946: Die Mörder sind unter Uns (*+s*). 1948: Die seltsamen Abenteuer des Herrn Fridolin B (*+s*). 1949: Rotation (*+s*); Schicksal aus zweiter Hand (*+s*). 1951: Der Untertan (*+co-s*). 1952: A Tale of Five Cities *ep* Wird Europa wieder lachen? (*uc*). 1953: Die Geschichte vom kleinen Muck – Little Mook (*+co-s*). 1954: Leuchtfeuer (*+co-s*). 1955: Mutter Courage und ihr Kinder (*+co-s*); Ciske-Ein Kind braucht Liebe (*+s*). 1957: Rose Bernd. 1958: Madeleine und der Legionär; Kanonen-Serenade (*+co-s*); Der Maulkorb. 1959: Rosen für den Staatsanwalt (*+st*). 1960: Kirmes (*+s*); Der letzte Zeuge – The Last Witness. 1962: Die glücklichen Jahre der Thorwalds (*co-d John Olden*); Die Rebellion (*+co-s*). 1963: Die Dreigroschenoper – The Threepenny Opera. 1964: Herrenpartie (*+co-s*); Das Lamm. 1966: Ganovenehre. 1968: Heimlichkeiten – Secrets (*+co-s*). 1970: Die Herren mit der weissen Weste. 1971: Heisse Spur St Pauli.

STEIGER, Rod

Actor. Westhampton, New York 1925–
1941: joined US Navy. 1946: clerk in Navy's Department of Dependents and Beneficiaries. 1947–49: New School for Social Research, Theatre Workshop, Actors' Studio. TV and theatre before first film as actor in 1951. On Broadway in 'Enemy of the People', 'Night Music', 'Seagulls over Sorrento', 'Rashomon' (with Claire Bloom, whom he married in 1958).

Films as actor include: 1951: Teresa. 1954: On the Waterfront. 1955: The Big Knife; Oklahoma!; The Court Martial of Billy Mitchell. 1956: The Harder They Fall; Jubal. 1957: Run of the Arrow. 1958: Cry Terror. 1959: Al Capone. 1960: Seven Thieves. 1961: The Mark. 1962: The Longest Day. 1963: Le Mani sulla città. 1964: Gli Indifferenti; E venne un uomo; The Loved One. 1965: The Pawnbroker; Dr Zhivago. 1966: La Ragazza e il generale. 1967: The Heat of the Night. 1968: No Way to Treat a Lady. 1969: 3 into 2 Won't Go; The Illustrated Man. 1970: Waterloo. 1971: Happy Birthday Wanda June.

STEINER, Max

Composer. Vienna 1888–
Imperial Academy of Music in Vienna under Gustav Mahler and others, winning Gold Medal. First operetta written when 14, ran a year in Vienna. Also published much symphonic and popular music. 1904: came to England as conductor. 1911: conducted at theatres in Paris. 1914: went to USA; conducted and orchestrated many musical shows on Broadway, including 'The Merry Widow', 'Ziegfeld Follies' and 'George White's Scandals'. 1929: Hollywood as musical director of RKO; started writing film scores. Later with Selznick and at Warner. Oscar for score of *The Informer* (1935).

Films as composer include: 1931: Cimarron. 1932: Bill of Divorcement. 1933: Little Women; King Kong. 1934: The Lost Patrol; Of Human Bondage. 1935: Alice Adams; The Informer. 1936: The Charge of the Light Brigade; The Garden of Allah. 1937: The Life of Emile Zola. 1938: Jezebel; The Dawn Patrol. 1939:

Sam Fuller's Merrill's Maurauders, *produced by Milton Sperling.*
Robert Stack (*left*) and Rock Hudson in Douglas Sirk's Written on the Wind.
Rod Steiger (*left*) *as* Al Capone, *directed by Richard Wilson.*

Gone With the Wind. 1940: The Letter. 1941: Sergeant York; They Died With Their Boots On. 1943: Casablanca. 1946: The Big Sleep; Cloak and Dagger; The Beast with Five Fingers. 1948: The Treasure of the Sierra Madre; Key Largo. 1949: The Fountainhead; White Heat. 1950: The Flame and the Arrow. 1951: Distant Drums. 1953: The Charge at Feather River. 1955: The Violent Men; Battle Cry. 1956: The Searchers; Bandido. 1957: Band of Angels; China Gate (co). 1959: The Hanging Tree; John Paul Jones; The FBI Story. 1960: A Summer Place; The Dark at the Top of the Stairs. 1961: Rachel Cade; Parrish; Susan Slade; A Majority of One. 1962: Rome Adventure. 1963: Spencer's Mountain. 1964: A Distant Trumpet; Youngblood Hawke.

STEINER, Ralph

Director and cinematographer. Cleveland, Ohio 1899–
Painter. Photographer in New York. Made amateur shorts. 1934: directed Elia Kazan and Irving Lerner in *Pie in the Sky*. 1936: founded company Frontier Films with Paul Strand, Pare Lorentz, Leo Hurwitz, Willard Van Dyke, Jay Leyda, Herbert Kline; in collaboration with Hurwitz and Strand photographed Lorentz's *The Plow That Broke the Plains*. 1939: made *The City* in collaboration with Van Dyke, for New York World's Fair under auspices of American Institute of Planners as propaganda for improvement of housing in America. 1942: dissolution of Frontier Films.

Films as director and cinematographer: 1929: H₂O. 1931: Mechanical Principle; Surf and Seaweed. 1934: Pie in the Sky. 1939: The City (+ co-p; co-c; co-d *Willard Van Dyke*).

STEINHOFF, Hans

Director. Pfaffenhofen, Germany 1882–1945 Luckenwalde, Germany
Gave up medical studies to work in theatre as actor and director. Directed films from 1922. From 1933: propaganda films at request of Goebbels. Died in air crash.

Films as director include: 1930: Rosenmontag. 1933: Hitlerjunge Quex. 1935: Der alte und der junge Könlg. 1937: Ein Volksfeind (+ co-s). 1938: Tanz auf dem Vulcan (+ co-s/co-st). 1939: Robert Koch der Bekämpfer des Todes. 1940: Die Geierwally. 1941: Ohm Krüger. 1942: Rembrandt (+ co-s).

STEN, Anna

(Anyushka Stenski) Actress. Kiev, Russia 1908–
1926: to Moscow. Enrolled on acting course. 1927–30: married to Grigori Alexandrov. 1930: to Germany; Ufa contract. 1931: first German film directed by Fedor Otsep. 1932: contract with Samuel Goldwyn. 1934: first Hollywood film. Also films in UK. 1962: last film *The Nun and the Sergeant*. New York stage with Actors Studio, and toured in 'The Threepenny Opera'.

Films as actress include: 1928: Potomok Chingis Khan; Moskva v Oktyabre. 1931: Salto Mortale. 1932: Stürme der Leidenschaft. 1934: We Live Again. 1935: The Wedding Night. 1940: The Man I Married. 1941: So Ends Our Night. 1943: They Came to Blow Up America. 1948: Let's Live a Little. 1955: Soldier of Fortune.

STENO

(Stefano Vanzina Steno) Director. Rome 1917–
Studied law; while a student, to Centro Sperimentale di Cinematografia. Contributor to and illustrator of journal Marc'Aurelio. Invited by Mario Mattoli to collaborate on scripts of several comedy films. After World War II, writer or assistant on films. 1946–49: writer in collaboration with Mario Monicelli. 1949–52: first film as director, in collaboration with Monicelli, first of several collaborations.

Films as writer include: 1941: La Scuola dei timidi (co). 1943: Tutta la città canta (co+ st). 1946: Aquila Nera (co). 1947: I Miserabile (co); L'Ebreo Errante; La Figlia del capitano (co). 1948: Il Cavaliere Misterioso (co).

Films as director in collaboration with Mario Monicelli: 1948: Al Diavolo la celeblrità – One Night of Fame – A Night of Fame; Totò cerca casa – Totò Wants a Home. 1950: E' arrivato il cavaliere; Vita da Cani – It's a Dog's Life. 1951: Totò e i re di Roma; Guardie e ladri – Cops and Robbers. 1952: Totò e le Donne; Le Infedeli – The Unfaithful; Totò a Colori (+ st/s).

Films as director: 1953: L'Uomo, La bestia e la virtù – Man, Beast and Virtue (+ co-s); Cinema d'altri tempi (+ co-st/co-s); Un Giorno in pretura (+ co-st/co-s). 1954: Un Americano a Roma – An American in Rome (+ co-st/co-s); Le Avventure di Giacomo Casanova (+ st/s). 1955: Piccola Posta (+ co-st/co-s). 1956: Mio Figlio Nerone – Nero's Weekend (+ co-st/co-s). 1957: Femmine tre volte – Female Three Times – Three Times a Woman (+ co-s); Susanna tutta panna. 1958: Mia Nonna Poliziotto (+ co-s); Guardia, ladro e cameriera (+ co-s). 1959: I Tartassati – The Overtaxed; Totò, Eva e il pennello proibito (+ st); Toto nella luna (+ co-st/co-s); Tempi Duri per i vampiri (+ co-st/co-s). 1960: A noi piace freddo – Some Like it Cold (+ co-s); Il Letto a tre piazze (+ co-s). Un Militare e mezzo (+ co-s). 1961: Psycosissimo (+ co-s); La Ragazza di mille mesi. 1962: Totò Diabolicus; I Moschettiere del mare; Copacabana Palace; I Due Colonelli – The Two Colonels. 1963: Totò contro i quattro. 1964: Gli Eroi del West (+ co-s). 1965: I Superdiabolici (+ co-s); Letti Sbagliati. 1966: Rose Rosse per Angelica (+ co-s). 1967: Arriva Dorellik. 1968: La Feldmarescialla – The Girl Field Marshal; Capriccio all' Italiana *ep* Il Maestro della domenica. 1969: I Trapianto. 1971: Il Vichingo Venuto dal Sud.

STERN, Stewart

Writer. New York 1922–
University of Iowa. World War II: rifle squad leader; Staff-Sergeant in US Infantry. 1943–45: actor and assistant stage manager on Broadway. 1945–46: dialogue director at Eagle Lion studios. 1950: contract as writer with MGM. Since worked for various companies. Much TV as writer and producer.

Films as writer include: 1951: Teresa (+ co-st); Benjy (+ st). 1955: Rebel Without a Cause. 1958: Thunder in the Sun (ad). 1961: The Outsider. 1967: Rachel, Rachel.

STEVENS, George

Director. Oakland, California 1904–
Parents owned West Coast touring theatre company;

as child acted for it. 1921: to Los Angeles with father, started in films as assistant cameraman. Cinematographer for Hal Roach on comedy shorts including Laurel and Hardy and 'Our Gang' series. 1928–32: gag writer and director of comedies for Roach e.g. on *Mama Loves Papa* (1931). Directed one feature at Universal (1933) before joining RKO. 1935: Katherine Hepburn accepted him as last resort to direct her in *Alice Adams,* which made his reputation. World War II: US Army Colonel in charge of film unit which covered 6th Army campaigns in North Africa and Europe (special citation for work on D-Day), and liberation of Dachau. 1945: with William Wyler, Frank Capra and Samuel Briskin formed Liberty Films Inc to produce 'message pictures'; company only made 1 film – Capra's *It's A Wonderful Life* – and Stevens abandoned the project after spending $100,000 on it.

Films as director: 1933: Cohens and Kellys in Trouble. 1934: Bachelor Bait. 1935: Alice Adams; Annie Oakley. 1937: A Damsel in Distress. 1938: Vivacious Lady (+ p). 1939: Gunga Din (+ p). 1941: Penny Serenade (+ p). 1942: Woman of the Year; The Talk of the Town (+ p). 1943: The More the Merrier (+ p). 1948: I Remember Mama (+ co-p). 1951: A Place in the Sun (+ p). 1952: Something to Live For (+ p). 1953: Shane (+ p). 1956: Giant (+ co-p). 1959: The Diary of Anne Frank (+ p). 1965: The Greatest Story Ever Told (+ p/co-s). 1968: The Only Game in Town.

STEVENS, Leith

Composer. Mount Moriah, Missouri 1909–70
Debut as pianist at 14 and as conductor at 16; then musical director for a ballet company. 1928: Juillard Foundation Fellowship. 1930: joined CBS as vocal arranger. 1933–41: composed and conducted for many radio shows, including those of Fred Allen and Abbott and Costello. 1939: Vitaphone short *Leith Stevens and the Saturday Night Swing Club on the Air*. 1941: first film score. 1942: radio director for Southwest Pacific area of Office of War Information. Returned to Hollywood to compose and conduct for radio. Since 1950: also TV. 1950: musical director at Paramount. 1970: died of heart attack after his wife killed in crash. Helped pioneer use of jazz in film background music.

Films as composer include: 1942: Syncopation. 1948: All My Sons. 1950: Destination Moon. 1951: When Worlds Collide. 1952: Beware, My Lovely; Eight Iron Men. 1953: The Hitch-Hiker; The Wild One. 1954: Private Hell 36. 1955: The Scarlet Hour. 1956: Julie; Great Day in the Morning. 1957: The Garment Center; The James Dean Story. 1959: The Gene Krupa Story. 1960: Hell to Eternity. 1961: Mantrap. 1962: The Interns. 1966: The Night of the Grizzly. 1967: Chuka.

STEVENS, Leslie

Director and writer. Washington DC 1924–
Educated at Westminster School, London and at a Washington high school from which he ran away to tour with Orson Welles. Brought back from Philadelphia by a Truant Officer. After 2 years in stock companies, entered Yale Drama School. Sold his first play, 'The Mechanical Rat' at 15 and wrote 6 more for summer stock groups (1941–2). 1943: US Air Force. Menial jobs until play 'Bullfight' (1954) became off-

Broadway hit. Author of many TV plays. President and executive producer of Daystar Productions which has made features and TV films; writer on e.g. 'The Aquarians'. Wife Kate Manx (died 1965) took leading parts in 2 of his films as director. Play 'The Lovers' was filmed as *The War Lord* (1965).

Films: 1958: The Left Handed Gun (*s*). 1960: Private Property (*d/co-p/s*); The Marriage-Go-Round (*p/s/fpl*). 1962: Hero's Island – The Land We Love (*d/p/s*). 1965: Incubus (*d/st/s*).

STEVENSON, Robert

Director. London 1905–
University of Cambridge. Began as journalist, then writer at Gainsborough e.g. on films directed by Victor Saville. 1930: first film as director; writer on films directed by others until 1937. 1940: to Hollywood, worked mainly for RKO until 1952. World War II: US Army. From 1957: contract with Walt Disney. TV includes episodes for 'Alfred Hitchcock Presents', 'Ford Theatre', 'Playhouse of Stars', 'Cavalcade of America'. 1934–44: married to actress Anna Lee, who appeared in some of his films.

Films as director include: 1933: Falling for You. 1936: Tudor Rose – Lady Jane Grey; The Man who Changed his Mind (*+s*). 1937: King Solomon's Mines. 1939: The Ware Case. 1940: Tom Brown's Schooldays. 1941: Back Street. 1942: Joan of Paris. 1943: Forever and a Day (*+co-p; co-d 6 others*). 1944: Jane Eyre (*+co-s*). 1947: Dishonored Lady. 1948: To the Ends of the Earth. 1949: I Married a Communist; Walk Softly, Stranger. 1950: My Forbidden Past. 1952: The Las Vegas Story. 1957: Old Yeller. 1960: The Absent-Minded Professor; Kidnapped. 1961: In Search of the Castaways – The Castaways. 1963: Son of Flubber. 1964: Mary Poppins. 1965: The Monkey's Uncle. 1966: The Gnome-Mobile. 1968: The Mickey Mouse Anniversary Show (*co-d Ward Kimball*). 1969: The Love-Bug. 1971: Bedknobs and Broomsticks.

STEWART, Donald Ogden

Writer. Columbus, Ohio 1894–
Yale University. Made his name as author of plays and books. 1930: acted in his play 'Rebound' on Broadway. Humorous books include 'Aunt Polly's Story of Mankind' and 'A Parody Outline of History'. During 1930s member of Algonquin Round Table with e.g. James Thurber, Ring Lardner, Harpo Marx. 1952: blacklisted; to England, wrote several scripts as Gilbert Holland. (Had been president of Anti-Nazi League in USA; refused to swear he was not a communist.) 1957: regained US passport; play 'The Kidders' produced in London. Oscar for screenplay *The Philadelphia Story* (1940).

Films as writer include: 1931: Tarnished Lady (*+fst*). 1934: The Barretts of Wimpole Street (*co*). 1937: The Prisoner of Zenda (*co*). 1938: Holiday (*co*); Marie Antoinette (*co*). 1939: Love Affair (*co*). 1940: The Philadelphia Story; Kitty Foyle (*co*); Smilin' Through (*co-di*). 1941: That Uncertain Feeling; A Woman's Voice (*co*). 1942: Tales of Manhattan (*co-st/co-s*); Keeper of the Flame. 1947: Life with Father. 1949: Edward, My Son.

STEWART, James

Actor. Indiana, Pennsylvania 1908–
Architecture at Princeton. Acted while a student. Summer stock in Falmouth, Massachusetts. Professional début in 'Goodbye Again', with it to Broadway. New York roles included 'Yellow Jack', 'Page Miss Glory', 'Journey at Night'. 3-year MGM contract: to Hollywood. 1935: first film as actor *The Murder Man*. 1935–41: worked mainly for MGM, but also for RKO, Warners, United Artists. 1940: Oscar as Best Actor for *The Philadelphia Story*. Subsequently worked mainly for Fox, Universal, Paramount, Columbia, Warners, MGM. 1941–45: USAAF service, reaching Colonel. 1957: directed, produced and narrated *Cowboy 57* for TV. 1959: promoted to Brigadier-General in Air Force Reserve. TV work also includes *Trail to Christmas* (1958) which he directed and John Ford's *Flashing Spikes* (1962). On Broadway acted in 'Harvey' in 1940 and 1970.

Films as actor include: 1936: Rose-Marie; Wife vs Secretary; Small Town Girl; The Gorgeous Hussy; Born to Dance; After the Thin Man. 1937: Seventh Heaven; The Last Gangster; Navy Blue and Gold. 1938: Of Human Hearts; Vivacious Lady; The Shopworn Angel; You Can't Take it With You. 1939: Made for Each Other; It's a Wonderful World; Mr Smith Goes to Washington; Destry Rides Again. 1940: The Shop Around the Corner; The Mortal Storm; No Time for Comedy; The Philadelphia Story. 1941: Come Live With Me; Pot O' Gold; Ziegfeld Girl. 1947: It's A Wonderful Life; Magic Town. 1948: Call Northside 777; A Miracle Can Happen; Rope; You Gotta Stay Happy. 1949: The Stratton Story; Malaya. 1950: Winchester '73; Broken Arrow; The Jackpot; Harvey. 1951: No Highway in the Sky. 1952: The Greatest Show on Earth; Bend of the River; Carbine Williams. 1953: The Naked Spur; Thunder Bay; The Glenn Miller Story. 1954: Rear Window; The Far Country. 1955: Strategic Air Command; The Man from Laramie. 1956: The Man Who Knew Too Much. 1957: The Spirit of St Louis; Night Passage. 1958: Vertigo; Bell, Book and Candle. 1959: Anatomy of a Murder; The FBI Story. 1960: The Mountain Road. 1961: Two Rode Together. 1962: The Man Who Shot Liberty Valance; Mr Hobbs Takes a Vacation; How the West was Won. 1963: Take Her, She's Mine. 1964: Cheyenne Autumn. 1965: Dear Brigitte; Shenandoah; The Rare Breed; The Flight of the Phoenix. 1968: Bandolero! 1970: The Cheyenne Social Club. 1971: Fool's Parade.

STIGLIC, France

Director. Kranj, Yugoslavia 1919–
Studied law in Ljubljana. World War II: resistance and journalism. Actor in avant-garde theatre. 1945: entered films. Several documentaries. 1948: first feature as director.

Features as director: 1948: Na Svoji Zemlji – On His Own Ground. 1952: Svet na Kajžarju – People of Kajzarju. 1955: Volča Nóč – The Living Nightmare. 1956: Dolina Miru – Peace Valley. 1958: Viza na Zloto – The False Passport. 1960: Deveti Krug – The Ninth Circle. 1961: Balada o trobenti i oblaku – Ballad of the Trumpet and the Cloud. 1963: Tistega Lepega Dne – That Fine Day. 1964: Ne placi Petre – Don't Cry, Peter. 1966: Amandus.

James Dean in Rebel Without a Cause. *directed by Nicholas Ray and written by Stewart Stern.*
Elizabeth Taylor and James Dean in Giant. *directed by George Stevens.*
James Stewart in Anthony Mann's The Man from Laramie.

STILLER, Mauritz

Director. Helsinki, Finland 1883–1928 Stockholm
Began as stage actor then director in Helsinki. 1910: took over Lilla Theatre, Stockholm. 1912: first films as director, 2- and 3-reelers for Svenska Bio. From 1917: directed features in Sweden. 1924: cast Greta Gustafsson in *Gösta Berlings Saga*, naming her Greta Garbo. 1925: with Garbo to Constantinople on unrealised film project; to Berlin where he coached her for *Die freudlose Gasse*; then to Hollywood, both under MGM contract. 1926: began 2 films for MGM, both completed by others. 1927–28: directed 3 films for Paramount; the last, *The Street of Sin*, was based on story by Josef von Sternberg who completed the film when Stiller returned to Sweden (after argument about reshooting requested by Paramount). 1933: Svensk Filmindustri asked Ragnar Hylten-Cavallius, script assistant on *Gösta Berlings Saga*, to adapt the 2 parts into shorter version with music; original no longer exists.

Films as director: 1912: Mor och dotter – Mother and Daughter (+ s/w). De Svarta Maskerna (+ co-s); Den Tyranniske Fastmännen (+ s/w); Vampyren eller en kvinnas slav; När kärleken dödar; Barnet; När larmklockan ljuder. 1913: Den Moderna Suffragetten – Den Suffragetten – Lily, den Suffragetten (+ s); Pa livets ödesvägar (+ s); Den Okända (+ s); Mannekängen (+ s); Gränsfolken; För sin kärleks skull (+ s); Livets konflikter – Life's Conflicts (+ s). 1914: När svärmor regerar eller sa tuktäsakta män (+ s/w); Kammarjunkaren (+ s); Stormfågeln; Skottet; Bröderna (+ st/s); Det Röda Tornet (+ co-s). 1915: När konstnärer älska – Mme Thora Fleming; Lekkamraterna (+ s); Hans Hustrus förflutna; Dolken; Mästertjuven; Madame de Thèbes. 1916: Hämnaren; Minlotsen; Hans Bröllopsnatt; Lyckonålen; Kärlek och journalistik; Vingarna (+ s); Kampen om hans hjärta (+ s); Balettprimadonnan – Wolo czarwienko. 1917: Thomas Graals Bästa Film; Alexander den store (+ s). 1918: Thomas Graals Bästa Barn (+ co-s). 1919: Sängen om dem eldröda blomman – Dans les remous – Song of the Scarlet Flower (+ co-s); Herr Arnes Pengar – Sir Arne's Treasure (+ co-s). 1920: Fiskebyn; Erotikon (+ co-s). 1921: Johan (co-d); De landsflyktige – In Self Defence (+ co-s). 1923: Gunnar Hedes saga (+ s). 1924: Gösta Berlings Saga – The Atonement of Gosta Berling (+ co-s). 1926: Ibanez' Torrent – The Torrent (co-d *Monta Bell*); The Temptress (co-d *Fred Niblo*). 1927: Hotel Imperial; The Woman on Trial (+ p). 1928: Street of Sin (co-d *Josef von Sternberg*).

STONE, Andrew L.

Director and writer. Oakland, California 1902–
UCLA. 1927: sold short film, which he had directed and scripted, to Paramount. Worked as writer and director for Sono Art. 1938–41: director and writer with Paramount. From 1943: own production company releasing through United Artists, then (from 1955) through MGM. From 1958: joint production company with wife Virginia Stone, who edited many of his films.

Films as director: 1927: The Elegy (+ s). 1928: Two O'Clock in the Morning: Liebenstraum. 1930: Sombras de Gloria – Shadows of Glory. 1932: Hell's Headquarters. 1937: The Girl Said No (+ p/st). 1938: Stolen Heaven (+ p); Say it in French (+ p); There's

Magic in Music – Magic in Music. 1939: The Great Victor Herbert (+ p/co-st). 1941: The Hard-Boiled Canary (+ p/co-st). 1943: Stormy Weather; Hi, Diddle Diddle (+ p). 1944: Sensations of 1945 – Sensations (+ p). 1945: Bedside Manner (+ p). 1946: The Bachelor's Daughters (+ p/s). 1947: Fun on a Weekend (+ p/s). 1950: Highway 301 (+ st/s). 1952: Confidence Girl (+ p/st/s); The Steel Trap (+ st/s). 1953: A Blueprint for Murder (+ s). 1955: The Night Holds Terror (+ p/s). 1956: Julie (+ s). 1958: Cry Terror (+ co-p/s); The Decks Ran Red (+ co-p/s). 1960: The Last Voyage (+ co-p/s). 1961: Ring of Fire (+ co-p/s). 1962: The Password is Courage (+ co-p/s). 1963: Never Put it in Writing (+ s). 1965: The Secret of My Success (+ s). 1970: Song of Norway (+ co-p/s).

STORCK, Henri

Director. Ostend, Belgium 1907–
1928: wrote on documentary films in Eclair Journal. From 1929: documentary director. 1933: assisted Jean Vigo on *Zéro de conduite* in which he acted. Over 130 documentaries. Founded Club de Cinéma d'Ostende. Author of book 'Le Film Récreatif pour Spectateurs Juveniles' (UNESCO, 1950).

Films as director include: 1931: Une Idylle à la plage. 1932: Histoire du soldat inconnu (+ s/e). 1933: Borinage – Misère au Borinage (+ co-s/co-c; co-d *Joris Ivens*). 1937: Les Maisons de la misère. 1946: Le Monde de Paul Delvaux – The World of Paul Delvaux. 1966: Le Bonheur d'être aimée (+ pc). 1971: Paul Delvaux ou les femmes défendues.

STOTHART, Herbert P.

Composer. Milwaukee, Wisconsin 1884–1949 Los Angeles
1910–15: taught music at University of Wisconsin. Then travelled in Europe. In New York theatre in 1920s, worked with Joseph Howard, George Gershwin, Bert Kalmar, Harry Ruby. 1930: original story for *The Lottery Bride*; worked entirely for MGM. 1934: adapted Franz Lehar's music for *The Merry Widow*.

Films as composer include: 1933: Rasputin and the Empress; The Barbarian. 1934: Queen Christina. 1935: Mutiny on the Bounty. 1936: Romeo and Juliet. 1937: Conquest; The Good Earth. 1938: Marie Antoinette. 1939: Idiot's Delight. 1940: Susan and God; Northwest Passage; Edison, the Man; Pride and Prejudice; Waterloo Bridge. 1941: They Met in Bombay. 1942: Mrs Miniver; Cairo; Tennessee Johnson. 1943: Madame Curie; The Human Comedy. 1944: A Guy Named Joe; Dragon Seed; Kismet; National Velvet; Thirty Seconds over Tokyo; The White Cliffs of Dover. 1945: The Picture of Dorian Gray; They Were Expendable. 1946: Adventure; The Green Years; Undercurrent; The Yearling; The Sea of Grass. 1947: High Barbaree; Desire Me (co); If Winter Comes. 1948: Hills of Home; The Three Musketeers.

STOUT, Archie

Cinematographer. Renwick, Iowa 1886–
Government hotel manager in forest service. 1914: worked for Mack Sennett. Moved to Fox (1917), Christie (1918). 1922: signed 5-year contract with Cecil B. De Mille at Paramount, remained there when

De Mille left in 1925 to form own company. Paramount to 1933, then freelance. 1952: contract with Batjac. 1954: last film *The High and the Mighty*; retired after a heart attack. Oscar for colour cinematography on *The Quiet Man* (with Winton C. Hoch; 1952).

Films as cinematographer include: 1928: Varsity. 1929: Men are Like That. 1930: Dangerous Paradise; Young Eagles; The Benson Murder Case; Manslaughter; The Sea God. 1931: It Pays to Advertise. 1933: Heritage of the Desert; Sunset Pass. 1934: The Last Round-Up. 1938: Professor Beware. 1939: Rulers of the Sea (co). 1944: It Happened Tomorrow (co); Summer Storm; Dark Waters (co). 1948: Fort Apache. 1950: Never Fear; Outrage. 1951: Hard, Fast, and Beautiful. 1952: The Quiet Man (co); Big Jim McLain. 1953: The Sun Shines Bright; Island in the Sky; Trouble Along the Way; Hondo (co). 1954: The High and the Mighty.

STRAND, Paul

Cinematographer. New York 1890–
1915: first one-man show of photographs at the Gallery of Photo Secession in New York. 1922–30: freelance work for newsreel companies and Hollywood studios. 1934: supervised and photographed *Redes*, for Department of Fine Arts of Mexican Government. 1935: joined the photographic staff of Pare Lorentz. Co-directed *Pay Day* (1938) and *Native Land* (1942) with Leo Hurwitz.

Films as cinematographer include: 1936: The Plow That Broke the Plains (co). 1942: Native Land (+ co-st/co-s/e; co-d *Leo Hurwitz*). 1948: Heart of Spain (+ co-e).

STRAUB, Jean-Marie

Director. Metz, France 1933–
Studied literature at Strasbourg and Nancy. 1950–55: ran film society in Metz. 1954–58: in Paris. Student and assistant with Abel Gance, Jean Renoir, Jacques Rivette, Robert Bresson, Alexandre Astruc. 1958: left France to avoid national service; from then in Germany. Married to Dainèle Huillet.

Films as director: 1963: Machorka-Muff (+ co-p/co-s). 1965: Nicht versoehnt *oder* es halft nur Gewalt, wo Gewalt herrscht – Unreconciled (+ co-s/co-e). 1967: Chronik der Anna Magdalena Bach (+ co-p/co-s/co-e). 1968: Der Braeutigam, die Komödiantin und der Zuhaelter (+ pc/co-s). 1970: Les Yeux ne peuvent pas en tout temps se fermer – Peut-être qu'un jour Rome se permettra de choisir à son tour – Othon (+ co-e).

STRICK, Joseph

Director. Pittsburgh, Pennsylvania 1923–
One year at UCLA. 1942–46: cameraman in USAAF. 1946–48: copy boy on Los Angeles Times. 1948: first film as director, in collaboration with Irving Lerner. Worked in TV. *The Savage Eye* took 5 years to make, in collaboration with Ben Maddow and Sidney Meyers; originally documentary only, then part for actress written in. 1963: first professional feature. 1965: directed 'Gallows Humour' on Dublin stage. 1966: for British TV made *The Hecklers*. 1968: began *Justine* for Fox, replaced by George Cukor. 1969: producer only

on *Ring of Bright Water.* 1970: Oscar for best documentary short, *Interviews with My Lai Veterans.*

Films as director: 1948: Muscle Beach (*co-d Irving Lerner*). 1953: The Big Break (*+p/co-pc*). 1959: The Savage Eye (*+co-p/co-s/co-e*; *co-d Ben Maddow, Sidney Meyers*). 1963: The Balcony (*+co-p*). 1967: Ulysses (*+p*). 1968: Justine (*uc*; *co-d George Cukor*). 1969: Tropic of Cancer (*+p/co-s*). 1970: Interviews with My Lai Veterans.

STRINDBERG, Göran

Cinematographer. Stockholm 1917–
Distantly related to August Strindberg. Apprenticed at 14 to photographers Bergn and Welinder. From 1937: assistant cameraman at Europa. From 1942: cinematographer at Sandrews and Terra Film. 1954–61: worked in Germany. 1964: instructor at the Swedish Film School. Some collaboration with Sven Nykvist.

Films as cinematographer include: 1946: Det regnar på vår kärlek (*co*). 1947: Skepp till Indialand; Musik i mörker. 1949: Fängelse. 1951: Fröken Julie. 1953: Barabbas (*co*); Dumbom. 1955: Die Ratten. 1960: La Grande Vie.

STROSS, Raymond

Producer. Leeds, Yorkshire 1917–
Oxford University. Odd jobs in London studios while a student, also theatrical work. Joined Columbia; became a sales supervisor for Midlands and branch manager for Ireland. Bought a theatre; eventually owned chain of 11. 1942: British Army; 18 months service. Became joint managing director of Garrick Theatre, London; sold theatre chain. 1948: returned to cinema. 1960: married actress Anne Heywood. Briefly associated in production with Robert Mitchum. 1964: managing director of production-distribution company releasing through British Lion. 1965: left for Hollywood.

Films as producer include: 1951: Hell is Sold Out. 1952: Rough Shoot; Tall Headlines. 1955: As Long as They're Happy; An Alligator Named Daisy. 1959: The Angry Hills. 1960: A Terrible Beauty. 1961: The Mark. 1963: The Leather Boys. 1968: The Fox.

STRUSS, Karl

Cinematographer. New York 1891–
Studied art at Columbia University. 1941: photographer for Bermuda government. 1914–17: own photographic studio, working on portraits and magazine illustrations; lens manufacturing. From 1919: with Cecil B. De Mille for 3 years. Then with B. P. Schulberg. 1927: received the first Oscar for cinematography on *Sunrise* (with Charles Rosher). 1927–30: with D. W. Griffith. 1931: joined Paramount. 1953–54: in Italy.

Films as cinematographer include: 1920: Something to Think About (*co*). 1921: The Affairs of Anatol; Fools Paradise. 1922: Saturday Night. 1927: Ben-Hur; Sunrise (*co*); The Battle of the Sexes (*co*). 1928: Drums of Love (*co*). 1929: Lady of the Pavements (*co*). 1930: Abraham Lincoln. 1931: Skippy. 1932: Dr Jekyll and Mr Hyde; Sign of the Cross. 1933: The Island of Lost Souls. 1934: Four Frightened People; Belle of the

Nineties. 1936: Anything Goes; Go West Young Man; Hollywood Boulevard. 1940: The Great Dictator (*co*). 1943: Journey into Fear. 1947: The Macomber Affair (*co*). 1952: Limelight.

STURGES, John

Director. Oak Park, Illinois 1911–
1932: began in films at RKO; worked as assistant art director, assistant editor, assistant to David O. Selznick, then editor. World War II: served in Signal Corps and Air Corps becoming Captain; made many army training films and documentaries e.g. *Thunderbolt* (1947) directed in collaboration with William Wyler. 1946: first features as director. Worked for Columbia until 1949. 1950–55: with MGM and RKO. Thereafter with various companies. 1960–67: one of the founders of production company Mirisch, releasing through United Artists.

Features as director: 1946: The Man who Dared; Shadowed. 1947: Alias Mr Twilight; For the Love of Rusty; Keeper of the Bees. 1948: The Best Man Wins; The Sign of the Ram. 1949: The Walking Hills. 1950: Mystery Street; The Capture; The Magnificent Yankee; Right Cross. 1951: Kind Lady; It's a Big Country (*co-d 5 others*); The People against O'Hara. 1952: The Girl in White. 1953: Jeopardy; Fast Company; Escape from Fort Bravo. 1954: Underwater!; Bad Day at Black Rock. 1955: The Scarlet Coat. 1956: Backlash. 1957: Gunfight at the O.K. Corral. 1958: The Old Man and the Sea (*co-d Fred Zinneman, uc*; *Henry King, uc*); The Law and Jake Wade; Last Train from Gun Hill. 1959: Never So Few. 1960: The Magnificent Seven (*+p*). 1961: By Love Possessed; Sergeants 3. 1962: A Girl Named Tamiko. 1963: The Great Escape (*+p*). 1964: The Satan Bug (*+p*). 1965: The Hallelujah Trail (*+p*). 1967: Hour of the Gun (*+p*). 1968: Ice Station Zebra. 1969: Marooned.

STURGES, Preston

Director and writer. Chicago 1898–1959 New York
Education in France, Germany, Switzerland, USA. At 16, became branch manager for mother's cosmetics firm, returning there after World War I service in US Air Corps. Freelance inventor. Stage manager in New York. Wrote 4 plays, including the successful 'Strictly Dishonorable' (1929); others failures. To Hollywood, wrote 15 screenplays, mainly for Paramount and Universal. 1940: first film as director and writer *The Great McGinty*. To 1944: worked for Paramount, left following disagreements over *The Great Moment*. Formed partnership with Howard Hughes for 3 films, released by RKO and Fox. 1954: to Paris, lived there for 3 years, made last film there. Oscar for original screenplay *The Great McGinty* (1940).

Films as writer include: 1930: Fast and Loose (*di*). 1933: The Power and the Glory. 1934: We Live Again (*co*); Imitation of Life (*di, uc*). 1935: The Good Fairy; Diamond Jim. 1937: Easy Living. 1938: Port of Seven Seas; If I Were King. 1939: Never Say Die (*co*). 1940: Remember the Night (*+st*). 1951: Strictly Dishonorable (*fpl*). 1956: The Birds and the Bees (*co*). 1958: Rock-a-Bye-Baby (*st*).

Films as director and writer: 1940: The Great McGinty (*+st*); Christmas in July (*+st*). 1941: The

James Mason and Inger Stevens in Andrew L. Stone's Cry Terror.

The Angry Hills, *directed by Robert Aldrich, produced by Raymond Stross.*

Spencer Tracy and Ernest Borgnine in Bad Day at Black Rock, *directed by John Sturges.*

Lady Eve. 1942: Sullivan's Travels (+ *st*); The Palm Beach Story (+ *st*). 1944: The Miracle of Morgan's Creek (+ *st*); Hail the Conquering Hero (+ *st*); The Great Moment. 1946: The Sin of Harold Diddlebock – Mad Wednesday (+ *st*). 1948: Unfaithfully Yours (+ *st*). 1949: The Beautiful Blonde from Bashful Bend. 1955: Les Carnets du Major Thompson – The Diary of Major Thompson – The French They are a Funny Race.

SUCKSDORFF, Arne

Director. Stockholm 1917–
Abandoned natural science at Stockholm University to study painting, then (1937–38) theatrical direction in Berlin. Took up photography. 1939: began first short film, which he scripted, photographed and edited. 1941–49: national film production contract to make series of documentaries. From 1951: freelance producer. 1953: first feature-length film. 1956–57: went to India to make *En Djungelsaga* in colour. 1971: directed animal sequences for *Mr Forbush and the Penguins*.

Films as director, writer, cinematographer and editor: 1939: Augustirapsodi (+ *p*). 1940: Din tillvaros land (*d/c only*). 1941: En Sommarsaga. 1942: Vinden från väster (*d only*); Sarvtid. 1944: Trut; Gryning. 1945: Skuggor över snön. 1947: Människor i stad; Den drömda dalen. 1948: En kluven värld; Uppbrott (*d/s/e only*). 1949: Strandhugg. 1950: Ett hörn i norr. 1951: Indisk by; Vinden och floden. 1953: Det Stora Äventyret – The Great Adventure. 1957: En Djungelsaga – The Flute and the Arrow (+ *p*). 1961: Pojken i trädet – The Boy in the Tree (*d/s*; + *p*). 1965: Mitt hem är Copacabana – My Home is Copacabana (*d only*).

SULLIVAN, Pat

Animator. Australia 1888–1933
To USA. From 1914: newspaper cartoonist, succeeding William F. Marriner on 'Wags – the Dog that Adopted a Man'. Started making film cartoons; worked with Otz Messmer on films for Universal Manufacturing Company e.g. *Motor Mat and his Fliv* (1916), *A Good Liar* (1917). Also worked on series of 'Hardrock Dome' cartoons for Bray studios. *c.* 1921: began 'Felix the Cat' series with Messmer at Pathé; then with Ideal Film Company. 1925–28: 78 Felix the Cat titles copyrighted. 1933: Sullivan died; Felix continued by Messmer until 1935. In 1940's, Messmer worked on 'Little Lulu' series for Dave Fleischer's studio.

SUMMERS, Manuel

Director. Seville, Spain 1935–
Family of English origin, son of painter Francisco Summers. Abandoned law studies. Art and drama in San Fernando. Moved to Madrid: Escuela de Bellas Artes; Instituto de Investigaçao e Experiencias Cinematograficas; Escuela Official de Cinematografia, 1958–59: first 2 films as director, both shorts, while student. 1960: graduated. Worked in TV, then as cartoonist for newspaper Pueblo, returned to TV. 1963: first feature *Del Rosa ... al Amarillo*. 1970: *Urtain, el Rey de la selva humana* distributed in Spain by Warners.

Films as director: 1958: El Muertin. 1959: El Viejecito. 1963: Del Rosa ... al Amarillo – The Rose and the Gold; La Niña de luto – The Girl in Mourning. 1964: El Juego de la oca (+ *co-s*). 1966: Juguetes Rotos – Broken Toys (+ *s*). 1968: No Somos de piedra – We're Not Made of Stone; Por que te engaña tu marido? Why Does Your Husband Leave You? (+ *co-s*). 1970: Urtain, el Rey de la selva humana – Urtain, His Family, His Friends.

SURTEES, Robert L.

Cinematographer. Covington, Kentucky 1906–
1927–29: assistant cameraman at Universal, including a period in Berlin. From 1930: cinematographer, worked for Warners, Pathé. 1943–62: cinematographer with MGM. Then for various companies. Oscars for colour cinematography *King Solomon's Mines* (1950), black-and-white cinematography *The Bad and the Beautiful* (1952).

Films as cinematographer include: 1944: Thirty Seconds Over Tokyo (*co*). 1945: Our Vines Have Tender Grapes. 1948: The Kissing Bandit; Act of Violence. 1949: Intruder in the Dust. 1951: The Light Touch; Quo Vadis (*co*); Mogambo (*co*); Escape from Fort Bravo. 1954: The Long, Long Trailer. 1955: Trial; Oklahoma!. 1956: The Swan (*co*); Tribute to a Bad Man. 1957: Les Girls; Raintree County. 1958: Merry Andrew; The Law and Jake Wade. 1959: Ben-Hur. 1960: Cimarron. 1962: Mutiny on the Bounty. 1964: The Collector (*co*). 1967: Doctor Dolittle; The Graduate. 1969: The Arrangement. 1970: The Liberation of L. B. Jones. 1971: Summer of '42.

SWANSON, Gloria

Actress. Chicago 1898–
Father US Army Captain. 1913: started as actress at Essanay. 1915: first credit on *The Fable of Elvira and Farina and the Meal Ticket*; abandoned plans to leave films and become a singer. 1916–17: worked for Sennett at Triangle-Keystone. 1918–21: under contract to Cecil B. De Mille. 1921: Paramount contract: made 10 films in 2 years. 1924: to France for *Madame Sans-Gêne* (1925). Turned down new Paramount contract. 1926: organised own company, releasing through United Artists. 1927: first film for own company, *The Love of Sunya*. Company financed and advised by Joseph P. Kennedy. 1928: on his advice *Queen Kelly* not released. 1932: dissolved company, left United Artists. Subsequently worked in films only occasionally. Toured in play 'Reflected Glory'; on Broadway and on tour in 'A Goose for the Gander'. 1948: 'Gloria Swanson Hour' on New York TV. 1956: last film. Five husbands include Wallace Beery (1916–19).

Films as actress include: 1916: Haystacks and Steeples. 1918: You Can't Believe Everything; Don't Change Your Husband. 1919: For Better, For Worse; Male and Female. 1920: Why Change Your Wife. 1921: The Affairs of Anatol; Under the Lash. 1922: Beyond the Rocks. 1923: Bluebeard's Eighth Wife; Prodigal Daughters; Zaza. 1924: A Society Scandal; Manhandled; Her Love Story; Wages of Virtue. 1925: Coast of Folly; Madame Sans-Gêne; Stage Struck. 1926: The Untamed Lady. 1928: Sadie Thompson; Queen Kelly (*ur*). 1929: The Trespasser. 1930: What a

Widow. 1931: Indiscreet; Tonight or Never. 1934: Music in the Air. 1950: Sunset Boulevard. 1956: Mio Figlio Nerone.

SWERLING, Jo (Joseph S.)

Writer. Russia 1894–
Journalist, playwright. Co-wrote play 'The Kibitzer' (1929) with Edward G. Robinson, filmed 1930; play 'The Understander' filmed as *Melody Lane* (1929). 1930: first film as writer, dialogue of *Around the Corner*. To 1936: almost all films for Columbia, many early films produced by Harry Cohn, many co-written with Dorothy Howell. Subsequently worked for numerous studios, including Fox, United Artists. 1950: co-wrote musical play 'Guys and Dolls,' filmed 1955. Work in TV includes episodes of 'The Lord Don't Play Favorites'; also producer e.g. on 'Bold Ones'.

Films as writer include: 1930: Ladies of Leisure (*ad/di*); Rain or Shine (*co-s/di*). 1931: Dirigible (*ad/di*); Ten Cents a Dance (*st/di*); The Miracle Woman; Platinum Blonde (*ad*). 1932: Washington Merry-Go-Round. 1933: Man's Castle. 1934: No Greater Glory. 1935: The Whole Town's Talking; Love Me Forever (*co*). 1936: The Music Goes 'Round; Pennies from Heaven. 1937: Double Wedding. 1938: Dr Rhythm (*co*). 1939: Made for Each Other; The Real Glory (*co*). 1940: The Westerner (*co*). 1941: Blood and Sand; Confirm or Deny. 1942: The Pride of the Yankees (*co*). 1943: Crash Dive. 1944: Lifeboat. 1946: Leave Her to Heaven. 1953: Thunder in the East.

SWIFT, David

Director. Minneapolis, Minnesota 1919–
World War II: served with 8th Air Force in England. Joined Walt Disney's animation studios. Wrote radio shows e.g. for Bob Hope. From 1949: TV work e.g. wrote 'Kraft Theatre', 'Studio One'; directed episodes of 'Wagon Train', 'Climax'. 1960: wrote first film as director, for Walt Disney. From 1962: worked mainly for Columbia. From 1964: also produced.

Films as director: 1960: Pollyanna (+ *s*). 1961: The Parent Trap (+ *s*). 1962: The Interns (+ *co-s*). 1963: Love is a Ball – All This and Money Too (+ *co-s*); Under the Yum Yum Tree (+ *co-s*). 1964: Good Neighbour Sam (+ *p/co-s*). 1967: How to Succeed in Business Without Really Trying (+ *p/s*).

T

TALMADGE, Constance

Actress. Brooklyn, New York 1900–
Sisters are actresses Norma and Natalie Talmadge. 1914: first film as actress *In the Latin Quarter*. 1917–19: mainly worked for Select. From 1919: worked mainly for First National. 1919–22: films with John Emerson and Anita Loos, as either writers or directors.

Films as actress include: 1916: Intolerance. 1917: Scandal. 1918: A Pair of Silk Stockings. 1919: A Temperamental Wife; The Virtuous Vamp. 1920: Two Weeks; The Love Expert. 1921: The Perfect Woman.

1922: Polly of the Follies; The Primitive Lover (+pc); East is West (+pc). 1924: Her Night of Romance. 1927: Venus of Venice; Breakfast at Sunrise. 1929: Venus.

TALMADGE, Norma

Actress. Niagara Falls 1897–1957 Las Vegas
Sisters are actresses Constance and Natalie Talmadge. 1911: at 14, first film as actress *The Four Poster Pest*. More than 200 silent films. Radio work with George Jessel. Married producer Joseph M. Schenk, and George Jessel.

Films as actress include: 1913: Under the Daisies. 1914: Goodbye Summer. 1915: The Battle Cry of Peace; The Criminal. 1917: Panthea; Poppy. 1918: The Forbidden City. 1919: The Probation Wife (+pc). 1920: The Branded Woman. 1921: The Sign on the Door. 1922: Smiling Through; The Eternal Flame. 1923: Ashes of Vengeance. 1924: The Song of Love; Secrets. 1925: The Lady. 1926: Kiki. 1927: Camille. 1928: The Dove; The Woman Disputed. 1930: New York Nights.

TAMIROFF, Akim

Actor. Baku, Russia 1899–
University and drama school in Moscow. 1923: went to USA on acting tour, and remained there. Worked as actor in theatre and nightclubs. 1933: first film appearance for MGM. 1938: first leading part in *The Buccaneer* for Paramount.

Films as actor include: 1934: Queen Christina; Sadie McKee; Chained; The Captain Hates the Sea. 1935: Naughty Marietta; Lives of a Bengal Lancer; Black Fury; Paris in Spring; China Seas; The Gay Deception; Two Fisted; The Story of Louis Pasteur. 1936: Desire; Anthony Adverse; The General Died at Dawn. 1937: King of Gamblers; The Great Gambini; High, Wide and Handsome. 1938: The Buccaneer; Spawn of the North. 1939: Union Pacific; The Magnificent Fraud; Disputed Passage. 1940: The Great McGinty; Northwest Mounted Police. 1941: New York Town. 1942: Tortilla Flat. 1943: Five Graves to Cairo; For Whom the Bell Tolls; His Butler's Sister. 1944: The Miracle of Morgan's Creek; Dragon Seed. 1946: A Scandal in Paris. 1948: My Girl Tisa. 1954: They Who Dare. 1955: Confidential Report. 1958: Touch of Evil; Me and the Colonel. 1960: Ocean's 11. 1961: Romanoff and Juliet. 1963: Le Procès. 1964: Topkapi. 1965: Le Bambole *ep* Monsignor Cupido; Alphaville, une étrange aventure de Lemmy Caution; Lord Jim; Marie-Chantal contre le docteur Kha; Campanadas a medianoche; Una Rosa per tutti. 1970: Sabra.

TARADASH, Daniel

Writer. Louisville, Kentucky 1913–
Graduated from Harvard (1933) and Harvard Law School (1936). 1937: passed New York State Bar exam but never practised. 1938: won first prize in a playwriting contest; hired by Columbia to collaborate on screenplay of *Golden Boy*. Officer in US Signal Corps; wrote training and industrial incentive films. 1956: directed *Storm Center* from own story and script in collaboration. 1971: president of AMPAS. Oscar for screenplay, *From Here to Eternity* (1953).

Films as writer include: 1949: Knock on Any Door (co). 1952: Rancho Notorious. 1953: From Here to Eternity. 1954: Desiree. 1955: Picnic. 1958: Bell, Book and Candle. 1965: The Saboteur—Code Name Morituri. 1966: Hawaii (co). 1968: Castle Keep (co).

TASHLIN, Frank

Director. Weehawken, New Jersey 1913–
Left school at 13. 1926–27: worked as newspaper seller, butcher's errand boy, junior employee in a brassière factory; took correspondence course in drawing. 1928: errand boy for Max Fleischer in New York. 1930: worked on *Aesop's Fables* cartoon series for RKO in New York, becoming animator. 1930–36: sold cartoons to leading picture magazines under pseudonym of Tish-Tash. 1933: to Hollywood as animator with Leon Schlesinger who was producing 'Merrie Melodies' and 'Looney Tunes' series for Warners. 1935: animator on 'Flip the Frog' series for MGM, then gagman and scriptwriter for Hal Roach at MGM e.g. Laurel and Hardy, Thelma Todd, Charlie Chase, 'Our Gang' series. Became writer and director on 'Merrie Melodies' and 'Looney Tunes' (including Porky Pig cartoons of which he subsequently directed one a month). 1939: joined Walt Disney as story director. 1941: executive in charge of production at Screen Gems studio (Columbia); supervised 3 teams producing 39 cartoons a year. From 1942: wrote and directed more 'Looney Tunes' (e.g. Porky Pig) and 'Merrie Melodies' (e.g. Bugs Bunny). 1944: first feature film as writer in collaboration; wrote and directed puppet series for United Artists. From 1945: anonymous gagman for Harpo Marx miming in *A Night in Casablanca* (1946), then gagman contract with Paramount e.g. on *Monsieur Beaucaire* (1946). 1947: wrote and directed puppet film *The Way of Peace*, made by Wartburg Press for the Lutheran Church. 1947–50: worked as writer usually in collaboration. 1951: first feature as director (uncredited) in collaboration. Has directed for various companies notably Paramount and Fox. Also radio scripts e.g. 'Eddie Bracken Show'; produced and directed for NBC and CBS TV e.g. 'Jack Benny Show', 'G-E Theatre'. Author of 4 picture books, 'The Bear that Wasn't', 'The Possum that Didn't' (published in London), 'The World that Isn't', 'The Turtle that Couldn't' published in New York. 1968: wrote story in collaboration of Alan Rafkin's *The Shakiest Gun in the West*.

Features as writer include: 1947: Variety Girl (co-st/co-s). 1948: The Paleface (co-st/co-s). 1949: Miss Grant Takes Richmond (co). 1950: Love Happy (co); Kill the Umpire (+st); The Good Humor Man; The Fuller Brush Girl. 1956: The Scarlet Hour (co-st/co-s).

Features as director, and writer in collaboration. 1951: The Lemon Drop Kid (uc, co-d Sidney Lanfield). 1952: The First Time; Son of Paleface. 1953: Marry Me Again (s alone). 1954: Susan Slept Here (uc, co-s). 1955: Artists and Models; The Lieutenant Wore Skirts. 1956: Hollywood or Bust (uc, co-s); The Girl Can't Help It (+p). 1957: Will Success Spoil Rock Hunter? – Oh for a Man! (+p/s alone). 1958: Rock-a-Bye Baby (s alone); The Geisha Boy (s alone). 1959: Say One for Me (+p/uc, co-s). 1960: Cinderfella (s alone). 1961: Bachelor Flat. 1962: It's Only Money (uc, co-s). 1963: The Man from the Diner's Club (d only); Who's

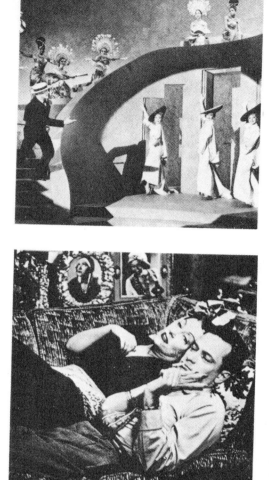

Les Girls, *directed by George Cukor and photographed by Robert L. Surtees.*
Gloria Swanson and William Holden in Billy Wilder's Sunset Boulevard.
Jacques Tati (left) in his own film, Les Vacances de Monsieur Hulot.

Minding the Store? 1964: The Disorderly Orderly (*s alone*). 1966: The Alphabet Murders (*d only*); The Glass Bottom Boat (*d only*). 1967: Caprice. 1968: The Private Navy of Sgt O'Farrell (*s alone*).

TATI, Jacques (Jacques Tatischeff)

Director, writer and actor. Pecq, France 1907–
Family of Russian descent; father a picture-frame maker. Educated in Paris. Played rugby for Racing Club de France. Travelled with father, then stage début in Paris cabaret (1931). Mime act. 1932–38: wrote, and acted in, 5 shorts. 1945–47: small roles in films directed by Claude Autant-Lara, *Sylvie et le fantôme* and *Le Diable au corps*. 1947: first film as director, writer and actor *L'Ecole des facteurs,* elaborated into first feature as director, writer in collaboration and actor *Jour de fête.* Own production company.

Short films as writer and actor: 1932: Oscar champion de tennis. 1934: On demande une brute (*co-s*). 1935: Gai Dimanche (*co-s/co-di*). 1936: Soigne ton gauche. 1938: Retour à la terre.

Films as director, writer in collaboration and actor: 1947: L'Ecole des facteurs (*s/st*). 1949: Jour de fête (*+ co-st*). 1953: Les Vacances de M Hulot – Mr Hulot's Holiday (*+ co-st*). 1958: Mon Oncle (*d/st/s*). 1967: Playtime (*+ co-st*). 1971: Trafic (*+ s/w*).

TAUROG, Norman

Director. Chicago 1899–
Began as stage actor at 13. From 1913: appeared as actor in films; then worked as property man. 1920–21: began directing and writing 2-reelers in collaboration with Larry Semon for Vitagraph (for titles *see* SEMON, Larry). 1924–28: directed over 45 2-reelers for Educational Films. 1929: first feature as director, *The Diplomats,* for Fox. 1929–30: director with Tiffany-Stahl, then Tiffany Productions. 1931–36: with Paramount. 1936–37: with Fox. 1938–51: mainly with MGM. 1952–60: returned to Paramount e.g. Dean Martin/Jerry Lewis films. Thereafter with various companies. Oscar for direction, *Skippy* (1930–31).

Features as director include: 1929: Lucky Boy (*co-d Charles C. Wilson*). 1931: Finn and Hattie (*co-d Norman Z. McLeod*); Huckleberry Finn; Skippy. 1932: Hold 'em Jail; If I Had a Million *ep* The Auto. 1934: We're Not Dressing; Mrs Wiggs of the Cabbage Patch. 1935: The Big Broadcast of 1936. 1936: Strike Me Pink (*co-d Robert Alton*); Reunion; Rhythm on the Range. 1937: Fifty Roads to Town; You Can't Have Everything. 1938: The Adventures of Tom Sawyer; Mad about Music; Boy's Town. 1939: Lucky Night. 1940: Young Tom Edison; Little Nellie Kelly, Broadway Melody of 1940. 1942: A Yank at Eton. 1943: Presenting Lily Mars; Girl Crazy. 1946: The Hoodlum Saint. 1948: The Bride Goes Wild; Big City; Words and Music. 1949: That Midnight Kiss. 1950: Please Believe Me. 1951: Rich, Young and Pretty. 1952: Room for One More. 1953: The Caddy. 1954: Living it Up. 1956: Bundle of Joy; The Birds and the Bees; Pardners. 1957: The Fuzzy Pink Nightgown. 1959: Don't Give up the Ship. 1960: Visit to a Small Planet; GI Blues. 1961: Blue Hawaii. 1963: Palm Springs Weekend. 1965: Tickle Me; Dr Goldfoot and the Bikini Machine; Sergeant Deadhead the Astronaut. 1966: Spinout—California Holiday.

TAVIANI brothers

Directors. Vittorio Taviani: Pisa, Italy 1930– ; Paolo Taviani: Pisa, Italy 1932–
Have always worked in collaboration. Began as critics and film club organisers. From 1948: long collaboration with Valentino Orsini with whom they ran the Teatro della Cronaco for the workers at the port of Leghorn. 1943: made first short film, *San Miniato, luglio 1944.* Several subsequent shorts. Assisted Luciano Emmer, Roberto Rossellini, Piero Nelli; with Orsini assisted Joris Ivens on direction of *L'Italia non è un paese povero* (1959). 1962: made first feature film.

Features as directors and writers (in collaboration with Valentino Orsini until 1963): 1962: Un Uomo da bruciare – A Man for Burning. 1963: I Fuorilegge del matrimonio (*+ co-st/co-s*). 1967: Sovversivi. 1968: Sotto il segno dello scorpione (*+ st*). 1971: San Michele aveva un gallo.

TAYLOR, Elizabeth

Actress. London 1932–
American parents, art dealer Francis Taylor and actress Sara Sothern. Ballet lessons under Vaccani at 3. World War II: at 7 evacuated to Pasadena, California. 1942: first film appearance in Harold Young's *There's One Born Every Minute,* for Universal. 1943: leading part as child actress in *Lassie Come Home* and long-term contract with MGM. Worked mainly for MGM. Husbands include (1952–57) actor Michael Wilding; (1957–58) Michael Todd; (1959–64) singer Eddie Fisher; (from 1964) Richard Burton. Wrote and illustrated children's book 'Nibbles and Me'. Oscars for best actress, *Butterfield 8* (1960), *Who's Afraid of Virginia Woolf?* (1966).

Films as actress include: 1944: Jane Eyre; The White Cliffs of Dover; National Velvet. 1947: Life with Father. 1948: Julia Misbehaves. 1949: Little Women. 1950: Father of the Bride. 1951: Father's Little Dividend; A Place in the Sun. 1952: Ivanhoe. 1954: Rhapsody; Elephant Walk; The Last Time I Saw Paris. 1956: Giant. 1957: Raintree County. 1958: Cat on a Hot Tin Roof. 1959: Suddenly Last Summer. 1963: Cleopatra; The VIPs. 1965: The Sandpiper. 1967: The Taming of the Shrew; Reflections in a Golden Eye; The Comedians. 1968: Dr Faustus; Boom; Secret Ceremony.

TAYLOR, Gilbert

Cinematographer. London 1914–
Camera assistant at 15. Became cinematographer during 1940s. 1954: special effects for *The Dambusters.*

Films as cinematographer include: 1948: The Guinea Pig. 1950: Seven Days to Noon. 1953: Singlehanded; The Weak and the Wicked. 1954: Seagulls over Sorrento. 1955: As Long as They're Happy; Josephine and Men. 1956: Yield to the Night; The Good Companions. 1957: Woman in a Dressing Gown. 1958: Ice Cold in Alex. 1962: It's Trad Dad! 1963: Dr Strangelove or, How I Learned to Stop Worrying and Love the Bomb. 1964: A Hard Day's Night; Hide and Seek. 1965: Repulsion; The Bedford Incident. 1966: Cul-de-Sac. 1969: Before Winter Comes. 1971: Macbeth.

TAYLOR, Robert

(Spangler Arlington Brough) Actor. Filley, Nebraska 1911–69 Santa Monica, California
College dramatics. Spotted by MGM talent scout. 1934: first film *Handy Andy.* 1939: married Barbara Stanwyck (divorced 1952). War service: flight instructor and director of training films. 1961: TV series, 'The Detectives'. Married actress Ursula Thiess. To 1955: almost all films for MGM.

Films as actor include: 1935: Buried Loot; Society Doctor; Times Square Lady; Broadway Melody of 1936; Magnificent Obsession. 1936: Small Town Girl; The Gorgeous Hussy; Private Number; His Brother's Wife; Camille. 1937: Broadway Melody of 1938; Personal Property. 1938: ·A Yank at Oxford; Three Comrades; The Crowd Roars; Stand Up and Fight. 1939: Lady of the Tropics; Remember?; Lucky Night. 1940: Waterloo Bridge; Escape; Flight Command. 1941: Billy the Kid; When Ladies Meet; Johnny Eager. 1942: Her Cardboard Lover; Stand By for Action. 1943: Bataan. 1944: Song of Russia. 1946: Undercurrent. 1948: The High Wall. 1949: The Bribe; Conspirator; Ambush. 1950: Devil's Doorway; Quo Vadis. 1951: Westward the Woman. 1952: Ivanhoe; Above and Beyond. 1953: Ride, Vaquero!; Knights of the Round Table; All the Brothers Were Valiant. 1954: Rogue Cop. 1955: Many Rivers to Cross; Quentin Durward. 1956: The Last Hunt; D-Day, the Sixth of June. 1957: Tip on a Dead Jockey. 1958: The Law and Jake Wade; Saddle The Wind; Party Girl. 1959: House of the Seven Hawks; The Hangman. 1960: Killers of Kilimanjaro. 1963: Cattle King. 1964: A House is Not a Home; The Night Walker. 1966: Pampa Salvaje; Johnny Tiger. 1968: Where Angels Go, Trouble Follows.

TAZIEFF, Haroun

Director. Varsovie, Poland 1914–
Began as agronomic engineer, then geologist specialising in volcanoes. Recorded all his expeditions on 16 mm, some only privately circulated or never shown. From 1952: 35 mm shorts. 1958: first feature-length documentary. 1960: formed production company, La Société Ciné-Documentó–Tazieff. Author of books, 'Cratères en feu', 'L'Eau et le feu', 'L'Enigme de la Pierre-Saint-Martin', 'Les Volcans'.

Films as director include: pre-1952: Records au gouffre de la Pierre-Saint-Martin; Stromboli; L'Eruption de l'Etna; Au milieu des cratères en feu. 1952: Grêle de feu. 1957: Eaux Souterraines. 1958: Les Rendez-vous du diable – Volcano (*+ co-p*). 1959: L'Exploration du lac de lave du Niragongo (*+p*). 1965: Le Volcan Interdit – Forbidden Volcano.

TEMPLE, Shirley

Actress. Santa Monica, California, 1929–
1932: first film as actress *Red Haired Alibi.* 1933: star in Educational Studios' 'Baby Burlesque Series'. 1934: first major part in a feature, *Stand up and Cheer*; under contract to Fox until 1940. Top of Motion Picture Herald box-office poll, 1936, '37, '38. 1940: Retired as child actress but returned to play a few teenage parts. TV: narrated own children's 'Storybook' series (1947) and (1960) hostess on 'Shirley Temple Show'. 1950: retired from films; became primarily

involved in charitable activities. Nominated to run as Republican candidate for Congress (1967). Special Oscar for 'her outstanding contribution to screen entertainment' during 1934. 1945–49: married to John Agar.

Films as actress include: 1934: Stand up and Cheer; Bright Eyes. 1935: The Little Colonel; Now and Forever; The Littlest Rebel. 1936: Captain January; Poor Little Rich Girl; Dimples. 1937: Wee Willie Winkie; Heidi. 1938: Little Miss Broadway; Rebecca of Sunnybrook Farm. 1939: The Little Princess. 1940: The Blue Bird. 1941: Kathleen. 1942: Miss Annie Rooney. 1947: The Bachelor and the Bobbysoxer. 1948: Fort Apache.

TESHIGAHARA, Hiroshi

Director. Tokyo 1927–
Father floral artist Sofu Teshigahara. Studied painting at Tokyo Art Institute. Wrote film criticism. 1953: made first documentary film. Assisted on 2 shorts. 1961: made first feature for own company. *Suna no Onna* (1964) also made independently, taken up by Toho. Contributed to multi-screen films at Osaka Festival (1970).

Films as director: 1953: Hokusai. 1957: Sofu Teshigahara. 1959: José Torres. 1961: Otoshi Ana – Pitfall – A Cheap Sweet and a Kid. 1964: Suna no Onna – Woman of the Dunes; La Fleur de l'âge ou les adolescentes *ep* Ako. 1965: Tanin no Kao – The Face of Another (+*p*). 1967: Bakuso – Explosion Course. 1968: Moetsukita Chizu – The Man Without a Map.

TESSARI, Duccio

Director and writer. Genoa 1926–
Chemistry at university. Documentary work in Genoa. 1958: in Germany; in collaboration with Wolfgang Staudte wrote *Kanonen-serenade*. 1959–63: writer in Rome; all scripts written in collaboration. 1962: first film as director. Also work in theatre, TV, journalism.

Films as writer in collaboration include: 1958: Kanonen-serenade. 1959: Cartagine Infiamme; Messalina, Venere Imperatrice; Gli Ultimi Giorni di Pompeii. 1960: La Vendetta di Ercole. 1961: Il Colosso di Rodi; Ercole alla conquista di Atlantide; Ercole al centro della terra; Maciste alla corto del Gran Khan; Marco Polo; Le Meraviglie di Aladino.

Films as director and writer: 1962: Arrivano I titani – Sons of Thunder (*co-s*). 1963: Il Fornaretto di Venezia. 1964: La Sfinga e sorride prima di morire, Stop—Londra. 1965: Una Voglio da morire; Una Pistola per Ringo – A Pistol for Ringo; Il Ritorno di Ringo – The Return of Ringo (*co-s*). 1967: Kiss Kiss … Bang Bang; Per amore … per magia – For Love … For Magic. 1968: Meglio vedova – Better a Widow (*co-s*); I Bastardi – Sons of Satan – The Cats (*co-s*). 1969: Vivi o preferibilmente morti (*co-s*); Matchball (*co-s*); Quella Piccola Differenza – That Little Difference (*co-s*). 1970: Forza G (*co-s*); La Morte risale a ieri sera – Death Occurred Last Night (*co-s*).

TETZLAFF, Ted

Director and cinematographer. Los Angeles 1903–
Began in photographic laboratory. 1922–27: in camera department at Fox. Cinematographer from 1927; with Columbia until 1933. Then with various companies including Paramount where he directed first film (1941). Continued as cinematographer until 1946. World War II: 2 years in USAAF, Major. 1945–50: with RKO as cinematographer then director. Then director with various companies.

Films as cinematographer include: 1929: The Younger Generation; The Donovan Affair. 1934: Fugitive Lovers. 1935: Paris in Spring. 1936: My Man Godfrey. 1938: Fools for Scandal. 1940: Remember the Night. 1941: The Road to Zanzibar. 1942: I Married a Witch. 1945: The Enchanted Cottage. 1946: Notorious.

Films as director: 1941: World Premiere. 1947: Riff Raff. 1948: Fighting Father Dunne. 1949: The Window; Johnny Allegro; A Dangerous Profession. 1950: The White Tower; Under the Gun. 1951: Gambling House; The Treasure of Lost Canyon. 1953: Terror on a Train – Time Bomb. 1955: Son of Sinbad. 1956: Seven Wonders of the World (*co-d 4 others*). 1957: The Young Land.

TEWKESBURY, Peter

Director. 1924–
Children's radio in California. Moved to TV; work as director included series 'It's a Man's World', 'My Three Sons', 'Peoples' Choice', 'Father Knows Best' and 'The Johnny Carson Show'. 1963: first film as director.

Films as director: 1963: Sunday in New York. 1964: Emil and the Detectives. 1967: Doctor, You've Got to be Kidding. 1968: Stay Away Joe. 1969: The Trouble with Girls.

THALBERG, Irving G.

Producer and studio head. New York 1899–1936 Hollywood
Father a Brooklyn lace importer. 1917: began in films as secretary at Universal's New York office. 1919: to Hollywood as Carl Laemmle's private secretary. 1920: general manager of Universal City. 1923: joined Louis B. Mayer as head of production. 1924: on merger with Metro and Goldwyn, became second-in-command of MGM production under Mayer. Controlled MGM's artistic policy in 1920s and '30s; fostered talents of diverse team of contract directors e.g. Clarence Brown, Sidney Franklin, Jack Conway, W. S. Van Dyke, Sam Wood, Victor Fleming; introduced the concept of the 'prestige picture'. Running battle with Erich von Stroheim whom he first met at Universal; executive producer on *Greed* (1923) and responsible with Mayer for having it cut down to what they regarded as a commercially manageable length. Argued box office potential of *The Big Parade* (1927) for which he got larger budget. Backed *Freaks* (1932) against considerable opposition. Worked closely with directors discussing scripts, attending rehearsals of major scenes, even re-editing after previews; but name appears as producer on very few films e.g. *A Night at the Opera* (1935), *Romeo and Juliet* (1936). Died of pneumonia; left widow Norma Shearer (married 1927). Last production (uncredited) *The Good Earth* (1937) carried foreword 'To the memory of Irving Grant Thalberg we dedicate this picture – his last great achievement'. 1937:

Un Uomo da Bruciare, *directed by Valentino Orsini and the Taviani brothers (Paolo and Vittorio Taviani). Elizabeth Taylor in Joseph L. Mankiewicz's* Cleopatra. Sunday in New York, *directed by Peter Tewkesbury.*

Academy of Motion Picture Arts and Sciences introduced new Oscar, the Irving G. Thalberg Memorial Award for distinguished production.

THEODORAKIS, Mikis

Composer. Chios, Greece 1925–

Athens Conservatory, Paris Conservatory. 1943: joined Resistance. 1947–52: arrested and deported during Greek Civil War. 1953: to Paris, studied under Oliver Messiaen. 1954: first public concert, in Paris. 1956: first major film score *Ill Met by Moonlight*. Ballet music for 'Antigone' and 'Les Amants de Teruel'. 1961: returned to Greece; first prize in Athens popular song festival. 1963: leader of Lambrakis youth movement; member of parliament. 1967–70: arrested for political activities. 1970: world tour of 80 concerts. Music for National Theatre of Greece; numerous songs, other compositions.

Films as composer include: 1958: Luna di miel. 1962: Les Amants de Teruel (*co*); Elektra; Phaedra. 1964: Zorba the Greek. 1968: Z. 1971: The Trojan Women.

THIELE, Rolf

Director. Redlice, Czechoslovakia 1918–

Studied in Berlin and Prague, then sociology at University of Göttingen. After World War II formed own production company with Hans Abich. Several films as producer, including Rudolf Jugert's *Es kommt ein Tag* (1950) which he co-wrote with Thea von Harbou and Hans Abich. 1951: produced own first film as director.

Films as director include: 1954: Sie (*+p/s*). 1955: Die Barrings (*+co-s*). 1956: Friederike von Barring (*+s*). 1958: Das Mädchen Rosemarie (*+co-s*). 1959: Labyrinth der Leidenschaft (*+co-s*). 1962: Lulu – No Orchids for Lulu (*+s*). 1963: Moral '63 (*+s*). 1964: DM-Killer (*+co-s*); Tonio Kröger. 1965: Das Liebeskarussell (*2 parts*). 1967: Der Lügner und die Nonne – The Liar and the Nun (*co-d Joseph Czech*). 1969: Ohrfeigen (*+s*).

THIRARD, Armand

Cinematographer. Mantes, France 1899–

Active service towards end of World War I, then still photographer. Entered film industry as actor, then production manager, becoming a camera operator at end of silent period.

Films as cinematographer include: 1932: Poil de Carotte. 1937: Gribouille (*co*). 1938: Hotel du Nord (*co*). 1942: L'Assassin habite au 21. 1946: La Symphonie Pastorale. 1947: Quai des Orfèvres; Le Silence est d'or. 1949: Manon. 1952: Les Belles de nuit. 1953: Le Salaire de la peur. 1955: Les Diaboliques. 1956: Et Dieu créa la femme. 1957: Sait-on jamais?. 1958: Les Bijoutiers du clair de lune. 1960: La Vérité. 1961: Goodbye Again. 1963: Le Repos du guerrier. 1964: Château en Suède; La Fabuleuse Aventure de Marco Polo. 1968: La Bataille de San Sebastian.

THOMAS, Ralph

Director. Hull, Yorkshire 1915–

Brother of director Gerald Thomas. Began as journalist. 1932: entered films as clapper boy at Sound City studios. 1934: assistant editor with British Lion, becoming editor. World War II: served in 9th Lancers. 1946–49: at Denham Studios in charge of trailer production for Rank. 1949: first feature as director. Films usually produced by Betty E. Box for Rank.

Films as director include: 1950: The Clouded Yellow. 1954: Doctor in the House. 1955: Above Us the Waves. 1957: Campbell's Kingdom. 1958: A Tale of Two Cities. 1959: The Thirty-Nine Steps. 1960: Conspiracy of Hearts. 1961: No Love for Johnnie; No, My Darling Daughter. 1962: The Wild and the Willing. 1964: The High Bright Sun. 1968: Nobody Runs Forever. 1970: Doctor in Trouble. 1971: Percy.

THOMPSON, J. Lee

Director. Bristol, Gloucestershire 1914–

1931–34: actor with the Nottingham Repertory Company; wrote 3 plays including 'Double Error', 'Murder Happened' both performed in London. 1934: began in films as actor; joined British International as writer. 1939: original script for Harold Huth's *East of Piccadilly*. World War II: radar operator, RAF. 1945: returned to films as writer e.g. on *For Them That Trespass* (1949). 1950: first film as director. Some American films.

Films as director: 1950: Murder Without Crime (*+st/s*). 1952: The Yellow Balloon (*+s*). 1953: The Weak and the Wicked (*+co-s*). 1954: For Better for Worse – Cocktails in the Kitchen (*+s*). 1955: As Long as They're Happy; An Alligator Named Daisy. 1956: Yield to the Night – Blonde Sinner; The Good Companions (*+co-p*). 1957: Woman in a Dressing Gown (*+co-p*). 1958: Ice Cold in Alex; No Trees in the Street (*+pc*). 1959: Tiger Bay; North West Frontier – Flame Over India. 1960: I Aim at the Stars. 1961: The Guns of Navarone; Cape Fear. 1962: Taras Bulba. 1963: Kings of the Sun. 1964: What a Way to Go; John Goldfarb, Please Come Home. 1965: Return from the Ashes (*+p*). 1966: Eye of the Devil. 1968: Before Winter Comes. 1969: The Chairman – The Most Dangerous Man in the World; Mackenna's Gold; Country Dance (*r 1971*).

THOMPSON, Virgil

Composer. Kansas City, Missouri 1896–

World War I: US Army service. Then studied at Harvard, and in Paris under Nadia Boulanger. Organist and choir-master in Boston; wrote music criticism for Vanity Fair and New York Herald-Tribune. After opera 'Four Saints in Three Acts' his work included occasional film scores.

Films as composer include: 1936: The Plow that Broke The Plains. 1937: The River; Spanish Earth (*co*). 1948: Louisiana Story. 1958: The Goddess.

THORNDIKE, Andrew *and* Annelie

Directors. Andrew: Frankfurt, Germany 1909– ; Annelie: Klützow, Germany 1925–

Andrew at first artist; became main representative for Ufa. 1942: soldier on eastern front, taken prisoner. 1948: to East Germany, joined DEFA. 1949: first film as director. 1950: directed *Der Weg nach Oben* written by Annelie, a teacher before becoming DEFA writer. From 1952: all films in collaboration, beginning with *Die Prüfung*. 1953: they married.

Andrew: films as director: 1949: Der Dreizehn Oktober; Aus unseren Tage *ep* Von Hamburg bis Stralsund (*+s*). 1950: Der Weg nach Oben (*+c*). 1951: Wilhelm Pieck-das Leben unseres Präsidenten (*+s*). 1952: Die Entfuhrung.

Andrew and Annelie: films as directors and writers in collaboration: 1952: Der Prüfung. 1954: Sieben vom Rhein. 1956: Du und mancher Kamerad – The German Story. 1957: Urlaub auf Sylt – Holiday on Sylt; General Speidel. 1958: Unternehmen Teutonenschwert. 1963: Das Russische Wunder – The Russian Miracle (*2 parts*). 1965: Tito in Deutschland. 1969: Du bist mein, ein Deutsches Tagebuch – A German Diary.

THORPE, Richard

(Rollo Smolt Thorpe) Director. Hutchinson, Kansas 1896–

Vaudeville, musical comedy until military service in World War I, then revue in Paris. Worked in films as gagman, actor, editor, art director. Extra for D. W. Griffith. Prop man, editor, assistant director on Johnny Hines comedies. 1923: first film as director for All Star Comedies. 1924–35: directed over 100 films for numerous companies including Artclass, Pathe, Tiffany, Chesterfield, Universal. 1935–65: worked for MGM.

Films as director: 1923: 3 O'Clock in the Morning. 1924: Rough Ridin'; Battling Buddy; Rarin' to Go; Fast and Fearless; Hard Hittin' Hamilton; Walloping Wallace; Rip Roarin' Roberts; Bringin' Home the Bacon; Gold and Grit. 1925: Thundering Romance; Fast Fightin'; On the Go; Tearin' Loose; Double Action Daniels. 1926: A Streak of Luck; Desert Demon; Trumpin' Trouble; Galloping On; The Fighting Cheat; Quicker 'n Lightnin'; Easy Going; Deuce High; Double Daring; Coming an' Going; The Roaring Rider; Speedy Spurs; Twin Triggers; Riding Rivals; The Saddle Cyclone; The Last Card; Rawhide; The Dangerous Dub; Bonanza Buckaroo; Twisted Triggers; College Days; Joselyn's Wife; The Bandit Busters (*+s*); The Cyclone Cowboy; A Soda Water Cowboy; Roarin' Broncs. 1927: The Ridin' Rowdy; The Galloping Gobs; The First Night; Tearin' into Trouble; Between Dangers; The Meddlin' Stranger; Skedaddle Gold; White Pebbles; The Obligin' Buckaroo; Ride 'em High; Pals in Peril; The Interferin' Gent. 1928: The Vanishing West (*10 eps*); Vultures of the Sea (*10 eps*); Desperate Courage; Cowboy Cavalier; The Ballyhoo Buster; The Valley of Hunted Men; Saddle Mates; The Desert of the Lost; The Flyin' Buckaroo. 1929: King of the Kongo; The Fatal Warning (*10 eps*); The Bachelor Girl. 1930: The Lone Defender (*12 eps*); Border Romance; The Dude Wrangler; Wings of Adventure; The Thoroughbred; Under Montana Skies; Utah Kid. 1931: The Lawless Woman (*+co-s*); Lady from Nowhere (*+e*); Wild Horses (*co-d Sidney Algier*); Sky Spider; Grief Street (*+e*); Neck and Neck; The Devil Plays (*+e*). 1932: Cross Examination; Murder at Dawn; Forgotten Women; Probation; Midnight Lady; Escapade; Forbidden Company; Beauty Parlour; The King Murder; The Thrill of Youth; Slightly Married. 1933:

Women Won't Tell; Secrets of Wu Sin (+ e); Love is Dangerous; Forgotten; Strange People; I Have Lived; Notorious But Nice; A Man of Sentiment; Rainbow over Broadway. 1934: Murder on the Campus; The Quitter; City Park (+ e); Stolen Sweets; Green Eyes; Cheating Cheaters; The Secret of the Chateau; Strange Wives. 1935: Last of the Pagans. 1936: The Voice of Bugle Ann; Tarzan Escapes. 1937: Dangerous Number; Night Must Fall; Double Wedding. 1938: Love is a Headache; Man-Proof; The First Hundred Years; The Toy Wife; The Crowd Roars; Three Loves Has Nancy. 1939: The Adventures of Huckleberry Finn; Tarzan Finds a Son. 1940: The Earl of Chicago; 20 Mule Team; Wyoming. 1941: The Bad Man; Barnacle Bill; Tarzan's Secret Treasure. 1942: Joe Smith, American; Tarzan's New York Adventure; Apache Trail; White Cargo. 1943: Three Hearts for Julia; Above Suspicion. 1944: Cry Havoc; Two Girls and a Sailor; The Thin Man Goes Home. 1945: Thriller of a Romance; Her Highness and the Bellboy; What Next, Corporal Hargrove?. 1947: Fiesta; This Time for Keeps. 1948: A Date With Judy; On an Island with You; The Sun Comes Up. 1949: Big Jack; Challenge to Lassie; Malaya. 1950: The Black Hand; Three Little Words. 1951: Vengeance Valley; The Great Caruso; The Unknown Man; It's a Big Country (co-d 5 others). 1952: Carbine Williams; Ivanhoe; The Prisoner of Zenda. 1953: The Girl Who Had Everything; All the Brothers were Valiant; Knights of the Round Table. 1954: The Student Prince; Athena. 1955: The Prodigal; Quentin Durward. 1957: Ten Thousand Bedrooms; Tip on a Dead Jockey; Jailhouse Rock. 1959: The House of the 7 Hawks. 1960: Killers of Kilimanjaro; The Tartars. 1961: The Honeymoon Machine. 1962: The Horizontal Lieutenant. 1963: Follow the Boys; Fun in Acapulco. 1965: The Golden Head; The Truth about Spring; That Funny Feeling. 1966: The Scorpio Letters (+ p). 1967: The Last Challenge (+ p).

THULIN, Ingrid

Actress. Sollefteå, Sweden 1929–
Studied acting at Norrköping City Theatre, and Royal Dramatic Theatre, Stockholm. From 1950: actress at Royal Dramatic Theatre. 1952–53: at Nya Theatre. 1953: Vasan. 1955–60: Malmö City Theatre. From 1960: Stockholm City Theatre. Also stage director. In films from 1948. 1965: directed and acted in short, Hängivelse. Married to director of Swedish Film Institute, Harry Schein.

Films as actress include: 1949: Kärleken segrar. 1956: Foreign Intrigue. 1957: Smultronstället. 1958: Nära livet; Ansiktet. 1960: Domaren. 1961: The Four Horsemen of the Apocalypse. 1962: Agostino. 1963: Nattvardsgästerna. 1963: Tystnaden. 1965: Return from the Ashes. 1966: La Guerre est finie. 1968: Vargtimmen. 1969: Riten. 1970: La Caduta degli dei.

TIERNEY, Gene

Actress. New York 1920–
1940: Fox contract after performance on Broadway in 'The Male Animal'; first film The Return of Frank James. 1955: nervous breakdown. No further films until Advise and Consent (1962). Worked mainly for Fox throughout career.

Films as actress include: 1941: Hudson's Bay; Tobacco Road; Sundown; The Shanghai Gesture; Son of Fury; Rings on Her Fingers. 1942: Thunder Birds; China Girl. 1943: Heaven Can Wait. 1944: Laura. 1945: A Bell for Adano. 1946: Leave Her to Heaven; Dragonwyck; The Razor's Edge. 1947: The Ghost and Mrs Muir. 1948: The Iron Curtain. 1949: Whirlpool. 1950: Night and the City; Where the Sidewalk Ends. 1951: The Mating Season; On the Riviera; The Secret of Convict Lake; Close to My Heart. 1952: Way of a Gaucho; Plymouth Adventure. 1953: Never Let Me Go. 1954: The Egyptian; Black Widow. 1955: The Left Hand of God. 1963: Toys in the Attic. 1965: The Pleasure Seekers.

TILLER, Nadja

Actress. Vienna 1929–
Mother opera singer Erika Korner, father actor Anton T. Tiller. Theatre and dance training then small roles at the Josefstadt Theatre. 1949: Miss Austria; then first film. Many films with Rolf Thiele.

Films as actress include: 1954: Sie. 1955: Die Barrings. 1956: Friederike von Barring. 1958: La Désordre et la nuit; Das Mädchen Rosemarie. 1959: The Rough and the Smooth; Labyrinth der Leidenschaft. 1961: La Chambre Ardente. 1962: Anima Nera; Lulu. 1963: Moral '63. 1964: Tonio Kröger. 1965: Das Liebeskarussell. 1966: The Poppy is also a Flower; Du Rififi à Paname. 1969: Ohrfeigen. 1970: Die Feuerzangenbowle.

TIOMKIN, Dmitri

Composer. St Petersburg, Russia 1899–
Child prodigy pianist, gave concerts in many European capitals. Earned money as student playing piano for silent films. Accompanied Max Linder on stage. 1925: went to USA as pianist. Entered films at beginning of sound period. Never under contract. World War II: musical director in US Signal Corps; music for army films. 1950: head of music department of Stanley Kramer Productions. Produced play 'Keeping Expenses Down' on Broadway. 1970: executive producer and musical supervisor on Tchaikovsky, made in Russia. Chevalier du Légion d'Honneur. Oscars for scores of High Noon (1952), The High and The Mighty (1954), The Old Man and The Sea (1958). Also Oscar for theme song of High Noon.

Films as composer include: 1937: Lost Horizon. 1938: You Can't Take it With You; The Great Waltz. 1939: Mr Smith Goes to Washington; Only Angels Have Wings (co). 1941: Meet John Doe. 1942: The Moon and Sixpence. 1943: Shadow of a Doubt. 1946: The Dark Mirror; Duel in the Sun. 1948: Red River. 1949: Champion. 1950: The Men; Cyrano de Bergerac. 1951: Strangers on a Train; The Thing. 1952: The Big Sky; High Noon; Angel Face. 1953: I Confess; Take the High Ground; Blowing Wild. 1954: Dial M for Murder; The High and the Mighty. 1955: The Court Martial of Billy Mitchell; Land of the Pharaohs. 1956: Friendly Persuasion; Giant. 1957: Wild is the Wind; Night Passage. 1958: The Old Man and the Sea. 1959: Rio Bravo. 1960: The Alamo; The Sundowners; The Unforgiven (co). 1963: Fifty-five Days at Peking. 1964: Circus World; The Fall of the Roman Empire. 1969: Mackenna's Gold (+ co-p).

Robert Mitchum and Gregory Peck in Cape Fear, directed by J. Lee Thompson.
Ingrid Thulin in Mai Zetterling's Nattlek.
Gene Tierney in Whirlpool, directed by Otto Preminger.

TISSÉ, Edward

Cinematographer. Stockholm 1897-1961 Moscow
Swedish father, Russian mother. Studied painting. Worked in Swedish films. Moved to Russia; newsreel cameraman in World War I. Filmed first May Day celebration in Red Square; photographed in collaboration the first Soviet film i.e. first produced by Moscow Cinema Committee, *Signal*. Worked on agit-trains, filmed Civil War battles. 1921: in absence of negative stock used washed and recoated positive stock to shoot *Golod ... Golod ... Golod*. 1925: first collaboration with Sergei Eisenstein on *Stachka*. 1927: photographed and played German officer in *Oktyabre*. With Eisenstein developed simultaneous use of several cameras. 1929: with Eisenstein and Grigori Alexandrov travelled to Berlin, Switzerland, Paris, London. In Switzerland directed and photographed fiction feature on abortion, *Frauennot-Frauenglück*. *1930: with Eisenstein to Mexico, shot 60,000 metres of Que Viva Mexico*, used in several edited versions. 1935: left Aleksander Dovzhenko's *Aerograd* to work on Eisenstein's *Bezhin Meadow*, unfinished. After *Aleksander Nevskii* worked on Eisenstein's project on building of Ferghana Canal in Central Asia; unfinished. 1944-45: photographed exteriors on both parts of *Ivan Groznyi*.

Films as cinematographer include: 1918: Ural. 1921: Agitpoezhd vtsika (*co*). 1924: Stachka. 1925: Bronenosets 'Potyomkin'. 1927: Oktyabre (+*w*). 1929: Staroie i Novoie. 1930: Romance Sentimentale. 1935: Aerograd (*co*). 1938: Aleksander Nevskii. 1944-45: Ivan Groznyi (*co*). 1946: V gorakh Yugoslavii. 1949: Vstrecha na Elbe. 1952: Kompozitor Glinka.

TODD, Michael (Mike)

(Avron Hirsch Golbogen) Producer. Minneapolis, Minnesota 1907-58
Father Polish rabbi. 1918: with family moved to Chicago. Many jobs while a child. 1917: president of construction company. Worked in sound-proofing Hollywood sound stages. Gag writer for Olsen and Johnson. From 1936: Broadway producer: shows include 'The Hot Mikado', 'The Streets of Paris' with Gypsy Rose Lee, 'Something for the Boys', 'Catherine the Great' with Mae West. Opened night club in Chicago, moved to New York. From 1945: in films. 1953: formed company with Joseph M. Schenk; with son Michael Todd Jr supervised European sequence of *This is Cinerama*. Developed 70 mm processes, Cinerama and Todd-AO. Only film as credited producer *Around the World in 80 Days* (1947-50: married to Joan Blondell. 1957: married Elizabeth Taylor.

TOLAND, Gregg

Cinematographer. Charleston, Illinois 1904-48 Hollywood
At 15, office boy at Fox. After a year, assistant cameraman on Al St John 2-reel comedies. 1926: assistant cinematographer to George Barnes at Goldwyn studios, then partner to Barnes. 1931: first film as solo cinematographer *Palmy Days*. World War II: Lieutenant in US Navy camera unit under Lieutenant-Commander John Ford: photographed and with him directed *December 7th*, in Honolulu; received Oscar for 2-reel release version (1943). Trained combat cameramen in Washington and worked for OSS and Navy in South America. Most of career under contract to Samuel Goldwyn. Oscar for black and white cinematography on *Wuthering Heights* (1939).

Films as cinematographer include: 1927-28: Life and Death of 9413, a Hollywood Extra (*co*). 1929: The Trespasser (*co*). 1930: Raffles (*co*). 1931: Indiscreet (*co*); Tonight or Never. 1932: Play Girl; Man Wanted; The Tenderfoot. 1933: The Kid from Spain; Tugboat Annie; The Nuisance; Roman Scandals. 1934: Lazy River; We Live Again; Forsaking All Others (*co*). 1935: The Wedding Night; Les Misérables; Mad Love (*co*); The Dark Angel; Splendor. 1936: These Three; Strike Me Pink (*co*); The Road to Glory; Come and Get It! (*co*). 1937: Beloved Enemy; History is Made at Night; Dead End. 1938: The Goldwyn Follies; The Cowboy and the Lady. 1939: Wuthering Heights; They Shall Have Music; Intermezzo. 1940: The Grapes of Wrath; Raffles; The Westerner; The Long Voyage Home; Citizen Kane; The Outlaw (*r* 1946). 1941: The Little Foxes; Ball of Fire. 1942: The Magnificent Ambersons (*co*). 1946: The Kid from Brooklyn. 1947: A Song is Born. 1948: Enchantment.

TONE, Franchot

Actor. Niagara Falls, New York 1906-68 New York
Father an applied chemist, president of Carborundum Company of America. Cornell University. Actor with stock company in Buffalo and first appearance on New York stage at 21. 1929-31: acted with Theatre Guild and Group Theatre. 1932: first films. Worked mainly for MGM until 1939 when he returned to Broadway in Irwin Shaw's 'The Gentle People' (for Group Theatre) and Hemingway's 'The Fifth Column'. From 1940: worked for various other companies in Hollywood. From 1945: more stage than film work. Married and divorced actresses Joan Crawford (1935-39); Jean Wallace (1941-48); Barbara Payton (1951-52); Dolores Dorn-Heft (1956-59), with whom he appeared in several Broadway productions.

Films as actor include: 1933: Dancing Lady; Today We Live; Bombshell; The Stranger's Return; Lady of the Night. 1934: The World Moves On; Sadie McKee. 1935: The Lives of a Bengal Lancer; Mutiny on the Bounty; Reckless; One New York Night. 1936: The King Steps Out; The Gorgeous Hussy. 1937: They Gave Him a Gun; Quality Street. 1938: Three Comrades. 1939: Fast and Furious. 1940: Trail of the Vigilantes. 1942: Star Spangled Rhythm. 1943: Pilot No 5; Five Graves to Cairo; True to Life; His Butler's Sister. 1944: The Hour Before the Dawn; Phantom Lady; Dark Waters. 1947: Honeymoon. 1949: Without Honor; The Man on the Eiffel Tower. 1951: Here Comes the Groom. 1958: Uncle Vanya (+ *co-d/co-p*; *co-d* John Goetz). 1962: Advise and Consent. 1964: In Harm's Way. 1965: Mickey One.

TONTI, Aldo

Cinematographer. Rome 1910-
1934: entered films. Camera assistant, then operator e.g. on *Scipione l'Africano* (1937) before becoming cinematographer in 1939.

Films as cinematographer include: 1938: Piccoli Naufraghi (*co*). 1942: Ossessione (*co*). 1947: Il Delitto de Giovanni Episcopo. 1948: Senza pietà. 1949: Il Mulino del Po. 1952: Europa '51; Dov'è la libertà? 1953: La Lupa. 1954: Ulisse (*co*). 1956: War and Peace (*co*). 1957: Le Notti di Cabiria. 1958: Tempestà (*co*); India; Fortunella. 1960: The Savage Innocents (*co*). 1962: Barabbas. 1963: Kali-Yug, la dea della vendetta. 1965: Operazione San Gennaro. 1967: Reflections in a Golden Eye. 1968: L'Uome dei palloncini. 1971: La Spina Dorsale del diavolo; Brancaleone alle crociate.

TORRE NILSSON, Leopoldo

Director. Buenos Aires, Argentina 1924-
Father, Argentinian film director Leopoldo Torres Ríos, originally Spanish Roman Catholic; mother Swedish Protestant. 1939-49: assistant director to father on 16 films and to Luis Bayón Herrara on 2; also occasionally e.g. assistant editor, camera assistant for father. 1944-45: philosophy at University of Buenos Aires. Book of poems 'Transito de la gota de agua' (published 1947). 1946-49: scripts for 9 of his father's films. 1947: first film as director and writer. 1950: directed feature (his first) in collaboration with father. 1954: 4 films for American TV. From 1957: wife novelist Beatriz Guido collaborated as writer, providing subjects for most of his films. 1958: directed Argentinian stage production of 'The Potting Shed'. Own production company. Many articles and reviews for Argentinian and Uruguayan film periodicals, contributed to 'Sight and Sound', 'Films and Filming'.

Films as director and writer: 1947: El Muro. 1950: El Crimen de Oribe (*co-s*; *co-d* Leopoldo Torres Ríos). 1953: El Hijo del crack (*co-s*; *co-d* Leopoldo Torres Ríos). 1954: Días de odio - Days of Hatred (*co-s*); La Tigra (*d only*). 1955: Para vestir santos - To Clothe the Saints (*d only*). 1956: Graciela (*co-s*); El Protegido - The Protégé. 1957: Precursores de la pintura Argentina; Los Arboles de Buenos-Aires; La Casa del angel - The House of the Angel - End of Innocence (*co-s*). 1958: El Secuestrador - The Kidnapper (*co-s*). 1959: La Caída - The Fall (*co-s*). 1960: Fin de fiesta - The Blood Feast - The Party is Over (*co-s*); Un Guapo del '900 - Tough Guy of 1900 (+ *co-p*; *co-s*). 1961: La Mano en la trampa - Hand in the Trap (+ *co-p*; *co-s*); Piel de verano - Summer Skin (*co-s*). 1962: Setenta veces siete - The Female - Seventy Times Seven (*co-s*); Homenaje a la hora de la siesta - Four Women for One Hero - Homage at Siesta Time (*co-s*). 1963: La Terraza - The Roof Garden - The Terrace (*co-s*). 1964: El Ojo de la cerradura - The Eavesdropper (*co-s*). 1966: Cavar un foso - To Dig a Pit; Monday's Child (*co-s*). 1967: Los Traidores de San Angel - Traitors of San Angel (*co-s*). 1968: Martin Fierro.

TOTHEROH, Rollie (Roland)

Cinematographer. San Francisco 1890-
Cartoonist for San Francisco newspaper when G. M. Anderson hired him as assistant cameraman for Essanay (1910). 1915: Charles Chaplin moved to Essanay from Keystone; Totheroh was cinematographer on his films until 1947. 1952: consultant on *Limelight*.

Films as cinematographer include: 1915: The Tramp. 1916: The Floorwalker (*co*); The Vagabond (*co*); The Pawnshop. 1917: Easy Street; The Cure; The Immigrant. 1918: A Dog's Life; Shoulder Arms. 1921: The Kid. 1923: The Pilgrim; A Woman of Paris (*co*); 1925: Gold Rush (*co*). 1928: The Circus (*co*). 1931: City Lights (*co*). 1936: Modern Times (*co*). 1940: The Great Dictator (*co*). 1947: Monsieur Verdoux (*co*).

TOTÒ

(Antonio de Curtis Gagliardi Ducas Comnuno di Bisanzio) Naples 1898–1967 Rome
Character actor in suburban theatres in Naples. 1917: at Jovinelli Theatre in Rome. Small variety theatres. 1933: became actor-manager. 1936: first film as actor *Fermo con le mani*. At outbreak of World War II had own company performing live acts in cinemas. Cesare Zavattini scripted *Totò il buono* for him: not made, but became *Miracolo a Milano* (1951). 1940: his third film *San Giovanni Decollato* written by Zavattini. 1941: began series of musical comedy revues which continued annually until 1949. 1945–46: only foreign tour, in Spain. Subsequently devoted himself mainly to films. 1952: acted in one of the first Italian colour films *Totò a colori*: published book 'Siamo uomini o caporali?'. 1955: married actress Franca Faldini.

Films as actor include: 1939: Animali Pazzi. 1948: Totò cerca casa. 1949: Totò le Moko. 1950: Napoli Milionaria; L'Imperatore di Capri; Totò cerca moglie; Figaro qua, Figaro là; Le Sei Moglie di Barbablù. 1951: Guardie e ladri; Totò e i re di Roma. 1952: Totò e le donne; Totò a colori. 1953: Dov'è la libertà?; L'Uomo, la bestia e la virtù; Tempi Nostri. 1954: Totò e Carolina; L'Oro di Napoli. 1957: La Loi c'est la loi. 1958: I Soliti Ignoti. 1959: Totò nella luna; Totò, Eva e il pennello proibito; I Tartassati; Arrangiatevi. 1960: Letto a tre piazze; Risate di Gioia. 1962: Totò Diabolicus; I Due Colonelli. 1963: Totò contro i quattro. 1964: Le Belle Famiglie *ep* Amare e un po' morire. 1965: La Mandragola; Operazione San Gennaro. 1966: Uccellacci e uccellini. 1967: Le Streghe *ep* La Terra vista della luna. 1968: Capriccio all'Italiana *eps* Il Maestro della domenica; Che cosa sono le nuvole?

TOURNEUR, Jacques

Director. Paris 1904–
Son of an actress, Van Doren, and Maurice Tourneur, then working as a stage manager in the theatre. 1913: emigrated to USA with father and (1919) became US citizen. 1922: after appearing in *Scaramouche,* started work for his father as script-boy, assistant and actor. 1926–28: after father returned to France, worked as actor in crowd scenes at MGM. Then returned to France; editor and assistant to father on 6 films, ending with *Le Voleur* (1933). 1931–34: directed 4 films in France. 1935: in USA directed sequences of *The Winning Ticket;* with 2nd-unit producer Val Lewton filmed the storming of the Bastille for *A Tale of Two Cities.* 1936–39: directed shorts for MGM in their regular series. 1939: *They All Come Out,* short semidocumentary made by MGM in collaboration with Department of Justice expanded to 4 reels, then 7, his first feature in USA. 1942: directed short *The Magic Alphabet* for John Nesbitt's Passing Parade. Worked on many TV series including 'Northwest Passage' (1958–59) of which he shot half the episodes. His among those assembled into features for theatrical release: *Frontier Rangers* ((1958, all 3 episodes), *Fury River* (1958, one episode 'The Vulture' out of 3),

Mission of Danger (1959, one episode 'The Breakout' in 3).

Features as director: 1931: Tout ça ne vaut pas l'amour. 1933: Toto; Pour être aimé. 1934: Les Filles de la concierge. 1939: They All Come Out; Nick Carter, Master Detective. 1940: Phantom Raiders. 1941: Doctors Don't Tell. 1943: Cat People; I Walked with a Zombie; The Leopard Man. 1944: Days of Glory; Experiment Perilous. 1946: Canyon Passage. 1947: Out of the Past – Build My Gallows High. 1948: Berlin Express. 1949: Easy Living. 1950: Stars in My Crown; The Flame and the Arrow. 1951: Circle of Danger; Anne of the Indies. 1952: Way of a Gaucho. 1953: Appointment in Honduras. 1955: Stranger on Horseback; Wichita. 1956: Great Day in the Morning; Nightfall. 1957: Night of the Demon – Curse of the Demon. 1958: The Fearmakers; Timbuktu. 1959: La Battaglia di Maratona – The Giant of Marathon (*co-d Mario Bava, Bruno Vailati*). 1964: The Comedy of Terrors. 1965: City in the Sea – War Gods of the Deep.

TOURNEUR, Maurice

Director. Paris 1876–1961 Paris
Sister actress Yvonne Tourneur; brother Robert Tourneur manager of Michodière Theatre, Paris. 1894: graduated from Lycée Condorcet. Became magazine and book illustrator, poster and fabric designer, then interior decoration designer. Assistant to Auguste Rodin. 1900–12: stage actor and director in France and UK. 1912: began in films as actor at Eclair e.g. in *La Dame de chez Maxim's, Occupe-toi d'Amélie, La Veuve Joyeuse.* 1913: began as director. 1914: went to USA as director at Eclair's studios, New Jersey; worked with own unit including art director Ben Carré (until 1919), cameraman John Van den Broek (until 1918), editor and assistant director Clarence Brown (until 1921), script clerk, casting director and leading man John Gilbert. 1915: production head at Paragon with contract to direct 8 features a year. 1917–18: films for Famous Players-Lasky and Artcraft. From 1918: formed own company, mainly distributing through Paramount. 1920: with Thomas H. Ince and others founded Associated Producers. 1921: became US citizen. 1926: left USA when MGM tried to make him work under a producer on *The Mysterious Island* (completed by Lucien Hubbard in 1929). From 1927: worked mainly in France. 1929: in Germany. 1930–35: director for Pathé-Natan. From 1941: with Continental A.C.E. 1948: last film as director. 1950: lost a leg in car accident. 1950–61: translated English novels into French. Married (1904) actress Fernande Petit; son Jacques Tourneur.

Films as director include: 1914: Mother; The Man of the Hour; The Wishing Ring. 1915: Alias Jimmy Valentine; The Ivory Snuff Box. 1917: Trilby; The Poor Little Rich Girl; Pride of the Clan; The Whip; Barbary Sheep. 1918: Prunella; A Doll's House; The Blue Bird; Sporting Life (+*p*); Woman (+*p*). 1919: Victory (+*p*); The White Heather. 1920: Deep Waters; Treasure Island (+*p*); The White Circle (+*p*); The Bait; The Last of the Mohicans (+*p; co-d Clarence Brown*). 1922: Lorna Doone (+*p/s*). 1923: The Christian; The Isle of Lost Ships (+*p*). 1925: Sporting Life (*rm* 1918). 1926: Aloma of the South Seas (+*p*). 1927: L'Equipage. 1929: The Mysterious Island (*co-d Lucien Hubbard, Benjamin Christensen*); Das Schiff der verlorene menschen (+*s*). 1930: Accusée, levez-

India, *directed by Roberto Rossellini, photographed by Aldo Tonti.*
Fin de Fiesta, *directed by Leopoldo Torre-Nilsson.*
Spencer Tracy (*right*) *in Frank Borzage's* The Big City.

vous. 1931: Partir; Maison de danses. 1932: Au nom de la loi; Les Gaîtés de l'escadron. 1933: Les Deux Orphelines; Le Voleur. 1935: Justin de Marseille. 1936: Koenigsmark – Crimson Dynasty (*English version*); Samson; Avec le sourire. 1938: Le Patriote – The Patriot – The Mad Emperor; Katia. 1939–41: Volpone. 1942: La Main du diable – Carnival of Sinners – The Devil's Hand. 1947: Après l'amour. 1948: L'Impasse des deux anges.

TRACY, Spencer

Actor. Milwaukee, Wisconsin 1900–
US Navy. American Academy of Dramatic Art. 1922: New York stage debut in 'RUR'. Short films then first feature as actor *Up The River* (1930). From 1934: most films for MGM. Oscars as Best Actor for *Captains Courageous* (1937) and *Boy's Town* (1938).

Films as actor include: 1932: Young American; Me and My Gal; Twenty Thousand Years in Sing Sing. 1933: The Power and the Glory; Man's Castle. 1934: Looking for Trouble; Bottoms Up; Marie Galante. 1935: Whipsaw. 1936: Libeled Lady; Fury; San Francisco. 1937: They Gave Him a Gun; Big City. 1938: Mannequin; Test Pilot. 1939: Stanley and Livingstone. 1940: Northwest Passage; I Take This Woman; Edison, the Man; Boom Town. 1941: Dr Jekyll and Mr Hyde. 1942: Woman of the Year; Tortilla Flat; Keeper of the Flame. 1944: A Guy Named Joe; The Seventh Cross; Thirty Seconds Over Tokyo. 1946: The Sea of Grass. 1947: Cass Timberlane. 1948: State of the Union. 1949: Edward, My Son; Malaya; Adam's Rib. 1950: Father of the Bride. 1951: Father's Little Dividend; The People Against O'Hara. 1952: Plymouth Adventure; Pat and Mike. 1953: The Actress. 1954: Broken Lance; Bad Day at Black Rock. 1956: The Mountain. 1957: Desk Set. 1958: The Old Man and the Sea; The Last Hurrah. 1960: Inherit the Wind. 1961: Judgment at Nuremburg; The Devil at Four O'Clock. 1962: How the West was Won. 1963: It's a Mad, Mad, Mad, Mad World. 1967: Guess Who's Coming to Dinner.

TRAUBERG, Ilya

Director. Odessa, Russia 1905–48 Berlin
Younger brother of Leonid Trauberg. 1927: entered films as writer; assistant on *Oktyabre*; first film as director, a documentary. 1929: for Sovkino, first feature as director. 1931: *Letun* is animated. 1936: made *Sin Mongolii* for Lenfilm, commissioned by Republic of Burat-Mongolia; made in Russian and Mongolian versions, crew from Leningrad. 1942: for Kino-Album series of shorts, in collaboration made *Pauki*.

Films as director: 1927: Leningrad Segodnya – Leningrad Today. 1929: Goluboi Ekspress – China Express – The Blue Express (+ *co-s*). 1931: Letun – Kites. 1934: Chastnyi Sluchai – An Unusual Case (+ *co-s*). 1936: Sin Mongolii – Son of Mongolia (*co-d R. Suslovich*). 1938: God Devyatnadtsatii – The Year 1919 (+ *co-s*). 1940: Kontsert-Vals – Concert Waltz (+ *co-s*; *co-d M. Dubson*). 1941: My zhdom vas s pobedoi – We Expect Victory There (*co-d A. Medvedkin*). 1942: Pauki – The Spider (*co-d I. Zemgano*).

TRAUBERG, Leonid

Director. Odessa, Russia 1902–
From 1917: collaboration with Grigori Kozintsev. They organised ambulant studio-theatre. 1921: in Petrograd issued manifestos of FEX (Factory of Eccentric Actor) and (with Sergei Yutkovich) co-founded the movement. 1923: their last stage production. Sevzapkino invited group to make short comedy, *Pokhozhdeniya Oktyabriny* (1924) which they wrote and directed. From 1926: Andrei Moskvin became their regular cinematographer. 1929: they took trip to Paris before making *Novyi Vavilon* in which Vsevolod Pudovkin acted. 1931: they made *Odna* as silent, then sound added with score by Dmitri Shostakovich. 1935–39: 'Maxim' trilogy. 1943: without Kozintsev directed and co-wrote *Aktrisa*. 1945: their film *Prostiye Lyudi* the first production finished after war's end to appear from restored Lenfilm; officially condemned, not released till 1956. 1947: end of collaboration with Kozintsev; scripted Herbert Rappoport's *Zhizn v tsitadeli*. 1949: among victims of official campaign against 'cosmopolitanism'. 1955: wrote script for Grigori Roshal's *Volnitsa*. 1960: for TV made *Mertvye Dushi*. Brother of Ilya Trauberg. For list as director in collaboration with Grigori Kozintsev, *see* KOZINTSEV.

Films as solo director: 1943: Aktrisa – The Actress (+ *co-s*). 1958: Shli Soldaty – Soldiers were Marching (+ *s*). 1960: Mertvye Dushi – Dead Souls (+ *s*). 1961: Volnyi Veter – Free Wind (*co-d A. Tontichkin*).

TRAUNER, Alexander

Designer. Budapest 1906–
Ecole des Beaux-Arts, Paris. 1929: worked as draughtsman on *Sous les toits de Paris*. Assistant to Lazare Meerson on e.g. *Le Million* (1931), *La Kermesse Heroïque* (1936). 1932: with P. Colombier adapted sets used on another film for *L'Affaire est dans le sac*. 1957: in Paris worked on *Love in the Afternoon*, invited by Billy Wilder to work in USA. Most subsequent work is American. Several credits as artistic director. Also work in theatre.

Films as designer include: 1937: Gribouille: Drôle de drame. 1938: Quai des brumes; Entrée des artistes; Hôtel du Nord. 1939: Le Jour se lève. 1941: Remorques. 1942: Lumière d'été; Les Visiteurs du soir (+ *co-st*). 1945: Les Enfants du paradis (*co*); Les Portes de la Nuit. 1946: Voyage – Surprise. 1949: Manèges; La Fleur de l'age (*uf*); La Marie du port (*co*); La Jeune Folle. 1950: Les Miracles n'ont lieu qu'une fois; La Marie du port (*co*); Juliette ou la clé des songes (*co*). 1951: Les Sept Péchés Capitaux *ep* La Luxure. 1952: Othello. 1955: L'Amant de Lady Chatterley; Land of the Pharoahs. 1956: En effeuillant la marguerite (*co*). 1957: Love in the Afternoon. 1958: Witness for the Prosecution. 1959: The Nun's Story; Once More with Feeling. 1960: The Apartment. 1961: Romanoff and Juliet; One, Two, Three; Paris Blues; Aimez-vous Brahms? 1962: Gigot; le Couteau dans la plaie. 1963: Irma la Douce; Behold a Pale Horse (+ *as-p*). 1964: Kiss Me, Stupid. 1966: How to Steal a Million. 1967: The Night of the Generals (*co*). 1969: Uptight! 1970: La Promesse de l'aube. 1971: Les Mariés de l'an II.

TRESSLER, Georg

Director. Vienna 1917–
Father actor Otto Tressler. Caricaturist. 1935–39: actor at Burgtheater, Vienna, then assistant director in Berlin theatre; also assistant and actor in Austrian films. 1945: as assistant editor, then editor. From 1947: directed documentary and educational shorts in Austria. 1956: began as feature director in Berlin. Subsequently worked also in Austria and USA. Also TV work.

Features as director: 1956: Die Halbstarken – Wolfpack (+ *co-s*). 1957: Unter 18; Noch minderjährig – Unter achzehn (+ *co-s*); Endstation Liebe – Terminus Love. 1958: Ein wunderbarer Summer. 1959: Lange Hosen, Kurze Haare; Das Totenschiff (+ *co-s*). 1960: Geständnis einer Sechzenhnjährigen. 1962: The Magnificent Rebel. 1965: Die lustigen Weiber von Windsor. 1966: Der Weibsteufel – A Devil of a Woman (+ *co-s*).

TREVOR, Claire

Actress. New York 1909–
American Academy of Dramatic Art; Columbia University. 1932: on Broadway in 'Whistling in the Dark'. 1933: seen in 'The Party's Over' by Warners talent scout; put under contract for series φ shorts. 1933: first feature *Life in the Raw*. To 1938: almost all films for Fox; then worked for numerous studios. 1947: on Broadway in 'The Big Two'. TV work includes 'Dodsworth'. Third husband Milton Bren (1948). Oscar as supporting actress for *Key Largo* (1948).

Films as actress include: 1934: Wild Gold. 1935: Spring Tonic; Black Sheep; Navy Wife. 1936: The Song and Dance Man; Human Cargo; To Mary-with Love; 15 Maiden Lane. 1937: Time Out for Romance; King of Gamblers; One Mile from Heaven; Dead End. 1938: The Amazing Dr Clitterhouse; Valley of the Giants. 1939: Stagecoach; I Stole a Million. 1940: Dark Command. 1941: Texas; Honky Tonk. 1942: Crossroads. 1943: The Desperadoes; Good Luck, Mr Yates. 1945: Murder My Sweet. 1946: Crack-Up; The Bachelor's Daughters. 1947: Born to Kill. 1948: Raw Deal; The Babe Ruth Story; Key Largo. 1951: Hard, Fast and Beautiful. 1952: My Man and I; Stop, You're Killing Me. 1953: The Stranger wore a Gun. 1954: The High and the Mighty. 1955: Man Without a Star; Lucy Gallant. 1956: The Mountain. 1958: Marjorie Morningstar. 1962: Two Weeks in Another Town. 1963: The Stripper. 1964: How to Murder Your Wife.

TRINTIGNANT, Jean-Louis

Actor. Pont-Saint-Esprit, France 1930–
Father and 4 uncles were racing drivers. 1950: to Paris; studied acting under Charles Dullin and Tania Balachova. 1951: began as stage actor with Raymond Hermantier's company. Then acted with various companies including productions of Shakespeare and Ionesco. 1955: began in films. 1956: established as screen actor by *Et Dieu créa la femme*. Also acted on French TV. Married to film director Nadine Trintignant.

Films as actor include: 1955: Si tous les gars du monde. 1956: Et Dieu créa la femme. 1959: Les Liaisons Dangereuses. 1960: Austerlitz; Coeur

Battant. 1961: Pleins Feux sur l'assassin; Les Sept Péchés Capitaux *ep* La Luxure. 1962: Le Combat dans l'île. 1963: Château en Suède. 1964: Mata Hari, agent H 21. 1965: Compartiment tueurs. 1966: La Longue Marche; Un Homme et une femme; Trans-Europ-Express. 1967: Col cuore in gola. 1968: Les Biches; Z. 1969: L'Homme qui ment; Ma Nuit chez Maud; Metti una sera a cena. 1970: Il conformista; Le Voyou.

TRNKA, Jiri

Animator and puppet-film maker. Pilsen, Czechoslovakia 1912–69 Prague
1921: won design competition organised by puppeteer Josef Skupa. 1923: began work as amateur at Skupa's puppet studios, designing and building puppets. 1929: work included in Paris puppet exhibition. 1929–35: School of Applied Arts, Prague. 1936: opened own puppet theatre for several months. 1938–42: designer for National Theatre, Prague. 1942–45: illustrator of children's books. 1945: first film as animator. 1947: first puppet film *Spaliček* (part animated) was also his first feature. 1958: commissioned by UNESCO to make *Proč UNESCO*. From 1947 most films made with animated puppets. Wrote own scripts, some in collaboration with Jiri Brdecka. Model work on films of e.g. Bretislav Pojar and Brdecka.

Films as director, writer and designer: 1945: Zasadil dědek repu – Grandpa Planted a Beet (*st*). 1946: Dárek – The Gift (*d/s/st only*); Pèrak a SS – Perak against the SS (*+ st/co-s; co-d Jiri Brdecka*); Zvířátku a petrovští – The Animals and the Brigands (*st*). 1947: Spaliček – The Czech Year (*st/s; + e*). 1948: Cisařův slavik – The Emperor's Nightingale (*co-s; + e*). 1949: Roman s Basou – The Story of a Double Bass; Arie prérie – The Song of the Prairie (*co-s*). 1950: Bajaja – Prince Bayaya (*co-s*). 1951: Veselý Cirkus – The Happy Circus (*co-s*); Certův Mlýn – The Devil's Mill; O Zlaté Rybce – The Golden Fish. 1952: Kutasek a Kutilka jak ráno vastavali – How Kutasek and Kutilka got up in the Morning; Jak stareček měnil až vyměnil – How Grandpa Changed Till Nothing was Left (*d/a only*). 1953: Stare Povesti Ceske – Old Czech Legends (*co-s*). 1954: Dva Mrazici – The Two Frosts; Dobrý Vojak Švejk – The Good Soldier Schweik (*3 parts*). 1955: Cirkus Hurvínek – The Hurvinek Circus (*co-s*). 1958: Proč UNESCO – Why UNESCO? (*d only*). 1959: Sen Noci Svatojanské – A Midsummer Night's Dream (*co-s/cy*). 1962: Vasen – Passion. 1963: Kybernetica Babička – Cybernetic Grandma. 1964: Ruka – The Hand. 1965: Archandel Gabriel a Pani Husa – The Archangel Gabriel and Mother Goose.

TROELL, Jan

Director, writer and cinematographer. Malmö, Sweden 1931–
School-teacher for 9 years in Malmö. 1958: first film as director, an amateur short later bought for TV. To 1965: directed shorts, including *Vär i Dalby hage* (1962) a 3-minute film used as TV interlude, *Pojken och draken* (1961) directed in collaboration with Bo Widerberg, and *Johan Ekberg* (1964) which won him a state scholarship. 1962: photographed Widerberg's *Barnvagnen*. 1965: first work as director in features, episode in *4 × 4*. Photographed and edited all own films and wrote all his features in collaboration.

Short films as director: 1958: Stad. 1960: Sommartäg – A Summer Day. 1961: Baten – The Boat; Nyärsafton pa Skanska slatten – New Year's Eve on the Plains of Scania; Pojken och draken – The Boy and the Kite (*co-d Bo Widerberg*). 1962: Vär i Dalby hage – Spring in the Meadows of Dalby; De Kom tillbaka – The Return; Den Gamla Kvarnen – The Old Mill. 1964: Johan Ekberg; Trakom – Trachoma (*co-d Lars Braw*). 1965: Porträtt av Åsa – Portrait of Asa.

Features as director, writer in collaboration, photographer and editor: 1965: 4 × 4 *ep* Uppehåll i Myrlandet – Interlude in the Marshland. 1966: Här har du ditt liv – Here is Your Life. 1967: Ole dole doff – Who Saw Him Die? 1970: Utvandrarna (*r 1971*); Invandrarna (*r 1972*).

TROTTI, Lamar

Writer and producer. Atlanta, Georgia 1900–52 Oceanside, California
Journalism at University of Georgia. From 1921: worked under Colonel Jason Joy in Hays Office, Atlanta; to Hollywood with Colonel Joy. From 1932: head of story department at Fox. Initially collaborated as writer with Dudley Nichols on e.g. 2 films directed by John Ford. From 1942: producer and writer with Fox, where he remained until his death. 1954: *There's No Business like Show Business* based on his story. Edited Motion Picture Monthly. Oscar for original screenplay, *Wilson* (1944).

Films as writer include: 1934: Judge Priest (*co*). 1935: Life Begins at Forty; Steamboat Round the Bend (*co*). 1936: Ramona; Can This Be Dixie? (*+ co-st*). 1937: Slave Ship (*co*). 1938: In Old Chicago (*co*); Alexander's Ragtime Band (*co*). 1939: Young Mr Lincoln; Drums along the Mohawk (*co*). 1940: Brigham Young. 1941: Hudson's Bay (*+ st*). 1942: Tales of Manhattan (*+ co-st; co-s*). 1946: The Razor's Edge. 1952: O. Henry's Full House *ep* The Cop and the Anthem.

Films as writer and producer include: 1942: Thunder Birds; Immortal Sergeant; The Ox-Bow Incident. 1945: A Bell for Adano (*co-s*). 1946: Colonel Effingham's Raid (*p only*). 1947: Captain from Castille. 1948: The Walls of Jericho; Yellow Sky. 1950: American Guerrilla in the Philippines.

TRUFFAUT, François

Director. Paris 1932–
At 15, office clerk; worked in factory. Saved from reformatory by André Bazin who got him work in film section of Travail et Culture. Journalist. 1951: drafted into French Army. Deserted; served prison term. 1953: discharged. Worked in film section of Ministry of Agriculture: sacked. 1954: first short film as director. 1956: assistant to Roberto Rossellini in preparation of 3 films; unmade. 1959: story writer on *A bout de souffle*; first feature film as director. 1961: signed *Manifeste des 121*, calling on soldiers to desert rather than serve in Algerian War. 1967: book consisting of interview with Alfred Hitchcock. 'Le Cinéma selon Hitchcock' (with Helen Scott). Production company Les Films du Carosse produced or co-produced e.g. *Le Testament d'Orphée* (1960), *Tire au flanc* (1961, also wrote), *Paris nous appartient* (1961), *Mata Hari, agent*

The Apartment *with Jack Lemmon, directed by Billy Wilder, art direction by Alexander Trauner.*
Francois Truffaut directing Jules et Jim.
Stanley Kubrick's Spartacus, *written by Dalton Trumbo.*

H 21 (1964, also wrote), *Deux ou trois choses que je sais d'elle* (1966), *Ma Nuit chez Maud* (1968), and all own films from 1959, except *Tirez sur le pianiste*, episode in *L'Amour à vingt ans*, and *Fahrenheit 451*. Book, 'Les Aventure d'Antoine Doinel' (1970).

Films as director: 1954: Une Visite. 1957: Les Mistons – The Mischief Makers (+ *s*). 1958: Histoire d'eau (+ *s; co-d Jean-Luc Godard*). 1959: Les Quatre Cents Coups – The 400 Blows (+ *st*). 1960: Tirez sur le pianiste – Shoot the Pianist – Shoot the Piano Player (+ *co-ad/co-di*). 1961: Jules et Jim (+ *co-ad/co-di*). 1962; L'Amour à vingt ans – Love at Twenty *ep* Paris (+ *s*). 1964: La Peau Douce – Silken Skin (+ *co-s/di*). 1966: Fahrenheit 451 (+ *co-s*). 1967: La Mariée était en noir – The Bride Wore Black (+ *co-di/co-ad*). 1968: Baisers Volés – Stolen Kisses (+ *co-s*). 1969: La Sirène du Mississippi – Mississippi Mermaid (+ *di/ad*); L'Enfant Sauvage (+ *co-ad/co-di/w*). 1970: Domicile Conjugal – Bed and Board (+ *co-s*). 1971: Les Deux Anglaises et le Continent (+ *co-ad/co-di*).

TRUMBO, Dalton

Writer. Montrose, Colorado 1905–
1921: moved with family to Los Angeles. Bread-wrapper in bakery. Manual work, then sold article to Vanity Fair. 1937: first work in films, contribution to treatment of *That Man's Here Again*. To 1940: most work for RKO. 1939: pacifist novel 'Johnny Got His Gun' won American Booksellers Award; filmed by him in 1971. 1940–45: worked mainly for MGM. 1950: imprisoned as one of 'Hollywood Ten' who refused to testify before 1947 House Committe on Un-American Activities. Blacklisted, wrote under pseudonyms. 1960: full credit for *Exodus* and subsequent work. 1960: reinstated as member of Writers Guild of America. Oscar for story of *The Brave One* (1956) under pseudonym Robert Rich. Book, 'Additional Dialogue: Letters of Dalton Trumbo 1942–1962' (1970).

Films as writer include: 1938: A Man to Remember. 1939: Sorority House; Five Came Back (*co*). 1940: A Bill of Divorcement; Kitty Foyle. 1941: You Belong To Me (*st*). 1942: The Remarkable Andrew (+ *st*). 1943: Tender Comrade (+ *st*). 1944: A Guy Named Joe; Thirty Seconds Over Tokyo. 1945: Jealousy (*st*); Our Vines Have Tender Grapes. 1960: Exodus; Spartacus. 1961: The Last Sunset. 1962: Lonely Are the Brave. 1965: The Sandpiper (*co*). 1966: Hawaii (*co*). 1968: The Fixer. 1971: The Horseman; Johnny Got His Gun (+ *d*).

TURIN, Victor

Director. St Petersburg, Russia 1895–
Sent by his wealthy family to USA. Massachusetts Institute of Technology. Worked at Vitagraph, then returned to Russia. 1926: first film as director. One of earliest members of VUFKU, in reorganisation of Ukrainian film industry. Joined Vostok-kino which made films for eastern republics. After *Turksib* (1929), given studio production post; little subsequent work as director. Invited to UK to address Workers' Film Society.

Films as director: 1926: Borba gigantov – Battle of the Giants. 1928: Provokator – The Provocateur. 1929: Turksib (+ *st/co-s*). 1938: Bakintsy – Men of Baku (+ *co-s*).

TURNER, Lana

(Julia Jean Frances Mildred Turner) Actress. Wallace, Idaho 1920–
To Los Angeles on death of father. Spotted and put under contract by Mervyn Leroy. 1937: first film as actress *They Won't Forget*. 1937–38: worked for Warners and United Artists. 1938–55: all films for MGM. From 1955: mainly Universal and MGM. 1969: TV series 'The Survivors'. Also stage. 6 husbands include Artie Shaw (1940–41) and Lex Barker (1953–57).

Films as actress include: 1937: A Star is Born; The Great Garrick. 1938: The Adventures of Marco Polo; Four's a Crowd; Love Finds Andy Hardy; Dramatic School. 1941: Ziegfeld Girl; Dr Jekyll and Mr Hyde; Honky Tonk; Johnny Eager. 1942: Somewhere I'll Find You. 1943: Slightly Dangerous. 1944: Marriage is a Private Affair. 1945: Weekend at the Waldorf. 1946: The Postman Always Rings Twice. 1947: Green Dolphin Street; Cass Timberlane. 1948: Homecoming; The Three Musketeers. 1950: A Life of her Own. 1952: The Merry Widow; The Bad and the Beautiful. 1953: Latin Lovers. 1954: The Flame and the Flesh; Betrayed. 1955: The Prodigal; The Sea Chase; The Rains of Ranchipur; Diane. 1957: Peyton Place; The Lady Takes a Flyer. 1959: Imitation of Life. 1960: Portrait in Black. 1961: By Love Possessed; Bachelor in Paradise. 1962: Who's Got the Action. 1965: Love Has Many Faces.

TURPIN, Ben

Actor. New Orleans, Louisiana 1874–1940 Hollywood
11 years in vaudeville. 1915: worked for Essanay, especially in 'Snakeville' series. 1917–27: worked mainly for Mack Sennett. 1927–28: to Columbia. Worked subsequently for Paramount, Warners, Pathe, RKO. 1933–38: no films. 1939–40: last 2 films for Fox and United Artists.

Films as actor include: 1916: Charlie Chaplin's Burlesque on Carmen. 1917: The Pawnbrocker's Heart. 1918: Whose Little Wife are You; Hide and Seek Detectives. 1919: Cupid's Day Off; East Lynne with Variations; When Love is Blind. 1921: Bright Eyes. 1923: When Summer Comes; Asleep at the Switch. 1924: The Hollywood Kid. 1925: The Wild Goose Chaser; The Raspberry Romance; Hogan's Alley. 1926: When a Man's a Prince; The Prodigal Bridegroom. 1927: The Jolly Jilter; The College Hero. 1930: The Love Parade. 1931: Cracked Nuts. 1932: Million Dollar Legs. 1940: Saps at Sea.

TUSHINGHAM, Rita

Actress. Liverpool, Lancashire 1942–
Acted in repertory and pantomime. Stage manager of Liverpool Players. 1961: first film as actress *A Taste of Honey*. Returned to stage for 'The Changeling' and 'The Kitchen', before second film. Played lead in Tony Richardson's Royal Court production of 'The Knack' and in film version (1965). Married TV cameraman Terry Bicknell who became her personal manager. 1970: formed production company with Desmond Davis. Also TV.

Films as actress include: 1963: The Leather Boys; A Place to Go; The Girl with Green Eyes. 1965: The

Knack—and How to Get It; Doctor Zhivago. 1967: Smashing Time. 1968: The Guru. 1969: The Bed Sitting Room.

TUTTLE, Frank

Director. New York 1892–1963 Hollywood
Yale University. 1915–17: an assistant editor on Vanity Fair magazine. 1917: publicity representative of the Metropolitan Musical Bureau, New York. 1918–19: press agent for New York Philharmonic Orchestra. 1919–20: writer with Paramount, on East Coast. 1922: directed first film. 1922–24: worked mainly with Film Guild. 1925–44: mainly with Paramount. Thereafter with various companies. One of founders of Screen Director's Guild.

Films as director include: 1922: The Cradle Buster (+ *s*). 1924: Grit. 1925: Lucky Devil. 1926: The American Venus; The Untamed Lady; Love 'em and Leave 'em; Kid Boots. 1927: Blind Alleys (+ *p*); One Woman to Another. 1928: Varsity; Easy Come Easy Go; The Greene Murder Case. 1929: The Studio Murder Mystery. 1930: Paramount on Parade (*co-d 10 others*); True to the Navy; Love Among the Millionaires; Her Wedding Night; Men Are Like That; The Benson Murder Case. 1931: No Limit; It Pays to Advertise. 1932: This Reckless Age (+ *co-s*); The Big Broadcast; This is the Night. 1933: Roman Scandals. 1934: Springtime for Henry (+ *co-s*); Here is My Heart. 1935: All the Kings Horses (+ *co-s*); The Glass Key; Two for Tonight. 1936: College Holiday. 1937: Waikiki Wedding. 1938: Dr Rhythm; Paris Honeymoon. 1939: I Stole a Million; Charlie McCarthy, Detective (+ *p*). 1942: This Gun for Hire; Lucky Jordan. 1943: Hostages. 1944: The Hour Before the Dawn. 1945: The Great John L; Don Juan Quilligan. 1946: Suspense; Swell Guy. 1950: Le Traqué – Gunman in the Streets. 1951: The Magic Face. 1955: Hell on Frisco Bay. 1956: A Cry in the Night. 1958: Island of Lost Women.

U

ULMER, Edgar G.

Director. Vienna 1904–
Academy of Arts and Sciences. Actor and assistant set designer in theatre; designer for conductor Arthur Nikisch and for Max Reinhardt. 1918–20: worked as film designer for Decla in Berlin and for Alexander Korda in Austria. 1923: designed Reinhardt's 'Das Mirakel' in Salzburg and USA; a year as art director at Universal for Cecil B. De Mille. From 1924: assistant art director and assistant director to F. W. Murnau on his last 7 films in Germany then USA. 1929: went to Germany to direct first film in collaboration with Robert Siodmak. 1930: art director at MGM, Hollywood; designer with Grand Opera Company, Philadelphia. 1933: directed first American film. 1934–42: New York, as theatre and film director. 1942–46: contract as director, writer, designer (sometimes on films by others) with Producer's Releasing Corporation. Subsequently worked for various companies in Europe and USA. 1954–57: director for Mexican TV. 1963: director for Martin Melcher's European productions.

Films as director include: 1929: Menschen am Sonntag – People on Sunday (co-d Robert Siodmak). 1933: Damaged Lives (+ co-st). 1934: The Black Cat – House of Doom (+ co-st). 1937: Green Fields (+ p; co-d Jacob Ben-Ami). 1938: The Singing Blacksmith. 1939: Moon over Harlem. 1942: Tomorrow We Live. 1943: My Son, the Hero (+ co-s/co-st); Girls in Chains (+ co-st); Isle of Forgotten Sins (+ co-st); Jive Junction. 1944: Bluebeard. 1945: Out of the Night – Strange Illusion; Club Havana; Detour. 1946: The Wife of Monte Cristo – Monte Cristo—Masked Avenger (+ co-s); Her Sister's Secret; The Strange Woman. 1947: Carnegie Hall. 1948: Ruthless. 1949: I Pirati di Capri – The Pirates of Capri – The Masked Pirate. 1951: St Benny the Dip; The Man from Planet X. 1952: Babes in Bagdad. 1954: Murder is my Beat – Dynamite Anchorage. 1955: Naked Dawn. 1957: Daughter of Dr Jekyll. 1959: Beyond the Time Barrier; The Amazing Transparent Man; Annibale – Hannibal (uc, co-d Carlo Ludovico Bragaglia). 1961: Antinea, l'amante della città – The Lost Kingdom (co-d Guiseppe Masini). 1964: Sette contro la morte – The Cavern (+ p).

UNSWORTH, Geoffrey

Cinematographer. London 1914–
From 1932: camera assistant at Gaumont British. 1937: joined Technicolor. 1946–59: cinematographer with the Rank Organisation. In 1960s worked for various companies including occasional US productions or co-productions.

Films as cinematographer include: 1949: The Spider and the Fly. 1951: Where No Vultures Fly. 1953: The Million Pound Note. 1954: The Purple Plain. 1955: Passage Home. 1956: Tiger in the Smoke; A Town Like Alice. 1957: Hell Drivers. 1958: A Night to Remember. 1959: North West Frontier. 1960: The World of Suzie Wong. 1962: The 300 Spartans. 1963: An Evening with the Royal Ballet (co). 1964: Becket. 1968: 2001, A Space Odyssey, 1970: Cromwell; Three Sisters.

USTINOV, Peter

Director, writer and actor. London 1921–
Parents Russian. Westminster School, then (1937) studied stagecraft at London Theatrical Studio under Michel St Denis. 1939: first appeared on stage in repertory and revue. 1940: dialogue director for British National Pictures; joined Royal Sussex Regiment. 1941: first film as actor Mein Kampf. From 1941: wrote plays including 'The Banbury Nose', 'The Love of Four Colonels' (1951), 'Romanoff and Juliet' (1956), 'Photo Finish' (1962). 1946: borrowed by Air Ministry to write and direct School for Secrets, a film about radar; appeared in John Gielgud's revival of 'Crime and Punishment'. Oscars as supporting actor for Spartacus (1960) and Topkapi (1964).

Films as director and writer: 1946: School for Secrets (+ co-p). 1947: Vice Versa (+ co-p/st). 1949: Private Angelo (+ co-p/w; co-d Michael Anderson). 1961: Romanoff and Juliet (+ p/fpl/w). 1962: Billy Budd (+ p/w; co-s). 1965: Lady L (+ w).

Films as actor include: 1942: One of Our Aircraft is Missing. 1944: The Way Ahead (+ co-s). 1951: Quo Vadis. 1954: The Egyptian. 1955: We're no Angels;

Lola Montès. 1960: The Sundowners. 1964: Topkapi. 1967: The Comedians.

V

VADIM, Roger

(Roger Vadim Plemmianikov) Director. Paris 1928–
Father Russian, mother French. After study at numerous schools acted on stage (1944–47). 1947–56: assistant to Marc Allégret starting with Blanche Fury in Britain. His penultimate film with Allégret was Futures Vedettes (1955) in which a second lead part was played by Brigitte Bardot, the female lead in En effeuillant la marguerite, which he also wrote for Allégret. Scripted a Bardot musical, Cette sacrée gamine (1955). Reporter-photographer for Paris Match and directed a French TV programme. 1957: directed a ballet, 'Le Rendez-vous Manqué', from story by Francoise Sagan. 1961: artistic supervisor on La Bride sur le cou, but sacked the director Jean Aurel and took over. 1962: produced Et Satan conduit le bal. His films have often starred his wives, Bardot, Annette Stroyberg (Annette Vadim) and Jane Fonda. Usually credited with collaboration on scripts of his films, sometimes with Roger Vailland.

Films as director: 1956: Et Dieu créa la femme – And God Created Woman – And Woman Was Created (+ co-s). 1957: Sait-on jamais? – When the Devil Drives – No Sun In Venice. 1958: Les Bijoutiers du clair de lune – Heaven Fell that Night (+ co-s). 1959: Les Liaisons Dangereuses (+ co-s). 1960: Et mourir de plaisir – Blood and Roses (+ co-s). 1961: Les Sept Péchés Capitaux ep L'Orgeuil; La Bride sur le cou – Please Not Now! (+ co-s). 1962: Le Repos du guerrier – Warrior's Rest – Love on a Pillow (+ co-s); Le Vice et la vertu – Vice and Virtue (+ co-s). 1963: Château en Suède – Nutty, Naughty Chateau. 1964: La Ronde. 1966: La Curée – The Game is Over – The Quarry (+ co-ad). 1967: Barbarella; Histoires Extraordinaires ep Metzengerstein. 1971: Pretty Maids All in a Row.

VAJDA, Ladislao or Ladislas

Director. Budapest 1905–65 Barcelona
Son of writer Ladislaus Vajda. 1925: joined Hunnia Film Company, Budapest. 1927: to Berlin, camera assistant, operator. Assistant to Pabst. 1933: first film as director in collaboration, in UK. 1935: returned to Hungary. Worked also in theatre. 1940–41: worked in Italy. 1943–48: in Spain. 1948–50: in UK. 1950–57: in Spain; became Spanish citizen. From 1958: worked in Switzerland, Germany and Spain. 1965: died during making of his last film.

Films as director: 1933: Where is this Lady? (co-d W. Victor Hanbury). 1935: Halló Budapest! 1936: Wings over Africa; Ember a híd alatt; Szenzáció (co-d Istvan Szekely). 1937: The Wife of General Ling; A kölcsönkert kastély; Az én lányom nem olyan. 1938: Magdát kicsapják; Döntö pillanat; Fekete Gyémántok; Péntek rézi; Rozmaring. 1940: Giuliano de' Medici. 1941: La Zia Smemorata (+ co-s). 1943: Se vende un

Tom Neal and Ann Savage in Detour by Edgar G. Ulmer.
Billy Budd, directed by Peter Ustinov.
Rudolph Valentino in The Four Horsemen of the Apocalypse by Rex Ingram.

palacio; Dolce Lunas de Miel. 1944: Te quiero para mi; El Testamento del Virrey. 1945: Cinco Lobitos. 1947: Tres Espejos; Barrio. 1948: Sin uniforme. 1949: The Golden Madonna. 1950: The Woman with no Name (+ co-s); Septima Pagina. 1951: Ronda Española. 1952: Doña Francisquitta (+ co-s). 1953: Carne de horca. 1954: Aventuras del Barbero de Sevilla. 1955: Marcelina, pan y vino (+ co-s); Tarde de toros. 1956: Mio Tio Jacinto (+ co-s). 1957: Un Angel e sceso por Brooklyn (+ co-s). 1958: Es geschah am hellichten Tage (+ co-s). 1959: Ein Mann geht durch die Wand. 1960: Maria, matricula de Bilbao. 1961: Der Lügner. 1962: Die Schatten werden Langer – Girls in the Shadows (+ co-s). 1963: Das Feuerschiff. 1965: La Signora di Beirut (uf).

VALENTINO, Rudolph

(Rodolfo Gugliemi) Actor. Taranto, Italy 1895–1926 New York
Failed course at Venice Military Academy. Trained in agriculture. 1913: to USA. Worked as gardener, then exhibition dancer in New York. Dancer with travelling music-hall troupe, to Hollywood. 1918: first film appearance in dance-hall scene. Subsequently played small film parts for various companies e.g. Universal, Vitagraph, Ince. 1921: first major role in *The Four Horsemen of the Apocalypse* for Metro; appeared in 3 more films for Metro then moved to Famous Players-Lasky until 1924. 1925–26: worked for independent companies; last 2 films released through United Artists. Died of peritonitis.

Films as actor include: 1919: The Delicious Little Devil; The Big Little Person; The Homebreaker. 1921: The Four Horsemen of the Apocalypse; The Uncharted Sea; The Conquering Power. 1922: Beyond the Rocks; Blood and Sand. 1925: The Eagle.

VALÈRE, Jean

Director. Paris 1925–
World War II: served in Army Film Unit. Then worked as apprentice in film laboratories. 1946: began as assistant director e.g. to Marcel Carné, Max Ophüls, Yves Allégret, André Cayatte. 1955: first short film as director, in collaboration. 1959: directed first feature. Also directed for TV e.g. 'Anatole'.

Films as director: 1955: Paris la nuit (*co-d Jacques Baratier*). 1957: Jours de fête à Moscou. 1959: La Sentence. 1960: Les Grandes Personnes (+ co-s). 1964: Le Gros Coup (+ co-s). 1969: La Femme Ecarlate – The Scarlet Woman (+ co-s). 1971: Mont-Dragon (+ co-s).

VALLI, Alida

(Alida Maria Altenburger) Actress. Pola, Italy 1921–
Centro Sperimentale di Cinematografia, Rome. In films from 1936. 1937: adopted screen name. 1943: refused to make propaganda films for reinstated fascist Republican party and spent 2 years in hiding. 1946: contract with David O. Selznick, continuing to work mainly in Italy where she made most of her films. 1956: took up stage acting in Rome and, for one season, in Philadelphia. Has appeared on Italian TV. Married (1941) musician Oscar de Mejo, later separated.

Films as actress include: 1940: Piccolo Mondo Antico. 1942: Noi Vivi. 1947: The Paradine Case. 1948: The Miracle of the Bells. 1949: The Third Man. 1950: Les Miracles n'ont lieu qu'une fois. 1952: Les Amants de Tolède. 1953: Siamo donne *ep* Alida Valli. 1954: Senso. 1957: Il Grido. 1958: Les Bijoutiers du clair de lune; La Diga sul Pacifico. 1959: Les Yeux sans visage. 1960: La Dialogue des Carmélites. 1961: Une Aussi Longue Absence. 1962: Homenaje a la hora de la siesta; Ophélia. 1967: Edipo Re. 1970: Strategia del ragno.

VALLONE, Raf

Actor. Catanzaro, Italy 1916–
Began as professional footballer for Turin, and journalist. 1948: first film as actor *Riso Amaro*. 1958: appeared on Paris stage in 'A View from the Bridge'. Subsequent stage appearances in Italy, France, USA. 1962: acted in series for Italian TV. Married (1952) actress Elena Varzi.

Films as actor include: 1949: Cuori senza frontiera. 1950: Non c'è pace tra gli ulivi; Il Cammino della speranza. 1951: Cristo Proibito; Anna; Camicie Rosse; Roma, ore undici. 1953: Thérèse Raquin. 1955: Il Segno di Venere. 1957: Guendalina; Rose Bernd. 1958: La Venganza. 1960: Recours en grâce; La Ciociara. 1961: El Cid. 1962: Vu du pont; Phaedra. 1963: The Cardinal. 1964: The Secret Invasion. 1965: Harlow. 1966: Nevada Smith. 1970: Cannon for Cordoba; La Morte risale a ieri sera.

VANCINI, Florestano

Director. Ferrara, Italy 1926–
Broke off scientific education to become journalist. 1949: began as documentary director. Made over 35 shorts. Worked as assistant to Valerio Zurlini, Mario Soldati e.g. assistant director and script-writer in collaboration on *La Donna del fiume* (1955). 1960: directed first feature and wrote script in collaboration with Pier Paolo Pasolini and Ennio de Concini.

Features as director: 1960: La Lunga Notte del '43 – The Long Night of '43 (+ co-s). 1961: Le Italiane e l'amore *ep* La Separazione Legale (+ co-s). 1962: La Banda Casaroli. 1964: La Calda Vita. 1965: I Lunghi Giorni della vendetta. 1966: Le Stagioni del nostro amore – Seasons of Our Love. 1968: L'Isola (+ co-s).

VAN DEN HORST, Herman

Director. Kinderdijk, Holland 1911–
Commercial college. Curator of biological museum. Nature photography. 1945: first film as director. 1960: first feature as director, made in Surinam. Produced most of his films; all are documentaries. Also poet.

Films as director: 1945: Metamorphose. 1948: Het Bijstere Land van Veluwen – Rape of a Country. 1949: Der Zee ontrukt – Wrested from the Sea. 1954: Vieren Maar – Lekko. 1965: Amsterdam.

Films as director and producer: 1952: Het Schot is te boord – Shoot the Nets. 1953: Houen zo – Steady Now. 1958: Prijs de maar – Praise the Sea. 1960: Faja Lobbi – Symphony of the Tropics – Fiery Love. 1961: Pan. 1967: Toccata.

VAN DYKE, Dick

Actor. West Plains, Missouri 1925–
Elder brother of nightclub comedian Jerry Van Dyke. 1947–53: comedy act with Philip Erickson. 1959: Broadway debut in 'The Girls Against the Boys'; also in 'Bye Bye Birdie'. TV series, 'The Dick Van Dyke Show' (1961–66).

Films as actor include: 1963: Bye Bye Birdie. 1964: What a Way to Go; Mary Poppins. 1965: The Art of Love. 1967: Divorce American Style; Fitzwilly. 1968: Chitty Chitty Bang Bang. 1969: Some Kind of a Nut.

VAN DYKE, Willard

Director. Denver, Colorado 1906–
University of California. Stills photographer. 1935: entered films as operator. 1937: cinematographer in collaboration on *The River*. 1939: with Ralph Steiner founded own company; in collaboration with Steiner made first film as director. 1942–46: commissions from US government. 1948: fled McCarthyism to Puerto Rico, set up documentary school there. From mid-1950s many films for TV. 1965: became director of department of film at Museum of Modern Art, New York. Almost all films are commissioned or sponsored. Films as producer include *Terribly Talented* (1948), Richard Leacock's *Toby and the Tall Corn* (1955), *Search into Darkness* (1962).

Films as director: 1939: The City (+ co-p/co-c; co-d Ralph Steiner). 1940: Valley Town (+ co-s); The Children Must Learn (+ s, co-c); Sarah Lawrence. 1941: To Hear Your Banjo Play; Tall Tales. 1942: The Bridge. 1943: Oswego; Steeltown. 1944: Pacific Northwest (+ co-c). 1945: San Francisco. 1946: Journey into Medicine. 1947: The Photographer. 1949: This Charming Couple; Mount Vernon. 1950: Years of Change. 1952: New York University. 1953: Working and Playing to Health; There is a Season. 1954: Recollections of Boyhood: an Interview with Joseph Welch; Cabos Blancos (co-d Angel F. Rivera); Excursion House. 1957: Life of the Molds. 1958: The Skyscraper (co-d Shirley Clarke); Tiger Hunt in Assam; Mountains of the Moon. 1959: Land of White Alice; The Procession. 1960: Ireland, the Tear and the Smile; Sweden. 1962: So That Men are Free; Harvest. 1963: Depressed Area, USA. 1964: Rice (co-d Wheaton Galentine); Frontiers of News (+ c). 1965: Pop Buell, Hoosier Farmer in Laos; Taming the Mekong; The Farmer, Feast or Famine (co-d Roger Barlow); Frontline Cameras 1935–1965 (+ p).

VAN DYKE, W. S.
or Woody

Director. San Diego, California 1887–1943 Hollywood
Began as stage actor in stock, vaudeville and road shows. 1915: entered films as extra; assistant on *The Birth of a Nation*. 1916: assistant director to D. W. Griffith on *Intolerance*. 1917: contract as director, writer, editor with Essanay in Chicago. 1918: military service during World War I. 1920–22: mainly, director of 15-episode serials for Pathe. 1923–24: director with various independent companies. 1924–26: mainly with Fox. 1927: with MGM and Pathe. From 1928: worked entirely with MGM. Was to direct *White Shadows in*

the *South Seas* in collaboration with Robert Flaherty, who resigned. World War II: Major in US Marine Corps Reserve.

Films as director from 1928: 1928: Wyoming (+ *st*); Under the Black Eagle; White Shadows in the South Seas. 1929: The Pagan. 1931: Trader Horn; Never the Twain shall Meet; Guilty Hands; The Cuban Love Song. 1932: Tarzan, the Ape Man; Night Court. 1933: Penthouse; The Prizefighter and the Lady (+ *p*). 1934: Eskimo; Manhattan Melodrama; The Thin Man; Forsaking all Others; Laughing Boy; Hide-Out. 1935: Naughty Marietta; I Live My Life. 1936: Rose-Marie; His Brother's Wife (+ *co-p*); San Francisco (+ *co-p*); The Devil is a Sissy; Love on the Run; After the Thin Man. 1937: Personal Property; They Gave Him a Gun; Rosalie. 1938: Marie Antoinette; Sweethearts. 1939: Stand Up and Fight; It's a Wonderful World; Andy Hardy Gets Spring Fever; Another Thin Man. 1940: I Love you Again; Bitter Sweet; I Take this Woman. 1941: Rage in Heaven; The Feminine Touch; Shadow of the Thin Man; Dr Kildare's Victory. 1942: Journey for Margaret; I Married an Angel; Cairo.

VANEL, Charles

Actor. Rennes, France 1885 –
1908: left naval academy. Joined amateur theatre companies, then provincial touring companies. From 1912: also acted in films. Paris stage. From 1920: acted only in films. 1935: directed and acted in *Dans la nuit*. 1949: several films in Italy.

Films as actor include: 1924: Pêcheurs d'islande; La Nuit de la revanche. 1926: La Proie du vent. 1931: L'Arlésienne. 1934: Le Grand Jeu. 1935: L'Equipage. 1936: La Belle Equipe; Jenny. 1937: Abus de confiance. 1939: L'Or du Cristobal. 1943: Le Ciel est à vous. 1949: In nome de la legge. 1953: Le Salaire de la peur. 1954: L'Affaire Maurizius; Si Versailles m'était conté. 1955: Les Diaboliques; To Catch a Thief. 1956: La Mort en ce jardin. 1959: Pêcheurs d'islande. 1960: La Vérité. 1962: La Steppa; Rififi à Tokyo. 1963: L'Aîné des ferchaux; Un Roi sans divertissement; Symphonie pour un massacre. 1965: Le Chant du monde. 1966: Un Homme de trop. 1968: La Prisonnière.

VAN PARYS, Georges

Composer. Paris 1902 – 70 Paris
Son of textile manufacturer. Educated in Paris, then law at Paris University. From 1924: composer. 1930: first film as composer in collaboration *Sous les toits de Paris*, first French sound film. Music for theatre includes 'Fra Diavolo', 'La Dame de Chez Maxim's', 'Mademoiselle Virginie' (operetta) and Marcel Achard's comedy-ballet 'Voulez-vous danser avec moâ?'. 1949: music for Achard's *Jean de la lune*. Numerous songs. Former president of composers' group in Syndicat National of authors and composers; former member of Comité des Variétés of ORTF. Chevalier de la Légion d'Honneur. Book, 'Les Jours comme ils viennent' (1969).

Films as composer include: 1931: Le Million (*co*); Un Soir de rafle. 1933: Cette Vieille Canaille. 1935: Quelle Drôle de gosse. 1937: Abus de confiance. 1941: Caprices. 1943: L'Homme de Londres. 1945: Le

Couple Idéal. 1947: Le Silence est d'or. 1949: Jean de la Lune; Lady Paname; Un Certain Monsieur. 1951: Fanfan la Tulipe (*co*); Le Grand Méliès; L'Amour, madame; Trois Femmes; Deux sous de violettes. 1952: Casque d'or; Les Belles-de-nuit; Adorables Créatures. 1953: Dortoir des grandes; Madame de . . .; Le Grand Jeu (*co*); Mam'zelle Nitouche; L'Affaire Maurizius; Rue de l'Estrapade (*co*). 1954: Avant le déluge (*co*); Madame DuBarry; Papa, Maman, la bonne et moi. 1955: French Can Can; Nana; Les Grandes Manoeuvres; Les Carnets du Major Thompson. 1956: The Happy Road. 1957: Les Misérables. 1958: Guinguette. 1959: Nathalie, Agent Secret. 1960: Tendre et Violente Elisabeth. 1961: Mister Topaze; Tout l'or du monde. 1962: Mandrin; Le Masque de fer. 1964: Monsieur. 1965: Les Fêtes Galantes. 1970: Elle boit pas, elle fume pas, elle drague pas, mais . . . elle cause!

VARDA, Agnès

Director. Brussels 1928 –
Sorbonne; Louvre art school; Vaugirard photographic school. From 1949: professional photographer. 1951–61: official photographer for Jean Vilar's Théâtre National Populaire; journalist/photographer for Réalités, Plaisir de France, Marie-France, travelling to China, Germany, UK, Portugal, Cuba. 1954: first film as director, edited by Alain Resnais. 1966: made *Elsa* for TV. Married to Jacques Demy.

Films as director: 1954: La Pointe Courte (+ *st/s/n*). 1957: O saisons, ô châteaux – Castles through the Ages (+ *st/s/n*). 1958: L'Opéra-Mouffe (+ *p/st/s/*); Du côté de la côte – The Riviera, Today's Eden (+ *st/s/n*). 1959: La Cocotte d'Azur. 1961: Cléo de 5 a 7 – Cleo from 5 to 7 (+ *st/s*). 1963: Salut les Cubains – Hello Cubans (+ *c*). 1964: Le Bonheur – Happiness (+ *st/s*). 1966: Loin du Vietnam – Far from Vietnam (*co-p only*); Les Créatures (+ *s*); Elsa. 1968: Black Panthers. 1969: Lions Love (+ *p/s*).

VASILIEV, Sergei and Georgi ('The Brothers Vasiliev')

Directors. Sergei: Moscow 1900 – 59 Moscow; Georgi: 1899 – 1945
Homonymous but unrelated. Sergei in Red Army from 1917 to end of World War I, then Leningrad Institute. Became editor at Sevzapkino specialising in re-editing foreign films. Together they were editors at Sovkino e.g. of footage shot by expedition to recover Nobile's Arctic dirigible. Both in Sergei Eisenstein's class. 1930: Grigori Alexandrov scripted their first film as directors. 1932: Leningrad studio gave them treatment written by widow of Dmitri Furmanov of her husband's novel; the Vasilievs rewrote it using widow's own records of the period; made the film, *Chapayev*, in 1934. 1943: Sergei became head of Lenfilm. 1944–46: official vacillations prevented realisation of projects. 1945: death of Georgi. 1956: Sergei visited UK to observe production techniques. They worked mainly for Lenfilm.

Films as directors together: 1930: Spyashchaya Krasavitsa – The Sleeping Beauty. 1932: Lichnoye Delo – A Personal Affair. 1934: Chapayev (+ *co-s*). 1938: Volochayevskie Dni – Volochayevsk Days (+ *s*). 1942: Oborona Tsaritsyna – The Defence of Tsaritsyn (+ *s*). 1943: Front. 1954: Geroi Chipki – The Heroes

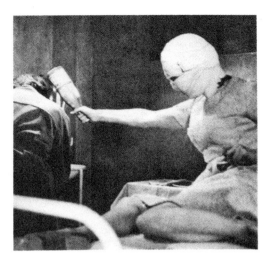

Alida Valli in Georges Franju's Les Yeux sans Visage.
Jean Harlow and Robert Taylor in W. S. Van Dyke's Personal Property.
Anna Karina and Jean-Luc Godard (right) in Agnès Varda's Cleo. de 5 à 7.

of Chipka (*Sergei alone*). 1958: V dni Oktyabrya – In the October Days (*Sergei alone*; + *co-s*).

VAUGHN, Robert

Actor. New York 1932–
Father radio actor Walter Vaughn. Mother stage actress Marcella Gaudel. Journalism at University of Minnesota. 1951: won radio acting contest. Drama at Los Angeles City College, acted and directed. Los Angeles State College; while there, resident director and actor at Albuquerque Summer House Theatre. Spotted in 'End as a Man' at Player's Ring Theatre, Hollywood; Hecht-Lancaster contract. Military service. 1958: loaned to Columbia for first film as actor *No Time to be Young*. TV series 'The Man From UNCLE'.

Films as actor include: 1959: The Young Philadelphians. 1960: The Magnificent Seven. 1968: Bullitt. 1969: The Bridge at Remagen.

VAVRA, Otakar

Director. Hraden Kralove, Czechoslovakia 1911–
Architecture at Brno and Prague University. Publicist. Made shorts throughout 1930s. Scriptwriter and assistant to several directors. 1937: first feature as director *Filosofská Historie*. Became senior professor in direction at FAMU.

Films as director: 1931: Svetlo pronika tmou (+ *s*). 1934: Zijeme v praze (+ *s*). 1935: Listopad (+ *s/e*). 1936: Velboud uchem jehly (+ *co-s*). 1937: Filosofská Historie (+ *s*); Panenstvi (+ *co-s*). 1938: Cech panen kutnohorskych (+ *co-s*). 1939: Humoreska (+ *s*); Kouzelný dům (+ *s*); Dívka v modrém (+ *s*). 1940: Maskovana milenka (+ *s*); Podved s runensem; Pacientka doctora Hegla (+ *s*); Pohadka maje (+ *s*). 1941: Turbina (+ *s*). 1942: Okouzlená (+ *s*); Prijdu hned (+ *co-s*). 1943: Štastnou cestu (+ *s*). 1945: Rozina Sebranec (+ *s*) – Rosina, the Foundling (+ *co-s*); Vlast vita. 1946: Cesta k barikadam; Nezbedny Bakalar – The Mischievous Tutor (+ *co-s*). 1947: Předtucha – Presentiment (+ *s*). 1948: Krakatit (+ *co-s*). 1949: Němá Barikáda – The Silent Barricade (+ *co-s*). 1952: Nastup – Fall In! (+ *co-s*). 1954: Jan Hus (+ *co-s*); Jan Žižka z trochova – The Hussite Warrior (+ *co-s*). 1957: Proti Všem – Against All (+ *co-s*). 1958: Občan Brych – Citizen Brych (+ *co-s*). 1959: První Parta – The First Rescue Party (+ *s*). 1960: Srpnová Neděle – August Sunday; Policejni hodina – Time, Gentlemen, Please (+ *s*). 1963: Horouci Srdce – The Passionate Heart – The Burning Heart. 1965: Zlata Renata – The Golden Queening. 1967: Romance pro Křidlovku – Romance for Trumpet. 1968: Třináctá Komanta – The Thirteenth Chamber. 1969: Kladivo na Čarodějnice – A Hammer against Witches.

VÈDRES, Nicole

Director. Paris 1911–65 Paris
Sorbonne. Published collection of photographs and engravings with essay, 'Une Siècle d'élégance francaise (1800–1900)'. Research for this led to album of photographs on history of French cinema from beginnings to 1945, 'Images du cinéma francais'. 1947: with assistance of Pierre Braunberger made first film, compilation of documentary material. 1950: *La Vie commence demain* contained footage of e.g. André Gide, Picasso,

Le Corbusier, Sartre, André Labarthe. After 1953 left cinema for TV and writing. Novels include 'Labyrinthe' and 'Christophe'.

Films as director: 1947: Paris 1900. 1950: La Vie commence demain. 1953: Aux Frontières de l'homme – The Border of Life (*co-d Jean Rostand*).

VEIDT, Conrad

(Conrad Weidt) Actor. Potsdam, Germany 1892–1943 Hollywood
Jewish parents. Stage training with Max Reinhardt. 1913: acted in Reinhardt's Deutsches Theatre in Berlin. 1917: first major film parts. Theatrical work in Germany and Austria. Acted in numerous films directed by Richard Oswald. 1922: directed, produced in collaboration, wrote and acted in *Lord Byron,* his only film as director. 1923: produced and acted in *Paganini*. 1927–29: several films in USA, mainly for Universal, including Paul Leni's *The Man Who Laughs*. 1932: to UK. 1938: in Paris acted in Richard Oswald's *Tempête sur l'Asie*. 1941–43: American films, including 2 produced by Victor Saville who had directed him in 2 British films.

Films as actor include: 1917: Das Rätsel von Bangalore; Die Seeschlacht. 1918: Das Tagebuch einer Verlorenen. 1919: Anders als die Andern; Das Kabinett des Dr Caligari; Prinz Kuckuck; Die Prostitution; Die Reise um die Erde in 80 Tagen; Unheimliche Geschichten. 1920: Satanas; Abend ... Nacht ... Morgen; Der Gang in die Nacht; Der Januskopf; Kurfurstendamm; Manolescus Memoiren; Patience; Der Reigen; Sehnsucht. 1921: Lady Hamilton; Das Indische Grabmal. 1922: Lukrezia Borgia. 1924: Carlos und Elisabeth; Nju; Das Wachsfigurenkabinett; Orlacs Hände. 1925: Ingmarsarvet. 1926: Durfen wir Schweigin?; Der Geiger von Florenz; Der Student von Prag. 1927: Beloved Rogue. 1929: Last Performance; Das Land ohne Frauen. 1930: The Virtuous Sin; Menschen im Käfig; Die Letzte Kompanie. 1931: Der Kongress tanzt; Der Mann, der den Mord beging. 1933: Ich und die Kaiserin; I Was a Spy; The Wandering Jew. 1937: Dark Journey; Under the Red Robe. 1939: The Spy in Black. 1940: Contraband; The Thief of Bagdad; Escape. 1941: A Woman's Face; The Men in Her Life. 1942: Nazi Agent; All Through the Night. 1943: Casablanca; Above Suspicion.

VELO, Carlos

Director. Spain 1905–
Teacher and lecturer. 1933–35: directed and wrote series of short documentaries in collaboration with Fernando Mantilla. 1936: made several shorts alone. 1937: emigrated to Mexico. From 1941: technical director of newsreels for cinema. From 1953: director of documentaries. From 1954: TV administrator in charge of newsreel production. 1955: in collaboration with the director wrote Benito Alazraki's *Raices,* and was technical supervisor on it. 1958: production adviser on *Nazarin*. 1959: made *Mexico Mio* at suggestion of Cesare Zavattini, with painter David Alfaro Siqueiros as artistic adviser.

Films as director and writer in collaboration with Fernando Mantilla: 1933: Castillos de Castilla; Terraco Augusta; Galicia y Compostela. 1934:

Almadrabas. 1935: Infinitos; Felipe II y el Escoriale; La Ciudad y el campo (*s alone*).

Films as director and writer: 1936: Saudade; En un lugarda Castilla; Romancero Marroquin. 1953: Pintura Mural Mexicana (*d only*). 1954: Tierra Caliente. 1955: Torero! (*co-s*). 1959: Mexico Mio. 1967: Pedro Paramo.

VENTURA, Lino

Actor. Parma, Italy 1918–
Moved to Paris as a child. Numerous early jobs included boxing. 1954: first film as actor *Touchez pas au Grisbi*.

Films as actor include: 1958: Marie-Octobre. 1959: Classe tous risques. 1960: La Ragazza en vetrina. 1961: Un Taxi pour Tobrouk. 1962: Le Bateau d'Emile. 1963: Le Diable et les dix commandements; Les Tontons Flingueurs; Die Dreigroschenoper. 1965: Les Barbouzes; L'Arme à gauche; Les Grandes Gueules; Le Deuxième Souffle. 1966: Avec la peau des autres. 1967: Les Aventuriers. 1969: L'Armée des ombres; Les Clan des Siciliens. 1971: Boulevard du Rhum.

VERA-ELLEN

(Vera-Ellen Westmeyr Rohe) Actress. Cincinnati, Ohio 1926–
Dancing lessons from 10 to improve her health. Sonia Serova School of Dancing, New York. Stage, night-clubs. 1939: Broadway debut 'Very Warm for Mary'. Also appeared in 'Higher and Higher', 'Panama Hattie', 'By Jupiter', 'A Connecticut Yankee'. 1945: first film *Wonder Man*. 1945–47: contract to Goldwyn. Later freelance and MGM contract. Married dancer Robert Hightower (1945–46, divorced).

Films as actor include: 1946: The Kid from Brooklyn; Three Little Girls in Blue. 1947: Carnival in Costa Rica. 1948: Words and Music. 1949: On the Town. 1950: Love Happy; Three Little Words. 1952: The Belle of New York. 1953: Call Me Madam; The Big Leaguer. 1954: White Christmas.

VERNEUIL, Henri

Director. Rodisto, Turkey 1920–
At 4 fled with American family from Turkey; settled in Marseille. Studied mechanical engineering, then worked in journalism and radio in Marseille. Entered film industry after the Liberation. 1946: directed first short in which Fernandel appeared. 1951: first feature as director, starring Fernandel.

Features as director include (complete from 1960): 1951: La Table aux crèves – The Village Feud (+ *co-s*). 1953: Ennemi Public No 1 – Public Enemy No 1. 1954: Le Mouton à cinq pattes – The Sheep has Five Legs (+ *co-s*). 1955: Les Amants du Tage – The Lovers of Lisbon. 1956: Pan's Palace – Hôtel. 1957: Une Manche et la belle – The Evil that is Eve (+ *co-s*). 1959: La Vache et le prisonnier. 1960: La Française et l'amour – Love and the Frenchwoman *ep* L'Adultère – Adultery; L'Affaire d'une nuit – It Happened All Night. 1961: Le Président (+ *co-s*); Les Lions sont lâchés. 1962: Un Singe en hiver – It's Hot in Hell; Mélodie en sous-sol – The Big Snatch (+ *co-s/e*). 1963:

Cent Mille Dollars au soleil – Greed in the Sun (+ *co-ad*). 1964: Weekend à Zuydcoote – Weekend in Dunkirk. 1966: La 25e heure – The 25th Hour (+ *co-s*). 1968: La Bataille de San Sebastian – Guns for San Sebastian. 1969: Le Clan des Siciliens – The Sicilian Clan (+ *co-s*). 1971: Le Casse (+ *p/co-ad/co-di*).

VERNON, Anne

(Edith Vignaud) Actress. St Denis, France 1925–
Studied painting. Worked at Marcel Rochas as fashion artist in early 1940s. 1943: designed costumes for *L'Eternel Retour*. Appearing in films by 1947. Also acted in French theatre. 1963: exhibited paintings in New York.

Films as actress include: 1951: Edouard et Caroline. 1952: Song of Paris. 1953: Rue de l'Estrapade. 1954: The Love Lottery; Bel Ami. 1955: La Donna più bella del mondo. 1959: Il Generale della Rovere. 1964: Les Parapluies de Cherbourg.

VERTOV, Dziga

(Denis Arkadievitch Kaufman) Director. Bialystock, Poland 1896–1954 Moscow
Father librarian. Studied music. Institute of Psycho-Neurology then University of Moscow. 1916: in Petrograd worked in laboratory of hearing. Soon after Revolution joined Committee of Cinematography in Moscow. Worked in titling and as editor. Edited footage on Revolution and Civil War. 1918–19: under Lev Kuleshov's supervision worked on *Kino Nedelya*, first Soviet film-journal, in 43 numbers. Became entirely responsible for it, organised groups of camera-men spread over Russia, travelled widely. 1919: made first feature length film *Godovshchina revolyutsii*. 1920–21: first experiments in mobile film units. 1922–25: made *Kino Pravda* film-journal in 23 numbers, some numbers appearing under other titles; collaborators included his brother cinematographer Mikhail Kaufman who worked with him on almost all his films until 1929; included first Soviet animation; particular emphasis on titles. 1924: *Kino Glaz*, documentary experiment, was co-directed by his wife Elizoveta Svilova; she collaborated on the scripts and editing of many of his films and co-directed *Chelovek s kinoapparatom* (1929) and his last 11 films (apart from the newsreels *Novosti dnya*). 1926: made 2 films for Kultkino, commissioned by organisations outside film industry; *Shestaya Chast mira* involved large number of travelling cameramen. 1928–30: worked for VUFKU based in Ukraine: films include *Chelovek s kinoapparatom* which used no titles or commentary. 1930: *Entuziazm* severely criticised in Russia. 1934: researched 100,000 metres of film for *Tri Pesni o Leninye*. 1937: last feature *Kolybelnaya*; after 're-organisation' of film industry, little employed. 1947–54: newsreels. Brother is cinematographer Boris Kaufman.

Films as director and writer: 1918–19: Kino Nedelya – Cine Weekly (*d/e/t only*; *43 numbers*). 1919: Godov-shchina revolyutsii – Anniversary of the Revolution (*d/e only*; *12 parts*); Boi pod Tsaritsynom – Fighting near Tsaritsin (+ *co-c/e*). 1920: Vskrytie moshchei Sergiya Radonezhskovo – The Exhumation of the Re-mains of Sergei Radonezhkovo (+ *co-c*); Vserossiiskii Starosta Kalinin – Kalinin, Starost of Russia (+ *c/e*); Protsess Mironova – The Trial of Mironov. 1921:

Agitpoezhd vtsika – Train of the Central Executive (*d only*). 1922: Istoriya grazhdanskoi voiny – History of the Civil War (+ *e*); Univermag – State Department Store (*d only*); Protsess eserov – The Trial of the Social Revolutionaries (+ *t*). 1922–25: Kino Pravda – Film Truth (+ *co-c/co-e/t*; *23 numbers*). 1923: Pyat let borby i pobedy – Five Years of Struggle and Victory. 1923–25: Goskino Kalendar – Goskino Journal (+ *e*; *55 numbers*). 1924: Dayesh vozdukh – Long Live the Air; Segodnya – Today; Sovetskie Igrushki – Soviet Toys; Grimaci Parizhi – Scowls of Paris; Zhumoreski – Humouresque. 1926: Shagai, Soviet! – Stride, Soviet! (*co-s*; + *e/t*); Shestaya Chast mira – A Sixth of the World (*co-s*; + *e/t*; *6 parts*). 1928: Odinnadtstyi – The Eleventh (*co-s*; + *co-e/t*; *5 parts*). 1930: Entuziazm – Simfoniya Donbassa – Enthusiasm– – Symphony of the Donbass (+ *co-e*). 1934: Tri Pesni o Leninye – Three Songs of Lenin (+ *e*). 1937: Kolybelnaya – Lullabye (+ *e/n*). 1947–54: Novosti dnya – Daily News (*d only*).

?Films as director with Elizoveta Svilova: 1924: Kino Glaz – Camera Eye (+ *e alone*; *6 parts*). 1929: Chelovek s kinoapparatom – Man with a Movie Camera (+ *s/co-e alone*). 1937: Pamyati Sergo Ordzhonikidzye – In Memory of Sergei Ordzhonikidzye (+ *co-s/co-e alone*); Sergo Ordzhoni-kidzye. 1938: Slava Sovetskim geroinyam – To the Glory of Soviet Heroines (+ *s*); Tri Geroini – Three Heroines (+ *s*). 1941: V raionye vysoty A – Height A (+ *s*); Krov za krov, smert za smert – Blood for Blood, Life for Life (+ *s/e*); Na linii ognya-operatory kino-khroniki – On the Line of Fire-Film Reporters (+ *s/e*). 1943: Tebye, front – Kazakhstan Frontu – To the Front – To the Kazakhstan Front (+ *s alone*). 1944: V gorakh Ala-tau – On Mount Ala-tau; Sovetskoi Iskusstvo – Soviet Art. 1947: Klyatva molodykh – The Oath of Youth.

VIDAL, Gore

Writer. New York 1925–
1943–46: US Army. 1946: first novel 'Williwaw'. 1952–53: wrote under pseudonym Edgar Box. Wrote for TV, including 'Omnibus', 'Studio One', 'Philco-Goodyear Playhouse'. 1956: edited 'Best TV Plays'; first film as writer *The Catered Affair* adapted from TV play by Paddy Chayefsky. 1957–58: TV play 'Visit to a Small Planet' produced on Broadway. 1958: TV play 'The Death of Billy the Kid' filmed as *The Left Handed Gun*. 1959: drama critic for Reporter magazine; in collaboration with Tennessee Williams adapted Williams' play for *Suddenly Last Summer*. 1960: Democratic-Liberal candidate for US Congress; 'Visit to a Small Planet' filmed. 1960–61: play 'The Best Man' produced on Broadway. 1961–63: member of President John F. Kennedy's Advisory Committee on the Arts. 1962: Play 'Romulus' on Broadway. 1963: adapted own play for *The Best Man*. 1968: play 'Weekend' on Broadway. 1970: co-wrote script of *Myra Breckenridge* from own novel. Novels include 'The Judgment of Paris' (1952) and 'Julian' (1964). Book of essays: 'Reflections Upon a Sinking Ship' (1968). Writer for Partisan Review, The Nation.

Films as writer include: 1956: The Catered Affair. 1958: I Accuse. 1959: The Scapegoat (*ad*); Suddenly Last Summer (*co*). 1964: The Best Man. 1966: Paris, brûle-t-il? (*co*). 1970: Myra Breckenridge (*co-s/fn*).

Conrad Veidt in Das Kabinett des Dr. Caligari.
Dziga Vertov's Three Songs of Lenin.
Joseph L. Mankiewicz's Suddenly, Last Summer, *written by Gore Vidal and Tennessee Williams.*

VIDOR, Charles

Director. Budapest 1900–59 Vienna
Universities of Budapest and Berlin, civil engineering and arts. Army service, reaching Lieutenant, wounded 3 times. Worked as labourer, singer. Odd job man at Ufa, Berlin; became assistant editor, editor, then assistant director. To USA. Sang 3 years in opera. To Hollywood. 1929: financed and directed short film *The Bridge*. 1932: first feature as director, uncredited in collaboration. 1932–37: worked for several studios including RKO, Paramount. 1939–48: worked mainly for Columbia. 1951–56: mainly MGM. 1957–60: Paramount, Fox and Columbia. Died during making of *Song Without End*; film completed by George Cukor.

Features as director: 1932: The Mask of Fu Manchu (*uc, co-d Charles Brabin*). 1933: Sensation Hunters. 1934: The Double Door. 1935: Strangers All; The Arizonian; His Family Tree. 1936: Muss 'em Up. 1937: A Doctor's Diary; The Great Gambini; She's no Lady. 1939: Blind Alley; Romance of the Redwoods; Those High Gray Walls. 1940: My Son, My Son!; The Lady in Question. 1941: New York Town; Ladies in Retirement. 1942: The Tuttles of Tahiti; The Desperadoes. 1943: Cover Girl. 1944: Together Again. 1945: A Song to Remember; Over 21. 1946: Gilda. 1948: Loves of Carmen. 1951: It's a Big Country (*co-d 5 others*). 1952: Thunder in the East; Hans Christian Anderson. 1953: Rhapsody. 1956: Love Me or Leave Me; The Swan. 1957: A Farewell to Arms; The Joker is Wild. 1960: Song Without End (*co-d George Cukor*).

VIDOR, King

Director. Galveston, Texas 1895–
Son of wealthy landowner. Peacock Military Academy, San Antonio and Tome Institute, Port Deposit. Labourer, then projectionist in Galveston's only cinema. Amateur shorts. Cameraman on Mutual newsreels. 1915–16: publicity films in New York; newsreel operator in San Francisco. 1917–18: small parts as actor in Hollywood, also assistant. Directed Universal shorts. 1918: first feature as director. 1918–22: own studio. To 1944: worked mainly for MGM. From 1946: worked for several companies, including Fox, Warners, Universal. 1953: wrote autobiography 'A Tree is a Tree'. 1954: TV director on 'Lights Diamond Jubilee'. Author of 'War and Peace of King Vidor'. Produced many of his films. From 1915: married to Florence Vidor, who acted in several of his early films.

Features as director and producer: 1919: The Jack-Knife Man (*+co-s*). 1920: The Family Honor. 1921: Love Never Dies; The Sky Pilot (*co-p*). 1922: Conquering the Woman; Woman, Wake Up; The Real Adventure; Dusk to Dawn. 1923: Alice Adams. 1925: Proud Flesh (*co-p*). 1926: La Bohème; Bardelys the Magnificent. 1927: The Big Parade. 1928: The Crowd (*+co-s*); Show People (*co-p*). 1929: Hallelujah. 1930: Not So Dumb (*co-p*); Billy the Kid. 1931: The Champ. 1933: The Stranger's Return. 1934: Our Daily Bread. 1936: The Texas Rangers (*+co-st*). 1941: H.M. Pulham, Esq. (*+co-s*). 1944: An American Romance (*+st*). 1952: Ruby Gentry (*co-p*). 1959: Solomon and Sheba (*ex-p*).

Films as director: 1918: The Turn in the Road (*+s*).

1919: Better Times (*+s*); The Other Half (*+s*); Poor Relations (*+s*). 1922: Wild Oranges (*+co-s*). 1923: Peg O' My Heart; The Woman of Bronze; Three Wise Fools (*+co-s*); Happiness. 1924: Wine of Youth; His Hour; Wife of the Centaur. 1928: The Patsy. 1931: Street Scene. 1932: Bird of Paradise; Cynara. 1935: The Wedding Night; So Red the Rose. 1937: Stella Dallas. 1938: The Citadel. 1940: Northwest Passage; Comrade X. 1946: Duel in the Sun (*co-d, uc William Dieterle, Joseph Von Sternberg*). 1948: A Miracle Can Happen – On Our Merry Way (*co-d Leslie Fenton*). 1949: The Fountainhead; Beyond the Forest. 1951: Lightning Strikes Twice. 1952: Japanese War Bride. 1955: Man Without a Star. 1956: War and Peace (*+co-s*).

VIERNY, Sacha

Cinematographer and director. Bois-le-Roi, France 1919–
After leaving university trained at e.g. IDHEC and ENPC. 1947: assisted Roger Leenhardt on *Les Dernières Vacances*. From 1948: assistant director, TV cameraman. 1950–51: directed 2 shorts. From 1953: cinematographer.

Films as director: 1950: Voyage en Algérie. 1951: L'Anthrose de la lanche.

Films as cinematographer include: 1958: Lettre de Sibérie; Le Chant du Styrène; L'Opéra-Mouffe. 1959: Hiroshima, mon amour (*co*). 1960: Le Bel Âge (*co*). 1961: Merci Natercia; La Morte-Saison des amours; L'Année Dernière à Marienbad. 1963: Muriel, ou le temps d'un retour. 1966: La Guerre est finie. 1967: Belle de jour.

VIGO, Jean

Director and writer. Paris 1905–34 Paris
Father, Eugène-Bonaventure de Vigo (known as Miguel Almereyda) was a leading anarchist. 1914: at 9 with father witnessed assassination of Jean Jaurès. Father's daily paper, Le Bonnet Rouge, involved in dubious financial arrangements with Germans during World War I; Almereyda arrested and died, probably suicide, in prison (1917). 1918: to the provinces; educated under assumed name. 1925: left *lycée* in Chartres to attend Sorbonne. 1926: fell ill and went to Pyrenees to recuperate. Illness recurred for rest of life; met his wife, Elisabeth Lozinska, 'Lydu', in a clinic. 1928: helped by Claude Autant-Lara and Germaine Dulac found film work as assistant to cinematographer L.-H. Burel on *Vénus*. 1929: married Lydu; financed by her father, commenced *A propos de Nice*. 1930: founded film society in Nice; followed part of shooting of *La Seine, la vie d'un fleuve* by Jean Lods (who had introduced him to Boris Kaufman, cinematographer on all his 4 films), with music by Maurice Jaubert. 1931: given job by Germaine Dulac, documentary on swimmer Jean Taris; health of Lydu prevented him taking film work in Paris. 1932: project for short on tennis-player to be made in 3 language-versions abandoned; introduced to Jacques-Louis Nounez, who financed and arranged distribution of last 2 films. *Zéro de conduite* banned totally and until 1945 shown only in film societies in France. Shooting of feature *L'Atalante* slowed by illness; unsuccessful trade-showing led to addition of popular song to score and change of name to that of song, *Le Chaland qui passe*.

This version a commercial failure; restored version had first public showing in 1940.

Films as director and writer: 1929: A propos de Nice, point de vue documentée (*+e*). 1931: Taris – La Natation – La Natation, par Jean Taris, champion de France – Taris, roi de l'eau – Jean Taris, champion de natation (*+e*). 1933: Zéro de conduite, jeunes diables au collège – Zero for Conduct (*+e*). 1934: L'Atalante – Le Chaland qui passe (*co-s*).

VISCONTI, Luchino

Director. Milan 1906–
Father was Giuseppe Visconti, Duke of Modrona, theatrical impresario. At 13, appeared in public, playing 'cello; also acted. Service in cavalry; founded racing stable. Through Coco Chanel met Jean Renoir in Paris and was assistant on *Une Partie de campagne* and *Les Bas-fonds*. Worked on adaptation of Sardou for Renoir's *La Tosca* and collaborated with Karl Koch on completion of film when, on outbreak of war, Renoir returned to France. 1942: first film as director adapted from James M. Cain's 'The Postman Always Rings Twice', a manuscript translation of which was sent to him by Renoir. 1945: assisted Mario Serandrei on *Giorno di gloria*. Also theatrical director and designer. In Italy has directed plays by e.g. Jean Cocteau, Tennessee Williams, Arthur Miller, and opera. In France directed ''Tis Pity She's a Whore' with Romy Schneider and Alain Delon and 'Two for the See-Saw' with Jean Marais and Annie Girardot. Opera productions at Covent Garden have included Verdi's 'Don Carlos'. His assistants on *La Terra trema* (1947) were Francesco Rosi and Franco Zeffirelli. Nephew is director Eriprando Visconti.

Films as director: 1942: Ossessione (*+co-s*). 1945: Giorni di gloria (*ep*). 1947: La Terra trema (*+s*). 1951: Bellissima (*+co-s*); Appunti su un fatto di cronaca. 1953: Siamo donne – We the Women (*ep*; *+co-s*). 1954: Senso – The Wanton Countess (*+co-s*). 1957: Le Notti Bianche – White Nights (*+co-s*). 1960: Rocco e i suoi fratelli (*+co-s*). 1962: Boccaccio '70 *ep* Il Lavoro – The Job (*+co-s*). 1963: Il Gattopardo – The Leopard (*+co-s*). 1965: Vaghe Stelle dell'Orsa – Of A Thousand Delights; Sandra (*+co-s*). 1966: Le Streghe *ep* La Strega Bruciata Viva. 1967: Lo Straniero (*+co-s*). 1970: La Caduta degli dei – Götterdämmerung – The Damned (*+co-s*). 1971: Morte a Venezia – Death in Venice (*+p/co-s*).

VITTI, Monica

(Maria Luisa Cociarelli) Actress. Rome 1931–
Rome Academy of Dramatic Art. 1954–60: mainly stage actress, in classical and modern roles for various companies. From 1955: also in TV drama. Small film parts from 1954. 1957: dubbed for actress Dorian Gray in *Il Grido*. 1960: first leading screen role in *L'Avventura*. Subsequently left theatre for films except for leading part in 'After the Fall' (1964).

Films as actress include: 1961: La Notte. 1962: L'Eclisse; Les Quatre Vérités. 1963: Château en Suède; Dragées au poivre. 1964: Alta Infedeltà; Il Deserto Rosso; Le Bambole *ep* La Minestra. 1965: Il Disco Volante; Fai in fretta ad uccidermi . . . ho freddo! 1966: Modesty Blaise; Le Fate *ep* Fata Sabina. 1967: La Ragazza con la pistola; La Civitura di castita – The Chastity Belt – On My Way to the Crusades I Met a Girl Who . . .; Tiho sposato per allegria. 1969: La Femme Ecarlate; Amore, mio aiutami. 1971: La Pacifista; Le Coppie eps Il Frigorifero and Il Leone.

VLADY, Marina

(Marina de Poliakoff-Baïdaroff) Actress. Clichy-la-Garenne, France 1937–

Russian ancestry. No dramatic training. 1947–49: worked at Paris Opéra. 1949: first film as actress Orage d'été. From 1952: acted regularly in films. 1952–55: many Italian films; a number since. 1970: married Russian comedian and singer, Vladimir Vyssotsky. Sister of Odile Versois.

Films as actress include: 1954: Avant le déluge; Giorni d'amore; Sie. 1955: Les Salauds vont en enfer; La Sorcière. 1958: Toi . . . le Vénin; La Nuit des espions; La Sentence. 1960: La Ragazza in vetrina; La Princesse de Clèves; Les Sept Péchés Capitaux ep L'Orgeuil. 1962: Adorable Menteuse; La Steppa. 1963: Les Bonnes Causes; Una Storia Moderna: L'Ape Regina; Dragées au poivre. 1966: Deux on Trois Choses que je sais d'elle; Campanadas a medianoche. 1968: Siuzhet dyla nebolshovo rasskaza. 1969: Sirokko. 1970: Contestazione Generale.

VON GERLACH, Arthur

Director. Vienna 1876–1925 Berlin

Stage producer in Leipzig. 1906–11: director of theatre in Bromberg, including productions of Shakespeare and Strindberg. 1910: produced Mozart and Wagner operas in Holland. Producer of 2 films with Fern Andra. 1922: first film as director, scripted by Carl Mayer. 1925: second film as director, scripted by Thea von Harbou; prepared Prinz von Hamburg: died of apoplexy before shooting began.

Films as director: 1922: Vanina. 1925: Zür Chronik von Grieshuus.

VON HARBOU, Thea

Writer. Tauperlitz, Bavaria 1888–1954 Berlin

Wrote best-selling novels. 1919: with Fritz Lang adapted own novel 'Das Indische Grabmal'; filmed by Joe May (1921) and in a new adaptation by Lang (1958). Collaborated with Lang on all his films from Das wandernde Bild (1920) until he left Germany in 1933. Married Lang during shooting of Der müde Tod (1921); divorced 1934. Remained in Germany, and worked on Nazi films including some by Veit Harlan. After the war wrote books and a few scripts.

Films as writer include (apart from all Fritz Lang's films from 1920 to 1932, beginning with Das wandernde Bild): 1921: Das Indische Grabmal (co). 1922: Der brennende Acker (co); Phantom. 1923; Die Finanzen des Grossherzogs. 1924: Mikaël (co). 1925: Zür Chronik von Grieshuus. 1935: Der alte und der junge Konig (co). 1937: Der Herrscher (co). 1938: Jugend; Verwechte Spuren (co).

Films as director and writer: 1933: Elizabeth und der Narr. 1934: Hanneles Himmelfahrt.

VON STERNBERG, Josef

(Josef Sternberg) Director. Vienna 1894–1969 Hollywood

To New York at 7 with parents; they returned to Vienna after 3 years. 1908: family returned to USA. At 17, apprentice to a cleaner, patcher and coater of film; also projectionist. World War I: US Army. Assistant director, also cutter, editor and writer. Assisted Emile Chautard whom he later cast in Morocco (1930) and Shanghai Express (1932). His translation from German of Karl Adolph's novel Daughters of Vienna was published in Vienna (1922). 1925: first film as director. 1926: made A Woman of the Sea for Charles Chaplin as vehicle for Edna Purviance; suppressed by Chaplin. To Paramount as assistant; after a week, directed retakes for Frank Lloyd's Children of Divorce (1927): reshot over half the film in 3 days. Apart from trip to Germany to direct Jannings' first film, Der blaue Engel (1930), stayed at Paramount until 1935. 2 reels of edited film from his unfinished UK film Claudius (1937) are in Cinemathèque Francais. 1938: directed some extra shots for The Great Waltz and began I Take This Woman on which he was replaced by Frank Borzage (and, after 2 years, by W. S. Van Dyke). Directed 1 week of Duel in the Sun (1946) while King Vidor ill; credited as Colour Consultant. Taught film classes at University of California. Autobiography 'Fun in a Chinese Laundry' (1965).

Films as director: 1925: The Salvation Hunters (+p/s/e). 1926: The Exquisite Sinner (+co-s); A Woman of the Sea – The Sea Gull (ur; +s). 1927: Children of Divorce (uc; co-d Frank Lloyd); Underworld. 1928: The Last Command (+s); The Dragnet; The Docks of New York. 1929: The Case of Lena Smith; Thunderbolt. 1930: Der blaue Engel – The Blue Angel (+s); Morocco. 1931: Dishonoured (+st); An American Tragedy (+co-s). 1932: Shanghai Express; Blonde Venus (+st). 1934: The Scarlet Empress. 1935: The Devil is a Woman (+c); Crime and Punishment. 1936: The King Steps Out. 1937: Claudius – I, Claudius (uf; +s). 1939: Sergeant Madden. 1941: The Shanghai Gesture (+co-s). 1943: The Town. 1946: Duel in the Sun (uc; co-d King Vidor, William Dieterle, uc). 1951: Jet Pilot (r 1957; co-d Jules Furthman, uc). 1952: Macao (co-d Nicholas Ray, uc); The Saga of Anatahan – Anatahan (+p/s/c/n).

VON STROHEIM, Erich

(Erich Oswald Stroheim) Director, writer and actor. Vienna 1885–1957 Paris

Father a Jewish merchant from Gleiwitz in Russian Silesia; mother from Prague. Brief military service, then emigrated to USA (about 1906). Various jobs; to Hollywood. Bit parts in Captain McLean (1914), Ghosts (1915); extra and assistant director on The Birth of a Nation (1915), Intolerance (1916). Larger part in Old Heidelberg (1915) for which also military adviser. Various films as assistant director, military adviser, art director, or actor: first major part, as Prussian officer, in For France (1917). 1918: first film as director, for Universal. 1921: Foolish Wives cut, partly for censorship reasons, to about two-thirds of its intended length. 1923: replaced on Merry-Go-Round by Rupert Julian. 1923: Greed, for Goldwyn, cut from 42 reels to 10 when Goldwyn merged with MGM. 1928: The Wedding March split into 2 parts, heavily truncated; second part released only in Europe; Queen

Lillian Gish, Walter Huston and Jennifer Jones in King Vidor's Duel in the Sun.
Zür Chronik von Grieshuus by Arthur von Gerlach.
Saga of Anatahan, directed by Josef Von Sternberg.

Kelly less than half finished when shooting was stopped: released in version edited by the producers, Joseph Kennedy and Gloria Swanson. Returned to acting and writing. His only sound film, *Walking Down Broadway* (1933), was largely made over without credit by Raoul Walsh; released as *Hello Sister*. 1936: to France. Was to direct *La Dame Blanche*; cancelled on outbreak of World War II. 1940: returned to USA. 1941–43: acted on stage in 'Arsenic and Old Lace'. 1946–57: lived in France. 3 novels: 'Paprika' (1935), 'Poto-Poto' (written in early 1930s but published 1956) and 'Les Feux de la Saint-Jean' (2 volumes; 1951, 1954).

Films as director: 1918: Blind Husbands (*+ st/s/a/w*). 1919: The Devil's Passkey (*+ co-st/s/a*). 1921: Foolish Wives (*+ st/s/co-a/co-cos/w*). 1923: Merry-Go-Round (*+ st/s/co-a/co-cos*; *co-d Rupert Julian*); Greed (*+ s/co-a/co-c*). 1925: The Merry Widow (*+ co-s/co-a/co-cos*). 1928: The Wedding March (part I: The Wedding March; part II: The Honeymoon) (*+ co-s/co-a/co-cos*); Queen Kelly (*+ co-st/co-s*). 1933: Walking Down Broadway (*ur*; *+ co-s*; *co-d Raoul Walsh, uc*).

Films as actor include: 1917: Panthea; For France. 1918: Hearts of the World. 1919: The Heart of Humanity (*+ technical adviser*). 1930: The Great Gabbo. 1932: As You Desire Me. 1937: La Grande Illusion; Mademoiselle Docteur. 1938: Les Disparus de Saint-Agil; Ultimatum. 1939: Les Pièges; Macao, L'Enfer du jeu; Menaces. 1940: I Was an Adventuress. 1941: So Ends Our Night. 1943: Five Graves to Cairo; The North Star. 1945: The Great Flamarion. 1947: La Danse de mort. 1950: Sunset Boulevard. 1953: L'Envers du paradis. 1955: Napoléon.

Films as writer include: 1936: San Francisco (*co-di*); Devil Doll (*co*). 1937: Between Two Women. 1947: La Danse de mort (*co-ad/co-di*).

VON SYDOW, Max

Actor. Lund, Sweden 1929–
Royal Dramatic Theatre drama school, Stockholm. 1949: first film while still a student, Alf Sjöberg's *Bara en mor*. 1951–53: actor at Norrköping-Linkoping city theatre. 1953–55: at Hälsingborg city theatre. 1955–60: at Malmö city theatre, directed by Ingmar Bergman e.g. in 'Cat on a Hot Tin Roof', 'Peer Gynt', 'Le Misanthrope'. 1956: first appearance in a Bergman film, *Det Sjunde Inseglet*. 1960–62 and 1964: at Royal Dramatic Theatre, Stockholm. 1965: went to Hollywood for *The Greatest Story Ever Told*. Subsequently in occasional films outside Sweden, also regular appearances for Bergman.

Films as actor include: 1951: Fröken Julie. 1957: Smultronstället. 1958: Ansiktet. 1959: Jungfrukällan. 1961: Sasom i en spegel. 1962: Älskarinnan. 1963: Nattvardsgästerna; 1965: The Reward. 1966: Hawaii. 1967: Svarta palmkronor. 1968: Vargtimmen; Skammen. 1970: En Passion; Utvandrarna. 1971: The Night Visitor; Beroringen.

VORKAPICH, Slavko

Montage expert and director. Dobrna, Yugoslavia 1895–
Educated in Belgrade, Budapest. To Paris, studied painting. 1927–28: collaboration with Robert Florey and Gregg Toland on 2 films. 1928–34: montage departments at RKO and Paramount. 1938: lecturer on montage at Museum of Modern Art, New York. 1941: directed shorts for Pathe's 'This is America' series. 1949–51: head of film department at University of Southern California. 1952–56: extensive travel in Europe. 1955: in Yugoslavia, feature as director, *Hanka*. Returned to Hollywood. 1960: edited *High Road*. 1965: lectured at Museum of Modern Art, New York.

Films as co-cinematographer and editor: 1927–28: Life and Death of 9413, a Hollywood Extra (*+ des*); The Loves of Zero (*+ s*).

Films as montage expert include: 1934: Manhattan Melodrama; Crime Without Passion. 1935: The Personal History, Adventures, Experience and Observations of David Copperfield, the Younger (*special effects*). 1936: Romeo and Juliet (*special effects*). 1937: The Good Earth; Maytime; Firefly; Broadway Melody of 1938; The Last Gangster. 1938: Test Pilot; Yellow Jack; Three Comrades; The Shopworn Angel; Marie Antoinette; Boys Town; Sweethearts. 1939: Idiot's Delight; Mr Smith Goes to Washington. 1940: The Howards of Virginia. 1948: Joan of Arc.

VUKOTIC, Dušan

Animator and director. Bileca, Yugoslavia 1927–
Architecture at Zagreb Technical University. Cartoonist for magazine Kerempuh. 1950: entered animation. Helped pioneer animation at Duga Studio. 1951: first film as animator. 1954–55: 13 advertising shorts. 1956: member of group who founded Zagreb-Film. 1961: directed *1001 Crtez*, documentary on animation. 1966: first feature as live-action director. Combined animation and live action in *Igra* (1962) and *Mrlja na savjesti* (1968). Lecturer at Belgrade Film Institute. Oscar for cartoon short subject *Surogat* (1961).

Films as director: 1951: Kićo; Začarani Dvorac u Dudincina – The Enchanted Castle in Dudinci. 1956: Nestašni Robot – The Playful Robot. 1957: Cowboy Jimmy; Carobni Zvuci – Charming Sounds; Abrakadabra. 1958: Osvetnik – The Revenger; Veliki Strah – The Great Fear. 1959: Koncert za Mašinsku Pušku – Concerto for Machine Gun; Krava na Mjesecu – The Cow on the Moon (*+ s*); Rep je ulaznica – My Tail is My Ticket (*+ co-s*). 1960: Piccolo (*+ s/a*). 1961: Surogat – Ersatz; 1001 Crtez – 1001 Drawings. 1962: Igra – The Play (*+ s/a*). 1963: Astromati – Astromuts; Veg zum nachbarn – The Way to the Neighbour. 1966: Sedmi Kontinent – The Seventh Continent (*co-d Joseph Medved*). 1968: Mrlja na savjesti – A Stain on His Conscience; Opera Cordis. 1969: Ars Gratia Artis.

WAGNER, Fritz Arno

Cinematographer. Schmiedefeld Rennsteig, Germany 1889–1958 Göttingen, Germany
Commercial training in Leipzig. Worked for business firm in Basle. Academy of Arts in Paris. 1909: joined Pathé in Paris; worked as newsreel cameraman in Berlin, Vienna and New York. Photographed the Huerta-Villa revolution in Mexico. 1919: to Berlin, to Decla-Bioscop. Worked on e.g. F. W. Murnau's first feature. Continued working in Germany through World War II and to his death.

Films as cinematographer include: 1921: Der müde Tod (*co*); Schloss Vogelöd (*co*). 1922: Nosferatu (*co*); Der brennende Acker (*co*). 1927: Die Liebe der Jeanne Ney (*co*). 1928: Spione. 1930: Westfront 1918 (*co*); Skandal um Eva. 1931: Die Dreigroschenoper (*co*); M (*co*); Kameradschaft (*co*). 1932: Das Testament des Dr Mabuse. 1941: Ohm Kruger (*co*). 1949: Die Brücke.

WAGNER, Robert

Actor. Detroit, Michigan 1930–
At 9 moved to Los Angeles. Failed stage audition. Spotted by talent scout at a family dinner party; screen test seen by Darryl F. Zanuck; contract. 1950: first film as actor *The Happy Years*. 1950–63: almost all films for Fox. 1957–63: married to Natalie Wood. From 1964: worked for several studios including Warners and MGM. 1967–68: TV series 'It Takes a Thief'.

Films as actor include: 1951: Halls of Montezuma; The Frogmen. 1952: With a Song in My Heart; What Price Glory. 1953: Titanic. 1954: Prince Valiant; Broken Lance. 1956: A Kiss Before Dying; The Mountain; Between Heaven and Hell. 1957: The True Story of Jesse James; Stopover Tokyo. 1958: The Hunters; In Love and War; Mardi Gras. 1959: Say One for Me. 1960: All the Fine Young Cannibals. 1962: The Longest Day; The War Lover. 1963: I Sequestrati di Altona. 1964: The Pink Panther. 1966: Harper. 1968: The Biggest Bundle of Them All.

WAJDA, Andrzej

Director. Suwalki, Poland 1926–
Father an officer in Polish Army. Education interrupted by World War II. From 1939: barrel-maker, joiner, ironsmith, assisted church painter-decorators. 1942: joined Resistance, taking orders from the exiled Polish government in London. After Liberation studied painting at the Cracow Academy of Fine Arts and direction at the Lódž Film School. While a student directed 3 shorts; assistant to Aleksander Ford e.g. on *Piatka z ulicy Barskiej* (1954). 1954: first feature as director *Pokolenie*, supervised by Aleksander Ford; Jerzy Lipman was cinematographer, also on several of his later films. Scriptwriter in collaboration on many of his films. 1967: made *Gates to Paradise* in UK. Also stage director in Poland.

Films as director: 1950: Zly chlopiec. 1951: Ceramika ilzecka. 1953: Kiedy ty spisz. 1954: Pokolenie – A Generation. 1955: Ide do Slonca – March Towards the Sun – I Go to the Sun (*+ st/s*). 1956: Kanal (*+ co-s*). 1958: Popiol i diament – Ashes and Diamonds (*+ co-s*). 1959: Lotna (*+ co-s*). 1960: Niewinni Czarodzieje – Innocent Sorcerers (*+ co-s*). 1961: Samson (*+ co-s*). 1962: Sibirska Ledi Magbet – The Siberian Lady Macbeth – Lady Macbeth of

Siberia; L'Amour à vingt ans – Love at Twenty *ep* Warsaw (*co-d Andrzej Zulawski*). 1966: Popioly – Ashes. 1967: Gates to Paradise. 1968: Wszystko na sprzedaz – Everything for Sale (*+s*); Przekladaniec – Roly Poly. 1969: Polowanie na muchy – Hunting Flies. 1970: Krajobraz po bitwie – Landscape After the Battle (*+ co-s*).

WAKHÉVITCH, Georges

Designer. Odessa, Russia 1907–
Pupil of Lazare Meerson. From 1927: worked in theatre. From 1935: alternated between theatre and films.

Films as designer or art director include: 1933: Baroud (*co*). 1934: Madame Bovary (*co*). 1937: La Grande Illusion (*co*). 1938: La Marseillaise (*co*). 1939: Louise. 1942: Les Visiteurs du soir (*co*). 1943: L'Eternel Retour. 1948: Dedée d'Anvers; L'Aigle à deux têtes (*co*). 1950: Miquette et sa mère. 1953: The Beggar's Opera. 1955: Ali Baba et les quarante voleurs. 1958: La Femme et le pantin; Marie – Octobre. 1960: Un, deux, trois, quatre! (*co*). 1964: Le Journal d'une femme de chambre; Par un beau matin d'été. 1965: Les Fêtes Galantes. 1969: King Lear (*r* 1971).

WALBROOK, Anton

(Adolph Anton Wilhelm Wohlbrück) Actor. Vienna 1900–
Father was clown Adolph Wohlbrück. 1920: first stage appearance. 1931: first film as actor. In UK from mid-1930s. 1939: London stage debut in 'Design for Living'. Theatrical work includes 'Watch on the Rhine', 'Call Me Madam'. From 1947: British subject.

Films as actor include: 1934: Maskerade. 1935: Der Student von Prag. 1937: Victoria the Great. 1938: Sixty Glorious Years. 1940: Gaslight. 1941: 49th Parallel. 1943: The Life and Death of Colonel Blimp. 1948: The Red Shoes. 1949: Queen of Spades. 1950: La Ronde. 1955: Oh, Rosalinda!; Lola Montès. 1957: Saint Joan. 1958: I Accuse.

WALD, Jerry

Producer. New York 1912–62 Hollywood
Columbia University. Radio editor for 4 years on New York Graphic. Wrote articles and books. Began film career by producing RKO shorts. From 1933: wrote feature scripts, often in collaboration, e.g. *The Roaring Twenties* (1939) and *They Drive by Night* (1940). 1941: associate producer. 1942: producer at Warner. 1950: formed a production company with Norman Krasna and made, e.g. *Clash by Night* and *The Lusty Men* (both 1952). 1953–56: executive producer and vice-president at Columbia. 1956: founded his own production company, working at and releasing through Fox. At the time of his death was planning a film of James Joyce's 'Ulysses'.

Films as producer include: 1943: Destination Tokyo. 1945: Objective Burma: Mildred Pierce. 1948: Key Largo; One Sunday Afternoon. 1949: Flamingo Road. 1950: Caged; The Breaking Point; The Glass Menagerie (*co*); Storm Warning. 1952: The Lusty Men (*co*). 1957: An Affair to Remember; No Down

Payment; Kiss Them for Me; Peyton Place. 1958: The Long, Hot Summer. 1959: The Sound and the Fury; Hound Dog Man; The Story on Page One. 1960: Sons and Lovers; Let's Make Love. 1961: Return to Peyton Place. 1963: The Stripper.

WALKER, Joseph

Cinematographer. Denver, Colorado 1902–
1914: entered films as cameraman. 1919: first feature as cinematographer *Back to God's Country*. 1938–39: photographed 18 of Frank Capra's 25 films of that period. 1929: applied for patent on invention of telephoto lens (issued 1933). 1934: photographed British film *The Lady is Willing*. Invented a Variable Diffusion and an imbibition double-exposure process. Many optical patents. Consultant to Todd-AO on 70 mm process.

Films as cinematographer include: 1927: The Great Mail Robbery; The College Hero; The Tigress. 1928: That Certain Thing; After the Storm; Ransom; Say it with Sables; Beware of Blondes; Submarine; Court Martial. 1929: Flight. 1930: Ladies of Leisure; Around the Corner; Midnight Mystery; Rain or Shine. 1931: Subway Express; The Miracle Woman; Platinum Blonde. 1932: Forbidden; American Madness; The Bitter Tea of General Yen. 1933: Lady for a Day. 1934: It Happened One Night; One Night of Love; Broadway Bill. 1935: Let's Live Tonight; Love Me Forever. 1936: The Music Goes 'Round; Mr Deeds Goes to Town; Theodora Goes Wild. 1937: Lost Horizon; The Awful Truth. 1938: Joy of Living; You Can't Take it with You. 1939: Only Angels Have Wings (*co*); Mr Smith Goes to Washington; His Girl Friday. 1940: Too Many Husbands; Arizona (*co*). 1941: Penny Serenade; Here Comes Mr Jordan; You Belong to Me. 1942: Tales of Manhattan. 1944: Together Again. 1945: Roughly Speaking. 1946: It's a Wonderful Life (*co*). 1948: The Mating of Millie. 1949: The Dark Past; Mr Soft Touch; Tell it to the Judge. 1950: No Sad Songs for Me; Never a Dull Moment. 1951: Born Yesterday; The Mob. 1952: The Marrying Kind.

WALKER, Robert

Actor. Salt Lake City, Utah 1918–51 Pacific Palisades, California
American Academy of Dramatic Art, New York. 1939: married Jennifer Jones, whom he met at drama school. In Greenwich Village theatricals. Couple went to Hollywood without success (1940) and returned to New York. Small success in radio before going back to Hollywood where (1943) both became stars, he with *Bataan*. 1945: she divorced him. 1948: appeared on drunken driving charges; 6 months in clinic for nervous disorders; marriage to John Ford's daughter Barbara lasted only 10 weeks. Died after injection of sodium amytal to calm an emotional outburst. Most films for MGM.

Films as actor include: 1943: Madame Curie. 1944: Since You Went Away; See Here, Private Hargrove; Thirty Seconds Over Tokyo. 1945: The Clock; Her Highness and the Bellboy; What Next, Corporal Hargrove. 1946: The Sea of Grass. 1949: Song of Love. 1950: Please Believe Me. 1951: Strangers on a Train; Vengeance Valley. 1952: My Son John.

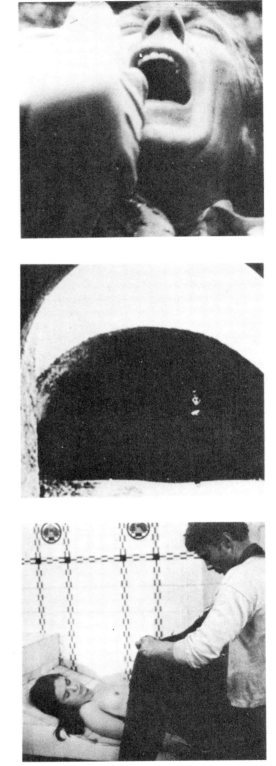

Max Von Sydow in Ingmar Bergman's Vargtimmen. Nosferatu (eine Symphonie des Grauens), *co-photographed by Fritz Arno Wagner.* Krajobraz po Bitwiej, *directed by Andrzej Wajda.*

285

WALLACH, Eli

Actor. New York 1915–

University of Texas; while a student worked as waiter-entertainer in Catskill Mountains, New York. City College of New York. 1938: Master's degree. Trained at Neighborhood Playhouse; acted minor roles on stage before World War II. 1941: enlisted as private; served 5 years in Medical Administrative Corps, reaching Captain. Acted in 'This Property is Condemned' in New York and in 1948 married the leading lady, Anne Jackson. 1948: one of earliest members of Actor's Studio. On Broadway in 'The Rose Tattoo' and 'Camino Real'. 1956: first film as actor *Baby Doll* for Warners. Subsequent Broadway appearances in 'Major Barbara' and with his wife in 'The Typist'. Worked for several studios, most frequently for Columbia.

Films as actor include: 1956: Baby Doll. 1958: The Lineup. 1960: Seven Thieves; The Magnificent Seven. 1961: The Misfits. 1962: Hemingway's Adventures of a Young Man; How the West was Won. 1963: The Victors. 1964: Act One; The Moon Spinners; Kisses for my President. 1965: Lord Jim. 1966: How to Steal a Million; The Poppy is also a Flower. 1967: Il Buono, il brutto, il cattivo. 1969: MacKenna's Gold. 1971: Romance of a Horse Thief.

WALLIS, Hal

Producer. Chicago 1899–

Left school at 14. Office boy with real estate firm, road salesman for electric-heating company. 1921: moved to Southern California; became manager of Tower Theatre, Los Angeles. 1922: joined Warners as assistant to the head of publicity department; in 3 months became publicity chief. 1924; worked for Sol Lesser's Principal Pictures Corp. 1925: returned to Warners; worked on publicity for *The Jazz Singer* (1927). 1928: promoted to studio manager, then executive producer at First National, which had been bought by Warners. From 1930: producer. 1933: succeeded Darryl F. Zanuck as Warners production chief. 1944: set up Hal Wallis Productions to make own films at Warners. 1945: moved production company to Paramount, which then released his films until 1968. 1967: married actress Martha Hyer. Twice received the Irving G. Thalberg Memorial Award (1938, 1943).

Films as producer include: 1930: Little Caesar; Five Star Final. 1932: I Am a Fugitive from a Chain Gang. 1933: The World Changes; Gold Diggers of 1933. 1934: Flirtation Walk; Captain Blood. 1935: Sweet Adeline; The Story of Louis Pasteur; G Men; A Midsummer Night's Dream. 1936: The Charge of the Light Brigade; God's Country and the Woman. 1937: Stolen Holiday; Green Light; The Prince and the Pauper; The Go Getter; Kid Galahad; The Life of Emile Zola; Confession; The Perfect Specimen; Tovarich; Hollywood Hotel. 1938: Gold is Where You Find It; The Adventures of Robin Hood; White Banners; Four Daughters; The Dawn Patrol; The Sisters; Brother Rat. 1939: Yes, My Darling Daughter (co); They Made Me a Criminal; Juarez; Daughters Courageous; The Roaring Twenties (co-p); The Private Lives of Elizabeth and Essex; We are not Alone (ex-p); The Old Maid. 1940: Four Wives; The Story of Dr Erlich's Magic Bullet; The Fighting 69th

(co); It All Came True (co); Virginia City (co); 'Til We Meet Again (co); Torrid Zone (co); All This and Heaven Too; The Sea Hawk (co); They Drive by Night; City for Conquest; No Time for Comedy (co); A Dispatch from Reuters; The Letter (co); Santa Fe Trail (co). 1941: The Great Lie (co); High Sierra (co); The Sea Wolf (co); The Strawberry Blonde (co); Out of the Fog; Manpower; The Bride Came C.O.D.; Sergeant York (co); Dive Bomber; The Maltese Falcon; They Died with their Boots On. 1942: The Man who Came to Dinner; King's Row; The Male Animal; Captains of the Clouds; In This our Life; Desperate Journey. 1943: Yankee Doodle Dandy (co); Casablanca; Air Force; This is the Army (co); Watch on the Rhine; Princess O'Rourke. 1944: Passage to Marseille. 1945: Love Letters; You Came Along. 1946: Saratoga Trunk; The Searching Wind; The Strange Love of Martha Ivers. 1947: I Walk Alone. 1948: Sorry, Wrong Number (co). 1949: The Accused; My Friend Irma; Rope of Sand; The File on Thelma Jordan. 1950: Paid in Full; The Furies; Dark City. 1951: The September Affair; Red Mountain; Peking Express. 1953: Come Back, Little Sheba; Scared Stiff; Money from Home. 1954: About Mrs Leslie. 1955: The Rose Tattoo; Artists and Models. 1956: Hollywood or Bust; The Rainmaker. 1957: Gunfight at the OK Corral; Loving You; The Sad Sack; Wild is the Wind. 1958: Hot Spell; King Creole; Last Train from Gun Hill. 1960: GI Blues. 1961: Summer and Smoke. 1964: Becket. 1965: The Sons of Katie Elder. 1969: True Grit.

WALPOLE, Sir Hugh Seymour

Writer. Auckland, New Zealand 1884–1941

Son of Reverend G. H. S. Walpole who became Bishop of Edinburgh. Emmanuel College, Cambridge. Intended for the ministry but became school-teacher. 1909–14: published 6 novels. Served in Russia during World War I, used material gathered there in 'The Dark Forest' (1916) and 'The Secret City' (1919). Lectured in America in 1919, 1922 and 1926. 1935: invited to Hollywood by MGM to work on script of *The Personal History, Adventures, Experience, and Observations of David Copperfield, the Younger*; also played small part in the film; MGM filmed play based on his short story 'The Silver Mask' as *Kind Lady*; in collaboration adapted his novel, one of the series 'The Herries Chronicle' (1930–33), for *Vanessa* (1935); worked briefly on *Kim* (unmade) and *The Prince and the Pauper* (made 1937) for Warners; for United Artists scripted *Little Lord Fauntleroy* (made 1936); returned to UK. Wrote *And So—Victoria* (unmade) for Victor Saville. 1937: knighted. 1938: wrote preface to symposium 'Behind the Screen'. Wrote 2 versions of *Jamaica Inn* for Paramount, both rejected. Posthumous adaptations of his work: *Mr Perrin and Mr Traill* (1948) and remake (1951) of *Kind Lady*. Wrote 42 novels including 'The Cathedral' (1922), 'The Fortress' (1932), 'John Cornelius' (1937) and the 'Jeremy' series (1919–27). Caricatured as Alroy Kear in W. S. Maugham's 'Cakes and Ale'.

WALSH, Raoul

Director. New York 1892–

University of Seton Hall. Spent 2 years in Europe, then studied acting in USA. 1910: debut as actor in New York theatre. 1912: joined Biograph studios as actor

and assistant to D. W. Griffith who sent him to Mexico to direct scenes for *Life of Villa*. 1915: played John Wilkes Booth in *The Birth of a Nation*. 1915–20: director with Fox, usually writing own scripts. Then with various companies. 1925–26: with Paramount. 1926–35: returned to Fox. Occasional appearances as actor until 1929 when he lost right eye in car accident; and replaced as actor in *In Old Arizona* by Warner Baxter. 1933: without credit reshot Erich von Stroheim's *Walking Down Broadway*; released as *Hello Sister*. 1935–39: with various companies, mainly Paramount; made 2 films in UK. 1939–51: mainly with Warners but made *Salty O'Rourke* for Paramount (1945). Then with various companies; most of last films for Fox. Formed Raoul Walsh Enterprises which produced *Come September* (1961). Uncredited for collaboration many films including *Helen of Troy* (1956) and for 2nd-unit direction on many films including *Edge of Darkness* (1943).

Films as director (complete from 1916 except for many uncredited collaborations): 1912: Life of Villa (co-d Christy Cabanne). 1915: The Regeneration (+p/co-s); Carmen (+p/s). 1916: The Honor System; Blue Blood and Red (+p/s). 1917: The Silent Lie; The Serpent (+p/s); Betrayed (+s); The Conqueror (+s); The Pride of New York (+s); The Innocent Sinner (+s); This is the Life. 1918: Woman and the Law (+s); The Prussian Cur (+s/st); I'll Say So; On the Jump (+s); Every Mother's Son (+s). 1919: Evangeline (+s); Should a Husband Forgive? (+s/st). 1920: The Strongest (+s); From Now On; The Deep Purple. 1921: The Oath (+p/s); Serenade. 1922: Kindred of the Dust (+pc/s). 1923: Lost and Found on a South Sea Island – Passions of the Sea. 1924: The Thief of Bagdad. 1925: East of Suez (+p); The Spaniard. 1926: The Wanderer (+p); The Lucky Lady (+p); The Lady of the Harem; What Price Glory. 1927: The Monkey Talks; Loves of Carmen (+s). 1928: Sadie Thompson – Rain (+s); The Red Dance; Me, Gangster. 1929: Hot for Paris (+st); The Cock-Eyed World; In Old Arizona (co-d Irving Cummings). 1930: The Big Trail; The Man Who Came Back. 1931: Women of All Nations; The Yellow Ticket. 1932: Wild Girl; Me and My Gal. 1933: Sailor's Luck; The Bowery; Going Hollywood. 1935: Under Pressure; Baby Face Harrington; Every Night at Eight. 1936: Klondike Annie; Big Brown Eyes (+co-s); Spendthrift (+co-s). 1937: OHMS – You're in the Army Now; Jump for Glory – When Thief Meets Thief; Artists and Models; Hitting a New High. 1938: College Swing. 1939: St Louis Blues; The Roaring Twenties. 1940: Dark Command; They Drive by Night – Road to Frisco. 1941: The Strawberry Blonde; Manpower; They Died with their Boots On; High Sierra. 1942: Desperate Journey; Gentleman Jim. 1943: Background to Danger; Northern Pursuit. 1944: Uncertain Glory. 1945: The Horn Blows at Midnight; Salty O'Rourke; Objective Burma. 1946: San Antonio (uc; co-d David Butler); The Man I Love. 1947: Pursued; Cheyenne. 1948: Silver River; Fighter Squadron. 1949: One Sunday Afternoon; Colorado Territory; White Heat. 1950: Montana (uc; co-d Ray Enright). 1951: Along the Great Divide; Captain Horatio Hornblower, RN – Captain Horatio Hornblower; Distant Drums; The Enforcer – Murder Incorporated (uc; co-d Bretaigne Windust). 1952: Glory Alley; The World in his Arms; The Lawless Breed; Blackbeard the Pirate. 1953: Sea Devils; A Lion is in the Streets; Gun Fury. 1954: Saskatchewan – O'Rourke of the Royal Mounted.

1955: Battle Cry; The Tall Men. 1956: The Revolt of Mamie Stover; The King and Four Queens. 1957: Band of Angels. 1958: The Naked and the Dead; The Sheriff of Fractured Jaw. 1959: A Private's Affair. 1960: Esther and the King – Esther e il re (+ p/co-s). 1961: Marines, Let's Go (+ p/st). 1964: A Distant Trumpet.

WALTERS, Charles

Director and choreographer. Pasadena, California
After University of Southern California, began stage career as actor and dancer for Fanchon and Marco shows in cinemas. 1934–39: actor and dancer. 1941: produced and choreographed musicals. 1942: first film as choreographer Seven Days Leave. 1947: first film as director. 1949: assisted Gene Kelly and Stanley Donen on dance sequences of Take Me Out to the Ball Game. Appeared as Joan Crawford's dance partner in Torch Song (1953).

Films as dance director or choreographer include: 1943: Girl Crazy (co). 1944: Meet Me in St Louis. 1948: Summer Holiday.

Films as director: 1947: Good News. 1948: Easter Parade. 1949: The Barkleys of Broadway. 1950: Summer Stock. 1951: Three Guys Named Mike; Texas Carnival. 1952: Belle of New York. 1953: Dangerous When Wet; Lili (+ co-chor); Torch Song (+ chor); Easy to Love. 1955: The Glass Slipper; The Tender Trap. 1956: High Society. 1957: Don't Go Near the Water. 1959: Ask Any Girl. 1960: Please Don't Eat the Daisies. 1961: Two Loves. 1962: Billy Rose's Jumbo. 1964: The Unsinkable Molly Brown. 1966: Walk Don't Run.

WALTON, Sir William

Composer. Oldham, Lancashire 1902–
Christ Church, Oxford; trained as cathedral chorister. At 18, to University and wrote first major work, a piano quartet. 1923–26: 'Facade', setting for recitation of poems of Edith Sitwell, also as pair of suites and ballet music. 1931: 'Balshazzar's Feast', biblical suite with libretto by Osbert Sitwell. 1935: First Symphony; first film as composer. 1940: ballet music 'The Wise Virgins'. 1942: incidental music for John Gielgud's production, 'Macbeth'. 1951: Knighted. 1953: Coronation March and Te Deum. 1960: Second Symphony. 1966: Missa Brevis. 1967: awarded Order of Merit; comic opera 'The Bear'. 1969: scored 'Battle in the Air' sequence of The Battle of Britain.

Films as composer: 1935: Escape Me Never. 1936: As You Like It. 1942: The Foreman Went to France. 1945: Henry V. 1948: Hamlet. 1955: Richard III. 1969: The Battle of Britain (co). 1970: Three Sisters.

WANGER, Walter

Producer. San Francisco 1894–
Dartmouth College; left to become assistant for a year to actor-manager Harley Granville-Barker, who was then touring USA. His first Broadway production, starring Nazimova, followed soon after. World War I: First-Lieutenant in Italy; then US Embassy, Rome. After Armistice, attaché to President Wilson's American Peace Mission. Produced 3

Broadway plays before meeting Jesse Lasky; worked as his assistant for a year. 3 years as stage producer in London; persuaded by Lasky to return as general manager of all Paramount film production. 1929: vice-president at Columbia. Then executive producer at MGM. 1934: returned to Paramount as independent producer for Walter Wanger Pictures Inc. 1936: changed releasing arrangements to United Artists. 1939–45: president of Academy of Motion Picture Arts and Sciences; became governor. 1940: married Joan Bennett. 1941: moved to Universal. 1945: with his wife and Fritz Lang formed Diana Productions which made Scarlet Street and Secret Beyond the Door. Later released through RKO, Eagle Lion, Allied Artists. 1951: shot Jennings Lang, his wife's agent; served 3 months and 9 days of a 4 month sentence, which led him to produce Riot in Cell Block 11 (1954). Began Cleopatra (1963) with Rouben Mamoulian as director in London; Darryl F. Zanuck sacked him as producer (although he retained the credit). 1962: divorced.

Films as producer include: 1934: Queen Christina. 1936: The Trail of the Lonesome Pine. 1937: You Only Live Once; History is Made at Night; Stand-In. 1939: Stagecoach (ex-p). 1940: Foreign Correspondent; The Long Voyage Home. 1941: Sundown. 1943: Gung Ho! 1946: Canyon Passage. 1948: Joan of Arc. 1949: Reign of Terror (co); The Reckless Moment. 1954: Riot in Cell Block 11; The Adventures of Hajji Baba. 1956: Invasion of the Body Snatchers. 1958: I Want to Live. 1963: Cleopatra.

WARHOL, Andy

Director. Pittsburgh, Pennsylvania 1928–
1945–49: Carnegie Institute of Technology, Pittsburgh. To New York. Commercial artist, then in late 1950s became 'pop' artist. 1963: made first film on trip to Los Angeles. 1953–65: all films silent, shot at 16 fps, except Harlot (1964). 1964–65: 8 films scripted by Ronald Tavel. 1966: first appearance of his mixed-media show The Exploding Plastic Inevitable (with the Velvet Underground). 1967: Four Stars shown once in 25 hour 2-screen version; subsequently shown only in segments. 1968: Valerie Solanis, who acted in I, a Man (1967), tried to kill him. 1969: made commercial for Schrafft's Ice Cream. Produced Paul Morrissey's Flesh (1968), Trash (1970) and Andy Warhol's Women (1971). Exact authorship of films difficult to ascertain.

Films as director include: 1963: Tarzan and Jane Regained Sort Of; Sleep; Kiss; Dance Movie – Roller Skate; Andy Warhol Films Jack Smith Filming Normal Love; Salome and Delilah; Haircut; Eat. 1964: Blow Job; Empire; Henry Geldzahler; Batman Dracula; Couch; Soap Opera – The Lester Persky Story; Taylor Mead's Ass; Mario Banana; Harlot. 1965: 13 Most Beautiful Women; 13 Most Beautiful Boys; Ivy and John; Suicide; Screen Test 1; Screen Test 2; The Life of Juanita Castro; Drunk; Horse; Poor Little Rich Girl; Vinyl; Bitch; Face; Restaurant; Kitchen; Prison; Afternoon; Beauty 2; Space; Outer and Inner Space; My Hustler; Camp; Paul Swan; Hedy – Hedy the Shoplifter – The 14 Year Old Girl; The Closet; More Milk, Evette – Lana Turner; Lupe. 1966: Bufferin – Gerard Malanga Reads Poetry; Eating Too Fast; The Velvet Underground and Nico; Chelsea Girls. 1967: Four Stars (for some segments see: International Velvet; Alan and Dickin; Imitation

Glory Alley, directed by Raoul Walsh.
Candy darling, an Andy Warhol 'superstar'.
Der Student von Prag, directed by Henrik Galeen, art direction by Hermann Warm.

of Christ; Courtroom; Gerard Has His Hair Removed With Nair; Katrina Dead; Sausalito; Alan and Apple; Group One; Sunset Beach on Long Island; High Ashbury; Tiger Moorse; The Loves of Ondine; I, a Man; Bike Boy; Nude Restaurant. 1968: Lonesome Cowboys; Blue Movie; Surfing Movie.

WARM, Hermann

Designer. Berlin 1889–
Studied commercial art in Berlin. Stage designer in Berlin and Dusseldorf. 1912: Vitaskop contract. Subsequently worked for Union, Decla, Decla-Bioskop, Greenbaum. Number of collaborations with Walter Röhrig, e.g. *Das Kabinett des Dr Caligari* (1919), *Der müde Tod* (1921). Also painter, member of Berlin 'Sturm' group. 1924–33: freelance architect and set designer in Hungary, France and UK. 1941–44: in Switzerland. After 1947: returned to Germany.

Films as designer include: 1919: Das Kabinett des Dr Caligari (*co*); Die Spinnen (*co*). 1921: Der müde Tod (*co*); Schloss Vogelöd. 1922: Phantom. 1924: Gräfin Donelli. 1926: Der Student von Prag. 1927: Die Liebe der Jeanne Ney; La Passion de Jeanne d'Arc; A Night in London. 1930: Dreyfus. 1931: Vampyr. 1935: Der Student von Prag (*co*).

WARNER Brothers

Studio heads. Harry: Poland 1881–1958 Los Angeles; Albert: Baltimore, Maryland 1884–1967 Miami Beach, Florida; Sam: 1888–1927; Jack L.: London, Ontario, Canada 1892–
Father a cobbler from Kraznashiltz, Poland, who opened a shop in Baltimore in 1883, subsequently travelled as a pedlar then settled with family in Youngstown, Ohio. Brothers worked mainly as salesmen of various commodities before setting up bicycle shop together. 1904: bought film projector; gave travelling shows with sister Rose playing the piano and Jack L. singing as boy soprano. 1905–07: ran 90-seat cinema at Newcastle, Pennsylvania; began as film distributors in Pittsburgh with branches in Maryland and Georgia. 1910: sold distribution rights to Patent Company and resumed as exhibitors with road show of *Dante's Inferno* (1911). 1912: Jack L. and Sam went into film production; made a number of films before and after service in World War I. 1923: formed Warner Brothers Pictures Incorporated with Jack L. in charge of production, Sam as technical chief, Albert handling distribution, Harry as business chief. 1924: absorbed Vitagraph company. 1925: opened cinema in Youngstown; began experiments in sound in association with Western Electric, culminating in showing of *Don Juan* (1926) with recorded musical accompaniment, and *The Jazz Singer* (1927) just after the death of Sam Warner who supervised sound campaign. 1929: absorbed First National production company and chain of cinemas. Company with permanent studio at Burbank outside Los Angeles continued with Jack as vice-president in charge of production, Harry and Albert in New York as president and treasurer until 1956 when presidency passed to Jack L. World War II: studio made many propaganda and recruitment films; Jack L. served as Colonel in US Air Force, organised first motion picture unit of Army Air Force, awarded CBE for services to Anglo-American relations. Jack L. continued as head of production into late 1960s, personally producing

occasional films, e.g. *My Fair Lady* (1964), *Camelot* (1967) and retaining independent unit after Warners taken over by Seven Arts in 1967. Became president of Warner Bros.-Seven Arts Studio, vice-chairman of the board. In collaboration with Dean Jennings wrote autobiography 'My First Hundred Years in Hollywood' (1965). Chevalier du Légion d'Honneur. Irving G. Thalberg Memorial Award (1958). Special Academy Award (1927–28) to Warner Brothers for producing 'the pioneer talking picture, which has revolutionised the industry', *The Jazz Singer*.

WARREN, Charles Marquis

Director. Baltimore, Maryland 1912–
Began as writer for magazines and novelist, e.g. 'Only the Valiant', 'Valley of the Shadow', 'Wilderness and Dead Heat'. 1942–45: Commander in US Navy. From 1948: writer with Paramount, e.g. collaborated on script of John Farrow's *Beyond Glory* (1948), then with Republic, Warners, e.g. co-wrote *Springfield Rifle* (1952). 1951: first film as director; his novel 'Only the Valiant' filmed. Worked for various companies. 1957–58: films released mainly through Fox. 1959–69: directed for TV, e.g. 'Gunsmoke', 'Gunslinger', 'Virginian' series.

Films as director: 1951: Little Big Horn (+ s). 1952: Hellgate (+ co-p/s). 1953: Arrowhead (+ s); Flight to Tangier (+ s). 1955: Seven Angry Men. 1956: Tension at Table Rock. 1957: Trooper Hook (+ co-s); Copper Sky (+ ex-p); Back from the Dead; The Unknown Terror; Ride a Violent Mile (+ ex-p/st). 1958: Cattle Empire; Desert Hell (+ ex-p/st); Blood Arrow (+ ex-p). 1969: Charro! (+ p/s).

WATKIN, David

Cinematographer. 1925–
1948: messenger boy for British Transport Films. 1955: first documentary as cinematographer. After 10 years with British Transport Films freelanced, worked on many documentaries. 1965: first feature as cinematographer. Woodfall contract. 1970: first American film, *Catch-22*.

Features as cinematographer: 1965: The Knack—and How to Get It; Help! 1966: The Persecution and Assassination of Jean-Paul Marat, as performed by the inmates of the Asylum of Charenton, under the direction of the Marquis de Sade; Mademoiselle. 1967: How I Won the War. 1968: The Charge of the Light Brigade. 1969: The Bed Sitting Room. 1970: Catch-22. 1971: The Boy Friend.

WATKINS, Peter

Director. Norbiton, Surrey 1935–
1956–59: Christ College, Cambridge. RADA assistant producer on advertising films; made 3 amateur films including *The Diary of an Unknown Soldier* (1959), *The Forgotten Faces* (1960). From 1959: editor with a documentary film company; directed 2 half-hour industrial films. At BBC: assistant editor, assistant director, and director. 1964–65: directed 2 feature-length films for TV.

Feature films as director: 1964: Culloden (+ s). 1965: The War Game (+ st/s). 1966: Privilege (+ co-s). 1968:

Gladiatorerna – The Peace Game (+ co-s). 1971: Punishment Park (+ co-s/e).

WATT, Harry

Director. Edinburgh, Midlothian 1906–
Edinburgh University. 1929: to Newfoundland; machine minder, waiter, balloon seller in Canada. Returned to UK; tried to set up manufacturing business; various jobs including demonstrator in London store. 1931: joined John Grierson's Empire Marketing Board film unit (later GPO Film Unit) as clerk. 1934: assistant director on *Man of Aran*. 1936: directed first short in collaboration with Basil Wright for GPO. 1939–42: associate producer and director with GPO Film Unit, from 1941 Crown Film Unit. 1942–43: director with Army Kinematograph Service. 1943: first feature as director, for Ealing. 1944: scripted *For Those in Peril*. 1955–56: producer with Granada TV. Then returned to Ealing. 1958: directed United Nations documentary, *People Like Maria*. From 1949: films in Australia and Africa.

Films as director: 1936: Night Mail (*co-d* Basil Wright); 6.30 Collection; Big Money (*co-d* Pat Jackson). 1937: The Savings of Bill Blewitt. 1938: North Sea; Health in Industry. 1939: Squadron 992; The First Days – A City Prepares (*co-d* Humphrey Jennings, Pat Jackson). 1940: London Can Take It (*co-d* Humphrey Jennings) – Britain Can Take It (*shortened UK version*); The Front Line; Britain at Bay. 1941: Target for Tonight (+ s); Christmas Under Fire. 1942: Dover Revisited; Twenty One Miles. 1943: Nine Men (+ s). 1944: Fiddlers Three. 1946: The Overlanders (+ s). 1949: Eureka Stockade (+ s). 1951: Where No Vultures Fly – Ivory Hunter. 1954: West of Zanzibar (+ st). 1958: People Like Maria. 1959: The Siege of Pinchgut (+ co-s).

WAXMAN, Franz

(Franz Wachsmann) Composer. Königshütte, Germany 1906–67 Los Angeles
Abandoned banking to attend Berlin Conservatory; also studied in Dresden; played in café dance bands. 1933: to France. German films as composer, including collaborations with Friedrich Hollander. 1934: in USA became head of music department at Universal. 1935–42: conductor of MGM orchestra. 1942–46: music director at Warners. 1947: founder and director of Los Angeles Music Festival. Oscars for scores of *Sunset Boulevard* (1950) and *A Place in the Sun* (1951).

Films as composer include: 1931: Der Mann, der seinen Mörder sucht (*co*). 1933: Ich und die Kaiserin (*co*). 1934: Liliom (*co*). 1935: Bride of Frankenstein. 1936: Fury; The Devil Doll. 1937: Captains Courageous; A Day at the Races. 1939: At the Circus. 1940: Rebecca; The Philadelphia Story. 1942: Woman of the Year. 1943: Air Force. 1945: The Horn Blows at Midnight; Pride of the Marines; Objective Burma. 1947: Dark Passage; The Paradine Case; Night Unto Night. 1950: Sunset Boulevard. 1951: A Place in the Sun. 1953: Come Back, Little Sheba; Stalag 17; A Lion is in the Streets. 1954: Rear Window; Prince Valiant; Elephant Walk. 1955: Mister Roberts; The Indian Fighter. 1956: Crime in the Streets. 1957: The Spirit of St Louis; Sayonara; Love in the Afternoon. 1959: The Nun's Story. 1960: Cimarron. 1961: King of the Roaring Twenties, The Story of Arnold Rothstein.

WAYNE, David

(Wayne McKeekan) Traverse City, Michigan 1916–
At 6 began acting in neighbourhood theatricals. Business administration at Michigan State University. Shakespearian repertory. Worked in marionette show. 1937: New York stage with Fredric March in 'The American Way'. World War II: volunteer ambulance driver in British Army. Returned to USA to act in 'The Merry Widow'; joined US Army as Lieutenant and instructor. Appeared in 'Park Avenue', 'Finian's Rainbow'. 1949: first film as actor *Portrait of Jennie*. Acted in 'Mr Roberts' in New York. Worked at Lincoln Theatre Centre. Also TV, e.g. 'Norby'.

Films as actor include: 1949: Adam's Rib. 1950: My Blue Heaven. 1952: With a Song in my Heart; Wait Till the Sun Shines, Nellie; O. Henry's Full House *ep* The Cop and the Anthem; We're Not Married; Down Among the Sheltering Palms. 1953: The I Don't Care Girl; How to Marry a Millionaire; Tonight We Sing. 1954: Hell and High Water. 1955: The Tender Trap. 1957: The Three Faces of Eve; The Sad Sack. 1959: The Last Angry Man. 1961: The Big Gamble.

WAYNE, John

(Marion Michael Morrison) Director and actor. Winterset, Iowa 1907–
University of Southern California. Prop man. 1928: first film as actor *Hangman's House*; stuntman on *Mother Machree*. 1930: lead in *The Big Trail*. 1923–33: worked for Fox, Columbia, Warners. 1934–36: worked for Monogram and Republic. 1936–41: mainly Universal and Republic. 1939: lead in *Stagecoach*. 1949: produced and acted in *The Fighting Kentuckian*. To 1950: worked for several companies, frequently for RKO, also Republic, MGM, United Artists. From 1951: frequently worked for Warners, several others. 1952: founded own company, Batjac. 1959: first film as director and actor *The Alamo*. 1968: directed in collaboration and acted in *The Green Berets*. Both films as director for own company. 1970: Oscar as Best Actor for *True Grit*.

Films as actor include: 1929: Salute. 1930: Men Without Women. 1931: Men are Like That. 1933: Central Airport; The Life of Jimmy Dolan; College Coach. 1940: Dark Command; The Long Voyage Home; Seven Sinners. 1941: The Shepherd of the Hills. 1942: Flying Tigers; Reap the Wild Wind; The Spoilers; Reunion in France. 1944: The Fighting Seabees. 1945: Back to Bataan; They Were Expendable. 1946: Without Reservations; Angel and the Badman (+*p*). 1948: Red River; Fort Apache; Three Godfathers. 1949: She Wore a Yellow Ribbon; Sands of Iwo Jima. 1950: Rio Grande. 1951: Jet Pilot (*r* 1957); Flying Leathernecks. 1952: Big Jim McLain; The Quiet Man. 1953: Trouble Along the Way; Hondo; Island in the Sky. 1954: The High and the Mighty. 1955: Blood Alley (+*pc*); The Conqueror; The Sea Chase. 1956: The Searchers. 1957: The Wings of Eagles; Legend of the Lost. 1958: The Barbarian and the Geisha. 1959: The Horse Soldiers; Rio Bravo. 1960: North to Alaska. 1961: The Comancheros. 1962: The Man Who Shot Liberty Valance; How the West Was Won *ep* The Civil War;

Hatari!; The Longest Day. 1963: McLintock! (+*pc*); Donovan's Reef. 1964: Circus World; In Harm's Way. 1965: The Sons of Katie Elder; The Greatest Story Ever Told. 1966: Cast a Giant Shadow. 1967: El Dorado; The War Wagon (+*pc*). 1969: Hellfighters; The Undefeated; True Grit. 1970: Chisum; Rio Lobo.

WEBB, Clifton

Actor. Indianapolis, Indiana 1891–1966 Beverly Hills, California
1898: picked out from dancing class to become actor with Children's Theatre. 1904: left school to paint and sing. In Aborn Opera Company. Taught dancing in New York. From 1917 in musical comedy. 1921–22: acted in London for C. B. Cochran. In Broadway plays and musicals. 3 seasons in 'Blithe Spirit'. Friendship with Otto Preminger led to first film as actor *Laura* (1944) and 5-year contract with Fox. All his films for Fox.

Films as actor include: 1946: The Dark Corner; The Razor's Edge. 1948: Sitting Pretty. 1949: Mr Belvedere Goes to College. 1953: Titanic. 1954: Woman's World; Three Coins in a Fountain. 1956: The Man Who Never Was. 1957: Boy on a Dolphin. 1959: The Remarkable Mr Pennypacker. 1962: Satan Never Sleeps.

WEBB, Jack

Director, producer and actor. Santa Monica, California 1920–
University of Southern California. 1943–45: US Army Air Force; USO. Radio drama, creating 'Dragnet' series based on film in which he acted *He Walked By Night* (1948). Director and actor on TV series 'Dragnet' and creator of 'Pete Kelly's Blues'. 1954: first film as director, producer and actor. Also producer, writer, TV executive, e.g. on 'Adam 12', 'The D.A.'. Married actress Julie London.

Films as director, producer, and actor: 1954: Dragnet (*d/w only*). 1955: Pete Kelly's Blues (*d/w only*). 1957: The D.I. 1959: Thirty – Deadline Midnight. 1961: The Last Time I Saw Archie. 1964: Purple is the Color.

Films as actor include: 1948: Hollow Triumph. 1950: Sunset Boulevard; Dark City; The Men. 1951: Appointment with Danger; The Halls of Montezuma; You're in the Navy Now.

WEBB, James R.

Writer. Denver, Colorado 1909–
1930: graduated Stanford University. From 1936: wrote fiction for e.g. Saturday Evening Post, Collier's, Cosmopolitan. From 1938: screenwriter. 1939–42: all films for Republic, most directed by Joseph Kane. 1942–46: US Army, reaching Major. 1949–55: worked mainly for Warners. 1950: Secretary of Screen Writer's Guild. 1956–59: wrote films released by United Artists. From 1962: worked for several studios, often MGM. 1963: Oscar for original story and screenplay, *How the West Was Won*.

Films as writer include: 1949: South of St Louis (*co-st/co-s*); Woman in Hiding (*fst*). 1950: Montana (*co*). 1951: Close to My Heart (+*fst*); Raton Pass (*co*). 1952: The Iron Mistress. 1953: The Charge at Feather

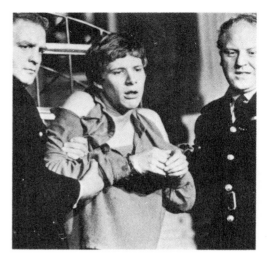

Paul Jones (centre) in Privilege, *directed by Peter Watkins.*
John Wayne and Claire Trevor (left) in John Ford's Stagecoach.
Der Golem by Paul Wegener and Carl Boese.

River (+ *st*). 1954: Phantom of the Rue Morgue (*co*); Apache; Vera Cruz (*co*). 1956: Trapeze. 1958: The Big Country (*co*). 1959: Pork Chop Hill. 1961: Cape Fear. 1962: How the West Was Won; Kings of the Sun (*co*). 1964: Cheyenne Autumn. 1968: La Bataille de San Sebastian. 1969: Alfred the Great (*st/co-s*; + *co-pc*); Sinful Davey (+ *st*). 1970: They Call me *Mister* Tibbs (*co*).

WEGENER, Paul

Director and actor. Bischdorf, Germany 1874–1948 Berlin
Law at Freiburg and Leipzig. 1895: toured in stock. 1905: to Max Reinhardt's Deutsches Theatre, Berlin. Became stage director, continued to act. 1913: entered films as writer and actor. 1916: first film as director was also first collaboration with Rochus Gliese. 1926: *The Magician* was made in France. 1937: last film as director; continued to act until death.

Films as director and actor: 1916: Rübezahls Hochzeit (+ *s*); Der Yoghi (+ *st/s*; *co-d Rochus Gliese*). 1917: Hans Trutz im Schlaraffenland; Der Golem und die Tanzerin (+ *st/s*; *co-d Rochus Gliese*). 1918: Rattenfänger von Hameln (+ *st/s*; *co-d Rochus Gliese*). 1920: Der Golem, wie er in die Welt kam (+ *s*; *co-d Carl Boese*). 1921: Der verlorene Schatten (*co-d Rochus Gliese*). 1923: Herzog Ferrantes Ende. 1924: Lebende Buddhas (+ *co-s*). 1934: Die Freundin eines grossen Mannes.

Films as director: 1934: Ein Mann nach Deutschland. 1935: August der Starke. 1936: Die Stunde der Versuchung; Moskau-Shanghai – Der Weg nach Shanghai. 1937: Krach und Gluck um Künneman; Unter Ausschluss der Öffentlichkeit.

Films as actor include: 1913: Der Student von Prag. 1914: Der Golem (+ *co-s*). 1920: Sumurun. 1922: Vanina; Lucrezia Borgia. 1926: The Magician. 1928: Alraune. 1942: Der grosse König.

WEILL, Kurt

Composer. Dessau, Germany 1900–50 New York
Berlin High School for Music, studied under Engelbert Humperdinck. 1919–20: operatic experience as coach and conductor at Dessau and Lüdenschied. 1921: settled in Berlin. 1921–24: studied under Giuseppe Busoni. 1926: first opera 'Der Protagonist'; married Lotte Lenya. 1927: first collaboration with Bertolt Brecht, first version of 'Aufstieg und Fall der Stadt Mahagonny' as *singspiel* with libretto by Brecht. 1928: collaborated with Brecht on cantata 'Der Lindburghflug' and topical opera 'Die Dreigroschenoper' a transposition of 'The Beggar's Opera'. 1929: wrote 'Happy End' to libretto by Brecht. 1930: operatic version of 'Mahagonny'; with Brecht wrote opera 'Der Jasager'. 1931: first film using his work *Die Dreigroschenoper*; with Brecht, sued Nero Film for changes; won; Brecht lost. 1932: opera 'Die Burgschaft'. 1933: ballet 'Die sieben Todsündens'; had to leave Germany because of Jewish descent; ballet produced in London as 'Anna-Anna'; 'Marie Galante' produced in Paris; wrote music to Robert Desnos' 'La Complainte de Fantômas'. 1935: 'A Kingdom for a Cow' produced in London; to USA. 1938: wrote 'Knickerbocker Holiday' to libretto by Maxwell Anderson; first American film as composer in collaboration *You and*

Me. 1943: became American citizen. 1944: music for Moss Hart's play 'Lady in the Dark'. 1947: incidental music for Elmer Rice's 'Street Scene'. 1948: American folk opera 'Down in the Valley'. 1949: music drama 'Lost in the Stars', libretto by Maxwell Anderson; died of heart attack.

Films as composer: 1931: Die Dreigroschenoper. 1938: You and Me (*co*). 1944: Lady in the Dark; Knickerbocker Holiday. 1945: Where Do We Go From Here (*co*; + *co-lyr*). 1947: One Touch of Venus. 1951: September Affair (*song*). 1962: Die Dreigroschenoper (*rm* 1931).

WEIS, Don

Director. Milwaukee, Wisconsin 1922–
Film studies at University of Southern California, then messenger boy at Warner Bros. 1943: in US Army; script supervisor on Army and Air Force films. From 1947: script supervisor on features, including *Body and Soul* (1947), *The Red Pony* (1949), *Champion* (1949), *Home of the Brave* (1949), *The Men* (1950), *The Prowler* (1951), and *M* (1951). 1951: first films as director; worked with MGM until 1954. Then with various companies, also TV including episodes of 'Dear Phoebe', 'The Thin Man,' 'Alfred Hitchcock Presents'. 'It Takes a Thief', 'A Man Called Ironside'. 1959: made *Mr Pharaoh and his Cleopatra* in Cuba; unreleased.

Films as director: 1951: Bannerline; It's a Big Country (*co-d 5 others*). 1952: Just This Once; You for Me. 1953: I Love Melvin; Remains to be Seen; A Slight Case of Larceny; The Affairs of Dobie Gillis; Half a Hero. 1954: The Adventures of Hajji Baba. 1957: Ride the High Iron; Deadlock. 1959: Mr Pharaoh and his Cleopatra (*ur*); The Gene Krupa Story – Drum Crazy – Gene Krupa Story. 1963: Critic's Choice. 1964: Looking for Love; Pajama Party. 1965: Billie (+ *p*). 1966: The Ghost in the Invisible Bikini. 1967: King's Pirate. 1968: Did You Hear the One About the Travelling Saleslady?

WEISBART, David

Producer. Los Angeles 1915–67
1935: abandoned pre-medical course at University of South Carolina when savings ran out. Became apprentice film editor in Warners trailer department. Then editor e.g. of *Edge of Darkness* (1943), *Mildred Pierce* (1945), *Johnny Belinda* (1948). Last film as editor was *A Streetcar Named Desire* (1951). 1952: first film as producer *Carson City*. Producer with Warners, Mirisch and Fox.

Films as producer include: 1953: The Charge at Feather River. 1955: Them; Rebel Without a Cause. 1956: Between Heaven and Hell. 1958: These Thousand Hills. 1959: A Private's Affair. 1960: Flaming Star. 1962: Follow That Dream; Kid Galahad. 1964: Rio Conchos; Goodbye Charlie. 1967: Valley of the Dolls.

WEISS, Jiri

Director. Prague 1913–
From 1934: director of documentary shorts. 1938: when Germans occupied Czechoslovakia, emigrated to UK. Spent World War II in Britain with Crown Film

Unit. 1945: returned to Czechoslovakia. 1947: first feature as director.

Short films as director include: 1939: The Rape of Czechoslovakia – Secret Allies. 1941: Eternal Prague. 1942: 100,000,000 Women. 1943: Before the Raid.

Features as director: 1947: Uluopena Hranice – The Stolen Frontier (+ *co-s*). 1948: Dravci – Wild Beasts (+ *co-s*). 1950: Posledni Výstřel – Last Shot; Vstanou novi bojovnici – New Heroes Will Arise. 1953: Můj Přítel fabián – My Friend the Gypsy (+ *co-s*). 1954: Punt'a a Čtyřlistek – Doggy and the Four (+ *co-s*). 1956: Hra o život – Life was the Stake (+ *co-s*). 1957: Vlči Jáma – Wolf Trap (+ *co-s*). 1959: Taková Láska – Appassionata (+ *co-s*). 1960: Romeo, Julie a tma – Romeo, Juliet and Darkness – Sweet Light in a Dark Room (+ *co-s*). 1961: Zbabělec – The Coward (+ *co-s*). 1963: Zlaté Kapradí – Golden Bracken (+ *s*). 1964: Tricetjedna ve stinu – Ninety in the Shade (+ *co-st*). 1967: Vražda po Cesku – Murder Czech Style (+ *co-s*).

WEISS, Peter

Director. Berlin 1916–
Swiss-Czech parents. Art Academy in Prague, then returned to Germany. 1934–36: lived in UK. 1936–38: Art Academy in Prague. 1939: to Sweden. 1952: first film as director. 1961: directed and wrote only feature *Hägringen*; made *Bag de ens fasader* in Denmark. 1966: adapted own play for Peter Brook who had directed it on London stage, for *The Persecution and Assassination of Jean-Paul Marat, as performed by the inmates of the asylum of Charenton under the direction of the Marquis de Sade*. Numerous plays and prose writings.

Films as director: 1952: Studie I; Studie II – Hallucinationer – Hallucinations. 1953: Studie III. 1954: Studie IV – Frigorelse. 1955: Studie V – Vaxelspel. 1956: Atel einterior – The Studio of Dr Faustus; Ansikten i skugga – Faces in the Shadows (*co-d Christer Stromholm*). 1957: Ingenting Ovanligt – Nothing Unusual; Enligt lag – According to the Law. 1958: Vad ska vi gora un da – What Shall We Do Now? 1961: Hägringen – The Mirage (+ *s*); Bag de ens fasader – Behind Uniform Facades.

WEISSMULLER, Johnny

Actor. Chicago 1904–
Olympic swimming champion. Swam with Esther Williams in Billy Rose's Aquacade at San Francisco International Exposition. 1932: first film *Tarzan the Ape Man*. TV series 'Jungle Jim'. Wives include actress Lupe Velez (1933–38, divorced).

Films as actor include: 1934: Tarzan and his Mate. 1936: Tarzan Escapes. 1939: Tarzan Finds a Son. 1941: Tarzan's Secret Treasure. 1942: Tarzan's New York Adventure. 1943: Stage Door Canteen; Tarzan Triumphs; Tarzan's Desert Mystery. 1945: Tarzan and the Amazons. 1946: Tarzan and the Leopard Woman. 1947: Tarzan and the Huntress. 1948: Tarzan and the Mermaids.

WELCH, Raquel

(Raquel Tejada) Actress. Chicago, Illinois 1942–
Father a Bolivian engineer. San Diego City College.

Beauty contests. To Hollywood; managed by Patrick Curtis. She married him; partners in own company. 1964: first film as actress *Roustabout*. Spotted by producer Saul David; after *Fantastic Voyage* (1966), Fox contract. Worked also for other studios, especially MGM. TV work includes 'Hollywood Palace', 'The Raquel Welch Show'.

Films as actress include: 1964: A House is not a Home. 1966: Fantastic Voyage; Le Fate *ep* Fata Elena. 1967: Bedazzled. 1968: The Biggest Bundle of Them All; Bandolero!; Lady in Cement. 1969: Flareup. 1970: Myra Breckinridge. 1971: Hannie Caulder.

WELD, Tuesday

(Susan Ker Weld) Actress. New York 1943–
Child model. 1956: first film as actress *Rock, Rock, Rock*. 1957: understudy in 'The Dark at the Top of the Stairs' on Broadway. 1959–62: TV series 'Dobie Gillis'. Worked for several studios.

Films as actress include: 1958: Rally 'Round the Flag, Boys! 1959: The Five Pennies. 1960: Because They're Young; High Time; Sex Kittens go to College; Private Lives of Adam and Eve. 1961: Return to Peyton Place; Wild in the Country; Bachelor Flat. 1963: Soldier in the Rain. 1965: The Cincinnati Kid. 1966: Lord Love a Duck. 1971: I Walk the Line.

WELLES, Orson

Director, actor and writer. Kenosha, Wisconsin 1915–
Studied painting at the Chicago Art Institute. 1931–33: in Dublin; actor at Gate Theatre (1931) as well as playing at Gaiety and Abbey Theatres; began as stage director. Returned to USA, acted on stage and radio. 1936–37: director and actor at Federal Theatre. 1937: with John Houseman formed own company, Mercury Theatre. 1938: for CBS radio, Mercury Company did series which continued until he left for Hollywood in 1939. One programme, on 30 October 1938, was 'The War of the Worlds', presented as news broadcasts and caused panic. Before going to Hollywood, ran films at Museum of Modern Art, New York. His RKO contract gave him 25% of gross takings of each film and 150,000 dollars in advance; the films were Mercury Productions. His first projects were *Heart of Darkness* (from Joseph Conrad) and *Smiler with a Knife* (from Nicholas Blake) but made *Citizen Kane* (1941). 1942: during making of *It's All True*, management of RKO changed; contract cancelled. *Journey into Fear* (1943) finished and re-edited by Norman Foster. Since then actor and director for films, theatre, radio and TV. In later films, often worked in chaotic conditions: *Othello* (1952) shot during 3 years as money kept running out and had 3 successive Desdemonas; shooting on *Confidential Report* (1955) not finished and released incomplete; not shown in USA until 1963. *Don Quixote* began shooting in Mexico in 1957, but is unfinished (2 episodes out of 3 made). Wrote 2 novels, one of which, 'Mr Arkadin' is basis of *Confidential Report*. Acted in all own films except *The Magnificent Ambersons* (1942).

Films as director and actor: 1941: Citizen Kane (+*p/co-st/co-s*). 1942: It's All True (*uf*; +*p*); The Magnificent Ambersons (*d/p/s* only). 1943: Journey Into Fear (+*co-s, uc*; *uc*, co-d Norman Foster). 1946: The Stranger (+*co-s*). 1948: Macbeth (+*p/s*); The Lady from Shanghai (+*p/s*). 1952: Othello (+*p/s*). 1955: Confidential Report – Mr Arkadin (+*p/s/a/co-st*). 1958: Touch of Evil (+*s*). 1959: Don Quixote (*uf*; +*s*). 1963: Le Procès – The Trial (+*s*). 1966: Campanadas a medianoche – Chimes at Midnight – Falstaff (+*s*). 1968: Histoire Immortelle – The Immortal Story.

Films as actor include: 1949: Prince of Foxes. 1950: The Black Rose. 1954: Si Versailles m'était conté. 1955: Napoléon. 1956: Moby Dick. 1958: The Roots of Heaven. 1959: Compulsion. 1960: Austerlitz; Crack in the Mirror. 1962: Rogopag *ep* La Ricotta. 1970: Catch-22; Waterloo. 1971: Ein Kampf um Rom; La Décade Prodigieuse.

WELLMAN, William A.

Director. Brookline, Massachusetts 1896–
1917: medical orderly in French Foreign Legion, then fighter pilot in the Lafayette Flying Corps. 1918: wounded in action and demobilised; wrote novel 'Go, Get 'Em'. Worked in cotton business in Boston. 1919: began in films as actor in *The Knickerbocker Buckaroo* for Douglas Fairbanks' company, and in *Evangeline*. 1921: joined Goldwyn studios as messenger. 1923: first films as director for Fox. 1926–30: mainly with Paramount. 1930–33: mainly with First National and Warners. Then with various companies. 1937: collaborated with Robert Carson on story for *The Last Gangster*. 1938–41: returned to Paramount. 1938–46: often produced own films. 1942–48: mainly with Fox. 1949–52: with MGM. Then Warners. 1958: retired after making *Lafayette Escadrille* in which son Bill Wellman, Jr appeared as actor.

Films as director: 1923: The Man Who Won; Second Hand Love; Big Dan; Cupid's Fireman. 1924: The Vagabond Trail; Not a Drum was Heard; The Circus Cowboy. 1926: When Husbands Flirt; The Boob – The Yokel; The Cat's Pajamas; You Never Know Women. 1928: The Legion of the Condemned; Ladies of the Mob; Beggars of Life. 1929: Wings; Chinatown Nights; The Man I Love; Woman Trap. 1930: Dangerous Paradise; Young Eagles; Maybe it's Love. 1931: Other Men's Women – The Steel Highway; The Public Enemy – Enemies of the Public; The Star Witness; Night Nurse; Safe in Hell – The Lost Lady. 1932: The Conquerors; Love is A Racket; The Hatchet Man – The Honourable Mr Wong; So Big; The Purchase Price. 1933: Frisco Jenny; Central Airport; Lady of the Night – Midnight Mary; Lilly Turner; Heroes for Sale; Wild Boys of the Road – Dangerous Days; College Coach – Football Coach. 1934: Looking for Trouble; Stingaree. 1935: The President Vanishes; The Call of the Wild. 1936: Small Town Girl; The Robin Hood of El Dorado (+*co-s*). 1937: A Star is Born (+*co-st*); Nothing Sacred. 1938: Men with Wings (+*p*). 1939: Beau Geste (+*p*); The Light that Failed (+*p*). 1941: Reaching for the Sun (+*p*). 1942: Roxie Hart; The Great Man's Lady (+*p*); Thunder Birds; The Ox-Bow Incident – Strange Incident. 1943: Lady of Burlesque – Striptease Lady. 1944: Buffalo Bill. 1945: This Man's Navy; The Story of GI Joe – War Correspondent (+*p*). 1946: Gallant Journey (+*p/co-s*). 1947: Magic Town. 1948: The Iron Curtain; Yellow Sky. 1949: Battleground. 1950: The Happy Years; The Next Voice You Hear. 1951: Across the Wide Missouri; Westward the Women; It's a Big Country (*co-d 5 others*). 1952: My Man and I. 1953: Island in the Sky. 1954: The High and the Mighty;

Terry Thomas and Tuesday Weld in Jack Cumming's production of Bachelor Flat, *directed by Frank Tashlin. Orson Welles (left) in his film,* Campanadas a medianoche.
The Story of G.I. Joe, *directed by William Wellman.*

Track of the Cat. 1955: Blood Alley. 1956: Goodbye, My Lady. 1958: Darby's Rangers – The Young Invaders; Lafayette Escadrille – Hell Bent for Glory (+ st).

WELLS, George

Writer and producer. New York 1909–
Father vaudeville actor and writer. Sciences at New York University. Radio work in 1930s. 1944: joined MGM as writer, also (from 1952) occasionally produced e.g. *Dangerous When Wet* (1953), *Jupiter's Darling* (1955). Oscar for original story and screenplay, *Designing Woman* (1957).

Films as writer include: 1947: Merton of the Movies (*co*); The Hucksters (*co-ad*). 1949: Take Me Out to the Ball Game (*co*). 1950: Three Little Words (+ *st*); Summer Stock (*co*). 1951: Angels in the Outfield (*co*); It's a Big Country (*co*); Texas Carnival (*co-st*). 1952: Lovely to Look At (*co*). 1953: I Love Melvin (+ *p*). 1957: Don't Go Near the Water (*co*). 1958: Party Girl. 1959: Ask Any Girl; The Gazebo. 1960: Where the Boys Are. 1968: The Impossible Years.

WENDKOS, Paul

Director. Philadelphia 1923–
Mass communication at Columbia University, New York and enrolled in Dramatic Workshop; film studies at New School for Social Research. Made documentaries: one on photographer Matthew Brady, one adapted from Edgar Allen Poe's 'The Raven' using woodcuts. Worked for State Department's Informational Film Programme, made about 35 films. 1957: directed and edited first feature *The Burglar,* led to Columbia contract. TV work includes several feature films and episodes in many series: 'Dr Kildare', 'Ben Casey', 'I Spy', 'The FBI', 'The Invaders', 'The Untouchables', 'The Fugitive', 'The 11th Hour', 'Breaking Point'; 'Hawaii 5-0'; 2 of his episodes in 'Naked City' written by Stirling Silliphant. TV work released as features: *Temple of the Swinging Doll* (1960), *Recoil* (1963), *Death of Innocence* (1971). 1968: 5-film contract with Mirisch began with *Guns of the Magnificent Seven.*

Films as director: 1957: The Burglar (+ *e*). 1958: The Case Against Brooklyn; Tarawa Beachhead. 1959: Gidget; Face of a Fugitive; Battle of the Coral Sea. 1960: Because They're Young. 1961: Angel Baby; Gidget Goes Hawaiian. 1963: Gidget Goes to Rome. 1966: Johnny Tiger. 1967: Attack on the Iron Coast. 1968: Guns of the Magnificent Seven. 1970: Hell Boats; Cannon for Cordoba. 1971: The Mephisto Waltz.

WERNER, Oskar

(O. Josef Bschliessmayer). Actor. Vienna 1922–
Studied acting at Helmuth Krauss' school. 1941–49: contract as actor with Vienna Burgtheatre. Subsequent appearances in a number of theatres in Austria and Switzerland, alternating films with stage work from 1948. 1955: first major film role. Has directed for German TV.

Films as actor include: 1955: Der letzte Akt; Lola Montès. 1961: Jules et Jim. 1965: Ship of Fools; The Spy Who Came in from the Cold. 1966: Fahrenheit 451. 1968: The Shoes of the Fisherman (*ur*).

WEST, Mae

Actress. Brooklyn, 1893–
1900: in a Brooklyn amateur talent show. 1901–04: child parts with stock companies. 1910: formed vaudeville team with Frank Wallace whom she married in 1911. Wrote material for own act and plays, including 'Sex' which led to arrest (with manager and producer) after campaign by Society for Suppression of Vice. Also wrote 'The Drag', 'The Wicked Age', 'Diamond Lil' (1928). 1932: under contract to Paramount; first film as actress *Night after Night*. Adapted some of own plays, including 'Diamond Lil', filmed as *She Done Him Wrong* (1933). 1943: retired from films; divorced. Returned to stage in own play, 'Catherine was Great'. 1946: on tour with 'Come on Up'. 1948: in London in 'Diamond Lil'. 1954: cabaret, Las Vegas. Since 1959: some TV appearances. 1970: return to cinema. Books include autobiography 'Goodness had Nothing to Do With It' (1956). Made recordings in 1930s and LP of Beatles songs.

Films include: 1932: Night after Night. 1933: She Done Him Wrong (+ *fpl*); I'm No Angel (+ *st/s/di*). 1934: Belle of the Nineties (+ *st/s*). 1935: Goin' to Town (+ *s/di*). 1936: Go West Young Man (+ *s*); Klondike Annie (+ *co-st/co-s*). 1937: Every Day's a Holiday (+ *s*). 1940: My Little Chickadee (+ *co-s*). 1943: The Heat's On. 1970: Myra Breckinridge (+ *co-s*).

WEXLER, Haskell

Director and cinematographer. Chicago 1923–
University of California. World War II: merchant seaman. Amateur documentaries. Father bought an armoury in Desplaines, Illinois for him to use as studio; used briefly. To Chicago, worked as assistant cameraman on documentaries also in South. To California. 1957: first feature as cinematographer *Stakeout on Dope Street* under pseudonym, to avoid trouble with union. 1960: photographic consultant on *Studs Lonigan*. 1965: producer in collaboration on *The Loved One*. 1969: first feature as director, writer, co-producer and cinematographer. Oscar for black and white cinematography on *Who's Afraid of Virginia Woolf?* (1966).

Features as cinematographer: 1958: Stakeout on Dope Street. 1959: The Savage Eye (*co*). 1960: Angel Baby (*co*). 1961: The Hoodlum Priest. 1963: A Face in the Rain; America, America. 1964: The Best Man. 1965: The Loved One (+ *co-p*). 1966: Who's Afraid of Virginia Woolf? 1967: In the Heat of the Night. 1968: The Thomas Crown Affair. 1970: Interviews with My Lai Veterans (*co*).

Films as director, writer, producer and cinematographer: 1965: The Bus. 1968: Nowsreel. 1969: Medium Cool (*co-p*). 1971: Brazil: a Report on Torture (*co-d Saul Landau*).

WHALE, James

Director. Dudley, Worcestershire 1896–1957 Hollywood
Cartoonist for The Bystander. Infantry officer in World War I. Started to act (1917) when a prisoner of war. 1918: acted in Birmingham repertory. Stage manager of Savoy Theatre (1923), then (from 1925) acted in West End. 1929: produced 'Journey's End', which moved to New York. Returned to UK for another London production and to film *Journey's End*, his first film as director. Almost all his films for Universal. Retired from cinema at the beginning of World War II to paint, but made *Hello, Out There* (1949) as part of a multi-episode film which was abandoned. 1951: directed a play 'Pagan in the Parlour' at Pasadena and brought it to UK (1952). Died after falling into swimming pool at his home.

Films as director: 1930: Journey's End. 1931: Waterloo Bridge; Frankenstein. 1932: The Old Dark House; The Impatient Maiden. 1933: The Invisible Man; The Kiss before the Mirror; By Candlelight. 1934: One More River. 1935: The Bride of Frankenstein; Remember Last Night? 1936: Show Boat. 1937: The Road Back; The Great Garrick. 1938: Sinners in Paradise; Port of Seven Seas; Wives Under Suspicion. 1939: The Man in the Iron Mask; Green Hell. 1941: They Dare Not Love. 1949: Hello Out There (*ep*; *ur*).

WHEELER, Lyle

Designer. Woburn, Massachusetts 1905–
University of Southern California. Magazine illustrator, industrial designer. 1936: first film as designer, in collaboration, *The Garden of Allah*. 1944: appointed supervising art director at Fox. Oscars for *Gone with the Wind* (1939), and (all subsequently in collaboration) *Anna and the King of Siam* (1946), *The Robe* (1953), *The King and I* (1956), *The Diary of Anne Frank* (1959).

Films as designer include (from 1944, almost all in collaboration): 1937: A Star is Born; The Prisoner of Zenda; Nothing Sacred. 1938: The Adventures of Tom Sawyer. 1939: Gone with the Wind; Intermezzo. 1940: Rebecca. 1944: Winged Victory; Wing and a Prayer. 1945: The House on 92nd Street; Fallen Angel; A Tree Grows in Brooklyn. 1946: Wake up and Dream; Cluny Brown; Centennial Summer; My Darling Clementine; Dragonwyck; Anna and the King of Siam. 1947: Forever Amber; The Foxes of Harrow; Daisy Kenyon; Kiss of Death; Gentleman's Agreement. 1948: Unfaithfully Yours; That Lady in Ermine; The Iron Curtain; Give My Regards to Broadway; Cry of the City; Call Northside 777; Street with no Name; The Snake Pit. 1949: Chicken Every Sunday; Thieves' Highway; Mother is a Freshman; Slattery's Hurricane; I Was a Male War Bride; House of Strangers; A Letter to Three Wives; Pinky; Whirlpool; The Fan; Down to the Sea in Ships; Twelve O'Clock High; Dancing in the Dark. 1950: An American Guerrilla in the Philippines; Two Flags West; When Willie Comes Marching Home; Panic in the Streets; No Way Out; All About Eve; Where the Sidewalk Ends; The Gunfighter; Broken Arrow. 1951: Halls of Montezuma; Fixed Bayonets; Rawhide; The House on Telegraph Hill; The Guy Who Came Back; Golden Girl; The Frogmen; Fourteen Hours; The Day the Earth Stood Still; Call me Mister; Bird of Paradise; Anne of the Indies; People Will Talk; Love Nest; The 13th Letter; You're in the Navy Now; The Desert Fox. 1952: Deadline USA; Viva Zapata!; Five Fingers; The Snows of Kilimanjaro; The Model and the Marriage Broker; Monkey Business; Return of the Texan; Red Skies of Montana; Diplomatic Courier; My Pal Gus; Pony

Soldier; Something for the Birds; Way of a Gaucho. 1953: The Robe; Treasure of the Golden Condor; Man in the Attic; How to Marry a Millionaire; Pickup on South Street; Gentlemen Prefer Blondes; Dangerous Crossing; White Witch Doctor; The I Don't Care Girl; Niagara; King of the Khyber Rifles. 1954: Hell and High Water; River of no Return; The Siege at Red River; Garden of Evil; Demetrius and the Gladiators; Désirée; There's No Business like Show Business. 1955: Daddy Long Legs; The Racers; Violent Saturday; House of Bamboo; The Seven Year Itch; The Tall Men; The Left Hand of God; The Girl in the Red Velvet Swing. 1956: The King and I; The Bottom of the Bottle; Carousel; The Lieutenant Wore Skirts; The Man in the Gray Flannel Suit; The Revolt of Mamie Stover; Bigger than Life; Bus Stop; The Last Wagon; The Girl Can't Help It; Between Heaven and Hell. 1957: A Hatful of Rain; Will Success Spoil Rock Hunter?; An Affair to Remember; The Three Faces of Eve; Stopover Tokyo; Kiss Them for Me; No Down Payment. 1958: South Pacific; The Young Lions; The Long, Hot Summer; Ten North Frederick; From Hell to Texas; The Bravados; The Hunters; The Barbarian and the Geisha; The Fiend who Walked the West; These Thousand Hills; Rally 'Round the Flag, Boys! 1959: Compulsion; The Diary of Anne Frank; The Sound and the Fury; Woman Obsessed; Say One for Me; A Private's Affair; Blue Denim; Hound Dog Man; The Man who Understood Women; Journey to the Centre of the Earth; The Story on Page One. 1960: From the Terrace; Wild River; Wake Me When it's Over; Seven Thieves; Can-Can. 1962: Advise and Consent. 1964: The Best Man. 1965: In Harm's Way. 1967: The Big Mouth. 1968: Where Angels Go, Trouble Follows. 1969: Marooned. 1970: Tell Me That You Love Me, Junie Moon.

WHITE, Pearl

Actress. Greenridge, Missouri 1889–1938 Neuilly, France
Acted in stock. 1910: first films for Powers. Worked for Pathe and Crystal, then returned to Pathe. 1914: first serial The Perils of Pauline. Numerous later serials. 1919: autobiography 'Just Me'. 1920–22: worked for Fox. 1923–25: in French films. Revues in London and Paris.

Films as actress include: 1915: The Exploits of Elaine; The New Exploits of Elaine. 1916: The Iron Claw. 1916–17: Pearl of the Army. 1917: The Fatal Ring. 1918: The House of Hate. 1918–19: The Lightning Raider. 1919: The Black Secret. 1922: Any Wife. 1922–23: Plunder. 1924: Le Terreur.

WHITNEY, John

Director
Astronomy at Pomona College, California. Spent a year in Europe, studied photography, musical composition. 1941: in collaboration with brother James began making animated abstract films. Some work with manipulated paper cut-outs shot at normal camera speed. From 1943: sound films, at first with existing records, then with synthetic sound created with pendulums, then by use of light beam making sound track directly on film. 1945: began working separately. 1949: entered Abstract Film Exercises at Brussels Experimental Film Festival under collective title Five Abstract Film Exercises: Studies in Motion.

Series of films set to existing musical compositions and using diffraction of light in an oil bath. From late 1940s, brothers worked separately. Early 1950s: experimental 16 mm work for TV. 1952: engineering films for Douglas Aircraft. 1957: collaborated with Charles and Ray Eames on multi-screen film Glimpses of USA for exhibition in Moscow. From 1957: constructed mechanical drawing machines for drawing abstract patterns: first machine used by Saul Bass on credits of Vertigo (1958). One year as director of animated films at UPA. Short musical films for CBS TV. Optically exposed images onto film, then used military surplus material, including analogue computers. 1961: 5 year grant from IBM; Catalogue is an informal selection of effects used in TV and film credits, using optical printer linked to analogue computer, produced by son John Whitney, Jr. Later used digital computer. 1960: set up own company for commissioned work. Title work includes 'The Chrysler Bob Hope Show', 'Dinah Shore Show', The Glass Bottom Boat (1966). Also e.g. Alcoa commercials. 1966: continuing grant from IBM. 1968: first complete film made with digital computer.

Films as director and cinematographer in collaboration with James Whitney: 1941–43: Variations (series). 1943: Abstract Film Exercise no 1; Abstract Film Exercise no 2 (uf); Abstract Film Exercise no 3 (uf). 1944: Abstract Film Exercise no 4 and 5. 1947–49: Mozart Rondo; Hot House.

Films as director: 1951–58: Celery Stalks at Midnight (+ c). 1959: Glimpses of USA (co-d Charles and Ray Eames). 1961: Catalogue (+ c). 1968: Permutations. 1970: 1–2–3. 1971: Matrix.

WICKI, Bernhard

Director and actor. St Pölten, Austria 1919–
Swiss father, Hungarian mother. Educated in Köthen, Berlin, and Vienna. From 1938: stage actor. From 1945: director in theatre in Switzerland, Monaco, Germany. From 1950: acted in films including several by Helmut Käutner with whom he also worked as assistant. 1958: first film as director. Has directed and acted in films in various parts of Europe. 1960: book of photographs 'Zwei Gramm Licht' with preface by Friedrich Dürrenmatt. 1965: directed in USA. Also TV work. Married to actress Agnes Fink.

Films as actor include: 1954: Die letzte Brücke. 1955: Es geschah am 20 Juli; Kinder, Mütter und ein General. 1957: Die Zürcher Verlobung. 1958: La Chatte. 1961: La Notte. 1963: Les Vacances Portugaises.

Films as director: 1958: Warum sind sie gegen uns? (+ s). 1959: Frau im besten Mannesalter; Die Brücke – The Bridge. 1961: Das Wunder des Malachias – Malachias (+ co-s). 1963: The Longest Day (German sequences). 1964: Der Besuch – La Vendetta della signora – La Rancune – The Visit. 1965: The Saboteur—Code Name Morituri. 1966: Transit (uf). 1971: Das falsche Gewicht (+ co-s).

WIDERBERG, Bo

Director. Malmö, Sweden 1930–
Began as author; novel and collection of short stories published at 20. 1960: film critic for Stockholm

Mae West and W. C. Fields in My Little Chickadee.
The Old Dark House, directed by James Whale, with Boris Karloff.
Richard Widmark in Madigan, directed by Don Siegel.

293

evening paper Expressen. 1961: directed, in collaboration with Jan Troell, and photographed, short *Pojken och draken*. From 1962: directed for the stage including Royal Dramatic Theatre, Stockholm. 1962: first feature as director. Wrote all own films; edited most.

Features as director, writer and (from 1965) editor: 1962: Barnvagnen – The Pram – The Baby Carriage. 1963: Kvarteret Korpen – Raven's End. 1965: Karlek 65 – Love 65. 1966: Heja Roland – Thirty Times Your Money. 1967: Elvira Madigan. 1969: Adalen '31. 1971: Joe Hill – The Ballad of Joe Hill (+*pc/s/e*).

WIDMARK, Richard

Actor. Sunrise, Minnesota 1914–
Speech and Political Science at Lake Forest University. 1936–38: instructor there in Speech and Drama. 1938: worked in New York radio. 1942: married writer Jean Hazelwood. 1943: Broadway debut in 'Kiss and Tell'. 1946–47: acted in 'Dream Girl' in Chicago. 1947: first film as actor *Kiss of Death*. To 1954: worked for Fox. Then worked for United Artists, MGM, Columbia and others. 1961: uncredited co-director of *The Secret Ways,* also produced and acted; script by his wife. 1965: in collaboration with James B. Harris produced *The Bedford Incident* and acted in it.

Films as actor include: 1948: Road House; The Street with No Name; Yellow Sky. 1949: Down to the Sea in Ships; Slattery's Hurricane. 1950: Night and the City; Panic in the Streets; No Way Out. 1951: Halls Of Montezuma; The Frogmen. 1952: O. Henry's Full House *ep* The Clarion Call; Don't Bother to Knock; Red Skies of Montana; My Pal Gus. 1953: Destination Gobi. 1954: Hell and High Water; Garden of Evil. 1955: The Cobweb; A Prize of Gold. 1956: Backlash; Run for the Sun; The Last Wagon. 1957: Saint Joan; Time Limit (+*co-p*). 1958: The Law and Jake Wade; The Trap; The Tunnel of Love. 1959: Warlock. 1960: The Alamo. 1961: The Secret Ways (+*p; uc, co-d Phil Karlson*); Two Rode Together; Judgment at Nuremberg. 1962: How the West Was Won. 1964: Cheyenne Autumn; Flight from Ashiya; The Long Ships. 1966: Alvarez Kelly. 1967: The Way West. 1968: Madigan. 1970: The Moonshine War.

WIENE, Robert

Director. Sasku, Sassonia 1881–1938 Paris
Son of a Czechoslovakian actor; brother of director Conrad Wiene. Began as stage actor in Germany and Czechoslovakia. 1914: began in films as scriptwriter. 1915: first film as director. Also wrote scripts for many of his own films and films by others. 1938: was working with Jean Cocteau in Paris on project for a sound version of *Das Kabinett des Dr Caligari*.

Films as director include: 1916: Frau Eva (+*s*). 1919: Das Kabinett des Dr Caligari. 1920: Genuine. 1921: Das Spiel mit dem Feuer (*co-d George Kroll*). 1922: Tragi-komödie. 1923: Raskolnikow (+*s*); I.N.R.I. (+*s*). 1924: Orlacs Hände; Pension Groonen. 1925: Der Rosenkavalier (+*s*). 1930: Der Andere. 1934: Polizeiakte 909. 1938: Ultimatum.

WIENER, Jean

Composer. Paris 1896–
Studied at Paris Conservatoire. Pianist for silent films. Wrote songs and music for the theatre and composed for films from 1932.

Films as composer include: 1932: L'Homme à l'Hispano. 1934: Les Affaires Publiques. 1936: Le Crime de Monsieur Lange (*co*); Les Bas-fonds; La Bandéra (*co*). 1945: Patrie. 1947: Les Frères Bouquinquant. 1948: Le Point de jour. 1949: Rendez-vous de Juillet (*co*); Le Parfum de la dame en noir. 1950: Maître après Dieu; Les Poussières. 1954: Touchez pas au grisbi. 1955: Futures Vedettes. 1957: Pot Bouille; Notre Dame, Cathédrale de Paris. 1959: La Femme et le pantin. 1960: Pantalaskas. 1966: Au Hasard, Balthazar. 1967: Mouchette.

WILCOX, Fred M.

Director. Tazewell, Virginia 1908–64
English and journalism at University of Kentucky. 1926: worked in MGM publicity department in New York. 1929: assisted King Vidor in New York in casting of *Hallelujah*; went with him to Hollywood. Became assistant director, test director. 1938: first film as director 1-reel (sepia) *Joaquín Murrieta*. 1943: for his first feature as director discovered Elizabeth Taylor and Lassie. 1949: *The Secret Garden* produced by Clarence Brown. To 1956: worked for MGM. 1960: last film, for Warners.

Feature films as director: 1943: Lassie Come Home. 1946: Blue Sierra; The Courage of Lassie. 1948: Three Daring Daughters – The Birds and the Bees; Hills of Home – Master of Lassie. 1949: The Secret Garden. 1951: Shadow in the Sky. 1953: Code Two. 1954: Tennessee Champ. 1956: Forbidden Planet. 1960: I Passed for White.

WILCOX, Herbert

Director and producer. Cork, Ireland 1892–
World War I: served in Royal Flying Corps. 1918: began in films as salesman to exhibitors in Yorkshire, then set up distribution company Astra Films with brother in Leeds. 1919: to London. 1920: expanded company to include film production. 1923: directed first film at Ufa studios, Berlin, as part of exchange arrangement by which Ufa distributed through Wilcox e.g. *Die Nibelungen*. 1925: founded Elstree Studios with J. D. Williams. 1928: in charge of production at British and Dominion Pictures. 1938–41: directed 4 films in USA. Films as producer include *The Beggar's Opera* (1953), *Yangtze Incident* (1957). Married (1943) Anna Neagle whom he established as an international star.

Films as director include: 1923: Chu Chin Chow. 1924: Decameron Nights – Dekameron Nächte. 1926: Nell Gwyn. 1927: Mumsie; Tip Toes; Madame de Pompadour. 1928: Dawn. 1929: The Woman in White. 1932: The Blue Danube; Goodnight Vienna. 1933: Bitter Sweet. 1934: Nell Gwyn. 1935: Peg of Old Drury. 1936: Limelight; The Three Maxims – The Show Goes On (+*p*). 1937: Victoria the Great. 1938: Sixty Glorious Years. 1939: Nurse Edith Cavell. 1940: Irene; No, No Nanette. 1941: Sunny (+*p*). 1942: They Flew Alone – Wings and the Woman (+*p*). 1943:

Forever and a Day (+*co-p; co-d 6 others*); The Yellow Canary. 1945: I Live in Grosvenor Square; A Yank in London. 1946: Piccadilly Incident. 1948: Spring in Park Lane. 1949: Maytime in Mayfair. 1950: Odette. 1951: The Lady with the Lamp (+*p*). 1952: Trent's Last Case (+*p*). 1954: Lilacs in the Spring – Let's Make It. 1955: King's Rhapsody (+*p*). 1957: These Dangerous Years. 1958: Wonderful Things. 1959: The Lady is a Square; Heart of a Man.

WILD, Harry J.

Cinematographer
Office boy at Paramount in New York. Assistant to George Folsey. To RKO as assistant. Worked in New York for 6 years, then to Hollywood. 1936: first film as cinematographer. Almost all films for RKO.

Films as cinematographer include: 1942: Valley of the Sun. 1943: Tarzan Triumphs; Stage Door Canteen; Tarzan's Desert Mystery (*co*). 1944: Mademoiselle Fifi. 1945: Murder My Sweet; First Yank into Tokyo; Cornered. 1946: Till the End of Time. 1947: They Won't Believe Me. 1948: Pitfall. 1949: The Big Steal; Easy Living. 1950: Walk Softly, Stranger. 1951: Gambling House; His Kind of Woman. 1952: The Las Vegas Story; Macao; Son of Paleface. 1953: Affair with a Stranger; Gentlemen Prefer Blondes; The French Line. 1954: She Couldn't Say No; Underwater. 1955: The Conqueror.

WILDE, Cornel

Director and actor. New York 1915–
1931: Columbia University. During break in studies caused by father's illness attended evening acting classes. Returned to pre-medical course; intercollegiate fencing champion. Newspaper reporter. New York stage; summer stock; On Broadway e.g. as Tybalt in Laurence Olivier's production of 'Romeo and Juliet'. Member of Actor's Studio. 1940: in Olympic training squad for fencing. To Hollywood in 'Romeo and Juliet': 6 months Warners contract; then Fox. First film as actor *The Lady with Red Hair* (1940); first starred in *A Song to Remember* (1944). To 1950: mainly at Fox. Then worked for several companies. 1956: first film as director, producer and actor. 1970: *No Blade of Grass* made in UK.

Films as actor include: 1942: Life Begins at 8.30. 1943: Wintertime. 1944: Guest in the House. 1947: It Had to Be You. 1950: Two Flags West. 1953: Treasure of the Golden Condor; Main Street to Broadway. 1954: Passion; The Big Combo. 1957: Omar Khayyam; Beyond Mombasa.

Films as director, producer and actor: 1956: Storm Fear. 1957: The Devil's Hairpin (+*co-s*). 1958: Maracaibo. 1962: Lancelot and Guinevere – Sword of Lancelot (*ex-p*). 1966: The Naked Prey. 1967: Beach Red. 1970: No Blade of Grass (*d/p only*).

WILDER, Billy

Director, producer and writer. Vienna 1906–
Journalist in Vienna; journalist and dancer in Berlin. 1929: among script collaborators on *Menschen am Sonntag*. German films as writer. 1934: in Mexico, then Hollywood where (1938) he began his collaboration with Charles Brackett on scripts (q.v. for

list) and then also on production of films he directed (until 1950). Since 1951 produced most of his films and scripted all (from 1957 mostly with I. A. L. Diamond).

Films as director, and writer in collaboration: 1934: Mauvaise Graine (st; co-d Alexander Esnay). 1942: The Major and the Minor. 1943: Five Graves to Cairo. 1944: Double Indemnity. 1945: The Lost Weekend. 1948: The Emperor Waltz; A Foreign Affair. 1950: Sunset Boulevard. 1951: Ace in the Hole – The Big Carnival (+p). 1953: Stalag 17 (+p). 1954: Sabrina (+p). 1955: The Seven Year Itch (+co-p). 1957: The Spirit of St Louis; Love in the Afternoon (+p). Witness for the Prosecution. 1959: Some Like it Hot (+p). 1960: The Apartment (+p). 1961: One, Two, Three (+p). 1963: Irma la Douce (+p). 1964: Kiss Me, Stupid (+p). 1966: The Fortune Cookie – Meet Whiplash Willie (+p). 1970: The Private Life of Sherlock Holmes (+p/co-s).

WILDER, Thornton

Writer. Madison, Wisconsin 1897–
Education in China and California. 1917–18: Coast Artillery Corps reaching corporal. 1920: Yale. 1920–21: American Academy in Rome. 1921–28: taught English in New Jersey. 1926: Princeton; first novel. 1927: Pulitzer Prize for novel 'The Bridge of San Luis Rey'. 1929: first film adaptation of his work *The Bridge of San Luis Rey*. 1930–36: member of faculty, University of Chicago. 1938: Pulitzer Prize for play 'Our Town'. 1940: first film as writer in collaboration *Our Town*. 1941: educational mission to South America for US Government. 1942: Pulitzer Prize for play 'The Skin of Our Teeth'. 1942–45: US Air Corps Intelligence, reaching Lieutenant-Colonel. 1943: in collaboration wrote *Shadow of a Doubt*. 1945: awarded MBE. 1950: Chevalier du Légion d'Honneur. 1958: play 'The Matchmaker' filmed by Joseph Anthony. 1964: turned 'The Matchmaker' into musical comedy 'Hello, Dolly!' (filmed in 1969).

WILLIAMS, Elmo

Director and editor. Lone Wolf, Oklahoma 1913–
Educated UCLA. 1933–39: assistant editor then editor in UK. 1935–39: with Merrill White ran editing service for British production companies. 1939–42: editor with RKO. 1942–46: civilian attached to US Army Signal Corps; directed and edited over 50 training films. 1946: produced and directed films and live shows for US TV, then returned to editing features. 1952: edited his first feature as director. 1958: with Yakima Canutt, was 2nd-unit director on *The Vikings*. 1962: associate producer and co-ordinator of battle episodes on *The Longest Day*. From 1963: managing director of Fox in Europe. 1970: took over from Richard Zanuck as head of production at Fox; also vice-president. Oscar with Harry Gerstad for editing of *High Noon* (1952).

Films as editor include: 1936: Limelight. 1937: Victoria the Great (co). 1939: Nurse Edith Cavell. 1940: Irene. 1943: Forever and a Day (co). 1948: The Miracle of the Bells. 1952: High Noon (co). 1954: 20,000 Leagues under the Sea.

Feature films as director: 1952: The Tall Texan (+e). 1954: The Cowboy (+p/e). 1957: Apache Warrior; Hell Ship Mutiny (+e; co-d Lee Sholem).

WILLIAMS, Emlyn

Actor and playwright. Pen-y-Ffordd, Wales 1905–
Much stage work (actor, writer and director) in UK and USA. 1934: adaptation and dialogue for *Evergreen*. Plays include 'Night Must Fall' filmed in 1937 and 1964, 'The Corn is Green' filmed in 1945, and 'Light of Heart' filmed as *Life Begins at 8.30* (1942). Actor in films from 1932; occasional scripts from 1934. 1949: directed and acted in *The Last Days of Dolwyn*, from own story and script. 1st volume of autobiography, 'George' (1971).

Films as actor include: 1932: Men of Tomorrow. 1936: Broken Blossoms (+s). 1937: Claudius (uf). 1938: The Citadel (+ad). 1939: Jamaica Inn; The Stars Look Down. 1940: The Girl in the News. 1941: Major Barbara. 1950: Three Husbands, 1951: The Scarf; The Magic Box. 1952: Another Man's Poison. 1955: The Deep Blue Sea. 1958: I Accuse. 1962: The L-Shaped Room.

WILLIAMS, Esther

Actress. Los Angeles 1923–
Swimming champion. University of Southern California. 1940: swam with Johnny Weissmuller in Billy Rose's Aquacade at San Francisco International Exposition. Modelling. 1942: first film as actress *Andy Hardy's Double Life*. To 1955: MGM contract. Then Universal and Fox. Married radio singer Ben Gage (1945–57, divorced) and actor Fernando Lamas (in 1963).

Films as actress include: 1944: A Guy Named Joe; Bathing Beauty. 1945: Thrill of a Romance. 1946: Ziegfeld Follies; The Hoodlum Saint. 1947: Fiesta; This Time for Keeps. 1948: On an Island With You. 1949: Take Me Out to the Ball Game. 1950: Duchess of Idaho; Pagan Love Song. 1951: Texas Carnival. 1952: The Million Dollar Mermaid. 1953: Dangerous When Wet; Easy to Love. 1955: Jupiter's Darling. 1956: The Unguarded Moment. 1958: Raw Wind in Eden.

WILLIAMS, Richard

Animator. Toronto 1933–
1948: began in films with Walt Disney. 1949: worked with UPA. 1949–53: commercial artist in Canada; worked with George Dunning at Graphic Associates; attended art school. 1953–55: in Spain; painted, played trumpet in jazz band. From 1955: lived in UK; ran own jazz band while making first animated films. 1958: first film released. Subsequently set up company Richard Williams Animated Films, financing original productions and making TV commercials e.g. 'Guinness at the Albert Hall'. From 1965: designed credit titles for feature films e.g. *What's New Pussycat?* (1965), *The Liquidator* (1965), *A Funny Thing Happened on the Way to the Forum* (1966), titles and animated sequences for *The Charge of the Light Brigade* (1968).

Films as animator include: 1958: The Little Island. 1959: The Story of the Motor Car Engine (co-d Erwin Broner). 1962: A Lecture on Man; Love Me, Love Me, Love Me. 1964: Circus Drawings. 1965: Diary of a Madman. 1966: The Dermis Probe; Pubs and Beaches. 1967: The Sailor and the Devil (co-d Errol Le Cain); I,

Raskolnikow. *directed by Robert Wiene.*
Cornel Wilde and Helen Stanton in Joseph H. Lewis' The Big Combo.
Jack Lemmon and Joe E. Brown in Billy Wilder's Some Like It Hot.

295

vor Pittfalks. 1970: Every Home Should Have One. 1971: A Christmas Carol.

WILLIAMS, Tennessee

(Thomas Lanier Williams) Writer. Columbus, Missouri 1914–

1931–33: University of Missouri. 1936–37: Washington University, St Louis. 1938: University of Iowa. Numerous jobs. 1940: play 'Battle of Angels' produced by Theatre Guild. 1948: Pulitzer Prize for 'A Streetcar Named Desire'. 1950: first film as writer in collaboration *The Glass Menagerie* based on own play. 1955: Pulitzer Prize for 'Cat on a Hot Tin Roof'; Wrote libretto for Raffaello de Banfield's opera 'Lord Byron's Love Letter'. 1956: only original screenplay *Baby Doll*. From 1958: film adaptations of his work mainly by others. 1960: *The Fugitive Kind* based on 'Orpheus Descending'.

Films based by others on his work include: 1958: Cat on a Hot Tin Roof. 1961: Summer and Smoke. 1962: The Roman Spring of Mrs Stone; Period of Adjustment; Sweet Bird of Youth. 1964: The Night of the Iguana. 1966: This Property is Condemned.

Films as writer: 1950: The Glass Menagerie (*co*). 1951: A Streetcar Named Desire. 1955: The Rose Tattoo. 1956: Baby Doll. 1959: Suddenly Last Summer (*co*); The Fugitive Kind (*co*). 1968: Boom.

WILSON, Michael

Writer. McAlester, Oklahoma 1914–

Script-writer since 1941: blacklisted after called before House Committee on Un-American Activities. 1956: uncredited work on *Friendly Persuasion*. 1957: wrote second and third versions of Carl Foreman's script for *The Bridge on the River Kwai*; film credited to Pierre Boule, who wrote the novel. 1962: uncredited work on *Lawrence of Arabia*. Oscar for screenplay, *A Place in the Sun* (with Harry Brown, 1951).

Films as writer include: 1941: The Man in Her Life. 1947: It's a Wonderful Life (*co*). 1951: A Place in the Sun (*co*). 1952: Five Fingers. 1953: Salt of the Earth. 1956: Friendly Persuasion (*uc*). 1957: The Bridge on the River Kwai (*co*, *uc*). 1963: Lawrence of Arabia (*co*, *uc*). 1965: The Sandpiper (*co*). 1968: Planet of the Apes (*co*). 1969: Che! (*co*).

WILSON, Richard

Director, writer and producer. McKeesport, Pennsylvania 1915–

Denver University, then announcer and actor for radio in Denver and New York. 1937–38: actor, stage manager and assistant producer for Orson Welles at Mercury Theatre. Worked on all Welles' films and radio shows to 1948. 1948: associate producer on *Lady From Shanghai* (in collaboration with William Castle), and *Macbeth*. Associate producer then producer at Universal-International. 1955: first film as director.

Films as director: 1955: Man with the Gun – Troubleshooter (*+co-s*). 1957: The Big Boodle – Night in Havana. 1958: Raw Wind in Eden (*+co-s*). 1959: Al Capone. 1960: Pay or Die (*+p*). 1963: Wall of Noise.

1964: Invitation to a Gunfighter (*+p/co-s*). 1968: Three in the Attic (*+p*).

WINDUST, Bretaigne

Director. Paris 1906–60 New York

Son of violinist Joseph Windust and singer Elizabeth Amory Day. Spent childhood in London. 1920: to USA. Studied at Princeton University. Co-founder of University Players at New Falmouth. From 1929: worked with Theatre Guild, New York. 1932: directed and acted in 'Strange Interlude' and 'The Taming of the Shrew'; directed Alfred Lunt and Lynne Fontanne on Broadway. Many other Broadway productions. Also TV director including 'Dear Arthur', 'Alfred Hitchcock Presents', 'Climax', 'Thin Man', 'Kitty Hawk'. From 1948: directed films mainly for Warners.

Films as director include: 1948: Winter Meeting; June Bride. 1950: Perfect Strangers; Pretty Baby. 1951: The Enforcer – Murder Incorporated (*co-d Raoul Walsh, uc*). 1952: Face to Face *ep* The Bride Comes to Yellow Sky. 1959: The Pied Piper of Hamelin.

WINTERS, Shelley

Actress. St Louis, Illinois 1922–

Drama Workshop of New School for Social Research, New York. Actor's Studio with Elia Kazan in New York, with Michael Chekhov, Charles Laughton in Hollywood. 1940: stage debut as understudy in 'Time of Your Life'. 1941: Broadway debut in 'The Night Before Christmas'. 1942: acted in 'Rosalinda'. 1943: Columbia contract; first film as actress, uncredited, What a Woman. 1947–48: Broadway in 'Oklahoma'. 1948–54: worked mainly for Universal. Then for numerous companies. Broadway parts include 'A Hatful of Rain' (1955) and 'Night of the Iguana' (1962) in which she replaced Bette Davis. Other stage roles include 'Born Yesterday', 'A Streetcar Named Desire', 'Two for the See Saw', 'A View from the Bridge'. TV work includes 'The Women' (1955), 'A Double Life' (1957). Also cabaret. Oscars as supporting actress for *The Diary of Anne Frank* (1959), *A Patch of Blue* (1965).

Films as actress include: 1944: She's a Soldier Too. 1945: Tonight and Every Night. 1948: A Double Life; Red River; Cry of the City. 1949: Johnny Stool Pigeon; The Great Gatsby. 1950: Winchester '73. 1951: He Ran All the Way; A Place in the Sun; Meet Danny Wilson. 1952: Phone Call from a Stranger; Untamed Frontier; My Man and I. 1954: Tennessee Champ; Saskatchewan; Executive Suite; Playgirl; Mambo. 1955: I Am a Camera; The Night of the Hunter; The Big Knife; I Died a Thousand Times. 1959: The Diary of Anne Frank; Odds Against Tomorrow; Let No Man Write My Epitaph. 1961: The Young Savages. 1962: Lolita; The Chapman Report. 1963: The Balcony. 1964: Gli Indifferenti; A House is not a Home. 1965: A Patch of Blue. 1966: Harper; Alfie. 1968: The Scalphunters; Buona Sera, Mrs Campbell. 1970: Bloody Mama; How Do I Love Thee?; Flap.

WISBAR, Frank

(Franz Wysbar) Director. Tilsit, East Prussia 1899–1967 Mainz, West Germany

Military service then writer and literary manager for film companies. Worked with Ufa then Terra. 1932:

first film as director. 1939: emigrated to USA where he changed his name. Worked as political writer, lecturer, wrote scripts and stories for films; directed films. 1949–53: produced and directed over 300 shorts for US TV; scripted and directed Fireside Theatre, General Electric Theatre; ran own company. 1955: returned to Germany. Made last film in Italy.

Films as director: 1932: Im Banne des Eulenspiegels. 1933: Anna und Elisabeth (*+co-s*). 1934: Rivalen der Luft. 1935: Hermin und die sieben Aufrechten (*+co-s*); Die Werft zum grauen Hecht (*+co-s*). 1936: Fährmann Maria (*+co-s*); Die Unbekannte (*+co-s*). 1937: Petermann ist dagegen (*+co-s*); Ball im Metropol (*+co-s*). 1945: Strangler of the Swamp (*rm Fährmann Maria 1936; +p/co-st/s*). 1946: Devil Bat's Daughter (*+p/co-s*); Lighthouse (*+p/s*). 1948: The Prairie. 1957: Haie und kleine Fische – U Boat 55 (*+s*). 1958: Nasser Asphalt. 1959: Hunde, wollt ihr ewig leben – Dogs, Do You Want to Live Forever – Battle Inferno. 1960: Fabrik der Offiziere; Nacht fiel über Gotenhaten. 1961: Barbara. 1962: Marcia o crepa (*+co-s*).

WISE, Robert

Director. Winchester, Indiana 1914–

Studied journalism but joined RKO (1933) and worked in sound department before becoming an editor. As editor worked on e.g. *Bachelor Mother* (1939), *My Favourite Wife* (1940), *Citizen Kane* (1941, with Mark Robson) and *The Magnificent Ambersons* (1942). Val Lewton let him finish *The Curse of the Cat People* (1944) as Gunther von Fritsch was not working fast enough. Produced most of own films since 1959.

Films as director: 1944: The Curse of the Cat People (*co-d Gunther von Fritsch*); Mademoiselle Fifi. 1945: The Body Snatchers; A Game of Death. 1946: Criminal Court; Born to Kill. 1948: Blood on the Moon; Mystery in Mexico. 1949: The Set-up. 1950: Three Secrets; Two Flags West. 1951: The House on Telegraph Hill; The Day the Earth Stood Still. 1952: The Captive City; Something for the Birds. 1953: Destination Gobi; The Desert Rats; So Big. 1954: Executive Suite. 1956: Helen of Troy; Tribute to a Badman; Somebody Up There Likes Me. 1957: This Could be the Night; Until They Sail. 1958: Run Silent, Run Deep; I Want to Live. 1959: Odds Against Tomorrow (*+p*). 1961: West Side Story (*+p; co-d Jerome Robbins*). 1962: Two for the Seesaw. 1963: The Haunting (*+p*). 1964: The Sound of Music (*+p*). 1966: The Sand Pebbles (*+p*). 1968: Star! (*+pc*). 1971: The Andromeda Strain (*+p*).

WOLFIT, Sir Donald

Actor. Newark upon Trent, Nottinghamshire 1902–68 London

1920: stage debut in 'The Taming of the Shrew'. 1924: London debut in 'The Wandering Jew' with Matheson Lang. 1927: repertory in Sheffield. 1928: on London stage in 'Such Men Are Dangerous'. 1929–30: at Old Vic. 1931–32: Canadian tour. 1933: producer with Margaret Rutherford, Margaret Webster, John Clements. 1934: first film as actor, as St Francis in Religious Film Society's *Inasmuch*. 1936: first Stratford season. 1937: first tour as actor-manager. 1944–45: toured France, Belgium, Italy for troops. 1947–48: in New York and Canada. 1950: CBE. 1951: Old Vic. 1952: re-formed his own company.

1955: autobiography 'First Interval'. 1957: Knighted. 1963: in South Africa. 1965: on Broadway. Also work in TV. Married Rosalind Iden, often his leading lady.

Films as actor include: 1952: The Ringer. 1955: A Prize of Gold; A Man on the Beach. 1958: I Accuse; Room at the Top. 1959: The Angry Hills; The Rough and the Smooth; The House of the Seven Hawks. 1962: Lawrence of Arabia. 1964: Becket.

WOOD, Natalie

(Natasha Gurdin) Actress. San Francisco 1938–
Father a set designer, mother a ballet dancer. 1943: first film, as extra in *Happy Land* under real name. 1949: Child Star of the Year. To 1954: worked mainly for RKO, Paramount, Fox, Columbia. Then mainly Warners. Married Robert Wagner (1957–63, divorced).

Films as actress include: 1945: Tomorrow is Forever. 1946: The Bride Wore Boots. 1947: Driftwood; The Ghost and Mrs Muir; Miracle on 34th Street. 1949: Chicken Every Sunday; Father was a Fullback; Our Very Own. 1950: No Sad Songs for Me; The Jackpot; Never a Dull Moment. 1951: The Blue Veil. 1952: Just for You. 1953: The Star. 1955: The Silver Chalice; Rebel Without a Cause. 1956: The Girl He Left Behind; A Cry in the Night; The Searchers; The Burning Hills. 1957: Bombers B-52. 1958: Kings Go Forth; Marjorie Morningstar. 1960: Cash McCall; All the Fine Young Cannibals. 1961: Splendour in the Grass. 1962: Gypsy. 1963: Love with the Proper Stranger. 1964: Sex and the Single Girl. 1965: The Great Race. 1966: Inside Daisy Clover; This Property is Condemned.

WOOD, Sam

Director. Philadelphia 1883–1949 Hollywood
Studied law. To Colorado then Nevada with gold rush. In Los Angeles during real estate boom; successful estate agent. Studied dramatic art in Los Angeles. Entered films as assistant to Cecil B. De Mille. Working as director with Famous Players-Lasky by 1919: with them until 1926. 1927–39: director with MGM. Then with various companies. 1949: last film *Ambush* completed and shown after his death. President of the Motion Picture Alliance for the Preservation of American Ideals.

Films as director: 1919: Double Speed. 1920: Excuse My Dust; The Dancin' Fool; What's Your Hurry?; Sick Abed. 1921: Don't Tell Everything; The Great Moment; Peck's Bad Boy (+ad); The Snob; Under The Lash. 1922: Beyond the Rocks; Her Gilded Cage; Her Husband's Trademark; The Impossible Mrs Bellew; My American Wife; 1923: Bluebeard's 8th Wife; His Children's Children; Prodigal Daughters. 1924: Bluff; The Female; The Mine With the Iron Door; The Next Corner; 1925: The Re-creation of Brian Kent. 1926: Fascinating Youth; One Minute To Play; 1927: The Fair Co-Ed; A Racing Romeo; Rookies. 1928: The Latest From Paris; Telling the World. 1929: It's a Great Life; So This Is College. 1930: Paid – Within the Law; They Learned About Women (co-d Jack Conway); The Richest Man in the World – Sins of the Children; The Girl Said No; Way for a Sailor; 1931: New Adventures of Get Rich Quick Wallingford; A Tailor Made Man; Man

in Possession. 1932: Huddle; Prosperity. 1933: Hold Your Man; The Barbarian; Christopher Bean – The Late Christopher Bean – Her Sweetheart. 1934: Stamboul Quest. 1935: A Night at the Opera; Whipsaw; Let 'em Have it. 1936: The Unguarded Hour. 1937: A Day at the Races (+p); Navy, Blue and Gold; Madame X. 1938: Lord Jeff; Stablemates. 1939: Goodbye, Mr. Chips. 1940: Rangers of Fortune; Raffles; Our Town; Kitty Foyle. 1941: The Devil and Miss Jones. 1942: King's Row; The Pride of the Yankees. 1943: For Whom The Bell Tolls (+p). 1944: Casanova Brown. 1945: Guest Wife. 1946: Saratoga Trunk; Heartbeat. 1947: Ivy. 1949: The Stratton Story; Command Decision; Ambush.

WOODWARD, Joanne

Actress. Thomasville, Georgia 1930–
Father publishing executive. Parents divorced while she was in high school in South Carolina. Modelling, then Louisiana State University. Became secretary, worked with Greenwich Little Theatre Group under Albert Macham. Neighbourhood Playhouse, New York with Sanford Meisner. Much TV work. Understudy to Janice Rule, Kim Stanley in 'Picnic'. 1954: 3 TV shows in Hollywood, spotted by Dick Powell, led to 7-year Fox contract. TV work continued, acted in 'The Lovers', including short Broadway run. 1958: married Paul Newman; acted with him in *The Long, Hot Summer*. With him in several films, directed by him in *Rachel, Rachel* (1968). Acted with him on New York stage in 'Baby Want a Kiss'. Oscar as Best Actress for *The Three Faces of Eve* (1957).

Films as actress include: 1955: Count Three and Pray. 1956: A Kiss Before Dying. 1957: The Three Faces of Eve; No Down Payment. 1958: The Long, Hot Summer; Rally 'Round the Flag, Boys. 1959: The Sound and the Fury; The Fugitive Kind. 1960: From the Terrace. 1961: Paris Blues. 1963: The Stripper; A New Kind of Love. 1966: A Big Hand for the Little Lady; A Fine Madness. 1968: Rachel, Rachel. 1969: Winning. 1970: WUSA.

WOOLF, John *and* James

Producers. John: London 1913– . James: London 1920–66 Beverley Hills, California
Father C. M. Woolf provided funds to prevent Gaumont-British closure, formed General Film Distributors which became nucleus of Rank Organisation. John: educated at Eton and in Switzerland. At 17 joined father's company. 1946: married actress Edana Romney. James: at 14 joined father's company in publicity department. To Hollywood, Universal publicity department. World War II: served in RAF. Set up own production company, joined by John; took over father's business on his death, then allowed it to pass to Rank. 1949: they founded Romulus Films and Remus Films. 1954: financial backers for Alexander Korda's London Films after British Lion placed in hands of receivers. Threatened with boycott by exhibitors when sold backlog of films to TV. 1958: their first credit as producers *Room at the Top*. 1962: James co-produced with Richard Attenborough *The L-Shaped Room*. 1966: James produced his only Hollywood film *King Rat* (though produced films in England for Hollywood studios). John director of Anglia TV. James' last film as producer William Kotcheff's *Life at the Top*. James died of heart attack;

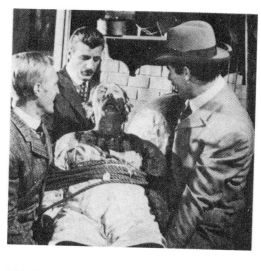

Pay or Die. produced and directed by Richard Wilson. Gary Cooper, Akim Tamiroff and Ingrid Bergman in Sam Wood's For Whom the Bell Tolls.
A Diary for Timothy. directed by Humphrey Jennings and photographed by Basil Wright.

John replaced him as producer of *Oliver!* (1968). John also financed London stage productions.

Films produced by their companies include: 1951: Pandora and the Flying Dutchman (*co*); African Queen (*co*); Lucky Nick Cain. 1952: Cosh Boy. 1953: Moulin Rouge (*co*). 1954: Beat the Devil (*co*). 1955: I am a Camera. 1956: Carrington VC; The Iron Petticoat; Three Men in a Boat. 1957: The Story of Esther Costello.

Films produced by James: 1958: Room at the Top (*co*). 1962: The L-Shaped Room (*co*); Term of Trial. 1964: The Pumpkin Eater; Of Human Bondage. 1966: King Rat.

Films produced by John: 1958: Room at the Top (*co*). 1968: Oliver!

WRIGHT, Basil

Director and producer. London 1907–
Sherborne and Corpus Christi College, Cambridge. From 1928: worked under John Grierson at Empire Marketing Board Film Unit, e.g. on *Conquest* (1929), then GPO Film Unit. 1931: directed first documentary. From 1930s many films as producer including Len Lye's *Rainbow Dance* (1936). 1937: founded Realist Film Unit. 1943–44: advisor to the Canadian Government on information technique and policy. 1944: producer in charge of Crown Film Unit. 1948: formed International Realist Ltd. 1953: in collaboration with Paul Rotha directed feature-length documentary *World Without End* for UN. Since directed art documentaries, also produced, e.g. *The Drawings of Leonardo da Vinci* (1953). From 1962: visiting professor of film art, University of California; produced many educational films for children. Author of book 'The Use of Film' (1948).

Films as director: 1931: O'er Hill and Dale. 1932: The Country Comes to Town. 1933: Windmill in Barbados; Cargo from Jamaica; Liner Cruising South. 1934: Song of Ceylon (*+ s/c*). 1936: Night Mail (*co-d Harry Watt*); 6.30 Collection (*co-d Harry Watt*). 1937: Children at School. 1938: The Face of Scotland. 1939: Evacuation. 1945: This Was Japan (*+ p*). 1946: The Story of Omolo (*+ p*). 1948: Bernard Miles on Gun Dogs. 1951: Waters of Time (*+ p/s*). 1953: World Without End – Je suis un homme (*+ co-s*; *co-d Paul Rotha*). 1956: The Stained Glass at Fairford (*+ p*). 1958: The Immortal Land (*+ co-p*). 1959: Greek Sculpture (*co-d Michael Ayrton*). 1960: A Place for Gold (*+ p*).

WRIGHT, Teresa

Actress. Maplewood, New Jersey 1919–
Acted in school plays. Apprentice at Wharf Theatre, Provincetown, Massachusetts. Graduated from school, returned to Wharf Theatre on scholarship. In 'Our Town' in New York as understudy and later on tour. On Broadway in 'Life with Father'. Spotted on stage by Lillian Hellman for first film as actress *The Little Foxes* (1941). Films mainly for RKO; also e.g. Paramount. Married Niven Busch (1942–52, divorced). 1942: Oscar as supporting actress for *Mrs Miniver*.

Films as actress include: 1942: Mrs Miniver; The Pride of the Yankees. 1943: Shadow of a Doubt. 1944:
Casanova Brown. 1946: The Best Years of Our Lives. 1947: Pursued. 1948: Enchantment. 1950: The Capture; The Men. 1952: Something to Live For; The Steel Trap. 1953: Count the Hours; The Actress. 1954: Track of the Cat. 1958: The Wonderful Years.

WYLER, William

Director. Mulhouse, Alsace 1902–
Swiss father, German mother. Trilingual (English, French, German) from childhood. Educated in Lausanne and Paris. 1919: press agent for Universal in Paris. 1920: to USA to work in Universal's foreign publicity department in New York. 1921: to Hollywood; office boy, property man, script clerk, assistant casting director, then assistant director with Universal. 1925: directed first of many 2-reelers for Mustang, a subsidiary of Universal. From 1926: also directed occasional 5-reel westerns for Universal. Remained with Universal as features director until 1935. From 1936: worked mainly for Samuel Goldwyn. World War II: commissioned as Major in US Army Air Force; made 3 documentaries including *The Fighting Lady* (1944); awarded Air Medal and promoted to Lieutenant-Colonel (1943); awarded Legion of Merit (1945). 1949–55: producer and director with Paramount. Thereafter independent director, also occasionally producing. 1934–36: was married to actress Margaret Sullavan. Oscars for direction: *Mrs Miniver* (1942, also Best Picture), *The Best years of Our Lives* (1946, also Best Picture), *Ben-Hur* (1959, also Best Picture). Irving G. Thalberg Memorial Award (1965).

Films as director: 1925: Crook Buster. 1926: Ridin' for Love (*+ st*); Lazy Lightning; The Fire Barrier; The Gunless Bad Man; The Horse Trader; Don't Shoot; Martin of the Mounted; The Two-Fister; The Stolen Ranch. 1927: Blazing Days; Hard Fists; Tenderfoot Courage; The Silent Partner; The Phantom Outlaw; The Haunted Homestead; The Lone Star; Gun Justice; Galloping Justice; The Ore Raiders; Straight Shootin'; Border Cavalier; Desert Dust; The Home Trail; The Square Shooter; Kelcy Gets his Man; Daze of the West; Thunder Riders. 1928: Anybody Here Seen Kelly?; The Shakedown. 1929: The Love Trap; Hell's Heroes. 1930: The Storm. 1931: A House Divided. 1932: The Old Dark House (*uc, co-d James Whale*); Tom Brown of Culver. 1933: Counsellor at Law; Her First Mate. 1934: Glamour. 1935: The Good Fairy; The Gay Deception. 1936: These Three; Come and Get It! (*co-d Howard Hawks*); Dodsworth. 1937: Dead End. 1938: Jezebel. 1939: Wuthering Heights. 1940: The Westerner; The Letter. 1941: The Little Foxes. 1942: Mrs Miniver. 1944: Memphis Belle (*+ p/s/co-c*). 1946: The Best Years of Our Lives – Glory for Me. 1947: Thunderbolt (*co-d John Sturges*). 1949: The Heiress (*+ p*). 1951: Detective Story. 1952: Carrie (*+ p*). 1953: Roman Holiday (*+ p*). 1955: The Desperate Hours (*+ p*). 1956: Friendly Persuasion (*+ p*). 1958: The Big Country (*+ co-p*). 1959: Ben-Hur. 1962: The Children's Hour – The Loudest Whisper (*+ p*). 1964: The Collector. 1966: How to Steal a Million. 1968: Funny Girl. 1970: The Liberation of L. B. Jones.

WYMAN, Jane

(Sarah Jane Fulks) St Joseph, Missouri 1914–
Radio vocalist. Chorus dancer in musical films. 1936:
first film as actress *Gold Diggers of 1937* (1936). Most films for Warners. Established scholarship at RADA. Also TV. Married Ronald Reagan (1940–48, divorced). Oscar as Best Actress for *Johnny Belinda* (1948).

Films as actress include: 1936: Cain and Mabel; Stage Struck. 1937: The King and the Chorus Girl; Ready Willing and Able; Slim; The Singing Marine. 1938: Brother Rat; The Spy Ring; The Crowd Roars; Fools for Scandal. 1939: Tail Spin. 1940: Brother Rat and a Baby; Angel from Texas; My Love Comes Back. 1941: Honeymoon for Three; Bad Men of Missouri. 1942: Larceny, Inc; My Favourite Spy; Footlight Serenade. 1943: Princess O'Rourke. 1945: Hollywood Canteen; The Lost Weekend. 1946: Night and Day; The Yearling. 1947: Magic Town; Cheyenne. 1948: A Kiss in the Dark; Johnny Belinda. 1949: Lady Takes a Sailor; It's a Great Feeling. 1950: Stage Fright; The Glass Menagerie. 1951: Here Comes the Groom; The Blue Veil; Three Guys Named Mike. 1952: Just For You. 1953: So Big. 1954: Magnificent Obsession. 1955: All That Heaven Allows; Lucy Gallant. 1956: Miracle in the Rain. 1960: Pollyanna. 1962: Bon Voyage!

Y

YAMADA, Isuzu

Actress. Osaka, Japan 1917–
Father actor Kasuo Youmada. School of music and dancing. At 14 entered films at Dai-Ichi, company formed by Kenji Mizoguchi and Masaichi Nagata. Acted in films of Mizoguchi and Teinosuke Kinugasa; she married the latter, one of 6 husbands. 1938: moved to Toho. After World War II joined Kazuo Hasegawa's theatre troupe; later freelanced, acting on radio, TV and theatre as well as in films. Daughter is actress Michiko Saga.

Films as actress include: 1934: Aize Toge; Orizuru Osen. 1935: Maria no Oyuki. 1936: Naniwa Ereji; Gion no Shimai. 1937: Osaka Natsu no Jin. 1938: Tsurahachi Tsurujiro. 1940: Hebihimesama. 1943: Uta Andon. 1945: Meito Bijomaru. 1946: Aru yo no Tonosama. 1947: Joyu. 1949: Kobanzame. 1953: Shukuzu. 1954: Okuman Choja. 1955: Takekurabe. 1956: Nagareru. 1957: Kumonosu-jo; Tokyo Boshoku; Kuroi Kawa; Donzoko. 1960: Yoru no Nagare. 1961: Yojimbo.

YATES, Herbert J.

Studio head. New York 1880–1966 Sherman Oaks, California
Columbia University. Tobacco millionaire by 30. From 1912: backed independent film production, e.g. Fatty Arbuckle shorts; ran film processing laboratories. 1932: merged 4 independent companies to set up Republic Pictures. Supervised all Republic's productions, notably 'singing cowboy' films with Gene Autry, Roy Rogers, John Wayne in 1930s and early 1940s; major features in late 1940s and 1950s. Married Czech skating star Vera Hruba Ralston who appeared in many Republic films. 1957: Republic abandoned film production and distribution to make TV films.

YATES, Peter

Director. Aldershot, Hampshire 1929–
Charterhouse. RADA. In repertory as actor, director, stage manager. Administrative work in motor-racing, also team manager, driver. Dubbing manager, then editor in documentaries. Assistant to e.g. Guy Hamilton, Tony Richardson, J. Lee Thompson, Jack Cardiff. Royal Court Theatre: directed 'An American Dream' and 'The Death of Bessie Smith'. 1962: first film as director. 1968: first American film. Mirisch contract. TV work includes episodes of 'The Saint' and 'The Secret Agent'.

Films as director: 1962: Summer Holiday. 1964: One Way Pendulum. 1967: Robbery (+ co-s). 1968: Bullitt. 1969: John and Mary. 1971: Murphy's War.

YEAWORTH, Irvin Shortess, Jr

Director
1950: entered films. 1958: first film as director, for Paramount. 1959–60: worked for Universal, associate producer on his own films. 1961–66: no films as director.

Films as director: 1958: The Blob. 1959: The 4-D Man (+ as-p). 1960: Dinosaurus! (+ as-p). 1967: Way Out (+ p).

YORDAN, Philip

Writer and producer. Chicago c. 1913–
University of Illinois; studied law at Kent College. Wrote plays for New York stage, e.g. 'Anna Lucasta'. 1941: uncredited work on script of *All That Money Can Buy*. 1942: collaborated on first film script, *Syncopation,* then contract to write films released through Monogram. Subsequently also producer. With Sidney Harmon formed production company, Security Pictures. Wrote novel 'Man of the West' filmed by Roy Rowland as *Gun Glory* (1957). In 1960s collaborated as writer on Samuel Bronston productions including *Circus World,* for which he wrote story with Nicholas Ray. President of Interplay Industries. Oscar for motion picture story *Broken Lance* (1954).

Films as writer include: 1944: When Strangers Marry (co). 1946: Suspense (+ st). 1949: House of Strangers; Anna Lucasta (+ p; co-s/fpl); Reign of Terror (co-st/co-s). 1950: Edge of Doom. 1951: Detective Story (co); Drums in the Deep South (co). 1952: Mara-Maru (co-st); Mutiny. 1953: Blowing Wild (+ st); Man Crazy (+ co-p; co-st/co-s). 1954: The Naked Jungle (co); The Big Combo; Johnny Guitar. 1955: Conquest of Space (co-ad); The Man from Laramie (co); The Last Frontier (co). 1956: The Harder They Fall (+ p); Joe Macbeth. 1957: Men in War (co); No Down Payment. 1958: God's Little Acre; The Bravados; The Fiend who Walked the West (co). 1959: Day of the Outlaw. 1960: Studs Lonigan (+ p). 1961: El Cid (co); King of Kings. 1963: Fifty-Five Days at Peking (co). 1964: The Fall of the Roman Empire (co). 1966: Battle of the Bulge (+ co-p; co-s). 1969: The Royal Hunt of the Sun (+ co-p). 1971: Captain Apache (+ co-p; co-s).

YORKIN, Bud

(Alan Yorkin) Director. Washington, Pennsylvania 1929–
English Literature at Columbia University. 1945: US Navy. After demobilisation worked for NBC. Much TV as writer and director including 'Henry Fonda and Family', 'Bobby Darin and Friends', 'An Evening with Fred Astaire', 'An Evening with Carol Channing', 'Spike Jones Show'; directed Dean Martin and Jerry Lewis on 'Colgate Comedy Hour'. 1963: first feature as director. Producer for TV e.g. on 'All in the Family'.

Films as director: 1963: Come Blow Your Horn (+ co-p). 1965: Never Too Late. 1967: Divorce American Style. 1968: Inspector Clouseau.

YOSHIMURA, Kozaburo
(or Kimisaburo)

Director. Hiroshima 1911–
Intended to study literature at Kyoto University: failed entrance examination. Failed examinations for post of assistant director. 1929: became assistant at Shochiku through influence of relative. Edited several films of Yasujiro Shimazu. 1934: first film as director; demoted to assistant. 1939: returned to direction with *Onna Koso Ie o Mamore.* 1944–45: Japanese Army; opportunity to study captured enemy films in Bangkok. 1950: left Shochiku to form independent company with Kaneto Shindo, who scripted several of his films, from 1948. 1957: completed Kenji Mizoguchi's *Osaka Monogatari.*

Films as director: 1934: Nukiashi Sashiashi. 1939: Onna Koso Ie o Mamore; Yoki no Uramachi – Lively Alley; Ashita no Odoriko – Tomorrow's Dancers; Gonin no Kyodai – Five Brothers and a Sister; Danryu – Warm Current. 1940: Nishizumi Senshacho-den – The Story of Tank-Commander Nishizumi. 1941: Hana – Blossom. 1942: Kancho Imada Shisezu – The Spy isn't Dead Yet; Minami no Kaze – South Wind (in 2 parts). 1943: Kaisen no Zenya – On the Eve of War. 1944: Kessen – Decisive Battle (co-d Ieruo Hagiyami). 1947: Zo o Kutta Renchu – The Fellows Who Ate the Elephant. 1948: Anjo-ke no Butokai – A Ball at the Anjo House; Yuwaku – Temptation; Waga Shogai no Kagayakeru Hi – The Day Our Lives Shine. 1949: Shitto – Jealousy; Mori no Ishimatsu – Ishimatsu of the Forest; Mahiru no Enbukyoku – Waltz at Noon. 1950: Shunsetsu – Spring Snow; Senka no Hate – End of War Disasters; Niju-sai Zengo – About Twenty Years Old. 1951: Itswareru Seiso – Clothes of Deception – Under Silk Garments; Jiyu Gakku – School of Freedom; Genji Monogatari – A Tale of Genji. 1952: Nishijin no Shimai – The Sisters of Nishijin; Boryoku – Violence. 1953: Senbazuru – Thousand Cranes; Yokubo – Desires; Yoake Mae – Before Dawn. 1954: Ashizuri Misaki – Cape Ashizuri; Wakai Hitotachi – People of Young Character; Aisurebakoso – Because I Love ep Hanauri Musume. 1955: Ginza no Onna – Women of the Ginza; Bijo to Kairyu – The Beauty and the Dragon. 1956: Totsuga Hi – Date for Marriage; Yoru no Kawa – Night River – Undercurrent; Yonju-hassai no Teiko. 1957: Osaka Monogatari – An Osaka story (co-d Kenji Mizoguchi); Yoru no Cho – Night Butter-flies; Chijo – On This Earth. 1958: Hitotsubu no Mugi – A Grain of Wheat; Yoru no Sugao – The Naked Face of Night – The Ladder of Success. 1959: Denwa wa Yugata ni Naru – A Telephone Ring in the Evening; Kizoku no Kaidan. 1960: Jokyo – A Woman's Testament (ep). 1961: Onna no Saka – Women of Kyoto; Konki – Marriageable Age; Onna no Kunsho – A Design for Dying. 1962: Katei no Jijyo

Samantha Eggar in William Wyler's The Collector.
Jane Wyman in Douglas Sirk's All that Heaven Allows.
Orson Welles and Loretta Young in The Stranger.

– Their Legacy; Sono yo wa Wasurenai – A Night to Remember – Hiroshima Heartache. 1963: Uso – Lies – When Women Lie (ep); Echizen Takeningyo – The Bamboo Doll. 1966: Kokoro no Sanmyaku – The Heart of the Mountains. 1967: Daraku suru Onna – A Fallen Woman. 1968: Nemureri Bijo – The House of the Sleeping Virgins; Atsui Yoru – A Hot Night.

YOUNG, Frederick A.

Cinematographer. London 1902–
Began as laboratory assistant with Gaumont British at 15. Cinematographer by 1930. Under contract to Herbert Wilcox during 1930s. World War II: Captain in army film unit; directed training films. Cinematographer, including a number of Anglo-American co-productions. 1970: awarded OBE. Oscars for colour cinematography, *Lawrence of Arabia* (1962), *Dr Zhivago* (1965).

Films as cinematographer include: 1930: The W Plan. 1932: The Little Damozel. 1939: Goodbye, Mr Chips. 1940: Contraband. 1941: 49th Parallel. 1942: The Young Mr Pitt. 1945: Caesar and Cleopatra (co). 1947: So Well Remembered. 1948: Escape; The Winslow Boy. 1949: Edward, My Son; Conspirator. 1950: Treasure Island. 1952: Ivanhoe. 1953: Knights of the Round Table (co); Terror on a Train. 1956: Invitation to the Dance (co); Bhowani Junction; Lust for Life (co). 1957: Beyond Mombasa; The Barretts of Wimpole Street; The Little Hut; Island in the Sun. 1958: I Accuse; Gideon's Day; Indiscreet: The Inn of the Sixth Happiness. 1959: Solomon and Sheba. 1965: Lord Jim; Rotten to the Core. 1966: The Deadly Affair. 1967: You Only Live Twice. 1969: The Battle of Britain (co); Sinful Davey (co). 1970: Ryan's Daughter. 1971: Nicholas and Alexandra.

YOUNG, Loretta

(Gretchen Young) Actress. Salt Lake City, Utah 1913–
Sisters are Sally Blane and Polly Ann Young. At 4, child extra; at 12, bit player; at 13, contract. To 1933: worked mainly for Warners. Then mainly Fox and Paramount. 1970: briefly board member of Technicolor Inc. Also TV. 1947: Oscar as Best Actress for *The Farmer's Daughter*.

Films as actress include: 1928: Laugh Clown Laugh; The Head Man. 1929: The Forward Pass; The Squall. 1930: Second Floor Mystery. 1932: The Hatchet Man. 1933: Heroes for Sale; Lady of the Night; She Had to Say Yes; Man's Castle. 1934: The House of Rothschild; Born to be Bad. 1935: The Call of the Wild; The Crusades; Clive of India. 1936: The Unguarded Hour; Ramona. 1937: Love is News. 1938: Kentucky; Four Men and a Prayer; Suez. 1939: Wife, Husband and Friend; Eternally Yours. 1941: The Men in Her Life; The Lady from Cheyenne. 1943: China. 1944: And Now Tomorrow. 1945: Along Came Jones. 1946: The Stranger. 1947: The Bishop's Wife. 1948: Rachel and the Stranger. 1949: The Accused; Mother is a Freshman; Come to the Stable. 1950: Key to the City. 1951: Cause for Alarm. 1952: Because of You; Paula. 1953: It Happens Every Thursday.

YOUNG, Robert

Actor. Chicago 1907–

1932: first film as actor *The Black Camel*. 1933: married his frequent co-star Betty Henderson. Worked mainly for MGM. Also TV.

Films as actor include: 1932: The Wet Parade; Strange Interlude. 1933: Hell Below; Tugboat Annie; The Kid from Spain; Today We Live. 1934: Carolina; Whom the Gods Destroy; Lazy River; The House of Rothschild; Spitfire. 1935: Remember Last Night? 1936: The Bride Comes Home; It's Love Again; Secret Agent. 1937: Navy Blue and Gold; I Met Him in Paris; Dangerous Number. 1938: Josette; Three Comrades; The Shining Hour. 1940: Northwest Passage; The Mortal Storm. 1941: Lady Be Good; Western Union; H. M. Pulham Esq. 1942: Cairo. 1943: Slightly Dangerous; Claudia; Sweet Rosie O'Grady. 1944: The Canterville Ghost. 1945: The Enchanted Cottage. 1946: The Searching Wind; Claudia and David. 1947: They Won't Believe Me; Crossfire. 1948: Sitting Pretty. 1949: That Forsythe Woman. 1951: Goodbye My Fancy. 1954: Secret of the Incas.

YOUNG, Terence

Director. Shanghai 1915–
History at St Catherine's College, Cambridge. 1936: began in films at British International Pictures studios; assistant director, scriptwriter, dialogue director, mainly on films directed by Brian Desmond Hurst. World War II: served in Guards Armoured Division; twice wounded in action. 1944: first film as director, in collaboration, a documentary, Scriptwriter. From 1948: feature director. Most films on foreign locations. 1966: made *The Poppy is also a Flower* for UN. 1967: first Hollywood film *Wait until Dark*.

Films as director: 1944: Men of Arnhem (co-d Brian Desmond Hurst). 1948: Corridor of Mirrors; One Night with You; Woman Hater. 1950: They Were not Divided (+p/s). 1951: Valley of the Eagles – Valley of Eagles (+p/s). 1952: Tall Headlines. 1953: The Red Beret – Paratrooper. 1955: That Lady; Storm over the Nile (co-d Zoltan Korda). 1956: Safari; Zarak. 1957: Action of the Tiger; No Time to Die – Tank Force (+ co-st/co-s). 1959: Serious Charge. 1960: Un, deux, trois, quatre! – Black Tights; Too Hot to Handle. 1961: Orazi e curiazi; Horatio – Duel of Champions. 1962: Dr No. 1963: From Russia with Love. 1965: The Amorous Adventures of Moll Flanders; Thunderball; La Guerra Segreta – The Dirty Game (co-d Carlo Lizzani, Christian-Jaque). 1966: Triple Cross; The Poppy is also a Flower – Danger Grows Wild. 1967: L'Aventuriero – The Rover; Wait until Dark. 1969: Mayerling (+ s); The Christmas Tree. 1971: De la part des copains; Soleil Rouge – Red Sun.

YOUNG, Victor

Composer. Chicago 1900–56 Palm Springs, Florida
Born in a tenement district of Chicago, began to play violin at 6. To live with grandfather in Warsaw, studied at Imperial Conservatory, graduating 1917. Debut as concert violinist with Warsaw Philharmonic Orchestra. 1918: to Paris and then (1920) to New York. 1921: American debut as concert violinist. 1922: concert master at Grauman's Million Dollar Theatre in Los Angeles. Then in vaudeville as arranger, conductor and violinist. Assistant musical director of the Balaban and Katz chain of theatres; composed and arranged silent film scores. 1929: worked in radio. 1931: musical

director at Brunswick Records. 1935: to Hollywood, joined Paramount music department; formed own orchestra and signed Decca recording contract. Wrote for radio and TV; scores for 2 Broadway musicals. Oscar nominations but only one Oscar, after death, for score of *Around the World in Eighty Days* (1956).

Films as composer include: 1939: The Light that Failed; Golden Boy. 1940: Northwest Mounted Police; The Outlaw (r 1946). 1942: The Great Man's Lady; Reap the Wild Wind; The Palm Beach Story. 1943: For Whom the Bell Tolls. 1944: The Ministry of Fear. 1948: The Emperor Waltz. 1949: The File on Thelma Jordan; Samson and Delilah. 1950: Rio Grande. 1951: Belle Le Grand; The Wild Blue Yonder; The Bullfighter and the Lady. 1952: Blackbeard the Pirate; Scaramouche; The Greatest Show on Earth; Something to Live for; One Minute to Zero; The Quiet Man. 1953: The Sun Shines Bright; Flight Nurse; Shane. 1954: Johnny Guitar; Three Coins in the Fountain. 1955: Strategic Air Command; The Tall Men. 1956: Around the World in Eighty Days. 1957: Run of the Arrow; China Gate (co).

YUTKEVICH, Sergei

Director. St Petersburg, Russia 1904–
Wrote book on Max Linder. Member of Grigori Kozintsev and Leonid Trauberg's ambulant studio theatre, with them co-founded FEX (1920). Theatrical writer and director. Collaborated with Sergei Eisenstein on stage production of 'Macbeth'. Assistant and designer to Abraham Room e.g. on *Predatel* (1926). 1927: directed street and factory scenes in Room's *Tretya Meschchanskaya*. 1928: first solo film as director. 1932: made *Vstrechnyi* in collaboration with Friedrich Ermler: directed scenes dealing with young people, Ermler those with old people. Began training programme: first film as supervisor co-directed by Marc Donskoi, *Pesnya o Schastye* (1934). Collaborated with Lev Arnshtam on documentary *Ankara, Serdtsye Turkii* (1934) and supervised Arnshtam's first feature *Podrugi* (1935). 1937: release of *Shakhtory* after 3 years spent in adjusting it to official requirements. 1938: *Chelovek s ruzhom* contained Maxim Strauch's first performance as Lenin; repeated in later films of Yutkevich. Became head of Soyuzdetfilm. 1941: made 3 shorts in series 'Fighting Film Album'. During World War II relieved of duties in order to work at Mosfilm. 1946: worked in documentaries. 1947: without open accusation, *Tvet nad Rossiei* banned and not released.

Films as director: 1927: Tretya Meschchanskaya – Three Meschchanskaya Street – Bed and Sofa (+ co-dec; co-d Abraham Room). 1928: Kruzheva – Lace (+ co-s). 1929: Chernyi Parus – The Black Sail. 1931: Zlatye Gory – Golden Mountains (+ co-s). 1932: Vstrechnyi – Counterplan (+ co-s; co-d Friedrich Ermler). 1934: Ankara, Serdtsye Turki – Ankara, Heart of Turkey (co-d Lev Arnshtam); Shakhtory – Miners (r 1937). 1938: Chelovek s ruzhom – The Man with a Gun. 1940: Yakov Sverdlov (+ co-s). 1943: Novye Pokhozhdeniya Shveika – New Adventures of Schweik. 1944: Dmitri Donskoi. 1946: Ozvobozhdennaya Frantsya – France Liberated; Zdravstvui Moskva – Greetings, Moscow!; Molodost nashi stranyi – Our Country's Youth. 1947: Tvet nad Rossiei – Light Over Russia (ur). 1948: Tri Vstrechi – Three Encounters (co-d Vsevolod Pudovkin, Alexander

Ptushko). 1951: Przhevalskii. 1954: Velikii Voin Albanii Skanderbeg – The Great Warrior Skanderbeg. 1956: Otello – Othello (+ *s*). 1958: Rasskazi o Leninye – Stories about Lenin. 1962: Banya – The Bath House (*co-d Anatoli Karanovich*). 1964: Lenin v Polshe – Lenin in Poland. 1968: Siuzhet dlya nebolshovo rasskaza – Lika, Le Grand Armour de Tchekhov – Lika, Chekhov's Love.

Z

ZAMPA, Luigi

Director. Rome 1905–
Studied architecture, then writer of short stories and plays; 3 plays performed in Rome. 1933: directed first short film; enrolled in Scuola Nazionale di Cinematografia dell'Accademia di Santa Cecilia. Then studied at Centro Sperimentale di Cinematografia. 1938–41: assistant director and script collaborator. 1941: first feature as director. 1944–45: in army film unit, Author of novel, 'Il Successo'.

Films as director: 1933: Risveglio di una città. 1940: Un Mare di guai (+ *co-st/co-s/co-di*; *co-d Carlo Bragaglia*). 1941: L'Attore Scomparso (+ *co-s*); Fra' Diavolo (+ *co-s*). 1942: Signorinette (+ *co-s/e*); C'è sempre un ma . . . (+ *co-st/s*). 1943: L'Abito Nero da sposa (+ *co-s*). 1945: Un Americano in vacanza – A Yank in Rome (+ *ad*). 1946: Vivere in pace (+ *co-st/co-s*). 1947: L'Onorevole Angelina – Angelina (+ *co-s*). 1948: Anni Difficili – Difficult Years – The Little Man (+ *co-s*). 1949: Campane a martello – Children of Change (+ *co-s*). 1950: È più facile che un cammelo – Twelve Hours to Live; Cuori senza frontiere – The White Line – The Heart knows no Frontiers. 1951: Signori in carrozza! – Rome-Paris-Rome (+ *co-s*). 1952: Processo alla città – A Town on Trial (+ *co-s*). 1953: Anni Facili – Easy Years (+ *co-s*); Siamo donne – We, the Women *ep* Isa Miranda (+ *co-s*). 1954: Questa è la vita *ep* La Patente (+ *co-s*); La Romana – Woman of Rome (+ *co-s*); L'Arte di arrangiarsi – The Art of Getting Along (+ *co-s*). 1955: Ragazze d'oggi (+ *st/s*). 1957: La Ragazza del Palio – The Love Specialist (+ *co-s*). 1958: Ladro lui, ladra lei (+ *st*). 1959: Il Magistrato – The Magistrate (+ *st/co-s*). 1960: Il Vigile – The Cop (+ *co-s*). 1962: Anni Ruggenti – Roaring Years (+ *co-st/co-s*). 1963: Frenesi de l'estate – Shivers in Summer. 1965: Una Questione d'onore – A Question of Honour (+ *co-s*). 1966: I Nostri Mariti *ep* Il Marito di Olga. 1967: Le Dolci Signore – Ladies and Ladies – Anyone Can Play. 1968: Il Medico della mutua – Be Sick . . . It's Free! (+ *co-s*). 1970: Contestazione Generale. 1971: Bello Onesto Emigrata Australia sposerebbe compaesan illibata.

ZANUCK, Darryl F.

Producer and studio head. Wahoo, Nebraska 1902–
When 8, at Military Academy in Los Angeles, played truant to earn a dollar a day as film extra. Nebraska National Guard in World War I, then shirt salesman, rivet catcher and poster tinter. Became writer. When studios announced they would only employ established writers, he persuaded a hair tonic firm to pay for publication of a book which he sent to studios.

Engaged to write Rin-Tin-Tin script for Warners, then given a contract to write all Rin-Tin-Tin movies (1924). Wrote many scripts, often under pen names. 1928: executive producer at Warner. 1929: wrote story for *Noah's Ark*. 1929–30: general executive and then (1931) chief executive in charge of all Warners productions. 1933: resigned to form 20th Century Productions with Joseph M. Schenk; vice-president in charge of production, releasing through United Artists. 1935: 20th Century amalgamated with Fox; post now covered whole of 20th Century Fox. 1941: Lieutenant-Colonel, then Colonel in Signal Corps supervising Army training films. 1942: resigned as vice-president and granted leave of absence as production head to work full-time for Army. 1943: returned as production chief. Later president. Resigned in 1952 to become independent producer releasing through Fox and, for *The Chapman Report* (1962, produced by son, Richard Zanuck), Warners. 1962: played important part as largest individual stockholder in Fox's crisis over *Cleopatra,* taking over production of the film from Walter Wanger and direction of studio from Spyros Skouras. Installed his son Richard (who worked under him as an independent) as head of production. 1970: Richard Zanuck resigned; became executive at Warners. 1971: Darryl Zanuck not re-elected Chairman; re-activated DFZ Productions Inc., releasing through Fox.

Films as producer include: 1935: Les Misérables. 1936: The Prisoner of Shark Island; The Road to Glory. 1937: Heidi. 1938: In Old Chicago; Four Men and a Prayer; Alexander's Ragtime Band; Suez. 1939: Jesse James. 1940: The Return of Frank James; The Grapes of Wrath. 1941: Tobacco Road; Blood and Sand; How Green Was My Valley. 1944: The Purple Heart; Wilson; Winged Victory. 1946: The Razor's Edge; Dragonwyck (*ex-p*). 1947: Gentleman's Agreement. 1949: Pinky; Twelve O'Clock High. 1950: All About Eve; No Way Out, 1951: David and Bathsheba; People Will Talk. 1952: Viva Zapata!; The Snows of Kilimanjaro. 1954: The Egyptian. 1956: The Man in the Gray Flannel Suit. 1957: Island in the Sun; The Sun Also Rises. 1958: Roots of Heaven. 1960: Crack in the Mirror. 1961: The Big Gamble. 1962: The Longest Day.

ZARKHI, Alexander

Director. St Petersburg, Russia 1908–
Leningrad Technicum of Screen Arts; to Sovkino in Leningrad, with Joseph Heifitz. They became script-writers in collaboration, ending with *Transport Ognya* (1930). 1928: their first film as directors in collaboration *Pesn o Metalle*. Moved to Lenfilm. They directed several films in which Nikolai Cherkasov acted. 1945: assigned by Gerasimov to make documentary compilation *Razgrom Japonii*. 1950: last film together *Ogni Baku*. Subsequently worked separately. For films directed in collaboration with Joseph Heifitz, *see* HEIFITZ, Joseph.

Films as solo director: 1952: Pavlinka. 1955: Nesterka. 1957: Vysota – The Heights. 1960: Lyudi na mostu – Men on the Bridge. 1962: Moi Mladshii Brat – My Younger Brother. 1967: Anna Karenina (+ *co-s*).

ZAVATTINI, Cesare

Writer. Luzzara Emilia, Italy 1902–
Journalist in Milan. Script reader. 1935: first film as

Sean Connery and Ursula Andress in Terence Young's Dr. No.
Nikolai Cherkasov in Deputat Baltiki, *directed by Joseph Heifitz and Alexander Zarkhi.*
John Huston, Daryl Zanuck and Orson Welles at the time of The Roots of Heaven.

writer (also story, in collaboration) *Darò un milione.* At beginning of World War II moved to Rome to concentrate on film work. Wrote for magazine *Cinema,* magazine published by Vittorio Mussolini for Fascist Film Organisation. 1942: first work with Vittorio de Sica, on *Teresa Venerdì.* Wrote monologue for theatre on writing of scripts, performed in Milan and Düsseldorf. 1961: supervised all episodes of *Le Italiane e l'amore,* including one unreleased.

Films as writer in collaboration include: 1941: Teresa Venerdì (*uc*). 1942: Don Cesare di Bazan; Quattro Passi fra le nuvole (+ *co-st*); I Bambini ci guardano. 1945: La Freccia nel fianco; La Porta del cielo (+ *co-st*); Il Testimone. 1946: Sciuscia (+ *st*); Un Giorno nella vita (+ *co-st*). 1947: Caccia Tragica. 1948: Ladri di biciclette (+ *st*). 1949: Au-delà des grilles. 1950: Miracolo a Milano (+ *st*); E primavera (+ *co-st*); Domenica d'agosto; Prima Comunione (+ *st*). 1952: Umberto D (+ *st*); Il Cappotto; Roma ore undici (+ *st*); Bellissima (*st*). 1953: Un Marito per Anna Zaccheo; Stazione Termini; Amore in città *eps* Tentato Suicidio (+ *co-st*), Paradiso per tre ore, Un Agenzia Matrimoniale (*p only*), La Storia di Caterina (*co-d Francesco Maselli*); Siamo Donne (*st all eps*). 1954: L'Oro di Napoli. 1955: Il Segno di Venere (+ *co-st*). 1956: Il Tetto (*alone*); Suor Letizia; La Donna del giorno. 1957: Era di venerdì 17 (*co-st*). 1961: La Ciociara; Il Giudizio Universale (*alone*). 1962: Boccaccio 70 *eps* Il Lavoro (*st*); Le Riffa (*alone*); La Isola di Arturo. 1963: Ieri, oggi e domani; I Sequestrati di Altona (*co-ad*); Il Boom (*alone*). 1964: Matrimonio all' Italiana (*uc*); Controsesso *ep* Cocaina di Domenica (*co-st/co-s*). 1965: Caccia alla volpe (+ *co-ad*; *s alone*). 1966: Le Streghe *eps* La Strega Bruciata Viva, Una Sera come le altre. 1970: I Girasoli; Il Giardino dei Finzi-Contini.

ZECCA, Ferdinand

Director. Paris 1864–1947 Paris
Father concierge at Théâtre de l'Ambigu. Began as café entertainer. In the 1890s made phonograph recordings for Charles Pathé. 1898: appeared in *Les Mésaventures d'une tête de veau* for Gaumont. 1899: acted in first Pathé films with phonograph cylinder accompaniment e.g. *Le Muet Mélomane.* From 1901: director with Pathé, also actor. 1905: his film *La Vie et la Passion de Jésus Christ* (1902) expanded by Lucien Nonquet. From 1905: director in charge of production at Pathé. From 1910: worked mainly in supervisory capacity as producer. 1912–14: producer on numerous films in series 'Scènes de la vie cruelle'. 1914: went to USA; American controller of Pathé Exchange. 1920–27: artistic director of Pathé-Baby in France.

Films as director include: 1901: Comment Fabien devient architecte (+ *w*); Les Sept Châteaux du diable (+ *w*); L'Histoire d'un crime (+ *w*); Idylle sous un tunnel (+ *w*); L'Assassinat de McKinley; Une Tempête dans une chambre à coucher (+ *w*); La Conquête de l'air (+ *w*); Quo Vadis? (+ *w*); La Baignade Impossible; Ali Baba et les 40 voleurs. 1902: La Catastrophe de la Martinique; Les Victimes de l'alcoolisme; La Poule Merveilleuse (+ *w*); La Belle au bois dormant (+ *w*); La Vie et la Passion de Jésus Christ – La Passion. 1903: Trente Ans ou la vie d'un joueur. 1904: La Grève; Au pays noir.

ZEFFIRELLI, Franco

Director. Florence 1923–
Accademia di Belle Arti, Florence. 1941–46: architecture at Florence University. Radio actor in Florence and Rome. 1947: acted in *L'Onorevole Angelina.* 1947–53: assistant to Luchino Visconti. Early theatre designs include 'A Streetcar Named Desire'. 1949: first professional theatre design, Visconti's production of 'Troilus and Cressida'. 1951: on stage directed 'Lulu'. Designer and costumist in opera. 1957: first film as director. Directed opera in Italy, Amsterdam, Tel Aviv, Dallas (Texas). 1958–59: directed opera in Rome and London. 1960: directed play 'Romeo and Juliet' in London. 1961: 'Falstaff' in London, 'Othello' in Stratford. 1962: 'Romeo and Juliet' in New York. 1963–64: designed and directed 'Lady of the Camelias' and 'Falstaff' in New York. 1964: 'Hamlet' in London. 1966: documentary on Florence floods, narration by Richard Burton. 1967: returned to films; 4-year contract with Paramount. Also work for Italian TV.

Films as director: 1957: Camping. 1967: The Taming of the Shrew (+ *co-p/co-s*). 1968: Romeo and Juliet (+ *co-s*).

ZEMAN, Karel

Director and writer. Ostroměř, Czechoslovakia 1910–
Business college. 1930: began working in France on Czech propaganda. 1943: began directing. Numerous puppet films, then animation, including publicity films. 1952: first feature as director. Continued to make shorts, including 'Mr Prokouk' series. Several features combine live-action and animation e.g. *Baron Prášil* (1962) and *Bláznova Kronika* (1964).

Features as director and writer: 1952: Poklad Ptaciko Ostrava – The Treasure of Birds' Island. 1954: Cesta do praveku – Journey into Primeval Times. 1958: Vynález zkazy – An Invention for Destruction. 1961: Baron Prášil – Baron Münchhausen. 1964: Bláznova Kronika – Dra Musketyri – The Jester's Tale (*co-s*). 1966: Vkradená Vzducholod – The Stolen Airship. 1970: Na komete.

ZETTERLING, Mai

Director and actress. Västerås, Sweden 1925–
Spent some of childhood in Australia, then moved to Stockholm. Made stage debut and first film as actress at 16. Studied at Royal Dramatic Theatre school. 1945–47: actress at Royal Dramatic Theatre; also in Swedish films. 1947: contract with Rank, and first British film as actress. Many stage appearances in UK in 1950s. 1960–63: directed 4 documentaries for BBC TV, 'The Polite Invasion', Lords of Little Egypt', 'The Prosperity Race', 'Do-it-yourself Democracy'. 1963: directed first short film for cinema, in UK. From 1964: directed features mainly for Sandrews. Married ballet dancer and ice-hockey player Tutte Lemkow, and writer David Hughes with whom she scripted *Nattlek* (1965, from her own novel) and *Flickorna* (1968).

Films as actress include: 1944: Hets. 1946: Iris och löjtnantshjärta. 1947: Frieda. 1948: Musik i mörker; Nu börjar livet; Hildegard; The Romantic Age. 1950: Blackmailed. 1953: The Ringer. 1954: Knock on

Wood. 1955: A Prize of Gold. 1961: Only Two Can Play. 1965: Lianbron.

Films as director: 1963: The War Game. 1964: Älskande Par – Loving Couples. 1965: Nattlek – Night Games (+ *co-s/fn*). 1967: Doktor Glas. 1968: Flickorna – The Girls.

ZINNEMANN, Fred

Director. Vienna 1907–
Law at Vienna University. 1927–28: course at l'Ecole Technique de Photographie et de Cinématographie, Paris. 1928: camera assistant on *La Marche des machines* in Paris. 1929: camera assistant and writer in collaboration on *Menschen am Sonntag* in Berlin; to Hollywood. 1930: extra in *All Quiet on the Western Front.* Became assistant to Berthold Viertel, then to Robert Flaherty on an unrealised project to have been filmed in Russia. 1931–32: assistant director on films including *The Kid from Spain* (1933). 1934: director in collaboration on documentary film for Mexican Department of Fine Arts. 1937–42: directed shorts for MGM e.g. 'Crime Does Not Pay', 'Pete Smith Speciality', 'John Nesbitt's Passing Parade' series. 1942–48: directed features for MGM. From 1949: freelance director working for various companies including Stanley Kramer, Warners, Columbia. 1956: began *The Old Man and the Sea* (1955) but withdrew; film finally directed by John Sturges. Oscars for short subject (1-reel) *That Mothers Might Live* (1938), documentary short subject *Benjy* (1951), and direction of *From Here to Eternity* (1953), *A Man for All Seasons* (1968).

Films as director: 1934: Redes – Pescados – The Wave (*co-d Emilio Gomez Muriel*). 1937: Friend Indeed. 1938: The Story of Doctor Carver; That Mothers Might Live; They Live Again; Weather Wizards; Tracking the Sleeping Death. 1939: While America Sleeps; Help Wanted!; One Against the World; Forgotten Victory; The Ash Can Fleet. 1940: A Way in the Wilderness; The Great Meddler; The Old South; Stuffie. 1941: Forbidden Passage; Your Last Act. 1942: The Lady or the Tiger?; Kid Glove Killer; Eyes in the Night. 1944: The Seventh Cross. 1946: Little Mister Jim; My Brother Talks to Horses. 1948: The Search – Die Gezeichneten; Act of Violence. 1950: The Men. 1951: Teresa; Benjy. 1952: High Noon; The Member of the Wedding. 1953: From Here to Eternity. 1955: Oklahoma! 1957: A Hatful of Rain. 1958: The Old Man and the Sea (*uc; co-d John Sturges, Henry King, uc*). 1959: The Nun's Story. 1960: The Sundowners. 1963: Behold a Pale Horse (+ *p*). 1967: A Man for All Seasons (+ *p*).

ZUCKMAYER, Carl

Writer. Mainz, Germany 1896–
Father farmer. From 1933: in Austria. 1938: to Switzerland. 1939: to USA, became factory manager. 1946–47: in Germany with US Army. From 1951: lived in Switzerland and USA. Plays include 'Der fröhliche Weinberg' (1925), 'Der Schinderhannes' (1927), 'Katherina Knie' (1928), 'Barbara Blomberg' (1949), 'Der Gesang im Feuerofen' (1950), 'Ulla Winblad' (1951), 'Des Teufels General' (1955). Also novelist, including 'Der Hauptmann von Köpenick' which was turned into play and filmed 4 times: co-scripted Richard Oswald's version (1931) which was

remade as *I Was a Criminal* in USA (1941). Other work in films includes adaptation in collaboration *Der blaue Engel* (1930). Autobiography (1938).

Films adapted from his work include: 1926: Qualen der Nacht (+ *co-s*). 1928: Schinderhannes. 1931: Der Hauptmann von Köpenick (+ *co-s*). 1941: I Was a Criminal. 1955: Des Teufels General. 1956: Der Hauptmann von Köpenick; Ein Mädchen aus Flandern. 1958: Der Schinderhannes.

ZUGSMITH, Albert

Director and producer. Atlantic City, New Jersey 1910–
University of Virginia. Reporter, editor on newspapers; wrote short stories. Chairman of radio-TV-newspaper brokers. Editor and publisher of Atlantic City Daily World. Printing executive. Executive of CBS and other TV companies. President, Famous Players Corporation. President, American Pictures Corporation. 1952–59: producer, beginning with *Invasion USA*. 1959: first film as director. Produced his other films as director. Films released by United Artists, Universal (1956–58), MGM and Allied Artists.

Films as producer include: 1955: Female on the Beach. 1956: Red Sundown; Star in the Dust; Written on the Wind. 1957: The Incredible Shrinking Man; The Tattered Dress; The Tarnished Angels; Man in the Shadow: Slaughter on 10th Avenue. 1958: The Female Animal (+ *st*); High School Confidential; Touch of Evil. 1959: The Beat Generation (+ *st*); The Big Operator; Girl's Town.

Films as director and producer: 1960: Private Lives of Adam and Eve (*co-d only*; *co-d Mickey Rooney*); College Confidential; Sex Kittens Go to College (+ *st*). 1961: Dondi (+ *co-s*; *co-p*). 1962: Confessions of an Opium Eater – Evils of Chinatown.

ZUKOR, Adolph

Studio head. Ricse, Hungary 1873–
Mother was daughter of a Hungarian rabbi. Orphaned in childhood. Apprenticed as clerk in Hungary; emigrated to USA at 16. Became furrier's apprentice; had own fur business in 4 years. 1903: with Marcus Loew opened penny arcade in New York, then branches in Newark, Philadelphia, Boston. 1904: opened cinema in New York; with Marcus Loew formed Loew's Consolidated. 1912: left Loew to form Engadine Corporation to show 4-reeler *Queen Elizabeth* starring Sarah Bernhardt. Set up Famous Players in Famous Plays to produce and distribute series of films directed by Edwin S. Porter, showing New York stage actors in their current successes; signed up Mary Pickford for Hollywood productions. 1916: merged Famous Players with Jesse L. Lasky Feature Plays, acting as president with Lasky as vice-president, Samuel Goldwyn as chairman, Cecil B. De Mille as director-general. From 1917: head of Famous Players-Lasky's distributing company, Paramount, later consolidated with production company and cinema chain. Worked mainly in New York. 1919: began extensive programme of theatre acquisition, 1935: replaced by Barney Balaban as president of Paramount; became chairman of the board. 1937: spent a year superintending several productions in Hollywood. Still chairman of Paramount board in his 90s. 1948: Special Academy Award 'for his services to the industry over a period of 40 years'.

ZURLINI, Valerio

Director. Bologna, Italy 1926–
While studying law in Rome, involved in university theatre. Directed shorts before making his first feature in 1954. Collaborated on script of Alberto Lattuada's *Guendalina* (1957).

Films as director: 1949: Sorrida prego; Racconto del quartiere; Favola del cappello. 1950: Pugilatori; Miniature. 1951: I Blues della domenica. 1952: Serenata da un soldo; Soldati in città; La Stazione; Il Mercato delle facce. 1953: Ventotte tonnellate. 1954: Ragazze di San Frediano. 1959: Estate Violenta (+ *co-s*). 1960: La Ragazza con la valigia – Girl with a Suitcase (+ *co-s*). 1962: Cronaca familiare – Family Diary (+ *co-s*). 1965: Le Soldatesse. 1968: Seduta alla sua destra – Out of Darkness – Black Jesus.

Ingrid Thulin in Mai Zetterling's Nattlek.
The Tarnished Angels. *directed by Douglas Sirk, produced by Albert Zugsmith.*
Valerio Zurlini's Cronaca Familiare.

A (1964) d/s Lenica anim* 9min
AAMU KAUPINGISSA (1955) d J Donner sh
AAN (1952) d/p Mehboob *129min (= Savage Princess)
AARDOLIE (1953) d/s Haanstra p Elton 9min (= The Changing Earth)
ABANDONED (1949) d J Newman p Bresler c Daniels co-a Boyle w Burr, J Chandler 78min
ABANDONADAS, LAS (1944) d/co-s/co-di Fernandez c Figueroa w Del Rio, Armendariz 95min
ABBASSO IL ZIO (c. 1965) d Bellocchio
ABBE CONSTANTIN, L' (1925) d/st Duvivier
ABBOTT AND COSTELLO MEET THE KILLER: BORIS KARLOFF (1949) d Charles T Barton w B Abbott, Costello, Karloff 94min U
ABC OF LOVE, THE (1920) d/s Perret Pat
ABDUCTORS, THE (1957 d A McLaglen c La Shelle w V McLaglen 80min Fox
ABDULLAH'S HAREM (1956) d/p/w Ratoff c Garmes w Kendall *88min Fox
ABE LINCOLN IN ILLINOIS (1940) d Cromwell c Howe w R Gordon 110min RKO
ABEND ... NACHT ... MORGEN (1920) d Murnau w Veidt 1700m Dec
Abenteuer des Doktor Dolittle, Das = DOKTOR DOLITTLE UND SEINE TIERE (1928)
Abenteuer des Prinzen Ahmed = GESCHICHTE DES PRINZEN AHMED, DIE (1926)
ABENTEUER EINER SCHONEN FRAU, DAS (1932) d Koster (as Kösterlitz) 89min
ABERGLAUBE (1940) d Ruttmann 504m
ABHIJAN (1962) d/s/m S Ray 150min (= Expedition)
ABIDJAN, PORT DE PECHE (1962) d/s Rouch 16mm
A BIENTOT J'ESPERE (1969) d Marker, Le Groupe Med-vedkine 16mm 32min
ABIE'S IRISH ROSE (1929) d/p V Fleming s Furthman c Rosson w Hersholt 3689m Par
ABIE'S IRISH ROSE (1946) d/p A Edward Sutherland c Mellor w Dru 96min pc B Crosby r UA
Abismos de pasion = CUMBRES BORRASCOSAS (1953)
ABITO NERO DA SPOSA, L' (1943) d/co-s Zampa co-s Freda
Able Seaman Brown = SINGLEHANDED (1951)
ABOMINABLE HOMME DES DOUANES, L' (1963) d M Allegret m Delerue w Brasseur, Blanche, Dalio 85min
A BOUT DE SOUFFLE (1959) d/s Godard st Truffaut c Coutard m Martial Solal technical adviser Chabrol w Seberg, Belmondo, Melville, (Godard) 89min (= Breathless)
ABOUT FACE (1952) d Del Ruth c Glennon *94min WB
ABOUT MRS LESLIE (1954) d Daniel Mann p Wallis co-s Kanter co-a Pereira c Laszlo w Ryan, Booth 104min Par
About Something Else (US) = ONECEM JINEM (1963)
About Twenty Years Old = NIJU–SAI ZENGO (1950)
Above All Law (US) = INDISCHE GRABMAL, DAS (1921)
ABOVE AND BEYOND (1952) d/p/co-s M Frank, Panama c June co-a Gibbons m Friedhofer w R Taylor, Parker 122min MGM
ABOVE SUSPICION (1943) d Thorpe p Saville a Gibbons m Kaper w B Crawford, MacMurray, Viedt, Rathbone, Lawford 90min MGM
ABOVE THE HORIZON (1966) d/p Kroitor, Hugh O'Connor *21min NFBC
ABOVE US THE WAVES (1955) d Thomas w J Mills 99min JAR
ABRAHAM LINCOLN (1930) d Griffith c Struss w W Huston 90min r UA
ABRAKADABRA (1957) d Vukotic anim
ABREGEONS LES FORMALITES! (1916) d/s Feyder 148m Gau
ABROAD WITH TWO YANKS (1944) d Dwan c Lawton w Bendix 80min r UA
ABSCHIED (1930) d Siodmak p Pommer co-s Pressburger 71min UFA (= So Sind die Menschen)
ABSCHIED VON DEN WOLKEN (1959) d G Reinhardt 101min (= Rebel Flight to Cuba)
ABSCHIED VON GESTERN (1966) d/p/s Kluge 90min (= Yesterday Girl)
ABSENT MINDED PROFESSOR, THE (1961) d Stevenson w MacMurray 97min
ABSINTHE (1913) d Brenon 1207m
ABSOLUTAMENTE CERTO! (1957) d/s/w Duarte
ABSTRACT FILM EXERCISE NO. 1 (1943); NO.2 (1943, uf); NO.3 (1943, uf); NOS 4 & 5 (1944) d/s Whitney, James Whitney Nos 1–3 8min; Nos 4–5 12min *16mm
ABUNA MESSIAS (1939) d Goffredo Alessandrini co-s Cottafavi
ACADIE, L'ACADIE, L' (1971) co-d/c Brault co-d Perrault 16mm 117min
ABUS DE CONFIANCE (1937) d/ad Decoin m Van Parys w Darrieux, Vanel 82min
ABU SERIES (1943) d Mackendrick 4 eps
Abwege = BEGIERDE (1928)
ABYSSES, LES (1962) d Papatakis 96min
A cancoa do berco Portugese version of TOUTE SA VIE (1930)
ACAPULCO (1951) d/co-st/co-s Fernandez
A CAUSE, A CAUSE D'UNE FEMME (1962) d/p/co-s/co-di Deville 110min

A CAVALLO DELLA TIGRE (1961) d/co-s Comencini w Manfredi 120min (= Jail Break On the Tiger's Back)
ACCATTONE (1961) d/s Pasolini m Bach 120min
ACCENT ON YOUTH (1935) d W Ruggles fpl Raphaelson c Shamroy w H Marshall, S Sidney 77min Par
ACCIAIO (1932) d/co-s Ruttmann co-s Pirandello (= Steel)
ACCIDENT, L' (1962) d/co-s Grenville c Badal 91min
ACCIDENT (1967) d/co-p Losey s Pinter w Bogarde, S Baker, Seyrig *105min
Accountant, The = REVISOR (1933)
ACCUSED, The (1936) d Thornton Freeland w Del Rio, Fairbanks Jr 84min r UA
ACCUSED, THE (1949) d Dieterle p Wallis c Krasner w L Young, R Cummings, Corey 101min Par
ACCUSEE, LEVEZ-VOUS (1930) d M Tourneur w Vanel
ACE IN THE HOLE (1951) d/p/co-s B Wilder c C Lang co-a Pereira m Friedhofer w K Douglas 111min Par (= The Big Carnival)
ACE OF THE SADDLE, THE (1919) d J Ford w Carey 6rs
A CHACUN SON PARADIS (1956) co-d/co-e/c Enrico co-d/co-s Emmer co-s Kast 90min (= Il Paradiso Terrestre/Ritual of Love)
ACHT ENTFESSELTEN, DIE (1939) d Kautner
ACHT MAL ACHT (1957) d/p/s/dec Richter w Duchamp, Arp, Cocteau, Tanguy, Hulsenbeck, Calder, Ernst *98min (= 8×8)
ACHTUNG, BANDITI! (1951) d/co-s Lizzani c Di Venanzo w Lollobrigida
A CIASCUNO IL SUO (1966) d/co-s Petri w Ferzetti *99min r UA (= To Each His Own)
A COEUR JOIE (1967) d/co-ad/co-di Bourguignon c Séchan w Bardot s *100min (= Two Weeks in September)
ACCIDENT VICTIM REVIVES, AN (1896) p Paul
Accordeur, L' = GONZAGUE (1933)
According to the Law = ENLIGT LAG (1957)
ACOMA, THE SKY CITY (1928, ur) d/s Flaherty c Shamroy
ACOSTATES FORSTE OFFER (1915) d Madsen
ACQUITTAL, THE (1923) d C Brown s Furthman 1988m U
ACROSS THE ATLANTIC (1915) d Brenon
ACROSS THE BRIDGE (1957) d Annakin st Greene w Steiger 103min JAR
ACROSS THE DEADLINE (1922) d Conway 1489m U
ACROSS THE PACIFIC (1926) d Del Ruth ad Zanuck c Haskin w M Loy 2103m WB
ACROSS THE PACIFIC (1942) d J Huston co-p Wald c Edeson co-e D Siegel w Bogart, Astor, Greenstreet 97min WB
ACROSS THE PLAINS (1911) (In 2 parts) d/s Ince (= War on the Plains)
ACROSS THE WIDE MISSOURI (1951) d Wellman c Mellor co-a Gibbons m Raksin w Gable, Menjou, Montalban *78min MGM
Acte d'amour, Un = ACT OF LOVE (1953)
ACTEON (1964) d/st/c Grau 75min
ACTION (1921) d J Ford 1376m U
ACTION FOR SLANDER (1937) d Tim Whelan p Saville w C Brook 8rs r UA
ACTION IN THE NORTH ATLANTIC (1943) d Bacon p Wald s Lawson c McCord w Bogart, Massey, R Gordon 127min WB
Action Man, The = SOLEIL DES VOYOUS, LE (1967)
ACTION OF THE TIGER (1957) d T Young w V Johnson, Carol, Connery CS* 93min MGM
ACTION STATIONS (1942) d/s/e Ivens 53min
ACTIVIST, THE (1969) d/co-p/co-s Napoleon *87min
ACT OF LOVE (1953) d/p/co-s Litvak co-s Shaw, w K Douglas, Reggiani, Bardot 108min r UA (= Un Acte d'amour)
ACT OF MURDER, AN (1948) d M Gordon m Amfitheatrof w March, E O'Brien 91min U
ACT OF VIOLENCE (1948) d Zinnemann c Surtees co-s Gibbons m Kaper w Heflin, Ryan, J Leigh, Astor 92min MGM
ACT ONE (1964) d/p/s Schary fab M Hart w Wallach 110min WB
ACTORS AND SIN (1952) co-d/p/s/fsts (Actor's Blood and Concerning a Woman of Sin) B Hecht as-d/c Garmes w Robinson 85min r UA
Actor's Revenge, An = YUKINOJO HENGE (1963)
ACTRESS, THE (1928) d Franklin co-s Lewin fpl (Trelawny of the Wells) Pinero c Daniels a Gibbons w Shearer 2134m MGM
Actress, The = AKTRISA (1943)
Actress = JOYU (1947)
ACTRESS, THE (1953) d Cukor s/fpl (Years Ago) R Gordon c Rosson co-a Gibbons m Kaper w Tracy, T Wright, Perkins, J Simmons 89min MGM
Actress and the Poet, The = JOYU TO SHINJI (1935)
ACTUALITES QUEBECOISES (1968) d Lamothe, Martial Filion, Alain Gélinas, Pascal Gélinas, Pierre Havel, François-Boris Kranjec, Pierre Larocque (series of 6) 70min
ADA (1961) d Daniel Mann c Ruttenberg w Martin, S Hayward, Meeker CS* 109min MGM
ADALEN '31 (1969) d/s/e Widerberg w Björk TS* 115min
ADAM AND EVALYN (1949) d/p Harold French w S Granger, J Simmons 93min

ADAM AND EVIL (1927) d Leonard a Gibbons, R Day w Hopper 2071m MGM
ADAM BEDE (1918) d Elvey fn George Eliot
ADAM HAD FOUR SONS (1941) d Ratoff c Marley w W Baxter, S Hayward, Ingrid Bergman 81min Col
ADAM'S RIB (1923) d De Mille 2904m FPL
ADAM'S RIB (1949) d Cukor s R Gordon, Kanin c Folsey co-a Gibbons m Rozsa w K Hepburn, Tracy, Holliday, Ewell, D Wayne 101min MGM
ADAM II (1968) d Lenica anim* 79min
ADAUCHI (1965 d Imai S (= Revenge)
ADDIO GIOVINEZZA (1918) d/ad/s Genina
ADDIO GIOVINEZZA (1927) d/co-ad/co-s Genina rm 1918
ADDIO GIOVINEZZA! (1940) d/co-s Poggioli
ADDIO MIMI (1950) d Gallone 92min
ADDRESS UNKNOWN (1944) d/p Menzies c Maté w Lukas 72min Col
ADEMAI BANDIT D'HONNEUR (1943) d Grangier 87min
ADEMAR LAMPIOT (1933) d Christian-Jaque, Paul Mesnier
ADHEMAR OU LE JOUET DE LA FATALITE (1951) co-d/s/lyr Guitry co-s/w Fernandel 89min
ADIEU LEONARD (1943) d/st/co-s P Prévert co-s/di/co-lyr J Prévert m Kosma (ps Georges Mouqué) w Brasseur, Carette, (Signoret) 90min Pat
ADIEU LES COPAINS (1930) d/s Joannon
ADIEU PHILIPPINE (1962) d/co-s/co-di/co-e Rozier w Caprioli 136min
ADMIRABLE CRICHTON (1957) d/s L Gilbert 93min Col
ADMIRAL NAKHIMOV (1946) d Pudovkin, Dmitri Vasiliev w Pudovkin 93min
ADMIRAL USHAKOV (1953) d Romm m Khatchaturian w Bondarchuk *108min
ADOLESCENZA (1959) d Maselli
ADORABLE (1933) d Dieterle co-st B Wilder c J Seitz w J Gaynor 88min Fox
ADORABLES CREATURES (1952) d/s Christian-Jaque di Charles Spaak c Matras m Van Parys w Carol, Darrieux, Gélin, Feuillère 110min
ADORABLE MENTEUSE (1961) d/p/co-s/co-di Deville w Vlady 120min
ADORATION (1928) d/p F Lloyd c J Seitz 2014m FN
A DOUBLE TOUR (1959) d Chabrol c Decaë dec Saulnier, Evein m Misraki w Belmondo *100min (= Web of Passion/Leda)
ADRES LENINA (1929) d Petrov 1713m (= Lenin's Address)
ADRIANA DI BERTEAUX (1910) d/s Guazzoni
ADRIENNE LECOUVREUR (1913) d Louis Mercanton fpl/w S Bernhardt
ADRIENNE LECOUVREUR (1938) d L'Herbier w Fresnay
ADUA E LE COMPAGNE (1960) d/co-s Petrangeli m Piccioni w Signoret, Riva, Mastroianni 150min (= Hungry for Love/Love à la Carte)
Adulterers, The = YORU NO TSUZUMI (1958)
ADULTERIO ALL' ITALIANA (1966) d/st/co-s Festa Campanile w Catherine Spaak, Manfredi, Caprioli, Tamiroff TS* 93min (= Adultery Italian Style)
Adultery Italian Style = ADULTERIO ALL' ITALIANA (1966)
ADVANCE TO THE REAR (1964) d G Marshall c Krasner w G Ford, M Douglas, Blondell PV* 86min MGM (= Company of Cowards?)
ADVENTURE (1925) d Fleming fst Jack London w Beery 2046m FPL
ADVENTURE (1946) d V Fleming c Ruttenberg co-a Gibbons m Stothart w Gable, Garson, Mitchell, Blondell 125min MGM
Adventure for Two = DEMI-PARADISE, THE (1943)
ADVENTURE IN HEARTS, AN (1919) d Cruze 5rs FPL
Adventure in the Bay of Gold, An = DOBRODRUZSTUI NO ZLATE ZATOCE (1955)
ADVENTURE IN THE HOPFIELDS (1954) d Guillermin 60min
Adventure is a Hard Life = TEZKY ZIVOT DOBROD-RUHA (1941)
ADVENTURER, THE (1917) d/s Chaplin co-c Totheroh w Chaplin, Purviance 2rs Mut
ADVENTURERS, THE (1969) d/p/co-s L Gilbert fn Harold Robbins c C Renoir w Aznavour, Borgnine, De Havilland PV* 171min Par
ADVENTURES IN SILVERADO (1948) d Karlson fn RL Stevenson 75min Col
ADVENTURES IN THE FAR NORTH (1923) d M Fleischer, Captain FE Keinschmidt 1494m
ADVENTURES OF AN ASTERISK (1956) d/co-s J Hubley co-s/e F Hubley anim
ADVENTURES OF A RAREBIT EATER (1917) d McCay anim series
ADVENTURES OF BARON MUNCHAUSEN, THE (1947, uf) d Dunning, Low
ADVENTURES OF BILLY, THE (1911) w Crisp Bio
ADVENTURES OF BULLWHIP GRIFFIN, THE (1967) d Neilson w Malden, Pleshette pc Disney *110min
Adventures of Doctor Dolittle, The = DOKTOR DOLITTLE UND SEINE TIERE (1928)
ADVENTURES OF DOLLIE, THE (1908) d Griffith 220m Bio

ADVENTURES OF DON JUAN, THE (1949) *d* V Sherman *p* Wald *co-s* Kurnitz *m* M Steiner *w* Flynn, Lindfors 110min WB

ADVENTURES OF GERARD, THE (1970) *d/co-s* Skolimowski *fn Arthur Conan Doyle w* Cardinale, Hawkins, Wallach PV* 91min (= *Le Avventure di Gerard*)

Adventures of Goopy and Bagha, The = GOOPY GYNE, BAGHA BYNE (1968)

ADVENTURES OF HAJJI BABA, THE (1954) *d* Weis *p* Wanger *c* Lipstein *w* Derek CS* 94min Fox

ADVENTURES OF HUCKLEBERRY FINN, THE (1939) *d* Thorpe *p* J Mankiewicz *s* H Butler *fn Mark Twain c* J Seitz *co-m* Waxman *w* Rooney 90min MGM

ADVENTURES OF HUCKLEBERRY FINN, THE (1960) *d* Curtiz *fn Mark Twain c* McCord *m* Moross *lyr* A Lerner *w* Randall, Keaton, Carradine CS* 107min MGM

ADVENTURES OF ICHABOD & MR. TOAD, THE (1949) *p* Disney *fst* (*The Legend of Sleepy Hollow*) *Washington Irving* and (*Wind in the Willows*) *Kenneth Graeme wv* B Crosby, Rathbone *68min *r* RKO

ADVENTURES OF JIMMY, THE (1951) *d/s/w/n* Broughton 12min

ADVENTURES OF MARCO POLO, THE (1938) *d* A Mayo *2nd /d* Ford (*uc*) *p* Goldwyn *c* Maté *m* Friedhofer *w* G Cooper, Rathbone, Turner 100min *r* UA

ADVENTURES OF MARK TWAIN, THE (1944) *d* Rapper *p* Lasky *c* Polito *m* M Steiner *w* March, Crisp, A Smith 130min WB

Adventure of Okyabrina, The = POKHOZHDENIYA OKTYABRINY (1924)

Adventures of Prince Achmed, The = GESCHICHTE DES PRINZEN AHMED, DIE (1926)

Adventures of Quentin Durward, The = QUENTIN DURWARD (1955)

ADVENTURES OF ROBIN HOOD, THE (1938) *d* Keighley, Curtiz *p* Wallis *as-p* Blanke *co-st/co-s* S Miller *co-c* Gaudio, Polito *m* Korngold *w* Flynn, de Havilland, Rains, Rathbone 105min WB

Adventures of Robinson Crusoe, The = ROBINSON CRUSOE (1952)

ADVENTURES OF RUTH, THE (1919–20) *co-d* G Marshall serial in 15eps Pat

ADVENTURES OF SHERLOCK HOLMES, THE (1905) *d* Blackton

ADVENTURES OF THE NEW FRONTIER (1959–63) *d* Pennebaker *w JF Kennedy* 16mm TV series

ADVENTURES OF THUD AND BLUNDER, THE (1962–65) *d* Dunning anim

ADVENTURES OF TOM SAWYER, THE (1938) *d* Taurog *p* Selznick *fn Mark Twain c* Howe *a* Wheeler *w* Brennan *93min *r* UA

Adventuress, The = I SEE A DARK STRANGER (1946)

Adversary, The = PRATIDWANDI (1971)

ADVISE AND CONSENT (1962) *d/p* Preminger *s* Mayes *fn Allen Drury c* Leavitt *a* Wheeler *cr* Bass *w* H Fonda, Laughton, Murray, Pidgeon, Lawford, Tierney, Tone, Ayres, Meredith PV 140min *r* Col

ADVOKATKA VERA (1937) *d* Fric (= *Vera the Lawyer*)

AELITA (1924) *d* Protazanov *w* Solntseva 1841m

AERELOSE, DEN (1916) *d/s* Madsen

AERESOPREJSNING, EN (1915) *d* Madsen

Aerial Antics = HOG WILD (1930)

AERO ENGINE (1933) *d/s/e* Elton *p* Grierson 55min

AEROGRAD (1935) *d/s* Dovzhenko *co-c* Tissé 80min (= *Frontier*)

Aeropuerto = BARAJAS, AEROPUERTO INTERNACIONAL (1950)

AESOP'S FABLES (1930) *co-anim* Tashlin series anim

AF ELSKOVS NAADE (1913) *d/co-s* Blom

AFFAIRE DES POISSONS, L' (1955) *d/co-ad* Decoin *dec* d'Eaubonne *w* Darrieux, Romance *110min

AFFAIRE DREYFUS, L' (1899) *d* Méliès 240m (12 parts)

AFFAIRE DU COLLIER DE LA REINE, L' (1946) *d* L'Herbier *s* Charles Spaak *m* Ibert *w* Romance, Mocky 118min

AFFAIRE D'UNE NUIT, L' (1960) *d* Verneuil *co-s* Aurenche *co-s/di* Jeanson 94min (= *It Happened All Night*)

AFFAIRE EST DANS LE SAC, L' (1932) *d* P Prévert *s/di* J Prévert *st/co-dec* (*uc*) Trauner *m* Jaubert *w* Carette, J Prévert, Le Chanois 45min Pat

AFFAIRE MANET, L' (1951) *d* Aurel *m* Van Parys 22min

AFFAIRE MAURIZIUS, L' (1954) *d/s/di* Duvivier *c* Lefebvre *co-m* Van Parys *w* Gélin, Rossi-Drago, Vanel 110min (= *On Trial*)

AFFAIRES PUBLIQUES, LES (1934) *d/co-c* Bresson *m* Wiener *w* Dalio

AFFAIR IN HAVANA (1957) *d* Benedek *w* Burr, Cassavetes 80min *r* AA

Affair in Monte Carlo (US) = 24 HOURS OF A WOMAN'S LIFE (1951)

AFFAIR IN TRINIDAD (1952) *d/p* V Sherman *c* J Walker *w* Hayworth, G Ford 98min Col

Affair of Madame Pompadour, The (UK) = AVVENTURE DI MANDRIN, LE (1952)

AFFAIR OF THE SKIN, AN (1964) *d* Maddow *w* Lindfors 102min

AFFAIRS OF ANATOL, THE (1921) *d* De Mille *c* Struss *w* Swanson 2684m FPL

AFFAIRS OF COLLINI, THE (1934) *d* La Cava *m* A Newman *w* Constance Bennett, March 80min *r* UA

AFFAIRS OF DOBIE GILLIS, THE (1953) *d* Weis *c* Mellor *co-a* Gibbons *w* D Reynolds, Fosse 74min MGM

AFFAIRS OF MARTHA, THE (1942) *d* Dassin *c* Lawton *a* Gibbons 65min MGM

Affaires of Messalina, The = MESSALINA (1951)

Affairs of Sally (UK) = FULLER BRUSH GIRL, THE (1949)

AFFAIR OF THE SKIN, AN (1964) *d/co-p/st/s* Maddow *co-p* Strick *w* Lindfors 102min

AFFAIR TO REMEMBER, AN (1957) *d/st/co-s* McCarey *p* Wald *co-s* Daves *rm* LOVE AFFAIR (1939) *c* Krasner *co-a* Wheeler *m* Friedhofer *w* C Grant, Kerr CS* 115min Fox

AFFAIR WITH A STRANGER (1953) *d* Rowland *c* Wild *w* J Simmons, Mature 89min RKO

AFFECTIONATELY YOURS (1941) *d* Bacon *p* Wallis *w* Oberon, A Smith, Hayworth 88min WB

AFFICHE, L' (1925) *d* J Epstein

AFFREUX, LES (1959) *d/co-s* M Allégret *m* Van Parys *w* Fresnay 90min

AFGRUNDEN (1910) *d Urban Gad* W Nielsen

A FIL DI SPADA (1952) *d* Bragaglia (= *At Sword's Point*)

A FLEUR DE PEAU (1961) *d/st/co-s* Bernard-Aubert 89min

AFRICA ADDIO (1965) *co-d/co-s* Jacopetti *co-d Franco Prosperi* S* 120min (= *Africa Blood and Guts*)

Africa Blood and Guts (US) = AFRICA ADDIO (1965)

African Fury (US) = CRY, THE BELOVED COUNTRY (1952)

AFRICAN QUEEN, THE (1951) *d/co-s* J Huston *p* Spiegel (*ps* SP Eagle) *co-s* Agee *fn C S Forester c* Cardiff *w* Bogart, K Hepburn *103min *pc* J Huston, Spiegel *co-pc* Woolf Bros *r* UA

AFRICA SOTTO I MARI (1953) *d Giovanni Roccardi w* Loren *87min

AFRICA—TEXAS STYLE (1967) *d/p* Marton *w* J Mills *106min Par

AFRIQUE ET LA RECHERCHE SCIENTIFIQUE, L' (1964) *d* Rouch 16mm

AFTER BUSINESS HOURS (1925) *d* St Clair 1707m Col

AFTER MANY YEARS (1908) *d* Griffith *c* Bitzer *fpm* (*Enoch Arden*) *Tennyson* 350m Bio

After Midnight (UK) = CAPTAIN CAREY, USA (1950)

AFTERNOON (1965) *d* Warhol 16mm 105min

AFTER OFFICE HOURS (1935) *d/co-p* Leonard *s* H Mankiewicz *w* Constance Bennett, Gable 75min MGM

AFTER THE BALL (1957) *d* Compton Bennett *w* Laurence Harvey 89min BL

After the Fox (1965) = CACCIA ALLA VOLPE (1965)

AFTER THE STORM (1928) *d* G Seitz *p* Cohn *c* J Walker 1664m Col

AFTER THE THIN MAN (1936) *d* WS Van Dyke *s* Goodrich, Hackett *fst* Hammett *co-m* Stothart *w* M Loy, W Powell, J Stewart 110m MGM

AFTER THE VERDICT (1929) *d* Galeen *c* Sparkuhl 2856m

AFTER TOMORROW (1932) *d* Borzage *c* Howe *w* J Gaynor 79min Fox

After Years of Study = GAKUSO O IDETE (1925)

Against All = PROTI VSEM (1937)

AGAINST THE WIND (1948) *d* Crichton *p* Balcon *w* Signoret 96min

AGA KHAN (1963) *d* R Leacock 16mm

AGE D'OR, L' (1930) *d/s* Buñuel *co-m* Van Parys *w* Modot, *Max Ernst*, P Prévert 60min

AGE FOR LOVE, THE (1931) *d* F Lloyd *co-c* J Seitz *m* A Newman *w* Horton 79min *r* UA

AGE INGRAT, L' (1964) *d* Grangier *m* Delerue *pc/w* Gabin, Fernandel S* 95min

AGENCE MATRIMONIALE (1952) *d/ad/di* Le Chanois *w* Michel, Carette 109min

AGENT FOR H.A.R.M. (1965) *d* G Oswald *w* Corey *84min U

AGE OF CONSENT, THE (1932) *d* La Cava 65min RKO

AGE OF CONSENT, THE (1968) *d/co-p* M Powell *co-p/w* Mason PV* 103min Col

AGE OF DESIRE, THE (1923) *d/p* Borzage 1571m FN

AGE OF THE BEAVER, THE (1951) *d* Low *e/cy* Kroitor 17min NFBC

AGGIE APPLEBY MAKER OF MEN (1933) *d* Sandrich *w* Constance Bennett, Roland, Pitts 73min RKO

AGGRESSOR, THE (1911) *co-d* Ince *w* Pickford

AGGUATO A TANGERI (1957) *d/co-s* Freda S 112min (= *Trapped in Tangiers*)

AGI MURAD, IL DIAVOLO BIANCO (1958) *d* Freda *fn* (*Adji Mourad, The White Devil*) *Leo Tolstoi c* Bava *w* Reeves FS* 98min (= *The White Warrior*)

AGITPOEZHD VTSIKA (1921) *d* Vertov *co-c* Tissé 750m (= *Train of the Central Executive*)

AGNESE VISCONTI (1910) *d* Pastrone

Agnus Dei (UK) = EGI BARANY (1971)

AGONIE DE JERUSALEM, L' (1926) *d/s* Duvivier

AGONY AND THE ECSTASY, THE (1965) *d/p* C Reed *s* P Dunne *c* Shamroy *w* Heston, Harrison TAO* 140min Fox

AGOSTINO (1962) *d/w* Bolognini *co-s/fn* Moravia *c* Tonti *w* Thulin 90min *pc* De Laurentiis

AGRICULTURE, L' (1955) *d* Dewever sh

AGRIPPINA (1910) *d/s/dec* Guazzoni

AGYU ES HARANG (1915) *d* Balasz

A-HAUNTING WE WILL GO (1942) *d Alfred Werker co-a* R Day *w* Laurel, Hardy, Cook 67min Fox

AH FURUSATO (1938) *d* Mizoguchi (= *Ah Kokyo/Ah, My Hometown*)

Ah Kokyo = AH FURUSATO (1938)

Ah, My Hometown = AH FURUSATO (1938)

AH, WILDERNESS! (1935) *d* C Brown *s* Goodrich, Hackett *fpl Eugene O'Neill m* Stothart *w* Beery, L Barrymore, Rooney 101min MGM

AI (1962) *d* Kuri anim 4min (= *Love*)

AIBU (1933) *d* Gosho (= *Caress*)

AIEN-KYO (1937) *d* Mizoguchi (= *Gorge Between Love and Hate*)

AI FUTATABI (1971) *d* Ichikawa PV* 95min (= *To Love Again*)

AIGLE A DEUX TETES, L' (1948) *d/s/fpl* Cocteau *c* Matras *dec/cos* Bérard, Wakhevitch *m* Auric *w* Feuillère, Marais 93min (= *Eagle with Two Heads*)

AI-JIN (1953) *d* Ichikawa Toho (= *The Lovers*)

AIJO NO KEIFU (1961) *d* Gosho

AI MARGINI DELLA METROPOLI (1953) *d/co-s* Lizzani *c* Di Venanzo *w* Girotti, Masina

AIMEZ-VOUS BRAHMS? (1961) *d/p* Litvak *fn Françoise Sagan c* Thirard *a* Trauner *m* Auric *w* Ingrid Bergman, Montand, Perkins 120min *r* UA (= *Goodbye Again*)

AINE DES FERCHAUX, L' (1963) *d/st/s/di* Melville *fn Georges Simenon c* Decaë *m* Delerue *w* Vanel, Belmondo FS* 104min (= *Un Jeune Homme/Magnet of Doom*)

AI NI YOMIGAERU HI (1922) *d* Mizoguchi Nik (= *The Day When Love Returns*)

AIN'T MISBEHAVING (1955) *d Edward Buzzell w* Laurie *82min U

AIR CADET (1951) *d* Pevney *p* A Rosenberg *w* Hudson 94min U

AIR CIRCUS, THE (1928) *d* Hawks, *Lewis B Seiler s* S Miller, McLeod 118min Fox

AIR DE PARIS, L' (1954) *d/co-s* Carné *w* Gabin, Arletty

AIR DERBY, THE (1929) *d/co-p* H Brown 2rs

AIR FORCE (1943) *d* Hawks *p* Wallis *s* D Nichols *di* Faulkner *c* Howe *m* Waxman *w* Garfield, Carey, A Kennedy 124min WB

AIR LEGION, THE (1929) *d* Glennon *si* 1938m *r* RKO

AIR MAIL (1932) *d* J Ford *c* Freund 83min U

AIRPORT (1970) *d/s* Seaton *p* R Hunter *fn Arthur Hailey c* Laszlo *co-a* Golitzen *m* A Newman *w* Lancaster, Martin, Seberg, G Kennedy, Hayes, Heflin, Nolan TAO* 136min

AIR PUR (1939 *uf*) *d/co-s/co-di* Clair *m* Jaubert

AIR RAID WARDENS (1943) *d* Edward Sedgwick *co-st/co-s* Rackin *a* Gibbons *w* Laurel, Hardy 67min

AISAI MONOGATARI (1951) *d/s* Shindo (= *The Story of a Beloved Wife*)

AISUREBAKOSO (1954) (= *Because I Love*)
ep d Imai
ep HANAURI MUSUME *d* Yoshimura

AI TO KIBO NO MACHI (1959) *d/s* Oshima 63min Sho (= *A Town of Love and Hope*)

AI TO SHI NO TANIMA (1954) *d* Gosho (= *The Valley Between Love and Death*)

AI WA CHIKARA DA (1930) *d* Naruse (= *Strength of Love*)

AIYOKO NO YORU (1930) *d* Gosho (= *Desire of Night*)

AIZO-TOGO (1934) *d* Mizoguchi *w* Yamada Nik (= *The Gorge Between Love and Hate*)

AKAHIGE (1965) *d/co-s* Kurosawa *w* Mifune S 185min *pc* Kurosawa *r* Toho (= *Red Beard*)

AKAI SATSUI (1964) *d* Imamura S 150min Nik (= *Unholy Desire*)

AKAI YUHI NI TERASARETE (1925) *d* Mizoguchi Nik (= *In the Red Rays of the Sleeping Sun*)

AKASEN CHITAI (1956) *d* Mizoguchi *c* Miyagawa *w* Kyo Dai (= *Street of Shame*)

AKATSUKI NO SHI (1925) *d* Mizoguchi Nik (= *Death at Dawn*)

AKATSUKI NO TSUISEKI (1950) *d* Ichikawa *s* Shindo Toho (= *Pursuit at Dawn*)

AKATSUKI NO YUSHI (1926) *d* Kinugasa (= *A Brave Soldier at Dawn*)

AKIBIYORI (1960) *d/co-s* Ozu *rm* BANSHUN (1949) *131min Sho (= *Late Autumn*)

AKIKET A PACSIRTA ELKISER (1959) *d* Ranódy 100min (= *For Whom the Lark Sings*)

AKI TACHINU (1960) *d* Naruse S 79min Toho (= *The Approach of Autumn*)

AKKARA PAHA (1969) *d* Peries 120min (= *Five Acres of Land*)

AKOGARE (1935) *d* Gosho (= *Yearning*)

AKROBET SCHO-O-ON (1943) *d/s* Staudte 86min Tob

AKTENSKAPSBYRAN (1912) *d/s* Sjöström 357m (= *Pa detta numera vanliga satt/Ni nagot att fortulla*)

AKTRISA (1943) *d/co-s* L Trauberg *c* Moskvin *m Offenbach* 68min (= *The Actress*)

AKUTO (1966) *d/s* Shindo S 122min Toho (= *Conquest*)

A LA BELLE ETOILE (1966) d/co-s P Prévert co-s/di J Prévert fn (The Cop and the Anthem) O'Henry m/w Wiener 60min ORTF
A LA CONQUETE DU POLE (1911) d Méliès 650m
ALADDIN (1953) d Reiniger fsts 1001 Nights anim 12min
ALADDIN'S LANTERN (1938) d G Douglas (1rl)
A LA MEMOIRE DU ROCK (1962) d Reichenbbach sh
ALAMO, THE (1960) d/p J Wayne s J Grant c Clothier m Tiomkin w J Wayne, Widmark, Laurence Harvey TAO 70* 193min
ALAN AND APPLE (1967) d Warhol 16mm *30min (segment of Four Stars)
ALAN AND DICKIN (1967) d Warhol 16mm *120min (segment of Four Stars)
A LA POURSUITE DU VENT (1943) d Leenhardt
ALARM, THE (1914) d/w Arbuckle 2rs Key
A LAS CINCO DE LA TARDE (1960) d/co-s Bardem 113min (= At Five o'clock in the Afternoon)
ALASKAN, THE (1924) d Brenon s Goldbeck c Howe 2052m FPL
A L'ASSAULT DES AIGUILLES DU DIABLE (1942) d/p/c Ichac 22min
A L'OUTRE DU MONDE (1952) d René Lucot, Georges Aden cy/n Cocteau 16mm *25min
A l'aube du troisième Jour = POLYORCHIA (1962)
ALBANIYA (1945) d/c Karmen
ALBATROS, L' (1971) d/co-s/w Mocky *90min
ALBERGO LUNA-CAMERA TRENTAQUATTRO (1947) d Bragaglia
Alberto Il Conquistatore = SCAPOLO, LO (1955)
ALBERT R.N. (1953) d L Gilbert 88min r UA (= Spare Man/Break to Freedom)
ALBINISME (1955) d Painlevé *
ALBUQUERQUE (1947) d Enright w R Scott, Chaney *90min Par
AL CAPONE (1959) d R Wilson c Ballard m Raksin w Steiger 105min WB
ALCHIME (1952) d/s Grémillon 7min
ALCOOL TUE, L' (1947) d/cy/c/e Resnais (ps Alzin Rezarail) 16mm sh
ALDEBARAN (1935) d/co-s-w Blasetti
ALEKSANDR NEVSKII (1935) d Eisenstein, Dmitri Vasiliev co-s Eisenstein c Tissé m Prokofiev w Cherkasov 112min (= Alexander Nevsky)
ALENKA (1961) d Barnet 89min
ALERTE EN MEDITERRANNEE (1938) d/st/s Joannon w Fresnay 104min (= Hell's Cargo)
ALESSANDRO, SEI GRANDE! (1941) d Bragaglia
ALEXANDER CALDER: FROM THE EARTH TO THE MOON (1963) d Richter
ALEXANDER DEN STORE (1917) d/s Stiller 2018m
Alexander Nevsky = ALEKSANDR NEVSKII (1938)
ALEXANDER'S RAGTIME BAND (1938) d H King p Zanuck as-p H Brown co-s Trotti c Marley songs Irving Berlin m A Newman w Power, Carradine, Fay, Hersholt 105min Fox
ALEXANDER THE GREAT (1956) d/p/s Rossen w Krasker w Burton, March, Darrieux, S Baker CS* 141min r UA
ALFA TAU (1942) d/st/s De Robertis
ALFIE (1966) d/p L Gilbert c Heller w Caine, Winters 114min Par
ALFRED THE GREAT (1969) d C Donner st/co-s J R Webb w Hemmings PV* 122min pc J R Webb r MGM
ALF'S BUTTON (1920) d/p Hepworth 7rs
ALF'S BUTTON (1930) d Will P Kellino w Oberon
ALGIERS (1938) d Cromwell p Wanger s Lawson rm PEPE-LE-MOKO (1937) c Howe w Lamarr, Boyer 95min r UA
AL HILAL (1932) d/st Mehboob
ALIAS JESSE JAMES (1959) d McLeod c Lindon co-a Pereira w Hope, R Fleming, Corey, (G Cooper) 92min r UA
ALIAS JIMMY VALENTINE (1915) d M Tourneur
ALIAS JIMMY VALENTINE (1928) d Conway a Gibbons w L Barrymore 88min MGM
ALIAS MIKE MORAN (1919) d Cruze 5rs FPL
ALIAS MR. TWILIGHT (1947) d J Sturges 69min Col
ALIAS NICK BEAL (1949) d J Farrow c Lindon co-a Dreier w Milland, Mitchell 93min Par
ALIAS THE DEACON (1928) d Edward Sloman w Hersholt 2094m U
ALIAS THE DEACON (1940) d Christy Cabanne c Cortez 72min U
ALIAS THE DOCTOR (1932) d Curtiz w Barthelmess, Karloff, Foster 69min FN
Ali-Baba (UK) = ALI-BABA ET LES QUARANTE VOLEURS (1955)
ALI BABA ET LES 400 VOLEURS (1901) d/w Zecca 50m Pat
ALI-BABA ET LES QUARANTE VOLEURS (1955) d/co-s Becker dec Wakhévitch m Misraki w Fernandel *90min (= Ali-Baba)
ALI BABA GOES TO TOWN (1937) d D Butler w Cantor, Cobb, G Lee 81min Fox
ALIBI, L' (1937) d Pierre Chenal w Jouvet, Préjean, Von Stroheim 82min
ALIBI IKE (1935) d Enright w De Havilland 73min WB
ALICE ADAMS (1923) d/p K Vidor c Barnes 1938m

ALICE ADAMS (1935) d G Stevens p Berman m M Steiner w K Hepburn, MacMurray, Hopper 99min RKO
ALICE BE GOOD (1926) d/co-s Cline p Sennett Pat
ALICE IN CARTOONLAND (1926–27) p Disney part anim series
ALICE IN SWITZERLAND d Cavalcanti *31min
ALICE IN WONDERLAND (1903) p Hepworth fst Lewis Carroll 244m
ALICE IN WONDERLAND (1933) d/co-s McLeod co-s J Mankiewicz, Menzies fst Lewis Carroll co-c Glennon m Tiomkin w G Cooper, Fields, Marsh, C Ruggles, Fazenda, C Grant, Horton, Oliver 90min Par
ALICE IN WONDERLAND (1951) p Disney fsts (Alice in Wonderland and Alice Through the Looking Glass) Lewis Carroll wv Haydn *75min r RKO
ALICE'S ADVENTURES IN WONDERLAND (1910) d Porter 4m
ALICE'S RESTAURANT (1969) d/co-s Penn fsong (The Alice's Restaurant Massacre) Arlo Guthrie songs Joni Mitchell, Woody Guthrie w Arlo Guthrie w Arlo Guthrie, (Pete Seeger) *110min r UA
ALIKI (1962) d/co-p Maté m Hadjidakis 100min
Alitet Leaves for the Hills = ALITET UKHODIT V GORI (1949)
ALITET UKHODIT V GORI (1949) d/co-s Donskoi 101min (= Zakonye bolshoi zemli/Alitet Leaves for the Hills)
ALL ABOUT EVE (1950) d/s J Mankiewicz p Zanuck c Krasner co-a Wheeler m A Newman w B Davis, A Baxter, G Sanders, Ritter, Monroe, Ratoff 138min Fox
ALL-AMERICAN CO-ED (1941) d/co-p/co-st Prinz co-p Roach w Langdon 50min r UA
ALL ASHORE (1953) d/co-s Quine co-st/co-s Edwards c Lawton w Rooney *80min Col
All Beginnings are Hard = MINDEN KEZDET NEHE (1966)
ALLEGORIA DI PRIMAVERA (1949) d/s Emmer, Enrico Gras 9min (= Botticelli/The Story of Spring)
ALLEGRETTO (1936) d Fischinger anim* 4min MGM
ALLEGRO (1939) d McLaren, Mary Ellen Bute *2½min
ALLEGRO, FANTASMA, L' (1941) co-d Amleto Palermi co-d/st Bragaglia (uc) w Toto
ALLEMAN (1964) d/n/pc Haanstra 90min (= The Human Dutch/Twelve Millions)
ALLER RETOUR (1948) d Astruc 16mm sh
ALLER SIMPLE, UN (1971) d/ad/di Giovanni *105min
ALLES DREHT SICH, ALLES BEWEGHT SICH! (1929) d/co-s Richter (= 'Everything Revolves, Everything Moves!')
ALLEZ OOP (1934) d Charles Lamont w Keaton (2rs)
ALLES FUR VERONICA (1936) d V Harlan 80min
ALL FALL DOWN (1962) d Frankenheimer p Houseman s Inge c Lindon m North w Saint, Beatty, Malden 110min MGM
ALL FOR HER (1970) d/s/w Brenon
All for Love = VSE PRO LASKA (1930)
ALL FOR THE LOVE OF A GIRL AND LAMPOONS (1920) pc Goldwyn-Bray 1rl
All Good Citizens = VSICHNI DOBRI RODACI (1968)
ALL I DESIRE (1953) d Sirk p R Hunter co-a Golitzen w Stanwyck, O'Sullivan 79min U
ALLIGATOR NAMED DAISY, AN (1955) d J Thompson p Stross w Boyd VV* 88min
ALLIGATOR PEOPLE, THE (1959) d Del Ruth co-a Wheeler CS 74min Fox
ALL IN A NIGHT'S WORK (1961) d Anthony p Wallis c La Shelle co-a Pereira m Previn w Martin, MacLaine, Robertson, C Ruggles *94min Par
ALL MY SONS (1948) d Reis fpl Arthur Miller c Metty m Leith Stevens w Robinson, Lancaster, Horton 94min U
ALL NIGHT LONG (1962) d Dearden 95min r JAR
ALLO, BERLIN! ICI PARIS! (1932) d/s Duvivier Tob
All of Myself = WATASHI NO SUBETE O (1954)
ALL QUIET ON THE WESTERN FRONT (1930) d Milestone di d Cukor ad/di Maxwell Anderson s G Abbott fn Erich Maria Remarque c Edeson w Ayres, (Parrish), (Zinnemann) 140min U
ALLTAGLICHE GESCHICHTE, EINE (1948) d Rittau 84min Tob
ALL THAT HEAVEN ALLOWS (1955) d Sirk p R Hunter c Metty co-a Golitzen w Wyman, Hudson, Moorehead *89min U
ALL THAT MONEY CAN BUY (1941) d/p Dieterle co-s/fst (The Devil and Daniel Webster) Stephen Vincent Benet co-s Yordan (uc) c August e Wise m Herrmann w W Huston, Darwell, S Simon 112min RKO (= Here is a Man)
ALL THE BROTHERS WERE VALIANT (1953) d Thorpe p Berman s H Brown rm 1922 c Folsey co-a Gibbons w R Taylor, S Granger, Blyth *101min MGM
ALL THE FINE YOUNG CANNIBALS (1960) d Michael Anderson p Berman c Daniels w N Wood, R Wagner CS* 122min MGM
ALL THE KING'S HORSES (1935) d/co-s Tuttle chor Prinz w Horton 86min Par
ALL THE KING'S MEN 1950 d/p/s Rossen fn Robert Penn Warren c Guffey co-e Parrish w B Crawford, Dru, Derek 109min Col

ALL THE WORLD TO NOTHING (1918) d H King 5rs
ALL THIS, AND HEAVEN TOO (1940) d Litvak p Wallis c E Haller w B Davis, Boyer 104min WB
All This and Money Too = LOVE IS A BALL (1962)
ALL THROUGH THE NIGHT (1942) d V Sherman as-p Wald w Bogart, c Veidt, Lorre 107min WB
ALL WOMEN HAVE SECRETS (1939) d Kurt Neumann w Lake (ps Constance Keane) 74min Par
ALLUMETTES ANIMEES, LES (1908) d Cohl anim 77m
ALMADRABAS (1934) d/s Velo, Fernando Mantilla (1rl)
ALMA MATER (1915) d/s Guazzoni
ALMOST A HUSBAND (1919) d Badger c Brodine 5rs pc Goldwyn
Almost a Man = UOMO A META, UN (1965)
ALMOST MARRIED (1932) d Menzies 67min Fox
AL NOSTRO SONNO INQUIETO (1965) d Mingozzi sh
ALOMA OF THE SOUTH SEAS (1926) d/p M Tourneur w W Baxter, W Powell 2094m FPL r Par
ALOMA OF THE SOUTH SEAS (1941) d Santell c Struss chor Prinz w Lamour *77min Par
Allone = ODNA (1931)
Alone on the Pacific = TAIHEIYO HITORIBOTCHI (1963)
ALONG CAME JONES (1945) d Heisler p G Cooper s N Johnson c Krasner w G Cooper, L Young, Duryea 90min RKO
ALONG CAME RUTH (1924) d Cline 1524m MGM
ALONG CAME YOUTH (1930) d McLeod, Lloyd Corrigan 63min Par
ALONG THE GREAT DIVIDE (1951) d Walsh c Hickox w K Douglas, V Mayo, Brennan 88min WB
ALOUETTE (1964) d McLaren 2min NFBC
ALPH (1970) d/s/c/e Markopoulos 16mm*
ALPHABET MURDERS, THE (1966) d Tashlin fn (The A.B.C. Murders) Agatha Christie w Randall, Ekberg 90min r MGM
ALPHAVILLE, UNE ETRANGE AVENTURE DE LEMMY CAUTION (1965) d/s Godard c Coutard m Misraki w Constantine, Karina, Tamiroff 98min
ALRAUNE (1928) d/s Galeen c Planer w Wegener, Helm 3346m (= Mandragore/Daughter of Destiny)
ALRAUNE (1930) d R Oswald c Krampf m Kaper w Helm
ALS ICH TOT WAR (1916) d/s/w Lubitsch 1rl (= When I was Dead)
ALSKANDE PAR (1964) d Zetterling c Nykvist w H Andersson, Björnstrand, Lindblom, Dahlbeck, Björk 118min San (= Loving Couples)
ALSKARINNAN (1962) d/s Sjöstrom w B Andersson, Von Sydow S 77min SF (= The Mistress)
ALSKLING, JAG GER MIG (1943) d Molander
ALS TWEE DRUPPELS WATER (1963) d Rademakers CS 119min (= The Spitting Image/The Dark Room of Damocles)
ALTA INFIDELTA (1964) co-c Di Venanzo 130min (= Sex in the Afternoon/High Infidelity)
  ep PECCATO NEL POMMERIGIO d/co-s Petri w Bloom, Aznavour
  ep LA SOSPIROSA d Salce w Vitti, Cassel
  ep SCANDALOSO d Rossi w Manfredi
ALTARS OF THE EAST (1955) p/s/n Ayres *
ALTE GESETZ, DAS (1923) d Dupont w Krauss 3028m (= Baruch)
ALTE UND DER JUNGE KONIG, DER (1935) d Steinhoff co-s Von Harbow w Jannings 122min
ALTGERMANISCHE BAUERNKULTUR (1934) d Ruttmann 17min
ALTITUDE 3,200 (1937) d Benoît-Lévy, Marie Epstein p Graetz m Jaubert w Barrault
ALTO CHIESE (1959) d Olmi *35min
ALTRA, L' (1947) d Bragaglia 99min
ALTRI TEMPI (1952) d/co-st/co-s Blasetti co-st/co-s Cecchi D'Amico co-s Rondi w Lollobrigida, De Sica, Caprioli 120min (= Infidelity)
ALVAREZ KELLY (1966) d Dmytryk p S Siegel c MacDonald w Holden, Widmark PV* 116min Col
ALWAYS AUDACIOUS (1920) d Cruze 5rs FPL
Always Further On = TARAHUMARA (1965)
ALWAYS GOODBYE (1931) co-d/d/a Menzies co-d Kenneth McKenna c Edeson 66min Fox
ALWAYS LEAVE THEM LAUGHING (1949) d Del Ruth p Wald co-s Shavelson c E Haller w V Mayo, Roman 116min WB
ALWAYS TELL YOUR WIFE (1922) d Seymour Hicks, Hitchcock sh
AMAKUSA SHIRO TOKISADA (1962) d/co-s Oshima 100min (= The Rebel)
AMAL, LE VOLEUR (1959) d Blue
AMAMI ALFREDO (1940) d Gallone m Verdi 91min
AMANAT (1955) co-d/p Roy co/d Arabind Sen
AMANDUS (1966) d Stiglic
AMANT DE CINQ JOURS, L' (1961) d/co-s De Broca m Delerue dec Evein w Cassel, Seberg, Presle 95min (= Infidelity)
AMANT DE LADY CHATTERLEY, L' (1955) d/s M Allégret fn D H Lawrence c Périnal dec Trauner m Kosma w Darrieux, Marquand 98min
AMANTE DI GRAMIGNA, L' (1969) d Lizzani *100min
AMANTE DI PARIDE, L' (1954) d/co-st/co-s M Allégret co-a Chiari m Rota w Lamarr *73min (= The Face that Launched a Thousand Ships/Helen of Troy)
AMANTE SEGRETA, L' (1941) d Gallone (= Troppo bella)

AMANTI, GLI (1969) d De Sica co-p Ponti co-s Zavattini fpl Rondi w Dunaway Mastroianni 88min (= A Place for Lovers)

AMANTI DI RAVELLO, GLI (1950) d/s De Robertis w Ferzetti 96min

AMANTS, LES (1958) d/co-s Malle c Decaë dec Evein, Saulnier m Brahms w Moreau, Modot FS 88min

AMANTS DE BRAS-MORT, LES (1951) d Pagliero

AMANTS DE MINUIT, LES (1931) d Genina, M Allégret co-c Sparkuhl

AMANTS DE TERUEL, LES (1961) d/s Rouleau c Renoir co-m Theodorakis CS* 94min

AMANTS DE TOLEDE, LES (1952) d Decoin fst (Le Coffre et le Revenant) Stendhal c Kelber w Valli, Armendariz, Arnoul 88min (= Lovers of Toledo)

AMANTS DE VERONE, LES (1948) d/st Cayatte s/di J Prévert c Alekan, Bourgoin m Kosma w Brasseur, Dalio, Reggiani, Aimée, Carol 81min

AMANTS DU PONT SAINT JEAN, LES (1947) d Decoin co-s/di Aurenche w M Simon

AMANTS DU TAGE, LES (1955) d Verneuil fn/di Joseph Kessel dec d'Eaubonne w Gélin, T Howard, Arnoul, Dalio 123min (= The Lovers of Lisbon)

AMANTS TERRIBLES, LES (1936) d M Allégret fpl (Private Lives) Coward

AMARILLY OF CLOTHES LINE ALLEY (1918) d Neilan 2rs FPL

AMATORFILMEN (1922) d Molander SF

AMAZING DR. CLITTERHOUSE, THE (1938) d/co-p Litvak co-s J Huston w Robinson, Bogart, Trevor, Crisp 87min WB

AMAZING TRANSPARENT MAN, THE (1959) d Ulmer 56min

AMAZONAS (1965) d Rocha *18min

AMAZONS, THE (1917) d Joseph Kaufman w Menjou 5rs

Amazons of Rome = VERGINE DI ROMA, LE (1960)

AMAZZONE MASCHERATA, L' (1914) d/w Ghione

AMBASSADOR'S DAUGHTER, THE (1956) d/p/s Krasna c Kelber w De Havilland, M Loy, Menjou CS* 102min r UA

AMBASSADOR'S ENVOY, THE (1913) d Ince w Borzage 950m

Ambiciosos, Los = FIEVRE MONTE A EL PAO, LA (1959)

AMBITIEUSE, L' (1958) d Allégret 95min

AMBITIOUS BUTLER, THE (1912) d/p/w Sennett w Normand ½rl Key

AMBUSH (1949) d S Wood c Lipstein w R Taylor, McIntire 89min MGM

AMBUSH AT TOMAHAWK GAP (1953) d Sears *73min Col

AMBUSHERS, THE (1967) d Levin co-c Guffey w Martin *102min Col

AMER CORSE (1908) d/s Jasset

AME D'ARTISTE (1925) d Dulac

Ame des Moulins, L' = MOULINS CHANTENT ET PLEURENT, LES (1912)

Amere Victoire: French version of BITTER VICTORY (1957) di Queneau 97min

AMERICA (1924) d/fpl (War) Griffith co-c Bitzer w L Barrymore 4481m r UA

AMERICA, AMERICA (1963) d/p/fn Kazan c Wexler m Hadjidakis 177min (= The Anatolian Smile)

AMERICAIN, UN (1958) d Cavalier 16mm

AMERICAIN, OU LE CHEMIN D'ERNOA, L' (1970) d/s Delluc

AMERICAIN SE DETEND, L' (1957) d Reichenbach m Legrand *13min

AMERICAN CITIZEN, AN (1913) d J Searle Dawley w J Barrymore

AMERICAN DREAM, AN (1966) d Robert Gist fn Mailer c Leavitt w Nolan, J Leigh, Parker *103 min WB (= See You in Hell, Darling)

AMERICAN GUERILLA IN THE PHILIPPINES (1950) d F Lang p/s Trotti co-a Wheeler m Mockridge w Power, Presle, Ewell *105min Fox (= I Shall Return)

AMERICAN HEIRESS, THE (1917) d/p Hepworth 3rs

AMERICAN IN PARIS, AN (1951) d Minneli p Freed st/s A Lerner co-c J Alton co-a Gibbons chor Gene Kelly m George Gershwin w Gene Kelly, Caron *113min MGM

American in Rome, An = AMERICANO A ROMA, UN (1954)

AMERICANIZATION OF EMILY, THE (1964) d Arthur Miller s Chayefsky c Lathrop w J Andrews, Garner, M Douglas, J Coburn 117min MGM (= Emily)

AMERICAN MADNESS (1932) d Capra s Riskin c J Walker w W Huston 76min Col

AMERICAN MARCH, AN (1941) d Fischinger m Souza anim* 4min

AMERICAN METHODS (1917) d/s F Lloyd 6rs Fox

AMERICANO, THE (1954) d Castle w G Ford, Romero *84min RKO

AMERICANO A ROMA, UN (1954) d/co-st/co-s Steno w Ponti, De Laurentiis w Sordi (= An American in Rome)

AMERICANO IN VACANZA, UN (1945) d/ad Zampa p Ponti w Cortese 100min (= A Yank in Rome)

AMERICAN ROMANCE, AN (1944) d/p/st K Vidor c Rosson a Gibbons *170min MGM

AMERICAN TRAGEDY, AN (1931) d/co-s Von Sternberg fn Theodore Dreiser c Garmes w S Sidney, Pichel 10rs Par

AMERICAN VENUS, THE (1926) d Tuttle w L Brooks, Oliver, Fairbanks Jr 2417m FPL

America through the Keyhole (UK) = AMERIQUE INSOLITE, L' (1960)

AMERIQUE INSOLITE, L' (1960) d/co-s Reichenbach co-cy Marker m Legrand FS* 88min (= America through the Keyhole)

AMERIQUE LUNAIRE, L' (1962) d/c Reichenbach m Legrand 13min

AMES DE FOUS (1917) d/s Dulac

AMES D'ENFANTS (1922) d Benoît-Lévy

AMES MORTES, LES (1960) d Allio

AMICA, L' (1915) d/co-s Guazzoni

AMICHE, LE (1955) d/co-s Antonioni co-s Cecchi D'Amico fst (Tra Donne Sole) Cesare Pavese c Di Venanzo m Fusco w Rossi-Drago, Cortese, Ferzetti 104min (= The Girl Friends)

A MI-CHEMIN DU CIEL (1931) d Cavalcanti Par

AMICI PER LA PELLE (1955) d/co-s Rossi m Rota 83min (= Friends for Life)

AMICO DELLE DONNE, L' (1942) d Poggioli

AMITIES PARTICULIERES, LES (1964) d Delannoy 105min (= This Special Friendship)

AMLETO E I SUO CLOWN (1920) d Gallone w Soava Gallone 1829m (= On with the Motley)

AMONG THE LIVING (1941) d Heisler p S Siegel c Sparkuhl w S Hayward, Carey 68min Par

Among the Ruins = HAIKYO NO NAKA (1923)

AMONG THOSE PRESENT (1921) w H Lloyd 3rs pc Roach

AMORE (1936) d Bragaglia w Feuillère

AMORE, L' (1948) 69min
ep UNA VOCE UMANA d/s/p Rossellini di/fpl (La Voix Humaine) Cocteau c Martelli dec Bérard w Magnani
ep IL MIRACOLA d/co-s Rossellini fst Fellini c Tonti w Magnani, Fellini

AMORE A PRIMA VISTA (1957) d/co-s Rossi * (= Buenos Dias, Amor)

AMORE A ROMA, UN (1960) d Risi w Martinelli, De Sica 113min

AMORE CANTA L' (1941) d Poggioli

AMORE DIFFICILE, L' (1962) 125min (= Sex Can Be Difficult)
ep L'AVVENTURA DI UN SOLDATO d/co-s/w Manfredi

AMORE E CHIACCHIERE (1957) d/co-s Blasetti co-s Zavattini w De Sica

AMORE E RABBIA (1967 r 1969) p Lizzani m Fusco TS* 102min (= Love and Anger/Vangelo 70)
ep L'INDIFFERENZA d/s Lizzani (= Indifference)
ep AGONIA d/s Bertolucci w The Living Theatre (= Agony)
ep LA SEQUENZA DEL FIORE DI CARTA d/s Pasolini 12min (= The Sequence of the Paper Flower)
ep L'ALLER ET RETOUR ANDANTE E RITORNO DES ENFANTS PRODIGUES DEI FIGLI PRODIGHI d/s Godard (= Love)
ep DISCUTIAMO, DISCUTIAMO d Bellocchio

AMORE IN CITTA (1953) c Di Venanzo
ep TENTATO SUICIDIO d/co-st/co-s Antonioni co-st/co-s Zavattini 20min
ep UN AGENZIA MATRIMONIALE d/co-st/co-s Fellini p Zavattini
ep GLI ITALIANI SI VOLTANO d/co-st/co-s Lattuada
ep L'AMORE CHE SI PAGA d Lizzani
ep LA STORIA DI CATERINA d Maselli, Zavattini
ep PARADISO PER TRE ORE d Risi co-s Zavattini, Ferreri

AMORE SI FA COSI, L' (1939) d Bragaglia

AMORE DI ERCOLE, GLI (1960) d Bragaglia w Mansfield FS* 98min (= The Loves of Hercules)

AMORE DI MEZZO SECOLO (1954) *
ep 1910 d/co-st/co-s Pietrangeli dec Chiari
ep GUERRA 1915-1918 d Germi co-s Pietrangeli
ep d/s Chiari
ep d Glauco Pellegrini
ep NAPOLI '43 d/s Rossellini dec Chiari 15min

AMORE MIO, AIUTAMI (1969) d Sordi c Di Palma m Piccioni w Sordi, Vitti *110min

AMORE NELL ARTE, L' (1950) d Bava sh

AMORI PERICOLOSI (1964) co-d Lizzani 115min

AMOROSA MENZOGNA, L' (1949) d/s Antonioni m Fusco 10min

AMOROUS ADVENTURES OF MOLL FLANDERS, THE (1965) d T Young fn Daniel Defoe c Moore w Novak, Lansbury, De Sica, G Sanders, Palmer 122min Par

A Morte Espreti No Mar = TIBERONEROS (1962)

AMOR UND DAS STANDHAFTE EHEPAAR (1920) d Reiniger anim 1rl

AMOUR A LA CHAINE, L' (1964) d/co-st De Givray m Delerue S 84min

AMOURA L'AMERICAINE, L' (1931) co-d Fejos s M Allégret w Carette 85min

AMOUR AVEC DES SI, L' (1963) d/co-p/s Lelouch 85min

AMOUR A VINGT ANS, L' (1962) supn De Baroncelli linking photographs Cartier Bresson, Aurel linking m Delerue CS 123min (= Love at Twenty)
ep PARIS d/s Truffaut c Coutard w Léaud
ep ROME d/s Renzo Rossellini w Rossi-Drago

ep TOKYO d/s Shintaro Ishihara
ep MUNICH d/s Marcel Ophuls
ep WARSAW d Wajda w Cybulski

AMOUR C'EST GAI, L'AMOUR C'EST TRISTE, L' (1968) d/co-s Pollet *90min

AMOUR CHANTE, L' (1930) d Florey artistic d M Allégret

AMOUR DE POCHE, UN (1957) d Kast c Cloquet w Brialy, Marais, Melville 85min

AMOUR D'UNE FEMME, L' (1953) d/st/co-s Grémillon w Presle, Girotti 109min

AMOUR EST EN JEU, L' (1957) d M Allégret w Girardot 90min (= Ma Femme, Mon Gosse et Moi)

AMOUREUX DU 'FRANCE', LES (1964) d/co-s Reichenbach, Pierre Grimblat co-c Reichenbach m Legrand FS* 96min

AMOUREUX SONT SEULS AU MONDE, LES (1947) d Decoin s/di Jeanson m Jouvet 94min

AMOUR FOU, L' d/co-s Rivette 255min (= Mad Love)

AMOUR, MADAME, L' (1951) d Grangier m Van Parys w Arletty 89min

AMOURS LE LA PIEUVRE (1967) d Painlevé *15min

AMOUR TENACE (1912) d/w Linder Pat

AMSTERDAM (1965) d Van der Horst 23min

AM TAG ALS DER REGEN KAM (1959) d G Oswald 85min (= The Day the Rains Came)

ANA (1957) d Ichikawa (= The Hole)

ANARCHIE CHEZ GUIGNOL, L' (1906) d Méliès 40m

ANASTASIA (1956) d Litvak p Adler m A Hildyard m A Newman w Ingrid Bergman, Brynner, Tamiroff, H Hayes CS* 105min Fox

Anatahan = SAGA OF ANATAHAN, THE (1953)

ANATA KAIMASU (1956) d Kobayashi (= I'll Buy You)

ANATA WA NANI O KANGAETE IRU KA? (1967) d/p Kuri anim* 10min (= What Do You Think?)

Anatolian Smile, The (UK) = AMERICA, AMERICA (1963)

ANATOMY OF A MURDER (1959) d/p Preminger s Mayes c Leavitt cr Bass m Duke Ellington w J Stewart, Remick, R Welch, G Scott, (Duke Ellington) 160min r Col

ANCHORS AWEIGH (1945) d G Sidney p Pasternak a Boyle chor Gene Kelly anim Hanna, Barbera w Sinatra, Gene Kelly 140min MGM

And All These Women = OCH ALLA DESSA KVINNOR (1944)

ANDALUSIAN DANCE (1897) p Paul 12m

ANDERE, DER (1930) d Wiene co-m Holländer 104min

ANDERS ALS DIE ANDERN (1919) d/p/co-s R Oswald w Veidt 2115m

Anders als und Ich = DRITTE GESCHLECHT, DAS (1957)

ANDERSON TAPES, THE (1971) d Lumet w Connery, Meeker *98min Col

ANDES NO HANAYOME (1966) d/s Mani S* 102min (= Bride of the Andes)

And God Created Woman = ET DIEU CREA LA FEMME (1956)

AND NOW TOMORROW (1944) d Pichel co-s R Chandler c Fapp a Dreier, Pereira m V Young w L Young, Ladd, S Hayward 85min Par

Andre Gidé = AVEC ANDRE GIDE (1950)

ANDREI KOZHUKHOV (1917) d/s Protazanov w Mozhukin 2264m

ANDRE MALRAUX (1958) d Kiegel 15min

ANDRE MASSON ET LES QUATRE ELEMENTS (1958) d/cy/m Grémillon *21min

ANDREUCCIO DA PERUGIA (1910) d/s/dec Guazzoni

ANDROCLES AND THE LION (1952) d/co-ad Chester Erskine p Pascal fpl G B Shaw m Hollander w J Simmons, Mature 98min RKO

ANDROMEDA STRAIN, THE (1971) d/p Wise PV* 127min U

AND SO THEY WERE MARRIED (1936) d E Nugent p B P Schulberg co-s Anthony w M Douglas, M Astor 74min Col

AND THE ANGELS SANG (1944) c G Marshall s M Frank, Panama c Struss a Dreier, Pereira m V Young w Lamour, MacMurray 96min Par

AND THEN THERE WERE NONE (1945) d/p/co-s Clair co-s D Nichols fn (Ten Little Niggers) Agatha Christie c Andriot w W Huston, L Hayward, Haydn 97min Fox (= Ten Little Niggers)

And There Came a Man = E VENNE UN UOMO (1964)

And There Was No More Sea = EN DER ZEE WAS NIET MEER (1956)

And Womas was Created = ET DIEU CREA LA FEMME (1957)

And Yet They Go On = SHIKAMO KAREA WA YUKU (1931)

And Yet We Live = DIKKOI IKITERU (1950)

ANDY HARDY COMES HOME (1958) d H W Koch w Rooney, Weissmuller 81min MGM

ANDY HARDY GETS SPRING FEVER (1939) d WS Van Dyke w Rooney 85min MGM

ANDY HARDY MEETS DEBUTANTE (1940) d G Seitz co-c Lawton w Rooney, Garland 86min MGM

ANDY HARDY'S BLONDE TROUBLE (1944) d G Seitz a Gibbons w H Marshall, Rooney 107min MGM

ANDY HARDY'S DOUBLE LIFE (1942) d G Seitz co-c Folsey a Gibbons m Amfitheatrof w Rooney, Esther Williams 92min MGM

ANDY HARDY'S PRIVATE SECRETARY (1941) *d* G Seitz *w* Rooney 101min MGM
ANDY WARHOL FILMS JACK SMITH FILMING *NORMAL LOVE* (1963) *d* Warhol 16mm si *3min
ANDY WARHOL'S WOMEN (1971) *d/c Paul Morrisey p* Warhol *90min (= *Sex/Women in Revolt*)
ANELLO DI SIVA, L' (1914) *d* Genina
ANEMIC CINEMA (1925) *d Marcel Duchamp as-d* Man Ray
ANFISA (1912) *d* Protazanov 860m
ANGE DE NOEL, L' (1905) *d* Méliès 200m (7 parts)
Angeklagt nach Paragraph 218 = ARZT STELLT FAST, DER (1966)
ANGEL (1937) *d/p* Lubitsch *s* Raphaelson *c* C Lang *co-a* Dreier *song* Holländer *w* Dietrich, H Marshall, Horton, M Douglas 91min Par
ANGEL AND THE BADMAN (1946) *d/s* J Grant *p* J Wayne *e* Keller *w* J Wayne, Carey 97min Rep
ANGEL BABY (1961) *d* Wendkos *co-c* Wexler *w* Blondell 97min
ANGELE (1934) *d/p/s* Pagnol *fn* (*Un de Baumuques*) *Jean Giono w* Fernandel 150min
ANGEL E SCESO POR BROOKLYN, UN (1957) *d/co-s* Vajda
ANGEL EXTERMINADOR, EL (1962) *d/co-st/s/di* Bunuel *co-st* Alcoriza *c* Figueroa 95min (= *The Exterminating Angel*)
ANGEL FACE (1952) *d* Preminger *p* H Hughes *co-s* F Nugent *c* Stradling *m* Tiomkin *w* Mitchum, J Simmons, H Marshall 90min RKO
ANGEL FROM TEXAS, AN (1940) *d* Enright *co-s* Niblo *fpl* G Kaufman *w* Reagan, Wyman 69min WB
Angelina = ONOREVOLE ANGELINA, L' (1947)
ANGEL IN EXILE (1948) *d* Dwan, *Philip Ford p* H Yates 90min Rep
ANGELO E IL DIAVOLO, L' (1946) *d/co-s* Camerini *st/co-s* Zavattini
ANGEL ON MY SHOULDER (1946) *d* A Mayo *m* Tiomkin *w* Muni, A Baxter, Rains 101min *r* UA
Angels and Pirates = ANGELS IN THE OUT FIELD (1951)
ANGELS IN THE OUTFIELD (1951) *d/p* C Brown *co-s* Wells *co-a* Gibbons *m* Amfitheatrof *w* J Leigh, P Douglas 102min MGM (= *Angels and Pirates*)
ANGELS OVER BROADWAY (1940) *co-d/p/st/s* B Hecht *co-d/c* Garmes *as-p* Fairbanks Jr *m* Antheil *w* Fairbanks Jr, Hayworth, Mitchell 80min Col
Angels' Pit, The = FOSSA DEGLI ANGELI, LA (1937)
ANGELS WASH THEIR FACES, THE (1939) *d* Enright *co-s* Busch *w* Sheridan, Reagan 76min WB
ANGELS WITH DIRTY FACES (1938) *d* Curtiz *c* Polito *m* M Steiner *w* Cagney, Bogart, Sheridan, G Bancroft (10rs) WB
Angel Wore Red, The = SPOSA BELLA, LA (1960)
ANGES DU PECHE, LES (1943) *d/co-s* Bresson *di jean Giraudoux c* Agostini 73min
ANGES GARDIENS (1964) *d* Reichenbach
ANGLAIS TEL QUE MAX LE PARLE, L' (1914) *d/s/w* Linder Pat
ANGLAR, FINNS DOM ... (1960) *d/s* Lindgren *w* Kulle *110min San (= *Do You Believe in Angels?/Love-Mates*)
ANGOISSANTE AVENTURE, L' (1923) *d* Protazanov *w* Mozhukin 1750m
ANGORA LOVE (1929) *d Lewis Foster p* Roach *st* McCarey *w* Laurel, Hardy 2rs *r* MGM
ANGRY HILLS, THE (1959) *d* Aldrich *p* Stross *s* Bezzerides *fn Leon Uris a* Adam *w* Mitchum, S Baker, Wolfit 105min *r* MGM
Angry Sea, The = IKARI NO UMI (1944)
ANGRY SILENCE, THE (1960) *d* G Green *co-p/s* Forbes *m* M Arnold *w* Attenborough 95min BL
ANGST, DIE (1954) *d* Rossellini *fst Stefan Zweig w* Ingrid Bergman 81min (= *La Paura/ Non Credo Piu All' Amore/Fear*)
ANGYALUK FOLDJE (1962) *d* Révész 98min (= *The Land of Angels*)
ANI IMOTO (1953) *d* Naruse *w* Kyo, Mori (= *Older Brother, Younger Sister*)
ANIMA DEL DEMI-MONDE, L' (1913) *d Baldassare Negroni w* Ghione
ANIMAL CRACKERS (1930) *d Victor heerman fco-mpl* G Kaufman *c* Folsey *w* C, G, H, Z, Marx, Dumont 99min Par
ANIMAL FARM (1954) *d/co-p* Halas, Batchelor *fn George Orwell* anim* 73min
ANIMALI PAZZI (1939) *d* Bragaglia *w* Toto
Animals, The = ANIMAUX, LES (1963)
Animals and the Brigands, The = ZVIRATKA A PETRO-VSTI (1946)
ANIMALS OF EDEN AND AFTER, THE (1970) *d* Brakhage 16mm* si 35min
ANIMA NERA (1962) *d/s* Rossellini *fpl* Patroni-*Griffi m* Piccioni *w* Gassman, Rossi-Drago, Tiller
ANIMAUX, LES (1963) *d* Rossif 90min (= *The Animals*)
ANIME BUIE (1915) *d/s/w* Guione
ANIOLY SPADAJA (1958) *d/s/w* Polanski *m* Komeda sh
ANJANGADH (1948) *d* Roy
ANJO-KE NO BUTOKAI (1948) *d* Yoshimura *s* Shindo *w* Mori (= *A BAll at the Anjo House*)

Ankara, Heart of Turkey = ANKARA, SERDTSYE TURKI (1934)
ANKARA, SERDTSYE TURKI (1934) *d* Yutkevich, *Leo Arnstam* (= *Ankara, Heart of Turkey*)
ANKLES AWAY (1938) *d/s/w* C Chase 2rs Col
AN-MAGRITT (1969) *d* Skouen *c* Nykvist S* 101min
ANNA (1951) *d* Lattuada *p* De Laurentiis, Ponti *co-st/co-s* Risi *c* Martelli *m* Rota *w* Mangano, Vallone, Gassman 111min
Anna = EDES ANNA (1958)
ANNA (1970) *d/s* J Donner *w* H Andersson *83min *co-pc* J Donner
ANNA AND THE KING OF SIAM (1946) *d* Cromwell *c* AC Miller *co-a* Wheeler *m* Herrmann *w* Harrison, Darnell, I Dunne, Cobb 128min Fox
ANNA ASCENDS (1922) *d* V Fleming 1816m FPL *r* Par
ANNABELLE'S AFFAIRS (1931) *d Alfred Werker as-p* Goetz *c* C Clarke *w* Jeannette Macdonald, V McLaglen 76min Fox
ANNA BOLEYN (1920) *d* Lubitsch *c* Sparkuhl *w* Jannings 100min UFA (= *Deception*)
ANNA CHRISTIE (1930) *d* C Brown *fpl Eugene O'Neill c* Daniels *a* Gibbons *w* Garbo, Bickford, Dressler 74min MGM (*German and Swedish versions: d* Feyder 10rs)
ANNA DI BROOKLYN (1958) *d Reginald Denham, C Lastricati supn/co-p* De Sica *co-p* Lollobrigida *c* Rotunno *w* Lollobrigida, De Sica *97min (= *Anna of Brooklyn/Fast and Sexy*)
ANNA KARENINA (1935) *d* C Brown *p* Selznick *fn Leo Tolstoy c* Daniels *a* Gibbons *m* Stothart *w* Garbo, March, O'Sullivan, Bartholomew, Rathbone 95min MGM
ANNA KARENINA (1948) *d/co-s/co-di* Duvivier *co-s/co-di* Anouilh *c* Alekan *cos* Beaton *w* V Leigh, R Richardson 128min *pc* A Korda
ANNA KARENINA (1967) *d/co-s* Zarkhi *fn Leo Tolstoy* 70* 135min
ANNA LA BONNE (1959) *d* Jutra *p* Truffaut *fsong* Cocteau
ANNA LUCASTA (1949) *d* Rapper *co-s/fpl* Yordan *c* Polito *w* Goddard, B Crawford 86min *r* Col
Ann and Eve = ANNA OCH EVA (1969)
ANNA OCH EVA (1969) *d* Mattson *100min (= *Ann and Eve*)
Anna of Brooklyn (UK) = ANNA DI BROOKLYN (1958)
ANNAPOLIS (1928) *d Christy Cabanne c* AC Miller 88min Pat
ANNAPOLIS STORY (1955) *d* D Siegel *p* W Mirisch *co-s* Mainwaring (*ps* Homes) *c* Leavitt *w* Derek *87min AA (= *The Blue and the Gold*)
ANNA THE ADVENTURESS (1920) *d/p* Hepworth *w* Wolman 1829m
ANNA UND ELISABETH (1933) *d/co-s* Wisbar 75min
ANNEE DERNIERE A MARIENBAD, L' (1961) *d* Resnais *s* Robbe-Grillet *c* Vierny *co-e* Colpi *a* Saulnier *cost* Evein, *Chanel w* Seyrig FS 94min
ANNE OF GREEN GABLES (1934) *d William D Taylor w* Hackett 6rs
ANNE OF THE INDIES (1951) *d* J Tourneur *co-s* P Dunne *co-a* Wheeler *m* Waxman *w* Peters, H Marshall *87min Fox
ANNIBALE (1959) *d* Bragaglia, Ulmer (*uc*) *w* Mature, Ferzetti, Girotti CS* 103min (= *Hannibal*)
ANNI DIFFICILE (1948) *d/co-s* Zampa *w* Girotti 90min (= *Difficult Years/The Little Man*)
ANNIE GET YOUR GUN (1950) *d* G Sidney *p* Freed *co-a* Gibbons *chor* R Alton *m/lyr Irving Berlin musical scoring Adolph Deutsch,* Edens, *Rodgers, Hammerstein w* Keel, Hutton *107min MGM
ANNIE LAURIE (1916) *d/p* Hepworth
ANNIE LAURIE (1927) *d John S Robertson co-a* Gibbons *w* L Gish 2661m MGM
ANNIE OAKLEY (1935) *d* G Stevens *w* Stanwyck, M Douglas 88min RKO
ANNI FACILI (1953) *d/co-s* Zampa *co-p* Ponti, De Laurentiis *c* Tonti 103min (= *Easy Years*)
ANNI RUGGENTI (1962) *d/co-st/co-s* Zampa *w* Manfredi 106min (= *Roaring Years*)
ANNIVERSARY, THE (1967) *d* R Baker *w* B Davis 95min WB
Anniversary of the Revolution = GODOVSHCHINA REVOLYUTSII (1919)
ANNUSHKA (1959) *d* Barnet 2444m
ANN VICKERS (1933) *d* Cromwell *s Sinclair Lewis w* I Dunne, W Huston, Oliver 69min RKO
A NOI PIACE FREDDO (1960) *d/co-s* Steno 105min (= *Some Like It Cold*)
ANONYME (1958) *d* Alexeiff anim
ANO TE KONO TE (1952) *d/co-s* Ichikawa Dai (= *This Way, that Way*)
ANOTHER DAWN (1937) *d* Dieterle *fst* (*The Ambassador's Wife*) *Somerset Maugham c* Gaudio *w* Flynn, K Francis 75min WB
ANOTHER FINE MESS (1930) *d James Parrott p* Roach *w* Laurel, Hardy (3rs) *r* MGM
ANOTHER MAN'S POISON (1952) *d* Rapper *co-p* Fairbanks Jr *w* B Davis, Emlyn Williams 89min *r* UA
ANOTHER MAN'S SHOES (1922) *d* Conway *c* B Reynolds 1296m U

ANOTHER PART OF THE FOREST (1948) *d* M Gordon *p* Bresler *fpl* Hellman *c* Mohr *m* Amfitheatrof *w* March, Blyth, Duryea, E O'Brien 107min U
ANOTHER SHORE (1948) *d* Crichton *c* Slocombe 77min
ANOTHER SKY (1958) *d/s* Lambert 85min
ANOTHER THIN MAN (1939) *d* WS Van Dyke *s* Goodrich, Hackett *fst* Hammett *co-c* Daniels *a* Gibbons *w* M Loy, W Powell
ANOTHER WILD IDEA (1934) *d* C Chase (*as* Parrott), *Eddie Dunn p* Roach *w* C Chase (2rs) MGM
A NOUS DEUX, PARIS! (1953) *d* Kast 26min Pat
A NOUS LA LIBERTE (1932) *d/s/di* Clair *c* Périnal *m* Auric *dec* Meerson 97min Tob (= *Liberté Chérie*)
ANSIGTET (1915) *d* Madsen
ANSIKTEN I SKUGGA (1956) *co-d* P Weiss (= *Faces in the Shadows*)
ANSIKTET (1958) *d/s* Ingmar Bergman *c* Fischer *w* Von Sydow, Thulin, B Andersson 101min SF (= *The Face/The Magician*)
ANTEFATTO (1971) *d/s/c* Bava *90min
ANTHONY ADVERSE (1936) *d* LeRoy *p* Blanke *c* Gaudio *m* Korngold *w* March, De Havilland, Rains, Tamiroff, L Hayward 136min WB
ANTHROSE DE LA LANCHE, L' (1951) *d* Vierny
ANTICIPATION OF THE NIGHT (1958) *d* Brakhage 16mm * si 42min
ANTINEA, L'AMANTE DELLA CITTA SEPOLTA (1961) *d* Ulmer, *Giuseppe Masini,* Borzage (*uc*) *s* Mainwaring *w* Trintignant TR* 100min (= *Atlantis, The Lost Continent/The Lost Kingdom*)
ANTOINE ET ANTOINETTE (1947) *d/co-s* Becker *w* Modot, (de Funès) 115min Gau
ANTOINETTE SABRIER (1927) *d* Dulac
Antonio das Mortes = SANTO GUERREIRO CONTRA O DRAGAO DA MALDADE, O (1969)
ANTONIO MEUCCI (1940) *d/co-s* Guazzoni
ANTONIO SAURA (1955) *d/p/c/e* Saura 16mm * 11min
ANTON SPELEC OSTROSTRELEC (1932) *d* Fric *c* Heller (= *Anton Spelec, the Thrower*)
Anton Spelec, the Thrower = ANTON SPELEC OSTRO-STRELEC (1932)
ANTONY AND CLEOPATRA (1950) *d* D Davis *fpl Shakespeare* 16mm 33min
ANUSCHKA (1942) *d* Kautner 101min
Anxious Years: reissue (1953) of DARK JOURNEY (1937)
ANYBODY HERE SEEN KELLY? (1928) *d* Wyler 1903m U
ANYBODY'S GOAT (1932) *d* Arbuckle (*ps* William Goodrich) 1rl
ANY NUMBER CAN PLAY (1949) *d* LeRoy *s* R Brooks *c* Rosson *co-a* Gibbons *w* Gable, Corey, Astor, A Smith 112min MGM
ANY OLD PORT (1932) *d James Horne p* Roach *w* Laurel, Hardy (2rs) *r* MGM
Anyone Can Kill Me = TOUS PEUVENT ME TUER (1957)
Anyone Can Play (US) = DOLCI SIGNORE, LE (1967)
ANYTHING CAN HAPPEN (1952) *d/co-s Seaton co-p* Perlberg *c* Fapp *co-a* Pereira *m* V Young *w* J Ferrer 107min Par
ANYTHING GOES (1936) *d* Milestone *c* Struss *chor* Prinz *lyr Cole Porter co-additional songs* Carmichael, Holländer *w* B Crosby, C Ruggles, Lupino, Dumont 92min Par
ANY WEDNESDAY (1966) *d Robert Miller p/s* JJ Epstein *c* Lipstein *m* Duning *w* J Fonda *109min WB
ANY WIFE (1922) *d* Brenon *w* White 1401m Fox
ANY WOMAN (1923) *d/p* H King *co-s* Furthman *co-c* E Haller 1818m FPL *r* Par
Anzio (US) = SBARCO DI ANZIO, LO (1968)
ANZUKKO (1958) *d/s* Naruse
AOIRO KAKUMEI (1953) *d* Ichikawa Toho (= *The Blue Revolution*)
AOI-SANMYAKU (1949) *d* Imai Toho (= *Blue Mountains*)
AOS (1964) *d* Kuri anim 9min
AOZORA NI MAKU (1931) *d* Naruse (= *Weeping Blue Sky*)
APACHE (1954) *d* Aldrich *p* H Hecht *s* JR Webb *c* Laszlo *m* Raksin *w* Lancaster, Peters, McIntire *92min *r* UA
APACHE AMBUSH (1955) *d* Sears 68min Col
APACHE DRUMS (1951) *d* Fregonese *p* Lewton *75min U
APACHEN, DIE (1919) *d* Dupont 1590m
APACHES, LES (1904) *d* Méliès 40m
APACHE'S LAST BATTLE (1964) *d* Fregonese 70* 122min (= *Old Shatterhand/Les Cavaliers Rouges*)
APACHE TRAIL (1942) *d* Thorpe *a* Gibbons *w* Nolan, D Reed 66min MGM
APACHE UPRISING (1966) *d* Springsteen *co-a* Pereira TS* 90min Par
APACHE WARRIOR (1957) *d* Elmo Williams 74min Fox
APACHE WARRIOR (1955) *d/p* Corman *c* F Crosby *69min
APARADHI KAUN (1958) *d* Roy
APARAJITO (1957) *d/s* S Ray *c* Mitra *m* Shanker 127min (= *The Unvanquished*)
Apart from You = KIMI TO WAKARETE (1932)
APARTMENT, THE (1960) *d/p/co-s* B Wilder *co-as-p/co-s* Diamond *c* La Shelle *a* Trauner *w* Lemmon, MacLaine, MacMurray PV 125min Mir *r* UA
APARTMENT FOR PEGGY (1948) *d/s* Seaton *p* Perlberg *co-a* Wheeler *m* Raksin *w* Crain, Holden 99min Fox

APENAS UN DELINCUENTE (1947) d Fregonese 92min

Ape Regina, L' = STORIA MODERNA: L'APE REGINA, UNA (1963)

APFUL IST AB, DER (1948) d/co-s/co-lyr/fpl Käutner 121min

APOCALYPSE DE SAINT-SEVRES, L' (1949) d Grémillon sh

A PORTE CHIUSE (1960) d/co-st Risi co-s Di Palma w Ekberg, Caprioli 103min (= *Behind Closed Doors*)

Apostasy = HAKAI (1948)

APOTHEOSIS (1970) d Lennon, *Yoko Ono* *18min

APPALOOSA, THE (1965) d Furie co-a Golitzen w Brando, Fernandez S* 98min (= *Southwest to Sonora*)

APPARTEMENT DES FILLES, L' (1963) d/co-s/co-di Deville p Graetz 95min

Appassionata = TAKOVA LASKA (1959)

APPEARANCES (1921) Crisp 1344m FPL r Par

APPLAUSE (1930) d Mamoulian c Folsey 85min Par

APPLE, THE (1962) d/p/co-anim Dunning *8min

APPOINTMENT, THE (1969) d Lumet c Di Palma des Gherardi m Barry w Aimée, Sharif, Lenya *100min MGM

APPOINTMENT IN HONDURAS (1953) d J Tourneur p Bogeaus c Biroc m G Ford, Sheridan *75min RKO

APPOINTMENT IN LONDON (1953) d P Leacock w Bogarde, Forbes, Finch 96min

Approach of Autumn, The = AKI TACHINU (1960)

APPUNTI PER UN FILM INDIANO (1968) d Pasolini RAI

APPUNII SU UN FATTO DI CRONACA (1951) d Visconti cy Vasco Pratolini 8min

APRES L'AMOUR (1947) d M Tourneur 90min

APRES LE BAL, LE TUB OU LE BAIN DE LA PARISIENNE (1897) d Méliès 20m

APRIL APRIL (1935) d Sirk (as Sierk) 82min

APRIL FOLLY (1919) d Leonard w Davies 1524m

April Fools = BOLOND APRILIS (1957)

APRIL FOOLS, THE (1969) d S Rosenberg w Lemmon, Deneuve, Lawford, M Loy, Boyer 95min Fox

APRIL IN PARIS (1952) d D Butler rm GOLD DIGGERS of 1937 w D Day 101min WB

APRIL LOVE (1957) d Levin co-a Wheeler m A Newman, Mockridge w S Jones CS* 97min Fox

A PROPOS DE JIVAGO (1961) d Alexeiff anim 5min

A PROPOS DE NICE, POINT DE VUE DOCUMENTEE (1929) d/s/e Vigo c B Kaufman 42min

A PROPOS D'UNE RIVIERE (1955) d/s Franju 25min (= *Au Fil de la Rivière/La Saumon Atlantique*)

APUR SANSAR (1959) d/s S Ray c Mitra m Shankar 117min (= *The World of Apu*)

AQUARIUM (1956) d Pintoff

A QUELQUES JOURS PRES (1968) d/co-st Ciampi *100min (= *O Par Dnu*)

AQUILA NERA (1946) d/co-s Freda p De Laurentiis co-s Monicelli fn (*Dubrovsky*) *Alexander Pushkin* w Lollobrigida 109min (= *The Black Eagle*)

ARAB, THE (1915) d/s De Mille pc Lasky

ARAB, THE (1924) d Ingram c J Seitz w Novarro 2057m MGM

ARABESQUE (1966) d/p Donen c Challis m Mancini w Peck, Loren PV* 105min pc Donen r U

ARABIAN NIGHTS (1942) d John Rawlins p Wanger c Krasner w Montez, Sabu 86min U

Arabie Inconnue = ARABIE INTERDITE (1937)

ARABIE INTERDITE (1937) d/s/c Clément * sh (= *Arabie Inconnue*)

ARAKURE (1957) d Naruse w Mori (= *Untamed Woman*)

ARANYER DIN RATRI (1970) d/s/m S Ray 120min (= *Day and Nights in the Forest*)

ARANYSARKANY (1966) d Ranódy S* 93min (= *The Golden Kite*)

ARBEIT MACHT GLUCKLICH (1933) d Ruttmann rm ACCIAIO (1932) (= *Stahl*)

ARBEJDET ADLER (1914) ds Blom

ARBEJDET KALDER (1941) d/s B Henning-Jensen

Arbetaren = STREJKEN (1913)

ARBOLES DE BUENOS AIRES, LOS (1953) d/s Torre-Nilsson * sh

Arbre de Noel, L' = CHRISTMAS TREE, THE (1969)

ARBRE GENEALOGIQUE (1947) d Dunning

ARBRES AUX CHAMPIGNONS (1951, *uf*) d/c Markopoulos 16mm

ARCADIAN MAID, AN (1910) d griffith w Pickford, Sennett 1rl Bio

ARCADIANS, THE (1927) d/p/s Saville 2134m Gau

ARCHANDEL GABRIEL A PANI HUSA (1965) d/s/a Trnka fst Bocaccio *29min (= *The Archangel Gabriel and Mother Goose*)

Archangel Gabriel and Mother Goose, The = ARCHANGEL GABRIEL A PANI HUSA (1965)

ARCHIMEDE, LE CLOCHARD (1959) d/co-ad Grangier f idea Gabin co-ad/di Audiard w Gabin 79min

ARCHITECTE MAUDIT, CLAUDE-NICOLAS LEDOUX, L' (1954) d Kast mf Scarlatti, Couperin 16mm 19min

ARCHITECTURE ET LUMIERE (1953) d Colpi, *J-P Ganancia* part * 20min

ARCH OF TRIUMPH, THE (1948) d/co-s Milestone co-s H Brown fn Erich Maria Remarque c Metty a Manzies w Ingrid Bergman. Boyer. Laughton 120min r UA

ARCTIC HARVEST (1946) d/co-s L Gilbert 11min

ARDOISE, L' (1969) d/co-s/ci Bernard-Aubert S* 90min

ARE GA MINATO NO HI DA (1961) d Imai (= *Pan Chopali*)

ARENA (1953) d R Fleischer co-a Gibbons 3-D* 83min MGM

ARENA (1969) d/co-s Samsonov 10rs

ARENICOLE (1965) d Painlevé 16mm *20min

ARE PARENTS PEOPLE? (1925) d St Clair c Glennon w Menjou 72m FPL r UA

Are We All Murderers? = NOUS SOMMES TOUS LES ASSASSINS (1952)

ARGENT, L' (1928) d L'Herbier fn Zola w Helm, Artaud, Jules Berry, Rouleau 4400m

ARGENTINE LOVE (1924) d/p Dwan fst *Vicente Blasco Ibanez* 1820m FPL r Par

Argonauti, Gli = GIGANTI DELLA TESSAGLIA, I (1960)

ARGYLL SECRETS (1948) d Endfield 63min

ARIANE (1931) d Czinner s Mayer w Bergner 70min

ARIE PRERIE (1949) d/co-s/a Trnka cps Brdecka anim Pojar *590m (= *Prairie*)

ARI NO MACHI NO MARIA (1958) d Gosho S* 110min Sho (= *Maria of the Ant Village*)

ARISE MY LOVE (1940) d Leisen s C Brackett, Wilder c C Lang w Colbert, Milland 113min Par

ARISTIDE MAILLOL, SCULPTEUR (1943) d Lods

ARISTOCRATES, LES (1955) d/co-s de la Patellière w Fresnay, Joannon, Ronet 100min

ARISTOTELE (1971) d Brdecka, *Max Massimino Garnier* *14min

ARIZONA (1931) d Gseitz ad/di Riskin c Tetzlaff w J Wayne 7rs Col

ARIZONA (1940) d/p W Ruggles co-c J Walker m V Young w Holden, Arthur 127min Col

ARIZONA COWBOY, THE (1950) d Springsteen e Keller 67min Rep

ARIZONIAN, THE (1935) d C Vidor st/s D Nichols 75min RKO

ARKANSAS TRAVELER, THE (1938) d Santell co-a Dreier 83min Par

ARLESIENNE, L' (1931) d De Baroncelli w Vanel

ARLESIENNE, L' (1942) d M Allégret s Archard fn *Alphonse Daudet* w Raimu

ARMA BIANCA (1936) d/e Poggioli

ARMA DEI VIGLIACCHI, L' (1913) d Baldessarre Negroni w Ghione

ARMATA BRANCALEONE, L' (1965) d/co-s Monicelli c Di Palma dec Gherardi w Gassman, Catherine Spaak 130min

ARME A GAUCHE, L' (1965) d Sautet w Ventura 103min (= *Guns for the Dictator*)

ARMEE DES OMBRES, L' (1969) d/s Melville w Signoret, Cassel, Ventura *140min

AR MIN MODELL, DET (1946) d Molander s Lindström w Kjellin SF

ARMORED CAR ROBBERY (1950) d R Fleischer 68min RKO

ARMORED COMMAND (1961) d Haskin c E Haller w Keel 98min AA

Army = RIKUGUN (1944)

ARNAUD, LES (1967) d/co-s Joannon w Bourvil *95min (= *The Arnauds*)

Arnauds, The = ARNAUD, LES (1967)

ARNELO AFFAIR, THE (1947) d/s Oboler p Bressler co-a Gibbons w G Murphy 86min MGM

AROUND IS AROUND (1950) d McLaren, *Evelyn Lambert* *10min NFBC

AROUND THE CORNER (1930) d Glennon p Cohn di Swerling c J Walker 72min Col

AROUND THE WORLD (1943) d/p Dwan c Metty 81min RKO

AROUND THE WORLD IN 80 DAYS (1956) d Michael Anderson p Todd as-p/des Menzies co-s Poe, J Farrow fn Jules Verne co-c Lindon co-a Adam cr Bass m V Young w Niven, Newton, MacLaine, Carol, Carradine, C Coburn, Colman, Coward, Dietrich, Fernandel, Gielgud, T Howard, Keaton, Lorre, V McLaglen, J Mills, Raft, Roland, Romero, Sinatra, Gardner TAO* 175min r UA

AROUND THE WORLD IN 80 MINUTES WITH DOUGLAS FAIRBANKS (1931) d/co V Fleming co-d/p Fairbanks Sr m A Newman w Fairbanks Sr 80min r UA

AROUND THE WORLD UNDER THE SEA (1966) d/p Marton PV* 117min MGM

ARRANGEMENT, THE (1969) d/p/s/fn Kazan c Surtees w K Douglas, Dunaway, Kerr PV* 125min WB

ARRANGIATEVI (1959) d Bolognini w Toto, Caprioli 105min

ARRETEZ LES TAMBOURS (1961) d Lautner m Delerue 108min

ARRIERE SAISON (1951) d/p/st Kirsanov fpm *Baudelaire* 17min

ARRIVA DORELLIK (1967) d Steno *

ARRIVANO I TITANI (1962) d/co-s Tessari *110min (= *Sons of Thunder*)

Arrividerci Baby = DROP DEAD DARLING (1966)

ARRIVISTA, L' (1913) d Baldessarre Negroni w Ghione

Arrow, the (UK) = FRECCIA NEL FIANCO, LA (1943)

ARROWHEAD (1953) d/s Warren c Rennahan co-a Periera w Heston, Palance, Keith 105min Par

ARROWSMITH (1932) d J Ford p Goldwyn fn Sinclair Lewis c June a R Day m A Newman w Colman, H Hayes, M Loy 108min r UA

ARRUZA (1959-68 r 1971) d/p/s Boetticher co-c Ballard n Quinn *73min

ARS (1959) d/s/cy Demy sh

ARSENAL (1929) d/s Dovzhenko 1820m

ARSENAL STADIUM MYSTERY, THE (1939) d T Dickinson 87min

ARSENE LUPIN (1932) d Conway w J Barrymore, L Barrymore 84min MGM

ARSENE LUPIN CONTRE ARSENE LUPIN (1962) d/co-s Molinaro w Brialy S 110min

-ARSENIC AND OLD LACE (1944) d/p Capra s JJ Epstein c Polito m M Steiner w C Grant, Lorre, Horton 118min WB

ARSEN LUPIN UTOLSO KALANDJA (1921) d Fejos

ARS GRATIA ARTIS (1969) d Vukotic *9min

ARTE COBODA (1954) d Barreto sh

ARTE DI ARRANGIARSI, L' (1954) d/co-s Zampa w Sordi 91min (= *The Art of Getting Along*)

ARTERES DE FRANCE (1939) d J Epstein 22min

ARTFUL KATE (1911) co-d Ince w Pickford

ARTHUR HONEGGER (1955) d Rouquier sh

ARTHUR PENN, 1922– : THEMES AND VARIANTS (1970) d Robert PSB Hughes w Penn, Bancroft, Beatty part * 86min

ARTHUR RUBENSTEIN: L'AMOUR DE LA VIE (1968) d Reichenback, *S Gérard Patris* co-p/co-s/c Reichenback m Beethoven, Brahms, Chopin etc. w Arthur Rubenstein *92min (= *Love of Life*)

ARTHUR TAKES OVER (1948) d St Clair 64min Fox

ARTICLE 330, L' (1934) d/p Pagnol

ARTIFICES (1963) d Reichenbach

ARTIST AND THE FLOWER GIRL, THE (1899) p Paul 24m

ARTISTEN IN DER ZIRKUSKUPPEL: RATLOS, DIE (1968) d/p/s Kluge part * 103min (= *Artistes at the Top of the Big Top: Disorientated*)

ARTISTS AND MODELS (1937) d Walsh c Milner co-m V Young, Hollländer chor Prinz w Lupino, Benny 97min Par

ARTISTS AND MODELS (1955) d/co-s Tashlin p Wallis co-s Kanter c Fapp co-a Pereira w Martin, J Lewis, Maclaine, Malone, Ekberg VV* 109min Par

ARTISTS AND MODELS (1938) d Leisen c Tetzlaff co-a Pereira chor Prinz w Benny, J Bennett 90min Par

Artistes at the Top of the Big Top: Disorientated (UK) = ARTISTEN IN DER ZIRKUSKUPPEL: RATLOS, DIE (1968)

ARTIST'S DREAM (OR) THE DACHSHUND AND THE SAUSAGE, THE (1910 r 1913) d Bray

Art of Getting Along, The (US) = ARTE DI ARRANGIARSI, L' (1954)

ART OF LOVE, THE (1965) d Jewison p R Hunter c Metty co-a Golitzen w Garner, A Dickinson, D Van Dyke *96min U

ART OF VISION, THE (1965) d Brakhage 16mm si *270min (includes *Prelude: Dog Star Man* and *Dog Star Man: Parts I – IV*)

Arturo's Island = ISOLA DI ARTURO, L' (1962)

ARU YO FUTATABI (1956) d/s Gosho (= *Twice on a Certain Night*)

ARU YO NO TONOSAMA (1946) d Kinugasa w Yamada (= *Lord for a Night*)

ARYAN, THE (1916) d Reginald Barker p Ince co-c August w W Hart 1350m Tri

ARZT AUS HALBERSTADT, EIN (1969) d Kluge

ARZT STELLT FAST, DER (1966) d A Ford c Schuftan part *89min (= *Angeklagt nach Paragraph 218/The Doctor Speaks*)

ASAHI WA KAGAYAKU (1929) d Mizoguchi (= *The Rising Sun is Shining*)

A SANGE FRIA (1946) d Daniel Tinayre p/st Saslavsky

ASA NO HAMON (1952) d Gosho (= *Morning Conflicts*)

ASA NO NAMIKI-MICHI (1936) d/s Naruse (= *Dawn in the Boulevard*)

As a Wife, as a Woman = TSUMA TOSHITE ONNA TOSHITE (1961)

ASCENSEUR POUR L'ECHAFAUD (1957) d/co-s Malle c Decaë m Miles Davis w Moreau, Ronet 92min (= *Lift to the Scaffold*)

ASCHENPUTTEL (1922) d Reiniger fst Brothers Grimm anim 109m (= *Cinderella*)

ASH CAN FLEET, THE (1939) d Zinnemann co-m Amfitheatrof (1rl) MGM

Ashes = POPIOLY (1966)

Ashes and Diamonds = POPIOL I DIAMENT (1958)

ASHES OF DESIRE (1919) d Borzage 6rs S & A

ASHES OF VENGEANCE (1923) d/s F Lloyd c Gaudio w N Talmadge, Beery 3015m FN

ASHI NI SAWATTA KOUN (1930) d Ozu Sho (= *Luck Touched My Legs*)

ASHI NI SAWATTA ONNA (1952) d/co-s Ichikawa (= *The Woman who Touched the Legs*)

ASHITA NO ODORIKO (1939) d Yoshimura (= *Tomorrow's Dancers*)

ASHIZURI MISAKI (1954) *d* Yoshimura (= *Cape Ashizuri*)
Ash Wednesday Confession = PASTNACHTSBEICHTE, DIE (1960)
ASK ANY GIRL (1959) *d* Walters *p* Pasternak *s* Wells *c* Bronner *w* Niven, MacLaine CS* 101min MGM
ASK A POLICEMAN (1939) *d* Marcel Varnel *s* Grilliat *w* Hay 83min
ASLEEP AT THE SWITCH (1923) *d* Del Ruth *w* Turpin 2 rs Pat
AS LONG AS THEY'RE HAPPY (1955) *d* J Thompson *p* Stross *c* G Taylor 91min
As Long as You're Healthy (UK) = TANT QU'ON A LA SANTE (1965)
ASPHALT (1929) *d/p* May *c* Rittau 2575m
ASPHALT JUNGLE, THE (1950) *d/co-s* J Huston *co-s* Maddow *fn* Burnett *c* Rosson *co-a* Gibbons *m* Rozsa *w* Hayden, McIntire, Monroe 112min MGM
Assassin, The = ASSASSINO, L' (1961)
ASSASSIN A PEUR DE LA NUIT, L' (1942) *d* Delannoy *m* Auric *w* Jules Berry
ASSASSINAT DE McKINLEY (1901) *d* Zecca 50m Pat
ASSASSINAT DU PERE NOEL (1941) *d* Christian-Jacque *di* Charles Spaak (= *The Murder of Father Christmas*)
ASSASSINATION BUREAU, THE (1968) *d* Dearden *c* Unsworth *w* Noiret *110min Par
ASSASSIN EST A L'ECOUTE, L' (1948) *d* Raoul André *co-s/di/u* Blanche 88min
ASSASSIN EST DANS L'ANNUAIRE, L' (1961) *d/co-ad* Joannon *w* Fernandel 98min Gau
ASSASSIN HABITE AU 21, L' (1942) *d/co-s* Clouzot *c* Thirard *w* Fresnay 90min
ASSASSINO, L' (1961) *d/co-s* Petri *co-s* Guerra, Festa Campanile *c* Di Palma *m* Piccioni *w* Mastroianni, Presle 105min (= *The Assassin*)
ASSASSINIO A SARAJEVO (1968) *d* Lizzani
ASSASSINS D'EAU DOUCE (1947) *d/c* Painlevé
ASSASSINS DE L'ORDE, LES (1971) *d/co-ad* Carné *c* Badal *100min
ASSASSINS ET VOLEURS (1956) *d/s* Guitry *m* Jean Français 85min Gau
ASSAULT ON A QUEEN (1966) *d* Jack Donohue *p* Goetz *as-p/c* Daniels *w* Sinatra, Conte, Kjellin PV* 106min Par
ASSEDIO DELL'ALCAZAR, L' (1940) *d/co-st/co-s* Genina
AS SEEN THROUGH A TELESCOPE (1900) *d* G Smith
ASSIGNED TO DANGER (1948) *d* Boetticher *c* O'Connell 66min EL
ASSIGNMENT IN BRITTANY (1943) *d* Conway *a* Gibbons *w* Lawford 96min MGM
ASSIGNMENT PARIS (1952) *d* Parrish *co-p* Bressler *co-c* Guffey *m* Duning *w* D Andrews, G Sanders 85min Col
ASSIGNMENT TO KILL (1968) *d/s* S Reynolds *c* Lipstein *w* Gielgud PV* 73min WB
Assistant to His Highness = POPBOCNIK JEHO VYSOSTI (1933)
ASSOLUTO NATURALE, L' (1969) *d* Pietrangeli *p* Laurence Harvey *co-s* Bolognini *w* Laurence Harvey *86min (= *He and She/She and He*)
ASSZONY A TELEPEN (1962) *d* Fehér (= *Woman at the Helm*)
As the Clouds Scatter = KUMO GA CHIGIRERU TOKI (1961)
ASTONISHED HEART, THE (1950) *d* T Fisher, *Anthony Darnborough s/fpl/m/w* Coward 89min
ASTROLOGIE (1952) *d/co-m* Grémillon 22min (= *Miroir de la Vie*)
ASTROMATI (1963) *d* Vukotic anim (= *Astromuts*)
Astromuts = ASTROMATI (1963)
ASTRONAUTES, LES (1959) *d/s* Borowczyk, Marker anim* 14min
ASTUTO BARONE, L' (1948) *d/co-p/co-s/e(uc)/wv* Freda *w* Manfredi, Salce (1rl) (= *L'Eredita Contesa*)
ASU O TSUKURU HITOBITO (1946) *co-d* Kurosawa *w* Mori 81min Toho (= *Those Who Make Tomorrow*)
AS YOU DESIRE ME (1932) *d* George Fitzmaurice *fpl* Pirandello *c* Daniels *w* Garbo, Von Stroheim, M Douglas, Hopper 71min MGM
AS YOU LIKE IT (1936) *d* Czinner *fpl* Shakespeare *dec* Meerson *m* Walton *w* Bergner, Olivier 97min
AS YOUNG AS YOU FEEL (1951) *d* Harmon Jones *p/s* Trotti *fst* Chayefsky *c* Joe MacDonald *co-a* Wheeler *w* Monroe, Ritter, D Wayne 77min Fox
ASZONYFALO (1918) *d* Balasz
At a High Cost = DOROGOI TSENOI (1958)
ATLANTE, L' (1934) *d/co-s/co-di* Vigo *c* B Kaufman *m* Jaubert *w* M Simon, Parlo 89min (= *Le Chaland Qui Passe*)
ATCHI WA KOTCHI (1962) *d* Kuri anim 28min (= *Here and There*)
AT CONEY ISLAND (1912) *d/p* Sennett *w* Sennett, Normand ½rl Key
ATEL EINTERIÓR (1956) *d* P Weiss (= *The Studio of Dr. Faustus*)
ATELIER DE FERNAND LEGER (1954) *d* Borowczyk
At Five O'Clock in the Afternoon = A LAS CINCO DE LA TARDE (1960)

ATHENA (1954) *d* Thorpe *p* Pasternak *w* D Reynolds, J Powell, Reeves *96min MGM
ATHLETE INCOMPLET, L' (1932) *d* Autant-Lara *French version · of* LOVE IS A RACKET *w* Fairbanks Jr 72min MGM
AT IT AGAIN (1912) *d/p* Sennett *w* Sennett, Normand ½rl Key
At it Again = CAUGHT IN THE RAIN (1914)
AT LAND (1944) *d/w* Deren 15min
ATLANTIC (1929) *d/p* Dupont (*German and English versions*) *w* Carroll 2503m (= *Atlantik*)
Atlantic Story, An = OPOWIESC ATLANTYCKA (1955)
ATLANTIDE, L' (1921) *d/s* Feyder *fn* Pierre Benoît
Atlantide, L': French version of HERRIN VON ATLANTIS, DIE (1932)
Atlantik = ATLANTIC (1929)
ATLANTIS (1913) *d/s* Blom
Atlantis the Lost Continent = SIREN OF ATLANTIS (1948)
ATLANTIS, THE LOST CONTINENT (1948) *d/p* Pal *90min MGM
Atlantis, the Lost Continent = ANTINEA, L'AMANTE DELLA CITTA SEPOLTA (1961)
ATLAS (1961) *d/p* Corman CS* 79min
AT LAST! THAT AWFUL TOOTH (1902) *d* G Smith 15m
At Midnight = EJFELKOR
ATOLL K (1950) *d/st* Joannon *c* Thirard *m* Misraki *w* Laurel, Hardy 93min (= *Robinson Crusoe/Utopia*)
Atom Age Vampire (US) = SEDDOK, SON OF SATAN (1963)
ATOME QUI VOUS VEUT DU BIEN, UNE (1959) *d/m* Gruel anim* 14min
Atonement of Gosta Berling, The : sound version of GOSTA BERLINGS SAGA (1924)
A TOUS LES VENTS (1944) *d* Decaë
A TOUT CASSER (1967) *d/co-s* John Berry *w* Constantine *90min
A TOUT PRENDRE (1963) *d/s/e/w* Jutra *co-c* Brault 100min (= *Take It All*)
ATSUI YORU (1968) *d* Yoshimura (= *A Hot Night*)
At Sword's Point = A FIL DI SPADA (1952)
ATTACK! (1956) *d/p* Aldrich *s* Poe *c* Biroc *w* Palance, Marvin 104min *pc* Aldrich *r* UA
ATTACK OF THE CRAB MONSTERS (1957) *d/p* Corman *c* F Crosby 64min AA
ATTACK ON THE IRON CAST (1967) *d* Wendkos 90min UA
ATT ALSKA (1964) *d/s* J Donner *c* Nykvist *w* H Andersson, Cybulski 95min (= *To Love*)
ATTAQUE NOCTURNE (1931) *d* M Allégret
ATTENTION! HELICOPTERES (1962) *d* Schoendoerffer sh
AT THE CIRCUS (1939) *d* Edward Buzzell *p* Le Roy *m* Waxman *w* C, G, H Marx, Dumont 87min
AT THE CROSSROADS OF LIFE (1908) *st/w* Griffith Bio
At the Photographer's = KOD FOTOGRAFIA (1959)
ATTI DEGLI APOSTOLI (1968) *co-d/p/co-s/e* Rossellini *co-d* Renzo Rossellini Jr *f* Acts of the Apostles 342min RAI
ATTORE SCOMPARSO, L' (1941) *d/co-s* Zampa
ATTRAPEZ MON CHAPEAU (1906) *d* Etienne Arnaud *s* Feuillade
ATTSEGLA AR NODUAANDIGT (1938) *d* Fejos 12min SF
AT TWELVE O'CLOCK (1913) *d* Sennett *w* Normand 1rl Key
AT ZIJE NEBOZTIK (1935) *d/co-st/co-s* Fric (= *Long Love Kindness*)
AUBERGE ROUGE, L' (1923) *d* J Epstein *fn* Balzac Pat
AUBERGE ROUGE L' (1951) *d* Autant-Lara *st/co-s/co-di* Aurenche *co-s/co-di* Bost *w* Fernandel, Rosay, Carette 100min (= *The Red Inn*)
AU BOIS PIGET (1956) *d* Dewever sh
AU BONHEUR DES DAMES (1929) *d/co-s* Duvivier *co-c* Thirard *dec* Christian-Jacque *w* Parlo
AU BONHEUR DES DAMES (1943) *d/co-s* Cayette *fst* Emile Zola *m* Simon, Préjean 88min
Aubusson = AUBUSSON ET JEAN LURCAT (1946)
AUBUSSON ET JEAN LURCAT (1946) *d* Lods 15min (= *Aubusson*)
AU COEUR DE LA VIE (1962) *d/s* Enrico *fst* Ambrose Bierce 94min
    ep LE RIVIERE DU HIBOU 26min (= *Incident at Owl Creek/An Occurrence at Owl Creek Bridge*)
    ep CHIKAMAUGA
    ep L' OISEAU MOQUEUR (= *The Mocking Bird*)
AU COEUR DE L' ILE DE FRANCE (1953) *d/co-m* Grémillon 22min
AU COEUR DE L'ORAGE (1947) *d/cy* Le Chanois *co-c* Bourgoin 100min
AUDACE COLPO DEI SOLITI IGNOTI (1959) *d/co-s* M Loy *w* Manfredi, Gassman, Cardinale 104min (= *Fiasco in Milan*)
AU-DELA DES GRILLES (1949) *d* Clément *co-s* Zavattini, Cecchi D'Amico *ad/di* Aurenche, Bost *w* Gabin, I Miranda (= *La Mura di Malapaga*)
AU-DELA DES MURS (1968) *d/s/cy/e* Lamothe *30min
AU DELA DU VISIBLE (1943) *d* Decaë
AUF EIS GEUHRT (1915) *d/w* Lubitsch 1rl (= *A Trip on the Ice*)
Au fil de la rivière = A PROPOS D'UNE RIVIERE (1955)
Au Fou! = SATSUJINKYO SHIDAI (1966)

AUF WIEDERSEHN, FRANZISKA (1941) *d/co-s* Käutner 100min
AUF WIEDERSEHN, FRANZISKA (1957) *d* Käutner *rm* 1941 104min
AUGEN DER MUMIE MA, DIE (1918) *d* Lubitsch *c* Sparkuhl *w* Negri, Jannings 55min (= *The Eyes of the Mummy Ma*)
AU GRAND BALCON (1949) *d* Decoin *c* Hayer *m* Kosma *w* Fresnay 116min
AUGUST DER STARKE (1935) *d* Wegener 107min
AUGUSTIRAPSODI (1939) *d/p/s/c/e* Sucksdorff 7min
August Sunday = SRPNOVA NEDELE (1960)
AU HASARD, BALTHAZAR (1966) *d/s* Bresson *c* Cloquet *m* Wiener *mf* Schubert 95min (= *Balthazar*)
AU LARGE DES COTES TUNISIENNES (1948–49) *d* Cousteau
AU MILIEU DES CRATERES EN FEU (*c* 1952) *d* Tazieff 16mm
AU NOM DE LA LOI (1932) *d* M Tourneur *w* Vanel
Aunt Green, Aunt Brown and Aunt Lilac = TANT GRUN, TANT BRUN OCH TANT GREDELIN (1946)
AUNTIE MAME (1958) *d* Da Costa *s* Comden, A Green *m* Kaper *w* R Russell, Dumont TR* 143min WB
Auntie's Fantasies = TETICKA (1941)
Aunt Zita = TANTE ZITA (1967)
AU PAYS DE GEORGES SAND (1926) *d/p* J Epstein *c* Périnal
AU PAYS DE NEUFVE-FRANCE (1959–60) *d/e* René Bounière *p/cy* Perrault 380min TV
AU PAYS DE PORGY AND BESS (1957) *d* Reichenbach
AU PAYS DES GRANDES CAUSSES (1952) *d* Mitry
AU PAYS DES MAGES NOIRS (1947) *d/s/c/e* Rouch, Jean Sauvy, Pierre Ponty 16mm
AU PAYS DU ROI LEPREUX (1927) *d/s* Feyder
AU PAYS NOIR (1904) Zecca Pat
AU PETIT BONHEUR (1945) *d* L'Herbier *w* Darrieux 95min
AUPRES DE MA BLONDE (1944) *d* Dunning
AURAT (1939) *d* Mehboob (= *Woman*)
AU RAVISSEMENT DES DAMES (1913) *d* Machin 265m
AURORA (1966) *d* Reichenbach
AU ROYAUME DES CIEUX (1949) *d/s/ad* Duvivier *di* Jeanson *w* Reggiani 108min (= *Woman Hunt*)
AUS DEN ERINNERUNGEN EINES FRAUENARZTES (1922) *Part 1: d* Gerhard Lamprecht *co/s/w* Lupu-Pick *Part 2: d/w* Lupu-Pick
AU SECOURS! (1923) *d/co-s* Gance *co-s/w* Linder 487m (= *The Haunted House*)
AUSGESTOSSENER, EIN (1913) *Part 1:* DER JUNGE CHEF *d* May 4rs *Part 2:* DER EWIGE FRIEDE *d* May, *Konrad Wieder* 3rs
AUSSI LOIN QUE L'AMOUR (1971) *d/co-s* Rossif *w* Dalio *90min
AUSSI LONGUE ABSENCE, UNE (1961) *d* Colpi *co-s/fn* Duras *m* Delerue *w* Valli S 94min
AUSTERLITZ (1960) *co-d/s/di* Gance *co-d* Roger Richebé *co-c* Alekan *w* Carol, Caron, Cardinale, Marais, Palance, M Simon, Welles, Trintignant, De Sica FS* 166min (= *The Battle of Austerlitz*)
AUSTERNPRINZESSEN, DIE (1919) *d/co-s* Lubitsch *c* Sparkuhl 4rs *r* UFA (= *The Oyster Princess*)
AUSTREIBUNG, DIE (1925) *d* Murnau *p* Pommer *fpl* G Hauptman *c* Freund *w* Dieterle 1557m Dec (= *Driven From Home/Expulsion*)
AUS UNSEREN TAGE (1949) 82min
    ep VON HAMBURG BIS STRALSUND *d/s* Andrew Thorndike
Auteur d'une enquete: French version of VORUNTERSUCHUNG (1931)
AUTHENTIQUE PROCES DE CARL EMMANUEL JUNG, L' (1967) *d/p/st/s/di* Hanoun 62min
AUTOMABOULISME ET AUTORITE (1899) *d* Méliès 40m
AUTOMANIA 2000 (1964) *d/p* Halas *s* Batchelor anim* 9½min
AUTOMATION (1958) *d* Alexeieff anim
AUTOUR D'UNE CABINE (1895) *d* Reynaud (paper)
AUTOUR D'UN RECIF (1948–49) *d/p* Cousteau 15min
Autumn = OSEN (1940)
Autumn Afternoon, An = SAMMA NO AJI (1962)
AUTUMN LEAVES (1956) *d* Aldrich *p* Goetz *c* C Lang *w* J Crawford, Robertson, Miles 107min Col
AUX DEUX COLOMBES (1949) *d/s/fpl/w* Guitry 95min
AUX FRONTIERES DE L'HOMME (1953) *d* Vedrès, *Jean Rostand* 20min (= *The Border of Life*)
AUX LIONS LES CHRETIENS (1911) *d/s* Feuillade 276m
AUX YEUX DU SOUVENIR (1948) *d/co-s* Delannoy *co-st/co-s/di* Jeanson *m* Auric *w* Marais, Morgan 102min
Avalanche = NADARE (1952)
... A VALPARAISO (1962) *d/s* Ivens *cy* Marker part * 34min
AVANT LE DELUGE (1954) *d/co-s* Cayatte *co-st/co-s/di* Charles Spaak *c* Bourgoin *co-m* Van Parys *w* I Miranda, Vlady 80min
AVANZI DI GALERA (1954) *d* Cottafavi *m* Fusco *w* Constantine, Cortese 102min
AVARE, L' (1960) *d* Blue, *R Hermantier*
Avarice = YOKU (1958)
AVATOR (1915) *d* Gallone
AVE CAESAR (1919) *d* A Korda

312

AVEC ANDRE GIDE (1951) d M Allégret w Philipe 98min (= André Gide)

AVEC LA PEAU DES AUTRES (1966) d/co-s Deray co-s Giovanni co-a D'Eaubonne m Ventura TS* 100min (= To Skin a Spy)

AVEC LE SOURIRE (1936) d M Tourneur w Chevalier

AVENGING CONSCIENCE, THE (1914) d Griffith fpms Edgar Allan Poe w Marsh 6rs Mut

AVE MARIA DE SCHUBERT (1936) d Ophuls c Planer mf Schubert 5min

AVENTURAS DEL BARBERO DE SEVILLA (1954) d Vajda

AVENTURE A PARIS (1936) d M Allégret dec Lourié

AVENTURE DE CABASSOU, L' (1945) d Grangier w Fernandel

AVENTURE MALGACHE (1944, ur) d Hitchcock w Krampf sh

AVENTURES AU RADIO-CIRCUS (1953) d Michel

AVENTURES D'ARSENE LUPIN, LES (1957) d/co-s Becker c Séchan *103min

AVENTURES DE MALTRACE (1913) d Cohl anim

AVENTURES DE PIEDS-NICKELES, LES (1917) d Cohl, Benjamin Rabier anim

AVENTURES DE ROBERT MACAIRE, LES (1925) d J Epstein 3000m

AVENTURES DE TILL L'ESPIEGLE, LES (1956) d/co-s/co-ad/w Philipe p Ivens c Matras m Auric Defa

AVENTURES DU BARON MUNCHAUSEN, LES (1911) d Méliès 235m

AVENTURES EXTRAORDINAIRES DE JULES VERNES, LES (1952) d Aurel 31min

AVENTURES EXTRAORDINAIRES D'UN BOUT DE PAPIER (1909) d Cohl anim

AVENTURIER, L' (1934) d L'Herbier

AVENTURIERS, LES (1967) d/co-s Enrico co-s/co-di/fn Giovanni w Delon, Reggiani, Ventura S* 112min

AVEU, L' (1970) d Costa-Gavras fst Lise and Arthur London c Coutard a Evein w Montand, Signoret, Ferzetti *160min (= The Confession)

AVEUX LES PLUS DOUX, LES (1971) d/co-ad/co-di Molinaro c Coutard w Noiret *90min

AVIATOR, THE (1929) d Del Ruth w Horton 75min WB

AVION DE MINUIT, L' (1938) d/co-ad/co-di Kirsanov w Jules Berry

AVVENTURA, L' (1960) d/st/co-s Antonioni m Fusco w Ferzetti, Vitti 145min

Avventura ad Algeri = MAN FROM CAIRO, THE (1953)

AVVENTURA DI DIO, L' (1920) d Genina

AVVENTURA DI SALVATOR ROSA, UN' (1940) d/co-s/co-e Blasetti

AVVENTURE DI BENVENUTO CELLINI, LE (1963) d Freda S*

Avventure di Dox, Le = CACCIA ALL' UOMO (1961)

Avventure di Gerard, Le = ADVENTURES OF GERARD, THE (1970)

AVVENTURE DI GIACOMO CASANOVA, LE (1954) d/st/s Steno c Bava w Ferzetti *105min

AVVENTURE DI MANDRIN, LE (1952) d/co-st/co-s Soldati w Vallone 81min (= The Affair of Madame Pompadour/Mountain Brigand/Don Juan's Night of Love)

AVVENTURE E GLI AMORI DI MIGUEL CERVANTES, LE (1967) d V Sherman w Buchholz, Lollobrigida, J Ferrer 70 * 119min (= Cervantes/The Young Rebel)

AVVENTURIERO, L' (1967) d T Young w Quinn, Hayworth *110min (= The Rover)

AWAKE AT GENERATION (1969, uf) d Pennebaker 16mm*

AWAKENING, THE (1909) d Griffith s/w Pickford 1rl Bio

AWAKENING, THE (1928) d V Fleming c Barnes a Menzies m Reisenfeld w Banky 90min pc Goldwyn r UA

Awakening, the = PRZEBUDZENIE (1934)

AWARA (1951) d/p Raj Kapoor s Abbas w Raj Kapoor (= The Vagabond)

AWARD PRESENTATION TO ANDY WARHOL (1964) d J Mekas c Markopoulos w Warhol, J Mekas 16mm 12min

AWAY ALL BOATS (1956) d Pevney c Daniels co-a Golitzen w J Chandler VV* 114min U

AWFUL TRUTH, THE (1929) d Neilan 68min Pat

AWFUL TRUTH, THE (1937) d/p McCarey c J Walker w I Dunne, C Grant 91min Col

AZ ELITELT (1917) d Balasz

AZ EN LANYOM NEM OLYAN (1937) d Vajda 85min

AZ PRIJDE KOCOUR (1963) d/co-s Jasny CS* 105min (= The Cat)

AZUR (1951) d Pagliero

AZUREXPRESS (1938) d Balasz

BAAP BETE (1954) d Roy

BABBAGE (1968) d/s C and R Eames c C Eames 3½min

BABBIT (1934) d Keighley co-ad Busch fn Sinclair Lewis 74min FN

BABE RUTH STORY, THE (1948) d/p Del Ruth w Bendix, Trevor, Bickford 106min AA

BABES IN ARMS (1939) d Berkeley p Freed fmpl Rogers and Hart c June w Garland, Rooney 97min MGM

BABES IN BAGDAD (1952) d Ulmer w Godard, G Lee *72min

BABES IN TOYLAND (1934) d Gus Meins, Charles Rogers p Roach w Laurel, Hardy (9rs) r MGM (= Wooden Soldiers)

BABES IN BROADWAY (1941) d Berkeley p Freed co-m Edens w Garland, Rooney, Quine, M O'Brien (D Reed, as Adams) 118min MGM

Babette Goes to War (UK) = BABETTE S'EN VA-T-EN GUERRE (1959)

BABETTE S'EN VA-T-EN GUERRE (1959) d Christian-Jacque di Audiard c Thirard w Bardot, Blanche CS* 100min (= Babette Goes to War)

Baby Carriage, the (UK) = BARNWAGNEN (1962)

BABY DAY (1913) d Sennett w Normand ½rl Key

BABY DOLL (1956) d/p Kazan s/fpl (The Long Stay Cut Short and 27 Wagons Full of Cotton) T Williams c B Kaufman co-a Sylbert m K Hopkins w Malden, C Baker, Wallach 114min r WB

BABY FACE HARRINGTON (1935) d Walsh co-s N Johnson additional as Lederer 61min MGM

BABY FACE NELSON (1957) d Siegel co-s Mainwaring c Mohr w Rooney, Cook 85min r UA

BABY MINE (1928) d/p Leonard co-a Gibbons 1566m MGM

BABY ON THE BARGE, THE (1915) d/p Hepworth

BABY, THE RAIN MUST FALL (1965) d Mulligan c Laszlo m E Bernstein w McQueen, Remick, Murray 93min co-pc McQueen r Col

BACHELOR AND THE BOBBY-SOXER, THE (1947) d Reis p Schary m Harline w C Grant, M Loy, Temple 95min RKO

BACHELOR APARTMENT (1931) d/w L Sherman w I Dunne 83min RKO

BACHELOR BAIT (1934) d G Stevens 75min RKO

BACHELOR BRIDES (1926) d W Howard c Andriot 2015m pc De Mille

BACHELOR FATHER, THE (1931) d/co-p Leonard co-p Davies w Davies, Milland 90min MGM

BACHELOR FLAT (1961) d/co-s Tashlin p J Cummings c Fapp w Weld CS* 92min r Fox

BACHELOR GIRL, THE (1929) d Thorpe p Cohn c J Walker 66min Col

BACHELOR IN PARADISE (1961) d J Arnold co-s Kanter st Caspary c Ruttenberg m Mancini w Hope, Turner, Moorehead CS* 109min MGM

BACHELOR MOTHER (1939) d Kanin s Krasna co-e Wise w G Rogers, Niven, C Coburn 81min RKO

BACHELOR PARTY, THE (1957) d Delbert Mann p H Hecht s/fpl Chayevsky c La Shelle w Murray 93min r UA

Bachelors Beware = DOKUSHIN-SHA GOYOJIN (1930)

BACHELOR'S DAUGHTERS, THE (1946) d/p/s Stone c Sparkuhl w Trevor, Menjou 89min r UA

BACIO DI CIRANO, IL (1913) d Gallone

BACK DOOR TO HEAVEN (1939) d/p/s W Howard co-c Mohr 85min Par

BACKFIRE (1950) d V Sherman co-s Goff, Roberts w Lindfors, V Mayo, E O'Brien 91min WB

BACK FROM ETERNITY (1956) d J Farrow c Mellor m Waxman w Ryan, Steiger, Ekberg 97min RKO

BACK FROM THE DEAD (1957) d Warren c E Haller S 79min Fox

BACKGROUND TO DANGER (1943) d Walsh p Wald co-s W Burnett c Gaudio m Hollander w Raft, Greenstreet, Lorre 80min WB

BACK IN CIRCULATION (1937) d Enright p Wallis fst Adela Rogers St John w Blondell 9rs WB

BACKLASH (1956) d J Sturges p A Rosenberg s B Chase c Glassberg w Widmark, D Reed, McIntire *84min

BACK PAY (1922) d Borzage 1969m r Par

BACKSTAGE (1919) d/s/w Arbuckle w Keaton 2rs FPL

BACK STREET (1932) Stahl c Freund w I Dunne, Pitts, Darwell 93min U

BACK STREET (1941) d Stevenson c Daniels w Boyer 89min U

BACK STREET (1961) d D Miller p R Hunter c Cortez a Golitzen w S Hayward, Miles *107min U

BACK TO BATAAN (1945) d Dmytryck c Musuraca w J Wayne, Quinn 95min RKO

BACK TO GOD'S COUNTRY (1919) c J Walker 6rs

BACK TO GOD'S COUNTRY (1953) d Pevney w Hudson, Cochran 78min U

BACKTRACK (1969) d Earl Bellamy s B Chase w R Fleming, Lupino *95min U

BACON GRABBERS (1929) d Lewis Foster p Roach st McCarey w Laurel, Hardy, Harlow 2rs r MGM

BAD AND THE BEAUTIFUL, THE (1952) d Minnelli p Houseman s Schnee c Surtees co-a Gibbons m Raksin w K Douglas, Turner, Pidgeon, D Powell, Grahame, Roland 118min MGM

BAD COMPANY (1931) d/co-s Garnett c AC Miller w Carey 68min RKO

BAD DAY AT BLACK ROCK (1954) d J Sturges p Schary c Mellor co-a Gibbons m Previn w Tracy, Ryan,

Brennan, Marvin, Borgnine, A Francis CS* 81min MGM

Bad Eggs = ROTAGG (1946)

BAD FOR EACH OTHER (1953) d Rapper c Planer w Heston, L Scott 83min Col

BAD GIRL (1931) d Borzage 90min Fox

Bad Girl, The = FURYO SHOJO

BADLANDERS, THE (1958) d Daves p A Rosenberg fn (The Asphalt Jungle) Burnett w J Seitz w Ladd, Borgnine CS* 83min MGM

Bad Luck (UK) = NODLANDING (1952)

Bad Luck = ZEZOWATE SZCZESCIE (1959)

BAD LUCK BLACKIE (1949) d Avery p Quimby anim* 7min MGM

BAD MAN, THE (1930) d Badger c J Seitz w W Huston 77min FN

BAD MAN, THE (1941) d Thorpe w Beery, L Barrymore, Reagan 70min

BADMAN'S COUNTRY (1958) d Sears 68min WB

BAD MEN OF MISSOURI (1941) d Enright w Wyman, A Kennedy 74min WB

Bad One, The (UK) = SORORITY GIRL (1958)

BAD SEED, THE (1956) d/p LeRoy s Mahin fpl Maxwell Anderson c Rosson m North 129min MGM

BAD SISTER (1931) d Hobart Henley c Freund w Pitts, Bogart, B Davis 73min U

Bad Sleep Well, the = WARUI YATSU HODO YOKU NEMURU (1960)

BAD DE ENS FASADER (1961) d P Weiss (= Behind Uniform Facades)

BAGNAIA, PAESE ITALICO (1949) d Maselli

Bag of Fleas, A = PYTEL BLECH (1962)

BAGUE, LA (1947) d Resnais w Marceau 16mm sh

BAHAMA PASSAGE (1941) d/p Edward H Griffith w Carroll, Hayden *83min Par

BAIE DES ANGES, LA (1962) d/s Demy c Rabier dec Evein m Legrand w Moreau CS 90min (= Bay of Angels)

BAIGNADE IMPOSSIBLE, LA (1901) d Zecca 50m Pat

BAILLON NEE, LA (1924) d Gaston Roudès w Fresnay

BAIN D'X (1956) d Alexeiff anim

BAISERS VOLES (1968) d/co-s Truffaut co-s De Givray w Léaud, Seyrig *91min co-pc Truffaut (= Stolen Kisses)

BAIT, THE (1920) d M Tourneur 1612m

Baited Trap, The (UK) = TRAP, THE (1958)

BAJAJA (1950) d/co-s/a Trnka anim Pojar *81min (= Prince Bayaya)

BAKARUHABAN (1957) d Feher c Badal 92min (= A Sunday Romance)

BAKER AND THE SWEEP, THE (1898) d G Smith

BAKINTSY (1938) d/co-s Turin 104min (= Men of Baku)

BAKUSHU (1951) d Ozu (= Early Summer)

BAKUSO (1967) d Teshigahara 74min (= Explosion Course)

BAL, LE (1931) d William Thiele w Darrieux

BALACLAVA (1930) d Elvey Milton Rosmer 11min

BALADA O TROBENTI I OBLAKU (1961) d Stiglic 75min (= Ballad of the Trumpet and the Cloud)

BALAO, L OU DES PAS AU PLAFOND (1913) d/s Jasset c Andriot

BALATUM (1938) d Alexeieff anim

BALCON DE LA LUNA, EL (1963) d Saslavsky

BALCONY, THE (1963) d/co-p Strick co-p/s Maddow fpl Jean Genet c Folsey w Winters 86min

BAL DU COMTE D'ORGEL, LE (1970) d/co-s M Allégret fn Raymond Radiguet co-di Francoise Sagan c Matras w Brialy, Presle *95min

BALLETPRIMADONNAN (1916) d Stiller 1072m (= Wolo Czarwieuko)

BALKED AT THE ALTAR (1908) d Griffith w Sennett 1rl Bio

BALLADA O SOLDATYE (1959) d/co-s Chukhrai 90min (= Ballad of a Soldier)

Ballad of the Narayama, The = NARAYAMA BUSHI-KO (1958)

Ballad of the Trumpet and the Cloud = BALADA O TROBENTI I OBLAKU (1961)

Ball at the Anjo House, A = ANJO-KE NO BUTOKAI (1948)

BALLAD OF CABLE HOGUE, THE (1970) d Peckinpah Ballard m Goldsmith *121min WB

Ballad of Joe Hill, The = JOE HILL

BALLAD OF JOSIE, THE (1968) d A McLaglen c Krasner co-a Golitzen w D Day, G Kennedy *102min U

BALLADE POUR UN VOYOU (1961) s Moussay

Ballad of a Soldier = BALLADA O SOLDATYE (1959)

Ballad of a Workman = FUTARI DE ARUITA IKUSHUNJU (1962)

BALLE AU COEUR UNE (1965) d/co-s Pollet co-s Kast m Theodorakis CS* 90min (= A Shot in the Heart)

BALLE DANS LE CANON, UNE (1958) d Deville, Charles Gérard 85min (= A Slug in the Heater)

BALLERINA (1939) d Benoit-Lévy

Ballerina (UK) = ROSEN FUR BETTINA (1956)

BALLERINE (1936) d Machaty

BALLET DANSERINDEN (1911) d Blom, Urban Gad w Nielsen

BALLETTENS DATTER (1913) d/s Madsen

Ballet Girl, The (UK) = MADEL VOM BALLET, DAS (1918)

Ballet Girl = BALLETTENS BORN (1954)
BALLET MECANIQUE (1924) d Leger, *Dudley Murphy* m Antheil
BALLET-OOP (1954) d Cannon * pc UPA r Col
BALLETTENS BORN (1954) d A Henning Jensen s B Henning Jensen 23min (= *Ballet Girl*; wv Bloom)
BALL IM METROPOL (1937) d/co-s Wisbar 84min
BALL OF FIRE (1941) d Hawks p Goldwyn co-st Wilder, co-s Brackett c Toland m A Newman w G Cooper, Stanwyck, D Andrews, Duryea, Haydn, Cook 111min r RKO
BALLON ROUGE, LE (1956) d/s Lamorisse c Sechan *36min (= *The Red Balloon*)
BALLOON (1960) co-d Pennebaker, R Leacock 16mm 28min
BALLOONATICS, THE (1923) d/s Keaton, Cline w Keaton 2rs pc Keaton
BALLYHOO BUSTER, THE (1928) d Thorpe w Brennan 1464m r Pat
Baltic Deputy = DEPUTAT BALTIKI (1937)
BAMBI (1942) p Disney *69min r RKO
BAMBINI (1951) d Maselli
BAMBINI AL CINEMA (1956) d Maselli sh
BAMBINI CI GUARDANO, I (1942) d/co-s De Sica co-s Zavattini (= *The Children are Watching Us*)
BAMBINI IN CITTA (1946) d Comencini 15min (= *Children in Cities*)
Bambino = TAXI DI NOTTE (1950)
BAMBOLE, LE (1964) 111min (= *Four Kinds of Love*)
ep LA TELEFONATA d Risi w Manfredi (= *The Telephone*)
ep IL TRATTATO DI EUGENETICA d Comencini st Steno (= *A Treatise on Eugenics*)
ep LA MINISTRA d Rossi w Vitti (= *The Supper*)
ep MONSIGNOR CUPIDO d Bolognini w Tamiroff, Lollobrigida
BAMBOO BLONDE, THE (1946) d A Mann 68min RKO
BAMBOO CROSS, THE (1955) d J Ford w Wyman 27min TV
Bamboo Doll, The = ECHIZEN TAKENINGYO (1963)
BAMBUALDERN PA MANTAIVEI (1957) d Fejos 11min SF
BAMSE (1969) d/co-s Mattsson w Jacobsson, Lindström *112min (= *The Teddy Bear*)
BANDA CASAROLI, LA (1962) d Vancini w Brialy
BANDA DELLE CIFRE, LA (1915) d/s/w Ghione (*3 parts*)
BANDE A PART (1964) d/s Godard c Coutard m Legrand w Karina 95min (= *Band of Outsiders/The Outsiders*)
BANDEIRANTES, OS (1960) d/co-s/co-di Camus *109min
BANDERA, LA (1935) d/co-s Duvivier co-s/di Charles Spaak m Weiner w Gabin, Annabella, P Renoir, Romance, Modot 100min
BANDIDO (1956) d R Fleischer c Laszlo m M Steiner w Mitchum, Roland 92min CS* r UA
BANDINI (1963) d Roy 120min
Bandit, The = CANGACEIRO, O (1953)
Bandit, The (US) = AMANTE DI GRAMIGNA, L' (1969)
BANDIT BUSTER, THE (1926) d/s Thorpe 1361m
Bandit General, The = TORCH, THE (1950)
BANDITI A MILANO (1967) d Lizzani p De Laurentiis w Thulin TS* 120min
BANDITI A ORGOSOLO (1961) d/p/co-s/c De Seta 98min
Bandit Island of Korabei = RETURN TO TREASURE ISLAND (1954)
BANDITO, IL (1946) d/st/co-s Lattuada p De Laurentiis c Tonti w Magnani
Bandits in Sardinia (US) = BARBAGIA (1969)
BANDITS OF THE WEST (1953) d Keller 54min Rep
BAND OF ANGELS (1957) d Walsh co-s Goff, Roberts c Ballard m M Steiner w Gable, De Carlo, Poitier S* 126min WB
Band of Ninja = NINJA BUGEICHO (1967)
Band of Outsiders (US) = BANDE A PART (1964)
BANDOLERO! (1968) d A McLaglen m Goldsmith c Clothier w J Stewart, Martin, G Kennedy, Welch PV* 106min Fox
BAND WAGON, THE (1953) d Minnelli p Freed as-p Edens s Comden, A Green co-a Gibbons chor Kidd w Astaire, Charisse (Gardner) *112min MGM
BANGIKU (1954) d Naruse (= *Late Chrysanthemums*)
BANJO (1947) d R Fleischer 68min RKO
BANJO ON MY KNEE (1936) d Cromwell as-p/s N Johnson w McCrea, Stanwyck, Brennan 80min Fox
BANK, THE (1915) d/s Chaplin c Totheroh w Chaplin, Purviance 2rs S & A
BANKA (1957) d Gosho w Mori (= *Elegy of the North*)
Bank Breaker, The = KALEIDOSCOPE (1966)
BANK DICK, THE (1940) d Cline s Fields (ps Mahatma Kane Jeeves) c Krasner w Fields 74min U
BANK HOLIDAY (1938) d C Reed w Lockwood 69min
BANKRAUB IN DER RUE LATOUR 61 (1961) d/w Jürgens 91min
BANNERLINE (1951) d Weis fst (*A Rose Is Not a Rose*) Raphaelson c Lipstein co-a Gibbons w L Barrymore 88min MGM
BANQUET DES FRAUDEURS (1952) d Storck tech adviser Cayatte 101min (= *The Smuggler's Ball*)
BANSHUN (1949) d/co-s Ozu 112min Sho (= *Late Spring*)
BANYA (1962) Yutkevich, *Anatoli Karanovich* fpl *Mayakovsky* anim S* 36min (= *The Bath House*)
BARABBAS (1953) d/co-s Sjöberg fn Per Lagerkvist co-c Strindberg, Nykvist w Dahlbeck, Kulle San
BARABBAS (1962) d R Fleischer p De Laurentiis fn *Per Lagerkvist* s Fry c Tonti a Chiari w Quinn, Mangano, Gassman, A Kennedy, Palance, Borgnine, Cortese 70TR* 134min r Col
BARA EN KYPARE (1960) d Kjellin * (= *Only a Waiter*)
BARA EN MOR (1949) d/co-s Sjöberg w Dahlbeck, von Sydow 99min SF (= *Only a Mother*)
BARA-GASSEN (1950) d Naruse
BARA IKUTABI (1955) d/s Kinugasa (= *A Girl Isn't Allowed To Love*)
BARAJAS, AEROPUERTO INTERNACIONAL (1950) d/s Bardem (= *Aeropuerto*)
BARANDE HAV (1951) d Mattsson d Strindberg w Dahlbeck, Jacobsson, Kjellin 108min (= *Rolling Sea*)
BARBABLU (1941) d/s Bragaglia
BARBAGIA (1969) d Lizzani p De Laurentiis S* 105min (= *Bandits in Sardinia*)
BARBARA (1961) d Wisbar w H Andersson *98min Ufa
BARBARELLA (1967) d Vadim p De Laurentiis c C Renoir w J Fonda, Hemmings, Marceau PV* 98min
BARBARIAN, THE (1933) d/p S Wood co-s/co-di Loos c Rosson m Stothart w M Loy, Novarro, Hopper 67min MGM
BARBARIAN AND THE GEISHA, THE (1958) d J Huston c C Clarke co-a Wheeler m Friedhofer w J Wayne CS* 102min Fox
Barbarians, The = REVAK, LO SCHIAVO DI CARTAGINE (1960)
BARBARY COAST (1935) d Hawks p Goldwyn st/s B Hecht, MacArthur c June a R Day m A Newman w M Hopkins, Robinson, McCrea, Brennan, Carey 91min UA (= *Port of Wickedness*)
BARBARY COAST GENT (1944) d Del Ruth a Gibbons w Beery, Carradine 87min MGM
BARBARY SHEEP (1917) d M Tourneur 6rs
BARBE-BLEU (1901) d Méliès fst *Charles Perrault* 225m
BARBE-BLEU (1936) d Painlevé, *René Bertrand* m Jaubert *10min
BARBED WATER (1969) d *Adrian J Wesley-Walker* ex-p Holt *50min
BARBED WIRE (1927) d/co-s *Rowland V Lee* p Pommer as-p BP Schulberg co-s/ad Furthman c Glennon w Negri, C Brook 2008m Par-FPL
BARBEREUSE (1916) d/s Gance
BARBER SHOP, THE (1933) d *Arthur Ripley* st/w Fields 2rs Par
BARBIER DE SEVILLE, LE (1904) d Méliès fpl *Beaumarchais* 420 m
BARBONI (1946) d Risi
BARBORA HLAVSOVA (1943) d Fric
BARBOUZES, LES (1965) d Lautner w Blanche, Darc, Ventura 109min
BARBUJAN A PANDRHOLA (1960) d/s Fric * (= *A Compact with Death*)
BARCELONA, VIEJA AMIGA (1961) d Grau
BAR DE JUFFROUW HEYENS, LA (1928) d/s/c/e Ivens 200m
BARDELYS THE MAGNIFICENT (1926) p/dd K Vidor c Daniels co-a Gibbons, R Day w J Gilbert 2610m MGM
BAR DI GIGI, IL (1961) d Baldi
BARDOT EN AMERIQUE (1965) d Reichenbach ORTF
BARE FISTS (1919) d J Ford w Carey 1676m U
BAREFOOT CONTESSA, THE (1954) d/p/s J Mankiewicz c Cardiff w Bogart, Gardner, E O'Brien, Cortese *128min r UA
BARGAIN OF THE CENTURY, THE (1933) d C Chase p Roach w C Chase, Pitts (2rs) MGM
BARIERA (1966) d/s Skolimowski m Komeda 83min (= *Barrier*)
BARIRI (1957) d Olmi *18min
BARKLEYS OF BROADWAY, THE (1949) d Walters p Freed st/s Comden, A Green co-a Gibbons chor R Alton w Astaire, G Rogers 109min MGM
BARNABY RUDGE (1915) d/p/ad Hepworth fn *Dickens* 1524m
BARNACLE BILL (1941) d Thorpe co-s H Butler a Gibbons m Kaper w Beery MGM
BARNACLE BILL (1957) d Frend p Balcon c Slocombe w Guinness 87min
BARN AV SOLEN (1955) d Skouen
BARNET (1912) d Stiller w Sjöstrom 635m
BARNET (1940) d/co-s Christensen (= *The Child*)
BARNET HORSE FAIR (1896) p Paul 43m
BARNETS MAGT (1914) d Madsen
BARNEY OLDFIELD'S RACE FOR LIFE (1913) d/p/w Sennett w Normand 1rl Key
BARNVAGNEN (1962) d/s Widerberg c Troell 91min (= *The Pram/The Baby Carriage*)
BARNYARD, THE (1923) d/s/w Semon 2rs Vit
BARNYARD BATTLE (1929) d Iwerks p Disney anim 1rl
BARON DE CRAC, LE (1913) d Cohl anim
BARON DE L'ECLUSE, LE (1959) d/co-s Delannoy fn *Georges Simenon* di Audiard w Gabin, Presle, Desailly 95min
BARONESS AND THE BUTLER, THE (1938) d W Lang p Zanuck co-s Trotti c AC Miller w W Powell 75min Fox
BARON FANTOME (1943) d/s Serge de Poligny di/wv Cocteau
Baron Munchhausen = BARON PRASIL (1961)
BARON OF ARIZONA, THE (1950) d/s Fuller c Howe w Price 93min
BARON PRASIL (1940) d Fric
BARON PRASIL (1961) d/s Zeman *80min (= *Baron Munchhausen*)
Baron-X = X-PARONI (1964)
BAROUD (1933) d/p/co-s/co-st Ingram co-c Burel co-dec Wakhévitch w Ingram 80min
BARQUERO (1969) d G Douglas *114min r UA
BARRABAS (1919) d/s Feuillade 1: La Maîtresse du juif errant (1579m); 2: La Justice des hommes (788m); 3: La Villa des glycines (825m); 4: Le Stigmate (798m); 5: Noëlle Maupré (797m); 6: La Fille du condamné (795m); 7: Les Ailles du Satan (800m); 8: Le Manoir Mystérieux (820m); 9: L'Otage (815m); 10: L'Oubliette (780m); 11: Le Revenant (782m); 12: Justice (782m)
BARRAGE DE L'AIGLE, LE (1946) d Leenhardt 15min
BARRAGE DU CHATELOT (1953) d Colpi
BARRAVENTO (1961) d/co-s Rocha 72min
BARRETTS OF WIMPOLE STREET, THE (1934) d Franklin co-s D Stewart c Daniels m Stothart w Shearer, March, O'Sullivan, Laughton 110min MGM
BARRETTS OF WIMPOLE STREET, THE (1957) d/p Franklin rm 1934 c F Young m Kaper w J Jones, Gielgud CS* 104min MGM
BARRICADE (1939) d Ratoff c Freund w Faye 71min Fox
Barrier = BARIERA (1966)
BARRINGS, DIE (1955) d/co-s Thiele w Dagover, Tiller 107min
BARRIO (1947) d Vajda
Bartered Bride, The (UK) = VERKAUFTE BRAUT, DIE (1932)
Baruch = ALTE GESETZ, DAS (1923)
BASAE (1964) d Pollet cy Astruc 16mm 10min
BAS-FONDS, LES (1936) d/co-ad/co-di J Renoir co-ad/co-di Charles Spaak fn *Maxim Gorki* c Bachelet co-dec Lourié m Wiener w Jouvet, Gabin 90min
BASHFUL BACHELOR, THE (1941) d St Clair w Pitts 75min RKO
BASHFUL JIM (1925) d Cline s Sennett
BASILISCHI, I (1963) d *L Wertmuller* c Di Venanzo 85min (= *The Lizards*)
BASILISK, THE (1914) d/p/s/c Hepworth 2500ft
BASTA GUARDALA (1971) d/co-s Salce co-s Steno w Salce *97min
BASTARDI, I (1968) d/co-s Tessari w Hayworth *102min (= *Sons of Satan/The Cats*)
BAT, THE (1926) d/p/ad *Roland West* c Edeson a Menzies w Fazenda 8219ft r UA
BATAAN (1943) d Garnett a Gibbons m Kaper w R Taylor, G Murphy, Mitchell, Nolan, R Walker 114min MGM
BATAILLE DE FRANCE, LA (1964) d/co-s Aurel
BATAILLE DE LA VIE, LA (1950) d Daquin sh
BATAILLE DE SAN SEBASTIAN, LA (1967) d Verneuil s JR Webb c Thirard w Quinn FS* 111min (= *Guns for San Sebastian*)
BATAILLE DES DIX MILLIONS, LA (1970) d Marker *Valerie Mayoux* s/n Marker 16mm 58min
BATAILLE DU RAIL, LA (1946) d/s Clément c Alekan 80min
BATAILLE SUR LE GRAND FLEUVE (1951) d/c Rouch *16mm (= *Chasse à l'hippopotame*) 45min
BATEAU D'EMILE, LE (1962) d De la Patellière s Audiard w Girardot, Ventura, Brasseur, M Simon FS 98min
BATEN (1961) d Troell (= *The Boat*)
Bath Harem, The = UKIYU BURO (1929)
Bath House, The=BANYA (1962)
BATHING BEAUTY (1944) d G Sidney p J Cummings gagman Keaton (uc) co-a Gibbons w Esther Williams, Rathbone, Dumont 101min MGM
BATIR A NOTRE AGE (1958) d/pc Leenhardt 22min
BATISSEURS, LES (1938) d J Epstein
BATMAN DRACULA (1964) d Warhol 16mm si 120min
BATTAGLIA DI ALGERI, LA (1961) d/co-st/co-m Pontecorvo 135min (= *The Battle of Algiers*)
BATTAGLIA DI MARATONA, LA (1959) co-d J Tourneur co-d/p/co-s *Bruno Vailati* co-d/c Bava co-dec Chiari w Reeves FS* 92min (= *The Giant of Marathon*)
BATTEMENTS DE COEUR (1939) d Decoin m Misraki w Darrieux 93min
BATTICUORE (1938) d/co-s Camerini w De Laurentiis
BATTLE, THE (1911) d Griffith 1rl Bio
BATTLE AT ELDERBUSH GULCH, THE (1913) d Griffith w L Gish, Marsh 2rs Bio
BATTLE CIRCUS (1953) d/s R Brooks p Berman c J Alton w Bogart, Allyson 87min MGM
BATTLE CRY (1955) d Walsh s/fn *Leon Uris* c Hickox m M Steiner w Heflin, A Ray, Malone, A Francis CS* 149min WB
BATTLE CRY OF PEACE, THE (1915) d/s/e Blackton w N Talmadge 9rs Vit
BATTLEFIELD (1899) p Paul 30m
Battle for Anzio, The = SBARCO DI ANZIO, LO (1968)
BATTLEGROUND (1949) d Wellman p Schary w V Johnson, G Murphy, Montalban 121min MGM
BATTLE HYMN (1957) d Sirk p R Hunter c Metty co-a Golitzen w Hudson, Duryea CS* 108min U

Battle Inferno = HUNDE, WOLLT IHR EWIG LEBEN (1959)

Battle of Algiers, The = BATTAGLIA DI ALGERI, LA (1965)

Battle of Austerlitz, The = AUSTERLITZ (1960)

BATTLE OF BRITAIN, THE (1943) *co-d* *Capra* *m* Tiomkin *n* W Huston 55min US Army

BATTLE OF BRITAIN, THE (1969) *d* Hamilton *co-p* Saltzman *co-c* F Young *co-m* Walton *w* Caine, T Howard, Jurgens, Olivier, Plummer, M Redgrave, R Richardson PV* 131min *r* UA

BATTLE OF BROADWAY (1938) *d* G Marshall *w* V McLaglen, Darwell 84min Fox

BATTLE OF CHINA, THE (1944) *d* Capra, Litvak *m* Tiomkin *n* W Huston US Army

Battle of Gallipoli (US) = TELL ENGLAND (1931)

BATTLE OF GETTYSBURG, THE (1914) *d* Ince *w* Borzage 1700m

Battle of Kawanakajima, The = KAWANAKAJIMA KASEN (1941)

BATTLE OF MIDWAY, THE (1942) *d/c/co-e* J Ford *co-e* Parrish *co-cy* J Ford, D Nichols *m* A Newman *wv* H Fonda, Darwell, Crisp 20min *r* Fox

BATTLE OF PARIS (1929) *d* Florey *w* C Ruggles, Lawrence 69min Par

BATTLE OF ROGUE RIVER (1954) *d* Castle *p* Katzman *70min Col

BATTLE OF RUSSIA, THE (1943) *d* Litvak *m* Tiomkin *n* W Huston 80min

BATTLE OF SAN PIETRO, THE (1944) *d/s/co-c/n* J Huston *m* Tiomkin 32min US Signal Corps

BATTLE OF SANTIAGO BAY, THE (1898) *d* Blackton

Battle of Stalingrad = STALINGRADSKAYA BITVA (1949)

Battle of Stalingrad = STALINGRADSKAYA BITVA (1970)

BATTLE OF THE BULGE (1966) *d* Annakin *p/co-s* Sperling, Yordan *c* Hildyard *a* Lourié *w* H Fonda, Ryan, D Andrews PV* 163min WB

BATTLE OF THE CENTURY, THE (1928) *d* Bruckman *supn* McCarey *p/s* Roach *w* Laurel, Hardy 2rs MGM

BATTLE OF THE CORAL SEA (1959) *d* Wendkos *m* Gold *w* Robertson 86min Col

Battle of the Giants = BORBA GIGANTOV (1926)

BATTLE OF THE RED MEN, THE (1912) *d* Ince *w* Conway (*2 parts*)

BATTLE OF THE RIVER PLATE, THE (1956) *d/p/s* M Powell, Pressburger *c* Challis *w* Finch (J Schlesinger) VV* 119min *r* JAR (= *Pursuit of the Graf Spee*)

BATTLE OF THE SEXES, THE (1914) *d* Griffith *c* Bitzer *w* L Gish, Crisp 5rs Mut

BATTLE OF THE SEXES, THE (1928) *d* Griffith *rm* 1914 *c* Struss, Bitzer *w* Hersholt 2480m *r* UA

BATTLE OF THE SEXES, THE (1960) *d* Crichton *fst* (*The Catbird Seat*) *James Thurber* *c* F Francis *e* Holt *w* Sellers 84min *r* BL

BATTLE OF THE VILLA FIORITA, THE (1964) *d/p/s* Davies *c* Morris *w* M O'Hara PV* 105min *r* WB

BATTLE OF WHO RUN, THE (1913) *d/p/w* Sennett *w* Normand $\frac{1}{2}$rl Key

Battleship Potemkin = BRONENOSETS 'POTYOMKIN' (1925)

BATTLING BUDDY (1924) *d* Thorpe 1402m

BATTLING BUTLER (1926) *d/p/w* Kenton 2124m *r* MGM

Bay of Angels = BAIE DES ANGES, LA (1962)

Beach, The (UK) = SPIAGGIA, LA (1953)

Beachcomber, The = VESSEL OF WRATH (1938)

BEACHHEAD (1954) *d* Heisler *p* HW Koch *w* Curtis *89min *r* UA

BEACH RED (1967) *d/p/w* Wilde *105min *r* UA

Bear, The = L'OURS (1960)

Bear and the Doll, The (US) = OURS ET LA POUPEE, L' (1970)

Beard of Strength = HIGE NO CHIKARA (1931)

BEAR ESCAPE, A (1912) *d/p/w* Sennett $\frac{1}{2}$rl Key

BEAR FACTS (1938) *d* G Douglas (1rl)

BEAR FEAT (1949) *d* C Jones anim* 7min WB

BEARS AND BAD MEN (1918) *d/s/w* Semon 2rs Vit

Beast, The = DUVAD (1959)

BEAST FROM 20,000 FATHOMS, THE (1953) *d* Lourié *st* Bradbury *c* JL Russell 80min WB

BEAST WITH FIVE FINGERS, THE (1947) *d* Florey *m* M Steiner *w* Lorre 88min WB

BEAT GENERATION, THE (1959) *d* Haas *p* Zugsmith *co-s* Matheson *w* Cochran, Danton S 95min MGM

BEAT GIRL (1959) *d* Greville *c* Lassally *m* Barry 85min

BEATNIK ET LE MINET, LE (1966) *d* Leenhardt

BEATRICE (1921) *d* Brenon

BEATRICE CENCI (1956) *d/co-s/co-e* Freda *w* Presle CS* 95min (= *I Maledetti*)

BEAT THE DEVIL (1954) *d/p/co-s* J Huston *co-p* Woolf Bros *as-p* Clayton *di Truman Capote* *c* Morris *w* Bogart, J Jones, Lollobrigida, Lorre 100min *r* UA

Beat 13 = 13 REVIR (1946)

BEAU BROADWAY (1928) *d* St Clair *a* Gibbons 1840m MGM

BEAU BRUMMEL (1924) *d* *Harry Beaumont* *w* J Barrymore, Astor 3018m WB

BEAU BRUMMEL (1954) *d* C Bernhardt *c* Morris *w* S Granger, E Taylor, Ustinov *111min MGM

Beau Chumps = BEAU HUNKS (1931)

BEAU GESTE (1926) *d* Brenon *m* Reisenfeld *w* Colman, W Powell, McLaglen part * 3231m FPL *r* Par

BEAU GESTE (1939) *d/p* Wellman *c* Sparkuhl *co-a* Dreier *m* A Newman *w* G Cooper, Milland, Preston, S Hayward, B Crawford, O'Connor 120min Par

BEAU HUNKS (1931) *d* *James Horne* *p* Roach *w* Laurel, Hardy (4rs) *r* MGM (= *Beau Chumps*)

BEAU IDEAL (1931) *d* Brenon *w* L Young 75min RKO

BEAU JAMES (1957) *d/co-s* Shavelson *co-a* Pereira *w* Miles, P Douglas, Hope, A Smith VV* 105min Par

BEAU PLAISIR, LE (1969) *d* Perrault *co-c* Brault 16mm *15min

BEAU SERGE, LE (1958) *d/p/s* Chabrol *c* Decaë *w* Brialy, Chabrol, de Broca 93min

BEAUTE DU DIABLE, LA (1950) *d/co-s/cp-di* Clair *c* Kelber *w* M Simon, Philipe, Modot 91min

BEAUTIFUL AND DAMNED, THE (1922) *d* *William A Seiter* *fst* Fitzgerald *w* Fazenda 7rs WB

BEAUTIFUL BLONDE FROM BASHFUL BEND, THE (1949) *d/p/s* P Sturges *co-a* L Wheeler *m* Mockridge *w* Grable, Romero *77min Fox

Beautiful Body = NIKUTAIBI (1928)

Beautiful but Dangerous = SHE HAD TO SAY YES (1953)

Beautiful but Dangerous (US) = DONNA PIU BELLA DEL MONDO, LA (1953)

Beautiful Days = URUWASHIKI SAIGETZU (1955)

BEAUTIFUL STRANGER, THE (1954) *d/st* D Miller *w* G Rogers, S Baker 89min *r* UA (= *Twist of Fate*)

Beautiful Swindlers, The = LES PLUS BELLES ESCROQUERIES DU MONDE (1963)

Beauty and the Beast = BELLE ET LA BETE, LA (1945)

BEAUTY AND THE BOSS (1932) *d* Del Ruth 66min WB

Beauty and the Dragon, The = BIJO TO KAIRYU (1955)

BEAUTY AND THE ROGUE (1918) *d* H King Mut

BEAUTY FOR SALE (1933) *d* Boleslavsky *c* Howe *w* Hopper 87min MGM

BEAUTY # 2 (1965) *d* Warhol 16mm 70min

BEAUTY PARLOR (1932) *d* Thorpe 64min

Beauty's Daughter = NAVY WIFE (1935)

Beauty's Sorrows = BIJIN AISHU (1931)

BEAUX JOURS, LES (1935) *d* M Allégret *s* Charles Spaak *w* Barrault, S Simon

BEBE (1910–13) *d/s* Feuillade (*series of over 60 films*)

BE BIG (1930) *d* *James Parrott* *p* Roach *w* Laurel, Hardy sh

Bebo's Girl = RAGAZZA DI BUBE, LA (1963)

Because I Love = AISUREBAKOSO (1955)

Be Careful = HANSOM CABMAN, THE (1924)

BECAUSE OF A WOMAN (1918) *d* Conway 5rs Tri

BECAUSE OF YOU (1952) *d* Pevney *c* Metty *w* L Young J Chandler 95min U

BECAUSE THEY'RE YOUNG (1960) *d* Wendkos *p* Bresler *w* Weld 102min Col

Because of my Hot Youth = FOR MIN HETA UNGDOMS SKULL (1952)

BECAUSE YOU'RE MINE (1952) *d* *Alexander Hall* *p* Pasternak *c* Ruttenberg *co-s* Gibbons *w* Lanza *103min MGM

BECKET (1964) *d* Glenville *p* Wallis *fpl* Anouilh *c* Unsworth *w* Burton, O'Toole, Wolfit, Gielgud PV* 148min *pc* O'Toole *r* Par

BECKONING TRAIL, THE (1916) *d* Conway 5rs U

BECKY SHARP (1935) *d/co-p* Mamoulian *co-p* Macgowan *fn* (*Vanity Fair*) *Thackeray* *c* Rennahan *w* M Hopkins *84min

Bed, The (UK) = SECRETS D'ALCOVE (1954)

BED, THE (1967) *d* Broughton 16mm *19min

Bed and Board (UK) = DOMICILE CONJUGAL (1970)

Bed and Sofa = TRETYA MESHCHANSKAYA (1927)

BEDAZZLED (1967) *d/p* Donen *w* Welch PV* 107min *pc* Donen *r* Fox

BEDEVILLED (1955) *d* Leisen *c* F Young *w* A Baxter CS* 85min MGM

BEDFORD INCIDENT, THE (1965) *d/co-p* J Harris *co-p* Widmark *s* Poe *c* G Taylor *w* Poitier, Widmark 102min Col

BEDKNOBS AND BROOMSTICKS (1971) *d* Stevenson *117min *pc* Disney

BEDLAM (1946) *d/co-s* Robson *p* Lewton *c* Musuraca *w* Karloff 79min RKO

BED OF ROSES (1933) *d/co-di* La Cava *w* Constance Bennett, McCrea 67min RKO

BEDROOM BLUNDER, A (1917) *d* Cline *p* Sennett 2rs Kay (= *Room 23*)

BEDSIDE (1934) *d* Florey *c* Hickox *w* Meek 65min FN

BEDSIDE MANNER (1945) *d/p* Stone *w* C Ruggles 78min *r* UA

BED SITTING ROOM, THE (1969) *d/co-p* Lester *c* Watkin *w* Tushingham

BEDTIME STORY (1964) *d* *Ralph Levy* *co-a* Golitzen *w* Brando, Niven, J Jones *99min U

Beethoven (UK) = GRAND AMOUR DE BEETHOVEN, UN (1936)

Beethoven 3rd Symphony – Eroica (UK) = SYMPHONIE NR 3 IN ES-DUR, OPUS 55 "EROICA" VON LUDWIG VAN BEETHOVEN (1967)

Before Dawn = REIMEI IZEN (1931)

BEFORE DAWN (1933) *d* Pichel *w* Darwell 60min RKO

Before Dawn = YOAKE MAE (1953)

Before October = PERED OKTIABRE (1965)

BEFORE THE FAIR (1962) *d/s* C and R Eames *c* C Eames *8min

BEFORE THE RAID (1943) *d* J Weiss 34min *r* MGM

BEFORE WINTER COMES (1968) *d* J Thompson *c* G Taylor *w* Niven, Karina *107min Col

BEGGAR MAID (1921) *w* Astor 2rs

BEGGAR ON HORSEBACK (1925) *d/p* Cruze *co-fpl* G Kaufman *w* Horton 2193m FPL *r* Par

BEGGARS OF LIFE (1928) *d* Wellman *w* Beery, L Brooks 84min Par

BEGGAR'S OPERA, THE (1953) *d* P Brook *p* Olivier, H Wilcox *ad from opera John Gay additional di/lyr* Fry *c* G Green *dec* Wakhévitch *w* Olivier *94min *r* BL

BEGIERDE (1928) *d* Pabst *w* Helm 107min (= *Abwege*)

BEGLETS (1932) *d/co-s* Petrov 1000m (= *The Fugitive*)

BEGONE, DULL CARE (1949) *d* McLaren, *Evelyn Lambert* *m Oscar Peterson* *$3\frac{1}{2}$min NFBC

Be Good unto Death = LEGY JO MINDHALALIG (1960)

BEGUILED, THE (1971) *d/p* Seigel *ex-p* Blaustein *a* Golitzen *w* Eastwood, Page *105min U

BEHEMOTH THE SEA MONSTER (1959) *d* Lourié, *Douglas Hickox* *s* Lourié 70min (= *The Giant Behemoth*)

Behind Closed Shutters = PERSIANE CHIUSE (1951)

Behind Closed Doors (UK) = A PORTE CHIUSE (1961)

BEHIND LOCKED DOORS (1948) *d* Boetticher *c* J Alton 61min EL

BEHIND THE DOOR (1919) *d* *Irvin V Willat* *w* Beery 7rs Par

BEHIND THE EIGHT BALL (1942) *d* Cline 60min U

Behind the Great Wall (UK) = MURAGLIA CINESE, LA (1918)

BEHIND THE MASK (1946) *d* Karlson 67min Mon

BEHIND THE MASK (1958) *d* *Brian Desmond Hurst* *w* M, V Redgrave *99min

BEHIND THE RISING SUN (1943) *d* Dmytryk *c* Metty *w* Ryan 89min RKO

BEHIND THE SCREEN (1916) *d/s* Chaplin *co-c* Totheroh *w* Chaplin, Purviance 2rs Mut

Behind the Shop Windows = ZA VITRINOI UNIVERMAGA (1956)

Behind Uniform Faces = BAG DE ENS FASADER (1961)

BEHOLD A PALE HORSE (1964) *d/p* Zinneman *as-p* Trauner *fn* (*Killing a Mouse on Sunday*) Pressburger *m* Jarre *w* Peck, Quinn, Sharif 118min Col

BEHOLD MY WIFE (1935) *d* Leisen *c* Shamroy *w* S Sidney, Sheridan 78min Par

Behold Thy Son = KIIRO KARASU (1957)

Being Two isn't easy = WATASHI WA NISAI (1962)

Bekännelsen på dödsbädden = ETT HEMLIGT GIFTERMAL (1912)

BEKENNTNIS DER INA KAHR, DAS (1954) *d* Pabst *w* Jurgens 102min

BEL AGE, LE (1960) *d/co-s* Kast *co-s* Doniol-Valcroze *fst* (*An Old Fool*) *Alberto Moravia* *c* Cloquet, Vierny *co-m* Delerue *w* *Boris Vian*, Brialy, Doniol-Valcroze, Pagliero 90min (= *Love is when you Make it*)

BEL AMI (1919) *d* Genina

BEL AMI (1954 *r* 1957) *d/co-s* Daquin *fn* *Guy de Maupassant* *c* Hayer *m* Eisler *w* Vernon S* 100min

BEL INDIFFERENT, LE (1957) *d* Demy *fst* Cocteau *c* Fradetal *dec* EVEIN *m* Jarre sh

Bella des Belles, La = DONNA PIU BELLA DEL MONDO, LA (1955)

BELLA DI ROMA, LA (1955) *d/co-s* Comencini *w* Sordi 108min (= *Roman Signorina*)

BELLA DONNA (1923) *d* *George Fitzmaurice* *c* AC Miller *w* Negri, Menjou 2409m FPL *r* Par

BELLA MUGNAIA, LA (1955) *d/co-s* Camerini *p* Ponti, De Laurentiis *rm* IL CAPELLO A TRE PUNTE (1934) *w* De Sica, Loren, Mastroianni CS* 92min (= *The Miller's Wife*)

BELL' ANTONIO, IL (1960) *d* Bolognini *co-s* Pasolini *fn* *Vitaliano Brancatis* *m* Piccioni *w* Mastroianni, Cardinale, Brasseur 100min

BELL, BOOK AND CANDLE (1958) *d* Quine *p* Blaustein *s* Taradash *m* Duning *w* J Stewart, Novak, Lemmon *103min Col

BELL BOY, THE (1918) *d/w* Arbuckle *w* Keaton 2rs Par

BELLBOY, THE (1960) *d/p/s* J Lewis *co-a* Pereira *w* J Lewis 72min Par

BELLE AU BOIS DORMANT, LA (1902) *d/w* Zecca 75m Pat

BELLE AU BOIS DORMANT, LA (1935) *d* Alexeieff anim

BELLE AVENTURE, LA (1944) *d* M Allégret *s* Achard

BELLE DAME SANS MERCI, LA (1921) *d* Dulac *fpm* Keats

BELLE DE JOUR (1967) *d/co-s* Buñuel *fn* *Joseph Kessel* *c* Vierny *w* Deneuve, Piccoli, Blanche

BELLE EQUIPE, LA (1936) *d/st/co-s* Duvivier co-s Charles Spaak *w* Gabin, Romance, Vanel 94min

BELLE ET LA BETE, LA (1946) *d/s* Cocteau *c* Alekan *dec/cos* Bérard *m* Auric *w* Marais, Marquand 89min (= *Beauty and the Beast*)

BELLE ETOILE (1938) *d* De Baroncelli *m* Misraki *w* M Simon

BELLE FAMIGLIE, LE (1964) *d/p* Gregoretti *w* Toto, N Loy, Girardot

BELLE HELENE, LA (1957) *d* Reiniger *m* *Offenbach* anim *(1rl)

BELLE LE GRAND (1951) d Dwan p H Yates c Keller m V Young 90min Rep

BELLE MA POVERE (1957) d/co-s Risi co-s Festa Campanile 98min (= Irresistible)

BELLE MEUNIERE, LA (1948) co-d/p/s Pagnol m Schubert *16mm

BELLE NIVERNAISE, LA (1923) d J Epstein fn Alphonse Daudet

BELLE O BRUTTE SI SPOSAN TUTTE (1939) d Bragaglia

BELLE OF NEW YORK, THE (1952) d Walters p Freed co-a Gibbons chor R Alton w Astaire *82min MGM

BELLE OF THE NINETIES (1934) d McCarey st/s West c Struss co-e Dmytryk w West 70min Par

BELLE QUE VOILA, LA (1950) d/di Le Chanois c Thirard m Kosma w Morgan 95min Pat

BELLES DE NUIT, LES (1952) d/s/di Clair co-c Thirard m Van Parys m Philipe, Carol, Lollobrigida 87min (= Night Beauties)

BELLES OF ST. TRINIANS, THE (1954) d/co-p/co-s Launder co-p/co-s Gilliat m M Arnold 91min BL

BELLE SOMMERS (1962) d Silverstein 63min Col

BELLES ON THEIR TOES (1952) d Levin c Arling w Carmichael. Hunter *89min Fox

BELLE STARR'S DAUGHTER (1948) d Lesley Selander st/s Burnett w Roman 86min r Fox

BELLE VIE, LA (1963) d/s Enrico 110min

BELL FOR ADANO, A (1945) d H King p/co-s Trotti fn John Hershey fpl Osborn co-a Wheeler m A Newman c La Shelle w Bendix, Dalio, Tierney, Conte 104min Fox

BELL HOP, THE (1921) d/st Semon, Taurog w Semon 2rs Vit

BELLISSIMA (1951) d/co-s Visconti co-s Cecchi d'Amico, Rosi fst Zavattini w Magnani, Blasetti 113min

BELLISSIMA NOVENBRE, UN (1968) d Bolognini w Lollobrigida, Piccoli, Ferzetti *101min (= That Splendid November)

BELLO ONESTO EMIGRATA AUSTRALIA SPOSEREBBE COMPAESAN ILLIBATA (1971) d Zampa c Tonti m Piccioni w Sordi, Cardinale *110min

BELLS, THE (1926) d James Young c O'Connell w L Barrymore, Karloff 1920m

BELLS ARE RINGING (1960) d Minnelli p Freed s/lyr Comden, A Green fmpl Comden, A Green, Jule Styne w Holliday, Martin CS* 125min MGM

BELLS GO DOWN, THE (1943) d Dearden p Balcon w Mason 89min r UA

Bells have gone to Rome, The (USA) = HARANGOK ROMABA MENTEK, A (1958)

BELLS OF ST. MARY'S, THE (1945) d/p/st McCarey s D Nichols c Barnes w B Crosby, Ingrid Bergman 127min RKO

BELOVED BOZO, THE (1925) d Cline co-s Sennett

BELOVED BRUTE, THE (1924) d Blackton c O'Connell w V McLaglen 7rs Vit

BELOVED ENEMY (1937) d Potter p Goldwyn c Toland m A Newman w Oberon, Niven 90min r UA

BELOVED INFIDEL (1959) d H King p Wald fab Sheila Graham co-a Wheeler c Shamroy m Waxman w Peck, Kerr CS* 123min Fox

BELOVED ROGUE, THE (1927) d Crosland c August w J Barrymore, Veidt 10rs r UA

BELOVED VAGABOND, THE (1936) d C Bernhardt rm (1923) c Planer w Chevalier, Lockwood 70min Col

BELOW ZERO (1930) d James Parrott p Roach st McCarey w Laurel, Hardy 21min r MGM

BELYI OREL (1928) d/co-s Protazanov w Meyerhold 185m (= The White Eagle)

Be Mine Tonight (US) = LIEU EINER NACHT, DAS (1932)

BE MY WIFE (1921) d/p/s/w Linder pc Goldwyn

BEND OF THE RIVER (1952) d A Mann p A Rosenberg s B Chase c Glassberg w J Stewart A Kennedy, Hudson *91min U (= Where the River Bends)

BENGAL BRIGADE (1954) d Benedek ad S Miller w Hudson *87min U

BENGASI (1942) d/co-st/co-s Genina co-st/co-s Ugo Betti

BENGAZI (1955) d Brahm c Biroc w Conte, V McLaglen S 79min RKO

BEN HUR (1927) d Niblo ad Mathis fn Lew Wallace co-c Struss co-a Gibbons w Novarro, M Loy 3654m MGM

BEN HUR (1959) d Wyler 2nd d Marton, Canutt, Soldati 3rd d Thorpe co-s Fry (uc) fn Wallace c Surtees m Rozsa w Heston, Hawkins, Boyd TAO PV* 217min MGM

BENI KOMORI (1951) d/s Kinugasa

BENITO CERENO (1969) d Serge Roullet fst Melville w Guerra *80min

BENITO MUSSOLINI (1961) d Pasquale Prunas supn Rossellini 92min (= Blood on the Balcony)

BENJAMIN (1967) d/co-st Deville c Cloquet w Morgan, Piccoli, Deneuve *100min

BENJY (1951) d Zinnemann st/s Stern sh

BENSAA SUONISSA (1971) d/s Jarva 97min (= Rally)

BENSON MURDER CASE, THE (1930) d Tuttle c Stout w W Powell 65min Par

BENTEN KOZO (1928) d Kinugasa (= Gay Masquerade)

BERCAIL, LE (1919) d L'Herbier

BERCEAUX, LES (1932) d J Epstein 300m

BERCEAUX, LES (1935) d Kirsanov

BERENICE (1954) d/s/e Rohmer fn Edgar Allan Poe c Rivette w Rohmer 16mm 15min

BERG DES SCHICKSALS, DER (1924) d/s/co-c Fanck 2432m

BERG-EJVIND OCH HANS HUSTRU (1917) d/co-s/w Sjöstrom 2781m

BERGERE ET LE RAMONEUR, LA (1952) d/co-s Grimault co-s/di J Prévert fst Hans Christian Andersen wv Brasseur, Aimée anim *95min

BERGKATZE, DIE (1921) d/co-s Lubitsch c Sparkuhl w Negri, Jannings 2743m r Union-UFA (= The Wildcat/The Mountain Cat)

BERKELEY SQUARE (1933) d F Lloyd p Lasky w L Howard 84min Fox

BERLIN (1945) d Yuli Raizman, Elizaveta Svilova co-c Karmen

BERLIN-ALEXANDERPLATZ (1931) d Jutzi co-s/fn Alfred Döblin 2440m

BERLIN, DIE SINFONIE DER GROSSTADT (1927) d/co-s Ruttmann co-s Freund f idea C Mayer 2000m (= Berlin, Symphony of a City)

BERLIN EXPRESS (1948) d J Tourneur co-p Schary c Ballard m Hollander w Oberon, Ryan, Lukas 87min RKO

BERLINO APPUNTAMENTO PER LE SPIE (1965) d Sala w D Andrews *105min (= Spy In Your Eye)

Berlin, Symphony of a City = BERLIN, DIE SINFONIE DER GROSSTADT (1927)

BERNARD-L'ERMITE (1927) d Painlevé

BERNARDINE (1957) d Levin co-a Wheeler w (J Gaynor) CS* 97min Fox

BERNARD MILUS ON GUN DOGS (1948) d B Wright 19min

BERORINGEN (1971) d/st/s Ingmar Bergman c Nykvist cr c Fischer w B Andersson, Von Sydow 117min (= The Touch)

BERSAGLIERI DELLA SIGNORA, I (1945) d Risi sh

BERTH MARKS (1929) d Lewis Foster p Roach st McCarey w Laurel, Hardy (2rs) r MGM

BE SAFE OR BE SORRY (1955) d Peries 15min

Be Sick . . . It's Free! = MEDICO DELLA MUTUA, IL (1968)

BESPOKE OVERCOAT, THE (1955) d/p Clayton m Auric 33min r BL

BEST FOOT FORWARD (1943) d Edward Buzzell p Freed a Gibbons chor Walters w Ball *95min MGM

Best Girl in my Life, The = NEJLEPSI ZENSKA MEHO ZIVOTE (1967)

BEST MAN, THE (1964) d Schaffner s/fpl Vidal c Wexler a Wheeler w H Fonda, Robertson, Sothern 104min r UA

BEST MAN WINS, THE (1948) d J Sturges fst Mark Twain 75min Col

Best of Enemies, The = DUE NEMICI, I (1962)

BEST OF EVERYTHING, THE (1959) d Negulesco p Wald c Mellor co-a Wheeler m A Newman w Boyd, J Crawford CS* 121min Fox

BEST THINGS IN LIFE ARE FREE, THE (1956) d Curtiz fn J O'Hara c Shamroy w Borgnine, Dailey CS 104min Fox

BEST YEARS OF OUR LIVES, THE (1946) d Wyler p Goldwyn fn (Glory for Me) MacKinlay Kantor c Toland m Friedhofer w March, T Wright, D Andrews, M Loy, V Mayo, Carmichael, Cochran 172min r RKO (= Glory for Me)

BESUCH, DER (1964) d Wicki s Barzman fpl Friedrich Durrenmatt w Ingrid Bergman, Quinn CS 100min Fox (= La Rancune/The Visit/La Vendetta della Signora)

Beta Som = FINCHE DURA LA TEMPESTA (1962)

BETE COMME LES HOMMES (1923) d/s Machin, Henri Wulschleger

BETE HUMAINE, LA (1938) d/ad/di J Renoir fn Zola c Courant dec Lourié m Kosma w Gabin, S Simon, F Renoir, Carette 105min (= Judas was a Woman)

BETE NOIRE, LA (1956) d Rouquier sh

BETIA, LA (1971) d/co-s De Bosio w Manfredi *102min

BETRAYAL (1929) d Milestone co-st Schertzinger a Dreier w Jannings, G Cooper 1979m Par

Betrayal, The = FRAULEIN DOKTOR (1968)

BETRAYED (1917) d/s Walsh 5rs Fox

BETRAYED (1954) d G Reinhardt w Turner, Gable, Mature *108min MGM

Betrayer, The = VANINA VANINI (1961)

BETTELGRAFIN, DIE (1918) d May, Bruno Ziener p/co-s May 4rs

Better a Widow = MEGLIO VEDOVA (1968)

BETTER TIMES (1919) d/s K Vidor w Pitts 1370m

BETTER WAY, THE (1909) d Griffith 1rl Bio

BETTINA LOVED A SOLDIER (1916) d Julian 5rs

BETTY OF GREYSTONE (1916) d Dwan p Griffith w D Gish 5rs r Tri

BETWEEN DANGERS (1927) d Thorpe 1382m

BETWEEN HEAVEN AND HELL (1956) d R Fleischer p Weisbart co-a Wheeler m Friedhofer w R Wagner, B Crawford CS* 94min Fox

Between Love and Duty (UK) = BOIS DES AMANTS, LE (1960)

BETWEEN MIDNIGHT AND DAWN (1950) d G Douglas w E O'Brien 89min Col

BETWEEN SHOWERS (1914) d Lehrman w Chaplin 1rl Key (= In Wrong/Charlie and the Umbrella/The Flirts)

BETWEEN THE ACTS (1919) d/s/w Semon 2rs Vit

BETWEEN TWO WOMEN (1937) d G Seitz fst (General Hospital) Von Stroheim c J Seitz a Gibbons w O'Sullivan 84min MGM

Between Two Worlds (US) = MUDE TOD, DER (1921)

Between Two Worlds = DELOVAK ATHARA (1966)

BETWEEN US GIRLS (1942) d/p Koster as-p Karlson (as Karlstein) 89min U

BEVERLY OF GRAUSTARK (1926) d Franklin co-a Gibbons w Davies 2128m MGM

BEWARE, MY LOVELY (1952) d Horner m Leith Stevens w Lupino, Ryan 77min RKO

BEWARE OF BACHELORS (1928) d Del Ruth co-c Brodine 8rs WB

BEWARE OF BLONDES (1928) d G Seitz p Cohn c J Walker a Wright 1722m Col

BEWARE OF LADIES (1936) d Pichel 64min Rep

BEWARE OF MARRIED MEN (1928) d A Mayo w M Loy 1652m WB

BEWARE OF PITY (1946) d Elvey fn Stefan Zweig cos Beaton w Palmer 103min r EL

BEWITCHED (1945) d/s Oboler p Bressler co-a Gibbons 65min MGM

BEYOND A REASONABLE DOUBT (1956) d F Lang w D Andrews, Fontaine 80min RKO

Beyond Decay = CHORAKU NO KANATA (1924)

BEYOND GLORY (1948) d J Farrow co-st/co-s Warren c J Seitz co-a Dreier m V Young w Ladd, D Reed, A Murphy 82min Par

BEYOND MOMBASA (1957) d G Marshall c F Young m Humphrey Searle w Wilde, D Reed *90min Col

BEYOND THE BLUE HORIZON (1942) d Santell c Mellor co-a Dreier w Lamour 76min PAR

BEYOND THE CURTAIN (1960) d Compton Bennett 88min JAR

BEYOND THE FOREST (1949) d K Vidor p Blanke c Burks m M Steiner w B Davis, Cotten, Roman 96min WB

BEYOND THE LAW (1968) d/co-p/co-e Mailer co-e Pennebaker w Mailer 16mm 110min

BEYOND THE LINE OF DUTY (1942) d Lewis Seiler n Reagan 22min WB

Beyond the River = BOTTOM OF THE BOTTLE, THE (1956)

BEYOND THE ROCKS (1922) d S Wood w Swanson, Valentino FPL r Par

BEYOND THE TIME BARRIER (1959) d Ulmer 75min

Beyond This Place = WEB OF EVIDENCE (1959)

BE YOUR AGE (1926) d McCarey Pat

BEZHIN LUG (1935, uf) d Eisenstein fst Turgenev c Tissé

BEZHIN LUG (1967) stills compiled by Yutkevich, Naum Kleimann m Prokofiev 25min (= Bezhin Meadow)

Bezhin Meadow = BEZHIN LUG (1967)

BEZPRIDANNITSA (1937) d/co-s Protazanov 87min (= Without Dowry)

BEZ VINY VINOVATYE (1945) d/s Petrov fpl Ostrovsky 98min (= Guilty Though Guiltless)

B.F.'s DAUGHTER (1948) d Leonard c Ruttenberg co-a Gibbons w Stanwyck, Heflin, C Coburn 108min MGM

BHARAT MATA (1957) d/p/st Mehboob *120min (= Mother India)

BHOWANI JUNCTION (1956) d Cukor p Berman fn John Masters c F Young colour consultant Hoyningen-Huene CS* 110min MGM

BIANCHI PASCOLI (1947) co-d/n Emmer co-d/co-s Enrico Gras 12min

BIBBIA, LA (1966) d/n J Huston, Ernst Haas (Creation sequence) p De Laurentiis s Fry c Rotunno a Chiari w R Harris, J Huston, Boyd, G Scott, Gardner, O'Toole, Ferzetti, Rossi-Drago 70* 175min r Fox (= The Bible . . . In the Beginning)

BIBI LA PUREE (1934) d Joannon

BICHES, LES (1968) d/co-s Chabrol c Rabier w Trintignant *90min (= The Does/The Girlfriends)

Bicycle, The = ROWER (1957, uf)

BIDONE, IL (1955) d/co-st/co-s Fellini c Martelli m Rota w B Crawford, Masina 94min (= The Swindle)

BIELINSKY (1953) d/co-s Kozintsev co-c Moskvin

BIEN AIMEE, LA (1966) d Doniol-Valcroze w Morgan * TV

BIEN AMADA, LA (1951) d/st Fernandez c Figueroa

BIENFAITEUR, LE (1942) d/ad Decoin m Van Parys w Raimu

BIENNER I NATT!, DET (1954) d Skouen

BIENVENIDO, MR MARSHALL! (1952) d/co-s Berlanga 2nd d/co-s Bardem 75min (= Welcome, Mr Marshall)

BIEVRE, LA (1939) d Clément sh

BIGAMIST, THE (1953) d/p/w Lupino w E O'Brien, Fontaine CS 83min

Bigamist, The = BIGAMO, IL (1956)

BIGAMO, IL (1956) d Emmer co-s Rosi w De Sica, Mastroianni 97min (= The Bigamist/A Plea for Passion)

Big Bankroll, The (UK) = KING OF THE ROARING TWENTIES, THE STORY OF ARNOLD ROTHSTEIN (1961)

BIG BLOCKADE, THE (1941) d Frend p Balcon as-p Cavalcanti co-c Slocombe w Hay, M Redgrave, (Frend) 68min pc

BIG BOODLE, THE (1957) d R Wilson c Garmes w Flynn, Armendariz 83min r UA

BIG BOY (1930) d Crosland w Jolson 70min WB

BIG BREAK, THE (1953) d/p Strick 73min

BIG BROADCAST, THE (1932) d Tuttle c Folsey w B Crosby 78min Par

BIG BROADCAST OF 1936, THE (1935) d Taurog w Tamiroff, B Crosby, G Ruggles 97min Par

BIG BROADCAST OF 1937, THE (1936) d Leisen e Heisler co-a Dreier sp eff Fischinger (uc) w Benny, Milland 97min Par

BIG BROADCAST OF 1938, THE (1938) d Leisen w Fields, Lamour, Hope 90min Par

BIG BROTHER (1923) d/p Dwan 2158m FPL

BIG BROWN EYES (1936) d/co-s Walsh p Wanger w C Grant, J Bennett, Pidgeon, Nolan 77min Par

BIG BUSINESS (1929) d James Horne p Roach supn/st McCarey w Laurel, Hardy 2rs r MGM

Big Carnival, The = ACE IN THE HOLE (1951)

BIG CAT, THE (1949) d Karlson 75min EL

BIG CIRCUS, THE (1959) d J Newman co-s Charles Bennett c Hoch w Mature, Price, R Fleming, Lorre, Roland CS* 108min co-pc Mature r AA

BIG CITY, THE (1928) d Browning a Gibbons w Chaney 2084m MGM

BIG CITY (1937) d Borzage p/st Krasna s Schary, H Butler c Ruttenberg w Tracy, Rainer 80min MGM

BIG CITY (1948) d Taurog p Pasternak c Surtees co-a Gibbons w M O'Brien, Preston, G Murphy 103min MGM

Big City, The = MAHANAGAR (1963)

BIG CITY BLUES (1932) d LeRoy w Bogart, Blondell 65min WB

BIG CLOCK, THE (1948) d J Farrow c J Seitz co-a Dreier w Milland, Laughton, O'Sullivan, Roman 95min Par

BIG COMBO, THE (1954) d J H Lewis s Yordan c J Alton m Raksin w Wilde, Conte 89min AA

BIG COUNTRY, THE (1958) d/co-p Wyler co-p Peck co-s JR Webb c Planer m Moross cr Bass w Peck, J Simmons, C Baker, Heston, Ives, Bickford TR* 166min r UA

BIG DAN (1923) d Wellman c August 6rs Fox

Big Deal at Dodge City = BIG HAND FOR THE LITTLE LADY, A (1966)

Big Fair, The = GRANDE FOIRE, LA (1960)

Big Family, The = BOLSHAIA SEMYA (1954)

Big Fish, The (UK) = DOBRODRUZSTVI NO ZLATE ZATOCE (1955)

BIG FISHERMAN, THE (1959) d Borzage c Garmes w Keel PV 70* 166min

Big Forest = DAI SHINRIN (1930)

BIG GAMBLE, THE (1931) d Niblo c Mohr w Pitts 60min RKO

BIG GAMBLE, THE (1961) d R Fleischer 2nd d Elmo Williams p Zanuck s Shaw c Mellor a d'Eaubonne m Jarre w Boyd, D Wayne, Ratoff CS* 100min r Fox

BIGGER THAN LIFE (1956) d N Ray c Mason co-st/co-s Maibaum c Joe MacDonald co-a Wheeler m Raksin w Mason, Rush, Matthau CS* 90min Fox

BIGGEST BUNDLE OF THEM ALL, THE (1968) d Annakin w De Sica, Robinson, R Wagner. Welch PV* 98min

BIG HAND FOR THE LITTLE LADY, A (1966) d/p Fielder Cook c Garmes w H Fonda, Bickford, Meredith, Woodward *95min WB (= Big Deal at Dodge City)

BIG HANGOVER, THE (1950) d/p/st/s Krasna c Folsey co-a Gibbons w E Taylor 82min MGM

BIG HEARTED HERBERT (1934) d Keighley 60min WB

BIG HEAT, THE (1953) d F Lang s Boehm c C Lang m Amfitheatrof w G Ford, Graham, Marvin 90min Col

BIG HOUSE, THE (1930) d George Hill a Gibbons w Beery, R Montgomery 87min r MGM (German and French versions: d Fejos)

BIG HOUSE, USA (1955) d HW Koch w B Crawford, Meeker 82min r UA

BIG IDEA, THE (1918) d Mohr w H Lloyd Pat

BIG JACK (1949) d Thorpe p G Reinhardt c Surtees m Stothart w Beery, Conte 85min MGM

BIG JAKE (1971) d George Sherman c Clothier m E Bernstein w J Wayne, M O'Hara PV* 110min

BIG JIM McLAIN (1952) d Edward Ludwig co-s J Grant c Stout w J Wayne 90min r WB

BIG KNIFE, THE (1955) d/p Aldrich s Poe fpl Odets c Laszlo cr Bass w Palance, Corey, Winters, Steiger, Lupino 104min pc r Aldrich UA

Big Land, The = BOLSHAYA ZEMLYA (1944)

BIG LAND, THE (1957) d G Douglas co-s Rackin c J Seitz w Ladd, V Mayo, E O'Brien *93min WB (= Stampeded)

BIG LEAGUER, THE (1953) d Aldrich c Mellor w Robinson, Vera-Ellen 70min MGM

BIG LIFT, THE (1950) d/st/s Seaton p Perlberg c C Clarke m A Newman w Clift, P Douglas 120min Fox

BIG LITTLE PERSON, THE (1919) d Leonard w (Valentino) 6rs U

BIG MONEY (1936) d Jackson, Watt p Cavalcanti 16mm GPO

BIG MOUTH, THE (1967) d/p/co-s J Lewis co-a Wheeler w J Lewis *107min Col

BIG NEWS (1929) d La Cava c AC Miller w Lombard 67min Pat

BIG NIGHT, THE (1951) d/co-s Losey co-s H Butler c Mohr w (Aldrich) 75min r UA

BIG NOISE, THE (1928) d/p Dwan st B Hecht 2259m FN

BIG NOISE, THE (1944) d St Clair c Joe Macdonald m Mockridge w Laurel, Hardy 67min Fox

BIG OPERATOR, THE (1959) d Haas fst Paul Gallico w Rooney, Cochran, Danton CS 91min pc Zugsmith r MGM

BIG PARADE, THE (1927) d/p K Vidor co-a Gibbons w J Gilbert, Adorée 3825m r MGM

BIG PUNCH, THE (1921) d/co-s J Ford st/co-s Furthman 5rs Fox

Big Race, The (US) = GRANDE FROUSSE, LA (1964)

BIG SHOT, THE (1942) d Lewis Seiler c Hickox w Bogart 82min WB

Big Shots, The (US) = GRANDES GUEULES, LES (1965)

BIG SKY, THE (1952) d/p Hawks s D Nichols c R Harlan m Tiomkin w K Douglas 140min r RKO

BIG SLEEP, THE (1946) d/p Hawks co-s Faulkner, Furthman fn R Chandler c Hickox m M Steiner w Bogart, Bacall, Malone, Cook 114min WB

Big Snatch, The = MELODIE EN SOUS SOL (1962)

BIG STEAL, THE (1949) d D Siegal co-s Mainwaring (ps Homes) c Wild m Harline w Mitchum, Bendix, Novarro 72min RKO

BIG STORE, THE (1941) d Charles Reisner c Lawton a Gibbons w H, G, C Marx, Dumont 80min

BIG STREET, THE (1942) d Reis c Metty w H Fonda, Ball, Moorehead, Conreid 88min RKO

BIG TIME (1929) d Kenneth hawks p Fox c O'Connell w J Ford 87min Fox

BIG TRAIL, THE (1930) d Walsh c Andriot, Edeson w J Wayne, Power 70mm 125min Fox

BIG TREES, THE (1952) d Felix Feist co-s JR Webb c Glennon w K Douglas *89min WB

Big Wash!, The = GRANDE LESSIVE, LA (1968)

BIJIN AISHU (1931) d Ozu sh (= Beauty's Sorrows)

Bijomaru Sword = MEITO BIJOMARU (1945)

BIJO TO KAIRYU (1955) d Yoshimura s Shindo (= The Beauty and the Dragon)

BIJOUTIERS DU CLAIR DU LUNE, LES (1958) d/co-s Vadim c Thirard m Auric w Bardot, Boyd, Valli CS* 90min (= Heaven Fell That Night)

BIJSTERE LAND VAN VELUWEN, HET (1948) d van der Horst 14min (= Rape of a Country)

BIKE BOY (1967) d Warhol 16mm *96min

BILA SPONA (1960) d/s Fric (= The White Slide)

BILDNIS EINER UNBEKANNTEN (1954) d/co-s Käutner 108min

BILJETT TILL PARADISET (1962) d Mattsson w Dahlbeck (= Ticket to Paradise)

BILLARD CASSE, LE (1916) d/s Feyder 115m Gau

BILLET DE BANQUE, LE (1906) d/s Feuillade

BILLIE (1965) d/p Weis S* 87min r UA

Billionaire, A = OKUMAN CHOJA (1954)

BILLION DOLLAR BRAIN (1967) d K Russell p Saltzman ex-p De Toth fn Len Deighton w Caine, Malden PV* 97min r UA

BILL OF DIVORCEMENT, A (1932) d Cukor p Selznick fpl Clemence Dane c Hickox m M Steiner w J Barrymore, K Hepburn 69min RKO

BILL OF DIVORCEMENT, A (1940) d J Farrow s Trumbo rm (1932) w M O'Hara, Menjou, H Marshall 74min RKO

BILLY BOY (1954) d Avery 6min * MGM

BILLY BUDD (1962) d/p Ustinov fst (Billy Budd, Foretopman) Herman Melville c Krasker w Stamp, Ryan, Ustinov, M Douglas CS* 125min r AA

BILLY JIM (1922) d Borzage 1493m

BILLY LIAR (1963) d J Schlesinger w Courtenay, Christie CS 98min

BILLY ROSE'S DIAMOND HORSESHOE (1945) d/s Seaton co-a Wheeler co-m A Newman w Grable, Dumont 104min Fox (= Diamond Horseshoe)

BILLY ROSE'S JUMBO (1962) d Walters 2nd d/chor (uc) Berkeley co-p Pasternak as-p Edens fn B Hecht, MacArthur c Daniels m/lyr Rodgers, Hart w D Day, Boyd PV* 124min MGM (= Jumbo)

BILLY THE KID (1930) d/p K Vidor di MacArthur a Gibbons w Beery 98min MGM

BILLY THE KID (1941) d D Miller w R Taylor 95min MGM

BIM, LE PETIT ANE (1950) d Lamorisse 36min

BINETTOSCOPE, LE (1910) d Cohl anim 113m

BIRAGHIN (1946) d Gallone

BIRAJ BAHU (1954) d Roy 150min

BIRD IN A BONNET, A (1958) d Freleng anim* 7min WB

BIRD MAN OF ALCATRAZ (1962) d Frankenheimer, Crichton ex-p H Hecht c Guffey m Bernstein w Lancaster, Malden, E O'Brien, Ritter 143min r UA

Bird of Heaven, A = EGI MADAR (1957)

BIRD OF PARADISE (1932) d K Vidor p Selznick chor Berkeley w Del Rio, McCrea 80min RKO

BIRD OF PARADISE (1951) d/s Daves c Hoch co-a Wheeler m Amfitheatrof w J Chandler *100min Fox

Bird of Prey = EPERVIER, L' (1933)

BIRDS, THE (1963) d/p Hitchcock s E Hunter fst Daphne du Maurier c Burks co-a Boyle sound consultant Herrmann w Pleshette *120min U

Birds and the Bees, The = THREE DARING DAUGHTERS (1947)

BIRDS AND THE BEES, THE (1956) d Taurog co-s P Sturges c Fapp co-a Pereira w M Gaynor, Niven VV* 94min Par

BIRDS ANONYMOUS (1957) d Freleng anim* 7min WB

Birds Come to Die in Peru, The (UK = OISEAUX VONT MOURIR AU PEROU, LES (1968)

BIRDS DO IT (1965) d Marton *95min Col

Birds in Peru (US) = OISEAUX VONT MOURIR AU PEROU, LES (1968)

Birds of Prey = RAPACE, LA (1968)

Birds, The Bees and the Italians, The (UK) = SIGNORE E SIGNORI (1965)

BIRTHDAY PARTY, THE (1968) d William Friedkin s/fpl Pinter *124min

BIRTHDAY PRESENT, THE (1957) d Jackson 100min BL

BIRTH OF A NATION, THE (1915) d/co-s Griffith fns (The Clansman, The Leopard's Spots) Thomas Dixon c Bitzer w Marsh, L Gish, Crisp, Walsh, Von Stroheim 3530m

BIRTH OF A SMILE, THE (1884) d Friese-Greene (4 slides)

BIRTH OF THE BLUES (1941) d Schertzinger c Mellor co-a Dreier w B Crosby 85min Par

BIRTH OF THE ROBOT, THE (1936) d Lye m Holst *6min

BIRUMA NO TATEGOTO (1956) d Ichikawa 106min Nik (= The Burmese Harp)

BISBETICA DOMATA, LE (1942) d Poggioli

BISCUIT EATER, THE (1940) d Heisler co-a Dreier 81min Par

BISHOP MISBEHAVES, THE (1953) d Dupont w O'Sullivan, Foster 85min MGM (= The Bishop's Misadventures)

Bishop's Misadventures, The = BISHOP MISBEHAVES, THE (1935)

BISHOP'S WIFE, THE (1947) d Koster p Goldwyn c Toland m Freidhofer w C Grant, L Young, Niven 108min RKO

BITCH (1965) d Warhol 16mm 70min

BITS OF LIFE (1921) d/co-st Neilan w Chaney 1932m pc Neilan r FN

Bitter Rice (UK) = RISO AMARO (1948)

Bitter Spirit, The = EIEN NO HITO (1961)

BITTER SWEET (1916) d Conway

BITTER SWEET (1933) d H Wilcox c F Young w Neagle 93min

BITTER SWEET (1940) d WS Van Dyke p Saville fpl Coward m Stothart w Jeanette MacDonald, G Sanders *92min MGM

BITTER SWEET (1959) d Siodmak

BITTER TEA OF GENERAL YEN, THE (1932) d/p Capra c J Walker w Stanwyck 89min Col

Bitter Victory = PAID IN FULL (1949)

BITTER VICTORY (1958) d/co-s N Ray p Graetz co-s Lambert c Kelber dec D'Eaubonne w Burton, Jurgens, Roman CS 90min r Col

BITVA ZA NASHU SOVETSKAYU UKRAINU (1943) d Solntseva, I Avdeyenko supn/s/cy Dovzhenko 80min (= The Fight for our Soviet Ukraine)

BITVA POD LENINO (1943) d A Ford

Bizarre Bizarre = DROLE DE DRAME (1937)

BJORN'S INFERNO (1964) d A King 16mm 53min

BLACK ARROW, THE (1948) d G Douglas fn R L Stevenson c Lawton w L Hayward 76min Col

BLACKBEARD THE PIRATE (1952) d Walsh m V Young w Newton, Darnell, Bendix *98min RKO

BLACK BIRD, THE (1926) d/st Browning dec Gibbons w Chaney, Adorée 2039m MGM

BLACKBOARD JUNGLE (1955) d/s R Brooks p Berman fn E Hunter c R Harlan co-a Gibbons w G Ford, A Francis, Poitier 94min MGM

BLACK CAMEL, THE (1931) d Hamilton MacFadden w R Young, Lugosi 71min Fox

Black Cargo = SCHWARZE FRACHT (1956)

BLACK CAT, THE (1934) d/co-st Ulmer fn Edgar Allan Poe w Karloff, Lugosi, Carradine 66min U (= House of Doom)

Black Cat = YABU NO NAKA NO KURONEKO (1968)

Black Eagle, The (UK) = AQUILA NERA (1946)

BLACK EYES (1939) d Brenon 71min

BLACK FOX, THE (1963) d/p/s Louis Stoumen n Dietrich 89min

BLACK FURY (1935) d Curtiz c Haskin w Muni, Tamiroff 92min FN

BLACK GOLD (1947) d Karlson w Quinn 90min r AA

BLACKGUARD, THE (1925) d Graham Cutts p Balcon s/dec Hitchcock 2804m

BLACK HAND, THE (1950) d Thorpe co-a Gibbons w Gene Kelly 92min MGM

BLACK HILLS AMBUSH (1952) d/as-p Keller 54min Rep

BLACK JACK (1949) d/co-s Duvivier co-s Charles Spaak m Kosma w G Sanders, H Marshall, Dalio 112min

Black Jesus (US) = SEDUTA ALLA SUA DESTRA (1968)

317

BLACK KNIGHT, THE (1954) d Garnett co-di Forbes (uc) w Ladd *85min Col
BLACK LEGION (1936) d A Mayo w Bogart, Sheridan 83min WB
BLACK MAGIC (1929) d G Seitz p Fox 66min Fox
BLACK MAGIC (1949) d/p Ratoff s Charles Bennett fn Dumas (Mémoires d'un Médecin) w Welles, Tamiroff, Cortese, Mangano 104min
BLACKMAIL (1929) d/co-s Hitchcock fpl/co-s Charles Bennett 2430m(si) 89min (sd)
BLACKMAIL (1939) d Potter w Robinson 81min MGM
BLACKMAILED (1951) d M Allégret co-s Vadim w Zetterling, Bogarde 85min
BLACK MIDNIGHT (1949) d Boetticher 60min Mon
Black Moritz = SCHWARZE MORITZ (1916)
BLACK NARCISSUS (1947) d/p/s M Powell, Pressburger c Cardiff w Sabu, Kerr, J Simmons *100min
Black on White = MUSTAA VALKOISELLA (1968)
Black on White = NERO SU BIANCO (1969)
BLACK ORCHID, THE (1958) d Ritt c Burks p Ponti w Loren, Quinn 96min Par
BLACK ORCHIDS (1916) d/s Ingram 5rs
Black Orpheus = ORFEU NEGRO (1958)
Blackout = CONTRABAND (1940)
BLACK OXEN (1923) d F Lloyd c Brodine w Bow 8rs pc F Lloyd r FN
Black Palm Trees, The = SVARTA PALMKRONOR (1967)
BLACK PANTHERS (1968) d Varda *25min
BLACK PIRATE, THE (1926) d Albert Parker st Fairbanks Sr (ps Elton Thomas) w Fairbanks Sr, Crisp 2587m pc Fairbanks r UA
Black River = KUROI KAWA (1957)
BLACK ROOTS (1971) d/pc Rogosin 16mm * 61min
BLACK ROSE, THE (1950) d Hathaway c Cardiff w Power, Welles, Hawkins, Laurence Harvey 120min Fox
Black Sabbath (UK) = TRE VOLTI DELLA PAURA, I (1963)
Black Sail, The = CHERNYI PARUS (1929)
BLACK SECRET, THE (1919) d G Seitz w White (serial in 15 eps) Pat
BLACK SHEEP (1935) d Dwan c AC Miller w Trevor 75min Fox (= Star for a Night)
BLACK SHEEP OF WHITEHALL, THE (1941) co-d Hay co-d Dearden w Hay, J Mills 80min r UA
BLACK SHIELD OF FALWORTH, THE (1954) d Maté c Glassberg a Golitzen w Curtis, J Leigh, H Marshall, Rush CS* 99min U
BLACKSMITH, THE (1922) d/s Keaton, St Clair w Keaton 2rs
BLACK SPURS (1965) d Springsteen w Darnell CS* 81min Par
Black Sun = SOLEIL NOIR (1966)
Black Sunday (US) = MASCHERA DEL DEMONIO, LA (1960)
BLACK SWAN, THE (1942) d H King co-s B Hecht co-s/ad S Miller fn Rafael Sabatini c Shamroy m A Newman w Power, M O'Hara, Mitchell, G Sanders, Carradine, Quinn *85min Fox
BLACK THIRTEEN (1953) d K Hughes 77min
Black Tights (UK) = UN DEUX TROIS QUATRE! (1960)
BLACKTON THE EVENING WORLD CARTOONIST (c 1897) d Edison w Blackton
BLACKTOP (1952) d/s C and R Eames c C Eames m JS Bach *11min
BLACK TUESDAY (1954) d Fregonese st/s Boehm c Cortez w Robinson 71min
Black Tulip, The = TULIPE NOIRE, LA (1963)
BLACK VISION (1965) d Brakhage 16mm si 3min
BLACK WATCH, THE (1929) co-d J Ford c August w V McLaglen, M Loy 93min Fox
BLACK WATERS (1929) d Neilan
BLACK WIDOW (1954) d/p/s N Johnson c C Clarke a Wheeler m Harline w G Rogers, Tierney, Raft, Heflin CS* 95min Fox
BLADE AF SATANS BOG (1919) d/ad/co-a Dreyer 3018m (= Leaves from Satan's Book)
BLAJACKOR (1964) d Mattsson TR* 107min (= Boys in Blue)
BLANC ET LE NOIR, LE (1930) d Florey, M Allégret fpl Guitry w Raimu, Fernandel
BLANCHE (1971) d/s Borowczyk w M Simon, Gassman *90min
BLANCHE FURY (1947) d M Allégret fn Joseph Shearing c G Green, Unsworth w S Granger 109min JAR
BLANDT MANGE, EEN (1961) d A Henning Jensen c Fischer
BLATT PAPIER, EIN (1916) d/p/co-s May 4rs
BLAUE ENGEL, DER (1930) d/s Von Sternberg p Pommer co-ad Zuckmayer fn (Professor Unrath) Heinrich Mann co-s Rittau songs Hollander w Jannings, Dietrich UFA-Par
BLAUE LICHT, DAS (1932) d/p/st Riefenstahl s Balasz w Riefenstahl 86min
-BLAUE STUNDE, DIE (1952) d V Harlan 100min
BLAZE OF NOON (1947) d J Farrow c Mellor co-a Dreier w A Baxter, Holden, Bendix, Hayden 91min Par
BLAZES (1961) d Breer anim* 16mm 3min
BLAZING DAYS (1927) d Wyler 2rs U
BLAZING FOREST, THE (1952) d Edward Ludwig c Lindon w Moorehead, Payne *90min Par

BLAZING SIX SHOOTERS (1940) d JH Lewis 61min Col
BLAZING THE TRAIL (1912) d Ince w Conway (2 parts)
BLAZNOVA KRONIKA (1964) d/co-s Zeman 80min (= Dra Musketyri/The Jester's Tale)
BLED, LE (1929) d J Renoir (Becker)
BLE EN HERBE, LE (1954) d/co-s Autant-Lara co-s/di Aurenche, Bost fn Colette w Feuillère, De Funès 105min (= Ripening Seed)
BLEKITNY KRZYZ (1955) d/s Munk 59min (= Men of the Blue Cross)
BLESSED EVENT (1932) d Del Ruth c Polito w D Powell 83min WB
BLESS THE BEASTS AND CHILDREN (1971) d/p Kramer *101min r Col
BLEUS DU CIEL, LES (1936) d/s/di Decoin m Van Parys w Préjean
Blind = SLEPAYA (1930)
BLIND ADVENTURE (1933) d Schoedsack 67min RKO
BLIND ALLEY (1939) d C Vidor 69min Col
BLIND ALLEYS (1927) d Tuttle p Zukor 1706m Par
BLIND DATE (1959) d Losey co-s Barzman c Challis des R MacDonald w S Baker, Presle 95min (= Chance Meeting)
BLIND FATE (1914) d/p Hepworth 610m
BLINDE KUH (1915) d/w Lubitsch 1rl (= Blind Man's Buff)
BLINDFOLD (1965) d/co-s P Dunne s Joe MacDonald m Schifrin w Hudson, Cardinale PV* 102min U
BLIND GODDESS, THE (1926) d V Fleming co-p Zukor 2244m FPL r Par
BLIND GODDESS, THE (1948) d Harold French w (Bloom) 88min
BLIND HUSBANDS (1918) d/st/s/a/w von Stroheim c B Reynolds 8rs U
Blind Man's Buff = BLINDE KUH (1915)
BLINDNESS OF DIVORCE (1918) d/s F Lloyd 6rs
BLINDNESS OF FORTUNE, THE (1918) d/p Hepworth 4rs
BLIND TERROR (1971) d R Fleischer m E Bernstein w M Farrow *89min (= See No Evil)
BLINKENDE FENSTER, DAS (1919) d/s Jutzi 1419m
BLINKITY BLANK (1955) d McLaren *5min NFBC
BLISS (1967) d/s/c/e Markopoulos 16mm *6min
BLITHE SPIRIT (1945) d Lean co-p/s/fpl Coward c Neame w Harrison *96min
BLIXT OCH DUNDER (1938) d Anders Henrikson s/w Ekman (= Thunder and Lightning)
BLOB, THE (1958) d Yeaworth w McQueen *85min Par
BLOCKADE (1928) d G Seitz 71min
BLOCKADE (1938) d Dieterle p Wanger s Lawson c Maté w Carroll, H Fonda 85min r UA
BLOCK BUSTERS (1944) d Wallace Fox co-p Katzman w Langdon 60min Mon
BLOCKHEADS (1938) d John G Blystone p Roach co-st/co-s Langdon w Laurel, Hardy 55min
BLODETS ROST (1913) d/w Sjöstrom 1800m
BLODIGA TIDEN, DEN (1960) d/s/e Leiser 118min (= Mein Kampf)
BLOMSTERTID..., DEN (1939) d/s Sjöberg (= Flowering Time)
BLONDE BANDIT, THE (1949) d Keller 59min Rep
Blonde Bombshell, The = BOMBSHELL (1933)
BLONDE CRAZY (1931) d Del Ruth w Cagney, Blondell, Milland 75min WB (= Larceny Lane)
BLONDE FEVER (1944) d Richard Whorf co-a Gibbons w Astor, Grahame 69min MGM
BLONDE FRAU DES MAHARADSCHA, DIE (1962) d V Harlan *90min
BLONDE FROM SINGAPORE, THE (1941) d Dmytryk c O'Connell 67min Col
Blonde in Love, A (UK) = LASKY JEDNE PLAVOV-LASKY (1965)
BLONDE INSPIRATION (1941) d Berkeley 72min MGM
BLONDE SAINT, THE (1926) d Svend Gade c Gaudio w Roland 2075m r FN
Blonde Sinner = YIELD TO THE NIGHT (1956)
BLONDE'S REVENGE, A (1926) d/co-s Cline p Sennett w Turpin Pat
BLONDE VENUS (1932) d/st Von Sternberg co-s Furthman c Glennon w Dietrich, H Marshall, C Grant 80min Par
BLONDIE JOHNSON (1933) d Enright c Gaudio w Blondell 75min WB
BLONDIE OF THE FOLLIES (1932) d Goulding p Davies di Loos c Barnes w Davies, R Montgomery, Pitts 90min MGM
BLOOD ALLEY (1955) d Wellman c Clothier w J Wayne, Bacall, Ekberg CS* 115min pc J Wayne r WB
Blood and Black Lace = SEI DONNE PER L'ASSASSINO (1964)
Blood and Roses (UK) = ET MOURIR DE PLAISIR (1960)
BLOOD AND SAND (1922) d Niblo ad Mathis fn Vincente Blasco Ibañez w Valentino 2472m FPL r Par
BLOOD AND SAND (1941) d Mamoulian co-p Zanuck s Swerling fn Ibañez rm 1922 co-c Rennahan co-a Day co-m A Newman co-chor Boetticher w Power, Darnell, Hayworth, Nazimova, Quinn, Carradine *125min Fox
Blood and Soul = CHI TO REI (1922)
BLOOD ARROW (1958) d/ex-p Warren S 75min Fox
Blood Feast, The (US) = FIN DE FIESTA (1959)

Blood For Blood, Life For Life = KROV ZA KROV, SMERT ZA SMERT (1941)
BLOOD MONEY (1933) d Roland Brown m A Newman w G Bancroft 65min r UA
Blood of a Poet, The = SANG D'UN POETE, LE (1930)
Blood on Easter Sunday = NON C'E PACE TRA GLI ULIVI (1950)
Blood on the Balcony = BENITO MUSSOLINI (1961)
BLOOD ON THE MOON (1948) d Wise c Musuraca w Mitchum, Preston 88min RKO
BLOOD ON THE SUN (1945) d F Lloyd c Sparkuhl m Rozsa w Cagney, S Sidney *98min r UA
BLOOD FROM THE MUMMY'S TOMB (1971) d Holt, Michael Carreras (uc) fn (Jewel of the Seven Stars) Bram Stoker *94min
BLOOD ORANGE (1913) d Fisher 76min
BLOOD SHIP, THE (1927) d G Seitz p Cohn 2086m Col
BLOODY MAMA (1970) d/p Corman co-ex-p Arkoff w Winters *84min AI
BLOOMFIELD (1971) d R Harris, Uri Zohar (uc) c Heller w R Harris, Schneider *105min
Blossom = HANA (1941)
Blossoming Port = HANA SAKU MINATO (1943)
BLOSSOMS IN THE DUST (1941) d LeRoy s Loos co-a Gibbons m Stothart w Garson, Pidgeon *100min MGM
BLOTTO (1930) d James Parrott p Roach st McCarey w Laurel, Hardy (2rs) r MGM
Blouse King, The (UK) = BLUSENKONIG, DER (1917)
BLOWING WILD (1953) d Fregonese p Sperling st/s Yordan c Hickox m Tiomkin w G Cooper, Stanwyck, Roman, Quinn 90min WB
BLOW JOB (1964) d Warhol si 16mm 30min
BLOW-UP (1966) d/co-s Antonioni co-di Edward Bond c Di Palma w Hemmings, V Redgrave *111min pc Ponti r MGM
BLUE (1968) d Silvio Narizzano c Cortez w Stamp, Malden, Montalban PV* 113min
Blue and the Gold, The (UK) = AN ANNAPOLIS STORY (1955)
Blue Angel, The: English version of BLAUE ENGEL, DER (1930)
BLUE ANGEL, THE (1959) d Dymtryk p J Cummings s Nigel Baldwin rm c Shamroy co-a Wheeler m Friedhofer w Jurgens 107min Fox
BLUEBEARD (1944) d Ulmer w Carradine 72min PRC
Bluebeard = LANDRU (1962)
BLUEBEARD'S CASTLE (1964) d M Powell 63min
BLUEBEARD'S EIGHTH WIFE (1923) d S Wood w Swanson 6rs FPL
BLUEBEARD'S EIGHTH WIFE (1938) d/p Lubitsch s B Wilder, Brackett co-a Dreier m Hollander w G Cooper, Colbert, Horton, Niven 85min Par
BLUEBEARD'S SEVEN WIVES (1926) d Santell c E Haller 2370m FN
BLUE BIRD, THE (1918) d M Tourneur FPL
BLUE BIRD, THE (1940) d W Lang p Zanuck c AC Miller co-a R Day m A Newman w Temple 188min Fox
BLUE BLAZES (1936) d Raymond Kane w Keaton 19min
BLUE BLAZES RAWDEN (1918) d/pc/w W Hart c August 5rs
BLUE BLOOD AND RED (1916) d/p/s Walsh 5rs Fox
BLUEBOTTLES (1928) d Ivor Montagu fst HG Wells c F Young w Laughton 800m
Blue Continent (UK) = SESTO CONTINENTO (1954)
BLUE DAHLIA, THE (1946) d G Marshall s R Chandler c Lindon co-a Dreier m V Young w Ladd, Lake, Bendix 96min Par
BLUE DANUBE, THE (1932) d H Wilcox w Helm 70min
BLUE DENIM (1959) d/co-s P Dunne p C Brackett fpl James Leo Herlihy, W Noble co-a Wheeler m Herrmann w Lynley CS 89min Fox (= Blue Jeans)
BLUE EAGLE, THE (1926) d J Ford p Fox w G O'Brien, J Gaynor d Butler 1890m Fox
Blue Express, The = GOLUBOI EKSPRESS (1929)
Bluefin Fury (UK) = CONTADINI DEL MARE (1955)
BLUE GARDENIA, THE (1953) d F Lang st Caspary c Musuraca w A Baxter, Conte, Sothern, Burr 90min r WB
BLUE HAWAII (1961) d Taurog p Wallis s Kanter c C Lang co-a Pereira w Presley PV* 101min Fox
BLUE JEANS (1958) d/co-s/co-e Rozier 22min
Blue Jeans (UK) = BLUE DENIM (1959)
BLUE LAGOON, THE (1948) d/co-s Launder co-s/p Gilliat c Unsworth w J Simmons 103min
BLUE LAMP, THE (1949) d Dearden p Balcon s T Clarke di Mackendrick w Bogarde 84min
BLUE MAX, THE (1966) d Guillermin ex-p Elmo Williams co-ad Barzman c Slocombe m Goldsmith w Peppard, Mason, Andress CS* 155min Fox
BLUE MOSES (1962) d Brakhage 16mm 11min
Blue Mountains = AOI-SANMYAKU (1949)
BLUE MOVIE (1968) d Warhol *16mm 90min
BLUE MURDER AT ST TRINIAN'S (1957) d/co-p/co-s Launder co-p/co-s Gilliat m M Arnold 86min BL
BLUEPRINT FOR MURDER, A (1953) d/s Stone co-a Wheeler w Cotten, Peters 77min Fox
Blue Revolution, The = AOIRO KAKUMEI (1953)
BLUES DELLA DOMENICA, (1951) d Zurlini sh
BLUES FOR LOVERS (1966) d/co-s Henreid 89min Fox

BLUE SIERRA (1946) *d* F Wilcox *co-m* Kaper (*10rs) MGM
BLUES IN THE NIGHT (1941) *d* Litvak *s* Rossen *c* E Haller *w* Nolan, Kazan 88min WB
BLUE SKIES (1946) *d* Heisler *p* S Siegel *co-c* C Lang *m Irving Berlin w* B Crosby, Astaire 104min Par
BLUES PATTERN (1956) *d* Pintoff
BLUE VEIL, THE (1951) *d* C Bernhardt *p* Wald, Krasna *c* Planer *w* Wyman, Laughton, Moorehead, N Wood 113min RKO
BLUFF, LE (1916) *d/s* Feyder 431m Gau
BLUFF (1924) *d* S Wood *co-p* Zukor *s* Goldbeck 1659m FPL *r* Par
BLUMEN AUS NIZZA (1936) *d* Genina *c* Planer
Blundering Boob, The = NEW JANITOR, THE (1914)
BLUSENKONIG, DER (1917) *d/w* Lubitsch (1rl) (= *The Blouse King*)
BLUSHING BRIDE, THE (1921) *d/st/s* Furthman (5rs) Fox
Blushing Charlie (UK) = LYCKLIGA SKITAR (1970)
Blüten, Gauner und die Nacht von Nizza = JARDINIER D'ARGENTEUIL (1966)
BOAT, THE (1921) *d/s* Keaton, Cline *w* Keaton (2rs)
Boat, The = BATEN (1961) *d* Troell
BOAT RACE (1899) *p* Hepworth
BOB AND CAROL AND TED AND ALICE (1969) *d/co-s Paul Mazursky p* Frankovich *c* C Lang *w* N Wood *105min
BOBBED HAIR (1925) *d* Crosland *s* Milestone (8rs)
BOB HAMPTON OF PLACER (1921) *d/p/pc* Neilan 2216m *r* FN
BOB LE FLAMBEUR (1955) *d/st/co-s/des/cy* Melville *c* Decaë 100min
BOBO, THE (1967) *d* Parrish *w* Sellers 105min WB
BOBS (1928) *d/e* Grémillon *c* Périnal 340m
BOCCACCIO '70 (1962) *p* Ponti *156min
ep IL LAVORA *d/co-s* Visconti *co-s* Cecchi D'Amico *st* Zavattini *fst* (*Au Bord du Lit*) *Maupassant c* Rotunno *m* Rota *w* Schneider 46min
ep LE TENTAZIONI DEL DOTTOR ANTONIO *d/co-st/co-s* Fellini *co-s* Rondi *c* Martelli *m* Rota *w* Ekberg
ep LE RIFFA *d* De Sica *s* Zavattini *c* Martelli *w* Loren
ep RENZO E LUCIANA *d/co-s* Monicelli *c* Martelli *m* Rota
BODAKUNGEN (1920) *d/s* Molander SF
BODY AND SOUL (1927) *d Reginald Barker co-dec* Gibbons *w* L Barrymore 1799m MGM
BODY AND SOUL (1931) *d* Santell *w* Bogart, M Loy 70min Fox
BODY AND SOUL (1947) *d* Rossen *s* Polonsky *c* Howe *e* Parrish *m* Friedhofer *w* Garfield, Palmer, Pevney 104min *r* UA
BODYGUARD (1948) *d* R Fleischer 62min RKO
BODY SNATCHER, THE (1945) *d* Wise *p* Lewton *fst R L Stevenson w* Karloff, Lugosi 77min RKO
BOEING THE LEADING EDGE (1966) *d/s* C and R Eames *c* C Eames *11min
BOHATERSTWO POLSKIEGO SKAVTO (1919) *d* Boleslavsky
BOHEME, LA (1926) *d/p* K Vidor *co-a* Gibbons *w* L Gish, J Gilbert, Horton, Adorée 2676m *r* MGM
BOHEMIAN GIRL, THE (1936) *d James Horne, Charles Rogers w* Laurel, Hardy (8rs) *r* MGM
BOIA DI LILLA, IL (1952) *d* Cottafavi 90min (= *La Vita Avventurosa di Milady*)
BOI POD TSARITSYNOM (1919) *d/s/co-c/e* Vertov (1rl) (= *Fighting Near Tsaritsin*)
BOIS DES AMANTS, LE (1960) *d* Autant-Lara *w* Rosay 96min (= *Between Love and Duty*)
BOITE A MUSIQUE (1961) *d* Borowczyk, Lenica *anim*
BOITE AUX REVES, LA (1943) *d/co-s* Y Allégret *w* Romance, Signoret
BOKHANDLAREN SOM SLUTADE BADA (1968) *d/s/w* Kulle *000min San (= *The Bookseller Who Gave Up Bathing*)
BOKU NO MARUMAGE (1933) *d* Naruse
BOL D'AIR A LOUE, UN (1962) *d/co-c* Reichenbach *m* Legrand *47min FS (= *La Douceur du village*)
Bold Seven, The = SEMERO SMELYKH (1936)
BOLERO (1934) *d* W Ruggles *chor* Prinz *w* Milland, Raft, Lombard, Sheridan (*as* Clara Lou Sheridan) 81min Par
BOLOND APRILIS (1957) *d/dec* Fábri (= *Summer Clouds/April Fools*)
BOLSHAYA SEMYA (1954) *d* Heifitz *w* Batalov 108min (= *The Big Family*)
BOLSHAYA ZEMLYA (1944) *d/s* Gerasimov 90min (= *The Big Land*)
BOLSHOI BALLET, THE (1957) *d* Czinner *100min
BOMBARDMENT OF MAFEKING (1899) *p* Paul 18m
BOMBAY TALKIE (1970) *d/co-s* Ivory *c* Mitra *112min
BOMBEN UBER MONTE CARLO *d Hans Schwartz w* Sten
BOMBERS B-52 (1957) *d* G Douglas *c* Clothier *w* Malden, N Wood CS* 106min WB (= *No Sleep Till Dawn*)
Bomb Mania = BOMBOMANIE (1958)
BOMBOMANIE (1958) *d/co-s* Pojar *co-s* Brdecka *anim** 14min (= *Bomb Mania*)
BOMBSHELL (1933) *d* V Fleming *p* H Hughes *s* Mahin, Furthman *co-c* Rosson *w* Harlow, Tone 93min MGM (= *The Blonde Bombshell*)
Bombsight Stolen (US) = COTTAGE TO LET (1941)
BOMBS OVER BURMA (1942) *d/co-s* JH Lewis 62min PRC
Bombs Over Japan = WILD BLUE YONDER, THE (1951)
BONANZA BUCKAROO, THE (1926) *d* Thorpe 1369m
BONAPARTE ET LA REVOLUTION (1971) *d/co-p/s/co-e* Gance *co-p* Lelouch *rm* NAPOLEON VU PAR ABEL GANCE (1926) *co-c* Burel *w* Artaud, Gance, Annabella 275min
BON BOCK, UN (1891) *d* Reynaud (paper)
BONCHI (1960) *d/co-s* Ichikawa *c* Miyagawa *w* Kyo S* 104min Dai
BOND, THE (1918) *d/s* Chaplin *c* Totheroh *w* Chaplin, Purviance (½rl) (= *Charles Chaplin in a Liberty Bond Appeal*)
BONDAGE (1933) *d* Santell *c* Andriot *w* Darwell 67min
BONDBOY, THE (1922) *d* H King (7rs)
BON DIEU SANS CONFESSION, LE (1953) *d/co-s* Autant-Lara *w* Darrieux 112min
BOND OF FEAR (1918) *d* Conway
Bone Head, The (re-issue) = HIS FAVOURITE PASTIME (1914)
BONHEUR, LE (1934) *d* L'Herbier *w* Boyer, Simon 98min Pat
BONHEUR, LE (1964) *d/st/s* Varda *co-c* Rabier *mf Mozart* *79min (= *Happiness*)
BONHEUR D'ETRE AIMEE, LE (1966) *d/pc* Storck 16min
BONJOUR, M LA BRUYERE (1956) *d* Doniol-Valcroze *ftexts La Bruyère* 21min
BONJOUR SOURIRE (1955) *d* Sautet 90min (= *Sourire aux lèvres*)
BONJOUR TRISTESSE (1958) *d/p* -*Preminger fn Françoise Sagan c* Périnal *des* Furse *cr* Bass *m* Auric *w* Kerr, Niven, Seberg CS part* 93min Col
BONNE CHANCE (1935) *d/s/fpl* Guitry *c* Bachelet *w* Guitry
BONNE CHANCE, CHARLIE (1962) *d/co-s* Richard *w* Constantine 89min
BONNES A TUER (1954) *d/co-ad/co-di* Decoin *dec* D'Eaubonne *w* Darrieux 90min
BONNES CAUSES, LES (1963) *d/co-s* Christian-Jaque *ad/di* Jeanson *c* Thirard *w* Bourvil, Brasseur, Vlady S 120min
BONNES FEMMES, LES (1960) *d/st* Chabrol *c* Decaë *co-m* Misraki 104min Pat
BONNIE AND CLYDE (1967) *d* Penn *p* Beatty *c* Guffey *w* Beatty, Dunaway *111min *r* WB
BONNIE BONNIE LASSIE (1919) *d/co-s* Browning (6rs) U
BONNIE SCOTLAND (1935) *d James Horne p* Roach *w* Laurel, Hardy 80min *r* MGM
BONS VIVANTS, LES (1965) *di* Audiard 105min (= *How to Keep the Red Lamp Burning*)
eps LA FERMATURE *and* LE PROCES *d* Grangier
ep LES BONS VIVANTS *w* De Funès, Darc
BON VOYAGE (1944) *d* Hitchcock *c* Krampf (4rs)
BON VOYAGE! (1962) *d* Neilson *w* Wyman, MacMurray *133min *pc* Disney
BOOB, THE (1926) *d* Wellman *c* Daniels *co-a* Gibbons *w* J Crawford 1530m MGM (= *The Yokel*)
BOOGIE DOODLE (1939–41) *d* McLaren *3½min
BOOK BARGAIN (1937–39) *d* McLaren *p* Grierson 10min GPO
Bookseller Who Gave up Bathing, The = BOKHANDLAREN SOM SLUTADE BADA (1968)
BOOM (1968) *d* Losey *s/fpl* (*The Milk Train Doesn't Stop Here Anymore*) T Williams *c* Slocombe *des* R MacDonald *m* Barry *w* Burton, E Taylor, Coward PV* 113min
BOOM, IL (1963) *d* De Sica *co-p* De Laurentiis *s* Zavattini *m* Piccioni *w* Sordi 97min
BOOM GOES THE GROOM (1939) *d/w* C Chase (2rs) Col
BOOMERANG, THE (1913) *d* Ince
BOOMERANG! (1947) *d* Kazan *p* De Rochemont *s* R Murphy *c* Brodine *co-a* R Day *w* D Andrews, Cobb, A Kennedy, Malden 88min Fox
BOOM TOWN (1940) *d* Conway *s* Mahin *fst* (*A Lady Comes to Burkburnett*) J Grant *a* Gibbons *m* Waxman *w* Gable, Tracy, Colbert, Lamour 116min MGM
BOOTS MALONE (1951) *d* Dieterle *s* Buchman *c* Lawton *w* Holden 103min Col
BOP GIRL (1957) *d* HW Koch 79min *r* UA
BORBA GIGANTOV (1926) *d* Turin 2785m (= *Battle of the Giants*)
BORDER CAVALIER (1927) *d* Wyler *p* Laemmle 1349m U
BORDER INCIDENT (1949) *d* A Mann *c* J Alton *m* Previn *w* Montalban, G Murphy 95min MGM
BORDER LEGION, THE (1924) *d* W Howard *fn Zane Grey* 2149m FPL *r* Par
Border of Life, The (UK) = AUX FRONTIERES DE L'HOMME (1953)
BORDER ROMANCE (1930) *d* Thorpe (7rs)
Border Street = ULICA GRANICZNA (1948)
BORDER TOWN (1935) *d* A Mayo *c* Gaudio *w* Muni, B Davis 90min WB
BORDER WIRELESS, THE (1918) *d/pc* W Hart *supn* Ince *c* August (5 rs)
BORDER WOLVES (1938) *d* JH Lewis 56min U
BORED OF EDUCATION (1937) *d* G Douglas *p* Roach (1 rl)
BORETS I KLOUN (1957) *d* Barnet, *K Yudin* 100min (= *The Wrestler and the Clown*)
BORINAGE (1933) *d/s/c* Ivens, Storck 26min (= *Misère au Borinage*)
Boring Afternoon, A = FADNI ODPOLEDNE (1965)
BORNENES SYND (1916) *d* Madsen
BORNEO (1954) *d* Bourguignon 16mm* 18min
BORNEVENNERNE (1914) *d* Madsen
BORN FREE (1965) *d Tom McGowan p* Foreman PV* 95min
BORN LUCKY (1932) *d* M Powell 78min
BORN RECKLESS (1930) *co-d* J Ford *s* D Nichols 82min Fox
BORN RECKLESS (1937) *d* St Clair 59min Fox
BORN RECKLESS (1959) *d* HW Koch *c* Biroc 79min WB
BORN TO BE BAD (1934) *d* L Sherman *m* A Newman *w* L Young, C Grant 61min *r* UA
BORN TO BE BAD (1950) *d* N Ray *co-ad* Schnee *c* Musuraca *m* Hollander *w* Fontaine, Ryan, M Ferrer 94min RKO
BORN TO DANCE (1936) *d* Del Ruth *p* J Cummings *c* June *m Cole Porter w* J Stewart (11rs) MGM
BORN TO KILL (1947) *d* Wise *w* Cook, Trevor 92min RKO
BORN TO SING (1942) *d Edward Ludwig chor* Berkeley *w* Dumont (8rs) MGM
BORN TO WIN (1971) *d/co-s* Passer *co-p/w* Segal *90min *r* UA
BORN YESTERDAY (1951) *d* Cukor *fpl* Kanin *c* J Walker *co-des* Horner *m* Hollander *w* Holliday, Holden, B Crawford 103min Col
BORO NO KESSHITAI (1942) *d* Imai (= *Suicide Troops of the Watch Tower*)
BORROWED HERO (1941) *d Lewis D Collins co-st* Roberts 65min Mon
BORSALINO (1970) *d/co-s* Deray *p* Delon *co-s* Sautet *w* Belmondo, Delon, (Darc) 126min *r* Par
BORSE, DIE (1939) *d/p* Richter (2½rs)
BORYOKU (1952) *d* Yoshimura *s* Shindo (= *Violence*)
Bosch = PARADISO PERDUTO, IL (1948)
BOSCHI SUL MARE (1942) *d* Chiari
BOSS, THE (1956) *d* Haskin *c* Mohr *w* Payne 89min *r* UA
BOSS OF BULLION CITY (1940) *d Ray Taylor w* Montez 59min U
BOSS OF HANGTOWN MESA, THE (1942) *d* JH Lewis 58min U
BOSSU, LE (1944) *d* Delannoy *c* Matras *m* Auric
BOSTON STRANGLER, THE (1968) *d* R Fleischer *co-a* R Day *w* Curtis, H Fonda, G Kennedy PV 114min Fox
BOTAN (1963) *d* Kuri *anim* 3min (= *The Button*)
BOTANY BAY (1953) *d* J Farrow *c* J Seitz *co-a* Pereira *w* Ladd, Mason *94min Par
Both Ends of the Candle (UK) = HELEN MORGAN STORY, THE (1957)
BOTTA E RISPOSTA (1950) *d/co-s* Soldati 80min
Botticelli = ALLEGORIA DI PRIMAVERA (1949)
BOTTLE IMP, THE (1917) *d* Neilan *fst Robert Louis Stevenson* (5 rs)
BOTTOM OF THE BOTTLE, THE (1956) *d* Hathaway *p* Adler *fn Georges Simenon c* Garmes *co-a* Wheeler *m* Harline *w* Cotten, Roman, V Johnson CS* 88min Fox (= *Beyond the River*)
BOTTOMS UP (1934) *d/co-st/co-s* D Butler *w* Faye, Tracy 86min Fox
BOUCHER, LE (1969) *d/s* Chabrol *c* Rabier *90min
BOUDOIR DIPLOMAT, THE (1930) *d* St Clair *p* Laemmle *c* Freund 68min U
BOUDU SAUVE DES EAUX (1932) *d/co-ad* J Renoir *co-p* M Simon *w* M Simon (Becker)
BOUGHT (1931) *d* A Mayo *c* June *w* Constance Bennett, Milland 92min WB
BOULANGERE DE MONCEAU, LA (1962) *d/s/e* Rohmer 16mm 26min
Boule de Suif = PUSHKA (1934)
BOULE DE SUIF (1945) *d* Christian-Jaque *s* Jeanson *c* Matras *w* Presle
BOULEVARD (1960) *d/co-ad* Duvivier *fn Robert Sabotier* 95min
BOULEVARD DU RHUM (1971) *d/co-ad/co-di* Enrico *w* Bardot, Ventura
BOUND AND GAGGED (1919) *d/w* G Seitz (series in 10 ep) Pat
BOUNDARY HOUSE (1918) *d/p/c* Hepworth (5rs)
BOUND IN MOROCCO (1918) *d/s* Dwan *p/w* Fairbanks Sr (4 rs) *r* FPL
Bountiful Summer = SHCHEDROYE LETO (1951)
BOUNTY HUNTER, THE (1954) *d* De Toth *w* R Scott, Borgnine * WB
BOUNTY KILLER, THE (1965) *d Spencer G Bennet w* G M Anderson, Duryea, *Buster Crabbe, Johnny Mack Brown* S* 93min
BOURGEOIS GENTILHOMME, LE (1958) *d Jean Meyer tech adviser* Deville *w Comédie Française* *97min
BOURGOGNE, LA (1936) *d* J Epstein 33min
Bourreau, Le = TETE DE TURC (1935)
BOURSE ET LA VIE, LA (1965) *d/co-s* Mocky *w* Fernandel *91min (= *Your Money or Your Life*)
BOUT-DE-ZAN (1912–16) *d/s* Feuillade (series of 45 films)
BOW BELLS (1954) *d/s* A Simmons *c* Lassally 14min
BOWERY, THE (1933) *d* Walsh *co-as-p* Goetz *a* R Day *m* A Newman *w* W Beery, Raft 90min *r* UA

BOWERY BOMBSHELL (1946) *d* Karlson 65min Mon
BOWLING MATCH, THE (1913) *d* Sennett *w* Normand 1rl Key
BOY AND HIS DOG, A (1947) *d* Prinz *10min WB
Boy = SHONEN (1969)
BOY . . . A GIRL, A (1969) *d/s/c/lyr* Derek *71min
Boy and the Kite, The (UK) = POJKEN OCH DRAKEN (1961)
Boyar's Plot, The = IVAN GROZNY, PART II (1945)
BOY, DID I GET A WRONG NUMBER! (1966) *d* G Marshall *co-s* Lewin *c* Lindon *w* Hope *99min *r* UA
BOY FRIEND, THE (1971) *d/p/s* K Russell *fpl* Sandy Wilson *c* Watkin *108min
BOY FROM OKLAHOMA, THE (1953) *d* Curtiz *p* Weisbart *c* Burks *88min WB
Boy in the Tree, The (UK) = POJKEN I TRADET (1960)
BOY MEETS GIRL (1938) *d* Bacon *p* Wallis *w* Cagney, Reagan 86min WB
BOY OF REVOLUTION, A (1911) *w* Cruze
BOY ON A DOLPHIN (1957) *d* Negulesco *c* Krasner *co-a* Wheeler *m* Friedhofer *w* Ladd, C Webb, Loren CS* 111min Fox
Boys, The = CHICOS, LOS (1960)
BOYS, THE (1962) *d* Furie *m* The Shadows CS 123m
Boys From the West Coast = VESTERHAUSDRENGE (1950)
Boys in Blue = BLAJACKOR (1964)
BOYS' NIGHT OUT (1962) *d* M Gordon *c* Arling *w* Novak, Garner, Randall, Bendix CS* 115min MGM
Boys of Paul Street, The = PAL ATCAI FIUK, A (1969)
BOYS OF THE CITY (1940) *d* JH Lewis *p* Katzman 65min Mon
BOYS RANCH (1946) *d* Rowland *co-a* Gibbons 97min MGM
BOY'S TOWN (1938) *d* Taurog *co-st/co-s* Schary *co-e* Vorkapich *w* Tracy, Rooney 9rs MGM
BOYS WILL BE BOYS (1921) *d* Badger *w* W Rogers 1311m Goldwyn
BOYS WILL BE BOYS (1935) *d* William Beaudine *co-s/w* Hay (8rs)
Boy 10 Feet Tall, A (US) = SAMMY GOING SOUTH (1963)
BOY WHO STOLE A MILLION, THE (1960) *d/co-s* Crichton *c* Slocombe 81min BL
BOY WITH GREEN HAIR, THE (1948) *d* Losey *ex-p* Schary *co-s* Barzman *c* Barnes *des consultant* J Hubley *m* Harline *w* Ryan *82min RKO
BRAEUTIGAM, DIE KOMOEDIANTIN UND DER ZUHAELTER, DER (1968) *d/co-s/pc* Straub 23min
BRA FLICKA REDER SIG SJALV (1915) *d/s* Sjostrom 850m
BRAHMINE ET LE PAPILLON, LE (1901) *d* Méliès 40m
BRAIN MACHINE, THE (1955) *d/s* K Hughes 83min
BRAINWASHED (1961) *d* G Oswald *w* Jurgens, Bloom 102min AA
BRANCALEONE ALLE CROCIATE *d* Monicelli *c* Tonti *w* Gassman *129min
BRAND, THE (1913) *d* Ince 1100m
BRANDED (1950)
  Maté *co-s* Boehm *c* C Lang *co-a* Dreier *w* Ladd, Bickford 95min Par
BRANDED WOMAN, THE (1920) *d/co-ad* Albert Parker *co-ad* Loos *w* N Talmadge 7rs
BRANDENDE STRAAL (1911) *d/w* Ivens 200m (= *De Wigwam*)
BRAND IM OZEAN (1939) *d* Rittau *w* Staudte 96min
BRANDING (1928) *co-d/c/e* Ivens *co-d/s* Mannus Franken 900m
BRANDING BROADWAY (1918) *d/co-pc/w* W Hart *c* August 5rs
BRAND NEW HERO, A (1914) *d/w* Arbuckle 1rl Key
BRASHER DOUBLOON, THE (1947) *d* Brahm *fnr* (*The High Window*) Chandler *w* G Montgomery 72min Fox
BRASIER ARDENT, LE (1923) *d/s/w* Mozhukhin *supn* Alexander Volkov
BRASS (1923) *d* Franklin *c* Brodine 2560m WB
BRASS BOTTLE, THE (1964) *d* Keller *w* Ives, Randall *89min U
BRASS BUTTONS (1919) *d* H King 5rs
BRASS KNUCKLES (1927) *d* Bacon *c* Brodine 1929m WB
BRASS LEGEND, THE (1956) *d* G Oswald *w* Burr 79min *r* UA
BRAT, THE (1919) *d* Herbert Blache *s* Mathis *w* Nazimova 7rs
BRAT, THE (1931) *d* J Ford *co-s* SN Behrman *c* August 81min Fox
BRAT GEROYA (1940) *d* Y Vasilchikov *a* Donskoi 76min
BRATISHKA (1927) *d/s* L Trauberg, Kozintsev *c* Moskvin *w* Gerasimov 1504m
BRATS (1930) *d* James Parrott *p* Roach *st* McCarey *w* Laurel, Hardy (2rs) *r* MGM
BRAVADOS, THE (1958) *d* H King *s* Yordan *c* Shamroy *co-a* Wheeler *m* Friedhofer, A Newman *w* Peck, Boyd CS* 98min Fox
Brave and the Beautiful, The (UK) = MAGNIFICENT MATADOR, THE (1955)
BRAVE CULLS, THE (1951) *d/p* Rossen *c* F Crosby, Howe *w* M Ferrer, Quinn 108min Col

BRAVE DON'T CRY, THE (1952) *d* P Leacock *p* Grierson 90min
BRAVE ONE, THE (1956) *d* Rapper *st* Trumbo (*ps* Robert Rich) *c* Cardiff *m* V Young CS* 100min RKO
Brave Soldier At Dawn, A = AKATSUKI NO YUSHI (1926)
BRAZEN BEAUTY, THE (1918) *d* Browning 5rs
BRAZIL: A REPORT ON TORTURE (1971) *d* Wexler, *Saul Landau* 60min
BRAZZA (1954) *d* Quilici sh
Bread = KHLEB (1918)
BREAD (1953) *d/s* C and R Eames *c* C Eames *6min
Bread of Love, The = KARLEKENS BROD (1953)
Break, The (UK) = RUPTURE (1961)
BREAKFAST AT SUNRISE (1927) *d* St Clair *p* C Talmadge *w* C Talmadge, Dressler 1897m FN
BREAKFAST AT TIFFANY'S (1961) *d* Edwards *s* Axelrod *fn* Truman Capote *c* Planer *co-a* Pereira *m* Mancini *w* A Hepburn, Peppard, Neal, Rooney *115min Par
BREAKING IT UP AT THE MUSEUM (1960) *d* Pennebaker *w* Tinguely 16mm 8min
BREAKING POINT, THE (1924) *d* Brenon *c* Howe 7rs Par
BREAKING POINT, THE (1950) *d* Curtiz *p* Wild *s* MacDougall *fn* (*To Have and Have Not*) Hemingway *c* McCord *w* Neal, Garfield 97min WB
BREAKING THE ICE (1938) *d* Cline *w* C Ruggles 81min RKO
Breaking the Sound Barrier = SOUND BARRIER, THE (1952)
BREAK THE NEWS (1938) *d/co-p/co-s* Clair *dec* Meerson *w* Chevalier 78min (= *Fausses Nouvelles*)
Break to Freedom (US) = ALBERT RN (1955)
BREAKING (1963) *d* Breer anim 16mm 6min
Breathless = A BOUT DE SOUFFLE (1959)
BREATH OF SCANDAL, A (1960) *d* Curtiz *w* Loren, Chevalier *90min
BREED OF MEN (1919) *d* Lambert Hillyer *supn* Ince *c* August *w* W Hart 5rs *pc* W Hart
BRENNENDES GEHEIMNIS (1933) *d* Siodmak *fst* Stefan Zweig *w* Richter 91min Ufa (= *The Burning Secret*)
BRENNENDE ACKER, DER (1922) *d* Murnau *co-s* Von Harbou *co-c* Freund, F Wagner *w* Krauss (= *The Burning Acre*)
BRENNER I NATT!, DET (1954) *d* Skouen 96min
BRESIL DES THEOPHILIENS, LE (1953) *d* Enrico TV
BRETAGNE, LA (1936) *d* J Epstein 44min
BREWSTER'S MILLIONS (1945) *d* Dwan *c* Lawton *m* Friedhofer 79min *r* UA
BRIBE, THE (1949) *d* Leonard *p* Berman *c* Ruttenberg *m* Rozsa *w* R Taylor, Gardner, Laughton, Price 98min MGM
BRIDAL PATH *d/co-p/s* Launder *co-p* Gilliat 95min BL
BRIDE CAME C.O.D., THE (1941) *d* Keighley *p* Wallis *s* JJ Epstein *c* E Haller *m* M Steiner *co-sp* *eff* Haskin *w* Cagney, B Davis 91min WB
BRIDAL SUITE (1939) *d* William Thiele *co-st* G Reinhardt *w* R Young, Annabella 69min MGM
BRIDE COMES HOME, THE (1936) *d/p* W Ruggles *w* Colbert, MacMurray, R Young 82min Par
Bride From Japan, The = HANAYOME-SANWA SE KAIICHI (1959)
BRIDE GOES WILD, THE (1948) *d* Taurog *c* June *co-a* Gibbons *w* V Johnson, Allyson 98min MGM
Bridegroom Talks in his Sleep, The = HANAMUKO NO NEGOTO (1934)
BRIDE OF FRANKENSTEIN (1935) *d* Whale *m* Waxman *w* Karloff, Carradine 80min U
Bride of Glomdal (UK) = GLOMDALSBRUDEN (1925)
Bride of the Andes (UK) = ANDES NO HANAYOME (1966)
BRIDE OF THE COLORADO (1927) *p* Bray
BRIDE OF THE STORM (1926) *d/p* Blackton *w* Power 7rs WB
BRIDE OF VENGEANCE (1949) *d* Leisen *c* Fapp *co-a* Dreier *m* Friedhofer *w* Goddard, Burr 91min Par
BRIDE'S AWAKENING, THE (1918) *d* Leonard 6rs
BRIDES OF DRACULA, THE (1960) *d* Fisher 85min JAR
BRIDE SUR LE COU, LA (1961) *d/co-s* Vadim *m* Jarre *w* Bardot, Darc CS 85min
Bride Talks in her Sleep, The = HANAYOME NO NEGOTO (1933)
Bride Wore Black, The = MARIEE ETAIT EN NOIR, LA (1967)
BRIDE WORE BOOTS, THE *d* Pichel *co-a* Dreier *w* Stanwyck, Cummings, N Wood, Benchley 86min Par
Bridge, The = BRUG, DE (1928)
BRIDGE, THE (1929) *d* C Vidor
BRIDGE, THE (1942) *d* W Van Dyke *s* Maddow 27min
Bridge, The (UK) = BRUCKE, DIE (1959)
Bridge Across No River = HASHI NO NAI KAWA (1969)
BRIDGE AT REMAGEN, THE (1969) *d* Guillermin *c* Cortez *m* E Bernstein *w* Segal, Vaughn PV* *r* UA
Bridge of Japan = NIHOMBASHI (1956)
BRIDGE OF SAN LUIS REY, THE (1929) *d* Charles Brabin *fn* T Wilder *a* Gibbons 88min MGM
BRIDGE OF SAN LUIS REY, THE (1944) *d* Rowland V Lee *p* Bogeaus *fn* T Wilder *m* Tiomkin *w* Tamiroff, Nazimova 106min *r* UA

BRIDGE ON THE RIVER KWAI, THE (1957) *d* Lean *p* Spiegel *co-s/fn* Pierre Boulle *co-s* Foreman (*uc*), M Wilson (*uc*) *c* Hildyard *m* M Arnold *w* Holden, Guinness, Hawkins CS* 161min *r* Col
BRIDGES AT TOKO-RI, THE (1955) *d* Robson *p* Perlberg *c* Griggs, C Clarke *co-a* Periera *w* Holden, Grace Kelly, March, Rooney *103min Par
BRIDGES-GO-ROUND (1958) *d/p/c/e* S Clarke *3½min
BRIDGE WIVES (1932) *d* Arbuckle (*ps* William Goodrich) 11min
BRIEF ECSTASY (1937) *d* Greville
BRIEF ENCOUNTER (1945) *d/co-s* Lean *co-p/co-s* Neame *co-p/ad/fpl* (*Still Life*) Coward *c* Krasker *w* T Howard 86min
BRIEF SEASON, A (1969) *d* Castellani *p* De Laurentiis
BRIG, THE (1964) *co-d/e* A Mekas *co-d/c* J Mekas *des* Julian Beck *w* The Living Theatre 68min
BRIGADEN O SVERIGE (1945) *d/s* B Henning Jensen
BRIGADE SAUVAGE, LA (1939) *d* L'Herbier 91min
BRIGADOON (1954) *d* Minnelli *p* Freed *s* Lerner *fmpl* A Lerner, *Loewe* *c* Ruttenberg *co-a* Gibbons *chor* Gene Kelly *w* Gene Kelly, V Johnson, Charisse CS* 102min MGM
BRIGAND, THE (1952) *d* Karlson *w* Quinn *94min Col
BRIGANTE, IL (1961) *d/co-s* Castellani *m* Rota 180min
BRIGANTE DI TACCA DEL LUPPO, IL (1953) *d/co-st/co-s* Germi *co-st* Fellini 103min
BRIGANTE MUSOLINO, IL (1950) *d/co-s* Camerini *p* Ponti, De Laurentiis *co-st/co-s* Monicelli, Steno *c* Tonti *w* Mangano 94min (= *Fugitive*)
BRIGANTI ITALIANAI, I (1961) *d/co-s* Camerini *w* Gassman, Borgnine, Tamiroff 106min (= *Seduction of the South*)
BRIGHAM YOUNG (1940) *d* Hathaway *as-p* MacGowan *s* Trotti *m* A Newman *w* Power, Darnell, Carradine, Price, Astor, Darwell 114min Fox
Brigham Young, Frontiersman = BRIGHAM YOUNG (1940)
BRIGHT EYES (1921) *d* St Clair *p/s* Sennett *w* Turpin 2rs
BRIGHT EYES (1934) *d/co-st* D Butler *c* AC Miller *w* Temple, Darwell 84min Fox
BRIGHT LEAF (1950) *d* Curtiz *p* Blanke *s* MacDougall *m* V Young *w* G Cooper, Bacall, Neal, Crisp 110min WB
BRIGHT LIGHTS, THE (1916) *d/w* Arbuckle *w* Normand 2rs Tri (= *The Lure of Broadway*)
BRIGHT LIGHTS (1925) *d* Leonard *c* J Arnold *co-a* Gibbons 1875m MGM
BRIGHT LIGHTS (1930) *d* Curtiz *c* Garmes *71min FN
BRIGHT LIGHTS (1935) *d* Berkeley *c* Hickox 83min WB
BRIGHTON ROCK (1947) *d* J Boulting *p* R Boulting *co-s/fn* Greene *co-s* Rattigan *w* Attenborough 95min ABC (= *Young Scarface*)
Bright Path, The = SVETLYI PUT (1940)
BRIGHT SHAWL, THE (1923) *d* John S Robertson *ad* Goulding *c* Folsey *w* Barthelmess, Robinson, Astor, W Powell, D Gish 2287m FN
BRIGHT VICTORY (1951) *d* Robson *c* Daniels *w* A Kennedy 97min U
BRIGHTY OF THE GRAND CANYON (1967) *d/s* Foster *w* Cotten *87min
BRINGING UP BABY (1938) *d/p* Hawks *co-s* D Nichols *c* Metty *w* C Grant, K Hepburn, C Ruggles 102min RKO
BRINGING UP FATHER (1928) *d* Conway *c* Daniels *co-a* Gibbons *w* Dressler 1933m MGM
BRINGING UP FATHER (1946) *d/co-st* Cline *c* O'Connell 68min Mon
BRINGING HOME THE BACON (1924) *d* Thorpe *w* Arthur 1426m
BRING YOUR SMILE ALONG (1955) *d/co-st/s* Edwards *co-st* Quine *c* Lawton *m* Duning *83min Col
Brink of Hell (UK) = TOWARD THE UNKNOWN (1956)
Brink of Life = NARA LIVET (1957)
BRINNER EN ELD, DET (1943) *d* Molander *w* Sjöström SF
BRITAIN AT BAY (1940) *d* Watt *cy* Priestley
Britain Can Take It: shortened version of LONDON CAN TAKE IT (1940)
BRITANNIA (1898) *p* Paul 18m
BRITANNIA MEWS (1949) *d* Negulesco *p* Perlberg *c* Périnal *m* M Arnold *w* D Andrews, M O'Hara 91min Fox (= *The Forbidden Street*)
BRITISH AGENT (1934) *d* Curtiz *c* E Haller *w* L Howard, K Francis, Romero 71min FN
BRITISH SOUNDS (1969, *ur*) *d/s* Godard 16mm *52min TV (= *See You at Mao*)
BROAD MINDED (1931) *d* LeRoy *w* Lugosi 72min FN
BROADWAY (1929) *d* Fejos *co-ad/co-s* Furthman *fpl* G Abbott, *Phillip Dunning* *c* Mohr part * 12rs *r* U
BROADWAY BABIES (1929) *d* LeRoy *p* Rowland *c* Polito 90min FN
BROADWAY BILL (1934) *d* Capra *st* Hellinger *s* Riskin, Buchman (*uc*) *c* J Walker *w* W Baxter, M Loy, Ball (11rs) Col
BROADWAY BY LIGHT (1957) *d/c* Klein *tech adviser* Resnais *11min
BROADWAY FEVER (1929) *d* Cline 1650m
BROADWAY GONDOLIER (1935) *d* Bacon *w* D Powell, J Blondell, Menjou, Fazenda 100min WB
BROADWAY LIMITED (1941) *d* G Douglas *p* Roach *w* V McLaglen. Pitts 75min *r* UA

BROADWAY MELODY OF 1936 (1935) d Del Ruth st M Hart co-m Freed w R Taylor, Benny 110min MGM

BROADWAY MELODY OF 1938 (1937) d Del Ruth p J Cummings c Daniels co-e Vorkapich a Gibbons w R Taylor, G Murphy, Garland, Benchley 12rs MGM

BROADWAY MELODY OF 1940 (1940) d Taurog co-st Schary co-c Ruttenberg w Astaire, G Murphy 102min MGM

BROADWAY MUSKETEERS (1938) d J Farrow c O'Connell w Sheridan 62min WB

BROADWAY NIGHTS (1927) d *Joseph C Boyle* c E Haller w Stanwyck 2062m r FN

BROADWAY RHYTHM (1944) d Del Ruth p J Cummings a Gibbons co-chor Walters, R Alton w G Murphy *115min MGM

BROADWAY ROSE (1922) d/pc Leonard st/s Goulding 6rs

BROADWAY SERENADE (1939) d/p Leonard s Lederer a Gibbons w Jeanette Macdonald, Ayres 114min MGM

BROADWAY THRU A KEYHOLD (1933) d L Sherman 90min r UA

BRODERNA (1914) d/st/s Stiller 632m

BROKEN ARROW (1950) d Daves p Blaustein co-a Wheeler m Friedhofer w J Stewart, J Chandler *93min Fox

BROKEN BLOSSOMS (1919) d/p/s Griffith co-c Bitzer w L Gish, Crisp, Barthelmess 1829m FPL

BROKEN BLOSSOMS (1936) d Brahm (as Hans Brahm) rm 1919 s/w Emlyn Williams

Broken Chains (USA) = YEVO PRIZYU (1925)

Broken Dishes = TOO YOUNG TO MARRY (1931)

BROKEN DOLL, A (1921) d/p/s Dwan co-c O'Connell 5rs

Broken Drum, The = YABURE-DAIKO (1949)

BROKEN FETTERS (1916) d/p/s Ingram 5rs

BROKEN HEARTS OF HOLLYWOOD (1926) d Bacon w Fairbanks Jr 2369m WB

BROKEN LANCE (1954) d Dmytryk p S Siegel st Yordan s R Murphy rm HOUSE OF STRANGERS (1949) co-c Joe MacDonald co-a Wheeler m Harline w Tracy, R Wagner, Widmark, E O'Brien, Peters CS* 96min Fox

Broken Lullaby (UK) = MAN I KILLED, THE (1932)

Broken Toys = JUGUETES ROTOS (1966)

Broken Vase, The = RAZBITAYA VAZA (1913)

BROLLOPSRESAN (1935) d Molander w Dagover SF

BRONCHO BILLY AND THE BABY (1908) d *GP Hamilton* w GM Anderson S & A

BRONCO BUSTER (1952) d Boetticher *80min U

BRONENOSETS 'POTYOMKIN' (1925) d Eisenstein c Tissé w Alexandrov 1740m (= *Battleship Potemkin*)

BROTHERHOOD, THE (1968) d Ritt p K Douglas c B Kaufman m Schifrin co-songs Mancini w K Douglas *98min Par

BROTHERHOOD OF MAN (1947) d Cannon co-st J Hubley 16mm *10min UPA

BROTHERHOOD OF THE BELL, THE (1970) d Wendkos w G Ford 120min TV

Brotherly Love = COUNTRY DANCE (1969 r 1971)

Brother of a Hero = BRAT GEROYA (1940)

BROTHER ORCHID (1940) d Bacon p J Warner, Wallis supn Hellinger w Robinson, Sothern, Bogart 87min WB

BROTHER RAT (1938) d Keighley p Wallis co-s Wald c E Haller w Reagan, Wyman 90min WB

BROTHER RAT AND A BABY (1940) d Enright p J Warner, Wallis co-s Wald w Wyman, Reagan 87min WB

BROTHERS (1930) d W Lang p Cohn 76min Col

BROTHERS IN LAW (1957) d R Boulting p J Boulting w Attenborough, (J Schlesinger) 74min BL

BROTHERS KARAMAZOV, THE (1957) d/s R Brooks p Berman ad JJ Epstein fn *Dostoïevski* c J Alton m Kaper w Brynner, Maria Schell, Bloom, Cobb *145min r MGM

BROTHERS RICO, THE (1957) d Karlson fn *George Simenon* c Guffey w Conte 91min Col

Brouillard sur la ville = GAZ MORTELS, LES (1916)

BROWNING VERSION, THE (1951) d Asquith s Rattigan w M Redgrave 90min BL

BROWN OF HARVARD (1926) d Conway tech adviser/w S Miller co-a Gibbons 2421m MGM

Brown on Resolution = SINGLEHANDED (1951)

BROWN WALLET, THE (1936) d M Powell 66min

BRUCKE, DIE (1949) d *Arthur Pohl* c F Wagner 84min

BRUCKE, DIE (1959) d Wicki 103min (= *The Bridge*)

BRUG, DE (1928) d/p/s/c/e Ivens 270m (= *The Bridge*)

BRUIT, LE (1955) d Leenhardt 26min

BRULURE DE MILLE SOLEILS, LA (1965) d/s Kast *26min (= *The Radiance of a Thousand Suns/The Fire of a Thousand Suns*)

BRUMES D'AUTOMNE (1929) d/s Kirsanov 270m

BRUNKUL (1941) d/s B Henning Jensen

BRUTALITAT IN STEIN (1960) d Kluge, *Peter Schamoni* sh

BRUTALITY (1912) d Griffith 1rl Bio

Brute, The = BRUTO, EL (1952)

Brute, The = DUVAD (1957)

BRUTE FORCE (1947) d Dassin p Hellinger s R Brooks c Daniels m Rozsa w Lancaster, Bickford, De Carlo, Blyth 98min U

BRUTO (1910) d/s/dec Guazzoni

BRUTO, EL (1952) d/co-s Buñuel co-s Alcoriza w Armendariz 83min (= *The Brute*)

BUBBLE, THE (1967) d/p/s Oboler (as Obler) 3-D* 112min

BUCCANEER, THE (1938) d/p De Mille c Milner co-a Dreier m Antheil w March, Tamiroff, Brennan, Quinn 90min Par

BUCCANEER, THE (1958) d Quinn rm 1938 c Griggs co-a Pereira m E Bernstein w Brynner, Heston, Bloom, Boyer VV* 120min pc De Mille r Par

BUCHANAN RIDES ALONE (1958) d Boetticher p H Brown as-p R Scott c Ballard a Boyle w R Scott *78min pc Scott, H Brown r Col

BUCHERONS DE LA MANOUANE (1962) d/s/cy/co-e Lamothe 28min

BUCHSE DER PANDORA, DIE (1928) d Pabst c Krampf w L Brooks 3254m Nero (= *Pandora's Box*)

BUCK BENNY RIDES AGAIN (1940) d/p Sandrich c C Lang co-a Dreier chor Prinz w Benny 82min Par

BUCKET OF BLOOD, A (1959) d/p Corman co-ex-p Arkoff a D Haller 65min

BUCKING BROADWAY (1917) d J Ford p/w Carey 5rs U

BUCKLIGE UND DIE TANZERIN, DER (1920) d Murnau c Freund s Mayer f ballet (Sumurum) M Reinhardt 1540m (= *The Hunchback and the Dancer*)

BUCK PRIVATES (1941) d *Arthur Lubin* c Krasner w B Abbott, Costello 84min U

BUD ABBOTT AND LOU COSTELLO IN HOLLYWOOD (1945) d *S Sylvan Simon* co-a Gibbons w B Abbott, Costello 83min r MGM

BUDDY'S SHOW BOAT (1934) p L Schlesinger (1rl)

Buenos Dias, Amor = AMORE A PRIMA VISTA (1957)

BUFFALO BILL (1944) d Wellman c Shamroy w McCrea, M O'Hara, Darnell, Mitchell, Price, Quinn 90min Fox

BUFFERIN (1966) d Warhol 16mm *35min (= *Gerard Malanga Reads Poetry*)

BUGAMBILIA (1944) d/co-s/st Fernandez c Figueroa w del Rio, Armendariz 98min

BUGIARDA, LA (1965) d Comencini w Catherine Spaak 95min

BUGLER OF ALGIERS, THE (1916) d Julian 5rs

BUGLES IN THE AFTERNOON (1951) d Rowland w Milland *85min r WB

BUGS AND THUGS (1953) d Freleng anim* 7min WB

BUGS BUNNY AND THE THREE BEARS (1944) d Freleng p L Schlesinger anim* 7min WB

BUGS BUNNY RIDES AGAIN (1947) d Freleng anim* 7min WB

BUG VAUDEVILLE (1916) d McCay anim

BUHUJEM NOWE WSIE (1946) d Jakubowska

BUILDERS (1942) Jackson 16mm 8min Crown

Build My Gallows High = OUT OF THE PAST (1947)

BUIO IN SALA (1949) d Risi

BUISSON ARDENT, LE (1955) d Alexeieff anim

BUKHTA SMERTI (1926) d Room 2284m (= *Death Bay*)

BULLDOG DRUMMOND (1929) d *F Richard Jones* c Barnes, Toland a Menzies w J Bennett, Colman 2554m r UA

BULLDOG DRUMMOND STRIKES BACK (1934) d Del Ruth s N Johnson c Marley m A Newman w Colman, L Young 84min r UA

BULLET IS WAITING, A (1954) d J Farrow c Planer w J Simmons *82min Col

BULLETS AND BROWN EYES (1916) d *Scott Sidney* supn Ince w Hersholt, Normand, J Gilbert 5rs Tri

BULLETS FOR O'HARA (1941) d W Howard c McCord rm PUBLIC ENEMY'S WIFE (1936) w Quinn 50min WB

BULLETS OR BALLOTS (1936) d Keighley co-st/s S Miller c Mohr w Robinson, Blondell, Bogart 77min FN

BULLFIGHT (1955) d/p/c/e S Clarke *9min

BULLFIGHT (1959) d A King 16mm 18min

BULL FIGHTER, THE (1927) d Cline p Sennett w Turpin Pat

BULLFIGHTER AND THE LADY, THE (1951) d Boetticher p J Wayne s J Grant co-e Ford m V Young w Stack, Roland 87min r Rep

BULLFIGHTERS, THE (1945) d St Clair c Brodine w Laurel, Hardy 41min Fox

BULLITT (1968) d P Yates c Fraker m Schifrin w McQueen *114min pc McQueen

BUMPING INTO BROADWAY (1920) w H Lloyd pc Roach r Pat 2rs

BUNDFALD (1957) d/s Kjaerulff-Schmidt (= *Dregs*)

BUNDLE OF JOY (1956) d Taurog co-s Krasna w D Reynolds, Menjou *98min RKO

BUNGAWAN SOLO (1951) d/co-s Ichikawa Toho (= *River Solo Flows*)

BUNNY HUGGED (1951) d C Jones anim* 7min WB

BUNNY LAKE IS MISSING (1965) d/p Preminger cr Bass w Lynley, Olivier, Coward PV 107min

BUNNY O'HARE (1970) d/p/co-s G Oswald co-c Griggs w B Davis, Borgnine *91min

BUONA SERA, MRS. CAMPBELL (1968) d/p/co-s M Frank w Lollobrigida, Lawford, Winters *111min r UA

BUONGIORNA NATURA (1955) d Olmi *10min

BUONO, IL BRUTO, IL CATTIVO, IL (1967) d/co-st/co-s *Sergio Leone* w Eastwood, Wallach TS* 180min (= *The Good, the Bad and the Ugly*)

Burden of Life = JINSEI NO ONIMOTSU (1935)

BUREAU OF MISSING PERSONS (1933) d Del Ruth w B Davis 79min WB

BURGLAR, THE (1957) d/e Wendkos w Duryea, Mansfield 90min Col

BURGLAR ON THE ROOF, THE (1898) d/s/dec/w Blackton

BURMA VICTORY (1945) d/cy R Boulting m Rawsthorne 62min Army Film Unit

Burmese Harp = BIRUMA NO TATEGOTO (1956)

Burn! = QUEIMADA! (1968)

Burning Acre, The = BRENNENDE ACKER, DER (1922)

Burning Court, The = CHAMBRE ARDENTE, LA (1961)

BURNING HILLS, THE (1956) d Heisler c McCord w N Wood CS* 94min WB

Burning Secret, The = BRENNEDES GEHEIMNIS (1933)

BURNING THE WIND (1929) d *Henry MacRae, Herbert Blache* w Karloff 5202ft U

BUS, THE (1965) d/p/s/c Wexler 62min

Bushido: Samurai Saga = BUSHIDO ZANKOKU MONOGATARI (1963)

BUSHIDO ZANKOKU MONOGATARI (1963) d Imai w Mori S 119min (= *Bushido: Samurai Saga/Oath of Obedience*)

BUSINESS AND PLEASURE (1932) d D Butler w W Rogers, McCrea, Karloff 97min Fox

BUS RILEY'S BACK IN TOWN (1965) d *Harvey Hart* co-s(uc) Inge c Metty co-a Golitzen *93min U

BUS STOP (1956) d Logan p Adler s Axelrod fpl Inge co-a Wheeler c Krasner m Mockridge, A Newman w Monroe, Murray CS* 96min Fox

Busted Johnny, A = MAKING A LIVING (1914)

BUSTER KEATON STORY, THE (1957) d/co-p/co-s *Sidney Sheldon* supn Keaton c Griggs w O'Connor, R Fleming, Lorre 91min Par

BUSTER SE MARIE (1930) d Autant-Lara *French version of SPITE MARRIAGE* (1929) a Gibbons w Keaton, Rosay 2148m MGM

BUSY BODIES (1933) d *Lloyd French* p Roach w Laurel, Hardy (2rs) r MGM

BUSY BODY, THE (1966) d/p Castle co-a Pereira w Ryan, A Baxter TS* 102min Par

BUSY DAY, A (1914) d/s/w Chaplin Key (= *Militant Suffragette*)

BUTA TO GUNKAN (1961) d Imamura S 100min Nik (= *Hogs and Warships*)

BUTCH CASSIDY AND THE SUNDANCE KID (1969) d Hill c C Hall w P Newman, Redford PV* 110min co-pc P Newman r Fox

BUTCHER BOY, THE (1917) d/w Arbuckle w Keaton 2 reels

BUT NOT FOR ME (1959) d W Lang p Perlberg, Seaton s JM Hayes st Raphaelson c Burks w Gable, C Baker, Cobb, Palmer 105min Par

BUTTERFLY, THE (1910, ur) p Paul

BUT THE FLESH IS WEAK (1932) d Conway st/s/fpl (*The Truth Game*) *Novello* w R Montgomery, Horton 77min MGM

BUTTERFIELD 8 (1960) d Daniel Mann p Berman s J Hayes, Schnee fn J O'Hara co-c Ruttenberg m Kaper w E Taylor, Laurence Harvey CS* 109min MGM

BUTTERFLY (1924) d C Brown c B Reynolds 2277m U

Button, The = BOTAN (1963)

BWANA DEVIL (1952) d/p/s Oboler c Biroc w Stack 3-D* 79min

BY CANDLELIGHT (1933) d Whale w Lukas 66min U

Bicycle Thieves = LADRI DI BICICLETTE (1948)

BYE BYE BARABARA (1968) d/co-s Deville *100min

BYE BYE BIRDIE (1963) d G Sidney p Kohlmar c Biroc w J Leigh, D Van Dyke PV* 112min Col

BYE BYE BRAVERMAN (1968) d/p Lumet c B Kaufman w Segal 94min WB

By Hook or by Crook (UK) = I DOOD IT (1943)

BY INDIAN POST (1919) d J Ford 2rs U

BYLO LO V MAJI (1951) d Fric, *Vaclav Berdych* (= *May Events*)

BYLONAS 120.000 (1956) d/c Fric

BY LOVE POSSESSED (1961) d J Sturges p W Mirisch fn *James Gould Cozzens* m E Bernstein c Metty w Turner, Mitchell *115min UA

BYL SOBIE RAZ (1957) d/s/dec Borowczyk, Lenica anim 11min (= *Once Upon A Time*)

BYN VID DEN TRIUSAMMA BRUNNEN (1930) d Fejos SF11min

By Rocket to the Moon (US) = FRAU IM MOND (1929)

BY SEA AND LAND (1944) d J Lee 14min

By the Bluest of Seas = U SAMOVO SINEVO MORYA (1936)

By the Lake = U OZERA (1970)

By the Law = PO ZAKONU (1926)

BY THE LIGHT OF THE SILVERY MOON (1953) d D Butler fsts *Booth Tarkington* m M Steiner w D Day *101min WB

BY THE SEA (1915) d/s Chaplin c Totheroh w Chaplin, Purviance 1rl S & A

BY WHOSE HAND? (1927) d W Lang p Cohn 1656m Col

BY WORD OF MOUSE (1955) d Freleng anim* 7min WB

CABEZAS CORTADAS (1970) d Rocha *90min
CABINET DE MEPHISTOPHELES, LE (1897) d Melies 60m
Cabinet of Dr Caligari, The (UK) = KABINETT DES DR CALIGARI, DAS (1919)
CABIN IN THE COTTON, THE (1932) d Curtiz w Barthelmess, B Davis 77min FN
CABIN IN THE SKY (1943) d Minnelli p Freed co-a Gibbons 99min MGM
CABIRIA (1914) d/co-s Pastrone co-s D'Annunzio m Pizzetti w Maciste 3000m
CABOS BLANCOS (1954) d W Van Dyke, *Angel F. Rivera* 30min
CABRIOLA (1965) d/p/co-s M Ferrer *90min (= *Every Day is a Holiday*)
CACCIA ALLA VOLPE (1965) d/co-ad De Sica s/co-ad Zavattini w Sellers, Mature, Tamiroff 102min r UA (= *After the Fox*)
CACCIA ALLA VOLPE NELLA CAMPAGNA ROMANA, LA (1938) d Blasetti c Cardiff * sh
CACCIA ALL'UOMO (1961) d Freda w Rossi-Drago 100min r Par (= *Le Avventure di Dox/Dox, caccia all'uomo*)
CACCIA TRAGICA (1947) d/co-st/co-s De Santis co-st Lizzani co-s/co-di Antonioni, Lizzani, Zavattini, Barbaro c Martelli w Girotti 89min
CAÇOULHA DO BARULHO, O (1949) d/s/e Freda w Duarte
CACTUS FLOWER (1969) d *Grene Saks* p Frankovitch s Diamond c C Lang w Matthau, Ingrid Bergman *104min
CADDY, THE (1953) d Taurog co-a Periera c Fapp w Martin, J Lewis, D Reed 95min Par
CADET ROUSSELLE (1946) d Dunning, Low 16mm *8min NFBC
CADETS DU CONSERVATOIRE, LES (1946) d Ciampi
CADUTA DEGLI DEI, LA (1970) d/co-s Visconti m Jarre w Bogarde, Thulin *152min (= *The Damned*)
CADUTA DI TROIA, LA (1910) d Pastrone 600m
CAESAR AND CLEOPATRA (1945) d/p Pascal fpl *G B Shaw* c F Young, Cardiff, Hildyard, Krasker m Auric cos Messel w V Leigh, Rains, S Granger, J Simmons 135min Jar
CAFAJESTES, OS (1962) d/co-s Guerra co-s Rocha 90min (= *The Unscrupulous Ones*)
CAF' CONC (1950, uf) d Grémillon
CAGED (1950) d Cromwell p Wald m M Steiner w Parker, Moorehead, Darwell 96min RKO
Caged (UK) = NELLA CITTA L'INFERNO (1959)
CAGE OF GOLD (1950) d Dearden p Balcon c Slocombe w J Simmons 83min
-*Cages* = KLATKI (1967)
CAGLIOSTRO (1928) d R Oswald cos Lourie
CAIDA, LA (1959) d/co-s Torre-Nilsson 84min (= *The Fall*)
CAIN AND MABEL (1936) d Bacon w Davies, Gable, (Wyman) 90min WB
CAINE (1968) d/s Fuller n A Kennedy *92min (= *Shark*)
CAINE MUTINY, THE (1954) d Dmytryk c Planer m M Steiner w Bogart, J Ferrer, MacMurray, V Johnson, Marvin *125min pc Kramer r Col
ÇA IRA (1964) d Brass 110mins (= *Il Fiume della Rivolta/Tell It Like It Is*)
CAIRO (1942) d W S Van Dyke c June a Gibbons m Stothart w Jeanette MacDonald, R Young 101min MGM
CAIUS GIULIO CESARE (1914) d/s/co-dec Guazzoni fpl (*Julius Caesar*) *Shakespeare*
CAKE-WALK INFERNAL (1903) d Melies 100m
CALABUCH (1956) d Berlanga w Cortese 93min
Calais-Douvres = NIE WIEDER LIEBE (1930)
CALAMITY JANE (1953) d D Butler w D Day, Keel *101min WB
CALCUTTA (1947) d J Farrow p/st/s S Miller co-a Dreier c J Seitz m V Young w Ladd, Bendix 83min Par
CALCUTTA (1969) d/cy Malle 16mm *97min
CALDA VITA, LA (1964) d Vancini w Ferzetti, Catherine Spaak *97min
CALENDAR GIRL (1947) d/as-p Dwan w V McLaglen 88min Rep
CALIFORNIA (1947) d J Farrow p S Miller c Rennahan m V Young w Milland, Stanwyck, Quinn, Paxinou *99min Par
California Holiday (UK) = SPINOUT (1966)
CALIPH STORK (1954) d Reiniger anim (1 rl)
CALL, THE (1910) d Griffith 1 rl Bio
CALL A COP (1921) d St Clair s Sennett 2rs Sen
CALLAWAY WENT THAT AWAY (1951) p/d/s M Frank, Panama c June co-a Gibbons w D Powell, Keel, MacMurray, McGuire 81min MGM
CALLE MAYOR (1956) d/co-s Bardem c Kelber m Kosma 95min (= *Grand Rue*)
CALL HER SAVAGE (1932) d *John F Dillon* c Garmes w Bow, Roland 88min Fox
CALLIGRAPHY (1953) d/s C and R Eames c C Eames
CALLING BULLDOG DRUMMOND (1951) d Saville w Pidgeon 80min MGM
CALLING DR GILLESPIE (1942) d *Harold S Bucquet* co-s Goldbeck c June m Amfitheatrof w L Barrymore, D Reed 82min MGM
CALL IT A DAY (1937) d A Mayo p Wallis c E Haller w De Havilland 90min WB
CALL ME BWANA (1963) d G Douglas p Saltzman c Moore w Ekberg, Hope *103min r UA
CALL ME MADAM (1953) d W Lang p S Siegel c Shamroy co-a Wheeler chor R Alton w Merman, G Sanders, O'Connor, Vera-Ellen *117min Fox
CALL ME MISTER (1951) d Bacon p Kohlmar co-s Lewin c Arling co-a Wheeler chor Berkeley m Harline w Grable, Dailey, J Hunter 96min Fox
CALL NORTHSIDE 777 (1948) d Hathaway c Joe MacDonald co-a Wheeler m A Newman w J Stewart, Conte, Cobb, Ritter 111min Fox
Call of Motherhood, The = MATER DOLEROSA (1917)
CALL OF THE CANYON, THE (1923) d V Fleming fn *Zane Grey* c Howe w LeRoy 2131m FPL r Par
CALL OF THE CUCKOO (1927) d Bruckman p Roach supn McCarey w Laurel, Hardy 2rs MGM
CALL OF THE FLESH (1930) d *Charles Brabin* w Adorée, Novarro 100min MGM
CALL OF THE NORTH, THE (1914) d/s De Mille pc Lasky
CALL OF THE ROAD, THE (1920) d *A E Coleby* w V McLaglen 6000 ft
CALL OF THE WILD, THE (1908) d Griffith fn *Jack London* 320m Bio
CALL OF THE WILD, THE (1935) d Wellman p Zanuck as-p Goetz fn *Jack London* a R Day, Golitzen m A Newman w Gable, L Young 95min r UA
"CALL TO ARMS", THE (1902) p Hepworth 46m
CALL TO ARMS, A (1913) d Ince 1200m
CALM YOURSELF (1935) d G Seitz w R Young 70min MGM
CALTIKI, IL MOSTRO IMMORTALE (1959) d Freda (ps Robert Hampton) c Bava (ps John Foam) sp eff Bava (ps Marie Foam) 75min (= *Caltiki, the Immortal Monster*)
Caltiki, the Immortal Monster = CALTIKI, IL MOSTRO IMMORTALE (1959)
CALYPSO (1958) co-d/co-st/co-s Rossi S* 90min
CALYPSO HEATWAVE (1957) d Sears e Katzman *86min
CAMELOT (1967) d Logan p J Warner s/lyr A Lerner fpl A Lerner, *Frederick Loewe* fn (*The Once and Future King*) *T. H. White* w V Redgrave, R Harris, Hemmings *179min WB
CAMEO KIRBY (1923) d J Ford w J Gilbert, Arthur 7rs Fox
Camera Eye = Kino Glaz (1924)
CAMERA MAKES WHOOPEE (1934–35) d McLaren 16mm 15min
CAMERAMAN, THE (1928) d *Edward Sedgwick* p Keaton co-st Bruckman w Keaton 8rs MGM
CAMERAMEN AT WAR (1943) d Lye
CAMERIERE, LE (1958) d Bragaglia, *Sergio Grieco* 90min
CAME THE BRAWN (1938) d G Douglas p Roach 1 rl MGM
CAMICIE ROSSE (1952) d Rosi, Alessandrini, Rossi dec Gherardi w Magnani, Vallone 90min (= *Red Shirts*)
CAMILLA (1954) d/co-s Emmer w Ferzetti
CAMILLE (1917) d *J Gordon Edwards* fpl (*La Dame aux Camélias*) *Dumas fils* w Bara 6rs Fox
CAMILLE (1921) d *Ray C Smallwood* p Nazimova s/ad Mathis fpl *Dumas* w Nazimova, Valentino 5600ft
CAMILLE (1927) d Niblo fpl *Dumas* w Roland, N Talmadge 2652m FN
CAMILLE (1936) d Cukor fpl *Dumas* c Daniels, Freund dec Gibbons m Stothart w Garbo, R Taylor, L Barrymore 108min MGM
CAMION BLANC, LE (1942) d/co-st/co-s Joannon di Cayatte w Jules Berry 112min
CAMISARDS, LES (1970) d/st/co-s/di Allio *105min
CAMMINO DELLA SPERANZA, IL (1950) d/co-s/co-st Germi co-st/co-s Fellini w Vallone 107min (= *The Road to Hope*)
CAMP (1965) d Warhol 16mm 70min
CAMPANE A MARTELLO (1949) d/co-s Zampa p Ponti w Lollabrigida, De Filippo (= *Children of Change*)
CAMPAGNE PREMIERE (1947) d/c/e Resnais 16mm sh
CAMPANADAS A MODIANOCHO (1966) d/s Welles fpls (*Henry IV parts 1 and 2, and Henry V*) *Shakespeare* w Welles, Moreau, Vlady, Gielgud, Tamiroff 119min co-pc Saltzman (= *Chimes at Midnight/Falstaff*)
CAMPBELL'S KINGDOM (1957) d Thomas w Bogarde, S Baker *100min Jar
CAMPING (1957) d Zeffirelli p Ponti co-st/co-s/w Manfredi
CAMPI SPERIMENTALI (1957) d Olmi *10min
CAMPO DEI FIORI (1943) d Mario Bonnard w Magnani
CANADA IS MY PIANO (1966) d Dunning, *Bill Sewell* 3-screen *5min
CANADIAN BUSINESS MAN, THE (1963) d Kroitor, Koenig
CANADIANS, THE (1961) d/s B Kennedy w Ryan CS* 85min Fox
CANALE, IL (1966) co-d Bertolucci *13min
CANARY MURDER CASE, THE (1929) d St Clair t H. Mankiewicz w W Powell, Arthur, L Brooks 79min Par
CANARY ROW (1951) d Freleng anim* 7min WB
CAN-CAN (1960) d W Lang p J Cummings co-s Lederer c Daniels co-a Wheeler w Sinatra, MacLaine, Chevalier, Dalio, Jourdan TAO* 131min Fox
Cancao do berco, A: Portuguese version of TOUTE SA VIE (1930)
CANCER, LE (1940) d Ciampi sh
CANDIDE (1960) d/co-s *Norbert Carbonnaux* fn *Voltaire* w Cassel, Brasseur, De Funès, M Simon 90min
Candle In The Wind = FUZEN NO TOMOSHIBI (1957)
CANDY (1968) d Marquand c Rotunno w Aznavour, Brando, Burton, Starr, J Coburn, J Huston, Matthau, Martinelli *124min
Candy Web, The = THIRTEEN FRIGHTENED GIRLS (1963)
CANGACEIRO, O (1953) d/st/s/w Barreto 105min (= *The Bandit*)
CANI DIETRO LE SBARRE (1955) d Pontecorvo sh
CANKER OF JEALOUSY, THE (1915) d/p Hepworth 3rs
CANNED FISHING (1938) d G Douglas p Roach (1rl)
CANNON FOR CORDOBA (1970) d Wendkos m E Bernstein w Peppard, Vallone PV* 104min Mir r UA
CANNSTATTER VOLKSFEST (1935) d Ruttmann
CANON (1964) d McLaren, *Grant Munro* *9min NFBC
Cantata (USA) = OLDAS ES KOTES (1963)
CANTAMAGGIO A CERVAREZZA (1954) d Maselli
CANTERBURY TALE, A (1944) d/p/s M Powell, Pressburger 125min
CANTERVILLE GHOST, THE (1944) d Dassin fst *Oscar Wilde* co-a Gibbons w Laughton, R Young, Lawford, M O'Brien 96min MGM
CAN THIS BE DIXIE? (1936) d/co-st G Marshall co-st/s Trotti co-c Glennon 70min Fox
CANTICO (1970) d Grau *95min
CANTICO DELLA CREATURE, IL (1942) co-d/co-s/n Emmer co-d/co-s *Enrico Gras, Tatiana Granding (1 rl)*
CANTIERE D'INVERNO (1955) d Olmi S* 9min
CANTIERI DELL'ADRIATICO, I (1933) d Barbaro
CANTO DELLA VITA, IL (1945) d Gallone
CANTO DO MAR, O (1952) d/p/co-st Cavalcanti 90min
CANYON PASSAGE (1946) d J Tourneur p Wanger as-p Golitzen c Cronjager songs Carmichael w D Andrews, S Hayward, Carmichael *92min U
CANZONI NEL MONDO (1963) d Sala
Cape Ashizuri = ASHIZURI MISAKI (1954)
CAPE FEAR (1961) d J Thompson s J R Webb c Leavitt a Boyle m Herrmann w Mitchum, Peck 103min U
CAPE FORLORN (1930) d/co-s Dupont w Veidt (*German version only*) 2336m (= *Love Storm Menschen im Käfig Le Cap Perdu*)
CAPELLO DA PRETE, IL (1943) d Poggioli
CAPER OF THE GOLDEN BULLS, THE (1966) d Rouse ex-p Levine co-a Pereira w Boyd *103min (= *Carnival of Thieves*)
CAPITAINE FRANCASSE, LE (1929) d/co-s/e Cavalcanti fn *Gautier* w Boyer
CAPITAINE FRACASSE, LE (1942) d/co-s Gance fn *Gautier* c Hayer m Honegger S* 105min
Capitaine Mollenard = MOLLENARD (1938)
CAPITAN BLANCO (1914) d Martoglio
CAPKOVY POVIDKY (1947) d/co-s Fric fsts *Karel Capek* (= *tales by Capek*)
CAPORALE DI GIORNATA (1958) d Braggaglia w Manfredi (= *Soldier On Duty*)
CAPORAL EPINGLE, LE (1962) d/co-ad/di J Renoir m Kosma w Cassel 105min
CAPPELLO A TRE PUNTE, IL (1934) d Camerini w De Filippo, Valli
Cap Perdu, Le French version of CAPE FORLORN (1930)
CAPPOTTO, IL (1952) d/co-s Lattuada co-s Zavattini fst *Nikolai V. Gogol* w Marceau 95min (= *The Overcoat*)
CAPRELLES (1931) d Painlevé m Jaubert
CAPRICCIO ALL' ITALIANA (1968) p De Laurentiis 6 eps *85min
ep IL MAESTRO DELLA DOMENICA d Steno w Toto
ep CHE COSA SONO LE NUVOLE? d/s/co-song Pasolini w Toto
CAPRICE (1967) d/co-s Tashlin co-p A Rosenberg c Shamroy w D Day, Harris CS* 98min Fox
CAPRICE (1941) d/st/co-ad/co-di Joannon co-s/co-di Cayatte m Van Parys
Caprices du Marie Les = FIGURANTS DU NOUVEAU MONDE, LES (1969)
Capricious Summer = ROZMARNE LETO (1968)
CAPTAIN APACHE (1971) d Singer p/s Sperling, Yordan as/p I Lerner e I Lerner (ps Leigh G Tallas) w C Baker CS* 94min
CAPTAIN BLOOD (1935) d Curtiz p H Brown, Wallis fn *Rafael Sabatini* c Mohr m Korngold w Flynn, De Havilland, Rathbone 119min FN
CAPTAIN BOYCOTT (1947) d/co-s Launder p Gilliat w S Granger, Donat 93min
CAPTAIN CAREY, USA (1950) d Leisen w Ladd 83min Par (= *After Midnight*)
CAPTAIN EDDIE (1945) d Bacon c Joe MacDonald w MacMurray, Bickford, Mitchell, Nolan 108min Fox
CAPTAIN FLY-BY-NIGHT (1923) d W Howard c Andriot 1506m
CAPTAIN FROM CASTILE (1947) d H King p/s Trotti c Arling, C Clarke co-a R Day m A Newman w Power, Romero, Peters, Cobb 140min Fox
CAPTAIN FURY (1939) d/p Roach c Brodine w Lukas, V McLaglen, Carradine 91min r UA
CAPTAIN HAREBLOWER (1954) d Freleng anim* 7min WB

CAPTAIN HATES THE SEA, THE (1934) d Milestone c August w V McLaglen, J Gilbert, Tamiroff 97min Par
CAPTAIN HORATIO HORNBLOWER RN (1951) d Walsh co-s Goff, Roberts fn C S Forester c G Green w Peck, V Mayo, S Baker *117min WB
CAPTAIN JANUARY (1924) d Cline 1888m
CAPTAIN JANUARY (1936) d D Butler w Temple, Darwell 77min Fox
CAPTAIN KIDD'S KIDS (1920) d H Lloyd 2rs pc Roach r Pat
CAPTAIN LIGHTFOOT (1955) d Sirk p R Hunter co-s/fst Burnett c Glassberg co-a Golitzen w Hudson, Rush CS* 91min U
CAPTAIN McLEAN (1914) d Conway w L Gish, Von Stroheim Tri
CAPTAIN NEWMAN M.D. (1963) d D Miller c Metty w Peck, Curtis, A Dickinson *126min U
CAPTAIN OF KOEPENICK, THE (1942) d R Oswald 71min (= I Was a Criminal)
CAPTAIN OF THE GUARD (1930) d Fejos (uc), John Stuart Robertson 83min U
CAPTAINS COURAGEOUS (1937) d V Fleming fst Rudyard Kipling co-s Mahin a Gibbons m Waxman w Tracy, L Barrymore, M Douglas, Bartholomew, Carradine, Rooney 12rs MGM
Captain's Daughter, The (UK) = FIGLIA DEL CAPITANO, LA (1947)
CAPTAIN SINBAD (1963) d Haskin w Armendariz *85min MGM
CAPTAINS OF THE CLOUDS (1942) d Curtiz p Wallis as-p William Cagney c Polito, Hoch w Cagney *113min WB
CAPTAIN'S TABLE, THE (1958) d J Lee co-s Forbes c Challis *89min JAR
CAPTAIN THUNDER (1930) d Crosland 66min WB
CAPTIVE, THE (1915) d/co-s De Mille pc Lasky
CAPTIVE CITY, THE (1952) d Wise c Garmes 91min r UA
Captive City, The (UK) = CITTA PRIGIONERA LA (1963)
CAPTIVE HEART, THE (1946) d Dearden p Balcon c Slocombe m Rawsthorne w M Redgrave 108min EL
CAPTIVE WILD WOMAN (1943) d Dmytryk 61min U
CAPTURE, THE (1950) d J Sturges c Cronjager m Amfitheatrof w Ayres, T Wright 81min RKO
CAPTURED! (1933) d Del Ruth w L Howard, Fairbanks Jr, Lukas 72min WB
CAPTURE OF AQUINALDO, THE (1914) w Darwell
CAPTURE OF YEGG BANK BURGLARS (1904) d Porter 30m Ed (in 4 parts: Capture & Death/Cellar Scene/ Dive Scene/Tracked)
CARABINIERE A CAVALLO, IL (1961) d Lizzani c Di Venanzo w Manfredi, Salce 95min
CARABINIERS, LES (1963) d/co-s Godard co-p Ponti co-s Rossellini c Coutard 80min (= The Soldiers)
CARAVAGGIO (1948) d Barbaro, R. Longhi
CARAVAN (1934) d Charrell s/di Raphaelson co-c Sparkuhl w Boyer, L Young 101min Fox
CARBINE WILLIAMS (1952) d Thorpe c Mellor w J Stewart, Corey 90min MGM
CARD, THE (1952) d/p Neame fn Arnold Bennett e C Donner w Guinness 91min JAR
CARDBOARD LOVER, THE (1928) d Leonard a Gibbons w Davies 2167m MGM
CARDINAL, THE (1963) d/p Preminger c Shamroy des Wheeler cr Bass m Moross w Lynley, D Gish, J Houston, Meredith, Vallone, Schneider PV70* 176min r Col
CARDINAL RICHELIEU (1935) d Rowland V Lee as-p Goetz c Marley m A Newman w G Arliss, O'Sullivan, Romero 83min r UA
CAREER (1959) d Anthony p Wallis c La Shelle co-a Pereira m Waxman w Martin, MacLaine 105min r Par
CAREFREE (1938) d Sandrich p Berman co-st D Nichols w Astaire, G Rogers 80min RKO
Careless = SOHO (1933)
Caress = AIBU (1933)
CARETAKER, THE (1963) d C Donner s/fpl Pinter c Roeg 105min BL
CARGAISONS BLANCHES (1937) d Siodmak s Jeanson w Dalio 76min Nero (= Le Chemin de Rio/Traffic in Souls/French White Cargo)
CARGO FROM JAMAICA (1933) d B Wright p Grierson 16min si 11min EMB
CARIBBEAN (1952) d/co-s Edward Ludwig c Lindon co-a Pereira w Payne *97min Par
CARICA EROICA (1952) d/st/s De Robertis 92min (= Heroic Charge)
CARL DREYER (1965) d Rohmer 16mm 60min ORTF
CARLOS UND ELISABETH (1924) d/p/s R Oswald co-c Sparkuhl w Dieterle, Veidt 3153m
CARLTON-BROWNE OF THE F.O. (1959) d R Boulting p J Boulting w Sellers 88min BL
CARMEN (1915) d/p/s Walsh fn Prosper Merimée w Bara 5rs Fox
CARMEN (1915) d De Mille fn Merimée pc Lasky
Carmen = CHARLIE CHAPLIN'S BURLESQUE ON CARMEN (1915)
CARMEN (1918) d Lubitsch fn Merimée w Negri 1650m UFA
CARMEN (1926) co-d/s/co-e Feyder co-d Rosay fn Merimée dec Meerson w Modot 3000m

CARMEN (1933) d/p Reiniger anim 11min
CARMEN (1942) d Christian-Jaque s Jeanson fopera Bizet fn Merimée w Romance 107min
CARMEN (1966) d Schorm 25min (= Carmen not only by Bizet)
CARMEN (1967) d Herbert von Karajan f opera Bizet co-c Reichenbach a/cos Wakhévitch *175min
Carmen Comes Home = KARUMEN KOKYO NI KAERU (1951)
CARMEN JONES (1954) d/p Preminger fpl Oscar Hammerstein II, Georges Bizet fn Merimée co-c Leavitt cr Bass chor Ross CS* 107min r Fox
Carmen Not Only By Bizet = CARMEN (1966)
Carmen's Pure Love = KARUMEN JUNJOSU (1952)
CARNAL KNOWLEDGE (1971) d/p M Nichols ex-p Levine c Rotunno PV* 97min
CARNAVAL A LA NOUVELLE ORLEANS (1957) d Reichenbach
CARNAVAL DES VERITES, LE (1919) d L'Herbier dec Autant-Lara
CARNAVAL PAULISTA (1936) d Barreto sh
CARNAVAL SACRE (1950) d Decae
CARNE DE HORCA (1953) d Vajda 85min
CARNEGIE HALL (1947) d Ulmer 133min IUA
CARNET DE BAL, UN (1937) d/co-ad/s Duvivier co-ad Jeanson c Kelber, Agostini m Jaubert w Rosay, Raimu, Jouvet, Fernandel 100min (= Christine)
CARNET DE PLONGEE (1950) d/p Cousteau *12min
CARNET DE VIAJE (1961) d/s Ivens
CARNETS DU MAJOR THOMPSON, LES (1955) d/s P Sturges co-c Matras m Van Parys w Carol (= The Diary of Major Thompson/The French They Are a Funny Race) 105min
CARNIVAL (1935) d W Lang st/s Riskin w Ball 76min Col
CARNIVAL IN COSTA RICA (1947) d Ratoff w Romero, Vera-Ellen *95min Fox
CARNIVAL IN THE CLOTHES CUPBOARD (1942) d Mackendrick sh
Carnival of Sinners (US) = MAIN DU DIABLE, LE (1942)
Carnival of Thieves = CAPER OF THE GOLDEN BULLS, THE (1966)
CARNIVAL ROCK (1957) d/p Corman 75min
CAROBNI ZVUCI (1957) d Vukotic anim (= Charming Sounds)
CAROL FOR ANOTHER CHRISTMAS (1964) d/p J Mankiewicz m Mancini w Hayden, Saint, Sellers TV
CAROLINA (1934) d H King c Mohr w J Gaynor, L Barrymore, R Young 85min Fox
CAROLINE CHERIE (1950) d Richard Pottier s Anouilh m Avric w Carol 105min
CAROLINE CHERIE (1967) d de la Patellière c Vierny w De Sica, Aznavour, Brialy S* 105min
CAROUSEL (1956) d H King fpl Rogers & Hammerstein c C Clarke co-a Wheeler w S Jones CS* 128min Fox
CARPACCIO (1947) d Barbaro, R. Longhi
Carpenter, The = PLOTINA (1932)
CARPETBAGGERS, THE (1964) d Dmytryk p Levine s J Hayes fn Harold Robbins c Joe MacDonald co-a Pereira m E Bernstein w Peppard, Ladd, Cummings, C Baker, Ayres PV* 150min Par
Carquenez Woods, The = HALF-BREED, THE (1916)
CARREFOUR (1939) d C Bernhardt w Vanel 74min
CARREFOUR DES ENFANTS PERDUS, LE (1943) d Joannon w Reggiani 110min
CARRIE (1952) d/p Wyler fn (Sister Carrie) Theodore Dreiser c Milner co-a Pereira w Olivier, J Jones, M Hopkins 118min Par
CARRIERE DE SUZANNE, LA (1963) d/s/e Rohmer 16mm 60min
CARRINGTON V.C. (1956) d Asquith p Woolf Bros w Niven 105min BL (= Court Martial)
Carrosse d'or, Le = CARROZZA D'ORO, LA (1953)
CARROZZA D'ORO, LA (1953) d/co-s J Renoir fn (Carrosse du Saint-Sacrement) Prosper Merimée c C Renoir dec Chiari m Vivaldi w Magnani *100min (= Le Carrosse d'or/The Golden Coach)
CARSON CITY (1952) d De Toth p Weisbart w R Scott *87min WB
CARSON CITY RAIDERS (1948) d Canutt (6rs) Rep
CARTAGINE IN FIAMME (1959) d/p/co-s Gallone s Tessari w Brasseur TR* 115min (= Carthage In Flames)
CARTOUCHE (1962) d/co-s de Broca co-s Charles Spaak c Matras m Delerue w Belmondo, Cardinale, Dalio S* 106min (= Swords of Blood)
Carthage In Flames = CARTAGINE IN FIAMME (1959)
CARVE HER NAME WITH PRIDE (1958) d/p/s L Gilbert w Scofield, Ronet 119min JAR
CASABLANCA (1943) d Curtiz p Wallis s H Koch, JJ Epstein c Edeson m M Steiner w Bogart, Ingrid Bergman, Henreid, Rains, Veidt, Lorre, Greenstreet 102min WB
CASABLANCA, NID D'ESPION (1963) d Decoin c Matras w Montiel, Ronet *90min
CASA DEI PULCINI, LA (1924) d/st Camerini
CASA DEL ANGEL (1957) d/co-s Torre-Nilsson 78min (= The House of the Angel/End of Innocence)
CASA DELLE VEDOVE, LA (1960) d Baldi *15min (= The Widows' Home)
CASA DEL RECUERDO, LA (1940) d Saslavsky

CASALS AT 88 (1964) d Pennebaker 16mm
CASANOVA (1927) d Alexander Wolkof w Mozhukhin
Casanova (US) — INFANZIA, VOCAZIONE E PRIMA ESPERIENZE DI GIACOMO CASANOVA, VENEZIANO (1969)
CASANOVA BROWN (1944) d S Wood p/s N Johnson c J Seitz w G Cooper, T Wright 94min RKO
CASANOVA FAREBBE COSI (1942) d/st/s Bragaglia w De Filippo, (Sordi)
CASANOVA'S BIG NIGHT (1954) d McLeod co-s Kanter co-a Pereira c Lindon w Hope, Fontaine, Rathbone, Burr, Price *86min Par
CASANOVA 70 (1964) d Moncelli ex-p Levine p Ponti c Tanti w Mastroianni *113min Par
CASA RICORDI (1954) d Gallone m Rossini, Verdi, Puccini, Donizetti, Bellini w Ferzetti *112min (= House of Ricordi (USA)
CASBAH (1948) d John Berry rm PEPE LE MOKO (1936) c Glassberg w De Carlo, Lorre 94min U
CAS DU DOCTEUR LAURENT, LE (1956) d/co-st Le Chanois c Alekan m Kosma w Gabin 110min
CASE AGAINST BROOKLYN, THE (1958) d Wendkos 81min Col
Case Against Paul Ryker, The = SERGEANT RYKER (1966)
CASE OF LENA SMITH, THE (1929) d von Sternberg s Furthman c Rosson technical adviser Dreier 2204m Par
CASE OF LUCKY LEGS, THE (1935) d A Mays c Gaudio (9rs) WB
CASE OF SERGEANT GRISCHA, THE (1930) d Brenon w Hersholt 91min RKO
CASE OF THE CURIOUS BIRDS, THE (1935) d Curtiz fn Earle Stanley Gardner w (Flynn) 80min FN
CASE OF THE HOWLING DOG, THE (1934) d Crosland fst Earle Stanley Gardner w Astor 75min WB
CASH (1933) d Z Korda w Donat 73min
CASH McCALL (1960) d Pevney p Blanke c Folsey m M Steiner w Garner, N Wood *102min WB
Casino de Paree = GO INTO YOUR DANCE (1935)
CASINO ROYALE (1967) d K Hughes, J Huston, Parrish, Joe McGrath, Val Guest p Bresler, Feldman c Hildyard cr R Williams w Niven, Andress, Sellers, Welles, Kerr, Holden, Boyer, J Huston, Raft, Belmondo, O'Toole (uc) PV *131min Col
Casket For Living, A = TOSEI TAMATEBAKO (1925)
CASO HALLER, IL (1933) d/co-e Blasetti w I Miranda
CASQUE D'OR (1952) d/co-s/di Becker dec D'Eauboune m Van Parys w Reggiani, Signoret, Modot 96min
CASSE, LE (1971) d/co-ad/co-di Verneuil fn David Goodis c Renoir w Belmondo, Sharif, Hossein PV* 120min
CASSIUS LE GRAND (1964) d Klein 42min
Cassowary = HIKUIDORI (1926)
CASS TIMBERLANE (1947) d G Sidney s D Stewart fn Sinclair Lewis co-a Gibbons w Tracy, Turner, Astor 119min MGM
CAST A DARK SHADOW (1955) d L Gilbert w Bogarde, Lockwood 83min
CASTA DIVA (1935) d Gallone m Bellini
CASTA DIVA (1954) d Gallone rm 1935 m Bellini
CAST A GIANT SHADOW (1966) d/co-p/s Shavelson w K Douglas, A Dickinson, Brynner, J Wayne PV* 141min r UA
CASTAGNE SONO BUONE, LE (1971) d/co-s Germi *104min
Castaways, The (US) = IN SEARCH OF THE CASTAWAYS (1961)
CASTELLI IN ARIA (1939) d/co-s Genina w De Sica, Lillian Harvey (German version: Ins Blaue Leben)
CASTELLO DELLA HALINCONIA, IL (1920 d Genina
CASTILLOS DE CASTILLA (1933) d/s Velo, Fernando Mantilla (1rl)
Cast Iron (UK) = VIRTUOUS SIN, THE (1930)
CASTLE KEEP (1968) d Pollack co-s Taradash c Decaë w Lancaster PV* 107min
CASTLE ON THE HUDSON (1940) d Litvak co-s S Miller c Edeson w Sheridan, Garfield, Meredith 77min WB
Castles Through the Ages (UK) = O SAISONS O CHATEAUX (1951)
Castle Within a Castle = SLOT I ET SLOT, ET (1954)
Catacombs = KATAKOMBY (1940)
CATALOGUE (1961) d/c Whitney *7min 16mm
CAT AND MOUSE (1958) d/p/s Rotha fn John Creasey
CAT AND THE CANARY, THE (1927) d Leni 2352m U
CAT AND THE CANARY, THE (1939) d E Nugent c C Lang co-a Dreier w Hope, Goddard 72min Par
CAT AND THE FIDDLE, THE (1934) d W Howard co-s Rosson, C Clarke w Novarro, Jeanette MacDonald *90min MGM
CATASTROPHE DE LA MARTINIQUE, LA (1902) d/w Zecca 75min Pat
CAT BALLOU (1965) d Silverstein p H Hecht 2nd d Canutt w J Fonda, Marvin *96min Col
Catch, The = SHIIKU (1961)
CATCH AS CATCH CAN (1931 d Neilan p Roach (2rs) r MGM
CATCH-22 (1970) d M Nichols co-2nd d Marton fn Joseph Heller c Watkin w Perkins, Welles, Dalio PV* 122min Par
CATCH US IF YOU CAN (1965) d Boorman r WB 91min

CAT CONCERTO, THE (1946) d Hanna, Barbera p Quimby anim* 7min MGM
CAT CREEPS, THE (1930) d Julian co-c Mohr w Hersholt 72min U
CATERED AFFAIR, THE (1956) d R Brooks s Vidal fpl Chayefsky c J Alton m Previn w B Davis, Borgnine, D Reynolds 94min MGM (= Wedding Breakfast)
Catherine = VIE SANS JOIE, UN (1924)
CATHERINE THE GREAT (1934) d Czinner co-st Biro c Périnal dec V Korda w Bergner, Fairbanks Jr 95min
CAT ON A HOT TIN ROOF (1958) d/co-s R Brooks co-s Poe fpl T Williams c Daniels w E Taylor, P Newman, Ives 108min r MGM
CAT PEOPLE (1943) d J Tourneur p/co-st(uc) Lewton c Musuraca e Robson w S Simon 73min RKO
CATS (1955) d Breer anim* 16mm 2min
Cats, The = KATTORNA (1965)
Cats, The (US) = BASTARDI, I (1968)
CAT'S CRADLE (1959) d Brakhage 16mm *5min (silent)
Cat Shows Her Claws, The = CHATTE SORT SES GRIFFES, LA (1960)
CAT'S MEOW, THE (1924) d Del Ruth w Langdon 2rs pc Sennett r Pat
CAT'S MEOW (1957) d Avery *7min MGM
CAT'S PAJAMAS, THE (1926) d Wellman c Milner 1765m FPL r Par
CAT'S PAW, THE (1934) d/s Sam Taylor m A Newman pc/w H Lloyd
CAT THAT HATED PEOPLE, THE (1948) d Avery p Quimby *7min MGM
CATTIVO SOGGETTO, UN (1933) d Bragaglia w De Sica
CATTLE EMPIRE (1958) d Warren w McCrea CS* 83min Fox
CATTLE KING, (1963) d Garnett w R Taylor *88min MGM (= Guns of Wyoming)
CATTLE QUEEN OF MONTANA (1954) d Dwan p Bogeaus c J Alton w Stanwyck, Reagan *88min r RKO
CAUCHEMAR, LE (1897) d Méliès 20m
CAUCHEMAR DE FANTOCHE, LA (1908) d Cohl anim 80m
CAUGHT (1949) d Ophuls c Garmes e Parrish m Hollander w Mason, Ryan 88min r MGM
CAUGHT IN A CABARET (1914) d/w Normand, Chaplin 2rs Key (= The Waiter/Jazz Waiter/Faking with Society)
CAUGHT IN THE DRAFT (1941) d D Butler c Struss w Hope, Lamour 82min Par
CAUGHT IN THE RAIN (1914) d/s/w Chaplin w Sennett 1rl Key (= At It Again)
CAUGHT WITH THE GOODS (1911) d/w Sennett ½rl r Bio
CAUSE FOR ALARM (1951) d Garnett c Ruttenberg co-a Gibbons m Previn w L Young 74min MGM
CA VA BARDER (1954) d/co-s John Berry w Constantine 90min
CAVALCADE (1933) d F Lloyd 2nd d Menzies fpl Coward w C Brook, Grable 110min Fox
CAVALCATA ARDENTE, LA (1923) d Gallone
Cavaliere di ferro, Il = CONTE UGOLINO, IL (1949)
CAVALIERE DI MAISON ROUGE, IL (1953) d Cottafavi 89min
CAVALIERE MISTERIOSO, IL (1948) d/co-s Freda p De Laurentiis co-s Moncelli w Gassmann 93min (= Le Cento Donne di Casanova)
CAVALIERI DELLA REGINA, I (1954) d/co-s Bolognini *79min
Cavaliers Rouges, Les = APACHES LAST BATTLE (1964)
CAVALLERIA (1936) d Goffredo Alessandrini w Magnani
CAVALLERIA RUSTICANA (1953) d Gallone w Quinn 3D* 80min (= Fatal Desire)
CAVALO DE OXUMARE, O (1961, uf) d Guerra sh
CAVAR UN FOSO (1966) d Torre-Nilsson (= To Dig a Pit)
CAVATORI DI MARMO (1950) d Nelli
CAVEMAN, THE (1926) d Milestone ad Zanuck w Hopper, M Loy 2055m WB
CAVE OF OUTLAWS (1951) d Castle c Glassberg w A Smith *75min U
Cavern, The = SETTE CONTRO LA MORTE (1964)
CAVE SE REBIFFE, LE (1961) d/w Grangier w Gabin, Carol 98min
CAVO AD OLIO FLUIDO A 220.000 VOLT (1959) d Olmi *13min
CAZA, LA (1965) d/co-s Saura 93min (= The Hunt)
CECH PANEN KUTNOHORSKYCH (1938) d/co-s Vavra
CE CORPS TANT DESIRE (1958) d Saslavsky w Ronet 100min (Way of the Wicked)
Ceiling (UK) = STROP (1962)
CEILING ZERO (1936) d Hawks p H Brown c Edeson w Cagney 95min r FN
CELA S'APPELLE L'AURORE (1956) d/co-s Brunel fn Emmanuel Robles m Kosma w Bosè, (Modot) 102min
CELEBRITY (1928) d/co-s Garnett c Marley a Leisen 1873m
CELERY STALKS AT MIDNIGHT (1951–58) d/c Whitney 16mm *4min
Celestina = SOLE NEGLI OCCHI, IL (1953)
CELESTINA, LA (1964) d/co-s Lizzani 126min
CELLE QUI DOMINE (1927) co-d Gallone
CELL 2455, DEATH ROW (1953) d Sears fab Caryl Chessman 77min Col
CELUI QUI DOIT MOURIR (1957) d/co-s Dassin co-s Barzman fn (The Great Passion) Nikos Kazantzakis m Auric w Mercouri, Ronet 122min (= He Who Must Die)
CENA DELLE BEFFE, LA (1941) d/co-s Blasetti w Cortese
CENDRILLON (1899) d Méliès fst Charles Perrault 140m
CENDRILLON OU LA PANTOUFLE MYSTERIEUSE (1911) d Méliès fst Charles Perrault rm CENDRILLON (1899) 1000m (45 parts)
CENERE (1916) d Febo Mari and Arturo Ambrosio w Duse
CENIZAS AL VIENTO (1942) d Saslavsky
CENPA (1939) d Alexeieff anim
CENTENNIAL SUMMER (1946) d/p Preminger co-a Wheeler m Jerome Kern w Darnell, Crain, Wilde, Brennan, Constance Bennett, D Gish *103min Fox
CENTINELA! ALERTA! (1936) d Grémillon ex-p Bunuel
CENT MILLE DOLLARS AU SOLEIL (1964) d Verneuil w Belmondo S* 100min (= Greed in the Sun)
CENTO DI QUESTI GIORNI (1933) co-d/st Camerini co-d Augusto Camerini s Soldati
Cento Donne di Casanova, Le = CAVALIERE MISTERIOSO, IL (1948)
CENTO HP (1915) d Genina
CENTOMILA DOLLARI (1940) d/co-s Camerini co-s Castellani
CENT POUR CENT (1957) d Alexeieff anim
CENTRAL AIRPORT (1933) d Wellman c Hickox w Barthelmess, (J Wayne) 70min FN
Centurions, The = LOST COMMAND (1966)
125, RUE MONTMARTE (1959) d/co-s Grangier 86min
CE QU LES FLOTS RACONTENT (1915) d/s Gance
CERAMIKA ILZECKA (1951) d/s Wajda 300m
C'ERA UNA VOLTA (1967) d/co-s Rosi p Ponti co-s Patroni-Griffi m Piccioni w Sharif, Loren, Del Rio FS* 103min (= More Than a Miracle/Cinderella, Italian Style)
C'ERA UNA VOLTA IL WEST (1969) d/co-st/co-s Sergio Leone co-st Bertolucci w H Fonda, Cardinale, Ferzetti TS* 165min (= Once Upon a Time in the West)
CERCLE ROUGE, LE (1970) d/s Melville c Decaë w Montand, Delon, Bourvil *140min
CEREMONY, THE (1963) d/p/s/di/w Laurence Harvey w Ireland 107min
Ceremony, The = GISHIKI (1971)
CERNY PETR (1964) d/st/co-s Forman 85min (= Peter and Pavla)
CERTAIN MONSIEUR, UN (1950) d Ciampi m Van Parys 90min
CERTAIN SMILE, A (1958) d Negulesco s Goodrich, Hackett fn Françoise Sagan c Krasner co-a Wheeler m A Newman w Fontaine, Seberg CS* 106min Fox
CERTAIN YOUNG MAN, A (1928) d/p Hobart Henley co-a Gibbons w Novarro, Adorée 5679 ft MGM
CERTO GIORNO, UN (1968) d/s/e Olmi *105min (= One Fine Day)
CERTOSA DI PARMA, LA (1947) d Christian-Jaque fn Stendhal c Aldo dec D'Eaubonne w Philipe, Casarès 170min (= La Chartreuse de Parme)
CERTUV MLYN (1951) d/s/a Trnka anim Pojar *21min (= The Devil's Mill)
Cervantes = AVVENTURE E GLI AMORI DI MIGUEL CERVANTES, LE (1967)
CESAR (1936) d/p/s/fpl Pagnol w Fresnay, Raimu 117min
CESAR CHEZ LES GAULOISES (1931) d Clément anim 16mm sh
CESAR GRANDBLAISE (1970) d/co-ad Dewever
C'E SEMPRE UN MA . . . (1942) d/st/co-s Zampa
CE SOIR-LA, GILLES VIGNEAULT (1968) d/co-e Lamothe co-c Brault, Jutra *70min
CE SOIR LES JUPONS VOLENT (1956) d Kirsanov w Vernon FS* 90min
CE SOIR OU JAMAIS (1960) d/p/co-s/co-di Deville w Karina 103min (= Tonight or Never)
CESTA DO HUBIN STUDAKOVY DUSE (1939) d/co-s Fric (= Searching the Hearts of Students)
CESTA DO PRAVEKU (1954) d/s Zeman *92min (= Journey into Primeval Times)
CESTA DUGA GODINA DANA (1957) d/co-s De Santis co-s Petri w Girotti, Rossi-Drago S 160min (= The Road a Year Long)
CESTA K BARIKADAM (1946) d Vavra
C'EST L'AVIRON (1945) d McLaren 3min NFBC
C'EST PAPA QUI PREND LA PURGE (1906) d/s Feuillade
CETTE SACREE GAMINE (1955) d Michel Boisrond w Bardot S* 87min (= Mam'zell Pigalle)
CETTE VIEILLE CANAILLE (1933) d/co-s Litvak m Van Parys 99min Pat
CEUX DE CHEZ NOUS (1915) d Guitry w S Bernhardt, Anatole France, Dégas, Rodin, Saint-Saens, Auguste Renoir, Rostand, Monet, Mirbeau, Lucien Guitry 600m Gau
CEUX DU RAIL (1942) d Clément c Alekan sh
CHA-CHA-CHA-BOOM! (1956) d Sears p Katzman 72min Col
CHAD HANNA (1940) d H King as-p/s N Johnson co-c Rennahan w Lamour, H Fonda, Darnell, Carradine, Darwell 86min Fox
CHAINED (1934) d C Brown s Mahin c Folsey w J Crawford, Gable, Tamiroff 71min MGM
CHAIN GANG, THE (1930) p Disney (1rl) r Col
CHAIN LIGHTNING (1950) d Heisler ex-p J Warner c E Haller w Bogart, Parker 94min WB
Chair, The = ISU (1962)
CHAIR, THE (1963) d R Leacock, Pennebaker, Gregory Shuker co-e R Leacock 16mm 72min
CHAIR DE POULE (1964) d/co-ad Duvivier fn (Come Easy go Easy) James Hadley Chase c Burel m Delerue w Hossein 110min (= Highway Pickup)
CHAIRMAN, THE (1969) d J Thompson s Maddow c Moore m Goldsmith w Peck PV* 99min Fox (= The Most Dangerous Man in the World)
CHAIRY TALE, A (1957) co-d McLaren co-d Jutra co-m Shankar w Jutra 10min (= Il Etait une chaise)
Chaland qui passe, Le = ATALANTE, L' (1934)
CHALICE OF SORROW, THE (1916) d/ad Ingram 5rs
CHALK GARDEN, THE (1963) d Neame p R Hunter s J Hayes m M Arnold w Kerr, H Mills, J Mills, Evans *106min JAR
CHALK RIVER BALLET (1950) d McLaren, René Jodoin
Challenge in the Snow (UK) = TREIZE JOURS EN FRANCE (1968)
CHALLENGE TO LASSIE (1949) d Thorpe co-a Gibbons m Previn w Crisp *76min MGM
CHAMADE, LA (1968) d/co-s/co-di Cavalier co-s/co-di Françoise Sagan w Deneuve, Piccoli *105min
CHAMBRE ARDENTE, LA (1961) d/co-ad Duvivier co-ad/di Charles Spaak m Auric w Brialy, Tiller 110min UFA (= The Burning Court/The Curse and the Coffin)
CHAMBRE BLANCHE, LA (1969) d/s/pc Lefebvre PV 80min
CHAMP, THE (1931) d/p K Vidor w Beery 87min r MGM
CHAMPAGNE (1928) d/ad Hitchcock 2387m
CHAMPAGNE CHARLIE (1944) d Cavalcanti p Balcon co-lyr T Clarke w Kendall 105min
Champagne Murders, The = SCANDALE LE (1966)
CHAMPION (1949) d Robson s Foreman c Planer m Tiomkin w K Douglas, A Kennedy, Roman 100min pc Kramer r UA
CHAMPION, THE (1915) d/s Chaplin c Totheroh w Chaplin, Turpin, Purviance, G M Anderson 2rs S & A (= Champion Charlie)
Champion Charlie = CHAMPION, THE (1915)
CHAMPI-TORTU (1921) d De Baroncelli
Champ of the Champs-Elysees, The = LE ROI DES CHAMPS-ELYSEES, LE (1934)
CHAMPS ELYSEES (1929) d Lods c B Kaufman
CHANBARA FUFU (1930) d/s Naruse (= Mr & Mrs Swordplay)
Chance Meeting (US) = YOUNG LOVERS, THE (1954)
Chance Meeting (US) = BLIND DATE (1959)
CHANCE OF A LIFETIME, THE (1943) d Castle 67min Col
CHANCES (1931) d Dwan c E Haller w Fairbanks Jr 71min FN
CHANDU, THE MAGICIAN (1932) d Menzies, Marcel Varnel c Howe w Lugosi 71min Fox
CHANG (1927) co-d/co-p/c Schoedsack co-d/co-p M Cooper 8rs Par-FPL
CHANGE OF SPIRIT (1911) d Griffith 1rl Biograph
Changing Countryside, The = GAMPERALIYA (1964)
Changing Earth, The (UK) = AARDOLIE (1953)
CHANGING HUSBANDS (1924) d Frank Orson, Paul Iribe supn De Mille c Glennon w Pitts 6799 ft FPL
CHANNEL INCIDENT (1940) d Asquith w Newton 9min
CHANSON D'ARMOR (1934) d/co-s J Epstein
CHANSON DE PEUPLIERS, LA (1931) d J Epstein c Matras 11min
Chanson du souvenir: French version of HOFKONZERT, DAS (1936)
CHANT DE LA MINE ET DU FEU, LE (1931) d Benoit-Lévy
CHANT D'ARMOUR, UN (1952) d Jean Genet p Papatakis si 25min
CHANT DES ONDES, LE (1943) d Leenhardt
CHANT DU MARIN, LE (1932) d Gallone
CHANT DU MONDE, LE (1965) d/s Camus fn Jean Giono w Deneuve, Vanel *105min
CHANT DU STYRENE, LE (1958) d/e Resnais cy Queneau c Vierny FS* 19min
CHANTEUR DE MINUIT, LE (1936) d Joannon co-c Matras, C Renoir m Misraki w S Simon
CHANTEUR INCONNU, LE (1946) d Cayatte 95min
CHANTIER EN RUINES, LE (1945) d Leenhardt 19min
CHANTONS FRANCAIS (1962) d P Prévert p De Rochemont 16mm * ORTF
CHAPAYEV (1934) d/co-s S & G Vasiliev 99min
Chapayev is With Us = CHAPAYEV S NAMI (1941)
CHAPAYEV S NAMI (1941) d Petrov co-s Gerasimov 256m (= Chapayev is With Us)
CHAPEAU DE MAX, LE (1913) d/s/w Linder Pat
CHAPEAU DE PAILLE D'ITALIE, UN (1927) d/s Clair fpl Eugene Labiche dec Meerson w Préjean 2950m (= The Italian Straw Hat)

CHAPMAN REPORT, THE (1962) d Cukor c Lipstein colour consultant Hoyningen-Huene m Rosenman w Winters, J Fonda, Bloom, Danton *125min pc Zanuck r WB

CHAPPAQUA (1966) d/p/s/w Conrad Rooks c R Frank co-in Shankar, Bach w Barrault, Shankar part* 82min

CHARADE (1963) d/p Donen c C Lang a D'Eaubonne m Mancini w C Grant, A Hepburn, J Coburn, Matthau, G Kennedy *113min U

CHARCUTIER DE MACHONVILLE, LE (1947) d Y. Vernel c Fradetal 95min

CHARGE AT FEATHER RIVER, THE (1953) d G Douglas p Weisbart st/s J R Webb c Marley m M Steiner w Miles 3D* 96min WB

CHARGE OF THE LANCERS (1953) d Castle p Katzman w Goddard *73min Col

CHARGE OF THE LIGHT BRIGADE, THE (1936) d Curtiz w Wallis fpm Tennyson co-c Polito m M Steiner w Flynn, De Havilland, Crisp, Niven 116min WB

CHARGE OF THE LIGHT BRIGADE, THE (1968) d T Richardson c Watkin cr R Williams w T Howard, V Redgrave, Gielgud, Hemmings, (Wolfit) PV* 141min r UA

Charles Chaplin in a Liberty Loan Appeal = BOND, THE (1918)

CHARLESTON (1927) d/p J Renoir c Bachelet 1200m

CHARLEY MOON (1956) d Hamilton *92min BL

CHARLEY'S AUNT (1941) d A Mayo p Perlberg s Seaton c Marley co-a R Day m A Newman w Benny, K Francis, A Baxter, Haydn 81min Fox

Charlie and the Sausages = MABEL'S BUSY DAY (1914)

Charlie and the Umbrella = BETWEEN SHOWERS (1914)

Charlie at the Bank = BANK, THE (1915)

Charlie at the Show = NIGHT IN THE SHOW, A (1915)

CHARLIE BUBBLES (1967) d/w Finney *89min

CHARLIE CHAN AT TREASURE ISLAND (1939) d Foster co-a R Day w Romero 70min Fox

CHARLIE CHAN IN PANAMA (1940) d Foster co-a R Day 75min Fox

CHARLIE CHAN IN RENO (1939) d Foster 70min Fox

CHARLIE CHAPLIN'S BURLESQUE ON CARMEN (1916) d/s Chaplin c Totheroh w Chaplin, W Ruggles, Turpin, Purviance 4rs S & A (= Carmen)

CHARLIE McCARTHY, DETECTIVE (1939) d/p Tuttle w R Cummings 77min U

Charlie's Recreation = TANGO TANGLES (1914)

Charlie the Perfect Lady = WOMAN, A (1915)

CHARLOTTE ET SON JULES (1959) d/s Goddard w Belmondo w Godard 20min

Charlotte et son Steak = PRESENTATION (1951–1961)

Charlotte et Veronique = TOUS LES GARCONS S'APPELLENT PATRICK (1957)

CHARLOTTE LOWENSKOLD (1931) d Molander r SF

CHARLY (1968) d/p Nelson s Silliphant m Shankar w Robertson, Bloom TS* 103min

CHARLY, DER WUNDERAFFE (1915) d/s May

CHARMANTS GARÇONS (1957) d Decoin s Charles Spaak m Van Parys, Legrand w Gélin *113min

CHARMER, THE (1917) d Conway

CHARMES DE L'EXISTENCE, LES (1949) co-d/co-s/cy Gremillon co-d/co-s Kast 22min

Charming Sounds = CAROBNI ZVUCI (1957)

CHARM SCHOOL, THE (1921) d Cruze 5rs FPL r Par

CHARRETTE FANTOME, LA (1939) d/s Duvivier p Graetz m Ibert w Jouvet, Fresnay, Modot 110min

CHARRO! (1969) p/d/s Warren w Presley PV* 98min

CHARRON, LE (1943) d/s Rouquier sh

Chartreuse de Parme, La = CERTOSA DI PARMA, LA (1947)

CHARULATA (1964) d/s/m S Ray c Mitra 112min (= The Lonely Wife)

CHASE, THE (1966) d Penn p Spiegel s Hellman c La Shelle des R Day m Barry w Brando, J Fonda, Redford, A Dickinson, M Hopkins PV* 135min

CHASE A CROOKED SHADOW (1958) d Michael Anderson p Fairbanks Jr 87min ABC

CHASED INTO LOVE (1917) d/s C Chase (as Parrott) w C Chase 2rs Fox

CHASE ME CHARLIE (1918) compilation film from Chaplin's S & A shorts 7rs

CHASER, THE (1928) d/pc/w Langdon 1751m r FN

CHASES OF PIMPLE STREET, THE (1935) d C Chase (as C Parrott) p Roach w C Chase (2rs) MGM

CHASING THROUGH EUROPE (1929) d D Butler, Alfred L Werker co-c Andriot, O'Connell 62min Fox

Chasse à courre à Villers-Cotterets = LA MORT DU CERF (1951)

Chasse à l'hippopotame = BATAILLE SUR LE GRAND FLEUVE (1951)

CHASSE A L'HOMME, LA (1953) d/s Kast 18min

CHASSE A L'HOMME, LA (1964) d Molinaro w Belmondo, Brialy, Deneuve, Darc, Presle 100min

CHASSE AU LION A L'ARC, LA (1965) d/s/c/n Rouch 16mm *91min (= The Lion Hunters)

CHASTNYI SLUCHAI (1934) d/co-s Ilya Trauberg 75min (= An Unusual Case)

CHAT DANS LA SAC, LE (1964) d/s/e Groulx m Coltrane, Vivaldi, Couperin 75min

CHATEAU DE VERRE (1950) d/co-s Clément co-s Bost w Morgan, Marais, Servais 95min

CHATEAU HANTE, LE (1897) d Méliès 20m

CHATEAUX DE FRANCE (1948) d/s/c/e Resnais 16mm *sh

CHATEAU EN SUEDE (1963) d Vadim fpl Françoise Sagan w Vitti, Brialy, Jurgens, Trintignant CS* 110min (= Nutty, Naughty Chateau)

Château Life = VIE DE CHATEAU, LA (1965)

CHATELAINE DU LIBAN, LA (1933) d J Epstein c Thirard, Matras

CHATTE, LA (1958) d/co-s Decoin m Kosma w Arnoul, Wicki 104min (= The Face of the Cat)

CHATTE SORT SES GRIFFES, LA (1960) d/co-ad Decoin m Kosma w Arnoul 105min (= The Cat Shows Her Claws)

CHAUDRONNIER, LE (1949) d Rouquier c Fradetal sh

Chauffören = HJARTAN SOM MOTAS (1914)

CHE! (1969) d R Fleischer co-s M Wilson m Schifrin w Sharif, Palance PV* 96min Fox

CHEAPER BY THE DOZEN (1950) d W Lang p/s Trotti c Shamroy co-a Wheeler w C Webb, M Loy 85min Fox

CHEAPER TO MARRY (1925) d Leonard p L Mayer a Gibbons w Fazenda 1981m MGM

Cheap Sweet and a Kid = OTOSHI ANA (1961)

CHEAT, THE (1915? d De Mille pc Lasky

CHEAT, THE (1931) d G Abbott c Folsey w Bankhead, Pichel 74min Par

CHEATING CHEATERS (1919) d Dwan c Edeson 5rs

CHEATING CHEATERS (1934) d Thorpe c Brodine w Romero 70min U

CHEERS FOR MISS BISHOP (1941) d Garnett p Rowland c Mohr 95min r UA

CHEESE MITES, OR LILLIPUTIANS IN A LONDON RESTAURANT (1902) p Paul 21m

CHEFS DE DEMAIN (1944) d Clément sh

CHE GIOIA VIVERE (1961) d/co-st/co-s Clément di Bost from idea Jacopetti c Decaë w Delon 132min (= Quelle Joie de Vivre)

CHELOVEK CHELOVEKU (1958) d Alexandrov * (= Man to Man)

CHELOVEK IZ RESTORANA (1927) d Protazanov 1700m (= The Restaurant Waiter)

CHELOVEK NO. 217 (1945) d/co-s Romm m Khatchaturian 101min (= Man No. 217)

CHELOVEK S KINOAPPARATOM (1929) d Vertov, Elizabeth Svilova s/co-e Vertov 1889m (= Man With a Movie Camera)

CHELOVEK S RUZHOM (1938) d Yutkevich m Shostakovich w Cherkasov 102min (= The Man With a Gun)

CHELSEA GIRLS (1966) d Warhol 16mm part *195min

CHEMIN DE BONHEUR, LE (1932 d May

Chemin de Rio, Le = CARGAISONS BLANCHES (1937)

CHEMINS DE KHATMANDU, LES (1969) d/st/co-s Cayatte w Martinelli 100min (= The Road to Katmandu)

CHEMIST, THE (1936) d Al Christie w Keaton 19min

CHERI-BIBI (1955) d Pagliero

CHERNYI PARUS (1929) d Yutkevich 1952m (= The Black Sail)

Chesscetera = PASSIONATE PASTIME (1957)

CHESS DISPUTE, A (1896) p Paul 24m

Chess Fever = SHAKHMATNAYA GORYACHKA (1925)

Chevalier de Maupin, Le = MADAMIGELLA DI MAUPIN (1965)

CHEVALIER DE MENILMONTANT (1954) d Baratier m Chevalier 13min

CHEVALIER DES NEIGES, LE (1913) d Méliès 400m

CHEVALIERS DU CHLOROPHORME, LES (1905) d Méliès 68m

CHEYENNE (1947) d Walsh c Hickox m M Steiner chor Prinz w Wyman, A Kennedy 100min WB

CHEYENNE AUTUMN (1964) d J Ford s J R Webb c Clothier a R Day m North w Widmark, C Baker, J Stewart, Robinson, Malden, Del Rio, Montalban, Roland, A Kennedy, Carradine, G O'Brien 70PV* 159min r WB

CHEYENNE SOCIAL CLUB, THE (1970) d/p Gene Kelly c Clothier w J Stewart, H Fonda, S Jones PV* 102min

CHEYENNE'S PAL (1917 d/st J Ford w Carey 2rs UA

Chicago, Chicago (UK) = GAILY, GAILY (1969)

CHICAGO SYNDICATE (1955) d Sears 83min Col

CHICHI ARIKI (1942) d/co-s Ozu Sho (= There Was A Father)

CHICKEN EVERY SUNDAY (1949) d/co-s Seaton co-fpl J J Epstein co-a Wheeler m A Newman w Dailey, N Wood 91min Fox

CHICKENS COME HOME (1931) d James Horne p Roach w Laurel, Hardy (3rs) r MGM

CHICOS, LOS (1960) d/co-s Ferreri (= The Boys)

CHICOT, DENTISTE AMERICAINE (1897) d Méliès 20m

CHI E DIO (1948) d Soldati 16mm

CHIEN ANDALOU, LE (1928) d/p/s Bunuel, Dali e Bunuel w Bunuel, Dali 24min

CHIEN DE PIQUE, LE (1960) d/co-s Y Allégret c Kelber m Legrand w Constantine 85min

CHIENNE, LA (1931) d/co-ad/co-di J Renoir co-c Sparkuhl w M Simon, Romance 100min

CHIEN QUI RAPPORTE, UNE (1930) d Jean Choux w Arletty

CHIENS PERDUS SANS COLLIER (1955) d/co-s Delannoy co-s Aurenche di Bost m Misraki w Gabin 93min

CHIISANS KUKAN (1964) d Kuri anim (= Small Space)

CHIISANA TOBOSHA (1967) d Kinugasa, N Kandrovich (= Little Runaway, The)

CHIISANA SASAYAKI (1966) d Kuri anim (= Little Murmur)

CHIJO (1957) d Yoshimura s Shindo (= On This Earth)

CHIKAGAI NIJUYOJIKAN (1947) d Imai, Hideo Sekigawa, Kiyoshi Kusuada Toho (= Twenty-Four Hours of a Secret Life)

CHIKAMATSU MONOGATARI (1954) d Mizoguchi c Miyagawa 109min Dai (= Story from Chikamatsu)

Chi Lavora e Perduto = IN CAPO AL MONDO (1963)

Child, The = BARNET (1940)

CHILDBIRTH (c. 1952) d Kershner US Information Service

Childhood of Gorky, The = DETSTVO GORKOVO (1938)

Child in Blue, The (UK) = KNABE IM BLAUE, DER (1919)

CHILD IN THE HOUSE (1956) d Charles de Lauteur, Endfield (uc) 88min

CHILD IS BORN, A (1939) d Bacon p Wallis s Rossen (9rs) WB

CHILDISH THINGS (1969) d/c Derek p/s/w Murray *93min

CHILD IS WAITING, A (1962) d Cassavetes c La Shelle e Kramer m Gold w Garland, Lancaster 102min pc Kramer

CHILD OF DIVORCE (1946) d R Fleischer 62min RKO

CHILD OF THE PRAIRIE, A (1915) d/w Mix 2rs Sel

CHILDREN AND CARS (1970) d/p Halas anim* 10min

Children are Watching Us, The (1942) = BAMBINI CI GUARDANO, I (1942)

CHILDREN AT SCHOOL (1937) d B Wright p Grierson 16mm 24min GPO

Children at Table = TWIN'S TEA PARTY 1898)

CHILDREN GALORE (1954) d Fisher 60min JAR

Children In Cities = BAMBINI IN CITTA (1946)

CHILDREN IN CONFLICT (1967) d A King (18-part series) 16mm

CHILDREN MUST LEARN, THE (1940) d/s/co-c W Van Dyke e I Lerner 12min

Children of Change = CAMPANE A MARTELLO (1945)

CHILDREN OF DIVORCE (1927) co-d/p F Lloyd co-d (uc) Von Sternberg c Milner w Bow, G Cooper, Hopper 2094m FPL r Par

Children of Divorce, The = SKILSMISSEN BØRN (1939)

CHILDREN OF DREAMS (1931) d Crosland 76min WB

CHILDREN OF DUST (1923) d/p Borzage 1898m r FN

Children of Hiroshima = GEMBAKU NO KO (1952)

Children of Paradise = ENFANTS DU PARADIS, LES (1945)

Children of the Sea = KAIKOKU DANJI (1926)

Children of the Soviet Arctic = ROMANTIKI (1941)

Children of the Storm = DETI BURI (1927)

CHILDREN OF THE SUN (1961) d/s J Hubley co-anim Cannon m Bach anim 10min

CHILDREN ON TRIAL (1946) d/co-s J Lee 62min

CHILDREN'S CORNER (1935) d L'Herbier sh

CHILDREN'S HOUR, THE (1962) d/p Wyler ad/fpl Hellman s J Hayes rm THESE THREE (1936) c Planer m North w A Hepburn, MacLaine, M Hopkins, Garner 108min Mir r UA (= The Loudest Whisper)

CHILDREN UPSTAIRS, THE (1955) d/s L Anderson c Lassally 4min

CHILD THOU GAVEST ME, THE (1921) d/p Stahl 1856m r FN (= Retribution)

CHILD WENT FORTH, A (1941) co-d/co-p/s Losey co-d/co-p/c John Ferno m Eisler 18min

CHILLY WILLY IN THE LEGEND OF ROCKABYE POINT (1955) d Avery p Lantz *6min U

Chimes at Midnight = CAMPANADAS A MEDIANOCHE (1966)

CHIMMIE FADDEN (1915) d/s De Mille pc Lasky

CHIMMIE FADDEN OUT WEST (1915) d/co-s De Mille pc Lasky

CHIMNEY'S SECRET, THE (1915) d/s/w Chaney 1rl U

Chimney Sweep, The = SOTAREN (1966)

CHIMP, THE (1932) d James Parrott p Roach w Laurel, Hardy (3rs) r MGM

CHINA (1943) d J Farrow co-a Dreier m V Young w L Young, Ladd, Bendix 79min Par

CHINA CLIPPER (1936) d Enright c Edeson w Bogart 85min WB

CHINA DOLL (1958) d Borzage c Clothier w Mature 88min pc J Wayne r UA

China Express = GOLUBOI EKSPRESS (1929)

CHINA GATE (1957) d/p/s Fuller c Biroc m V Young, M Steiner w A Dickinson CS 97min

CHINA GIRL (1942) d Hathaway p/s B Hecht c Garmes co-a R Day m A Newman w Tierney, V McLaglen 96min Fox

China is Near (UK) = CINA E VICINA, LA (1967)

China Liberated = OSVOBOZHDENNYI KITAI (1952)

CHINA SEAS (1935) d Garnett as-p Lewin co-s Furthman c June m Stothart w Gable, Harlow, Beery, R Russell, Meek, Tamiroff, Benchley 90min MGM

CHINA SKY (1945) d Enright fn Pearl S Buck c Musuraca m Harline w R Scott, Quinn 78min RKO

CHINA STRIKES BACK (1937) p/s Meyer 16mm 23min

CHINATOWN NIGHTS (1929) *d* Wellman *as-p* Selznick *w* Beery 83min Par
CHINA VENTURE (1953) *d* D Siegel *c* Leavitt *w* E O'Brien 80min Col
CHINESE PARROT, THE (1927) *d* Leni 2260m U
CHINOISE, LA (1967) *d/s* Godard *c* Coutard *m* Stockhausen *w* Léaud *95min
CHINY I LYUDI (1929) *d* Protazanov, *Mikhail Doller co-s* Protazanov *fst* Anton Chekov 1770m (= *Ranks and People*)
CHIRGWIN, THE 'WHITE-EYED KAFFIR' (1897) *p* Paul 80ft
CHIRIAKHANA (1967) *d/s/m* S Ray (= *The Zoo/The Menagerie*)
CHIRURGIE CORRECTRICE ET REPARATRICE, LA (1939) *d* Painlevé
CHIRURGIEN AMERICAIN, LE (1897) *d* Méliès 20m
CHISTOYE NEBO (1961) *d* Chukhrai *110min (= *Clear Skies*)
CHISUM (1970) *d* A McLaglen *c* Clothier *w* J Wayne *110min *pc* J Wayne *r* WB
CHI TO REI (1922) *d/s* Mizoguchi (= *Blood and Soul*)
CHITTY CHITTY BANG BANG (1968) *d/co-s* K Hughes *co-s* Ronald Dahl *fst* Ian Fleming *ad* Maibaum *c* Challis *des* Adam *w* D Van Dyke PV70* 145min *r* UA
CHLEN PRAVITELSTVA (1940) *d/st* Heifitz, Zarkhi 106min (= *Member of the Government/The Great Beginning*)
CHLOE, LOVE IS CALLING YOU (1934) *d* Neilan 62min
Chnouf = RAZZIA SUR LA CHNOUF (1954)
CHOCOLATE SOLDIER, THE (1941) *d* Del Ruth *p* Saville 102min *r* MGM
CHOKON YASHA(1928) *d* Kinugasa (= *Female Demon*)
Choose Life = WAHLE DAS LEBEN (1963)
CHOPIN (1957) *d/e* Mitry 20min
CHORAKU NO KANATA (1924) *d/s* Kinugasa (= *Beyond Decay*)
CHOREOGRAPHY FOR CAMERA: PAS DE DEUX (1945) *d* Deren 2min
CHORTOVO KOLESO (1926) *d* L Trauberg, Kozintsev *c* Moskvin *w* Gerosimov 2600m (= *The Devil's Wheel*)
Chorus of Tokyo = TOKYO NO GASSHO (1931)
CHOSES DE LA VIE, LES (1970) *d/co-s* Sautet *w* Piccoli, Schneider 90min
CHOTARD ET COMPAGNIE (1933) *d/co-ad* J Renoir
CHOUANS, LES (1946) *d* Henri Calef *fn* Balzac *w* Jouvet Marais 99min
CHRIST DANS LA CITE, LA (1963) *d/c* Hanoun TV
Christian = KRISTIAN (1939)
Christian IV, Master Builder = CHRISTIAN IV, SOM BYGHERRE (1941)
CHRISTIAN IV, SOM BYGHERRE (1941) *d/co-s* B Henning Jenson *co-s* A Henning Jenson 9min (= *Christian IV, Master Builder*)
CHRISTIAN, THE (1923) *d* M Tourneur *a* Gibbons 2438m *pc* Goldwyn
CHRISTINA (1929) *d* W Howard *c* Andriot *w* J Gaynor 85min Fox
Christine = CARNET DE BAL, UN (1937)
CHRISTINE JORGENSEN STORY, THE (1970) *d* Rapper *fab* Christine Jorgensen *89min *r* UA
CHRISTINE OF THE BIG TOPS (1926) *d* A Mayo 1768m
CHRISTINE OF THE HUNGRY HEART (1924) *d* George Archainbaud *w* C Brook, W Baxter 7500ft *pc* Ince *r* FN
CHRIST MARCHANT SUR LES EAUX OU LE MIRACLE DES FLOTS, LE (1899) *d* Méliès 20m
CHRISTMAS (1922) *d* St Clair 2rs
CHRISTMAS CAROL, A (c 1938) *d* Bradley 16mm *si sh*
CHRISTMAS CAROL, A (1940) *d/s/c/e/w* Markopoulos *fst* Charles Dickens 8mm 3min
CHRISTMAS CAROL, A (1971) *d/p* R Williams *ex-p* C Jones *fst* Dickens *wv* M Redgrave anim* 30min
CHRISTMAS CRACKER (1964) *d* McLaren, G Munro, J Hall, G Potterton *9min NFBC
CHRISTMAS HOLIDAY (1944) *d* Siodmak *s* H Mankiewicz *fn* W Somerset Maugham *w* Gene Kelly, Durbin 93min Par
CHRISTMAS IN JULY (1940) *d/st/s* P Sturges *c* Milner *co-a* Dreier *w* D Powell 70min Par
CHRISTMAS TREE, THE (1969) *d/s* T Young *c* Alekan *m* Auric *w* Holden, Bourvil *108min (= *L'Arbre de Noel*)
CHRISTMAS UNDER FIRE (1941) *d* Watt 10min
CHRISTMAS VISITOR, THE (1958) *d* Halas *p* Halas, Batchelor anim 8min
CHRISTOPHER BEAN (1933) *d* S Wood *c* Daniels *w* Dressler, L Barrymore, Hersholt 75min MGM (= *The Late Christopher Bean/Her Sweetheart*)
CHRISTOPHER COLUMBUS (1949) *d* David MacDonald *m* Arthur Bliss *w* March *104min
CHRISTOPHER CRUMPET (1953) *d* Cannon *pc* UPA *r* Col
CHRISTOPHER CRUMPET'S PLAYMATE (1955) *d* Cannon * *pc* UPA *r* Col
CHRISTOPHER PLUMMER (1964) *d* A King, *Wm* Brayne 16mm 53min
Chronicle of a Summer = CHRONIQUE D'UN ETE (1961)

CHRONIK DER ANNA MAGDALENA BACK (1967) *d/co-p/co-s/co-e* Straub *co-p* Baldi 93min
CHRONIQUE D'UN ETE (1961) *co-d/p/co-s/w* Rouch *co-d/co-s/w* Morin *co-c* Coutard, Brault 16mm 90min (= *Chronicle of a Summer*)
CHRONIQUE PROVINCIAL (1958) *d/s* Rappeneau *sh*
CHU CHIN CHOW (1923) *d* H Wilcox 2743m
CHUDA HOLKA (1932) *d* Fric
CHUKA (1967) *d* G Douglas *co-a* Pereira *m* Leith Stevens *w* Borgnine, J Mills, L Hayward *91min Par
CHUMLUM (1964) *d* Rice 16mm 26min
CHUMP AT OXFORD, A (1940) *d* Alfred Goulding *as-p* Roach *co-s/co-st* Langdon *w* Laurel, Hardy 63min *r* UA
CHURCHILL'S ISLAND (1941) *p* Grierson NFBC
CHUSHINGURA (1932) *d/s/w* Kinugasa (= *The Royal 47 Ronin/The Vengeance of the 47 Ronin*)
CHUTE DE LA MAISON USHER, LA (1928) *d* J Epstein *fst* Poe 1830m (= *The Fall of the House of Usher*)
CHUZHOI BEREZ (1930) *d* Donskoi *si* (= *The Other Shore*)
CIAO, FEDERICO! (1970) *d/s/c/co-song* Gideon Bachmann *w* Fellini 16mm 61min
CIBOULETTE (1933) *d/co-s* Autant-Laura *s/di* J Prévert *fpl* Reynoldo Hahn *c* Courant *des* Meerson *w* Romance
CICERNACCHIO (1915) *d/s* Chione
CIECCA DI SORRENTO (1934) *d* Nunzio Malasomina *w* Magnani
CIEL EST A VOUS, LE (1943) *d* Grémillon *co-s* Charles Spaak *w* Vanel 106min
CIE, LA TERRE, LE (1966) *d* Ivens *n* L Anderson 28min (= *Threatening Sky, The*)
CIEL SUR LA TETE, LE (1964) *d* Ciampi *co-c* Séchan CS* 107min Gau
CIELO SULLA PALUDE (1949) *d/ad/co-s* Genina *co-s* Cecchi d'Amico *c* Aldo 97min (= *Heaven Over the Marshes*)
CIEN (1956) *d* Kawalerowicz 100min (= *The Shadow*)
CIEN CABALLEROS, LOS (1965) *d/co-s* Cottafavi S* 125min (= *The Hundred Horsemen*)
CIGALE ET LA FOURMI, LA (1897) *d* Méliès 20m
CIGALON (1935) *d/p/s/di* Pagnol
CIGARETPIGEN (1915) *d/s* Madsen
CIGARETTE, LA (1919) *d* Dulac 1463m
CIGARETTE POUR UN INGENU, UNE (1967, *uf*) *d* Grangier
CIMARRON (1931) *d* W Ruggles *fn* Edna Ferber *c* Cronjager *m* Steiner *w* I Dunne, Oliver 13rs RKO
CIMARRON (1960) *d* A Mann *fn* Edna Ferber *c* Surtees *m* Waxman *w* G Ford, Maria Schell, A Baxter CS* 145min MGM
CIMARRON KID, THE (1951) *d* Boetticher *w* A Murphy *84min U
CIMETIERE DANS LA FALAISE, LA (1951) *d/c* Rouch 16mm *25min
CINA E VICINA, LA (1967) *d/st/co-s* Bellochio 110min (= *China is Near*)
CINCINNATTI KID, THE (1965) *d* Jewison *c* Lathrop *m* Schifrin *w* McQueen, Robinson, Malden, Weld, Blondell *113min *co-pc* McQueen *r* MGM
CINCO BESOS (1946) *d* Saslavsky
CINCO LOBITOS (1945) *d* Vajda
Cinderella = ASCHENPUTTEL (1922)
CINDERELLA (1949) *p* Disney *75min *r* RKO
CINDERELLA (1963) *d* Reiniger anim* 10min
CINDERELLA AND THE FAIRY GODMOTHER (1898) *d* G Smith
Cinderella, Italian Style = C'ERA UNA VOLTA (1967)
CINDERELLA JONES (1960) *d* Berkeley *c* Polito *w* Cook, Horton 92min WB
CINDERFELLA (1960) *d/s* Tashlin *p/w* J Lewis *88min *r* Par
CINEMA D'ALTRI TEMPI (1953) *d/co-st/co-s* Steno *95min
CINERAMA HOLIDAY (1955) *d* Robert Bendick, Phillipe de Lacey *p* De Rochemont *co-a* Halas, Batchelor *119min
Cine Weekly = KINO NEDELYA (1918–1919)
CINQ GENTLEMEN MAUDITS, LES (1931) *d/s* Duvivier *c* Thirard *m* Ibert Tob (= *Die Vunf Verfluchten Gentlemen*)
CINQ SEPTEMBRE A SAINT-HENRI, LE (1962) *d* Hubert Auquin *c* Groulx
CINQUE BAMBOLE PER LA LUNA DI AGOSTO (1970) *d* Bava *85min (= *Five Dolls for an August Moon*)
CINTURA DI CASTITA, LA (1967) *d* Festa Campanile *c* Di Palma *w* Curtis, Vitti TC* 110min *r* WB (= *The Chastity Belt/On My Way to the Crusades, I Met a Girl Who . . .*)
CIOCIARA, LA (1961) *d/co-s* De Sica *p* Ponti *co-s* Zavattini *fn* Alberto Moravia *w* Loren, Belmondo, Vallone 110min (= *Two Women*)
CIRANO DI BERGERAC (1923) *d* Genina *s* Camerini
CIRCE, THE ENCHANTRESS (1924) *d/co-pc* Leonard *st* Vicente Blasco Ibanez *a* Gibbons 2097m *r* MGM
CIRCLE, THE (1925) *d* Borzage *fst* W Somerset Maugham *co-a* Gibbons 1680m MGM
CIRCLE OF DANGER (1951) *d* J Tourneur *c* Morris *w* Milland 104min *r* UA
CIRCLE OF DECEPTION (1960) *d* J Lee CS 110min

CIRCLE OF THE SUN (1960) *d/s* Low *30min NFBC
Circles = KREISE (1933)
CIRCO (1950) *d* Berlanga
CIRCOLO PICKWICK, IL (1967) *d* Gregoretti *fn* Dickens TV
CIRCO MAS PEQUENO DEL MUNDO, EL (1962) *d/s* Ivens *cy* J Prévert 6min
CIRCONCISION, LA (1949) *d/p/c* Rouch 16mm 30min
Circus = CiRK (1936)
CIRCUS, THE (1928) *d/p/s/m/e* Chaplin *co-c* Totheroh *w* Chaplin 1950m, *r* UA
CIRCUS CLOWN (1934) *d* Enright *c* Hickox 63min WB
CIRCUS COWBOY, THE (1924) *d* Wellman 1272m Fox
CIRCUS DAYS (1923) *d/co-ad* Cline *p* Lesser 1885, *r* FN
CIRCUS DRAWINGS (1964) *d* R Williams
Circus Fandango = CIRKUS FANDANGO (1954)
CIRKUS HURVINEK (1955) *d/co-s/c* Trnka *27min (= *The Hurvinek Circus*)
CIRCUS KID, THE (1928) *d* G Seitz 68min
CIRCUS NOTEBOOK (1966) *d* Mekas *12min (extract from DIARIES NOTES & SKETCHES)
Circus of Love = YOTTSU NO KOI NO MONOGATARI (1947)
CIRCUS WORLD (1964) *d* Hathaway *p* Bronston *co-s* B Hecht, J Grant *st* N Ray, Yordan *c* Hildyard *2nd c* C Renoir *m* Tiomkin *w* J Wayne, Cardinale, Hayworth, Conte, Nolan *135min Par (= *The Magnificent Showmen*)
CIRK (1936) *d* Alexandrov 89min (= *Circus*)
CISARUV PEKAR (1951) *d* Fric *125min (= *The Emperor's Baker*)
CISARUV SLAVIK (1948) *d/co-s/e/a* Trnka *co-s* Brdecka *fst* Hans Christian Andersen anim Pojar *73min (= *The Emperor's Nightingale* French version: LE ROSSIGNOL DE L'EMPEREUR DE CHINE (1951) *cy/wv* Cocteau)
CISKE EIN KIND BRAUCHT LIEBE (1955) *d* Staudte 96min
CITA DE AMOR, UNA (1956) *d* Fernandez *c* Figueroa
CITADEL, THE (1938) *d* K Vidor *p* Saville *ad* Emlyn Williams *c* Stradling *co-dec* Meerson *e* Frend *w* Donat, R Russell, Harrison, R Richardson, Emlyn Williams 112min MGM
CITADELLE DU SILENCE, LA (1937) *d* L'Herbier *co-c* Thirard *co-m* Honegger, Milhaud *w* Annabella, P Renoir
CITE DU MIDI, LA (1951) *d* Baratier *w* M Simon 26min
Citizen Brych = OBCAN BRYCH (1958)
CITIZEN KANE (1941) *d/p/co-st/co-s* Welles *co-st/co-s* H Mankiewicz *c* Toland *e* Wise, Robson *m* Herrmann *w* Welles, Cotten, Moorehead, (R Wilson) 119min *r* RKO
CI TROVIAMO IN GALLERIA (1953) *d* Bolognini *w* Sordi, Loren *
Citta Canora, La = CITY OF SONG (1931)
CITTA CHE DORME (1953) *d* Maselli
CITTA DEL CINEMA, LA (1955) *d* Sala *sh*
CITTA PRIGIONERA, LA (1963) *d* Anthony *m* Piccioni *w* Niven *r* Par 110min (= *Conquered City/Captive City*)
CITTA SI DIFENDE, LA (1951) *d/co-s* Genina *co-s* Fellini, Comencini *w* Lollobrigida 90min (= *Four Ways Out/Passport to Hell*)
CITY, THE (1939) *d/p/c* W Van Dyke, R Steiner *st* Lorentz *co-s* Lewis Mumford *m* Copland, Rawsthorne 44min
CITY BENEATH THE SEA (1953) *d* Boetticher *co-a* Golitzen *w* Ryan, Quinn *87min U
CITY FOR CONQUEST (1940) *d* Litvak *p* Wallis *c* Polito, Howe *m* M Steiner *w* Cagney, Sheridan, Quinn, A Kennedy, Kazan 101min WB
City Girl (re-issue) = OUR DAILY BREAD (1930)
CITY GONE WILD, THE (1927) *d* Cruze *co-st/s* Furthman *t* H Mankiewicz *c* Glennon *w* L Brooks 1648m Par
City Government = CITY SPEAKS, A (1946)
CITY IMPERIAL VOLUNTEERS LEAVING FOR SOUTH AFRICA (1900) *p* Hepworth
CITY IN THE SEA (1965) *d* J Tourneur *co-p* Arkoff *co-s* Charles Bennett *fpm* Edgar Allan Poe *w* Price PV* (= *War Gods of the Deep*)
CITY IS DARK, THE (1954) *d* De Toth *c* Glennon *w* Hayden 73min WB (= *Crime Wave*)
CITY LIGHTS (1931) *d/p/s/m* Chaplin *co-c* Totheroh *w* Chaplin (Parrish) 81min UA
CITY OF FEAR (1959) *d* I Lerner *c* Ballard *m* Goldsmith 81min Col
CITY OF GOLD (1957) *d/c* Low, Koenig *s* Kroiter 23min NFBC
CITY OF SONG, THE (1931) *d* Gallone *w* Helen 100min (= *La Citta canora*)
CITY OUT OF TIME (1959) *d* Low *15min NFBC
CITY PARK (1934) *d/e* Thorpe 72min
City Prepares, A = FIRST DAYS, THE (1939)
CITY SPEAKS, A (1947) *d/p/co-s* Rotha 69min
CITY STREETS (1931) *d* Mamoulian *fst* Hammett *c* Garmes *w* G Cooper, S Sidney, Lukas 74min Par
CITY THAT NEVER SLEEPS, THE (1924) *d/p* Cruze 1858m FPL *r* Par
CIUDAD Y EL CAMPO, LA (1935) *d* Velo, Fernando Mantilla *s* Velo (2rs)
CIVILISATION (1916) *co-d* Ince *co-a* August *m* Schertzinger 2500m Tri

CIVILISATION A TRAVERS LES AGES, LA (1908) d Méliès 380m (11 parts)

Claire's Knee (UK) = GENOU DE CLAIRE, LE (1970)

CLAN DES SICILIENS, LE (1969) d/co-s Verneuil co-s Giovanni c Decaë a Saulnaier w Gabin, Belmondo, Delon, Ventura PV* 120min (= *The Sicilian Clan*)

Clap Vocalism = NINGEN DOBUTSUEN (1961)

CLARA DE MONTARGIS (1951) d/s/ad/di Decoin c Renoir 98min

CLARENCE THE CROSS-EYED LION (1965) d Marton w Hayden *98min MGM

CLASH BY NIGHT (1952) d F Lang ex-p Wald fpl Odets c Musuraca w Stanwyck, P Douglas, Ryan, Monroe 105min r RKO

CLASSE TOUS RISQUES (1959) d/co-s Sautet co-s/fn Giovanni c Cloquet m Delerue w Belmondo, Ventura 110min

CLAUDELLE INGLISH (1961) d G Douglas w A Kennedy 99min WB (= *Young and Eager/Jilted*)

CLAUDIA (1943) d Goulding c Shamroy m A Newman w McGuire, R Young 91min Fox

CLAUDIA AND DAVID (1946) d W Lang ad Caspary c La Shelle m Mockridge w R Young, McGuire, Astor 78min Fox

CLAUDIUS (1937, uf) d/s Von Sternberg p A Korda fn (I Claudius) *Robert Graves* c Périnal dec V Korda w Laughton, Oberon, Newton, R Richardson, Emlyn Williams (= *I, Claudius*)

CLAY PIGEON, THE (1949) d R Fleischer s Foreman w Quine 63min RKO

CLEANING UP (1926) d/s Arbuckle (ps William Goodrich) (2rs)

Clear Skies = CHISTOYE NEBO (1961)

CLEMENCEAU CASE, THE (1915) d/s Brenon Fox

CLEO DE 5 A 7 (1961) d/st/s Varda p Ponti c Rabier dec Evein m Legrand w Legrand, (Godard, Karina, Constantine, Brialy)

Cleo From 5 to 7 (UK) = CLEO DE 5 A 7 (1961)

CLEOPATRA (1934) d/p De Mille c Milner co-a Dreier chor Prinz w Colbert, Pichel, Carradine (as John Peter Richmond) 98min Par

CLEOPATRA (1963) d/co-s J Mankiewicz co-2nd d Marton p Wanger co-s Buchman, MacDougall, L Durrell (uc), N Johnson (uc) f histories Plutarch, Suetonius, Appian and (The Life and Times of Cleopatra) C M Franzero c Shamroy, Hildyard, m North co-e Elmo Williams w E Taylor, Burton, Harrison TAO* 243min Fox

CLEOPATRE (1899) d Méliès 40m

CLIENT SERIEUX, UN (1932) d Autant-Lara

Cliff, The = SHIROI GAKE (1961)

Climates of Love (UK) – CLIMATS (1961)

CLIMATS (1961) d/co-s Stellio Lorenzi fn André Maurois c Vierny w Riva, Piccoli, V Lady 143min (= *Climates of Love*)

CLIMBING HIGH (1939) d C Reed w M Redgrave 79min r MGM

CLIVE OF INDIA (1935) d Boleslavsky p Zanuck as-p Goetz m A Newman c Marley a R Day w Colman, L Young, Romero 100min r UA

Cloak, The = SHINEL (1926)

CLOAK AND DAGGER (1946) d F Lang p Sperling c Polito m M Steiner w G Cooper, Palmer 106min r WB

CLOCK, THE (1945) d Minnelli p Freed c Folsey co-a Gibbons w Garland, R Walker 90min MGM

CLOCKWORK ORANGE, A (1971) d/p/s Kubrick *137min

CLOD, THE (1912) d Ince

CLOISTER'S TOUCH, THE (1910) d Griffith (1rl) Bio

Closed Doors = SUYLOVCENIM VEREJNOSTI (1933)

CLOSE HARMONY (1929) d Cromwell, *Edward A Sutherland* t J Mankiewicz 1911m Par

Closely Observed Trains = OSTRE SLEDOVANE VLAKY (1966)

CLOSE QUARTERS (1943) d/s J Lee 75min

CLOSET, THE (1965) d Warhol 70min 16mm

CLOSE TO MY HEART (1951) d/s Keighley s/fst (A Baby for Midge) JR Webb c Burks m M Steiner w Milland, Tierney 90min WB

CLOTHES MAKE THE PIRATE (1925) d M Tourneur w D Gish 2438m FN

Clothes of Deception = ITSWARERU SEISO (1951)

CLOUDED YELLOW, THE (1950) d Thomas c Unsworth w J Simmons, T Howard 96min JAR

CLOUD PATROL, THE (1928) d/co-p H Brown (2rs)

Clouds At Twilight = YUYAKE-KUMO (1956)

Clouds Will Roll Away, The = NENI STALE ZAMRACENO (1950)

CLOVEK PODVODON (1961) co-d/s Brdecka co-d Ladislav Capek (= *Man Underwater*)

CLOWN, THE (1953) d Leonard s Rackin co-a Gibbons 92min MGM

CLOWN ET SES CHIENS (1892) d Reynaud (paper)

CLOWN PRINCES (1939) d G Sidney (1rl) MGM

CLOWNS, I (1970) d/co-p/co-s Fellini m Rota w (Etaix, Ekberg) *91min RAI-ORTF

CLUB HAVANA (1945) d Ulmer 61min PRC

Club of the Big Deed, The = SVD (1927)

CLUNY BROWN (1946) d/n Lubitsch c La Shelle co-a Wheeler m Mockridge w Boyer, J Jones, Lawford, Hayden 101min Fox

C. MAN (1949) d/p I Lerner w Carradine 75min

C'MON LET'S LIVE A LITTLE (1967) d D Butler S 85min Par

COAL FACE (1936) d/s Cavalcanti p Grierson m Britten cy W H Auden 12min

COAST OF FOLLY, THE (1925) d/p Dwan w Swanson 2130m FPL

COBRA WOMAN (1944) d Siodmak co-s R Brooks co-a Golitzen w Montez, Sabu, Choney 70min U

COBWEB, THE (1917) d/p Hepworth (5rs)

COBWEB, THE (1955) d Minnelli p Houseman s Paxton c Folsey co-a Gibbons m Rosenman w Widmark, Grahame, Bacall, Boyer, L Gish CS* 124min MGM

COCHECITO, EL (1969) d/co-s Ferreri 81min

COCINOR (1958) cr Alexeieff anim

Cock Crows Twice, The = NIWATORI WA FUTATABI NAKU (1954)

COCKEYED CAVALIERS (1934) d Sandrich 72min RKO

COCK-EYED WORLD, THE (1929) d Walsh c Edeson w V McLaglen 118min Fox

COCKLESHELL HEROES (1956) d J Ferrer s Forbes, Maibaum co-c Moore w J Ferrer, T Howard CS* 97min Col

COCKTAIL HOUR (1933) d Schertzinger c August w R Scott 74min Col

Cocktails in the Kitchen = FOR BETTER OR WORSE (1954)

COCOANUTS, THE (1929) d Florey, *Joseph Santley* fpl G Kaufman, *Irving Berlin* c Folsey m Irving Berlin w C, G, H, Z Marx, Dumont, K Francis 96min Par

COCOTIERS, LES (1963) d Rouch 16mm

COCOTTE D'AZUR, LA (1959) d Varda

C.O.D. (1932) d M Powell 66min

Code, The = SZYFRY (1966)

CODE OF HONOR, THE (1916) d/w Borzage Tri

CODE OF MARCIA GRAY, THE (1916) d/s F Lloyd (5rs)

CODE OF THE SCARLET (1928) d H Brown c McCord w R Walker 1707m FN

CODE OF THE SEA (1924) d V Fleming 1840m FPL

CODE OF THE WEST (1925) d W Howard fn Zane Grey c Andriot w Constance Bennett, D Butler, G Bancroft 2066m FPL r Par

Code of Women = JOKYO (1960)

CODE TWO (1953) d F Wilcox c June co-a Gibbons w Meeker 68min MGM

CODINE (1962) d/co-st/co-m/e Colpi 80min

COEUR BATTANT, LE (1960) d/st Doniol Valcroze c Matras m Legrand w Trintignant 86min

COEUR D'AMOUR EPRIS (1952) d Aurel 16mm 15min (= *The Searching Heart*)

COEUR DE CRISTAL (1957) d Gruel anim

COEUR DE GUEUX (1936) d J Epstein (= *Cuor di Vaga Sancto*)

COEUR DE LA FRANCE, LE (1966) d Leenhardt

COEUR DE LILAS (1932) d/s Litvak fpl Tristan Bernard w Gabin, Fernandel

COEUR DE PARIS, LE (1933) d Benoît-Lévy

COEUR DES GUEUX, LE (1925) d/s Machin, *Henri Wulschleger* 2500m

COEUR FIDELE (1923) d/st J Epstein Pat

COEUR GROS COMME CA, UN (1961) d/co-c Reichenbach m Legrand, Delerue 82min

COEURS FAROUCHES (1924) d/s Duvivier

Coffin, The = TRAFRACKEN (1966)

COMBAT SANS HAINE (1948) d Michel

COHENS AND KELLYS IN TROUBLE (1933) d G Stevens w O'Sullivan 68min U

COHEN SAVES THE FLAG (1913) d Sennett w Normand (1rl) Key

Coin is a Coin, A = SLANT AR EN SLANT, INTE SANT?, EN (c 1955)

COL CUORE IN GOLA (1967) d/st/co-s/e Brass w Trintignant *107min (= *With Bated Breath*)

Cold Feast, The = LEDYANAYA SUDBA (1930)

COLDITZ STORY, The (1955) d/co-s Hamilton w J Mills, Forbes 97min BL

COLD TURKEY (1925) d Cline s Sennett (2rs)

COLD WIND IN AUGUST, A (1961) d Singer c F Crosby 80min

COLLECTION MENARD, LA (1943) d Bernard Roland p Joannon 86min

COLLECTIONNEUSE, LA (1966) d/s Rohmer *90min

COLLECTOR, THE (1964) d Wyler c Surtees, Krasker m Jarre w Stamp *119min r Col

COLLEEN (1936) d Alfred E Green c Polito, Haskin w Fazenda, D Powell 89min WB

COLLEGE (1927) d James Horne p/w Keaton 1803m r UA

COLLEGE COACH (1933) d Wellman co-s Busch w D Powell, (J Wayne) 75min WB

COLLEGE CONFIDENTIAL (1960) d/p Zugsmith co-a Golitzen w H Marshall 91min U

COLLEGE DAYS (1926) d Thorpe 2225m

COLLEGE HERO, THE (1927) d W Lang p Cohn c J Walker w Turpin 1715m Col

COLLEGE HOLIDAY (1936) d Tuttle c Sparkuhl w Benny 86min Par

COLLEGE HUMOR (1933) d W Ruggles w B Crosby 80min Par

College Is a Nice Place = DAIGAKU YOI TOKO (1936)

COLLEGE SCANDAL (1935) d E Nugent co-s Brackett 76min Par

COLLEGE SWING (1938) d Walsh c Milner song Carmichael w Hope, Horton, Grable, Payne, R Cummings 86min Par

COLLEGE WIDOW, THE (1927) d A Mayo w Ryan 2017m WB

COLLIER'S LIFE, A (1904) d Paul 315 ft

COLONEL BOGEY (1948) d Fisher 51min

COLONEL CHABERT (1943) d René La Henaff fn Balzac w Raimu 105min

COLONEL EFFINGHAM'S RAID (1945) d Pichel c Cronjager co-a Wheeler m Mockridge w J Bennett, C Coburn 70min Fox

COLONEL HEEZA LIAR (1922–23) d Vernon Stallings anim series pc Bray

COLONEL HEEZA LIAR WINS THE PENNANT (1916) d/pc Bray (1rl)

COLONEL'S PERIL, THE (1912) d Ince

COLONEL'S SON, THE (1912) d Ince

COLONEL'S WARD, THE (1912) d Ince

COLONIE SICEDISON (1958) d Olmi 13min

COLONNA TRAIANA, LA (1949) co-d/co-s/n Emmer co-d/co-s Enrico Gras 13min

COLORADO PLUCK (1921) d/ad Furthman 1432m Fox

COLORADO TERRITORY (1949) d Walsh c Hickox w McCrea, V Mayo, Malone 94min WB

COLORATURA (1931) d Fischinger 1min anim

COLOR IS RED, THE (c 1952) d Cornfield 16mm

COLOR ME DEAD (1969) d/p Eddie Davis co-s Rouse *97min

COLOSSUS OF NEW YORK, THE (1958) d Lourié st Goldbeck co-a Pereira 70min Par

COLOUR BOX (1935) d Lye *min GPO

COLOUR COCKTAIL (1934–35) d McLaren 16mm *5min

COLOUR CRY (1952) d Lye *4min

COLOUR FLIGHT (1939) d Lye

COLPA E LA PENA, LA (c1965) d Bellocchio sh

COLPO DI PISTOLA, UN (1942) d/co-s Castellani co-s Soldati fn Pushkin (= *A Pistol Shot*)

COLPO DI STATO (1968) d/co-s Salce p Ponti 105min

COLTER CRAVEN STORY, THE (1960) d J Ford w Carradine, Marsh, J Wayne (ps Michael Morris) 53min TV (ep in series Wagon Train)

"COLUMBIA" AND "SHAMROCK II" (1901) d Porter (in 5 parts) Ed

"COLUMBIA" WINNING THE CUP (1899) d Porter 37ft Ed

COMANCHEROS, THE (1961) d Curtiz s J Grant, Huffaker c Clothier m E Bernstein w J Wayne, Marvin CS* 107min Fox

COMANCHE STATION (1960) d/p/st Boetticher ex-p H Brown s B Kennedy c Lawton w R Scott CS* 73min pc Scott, H Brown r Col

COMBAT DANS L'ILE, LE (1962) d/co-st Cavalier supn Malle di Rappeneau dec Evein w Trintignant, Schneider 100min

COMBAT NAVAL DEVANT MANILLE (1898) d Méliès 20m

COME ALONG, DO! (1898) p Paul 80 ft

COME AND GET IT! (1936) d Hawks, Wyler p Goldwyn co-s Furthman fn Edna Ferber c Toland, Maté a R Day m A Newman w McCrea, Brennan 105min r UA (= *Roaring Timber*)

COME AND PLAY, SIR (1965–67) d Pojar (series of 3)

COME BACK AFRICA (1958) d/pc/e Rogosin 90min

COME BACK, LITTLE SHEBA (1953) d Daniel Mann p Wallis fpl Inge c Howe co-a Pereira m Waxman w Lancaster, Temple, Booth 99min Par

COME BLOW YOUR HORN (1963) d/co-p Yorkin ex-p HW Koch c Daniels co-a Pereira w Sinatra, Cobb, Rush PV* 112min Par

COME CLEAN (1931) d James Horne p Roach w Laurel, Hardy (2rs) r MGM

COMEDIANS, THE (1967) d/p Glenville s/fn Greene c Decaë w Burton, E Taylor, Guinness, Ustinov, L Gish PV* 160min MGM

COMEDIE DU BONHEUR, LA (1940) d L'Herbier di Cocteau w M Simon

COMEDIEN, LE (1947) d/s/fpl/w Guitry 95min

COMEDY OF TERRORS, THE (1964) d J Tourneur co-p Arkoff as-p/s Matheson c F Crosby a D Haller w Price, Lorre, Karloff, Rathbone PV* 88min AI

COME FILL THE CUP (1951) d G Douglas p Blanke s Goff, Roberts c Burks w Cagney 113min WB

COME FLY WITH ME (1963) d Levin p De Grunwald w Malden PV* 109min MGM

COME LE FOGLIE (1934) d/co-s Camerini w I Miranda

COME LIVE WITH ME (1941) d/p C Brown c Folsey w J Stewart, Lamarr 86min MGM

COME NEXT SPRING (1955) d Springsteen m M Steiner w Cochran, Sheridan 92min Rep

COME ON IN (1918) d/co-p/co-s Emerson co-p/co-s Loos (5 rs) FPL

COME ON, LEATHERNECKS (1938) d Cruze w Ladd 65min Rep

COME ON MARINES! (1934) d Hathway c B Reynolds chor Prinz w Lupino, Sheridan (as Clara Lou Sheridan) 70min Par
COME SEPTEMBER (1961) d Mulligan c Daniels w Hudson, Lollobrigida CS* 112min pc Walsh U
COME THROUGH (1917) d Conway (7rs) U
COME TO THE STABLE (1949) d Koster m Mockridge w L Young 94min Fox
COMET OVER BROADWAY (1938) d Berkeley co-s Hellinger c Howe w Crisp, (S Hayward) 69min WB
COMIC FACES (1898) d G Smith 23m
Comic History of Aviation, A = JAK SE CLOVEK NAUCIL LETAT (1958)
COMICOS (1954) d/s Bardem
Comic Strip Hero = JEU DE MASSACRE (1967)
COMING AN' GOING (1926) d Thorpe 1463m
Coming of Age in Ibiza = RUNNING AWAY BACKWARDS (1964)
COMING OF ANGELO, THE (1913) d Griffith (1rl) Bio
COMIN' THRO' THE RYE (1916) d Hepworth 5000ft
COMIN' THRO' THE RYE (1923) d/p Hepworth rm 1916 (6rs)
COMIZI D'AMORE (1964) d/cy/co-n/w Pasolini 90min
COMMAND, THE (1954) d D Butler p Katzman st/ad Fuller CS 94min WB (= *Rear Guard*)
COMMAND DECISION (1949) d S Wood p Franklin c Rosson co-a Gibbons m Rozsa w Gable, Pidgeon, V Johnson, Bickford, Quine 112min MGM
COMMANDING OFFICER, THE (1915) d Dwan w Neilan, Crisp (4rs) FP
Commando (US) = MARCIA O CREPO (1962)
COMMANDOS STRIKE AT DAWN (1943) d J Farrow st C S Forester s Shaw c Mellor w Muni, L Gish 99min Col
COMMARE SECCA, LA (1962) d/co-s Bertolucci st/co-s Pasolini m Piccioni 100min
COMMENT FABIEN DEVIENT ARCHITECTE (1901) d Zecca 50m Pat
COMMENT MAX FAIT LE TOUR DU MONDE (1913) d/s/w Linder Pat
COMMENT SAVOIR (1966) d Jutra 70min
COMMENT TUER UNE CADILLAC (1959) d Klein sh
COMME UN POISSON DANS L'EAU (1962) d Michel m Legrand w Noiret 82min
COMMISSAIRE EST BON ENFANT, LE (1934) d/co-s P Prévert, Becker c Kelber w P Prévert 43min (= *Le Gendarme est sans pitié*)
COMMISSARIO, IL (1962) d/co-s Comencini p De Laurentiis w Sordi 101min
COMMON CLAY (1930) d V Fleming s Furthman w Constance Bennett, Ayres 89min Fox
Communicants, The = NATTVARDSGASTERNA (1962)
COMMUNICATIONS PRIMER (1953) d/s C & R Eames c C Eames *22½min
Compact With Death, A = BARBUJAN A PANDRHOLA (1960)
COMPAGNI, I (1963) d/co-s Monicelli c Rotunno w Mastroianni, Girardot 127min r Par (= *The Strikers/The Organizer*)
COMPAGNO DON CAMILLO, IL (1965) d Comencini w Fernandel 109min
COMPAGNONS DE LA GLOIRE, LES (1945) d Ciampi 16mm sh
COMPAGNONS DE LA MARGUERITE, LES (1966) d/co-s Mocky w Blanche 90min (= *The Order of the Daisy*)
COMPANERAS AND COMPANEROS (1970) d/s A Mekas, *Barbara and David Stone* 16mm *90min
Company of Cowards? = ADVANCE TO THE REAR (1964)
COMPANY SHE KEEPS, THE (1950) d Cromwell c Musuraca m Harline w L Scott 83min RKO
COMPARTMENT TUEURS (1965) d/s Costa-Garras w Montand, Gélin, Piccoli, Signoret, Trintignant S 95min (= *The Sleeping Car Murders*)
COMPLESSI, I (1965) 100min (= *Complexes*)
   ep UNA GIORNATA DECISIVA d Risi w Manfredi
   ep IL COMPLESSO DELLA SCHIAVA NUBIANA d Rossi
Complexes (US) = I COMPLESSI (1965)
Composition in Blue = KOMPOSITION IN BLAU (1934)
COMPROMISE (1925) d Crosland w C Brook, Fazenda 2070m WB
COMPULSION (1959) d R Fleischer s R Murphy c Mellor co-a L Wheeler w Welles CS 103min Fox
COMPUTER GLOSSARY, A (1967) d/s C and R Eames c C Eames m E Bernstein *10½min
COMRADES (1911) d/w Sennett (1rl) Bio
COMRADESHIP (1919) d Elvey 1829m (= *Comrades in Arms*)
Comrades in Arms = COMRADESHIP (1919)
COMRADE X (1940) d K Vidor p G Reinhardt s B Hecht, Lederer c Ruttenberg m Kaper w Gable, Lamarr 90min r MGM
COMTE DE MONTE CRISTO, LE (1960) d Autant-Lara S* 130min (= *The Story of the Count of Monte Cristo*)
CONCEALMENT (1935) d Dieterle w Stanwyck 63min WB
CONCERT DE MONSIEUR ET MADAME KABAL, LE (1962) d/s Borowczyk anim* 6½min (= *The Concert of Mr and Mrs Kabal*)

Concert of Mr and Mrs Kabal, The = CONCERT DE MONSIEUR ET MADAME KABAL, LE (1962)
Concerto for a Machine Gun = KONCERT ZA MASINSKU PUSKU (1959)
Concert of the Masters of Ukrainian Art = KONTSERT MASTEROV UKRAINSKOVO ISKUSSTVA (1952)
Concert Waltz = KONTSERT-VALS (1940)
Concrete Jungle, The (US) = CRIMINAL, THE (1960)
CONDAMNE A MORT S'EST ECHAPPE, UN (1956) d/s Bresson c Burel mf Mozart 102min (= *A Man Escaped*)
CONDEMNED (1929) d W Ruggles p Goldwyn c Barnes, Toland a Menzies e Heisler w Colman (10rs) r UA
Condemned of Altona, The = SEQUESTRATI DI ALTONA, I (1962)
Conduct Report on Professor Ishinaka = ISHINAKA SRNSEI GYOJOKI (1950)
Conduct Unsatisfactory = KANTOR IDEAL (1932)
CONE OF SILENCE (1960) d Frend w G Sanders 92min BL
CONEY ISLAND (1917) d/w Arbuckle w Keaton (2rs) (= *Fatty at Coney Island*)
CONEY ISLAND (1943) d W Lang p Perlberg st/s Seaton co-a R Day chor Pan m A Newman w Grable, Romero, G Montgomery 96min Fox
CONFESSION (1937) d May p Wallis co-ad JJ Epstein c Hickox w Rathbone, K Francis, Crisp 88min WB
CONFESSION (1953) d/s K Hughes 90min
CONFESSION, THE (1964, ur) d/p William Marshall w G Rogers, Milland, Dieterle (= *Quick, Let's Get Married*)
Confession, The = AVEU, L' (1970)
CONFESSIONE DI UN COMMISARIO DI POLIZIA AL PROCURATORE DELLA REPPUBBLICA (1971) d/co-s Damiani *101min
Confessions of a Counter-spy (UK) = MAN ON A STRING (1960)
CONFESSIONS OF A NAZI SPY (1939) d Litvak w G Sanders, Robinson, Lukas 102min WB
CONFESSIONS OF AN OPIUM EATER (1962) d/p Zugsmith fn Thomas De Quincey c Biroc a Lourié w Price 85min AA (= *Evils of Chinatown*)
CONFESSIONS OF A QUEEN (1925) d Sjöström fn Alphonse Daudet co-a Gibbons 1774m MGM
CONFESSIONS OF BOSTON BLACKIE (1941) d Dmytryk 65min Col
CONFIDENCE GIRL (1952) d/p/st/s Stone c Clothier 81min pc Stone r UA
CONFIDENCES ENTRE QUATRE YEUX (1954) d Michel w Neff
CONFIDENTIAL AGENT (1945) d Shumlin fn Greene c Howe m Waxman w Bacall, Boyer, Paxinou, Lorre 118min WB
Confidential File = CONFIDENTIAL REPORT (1955)
CONFIDENTIAL REPORT (1955) d/p/s/a/cos Welles c Bourgoin m Misraki w Welles, M Redgrave, Tamiroff, Paxinou 99min r WB (= *Confidential File/Mr. Arkadin*)
CONFIRM OR DENY (1941) d A Mayo, F Lang (uc) s Swerling fco-st Fuller c Shamroy w J Bennett 73min Fox
Conflagration = ENJO (1958)
CONFLICT (1945) d C Bernhardt co-st Siodmak w Weisbart m Hollander w Bogart. Greenstreet, A Smith 86min WB
CONFORMISTA, IL (1970) d/s Bertolucci fn Alberto Moravia m Delerue w Trintignant *110min
Confrontation, The = FENYES SZELEK (1969)
CONGO CROSSING (1956) d Pevney c Metty w V Mayo, Lorre *87min U
CONGO MAISIE (1940) d Potter c Lawton a Gibbons w Sothern 70min MGM
CONGRES DER VAKVEREENIGINGEN (1930) d/s/co-c/e Ivens 300m
CONGRES DES NATIONS EN CHINE (1901) d Méliès 20m
Congress Dances, the = KONGRESS TANZT, DER (1931)
CON IL CUORE FERMO SICILIA (1966, uf) d Mingozzi sh
Conjugal Bed, The (UK) = STORIA MODERNA: L'APE REGINA, UNA (1963)
CONNECTICUT YANKEE, A (1931) d D Butler fn Mark Twain w M Loy, O'Sullivan, W Rogers 78min Fox
CONNECTICUT YANKEE AT KING ARTHUR'S COURT, THE (1920) d Emmett J Flynn fn Mark Twain c Andriot 8291ft Fox
CONNECTICUT YANKEE IN KING ARTHUR'S COURT, A (1949) d Garnett fn Mark Twain c Rennahan co-a Dreier m V Young w B Crosby, Bendix, R Fleming 107min Par
CONNECTION, THE (1960) d/co-p S Clarke w The Living Theatre 110min
CON QUALE AMORE, CON QUANTO AMORE (1969) d/co-s Festa Campanile w Catherine Spaak TS* 107min
Conquered City US) = CITTA PRIGIONERA, LA (1963)
Conquered Seas = POKORITELI MORYA (1959)
CONQUERING POWER, THE (1921) d/p Ingram fn (*Eugénie Grandet*) Balzac ad Mathis c J Seitz w Valentino 1935m MGM

CONQUERING THE WOMAN (1922) d/p K Vidor c Barnes w D Butler 1794m
CONQUERER, THE (1917) d/s Walsh (8rs) Fox
CONQUERER, THE (1955) d/p D Powell co-c La Shelle, Wild m V Young w J Wayne, S Hayward, Armendariz, Moorehead CS* 111min RKO
CONQUERERS, THE (1932) d Wellman c Cronjager w Oliver 84min RKO
CONQUEST (1928) d Del Ruth w H Warner 75min WB
CONQUEST (1929) d B Wright p Grierson
CONQUEST (1937) d C Brown c Freund a Gibbons m Stothart w Garbo, Boyer, Ouspenskaya 112min MGM (= *Marie Walewska*)
Conquest = AKUTO (1966)
Conquest of Annapurna = VICTOIRE SUR L'ANNAPURNA (1953)
CONQUEST OF COCHISE (1953) d Castle p Katzman w Stack *70min Col
CONQUEST OF SPACE (1955) d Haskin p Pal co-ad Yordan c Lindon co-a Pereira *80min Par
CONQUEST OF THE AIR (1935) d Z Korda 25min
CONQUEST OF THE DRY ZONE (1954) d Peries 14min
CONQUETE DE L'AIR, LA (1901) d/w Zecca 50m Pat
CONQUETE DE L'ANGLETERRE, LA (1955) d Leenhardt 27min
CONQUETE DE GAULES, LA (1922) co-d Burel
CONQUISTA DEI DIAMANTI, LA (1916) d Genina
CONSEIL D'AMI, UN (1916) d/s Feyder 243m Gau
CONSIDER YOUR VERDICT (1938) d R Boulting p J Boulting 38min
CONSPIRACY, THE (1914) d Dwan w Emerson (4rs) FP
CONSPIRACY OF HEARTS (1960) d Thomas w Palmer 111min JAR
Conspiracy of the Doomed = ZAGOVOR OBRECH-YONNIKH (1950)
CONSPIRATOR (1949) d Saville c F Young w R Taylor, E Taylor 87min MGM
CONSPIRATORS, THE (1944) d Negulesco c Edeson w Lamarr, Henreid, Greenstreet 101min WB
CONSTANCE (1957) cr Alexeieff anim* 1min
CONSTANT HUSBAND, THE (1955) d/co-p/co-s Gilliat co-p Launder m M Arnold w Kendall, Harrison 88min BL
CONSTANT NYMPH, THE (1943) d Goulding p Blanke c Gaudio e Weisbart m Korngold w Boyer, Fontaine, C Coburn, Dalio, Lorre, A Smith 112min WB
CONSTRUIRE UN FEU (1927 r 1930) d Autant-Lara sh
CONTACT (1932) d Rotha 42min
CONTADINI DEL MARE (1955) d/c/e De Seta 7min (= *Bluefin Fury*)
CONTE DI LUNA, IL (1943) d Emmer
Contemporary Story, A = HISTORIA WSPOLCZESNA (1960)
Contempt = MEPRIS, LE (1963)
CONTESSA DI PARMA, LA (1937) d/co-s/co-e Blasetti co-s Soldati c Martell co-m Fusco
CONTESTAZIONE GENERALE (1970) d Zampa m Piccioni w Gassman, Manfredi, Sordi, M Simon, Vlady *125min
CONTES ZAGHAWA, LES (1966) d Gruel, *André Fontaine* anim
CONTE UGOLINO, IL (1949) d/co-s Freda co-s Monicelli fpm (*L'Inferno*) Dante 90min (= *Il Cavaliere di Ferro*)
CONTRABAND (1925) d/p Crosland 2065m FPL r Par
CONTRABAND (1940) d/co-s M Powell st Pressburger c F Young w Veidt, Kerr 91min (= *Blackout*)
CONTRASTES (1959) d Dewever, *Robert Menegoz* * sh
CONTREPOINT (1964) d Enrico
CONTROFAGOTTO (1961) d Gregoretti TV
CONTROSESSO (1964) p Ponti 110min
   ep COCAINA DI DOMENICA d Rossi co-st/co-s Zavattini w Manfredi
   ep IL PROFESSORE d/co-st/co-s Ferreri
   ep UNA DONNA D'AFFARI d/co-st/co-s Castellani w Manfredi
Convention City = SONS OF THE DESERT (1933)
CONVENTION CITY (1933) d A Mayo w Menjou, Astor, D Powell, Blondell 69min FN
CONVERSATIONS IN VERMONT (1971) d R Frank c 25min
CONVICT 99 (1938) d Marcel Varnel w Hay 87min
CONVICT 13 (1920) d/s Keaton, Cline w Keaton (2rs) Metro
COOGAN'S BLUFF (1968) d/p D Siegel co-a Golitzen m Schrifrin w Eastwood, Cobb *94min U
COOK, THE (1918) d/s/w Arbuckle w Keaton (2rs) r Par
COOL HAND LUKE (1967) d S Rosenberg c C Hall m Schifrin w P Newman, G Kennedy PV* 127min
COOL SOUND FROM HELL, A (1959) d/s Fric 71min
COOL WORLD, THE (1963) d/co-s/e S Clarke 125min
COP, THE (1928) d/p Crisp s Garnett c A C Miller 2150m Pat
Cop, The = VIGILE, IL (1960)
COPACABANA (1947) d Alfred W Green c Glennon w G Marx, C Miranda, Cochran 92min r UA
COPACABANA PALACE (1962) d Steno PS* 122min
COPPELIA OU LA POUPEE ANIMEE (1900) d Méliès fst Hoffman 40m
COPPER CANYON (1950) d J Farrow c C Lang co-a Dreier w Milland. Lamarr 83min Par

COPPER SKY (1957) d/ex-p Warren S 77min Fox
COPPIA TRANQUILLA, UNA (1968) d/co-s Maselli w Hudson, Cardinale *88min (= A Fine Pair)
COPPIE, LE (1971) *130min
ep IL FRIGORIFERO d Monicelli c Di Palma w Vitti
ep LA CAMERA d Sordi m Piccioni w Sordi
ep IL LEONE d De Sica w Sordi, Vitti
COPS (1922) d/s Keaton, Cline w Keaton (2rs)
Cops and Robbers = GUARDIE E LADRI (1951)
Cops and Watches = TWENTY MINUTES OF LOVE (1914)
COQUETTE D'ANGLETERRE, LA (1935) d Cohl anim
COQUETTE (1929) d/di Sam Taylor fco-pl G Abbot c Struss w Pickford 6993ft pc Pickford
COQUILLE ET LE CLERGYMAN, LA (1928) d Dulac s Artaud (3rs) (= The Seashell and the Clergyman)
COR, LE (1931) d J Epstein c Matras 300m
CORALIE ET CIE (1934) d/s Cavalcanti
CORBARI (1970) d Orsini *109min
CORBEAU, LE (1943) d/co-s Clouzot c Hayer w Fresnay 92min
CORBEILLE ENCHANTEE, LA (1903) d Méliès 25m
CORBUSIER, L'ARCHITECTE DU BONHEUR, LE (1956) d Kast m Delerue 20min
CORDE . . . UN COLT, UNE (1968) d/s/w Hossein *90min
CORIOLAN (1950) d/s Cocteau w Marais 16mm
CORNERED (1945) d Dinytryk s Paxton c Wild w D Powell 102min RKO
CORNER IN WHEAT, A (1909) d Griffith fn (The Pit) Frank Norris w Mack Sennett (1rl) Bio
Corn = KORN (1943)
Corner of Great Tokyo, A = DAI-TOKYO NO IKKAKU (1930)
CORN IS GREEN, THE (1945) d Rapper fpl Emlyn Williams c Polito m M Steiner w B Davis 114min WB
CORONA DI FERRO, LA (1941) d/co-st/co-s Blasetti w Girotti 138min (= The Iron Crown)
CORONA NEGRA, LA (1952) d Saslavsky s Cocteau w Gassman 94min
CORONATION OF KING EDWARD VII, THE (1901) p Hepworth 750ft (6 parts)
CORONER CREEK (1948) d Enright p H Brown w R Scott 93min Col
COROT (1965) d Leenhardt 18min
Corporal Dolan AWOL (UK) = RENDEZVOUS WITH ANNIE (1946)
CORPS DE DIANE (1968) d Jean-Louis Richard w Moreau *95min
CORPSE CAME C.O.D., THE (1947) d Levin c Andriot m Duning w Blondell 87min Col
CORRAL (1954) d/s Low c Koenig 12min NFBC
CORREDO DI SPOSA, IL (1961) d Baldi
Corridor, The = KORRIDOREN (1968)
CORRIDOR OF MIRRORS (1948) d T Young m Auric 105min
Corrupt, The = SYMPHONIE POUR UN MASSACRE (1963)
CORRUZIONE, LA (1963) d Bolognini m Fusco 87min
CORSAIRE, LE (1939) d M Allégret
CORSARO, IL (1924) d Gallone, Genina
CORSICAN BROTHERS, THE (1898) d G Smith
CORSICAN BROTHERS, THE (1941) d Ratoff c Stradling m Tiomkin w Fairbanks Jr, Tamiroff 112min r UA
CORTIGIANA DI BABILONIA, LA (1955) d/s Bragaglia w R Fleming *105min (= Queen of Babylon, The/Slave Woman, The)
CORTILI, IL PITTORE DELLA MONTAGNE (1948) d Risi sh
CORVETTE K–225 (1943) d Richard Rosson p Hawks co-c Gaudio w R Scott, (Lawford), (Mitchum) 99min (= The Nelson Touch)
CORY (1898) p Paul
COSSACKS, THE (1928) d/p George Hill fn Tolstoi co-a Gibbons w Adorée, J Gilbert (10rs) MGM
COSTA BRAVA '59 (1959) d Grau
COSE DA PAZZI (1954) d Pabst co-c Bava mf Verdi
COSH BOY (1952) d/co-s L Gilbert p Woolf Bros 73min (= The Slasher)
COSTA AZZURA (1959) d/co-st/co-s Sala w Sordi, Martinelli FS* 93min
COSTANZA DELLA RAGIONE, LA (1964) d/co-s Festa Campanile fn Vasco Pratolini w Deneuve 86min
COSTRUZIONI MECCANICHE RIVA (1956) d Olmi *23min
COTE D'AZUR, LA (1954) d/s Leenhardt 25min
COTTAGE ON DARTMOOR, A (1930) d Asquith 109min
COTTAGE TO LET (1941) d Asquith co-s De Grunwald w J Mills 90min BL (= Bombsight Stolen)
COUCH (1964) d Warhol 16mm si 40min
COUNSEL FOR CRIME (1937) d Brahm 61min Col
COUNSELLOR AT LAW (1933) d Wyler s/fpl Elmer Rice c Brodine w J Barrymore, M Douglas, (Quine), (V Sherman) 78min U
COUNSEL'S OPINION (1933) d Dwan 71min
COUNT, THE (1916) d/s Chaplin co-c Totheroh w Chaplin, Purviance (2rs) Mut
Counted Out = KNOCKOUT, THE (1914)
COUNTER-ATTACK (1945) d Z Korda s Lawson c Howe w Muni 90min Col (= One Against Seven)
COUNTER-ESPIONAGE (1942) d Dmytryk 72min Col

COUNTERFEIT CAT, THE (1949) d Avery p Quimby anim* 7min MGM
COUNTERFEIT TRAITOR, THE (1961) d/s Seaton c Bourgoin w Holden, Palmer, Dahlbeck *140min Par
Counterplan = VSTRECHNYI (1932)
COUNTERPOINT (1967) d Nelson c Metty m Kaper w Heston, Maximilian Schell, (Nelson) *107min U
COUNTESS CHARMING, THE (1917) d Crisp (5rs) pc Lasky
COUNTESS FROM HONG KONG, A (1967) dp/s/di/m Chaplin w Brando, Loren, (Chaplin) 120min U
COUNTESS OF MONTE CRISTO, THE (1934) d Freund w Lukas 78min U
COUNT OF MONTE CRISTO (1912) d Porter 5rs FP
COUNT OF MONTE CRISTO, THE (1934) d/co-s/co-di Rowland V Lee co-s/co-di P Dunne fn Dumas c Marley w Donat 115min r UA
COUNTRY COMES TO TOWN, THE (1932) d B Wright p Grierson
COUNTRY DANCE (1969 r 1971) d Thompson c Moore w O'Toole *112min
COUNTRY DOCTOR, THE (1927) d Julian c Marley 2286m r Pat
COUNTRY DOCTOR, THE (1936) d H King p Zanuck co-c J Seitz w Darwell, Hersholt 110min Fox
Country Doctor, The = SELSKII VRACH (1952)
COUNTRY GIRL, THE (1954) d/co-p/s Seaton co-p Perlberg fpl Odets a Periera w Grace Kelly, B Crosby, Holden 104min Par
COUNTRY HERO, A (1920) d/w Arbuckle w Keaton 2rs FPL
COUNTRY HUSBAND, THE (1958) d Neilson 75min Col
COUNTRY THAT GOD FORGOT, THE (1916) d/s Neilan 5rs Sel
COUNT TAKES THE COUNT, THE (1936) dc Chase (as Parrott), Harold Law p Roach w C Chase (2rs) MGM
COUNT THE HOURS (1953) d D Siegel p Bogeaus c J Alton w T Wright 70min RKO (= Every Minute Counts)
COUNT THREE AND PRAY (1955) d George Sherman c Guffey m Duning w Heflin, Woodward S* 102min Col
COUNTY CHAIRMAN, THE (1914) d/s Dwan 5rs
COUNTY HOSPITAL (1932) d James Parrott p Roach w Laurel, Hardy (2rs) r MGM
COUNT YOUR BLESSINGS (1959) d Negulesco c Folsey, Krasner m Waxman w Chevalier, Kerr CS* 102min MGM
COUP DE GRACE, LE (1965) co-d/s Cayrol co-d Claude Durand w Piccoli, Riva, Darrieux 105min
COUP DU BERGER, LE (1956) d Rivette w Brialy, Doniol-Valcroze sh pc Chabrol
COUPLE, UN (1960) d/co-s Mocky co-s Queneau c Schuftan w Blanche 84min (= The Love Trap)
COUPLE IDEAL, LE (1945) d Rouleau, Bernard-Roland m Van Parys w Rouleau
Couple On The Move, A = HIKKOSHI FUFU (1928)
COURAGE (1930) d A Mayo 73min WB
COURAGE OF LASSIE, THE (1946) d F Wilcox co-a Gibbons m Kaper w E Taylor 92min MGM
COURAGE OF THE WEST (1937) d JH Lewis 58min U
COURONNEMENT DU ROI EDOUARD VII (1902) d Méliès
COURSE AUX POTIRONS (1907) d Cohl anim
COURSE DES BELLES-MERES, LA (1907) d/s Feuillade 100m
COURTE-TETE (1956) d Norbert Carbonneaux w De Funès 74min
COURTIN' OF CALLIOPE CLEW, THE (1916) d/w Borzage Tri
COURT JESTER, THE (1956) d/p/st/s M Frank, Panama c June co-a Periera w Kaye, Rathbone VV* 101min Par
COURT-MARTIAL (1928) d G Seitz p Cohn c J Walker 1833m Col
Court Martial (US) = CARRINGTON V.C. (1956)
COURT-MARTIAL OF BILLY MITCHELL, THE (1955) d Preminger p/co-st/co-s Sperling c Leavitt m Tiomkin w G Cooper, Bickford, Steiger CS* 100min r WB (= One Man Mutiny)
Court Martial of Sergeant Ryker, The = SERGEANT RYKER (1966)
COURTROOM (1966) d Warhol 16mm *30min (segment of Four Stars)
COURTSHIP (1898) p Paul 80ft
COURTSHIP OF ANDY HARDY, THE (1942) d G Seitz w Rooney, D Reed 93min
COURTSHIP OF EDDIE'S FATHER (1963) d Minnelli p Pasternak c Krasner w G Ford, S Jones PV* 118min r MGM
COUSINS, LES (1958) d/p/s Chabrol c Decaë dec Saulnier, Evein m Misraki w Brialy 110min
COUTEAU DANS LA PLAIE, LE (1962) d Litvak c Alekan dec Trauner w Loren, Perkins 110min (= Five Miles to Midnight)
COVEK NIJE TIJKA (1966) d/s Makavejev 80min
COVERED WAGON, THE (1923) d/p Cruze co-m Reisenfeld 2867m FPL
COVER GIRL (1944) d C Vidor co-c Maté chor Gene Kelly w Hayworth, Gene Kelly *107min Col

COVER TO COVER (1936) d Alexander Shaw p Rotha 21min
COWARD, THE (1915) co-d Ince w J Gilbert 1800m Tri
Coward, The = ZBABELEC (1961)
Coward and the Holy Man, The = KAPURUSH-O-MAHAPURUSH (1965)
COWBOY (1958) d Daves p Blaustein co-s H Butler (uc) c Lawton cr Brass m Duning w G Ford, Lemmon *92min Col
COWBOY, THE (1954) d/p/e Elmo Williams *67min
COWBOY AND THE LADY, THE (1938) d Potter p Goldwyn rm 1929 co-st McCarey c Toland a R Day m A Newman w G Cooper, Oberon (9rs) r UA
COWBOY CAVALIER, THE (1928) d Thorpe w R Walker 1379m
COWBOY 57 (1957) d/p/n J Stewart TV
COWBOY FROM BROOKLYN (1938) d Bacon p Wallis w D Powell, Reagan, Sheridan 8rs WB
COWBOY JIMMY (1957) d Vukotic *13min anim
COWBOY MILLIONAIRE, THE (1935) d Cline p Lesser w G O'Brien 65min Fox
Cow on the Moon, The = KRAVA NA MJESECU (1959)
CRABES, LES (1929) d Painlevé m Delannoy
CRACKED ICE MAN, THE (1934) d C Chase (as Parrott), Eddie Dunn p Roach w C Chase 22rs MGM
CRACKED NUTS (1931) d Cline c Musuraca w Turpin 8rs RKO
CRACK IN THE MIRROR (1960) d R Fleischer p Zanuck c Mellor a D'Eaubonne m Jarre w Welles
CRACK IN THE WORLD (1965) d Marton a Lourié w D Andrews *96min Par
CRACK-UP (1936) d St Clair w Lorre 70min Fox
CRACK UP (1946) d Reis co-s Paxton m Harline w H Marshall, Trevor 93min RKO
CRADLE BUSTER, THE (1922) d/co-p/st/s Tuttle 6rs
CRADLE OF COURAGE, THE (1920) d/s Lambert Hillyer c August w W Hart 5rs pc W Hart
CRADLE OF GENIUS (1959) d Rotha w Sean O'Casey
CRADLE SNATCHERS, THE (1927) d Hawks c O'Connell w Fazenda 1915m Fox
CRADLE SONG (1933) d Leisen c C Lang 76min Par
CRAIG'S WIFE (1936) d Dorothy Arzner w Mitchell, R Russell 74min Col
CRAINQUEBILLE (1923) d/p/des Feyder fn Anatole France co-c Burel w Rosay 1650m
CRAINQUEBILLE (1934) d de Baroncelli rm by Feyder w Modet 65min
Cranes are Flying, The = LETYAT ZHURAVLI (1957)
CRANEUR, LE (1955) d Kirsanov w Vlady 92min
CRASH, THE (1928) d Cline c McCord 1898m FN
CRASH, THE (1932) d Dieterle c E Haller 65min FN
CRASH DIVE (1943) d A Mayo st Burnett s Swerling c Shamroy w Power, A Baxter, D Andrews *105min Fox
CRASH LANDING (1958) d Sears p Katzman 76min Col
Crash of Silence, The (US) = MANDY (1932)
Crazy Desire = VOGLIA MATTA, LA (1962)
CRAZY HOUSE (1943) d Cline w Olsen, Johnson 80min U
Crazy Page, A = KURUTTA IPPEIJI (1926)
Crazy Pete = PIERROT LE FOU (1965)
Crazy Ray, The (UK) = PARIS QUI DORT (1924)
CRAZY TO MARRY (1921) d Cruze w Arbuckle 1647m FPL r Par
CRAZY WORLD OF LAUREL AND HARDY, THE (1966) p Roach (compilation)
CREAM PUFF ROMANCE, A (1916) d/w Arbuckle 2rs (= A Reckless Romeo)
CREATIVE PERSON, THE (1967) co-d/ex-p A King (in 13 parts) TV
CREATURE FROM THE BLACK LAGOON (1954) d J Arnold 3–D 79min U
CREATURE FROM THE HAUNTED SEA (1960) d/p Corman 60min
CREATURES, LES (1966) d/s Varda w Deneuve, Piccoli, Dahlbeck FS 105min
CREDO (1924) d/p Duvivier (= La Tragédie de Lourdes)
CREME SIMON, LA (1937) d Alexeieff anim (3 films)
CREOSOOT (1913) d/e Ivens 54min
CREPUSCOLO DI UM MONDO (1953) d Nelli sh
Crest of the Wave = SEAGULLS OVER SORRENTO (1954)
CRESUS (1960) d/p Jean Criono w Fernandel S 100min
CREVETTES, LES (1929) d Painlevé m Delannoy
CRICCA DORATA, LA (1913) d/s/w Ghione
CRICKET ON THE HEARTH, THE (1909) d Griffith fn Charles Dickens 1rl Bio
Cri du cormoran le soir au-dessous des jonques, Le = PAUME, LE (1971)
CRIME AND PUNISHMENT (1935) d Von Sternberg p BP Schulberg co-s Anthony fn Dostoievsky c Ballard w Lorre 89min Col
CRIME AND PUNISHMENT, USA (1959) d D Sanders p T Sanders fn Dostoievsky c F Crosby 78min AA
Crime at the Girl's School = ZLOCIN V DIVCI SKOLE (1965)
CRIME DE MONSIEUR LANGE, LE (1936) d/co-s J Renoir co-ad/di J Prévert c Bachelet co-m Wiener, Kosma w Jules Berry 80min
CRIME DOCTOR (1943) d M Gordon w W Baxter 66min Col

CRIME DOCTOR'S GAMBLE, THE (1947) d Castle w W Baxter 66min

CRIME DOCTOR'S MANHUNT, THE (1946) d Castle w W Baxter 60min Col

CRIME DOCTOR'S WARNING, THE (1945) d Castle c O'Connell w W Baxter 64min Col

CRIME IN THE STREETS (1956) d D Siegel s/st Rose c Leavitt m Waxman w Cassavetes 91min AA

CRIMEN (1960) d Camerini p De Laurentiis c Di Venanzo w Sordi, Gassmann, Manfredi, Mangano CS 110min (= Killing at Monte Carlo)

CRIMEN A LAS TRES (1935) d Saslavsky

CRIMEN DE ORIBE (1950) co-d/co-s Torre-Nilsson 85min

CRIME OF DOCTOR FORBES, THE (1936) d G Marshall 75min Fox

CRIME AND PASSION (1957) d G Oswald c La Shelle w Stanwyck, Hayden, Burr 84min UA

CRIME UNLIMITED (1935) d Ralph Ince w Palmer 73min WB

Crime Wave = CITY IS DARK, THE (1953)

CRIME WITHOUT PASSION (1934) d/p/st/s B Hecht, MacArthur as-d/c Garmes co-e Vorkapich w Rains, (H Hayes) 80min Par

CRIMINAL, THE (1915) d Van Dyke Brooke w N Talmadge 3rs Vit

CRIMINAL, THE (1960) d Losey c Krasker design consultant R MacDonald w S Baker 97min (= The Concrete Jungle)

CRIMINAL CODE, THE (1931) d Hawks p Cohn co-ad/co-di S Miller c Howe w W Huston, Karloff 97min Col

CRIMINAL COURT (1946) d Wise 63min RKO

Criminal Life of Archibaldo de la Cruz, The = ENSAYO DE UN CRIMEN (1955)

CRIMINALS WITHIN (1941) d JH Lewis 67min

CRIMSON CITY, THE (1928) d A Mayo w M Loy 1642m WB

Crimson Dynasty (UK) = KOENIGSMARK (1935)

CRIMSON KIMONO, THE (1959) d/p/s Fuller c Leavitt co-a Boyle 82min Col

CRIMSON PIRATE, THE (1952) d Siodmak co-p H Hecht c Heller m Alwyn w Lancaster 109min r WB

CRIN BLANC, LE CHEVAL SAUVAGE (1935) d Lamorisse c Sechan 47min (= The White Stallion)

CRISE DU LOGEMENT, LA (1955) d/s Dewever sh

CRISE EST FINIE, LA (1934) d Siodmak w Darrieux, Préjean 74min (= Finie La Crise/The Slump is Over)

CRISI (1921) d Genina

Crisis = KRIS (1945)

CRISI (1950) d/s R Brooks p Freed c June m Rozsa w C Grant, J Ferrer, Novarro, Roland 95min MGM

CRISIS (1963) d/c Pennebaker w John F Kennedy and Robert F Kennedy 16mm 55min

CRISS CROSS (1948) d Siodmak c Planer m Rozsa w Lancaster, De Carlo, Duryea, (Curtis) 87min U

CRISTOFORO COLOMBO (1937) d Gallone

CRISTO NON SI E FERMATO A EBOLI d Michele Gaudin c Rotunno

CRISTO PROIBITO, IL (1950) d Curzio Malaparte w Vallone 100min (= Strange Deception/Forbidden Christ)

CRITIC, THE (1963) d/p Pintoff mf Bach *5min

CRITIC'S CHOICE (1963) d Weis m Duning c C Lang w Hope, Ball PV* 100min WB

CROCIATA DEGLI INNOCENTI, LA (1916) d Alessandro Boulet, Gino Rosselli fpl D'Annunzio

CROMWELL (1911) D Henri Desfautaines w Jules Berry

CROMWELL (1970) d/s K Hughes c Unsworth w R Harris, Guinness PV* 139min Col

CRONACA DI UN AMORE (1950) d/co-s/st Antonioni co-s Maselli m Fusco w Bosè, Girotti 96min

CRONACA FAMILIARE (1962) d/co-s Zurlini fn Vasco Pratolini c Rotunno w Mastroianni *122min (= Family Diary)

CRONACHE DI POVERI AMANTI (1954) d/co-s Lizzani c Venanzo w Mastroianni 102min

CRONJE'S SURRENDER TO LORD ROBERTS (1900) p Paul 60ft

CROOK BUSTER (1925) d Wyler 2rs U

CROOKED WAY, THE (1949) d Florey p Bogeaus w Payne 90min r UA

CROOKS AND CORONETS (1969) d/s Jim O'Connolly w Evans, Romero *106min WB

CROONER (1932) d Bacon 68min WB

CROP CHASERS (1939) d Iwerks anim* 1rl r Col

CROQUIS DE L'ISLANDE (1956) d Hanoun sh TV

CROSS AND THE SWITCHBLADE, THE (1970) d/co-s Murray *106min

CROSS EXAMINATION (1932) d Thorpe 74min

Cross-Eyed Fortune = ZEZOWATE SZCZESCIE (1959)

CROSSFIRE (1947) d Dmytrysk s Paxton fn (The Brick Foxhole) R Brooks w Mitchum, Ryan, R Young. Grahame 86min RKO

Crossing of the Rhine, The = LE PASSAGE DU RHIN (1960)

CROSSING THE AMERICAN PRAIRIES IN THE EARLY FIFTIES (1911) d Griffith 1rl Bio

CROSS MY HEART (1947) d John Berry c C Lang 83min Par

CROSS OF LORRAINE, THE (1943) d Garnett a Gibbons m Kaper w Gene Kelly, Lorre 90min MGM

Crossroads = JUJIRO (1928)

CROSSROADS (1942) d Conway c Ruttenberg a Gibbons w Lamarr, Rathbone, W Powell, Trevor 84min MGM

CROSSROADS OF NEW YORK, THE (1922) d Richard Jones p/s/st Sennett 6rs FN

Cross Up = TIGER BY THE TAIL (1955)

Crossways = JUJIRO (1928)

CROWD, THE (1928) d/p/st/co-s K Vidor co-a Gibbons 2540m MGM

CROWDED DAY, THE (1954) d Guillermin 82min

CROWDED SKY, THE (1950) d Pevney s Schnee c Stradling w D Andrews, R Fleming, A Francis *105min WB

Crowded Train, The = MANIN DENSHA (1957)

CROWD ROARS, THE (1932) d/st Hawks co-s S Miller, Busch c Hickox w Cagney, Blondell 85min WB

CROWD ROARS, THE (1938) d Thorpe w O'Sullivan, R Taylor, Wyman MGM

CROWN V. STEVENS (1934) d M Powell 65min

CRUEL, CRUEL LOVE (1914) d Sennett w Chaplin 1rl Key (= Lord Help Us)

CRUEL SEA, THE (1953) d Frend p Balcon s Eric Ambler fn Nicholas Monsarrat m Rawsthorne w Hawkins, S Baker 126min

CRUISE OF THE ZACA, THE (1952) d/n Flynn *18min WB

CRUISIN' DOWN THE RIVER (1953) d/co-st/co-s Quine co-st/co-s Edwards c Lawton w De Carlo *81min Col

CRUSADES, THE (1953) d De Mille p Zukor co-s D Nichols, Brackett c Milner a Dreier chor Prinz w Young, Carradine, Sheridan 125min Par

CRUZ NA PRACA, A (1960) d Rocha 8min

Cry, The = IL GRIDO (1957)

CRY DANGER (1951) d Parrish c Biroc a R Day w D Powell, R Fleming 79min RKO

CRY FOR HAPPY (1961) d G Marshall p Goetz m Duning c Guffey w G Ford, O'Connor CS* 110min Col

CRY FOR HELP, A (1912) d Griffith w L Gish, D Gish 1rl Bio

CRY FROM THE STREETS, A (1958) d/p L Gilbert 99min

CRY HAVOC (1944) d Thorpe s Osborn m Amfitheatrof c Freund a Gibbons w Blondell, Sothern, (Mitchum) 97min MGM

CRY IN THE NIGHT, A (1956) d Tuttle c J Seitz w E O'Brien, N Wood, Burr 75min WB

Cry of Battle = TO BE A MAN (1963)

CRY OF THE CITY (1948) d Siodmak p S Siegel s R Murphy fn (The Chair for Martin Rome) Henry Edward Halseth co-a Wheeler m A Newman w Conte, Mature, Winters 96min Fox

CRY OF THE HUNTED (1953) d JH Lewis c Lipstein co-a Gibbons w Gassman 80min MGM

CRYSTAL BALL, THE (1943) d E Nugent co-ad Dreier w Goddard, Milland, Bendix 81min U

CRY TERROR (1958) d/co-p/s Stone co-p/e Virginia Stone w Mason, Stringer, A Dickinson, Marsh 96min MGM

CRY, THE BELOVED COUNTRY (1952) d/co-p Z Korda s/fn Alan Paton c Krasker w Poitier 103min (= African Fury)

CSASZAR KATONAI (1918) d Balasz

CSEND ES KIALTAS (1968) d/co-s Jancsó S 85min (= Silence and Cry)

CSILLAGOSOK (1950, ur) d/co-s Ranody (= Stars)

CSILLAGOSOK, KATONAK (1967) d/co-s Jancsó S 90min (= The Red and the White)

CUANDO LEVANTA LA NIEBLA (1952) d Fernandez c Figueroa

CUBAN LOVE SONG, THE (1931) d W S Van Dyke as-p Lewin c Rosson m Stothart w Fazenda 90min MGM

CUBAN REBEL GIRLS (1959) d Barry Mahon w Flynn 63min

CUBA SEGODNYA (1960) d/c Karmen (= Cuba Today)

CUBA SI! (1961) d/s/c Marker 55min

Cuba Today = CUBA SEGODNYA (1960)

CUCARACHA, LA (1934) d/co-st Lloyd Corrigan p Macgowan c Rennahan * (2rs) r RKO

CUCCAGNA, LA (1962) d/co-s/w Salce (= The Land of Plenty)

Cuckold, The = PAROHY (1947)

Cuckoo = HOTOTOGISU (1932)

CUCKOO CLOCK, THE (1950) d Avery anim* 7min MGM

CUD NAD WISLA (1921) d Boleslavsky

CUENCA (1958) d/s/e Saura *49min

CUISINE AU BEURRE, LA (1963) d Grangier w Fernandel, Bourvil 82min

CUISINE DE L'OGRE, LA (1908) d Méliès 115m

CUISINE EXPRESS (1912) d Cohl anim

CUL-DE-SAC (1966) d/co-s Polanski c G Taylor m Komeda 111min

CULTURE DES TISSUS ET FORMATION DE MACROCYTES, LA (1935) d Painlevé

Culture du Mil, La = GENS DU MIL, LES (1951)

CULLODEN (1964) d/s Watkins 16mm 73½min BBC

CUMBERLAND STORY, THE (1947) d/s Jennings 39min

CUMBRES BORRASCOSAS (1953) d/s Bunuel fn (Wuthering Heights) Emily Brontë 90min (= Abismos de pasion)

Cuor di Vagabondo = COEUR DU GUEUX (1936)

CUORE RIVELATORE (1947) d Risi sh

CUORI INFRANTI. I (1962)

ep LA MANINA DE FATMA d/co-s/w Caprioli co-s Patroni Griffi 90min (all film)

CUORI SENZA FRONTIERE (1950) d Zampa p Ponti w Lollobrigida 86min (= The White Line/The Heart Knows No Frontier)

CUPID'S DAY OFF (1919) d Cline s Sennett w Turpin 2rs pc Sennett

CUPID'S FIREMAN (1923) d Wellman c August 1281m Fox

CURATE'S DILEMMA, OR THE STORY OF AN ANT HILL, THE (1906) p Paul 290ft

CURE, THE (1917) d/s/w Chaplin c Totheroh w Purviance 2rs Mut

CUREE, LA (1966) d/co-ad Vadim fn Emile Zola c C Renoir w J Fonda, Piccoli PV* 95min

CURE FOR LOVE, THE (1949) d/p/co-s/w Donat 98min

CURE THAT FAILED, THE (1913) d Sennett w Normand +rl Key

CURLYTOP (1924) d Elvey 1776m Fox

Curse and the Coffin, The (UK) = CHAMBRE ARDENTE, LA

Cursed Millions = PROKLYATYE MILLIONY (1917)

CURSE OF FRANKENSTEIN, THE (1957) d Fisher *83min WB

CURSE OF IKU, THE (1918) d Borzage S & A

CURSE OF THE CAT PEOPLE, THE (1944) d Wise, Gunther von Fritsch p Lewton c Musuraca m Bakaleinikoff w S Simon 70min RKO

Curse of the Dead = OPERAZIONE PAURA (1966)

Curse of the Demon (us) = NIGHT OF THE DEMON (1957)

CURSE OF THE WEREWOLF, THE (1961) d Fisher *88min JAR

CURTAIN POLE, THE (1909) d Griffith w Sennett 250m Bio

CUSTARD CUP, THE (1923) d Brenon 1879m Fox

CUSTER OF THE WEST (1968) d Siodmak 2nd d/p I Lerner a Lourié w J Hunter, Ryan 70* 146min

Custer's Last Fight = LIEUTENANT'S LAST FIGHT (1912)

CUSTER'S LAST RAID (1912) d Ince

CYBELE, OU LES DIMANCHES DE VILLE D'AVRAY (1962) d/co-s Bourguignon m Jarre S 110min (= Sundays and Cybele)

Cybernetic Grandma = KYBERNETICKA BABICKA (1963)

CYCLE OF FATE, THE (1916) d/s Neilan 5rs

CYCLONE COWBOY, THE (1927) d Thorpe 1355m

CYKLEDRENGENE I TORVEGRAVEN (1940) d/s B Henning-Jensen

CYNARA (1932) d K Vidor p Goldwyn c June m A Newman w Colman, K Francis 75min pc Goldwyn r UA

CYNTHIA (1947) d Leonard co-a Gibbons m Kaper w E Taylor, G Murphy 98min MGM

CYRANO DE BERGERAC (1950) d M Gordon s Foreman c Planer m Tiomkin w J Ferrer 112min r UA

CYRANO ET D'ARTAGNAN (1963) d/s Gance c Martelli w J Ferrer, Cassel, Noiret, M Simon *145min

Czarina (UK) = ROYAL SCANDAL, A (1945)

CZECHOSLOVAKIA 1918–1968 (1968) d D Sanders *10min

Czech Year, The = SPALICEK (1947)

CZLOWIEK NA TORZE (1956) d/co-s Munk 89min (= Man on the Track)

DACTYLO SE MARIE, LE (1933) d May

DADASCOPE Part I 1956, Part II 1967) d Richter w Duchamp, Tanguy, Arp, Hulsenbeck 19min

DADDY LONG LEGS (1919) d Neilan w Pickford 7rs FN

DADDY LONG LEGS (1931) d Santell c Andriot w J Gaynor W Baxter 73min Fox

DADDY LONG LEGS (1955) d Negulesco c Shamroy co-a Wheeler co-chor Astaire w Astaire, Caron, Ritter, F Clark CS* 126min Fox

DADDY'S GONE A-HUNTING (1925) d/p Borzage a Gibbons 1783m MGM

DADDY'S GONE A-HUNTING (1969) d/p Robson c Laszlo *108min WB

DAFFY DUCK AND EGGHEAD (1937) supn Avery p L Schlesinger *7min WB

DAGFIN (1926) d/p/co-s May w Wegener 3407m

DAGLI APPENNINI ALLE ANDE (1959) d/co-s Quilici w Rossi-Drago CS* 100min

DIABUTSU KAIGEN (1952) d/s Kinugasa w Kyo Dai (= Saga of the Great Buddha)

DAICHI WA HOHOEMU (1925) ep d Mizoguchi (= Smile of our Earth)

DAIGAKU WA DETA KEREDO (1929) d Ozu Sho (= I Graduated, But . . .)

DAIGAKU WA DETA (1929) d Ozu

DAIGAKU YOI TOKO (1936) d/st Ozu Sho (= College is a Nice Place)

DAIGO FUKURYU MARU (1958) d/s Shindo (= Lucky Dragon No. 5)

Daily News = NOVOSTI DNYA (1947–54)

DAINAH LA METISSE (1931) d Grémillon s Charles Spaak co-c Périnal w Vanel 80min

DAI SHINRIN (1930) d Gosho (= Big Forest)
Daisies (UK) = SEDMIKRASKY (1966)
DAISY KENYON (1947) d/p Preminger c Shamroy co-a Wheeler m Raksin w J Crawford, D Andrews, H Fonda 99min Fox
DAITOA SENSO (1968) cy/e Oshima (= The Pacific War)
DAI-TOKYO NO IKKAKU (1930) d/s Gosho (= A Corner of Great Tokyo)
DALEKA CESTA (1949) d/co-s Radok 90min (= Distant Journey)
DALLAS (1950) d Heisler c E Haller m M Steiner w G Cooper, Roman, Cochran 94min WB
DAMAGED LIVES (1933) d/cos Ulmer 120min
DAMA S MALOU NOZKOU (1919) d J S Kolar co-s/w Machaty
DAMA S SOBACHKOI (1960) d/s Heifitz fst Anton Chekov c Moskvin w Babalov 90min (= The Lady with a Little Dog)
DAMBUSTERS, THE (1954) d Michael Anderson sp eff G Taylor w M Redgrave 125min ABC
DAME AUX CAMELIAS, LA (1911) d André Calmettes w S Bernhardt 900m
DAME AUX CAMELIAS, LA (1934) d/s Gance fn Dumas w Fresnay 110min
DAME DANS L'AUTO AVEC DES LUNETTES ET UN FUSIL, LA (1969) d/co-ad Litvak c C Renoir m Legrand PV* 105min Col (= The Lady in the Car with Glasses and a Gun)
DAME DE CHEZ MAXIM'S, LA (1912) d Emile Chautard w M Tourneur
DAME DE MALACCA, LA (1938) d M Allégret w Feuillère
DAME DE PIQUE, LA (1965) d Keigel fst Pushkin w Parlo 92min (= The Queen of Spades)
DAME MIT DEN SCHWARWN HANDSCHUHEN, DIE (1919) d Curtiz
DAME MIT SONNENBLUMEN, DIE (1919) d Curtiz
DAMEN I SVART (1958) d Mattsson c Nykvist w Bjork 85min (= Woman in Black)
DAMEN MED DE LYSE HANDSKER (1942) d Christensen (= The Lady with the Coloured Gloves)
DAMES (1934) d Enright co-st/s Daves c Hickox, Barnes chor Berkeley w Blondell, D Powell, Pitts, (Quine) 90min WB
DAMES DU BOIS DE BOULOGNE, LES (1945) d/s Bresson di Cocteau fn (Jacques le Fataliste) Denis Diderot c Agostini w Casarès 90min
DAMNATION DE FAUST, LA (1898) d Méliès fpm Berlioz 20m
DAMNED, THE (1962) d Losey design consultant R MacDonald w Lindfors S 87min Col (= These are the Damned)
Damned, the = CADUTA DEGLI DEI, LA (1970)
DAMNED DON'T CRY, THE (1950) d V Sherman p Wald c McCord w J Crawford, Cochran 103min WB
Damn the Defiant (US) = H.M.S. DEFIANT (1961)
DAMN YANKEES (1959) d/p G Abbott, Donen s/pco-mpl G Abbott c Lipstein chor/w Fosse cr Binder *109min WB (= What Lola Wants)
DAMON AND PYTHIAS (1961) d C Bernhardt *99min MGM
DAMON DES MEERES (1930) d Curtiz fn (Moby Dick) Herman Melville c Hickox w Dieterle 80min WB (German version of Lloyd Bacon's Moby Dick)
DAMSEL IN DISTRESS, A (1937) d G Stevens p Berman co-s/fst P G Wodehouse c August m George Gershwin w Astaire, Fontaine 100min RKO
DANCE, GIRL, DANCE (1940) d Dorothy Arzner co-p Pommer c Metty e Wise w L Hayward, M O'Hara, Ouspenskaya, Ball 90min RKO
DANCE HALL (1941) d Pichel c Andriot w Romero 68min Fox
DANCE HALL (1950) d Crichton p Balcon co-s Mackendrick c Slocombe e Holt w Kendall 80min
DANCE IN THE SUN (1953) d/p/c/e S Clarke 7min
DANCE MADNESS (1926) d Leonard co-c Daniels co-a Gibbons w Hopper 1950m MGM
DANCE MOVIE (1963) d Warhol 16mm si 45min (= Roller Skate)
The Dance of Death = PLYASKA SMERTI (1916)
DANCE OF LIFE, THE (1929) d Cromwell, Edward A Sutherland as-p Selznick w Cromwell, Sutherland * sd: 118min si: 2282m Par
Dance of the Heron = DANS VAN DE REIGER, DIE (1966)
DANCE OF THE VAMPIRES (1967) d/co-p/co-s/w Polanski c Slocombe m Komeda PV* 91min MGM (= The Fearless Vampire Killers/Pardon Me, but your teeth are in my neck)
DANCE, PRETTY LADY (1931) d Asquith 64min
DANCER OF PARIS, THE (1926) d Santell c E Haller 6220ft FN
DANCER'S DREAM, THE (1906) p Paul 180ft
DANCE SQUARED (1963) d McLaren anim NFBC
Dance Training = KYOREN NO BUTO (1924)
DANCE WITH ME, HENRY (1956) d Charles T Barton w B Abbott, Costello
DANCIN' FOOL, THE (1920) d S Wood 5rs
Dancing Girls of Izu = IZU NO ODORIKO (1933)
DANCING GIRL, THE (1915) d Dwan 4rs FP

DANCING IN THE DARK (1949) d Reis fco-pl (The Bandwagon) G Kaufman co-a Wheeler m A Newman w W Powell, Menjou, Hersholt *92min Fox
DANCING LADY (1933) d Leonard w J Crawford, Gable, Tone, Astaire, Benchley 82min MGM
DANCING MASTERS, THE (1943) d St Clair c Brodine w Laurel, Hardy, Dumont, Mitchum 64min Fox
Dancing Master, The (1961, uf) part included in SENSELESS (1962)
DANCING MOTHERS (1926) d Brenon co-st Goulding w Bow 2186m FPL r Par
Dancing Princess = MAIHIME (1951)
DANCING SWEETIES (1930) d Enright 62min WB
DANDY DICK (1935) d William Beaudine w Hay 73min
DANDY IN ASPIC, A (1968) d A Mann, Laurence Harvey(uc) p A Mann c Challis m Quincy Jones w Laurence Harvey, Courtenay, M Farrow PV* 107min Col
DANGER AHEAD (1923) d W Howard 5rs
Danger: Diabolik = DIABOLIK (1967)
DANGER, GO SLOW (1918) d/co-s Leonard 6rs U
Danger Grows Wild (UK) = POPPY IS ALSO A FLOWER, THE (1966)
Danger is a Woman (US) = QUAI DE GRENELLE (1950)
DANGER LIGHTS (1930) d G Seitz co-c Struss w Arthur 73min RKO
DANGER – LOVE AT WORK (1937) d Preminger co-s/st J Grant w Sothern, Horton, Carradine, Cook 81min Fox
Danger on the Danube = NEGYEN AZ ARBAN (1961)
DANGEROUS NUMBER (1937) d Thorpe w R Young, Sothern 71min MGM
DANGEROUS YEARS (1947) d Arthur Pierson w (Monroe) 62min Fox
Danger Stalks Near = FUZEN NO TOMOSHIBI (1957)
DANGEROUS AGE, A (1957) d/s Furie 69min pc Furie
DANGEROUS AGE, THE (1922) d/p Stahl 7rs FN
DANGEROUS CROSSING (1953) d J Newman c La Shelle co-a Wheeler w Crain 75min Fox
DANGEROUS DAN McFOO (1959) supn Avery p L Schlesinger *7min WB
DANGEROUS DUB, THE (1926) d Thorpe 1363m
DANGEROUS FLIRT, THE (1924) d Browning co-c Andriot 6rs
DANGEROUS HOURS (1919) d Niblo 7rs
DANGEROUSLY THEY LIVE (1942) d Florey c O'Connell 77min WB
DANGEROUSLY YOURS (1937) d St Clair w Romero, Darwell 63min Fox
DANGEROUS NAN McGREW (1930) d St Clair c Folsey 73min Par
DANGEROUS PARADISE (1930) d Wellman fn (Victory) J Conrad c Stout 59min Par
DANGEROUS PROFESSION, A (1949) d Tetzlaff co-s/co-st Rackin w Raft 79min RKO
Dangerous Spring = FARLIG VAR (1948)
DANGEROUS TO KNOW (1938) d Florey w Tamiroff, Nolan, Quinn 70min Par
DANGEROUS WHEN WET (1953) d Walters p Wells c Rosson co-a Gibbons anim sequences Quimby, Hanna, Barbera w Esther Williams *95min MGM
Danger Route = ESCAPE ROUTE (1967)
DANGER SIGNAL (1945) d Florey c Howe 78min WB
DANIELE CORTIS (1947) d/co-s Soldati co-s Comencini w Gassman
Danish Village Church, The = LANDSBYKIRKEN (1947)
DANJURO SANDAI (1944) d Mizoguchi Sho (= Three Generations of Danjuro)
DANNATI DELLA TERRA, I (1968) d Orsini fbook Franz Fanon * part 90min
DANN SCHON LIEBER LEBERTRAN (1930) d/co-s Ophuls co-s Pressburger c Schuftan 100min Ufa
DANRYU (1939) d Yoshimura (= Warm Current)
DANSE DE MORT, LA (1947) d Marcel Cravenne co-ad/co-di Von Stroheim fpl August Strindberg w Von Stroheim 88min
Danse Macabre = TETTES ISMERETLEN, A (1957)
DANSERINDENS HAEVN (1915) d/co-s Madsen
DANSE SERPENTINE (1896) d Méliès 20m
DANSEUSES DE LA MER (1960) d Painlevé *
DANSKE SYDHAVSOER, DE (1944) d B Henning Jensen s A Henning Jensen
DANSK POLITI I SVERIGE (1945) d/s A Henning Jensen
DANS LA NUIT (1935) d/w Vanel
Dans les Remous = SANGEN OM DEN ELDRÖDA BLOMMAN (1919)
DANS LE VENT (1963) d/co-s/co-e Rozier 9min TV
DANS L'OURAGAN DE LA VIE (1918) d Dulac
Danstavlingen i esira ep in SVARTA HORISONTER (1936)
DANS UNE ILE PERDUE (1931) d Cavalcanti fn (Victory) Joseph Conrad Par
DANS VAN DE REIGER, DE (1966) d Rademakers CS 80min (= The Dance of the Heron)
DANTON (1921) d/s Dimitri Buchowetzki dec Dreier w Jannings, Krauss 6000ft
DANZATRICE DELLA TAVERNA NERA (1914) d/w Ghione
DAPHNE (1936) d Rossellini sh
DAPHNE (1964) d Enrico TV

DAPHNE AND THE PIRATE (1916) d Christy Cabanne w L Gish 5rs Tri
DAPHNIE, LA (1925) d Painlevé
DA QUI ALL'EREDITA (1955) d/co-s Freda part *
DARAKU SURU ONNA (1967) d Yoshimura s Shindo 95min Sho (= A Fallen Woman)
DARBY O'GILL AND THE LITTLE PEOPLE (1959) d Stevenson c Hoch w Connery *93min pc Disney
DARBY'S RANGERS (1958) d Wellman p Rackin c Clothier m M Steiner w Garner 121min WB (= The Young Invaders)
DAREDEVIL, THE (1920) d/st/s/w Mix 5rs Fox
DARK ALIBI (1946) d Karlson 61min Mon
DAREK (1946) d/st/s Trnka anim Pojar anim 452m (= The Gift)
DARK ANGEL, THE (1925) d George Fitzmaurice c Barnes w Banky, Colman 7311ft FN
DARK ANGEL, THE (1935) d Franklin p Goldwyn co-s Hellman c Toland e Heisler a R Day m A Newman w March, Oberon, H Marshall 108min UA
DARK AT THE TOP OF THE STAIRS, THE (1960) d Delbert Mann fpl W Inge m M Steiner w McGuire, Preston *123 WB
DARK AVENGER (1955) d Levin p Mirisch w Flynn, Finch S* 85min (= The Warriors)
DARK CITY (1950) d Dieterle p Wallis c Milner m Waxman w Heston, L Scott, Lindfors 88min Par
DARK COMMAND (1940) d Walsh p S Siegel fn Burnett m V Young w J Wayne, Pidgeon, R Rogers, Trevor 93min Rep
DARK CORNER, THE (1946) d Hathaway p Kohlmar c Joe Macdonald m Mockridge w Ball, Bendix, C Webb 99min Fox
Dark Dreams of August = OSCUROS SUENOS DE AGOSTO (1967)
DARK HAZARD (1934) d Alfred E Green fn Burnett c Polito w Robinson 72min FN
DARK JOURNEY (1937) d/p Saville w V Leigh, Veidt, Newton 81min BL (Reissue 1953 as Anxious Years)
DARK MIRROR, THE (1946) d Siodmak p/s N Johnson m Tiomkin w De Havilland, Ayres, Mitchell 85min U
Darkness at Noon = MAHIRU NO ANKOKU (1956)
Darkness in Daytime = NAPPALI SÖTETSÉG (1963)
Dark Age (UK) = SCANDAL SHEET (1952)
DARK PASSAGE (1947) d/s Daves p Wald c Hickox e Weisbart m Waxman w Bogart, Bacall, Moorhead 106min WB
DARK PAST, THE (1949) d Maté p Adler c J Walker m Duning w Holden, Cobb 75min Col
Dark Purpose = L'INTRIGO (1963)
DARK PURPOSE (1964) d G Marshall w G Sanders, S Jones *97min U
Dark Room of Damocles, The = ALS TWEE DRUPPELS WATER (1963)
DARK SECRETS (1923) d V Fleming st/s Goulding c Rosson 6rs FPL
DARK STAR, THE (1919) d Dwan w Davies 7rs r FPL
DARK STREETS (1929) d/p F Lloyd c E Haller Sd: 60min Si: 1680m FN
Dark Sunlight = SOLEIL NOIR (1966)
DARK VICTORY (1939) d Goulding c E Haller w B Davis, Bogart, Reagan 106min WB
DARK WATERS (1944) d De Toth p Bogeaus co-c Stout m Rozsa w Oberon, Tone, Mitchell, Cook 90min UA
DARLING (1965) d J Schlesinger w Bogarde, Laurence Harvey, Christie 127min r WB
DARLING, HOW COULD YOU! (1951) d Leisen fpl (Alice Sit by the Fire) J M Barrie c Fapp co-a Periera w Fontaine 96min Par
DARLING LILI (1970) d/p/co-s Edwards c R Harlan m Mancini w J Andrews, Hudson PV* 136min r Par
DARÒ UN MILIONE (1935) d/co-s Camerini co-st/co-s Zavattini co-c Martelli w De Sica
DASH THROUGH THE CLOUDS, A (1912) d Sennett w Normand ½rl Bio
Date for Marriage = TOTSUGA HI (1956)
DATE WITH DIZZY, A (1958) d J Hubley anim 10min
DATE WITH JUDY, A (1948) d Thorpe p Pasternak c Surtees w Beery, J Powell, E Taylor, C Miranda, Stack *113min MGM
DATE WITH THE FALCON, A (1941) d Reis w G Sanders 63min RKO
Daughters, Wives and a Mother = MUSUME TSUMA HAHA (1960)
Daughter = MUSUME (1926)
Daughter of Destiny = ALRAUNE (1928)
DAUGHTER OF DR. JEKYLL (1957) d Ulmer 69min
DAUGHTER OF ROSIE O'GRADY, THE (1950) d D Butler chor Prinz w D Reynolds Darwell 103min WB
DAUGHTER OF SHANGHAI (1937) d Florey w Bickford, Quinn 7rs Par
DAUGHTER OF THE GODS, A (1916) d/st/s Brenon 10rs
DAUGHTER OF THE LAW, A (1921) d Conway c Glennon 5rs U
Daughter of the Sands = NOCES DE SABLE, LES (1948)
DAUGHTERS COURAGEOUS (1939) d Curtiz p Wallis as-p Blanke st/s JJ Epstein c Howe m M Steiner w Rains, Garfield 107min WB
Daughters of Yoshiwara = TAKEKURABE (1955)
DAUMIER (1959) d/pc Leenhardt 19min

DAUPHINS ET CETACES (1948–49) d Cousteau
DAVANTI A LUI TREMAVA TUTTA ROMA (1946) d Gallone
DAVID (1962) d R Leacock, Pennebaker p Drew 16mm 54min
DAVID AND BATHSHEBA (1951) d H King p Zanuck s P Dunne c Shamroy co-a Wheeler chor Cole m A Newman w Peck, S Hayward *116min Fox
DAVID AND LISA (1962) d Perry w Dullea 94min
David Copperfield (UK) = PERSONAL HISTORY, ADVENTURES, EXPERIENCE AND OBSERVATIONS OF DAVID COPPERFIELD THE YOUNGER, THE (1934)
DAVID COPPERFIELD (1970) d Delbert Mann fn Dickens w Attenborough, Evans, Olivier, M Redgrave, R Richardson *118min
DAVID GOLDER (1930) d/s/di Duvivier c Périnal des Meerson 2244m
DAVID HARUM (1915) d Dwan c Rosson 5rs FP
DAVID HARUM (1934) d Cruze c Mohr w Darwell, W Rogers 83min Fox
DAVY CROCKETT AND THE RIVER PIRATES (1956) d/co-s Foster c Glennon *81min pc Disney
DAVY CROCKETT, KING OF THE WILD FRONTIER (1955) d Foster *93min
DAWN, THE (1914) d Crisp
DAWN (1928) d H Wilcox w Thorndyke 2225m
DAWN GUARD (1941) d R Boulting p J Boulting 6min
Dawn of the Founding of Manchukuo and Mongolia, The = MANMO KENROKU NO REIMEI (1932)
Dawn in the Boulevard = ASA NO NAMIKI – MICHI (1936)
DAWN PATROL, THE (1930) d/co-s Hawks co-s S Miller c E Haller w Barthelmess, Fairbanks Jr 95min FN (= *The Flight Commander*)
DAWN PATROL, THE (1938) d Goulding rm 1930 p Wallis co-s S Miller c Gaudio m M Steiner w Niven, Flynn, Rathbone, Crisp 103min WB
DAY, THE (1961) d/p/s Finch 26min
Day After Tomorrow = STRANGE HOLIDAY (1945)
DAY AT THE RACES (1937) d/p S Wood co-st/co-s Seaton c Ruttenberg a Gibbons m Waxman w H, G & C Marx, O'Sullivan, Dumont 109min MGM
DAYBREAK (1931) d Feyder w Novarro, Hersholt MGM
Daybreak = JOUR SE LEVE, LE (1939)
DAYBREAK (1947) d Compton Bennett 81min GF
DAYBREAK AND WHITEYE (1957) d Brakhage 16mm 8min
DAYBREAK EXPRESS (1953) d/p Pennebaker m Duke Ellington 16mm *6min
DAY DREAMS (1922) d/s Keaton, Cline w Keaton 3rs pc Keaton FN
DAYESH VOZDUKH (1924) d/s Vertov 1rl (*Long Live the Air*)
Day in the New World, A = DEN NOVOGO MIRA (1940)
DAY OF FAITH, THE (1923) d Browning co-s Mathis w Power 7rs pc Goldwyn
Day of Happiness, A = DEN SCHASTYA (1963)
Day of Sin (UK) = GIORNATA BALORDA, LA (1960)
DAY OF THE BADMAN (1958) d Keller c Glassberg co-a Golitzen w MacMurray CS* 81min U
DAY OF THE DEAD (1957) d/s C and R Eames c C Eames *18min
DAY OF THE FIGHT (1951) d Kubrick 16mm 16min RKO
DAY OF THE OUTLAW (1959) d De Toth s Yordan c R Harlan w Ives, Ryan, Cook 92min r UA
DAY OF TRIUMPH (1954) co-d Pichel c June w Cobb, Dru *110min
Day of Wrath (US) = MODREHJAEL-PEN (1942) (= *Vredens Dag/Dies Irae*)
Day our Lives Shine, The = WAGA SHOGAI NO KAGAYAKERU (1948)
Days and Nights in the Forest (UK) = ARANYER DIN RATRI (1970)
Days are Numbered (UK) = GIOANI CONTATI, I (1967)
DAY SHE PAID, THE (1919) d Ingram 1829m U
DAYS OF '49 (1913) d Ince w Borzage
DAYS OF GLORY (1944) d J Tourneur c Gaudio m Amfitheatrof w Peck 86min RKO
Days of Hatred (UK) = DIAS DE ODIO (1954)
DAYS OF WHISKY GAP (1961) d Low p Kroitor, Koenig 16mm 29min NFBC
DAYS OF WINE AND ROSES (1963) d Edwards c Lathrop m Mancini w Lemmon, Remick, Bickford 116min WB
Days of Youth = WAKAKI HI (1929)
DAYS PLEASURE, A (1919) d/s Chaplin c Totheroh w Chaplin, Purviance 2rs FN
DAY THE EARTH STOOD STILL, THE (1951) d Wise p Blaustein co-a Wheeler m Herrmann w Neal 92min Fox
DAY THE FISH CAME OUT, THE (1967) d/p/s/cos Cacoyannis c Lassally m Theodorakis w Courtenay *109min Fox
Day the Rains came, The (1959) = AM TAG ALS DER TEGEN KAM
DAY THE WORLD ENDED, THE (1955) d/p Corman S 81min
DAY THEY ROBBED THE BANK OF ENGLAND, THE (1960) d Guillermin co-ad Maibaum c Périnal w A Ray, O'Toole 85min r MGM
DAY-TIME WIFE (1939) d Ratoff p Zanuck c Marley m Mockridge w Power Darnell 71min Fox
Day when Love Returns, the = AI NI YOMIGAERU HI (1922)
DAZE OF THE WEST (1927) d Wyler 2rs U
D-DAY, THE SIXTH OF JUNE (1956) d Koster p Brackett c Garmes co-a Wheeler w R Taylor, O'Brien CS* 106min Fox
DEACON'S TROUBLES, THE (1912) d Sennett w Normand ½rl Key
DEAD, THE (1960) d Brakhage 16mm si* 11min
DEAD END (1937) d Wyler p Goldwyn s Hellman c Toland a R Day m A Newman w S Sidney, McCrea, Bogart, Trevor 93min r UA
DEAD END CREEK (1965) d/co-s Jackson 94min (serial in 6 parts)
DEADFALL (1968) d/s Forbes m Barry w Caine, Barry 120min r Fox
Dead Image = DEAD RINGER (1964)
DEADLIER SEX, THE (1920) d Robert Thornby w (Karloff) 1646m Pat
Deadline (UK) = DEADLINE U.S.A. (1952)
DEADLINE AT DAWN (1946) d Clurman s Odets c Musuraca m Eisler w S Hayward Lukas 83min RKO
Deadline Midnight (UK) = THIRTY (1959)
DEADLINE USA (1952) d/s R Brooks p S Siegel c Krasner co-a Wheeler m Mockridge w Bogart, E Barrymore 87min Fox (= *Deadline*)
DEADLOCK (1957) d Weis w Dalio 44min WB (US TV movie given UK release)
DEADLY AFFAIR, THE (1966) d/p Lumet fn John Le Carré c F Young w Mason, Signoret, Maxmilian Schell, H Anderson 107min Col
DEADLY BEES, THE (1966) d F Francis *123min Par
DEADLY COMPANIONS, THE (1961) d Peckinpah c Clothier w M O'Hara, Keith, Cochran PV* 90min
DEADLY IS THE FEMALE (1949) d JH Lewis c R Harlan 87min r UA (= *Gun Crazy*)
DEAD OF NIGHT (1945) p Balcon additional di T Clarke c Slocombe m Auric w M Redgrave 104min
ep THE HAUNTED MIRROR d/s Hamer
ep THE HEARSE DRIVER d Dearden
ep THE GOLFING STORY d Crichton
ep THE VENTRILOQUIST'S DUMMY d Cavalcanti
DEAD ONES, THE (1948) d/s/c/e Markopoulos 35min
DEAD RECKONING (1947) d Cromwell w Bogart, L Scott 100min Col
DEAD RINGER (1964) rm LA OTRA (1947) d Henreid c E Haller m Previn w B Davis, Malden, Lawford 115min WB (= *Dead Image*)
Dead Run = QUI VEUT TUER CARLOS? (1969)
Dead Souls = MERTVYE DUSHI (1960)
DEAR BRIGITTE (1965) d Koster p Kohlmar s Kanter c Ballard w J Stewart CS* 100min Fox
DEAR HEART (1964) d Delbert Mann c R Harlan m Mancini w Page, G Ford 114min WB
Dearly Loved Face, A = NATSUKASHI NO KAO (1941)
DEARIE (1927) d A Mayo as-d Blanke 1797m WB
Dear John = KÄRE JOHN (1964)
DEAR WIFE (1950) d Haydn w Holden 88min Par
Death at Dawn = AKATSUKI NO SHI (1925)
Death Bay = BUKHTA SMERTI (1926)
Death by Hanging = KOSHIKEI (1968)
DEATH DAY (1933) p Sol Lesser (see *Que Viva Mexico* (1931))
DEATH IN SMALL DOSES (1957) d J Newman 78min Col
Death in Venice = MORTE A VENEZIA (1971)
Death Occurred Last Night = MORTE RISALE A IERI SERA, LA (1970)
DEATH OF A CHAMPION (1939) d Florey w O'Connor 67min Par
Death of a Cyclist = MUERTE DE UN CICLISTA (1955)
Death of a Friend (UK) = MORTE DI UN AMICO (1960)
Death of a Maiden = SHOJO NO SHI (1927)
Death Ray, The = LUCH SMERTI (1925)
DEATH OF A SALESMAN (1951) d Benedek fpl Arthur Miller c Planer m North w March 112min pc Kramer r Col
DEATH OF HEMINGWAY, THE (1965, uf) d/s/c/e Markopoulos 12min
DEATH OF INNOCENCE (1971) d Wendkos w Winters, A Kennedy *90min TV
DEATH ON THE ROAD (1935) d Rotha 17min
DEATH TAKES A HOLIDAY (1934) d Leisen c Lang w March 78min Par
DE BABORD A TRIBORD (1926) d/s/c Matras
Debauchery is Wrong = DORAKU GOSHINAN (1928)
DEBITO D'ODIO (1919) d Genina
DEBUREAU (1950) d/s/fpl/w Guitry 93min
Decadent Influence, The = UNE FILLE ET DES FUSILS (1964)
DECADE PRODIGIEUSE, LA (1971) d Chabrol c Rabier w Welles, Perkins, Piccoli *105min
Decameron, The = DECAMERONE, IL (1971)
DECAMERONE, IL (1971) d/s/co-m Pasolini fsts Boccaccio w Pasolini, Mangano *112min (= *The Decameron*)
DECAMERON NIGHTS (1924) d H Wilcox fsts Boccaccio w L Barrymore, Krauss (= *Dekamera Nächte*)
DECAMERON NIGHTS (1952) d Fregonese p Frankovitch c Green w Fontaine *94min
DECEMBER 7TH (1943) co-d J Ford co-d/c Toland e Parrish m A Newman 20min
DECEPTION (1946) d Rapper p Blanke c E Haller w Rains, B Davis, Henreid 112min WB
Deception (USA) = ANNA BOLEYN (1920)
DECHAINES, LES (1950) d Kiegel
DECIDING KISS, THE (1918) d Browning 5rs
DECIMA VITTIMA, LA (1965) d/co-s Petri p Ponti ex-p Levine c Di Venanzo m Piccioni w Mastroianni, Andress, Martinelli *92min (= *The 10th Victim*)
DECISION AT SUNDOWN (1957) d Boetticher p H Brown c Guffey w R Scott *77min pc Scott, H Brown r Col
DECISION BEFORE DAWN (1951) d/co-p Litvak c Planer m Waxman w Malden, Neff 119min Fox
DECISION OF CHRISTOPHER BLAKE, THE (1948) d Peter Godfrey p/s MacDougall fpl (*Christopher Blake*) M Hart c Freund m M Steiner w A Smith 75min WB
Decisive Battle = KESSEN (1944)
DECKS RAN RED, THE (1958) d/co-p/s Stone co-p/e Virginia Stone w Mason, B Crawford 84min pc Stone r MGM
DECREE OF DESTINY, A (1911) d Griffith w Pickford 1rl Bio
DEDE (1934) d René Guissart w Préjean, Darrieux
DEDECEK AUTOMOBIL (1956) d/co-s d/co-s Radok co-s Forman 90min (UK = *Old Man Motor Car*)
DEDEE D'ANVERS (1948) d/co-s Y Allégret c Bourgoin des Wakhévitch w Signoret, Paglino, Dalio 100min
DEEP BLUE SEA, THE (1955) d/p Litvak s/fpl Rattigan c Hildyard dec V Korda m Arnold w V Leigh, Emlyn Williams CS* 99min Fox
DEEP END (1970) d/co-s Skolimowski *88min
DEEP IN MY HEART (1954) d Donen p Edens c Folsey co-a Gibbons co-chor Donen w J Ferrer, Oberon, Pidgeon, Henreid, Charisse, Ann Miller, Keel, F Powell, Gene Kelly *132min MGM
DEEP PURPLE, THE (1920) d Walsh 7rs
DEEP SIX, THE (1958) d Maté p/co-s Rackin c J Seitz w Ladd, Bendix *105min WB
DEEP VALLEY (1947) d Negulesco st Totheroh c McCord m M Steiner w Lupino 104min WB
DEEP WATERS (1920) d M Tourneur w J Gilbert 5rs FPL
DEEP WATERS (1948) d H King s R Murphy c La Shelle co-a Wheeler w Peters, D Andrews, Romero 85min Fox
DEESSE (1966) d/s Cayrol sh
DEFEATED PEOPLE, A (1945) d/s Jennings p B Wright 19min
Defeat of Japan, The = RAZGROM JAPONII (1945)
Defector, The = ESPION, L' (1966)
Defence of Tsaritsyn, The = OBORONA TSARITSYNA (1942)
DEFIANT ONES, THE (1958) d/p Kramer c Leavitt m Gold w Curtis, Poitier 93min pc Kramer r UA
DEFROQUE, LE (1953) d/st/co-ad/w Joannon co-ad De La Patellière w Fresnay 116min
De Gais Ivrons en Congrès = RAQUETTEURS, LES (1958)
DE GAULLE SKETCH (1959) d/s C and R Eames c Eames 1½min
DE GOURDIS DE LA ONZIEME, LES (1936) d Christian-Jaque co-s Anouilh w Fernandel
DEJEUNER SU L'HERBE, LE (1959) d/p/s J Renoir m Kosma *92min (= *Lunch on the Grass*)
Decameron Nächte (1924) = DECAMERON NIGHTS
DEKIGOKORO (1933) d/fn Ozu Sho (= *Passing Fancy*)
DE L'AMOUR (1964) d/co-st Aurel fn Stendhal w Karina, Piccoli, Martinelli 90min
DE LA PART DES COPAINS (1971) d T Young w Mason *90min
DELFINI, I (1960) d/co-s/co-st Maselli c Di Venanzo m Fusco w Cardinale 110min
DELHI DURBAR (1903) p Paul 240ft
DELHI WAY, THE (c 1960) d Ivory 16mm * 45min
DELICATE DELINQUENT, THE (1957) d/st/s Don McGuire pc/w J Lewis VV 100min Par
DELICIOUS d D Butler w J Gaynor 101min Fox
DELICIOUS LITTLE DEVIL, THE (1919) d Leonard w (Valentino) 1524m U
DELITTO DI GIOVANNI EPISCOPO, IL (1947) rm GIOVANNI EPISCOPO (1916) d/co-s Lattuada co-s Fellini, Cecchi D'Amico fn D'Annunzio c Tonti co-m Rota w Sordi 94min (= *Giovanni Episcopo/-Flesh Will Surrender*)
DELO RUMIANTSEVA (1956) d/co-s Heifitz 102min (= *The Rumiantsev Case*)
DELOVAK ATHARA (1966) d/co-s Peries 105min (= *Between Two Worlds*)
DEL ROSA . . . AL AMARILLO (1963) d Summers 94min (= *The Rose and the Gold*)
DELTA FACTOR, THE (1970) d/p Garnett fn Mickey Spillane
DELTA-PHASE ONE (1962) d/s Haanstra *20min pc Haanstra
DEMAIN A NANGUILA (1960) d Ivens
DEMANTY NOCI (1964) d/co-s Nemec 64min (= *Diamonds of the Night*)
DE MAYERLING A SARAJEVO (1940) d/co-s Ophuls st Zuckmayer c Courant, Heller (supn: Schuftan) dec D'Eaubonne w Feuillère 89min

DEMENT DU LAC JEAN JAUNE, LE (1947) d Jutra, Brault

DEMENTIA 13 (1963) d/s Coppola ex-p Corman 81min (= The Haunted and the Hunted)

DEMETRIUS AND THE GLADIATORS (1954) d Daves p/s Dunne c Krasner co-a Wheeler co-m Waxman, A Newman w Mature, S Hayward, A Bancroft, Borgnine CS* 101min Fox

DEMI-BRIDE, THE (1927) d/p Leonard co-a Gibbons w Shearer 2099m MGM

DEMI-PARADISE, THE (1943) d Asquith p/s De Grunwald w Olivier 115min BL (= Adventure for Two)

DEMOISELLE ET LE VIOLONCELLISTE, LA (1964) d Jean-François Lagvionie p Grimault anim* 9min

DEMOISELLE ET SON REVENANT, LA (1952) d M Allégret s Vadim

DEMOISELLES DE ROCHEFORT, LES (1967) d/s Demy c Cloquet dec Evein m Legrand w Deneuve, Darrieux, Piccoli, Gene Kelly, Varda FS* 120min

Demon, The = ONIBABA (1965)

DEMON DE MINUIT, LE (1962) d M Allégret w Boyer 85min

DEMONIO, IL (1963) d/st/co-s Rondi m Piccioni 100min

Demonio y carne = SUSANA (1951)

DEMON OF FEAR, THE (1916) d/w Borzage Tri

DEMONS DE L'AUBE, LES (1945) d Y Allégret co-m Honegger 100min

DEMONS ET MERVEILLES DE BALI (1954) d Bourguinon 16mm* 18min

DE MONTREAL A MANICOUAGAN (1963) d/s/cy Lamothe 28min

DEMUTIGE UND DIE SANGERIN, DER (1925) d/co-s Dupont w Dagover 3819m

DENMARK GROWS UP (1947) d A Henning Jensen, Hagan Hasselbalch, Søren Melson 21min

DEN NOVOGO MIRA (1940) d/c Karmen (= A Day in the New World)

DEN OF THIEVES, A (1904) p Hepworth 425ft

DENONCIATION, LA (1962) d/st Doniol-Valcroze m Delerue w Ronet 110min

DE NOTRE TEMPS (1962) d Rossif S 9min

DEN SCHASTYA (1963) d/co-s Heifitz w Batalov S 101min (= A Day of Happiness)

DEN SEDMY, OSMA NOC (1969) d Schorm (= Seventh Day, Eighth Night)

Dentist, The = LAUGHING GAS (1914)

DENTIST, THE (1932) d Leslie Pearce w Fields (2rs) Par

DENTS LONGUES, LES (1952) d/w Gélin 110min

DENVER & RIO GRANDE (1952) d Haskin c Rennahan co-a Pereira w Hayden, Pitts, E O'Brien *89min Par

DENWA WA YUGATA NI NARU (1959) d Yoshimura (= A Telephone Ring in the Evening)

DEONZO BROS IN THEIR WONDERFUL TUB-JUMPING ACT, THE (1897) d Paul 120ft

DEPART, LE (1967) d/co-s Skolimovski m Komeda w Léaud 91min

Departure of a Grand Old Man = UKHOD VELIKOVO STARTSA (1912)

DEPORTED (1950) d Siodmak c Daniels w J Chandler 89min U

DEPRESSED AREA, USA (1963) d W Van Dyke 30min

Depression Period = FUKEIKI JIDAI (1930)

Depth Charge Flotilla = ASH CAN FLEET (1939)

DEPUTAT BALTIKI (1937) d/co-s Heifitz, Zarkhi w Cherkasov 96min (= Baltic Deputy)

DEPUTY DROOPY (1955) d Avery p Quimby anim* 7min MGM

DERMIS PROBE, THE (1966) d Williams anim* 5min

DERNIER AMOUR (1948) d Jean Stelli w Annabella

DERNIER ATOUT (1942) d/co-s/co-e Becker di Bost c Hayer w Rouleau, P Renoir, Modot 105min

DERNIERES VACANCES, LES (1948) d/s Leenhardt c Agostini 95min

DERNIER MILLIARDAIRE, LE (1934) d/s/di Clair co-c Maté m Jaubert 90min Pat

DERNIERS JOURS DE POMPEÏ, LES (1948) d/co-ad/di L'Herbier fn E Bullwer Lytton w Presle 110min (= Gli Ultimi giorni di Pompei)

DERNIER SOU, LE (1944) d/st Cayatte 88min

DERNIER VOYAGE DE GULLIVER, LE (1960 uf) d/s Borowczyk anim

DEROUTE, LA (1958) d Ado Kyrou supn Franju

DER VAR ENGANG EN KRIG (1966) d Kjaerrulf-Schmidt 95min (= Once there was a War/Once Upon a War)

DE SADE (1969) d Endfield, Corman(uc) co-p Arkoff s Matheson w Palmer, J Huston *113min AI

DESASTRES DE LA GUERRE, LES (1951) d/co-s Kast co-s/m Grémillon 16mm 20min

DESCRIPTION D'UN COMBAT (1960) d/s Marker c Cloquet *57min

Descendants of Taro Urashima, The = URASHIMA TARO NI KŌEI (1946)

Deserter, The = DEZERTER (1965)

DESERT BRIDE, THE (1928) d W Lang p Cohn c June 1646m Col

DESERT DEATH (1935) d G Seitz 2rs

DESERT DEMON, THE (1926) d Thorpe

DÉSERT DE AGALLE, LE (1958) d/co-s/w Joannon w Girardot 100min

DESERT DUST (1927) d Wyler 1325m U

DESERTED AT THE ALTAR (1922) d W Howard, Al Kelly fp Pierce Kingsley 2088m

DESERTER (1898) p Paul 1rl 80ft

DESERTER, THE (1913) d Ince

DESERTER, THE (1916) co-d Ince Tri

Deserter = DESERTIR (1933)

Deserter, The = SPINA DORSALE DEL DIAVOLO, LA (1971)

DESERT FOX, THE (1951) d Hathaway p/s N Johnson c Brodine co-a Wheeler m Amfitheatrof w Mason 88min Fox (= Rommel – Desert Fox)

DESERT FURY (1947) d Lewis Allen p Wallis s Rosson c Cronjager, C Lang m Rozsa w Corey, Lancaster, L Scott, Astor *95min Par

DESERT GOLD (1926) d G Seitz co-supn B P Schulberg fn Zane Grey (1913) w W Powell 2103m FPL r Par

DESERT HELL (1958) d/ex-p/st Warren w Keith S 82min Fox

DESERT HERO, A (1919) d/s/w Arbuckle w Keaton 2rs Par

DESERTIR (1933) d Pudovkin w Gerasimov, Pudovkin 2661m (= Deserter)

DESERT LAW (1919) d Conway 5rs

DESERT LEGION (1953) d Pevney c J Seitz w Ladd, Conte, Tamiroff *87min RKO

DESERT LOVE (1920) d/s Jacques Jaccard st/w Mix 5rs Fox

DESERT OF THE LOST, THE (1927) d Thorpe 1520m r Pat

DESERT OF LOST MEN (1951) d/as-p Keller 54min Rep

DESERT OF WHEAT (1918) d Conway

DESERTO ROSSO (1964) d/co-st/co-s Antonioni c Di Palma m Fusco w Vitti, R Harris *120min (= The Red Desert)

DESERT RATS, THE (1953) d Wise st/s R Murphy co-a Wheeler c Ballard m Harline w Burton, Mason, Newton 88min Fox

DESERT SONG, THE (1929) d Del Ruth fco-mpl/co-m Oscar Hammerstein II w M Loy, Fazenda 123min WB

DESERT SONG, THE (1943) d Florey pco-mpl/co-m Oscar Hammerstein II c Glennon 96min WB

DESERT VICTORY (1943) d (uc) R Boulting co-m (uc) Alwyn 60min

DES FEMMES DISPARAISSENT (1958) d Molinaro w Hossein 85min

DES FEMMES ET LES FLEURS (1963) d Leenhardt

DES HOMMES QUI ONT PERDU RACINE (1956) d Hanoun sh TV

DESIDERIO (1943 r 1946) d/co-s Rossellini, Pagliero co-s De Santis w Girotti 102min

DESIGN FOR DEATH (1948) d/co-p R Fleischer co-e Elmo Williams 48min RKO

DESIGN FOR LIVING (1933) d Lubitsch s B Hecht fpl Coward c Milner a Dreier w March, G Cooper, M Hopkins, Horton, Darwell 85min Par

Design For Dying, A = ONNA NO KUNSHO (1961)

DESIGNING WOMAN (1957) d Minnelli p Schary st/s Wells c J Alton chor Cole m Previn w Peck, Bacall, Cole, CS* 117min MGM

Design of a Human Being = NINGEN MOYO (1949)

DESIRABLE (1934) d A Mayo c E Haller w Darwell 68min WB

DESIRE (1936) d Borzage supn Lubitsch c C Lang, Milner, co-a Dreier m Hollander w Dietrich, G Cooper, Tamiroff 89min Par

DESIRE (1938) d/s Guitry c Bachelet w Guitry, Arletty 106min

Desire = TOUHA (1958)

DESIRED WOMAN, THE (1927) d Curtiz as-d Blanke 1953m WB

DESIREE (1954) d Koster p Blaustein s Taradash c Krasner co-a Wheeler m North song A Newman w Brando, J Simmons, Oberon CS* 110min Fox

DESIRE ME (1947) d Conway, Cukor (uc) c Ruttenberg, C Lang, Cronjager co-a Gibbons w Garson, Mitchum 91min MGM

Desire of Night = AIYOKO NO YORU (1930)

Desires = YOKUBO (1953)

DESIR ET L'AMOUR, LE (1951) d/di Decoin c Kelber w Carol, Arnoul, Préjean 88min

DESIRE UNDER THE ELMS (1958) d Delbert Mann fpl Eugene O'Neill c Fapp co-a Pereira m E Bernstein w Loren, Perkins, Ives VV 114min Par

DESISTFILM (1954) d Brakhage 16mm 7min

DESK SET, THE (1957) d W Lang c Shamroy co-a Wheeler co-m Mockridge w Tracy, K Hepburn, Blondell CS* 103min Fox

DESORDRE (1949) d Baratier w (Annabella, Welles, Cocteau) 18min (= Disorder)

DESORDRE A VINGT ANS, LE (1967) [incorporates DESORDRE (1949)] d Baratier w Artaud, Cocteau, Riva, Arrabal, Jean-Paul Sartre, Simone De Beauvoir *60min (Disorder is Twenty Years Old)

DESORDRE ET LA NUIT, LE (1958) d Grangier w Gabin, Darrieux, Tiller 93min

DESPERADOES, THE (1943) d C Vidor p H Brown w G Ford, R Scott, Trevor *85min Col

DESPERATE (1947) d/co-st A Mann ad Rackin w Burr 73min RKO

DESPERATE ADVENTURE, A (1938) d/as-p John M Aver w Novarro 67min Rep

DESPERATE COURAGE (1928) d Thorpe 5rs r Pat

DESPERATE HOURS, THE (1955) d/p Wyler c Garmes co-a Pereira w Bogart, March, A Kennedy VV* 112min Par

DESPERATE JOURNEY (1942) d Walsh p Wallis c Glennon m M Steiner w Reagan, A Kennedy, Flynn 107min WB

DESPERATE LOVER, A (1912) d Sennett w Normand ½rl Key

DESPERATE MOMENT (1953) d Compton Bennett w Bogarde, Zetterling 88min JAR

DESPERATE SEARCH (1952) d JH Lewis co-a Gibbons c Lipstein w Keel 73min MGM

DESPERATE TRAILS (1921) d J Ford w Carey 5rs U

DES PISSENLITS PAR LA RACINE (1964) d/co-s Lautner m Delerue w de Funès, Darc, Blanche 95min

DESPOILER, THE (1915) d Ince c August 1600m Tri

DES RAILS SOUS LES PALMIERS (1951) co-d/e Colpi co-d M-A Colson Malleville 19min

DES RUINES ET DES HOMMES (1958) co-d Kast sh

DESSOUS DES CARTES, LE (1947) d/co-s Cayette co-s Charles Spaak c Thirard w Reggiani 90min

DESTINATION GOBI (1953) d Wise c C Clarke co-a Wheeler w Widmark *89min Fox

DESTINATION MOON (1950) d Pichel p Pal c Lindon m Leith Stevens 90min EL

DESTINATION TOKYO (1944) d/co-s Daves p Wald c Glennon m Waxman w C Grant, Garfield 135min WB

DESTINATION UNKNOWN (1933) d Garnett 67min U

DESTINEES (1953) 96min (= Love, Soldiers and Women)
ep DUE DONNE d Pagliero w Rossi-Drago
ep JEANNE d Delannoy st Aurenche, Bost m Auric w Morgan, Piccoli

DESTIN FABULEUX DE DESIREE CLARY, LE (1941) d/s Guitry c Bachelet w Guitry, Barrault 113min

DESTINO D'AMORE (1943, ur) d/s Emmer, Enrico Gras, Tatiana Grauding

Destiny = MUDE TOD, DER (1921)

DESTROYER (1943) d William A Seiter co-s B Chase c Planer w G Ford, Robinson 99min Col

Destroy, She Said = DETRUIRE, DIT-ELLE (1969)

DESTRY (1954) d G Marshall rm DESTRY RIDES AGAIN (1939) w A Murphy, Mitchell *95min U

DESTRECTEURS MARINS DES BOIS (1954) d Painlevé 16mm* 55min

DESTRY RIDES AGAIN (1932) d Ben Stoloff w Mix, Pitts 55min U

DESTRY RIDES AGAIN (1939) d G Marshall p Pasternak c Mohr w J Stewart, Dietrich 94min U

DET ÄR HOS MIG HAN HAR VARIT (1963) d Mattsson 106min (= Yes he has been with me)

DETECTIVE, THE (1968) d G Douglas p A Rosenberg c Biroc m Goldsmith w Sinatra, Remick, Meeker PV* 114min Fox

DETECTIVE STORY (1951) d Wyler co-s Yordan c Garmes a Pereira w K Douglas, Parker, Bendix 103min Par

DETENUTO IN ATTESA DI GIUDIZIO (1971) d N Loy w Sordi *102min

DETI BURI (1927) d Ermler, Elward Johanson 1547m (= Children of the Storm)

DET KON EN GÄST (1947) d Mattsson w Bjork (= A Guest Came)

DET KOM TVÅ MÄN (1958) d Mattsson w Jacobson, Marquand (= There Came Two Men)

DETOUR (1945) d Ulmer 68min

DETOURING AMERICA (1939) supn Avery p L Schlesinger (1rl) WB

DE TOUT POUR FAIRE UN MONDE (1962) d Cayrol 15min

DET REGNAR PÅ VÅR KÄRLEK (1946) d/co-s Ingmar Bergman co-c Strindberg w Björnstrand (= It Rains on Our Love)

DETRUIRE, DIT-ELLE (1969) d/s/fn Duras 100min (= Destroy, She Said)

DETSTVO GORKOVO (1938) d/co-s Donskoi fab Maxim Gorky 110min (= The Childhood of Gorky)

DEUCE HIGH (1926) d Thorpe w R Walker

DEUS E O DIABO NA TERRA DEL SOL (1964) d/s/a/lyr Rocha mf Heitor Villa-Lobos, J S Bach 110min (= Black God, White Devil)

DEUSES E OS MORTOS, OS (1970) d/co-s/co-e Guerra *129min (= Gods and the Dead)

DEUS EX (1970) d Brakhage 16mm*

DEUTSCHE PANZER (1940) d Ruttmann 12½min Ufa

DEUTSCHER RUNDFUNK (1928) d Ruttmann

DEUTSCHLAND, ERWACHE! (1966) d/p Leiser 87min

DEUX AMIS (1946) d Kirsanov

DEUX ANGLAISES ET LE CONTINENT, LES (1971) d/co-ad/co-di Truffaut m Delerue w Léaud *130min

DEUX AOÛT 1914, LE (1914) d/w Linder Pat

DEUX CENT MILLE LIEUES SOUS LES MERS OU LE CAUCHEMAR D'UN PECHEUR (1907) d Méliès fn Jules Verne 265m (30 parts)

DEUX COUVERTS (1935) d Perret fpl Guitry

DEUX GAMINES, LES (1920) d/s Feuillade 1: Fleurs de Paris; 2: La Nuit de Printemps (760m); 3: La Fugitive (790m); 4: La Morte Vivante (800m); 5: Le Lis sous L'orage (720m); 6: L'Accalmie (780m); 7: Celle

DEUX GAMINES, LES—cont.
qu'on n'attendait plus (800m); 8: Parmi les Coups (800m); 9: Le Serment de Ginette (800m); 10: Le Candidat à la Mort (815m); 11: La Cité des Chiffons (810m); 12: Le Retour (815m)
DEUX HOMMES DANS MANHATTAN (1958) *d/s/di/co-c/w* Melville *co-c* Hayer 84min *r* Col
DEUXIEME SOUFFLE, LE (1965) *d/s/co-di* Melville *co-di/fn* Giovanni *w* Ventura 150min (= *Second Wind/The Second Breath*)
DEUX ORPHELINES, LES (1933) *d* M Tourneur 104min
DEUX OU TROIS CHOSES QUE JE SAIS D'ELLE (1966) *d/s* Godard *c* Coutard *mf Beethoven w* Vlady TS* 95min *co-pc* Truffaut (= *Two or Three Things I Know About Her*)
DEUX SOUS DE BIOLETTES (1951) *d* Anouilh *m* Van Parys 120min
DEUX TIMIDES, LES (1928) *d/s* Clair *fpl Labiche des Meerson w* Rosay 2620m
Deux Timides, Les = JEUNES TIMIDES (1941)
DEVANT'S HAND SHADOWS (1897) *p* Paul 80ft
DEVDAS (1935) *d Pramathesh Chandra Barua c* Roy
DEVDAS (1956) *d/p* Roy *rm* (*d Barua* 1935) *fn Chatterjee* 150min
DEVETI KRUG (1960) *d* Stiglic 107min (= *The Ninth Circle*)
DEVI (1960) *d/s* S Ray *c* Mitra 94min *pc* Ray (= *The Goddess*)
DEVIL AND MISS JONES, THE (1941) *d* S Wood *co-p/st/s* Krasna *c* Stradling *w* R Cummings, Arthur, C Coburn 92min RKO
DEVIL AND THE DEEP, THE (1932) *d Marion Gering c* C Lang *w* Bankhead, G Cooper, Laughton, C Grant 78min Par
Devil and the Nun, The = MATKA JOANNA OD ANIOLOW (1961)
Devil and the Ten Commandments, The (UK) = DIABLE ET LES DIX COMMANDEMENTS, LE (1963)
DEVIL AT FOUR O'CLOCK, THE (1961) *d* LeRoy *p* Kohlmar *c* Biroc *m* Duning *w* Tracy, Sinatra *111min Col
DEVIL BAT'S DAUGHTER (1946) *d/p/co-s* Wisbar *w* Lugosi 60min
Devil by the Tail, The = DIABLE PAR LA QUEUE, LA (1969)
DEVIL COMMANDS, THE (1941) *d* Dmytryk *w* Karloff 65min Col
DEVIL DANCER, THE (1927) *d/p* Niblo *co-c* Barnes *w* C Brook 2316m AA
DEVIL DOGS OF THE AIR (1935) *d* Bacon *c* Edeson *w* Cagney 84min WB
DEVIL DOLL, THE (1936) *d/st* Browning *co-s* Von Stroheim *m* Waxman *w* L Barrymore, O'Sullivan 78min MGM
Devil in the Flesh (UK) = DIABLE AU CORPS, LE (1947)
DEVIL IS A SISSY, THE (1936) *d* W S Van Dyke *co-s* Mahin *c* Rosson *co-m/lyr* Freed *co-m* Stothart *w* Rooney, Bartholemew 92min MGM
DEVIL IS A WOMAN, THE (1935) *d/c* Von Sternberg *s John Dos Passos fn* (*La Femme et le Pantin*) *Pierre Louys as-c* Ballard *a* Dreier *w* Dietrich, Romero, Horton 85min Par
DEVIL MAKES THREE, THE (1952) *d* Marton *w* Gene Kelly 96min MGM
DEVIL-MAY-CARE (1929) *d* Franklin *as-p* Lewin *a* Gibbons *co-m* Stothart *m* Tiomkin *w* Novarro 98min MGM
Devil Never Sleeps, The (UK) = SATAN NEVER SLEEPS (1961)
DEVIL PLAYS, THE (1931) *d/e* Thorpe 63min
DEVIL RIDES OUT, THE (1968) *d* Fisher *fn Dennis Wheatley s* Matteson *95min
DEVILS, THE (1971) *d/co-p/s* K Russell *fpl John Whiting and fbk* (*The Devils of Loudon*) *Aldous Huxley w* V Redgrave *115min *r* WB
DEVIL'S ANGELS (1967) *d* D Haller *co-ex-p* Arkoff *w* Cassavetes PV* 84min *pc* Corman *r* AI
DEVIL'S BRIGADE, THE (1968) *d* A McLaglen *c* Clothier *m* North *w* Robertson, W Holden, D Andrews PV* 128min UA
DEVIL'S BROTHER, THE (1933) *co-d/p* Roach *co-d Charles Rogers w* Laurel, Hardy 88min *r* MGM (= *Fra Diavolo*)
DEVIL'S CARGO, THE (1925) *d* V Fleming *w* Beery (8rs) FPL *r* Par
DEVIL'S CIRCUS, THE (1926) *d/st/s* Christensen *c* B Reynolds *w* Shearer 2057m MGM
DEVIL'S DISCIPLE, THE (1959) *d* Hamilton, Mackendrick(*uc*) *p* H Hecht *fpl G B Shaw c* Hildyard *m Richard Rodney Bennett w* Lancaster, K Douglas, Olivier 82min *r* UA
DEVIL'S DOORWAY (1950) *d* A Mann *c* J Alton *m* Amfitheatrof *w* R Taylor, *Calhern* 81min MGM
Devil's Envoys, The = VISITEURS DU SOIR, LES (1942)
Devil's Eye, The = DJÄVULENS ÖGA (1960)
DEVIL'S HAIRPIN, THE (1957) *d/p/co-s* Wilde *c* Fapp *co-a* Pereira *w* Wilde VV* 82min Par
Devil's Hand, The (UK) = MAIN DU DIABLE, LA (1942)
DEVIL'S HOLIDAY, THE (1930) *d/st/s/m* Goulding *w* Lukas, Pitts 74min Par
DEVIL'S IN LOVE, THE (1933) *d* Dieterle *c* Mohr *w* L Young 70min Fox
Devil's Mill, The = CERTUV MLYN (1951)
DEVIL'S PARTY, THE (1938) *d Ray McCarey fn* (*Hell's Kitchen has a Pantry*) B Chase *w* V McLaglen 65min U
DEVIL'S PASSKEY, THE (1919) *d/co-st/s/a* Von Stroheim *c* B Reynolds (12rs) U
DEVIL-STONE, THE (1917) *d* De Mille *co-st Beatrice de Mille* (6rs) FPL
Devil Strikes at Night, The = NACHTS, WENN DER TEUFEL KAM (1957)
Devil's Wanton, The = FÄNGELSE (1949)
Devil's Weapon, The = DJAVULENS INSTRUMENT (1965)
Devil's Wheel, The = CHORTOVO KOLESO (1926)
DEVIL WITH HITLER, THE (1944) *d* G Douglas *co-p* Roach 45min UA
DEVIL WITH WOMEN, A (1930) *d Irving Cummings co-s/co-di* D Nichols *w* Bogart, V McLaglen 64min Fox
DEVOTION (1946) *d* C Bernhardt *c* E Haller *m* Korngold *w* Lupino, De Havilland, Henreid, Greenstreet 107min WB
Devotion (UK) = EDERA, L' (1950)
Devotion = HANGIVELSE (1965)
DEVUSHKA S KOROBKO (1927) *d* Barnet *w* Sten 1650m (= *The Girl with the Hat Box*)
DEVYAT DNI ODNOVO GODA (1961) *d/co-s* Romm *w* Batalov 110min (= *Nine Days of One Year*)
DEZERTER (1965) *d* Brdecka (= *Deserter*)
DHARTI KE LAL (1949) *d/s* Abbas *m* Shankar
D'HOMMES A HOMMES (1948) *d/co-s* Christian-Jaque *co-s* Charles Spaak *c* Matras *w* Barrault 96min
D I, The (1957) *d/p/w* J Webb 106min WB
DIABLE AU COEUR, LE (1927) *d* L'Herbier *dec* Autant-Lara
DIABLE AU CORPS, LE (1947) *d* Autant-Lara *p* Graetz *s/di* Aurenche, Bost *fn Raymond Radiguet c* Kelber *w* Philipe, Presle, Tati 122min *r* U (= *Devil in the Flesh*)
DIABLE AU COUVENT, LE (1899) *d* Méliès 65m
DIABLE BOITEUX, LE (1948) *d/s/fpl w* Guitry *w* (Hossein) 120min
DIABLE DANS LA VILLE, LE (1924) *d* Dulac
DIABLE ET LES DIX COMMANDEMENTS, LE (1963) *d/co-s* Duvivier *co-di* Audiard, Jeanson *w* M Simon, Arnoul, Presle, Aznavour, Fernandel, Modot, Darrieux, Delon, Brialy, de Funès, Ventura 120min (= *The Devil and the Ten Commandments*)
DIABLE PAR LA QUEUE, LE (1969) *d* De Broca *m* Delerue *w* Montand, Maria Schell *92min (= *The Devil by the Tail*)
Diabolically Yours (UK) = DIABOLIQUEMENT VOTRE (1967)
DIABOLICI, I (1920) *d/s* Genina
DIABOLIK (1967) *d/co-s* Bava *co-p* De Laurentiis *w* Piccoli *105min (= *Danger: Diabolik*)
DIABOLIQUEMENT VOTRE (1967) *d/co-ad* Duvivier *fn Louis Thomas c* Decaë *w* Delon 95min (= *Diabolically Yours*)
DIABOLIQUES, LES (1955) *d/co-s* Clouzot *fn* (*Celle qui n'était plus*) *Boileau, Narcejac c* Thirard *w* Signoret, Vanel 115min
DIA DE VIDA, UN (1950) *d/st* Fernandez *c* Figueroa
DIAL M FOR MURDER (1954) *d/p* Hitchcock *c* Burks *m* Tiomkin *w* Milland, Grace Kelly, R Cummings (2 versions: one 3D)* 105min WB
DIALOG (1968)
ep d/s Skolimowski *w* Léaud
DIALOGUE DES CARMELITES, LE (1960) *d* Agostini, *R Bruckberger fn Georges Bernanos w* Moreau, Brasseur, Valli, Barrault 110min
DIAL 17 (1953) *d* Michael Anderson 26min BL
DIAMANT NOIR, LE (1940) *d* Delannoy *w* Vanel
DIAMOND, CUT DIAMOND (1932) *d* Niblo *w* Menjou 71min MGM
DIAMOND HEAD (1963) *d* G Green *c* Leavitt *w* Heston PV* 106min BL
Diamond Horseshoe = BILLY ROSE'S DIAMOND HORSESHOE (1945)
DIAMOND JIM (1935) *d A Edward Sutherland co-s* P Sturges *w* Arthur, Romero 93min U
DIAMOND QUEEN, THE (1953) *d* Brahm *c* Cortez *c* Lourié *w* Roland *80min WB
DIAMONDS ARE FOREVER (1971) *d* Hamilton *co-p* Saltzman *co-s* Maibaum *c* Moore *m* Barry *des* Adam *w* Connery *119min
Diamonds of the Night = DEMANTY NOCI (1964)
DIANE (1955) *d* D Miller *s C Isherwood c* Planck *co-a* Gibbons *m* Rozsa *w* Turner, Armendariz CS* 110min MGM
DIANE OF THE FOLLIES (1916) *w* L Gish
DIARIES, NOTES AND SKETCHES (ALSO KNOWN AS 'WALDEN') (1964–69) *d/c* J Mekas *w* J Mekas, A Mekas, Brakhage, S Clarke, Dreyer, Markopoulos, Richter, Warhol, John Lennon 16mm* 175½min (1st draft edition)
DIARY FOR TIMOTHY, A (1945) *d/s* Jennings *p* B Wright *s EM Forster cy* M Redgrave 38min Comm
DIARY OF A CHAMBERMAID, THE (1946) *d/co-s* J Renoir *co-p/co-s* Meredith *co-p* Bogeaus *c* Andriot *a* Lourié *w* Goddard, Meredith, Lederer 76min *r* UA (= *Le journal d'une femme de chambre*)
Diary of a Chambermaid = JOURNAL D'UNE FEMME DE CHAMBRE, LE (1964)
Diary of a Country Priest = JOURNAL D'UN CURÉ DE CAMPAGNE (1950)
DIARY OF A HIGH SCHOOL BRIDE (1959) *d/p/co-s* Topper 72min AI
DIARY OF A MAD HOUSEWIFE (1970) *d/p* Perry *95min *r* U
DIARY OF A MADMAN (1963) *d Reginald Le Borg fst Maupassant a* D Haller *w* Price 96min *r* UA
DIARY OF A MADMAN (1965) *d* R Williams anim
DIARY OF ANNE FRANK, THE (1959) *d/p* G Stevens *s/fpl* Goodrich, Hackett *c* Mellor *co-a* Wheeler *m* A Newman *w* Winters CS 170min Fox
DIARY OF AN UNKNOWN SOLDIER, THE (1959) *d* Watkins 16mm 17min
DIARY OF A SERGEANT (1945) *d* J Newman 16mm 20min
Diary of a Shinjuku Thief = SHINJUKU DOROBO NIKKI (1968)
Diary of a Tired Man = NIPPON NO SEISHUN (1968)
Diary of Major Thompson, The (UK) = CARNETS DU MAJOR THOMPSON, LES (1955)
Diary of Sueko, The = NIANCHAN (1959)
Diary of Yunbogi, The = YUNBOGI NO NIKKI (1965)
DIAS DE ODIO (1954) *d/co-s* Torre Nilsson *co-s/fst* (*Emma Zunz*) *Jorge Luis Borges* 70min (= *Days of Hatred*)
DIAVOLO CON CELEBRITA, AL (1948) *d* Steno, Monicelli 80min (= *One Night of Fame/A Night of Fame*)
DICE OF DESTINY (1920) *d* H King (5rs) Pat
DICK TRACY VS CUEBALL (1946) *d* G Douglas 62min RKO
DICK TURPIN (1925) *d John G Blystone w* Mix (7rs) Fox
DICTATOR, THE (1922) *d* Cruze (6rs) FPL *r* Par
DICTATOR, THE (1935) *d* Saville *c* Planer *w* C Brook, Carroll, Emlyn Williams 85min (= *The Love Affair of the Dictator/Loves of a Dictator*)
DICTIONNAIRE DE JOACHIM, LE (1965) *d/s* Borowczyk *anim** 9min (= *Joachim's Dictionary*)
DID YOU HEAR THE ONE ABOUT THE TRAVELLING SALESLADY? (1968) *d* Weis S* 96min U
DIE DAS LICHT SCHEUEN . . . (1920) *d/s* Jutzi
Die, Monster, Die (USA) = MONSTER OF TERROR (1965)
DIER YOGHI (1916) *co-d/st/s/w* Wegener *co-d Rochus Gliese*
Dies Irae = VREDENS DAG (1942)
DIEU A BESOIN DES HOMMES (1950) *d* Delannoy *p* Graetz *s/di* Aurenche, Bost *fn* (*Un Recteur De l'Ile de Sein*) *Henri Queffelec c* Lefebvre *w* Fresnais, Gélin, Mocky 100min (= *Isle of Sinners*)
Difficult Life, A (UK) = VITA DIFFICILE, UNA (1961)
Difficult Years (US) = ANNI DIFFICILI (1948)
DIGA DEL GHIACCIAIO, LA (1954) *d* Olmi 10min
DIGA SUL PACIFICO, LA (1958) *d/co-ad* Clément *p* De Laurentiis *co-ad* Shaw *fn* Duras *c* Martelli *dec* Gherardi *m* Rota *w* Mangano, Perkins, Conte, Valli TR* 106min Col (= *The Sea Wall*)
DIGUE, LA (1911) *d/s* Gance *w* P Renoir (= *Pour Sauver la Hollande*)
DIJKBOUW (1952) *d/s/co-c/e* Haanstra *p* Elton (= *The Dike Builders*)
DIKKOI IKITERU (1950) *d* Imai (= *And Yet We Live/We Are Living*)
Dike Builders, The = DIJKBOUW (1952)
DILEMMA (1962) *d/s/e* Carlsen 88min (= *A World of Strangers*)
DILLINGER È MORTO (1969) *d* Ferreri *w* Piccoli, Girardot *95min (= *Dillinger is Dead*)
Dillinger is Dead = DILLINGER È MORTO (1969)
DIMANCHE A PEKIN (1956) *d/s/c* Marker *20min
DIMENTICATI, I (1953) *d/c/e* De Seta
DIM LITTLE ISLAND, THE (1949) *d/p* Jennings *m Ralph Vaughan Williams* 11min
DIMPLES (1936) *d William A Seiter p* Zanuck *as-p* N Johnson *w* Temple 78min Fox
DINKY DOODLE (1925–26) *d/s* Lantz anim series *pc* Bray
DINNER AT EIGHT (1933) *d* Cukor *p* Selznick *co-s* H Mankiewicz *fpl Edna Ferber* G *Kaufman co-di* D Stewart *c* Daniels *a* Gibbons *w* J Barrymore, Dressler, Harlow, L Barrymore, Beery, Hersholt 108min MGM
DINNER HOUR (1935) *d* Anstey *p* Elton 20min
DINOSAURUS! (1960) *d/as-p* Yeaworth *c* Cortez CS* 85min JAR-U
DIN TILLVAROS LAND (1940) *d/c* Sucksdorff
DINTY (1921) *d* Neilan, *John McDermott* 1829m
DIPLOMACY (1926) *d* Neilan 2122m FPL *r* Par
DIPLOMATIC COURIER (1952) *d* Hathaway *fn* (*Similar Errand*) *Peter Cheyney c* Ballard *co-a* Wheeler *w* Power, Neal, Malden, Marvin, Neff 97min Fox
DIPLOMATIC MISSION (1919) *d* Conway (5rs) Vit
Diplomatic Pouch, The = SOUMKA DIPKOURIERA (1927)
DIPLOMATS, THE (1929) *d* Taurog Fox

Diptych = DIPTYQUE (1967)
DIPTYQUE (1967) *d/st/c* Borowczyk *8½min (= *Diptych*)
DIRECTED BY JOHN FORD (1971) *d/s Peter Bogdanovich n* Welles *w* J Wayne, Stewart, H Fonda, J Ford *95min
DIRIGEABLE FANTASTIQUE OU LE CAUCHEMAR D'UN INVENTEUR, LE (1906) *d* Méliès 60m
DIRIGIBLE (1931) *d* Capra *p* Cohn *ad/di* Swerling 102min Col
DIRTY DINGUS MAGEE (1970) *d* B Kennedy *w* Sinatra, G Kennedy PV* 90min MGM
DIRTY DOZEN, THE (1967) *d* Aldrich *co-s* N Johnson *w* Marvin, Borgnine, G Kennedy, Cassavetes, Meeker, Ryan *149min MGM
Dirty Games, The = GUERRA SECRETA, LA (1965)
DIRTY HARRY (1971) *d/p* Siegel *m* Schifrin *w* Eastwood *102min
DIRTY WORK (1933) *d Lloyd French p* Roach *w* Laurel, Hardy (sd) (2rs) *r* MGM
DISASTER, LAUNCHING OF HMS ALBION (1898) *p* Paul 40ft
DISBARRED (1939) *d* Florey *co-a* Dreier *w* Preston 58min Par
DISCARDED LOVERS (1932) *d* Newmeyer 60min
DISCIPLE, THE (1915) *d/p/w* W Hart (5rs) Tri
Discovery of Zero, The = ZERO NO HAKKEN (1963)
DISCO VOLANTE, IL (1965) *d* Brass *m* Piccioni *w* Sordi, Rossi-Drago, Mangano, Vitti 93min *pc* De Laurentiis (= *The Flying Saucer*)
Discord (US) = SZAKADEK (1955)
DISHONORED (1931) *d/st* Von Sternberg *c* Garmes *dec* Dreier *w* Dietrich, V McLaglen 91min Par
DISHONORED LADY (1947) *d* Stevenson *c* Andriot *w* Lamarr 85min UA
Disorder (UK) = DESORDRE (1949)
Disorder is Twenty Years Old (UK) = DESORDRE A VINGT ANS, LE (1967)
DISORDERLY ORDERLY, THE (1964) *d/s* Tashlin *co-a* Pereira *w* J Lewis 90min Par
DISPARUS DE SAINT-AGIL, LES (1938) *d* Christian-Jaque *co-s* J Prévert(*uc*) *w* Von Stroheim, M Simon 103min
DISPATCH FROM REUTERS, A (1940) *d* Dieterle *p* Wallis *as-p* Blanke *c* Howe *m* M Steiner *w* Robinson 89min WB (= *This Man Reuter*)
Dispersing Clouds = WAKARE-GUMO (1951)
Dishevelled Hair = MIDARE-GAMI (1961)
Disprezzo, Il = LE MEPRIS (1963)
DISPUTED PASSAGE (1939) *d* Borzage *c* Mellor *w* Lamour, Tamiroff 91min Par
DISQUE 927 (1929) *d* Dulacsh
DISRAELI (1921) *d Henry Kolker w* G Arliss 6800ft *r* UA
DISRAELI (1929) *d Alfred E Green rm* 1921 *c* Garmes *w* G Arliss, J Bennett 90min WB
Distant Clouds = TOI KUMO (1955)
DISTANT DRUMS (1951) *d* Walsh *p* Sperling *fst/co-s* Busch *co-s* Rackin *c* Hickox *m* M Steiner *w* G Cooper *101min WB
Distant Journey = DALEKA CESTA (1949)
DISTANT TRUMPET, A (1964) *d* Walsh *c* Clothier *m* M Steiner *w* Pleshette PV* 117min WB
Ditte, Child of Man = DITTE, MANNESKEBARN (1946)
DITTE MENNESKEBARN (1946) *d/s* B Henning Jensen 102min (= *Ditte, Child Of Man*)
DITTO (1937) *d Lamont w* Keaton 17min
DIVE BOMBER (1941) *d* Curtiz *p* Wallis *c* Glennon, Hoch *w* Flynn, MacMurray, A Smith 133min WB
DIVERTISSEMENT, LE (1952) *d* Rivette *sh*
DIVERTISSEMENT (1960) *d* Alexeieff anim* 1min
DIVIDE AND CONQUER (1943) *d* Capra, Litvak *m* Tiomkin *n* W Huston US War Department
DIVIDED HEART, THE (1954) *d* Crichton *p* Balcon *c* Heller *m* Auric 89min
DIVIDEND, THE (1916) *co-d* Ince Tri
Dividing Line, The (UK) = THE LAWLESS (1949)
DIVINE (1935) *d/co-s* Ophuls *fn/di* (*L'Envers du Music-Hall*) Colette 80min
DIVINE CROISIERE, LA (1928) *d/s* Duvivier
DIVINE DAMNATION, THE (1967) *d/s/c/e* Markopoulos 16mm* 60min
DIVINE LADY, THE (1929) *d/p* F Lloyd *c* J Seitz *w* Dressler, (Parrish) 109min FN
DIVINE WOMAN, THE (1928) *d* Sjöström *fpl* (*Starlight*) *Gladys Unger co-a* Gibbons *w* Garbo, L Sherman 2225m MGM
DIVING GIRL, THE (1911) *d* Sennett *w* Normand (½rl) Bio
DIVKA V MODREM (1939) *d/s* Vavra
DIVORCE (1945) *d William Nigh co-p/w* K Francis 70min Mon
DIVORCE AMERICAN STYLE (1967) *d* Yorkin *c* C Hall *w* D Van Dyke, D Reynolds, V Johnson, J Simmons *109min Col
DIVORCE AMONG FRIENDS (1930) *d* Del Ruth 68min WB
Divorced = FRANSKILD (1951)
DIVORCEE, THE (1919) *d Herbert Blache supn Maxwell Karger co-s* Mathis *fpl* (*The Lady*) *Somerset Maugham w* E Barrymore (5rs)
DIVORCEE, THE (1930) *d/p* Leonard *c* Brodine *a* Gibbons *w* Shearer, Montgomery 84min MGM
Divorce, Italian Style (UK) = DIVORZO ALL'ITALIANA (1961)
DIVORZIO ALL'ITALIANA (1961) *d/co-st/co-s* Germi *w* Mastroianni 108min (= *Divorce, Italian Style*)
DIVOTVORNY KLOBOUK (1952) *d/s* Radok (= *The Magic Hat*)
DIX DE HOLLYWOOD (1951) *d* John Berry *c* Hayer
DIXIELAND DROOPY (1954) *d* Avery *p* Quimby *7min MGM
DIXIE MERCHANT, THE (1926) *d* Borzage 1563m Fox
DIXIÈME SYMPHONIE, LA (1918) *d/s* Gance *c* Burel
DIX MINUTES SUR LE F.F.I. (1944) *d* Michel *sh*
Dix Petits Indiens (France) = AND THEN THERE WERE NONE (1945)
DIX-SEPTIEME PARALLELE (1968) *d* Ivens, *Marceline, Loridan* 115min
DJAVULENS INSTRUMENT (1965) *d* Fischer sh (= *The Devil's Weapon*)
DJÄVULENS ÖGA (1960) *d/s* Ingmar Bergman *c* Fischer *mf Scarlatti w* B Andersson, Björnstrand, Kulle 90min SF (= *The Devil's Eye*)
DJERBA (1947) *d/cy* Lamorisse 15min
Djungeldansen ep in SVARTA HORISONTER (1936)
EN DJUNGELSAGA (1955) *d/p/s/c/e* Sucksdorff *m* Shankar S* 75min (= *The Flute and the Arrow*)
DMITRI DONSKOI (1944) *d* Yutkevich
D-M KILLER (1964) *d/co-s* Thiele *w* Jürgens 110min
DNES NAPOSLED (1958) *d/co-s* Fric (= *Today for the Last Time*)
DNES VECER VSECHNO SKONCĬ (1955) *d* Jasny, *Karel Kachyna* (= *Everything Ends Tonight*)
D O A (1949) *d* Maté *co-st/co-s* Rouse *c* Laszlo *m* Tiomkin *w* E O'Brien 83min *r* UA
DO BIGHA ZAMIN (1953) *d/p* Roy 94min (= *Two Acres of Land*)
DOBRE BYDLENI (1960) *d* Pojár anim (= *A Good Place to Live*)
DOBRODRUZSTUI NO ZLATE ZATOCE (1955) *d* Pojar 54min (= *An Adventure in the Bay of Gold*) or (= *The Big Fish* (UK))
DOBRY VOJAK SVEJK (1931) *d* Fric *fn Jaroslav Haček* (= *Good Soldier Schweik*)
DOBRY VOJAK SVEJK (1954) *d/s/a* Trnka Part 1: 650m; Part 2: 680m; Part 3: 620m (= *The Good Soldier Schweik*)
DOBU (1954) *d/s* Shindo (= *Gutter*)
DOC (1971) *d/p* Perry *w* Dunaway *95min *r* UA
DOCHU SUGORUKU KAGO (1926) *d* Kinugasa (= *The Palanquin*)
DOCHU SUGORUKU BUNE (1926) *d* Kinugasa
DOCKS OF NEW YORK, THE (1928) *d* Von Sternberg *s* Furthman *c* Rosson *dec* Dreier *w* G Bancroft 2195m Par
DOCKS OF SAN FRANCISCO (1932) *d* G Seitz *c* Cronjager 64min
DOCTOR AND THE GIRL, THE (1949) *d* C Bernhardt *p* Berman *co-a* Gibbons *w* G Ford, C Coburn, J Leigh 98min MGM
DR BLOOD'S COFFIN (1960) *d* Furie *92min *r* UA
DR BROADWAY (1942) *d* A Mann *p* S Siegel *st* B Chase *c* Sparkuhl 67min Par
DR BULL (1933) *d* J Ford *fn* (*The Last Adam*) *James Gould Cozzens w* W Rogers (Parrish) 76min Fox
DR CYCLOPS (1940) *d* Schoedsack *co-a* Dreier 78min Par
DOCTOR DOLITTLE (1967) *d* R Fleischer *fsts Hugh Lofting c* Surtees *des* Chiari *chor* Ross *w* Harrison, Attenborough TAO* 152min *r* Fox
DOCTORED AFFAIR, A (1913) *d* Sennett *w* Normand (½ rl) Key
Dr Ehrlichs Magic Bullet = STORY OF DR EHRLICH'S BULLET, THE (1940)
DR FAUSTUS (1968) *d/p -Burton, Neville Coghill fpl* Marlowe *w* Burton, (E Taylor) *93min
Dr G and the Love Bombs = DR GOLDFOOT AND THE GIRL BOMBS (1966)
DR GILLESPIE'S CRIMINAL CASE (1943) *d* Goldbeck *c* Brodine *a* Gibbons *m* Amfitheatrof *w* L Barrymore, V Johnson, M O'Brien 89min MGM
DR GILLESPIE'S NEW ASSISTANT (1942) *d/co-s* Goldbeck *c* Folsey *a* Gibbons *m* Amfitheatrof *w* L Barrymore, V Johnson, Quine 87min MGM
DR GOLDFOOT AND THE BIKINI MACHINE (1965) *d* Taurog *co-p* Arkoff *c* Leavitt *w* Price PV* 90min AI
DR GOLDFOOT AND THE GIRL BOMBS (1966) *d* Bava *w* Price CS* 85min AI (= *Dr G and the Love Bombs/I Due Mafiosi dell F B I/Le Spie Vengone dal Semifreddo*)
DOCTOR IN THE HOUSE (1954) *d* Thomas *fn Richard Gordon w* Bogarde, Kendall *91min JAR
Doctor in the Village = DORP AAN DE RIVEIR (1958)
DOCTOR IN TROUBLE (1970) *d* Thomas *90min *r* JAR
DOCTOR JACK (1922) *d* Newmeyer *p/co-st* Roach *w* H Lloyd 1432m *pc* Roach
DR JEKYLL AND MR HYDE (1920) *d John S Robertson fn* (*The Strange Case of Dr Jekyll and Mr Hyde*) *w* J Barrymore (7 rs) FPL
DR JEKYLL AND MR HYDE (1932) *d/p* Mamoulian *fn Stevenson c* Struss *a* Dreier *w* March, M Hopkins, Horton 81min Par
DR JEKYLL AND MR HYDE (1941) *d/p* Fleming *s* Mahin *fn Stevenson c* Ruttenberg *m* Waxman *w* Ingrid Bergman, Turner, Tracy, Crisp 122min MGM
DR JEKYLL AND SISTER HYDE (1971) *d* R Baker *97min
DR KILDARE'S VICTORY (1941) *d* W S Van Dyke *c* Daniels *w* Ayres, Barrymore 92min MGM
Doctor Knock (UK) = KNOCK (1951)
DR MABUSE DER SPIELER (1922) Part 1: DR MABUSE DER SPIELER - EIN BILD DER ZEIT; Part 2: INFERNO - MENSCHEN DER ZEIT *d/co-s* F Lang *co-s* Von Herbou Part 1: *p* Pommer 2620m; Part 2: 2753m Dec/*Ufa*
DR MONICA (1934) *d* Keighley *c* Polito *w* K Francis 61min WB
DR NO (1962) *d* T Young *p* Saltzman *co-s* Maibaum *fn I Fleming c* Moore *des* Adam *w* Connery, Andress *105min UA
DR RHYTHM (1938) *d* Tuttle *co-s* Swerling *fst O'Henry c* C Lang *w* B Crosby 80min Par
DOCTOR'S DIARY, A (1937) *d* C Vidor *p* B P Schulberg *w* G Bancroft 70min Par
DOCTOR'S DILEMMA, THE (1959) *d* Asquith *p/s* De Grunwald *fpl G B Shaw c* Krasker *co-s* Beaton *m* Kosma *w* Bogarde, Caron 98min MGM
DOCTORS DON'T TELL (1941) *d* J Tourneur 65min Rep
DR SOCRATES (1935) *d* Dieterle *st* Burnett *c* Gaudio *w* Muni 70min WB
Doctor Speaks, The = ARZT STELLT FAST, DER (1966)
DR STRANGELOVE, OR, HOW I LEARNED TO STOP WORRYING AND LOVE THE BOMB (1963) *d/p co-s* Kubrick *co-s T Southern, Peter George fn* (*Red Alert/Two Hours to Doom*) *P George c* G Taylor *des* Adam *w* Sellers, G Scott, Hayden, K Wynn 94min Col
DOCTORS' WIVES (1931) *d* Borzage *c* Edeson *w* J Bennett, W Baxter 80min Fox
DOCTOR'S WIVES (1971) *d George Schaeffer p* Frankovich *s* Taradash *c* Chang *des* Wheeler *m* E Bernstein *102min
DROPOUT (1970) *d* Brass *w* V Redgrave
DR SYN (1937) *d Roy William Neill w* G Arliss, Lockwood 81min Gaw
DR SYN, ALIAS THE SCARECROW (1963) *d* Neilson *98min *pc* Disney
DR TERROR'S HOUSE OF HORRORS (1965) *d* F Francis TS 98min
DOCTOR X (1932) *d* Curtiz *co-c* Rennahan 80min FN
DR X (*c*1938) *d* Bradley *sh*
DOCTOR, YOU'VE GOT TO BE KIDDING (1967) *d* Tewkesbury *m* K Hopkins PV* 94min MGM
DR ZHIVAGO (1965) *d* Lean *p* Ponti *s* Bolt *fn B Pasternak c* F Young *m* Jarre *w* Sharif, Christie, Steiger, Guinness, Courtenay, R Richardson PV70* 193min *r* MGM
DOCUMENTARY ON A HURRICANE IN GALVESTON (1913) *co-d/co-p* Vidor 1min *pc* Vidor
DOCUMENTO, IL (1939) *d/co-s/e* Camerini *co-s* Castellani, Soldati
DOCUMENTS SECRETS(1940) *d* Joannon
DODDET HALSBAND, DEN (1910) *d/s* Blom
Dödens Besegrare = HON SEGRADE (1915)
DÖDENS BRUD (1911) *d/s* Blom
DODESKA-DEN (1970) *d/co-s* Kurosawa *139min
DO DETECTIVES THINK? *d* Fred Guiol *w* Laurel, Hardy Pat
DODGE CITY (1939) *d* Curtiz *c* Polito *w* Flynn, De Havilland, Sheridan 105min WB
DÖDSKYSSEN (1916) *d/co-s/w* Sjoström 1185m
DODSWORTH (1936) *d* Wyler *p* Goldwyn *fn Sinclair Lewis c* Maté *a* R Day *m* A Newman *w* W Huston, Lukas, Astor, Niven, Ouspenskaya, Payne 90min *r* UA
Does, The = BICHES, LES (1968)
DOGADAJ (1969) *d/co-s* Mimica *88min (*The Event*)
DOG CATCHER'S LOVE, THE (1917) *d* Cline *p* Sennett Tri-Key
Doggy and the Four (*tr*) = PUNT'A A CTYRLISTEK (1954)
DOG POUNDED (1954) *d* Freleng anim* 7min WB
Dogs, Do you want to Live Forever (UK) = HUNDE WOLLT IHP EWIG LEBEN(1959)
Dog's Heads = PSOHCAUCĬ (1954)
Dog's Life = ZIVOT JE PES (1933)
DOG'S LIFE, A (1918) *d/s/w* Chaplin *c* Totheroh *w* Purviance (3rs) FN
Dog's Life, A (UK) = MONDO CANE No 1 (1961)
DOG STAR MAN: PART I (1962) *d* Brakhage 16mm* si 30min
DOG STAR MAN: PART II (1963) *d* Brakhage 16mm* si 7min
DOG STAR MAN: PART III (1964) *d* Brakhage 16mm* si 11min
DOG STAR MAN: PART IV (1964) *d* Brakhage 16mm* si 5min
DOG'S TALE, A (1911) *co-d* Ince *w* Pickford
Do I Love You? = LYUBLYU LI TEBYA (1934)
Doing His Best = MAKING A LIVING (1914)
DOKA-O (1926) *d/s* Mizoguichi Nik (= *King of a Penny*)
DOKOVJOMONOGOTARI - ZENI NO ODORI (1964) *d* Ichikawa *c* Miyagawa S* 90min Dai (= *Money Talks*)

DOKTOR DOLITTLE UND SEINE TIERE (1928) d Reiniger co-anim Bartosch fn Hugh Lofting anim 25min (= Das Abenteuer des Doktor Dolittle/The Adventures of Doctor Dolittle)

DOKTOR GLAS (1967) d Zetterling

DOKUSHIN-SHA GOYOJIN (1930) d/s Gosho (= Bachelors Beware)

DOLCE LUNAS DE MIEL (1943) d Vajda

DOLCE VITA, LA (1959) d/st/co-s Fellini co-s Rondi c Martelli dec Gherardi m Rota w Mastroianni, Aimée, Ekberg 178min Pat

DOLCI INGANNI, I (1960) d/st/co-s Lattuada m Piccioni w Catherine Spaak, Marquand 91min

DOLCI SIGNORE, LE (1967) d Zampa w Andress *102min (= Ladies & Ladies/Anyone Can Play)

DOLDERTAL 7 (1971) d/s/c/e Markopoulos 16mm*

DOLINA MIRU (1956) d Stiglic (= Peace Valley)

DOLKEN (1915) d Stiller 992m

Doll, The (UK) = PUPPE, DIE (1919)

Doll, The = VAXDOCKAN (1962)

Doll, The = LALKA (1969)

DOLLAR (1937) d Molander w Ingrid Bergman SF

DOLLAR-A-YEAR MAN, THE (1921) d Cruze w Arbuckle 1404m FPL r Par

DOLLAR DANCE (1941) d/cr McLaren anim* 6min NFBC

DOLLAR DOWN (1925) d Browning 1925m

DOLLARI E FRAKS (1919) d/p/s/w Ghione

DOLLARS (1971) d/st/s R Brooks p Frankovich w Beatty *120min

DOLL FACE (1946) d Lewis Seiler fpl G Lee (as Louise Hovick) co-a Wheeler w G Lee, C Miranda 80min Fox

DOLL'S HOUSE, A (1918) d M Tourneur fpl Henrik Ibsen (5rs) FPL

DOLL'S HOUSE, A (1922) d Charles Bryant p Nazimova fpl Ibsen w Nazimova 6650ft r UA

DOLLY MACHT DAS KARRIERE (1930) d Litvak Ufa

DOLOROSA, LA (1934) 102min

DOM (1958) d/s/dec Borowczyk, Lenica anim* 14min (= House)

DOMANI NON SIAMO PIU QUI (1966) d Rondi w Thulin 112min

DOMAREN (1960) d/co-s Sjöberg c Nykvist w Thulin 109min San (= Judge)

DOMBEY AND SON (1918) d/p Elvey (6rs)

DOMENICA D'AGOSTO (1950) d/co-s Emer co-s Zavattini, Rosi w Mastroianni 75min (= Sunday in August)

DÖMEN ICKE (1914) d Sjöström 1176m

DOMESTIC TROUBLES (1928) d Enright w Fazenda 58min WB

DOMICILE CONJUGAL (1970) d/co-s Truffaut co-s De Givray w Léaud *100min co-pc Truffaut (= Bed and Board)

DOMINANT SEX, THE (1937) d Brenon 74min ABC

DOMINO VERT, LE (1935) d Decoin w Darrieux

DOM NA TRUBNOI (1928) d Barnet co-s Victor Shklovsky 1757m (= The House on Trubnaya Square)

DOMO DEL MATTINO, IL (1932) d/s Guazzoni

DOM V SUGRIBAKH (1928) d Ermler 1757m (= The House in the Snow Drifts)

DONA FRANCISQUITTA (1952) d/co-s Vajda *85min

DONATELLA (1956) d Monicelli w Martinelli, Ferzetti CS* 100min

Don Camillo = PETIT MONDE DE DON CAMILLO, LE (1952)

DON CAMILLO E L'ONOREVOLE PEPPONE (1955) d Gallone w Fernandel 98min (= Don Camillo's Last Round)

Don Camillo's Last Round = DON CAMILLO E L'ONOREVOLE PEPPONE (1955)

DON CESARE DI BAZAN (1942) d/co-s Freda co-s Zavattini 78min r AA (= La Lamadel Giustiziere)

DON DEL MAR, EL (1957) d Grau

DONDE MUEREN LAS PALABRAS (1946) d Fregonese r MGM (= When Words Fail)

DONDI (1961) d/co-p/co-s Zugsmith 100min AA

Don Diego and Pelagia = DON DIEGO I PELAGEYA (1928)

DON DIEGO I PELAGYEA (1928) d Protazanov 1900m (= Don Diego and Pelagia)

DON GIOVANNI (1955) d Czinner *170min

DON GIOVANNI DELLA COSTA AZZURA, I (1962) d/co-st/co-s Sala w Jurgens, Ferzetti, Rossi-Drago FS* 98min

DON GIOVANNI IN SICILIA (1967) d Lattuada 100min

DON JUAN (1926) d Crosland c Haskin w J Barrymore, Astor, M Loy, Hopper 111min WB

DON JUAN (1955) d/co-s John Berry 95min

DON JUAN ET FAUST (1922) d L'Herbier dec Autant-Lara

DON JUAN QUILLIGAN (1945) d Tuttle c Brodine co-a Wheeler w Blondell, Bendix 75min Fox

Don Juan's Night of Love (US) = AVVENTURE DI MANDRIN, LE (1952)

DONKEY RACE (1898) d Hepworth 50ft

DON LORENZO (1953) d Bragaglia co-st Steno

DONNA CHE VENNE DEL MARE, LA (1956) d/st/co-s De Robertis co-s Festa Campanile w De Sica m Piccioni S 90min

DONNA DEL FIUME, LA (1955) d Soldati p Ponti, De Laurentiis co-s Pasolini, Vancini c Martelli w Loren *95min (= Woman of the River)

DONNA DEL GIORNO, LA (1956) d/co-s Maselli co-s Zavattini w Reggiani

DONNA DELLA MONTAGNA, LA (1943) d/co-s Castellani

DONNA DEL MONDO, LA (1962) co-d/cy/e Jacopetti co-d Franco Prosperi * (= Eva Sconosciuta/Women of the World)

DONNA DUENDE, LA (1945) d Saslavsky

DONNA E IL CADAVERE, LA (1919) d/s Genina

DONNA E UNA COSA MERAVIGLIOSA, LA (1964) d Bolognini c Di Venanzo, Martelli co-m Piccioni w Caprioli part* 190min

DONNA HA UCCISO, UNA (1951) d/co-s Cottafavi 87min

DONNA JUANA (1927) d/co-s Czinner co-c Freund w Bergner 3081m r Ufa

DONNA LIBERA, UNA (1954) d Cottafavi 87min r Fox

DONNA NUDA, LA (1914) d Gallone

DONNA PASSO, UNA (1922) d Genina

DONNA PIU BELLA DEL MONDO, LA (1955) d Leonard c Bava w Lollobrigida, Gassman, Vernon 115min (= Beautiful but Dangerous/La Bella des Belles)

DONNA SCIMMIA, LA (1963) d/co-s Ferrari p Ponti w Girardot 100min (= Monkey Woman)

DONNE E BRIGANTI (1950) d/co-st/co-s Soldati 93min

DONNE-MOI TES YEUX (1943) d/s Guitry w Guitry, André Dunoyer de Segonzac, (Othon Friesz), (André Derain), (Raoul Dufy), (Maurice de Vlaminck), (Maurice Utrillo) 101min

DONNE SOLE (1956) d/st/co-s Sala w Rossi-Drago

DO NOT DISTURB (1965) d Ralph Levy co-p A Rosenberg c Shamroy co-a Boyle w D Day S* 102min Fox

DONOVAN AFFAIR, THE (1929) d Capra p Cohn c Tetzlaff 79min Col

DONOVAN'S REEF (1963) d/p J Ford s F Nugent, J Grant c Clothier co-a Pereira m Mockridge w J Wayne, Marvin, Romero, Lamour, Dalio (Marsh) *109min r Par

DON PIETRO CARUSO (1916) d/w Ghione

Don Quintin El Amargoo = HIJA DEL ENGANO, LA (1951)

DON QUIXOTE (1923) d Elvey fn Cervantes (5rs)

DON Q, SON OF ZORRO (1925) d/w Crisp w Astor, Fairbanks Sr, Hersholt 3129m r UA

DON QUICHOTTE (1909) d Cohl anim 200m

DON QUICHOTTE (1933) d Pabst fn Cervantes m Ibert anim Reiniger 83min (= Don Quixote)

Don Quixote (UK) = DON QUICHOTTE (1933)

DON QUIXOTE (1934) d Iwerks anim* (1rl)

DON QUIXOTE (1955, uf) d/s Welles fn Cervantes w Welles, Tamiroff

DON QUIXOTE (1957) d/co-s Kozintsev fn Cervantes co-c Moskvin w Cherkasov CS* 105min

DON'T BET ON BLONDES (1935) d Florey w Flynn 60min WB

DON'T BET ON WOMEN (1931) d W Howard c Andriot w Jeanette MacDonald 70min Fox

DON'T BITE YOUR DENTIST (1930) d Cline s Sennett (2 rs) pc Sennett

DON'T BOTHER TO KNOCK (1952) d R Baker w Widmark, Monroe, A Bancroft, Cook 76min Fox

DON'T CHANGE YOUR HUSBAND (1918) d De Mille w Swanson (6rs) FPL

Don't Cry Peter = NE PLACI PETRE (1964)

DON'T EVER MARRY (1921) d Neilan, Victor Heerman 1829m pc Neilan

DON'T GIVE UP THE SHIP (1959) d Taurog p Wallis co-a Pereira w J Lewis 89min Par

DON'T GO NEAR THE WATER (1957) d Walters co-s Wells c Bronner m Kaper w G Ford, A Francis CS* 102min MGM

DON'T KNOCK THE ROCK (1957) d Sears p Katzman 80min Col

DON'T KNOCK THE TWIST (1962) d Oscar Rudolph p Katzman 87min Col

DON'T LOOK BACK (1967) d/s/co-c/e Pennebaker co-p R Leacock, Pennebaker songs/w Bob Dylan 16mm 96min

Don't Make War Make Love = NON FACCIO LA GUERRA, FACCIO L'AMORE (1966)

DON'T MAKE WAVES (1967) d Mackendrick c Lathrop w Curtis, Cardinale PV* 100min MGM

DON'T MARRY FOR MONEY (1923) d C Brown (6rs)

DÖNTÖ PILLANAT (1938) d Vajda 84min

DON'T SHOOT (1922) d Conway (6rs) U

DON'T SHOOT (1926) d Wyler (2 rs) U

DON'T TALK TO STRANGE MEN (1962) d Jackson 65min BL

DON'T TELL EVERYTHING (1921) d S Wood w Swanson 1505m FPL r Par

Don't Trust Your Husband = AN INNOCENT AFFAIR (1968)

DON'T WEAKEN (1920) d St Clair s/supn Sennett (2rs) pc Sennett

DONZOKO (1957) d/co-p/co-s Kurosawa fpl (The Lower Depths) Maxim Gorky w Mifune, Yamada 137min Toho (= The Lower Depths)

DOOLINS OF OKLAHOMA, THE (1949) d G Douglas p H Brown c Lawton w R Scott, Ireland 90min Col (= The Great Manhunt)

Doomed = IKIRU (1952)

Door to the open sea = PORTE DU LARGE, LA (1936)

DOORWAY TO HELL, THE (1930) d A Mayo w Cagney, Ayres 79min WB

DOPO IL VEGLIONE (1914) d Genina

DOPPELGANGER (1969) d Parrish *100min U

DOPPIA FERITA, LA (1915) d/st/s Genina

DORAKU GOSHINAN (1928) d/s Gosho (= Debauchery is Wrong)

DORA NELSON (1940) d/co-st/co-s Soldati co-st/co-s Zampa

DORNRÖSCHEN (1918) d/s/c/dec/cos Leni w Wegener

DORNRÖSCHEN (1922) d Reiniger anim (1rl)

DOROGOI MOI CHELOVEK (1958) d/co-s Heifitz w Batalov 108min (= My Dear Fellow)

DOROGOI TSENOI (1958) d Donskoi *95min (= At a High Cost)

DOROTHEA ANGERMANN (1959) d/p Siodmak fpl Gerhardt Hauptmann 93min

DOROTHY'S DREAM (1902) d G Smith

DOROTHY VERNON OF HADDON HALL (1924) d Neilan w Pickford (10rs) r UA

DORP AAN DE RIVEIR (1958) d Rademakers 91min (= Doctor in the Village)

DORTOIR DES GRANDES (1953) d/co-ad Decoin m Van Parys w Marais, Moreau, Arnoul 96min (= Girl's Dormitory)

DOS AU MUR, LE (1957) d Molinaro w Moreau 93min

DOSSIER NOIR, LE (1955) d/co-s Cayatte co-s/di Charles Spaak c Bourgoin 115min

DOT AND THE LINE, THE (1965) d C Jones anim* 10min MGM

DOTS (1939–41) d McLaren anim* 2½min

DOTTOR ANTONIO, IL (1938) d/s Guazzoni

DOUBLE ACTION DANIELS (1925) d Thorpe

DOUBLE AMOUR, LE (1925) d J Epstein

DOUBLE-BARRELLED DETECTIVE STORY (1965) d A Mekas w J Mekas 90min

Double Bed, The = LIT A DEUX PLACES, LE (1965)

DOUBLE DARING (1926) d Thorpe w Arthur (5rs)

DOUBLE DOOR, THE (1934) d C Vidor 70min Par

DOUBLE DYNAMITE (1951) d Irving Cummings w G Marx, J Russell, Sinatra 80min RKO

DOUBLE HARNESS (1933) d Cromwell as-p Macgowan w W Powell 70min RKO

DOUBLE INDEMNITY (1944) d/co-s B Wilder co-s R Chandler fst James M Cain c J Seitz a Dreier, Pereira m Rozsa w MacMurray, Stanwyck, Robinson 107min Par

DOUBLE LIFE, A (1948) d Cukor s Kanin, R Gordon c Krasner c Parrish m Rozsa w Colman, E O'Brien, Winters 101min U

DOUBLEMAN, THE (1967) d/w Schaffner w Brynner, Nolan 105min WB

DOUBLE REWARD, A (1912) d Ince

DOUBLE SPEED (1919) d S Wood (5rs)

DOUBLE WEDDING (1937) d Thorpe p J Mankiewicz s Swerling c Daniels a Gibbons w W Powell, M Loy

DOUBLE WHOOPEE (1929) d Lewis Foster p Roach st McCarey w Laurel, Hardy, Harlow (2rs) r MGM

DOUBLING FOR ROMEO (1921) d Badger pc Goldwyn w W Rogers 5304ft pc Goldwyn

DOUBTING THOMAS (1935) d D Butler w W Rogers 75min Fox

DOUCE (1943) d Autant-Lara s/di Aurenche, Bost c Agostini 104min

DOUCEMENT LES BASSES! (1971) d/co-di D Gray w Delon *90min

Douceur du Village, La = BOL D'AIR A LOUE, UN (1962)

DOUGH AND DYNAMITE (1914) d/s/w Chaplin w C Chase (2rs) Key (= The Doughnut Designer)

DOUGHBOYS (1930) d Edward Sedgwick p Keaton a Gibbons w Keaton, Sothern 82min MGM

Doughnut Designer, the = DOUGH AND DYNAMITE (1914)

DOULOS, LE (1962) d/p/s/di Melville co-p Ponti c Hayer m Misraki w Belmondo, Piccoli, Reggiani, Desailly 108min

DOULOUREUSE, LA (1920) d Genina

DOUZE MOIS (1959) d Gruel anim

DOVE, THE (1928) d/p/co-ad Ronald West a Menzies w Talmadge, Roland 9100ft r UA

Dove, The = GIRL OF THE RIO, THE (1932)

DOV'E LA LIBERTA? (1953) d/st Rossellini p Ponti, De Laurentiis co-s Pietrangeli c Tonti w Toto 84min

DOVER REVISITED (1942) d Watt Moi

DOWN AMONG THE SHELTERING PALMS (1952) d Goulding, p Kohlmar co-s Lewin w Harold Arlen w Greer, M Gaynor, Marvin, D Wayne TC* 86min Fox

Down and Out = LAUGHING GAS (1914)

DOWN ARGENTINE WAY (1940) d Irving Cummings p Zanuck c Shamroy, Rennahan w Grable, C Miranda 94min Fox

DOWNHILL (1927) d Hitchcock p Balcon 2632m

DOWNHILL RACER, THE (1969) d Michael Ritchie m K Hopkins w Redford *101min

DOWN MEMORY LANE (1949) *d* Karlson (compilation) 71min EL

DOWN ON THE FARM (1920) *d* Erle Kenton, Ray Gray *p* Sennett *w* Fazenda, Turpin (2rs) *r* UA

DOWN ON THE FARM (1938) *d* St Clair *w* Fazenda 61min Fox

DOWNSTAIRS (1932) *d/p* Monta Bell *st* J Gilbert *c* Rosson *w* J Gilbert, Lukas 75min MGM

DOWN TO EARTH (1917) *d/co-s* Emerson *p/st/w* Fairbanks *co-s* Loos (5rs)

DOWN TO EARTH (1932) *d* D Butler *w* W Rogers 81min Fox

DOWN TO THE SEA IN SHIPS (1922) *d/p* Elmer Clifton *w* Bon (12rs)

DOWN TO THE SEA IN SHIPS (1949) *d* Hathaway *rm* (1922) *co-s* Mahin *c* Joe MacDonald *a* Wheeler *m* A Newman *w* Widmark, L Barrymore, McIntire 120min Fox

Dox, Caccia All'Uomo = CACCIA ALLUONO (1961)

Do You Believe in Angels? (UK) = ANGLAR, FINNS DOM . . . (1961)

DO YOU LOVE ME? (1946) *d* Ratoff *c* Cronjager *co-a* Wheeler *w* M O'Hara, Grable(uc) 91min Fox

DRACOS (1956) *d* Koundouros 110min (= *The Ogre of Athens*)

DRACULA (1931) *d* Browning *fn* Bram Stoker *c* Freund *w* Lugosi 85min U

DRACULA (1958) *d* Fisher *82min JAR

DRACULA HAS RISEN FROM THE GRAVE (1968) *d* F Francis *w* C Lee TC* 92min WB-Pat

DRACULA, PRINCE OF DARKNESS (1965) *d* Fisher S* 90min

DRAG (1929) *d* F Lloyd *c* E Haller *w* Barthelmess 85min FN

DRAG-A-LONG DROOPY (1954) *d* Avery *p* Quimby anim* 8min MGM

DRAGEES AU POIVRE (1963) *d/co-st* Baratier *c* Decaë *w* Belmondo, Blanche, Brasseur, Vadim, Vitti, Vlady, Signoret 94min (= *Sweet and Sour*)

Dragers Juveler = LOJEN OCH TÅRAR (1912)

DRAGNET, THE (1928) *d* Von Sternberg *co-s* Furthman *t* H Mankiewicz *c* Rosson *dec* Dreier *w* G Bancroft, W Powell 2398m Par

DRAGNET (1954) *d/w* J Webb *w* Boone *89min *r* WB

DRAGONNADES SOUS LOUIS XIV, LES (1909) *d/s* Jasset

DRAGON SEED (1944) *d* Conway, *Harold S Bucquet p* Berman *fn* Pearl Buck *a* Gibbons, Wheeler *m* Stothart *w* K Hepburn, Tamiroff, W Huston, Moorehead 145min MGM

DRAGONWYCK (1946) *d/s* J Mankiewicz *p* Lubitsch *ex-p* Zanuck *c* AC Miller *co-a* Wheeler *m* A Newman *w* Tierney, W Huston, Price 103min Fox

DRAGOTSENNYE ZERNA (1948) *d* Heifitz, Zarkhi 2485m (= *The Precious Seeds*)

DRAGSTRIP RIOT (1958) *d* Bradley 68min AI

DRAGUERS, LES (1959) *d/s* Mocky *c* Sechan *m* Jarre *w* Aznavour, Aimée 75min (= *The Young Have no Morals*)

DRAKEN PA KOMODO (1937) *d* Fejos 13min SF

DRAMATIC SCHOOL (1938) *d* Robert B Sinclair *p* LeRoy *c* Daniels *m* Waxman *w* Goddard, Turner 80min

DRAME AU CHATEAU D'ACRE, UN (1912) *d/s* Gance (= *Les Morts, Reviennentils?*)

DRAME AU PAYS BASQUE, UN (1913) *d/s* Feuillade *917m

DRAME CHEZ LES FANTOCHES, UNE (1908) *d* Cohl anim 72m

DRAME DE SHANGHAI, LE (1938) *d* Pabst *c* Schuftan *w* Jouvet 100min

DRAMMA A 16 ANNI, UN (1929) *d* Genina

DRAMMA DELLA CORONA, IL (1916) *d* Genina

DRAMMA DI CRISTO (1948) *co-d/co-s/n* Emmer *co-d/co-s* Enrico Gras 257m

DRAMMA IGNORATO, UN (1916) *d/s/w* Ghione

Dra Musketyri = BLAZNOVA KRONIKA (1964)

DRANGO (1957) *co-d/co-p/s* Hall Bartlett *co-d* Jules Bricken *c* Howe *m* E Bernstein *w* J Chandler, Dru 96min *r* UA

DRAPEAU NOIR FLOTTE SUR LA MARMITE, LE (1971) *d/co-ad/d* Audiard *a* D'Eaubonne *w* Gabin *80min

DRASTIC DEMISE (1945, *ur*) *d/c/e* Anger 5min

DRAVCI (1948) *d/co-s* J Weiss (= *Wild Beasts*)

DRAWINGS OF LEONARDO DA VINCI, THE (1953) *d* Adrian de Potier *p* B Wright *wv* C Day Lewis *23min

DREAM, A (1911) *co-d* Ince *w* Pickford

Dream = MECHTA (1943)

DREAM CIRCUS (1939 *uf*) *d* Reiniger *m* Stravinsky anim

Dreamer's Walk, A = DRÖMMARES VANDRING, EN (1957)

DREAM GIRL, THE (1916) *d* De Mille (5rs) FPL

DREAM GIRL (1948) *d* Leisen *st* Elmer Rice *c* Fapp *co-a* Dreier *m* V Young 85min Par

DREAMING LIPS (1932) *d* Czinner *rm* Traumende Mund, Der (1932) *co-p/technical supn* Garmes *w* Bergner 94min

DREAM OF A RAREBIT FIEND (1906) *d* Porter Ed

Dream of Freedom, A = EN DRÖM OM FRIHET (1969)

DREAM OF KINGS, A (1969) *d* Daniel Mann *m* North *w* Quinn *110min

DREAM OF KINGS, A (1970) *d* Peries *20min

DREAM OF LOVE (1928) *d* Niblo *co-c* Daniels *a* Gibbons *w* J Crawford 1757m MGM

Dreams = KVINNODRÖM (1955)

DREAMS (1961) *d* A King 16mm 28min

Dreams of Youth = SEISHUN NO YUMEJI (1922)

Dreams of Youth = WAKODO NO YUME (1928)

Dreams of Youth = SEISHUN NO YUMEJI (1922)

DREAMS THAT MONEY CAN BUY (1944–46) *p* Richter *84min

    ep THE GIRL WITH THE PREFABRICATED HEART *d/s* Leger

    ep 'ROTORELIEFS' AND 'NUDE DESCENDING A STAIRCASE' *d/s* Duchamp

    ep LA SEMAINE DE LA BONTE *d/s/w* Ernst

    ep BALLET *d/s* Calder

    ep RUTH ROSES AND REVOLVERS *d/s* Man Ray *w* Milhaud

    ep NARCISSUS *d/s* Richter

DREAM STREET (1921) *d/p* Griffith *c* Bitzer *w* Power 33352m UA

DREAM WIFE (1953) *d/co-s* Sidney Sheldon *c* Krasner *co-a* Gibbons *w* C Grant, Kerr, Pidgeon 101min MGM

Dregs = BUNDFALD (1957)

DREIGROSCHENOPER, DIE (1931) *d* Pabst *co-s* Balasz, Brecht(uc), Dudow(uc) *fpl* Brecht, Weill *co-c* F Wagner *m* Weill *w* Lenya 111min WB-Nero (= *L'Opera de Quat' sous/The Threepenny Opera*)

DREIGROSCHENOPER, DIE (1963) *d* Staudtz *fpl* Brecht, Weill *w* Jurgens, Neff, Ventura S* 124min (= *The Threepenny Opera*)

DREIZEHN OKTOBER, DER (1949) *d* Andrew Thorndike

Dress, The (UK) = KLANNINGEN (1964)

DRESS PARADE (1927) *d/p* Crisp *c* Marley *a* Leisen 2012m Pat

DREYFUS (1930) *d/p* R Oswald *dec* Warm (sd)

DRIFTER, THE (1929) *d/co-st* Robert DeLacy *w* Mix 1797m *r* RKO

DRIFTERS (1929) *d/p/s/e* Grierson 50min

DRIFTING (1923) *d/co-s* Browning *w* Beery (7rs) U

Drifting Clouds = WAKARE-GUMO (1951)

DRIFTWOOD (1947) *d* Dwan *c* J Alton *w* Brennan, N Wood 90min Rep

DRITTE GESCHLECHT, DAS (1957) *d* V Harlan 103min (= *The Third Sex/Anders als du und ich*)

DRIVE A CROOKED ROAD (1954) *d* Quine *s* Edwards *c* Lawton *w* Rooney 82min Col

Driven From Home (UK) = AUSTREIBUNG (1923)

DRIVING PAST OF FOUR-IN-HEADS (1898) *p* Hepworth 50ft

DROGA MLODYCH (1936) *d* A Ford *sh* (= *Youth's Journey*)

DROIT A LA VIE, LE (1916) *d/s* Gance *c* Burel (5rs) (= *Right to Live*)

DROLE DE DIMANCHE, UN (1959) *d* M Allégret *m* Misraki *w* Arletty, Darrieux, Bourvil, Belmondo 90min

DROLE DE DRAME (1937) *d* Carné *s/di* J Prévert *c* Schuftan *dec* Trauner *m* Jaubert *w* Rosay, Simon, Jouvet, Barrault (= *Bizarre Bizarre*)

DROLE DE JEU (1967) *d* Kast *105min ORTF (= *The Most Dangerous Game*)

DROLE DE NOCE (1951) *d/co-p/co-st/co-s* Joannon *w* Carette, Richard 73min

DROLE DE PAROISSIEN, UN (1963) *d/s* Mocky *c* Burel *w* Bourvil, Blanche 83min (= *Heaven Sent*)

DROMDA DALEN, DEN (1947) *d/s/c/e* Sucksdorff 12min SF

DROMMARES VANDRING, EN (1957) *d* Lindgren *c* Nykvist *w* Kulle San (= *A Dreamer's Walk*)

DROM OM FRIHET, EN (1969) *d/co-s* Halldoff S 86min (= *A Dream of Freedom*)

DROOPY'S DOUBLE TROUBLE (1951) *d* Avery *p* Quimby anim* 7min MGM

DROOPY'S GOOD DEED (1951) *d* Avery *p* Quimby anim* 7min MGM

DROP DEAD DARLING (1966) *d/p/co-st/s* Hughes *w* Curtis PV* 100min Par (= *Arivederci Baby*)

Drop Dead, My Love = MARITO E MIO L'AMAZZO O QUANDO MI PARE, IL (1967)

Drottningholm Court Theatre = DROTTNINGSHOLM-TEATERN (1965)

DROTTNINGSHOLMTEATERN (1965) *co-d/c* Fischer *co-d* Lindroth 16mm *28min (= *Drottningholm Court Theatre*)

DRUH A SMENA (1940) *d* Fric (= *Second Lawyer*)

DRUM, THE (1938) *d* Z Korda *c* Périnal *dec* V Korda *w* Sabu *102min (= *Drums*)

DRUM BEAT (1954) *d/s* Daves *c* Morley *m* V Young *w* Ladd, Cook CS* 111min WB

Drum Crazy – The Gene Krupa Story (UK) = GENE KRUPA STORY, THE (1959)

DRUMMER OF THE 8TH, THE (1913) *d* Ince *w* Borzage 900m

Drums (US) = DRUM, THE (1938)

DRUMS ALONG THE MOHAWK (1939) *d* J Ford *ex-p* Zanuck *co-s* Trotti *c* Glennon, Rennahan *co-a* R Day *m* A Newman *w* Colbert, H Fonda, Oliver, Carradine (Marsh) *103min Fox

DRUMS IN THE DEEP SOUTH (1951) *d/a* Menzies *co-s* Yordan *m* Tiomkin *c* Lindon *87min RKO

DRUMS OF FATE (1922) *d* Charles Maigne *c* Howe 5716ft FPL *r* Par

DRUMS OF JEOPARDY, THE (1931) *d* G Seitz 75min

DRUMS OF LOVE (1928) *d/p/d* Griffith *co-c* Bitzer, Struss *dec* Menzies *w* L Barrymore 2545m *r* UA

DRUMS OF TAHITI (1953) *d* Castle *p* Katzman *73min Col

DRUNK (1965) *d* Warhol 16mm 70min

DRUNKARD'S REFORMATION, A (1909) *d* Griffith *c* Bitzer 165m Bio

DRY MARTINI (1928) *d* D'Arrast *w* Astor 80min Fox

DRY ROT (1956) *d* Elvey *p* Clayton 87min *r* BL

DUB, THE (1918) *d* Cruze (5rs) FPL

DUBARRY VON HEUTE, EINE (1926) *d* A Korda *w* Dietrich 3004m

DU BARRY WAS A LADY (1943) *d* Del Ruth *p* Freed *c* Freund *a* Gibbons *w* Ball, Gene Kelly, Gardner *101min *r* MGM

Dubious patriots, the (1964) = SECRET INVASION, THE (1964)

DU BIST MIN, EIN DEUTSCHES TAGEBUCH (1969) *d/s* Thorndike 70* 118min (= *A German Diary*)

Dubrowsky = VENDICATORE, IL (1958)

DU CHARBON ET DES HOMMES (1953) *d* Leenhardt 22min

DUCHESSE DE LANGEAIS, LA (1942) *d* de Baroncelli *s/di Giraudoux w* Feuillère

DUCHESS OF BUFFALO, THE (1926) *d* Franklin *w* C Talmadge 2115m WB

DUCHESS OF IDAHO (1950) *d* Leonard *p* Pasternak *co-a* Gibbons *w* Esther Williams, V Johnson 98min MGM

DUCK AMUCK (1953) *d* C Jones anim* 7min WB

DUCK SOUP (1927) *w* Laurel, Hardy Pat

DUCK SOUP (1933) *d* McCarey *ex-p* H Mankiewicz *w* H, G, C, Z Marx, Dumont 70min Par

DU COTE DE LA COTE (1958) *d/st/s/n* Varda *e* Colpi *27min (= *The Riviera – Today's Eden*)

DU COTE D'OROUET (1971) *d/s* Rozier 16mm* 125min

DUDE RANGER, THE (1934) *d* Cline *p* Lesser *w* G O'Brien 63min Fox

DUDE WRANGLER, THE (1930) *d* Thorpe 69min

DUE COLONNELLI, I (1962) *d* Steno *w* Toto, Pidgeon 103min (= *The Two Colonels*)

DUE CROCIFISSI, I (1918) *d/s* Genina

DUE CUORI SOTTO SEQUESTRO (1941) *d/s* Bragaglia

DUAL, THE (1912) *d/p* Sennett *w* Sennett, Normand (½rl) Key

DUE FOSCARI, I (1942) *d* Enrico Fulchignoni *co-s* Antonioni

DUEL (1927) *d* De Baroncelli

DUEL, LE (1939) *d* Fresnay *s* Clouzot *c* Matras *w* Fresnay 2300m

Duel, The = POEDINOK (1957)

DUEL A MORT, UN (1948) *w* Keaton *sh*

DUEL AT DIABLO (1966) *d/co-p* Nelson *w* Garner, Poitier, B Andersson *103min UA

DUEL AT SILVER CREEK (1952) *d* D Siegel *c* Glassberg *co-a* Golitzen *w* A Murphy, (Marvin) 77min U

DUEL DE MAX, LE (1913) *d/w* Linder Pat

DUEL D'HAMLET, LE (1900) *d* Clement Maurice *w* S Bernhardt

DUE LETTERE ANONIME (1945) *d/co-s* Camerini *p* Ponti

DUEL IN THE JUNGLE (1954) *d* G Marshall *w* D Andrews, Crain *102min WB

DUEL IN THE SUN (1946) *d* K Vidor, Dieterle(uc), Von Sternberg(uc) *p* Selznick *fn* Busch *c* Garmes, Rosson, Rennahan *m* Tiomkin *colour consultant* Von Sternberg *w* Peck, Cotton, L Barrymore, J Jones, H Marshall, L Gish, W Huston, Pickford, Cary *138min *pc* Selznick *r* UA

DUELO EN LAS MONTANAS (1949) *d* Fernandez *fst* (*Spring Rains*) Ivan Turgenev *e* Figueroa

Duel of Champions (US) = ORAZI E CURIAZI (1961)

Duel of a Snowy Night, The = YUKI NO YO NO KETTO (1954)

DUEL ON THE MISSISSIPPI (1955) *d* Castle *71min Col

Due Mafiosi dell F B I, I = DR GOLDFOOT AND THE GIRL BOMBS (1966)

DUE ORFANELLE, LE (1942) *d* Gallone *w* Valli 92min (= *The Two Orphans*)

DUE MILLIONI PER UN SORRISO (1940) *d* Soldati, *Carlo Borghesio*

DUE MOGLIE SONO TROPPE (1950) *d/co-s* Camerini *m* Rota

DUE NEMICI, I (1962) *d* Hamilton *p* De Laurentiis *c* Rotunno *m* Rota *w* Niven, Sordi TR* 104min BL/Col (= *The Best of Enemies*)

DUE SERGENTI, I (1936) *d* Guazzoni *w* Valli

DUE SOLDI DI SPERANZA (1951) *d/co-st/co-s* Castellani 95min (= *Two Pennies of Hope/Two Pennyworth of Hope*)

DUFFY (1968) *d* Parrish *c* Heller *w* J Coburn, Mason, *J Fox* *101min Col

DU HAUT EN BAS (1933) *d* Pabst *c* Schuftan *w* M Simon, Gabin, Lorre 79min

DUKE COMES BACK, THE (1937) *d* Pichel Rep

DUKE ELLINGTON IN PARIS (1960) *d* Kiegel TV

DUKE OF CHIMNEY BUTTE, THE (1921) *d* Borzage (5 rs)

DUKE OF WEST POINT, THE (1938) *d* Alfred E Green *w* L Hayward, Fontaine 96min *r* UA

DUKE STEPS OUT, THE (1929) d/p Cruze w J Crawford, Daves a Gibbons 69min MGM

Dulcimer Street = LONDON BELONGS TO ME (1948)

DULCY (1923) d Franklin co-s Loos, Emerson c Brodine w C Talmadge (7rs)

Dull Clang, A = HARD KLANG (1952)

DUMB GIRL OF PORTICI, THE (1916) p The Smalleys w Karloff, Julian (10rs) U

DUMB-HOUNDED (1943) d Avery anim* 8min MGM

DUMBO (1941) p Disney anim* 64min r RKO

DUMBOM (1953) d Hans Lagerkvist, Nils Poppe c Strinberg w Poppe, B Andersson

DUMKY (1965) d Jasny

DUMMKOPF, DER (1921) d/w Lupu-Pick fn (The Idiot) Dostoievski

DUMMY, THE (1929) d Robert Milton ad/di H Mankiewicz w Cromwell, March, Pitts 5357ft Par

DU MOURON POUR LES PETITS OISEAUX (1962) d/co-s Carné dec Saulnier co-m Aznavour

DUNOYER DE SEGONZAC (1965) d Reichenbach, Monique Lepeuve

Dura Lex = PO ZAKONU (1926)

DURANTE L'ESTATE (1971) d/co-st/co-s Olmi *105min RAI

DURCH DIE WALDER, DURCH DIE AVEN (1956) d/s Pabst w E Bartok S* 95min

DURFEN WIR SCHWEIGIN? (1926) d/s Roswald w Veidt 2686m

DU RIFIFI A PANAME (1966) d De La Patellière w Gabin, Raft, Tiller, Darc S* 100min (= Rififi in Paris/The Upper Hand)

DU RIFIFI CHEZ LES HOMMES (1954) d/co-s Dassin c Agostini m Auric w Dassin, Hossein 117min (= Rififi (Means Trouble) UK

DURING ONE NIGHT (1961) d/p/s Furie 80min Gala

DU SANG, DE LA VOLUPTE ET DE LA MORT (1947) d/s/c/e/w Markopoulos

Part I PSYCHE m R Vaughan Williams fn Pierre Louys 16mm* 25min

Part II LYSIS f Plato m Honegger 16mm* 30min

Part III CHARMIDES f Plato m Milhaud 16mm* 15min

DU SKAL AERE DIN HUSTRU (1925) d/co-s/a Dreyer

DUSK TO DAWN (1922) d/p K Vidor c Barnes w Franklin 1585m Vidor

Du Sollst Nicht Ehe Brechen (Germany) = THERÈSE RAQUIN (1928)

DUSSELDORF (1936) d/co-s Ruttmann 14min

DUST AND GOLD (1955) d Guillermin 61min

DUST BE MY DESTINY (1939) d Lewis Seiler s Rossen c Howe w Garfield 88min WB

DUTCH GOLD MINE, A (1911) d/w Sennett ($\frac{1}{2}$rl) Bio

DU UND MANCHUR KAMERAD (1956) d/s A & A Thorndike 110min (= The German Story)

DÚVAD (1959) d/s/dec Fabri 90min (= The Brute/The Beast)

DVA-BULDI DVA (1929) d Kuleshov, Nina Agadzhanova - Shutko s Osip Brik 1519m (= Two-buldi-Two)

DVADTSAT DVA NESCHASYA (1930) d Gerasimov, C Bartenev 1500m (= Twenty Two Misfortunes)

DVA MRAZKI (1954) d/s/a Trnka anim* 341m (= The Two Frosts)

DWELLING PLACE OF LIGHT (1921) d Conway (7rs)

DYNAMIQUE DE L'ÉVOLUTION DE L'OEUF DE PIEUVRE (1967) d Painlevé 16mm 45min

DYNAMITE (1929) d/p De Mille co-d Lawson c Marley co-a Gibbons, Leisen m Stothart w Bickford, McCrea, Holden 119min MGM

Dynamite Anchorage = MURDER IS MY BEAT (1954)

DYNAMITE CHICKEN (1971) d Pintoff 90min

DZHOI I DRUZHOK (1928) d/s Petrov, M Khukhunashvili 1600m (= Dzhoi and his Friend)

Dzhoi and his Friend = DZHOI I DRUZHOK (1928)

EACH DAWN I DIE (1939) d Keighley c Edeson w Raft, Cagney, G Bancroft 92min WB

EADIE WAS A LADY (1945) d Arthur Dreifuss c Guffey w Ann Miller 68min Col

EAGLE, THE (1925) d C Brown fst (Dubrovsky) Pushkin co-c Barnes a Menzies w Valentino, Banky 2059m r UA

EAGLE OF THE SEA, THE (1926) d F Lloyd as-p BP Schulberg c Brodine 2210m FPL r Par

Eagle with Two Heads, The = AIGLE A DEUX TÊTES, L' (1947)

EAMES LOUNGE CHAIR (1956) d/s C and R Eames c C Eames m E Bernstein 2$\frac{1}{2}$min

EARL OF CHICAGO, THE (1940) d Thorpe p Saville c June a Gibbons w Montgomery 85min MGM

Early Autumn = KOHAYAGAWA-KE NO AKI (1961)

Early Spring = SOSHUN (1956)

Early Summer = BAKUSHU (1951)

EARLY TO BED (1928) d Emmett Flynn p Roach supn/st McCarey w Laurel, Hardy (2rs) r MGM

EARLY TO BED (1936) d McLeod w C Ruggles 73min Par

EARLY TO WED (1926) d Borzage w Pitts 1802m Fox

E'ARRIVATO IL CAVALIERE (1950) d Steno, Monicelli p Ponti c Bava

Earth = ZEMLYA (1930)

EARTH AND ITS PEOPLES, THE (1948–52) p De Rochemont (series)

EARTHBOUND (1940) d Pichel cp-s Lawson m A Newman w W Baxter 67min Fox

EARTH DIES SCREAMING, THE (1964) d Fisher 62min Fox

Earth's Sap, The = SÈVE DE LA TERRE (1955)

EARTH VS THE FLYING SAUCERS (1956) d Sears p Katzman 83min Col

EARTH WOMAN, THE (1926) d W Lang 1777m

EARTHWORM TRACTORS (1936) d Enright 63min WB

EASIEST WAY, THE (1931) d Conway w Constance Bennett, Menjou, R Montgomery, Gable 86min MGM

EAST AFRICAN SAFARI (1965) d Reichenbach

Easter In Sicily (US) = PASQUA IN SICILIA (1955)

Easter Island = ÎLE DE PÂQUES, L' (1934)

EASTERN WESTERNER, AN (1920) w H Lloyd 2rs r Pat

EASTER PARADE (1948) d Walters p Freed st/co-s Goodrich, Hackett chor R Alton w Astaire, Garland, Lawford, Ann Miller 103min MGM

EAST IS WEST (1922) d Franklin c Gaudio w C Talmadge 2359m pc C Talmadge r FN

EAST LYNNE (1931) d F Lloyd c J Seitz w C Brook 72min Fox

EAST LYNNE WITH VARIATIONS (1919) d Cline p/s Sennett w Turpin 2rs r Par

EAST OF BROADWAY (1924) d W Howard c Andriot 1760m

EAST OF EDEN (1955) d/p Kazan s Osborn fn John Steinbeck c McCord m Rosenman w Dean, Ives CS* 115min WB

EAST OF PICCADILLY (1939) d Harold Huth se/s J Thompson 79min ABC (= The Strangler)

EAST OF SUEZ (1925) d/p Walsh fst Somerset Maugham c Milner w Negri 2047m FPL r Par

EAST OF SUMATRA (1953) d Boetticher w J Chandler, Quinn 82min *U

EAST SIDE OF HEAVEN (1939) d/co-st Butler w B Crosby, Blondell 88min U

EAST SIDE, WEST SIDE (1927) d/s Dwan w G O'Brien 2485m Fox

EAST SIDE, WEST SIDE (1949) d LeRoy co-a Gibbons m Rozsa w Stanwyck, Gardner, Mason, Charisse, Heflin 108min MGM

East Wind = VENT D'EST (1969)

EASY COME, EASY GO (1928) d Tuttle c Cronjager 1635m Par

EASY COME, EASY GO (1947) d J Farrow p Macgowan c Fapp co-a Dreier 77min Par

EASY GOING (1926) d Thorpe 1494m

Easy Life = SORPASSO, IL (1962)

EASY LIVING (1937) d Leisen st Caspary s P Sturges c Tetzlaff co-a Dreier w Arthur, Milland 88min Par

EASY LIVING (1949) d J Tourneur s Schnee fst (Education of the Heart) Shaw c Wild w Mature, Ball, L Scott, Nolan 77min RKO

EASY MILLIONS (1933) d Newmeyer 56min

EASY STREET (1917) d/s Chaplin c Totheroh w Chaplin, Purviance 2rs Mut

EASY TO LOVE (1933) d Keighley c E Haller w Menjou, Astor, Horton 65min WB

EASY TO LOVE (1953) d Walters 2nd d Berkeley p Pasternak c June co-a Gibbons w Esther Williams, V Johnson, C Baker *96min MGM

EASY VIRTUE (1927) d Hitchcock p Balcon fpl Coward

Easy Years (US) = ANNI FACILI (1953)

EAT (1963) d Warhol 16mm si 45min

EATING TOO FAST (1966) d Warhol 16mm 70min

EAU, L' (1966) d Alexeieff anim*

EAU A LA BOUCHE, L' (1959) d/st/s Doniol-Valoroze w Chabrol 83min (= The Game of Love)

EAU D'EVIAN, L' (1937) d Alexeieff anim

EAU VIVE (1938) d/s J Epstein co-c Bachelet 44min

EAUX D'ARTIFICE (1953) d/s/c/e/cos Anger m Vivaldi 16mm* 13min

EAUX SOUTERRAINES (1957) d Tazieff

EAUX VIVES (1941) d Decaë, Cl. Decaë

Eavesdropper, The = OJO DE LA CERRADURA, EL (1964)

ECCE HOMO – NAME, AGE AND OCCUPATION (1941, uf) d Lorentz

ECHEC AU PORTEUR (1957) d/co-s Grangier w Moreau, Reggiani 86min

ECCENTRIC DANCER, THE (1900) p Hepworth 15m

ECHIGO TSUTSUISHI OYASHIRAZU (1964) d Imai S 112min (= Story from Echigo)

ECHIZEN TAKENINGYO (1963) d Yoshimura c Miyagawa S 102min Dai (= The Bamboo Doll)

Echiquier de Dieu, L': Original title for FABULEUSE AVENTURE DE MARCO POLO, LA (1964)

Echo, The = YAMA NO OTO (1954)

Echo School = YAMABIKO GEKKO (1952)

Eclipse, The = ECLISSE, L' (1962)

ECLIPSE DEL SOL (1943) d Saslavsky

ECLISSE, L' (1962) d/co-st/co-s Antonioni c Di Venanzo m Fusco w Delon, Vitti 125min (= The Eclipse)

ECOLE BUISSONNIERE, L' (1949) d/st/co-s Le Chanois m Kosma 115min

ECOLE DES FACTEURS, L' (1947) d/st/s/w Tati

ECOLE DES FEMMES. L' (1940, uf) d Ophuls fpl Molière c Kelber w Jouvet

ECOLES DE PILOTAGE (1956) d Mitry

ECONOMIE DES METAUX, L' (1957) d Rouquier sh

ECRIRE EN IMAGES (1957) d/s/e Mitry

ECRITURE DU MOUVEMENT (1947) d Painlevé 27min

E C S (1962) d/s C and R Eames c Eames *7min

Ectasy = EXTASE (1933)

Eddie = EDDIE SACHS AT INDIANAPOLIS (1961)

EDDIE SACHS AT INDIANAPOLIS (1961) d R Leacock, Drew 16mm 58min (= Eddie)

EDDY DUCHIN STORY, THE (1956) d G Sidney p Wald w Power, Novak CS* 123min Col

EDEN ET APRES, L' (1970) d/s Robbe-Grillet *98min

EDERA, L' (1950) d/co-s Genina 94min (= Devotion)

ÉDES ANNA (1958) d/co-s/dec Fábri 87min (= Anna)

EDES MOSTOHA (1935) d Balazs

EDGAR ALLAN POE (1909) d Griffith 1rl Bio

EDGAR ET SA BONNE (1949) d Michel sh

EDGE OF DARKNESS (1943) d Milestone 2nd d Walsh p Blanke ex-p J Warner s Rossen c Hickox e Weisbart w Flynn, Sheridan, W Huston, R Gordon 120min WB

EDGE OF DOOM (1950) d Robson s Yordan a R Day m Friedhofer w D Andrews, F Granger 99min RKO

EDGE OF ETERNITY (1959) d/as-p D Siegel c Guffey m Amfitheatrof w Wilde CS* 80min Col

EDGE OF FURY (1958) d I Lerner, Robert Gurney Jr co-c C Hall 70min r UA

EDGE OF THE CITY (1956) d Ritt co-p/s Aurthur c Brun e Meyers cr Bass m Rosenman w Cassavettes, Poitier 85min MGM (= A Man is Ten Feet Tall)

EDIPO RE (1967) d/s Pasolini fpls (Oedipus Rex and Oedipus Coloneus) Sophocles w Mangano, Valli, Pasolini *110min (= Oedipus Rex)

EDISON KINETOSCOPIC RECORD OF A SNEEZE, JANUARY 7, 1894 (1894) d Dickson (= Fred Ott's Sneeze)

EDGE OF THE WORLD, THE (1937) d/s M Powell 81min

EDISON, THE MAN (1940) d C Brown st Schary, H Butler c Rosson a Gibbons m Stothart w Tracy, c Coburn 107min MGM

EDOUARD ET CAROLINE (1951) d/co-s Becker w Vernon, Gélin 100min

EDUCATION SENTIMENTALE 61 (1962) d Astruc fn Flaubert c Badal dec Saulnier w Brialy FS 92min

EDWARD, MY SON (1949) d Cukor s D Stewart c F Young w Tracy, Kerr 112min MGM

Effeminate One, The = MAZLICEK (1934)

EFFET DE MER SUR LES ROCHERS (1896) d Méliès 20m

E-FLAT MAN, THE (1935) d Lamont w Keaton 2rs

Egg, The = JAJE (1959)

Eggs. The = SADO-NO TAMAGO (1966)

EGI BARANY (1971) d/co-s Jancsó 92min (= Agnus Dei)

EGI MADAR (1957) d Fehér (= A Bird of Heaven)

EGRI CSILLAGOK (1923, uf) d Fejos

EGYENLOSEG (1918) d Balazs

EGYPTIAN, THE (1954) d Curtiz p Zanuck co-s P Dunne c Shamroy co-a Wheeler m Herrmann, A Newman w J Simmons, Mature, Tierney, Ustinov, Carradine CS* 140min Fox

EICHMANN UND DAS DRITTE REICH (1961) d/s Leiser 90min (= Murder by Signature)

EIEN NO HITO (1961) d/s Kinoshita w Nakadai S 107min Sho (= The Bitter Spirit/Immortal Love)

$8\frac{1}{2}$ = OTTO E MEZZO (1963)

1860 (1934) d/co-s/co-e Blasetti

Eighth Day of the Week, The = OSMY DZIEN TYGODNIA (1957)

EIGHTH PLAGUE, THE (1945) d J Lee 16mm 11min MOI

EIGHT IRON MEN (1952) d Dmytryk m Leith Stevens w Marvin 80min pc Kramer r Col

813 (1922) d Mizoguchi Nik (= Ripimono)

8 ON THE LAM (1967) d G Marshall co-s Lewin w Hope 106min r UA

8 × 8 = ACHT MAL ACHT (1957)

80 DAYS, THE (1944) d/p Jennings 14min

80 STEPS TO JONAH (1969) d/p/co-s G Oswald c La Shelle w Rooney

Einsam Grab, Ein = TAT DER GRAFIN WORMS, DIE (1916)

EISENSTEIN IN MEXICO (1933) p Lesser [see QUE VIVA MEXICO (1931)]

EISENSTEIN'S MEXICAN PROJECT (1958) compiled by Jay Leyda [see QUE VIVA MEXICO (1931)]

EINSTEIN THEORY OF RELATIVITY, THE (1923) M Fleischer anim 1219m

EJFELKOR (1957) d Révész 92min (= At Midnight)

EL (1952) d/co-s Bunuel co-s Alcoriza c Figueroa 100min

E L'AMOR CHE MI ROVINA (1951) d Soldati 106min

EL CID (1961) d A Mann 2nd d Canutt p Bronston co-s Yordan, Barzman (uc) c Krasker m Rozsa w Heston, Loren, Vallone TR70* 185min MGM

EL CONDOR (1970) d Guillermin p De Toth m Jarre w Cook *102min

ELD OMBORD (1923) d/s/w Sjöström 2270m SF

ELDORA (1952) d/s/c/e Markopoulos 8mm *7min

ELDORADO (1921) d L'Herbier Gaul

EL DORADO (1967) d/p Hawks c Rosson co-a Pereira w J Wayne, Mitchum *110min r Par

ELDRIDGE CLEAVER. BLACK PANTHER (1970) d/c/e
    Klein 73min
ELECTRA (1961) d/p/s Cacoyannis fpl Euripides˘c Lassally
    m Theodorakis 113min
ELECTRIC HOUSE, THE (1922) co-d Cline co-d/pc/w
    Keaton 2rs
ELECTRICITÉ (1937) d Grimault anim
ELECTROLYSE DU NITRATE D'ARGENT (1935) d
    Painlevé
ELEGY, THE (1927) d/s Stone
Elegy of the North = BANKA (1957)
ELEMENTS OF THE AUTOMOBILE (1920) p Bray (series
    of 13) US Army
Eléments pour une Etude de Rhythme = TAMBOURS DE
    PIERRE (1964)
ELÉNA ET LES HOMMES (1956) d/co-ad/di/lyr J Renoir c
    C Renoir m Kosma w Ingrid Bergman, Marais, M
    Ferrer, (Modot), (Brialy) *95min
ELEPHANT BOY (1936) d Flaherty, Z Korda fn (Toomai of
    the Elephants) R Kipling e Crichton w Sabu 84min r
    UA
Elephants Never Forget = ZENOBIA(1939)
ELEPHANT WALK (1954) d Dieterle s Mahin c Griggs co-a
    Pereira m Waxman w E Taylor, D Andrews, Finch
    *103min Par
ELETJEL (1954) d Fábri (= Fourteen Lives Saved)
ELEUTHERIA EN CULTURE (1958) d Painlevé
Eleven Men = KET FELIDO A POKOLBAN (1961)
/Eleventh, The/=ODINNADTSATYI(1928)
Eleventh Commandment, The = JEDENÁCTÉ PRIKÁZÁNI
    (1935)
EL FRAYLE (1953) d Olmi *13min
ELF TEUFEL, DIE (1927) d Z Korda 2476m
EL GRECO (1964) d/co-s Salce p/m/w Ferrer CS* 95min
Elisabeth, Reine d'Angleterre = REINE ELISABETH, LA
    (1912)
ELISIR D'AMORE, L' (1939) d Reiniger anim 1rl
ELITELT, AZ (1917) d Balasz
ELIZABETH AND MARY (1964) d/co-c/co-e Pennebaker
    16mm 60min
Elizabeth the Queen = PRIVATE LIVES OF ELIZABETH
    AND ESSEX, THE (1939)
ELIZABETH UND DER NARR (1933) d/s Von Harbou
    78min
ELLA CINDERS (1926) d Alfred E Green co-s LeRoy w
    Langdon 1993m r FN
ELLE BOIT PAS, ELLE FUME PAS, ELLE DRAGUE
    PAS, MAIS ... ELLE CAUSE! (1970) d/co-s
    Audiard dec D'Eaubonne m Van Parys w Girardot,
    Darc *80min
ELMER GANTRY (1960) d/s R Brooks fn Sinclair Lewis c
    J Alton m Previn w Lancaster, J Simmons, A
    Kennedy, S Jones, McIntire *145min r UA
ELMER'S CANDID CAMERA (1940) d C Jones p L
    Schlesinger anim (1rl)
ELMER'S PET RABBIT (1940) d C Jones p L Schlesinger
    anim (1rl)
ELMER THE GREAT (1933) d LeRoy w Wyman 74min FN
ELNEMUT HARANGOK (1916) d Balasz
ELOGE DU CHIAK (1970) d/st/co-c/e Brault wv Perrault
    16mm
EL PASO STAMPEDE (1953) d Keller 54min Rep
ELSA (1966) d Varda 26min ORTF
ELSKOVLEG (1913) d/s Madsen
ELSKOVS MAGT (1913) d Madsen
ELSTREE CALLING (1930) d Hitchcock, Adrian, Brunel
    86min
E LUCEAN LE STELLE (1935) d Gallone
Elusive Jan, The = NEULOVIMYI YAN (1943)
ELUSIVE PIMPERNEL, THE (1950) d/p/s M Powell, Press-
    burger fn Baroness Orczy c Challis w Niven, Hawkins
    *109min r BL (= The Scarlet Pimpernel)
ELVIRA MADIGAN (1967) d/s/e Widerberg m Mozart
    95min
EMAK BAKIA (1926) d/p/c Man Ray 17min
EMAN FIALA (1961) d/co-st Fric
EMBARQUEMENT POUR LE CIEL, L' (1953) d/s Aurel
    13min
EMBER A HID ALATT (1936) d Vajda 81min
EMBROGYNÈSE D' ORIZIAS LATIPES (1959) d Painlevé
    16mm
EMERGENCY CALL (1952) d/co-s L Gilbert 92min
    (= Hundred Hour Hunt)
EMERGENCY SQUAD (1940) d Dmytryk co-a Dreier w
    Quinn 60min Par
EMIGRANTE, L' (1939) d Joannon st Aurenche, Y Allégret
    c Schuftan w Feuillère
EMIGRATA, L' (1918) d Genina
EMIL AND THE DETECTIVES (1964) d Tewkesbury
    *99min
EMILIE HOGQVIST (1939) d/co-s Molander SF
Emily = AMERICANIZATION OF EMILY, THE (1964)
EMMA (1932) d C Brown w Dressler, Hersholt, M Loy
    72min MGM
Emma Hamilton (UK) = LADY HAMILTON -
    ZWISCHEN SCHMACH UND LIEBE (1968)
EMPEROR JONES (1933) d Bradley sh
EMPEROR'S CANDLESTICKS, THE (1937) d George
    Fitzmaurice c Rosson co-e Vorkapich a Gibbons m
    Waxman w Rainer, W Powell 89min MGM

Emperor's Nightingale, The = CISARUV SLAVIK (1948)
EMPEROR WALTZ, THE (1948) d/co-s B Wilder p/co-s
    Brackett c Barnes co-a Dreier m V Young w Crosby,
    Fontaine, Haydn *106min Par
Emperor and His Baker, The = CISARUV PEKAR (1951)
EMPIRE OF DIAMONDS, THE (1920) d/p/s Perret Pat
EMPLOYEES' ENTRANCE (1933) d Del Ruth w L Young
    75min WB
Empty Canvas, The (US) = NOIA, LA (1963)
EMPTY HANDS (1924) d/p V Fleming w Shearer 7rs FPL
EMPTY HEARTS (1924) d Santell c E Haller 6rs
EMPTY POCKETS (1917) d Brenon 6rs FN
ENAMORADA (1946) d Fernandez p/co-s Alazraki c
    Figueroa w Felix, Armendariz
EN AV DE MÅNGA (1915) d/s Sjöström 840m (= One out
    of Many)
EN BATEAU (1951) d Mitry m Débussy
EN CAS DE MALHEUR (1958) d Autant-Lara s/di
    Aurenche, Bost fn Georges Simenon w Gabin, Bardot,
    Feuillère 105min (= Love is my Profession)
Enchanted Castle at Dudinci, The = ZACARANI DVORAC
    V DUDINCIMA (1951)
ENCHANTED COTTAGE, THE (1945) d Cromwell co-s h
    Mankiewicz fpl Pinero c Tetzlaff w R Young, H
    Marshall, McGuire 91min RKO
Enchanted Desna, The = ZACHAROVANAYA DESNA
    (1965)
ENCHANTED ISLAND (1958) d Dwan p Bogeaus fn
    (Typee) Herman Melville w D Andrews, J Powell
    *87min r WB
Enchanted Walk = FORTROLLAD VANDRING (1954)
ENCHANTMENT (1948) d Reis p Goldwyn c Toland m
    Friedhofer w Niven, T Wright, F Granger 102min
    RKO
ENCLOS, L' (1960) d/co-s Gatti 106min (= The Enclosure)
Enclosure, The = ENCLOS, L' (1960)
EN COMPAGNIE DE MAX LINDER (1963) compilation:
    includes extracts from SEVEN YEARS BAD LUCK
    (1921), BE MY WIFE (1921), THE THREE
    MUST-GET-THERES (1922) 88min (= Laugh with
    Max Linder)
ENCORE (1951) d Jackson, Anthony Pelissier, Harold
    French fsts Somerset Maugham 89min
    ep THE ANT AND THE GRASSHOPPER s T Clarke
Encounter (UK) = STRANGER ON THE PROWL (1952)
Encounters at Dusk = MÖTEN I SKYMNINGEN (1957)
Encounters in the Dark = SPOTKANIA W MROKU
    (1960)
ENCYCLOPEDIE DE GRAND' MAMAN EN 13
    VOLUMES, L' (1963) d Borowczyk anim
ENCYCLOPEDIE FILMEE ARITHMETIQUE (1951) d
    Kast sh
ENDA NATT, EN (1938) d Molander w Ingrid Bergman SF
End as a Man (UK) = STRANGE ONE, THE (1957)
ENDELIG ALENE (1914) d/s Madsen
EN DER ZEE WAS NIET MEER (1956) d/pc/s/e Haanstra
    *22min (= And There was no more Sea)
Endless Desire = HATESHINAKI YOKUBO (1958)
End of a Priest = FARARUV KONEC (1969)
End of a Prolonged Journey = HANA NO NAGADOSU
    (1954)
End of Innocence (US) = CASA DEL ANGEL, LA (1957)
End of St. Petersburg, The = KONETS SANKT-
    PETERBURGA (1927)
END OF THE AFFAIR, THE (1954) d Dmytryk fn Greene
    w Kerr, J Mills, V Johnson 105min r Col
End of War Disasters = SENKA NO HATE (1950)
ENDSTATION LIEBE (1957) d Tressler w Buchholz 85min
    (= Terminus Love)
Endstation 13 Sahara = STATION 6 SAHARA (1964)
EN EFFEUILLANT LA MARGUERITE (1956) d/co-s
    M Allégret co-s Vadim co-dec Trauner m Misraki
    w Bardot, Gelin 100min (= Mamzelle Strip-
    Tease)
En el Viejo Tampico = GRAN CASINO (1947)
ENEMIES OF WOMEN, THE (1923) d Crosland fst Vicente
    Blasco-Ibáñez w L Barrymore 3200m
ENEMY, THE (1928) d/p Niblo co-s/ad Goldbeck a
    Gibbons, R Day w L Gish 2495m
ENEMY BELOW, THE (1957) d/p D Powell s Mayes c
    Rosson co-a Wheeler m Harline w Mitchum, Jurgens
    98min Fox
Enemy of the People = MINSHU NO TEKI (1946)
ENEMY SEX, THE (1924) d Cruze 2415m FPL r Par
ENERGIA ELETTRICA NELL' AGRICOLTURA, L'
    (1955) d Olmi *10min
ENERGY FIRST (1955) d L Anderson 5min
ENFANCE DE L'ART, L' (1910) d Cohl anim105m
ENFANT D'AMOUR, L' (1931) d L'Herbier w M Simon
    Gau
ENFANT DE PARIS, L' (1913) d/s Perret (4 parts) 600m
ENFANT DU CARNAVAL, L' (1921) d/s/w Mozhukhin
ENFANT SAUVAGE, L' (1970) d/co-ad/co-c Truffaut f
    (Mémoire et Rapport sur Victor de l'Aveyron) Jean
    Itard m Vivaldi w Truffaut 85min co-pc Truffaut
    (= Wild Child)
ENFANTS DE NEANT, LES (1967) co-d/c Brault co-d
    Annie Tresgot 45min
ENFANTS DU PARADIS, LES (1945) d Carné s/di J

Prevert co-dec Trauner co-m Kosma w Arletty, Bar-
    rault, Brasseur, Casarès, Modot, P Renoir 195min
    Pat (= Children of Paradise)
ENFANTS DU SILENCE, LES (1963) co-d/e/cy Jutra co-
    d/c Brault 24min
ENFANTS TERRIBLES, LES (1950) d/co-s/dec/cy Melville
    co-s/p/di Cocteau c Decaë mf Bach, Vivaldi 107min
    pc Melville
ENFER, L' (1964, uf) d Clouzot co-c C renoir, Thirard w
    Schneider, Reggiani *
Engagement, The (UK) = FIDANZATI, I (1962)
Engagement Ring = KONYAKU YUBIWA (1950)
Engineer Prite's Project = PROEKT INZHENERA
    PRAITA (1918)
ENGINEER'S WORKSHOP, AN (1896) p Paul 1·28m
ENGLISHMAN AND THE GIRL (1910) d Griffith w
    Sennett, Pickford 1rl Bio
ENGLISH SOLDIER TEARING DOWN THE BOER
    FLAG (1899) p Hepworth
ENHORNINGEN (1955) d Molander
Enigma = FRAU NACH DER MAN SICH SEHNT, DIE
    (1929)
ENIGME (1919) d/s Feuillade 4135m (= Le Mot de
    l'enigme)
ENIGME AUX FOLIES-BEGÈRE (1959) d Mitry 82min
ENIGME DE DIX HEURES, L' (1912) d/s Gance
ENIGME DU MONT AGEL, L' (1924) d/s Machin, Henri
    Wulschleger 1586m
ENJO (1958) d Ichikawa c Miyagawa S 96min Dai (= Flame
    of Torment/Conflagration)
EN LANYOM NEM OLYAN, AZ (1937) d Vajda 85min
ENLEVEMENT EN HYDROPLANE, UN (1913) d/s/w
    Linder Pat
ENLIGT LAG (1957) co-d/co-s P Weiss (= According to the
    Law)
EN LISANT LE JOURNAL (1932) d Cavalcanti
ENNEMI PUBLIC NO. 1 (1953) d Verneuil co-s Audiard c
    Thirard m Rota w Gabin, Fernandel 95min (= Public
    Enemy No. 1)
ENOCH ARDEN (1911) d Griffith fpm Alfred Lord
    Tennyson rm AFTER MANY YEARS (2 parts) 1rl
    Bio
ENOCH ARDEN (1915) d Christy Cabanne fpm Tennyson
    w L Gish, Griffith
Enough Rope (UK) = MEURTRIER, LE (1962)
EN PASSANT (1943) d Alexeieff anim 5min
EN PASSANT PAR LA LORRAINE (1950) d/s Franju c
    Fradetal m Kosma 31min
EN PLEIN CIRAGE /61/ d Lautner m Delerue w Carol
    104min
EN PLEIN MIDI (1958) d/pc Leenhardt 403m
EN RADE (1928) d/co-s/e Cavalcanti
ENSAYO DE UN CRIMEN (1955) d/co-s Bunuel 91min
    (= Criminal Life of Archibaldo de la Cruz)
ENSIGH PULVER (1964) d/p/co-s Logan c Lawton m
    Duning w Ives, Matthau PV* 104min WB
ENTENTE CORDIALE (1938) d L'Herbier m Milhaud
    110min
ENTER LAUGHING (1967) d/co-s Carl Reiner c Biroc w J
    Ferrer, Winters *112min Col
ENTER MADAM (1935) d E Nugent co-s Brackett w Grant
    83min Par
ENTERTAINER, THE (1960) d T Richardson p Saltzman
    co-s/fpl Osborne c Morris e Holt (uc) w Olivier,
    Finney 96min BL
ENTERTAINING THE BOSS (1922) d St Clair 2rs
Enthusiasm = ENTUZIAZM (1930)
ENTOTSU NO MIERU BASHO (1953) d Gosho 110min
    (= Where Chimneys are Seen/Four Chimneys)
ENTR'ACTE (1924) d/e Clair st Francis Picabia m Erik
    Satie w Picabia, Auric, Satie, Marcel Duchamp
    325m
ENTREE DES ARTISTES (1938) d M Allégret co-s/ad/di
    Jeanson co-s Cayatte c Matras dec Trauner m Auric
    w Louvet, Dalio 90min
ENTRE LA MER ET L'EAU DOUCE (1966) d/co-s/co-c
    Brault 90min (= Genevieve)
ENTRE LA TERRE ET LE CIEL (1958) d Carlos Vilardebo
    s Rappeneau m
ENTRE ONZE HEURES ET MINUIT (1948) d/co-ad
    Decoin di Jeanson c Hayer w Jouvet 92min
    (= Between Eleven o'clock and Midnight)
ENTRE SEINE ET MER (1960) d/pc Leenhardt
ENTRE TU ET VOUS (1969) d Groulx c Brault 65min
ENTREZ DANS LA DANSE (1948) d/s Leenhardt
ENTSAGUNGEN (1913) d May 1246m
ENSTEHUNG DER FARBE, DIE (1938) d/p Richter part*
    2rs
ENTUZIAZM (1930) d/s/co-e Vertov 95min (= Simfoniya
    Donbassa/Enthusiasm/Symphony of the Donbass)
EN UN LUGARDA CASTILLA (1936) d/s Velo 2rs
ENVERS DU PARADIS, L' (1953) d/s Grevil m Misraki w
    Von Stroheim 100min
EPAVE, L' (1949) d Willy Rozier w Arnoul 94min
EPAVES (1945) d/p Cousteau 30min
E PERMESSO MARESCIAL – LO? (1958) d Bragaglia

EPERVIER, L' (1933) d L'Herbier w Boyer 94min (= Bird of Prey)
EPILOG (1950) d/co-s Kautner
EPINE AU PIED, UNE (1954) d Rozier sh
Epitome = SHUKUZU (1953)
E' PIU FACILE CHE UN CAMELLO ... (1950) d Zampa s Zavattini w Gabin 98min (= Twelve Hours to Live)
Epoch of Loyalty = KINNO JIDAI (1926)
EPOUVANTAIL, L' (1943) d/st Grimault anim* 9min
E PRIMAVERA (1950) d/co-st/co-s Castellani co-st/co-s Zavattini, Cecchi d'Amico m Rota 87min (= Springtime in Italy)
Equinox Flower = HIGANBANA (1958)
EQUIPAGE, L' (1927) d M Tourneur c Burel
EQUIPAGE, L' (1935) d Litvak rm 1927 m Honnegger w Annabella, Vanel 111min Pat
ERA DI VENERDI 17 (1957) d/co-s Soldati co-s Zavattini w Fernandel
ERAKU NARU (1932) d/s Naruse (= Erroneous Practice)
ERA NOTTE A ROMA (1960) d/co-s Rossellini co-s Rondi w Bondarchuk 120min
ERCOLE AL CENTRO DELLA TERRA (1961) d/co-s/c Bava S* 83min (= Hercules in the Centre of the Earth)
ERCOLE ALLA CONQUISTA DI ATLANTIDE (1961) d Cottafavi TR* 104min (= Hercules Conquers Atlantis)
ERCOLE E LA REGINA DI LIDIA (1959) d/co-s Pietro Francisci c Bara w Reeves FS* 105min (= Hercules Unchained)
Eredita Contesa, L' = ASTUTO BARONE, L' (1948)
ER I BANGE (1971) d/p/co-s Carlsen 94min
Erik the Conqueror = INVASORI, GLI (1961)
Erik the Great = LAST PERFORMANCE, THE (1929)
Erik the Great Illusionist = LAST PERFORMANCE, THE (1929)
ERNIE GAME, THE (1967) d/s Owen *86min NFBC
EROE DI NOSTRI TEMPI, UN (1955) d/co-st Monicelli w Sordi, Lattuada
EROE SONO IO, L' (1952) d Bragaglia 89min (= I'm the Hero)
EROGAMI NO ONRYO (1930) d Ozu Sho (= The Revengeful Spirit of Eros)
EROICA (1957) d Munk 87min
EROICA (1960) d/p/co-s Cacoyannis c Lassally 121min WB (= Our Last Spring)
EROI D'ARTIDE, GLI (1954) supn Emmer *
EROI DELLA DOMENICA, GLI (1953) d/co-st/co-s Camerini co-s Risi c Bava w Vallone, Mastroianni
EROI DEL WEST, GLI (1964) d/co-s Steno *
EROS, O BASILEUS (1967) d/s/c/e Markopoulos 16mm *45min
EROTIKON (1920) d/co-s Stiller co-s Molander
EROTIKON (1929) d/s Machaty
ERRAND BOY, THE (1961) d/co-s/w J Lewis co-a Pereira 92min pc J Lewis r Par
ERREUR TRAGIQUE (1913) d/s Feuillade 530m
Erroneous Practice = ERAKU NARU (1932)
Ersatz = SUROGAT (1961)
ERSTE KUSS, DER (1928) d Carl Lamac c Heller 2490m
ERSTE LIEBE (1970) d/co-p/co-s Maximilian Schell fst Turgenev c Nykvist w Maximilian Schell, Cortese, Osborne *92min
ERUPTION DE L'ETNA, L' (pre- 1952) d Tazieff 16mm
ERUPTION VOLCANIQUE A LA MARTINIQUE (1902) d Méliès 30m
ESA PAREJA FELIZ (1951 r 1953) d/s Berlanga, Bardem
ESCALA EN LA CIUDAD (1936) d Saslavsky
ESCALE (1959) d Bourguignon m Delerue *18min
ESCALE AU SOLEIL (1946) d/s Verneuil w Fernandel 26min
ESCAMOTAGE D'UNE DAME CHEZ ROBERT HOUDIN (1896) d Méliès 20m
ESCAPADE (1932) d Thorpe 67min
ESCAPADE (1935) d/co-p Leonard s H Mankiewicz c E Haller w W Powell, Rainer 87min MGM
ESCAPADE (1955) d P Leacock w J Mills 87min
ESCAPE, THE (1914) d Griffith w Marsh, Crisp 7rs Mut
ESCAPE (1938) d Joannon
ESCAPE (1940) d/co-s LeRoy co-s Oboler a Gibbons m Waxman w Shearer, R Taylor, Veidt, Nazimova 104min MGM (= When the Door Opened)
ESCAPE (1948) d J Mankiewicz p Perlberg s P Dunne fpl Galsworthy c F Young m Alwyn w Harrison 78min Fox
ESCAPE EPISODE (1944) (ur) d/s/c/e Anger si 35min
ESCAPE EPISODE (1946) d/s/c/e Anger rm 1944 m Scriabin 27min
ESCAPE FROM EAST BERLIN (1962) d Siodmak co-p/w Murray (= Tunnel 28)
ESCAPE FROM FORT BRAVO (1953) d J Sturges c Surtees co-a Gibbons w Parker, Holden *98min MGM
ESCAPE FROM SAN QUENTIN (1957) d Sears p Katzman 81min Col
ESCAPE FROM ZAHRAIN (1961) d/p Neame w Brynner, Mason PV* 89min Par
ESCAPE IN THE FOG (1945) d Boetticher 63min Col
ESCAPE ME NEVER (1935) d Czinner e Lean m Walton w Bergner 91min

ESCAPE OF JIM DOLAN, THE (1913) s/w Mix Sel
ESCAPE ROUTE (1967) d Holt w Lynley 92min r UA (= Danger Route)
ESCAPE TO BURMA (1955) d Dwan p Bogeaus c J Alton w Ryan, Stanwyck S* 87min r RKO
ESCAPE TO GLORY (1940) d Brahm w Constance Bennett 73min Col (= Submarine Zone)
ESCARPINS DE MAX, LES (1913) d/s/w Linder Pat
ESCLAVE, L' (1953) d Ciampi m Auric w Gélin, Rossi-Drago 99min Pat
ES GESCHAH AM HELLICHTEN TAGE (1958) d/co-s Vajda fpl Friedrich Dürrenmatt w M Simon
ES GESCHAH AM 20 JULI (1955) d Pabst co-s Machaty w Wicki 87min
ESKADRILYA N. 5 (1939) d Room 2456m (= Five Squadron)
ESKIMO (1934) d WS Van Dyke s Mahin 117min MGM (= Der Eskimo/Flucht ins Weisse Land)
ESKIMO VILLAGE (1934) d Anstey
ESPAGNE 39 (1937) d Le Chanois supn Bunuel
ESPANA LEAL EN ARMAS (MADRID 36) (1937) co-d Bunuel
ESPION, L' (1966) d/p/co-s/co-d Raoul Lévy c Coutard w Clift, Godard *100min (= The Defector)
ESPIONAGE AGENT (1939) d Bacon w McCrea 84min WB
ESPIONS, LES (1957) d/co-s Clouzot c Matras m Auric w Jurgens, Ustinov 135min
ESPOIR, L' (1939 r 1945) d/s Malraux m Milhaud 90min (= Sierra de Teruel)
ESPONTANEO, EL (1963) d/co-st/co-s Grau 92min
ESSAI DE SIMULATION DE DELIRE CINEMATOGRAPHIQUE (1935) d Man Ray, André Breton, Paul Eluard
ESTATE VIOLENTA (1959) d/co-s Zurlini w Trintignant, Rossi-Drago 105min
ESTERINA (1959) d Lizzani 90min (= L'Herbe Folle)
ESTHER AND THE KING (1960) d/p/co-s Walsh c Bava f The Book of Esther CS* 110min r Fox (= Esther e il Re)
Esther e il re (1960) = ESTHER AND THE KING
Estrellados: Spanish version of FREE AND EASY (1930)
ES WERDE LICHT! (1917-18)
  Part 1 (1917) d/p R Oswald s R Oswald, Lupu-Pick st/w Lupu-Pick 1777m
  Part 2 (1918) d/p R Oswald s R Oswald, Dupont
  Part 3 (1918) d R Oswald w Krauss 5rs
ETA DEL FERRO, L' (1964) d Renzo Rossellini Jr. s Rossellini 300min
ETALON, L' (1969) d/co-s/w Mocky w Bourvil *90min (= The Stud)
Etang Tragique, L' = SWAMP WATER (1941)
ET DIEU CREA LA FEMME (1956) d/co-s Vadim c Thirard m Misraki w Bardot, Jurgens, Marquand, Trintignant CS* 90min (= And Woman was Created/And God Created Woman)
ETE INDIEN, L' (1957) d Reichenbach S*
ETERNAL FLAME, THE (1922) d F Lloyd fn (La Duchesse de Langeais) Balzac c Gaudio w N Talmadge, Menjou 8rs
Eternal Generation, The = ONNA NO SONO (1954)
ETERNAL LOVE (1929) d Lubitsch e Marton m Reisenfeld w J Barrymore 6374ft r UA
Eternal Love (UK) = ETERNEL RETOUR, L' (1943)
ETERNALLY YOURS (1939) d Garnett p Wanger w L Young, Niven, B Crawford, Pitts r UA
ETERNAL PRAGUE (1941) d J Weiss 9min
Eternal Rainbow, The = KONO TEN NO NIJI (1958)
ETERNAL SIN (1917) d Brenon Gau
ETERNAL THREE, THE (1923) d Neilan, Frank Urson st Neilan 6854ft pc Goldwyn
ETERNEL RETOUR, L' (1943) d Delannoy st/s/di Cocteau dec Wakhévitch m Auric w Marais 111min (= Eternal Love)
ETE SAUVAGE, UN (1970) d/co-s Camus w Paxinou *90min
ETES-VOUS FIANCEE A UN MARIN GREC OU A UNE PILOTE DE LIGNE (1970) d/co-s Aurel c Coutard 100min
ET MOURIR DE PLAISIR (1960) d/co-s Vadim c C Renoir w M Ferrer, M Allégret, Martinelli TR* 84min (= Blood and Roses)
ETOILE DE MER, L' (1928) d/p/c Man Ray fmp Robert Desnos 15min
ETOILE DE MER, L' (1959) d Bourguignon m Delerue *21min Pat
ETOILES DE MIDI, LES (1919) d/co-s/co-di Ichac m Jarre *78min
ETRANGE MADAME X, L' (1950) d Grémillon w Morgan 2750m
ETRANGE MONSIEUR VICTOR, L' (1938) d Grémillon ad/co-di Charles Spaak co-di Achard w Raimu, Romance 102min
ETROITS SONT LES VAISSEAUX (1962) d Gruel, Laure Garcin fpm Saint John Perse anim 11min
ETSURAKU (1965) d Oshima 96min pc Oshima r Sho (= The Pleasures of the Flesh)
ETTORE FIERAMOSCA (1939) d/co-st/co-s/co-e Blasetti
ETUDE CINEMATOGRAPHIQUE SUR UNE ARABESQUE (1928) d Dulac sh

ETUDE DE MOUVEMENTS (1928) d/s/c/e Ivens 200m
ETUDIANTE D'AUJOURD'HUI, UNE (1966) d/s/e Rohmer 16mm 13min
EUGENIA GRANDET (1946) d/co-s Soldati fn Balzac
EUREKA STOCKADE (1949) d/s Watt p Balcon w Finch 103min
EUROPA DI NOTTE (1958-59) d/co-s Blasetti *100min (= European Nights)
EUROPA '51 (1952) d/st/co-s Rossellini p Ponti, De Laurentiis co-s Pietrangeli, Rondi c Tonti w Ingrid Bergman, Masina 110min
EUROPA-POSTLAGERND (1918) d/s Dupont
EUROPA RADIO (1931) d Richter p Philips-Radio 1rl
European Nights (UK) = EUROPA DI NOTTE (1958-59)
Eva = EVE (1962)
EVA (1962) d/co-s Molander st/co-s Ingmar Bergman w Dahlbeck 84min
EVACUATION (1939) d B Wright
EVADÉE, L' (1929) co-d Burel
EVADES, LES (1954) d/co-ad/co-di Le Chanois m Kosma w Fresnay 100min
EVANGELIEMANDENSLIV (1914) d/s Madsen
EVANGELIMANN, DER (1925) d/s/w Madsen
EVANGELINE (1919) d/s Walsh fpm Henry W Longfellow w Wellman 5rs Fox
Evangeline et le Tonnerre = TONNERRE, LE (1921)
Eva Plays the Fool = EVA TROPI HLOUPOSTI (1939)
Eva Sconosciuta = DONNA DEL MONDO, LA (1962)
EVA TROPI HLOUPOSTI (1939) d Fric (= Eva Plays the Fool)
EVE (1962) d Losey co-s H Butler fn James Hadley Chase c Di Venanzo co-a R MacDonald m Legrand w Moreau, S Baker, (Losey, De Sica) 118min (= Eva)
EVELYN PRENTICE (1934) d W Howard c C Clarke w W Powell, R Russell, M Loy 80min MGM
EVENING WITH THE ROYAL BALLET, AN (1963) d Asquith, Anthony Havelock Allan c Unsworth, Challis 16mm 85min
E VENNE UN UOMO (1964) d/co-s Olmi w Steiger *90min co-pc Saltzman (= A Man Named John/And There Came a Man)
EVENSONG (1934) d Saville w Emlyn Williams 87min Gau
Event, The = DOGADAJ (1969)
EVE OF ST. MARK, THE (1944) d Stahl s Seaton fpl Maxwell Anderson w A Baxter, Price 96min Fox
EVER CHANGING MOTOR CAR, THE (1962) d Dunning, Alan Ball p Dunning co-st/anim R Williams 11min
EVERGREEN (1934) d Saville ad/di Emlyn Williams 90min
EVER IN MY HEART (1933) d A Mayo w Stanwyck 68min WB
EVER SINCE EVE (1934) d G Marshall c AC Miller w G O'Brien 72min Fox
EVER SINCE EVE (1937) d Bacon w Davies, R Montgomery, Fazenda 80min WB
EVERYBODY DOES IT (1949) d Goulding s N Johnson fst James M Cain co-m A Newman w Darnell, C Coburn, P Douglas 98min Fox
Everybody Go Home (US) = TUTTI A CASA (1960)
Everybody in Love (US) = TUTTI INAMORATI (1959)
EVERYBODY'S ACTING (1926) d/st Neilan 6139ft FPL
EVERYBODY'S BABY (1938) d St Clair 62min Fox
EVERYBODY SING (1938) d Edwin L Marin co-m Kaper w Garland 80min
EVERYDAY (1929) d/p/s Richter w Eisenstein, Lye 30min
Everyday Chronicle = MALA KRONIKA (1962)
Everyday Courage = KAZDY DEN ODVAHU (1964)
EVERY DAY EXCEPT CHRISTMAS (1957) d L Anderson co-p Reisz c Lassally 40min
Every Day's a Holiday (US) = CABRIOLA (1965)
EVERY HOME SHOULD HAVE ONE (1970) d/p/co-anim/co-des R Williams anim* 7min
Every Man's Woman (UK) = ROSA PER TUTTI, UNA (1965)
Every Minute Counts (UK) = COUNT THE HOURS (1953)
EVERY MOTHER'S SON (1918) d/s Walsh 5rs Fox
EVERY NIGHT AT EIGHT (1935) d Walsh p Wagner w Raft, Faye 80min Par
Everynight Dreams = YOGOTO NO YUME (1933)
EVERY SUNDAY (1936) d Felix E Feist w Garland, Durbin 1rl MGM
EVERY SUNDAY AFTERNOON (1936) d Felix E Feist w Garland, Durbin 1rl MGM
Everything Ends Tonight = DNES VECER VSECHNO SKONCI (1955)
Everything for Sale = WSZYSTKO NA SPRZEDAZ (1968)
EVERYTHING I HAVE IS YOURS (1952) d Leonard p/st/s Wells co-a Gibbons w G Champion * 92min MGM
Everything Revolves, Everything Moves! = ALLES DRECHT SICH, ALLES BEWEGT SICH! (1929)
EVERYTHING'S ROSIE (1931) d Bruckman c Musuraca 67min RKO
Everything That Lives = IKITOSHI IKERUMONO (1934)
EVES FUTURES (1966) d Baratier 20min
EVE'S LOVER (1925) d Del Ruth ad Zanuck w Bow 6010ft WB
Evil Eden = MORT EN CE JARDIN, LA (1956)
Evil Eye, The (UK) = RAGAZZA CHE SAPEVA TROPPO, LA (1962)

EVIL OF FRANKENSTEIN. THE (1963) d F Francis 84min JAR
Evil that is Eve, The = MANCHE ET LA BELLE, UNE (1957)
Evils of Chinatown (UK) = CONFESSIONS OF AN OPIUM EATER (1962)
EVIL WOMEN DO, THE (1916) d Julian 5rs
EVOCATION (1938) d Ciampi sh
EVOLUTION (1923) co-d M Fleischer 6rs
EVOLUTION DE L'OEUF D'EPINOCHE (GASTRO-TEUS ACULEATUS) DE LA FECONDATION A L'ECLOSION (1925) d/c Painlevé
EVOLUTION D'UN GRAIN D'ARGENT DANS UNE EMULSION PHOTOGRAPHIQUE (1933) d Painlevé
EVOLUTION GEOLOGIQUE DE LA CHAINE DES ALPES, L' (1936) d Painlevé *
EWAG LUDZIE Z SZASA (1959) d/s Polanski m Komeda sh (= *Two Men and a Wardrobe*)
EWIGE KLANG, DER (1943) d/co-s Rittau 87min (= *Der Geiger*)
EWIGE TRAUM, DER (1934) d/s Fanck 85min UFA (= *Der König des Mont-Blanc*)
EXCELSIOR! (1901) d Méliès 40m
EXCESS BAGGAGE (1928) d/p Cruze 8rs MGM
EXCLUSIVE STORY (1936) d G Seitz 73min MGM
EX-CONVICT, THE (1904) d Porter 293ft Ed
EXCURSION HOUSE (1954) d W Van Dyke n Meredith 60min (2 parts)
EXCUSE MY DUST (1920) d S Wood 5rs
EXCUSE MY DUST (1951) d Rowland p Conway st/s Wells co-a Gibbons *82min MGM
EXECUTION D'UN ESPION (1897) d Méliès 20m
Executioner, The = VERDUGO, EL (1963)
EXECUTIVE SUITE (1954) d Wise p Houseman s Lehman c Folsey co-a Gibbons w Holden, Allyson, Stanwyck, March, Winters, P Douglas 104min MGM
Exhumation of the Remains of Sergei Radonezhkovo, The = VSKRYTIE MOSHCHEI SERGIYA RADONEZHSKOVO (1920)
EXILE, THE (1948) d/co-s(uc) Ophuls p/co-s Fairbanks Jr c Planer w Fairbanks Jr, Montez 92min U
EX-LADY (1933) d Florey c Gaudio w B Davis 65min WB
EXODUS (1960) d/p Preminger s Trumbo fn Leon Uris c Leavitt a R Day cr Bass m Gold w P Newman, Saint, R Richardson, Lawford, Cobb, Derek, Ratoff PV70* 212min r UA
EXPANDING AIRPORT, THE (1958) d/s C and R Eames c C Eames *10min
Expedition = ABHIJAN (1962)
EXPERIMENT (1943) d Fric
Experiment in Evil = TESTAMENT DU DOCTEUR CORDELIER, LE (1961)
EXPERIMENT IN TERROR (1962) d/p Edwards c Lathrop m Mancini w G Ford, Remick 122min Col (= *Grip of Fear*)
EXPERIMENT PERILOUS (1944) d J Tourneur c Gaudio w Lamarr, Lukas 91min RKO
EXPERT, THE (1932) d A Mayo 68min WB
EXPLOITS OF ELAINE, THE (1915) co-d Arthur B Reeve, CW Goddard w White (serial in 14 eps) Pat
EXPLORATION DU LAC DE LAVE DU NIRAGONGO (1959) d/p Tazieff
Explosion Course = BAKUSO (1967)
EXPLOSION DE LA POPULATION (1967) d Hebert anim
EXPLOSION OF A MOTOR CAR, THE (1900) p Hepworth 100ft
EXPLOSIVE GENERATION, THE (1961) d Kulik c F Crosby 89min r UA
EXPRESS TRAINS (IN A RAILWAY CUTTING) (1898) p Hepworth 50ft
Expulsion (UK) = AUSTREIBUNG, DIE (1923)
EXQUISITE SINNER, THE (1926) d/co-s Von Sternberg w Adoré 5977ft MGM
EXQUISITE THIEF, THE (1919) d Browning 6rs U
EXTASE (1933) d/co-s Machaty w Lamarr (as Kiesler) 81min (= *Ecstasy*)
Exterminating Angel, The = ANGEL EXTERMINADOR, EL (1962)
EXTRA! EXTRA! (1922) d W Howard p Fox 4160ft Fox
EXTRA GIRL, THE (1923) d Richard Jones st Sennett w Normand 6rs
Extraordinary Adventures of Mr. West in the Land of the Bolsheviks, the = NEOBYCHAINIYEPRIKLUCHENIYA MISTERA VESTA V STRANYE BOLSHEVIKOV (1924)
EXTRAORDINARY, CHILD, THE (1954) d Brakhage, Larry Jordan 16mm si 10min
EXTRAORDINARY SEAMAN, THE (1967 R 1969) d Frankenheimer c Lindon m Jarre w Niven, Dunaway, Rooney PV* 80min MGM
Eye for an Eye, An = OEIL POUR OEIL (1956)
EYE FOR EYE (1918) d/co-ad Albert Capellani co-ad Mathis p/w Nazimova 7rs MGM
EYE OF THE DEVIL (1966) d J Thompson w Niven, Kerr, Pleasance 90min MGM
EYES (1970) d Brakhage 16mm* si
Eyes, The Sea and a Ball = NATSUKASHIKI FUEYA TAIKO (1967)

EYES IN THE NIGHT (1942) d Zinnemann w D Reed 80min MGM
EYES OF MYSTERY, THE (1918) d Browning 5rs Metro
Eyes of the Mummy Ma, The = AUGEN DER MUMIE MA, DIE (1918)
EYES OF THE WORLD, THE (1930) d/p H King 80min r UA
Eyes Without a Face (UK) = YEUX SANS VISAGE, LES (1959)
EYEWASH (1958–59) d Breer 16mm * part anim si 3min
EYE WITNESS (1950) d R Montgomery co-st/co-s H Butler m M Arnold w R Montgomery 104min EL

FABIOLA (1918) d Guazzoni
FABIOLA (1949) d Blasetti co-s Pietrangeli, Zavattini, Cecchi D'Amico w Girotti, Morgan, Ferzetti, M Simon 97min
FABLE OF ELVIRA AND FARINA AND THE MEAL TICKET, THE (1915) d George Ade w Swanson 1rl S & A
FABLE OF THE FABRICS (1942) d Mackendrick sh
FABRIK DER OFFIZIERE (1960) d Wisbar 97min
FABULEUSE AVENTURE DE MARCO POLO, LA (1964) d Christian-Jacque, De la Patellière, Noel Howard co-s/co-ad De la Patellière co-ad Rappeneau c Thirard a Saulnier w Bucholz, Quinn, Tamiroff, Hossein, Sharif, Martinelli, Welles, Girotti S* 115min (= *L'Echiquier de Dieu/The Fabulous Adventures of Marco Polo*)
Fabulous Adventures of Marco Polo, The (UK) = FABULEUSE AVENTURE DE MARCO POLO, LA (1964)
FABULOUS FIFTIES (1960) co-d C Eames TV
FACE (1965) d Warhol 16mm 70min
Face, The = KAO (1965)
Face, The = ANSIKTET (1958)
FACE AT THE WINDOW, THE (1910) d Griffith w Pickford, Irl Bio
FACE BEHIND THE MASK, THE (1941) d Florey c Planer w Lorre 69min
FACE IN THE CROWD, A (1967) d/p Kazan s/fst (*Your Arkansas Traveller*) B Schulberg w Neal, Matthau, Remick, Neilan 126min r WB
FACE IN THE RAIN, A (1963) d Kershner co-ad H Butler c Wexler 81min r Fox
Face of Another, The = TANIN NO KAO (1965)
FACE OF A FUGITIVE (1959) d Wendkos w MacMurray, J Coburn 81min Col
Face of a Murderer, The = SATSUJINSHA NO KAO (1950)
FACE OF BRITAIN, THE (1935) d Rotha 18min
FACE OF SCOTLAND, THE (1938) d B Wright p Grierson 20min
Face of the Cat, The = CHATTE, LA (1958)
Face of the Medusa = PROSOPO TES MEDOUSAS, TO (1967)
FACE ON THE BAR ROOM FLOOR, THE (1914) d/s/w Chaplin 1rl (= *The Ham Artist*)
FACE ON THE BAR ROOM FLOOR, THE (1923) d J Ford 1763m Fox
FACES (1968) d/s Cassavetes 130min
Faces in the Shadows = ANSIKTEN I SKUGGA (1956)
Face That Launched a Thousand Ships, The = AMANTE DI PARIDE, L' (1954)
FACE THE MUSIC (1954) d Fisher 84min
FACE TO FACE (1952) 90min RKO
ep THE SECRET SHARER d Brahm fn Joseph Conrad c Struss m Friedhofer w Mason
ep THE BRIDE COMES TO YELLOW SKY d Windust s Agee fn Stephen Crane w Preston, Agee
FACE VALUE (1917) d/co-st Leonard 5rs
FACE VALUE (1927) d Florey 1339m
FACIAL EXPRESSIONS (1902) p Paul 18m
Facing the Wind = VETER V LITSO (1930)
FACTEUR S'EN VA-T-EN GUERRE, LE (1966) d Bernard-Aubert w Aznavour S* 95min
FACTEUR TROP FERRE, UN (1907) d L Feuillade 165m
FACTS OF LIFE, THE (1960) d/co-s M Frank p/co-s Panama c C Lang cr Bass m Harline w Hope, Ball 103min pc Panama, M Frank r UA
FADA, LA (1932) d Burel
FADERN (1969) d/s Sjöberg w Lindblom 106min TV (= *The Father*)
FADER OG SON (1911) d Blom
FADNI ODPOLEDNE (1916) d/co-s Passer co-s/fst Bohumil Hrabal 14min (= *A Boring Afternoon*)
FAGYOSSZENLEK (1962) d Révész 77min (= *Hail Days*)
FAHRENDES VOLK (1938) d/co-s Feyder dec D'Eaubonne w Rosay 107min Tob (= *Les Gens Du Voyage*)
FAHRENHEIT 451 (1966) d/co-s Truffaut co-s Richard fn Bradbury c Roeg m Herrmann w Werner, Christie *112min U
FAIBLES FEMMES (1958) d/co-s Michel Boisrond p Graetz m Misraki w Delon *100min (= *Women are Weak*)
FAI IN FRETTA AD UCCIDERMI ... HO FREDDO! (1966) d/co-s Maselli w Vitti (= *Kill me Quick, I'm Cold*)

FAIL SAFE (1963) d Lumet w H Fonda, Matthau 112min Col
FAIM DU MONDE, LA (1958) d/p Grimault s J Prévert anim
FAIR CO-ED, THE (1927) d S Wood c J Seitz co-a Gibbons w Davies 1952m
Fair Exchange, A = GETTING ACQUAINTED (1914)
Fairies, The (UK) = FATE, LE (1966)
FAIR WARNING (1937) d/s Foster w Payne 68min Fox
Faiseurs De Pluie, Ees = HOMMES QUI FONT LA PLUIE, LES (1951)
FAISONS UN REVE (1936) d/s/fpl Guitry w Guitry, Rainer, (Arletty, M Simon) 86min
FAIT DIVERS (1923) d Autant-Lara m Honegger w Artaud
FAITES-MOI CONFIANCE (1953) d Grangier 85min
FAITHFUL HEART, THE (1932) d Saville w H Marshall 83min
FAITHLESS (1932) d Harry Beaumont w Bankhead, Montgomery 76min MGM
FAITS DIVERS A PARIS (1950) d/p Kirsanov c Fradetal 84min
FAJA LOBBI (1960) d/p Van Der Horst *70min (= *Symphony of the Tropics/Fiery Love*)
Faking with Society = CAUGHT IN A CABARET (1914)
FAKIR, MYSTERE INDIEN, LE (1896) d Méliès 20m
FALBALAS (1945) d/co-s Becker c Hayer w Rouleau, Presle 95min
FALCO D'ORO, IL (1956) d Bragaglia
FALCON AND THE CO-EDS, THE (1943) d William Clemens w Malone (as Maloney) 68min RKO
FALCON IN HOLLYWOOD, THE (1944) d G Douglas c Musuraca 67min RKO
FALCON IN SAN FRANCISCO, THE (1945) d JH Lewis 66min RKO
FALCON STRIKES BACK, THE (1945) d Dmytryk 66min RKO
FALCON TAKES OVER THE (1942) d Reis fn (*Farewell My Lovely*) R Chandler w G Sanders 63min RKO
FALCO ROSSO, IL (1950) d Bragaglia 88min
FALENA, LA (1916) d Gallone
Falkentraum, Der Sequence in Part 1 of NIBELUNGEN, DIE (1924)
Fall, The (US) = CAIDA, LA (1959)
FALLEN ANGEL (1945) d/p Preminger c La Shelle co-a Wheeler m Raksin w D Andrews, Faye, Darnell, Bickford, Carradine 97min Fox
FALLEN IDOL, THE (1948) d C Reed st/s (*The Basement Room*) Greene c Périnal dec V Korda m Alwyn w Morgan, R Richardson, Hawkins 94min
Fallen Woman, A = DARAKU SURU ONNA (1967)
Fall In! = NASTUP (1952)
FALLING FOR YOU (1933) d Stevenson, Jack Hulbert s Gilliat 78min
FALL MOLANDER, DER (1944) d Pabst
Fall of Berlin, The = PADENIE BERLINA (1949)
Fall of Rome, The (US) = SOLO CONTRO ROMA (1966)
Fall of the House of Usher, The (UK) = CHUTE DE LA MAISON USHER, LA (1928)
FALL OF THE HOUSE OF USHER, THE (1960) d/p Corman s Matheson fst Poe c F Crosby a D Haller w Price CS* 79min (= *The House of Usher*)
Fall of the Romanov Dynasty = PADENE DINASTI ROMAVOUIKH (1927)
FALL OF THE ROMAN EMPIRE, THE (1964) d A Mann 2nd d Canutt, Marton p Bronston co-s Barzman, Yordan c Krasker m Tiomkin w Loren, Boyd, Guinness, Mason, Plummer, M Ferrer, Sharif PV* 185min JAR
FALL OF THE ROMANOFFS, THE (1917) d Brenon
FALL ROSENTOFF, DER (1918) d/w Lubitsch 1rl (= *The Rosentopf Case*)
FALSARI, I (1950) d/co-s Rossi w Ferzetti
FALSCHE GEWICHT, DAS (1971) d/co-s Wicki *150min
FALSE FACES (1932) d/p L Sherman c McCord w L Sherman
False Passport, The = VIZA NA ZLOTO (1958)
FALSE ROAD, THE (1920) d Niblo 6rs
False Alarm = TRADGARDSMASTAREN (1912)
Falstaff (US) = CAMPANADAS A MEDIANOCHE (1966)
Fame = SLAVA (1958)
FAME IS THE SPUR (1947) d R Boulting co-p J Boulting co-p Del Giudice fn Howard Spring c Krampf w M Redgrave 116min
FAMIGLIA IMPOSSIBILE, UNA (1940) d Bragaglia
FAMILIE BENTHIN (1950) co-d/co-s Dudow co-d Kurt Matzig 2684m Defa
FAMILJENS HEMLIGHET (1936) d Molander SF
FAMILY AFFAIR, A (1937) d G Seitz w L Barrymore, Rooney 69min MGM
Family Diary = CRONACA FAMILIARE (1962)
FAMILY HONOUR, THE (1920) d/p K Vidor 1350m r FN
FAMILY JEWELS, THE (1965) d/c/co-s J Lewis co-a Pereira w J Lewis, A Baxter *100min Par
FAMILY MIXUP, A (1912) d/p Sennett w Sennett, Normand ½rl Key
FAMILY PORTRAIT (1950) d/s Jennings 24min
FAMILY WAY, THE (1966) d R Boulting m McCartney w H Mills, J Mills *114min BL

FAMOUS FERGUSON CASE (1932) d Bacon w Blondell 70min WB
FAMOUS MRS FAIR, THE (1923) d Niblo 6100ft
FAN, THE (1949) d/p Preminger co-s *Dorothy Parker fpl* (*Lady Windermere's Fan*) *Oscar Wilde* c La Shelle co-a Wheeler m Amfitheatrof w Crain, Carroll, G Sanders 79min Fox (= *Lady Windermere's Fan*)
FANATIC (1964) d *Silvio Narizzano* w Bankhead *96min r Col (= *Die! Die! My Darling*)
FANCHON THE CRICKET (1915) w Pickford, Astaire 1rl
FANCY PANTS (1950) d G Marshall co-a Dreier c C Lang w Hope, Ball 92min Par
FANFAN LA TULIPE (1951) d/co-s Christian-Jacque c Matras co-s Jeanson co-m Van Parys w Philipe, Lollobrigida 102min
FANFARE (1958) d/co-s/co-e Haanstra 93min
Fanfare for Figleaves = IT STARTED IN PARADISE (1952)
FANGELSE (1949) d/s Ingemar Bergman c Strindberg w Ekman 80min (= *The Devil's Wanton/Prison*)
FANGE NR 1 (1935) d/st Fejos
FANGE NR 113 (1916) d/s Madsen
FANNY (1932) d M Allégret p/fst Pagnol w Rainer, Fresnay 120min
FANNY (1961) p/d Logan c Cardiff s JJ Epstein *fco-pl* Logan *fs* (*Marius/Caeser/Fanny*) Pagnol w Boyer, Chevalier, Caron 133min WB
FANNY BY GASLIGHT (1944) d Asquith w Mason, S Granger 108min BL (= *Man of Evil*)
FANTASIA (1940) p Disney m *Bach* (*Toccata & fugue in D minor*), *Tchaikovsky* (*Nutcracker Suite*), *Dukas* (*Sorcerer's Apprentice*), Stravinsky (*Rite of Spring*), *Moussorgsky* (*Night on the Bald Mountain*), *Beethoven* (*Pastoral Symphony*), *Ponchelli* (*Dance of the Hours*), *Schubert* (*Ave Maria*) *120min
FANTASIA SOTTOMARINA (1939) d Rossellini sh
FANTASMAGORIE (1908) d Cohl 36m anim
FANTASMI A ROMA (1961) d/co-s Pietranngeli c Rotunno co-des *Chiari* m Rota w Mastroianni, Gassman *101min
FANTASMI DEL MARE (1948) d De Robertis co-s Cottafavi, De Santis 102min
Fantastic Night = NUIT FANTASTIQUE, LA (1942)
Fantastic Tale of Naruto, A = NARUTO HICHO (1957)
FANTASTIC VOYAGE (1966) d R Fleischer c Laszlo m Rosenman w Boyd, Welch, O'Brien, A Kennedy CS* 100min Fox
FANTOMAS (1913) d/s Feuillade 1: Le Vol du Royal-Palace Hôtel 2: La Disparition de Lord Beltham 3: Autour de l'echafaud 1146m
Fantomas II = JUVE CONTRE FANTOMAS (1913)
Fantomas III = MORT QUI TUE, LE (1913)
Fantomas IV = FANTOMAS CONTRE FANTOMAS (1914)
Fantomas V = FAUX MAGISTRAT, LE (1914)
FANTOMAS (1931) d/s Fejos w Modot
FANTOMAS CONTRE FANTOMAS (1914) d/s Feuillade 1: Fantômas et l' opinion publique; 2: Le Mur qui saigne; 3: Fantômas contre Fantômas; 4: Règlement de comptes 1274m (= *Fantômas, IV*)
Fantôme A Vendre (France) = GHOST GOES WEST, THE (1935)
FANTOME DU MOULIN ROUGE, LE (1925) d/s Clair w Préjean 90min
FARAON (1965) d/co-s Kawalerowicz CS* 183min (= *Pharaoh*)
FARARUV KONEC (1969) d/co-s Schorm 95min (= *End of a Priest*)
FAR CALL, THE (1929) d Dwan co-s S Miller c Rosson w (R Scott) 59min Fox
FARCEUR, LE (1960) d/co-s De Broca dec Saulnier m Delerue w Cassell, Aimée 90min pc Chabrol (= *The Joker*)
FAR COUNTRY, THE (1954) d A Mann p A Rosenberg s B Chase c Daniels co-a Golitzen w J Stewart, Roman, Brennan, McIntire 97min * U
Farewells = POZENGNANIA (1958)
Farewell My Lovely = MURDER MY SWEET (1945)
FAREWELL TO ARMS, A (1933) d Borzage *fn* Hemingway c C Lang w G Cooper, H Hayes, Menjou 78min Par
FAREWELL TO ARMS, A (1957) d C Vidor *2nd d* Marton p Selznick s B Hecht *fn* Hemingway co-c Morris w Hudson, J Jones, De Sica, Sordi CS* 152min Fox
FAREWELL TO CHILDHOOD (1950) d Peries, *Hereward Janez 16mm* 14min
Farewell to Dreams = YUAKE-KUMO (1956)
Farewell to the Devil = POGEGNANIE Z DIABLEM (1957)
FAR FROM THE MADDING CROWD (1967) d J Schlesinger c Roeg *fn Thomas Hardy* des R Macdonald m *Richard Rodney Bennett* w Christie, Stamp, Finch PV 70* 168min
Far From Vietnam = LOIN DU VIETNAM (1967)
FARHMANN MARIA (1936) d/co-s Wisbar 2285m
FAR HORIZON, THE (1955) d Maté c Fapp co-s Pereira w MacMurray, Heston, D Reed Par VV* 108min
FAR JAG LANA DIN FRU? (1959) d Mattson c Nykvist 104min (= *May I Borrow your Wife?*)
FARLIGE ADLER, DEN (1913) d/s Blom
Farlig Pant, En = MASTERMAN (1910)
FARLIG VAR (1948) d Mattson s Lindstrom w Sjöstöm
FARM CALENDAR (1955) d/s/cy Kroitor co-c Koenig 16mm 44min NFBC
FARMER AUS TEXAS, DER (1925) d/p/co-s May dec Leni 2540m
FARMER, FEAST OR FAMINE, THE (1965) d W Van Dyke, *Roger Barlow* 30min
FARMER'S DAUGHTER, THE (1947) d Potter p Schary c Krasner m Harline w L Young, Cotten, E Barrymore, Bickford 97min RKO
FARMER'S WIFE, THE (1928) d/ad Hitchcock 67min
FARMER'S WIFE, THE (1941) d L Arness, Norman Lee Pat 82min
FARMER TAKES A WIFE, THE (1935) d V Fleming s H Mankiewicz co-m Kaper w J Gaynor, H Fonda, Bickford
FARMER TAKES A WIFE, THE (1953) d Levin co-a Wheeler c Arling w Grable, Ritter *81min Fox
FARREBIQUE (1946) d/s Rouquier
FASCINATING YOUTH (1926) d S Wood w (Menjou), (Bow), (Milestone), (St Clair) 6882ft FPL r Par
FASCINATION (1922) d/pc Leonard st/ad Goulding
Fascist, The (UK) = FEDERALE, IL (1961)
FASHION OF 1934 (1934) d Dieterle chor Berkeley w W Powell, B Davies, Darwell 78min FN
Fashion = FASSHON (1960)
FASHION ROW (1923) d/p/pc Leonard (7rs)
FASHIONS IN LOVE (1929) d/co-songs Schertzinger c Cronjager w Menjou 73min Par
FASSHON (1960) d Kuri 5min anim (= *Fashion*)
FAST AND FEARLESS (1924) d Thorpe w Arthur 4600ft
FAST AND FURIOUS (1939) d Berkeley s Kurnitz c June w Tone, Sothern 73min MGM
FAST AND LOOSE (1930) d Newmayer di P Sturges w M Hopkins, Lombard 6138 ft Par
Fast and Sexy (US) = ANNA DI BROOKLYN (1958)
FAST COMPANY (1953) d J Sturges co-a Gibbons c Lipstein w Keel 67min MGM
FASTERS MILJONER (1939) d Molander SF (= *Fasters Miljoner*)
FASTEST GUN ALIVE, THE (1956) d/co-s Rouse m Previn c Folsey w M O'Hara, G Ford, B Crawford, Crain 92min MGM
FAST FIGHTIN' (1925) d Thorpe
FAST LADY, THE (1962) d Annakin w (Christie) r JAR *95min
FASTMO UTHYRES (1951) d Molander w Dahlbeck 2485m
FASTNACHTSBEICHTE, DIE (1960) d Dieterle *99min (= *Ash Wednesday Confession*)
FAST WORKERS (1933) d Browning c Marley w J Gilbert 66min MGM
FATAL CHOCOLATE, THE (1912) d/w *Sennett* w Normand (½rl) Bio
Fatal Desire = CAVALLERIA RUSTICANA (1953)
FATALE MEPRISE (1900) d Méliès 20m
FATAL GLASS OF BEER, THE (1933) d Bruckman s Sennett w Fields 21min Par
FATAL LADY (1936) d Edward Ludwig p Wanger c Shamray w Pidgeon, Foster 73min Par
FATAL MALLET, THE (1914) co-d/w Chaplin co-d/p-w Sennett w Normand (1rl) KEY (= *Pile Driver*)
FATAL RING, THE (1917) d G Seitz w White 20eps Pat
FATAL WARNING, THE (1929) d Thorpe w Karloff 10eps
FATE (1913) d Griffith w Pickford, Marsh (1rl) Bio
Fate = TAQDEER (1943)
FATE, LE (1966) *110min (= *The Fairies/The Queens/Sex Quartet*)
ep FATA MARTA d Pietrangeli des Chiari w Sordi
ep FATA ELENA d Bolognini w Welch
ep FATA ARMENIA d Monicelli w Cardinale
ep FATA SABINA d/co-s Salce c Di Palma w Vitti
FATE IS THE HUNTER (1964) d Nelson p A Rosenberg m Goldsmith c Krasner w G Ford, J Russell, Pleshette, Malone CS 106min Fox
FATE'S FATHEAD (1934) d C Chase (as Parrott) p Roach w C Chase (2rs) MGM
Father, The = FADERN (1969)
FATHER BROWN (1954) d Horner *fst GK Chesterton* m Auric w Guinness, Greenwood, Finch 91min r Col
FATHER GOOSE (1964) d Nelson c C Lang w C Grant, T Howard, Caron *115min U
FATHER IS A BACHELOR (1950) d Foster, *Abby Berlin* co-s/st J Grant c Guffey w Holden 84min Col
FATHER NILE (1931) p/pc Bray (1rl) r Col
FATHER OF THE BRIDE (1950) d Minnelli p Berman s Goodrich, Hackett c J Alton w Tracy, J Bennett, E Taylor 92min MGM
Father Sergius = OTETS SERGII (1918)
FATHER'S CHOICE (1913) d Sennett w Normand (½rl) Key
Father's Dilemma (US) = PRIMA COMMUNIONE (1910)
FATHER'S LITTLE DIVIDEND (1951) d Minnelli p Berman s Goodrich, Hackett c J Alton co-a Gibbons w Tracy, J Bennett, E Taylor 81min MGM
FATHER VOITECH = PATER VOJTECH (1929)
FATHER VOTTECH = PATER VOJTECH (1936)
Father Wanted, A = PAPPA SOKES (1947)
FATHER WAS A FULLBACK (1949) d/Stahl p Kohlmar co-a Wheeler w MacMurray, M O'Hara, N Wood, Ritter 79min Fox
FATICHE DI ERCOLE, LE (1957) d/co-s *Pietro Francisci* c Bava w Reeves FS* 105min (= *Hercules*)
FAT MAN, THE (1951) d Castle c Glassberg w Hudson 77min U
FATTY AGAIN (1914) d/w Arbuckle (1rl) Key
FATTY AND MABEL ADRIFT (1916) d/w Arbuckle p Sennett w Normand (3rs) Tri
FATTY AND MABEL AT THE SAN DIEGO EXPOSITION (1915) d/w Arbuckle w Normand (1rl) Key
FATTY AND MABEL'S SIMPLE LIFE (1915) d/w Arbuckle p Sennett w Normand (2rs) Key (= *Mabel and Fatty's Simple Life*)
FATTY AND MINNIE-HE-HAW (1914) d/w Arbuckle p Sennett (2rs) Key
FATTY AND THE BROADWAY STARS (1915) d/w Arbuckle w Sennett (2rs) Tri
FATTY AND THE HEIRESS (1914) d/w Arbuckle (1rl) Key
Fatty at Coney Island = CONEY ISLAND (1917)
FATTY'S CHANCE ACQUAINTANCE (1915) d/w Arbuckle p Sennett (1rl) Key
FATTY'S DEBUT (1914) d/w Arbuckle (1rl) Key
FATTY'S FAITHFUL FIDO (1915) d/w Arbuckle p Sennett (1rl) Key
FATTY'S FINISH (1914) d/w Arbuckle (1rl) Key
FATTY'S FLIRTATION (1913) d (unknown) w Arbuckle, Normand (½rl) Key
FATTY'S GIFT (1914) d/w Arbuckle (1rl) Key
FATTY'S JONAH DAY (1914) d/w Arbuckle p Sennett w Normand (1rl) Key
FATTY'S MAGIC PANTS (1914) d/w Arbuckle p Sennett (1rl) Key
FATTY'S NEW ROLE (1915) d/w Arbuckle p Sennett (1rl) Key
FATTY'S PLUCKY PUP (1915) d/w Arbuckle p Sennett (2rs) Key (= *Foiled by Fido*)
FATTY'S RECKLESS FLING (1915) d/w Arbuckle p Sennett (1rl) Key
FATTY'S TINTYPE TANGLE (1915) d/w Arbuckle p Sennett w Normand (2rs) Key (= *Fido's Tintype Tangle*)
FATTY'S WINE PARTY (1914) d/w Arbuckle p Sennett w Normand (1rl) Key
FAUN (1917) d A Korda
FAUSSE MAITRESSE, LA (1942) d Cayatte *fst Honoré de Balzac* w Darrieux 85min
Fausses Nouvelles = BREAK THE NEWS (1937)
FAUST (1926) d Murnau co-s Rohrig *fpls Goethe, Marlowe* p Pommer w Jannings, Dieterle 6500 ft UFA
FAUST AND MEPHISTOPHELES (1898) d G Smith
Faust and the Devil = LEGGENDA DI FAUST, LA (1949)
FAUST AUX ENFERS OU LA DAMNATION DE FAUST d Méliès *fpm Hector Berlioz* 170m (15 parts)
FAUST ET MARGUERITE (1897) d Méliès *fst* (*Le Malade Imaginaire*) *Molière* 20m
FAUTE DE L'ABBE MOURET, LA (1970) d/co-s Franju *fn Emile Zola* co-pc Truffaut c Fradetal *100min
FAUTE D'ORTHOGRAPHE, LA (1919) d/s Feyder 679m
FAUT PAS PRENDRE LES ENFANTS DU BON DIEU POUR DES CANARDS SAUVAGES (1968) d/co-ad/s Audiard co-dec D'Eabonne co-m Van Parys w Rosay FS* 80min
FAUX MAGISTRAT, LE (1914) d/s Feuillade 1881m (= *Fantômas, V*)
FAVOLA DEL CAPPELLO (1949) d Zurlini
FAVORITE SON, THE (1913) d Ince
FAZIL (1928) d Hawks co-s S Miller c O'Connell 7217 ft Fox
FBI STORY, THE (1959) p/d LeRoy c Biroc m M Steiner co-s Breen w J Stewart, Miles *149min WB
Fear = ANGST, DIE (1954)
FEAR AND DESIRE (1953) d/p/c/e Kubrick 68min
FEARLESS FAGAN (1952) d Donen co-p Franklin s Lederer c Lipstein co-a Gibbons w J Leigh 78min MGM
Fearless Vampire Killers, or Pardon Me, but your Teeth are in my Neck, The (US) = DANCE OF THE VAMPIRES (1967)
FEARMAKERS, THE (1958) d J Tourneur c Leavitt w D Andrews 83min r UA
FEAR STRIKES OUT (1957) d Mulligan co-a Pereira m E Berstein w Malden, Perkins 100min VV Par
FEAST AT ZHIRMUNKA = PIR Y SHIRMUNKA (1941)
Feast of St Jorgen, The = PRAZDNIK SVYATOVO YORGENA (1930)
FEDERALE, IL (1961) d/co-s/w Salcs 102min (= *The Fascist*)
FEED 'EM AND WEEP (1938) G Douglas p Roach (1rl) MGM
FEED THE KITTY (1952) C Jones anim* 7min WB
FEEL MY PULSE (1928) d/p La Cava 5808ft Par
FEET FIRST (1930) d Bruckman w H Lloyd pc H Lloyd 90min r Par
FEET OF CLAY (1928) d De Mille c Marley 9746ft FPL
FEHER EJSZAKAK (1916) d/s A Korda
FEHER GALAMBOK FEKETE VAROSBAN (1922) d Balàsz
FEIND IM BLUT (1931) d/s Ruttmann 2084m
FEKETE GYMANTOK (1938) d Vajda 2349m
FEKETE KAPITANY (1921) d Fejos

FELDMARESCIALLA, LA (1968) d Steno *80min (= Girl Field Marshal)
FELICES PASCUAS (1954) d/co-s Bardem
FELICIE NANTEUIL (1945) d M Allégret s Achard fn Anatole France w P Prévert
FELINS, LES (1964) d/co-s Clément c Decaë m Schifrin cr Borowczyk w Delon, J Fonda 110min MGM (= The Love Cage/Joy House)
FELIPE II Y EL ESCORIALE (1935) d/s Velo, Fernando Mantilla
FELIX DZERZHINSKY (1957) d Kalatozov
FELIX KRULL (1957) d Kurt Hoffman fn Thomas Mann w Buchholz
FELIX LECLERC, TROUBADOUR (1959) d Jutra c Brault 30min
FELLINI – SATYRICON (1969) d/co-st/co-s/co-dec Fellini co-s Rondi fn Satyricon C. Petronius Arbiter c Rotunno co-m Rota w Bosè PV* 129min Bio
Fellows Who Ate The Elephant, The = ZO O KUTTA RENCHU (1947)
FEMALE (1933) d Curtiz c Hickox 60min FN
FEMALE, THE (1924) d S Wood w W Baxter 6167ft FPL r Par
Female, The (US) = SETENTA VELES SIETE (1962)
FEMALE ANIMAL, THE (1958) d Keller p Zugsmith c Metty co-a Golitzen w Lamarr, J Powell CS 84min U
Female Demon = CHOKON YASHA (1928)
Female Impersonater, The = MASQUERADE, THE (1914)
FEMALE OF THE SPECIES, THE (1912) d Griffith w Pickford (1rl) Bio
FEMALE ON THE BEACH (1955) d Pevney p Zugsmith c C Lang w J Crawford, J Chandler 97min U
Female Three Times = FEMMINE TRE VOLTE (1957)
Femina = FEMMINA (1918)
FEMININE TOUCH, THE (1941) d WS Van Dyke p J Mankiewicz a Gibbons m Waxman w June w K Francis, Heflin, R Russell 97min MGM
FEMININE TOUCH, THE (1957) d Jackson *91min JAR
FEMME FLEUR, LA (1965) d Lenica anim* 12min (= Woman is a Flower)
FEMMINE TRE VOLTE (1957) d/co-s Steno p Ponti w Manfredi 85min (= Female Three Times/Three Times A Woman)
FEMME COQUETTE, UNE (1955) d/s/c Godard (ps Hans Lucas) fst Guy de Maupassant 10min
FEMME DANS LA NUIT, UNE (1951) d Gréville, Gance s Gance co-a Alekan w Romance 100min
FEMME DE NULLE PART, LA (1922) d/s Delluc
FEMME DISPARAIT, UNE (1942) d/s/co-p Feyder co-p Rosay c Kelber dec D'Eaubonne w Rosay
FEMME DOUCE, UNE (1969) d/s Bresson fst Fyodor Dostoievsky c Cloquet *87min (= A Gentle Creature)
FEMME DU BOULANGER, LA (1938) d/p/s/di Pagnol w Rainer 119min
FEMME DU BOUT DU MONDE, LA (1937) d J Epstein w Vanel
FEMME ECARLATE, LA (1969) d/co-s Valère w Vitti, Ronet *100min (= The Scarlet Woman)
FEMME EN HOMME, LA (1931) d Genina w Rosay
FEMME EST UNE FEMME, UNE (1961) d/s Godard co-p Ponti c Coutard dec Evein m Legrand w Karina, Brialy, Belmondo, (Moreau) FS* 85min
FEMME ET LE PANTIN, LA (1929) d De Baroncelli
FEMME ET LE PANTIN, LA (1958) d/co-ad Duvivier co-ad/di Achard fn Pierre Louys dec Wakhévitch m Wiener w Bardot *100min Pat (= A Woman like Satan)
FEMME FLEUR, LA (1965) d Lenica anim* 12min (= Woman is a Flower)
FEMME INFIDELE, LA (1968) d/s Chabrol c Rabier w Ronet *95min
FEMME MARIEE, LA or UNE (1964) d/s Godard c Coutard w Leenhardt 98min (= A or The Married Woman)
FEMME NUE, LA (1926) d/s Perret
FEMMES, LES (1969) d/co-ad Aurel w Bardot, Ronet 90min
FEMMES DU LOUVRE, LES (1951) d/co-s Kast co-s Grémillon 22min
FEMME SPECTACLE, LA (1964) d/s Lelouch 63min
Femme sur la Plage, La (1946) = WOMAN ON THE BEACH, THE FEMMINA (1918) d/st Genina (= Femina)
FEMMINA (1954) d M Allégret w Lamarr *
FEMMINE TRE VOLTE (1957) d/co-s Steno p Ponti w Manfredi 85min (= Female Three Times/Three Times A Woman)
FENYES SZELEK (1969) d Jancso S* 86min (= The Confrontation)
FERIEN AUF SYLT (1958) d Thorndikes 20min DEFA (= Holiday on Sylt)
FERME AUX LOUPS, LA (1943) d Richard Pottier w Carol (ps Maryse Arley) 96min
FERMIERE A MONTFAUCON (1968) d/s Rohmer 13min
FERMO CON LE MANI (1936) d/co-s Gero Zambuto w Toto
FERRO, IL (1917) fpl D'Annunzio
FERROVIERE, IL (1916) d/co-s/w Germi p Ponti 116min
FERRY PILOT (1941) d Jackson 31min
FERRY TO HONG KONG (1959) d/s L Gilbert c Heller w Welles, C Jurgens 113min JAR

FERTILIZZANTI COMPLESSI (1916) d Olmi *22min
FERTILIZZANTI PRODOTTI DALLA SOCIETA DEL GRUPPO EDISON (1959) d Olmi *3min
FESTA A CASTELLUCCIO (1954) d Pontecorvo
FESTA A PAMPLONA (1959) d Mingozzi
FESTA DEI MORTI IN SICILIA (1953) d Maselli
Festa a Isidoro = GOYA (1950)
FESTIVAL IN LONDON (1951) d P Leacock *10min
FESTIVAL PANAFRICAIN (1969) d/s Klein *125min
FESTIVAL IN PUERTO RICO (1961) d/e Kroitor, Koenig p Kroitor 16mm 27min NFBC
FETE A HENRIETTE, LA (1953) d/st/co-s Duvivier co-s/di Jeanson dec D'Eaubonne m Auric w Neff, Carette 118min (= Henriette)
FETE ESPAGNOLE, LA (1919) d Dulac s Delluc w Modot
FETES DE FRANCE (1940) d Leenhardt, René Zaber 20min
FETES GALANTES (1950) d Aurel 16mm 15min
FETES GALANTES, LES (1965) d/s/di Clair c Matras dec Wakhévitch m Van Parys w Cassell 101min
FEU (1937) d De Baroncelli w Vanel, Brasseur
FEU AUX POUDRES, LE (1956) d/ad Decoin co-m Jarre DS 98min
FEU DE PAILLE (1939) d Benoit-Lévy
FEUD IN THE KENTUCKY HILLS, A (1913) d Griffith w Pickford (1rl) Bio
FEUERLOSCHER E.A. WINTERSTEIN (1970) d Kluge (short)
FEUERWERK (1954) d Kurt Hoffman p/co-s/co-fn Charell w Palmer, Schneider *83min (= Oh! My Papa)
FEUERZANGENBOWLE, DIE (1970) d/s Kautner w Tiller *100min
FEU FOLLET, LE (1963) d/co-s Malle fn Drieu La Rochelle c Cloquet mf Satie dec Evein w Ronet, Moreau 121min (= Will of the Wisp)
FEU MATHIAS PASCAL (1925) d L'Herbier fn (Il Fu Mattia Pascal) Luigi Pirandello dec Cavalcanti, Meerson w Mozhukhin, M Simon 4600m (= Late Matthew Pascal, The)
FEU SACRE, LE (1920) d Henri Diamant-Berger s/w Linder
FEUX DE LA MER, LES (1948) d J Epstein 4600m
EEVER IN THE BLOOD, A (1960) d V Sherman c Marley w A Dickinson, Danton H Marshall 117min WB
FEVERSCHIFF, DAS (1963) d Vajda 84min
FEW NOTES ON OUR FOOD PROBLEM, A (1968) d Blue
Few Words of Introduction, A = UVODNI SLOVO PRONESE (1964)
F 100 (1956) d R Leacock
FIACCOLA SOTTO IL MOGGIO (1911) fpl D'Annunzio 215m
FIACCOLA SOTTO IL MOGGIO (1916) fpl D'Annunzio rm 1911
FIAKER N 13 (1926) d Curtiz dec Leni 2502m
FIAMMA CHE NON SI SPEGNE (1949) d Cottafavi 2897m
FIAMMATA, LA (1913) d/co-s Blasetti w Rossi-Drago 89min (= Pride, Love and Suspicion)
Fiasco in Milan (US) = AUDACE COLPO DEI SOLITI IGNOTI (1919)
FIBRE E CIVILTA (1957) d Olmi *23min
FICKLE FATTY'S FALL (1915) d/w Arbuckle (2rs) Tri
Fickleness Gets On The Train = UWAKI WA KISHA NOTTE (1931)
FICKLE SPANIARD, THE (1912) d Sennett w Normand (½rl) Bio
FIDANZATI, I (1962) d/p/s Olmi 84min (= The Engagement)
FIDANZATO DI MIA MOGLIE, IL (1943) d/s/st Bragaglia
FIDDLE DE DEE (1947) d McLaren 3½min NFBC
FIDDLER ON THE ROOF (1971) d/p Jewison c Morris des Boyle PV* 180min r UA
FIDDLERS THREE (1944) d Watt as-p Hamer w Kendall 89min
FIDELE GEFANGNIS, DAS (1917) d Lubitsch fm Johann Strauss w Jannings (1rl) (= The Merry Jail)
Fido's Tintype Tangle = FATTY'S TINTYPE TANGLE (1915)
FIELD DAY, THE (1963) d A King excerpt fpl (The Brig) Kenneth Brown 16mm 12min
FIEND WHO WALKED THE WEST, THE (1958) d G Douglas co-s Yordan fs KISS OF DEATH (1947) B Hecht, Lederer c Joe MacDonald co-a Wheeler 101min CS Fox
Fiery Love = FAJA LOBBI (1960)
Fiery Miles = OGNENNYE VERSTY (1957)
FIESKO (1913) w Dieterle
FIESKO (1920) d/co-dec Leni
FIESTA (1947) d Thorpe p J Cummings w Esther Williams, Montalban, Tamiroff, Charisse, Astor *102min MGM
FIESTA BRAVA (1956, uf) d/co-s Cottafavi
FIESTA DE SANTA BARBARA, LA (1936) d Lewis Lewyn w Keaton, Cooper MGM
FIEVRE (1921) d/s Delluc w Modot
FIEVRE MONTE A EL PAO, LA (1959) d/co-s Buñuel co-s Alcoriza c Figueroa m Misraki w Philipe 97min Los Ambiciosos/Republic of Sin)
FIEVRES (1941) d Delannoy 98min
FIFI LA PLUME (1965) d/s LAMORISSE 80min

15 MAIDEN LANE (1936) d Dwan c J Seitz w Trevor, Romero, Nolan 64min Fox
FIFTH AVENUE GIRL (1939) d/p La Cava w G Rogers 83min RKO
50 FANTASTICS AND 50 PERSONALITIES (1964–66) d Warhol
FIFTY-FIFTY (1916) d/st Dwan p Griffith w N Talmadge (5 rs) r Tri
50–50 (1932) d Florey
FIFTY-FIVE DAYS AT PEKING (1963) d N Ray 2nd d Marton p Bronston co-s Yordan c Hildyard m Tiomkin w Heston, Gardner, Niven, Lukas TR70* 150min r JAR
FIFTY MILLION FRENCHMEN (1931) d Bacon w Olson & Johnson 65min WB
FIFTY ROADS TO TOWN (1937) d Taurog c August 81min Fox
FIGARO E LA SUA GRAN GIORNATA (1931) d Camerini
FIGARO QUA, FIGARO LA (1950) d Bragaglia w Toto 86min
Fight, The = LUTTE, LA (1961)
FIGHTER SQUADRON (1948) d Walsh p/st/s S Miller ad Rackin co-c Hickox e Nyby m M Steiner w E O'Brien, Stack, Hudson 96min WB
FIGHT FOR LIFE, THE (1940) d/s Lorentz c F Crosby 68min
Fight for our Soviet Ukraine = BITVA ZA NASHU SOVETSKAYU UKRAINU (1943)
FIGHTING BACK (1940) d St Clair 62min Fox
FIGHTING BLOOD (1923) d St Clair (serial in 12eps) (12 rs)
FIGHTING BLOOD (1911) d Griffith w L Barrymore (1rl) Bio
FIGHTING BROTHERS, THE (1919) d J Ford (2rs) U
FIGHTING CHEAT, THE (1926) d Thorpe w Arthur 4626ft
FIGHTING COWARD, THE (1924) d/p Cruze FPL
FIGHTING EAGLE, THE (1927) d/p Crisp c AC Miller 8000ft Pat
FIGHTING FATHER DUNNE (1948) d Telzlaff co-s Rackin 93min RKO
Fighting Friends = WASEI KENKA TOMODACHI (1929)
FIGHTING GENTLEMAN, THE (1932) d Newmayer 68min
FIGHTING HEART, THE (1925) d J Ford c August w G O'Brien 6897ft Fox
FIGHTING KENTUCKIAN, THE (1949) d/st/s George Waggner p J Wayne c Garmes m Antheil w J Wayne, Hardy 100min Rep
FIGHTING LADY, THE (1944) d Wyler p De Rochemont *61min Fox
Fighting near Tsaritsin = BOI POD TSARITSYNOM (1919)
FIGHTING ODDS, THE (1917) d Dwan p Goldwyn (5rs)
Fighting O'Flynn, The = O'FLYNN, THE (1948)
FIGHTING SEABEES, THE (1944) d Edward Ludwig st/co-s B Chase w J Wayne, S Hayward 100min Rep
FIGHTING 69TH, THE (1940) d Keighley p J Warner, Wallis c Gaudio co-sp eff Haskins w Cagney 90min WB
FIGHT ON FOR OLD (1956) d Pintoff
FIG LEAVES (1926) d/st Hawks c August co-a Menzies w G O'Brien part* 6498ft Fox
FIGLIA DEL CAPITANO, LA (1947) d/co-s Camerini p De Laurentiis co-s Monticelli fn Alexander Puskin c Toni w Gassman 75min (= The Captain's Daughter)
FIGLIA DEL CORSARO VERDE, LA (1940) d Guazzoni
FIGLIA DI JORIO, LA (1911) d Edoardo Bencivenga fpl D'Annunzio 575m
FIGLIA DI JORIO, LA (1916) d Edoardo Bencivenga fpl D'Annunzio rm 1911
FIGLIO DI D'ARTAGNAN, IL (1949) d/s Freda 86min
FIGLIO DI SPARTACUS, IL (1962) d Sergio Corbucci w Piccioni w Reeves CS* 102min (= The Slave)
FIGURANTS DU NOUVEAU MONDE, LES (1969) d De Broca w Noiret *90min (= Les Caprices du Marie/Give Her the Moon)
FIGURE HEAD, THE (1953) d/p Halas, Batchelor anim* 81min
FIGURES IN A LANDSCAPE (1970) d Losey c Alekan PV* 85min
FILE ON THELMA JORDAN, THE (1949) d Siodmak p Wallis m V Young w Stanwyck, Corey 100min r Par (= Thelma Jordan)
FILLE AU DIABLE, LA (1946) d/ad Decoin w Fresnay
FILLE BIEN GARDEE, LA (1924) d/s Feuillade 1500m
FILLE DE HAMBOURG, LA (1958) d Y Allégret c Thirard w Gélin 86min Pat
FILLE DE L'EAU, LA (1924) d/p/dec J Renoir co-c Bachelet w P Renoir, Brasseur 80min
FILLE DU DIABLE, LA (1946) d Decoin w Fresnay 100min
FILLE DU PUISATIER, LA (1940) d/p/s/di Pagnol w Fernandel, Raimu 131min
FILLE ET DES FUSILS, UNE (1964) d/co-s Lelouch 110min (= The Decadent Influence)
FILLE POUR L'ETE, UNE (1960) d/co-s Molinaro w Presle S* 80min

343

FILLES DE LA CONGIERGE, LES (1943) d J Tourneur co-c Kelber co-dec Wakhévitch m Van Parys

FILLES DU SOLEIL, LES (1949) d Baratier *35min

FILM (1965) d Alan Schneider s Samuel Beckett w Keaton 24min

FILM AND REALITY (1942) d Cavalcanti (compilation) 105min

Film aus dem Sueden, Ein = GRUENE MANUELA, DIE (1923)

FILM COMME LES AUTRES, UN (1968) d Godard 120min (= A Film Like All the Others)

Film is Rhythm = RHYTHMUS 21 (1921)

FILM JOHNNIE, A (1914) d Sennett w Chaplin, Arbuckle (1rl) Key (= Movie Nut)

Film Like All the Others, A = FILM COMME LES AUTRES, UN (1968)

FILM MAGAZINE OF THE ARTS (1963) d/co-c/co-e J Mekas w Warhol 16mm part *20min

FILM OMNE TITEL (1948) d/co-s Kautner w Neff 2810m

FILMS BY STAN BRAKHAGE: AN AVANT-GARDE HOME MOVIE (1961) d Brakhage 16mm* Si 5min

FILMSTUDIE (1925) d/co-c/dec Richter 600ft

Film Truth = KINO PRAVDA (1922–25)

FILOSOFSKA HISTORIE (1937) d/s Vavra c Heller

FILS D'AMERIQUE, UN (1932) d Gallone w S Simon

FILS DE L'EAU, LES (1958) edited from: BATAILLE SUR LE GRAND FLEUVE/LA CIMETIERE DANS LA FALAISE/LES HOMMES QUI FONT LA PLUIE/LES GENS DU MIL/LA CIRCON-CISION 16mm* 88/80/60min

FILS DU FLIBUSTIER, LE (1922) d/s Feuillade 1: La Flibuste (1300m); 2: Le Pavillon Noir (740m); 3: Le Vaisseau Maudit (780m); 4: Maman (820m) 5: La Noce d'Anais (800m); 6: La Mission d'un fils (800m); 7: Le Justicier (800m); 8: La Drogue Blanche (800m); 9: Le Passé (800m); 10: Le Revenant de Saint-Fons (800m); 11: Le Maître Chanteur (800m); 12: Le Testament

FILUMENA MARTURANO (1911) d/co-s/fpl/w De Filippo m Rota

FINAL APPOINTMENT (1954) d Fisher 69min BL

FINAL TEST, THE (1952) d Asquith st/s Rattigan 16mm 91min BL/JAR

Finances Of The Grand Duke (UK) = FINANZEN DES GROSSHERZOGS, DIE (1923)

FINANZEN DES GROSSHERZOGS, DIE (1932) d Murnau p Pommer s Von Harbou c Freund, Planer 2500m (= Finances of the Grand Duke)

FINCHE DURA LA TEMPESTA (1963) d Frend w Mason, Palmer, Ferzetti 105min (= Beta Som/Torpedo Bay)

FIN DE DON JUAN, LA (1911) d/s Jasset

FIN DE FIESTA (1960) d/co-s Torre Nilsson 100min (= The Blood Feast/The Party is Over)

FIN DE JOURNEE (1968) d Grangier

FIND, FIX AND STRIKE (1942) d Compton Bennett p Cavalcanti 37min

FINDLING, DER (1967) d/co-s Moorse fn Von Kleist 80min (= The Foundling/The Orphan)

FIND THE LADY (1936) d Roland Grillette w G Sanders 70min

FIN DU JOUR, LA (1939) d/s/co-ad Duvivier co-ad/di Charles Spaak c Matras m Jaubert w Jouvet, M Simon, Modot 93min

FIN DU MONDE, LA (1931) d/s/c/w Gance artistic collaboration Ruttman 90min

FIND YOUR MAN (1924) d St Clair c Garmes w Rin Tin Tin 6100ft WB

FINE CLOTHES (1925) d/p Stahl 6971ft FN

FINE MADNESS, A (1966) d Kershner c McCord w Connery, Woodward, Seberg *104min WB

Fine Pair, A (US) = COPPIA TRANQUILLA, UNA (1969)

FINESTRA SUL LUNA PARK, LA (1956) d/co-s Comencini 97min

FINESTRE (1950) d Maselli

FINESTRE, LE (1962) d Mingozzi sh

Finger Of Guilt (US) = INTIMATE STRANGER, THE (1956)

FINGER PRINTS (1926) Bacon w Fazenda 6400ft WB

FINGERS AT THE WINDOW (1942) d Lederer co-c Lawton m Kaper w Rathbone 80min MGM

FINIAN'S RAINBOW (1968) d Coppola c Lathrop w Astaire 70PV* 144min WB

Finie La Crise = CRISE EST FINIE, LA (1934)

FINISHING TOUCH, THE (1928) d Bruckman p Roach supn McCarey w Laurel, Hardy (2rs) MGM

FINIS TERRAE (1929) d J Epstein

FINN AND HATTIE (1939) co-d Taurog co-d/co-s McLeod co-s J Mankiewicz w Pitts

FIOR DI MALE (1915) d Gallone

FIORI, I (1953) d Maselli

FIORITURES (1915) d/s Gance (= La Source de Beauté)

Fire = FUOCO (1968)

Fire, The = OGON (1930)

FIREBALL, THE (1950) d/co-s Garnett m V Young w Rooney, Monroe 84min Fox

FIRE BARRIER, THE (1926) d Wyler (2rs) U

FIREBIRD, THE (1934) d Dieterle f Opera Stravinsky c E Haller w Darwell WB

FIRECREEK (1968) d Vincent McEveety p P Leacock w J Stewart, H Fonda PV* 104min

FIRE DOWN BELOW (1957) d Parrish co-m Lemmon w Hayworth, Mitchum, Lemmon CS* 116min Col

FIRE FLINGERS, THE (1919) d/w Julian (6rs)

FIREFLY, THE (1937) d/co-p Leonard s Goodrich, Hackett ad Ogden Nash a Gibbons co-e Vorkapich w Jeannette MacDonald 135min MGM

Firefly Light = HOTARUBI (1958)

FIREMAN, THE (1916) d/s/w Chaplin co-c Totheroh w Purviance, Bacon (2rs) Mut

FIREMAN, SAVE MY CHILD (1932) d Bacon 66min WB

Fireman's Ball, The (UK) = HORI MA PENENKO (1967)

FIREMEN TO THE RESCUE (1903) p Hepworth 325ft

Fire of a Thousand Suns, The (UK) = BRULER DE MILLE SOLEILS, LA (1965)

FIRE OF WATERS (1965) d Brakhage 16mm 10min

FIRE OVER AFRICA (1954) d Richard Sale p Frankovich co-c Challis w M O'Hara *84min r Col

FIRE OVER ENGLAND (1937) d W Howard c Howe w Olivier, V Leigh, Mason, Newton 91min UA

FIRE RAISERS, THE (1933) d/co-s M Powell 77min

Fires On The Plain = NOBI (1959)

FIRES WERE STARTED (1943) d/s Jennings 63min

FIREWORKS (1947) d/s/c/e/w Anger 15min

FIRST A GIRL (1936) d Saville 93min Gau

FIRST AUTO, THE (1927) d Del Ruth st Zanuck 6931ft WB

First Communion (UK) = PRIMA COMUNIONE (1910)

First Day, The = PERVYI DEN (1958)

First Day of Freedom, The = PIERWSZY DZIEN WOLNOSCI (1964)

FIRST DAYS, THE (1939) d Jennings, Watt, Jackson p Cavalcanti 23min (= A City Prepares)

First Echelon, The = PERVYI ESHELON (1956)

FIRST GENTLEMAN, THE (1947) d Cavalcanti 110min

FIRST 100 YEARS, THE (1924) d Richard Jones w Langdon (2rs) pc Sennett r Pat

FIRST HUNDRED YEARS, THE (1938) d Thorpe st/p -Krasna c Ruttenberg a Gibbons w R Montgomery 75min MGM

First Kiss, The = KUCHIZUKE (1955)

FIRST LEGION, THE (1951) d/co-p Sirk w Boyer, Rush 86min UA

First Love = HATSUKOI (1926)

FIRST LOVE (1939) d Koster p Pasternak w Durbin, Stack 84min

First Love (1939) d Koster p Pasternak w Durbin, Stack 84min

First Mass, The = PRIMEIRA MISSA, A (1961)

FIRST NIGHT, THE (1927) d Thorpe

FIRST OF THE FEW, THE (1942) d L Howard s De Grunwald c Périnal w L Howard, Niven 118min (= Spitfire)

FIRST ON THE ROAD (1960) d Losey 12min

First Rescue Party, The = PRVNI PARTA (1959)

FIRST TEXAN, THE (1956) d Haskin p Mirisch w McCrea 82min AA

FIRST TIME, THE (1952) d/co-s Tashlin p H Hecht co-s/co-st H Butler c Laszlo m Hollander w R Cummings 89min

FIRST TIME, THE (1968) d Neilson c Laszlo m K Hopkins 90min Mir r UA (= You Don't Need Pyjamas at Rosie's)

FIRST YANK INTO TOKYO (1940) d G Douglas c Wild m Harline 82min RKO

FIRST YEAR, THE (1926) d Borzage 5038ft Fox

FIRST YEAR, THE (1932) d W Howard c Mohr w J Gaynor 80min Fox

First Years, The = PIERWSZE LATA (1947)

FISHER MAID, THE co-d Ince w Pickford

Fishermen (UK) = PESCHERECCI (1957)

FISHY TALES (1937) d G Douglas p Roach 1rl MGM

FISKEBYN (1920) d Stiller 1833m

Fists In The Pocket (UK) = PUGNI I TASCA (1966)

FIST FIGHT (1964) d Breer anim 16mm* 11min

FITZWILLY (1967) d Delbert Mann p/w Mirisch c Biroc a Boyle w D Van Dyke, Evans PV* 102min r UA (= Fitzwilly Strikes Back)

Fitzwilly Strikes Back (UK) = FITZWILLY (1968)

Fiume Della Rivolta, Il = ÇA IRA (1964)

Fiume Giallo, Il = MURAGLIA CINESE, LA

FIVE (1951) d/p/s Oboler 93min Col

Five Acres Of Land = AKKARA PAHA (1969)

FIVE AGAINST THE HOUSE (1955) d Karlson co-p/co-s Silliphant m Duning w Novak 84min Col

FIVE AND TEN (1931) d/co-p Leonard co-p Davies c Barnes w Davies, L Howard 88min MGM

FIVE AND TEN CENT ANNIE (1928) d Del Ruth w Brodine 6rs WB

Five Angles On Murder (UK) = WOMAN IN QUESTION (1950)

Five Boys From Barska Street = PIATKA Z ULICY BARSKIEJ (1954)

Five Branded Woman = JOVANKA E L'ALTRI

Five Brothers and a Sister = GONIN NO KYODAI

FIVE CAME BACK (1939) d J Farrow co-s Trumbo c Musuraca w Ball, Carradine 74min RKO

FIVE CARD STUD (1968) d Hathaway p Wallis c Fapp m Jarre w Martin, Mitchum Par 103min

Five Dolls for an August Moon = CINQUE BAMBOLE PER LA LUNA DI AGOSTO (1970)

FIVE FINGER EXERCISE (1962) d Daniel Mann s Goodrich, Hackett fpl Peter Shaffer m Moross w R Russell, Hawkins, Maximilian Schell 109min Col

FIVE FINGERS (1952) d J Mankiewicz s M Wilson co-a Wheeler c Brodine m Herrman w Mason, Darrieux 108min Fox

FIVE FOR FOUR (1941–43) d McLaren *4min NFBC

FIVE GATES TO HELL (1959) d/p/s Clavell co-a Wheeler c Leavitt 98min CS Fox

Five Girls Equals a Millstone Round One's Neck = PET HOLEK NA KRKU (1967)

FIVE GRAVES TO CAIRO (1943) d/co-s B Wilder p/co-s C Brackett fpl (Hotel Imperial) Biro c J Seitz co-a Dreier m Rozsa w Tone, A Baxter, Tamiroff, Von Stroheim 96min Par

FIVE GUNS WEST (1954) d/p Corman c F Crosby w Malone *78min

Five Miles To Midnight (US) = COUTEAU DANS LE PLAIE, LE (1962)

Five Million Years To Earth (US) = QUATERMASS AND THE PIT (1967)

FIVE PENNIES, THE (1959) d/co-s Shavelson co-s Pereira c Fapp w Kaye, Weld, Hope 117min VV* Par

Five Squadron = ESKADRILYA N 5 (1939)

FIVE STAR FINAL (1931) d LeRoy p Wallis c Polito w Robinson, Karloff 89min FN

Five-Storied Pagoda, The = GOJU NO TO (1944)

Five Years Of Struggle And Victory = PYAT LET BORBY I POBEDY (1923)

5,000 FINGERS OF DR T, THE (1952) d Rowland c Planer *88min pc Kramer r Col

FIXED BAYONETS (1951) d/s Fuller c Ballard co-a Wheeler w Basehart, (Dean 92min Fox

FIXER, THE (1968) d Frankenheimer s Trumbo fn Bernard Malamud m Jarre w Bogarde *133min MGM

FIXER UPPERS, THE (1935) d Charles Rogers p Roach w Laurel, Hardy (2rs) r MGM

FLAG LIEUTENANT, THE (1925) d Elvey 8900ft

FLAME AND THE ARROW, THE (1950) d J Tourneur co-p H Hecht c E Haller m M Steiner w Lancaster, V Mayo *88min WB

FLAME AND THE FLESH, THE (1954) d R Brooks p Pasternak c Challis w Turner *104min MGM

FLAME IN THE STREETS (1961) d R Baker c Challis w J Mills CS 93min JAR

Flame of My Love = WOGA KOI WA MOENU (1948)

FLAME OF NEW ORLEANS, THE (1941) d/co-s Clair p Pasternak co-s/st Krasna c Maté w Dietrich 80min U

Flame of Torment = ENJO (1958)

Flame over India = NORTHWEST FRONTIER (1959)

FLAME WITHIN, THE (1935) d/s Goulding c Howe w L Hayward, H Marshall, O'Sullivan 71min MGM

Flames Over Baku = OGNI BAKU (1950)

FLAMING FEATHER (1951) d Enright c Rennahan w Hayden, Rush *77min Par

FLAMING ROAD (1949) d Curtiz p Wald c McCord w J Crawford, Greenstreet 74min WB

FLAMING STAR (1960) d D Seigel p Weisbart co-s/fn (Flaming Lance) Huffaker co-s N Johnson c C Clarke m Mockridge w Presley, Del Rio, McIntire CS* 101min Fox

Flaming Years, The = POVEST PLANMENYCH LET (1961)

FLAMME, DIE (1923) d Lubitsch fpl Hans Muiler co-c Sparkuhl w Negri UFA (= Montmarte)

FLAP (1970) d C Reed s/fn (Nobody Loves a Drunken Indian) Huffaker w Quinn, Winters PV* 107min WB (= The Last Warrior)

FLAPPER, THE (1920) d Crosland w (Shearer) 6rs pc Selznick

FLAREUP (1969) d Neilson w Welch 90min MGM

FLASHING SPIKES (1962) d J Ford c Clothier cr Bass w J Stewart, (J Wayne) 53min TV

FLAT FOOT STOOGES (1938) d/w C Chase 2rs Col

Flavour of Green Tea Over Rice, The = OCHAZUKE NO AJI (1952)

FLAW, THE (1955) d Fisher 61min

FLEA CIRCUS, THE (1954) d Avery *7min MGM

FLEBUS (1957) d Pintoff CS* 7min WB

Fledermaus 55 = OH, ROSALINDA (1955)

FLEET'S IN, THE (1928) d St Clair w Bow 6730ft FPL-Par

FLEET'S IN, THE (1942) d Schertzinger c Mellor w Lamour, Holden 93min Par

FLEET THAT CAME TO STAY, THE (1946) d Boetticher for US Navy r Par

FLESH (1932) d J Ford st Goulding di M Hart c Edeson w Hersholt, Beery 95min MGM

FLESH (1968) d Paul Morrissey p Warhol *105min

FLESH AND FANTASY (1943) co-p Duvivier fst Oscar Wilde co-p/w Boyer co-c Cortez des Boyle w Robinson, Mitchell, Stanwyck, R Cummings, Lawford 98min U (= Obsessions)

FLESH AND FURY (1952) d Pevney c Glassberg w Curtis 82½min U

FLESH AND THE DEVIL (1927) d C Brown c Daniels w Garbo, J Gilbert 9rs MGM

Flesh and Woman = GRAND JEU, LE (1954)

FLESH OF MORNING (1956) d Brakhage 16mm 25min

Flesh Will Surrender (UK) = DELITTO DI GIOVANNI EPISCOPO (1947)

FLEUR DE L'AGE, LA (1947, *uf*) *d* Carné *s/di* J Prévert *dec* Trauner *m* Kosma *w* Aimée, Reggiani, Arletty, Carol
FLEUR DE L'AGE OU LES ADOLESCENTES, LA (1964) 110min
ep GENEVIEVE *d* Brault
ep MARIE-FRANCE ET VERONIQUE *d/s* Rouch
ep FIAMMETTE *d/s* Baldi 34min
ep AKO *d* Teshigahara
FLEUR DES RUINES, LA (1916) *d/s* Gance
FLEUR D' OSEILLE (1967) *d/co-s* Lautner *w* Darc S* 90min
FLEUR SANGLANTE, LA (1912) *d* Machin Pat
Fleuve, Le = RIVER, THE (1950)
FLEUVE, LE (1952) *d* Mitry *c* Fradetal
FLICKAN I FRACK (1956) *d* Mattson *c* Nykvist *m Johann Strauss w* Kjellin *98min (= *Girl in a Dress Coat*)
FLICKAN I REGNET (1955) *d/co-s/w* Kjellin San (= *Girl In The Rain*)
FLICKA OCH HYACINTER (1970) *d* Ekman 89min
FLICKERING YOUTH (1924) *d Erle Kenton w* Langdon, Sennett 2rs *pc* Sennett *r* Pat
FLICKORNA (1968) *d/co-s* Zetterling *w* B Anderson, H Anderson, Lindblom, Bjornstrand 93min (= *The Girls*)
FLIEGENDE KOFFER, DER (1921) *d* Reiniger anim 299ft
FLIGHT (1929) *d/di* Capra *p* Cohn *c* J Walker Col
FLIGHT COMMAND (1940) *d* Borzage *c* Rosson *m* Waxman *a* Gibbons *w* R Taylor, Pidgeon 113min MGM
Flight Commander, The = DAWN PATROL, THE (1930)
FLIGHT FROM ASHIYA (1964) *d* Michael Anderson *p* H Hecht *c* Guffey, Joe Macdonald *des* Lourié *w* Brynner, Widmark PV* 102min *r* UA
FLIGHT FROM DESTINY (1941) *d* V Sherman *p* J Warner WB 73min
Flight Into France (UK) = FUGA IN FRANCIA (1948)
FLIGHT NURSE (1953) *d/co-lyr* Dwan *p* H Yates *m* V Young 90min Rep
FLIGHT OF THE DOVES (1971) *d/p/co-s* Nelson *w* McGuire *101min Col
FLIGHT OF THE PHOENIX, THE (1965) *d/p/pc -Aldrich c* Biroc *w* J Stewart, Attenborough, Finch, Borgnine, Duryea, Marquand, G Kennedy *149min Fox
FLIGHT TO HONG KONG (1956) *d/p/co-s* J Newman *w* Rush 88min UA
FLIGHT TO TANGIER (1953) *d/s* Warren *co-a* Periera *c* Rennahan *w* Fontaine, Palance, Dalio 3-D* 90min Par
FLIM FLAM MAN, THE (1967) *d* Kershner *2nd/d* Canutt *c* C Lang *m* Goldsmith *w* G Scott PV* 104min Fox (= *One Born Every Minute*)
FLIRTATION WALK (1934) *d/p* Borzage *co-p* Wallis *s* Daves *c* Polito, Barnes *w* Powell, Power 97min WB
FLIRTING HUSBAND, THE (1912) *d* Sennett *w* Normand ½rl Key
Flirts, The = BETWEEN SHOWERS (1914)
FORTY FOUR FLUSHERS (1926) *d* Cline *s* Sennett
Floating Clouds = UKIGUMO (1955)
Floating Reeds, The = UKIGUSA (1959)
Floating Vessel = UKIFUNE (1957)
Floating Weeds = UKIGUSA (1959)
Flood, The = POVODEN (1958)
FLOODS OF FEAR (1968) *d/s* Crichton *c* Challis *m Alan Rawsthorne w* Keel 84m JAR
FLOOR BELOW, THE (1918) *d* Badger *w* Normand 6rs
FLOORWALKER, THE (1916) *d/s* Chaplin *co-c* Totheroh *w* Chaplin, Purviance, Bacon 2rs Mut
FLORADAS NA SERRA (1953) *d* Salce
FLORENCE NIGHTINGALE (1915) *d/p* Elvey 3700ft
FLORENTINE DAGGER, THE (1935) *d* Florey *p* H Brown *fn* B Hecht 70min WB
FLOR SILVESTRE (1943) *d/co-s* Fernadez *c* Figueroa *w* Del Rio, Armendariz, Fernandez 96min
Flower, The = HANA (1967)
Flower Blooms, A = HANA HIRAKU (1948)
FLOWER DRUM SONG (1961) *d* Koster *p* R Hunter *fmpl Rogers, Hammerstein co-a* Golitzen 133min PV* U
Flowering Time = BLOMSTER TID . . . . ., DEN (1939)
FLOWER OF DOOM, THE (1917) *d/s* Ingram U
FLOWERS OF ASPHALT (1951) *d/s/c/e* Markopoulos 16mm 10min
FLOWER THIEF, THE (1960) *d* Rice, *Vernon Zimmerman* 16mm 75min
Flowing = NAGARERU (1956)
Flowing Night = YORU NO NAGARE (1969)
FLUGTEN FRA MILLIONERNE (1934) *d/s* Fejos
Flute And The Arrow, The (UK) = DJUNGELSAGA, EN (1955)
FLUTE MAGIQUE, LE (1946) *d/co-s* Grimault *co-s* Leenhardt anim* 10min
FLY, THE (1958) *d/p Kurt Neumann s* Clavell *c* Struss *co-a* Wheeler *w* H Marshall, Price CS* 94min Fox
FLY, THE (1971) *d* Lennon, *Yoko Ono* *45min
FLY-BY-NIGHT (1942) *d* Siodmak *p* S Siegel *c* J Seitz 74min Par
FLY COP, THE (1920) *d/st* Semon, Taurog, *Mort Peebles w* Semon, Hardy 2rs Vit
FLYIN' BUCKAROO, THE (1928) *d* Thorpe
FLYING COLOURS (1917) *d* Borzage Tri
FLYING DEUCES, THE (1939) *d Edward A Sutherland co-st/co-s* Langdon *w* Laurel, Hardy 69min
FLYING DOWN TO RIO (1933) *d Thornton Freeland w* Astaire, G Rogers 89min RKO
FLYING ELEPHANTS (1927) *d Frank Butler w* Laurel, Hardy Pat
FLYING FOOL, THE (1929) *d/co-s* Garnett *c* AC Miller 5715ft Pat
FLYING HOUSE, THE (1920) *d* McCay anim
FLYING LEATHERNECKS (1951) *d* N Ray *s* J Grant *w* J Wayne, Ryan *102min RKO
FLYING MAN, THE (1962) *d/p* Dunning anim* 3min
FLYING MISSILE, THE (1950) *d* Levin *w* Lindfors, G Ford, Quine 93min Col
FLYING PADRE (1951) *d* Kubrick 16mm 9min RKO
FLYING ROMEOS (1928) *d* LeRoy *co-s* Conway 6184 FN
Flying Saucer, The (UK) = DISCO VOLANTE, IL (1961)
FLYING SCOT, THE (1957) *d* Compton Bennett 69min AA (= *Mail Bag Robbery*)
FLYING SQUAD, THE (1940) *d* Brenon 63min
FLYING TIGERS (1942) *d* D Miller *w* J Wayne 102min Rep
Flying Trapeze (UK) = CITE DU MIDI, LA (1951)
FLYKTINGAR FINNER EN HAMN (1945) *d/s* A and B Henning-Jensen
FLYVEREN OG JOURNALISTENS HUSTRU (1911) *d* Blom
F-MAN *d* Cline *co-a* Dreier 62min Par
FOCOLARE SPENTO, IL (1925) *d/pc* Genina (= *Piu Grande Amore, Il*)
Fog And Rain = KIRI NO AME (1924)
Foggy Harbour = KIRI NO MINATO (1923)
FOG OVER FRISCO (1934) *d* Dieterle *c* Gaudio *w* B Davis 68min FN
Foiled By Fido = FATTY'S PLUCKY PUP (1915)
FOILING FICKLE FATHER (1913) *d/w* Normand ½rl Key
FOLIE DES VAILLANTS, LA (1926) *d* Dulac
FOLIE DU DOCTEUR TUBE, LA (1915) *d/s* Gance *c* Burel
FOLIES BERGERE (1935) *d* Del Ruth *p* Zanuck *as-p* Goetz *co-c* Marley *w* Chevalier, Sothern, Oberon 84min *r* UA (French version *di* Achard)
FOLIES-BERGERE (1956) *d* Decoin *w* Constantine *102min
FOLKETS VAN (1918) *d/s* Madsen
FOLLET (1943) *d/co-s* B Henning-Jensen
FOLLOW ME, BOYS (1966) *d Norman Tokar w* MacMurray, C Ruggles, L Gish *133min
FOLLOW ME QUIETLY (1949) *d* R Fleischer, A Mann (*uc*) *co-st* A Mann *e* Elmo Williams 59min RKO
FOLLOW THAT DREAM (1962) *d* G Douglas *p* Weisbart *s* Lederer *w* Presley PV* 110min *r* UA
FOLLOW THE BOYS (1944) *d Edward Sutherland p* Feldman *w* Fields, Jeannette MacDonald, Montez, O'Connor, Raft, R Scott, Welles, Dietrich 122min U
FOLLOW THE BOYS (1963) *d* Thorpe PV* 95min *r* MGM
FOLLOW THE FLEET (1936) *d* Sandrich *w* Astaire, G Rogers, R Scott, Ball, Grable 110min RKO
FOLLY TO BE WISE (1952) *d/co-p/co-s* Launder *co-p* Gilliat *c* Hildyard 91min BL
FOMA GORDEYEV (1959) *d/co-s* Donskoi *fn Maxim Gorky* 95min (= *Thomas Gordeyev*)
FONDERIES MARTIN, LES (1938) *d* Alexeieff anim
FONTAINE D'ARETHUSE, LA (1936) *d* Kirsanov
FONTAINE DE VAUCLUSE (1953) *d* Malle sh
FOOD FOR SCANDAL (1920) *d* Cruze 5rs
FOOLISH MATRONS, THE (1921) *d* C Brown, M Tourneur 6rs
FOOLISH WIVES (1921) *d/st/s/w* Von Stroheim *c* B Reynolds, Daniels *a/cos* Von Stroheim, R Day *m Sigmund Romberg* 12rs U
FOOL KILLER, THE (1965) *d Serrando Gonzalez w* Perkins
FOOLS FIRST (1922) *d/p/pc* Neilan *co-c* Struss 5773ft *r* FN
FOOLS FOR LUCK (1928) *d/p Charles F Reisner w* Fields 5758ft FN
FOOLS FOR SCANDAL (1938) *d/p* LeRoy *c* Tetzlaff *m* Rogers, Hart *w* Lombard, Wyman 81min WB
FOOL'S PARADE (1971) *d/p* A McLaglen *w* Stewart, G Kennedy, A Baxter 97min *r* Col
FOOL'S PARADISE (1921) *d* De Mille *c* Struss 9rs FPL
FOOL'S REVENGE, A (1909) *d* Griffith (*Rigoletto*) *Verdi* 1rl Bio
FOOL THERE WAS, A (1915) *d/s Frank Powell w* Bara 6rs
FOOT AND MOUTH (1955) *d/s/n* Anderson *c* Lassally 20min
FOOTBALL (1961) *d* R Leacock, *Robert Drew* 16mm 57min (= *Mooney vs Fowle*)
Footbridge, The (UK) = LEVIATHAN (1961)
FOOTLIGHT FEVER (1941) *d* Reis 69min RKO
FOOTLIGHT PARADE (1933) *d* Bacon *c* Barnes *chor* Berkeley *w* Cagney, Blondell, D Powell, Garfield 100min WB
FOOTLIGHT SERENADE (1942) *d* Ratoff *c* Garmes *w* Payne, Mature, Grable, Wyman 81min Fox
FOOTLOOSE WINDOWS (1926) *d* Del Ruth *s* Zanuck 7rs WB
FOOTSTEPS IN THE DARK (1941) *d* Bacon *p* Wallis *c* E Haller *m* Hollander *w* Flynn 96min WB
FOOTSTEPS IN THE FOG (1955) *d Arthur Lubin co-p* Frankovich *c* Challis *w* S Granger, J Simmons *90min *r* Col
Fop, The = PIZHON (1929)
For a Few Dollars More (UK) = PER QUALCHE DOLLARO IN PIU (1965)
For a Fistful of Dollars (UK) = PER UN PUGNO DI DOLLARI (1964)
FOR ATT INTE TALA OM ALLA DESSA KVINNOR (1964) *d* Ingmar Bergman *co-s* (*ps* Buntel Ericsson) *c* Nykvist *w* Kulle, Dahlbeck, B Andersson, H Andersson *80min SF (= *Now About These Women*)
FOR BETTER FOR WORSE (1919) *d* De Mille *w* Swanson 7rs FPL
FOR BETTER FOR WORSE (1954) *d/s* J Thompson *w* Bogarde *84min (= *Cocltails in the Kitchen*)
FOR BETTER, FOR WORSE (1961) *d/p* Halas *co-s* Halas, Batchelor anim* 11min
FORBIDDEN (1932) *d/st* Capra *ad/di* Swerling *c* J Walker *w* Stanwyck, Menjou 33min Col
FORBIDDEN (1953) *d* Maté *c* Daniels *w* Curtis, Dru 85min U
FORBIDDEN CARGO (1925) *d Tom Buckingham w* Karloff 1478m
Forbidden Christ (UK) = CRISTO PROIBITO, IL (1950)
FORBIDDEN CITY, THE (1918) *d* Franklin *w* N Talmadge 5rs
FORBIDDEN COMPANY (1932) *d* Thorpe 67min
FORBIDDEN FRUIT (1921) *d* De Mille 8rs FPL
Forbidden Games = JEUX INTERDITS (1951)
FORBIDDEN PARADISE (1924) *d* Lubitsch *co-fpl* (*The Czarina*) Biro *dec* Dreier *w* Negri, Menjou, (Gable) 60min Par
FORBIDDEN PASSAGE (1941) *d* Zinnemann 21min MGM
FORBIDDEN PLANET (1956) *d* Wilcox *c* Folsey *co-a* Gibbon *w* Pidgeon, H Francis CS* 98min MGM
Forbidden Street, The = BRITANNIA MEWS (1949)
FORBIDDEN THING, THE (1920) *d/p/co-s* Dwan *c* Gaudio 6rs
Forbidden Volcano, The = VOLCAN INTERDIT, LE (1965)
FOR CASH (1915) *d* Chaney 2rs U
FORCE DOIT RESTER A LA LOI (1899) *d* Méliès 20m
FORCE OF ARMS (1951) *d* Curtiz *c* McCord *w* Holden 100min WB
Force of Destiny, The = FORZA DEL DESTINO, LA (1949)
FORCE OF EVIL (1948) *d/co-s* Polonsky *c* Barnes *co-a* R Day *m* Raksin *w* Garfield 78min MGM
FOREIGN AFFAIR, A (1948) *d/co-s* B Wilder *p/co-s* Brackett *co-s* Breen *c* C Lang *co-a* Dreier *m* Hollander *w* Arthur, Dietrich 116min Par
FOREIGN CORRESPONDENT (1940) *d* Hitchcock *p* Wagner *co-s* Charles Bennett, Benchley (*uc*) *c* Maté *a* Golitzen *des* Menzies *m* A Newman *w* McCrea, H Marshall, G Sanders, Benchley 120min *r* UA
FOREIGN INTRIGUE (1956) *d/p/s -S Reynolds w* Mitchum, Thulin 100min UA
FOREMAN OF THE JURY, THE (1913) *d* Sennett *w* Normand 1rl Key
FOREMAN WENT TO FRANCE, THE (1942) *d* Frend *p* Balcon *s* L Arliss, *st* Priestley *e* Hamer *m* Watton 87min
FOREST ON THE HILL, THE (1919) *d/p* Hepworth 6000ft
FOREST RANGERS, THE (1942) *d* G Marshall *c* C Lang *co-a* Dreier *w* MacMurray, Goddard, S Hayward 87min Par
FOREVER AMBER (1947) *d* Preminger *p* Perlberg *co-s* P Dunne *fn Kathleen Winsor c* Shamroy *s* Wheeler *m* Raksin *w* Darnell, Wilde, G Sanders, Haydn *140min Fox
FOREVER AND A DAY (1943) *d/p* Clair, Goulding, Saville, F Lloyd, Stevenson, *Hardwicke*, H Wilcox *co-s* Charles Bennett, *C S Forrester, Christopher Isherwood*, D Stewart *co-c* Garmes, Metty, Musuraca *co-e* Elmo Williams *w* R Cummings, Laughton, Lupino, H Marshall, Milland, Neagle, Oberon, Rains, Crisp, V McLaglen, Keaton, Horton 105min RKO
FOREVER ENGLAND (1935) *d* Asquith
FOREVER FEMALE (1953) *d* Rapper *s* JJ Epstein *co-a* Pereira *c* Stradling *w* Holden, G Rogers, P Douglas 93min Par
FORFAITURE (1937) *d* L Herbier *c* Schuftan *dec* Y Allégret *w* Jouvet
FOR FRANCE (1917) *d* W Ruggles *w* Von Stroheim 5rs Vit
FOR FREEDOM (1918) *d* F Lloyd 6rs Fox
FOR FREEDOM OF CUBA (1912) *d* Ince *w* F Lloyd
FORGET ME NOT (1936) *d* Z Korda 73min
FORGOTTEN (1933) *d* Thorpe 65min
FORGOTTEN FACES (1928) *d/p* Schertzinger *e* Selznick *w* C Brook 7640ft Par
FORGOTTEN FACES (1935) *d* Dupont *c* Sparkuhl *w* H Marshall, R Cummings 71min Par
FORGOTTEN FACES, THE (1960) *d/p/s* Watkins 16mm 17min
FORGOTTEN PRAYER, THE (1916) *d/w* Borzage Tri
FORGOTTEN VICTORY (1939) *d* Zinnemann 1rl MGM
FORGOTTEN WOMEN (1932) *d* Thorpe 69min *r* Mon
FOR HEAVEN'S SAKE (1926) *d Sam Taulor co-st* Bruckman *w* H Lloyd 5356ft *pc* H Lloyd *r* Par
FOR HEAVEN'S SAKE (1950) *d/s* Seaton *p* Perlberg *m* A Newman *w* J Bennett, R Cummings 92min Fox
FOR HER BROTHER'S SAKE (1911) *co-d* Ince *w* Pickford
FOR LIFE, AGAINST THE WAR (1967) *co-d* Breer, Hurwitz, J Mekas 16mm part* 180min

FOR LIZZIE'S SAKE (1913) d Sennett w Normand ½rl Key

For Love . . . For Magic = PER AMORE . . . PER MAGIA (1967)

FOR LOVE OF IVY (1968) d Daniel Mann st/w Poitier s Aurthur *100min

FOR LOVE OF MABEL (1913) d Sennett w Normand 1rl Key

FOR LOVE OF MEAT (1908) d Griffith fst (*Just Meat*) *Jack London* 165m Bio

FOR LOVE OF YOU (1934) d Gallone 77min

FOR LOVE OR MONEY (1963) d M Gordon co-a Golitzen w K Douglas, M Gaynor, Bendix, Ritter *108min U

FOR ME AND MY GAL (1942) d Berkeley p Freed c Daniels co-m Edens w Garland, Gene Kelly, Quine, G Murphy 104min MGM

FOR MEN ONLY (1952) d/p/w Henreid w Miles 93min

FOR MIN HETA UNGDOMS SKULL (1952) d Mattsson co-s Lindstrom 95min (= *Because of My Hot youth*)

FORM PHASES I (1952) d Breer anim 16mm 2min

FORM PHASES II AND III (1953) d Breer anim* 16mm 2½min

FORM PHASES IV (1954) d Breer anim* 16mm 4min

FORNARETTO DI VENEZIA, IL (1961) d/s Tessari w Morgan *83min

FORNARINA, LA (1942) d Guazzoni

FORSAKING ALL OTHERS (1934) d WS Van Dyke s J Mankiewicz c Toland, Folsey w Gable, Montgomery, J Crawford 84min MGM

FOR SCENT-IMENTAL REASONS (1949) d C Jones anim* 7min WB

FORSE CHE SI FORSE CHE NO (1916) d *M Gardiulo fpl* D'Annunzio

FORSEGLADE LAPPAR (1927) d Molander SF

FOR SIN FADERS SKYLD (1916) d/co-s Madsen

FOR SIN KARLEKS SKULL (1913) d/p Stiller w Sjoström

FOR SIT LANDS AERE (1915) d Blom

Forsyte Sage, The (UK) = THAT FORSYTE WOMAN (1949)

FORT APACHE (1948) d/co-p J Ford co-p M Cooper s F Nugent c Stout w J Wayne, H Fonda, Temple, G O'Brien, V McLaglen, Armendariz, (March) 127min r RKO

FORT BOWIE (1958) d H W Koch

FORT DOBBS (1958) d G Douglas p Rackin co-st/co-s B Kennedy c Clothier m M Steiner w V Mayo, Keith 90min WB

FORT DODGE STAMPEDE (1951) d/as-p Keller 60min Rep

FORT DU FOU (1962) d/co-ad Joannon S 86min

FOR THE CAUSE (1913) d Ince

FOR THE DEFENCE (1930) d Cromwell c C Lang w W Powell, K Francis 65min Par

FOR THE FIRST TIME (1959) d Maté c Tonti w Lanza TR* 92min MGM

FOR THE LOVE OF MIKE (1927) d Capra c E Haller w G Sidney, Colbert 7rs FN

FOR THE LOVE OF RUSTY (1947) d J Sturges 69min Col

FOR THEM THAT TRESPASS (1949) d Cavalcanti s Thompson 95min ABC

FOR THOSE IN PERIL (1944) d Crichton co-s T Clarke, Watt 67min

FORTIETH DOOR, THE (1924) d G Seitz serial in 10ep Pat

FORT MASSACRE (1958) d J Newman p W Mirisch w McCrea CS* 80min UA

FORTROLLAD VANDRING (1954) d Mattsson s Lindstrom (= *Enchanted Walk*)

FORT TI (1953) d Castle p Katzman *73min Col

FORTUNA DI ESSERE DONNA, LA (1956) d/co-s Blasetti co-s Cecchi d'Amico c Martelli w Loren, Boyer, Mastroianni 92min (= *Lucky to be a Woman*)

FORTUNE COOKIE, THE (1966) d/p/co-s B Wilder co-as-p/co-s Diamond c La Shelle m Previn w Lemmon, Matthau PV 126min co-pc Mir r UA (= *Meet Whiplash Willie*)

FORTUNE IS A WOMAN (1956) d/co-p/co-s Gilliat co-p/co-s Launder m Alwyn w Hawkins 95min Col (= *She Played With Fire*)

FORTUNELLA (1958) d Filippo co-s Fellini c Tonti m Rota w De Filippo, Masina, Sordi, P Douglas 96min pc De Laurentiis

FORTUNES OF CAPTAIN BLOOD, THE (1950) d G Douglas p H Brown w L Hayward 96min Col

Forty-first, The = SOROK PERVYI (1927)

Forty-first, The = SOROK PERVYI (1956)

45 MINUTES FROM HOLLYWOOD (1926) w Laurel, Hardy Pat

FORTY GUNS (1957) d/p/s Fuller c Biroc w Stanwyck CS 79min Fox

Forty Hearts = SOROK SERDETS (1931)

FORTY LEAGUES FROM PARADISE (1970) d Peries *27min

FORTY LITTLE MOTHERS (1940) d Berkeley c Lawton w Cantor, Lake (ps Constance Keane) 94min MGM

FORTY NAUGHTY GIRLS (1937) d Cline c Metty w Pitts 64min RKO

49TH PARALLEL (1941) d/p M Powell c F Young e Lean w Olivier, Walbrook, L Howard 123min (= *The Invaders*)

FORTY POUNDS OF TROUBLE (1962) d Jewison w Curtis, Pleshette PV* 106min

42ND STREET (1933) d Bacon c Polito chor Berkeley w Baxter, D Powell, G Rogers 85min WB

Forward Flag Of Independence = SUSUME DOKURITSUKI (1943)

FORWARD INTO THE FUTURE (1964) d Peries 24min

FORWARD PASS, THE (1929) d Cline w Fairbanks Jr, L Young 7212ft WB

FOR WHOM THE BELL TOLLS (1943) d/p S Wood fn Hemingway s D Nichols c Rennahan co-a Dreier des Menzies m V Young w G Cooper, Ingrid Bergman, Tamiroff, De Carlo, Paxinou *170min Par

For Whom the Larks Sing = AKIKET A PACSIRTA ELKISER (1959)

FORZA BRUTA, LA (1941) d Bragaglia

FORZA DEL DESTINO, LA (1949) d Gallone m Verdi w Gobbi 110min (= *The Force of Destiny*)

FORZA G (1970) d/co-s Tessari

FOSSA DEGLI ANGELI, LA (1937) d/co-s Bragaglia (= *The Angels' Pit*)

FOU DE LA FALAISE, LE (1915) d/s Gance

FOUNDLING, THE (1915, ur) d Dwan p/w Pickford 5rs FP

Foundling, The = FINDLING, DER (1967)

FOUNTAIN, THE (1934) d Cromwell c Toland, Folsey w Lukas, Hersholt 83min RKO

FOUNTAINHEAD, THE (1949) d K Vidor p Blanke c Burks e Weisbart m M Steiner w G Cooper, Neal 119min WB

Fountainhead, The = IZUMI (1956)

FOUR BARRIERS (1938) d/s Cavalcanti p Grierson, Watt 8min

4 × 4 ep UPPEHALL I MYRLANDET (1964) d/co-s/c/e Troell w Von Sydow CS 30min (= *Interlude in the Marshland*)

Four Children in the Flood = NEGYEN AZ ARBAN (1961)

Four Chimneys = ENTOTSU NO MIERU BASHO (1953)

FOUR DAUGHTERS (1938) d Curtiz p Wallis di Rapper co-s JJ Epstein c E Haller m M Steiner w Rains, Garfield 90min WB

FOUR DAYS (1951) d Guillermin 55min

Four Days of Naples, The (UK) = QUATTRO GIORNATE DI NAPOLI, LE (1962)

FOUR DAYS WONDER (1937) d *Sidney Salkow* c Cortez U

FOUR DEVILS (1928) d Murnau co-s C Mayer co-c O'Connell w J Gaynor 2547m Fox

4–D MAN, THE (1959) d/as-p Yeaworth *85min U

FOUR FEATHERS, THE (1929) d/p Schoedsack, M Cooper, *Lothar Mendes* w C Brook, W Powell sd 7580ft Par

FOUR FEATHERS, THE (1939) d Z Korda p A Korda co-di Biro c Périnal m Rozsa w R Richardson *126min r UA

4 FOR TEXAS (1963) d/p/co-s Aldrich ex-p H W Koch c Laszlo co-2nd c Guffey, Biroc w Sinatra, Martin, Andress, Ekberg *124min WB

FOUR FRIGHTENED PEOPLE (1934) d De Mille c Struss co-a Dreier w Colbert, H Marshall 78min Par

FOUR HORSEMEN OF THE APOCALYPSE, THE (1921) d Ingram s Mathis fn *Vicente Blasco Ibañez* c J Seitz w Valentino, Beery 11rs MGM

FOUR HORSEMEN OF THE APOCALYPSE, THE (1962) d Minnelli p Blaustein co-s Ardrey fn *Vicente Blasco Ibañez* c Krasner m Previn w G Ford, Thulin, Boyer, Cobb, Henreid, Lukas CS* 153min r MGM

FOUR HOURS TO KILL (1935) d Leisen s/fpl (*Small Miracle*) *Krasna* w Barthelmess, Milland 73min Par

Four Hundred Blows, The (UK) = QUATRE CENT COUPS, LES (1959)

FOUR IN THE AFTERNOON (1951) d/s/c/wv Broughton fpms (in *Musical Chairs*) Broughton 16min

4 IN THE MORNING (1965) d/s A Simmons m Barry 94min

Four Kinds Of Love (UK) = BAMBOLE, LE (1964)

Four Love Stories = YOTTSU NO KOI NO MONOGATARI (1950)

Four Love Stories = YOTTSU NO KOI NO MONOGATARI (1947)

FOUR MEN AND A PRAYER (1938) d J Ford p Zanuck as-p Macgowan w L Young, G Sanders, Niven, Carradine 85min Fox

Four Monks, The = QUATTRO MONACI, I (1962)

FOUR MOTHERS (1941) d Keighley w Rains 86min WB

Four Musketeers, The = QUATTRO MOSCHETTIERI, I (1963)

4 9 1 (1964) d Sjöman c Fischer 105min SF

FOUR PARTS (1934) d C Chase (as Parrott) *Eddie Dunn* p Roach w C Chase 2rs MGM

FOUR POSTER, THE (1952) d Reis anim J Hubley c Mohr m Tiomkin w Harrison, Palmer 103min pc Kramer r Col

FOUR POSTER PEST, THE (1911) w N Talmadge

FOUR'S A CROWD (1938) d Curtiz c E Haller w Flynn, De Havilland, R Russell, Turner 91min WB

FOUR-SIDED TRIANGLE (1953) d Fisher m Arnold 81min

FOUR SONS (1928) d J Ford co-c C Clarke co-m Rothafel, Rapee w (Parrish) 9412ft Fox

FOUR SONS (1940) d A Mayo p Zanuck as-p H Brown ad Sperling s Lawson c Shamroy 89min Fox

Four Stars (1967) d Warhol 2 screens 25 hours subsequently fragmented; for some fragments see International Velvet; Alan and Dickin; Imitation of Christ; Courtroom; Gerard has his hair removed with Nair; Katrina Dead; Sausalito; Alan and Apple; Group One; Sunset Beach on Long Island; High Ashbury; Tiger Moorse; The Loves of Ondine *Other segments were*: Ondine and Ingrid; Ivy and Susan; Sunset in California; Ondine in Yellow Hair; Philadelphia Story; Katrina; Barbara and Ivy; Ondine and Edie; Susan and David; Orion; Emanuel; Rolando; Easthampton Beach; Swimming Pool; Nico-Katrina; Tally and Ondine; Ondine in Bathroom; Susan Screen Test; Susan Bottomly

Four Steps In The Clouds (UK) = QUATTRO PASSI FRA LE NUVOLE (1942)

FOURTEEN HOURS (1951) d Hathaway p S Siegel s Paxton c Joe MacDonald co-a Wheeler m A Newman w P Douglas, Moorehead, Grace Kelly, J Hunter 92min Fox

Fourteen Lives Saved = ELETJEL (1959)

Fourteen Year Old Girl, The = HEDY (1965)

FOURTH ESTATE, THE (1940) d/s *Rotha* co-cy B Wright 45min

FOURTH MUSKETEER, THE (1923) d W Howard c O'Connell 5800ft

Four Truths, The = QUATRES VERITES, LES (1962)

|Four Ways Out (US) = CITTA SI DIFENDE, LA (1952)

FOUR WIVES (1940) d Curtiz p Wallis as-p Blanke s JJ Epstein c Polito m Steiner w Rains 101min WB

Four Women For One Hero (UK) = HOMENAJE A LA HORA DE LA SIESTA (1902)

FOX, THE (1968) d *Mark Rydell* p Stross co-s H Koch c Fraker m Schifrin *110min

FOX CHASE, THE (1952) d Lye

FOXES OF HARROW, THE (1947) d Stahl c La Shelle co-a Wheeler w Harrison, M O'Hara, Haydn, V McLaglen 117min Fox

FOX FIRE (1955) d Pevney p A Rosenberg c Daniels w J Russell, J Chandler, Duryea *91½min U

FOX FIRE CHILD WATCH (1971) d Brakhage 16mm *

FOX HUNT (1937) d Gross, *Hector Hoppin* anim* 8min

FOXY PUP, THE (1937) d Iwerks anim* 603ft r Col

Fra' Diavolo = DEVIL'S BROTHER, THE (1933)

FRA' DIAVOLO (1941) d/co-s Zampa

FRA FYRSTE TIL KNEJPEVAERT (1913) d/s Madsen

Fragments of an Empire = OBLOMOK IMPERII (1929)

FRAMED (1947) d *Richard Wallace* s Maddow w G Ford 81min Col

FRAMING YOUTH (1937) d G Douglas p Roach 1rl MGM

FRANCAISE ET L'AMOUR, LA (1960) 135min (= *Love and the Frenchwoman*)

ep L'ENFANCE d Decoin m Kosma (= *Infancy*)

ep L'ADOLESCENCE d Delannoy m Misraki (= *Adolescence*)

ep LA VIRGINITE d *Michel Boisrond*

ep LE MARIAGE d/co-s Clair co-s Rappeneau 28min (= *Marriage*)

ep L'ADULTERE d Verneuil co-s Audiard w Belmondo (= *Adultery*)

ep LE DIVORCE d Christian-Jaque s Charles Spaak w Girardot (= *Divorce*)

ep LA FEMME SEULE d/ad/di Le Chanois m Delerue w Carol (= *A Woman Alone*)

FRANCE EST UN JARDIN, LA (1953) d/p Leenhardt *32min (= *France is a Garden*)

France is a Garden = FRANCE EST UN JARDIN (1953)

France Liberated = OZVOBOZHDENNAYA FRANTSYA (1946)

FRANCESCO, GIULLARE DI DIO (1950) d/co-s Rossellini co-s Fellini f (*I Fioretti di San Francesco*) c Martelli 75min

FRANCE SUR UN CAILLOU, LA (1960) d Groulx, *Claude Fournier* e Groulx

FRANCHE LIPPEE (1933) d Delannoy sh

FRANCISCAIN DE BOURGES, LE (1968) d Autant-Lara *100min

FRANCIS IN THE NAVY (1955) d *Arthur Lubin* w Eastwood, O'Connor 80min U

FRANCIS OF ASSISI (1961) d Curtiz w Armendariz CS* 111min Fox

FRANCK AROMA (1937) d Alexeieff anim

FRANCO DE PORT (1937) d/s/di Kirsanov 75min

Françoise Steps Out (UK) = RUE DE L'ESTRAPADE (1953)

FRANCOIS MAURIAC (1954) d Leenhardt 36min

FRANCOIS Ier (1936) d Christian-Jaque w Fernandel

FRANKENSTEIN (1931) d Whale fn *Mrs P B Shelley* c Edeson w Karloff 67min U

FRANKENSTEIN CREATED WOMAN (1967) d Fisher *86min

FRANKENSTEIN MUST BE DESTROYED (1969) d Fisher *97min WB

FRANKENSTEIN–1970 (1958) d H W Koch w Karloff

FRANSKILD (1951) d Molander co-st/s Ingmar Bergman w Kjellin 2820m SF (= *Divorced*)

FRAN YTTERSTA SKAREN (1931) d Molander

FRATELLI MIRACOLOSI, I (1949) co-d/co-s/s/n Emmer co-d/co-s *Enrico Gras* 10min (= *The Miraculous Brothers*)

Fraternally Yours = SONS OF THE DESERT (1933)

FRAU BLACKBURN WIRD GEFILMT (1967) *d* Kluge sh
FRAUENLIEBE – FRAUENLEID (1937) *d/st/s* Genina
FRAUENNOT – FRAUENGLUCK (1929) *d/c* Tissé
FRAUENSCHICKSALE (1952) *d/cos* Dudow *m* Eisler 2850m Defa
FRAU EVA (1916) *d/s* Wiene *fn* (*Fromont Jeune et Risler aîné*) *Alphonse Daudet* *c* Freund *w* Jannings
FRAU IM BESTEN MANNESALTER (1959) *d* Wicki
FRAU IM MOND (1929) *d/p/co-s* F Lang *co-s* Von Harbou *co-c* Courant *co-c/co-sp eff* Fischinger 4356m *r* Ufa (= *By Rocket to the Moon/The Girl in the Moon*)
FRAULEIN DOKTOR (1968) *d/co-s* Lattuada *98min *co-pc* De Laurentiis Par (= *The Betrayal*)
FRAULEIN ELSE (1929) *d* Czinner *co-c* Freund *w* Bergner 1815m
FRAULEIN SEIFENSCHAUM (1914) *d/s/w* Lubitsch 1rl (= *Miss Soapsuds*)
FRAULEIN ZAHNARZT (1919) *d/p/co-s* May 1494m
FRAU MIT DEM SCHLECHTEN RUF, DIE (1925) *d* Christensen *w* L Barrymore 1894m Ufa (= *The Woman Who Did*)
FRAU NACH DER MAN SICH SEHNT, DIE (1929) *d* C Bernhardt *c* Courant *w* Dietrich 2360m (= *Enigma*)
FRAU NACH MASS (1940) *d/s* Kautner 2571m
FRAU UBER BORD (1945, *uf*) *d* Staudte Tob
FREAKS (1932) *d* Browning *co-s* Goldbeck 61min MGM
Freccia, La = FRECCIA NEL FIANCO, LA (1943)
FRECCIA NEL FIANCO, LA (1943) *d/co-s* Lattuada *p* Ponti *co-s* Zavattini, *Moravia* *m* Rota (= *La Freccia/The Arrow*)
FRECKLES (1917) *d* Neilan 5rs FPL
FRECKLES (1960) *d* A McLaglen *c* F Crosby CS* 84min Fox
FRED BARRY, COMEDIAN (1959) *d/s* Jutra 30min
FREDLOS (1935) *d* Fejos
FREE AND EASY (1930) *d/p* *Edward Sedgwick* *dec* Gibbons *w* Keaton, L Barrymore, Montgomery, Niblo 10rs MGM (= *Estrellados*)
FREE AND EASY (1941) *d* G Sidney *st* *I Novello* *c* Lawton, Folsey *w* R Cummings 56min MGM
FREE RADICALS (1958) *d* Lye 16mm 5min
Fred Ott's Sneeze = EDISON KINETOSCOPIC RECORD OF A SNEEZE, JANUARY 7, 1894 (1894)
FREEDOM RADIO (1941) *d* Asquith *co-s* De Grunwald *w* C Brook 90min Col (= *The Voice in the Night*)
FREE SOUL, A (1931) *d* C Brown *c* Daniels *w* J Crawford, Gable, L Barrymore, Shearer, L Howard 91min MGM
Free to Live (UK) = HOLIDAY (1938)
Free Wind = VOLNYI VETER (1961)
FREEZE OUT, THE (1921) *d* J ford *w* Carey 4400ft U
FRELSENDE FILM, DEN (1915) *d* Madsen
FRENCH CANCAN (1955) *d/s* J Renoir *m* Van Parys *w* Gabin, Arnaud, *Edith Pial* Modot, Piccoli *
FRENCH DOLL, THE (1923) *d/pc* Leonard 7rs Metro
FRENCH DRESSING (1927) *d/p* Dwan *c* E Haller *w* C Brook, Hopper 6344ft FN
FRENCH DRESSING (1963) *d* K Russell *m* Delerue 86min
FRENCH LINE, THE (1953) *d* Bacon *c* Wild *w* J Russell, Roland 3-D 102min RKO
FRENCHMAN'S CREEK (1944) *d* Leisen *fn* *D du Maurier* *c* Barnes *co-a* Dreier *w* Fontaine, Rathbone 113min Par
FRENCH MISTRESS, A (1960) *d/co-p* R Boulting *co-p* J Boulting 98min BL
French They Are a Funny Race, The (US) = CARNETS DU MAJOR THOMPSON, LES (1955)
French White Cargo (US) = CARGAISONS BLANCHES (1937)
FRENCH WITHOUT TEARS (1939) *d* Asquith *co-s* De Grunwald *fpl* Rattigan *e* Lean *w* Milland 84min Par
FRENESIA DELL'ESTATE (1963) *d* Zampa *w* Manfredi, Gassman (= *Shivers in Summer*)
Frenzy (UK) = HETS (1944)
FRERE DE LAIT, LE (1916) *d/s* Feyder 180m Gau
FRERES BOUQUINQUANT, LES (1947) *d/co-s* Daquin *m* Wiener *w* Préjean 99min
Fresh Air = JINY VZDUCH (1939)
FRESH AIREDALE (1945) *d* C Jones anim* 7min WB
FRESHMAN, THE (1925) *co-d* Newmayer *co-d/s* *Sam Taylor* *w* H Lloyd 6883ft *pc* H Lloyd *r* Pat
FREUDLOSE GASSE, DIE (1925) *d* Pabst *w* Garbo, Nielsen, Krauss, (Dietrich) 110min (post-synchronized version *r* 1937: *Streets of Sorrow*)
FREUD, THE SECRET PASSION (1962) *d/co-s* J Huston *c* Slocombe *m* Goldsmith *w* Clift 120min *r* U
FREUNDIN EINES GROSSEN MANNES, DIE (1934) *d/w* Wegener 2638m Ufa
Freundschaft siegt = MY ZA MIR (1951)
FRIC FRAC (1939) *d* Autant-Lara *w* Arletty, Fernandel, M Simon 105min
FRIDAS VISOR (1930) *d/co-s* Molander SF
FRIDAY THE THIRTEENTH (1933) *d* Saville *w* R Richardson, Emlyn Williams 89min GB
FRIEDA (1947) *d* Dearden *p* Balcon *w* Zetterling 98min
FRIEDERIKE VON BARRING (1956) *d/s* Thiele *w* Tiller
FRIEND INDEED (1937) *d* Zinnemann 10min MGM
FRIENDLY ENEMIES (1942) *d* Dwan *c* Cronjager *w* C Ruggles 95min *r* UA
FRIENDLY PERSUASION (1956) *d/p* Wyler *s* M Wilson (*uc*) *m* Tiomkin *w* G Cooper, McGuire, Perkins *139min *r* AA
FRIENDS (1912) *d/s* Griffith *w* Pickford, L Barrymore 1rl Bio
FRIENDS (1971) *d/p/st* L Gilbert *102min
FRIENDS AND LOVERS (1931) *d* Schertzinger *w* Olivier, Menjou, Von Stroheim 76min RKO
Friends For Life = AMICI PER LA PELLE (1955)
FRIENDS OF MR. SWEENEY (1934) *d* *Edward Ludwig* *w* MacMurray, C Ruggles 70min WB
Frigorelse = STUDIE IV (1954)
FRIHEDSFONDEN (1945) *d/s* B Henning Jensen
FRISCO JENNY (1933) *d* Wellman *c* Hickox 70min FN
FRISCO KID (1935) *d* Bacon *co-st/co-s* S Miller *c* Polito *w* Cagney 76min WB
FRITZ BAUER (1930) *d/s* Petrov 1843m
Frogman Spy = MIZAR (1954)
FROGMEN, THE (1951) *d* Bacon *c* Brodine *co-a* Wheeler *m* Mockridge *w* Widmark, D Andrews, J Hunter, R Wagner 97min Fox
FROG POND, THE (1938) *d* Iwerks anim* 1rl *r* Col
FROG PRINCE, THE (1954) *d* Reiniger *fst* *Brothers Grimm* anim 10min
FROG PRINCE, THE (1961) *d* Reiniger anim* 10min
FROKEN JULIE (195?) *d/s* Sjöberg *fpl* *August Strindberg* *c* Strindberg *w* Björk, (Von Sydow) 87min San (= *Miss Julie*)
From A Roman Balcony (US) = GIORNATA BALORDA, LA (1965)
FROM DADA TO SURREALISM: 40 YEARS OF EXPERIMENT (1961) *a compilation of Richter films, prepared for Museum of Modern Art, New York*
FROM A TO Z-Z-Z (1955) *d* Freleng anim* 7min WB
FROM HAND TO MOUTH (1920) *w* H Lloyd 2rs *pc* Roach *r* Pat
FROM HEADQUARTERS (1933) *d* Dieterle 7rs FN
FROM HELL TO TEXAS (1958) *d* Hathaway *co-s* Mayes *co-a* Wheeler *m* Amfitheatrof *w* Murray CS* 100min Fox (= *Manhunt*)
FROM HERE TO ETERNITY (1953) *d* Zinnemann *p* Adler *s* Taradash *fn* *James Jones* *c* Guffey *w* Lancaster, Clift, Kerr, Sinatra, D Reed, Borgnine 118min Col
FROM HERE TO THERE (1964) *d* Bass S* 8min
FROM NOW ON (1920) *d* Walsh *co-c* Ruttenberg 7rs Fox
FROM PADDINGTON TO PENZANCE (TOUR OF THE WEST OF ENGLAND BY GWR) (1905) *p* Paul 1005ft 11 parts
FROM RUSSIA WITH LOVE (1963) *d* T Young *co-p* Saltzman *s* Maibaum *fn* *I Fleming* *c* Moore *m* Barry *w* Connery, Armendariz, Lenya *116min
From Saturday to Sunday = ZE SOBOTY NA NEDELI (1931)
FROM SOUP TO NUTS (1928) *d* *Edgar Kennedy* *p* Roach *st* McCarey *w* Laurel, Hardy sd 2rs *r* MGM
FROM THE EARTH TO THE MOON (1958) *d* Haskin *p* Bogeaus *fn* *Jules Verne* *w* Cotten, G Sanders *100min WB
FROM THE TERRACE (1960) *d/p* Robson *s* Lehman *fn* *John O'Hara* *co-a* Wheeler *m* E Bernstein *w* P Newman, Woodward, M Loy CS* 144min Fox
FROM THIS DAY FORWARD (1946) *d* John Berry *p* Pereira *ad* Kanin *s* H Butler *c* Barnes *m* Harline *w* Fontaine 95min RKO
FROM WHENCE COMETH HELP (1949) *w* Poitier US Army
FRONT (1943) *d* S and G Vasiliev
Frontier (US) = AEROGRAD (1935)
FRONTIERE, LA (1961) *d/co-s/co-c* *Cayrol* 17min
FRONTIER MARSHAL (1939) *d* Dwan *c* C Clarke *co-a* R Day *w* R Scott, Romero, Carradine 71min Fox
FRONTIER RANGERS (1959) *d* J Tourneur 3ep US TV series *Northwest Passage* *83min MGM
FRONTIERS OF NEWS (1964) *d/c* W Van Dyke 11min
FRONT LINE, THE (1940) *d* Watt GPO
FRONTLINE CAMERAS (1935–1965) *d/p* W Van Dyke 16min
FRONT PAGE, THE (1931) *d* Milestone *p* H Hughes *fpl* B Hecht, MacArthur *co-di* Lecerer *a* R Day *w* Menjou, Horton, (Milestone) 101min UA
FROU FROU (1955) *d/co-ad/co-s* Genina *c* Alekan *w* De Funès, Bardot CS* 108min
FRONT PAGE WOMAN (1935) *d* Curtiz *c* Gaudio *w* B Davis 82min WB
FROZEN JUSTICE (1929) *d* Dwan *c* Rosson sd 7170ft Fox
FROZEN NORTH, THE (1922) *d/s* Keaton, Cline *w/co-pc* Keaton
FRUHLINGS ERWACHEN (1929) *d/p* R Oswald *w* (Lorre) 2309m
FRUHLINGSRAUSCHEN (1929) *d/w* Dieterle 2609m
FRUHLINGSTIMMEN (1934) *d* Fejos
FRUIT DEFENDU, LE (1951) *d/co-s* Verneuil *fn* (*Lettre à ma juge*) *Georges Simenon* *w* Fernandel 103min
FRUITFUL VINE, THE (1921) *d* Elvey *w* Rathbone 7000ft
FRUITS AMERS (1966) *d* *Jacqueline Audry* *w* Riva *108min (= *Bitter Fruit*)
FRUMENTO, IL (1958) *d* Olmi *20min
FRUSTA E IL CORPO, LA (1963) *d* Bara (*ps* John M Old) *90min (= *Night is the Phantom*)
FRUTTO ACERBO (1934) *d* Bragaglia
FUDGET'S BUDGET (1954) *d* Cannon * *pc* UPA *r* Col
FUEFUKI-GAWA (1960) *d* Kinoshita S* Sho (= *The River Fuefuki*)
FUFU (1953) *d* Naruse (= *Husband and Wife*)
FUGA, LA (1937) *d* Saslavsky
FUGA A DUE VOCI (1943) *d/st/s* Bragaglia
FUGA DEGLI AMANTI, LA (1914) *d* Genina
FUGA IN FRANCIA (1948) *d/co-st/co-s* Soldati *p* Ponti *w* Germi 91min (= *Flight Into Francia*)
Fugitive (UK) = BRIGANTE MUSOLINO, IL (1950)
Fugitive, The = BEGLETS (1932)
FUGITIVE, THE (1947) *d/co-p* J Ford *co-p* M Cooper *as-p* Fernandez *s* D Nichols *fn* Greene (*The Power and the Glory*) *c* Figueroa *w* H Fonda, Del Rio, Armendariz, (M Ferrer) 104min *r* RKO
FUGITIVE FROM MATRIMONY, A (1919) *d* H King 5rs
Fugitive in Saigon = MORT EN FRAUDE (1956)
FUGITIVE KIND, THE (1959) *d* Lumet *co-s/fpl* (*Orpheus Descending*) T Williams *c* B Kaufman *m* K Hopkins *w* Brando, Magnani, Woodward
FUGITIVE LADY (1951) *d* *Sidney Salkow* *p* Frankovich 78min Rep 119min *r* UA
FUGITIVE LOVERS (1934) *d* Boleslavsky *s* Hackett, Goodrich, G Seitz *c* Tetzlaff *w* Montgomery, (Tamiroff) 84min MGM
FUGUE DE MAHMOUD, LA (1950) *d/s* Leenhardt 30min
FUHRMANNHENSCHEL (1918) *d* Lubitsch *fst* *Gerhard Hauptmann* *c* Sparkuhl *w* Jannings
FUITE DE GAZ, LA (1912) *d/w* Linder Pat
FUJICHO (1947) *d* Kinoshita (= *Phoenix*)
FUKEIKI JIDAI (1930) *d/s* Naruse (= *Depression Period*)
FUKEYO KOIKAZE (1935) *d* Gosho
FULL CONFESSION (1939) *d* J Farrow *w* V McLaglen 75min RKO
FULLER BRUSH GIRL, THE (1950) *d* Bacon *s* Tashlin *c* Lawton *w* Ball 89min Col (= *Affairs of Sally*)
Full House = O'HENRY'S FULL HOUSE (1952)
FULL HOUSE, A (1920) *d* Cruze 5rs
FULL OF LIFE (1957) *d* Quine *p* Kohlmar *c* Lawton *m* Duning *w* Holliday, Conte 91min Col
FULTAH FISHER'S BOARDING HOUSE (1923) *d* Capra *fpm* *Rudyard Kipling* Pat
FUMEE NOIRE (1920) *co-d/s* Delluc *co-d* *René Coiffart*
FUMEES (1915) *d* Alexeieff, *Georges Violet* anim* 1min
FUMO DI LONDRA (1965) *d/co-s/w* Sordi *m* Piccioni S* 118min
FUN AT ST. FANNY'S (1956) *d* Elvey S 80min
FUNERAL IN BERLIN (1966) *d* Hamilton *p* Saltzman *fn* *Len Deighton* *c* Heller *w* Caine PV* 102min Par
FUNERAL OF QUEEN VICTORIA, THE (1901) *p* Paul 360ft
Funf Verfluchten Gentlemen, Die (1932): German version of CINQ GENTILHOMMES MAUDITS (1931)
Funf vom Titan, Die = VOR UNS LIEGT DAS LEBEN (1948)
FUN IN ACAPULCO (1963) *d* Thorpe *p* Wallis *c* Fapp *co-a* Pereira *w* Presley, Andress, Lukas *97min *r* Par
FUNNIA DEL FALORIA, LA (1950) *d/s* Antonioni 10min
FUNKZAUBER (1927) *d/p* R Oswald *w* Krauss 2486m
FUNNY FACE (1957) *d/co-chor* Donen *p/co-m/co-lyr* Edens *co-m/co-lyr* *George and Ira Gershwin* *c* June *co-a* Pereira *co-chor* Astaire, Loring *w* Astaire, A Hepburn VV* 104min Par
FUNNY GIRL (1968) *d* Wyler *p* Stark *c* Stradling *des* Callahan *chor* Ross *w* Sharif, A Francis, Pidgeon PV70* 146min *pc* Stark *r* Col
FUNNY THING HAPPENED ON THE WAY TO THE FORUM, A (1966) *d* Lester *p/co-s* M Frank *c* Roeg *cr* R Williams *w* Keaton *99min *r* UA
FUN ON A WEEKEND (1947) *d/p/s* Stone 93min UA
FUOCO, IL (1915) *d* Pastrone, *Zacconi* *s* D'Annunzio
FUOCO (1968) *d/co-p/s* Baldi *100min (= *Fire*)
FUORILEGGI DEL MATRIMONIO, I (1963) *d/co-st/co-s* Orsini, P and V Taviani *m* Fusco *w* Giraudot 105min
FURIES, THE (1950) *d* A Mann *p* Wallis *s* Schnee *fn* Busch *c* Milner *m* Waxman *w* Stanwyck, Corey, W Huston, Roland 109min Par
FURTHER DETAILS OF LAUREL AND HARDY, THE (1967) *d* *Robert Youngson compilation* *w* Laurel, Hardy 100min *pc* *Robert Youngson* *r* Fox
FURUSATO (1922) *d/s* Mizoguchi Nik (= *Hometown*)
FURUSATO (1930) *d* Mizoguchi *rm* 1922 Nik (= *Hometown*)
FURUSATO NO UTA (1925) *d* Mizoguchi Nik
FURY (1922) *d/st/fn* Goulding 9rs
FURY (1936) *d/co-s* Lang *p* J Mankiewicz *st* Krasna *c* Ruttenberg *m* Waxman *w* Tracy, S Sidney, Brennan 94min MGM
FURY AT GUNSIGHT PASS (1956) *d* Sears 68min Col
FURY AT SHOWDOWN (1957) *d* G Oswald *c* La Shelle *w* Derek 75min UA
Fury Of The Vikings = INVASORI, GLI (1961)
FURYO SHOJO (1949) *d/s* Naruse (= *The Bad Girl*)
FURY RIVER (1959) ep THE VULTURE *d* J Tourneur 3ep from US TV series *Northwest Passage* *74min MGM
FUSHIN NO TOKI (1968) *d* Imai S* 120min Dai (= *Time Of Reckoning/When You Can't Believe Anyone*)
FUSS AND FEATHERS (1918) *d* Niblo 5rs FPL
FUTARI DE ARUITA IKUSHUNJU (1962) *d* Kinoshita S 110min Sho (= *Ballad of a Workman*)

FUTATSU DORO (1933) d/s Kinugasa (= Two Stone Lantern)
FUTATSU-NO YAKIZAKANA (1968) p/d/st Kuri anim* 13min (= Two Grilled Fish)
FUTURE'S IN THE AIR, THE (1936) d Alexander, Ralph Keene p Rotha m Alwyn
FUTURES VEDETTES (1954) d/co-s M Allégret co-s/di Vadim m Wiener w Marais, Bardot 95min Col
Futurismo = INHUMAINE, L' (1924)
FUYAKI SHINJU (1934) d/s Kinugasa
FUZEN NO TOMOSHIBI (1957) d/s Kinoshita Sho (= Candle In The Wind/Danger Stalks Near)
FUZIS, OS (1964) d/st/co-s/e Guerra 110min (= The Guns)
FUZZY PINK NIGHTGOWN, THE (1957) d Taurog c La Shelle w J Russell, Meeker, Menjou 87min r UA

GAA MED MIG HJEM (1941) d Christensen
GABRIEL OVER THE WHITE HOUSE (1933) d La Cava c Glennon w W Huston, Tone, (Tamiroff) 87min MGM
GABY (1956) d C Bernhardt s Goodrich, Hackett, Lederer co-a Gibbons w Caron CS* 97min MGM
Gadfly, The = POPRIGUNYA (1955)
GAGNANT, LE (1935) d Y Allégret sh
GAI DIMANCHE (1935) d Jacques Berr co-s/co-di/w Tati
GAIJO NO SUKECHI (1925) d Mizoguchi Nik (= Street Sketches)
GAILY, GAILY (1969) d/p Jewison fn B Hecht des Boyle m/co-songs Mancini w Mercouri, Keith, Kennedy *117min r UA (= Chicago, Chicago)
GAINES ROUSSEL, LES (1939) d Alexeieff anim
GAI SAVOIR, LE (1969) d/s Godard fn (Emile) Rousseau w Léaud *91min ORTF
GAITES DE L'ESCADRON, LES (1932) d M Tourneur w Raimu, Gabin
GAITO NO KISHI (1928) d Gosho
GAKUSO O IDETE (1925) d/co-s Mizoguchi Nik (= After Years Of Study)
GALA (1961) d/p/s Pollet CS 20min sh
Gala Dinner = UNNEPI VACSORA (1956)
GALATHEA (1935) d/p Reiniger anim 1rl 960ft
GALAXIE (1966) d/s/c/e Markopoulos w S Clarke, J Mekas 16mm* 90min
GALERIES DE MALGOVERT, LES (1950) d Rouquier 1200m
GALGMANNEN (1945) d Molander SF
GALIA (1965) d/co-s Lautner mf Bach w Darc 105min
GALICIA Y COMPOSTELA (1933) d/s Velo, Fernando Mantilla 1rl
GALLANT BESS (1946) d Marton a Gibbons 101min MGM
GALLANT HOURS, THE (1960) d/p Montgomery c Joe Macdonald w Cagney 115min pc Cagney, Montgomery r UA
GALLANT JOURNEY (1946) d/p/co-s Wellman co-c Guffey w G Ford, C Ruggles 85min Col
GALLANT LADY (1934) d La Cava p Zanuck c Marley m A Newman w C Brook 84min UA
GALLANT LITTLE TAILOR, THE (1954) d Reiniger fst Brothers Grimm anim 10min
GALLANT SONS (1940) d G Seitz 73min MGM
GALLOPIN' GALS (1940) d Hanna, Barbera p Quimby anim 681 MGM
GALLOPIN' GAUCHO, THE (1930) d Iwerks p Disney anim 1rl
GALLOPING BUNGALOWS (1924) d Cline p Sennett s Cline, Garnett Pat
GALLOPING GOBS, THE (1927) d Thorpe
GALLOPING HOOFS (1924-25) d G Seitz serial in 10ep Pat
GALLOPING JUSTICE (1927) d Wyler 2rs U
GALLOPING MAJOR, THE (1951) d/co-s Cornelius
GALLOPING ON (1926) d Thorpe
GAMBIT (1966) d Neame co-a Golitzen w MacLaine, Caine *108min U
GAMBLER'S FATE, OR THE ROAD TO RUIN, THE (1901) p Paul 200ft
GAMBLERS, THE (1929) d Curtiz 6611ft WB
GAMBLING HOUSE (1951) d Tetzlaff c Wild w Mature, Bendix 80min RKO
GAMBLING LADY (1934) d A Mayo w Stanwyck, McCrea 67min WB
GAMBLING SEX, THE (1932) d Newmeyer 59min
Game, The = GRA (1968)
Game Is Over, The = CURÉE, LA (1966)
GAME OF DEATH, A (1945) d Wise 72min RKO
Game of Love, The (UK) = EAU A LA BOUCHE, L' (1959)
Game Of Luck = ONNENPELI (1965)
GAME OF WITS, A (1917) d H King Mut
GAME OLD KNIGHT, A (1915) d Dick Jones p Sennett w Fazenda 2rs Tri-Key
GAMES (1967) d/co-st Curtis Harrington c Fraker co-a Golitzen w Signoret S* 100min U
GAMIN DE PARIS, LE (1923) d/s Feuillade 1900m
GAMLA KUARNEN, DEN (1962) d Troell (= The Old Mill)
GAMMELION (1967) d/s/c/e Markopoulos 16mm *60min
GAMLET (1964) d/s Kozintsev fpl Shakespeare m

Shostakovich (trans Boris Pasternak) S 150min (= Hamlet)
GAMPERALIYA (1964) d Peries 105min (= The Changing Countryside)
GANCHEROS, LOS (1956) d Berlanga
GANG IN DIE NACHT, DER (1920) d Murnau s Mayer fn (Dr Jekyll and Mr Hyde) Stevenson w Veidt, Lugosi 2000m (= Love's Mockery/The Walk in the Night)
GANG'S ALL HERE, THE (1943) d Berkeley c Cronjager m A Newman w Faye, C Miranda, Crain, Horton *103min Fox
GANGS OF NEW YORK, THE (1938) d Cruze st/co-s Fuller w Bickford 67min Rep
GANGSTER, EL (1964) d Alcoriza
GANGSTERPREMIERE (1951) d/co-s/w Jurgens
GANGSTER STORY (1961) d/w Matthau
Gangster We Made, The = VICIOUS YEARS, THE (1950)
GANG WAR (1928) d Glennon 6365ft
GANS VON SEDAN, DIE (1959) d/co-s Käutner 2455m Ufa
GARAGE, THE (1919) d/s Arbuckle w Arbuckle, Keaton 2rs FPL
Garçon divorcé, Le = MARI DIVORCE, LE (1933)
GARCON SAUVAGE, LE (1951) d Delannoy fn Edouard Peisson ad/di Jeanson c Lefebvre m Misraki
GARDEN GOPHER (1950) d Avery anim *6min MGM
GARDEN OF ALLAH, THE (1927) d/p Ingram c Garmes 8200m MGM
GARDEN OF ALLAH, THE (1936) d Boleslavsky di-d Logan (uc) p Selznick co-s Goldbeck c Rosson co-a Wheeler m M Steiner w Dietrich, Boyer, Rathbone, Carradine *85min r UA
Garden of Delights, The = JARDIN DE LOS DELICES, EL (1970)
GARDEN OF EDEN, THE (1928) d/p Milestone w L Sherman
GARDEN OF EVIL (1954) d Hathaway p Brackett co-c Krasner co-a Wheeler m Herrman w G Cooper, S Hayward, Widmark CS* 100min Fox
GARDEN OF THE MOON (1938) d Berkeley co-s Wald c Gaudio w Payne 94min WB
GARDEN OF WEEDS, THE (1924) d/p Cruze 6230ft FPL
Garden Of Women, The = ONNA NO SONO (1954)
GARDIENS DE PHARE (1929) d/e Grémillon s Feyder c Périnal 2400m
UN GARIBALDINO AL CONVENTO (1941) d/co-ad/w De Sica
GARMENT CENTER, THE (1957) d V Sherman, Aldrich (uc) c Biroc m Leith Stevens w Cobb 87min Col (= The Garment Jungle)
Garment Jungle, The = GARMENT CENTER, THE (1957)
GASLIGHT (1940) d T Dickinson w Walbrook, Newton
GASLIGHT (1944) d Cukor fpl (Angel St) Patrick Hamilton rm 1940 c Ruttenberg a Gibbons m Kaper w Boyer, Ingrid Bergman, Cotten 114min MGM (= The Murder in Thornton Square)
GAS-OIL (1955) d Grangier s Audiard w Gabin, Moreau 89min
GASOLINE GUS (1921, ur) d Cruze
GASSEN MAUER (1931) d Lupu-Pick co-c Schuftan w Staudte sd 2654m
GAS-S-S (1970) d/p Corman *97min (= Gas-s-s or how it became necessary to destroy the world in order to save it)
Gas-s-s or how it became necessary to destroy the world in order to save it = GAS-S-S (1970)
GATANS BARN (191?) d Sjöström 1103m
GATEGUTTER (1949) d Skouen, Uif Greber s/fn Skouen (= Guttersnipes/Gods of the Street)
Gate of Hell = JIGOKUMON (1953)
GATES TO PARADISE (1967) d Wajda TS* 89min
GATHERING OF EAGLES, A (1963) d Delbert Mann m Goldsmith c R Harlan w Hudson *115min U
GATTOPARDO, IL (1963) d/co-s Visconti co-s Cecchi d'Amico, Festa Campanile fn Giuseppe Tomasi di Lampedusa c Rotunno m Rota w Lancaster, Delon, Cardinale, Reggiani TR* 205min (= The Leopard)
GAUCHO, LE (1964) d Risi w Gassman, Manfredi 115min
GAUCHO, THE (1928) d F Richard Jones p Fairbanks Sr st Fairbanks Sr (ps Elton Thomas) c Gaudio w Pickford, Fairbanks Sr, (Fernandez) part * 9358ft r UA
GAUGUIN (1950) d/c Resnais p Braunberger m Milhaud 11min
GAVOTTE (1967) d/st Borowczyk *10min
GAY BRIDE, THE (1934) d Conway c June w Lombard, Pitts 80min MGM
Gay Canary, The = VESELAYA KANAREIKA (1929)
GAY DECEIVER, THE (1926) d Stahl 6671ft MGM
GAY DECEPTION, THE (1935) d Wyler p Lasky w Tamiroff 79min Fox
GAY DEFENDER, THE (1927) d/p La Cava c Cronjager 6230ft FPL
GAY DESPERADO, THE (1936) d Mamoulian co-p Lasky c Andriot a R Day m A Newman w Lupino 88min pc Pickford-Lasky r UA
GAY DIPLOMAT, THE (1931) d Boleslavsky 70min RKO
GAY DIVORCEE, THE (1934) d Sandrich p Berman w G Rogers, Astaire, Grable, Horton 107min RKO
GAY FALCON, THE (1941) d Reis c Musuraca w G Sanders 67min RKO

Gay Lady, The = BATTLE OF PARIS (1929)
Gay Mrs Trexal, The (UK) Ô SUSAN AND GOD (1939)
Gay Masquerade = BENTEN KOZO (1928)
GAY PURR-EE (1962) d Abe Levitow co-s C Jones wv Garland *86min WB
GAY SISTERS, THE (1942) d Rapper p Blanke c Polito m M Steiner w Stanwyck, Crisp 108min WB
GAZ, LE (1939, uf) d Alexeieff anim*
GAZEBO, THE (1959) d G Marshall s Wells w D Reynolds, G Ford, Pitts CS 100min MGM
GAZ MORTELS, LES (1916) d/s Gance c Burel (= Brouillard sur la Ville)
GEBISSEN WIRD NUR NACHTS – HAPPENING DER VAMPIRE (1971) d F Francis *97min
GEFANGENE DES MAHARADSCHA, DIE (1953) d V Harlan 2832m
GEFANGENE VON SHANGHAI, DIE (1927) co-d/st Genina co-d Geza Von Bolvary
GEHEIMNIS DES ABBE X, DAS (1927) d/s/w Dieterle 2205m (= Der Mann, der nicht Lieben darf/Secret of Abee X)
GEHEIMNIS DER AMERIKA-DOCKS, DAS (1918) d/s Dupont 1446m
GEHEIMNIS DER LEEREN WASSERFLASCHE, DAS (1917) d/p May 4rs
GEHEIMNISSE EINER SEELE (1926) d Pabst w Krauss 95min Ufa
GEHEIMNISVOLLE TIEFEN (1949) d Pabst 109min
GEHEIMNISVOLLE VILLA, DIE (1914) d May 1322m
GEHEIMSEKRETAR, DER (1915) d/p/co-s may 4rs
GEHETZTE FRAUEN (1927) d/p R Oswald w Nielsen 2447m
GEIDO ICHIDAI OTOKO (1940) d Mizoguchi Sho (= The Life of an Artist)
GEIER-WALLY DER (1921) d/s Dupont dec Leni w Dieterle 2155m r Ufa (= Ein Roman aus den Burgen/Geyerwally)
GEIERWALLY, DIE (1940) d Steinhoff 2840m Tob
Geiger, Der = EWIGE KLANG, DER (1943)
GEIGER VON FLORENZ, DER (1926) d/s Czinner w Bergner, Veidt 2260m Dec
GEISHA BOY, THE (1958) d/st/s Tashlin p J Lewis w J Lewis, Pleshette VV* 98min r Par
Geisha-Girl Ginko = SHUKUZU (1953)
GEKKA NO KYOJIN (1926) d Kinugasa (= Moonlight Madness)
GELOSIA, LA (1915) d Genina
GELOSIA (1942) d Poggioli
GELOSIA (1954) d/co-s Germi
GEMBAKO NO ZU (1951) d Imai (= Pictures of the Atom Bomb)
GEMBAKU NO KO (1952) d/s Shindo p Yoshimura 85min (= Children of Hiroshima)
GEMISCHTE FRAUENCHOR, DER (1916) d/w Lubitsch 1rl (= The Mixed Ladies Chorus)
GENDAI NO JOWO (1924) d Mizoguchi Nik (= Queen of Modern Times)
GENDRE DE MONSIEUR POIRIER, LE (1933) d/p/s Pagnol co-c Hayer 100min
Gendarme est sans pitié = COMMISSAIRE EST BON ENFANT, LE (1934)
GENE KRUPA STORY, THE (1959) d Weis c Lawton m Leith Stevens 100min Col (= Drum Crazy – The Gene Krupa Story)
GENERAL, THE (1926) co-d/co-st/co-ad Bruckman co-d/p/co-st/w Keaton 8rs r UA
General, The = KAKKA (1940)
GENERAL CRACK (1929) d Crosland c Gaudio w J Barrymore, L Sherman 149min WB
GENERAL DIED AT DAWN, THE (1936) d Milestone s Odets c Milner w G Cooper, Carroll, Tamiroff 97min Par
GENERALE DELLA ROVERE, IL (1959) d/co-s Rossellini w De Sica, Caprioli, Vernon 130min
Generalnaya Linnia = STAROIE I NOVOIE (1929)
General Line, The = STAROIE I NOVOIE (1929)
GENERAL NUISANCE (1941) d Jules White co-s Bruckman w Keaton 18min Col
GENERAL SPANKY (1936) d Newmayer, G Douglas p Roach 73min MGM
GENERAL SPEIDEL (1957) d/s A and A Thorndike Defa
Generation, A = POKOLENIE (1954)
GENERATION SPONTANEE (1909) d Cohl anim 103m
Genevieve = ENTRE LA MER ET L'EAU DOUCE (1966)
GENIUS (1970) d/s/c/e Markopoulos 16mm * c 90min
GENJI MONOGATARI (1951) d Yoshimura s Shindo fn Murasaki Shikibu c Miyagawa w Kyo 124min Dai (= A Tale of Genji)
GENNAMA TO BIJO TO SAN-AKUNIN (1958) d Ichikawa (= Money and Three Bad Men)
GENOU DE CLAIRE, LE (1970) d/s Rohmer w Brialy *107min (= Claire's Knee)
GENROKU CHUSHINGURA (I and II) (1942) d Mizoguchi r Sho (= Loyal 47 Ronin)
GENS DU MIL, LES (1951) d/c Rouch 16mm * 45min (= La Culture du Mil)
Gens du voyage, Les: French version of FAHRENDES VOLK (1938)
GENTE DEL PO (1943 r 1947) d/s Antonioni 9min

GENTLE ANNIE (1944) *d* Morton *co-a* Gibbons *w* D Reed 80min MGM
GENTLE CORSICAN, THE (1956) *d/s* A Simmons *c* Lassally *25min
Gentle Creature, A = FEMME DOUCE, UNE (1969)
GENTLE GIANT (1967) *d* Neilson *w* Miles, Meeker *93min Par
GENTLE GUNMAN, THE (1952) *d* Dearden *w* J Mills, Bogarde 86min
GENTLEMAN AFTER DARK (1942) *d* Edward L Marin *c* Krasner *m* Tiomkin *w* M Hopkins 74min *r* UA
GENTLEMAN D'EPSOM (1962) *d/co-s* Grangier *w* Gabin 82min *r* Ufa
GENTLEMAN FROM LOUISIANA (1936) *d* Pichel 70min Rep
GENTLEMAN FROM NOWHERE, THE (1948) *d* Castle *w* W Baxter 65min Col
GENTLEMAN JIM (1942) *d* Walsh *c* Hickox *w* Flynn, A Smith 104min WB
GENTLEMAN JOE PALOOKA (1946) *d/s* Enfield 69min Mon
GENTLEMAN OF FRANCE, A (1903) *d* Blackton
GENTLEMAN OF PARIS, A (1927) *d* D'Arrast *c* Rosson 5927ft Par
GENTLEMAN'S AGREEMENT (1934) *d* George Pearson *w* V Leigh
GENTLEMEN'S AGREEMENT (1947) *d* Kazan *p* Zanuck *s* M Hart *c* AC Miller *co-a* Wheeler *m* A Newman *w* Peck, McGuire, Garfield 118min Fox
GENTLEMAN'S FATE, A (1931) *d* LeRoy *w* J Gilbert 90min MGM
GENTLEMAN OF NERVE (1914) *d/s* Chaplin *w* Chaplin, Normand, C Chase 1rl Key (= *Some Nerve*)
GENTLEMEN OF THE PRESS (1929) *d* Millard Webb *c* Folsey *w* K Francis, W Huston, C Ruggles, Foster 7176ft FPL *r* Par
GENTLEMEN PREFER BLONDES (1928) *s* St Clair *fst/co-ad/fco-pl* Loos *co-ad/fco-pl* Emerson *c* Rosson 6787ft Par
GENTLEMEN PREFER BLONDES (1953) *d* Hawks *p* S Siegel *s* Lederer *fpl* Loos, *Joseph Fields c* Wild *co-a* Wheeler *chor* Cole *co-songs Jules Styne*, Carmichael *w* J Russell, Monroe, C Coburn, Dalio *91min Fox
Gentle Sergeant, The = THREE STRIPES IN THE SUN (1955)
GENUINE (1920) *d* Wiene *s* C Mayer 2286m Dec
GEO LE MYSTERIEUX (1916) *d* Dulac
GEORDIE (1955) *d/co-p/co-s* Launder *co-p/co-s* Gilliat *m* Alwyn 98min BL
GEORGE (1963) *d* Leenhardt
GEORGE RAFT STORY, THE (1961) *d* J Newman *w* Danton, Mansfield 106min AA (= *Spin of a Coin*)
GEORGE WASHINGTON, JR (1924) *d* St Clair
GEORGE WASHINGTON SLEPT HERE (1942) *d* Keighley *p* Wald *fpl* G Kaufman, M Hart *c* E Haller *w* Benny, C Coburn, Sheridan 93min WB
GEORGE WHITE'S SCANDALS (1934) *d* George White, Thornton Freeland, Harry Lachman *co-c* Garmes *w* Faye 79min Fox
GERALD McBOING BOING (1951) *d* Cannon *p* Bosustow *co-anim* Hubley *8min pc* UPA *r* Col
GERALD McBOING BOING ON PLANET MOO (1956) *d* Cannon *m* Gold anim* *pc* UPA *r* Col
GERALD McBOING BOING'S SYMPHONY (1953) *d* Cannon anim* *pc* UPA *r* Col
GERARD DE LA NUIT (1955) *d* Hanoun 579m
GERARD HAS HIS HAIR REMOVED WITH NAIR (1967) *d* Warhol 16mm *30min (segments of *Four Stars*)
Gerard Malanga Reads Poetry = BUFFERIN (1966)
GERMAINE (1923) *d* Genina
German Diary, A = DU BIST MIN, EIN DEUTSCHES TAGEBUCH (1969)
GERMANIA, ANNO ZERO (1947) *d/st/co-s* Rossellini *co-s* Lizzani 75min (= *Germany, Year Zero*)
Germany Story, The (UK) = DU UND MANCHUR KAMERAD (1956)
Germany, Year Zero = GERMANIA, ANNO ZERO (1947)
GERMINAL (1963) *d* Y Allégret *s* Charles Spaak *c* Bourgoin S 110min
GERONIMO'S REVENGE (1962) *d* Neilson, Keller *77min *pc* Disney
GEROI CHIPKI (1954) *d* S Vasiliev *112min (= *The Heroes of Chipka*)
GERTIE (1914) *d* McCay anim
GERTIE ON TOUR (1917) *d* McCay anim
GERTIE THE TRAINED DINOSAUR (1910) *d* McCay anim
GERTRUD (1964) *d/s* Dreyer 115min
GERUSALEMME LIBERATA, LA (1911) *d/s/dec* Guazzoni *w* Ghione
GERUSALEMME LIBERATA (1957) *d* Bragaglia CS* 93min (= *Jerusalem Set Free/The Mighty Crusaders*)
GERVAISE (1956) *d* Clément *fn* (*L'Assomoir*) Emile Zola *ad/di* Aurenche, Bost *m* Auric *w* Maria Schell 102min
GESCHICHTE DER STILLEN MUHLE, DIE (1914) *s* R Oswald 1208m
GESCHICHTE DES PRINZEN AHMED, DIE (1926) *d* Reiniger *co-anim* Ruttman, Bartosch anim 1800m

(= *Das Aventeuer des Prinzen Ahmed/The Adventures of Prince Ahmed*)
GESCHICHTE EINER KLEINER PARISERIN, DIE (1927) *d* Genina (= *Sprung ins Glück/Totte et Sa Chance*)
GESCHICHTE VOM KLEINEN MUCK, DIE (1953) *d/co-s* Staudte *75min Defa (= *Little Mook*)
GESCHLECHT IN FESSELN (1928) *d/w* Dieterle 2724m (= *Sex in Chains*)
GESETZ DER MINE, DAS (1915) *d/p/s* May 1230m
GESOLEI (1923) *d* Ruttmann
GESPENSTERUHR, DIE (1916) *d/p/co-s* May
GESTANDNIS UNTER VIER AUGEN (1954) *d* Michel *w* Neff 100min
GESTANDNIS EINER SECHZEHNJAHRIGEN (1960) *d* Tressler
Gestapo = NIGHT TRAIN TO MUNICH
GESTOHLENE HERZ, DAS (1934) *d/p* Reiniger anim 10min (= *The Stolen Heart*)
GET-AWAY, THE (1941) *d* Edward Buzzell *a* Gibbons *m* Amfitheatrof *w* D Reed 89min MGM
GETAWAY KATE (1918) *d* G Seitz Pat
GET 'EM YOUNG (1926) *d* Laurel *Fred Guiol p* Roach *s/w* Laurel Pat
Get Married Mother = KAACHAN KEKKON SHIROYO (1962)
Get off My Back (UK) = SYNANON (1965)
GET OUT AND GET UNDER (1920) *w* H Lloyd 2rs *pc* Roach *r* Pat
GET RICH QUICK WALLINGFORD (1921) *d* Borzage 7rs FPL
GETTING ACQUAINTED (1914) *d/s/w* Chaplin *w* Normand 1rl Key (= *A Fair Exchange*)
GETTING EVEN (1909) *d* Griffith *w* Pickford 1rl Bio
GETTING GERTIE'S GARTER (1945) *d/co-s* Dwan *c* Lawton *m* Friedhofer 73min *r* UA
Getting His Goat = THE PROPERTY MAN (1914)
GETTING HARRY MARRIED (1919) *d* Dwan *p/w* Davies *s* Emerson, Loos 5rs
GEZEICHNETEN, DIE (1922) *d/s* Dreyer *w* Boleslavsky
Geyerwally = GEIER-WALLY, DER (1921)
Ghost, The (UK) = SPECTRO, LO (1962)
GHOST AND MRS MUIR, THE (1947) *d* J Mankiewicz *p* Kohlmar *s* P Dunne *c* C Lang *co-a* R Day *m* Herrmann *w* Harrison, Tierney, G Sanders, N Wood 104min Fox
Ghost at Noon, A = LE MEPRIS (1963)
GHOST BREAKERS, THE (1940) *d* G Marshall *c* C Lang *w* Lukas, Quinn, Goddard, Hope 82min Par
GHOST CATCHERS (1944) *d* Cline *w* Olsen, Johnson 67min U
GHOST FLOWER, THE (1918) *d* Borzage Tri
GHOST GOES WEST, THE (1935) *d/co-s* Clair *p* A Korda *fn* Eric Keown (*Sir Tristan Goes West*) *c* Rosson *des* V Korda *w* Donat 98min (= *Fantome à Vendre*)
GHOST IN THE INVISIBLE BIKINI, THE (1966) *d* Weis *co-p* Arkoff *c* Cortez *w* Karloff, Rathbone PV* 82min AI
GHOST OF FOLLY, THE (1926) *d* Cline *s* Sennett
GHOST OF ST. MICHAEL'S, THE (1941) *d* Marcel Varnel *w* Hay 82min
GHOST OF THE CHINA SEA (1958) *d* Sears 79min Col
GHOSTS (1915) *d* Emerson *fpl* Ibsen *w* Von Stroheim Mut
Ghosts Before Breakfast = VORMITTAGSSPUK (1928)
GHOST SHIP, THE (1943) *d* Robson *p* Lewton *c* Musuraca 69min RKO
Ghosts in Rome (UK) = FANTASMI A ROMA (1961)
Ghosts – Italian Style (UK) = QUESTI FANTASMI (1967)
Ghost Story of Youth = SEISHUV ICAIDAN (1955)
Ghost That Will Not Return, The = PRIVIDENIE, KOTOROYE NE VOZVRASHCHAYETSYA (1930)
GHOUL, THE (1933) *d* T Hayes Hunter *w* R Richardson, Karloff 77min
GIACOMO L'IDEALISTA (1942) *d/co-s* Lattuada *p* Ponti AA
GIALLO (1933) *d* Camerini *s* Soldati
GIANT (1956) *d/co-p* G Stevens *fn* Edna Ferber *c* Mellor *m* Tiomkin *w* E Taylor, Hudson, Dean, C Baker *198min *r* WB
Giant Behemoth, The = BEHEMOTH THE SEA MONSTER (1959)
GIANT CLAW, THE (1957) *d* Sears *p* Katzman 76min Col
Giant of Marathon, The = LA BATTAGLIA DI MARATONA (1959)
Giant of Thessaly, The (US) = I GIGANTI DELLA TESSAGLIA (1960)
GIARDINO DEI FINZI-CONTINI, IL (1970) *d* De Sica *co-s* Zavattini *103min
G.I. BLUES (1960) *d* Taurog *p* Wallis *c* Griggs *w* Presley *104min Par
Gideon of Scotland Yard (US) = GIDEON'S DAY (1959)
GIDEON'S DAY (1958) *d* J Ford *s* T Clarke *c* F Young *a* Adam *w* Hawkins *91min Col (= *Gideon of Scotland Yard*)
GIDGET (1959) *d* Wendkos *c* Guffey *w* Robertson CS 95min Col
GIDGET GOES HAWAIIAN (1961) *d* Wendkos *p* Bresler *c* Bronner *m* Duning 101min Col

GIDGET GOES TO ROME (1963) *d* Wendkos *p* Bresler *co-c* Bronner 109min Col
The Gift = DAREK (1946)
GIFT HORSE, THE (1952) *d* Compton Bennett *co-s* Goff, Roberts *w* T Howard, Attenborough 100min BL
GIFT OF GAB (1934) *d* Freund *co-st* Wald *w* Lukas, Karloff, Lugosi 70min U
GIFT OF LOVE, THE (1958) *d* Negulesco *p* Brackett *s* Krasner *co-a* Wheeler *m* Mockridge *w* Stack, Bacall CS* 105min Fox
GIFTPILEN (1915) *d/s* Blom
GIGANTI DELLA TESSAGLIA, I (1960) *d/co-s* Freda *w* Girotti S* 87min (= *Gli Argonanti/The Giant of Thessaly*)
GIGI (1958) *d* Minnelli *p* Freed *s/lyr* Lerner *fn* Colette *c* Ruttenberg *des/cos* Beaton *w* Caron, Chevalier CS* 115min *r* MGM
GIGOLO (1926) *d* W Howard *c* Androit 7295ft *pc* De Mille
GIGOLO, LE (1960) *d/co-s/co-di* Demy *w* Valli, Brialy 95min Pat
Gigolo and Gigolette = ENCORE (1951)
GIGOT (1962) *d* Gene Kelly *c* Bourgoin *a* Trauner *104min Fox
GIGUE MERVEILLEUSE, LA (1909) *d* Méliès
G.I. HONEYMOON (1945) *d* Karlson 70min Mon
GILDA (1946) *d* C Vidor *c* Maté *w* Hayworth, G Ford 110min Col
GILDED LILY, THE (1921) *d/p* Leonard *c* E Haller 6100ft FPL
GILDED LILY, THE (1935) *d* W Ruggles *c* Milner *w* Colbert, MacMurray, Milland 80min Par
GILDERSLEEVE ON BROADWAY (1943) *d* G Douglas *a* D'Agostino 65min RKO
GILDERSLEEVE'S BAD DAY (1943) *d* G Douglas *co-a* D'Agostino *a* Darwell 62min RKO
GILDERSLEEVE'S GHOST (1944) *d* G Douglas *co-a* D'Agostino 63min RKO
GILLEKOP (1916) *d/s* Blom
GIMME SHELTER (1971) *co-d/co-c* A and D Maysles *co-d* Charlotte Zwerin *90min
Gimpei From Koina = KOINA NO GINPEI (1933)
GINEPRO FATTO UOMO (c 1963) *d* Bellocchio
The Gingerbread Cottage = PERNIKOVA CHALOUPKA (1951)
GINSBERG THE GREAT (1927) *d* Haskin 5390ft WB
GINZA-GESHO (1951) *d* Naruse
GINZA NO MOSA (1960) *d* Ichikawa (= *A Ginza Veteran*)
GINZA NO ONNA (1955) *d* Yoshimura (= *Women of The Ginza*)
GINZA NO YANAGI (1932) *d* Gosho (= *Willows of Ginza*)
GINZA SANSHIRO (1950) *d* Ichikawa Toho (= *Sanshiro at Ginza*)
Ginza Veteran, A = GINZA NO MOSA
GIOCHI IN COLONIA (1958) *d* Olmi *27min
GIOCONDA, LA (1911) *fpl* D'Annunzio 205m
GIOCONDA, LA (1916) *d* E Rodolfi *fpl* D'Annunzio *rm* 1911
GION BAYASJI (1953) *d* Mizoguchi *c* Miyagawa (= *Gion Music*)
Gion Festival = GION MATSURI (1933)
GION MATSURI (1933) *d/s* Mizoguchi (= *Gion Festival*)
Gion Music = GION BAYASHI (1933)
GION NO SHIMAI (1936) *d* Mizoguchi *w* Yamada (= *Sisters of Gion*)
GIORDANO BRUNO, EROE DI VALMY (1908) *d* Pastrone
GIORNATA BALORDA, LA (1960) *d* Bolognini *co-s* Pasolini *co-s/fst* (*Racconti Romain, Nuovi Racconti Romain*) Moravia *m* Piccioni 85min (= *From a Roman Balcony/A Day of Sin*)
GIORNI CONTATI, I (1962) *d/co-s* Petri *co-s* Guerra *w* Caprioli 102min (= *Days are Numbered*)
GIORNI D'AMORE (1954) *d/co-s* De Santis *co-s* Petri *c* Martelli *w* Vlady, Mastroianni *
GIORNO DA LEONI, UN (1961) *d/co-st/co-s* N Loy 100min
GIORNO DELLA CIVETTA, IL (1968) *d/co-s* Damiani *m* Fusco *w* Cardinale, Cobb, Reggiani S* 113min
GIORNO IN BARBAGIA, UN (1958) *d/c/e* De Seta *
GIORNO IN PRETURA, UN (1953) *d/co-st/co-s* Steno *w* Sordi
GIORNO NELLA VITA, UN (1946) *d/co-st/co-s* Blasetti *co-st/co-s* Zavattini *co-s* Chiari *w* Girotti 95min
Giotto = RACCONTO DA UNA AFFRESCO (1940)
GIOVANE ATTILA, IL (1971) *d/co-s* Jancso *90min RAI
GIOVANI MARITI (1958) *d/co-s* Bolognini *co-s* Festa, Campanile, Pasolini 101min (= *Young Husbands*)
GIOVANNA D'ARCO AL ROGO (1954) *d/s* Rossellini *f oratorio* Paul Claudel, Honegger *w* Ingrid Bergman *80min
GIOVANNI EPISCOPO (1916) *d* M Gargiulo *fn* D'Annunzio
Giovanni Episcopo = IL DELITTO DI GIOVANNI EPISCOPO (1947)
GIC VEDI, IL (1962) *d/co-s* Risi (= *Thursday*)
GIOVENTU PERDUTA (1948) *d/st/co-s* Germi, *p* Ponti *co-s* Pietrangeli, Monicelli *w* Girotti 80min (= *Lost Youth*)

GIRASOLI, I (1970) *d* De Sica *ex-p* Levine *co-p* Ponti *co-st/co-s* Zavattini *c* Rotunno *m* Mancini *w* Loren, Mastroianni *107min (= *Sunflower*)
GIRL, A GUY AND A GOB, A (1941) *d Richard Wallace p* H Lloyd *c* Metty *w* G Murphy, Ball, E O'Brien 91min RKO
Girl and the General, The (UK) = RAGAZZA E IL GENERALE, LA (1966)
Girl at Dojo Temple, A = MUSUME DOJOJI (1946)
GIRL AT HOME, THE (1917) *d* Neilan 5rs
GIRL CAN'T HELP IT, THE (1956) *d/p/co-s* Tashlin *fst* (*Do Re Mi*) Kanin *c* Shamroy *co-a* Wheeler *w* Ewell, Mansfield, E O'Brien CS* 99min Fox
GIRL CRAZY (1943) *d* Taurog *p* Freed *a* Gibbons *co-c* Daniels *chor* Berkeley, Walters *w* Rooney, Garland, Lawford (Allyson) 99min MGM
Girl Field Marshall, The = FELDMARESCIALLA, LA (1968)
Girl Friends, The = AMICHE, LE (1955)
Girlfriends, The = BICHES, LES (1968)
GIRL FROM CHICAGO (1927) *d* Enright 7rs WB
GIRL FROM MAXIM'S, THE (1933) *d/p* A Korda *fpl Georges Feydeau c* Périnal *w* Romance 79min *r* UA
GIRL FROM MISSOURI, THE (1934) *d* Conway *s* Loos, Emerson *c* June *w* Harlow, J Barrymore, Tone 75min MGM
Girl From Swabia, The = SCHWABENMADLE (1919)
Girl From Texas, The = TEXAS, BROOKLYN, AND HEAVEN (1948)
GIRL HABIT, THE (1931) *d* Cline *w* Dumont, C Ruggles, (Goddard) 8rs Par
GIRL HE LEFT BEHIND, THE (1956) *d* D Butler *c* McCord *w* N Wood, Garner 102min WB
GIRL HUNTERS, THE (1963) *d/co-s* Rowland *st/co-s Mickey Spillane w Mickey Spillane,* Nolan PV 103min
Girl I Loved, The = WAGA KOISESHI OTOME (1946)
Girl In A Bikini (UK) = POVERI MA BELLI (1956)
Girl in a Dress Coat = FLICKAN I FRACK (1956)
Girl in Black, The = KORITSI ME TA MAURA, TO (1955)
GIRL IN BLACK STOCKINGS, THE (1957) *d* H W Koch *ex-p* Schenk *w* A Bancroft 73min UA
GIRL IN EVERY PORT, A (1928) *d/st* Hawks *s* S Miller *c* O'Connell *w* V McLaglen, L Brooks 5500ft Fox
GIRL IN EVERY PORT, A (1952) *d* Endfield *c* Musuraca *w* G Marx 87min RKO
Girl in Mourning, The (UK) = NINA DE LUTO, LA (1963)
GIRL IN No. 29, THE (1920) *d* J Ford 5rs U
Girl in Overalls = SWING SHIFT MAISIE (1945)
GIRL IN THE CROWD, THE (1934) *d* M Powell 52min
GIRL IN THE LIMOUSINE, THE (1924) *d/w* Semon *w* Hardy 5630ft *r* FN
Girl in the Moon, The (UK) = FRAU IM MOND (1929)
GIRL IN THE NEWS, THE (1940) *d* C Reed *s* Gilliat *w* Lockwood, Emlyn Williams 78min *r* MGM
Girl in the Rain = FLICKAN I REGNET (1955)
GIRL IN THE RED VELVET SWING, THE (1955) *d* R Fleischer *p/co-s* Brackett *c* Krasner *co-a* Wheeler *m* Friedhofer *w* Milland, F Granger CS* 109min Fox
Girl In The Rumour, The = UWASA NO MUSUME (1935)
Girl in the Shadows = SCHATTEN WERDEN LANGER, DIE (1962)
GIRL IN WHITE, THE (1952) *d* J Sturges *co-a* Gibbons *m* Raksin *w* Allyson, A Kennedy 93min MGM
Girl Isn't Allowed To Love, A = BARA IKUTABI (1955)
Girlfriend = KANOJO (1926)
Girlfriends = PODRUGI (1935)
GIRL MISSING (1933) *d* Florey *st* Furthman *c* Struss 69min WB
GIRL MOST LIKELY, THE (1957) *d* Leisen *w* J Powell, Robertson *98min U
GIRL MUST LIVE, A (1939) *d* C Reed *s* Launder *w* Lockwood, Palmer 93min *r* Fox
GIRL NAMED TAMIKO, A (1963) *d* J Sturges *p* Wallis *c* C Lang *co-a* Pereira *m* E Bernstein PV* 110min Par
Girl Nyuyo, The = SHOJO NYUYO (1930)
GIRL OF THE GOLDEN WEST, THE (1915) *d/s* De Mille *pc* Lasky
GIRL OF THE GOLDEN WEST, THE (1938) *d* Leonard *st* Belasco *a* Gibbons *e* Vorkapich *m* Romberg *w* Jeannette MacDonald, Pidgeon 120min
GIRL OF THE LIMBERLOST, THE (1945) *d* M Ferrer *c* Guffey *m* Gold 60min Col
GIRL OF THE PORT (1930) *d* Glennon 6174ft RKO
GIRL OF THE RIO, THE (1932) *d* Brenon *w* Del Rio 78min RKO (= *The Dove*)
GIRL OF YESTERDAY, A (1915) *d* Dwan *p/s* Pickford *w* Pickford, Neilan, Crisp 5rs FP
GIRL ON A MOTORCYCLE (1968) *d/co-s* Cardiff *w* Delon *91min *r* Bl
GIRL ON APPROVAL (1962) *d* Frend 75min BL
GIRL RUSH (1944) *d* G Douglas *c* Musuraca *co-a* D'Agostino *w* Mitchum 65min RKO
GIRLS, LES (1957) *d* Cukor *p* S Siegel *st* Caspary *c* Surtees *colour consultant* Hoyningen-Huene *m/lyr Cole Porter chor* Cole *w* Gene Kelly, Kendall, M Gaynor CS* 114min MGM
Girls, The = FLICKORNA (1968)
GIRLS ABOUT TOWN (1931) *d* Cukor *c* E Haller *w* K Francis, McCrea 66min Par
GIRL SAID NO, THE (1930) *d/s* Wood *di* MacArthur *a* Gibbons *w* Dressler 92min
GIRL SAID NO, THE (1937) *d/p/st* Stone 64min
Girl's Dormitory (UK) = DORTOIR DES GRANDES (1953)
GIRL FROM EVERYWHERE, THE (1927) *d* Cline
Girls of Izu, The = IZU NO MUSUMETACHI (1945)
Girls of Okinawa, The = HIMEYURI NO TO (1953)
GIRL SHY (1924) *co-d* Newmayer *co-d/co-st Sam Taylor w* H Lloyd 4457ft *pc* H Lloyd
GIRLS IN CHAINS (1943) *d/cos* Ulmer 72min
GIRLS IN THE NIGHT (1953) *d* J Arnold *co-a* Boyle 83min U (= *Life After Dark*)
Girls Marked Danger = TRATTA DELLE BIANCHE, LA (1952)
Girls of the Piazza di Spagna = RAGAZZE DI PIAZZA DI SPAGNA, LE (1952)
GIRLS ON THE LOOSE (1958) *d* Henreid *c* Lathrop *co-a* Golitzen 78min U
GIRLS' SCHOOL (1938) *d* Brahm *c* Planer 63min Col
GIRLS' TOWN (1959) *d* Haas *p* Zugsmith *c* JL Russell 92min MGM
Girl Was Young, The (US) = YOUNG AND INNOCENT (1937)
GIRL WHO HAD EVERYTHING, THE (1953) *d* Thorpe *fn Adela Rogers St Johns co-a* Gibbons *m* Previn *w* E Taylor, W Powell *69min MGM
GIRL WHO RAN WILD, THE (1922) *d/s* Julian *fst* (*M'Liss*) *Bret Harte* 5rs
GIRL WHO STAYED AT HOME, THE (1919) *d/p* Griffith *c* Bitzer *w* D Butler 7rs *co-pc* Griffith
Girl With A Pistol, The (US) = RAGAZZA CON LA PISTOLA, LA (1967)
Girl with a Suitcase = RAGAZZA CON LA VALIGIA, LA (1960)
GIRL WITH GREEN EYES, THE (1963) *d* D Davis *ex-p* T Richardson *s/fn* (*The Lonely Girl*) *Edna O'Brien w* Finch, Tushingham 91min *r* UA
Girl with the Hat Box, The = DEVUSHKA S KOROBKOI (1927)
GIROVAGHI, I (1956) *d* Fregonese *w* Ustinov S* 95min
GISHIKI (1971) *d/co-st/co-s* Oshima S* 122min (= *The Ceremony*)
GITANES (1924) *d* De Varoncelli
GITANOS ET PAPILLONS (1954) *d/co-c/co-anim/cy* Gruel *p* Papatakis anim* 20min
GIUDIZIO UNIVERSALE, IL (1961) *d* De Sica *co-p* De Laurentiis *s* Zavattini *w* De Sica, Aimée, Borgnine, Fernandel, Gassman, Manfredi, Mangano, Mercouri, Sordi, Palance
GIULETTA DELLI SPIRITI (1965) *d/co-s* Fellini *co-s* Rondi *c* Di Venanzo *dec* Gheradi *m* Rota *w* Masina, Cortese *145min (= *Juliet of the Spirits*)
GIULETTA E ROMEO (1954) *d/co-st/co-s* Castellani *fpl Shakespeare c* Krasker *w* Laurence Harvey (= *Romeo and Juliet*)
GIULETTA E ROMEO (1964) *d/s* Freda S* 90min (= *Romeo and Juliet*)
GIULIANO DE' MEDICI (1940) *d* Vajda
GIUSEPPE VENDUTO DAI FRATELLI (1960) *d* Rapper, *Luciano Ricci* *103min (= *Sold into Egypt/Joseph and his Brethren*)
GIUSEPPE VERDI (1938) *d* Gallone *m Verdi*
GIVE A GIRL A BREAK (1953) *d* Donen *p* F Cummings *st* Caspary *s* Goodrich, Hackett *c* Mellor *co-chor* Donen, Champion *w* Champion, D Reynolds, Fosse *82min MGM
Give Her the Moon (US) = FIGURANTS DU NOUVEAU MONDE, LES (1969)
GIVE ME A SAILOR (1938) *d* E Nugent *c* Milner *co-a* Dreier *chor* Prinz *w* Hope, Grable 80min Par
GIVE ME YOUR HEART (1936) *d* A Mayo *w* K Francis 9rs WB
GIVE MY REGARDS TO BROADWAY (1948) *d* Bacon *co-a* Wheeler *w* Dailey, C Ruggles 89min Fox
GIVE OUT, SISTERS (1942) *d* Cline *w* O'Connor 65min U
GIVE US THE MOON (1944) *d/s Val Guest w* J Simmons, Lockwood 95min
GIVE US THIS DAY (1949) *d* Dmytryk *s* Barzman 120min Eagle Lion-Rank
GLACE A TROIS FACES (1927) *d/p* J Epstein
GLACIERS (1942) *d* Decaë 10min
GLAD-EYE, THE (1928) *co-d/p/s* Saville *co-d* Elvey 7700ft Gau
GLADIATORERNA (1969) *d/co-s* Watkins *91min San (= *The Peace Game*)
GLAD RAG DOLL, THE (1929) *d* Curtiz *c* Haskin 6885ft WB
GLAIVE ET LA BALANCE, LE (1962) *d/st* Cayatte *s* Charles Spaak *di* Jeanson *w* Perkins, Brialy CS 120min Gau (= *Two Are Guilty*)
GLAMOUR (1934) *d* Wyler *fst Edna Ferber w* Lukas 74min U
GLAS (1958) *d/s* Haanstra *12min *pc* Haanstra (= *Glass*)
GLASBERGET (1953) *d* Molander *s/w* Ekman *w* Björnstrand 2770m SF
GLASGOW FIRE BRIGADE (1898) *p* Paul 100ft
Glass = GLAS (1958)
GLASS-BOTTOM BOAT, THE (1966) *d* Tashlin *c* Shamroy *w* D Day PV* 110min MGM
GLASS KEY, THE (1935) *d* Tuttle *fn* Hammett *w* Raft, Milland, Sheridan 80min Par
GLASS KEY, THE (1942) *d* Fleischer *as-p* Kohlmer *fn* Hammett *rm* 1935 *co-a* Dreier *m* V Young *w* Ladd, Lake 85min Par
GLASS MENAGERIE, THE (1950) *d* Rapper *p* Wald, Feldman *co-s/fpl* T Williams *c* Burks *m* M Steiner *w* Wyman, K Douglas, A Kennedy, Lawrence 107min WB
GLASS MOUNTAIN, THE (1948) *d Henry Cass w* Cortese 97min
GLASS SLIPPER, THE (1955) *d* Walters *c* Arling *co-a* Gibbons *m* Kaper *w* Caron *94min MGM
GLASS WEB, THE (1953) *d* J Arnold *w* Robinson 3D 81min U
GLAS WASSER, DAS (1960) *d/s* Käutner 2335m
GLENN GOULD – ON THE RECORD (1960) *d/p* Kroitor, Koenig *c* Koenig 16mm 30min NFBC
GLENN GOULD – OFF THE RECORD (1960) *d/p* Kroitor, Koenig *c* Koenig 16mm 30min NFBC
GLEN MILLER STORY, THE (1953) *d* A Mann *p* A Rosenberg *c* Daniels *co-a* Golitzen *m Glenn Miller w* J Stewart, Allyson *118min U
GLIMPSES OF THE MOON, THE (1923) *d/p* Dwan *c* Rosson 6502ft FPL
GLIMPSES OF USA (1959) *d* Whitney, C and R Eames *7screens 12min
Glinka = KOMPOZITOR GLINKA (1952)
Glinka – Man of Music = KOMPOZITOR GLINKA (1952)
Glumov's Film-Diary = KINODNEVIK GLUMOVA (1923)
GLOBAL AFFAIR, A (1964) *d* J Arnold *co-s* Lederer *c* Ruttenberg *w* Hope, De Carlo CS 84min MGM
GLOMDALSBRUDEN (1925) *d/a* Dreyer
GLORIA, LA (1913) *d Baldassare Negroni w* Ghione
GLORIOUS ADVENTURE, THE (1922) *d/p/s* Blackton *w* V McLaglen 7rs
GLORIFYING THE AMERICAN GIRL (1929) *d/co-st Millard Webb c* Folsey *w* Cantor, Zukor, Weissmuller, (G Douglas) part * 8071ft FPL *r* Par
GLORIOUS BETSY (1928) *d* Crosland *c* Mohr 7rs WB
GLORIOUS EIGHTH OF JUNE, THE (1934) *w* Jennings
GLORY (1955) *d/p* D Butler *w* M O'Brien, Brennan S 100min RKO
GLORY ALLEY (1952) *d* Walsh *c* Daniels *w* Caron, Meeker, McIntire, Roland 79min MGM
Glory At Sea (US) = GIFT HORSE, THE (1952)
Glory For Me = BEST YEARS OF OUR LIVES, THE (1946)
GLORY GUYS, THE (1966) *d/co-p Arnold Laven s* Peckinpah *c* Howe PV* 112min *r* UA
GLOVE TAPS (1937) *d* G Douglas *p* Roach 1rl MGM
GLOWA (1953) *d* Borowczyk
GLUCKLICHE MUTTER, DIE (1924) *d Rudolf Sieber w* Dietrich
GLUCKLICHEN JAHRE DER THORWAL, DIE (1962) *d* Staudte, *John Olden w* Bergner 88m
GLUTTON'S NIGHTMARE, THE (1901) *p* Hepworth 150ft
G.M.B.H. TENOR, DER (1916) *d/w* Lubitsch *c* Sparkuhl 3rs (= *The Tenor, Inc*)
G MEN (1935) *d* Keighley *p* Wallis *st/s* S Miller *c* Polito *w* Cagney, Nolan 85min WB
G-MEN NEVER FORGET (1947) *d* Canutt, *Fred Brannon as-p* Frankovich series of 12ep 2rs each Rep
GNEV DIONISA (1914) *d/s* Protazanov 1650m (= *The Wrath of Dionysus*)
GNOME-MOBILE, THE (1966) *d* Stevenson *p* Disney *fn* (*Gnomobile*) Sinclair *w* Brennan *84min
GO AND GET IT (1920) *d* Neilan, *Henry Symonds pc* Neilan
GOAT, THE (1918) *d* Crisp *w* Novarro 5rs
GOAT, THE (1921) *d/s/w* Keaton, St Clair 2rs *pc* Keaton *r* Metro
GOBBO, IL (1960) *d/co-s* Lizzani *co-c* Tonti *dec* Gherardi *m* Piccioni 103min *pc* De Laurentiis (= *The Hunchback of Rome*)
GO-BETWEEN, THE (1971) *d* Losey *s* Pinter *fn L P Hartley cr* R Macdonald *m* Legrand *w* Christie, M Redgrave *116min
GO CHASE YOURSELF (1938) *d* Cline *w* Ball 70min RKO
GO CHEZ LES OISEAUX (1937–39) *d* Grimault anim
God and his Servants, A = HERREN OG HANS TJENERE (1959)
GODARD ON GODARD (1969) *d* Pennebaker, *Mark Woodcock* 16mm part * 40min (= *Two American Audiences*)
GODDESS, THE (1958) *d* Cromwell *s* Chayefsky *m* V Thompson 105min Col
GOD DEVYATNADISATII (1938) *d/co-s* I Trauberg 2327m (= *The Year 1919*)
Goddess, The (UK) = DEVI (1960)
GODELUREAUX, LES (1960) *d/co-s* Chabrol *c* Rabier *w* Brialy 99min
GOD GAVE HIM A DOG (1940) *d* Heisler 81min *r* Par
GOD GAVE ME 20 CENTS (1926) *d* Brenon 6532ft FPL
GOD IS MY CO-PILOT (1940) *d* Florey *c* Hickox *w* Massey 90min WB
GODDESS GIRL, THE (1928) *d* De Mille *c* Marley *a* Leisen 12rs
Gods and the Dead = DEUSES E OS MORTOS, OS (1970)

GOD'S COUNTRY AND THIS WOMAN (1936) d
Keighley p Wallis c Gaudio *80min WB
GOD'S GIFT TO WOMEN (1931) d Curtiz w Blondell, L
Brooks 71min WB (= Too Many Women)
GOD SHIVA (1955) d/s/e Haanstra
GOD'S LITTLE ACRE (1958) d/co-p A Mann s Yordan fn
Erskine Caldwell c E Haller m E Bernstein w Ryan, A
Ray 118min AA
Gods Of The Street = GATEGUTTER (1949)
God's Thunder = LA TONNERRE DE DIEU (1965)
GODOVSHCHINA REVOLYUTSII (1919) d/e Vertov
150–180min (12 parts) (= Anniversary of the Revolu-
tion)
GO GET 'EM HUTCH (1922) d/p G Seitz serial 15ep Pat
GO GETTER, THE (1937) d Berkeley p Wallis s Daves c
Edeson 92min WB
GOGLEREN (1912) d/s Madsen
GOHA (1958) d Baratier c Bourgoin w Sharif, (Cardinale)
*83min
GOING BYE-BYE (1934) d Charles Rogers p Roach w
Laurel, Hardy (sd) 2rs r MGM
GOING GAY (1933) d Gallone 78min
GOING HIGHBROW (1935) d Florey w Horton, Pitts
67min WB
GOING HOLLYWOOD (1933) d Walsh s D Stewart c
Folsey w B Crosby, Davies 80min MGM
GOING MY WAY (1944) d/p/st -McCarey c Lindon w B
Crosby 124min Par
GOING PLACES (1938) d Enright p Wallis co-s Wald w D
Powell, Reagan 85min WB
GOING STEADY (1958) d Sears p Katzman 79min Col
GOIN' TO TOWN (1935) d Alexander Hall s/di West c
Struss w West 74min Par
GO INTO YOUR DANCE (1935) d A Mayo c Polito w
Jolson, Tamiroff 98min WB (= Casino de Paree)
GOJUMAN-NIN NO ISAN (1963) d Mifune w Mifune,
Nakadai S* 98min pc Mifune (= Legacy of the Five
Hundred Thousand)
GOJU NO TO (1944) d Gosho (= The Five-Storied Pagoda)
GOLD (1955) d Low cy/c/e Koenig 16mm 10min NFBC
Gold = ZLOTO (1962)
GOLD AND GLITTER (1912) d Griffith w D Gish, L Gish,
L Barrymore 1rl Bio
GOLD AND GRIT (1924) d Thorpe
GOLD DIGGERS, THE (1923) d Harry Beaumont w
Fazenda 5600ft WB
GOLD DIGGERS IN PARIS (1937) d Enright p Wallis co-st
Wald c Polito, Barnes 97min WB
GOLD DIGGERS OF BROADWAY (1929) d Del Ruth
* 11rs WB
GOLD DIGGERS OF 1933 (1933) d LeRoy p Wallis c
Polito chor Berkeley w Blondell, D Powell, G Rogers
96min WB
GOLD DIGGERS OF 1935 (1935) d Berkeley c Barnes w D
Powell, Menjou 98min FN
GOLD DIGGERS OF 1937 (1936) d Bacon p Wallis fco-pl
Maibaum c Edeson chor Berkeley w D Powell,
Blondell, (Wyman) 100min WB
GOLD DUST GERTIE (1931) d Bacon co-s Enright w
Olsen, Johnson 2rs WB
GOLDEN BED, THE (1925) d De Mille c Marley 8584ft
FPL
GOLDEN BLADE, THE (1953) d Nathan Juran w Laurie,
Hudson, Ekberg *81min U
GOLDEN BOY (1939) d Mamoulian p Perlberg co-s
Taradash fpl Odets c Musuraca, Freund m V Young
w Stanwyck, Holden, Menjou, Cobb 91min Col
Golden Bracken (UK) = ZLATE KAPRADI (1963)
GOLDEN CHANCE, THE (1916) d De Mille pc Lasky
Golden Coach, The = CARROZZA D'ORO, LA (1953)
GOLDEN DAWN (1930) d Enright 82min WB
Golden Demon, The = KONJIKI YASHA (1923)
GOLDEN EARRINGS (1947) d Leisen cos Polonsky c Fapp
co-a Dreier m V Young w Milland, Dietrich 95min
Par
GOLDENE GANS, DIE (1944, uf) d Reiniger fst Brothers
Grimm anim
Golden Honey = ZOLOTOI MED (1928)
Golden Mountains = ZLATYE GORY (1931)
GOLDENE PEST, DIE (1954) d Brahm 93min
GOLDENE SCHMETTERLING, DER (1926) d Curtiz dec
Leni 6040ft
GOLDENE STADT, DIE (1942) d/co-s V Harlan * 3004m
Ufa
Golden Fish, The = ZLATE RYBCE O (1951)
Golden Fish, The = HISTOIRE D'UN POISSON ROUGE,
L' (1959)
GOLDEN GIRL (1951) d Bacon c C Clarke co-a Wheeler w
M Gaynor 107min Fox
GOLDEN CLOUDS (1940) d Dmytryk co-a Dreier w Ryan
69min Par
GOLDEN GLOVES (1961) d/c/e Groulx 29min
GOLDEN HEAD, THE (1965) d Thorpe w G Sanders
70-TR-Cinerama* 115min
Golden Kite, the = ARANYSARKANY (1966)
GOLDEN MADONNA, THE (1949) d Vajda 91min r WB
Golden Mark, The = SOUTH OF ALGIERS (1952)
GOLDEN POSITIONS, THE (1970) d Broughton 16mm
part * 32min
Golden Queening, The = ZLATA RENATA (1965)

GOLDEN SALAMANDER, THE (1950) d/co-s Neame m
Alwyn w T Howard, Aimée 87min JAR
GOLDEN SUPPER, THE (1910) d Griffith fpm The Lover's
Tale Tennyson 1rl Bio
Golden Virgin, The (US) = THE STORY OF ESTHER
COSTELLO (1957)
GOLDEN WEBB (1926) d W Lang c June w Karloff 6224ft
Gold Fever = HOMME DE MARRAKECH, L' (1965)
GOLDFINGER (1964) d Hamilton co-p Saltzman co-s
Maibaum fn Ian Fleming c Moore des Adam m
Barry w Connery *109min UA
Gold for the Caesars (US) = ORO PER I CESARI (1962)
GOLD GHOST, THE (1934) d Lamont w Keaton 2rs
GOLDIE GETS ALONG (1933) d St Clair 67min RKO
GOLD IS NOT ALL (1910) d Griffith 1rl Bio
GOLD IS WHERE YOU FIND IT (1938) d Curtiz p Wallis
c Polito sp eff Haskin w De Havilland, Rains 90min
WB
Gold of Naples = L'ORO DI NAPOLI (1954)
GOLD OF THE SEVEN SAINTS (1961) d G Douglas c
Biroc S 88min WB
GOLD RUSH, THE (1925) d/s/p Chaplin assist d D'Arrast
(uc) w Chaplin 9rs UA
GOLDWYN FOLLIES, THE (1938) d G Marshall p
Goldwyn st/s B Hecht c Toland a R Day m George
Gershwin lyr Ira Gershwin w Menjou, Ladd 120min r
UA
GOLEM, DER (1914) d Galeen s/w Wegener, Galeen 1250m
GOLEM, LE (1936) d/co-s Duvivier w Dalio, Carette 83min
(= The Legend of Prague)
GOLEM UND DIE TÄNZERIN, DER (1917) co-d/st/s/w
Wegener co-d Rochus Gliese
GOLEM, WIE ER IN DIE WELT KAM, DER (1920) d
Wegener, Carl Boese s/w Wegener c Freund dec
Poelzig 1922m Ufa
GOLFOS, LOS (1959) d/co-s Saura 90min (= The
Hooligans)
GOLF SPECIALIST, THE (1930) d Monte Brice w Fields
2rs RKO
GOLGOTHA (1935) d/s Duvivier m Ibert w Gabin, Feuillère
91min
Goliath And The Dragon (UK) = VENDETTA DI
ERCOLE, LE (1960)
GOLOD ... GOLOD ... GOLOD (1921) d/s Vladimir
Gardin, Pudovkin c Tissé 500min (= Hunger ...
Hunger ... Hunger)
GOLUBOI EKSPRESS (1929) d/co-s I Trauberg 1700m
(= China Express/The Blue Express)
GOLU HADAWATHA (1968) d Peries 110min (= The
Silence of the Heart)
GO MAN GO (1954) d Howe m North w Poitier 85min r UA
GO NAKED IN THE WORLD (1961) d/s Macdougall p
A Rosenberg c Krasner w Lollobrigida, Borgnine CS*
103min MGM
GONDOLE AUX CHIMERES, LA (1936) d Genina c Burel
GONE TO EARTH (1951) d/p/s M Powell, Pressburger ex-p
A Korda, Selznick c Challis w J Jones *110min r BL
(= The Wild Heart)
GONE WITH THE WIND (1939) d V Fleming, Cukor (uc),
S Wood (uc) co-s Fitzgerald (uc) fn Margaret Mitchell
c Rennahan, Garmes (uc), E Haller a Wheeler des
Menzies m M Steiner w Gable, V Leigh, L Howard,
De Havilland, Mitchell, Darwell, Canutt *220min r
MGM
GONIN NO KYODAI (1939) d Yoshimura s Kinoshita
(= Five Brothers And A Sister)
GONKA ZA SAMOGONKOI (1924) d Room 1200m
GONZAGUE (1933) d/ad/s/di Grémillon (= L'Accordeur)
GOOD AND NAUGHTY (1926) d St Clair c Glennon w
Negri 5503ft FPL r Par
GOOD BAD BOY, THE (1924) d Cline
GOOD BAD MAN, THE (1916) d Dwan p Griffith s/w
Fairbanks Sr c V Fleming 5rs r Tri (= Passing
Through)
GOODBYE AGAIN (1933) d Curtiz c Barnes w Blondell
65min FN
Good/ve Again (US) = AIMEZ VOUS BRAHMS? (1961)
GOODBYE, BILL (1918) d/co-p/co-st Emerson p/co-st Loos
5rs FPL
GOODBYE CHARLIE (1964) d Minnelli p Weisbart st
Axelrod s Kurnitz c Krasner a R Day m Previn w
Curtis, Matthau, D Reynolds CS* 117min Fox
Goodbye, Goodday = SAYONARA KANNICHIWA (1959)
GOODBYE KISS, THE (1928) d/s Sennett 9rs FN (The
Romance of a Bathing Girl)
GOODBYE, MR CHIPS (1939) d S Wood p Saville fpl
James Hilton c F Young e Frend w Donat, Garson, J
Mills, Henreid 114min MGM
GOODBYE, MR CHIPS (1969) d/chor Ross s Rattigan rm
1939 c Morris w O'Toole, M Redgrave PV70*
147min
GOODBYE MY FANCY (1951) d V Sherman p Blanke c
McCord w J Crawford, R Young 107min WB
Goodbye, My Girl = SHOJO-YO SAYONARA (1933)
GOODBYE, MY LADY (1956) d Wellman c Clothier w
Brennan, Poitier 95min pc J Wayne r WB
GOODBYE SUMMER (1914) d Van Dyke Brooke w N
Talmadge 2rs Vit
GOOD COMPANIONS, THE (1933) d Saville p Balcon fn
JB Priestley w Gielgud, Hawkins 113min Gau

GOOD COMPANIONS, THE (1956) d/co-p J Thompson fn
JB Priestley c G Taylor CS* 104min
GOOD DIE YOUNG, THE (1954) d/co-st L Gilbert as-p
Clayton w Laurence Harvey, Grahame 98min BL
GOOD EARTH, THE (1937) d George Hill (uc), Machaty
(uc), V Fleming (uc), Franklin as-p Lewin c Freund
montage expert Vorkapich a Gibbons m Stothart w
Muni, Rainer 136min MGM
GOOD FAIRY, THE (1935) d Wyler s P Sturges fpl Ferenc
Molnar c Brodine w H Marshall, Romero 90min U
Good Fairy, The = ZENMA (1951)
Good For Nothing, The = HIS NEW PROFESSION (1914)
GOOD GUYS AND THE BAD GUYS, THE (1969) d B
Kennedy c Stradling w Mitchum, G Kennedy,
Carradine PV* 90min WB
GOOD HUMORMAN, THE (1950) d Bacon s Tashlin
80min Col
GOOD INTENTIONS (1930) d/s/di W Howard 69min Fox
GOOD LIAR, A (1917) d Sullivan, Otz Messmer anim ½rl
GOOD LITTLE DEVIL, A (1913) d J Searle Dawley w
Pickford
GOOD LUCK, MR YATES (1943) d Enright w Trevor 7rs
Col
Good Morning = OHAYO (1959)
GOOD MORNING, BOYS (1937) d Marcel Varnel w Hay,
Palmer 8rs (= Where There's a Will)
GOOD MORNING, MISS DOVE (1955) d Koster c
Shamroy co-a Wheeler m Harline w J Jones, Stack
CS* 107min Fox
Good Mothers = ØDREHJAELPEN (1942)
GOOD NEIGHBOUR SAM (1964) d/p/co-s Swift c Guffey
w Lemmon, Schneider, Robinson *130min Col
GOOD NEWS (1947) d Walters co-p Freed s/co-lyr Comden,
A Green co-a Gibbons co-p/co-m/co-lyr Edens m
Allyson, Lawford 95min MGM
GOODNIGHT NURSE (1918) d/s Arbuckle w Arbuckle,
Keaton 2rs Par
GOODNIGHT VIENNA (1932) d H Wilcox w Neagle
75min
GOOD OLE COUNTRY MUSIC (1956) d Pintoff
Good Place to Live, A = DOBRE BYDLENI (1960)
GOOD PROVIDER, THE (1922) d Borzage fst Fannie
Hurst 8rs
GOOD SAM (1948) d/p/co-st McCarey c Barnes w G
Cooper, Sheridan, Roman 114min RKO
Good Soldier Schweik = DOBRY VOJAK SUEJK (1931)
Good Soldier Schweik, The = DOBRY VOJAK SUEJK
(1954)
Good, The Bad And The Ugly, The (UK) = BUONO, IL
BRUTTO, IL CATTIVO, IL (1967)
GOOD TIME CHARLEY (1927) d Curtiz 6302ft WB
GOOD TIMES, WONDERFUL TIMES (1966) d/p Rogosin
70min pc Rogosin
GOOD YEARS, THE (1962) d C Eames TV
GOOPY GYNE, BAGHA BYNE (1968) d S Ray part
*120min (= The Adventures of Goopy and Bagha)
GOOSE HANGS HIGH, THE (1925) d/p Cruze 6172ft FPL
GOOSELAND (1926) d/s Cline p Sennett Pat
GOOSE STEPS OUT, THE (1942) d Hay, Dearden w
Hay 75min r UA
GOOSE WOMAN, THE (1925) d C Brown c Constance Bennett
7500ft U
GORACA LINIA (1965) d Jakubowska 107min (= Hot
Mine)
Gorge Between Love and Hate, The = AIZO-TOGE (1934)
Gorge Between Love and Hate = AIEN-KYO (1937)
GORGEOUS HUSSY, THE (1936) d C Brown p J Man-
kiewicz c Folsey a Gibbons m Stothart w R Taylor, J
Crawford, L Barrymore, Tone, M Douglas, J Stewart
102min MGM
GORGO (1961) d/co-st Lourié c F Young *78min MGM-BL
GORGON, THE (1964) d Fisher *83min
GORILLA, THE (1939) d Dwan p Zanuck as-p H Brown c
Cronjager co-a R Day w Lugosi 66min Fox
GORILLA HUNT, THE (1939) d Iwerks anim* 696ft r Col
GORIZONT (1933) d/co-s/e Kuleshov co-s Victor Skhlovsky
7rs (= Horizon)
GORIZONT (1962) d Heifitz 108min (= Horizon)
GORYACHIE DENECHKI (1935) d/s Heifitz, Zarkhi
98min (= Hectic Days)
GOSH-DARN MORTGAGE, THE (1926) d Cline s Sennett
Goskino Journal = GOSKINO KALENDAR (1923–25)
GOSKINO KALENDAR (1923–25) d/s/e Vertov 55x 1rl
(300m each) (= Goskino Journal)
Gospel According to St Matthew, The (UK) = VANGELO
SECONDO MATTEO, IL (1964)
GOSSELINE, LA (1923) d/s Feuillade 1376m
GOSSETTE (1922) d Dulac
GOSTA BERLINGS SAGA (1924) d/co-s Stiller w Garbo (2
parts) 2775m SF [sound version The Atonement of
Gosta Berling (1933)]
GOST O OSTROVA SVOBODY (1963) d/c Karmen
(= Question Freedom Island)
GOTAMA THE BUDDHA (1955) d Roy, Rajbans Khanna
p Roy 83min
Goto, Island of Love = GOTO, L'ISLE D'AMOUR (1968)
GOTO L'ILE D'AMOUR (1968) d/s/di Borowczyk w
Brasseur *93min (= Goto, Island of Love)
GOTTESGEISSEL (1919) d Curtiz
GOUMBE (1957) d/s Rouch 16mm

351

GOUMBE DES JEUNES NOCEURS, LA (1966) d/c Rouch 16mm 27min

GOUPI MAINS-ROUGES (1943) d/co-s Becker co-c Bourgoin 95min (= It happened at the Inn)

GOUT DU LA VIOLENCE, LE (1960) d/s/w Hossein S 80min

GOUTTE DE SANG, LA (1924) d J Epstein Pat

GOVERNMENT GIRL (1943) d/p/s D Nichols ad B Schulberg m Harline w De Havilland, Darwell, Moorehead 93min RKO

GO WEST (1925) d/p/st-w Keaton 7rs MGM

GO WEST (1940) d Edward Buzzell m Edens w C, G, H Marx 81min MGM

GO WEST, YOUNG MAN (1936) d Hathaway s West c Struss w West, R Scott 82min Par

GOWN SHOP, THE (1923) d/s/w Semon 2rs Vit

GOYA (1950) d/s Emmer c Bava 21min (= Festa di S. Isidoro)

GOYA OU LES DESASTRES DE LA GUERRE (1951) co-d/cy/m Grémillon co-d/s Kast 22min

GOYOSEN (1926) d Kinugasa

GRA (1968) d Kawalerowicz *94min (= The Game)

GRACIELA (1936) d/co-s Torre-Nilsson 87min

Grace Moore Story, The (UK) = SO THIS IS LOVE (1935)

GRADENICO E TIEPOLO OVVERO AMORI E CONGIURE A VENEZIA (1911) d/s Guazzoni

GRADUATE, THE (1967) d M Nichols c Surtees songs Simon and Garfunkel w A Bancroft PV* 108min r UA

GRAFIN DONELLI (1924) d Pabst dec Warm 81min

GRAF VON CARABAS, DER (1934) d/p Reiniger fst Brothers Grimm anim 1rl

GRAIN DE SABLE, LE (1965) d/co-s Kast co-s de Givray w Palmer, Brasseur 98min ORTF

Grain of Wheat, A = HITOTSUBA NO MUGI (1958)

GRAMO VON BALLET (c 1963) d Schorm part anim TV

GRAN CALAVERA, EL (1949) d Bunuel co-s/w Alcoriza 90min

GRAN CASINO (1947) d Buñuel 85min (= En el viejo tampico)

GRAND AMOUR, LE (1968) d/w Etaix *85min Fox (= The Great Love)

GRAND AMOUR DE BEETHOVEN, UN (1936) d/s Gance w Barrault 7261ft (= Beethoven)

GRAND BARRAGE, LE (1961) d Olmi

GRAND DUCHESS AND THE WAITER, THE (1926) d St Clair c Garmes w Menjou 6300ft FPL

GRANDE APPELLO, IL (1936) d/st/co-s Camerini

GRAND CHARTREUSE, LA (1938) d Clément sh

GRANDE CIDADE, A (1966) d Carlos Diegues p Rocha

GRANDE FOIRE, LA (1960) d Mitry 15min (= The Big Fair)

GRANDE FROUSSE, LA (1964) d/s Mocky w Bourvil, Barrault, Blanche 92min (= The Big Scare)

GRANDE GUERRA, LA (1960) d/co-s Monicelli p De Laurentiis co-c Rotunno w Sordi, Gassmann, Mangano CS 113min (= The Great War)

GRANDE ILLUSION, LA (1937) d/co-s J Renoir co-s/co-di Charles Spaak c Matras dec Lourié, Wakhévitch m Kosma w Gabin, Fresnay, Von Stroheim, Dalio, Parlo, Carette, Modot, Becker 3542m

GRANDE LESSIVE, LA (1968) d/co-s Mocky w Blanche, Bourvil *95min r UA (= The Big Wash!)

GRANDE PAESE D'ACCIAIO, IL (1960) d Olmi S* 13min

GRANDE PASTORALE, LA (1943) d Clément sh

GRANDE SAUTERELLE, LA (1966) d/co-s Lautner S* 100min

GRANDE FAMILLES, LES (1959) d/co-ad De la Patellière co-ad/di Audiard fn Maurice Druon w Gabin, Brasseur, Desailly, (Riva) 90min

GRANDES GUEULES, LES (1965) d/co-s Enrico w Bourvil, Ventura *130min (= The Wise Guys/The Big Shots)

GRANDES MANOEUVRES (1896) d Méliès 20m

GRANDES MANOEUVRES, LES (1955) d/s/di Clair m Van Parys w Philipe, Morgan, Desailly, Bardot 98min (= Summer Manoeuvres)

GRANDES PELOUSES, LES (1961) d/s Moussy *22min (= The Great Fields)

GRANDES PERSONNES, LES (1960) d/cos Valère c Coutard dec Evein w Seberg 96min

GRANDE STRADA, LA (1948) d Cottafavi, M Waszinsky

GRANDE STRADA AZZURRA, LA (1957) co-d Pontecorvo w Montand, Valli, Girotti S* (= Squarcia)

GRANDE VERGOGNA, LA (1916) d/s/w Ghione

GRANDE VIE, LA (1960) d/co-ad/co-di Duvivier c Strindberg w Masina 88min Pat

GRAND HOTEL (1932) d Goulding fn Vicki Baum c Daniels a Gibbons w J Barrymore, Garbo, Beery, Hersholt, L Barrymore, J Crawford 105min MGM

GRAND HOTEL BABYLON, DAS (1919) d Dupont 1545m

GRANDI MAGAZZINI, I (1939) d/co-st/co-s Camerini co-s Castellani w De Sica

GRAND JEU, LE (1934) d/co-s Feyder co-s Charles Spaak des Meerson m Eisler w Rosay, Vanel 115min

GRAND JEU, LE (1953) d Siodmak co-s Charles Spaak, Feyder(uc) co-m Van Parys w Lollobrigida, Arletty 103min (= Flesh and Woman)

GRANDMA'S BOY (1922) d Newmayer p/co-st Roach w H Lloyd 4841ft

GRANDMA'S READING GLASS (1900) d G Smith 100ft

GRAND MELIES, LE (1952) d/s Franju m Van Parys 30min

GRAND MILITARY PARADE, THE (1913) d K Vidor 1rl Mut

Grandpa Planted a Beet = ZASADIL DEDEK RERU (1945)

GRAND PARADE, THE (1930) d Newmayer p/s Goulding 8rs Pat

GRAND PATRON, UN (1951) d Clampi w Fresnay, Ronet 95min

GRAND PRIX (1966) d Frankenheimer s Aurthur c Lindon cr Bass m Jarre w Garner, Saint, Mifune, Montand 70* 175min MGM

GRAND REFRAIN, LE (1936) d/s Yves Mirande supn Siodmak dec Lourié Grand Rue = CALLE MAYOR (1956)

GRAND SAUTERELLE, LA (1966) d/co-s Lautner w Darc, Blanche *95min

GRANDS CHEMINS, LES (1962) d/co-s Marquand supn Vadim S* 95min (= Of Flesh and Blood)

GRAND SLAM (1933) d Dieterle c Hickox w Lukas, L Young 67min WB

GRAND SLAM OPERA (1936) d/co-s Charles Lamont co-s/w Keaton 1860ft

GRANDS MOMENTS, LES (1965) d/s Lelouch S 100min

GRAND STREET (1953) d J Mekas

GRAND SUD, LE (1956) d Reichenbach *9min

GRANDUCHESSA SI DIVERTI (1940) d Giacomo Gentilomo s Monicelli

GRANNY (1912) d Griffith w Pickford 1rl Bio

GRANSFOLKEN (1913) d Stiller fn (Benvenuti) Zola 965m

GRANTON TRAWLER (1934) d Anstey p Grierson 11min EMB

GRAPES OF WRATH, THE (1940) d J Ford p Zanuck as-p/s N Johnson fn John Steinbeck c Toland co-a R Day m A Newman w H Fonda, Darwell, Carradine, (Marsh) 129min Fox

GRASS (1926) d/co-p/c Schoedsack, M Cooper co-p/s Marguerite Harrison 1580ft FPL

GRASSHOPPER AND THE ANT, THE (1954) d Reiniger fst La Fontaine anim 10min

Grasshopper, The = POPRIGUNYA (1955)

GRASS IN GREENER, THE (1960) d/co-p Donen c Challis m Coward w C Grant, Kerr, Mitchum, J Simmons TR* 104min U

Gratitude To The Emperor = KOON (1927)

GRATUITIES (1927) d/e Grémillon c Périnal 400m

GRAUSIGE NACHTE (1920) d Lupu-Pick

Great Adventure, The (UK) = STORA AVENTYRET, DET (1943)

GREAT AMERICAN BROADCAST, THE (1941) d A Mayo as-p Macgowan c Marley, Shamroy w Faye, Payne, Romero 91min Fox

GREAT BANK ROBBERY, THE (1969) d Hy Averback w Novak, Tamiroff, Cook PV* 95min

Great Beginning, The (US) = CHLEN PRAVITELSTVA (1940)

GREAT CARUSO, THE (1951) d Thorpe p Pasternak a Gibbons w Lanza, Blyth *109min MGM

GREAT CATHERINE (1968) d Gordon Flemyng fpl GB Shaw c Morris m Tiomkin w O'Toole, Moreau, Hawkins, Tamiroff *98min pc O'Toole

Great Citizen, A = VELIKII GRAZHDANIN (1938–39)

GREAT COMMANDMENT, THE (1939) d Pichel 85min Fox

Great Consoler, The = YELIKII UTESHITEL (1933)

GREAT GAME, THE (1930) d Jack Raymond w Harrison 7036ft

GREAT DAN PATCH, THE (1949) d J Newman 94min (= Ride a Reckless Mile)

GREAT DAY IN THE MORNING (1956) d J Tourneur m Leith Stevens w V Mayo, Stack, Roman, Burr S* 92min RKO

GREAT DIAMOND ROBBERY, THE (1953) d Leonard co-s Rackin c Ruttenberg co-a Gibbons 69min MGM

GREAT DICTATOR, THE (1940) d/p/s/m Chaplin c Totheroh, Struss w Chaplin, Goddard 126min r UA

GREATER THAN LOVE (1921) d Niblo 7rs

GREAT ESCAPE, THE (1963) d/p -J Sturges s Clavell, Burnett fn Paul Brickhill c Fapp m E Bernstein w McQueen, J Coburn, Attenborough, Pleasance, Garner PV* 168min UA

GREATEST QUESTION, THE (1919) d/p Griffith co-c Bitzer w L Gish, Barthelmess 6rs FN

GREATEST SHOW ON EARTH, THE (1952) d/p/cy De Mille co-c Barnes, Marley co-a Pereira m V Young w Heston, Wilde, Lamour, Grahame, J Stewart, (B Crosby, Hope, E O'Brien, De Mille) *153min Par

GREATEST STORY EVER TOLD, THE (1965) d/p/co-s G Stevens c Mellor, Griggs co-a R Day w Von Sydow, McGuire, Heston, Poitier, C Baker, Heflin, J Wayne, J Ferrer, Rains, Conte PV70* 195min r UA

GREATEST THING IN LIFE, THE (1918) d/p/s Griffith c Bitzer w L Gish, D Butler 7rs

GREAT EXPECTATIONS (1946) d/co-s Lean co-s/co-p Neame fn Dickens c G Green w J Mills, Guinness, J Simmons 118min

Great Fear, The = VELIKII STRAH (1958)

Great Fields, The = GRANDES PELOUSES, LES (1961)

GREAT FLAMARION, THE (1945) d A Mann w Von Stroheim, Duryea 68min Rep

GREAT GABBO, THE (1930) d Cruze st B Hecht w Von Stroheim 70min

GREAT GAMBINI, THE (1937) d C Vidor p BP Schulberg c Shamroy w Tamiroff 70min Par

GREAT GARRICK, THE (1937) d Whale p LeRoy c E Haller w De Havilland, Harlow, Turner 91min WB

GREAT GATSBY, THE (1926) d Brenon fn Fitzgerald w W Baxter, W Powell 7296ft FPL

GREAT GATSBY, THE (1949) d E Nugent p/co-s Maibaum fn Fitzgerald c J Seitz a Dreier w Ladd, Cook, Winters 92min Par

GREAT GILDERSLEEVES, THE (1942) d G Douglas w Darwell 62min RKO

GREAT GOLD ROBBERY, THE (1913) d Elvey 2300ft

GREAT GUNS (1941) d Monty Banks w Laurel, Hardy, Marsh 74min Fox

GREAT IMPERSONATION, THE (1936) d Crosland 77min U

GREAT IMPOSTER, THE (1960) d Mulligan c Burks co-a Golitzen m Mancini w Curtis, E O'Brien, Malden 112min U

GREAT JOHN L, THE (1945) d Tuttle co-p/s J Grant m V Young w Darnell 96min r UA

GREAT LIE, THE (1941) d Goulding p J Warner, Wallis as-p Gaudio m M Steiner w B Davis, Astor 108min WB

GREAT LOVE, THE (1925) d/st Neilan 4521ft MGM

Great Love, The = GRAND AMOUR, LE (1968)

GREAT LOVER, THE (1918) d/p/s Griffith c Bitzer w L Gish 7rs

GREAT LOVER, THE (1920) d F Lloyd 6rs pc Goldwyn

GREAT MCGINTY, THE (1940) d/st/s P Sturges c Mellor co-a Dreier w Tamiroff 81min Par

GREAT MAIL ROBBERY, THE (1927) d G Seitz c J Walker 6504ft

GREAT MAN, THE (1956) d/co-s/w J Ferrer p A Rosenberg c Lipstein 92min U

Great Manhunt, The = DOOLINS OF OKLAHOMA, THE (1949)

GREAT MAN'S LADY, THE (1942) d/p Wellman c Mellor co-a Dreier m V Young w Stanwyck, McCrea 90min Par

GREAT MAN VOTES, THE (1939) d Kanin c Metty w J Barrymore 70min RKO

GREAT MEDDLER, THE (1940) d Zinnemann 11min MGM

GREAT MISSOURI RAID, THE (1951) d G Douglas 2nd d Canutt c Rennahan w Corey 83min Par (= The Great Manhunt)

GREAT MOMENT, THE (1921) d S Wood w Swanson 6372ft FPL r Par

GREAT MOMENT, THE (1944) d/s P Sturges c Milner co-a Dreier m V Young w McCrea, Carey 83min Par

GREAT O'MALLEY, THE (1936) d Dieterle p H Brown c E Haller w Bogart, Crisp, Sheridan 71min WB

Great Patriotic War, The = VELIKAYA OTECHEST-VENNAYA (1965)

GREAT PLAINS, THE (1957) d Kroitor 16mm* 24min NFBC

GREAT PROBLEM, THE (1916) d/p/s Ingram 5rs

GREAT PROFILE, THE (1940) d W Lang p Zanuck co-st/co-s Sperling co-a R Day m Mockridge w J Barrymore, Ratoff, Payne, A Baxter 82min Fox

GREAT RACE, THE (1965) d/co-st Edwards c R Harlan m Mancini w Lemmon, Curtis, N Wood PV* 163min r WB

GREAT REDEEMER, THE (1920) d C Brown s Furthman, J Gilbert w J Gilbert 5rs Metro

Great Road, The = VELIKII PUT (1927)

GREAT RUPERT, THE (1950) d Pichel p Pal c Lindon 86min EL

GREAT ST. LOUIS BANK ROBBERY, THE (1959) d Charles Guggenheim, John Stix w McQueen 86min r UA

GREAT ST TRINIAN'S TRAIN ROBBERY, THE (1966) d Gilliat, Launder p Gilliat co-s Launder *93min BL

GREAT SINNER, THE (1949) d Siodmak p G Reinhardt fn (The Gambler) Dostoievski c Folsey m Kaper w Peck, Gardner, W Huston, M Douglas, E Barrymore, Moorehead 110min MGM

Great Strength = VELIKAYA SILA (1950)

GREAT TRAIN ROBBERY, THE (1903) d Porter w GM Anderson 302ft Ed

Great Turning Point, The = VELIKII PERELOM (1946)

GREAT VICTOR HERBERT, THE (1939) d/p/co-st Stone c Milner co-a Dreier chor Prinz 84min Par

GREAT WALTZ, THE (1938) d Duvivier st G Reinhardt c Ruttenberg des Gibbons m Tiomkin f Johann Strauss w Rainer 104min MGM

Great War, The (UK) = GRANDE GUERRA, LA (1959)

Great Warrior Standerberg, The = VELIKII VOIN ALBANII SKANDERBERG (1954)

GREAT WHITE HOPE, THE (1970) d Ritt c Guffey w Dalio PV* 102min

Great White Silence, The (1911) 1st version of 90 DEGREES SOUTH (1930)

GREAT ZIEGFELD, THE (1936) d/co-p Leonard w M Loy, W Powell 180min MGM

GREED (1923) d/s Von Stroheim fn (McTeague) Frank Norris c B Reynolds, Daniels a R Day, Von Stroheim E von Stroheim, Ingram, Mathis w Pitts, Hersholt 10 rs r MGM

Greediness Punished = TRAMP AND TURPENTINE BOTTLE (1902)

Greed in the Sun = CENT MILLE DOLLARS AU SOLEIL (1963)

GREEDY FOR TWEETY (1957) d Freleng anim* 7min WB

GREEK SCULPTURE (1959) d B Wright, Michael Ayrton *22min

GREEKS HAD A WORD FOR THEM, THE (1932) d/p L Sherman c Barnes e Heisler m A Newman w Blondell, Grable 79min r UA

GREEN AND PLEASANT LAND (1955) d/s L Anderson c Lassally 4min

GREEN BERETS, THE (1968) d J Wayne, Ray Kellogg p J Wayne c Hoch m Rozsa w J Wayne, A Ray PV* 138min

GREEN COCKATOO, THE (1940) d Menzies st Greene w J Mills, Newton 65min

GREEN DOLPHIN STREET (1947) d Saville s Raphaelson c Folsey m Kaper w Turner, Heflin, D Reed 141min r MGM

GREENE MURDER CASE, THE (1929) d Tuttle w W Powell, Arthur 6383ft

GREEN EYES (1934) d Thorpe 63min

GREEN FIELDS (1937) co-d/p Ulmer co-d Jacob Ben-Ami 11rs

GREEN FIRE (1954) d Marton s Goff, Roberts co-a Gibbons w Grace Kelly, S Granger, P Douglas CS 100min MGM

GREEN FOR DANGER (1946) d/s Gilliat co-s Launder m Alwyn w T Howard 91min JAR

GREENGAGE SUMMER, THE (1961) d L Gilbert p Saville s H Koch c F Young w Darrieux 99min BL (= Loss of Innocence)

GREEN GHOST, THE (1929) d L Barrymore

GREEN GLOVE, THE (1952) d Maté s/s Charles Bennett c C Renoir a Trauner m Kosma w G Ford 88min UA

GREEN GRASS OF WYOMING (1948) d Louis King c C Clarke co-a Wheeler w C Coburn, Ives, Nolan 89min Fox

GREEN MILL (1940) d Whale w Fairbanks Jr, J Bennett, Price, G Saunders, G Bancroft 87min U

GREEN LIGHT (1937) d Borzage p Wallis c Haskin m M Steiner w Flynn 85min FN-WB

GREEN MANSIONS (1959) d M Ferrer fn WH Hudson c Ruttenberg m Kaper w A Hepburn, Perkins, Cobb CS* 101min MGM

Green Mare's Nest, The (UK) = JUMENT VERTE, LA (1959)

GREEN PASTURES, THE (1936) co-d/fpl Marc Connolly co-d Keighley p Blanke c Mohr m Korngold 90min WB

GREENWICH VILLAGE (1944) d W Lang co-c Shamroy w Gable, Bendix, Holliday, C Miranda 82min Fox

GREEN YEARS, THE (1946) d Saville co-s Ardrey c Folsey m Stothart w C Coburn 125min MGM

Greetings Moscow! = ZDRAVSTVUI MOSKVA (1946)

GREGORY RATOFF IN 'FOR SALE' (1929) w Ratoff 1rl Vit

GREKH (1916) d Protazanov s/w Mozzhukin 1940m (in 3 parts) (= Sin)

GRELE DE FEU (1952) d Tazieff *16min

GREUX AU PARADIS, LES (1945) d René Le Menaff w Raimu, Fernandel

GREVE, LA (1904) d Zecca

GREVINDE HJERTELOS (1915) d Madsen

GREVINDENS AERE (1918) d Blom s Dreyer

GRIBICHE (1875) d/s Feyder des Meerson w Rosay 90min

GRIBOUILLE (1937) d M Allegret s/di Achard m Auric co-c Kelber, Thirard dec Trauner w Raimu, Morgan, Carette 85min

GRIDO, IL (1957) d/co-s/st Antonioni c Di Venanzo m Fusco w Cochran, Valli 116min

GRIDO DELLA CITTA, IL (1949) d Risi

GRIEF STREET (1931) d/e Thorpe 70min

GRIFF NACH DEN STERNEN (1955) d Käutner 92min

GRILLER, DER (1968) d Moorse

GRIMACI PARIZHI (1924) d/s Vertov anim 60m (= Scowls of Paris)

GRIM COMEDIAN, THE (1921) d F Lloyd c Brodine 6rs pc Goldwyn

GRIM PASTURES (1943) d Dunning anim

Grip of Fear, The = EXPERIMENT IN TERROR (1962)

GRISSOM GANG, THE (1971) d/p Aldrich fn (No Orchids for Miss Blandish) James Hadley Chase c Biroc *128min pc Aldrich

GRIT (1924) d Tuttle w Bow 5800ft

GROCERY CLERK'S ROMANCE, THE (1912) d Sennett w Normand ½rl Key

GROENLAND (1952) co-d/p Ichac co-d Jean-Jacques Languepin 69min RKO (= Groënland, Terre des Glaces)

Groënland, Terre Des Glaces = GROENLAND (1952)

GROMADA (1952) d Kawalerowicz, Kazimierz Sumerski 105min (= The Village Mill)

GROS COUP, LE (1964) d/co-s Valere w Riva, Kruger 99min

GROS ET LE MAIGRE, LE (1961) d/co-s/w Polanski m Komeda 16min

GROSSE FREIHEIT Nr 7 (1944) d/co-s Käutner 3060m (= La Paloma)

GROSSE KONIG, DER (1942) d/s V Harlan w Wegener 3233m Tob

GROSSE LIEBE, DIE (1931) d Preminger 76min

GROSSE LIEBESSPIEL (1963) d Alfred Weidenmann w Neff 133min

GROSSE LOS, DAS (1928) d C Bernhardt

GROSSE RAUSCH, DER (1932) d C Bernhardt

GROSSE SPRUNG, DER (1927) d/s Fanck w Riefenstahl 2931m Ufa

GROSSE TETE, UNE (1962) d/co-s De Givray co-s Truffaut c Kelber m Legrand w Constantine, Etaix 96min

GROSSE VERHAU, DER (1971) d/p/s Kluge *90min

Grotesque Chicken, The = SPATNE NAMALOVANA SLEPICE (1963)

GROTTE AUX SURPRISES, LA (1905) d Méliès 40m

GROUNDS FOR MARRIAGE (1950) d Leonard c J Alton co-a Gibbons m Kaper w V Johnson 91min MGM

GROUP, THE (1945) d Lumut p/s Buchman presented by Feldman fn M McCarthy c B Kaufman des Callahan *150min UA

Group Kamikaze = KAMIKAZE REN (1933)

GROUP ONE (1967) d Warhol 16mm *30min (segment of Four Stars)

Growing Up = TAKEKURABE (1955)

GROZA (1934) d/s Petrov fpl Ostrovsky 84min (= Thunderstorm)

GRUMPY (1930) d Cukor, Cyril Gardner w Lukas 5591ft 74min Par

GRUNE MANUELA, DIE (1923) d Dupont w Dieterle 2651m r UFA (= Ein Film aus dem Sueden)

GRUNYA KORNAKOVA (1936) d/co-s Ekk* 105min (= Nightingale, Little Nightingale)

GRYNING (1944) d/s/c/e Sucksdorff 8min SF

GUADALCANAL DIARY (1943) d Lewis Seiler s Trotti c C Clarke w Conte, Bendix, Quinn, Nolan 93min Fox

GUAPO DEL '900, UN (1960) d/co-p Torre-Nilsson 84min (= Tough Guy of 1900)

GUARANY (1948) d/s Freda fab/m Carlos Gomez

GUARDIA, GUARDIA SCELTA, BRIGADIERE E MARESCIALLO (1956) d Bolognini w Sordi, Manfredi 100min

GUARDIA DEL CORPO, LA (1942) d/co-s Bragaglia co-s/w De Sica 84min

GUARDIA, LADRO E CAMERIERA (1958) d/co-s Steno w Manfredi

GUARDIE E LADRI (1951) d/s Steno, Monicelli p Ponti, De Laurentiis c Bava w Toto 100min (= Cops and Robbers)

GUARDSMAN, THE (1931) d Franklin as-p Lewin c Brodine w Pitts 80min MGM

GUBIJINSO (1935) d Mizoguchi (= Poppies)

GUDERNES YNDLING (1920) d/s Madsen

GUENDALINA (1957) d/co-s Lattuada p Ponti co-s Zurlini c Martelli m Piccioni w Vallone 91min

GUERISSEUR, LE (1913) d Ciampi w Marais 98min

GUERNICA (1950) d/c Resnais p Braunberger cy Paul Eluard w Casarès 12min

GUERRA SEGRETA, LA (1965) d T Young, Lizzani, Christian-Jaque w H Fonda, Gassmann, Girardot, Bourvil (= The Dirty Game)

GUERRE EN DENTELLES, LA (1952) d/s/m Kast 800ft (= Jacques Callot, Correspondant de Guerre)

GUERRE EST FINIE, LA (1966) d Resnais s/n Jorge Semprun c Vierny a Saulnier m Fusco w Montand, Thulin, Piccoli 121min

GUERRIERI (1942) co-d/co-s/n Emmer co-d/co-s Enrico Gras, Tatiana Grauding

GUESS WHO'S COMING TO DINNER (1967) d/p Kramer c Leavitt w Tracy, Poitier, K Hepburn 108min

Guest Game, A = DET KOM EN GAST (1947)

GUEST IN THE HOUSE (1944) d Brahm c Garmes w A Baxter, Wilde 121min r UA

Guest on Freedom Island = GOST O OSTROVA SVOBODY (1963)

GUEST WIFE (1945) d S Wood m Amfitheatrof w Colbert 90min UA

GUEULE D'AMOUR (1937) d Grémillon s/di Charles Spaak c Rittau w Gabin 2800m

GUGLIELMO OBERDAN, IL MARTIRE DI TRIESTE (1915) d/s/w Ghione

GUIDE FOR THE MARRIED MAN, A (1967) d Gene Kelly c J MacDonald w Matthau, Ball, Benny, F Hunter PV* 89min Fox

GUILLAUME (1896) d Reynaud

GUILT OF JANET AMES, THE (1947) d Levin c J Walker m Duning w R Russell, M Douglas 83min Col

GUILTY? (1930) d G Seitz p Cohn c Tetzlaff * 6371ft

GUILTY HANDS (1931) d WS Van Dyke w L Barrymore, K Francis 21min

Guilty Though Guiltless = BEZ VINY VINOVATYE (1945)

GUINEA PIG, THE (1948) d/co-s R Boulting p J Boulting as-p Del Giudice c G Taylor w Attenborough 97min

GUINGUETTE (1958) d/co-s Delannoy co-s/co-st/di Jeanson m Van Parys 104min

GULA BILEN, DEN (1963) d Mattson (= The Yellow Ca

GULA DIVISIONEN (1954) d Stig Olin w Ekman

GULDET OG VORT MJERTE (1912) d Madsen

GULDETS GIFT (1915) d Madsen co-s Dreyer

GULF BETWEEN, THE (1918) d/p Kalmus

GULLIVER'S TRAVELS (1938) d/p M and D Fleischer Swift *77min Par

GUMSHOE (1971) d Stephen Frears pc/w Finney 84min

Gun Crazy = DEADLY IS THE FEMALE (1949)

GUNFIGHT, A (1971) d Lamont Johnson w K Dougla Vallone *89min

GUNFIGHT AT DODGE CITY, THE (1959) d J Newma p W Mirisch w McCrea, McIntyre CS* 81min UA

GUNFIGHT AT THE O.K. CORRAL (1957) d J Sturges Wallis c C Lang co-a Pereira w Lancaster, Douglas, R Fleming, Ireland VV* 122min Par

GUNFIGHTER, THE (1950) d H King p N Johnson co-s De Toth c AC Miller co-a Wheeler m A Newman w Peck, Malden, Marsh 84min Fox

GUNFIGHTERS OF THE CASA GRANDE (1965) Rowland st/co-s B and Patricia Chase CS* 92mi MGM

GUN FIGHTIN' GENTLEMAN, A (1919) d/co-st J For co-st/w Carey 5rs U

GUN FURY (1953) d Walsh w Hudson, Marvin, D Reed *83min

GUNGA DIN (1939) d/p G Stevens co-st B Hecht MacArthur fpl Rudyard Kipling c August m A Newman w C Grant, V McLaglen, Fairbanks Jr Fontaine 117min RKO

GUNG HO! (1943) d Enright p Wangner c Krasner co-a Golitzen w R Scott, Mitchum, Beery 88min U

GUN GLORY (1957) d Rowland fn (Man of the West) Yordan w S Granger, R Fleming CS* 89min MGM

GUN GOSPEL (1927) d H Brown 6273ft FN

GUN IN HIS HAND, A (1945) d Losey 19min MGM

GUN JUSTICE (1927) d Wyler 2rs U

GUN LAW (1919) d J Ford 2rs U

GUNLESS BAD MAN, THE (1926) d Wyler 2rs U

Gunman in the Street = TRAQUE, LE (1950)

GUNMAN'S WALK (1958) d Karlson p Kohlmar s F Nugent c Lawton w Heflin CS* 97min Col

GUNN (1967) d/st/co-s Edwards c Lathrop m Mancini *94min r Par

GUNNAR HEDES SAGA (1923) d/s Stiller fn Selma Lagerlof 1840m SF

GUN PACKER, THE (1919) d/co-st J Ford 2rs U

Gun Runner, The = SANTIAGO (1956)

GUN RUNNERS, THE (1958) d D Siegel fn (To Have and Have Not) Hemingway co-s Mainwaring c Mohr m Leith Stevens w A Murphy 83min r UA

Guns, The = FUZIS, OS (1964)

GUNS AT BATASI (1964) d Guillermin c Slocombe w Attenborough, M Farrow, Hawkins 103min Fox

Guns for San Sebastian = BATAILLE DE SAN SEBASTIAN, LA (1968)

Guns for the Dictator = ARME A GAUCHE, L' (1965)

Guns in the Afternoon (UK) = RIDE THE HIGH COUNTRY (1962)

GUNSLINGER (1956) d/p Corman *71min

GUNS OF DARKNESS (1962) d Asquith c Krasker w Caron, Niven 103min

GUNS OF FORT PETTICOAT, THE (1957) d G Marshall p H Brown c Rennahan w A Murphy *82min pc H Brown, A Murphy r Col

GUNS OF THE LOOS, THE (1928) d Sinclair Hill w Carroll 7900ft

GUNS OF NAVARONE, THE (1961) d J Thompson ex-p/s Foreman c Morris w Peck, Niven, Quinn, S Baker, R Harris, Forbes CS* 151min Col

GUNS OF THE MAGNIFICENT SEVEN (1968) d Wendkos m E Bernstein w G Kennedy PV* 105min Mir r UA

GUNS OF THE TREES (1961) d J Mekas w A Mekas 85min

Guns of Wyoming, The (UK) = CATTLE KING (1963)

GUN THAT WON THE WEST, THE (1955) d Castle p Katzman *70min Col

GUN THE MAN DOWN (1956) d A McLaglen s B Kennedy c Clothier w Dickinson 78min pc J Wayne r UA

GUN WOMAN, THE (1915) d Borzage

GURU, THE (1968) d/co-s Ivory c Mitra w Tushingham *112min

GUSHER, THE (1913) w Normand 1rl Key

GUTEI KENKEI (1931) d/s Gosho

Gutter = DOBU (1954)

Guttersnipes = GATEGUTTER (1949)

GUVERNORENS DATTER (1912) d/s Blom

GUY, A GAL AND A PAL, A (1945) d Boetticher co-p/w R Hunter 63min Col

GUY COULD CHANGE, A (1945) d/as-p W Howard 65min Rep

GUY NAMED JOE, A (1944) d V Fleming co-st Boehms s Trumbo c Folsey, Freund a Gibbons m Sothart w Tracy, I Dunne, V Johnson, L Barrymore, Esther Williams, (Edwards) 120min MGM

GUYS AND DOLLS (1955) d/s J Mankiewicz p Goldwyn fmpl Swerling, Abe Burrows fst Damon Rynyon chor Kidd m Mockridge w Brando, J Simmons, Sinatra CS* 150min MGM

GUY WHO CAME BACK, THE (1951) d J Newman p Blaustein, La Shelle co-a Wheeler m L Newman w P Douglas, Darnell, J Bennett, Z Mostel 87min Fox

GVOZD V SAPOGYE (1932, ur) d Kalatozov (= Nail in the Boot)

GWIAZDY MUSZA PLONAC (1954) co-d/co-s Munk co-d Witold Lesiewicz 66min

GYALOG A MENNYORSZAGBA (1959) d Feher 100min (= Walking to Heaven)

GYCKLARNAS AFTON (1953) d/s Ingmar Bergman co-c Nykvist w H Andersson, Ekman, Björnstrand 95min San (= The Naked Light/Sawdust and Tinsel)

GYLDNE SMIL, DET (1935) d/s Fejos

GYPPO LOGGERS (1957) d A King 16mm 29min

GYPSY (1962) p/d LeRoy fpl f memoirs G Lee w R Russell, N Wood, Malden, (Benny) TR* 149min WB

GYPSY AND THE GENTLEMAN, THE (1958) d Losey c Hildyard des consultant R MacDonald w Mercouri *107min JAR

Gypsy Blood (US) = CARMEN (1918)

GYPSY COLT (1954) d Marton co-a Gibbons c Lipstein *72min MGM

GYPSY MOTHS, THE (1969) d Frankenheimer c Lathrop m E Bernstein w Lancaster, Kerr *106min MGM

GYPSY QUEEN, THE (1913) d Sennett w Normand, Arbuckle 1rl Key

HAARLEM (1943) d Gallone w Girotti 80min (= Knock Out)

HABANERA LA (1937) d Sirk 98min

HABEAS CORPUS (1929) d James Parrott p Roach supn/st McCarey 2rs r MGM

HABITACION DE ALQUILAR (1960) d Picazo

HABIT OF HAPPINESS, THE (1916) d/co-s/st Dwan p Griffith co-s/w Fairbanks Sr 5 rs r Tri (= Laugh and the World Laughs)

HACELDAMA (1919) d/s Duvivier (= Le Prix de Sang)

HADAKA NO SHIMA (1960) d/co-p/s Shindo 92min S (= The Island)

Hadimrsku Doesn't Know = TO NEZNATE HADIMRSKU (1931)

HAEVNENS NAT (1915) d/s/w Christensen (= The Night of Revenge)

HAGIOGRAPHIA (1971) d/s/c/e Markopoulos 16mm*

HÄGRINGEN (1958–59) d P Weiss 72min (= The Mirage)

HAHA (1964) d/s Shindo (= Mother)

HAHA O KOWAZUYA (1934) d Ozu Sho (= A Mother Ought To Be Loved)

HAHA WA SHINAZU (1942) d Naruse

HAHA-YO KOISHI (1926) d Gosho (= Mother's Love)

HAIE UND KLEINE FISCHE (1957) d/s Wisbar 3274m (= U-Boat 55)

HAIKYO NO NAKA (1923) d/s Mizoguchi Nik (= Among the Ruins)

Hail Days = FAGYOSSZENLEK (1962)

HAIL THE CONQUERING HERO (1944) d/s/st P Sturges c J Seitz co-a Dreier 101min Par

HAIRCUT (1963) d Warhol 16mm si 33min

HAIRPINS (1920) d Niblo p Ince 5000ft

HAIR RAISING HARE (1945) d C Jones anim* 7min WB

HAIRY APE, THE (1944) d Santell fpl Eugene O'Neill c Andriot w Bendix, S Hayward 90min UA

HAIZAN NO UTA WA KANASHI (1922) d/s Mizoguchi Nik (= Sad Song of the Defeated)

HAKAI (1948) d Kinoshita (= Apostasy)

HAKAI (1962) d Ichikawa c Miyagawa S Dai (= The Sin)

HAKOIRI MUSUME (1935) d Ozu Sho (= Young Virgin)

HAKUCHI (1951) d/co-s Kurosawa fn (The Idiot) Dostieovski w Mori, Mifune 166min Sho (= The Idiot)

HAKUCHU NO TORIMA (1966) d Oshima 99min pc Oshima r Sho (= Violence at Noon)

HALALOS CSOND (1918) d Balasz

HALB BLUT (1919) d/s F Lang p Pommer Dec

HALBSTARKEN, DIE (1956) d/co-s Tressler w Buchholz 97min (= Wolfpack)

HALF A BRIDE (1928) d La Cava c Milner w G Cooper 6263ft Par

HALF A HERO (1953) d Weis co-a Gibbons 71min MGM

HALF A SIXPENCE (1967) d/co-p G Sidney co-ex-p Perlberg fn (Kipps) H G Wells c Unsworth PV* 146min Par

Halfbreed = HALVBLOD (1913)

HALF-BREED, THE (1916) d Dwan p Griffith s Loos fst Bret Harte w Fairbanks Sr 5rs r Tri (= The Carquenez Woods)

HALF NAKED TRUTH, THE (1932) d/co-s La Cava c Glennon 67min RKO

HALF-PINT PYGMY (1948) d Avery p Quimby anim* 7min MGM (= George and Junior)

HALFWAY HOUSE (1944) d Dearden p Balcon as-p Cavalcanti w Rosay 95min

HALFWAY TO HEAVEN (1929) d/s G Abbott w Arthur, Lukas 6180ft Par

HALFWAY TO HOLLYWOOD (1938) d/w C Chase 2rs Col

HALLELUJAH (1929) d/p K Vidor a Gibbons 101min

HALLELUJAH, I'M A BUM (1933) d Milestone st B Hecht c Andriot m/di Rodgers and Hart w Jolson, Langdon 82min UA (= Hallelujah, I'm a Tramp)

Hallelujah, I'm a Tramp (UK) = HALLELUJAH, I'M A BUM (1933)

HALLELUJAH THE HILLS (1963) d/s/e A Mekas 88min

HALLELUJAH TRAIL, THE (1965) d/p J Sturges c Surtees m E Bernstein w Lancaster, Remick, Pleasance CR* 165min UA

HALLIDAY BRAND, THE (1957) d JH Lewis c Rennahan w Cotten, Lindfors 77min UA

HALLO BUDAPEST! (1935) d Vajda 2153m

HALLO EVERYBODY! (1933) d Richter m Milhaud 2½ rs

HALLS OF MONTEZUMA (1951) d Milestone co-c Hoch co-a Wheeler w Widmark, Palance, R Wagner, Malden, Webb *133min Fox

Hallucinationer = STUDIE II (1953)

HALLUCINATION DE L'ALCHIMISTE, L' (1897) d Méliès 20m

Hallucinations = STUDIE II (1953)

HALTIMME (1965) d Halldoff 12min (= Time Out)

HALVBLOD (1913) d Sjöström 1266m (= Halfbreed)

Ham and Eggs = HAM AND EGGS AT THE FRONT (1927)

HAM AND EGGS AT THE FRONT (1927) d Del Ruth st Zanuck c C Clarke 5500ft WB (= Ham and Eggs)

Ham Artist, The = FACE ON THE BARROOM FLOOR, THE (1914)

Hamburg = WELTSTRASSE SEE (1938)

HAMLET (1948) d/co-p Olivier co-p Del Giudice fpl Shakespeare m Walton w Olivier, J Simmons 155min

HAMLET (1913) d Blackton fpl Shakespeare 5rs Gau

HAMLET (1910) d/s Blom fpl Shakespeare

HAMLET (1920) d Svend Gade c Courant w Nielsen 2367m

Hamlet = GAMLET (1964)

HAMLET (1969) d T Richardson fpl Shakespeare *117min

HAMLET, PRINCE DE DANEMARK (1907) d Méliès fpl Shakespeare 165m

Hammer Against Witches, A = KLADIVO NA CÄRODĚJNICE (1969)

HAMMERFEST (1903) p Paul 80ft

HAMMERHEAD (1968) d D Miller *99min Col

HÄMNAREN (1916) d Stiller 1011m

HAMNSTAD (1948) d/s Ingmar Bergman c Fischer 100min SF (= Port of Call)

HAMPI (1960) d/s Rouch 16mm

HANA (1914) d Yoshimura (= Blossom)

HANA (1967) d/p/st Kuri anim* 50seconds (= Flower, The)

HANA HIRAKU (1948) d Ichikawa Toho (= A Flower Blooms)

HANAKOGO NO UTA (1937) d/s Gosho (= Song of A Flower Basket)

HANAMUKO NO NEGOTO (1934) d Gosho (= The Bridegroom Talks In His Sleep)

HANA NO NAGADOSU (1954) d/s Kinugasa (= End Of A Prolonged Journey)

HANADAKA JIJII (1923) d/s Kinugasa

HANA SAKU MINATO (1943) d Kinoshita (= The Blossoming Port)

HANAYOME NO NEGOTO (1933) d Gosho (= The Bride Talks In Her Sleep)

HANAYOME-SAN WA SEKAI ICHI (1959) d/s Shindo (= The Bride From Japan)

The Hand = PUKA (1964)

HAND, THE (1968) d/s Brdecka *14min

HANDFULL RIS, EN (1938) d Fejos 73min SF (= Man och Kvinna)

HAND IN HAND (1960) d P Leacock w Sybil Thorndike 80min

Hand in the Trap (UK) = MANO EN LA TRAMPA (1961)

HANDLE WITH CARE (1932) d D Butler 72min Fox

HAND OF DEATH (1962) d Neilson c F Crosby 60min Fox

HANDS ACROSS THE TABLE (1935) d Leisen c Tetzlaff co-s Krasna w Lombard, MacMurray 80min Par

HANDS, KNEES AND BOOMPS-A-DAISY (1969) d Dunning anim* 3min

Hands Of Orlac, The (UK) = ORLACS HANDE (1924)

Hands of Orlac, The = MAD LOVE (1935)

Hands of Orlac, The (UK) = LES MAINS D'ORLAC (1959)

Hands Over The City (UK) = MANI SULLA CITTÀ, LE (1963)

HAND-PAINTED ABSTRACTION (1934) d McLaren anim* 3min

Hands Up! = RĘCE DO GORY (1967)

HANDY ANDY (1934) d D Butler w W Rogers, R Taylor 83min Fox

HANGED MAN, THE (1964) d D Siegel rm RIDE THE PINK HORSE (1947) w E O'Brien, Miles *87min U

HANG 'EM HIGH (1968) d Ted Post w Eastwood *114min

HANGING OUT THE CLOTHES, OR MASTER MISTRESS AND MAID (1898) d G Smith 69ft

Hanging Stockings On A Christmas Tree = NIGHT BEFORE CHRISTMAS (1902)

HANGING TREE, THE (1959) d Daves co-s Mayes c McCord m M Steiner w G Cooper, Maria Schell, Malden, G Scott *106min WB

HANGIVELSE (1965) d/w Thulin sh (= Devotion)

HANGMAN, THE (1959) d Curtiz s D Nichols c Griggs w R Taylor 87min Par

HANGMAN'S HOUSE (1928) d J Ford w V McLaglen, J Wayne 7rs Fox

HANGMEN ALSO DIE! (1943) d/p/co-st/co-s F Lang co-st/co-s Brecht c Howe m Eisler w Brennan 140min r UA (= Lest We Forget)

HANGOVER SQUARE (1945) d Brahm c La Shelle co-a Wheeler m Herrmann w Darnell, G Sanders 77min Fox

HANKA (1955) d Vorkapich

HANNA AMON (1951) d V Harlan 106min

HANNELES HIMMELFAHRT (1934) d/s Von Harbou 64min

Hannibal (UK) = ANNIBALE (1959)

HANNIBAL TANAR UR (1956) d/co-s Fabri 90min (= Professor Hannibal)

HANNIE CAULDER (1971) d B Kennedy co-s B Kennedy (ps ZX Jones) w Welch, Borgnine PV 85min

HANS BRÖLLOPSNATT (1916) d Stiller 1019m

HANS CHRISTIAN ANDERSEN (1952) d C Vidor p Goldwyn s M Hart c Stradling co-a R Day w Kaye, F Granger *120min RKO

HANSEL AND GRETEL (1955) d Reiniger fst Brothers Grimm anim 1rl

HANS ENGELSKA FRU (1926) d Molander w Dagover SF

HANS GODE GENIUS (1920) d/s Blom

HANS HUSTRUS FÖRFLUTNA (1915) d Stiller 1090m

HANS IM GLUCK (1936) d/s Rohrig, Robert Herth co-dec Rohrig 2413m

HANS IM GLUCK (1938) d/p Richter 600ft

HANS NÄDS TESTAMENTE (1919) d/co-s Sjöström fn Hjalman Bergman 1536m

HANSOM CABMAN, THE (1924) d Harry Edwards w Langdon 2rs pc Sennett r Pat (= Be Careful)

HANSOM DRIVER, THE (1913) d/p Sennett w Sennett, Normand ½rl Key

HANS RIGTIGE KONE (1916) d/s Madsen

HANS TRUTZ IN SCHLARAFFONLAND (1917) d/w Wegener

Happening, The = IT'S WHAT'S HAPPENING (1967)

HAPPIEST DAYS OF YOUR LIFE (1950) d/p/co-s Launder 81min BL

HAPPINESS (1923) d K Vidor w Hopper 76min 8rs Metro

Happiness (UK) = BONHEUR, LE (1964)

HAPPINESS AHEAD (1934) d LeRoy c Gaudio w D Powell, Darwell 86min FN

HAPPINESS OF THREE WOMEN, THE (1954) d Elvey 78min

HAPPY ANNIVERSARY (1959) d D Miller c Garmes w M Gaynor, Niven 81min UA

Happy Anniversary (UK) = HEUREUX ANNIVERSAIRE (1962)

HAPPY BIRTHDAY, BLACKIE (1963) d R Leacock 16mm

HAPPY BIRTHDAY WANDA JUNE (1971) d Robson s/fpl Kurt Vonnegut w Steiger *105min

Happy Circus, The = VESELY CIRKUS (1951)

HAPPY ENDING, THE (1969) d/p/s R Brooks c C Hall m Legrand w F Simmons, S Jones, T Wright PV* 117min r UA

HAPPY GO LUCKY (1943) d C Bernhardt co-s Panama, M Frank co-c Struss w D Powell 81min Par

HAPPY-GO-NUTTY (1944) d Avery anim* 668ft MGM

HAPPY HOOLDINI (AND) LAMPOONS (1920) pc Goldwyn-Bray 1rl

HAPPY HOOLYN (1900) d/w Blackton

HAPPY HOOLIGAN (1901–03) d Porter 19ft Ed (7eps)

HAPPY HOOLIGAN APRIL-FOOLED (1901) d Porter 24ft Ed

HAPPY HOOLIGAN IN A TRAP (1903) d Porter 20ft Ed

HAPPY HOOLIGAN'S INTERRUPTED LUNCH (1903) d Porter 37ft Ed

HAPPY HOOLIGAN SURPRISED (1901) d Porter 24ft Ed

HAPPY HOOLIGAN TURNS BURGLAR (1902) d Porter 47ft Ed

HAPPY IN THE MORNING (1938) d Jackson p Cavalcanti 13min

HAPPY IS THE BRIDE (1957) d R Boulting p J Boulting 84min BL

HAPPY LAND (1943) d Pichel as-p Macgowan c La Shelle m Mockridge w (N Wood, as Natasha Gurdin) 75min Fox

HAPPY LANDING (1938) d Del Ruth co-st/co-s Sperling w Romero, Hersholt 102min Fox

Happy Mothers' Day, Mrs Fisher = QUINT CITY USA (1963)

HAPPY ROAD, THE (1956) d/p/w Gene Kelly co-s Kurnitz m Van Parys w M Redgrave, (Cassel) 100min MGM

HAPPY THIEVES, THE (1962) d G Marshall w Harrison, Hayworth, Blanche 88min UA

HAPPY THOUGH MARRIED (1918) d Niblo 5rs FPL

HAPPY TIME, THE (1952) d R Fleischer c Lawton m Tiomkin w Boyer 94min pc Kramer Col

HAPPY WARRIOR, THE d F Martin Thornton w L Howard

HAPPY YEARS, THE (1950) d Wellman co-a Gibbons w R Wagner 86min MGM

Harakiri = SEPPUKU (1963)

HARA-KIRI (1919) d F Lang w Dagover 2525m Dec

HARANGOK ROMABA MENTEK, A (1958) d Jansco
  (= The Bells Have Gone to Rome)
HAR BORJAR AVENTYRET (1965) d/s J Donner c Badal
  w H Andersson FS 90min San
Harbour Rats = UMI NO YARODOMO (1957)
HARD-BOILED CANARY, THE (1941) d/p/co-st Stone
  Par
HARD DAY'S NIGHT, A (1964) d Lester c G Taylor
  songs/w The Beatles 87min r UA
HARDER THEY FALL, THE (1956) d Robson p/s Yordan
  fn B Schulberg c Guffey m Friedhofer w Bogart,
  Steiger 109min Col
HARD, FAST, AND BEAUTIFUL (1951) d/p Lupino c
  Stout w Trevor 79min RKO
HARD FISTS (1927) d Wyler 2rs U
HARD HITTIN' HAMILTON (1924) d Thorpe pc Artclass
HARD KLANG (1952) d Mattsson w Sjostrom (= A Dud
  Clang)
Hard Life = UKHABY ZHIZNI (1928)
HARD LUCK (1921) d/s Keaton, Cline w Keaton 2rs Metro
Hard Summer, A = VIZIVAROSI NYAR (1965)
HARD TO GET (1938) d Enright p Wallis co-s Wald w D
  Powell, De Havilland 80min WB
HARD TO HANDLE (1933) d LeRoy w Cagney 75min WB
HARD WAY, THE (1942) d V Sherman p Wald c Howe w
  Lupino 109m WB
Hardworking Clerk = KOSHIBEN GANBARE (1931)
HARDYS RIDE HIGH, THE (1939) d G Seitz w Rooney
  80min
HARE CONDITIONED (1945) d C Jones anim Cannon *
  7min WB
HARE KRISHNA (1966) d J Mekas m Allen Ginsberg
  16mm * 4min extract from DIARIES, NOTES and
  SKETCHES
HAREM, L' (1967) d Ferreri w C Baker CS* 100min (= The
  Harem)
Harem, The = HAREM, L' (1967)
HAREM KNIGHT, A (1926) d/co-s Cline p Sennett w
  Turpin Pat
HAREM'S EVENTYR, ET (1914) d Madsen
HAR HAR DU DITT LIV (1966) d/co-s/co/co/e Troell w Von
  Sydow 167min part * SF (= Here is Your Life)
HARICOT, L' (1962) d/s/c Sechan part *17min
HAR JEG RET TIL AT TAGE MIT EGET LIV? (1919) d/s
  Madsen
HAR KOMMER BARSARKARNA (1965) d Mattson TR*
  (= The Two Vikings)
HARLEKIN (1931) d Reiniger anim 490ft
HARLEKIN ES SZERELMESE (1966) d Feher (=
  Harlequin and Her Love)
HARLEM WEDNESDAY (1957) d/e J and F Hubley anim
  10min
Harlequin and Her Love = HARLEKIN ES SZERELMESE
  (1966)
HARLOT (1964) d Warhol s Ronald Tavel 70min 16mm
HARLOW (1965) d G Douglas s J Hayes c Ruttenberg co-a
  Pereira p Levine w C Baker, Lawford, Vallone PV*
  125min Par
HARLOW (1965) d Alex Segal w Lynley, G Rogers 108min
Harmony Parade = PIGSKIN PARADE (1936)
HAROLD TEEN (1928) d LeRoy p Dwan c E Haller w
  (Hopper) 8rs FN
HAROM CSILLAG (1960) (3 ep) d Jancso, Karoly Wieder-
  mann, Zoltan Varkonyi (= Three Stars)
HARPER (1966) d Smight c C Hall co-m (song) Previn w P
  Newman, Bacall, J Leigh, R Wagner, Winters PV*
  121min WB (= The Moving Target)
HARRIET CRAIG (1950) d V Sherman w J Crawford,
  Corey 94min Col
HARRISON ES BARRISON (1917) d A Korda
Harry Black = HARRY BLACK AND THE TIGER (1958)
HARRY BLACK AND THE TIGER (1958) d Fregonese s
  Boehm w S Granger, Rush CS* 107min Fox
  (= Harry Black)
HARRY MUNTER (1970) d/s Grede m Dvorak *101min
HARU KORO NO HANA NO EN (1958) d/s Kinugasa
  (= A Spring Banquet)
HARU NO MEZAME (1947) d/s Naruse (= Spring
  Awakening)
HARU NO YUME (1960) d/s Kinoshita S* 104min Sho
  (= Spring Dreams)
HARU WA GOFUJIN KARA (1932) d/st Ozu Sho
  (= Spring Comes With The Ladies)
Harvest = REGAIN (1937)
HARVEST (1962) d W Van Dyke *27min
HARVEY (1950) d Koster c Daniels w J Stewart 104min U
HARVEY GIRLS, THE (1945) d G Sidney p Freed as-p
  Edens co-s Raphaelson c Folsey co-a Gibbons chor R
  Alton w Garland, Charisse 101min MGM
HARVEY MIDDLEMAN, FIREMAN (1965) d/p/s/m
  Pintoff *76min r Col
HAS ANYBODY SEEN MY GAL? (1952) d Sirk w C
  Coburn, Hudson, Dean, Laurie 89min U
HASARD ET L'AMOUR, LE (1913) d/s/w Linder
Hash House Hero (re-issue) = STAR BOARDER, THE
  (1914)
HASHI NO NAI KAWA (1969) d Imai *125min (= Bridge
  Across No River/River Without a Bridge)
HASTY HEART, THE (1949) d V Sherman w Reagan, Neal
  99min WB

HAT, THE (1964) d/s J and F Hubley co-di/wv Dizzy
  Gillespie anim*
HATARI! (1962) d/p Hawks st Kurnitz c R Harlan, Brun
  (uc) co-a Pereira m Mancini co-song Carmichael w J
  Wayne, Martinelli *159min r Par
HATARAKU IKKA (1939) d/s Naruse (= The Whole
  Family Works)
HATCHET MAN, THE (1932) d Wellman c Hickox w
  Robinson, L Young 74min FN
HATEFUL GOD, THE (1913) d Ince w Hayakawa
HATESHINAKI JONETSU (1949) d Ichikawa Toho
  (= Passion Without Limit)
HATESHINAKI YOKUBO (1958) d Imamura S 100min
  Nik (= Endless Desire)
HATFUL OF RAIN, A (1957) d Zinnemann p Adler c Joe
  Macdonald co-a Wheeler m Herrmann w Saint,
  Nolan, Murray CS* 109min Fox
Hatred = MOLLENARD (1938)
HATS OFF (1927) d Hal Yates p Roach supn McCarey w
  Laurel, Hardy 2rs r MGM
HATSUKOI (1926) d/s Gosho (= First Love)
HATTER'S CASTLE (1942) d Lance Comfort w Kerr,
  Mason, Newton 100min
Haunted and the Hunted, The = DEMENTIA 13 (1962)
HAUNTED BEDROOM, THE (1919) d Niblo p Ince c
  Barnes 5rs FPL
Haunted Castle, The = SCHLOSS VOGELOD (1921)
HAUNTED CURIOSITY SHOP, THE (1899) p Paul 140ft
HAUNTED HOMESTEAD, THE (1927) d Wyler 2rs U
HAUNTED HOTEL, THE (1907) d Blackton 100m Vit
HAUNTED HOUSE, THE (1921) d/w Keaton, Cline 2rs
  Metro
Haunted House, The = AU SECOURS! (1923)
HAUNTED HOUSE, THE (1928) d Christensen co-s Biro c
  Polito 5755ft FN
HAUNTED NIGHT, THE (1957) d Pintoff
HAUNTED PALACE, THE (1963) d/p Corman co-ex-p
  Arkoff fsts Poe, Lovecraft c F Crosby a D Haller w
  Price, Cook PV* 85min AI
HAUNTED SPOOKS (1920) w H Lloyd 2rs pc Roach r Pat
HAUNTING, THE (1963) d/p Wise w Bloom PV 112min
  MGM
HAUNTING SHADOWS (1919) d H King 5rs
HAUPTMANN VON KOEPENICK, DER (1931) d R
  Oswald co-s/fn Zuckmayer 2945m
HAUPTMANN VON KOLN, DER (1956) d/co-s Dudow fn
  Zuckmayer 3228m Defa
HAUPTMANN VON KOPENICK, DER (1956) d/co-s
  Kautner fn Zuckmayer rm 1931 93min
HAUS DER LUGE (1925) d/co-s Lupu-Pick fpl Ibsen w
  Krauss 3037m r Ufa
HAUS IN MONTEVIDEO, DAS (1964) d Käutner
HAUT DE VENT (1942) d De Baroncelli
HAUTE LISSE (1956) d/m Grémillon +450m
HAUTETERRE (1952) d Mitry m P. De la Forêt-Divonne
HAVANA WIDOWS (1933) d Enright c Barnes w Blondell
  62min WB
HAVE A HEART (1934) d/co-st D Butler c Howe 85min
  MGM
HAVING WONDERFUL TIME (1938) d Santell w Fair-
  banks Jr, G Rogers, Ball, Ann Miller 21min RKO
HAVI ZOO FIX (1936) d Balazs
HAVSGAMARNA (1915) d Sjöström 1000m (=
  Smugglarens Dotter/Rosen på tistelön/Sea Vultures)
HAWAII (1966) d Hill prologue supn Blue p W Mirisch s
  Trumbo, Taradash fn James Michener c R Harlan m
  E Bernstein w J Andrews, Von Sydow, R Harris PV*
  179min r UA
HAWAIIANS, THE (1970) d Tom Gries p W Mirisch s JR
  Webb fn (Hawaii) Michener c Lathrop, Ballard m
  Mancini w Heston PV* 134min Mir r UA (= Master
  of the Islands)
HAWAII CALLS (1938) d Cline 91min RKO
HAWK, THE (1935) d Dmytryk 55min
HAWK OF WILD RIVER, THE (1952) d Sears 54min Col
Hawks and the Sparrows, The = UCCELLACCI E
  UCCELLINI (1966)
HAWKS NEST, THE (1928) d Christensen c Polito 7433ft
  FN
HAWTHORNE OF THE USA (1919) d Cruze 5rs FPL
HAXAN (1921) d/s/w Christensen 6840ft SF (= Witchcraft
  Through the Ages)
HAYSEED, THE (1919) d/s/w Arbuckle 2rs FPL
HAYSEED ROMANCE (1935) d Charles Lamont w Keaton
  2rs
Haystack, the = MEULE, LA (1962)
HAYSTACKS AND STEEPLES (1916) d Badger w
  Swanson
HAZARD (1948) d G Marshall c Fapp co-a Dreier w
  Goddard 95min Par
HAZUKASHII YUME (1927) d Gosho (= Intimate Dream)
HEADIN' SOUTH (1918) d Arthur Rosson supn Dwan p/w
  Fairbanks Sr 5rs r FPL
HEAD MAN, THE (1928) d Cline w L Young 4174ft WB
Head of the Family = PADRE DI FAMIGLIA (1967)
HEAD OVER HEELS (1922) d Schertzinger, Paul Bern w
  Normand 5rs pc Goldwyn
HEALTH IN INDUSTRY (1938) d Walt Gau
HEALTH IN WAR (1940) d Jackson 13min MOI
He and His Sister = ON A JEHO SESTRA (1931)

He and She = ASSOLUTO NATURALE, L' (1969)
Heart, The = KOKORO (1955)
HEARTBEAT (1946) d S Wood p Hakim Bros w G Rogers,
  Menjou, Rathbone 102min RKO
HEART BUSTER, THE (1924) d Conway w Mix 5rs Fox
Heart Knows No Frontier, The = CUORI SENZA
  FRONTIERE (1950)
Heart In Mouth = CUORE IN GOLA, IL (1964)
HEART OF A CHILD, THE (1920) d Ray C Smallwood w
  Nazimova 6rs
HEART OF A CHILD (1958) d C Donner 77min JAR
HEART OF A LION, THE (1917) d/s F Lloyd 7rs Fox
HEART OF A MAN (1959) d H Wilcox p Neagle 92min
Heart of a Mother = SERDTSE MATERI (1967)
Heart of a Nation = UNTEL, PERE ET FILS (1940)
HEART OF BRITAIN, THE (1941) d Jennings cy Ed
  Merrow 9min Crown
HEART OF HUMANITY, THE (1919) d Allen Hollubar
  technical adviser/w Von Stroheim 8rs
HEART OF MARYLAND, THE (1927) d Bacon c Mohr
  5800ft WB
HEART OF NEW YORK (1932) d LeRoy 78min WB
HEART OF NORA FLYNN, THE (1916) d De Mille 5rs pc
  Lasky
Heart of Solomon, The = SERDTSE SOLOMONA (1932)
HEART OF SPAIN (1948) co-c/co-e Strand co-e Hurwitz
Heart of the Mountains, The = KOKORO NO
  SANMYAKU (1966)
HEART OF THE SHERIFF, THE (1915) p/s/w Mix 1rl Sel
HEART OF THE WILDS (1918) d Neilan 5rs FPL
HEART O' THE HILLS (1919) d Franklin w Pickford, J
  Gilbert 6135ft WB
HEARTS ADRIFT (1914) d Porter w Pickford
Hearts and Dollars = TATIANA (1923/24) d Litvak w
  Petrov
HEARTS AND FLOWERS (1919) d Cline s Sennett w
  Fazenda 2rs Sen
HEARTS AND PLANETS (1915) d/p/w Sennett 1rl Key
HEARTS AND SPURS (1925) d WS Van Dyke w Lombard
  4600ft Fox
HEARTS ARE TRUMPS (1937) d G Douglas p Roach (1rl)
  MGM
HEARTS ARE TRUMPS (1920) d Ingram s Mathis c J Seitz
  6rs MGM
HEARTS DIVIDED (1936) d Borzage p H Brown c Folsey w
  D Powell, Rains, Davies, C Ruggles, Horton 87min
  WB
HEARTS IN BONDAGE (1936) d Ayres m Reisenfeld
  69min Rep
HEARTS IN EXILE (1929) d Curtiz sd 7877ft WB·
HEARTS OF OAK (1924) d J Ford 5336ft Fox
HEARTS OF THE WORLD (1918) d/p Griffith c Bitzer,
  Machin w L Gish, D Gish, Von Stroheim, Coward
  13rs pc Griffith
HEARTS OR DIAMONDS (1918) d H King 5rs
HEART TROUBLE (1928) d/w Langdon 5400ft pc Langdon
  r FN
HEAT LIGHTNING (1934) d LeRoy co-st G Abbott c
  Hickox w Darwell 63min WB
HEAT'S ON, THE (1943) d Ratoff w West 80min Col
HEAVE AWAY MY JOHNNY (1949) d/p/s Halas,
  Batchelor anim* 10min
Heaven and Hell = TENGOKU TO JIGOKO (1963)
HEAVEN CAN WAIT (1943) d/p Lubitsch s Raphaelson c
  Cronjager m A Newman w Tierney, C Coburn
  112min Fox
Heaven Fell That Night = BIJOUTIERS DU CLAIR DE
  LUNE, LES (1957)
HEAVEN KNOWS, MR ALLISON (1957) d/co-s J Huston
  p Adler co-s Mahin c Morris, Cardiff m Auric w
  Mitchum, Kerr CS* Fox
Heaven Linked with Love = TENGOKU NI MUSUME KOI
  (1933)
Heaven Over the Marshes = CIELO SULLA PALUDE
  (1949)
HEAVENS ABOVE! (1963) d/co-s J Boulting p R Boulting w
  Sellers 118min BL
Heaven Sent = DROLE DE PAROISSEN, UN (1963)
HEAVEN WITH A BARBED WIRE FENCE (1940) d
  Ricardo Cortez st/co-s Trumbo c Cronjager w G Ford
  62min Fox
HEBIHIMESAMA (1940) d/s Kunugasa w Yamada (2 parts)
  (= Miss Snake Princess)
HE CANNOT GET A WORD IN EDGEWAYS (1906) p
  Paul 170ft
HECKLERS, THE (1966) d Strick 50min TV
HE COMES UP SMILING (1918) d Dwan p/w Fairbanks Sr
  c August 5rs r FPL
Hectic Days = GORYACHIE DENECHKI (1935)
HEDDA GABLER (1919) d Pastrone fpl Ibsen
HE DID AND HE DIDN'T (1916) d/w Arbuckle w
  Normand 2rs Tri (= Love and Lobsters)
He Died After the War = TOKYO SENSO SENGO HIWA
  (1971)
HEEDLESS MOTHS (1921) d Leonard 6rs
HEDY (1965) d Warhol s Ronald Tavel 16mm 70min
  (= Hedy the Shoplifter/The 14 Year Old Girl)
Hedy the Shoplifter = HEDY (1965)
HEIDI (1937) d Dwan p Zanuck c AC Miller w Temple,
  Hersholt 88min Fox

Heidi = SON TORNATA PER TE (1953)
Height, A = V RAIONYE VYSOTY A (1941)
Heights, A = VYSOTA (1957)
HEILIGE BERG, DER (1926) d/s Fanck w Riefenstahl 3100m UFA
HEILIGE UND IHR NARR, DIE (1928) d Dieterle c Rittau w Dieterle 3006m (= The Saint and Her Fool)
HEIMAT UND FREMDE (1913) d/s May 1666m
HEIMKEHR (1928) d/p May c Rittau 3006m (= Homecoming)
HEIMLICHKEITEN (1968) d Staudte *84min (= Secrets)
HEINZE'S RESURRECTION (1913) d Sennett w Normand 1rl Key
HEIRESS, THE (1949) d/p Wyler fn (Washington Square) Henry James co-a Horner m Copland w De Havilland, M Hopkins, Clift, R Richardson
Heir to Gengis Khan, The = POTOMOK GHINGIS KHAN (1928)
HEISSE SPUR ST PAULI (1971) d Staudte *90min
HEJ (1965) d/s Cornell
HEJA ROLAND (1966) d/s/e Widerberg 96min (= 30 Times Your Money)
HEJ RUP! (1934) d/co-st/co-s Fric c Heller
HE LAUGHED LAST (1956) d/co-st/s Edwards co-st Quine *77min Col
HELD BY THE ENEMY (1920) d Crisp 6rs FPL
HELENE (1936) d Benoit-Lévy w Barrault 130min
HELEN MORGAN STORY, THE (1957) d Curtiz p Rackin c McCord chor Prinz w Blyth, P Newman CS* 118min WB (= Both Ends of the Candle)
HELEN OF FOUR GATES (1920) d/p Hepworth 5880ft
Helen of Troy = AMANTE DI PARIDE, L' (1954)
HELEN OF TROY (1956) d Wise, Walsh (uc) c Stradling m M Steiner w S Baker, Bardot CS* 118min WB
HELIOGABALE (1919) d Pastrone
HELL AND HIGH WATER (1954) d/co-s Fuller co-s Lasky c Joe Macdonald co-a Wheeler m A Newman w Widmark, D Wayne CS* 103min Fox
HELL BELOW (1933) d Conway co-di Mahin c Rosson w Montgomery, W Huston, R Young, Mahin 100min MGM
HELL BELOW ZERO (1954) d Robson ad Maibaum w Ladd, S Baker *91min Col
HELL BENT (1918) d/co-s J Ford c B Reynolds co-s/w Carey 5700ft U
HELL BENT FOR ELECTION (1944) d C Jones p Bosustow* 1rl
Hell Bent for Glory = LAFAYETTE ESCADRILLE (1958)
HELLBOUND (1931) d W Lang 81min
HELLDORADO (1934) d Cruze p Lasky c J Seitz 74min Fox
HELL DRIVERS (1957) d/s Endfield c Unsworth w Connery 108min JAR
HELLER IN PINK TIGHTS (1960) d Cukor co-p Ponti co-s D Nichols fn (Heller with a Gun) Louis L'Amour c Lipstein co-colour consultant Hoyningen-Huene m Amfitheatrof w Loren, Quinn, M O'Brien, Novarro *100min r Par
HELLFIGHTERS (1969) d A McLaglen s Huffaker c Clothier co-a Golitzen m Rosenmann w J Wayne, Miles PV* 121min U
HELLGATE U.S.A. (1952) d/co-p/s Warren e Elmo Williams w Hayden 87min
HELL HARBOR (1930) d/p H King w Hersholt 90min r UA
HELLIGE LOGNE (1925) d/s Madsen fn Gerhardt Hauptmann
HELL IN THE PACIFIC (1968) d Boorman c C Hall m Schifrin w Marvin, Mifune PV* 103min
HELLIONS, THE (1963) d Annakin c Moore TR* 80min r Col
HELL IS FOR HEROES (1962) d D Siegel p Blanke c Lipstein co-a Pereira m Rosenman w McQueen, J Coburn 89min Par
HELL IS SOLD OUT (1951) d Michael Anderson p Stross w Attenborough, Zetterling 84min
Hello Beautiful = POWERS GIRLS, THE (1942)
Hello Children! = ZDRAVSTVUITYE DETI! (1962)
Hello Cubans = SALUT LES CUBAINS (1964)
HELLO, DOLLY! (1969) d Gene Kelly p/s Lehman as-p Edens fmpl Jerry Herman, Michael Stewart fpl (Matchmaker, The) T Wilder chor Kidd w Matthau TAO* 148min Fox
HELLO DOWN THERE (1968) d J Arnold w Randall, J Leigh *98min
HELLO-GOODBYE (1970) d Negulesco c Decaë w Jurgens *107min Fox
HELLO MABEL (1914) d Normand(?) w Normand 1rl Key
HELL ON FRISCO BAY (1956) d Tuttle s Boehm, Rackin c J Seitz m M Steiner w Ladd, Robinson, Dru CS* 98min WB
HELLO OUT THERE (1949, (ur) d Whale fpl Saroyan 40min
HELLO SISTER (1930) d W Lang 80min pc Cruze
Hello, Sister = WALKING DOWN BROADWAY (1933)
HELLO SUCKER (1941) d Cline 62min U
HELLO TROUBLE (1918) d C Chase (as C Parrott) w C Chase 2rs
HELL'S ANGELS (1930) d/p H Hughes di/d Whale co-st Neilan co-c Gaudio w Harlow *(ball and battle sequences) 135min r UA

HELL'S BELLS (1930) d Iwerks p Disney anim (1rl)
Hell's Cargo = ALERTE EN MÉDITERANEE (1938)
HELL'S HEADQUARTERS (1932) d Stone 63min
HELL'S HEROES (1929) d Wyler rm Marked Men (1919) w Bickford, J Huston 78min U
HELL'S HIGHROAD (1925) d Julian c Marley 6084ft
Hell's Highway = VIOLENT ROAD (1958)
HELL'S HINGES (1916) d Ince w W Hart 5rs Tri
HELL SHIP MUTINY (1957) d Lee Sholem, Elmo Williams co-c Leavitt e Elmo Williams w Carradine, Lorre 60min
HELL'S ISLAND (1954) d Karlson c Lindon w Payne VV* 84min Par
HELL'S KITCHEN (1939) d Dupont, Lewis Seiler w Reagan WB
HELL SQUAD (1958) d/p/s Topper 73min
HELL TO ETERNITY (1960) d Karlson c Guffey m Leith Stevens w J Hunter 132min AA
HELL UNLIMITED (1936-37) d McLaren, Helen Biggar 15min 16mm
HELLZAPOPPIN' (1941) d Potter w Olsen, Johnson 84min
He Loved Her So = TWENTY MINUTES OF LOVE (1914)
HE LOVED LIKE HE LIED (1920) d St Clair 2rs U
HELP! (1965) d Lester c Watkin songs/w The Beatles *92min r UA
Helping Himself = HIS NEW PROFESSION (1914)
HELPMATES (1931) d James Parrott p Roach w Laurel, Hardy (2rs) r MGM
HELP WANTED! (1939) d Zinnemann 21min MGM
HELP WANTED - MALE (1920) d/w H King Pat
HE MARRIED HIS WIFE (1940) d Del Ruth p Zanuck co-s J O'Hara co-a R Day w McCrea, Romero, Cook 83min Fox
HEM FRAN BABYLON (1941) d/co-s Sjoberg (= Home From Babylon)
HEMINGWAY'S ADVENTURES OF A YOUNG MAN (1962) d Ritt p Wald f (Nick Adam's Stories) Hemingway c Garmes m Waxman w Dailey, A Kennedy, Montalban, P Newman, Wallach 145min Fox
HEMLIGT GIFTERMAL, ETT (1912) d Sjöström 1650m (= Bekännelsen på dödsbädden/Em Moder)
HEMMELIGHEDSFULDE X, DET (1913) d/s/w Christensen (= Mysterious X, The)
HEMSLAVINNOR (1933) d Ragnor Widestedt w Ekman
HEMSOBORNA (1955) d Mattson s Lindstrom fn August Strindberg *100m (= The People of Hemso)
HENDES HELT (1917) d/s Madsen
HENDES MODERS LOFTE (1916) d/s Madsen
HENDES NAADE DRAGONEM (1925) d/s Blom
HEN HOP (1941-43) d McLaren anim* 3min NFBC
Hen In The Wind, A = KAZE NO NAKA NO MENDORI (1948)
HENKEL (1938) d Ruttmann
HENLEY REGATTA (1898) p Hepworth 300ft (6 parts)
HEN PECKED HOBOES (1946) d Avery p Quimby anim* 744ft MGM
Henriette = FETE A HENRIETTE, LA (1957)
HENRY (1955) d/s L Anderson c Lassally 5½min
HENRY V (1945) d/w Olivier fpl Shakespeare c Krasker cos Furse m Walton w Newton *137min
HENRY GELDZAHLER (1964) d Warhol 100min si 16mm
HE RAN ALL THE WAY (1951) d John Berry c Howe m Waxman w Winters, Garfield 77min UA
HER AWAKENING (1911) d Griffith w Pickford 1rl Bio
HERB ALPERT AND THE TIJUANA BRASS DOUBLE FEATURE (1966) d J and F Hubley anim* 5min
Herbe Folle, L' = ESTERINA (1959)
HER BELOVED VILLAIN (1920) d S Wood 5rs
HER BODY IN BOND (1918) d Leonard 6rs U
Her Brother = OTOTO (1960)
HER CARDBOARD LOVER (1942) d Cukor co-dec Gibbons m Waxman w Shearer, R Taylor, G Sanders 93min MGM
HER CODE OF HONOR (1919) d Stahl
Hercules = FATICHE DI ERCOLE, LE (1957)
Hercules Conquers Atlantis = ERCOLE ALLA CONQUISTA DI ATLANTIDE (1961)
Hercules In The Centre Of The Earth = ERCOLE AL CENTRO DE LA TERRA (1961)
Hercules Unchained = ERCOLE E LA REGINA DI LIDIA (1959)
HER DECISION (1918) d Conway w Swanson 5rs Tri
Here and There = ATCHI WA KOTCHI (1962)
HERE COMES COOKIE (1935) d McLeod 7rs Par
HERE COMES MR JORDAN (1941) d Alexander Hall s S Miller, Buchman c J Walker w Montgomery, Rains, Horton 93min Col
HERE COMES THE GROOM (1951) d/p Capra co-st Riskin c Barnes co-a Pereira song Carmichael w B Crosby, Wyman, Tone, A Smith, Lamour (uc)
HERE COMES THE NAVY (1934) d Bacon w Cagney 87min WB
HERE COMES THE GIRLS (1953) d Claude Binyon co-s Kanter c Lindon w Hope *78min Par
HERE COME THE MARINES (1952) d A McLaglen, W Beaudine 66min Mon
HERE COME THE WAVES (1944) d/p Sandrich c C Lang co-a Dreier w B Crosby, Hutton, De Carlo 99min Par

HERE I AM A STRANGER (1939) d Del Ruth co-s Sperling c Arthur e Miller 83min Fox
Here Is a Man = ALL THAT MONEY CAN BUY (1941)
Here Is a Spring = KOKO NI IZUMI ARI (1955)
HERE IS MY HEART (1934) d Tuttle c Struss w B Crosby, Tamiroff 77min Par
Here Is Your Life = HAR HAR DU DITT LIV (1966)
Here's To The Girls = OJOSAN KAMPAI (1949)
Here They Come Down the Street = PARADE (1952)
HERE WE GO AGAIN (1942) d/p Dwan 77min RKO
HERE WE GO ROUND THE MULBERRY BUSH (1967) d/p C Donner cr R Williams 94min r UA
HER GILDED CAGE (1922) d S Wood w Swanson 6338 ft FPL r Par
HER FIRST AFFAIRE (1933) d Dwan w Lupino 71min
HER FIRST BEAU (1916) d Cline p Sennett Tri-Key
-HER FIRST BISCUITS (1909) d Griffith w Pickford 1rl Bio
HER FIRST MATE (1933) d Wyler w Pitts 66min U
HER FIRST ROMANCE (1940) d Dmytryk w Ladd 77min Mon
HER FIRST ROMANCE (1951) d Seymore Friedman c Lawton w M O'Brien 72min Col
HER FRIEND THE BANDIT (1914) d/w Chaplin, Normand 1rl Key
HER HIGHNESS AND THE BELLBOY (1945) d Thorpe p Pasternak w Lamarr, R Walker, Allyson, Moorehead 111min MGM
HER HUSBAND'S FRIEND (1920) d Niblo 4453ft Par
HER HUSBAND'S SECRET (1925) d/pc F Lloyd c Brodine 6150ft FN
HER HUSBAND'S TRADEMARK (1922) d S Wood w Swanson 5101ft FPL r Par
HER INDIAN HERO (1909) d/w Conway
HERITAGE OF THE DESERT (1933) d Hathaway fn Zane Grey rm 1924 s Stout w R Scott 60min Par
HERITIERS, LES (1955) d Groulx
Heritiers de L'Oncle James, Les = MILLIONS DE L'ONCLE JAMES, LES (1924)
HER KINGDOM OF DREAMS (1920) d Neilan 7rs
HER LAST AFFAIRE (1934) d M Powell 77min
HER LAST TRIP (1939) d Jennings GPO (= S.S. Ionian)
HER LOVE STORY (1924) d/p Dwan s Tuttle w Swanson 6750ft FPL
HER MAJESTY, LOVE (1931) d Dieterle w Fields 78min FN
HER MAN (1930) d Garnett 83min Pat
HERMAN MILLER AT THE BRUSSELS FAIR (1958) d/s C & R Eames c R Eames 4½min
HERMINE UND DIE SIEBEN AUFRECHTEN (1935) d/co-s Wisbar 3035m
HER MOTHER'S OATH (1913) d Griffith w D Gish 1rl Bio
HER NATURE DANCE (1917) d Cline p Sennett Tri-Kay
HER NEW BEAU (1913) d/p Sennett w Sennett, Normand ½rl Key
HER NIGHT OF ROMANCE (1924) d Franklin w C Talmadge, R Colman 7019ft WB
Hero, The = NAYAK (1966)
HEROES, THE (1969) d Negulesco w Jurgens CS* 9270ft
Heroes and Sinners (1955) = HEROS SONT FATIGUES, LES (1955)
HEROES FOR SALE (1933) d Wellman w Barthelmess, L Young 73min FN
Heroes of Chipka, The = GEROI CHIPKI (1954)
HEROES OF TELEMARK, THE (1965) d A Mann co-s Barzman c Krasker m M Arnold w K Douglas, R Harris, Jacobsson, M Redgrave PV* 131min Col
Hero For a Night = HRDJA JEDNE NOCI (1935)
Heroic Charge = CAPRICA EROICA (1952)
HEROISME DE PADDY, L' (1916) d/s Gance
HERO'S ISLAND (1962) d/p/s Leslie Stevens c McCord w Mason PV* 94min UA (= The Land We Love)
HEROS SONT FATIGUES, LES (1955) d Ciampi c Alekan w Montand, Felix, Jurgens 115min (= Heroes and Sinners)
HER PRIVATE LIFE (1929) d A Korda c J Seitz w Pidgeon, Pitts 6488ft FN
HERR ARNES PENGAR (1919) d/co-s Stiller co-s Molander fn Selma Lagerlof 2219m (= Sir Arne's Treasure)
HER ARNES PENGAR (1954) d/co-s Molander w Jacobsson, B Andersson *91min SF
HERR DER LIEBE, DER (1919) d/w F Lang p Pommer 1316m Dec
HERREN MIT DER WEISSEN WESTE, DIE (1970) d Staudte *92min
HERREN OG HANS TJENER (1959) d Skouen 84min (= Master and His Servants, The/A God and His Servants)
HERREN PARTIG (1964) d/co-s Staudte 94min
HERRIN DER MEERE (1922) d A Korda
HERRIN DER WELT, DIE (1919-20) (8 parts) Parts 1/2/3 d/p/co-s May 1894m/1929m/1605m Parts 4/5/6/7 p/co-s & artistic advisor May Part 8 d/p/co-s May 2181m
HERRIN DER WELT (1960) d Dieterle *98min
HERRIN VON ATLANTIS, DIE (1932) d Pabst co-c Shuftan w Helm 90min Nero (= L'Atlantide)
HERR PUNTILA UND SEIN KNECHT MATTI (1956) d/co-ad Cavalcanti co-ad/fpl Brecht m Eisler 95min

HERRSCHER, DER (1937) *d* V Harlan *co-s* von Harbou *w* Jannings 2918m
HERR STRAUSS (1966) *d* Pennebaker 30min 16mm TV
HERR UBER LEBEN UND TOD (1919) *d/co-s* Lupu-Pick
HER SISTER FROM PARIS (1925) *d* Franklin *w* C Talmadge, R Colman 6900ft WB
HER SISTER'S SECRET (1946) *d* Ulmer *c* Planer 83min
HER SOUL'S INSPIRATION (1917) *d* Conway 5rs
Her Sweetheart = CHRISTOPHER BEAN (1933)
HER TWELVE MEN (1954) *d* Leonard *p* Houseman *c* Ruttenberg *co-a* Gibbons *w* Garson, Ryan, Haydn 91min MGM
HER WEDDING NIGHT (1930) *d* Tuttle *w* Bow, C Ruggles 6294ft Par
HER WILD OAT (1927) *d* Neilan *c* Folsey 6118ft FN
HERZOG FERRANTES ENDE (1923) *d/w* Wegener
HERZOG IN SATANELLA (1920) *d* Curtiz
He, She, Or It = POUPEE, LA (1962)
HE'S MY GUY (1943) *d* Cline 64min U
HETS (1944) *d* Sjoberg *s* Ingmar Bergman *w* Kjellin, Zetterling, Bjornstrand 101min SF (= *Frenzy/Torment*)
HESTE (1943) *d/co-s* B Henning Jensen 39min (= *Horses*)
HESTEN PA KONGENS NYTORU (1941) *d/s* B Henning Jensen
HEURES, LES (1909) *d/s* Feuillade Part 1 *L'Aube, L'Aurore* 58m Part 2 *Le Matin, Le Jour* 50m Part 3 *Midi La Vespree, Le Crepuscule* 83m Part 4 *Le Soir, La Nuit* 53m
HEUREUX ANNIVERSAIRE (1962) *co-d/co-s/w* Etaix *co-d/co-s* Jean-Claude Carrière 12min (= *Happy Anniversary*)
HEUREUX QUI COMME ULYSSE ... (1970) *d/co-s* Colpi *m* Delerue *w* Fernandel *90min
HEUT' KOMMT'S DRAUF AN (1933) *d* Kurt Gerron *w* Rainer 86min
HE WALKED BY NIGHT (1948) *d* Alfred Werker, A Mann (uc) *c* J Alton *w* J Webb 80min EL
HE WAS HER MAN (1934) *d* Bacon *w* Cagney, Blondell 90min WB
HE WHO GETS SLAPPED (1924) *d/co-s* Sjöström *fpl* Leonid Andreiev *des* Gibbons *w* Chaney, Shearer, J Gilbert 6800ft MGM
He Who Must Die = CELUI QUI DOIT MOURIR (1957)
HE WHO RIDES A TIGER (1965) *d* Crichton 103min BL
HEYA (1967) *d/p* Kuri *anim** 5min (= *The Room*)
HEY, HEY USA (1938) *d* Marcel Varnel *w* Hay 92min
HEY RUBE! (1928) *d* G Seitz 6290ft
HIBANA (1922) *d/s* Kinugasa (= *Spark*)
HIBANA (1956) *d/s* Kinugasa *rm* 1922 (= *Spark*)
HIBARI NO TAKEKURABE (1958) *d* Gosho
HIBERNATUS (1969) *d* Molinaro *w* De Funes S* 80min Gau
HICK, THE (1921) *d/s* Semon, Taurog *w* Semon 2rs Vit
HIGH BRIGHT SUN, THE (1964) *d* Thomas *w* Bogard *114min JAR
HIGH COMMAND, THE (1937) *d* T Dickinson *co-c* Jeller *w* Mason 74min
HIGH COST OF LOVING, THE (1958) *d/w* J Ferrer *c* Folsey CS 87min MGM
HIGH FLYERS (1937) *d* Cline *w* Dumont 70min RKO
High Infidelity = ALTA INFIDELTA (1964)
HIGHLY DANGEROUS (1950) *d* R Baker *w* Lockwood 88min BL
HIGH NOON (1952) *d* Zinnemann *s* Foreman *c* F Crosby *co-e* Elmo Williams *m* Tiomkin *w* G Cooper, Grace Kelly, Mitchell 85min *pc* Kramer *r* UA
HIGH PRESSURE (1932) *d* LeRoy *w* W Powell 74min WB
HIGH ROAD (1960) *d* John Gunther *c* Vorkapich
High Road, The = LADY OF SCANDAL, THE (1930)
High School = TERZA LICEO (1953)
HIGH SCHOOL CONFIDENTIAL (1958) *d* J Arnold *p* Zugsmith CS 85min MGM
HIGH SCHOOL HERO (1927) *d/co-st* D Butler *w* D Fairbanks Jr 5498ft Fox
HIGH SIERRA (1941) *d* Walsh *p* J Warner, Wallis *as-p* Hellinger *co-s* J Huston *co-s/fn* Burnett *c* Gaudio *w* Bogart, Lupino, Wilde, A Kennedy 110min WB
HIGH SIGN, THE (1921) *d/s* Keaton, Cline *w* Keaton 2rs Metro
HIGH SOCIETY (1956) *d* Walters *p* S Siegel *co-a* Gibbons *w* B Crosby, Grace Kelly, Sinatra, *L Calhern, L Armstrong* VV* 107min MGM
HIGH SOCIETY BLUES (1930) *d* D Butler *w* J Gaynor, Hopper 102min Fox
HIGH STAKES (1931) *d/w* L Sherman 72min RKO
HIGH STEEL (1966) *d* Owen *sh* 14min Par
HIGH TENSION (1936) *d* Dwan *w* Foster 63min Fox (= *Trouble Makers*)
High Tension = SANT HANDER INTE HAR (1950)
HIGH TIDE AT NOON (1957) *d* P Leacock 109min
HIGH TIME (1960) *d* Edwards *p* C Brackett *st* Kanin *c* Fredericks *m* Mancini *w* B Crosby, Weld CS* 103min Fox
HIGH TREASON (1929) *d* Elvey 8350ft sd
HIGH TREASON (1951) *d/co-s* R Boulting *p* J Boulting 93min Gau
High Vermilion = SILVER CITY (1951)
HIGH WALL, THE (1948) *d* C Bernhardt *co-s* Boehm *co-a* Gibbons *m* Kaper *w* R Taylor, H Marshall 99min MGM

HIGHWAY DRAGNET (1954) *d* Nathan Juran *co-p/co-s* Corman *w* Conte, J Bennett 71min AA
Highway Pickup = CHAIR DE POULE (1964)
HIGHWAY 301 (1950) *d/st/s* Stone *w* Cochran 83min WB
HIGH, WIDE AND HANDSOME (1937) *d* Mamoulian *s/lyr* Oscar Hammerstein II *c* Milner, Sparkuhl *co-a* Dreier *m* Jerome Kern *chor* Prinz *w* I Dunne, R Scott, Lamour, Tamiroff, Bickford, Pichel 110min Par
HIGH WIND IN JAMAICA, A (1965) *d* Mackendrick *fn* Richard Hughes *w* Quinn, J Coburn CS* 104min Fox
HIJA DEL ENGANO, LA (1951) *d* Bunuel *co-s* Alcoriza 80min (= *Don Quintin el Amargao*)
HIJO DEL CRACK, EL (1953) *co-d/co-s* Torre-Nilsson 77min
HIJOSEN NO ONNA (1933) *d/st* Ozu Sho (= *Women On The Firing Line*)
HIKINIGE (1966) *d* Naruse S 100min Toho (= *Moment of Terror/Hit-And-Run*)
HIKKOSHI FUFU (1928) *d* Ozu Sho (= *A Couple On The Move*)
HIKUIDORI (1926) *d* Kinugasa (= *Cassowary*)
HILDA CRANE (1956) *d/s* P Dunne *fpl* Raphaelson *c* Joe Macdonald *co-a* Wheeler *w* J Simmons CS* 87min Fox
HILDE WARREN UND DER TOD (1917) *d/p* May *s* F Lang *c* Courant 4rs
HILL, THE (1965) *d* Lumet *c* Morris *w* Connery, M Redgrave 123min MGM
HILL IN KOREA, A (1956) *d* Julian Amyes *c* F Francis *m* M Arnold *w* S Baker, (Caine) 81min
HILLS OF HOME (1948) *d* F Wilcox *s* Ludwig *m* Stothart *w* Crisp, J Leigh *97min MGM (= *Master of Lassie*)
HILL 24 DOESN'T ANSWER (1955) *d/co-p* T Dickinson 101min
HIMEYURI NO TO (1953) *d* Imai (= *Tower of Lilies/The Girls of Okinawa*)
HIMLASPELET (1942) *d/co-s* Sjoberg *co-s/st/w* Lindstrom *w* Bjork 105min (= *Road to Heaven, The*)
HIMMEL OHNE STERNE (1955) *d/co-s* Käutner *w* Buchholz 2951m
HIMMELSKIBBET (1918) *d* Madsen
HIMSELF AS HERSELF (1967) *d/s/c/e* Markopoulos *fn* (Seraphita) Balzac 16mm *60min
HINDLE WAKES (1918) *d/p* Elvey 5000ft
HINDLE WAKES (1929) *co-s/p/s* Saville *co-d* Elvey 8800ft
HINDLE WAKES (1932) *d/s* Saville 77min
HI, NELLIE! (1934) *d* LeRoy *c* Polito *w* Muni 75min WB
HINTER DEN ZAHLEN (1939) *d/co-s* Ruttmann
HINTERTREPPE (1921) *d* Leni, *Leopold Jebner s* Mayer *w* Dieterle UFA
HINTON JARO SZERELEM (1954) *d* Ranody (= *Love Travels By Coach*)
HIPPOCAMPE, L' *d* Painlevé *m* Milhaud 15min
HIPS, HIPS, HOORAY! (1934) *d* Sandrich 68min RKO
Hiroshima Heartache = SONO YO WA WASURENAI (1962)
HIROSHIMA MON AMOUR (1959) *d* Resnais *s* Duras *co-c* Vierny *co-e* Colpi *m* Fusco, Delerue *w* Riva 91min
HIS ALIBI (1916) *d/w* Arbuckle 2rs
HIS BREAD AND BUTTER (1916) *d* Cline *p* Sennett Tri-Key
HIS BROTHER'S WIFE (1936) *d/co-p* WS Van Dyke *w* R Taylor, Stanwyck, Hersholt 90min MGM
HIS BUTLER'S SISTER (1943) *d* Borzage *w* Tone, Durbin, Tamiroff 94min U
His Call = YEVO PRIZYU (1925)
HIS CHILDREN'S CHILDREN (1923) *d* S Wood *c* 8300ft FPL *r* Par
HIS CROOKED CAREER (1913) *d/p/w* Sennett ½rl Key
His Daredevil Queen = MABEL AT THE WHEEL (1914)
HIS DOUBLE LIFE (1933) *d* Arthur Hopkins *c* Edeson *w* L Gish 72min Par
HIS EXCELLENCY (1952) *d/s* Hamer *c* Slocombe *e* Holt 84min
HIS EX MARKS THE SPOT (1941) *d* Jules White *w* Keaton 18min Col
HIS FAMILY TREE (1935) *d* C Vidor *c* Andriot 69min RKO
HIS FAVORITE PASTIME (1914) *d* G Nichols *w* Chaplin, Arbuckle 1rl Key (= *Bare Head, The*)
HIS FIRST COMMAND (1930) *d* La Cava *co-c* AC Miller 65min Pathe
HIS FIRST FLAME (1927) *d* Harry Edwards *co-s* Capra *w* Langdon 4700ft *pc* Sennett
HIS GIRL FRIDAY (1939) *d/p* Hawks *s* Lederer *fpl* (The Front Page) B Hecht, MacArthur *c* J Walker *w* C Grant, R Russell 92min Col
HIS GLORIOUS NIGHT (1930) *d/p/m* L Barrymore *w* J Gilbert, Hopper 80min MGM (= *Si L'Empereur Sauvait Ça!*)
HIS HOUR (1924) *d* K Vidor *p* L Mayer *w* J Gilbert 7rs MGM
HIS HOUSE IN ORDER (1928) *d* Randal Ayrton *fpl* Pinero *w* Bankhead 7400ft Gau
HIS KIND OF WOMAN (1951) *d* J Farrow, R Fleischer(uc) *c* Wild *w* Mitchum, Jane Russell, Price 120min RKO
HIS LAST MAUL (1928) *d* Neilan 5797ft
HIS LORDSHIP (1932) *d* M Powell 77min
HIS LORDSHIP'S DILEMMA (1915) *d* Edwin Middleton *w* Fields

HIS LUCKY DAY (1929) *d* Cline 5466ft European
His Majesty Mr Jones = PRIMA COMUNIONE (1950)
HIS MAJESTY O'KEEFE (1953) *d* Haskin *p* H Hecht *c* Heller *w* Lancaster *92min WB
HIS MARRIAGE WOW (1925) *d* Harry Edwards *w* Langdon 2rs *pc* Sennett *r* Pat
HIS MESSAGE (1911) *d* Ince
HIS MUSICAL CAREER (1914) *d/s/w* Chaplin 1rl Key (= *Musical Tramps/The Piano Movers*)
His Mysterious Adventure = SEINE FRAU DIE UNBEKANNTE (1923)
His Name is Sukhe-Bator = YEVO ZOVUT SUKHE-BATOR (1942)
HIS NEMESIS (1912) *d* Ince
HIS NEW JOB (1915) *d/s/w* Chaplin *c* Totheroh *w* Turpin 2rs S & A
HIS NEW MAMMA (1924) *d* Del Ruth *w* Langdon 2rs *pc* Sennett *r* Pat
HIS NEW PROFESSION (1914) *d/s* Chaplin *w* Chaplin, C Chase 1rl Key (= *The Good For Nothing/Helping Himself*)
HIS PICTURE IN THE PAPERS (1916) *d/co-s* Emerson *co-s* Loos *w* Fairbanks Sr 5rs Tri
HIS PREHISTORIC PAST (1914) *d/s/w* Chaplin 2rs Key
HIS ROBE OF HONOR (1918) *d* Ingram
HIS ROYAL SLYNESS (1919) *w* H Lloyd 2rs *pc* Roach *r* Pat
HIS SMOTHERED LOVE (1918) *d* Cline *p* Sennett 2rs Par
HISSYO KA (1945) *co-d* Mizoguchi Sho
HIS TALENTED WIFE (1914) *d/p/w* Sennett 1rl Key
Histoire d'Amour, Une: French version of LIEBELEI (1932)
HISTOIRE D'EAU, UNE (1958) *co-d/s* Truffaut *co-d* Godard *w* Brialy 18min
HISTOIRE D'ELEPHANTS, UNE (1958) *d* Rossif *550m
HISTOIRE DE RIRE (1941) *d* L'Herbier *w* Presle, P Renoir
HISTOIRE D'O (1961, *uf*) *d* Anger
HISTOIRE D'ODESSA (1934–35) *d* Lods
HISTOIRE D'UN CRIME, L' (1901) *d/w* Zecca 25–50m Pat
HISTOIRE D'UNE PEPITE (1962) *d* Hebert anim
HISTOIRE D'UN PETIT GARCON DEVENU GRAND (1963) *d* Reichenbach 12min
HISTOIRE D'UN PIERROT (1914) *d* Baldassare Negroni *w* Ghione
HISTOIRE D'UN POISSON ROUGE, L' (1959) *d/s* Séchan *p* Jacques Cousteau *20min (= *Golden Fish, The*)
HISTOIRE GRISE (1962) *d* Hebert anim
HISTOIRE DU PALAIS IDEAL (1954) *d* Baratier
HISTOIRE DU SOLDAT INCONNU (1932) *d/s/e* Storck 12min
HISTOIRE IMMORTELLE (1968) *d/w* Welles *fst* Dinesen *cos* Pierre Cardin *m* Satie *w* Moreau *58min ORTF
HISTOIRES EXTRAORDINAIRES (1967) *120min
  ep TOBY DAMMIT *d* Fellini *fst* (Never Bet the Devil Your Head) Edgar Allan Poe *m* Rota *w* Stamp
  ep METZENGERSTEIN *d* Vadim *c* C Renoir *w* J Fonda
  ep WILLIAM WILSON *d* Malle *w* Bardot, Delon *120min
HISTORIA DE AMOR, UNA (1967) *d/co-s* Grau 108min
HISTORIA DE UNA CHICA SOLA (1969) *d/co-s* Grau *100min
HISTORIA DE UNA NOCHE (1941) *d* Saslavsky
HISTORIA DE UNA NOCHE (1961) *d* Saslavsky
HISTORIA DI UNA MALE MUJER (1948) *d* Saslavsky *w* Del Rio
HISTORIA WSPOLCZESNA (1960) *d* Jakubowska 90min (= *A Contemporary Story/It Happened Yesterday*)
HISTORIEN OM BARBARA (1967) *d* Kjaerrulf-Schmidt 84min (= *Story Of Barbara*)
HISTORY AND ROMANCE OF TRANSPORTATION, THE (1941) *co-d* Meyers
HISTORY IS MADE AT NIGHT (1937) *d* Borzage *p* Wanger *c* Toland *m* A Newman *w* Boyer, Arthur 95min *r* UA
HISTORY OF THE CINEMA, THE (1956) *d/p* Halas anim* 10min
History of the Civil War = ISTORIYA GRAZHOANSKOI VOINY (1922)
HIS TRUST FULFILLED (1911) *d* Griffith in 2 parts 600m Bio
HIS TRYSTING PLACE (1914) *d/s/w* Chaplin *w* Normand 2rs Key
His Two Loves = PUCCINI (1952)
HIS WEDDING NIGHT (1917) *d/w* Arbuckle *w* Keaton 2rs Par
HIS WIFE'S MISTAKE (1916) *d/w* Arbuckle 2rs Tri
Hit-And-Run = HIKINIGE (1966)
HITCH-HIKER, THE (1953) *d/p/co-s* Lupino *c* Musuraca *m* Leith Stevens *w* E O'Brien 71min RKO
HITCHIN' POSTS (1920) *d* J Ford 5rs U
HITLER (1962) *d* Heisler *c* Biroc 107min
HITLER GANT, THE (1944) *d* J Farrow *s* Goodrich, Hackett *c* Laszlo *co-a* Dreier 101min Par
HITLERJUNGE QUEX (1933) *d* Steinhoft 2609m UFA
HITLER LIVES? (1945) *d* D Siegel 20min
HITLER'S CHILDREN (1943) *d* Dmytryk *c* Metty 83min RKO
Hitler's Hangman = HITLER'S MADMAN (1943)
HITLER'S MADMAN (1943) *d* Sirk *w* Carradine, Gardner 85min MGM (= *Hitler's Hangman*)
HITO NO ISSHO (1928) (I) *d* Mizoguchi Nik (in 3 parts) (= *Life of a Man*)

HITO NO YO NO SUGATA (1928) d Gosho
HITORI MUSUKO (1936) d/st Ozu Sho (= The Only Son)
HITOTSUBU NO MUGI (1958) d Yoshimura (= A Grain of Wheat)
HITTEBARNET (1915) d Madsen
HIT THE DECK (1955) d Rowland c Folsey co-a Gibbons w J Powell, D Reynolds, Pidgeon CS* 112min MGM
HIT-THE-TRAIL HOLIDAY (1918) d Neilan s Emerson, Loos 5rs FPL
HIT THE ROAD (1941) d May 61min U
HITTING A NEW HIGH (1937) d Walsh p Lasky w Horton 85min RKO
HIVER, L' (1969) d Hanoun
HJARTAN SOM MOTAS (1914) d Sjöström 790m (= Chauffaren)
HJARTATS TRIUMF (1929) d Molander SF
HJERTERNES KAMP (1912) d Blom
H.M.PULHAM, ESQ (1941) d/p/co-s K Vidor c June a Gibbons m Kaper w Lamour, R Young, C Coburn, Heflin 120min pc K Vidor r MGM
H.M.S. DEFIANT (1962) d L Gilbert c Challis w Guinness, Bogarde 101min BL (= Damn the Defiant)
HO! (1968) d/co-s Enrico fn Giovanni a Saulnier w Belmondo *107min (= Ho! Criminal Face)
HOA-BINH (1970) d/ad Coutard *90min
HOBBS IN A HURRY (1918) d H King 6rs
HOBSON'S CHOICE (1954) d/p/co-s Lean fpl Harold Brighouse c Hildyard m M Arnold w Laughton, J Mills 107min pc A Korda r BL
HOCH ZEIT EXCENTRICCLUB, DIE (1917) d/p May s F Lang 4rs
Ho! Criminal Face = HO! (1968)
HOFFMANS ERZAHLUNGEN (1916) d/p/co-s R Oswald w Krauss
HOFKONZERT, DAS (1936) d/co-s Sirk 85min (= Chanson du Souvenir)
HOGAN'S ALLEY (1925) d Del Ruth ad Zanuck w Fazenda, Turpin 5600ft WB
HOGARAKA NI AYUME (1930) d Ozu Sho (= Walk Cheerfully)
HOGFJALLETS DOTTER (1914) d/s/w Sjöström 636m (= Lappflickan)
Hogs & Warships = BUTA TO GUNKAN (1961)
HOG WILD (1930) d James Parrott st McCarey w Laurel, Hardy (2rs) r MGM (= Aerial Antics)
HOGY ALLUNK, FIATALEMBER? (1963) d Revesz 85min (= Well, Young Man?)
HOHOEMO HINSEI (1930) d Gosho (= A Smiling Character)
HOJT SPIL (1913) d/s Blom
HOKUSAI (1953) d Teshigahara sh
HOLD BACK THE DAWN (1941) d Leisen s Brackett, Wilder co-a Dreier w Boyer, De Havilland, Goddard, Leisen, (Holden, Lake) 115min Par
HOLD BACK THE NIGHT (1956) d Dwan c Fredericks w Payne 75min AA
HOLD 'EM JAIL (1932) d Taurog ex-p Selznick co-s SJ Perelman w Grable, Oliver 73min RKO
HOLD EVERYTHING (1930) d Del Ruth *74min WB
HOLD ME TIGHT (1932) d D Butler c AC Miller 72min Fox
HOLD ONTO YOUR HATS (1967) d Pojar anim NFBC
HOLD THAT CO-ED (1938) d G Marshall p Zanuck c Planck w J Barrymore, G Murphy 80min Fox
HOLD THAT GHOST (1941) d Arthur Lubin w B Abbott, Costello 86min U
HOLD YOUR MAN (1933) d S Wood st/co-s Loos w Gable, Harlow 89min
HOLE, THE (1962) d/s J Hubley co-di/wv Dizzy Gillespie anim* 15min
Hole, The = ONIBABA (1966)
Hole, The = ANA (1951)
Hole, The = TROU, LE (1959)
HOLE IN THE HEAD, A (1959) d/p Capra c Daniels w Sinatra, Robinson, Parker, Ritter CS* 120min r UA
HOLE IN THE WALL, THE (1929) d Florey c Folsey w Colbert, Robinson 65min Par
HOLIDAY (1938) d Cukor s D Stewart, Buchman fpl Philip Barry c Planer w K Hepburn, C Grant, Horton, Ayres 95min Col (= Free To Live)
HOLIDAY AFFAIR (1949) d/p Don Hartman c Krasner w Mitchum, J Leigh, Corey 87min RKO
HOLIDAY CAMP (1947) d Annakin w J Warner 97min BL r JAR
HOLIDAY IN MEXICO (1946) d G Sidney p Pasternak c Stradling co-a Gibbons w Pidgeon, J Powell 127min MGM
HOLIDAY INN (1942) d/p Sandrich co-a Dreier w B Crosby, Astaire 101min Par
Holiday in Spain = SCENT OF MYSTERY (1960)
Holiday on Sylt = FERIERN AUF SYLT (1958)
HOLLYWOOD (1923) d Cruze w Arbuckle, Astor, De Mille, W Hart, Negri, W Rogers, Swanson, Turpin 8100ft FPL r Par
HOLLYWOOD BOULEVARD (1936) d Florey c Struss w R Cummings, G Cooper 68min Par
HOLLYWOOD CANTEEN (1945) d/s Daves c Glennon chor Prinz e Nyby w Benny, Cantor, J Crawford, B Davis, Garfield, Greenstreet, Henreid, Lorre, Lupino,

Parker, R Rogers, A Smith, Stanwyck, Wyman, Malone 124min WB
HOLLYWOOD CAVALCADE (1939) co-d (d comic sequence) St Clair w Faye, Jolson 97min Fox
Hollywood Extra, A = LIFE AND DEATH OF 9413 (1928)
HOLLYWOOD HANDICAP (1938) d/w Keaton 1rl MGM
HOLLYWOOD HOTEL (1937) d Berkeley p Wallis co-st/co-s Wald co-c Barnes w D Powell, Parsons, Benny Goodman and his Orchestra, (S Hayward) Reagan 109min WB
HOLLYWOOD KID, THE (1924) d Del Ruth w Sennett, Turpin 2rs Pat
HOLLYWOOD LUCK (1932) d Arbuckle (ps William Goodrich) 21min
HOLLYWOOD OR BUST (1956) d/co-s (uc) Tashlin p Wallis c Fapp co-a Pereira w Martin, J Lewis, Ekberg VV* 95min Par
HOLLYWOOD PARTY (1934) d Boleslavsky(uc), Dwan (uc), Rowland (uc) c Howe co-m Freed w Laurel, Hardy 70min MGM (includes animated section in colour by Disney)
HOLLYWOOD REVUE, THE (1929) d Charles F Reisner a Gibbons, R Day w Benny, Keaton, J Crawford, Gilbert, Laurel, Hardy, Shearer, Davies, Dressler, L Barrymore part * 13rs MGM
HOLLYWOOD STORY (1951) d Castle w Conte, McCrea (uc) 76min U
HOLY MATRIMONY (1943) d Stahl p/s N Johnson c Ballard 87min Fox
HOLY SMOKE (1963) d/s/dec Borowczyk anim* 15min
HOLY TERROR, A (1931) d Irving Cummings w G O'Brien, Bogart 53min Fox
Homage at Siesta Time = HOMENAJE A LA HORA DE LA SIESTA (1962)
HOMAGE TO JEAN TINGUELY'S HOMAGE TO NEW YORK (1960) d Breer 11min 16mm
HOMBORI (1949) d/s Rouch 16mm
HOMBRE (1967) d/co-p Ritt c Howe m D Rose w P Newman, March, Rush PV* 111min Fox
HOME (1916) co-d Ince Tri
HOME AT SEVEN (1951) d R Richardson p/s De Grunwald w R Richardson, Hawkins 85min (= Murder on Monday)
HOME BEFORE DARK (1958) d/p LeRoy c Biroc m Waxman w J Simmons, R Fleming 136min WB
HOMEBREAKER, THE (1919) d Schertzinger supn Ince w (Valentino) 5rs pc Ince
Homecoming = HEIMKEHR (1928)
HOMECOMING (1948) d LeRoy p Franklin s Osborn c Rosson co-a Gibbons m Kaper w Gable, Turner, A Baxter 113min MGM
HOME FOLKS (1912) d Griffith w Pickford 1rl Bio
HOME FROM THE HILL (1960) d Minnelli s H Frank, Ravetch c Krasner m Kaper w Mitchum, Peppard, Parker CS* 148min pc S Siegel MGM
HOME FROM THE SEA (1962) d Peries 40min
HOME IN INDIANA (1944) d Hathaway c Cronjager m Friedhofer w Brennan, Crain 103min Fox
Home From Babylon = HEM FRAN BABYLON (1941)
HOMENAJE A LA HORA DE LA SIESTA (1962) d/co-s Torre Nilsson w Valli 85min (= Homage at Siesta Time/Four Women for One Hero)
HOMENAJE PARA ADRIANA (1968) d Picazo
HOME OF THE BRAVE (1949) d Robson s Foreman m Tiomkin w K Douglas 85min pc Kramer r UA
HOMESTEADER DROOPY (1954) d Avery p Quimby anim* 8min MGM
HOME SWEET HOME (1914) d Griffith w L Gish, Marsh, Crisp, D Gish 6rs Mut
HOME, SWEET HOMICIDE (1946) d Bacon w R Scott 90min Fox
HOME TO DANGER (1951) d Fisher 66min
Hometown = FURUSATO (1922)
Hometown = FURUSATO (1930)
HOME TOWN STORY (1951) d/st/s Arthur Pierson c Andriot w Monroe 61min MGM
HOME TRAIL, THE (1927) d Wyler 2rs U
HOMICIDAL (1961) d/p/n Castle c Guffey m Friedhofer 87min Col
HOMMAGE A ALBERT EINSTEIN (1955) d Lods 11min
HOMME AIMANTE, L' (1907) d/s Feuillade 135m
HOMME A LA BUICK, L' (1966) d/s Grangier m Legrand w Fernandel, Melville, Darrieux S* 85min
HOMME A LA PIPE, L' (1962) d Leenhardt *16min
HOMME A L'HISPANO, L' (1927) d Duvivier
HOMME A L'HISPANO, L' (1932) d J Epstein c Agostini, Thirard m Wiener
HOMME A L'IMPERMEABLE, L' (1957) d/co-s Duvivier fn James Hadley Chase m Van Parys w Fernandel 106min (= The Man in the Raincoat)
HOMME AU CHAPEAU ROUGE (1946) d Pierre Billon s Charles Spaak fn (The Eternal Husband) Dostoievski w Raimu 91min
HOMME AUX CLEFS D'OR, L' (1956) d/st/co-ad Joannon co-a D'Eaubonne s Fresnay, Girardot 92min
HOMME DE COMPAGNIE, L' (1916) d Feyder s Tristan Bernard 759/842m Gau
HOMME DE LONDRES, L' (1943) d/ad Decoin fn Georges Simenon m Van Parys 98min

HOMME DE MARRAKECH, L' (1965) d/co-st Deray *95min (= Gold Fever)
HOMME DE NEW YORK, L' (1967) d Camus
HOMME DE RIO, L' (1963) d De Broca co-s Rappeneau c Séchan m Delerue w Belmondo *110min AA (= That Man From Rio)
HOMME DE TROP, UN (1966) d Costa-Gavras w Piccoli, Brialy, Brasseur, Vanel 110min (= Shock Troops)
HOMME DU JOUR, L' (1937) d/co-s Duvivier di Charles Spaak m Wiener w Chevalier 94min
HOMME DU LARGE, L' (1920) d L'Herbier dec Autant-Lara w Boyer
Homme du Sud, L' = SOUTHERNER, THE (1945)
HOMME EN MARCHE, L' (1952) d Joseph Rivoalen c Fradelat 30min
HOMME ET SON BOSS, UN (1970) co-d/c Guy Borremans co-d Lamothe 6min
HOMME ET UNE FEMME, UN (1966) d/st/co-ad/co-di/c Lelouch w Aimee, Trintignant *102min (= A Man and a Woman)
HOMME MARCHE DANS LA VILLE, UN (1950) d Pagliero
HOMME NU (1910) d Henri Desfontaines w Raimu
HOMME QUI ASSASSINA, L' (1930) d C Bernhardt
HOMME QUI MENT, L' (1969) d/s Robbe-Grillet w Trintignant 98min co-pc Saltzman (= Muz Ktery Lze/The Man Who Lies/Shock Troops)
HOMME QUI ME PLAIT, UN (1969) d Lelouch w Girardot, Belmondo *95min
HOMME-MOUCHE, L' (1902) d Méliès 40m
Homme Noir, L' = MANOIR DE LA PEUR, LE (1927)
HOMME-ORCHESTRE, L' (1900) d/w Méliès 40m
HOMME PROTEE, L' (1899) d Méliès 40m
HOMME QUI ME PLAIT, UN (1969) d/co-st/co-s Lelouch w Girardot, Belmondo *95min
HOMME SANS COEUR, L' (1937) d Joannon c B Kaufman w P Renoir
HOMME SANS TETE, L' (1912) d Cohl anim
HOMME SANS VISAGE, L' (1919) d/s Feuillade 1560m
HOMMES EN BLANC, LES (1955) d Ralph Habib p Graetz w Moreau 102min
HOMMES NOUVEAUX, LES (1936) d L'Herbier fn Claude Farrere co-a Lourié 120min
HOMMES QUI FONT LA PLUIE, LES (1951) d/c Rouch *35min 16mm (= Yenendi/Les Faiseurs de Pluie/Rainmakers)
HOMMES QUI ONT PERDU RACINE, DES (1956) d Hanoun sh TV
HOMOMAN, J' (1964) d/p/s Lefebvre 24min
HON DANSADE EN SOMMAR (1951) d Mattsson p Strindberg w Jacobsson 93min (= One Summer of Happiness)
HON, DEN ENDA (1926) d/co-s Molander SF
HONDO (1953) d J Farrow co-p J Wayne s J Grant c Stout, Burks 2nd, ur Ford co-m Friedhofer w J Wayne, page 3D* 93min r WB
HONEST THIEF, THE (1918) d G Seitz Pat
HONEY (1930) d W Ruggles ad/t H Mankiewicz w Pitts 6701 ft Par
Honeycomb, The = MADRIGUERA, LA (1969)
HONEYMOON (1947) d Keighley c Cronjager w Temple, Tone 74min RKO
Honeymoon, The part 2 of WEDDING MARCH, THE (1928)
Honeymoon = LUNA DE MIEL (1958)
HONEYMOON FOR THREE (1941) d Bacon s JJ Epstein c E Haller w Sheridan, C Ruggles, Wyman 94min WB
HONEYMOON HARDSHIPS (1924) d Ralph Cedar co-s Garnett 2rs
HONEYMOON MACHINE, THE (1961) d Thorpe s Wells c La Shelle m Harline w McQueen CS* 88min r MGM
HONEY POT, THE (1967) d/co-p/s J Mankiewicz co-p Feldman co-c Di Venanzo w Harrison, S Hayward, Robertson *150min pc Feldman r UA
HONKY TONK (1929) d Bacon c B Reynolds 7rs WB
HONKY TONK (1941) d Conway p Berman c Rosson a Gibbons m Waxman w Gable, Turner, Trevor 105min MGM
HONNEURS DE LA GUERRE, LES (1961) d Dewever co-c Cloquet 85min
HONNEUR EST SATISFAIT, L' (1906) d Méliès 100m
HONNO (1966) d/s Shindo 103min (= Instinct/Last Sex/Impotence)
HONORABLE CATHERINE, L' (1942) d L'Herbier w Feuillère, Rouleau
HONOR OF THE FAMILY (1931) d Bacon fn Balzac c E Haller 45min FN
HONORS EASY (1935) d Brenon w Lockwood 62min
HONOR SYSTEM, THE (1916) d Walsh 10rs Fox
HONRYU (1926) d Gosho (= A Rapid Stream)
Honour Among Thieves = TOUCHEZ PAS AU GRISBI (1954)
HON SEGRADE (1915) d/s/w Sjöström 900m
HOODLUM, THE (1919) d Franklin 6rs FN
HOODLUM PRIEST, THE (1961) d Kershner c Wexler w Murray 101min r UA
HOODLUM SAINT, THE (1946) d Taurog c June co-a Gibbons w W Powell, Esther Williams 91min MGM
HOODMAN BLIND (1923) d J Ford w D Butler 5434ft Fox

HOOK, THE (1962) d Seaton p Perlberg c Ruttenberg w K
Douglas, R Walker MGM
HOOK, LINE AND SINKER (1969) d G Marshall p J Lewis
w J Lewis, Lawford, A Francis *92min
Hooligans, The = GOLFOS, LOS (1959)
HOOP-LA (1933) d F Lloyd w Bow 78min Fox
HOOSE-GOW, THE (1929) d *James Parrott* p Roach *st*
McCarey w Laurel, Hardy (2rs) r MGM
HO PERDUTO MIO MARITO (1936) d/s Guazzoni
Hoppity Goes To Town = MR BUG GOES TO TOWN
(1941)
HOPPITY HOP (1946) d McLaren anim* 2½min NFBC
HOPPLA WIR LEBEN (1927) d Piscator, Ruttmann
HOPPY SERVES A WRIT (1942) d George Archainbaud c
R Harlan w Mitchum 66min r UA
HORA DE LA VERDAD (1945) d Foster
Horatio = ORAZI E CURIAZI (1961)
Hordubal Brothers, The = HORDUBALOVE (1937)
HORDUBALOVE (1937) d Fric *fn* Karel Capek (= *The
Hordubal Brothers*)
HORI MA PENENKO (1967) d Forman co-s Forman,
Passer c Ondricek *73min (= *The Fireman's Ball/
Like a House on Fire*)
Horizon = GORIZONT (1933)
Horizon = GORIZONT (1962)
HORIZONS WEST (1952) d Boetticher w Ryan, Hudson,
McIntire *81min *
HORIZONTAL LIEUTENANT, THE (1962) d Thorpe p
Pasternak s Wells c Bronner S* 90min r MGM
HORLA, LE (1967) d/s Pollet *fn* Guy de Maupassant m
Ravel *38min
HORN BLOWS AT MIDNIGHT, THE (1945) d Walsh p
Hellinger c Hickox m Waxman *chor* Prinz w Benny,
Dumont, A Smith 80min WB
HORNETS' NEST (1970) d Karlson w Hudson *109min r
UA
HORN I NORR, ETT (1950) d/s/c/e Sucksdorff 26min SF
HOROKI (1962) d Naruse 124min Toho (= *Lonely Lane*)
HOROLGER AMOUREUX (1935) w Keaton
HOROUCI SRDCE (1963) d Vavra (= *The Passionate
Heart*)
Horror Chamber of Dr Faustus, The = YEUX SANS
VISAGE, LES (1959)
HORROR OF IT ALL, THE (1964) d Fisher 75min Fox
HORSE (1965) d Warhol s Ronald Tavel 105min 16mm
HORSE FEATHERS (1932) d McLeod *ex-p* H Mankiewicz c
June *dance* H Hecht w H, G, C, Z Marx 70min Par
HORSEMAN OF THE PLAINS, A (1928) d *Benjamin
Stoloff* w Mix 4399ft Fox
HORSEMEN OF THE SIERRA (1949) d Sears 56min Col
HORSEMEN, THE (1971) d Frankenheimer s Trumbo c C
Renoir m Delerue w Sharif, Palance PV* 109min
co-pc Frankenheimer r Col
HORSE OVER TEA KETTLE (1962) d Breer anim* 7min
16mm
Horses = HESTE (1943)
HORSE SHOES (1927) d Bruckman w Arthur 5668ft Pat
HORSE'S MOUTH, THE (1959) d Neame s/w Guinness *fn*
Joyce Cary *95min r UA
HORSE SOLDIERS, THE (1959) d J Ford p/s Mahin,
Rackin c Clothier w J Wayne, Holden *119min Mir r
UA
HORSE TRADER, THE (1926) d Wyler 2rs U
HOSTAGES (1943) d Tuttle *as-p* S Siegel c Milner *co-a*
Dreier m V Young w Bendix, Lukas, Rainer 88min
Par
Hostile Wind, The = VIKHRI VRAZHDEBYNE (1956)
HOSTILE WITNESS (1967– r 1970 d/w Milland *101min r
UA
HOTARUBI (1958) d Gosho (= *Firefly Light*)
HOT BLOOD (1956) d N Ray c June w J Russell, Wilde CS*
85min Col
HOT DOG CARTOONS (1926–27) d Lantz, *Clyde Geronini
pc* Bray anim series
HOTEL (1967) d Quine p/s Mayes c C Lang w Catherine
Spaak, Malden, M Douglas, Conte, Oberon *124min
WB
Hotel At Osaka = OSAKA NO YADO (1954)
HOTEL DES INVALIDES (1952) d/s Franju c Fradetal m
Jarre w M Simon
HOTEL DU LIBRE ECHANGE, L' (1934) d M Allégret
HOTEL DU NORD (1938) d Carné *ad/di* Jeanson,
Aurenche c Thirard *dec* Trauner m Jaubert w
Annabella, Arletty, Jouvet
HOTEL FOR WOMEN (1939) d Ratoff w Sothern, Darnell
84min Fox
HOTEL IMPERIAL (1927) d Stiller p/co-s Pommer, B.P.
Schulberg s Furthman *fpl* Biro c Glennon w Negri
7091ft FPL r Par
HOTEL IMPERIAL (1939) d Florey *fpl* Biro c Mellor w
Milland, I Miranda 67min Par
HOTEL MODRAHVEZDA (1941) d/co-s Fric
HOTEL PARADISO (1966) d/p/s/w Glenville *fpl (L' Hôtel
du Libre Echange) Georges Feydeau* w Guinness,
Lollobrigida, Tamiroff PV* 96min MGM
HOTEL SAHARA (1951) d Annakin c Hildyard w De Carlo,
Ustinov 96min BL r JAR
HOTEL SPLENDIDE (1932) d M Powell 53min
Hot Finish (re-issue) = MABEL AT THE WHEEL (1914)
HOT FOR PARIS (1929) d/st Walsh w V McLaglen 6570ft

HOT HEIRESS, THE (1931) d Badger c Polito *m/lyr*
Richard Rodgers, Lorenz Hart w Pidgeon 85min FN
HOT HOUSE (1947–49) d/c Whitney, *James Whitney* *4min
16mm
Hot Mine, The = GORACA LINIA (1965)
Hot Marshland, The = NETSUDEI-CHI (1950)
HOT NEWS (1928) d Badger 6528ft Par
Hot Night, A = ATSUI YORU (1968)
HOTOTOGISH (1932) d Gosho (= *Cuckoo*)
HOT RODS TO HELL (1967) d Brahm p Katzman w D
Andrews, Crain * r MGM
HOT SPELL (1958) d Daniel Mann p Wallis s Poe c Griggs
co-a Pereira m North w Quinn, MacLaine, Booth VV
86min Par
HOT STUFF (1929) d LeRoy c Hickox part sd 6725ft si
6337ft FN
HOTSY-TOTSY (1925) d/s Cline p Sennett Pat
HOTTENTOT, THE (1929) d Del Ruth w Horton 8rs
HOT WATER (1924) co-d Newmeyer co-d/co-st Sam Taylor
w H Lloyd 4899ft *pc* H Lloyd r Pat
HOUDINGENS SON AR DOD (1937) d Fejos SF
HOUDINI (1953) d G Marshall p Pal s Yordan c Laszlo *co-a*
Pereira w J Leigh, Curtis *106min Par
HOUEN ZO (1953) d/p Van den Horst 20min (= *Steady
Now*)
HOUND DOG MAN (1959) d D Siegel p Wald c C Clarke
co-a Wheeler m Mockridge w Lynley, Darwell CS*
87min Fox
HOUND OF THE BASKERVILLES, THE (1921) d Elvey
fn Conan Doyle 5000ft
HOUND OF THE BASKERVILLES, THE (1959) d Fisher
fn Conan Doyle *87min r UA
Hounds of Zaroff, The = MOST DANGEROUS GAME,
THE (1932)
HOUR BEFORE THE DWAN, THE (1944) d Tuttle *fn*
Somerset Maugham c J Seitz *co-a* Dreier m Rozsa w
Lake, Tone 75min Par
Hour of Glory = SMALL BACK ROOM, THE (1948)
HOUR OF RECKONING, THE (1914) d Ince
HOUR OF THE GUN (1967) d/p J Sturges c Ballard m
Goldsmith w Garner, Ryan PV* 100min Mir r UA
Hour of the Wolf = VARGTIMMEN (1968)
Hours of Love, The = ORE DELL'AMORE, LE (1963)
House = DOM (1958)
HOUSE (1955) d/s C and R Eames c C Eames m E Bernstein
*11min
HOUSE ACROSS THE BAY, THE (1940) d A Mayo p
Wanger w Raft, J Bennett, Nolan, Pidgeon 88min UA
HOUSE ACROSS THE LAKE, THE (1954) d/s/fn (High
Wray) K Hughes 69min
House at the End of the World, The = MONSTER OF
TERROR (1965)
HOUSEBOAT (1958) d/co-s Shavelson c June *co-a* Pereira m
Duning w C Grant, Loren *110min Par
HOUSE BUILT UPON SAND, THE (1917) d Edward
Morrisey w L Gish Tri
HOUSE BY THE RIVER (1950) d F Lang *fn AP Herbert* c
Cronjager m Antheil w L Hayward 88min r Rep
HOUSE DIVIDED, A (1919) d Bess Meredyth w Fazenda
HOUSE DIVIDED, A (1931) d Wyler *di* J Huston w W
Huston 66min U
HOUSEHOLDER, THE (1963) d/co-s Ivory c Mitra
HOUSE I LIVE IN, THE (1945) d/co-p LeRoy w Sinatra
10min RKO
House in the Snow Drifts, The = DOM V SUGRIBAKH
(1928)
HOUSE IN THE SQUARE, THE (1951) d R Baker w
Power, Blyth part * 91min Fox (= *I'll Never Forget
You*)
HOUSE IS NOT A HOME, A (1964) d/co-s Rouse w
Winters, R Taylor, Romero, B Crawford (R Welch)
95min
HOUSEKEEPER'S DAUGHTER, THE (1939) d/p Roach
co-s G Douglas c Brodine w Menjou, Mature 71min r
UA
HOUSEMASTER, THE (1938) d Brenon w (Michael
Anderson) 96min
HOUSE OF BAMBOO (1955) d/di Fuller p Adler c Joe
Macdonald *co-a* Wheeler m Harline w Ryan, Stack
CS* 102min Fox
HOUSE OF BLACKMAIL (1953) d Elvey 72min
HOUSE OF CARDS (1969) d Guillermin *co-a* Golitzen w
Peppard, Welles TS* 105min r JAR
HOUSE OF DARKNESS, THE (1913) d Griffith w L Gish,
L Barrymore 1rl Bio
HOUSE OF DARKNESS (1948) d Oswald Mitchell w
Laurence Harvey 77min
House of Doom = BLACK CAT, THE (1934)
HOUSE OF FEAR, THE (1939) d May c Krasner 67min U
House of Fright = 2 FACES OF DR JEKYLL, THE (1960)
HOUSE OF HATE, THE (1918) d G Seitz w White serial in
20 eps Pat
HOUSE OF HORROR, THE (1929) d Christensen c E
Haller, Polito w Fazenda 5919ft sd FN
House of Light, The = CHAMBRE BLANCHE, LA (1969)
House of Lovers, The = POT BOUILLE (1951)
HOUSE OF MARNEY, THE (1927) d Hepworth 6600ft
HOUSE OF NUMBERS (1957) d/co-s Rouse c Folsey m
Previn w Palance CS 92min MGM
House of Ricordi = CASA RICORDI (1954)

HOUSE OF ROTHSCHILD, THE (1934) d Alfred Werker p
Zanuck *as-p* Goetz s N Johnson c Marley a R Day m
A Newman w G Arliss, Karloff, L Young, R Young
part * 86min Fox r UA
HOUSE OF SCIENCE (1962) d/s C and R Eames c C
Eames *15½min
HOUSE OF SECRETS (1956) d G Green *co-s* Forbes VV*
97min JAR
House of Silence, The = VOCE DEL SILENZIO (1952)
HOUSE OF STRANGERS (1949) d J Mankiewicz p S Siegel
s Yordan c Krasner *co-a* Wheeler m Amfitheatrof w
Robinson, Conte, Hayward 101min Fox
House of the Angel = CASA DEL ANGEL, LA (1957)
HOUSE OF THE ARROW, THE (1953) d Michael
Anderson 73min AOC
House of the Bories, The = MAISON DES BORIES, LA
(1970)
HOUSE OF THE SEVEN GABLES, THE (1940) d May *fst*
Nathaniel Hawthorne c Krasner w G Sanders, Price
89min U
HOUSE OF THE SEVEN HAWKS, THE (1959) d Thorpe
w R Taylor, Wolfit 92min r MGM
House of the Sleeping Virgins, The = NEMURERU BIJO
(1968)
House of Usher, The = FALL OF THE HOUSE OF
USHER, THE (1960)
HOUSE OF WAX (1953) d De Toth c Glennon, Marley w
Price 3-D* 88min WB
HOUSE ON 56th STREET (1933) d Florey c E Haller *di*
Keighley w K Francis 68min WB
HOUSE ON HAUNTED HILL, THE (1958) d/p Castle w
Price, Cook 75min AA
HOUSE ON 92nd STREET, THE (1945) d Hathaway p De
Rochemont c Brodine *co-a* Wheeler w Nolan 88min
Fox
HOUSE ON TELEGRAPH HILL, THE (1951) d Wise c
Ballard *co-a* Wheeler m A Newman w Basehart,
Cortese 93min Fox
House on Trubnaya Square, The = DOM NA TRUBNOI
(1928)
HOUSE THAT JACK BUILT, THE (1901) d G Smith
HOUSE THAT JACK BUILT, THE (1911) co-d Ince w
Pickford
HOUSING PROBLEMS (1935) d Anstey, Elton 13min
HOUSTON STORY, THE (1956) d Castle p Katzman 79min
Col
HOUSTON, TEXAS (1956) d/c Reichenback *8min
HO VISTO BRILLARE LE STELLE (1939) d/s Guazzoni
How About Us? = HUAD MED OS? (1964)
HOW A MOSQUITO OPERATES (1910) d McCay anim
HOWARDS OF VIRGINIA, THE (1940) d/p F Lloyd s
Sidney Buchman c Glennon *montage expert*
Vorkapich w C Grant, Ladd 122min Col
HOW COULD YOU JEAN? (1918) d William Desmond
Taylor w Pitts 5rl FPL
HOW DO YOU LIKE THEM BANANAS (1966) d/pc
Rogosin 10min
How Fine, How Fresh the Roses Were = KAK KHOROSHI,
KAK SVEZHI BYLI ROZY (1913)
HOW DO I LOVE THEE? (1970) d M Gordon c Metty w M
O'Hara, Winters *110min
How Grandpa Changed Till Nothing Was Left = JAK
STARECEK MENIL AZ VYMENIL (1952)
HOW GREEN WAS MY VALLEY (1941) d J Ford p
Zanuck s P Dunne c AC Miller *co-a* R Day *song* A
Newman w Pidgeon, M O'Hara, Crisp 118min Fox
HOW IT FEELS TO BE RUN OVER (1900) p Hepworth
50ft
HOW I WON THE WAR (1967) d/p Lester c Watkin w John
Lennon *110min r UA
How Kutashek and Kutilka Got Up in the Morning =
KUTASHEK A KUTILKA JAK RANO
VASTAVAZI (1952)
How Man Learned to Fly = NEZ NAM NAROSTA
KRIDLA (1958)
HOW NOW BOING BOING (1954) d Cannon anim* *pc*
UPA r Col
HOW SHE TRIUMPHED (1911) d Griffith 7rl Bio
How the Baby's Soul Sobs = KAK RYDALA DUSHA
REBENKA (1913)
HOW THE BURGLAR TRICKED THE BOBBY (1901) d
Hepworth 100ft
How the Steel was Tempered = KAK ZAKAL YALAS
STAL (1942)
HOW THE WEST WAS WON (1962) s JR Webb c Daniels,
Krasner, C Lang m A Newman w Cobb, H Fonda,
Malden, Peck, Preston, D Reynolds, J Stewart,
Wallach, Widmark, Brennan, Moorehead, Ritter,
Tracy Cinerama* 165min MGM
ep THE CIVIL WAR d J Ford c La Shelle m A Newman w J
Wayne, Peppard, C Baker
ep THE RAILROAD d G Marshall
ep THE RIVERS, THE PLAINS, THE OUTLAWS d Hathaway
How to be Loved = JAK BYC KOCHANA (1963)
HOW TO BE VERY, VERY POPULAR (1955) d/p/s N
Johnson c Krasner *co-a* Wheeler m Mockridge w
Grable, R Cummings, C Coburn CS* 90min Fox
HOW TO COMMIT MARRIAGE (1969) d Panama c C
Lang w Hope, Wyman *98min
How to Furnish a Flat = JAK SI ZARIDIT BYT (1960)

359

LES (1965)
HOW TO MAKE IT (1968, *ur*) *d* Corman *w* Pleshette, Romero * (= *What's In It For Harry?*)
HOW TO MARRY A MILLIONAIRE (1953) *d* Negulesco *p/s* N Johnson *c* Joe Macdonald *co-a* Wheeler *w* Grable, Monroe, Bacall, W Powell, D Wayne CS* 95min Fox
HOW TO MURDER YOUR WIFE (1964) *d* Quine *p/s* Axelrod *w* Lemmon *118min *r* UA
HOW TO SLEEP (1935) *d* Nick Grinde *w* Benchley 1rl MGM
HOW TO STEAL A MILLION (1966) *d* Wyler *p* Kohlmar *s* Kurnitz *c* C Lang *des* Trauner *w* A Hepburn, O'Toole, Wallach, Boyer PV* 127min *r* Fox
HOW TO SUCCEED IN BUSINESS WITHOUT REALLY TRYING (1967) *d/p/s* Swift *c* Guffey *a* Boyle PV* 119min UA
HOW TO UNDRESS IN PUBLIC WITHOUT UNDUE EMBARRASSMENT (1965) *d* Compton Bennett 50min
HOW WE BREATHE (1919) *d/pc* Bray
HRANJENIK (1970) *d* Mimica *90min
HRA O ZIVOT (1956) *d/co-s* Weiss 100min (= *Life was the Stake*)
HRDJA JEDNE NOCI (1935) *d* Fric (= *Hero For a Night*)
H₂O (1929) *d/c* R Steiner 14min
HUCKLEBERRY FINN (1931) *d* Taurog *fn* M Twain *w* Darwell 73min Par
HUCKSTERS, THE (1947) *d* Conway *p* Hornblow *co-ad* Wells *c* Rosson *co-a* Gibbons *w* Gable, Kerr, Greenstreet, Menjou, Gardner 115min MGM
HUD (1963) *d/co-p* Ritt *c* Howe *co-a* Pereira *m* E Bernstein *w* P Newman, M Douglas, Neal PV 112min Par
HUDDLE (1932) *d* S Wood *w* Navarro 104min
HUDSON'S BAY (1941) *d* Pichel *as-p* Macgowan *st/s* Trotti *c* Marley, Barnes *m* A Newman *w* Muni, Tierney, Price 95min RKO
HUE AND CRY (1947) *d* Chrichton *p* Balcon *as-p* Cornelius *st/s* T Clarke *c* Slocombe 82min *pc* Ealing
Hugo and Josefin = HUGO OCH JOSEFIN (1968)
HUGO OCH JOSEFIN (1968) *d/co-s* Grede *82min (= *Hugo and Josefin*)
Hugs and Kisses = PUSS OCH KRAM (1967)
HUILOR (1937) *d* Alexeieff *m* Auric anim
HUIS CLOS (1954) *d* Jacqueline Audry *fpl* Jean-Paul Sartre *w* Arletty 95min
HUITIEME JOUR, LE (1959) *d/st/co-s* Hanoun *c* Fradetal *m* Kosma *w* Riva 78min
HULA (1927) *d* V Fleming *w* Bow, C Brook 5862ft Par
HUMAN CARGO (1936) *d* Dwan *w* Trevor, Hayworth (as Rita Cansino) 66min Fox
HUMAN COMEDY, THE (1943) *d/p* C Brown *fpl* William Saroyan *c* Stradling *a* Gibbons *m* Stothart *w* Rooney, V Johnson, D Reed (Mitchum) 118min MGM
Human Condition, The = NINGEN NO JOKEN Parts 1–3 (1957–61)
HUMAN DESIRE (1954) *d* F Lang *ex-p* Wald *fn* (*La Bête Humaine*) Emile Zola *c* Guffey *m* Amfitheatrof *w* G Ford, Grahame, B Crawford 90min Col
Human Dutch, The = ALLEMAN (1964)
HUMAN FISH, THE (1933) *d* Bruckman 2rs Par
HUMAN FLY, THE (1896) *p* Paul 1rl (80ft) (= *Upside Down*)
HUMAN JUNGLE, THE (1953) *d* J Newman 82min AA
Human Zoo = NINGEN DOBUTSEN (1961)
HUMDRUM BROWN (1918) *d* Ingram 5000ft
HUMORESKA (1939) *d/s* Vavra
Humouresque = ZHUMORESKI (1924)
HUMORESQUE (1920) *d* Borzage *fst* Fannie Hurst *m* Reisenfeld 6rs FPL
HUMORESQUE (1947) *d* Negulesco *p* Wald *s* Odets *c* E Haller *chor* Prinz *w* J Crawford, Garfield 125min WB
HUMOROUS PHASES OF FUNNY FACES (1906) *d* Blackton Vit
HUMRAHI (1945) *d* Roy
HUNCHBACK, THE (1914) *w* L Gish 2rs
Hunchback and the Danger = BUCKLIGE UND DIE TANZERIN, DER (1920)
HUNCHBACK OF NOTRE DAME, THE (1923) *d* Wallace Worsley *dec* Dreier *w* Chaney 12rs U
HUNCHBACK OF NOTRE DAME, THE (1939) *d* Dieterle *p* Berman *fn* Victor Hugo *c* August *co-e* Wise *m* A Newman *w* Laughton, Mitchell, M O'Hara, E O'Brien 117min RKO
Hunchback of Notre Dame, The = NOTRE DAME DE PARIS (1957)
Hunchback of Rome, The = GOBBO, IL (1960)
HUNDE, WOLLT IHR EWIG LEBEN! (1959) *d* Wisbar 97min (= *Dogs, Do You Want To Live For Ever/Battle Inferno*)
Hundred Horsemen, the = CIEN CABALLEROS, LOS (1965)
Hundred Hour Hunt = EMERGENCY CALL (1952)
100,00,00 WOMEN (1942) *d* J Weiss 8min
HUNDRED THOUSAND CHILDREN, A (1955) *d/s* L Anderson *c* Lassally 4min
100,000 DOLLARS AU SOLEIL (1963) *d/co-ad* Verneuil *di* Audiard *w* Belmondo FS 128min (= *Greed in the Sun*)
Hunger = SULT (1966)

Hunger – Hunger – Hunger = GOLOD – GOLOD – GOLOD (1921)
HUNGER IN WALDENBURG (1928) *d/c* Jutzi
Hungry For Love = ADUA E LE CAMPAGNE
HUNT, THE (1915) *d* C Chase (as C Parrott), Ford Sterling *p* Sennett 2rs Tri-Key
Hunt, The = CAZA, LA (1965)
HUNTED (1952) *d* Chrichton *w* Bogarde 84min JAR (= *Stranger in Between*)
Hunted, The = PARANOMI, I (1958)
HUNTED WOMAN, THE (1925) *d* Conway 4954ft Fox
HUNTERS, THE (1958) *d/p* D Powell *s* Mayes *c* C Clarke *co-a* Wheeler *w* Mitchum, R Wagner CS* 108min Fox
Hunting Flies = POLOWANIE NA MUCHY (1969)
Hunting Rifle = RYOJU (1961)
HURDES, LA (1932) *d/e* Bunuel *c* Lotar *m* Brahms 27min (= *Terre Sans Pain/Land Without Bread*)
HURRICANE, THE (1938) *d* J Ford, Heisler *p* Goldwyn *s* D Nichols *c* Glennon, Stout (2nd) *a* R Day, Golitzen *m* A Newman *w* Lamour, Astor, Mitchell (Carradine) 102min *r* UA
HURRICANE HUTCH (1921) *d* G Seitz serial in 15 eps Pat
HURRY SUNDOWN (1967) *d/p* Preminger *c* Krasner, Griggs *w* Caine, J Fonda, Meredith, Dunaway, G Kennedy PV* 146min Par
Hurvinek Circus, The = CIRKUS HURVINEK (1955)
Husband and Wife = FUFU (1953)
Husband and Wife = MARITO E MOGLIE (1952)
Husband for Anna, A = MARITO PE ANNA ZACCHEO, UN (1953)
HUSBANDS (1970) *d/s/w* Cassavetes *154min
HUSBANDS AND LOVERS (1924) *d/p* Stahl 8rs FN
HUSH, HUSH SWEET CHARLOTTE (1964) *d/p/pc* Aldrich *c* Biroc *w* B Davis, De Havilland, Cotten, Moorehead, Astor, G Kennedy 133min Fox
HUSHING THE SCANDAL (1915) *d* Sennett *w* C Ruggles 2rs Key
HUSH MONEY (1932) *d* Sidney Lanfield *di* D Nichols *c* J Seitz *w* M Loy, J Bennett, Raft 68min Fox
HUSKORS, ET (1914) *d* Madsen
Hussite Warrior, The = JAN ZIZKA Z TROCNOVA (1955)
HUSTLER, THE (1961) *d/p/co-s* Rossen *c* Schuftan *des* Horner *dec* Callahan *m* K Hopkins *w* P Newman, Laurie, G Scott CS 135min Fox
HUSZ EVRE EGYMASTOL (1962) *d* Feher (= *The Truth Cannot Be Hidden*)
HUSZ ORA (1964) *d* Fabri 112min (= *Twenty Hours*)
HUTTERITES, THE (1965) *d* Low *co-p* Kroiter 27min 16mm NFBC (for TV)
HVAD MED OS? (1964) *d* Carlsen (= *How About Us*)
HVEM ER GENTLEMANTYVEN? (1915) *d* Madsen
HVEZDA ZYANA PELYNEK (1964) *d* Fric (= *Star Named Wormwood, A*)
HVIDE DAME, DEN (1913) *d/s* Madsen
HVOR BJERGENE SEJLER (1955) *d/s* B Henning Jensen (= *Where Mountains Float*)
HVOR SORGENE GLEMMES (1915) *d* Madsen
HVO SOM ELSKER SIN FADER (1915) *d* Madsen
HYAKUMAN-NIN NO MUSUMETACHI (1963) *d/s* Gosho (= *A Million Girls*)
HYAS ET STENORINQUE (1930) *d* Painlevé *m* Scarlatti
Hymn To a Tired Man = NIPPON NO SEISHUN (1968)
HYSTERIA (1966) *d* F Francis 85min MGM
HIDARI UCHIWA (1935) *d* Gosho
HIDDEN FEAR (1957) *d/co-s* De Toth *w* Payne 83min UA
Hidden Fortress, The = KAKUSHI TORIDE NO SAN-AKUNIN
Hidden Room, The = OBSESSION (1949)
HIDDEN TRAIL, THE (1911) *d* Ince
HIDDEN WOMAN, THE (1922) *d* Dwan 4626ft
Hide and Seek = KURRAGOMMA (1963)
HIDE AND SEEK (1964) *d* Enfield *c* G Taylor *w* Jurgens 90min BL
HIDE AND SEEK, DETECTIVES (1918) *d* Cline *s* Sennett *w* Turpin 2rs *pc* Sennett *r* Par
HIDE AND SHRIEK (1938) *d* G Douglas *p* Roach 11min
HIDEKO NO SHASHO-SAN (1941) *d/s* Naruse
HIDE-OUT (1934) *d* WS Van Dyke *s* Goodrich, Hackett *co-c* June *w* O'Sullivan, Montgomery 82min MGM
HIDEOUT (1949) *d* Peter Graham Scott *w* Keel
HI, DIDDLE DIDDLE (1943) *d/p* Stone *w* Menjou, Negri 72min *r* UA
HIERRO MUERE, A (1963) *d* Manuel Mur-Oti *fst* (*A Sangre Fria*) Saslavsky
HIGANBANA (1958) *d/co-s* Ozu *164min Sho (= *Equinox Flower*)
HIGE NO CHIKARA (1931) *d/s* Naruse (= *Beard Of Strength*)
Higgins Family, The = MEET THE MISSUS (1940)
HIGH AND DIZZY (1920) *w* H Lloyd 2rs *r* Pat
High and Dry = MAGGIE, THE (1954)
High and Low = TENGOKU TO JIGOKU (1963)
HIGH AND THE MIGHTY, THE (1954) *d* Wellman *c* Stout *m* Tiomkin *w* J Wayne, Strick, Newton, Trevor CS* 147min WB
HIGH ASHBURY (1967) *d* Warhol *30min 16mm (segment of *Four Stars*)
HIGH BARBAREE (1947) *d* Conway *co-a* Gibbons *m*

Stothart *w* V Johnson, Allyson, Mitchell 91min MG
I ACCUSE (1958) *d* J Ferrer *s* Vidal *c* F Young *m* Alwyn *w* Ferrer, Walbrook, Lindfors, Emlyn Williams, Wo CS 99min MGM
I AIM AT THE STARS (1960) *d* J Thompson *w* Jurge 106min Col
I AM A CAMERA (1955) *d* Cornelius *p* Woolf Bros *as* Clayton *c* G Green *e* Donner *m* M Arnold *w* Lauren Harvey, Winters 99min Mon
I AM A FUGITIVE FROM A CHAIN GANG (1932) LeRoy *p* Wallis *c* Polito *w* Muni 76min WB
I, A MAN (1967) *d* Warhol 16mm 100min
I AM A THIEF (1935) *d* Florey *c* Hickox *w* Astor, Pick 64min WB
I am Cuba = O SOY CUBA (1964)
I am Curious, Blue (1968) JAG ÄR NYFIKEN-BLÅ
I am Curious, Yellow (UK) = JAR ÄR NYFIKEN, GU (1967)
I AM SUZANNE (1934) *d* Rowland V Lee *p* Lasky Garmes *w* Lillian Harvey 98min Fox
I, A Negro = MOI, UN NOIR (1958)
IBANEZ' TORRENT (1926) *d* Stiller, Monta Bell *fn* Iban *w* Garbo 6450ft MGM (= *The Torrent*)
I Became a Criminal (USA) = THEY MADE ME FUGITIVE (1947)
I BELIEVE IN YOU (1951) *d/p/s* Dearden, *Michael Relph* Laurence Harvey 95min
IBM AT THE FAIR (1965) *d/s* C and R Eames *c* C Eames E Bernstein 7½min
IBM FAIR PRESENTATION FILM I AND II (1962–6 *d/s* C and R Eames *c* C Eames
IBM MATHEMATICS PEEP SHOW (1961) *d/s* C and Eames *c* C Eames *m* E Bernstein *11min
IBM MUSEUM (1967) *d/s* C and R Eames *c* C Eames 10m
I CAN GET IT FOR YOU WHOLESALE (1951) *d* Gordon *p* S Siegel *ad* Caspary *s* Polonsky *c* Kras *co-a* Wheeler *m* L Newman *w* S Hayward, G Sand 90min Fox (= *This is My Affair*)
ICEBOUND (1924) *d* William De Mille *w* Olivier 647 FPL *r* Par
ICE COLD IN ALEX (1958) *d* J Thompson *c* G Taylor *w* Mills 129min ABC
ICE FLOOD, THE (1926) *d/co-s* G Seitz 5747ft U
ICE PALACE (1960) *d* V Sherman *p* Blanke *c* Biroc *m* Steiner *w* Burton, Ryan, Danton *113min WB
ICE STATION ZEBRA (1968) *d* J Sturges *c* Fapp Legrand *w* Hudson, Borgnine, Kjellin, Nolan PV 148min MGM
ICH HAB VON DIR GETRAUMT (1944) *d* Staudte 199 Tob
ICHIBAN UTSUKUSHIKU (1944) *d/s* Kurosawa 85m Toho
ICH LEBE FUR DICH (1929) *d/w* Dieterle 2723m
ICH MÖCHTE KEIN MANN SEIN (1919) *d/co-s* Lubits *c* Sparkuhl 3rs (= *I Don't Want to be a Man*)
ICH UND DIE KAISERIN (1933) *d* Hollander *co-a* Rohrig *m* Waxman *w* Lillian Harvey, Veidt
ICH WERDE DICH AUF HANDEN TRAGEN (1958) *d* Harlan 2496m
I, Claudius = CLAUDIUS (1937)
I CONFESS (1953) *d/p* Hitchcock *c* Burks *m* Tiomkin Clift, A Baxter, Malden 95min WB
ICONOCLAST, THE (1910) *d* Griffith 1rl Bio
I COULD GO ON SINGING (1962) *d* Neame *w* Garla Bogarde PV* 100min UA
I COVER CHINATOWN (1936) *d/w* Foster 65min
I COVER THE UNDERWORLD (1955) *d* Springste 70min Rep
I COVER THE WATERFRONT (1933) *d* Cruze *c* June *m* Newman *w* Colbert 70min *r* UA
I'D CLIMB THE HIGHEST MOUNTAIN (1951) *d* H K *c* Cronjager *w* S Hayward *88min Fox
IDEA DI UN'ISOLA (1967) *d/p* Rossellini *60min (American TV)
IDEAL (1965) *d* Pojar *15min
IDEALER GATTE, EIN (1935) *d* Hubert Selpin *w* He 2330m
IDEAL HUSBAND, AN (1948) *d/p* A Korda *s* Biro *fpl* Oscar Wilde *a* Périnal *a* V Korda *cos* Beaton Goddard *96min *r* BL
IDE DO SLONCA (1955) *d/s/st* Wajda 380m (= *Ma Towards The Sun/I Go To The Sun*)
IDÉE, L' (1931) *d* Bartosch *m* Honegger
IDÉE À L'EAU, UNE (1939) *d* Le Chanois *w* Mo (= *L'Irrésistible Rebelle*)
I DEN GRØNNE SKOV (1968) *d* Kjaerulff-Schmidt *92 (= *In The Green Of The Woods*)
Identification Marks None = RYSOPIS (1964)
I DIED A THOUSAND TIMES (1955) *d* Heisler *p* Goldb *s* Burnett *fn* High Sierra *rm* HIGH SIERRA 194 McCord *w* Palance, Winters, Marvin CS* 109m WB
IDILLIO TRAGICO (1912) *d* Baldassare Negroni *w* Ghic
IDIOT, L' (1946) *d* Georges Lampin *s* Charles Spaak Dostoievski *w* Philipe, Feuillère 98min

Idiot, The (1951)= HAKUCHI (1951)
IDIOT'S DELIGHT (1939) *d* C Brown *c* Daniels *m* Stothart *w* Gable, Shearer, C Coburn, Meredith 105min MGM
IDLE CLASS, THE (1921) *d/s/w* Chaplin *c* Totheroh *w* Purviance 2rs FN
IDLERS THAT WORK (1949) *d/n* L Anderson *mf* Ralph Vaughan Williams, Copland 17min
I'D LOVE TO TAKE ORDERS FROM YOU (1936) *supn* Avery *p* L Schlesinger *anim* 7min WB (= *Merry Melody*)
I DO (1921) *d/st* Roach, Sam Taylor *w* H Lloyd 2rs
I DODENS VANTRUM (1946) *d* Ekman *w* Lindfors 92min
IDOL DANCER, THE (1920) *d/p* Griffith *c* Bitzer *w* Barthelmess 7rs FN
IDOL OF PARIS (1948) *d* L Arliss 105min WB
IDOLO INFRANTO (1913) *d/s* Ghione
Idols in the Dust = SATURDAY'S HERO (1951)
I DON'T CARE GIRL, THE (1953) *d* Bacon *c* Arling *co-a* Wheeler *w* M Gaynor, D Wayne *78min Fox
I Don't Want To Be A Man (1919) = ICH MOCHTE KEIN MANN SEIN
I DOOD IT (1943) *d* Minnelli *p* J Cummings *c* June *co-a* Gibbons 102min MGM (= *By Hook or by Crook*)
I'D RATHER BE RICH (1964) *d* Smight *p* R Hunter *c* Metty *w* Chevalier, C Ruggles *96min U
I DREAM OF JEANIE (1952) *d* Dwan *p* H Yates *90min Rep
I DREAM TOO MUCH (1935) *d* Cromwell *w* H Fonda 95min RKO
IDYLLE A LA FERME UNE (1912) *d/s/w* Linder Pat
IDYLLE A LA PLAGE, UNE (1931) *d* Storck *w* Rouleau 22min
IDYLLE SOUS UN TUNNEL (1901) *d/w* Zecca 25-50m Pat
IERI, OGGI E DOMANI (1963) *d* De Sica *p* Ponti *co-s* Zavattini, De Filippo, *Alberto Moravia* *c* Rotunno *w* Loren, Mastroianni *119min (= *Yesterday, Today and Tomorrow*)
IF .... (1968) *d/co-p* L Anderson *c* Ondricek part *112min *r* Par
IF I HAD A MILLION (1932) *co-s* Buchman, J Mankiewicz, S Miller *w* G Cooper, C Ruggles 88min Par
    ep THE STREETWALKER *d* Cruze
    ep THE OLD LADIES HOME *d* Cruze
    ep THE FORGER *d* McLeod *w* Raft
    ep THE AUTO *d* Taurog *s* J Mankiewicz *w* Fields
    ep THE CLERK *d/s* Lubitsch *w* Laughton
IF I HAD MY WAY (1940) *d/p/co-st* D Butler *w* B Crosby 95min U
IF I WERE FREE (1933) *d* E Nugent *as-p* Macgowan *c* Cronjager *w* I Dunne, C Brook 66min RKO
IF I WERE KING (1938) *d/p* F Lloyd *s* P Struges *c* Sparkuhl *w* Rathbone, Colman 100min Par
IF I WERE QUEEN (1922) *d* W Ruggles *w* W Baxter 6092ft
IF I WERE SINGLE (1927) *d* Del Ruth *w* Loy 6175ft WB
I Flunked, But ... = RAKUDAI WA SHITA KEREDO (1930)
I FOUND STELLA PARISH (1935) *d* LeRoy *p* H Brown *c* Hickox *w* K Francis, Lukas 84min FN
If There was no Music (GB) = KDYBY TY MUZIKY NEBLY (1963)
If this be Sin = THAT DANGEROUS AGE (1950)
IF WINTER COMES (1947) *d* Saville *p* Bergman *c* Folsey *m* Stothart *w* Pidgeon, Kerr, J Leigh 97min MGM
If You Feel Like Singing = SUMMER STOCK (1950)
IF YOU KNEW SUSIE (1948) *d* G Douglas *p/w* Cantor 90min RKO
If You Like It = SUKI NAREBA KOSO (1928)
IGEN (1964) *d* Révész 75min (= *Yes*)
I GOPHER YOU (1954) *d* Freleng *anim* 7min WB
IGOR STRAVINSKY: A PORTRAIT (1966) *d* R Leacock
I Go to the Sun = IDE DO SLONCA (1955)
I GIVE MY HEART (1935) *d* Marcel Varnel *s* Launder 90min
I GIVE MY LOVE (1934) *d* Freund *st* Vicki Baum *w* Lukas 70min U
IGRA (1962) *d/s/a* Vutovic *anim* 310m (= *The Play*)
I Graduated, But ... = DAIGAKU WA DETA KEREDO (1929)
IGY JOTTEM (1964) *d* Jancso 109min (= *My Way Home*)
I HAVE LIVED (1933) *d* Thorpe 65min
IHRE MAJESTÄT, DIE LIEBE (1931) *d/p* May 2789m
IHR GROSSES GEHEIMNIS (1935) *d/p* May 4rs
IKARI NO MACHI (1950) *d* Naruse (= *Town of Anger*)
IKARI NO UMI (1944) *d* Imai 2497m Toho (= *The Angry Sea*)
IK-FILM (1929) *d/s/c/e* Ivens, Hans Van Meerten 200m
IKIMONO NO KIROKU (1955) *d/co-s* Kurosawa *w* Mifune 113min Toho
IKIRU (1952) *d/co-s* Kurosawa 143min Toho (= *Doomed/Living*)
IKITEIRU MAGOROKU (1943) *d* Kinoshita (= *Magoroku Is Still Alive*)
IKITOSHI IKERUMONO (1934) *d* Gosho (= *Everything That Lives*)
I Knew Her Well (US) = IO LA CONOSCERO BENE (1965)
I KNOW WHERE I'M GOING (1945) *d/p/s* M Powell, Pressburger 91min
IKONOKOTTA SHINSENGUMI (1932) *d/s* Kinugasa (= *The Surviving Shinsengumi*)

ILE DE CALYPSO: ULYSSE ET POLYPHEME, L' (1905) *d* Méliès 70m
ILE DE PAQUES, L' (1934) *d* Storck *m/n* Jaubert 30min (= *Easter Island*)
ILE DU BOUT DU MONDE, L' (1958) *d/co-s* Gréville *co-m* Aznavour *w* Marquand 104min
ILE DU PÉCHÉ, L' (1939) *d* Gréville
Il était une Chaise = CHAIRY TALE, A (1957)
I LIVE FOR LOVE (1935) *d* Berkeley *co-st/co-s* Wald, JJ Epstein *c* Barnes *m* Tiomkin *w* Del Rio 8rs WB
I LIVE IN GROSVENOR SQUARE (1945) *d* H Wilcox *c* Heller *w* Neagle, Harrison 114min ABC
I LIVE MY LIFE (1935) *d* WS Van Dyke *s* J Mankiewicz *co-st* G Reinhardt *c* Folsey *m* Tiomkin *w* J Crawford 81min MGM
I LIVETS BRANDING (1915) *d* Madsen
I'LL BE SEEING YOU (1944) *d* Dieterle *p* Schary *c* Gaudio *m* Amfitheatrof *w* G Rogers, Cotten, Temple 85min *pc* Selznick *r* UA
I'll Buy You = ANATA KAIMASU (1956)
I'LL CRY TOMORROW (1956) *d* Daniel Mann *c* Arling *co-a* Gibbons *m* North *w* Conte, S Hayward, Danton 117min MGM
I'll Get You For This (GB) = LUCKY NICK CAIN (1951)
I'LL GIVE A MILLION (1938) *d* W Lang *co-st* Zavattini *co-s* Sperling *c* Andriot *w* W Baxter, Hersholt, Lorre, Carradine 75min Fox
ILLIAC PASSION, THE (1967) *d/s/c/e* Markopoulos *w* Markopoulos, Warhol 16mm*90min
ILLICIT (1931) *d* A Mayo *w* Stanwyck 6041ft WB
Illicit Interlude = SOMMARLEK (1950)
ILL MET BY MOONLIGHT (1956) *d/p/s* M Powell, Pressburger *c* Challis *m* Theodorakis *w* Bogarde VV 104min *r* JAR (= *Night Ambush*)
I'll Never Forget You (US) = HOUSE IN THE SQUARE, THE (1951)
I'LL SAY SO (1918) *d* Walsh 5rs Fox
I'LL SEE YOU IN MY DREAMS (1951) *d* Curtiz *c* McCord *w* D Day 109min WB
I'LL TAKE VANILLA (1934) *d* C Chase (as Parrott) *p* Roach *w* C Chase 2rs MGM
ILLUMINATIONS (1963) *d/c* Reichenbach *fpm* Arthur Rimbaud *m* Legrand *10min
Illusion Of Blood = YOTSUYA KAIDAN (1949)
ILLUSTRATED MAN, THE (1969) *d* Smight *fn* Bradbury *c* Lathrop *a* Sylbert *m* Goldsmith *w* Steiger, Bloom PV* 103min WB
IL NE FAUT PAS MOURIR POUR ÇA (1967) *d/s/pc* Lefebvre 75min
I LOVE A MYSTERY (1945) *d* Levin *c* Goffey 70min Col
I LOVE A SOLDIER (1944) *d/p* Sandrich *c* C Lang *co-a* Dreier *w* Goddard 106min Par
I LOVED A SOLDIER (1936, uf) *d* Hathaway *supn* Lubitsch *c* C Lang *w* Dietrich, Boyer, Tamiroff, Stander, Sullavan Par
I LOVED YOU WEDNESDAY (1933) *d* H King, Menzies *c* Mohr *w* W Baxter 80min Fox
I LOVE MELVIN (1953) *d* Weis *p/s* Wells *c* Rosson *co-a* Gibbons *chor* R Alton *w* R Taylor, D Reynolds, O'Connor, Keel(uc) *76min MGM
I LOVE YOU AGAIN (1940) *d* WS Van Dyke *co-s* Lederer *a* Gibbons *m* Waxman *w* W Powell, M Loy 99min MGM
I LOVE YOU, ALICE B TOKLAS (1968) *d* Hy Averback *c* Lathrop *w* Sellers *93min WB
I Love, You Love (UK) = IO AMO, TU AMI (1960)
ILS ETAIENT NEUF CELIBATAIRES (1939) *d/s/w* Guitry
ILUSION VIAJA EN TRANVIA, LA (1953) *d* Buñuel 90min
IL Y A DES PIEDS AU PLAFOND (1911) *d/s* Gance
IMAGE, L' (1925) *d/s/co-st* Feyder *co-c* Burel 90min
IMAGES D'OSTENDE (1930) *d/p* Storck 15min
IMAGES POUR BAUDELAIRE (1958) *d* Kast *m* Delerue 550m Pat
Image = OMOKAGE (1948)
IMAGE BY IMAGES I (1954) *d* Breer *anim* 16mm 10seconds
IMAGE BY IMAGES II AND III (1955) *d* Breer *anim* 16mm 7min
IMAGE BY IMAGE IV (1955) *d* Breer *anim* 16mm*3min
IMAGES MATHEMATIQUES DE LA LUTTE POUR LA VIE (1936) *d* Painlevé
IMAGES MATHEMATIQUES DE LA QUATRIEME DIMENSION (1936) *d* Painlevé
IMAGES POUR DEBUSSY (1951) *d/s* Mitry *m* Claude Debussy 11min
IMA HITOTABI NO (1947) *d* Gosho (= *One More*)
I'M ALL RIGHT JACK (1959) *d/co-p* R Boulting *co-p* J Boulting *w* Sellers, Attenborough 105min BL
I MARRIED A COMMUNIST (1949) *d* Stevenson *c* Musuraca *w* Ryan 73min RKO
I MARRIED A DOCTOR (1936) *d* A Mayo 83min WB
I MARRIED AN ANGEL (1942) *d* WS Van Dyke *s* Loos *c* June *a* Gibbons *w* Jeanette MacDonald, Horton 84min MGM
I MARRIED A WITCH (1942) *d/co-p* Clair *c* Tetzlaff *co-des* Dreier *w* March, Lake, Benchley, S Hayward 78min AA

IM BANNE DES EVLENSPIEGELS (1932) *d* Wisbar 2124m
Imbarco a mezzanotte = STRANGER ON THE PROWL (1952)
Imboscata, L' = BANDA DELLE CIFRE, LA (1915)
I'M COLD (1955) *d* Avery *p* Lantz *anim* 7min U (= *Chilly Willy*)
IM DIENSTE DER MENSCHHEIT (1938) *d/co-s* Ruttmann
I MET HIM IN PARIS (1937) *d/p* C Ruggles *co-a* Dreier *w* Colbert, M Douglas, R Young 86min Par
I MET MY LOVE AGAIN (1938) *d* Logan, *Arthur Kipley* *p* Wanger *c* Mohr *w* J Bennett, H Fonda 77min *r* UA
IMITATION GENERAL (1958) *d* G Marshall *c* Folsey *w* G Ford CS 88min MGM
IMITATION OF CHRIST (1967) *d* Warhol 16mm *480min/120min (segment of FOUR STARS)
IMITATION OF LIFE (1934) *d* Stahl *di* P Sturges (uc) *w* Colbert 106min U
IMITATION OF LIFE (1959) *d* Sirk *p* R Hunter *rm* (1934) *c* Metty *co-a* Golitzen *w* Turner, *Mahalia Jackson* *124min U
IM KAMPFE MIT DEM BERGE (1921) *d/s/co-c* Franck 1536m
IMMACULATE ROAD, THE (1960) *d* Maté *w* L Young 51min
IMMAGINI E COLORE (1938) *d* Sala sh
IMMEDIATE DISASTER (1954) *d* Burt Balaban *w* Neal 16mm
IMMENSEE (1943) *d/co-s* V Harlan *2592m Ufa
IMMIGRANT, THE (1917) *d/s/w* Chaplin *c* Totheroh *w* Purviance 2rs Mut
IMMOLAZIONE (1914) *d/s/dec* Guazzoni
IMMORALE, L' (1967) *d* Germi
IMMORTAL LAND, THE (1958) *d/co-p* B Wright *40min
Immortal Love = EIEN NO HITO (1961)
IMMORTAL SERGEANT (1942) *d* Stahl *p/s* Trotti *co-c* AC Miller *co-a* R Day *w* H Fonda, M O'Hara, Lawford, Mitchell 91min Fox
Immortal Story, The (UK) = HISTOIRE IMMORTELLE (1968)
IMMORTELLE, L' (1962) *d/s* Robbe-Grillet *co-m* Delerue *w* Doniol Valcroze 100min *co-pc* De Laurentiis
Im Namen der Menschlipchkeit = DER PROZESS (1947)
I'M NO ANGEL (1933) *d* W Ruggles *st/s/di* West *w* West, C Grant 87min Par
I, MOBSTER (1958) *d/co-p* Corman *c* F Crosby *a* D Haller *w* Cochran CS 80min Fox (= *The Mobster*)
IMPASSE DES DEUX ANGES, L' (1948) *d* M Tourneur *s* Le Chanois *c* C Renoir *w* Signoret 84min
IMPATIENT MAIDEN, THE (1932) *d* Whale *c* Edeson *w* Ayres 72min U
IMPERATORE DI CAPRI, L' (1950) *d* Comencini *p* Ponti *w* Toto
IMPIEGATA DI PAPA, L' (1934) *d/co-e* Blasetti
IMPORTANCE OF BEING EARNEST, THE (1952) *d/s* Asquith *fpl* Wilde *w* Greenwood, M Redgrave, Evans 92min BL
IMPOSSIBLE MRS BELLEW, THE (1922) *d* S Wood *w* Swanson 7155ft FPL *r* Par
IMPOSSIBLE YEARS, THE (1968) *d* M Gordon *s* Wells *c* Daniels *w* Niven PV* 99min MGM
IMPOSSIVEL ACONTECE, O (1969) 90min (3eps)
    ep O REIMPLANTE *d/st/s* Duarte
IMPOSTER, THE (1944) *d/st/s* Duvivier *co-a* Lourié *m* Tiomkin *w* Gabin 90min U
IMPFOSTER, EL (1957) *d/co-s* Fernandez *w* Armendariz 90min
IMPRESSIONI SICILIANE (1931) *d* Poggioli sh
Impotence = HONNO (1966)
IMPRESSIONS DE NEW YORK (1955) *d/c* Reichenbach *cy* Doniol Valcroze *m* Bela Barlok *330m
IMPRESSIONS DE PARIS (1967) *d* Reichenbach
IMPREVISIBLES NOUVEAUTES (1961) *d* Rossif * sh (= *Unforeseeable Novelties*)
IMPREVISTO, L' (1961) *d* Lattuada *m* Piccioni *w* Aimée 106min *r* Col (= *The Unexpected*)
IMPULSU (1955) *d* Charles de Lautow, Endfield (uc) *w* A Kennedy 80min
I'M STILL ALIVE (1940) *d* Reis 72min RKO
I'm the Hero = EROE SONO IO, L' (1952)
IM WEISSEN ROSSL (1952) *d* Werner Jacobs *s* Charrell 103min
IM ZEICHEN DES VERTRAUENS (1938) *d* Ruttmann
INADMISSIBLE EVIDENCE (1968) *d* Anthony Page *s/fpl* Osborne 96min
IN AGAIN, OUT AGAIN (1917) *d/p* Emerson *st/s* Loos *c* Edeson *w* Fairbanks Sr 5rs
IN A LONELY PLACE (1950) *d* N Ray *c* Guffey *m* Antheil *w* Bogart, Grahame 94min *r* Col
INAMORATI, GLI (1955) *d/co-s* Bolognini (= *Wild Love*)
IN AMORE SI PECCA IN DUE (1953) *d* Cottafavi 2470m *r* MGM
INASMUCH (1934) *d* Alec Saville *w* Wolfit 22min
I NATT ELLER ALDRIG (1941) *d* Molander SF
INAUGURATION OF THE PLEASURE DOME (1954, 1958, 1966) *d/s/c/e/w* Anger *w* Anias Nin 16mm *39min
    1st version: single screen *m* Harry Partch
    2nd version: triple screen

3rd version: single screen m Janacek (= Sacred Mushroom)

INAZUMA (1952) d Naruse (= *Lightning*)

IN BETWEEN (1955) d Brakhage m John Cage 16mm *10min

IN CALIENTE (1935) d Bacon s Wald, JJ Epstein c Polito w Horton, Del Rio 85min WB

IN CAMPAGNA E CADUTA UNA STELLA (1940) d/st/co-s/w De Filippo co-s Freda

IN CAPO AL MONDO (1963) d/s/e Brass 98min (= *Chi Lavora e Perduto*)

INCATENATA, L' (1921) d Genina

INCENDIARY BLONDE (1945) d G Marshall c Rennahan co-a Dreier w Hutton, C Ruggles, Roman 113min Par

In China = V KITAI (1941)

Incident at Owl Creek (UK) = RIVIERE DU HIBOU, LA (1961)

Incident in a Volcano = SLUCHAI V VULKANYE (1941)

IN COLD BLOOD (1967) d/p/s R Brooks fn Truman Capote c C Hall a Boyle PV 134min Col

INCOMPRESO (1966) d Comencini w Quayle *105min (= *Misunderstood*)

INCOMPETANT HERO, AN (1914) d/w Arbuckle p Sennett 1rl Key

IN CONFERENCE (1931) d Cline s Sennett 1898ft

INCONNUS DANS LA MAISON, LES, (1942) d Decoin, ad/di Clouzot fn Georges Simenon w Raimu 90min (= *Strangers in the House*)

INCREDIBLE SHRINKING MAN, THE (1957) d J Arnold p Zugsmith s Matheson co-a Golitzen 81min U

INCUBUS (1965) d/st/s Leslie Stevens c C Hall 78min

INDAGINE SU UN CITTADINO AL DI SOPRA DI OGNO SOSPETTO (1970) d/co-s Petri *115min (= *Investigation of a Citizen Above Suspicion*)

IN DER NACHT (1931) d Ruttmann 350m

IN DER FIEFE DES SCHACHTES (1912) d/s May 770m

INDE 68 (1969) d Malle 7 parts × 50min TV (= *Louis Malle's India/Phantom India*)

INDEX-HANS RICHTER (1969) d/s/c/e Markopoulos w Richter 16mm *30min

INDIA (1958) d/st/co-s Rossellini c Tonti *90min

Indianapolis = TO PLEASE A LADY (1950)

INDIANAPOLIS SPEEDWAY (1939) d Bacon st Hawks c Hickox w Sheridan, Payne 85min WB

INDIAN FANTASY (1938) d Gross, *Hector Hoppin* anim* 17min

INDIAN FIGHTER, THE (1955) d De Toth co-s B Hecht m Waxman w K Douglas, Matthau, Cook, Chaney, Martinelli CS* 88min UA

INDIAN MASSACRE, THE (1912) d Ince w Conway (in 2 parts)

Indian Morning = UTRO INDII (1959)

INDIAN PAINT (1966) d/s Foster c Crosby *91min Col

Indian Summer = ROZMARNE LETO (1968)

INDIA VISTA DA ROSSELLINI, L' (1959) d/p Rossellini 16mm RAI 10eps 1 *India Senza Miti*; 2 *Bombay, La Porta Dell'India*; 3 *Architettura e Costume di Bombay*; 4 *Varsova*; 5 *Verso Il Sud*; 6 *Le Lagune Del Malabar*; 7 *Il Kerala*; 8 *Hirakud, La Diga Sul Fiume Mahadi*; 9 *Il Pandit Nehru*; 10 *Gli Animali Dell'India* 18–29min Each

INDIFFERENTI, GLI (1964) d Maselli s Cecchi d'Amico fn Moravia c Di Venanzo m Fusco w Cardinale, Goddard, Steiger, Winters 100min (= *Time of Indifference*)

INDISCHE GRABMAL, DAS (1921) d/p May co-s/fn Von Harbou co-s F Lang w Veidt (in 2 parts) (= *Above All Law*)

INDISCHE GRABMAL, DAS (1959) d/co-s F Lang fn Von Harbou rm (DAS INDISCHE GRABMAL part II 1921) *101min

INDISCREET (1931) d/co-s McCarey c June, Toland m A Newman w Swanson 90min UA

INDISCREET (1958) d Donen co-p Donen, C Grant s/fpl Krasna c F Young w C Grant, Ingrid Bergman *98min WB

INDISCRET, L' (1969) d Reichenbach *85min

Indiscretion Of An American Wife = STAZIONE TERMINI (1953)

INDISK BY (1951) d/s/c/e Sucksdorff 25min SF

INDONESIA CALLING (1946) d/s/e Ivens n Finch 23min

INDUSTRIAL BRITAIN (1931) d/c Flaherty p/e Grierson 22min EMB

Industrial Symphony = PHILIPS-RADIO (1931)

IN ENEMY COUNTRY (1968) d/p Keller c Griggs co-a Golitzen *107min U

IN FACCIA AL DESTINO (1913) d Baldessare Negroni w Ghione

INFANZIA, VOCAZIONE E PRIMA ESPERIENZE DI GIACOMO CASANOVA, VENEZIANO (1969) d/co-s Comencini *119min (= *Casanova*)

LE INFEDLI (1952) d Steno, Monicelli p Ponti, De Laurentiis c Tonti w Lollobrigida 97min (= *The Unfaithful*)

Infedility (UK) = ALTRI TEMPI (ZIBALDONE NO 1) (1952)

INFERNO (1953) d R Baker c Ballard co-a Wheeler m L Newman w Ryan, R Fleming 3D 83min Fox

INFERNO DE ALMAS (1958) d Alazraki

INFERNO DI AMORE (1928) d Gallone

Infidelity = L'AMANT DE CINQ JOURS (1961)

INFINITOS (1935) d/s Velo, *Fernando Mantilla* 1rl

INFLATION (1927) d/s/dec Richter 900ft (20min originally, 8min finally) Ufa

INFLUENCE DE LA LUMIERE SUR LES MOUVEMENTS DE L'OEUF DE TRUITE (1957) d Painlevé 16mm part *

INFORMATION MACHINE, THE (1957) d/s C & R Eames c C Eames m E Bernstein *10min

INFORMER, THE (1912) d Griffith w Pickford, D Gish 1rl Bio

INFORMER, THE (1935) d J Ford s D Nichols c August m M Steiner w V McLaglen (Parrish) 91min RKO

IN GAY MADRID (1930) d/p Leonard w Novarro 71min MGM

INGEBORG HOLM (1913) d/s Sjöström 2006m

INGEN MORGONDAG (1957) d Mattsson, w Kulle (= *No Tomorrow*)

INGENTING OVANLIGT (1957) d P Weiss (= *Nothing Unusual*)

INGMARSARVET (1925) d Molander w Veidt SF

INGMARSSONERNA (I) (1918) d/s/w Sjöström fn Selma Layerlof 2020m

INGMARSSONERNA (II) (1918) d/s/w Sjöström 2183m

IN HARM'S WAY (1964) d/p Preminger s Mayes c Griggs, 2nd c Lathrop dec Wheeler cr Bass m Goldsmith w J Wayne, K Douglas, Neal, D Andrews, Meredith, Tone, H Fonda, (G Kennedy) PV 165min r Par

Inheritance, The = KARAMI-AI (1962)

INHERIT THE WIND (1960) d/p Kramer c Laszlo m Gold w Tracy, March, Gene Kelly pc Kramer r UA

L'INHUMAINE (1924) d/s L'Herbier co-dec Cavalcanti, Léger, Autant-Lara m Milhaud 1800m (= *Futurisme*)

INITIATION A LA DANSE DES POSSEDES (1949) d/p/c Rouch 16mm *36min

IN JENEN TAGEN (1947) d/co-s Käutner 3035m

IN LIKE FLINT (1967) d G Douglas c Daniels m Goldsmith w Cobb, J Coburn CS* 114min Fox

IN LINE OF DUTY (1931) d Glennon c Stout w Beery 60min

IN LOVE AND WAR (1958) d P Dunne p Wald co-a Wheeler m Friedhofer w F Hunter, R Wagner CS* 105min Fox

In Memory of Sergei Ordzhonikidzye = PAMYATI SERGO ORDZHONIKIDZYE (1937)

IN NAME ONLY (1939) d Cromwell w Lombard, C Grant, K Francis, C Coburn 102min RKO

INNAMORATA, L' (1921) d Genina

INNAMORATI, GLI (1955) d/co-s Bolognini co-s Festa Campanile w Manfredi 93min (= *Wild Love*)

Inn At Osaka, An = OSAKA NO YADO (1954)

INNER AND OUTER SPACE (1960) d Breer anim 16mm *5min

Inn In Tokyo, An = TOKYO NO YADO (1953)

Innocence is Bliss = MISS GRANT TAKES RICHMOND (1949)

Innocence unprotected = NEVINOST BEZ ZASTITE (1968)

INNOCENT AFFAIR, AN (1948) d Bacon c Cronjager w MacMurray, Carroll 90min UA (= *Don't Trust your Husband*)

Innocent Witch, An = OSOREZAN NO ONNA (1965)

INNOCENT EYE, THE (1958) d J Schlesinger 36min BBC

INNOCENT MAGDALENE, AN (1916) d Dwan, p Griffith st Griffith (ps Granville Warwick) w L Gish 5rs r Tri

INNOCENTS, THE (1961) d/p Clayton co-s Truman Capote fst (*The Turn of the Screw*) Henry James c F Francis m Auric w Kerr, M Redgrave CS 99min Fox

INNOCENTS OF PARIS (1929) d Richard Wallace c C Lang w Chevalier 6148ft Par

INNOCENT SINNER, THE (1917) d/ad Walsh 6rs Fox

INNOCENT SINNERS (1958) d P Leacock w David Kossoff, Flora Robson 95min

Innocent Sorcerers = NIEWINNI CZARODZIEJE (1960)

INN OF EVIL = INOCHI BONIFURO (1971)

INN OF THE SIXTH HAPPINESS, THE (1958) d/p Robson p Adler c F Young m M Arnold w Ingrid Bergman, Jurgens, Donat CS* 158min Fox

IN NOME DELLA LEGGE (1949) d/co-s Germi co-s Fellini, Monicelli w Girotti, Vanel 103min (= *In the Name of Law*)

IN NOME DEL PADRE (1971) d/s Bellocchio *115min

IN NOME DEL POPOLO ITALIANO (1971) d Risi w Gassman *101min

INOCENTES, LOS (1962) d/co-s Bardem 110min

INOCHI BONIFURO (1971) d Kobayashi w Nakadai 120min (= *Inn of Evil*)

IN OLD ARIZONA (1929) co-d Walsh co-c Edeson w W Baxter 8724ft Fox

IN OLD CALIFORNIA (1910) d Griffith 1rl Bio

IN OLD CHICAGO (1938) d H King p Zanuck as-p Macgowan co-s Trotti fst Busch c Marley w Power, Faye 115min Fox

In Old Heidelberg (UK) = STUDENT PRINCE, THE (1927)

IN OLD KENTUCKY (1909) d Griffith w Pickford 1rl Bio

IN OLD KENTUCKY (1920) d Neilan 7rl FN

IN OLD KENTUCKY (1927) d/p Stahl 6646ft MGM

IN OLD KENTUCKY (1935) d G Marshall c O'Connell w W Rogers 86min Fox

IN OLD MADRID (1911) co-d Ince w Pickford

IN OLD SANTA FE (1934) d David Howard w Autry 65min

INONDATION, L' (1924) d/s Delluc

IN OUR TIME (1944) d V Sherman p Wald co-s H Koch w Lupino, Henreid, Nazimova 110min WB

IN PARIS PARKS (1954) d/p/c/e S Clarke *13½min

IN PREHISTORIC DAYS (1913) d Griffith 1rl Bio

INQUEST (1940) d R Boulting p J Boulting 60min BL

I.N.R.I. (1923) d/s Wiene w Krauss, Nielsen 3444m

Ins Blaue Leben = CASTELLI IN ARIA (1939)

IN SEARCH OF THE CASTAWAYS (1961) d Stevenson p Disney fns (*In Search of the Castaways* and *Captain Grant's Children*) Jules Verne w H Mills, G Sanders, Chevalier *100min pc Disney (= *The Castaways*)

Insect Woman, The = NIPPON KONCHUKI (1963)

INSEL DER SEELIGEN (1913) d M Reinhardt

In Self-Defence (1921) = LANDSFLYKTIGE, DE

INSIDE DAISY CLOVER (1966) d Mulligan s/fn Lambert c C Lang m Previn w N Wood, Plummer, R Gordon, Redford PV* 128min WB

INSIDE DETROIT (1955) d Sears 82min Col

INSIDE OUT (1964) d Moorse 16min

INSIDE STORY, THE (1948) d/p Dwan co-st Lehman 87min Rep

Insomnia = INSOMNIE (1965)

INSOMNIE (1965) d/co-s/w Etaix c Boffety *17min (= *Insomnia*)

INSOUMIS, L' (1964) d/s/co-ad Cavalier c C Renoir dec Evein w Delon 110min MGM

INSPECTOR, THE (1961) d P Dunne p Robson fn Jan de Hartog m M Arnold w Boyd CS* 111min pc Robson r Fox (= *Lisa*)

INSPECTOR CALLS, AN (1954) d Hamilton s Davis fpl Priestley w Forbes 79min BL

INSPECTOR CLOUSEAU (1968) d Yorkin c Ibbetson PV* 105min Mir r UA

INSPECTOR GENERAL, THE (1949) d Koster p Wald co-s Kurnitz fpl Gogol w Kaye 102min WB

Inspector Returns Home, The = INSPEKTOR SE VRACA KUCI (1959)

INSPEKTOR SE VRACA KUCI (1959) d/s Mimica anim* 10min (= *The Inspector Returns Home*)

INSPIRATION (1931) d C Brown c Daniels w Garbo, Montgomery 74min MGM

Instinct = HONNO (1966)

INSTINCT EST MAITRE, L' (1916) d Feyder 1192m Gau

INTENT TO KILL (1958) d Cardiff CS 89min r Fox

INTERFERIN' GENT, THE (1927) d Thorpe

INTERIM (1953) d Brakhage 16mm 25min

INTERLUDE (1957) d Sirk p R Hunter c Daniels co-a Golitzen mf Beethoven, Wagner, Liszt, Brahms, Mozart, Schumann w Allyson, Rosay CS* 90min U

Interlude In The Marshland (1964) = UPPEHALL I MYRLANDET

INTERMEZZO (1936) d/co-s Molander w Ingrid Bergman, Ekman SF

INTERMEZZO (1939) d Ratoff p Selznick as-p L Howard c Toland a Wheeler w L Howard, Ingrid Bergman 60min UA

INTERNATIONAL HOUSE (1933) d Edward Sutherland c E Haller w Fields, Lugosi 70min Par

International Spy = SPY RING, THE (1938)

INTERNATIONAL VELVET (1967) d Warhol 16mm *30min (segment of *Four Stars*)

INTERNS THE (1962) d/co-s Swift c Metty m Leith Stevens w Robertson 120min Col

INTERRUPTED ELOPEMENT, AN (1912) d Sennett w Normand ½rl Bio

INTERUPTED MELODY (1955) d C Bernhardt co-a Gibbons co-c Ruttenberg w G Ford, Parker CS* 106min MGM

INTERVIEW, THE (1961) d/p Pintoff *5min pc Pintoff

INTERVIEWS WITH MY LAI VETERANS (1970) d Strick co-c Wexler 22min

IN THE AISLES OF THE WILD (1912) d Griffith w L Gish, Carey 1rl Bio

In the Big City = V BOLSHOM GORODYE (1927)

IN THE CLUTCHES OF THE GANG (1914) d Sennett (?) w Arbuckle, Normand 1rl Key

IN THE FRENCH STYLE (1963) d Parrish p/s Shaw c Kelber m Kosma w S Baker, Seberg, *James Leo Herlihy* 105min Col

IN THE GOOD OLD SUMMERTIME (1949) d Leonard p Pasternak co-ad Goodrich, Hackett s Raphaelson co-a Gibbons w Garland, V Johnson, Keaton 102min MGM

In The Green of The Woods = I DEN GRØNNE SKOV (1968)

IN THE HEART OF A FOOL (1921) d/p Dwan 7rs r FN

IN THE HEAT OF THE NIGHT (1967) d Jewison p W Mirisch s Silliphant c Wexler w Poitier, Steiger * r UA

IN THE LATIN QUARTER (1914) d Lionel Belmore w C Talmadge 2rs Vit

IN THE MEANTIME, DARLING (1944) d/p Preminger c Joe MacDonald w Crain, Edwards 72min Fox

In the Mountains of Yugoslavia = V GORAKH YUGOSLAVII (1946)

In the Name of Life = VO IMYA ZHIZNI (1947)

In the Name of the Fatherland = VO IMYA RODINY (1943)

In the Name of the Law (UK) = INOME DELLA LEGGE (1949)

IN THE NEXT ROOM (1930) *d* Cline *c* J Seitz 69min FN
IN THE NICK (1960) *d/s* K Hughes CS 105min *r* Col
In the October Days = V DNI OKTYABRYA (1958)
IN THE PARK (1915) *d/s/w* Chaplin *c* Totheroh *w* Turpin, Purviance Bacon 1rl S&A
In the Presence of Life = MIMO ZHIZHNI (1914)
In the Red Rays of the Sleeping Sun = AKAI YUHI NI TERASARETE (1925)
In the Storm = U OLUJI (1952)
IN THE STREET (1948) *p* Agee, Helen Levitt, Janice Loeb
IN THE SULTAN'S GARDEN (1911) *co-d* Ince *w* Pickford
In the Town of S = V GORODYE S (1966)
IN THE WAKE OF THE BOUNTY (1933) *d Herman F Erben w* Flynn 70min
IN THIS OUR LIFE (1942) *d/co-s* J Huston *co-s* H Koch *p* Wallis *c* E Haller *sp eff* Haskin *m* M Steiner *w* B Davis De Havilland, C Coburn, W Huston, Bogart (*uc*) 97min WB
Intimate Dream = HAZUKASHII YUME (1927)
Intimate Lighting = INTIMNI OSVETLENI (1966)
INTIMATE STRANGER, THE (1956) *d* Losey (*ps* J Walton) *s* H Koch (*ps* Peter Howard) *des* R MacDonald *w* Losey (*uc*) 95min (= *Finger of Guilt*)
IN TIME WITH INDUSTRY (1937) *d* Lye
INTIMNI OSVETLENI (1966) *d/co-s* Passer *co-c* Ondricek 72min (= *Intimate Lighting*)
INTOLERANCE (1916) *d* Griffith *as-d* WS Van Dyke, Von Stroheim, Browning *co-c* Bitzer *w* Marsh, L Gish, Browning, Von Stroheim, C Talmadge, Fairbanks Sr, Crisp 13rs *pc* Griffith (modern ep = THE MOTHER AND THE LAW)
Into the Blue = PARIS-MEDITERRANEE (1931)
INTO THE NET (1924) *d* G Seitz Pat (serial in 10eps)
IN TOW (1914) *d/p/s/w* Vidor 20min *pc* Vidor
Intoxication (UK) = RAUSCH (1919)
INTREPID MR TWIGG, THE (1968 *r* 1971) *d* F Francis *36min BL
INTRIGANTES, LES (1954) *d* Decoin *c* Kelber *m* Van Parys *w* Moreau, Rouleau 100min
INTRIGO, L' (1964) *d* Sala, G Marshall *w* S Jones *97min U (= *Dark Purpose*)
Introduction to Anthropology, An = JINRUGAKU NYUMON (1966)
INTRODUCTION TO FEEDBACK (1960) *d/s* C & R Eames *c* C Eames *m* E Bernstein *11min
INTRODUCTION TO JAZZ (1953) *d* D Sanders 16mm 12min
Introduction To Marriage = KEKKON GAKU NYUMON (1930)
INTRUDER, THE (1953) *d* Hamilton *w* Hawkins 84min BL
INTRUDER, THE (1961) *d/p* Corman 84min (= *The Stranger*)
INTRUDER IN THE DUST (1949) *d/p* C Brown *s* Maddow *fn* Faulkner *c* Surtees *co-a* Gibbons 87min MGM
INTRUSE, L' (1913) *d/s* Feuillade 815m
INVADERS, THE (1912) *d* Ince
INVADERS, THE (1934) *d Adrian Brunel w* Keaton 6rs (= *An Old Spanish Custom*)
Invaders, The = FORTYNINTH PARALLEL (1941)
INVADERS FROM MARS (1953) *d/des* Menzies *c* J Seitz 81min BL
INVANDRARNA (1970 *r* 1972) *d/co-s/c/e* Troell *w* Von Sydow CS* SF
Invasion, The = NASHESTVIE (1945)
INVASION, L' (1970) *d* Y Allégret *w* Piccoli *91min
INVASION OF THE BODY SNATCHERS (1956) *d* D Siegel *p* Wanger *s* Mainwaring *di d* Peckinpah *c* Fredericks S 80min RKO
Invasion Pacifique, L' = QUEBEC-USA (1962)
INVASORE, L' (1943) *d/st/co-s Nino Giannini co-s/supn* Rossellini
INVASORI, GLI (1961) *d/co-s/co-c* Bava S* 98min (= *Erik the Conqueror/Fury of the Vikings*)
An Invention for Destruction = UYNALEZ ZKAZY (1958)
INVENZIONE DELLA CROCE, L' (1949) *co-d/co-s/n* Emmer *co-d/co-s Enrico Gras* 10min (= *Legend of the True Cross*)
Investigation of a Citizen Above Suspicion = INDAGINE SU UN CITTADINO AL DI SOPRA DI OGNO SOSPETTO (1970)
Invincibles, The = NEPOBEDIMYE (1943)
INVINCIBLE SIX, THE (1970) *d* Negulesco *m* Hadjidakis *w* Jurgens *103min
INVISIBLE AVENGER, THE (1957) *d John Sledge*, Howe 60min Rep
INVISIBLE GHOST (1941) *d* JH Lewis *p* Katzman *w* Lugosi 64min Mon
INVISIBLE MAN, THE (1933) *d* Whale *fn H G Wells c* Edeson *w* Rains, Carradine 71min U (Russian version *d* Donskoi 1935)
INVISIBLE MAN RETURNS, THE (1940) *d/co-st* May *c* Krasner *w* Price 81min U
INVISIBLE MENACE, THE (1938) *d* J Farrow *c* O'Connell *w* Karloff 55min WB (= *Without Warning*)
INVISIBLE POWER, THE (1921) *d/p* F Lloyd *c* Brodine 6500ft *pc* Goldwyn
Invisible Power (UK) = WASHINGTON MERRY-GO-ROUND (1932)
INVISIBLE STRIPES (1939) *d* Bacon *p* Wallis *c* E Haller *w* Raft, Holden, Bogart 82min WB
INVISIBLE WOMAN, THE (1940) *d Edward Sutherland st* Siodmak, May *w* Montez, J Barrymore, C Ruggles 72min U
INVITATA, L' (1969) *d* De Seta *w* Piccoli *115min (= *L'Invitée*)
INVITATION (1952) *d* G Reinhardt *s* Osborn *c* June *co-a* Gibbons *w* V Johnson, McGuire, Roman 84min MGM
INVITATION AU VOYAGE, L' (1927) *d* Dulac sh
INVITATION TO A GUNFIGHTER (1964) *d/p/co-s* R Wilson *c* Joe MacDonald *m* Raksin *w* Brynner, Segal 93min *pc* Kramer *r* UA
INVITATION TO HAPPINESS (1939) *d/p* W Ruggles *co-a* Dreier *m* Hollander *w* C Ruggles, I Dunne, MacMurray 95min Par
INVITATION TO THE DANCE (1956) *d/s/chor/w* Gene Kelly *p* Freed *c* F Young, Ruttenberg *co-a* Gibbons *anim* Hanna, Barbera *m* Previn, Ibert, Edens *93min MGM
Invitée, L' = INVITATA, L' (1969)
INVITE MONSIEUR A DINER (1932) *d* Autant-Lara
INVITO A PRANZO, UN (1907) *d/s* Guazzoni
INVOCATION OF MY DEMON BROTHER (1969) *d/s/c/e* Anger *m Mick Jagger* 16mm *12min
IN WHICH WE SERVE (1942) *co-d/p/s/m/w* Coward *co-d* Lean *c* Neame *w* J Mills, Attenborough 114min BL
In Wrong = BETWEEN SHOWERS (1914)
IO AMO, TU AMI (1960) *d* Blasetti *c* Tonti S* 95min *pc* De Laurentiis (= *I Love, You Love*)
IO, IO, IO, . . . EGLI ALTRI (1965) *d/co-s* Blasetti *co-s* Cecchi d'Amico, Rossi *w* Lollobrigida, De Sica Mangano, Manfredi, Mastoianni, Caprioli 125min (= *Me, me, Me, . . . and No Others*)
IO LA CONOSCEVO BENE (1965) *d/co-st/co-s* Pietrangeli *des/cos* Chiari *m* Piccioni *w* Manfredi, Brialy 115min Pat (⇌ *I Knew Her Well*)
I PASSED FOR WHITE (1960) *d* F Wilcox *c* Folsey 93min WB
IPCRESS FILE, THE (1965) *d* Furie *p* Saltzman *fn Len Deighton c* Heller *des* Adam *m* Barry *w* Caine *109min JAR
IPPON GATANA DOHYOIRI (1934) *d/s* Kinugasa (= *Sword and the Sumo Ring, A*)
IRAN (1971) *d* Lelouch *18min
I.R.A.S. (1966) *d* Gregoretti TV
IRELAND, THE TEAR AND THE SMILE (1960) *d* W Van Dyke 60min
I REMEMBER MAMA (1948) *d/co-p* G Stevens *ad John van Druten c* Musuraca *w* I Dunne 134min RKO
IRENE (1940) *d* J Wilcox *c* Metty *e* Elmo Williams *w* Milland, Neagle 101min RKO
IRIS (1916) *d/p/c* Hepworth 5600ft
Iris and the Lieutenant = IRIS OCH LÖJTNANTSHJÄRTA (1946)
IRISH EYES ARE SMILING (1944) *d* Ratoff *p Damon Runyon co-a* Wheeler *w* Quinn 90min Fox
IRISH IN US, THE (1935) *d* Bacon *w* Cagney, De Havilland 84min WB
IRIS OCH LÖJTNANTSHJÄRTA (1946) *d/s* Sjöberg *w* Kjell in, Zetterling 80min SF (= *Iris and the Lieutenant*)
IRMA LA DOUCE (1963) *d/p/co-s* B Wilder *co-as-p/co-s* Diamond *c* La Shelle *a* Trauner *m* Previn *w* Lemmon, MacLaine PV* 147min *co-pc* Mir *r* UA
IRON CLAW, THE (1916) *d Edward José w* White (serial in 20 eps) Pat
Iron Crown, The (UK) = CORONA DI FERRO (1941)
IRON CURTAIN, THE (1948) *d* Wellman *p* S Siegel *c* C Clarke *co-a* Wheeler *fm* Prokofiev *w* D Andrews, Tierney 87min Fox
IRON DUKE, THE (1934) *d* Saville *c* Courant *w* G Arliss, Emlyn Williams 88min Gau
IRON GLOVE, THE (1959) *d* Castle *p* Katzman *w* Stack *77min Col
IRON HORSE, THE (1924) *d* J Ford *co-c* Guffey *m* Rapee *w* G O'Brien 11335ft Fox
IRONIE DU DESTIN, L' (1923) *d/s/w* Kirsanov 5600ft
IRON MAJOR, THE (1943) *d* Enright *e* Wise *w* Ryan 85min RKO
IRON MAN, THE (1931) *d/p* Browning *fst* Burnett *w* Ayres, Harlow 73min U
IRON MAN (1951) *d* Pevney *p* A Rosenberg *co-s* B Chase *fst* Burnett *w* J Chandler, Hudson 82min U
IRON MASK, THE (1929) *d* Dwan *p* Fairbanks Sr *co-s* Fairbanks Sr (*ps* Elton Thomas) *fn* (*Trois Mousquetaires, Vingt Ans Après, L'Homme au Masque de Fer*) *Alexandre Dumas Père a* Menzies *w* Fairbanks Sr, (Parrish) 8659ft (silent) 8855ft (with spoken prologue and epilogue)
IRON MISTRESS, THE (1952) *d* G Douglas *p* Blanke *s* J R Webb *m* M Steiner *c* J Seitz *w* V Mayo, Ladd, Kjellin *110min WB
IRON PETTICOAT, THE (1956) *d* Thomas *st/s* B Hecht *p* Woolf Bros *w* K Hepburn, Hope VV* 87min MGM
IRONSIDE (1970) *d* Weis *w* Burr 60min TV
IRON STRAIN, THE (1915) *d* Reginald Barker *p/Supn* Ince Tri
Irony of Fate, The (UK) = IRONIE DU DESTIN, L' (1923)
IROQUOIS TRAIL, THE (1950) *d* Karlson 85min *r* UA
Irresistible (UK) = BELLE MA POVERE (1957)
Irrésistible rebelle L' = IDEE A L'EAU, UNE (1939)
ISADORA (1968) *d* Reisz *m* Jarre *w* V Redgrave PV* 138min U (= *The Loves of Isadora*)
I SAW WHAT YOU DID (1965) *d/p* Castle *c* Biroc *w* J Crawford 82min U
ISCHIA OPERAZIONE AMORE (1966) *d/co-s* Sala *co-s* De Santis *
I SEE A DARK STRANGER (1946) *d/co-s* Launder *p/co-s* Gilliat *w* Kerr, T Howard 112min (= *The Adventuress*)
I SELL ANYTHING (1934) *d* Florey *w* P O'Brien 71min WB
IS EVERYBODY HAPPY? (1929) *d* A Mayo 7394ft WB
I Shall Return (UK) = AMERICAN GUERRILLA IN THE PHILIPPINES (1950)
Ishimatsu Of The Forest = MORI NO ISHIMATSU (1949)
ISHINAKA SENSEI GYOJOKI (1950) *d* Naruse *w* Mifune (= *Conduct Report On Professor Ishinaku*)
I SHOT JESSE JAMES (1948) *d/s* Fuller 81min
ISLA DE LA PASION, LA (1941) *d/st/s* W Fernandez *w* Armendariz
Island, The = HADAKA NO SHIMA (1960)
Island, The = ÖN (1964 *r* 1966)
ISLAND IN THE SKY (1953) *d* Wellman *c* Stout *m* Friedhofer *w* J Wayne, Nolan 109min WB
ISLAND IN THE SUN (1957) *d* Rossen *p* Zanuck *c* F Young *m* M Arnold *w* Mason, Fontaine, Boyd CS* 119min Fox
Island of Desire = SATURDAY ISLAND (1951)
ISLAND OF LOST SOULS, THE (1933) *d Erle C Kenton fn H G Wells c* Struss *w* Laughton, Lugosi 70min Par
ISLAND OF LOST WOMEN (1958) *d* Tuttle 66min
ISLAND OF LOVE (1963) *d/p* Da Costa *c* Stradling *m* Duning *w* Preston, Matthau, Randall PV* 101min WB
Island of Naked Scandal = SHIMA NO RATAI JIKEN (1931)
Island of Shame = THE YOUNG ONE (1960)
ISLAND OF TERROR (1966) *d* Fisher *89min
ISLAND PEOPLE (1940) *d* P Leacock, Rotha sh
ISLANDS OF THE SEA (1959) *co-c* C Hall *28min *pc* Disney
Islands on the Lagoon = ISOLE DELLA LAGUNA (1947)
ISLAS MARIAS (1950) *d* Fernandez *c* Figueroa
The Isle of Death = SOROKH PERVYI (1927)
ISLE OF FORGOTTEN SINS (1943) *d/co-st* Ulmer *w* Carradine 83min
ISLE OF FORGOTTEN WOMEN (1927) *d* G Seitz *p* Cohn *st* Parsons *c* J Walker 5645ft Col
ISLE OF FURY (1936) *d* Frank McDonald *fn* (*Three in Eden*) *S Maugham w* Bogart 60min WB
ISLE OF LOST SHIPS, THE (1923) *d/p* M Tourneur 8rs FN
ISLE OF MISSING MEN (1947) *d* R Oswald *w* Roland 5904ft Mon
ISLE OF PINGO PONGO, THE (1938) *d* Avery 1rl WB
Isle of Sinners (UK) = DIEU A BESION DES HOMMES (1950)
ISLE OF THE DEAD (1945) *d* Robson *p* Lewton *m* Harline *w* Karloff 72min RKO
Isle of the Lion = OROSZLAN UGRANI KESKUL, AZ (1969)
IS MATRIMONY A FAILURE? (1922) *d* Cruze 6rs FPL
ISN'T IT ROMANTIC (1948) *d* McLeod *c* Lindon *w* Lake 67min Par
ISN'T LIFE WONDERFUL (1924) *d* Griffith 9rs UA
ISOLA, L' (1968) *d/co-s* Vancini
ISOLA DI ARTURO, L' (1962) *d/co-s* Damiani *co-p* Ponti *co-s* Zavattini *m* Rota 102min (= *Arturo's Island*)
ISOLE DELLA LAGUNA (1947) *d/s* Emmer, *Enrico Gras* 377m (= *Islands on the Lagoon*)
ISOLE DI FUOCO (1954) *d/c/e* De Seta
I SOM HÅR INTRÅDEN (1945) *d* Mattsson *w* Bjornstrand (= *You who are about to Enter*)
ISPANIYA (1939) *d/e* Shub *co-c* Karmen 2090m (= *Spain*)
Is Paris Burning? (1966) = PARIS BRÛLE-T-IL?
I SPY (1934) *d* Dwan 62min (= *The Morning After*)
ISTANBUL (1956) *d* Pevney *co-s/st/c* S Miller *c* Daniels *w* Flynn CS* 94min U
I Stand Condemned (US) = MOSCOW NIGHTS (1936)
I STOLE A MILLION (1939) *d* Tuttle *s Nathaniel West c* Krasner *w* Raft, Trevor 80min U
ISTORIYA GRAZHDANKOI VOINY (1922) *d/s/e* Vertov 13rs (approx 3900m) (= *History of the Civil War*)
ISTRUTTORIA, L' (1914) *d/s* Guazzoni
ISU (1962) *d* Kuri anim 10min (= *The Chair*)
I Survived Certain Death = PREZIL JSEM SUOU SMRT (1960)
IS YOUR HONEYMOON REALLY NECESSARY (1953) *d* Elvey 79min
IT (1927) *d/co-p* Badger *co-p/fn/ad Elinor Glyn w* Bow, G Cooper 6452ft Par
I TAKE THIS WOMAN (1940) *d* WS Van Dyke *st* MacArthur *c* Rosson *a* Gibbons *w* Lamarr, Tracy 97min MGM
ITALIA 61 (1961) *d* Lenica anim
ITALIAN BARBER, THE (1911) *d* Griffith *w* Pickford, Sennett 1rl Bio
Italian Brigands (UK) = BRIGANTE, IL (1961)
ITALIANE E L'AMORE, LE (1961) *overall d/idea* Zavattini 100min (= *Latin Lovers*)

ep L'EDUCAZIONE SESSUALE DEI FIGLI d/s Lorenzo Mazzetti (= *Children*)

ep LE ADOLESCENTI E L'AMORE d Maselli (= *Adolescents*)

ep LA SFREGIATA d Nelli (= *The Slasher*)

ep LA PROVA D'AMORE d Baldi (= *Proof of Love*)

ep LE RAGAZZE-MADRI d Nelo Risi

ep IL MATRIMONIO ASSURDO d Carlo Musso (= *Marriage*)

ep LA PRIMA NOTTE d Giulio Questi (= *Honeymoon*)

ep LA FRENESIA DEL SUCCESSO d Guilio Macchi (= *Success*)

ep L'INFIDELTA CONIUGALE d/s Ferreri c Gatti (= *The Adultress*)

ep LA SEPERAZIONE LEGALE d/co-s Vancini

ep LA VEDOVA BIANCA d Mingozzi

ITALIANO, BRAVA GENTE (1964) d/co-s De Santis w A Kennedy CS 150min (= *They Went To Vostok/Oni Shli na Vostok*)

ITALIANO IN AMERICA, UN (1968) d/co-st/co-s Sordi m Piccioni w Sordi, De Sica *118min

ITALIA NON E'UN PAESE POVERO, L' (1959) d/co-s/co-a Ivens 135min TV

ITALIAN SECRET SERVICE (1967) d Comencini w Manfredi *105min

Italian Straw Hat, The = CHAPEAU DE PAILLE D'ITALIE (1927)

ITALIA PICCOLA (1957) d/co-s Soldati S*

IT ALL CAME TRUE (1940) d Lewis Seiler co-p Wallis as-p Hellinger c E Haller w Bogart, Pitts, Sheridan 97min WB

IT ALWAYS RAINS ON SUNDAY (1948) d/co-s Hamer p Balcon as-p/co-s Cornelius c Slocombe m Auric 92min

IT CAME FROM OUTER SPACE (1953) d J Arnold fst Bradbury co-a Boyle w Rush 3D 80min U

IT CAN BE DONE (1929) d Newmayer 6560ft (m & sd eff added) U

IT CONQUERED THE WORLD (1956) d/p Corman 68min

ITEL A BALATON (1932) d Fejos co-a Marley 66min

IT GROWS ON TREES (1952) d Arthur Lubin w I Dunne 84min U

IT HAD TO BE YOU (1947) co-d/co-p Don Hartman co-d/co-c Maté s Panama m Frank w G Rogers, Wilde 98min Col

IT HAD TO HAPPEN (1936) d Del Ruth p Zanuck c Marley w Raft, R Russell 79min Fox

It Happened All Night = AFFAIRE D'UNE NUIT, L' (1960)

It Happened at the Inn = GOUPI MAINS-ROUGES (1943)

IT HAPPENED IN ATHENS (1962) d Marton c Courant w Mansfield CS* 92min Fox

IT HAPPENED IN NEW YORK (1935) d Crosland co-s S Miller 75min U

IT HAPPENED IN PARIS (1935) d C Reed, Robert Wyler 6120ft

It Happened in Rome (UK) = SOUVENIR D'ITALIE (1957)

It Happened in Tokyo = KAWA NO ARU SHITAMACHI NO HANSHI (1955)

IT HAPPENED ONE DAY (1934) d C Chase (as Parrott), Eddie Dunn p Roach w C Chase 2 rs MGM

IT HAPPENED ONE NIGHT (1934) d Capra s Riskin c J Walker w Gable, Colbert 105min Col

IT HAPPENED ON FIFTH AVENUE (1947) d/p Del Ruth w C Ruggles 115min AA

IT HAPPENED TO JANE (1959) d/p Quine c Lawton m Duning w D Day, Lemmon *98min Col (= *That Jane from Maine*)

IT HAPPENED TOMORROW (1944) d/co-s/co-di Clair co-s/co-di D Nichols c Stout technical adviser Schuftan w D Powell, Darnell 85min UA

It Happened Yesterday = HISTORIA WSPOLCZESNA (1960)

IT HAPPENS EVERY SPRING (1949) d Bacon p Perlberg co-a Wheeler c Joe MacDonald m Harline w Milland, P Douglas, Peters 89min Fox

IT HAPPENS EVERY THURSDAY (1953) d Pevney c Metty w L Young, Darwell 80min U

Itinerant Actor, An = TABIUAKUSHA (1940)

ITIVATALNOK URAK (1918) d Balasz

ITOSHINO WAGAKO (1926) d/s Gosho (= *My Beloved Child*)

IT PAYS TO ADVERTISE (1919) d Crisp 5rs FPL

IT PAYS TO ADVERTISE (1931) d Tuttle c Stout w Lombard, L Brooks, Foster 75min Par

It Rains On Our Love = DET REGNAR PÅ VÅR KÅRLEK (1946)

IT'S A BIG COUNTRY (1951) d Thorpe, J Sturges, Weis, Wellman, C Brown co-st Schary co-s Wells c Vidor, J Alton, June, Mellor co-a Gibbons co-m Kaper, Raksin w E Barrymore, March, Gene Kelly, G Murphy, V Johnson, J Leigh, W Powell, G Cooper 88min MGM

IT'S A CRIME (1957) d Koenig anim 13min

IT'S A CINCH (1932) d Arbuckle (ps William Goodrich) 20min

IT'S A DATE (1940) d William A Seiter p Pasternak s Krasna w K Francis, Pidgeon, Durbin 103min U

It's A Dog's Life = VITA DA CANI (1950)

IT'S A GIFT (1934) d McLeod st Fields (ps Charles Bogle) w Fields 7rs Par

IT'S A GREAT FEELING (1949) d D Butler st Diamond co-s Shavelson w D Day, G Cooper, Bogart, Flynn, Kaye, Neal, Reagan, Robinson, Wyman 84min WB

IT'S A GREAT LIFE (1929) d S Wood c Marley a Gibbons part *95min MGM

IT'S A GREAT LIFE (1935) d Cline p Zukor c B Reynolds, co-songs Hollander 64min Par

IT'S ALL TRUE (1942, uf) d/p Welles w Duarte

IT'S ALL YOURS (1937) d E Nugent p Perlberg w Carroll 80min Col

IT'S ALWAYS FAIR WEATHER (1955) co-d Donen co-d/chor Gene Kelly p Freed st/s/ly Comdon, A Green, C Bronner co-a Gibbons m Previn w Gene Kelly, Charisse, Dailey, Kidd S* 101min MGM

IT'S A MAD, MAD, MAD, MAD WORLD (1963) d/p Kramer c Laszlo cr Bass m Gold w Tracy, Rooney, Horton, Pitts, Keaton PV 70* 192min r UA

IT'S A SMALL WORLD (1950) d/co-s Castle, Struss EL 74min

IT'S A WISE CHILD (1931) d/co-p Leonard co-p/w Davies 83min MGM

IT'S A WONDERFUL LIFE (1947) d/p/co-s Capra co-s Goodrich, Hackett, M Wilson, Swerling c J Walker, Biroc m Tiomkin w J Stewart, D Reed, L Barrymore, Grahame 129min r RKO

IT'S A WONDERFUL WORLD (1939) d WS Van Dyke co-st H Mankiewicz s/co-st B Hecht w Colbert, J Stewart 86min MGM

IT'S HARD TO RECOGNISE A PRINCESS (1966) d Pojar anim NFBC

It's Hot In Hell = SINGE EN HIVER, UN (1962)

IT SHOULD HAPPEN TO YOU (1954) d Cukor p Kohlmar s Kanin c C Lang m Hollander w Holliday, Lawford, Lemmon, Constance Bennett 86min Col

IT'S IN THE BAG (1945) d Richard Wallace co-s Reville c Metty w Benny, Bendix, Benchley 90min r UA

IT'S LOVE AGAIN (1936) d Saville w R Young 84min Gau

IT'S LOVE I'M AFTER (1937) d A Mayo p Wallis w B Davies, De Havilland, L Howard 90min WB

It's Magic (UK) = ROMANCE IN THE HIGH SEAS

It's My Life (UK) = VIVRE SA VIE (1962)

IT'S ONLY MONEY (1962) d/co-s Tashlin (uc) co-a Pereira w J Lewis 84min co-pc J Lewis r Par

IT STARTED IN NAPLES (1960) d/co-s Shavelson c Surtees co-a Pereira w Gable, Loren, De Sica VV* 100min Par

IT STARTED IN PARADISE (1952) d Compton Bennett w Kendall 94min BL (= *Fanfare For Figleaves*)

It Started in Tokyo (B) = TWENTY PLUS TWO (1961)

IT STARTED WITH A KISS (1959) d G Marshall p A Rosenberg s Lederer c Bronner w G Ford, D Reynolds CS* 104min MGM

IT STARTED WITH EVE (1941) d Koster p Pasternak co-s Krasna c Maté w Durbin, Laughton, R Cummings 90min U

IT'S THE OLD ARMY GAME (1926) d/p Edward Sutherland w Fields, L Brooks 6889ft FPL r Par

IT'S TRAD, DAD (1962) d Lester c G Taylor 73min r Col (= *Ring-a-Ding Rhythm* (US))

IT'S UP TO YOU (1941) d Kazan approx 120min US Dept of Agriculture

ITSWARERU SEISO (1951) d Yoshimura s Shindo (= *Clothes of Deception/Under Silk Garments*)

IT'S WHAT'S HAPPENING (1967) d Silverstein ex-p Spiegel c Lathrop des R Day w Quinn, Dunaway, R Walker 1101m Col (= *The Happening*)

ITTO (1934) d Benoît-Levy, Marie Epstein c Agostini

IVAN (1932) d/s Dovzhenko 2800m

IVAN GROZNYI (I) (1944) d/s Eisenstein c Tissé (exteriors), Moskvin (interiors) m Prokofiev w Cherkassov, Pudovkin 100min 2745m (= *Ivan The Terrible; Part I*)

IVAN GROZNYI: BOYARSKII ZAGOVOR (1945 r 1958) d/s Eisenstein c Tisse (exteriors), Moskvin (interiors & colour sequences) m Prokofiev w Cherkassov part *88min 2373m (= *Ivan The Terrible (Part II): The Boyars Plot*)

IVANHOE (1913) d Brenon fn Sir Walter Scott 600ft

IVANHOE (1952) d Thorpe 2nd d Canutt p Berman fn Sir Walter Scott c F Young co-a Furse w R Taylor, E Taylor, Fontaine, G Sanders, Emlyn Williams *107min MGM

IVAN IL TERRIBILE (1915) d Guazzoni

Ivan the Terrible (Part I) = IVAN GROZNYI (1944)

Ivan The Terrible (Part II): The Boyars Plot = IVAN GROZNYI: BOYARSKII ZAGOVOR (1945 r 1958)

I'VE ALWAYS LOVED YOU (1946) d Borzage s/fst (Concerto) B Chase c Gaudio w Ouspenskaya *68min Rep

I'VE GOT YOUR NUMBER (1934) d Enright w Blondell 68min WB

I, VOR PITTFALKS (1967) d Williams

Ivory Hunter = WHERE NO VULTURES FLY (1951)

IVORY SNUFF BOX, THE (1915) d M Tourneur

IVY (1947) d S Wood p Menzies s Charles Bennett c Metty m Amfitheatrof w Fontaine, H Marshall 99min U

IVY AND JOHN (1965) d Warhol 16mm 35min

I WAKE UP SCREAMING (1941) d Bruce Humberstone p Sperling c Cronjager w Cook, Mature, Grable 82min Fox

I WALK ALONE (1947) d Haskin p Wallis s Schnee co-a Dreier w Lancaster, K Douglas, L Scott, Carey 98min Par

I WALKED WITH A ZOMBIE (1943) d J Tourneur p Lewton e Robson 68min RKO

I WALK THE LINE (1971) d Frankenheimer songs Johnny Cash w Peck, Weld, Meeker PV* 96min co-pc Frankenheimer r Col

I WANTED WINGS (1941) d Leisen co-s Maibaum co-a Dreier w Milland, Holden, Wayne, Lake, Hopper 131min Par

I WANT TO LIVE (1958) d Wise p Wanger c Lindon w S Hayward 120min pc J Mankiewicz r UA

I WANT YOU (1951) d Robson p Goldwyn c Stradling m Harline w D Andrews, F Granger, McGuire 102min RKO

I WAS A COMMUNIST FOR THE FBI (1952) d G Douglas 82min WB

I Was A Criminal = CAPTAIN OF KOEPENICK, THE (1942)

I Was A Fireman = FIRES WERE STARTED (1943)

I WAS A MALE WAR BRIDE (1949) d Hawks p S Siegel co-s Brodine co-a Wheeler m Mockridge w C Grant, Sheridan 105min Fox (= *You Can't Sleep Here*)

I WAS AN ADVENTURESS (1940) d Ratoff as-p N Johnson co-s J O'Hara c Cronjager, Shamroy w Von Stroheim, Lorre 81min Fox

I WAS A SPY (1933) d Saville p Balcon w Veidt w H Marshall, Veidt, Carroll 89min Gau

I Was Born, But ... = UMARETE WA MITA KEREDO (1932)

I WAS HAPPY HERE (1965) d/co-s D Davis st/co-s Edna O'Brien 91min r JAR (= *Time Lost And Time Remembered*)

IWASHIGUMO (1958) d Naruse S* 130min Toho (= *The Summer Clouds*)

I WAS MONTY'S DOUBLE (1958) d Guillermin s Forbes w J Mills, Forbes 100min r ABC

I WONDER WHO'S KISSING HER NOW? (1947) d Bacon co-a R Day m A Newman 105min Fox

IZUMI (1956) d Kobayashi (= *The Fountainhead*)

IZU NO MUSUMETACHI (1945) d Gosho (= *Girls Of Izu, The*)

IZU NO ODORIKO (1933) d Gosho (= *Dancing Girls of Izu*)

J'UCCUSE! (1918) d/s Gance co-c Burel w (Blaise Cendrars) 7000ft Pat

J'ACCUSE (1937) d/s Gance rm 1918 104min (= *That They May Live*)

JACK AND THE BEANSTALK (1952) d Jean Yarbrough w B Abbott, Costello *78min r WB

JACK AND THE BEANSTALK (1955) d Reiniger anim* 10min (= *Jack the Giant Killer*)

JACKASS MAIL (1941) d McLeod w Beery 80min MGM

JACKIE (1921) d J Ford 5 rs Fox

JACK-KNIFE MAN, THE (1919) d/p/cos K Vidor 6rs 60min pc Vidor r FN

JACK LE RAMONEUR (1906) d Méliès 33m (25 parts)

JACK LONDON (1943) d Santell w Hayward, V Mayo 94min pc Bronston r UA

JACKPOT, THE (1950) d W Lang c La Shelle co-a Wheeler w J Stewart, N Wood 85min Fox

Jack the Giant Killer = JACK AND THE BEANSTALK (1955)

JACOBS STEGE (1942) d Molander c Fischer SF

JACQUELINE (1956) d R Baker 92min JAR

Jacques Callot, Correspondant de Guerre = GUERRE EN DETELLES, LA (1952)

JA, DER HIMMEL UBER WIEN (1930) w Rainer

JAG AR NYFIKEN, BLA (1968) d/s Sjöman 103min (= *I am Curious, Blue*)

JAG AR NYFIKEN, GUL (1967) d/s Sjöman 110min San (= *I am Curious, Yellow*)

JAGD NACH DEM GLUCK, DIE (1930) d/co-s Rochus Gliese co-s/co-anim Reiniger co-anim Bartosch 96min

JAGIRDAR (1937) d Mehboob

JAGUAR (1967) d/s Rouch 16mm *110min

JAGUAR'S CLAWS, THE (1917) d Neilan 5rs

JAHRE VERGEHEN, DIE (1945) d Rittau 82min Tob (= *Der Senator*)

JAIL BAIT (1937) d Charles Lamont w Keaton 2rs

Jailbirds = PARDON US (1931)

Jail Break (UK) = A CAVALLO DELLA TIGRE (1961)

JAILHOUSE ROCK (1957) d Thorpe p Berman c Bronner w Presley 97min MGM

J'AI QUELQUE CHOSE A VOUS DIRE (1930) d M Allégret

J'AI TANT DANSE (1944) d Dunning

J'AI TUE RASPOUTINE (1967) d/s/w Hossein FS* 100min

Ja, Ja Mein General! But Which Way to the Front? (UK) = WHICH WAY TO THE FRONT? (1970)

JAJE (1959) d/s Mimica anim* 11min (= *The Egg*)

JAK BYC KOCHANA (1963) d Has w Cybulski 100min (= *How to be Loved*)

JAK SE CLOVEK NAUCIL LETAT (1958) d Brdecka (= *A Comic History of Aviation*)

JAK SI ZARIDAT BYT (1960) d Pojar anim (= *How to Furnish a Flat*)

JAK STARECEK MENIL AZ VYMENIL (1952) d/a Trnka

anim* 255m (= *How Grandpa changed till Nothing Was Left*)

Ja-Kuba = O SOY CUBA (1964)

JALNA (1935) *d* Cromwell *p* Macgowan *c* Cronjagger 77min RKO

JALOUSIE DE BARBOUILLE, LA (1929) *d/s/e/dec* Cavalcanti

JALSAGHAR (1958) *d/s* S Ray *c* Mitra *m Ustad Vilayat Khan* 100min *pc* Ray (= *The Music Room*)

JAMAICA INN (1939) *d* Hitchcock *co-p* Pommer, Laughton *fn Daphne du Maurier co-s* Gilliat, Priestley *e* Hamer *w* Laughton, M O'Hara, Newton, Emlyn Williams 108min

James Brothers, The (UK) = THE TRUE STORY OF JESSE JAMES (1957)

JAMES DEAN STORY, THE (1957) *d/p/e Robert Altman, George W George st/s* Stern *m* Leith Stevens *w* Dean 82min *r* WB

JAMESTOWN BALOOS (1957) *d* Breer anim 16mm *6min

JAM-MAKING (1906) *p* Paul 230ft

JANE (1963) *d Hope Ryden p* R Leacock, Drew *w* J Fonda 50min

JANE EYRE (1944) *d/co-s* Stevenson *p* Goetz *co-s Aldous Huxley,* Houseman *fn Charlotte Bronte c* Barnes *w* Welles, Fontaine, Moorehead, M O'Brien, E Taylor 96min Fox

JANE EYRE (1971) *d* Delbert Mann *fn* Bronte *w* G Scott, Hawkins *110min *r* BL

JAN HUS (1954) *d/co-s* Vavra*

JANICE MEREDITH (1925) *d E Mason Hopper co-c* Barnes *w* Davies, Power, Fields 10655ft *pc* Hearst *r* MGM

JANIE (1944) *d* Curtiz 106min WB

JANOSIK (1936) *d/co-s* Frič

Janus Faced (UK) = JANUSKOPF (1920)

JANUSKOPF, DER (1920) *d* Murnau *co-c* Freund *a* Richter *w* Veidt, Lugosi 2300m Dec (= *Janus Faced*)

JAN ZIZKA Z TROCNOVA (1955) *d/co-s* Vavra* (= *The Hussite Warrior*)

JAPANESE NIGHTINGALE, A (1918) *d George Fitzmaurice c* AC Miller

Japanese Summer: Double Suicide = MURI SHINJU NIHON NO NATSU (1967)

Japanese Tragedy, A = NIHON NO HIGEKI (1953)

JAPANESE WAR BRIDE (1952) *d* K Vidor *c* Linden *co-m* A Newman 91min Fox

JAPON D'HIER ET D'AUJOURDHUI (1959) *co-d* Kast *13min Pat

JARDIN DE LAS DELICIAS, EL (1970) *d/co-s* Saura *95min (= *Garden of Delights, The*)

JARDINIER D'ARGENTEUIL (1966) *d* Le Chanois *w* Jurgens, Gabin S* 85min (= *Bluten, Gauner und die Nacht von Nizza*)

JARDIN PUBLIC, UN (1955) *d Paul Paviot w* Marceau 17min .

JARDINS DE PARIS, LES (1948, uf) *d/c/e* Resnais *sequence d* Bazin

JASHUMON NO ONNA (1924) *d/s* Kinugasa (= *A Woman's Heresy*)

JAUNE LE SOLEIL (1971) *d/s/fn* (*Abahn, Sabana, David*) *co-e* Duras 16mm 95min

JAWS OF STEEL (1927) *d* Enright 6rs WB

JAYHAWKERS, THE (1959) *d/co-p/co-s* M Frank *co-p* Panama *co-s* Bezzerides *c* Griggs *co-a* Pereira *m* Moross *w* J Chandler VV* 110min *pc* M Frank, Panama *r* Par

JAY WALKER, THE (1956) *d* Cannon anim* 7min *pc* UPA *r* Col

JAZZBOAT (1960) *d/co-s* K Hughes *c* Moore CS 96min *r* Col

JAZZ CHAIR (1960) *d/s* C & R Eames *c* C Eames 6½min

Jazz Comedy = VESYOLYE REBYATA (1934)

JAZZ FOOL, THE (1929) *d* Iwerks *p* Disney anim 1rl

JAZZMANIA (1923) *d/pc* Leonard *st/s* Goulding 8rs Metro

JAZZ SINGER, THE (1927) *d* Crosland *fpl* Raphaelson *c* Mohr *w* Jolson, M Loy 98min WB

JAZZ SINGER, THE (1952) *d* Curtiz *fpl* Raphaelson *107min WB

Jazz Waiter = CAUGHT IN A CABARET (1914)

JEALOUSY (1945) *d/p/co-s* Machaty *st* Trumbo *m* Eisler 71min Rep

Jealousy = SHITTO (1949)

JEAN COTON (1952) *d/s* M Allégret 750m

JEAN DE LA LUNE (1931) *d Jean Choux st/s* Achard *dec* Meerson *w* M Simon 7708ft

JEAN DE LA LUNE (1949) *d/st/s/di* Achard *c* Kelber *m* Van Parys *w* Darieux 94min

JEAN-JACQUES ROUSSEAU (1958) *co-d* Leenhardt, *Jean-Paul Vivet* *20min

JEAN-LUC GODARD (1964) *d* Doniol-Valcroze TV

JEAN MIRO (1948) *d* Aurel sh

JEANNE A ROUEN (1952–53) *d* Enrico TV

JEANNE D'ARC (1900) *d/w* Méliès 275m (12 parts)

Jeanne d'Arc (US) = PASSION DE JEANNE D'ARC, LA (1927)

JEANNE DORE (1916) *d Louis Mercanton w* S Bernhardt

JEANNE EAGELS (1957) *d/p* G Sidney *m* Duning *w* Novak, J Chandler, Moorehead 109min Col

Jean Taris, Champion de Natation = TARIS (1931)

JEDENACTE PRIKAZANI (1935) *d* Fric *c* Heller (= *The Eleventh Commandment*)

Jeder Achte = VOLKSKRANKHEIT KREBS (1940)

JEFFREYS AND RUHLIN SPARRING CONTEST AT SAN FRANCISCO (1901) *d* Porter Ed

JEHANNE (1916) *d* Enrico *580m

JE L'AI ETE TROIS FOIS (1952) *d/s* Guitry *c* Bachelet *w* Guitry, De Funes 83min

JENNY (1936) *d* Carné *co-st/di* J Prévert *co-m* Kosma *w* Rosay, Préjean, Barrault, Vanel

Jenny Lind = LADY'S MORALS, A (1930)

JEOPARDY (1953) *d* J Sturges *co-a* Gibbons *c* Milner *w* Stanwyck, Meeker 69min MGM

JEROME PERREAU, HEROS DES BARRICADES (1936) *d* Gance

Jerusalem Set Free = GERUSALEMME LIBERATA (1957)

Jesien (1956) *d* Borowczyk

JE SEME A TOUT VENT (1952) *d/cos -Kast* 900m

JESSE JAMES (1939) *d* H King *p* Zanuck *as-p/st/s* N Johnson *c* Barnes *w* Power, H Fonda, R Scott, Carradine, Darwell *105min Fox

JESSE JAMES VS THE DALTONS (1953) *d* Castle *p* Katzman *65min Col

JESSICA (1962) *d/p* Negulesco *w* A Dickinson, Chevalier, Moorehead, Dalio, Ferzetti PV* 112min UA

The Jester's Tale = BLAZNOVA KRONIKA (1964)

JE SUIS AVEC TOI (1943) *d* Decoin *w* Fresnay 95min

Je Suis Un Homme = WORLD WITHOUT END (1953)

JE SUIS UN SENTIMENTAL (1955) *d/co-s* John Berry *w* Constantine 97min

JE T'AIME, JE T'AIME (1968) *d/co-ad/co-di* Resnais *co-m Krzysztof Penderecki w* (Robbe-Grillet), (Richard), Doniol Valcroze) 94min

J'ETAIS UNE AVENTURIERE (1938) *w* Feuillère

JETEE, LA (1963) *d/s* Marker *w* Klein 29min

JET OVER THE ATLANTIC (1959) *d* Haskin *p* Bogeaus *w* V Mayo, Raft 91min

JET PILOT (1951 *r* 1957) *co-d* Von Sternberg *co-d(uc)/p/s* Furthman *c* Hoch *m* Kaper *w* J Wayne, J Leigh 112min RKO *r* U

JET STORM (1959) *d/cos* Endfield *c* Hildyard *w* Attenborough, Zetterling 99min BL

JEU I (1962) *d* Reichenbach, *Dirk Sanders*

JEU DE LA VERITE, LE (1961) *d/s/w* Hossein S 92min

JEU DE MASSACRE (1957) *d/s* Jessua *w* Cassel *95min (= *Comic Strip Hero*)

JEUNE FILLE AU JARDIN, LA (1936) *d* Kirsanov 35mm

JEUNE FILLE DE FRANCE (1938) *d* Y Allégret sh

JEUNE FOLLE, LA (1952) *d* Y Allégret *m* Misraki 95min

Jeune Homme, Un = AINE DES FERCHAUX L' (1962)

JEUNE HOMME ET LA MORT, LE (1953) *d/c* Anger *f ballet* Cocteau *chor Roland Petit*

JEUNE PATRIARCHE (1957) *d* Bourguignon *589m

JEUNES FILLES EN DETRESSE (1939) *d* Pabst *w* Presle

JEUNES LOUPS, LES (1968) *d* Carné *111min (= *The Young Wolves*)

JEUNESSES MUSICALES, LES (1956) *d/s* Jutra 44min

JEUNES TIMIDES (1941) *d* Y Allégret (*ps* Champlain) *rm* LES DEUX TIMIDES (1928) *c* Agostini *w* Brasseur, P Prévert 83min (= *Les Deux Timides*)

JEU SI SIMPLE, UN (1964) *d/e* Groulx *30min

JEUVES, MILAGRO, LOS (1957) *co-d/s* Berlanga

JEUX DE L'AMOUR, LES (1959) *d/co-s* De Broca *dec* Saulnier, Evein *m* Delerue *w* Cassel 90min *pc* Chabrol

JEUX D'ENFANTS (1946) *d* Painlevé *m Bizet* 10min

JEUX DES ANGES, LES (1964) *d* Borowczyk anim* 13min

JEUX DES ENFANTS (1947) *c* Fradetal

JEUX INTERDITS (1952) *d/co-s/co-di* Clément *co-s/co-di* Aurenche, Bost 102min (= *Forbidden Games*)

JEUX SONT FAITS, LES (1947) *d/co-s* Delannoy *st/di Jean Paul Sartre c* Matras *m* Auric *w* Pagliero, Presle 91min

JE VOUS AIMERAI TOUJOURS (1933) *d* Decoin

JEWEL IN PAWN (1917) *d* Conway

JEWEL ROBBERY (1932) *d* Dieterle *w* W Powell, F Francis 70min WB

JEZEBEL (1938) *d* Wyler *as-p* Blanke *co-s* J Huston *c* E Haller *m* M Steiner *w* B Davis, H Fonda, Crisp, Pichel 103min WB

JIGGS AND MAGGIE IN COURT (1948) *d* Cline, *William Beaudine co-st/co-s* Cline *c* O'Connell 71min Mon

JIGGS AND MAGGIE IN SOCIETY (1948) *d/co-st/co-s* Cline *c* O'Connell 66min Mon

JIGOKUMON (1953) *d/s* Kinugasa *p* Nagata *w* Kyo *90min Dai (= *Gate of Hell*)

JIHI SHINCHO (1927) *d* Mizoguchi Nik (= *Like the Changing Heart of a Bird*)

Jilted UK) = CLAUDELLE INGLISH (1961)

JIM BLUDSO (1917) *d* Browning Tri

JIMENA (1961) *d* Picazo

JIMMY THE GENT (1934) *d* Curtiz *w* Cagney, B Davis 67min WB

JIM THE CONQUEROR (1927) *d* G Seitz *c* Rosson 5324ft *r* PRC

JIM THORPE – ALL AMERICAN (1951) *d* Curtiz *c* E Haller *m* Steiner *w* Lancaster, Bickford, Cochran 107min WB (= *Man of Bronze*)

JIN KYO (1924) *d* Mizoguchi Nik (= *World Down Here*)

JINGUIGAKU MYUMON (1966) *d/co-s* Imamura *as-p Drs Phyllis and Eberhart Kronhausen* S 128min Nik (= *The Pornographer/An Introduction to Anthropology*)

JINSEI NO ONIMOTSU (1935) *d* Gosho (= *Burden of Life*)

JINSEI O MITSUMETE (1923) *d/s* Kinugasa

JINSEI TOMBOGAERI (1946) *d* Imai Toho (= *Life Is Like A Somersault*)

JINX (1919) *d* Schertzinger *w* Normand 5rs *pc* Goldwyn

JINY VZDUCH (1939) *d* Frič (= *Fresh Air*)

JITNEY ELOPEMENT, THE (1915) *d/s* Chaplin *c* Totheroh *w* Chaplin, Purviance, Bacon 2rs S&A

JITTERBUGS (1943) *d* St Clair *c* Andriot *w* Laurel, Hardy 75min Fox

JIVARO (1954) *d Edward Ludwig c* Lindon *co-a* Pereira *w* Keith, R Fleming *91min Par

JIVE JUNCTION (1943) *d* Ulmer 62min

JIYU GAKKU (1951) *d* Yoshimura (= *School of Freedom*)

Joachim's Dictionary = DICTIONNAIRE DE JOACHIM, LE (1965)

JOAN MIRO (1948) *d* Aurel sh

JOANNA (1925) *d Edwin Carewe w* Del Rio 7762ft *r* FN

JOAN OF ARC (1948) *d* V Fleming *p* Wanger *co-s/fpl* (*Joan of Lorraine*) Maxwell Anderson *co-c* Hoch *a* R Day *m* Friedhofer *montage expert* Vorkapich *w* Ingrid Bergman, J Ferrer 145min RKO

JOAN OF PARIS (1942) *d* Stevenson *c* Metty *w* Henreid, Mitchell, Ladd, Morgan 95min RKO

JOAN THE WOMAN (1916) *d/p* De Mille

JOAQUIN MURRIETA (1938) *d* F Wilcox 1rl MGM

Job, The (UK) = IL POSTO (1961)

Job, The = IL LAVO ep in BOCCACCIO '70 (1962)

JOCONDE, LA (1957) *d/m* Gruel *fst Boris Vian* anim* 16mm (= *Mona Lisa: The Story Of An Obsession*)

JOE HILL (1971) *d/s/e* Widerberg *115min *pc* Widerberg (= *The Ballad of Joe Hill*)

JOE MACBETH (1956) *d* K Hughes *p* Frankovich *s* Yordan *w* P Douglas 90min Col

JOEN (1959) *d/s* Kinugasa (= *Tormented Flame*)

JOEN NO CHIMATA (1922) *d* Mizoguchi Nik (= *Town of Fire*)

JOE PALOOKA IN THE BIG FIGHT (1949) *d* Endfield Mon

JOE SMITH, AMERICAN (1942) *d* Thorpe *fst Paul Gallico c* Lawton *a* Gibbons *w* R Young, Anthony, Gardner MGM

JOFROI (1934) *d/p/s/di* Pagnol 65min

Jôgo Peligroso = JUEGO PELIGROSO (1966)

JOHAN (1921) *co-d* Stiller 2204m SF

JOHAN EKBERG (1964) *d* Troell 21min

JOHANN MOUSE (1952) *d* Hanna, Barbera *p* Quimby anim* 8min MGM

JOHANN THE COFFINMAKER (1927–28) *d/st* Florey *s/co-c/e* Vorkapich *co-c* Toland sh

JOHN AND MARY (1969) *d* P Yates *w* M Farrow PV* 92min *r* Fox

John Doe, Dynamite = MEET JOHN DOE (1941)

JOHN GOLDFARB, PLEASE COME HOME (1964) *d* J Thompson *c* Shamroy *w* MacLaine, Ustinov CS* 96min *r* Fox

JOHN LOVES MARY (1949) *d* D Butler *c* Marley *w* Reagan, Neal 87min WB

JOHNNY ALLEGRO (1949) *d* Tetzlaff *st* F Grant *c* Biroc *w* Raft 81min Col

JOHNNY APOLLO (1940) *d* Hathaway *co-s* P Dunne *c* AC Miller *w* Power, Lamour, Nolan 93min Fox

JOHNNY BANCO (1967) *d/co-s* Y Allégret *c* Kelber *dec* D'Eaubonne *w* Buchholz *95min

JOHNNY BELINDA (1948) *d* Negulesco *p* Wald *c* McCord *e* Weisbart *w* Wyman, Ayres, Bickford, Moorehead 102min WB

JOHNNY COME LATELY (1943) *d* W Howard *c* Sparkuhl *w* Cagney 97min *r* UA (= *Johnny Vagabond*)

JOHNNY COOL (1963) *d/co-p William Asher co-p* Lawford *c* Leavitt *w* Cook 101min *r* UA

JOHNNY DOESN'T LIVE HERE ANYMORE (1944) *d* May *w* S Simon, Mitchum 77min Mon

JOHNNY EAGER (1941) *d* LeRoy *st/co-s* F Grant *co-s* Mahin *c* Rosson *m* Kaper *w* R Taylor, Turner, Heflin 107min MGM

JOHNNY FRENCHMAN (1945) *d* Frend *st/s* Clarke *w* Rosay 11min EL

JOHNNY GET YOUR HAIR CUT (1927) *d* A Mayo, *B Reaves Eason* 6396ft MGM

JOHNNY GOT HIS GUN (1971) *d/s* Trumbo *100min

JOHNNY GUITAR (1954) *d/as-p* N Ray *s* Yordan *c* Stradling *m* V Young *w* J Crawford, Hayden, Borgnine, Carradine(*uc*) *110min Rep

JOHNNY HOLIDAY (1950) *d/co-s* Goldbeck *c* Mohr *m* Waxman *w* Bendix, Carmichael 92min *r* UA

Johnny In the Clouds (US) = WAY TO THE STARS (1945)

JOHNNY O'CLOCK (1947) *d/s* Rossen *c* Guffey *m* Duning *w* D Powell, Cobb, J Chandler 85min Col

JOHNNY ONE EYE (1950) *d* Florey *p* Bogeaus *st Damon Runyon c* Andriot 78min *r* UA

JOHNNY ON THE RUN (1953) *d/p* L Gilbert 68min ABC

JOHNNY STOOL PIGEON (1949) *d* Castle *p* A Rosenberg *w* Duryea, McIntire, Winters, Curtis 75min U

JOHNNY TIGER (1966) *d* Wendkos *w* R Taylor *102min U

JOHNNY TROUBLE (1957) *d/p John H Aver c* Marley *w* E Barrymore 80min *r* WB

Johnny Vagabond (UK) = JOHNNY COME LATELY (1943)

JOHN PAUL JONES (1959) d/co-s Farrow p Bronston c Kelber m Steiner w Stack, C Coburn, B Davis TR* 126min WB

JOHN SMITH WAKES UP (1941) d J Weiss 43min

JOIE DE VIVRE (1934) d Gross, Hector Hoppin anim 10min

JOI-UCHI (1967) d Kobayashi w Mifune, Nakadai S 128min Toho/Mifune (= Rebellion)

Joker, The = LE FARCEUR (1960)

JOKER IS WILD, THE (1957) d C Vidor c Fapp co-a Pereira w Sinatra, M Gaynor, Crain VV* 123min Par

JOKYO (1960) S* 94min Dai (= A Woman's Testament/ Code of Women)
ep d Ichikawa
ep d Yoshimura c Miyagawa w Kyo

YOKYU AISHI (1930) d Gosho (= Sad Story Of A Bar-maid)

JOLANDA, LA FIGLIA DEL CORSARO NERO (1952) d Soldati m Rota pc Ponti, De Laurentiis

JOLIFOU INN (1955) d Low *11min NFBC

JOLI MAI, LE (1963) d/cy Marker m Legrand n Montand 180min (English version: n Signoret)

JOLLY BAD FELLOW, A (1963) d Don Chaffey p Balcon s Hamer m Barry 96min

JOLLY, CLOWN DA CIRCO (1923) d/co-s Camerini st Genina

Jolly Fellows, The = VESYOLYEREBYATA (1939)

JOLLY JILTER, THE (1927) d Cline co-s Sennett w Turpin

JOLSON SINGS AGAIN (1949) d Levin w Larry Parks 96min r Col

JOLSON STORY, THE (1946) d Alfred E Green, JH Lewis c J Walker chor Cole *128min Col

JONES FAMILY IN HOLLYWOOD, THE (1939) d St Clair co-st Keaton 60min Fox

JONES FAMILY IN QUICK MILLIONS, THE (1939) d St Clair co-st Keaton 61min Fox

JONETSU NO ICHIYA (1929) d/s Gosho (= One Night of Passion)

JORDAN IS A HARD ROAD (1915) d/s Dwan p Griffith w D Gish 5rs r Tri

JOSEF DRENTERS (1960) d A King 16mm 30min

JOSEI NI KANSURU JUNISHO (1954) d Ichikawa Toho (= Twelve Chapters About Women)

JOSEI NO SHORI (1946) d Mizoguchi Sho (= Women's Victory)

JOSEI WAT SUYOSHI (1924) d Mizoguchi Nik (= Women are Strong)

JOSELYN'S WIFE (1926) d Thorpe

Joseph and His Brethren = GIUSEPPE VENDUTTO DAI FRATELLI (1960)

JOSEPH MANES (1952) d Pojar (in 2 parts)

JOSEPHINE AND MEN (1955) d R Boulting p J Boulting c G Taylor w Finch *98min BL

JOSE TORRES (1959) d Teshigahara w Jose Torres 54min

JOSETTE (1938) d Dwan s J Grant w S Simon R Young 73min Fox

JOSHUA, A NIGERIAN PORTRAIT (1962) d A King 16mm 57min

JOUETS ANIMES, LES (1912) d Cohl anim

JOUEUR, LE (1958) d Autant-Lara co-s/co-di Aurenche, Bost fn Fyodor Dostoievski w Philipe, Rosay, Carette *105min

JOUR COMME LES AUTRES, UN (1952) d Rouquier 680m

JOUR DE FETE (1947) d/co-st/co-di/w Tati 70min

JOUR DU FROTTEUR, LE (1932) d/s/e Cavalcanti

JOUR ET L'HEURE, LE (1963) d/co-ad Clément c Cecaë dec Evein w Signoret, Piccoli S 110min MGM

JOURNAL D'UN CURE DE CAMPAGNE, LE (1950) d/s Bresson fn Georges Bernanos c Burel 120min (= Diary of a Country Priest)

Journal d'une Femme de Chambre, Le (1946) = THE DIARY OF A CHAMBERMAID

JOURNAL D'UNE FEMME DE CHAMBRE, LE (1964) d/co-s Bunuel fn Octave Mirbeau dec Wakhevitch w Moreau, Piccoli FS 95min (= Diary of a Chamber-maid)

JOURNAL D'UNE FEMME EN BLANC, LE (1965) d Autant-Lara co-s/co-di Aurenche c Kelber 110min Gau

JOURNAL D'UN SCELERAT (1950) d/s/e Rohmer 16mm sh

Journalist = VASHA ZNAKOMAYA (1927)

Journalist, The = ZHURNALIST (1967)

JOURNAL ANIME, LE (1908) d Cohl anim 78m

JOURNAL OF A CRIME (1934) d Keighley c E Haller w Menjou, Darwell, Pidgeon 66min FN

Journal of The Orange Flower = KARATACHI NIKKI (1959)

JOURNEE NATURELLE (1947) d Resnais 16mm * sh (= Visite a Max Ernst)

Journey Out = RESAN BORT (1945)

JOURNEY TO JERUSALEM, A (1968) d Michael Mindlin co-c A and D Maysles, R Leacock w Leonard Bernstein *84min

JOURNEY, THE (1958) d/p Litvak c Hildyard w Brynner, Kerr, G Marshall, Aimée 127min MGM (= Some of Us May Die)

JOURNEY FOR MARGARET (1942) d WS Van Dyke p Schary c June a Gibbons m Waxman w M O'Brien, R Young 81min MGM

Journey into Autumn = KVINNODROM (1955)

JOURNEY INTO FEAR (1943) d Foster, Welles(uc) p/co-s (uc) Welles co-s Cotten c Struss e Robson w Welles, Cotten, Del Rio, Moorehead 69min RKO

JOURNEY INTO LIGHT (1951) d Heisler w Hayden, Darwell, Mitchell, Lindfors 87min Fox

JOURNEY INTO MEDICINE (1946) d W Van Dyke c B Kaufman 30min

Journey into Primeval times = CESTA DO PRAVEKO (1954)

Journey Round My Skull = UTAZAS A KOPONYAM KORUL (1970)

JOURNEY'S END (1930) d Whale 130min

JOURNEY TOGETHER (1945) d/s J Boulting fst Rattigan w Attenborough, Robinson 95min

JOURNEY TO THE CENTER OF THE EARTH (1959) d Levin p/co-s Brackett fn Jules Verne co-a Wheeler m Herrmann w Mason CS* 132min Fox

Journey to the Lost City (US) = DER TIGER VON ESCHNAPUR and DAS INDISCHE GRABMAL (1959) 95min version

JOURS DU FETE A MOSCOU (1957) d Valère

JOUR SE LEVE, LE (1939) d Carné di J Prévert c Courant dec Trauner m Jaubert w Gabin, Arletty, Jules Berry (= Daybreak)

JOVANKA É L'ALTRI (1960) d Ritt p De Lautentiis c Rotunno dec Chiari w Moreau, Heflin, Miles, Mangano, Germi 106min Par (= Five Branded Women)

Joven, La = THE YOUNG ONE (1960)

JOVENES, LOS (1961) d/st/s/ad Alcoriza 95min (= The Young Ones)

JOYEUX MICROBES, LES (1909) d Cohl anim 102m

JOY GIRL, THE (1927) d/p Dwan w Dressler 5877ft Fox

Joy House = LES FELINS (1964)

JOY OF LIVING (1938) d Garnett c J Walker m Jerome Kern w I Dunne, Fairbanks Jr 90min RKO

JOYU (1947) d/s Kinugasa wYamada (= Actress)

JOYU SUMAKO NO KOI (1947) d Mizoguchi Sho (= Love of Actress Sumako)

JOYU TO SHINJI (1935) d Naruse (= The Actress and the Poet)

JUAREZ (1939) d Dieterle d/di Rapper p Wallis as-p Blanke co-s J Huston c Gaudio m Korngold w Muni, B Davis, Rains, Crisp, Garfield, Roland, Pichel 132min WB

JUBAL (1956) d Davies c Lawton co-m Rakson w G Ford, Borgnine, Steiger CS* 100min Col

Jubilation Street = KANKO NO MACHI (1944)

JUBILEE (1897) p Paul

Jubilee = YUBILEI (1944)

JUBILEJ G IKLA (1955) d Mimica (= Mr Ikle's Jubilee)

JUBILA (1919) d Badger 6rs pc Goldwyn

JUDASPENGAR (1915) d Sjöström 799m (= Judas-pengene)

Judas Pengene (= JUDAS PENGAR (1915)

Judas was a Women = HUMAINE BETE, LA (1938)

JUDEX (1916) d/co-s Feuillade 1 L'Ombre Mysterieuse 1262m; 2 L'Expiation 660m; 3 La Meute Fantastique 762m; 4 Le Secret De La Tombe 488m; 5 Le Moulin Tragique 742m; 6 Le Môme Régliss 816m; 7 La Femme En Noir 853m; 8 Les Souter-rains Du Château Rouge 638m; 9 Lorsque L'Enfant Parut 600m; 10 Le Coeur De Jacqueline 484m; 11 L'Ondine 427m; 12 Le Pardon D'Amour 436m (= Le Plus Grand Succes de René Cresté)

JUDEX (1963) d Franju rm 1916 c Fradetal m Jarre 95min

Judge = DOMAREN (1960)

JUDGE HARDY AND SON (1939) d G Seitz a Gibbons w Rooney, Ouspenskaya 87min MGM

JUDGE HARDY'S CHILDREN (1938) d G Seitz w Rooney 78min MGM

JUDGEMENT AT NUREMBERG (1961) d/p Kramer c Laszlo w Tracy, Lancaster, Widmark, Dietrich, Maximilian Schell, Clift, Garland 178min pc Kramer r UA

JUDGEMENT OF THE GUILTY (1916) d Conway

JUDGE PRIEST (1934) d J Ford s D Nichols, Trotti w W Rogers Parrish (uc) 80min Fox

JUDITH (1965) d Daniel Mann s J Hayes, Lawrence Durrell w Loren, Finch, Hawkins PV* 109min Par

JUDITH OF BETHULIA (1913) d Griffith c Bitzer w Marsh, L Gish 4rs Bio

JUDITH TRACHTENBERG (1920) d Galeen 2373m

Judo Saga = SUGATA SANSHIRO (1943)

JUD SUSS (1940) d/s V Harlan w Krauss, Staudte 2663m

JUEGO DE LA OCA, EL (1964) d/co-s Summers 120min

JUEGO PELIGROSO (1966) co-d Alcoriza, Arturo Ripstein * (= Jogo Peligroso)

JUEVES MILAGRO, LOS (1957) d/s Berlanga 90min

JUGEND (1938) d V Harlan s Von Harbou 2552m Tob

JUGGLER, THE (1953) d Dmytryk m Antheil w K Douglas, Kjellin 86min pc Kramer r Col

JUGUETES ROTOS (1966) d/s Summers 84min (= Broken Toys)

JUIF ERRANT, LE (1904) d Méliès 65m

JUJIRO (1928) d/s/w Kinugasa 97min Sho (= Crossways-/Crossroads/Shadows over Yoshiwara)

JULE GIRL (1942) d C Bernhardt p Wallis as-p Wald c Glennon w Sheridan, Reagan 90min WB

JUKU NO HARU (1933) d Gosho (= The Nineteenth Spring)

JULES ET JIM (1961) d/co-ad/co-di Truffaut c Coutard m Delerue w Moreau, Werner CS 105min co-pc Truffaut

JULIA MISBEHAVES (1948) d Conway c Ruttenberg co-a Gibbons w Garson, Pidgeon, Lawford, E Taylor, Romero 99min MGM

JULIE (1956) d/s Stone e Virginia Stone m Leith Stevens w D Day, Jourdan, Marsh 99min MGM

Juliet of the Spirits = GIULIETTA DEGLI SPIRITI (1965)

JULIETTA (1953) d M Allégret c Alekan des D'Eaubonne w Mariais, Moreau 99min Col

JULIETTE OU LA CLE DES SONGES (1951) d/co-s Carné c Alekan co-dec Trauner m Kosma w Philipe

JULIUS CAESAR (1949) d/p/ad/w Bradley fpl Shakespeare w Heston 16mm 90min

JULIUS CAESAR (1950) d D Davis 16mm 32min

JULIUS CAESAR (1953) d/s J Mankiewicz p Houseman fpl Shakespeare ad H Koch c Ruttenberg co-a Gibbons m Rozsa w Brando, Mason, E O'Brien, Kerr, Gielgud, Garson 120min MGM (1969: 70mm version)

JULIUS CAESAR (1970) d Stuart Burge w Heston, Gielgud, Vaughn PV* 116min

Jumbo (UK) = BILLY ROSE'S JUMBO (1962)

JUMENT VERTE, LA (1959) d/p Autant-Lara s/di Aurenche, Bost fn Marcel Ayme w Bourvil, Blanche FS* 105min (= The Green Mare's Nest)

JUMP FOR GLORY (1937) d Walsh w Fairbanks Jr 90min r UA (= When Thief Meets Thief)

JUMP INTO HELL (1955) d D Butler p Weisbart c Marley 82min WB

JUN-AI MONOGATARI (1957) d Imai S* 134min (= Story of Pure Love)

JUNE BRIDE (1948) d Windust p Blanke c McCord w B Davis, Montgomery, D Reynolds 97min WB

JUNGE MEDARDUS, DER (1925) d Curtiz Ufa

Jungerau auf dem Dach, Die German version of THE MOON IS BLUE (1953) di Zuckmayer

JUNGERUKALLEN (1959) d Ingmar Bergman c Nykvist w Von Sydow, Lindblom 85min SF (= The Virgin Spring)

Jungle Book, The (UK) = RUDYARD KIPLING'S JUNGLE BOOK (1942)

JUNGLE BOOK, THE (1967) p Disney f ('Mowgli' books) Rudyard Kipling wv G Sanders *78min

JUNGLE HEAT (1957) d HW Koch 75min r UA

JUNGLE PATROL (1948) d J Newman 72min Fox

JUNGLE PRINCESS (1936) d William Thiele m/lyr Hollander w Lamour, Milland, Tamiroff 85min Par

JUNGLE QUEEN (1945) d Ray Taylor, Lewis D Collins w Roman (serial in 13eps) U

JUNGLE RHYTHM (1929) d Iwerks p Disney anim 1rl

JUNIOR MISS (1945) d/s Seaton c C Clarke co-a Wheeler 94min Fox

JUNTO (1930) d Naruse (= Pure Love)

JUNO AND THE PAYCOCK (1930) d/co-s Hitchcock co-s Reville fpl Sean O'Casey 85min

JUPITER (1952) d Grangier m Van Parys (= Douze Heures de Bonheur)

JUPITER'S DARLING (1955) d G Sidney p Wells co-a Gibbons w Esther Williams, Keel, Sanders, Champion, Haydn CS* 96min MGM

JURY OF FATE, THE (1917) d Browning 5rs Metro

JUSQU' AU COEUR (1968) d/s Lefebvre anim Hebert part * 93min

JUST ACROSS THE STREET (1952) d Pevney w Sheridan 78½min U

JUST ANOTHER BLONDE (1926) d Santell c Edeson w L Brooks 5603ft r FN

JUST A GIGOLO (1931) d Conway w Milland 66min MGM

JUST BEFORE DAWN (1946) d Castle w W Baxter 65min Col

JUST BROWN'S LUCK (1913) d Sennett w Normand ½rl Key

JUSTE AVANT LA NUIT (1971) d/s Chabrol c Rabier *100min

JUST FOR YOU (1952) d E Nugent fst (Francois) Stephen Vincent Benet c Barnes co-a Pereira w B Crosby, Wyman, E Barrymore, N Wood *104min Par

JUST GOLD (1913) d Griffith w L Gish, D Gish, L Barrymore 1rl Bio

JUSTICE D'ABORD (1921) d Protazanov w Mozhukhin 1544m

JUSTICE EST FAITE (1950) d/co-s Cayatte co-s/di Charles Spaak c Bourgoin w Parlo 106min (= Justice Has Been Done)

Justice Has Been Done = JUSTICE EST FAITE (1950)

JUST IMAGINE (1930) d/s D Butler w O'Sullivan 9695ft Fox

JUSTIN DE MARSEILLE (1935) d M Tourneur

JUSTINE (1969) d Cukor, Strick (uc) p Berman fn (The Alexandria Quartet) Lawrence Durrell c Shamroy m Goldsmith w Aimée, Bogarde, Karina, Noiret, Dalio PV* 116min Fox

JUST PALS (1920) d J Ford 5rs Fox

JUST THIS ONCE (1952) d Weis c June co-a Gibbons w J Leigh, Lawford 90min MGM

JUVE CONTRE FANTOMAS (1913) d/s Feuillade 1 La Catastrophe du Simplon Express; 2 Au Crocodile

3 *La Ville Hantée*; 4 *L'Homme Noir* 1288m
(= *Fantomas, II*)
J.W. COOP (1971) *d/p/s* Robertson *w* Robertson, Page
*112min Col

KAACHAN KEKKON SHIROYO (1962) *d/s* Gosho
(= *Get Married Mother*)
KAACHAN TO JUICHI-NIN NO KODOMO (1966) *d*
Gosho S* 106min Sho (= *Our Wonderful Years*)
KABE ATSUKI HEYA (1953) *d* Kobayashi *w* Nakadai
(= *Room with Thick Walls*)
KABINETT DES DR CALIGARI, DAS (1919) *d* Wiene *p*
Pommer *co-s* C Mayer *dec* Warm, Röhrig *w* Veidt,
Krauss, Dagover 1500m 6rs DEC-UFA (= *The
Cabinet of Dr Caligari*)
KABOCHA (1928) *d/st* Ozu Sho (= *Pumpkin*)
KABULIWALA (1961) *d/p* Roy *fst* Tagore 95min
KAERANU SASABUE (1926) *d* Goshu
KAERLIGHEDENS TRIUMPH (1915) *d* Madsen
KAERLIGHED PA KREDIT (1955) *d/s* A Henning Jensen
KAERLIGHEDSLAENGEL (1915) *d* Blom
KAETTEKITA YOPPARAI (1968) *d/pc/co-s* Oshima *80m
r Sho (= *Three Resurrected Drunkards*)
KAFUKU (1937) *d* Naruse (2 parts)
KAGERO (1969) *d/s* Shindo (= *Heat Wave Island*)
KAGERO EZU (1959) *d/s* Kingasa (= *Stop the Old Fox*)
KAGI (1959) *d/cy* Ichikawa *c* Miyagawa *w* Kyo, Nakadai S*
107min (= *Odd Obsessions/The Key*)
KAGIRINAKI HODO (1934) *d* Naruse
KAIDAN (1964) *d* Kobayashi *fs* Lafcadio Hearn *w* Nakadai
S* 164min (= *Kwaidan*) 4 eps: Kurokami (= *Black
Hair, The*): Yuki-Onna (= *The Woman of the Snow*);
Miminashi Hoicho-Hoichi (= *The Earless*); *Chawan
no Naka* (= *In a Cup of Tea*)
KAIKOKU DANJI (1926) *d* Mizoguchi Nik (= *Children of
the Sea*)
KAIKOKUKI (1928) *d/w* Kinugasa (= *Tales From a
Country by the Sea*)
KAISEN NO ZENYA (1943) *d* Yoshimura (= *On the Eve of
War*)
KAISER, THE (1918) *d/w* Julian 7rs (= *The Kaiser, the
Beast of Berlin*)
Kaiser, the Beast of Berlin, The = KAISER, THE (1918)
KAISHAIN SEKATSU (1929) *d* Ozu Sho (= *The Life of an
Office Worker*)
KAISHAM SEIKATSU (1930) *d* Ozu
KAJA, UBIT CU TE! (1967) *d/co-s* Mimica *80min
(= *Kaya, I'll Kill You*)
KAK KHOROSHI, KAK SVEZHI BYLI ROZY (1913) *d/s*
Protazanov 715m (= *How Fine, How Fresh the
Roses Were*)
KAKKA (1940) *d* Imai (= *The General*)
KAK RYDALA DUSHA REBENKA (1913) *d/s*
Protazanov 260m (= *How the Baby's Soul Sobs*)
KAKUSHI TORIDE NO SAN-AKUNIN (1958) *d/co-p/co-s*
Kurosawa *w* Mifune S 139min Toho (= *The Hidden
Fortress*)
KAK ZAKALYALAS STAL (1942) *d/s* Donskoi 92min
(= *How the Steel Was Tempered*)
KALEIDOSCOPE (1935) *d* Lye *4min
KALEIDOSCOPE (1961) *d/s* C and R Eames *c* C Eames
KALEIDOSCOPE (1966) *d* Smight *c* Challis *w* Beatty
*103min (= *The Bank Breaker*)
KALEIDOSCOPE SHOP (1961) *d/s* C and R Eames *c* C
Eames 3½min
KALIDAA (1918) *d* Genina (= *La Storia di una Huhmia*)
Kalinin, Starost of Russia = VSEROSSIISKII STAROSTA
KALININ (1920)
KALI-YUG, LA DEA DELLA VENDETTA (1963) *d*
Camerini *c* Tonti * (= *Kali-Yug, Goddess of
Vengeance*)
Kali-Yug, Goddess of Vengeance (UK) = KALI-YUG, LA
DEA DELLA VENDETTA
KAMERADSCHAFT (1931) *d* Pabst *co-c* FA Wagner
93min Gau-Nero
KAMI ENO MICHI (1928) *d* Gosho (= *Road to God*)
KAMIGAMI NO FUKAKI YOKUBO (1968) *d* Imamura
S* 180min Nik (= *Kuragejima: Legends from
a Southern Island/A Profound Longing of the Gods*)
KAMIKAZE REN (1933) *d* Mizoguchi (= *Group Kamikaze*)
KAMI-NING YO HARU NO SASAYAKI (1926) *d*
Mizoguchi Nik (= *Paper Doll's Whisper of Spring*)
KAMMARJUNKAREN (1914) *d/s* Stiller
KAMPEN MOD KRAEFTEN (1947) *d/co-s* Dreyer 315m
KAMPEN OM HANS HJÄRTA (1916) *d/s* Stiller 895m
Kampf des Unabhangigen gegen den Kommerziellen Film =
STURM ÜBER LA SARRAZ (1929)
KAMPF UM ROM, DER (1969) *d* Siodmak *w* Welles,
Laurence Harvey TS* 103min
KANAL (1956) *d/co-s* Wajda 2612m
KANASHIKI HAKUCHI (1924) *d/co-s* Mizoguchi Nik
(= *Sad Idiot*)
KANASHIMI WA ONNA DAKENI (1958) *d/s* Shindo
(= *Only Women have Trouble*)
KANCHENJUNGA (1962) *d/s/m* S Ray *c* Mitra *102min *pc*
S Ray

KANCHO IMADA SHISEZU (1942) *d* Yoshimura (= *The
Spy isn't Dead Yet*)
KANE (1926) *d/co-s* Mizoguchi (= *Money*)
KANGAROO (1952) *d* Milestone *c* C Clarke *co-a* Wheeler *w*
M O'Hara, Lawford *84min Fox
KANKO NO MACHI (1944) *d* Kinoshita (= *Jubilation
Street*)
KANMAN KALLA KARLEK, DET (1937) *d* Molander
KANOJO (1926) *d/s* Gosho (= *Girlfriend*)
KANOJO TO UNMEI (1924) *d/s* Kinugasa (2 parts) (= *She
has Lived her Destiny*)
KANONENSERENADE (1958) *d/co-s* Staudte *co-s* Tessari
w De Sica 90min
KANRAKU NO ONNA (1924) *d/co-s* Mizoguchi Nik
(= *Woman of Pleasure*)
KANSAS CITY CONFIDENTIAL (1952) *d* Karlson *w*
Payne 87min *r* UA (= *The Secret Fear*)
KANSAS CITY PRINCESS, THE (1934) *d* Keighley *c*
Barnes *w* Blondell 64min WB
KANSAS RAIDERS (1950) *d* Enright *c* Glassberg *w* A
Murphy, Curtis 80min U
KANTOR IDEAL (1932) *d* Frič *c* Heller (= *Conduct
Unsatisfactory*)
'KANTOROWITZ-LIKÖRE' (1923) *d* Ruttman 60m
KAO (1965) *d* Kuri anim (= *The Face*)
KAPO (1959) *d* Pontecorvo *dec* Gherardi *w* Riva 118min
KAPT'N BAY-BAY (1952) *d/co-s* Käutner 101min
KAPURUSH-O-MAMAPURUSH (1965) *d/s/m* S Ray
74min (= *The Coward and the Holy Man*)
KARAKORAM (1936) *d/c/e* Ichac 950m
KARAKURI MUSUME (1927) *d/s* Gosho (= *Tricky
Girl*)
KARAMI-AI (1962) *d* Kobayashi *w* Nakadai 107min Sho
(= *The Inheritance*)
KARA SLAKTEN (1933) *d/s* Molander *w* Ekman SF
KARATACHI NIKKI (1959) *d* Gosho (= *Journal of the
Orange Flower*)
KARD ES KOCKA (1959) *d* Fehir (= *Sword and Dice*)
KARE JOHN (1964) *d/s* Lindgren *w* Kulle 111min San
(= *Dear John*)
KARIN INGSMARSDOTTER (1919) *d/co-s/w* Sjöström *fn*
(*Jerusalem II Selma Layerlof* 2304m
KARIN MÅNSDOTTER (1954) *d/s* Sjöberg *fpl* (*Erik XIV*)
August Strindberg *c* Nykvist *w* Jacobson, Kulle part *
San
KARLEK (1952) *d* Molander *co-s* Lindstrom *w* Sjöström,
Kulle, Lindblom SF 2920m
KARLEKENS BROD (1935) *d* Mattsson 90min (= *The
Bread of Love*)
KARLEKEN SEGRAR (1949) *d* Molander *w* Thulin SF
104min
KARLEK OCH JOURNALISTIK (1916) *d* Stiller 834m
KARLEK OCH KASSABRIST (1932) *d/s* Molander SF
KARLEK OCH STATISTIK (c 1955) *c* Lindgren (= *Love
and Statistics*)
KARLEK 65 (1965) *d/s/e* Widerberg *co-m* Vivaldi *95min
(= *Love 65*)
KARLEK STARKARE AN HAT (1913) *d* Sjöström 625m
(= *Skogsdotterns Hemlighet/Tjuvskyften*)
KARNIVAL KID, THE (1929) *d* Iwerks *p* Disney anim 1rl
KAROSZEK (1939) *d* Balasz
KARUMEN JUNJOSU (1952) *d* Kinoshita (= *Carmen's
Pure Love*)
KARUMEN KOKYO NI KAERU (1951) *d/st/s* Kinoshita
*87min Sho (= *Carmen Comes Home*)
KASPICHY (1944) *d* Alexandrov (= *Men of the Caspian*)
KASTRULLRESAN (1950) *d* Mattsson *a* Dahlbeck (= *The
Saucepan Journey*)
KATAKOMBY (1940) *d* Frič (= *Catacombs*)
KATEI NO JIJYO (1962) *d* Yoshimura *s* Shindo *w* Kyo
(= *Their Legacy*)
KATERLAMPE (1936) *d* V Harlan 2421m
KATHLEEN (1941) *d* Harold S Bucquet *a* Gibbons *m*
Waxman *w* Temple, H Marshall 88min MGM
KATHLEEN MAVOURNEEN (1913) *d* Brenon 1000ft
KATIA (1938) *d* M Tourneur *w* Darrieux 89min
KATJA (1938) *d* Siodmak *co-s* Charles Spaak *w* Jurgens,
Schneider 90min (= *The Magnificent Sinner*)
KATTORNA (1965) *d/co-s* Carlsen *m* Komeda *w* Dahlbeck
93min (= *The Cats*)
KATKA-BUMAZMNYI RANET (1926) *d* Ermler, *Edward
Johanson co-c* Moskvin 2010m (= *Katka's Reinette
Apples*)
KAUKASIERIN, DIE (1918) *d* May, *Jens W Krafft p/s* May
4rs
Katka's Reinette Apples = KATKA-BUMAZMNYI RANET
(1926)
KATRINA DEAD (1967) *d* Warhol 16mm * 30min (segment
of *Four Stars*)
KAWANAKAJIMA KASEN (1941) *d/s* Kinugasa (= *The
Battle of Kawanakajima*)
KAWA NO ARU SHITAMACHI NO HANSHI (1955) *d/s*
Kinugasa (= *It happened in Tokyo*)
Kaya, I'll Kill You = KAJA, UBIT CU TE! (1967)
KAZAHANA (1959) *d* Kinoshita (= *Snow Flurry*)
Kazakhstan Frontu = TEBYE, FRONT (1943)
KAZDY DEN ODVAMU (1964) *d/s* Schorm *w* Menzel
105min (= *Everyday Courage*)
KAZE NO NAKA NO MENDORI (1948) *d/co-s* Ozu Sho
(= *A Hen In The Wind*)

KDYBY TY MUZIKY NEBLY (1963) *d/co-s* Forman *st/co-s*
Passer *c* Ondricek *45min (= *If There was No Music*)
Added to KONKURS (1963) to make KONKURS
(= *Talent Competition*) Feature Length
KEAN (1922) *d* Alexandre Wolcoff *fpl* Dumas *w* Mozhukhin
KEAN (1957) *d/co-s* Gassman, Rosi *co-s* Cecchi D'Amico
fpl Dumas *c* Di Venanzo *w* Gassman, Rossi-Drago
Keep an Eye on Amelia (UK) = OCCUPE TOI D'AMELIE
(1949)
KEEP 'EM HOME (1922) *d* St Clair 2rs
KEEPER OF THE BEES (1947) *d* J Sturges *w* Darwell
68min Col
KEEPER OF THE FLAME (1942) *d* Cukor *p* Saville *s* D
Stewart *c* Daniels *co-des* Gibbons, Wheeler *m* Kaper
w K Hepburn, Tracy 100min MGM
Keepers, The = TETRE CONTRE LES MURS, LA (1958)
KEEP LAUGHING (1932) *d* Arbuckle (ps William
Goodrich) 20min
KEEP YOUR MOUTH SHUT (1945) *d* McLaren, Dunning
anim 3min NFBC
KEIRAKU HICHU (1928) *d* Kinugasa
KEIJATSUKAN TO BOROYOKU-DAN (1959) *d* Ichikawa
(= *Police and Small Gangsters*)
KEJSAREN AV PORTUGALLIEN (1945) *d/co-s* Molander
co-s Lindström *w* Sjöström SF
KEKKON (1947) *d* Kinoshita (= *Marriage*)
KEKKON-GAKU NYUMON (1930) *d* Ozu Sho (= *Intro-
duction to Marriage*)
KEKKON KOSHIN-KYOKU (1951) *d/co-s* Ichikawa Toho
(= *Wedding March*)
KEKKON NO SEITAI (1941) *d* Imai (= *Married Life*)
KELCY GETS HIS MAN (1927) *d* Wyler 2rs U
KELLY AND ME (1957) *d* Leonard *co-a* Golitzen *w* V
Johnson, Laurie CS* 86min U
KELLY'S HEROES (1968) *d* Brian G Hutton 2nd *d* Marton *w*
Eastwood PV* 143min
KELLY THE SECOND (1936) *d* Gus Meins *p* Roach
co-ad/co-di G Douglas *w* C Chase 85min MGM
KENTUCKIAN, THE (1955) *d* Lancaster *p* H Hecht *c*
Laszlo *m* Herrmann *w* Lancaster, Carradine,
McIntire, Matthau S* 104min *r* U
KENTUCKY (1938) *d* D Butler *co-s* Trotti *c* Cronjager *w* L
Young, Brennan 96min Fox
KENTUCKY CINDERELLA, A (1917) *d* Julian 5rs
KENTUCKY KERNELS (1934) *d* G Stevens *c* Cronjager *w*
Dumont 75min RKO
KENTUCKY MOONSHINE (1938) *d* D Butler *as-p*
Macgowan 80min Fox (= *Three Men and a Girl*)
KENNEL MURDER CASE, THE (1933) *d* Curtiz *w* Astor,
W Powell 73min WB
KENTUCKY PRIDE (1925) *d* J Ford 6597ft Fox
KENYA (1961) *d/c* A and D Maysles, R Leacock
KEPT HUSBANDS (1931) *d* Bacon *w* McCrea 79min RKO
KERMESSE HEROIQUE, LA (1935) *d/co-s* Feyder *co-s/fn*
Charles Spaak *dec* Meerson *w* Rosay, Jouvet 115min
Tob (= *Die Klugen Frauen*)
KESSEN (1944) *d* Yoshimura, *Teruo Hagiyami* (= *Decisive
Battle*)
KÉT FÉLIDÖ A POKOLBAN (1961) *d/dec* Fábri 122min
(= *The Last Goal/Eleven Men/Two Half Times in
Hell*)
KETSZER KETTO NEHA OT (1954) *d* Révész (= *2 Times
2 are sometimes 5*)
KEY, THE (1934) *d* Curtiz *c* E Haller *w* W Powell 70min WB
KEY, THE (1958) *d* C Reed *ex-p/s* Foreman *c* Morris *m* M
Arnold *w* Holden, Loren, T Howard, Forbes CS
134min Col
Key, The = KAGI (1959)
KEYHOLD, THE (1933) *d* Curtiz *w* K Francis 66min WB
KEY LARGO (1948) *d/co-s* J Huston *p* Wald *fpl* Maxwell
Anderson *co-s* R Brooks *c* Freund *m* M Steiner *w*
Bogart, Bacall, Robinson, L Barrymore, Trevor
102min WB
KEYS OF THE KINGDOM, THE (1944) *d* Stahl *p/co-s* J
Mankiewicz *co-s* N Johnson *fn* AJ Cronin *c* AC
Miller *m* A Newman *w* Peck, Price, Mitchell
Keys to Happiness, The = KLYCHI SCHASTYA (1913)
KEY TO THE CITY (1950) *d* G Sidney *c* Rosson *co-a*
Gibbons *m* Kaper *w* Gable, Burr, L Young 99min
MGM
KEY WITNESS (1960) *d* Karlson *w* J Hunter CS 82min
MGM
KHARTOUM (1966) *d* Dearden 2nd *d* Canutt *p* Blaustein *s*
Ardrey *w* Heston, Olivier, R Richardson PV70*
128min *r* UA
Khazdeni Za Tri Morya = PARDESI (1957)
KHLEB (1918) *d* co-d/w Boleslavsky *co-d* Boris Sushkevich
(= *Bread*)
KICO (1951) *d* Vukotic anim
KID, THE (1921) *d/s/w* Chaplin *assist d* Reisner *c* Totheroh
w Coogan, Purviance 6rs FN
KID AUTO RACES AT VENICE (1914) *d* Lehrman *w*
Chaplin ½rl Key
KID BOOTS (1926) *d* Tuttle *w* Cantor, Bow 7114ft FPL
KID BROTHER, THE (1927) *d* Ted Wilde *w* H Lloyd 7654ft
pc H Lloyd *r* Par
KIDDIES' CAKE WALK (1896) *p* Paul 62ft
KID FOR TWO FARTHINGS, A (1955) *d* C Reed *s/fn*
Wolf Mankowitz *96min *r* BL
KID FROM BROKEN GUN, THE (1952) *d* Sears 56min Col

KID FROM BROOKLYN, THE (1946) d McLeod p Goldwyn c Toland w Kaye, V Mayo, Cochran, Vera-Ellen 104min RKO

KID FROM SPAIN, THE (1933) d/st McCarey p Goldwyn c Toland e Heisler chor Berkeley w Cantor, R Young, Franklin, Grable, Goddard 98min r UA

KID GALAHAD (1937) d Curtiz p Wallis s S Miller c Gaudio w Robinson, B Davis, Bogart 102min WB

KID GALAHAD (1962) d Karlson p Weisbart c Guffey w Presley *95min r UA

KID GLOVE KILLER (1942) d Zinnemann a Gibbons w Heflin, Gardner 74min MGM

KID GLOVES (1929) d Enright c B Reynolds 7rs WB

KID MILLIONS (1934) d Del Ruth co-st/co-s N Johnson c June e Heisler m A Newman w Cantor, Sothern, G Murphy part * 10rs r UA

KIDNAPPED (1917) d Crosland fn RL Stevenson 5rs Ed

KIDNAPPED (1960) d/s Stevenson Disney fn RL Stevenson w Finch, O'Toole *95min pc Disney

KIDNAPPED (1971) d Delbert Mann fns (Kidnapped and David Balfour) RL Stevenson w Caine, T Howard *100min

Kidnapper, The (UK) = SECUESTRADOR, EL (1958)

KIDNAPPERS, THE (1953) d P Leacock 93min (= Little Kidnappers)

KIDS IS KIDS (1920) d C Chase (as C Parrott) w C Chase 2rs FPL

KID SPEED (1924) d/s Semon, Noel Mason Smith w Semon, Hardy 2rs

KIEDY TY SPISZ (1953) d/s Wajda 302m

KIERUNEK NOWA HUTA (1951) d Munk 13min

KIFF TEBBI (1927) d Camerini

KIIROI KARASU (1957) d Gosho *104min Sho (= Behold Thy Son/Yellow Crow)

KIKI (1926) d C Brown w N Talmadge, Colman 8299ft FN

KIKI (1931) d/s/ad Sam Taylor c Struss m A Newman w Pickford, (Grable) 87min r UA

Kiki and Isamu = KIKU TO ISAMU (1959)

KIKU TO ISAMU (1959) d Imai S* 117min (= Kiky and Isamu)

KILL (1971) d/s Gary w Seberg, Mason, Boyd, Jurgens *102min

KILLER, THE (1921) d/w Conway 6000ft Pat

Killer! = QUE LA BETE MEURE (1969)

KILLER IS LOOSE, THE (1956) d Boetticher c Ballard w Cotten, R Fleming, Corey 73min r UA

KILLER McCOY (1947) d Rowland c Ruttenberg co-a Gibbons w Rooney, Blyth, (Winters) 104min MGM

Killer on a Horse = WELCOME TO HARD TIMES (1967)

KILLERS, THE (1946) d Siodmak p Hellinger s J Huston (uc) fns Hemingway m Rozsa w Lancaster, Gardner, E O'Brien 102min U

KILLERS, THE (1964) d/p D Siegel fst Hemingway rm 1946 w Marvin, A Dickinson, Cassavetes, Reagan *95min U

KILLER SHARK (1950) d Boetticher 76min Mon

KILLER'S KISS (1955) d/co-p/as/t/s/c/e Kubrick 64min r UA

KILLERS OF KILIMANJARO (1960) d Thorpe co-st Maibaum c Moore m Alwyn w R Taylor CS* 90min r Col

KILLING, THE (1956) d/s Kubrick as-d A Singer c Ballard w Hayden, Cook 83min r UA

Killing at Monte Carlo (UK) = CRIMEN (1960)

KILLING OF SISTER GEORGE, THE (1968) d/p/pc Aldrich fpl Frank Marcus w Reid *140min

Kill me Quick, I'm Cold = FAI IN FRETTA AD UCCIDERMI ... HO FREDDO! (1966)

KILL ME TOMORROW (1957) d Fisher 80min

KILL OR BE KILLED (1942) d Lye 15min

KILL THE UMPIRE (1950) d Bacon st/s Tashlin c Lawton w Bendix 78min Col

KILROY WAS HERE (1947) d Karlson 68min Mon

KIM (1950) d Saville fn Rudyard Kipling co-a Gibbons m Previn w Flynn, Lukas 112min MGM

KIMI TO WAKARETE (1932) d/s Naruse (= Apart from you)

KIMI TO YUKU MICHI (1936) d/s Naruse

KINDER DER FINSTERNIS (1921) Part 1 Das Mann aus Nepal; Part 2 Kämpfende Welten d/co-s Dupont co-c Freund dec Leni Part 1: 1785m; Part 2: 1375m r Ufa

KINDER, MUTTER UND EIN GENERAL (1955) d Benedek p Pommer c Rittau w Maximilian Schell 110min

KINDERTRAGODIE (1927) d Jutzi 1989m

KIND HEARTS AND CORONETS (1949) d/co-s Hamer p Balcon c Slocombe co-e (uc) Holt w Guinness, Greenwood 106min

KIND LADY (1935) d G Seitz fst Walpole c Folsey w Rathbone 77min MGM

KIND LADY (1951) d J Sturges co-s Charles Bennett fst Walpole c Ruttenberg co-a Gibbons w E Barrymore 78min MGM

KINDLING (1915) d/s De Mille pc Lasky

KIND OF LOVING, A (1967) d J Schlesinger s Waterhouse & Hall fn Stan Barstow 112min

KINDRED OF THE DUST (1922) d Walsh 8rs pc Walsh r FN

KING: A FILMED RECORD ... MONTGOMERY TO MEMPHIS (1970) co-d Lumet, J Mankiewicz p Landau n/w P Newman, Woodward, Heston, Lancaster, Poitier 153min

KING AND COUNTRY (1964) d/co-p Losey design consultant Richard Macdonald w Bogarde, Courtenay 86min

KING AND FOUR QUEENS, THE (1956) d Walsh c Ballard m North w Gable, Parker CS* 84min pc Gable r UA

KING AND I, THE (1956) d W Lang p Brackett s Lehman fmpl Rodgers & Hammerstein c Shamroy co-a Wheeler chor Robbins w Kerr, Brynner CS55* 133min Fox

KING AND THE CHORUS GIRL, THE (1937) d LeRoy st/s Krasna, G Marx c Gaudio w Blondell, Horton, Wyman 10rs WB

KING CREOLE (1958) d Curtiz p Wallis fn (A Stone for Danny Fisher) Harold Robbins c R Harlan w Presley, Mattau VV* 116min Par

KINGDOM OF LOVE, THE (1917) d/s F Lloyd 5rs Fox

KING IN NEW YORK, A (1957) d/p/s/m/w Chaplin c Périnal e Colpi 105min

KING KONG (1933) co-d/co-p Schoedsack co-d/co-p/co-st/fidea M Cooper ex-p Selznick co-st Edgar Wallace m M Steiner 100min RKO

KING LEAR (1969 r 1971) d P Brook fpl Shakespeare des Wakhévitch w Scofield 136min

King Lear = KOROL LIR (1971)

King Matthew I = KROL MACIUS PIERWSZY (1958)

KING MURDER, THE (1932) d Thorpe 64min

KING OF ALCATRAZ (1938) d Florey st/s Reis w Nolan, Carey, Quinn, Preston 56min Par

King of a Penny = DOKA-O (1926)

KING OF GAMBLERS (1937) d Florey co-a Dreier w Nolan, Tamiroff, L Brooks, Trevor 78min Par

King of Hearts = ROI DE COEUR, LE (1966)

KING OF JAZZ (1930) d John Murray Anderson co-c Mohr w (B Crosby) 105min U

King of Kings = KRAL KRALU (1963)

KING OF KINGS, THE (1927) d/p/co-s De Mille f (The Gospels) c Marley a Leisen m Riesenfeld 13500ft part * pc De Mille

KING OF KINGS (1961) d N Ray p Bronston s Yordan co-c Planer, Krasner a Wakhévitch m Rozsa w J Hunter, Ryan, Lindfors, Welles TR70* 168min r MGM

KING OF THE KHYBER RIFLES (1953) d H King s Goff, Roberts c Shamroy co-a Wheeler m Herrmann w Power *99min Fox

KING OF THE KONGO (1929) d Thorpe w Karloff serial in 10 eps

KING OF THE ROARING TWENTIES – THE STORY OF ARNOLD ROTHSTEIN (1961) d J Newman s Swerling m Waxman w Rooney 105min AA (= The Big Bankroll)

KING OF THE UNDERWORLD (1939) d Lewis Seiler st Burnett co-s V Sherman w Bogart, K Francis 8rs WB

KING OF THE WILD STALLIONS (1959) d Springsteen CS* 75½min AA

KING RAT (1966) d Forbes p James Woolf fn Clavell c Guffey m Barry w Segal, Courtenay, J Mills 134min r Col

KING RELUCTANT, THE (1956) d Lee Thompson

KING RICHARD AND THE CRUSADERS (1954) d D Butler p Blanke fn (The Talisman) Sir Walter Scott c Marley m M Steiner w G Sanders, V Mayo, Harrison, Laurence Harvey CS 114min WB

KINGS AND QUEENS (1956) d Czinner n M Redgrave sh *

KING'S BREAKFAST, THE (1936) d Reiniger fpm AA Milne anim

KINGS GO FORTH (1958) d Daves c Fapp m E Bernstein w Sinatra, Curtis, N Wood 109min r UA

KING-SIZED CANARY (1947) d Avery p Quimby anim* 8min MGM

KINGS OF THE SUN (1963) d J Thompson co-s JR Webb c Joe Macdonald m E Bernstein w Brynner PV* 107min UA

KING SOLOMAN OF BROADWAY (1935) d Crosland 75min U

KING SOLOMON'S MINES (1937) d Stevenson co-s Charles Bennett fn Rider Haggard 80min Gau

KING SOLOMON'S MINES (1950) d Compton Bennett, Marton, fn Rider Haggard c Surtees co-a Gibbons w Kerr, S Granger 102min MGM

KING'S PRIVATE (1967) d Weis co-a Golitzen *99min U-JAR

KING'S RHAPSODY (1955) d/p J Wilcox fpl Ivor Novello w Flynn, Neagle CS* 93min r BL

KING'S ROW (1942) d S Wood p Wallis c Howe w Sheridan, Reagan, R Cummings, C Coburn, Ouspenskaya, Rains 127min WB

KING STEPS OUT, THE (1936) d Von Sternberg p Perlberg s Buchman c Ballard m Fritz Kreisler w Tone 85min Col

KING'S THIEF, THE (1955) d Leonard co-a Gibbons w Blyth, Niven, G Sanders CS* 78min MGM

KINNO JIDAI (1926) d Kinugasa (= Epoch of Loyalty)

KINODNEVIK GLUMOVA (1923) d Eisenstein w Alexandrov sh (= Glunov's Film-Diary)

KINO GLAZ (1924) d Vertov, Elizabeth Svilova e Vertov 6rs (6 parts) (= Camera Eye)

KINO NEDELYA (1918-19) d/e/t Vertov (= Cine Weekly) (43 no's)

KINO PRAVDA (1922-25) d/s/co-c/co-e/t Vertov 300m per no. (23 numbers) (= Film Truth)

KIN OU KANE (1926) d/cos Mizoguchi Nik

KINO ZA DVADTSAT LET (1940) d/e Pudovkin, Shub 89min (= Twenty Years of Soviet Cinema)

KINUYO MONOGATARI (1930) d Gosho (= Story of Kinuyo)

KIPPS (1941) d C Reed s Gilliat fn HG Wells w M Redgrave 112min r Fox

KIRINJI (1926) d Kinugasa

KIRI NO AME (1924) d/s/w Kinugasa (= Fog and Rain)

KIRI NO MINATO (1923) d Mizoguchi fpl (Ann Christie) Eugene O'Neill Nik

KIRMES (1960) d/co-s Staudte 103min

KISEKI (1963) d Kuri anim 3min (= Locus)

Kisenga, Man of Africa = MEN OF TWO WORLDS (1946)

KISHIN YURI KEIJI (1924) d/s Kinugasa

KISMET (1944) d Dieterle co-a Gibbons m Stothart chor Cole w Dietrich, Colman, De Carlo, Cole 100min MGM

KISMET (1955) d Minnelli p Freed co-s/fco-mpl Lederer fm Borodin c Ruttenberg co-a Gibbons chor Cole w Keel, Blyth CS* 113min MGM

KISS (1963) d Warhol 16mm sil 50min

KISS, THE (1900) p Hepworth

KISS, THE (1921) d Conway c Glennon 4488ft U

KISS, THE (1929) d/s Feyder as-p Lewin c Daniels des Gibbons w Garbo, Ayres 90min MGM

KISS BEFORE DYING, A (1956) d G Oswald c Ballard w R Wagner, J Hunter, Woodward, Astor CS* 94min UA

KISS BEFORE THE MIRROR, THE (1933) d Whale w Lukas, Pidgeon 66min U

KISSES FOR MY PRESIDENT (1964) d/p C Bernhardt c Surtees m Kaper w MacMurray, Wallach 113min WB

KISS FOR CINDERELLA, A (1926) d Brenon 9686ft FPL

Kiss from the Stadium, A = POLIBEK ZE STADIONU (1948)

KISS IN A TAXI, A (1927) d Badger 6349ft Par

KISSING BANDIT, THE (1948) d Benedek p Pasternak c Surtees w Sinatra, Charisse, Montalban, Ann Miller *102min MGM

KISS IN THE DARK, A (1948) d Daves p/s Kurnitz c Burks e Weisbart m M Steiner w Niven, Wyman, B Crawford, Ouspenskaya 87min WB

KISS KISS ... BANG BANG (1967) d/s Tessari *110min

KISS ME AGAIN (1925) d Lubitsch w Bow 6455ft WB

KISS ME DEADLY (1955) d/p Aldrich s Bezzerides fn Mickey Spillane c Laszlo w Meeker 96min r UA

Kiss Me General = MARTIN SOLDAT (1966)

KISS ME KATE (1953) d G Sidney p J Cummings co-a Gibbons w Keel, Fosse, Ann Miller *109min MGM

KISS ME, STUPID (1964) d/p/co-s B Wilder co-as-p/co-s Diamond c La Shelle a Trauner m Previn w Martin, Novak PV 124min co-pc Mir r UA

KISS OF DEATH (1947) d Hathaway p Kohlmar s Hecht, Lederer c Brodine co-a Wheeler m A Newman w Mature, Widmark 98min Fox

KISS OF FIRE (1955) d J Newman co-a Boyle w Palance, Rush *87min U

Kiss on the Cruise, The = KYSSEN PA KRYSSEN (1950)

KISS THE BLOOD OFF MY HANDS (1948) d Foster co-ad Maddow c Metty m Rozsa w Fontaine, Lancaster, Newton 79min pc H Hecht, Lancaster r U

KISS THE BOYS GOODBYE (1941) d Schertzinger c Tetzlaff 85min Par

KISS THE GIRLS AND MAKE THEM DIE (1967) d Levin p De Laurentiis w Vallone 106min r Col

KISS THEM FOR ME (1957) d Donen p Wald s JJ Epstein c Krasner co-a Wheeler w C Grant, Mansfield CS* 102min Fox

KISS TOMORROW GOODBYE (1950) d G Douglas e Marley w Cagney 102min pc Cagney r WB

KIT CARSON (1940) d G Seitz w D Andrews 97min UA

KITCHEN (1965) d Warhol s Ronald Tavel 16mm 70min

KITCHEN LADY, THE (1918) d Cline s Sennett w Fazenda 2rs Sen

Kites = LETUN (1931)

KITSCH (1919) d Lupo-Pick 2140m

KITTE-NO GENSO (1959) d Kuri anim 7min (= Stamp Fantasia)

KITTY (1929) d Saville 2rs

KITTY (1945) d Leisen c Fapp co-a Dreier m V Young w Goddard, Milland 103min Par

KITTY FOYLE (1940) d S Wood s Trumbo, D Stewart w G Rogers 107min RKO

KITTY UND DIE WULTKONFURUNZ (1939) d/s Käutner 96min

KIZOKU NO KAIDAN (1959) d Yoshimura

KLABAUTERMANNEN (1969) d/p/co-s Carlsen 92min (= We are All Demons!)

KLADIVO NA CARODEJNICE (1969) d Vavra 110min (= A Hammer against Witches)

KLANNINGEN (1964) d Sjöman c Nykvist 85min SF (= The Dress)

KLASS UND DATSCH, DIE PECHVÖGEL (1926) d/s/c/dec Jutzi 1602m

KLATKI (1967) d Miroslaw Kijowicz m Komeda 7min (= Cages)

KLEIDER MACHEN LEUTE (1940) *d/s* Käutner 106min
KLEINE NAPOLEON, DER (1923) *d Georg Jacoby w* Dietrich Ufa
KLEINE SCHORNSTEINFEGER, DER (1935) *d/p* Reiniger anim 625ft (= *The Little Chimney Sweep*)
KLEINE WELT IM DUNKELN, EINE (1938) *d/p* Richter 700ft
KLEPTOMANIAC, THE (1905) *d* Porter 315ft Ed
KLIMA VON VANCOURT, DAS (1917) *d/p* May
KLONDIKE ANNIE (1936) *d* Walsh *co-st/co-s* West *e* Heisler *w* West, V McLaglen 80min Par
KLONDIKE FURY (1942) *d* W Howard *c* O'Connell 67min Mon
KLOSTRET I SENDORMIR (1919) *d/s* Sjöström 1565m
Klugen Frauen, Die (1935) German version of LA KERMESSE HÉROIQUE (1935)
KLYATVA MOLODYKH (1947) *d* Vertov, Elisabeth Svilova 3rs (= *The Oats of Youth*)
KLYATVA TIMURA (1942) *d* Kuleshov 6rs (= *The Oath of Timur*)
KLYUCHI SCHASTYA (1913) *d* Protazanov, *Vladimir Gardin* 4700m (2 parts) (= *The Keys to Happiness*)
KLUVEN VARLD, EN (1948) *d/s/c/e* Sucksdorff *m* JS Bach 9min SF
KNABE IN BLAU DER (1919) *d* Murnau (= *The Child in Blue*)
KNACK – AND HOW TO GET IT, THE (1965) *d* Lester *c* Watkin *m* Barry *w* Tushingham 86min *r* UA
KNAVE OF HEARTS (1954) *d/co-s p* Graetz *co-di* Queneau *c* Morris *w* Philipe, Greenwood 100min (= *Monsieur Ripois/Lovers, Happy Lovers*)
KNICKERBOCKER BUCKAROO, THE (1919) *d* Albert Parker *w* Wellman 6rs *pc* Fairbanks Sr
KNICKERBOCKER HOLIDAY (1944) *d/p* H Brown *co-s* Boehm *fpl* Maxwell Anderson, Weill *m* Weill *w* C Coburn 85min *r* UA
Knife, The = HET MES (1961)
Knife in the Water = NOZ W WODZIE (1962)
KNIGHTS OF THE ROUND TABLE (1953) *d* Thorpe *p* Berman *fpm* (*Le Mort D'Arthur*) Sir Thomas Malory *co-c* F Young *cos* Furse *m* Rozsa *w* R Taylor, Gardner, M Ferrer, S Baker CS* 115min MGM
Knights of the Teutonic Order = KRZYZACY (1960)
KNIGHT WITHOUT ARMOUR (1937) *d* Feyder *s* Biro *co-c* Cardiff *des* Meerson *m* Rozsa *w* Dietrich, Donot 90min *pc* A Korda
KNIPLINGER (1926) *d/s* Madsen
KNOCK (1951) *d* Guy Le France *c* C Renoir *w* Jouvet, P Renoir 98min (= *Doctor Knock*)
KNOCK ON ANY DOOR (1949) *d* N Ray *co-s* Taradash *c* Guffey *m* Antheil *w* Bogart, Derek 100min *r* Col
KNOCK ON WOOD (1954) *d/p/s* M Frank, Panama *c* Fapp *co-a* Pereira *chor* Kidd *w* Kaye, Zetterling 103min Par
KNOCK OUT, THE (1914) *d* Sennett *w* Chaplin, Sennett, Arbuckle, C Chase 2rs Key (= *Counted Out/The Pugilist*)
Knock Out = HAARLEM (1943)
KNOCKOUT REILLY (1927) *d/p* St Clair *c* Cronjager 7rs FPL
KNOW YOUR ENEMY: JAPAN (1945) *d* Capra, Ivens *m* Tiomkin *n* W Huston US Army Pictorial Service
KNUTE ROCKNE – ALL-AMERICAN (1940) *d* Bacon *w* Reagan 11rs WB
KOBANZAME (1949) *d/s/w* Yamada (Part 2)
KOBENHAUN-KALUNDBORG (1934) *d* Madsen
KOCICI SKOLA (1963) *d* Pojar anim* 15min (series of 3) (= *School for Cats*)
Kodak, Un = SIX ET DEMI-ONZE (1927)
KOD FOTOGRAFA (1959) *d/s* Mimica anim* 9min (= *At the Photographer's*)
KOENIGSMARK (1923) *d/s* Perret *pc* Perret-Pat
KOENIGSMARK (1935) *d* M Tourneur *m* Ibert *w* Fresnay 95min (= *Crimson Dynasty*)
Koga Mansion = KOGA YASHIKI (1949)
KOGA YASHIKI (1949) *d/s* Kinugasa (= *Koga Mansion*)
KOGE (1964) *d* Kinoshita S 205min Sho (= *The Scent of Incense*)
Kohana = YOSHIWARA (1937)
KOHAYAGAWA-KE NO AKI (1961) *d/co-s* Ozu *103min Toho (= *Early Autumn*)
Kohlhiesel's Daughters (UK) = KOHLHIESEL'S TÖCHTER (1920)
KOHLHIESELS TÖCHTER (1920) *d/co-s* Lubitsch *c* Sparkuhl *w* Jannings 70min *r* UFA (= *Kohlhiesel's Daughters*)
KOI (1924) *d/w* Kinugasa (= *Love*)
KOIBITO (1951) *d/cos* Ichikawa Toho (= *The Lover*)
KOINA NO GINPEI (1933) *d/s* Kinugasa (= *Gimpei from Koina*)
KOI NO TOKYO (1932) *d* Gosho (= *Love in Tokyo*)
KOI TO BUSHI (1925) *d/s* Kinugasa (= *Love and a Warrior*)
KOI TO WA NARINU (1924) *d* Kinugasa
KOKO NI IZUMI ARI (1955) *d* Imai (= *Here is a Spring*)
KOKORO (1955) *d* Ichikawa *w* Mori 120min Nik (= *The Heart*)
KOKORO NO SANMYAKU (1966) *d* Yoshimura (= *The Heart of the Mountains*)
KOLBERG (1945) *d/co-s* V Harlan *110min UFA

KÖLCSÖNKERT KASTÉLY, A (1937) *d* Vajda 2444m
KOLDUSGROF, A (1917) *d* Balasz
KOLEJARSKIE SLOWO (1953) *d/s* Munk 22min
KOLYBELNAYA (1937) *d/s/e/n* Vertov 1622m (= *Lullabye*)
KOME (1957) *d* Imai *118min (= *Rice*)
KOMEDIE OM GELD (1936) *d/co-s* Ophuls *c* Schuftan 81min
Komm'zu Mirzum Rendez-vous: German version of L'AMOUR CHANTE (1930)
KOMODIANTEN (1941) *d/co-s* Pabst 120min
KOMPOSITION IN BLAU (1934) *d* Fischinger *m* Nicolai anim* 5min (= *Composition in Blue*)
KOMPOZITOR GLINKA (1952) *d/co-s* Alexandrov *c* Tissé * 112min (= *Glinka/Glinka – Man of Music*)
KOMSOMOL (1932) *d/co-s* Ivens *m* Eisler 1500m (= *Pem o Gerojach/Youth Speaks*)
Komosomol – Patron of Electrification = KSE (1932)
KOMSOMOLSK (1938) *d/co-s* Gerasimov 108min
KOM TILLBACKA, DE (1962) *d* Troell (= *The Return*)
KONCERT ZA MASINSKU PUSKU (1959) *d* Vukotic anim* 12min (= *Concerto for Machine Gun*)
KONEC NASEHO CASU (1964) *d* Jakubowska
KONETS SANKT-PETERBURGA (1927) *d* Pudovkin, *Mikhail Doller w* Pudovkin 2500m (= *The End of St Petersburg*)
KONGA YO (1962) *d/co-s* Y Allégret *108min
KONGRESS TANZT, DER (1931) *d* Charrell *p* Pommer *co-dec* Rohrig *w* Veidt, Dagover, Lillian Harvey 2773m UFA (= *The Congress Dances*)
König des Mont-Blanc, Der = EWIGE TRAUM, DER (1934)
KONIGSKINDER (1949) *d/cos* Käutner 95min
KONIGSWALTZER, DER (1935) *d* Herbert Maisch *w* Jurgens 2286m UFA
KONJIKI YASHA (1923) *d/s* Kinugasa (= *The Golden Demon*)
KONKI (1961) *d* Yoshimura *c* Miyagawa *w* Kyo S* 98min Dai (= *Marriageable Age*)
KONKURS (1963) *d/co-s* Forman *st/co-s* Passer *c* Ondricek 16mm 45min KDBY TY MUZIKY NEBLY (1963) added to make KONKURS (= *Talent Competition*) Feature length
KONO HIROI SORA NO DOKOKANI (1954) *d* Kobayashi Sho (= *Somewhere Beneath The Wide Sky*)
KONO TEN NO NIJI (1958) *d/s* Kinoshita S* 106min Sho (= *The Eternal Rainbow*)
KONTSERT MASTEROV UKRAINSKOVO ISKUSSTVA (1952) *d/s* Barnet 86min (= *Concert of the Masters of Ukrainian Art*)
KONTSERT-VALS (1940) *d/s* Ilya Trauberg, *M Dobson* 70min (= *Concert Waltz*)
KONYAKU YUBIWA (1950) *d* Konoshita *w* Mifune (= *Engagement Ring*)
KOON (1927) *d* Mizoguchi Nik (= *Gratitude to the Emperor*)
KORABLI SHTURMUYUT BASTIONY (1953) *d* Romm *m* A Khatchaturian *94min (= *Ships Attacking Forts*)
KOREA (1959) *d/co-p* J Ford *co-p/w* G O'Brien *30min US Defence Dept
KÖRHINTA (1955) *d/co-s/dec* Fábri 100min (= *Merry-Go-Round/Little Fairground Swing*)
KORITSI ME TA MAURA, TO (1955) *d/s* Cacoyannis *c* Lassally *m* Hadjidakis *w* Lambetti 93min (= *The Girl in Black*)
KÖRKARLEN (1920) *d/s/w* Sjöström 1866m SF
KÖRKARLEN (1958) *d* Mattsson *s* Lindstrom *w* Jacobsson, Bjork S 109min (= *The Phantom Carriage*)
KORN (1943) *d/s* B Henning Jensen (= *Corn*)
KORNSPEKULANTENS DATTER (1915) *d/s* Madsen
KOROL LIR (1971) *d* Kozintsev *fpl* Shakespeare (translation: *Boris Pasternak*) *m* Shostakovich 124min (= *King Lear*)
KORRIDOREN (1968) *d/co-s* Halldoff *87min (= *The Corridor*)
KORT AR SOMMAREN (1962) *d* B Henning Jensen *c* Fischer *w* Kulle, B Andersson S* 110min (= *Pan*)
KOSAR UND DIE NACHTIGALL (1935) *d* Jutzi 2385m
KOSHIBEN GANBARE (1931) *d/s* Naruse (= *Hardworking Clerk*)
KOSHIKEI (1968) *d/p/pc/co-s* Oshima 117min (= *Death by Hanging*)
KOTAN NO KUCHIBUE (1959) *d* Naruse *w* Mori (= *A Whistle In My Heart*)
KOTCH (1971) *d* Lemmon *w* Matthau *113min
KOTOSHI NO KOI (1962) *d* Kinoshita S 82min Sho (= *New Year's Love*)
KOUZELNY DUM (1939) *d/s* Vavra
KRACH IM INTERHAUS (1935) *d* V Harlan 2283m
KRACH UND GLUCK UM KUNNEMANN (1937) *d* Wegener 2442m Dec
KRAHEN FLIEGEN UM DEN TURN (1917) *d/p/co-s* May 4rs
KRAJOBRAZ PO BITWIE (1970) *d/co-s* Wajda *co-m* Vivaldi, Chopin (= *Landscape After Battle*)
KRAKATIT (1948) *d/co-s* Vavra *fn* Kavel Capek
KRAL KRALU (1963) *d* Fric *fst* J Weiss (= *King of Kings*)
KRANES KONDITORI (1951) *d/s* A Henning Jensen

KRANKHEITS BILD DES SCHLACHTENERPROBTEN UNTEROFFIZIERS IN DER ENDSCHLACHT, DAS (1971) *d* Kluge, *O Mai, A Zemann*
KRASNAYA PALATKA (1971) *d* Kalatozov *w* Connery, Cardinale, Finch, Girotti *121min (= *The Red Tent*)
KRASNAYA PRESNYA (1926) *d* Room, *L Sheffer* 654m (= *Red Presnya*)
KRAVA NA MJESECU (1959) *d/s* Vukotic anim* 310m (= *The Cow on the Moon*)
KREISE (1933) *d* Fischinger *m* Greig, Wagner anim* 2min (= *Circles*)
KREMLIN LETTER, THE (1970) *d/co-s* J Huston *w* B Andersson, G Sanders, Von Sydow, Welles, J Huston PV* 121min Fox
KRESTYANYE (1935) *d/co-s* Ermler 113min (= *Peasants*)
KREUTZER SONATA (1915) *d/s* Brenon 5rs Fox
KREUTZEROVA SONATA (1926) *d/s* Machaty *fst* Tolstoi *c* Heller (= *The Kreutzer Sonata*)
Kreutzer Sonata, The = KREUTZEROVA SONATA (1926)
KREUTZERSONATE, DIE (1937) *d* V Harlan *w* Dagover 2320m *r* UFA
Kriemhild's Revenge = KRIEMHILDS RACHE (1924)
Kriemhilds Rache Part 2 of DIE NIBELUNGEN (1924) (= *Kriemhild's Revenge*)
KRIGENS FJENDE (1915) *d* Madsen
KRIG OG KAERLIGHED (1914) *d* Madsen *s* Dreyer
KRIS (1945) *d* Ingmar Bergman SF (= *Crisis*)
KRISTIAN (1939) *d/co-st* Fric (= *Christian*)
KRISTINUS BERGMAN (1948) *d/s* A and B Henning Jensen 90min
Krogen Og Kronborg = ET SLOT I ET SLOT (1954)
KRÓK DO TMY (1938) *d* Fric *c* Heller (= *Madmen in the Dark*)
KROL MACIUS PIERWSZY (1958) *d/co-s* Jakubowska * (= *King Matthew I*)
KROV ZA KROV, SMERT ZA SMERT (1941) *d/s/e* Vertov, Elisabeth Svilova 1rl (= *Blood for Blood, Life for Life*)
KRUZHEVA (1928) *d/co-s* Yutkevich 2100m (= *Lace*)
KRZYZACY (1960) *d/co-s* A Ford S* 180min (= *Knights of :he Teutonic Order*)
KSE (1932) *d/s/e* Shub 100min (= *Komsomol – Patron of Electrification*)
KUCHIZUKE (1955) (ep) *d* Naruse 115min (all eps) (= *The First Kiss*)
KUCKUCKSJAHRE (1967) *d/co-s* Moorse *100min
KUHLE WAMPE (1932) *d* Dudow *st/co-s/lyr* Brecht *c* Krampf *m* Eisler 2017m
KUMO GA CHIGIRERU TOKI (1961) *d* Gosho (= *As the Clouds Scatter*)
KUMONOSU-JO (1957) *d/co-p/co-s* Kurosawa *fpl* (*Macbeth*) Shakespeare *w* Mifune, Yamada 110min Toho (= *Throne of Blood*)
KUNGAJAKT (1944) *d/st* Sjöberg SF (= *Royal Hunt*)
KUNSTEN AT LEVE LIVET (1927) *d/s* Madsen
KUNSTNERS GENEMBRUD, EN (1915) *d* Madsen
KUNSTSEIDERNE MADCHEN, DAS (1960) *d* Duvivier *w* Masina 104min
KURFURSTENDAMM (1920) *d/p/s* R Oswald *w* Nielsen, Veidt 2424m
KUROL JUNIN NO ONNA (1961) *d* Ichikawa Toho (= *Ten Black Women*)
Kuragejima: Legends from a Southern Island = KAMIGAMI NO FUKAKI YOKUBO (1968)
KURAYAMI NO USHIMATSU (1935) *d/s* Kinugasa
KURODA SEICHUROKU (1938) *d/s* Kinugasa
KUROI KAWA (1957) *d* Kobayashi *w* Nakadai, Yamada (= *Black River*)
Kuroneko = YABU NO NAKA NO KURONEKO (1968)
KURRAGÖMMA (1963) *d/p* Lindgren San (= *Hide and Seek*)
KURUTTA IPPEIJI (1926) *d/w* Kinugasa (= *A Crazy Page*)
KUSTOM KAR KOMMANDOS (1965) *d/c/e* Anger 16mm *5min
KUTASEK A KUTILKA JAR RANO VASTAVALI (1952) *d/co-s* Trnka *487m (= *How Kustasek and Kutilka Got Up in the Morning*)
KUTSUKATE TOKIJIRO (1934) *d/s* Kinugasa
KUTUZOV (1944) *d* Petrov 113min
KVARTERET KORPEN (1963) *d/s* Widerberg *m* Torelli 100min (= *Raven's End*)
KUARTETTEN SOM SPRÄNGDES (1950) *d* Molander *w* Björk *w* Kulle, Sjöström
KVINNA I VITT (1949) *d* Mattsson *s* Lindstrom *w* Dahlbeck (= *Woman in White*)
KVINNAS ANSIKTE, EN (1938) *d* Molander *w* Ingrid Bergman SF
KVINNA UTAN ANSIKTE (1947) *d* Molander *s* Ingmar Bergman *w* Kjellin, Björk 101min (= *The Woman without a Face*)
KVINNODRÖM (1955) *d/s* Ingmar Bergman *w* Dahlbeck, Andersson, Björnstrand 86min San (= *Dreams/Journey into Autumn*)
KVINNORS VÄNTAN (1952) *d/s/fpl* (*Rakel och Biografvaktmästaren*) Ingmar Bergman *c* Fischer *w* Björk, Dahlbeck, Björnstrand, Kulle 105min SF (= *Secrets of Women/Waiting Women*)
Kwaidan = KAIDAN (1964)
KYBERNETICKA BABICKA (1963) *d/s/a* Trnka *803m (= *Cybernetic Grandma*)

KYOKUBADAN NO JOWO (1925) *d* Mizoguchi Nik (= *Queen of Circus*)

KYO MO MATA KAKUTE ARINAN (1959) *d* Kinoshita (= *Thus Another Day*)

KYOREN NO BUTO (1924) *d/s* Kinugasa (= *Dance Training*)

KYOREN NO ONNA SHISHO (1926) *d* Mizoguchi Nik (= *Passion of a Woman Teacher*)

KYOTO (1968) *d* Ichikawa sh

KYRIAKATIKO XYPNIMA (1953) *d/st/s* Cacoyannis 94min (= *Windfall in Athens*)

KYSSEN PÅ KRYSSEN (1950) *d/co-s* Mattsson co-s Ekman w Björnstrand (= *The Kiss on the Cruise*)

LABIRYNT (1962) *d/s/dec* Lenica anim* 15min (= *Labyrinth*)

LABURNUM GROVE (1936) *d* C Reed 73min

Labyrinth = LABIRYNT (1962)

LABYRINTH DER LEIDEN SCHAFT (1959) *d/co-s* Thiele w Tiller 2570m UFA

LABYRINTH DES GRAUENS (1920) *d* Curtiz

LAC-AUX-DAMES, LE (1934) *d* M Allégret *fst* Vicky Baum w M Simon, S Simon 88min

Lace = KRUZHEVA (1928)

LACHENDEN ERBEN, DIE (1931 *r* 1933) *d/co-s* Ophuls *fpl* (*Romeo and Juliet*) Shakespeare 75min UFA

LÂCHES VIVENT D'ESPOIR, LES (1960) *d/co-st* Bernard-Aubert 90min

LACRIME E SORRISI (1912) *d* Baldassare Negroni w Ghione

LADDIE (1935) *c* G Stevens *p* Berman w Crisp 70min RKO

LADDER, THE (1967) *d/p/anim* Dunning *5min

Ladder of Success, The = YORU NO SUGAO (1958)

LADIES IN RETIREMENT (1941) *d* C Vidor *c* Barnes w Lupino, L Hayward 92min Col

LADIES' MAN (1931) *d* Lothar Mendes *s* H Mankiewicz *c* Milner w K Francis, Lombard, W Powell 70min Par

LADIES' MAN, THE (1961) *d/p/co-s* J Lewis co-a Pereira w J Lewis Raft *106min Par

LADIES MUST LOVE (1933) *d* Dupont *c* Gaudio 69min U

LADIES NIGHT IN A TURKISH BATH (1928) *d* Cline 7rs FN

LADIES OF LEISURE (1930) *d* Capra *p* Cohn *ad/s* Swerling *c* J Walker w Stanwyck, L Sherman 98min Col

LADIES OF THE CHORUS (1949) *d* Karlson w Monroe 61min Col

LADIES OF THE JURY (1932) *d* L Sherman w Oliver 65min RKO

LADIES OF THE MOB (1928) *d* Wellman *s* J Farrow w Bow 6792ft Par

LADIES THEY TALK ABOUT (1933) *co-d* Keighley *c* J Seitz w Stanwyck 68min WB

LADIES' "TORTOISE" RACE (1898) *p* Hepworth 50ft

LADRI DI BICICLETTE (1948) *d/p/co-ad* De Sica *st/s/co-ad* Zavattini *fn* Luigi Bartolini *co-ad* Cecchi d'Amico 85min (= *Bicycle Thieves*)

LADRO DI BAGDAD, IL (1960) *d* Arthur Lubin w Reeves CS* 100min (= *The Thief of Bagdad*)

LADRO DI VENEZIA, IL (1951) *d* Brahm w Montez 87min Fox (= *The Thief of Venice*)

LADRO LUI, LADRA LEI (1958) *d/st* Zampa w Sordi

Ladies and Ladies = DOLCI SIGNORE, LE (1967)

Lady = LADY, THE (1925)

Lady, And Her Favorites, The = SHUKUJO TO HIGE (1931)

LADY, THE (1925) *d/p* Borzage *c* Gaudio w N Talmadge 2350m FN (= *Lady*)

LADY AND THE BANDIT, THE (1951) *d* Ralph Murphy *fpm* Alfred Noyes w L Hayward 79min Col

LADY AND THE MOUSE, THE (1913) *d* Griffith w L Gish, D Gish, L Barrymore 1rl Bio

LADY AND THE TRAMP (1955) *p* Disney *fst* Ward Greene *sp* *eff* Iwerks *wv* Peggy Lee CS anim* 76min

LADY BE GOOD (1941) *d* McLeod *c* Folsey *chor* Berkeley w Sothern, R Young Dailey 111ft MGM

LADYBIRD (1927) *d* W Lang

LADYBUG, LADYBUG (1963) *d/p* Perry 84min UA

LADY EVE, THE (1941) *d/s* P Sturges *c* Milner w Stanwyck, H Fonda, C Coburn 97min Par

LADY FOR A DAY (1933) *d* Capra *p* Cohn *s* Riskin *fst* Damon Runyon *c* J Walker 83min Col

LADY FROM CHEYENNE, THE (1941) *d* F Lloyd *c* Krasner w L Young, Preston 87min U

LADY FROM NOWHERE (1931) *d/e* Thorpe 65min

LADY FROM SHANGHAI, THE (1948) *d/p/s* Welles *as-p* R Wilson, Castle *c* Lawton w Welles, Hayworth 86min Col

LADY FROM TEXAS, THE (1951) *d* Pevney 77min U

LADY GAMBLES, THE (1949) *d* M Gordon *c* Metty *a* Golitzen w Stanwyck, Preston, Curtis 99min U

LADY GANGSTER (1942) *d* Florey (*ps* Florey and Roberts) 62min WB

LADY GODIVA RIDES AGAIN (1951) *d/co-p/co-s* Launder *co-p* Gilliat *m* Alwyn w Kendall 90min BL

LADY HAMILTON (1921) *d/pc* R Oswald w Veidt, Krauss

Lady Hamilton (UK) = THAT HAMILTON WOMAN (1941)

LADY HAMILTON – ZWISCHEN SCHMACH UND LIEBE (1968) *d* Christian-Jaque *fn* Dumas w Tiller, J Mills PV* 98min (= *Emma Hamilton*)

LADY IN A CAGE (1964) *d* Walter Grauman *c* Garmes w De Havilland 93min Par

LADY IN A JAM (1942) *d/p* La Cava w I Dunne 78min U

LADY IN CEMENT (1968) *d* G Douglas *p* A Rosenberg *c* Biroc w Sinatra, Welch, Conte PV* 93min Fox

LADY IN QUESTION, THE (1940) *d* C Vidor *fst* Achard *c* Andriot w Hayworth, G Ford 81min Col

Lady in the Car with Glasses and a Gun, The = DAME DANS L'AUTO AVEC DES LUNETTESE ET UN FUSIL, LA (1970)

LADY IN THE DARK (1944) *d* Leisen *s* Goodrich, Hackett *fpl* M Hart *c* Rennahan *a* Dreier *m* Weill w G Rogers, Milland W Baxter 100min Par

LADY IN THE LAKE (1946) *d* R Montgomery *fn* R Chandler *co-a* Gibbons w R Montgomery, Nolan, 103min MGM

Lady in White = VITA FRUN (1962)

LADY IS A SQUARE, THE (1959) *d* H Wilcox w Neagle 98min

LADY IS WILLING, THE (1934) *d* Gilbert Miller *c* J Walker w L Howard 67min Col

LADY IS WILLING, THE (1942) *d/p* Leisen *st/co-s* J Grant *c* Tetzlaff w Dietrich, MacMurray 92min Col

Lady Jane Grey = TUDOR ROSE (1936)

LADY KILLER (1933) *d* Del Ruth *c* Gaudio w Cagney 76min WB

LADYKILLERS, THE (1955) *d* Mackendrick *p* Balcon *as-p* Holt *c* Heller w Guinness, Sellers 97min JAR

Lady Knows a Little of it – from the Devil, The = ZHENSHCHINA ZAKHOCHET – CHORTA OBMOROCHIT (1964)

LADY L (1965) *d/w* Ustinov *p* Ponti *fn* Gary *c* Alekan w Loren, P Newman, Niven, Noiret, Piccoli PV* 124min MGM

LADY MACBETH (1918) *d* Guazzoni

Lady Macbeth of Siberia = SIBIRSKA LEDI MAGBET (1962)

Lady Margon = LADY MARIONS SOMMARFLIRT (1912)

LADY MARIONS SOMMARFLIRT (1912) *d* Sjöström (= *Lady Margon*)

LADY OF BURLESQUE (1943) *d* Wellman *fn* (*The G-String Murders*) G Lee w Stanwyck 91min *r* UA (= *Striptease Lady*)

LADY OF CHANCE, A (1929) *d/p* Leonard *ad* Goulding *c* Marley, Daniels w L Sherman 8rs MGM

LADY OF LOVE, A (1930) *d/p* Sjöström w Banky, Robinson 92min MGM

LADY OF SCANDAL, THE (1930) *d* Franklin *co-c* A C Miller w Rathbone 6855ft MGM (= *The High Road*)

LADY OF THE HAREM, THE (1926) *d* Walsh *c* Milner w Fazenda 5717ft FPL

LADY OF THE NIGHT (1933) *d* Wellman *st* Loos w L Young, Tone 71min MGM (= *Midnight Mary*)

LADY OF THE PAVEMENTS (1929) *d* Griffiths *c* Struss, Bitzer 85min UA

LADY OF THE TROPICS (1939) *d* Conway *st/s* Hecht *c* Folsey w R Taylor, Lamarr 92min MGM

LADY ON A TRAIN (1945) *d* Charles David *fn* Leslie Charteris *m* Rozsa w Durbin, Horton, Duryea 93min U

LADY OR THE TIGER?, THE (1942) *d* Zinnemann 9min MGM

LADY PANAME (1949) *d/p/co-s* Jeanson *co-s* P Prévert, J Prévert *m* Van Parys w Jouvet 95min

LADY PAYS OFF, THE (1951) *d* Sirk *c* Daniels w Darnell 80min U

Lady President, The (UK) = PRESIDENTESSA, LA (1913)

LADY'S MORALS, A (1930) *d* Franklin w Beery 10rs MGM (= *Jenny Lind*)

LADY'S PROFESSION, A (1933) *d* McLeod 68min Par

LADY SURRENDERS, A (1930) *d* Stahl w Rathbone 8772ft U

Lady Surrenders, A = LOVE STORY (1944)

LADY TAKES A FLYER, THE (1957) *d* J Arnold *c* Glassberg w Turner, J Chandler CS* 95min U

LADY TAKES A SAILOR, THE (1949) *d* Curtiz *p* Kurnitz *c* McCord *e* Weishart *m* M Steiner w Wyman 99min WB

LADY TO LOVE, A (1930) *d* Sjöström w Banky, Robinson MGM

LADY VANISHES, THE (1938) *d* Hitchcock *s* Launder, Gilliat, Reville w M Redgrave, Lockwood, Lukas 97min

LADY WINDERMERE'S FAN (1925) *d* Lubitsch *fpl* Oscar Wilde w Colman 80min WB

Lady Windermere's Fan = FAN, THE (1949)

Lady with a Little Dog, The = DAMA S SOBACHKOI (1960)

LADY WITHOUT PASSPORT, A (1950) *d* JH Lewis *m* Raksin *co-a* Gibbons w Lamarr 73min MGM

LADY WITH RED HAIR, THE (1940) *d* C Bernhardt *p* J Warner *c* Edeson w Rains, M Hopkins, A Smith, (Wilde) 84min WB

Lady with the Coloured Gloves, The = DAMEN MED DE LYSER HANDSKER (1942)

LADY WITH THE LAMP, THE (1951) *d/p* H Wilcox w Neagle 110min *r* BL

LAENGSLERNES NAT (1929) *d/s* Madsen

LAFAYETTE ESCADRILLE (1958) *d/st* Wellman *c* Clothier *m* Rosenman 93min WB

LAFAYETTE! WE COME! (1918) *d/s* Perret *c* Andriot Pat

LA-HAUT SUR CES MONTAGNES (1946) *d* MacLaren 3min NFBC

LAISSE ALLER, C'EST UNE VALSE (1971) *d/co-s* Lautner w Darc, N Loy *100min

LALKA (1968) *d/s* Has FS 159min (= *The Doll*)

Lama del Guistiziere, La = DON CESARE DI BAZAN (1942)

LAMB, THE (1915) *d/s* Christy Cabanne w Fairbanks Sr 5rs Tri

LAMBERT & CO (1964) *d* Pennebaker 15min

Lament of a White Lily = SHIRAYURI WA NAGEKU (1925)

LAMIEL (1967) *d/co-s* Aurel *fn* Stendhal *mf* Mozart w Karina, Brialy, Hossein 95min

LAMM, DAS (1964) *d* Staudte 90min

LAMPE QUI FILE, LA (1909) *d* Cohl anim 100m

LAMP STILL BURNS, THE (1943) *d* Elvey w S Granger 90min

Lana Turner = MORE MILK, EVETTE (1965)

LANCELOT AND GUINEVERE (1962) *d/ex-p/w* Wilde PV* 117min U (= *Sword of Lancelot*)

LANCER SPY, THE (1937) *d* Ratoff *sp* Dunne w Del Rio, G Sanders, Lorre Fox

LAND, THE (1942) *d/s/co-cy/co-c/n* Flaherty *co-c* F Crosby, I Lerner 43min US Dept of Agriculture

LAND BEYOND THE LAW, THE (1927) *d* H Brown 6195ft FN

LANDFALL (1949) *d* Annakin 87min

LANDLADY, THE (1938) *d* R Boulting *p* J Boulting 36min

LANDLORD, THE (1970) *d* Hal Ashby *p* Jewison *110min

Land of Angels, The = ANGYALUK FÖLDJE (1962)

Land of Desire, The = SKEPP TILL INDIALAND (1947)

LAND OF JAZZ, THE (1920) *d/co-st/ad* Furthman 5rs Fox

LAND OF LIBERTY (1940) *p/n/e* De Mille 137min

Land of Plenty, The = CUCCAGNA, LA (1962)

LAND OF PROMISE (1945) *d* Rotha w J Mills 67min

LAND OF THE PHARAOHS (1955) *d/p* Hawks *co-st/co-s* Faulkner, Kurnitz, *c* Garmes, R Harlan *a* Trauner *m* Tiomkin w Hawkins CS* 106min WB

LAND OF THE SILVER FOX (1928) *d* Enright 7rs

LAND OF WHITE ALICE (1959) *d* W Van Dyke 27min

Land ohne Frauen, Das = TERRA SENZA DONNE (1929)

LANDRU (1962) *d* Chabrol *co-p* Ponti *s* Sagan *c* Rabier *dec* Saulnier w Darrieux, Morgan Neff, Queneau, Melville *115min (= *Bluebeard*)

LANDSBYKIRKEN (1947) *d/co-s* Dreyer 14min (= *The Danish Village Church*)

Landscape After the Battle = KRAJOBRAZ PO BITWIE (1970)

LANDSFLYKTIGE, DE (1921) *d/co-s* Stiller 1973 *m* SF (*In Self-Defence*)

LANDSHÖVDINGENS DOTTRAR (1915) *d/s* Sjöström 1100m (= *Tvillingsystravna*)

Land We Love, The = HERO'S ISLAND (1962)

Land Without Bread = HURDES, LAS (1932)

LANE THAT HAD NO TURNING, THE (1922) *d* Fleming 5rs FPL

LANGAGE DE L'ECRAN (1947) *d* Rozier sh

LANGAGE DES FLEURS, LE (1959) *d* Lenica anim

LANGLOIS (1970) *d/p/c* Eila Hershon, Roberto Guerro w L Gish, Ingrid Bergman, Moreau, Signoret, Deneuve, Truffaut *52min

LANGE HOSEN, KURZE HAARE (1959) *d* Tressler

Language du Sourire, Le = SIKKIM, TERRE SECRETE (1916)

Lantern, The = UTA ANDON (1960)

Lantern Under a Full Moon = MEIGATSU SOMATO (1951)

LAPIQUE (1965) *d* Reichenbach

Lappflickan = HOGFJALLETS DOTTER (1914)

LARCENY, INC (1942) *d* Bacon *p* Wallis *c* Gaudio w Robinson, Wyman, B Crawford, Quinn 95min WB

Larceny Lane = BLONDE CRAZY (1931)

LAREDO, COSTA DE ESMERELDA (1961) *d* Grau

LARCENY ON THE AIR (1937) *d* Pichel 61min Rep

Larks on a Thread = SKRIVANCI NA NITICH (1969)

LASH, THE (1930) *d/p* F Lloyd *c* E Haller w Barthelmess, Astor 75min FN

LASKY JEDNE PLAVOVLASKY (1965) *d/st* Forman *co-s* Forman, Passer *c* Ondricek 85min (= *A Blonde in Love/Loves of a Blonde*)

LASSIE COME HOME (1943) *d* F Wilcox *s* H Butler *m* Amfitheatrof w E Taylor Crisp *9rs MGM

LAST ANGRY MAN, THE (1959) *d* Daniel Mann *p* Kohlmar *ad* R Murphy *c* Howe *m* Duning w Muni, D Wayne 100min Col

LAST BOMB, THE (1947) *d* F Lloyd *20min USAAF *r* WB

LAST CARD, THE (1926) *d* Thorpe

LAST CHALLENGE, THE (1967) *d/p* Thorpe w G Ford, A Dickinson PV* 96min MGM (= *Pistolero/ Pistolero of Red River*)

LAST COMMAND, THE (1928) d/s Von Sternberg st Lubitsch c Glennon dec Dreier t H Mankiewicz w Jannings, W Powell 8154ft Par
LAST COMMAND, THE (1955) d/p F Lloyd m M Steiner w Hayden *110min Rep
Last Company, The (UK) = LETZTE KOMPANIE, DIE (1930)
LAST DAYS OF DOLWYN, THE (1949) d/st/s Emlyn Williams p De Grunwald c Heller w Burton, Emlyn Williams, Evans 95min BL
Last Days of Pompeii, The = ULTIMI GIORNI DI POMPEI, GLI (1926)
LAST DAYS OF POMPEII, THE (1935) d Schoedsack p M Cooper w Rathbone 92min RKO
Last Days of Pompeii, The = ULTIMI GIORNI DI POMPEI, GLI (1959)
LAST DROP OF WATER, THE d Griffith 1rl Bio
LAST FLIGHT, THE (1931) d Dieterle c Hickox w Barthelmess 80min FN
LAST FRONTIER, THE (1926) d G Seitz 7800ft PRC
LAST FRONTIER, THE (1956) d A Mann co-s Yordan, Maddow (uc) c Mellor m Harline w Mature, A Bancroft, Preston CS* 98min Col
LAST GANGSTER, THE (1937) d Edward Ludwig co-st Wellman s Mahin c Daniels co-s Vorkapich w J Stewart, EG Robinson, Carradine 81min MGM
Last Goal, The = KET FELIDO A POKOLBAN (1961)
LAST HOLIDAY (1950) d Henry Cass co-p/s Priestley w Guinness 88min
LAST HUNT, THE (1956) d/s R Brooks p Schary c R Harlan m Amfitheatrof w R Taylor, S Granger, Nolan CS* 98min MGM
LAST HURRAH, THE (1958) d/p J Ford s F Nugent c Lawton w Tracy, J Hunter, Rathbone, Crisp, Darwell, Carradine 121min Col
Last Laugh, The = LETZTE MANN, DER (1923)
Last Man, The = POSLEDNI MUZ (1934)
LAST MAN TO HANG, THE (1956) d Fisher co-ad Elvey w Forbes 75min r Col
LAST MILE, THE (1932) d Sam Bischoff s S Miller c Edeson 75min
LAST MILE, THE (1959) d H W Koch co-s S Miller rm 1932 c Brun 81min r UA
LAST MOMENT, THE (1928) d/st/s/e Fejos c Shamroy 5600ft
LAST NIGHT OF THE BARBARY COAST (pre-1915) d/c Mohr 1rl
LAST OF MRS CHEYNEY, THE (1929) d Franklin c Daniels w Shearer, Rathbone 95min MGM
LAST OF MRS CHEYNEY, THE (1937) rm 1929 d Boleslavsky, George Fitzmaurice co-s Raphaelson rm 1929 c Folsey a Gibbons w J Crawford, W Powell, R Montgomery 98min MGM
LAST OF THE COMANCHES (1952) d De Toth p Adler c Lawton m Duning w B Crawford *84min Col (= Sabre and the Arrow)
LAST OF THE LINE, THE (1914) d Ince
LAST OF THE LONE WOLF, THE (1930) d Boleslavsky p Cohn 65min Col
LAST OF THE MOHICANS, THE (1920) d C Brown, M Tourneur fn James Fenimoore Cooper p Brown w Beery, Karloff 6rs
LAST OF THE MOHICANS, THE (1936) d G Seitz sp Dunne fn James Fenimoore Cooper w R Scott 91min UA
LAST OF THE PAGANS (1935) d Thorpe 72min MGM
LAST OUTLAW, THE (1919) d J Ford 2rs U
LAST PAGE, THE (1952) d Fisher 84min
Last Pair Out = SISTA PARET UT (1955)
Last Paradise, The = ULTIMO PARADISO, L' (1956)
LAST PERFORMANCE, THE (1929) d Fejos c Mohr w Veidt 7rs r U (= Erik The Great/Erik The Great Illusionist)
LAST ROUND-UP, THE (1934) d Hathaway fn (The Border Legion) Zane Grey c Stout w R Scott 61min Par
LAST RUN, THE (1971) d R Fleischer c Nykvist w G Scott *95min MGM
LAST SAFARI, THE (1967) d/p Hathaway c Moore w S Granger *115min Par
Last Shot = POSLEDNI VYSTREL (1950)
Last Stage, The = OSTATNI ETAP (1948)
LAST STAND, THE (1938) d JH Lewis 56min Col
LAST SUMMER (1969) d Perry fn E Hunter *97min Fox
LAST SUNSET, THE (1961) d Aldrich s Trumbo c Laszlo co-a Golitzen m Gold co-song Tiomkin w Hudson, K Douglas, Cotten, Malone, Lynley *112min r U
Last Temptation (UK) = SUOR LETIZIA (1916)
LAST TIME I SAW ARCHIE, THE (1961) d/p/w J Webb c Joe MacDonald w Mitchum 98min AA
LAST TIME I SAW PARIS, THE (1954) d/co-s R Brooks p J Cummings co-s JJ Epstein fst (Babulon Revisited) Fitzgerald c Ruttenberg w E Taylor, V Johnson, Pidgeon, D Reed *116min MGM
LAST TRAIL (1927) d Lewis Seiler fn Zane Grey w Mix 5190ft Fox
LAST TRAIN FROM GUN HILL (1958) d J Struges p Wallis s Poe co-a Pereira m Tiomkin c C Lang w K Douglas, Quinn VV* 94min Par

LAST VALLEY, THE (1971) d/p/ad Clavell m Barry w Caine, Sharif TAO 70* 125min
LAST VOYAGE, THE (1960) d/co-p/s Stone co-p/e Virginia Stone c Mohr w Stack, Malone, G Sanders, E O'Brien *91min r MGM
LAST WAGON, THE (1956) d/co-s Daves co-s J Grant co-a Wheeler m L Newman w Widmark CS* 99min Fox
LAST WARNING, THE (1929) d Lewis c Mohr 8rs
Last Warrior, The = FLAP (1970)
Last Will of Dr Mabuse, The (US) = TESTAMENT DES DR MABUSE, DAS (1932)
Last Witness, The (UK) = LETZTE ZEUGE, DER (1961)
LAST WOMAN ON EARTH, THE (1960) d/p Corman S* 71min
LAS VEGAS NIGHTS (1941) d Ralph Murphy c Mellor w Sinatra 89min Par
LAS VEGAS STORY, THE (1952) d Stevenson c Wild w J Russell, Mature, Price, Carmichael 88min RKO
Late Autumn = AKIBYORI (1960)
Late Christopher Bean, The = CHRISTOPHER BEAN (1933)
Late Chrysanthemums = BANGIKU (1954)
LATE EDWINA BLACK, THE (1951) d Elvey 78min r BL
LATE EXTRA (1935) d Albert Parker w Mason, (Wolfit) 69min
LATE GEORGE APLEY, THE (1947) d J Mankiewicz p Kohlmar s P Dunne fco-pl G Kaufman fco-pl/fn John P Marquand m Mockridge c La Shelle w Colman, Haydn 98min Fox
Late Matthew Pascal, the = FEU MATHIAS PASCAL (1925)
Late Season = U TOSZEZON (1967)
Late Spring = BANSHUN (1949)
LATEST FROM PARIS, THE (1928) d S Wood c Daniels w Shearer 7743ft MGM
LATIN LOVERS (1953) d LeRoy p Pasternak c Ruttenberg co-a Gibbons w Turner, Montalban *104min MGM
Latin Lovers (UK): 8 eps of ITALIANE E L'AMORE, LE (1961)
LAUFER VON MARATHON, DER (1933) d Dupont s Von Harbou c Schuftan w Helm 100min
LAUGH AND GET RICH (1931) d/s La Cava w Oliver 73min RKO
Laugh and the World Laughs = HABIT OF HAPPINESS, THE (1916)
LAUGH CLOWN LAUGH (1928) d/p Brenon c Howe w Chaney, L Young 5916ft
LAUGHING BILL HYDE (1918) d Hobart Henley w W Rogers 6rs pc Goldwyn
LAUGHING BOY (1934) d WS Van Dyke co-s Mahin m Stothart w Novarro 78min MGM
LAUGHING GAS (1914) d/s/w Chaplin 2rs Key (= Tuning His Ivories/The Dentist/Down and Out)
LAUGHING GRAVY (1931) d James Horne p Roach w Laurel, Hardy (2rs) r MGM
LAUGHTER (1930) d/co-st D'Arrast c Folsey w March 7089ft Par
LAUGHTER IN PARADISE (1951) d Mario Zampi w A Hepburn 93min
LAUGHTER IN THE DARK (1969) d T Richardson s Edward Bond fn Vladimir Nabokov w Karina *104min r UA
Laugh with Max Linder = EN COMPAGNIE DE MAX LINDER (1963)
LAUNCHING OF JAPAN'S NEW WARSHIP 'KATORI' (1905) p Paul 200ft
LAURA (1944) d/p Preminger fn Caspary c La Shelle co-a Wheeler m Raksin w Tierney, D Andrews, C Webb, Price 88min Fox
LAUREL-HARDY MURDER CASE, THE (1930) d James Parrott p Roach w Laurel, Hardy 3rs r MGM
LAVENDER HILL MOB, THE (1951) d Crichton p Balcon c Slocombe a Holt st/s T Clarke w Guinness, A Hepburn 78min
LAW AND IDSORDER (1958) d Cornelius, Crichton w M Redgrave 76min BL
LAW AND JAKE WADE, THE (1958) d J Sturges c Surtees w R Taylor, Widmark CS* 86min MGM
LAWBREAKERS, THE (1960) d J Newman co-s Burnett c Musuraca w Miles 79min MGM (TV pilot released theatrically outside US)
LAWFUL LARCENY (1932) d Dwan p Zukor c Rosson 5503ft FPL
LAWFUL LARCENY (1930) d/w L Sherman 66min RKO
LAWLESS, THE (1950) d Losey s/fn (The Voice of Stephen Wilder) Mainwaring (ps Homes) des consultant J Hubley 83min Par (= The Dividing Line)
LAWLESS BREED, THE (1952) d Walsh c Glassberg w Hudson, McIntire 83min U
LAWLESS REGION, THE (1929) d H Brown 6100ft FN
LAWLESS STREET (1955) d JH Lewis p H Brown as-p/w R Scott c Rennahan *78min Col
LAWLESS WOMAN, THE (1931) d/co-s Thorpe 63min
LAW OF MEN, THE (1919) d Niblo 5rs FPL
Law of Survival, The = LOI DU SURVIVANT, LA (1966)
LAW OF THE LAWLESS, THE (1923) d Fleming 7rs FPL
LAW OF THE TROPICS (1941) d Enright c Hickox w Constance Bennett 76min WB
LAW OF THE WEST, THE (1912) d Ince

LAWRENCE OF ARABIA (1962) d Lean p Spiegel s Bolt, M Wilson (uc) c F Young co-2nd c Roeg in Jarre w O'Toole, Guinness, Quinn, Hawkins, J Ferrer, Rains, A Kennedy, Sharif, Wolfit PV 70* BL/Col
LAW VS BILLY THE KID, THE (1954) d Castle p Katzman *73min Col
LAWYER, THE (1968) d/co-s Furie *120min Par
LAWYER MAN (1932) d Dieterle w W Powell 72min WB
LAZYBONES (1925) d Borzage w Pitts 7234ft Fox
LAZY BONES (1935) d M Powell 66min
LAZY LIGHTNING (1926) d Wyler 2rs U
LAZY RIVER (1934) d G Seitz c Toland w R Young 75min MGM
LAZZARELLA (1957) d Bragaglia w Girotti
LEADING LIZZIE ASTRAY (1914) d/w Arbuckle p Sennett 1rl Key
LEADVILLE GUNSLINGER (1952) d/as-p Keller 54min Rep
LEAGUE OF GENTLEMEN, THE (1960) d Dearden co-p/w Attenborough s Forbes w Hawkins, Forbes 113min Jar
LEAH, THE FORSAKEN (1914) d Brenon
LEARNING TO LOVE (1925) d Franklin st/ad Emerson, Loos w C Talmadge 5400ft WB
LEASE OF LIFE (1954) d Freund c Slocombe m Rawsthorne w Donat *94min
LEATHER BOYS, THE (1963) d Furie p Stross w Tushingham CS 108min r BL
LEATHER GLOVES (1948) d/p Quine, William Asher w Edwards 75min Col (= Loser Take All)
LEATHERNECKING (1930) d Cline w I Dunne 79min RKO
LEATHERSTOCKING (1924) d G Seitz fns James Fennimore Cooper Pat (serial in 10 eps)
LEAVE 'EM LAUGHING (1928) d Bruckman supn McCarey p/s Roach w Laurel, Hardy 2 rs MGM
LEAVE HER TO HEAVEN (1946) d Stahl s Swerling c Shamroy co-a Wheeler m A Newman w Tierney, Wilde, Price, Crain 110min Fox
Leave it to Me = NECHTE TO NA MNE (1955)
Leaves From Satan's Book (US) = BLADE AF SATANS BOG (1919)
LEBENDE BUDDHAS (1924) d/co-s/w Wegener sp eff Ruttmann co-dec Poelzig w Nielson 2547m Terra
LEBENDE LEICHNAM, DER (1929) d/s Fedor Otsep fpl Tolstoi co-c Jutzi w Pudovkin 3532m
LEBEN VON ADOLF HITLER, DAS (1961) d/cy/e Rotha 102min (= Life of Adolf Hitler, The)
LECTURE ON MAN, A (1962) d R Williams anim 5min
Leda = A DOUBLE TOUR (1959)
LEDOLOM (1931) d Barnet 1792m (= Thaw)
LEDYANAYA SUDBA (1930) d/co-s Petrov 1940m (= Cold Feast, The)
LEFT HANDED GUN, THE (1958) d Penn s Leslie Stevens fpl Vidal c Marley w P Newman 102min r WB
LEFT HAND OF GOD, THE (1955) d Dmytryk p Adler c Planner co-a Wheeler m V Young w Bogart, Moorehead, Cobb, Tierney CS* 87min Fox
LEFT, RIGHT AND CENTRE (1958) d/co-p/co-s Gilliat co-p Launder 95min
Legacy of the Five Hundred Thousand = GOJUMAN-NIN NO ISA (1963)
LEGENDA O KRASNE JULICE (1968) d Passer (= The Legend of Beautiful Julia)
LEGENDA SINFONICA (1947) d Bava, M Melani c Bava
LEGENDE VON DER HEILIGEN SIMPLICIA (1920) d/p May s Von Harbou 2310m
Legend of Beautiful Julia, The = LEGENDA O KRASNE JULICE (1968)
LEGEND OF LYLAH CLARE, THE (1968) d/p/pc Aldrich co-s H Butler c Biroc w Finch, Novak, Borgnine, Cortese *127min r MGM
Legend of Prague, The (UK) = GOLEM, LE (1936)
Legend of St Ursula, The = LEGGENDA DI SANT' ORSOLA, LA (1948)
LEGEND OF THE LOST (1957) d/p Hathaway co-st/co-s B Hecht c Cardiff w J Wayne, Loren TR* 109min pc J Wayne r UA
Legend of the True Cross = INVENZIONE DELLA CROCE, L' (1949)
LEGEND OF YOUNG TURPIN, THE (1965) d Neilson *83min pc Disney
LEGGENDA DEL PIAVE, LA (1952) d/st/co-s Freda
LEGGENDA DI FAUST, LA (1949) d Gallone fpl Goethe 86min (= Faust and the Devil)
LEGGENDA DI SANT' ORSOLA, LA (1948) co-d/s Emmer co-d Enrico Gras cy/wv Cocteau 11min (= The Legend of St Ursula)
LEGIONI DI CLEOPATRA, LE (1959) d Cottafavi w G Marshall 102min
LEGION OF DEATH, THE (1918) d Browning 7 rs
LEGION OF THE CONDEMNED, THE (1928) d/p Wellman w G Cooper 7415ft Par
Legion of the Street, The = LEGION ULICY (1932)
Legend Or Was It?, A = SHITO NO DENSETSU (1963)
Legion's Last Patrol (UK) = MARCIA O CREPO (1962)
LEGION ULICY (1932) d A Ford (= The Legion of the Street)
LEGS (1970) d/wv Lennon, Yoko Ono wv J Mekas *50min (= Up Your Legs Forever)

LEGY JO MINDHALALIG (1960) *d* Ranódy (= *Be Good unto Death*)
LEHRER IM WANDEL (1963) *d* Kluge sh
LEIBE (1928) *d* Czinner
LEIDENSCHAFT (1925) *d/p Richard Eichberg w* Lillian Harvey 2345m
LEITH STEVENS AND THE SATURDAY NIGHT SWING CLUB ON THE AIR (1939) *d Lloyd French w* Leith Stevens 10min
LEKKAMRATERNA (1915) *d/s* Stiller 693m
Lekko = VIEREN MAAR (1954)
LEKTION I KÄRLEK, EN (1954) *d/s* Bergman *w* Dahlbeck, Björnstrand, H Andersson 95min SF
LEMON DROP KID, THE (1934) *d* Neilan *fst Damon Runyon* 71min Par
LEMON DROP KID, THE (1951) *d Sidney Lanfield,* Tashlin (*uc*) *co-s* Tashlin *fst Damon Runyon c* Fapp *co-a* Pereira *w* Hope, Nolan, Darwell 91min *r* Par
LENA AND THE GEESE (1912) *d* Griffith *w* Marsh, Pickford 1 rl Bio
LENDEMAIN, LE (1950) *d* Queneau
Leningrad in Combat = LENINGRAD V BORBYE (1942)
LENINGRAD SEGODNYA (1927) *d* Ilya Trauberg 1100m (= *Leningrad Today*)
Leningrad Today = LENINGRAD SEGODNYA (1927)
LENINGRAD V BORBYE (1942) *d* Karmen, *N Komarevstev, V Solostov, Y Uchitel co-c* Karmen 7 rs (= Leningrad in Combat)
Lenin in 1918 = LENIN V 1918 GODU (1939)
Lenin in October = LENIN V OKTYABRE (1937)
Lenin in Poland = LENIN W POLSCE (1961)
Lenin in Poland = LENIN V POLSHO (1964)
LENIN IN SWITZERLAND (1966) *d* Alexandrov
Lenin Lives = ZHIVOI LENIN (1948)
Lenin's Address = ADRES LENINA (1929)
LENIN V 1918 GODU (1939) *d* Romm *w* Cherkasov 132min (= *Lenin in 1918*)
LENIN V OKTYABRE (1937) *d* Romm, *Dmitri Vasiliev* 111min (= *Lenin in October*)
LENIN V POLSHO (1964) *d* Yutkevich S 97min (= *Lenin in Poland*)
LENIN IN POLSCE (1961) *d* Alexandrov 105min (= *Lenin in Poland*)
LENZ (1971) *d/s* Moorse *fst Büchner* *125min
LEO LA LUNE (1957) *co-d/p* Jessua *co-d Robert Giraud* 16min (= *Leo The Moon*)
LEONARDO DA VINCI (1952) *d/s* Emmer 62min
LEONE HAVE SEPT CABECAS, DER (1970) *d/co-s/co-e* Rocha *w* Léaud *103min *pc* Ferreri
LEONI AL SOLE (1961) *d/co-s/w* Caprioli *c* Di Palma *100min
LEON MORIN, PRETRE (1961) *d/s/di* Melville *p* Ponti *c* Decaë *w* Belmondo, Riva 125min
Leopard, The = GATTOPARDO, IL (1963)
LEOPARD LADY (1928) *d* Julian 6650ft Pat
LEOPARD MAN, THE (1943) *d* J Tourneur *p* Lewton *e* Robson 59min RKO
LEO THE LAST (1970) *d/co-s* Boorman *fpl* (*The Prince*) *George Tabori w* Mastroianni *104min *r* UA
Leo the Moon = LÉO LA LUNE (1957)
Lester Persky Story, the = SOAP OPERA (1964)
LEST WE FORGET (1918) *d/s* Perret Pat
Lest We Forget = HANGMEN ALSO DIE! (1943)
LET 'EM HAVE IT (1935) *d* S Wood 90min
LET FREEDOM RING (1939) *d* Conway *st/s* Hecht *w* Eddy, V McLaglen, L Barrymore 100min MGM
LET IT BE (1970) *d Michael Lindsay-Hogg ex-p/songs/w* The Beatles *81min
LET IT RAIN (1927) *d* Cline 5 rs FPL
LET ME DREAM AGAIN (1900) *d* G Smith
LET NO MAN WRITE MY EPITAPH (1959) *d* P Leacock *c* Guffey *w* Ives, Winters, Seberg 106min
LET'S DANCE (1950) *d* McLeod *c* Barnes *a* Dreier *w* Hutton, Astaire 112min Par
LET'S FACE IT (1943) *d Sidney Lanfield as-p* Kohlmar *c* Lindon *w* Hope, Pitts 76min Par
LET'S GET MARRIED (1926) *d* La Cava *c* Cronjager *w* Oliver 6664ft FPL
LET'S GO (1923) *d* W Howard 5198ft
LET'S GO NATIVE (1930) *d* McCarey *c* Milner *w* Jeanette MacDonald, K Francis 6788ft Par
LET'S GO PLACES (1929) *d Frank Strayer w* Grable 6787ft Par
LET'S KILL UNCLE (1966) *d/p* Castle *c* Lipstein *92min U
LET'S LIVE A LITTLE (1948) *d Richard Wallace co-p* R Cummings *c* Laszlo *w* Lamarr, R Cummings, Sten 85min EL
LET'S LIVE TONIGHT (1935) *d* Schertzinger *c* J Walker *w* Lillian Harvey 69min Col
LET'S MAKE IT LEGAL (1951) *d Richard Sale co-s* Diamond *c* Ballard *co-a Wheeler w* Colbert, Carey, Wagner, Monroe 77min Fox
LET'S MAKE LOVE (1960) *d* Cukor *p* Wald *st/s* Krasna *additional di* Kanter *c* Fapp *colour consultant* Hoyningen-Huene *a* Wheeler *chor* Cole *w* Monroe, Montand, Randall (B Crosby, Gene Kelly) CS* 118min *r* Fox
Let's Make Up (US) = LILACS IN THE SPRING
Let's Play Hide-and-Seek = SKAL VI LEGE SKJUL (1969)

LETTER, THE (1940) *d* Wyler *p* J Warner, Wallis *s* H Koch *fst W Somerset Maugham c* Gaudio *m* M Steiner *w* B Davies, H Marshall 95min WB
Letter M, The = SLOWCE M (1963)
LETTERE DI UNA NOVIZIA (1960) *d/co-s* Lattuada *w* Girotti, Belmondo 102min
LETTER FOR EVIE (1945) *d* Dassin *c* Freund *co-a* Gibbons 89min MGM
LETTER FROM AN UNKNOWN WOMAN (1948) *d/co-s* Ophuls *p* Houseman *co-s* H Koch *fst* (*Briefe einer Unbekannten*) *Stefan Zweig c* Planer *a* Golitzen *m* Amfitheatrof *w* Fontaine 90min *r* U
LETTER FROM COLOMBIA (1963) *d* Blue
LETTER FROM HOME, A (1941) *d* C Reed sh
LETTER OF INTRODUCTION (1938) *d/p* Stahl *c* Freund *w* Menjou, G Murphy, Sheridan 104min U
Letter That Was Not Sent, The = NEOTPRAVLENNOE PISMO (1960)
LET THERE BE LIGHT (1956, *ur*) *d/co-s/co-c* Huston *co-c* Cortez *m* Tiomkin *c* 45min US Signal Corps
LET THE WORLD GO FORTH (1965) *n* Reagan sh
LETTER TO THREE WIVES, A (1949) *d/s* J Mankiewicz *p* S Siegel *ad* Caspary *c* AC Miller *co-a* Wheeler *m* A Newman *w* Darnell, Crain, Sothern, K Douglas, P Douglas, Ritter, Marsh 103min Fox
LETTINO VUOTO, IL (1913) *d/s* Guazzoni
LETTI SBAGLIATI (1965) *d* Steno *
Letto, Il = SECRETS D'ALCOVE (1954)
LETTO A TRE PIAZZE, IL (1960) *d/co-s* Steno *w* Toto 95min
LETTRE DE PARIS (1933) *d* Leenhardt
LETTRE DE PARIS (1945) *d/s* Leenhardt 21min
LETTRE DE SIBERIE (1958) *d/s* Marker *c* Vierny *80min
LETTRES D' AMOUR (1942) *d* Autant-Lara *co-s/di* Aurenche *c* Agostini 85min
LETTRES DE CHINE (1957) *d/s* Ivens 1138m *41min (3 parts: *L'Hiver/L'Eveil du printemps/La Fête du printemps*)
LETTRES DE MON MOULIN, LES (1954) *d/s* Pagnol *fst Daudet* 180min
LETTY LYNTON (1932) *d* C Brown *w* R Montgomery, J Crawford 62min MGM
LETUN (1931) *d* Ilya Trauberg anim 406m (= *Kites*)
LET US BE GAY (1930) *d/p* Leonard *c* Brodine *w* Shearer, Dressler, Hopper, Rosay 78min MGM
LET US LIVE (1939) *d* Brahm *c* Ballard *w* H Fonda, O'Sullivan 68min Col
LETYAT ZHURAVLI (1957) *d* Kalatozov *w* Batalov 92min (= *The Cranes Are Flying*)
LETZTE AKT, DER (1955) *d* Pabst *fst EM Remarque w* Werner 109min
LETZTE BRUCKE, DIE (1954) *d/s* Kautner *w* Wicki, Maximilian Schell
LETZTE FORT, DAS (1927) *d* C Bernhardt 2281m
LETZTE KOMPANIE, DIE (1930) *d* C Bernhardt *c* Krampf *w* Veidt UFA (= *The Last Company*)
LETZTE MANN, DER (1924) *d* Murnau *p* Pommer *s* C Mayer *c* Freund *co-dec* Rohrig *w* Jannings 2036m UFA (= *The Last Laugh*)
LETZTE ZEUGE, DER (1960) *d* Staudte 102min (= *The Last Witness*)
LEUCHFEUER (1954) *d/co-s* Staudte 95min Defa
LEUTNANT AUF BEFEHL (1916) *d/w* Lubitsch 1 rl (= *Lieutenant by Command*)
LEV A PISNICKA (1959) *d* Pojar anim* 17min (= *The Lion and the Ditty*)
LEVIATHAN (1961) *d/co-s* Kiegel *c* Hayer *m Arnold Schoenberg w* Palmer 93min (= *The Footbridge*)
Ley del Forestero, La = SIE NANNTEN IHN GRINGO (1966)
LIANA (1955) *d/co-s* Barnet 77min
Liaisons Amoureuses, Les = MORTE-SAISON DES AMOURS, LA (1961)
LIAISONS DANGEREUSES, LES (1959) *d/co-s* Vadim *fn Laclos m Thelonius Monk, Art Blakey w* Moreau, Philipe, Trintignant CS 106min
Liar and the Nun, The = LUGNER UND DIE NONNE, DER (1967)
LIBEL (1959) *d* Asquith *p/co-s* De Grunwald *w* Bogarde, De Havilland 100min MGM
LIBELED LADY (1936) *d* Conway *c* Brodine *w* Harlow, Tracy, M Loy, W Powell 98min MGM
Liberation = OSVOBOZHDENIE (1940)
LIBERATION OF LB JONES, THE (1970) *d* Wyler *co-s* Silliphant *c* Surtees *m* E Bernstein *w* Cobb *102min Col
Liberté = PAQUEBOT LIBERTE, LE (1950)
Liberté = PUNITION, LA (1962)
Liberté Cherie = A NOUS LA LIBERTE (1931)
LIBERTE EN CROUPE, LA (1970) *d/co-s* Molinaro *c* Coutard *86min
LIBERTE I (1962) *d/co-st* Ciampi *w* Ronet S 90min Pat
Libertine, The (US) = MATRIARCA, LA (1968)
LIBERTY (1929) *d* McCarey *p* Roach *w* Laurel, Hardy, Harlow 2 rs *r* MGM
Libido = SEI NO KIGEN (1967)
Licht in der Finsternis = ROSEN FUR BETTINA (1956)
LICHNOYE DELO (1932) *d* S & G Vasiliev (= *A Personal Affair*)
LICHTSRAHL IM DUNKEL, EIN (1917) *d/p* May 4 rs

LICK OBSERVATORY (1968) *d/s* C & R Eames *c* C Eames *10min
LIDECNYOMAS (1920) *d/co-s* Fejos *fst* (*The Crime of Lord Arthur Saville*) *Oscar Wilde*
LIDE NA KOLEKACH (1966) *d* Fric *87min (= *People on Wheels*)
LIDE NA KRE (1937) *d* Fric (= *Lost on Ice*)
LIEBE (1928) *d* Czinner *w* Bergner
LIEBE DER HETTY RAYMOND, DIE (1917) *d/p* May
LIEBE DER JEANNE NEY, DIE (1927) *d* Pabst *co-s* Vajda *co-c* F Wagner *dec* Warm *w* Helm 2320m UFA
Liebe der Mitsu, Die = TOCHTER DES SAMURAI, DIE (1937)
LIEBE DES VAN ROYK, DIE (1918) *d/co-s* Lupu-Pick 4 rs
LIEBE KANN WIE GIFT SEIN (1958) *d* V Harlan 91min
LIEBELEI (1932) *d/co-s* Ophuls *fpl Arthur Schnitzler c* Planer *mf Mozart, Brahms, Beethoven* 88min (= *Une Histoire d'amour*)
LIEBENSTRAUM (1928) *d* Stone
LIEBESBREIFE DER BARONIN VON S . . ., Die (1924) *d/co-s* Galeen 2381m UFA
LIEBESKARNAVAL (1928) *d/s* Genina
LIEBESKARUSSEL, DAS (1965) *d* Thiele *w* Jurgens, Deneuve, Ekberg, Tiller *112min (2 parts)
LIEBES PILGERFAHRT (1923) *d* Protozanov 2000m
LIEBESSPIEL (1931) *d* Fischinger anim si
LIEBE UND SO WEITER (1968) *d/co-s* Moorse *84min
LIED DER STROME, DAS (1954) *d/co-s* Ivens *songs* Brecht *m* Shostakovitch 102min (contains extracts from BORINAGE, NIEUWE GRONDEN)
LIED EINER NACHT, DAS (1932) *d* Litvak 85min Gau (= *Tell Me Tonight/Be Mine Tonight*)
LIED FUR DICH, EIN (1933) *d/p* May 2431m
Lies = USO (1963)
Lieutenant by Command = LEUTNANT AUF BEFEHL (1916)
Lieutenant Kizhe = PORUCHIK KIZHE (1934)
LIEUTENANT'S LAST FIGHT (1912) (2 parts) (= *Custer's Last Fight*)
LIEUTENANT WORE SKIRTS, THE (1956) *d/co-s* Tashlin *p* Adler *co-a* Wheeler *m* Mockridge *w* Ewell CS* 99min Fox
LIFE (1915, *uf*) *d/s/w* Chaplin
Life After Dark = GIRLS IN THE NIGHT (1953)
LIFE AND DEATH OF COLONEL BLIMP, THE (1943) *d/p/s* M Powell, Pressburger *c* Périnal *w* Kerr, Walbrook *163min
LIFE AND DEATH OF 9413, A HOLLYWOOD EXTRA (1927–28) *d/st/s* Florey *des/co-c/e* Vorkapich *co-c* Toland si 1 rl (= *A Hollywood Extra/Hollywood Rhapsody*)
LIFE AT THE TOP (1965) *d Ted Kotcheff fn John Braine c* Morris *w* Laurence Harvey, J Simmons, Wolfit 117min
LIFE BEGINS (1932) *d* E Nugent, *James Flood w* L Young, G Farrell 71min FN
LIFE BEGINS AT 8.30 (1942) *d* Pichel *p/s* N Johnson *fpl* (*The Light of Heart*) Emlyn Williams *c* Cronjager *w* Wilde, Lupino 85min Fox
LIFE BEGINS AT FORTY (1935) *d* G Marshall *s* Trotti *w* W Rogers, Darwell 85min Fox
LIFE BEGINS FOR ANDY HARDY (1941) *d* G Seitz *a* Gibbons *w* Rooney, Garland 100min MGM
LIFEBOAT (1944) *d* Hitchcock *p* Macgowan *s* Swerling *fst John Steinbeck m* Friedhofer *w* Bankhead, Bendix 96min Fox
LIFE DRAMA OF NAPOLEON BONAPARTE AND EMPRESS JOSEPHINE OF FRANCE, THE (1909) *d* Blackton Vit
LIFE FOR RUTH (1962) *d* Dearden 91min JAR
LIFE HESITATES AT 40 (1935) *d* C Chase (*as* Parrott), *Harold Law p* Roach *w* C Chase 2 rs MGM
LIFE IN HER HANDS (1951) *d* P Leacock 58min
LIFE IN SOMETOWN, U.S.A. (1938) *d/w* Keaton 1 rl MGM
LIFE IN THE BALANCE, A (1955) *d* Horner *fst Georges Simenon w* Marvin, A Bancroft, Montalban 74min Fox
Life in the Citadel = ZHIZN V TSITADELI (1947)
LIFE IN THE RAW (1933) *d Louis King fn Zane Grey w* G O'Brien, Trevor 59min Fox
Life is Good = PROSTOI SLUCHAI (1932)
Life is Like a Somersault = JINSEI TOMBOGAERI (1946)
Life, Love, Death = VIE, L'AMOUR, LA MORT, LA (1969)
LIFE OF A COWBOY, THE (1906) *d* Porter Ed
Life of Adolf Hitler, The (UK) = LEBEN VON ADOLF HITLER, DAS (1961)
Life of a Man = HITO NO ISSHO (1928)
LIFE OF AN AMERICAN FIREMAN (1903) *d* Porter 169ft Ed
Life of an Artist, The = GEIDO ICHIDAI OTOKO (1941)
Life of an Office Worker, The = KAISHAIN SEIKATSU (1929)
LIFE OF EMILE ZOLA, THE (1937) *d* Dieterle *p* Wallis *as-p* Blanke *di d* Rapper *m* M Steiner *w* Muni, Crisp 116min WB
LIFE OF HER OWN, A (1950) *d* Cukor *c* Folsey *co-a* Gibbons *m* Kaper *w* Turner, Milland, Ewell 108min Fox

LIFE OF JIMMY DOLAN, THE (1933) d A Mayo w L Young, (J Wayne) 9 rs WB
LIFE OF JUANITA CASTRO, THE (1965) d Warhol 16mm 70min
Life of O-Haru, The = SAIKAKU ICHIDAI ONNA (1952)
LIFE OF THE MOLDS (1957) d W Van Dyke 20min
LIFE OF THE PARTY, THE (1930) d Del Ruth 78min WB
LIFE OF VILLA (1912) d Christy Cabanne, Walsh supn Griffith
Life's Conflicts = LIVETS KONFLIKTER (1913)
LIFE'S GREATEST PROBLEM (1919) d/p Blackton 6 rs
LIFE'S HARMONY (1916) d/w Borzage Tri
Life's Just Great = LIVET AR STENKULL (1967)
Life Upside Down = VIE A L'ENVERS, LA (1964)
Life was the Stake = HRA O ZIVOT (1956)
LIFE WITH FATHER (1947) d Curtiz c Marley m M Steiner w I Dunne, E Taylor, Pitts, W Powell 118min WB
LIFTING SHADOWS (1920) d/s Perret Pat
Lift to the Scaffold (UK) = ASCENSEUR POUR L'ECHAFAUD (1957)
Ligeia = TOMB OF LIGEIA, THE (1964)
Light Fantastic, The = LOVE IS BETTER THAN EVER (1951)
LIGHTHOUSE (1946) d/p/s Wisbar 60min
Lighthouse, The = YOROKUBI MO KANASHIMI MO IKUTOSHITSUKI (1957)
LIGHTHOUSE BY THE SEA, THE (1925) d St Clair w Fazenda 5800ft WB
LIGHT IN THE DARK, THE (1922) d/co-s C Brown w Chaney 7 rs
LIGHT IN THE FOREST, THE (1958) d Herschel Daugherty w Lynley, Corey, Dru, McIntire *93min pc Disney
LIGHT IN THE PIAZZA (1962) d G Green p Freed s JJ Epstein c Heller w De Havilland S* 101min MGM
LIGHTNIN' (1925) d J Ford c August 8050ft Fox
LIGHTNIN' (1930) d H King w McCrea w Rogers 85min Fox
Lightning = INAMUMA (1952)
LIGHTNING GUNS (1950) d Sears 55min Col
LIGHTNING RAIDER, THE (1918–19) d/co-s G Seitz w White (serial in 15 eps)
LIGHTNING STRIKES TWICE (1951) d K Vidor p Blanke c Hickox m M Steiner w Roman 91min WB
LIGHT OF WESTERN STARS, THE (1925) d W Howard fn Zane Grey c Andriot 6859ft Par-FPL
Light Over Russia = TSVET NAD ROSSIEI (1947)
Lights of Night = NISHIGINZA ESKIMAU (1958)
Lights of Variety = LUCI DEL VARIETA (1950)
LIGHT THAT FAILED, THE (1939) d/p Wellman co-a Dreier m V Young w Colman, Lupino, W Huston 97min Par
LIGHT TOUCH, THE (1951) d/s R Brooks p Berman c Surtees m Rozsa w S Granger, G Sanders 107min MGM
LIGHT UP THE SKY (1960) d/p L Gilbert 90min BL
LIGNE DE DEMARCATION, LA (1966) d/co-s Chabrol c Rabier w Seberg, Gélin, Ronet 90min (= The Line of Demarcation)
LIGNE DE MIRE, LA (1960, u/f) d Pollet
Lika, Chekhov's Love = SIUZHET DLYA NEBOLSHOVO RASSKAZA (1968)
Lika, le Grand Amour de Tchekhov = SIUZHET DLYA NEBOLSHOVO RASSKAZA (1968)
Like a House on Fire (US) = HORI MA PENENKO (1967)
Like Father, Like Son (UK) = PADRI E FIGLI (1957)
LIKELY STORY, A (1947) d Potter m Harline 89min RKO
Like Night and Day = SOM NATT OCH DAG (1969)
Like The Changing Heart of a Bird = JIHI SHINCHO (1927)
LI'L ABNER (1940) d Albert S Rogell st Al Capp w Keaton 78min r RKO
LI'L ABNER (1959) d/co-s/co-fpl M Frank p/co-s/co-fpl Panama c Fapp co-a Pereira VV* 114min pc M Frank, Panama r Par
LILACS IN THE SPRING (1954) d H Wilcox w Neagle, Flynn *94min (= Let's Make Up)
LILAC TIME (1928) d George Fitzmaurice ad Goldbeck
LILI (1953) d/co-chor Walters co-a Gibbons m Kaper w Caron, M Ferrer *81min MGM
LILIES OF THE FIELD (1930) d A Korda c Garmes 5979ft FN
LILIES OF THE FIELD (1963) d/p Nelson S Poe c E Haller m Goldsmith w Poitier 94min MGM
LILIOM (1930) d Borzage 90min Fox
LILIOM (1934) d/co-s F Lang p Pommer fpl Ferenc Molnar co-c Maté co-m Waxman w Boyer, Artuaud, Romance 120min
LILITH (1963) d/p/co-s Rossen co-s Aurthur c Schuftan m K Hopkins w Beatty, Seberg 96min r Col
Lilly, den Suffragetten = MODERNA SUFFRAGETTEN, DEN (1913)
LILLY TURNER (1933) d Wellman c Hickox 75min FN
LILY OF THE TENEMENTS, THE (1911) d Griffith 1rl Bio
LIMELIGHT (1936) d H Wilcox e Elmo Williams w Neagle 80min
LIMELIGHT (1952) d/p/s/chor/m/songs Chaplin technical consultant Totheroh c Struss a Lourié w Chaplin, Bloom, Keaton, Purviance 143min UA

LIMONADOVY JOE (1964) d Oldrich Lipsky fpl Brdecka
LIMPING MAN (1953) d Charles de Lautour, Endfield (uc) 76min
Line of Demarcation, The = LIGNE DE DEMARCATION, LA (1966)
Line of Destiny, The = REKAVA (1956)
LINER CRUISING SOUTH (1933) d B Wright GPO
LINES HORIZONTAL (1960) d McLaren, Evelyn Lambert S* anim 6min NFBC
LINES OF WHITE ON A SULLEN SEA (1909) d Griffith 1 rl Bio
LINES VERTICAL (1960) d McLaren, Evelyn Lambert S* anim 6min NFBC
LINE TO TCHERVA HUT, THE (1937) d Cavalcanti p Grierson, Watt m Britten 10min
LINEUP, THE (1958) d D Siegel s Silliphant c Mohr w Wallach 86min Col
LINGNER WERKE (1935) d Alexeieff anim
LIOLA (1963) d/co-s Blasetti fpl Luigi Pirandello w Brasseur, Aimée 95min (= A Very Handy Man)
LION, THE (1962) d Cardiff m Arnold w Holden, T Howard CS* 96min Fox
Lion and the Ditty, The = LEV A PISNICKA (1959)
LION AND THE LAMB, THE (1931) d G Seitz 74min Col
LION AND THE MOUSE, THE (1928) d Bacon c Brodine w L Barrymore 6251ft WB
LION DES MOGOLS, LE (1924) d/e J Epstein s/w Mozhukhin
LION HAS WINGS, THE (1939) d M Powell, Brian Desmond-Hurst, Adrian Brunel dec V Korda w Oberon, R Richardson 70min pc A Korda r UA
Lion Hunters, The = CHASSE AU LION A L'ARC, LA (1965)
LION IN WINTER, THE (1968) d Anthony Harvey ex-p Levine c Slocombe m Barry w O'Toole, K Hepburn PV* 134min
LION IS IN THE STREET, A (1953) d Walsh m Waxman w Cagney, A Francis, McIntyre *88min WB
LIONS LOVE (1969) d/p/s Varda w S Clarke *115min
LIONS SONT LACHES, LES (1961) d Verneuil di Audiard c Matras w Cardinale, Darrieux, Morgan, Brialy FS 98min
LIQUIDATOR, THE (1965) d Cardiff cr R Williams m Schifrin w T Howard, Tamiroff PV* 104min MGM
Lisa (US) = INSPECTOR, THE (1961)
LISBON (1956) d/as-p/w Milland st Rackin w M O'Hara, Rains *90min Rep
LISTEN, DARLING (1938) Edwin L Marin p J Cummings c Lawton a Gibbons w Garland, Pidgeon, Bartholomew, Astor 70min MGM
Listen, Let's Make Love = SCUSI, FACCIAMO L'AMORE? (1968)
LISTEN TO BRITAIN (1941) d/e Jennings, McAllister s Jennings 70min
LIST OF ADRIAN MESSENGER, THE (1963) d J Huston c Joe MacDonald co-a Golitzen m Goldsmith w G Scott, K Douglas, Curtis, Lancaster, C Brook, H Marshall, Sinatra, Mitchum, Dalio, (J Huston) 98min r UA
LISTOPAD (1935) d/s/e Vavra
Liszt Rhapsody = WENN DIE MUSIK NICHT WAR (1935)
LIT A COLONNE, LE (1942) d Roland Tual w Marais
LIT A DEUX PLACES, LE (1965) d Delannoy, Francois Dupont-Midi, Gianni Puccini fst La Fontaine 120min (= The Double Bed)
LITET BO (1956) d Mattson (= A Little Place of One's Own)
LITTLE AMERICAN, THE (1917) d De Mille w Pickford, Novarro, Beery, S Wood 6rs r FPL
LITTLE BALLERINA, THE (1947) d/co-s L Gilbert w Margot Fonteyn 62min
LITTLE BIG HORN (1951) d/s Warren 86min
LITTLE BIG MAN (1970) d Penn fn Thomas Berger w Dunaway PV* 147min
LITTLE BIG SHOT (1935) d Curtiz co-s Wald, JJ Epstein c Gaudio w Horton 78min WB
LITTLE BIT OF HEAVEN, A (1940) d Marton p Pasternak co-s Taradash c J Seitz e Benedek w Stack 87min U
LITTLE BOY LOST (1953) d/s Seaton p Perlberg c Barnes co-a Pereira w B Crosby 95min Par
LITTLE BOY WITH A BIG HORN, THE (1953) d Cannon anim* 7min UPA r Col
LITTLE BROTHER RAT (1939) d C Jones p L Schlesinger anim* 7min
LITTLE CAESAR (1930) d LeRoy p Wallis fn Burnett c Gaudio w Robinson, Fairbanks Jr 80min FN
Little Chimney Sweep, The = KLEINE SCHORN- STEINFEGER, DER (1935)
LITTLE COLONEL, THE (1935) d Butler c AC Miller w Temple 82min Fox
LITTLE DOCTOR, THE (1901) d G Smith 100ft
Little Drop Too Much, A = SKLENICKU VIC, O (1953)
Little Fairground Swing = KORHINTA (1955)
LITTLE FAUSS AND BIG HALSY (1970) d Furie w Redford PV* 99min Par
LITTLE FOXES, THE (1941) d Wyler p Goldwyn s/fpl Hellman c Toland w B Davis, H Marshall, T Wright, Duryea 116min r RKO
LITTLE FRANCH GIRL, THE (1925) d Brenon c Rosson 5628ft FPL

LITTLE FUGITIVE, THE (1953) co-d/co-p/co-s/c Engel co-d Ruth Orkin 75min
LITTLE GIANT, THE (1933) d Del Ruth w Robinson, Astor 75min WB
LITTLE GIANT (1946) d William A Seiter w Dumont, B Abbot, Costello 91min U
LITTLE HERMAN (1914) d/p Terry anim
LITTLE HERO, A (1913) d Sennett w Normand ½rl Key
LITTLE HUT, THE (1957) d/co-p Robson c F Young w Gardner, Niven, S Granger *78min MGM
LITTLE IRISH GIRL, THE (1926) d Del Ruth ad Zanuck 6100ft WB
LITTLE ISLAND, THE (1958) d R Williams S* anim 29min
LITTLE JOHNNY JONES (1929) d LeRoy 74min FN
LITTLE JOURNEY, A (1927) d/p Leonard s Lewin 6088ft MGM
Little Kidnappers = KIDNAPPERS, THE (1953)
LITTLE LORD FAUNTLEROY (1921) d Alfred E Green, Jack Pickford pc/w Pickford 10rs r UA
LITTLE LORD FAUNTLEROY (1936) d Cromwell p Selznick s Walpole w Bartholomew 98min r UA
Little Man, The (UK) = ANNI DIFFICILI (1948)
LITTLE MAN WHAT NOW? (1934) d Borzage c Brodine 97min U
LITTLE MEN (1940) d McLeod c Musuraca w K Francis, G Bancroft 84min RKO
LITTLE MISS BROADWAY (1938) d Irving Cummings w Temple, G Murphy 72min Fox
LITTLE MISS SMILES (1922) d J Ford 5rs Fox
LITTLE MISS THOROUGHBRED (1938) d J Farrow c O'Connell w Sheridan 65min WB
LITTLE MR. JIM (1946) d Zinnemann co-a Gibbons 92min MGM
Little Mook = GESCHICHTE VOM KLEINEN MUCK, DIE (1953)
Little Murmur = CHIISANA SASAYAKI (1966)
LITTLE NELLIE KELLY (1940) d Taurog p Freed c June w Garland, G Murphy 100min MGM
LITTLE NELL'S TOBACCO (1911) co-d Ince w Pickford
LITTLE NEMO (1909) d McCay anim
Little Nuns, The (UK) = MONACHINE, LE (1963)
Little Old-Fashioned World UK) = PICCOLO MONDO ANTICO (1940)
LITTLE OLD NEW YORK (1940) d H King p Zanuck c Shamroy m A Newman w Faye, MacMurray 100min Fox
LITTLE ORPHAN, THE (1917) d Conway 5rs
LITTLE ORPHAN, THE (1948) d Hanna, Barbera p Quimby anim* 8min MGM
LITTLE PHANTASY ON A NINETEENTH CENTURY PAINTING, A (1946) d McLaren anim 4min NFBC
Little Place of One's Own, A = LITTLE BO (1956)
LITTLE PRINCESS, A (1917) d Neilan 5rs
LITTLE PRINCESS, THE (1939) d W Lang p Zanuck co-c AC Miller w Temple, Romera 91min Fox
LITTLE RANGER, THE (1938) d G Douglas 1rl
LITTLE RED DECIDES (1918) d Conway 5rs
LITTLE RED MONKEY (1953) d/co-s K Hughes 74min
LITTLE ROBINSON CRUSOE (1924) d Cline 6216ft r MGM
Little Runaway, the = CHIISANA TOBOSHA (1967)
LITTLE RURAL RED RIDING HOOD (1949) d Avery p Quimby anim* 6min MGM
LITTLE SAVAGES, THE (1959) d Haskin w Armendariz S 72min r Fox
LITTLE SHEPHERD OF KINGDOM COME, THE (1928) d/p Santell c Garmes w Barthelmess 7700ft FN
LITTLE SHEPHERD OF KINGDOM COME, THE (1961) d A McLaglen c F Crosby CS* 108min Fox
LITTLE SHOP OF HORRORS, THE (1960) d/p Corman 70min
Little Soldier, The = PETIT SOLDAT, LE (1960)
LITTLEST OUTLAW, THE (1955) d Roberto Gavaldon w Armendariz *75min pc Disney
LITTLEST REBEL, THE (1935) d D Butler w Temple 73min Fox
LITTLE TEACHER, THE (1909) d Griffith w Pickford 1rl Bio
LITTLE TEACHER, THE (1914) d/p Sennett w Sennett, Normand, Arbuckle 2rs Key
LITTLE TEASE, THE (1913) d Griffith 1rl Bio
LITTLE TERROR, THE (1917) d/s Ingram 5rs
LITTLE 'TINKER (1948) d Avery p Quimby anim* 1rl MGM
Little Umbrella, The = PARAPLICKO (1957)
LITTLE WIDOW, THE (1919) co-d St Clair p/supn/s Sennett 1913ft
LITTLE WILDCAT (1928) d Enright c B Reynolds 7rs WB
LITTLE WOMEN (1933) d Cukor s Mason ex-p H Cooper as-p Macgowan fn Louisa May Alcott m M Steiner w K Hepburn, J Bennett, Lukas, Oliver 113min RKO
LITTLE WOMEN (1949) d/p LeRoy fn Alcott co-a Gibbons w E Taylor, Lawford, Allyson, Astor, J Leigh, M O'Brien 121min MGM
Little World of Don Camillo, The (UK) = PETIT MONDE DE DON CAMILLO, LE (1951)
LIVE FAST, DIE YOUNG (1958) d Henreid c Lathrop co-a Golitzen 82min U
Live for Life (UK) = VIVRE POUR VIVRE (1967)

373

LIVE GHOST, THE (1934) *d Charles Rogers p* Roach *w* Laurel, Hardy 2rs *r* MGM

LIVE IN FEAR (1958) *d/p/co-s* Fregonese 68min

Lively Alley = YOKI NO URAMACHI (1939)

LIVELY SET, THE (1964) *d* J Arnold *95min U

LIVES OF A BENGAL LANCER, THE (1935) *d* Hathaway *c* C Lang *w* G Cooper, Tone, Tamiroff 109min Par

LIVER AR STENKULL (1967) *d/co-s* Halldorff 84min (= *Life's Just Great*)

LIVETS GOGLRSPIL (1916) *d/s* Madsen

LIVETS KONFLIKTER (1913) *d/s* Stiller *w* Sjöström (= *Life's Conflicts*)

LIVETS STORME (1911) *d/s* Blom *w* Nielsen

LIVETS VAR (1957) *d* Mattson (= *Spring of Life*)

LIVE WIRE, THE (1937) *d* Brenon 69min BL

LIVE WIRES (1946) *d* Karlson 64min Mon

Living = IKIRU (1952)

Living Camera, The = NEHRU (1962)

Living Corpse, The = ZHIVOI TRUP (1929)

LIVING DANGEROUSLY (1936) *d* Brenon 69min

Living Dead, The (UK) = UNHEIMLICHE GESCHICHTEN (1932)

LIVING DESERT (1953) *d James Algar co-c* C Hall *pc* Disney *72min

LIVING IDOL, THE (1957) *d/co-p/st/s* Lewin *c* Hildyard CS* 101min *co-pc* Lewin *r* MGM

LIVING IT UP (1954) *d* Taurog *st* B Hecht *c* Fapp *co-a* Pereira *w* Martin, J Lewis, J Leigh *95min Par

LIVING MACHINE, THE (1961) *d/p* Kroitor *c* Koenig 16mm 29min (Part 1)/30min (Part 2) NFBC

Living Nightmare, The = VOLCA NOC (1955)

LIVING ON VELVET (1935) *d* Borzage *st/s* Wald, JJ Epstein *c* Hickox 80min WB

LIVRO, O (1954) *d* Barreto sh

Lizards, The = BASILISCHI, I (1963)

LJUBAVNI SLUCAJ, TRAGEDIJA SLUZBENICE P.T.T (1967) *d/s* Makavejev 69min (= *Love Dossier, or the Tragedy of a Switchboard Operator/Switchboard Operator*)

LJUSNANDE FRAMTID, DEN (1940) *d/co-s* Molander *w* Kjellin SF

LJUVLIG AR SOMMARNATTEN (1961) *d* Mattson (= *The Summer Night is Sweet*)

LLANTO POR UN BANDIDO (1964) *d/co-s* Saura *w* Bunuel CS* 95min (= *Weeping for a Bandit*)

LLOYD'S OF LONDON (1936) *d* H King *as-p* Macgowan *c* Glennon *w* Carroll, Power, G Sanders, Bartholemew 115min Fox

Loafers, The (UK) = VITELLONI, I (1953)

LOCAL BOY MAKES GOOD (1931) *d* LeRoy *co-ad* Enright *fpl* (*The Poor Nut*) *JC Nugent*, E Nugent *c* Polito 67min FN

LOCKED HEART (1918) *d* H King

LOCKET, THE (1946) *d* Brahm *c* Musuraca *w* Mitchum 86min RKO

LOCKSPITZEL (1935) *d* Jutzi 1993m

Locomotive No B-1000 = PAROVOZ NO B-1000 (1927)

LOCOMOTIVES (1934) *d* Jennings 9min

Locus = KISEKI (1963)

LOCUST PLAGUE (*c* 1952) *d* Kershner

LODGER, THE (1926) *d/co-s* Hitchcock *p* Balcon 7685ft

LODGER, THE (1931) *d* Elvey 7605ft

LODGER, THE (1944) *d* Brahm *c* Ballard *m* Friedhofer *w* Oberon, G Sanders 80min Fox

LODGING FOR THE NIGHT, A (1912) *d* Griffiths *w* Pickford 1rl Bio

LOGIS ET DES HOMMES, LES (1958) *d* Dewever sh

LOI, LA (1958) *d/s* Dassin *c* Martelli *w* Mastroianni, Mercouri, Montand, Lollabrigida, Brasseur 120min MGM

LOI C'EST LA LOI, LA (1957) *d/co-ad* Christian-Jaque *c* Di Venanzo *m* Rota *w* Fernandel, Toto 95min

LOI DU NORD, LA (1939) *d* Feyder *fn* (*Telle qu'elle était en son vivant*) *Maurice-Constantin Weyer dec* D'Eaubonne *w* Morgan 100min (= *La Piste du Nord*)

LOI DU SURVIVANT, LA (1966) *d/s/fn* (*Les Aventuriers*) Giovanni *100min (= *The Law of Survival*)

LOIN DU VIETNAM (1967) *d/co-p* Godard, Ivens, Klein, Resnais, Lelouch *co-p* Varda *co-c* Cloquet *e* Marker part 16mm part * (= *Far From Vietnam*)

LOJEN OCH TARAR (1912) *d* Sjöström 668m (= *Dragers Juveler*)

LOLA (1961) *d/s* Demy *c* Coutard *dec* Evein *m* Legrand *w* Aimée S 85min

LOLA MONTES (1955) *d/co-s* Ophuls *fn Cécil Saint-Laurent c* Matras *co-dec* D'Eaubonne *m* Auric *w* Carol, Ustinov, Werner, Walbrook CS* 140min (= *Lola Montez/The Sins of Lola Montes*)

Lola Montez = LOLA MONTES (1955)

LOLITA (1962) *d* Kubrick *p* J Harris *s/fn Vladimir Nabokov c* Morris *w* Mason, Sellers, Winters 153min *r* MGM

LOMBARDI, LTD (1929) *d* Conway 1000ft

LOMELIN (1965) *d/c* Reichenbach 22min

LONDON AFTER MIDNIGHT (1927) *d/p/st* Browning *w* Chaney 5687ft MGM

LONDON CAN TAKE IT (1940) *d* Jennings, Watt *co-e* J Lee 10min GPO

LONDON BELONGS TO ME (1948) *d/co-s* Gilliat *p* Launder *w* Attenborough 112min JAR (= *Dulcimer Street*)

LONDON EXPRESS AT WOOD GREEN (1896) *p* Paul 40ft

LONDON POP (1964) *d* Moorse

London Smoke (UK) = FUMO DI LONDRA (1965)

LONDON TOWN (1946) *d/p/st* W Ruggles *w* Kendall *119min *r* EL (= *My Heart Goes Crazy*)

LONEDALE OPERATOR, THE (1911) *d* Griffith 1rl Bio

LONE DEFENDER (1930) *d* Thorpe (serial in 12eps)

LONELINESS OF THE LONG DISTANCE RUNNER, THE (1962) *d/p* T Richardson *s/fst Alan Sillitoe c* Lassally *w* Courtenay, M Redgrave 104min BL

LONELY ARE THE BRAVE (1962) *d* D Miller *s* Trumbo *c* Lathrop *m* Goldsmith *w* K Douglas, Matthau PV 107min U

LONELY BOY (1962) *d* Kroitor, Koenig *p* Kroitor *c* Koenig *m/w Paul Anka* 16mm 28min NFBC

LONELYHEARTS (1958) *d Vincent J Donehue p/s* Schary *c* J Alton *w* Clift, M Loy, Ryan 108min *r* UA

Lonely Lane = HOROKI (1962)

LONELY MAN, THE (1957) *d* Levin *c* Lindon *co-a* Pereira *w* Perkins, Palance, Cook VV 87min Par

Lonely Roughneck, The = SABISHII RANBOMONO (1927)

Lonely Village = SABISHIKI MURA (1924)

LONELY VILLA (1909) *d* Griffith *s* Sennett *c* Bitzer *w* Sennett, Pickford 200m Bio

Lonely Wife, The = CHARULATA (1964)

Lonely Woman, The = VIAGGIO IN ITALY (1953)

LONE RANGER, THE (1956) *d* Heisler *p* Goldbeck *86min WB

LONESOME (1928) *d* Féjos part * 7rs *r* U

LONESOME COWBOYS (1968) *d* Warhol 16mm* 110min

LONE STAR, THE (1927) *d* Wyler 2rs U

LONE STAR (1951) *d* V Sherman *s/fst* B Chase *c* Rosson *co-a* Gibbons *w* Gable, Gardner, B Crawford, L Barrymore 94min MGM

LONE WOLF, THE (1917) *d* Brenon 6rs Gau

Long Ago, Tomorrow (US) = RAGING MOON, THE (1971)

LONG ARM, THE (1956) *d* Frend *p* Balcon *w* Hawkins 96min JAR

LONG CHANCE, THE (1922) *d* Conway 5rs U

LONG DAY'S JOURNEY INTO NIGHT (1962) *d* Lumet *p* Landau *fpl Eugene O'Neill c* B Kaufman *m* Previn *w* K Hepburn, R Richardson 136min Fox

LONG DUEL, THE (1967) *d/p* Annakin *c* Hildyard *w* Brynner, T Howard PV* 115min JAR

LONGEST DAY, THE (1962) *d* Marton, Annakin, Wicki, G Oswald (*uc*) *p* Zanuck *Battle co-ordinator/as-p* Elmo Williams *s/fn Cornelius Ryan co-additional s* Gary *co-c* Bourgoin *co-a* V Korda *m* Jarre *w* Arletty, Barrault, Bourvil, Burton, Connery, Danton, M Ferrer, H Fonda, Holden, J Hunter, Jurgens, Lawford, Mitchum, Marquand, E O'Brien, Ryan, Steiger, R Wagner, J Wayne CS 180min Fox

LONG GRAY LINE, THE (1955) *d* J Ford *c* Lawton *m* Duning *w* Power, M O'Hara, Crisp CS* 138min *r* Col

LONG-HAIRED HARE (1949) *d* C Jones anim* 7min WB

LONG HAUL, THE (1957) *d/s* K Hughes *w* Mature 100min *r* Col

LONG HOT SUMMER, THE (1958) *d* Ritt *p* Wald *fn* (*The Hamlet*) Faulkner *c* La Shelle *co-a* Wheeler *m* North *w* P Newman, Woodward, Welles, Remick CS* 117min Fox

Longing (UK) = SEHNSUCHT (1921)

LONG JOHN SILVER (1955) *d* Haskin *st/s* Rackin *w* Newton CS* 109min

Long Live Kindness = AT ZIJE NEBOZTIK (1935)

Long Live the Air = DAYESH VOZDUKH

LONG, LONG TRAILER, THE (1954) *d* Minnelli *p* Berman *s* Goodrich, Hackett *c* Surtees *co-a* Gibbons *w* Ball *96min MGM

LONG LOST FATHER (1934) *d* Schoedsack *as-p* Macgowan *w* J Barrymore 61min RKO

LONG MEMORY, THE (1952) *d/s* Hamer *w* J Mills 96min JAR

LONG NIGHT, THE (1947) *d/co-p* Litvak *rm* LE JOUR SE LEVE (1937) *c* Polito *a* Lourié *m* Tiomkin *w* H Fonda, Price, Cook 97min RKO

Long Night of '43, The = LUNGA NOTTE DEL '43, LA (1960)

LONG PANTS (1927) *d* Capra *w* Langdon 6rs *pc* Langdon *r* FN

Long Ride Home, The = TIME FOR KILLING, A (1967)

LONG SHIPS, THE (1964) *d* Cardiff *c* Challis *w* Widmark, Poitier TR* 124min *r* Col

LONGUE MARCHE, LA (1966) *d/co-s* Astruc *w* Hossein, Ronet, Trintignant FS 90min

LONG VOYAGE HOME, THE (1940) *d* J Ford *p* Wanger *s* D Nichols *fpl* (*four one-act plays*) *Eugene O'Neill c* Toland *w* Mitchell, J Wayne 105min *r* UA

LONG WAIT, THE (1954) *d* Saville *fst Mickey Spillane c* Planer *w* Quinn, C Coburn 89min *r* UA

LOOK BACK IN ANGER (1959) *d* T Richardson *p* Saltzman *additional di/fpl* Osborne *c* Morris *w* Burton, Evans, Bloom 101min ABC

LOOK FOR THE SILVER LINING (1949) *d* D Butler *c* Marley *chor* Prinz *w* C Ruggles 105min WB

LOOKING FOR LOVE (1964) *d* Weis *p* Pasternak *c* Krasner PV* 83min MGM

LOOKING FOR TROUBLE (1934) *d* Wellman *a* R Day *m* A Newman *w* Tracy 77min *r* UA

LOOKING FORWARD (1933) *d* C Brown *w* L Barrymore 82min MGM

Look Out! = POZOR! (1959)

LOOK WHO'S LAUGHING (1941) *d/p* Dwan *w* Ball 78min RKO

Loony Tom = LOONY TOM, THE HAPPY LOVER (1954)

LOONEY TOM, THE HAPPY LOVER (1954) *d/s/c* Broughton 10min (= *Loony Tom*)

LOOPS (1939–41) *d* McLaren anim* 2½min

LOOPS (1958) *d/p/c/e* S Clarke

LORD BYRON (1922) *d/co-p/s/w* Veidt

LORD CAMBER'S LADIES (1932) *d Benn Levy p* Hitchcock *w* Lawrence 80min

Lord for a Night = ARU YO NO TONOSAMA (1964)

Lord Help Us = CRUEL, CRUEL LOVE (1914)

LORD JEFF (1938) *d* S Wood *c* J Seitz *a* Gibbons *w* Rooney, Bartholemew, C Coburn, Lawford 78min MGM

LORD JIM (1925) *d* Fleming 6702ft FPL

LORD JIM (1965) *d/s* R Brooks *fn Joseph Conrad c* F Young *w* O'Toole, Tamiroff, Hawkins, Mason, Jurgens, Lukas, Wallach 70PV* 154min Col

LORD LOVE A DUCK (1966) *d/p/co-s* Axelrod *c* Fapp *w* Weld, R Gordon 91min *r* UA

LORD OF THE FLIES, THE (1962) *d/s* P Brook *fn William Golding* 91min BL

LORNA DOONE (1922) *d/p/s* M Tourneur *fn R D Blackmore* 8rs

LORNA DOONE (1934) *d/p Basil Dean fn Blackmore w* Lockwood 80min

LORNA DOONE (1951) *d* Karlson *fn Blackmore m* Duning *88min Col

LORO SERENATA, EL (1939) *d* Saslavsky

Loser Take All (UK) = LEATHER GLOVES (1948)

LOSER TAKES ALL (1956) *d* Annakin *s/fn* Greene *c* Périnal CS* 88min BL

Loss of Innocence (US) = GREENGAGE SUMMER, THE (1961)

LOST (1956) *d* G Green *89min JAR

LOST AND FOUND ON A SOUTH SEA ISLAND (1923) *d* Walsh 7rs (= *Passions of the Sea*)

LOST ANGEL (1943) *d* Rowland *a* Gibbons *m* Amfitheatrof *w* M O'Brien 91min MGM

LOST COMMAND (1966) *d/p* Robson *c* Surtees *m* Waxman *w* Quinn, Delon, Cardinale, Segal, Ronet PV* 129min Col (= *The Centurions*)

LOST HORIZON (1937) *d/p* Capra *s* Riskin *c* J Walker *m* Tiomkin *w* Colman, Horton, Mitchell 132min Col

Lost Kingdom, The (UK) = ANTINEA, L'AMANTE DELLA CITTA SEPOLTA (1961)

LOST MAN, THE (1969) *d/s* Aurthur *co-a* Golitzen *w* Poitier *122min *r* U

Lost One, The = TRAVIATA, LA (1949)

Lost on Ice = LIDE NA KRE (1937)

LOST PATROL, THE (1934) *d* J Ford *ex-p* M Cooper *co-s* D Nichols *m* M Steiner *w* V McLaglen, Karloff 74min RKO

Lost Property (UK) = SOUVENIRS PERDUS (1949)

Lost Sex = HONNO (1966)

Lost Spring = MUSHIBAMERU HARU (1932)

LOST WEEKEND, THE (1945) *d/co-s* B Wilder *p/co-s* C Brackett *c* J Seitz *co-a* Dreier *m* Rozsa *w* Milland, Wyman 99min Par

LOST WORLD, THE (1960) *d/co-s Irwin Allen co-s* Charles Bennett *fn Conan Doyle c* Hoch *w* Rains S* 98min Fox

Lost Youth (UK) = GIOVENTU PERDUTA (1947)

LOTNA (1959) *d/co-s* Wajda *93min

LOTTA DELL' UOMO PER LA SUA SOPRAVVIVENZA, LA (1967) *d Renzo Rossellini Jr p/supn/s* Rossellini

LOTTE IN ITALIA (1969) *d* Godard *60min RAI (= *Struggle in Italy*)

LOTTERY BRIDE, THE (1930) *d Paul L Stein st* Stothart *w* Jeanette Macdonald, Pitts 80min *r* UA

LOTTERY MAN, THE (1919) *d* Cruze 5rs FPL

LOTTI ESREDESI (1917) *d* Balasz

LOTUS EATER, THE (1921) *d/pc* Neilan 7rs FN

Loudest Whisper, The (UK) = CHILDREN'S HOUR, THE (1961)

LOUISA (1950) *d Alexander Hall w* Laurie, Reagan, C Coburn 90min U

LOUIS CAPET (1959) *d* Leenhardt, *Jean-Paul Vivet* 27min (= *Louis XVI*)

LOUISE (1939) *d/co-s* Gance *c* Courant *dec* Wakhévitch 90min

LOUISIANA (1947) *d* Karlson 82min Mon

LOUISIANA STORY (1948) *d/s* Flaherty *c* Leacock *m* V Thompson 77min

Louis Malle's India = INDE 68 (1969)

Louis WVI = LOUIS CAPET (1954)

LOURDES ET SES MIRACLES (1955) *d* Rouquier 91min (3parts: *Temoignages* 40min *Perlerinage* 36min *Imprévu* 15min)

LOUVES, LES (1957) *d* Saslavsky *w* Presle, Moreau 105min (= *The She-Wolves*)

LOVABLE CHEAT, THE (1949) *d* R Oswald *fpl Balzac w* C Ruggles, Keaton 78min

Love = MIRSU (1924)

Love = KOI (1924)
LOVE (1928) *d/p* Goulding *fn* (*Anna Karenina*) Tolstoi *c* Daniels *w* Garbo, J Gilbert 7365ft MGM
Love = AI (1962)
LOVE AFFAIR (1932) *d Thornton Freeland ad/di* Swerling *c* Tetzlaff *w* Bogart 68min Col
LOVE AFFAIR (1939) *d/co-st* McCarey *s* Daves, D Stewart *c* Maté *co-e* Dmytryk *w* I Dunne, Boyer, Ouspenskaya 88min RKO
Love Affair of the Dictator, The (UK) = DICTATOR, THE (1935)
Love à la Carte (US) = ADUA E LE CAMPAGNE (1960)
LOVE AMONG THE MILLIONAIRES (1930) *d* Tuttle *di* H Mankiewicz *w* Bow 6910ft Par
Love and a Warrior = KOI TO BUSHI (1925)
Love and Anger (UK) = 4 eps of AMORE E RABBIA (1967 *r* 1969) 78min
LOVE AND COURAGE (1913) *d* Sennett *w* Normand ½rl Key
LOVE AND GLORY (1924) *d/co-s* Julian 7094ft U
LOVE AND KISSES (1925) *d* Cline *s* Sennett
Love and Larceny (UK) = MATTATORE, IL (1959)
Love and Lobsters = HE DID AND HE DIDN'T (1916)
Love and Lunch = MABEL'S BUSY DAY (1914)
LOVE AND PAIN (1913) *d* Sennett *w* Normand ½rl Key
Love and Statistics = KARLEK OCH STATISTIK (*c* 1955)
LOVE AND THE DEVIL (1929) *d* A Korda *c* Garmes 6588ft FN
Love and the Frenchwoman (UK) = FRANCAISE ET L'AMOUR, LA (1960)
LOVE AT FIRST FLIGHT (1928) *d* Cline *p* Sennett 2rs Pat
Love at Twenty (UK) = AMOUR A VINGT ANS, L' (1962)
LOVE BEFORE BREAKFAST (1936) *d* W Lang *c* Tetzlaff *w* Lombard, Romero 70min U
LOVE-BUG, THE (1969) *d* Stevenson *107min pc* Disney
LOVE BURGLAR, THE (1919) *d* Cruze 5rs FPL
Love Cage, The = FELINS, LES (1964)
Love Circle, The = METTI UNA SERA A CENA (1969)
LOVE COMES ALONG (1930) *d* Julian 7048ft RKO
LOVE CRAZY (1941) *d* Conway *co-st/co-s* Ludwig *co-s* Lederer *c* June *a* Gibbons *w* W Powell, M Loy 100min MGM
LOVED ONE, THE (1964) *d* T Richardson *co-p/s* Wexler *s* Christopher Isherwood, Terry Southern *fn* Evelyn Waugh *w* Steiger, J Coburn, Gielgud 117min MGM
Love Dossier, or the Tragedy of a Switchboard Operator = LJUBAVNI SLUČAJ, TRAGEDIJA SLUZBENICE (1967)
LOVE 'EM AND FEED 'EM (1927) *d* Bruckman *supn* McCarey *p* Roach 2rs MGM
LOVE 'EM AND LEAVE 'EM (1926) *d* Tuttle *w* L Brooks 6075ft FPL
LOVE 'EM AND WEEP (1927) *d* Fred Guiol *w* Laurel, Hardy Pat
LOVE EXPERT, THE (1920) *d* David Kirkland *p* Emerson, Loos *w* C Talmadge 6rs
LOVE FINDS ANDY HARDY (1938) *d* G Seitz *w* Rooney, Garland, Turner 90min MGM
LOVE FLOWER, THE (1920) *d/p* Griffith *w* Barthelmess 7rs UA
LOVE HAPPY (1950) *d* D Miller *st* H Marx *co-s* Tashlin *c* Mellor *w* C, G, H Marx, Burr, Vera-Ellen 91min *r* UA
LOVE HAS MANY FACES (1965) *d* Singer *p* Bresler *c* Ruttenberg *m* Raksin *w* Turner, Roman, Robertson *105min Col
LOVE, HONOR AND OBEY (1921) *d* Richard Jones, Erle Kenton *p* Sennett 5rs *r* FN
LOVE IN BLOOM (1935) *d* E Nugent 75min Par
Love in Las Vegas = VIVA LAS VEGAS (1964)
LOVE INSURANCE (1919) *d* Crisp 5rs FPL
LOVE IN THE AFTERNOON (1957) *d/p/s* Wilder *co-s* Diamond *c* Mellor *a* Trauner *m* Waxman *w* G Cooper, A Hepburn, Chevalier, (Trauner) 125min *r* AA
Love in Tokyo = KOI NO TOKYO (1932)
LOVE IS A BALL (1963) *d/co-s* Swift *c* Séchan *dec* D'Eaubonne *m* Legrand *w* G Ford, Boyer, Montalban, Jacobsson PV* 111min UA (= *All This and Money Too*)
LOVE IS A HEADACHE (1938) *d* Thorpe *c* J Seitz *a* Gibbons *w* Tone, Rooney 68min MGM
LOVE IS A MANY-SPLENDORED THING (1955) *d* H King *p* Adler *c* Shamroy *co-a* Wheeler *m* A Newman *w* Holden, J Jones CS* 102min Fox (= *A Many-Splendored Thing*)
LOVE IS A RACKET (1932) *d* Wellman *c* Hickox *w* Fairbanks Jr 72min FN
LOVE IS BETTER THAN EVER (1951) *d* Donen *c* Rosson *a* Gibbons *w* E Taylor, G Kelly 81min MGM (= *The Light Fantastic*)
LOVE IS DANGEROUS (1933) *d* Thorpe 67min (= *Love is Like That*)
Love is Like That = LOVE IS DANGEROUS (1933)
Love is My Profession (UK) = EN CAS DE MALHEUR (1958)
LOVE IS NEWS (1937) *d* Garnett *p* Zanuck *w* Power, L Young, G Sanders, Darwell 78min Fox
LOVE IS ON THE AIR (1937) *d* Nick Grinde *w* Reagan 6rs WB

Love is When You Make It (UK) = BEL AGE, LE (1960)
LOVE LAUGHS AT ANDY HARDY (1946) *d* Goldbeck *a* Gibbons *w* Rooney 93min MGM
LOVE LETTERS (1945) *d* Dieterle *p* Wallis *c* Garmes *m* V Young *w* Oberon, J Jones, Cotten 101min Par
LOVE, LIVE AND LAUGH (1929) *d* W Howard *co-c* Andriot Fox
Lovelorn Geisha, The = YORU NO NAGARE (1960)
LOVE LOTTERY (1954) *d* Crichton *s* Kurnitz *c* Slocombe *e* Holt *w* Niven, Vernon, (Bogart) *89min
LOVELY TO LOOK AT (1952) *d* LeRoy *p* J Cummings *co-s* Wells *c* Folsey *co-a* Gibbons *w* Keel, Champion, Ann Miller *112min MGM
LOVELY WAY TO DIE, A (1968) *d* David Lowell Rich *w* K Douglas, Wallach S* 103min U
LOVE MACHINE, THE (1971) *d* Jack Haley Jr *p* Frankovich *c* C Lang *des* Wheeler *w* Ryan, Hemmings *108min
Love Makers, The (UK) = VIACCIA, LA (1961)
LOVEMAKING (1968) *d* Brakhage 16mm *si* *36min
Love-Mates (US) = ANGLAR, FINNS DOM ... (1960)
LOVE ME AND THE WORLD IS MINE (1927) *d/co-s* Dupont *p* Laemmle 6813ft U
LOVE ME FOREVER (1935) *d/st* Schertzinger *co-s* Swerling *c* J Walker 90min Col
LOVE ME, LOVE ME, LOVE ME (1962) *d* R Williams anim* 8min
LOVE ME OR LEAVE ME (1955) *d* C Vidor *p* Pasternak *c* Arling *co-a* Gibbons *w* D Day, Cagney CS* 122min MGM
LOVE ME TENDER (1956) *d* Robert D Webb *w* Presley 89min Fox
LOVE ME TONIGHT (1932) *d/p* Mamoulian *c* Milner *a* Dreier *m* Rodgers and Hart *w* Chevalier, Jeanette Macdonald, M Loy, C Ruggles 89min Par
LOVE NEST, THE (1923) *d/pc/w* Keaton
LOVE NEST (1951) *d* J Newman *s* Diamond *co-a* Wheeler *w* Monroe 84min Fox
LOVE NEST ON WHEELS (1937) *d* Charles Lamont *w* Keaton 1604ft
LOVE NEVER DIES (1921) *d/p/ad* K Vidor 60min 6751ft
Love of Actress Sumako = JOYU SUMAKO NO KOI (1947)
Love of Life = AUTHUR RUBENSTEIN, L'AMOUR DE LA VIE (1968)
LOVE OF SUNYA, THE (1927) *d* Albert Parker *pc/w* Swanson 7311ft *r* UA
Love on a Pillow = REPOS DU GUERRIER, LE (1962)
Love One Another (UK) = GEZEICHNETEN, DIE (1922)
LOVE ON THE DOLE (1941) *d* John Baxter *w* Kerr 100min
LOVE ON THE RUN (1936) *d* WS Van Dyke *p* J Mankiewicz *s* Mahin *w* Gable, Tone, J Crawford 80min MGM
LOVE ON THE WING (1937–39) *d* McLaren *p* Cavalcanti *5½min GPO
LOVE ON TOAST (1937) *d* Dupont 65min Par
LOVE ON WHEELS (1932) *d* Saville 86min
LOVE PARADE, THE (1930) *d* Lubitsch *c* Milner *dec* Dreier *m* Schertzinger *w* Chevalier, Jeanette Macdonald, Turpin, L Barrymore, Harlow 12rs Par
Lover, The = KOIBITO (1951)
LOVER COME BACK (1961) *d* Delbert Mann *c* Arling *w* Hudson, D Day, Randall *107min U
Love Rewarded = NAGRODZONE UCZUCTE (1957)
LOVE ROUTE, THE (1915) *d* Dwan 4rs FP
Lovers, The = AIJIN (1953)
LOVERS? (1927) *d/p* Stahl *w* Novarro 5291ft MGM
LOVERS AND LOLLYPOPS (1955) *co-d/p/co-s/c* Engel *co-d* Ruth Orkin 80min
LOVERS COURAGEOUS (1932) *d/p* Leonard *w* Montgomery 8rs MGM
Lovers, Happy Lovers = KNAVE OF HEARTS (1954)
Lovers Must learn = ROME ADVENTURE (1962)
Lovers of Lisbon, The = AMANTS DU TAGE, LES (1954)
Lovers of Montparnasse, The (UK) = MONTPARNASSE 19 (1957)
Lovers of Toledo = AMANTS DE TOLEDE, LES (1952)
Love's Berries = YAGODKA UCZUCTE (1957)
Lovesicxness at Sea = LOVESICKNESS AT SEA (1913)
Love 65 (UK) = KARLEK 65 (1965)
LOVESICKNESS AT SEA (1913) *d/p* Sennett *w* Sennett, Normand 1rl Key (= *Lovesicxness at Sea*)
Loves Mockery (US) = GANG IM DIE NACHT, DER (1920)
Loves of a Blonde (US) = LASKY JEDNE PLAVOV-LASKY (1965)
Loves of a Dictator (US) = DICTATOR, THE (1935)
LOVES OF CARMEN (1927) *d/s* Walsh *fst* (*Carmen*) Prosper Merimée *co-c* Andriot *w* Del Rio, V McLaglen 9rs Fox
LOVES OF CARMEN, THE (1968) *d/p* C Vidor *fst* (*Carmen*) Prosper Merimée *w* Hayworth, G Ford *88min Col
Loves of Hercules, The = AMORI DI ERCOLE, GLI (1960)
Loves of Isadora, The (US) = ISADORA (1967)
LOVES OF JOANNA GODDEN, THE (1947) *d* Frend *s* H E Bates *c* Slocombe 89min
LOVES OF LETTY, THE (1919) *d* F Lloyd 6000ft *pc* Goldwyn

LOVES OF ONDINE, THE (1967) *d* Warhol 16mm 86min (segment of FOUR STARS)
Loves of Pharaoh, The (US) = WEIB DES PHARAO, DAS (1922)
LOVES OF ZERO, THE (1927–28) *d/st* Florey *s/co-c/e* Vorkapich *co-c* Toland *dec* Menzies sh
Love, Soldiers and Women (UK) = DESTINEES, LES (1953)
Love Specialist, The = RAGAZZA DEL PALIO, LA (1957)
Love Storm (US) = CAPE FORLORN (1930)
LOVE STORY (1944) *d* L Arliss *w* Lockwood, S Granger 113min EL *r* U (= *A Lady Surrenders*)
LOVE SUNDAE, A (1926) *d* Cline *s* Sennett
LOVE'S WILDERNESS (1924) *d* Leonard 7rs FN
LOVE TEST, THE (1935) *d* M Powell 63min
LOVE THY NEIGHBOUR (1940) *d/p* Sandrich *c* Tetzlaff *co-a* Dreier *w* Benny 82min Par
LOVE TRAP, THE (1929) *d* Wyler 71min U
Love Trap, The (UK) = COUPLE, UN (1960)
Love Travels by Coach = HINTON JARO SZERELEM (1954)
LOVE UNDER FIRE (1937) *d* G Marshall *p* Zanuck *as-p* N Johnson *w* L Young, Carradine 76min Fox
LOVE WITH THE PROPER STRANGER (1963) *d* Mulligan *c* Krastner *co-a* Pereira *m* E Bernstein *w* McQueen, N Wood 100min Par
LOVING (1956) *d* Brakhage 16mm * *si* 6min
LOVING (1970) *d* Kershner *w* Segal, Saint, Hayden *89min *r* Col
Loving Couples = ALSKANDE PAR (1964)
LOVING YOU (1957) *d/co-s* Kanter *p* Wallis *c* C Lang *w* Presley, Corey, L Scott VV* 101min Par
Lower Depths, The = DONZOKO (1957)
Loyal 47 Ronin, The = CHUSHINGURA (1932)
Loyal 47 Ronin = GENROKU CHUSHINGURA (1942)
L-SHAPED ROOM, THE (1962) *d/s* Forbes *p* Attenborough, James Woolf *fn* Lynne Reid Banks *m* Brahms *c* Slocombe *w* Caron, Emlyn Williams 142min BL
LUCCIOLA (1917) *d/co-st* Genina
LUCE NEGLI IMPRESSIONISTI, LA (1938) *d* Sala sh
LUCETTE (1924) *d co-d/s* Feuillade *co-d/e* Maurice Champreux 1600m
LUCH SMERTI (1925) *d/w* Kuleshov *s/dec/w* Pudovkin 2995m (= *The Death Ray*)
LUCIANO (1962) *d/co-s* Baldi 80min
LUCIANO SERRA, PILOTA (1938) *d/co-s* Goffredo Alessandrini *supn* Vittorio Mussolini *co-s* Rossellini
LUCIANO (VIA DEI CAPELLARI) (1960) *d* Baldi
LUCI DEL VARIETA (1950) *co-d/co-s* Lattuada *co-d/st/co-s* Fellini *c* Martelli *w* Masina, Caprioli 90min
LUCIE DE TRECOEUR (1922) *d* Genina
LUCIFER RISING (1966), *uf*) *d* Anger
LUCIFER RISING, CHAPTER ONE (1971) *d/s/c/e/w* Anger 16mm *7min
LUCK OF GINGER COFFEY, THE (1964) *d* Kershner *a* Horner 99min BL
LUCK OF THE FOOLISH, THE (1924) *d* Harry Edwards *w* Langdon 2rs *pc* Sennett *r* Pat
LUCK OF THE IRISH, THE (1919) *d* Dwan 7rs
Luck Touched My Legs = ASHI NI SAWATTA KOUN (1930)
LUCKY BOY (1929) *d* Taurog, Charles C Wilson 10rs
LUCKY DAN (1922) *d* W Howard 4700ft
LUCKY DEVIL (1925) *d* Tuttle *w* Oliver 5935ft FPL *r* Par
Lucky Dragon No 5 = DAIGO FUKURYU MARU (1958)
LUCKY DUCKY (1948) *d* Avery *p* Quimby anim* 8min MGM
LUCKY JIM (1957) *d/co-p* J Boulting *co-p* Boulting 95min BL
LUCKY JO (1964) *d/co-st* Deville *m* Delerue *w* Constantine, Brasseur, Arnoul 95min
LUCKY JORDAN (1942) *d* Tuttle *p* Kohlmar *c* J Seitz *a* Dreier *w* Ladd 84min Par
LUCKY LADY, THE (1926) *d/p* Walsh *c* Milner *w* L Barrymore 6rs FPL
LUCKY ME (1955) *d* Jack Donahue *w* D Day CS* 100min WB
LUCKY NICK CAIN (1951) *d* J Newman *p* Woolf Bros *c* Heller *w* Raft 87min Fox (= *I'll Get You for This*)
LUCKY NIGHT (1939) *d* Taurog *c* June *w* R Taylor 90min MGM
LUCKY NUMBER, THE (1933) *d* Asquith 6535ft
LUCKY PARTNERS (1940) *d* Milestone *fpl* (*Bonne Chance*) Guitry *m* Tiomkin *w* Colman, G Rogers 102min RKO
LUCKY SAN (1952) *d/co-s* Ichikawa Toho (= *Mr Lucky*)
LUCKY STAR (1929) *d* Borzage *w* J Gaynor 2800 Fox
LUCKY STARS (1925) *d* Harry Edwards *w* Langdon 2rs *pc* Sennett *r* Pat
Lucky to be a Woman (UK) = FORTUNA DI ESSERE DONNA, LA (1956)
LUCRECE (1943) *d* Joannon 100min
LUCRECE BORGIA (1935) *d/s* Gance *co-c* B Kaufman *w* Feuillade 96min
Lucrèce Borgia = LUCREZIA BORGIA (1952)
LUCRETIA LOMBARD (1923) *d* Conway 7rs WB
LUCREZIA BORGIA (1919) *d* Genina
LUCREZIA BORGIA (1922) *d/p/s* R Oswald *co-c* Freund *w* Veidt, Wegener, Dieterle 3286m

LUCREZIA BORGIA (1952) d/co-st/co-s Christian-Jaque c Matras w Carol, Armendariz, Marquand, Ronet *120min

LUCY GALLANT (1955) d Parrish co-s Mahin c Lindon co-a Pereira w Heston, Wyman, Ritter, Trevor VV* 104min Par

LUDWIG II (1954) d Kautner c Slocombe fm Wagner *115min

LUDWIG DER ZWEITE, KONIG VON BAYERN (1929) d/w Dieterle 3929m

LUDZIE WISLY (1937) co-d A Ford

LUFFAR-PETER (1922) d/p/s/w Erik A Petschler w Garbo

LUGNER, DER (1961) d Vajda 93min

LUGNER UND DIE NONNE, DER (1967) d Thiele, Joseph Czech w Jurgens *99min (= The Liar and the Nun)

Lullabye = KOLYBELNAYA (1937)

LULLI OU LE VIOLON BRISE (1908) d Méliès * 208m (4 parts)

LULLABY OF BROADWAY (1951) d D Butler co-chor Prinz w D Day 92min WB

LULU (1915) d Genina

LULU (1962) d Thiele w Tiller, Neff 100min (= No Orchids for Lulu)

LULU BELLE (1948) d Leslie Fenton p Bogeaus fco-pl MacArthur c Laszlo w Lamour, G Montgomery 87min Col

LUMIERE D'EN FACE, LA (1955) d Georges Lacombe st Aurel w Bardot 100min (= The Light Across the Street)

LUMIERE D'ETE (1942) d Grémillon co-s/co-di J Prévert dec Trauner w Brasseur 118min

LUMIGRAPH TEST REEL (1951) d Fischinger anim

LUMMOX (1930) d Brenon c Struss 86min UA

LUNA DE MIEL (1958) d/co-p/co-s M Powell co-c Périnal m Theodorakis *109min (= Honeymoon)

LUNATIC AT LARGE, THE (1926) d Newmayer c O'Connell 5521ft FN

LUNCHEON AT TWELVE (1933) d C Chase (as Parrott) p Roach w C Chase 2rs MGM

Lunch on the Grass = DEJEUNER SUR L'HERBE, LE (1959)

LUNE DES LAPINS, LA (1950) d/s/e/a/cos Anger part * 10min (= Rabbits' Moon)

LUNEGARDE (1964) d M Allégret s Achard fn Pierre Benoit 72min Pat

LUNETTES FEERIQUES, LES (1909) d Cohl anim 122m

LUNGA NOTTE DEL '43, LA (1960) d/co-s Vancini co-s Pasolini c Di Palma w Ferzetti 110min (= The Long Night of '43)

LUNGHI GIORNI DELLA VENDETTA, I (1965) d Vancini *120min

LUOGHI VERDIANI (1948) d/s Emmer, Enrico Gras (= Sulle Rome di Verdi)

LUPA, LA (1953) d/co-s/ad Lattuada p Ponti, De Laurentiis co-s Pietrangeli c Tonti 90min (= The Vixen/The She-Wolf)

LUPE (1965) d Warhol 16mm *70min

LURED (1947) d Sirk c Daniels w G Sanders, Ball, C Coburn, Karloff 102min r UA

Lure of Broadway, The = BRIGHT LIGHTS, THE (1916)

LURE OF THE ORIENT, THE (1921) d/w Conway

LURE OF THE SWAMP (1957) d Cornfield S 74min Fox

LURE OF THE WILDERNESS (1952) d Negulesco c Cronjager co-a Wheeler m Waxman w J Hunter, Peters *92min Fox

LUST FOR LIFE (1956) d Minnelli p Houseman c F Young, R Harlan co-a Gibbons m Rozsa w K Douglas, Quinn CS* 122min MGM

LUSTGARDEN (1961) d Kjellin s Ingmar Bergman, Erland Josephson (ps (both) Buntel Ericsson) c Fischer w Björnstrand, B Andersson * (= Pleasure Garden)

LUSTIGE EHEMANN, DER (1919) d/s Lubitsch c Sparkuhl 3rs (= The Merry Husband)

LUSTIGEN WEIBER VON WINDSOR, DIE (1965) d Tressler f operetta Nicolai fpl (The Merry Wives of Windsor) Shakespeare w Foster *94min

Lust of the Vampire (UK) = VAMPIRI, I (1956)

LUTTE CONTRE LE FROID, LA (1960) d Gruel *anim

LUSTY MEN, THE (1952) d N Ray p Wald, Krasna c Garmes w S Hayward, Mitchum, A Kennedy 113min r RKO

LU TEMPU DI LI PISCI SPATA (1954) d/c/e De Seta

LUTRING (1966) d/cò-st Lizzani 118min (= Svegliata e uccidi/Wake Up and Kill/Too Soon to Die)

LUTTE, LA (1961) d/c/e Jutra, Brault, Marcel Carrière, Claude Fournier m J S Bach, Vivaldi 28min (= The Fight)

LUV (1967) d C Donner c Laszlo w Lemmon PV* 96min Col

LYCEE SUR LA COLLINE, LE (1952) d Rouquier 26min

LYCKLIGA SKITAR (1970) d/co-s Sjoman *97min (= Blushing Charlie)

LYCKONALEN (1916) d Stiller 709m

LYDIA (1916) d Madsen

LYDIA (1941) d/co-st Duvivier p A Korda co-s B Hecht as-p/c Garmes m Rozsa w Oberon, Cotten, Olivier 90min r UA

LYDIA BAILEY (1952) d Negulesco co-a Wheeler chor Cole w A Francis *89min Fox

LYKKEN (1916) d/s Madsen

LYKKEN DRABER (1913) d Madsen

LYNN SEYMOUR (1964) d A King m Matyas Seiber 16mm 26min

LYUBLYU LI TEBYA (1934) d/s Gerasimov 70min (= Do I Love You?)

LYUDI (1966) d Chukhrai (= People)

LYUDI I ZVERI (1962) d/s Gerasimov 2 parts: 101min and 110min (= Men and Beasts)

LYUDI NA MOSTU (1960) d Zarkhi 101min (= Men on the Bridge)

M (1931) d/co-s F Lang co-s Von Harbou co-c F Wagner w Lorre 120min Nero (= Mörder unter Uns)

M (1951) d Losey rm 1931 c Laszlo des consultant J Hubley w D Wayne, Burr 88min Col

MAA (1951) d Roy

MAANEPRINSESSEN (1916) d Madsen

MABEL AND FATTY'S MARRIED LIFE (1915) d/w Arbuckle p Sennett w Normand 1rl Key

Mabel and Fatty's Simple Life = FATTY AND MABEL'S SIMPLE LIFE (1915)

MABEL AND FATTY'S WASH DAY (1915) d/w Arbuckle p Sennett w Normand 1rl Key

MABEL AND FATTY VIEWING THE WORLD'S FAIR AT SAN FRANCISCO, CAL (1915) d Arbuckle p Sennett w Arbuckle, Normand 1rl Key

MABEL AT THE WHEEL (1914) co-d/p Sennett co-d Normand w Chaplin, Sennett, Normand 2rs Key (= His Dare Devil Queen/Hot Finish)

MABEL, FATTY AND THE LAW (1915) d/w Arbuckle w Normand 1rl Key

MABEL'S ADVENTURES (1912) d Sennett w Normand ½rl Key

MABEL'S AWFUL MISTAKE (1913) d/p Sennett w Sennett, Normand 1rl Key

MABEL'S BARE ESCAPE (1914) d Normand (?) w Normand 1rl Key (= Mabel's Bear Escape)

Mabel's Bear Escape = MABEL'S BARE ESCAPE (1914)

MABEL'S BLUNDER (1914) d Normand (?) w Normand 1rl Key

MABEL'S BUSY DAY (1914) d/w Normand, Chaplin 1rl Key (= Love and Lunch/Charlie and the Sausages)

MABEL'S DRAMATIC CAREER (1913) d/p Sennett w Normand, Arbuckle, Sennett 1rl Key

MABEL'S HEROES (1913) d/p Sennett w Normand, Sennett ½rl Key

MABEL'S LATEST PRANK (1914) d Normand (?) w Normand 1rl Key

MABEL LOST AND WON (1915) w Normand 1rl Key

MABEL'S LOVERS (1912) d Sennett w Normand ½rl Key

MABEL'S MARRIED LIFE (1914) d/w Normand, Chaplin 1rl Key

MABEL'S NERVE (1914) d/w Normand 1rl Key

MABEL'S NEW HERO (1913) d Sennett w Normand 1rl Key

MABEL'S NEW JOB (1914) d/w Normand 2rs Key

MABEL'S STORMY LOVE AFFAIR (1913) w Normand 1rl Key

MABEL'S STRANGE PREDICAMENT (1914) d Henry Lehrman, Sennett w Chaplin, Normand 1rl Key

MABEL'S STRATAGEM (1912) d Sennett w Normand ½rl Key

MABEL'S WILFUL WAY (1915) w Normand 1rl Key

MACABRE (1958) d/p Castle co-a Kinoshita 73min AA

MACADAM (1946) d Marcel Blistène supn/s Feyder s Camus dec D'Eaubonne m Wiener w Rosay, Signoret

MACAO (1952) d Von Sternberg, N Ray c Wild w Mitchum, J Russell, Bendix, Grahame 81min RKO

MACAO, L'ENFER DU JEU (1939) d Delannoy co-c Hayer m Auric w Von Stroheim, P Renoir

MACBETH (1946) d Thomas Blair p/s/c/e/w Bradley fpl Shakespeare co-s Heston

MACBETH (1948) d/p/s/w Welles as-p R Wilson fpl Shakespeare c JL Russell m Ibert 86min pc Feldman

MACBETH (1971) d/co-s Polanski fpl Shakespeare c G Taylor *140min

MACCABEI, I (1911) d/s/dec Guazzoni

MACCHINA AMMAZZACATTIVI LA (1948) d/co-p/co-s Rossellini fco-st De Filippo 80min

McCONNELL STORY, THE (1955) d G Douglas p Blanke c J Seitz m M Steiner w Allyson, Ladd CS* 101min WB (= Tiger in the Sky)

MccDonald of the Canadian Mounties = PONY SOLDIER (1952)

MACHINE A REFAIRE LA VIE, LA (1924) co-d Duvivier 4950m

MACHINE A REFAIRE LA VIE, LA (1933) d Duvivier rm 1924 180min

MACHINE ET L'HOMME, LA (1956) d Mitry 20min

MACHINE GUN KELLY (1958) d/p Corman c F Crosby 80min AI

MACHINE OF EDEN, THE (1970) d Brakhage 16mm* si 11min

MACHI NO HITOBITO (1926) d Gosho (= Town People)

MACHNOWER SCHLEUSEN, DIE (1927) d/s/c Jutzi sh

MACHORKA-MUFF (1963) d/co-p/co-s Straub 17min

MACISTE (1915) d Pastrone w Maciste 2010m

MACISTE ALLA CORTE DEL GRAN KHAN (1961) d Freda co-s Tessari CS* 95min (= Samson and the Seven Miracles of the World)

MACISTE ALL' INFERNO (1962) d Freda CS* 85min

MACISTE ALPINO (1916) d Pastrone, Romano Borgnetto, Luigi Maggi w Maciste 2600m

MACISTE CONTRO LO SCEICCO (1925) d/st Camerini w Maciste

MACISTE UND DIE CHINESISCHE TRUHE (1923) d Carl Boese w Maciste 2072m

MACK AT IT AGAIN (1914) d/p Sennett w Normand, Sennett 1rl Key

MACKENNA'S GOLD (1969) d J Thompson co-p/s Foreman co-p m Tiomkin c Joe Macdonald w Wallach, Sharif, Peck, Robinson, Meredith, Cobb PV* 136min Col

McLINTOCK! (1963) d A McLaglen st/s J Grant c Clothier co-a Pereira w J Wayne, M O'Hara, De Carlo PV* 127min pc J Wayne r UA

MACLOVIA (1948) d/co-s Fernandez c Figueroa w Felix, Armendariz 90min

McMASTERS, THE (1970) d Kjellin w Ives, Palance, Carradine *90min (= The McMasters ... Tougher than the West Itself!)

McMasters ... Tougher than the West Itself!, The (UK) = McMASTERS, THE (1970)

MACOMBER AFFAIR, THE (1947) d Z Korda co-p Bogeaus fst (The Short Happy Life of Francis Macomber) Hemingway co-c Struss m Rozsa w Peck, J Bennett, Preston 90min r UA

MA COUSINE DE VARSOVIE (1932) d Gallone co-s Clouzot

MAD ABOUT MUSIC (1938) d Taurog p Pasternak w H Marshall, Durbin 98min U

MADAMA BUTTERFLY (1955) d Gallone c C Renoir m Puccini *114min (= Madame Butterfly)

Madame (UK) = MADAME SANS-GENE (1961)

Madame and Wife = MADAMU TO NYOBO (1931)

MADAME BOVARY (1934) d/s J Renoir fn Flaubert c Bachelet co-dec Lourié, Wakhévitch m Milhaud w P Renoir, Negri 117min

MADAME BOVARY (1949) d Minnelli p Berman s Ardrey fn Flaubert co-a Gibbons m Rozsa w J Jones, Mason, Heflin, Kjellin 114min MGM

Madame Butterfly = MADAMA BUTTERFLY (1955)

MADAME CURIE (1943) d LeRoy s Franklin co-s Osborn, Fitzgerald(uc) c Ruttenberg a Gibbons m Stothart w Garson, Pidgeon, R Walker, V Johnson, M O'Brien 124min MGM

MADAME DE ... (1953) d/co-s Ophuls co-s/di Achard fn Louise de Vilmorin c Matras dec D'Eaubonne m Van Parys, Oscar Strauss w Darrieux, Boyer, De Sica 102min

MADAME DE POMPADOUR (1927) d H Wilcox s Dupont w D Gish 7rs

MADAME DE THEBES (1915) d Stiller 1342m

MADAME DUBARRY (1919) d Lubitsch c Sparkuhl w Negri, Jannings 85min r Ufa (= Passion)

MADAME DUBARRY (1934) d Dieterle c Polito w Del Rio 79min WB

MADAME DUBARRY (1954) d/co-s Christian-Jaque co-s Jeanson c Matras m Van Parys w Carol *106min

MADAME ET LE MORT (1942) d Daquin w P Renoir 103min

MADAME PUTIPHAR (1911) d/co-s Blom

MADAME SANS-GENE (1925) d Perret c Marley w Brasseur, Swanson 9994ft FPL

MADAME SANS-GENE (1941) d/p co-ad Roger Richebe co-ad Aurenche w Arletty

MADAME SANS-GENE (1961) d/co-s Christian-Jaque p Ponti co-s Jeanson dec D'Eaubonne w Hossein, Loren 70* 97min (= Madame)

MADAME SE MEURT (1961) d/s/cy Cayrol, Claude Durand m Bartok, Mendelssohn 17min

MADAME SPY (1934) d Freund 70min U

MADAME TALLIEN (1916) d/s/dec/cos Guazzoni

Mme Thora Fleming = NAR KONSTNARER ALSKA (1915)

MADAME WUNSCHT KEINE KINDER (1926) d A Korda s Balasz 2166m

MADAME X (1920) d/co-s F Lloyd 7rs pc Goldwyn

MADAME X (1929) d L Barrymore 10rs

MADAME X (1937) d S Wood c J Seitz co-a Gibbons 72min MGM

MADAME X (1965) d David Lowell Rich p R Hunter w Constance Bennett, Meredith, Montalban, Turner 100min

MADAMIGELLA DI MAUPIN (1965) d Bolognini fn Théophile Gautier w Catherine Spaak, Hossein S* 95min Pat (= Le Chevalier de Maupin)

MADAM SATAN (1930) d/p De Mille c Rosson a Leisen co-m Stothart 80min MGM

MADAMU TO NYOBO (1931) d Gosho (= The Neighbour's Wife and Mine/Madame and Wife)

MADCHEN AUS FLANDERN, EIN (1956) d/co-s Kautner fpl Zuckmayer w Maximilian Schell 108min

MADCHEN IN UNIFORM (1931) d Sagan 2682m

MADCHEN ROSEMARIE, DAS (1958) d/co-s Thiele w Tiller 100min

MADCHEM VOM MOORHOF, DAS (1935) d Sirk 82min
MADDALENA (1953) d/co-s Genina co-s Bost c C Renoir w Vanel *102min
MADDALENA (1971) d/co-s Kawalerowicz *105min
MADDALENA ZERO IN CONDOTTA (1940) d/co-s/w De Sica
MAD DOCTOR OF MARKET STREET, THE (1941) d JH Lewis 61min U
MADE FOR EACH OTHER (1939) d Cromwell p Selznick s Swerling a Wheeler w J Stewart, Lombard, C Coburn 85min r UA
MADE IN ITALY (1965) d/co-s N Loy w Manfredi, Magnani, Sordi, Catherine Spaak S* 102min
MADE IN U.S.A. (1966) d/s Godard c Coutard m Schumann, Beethoven w Karina, Léaud TS* 85min
MADELEINE (1950) d Lean c G Green 114min
MADELEINE UND DER LEGIONAR (1958) d Staudte w Neff, Wicki 102min
MADELINE (1952) d Cannon anim* Col
MADEL VOM BALLET, DAS (1918) d Lubitsch c Sparkuhl 3rs (= The Ballet Girl)
MADEMOISELLE (1966) d T Richardson st/s Jean Genet c Watkins w Moreau PV 103min r UA
MADEMOISELLE DOCTEUR (1936) d Pabst co-s H Mankiewicz co-c Schuftan co-m Honegger w Parlo, Fresnay, Jouvet, Romance, Barrault, Modot 95min
MADEMOISELLE DOCTEUR (1937) d Gréville c Schuftan m Honegger w Von Stroheim, Parlo, Modot, Romance (English version of MADEMOISELLE DOCTEUR (1936))
MADEMOISELLE FIFI (1944) d Wise p Lewton fst Guy de Maupassant c Wild w S Simon 69min RKO
Mademoiselle France = REUNION IN FRANCE (1942)
MADEMOISELLE MA MERE (1937) d Decoin fpl Louis Verneuil w Darrieux 96min
MADEMOISELLE MIDNIGHT (1924) d/pc Leonard 7rs
MADEMOISELLE MODISTE (1926) d Leonard 6230ft FN
Mad Emperor, The (US) = PATRIOTE, LE (1938)
MAD GENIUS, THE (1931) d Curtiz w J Barrymore, Karloff 81min WB
MAD HOLIDAY (1936) d G Seitz c Ruttenberg w Pitts 71min MGM
MADHUMATI (1958) d/p Roy 110min
MADIGAN (1968) d D Siegel co-s Polonsky c Metty co-a Golitzen w Widmark, H Fonda TS* 101min U
MADISON AVENUE (1962) d/p H Bruce Humberstone c C Clarke w D Andrews, Crain 94min Fox
MADISON SQUARE GARDEN (1932) d H Brown w Pitts 74min Par
MAD LOVE (1935) d Freund co-c Toland w Lorre 83min MGM (= The Hands of Orlac)
Mad Love = AMOUR FOU, L' (1969)
MAD MAGICIAN, THE (1954) d Brahm c Glennon w Price 3D 72min Col
Madmen in the Dark = KROK DO TMY (1938)
MADNESS OF THE HEART (1949) d/s Charles Bennett w Lockwood 101min JAR
MADO (1965) d Kuri anim 10min (= The Window)
MADONNA OF AVENUE A, THE (1929) d Curtiz c Haskin 5249ft WB
MADONNA OF THE STREETS (1924) d Edwin Carewe w Nazimova, Beery 7507ft r FN
MADRIGUERA, LA (1969) d/co-s Antonio Saura co-s Saura 95min (= The Honeycomb)
Mad Wednesday = SIN OF HAROLD DIDDLEBOCK, THE (1946)
MADWOMAN OF CHAILLOT, THE (1969) d Forbes p Landau fpl Jean Giraudoux c Guffey, C Renoir w Boyer, K Hepburn, Evans, Heinreid, Masina, Brynner, Kaye PV* 142min r FN
MAESTRINA, LA (1913) d Baldassare Negroni w Ghione
MAESTRO DI VIGEVANO, IL (1963) d/co-s Petri c Martelli m Rota w Bloom, Sordi 112min pc De Laurentiis
Ma Femme, Mon Gosse et Moi = AMOUR EST EN JEU, L' (1957)
MAFIOSO (1962) d Lattuada co-s Ferreri m Piccioni w Sorda 105min
MAGAKORO (1953) d Kobayashi (= Sincere Heart)
MAGDAT KICSAPJAK (1938) d Vajda 89min
MAGGIE, THE (1954) d Mackendrick co-p Balcon w P Douglas 92min JAR
MAGIA (1917) d A Korda
MAGICAL MYSTERY TOUR (1966) d/p/s/e/w The Beatles * TV
MAGIC ALPHABET, THE (1942) d J Tourneur 11min
MAGIC BOX, THE (1951) d J Boulting p Neame c Cardiff w Donat, Attenborough, Olivier, M Redgrave, Emlyn Williams, Maria Schell *118min r BL
MAGIC CANVAS (1946) d Halas p Halas Batchelor anim 10min
Magic City, The = MAIJIKI POLIS, I (1954)
MAGIC FACE, THE (1951) d Tuttle 89min Col
MAGIC FIRE (1955) d/p Dieterle co-s Dupont fb (Richard Wagner) Bertita Harding c E Haller mf Wagner arranged by Korngold w R Fleming, De Carlo, Cortese, (Korngold) *94min r Rep

MAGIC FLAME, THE (1927) d/p H King co-s Mathis fpl (King Harlequin) Rudolph Lothar w Colman, Banky 9rs
MAGIC FLUKE (1949) d J Hubley ex-p Bosustow co-anim Cannon anim* 7min Col
MAGIC FOUNTAIN PEN, THE (1909) d Blackton Vit
Magic Hat, The = DIVOTVORNY KLOBOUK (1952)
MAGIC HORSE, THE (1953) Reiniger fst 1001 Nights anim 10min
MAGICIAN, THE (1926) d/ad Ingram c J Seitz w Wegener 6960ft MGM
Magician, The (US) = ANSIKTET (1958)
MAGICIEN, LE (1959) d/p/c/w Borowczyk *3min
Magiciens de Wanzerbé = MAGICIENS NOIRS, LES (1949)
MAGICIENS NOIRS, LES (1949) d/p/c Rouch, Marcel Griaule 16mm* 38min (= Magiciens de Wanzerbé/Ouanzerbé, Capitale de la Magie)
Magic in Music = THERE'S MAGIC IN MUSIC (1938)
Magic Mountains = MONTAGNES MAGIQUES (1962)
MAGIC SWORD, THE (1902) p Paul 180ft
MAGIC TOWN (1947) d Wellman p/co-st/s Riskin c Biroc w J Stewart, Wyman 103min RKO
MAGIRAMA (1956) d Gance, Nelly Kaplan compilation of films by Gance including J'ACCUSE (1918), QUATORZE JUILLET 1953 (1953) PV
Magistrate, The = MAGISTRATO, IL (1959)
MAGISTRATO, IL (1959) d/st/co-s Zampa w Cardinale 100min (= The Magistrate)
MAGLIARI, IL (1959) d/co-st/co-s Rosi co-st/co-s Cecchi D'Amico, Patroni Griffi c Di Venanzo m Piccioni w Sordi 107min
MAGNAS MISKA (1917) d A Korda
MAGNET, THE (1949) d Frend p Balcon 79min
MAGNETISEUR, LE (1897) d Méliès 20m
Magnet of Doom (US) = AINE DES FERCHAUX, L' (1962)
Magnificent Adventurer (UK) = MAGNIFICO AVVENTURIERO, IL (1963)
MAGNIFICENT AMBERSONS, THE (1942) d/p/s Welles fn Booth Tarkington c Cortez, Toland m Hermann e Wise w Cotton, Moorehead, A Baxter, (L Hayward) 88min RKO
Magnificent Cuckold, the (UK) = MAGNIFICO CORNUTO, IL (1964)
MAGNIFICENT DOLL (1946) d Borzage a Golitzen w G Rogers, Niven, Meredith 95min U
MAGNIFICENT DOPE, THE (1942) d W Lang s Seaton c Marley w H Fonda 83min Fox
MAGNIFICENT FLIRT, THE (1928) d/co-s D'Arrast w L Young 4998 Par
MAGNIFICENT FRAUD, THE (1939) d Florey c Mellor chor Prinz w Tamiroff, Nolan 78min Par
MAGNIFICENT MATADOR, THE (1955) d/st Boetticher s C Lang c Ballard w Quinn, M O'Hara CS* 94min (= The Brave and the Beautiful)
MAGNIFICENT OBSESSION (1935) d Stahl st Lloyd C Douglas w I Dunne, R Taylor 112min U
MAGNIFICENT OBSESSION (1954) d Sirk p R Hunter rm (1935) w Wyman, Hudson, Moorehead, Rush *108min U
MAGNIFICENT REBEL, THE (1962) d Tressler m Beethoven *94min pc Disney
Magnificent Seven, The = SHICHININ NO SAMURAI (1954)
MAGNIFICENT SEVEN, THE (1960) d/p J Sturges c C Lang m E Bernstein w Brynner, McQueen, J Coburn, Bucholz, Vaughn, Wallach PV* 126min UA
Magnificent Showman, The = CIRCUS WORLD (1964)
Magnificent Sinner, The = KATJA (1959)
MAGNIFICENT YANKEE, THE (1950) d J Sturges c Ruttenberg co-a Golitzen m Raksin 89min MGM
MAGNIFICO AVVENTURIERO, IL (1963) d Freda *93min (= Magnificent Adventurer)
MAGNIFICO CORNUTO, IL (1964) d Pietrangeli des Chiari w Cardinale 123min (= The Magnificent Cuckold)
MAGOKORO (1939) d/s Naruse (= Sincerity)
MAGOO'S PUDDLE JUMPER (1956) p Bosustow CS* 1rl UPA r Col
Magoroku is Still Alive = IKITEIRU MAGOROKU (1943)
MAGOT DE JOSEFA, LE (1963) d Autant-Lara s Aurenche, Bost w Magnani, Bourvil, Brasseur S* 90min
MAGUS, THE (1968) d G Green fn John Fowles w Quinn, Caine, Karina PV* 116min Fox
MAHANAGAR (1963) d/m S Ray c Mitra 122min (= The Big City)
MAHARAJAENS UNDLINGSHUSTRU (1918) d Blom
MAHIRU NO ANKOKU (1956) d Imai 107min (= Darkness at Noon/Shadows in Sunlight)
MAHIRU NO ENBUKYOKU (1949) d Yoshimura (= Waltz at Noon)
Maiden for a Prince (US) = VERGINE PER IL PRINCIPE, UNA (1965)
MAID OF SALEM (1937) d/p F Lloyd m V Young w Colbert, MacMurray 85min Par
MAIDSTONE (1970) d/p/st/co-e/w Mailer co-c R Leacock, Pennebaker 16mm *110min

MAIGRET ET L'AFFAIRE SAINT-FIACRE (1959) d/co-s Delannoy fn Georges Simenon di Audiard w Gabin 98min
Maigret Sets a Trap (UK) = MAIGRET TEND UN PIEGE (1958)
MAIGRET TEND UN PIEGE (1958) d/co-s Delannoy fn Georges Simenon di Audiard w Gabin, Desailly, Girardot 120min (= Maigret Sets a Trap)
MAIGRET VOIT ROUGE (1963) d Grangier fn (Maigret, Loquan et les Gangsters) w Gabin 90min
MAIHIME (1951) d Naruse (= Dancing Princess)
MAIJIKI POLIS, I (1954) d Koundouros (= The Magic City)
MAIL AND FEMALE (1937) d G Douglas p Roach 1rl MGM
Mailbag Robbery (US) = FLYING SCOT, THE (1957)
MAIL EARLY (1941–43) d McLaren *2min NFBC
MAIL EARLY FOR CHRISTMAS (1959) d McLaren *¼min NFBC
MAIL ORDER BRIDE (1963) d/s B Kennedy PV* 83min MGM (= West of Montana)
MAIN DU DIABLE, LA (1942) d M Tourneur s Le Chanois w Fresnay 82min (= Carnival of Sinners/The Devil's Hand)
MAIN EVENT, THE (1927) d W Howard Pat
MAINS D'ORLAC, LES (1959) d/co-s Greville w M Ferrer 105min (= The Hands of Orlac)
MAINS NETTES, LES (1958) d Jutra co-c Brault 75min
MAINSPRING, THE (1916) d Conway
MAIN STREET TO BROADWAY (1953) d Garnett s Raphaelson c Howe w Bankhead, L Barrymore, Harrison, Palmer, Logan, Moorehead, E Barrymore, Booth, Wilde 102min MGM
MAISIE GETS HER MAN (1942) d Del Ruth a Gibbons w Sothern 85min r MGM
MAIS N' TE PROMENE DONC PAS TOUTE NUE (1936) d Joannon fpl Feydeau
MAISON AUX IMAGES, LA (1955) d/s Grémillon *18min
MAISON DE DANSES (1931) d M Tourneur w Vanel
MAISON DE L'ESPOIR, LA (1915) d/p/s De Baroncelli
MAISON DES BORIES, LA (1970) d Doniol-Valcroze c Cloquet *87min ORTF (= The House of the Bories)
MAISON DU PASSEUR, LA (1965) d/s P Prévert di J Prévert 16mm 80min ORTF
MAISONS DE LA MISERE, LES (1937) d Storck m Jaubert 10min
MAISON SOUS LA MER, LA (1947) d Jenri Calef c C Renoir w Aimée, Romance 105min
MAISON SOUS LES ARBRES, LA (1971) d/co-s /co-ad Clément w Dunaway, Ronet *100min
MAITRE APRES DIEU (1950) d Daquin m Wiener w Brasseur 92min
MAITRE DE MONTPELLIER, LE (1960) d/pc Leenhardt
MAITRE DES FORGES, LA (1933) d/s Gance 90min
MAITRE DU TEMPS, LE (1969) d Pollet s/di Pollet, Kast
MAITRES-FOUS, LES (1955) d/c/n Rouch 16mm* 36min
MAJA DESNUDA, LA (1958) d Kosten c Rotunno w Gardner *112min (= The Naked Maja)
MAJDANEK, OBOZ SMIERCI (1944) d A Ford
MAJOR AND MINOR, THE (1942) d/co-s B Wilder co-s C Brackett co-a Dreier w G Rogers, Milland, Benchley 100min Par
MAJOR BARBARA (1941) d/p Pascal s/fpl/di GB Shaw c Neame e Frend m Walton w Harrison, Kerr, Newton, Emlyn Williams 121min
MAJORDOME, LE (1965) d/co-s Delannoy co-s Jeanson 93min (= The Majordomo)
Majordomo, The = MAJORDOME, LE (1965)
MAJOR DUNDEE (1965) d/co-s Peckinpah p Bresler c Leavitt m Amfitheatrof w Heston, J Coburn, R Harris PV* 134min Col
MAJORITY OF ONE, A (1961) d/p LeRoy m M Steiner w R Russell, Guinness, Danton *156min WB
MAKE MINE LAUGHS (1949) d R Fleischer 64min RKO
MAKE MINE MUSIC (1946) p Disney sp eff Iwerks co-m Prokofiev part anim* 74min
MAKE WAY FOR TOMORROW (1937) d/p McCarey c Mellor co-a Dreier m Antheil w Mitchell 91min Par
MAKI ALLAST VALLAL (1916) d Balasz
MAKING A LIVING (1914) d Lehrman w Chaplin 1rl Key (= Troubles/A Busted Johnny/ Doing His Best)
MAKING MOVING PICTURES (1908) d Blackton Vit
MAKKERS STAAKT UW WILD GERAAS (1960) d Rademakers 99min (= That Joyous Eve)
Malachias (UK) = WUNDER DES MALACHIAS, DAS (1961)
MALACHOV KIRGAN (1944) d/co-s Heifitz, Zarkhi 89min
MALADE HYDROPHOBE OU L'HOMME QUI A DES ROUES DANS LA TETE, LA (1900) d Méliès 20m
Malaga (UA) = MOMENT OF DANGER (1959)
MALA KRONIKA (1962) d/co-s Mimica anim* 10min (= Everyday Chronicle)
MALARIA (1923) d Kershner
MALARPIRATER (1923) d/s Molander SF
MALAYA (1949) d Thorpe c Fosey m Kaper w Tracy, J Stewart, Cortese, Greenstreet, Roland 95min MGM
MAL DE MER, LE (1912) d/s/w Linder Pat
MALDONE (1927) d Grémillon c Périnal, Matras co-accompanying m Delannoy on themes from Grémillon, Satie, Honegger, Debussy 2800m

MALE AND FEMALE (1919) *d* De Mille *fpl* (*The Admirable Crichton*) *JM* Barrie *co-s* Leisen *w* Swanson 9rs FPL

MALE ANIMAL, THE (1942) *d/fco-pl* E Nugent *p* Wallis *co-s* JJ Epstein *fco-pl* James Thruber *c* Edeson *w* H Fonda, De Havilland 101min WB

Maledetti, I = BEATRICE CENCI (1956)

MALEDETTO IMBROGLIO, UN (1959) *d/co-s/w* Germi *w* Cardinale, Rossi-Drago 114min

MALEFICES (1961) *d/co-s* Decoin FS 104min (= *Where the Truth Lies*)

MALENCONTRE (1920) *d* Dulac

MALFRAY (1948) *d* Resnais, *Robert Hessens* 16mm

MALIBRAN, LA (1943) *d/s* Guitry *co-c* Bachelet *w* Guitry, Cocteau 106min

MALI MESTIERI, IL (1963) *d* Mingozzi *sh*

MALLARME (1960) *d* Lods 17min *pat*

MALLE AU MARIAGE, LA (1912) *d/s/w* Linder Pat

MALOMBRA (1916) *d* Gallone

MALOMBRA (1942) *d/co-ad/co-s* Soldati *w* I Miranda 135min

MALQUERIDA, LA (1949) *d/co-s* Fernandez *c* Figueroa *w* Del Rio, Armendariz 83min

MALTESE BIPPY, THE (1969) *d* Panama *c* Daniels *w* Lynley PV* 92min

MALTESE FALCON, THE (1931) *d* Del Ruth *fn* Hammett 75min WB

MALTESE FALCON, THE (1941) *d/s* Huston *p* Wallis *as-p* Blanke *fn* Hammett *c* Edeson *w* Bogart, Astor, Lorre, Greenstreet, Cook, (W Huston) 100min WB

MAMA LOVES PAPA (1931) *d* G Stevens *p* Roach 2rs *r* MGM

MAMA LOVES PAPA (1933) *d* McLeod *w* C Ruggles 68min Par

MAMAN COLIBRI (1929) *d/co-s* Duvivier *co-c* Thirard *des* Christian-Jaque

MAMAN POUPEE (1919) *d* Gallone

MAMA STEPS OUT (1937) *d* G Seitz *st/s* Loos 65min MGM

MAMBO (1954) *d/co-s* Rossen *p* Ponti, De Laurentiis *c* Rosson *co-m* Rota *w* Mangano, Gassman, Winters 94min *r* Par

MAMMA ROMA (1962) *d/s* Pasolini *m* Vivaldi *w* Magnani 110min

MAMMY (1930) *d* Curtiz *st/songs* Irving Berlin *w* Jolson, L Sherman 84min WB

MAMSELL JOSEBETH (1963) *d/c* Fischer *sh*

MAMY WATER (1955) *d/s/c* Rouch 16mm 19min (= *Pêche et le Culte de la Mer*)

MAM'ZELLE NITOUCHE (1931) *d* M Allégret *m* Van Parys *w* Raimu , Feuillère. S Simon

MAM'ZELLE NITOUCHE (1953) *d/co-s* Y Allégret *co-s/di* Achard *co-s* Aurenche *fmpl* Meilhac, Milhaud *c* Thirard *dec* D'Eaubonne *m* Van Parys *w* Fernandel *90min

Mamzelle Strip-tease = EN EFFEUILLANT LA MARGUERITE (1956)

Mam'zelle Pigalle = CETTE SACREE GAMINE (1955)

Man = NINGEN (1925)

Man, The = NINGEN (1962)

MAN ABOUT THE HOUSE, A (1947) *d/co-s* L Arliss *w* (Donat) 95min BL

MAN ABOUT TOWN (1939) *d* Sandrich *c* Tetzlaff *co-a* Dreier *chor* Prinz *m* V Young *w* Lamour, Grable, Benny 85min Par

MAN AFRAID (1957) *d* Keller *c* Metty *co-a* Golitzen *m* Mancini CS 84min U

MAN ALIVE (1945) *d* Enright *m* Harline *w* Menjou 70min RKO

MAN ALONE, A (1955) *d* Milland *c* Lindon *m* V Young *w* Milland *96min Rep

Man and a Woman, A (UK) = HOMME ET UNE FEMME, UN (1966)

MAN AND HIS DOG OUT FOR AIR, A (1957) *d* Breer *anim* 16mm 3min

MAN AND POLAR REGIONS (1967) *co-d* S Clarke 11-*screen* Expo '67

MAN BAIT (1926) *d* Crisp *c* Rosson *w* Fairbanks Jr 5865ft

Man, Beast and Virtue, L' (1952) = UOMO, LA BESTIA E LA VIRTU, L' (1952)

MAN BEHIND THE MASK, THE (1936) *d* M Powell 70min *r* MGM

MAN BETWEEN, THE (1953) *d* C Reed *s* Kurnitz *w* Bloom, Mason, Neff 101min *pc* C Reed *r* UA

MAN CALLED BACK (1932) *d* Florey 79min

MAN CALLED FLINTSTONE, THE (1966) *d/p* Hanna, Barbera *anim* 87min *r* Col

Man Called Gringo (US) = SIE NANNTEN IHN GRINGO (1966)

MAN CALLED HORSE, A (1970) *d* Silverstein *m* Rosenman *w* R Harris PV* 114min

MAN CALLED PETER, A (1955) *d* Koster *c* Lipstein *m* A Newman *w* Peters CS* 119min Fox

MANCHE ET LA BELLE, UNE (1957) *d/co-s* Verneuil *c* Matras *dec* D'Eaubonne *w* I Miranda 101min (= *The Evil that is Eve*)

MANCHURIAN CANDIDATE, THE (1962) *d/co-p* Frankenheimer *ex-p* HW Koch *s/co-p* Axelrod *fn* Richard Condon *c* Lindon *w* Sinatra, J Leigh, Laurence Harvey 126min *r* UA

MAN COULD GET KILLED, A (1966) *d* Neame, *Cliff Owen w* Garner, Mercouri PV* 98min JAR

MAN CRAZY (1953) *d* I Lerner *co-pl/co-st/co-s* Yordan 79min Fox

MANDALAY (1934) *d* Curtiz *c* Gaudio *w* K Francis 65min FN

MANDEN DER SEJREDE (1918) *d/s* Madsen

MANDEN UDEN FREMTID (1915) *d* Madsen

MANDEN UDEN SMIL (1916) *d/s* Madsen

MAN DIE ZIJN HAAR KORT LIET KNIPPEN, DE (1966) *d/co-s* Delvaux *al* Cloquet 95min (= *The Man Who Had His Hair Cut Short*)

MANDRAGOLA, LA (1965) *d* Lattuada *fpl* Niccolò Machiavelli *w* Brialy, Toto 99min (= *The Mandrake*)

Mandragore = ALRAUNE (1928)

Mandrake, The (UK) = MANDRAGOLA, LA (1965)

MANDRIN (1962) *d/co-s/di* Le Chanois *m* Von Parys S* 130min Pat (= *Mandrin, Bandit Gentilhomme*)

Mandrin, Bandit Gentilhomme = MANDRIN (1962)

MANDY (1952) *d* Mackendrick *p* Balcon *c* Slocombe *e* Holt *w* Hawkins 92min (= *The Crash of Silence*)

MAN-EATER OF KUMAON (1948) *d* Haskin *fn* Jim Corbett *c* Mellor *w* Sabu, Corey 79min U

MANEGE (1938) *d* Gallone

MANEGES (1949) *d* Y Allégret *c* Bourgoin *co-dec* Trauner *w* Signoret 90min

MAN FOR ALL SEASONS, A (1966) *d/p* Zinnemann *s/fpl* Bolt *c* Moore *m* Delerue *w* Scofield, V Redgrave *120min Col

Man for Burning, A = UOMO DA BRUCIARE, UN (1962)

MAN FROM BITTER RIDGE, THE (1955) *d* J Arnold *c* Metty *80min U

MAN FROM CAIRO, THE (1953) *d* Enright *w* Raft 82min (= *Avventura ad Algeri*)

MAN FROM COLORADO, THE (1948) *d* Levin *st* B Chase *co-s* Maddow *m* Duning *w* G Ford, Holden 99min Col

MAN FROM DEL RIO (1956) *d* Horner *c* Cortez *w* Quinn 82min *r* UA

MAN FROM DOWN UNDER, THE (1943) *d/co-p* Leonard *a* Gibbons *w* Laughton, D Reed, Lawford 103min MGM

MAN FROM EGYPT, THE (1916) *d/co-s/w* Semon 1rl Vit

MAN FROM FRISCO (1944) *d* Florey *w* Duryea 91min Rep

MAN FROM HOME, THE (1914) *d/p/s* De Mille *co-fpl* Booth Tarkington 5rs *pc* Lasky

MAN FROM LARAMIE, THE (1955) *d* A Mann *p* Goetz *co-s* Yordan *c* C Lang *m* Duning *w* J Stewart, A Kennedy, Crisp CS* 104min Col

MAN FROM LOST RIVER, THE (1921) *d* F Lloyd *c* Brodine 6rs *pc* Goldwyn

Man from Nevada (UK) = NEVADAN, THE (1950)

MAN FROM PLANET X, THE (1951) *d* Ulmer *c* JL Russell 70min *r* UA

MAN FROM THE ALAMO, THE (1953) *d* Boetticher *p* A Rosenberg *c* Metty *co-a* Golitzen *w* G Ford *79min U

MAN FROM THE DINER'S CLUB, THE (1963) *d* Tashlin *c* Mohr *w* Kaye, G Kennedy 96min Col

MAN FROM THE EAST, THE (1914) *d/s/w* Mix 1rl Sel

MAN FROM TUMBLEWEEDS, THE (1940) *d* JH Lewis 59min Col

MANHANDLED (1924) *d/p* Dwan *s* Tuttle *c* Rosson *w* Swanson 6998ft FPL

MANHATTAN MADNESS (1916) *d* Dwan *p* Griffith *w* Fairbanks Sr 5rs *r* Tri

MANHATTAN MONKEY BUSINESS (1935) *d* C Chase (*as* Parrott), *Harold Law p* Roach *w* C Chase 2rs MGM

MANHATTAN MELODRAMA (1934) *d* WS Van Dyke *p* Selznick *co-s* J Mankiewicz *c* Howe *co-e* Vorkapich *w* W Powell, Gable, M Loy, Rooney 93min MGM

MANHATTAN PARADE (1932) *d* Bacon 8rs WB

Manhood = MUZHESTVO (1955)

MAN HUNT (1941) *d* F Lang *as-p* Macgowan *s* D Nichols *c* AC Miller *co-a* R Day *m* A Newman *w* Pidgeon, J Bennett, G Sanders, Carradine 102min Fox

Manhunt = FROM HELL TO TEXAS (1958)

MAN HUNTER, THE (1919) *d/st/s* F Lloyd 6rs Fox

MANIACI, I (1963) *d* Caprioli

MANICURE LADY, THE (1911) *d/w* Sennett 1rl Bio

MAN I KILLED, THE (1932) *d* Lubitsch *co-s* Raphaelson *c* Milner *dec* Dreier *w* L Barrymore, Pitts 76min Par (= *Broken Lullaby*)

MAN I LOVE, THE (1929) *d* Wellman *st/di* H Mankiewicz *t* J Mankiewicz 6524ft Par

MAN I LOVE, THE (1946) *d* Walsh *c* Hickox *m* M Steiner *w* Lupino 96min WB

MAN I MARRIED, THE (1940) *d* Pichel *c* Marley *w* J Bennett, Nolan, Ouspenskaya, Sten 72min Fox

MANIN DENSHA (1957) *d/co-s* Ichikawa Dai (= *The Crowded Train*)

MAN IN GREY, THE (1943) *d/co-s* L Arliss *w* Mason, Lockwood, S Granger 116min

MAN IN POSSESSION (1931) *d* S Wood *co-di* PG Wodehouse *w* Montgomery 79min

MAN IN THE ATTIC (1953) *d* Fregonese (*uc*), *RL Jacks co-a* Wheeler *w* Palance 82min Fox

MAN IN THE GRAY FLANNEL SUIT, THE (1956) *d/s* N Johnson *p* Zanuck *fn* Sloan Wilson *c* C Clarke *co-a* Wheeler *m* Herrmann *w* Peck, J Jones, March, Cobb CS* 152min Fox

MAN IN THE IRON MASK, THE (1939) *d* Whale *fn* Dumas *w* L Hayward, J Bennett 110min U

MAN IN THE MIDDLE, THE (1963) *d* Hamilton *w* Mitchum, T Howard CS 94min Fox

MAN IN THE MIRROR, THE (1936) *d* Elvey *c* Courant *w* Horton 85min

MAN IN THE MOON (1960) *d* Dearden *co-s* Forbes 99min JAR

MAN IN THE NET, THE (1959) *d* Curtiz *p* W Mirisch *s* Rose *c* J Seitz *w* Ladd 97min *r* UA

Man in the Raincoat, The (UK) = HOMME A L'IMPERMEABLE, L' (1956)

MAN IN THE SADDLE (1951) *d* De Toth *p* H Brown *c* Lawton *w* R Scott *87min Col

MAN IN THE SHADOW (1957) *d* J Arnold *p* Zugsmith *c* Arling *w* J Chandler, Welles CS 80min U (= *Pay the Devil*)

MAN IN THE SKY (1956) *d* Crichton *p* Balcon *as-p* Holt *c* Slocombe *w* Hawkins S 86min

MAN IN THE TRUNK, THE (1942) *d* St Clair 70min Fox

MAN IN THE VAULT (1955) *d* A McLaglen *s* B Kennedy *c* Clothier *w* Ekberg 73min *pc* J Wayne *r* RKO

MAN IN THE WHITE SUIT, THE (1951) *d/co-s* Mackendrick *co-p* Balcon *c* Slocombe *w* Guiness, Greenwood 85min

Man is not a Bird = COVEK NIJE TIJKA (1966)

Man is Ten Feet Tall, A = EDGE OF THE CITY (1956)

MANI SULLA CITTA, LE (1963) *d/co-st/co-s* Rosi *c* Di Venanzo *m* Piccioni *w* Steiger 110min *r* WB (= *Hands over the City*)

MANLY MAN, A (1911) *co-d* Ince *w* Pickford

MANMO KENROKU NO REIMEI (1932) *d* Mizoguchi (= *The Dawn of the Founding of Manchukuo and Mongolia*)

Man Named John, A (UK) = E VENNE UN UOMO (1964)

MANN, DEM MAN SEINEN NAMEN STAHL, DER (1945, *uf*) *d/co-s* Staudte Tob

MANN, DER DEN MORD BEGING, DER (1931) *d* C Bernhardt *w* Veidt

Mann, der nicht Lieben darf, Der = GEHEIMNIS DES ABBE X, DAS (1927)

Mann, der nicht nein Sagen kann, Der: German version of MA NON E UNA COSA SERIA (1936)

MANN DER SEINEN MORDER SUCHT, DER (1931) *d* Siokmak *p* Pommer *co-s* B Wilder *co-dec* Rohrig *m* Hollander, Waxman 95min UFA

MANNEKANGEN (1913) *d/s* Stiller

MANNEKANG I ROTT (1958) *d* Mattson *w* Björk *110min (= *Mannequin in Red*)

MANNEN I MORKER (1955) *d* Mattson *co-s* Lindström *w* Sjöström (= *Men in Darkness*)

MANNEQUIN (1926) *d/p* Cruze *w* W Baxter, Pidgeon, Pitts 7rs Par

MANNEQUIN (1938) *d* Borzage *p* J Mankiewicz *c* Folsey *w* Tracy, J Crawford 92min MGM

Mannequin in Red = MANNEKANG I ROTT (1958)

MANNESMANN (1937) *d* Ruttmann 15min

Man Next Door, The = TONARI-NO YARO (1965)

MANN GEHT DURCH DIE WAND, EIN (1959) *d* Vajda 98min

MANN IM KELLER, DER (1914) *d* May 1412m

Manniskor möts och ljuv musik uppstäri i hjartat = MENNESKER MØDES OG SØD MUSIK OPSTAAR I HJERTET (1968)

MANN NACH DEUTSCHLAND, EIN (1934) *d* Wegener 61min UFA

Man No 217 = CHELOVEK No 217 (1945)

Man och Kvinna = HANDFULL RIS, EN (1938)

MANO DELLO STRANIERO, LA (1953) *d/co-s* Soldati *w* Valli, T Howard 85min (= *The Stranger's Hand*)

MANO EN LA TRAMPA, LA (1961) *d/co-p/co-s* Torre-Nilsson 90min (= *Hand in the Trap*)

MAN OF ARAN (1934) *d/s/c* Flaherty *p* Balcon 70min Gau

MAN OF A THOUSAND FACES (1957) *d* Pevney *co-s* Goff, Roberts, *c* Metty *w* Cagney, Malone CS 122min U

Man of Bronze (UK) = JIM THORPE – ALL AMERICAN (1951)

Man of Evil (US) = FANNY BY GASLIGHT (1944)

Man of Iron (UK) = FERROVIERE, IL (1956)

MAN OF SENTIMENT, A (1933) *d* Thorpe 62min

Man of the Century = ROVESNIK VEKA (1960)

MAN OF THE FOREST (1933) *d* Hathaway *fn* Zane Grey *c* B Reynolds *w* R Scott, Carey 59min Par

MAN OF THE HOUR, THE (1914) *d* M Tourneur

MAN OF THE WEST (1958) *d* A Mann *p* W Mirisch *s* Rose *c* E Haller *a* Boyle *m* Harline *w* G Cooper, Cobb CS* 96min AA

MA NO IKE (1923) *d/s* Kinugasa (= *The Spirit of the Pond*)

MANOIR DE LA PEUR, LE (1927) *d/s* Machin, *Henri Wulschleger* 1615m (= *L'Homme Noir*)

MANOLESCUS MEMOIREN (1920) *d/p* R Oswald *w* Veidt 2346m

MANOLETE (1944, *uf*) *d/s* Gance

MANOMETR No 1 (1930) *d* Room 878m

MANOMETR No 2 (1931) *d* Room 1540m

MANON (1948) *d/co-s* Clouzot *fn* (*Manon Lescaut*) *Abbé Prévost c* Thirard *m* Misraki *w* Reggiani 100min

MAN ON A STRING (1960) *d* De Toth *p* De Rochemont *co-c* Lawton *m* Duning *w* Borgnine 92min Col (= *Confessions of a Counterspy*)

MAN ON A TIGHTROPE (1953) *d* Kazan *as-p* G Oswald *m* Waxman *w* March, Grahame, Menjou 105min Fox

MANON DES SOURCES (1952) *d/p* Pagnol 144min

MA NON E UNA COSA SERIA (1936) *d* Camerini *co-s* Soldati *fpl Luigi Pirandello w* De Sica (= *Der Mann der nicht nein Sagen kann*)

MANON: FINESTRA 2 (1956) *d* Olmi *13min

MAN ON FIRE (1957) *d/s* Macdougall *p* S Siegel *c* Ruttenberg *m* Raksin *w* B Crosby 95min MGM

MANON LESCAUT (1939) *d* Gallone *fn Abbé Prévost*

MANON 70 (1968) *d/co-s/co-di* Aurel *fn* (*Manon Lescaut*) *Abbé Prévost mf Vivaldi w* Deneuve, Brialy, Martinelli *110min

MAN ON THE BEACH, A (1955) *d* Losey *des consultant* R Macdonald *w* Wolfit S* 29min

MAN ON THE EIFFEL TOWER, THE (1949) *d* Meredith *fn* (*La Tête d'un Homme*) *Georges Simenon c* Cortez *w* Laughton, Meredith, Tone *97min *r* RKO

MAN ON THE FLYING TRAPEZE (1935) *d* Bruckman *co-st* Fields (*ps* Charles Bogle) *w* Fields, Brennan 66min Par

MAN ON THE PROWL (1957) *d/p/co-s* Napoleon *c* Musuraca *m* Gold 85min *r* UA

Man on the Track = CZLOWIEK NA TORZE (1956)

MANPOWER (1927) *d* Badger *c* Cronjager 5617ft Par

MANPOWER (1941) *d* Walsh *p* Wallis *as-p* Hellinger *co-s* Wald *c* E Haller *w* Robinson, Raft, Dietrich 104min WB

MAN-PROOF (1937) *d* Thorpe *c* Freund *m* Waxman *w* M Loy, Tone, R Russell, Pidgeon 74min MGM

MAN'S CASTLE (1933) *d* Borzage *s* Swerling *c* August *w* Tracy, L Young 75min Col

MAN'S FAVORITE SPORT? (1964) *d/p* Hawks *c* R Harlan *co-a* Golitzen *m* Mancini *w* Hudson *127min *r* U

MAN'S GENIUS (1912) *d* Griffith *w* Marsh 1rl Bio

Man's Heart = OTOKO GOKORO (1925)

MANSLAUGHTER (1922) *d* De Mille 10rs FPL

MANSLAUGHTER (1930) *d/s* G Abbott *rm* 1922 *c* Stout *w* March, Colbert 75min Par

MAN'S MAN, A (1929) *d/p* Cruze 8rs MGM

MAN SPELT NICHT MIT DER LIEBE (1926) *d* Pabst *w* Krauss 2500m

Man's Value = TSENA CHELOVEKA (1928)

MAN TO MAN (1930) *d* Dwan 68min FN

Man to Man = CHELOVEK CHELOVEKU (1958)

MAN TO REMEMBER, A (1938) *d* Kanin *s* Trumbo 80min RKO

MANTRA MUGDH (1949) *d* Roy

MANTRAP (1926) *d* V Fleming *c* Howe *w* Bow 6077ft FPL

MANTRAP (1953) *d* Fisher *w* Henreid, Kendall 78min

MANTRAP (1961) *d/co-p* E O'Brien *c* Griggs *m* Leith Stevens *w* J Hunter 93min Par

MANUELA (1957) *d* Hamilton *c* Heller *m* Alwyn *w* T Howard, Armendariz, Martinelli 95min BL

MA NUIT CHEZ MAUD (1968) *d/st/s/di* Rohmer *w* Trintignant 110min *co-pc* Truffaut (= *My Night with Maud/My Night at Maud's*)

MAN UNDER COVER, THE (1922) *d* Browning 5rl U

Man Underwater = CLOVEK PODVODON (1961)

MAN UPSTAIRS, THE (1926) *d* Del Ruth 5800ft WB

Man Vanishes, A = NINGEN JOHATSU (1967)

MAN WANTED (1932) *d* Dieterle *c* Toland *w* K Francis 63min WB

MAN WHO CAME BACK, THE (1924) *d/p Emmett J Flynn s* Goulding *c* Andriot *w* G O'Brien 8293ft Fox

MAN WHO CAME BACK, THE (1930) *d* Walsh *c* Edeson *w* J Gaynor 74min Fox

MAN WHO CAME TO DINNER, THE (1942) *d* Keighley *p* Wallis *co-as-p* Wald *co-s* JJ Epstein *fpl* G Kaufman, M Hart *c* Gaudio *w* B Davis, Sheridan 166min WB

MAN WHO CHANGED HIS MIND, THE (1936) *d* Stevenson *s* Gilliat *w* Karloff 66min

MAN WHO COULD CHEAT DEATH, THE (1959) *d* Fisher 83min *r* Par

MAN WHO DARED, THE (1946) *d* J Sturges 65min Col

Man who had his Hair Cut Short, The = MAN DIE ZIJN HAAR KORT KIET KNIPPEN, DE (1966)

MAN WHO HAUNTED HIMSELF, THE (1970) *d/co-s* Dearden *94min

MAN WHO KNEW TOO MUCH, THE (1934) *d* Hitchcock *co-p* Balcon *st* Charles Bennett, *DB Wyndham-Lewis c* Courant *w* Lorre, Fresnay 74min Gau

MAN WHO KNEW TOO MUCH, THE (1956) *d/p* Hitchcock *as-p* H Coleman *co-s* J Hayes *st* Charles Bennett, *DB Wyndham-Lewis rm* 1934 *c* Burks *co-a* Pereira *m* Herrmann *w* J Stewart, D Day, Gélin, (Herrmann) *119min Par

MAN WHO LAUGHS, THE (1928) *d* Leni *fn Victor Hugo w* Veidt 3000m U

Man who Lies, The = HOMME QUI MENT, L' (1968)

MAN WHO NEVER WAS, THE (1956) *d* Neame *s Nigel Balchin m* Rawsthorne *c* Morris *w* Boyd, Grahame, C Webb CS* 103min *r* Fox

MAN WHO PLAYED GOD, THE (1922) *d Harmon Weight w* G Arliss, Astor 5855ft *r* UA

MAN WHO PLAYED GOD, THE (1932) *d John D Adolfi rm* 1922 *w* G Arliss, B Davis, Milland, Hopper 81min WB

MAN WHO SHOT LIBERTY VALANCE, THE (1962) *d* J Ford *p/co-s* Goldbeck *c* Clothier *m* Mockridge *w* J Stewart, J Wayne, Miles, Marvin, E O'Brien, Carradine 122min *r* Par

MAN WHO STAYED AT HOME, THE (1915) *d/p/c* Hepworth 3500ft

MAN WHO TALKED TOO MUCH, THE (1940) *d* V Sherman *w* Barthelmess 75min WB

MAN WHO UNDERSTOOD WOMEN, THE (1959) *d/s/e* N Johnson *fn* Gary *c* Krasner *co-a* Wheeler *w* Caron, H Fonda, Dalio CS* 105min Fox

MAN WHO WON, THE (1923) *d* Wellman *c* August 5rs Fox

Man with a Gun, The = CHELOVEK S RUZHOM (1938)

Man with a Movie Camera = CHELOVEK S KINOAPPARATOM (1929)

MAN WITHIN, THE (1947) *d Bernard Knowles fn* Greene *c* Unsworth *w* Greenwood, M Redgrave, Attenborough *88min

Man without a Map, The = MOETSUKITA CHIZU (1968)

Man without a Nationality, The = MUKOKUSEKI-MONO (1951)

MAN WITHOUT A STAR (1955) *d* K Vidor *p* A Rosenberg *co-s* B Chase *c* Metty *co-a* Golitzen *w* K Douglas, Crain, Trevor *89min U

MAN WITH THE GOLDEN ARM, THE (1955) *d/p* Preminger *fn Nelson Algren c* Leavitt *m* E Bernstein *cr* Bass *w* Sinatra, Novak, Parker 119min *r* UA

MAN WITH THE GUN (1955) *d/co-s* R Wilson *c* Garmes *m* North *w* Mitchum, A Dickinson 89min *r* UA (= *Troubleshooter*)

Man with the X-Ray Eyes, The (UK) = X – THE MAN WITH THE X-RAY EYES (1967)

MAN WITH TWO FACES, THE (1934) *d* A Mayo *co-s* Busch *fco-pl* (*The Dark Tower*) G Kaufman *w* Robinson 73min WB

Man, Woman and Dog = OTOKO TO ONNA TO INU (1964)

MANXMAN, THE (1929) *d* Hitchcock 8163ft

MANY A PICKLE (1937–39) *d* McLaren *p* Grierson 2min GPO

MANY HAPPY RETURNS (1934) *d* McLeod *w* Milland 64min Par

MANY RIVERS TO CROSS (1955) *d* Rowland *p* J Cummings *c* J Seitz *co-a* Gibbons *m* Mockridge *w* R Taylor, Parker, V McLaglen CS* 92min MGM

Many-Splendored Thing, A = LOVE IS A MANY-SPLENDORED THING (1955)

Mao Tse-Tung and the Cultural Revolution = MO TAKU-TO TO BUNKADAI-KAKUMEI (1969)

MARACAIBO (1958) *d/p* Wilde *fn* Silliphant *w* Wilde VV* 88min Par

MARU MARU (1952) *d* G Douglas *co-st* Yordan *c* Burks *m* M Steiner *w* Flynn, Roman, Burr 98min WB

MARANHOA '66 (1969) *d* Rocha 10min

MARBLE HEART (1916) *d/s* Brenon 5rs Fox

MARC ANTONIO E CLEOPATRA (1913) *d/s/dec* Guazzoni *fpl Shakespeare*

MARC ANTONIO E CLEOPATRA (1916) *d/s* Guazzoni *fpl* Shakespeare

MARCEL ALLAIN (1966) *d* Franju TV

MARCELINO, PAN Y VINO (1955) *d/co-s* Vajda 90min

MARCELLA (1922) *d* Gallone

MARCH, THE (1963) *d* Blue 33min (= *The March to Washington*)

MARCHAND DE NOTES, LE (1942) *d* Grimault anim*

MARCHE, LA (1951) *d* Audiard sh

MARCHE DES MACHINES, LA (1928) *d Eugene Deslaw c* B Kaufman 6min

MARCHE OU CREVE (1959) *d* Lautner *m* Delerue 100min

MARCH OF THE YEARS (1933–34) *p* De Rochemont series in 10 parts

MARCH OF TIME (1935–42) *p* De Rochemont series in 68 parts

March towards the Sun = IDE DO SLONCA (1955)

March to Washington, The = MARCH, THE (1963)

MARCIA NUZIALE (1965) *d/co-s* Ferreri 105min

MARCIA O CREPA (1962) *d/co-s* Wisbar *w* S Granger 98min (= *Commando/Legion's Last Patrol*)

MARCIA SU ROMA, LA (1963) *d* Risi *m* Piccioni *w* Gassman 95min

MARCO POLO (1961) *d* Fregonese *co-s* Tessari CS* 104min

MARDI GRAS (1958) *d* Goulding *p* Wald *co-s* Kanter *co-a* Wheeler *w* J Hunter, R Wagner CS* 107min Fox

MARE, IL (1962) *d/st/s* Patroni-Griffi *m* Fusco 110min

MARE DI GUA, UN (1940) *d/co-st/co-s/co-di* Bragaglia, Zampa

MARE DI NAPOLI, IL (1921) *d* Gallone

MARE MATTO (1963) *d/co-st/co-s* Castellani *w* Lollobrigida, Belmondo 120min

MARE NOSTRUM (1926) *d* Ingram *c* J Seitz 9894ft MGM

MARGIE (1946) *d* H King *c* C Clarke *m* A Newman *w* Crain 94min Fox

MARGIN FOR ERROR (1943) *d* Preminger *fpl Claire Booth Luce c* Cronjager *co-a* R Day *w* J Bennett, Preminger 74min Fox

MARGUERITE DE LA NUIT (1955) *d* Autant-Lara *s* Jeanson *fn Pierre Mac Orlan w* Montand, Morgan, Girotti *126min

MARIA CANDELARIA (1943) *d/st/co-s* Fernandez *c* Figueroa *w* Del Rio, Armendariz 110 (= *Portrait of Maria*)

MARIA CHAPDELAINE (1934) *d/s* Duvivier *co-c* Périnal *m* Wiener *w* Gabin 110min (= *The Naked Heart*)

Maria Chapdelaine = NAKED HEART, THE (1949)

MARIA DER MAGD (1936) *d/co-s* V Harlan 2474m

MARIA DI MAGDALA (1915) *d* Gallone

MARIAGE AU TELEPHONE, UN (1912) *d/s/w* Linder Pat

MARIAGE D'AMOUR (1942) *d/co-ad/co-di* Decoin 82min

MARIAGE DE CHIFFON, LE (1942) *d* Autant-Lara *co-s/di* Aurenche *c* Agostino *m* Wiener 100min

MARIAGE DE FIGARO, LE (1959) *d Jean Meyer technical adviser* Deville *fpl Beaumarchais m Mozart w Comédie Française* *105min

MARIAGE DE MADEMOISELLE BEULEMANS, LE (1926) *d/s* Duvivier *c* Thirard

MARIAGE IMPREVU, UN (1913) *d/s/w* Linder Pat

MARIA KET EJSZA KAJA (1940) *d* Balasz

MARIA MARTEN (1913) *d/p* Elvey 2850ft

MARIA, MATRICULA DE BILBAO (1960) *d* Vajda *w* Vanel S*

MARIANNE (1929) *d/p* Leonard *w* Davies 10000ft MGM

MARIANNE DE MA JEUNESSE (1955) *d/s* Duvivier *fn* (*Douloureuse Arcadie*) *Peter de Mendelssohn des* D'Eaubonne *m* Ibert 110min

MARIA NO OYUKI (1935) *d* Mizoguchi *fn* (*Boule de Suif*) *Maupassant w* Yamada (= *Virgin from Oyuki*)

Maria of the Ant Village = ARI NO MACHI NO MARIA (1958)

MARIA PA KVARNGARDEN (1945) *d* Mattson *w* Lindfors (= *Marie in the Windmill*)

MARI A PRIX FIXE, UN (1963) *d* De Givray *w* Karina FS 80min

MARIA ROSA (1915) *d* De Mille 5rs *pc* Lasky

MARI DIVORCE, LE (1933) *d* Cavalcanti (= *Le Garçon Divorcé*)

MARIE ANTOINETTE (1938) *d* WS Van Dyke *co-s* D Stewart *c* Daniels *a* Gibbons *co-e* Vorkapich *m* Stothart *w* Shearer, Power, J Barrymore 160min MGM

MARIA-ANTOINETTE (1953) *d* Delannoy *w* Morgan, Piccoli S* 125min (= *Shadow of the Guillotine*)

MARIE-CHANTAL CONTRE LE DOCTEUR KHA (1965) *d/co-s* Chabrol *c* Rabier *w* Reggiani, Tamiroff *110min

MARIE-CHRISTINE (1970) *co-d* Jutra *co-d/w Geneviève Bujold c* Brault *10min

MARIE DU PORT, LA (1950) *d* Carné *co-s/co-di* J Prévert *fn Georges Simenon c* Alekan *co-dec* Trauner *m* Kosma *w* Gabin

MARIEE ETAIT EN NOIR, LA (1967) *d/co-ad/co-di* Truffaut *co-ad/co-di* Richard *fn* (*The Bride Wore Black*) *William Irish c* Coutard *m* Herrmann *w* Moreau, Brialy *107min *co-pc* De Laurentiis, Truffaut *r* UA (= *The Bride Wore Black*)

MARIE GALANTE (1934) *d* H King *c* J Seitz *w* Tracy 88min Fox

Marie in the Windmill = MARIA PA KVARNGARDEN (1945)

MARIE LA MISERIE (1945) *d* De Baroncelli

Marie, Legend Hongroise = TAVASZI ZAPOR (1932)

MARIE-OCTOBRE (1958) *d/co-ad* Duvivier *di* Jeanson *dec* Wakhévitch *w* Darrieux, Reggiani, Ventura 90min

MARIES DE L'AN II, LES (1971) *d/s/co-ad* Rappeneau *co-ad* Sautet *c* C Renoir *des* Trauner *m* Legrand *w* Belmondo, Brasseur *100min

Marie Walewska = CONQUEST (1937)

MARINAI SENZA STELLA (1943) *d/st/s* De Robertis

MARINES, LES (1957) *d/co-c* Reichenbach *m* Delerue, *Beethoven* 22min

MARINES ET CRISTAUX (1928) *d/s* Gance sh

MARINES, LETS GO (1962) *d/p/st* Walsh *c* Ballard CS* 103min Fox

MARIO BANANA (1964) *d* Warhol 16mm si 4min

MARIONETKI (1934) *d/s* Protazanov 2500m (= *Puppets*)

MARIONETTE (1938) *d* Gallone

MARIONETTEN (1918) *d* Lubitsch

MARIONETTEN DER LEIDENSCHAFT (1919) *d/co-s* Lupu-Pick

MARISA LA CIVETTA (1957) *d/co-s* Bolognini *co-s* Pasolini *pc* Ponti

MARITI IN CITTA (1957) *d/co-s* Comencini

MARITO, IL (1958) *co-d/co-s* N Loy *co-st/co-s/w* Sordi

MARITO E MIO .... L'AMAZZO O QUANDO MI PARE, IL (1967) *d/s* Festa Campanile *w* Catherine Spaak *100min (= *Drop Dead, My Love*)

MARITO E MOGLIE (1952) *d/co-s/fpl/w* De Filippo 91min *r* RKO (= *Husband and Wife*)

MARITO PER ANNA ZACCHEO, UN (1953) *d/s* De Santis *co-s* Zavattini *c* Martinelli *w* Girotti 75min (= *A Husband for Anna*)

MARIUS (1931) *d* A Korda *p/s/fpl* Pagnol *w* Raimu, Fresnay 120min Par

MARIUS ET OLIVE A PARIS (1935, ur) d J Epstein (uc)
Marizza, Called the Smuggler-Madonna (UK) = MARRIZA, GENANNT DIE SCHMUGGLER MADONNA (1922)
MARIZZA, GENANNT DIE SCHMUGGLER MADONNA (1922) d Murnau c Freund 1800m (= Marizza, Called the Smuggler-Madonna)
MARJORIE MORNINGSTAR (1958) d Rapper p Sperling m M Steiner w Gene Kelly, N Wood, Trevor *123min WB
MARK, THE (1961) d G Green p Stross co-s Buchman c Slocombe w Maria Schell, Steiger CS 127min co-pc Stross, Buchman r Fox
MARKED MAN, A (1917) d/st J Ford w Carey 5rs U
MARKED MEN (1919) d J Ford w Carey 5rs U
MARKED WOMAN (1937) d Bacon p Wallis co-st/co-s Rossen ad S Miller w B Davis, Bogart 97min WB
MARK OF THE RENEGADES (1951) d Fregonese w Charisse, Roland, Montalban *81min U
MARK OF THE VAMPIRE (1935) d Browning c Howe w L Barrymore, Lugosi, Hersholt 85min MGM
MARK OF THE WHISTLER (1944) d Castle 60min Col
MARK OF ZORRO, THE (1920) d Niblo c Gaudio w Fairbanks Sr 8rs r UA
MARK OF ZORRO, THE (1940) d Mamoulain c AC Miller m A Newman w Power, Rathbone, Darnell 93min Fox
MARKURELLS I WADKOPING (1930) d/w Sjöström s/fn Hjalmar Bergman SF (= Väter und Söhne)
MARNIE (1964) d/p Hitchcock c Burks co-a Boyle m Herrmann w Connery *130min r UA
MAROC D'AUJOURD'HUI (1949) d Michel sh
MAROONED (1969) d J Sturges p Frankovitch c Fapp des Wheeler w Peck PV70* 133min Col
MARQUITTA (1927) d J Renoir co-c Bachelet 2200m
Marriage = KEKKON (1947)
Marriageable Age = KONKI (1961)
MARRIAGE CIRCLE, THE (1924) d Lubitsch fpl (Only a Dream) Lothar Schmidt w Menjou 8rs WB
MARRIAGE-GO-ROUND (1960) d W Lang p/s/fpl Leslie Stevens w S Hayward, Mason CS* 98min Fox
MARRIAGE IS A PRIVATE AFFAIR (1944) d Leonard p Berman co-a Gibbons m Kaper w Turner 116min MGM
Marriage, Italian Style = MATRIMONIO ALL'ITALIANA (1964)
MARRIAGE LICENSE? (1926) d Borzage w Pidgeon 7168ft Fox
MARRIAGE OF CONVENIENCE (1960) d C Donner 58min
MARRIAGE OF WILLIAM ASHE, THE (1916) d/p/c Hepworth 5rs
MARRIAGE ON THE ROCKS (1965) d Jack Donohue p/c Daniels w Kerr, Romero, Sinatra, Martin PV* 109min WB
MARRIAGE RING, THE (1918) d Niblo 5rs FPL
MARRIED AND IN LOVE (1940) d J Farrow 58min RKO
MARRIED COUPLE, A (1969) d/p A King 16mm * 112min
Married Lady Borrows Money, A = OKUSAMA SHAKUYOSHO (1936)
MARRIED LIFE (1920) d Erle Kenton p Sennett w Fazenda, Turpin 5rs r FN
Married Life = KEKKON NO SEITAH (1941)
Married Life, A = MESHI (1951)
Married Woman, The or *A* = FEMME MARIEE, UNE (1964)
MARRYING KIND, THE (1952) d Cukor s R Gordon, Kanin c J Walker m Friedhofer w Holliday, A Ray 98min Col
MARRY ME (1925) d/p Cruze w Horton 5526ft FPL
MARRY ME (1932) d/s Asquith 85min
MARRY ME (1949) d Fisher co-s L Gilbert 97min
MARRY ME AGAIN (1953) d/s Tashlin w R Cummings 73min RKO
MARSEILLAISE, LA (1938) d/co-s J Renoir co-c Bourgoin co-dec Wakhévitch m (classical) Lalande, Giétry, Rameau, Mozart, Bach, Rouget de Lisle co-m (modern) Kosma shadow theatre Reiniger w P Renoir, Jouvet, Carette, Modot 132min
MARSHAL OF CEDAR ROCK (1953) d Keller 54min Rep
MARTHA'S VINDICATION (1916) co-d Franklin w N Talmadge 5rs Tri
MARTHE RICHARD AU SERVICE DE LA FRANCE (1937) d/co-ad/co-di Raymond Bernard m Honegger w Feuillère, Von Stroheim, Dalio
MARTIANS COME BACK (1956) d Pintoff
MARTIN ET GASTON (1953) d/co-m Gruel p Papatakis anim* 10min
MARTIN FIERRO (1968) d/p Torre Nilsson 70* 136min
MARTIN LUTHER (1953) d/w Pichel c Brun 103min
MARTIN OF THE MOUNTED (1926) d Wyler 2rs U
MARTIN ROUMAGNAC (1946) d/s Georges Lacombe m Fusco w Gabin, Gélin, Dietrich 99min
MARTIN SOLDAT (1966) d/co-st Deville *90min (= Kiss Me General)
MARTY (1955) d Delbert Mann p H Hecht s/fpl Chayevsky c La Shelle w Borgnine 91min r UA
Martyrs of Love = MUCEDNINI LASKY (1966)
MARY BURNS, FUGITIVE (1935) d W Howard p Wanger c Shamroy w S Sidney, M Douglas 84min Par
MARY JANE'S MISHAP (1901) d G Smith
MARY JANE'S PA (1935) d Keighley c E Haller 71min FN
MARYLAND (1940) d H King c Barnes, Rennahan m A Newman w Brennan, Payne, C Ruggles *92min Fox
MARY, MARY (1963) d/p LeRoy s Breen w D Reynolds *126min WB
MARY OF SCOTLAND (1936) d J Ford p Berman s D Nichols fpl Maxwell Anderson c August m M Steiner w K Hepburn, March, Carradine, Crisp 123min RKO
MARY POPPINS (1964) d Stevenson w J Andrews, D Van Dyke, Darwell *139min
MARY'S BIRTHDAY (1951) d Reiniger anim* 1rl Crown
MARY STEVENS, M.D. (1933) d Bacon c Hickox w K Francis 70min WB
MAR Y TU, EL (1951) d/st Fernandez c Figueroa
MARZIA NUZIALE (1915) d Gallone
MASCHERA DEL DEMONIO, LA (1960) d/co-s/c Bava co-p Arkoff fn(Vij) Nikolai Gogol 88min (= Black Sunday/Revenge of the Vampire/Mask of the Demon)
MASCHERA E IL VOLTO, LA (1919) d Genina
MASCHIACCIO (1917) d/st Genina
MASCOTTE (1930) d A Ford
MASCULIN FEMININ (1966) d/s Godard fsts (La Femme de Paul and Le Signe) Guy de Maupassant w Léaud, (Bardot) 110min
Mask and the Sword = SINGOALLA (1949)
MASKARAD (1941) d/s/w Gerasimov fpl Lermontov 100min (= Masquerade)
MASKED EMOTIONS (1927) d D Butler, Kenneth Hawks w G O'Brien 5365ft Fox
Masked Pirate, The = PIRATI DI CAPRI, IL (1949)
MASKERADE (1934) d/s Willi Forst w Walbrook 101min
MASKIERTE SCHRECKEN, DER (1919) d/s Jutzi 1568m
MASK OF DIMITRIOS, THE (1944) d Negulesco p Blanke fn(Coffin for Demetrius) Eric Ambler c Edeson w Greenstreet, Lorre 95min WB
MASK OF DUST (1954) d Fisher 79min
MASK OF FU MANCHU, THE (1932) d Charles Brabin, C Vidor(uc) fst Sax Rohmer w Hersholt, Karloff, M Loy 7rs MGM
MASK OF THE AVENGER (1951) d Karlson c Lawton w Derek, Quinn *83min Col
Mask of the Demon = MASCHERA DEL DEMONIO, LA (1964)
MASKOVANA MILENKA (1940) d/s Vavra fn (L'Amour Masquée) Balzac
MASKS OF THE DEVIL (1928) d Sjöström fst Jacob Wasserman a Gibbons w J Gilbert 5575ft MGM
MASQUE DE FER, LE (1962) d Decoin m Van Parys w Marais FS* 127min
MASQUE D'HONNEUR, LE (1912) d/s Gance
MASQUE OF THE RED DEATH, THE (1964) d/p Corman fst Poe c Roeg w Price S* 89min
Masquerade = MASKARAD (1941)
MASQUERADE (1964) d Dearden c Heller w Hawkins, Robertson *102min r UA
MASQUERADE IN MEXICO (1945) d Leisen c Lindon co-a Dreier m V Young w Lamour 96min Par
MASQUERADER, THE (1914) d/s/w Chaplin w Arbuckle 1rl Key (= Putting One Over/The Female Impersonator)
MASQUES (1952) d Alexeieff anim* 1min
MASSACRE, THE (1912) d Griffith 1rl Bio
MASSACRE (1934) d Crosland c Barnes w Barthelmess 74min WB
MASSACRE CANYON (1954) d Sears 66min Col
Master and his Servants, The = HERREN OG HANS TJENERE (1959)
MASTERMAN (1920) d/w Sjöström 2400m SF (= En Farlig Pant)
MASTER OF BALLANTRAE, THE (1953) d Keighley fn RL Stevenson c Cardiff w Flynn *89min WB
Master of Lassie = HILLS OF HOME (1948)
Master of the Islands (UK) = HAWAIIANS, THE (1970)
Master of Winter Sports = MISTUI ZIMICH SPORTU (1955)
MASTER PLAN, THE (1954) d/s Endfield (ps Hugh Baker) 78min
MASTER RACE, THE (1949) d/st/co-s Biberman c Metty 96min RKO
MASTERSON OF KANSAS (1954) d Castle p Katzman *72min Col
MASTERTJUVEN (1915) d Stiller 928m
MAT (1926) d/w Pudovkin fn Maxim Gorky 1850m (= Mother)
MAT (1956) d/co-s Donskoi fn Maxim Gorky w Batalov *103min (= Mother)
MATA AU HI MADE (1932) d Ozu sho (= Until the Day We Meet Again)
MATA AU HI MADE (1950) d Imai Toho (= Until the Day We Meet Again/Until Our Next Meeting)
MATA HARI (1932) d George Fitzmaurice c Daniels w Garbo, Novarro, L Barrymore 90min MGM
MATA-HARI, AGENT H21 (1964) d/co-s Richard co-s Truffaut m Delerue w Trintignant, Moreau 93min pc Truffaut
MATCHBALL (1969) d/co-s Tessari
MATCH CONTRE LA MORT (1959) d Bernard-Aubert w Blanche 87min Pat
MATCHE DE BOXE ENTRE PATINEURS A ROULETTES (1912) d/s/w Linder Pat
MATCH KING, THE (1932) d Keighley, Howard Bretherton 70min FN
MATCHLESS (1966) d/co-s Lattuada co-m Piccioni *104min r UA
MATCHMAKER, THE (1958) d Anthony s J Hayes fpl T Wilder c C Lang co-a Pereira w Booth, Perkins, MacLaine VV 101min Par
MATE OF THE SALLY ANN, THE (1917) d H King Mut
MATER DOLOROSA (1917) d/s Gance c Burel w Artaud, Modot 4400ft (= The Call of Motherhood/The Sorrowing Mother)
MATER DOLOROSA (1933) d/s Gance rm 1917 c Burel w Artaud, Modot 49min
MATERIAUX NOUVEAUX, DEMEURES NOUVELLES (1956) d Colpi sh
MATERNELLE, LA (1933) co-d/s Benoît-Lévy co-d Marie Epstein 77min (= Nursery School)
MATERNITE (1929) d Benoît-Lévy
MATINEE IDOL, THE (1928) d Capra p Cohn 6rs Col
MATING CALL, THE (1928) d Cruze t H Mankiewicz 6325ft Par
MATING GAME, THE (1959) d G Marshall fn(The Darling Buds of May) HE Bates c Bronner w D Reynolds, Randall, Douglas CS* 96min MGM
MATING OF MILLIE, THE (1948) d Levin c J Walker w G Ford 87min Col
MATING SEASON, THE (1951) d Leisen p/co-s c Brackett co-s Breen c C Lang co-a Pereira w Tierney, M Hopkins, Ritter 101min Par
MATKA JOANNA OD ANIOLOW (1961) d/co-s Kawalerowicz 108min (= Mother Joan of the Angels/The Devil and the Nun)
MATRIARCA, LA (1968) d Festa Campanile w Catherine Spaak, Trintignant, Caprioli *90min (= The Libertine)
MATRIMONIAL BED, THE (1930) d Curtiz 98min WB
MATRIMONIO ALLA MODA (1951) d/s/n Emmer 10min
MATRIMONIO ALL'ITALIANO (1964) d De Sica p Ponti ex-p Levine co-s De Filippo, Zavattini(uc) fpl (Filumena Marturano) De Filippo w Loren, Mastroianni *100min (= Marriage, Italian Style)
MATRIX (1971) d Whitney 16mm *
MATTATORE, IL (1959) d Risi w Gassman S 105min (= Love and Larceny)
Matter of Dignity, A = TELEFTEO PSEMMA, TO (1957)
Matter of Innocence, A (US) = PRETTY POLLY (1967)
MATTER OF LIFE AND DEATH, A (1946) d/p/s M Powell, Pressburger c Cardiff 2nd c Challis w Niven, Attenborough *104min
Matter of Morals, A = SISTA STEGEN, DE (1960)
MATTER OF PRIDE, A (1961) d A King 16mm 17min
MATURA REISE (1943) d S Steiner supn Feyder 106min
MAUDITE SOIT LA GUERRE (1914) d Machin 1050m (= Le Moulin Maudit)
MAUDITS, LES (1947) d/co-ad Clément di Jeanson c Alekan w Dalio 105min
MAUDITS SAUVAGES, LES (1971) d/s Lefebvre S* 107min
MAULKORB, DER (1958) d Staudte 94min
MAUPRAT (1926) d/p J Epstein fn G Sand pc J Epstein
MAUVAIS COUPS, LES (1960) d Francois Leterrier fn Roger Vailland c Badal w Signoret S110min (= Naked Autumn)
MAUVAISE GRAINE (1934) co-d/st B Wilder co-d/co-s Alexander Esway w Darrieux
MAUVAISES RENCONTRES, LES (1955) d/co-s/co-di Astruc w Aimée, Piccoli 90min
MAVROST NADE VSE (1937) d/co-s Frič (= Morality Above All)
MAX A MONACO (1913) d/s/w Linder Pat
MAX AMOUREUX DE LA TEINTURIERE (1911) d/s/w Linder Pat
MAX A PEUR DE L' EAU (1913) d/s/w Linder Pat
Max Assassiné = QUI A TUE MAX? (1913)
MAX ASTHMATIQUE (1913) d/s/w Linder Pat
MAX AU COUVENT (1913) d/w Linder Pat
MAX A UN DUEL (1911) d/w Linder Pat
MAX BANDIT PAR AMOUR (1912) d/w Linder Pat
MAX BOXEUR PAR AMOUR (1912) d/w Linder Pat
MAX COCHER DE FIACRE (1912) d/s/w Linder Pat
MAX COLLECTIONNEUR DE CHAUSSURES (1912) d/w Linder Pat
MAX COMES ACROSS (1917) d/s/w Linder 830m S & A
MAX CONTRE NICK WINTER (1912) d/w Linder w Gance Pat
MAX CUISINIER PAR AMOUR (1911) d/s/w Linder Pat (= Max et Jane Font des Crêpes)
MAX DANS LES AIRS (1914) d/s/w Linder Pat
MAX DANS SA FAMILLE (1911) d/s/w Linder Pat
Max Décoré = MEDAILLE DE SAUVETAGE, LA (1914)
MAX DEVRAIT PORTER DES BRETELLES (1915) d/s/w Linder Pat
MAX EMULE DE TARTARIN (1912) d/w Linder Pat
MAX EN CONVALESCENCE (1911) d/s/w Linder Pat
Max entre deux femmes = MAX ENTRE DEUX FEUX (1916)
MAX ENTRE DEUX FEUX (1916) d/s/w Linder Pat (= Max entre deux femmes)
Max Escamoteur = SUCCES DE LA PRESTIDIGITATION, LE (1912)

MAX EST CHARITABLE (1911) d/w Linder Pat
MAX EST DISTRAIT (1911) d/w Linder Pat
MAX ET JANE EN VOYAGE DE NOCES (1911) d/s/w Linder Pat
Max et Jane Font des Crêpes = MAX CUISINIER PAR AMOUR (1911)
MAX ET LA DOCTORESSE (1914) d/s/w Linder Pat
MAX ET LA MAIN QUI ETREINT (1916) d/s/w Linder Pat
MAX ET LE BATON DE ROUGE (1914) d/w Linder Pat
MAX ET LE BILLET DOUX (1913) d/s/w Linder Pat
MAX ET LE COMMISSAIRE (1914) d/w Linder Pat
MAX ET LE MARI JALOUX (1914) d/s/w Linder Pat
MAX ET L'ENTENTE CORDIALE (1912) d/s/w Linder Pat
MAX ET LE SAC (1915) d/s/w Linder
MAX ET LES FEMMES (1912) d/s/w Linder Pat (= *Oh! Les Femmes!*)
MAX ET LES FERRAILLEURS (1971) d/co-s Sautet w Piccoli, Schneider *110min
MAX ET L'ESPION (1915) d/s/w Linder Pat
MAX ET SON CHIEN DICK (1911) d/s/w Linder Pat
MAX ET SON ANE (1911) d/w Linder Pat
MAX FAIT DES CONQUETES (1913) d/s/w Linder Pat
MAX ILLUSIONISTE (1914) d/s/w Linder Pat
MAX IN A TAXI (1917) d/s/w Linder 2rs S & A
MAX JOCKEY PAR AMOUR (1912) d/w Linder Pat
MAX LANCE LA MODE (1911) d/s/w Linder Pat
MAX MAITRE D'HOTEL (1914) d/s/w Linder Pat
MAX MEDECIN MALGRE LUI (1914) d/s/w Linder Pat
MAX N'AIME PAS LES CHATS (1913) d/s/w Linder Pat
MAX PART EN VACANCES (1913) d/s/w Linder Pat (= *Les Vacances de Max*)
MAX PEDICURE (1914) d/w Linder Pat
MAX PEINTRE PAR AMOUR (1912) d/s/w Linder Pat
MAX PRATIQUE TOUS LES SPORTS (1912) d/co-s/w Linder Pat
MAX PROFESSEUR DE TANGO (1912) d/s/w Linder Pat
MAX REPREND SA LIBERTE (1911) d/w Linder Pat
MAX SAUVETEUR (1914) d/w Linder Pat
MAX TOREADOR (1912) d/w Linder Pat
MAX VEUT FAIRE DU THEATRE (1911) d/w Linder Pat
MAX VEUT GRANDIR (1912) d/w Linder Pat
MAX VICTIME DU QUINQUINA (1911) d/w Linder Pat
MAX VIRTUOSE (1913) d/s/w Linder Pat
MAX WANTS A DIVORCE (1917) d/s/w Linder 830m S & A
MAYA (1964) d John Berry PV* 91min MGM
MAYBE IT'S LOVE (1930) d Wellman w J Bennett 74min WB
MAY BLOSSOM (1915) d Dwan w Neilan, Crisp 4rs r FPL
MAYERLING (1936) d Litvak s Joseph Kessel, Achard m Honegger w Boyer, Darrieux 93min Nero
MAYERLING (1957) d Litvak rm 1936 w Ferrer, A Hepburn 90min
MAYERLING (1969) d/s T Young c Alekan des Wakhévitch w Sharif, Deneuve, Mason, Gardner PV* 141min r WB
May Events = BYLO LO V MAJI (1951)
May I Borrow Your Wife = FAR JAG LANA DIN FRU? (1959)
MAYIKI POLIS, I (1955) d Koundouros m Hadjidakis
MAYOR OF HELL (1933) d A Mayo w Cagney 86min WB
May Rain and Silk Paper = SAMIDARE SOSHI (1924)
MAYTIME (1937) d/co-p Leonard a Gibbons co-e Vorkapich w J Barrymore, Jeanette Macdonald 113min MGM
MAYTIME IN MAYFAIR (1944) d H Wilcox w Neagle *95min BL
MAZE, THE (1953) d/a Menzies ex-p Mirisch 3D 81min AA
MAZLICEK (1934) d/co-st/co-s Frič (= *The Effeminate One*)
ME AND MARLBOROUGH (1935) d Saville 84min Gau
ME AND MY BROTHER (1968) d/s/c R Frank part *95min
ME AND MY GAL (1932) d Walsh c AC Miller w Tracy, J Bennett 78min Fox
ME AND MY PAL (1933) d Charles Rogers p Roach w Laurel, Hardy (2rs) r MGM
ME AND THE BOYS (1929) d/p Saville sh
ME AND THE COLONEL (1958) d Glenville p Goetz c Guffey m Duning w Kaye, Jurgens, Tamiroff 109min Col
Me and You = MEJ OCH DEJ (1968)
MEANEST MAN IN THE WORLD (1923) d Cline 5860ft WB
MEASURE OF A MAN, THE (1916) d Conway 5rs
MECHANICAL PRINCIPLE (1931) d/c R Steiner 11min
Mechanics of the Brain = MEKHANIKA GOLOVNOVO MOZGA (1926)
MECHTA (1943) d/co-s Romm 99min (= *Dream*)
MEDAILLE DE LA SAUVETAGE, LA (1914) d/w Linder Pat (= *Max Décoré*)
MEDAL FOR BENNY, A (1945) d Pichel co-st John Steinbeck c Lindon co-a Dreier m V Young w Lamour 77min Par
MEDAL FOR THE GENERAL (1944) d Elvey 90min
MEDAN STADEN SOVER (1950) d/s Lars-Eric Kjellgren st PA Fogelström, Ingmar Bergman

MEDDLIN' STRANGER, THE (1927) d Thorpe
MEDEA (1969) d/s Pasolini fpl Euripides w Girotti *120min
MEDECIN DES SOLS (1953) d Bourguignon 16mm 200m
MEDECINE BALL CARAVAN (1971) d/co-p Reichenbach TS* 88min r WB
MEDICO CONDOTTO (1952) d Giuliano Bizetti supn co-st/co-s Rossellini co-st/co-s Pietrangeli
MEDICO DELLA MUTUA, IL (1968) d/co-s Zampa co-s/w Sordi *98min (= *Be Sick . . . It's Free!*)
MEDICO E LO STREGONE, IL (1957) d Monicelli w De Sica, Mastroianni S 98min
Medieval Dutch Sculpture = NEDERLANDSE BEELDHOUWKUNST TIJDENS DE LATE MIDDELEEUWENEN (1951)
MEDIO SIGLO EN UN PINCEL (1960) d Grau
MEDITATION ON VIOLENCE (1948) d Deren 12min
MEDITERRANEE (1963) d Pollet 16mm 40min
MEDIUM COOL (1969) d/c/co-p Wexler m Mike Bloomfield, the Mothers of Invention *111min
MED LIVET SOM INSATS (1939) d/co-s Sjöberg (= *They Staked Their Lives*)
MEET BOSTON BLACKIE (1941) d Florey c Planer 61min Col
MEET DANNY WILSON (1951) d Pevney w Sinatra, Winters, Burr 86min U
MEET ME TONIGHT (1952) d Anthony Pelissier s/fpls(Red Peppers/Fumed Oak/Ways and Means)/w Coward *85min
MEET THE CHUMP (1941) d Cline 60min U
Meeting on the Elbe = VSTRECHA NA ELBE (1949)
MEET JOHN DOE (1941) d/p Capra s Riskin c Barnes m Tiomkin w G Cooper, Stanwyck, Brennan 123min WB (= *John Doe Dynamite*)
MEET MARLON BRANDO (1965) d/c A and D Maysles w Brando 29min
MEET ME AT THE FAIR (1952) d Sirk w Dailey *87min U
MEET ME IN LAS VEGAS (1956) d Rowland p Pasternak c Bronner co-a Gibbons w Dailey, Charisse, Moorehead, Henreid, (D Reynolds) CS* 112min MGM
MEET ME IN ST LOUIS (1944) d Minnelli p Freed co-c Folsey co-a Gibbons chor Walters w Garland, M O'Brien, Astor *113min MGM
MEET NERO WOLFE (1936) d Biberman p BP Schulberg co-s Anthony fn Rex Stout w Hayworth (as Cansino) 73min Col
MEET THE MISSUS (1940) d St Clair 67min Rep (= *The Higgins Family*)
MEET THE PIONEERS (1948) d/co-e/n L Anderson 33min
Meet Whiplash Willie (UK) = FORTUNE COOKIE, THE (1966)
ME FAIRE CA A MOI (1961) d Pierre Grimblat co-s Richard (uc)
MEFIEZ VOUS, FILLETTES (1957) d Y Allégret fn James Hadley Chase m Misraki w Hossein 87min
MEGFELELO EMBER, A (1959) d Révész (= *The Right Man*)
MEGLIO VEDOVA (1968) d/co-s Tessari w Ferzetti *101min (= *Better a Widow*)
ME, GANGSTER (1928) d Walsh c Edeson w Lombard 6042ft Fox
MEGFAGYOTTGYERMEK, A (1921) d Balasz
MEIER AUS BERLIN (1919) d/w Lubitsch sh (= *Meyer From Berlin*)
MEIGATSU SOMATO (1951) d/s Kinugasa (= *Lantern Under a Full Moon*)
MEIJI HARU AKI (1968) d Gosho
MEILLEUR BOBONNE, LA (1930) d M Allégret
MEILLEURE PART, LA (1955) d/co-s Y Allégret c Alekan m Misraki w Philipe CS* 90min Col
MEINE FRAU, DIE FILMSCHAUSPIELERIN (1919) d/co-s Lubitsch c Sparkuhl 1200m (= *My Wife, the Film Star*)
MEINE VIER JUNGENS (1944) d Rittau 85min Tob
MEIN KAMPF (1959) d/s/e Leiser 118min (= *Den Blodiga Tiden*)
MEIN KAMPF – MY CRIMES (1940) d Norman Lee w Ustinov
Mein Schulfreund = SCHULFREUND, DER (1960)
MEIN SOHN, DER HERR MINISTER (1937) d V Harlan w Rosay 81min UFA
MEIN VATER, DER SCHAUSPIELER (1956) d/p Siodmak fst Hans Grimm 105min
MEIN WILLIE IST GESETZ (1919) d Lupu-Pick
MEITO BIJOMARU (1945) d Mizoguchi w Yamada Sho (= *Bijomaru Sword*)
MEJ OCH DEJ (1968) d A Henning Jensen *92min (= *Me and You*)
MEKHANIKHA GOLOVNOVO MOZGA (1926) d/s Pudovkin 1850m (= *Mechanics of the Brain*)
MELBA (1953) d Milestone p Spiegel (ps S P Eagle) st/s Kurnitz *115min r UA
MEL B SPURR GIVES 'THE VILLAGE BLACKSMITH' (1897) p Paul 60ft
MELODIE DER WELT, DIE (1929) d Ruttmann 2000m (= *World Melody/The Melody of the World*)
MELODIE EN SOUS-SOL (1962) d/co-s/e Verneuil co-s/di Audiard w Gabin, Delon, Romance FS 117min (= *The Big Snatch*)
MELODIE ETERNE (1940) d Gallone

MELODY CRUISE (1933) d/co-s Sandrich c Glennon w C Ruggles 76min RKO
Melody Inn (UK) = RIDING HIGH (1943)
MELODY IN SPRING, A (1934) d McLeod w C Ruggles, Sothern 75min Par
MELODY LANE (1929) d/co-ad Robert F Hill fpl(The Understander) Swerling 6760ft U
Melody of Life (UK) = SYMPHONY OF SIX MILLION (1932)
Melody of the World, The = MELODIE DER WELT, DIE 29
Melody of Youth = THEY SHALL HAVE MUSIC (1939)
MELOMANE, LE (1903) d/w Méliès 55m
MELONS BALADEURS, LES (1911) d Cohl anim
Member of the Government = CHLEN PRAVITELSTVA (1940)
MEMBER OF THE WEDDING, THE (1953) d Zinnemann fn Carson McCullers c Mohr 91min pc Kramer r Col
Memories of Young Days = WAKAKI HI NO KANGEKI (1931)
Me, Me, Me . . . and the Others (UK) = IO, IO, IO . . . E GLI ALTRI (1965)
MEMORY LANE (1926) d/p/co-s Stahl 6825ft FN
Memory of Love = NIGHT SONG (1947)
Me, Mother and You = IO, MAMMETA E TU (1958)
MEMPHIS BELLE (1944) d/p/c Wyler *40min
MEN, THE (1950) d Zinnemann st/s Foreman m Tiomkin w Brando, T Wright, J Webb 85min pc Kramer r UA
MENACES (1939) d Greville w Von Stroheim
Menagerie, the (UK) = CHIRIAKHANA (1967)
Men and Beasts = LYUDI I ZVERI (1962)
MEN ARE LIKE THAT (1930) d Tuttle co-s/di H Mankiewicz c Stout 105min Par
MEN ARE LIKE THAT (1931) d G Seitz s/di Riskin c Tetzlaff w J Wayne 70min Col
MEN ARE SUCH FOOLS (1938) d Berkeley c Hickox w Bogart 70min WB
Men at the Crossroads = MENSCHEN AM WEGE, DER (1923)
MEN BEHIND THE METERS (1940) d Elton
MENDER OF NETS, THE (1912) d Griffith w Pickford, Normand 1rl Bio
MEN ETT LEJON, EN (1940) d Molander SF
MENILMONTANT (1924) d/p/s/co-c Kirsanov 2854ft
MEN IN DANGER (1938) d Jackson p Cavalcanti 38min
Men in Darkness = MANNEN I MORKER (1955)
MEN IN EXILE (1937) d J Farrow (6rs) WB
MEN IN HER LIFE, THE (1941) d/p Ratoff co-s M Wilson co-c AC Miller w L Young, Veidt 90min Col
MENINO DE ENGENHO (1965) d Walter Lima Jr p Rocha 86min
MEN IN WAR (1957) d A Mann s Yordan, Maddow (uc) c E Haller m E Bernstein w Ryan, A Ray 104min AA
MEN IN WHITE (1934) d Boleslavsky c Folsey a Gibbons w Gable, M Loy, Hersholt 80min MGM
MENNESKER MØDES OG SØD MUSIK OPSTAAR I HJERTET (1968) d/co-p/co-e Carlsen m Komeda w H Andersson, Dahlbeck 105min San (= *People Meet/Människor Möts och Ljuv Musik Uppstär i Hjartat*)
MEN OF ARNHEM (1944) d T Young, Brian Desmond Hurst
Men of Baku = BAKINTSY (1938)
MEN OF ROCHDALE (1946) d Compton Bennett 38min
MEN OF TEXAS (1942) d Enright w Stack, B Crawford 82min U
MEN OF THE ALPS (1939) d Cavalcanti 10min
Men of the Blue Cross = BLEKITNY KRZYZ (1955)
Men of the Caspian = KASPICHY (1944)
MEN OF THE FIGHTING LADY (1954) d Marton a Gibbons w V Johnson, Pidgeon *80min MGM
Men of Tohoku, The = TOHOKU NO ZUNMUTACHI (1957)
MEN OF TOMORROW (1932) d Sagan w Oberon, Donat, Emlyn Williams 8000ft
MEN OF TWO WORLDS (1946) d/co-s Dickinson co-p Del Giudice *109min JAR (= *Kisenga, Man of Africa*)
Men on the Bridge = LYUDI NA MOSTU (1960)
MEN O' WAR (1929) d Lewis Foster p Roach st McCarey 2rs(sd) r MGM
MENSCHEN AM SONNTAG (1929) co-d Ulmer co-d/p/co-s Siodmak co-s B Wilder, Zinnemann c Schuftan 2460m (= *People on Sunday*)
MENSCHEN AM WEGE (1923) d/s Dieterle fst Tolstoi w Dieterle, Dietrich 1657m (= *Men at the Crossroads*)
Menschen Hinter Gittern: German version of BIG HOUSE (1930)
Menschen in Käfig = CAPE FORLORN (1930)
MENSCHEN IM STURM (1934) d Fejos
MENS PESTEN RASER (1913) d/s Madsen
MENUET LILLIPUTIEN, LE (1905) d Méliès 65m
MEN WITHOUT NAMES (1935) d Ralph Murphy c B Reynolds e Heisler w MacMurray 66min Par
MEN WITHOUT WOMEN (1930) d/st J Ford s D Nichols co-c August w (J Wayne, Parrish) 77min Fox
MEN WITH WINGS (1938) d/p Wellman song Carmichael w MacMurray, Milland, O'Conner *105min Par
MENZOGNA, LA (1916) d/st/s Genina
MEOTO BOSHI (1926) d/w Kinugasa (= *Star of Married Couples*)

381

MEPHISTO WALTZ, THE (1971) d Wendkos s Maddow m Goldsmith w Jurgens *115min Fox

MEPRIS, LE (1963) d/s Godard co-p Ponti, Levine fn Albert Moravia c Coutard m Delerue w Bardot, Palance, Piccoli, F Lang, (Godard) FS* 100min (= Il Disprezzo/A Ghost at Noon/Contempt)

MEPRIS N'AURA QU'UN TEMPS, LE (1970) d/s/cy Lamothe part* 95min

MERAVIGLIE DI ALADINO, LE (1961) d Levin 2nd d Bava w De Sica, O'Connor S* 92min (= Wonders of Aladdin)

MERCATO DELLE FACCE, IL (1952) d Zurlini sh
MERCENARIES, THE (1967) d Cardiff PV* 100min MGM
MERCI, NATERCIA (1960) d Kast c Vierny m Delerue
Mer Des Corbeaux, La = MOR' VRAN (1930)
MERE ET L'ENFANT, LA (1959) co-d Demy 18min
MERELY MARY ANN (1931) d H King s Furthman c J Seitz w J Gaynor 72min Fox
MERE FRANCAISES (1917) d Louis Mercanton w S Bernhardt
MERLE, LE (1958) d McLaren, Evelyn Lambert *5min NFBC
MERLUSSE (1935) d/p/di Pagnol 74min
MERRILL'S MARAUDERS (1962) d/co-s Fuller p/co-s Sperling c Clothier w J Chandler *98min
MERRILY WE GO TO HELL (1932) d Dorothy Arzner w C Grant, March, S Sidney 78min Par
MERRILY WE LIVE (1938) d McLeod p Roach c Brodine w Constance Bennett 95min MGM
MER ROUGE, LA (1952) d/p Cousteau 16min *60min
MERRY ANDREW (1958) d/chor Kidd p S Siegel co-s Diamond fst Paul Gallico c Surtees w Kaye S* 103min MGM
MERRY-GO-ROUND (1923) d Von Stroheim, Julian st/s Von Stroheim c B Reynolds, Daniels a/cos Von Stroheim, R Day c10rs U
Merry-Go-Round (1955) = KORHINTA (1955)
Merry Husband, The = LUSTIGE EHEMANN, DER (1919)
Merry Jail, The = FIDELE GEFANGNIS, DAS (1917)
MERRY MANNEQUINS (1937) d Iwerks anim* 7½min r Col
MERRY WIDOW, THE (1925) d/co-s Von Stroheim a/cos Von Stroheim, R Day co-c B Reynolds, Daniels mf Franz Lehar w J Gilbert (Gable) c12rs MGM
MERRY WIDOW, THE (1934) d Lubitsch co-s Raphaelson a Gibbons mf Lehar w Chevalier, Jeannette Macdonald, Horton, Tamiroff 97min MGM (French version: di Achard)
MERRY WIDOW, THE (1952) d C Bernhardt p Pasternak c Folsey co-a Gibbons mf Lehar chor Cole w Turner, Haydn *105min MGM
MERTON OF THE MOVIES (1924) d/p Cruze fco-pl G Kaufman 7655ft FPL
MERTON OF THE MOVIES (1947) d R Alton co-s Wells fco-pl G Kaufman rm 1924 co-a Gibbons w Skelton, Grahame 83min MGM
MERTVYE DUSHI (1960) d/s L Trauberg fn NV Gogol 103min (= Dead Souls)
MESAVENTURES D'UN AERONAUTE (1901) d Méliès 20m
MESAVENTURES D'UNE TETE DE VEAU, LES (1898) d Alice Guy p Gaumont w Zecca
MESEK AZ IVOGEPRAL (1916) d/s A Korda
MESHES OF THE AFTERNOON (1943) d Deren, Alexander Hammid w Deren 16mm 14min
MES, HET (1961) d Rademakers 90min (= The Knife)
MESHI (1951) d Naruse Toho (= Repast/A Married Life)
MESKAL LE CONTREBANDIER (1908) d/s Jasset
MESMERIST, THE (1898) d G Smith
MESSA DA REQUIEM (1969) d Clouzot m Verdi *85min
Message, The = SANDESAYO (1960)
MESSAGE FROM GENEVA (1936) d/s Cavalcanti 9min
MESSAGER, LE (1937) d Rouleau s Achard dec Lourié w Gabin
MESSAGE IN THE BOTTLE, THE (1911) co-d Ince w Pickford
MESSAGE TO GARCIA, A (1936) d G Marshall p Zanuck c Maté w Beery, Stanwyck, Hayworth (as Cansino) 77min Fox
MESSALINA (1923) d/co-s Guazzoni
MESSALINA (1951) d/co-s Gallone 102min (= The Affairs of Messalina)
MESSALINA (1950) d Cottafavi TR* 94min r WB (= Messalina, Venere Imperatrice)
Messalina, Venere Imperatrice = MESSALINA (1959)
MESSIEURS LUDOVIC (1946) d/ad/di Le Chanois m Kosma w Jules Berry, Carette
METALL (1933, uf) d/s Richter 8rs
METALL DES HIMMELS (1934) d Ruttmann 372m
METAMORPHOSE (1945) d Van den Horst 20min
METELLO (1970) d/co-s Bolognini co-s Cecchi d'Amico fn Vasco Pratolini w Bosè *102min
METHODE DE GYMNASTIQUE PENCHENAT (1965) d Painlevé 45min
METIER DE DANSEUR (1953) d Baratier 22min
METIER DE FOUS (1948) d André Hunebelle technical advisor Ciampi
METIER DES AUTRES, LE (1960) d/cy Enrico 25min
METRO, LE (1934) d Franju, Langlois 16mm
METRO (1950) d Leenhardt 21min

METRO LUNGO CINQUE, UN (1961) d Olmi *
METROPOLIS (1927) d/co-s F Lang p Blanke, Pommer co-s Von Harbou c Freund, Rittau sp eff Schuftan w Helm 4189m UFA
METROPOLITAN (1935) d Boleslavsky p Zanuck c Maté w Romero, Darwell 80min Fox
METROPOLITAIN (1958) d Gruel, Lauré Garcin fpm (Illuminations) Rimbaud anim* 10min
Metropolitan Symphony = TOKAI KOKYOGAKU (1929)
METTI UNA SERA A CENA (1969) d/s Patroni-Griffi w Trintignant, Girardot S* 125min (= The Love Circle)
MEULE, LA (1962) d/s Allio 21min (= The Haystack)
MEURTRIER, LE (1962) d Autant-Lara s/di Aurenche, Bost w Vlady, Hossein, Ronet S 115min (= Enough Rope)
MEXICANA (1945) d/p Santell 83min Rep
MEXICAN FOOTAGE, THE (1964) d Rice 16mm si 10min
MEXICAN TRAGEDY, A (1912) d Ince
MEXICO MIO (1959) d/co-s Velo co-s Zavattini
Meyer from Berlin (UK) = MEIER AUS BERLIN (1919)
MEZZANOTTE (1915) d/st/s Genina
MIAMI (1924) d Crosland 7rs
MIAMI STORY, THE (1954) d Sears p Katzman 75min Col
MIA NONNA POLIZIOTTO (1958) d/co-s Steno 97min
MIA SIGNORA, LA (1964) 115min pc De Laurentiis (5 eps)
ep LUCIANA d Bolognini c Martelli w Mangano, Sordi
eps I MIEI CARI and L'UCCELLINO d Brass c Martelli w Mangano, Sordi
ep ERITREA d/s Comencini w Mangano
MIA VALLE, LA (1955) d Olmi *9min
MICE WILL PLAY, THE (1938) supn Avery p L Schlesinger anim* 7min WB
MICHAEL AND MARY (1931) d Saville w H Marshall 83min
Michael Strogoff = MICHAEL STROGOFF (1956)
MICHELANGELO ANTONIONI, STORIA DI UN AUTORE (1966) d Mingozzi sh
MICHELANGELO, DAS LEBEN EINES TITANEN (1940) d/s Curt Oertel US version: TITAN – THE STORY OF MICHELANGELO (1950) e Flaherty 86min
MICHELINE L B (1957) d Olmi *45min
MICHEL STROGOFF (1937) d De Baroncelli
MICHEL STROGOFF (1956) d Gallone fn Verne w Jurgens CS* 94min (= Michael Strogoff)
MICHEL STROGOFF (1968) d Lautner
MICHURIN (1948) d/s/fpl (Zhiza v Tsveton) Dovzhenko m Shostakovich *101min
MICKEY (1918) d Richard Jones w Normand 8rs Par
MICKEY MOUSE ANNIVERSARY SHOW, THE (1968) co-d Stevenson co-d/p/s Ward Kimball part anim part* 81min pc Disney
MICKEY ONE (1965) d/p Penn c Cloquet w Beatty, Tone 93min r Col
MICKEY'S CHOO CHOO (1930) d Iwerks p Disney anim (1rl)
MICSODA EJSZAKA (1958) d/co-s Révesz (= What a Night!)
MIDARE-GAMI (1961) d/s Kinugasa (= Dishevelled Hair)
MIDARE-GUMO (1967) d Naruse w Mori S* 110min Toho (= Two in the Shadow/Scattered Clouds)
MIDARERU (1964) d Naruse 95min Toho (= Yearning)
MIDAS RUN, THE (1969) d Kjellin co-song E Bernstein w Astaire, R Richardson, Romero *104min
MIDDLE OF THE NIGHT (1959) d Delbert Mann s/fpl Chayevsky c Brun w March, Novak 118min Col
MIDNATSGAESTEN (1924) d/s Madsen
MIDNATSJAEGERNEN (1917) d/s Madsen
MIDNIGHT (1934) d/p/s Chester Erskin w Bogart 76min U
MIDNIGHT (1939) d Leisen s B Wilder, Brackett c C Lang chor Prinz w Colbert, J Barrymore, Astor, Hopper 94min Par
MIDNIGHT ALIBI (1934) d Crosland fst (The Old Doll's House) Damon Runyon w Barthelmess 60min WB
MIDNIGHT COWBOY (1969) d K Schlesinger m Barry *119min r UA
MIDNIGHT ELOPEMENT, A (1912) d Sennett w Normand ½rl Key
MIDNIGHT FROLICS (1938) d Iwerks anim* (1rl) r Col
Midnight Incident, A = PULNOCNI DOBRUDRUZSTVI (1960)
MIDNIGHT LACE (1960) d D Miller co-p R Hunter s Goff, Roberts c Metty co-a Golitzen w D Day, Harrison, M Loy, H Marshall *108min U
MIDNIGHT LADY (1932) d Thorpe 65min
Midnight Mary = LAY OF THE NIGHT (1933)
MIDNIGHT MYSTERY (1930) d G Seitz c J Walker w L Sherman 6463ft RKO
MIDNIGHT PATROL, THE (1933) d Lloyd French p Roach w Laurel, Hardy 9½min r MGM
MIDNIGHT STORY, THE (1957) d Pevney c Metty w Curtis, Roland 89min U
Midnight Sun at Scaro, The = SUN, THE (1903)
MIDSHIPMAID, THE (1932) d Albert De Courville w J Mills 82min
MIDSHIPMAN, THE (1925) d Christy Cabanne w Novarro 7498ft MGM
MIDSHIPMAN EASY (1935) d C Reed p/e T Dickinson w Lockwood 100min
MIDSUMMER DAY'S WORK, A (1939) d/s/dec Cavalcanti m Grieg

MIDSUMMER MUSH (1933) d C Chase (as Parrott) Roach w C Chase (2rs) MGM
MIDSUMMER NIGHT'S DREAM, A (1935) d Dieterle, Reinhardt p Wallis fpl Shakespeare co-c Mohr Haskin m Mendelssohn arranged by Korngold Rooney, Cagney, D Powell, De Havilland, (Ange 132min WB
MIDSUMMER NIGHT'S DREAM, A (1968) d P Hall f Shakespeare w Royal Shakespeare Compan *124min
Midsummer Night's Dream, A (1971): English version SEN NOCI SVATOJANSKE (1959) wv Burton
MIGHTY, THE (1929) d Cromwell w G Bancroft 6802ft Pa
MIGHTY BARNUM, THE (1934) d W Lang c Marley m Newman w Beery, Menjou 85min r UA
Mighty Crusaders, The = GERUSALEMME LIBERAT (1957)
MIGHTY JOE YOUNG (1949) d Schoedsack co-p/st Cooper 93min RKO
Migratory Birds Under the Moon = TSUKI NO WATAR DORI (1951)
MIKADO, THE (1939) d Schertzinger 2nd d T Dickinson opera Gilbert, Sullivan 90min U
MIKAEL (1924) d/co-s Dreyer p Pommer co-s Von Harb rm VINGARNA (1916) c Freund, Maté Christensen 1966m Dec
MIKE (1926) d/st Neilan 6775ft MGM
MIKRES AFRODITES (1963) d/co-p Koundouros f (Daphnis and Chloe) Longus and fpms (Idyl Theocritus 98min (= Young Aphrodites)
MIL, LE (1962) d/s Rouch 16min
MILDRED PIERCE (1945) d Curtiz p Wald s Macdougall James M Cain c E Haller e Weisbart m M Steiner w Crawford, Blyth 111min WB
MILE AVEC JULES LADOUMEGUE, LE (1932) d Lods
Militant Suffragette = BUSY DAY (1914)
MILITARE E MEZZO, UN (1960) d/co-s Steno *110min
MILKY WAY, THE (1936) d McCarey p Quimby w Lloyd, Menjou 83min Par
Milky Way, The = VOIE LACTEE, LA (1968)
MILLET ET DEUXIEME NUIT, LA (1933) d Alexand Wolcoff w Mozhukhin
MILLER AND THE SWEEP, THE (1898) d G Smith 40ft
MILLER'S DAUGHTER, THE (1905) d Porter Ed
Miller's Wife, The (UK) = BELLA MUGNAIA, L (1955)
MILLION, LE (1931) d/s/di Clair co-c Périnal dec Meersc co-m Van Parys w Annabella 90min Tob
MILLIONAIRE, THE (1922) d Conway
MILLIONAIRE COWBOY, THE (1935) d Cline 4900ft
MILLIONAIRE DROOPY (1956) d Avery p Quimby anim 7min MGM
MILLIONAIRE FOR CHRISTY, A (1951) d G Marshall MacMurray, Parker 91min Fox
MILLIONAIRES D'UN JOUR (1949) d André Hunebe technical advisor Ciampi w Brasseur 106min
MILLIONAIRESS, THE (1960) d Asquith fpl GB Shaw Hildyard w Loren, Sellers, De Sica CS* 90min Fox
MILLIONARDRENGEN (1913) d Madsen
MILLION BID, A (1927) d Curtiz c Mohr 6310ft WB
MILLION DOLLAR BABY (1941) d C Bernhardt p Warner, Wallis co-s Wald w Reagan 100min WB
MILLION DOLLAR DOLLIES, THE (1918) d/s Perr serial Pat
MILLION DOLLAR LEGS (1932) d Cline co-s Mankiewicz w Fields, Turpin 64min Par
MILLION DOLLAR LEGS (1939) d Nick Grinde, Dmytry (uc) e Dmytryk w Grable, O'Connor 59min Par
MILLION DOLLAR MERMAID (1952) d LeRoy c Fols a Gibbons chor Berkeley w Mature, Pidgeon, Esth Williams *115min MGM
MILLION DOLLAR MYSTERY (1914) w Cruze series 23 eps
Million Girls, A = HYAKUMAN-NIN N MUSUMETACHI (1963)
MILLION POUND NOTE, THE (1953) d Neame fst Ma Twain c Unsworth e C Donner m Alwyn w Pec Forbes *91min JAR
MILLIONS DE L'ONCLE JAMES, LES (1924) d/s Machi Henri Wulschleger 1700m (= Les Heritiers de l'onc James)
MILLIONS LIKE US (1943) d/s Launder, Gilliat 103m JAR
MILLS OF THE GODS, THE (1909) d Griffith 1rl Bio
MIMO ZHIZNI (1914) d Protozanov 1258m (= In t Presence of Life)
MINAMI NO KAZE (1942) d Yoshimura (2 parts) (= Sou Wind)
MIN AND BILL (1930) d George Hill w Beery, Dress 70min MGM
MINDBENDERS, THE (1963) d Dearden w Bogar 113min WB
MINDEN KEZDET NEHE (1966) d Révész 120min (= A Beginnings are Hard)
MIND READER, THE (1933) d Del Ruth c Polito 69m WB
MIND YOUR OWN BUSINESS (1936) d McLeod w Ruggles 75min Par
MINE IN VISTA (1940) d/s De Robertis
Miners = SHAKHTORY (1934 r 1937)

MINE WITH THE IRON DOOR, THE (1924) d S Wood 6180ft pc Lesser
MING GREEN (1966) d/s/c/e Markopoulos 16mm * 9min
MINIATURE (1950) d Zurlini sh
Minin and Pojarsky = MININ I POZHARSKII (1939)
MININ I POZHARSKII (1939) d Pudovkin, Mikhail Doller 3647m (= Minin and Pojarsky)
MINISTERN (1970) d/s/w Kulle *95min San
MINISTRY OF FEAR, THE (1944) d F Lang p/s S Miller fn Greene a Dreier, Pereira m V Young w Milland, Duryea 84min Par
MINIVER STORY, THE (1950) d Potter p Franklin c Ruttenberg m Stothart, Rozsa w Pidgeon, Garson, Finch 104min MGM
MINLOTSEN (1916) d Stiller 746m
MINNIE (1922) d Neilan, Frank Urson s Neilan co-c Struss 6696ft pc Neilan r FN
MINNIE AND MOSKOWITZ (1971) d/s/w Cassavetes *114min
MINOTAUR (1954) d Richter
MINSHU NO TEKI (1946) d Imai Toho (= Enemy of the People)
MINISTREL MAN (1944) d JH Lewis des Ulmer 69min
MINUTE DE VERITE, LA (1952) d/co-s Delannoy co-s/di Jeanson m Misraki w Gabin, Morgan, Gélin 109min Gau (= The Moment of Truth)
MIO FIGLIO NERONE (1956) d/co-st/co-s Steno c Bava w Sordi, Swanson, De Sica, Bardot CS* 89min (= Nero's Weekend)
MIO FIGLIO PROFESSORE (1946) d/co-s Castellani co-s Cecchi d'Amico 88min (= My Son, the Professor)
MIO TIO JACINTO (1956) d/co-s Vajda
MIQUETTE ET SA MERE (1950) d/co-s Clouzot c Thirard dec Wakhévitch w Jouvet, Bourvil 95min
MIRA (1971) d/co-p/w Rademakers m Delerue *93min
MIRACLE, THE (1959) d Rapper p Blanke c E Haller m E Bernstein w C Baker, Paxinov S* 121min WB
MIRACLE, UN (1954) d Breer, Pontus Hulten anim* 16mm 18seconds
MIRACLE CAN HAPPEN, A (1948) d K Vidor, Leslie Fenton p Bogeaus, Meredith st Oboler co-s J O'Hara co-c Cronjager, Biroc, Laszlo, J Seitz w Meredith, Goddard, MacMurray, J Stewart, H Fonda, Lamour 107min r UA (= On Our Merry Way)
MIRACLE DES AILES, LE (1956) d Mitry 30min
MIRACLE DES LOUPS, LE (1924) d Raymond Bernard w Préjean
MIRACLE DU BRAHMINE, LE (1900) d Méliès 80m
Miracle in Milan = MIRACOLO A MILANO (1950)
MIRACLE IN SOHO (1957) d Julian Amyes s Pressburger *98min
MIRACLE IN THE RAIN (1958) d Maté s/fn B Hecht c Metty m Waxman w Wyman, Dalio, V Johnson 107min WB
MIRACLE, MAN, THE (1919) d George Loane Tucker w Chaney 9rs Par
MIRACLE MAN, THE (1932) d McLeod w S Sidney, Pichel, Karloff 85min Par
MIRACLE OF LOVE, THE (1919) d Leonard 7rs
MIRACLE OF MORGAN'S CREEK, THE (1944) d/st/s P Sturges c J Seitz co-a Dreier w Tamiroff 99min Par
MIRACLE OF OUR LADY OF FATIMA, THE (1952) d Brahm m M Steiner w Roland *102min WB
MIRACLE OF THE BELLS, THE (1948) d Pichel p Lasky s B Hecht e Elmo Williams m Harline w MacMurray, Sinatra, Valli, Cobb 120min RKO
MIRACLE ON 34th STREET (1947) d/s Seaton p Perlberg c C Clarke m Mockridge w Payne, M O'Hara, N Wood, Ritter 96min Fox
MIRACLES FOR SALE (1939) d Browning co-s J Grant Lawton w R Young 71min MGM
MIRACLES N'ONT LIEU QU'UNE FOIS, LES (1950) d Y Allégret w Marais, Valli 98min
MIRACLE WOMAN, THE (1931) d Capra p Cohn s/di Swerling fco-pl (Bless You Sister) Riskin c J Walker w Stanwyck 90min Col
MIRACLE WORKER, THE (1962) d Penn s/fpl William Gibson w A Bancroft 106min r UA
MIRACOLO A MILANO (1951) d/p/co-ad De Sica co-ad/fst(Toto il Buone) Zavattini co-ad Cecchi D'Amico, Chiari c Aldo 96min (= Miracle in Milan)
Miraculous Brothers, The = FRATELLI MIRACOLOSI, I (1949)
MIRAGE, THE (1958–59) d P Weiss 72min (= Hägringen)
MIRAGE (1965) d Dmytryk p Keller c Joe Macdonald co-a Golitzen w Peck, Matthau, G Kennedy 109min U
MIRAKLET (1913) d Sjöström fn(Lourdes) Emile Zola 1045m (= Underverket)
MIRANDA (1948) d Annakin 80min BL
MIREILLE (1907) d Perret s Gance
MIROIR A DEUX FACES, LES (1958) d/co-st/ad Cayatte c Matras w Morgan, Bourvil, (Carette) 96min Gau
Miroir de la Vie = ASTROLOGIE (1952)
MIROIR DE VENISE OU LES MESAVENTURES DE SHYLOCK, LE (1905) d Méliès 66m
Mirror of Holland = SPIEGEL VON HOLLAND (1950)
MIRSU (1954) d/s Kinugasa (= Love)
Mischief Makers, The = MISTONS, LES (1957)
Mischievous Tutor, The = NEZBEDNY BAKALAR (1946)

MISE A SAC (1967) d/co-st/co-s Cavalier *98min AA
MISERABILI, I (1947) d/co-s Freda p Ponti co-s Monicelli fn(Les Miserables) Victor Hugo w Cortese, Ferzetti, Mastroianni 2 parts: Caccia all'uomo 95min; Tempesta su Parigi
MISERABLES, LES (1918) d/co-s/co-ad F Lloyd fn Victor Hugo 10rs Fox
MISERABLES, LES (1935) d Boleslavsky p Zanuck co-as-p Goetz fn Hugo c Toland a R Day m A Newman w March, Laughton, Carradine 110min r UA
MISERABLES, LES (1952) d Milestone p Kohlmar s R Murphy fn Hugo c La Shelle co-a Wheeler m North w Newton, S Sidney 106min Fox
MISERABLES, LES (1957) d/co-s Le Chanois co-s Audiard fn Hugo w Gabin, Bourvil, Reggiani TR* Part 1: 97min; Part 2: 120min Par
Misère au Borinage = BORINAGE (1933)
MISERICORDIA (1960) d Lupu-Pick (= Tötet nicht mehr)
MISERIE DEL SIGNOR TRAVET, LE (1945) d/co-s/co-di Soldati fpl Bersezio w Sordi
MISFITS, THE (1961) d J Huston s A Miller c Metty m North w Monroe, Gable, Clift, Ritter, Wallach 125min r UA
Mishrka against Yudenich = MISHKI PROTIV YUDENICHKA (1925)
MISHKI PROTIV YUDENICHKA (1925) d/co-s L Trauberg, Kozintsev w Gerasimov 680m (= Mishka against Yudenich)
MISPLACED FOOT, A (1914) w Normand ½rl Key
MISS ANNIE ROONEY (1942) d Edward L Marin w Temple 84min UA
MISS BREWSTER'S MILLIONS (1926) d Badger w W Baxter 6457ft FPL
MISS CATASTROPHE (1957) d Kirsanov
MISS DOROTHY'S BEKENNTNIS (1920) d Curtiz
MISS ELLEN TERRY AT HOME (1900) d G Smith
MISS FATTY'S SEASIDE LOVERS (1915) d/w Arbuckle p Sennett 1rl Key
MISS GRANT TAKES RICHMOND (1959) d Bacon co-s Tashlin c Lawton w Ball, Holden 89min Col (= Innocence is Bliss)
MISS HOBBS (1920) d Crisp 6 rs
MISSING JUROR, THE (1944) d Boetticher c O'Connell 66min Col
MISSING LADY, THE (1946) d Karlson 60min Mon
MISSION A TANGIERS (1949) d André Hunebelle technical advisor Ciampi s Audiard 100min
MISSIONE TIMIRIAZEV (1953) d Pontecorvo sh
MISSION OF DANGER (1959) ep THE BREAK OUT d J Tourneur *79min MGM (film of 3eps from US TV series Northwest Passage)
MISSION OVER KOREA (1953) d Sears c Leavitt w O'Sullivan 85min Col
MISSIONS DE FRANCE (1939) d Ichac
MISSION TO MOSCOW (1943) d Curtiz s H Koch c Glennon chor Prinz w W Houston, Parker, Charisse (ps Lily Norwood) 123min MGM
MISSISSIPPI (1935) d A Edwards Sutherland fst Booth Tarkington c C Lang m/lyr Rogers, Hart w Fields, B Crosby, J Bennett, (Sheridan) 73min Par
MISSISSIPPI GAMBLER, THE (1953) d Maté st/s S Miller c Glassberg co-a Golitzen w Power, Laurie, McIntyre *98min U
Mississippi Mermaid (US) = SIRENE DU MISSISSIPPI, LA (1969)
MISS ITALY (1949) d Duilio Colette w Lollobrigida 90min
Miss Julie = FROKEN JULIE (1950)
MISS MEND (1926) d/co-s Barnet, Fyodor Otsep w Barnet 5100m (in 3 series)
Miss Oyu = OYUSAMA (1951)
MISS PACIFIC FLEET (1935) d Enright w Blondell 66min WB
MISS PINKERTON (1932) d Bacon w Blondell 66min WB
MISS PROVIDENT (1935) d Marton
MISS ROBIN HOOD (1952) d Guillermin 78min
MISS SADIE THOMPSON (1953) d C Bernhardt p Wald c Lawton w Hayworth, J Ferrer, A Ray 3D* 91min Col
Miss Snake Princess = HEBIHIMESAMA (1940)
Miss Soapsuds = FRAULEIN SEIFENSCHAUM (1914)
MISS SUSIE SLAGLE'S (1946) d John Berry co-s H Butler c C Lang m Amfitheatrof w Lake, L Gish 88min Par
MISS TATLOCK'S MILLIONS (1948) d Haydn p/co-s Brackett co-s Breen c C Lang co-a Dreier m V Young w Stack, Haydn, Leisen 101min Par
MISS TULIP STAYS THE NIGHT (1955) d L Arliss 68min
MISS TUTTI FRUTTI (1921) d Curtiz
MISTAKE, THE (1913) d Griffith 1 rl Bio
MISTAKEN MASHER, THE (1913) d/p/w Sennett w Normand ½rl Key
MR AND MRS SMITH (1941) d Hitchcock st/s Krasna w Lombard, Montgomery 95min RKO
Mr and Mrs Swordplay = CHANBARA FUFU (1930)
Mr Arkadin = CONFIDENTIAL REPORT (1955)
MR BELVEDERE GOES TO COLLEGE (1949) d E Nugent co-a Wheeler m A Newman w C Webb, Temple, J Chandler 83min Fox
MR BELVEDERE RINGS THE BELL (1951) d Koster c La Shelle co-a Wheeler w C Webb, Dru 87min Fox

MR BLANDINGS BUILDS HIS DREAM HOUSE (1948) d Potter p/s Panama, M Frank c Howe m Harline w C Grant, M Loy, M Douglas 94min pc Selznick r RKO
MRS ERRICKER'S REPUTATION (1920) d/p Hepworth 5780ft
MISTER BUDDWING (1965) d Delbert Mann fn (Buddwing) E Hunter w Garner, Pleshette, J Simmons S 100min MGM
MR BUG GOES TO TOWN (1941) d M and D Fleischer anim* 78min Par (= Hoppity Goes to Town)
MISTER CORY (1957) d/s Edwards c Metty a Golitzen w Curtis, Bickford CS* 92min U
MR DEEDS GOES TO TOWN (1936) d/p Capra s Riskin c J Walker w G Cooper, Arthur, G Bancroft 115min Col
MR DYNAMITE (1935) d Crosland 67min U
MISTER 880 (1950) d Goulding s Riskin co-a Wheeler w Lancaster, McGuire 90min Fox
Mr Fixer = MR FIX IT (1912)
MR FIX IT (1912) d/p/w Sennett w Normand ½rl Key (= Mr Fixer)
MR FIXIT (1918) d/s Dwan p/w Fairbanks Sr 5 rs FPL
MISTER FLOW (1936) d Siodmak s Jeanson fn Gaston Leroux w Jouvet, Feuillère 94min
MR FORBRUSH AND THE PENGUINS (1971) d Al Viola d (animal sequences) Sucksdorff w H Mills *101min BL
MR FREEDOM (1968) d/s Klein w Noiret, Seyrig, Montand *110min
MR HOBBS TAKE A VACATION (1962) d Koster p Wald s N Johnson c Mellor m Mancini w J Stewart, M O'Hara CS* 116min Fox
Mr Ikle's Jubilee = JUBILEJ G. IKLA (1955)
MR JONES AT THE BALL (1908) d Griffith w Sennett 1rl Bio
Mr Kinky = PROFETA, IL (1967)
MR LUCKY (1943) d Potter c Barnes w C Grant, Bickford 100min RKO
My Lucky = LUCKY SAM (1952)
MR MASKELYNE (OF THE EGYPTIAN HALL) SPINNING PLATES AND BASINS (1897) p Paul 40ft
MISTER MOSES (1964) d Neame c Morris m Barry w Mitchum, C Baker PV* 116min r UA
MR MOTO TAKES A CHANCE (1938) d/co-st Foster w Lorre 63min Fox
MR MOTO TAKES A VACATION (1939) d/co-s Foster c C Clarke w Lorre 61min Fox
MR MUSIC (1951) d Haydn fpl Raphaelson c Barnes co-a Dreier w B Crosby, G Marx, C Coburn, Champion, Ewell, Stack 113min Par
MISTERO DEL TEMPIO INDIANO, IL (1963) d Camerini c Tonti *
MR PEABODY AND THE MERMAID (1948) d Pichel p/s N Johnson c Metty w W Powell, Blyth 89min U
MR PEARSON (1963) d Richard Ballentine c Pennebaker 16mm 56min
MR PECKSNIFF FETCHES THE DOCTOR (1896) p Paul 145ft
Mr Poo = PU SAN (1953)
MISTER ROBERTS (1955) d J Ford, LeRoy s F Nugent, Logan fco-pl Logan c Hoch m Waxman w H Fonda, Cagney, Lemmon, W Powell CS* 123min r WB
MR ROBINSON CRUSOE (1932) d Edward Sutherland st Fairbanks Sr (ps Elton Thomas) m A Newman w Fairbanks Sr 70min r UA
MR SARDONICUS (1961) d/p Castle c Guffey 89min Col
MR SKEFFINGTON (1945) d V Sherman co-p/co-s JJ Epstein c E Haller m Waxman w B Davis, Rains 146min WB
MR SKITCH (1933) d Cruze c J Seitz w W Rogers, Pitts 70min Fox
MR SMITH GOES TO WASHINGTON (1939) d/p Capra s Buchman c J Walker co-e Vorkapich m Tiomkin w Arthur, J Stewart, Rains, Mitchell, Carey 129min Col
MR SOFT TOUCH (1949) d G Douglas, Levin c Lawton, J Walker w G Ford 93min Col
MR TOPAZE (1961) d Sellers fpl(Topaze) Pagnol m Van Parys w Sellers *84min Fox
Mister V = PIMPERNEL SMITH (1941)
MIST IN THE VALLEY (1923) d/p Hepworth 6820ft
MISTONS, LES (1957) d/s/pc Truffaut 26min (= The Mischief Makers)
MISTRAL, LE (1966) d/co-s Ivens cy Gatti
Mistress, The (UK) = ALSKARINNAN (1962)
MISTRESS OF SHENSTONE (1921) d H King 6rs
MISTVI ZIMNICH SPORTU (1955) d/co-s Frič (= Master of Winter Sports)
Misunderstood = INCOMPRESO (1966)
MITT HEM AR COPACABANA (1965) d Sucksdorff 88min SF
MITTSU NO AI (1954) d Kobayashi (= Three Loves)
Mixed Ladies' Chorus, The (UK) = GEMISCHTE FRAUENCHOR, DER (1916)
MIXED MAGIC (1936) Raymond Kane w Keaton 2rs
MIYAMOTO MUSASHI (1942) d Mizoguchi
MIZAR (1954) d/s De Robertis *85min (= Frogman Spy)
MLADE DNY (1956) d/c Frič
MLADI NASI VLASTI (1956) d/c Frič
M'LISS (1918) d Neilan fst Bret Harte 5rs FPL

MLODOSC SZOPIN (1952) *d/s* A Ford *m Chopin, Bach, Mozart, Paganini* 97min (= *The Young Chopin*)
MOANA (1926) *d/s/c/e* Flaherty, *Frances Flaherty* 90min FPL
MOB, THE (1951) *d* Parrish *p* Bresler *c* J Walker *m* Duning *w* B Crawford, Borgnine 87min Col
Mobster, The (UK) = I, MOBSTER (1958)
MOBY DICK (1930) *d* Bacon *fn Herman Melville w* J Barrymore, J Bennett 7160ft WB (German version: *d* Bacon, Curtiz)
MOBY DICK (1956) *d/co-p/co-s* J Huston *co-s* Bradbury *fn Herman Melville c* Morris *2nd c* F Francis *w* Peck, Welles *115min WB
MOCKERY (1927) *d/st* Christensen *co-a* Gibbons *w* Chaney 5957ft MGM
MODEL AND THE MARRIAGE BROKER, THE (1952) *d* Cukor *p/co-s* Brackett *co-s* Breen *c* Krasner *co-a* Wheeler *m* Mockridge *w* Crain, Ritter 103min Fox
MODEL SHOP (1969) *d/s* Demy *w* Aimée *92min
MODENA, CITTA DELL'EMILIA ROSSA (1950) *d* Lizzani
Moder, Em = HEMLIGT GIFTERMAL, ETT (1912)
MODERATO CANTABILE (1960) *d/co-s* P Brook *co-s/fn* Duras *w* Moreau, Belmondo CS* 90min (= *Seven Days . . . Seven Nights*)
MODE RÊVEE, LA (1939) *d* L'Herbier *c* Bachelet *m* Auric, *Claude Débussy* sh
MODERNA SUFFRAGETTEN, DEN (1913) *d/s* Stiller 464m (= *Den Suffragetten/Lily, den Suffragetten*)
MODERN HERO, A (1934) *d* Pabst *a* Gibbons *w* Barthelmess 71min WB
MODERN LOVE (1918) *d/co-st* Leonard 6rs U
MODERN MUSKETEER, A (1917) *d/s* Dwan *p/w* Fairbanks Sr *c* V Fleming 5rs *r* FPL
MODERNO BARBA AZUL, EL (1946) *d Jaime Salvador w* Keaton 90min
MODERN SALOME, A (1919) *d/s* Perret *fpl* (*Salome*) *Oscar Wilde* Pat
MODERN TIMES (1936) *d/p/s/m* Chaplin *co-c* Totheroh *w* Chaplin, Goddard 85min *r* UA
MODESTY BLAISE (1966) *d* Losey *c* Hildyard *des* R Macdonald *w* Vitti, Bogarde, Stamp *119min Fox
MOD LYSET (1918) *d/s* Madsen *w* Nielsen
MODREHJAELPEN (1942) *d/s* Dreyer 12min (= *Good Mothers*)
MOETSUKITA CHIZU (1968) *d* Teshigahara S* 118min (= *The Man Without a Map*)
MOGAMBO (1953) *d* J Ford *s* Mahin *rm* RED DUST (1932) *c* Surtees, F Young *w* Gable, Gardner, Grace Kelly *116min MGM
MOGLIE BELLA, LA (1924) *d* Genina
MOGLIE DEL PRETE, LA (1971) *d* Risi *p* Ponti *w* Loren, Mastroianni *106min (= *The Priest's Wife*)
MOGLIE DI SUA ECCELLENZA, LA (1913) *d* Genina
MOGLIE, MARITO E . . . (1920) *d/st* Genina *s* Camerini
MOGLIE PERICOLOSE (1958) *d/co-s* Comencini 105min
MOGLIE PER UNA NOTTE (1952) *d* Camerini
MOIRES (1963) *d/c* J Mekas *w* Dali 16mm 3½min
MOIA RODINA (1933) *d/co-s* Heifeitz, Zarkhi 2175m (= *My Fatherland*)
MOI MLADSHII BRAT (1962) *d* Zarkhi 104min (= *My Younger Brother*)
MOIRES (1963) *d/c* J Mekas *w* Dali 16mm 3½min
MOISSON, LA (1966) *d* Lamothe *10min
MOI UNIVERSITETI (1940) *d/co-s* Donskoi *fab Maxim Gorki* 102min (= *My Universities*)
MOI, UN NOIR (1958) *d/s/c* Rouch 16mm *77min (= *I, a Negro/Treichville*)
MOKUSEKI (1940) *d* Gosho (= *Wooden Head*)
MOLIERE (1909) *d* Perret *w* Gance
MOLLENARD (1938) *d* Siodmak *co-s* Charles Spaak *m* Milhaud *w* Préjean, P Renoir, P Prévert Dalio 89min (= *Capitaine Mollenard/Hatred*)
MOLLY BAWN (1916) *d/p* Hepworth 4rs
MOLLYCODDLE, THE (1920) *d* V Fleming *p/w* Fairbanks Sr *w* Beery 6rs
MOLLY MAGUIRES, THE (1968) *d* Ritt *c* Howe *m* Mancini *w* R Harris, Connery PV* 125min Par
MOLLY O' (1921) *d F Richard Jones p/st* Sennett *w* Normand, L Sherman 8rs
MOLODAYA GUARDIYA (1948) *d/s* Gerasimov *m* Shostakovich *w* Bondarchuk 2 parts: 101min and 86min (= *The Young Guard*)
MOLODOST NASHI STRANYI (1946) *d* Yutkevich (= *Our Country's Youth*)
MOLTI SOGNI PER LE STRADE (1948) *d/co-s* Camerini *p* De Laurentiis *c* Tonti *m* Rota *w* Magnani, Girotti 84min
MOME AUX BOUTONS, LA (1958) *d* Lautner S* 98min
MOMENT (1969) *d/s/c/e* Markopoulos *w Barbara Hepworth* 16mm* 8min
MOMENT IN LOVE, A (1957) *d/p* S Clarke 9min
MOMENTO DELLA VERITA, IL (1965) *d/co-p/st/s* Rosi *c* Di Venanzo *m* Piccioni S* 110min
MOMENT OF DANGER (1959) *d* Benedek *d* D Stewart *w* T Howard 79min (= *Malaga*)
Moment of Terror = HIKINIGE (1966)
Moment of Truth, The (UK) = MINUTE DE VERITE, LA (1951)
MOMENTO PIU BELLO, IL (1957) *d* Emmer *m* Rota *w* Mastroianni 90min (= *The Most Wonderful Moment*)
MOMENT TO MOMENT (1965) *d/p* LeRoy *co-s* Mahin *co-a* Golitzen *m* Mancini *w* Seberg *108min U
MOMMA DON'T ALLOW (1955) *d/s* Reisz, T Richardson 22min
MONACHINE, LE (1963) *d* Salce *w* Catherine Spaak 105min (= *The Little Nuns*)
MONA, L'ETOILE SANS NOM (1966) *d* Colpi *m* Delerue *w* Vlady 85min
MON AMIE PIERRETTE (1967) *d/s* Lefebvre *68min
MON CHIEN (1956) *d/s* Franju *cy* J Prévert 25min
MON COEUR T' APPELLE (1936) *d* Gallone
MONCTON (1970) *co-d* Perrault *co-d/c* Brault
Monday or Tuesday = PONELJAK ILI UTORAK (1966)
MONDAY'S CHILD (1966) *d/co-s* Torre Nilsson *w* A Kennedy, Page 85min
MONDE DE L'ENFANCE, LE (1970, *uf*) *d/s/co-cy* Lamothe
MONDE DE PAUL DELVAUX, LE (1946) *d* Storck 11min (= *The World of Paul Delvaux*)
MONDE DU SILENCE, LE (1956) *co-d/p* Cousteau *co-d/co-c* Malle *co-c* Séchan *86min (= *The Silent World*)
MONDE INSTANTANE, LE (1960) *d* Rossif 17min Pat
MONDE SANS SOLEIL, LE (1964) *d/p* Cousteau 94min Col (= *World Without Sun*)
MONDO CANE No 1 (1961) *d/cy/e* Jacopetti *as-d Franco Prosperi, Paolo Cavara* *105min (= *A Dog's Life*)
MONDO CANE No 2 (1963) *co-d/co-p/co-s/cy* Jacopetti *co-d Franco Prosperi* *97min
MONDO NUOVO, UN (1965) *d* De Sica *s/di* Zavattinni *w* Brasseur, I Miranda 90min *co-pc* Saltzman
Money = KANE (1926)
MONEY AND THE WOMAN (1940) *d* W Howard *c* O'Connell 67min WB
Money and Three Bad Men = GENNAMA TO BIJO TO SAN-A-KUNIN (1958)
MONEY CHANGERS (1921) *d* Conway
MONEY CORRAL, THE (1919) *d/co-st Lambert Hillyer co-st/w* W Hart *c* August 5rs *pc* W Hart
MONEY FROM HOME (1953) *d* G Marshall *p* Wallis *s* Kautner *fst Damon Runyan c* Fapp *co-a* Pereira *w* Martin, J Lewis, Haydn 3D* 100min Par
MONEY MANIAC, THE (1921) *d/p/s* Perret Pat
Money or Your Life (UK) = BOURSE ET LA VIE, LA (1965)
MONEY TALKS (1926) *d* A Mayo 70min
Money Talks = DOKONJO MONOGOTARI - ZENI NO ODORI (1963)
MONEY TO BURN (1926) *d* W Lang *c* June 5900ft
MONEY TRAP, THE (1965) *d* B Kennedy *w* G Ford, Hayworth, Cotten, Montalban PV* 92min MGM
MONEY, WOMEN AND GUNS (1958) *d Richard Bartlett c* Lathrop S* 80min U
MON FRERE JACQUES (1961) *d/s* P Prévert *w* Arletty, Brasseur, Carné, Gabin, J Prévert, P Prévert ORTF 6 eps of 50min
MONGOLI, I (1961) *d* De Toth, Freda *w* Palance, Ekberg CS* 115min (= *The Mongols*)
Mongols, The = MONGOLI, I (1961)
MONORAIL (1898) *p* Paul 40ft
Monika = SOMMAREN MED MONIKA (1952)
MONKEY BUSINESS (1931) *d* McLeod *ex-p* H Mankiewicz *w* C, G, H, Z Marx 68min Par
MONKEY BUSINESS (1952) *d* Hawks *p* S Siegel *s* B Hecht, Diamond, Lederer *c* Krasner *co-a* Wheeler *m* Harline *w* C Grant, G Rogers, C Coburn, Monroe 97min Fox
MONKEY ON MY BACK (1957) *d* De Toth 93min *r* UA
MONKEYS, GO HOME! (1966) *d* A McLaglen *w* Chevalier *101min
MONKEYSHINES (1891) *d* Dickson
MONKEY'S UNCLE, THE (1965) *d* Stevenson *87min *pc* Disney
MONKEY TALKS, THE (1927) *d* Walsh *c* O'Connell 6rs Fox
Monkey Woman (UK) = DONNA SCIMMIA, LA (1963)
MONOCLEN (1906) *w* Blom
MONOCLE NOIR, LE (1961) *d* Lautner 88min
MONOCLE RIT JAUNE, LE (1964) *d* Lautner *w* Dalio 100min
MON OEIL (1966, *uf*) *d/s* Lefebvre
MON ONCLE (1958) *d/st/s/w* Tati *c* Bourgoin *120min
MON ONCLE ANTOINE (1971) *d* Jutra *c* Brault *110min
MON ONCLE BENJAMIN (1969) *d* Molinaro *92min
MONORAIL (1898) *p* Paul 40ft
MON PERE AVAIT RAISON (1936) *d/s/fpl/w* Guitry
MONPTI (1957) *d/co-s* Käutner *w* Buchholz, Schneider 101min
MONSIEUR (1964) *d* Le Chanois *co-s* Sautet *m* Van Parys *w* Gabin, Darc, Noiret 91min
MONSIEUR ALBERTE PROPHETE (1962) *d/s/n* Rouch 16mm 33min
MONSIEUR BEAUCLAIRE (1946) *d* G Marshall *s* M Frank, Panama *fst Booth Tarkington co-a* Dreier *w* Hope 93min Par
MONSIEUR CORDON (1933) *d* P Prévert *s/w* Aurenche *c* Kelber 9min Pat
MONSIEUR DE COMPAGNIE, UN (1964) *d* De Broca *c* Coutard *m* Delerue *w* Brialy, Deneuve, Girardot, Cassell *84min Fox
MONSIEUR DE VOLTAIRE (1963) *d* Leenhardt 28min
MONSIEUR ET MADAME CURIE (1953) *d/s* Franju *fbio* (*Pierre Curie*) *Marie Curie m Beethoven* 16min
Monsieur Hulot's Holiday = LES VACANCES DE M HULOT (1951)
MONSIEUR LE DUC (1932) *d* Autant-Lara
MONSIEUR LECOQ (1968, *uf*) *d* Holt *w* Tamiroff
MONSIEUR PINSON, POLICIER (1915) *d* Feyder, *Gaston Ravel* 950m Gau
MONSIEUR PIPE (1936, *uf*) *d* Grimault anim
MONSIEUR STOP (1913) *d* Cohl anim
MONSIEUR TETE (1959) *d* Gruel, Lenica *cy Eugene Ionesco* anim* 13min
Monsieur Ripois = KNAVE OF HEARTS (1954)
MONSIEUR ROBIDA, PROPHETE ET EXPLORATEUR DU TEMPS (1954) *d* Kast 25min
MONSIEUR VERDOUX (1947) *d/p/s/m/w* Chaplin *as-d* Florey, *Wheeler Dryden co-c* Totheroh, Courant 123min *r* UA
MONSIEUR VINCENT (1947) *d Maurice Cloche co-s* Anouilh *c* C Renoir *w* Fresnay 113min
MONSOON (1952) *d* Rodney Amateau *fpl* (*Romeo and Jeanette*) Anouilh *86min
MONSTER AND THE GIRL, THE (1941) *d* Heisler *c* Milner *w* Lukas 65min Par
MONSTER OF HIGHGATE PONDS, THE (1960) *d* Cavalcanti *p* Halas *st* J Batchelor 45min *pc* Halas and Batchelor
MONSTER OF TERROR (1965) *d* D Haller *co-ex-p* Arkoff *w* Karloff S* 81min (= *Die, Monster, Die/The Movie at the End of the World*)
MONSTER OF THE PIEDRAS BLANCAS (1958) *d Irvin Berwick c* Lathrop 71min
MONSTER ON THE CAMPUS (1958) *d* J Arnold *c* Metty 76min U
MONTAGNE INFIDELE, LA (1923) *d* J Epstein Pat
MONTAGNES MAGIQUES (1962) *d* Enrico *20min (= *Magic Mountains*)
MONTANA (1950) *d* Enright, Walsh(*uc*) *co-s* JR Webb, B Chase *c* Freund *w* Flynn, A Smith 76min WB
MONTANA BELLE (1952) *d* Dwan *w* J Russell *82min RKO
MONTANA MOON (1930) *d* St Clair *w* J Crawford 8115ft MGM
MONT-DRAGON (1971) *d/co-s* Valère *88min
MONTE CARLO (1926) *d Christy Cabanne c* Daniels *co-a* Gibbons *w* Pitts 6129ft MGM
MONTE CARLO (1930) *d* Lubitsch *c* Milner *dec* Dreier *w* Jeanette Macdonald, Pitts 8026ft Par
Monte Carlo or Bust (UK) = THOSE DARING YOUNG MEN IN THEIR JAUNTY JALOPIES (1968)
MONTE CRISTO (1922) *d* Emmett J Flynn *technical adviser* Florey *fn* (*The Count of Monte Cristo*) *Alexandre Dumas c* Andriot *w* J Gilbert, Adorée 9828ft Fox
Monte Cristo - Masked Avenger = WIFE OF MONTE CRISTO, THE (1946)
MONTEREY POP (1969) *d/s/co-c* Pennebaker *co-c* R Leacock, A Maysles *w* Shankar 16mm* 82min
MONTE SANT' ANGELO (1942) *d* Chiari
MONT WALSH (1970) *d* Fraker *m* Barry *w* Marvin, Moreau, Palance *99min
Montmartre (USA) = FLAMME, DIE (1923)
MONTPARNASSE 19 (1958) *d/s* Becker *c* Maltras *dec* D'Eaubonne *m* Misraki *w* Philipe, Aimée, Palmer 102min
MONTREUR D'OMBRE, LE (1959) *d* Bourguignon *m* Delerue *444m Pat
MOOCHING THROUGH GEORGIA (1939) *d Jules White s* Bruckman *w* Keaton 18min Col
MOON AND SIXPENCE, THE *d/a* Lewin *fn W Somerset Maugham c* J Seitz *m* Tiomkin *w* G Saunders, H Marshall 89min *co-pc* Lewin *r* UA
MOONBIRD (1959) *d/co-s* J Hubley *co-s/e* F Hubley anim 10min
Mooney vs Fowle = FOOTBALL (1961)
Moon-faced = OKAMA (1927)
MOONFLEET (1955) *d* F Lang *p* Houseman *co-a* Gibbons *m* Rozsa *w* S Granger, G Sanders, Greenwood, Lindfors CS* 87min MGM
MOON IS BLUE, THE (1953) *d/co-p* Preminger *c* Laszlo *w* Holden, Niven, Ratoff 99min *r* UA (= *Die Jungfrau auf dem Dach*)
MOON IS DOWN, THE (1943) *d* Pichel *p/s* N Johnson *fn J Steinbeck c* AC Miller *m* A Newman *w* Cobb 90min Fox
MOONLIGHT AND CACTUS (1932) *d* Arbuckle (*ps* William Goodrich) 2rs
Moonlight and Melody = MOONLIGHT AND PRETZELS (1933)
MOONLIGHT AND PRETZELS (1933) *d* Freund 82min U (= *Moonlight and Melody*)
MOONLIGHTER, THE (1953) *d* Rowland *st/s* Brusch *c* Glennon *w* MacMurray, Stanwyck 3D 77min WB
MOONLIGHT IN HAVANA (1942) *d* A Mann 63min U
Moonlight Madness = GEKKA NO KYOJIN (1926)
MOONLIGHT SONATA (1937) *d Lothar Mendes w* Paderewski 86min

Moon of Israel = SKLAVENKONIGIN, DIE (1924)
MOON OVER HARLEM (1939) *d* Ulmer 8rs
MOON OVER MIAMI (1941) *d* W Lang *p* H Brown *co-ad* Seaton *co-c* Marley, Shamroy *chor* Cole *co-a* R Day *m* A Newman *w* Grable, R Cummings, Cole *91min Fox
Moon Over Shanghai, The = SHANAI NO TSUKI (1941)
MOON PILOT (1961) *d* Neilson *w* E O'Brien *98min pc* Disney
MOONRISE (1948) *d* Borzage *p/s* Haas *c* JL Russell *w* Ingram, E Barrymore 90min Rep
MOONSHINE (1918) *d/w* Arbuckle *w* Keaton 2rs Par
MOONSHINERS, THE (1916) *d* Arbuckle 2rs
MOONSHINE VALLEY (1922) *d* Brenon 5rs Fox
MOONSHINE WAR, THE (1970) *d* Quine *w* Widmark *99min r* MGM
MOON-SPINNERS, THE (1964) *d* Neilson *w* H Mills, Wallach, Negri, Greenwood *118min pc* Disney
MOONTIDE (1942) *d* A Mayo, F Lang(*uc*) *p* Hellinger *s* J O'Hara *c* C Clarke *m* Mockridge, A Newman *w* Lupino, Gabin, Mitchell, Rains 94min Fox
Moontrap, The = POUR LA SUITE DU MONDE (1962)
MOON ZERO TWO (1969) *d* R Baker *100min
MORAL '63 (1963) *d/s* Thiele *w* Tiller S 100min
Morality Above All = MAVROST NADE USE (1937)
MORANBON (1958) *d* Jean-Claude Bonnardot *s* Gatti S 90min
MORECTWO (1957) *d* Polanski *sh* (= *The Crime*)
MORDAREN-*EN HELT VANLIG PERSON* (1957) *d* Mattsson 88min (= *The Murderer – An Ordinary Person*)
MORDER SIND UNTER UNS DIE (1946) *d/s* Staudte *w* Neff (as *Knef*) (= *The Murderers are Amongst us*) 2400m Defa
Mörder Unter Uns = M (1931)
MORD OHNE TATER, DER (1920) *d/co-s* Dupont 1603m
MORE MILK, EVETTE (1965) *d* Warhol 16m 70min (= *Lana Turner*)
More than a Miracle = C'ERA UNA VOLTA (1967)
MORE THE MERRIER, THE (1943) *d/p* G Stevens *c* Tetzlaff *m* Harline *w* Arthur, C Coburn, McCrea 104min Col
MORGAN, A SUITABLE CASE FOR TREATMENT (1966) *d* Reisz *w* V Redgrave 97min BL
MORGAN IL PIRATA (1960) *d/s* De Toth *w* Reeves CS* 95min MGM (= *Morgan the Pirate*)
MORGAN LE PIRATE (1909) *d/s* Jasset
Morgan the Pirate = MORGAN ZI PIRATA (1960)
MORIANERNA (1965) *d* Mattsson *w* Dahlbeck 100min (= *Morianna*)
Morianna = MORIANERNA (1965)
MORI NO ISHIMATSU (1949) *d* Yoshimura (= *Ishimatsu of the Forest*)
NORMAN MAID, A (1917) *d* Leonard
The Morning After = I SPY (1934)
Morning Conflicts = ASA NO HAMON (1952)
MORNING DEPARTURE (1950) *d* R Baker *w* J Mills, Attenborough 102min BL (= *Operation Disaster*)
MORNING GLORY (1933) *d* L Sherman *p* Berman *c* Glennon *m* M Steiner *w* K Hepburn, Fairbanks Jr, Menjou 74min RKO
Morning With the Osone Family, a = OSONE-KE NO ASA (1946)
MOROCCO (1930) *d* Von Sternberg *s* Furthman *c* Garmes *dec* Dreier *w* G Cooper, Dietrich, Menjou 90min Par
MOROCCO (1958) *d* A King 16mm 58min
MOR OCH DOTTER (1912) *d/s/w* Stiller 480m
MORO NABA (1957) *d/c* Rouch 16mm
MORTADELLA, LA (1971) *d/co-s* Monicelli *co-s* Cecchi D'Amico *w* Loren *103min
MORTAL STORM, THE (1940) *d* Borzage *p* Saville *c* Daniels *a* Gibbons *w* J Stewart, R Young. Stack, Dailey, Ouspenskaya 100min MGM
MORT DU CERF, LA (1951) *d* Kirsanov 14min (= *Chasse à Courre à Villers-Cotterets*)
MORT DU CYGNY, LA (1937) *d* Benoît-Lévy *c* Burel 95min
MORT D'UN TUEUR, LA (1963) *d/s/w* Hossein 75min
MORT DU SOLEIL, LA (1921) *d* Dulac
MORTE A VENEZIA (1971) *d/p/co-s* Visconti *fst* Thomas Mann *m* Mahler *w* Bogarde, Mangano PV* 130min (= *Death in Venice*)
MORTE DI UN AMICO (1960) *d/co-s* Rossi 97min
MORTE CIVILE, LA (1942) *d* Poggioli
MORT EN CE JARDIN, LA (1956) *d/co-s* Buñuel *co-s* Alcoroza, queneau *m* Misraki *w* Signoret, Piccoli, Vanel *97min (= *Evil Eden/La Muerte en esta Jardin*)
MORT EN FRAUDE (1916) *d/co-s/co-di* Camus *co-s/co-di* Audiard *c* Sechan *w* Gélin 105min (= *Fugitive in Saigon*)
MORTE RISALE A IERI SERA, LA (1970) *d/co-s* Tessari *w* Vallone *96min (= *Death Occurred Last Night*)
MORTE-SAISON DES AMOURS, LA (1961) *d/co-s* Kast *c* Vierny *dec* Saulnier *m* Delerue *w* Arnoul, Gélin 100min (= *Les Liaisons Amoureuses/The Season for Love*)
MORT INTERDITE (1941) *d* Ciampi *sh*
MORT QUI TUE, LE (1913) *d/s* Feuillade 1945m In 6 parts (= *Fantomas, III*)

Morts Reviennent-Ils?, Les = DRAME AU CHATEAU D'ACRE, UN (1912)
MOR'URAN (1930) *d* J Epstein 26min (= *La Merdes Corbeaux*)
MOSAIC (1965) *d* McLaren, *Evelyn Lambert* *6min NFBC
MOSAIC LAW, THE (1912) *d* Ince *w* Conway
MOSCHETTIERE DEL MARE, I (1962) *d* Steno *w* A Ray *115min
Moscow = MOSKVA (1932)
Moscow Builds the Metro = MOSKVA STROYIT METRO (1934)
Moscow in October = MOSKVA V OKTYABRE
Moscow Laughs = VESYOLYE REBYATA (1934)
MOSCOW NIGHTS (1935) *d* Asquith *w* Olivier 74min BL (= *I Stand Condemned*)
MOSCOW – TEN YEARS AFTER (1969) *d* Pennebaker
MOSE (1963) *d* Gruel anim 3min
MOSKAU-SHANGHAI (1936) *d* Wegener *w* Negri 2345m (= *Der Weg nach Shanghai*)
MOSKVA (1932) *d/c* Karman (= *Moscow*)
MOSKVA STROYIT METRO (1934) *d/s/e* Shub 400m (= *Moscow Builds the Metro*)
MOSKVA V OKTYABRE (1927) *d* Barnet *dec* Alexander Rodchenko *w* Barnet, (Sten) (= *Moscow in October*)
MOSS ROSE (1947) *d* Ratoff *co-s* Furthman *c* Joe Macdonald *ad* Busch *w* Mature, E Barrymore, Price 82min Fox
MOST DANGEROUS GAME, THE (1932) *d/p* Schoedsack, Pichel *w* McCrea 66min RKO (= *The Hounds of Zaroff*)
Most Dangerous Game, The (UK) = DROLE DE JEU (1967)
MOST DANGEROUS MAN ALIVE, THE (1958 *r* 1961) *d* Dwan *p* Bogeaus 82min Col
Most Dangerous Man in the World, The (UK) = CHAIRMAN, THE (1969)
MOSTRI, I (1963) *d/co-s* Risi *w* Gassman
MOST UNLIKELY MILLIONAIRE, THE (1965) *d* A King 16mm 27min
Most Wonderful Moment, The = MOMENTO PIU BELLO, IL (1957)
MO TAKU-TO TO BUNKADAI-KAKUMEI (1969) *d* Oshima (= *Mao Tse-Tung and the Cultural Revolution*)
MOT DE CAMBRONNE, LE (1936) *d/s/fpl/w* Guitry Pat *r*
Mot de L'Enigme, Le = ENIGME (1919)
MOTEN I SKYMNINGEN (1957) *d* Kjellin *c* Fischer *w* Dahlbeck (= *Encounters at Dusk*)
MOTH, THE (1934) *d* Newmeyer 64min
Mother = MAT (1926)
MOTHER (1914) *d* M Tourneur
Mother = MAT (1956)
Mother = HAHA (1964)
Mother and the Law, The = modern ep in INTOLERANCE (1916)
MOTHERING HEART, THE (1913) *d* Griffith *w* L Gish 1rl Bio
Mother India = BHARAT MATA (1957)
MOTHER IS A FRESHMAN (1949) *d* Bacon *c* Arling *co-a* Wheeler *w* L Young, V Johnson 81min Fox (= *Mother Knows Best*)
Mother Joan of the Angels = MATKA JOANNA OD ANIOLOW (1961)
Mother Knows Best = MOTHER IS A FRESHMAN (1949)
MOTHER MACHREE (1928) *d* J Ford *w* V McLaglen (Parrish, J Wayne) 75min Fox
MOTHER OF MINE (1917) *d/co-s* Julian 5rs
MOTHER O'MINE (1921) *d* Niblo *supn* Ince 7rs
Mother Ought to be Loved, A = MAMA O KOWAZUYA (1934)
MOTHER'S DAY (1948) *d/p/s* Broughton 22min
Mother's Devotion, A = VERNOST MATERI (1967)
MOTHER'S HOLIDAY (1932) *d* Arbuckle (*ps* William Goodrich) 1rl
Mother's Love = HAHA-YO KOISHI (1926)
MOTHER WORE TIGHTS (1947) *d* Lang *p* Trotti *co-a* R Day *m* A Newman *w* Grable, Dailey 107min Fox
Mother = OKASAN (1952)
MOTHLIGHT (1963) *d* Brakhage 16mm* si 4min
MOTION PAINTING (1948) *d* Fischinger *m* Bach anim* 11min
MOTION PICTURES (1955) *d* Breer anim* 16mm 3min
Motor Cycles = PETISTOVKA (1949)
? MOTORIST, THE (1906) *p* Paul 190ft (= *P.A.K.*)
MOTOR MAT AND HIS FLIV (1916) *d* Sullivan, *Otz Messmer* anim 3/4rs
MOUCHETTE (1967) *d/s* Bresson *fn* (*Nouvelle Histoire de Mouchette*) Georges Bernanos *c* Cloquet *song* Wiener *mf* Monteverdi 90min
MOTS ONT UN SENS, LES (1970) *d* Marker 16mm 45min
Le Moulin Maudit = MAUDITE SOIT LA GUERRE (1914)
MOULIN ROUGE (1928) *d/s* Dupont 10500ft
MOULIN ROUGE (1953) *d/p/co-s* J Huston *co-p* Woolf Bros *as-p* Clayton *c* Morris *m* Auric *w* J Ferrer *120min *r* UA
MOULINS CHANTENT ET PLEURENT, LES (1912) *d* Machin 180m (= *L'Ame des Moulins*)
MOUNTAIN, THE (1956) *p/d* Dmytryk *s* Macdougall *c* Planer *co-a* Pereira *w* Tracy, R Wagner, Trevor VV* 105min Par

Mountain Brigand (UK) = AVVENTURE DI MANDRIN, LE (1952)
Mountain Cat, The = DIE BERGKATZE (1921)
MOUNTAIN EAGLE, THE (1926) *d* Hitchcock *p* Balcon 7503ft
MOUNTAIN JUSTICE (1936) *d* Curtiz *c* E Haller 82min WB
MOUNTAIN MUSIC (1937) *d* Florey *p* Glazer *co-s* S Lederer *c* Struss *co-a* Dreier *chor* Prinz 8rs Par
MOUNTAIN RAT, THE (1914) *w* Crisp
MOUNTAIN ROAD, THE (1960) *d* Daniel Mann *p* Goetz *c* Guffey *m* Moross *w* J Stewart 102min *pc* Goetz *r* Col
MOUNTAINS OF THE MOON (1958) *d* W Van Dyke *60min
MOUNT VERNON (1949) *d* W Van Dyke *c* R Leacock 14min
MOURIR A MADRID (1963) *d* Rossif *m* Jarre 85min (= *To Die in Madrid*)
MOURIR D'AIMER (1970) *d/co-s* Cayatte *w* Girardot *110min
MOURNING BECOMES ELECTRA (1947) *d/co-p* D Nichols *fpl* Eugene O'Neill *c* Barnes *w* R Russell, M Redgrave, Paxinou, K Douglas 160min RKO
MOUSE IN THE ART SCHOOL, THE (1901) *d* G Smith
MOUSE ON THE MOON, THE (1963) *d* Lester *cr* Binder *85min *r* Col
MOUSE THAT ROARED, THE (1959) *d* J Arnold *w* Sellers, Seberg *90min *r* Col
MOUSE TROUBLE (1944) *d* Hanna, Barbera *p* Quimby anim* 8min MGM
MOUSQUETAIRES DE LA REINE, LES (1903) *d* Méliès 50m
MOUTHPIECE, THE (1932) *d* E Nugent, *James Flood* *w* (Goddard) 90min WB
MOUTON A CINQ PATTES, LE (1954) *d/co-s* Verneuil *w* Fernandel, Arnoul, De Funès 100min (= *The Sheep has Five Legs*)
Moutons de Praxos, Les = POLYORCHIA (1962)
MOVE (1970) *d* S Rosenberg *p* Berman *c* Daniels PV* 90min Fox
MOUVEMENT PERPETUEL (1949) *co-d/s* Jutra *co-d* Brault
MOVE OVER, DARLING (1963) *d* M Gordon *co-p* A Rosenberg *co-s* Kanter *c* Fapp *w* D Day, Garner, Ritter CS* 103min Fox
MOUVEMENTS PROTOPLASMIQUES DANS LES CELLULES D'ELODEA CANNADENSIS EN MILIEUX ISOTONIQUE, HYPERTONIQUE, HYPOTONIQUE (1929) *d* Painlevé
MOVIE CRAZY (1932) *d* Bruckman *w* H Lloyd 94min Par
Movie Nut = FILM JOHNNIE, A (1914)
MOVIES TAKE A HOLIDAY, THE (1944) *co-d/e* Richter *co-d* Herman Weinberg compilation of films by Clair, J Renoir, *Marcel Duchamp*, Léger, Man Ray, Richter
Moving Target, The (UK) = HARPER (1966)
MOZART RONDO (1947–1949) *d/c* Whitney, *James Whitney* 16mm *4min (with HOT HOUSE)
M.P. Case, The = ZAAK M.P., DE (1960)
MRLJA NA SAVJESTI (1968) *d* Vukotic *454m (= *A Stain on his Conscience*)
MRS KENNEDY'S WHITE HOUSE TOUR (c1962) *d* Schaffner *w* Jacqueline Kennedy TV
MRS MINIVER (1942) *d* Wyler *p* Franklin *c* Ruttenberg *a* Gibbons *m* Stothart *w* Garson, T Wright, Pidgeon, Lawford 134min MGM
MRS PARKINGTON (1944) *d* Garnett *c* Ruttenberg *co-a* Gibbons *m* Kaper *w* Garson, Pidgeon, Moorehead, Duryea, Lawford, D Reed 124min MGM
MRS TEMPLE'S TELEGRAPH (1920) *d* Cruze 5rs FPL
MRS WIGGS OF THE CABBAGE PATCH (1934) *d* Taurog *c* C Lang *w* Fields, Pitts, Sheridan (as Clara Lo Sheridan) 80min Par
MUCEDNINI LASKY (1966) *d/co-s* Nemec *c* Ondricek *w* L Anderson 3 parts (= *Martyrs of Love*)
MUDDY ROMANCE, A (1913) *d* Sennett *w* Normand 1rl Key
Muddy Waters = NIGORIE (1953)
MÜDE THEODOR, DER (1936) *d* V Harlan 2265m
MÜDE TOD, DER (1921) *d/co-s* F Lang *p* Pommer *co-s* Von Harbou *co-c* F Wagner *co-a* Warm, Röhrig *w* Dagover 2306m Dec (= *Between Two Worlds/ Destiny*)
MUDLARK, THE (1950) *d* Negulesco *p/s* N Johnson *c* Périnal *w* Guinness, I Dunne 99min Fox
MUERTE DE PIO BAROJA, LA (1957, *ur*) *d* Bardem
MUERTE DE UN CICLISTA (1955) *d/s* Bardem *w* Bosè 85min (= *Death of a Cyclist*)
MUERTIN, EL (1958) *d* Summers *sh*
Muerte en esta jardin, La = LA MORT EN CE JARDIN (1956)
MUET MELOMANE, LE (1899) *w* Zecca Pat
Muiden Circle Lives Again, The = MUIDERKRING HERLEEFT, DE (1949)
MUIDERKRING HERLEEFT, DE (1949) *d/s/e* Haanstra (= *The Muiden Circle Lives Again*)
MUJERES LOS PREFIEREN TANTOS, LAS (1966) *d* Saslavsky
MUJER SIN AMOR, UNA (1951) *d* Buñuel *fst* (*Pierre et Jean*) Guy de Maupassant

MUJ PRIEL FABIAN (1953) d/co-s J Weiss * (= *My Friend the Gypsy*)

MUKOKUSEKI – MONO (1951) d Ichikawa (= *The Man without a Nationality*)

MUKOKUSEKI-SHA (1951) d/co-s Ichikawa

MUKTI (1937) d Pramathesh Chandra Barva c Roy

MULHER DE VERDADE (1954) d/p Cavalcanti

MULINO DEL PO, IL (1949) d/co-ad Lattuada p Ponti co-s Fellini fn Ricardo Bacchelli c Tonti m Pizzette 107min

MUMMY, THE (1932) d Freund w Karloff 72min U

MUMMY, THE (1959) d Fisher *88min JAR

MUMSIE (1927) d H Wilcox w H Marshall

MUMSY, NANNY, SONNY AND GIRLY (1969) d F Francis 102min

MUNCHEN-BERLIN WANDERUNG (1927) d Fischinger

MUNEKATA SHIMAI (1950) d/co-s Ozu (= *The Munekata Sisters*)

Munekata Sisters, The = MUNEKATA SHIMAI (1950)

MUNNA (1954) d/p/s Abbas

MUNTZ TV (1953) d Fischinger anim 1min

Mura di Malapaga = AU-DELA DES GRILLES (1948)

MURAGLIA CINESE, LA (1958) d Lizzani *100min (= *Behind the Great Wall/Il Fiume Gallo*)

MURA NO HANAYOME (1927) d Gosho (= *The Village Bride*)

MURATO, IL (1949) d/s De Robertis

MURATTI GREIFT EIN (1934) d Fischinger anim* 2¼min

MURATTI PRIVAT (1934) d Fischinger anim

MUR DE L'ATLANTIQUE, LE (1970) d/co-s Camus w Bourvil *100min

MURDER (1930) d Hitchcock s Reville w H Marshall 92min

Murder a la Carte (UK) = VOICI LE TEMPS DES ASSASSINS (1955)

MURDER AT DAWN (1932) d Thorpe 61min

MURDER AT MONTE CARLO (1935) d Ralph Ince w Flynn

MURDER AT THE VANITIES (1934) d Leisen chor Prinz w V McLaglen, Sheridan (as Clara Lou Sheridan) 70min Par

MURDER BY CONTRACT (1958) d Lerner c Ballard 81min Col

MURDER BY PROXY (1955) d Fisher 87min

Murder by Signature = EICHMANN UND DAS DRITTE REICH (1961)

Murder Czech Style (UK) = VRAZDA PO CESKU (1967)

Murder on Dante Street = UBIISTVO NA ULITSYE DANTE (1956)

Murder – An Ordinary Person, The = MORDAREN – ENHELT VANLIG PERSON (1967)

Murderers are Amongst us, The = DIE MORDER SIND UNTER UNS (1946)

Murderers at Large = UBIITSI UYKHODYAT NA DOROGU (1942)

MURDERER'S ROW (1966) d Levin m Schifrin c Leavitt w Martin, Malden *108min Col

MURDER HE SAYS (1945) d G Marshall c Sparkuhl co-a Dreier w MacMurray 91min Par

Murder Inc = ENFORCER, THE (1951)

MURDER INCORPORATED (1960) co-d/s Rosenberg co-d/p Balaban CS 103min Fox

MURDER IN THE BIG HOUSE (1942) d B Reaves Eason w V Johnson 59min WB

MURDER IN THE BLUE ROOM (1944) d Leslie Goodwins co-s Diamond 61min U

Murder in Thornton Square, The (UK) = GASLIGHT (1944)

MURDER IS MY BEAT (1954) d Ulmer 77min AA (= *Dynamite Anchorage*)

MURDER MAN, THE (1935) d/co-st/co-s Tim Whelan w J Stewart, Tracy 70min MGM

MURDER MY SWEET (1945) d Dmytryk s Paxton fn (*Farewell My Lovely*) R Chandler c Wild w D Powell, Trevor 89min RKO (= *Farewell My Lovely*)

Murder of Father Christmas, The (UK) = L'ASSASSINAT DU PERE NOEL (1941)

Murder on Diamond Row (US) = SQUEAKER, THE (1937)

Murdon on Monday = HOME AT SEVEN (1951)

MURDER ON THE CAMPUS (1934) d Thorpe 7rs

MURDER ON THE ROOF (1930) d G Seitz p Cohn c J Walker 5400ft Col

MURDERS IN THE RUE MORGUE (1932) d Florey fst E A Poe di J Huston w Lugosi 75min U

MURDER WILL OUT (1930) d Badger w Hopper 6200ft FN

MURDER WITHOUT CRIME (1950) d/st/s J Thompson 76min

MURI DI SANA, I (1971) d Pasolini 14min RAI

MURIEL, OU LE TEMPS D'UN RETOUR (1963) d Resnais s Cayrol c Vierny a Saulnier m Hans Werner Henze cr Lenica w Seyrig *116min

MURI SHINJU NIHON NO NATSU (1967) d/co-s Oshima *98min pc Oshima r Sho (= *Japanese Summer/-Double Suicide*)

MURO. EL (1947) d/s Torre-Nilsson 8min

MURPHY'S WAR (1971) d P Yates s Silliphant c Slocombe m Barry w O'Toole, Noiret *108min

Musashi Miyamoto = MIYAMOTO MUSASHI (1942)

MUSASHINO FUJIN (1951) d Mizoguchi w Mori Toho (= *Woman of Musashino*)

MUSCLE BEACH (1948) d I Lerner, Strick 10min

MUSÉE DANS LA MER, UN (1953) d/p Cousteau *

MUSÉE GRÉVIN (1958) co-d Demy c Fradetal 600m

MUSEO DEI SOGNI, IL (1949) d Comencini

MUSHIBAMERU HARU (1932) d Naruse (= *Lost Spring*)

MUSICA, LA (1966) co-d/s/fpl Duras co-d Paul Seban c Vierny w Hossein, Seyrig 82min

MUSICAL POSTER (1940) d Lye *2min

Musical Tramps = HIS MUSICAL CAREER (1914)

Music Blasters = YOU'RE DARN TOOTIN' (1928)

MUSIC BOX, THE (1932) d James Parrott p Roach w Laurel, Hardy 3rs (sd) r MGM

MUSIC FOR MILLIONS (1944) d Koster p Pasternak c Surtees co-a Gibbons w M O'Brien, Allyson

MUSIC GOES 'ROUND, THE (1936) d Schertzinger s Swerling c J Walker 80min Col

Music Hall = TANGO TANGLES (1914)

Musician's Girl, The = MUZIKANTSKA LIDUSKA (1940)

MUSIC IN THE AIR (1934) d May co-s B Wilder w Swanson 85min Fox

MISIC IS MAGIC (1935) d G Marshall c O'Connell w Faye 65min Fox

MUSIC LOVERS, THE (1971) d/p K Russell c Slocombe m Tchaikovsky *122min r UA

MUSIC MAN, THE (1962) d/p Da Costa c Burks w Preston, S Jones TR* 151min WB

MUSIC MASTER, THE (1908) d Wallace McCutcheon w Griffith Bio

MUSIC MASTER, THE (1927) d/p Dwan fpl David Belasco 7754ft Fox

Music Room, The (UK) = JALSAGHAR (1958)

MUSIK I MÖRKER (1947) d Ingmar Bergman c Strindberg w Zetterling, Björnstrand 90min (= *Night is My Future*)

MUSKETEERS OF PIG ALLEY, THE (1912) d Griffith s Loos w L Gish, Carey 1rl Bio

MUSUKO NO SEISHUN (1952) d Kobayashi 3999ft (= *My Son's Youth*)

MUSUME (1926) d/s Gosho (= *Daughter*)

MUSUME TSUMA HAHA (1960) d Naruse w Mori S* 122min Toho (= *Daughters, Wives and a Mother*)

MUSS 'EM UP (1936) d Vidor p Berman st J Grant 70min RKO

MUSTAA VALKOISELLA (1968) d/pc/s/e/w J Donner *95min (= *Black on White*)

MUSUME DOJOJI (1946, ur) d Ichikawa (= *A Girl at Dojo Temple*)

MUTINEERS, THE (1961) d L Gilbert 60min Col

MUTINY (1952) d Dmytryk co-s Yordan c Laszlo m Tiomkin 77min r UA

MUTINY ON THE BODY! (1939) d/w C Chase 2rs Col

MUTINY ON THE BOUNTY (1935) d/p F Lloyd p Thalberg as-p Lewin co-s Furthman c Edeson a Gibbons m Stothart co-song Kaper w Laughton, Gable, Tone, Crisp 132min MGM

MUTINY ON THE BOUNTY (1962) d Milestone p A Rosenberg s Lederer c Surtees m Kaper w Brando, T Howard, R Harris, Haydn PV* 179min MGM

MUTTER COURAGE UND IHRE KINDER (1955) d/co-s Staudte co-s/fpl Brecht w Signoret 4125m

MUTTER KRAUSENS FAHRT INS FLUCK (1929) d/c Jutzi 3297m

MUTTS TO YOU (1938) d/w C Chase 2rs Col

MUZHESTVO (1939) d Kalatozov 2008m (= *Manhood*)

MUZIKANTSKA LIDUSKA (1940) d Frič (= *The Musician's Girl*)

Muz Ktery Lze = L'HOMME QUI MENT (1969)

MUZ Z NEZNAMA (1939) d Frič (= *Reluctant Millionaire*)

MY AMERICAN WIFE (1922) d S Wood w Swanson 6091ft FPL r Par

My Apprenticeship = V LYUDYAKM (1939)

MY BABY (1912) d Griffith 1rl Bio

My Beloved Child = ITOSHINO WAGAKO (1926)

MY BEST GAL (1944) d A Mann st R Brooks 67min Rep

MY BILL (1938) d J Farrow c Hickox w K Francis 65min WB

MY BLUE HEAVEN (1950) d Koster p S Siegel c Arling co-a Wheeler m A Newman w M Gaynor, Grable, D Wayne *96min Fox

My Brother Down There = RUNNING TARGET (1956)

MY BROTHER TALKS TO HORSES (1946) d Zinnemann c Rosson co-a Gibbons w Lawford, C Ruggles 92min MGM

My Brother, The Outlaw = MY OUTLAW BROTHER (1952)

MY COUSIN RACHEL (1952) d Koster p/s N Johnson fn D Du Maurier c La Shelle co-a Wheeler m Waxman w De Havilland, Burton 98min Fox

MY DARLING CLEMENTINE (1946) d J Ford c Joe MacDonald co-a Wheeler m Mockridge w H Fonda, Darnell, Mature, Brennan, Darwell, (Marsh) 97min Fox

My Daughter Joy = OPERATION X

My Dear Fellow = DOROGOI MOI CHELOVEK (1958)

MY DEAR MISS ALDRICH (1937) d G Seitz p/st/s H Mankiewicz c Lawton a Gibbons w O'Sullivan, Pidgeon, Oliver 74min MGM

MY DEAR SECRETARY (1948) d/st/s Charles Martin c Biroc w K Douglas 94min r UA

MY DREAM IS YOURS (1949) d/p Curtiz co-s Kurnitz c E Haller w D Day, Menjou 101min WB

My Enemy The Sea = TAIHEIYO HITOSI SOTCHI (1963)

MY FAIR LADY (1964) d Cukor p J Warner s A Lerner fmpl A Lerner, Frederick Loewe fpl (*Pygmalion*) George Bernard Shaw c Stradling co-des/cos Beaton w A Hepburn, Harrison PV70* 175min WB

My Fatherland = MOIA RODINA (1932)

MY FATHER'S HOUSE (1947) d/co-p Herbert Kline c F Crosby 85min

My Fault Continued = SHIN ONOGA TSUMI (1926)

MY FAVORITE BLONDE (1942) d Sidney Lanfield st Panama, Frank c Mellor a Drier w Hope 78min Par

MY FAVORITE BRUNETTE (1947) d E Nugent co-a Drier c Lindon w Hope, Lamour, Lorre, Ladd(uc) 87min pc Hope r Par

MY FAVORITE SPY (1942) d Garnett p H Lloyd w Wyman 86min RKO

MY FAVORITE SPY (1951) d McLeod a Pereira, Dreier c Milner m V Young w Lamarr, Hope 93min Par

MY FAVORITE WIFE (1940) d Kanin supn/p/co-st McCarey c Maté e Wise w C Grant, I Dunne, R Scott 88min RKO

My First Love Affair = NOGIKU NO GOTOKI KIMI NARIKI (1955)

MY FOOLISH HEART (1949) d Robson p Goldwyn s JJ Epstein c Garmes a R Day w D Andrews, S Hayward 98min RKO

MY FORBIDDEN PAST (1950) d Stevenson c Wild w M Douglas, Gardner, Mitchum 81min RKO

MY FRIEND IRMA (1949) d G Marshall p Wallis co-a Dreier w Martin, J Lewis *103min Par

My Friend the Gypsy = MUJ PRITEL FABIAN (1953)

MY FRIEND THE KING (1931) d/s M Powell 47min

MY GAL SAL (1942) d Irving Cummings co-s Miller fn Theodore Dreiser co-a R Day m A Newman w Hayworth, Mature *103min Fox

MY GEISHA (1962) d Cardiff s Kramer a Periera w MacLaine, Montand, Robinson, R Cummings TR* 120min Par

MY GIRL TISA (1948) d E Nugent p Sperling c E Haller e Nyby m M Steiner w Palmer, Tamiroff 95min

MY HEART BELONGS TO DADDY (1942) d Siodmak p S Siegel c Fapp a Dreier 75min Par

My Heart Goes Crazy (US) = LONDON TOWN (1946)

MY HEART IS CALLING (1934) d Gallone s Gilliat

MY HERO (1912) d Griffith 1rl Bio

My Home is Copacabana = MITT HEM AR COPACABANA (1965)

MY HUSBAND'S WIVES (1924) d Elvey 4609ft Fox

MY HUSTLER (1965) d/p/c Warhol 16mm 70min

MY LEARNED FRIEND (1943) co-d Dearden co-d/w Hay 74min

My Life to Live (US) = VIVRE SA VIE (1962)

MY LIFE WITH CAROLINE (1941) d/p Milestone c Milner w Colman, Roland 81min RKO

MY LIPS BETRAY (1933) d John Blystone c Garmes w Lillian Harvey 76min Fox

MY LITTLE CHICKADEE (1940) d Cline s/w West, Fields 83min U

MY LOVE CAME BACK (1940) d C Bernhardt p J Warner, Wallis co-s Goff s Goetz w De Havilland, Wyman 81min WB

MY LUCKY STAR (1938) d Del Ruth w Romero, Cook, G Lee 84min Fox

MY MAN (1929) d A Mayo 9000ft WB

MY MAN AND I (1952) d Wellman c Mellor co-a Gibbons v Winters, Corey, Montalban, Trevor 99min MGM

MY MAN GODFREY (1936) d/p La Cava c Tetzlaff w Lombard, W Powell, (Wyman) 95min U

MY MAN GODFREY (1957) d Koster p R Hunter c Daniels co-a Golitzen w Niven, Allyson CS* 92min U

MY NAME IS JULIA ROSS (1945) d JH Lewis c Guffey 65min Col

My Night at Maud's = MA NUIT CHEZ MAUD (1968)

My Night with Maud (UK) = MA NUIT CHEZ MAUD (1968)

MY OUTLAW BROTHER (1951) d E Nugent p Bogeaus w Rooney, Preston, Stack 82min r EL (= *My Brother, The Outlaw*)

MY OWN PAL (1926) d John G Blystone w Mix 6rs Fox

MY OWN TRUE LOVE (1949) d Compton Bennett p Lewton w M Douglas 84min Par

MY PAL GUS (1952) d Parrish co-a Wheeler m Harline w Widmark, Dru 83min Fox

MY PARTNER MR DAVIS (1936) d Autant-Lara s/di J Prévert 60min

MY PAST (1931) d Del Ruth w Blondell 83min WB

MYRA BRECKINRIDGE (1970) d/co-s Michael Sarne co-s/fn Vidal co-s West w West, J Huston, Welch, Carradine PV* 94min Fox

MY REPUTATION (1946) d C Bernhardt p Blanke c Howe m M Steiner w Stanwyck 94min WB

MYRIAM (1929) d/co-s Guazzoni

M₃ Second Brother = NIANCHAN (1959)

MY SIN (1931) d/co-s G Abbott c Folsey w Bankhead, March 80min Par

MY SISTER EILEEN (1955) d/co-s Quine p Kohlmar co-s Edwards c Lawton chor Fosse w J Leigh, Fosse, Lemmon S* 108min Col
My Sister, My Love = SYSKONBADD 1782 (1966)
MY SIX CONVICTS (1952) d Fregonese m Tiomkin w Roland, Kjellin 104min pc Kramer r Col
MY SIX LOVES (1963) d Champion c Arling w Robertson, D Reynolds *101min Par
MY SON JOHN (1952) d/st/co-s/p McCarey ad Mahin c Stradling co-a Pereira w H Hayes, R Walker, Heflin 90min Par
MY SON, MY SON! (1940) d C Vidor c Stradling w Carroll, L Hayward 115min UA
My Son's Youth = MUSUKO NO SEISHUN (1952)
MY SON, THE HERO (1943) d/co-st/co-s Ulmer 65min
My Son, The Professor = MIO FIGLIO PROFESSORE (1946)
MYSTERE BARTON, LE (1949) d/s Charles Spaak
MYSTERE DE LA CHAMBRE JAUNE, LE (1931) d L'Herbier
MYSTERE DE L'ATELIER 15, LE (1957) co-d Resnais cy Marker c Cloquet, Vierny 18min
MYSTERE DE LA TOUR EIFFEL, LE (1927) d Duvivier co-c Thirard sh (= *Tramel's'en Fiche*)
MYSTERE DE PARIS (1934) d De Baroncelli
MYSTERE KOUMIKO, LE (1965) d/s/c/e Marker 16mm * 45min
MYSTERE PICASSO, LE (1956) d/s Clouzot c C Renoir e Colpi m Auric w *Pablo Picasso*, Clouzot 78min
MYSTERES DE PARIS, LES (1943) d De Baroncelli
MYSTERES DU CHATEAU DU DE, LES (1929) d/c Man-Ray 22min
MYSTERIES, THE (1968) d/s/c/e Markopoulos 16mm *80min
Mysteries of India (USA) = INDISCHE GRABMAL, DAS (1921)
MYSTERIOUS DR. FU MANCHU, THE (1929) d Rowland V Lee w Arthur 86min Par
MYSTERIOUS INTRUDER, THE (1946) d Castle 62min Col
MYSTERIOUS ISLAND, THE (1929) co-d/s Lucien Hubbard co-d M Tourneur, Christensen fst (*L'Isle Mysterieuse*) Jules Verne a Gibbons w L Barrymore part * 8569ft (sd/si) MGM
MYSTERIOUS ISLAND (1961) d Endfield fn Jules Verne m Herrmann w Greenwood *100min Col
MYSTERIOUS LADY, THE (1928) d Niblo c Daniels w Garbo 7750ft MGM
Mysterious Mr Davis, The = MY PARTNER MR DAVIS (1936)
MYSTERIOUS MR MOTO (1938) d/co-s Foster w Lorre 62min Fox
Mysterious X, The = HEMMELIGHEDSFULD X, DET (1913)
MYSTERY IN MEXICO (1948) d Wise 66min RKO
Mystery of Blood, The = FAJEMSTUI KRUE (1953)
MYSTERY OF MARIE ROGET (1942) d Phil Rosen fst Poe w Montez, Ouspenskaya 61min U
MYSTERY OF THE WAX MUSEUM, THE (1933) d Curtiz c Rennahan 73min WB
MYSTERY SEA RAIDER (1940) d Dmytryk co-a Dreier 75min Par
MYSTERY STREET (1950) d J Sturges c J Alton s Boehm, R Brooks c Gibbons w Montalban 93min MGM
MYSTERY SUBMARINE (1950) d Sirk co-a Boyle 78min U
MYSTIC, THE (1925) d Browning 7rs MGM
MYSTIKE FREMMEDE, DEN (1914) d Madsen
My Stupid Brother = NIISAN NO BAKA (1932)
MY S URALA (1944) d Kuleshov 9rs (= *We of the Urals*)
My Rail is my Ticket = REP JE ULAZNICA (1959)
MYTEN (1966) d/co-s Halldoff 84min (= *The Myth*)
Myth, The = MYTEN (1966)
My Universities = MOI UNIVERSITETI (1940)
MY VALET (1915) d/p/w Sennett w Normand 3rs Tri
My Way Home (UK) = IGY JOTTEM (1964)
MY WEAKNESS (1933) d/co-s D Butler c AC Miller w Lillian Harvey, Ayres 73min Fox
MY WIFE'S RELATIONS (1922) d/s Keaton, Cline w Keaton 2rs co-pc Keaton
My Wife, The Film Star (UK) = MEINE FRAU, DIE FILMSCHAUSPIELERIN (1919)
MY WILD IRISH ROSE (1947) d D Butler chor Prinz w G O'Brien 101min WB
My Younger Brother = MOI MLADSHII BRAT (1962)
MY ZA MIR (1951) d Ivens, Ivan Pyriev *2700m Defa (= *Freundschaft siegt*)
MY ZHDOM VAS S POBEDOI (1941) co-d Ilya Trauberg co-d/s A Medvedkin 975m (= *We Expect Victory There*)

NAAEDE FAERGEN, DE (1948) co-d/s Dreyer co-d Jorgen Roos 12min (= *They Caught the Ferry*)
NACERADEC, KRAL KIBICU (1913) d/co-s Machaty
Nacht des Gravens, Eine (1930) Alternative Title of *Die Zwolfte Stunde* (1930) sound version of NOSFERATU, EINE SYMPHONIE DES GRAVENS (1922)

NACHT FIEL UBER GOTENHATEN (1960) d Wisbar 102min
NACHT IN VENEDIG, EINE (1933) d Gallone m Johan Strauss (= *Una Notte a Venezia*)
NACHMITTAG ZU DEN WETTRENNEN (1929) d Richter
NACHT OHNE PAUSE, DIE (1931) d Morton, Fritz Wenzler 2379m
NACHTS, WENN DERTEUFFEL KAM (1957) d/p Siodmak 104min (= *The Devil Strikes At Night*)
NADARE (1937) d/s Naruse (= *Avalanche*)
NADARE (1952) d/s Shindo (= *Avalanche*)
NADEZHDA (1955) d/s Gerasimov 1353m
NADJA A PARIS (1964) d/p/e Rohmer 16mm 13min
NAD NIEMNEM (1939) d Jakabowska, Karol Szolowski (= *On the Banks of the Niemen*)
NAD RANEM (1928) d A Ford sh
NAGARERU (1956) d Naruse w Yamada (= *Flowing*)
NAGAYA SHINSHI-ROKU (1947) d/co-s Ozu Sho (= *Record of a Tenement Gentleman*)
NAG IN THE BAG, A (1938) d/w C Chase 2rs Col
NAGRODZONE UCZUCTE (1957) d/s Borowczyk, Lenica anim* 10min (= *Love Rewarded*)
NAGURARETA KOCHIYAMA (1934) d/s Kinugasa
NAIF AUX QUARANTE ENFANTS, LE (1957) d/co-s Agostini 98min
Nail in the Boot = GVOZD V SAPOGE (1932)
NAINA PAIVINA (1955) d J Donner sh
NAIN ET GEANT (1902) d Méliès 20m
NAIS (1946) d Raymond Lebourier s Pagnol fst (*Nais Micoulin*) Emile Zola w Fernandel 127min
NAISENKUVIA (1970) d/s/co-t/w J Donner *90min co-pc J Donner (= *Portraits of Women*)
NAISSANCE DE LA PHOTO (1965) d Leenhardt
NAISSANCE DES HEURES, LA (1927) d Greville
NAISSANCE DU CINEMA (1946) d Leenhardt 40min
NAKED AND THE DEAD, THE (1958) d Walsh s D and T Sanders fn Mailer c La Shelle m Herrmann w A Ray, Robertson S* 135min RKO
Naked Autumn (US) = MAUVAIS COUPS, LES (1960)
NAKED CITY, THE (1948) d Dassin p Hellinger c Daniels co-m Rozsa 96min r U
NAKED DAWN, THE (1955) d Ulmer w A Kennedy *81min r U
NAKED EARTH, THE (1958) d V Sherman S 96min Fox
NAKED EDGE, THE (1961) d Michael Anderson ex-p Brando w G Cooper, Kerr 99min r UA
Naked Face of Night, The = YORU NO SUGAO (1958)
Naked Heart, The (UK) = MARIA CHAPDELAINE (1934)
NAKED HEART, THE (1949) d/s M Allégret di Vadim c Thirard w Morgan, Rosay 96min (= *Maria Chapdelaine*)
NAKED JUNGLE, THE (1954) d Haskin p Pal s Yordan, Macdougall c Laszlo co-a Pereira m Amfitheatrof w Heston, Parker *95min Par
NAKED KISS, THE (1963) d/co-p/s Fuller c Cortez co-a Lourie 92min Allied
Naked Light, The (US) = GYCKLARNAS AFTON (1953)
NAKED MAJA, THE (1959) d Koster c Rotunno w Gardner TR* 111min r UA (= *La Maja Desnuda*)
NAKED PARADISE (1956) d/p Corman c F Crosby *62min pc Corman (= *Thunder Over Hawaii*)
NAKED PREY, THE (1966) d/p/w Wilde PV* 94min Par
NAKED RUNNER, THE (1967) d Furie w Sinatra *102min WB
NAKED SPUR, THE (1953) d A Mann c Mellor co-a Gibbons m Kaper w J Stewart, J Leigh, Ryan, Meeker *91min MGM
Naked Youth, a Story of Cruelty = SEISHUN ZANKOKU MONOGATARI (1960)
NAKODO NO YUME (1928) d Ozu (= *Dreams of Youth*)
NA KOMETE (1970) d/s Zeman fn Jules Verne *85min
NA KRASNOM FRONTYE (1920) d/s/e/w Kuleshov 700m (= *On The Red Front*)
NA LINII OGNYA-OPERATORY KINOKHRONIKI (1941) d/s/e Vertov, Elisabeth Svilova (= *On the Line of Fire – Film Reporters*)
NAME THE MAN (1924) d Sjöström fn (*The Master of Man*) Hall Caine pc Goldwyn
NAMU, THE KILLER WHALE (1965) d/p Benedek *89min UA
NANA (1926) d/p J Renoir fn Zola co-c Bachelet dec Autant-Lara w Krauss
NANA (1934) d Dorothy Arzner p Goldwyn fn Zola c Toland m A Newman w Sten 89min r UA
NANA (1955) d/co-s Christian-Jacque co-s Jeanson c Matras m Van Parys w Carol, Boyer *120min
NANCY GOES TO RIO (1950) d Leonard p Pasternak co-a Gibbons w J Powell, C Miranda, Sothern 99min MGM
NANCY STEELE IS MISSING (1937) d G Marshall p Johnson w J McLaglen, Lorre, Carradine, Darwell 7819ft Fox
Naniwa Elegy = NANIWA EREJI (1936)
NANIWA EREJI (1936) d/co-s Mizoguchi w Yamada Dai (= *Naniwa Hika/Naniwa Elegy*)
Naniwa Hika = NANIWA EREJI (1936)
NANIWA ONNA (1940) d/co-s Mizoguchi Sho (= *Woman of Osaka*)

NANNY, THE (1965) d Holt m Rodney Bennett w B Davis 93min r WB
NANOOK OF THE NORTH (1922) d/s/c/co-t Flaherty 70min r Pat
NANTO NO HARU (1925) d/s Gosho (= *Spring In Southern Islands*)
NAPLES AU BAISER DE FEU (1937) d Genina co-s/di Jeanson w Romance, M Simon, Dalio 81min
NAPLES IS A BATTLEFIELD (1944–46) d Clayton 15min
NAPOLEON (1955) d/s Guitry technical adviser Lourié m Jean Françaix w Guitry, Brasseur, Darrieux, Gabin, Gélin, Marais, Montand, Morgan, Presle, Reggiani, Rossi-Drago, Maria Schell, Von Stroheim, Welles *182min
NAPOLEON AUF ST HELENA (1929) d Lupu-Pick s Gance w Krauss
NAPOLEON BONAPARTE (1934) sound version Napoleon Vu Par Abel Gance (1926)
NAPOLEON'S BARBER (1928) d J Ford 32min Fox
NAPOLEON VU PAR ABEL GANCE (1926) d/s/e/w Gance co-c Burel m Honegger w Artaud, Annabella 11400ft
NAPOLETANI A MILANO (1953) d/co-s/w De Filippo 105min
Napoli '43 ep in AMORI DI MEZZO DECOLO (1954)
NAPOLI MILIONARIA (1950) d/co-p/co-s/fpl/w De Filippo w Toto co-pc De Laurentiis 98min
NAPPALI SOTETSEG (1963) d/s/dec Fabri S 100min (= *Darkness in Daytime*)
NARA LIVET (1958) d/co-s Ingmar Bergman w Dahlbeck, Thulin, B Andersson von Sydow 83min (= *Brink of Life/So Close to Life*)
NARAYAMA BUSHI-KÔ (1958) d Kinoshita S* 98min Sho (= *The Ballad of the Narayama*)
NAR KARLEKEN DODAR (1912) d/co-s/fst Stiller w Sjöström 842m
NAR KARLEKEN KOM TILL BYN (1950) d/s Mattsson w Thulin 3020m (= *When Love Comes to the Village*)
NAR KONSTNARER ALSKA (1915) d Stiller 1015m (= *Mme Thora Fleming*)
NAR LARMKLOCKZN LJUDER (1912) d Stiller
NAR MAN KUN ER UNG (1943) d B Henning Jensen co-s A and B Henning Jensen
NAR MORKRET FALLER (1960) d Mattsson 113min (= *When Darkness Falls*)
NARROW MARGIN, THE (1952) d R Fleischer 70min RKO
NARROW TRAIL, THE (1917) d/p/pc/st/w W Hart c August 7rs
NARROW VALLEY (1921) d/p Hepworth 5000ft
NAR SVARMOR REGERAR ELLER SA TUKTASAKTA MAN (1914) d/s/w Stiller 405m
NARUTO HICHO (1957) d/s Kinugasa (= *A Fantastic Tale of Naruto*)
NASANU NAKA (1932) d Naruse (= *Stepchild*)
Nasreddin in Bukhard = NASREDDIN U BUKHARYE (1943)
NASE KARKULKA (1960) d/s Brdecka (= *Our Little Red Hiding Hood*)
NASHESTVIE (1945) d Room 2745m (= *The Invasion*)
NASHI CHEMPIONY (1950) d Donskoi (= *Sportivnaya Slava/Sporting Fame/Our Champions*)
NASHORNER, DIE (1963) d Lenica fst Ionesco anim* 11min (= *The Rhinoceros*)
NASILJE NA TRGU (1961) d Leonardo Bercorici w B Crawford, B Andersson, Björk 120min (= *Square of Violence*)
NASREDDIN U BUKHARYE (1943) d Protazanov 2399m (= *Nasreddin in Bukhara*)
NASSER ASPHALT (1958) d Wisbar 2423m
NA START (1935) d Jakabowska, Eugeniesz Cekalski sh
NASTUP (1952) d/co-s Vavia * (= *Fall In!*)
NA SVOJI ZEMLJI (1948) d Stiglic (= *On His Own Ground*)
NATA DI MARZO (1957) d/co-s/st Pietrangeli p Ponti m Piccioni w Ferzetti*
Nation, La = TARIS (1931)
Natation, Par Jean Taris, Champion de Taris, La = TARIS (1931)
NATHALIE, AGENT SECRET (1959) d Decoin di Jeanson m Van Parys w Carol 95min
NATIONAL AQUARIUM PRESENTATION (1967) d/s Eames c C Eames *10½min
NATIONAL VELVET (1944) d C Brown m Stothart co-a Gibbons w Rooney, E Taylor, Crisp 125min MGM
NATIVE LAND (1942) d/co-st/co-s Hurwitz, Strand e Hurwitz n Paul Robeson 16mm 105min
NATSUKASHIKI FUEYA TAIKO (1967) d Kinoshita S* 115min Toho (= *Eyes, The Sea and a Ball*)
NATSUKASHI NO KAO (1941) d/s Naruse (= *A Dearly Beloved Face*)
NATT, EN (1931) d Molander SF
NATTENS MYSTERIUM (1916) d/s Madsen
NATT EVANDREREN (1916) d/s Madsen
NATTLEK (1965) d/co-s/fn Zetterling w Thulin, Lindstrom 102min San (= *Night Games*)
NATTMARA (1965) d/co-s Mattsson w Jacobsson 88min (= *Nightmare*)
NATTVARDSGASTERNA (1963) d/s Ingmar Bergman c Nykvist as-d Sjoman w Björnstrand, Thulin, Von

Sydow, Lindblom 80min SF (= *Winter Light/The Communicants*)
NATURA E CHIMICA (1919) *d* Olmi S* 17min
NATURE OF THE BEAST, THE (1919) *d/p/c* Hepworth
NAUFRAGATORE, IL (1915) *d/s/w* Ghione
NAUGHTY BABY (1928) *d* LeRoy *c* E Haller part sd 6360ft si 6906ft FN
NAUGHTY BUT NICE (1939) *d* Enright *co-s* Wald *w* Sheridan, D Powell, Reagan, Pitts 90min WB
NAUGHTY FLIRT, THE (1931) *d* Cline *w* M Loy 5125ft WB
NAUGHTY MARIETTA (1935) *d* WS Van Dyke *s* Mahin, Goodrich, Hackett *c* Daniels *m adaptation* Stothart *w* Jeanette Macdonald, Tamiroff 80min MGM
NAUKA BLIZEJ ZYCIA (1951) *d/co-c* Munk 12min
NAUKARI (1954) *d/p* Roy
NAVAJO (1951) *d/s* Foster 70min
NAVE, LA (1911) *fpl* D'Annunzio 525m
NAVE, LA (1920) *co-d/fpl* D'Annunzio *co-d Mario Roncorouis rm* 1911
NAVE BIANCA, LA (1941) *d/co-s* Rossellini *st/co-s/supn* De Robertis 77min
NAVIGATION MARCHANDE (1954) *d/cy* Franju *c* Decaë
NAVIGATOR, THE (1924) *co-d/p* Keaton *co-d* Crisp *co-s* Bruckman *w* Keaton 6rs Metro-Goldwyn
NAVRAT DOMU (1948) *d* Frič (= *Return Home*)
NAVRAT ZTRACENEHO SYNA (1966) *d/st/s* Schorm *w* Menzel 90min (= *The Return of the Prodigal Son*)
NAVY BLU AND GOLD (1937) *d* S Wood *c* J Seitz *a* Gibbons *w* R Young, J Stewart, L Barrymore 10rs MGM
NAVY BLUES (1930) *d* C Brown *co-di* E Nugent 9rs MGM
NAVY BLUES (1941) *d* Bacon *p* Wallis *w* Sheridan 108min WB
NAVY SPY (1937) *co-d* JH Lewis *co-d/s Crane Wilbur* 6rs
NAVY WIFE (1935) *d* Dwan *c* J Seitz, Maté, Trevor, Darwell, 69min Fox (= *Beauty's Daughter*)
NAYAK (1966) *d/s/m* S Ray *c* Mitra 120min Ray (= *The Hero*)
NAYA SANSAR (1941) *s* Abbas
NAZARIN (1958) *d/co-s* Buñuel *production adviser* Velo *c* Figueroa 94min
NAZI AGENT (1942) *d* Dassin *w* Veidt 82min MGM
NAZIS STRIKE, THE (1942) *d* Capra, Litvak *m* Tiomkin *n* W Huston 40min US War Department
NEANDERTHAL MAN, THE (1953) *d* Dupont *c* Cortez 78min UA
NEARER MY GOD TO THEE (1918) *d/p* Hepworth 5rs
NEBBIA A VENEZIA (1938) *d* Sala sh
NEBEL UND SONNE (1916) *d/p/s* May 5rs
NEBRASKAN, THE (1953) *d* Sears 3-D* 68min Col
NECHTE TO NA MNE (1955) *d* Frič *s* Frič, Forman (= *Leave it to me*)
NECK AND NECK (1931) *d* Thorpe *w* Brennan 63min
NEDERLANDSE BEELDHOUWKUNST TIJDENS DE LATE MIDDELEEUWENEN (1951) *d/e* Haanstra 12min (= *Medieval Dutch Sculpture*)
NED KELLY (1970) *d/co-s* T Richardson *103½min
NED MED VAABNENE (1914 *r* 1916) *d* Madsen *s* Dreyer
NEGRO BLANC, LE (1911) *co-d/co-s/w* Gance 545ft Pat
NEGRO SOLDIER, THE (1944) *d* Heisler 40min
NEGYEN AZ ARBAN (1961) *d* Révész 54min (= *Four Children in the Flood/Danger on the Danube*)
NEHRU (1962) *d* R Leacock, *Gregory Shuker c* R Leacock 60min (= *The Living Camera*)
NEIGE A FONDU SUR LA MANICOUA GAN, LA (1965) *d/s/di/e* Lamothe 58min
NEIGE ETAIT SALE, LE (1953) *d* Saslavsky
NEIGHBORHOOD HOUSE (1936) *d* C Chase (*as* Parrott), *Harold Law p* Roach *w* C Chase 2rs MGM
NEIGHBORS (1921) *d/s* Keaton, Cline *w* Keaton 2rs Metro
NEIGHBOURS (1952) *d* McLaren *c* Koenig 16mm *8min NFBC
Neighbour's Wife and Mine, The = MADAMU TO NYOBU (1931)
NEIN, NEIN, NANETTE (1930) *d* Madsen
NEJLEPSI ZENSKA MEHO ZIVOTTE (1967) *d* Frič (= *The Best Girl in my Life*)
NE KERDEZD KI VOLTAM (1941) *d* Balasz
NE KOFUN SHICHA IYAYO (1931) *d* Naruse (= *Now Don't Get Excited*)
NEL GORGO (1918) *d/s/w* Ghione
NEL GORGO DE PECCATO (1952) *d* Cottafavi 2470m
NELLA CITTA L'INFERNO (1959) *d/co-s* Castellani *co-s* Cecchi d'Amico *w* Magnani, Masina, Sordi 110min (= *Caged*)
NELL DALE'S MEN FOLKS (1916) *d/w* Borzage Tri
NEL GWYN (1926) *d* H Wilcox *w* D Gish 7760ft
NELL GWYN (1934) *d* H Wilcox *rm* 1926 *c* F Young *w* Neagle 85min
NELL'S YELLS (1939) *d* Iwerks anim* 1rl *r* Col
NEL MEZZOGIORNO QUALCOSA E CAMBIATO (1950) *d* Lizzani sh
NEL SEGNO DI ROMA (1958) *d Guido Brignone,* Freda (2nd), Antonioni(*uc*) *w* Ekberg *100min (= *La Regina del Deserto*)
NELSON (1918) *d/p* Elvey 7rs
Nelson Touch, The = CORVETTE K-225 (1943)
NEM (1965) *d* Révész 76min (= *No*)
NEMA BARIKADA (1949) *d/co-s* Vavra (= *The Silent Barricade*)
N'EMBARASSEZ PAS VOTRE BONNE (1914) *d/s* Linder Pat
NEMESIS (1921) *d* Gallone *w Soava Gallone* 6500ft
NEMURERU BIJO (1968) *d* Yoshimura *s* Shindo S 95min (= *The House of the Sleeping Virgins*)
NENE (1923) *d* De Baroncelli
NENI STALE ZAMRACENO (1950) *d/c* Jasny, *Karel Kachyna co-s* Jasny (= *The Clouds will Roll Away*)
NE NOUS FACHONS PAS (1965) *d* Lautner *w* Darc 100min
NEOBYCHAINYE PRIKLUCHENIYA MISTERA VESTA V STRANYE BOLSHEVIKOV (1924) *d/co-s/e* Kuleshov *co-s/dec/w* Pudovkin *w* Barnet 2680m (= *The Extraordinary Adventures of Mr West in the Land of the Bolsheviks*)
NEOKONCHENNAYA POVEST (1955) *d* Ermler *w* Bondarchuk 2712m (= *Unfinished Story*)
NEOTPRAVLENNOE PISMO (1960) *d* Kulatazov 88min (= *The Letter that was not Sent*)
NE PLACI PETRE (1964) *d* Stiglic (= *Don't Cry, Peter*)
NEPOBEDIMYE (1943) *d* Gerasimov, Kalatozov *co-s* Kalatozov *w* Cherkasov 2594m (= *The Invincibles*)
NEPOKORENNIYE (1945) *d/co-s* Donskoi 2590m (= *Semia Tarassa/Unconquered*)
NEPTUNE'S DAUGHTER (1914) *d* Brenon
NEPTUNE'S DAUGHTER (1949) *d Edward Buzzell gagman* Keaton(*uc*) *co-a* Gibbons *w* Esther Williams, Montalban *93min MGM
NERONE (1930) *d/co-e* Blasetti
NERO SU BIANCO (1969) *d* Brass *89min (= *Black on White*)
Nero's Weekend = MIO FIGLIO NERONE (1956)
NE SOI PAS JALOUSE (1932) *d/co-s/st* Genina
NESSUNO TORNA INDIETRO (1944) *d/co-s* Blasetti *w* Cortese, De Sica AA
NEST, THE (1943, *ur*) *d/s/c/e* Anger *w* Derek 20min
NESTASNI ROBOT (1956) *d* Vukotic anim (= *The Playful Robot*)
NESTERKA (1955) *d* Zarkhi 2595m
NET, THE (1952) *d* Asquith 86m in Bl (= *Project M7*)
NE TIREZ PAS DOLLY! (1937) *d* Delannoy
NETSUDEI-CHI (1950) *d/co-s* Ichikawa Toho (= *The Hot Marshland*)
Nettezza Urbana = N U (1948)
NEUES LEBEN (1930) *d/s* Richter 2rs
NEULOVIMYI YAN (1943) *d* Petrov, *I Annenskii* 1630m (= *The Elusive Fan*)
NEVADAN, THE (1950) *d* G Douglas *p* H Brown *c* Lawton *w* Malone, R Scott 81min Col (= *Man from Navada*)
NEVADA SMITH (1966) *d/p* Hathaway *ex-p* Levine *st/s* J Hayes *c* Ballard *co-a* Pereira *m* A Newman *w* McQueen, Malden, A Kennedy, Vallone, Keith, Pleshette PV* 128min *pc* McQueen *r* Par
NEVER A DULL MOMENT (1950) *d* G Marshall *c* J Walker *w* I Dunne, MacMurray, N Wood 89min RKO
NEVER FEAR (1950) *d/p/co-s* Lupino *c* Stout 81min EL
NEVER GIVE A SUCKER AN EVEN BREAK (1941) *d* Cline *s* Fields (*ps* Otis Criblecoblis) *w* Fields, Dumont 71min U
NEVER LET GO (1960) *d/co-st* Guillermin *c* Challis *m* Barry *w* Sellers 91min JAR
NEVER LET ME GO (1953) *d* Daves *p* C Brown *c* Krasker *w* Gable, Tierney 94min MGM
NEVER LOVE A STRANGER (1958) *d Robert Stevens c* Garmes *w* J Barrymore, McQueen 91min AA
Never On Sunday = POTE TIU KYRIAKI
NEVER PUT IT IN WRITING (1963) *d/s* Stone *e Virginia Stone* 93min *pc* A and V Stone AA
NEVER SAY DIE (1939) *d* E Nugent *co-s* P Sturges *co-a* Dreier *chor* Prinz *w* Hope 80min Par
NEVER SAY GOODBY (1956) *d J Hopper,* Sirk (*uc*) *w* Hudson, Sanders *96min
NEVER SO FEW (1959) *d* J Sturges *c* Daniels *m* Friedhofer *w* Sinatra, Lollobrigida, Lawford, McQueen, Henreid CS* 124min MGM
NEVER STEAL ANYTHING SMALL (1958) *d* Lederer *p* A Rosenberg *fpl* (*The Devil's Hornpipe*) Maxwell Anderson, Mamoulian *lyr* Maxwell Anderson *e* Lipstein *co-a* Golitzen *w* Cagney, S Jones CS* 94min U
NEVER THE TWAIN SHALL MEET (1931) *d* WS Van Dyke *w* L Howard 79min MGM
NEVER TOO LATE (1965) *d* Yorkin *c* Lathrop *w* O'Sullivan, Nolan PV* 105min WB
NEVER WAVE AT A WAC (1953) *d* McLeod *m* Bernstein *w* J Russell, P Douglas 87min *r* RKO (= *The Private Wore Skirts/The Newest Profession*)
NEVER WEAKEN (1921) *d* Newmeyer *p/co-st* Roach *w* H Lloyd 3rs
NEVINOST BEZ ZASTITE (1968) *d/s/dec* Makavejev *78min (= *Innocence Unprotected*)
NEW ADVENTURES OF GET RICH QUICK WALLINGFORD (1931) *d* S Wood *s/di* MacArthur 96min MGM
New Adventures of Schweik = NOVYE POKHOZHDENIYA SHVEIKA (1943)
New Angels, The = NUOVI ANGELI, I (1961)
New Babylon, The = NOVYI VAVILON (1929)
NEW COOK, THE (1911) *d/s/w* Ince
New Earth = NIEUWE GRONDEN (1934)
Newest Profession, The = NEVER WAVE AT A WAC (= *The Private Wore Skirts*)
NEW EXPLOITS OF ELAINE, THE (1915) *d* Louis Gasnier, Donald Mackenzie *w* White serial in 10eps Pat
New Face in Hell = P J (1968)
NEW FACES (1954) *d* Horner *c* Ballard CS* Fox
NEW FACES OF 1937 (1937) *d Leigh Jason w* Ann Miller 100min RKO
NEW FRONTIERS (1941, *uf*) *d* Ivens
New Grief = NYONIN AISHU (1937)
New Heart, A = SERDTSYE BETSYA VNOV (1956)
New Heroes Will Arise (UK) = VSTANOV NOVI BOJOVNICI (1950)
NEW JANITOR, THE (1914) *d/s/w* Chaplin 1rl Key (= *The Porter/The Blundering Boob*)
NEW KIND OF LOVE, A (1963) *d/p/s* Shavelson *c* Fapp *a* Pereira *w* P Newman, Woodward, Ritter, Chevalier *110min Par
New Kind of Woman, A = SHIN JOSEIKAN (1928)
NEW KLONDIKE, THE (1926) *d* Milestone *fst Ring Lardner* 7221ft FPL
NEW LOT, THE (1943) *d* C Reed 44min
NEW MEXICO (1951) *d* Reis *w* Ayres, Burr *76min *r* UA
NEW MOON (1930) *d* Conway *w* Menjou 78min MGM
NEW MOON (1940) *d/p* Leonard *co-s Hammerstein a* Gibbons *w* Jeanette Macdonald 105min MGM
NEW NEIGHBOR, THE (1912) *d* Sennett *w* Normand ½rl Key
NEW ORLEANS UNCENSORED (1955) *d* Castle *p* Katzman 76min Col (= *Riot on Pier Six*)
NEW RATES (1934) *d* Cavalcanti
New Road, The = SHINDO (1936)
NEW SCHOOL TEACHER, THE (1923) *d* La Cava 6rs
NEWS FOR THE NAVY (1937–39) *d* McLaren *p* Grierson 10min GPO
New Snow = SHINSETSU (1942)
NEWSPAPER TRAIN (1941) *d* Lye
NEW PARADE, THE (1928) *d/co-st* D Butler 6640ft Fox
New Tales of the Taira Clan = SHIN HEIKE MONOGATARI (1955)
NEW WOMAN, THE (1968) *d* A King 16mm *60min
New Year's Eve on the Plains of Scania = NYARSAFTON PA SKANSKA SLATTEN (1961) (= *New Year's Eve on the Scanian Plains*)
New Year's Eve on the Scanian Plains = NYARSAFTON PA SKANSKA SLATTEN (1961)
New Year's Love = KOTOSHI NO KOI (1962)
NEW YORK BALLADE (1955) *d/c* Reichenbach *cy* Doniol-Valcroze *n* Desailly *18min
NEW YORK CONFIDENTIAL (1955) *d/co-s* Rouse *w* Conte, B Crawford 87min
NEW YORK HAT, THE (1905) *s* Loos
NEW YORK HAT, THE (1912) *d* Griffith *s* Loos *w* Pickford, L Barrymore, D and L Gish, Marsh 1rl Bio
NEW YORK LIGHTBOARD (1961) *d* McLaren *10min NFBC
NEW YORK LIGHT RECORD (1961) *d* McLaren 16mm 10min NFBC
NEW YORK NIGHTS (1929) *d* Milestone *s* Furthman *c* June *w* N Talmadge, Roland (Harlow) 9rs (sd) *r* UA
NEW YORK TOWN (1941) *d* C Vidor *st/co-s* Swerling *co-a* Dreier *w* MacMurray, Preston, Tamiroff 94min Par
NEW YORK UNIVERSITY (1952) *d* W Van Dyke *co-c* R Leacock 20min
NEXT CORNER, THE (1924) *d* S Wood *w* Chaney 7081ft FPL *r* Par
NEXT OF KIN (1942) *d* Dickinson *p* Balcon *w* Hawkins 101min
NEXT TIME I MARRY (1938) *d* Kanin *c* Metty *w* Ball 64min RKO
NEXT TO NO TIME (1958) *d/s* Cornelius *fst* (*The Enchanted Hour*) *Paul Gallico c* F Francis *m* Auric *93min BL
NEXT VOICE YOU HEAR, THE (1950) *d* Wellman *p* Schary *s* Schnee *c* Mellor *m* Raksin *co-a* Gibbons 80min MGM
NEZBEDNY BAKALAR (1946) *d/co-s* Vavra (= *The Mischievous Tutor*)
NEZ DE CUIR (1951) *d/s* Y Allégret *des* Wakhévitch *m* Auric *w* Marais, Girotti 92min Pat
NEZ, LE (1963) *d* Alexeieff anim 11min (= *The Nose*)
NEZ NAM NAROST A KRIDLA (1958) *d/s* Brdecka (= *How Man Learned to Fly*)
NIANCHAN (1959) *d* Imamura S 102min Nik (= *My Second Brother/The Diary of Sueko*)
NIAGRA (1953) *d* Hathaway *p/co-s* Brackett *co-s* Breen *c* Joe Macdonald *co-a* Wheeler *w* Monroe, Cotton, Peters *87min Fox
NIAGRA FALLS (1941) *d* G Douglas *p* Roach *w* Pitts 43min *r* UA
NIBELUNGEN, DIE (1924) Part I SIEGFRIED; Part II KRIEMHILDS RACHE *d/co-s* F Lang *co-s* Von Harbou *co-c* Rittau, Ruttmann (*Der Falkentraum* sequence) *p* Pommer Part I 3216m; Part II 3576m Dec/*Ufa*

NICE GIRL LIKE ME, A (1969) d/co-s D Davis co-c G Taylor *91min
NICHIRIN (1925) d Kinugasa (= The Sun)
NICHOLAS AND ALEXANDRA (1971) d Schaffner p Spiegel c F Young w Olivier, M Redgrave, Jurgens PV* 185min pc Schaffner, Spiegel r Col
NICHOLAS NICKLEBY (1947) d Cavalcanti p Balcon fn Dickens 108min JAR
NICHT VERSOEHNT (1965) or ES HELFT NUR GEWALT, WO GEWALT HERRSCHT d/co-s/co-e Straub 1500m (= Unreconciled)
NICK CARTER (1908) d/s Jasset serial of six eps
NICK CARTER CONTRE PAULIN BROQUET (1911) serial d/s Jasset c Andriot
NICK CARTER, MASTER DETECTIVE (1939) d J Tourneur c Lawton co-a Gibbons w Pidgeon 60min MGM
NICK CARTER VA TOUT CASSER (1964) d Decoin w Constantine 95min
NICKEL HOPPER, THE (1926) st (?) Roach w Normand Pat
NIEDZIELNY PORANIK (1955) d/s Munk *20min (= One Sunday Morning)
NIEMAND WEISS ES (1920) d/co-s-w Lupu-Pick 2280m
NIEUWE GRONDEN (1934) d/s/co-c/e/cy/n Ivens co-c Lotar m Eisler (contains sequences from Borinage) 900m (= New Earth)
NIE WIEDER LIEBE (1930) d Litvak co-dec Rohrig w Ophuls, Lillian Harvey 80min UFA (= Calais-Douvres)
NIEWINNI CZARODZIEJE (1960) d Wajda s Wajda, Skolimowski m Komeda w Cybulski 2480m (= Innocent Sorcerers)
NIGER-JEUNE REPUBLIQUE, LE (1961) d/e Jutra documentation Rouch 58min
Night = YORU (1923)
Night, The = LA NOTTE (1961)
NIGHT AFTER NIGHT (1932) d A Mayo c E Haller w Raft, West 70min Par
Night Ambush = ILL MET BY MOONLIGHT (1957)
NIGHT AND DAY (1946) d Curtiz co-c Marley sp eff Burks additional m M Steiner e Weisbart chor Prinz w C Grant, Malone, A Smith, Wyman 128min WB
Night and Fog in Japan = NIHON NO YORU TO KIRI (1960)
NIGHT AND THE CITY (1950) d Dassin w Widmark, Tierney 95min Fox
NIGHT ANGEL, THE (1931) d/s Goulding w March 86min Par
NIGHT AT THE OPERA, A (1935) d S Wood p Thalberg co-st/co-s G Kaufman co-a Gibbons m Stothart w H, G and C Marx, Dumont 90min MGM
NIGHT BEAT (1931) d G Seitz c Cronjager 61min
Night Beauties (UK) = BELLES-DE-NUIT, LES (1952)
NIGHT BEFORE, THE (1921) d St Clair 2rs Fox
NIGHT BEFORE CHRISTMAS, THE (1905) d Porter 17ft Ed (= Hanging Stockings on a Christmas Tree)
NIGHT BEFORE THE DIVORCE, THE (1942) d Siodmak c Marley 67min Fox
NIGHT BIRD, THE (1928) d Newmayer 6702ft (si) U
Night Butterflies = YORU NO CHO (1957)
NIGHTCATS (1956) d Brakhage 16mm * si 8min
NIGHT CLUB, THE (1925) d Frank Urson, Paul Iribe c Marley co-fpl (After Five) De Mille w Beery, Fazenda 5732ft FPL
NIGHT CLUB (1928) d Florey
NIGHT CLUB GIRL (1944) d Cline 61min U
NIGHT COURT (1932) d WS Van Dyke fco-pl Hellinger c Brodine w W Huston, Hersholt 90min MGM
Night Drum = YORU NO TSUZUMI (1958)
NIGHTFALL (1958) d J Tourneur s Silliphant fn (The Dark Chase) David Goodis c Guffey m Duning w A Bancroft, A Ray, Keith 78min r Col
Night Fighter, The (US) = TERRIBLE BEAUTY, A (1960)
NIGHT FLIGHT (1933) d C Brown ex-p Selznick fn (Vol de Nuit) Antoine de Saint-Exupéry m Stothart w J & L Barrymore, Gable, H Hayes, M Loy, Montgomery 84min MGM
NIGHT FLYER, THE (1928) d W Lang 5954ft pc Cruze r Pat
Night Games = NATTLEK (1965)
NIGHT HAS A THOUSAND EYES, THE (1948) d J Farrow c Seitz co-a Dreier m V Young w Robinson, Roman 80min Par
NIGHT HAS EYES, THE (1942) d L Arliss w Mason 79min
Night Heat (UK) = NOTTE BRAVA, LA (1959)
NIGHT HOLDS TERROR, THE (1955) d/p/s Stone e Virginia Stone w Cassavetes 86min MGM
NIGHT IN CASABLANCA, A (1946) d A Mayo w H, G, & C Marx, Roman 85min UA
NIGHTINGALE, THE (1914) d Augustus Thomas w E Barrymore
Nightingale, Little Nightingale = GRUNYA KORNAKOVA (1936)
Night in Havana = BIG BOODLE, THE (1957)
NIGHT IN LONDON, A (1927) d Lupu-Pick dec Warm w Lillian Harvey 2371m (= Eine Nacht in London)
Night in September, A = NOCH V SENTYABRE (1939)
NIGHT IN THE SHOW, A (1915) d/s/w Chaplin c Totheroh w Purviance 2rs S & A (= Charlie at the Show)

Night is My Future = MUSIK I MORKER (1947)
Night is the Phantom (UK) = FRUSTA E IL CORPO, LA (1963)
NIGHT LIFE OF NEW YORK (1925) d/p Dwan w D Gish 6998ft FPL
NIGHT LIFE OF THE GODS (1935) d L Herman fn Thorne Smith 73min U
NIGHT MAIL (1936) d B Wright, Watt p Grierson m Benjamin Britten cy W H Auden
NIGHTMARE (1963) d F Francis 82min Jar
Nightmare = NATTMARA (1966)
NIGHTMARE ALLEY (1947) d Goulding p Jessel s Furthman c Garmes co-a Wheeler m Mockridge w Power, Blondell 111min Fox
NIGHT MUST FALL (1937) d Thorpe fpl Emlyn Williams c June a Gibbons w Montgomery, R Russell MGM
NIGHT MUST FALL (1964) d/co-p Reisz co-p/w Finney fpl Emlyn Williams c F Francis 105min MGM
NIGHT N' GALES (1937) d G Douglas p Roach 1rl MGM
NIGHT NURSE (1931) d Wellman w Stanwyck, Blondell, Gable 72min WB
NIGHT OF ADVENTURE, A (1944) d G Douglas 65min RKO
Night of Fame, A (UK) = AL DIAVOLO CON CELEBRITA (1948)
NIGHT OF LOVE, THE (1927) d George Fitzmaurice co-c Barnes w Colman, Banky 7600ft pc Goldwyn r UA
NIGHT OF MYSTERY, A (1936) d Dupont 65min Par
NIGHT OF NIGHTS, THE (1939) d Milestone s D Stewart 86min Par
Night of Remembrance, A = PAMIATKA Z CELULOZY (1954)
Night of Revenge, The = HAEVNENS NAT (1915)
NIGHT OF THE BIG HEAT (1967) d Fisher *94min
NIGHT OF THE DEMON (1957) d J Tourneur co-s Charles Bennett, Endfield (uc) a Adam e M Gordon w D Andrews 83min r Col (= Curse of the Demon)
NIGHT OF THE FOLLOWING DAY (1968) d/co-s Cornfield w Brando *93min U
NIGHT OF THE GENERALS, THE (1967) d Litvak p Spiegel co-s Joseph Kessel fn Hans Helmut Kirst c Decaë co-a Trauner m Jarre w Sharif, O'Toole, Noiret, Plummer, Courtenay, Greco PV* 148min Col
NIGHT OF THE GRIZZLY, THE (1966) d Pevney c Lipstein, Griggs co-a Pereira m Leith Stevens 102min Par
NIGHT OF THE HUNTER, THE (1955) d Laughton 2nd d D Sanders s Agee c Cortez w Mitchum, Winters, L Gish 93min r UA
NIGHT OF THE IGUANA (1964) d/co-p/co-s J Huston co-p Stark c Figueroa fpl T Williams w Burton, Gardner, Kerr 118min r MGM
NIGHT OF THE PARTY, THE (1933) d M Powell 61min
Night on Bare Mountain, A = NUIT SUR LE MONT CHAUVE, UNE (1933)
Night or Day = YO VAI PAIVA (1962)
NIGHT OUT, A (1915) d/s/w Chaplin c Totheroh w Turpin, Purviance 2rs S & A
NIGHT OWLS (1930) d James Parrott p Roach st McCarey w Laurel, Hardy 2rs (sd) r MGM
NIGHT PARADE (1929) d St Clair co-fpl G Abbott 8rs RKO
NIGHT PASSAGE (1957) d Neilson, A Mann (uc) p A Rosenberg s B Chase c Daniels m Tiomkin w J Stewart, A Murphy, Duryea 90min TR* U
NIGHT PEOPLE (1954) d/p/s N Johnson as-p G Oswald c C Clarke m Mockridge w Peck, B Crawford, Björk CS* 93min Fox
Night River = YORU NO KAWA (1956)
Nightshade Flower = YE-RAI-SHANG (1951)
Nights of Cabiria = NOTTI DI CABIRIA, LE (1956)
NIGHT SONG (1947) d Cromwell c Ballard w Oberon, E Barrymore, D Andrews, Carmichael 101min RKO
NIGHT THE WORLD EXPLODED, THE (1957) d Sears p Katzman 64min Col
NIGHT TO REMEMBER, A (1958) d R Baker c Unsworth 123min JAR
Night to Remember, A = SONO YO WA WASURENAI (1962)
Night Train = POLIAG (1959)
NIGHT TRAIN TO MUNICH (1940) d C Reed s Gilliat, Launder w Lockwood, Harrison, Henreid 95min
NIGHT UNTO NIGHT (1947) d D Siegel c Marley m Waxman w Reagan, Lindfors, B Crawford 92min WB
NIGHT VISITOR, THE (1971) d Benedek m Mancini w Von Sydow, T Howard, Ullman *102min
NIGHT WALKER, THE (1964) d/p Castle w Stanwyck, R Taylor 86min U
NIGHT WAS OUR FRIEND (1952) d Michael Anderson 61min
NIGHT WATCH, THE (1928) d A Korda s Biro c Struss w Lukas 6676ft FN
NIGHT WATCHMAN, THE (1938) d C Jones p L Schlesinger anim* 7min
NIGHT WITHOUT SLEEP (1952) d R Baker m A Newman w Darnell, Neff 77min Fox
NIGORIE (1953) d Imai fs Ichiyo Higuchi (= Muddy Waters/Troubled Waters)
NIHIKI-NO SAMA (1959) d Kuri anim (= Two Sauries)

NIHON-BASHI (1929) d/s Mizoguchi Nik (= The Nihon Bridge)
NIHONBASHI (1956) d Ichikawa * Dai (= Bridge of Japan)
Nihon Bridge, The = NIHON BASHI (1929)
NIHON NO HIGEKI (1953) d Kinoshita (= A Japanese Tragedy)
NIHON NO YORU TO KIRI (1960) d/co-s Oshima *107min Sho (= Night and Fog in Japan)
NIHON SHUNKA-KO (1967) d/pc/co-s Oshima *103min Sho (= A Treatise on Japanese Bawdy Song)
NIISAN NO BAKA (1932) d Gosho (= My Stupid Brother)
NIJU-SAI ZENGO (1950) d Yoshimura (= About Twenty Years Old)
NIJUSHI NO HITOMI (1954) d/s Kinoshita 110min Sho (= Twenty Four Eyes)
NIKAI NO HIMEI (1931) d/s Naruse
NIKOLAI STAVROGIN (1915) d/co-s Protazanov fn (The Possessed) Fydor Dostoevski w Mozhukhin 2200m
NIKUTAIBI (1928) d Ozu Sho (= Beautiful Body)
NI LIV (1957) d/s Skonen 97min (= Nine Lives/We Die Alone)
NI LJUGER (1970) d/s Sjöman 107min (= You're Lying)
NILSSON (1951) d Halldoff 14min
Nina B Affair, The = AFFAIRE NINA B, L' (1961)
NINA DE LUTO, LA (1963) d Summers *84min (= The Girl in Mourning)
Ni Nagot Att Fortulla = AKTENSKAPSBYRAN (1912)
Nine Days of One Year = DEVYAT DNI ODNOVO GOPA (1961)
NINE HOURS TO RAMA (1963) d/p Robson m M Arnold cr Bass w Buchholz, J Ferrer CS* 125min Fox
Nine Lives (US) = NI LIV (1957)
NINE LIVES OF ELFEGO BACA, THE (1959) d/s/co-songs Foster *79min pc Disney
NINE MEN (1943) d/s Watt p Balcon as-p/e Crichton 67min r UA
1984 (1956) d Michael Anderson fn George Orwell m M Arnold w M Redgrave, E O'Brien 90min ABC
Nineteenth Spring, The = JUKU NO HARU (1933)
90 DEGREES SOUTH (1930) s/c/e Ponting 1st version: THE GREAT WHITE SILENCE (1911)
Ninety in the Shade (UK) = TRICETJEDNA VE STINU (1964)
99 RIVER STREET (1953) d Karlson c Planer w Payne 83min r UA
NINGEN (1925) d Mizoguchi Nik (= Man)
NINGEN (1962) d/s Shindo 120min (= The Man)
NINGEN DOBUTSUEN (1961) d Kuri anim (= Human Zoo/Clap Vocalism)
NINGEN JOHATSU (1967) d Imamura 130min Nik (= A Man Vanishes)
NINGEN MOYO (1949) d Ichikawa Toho (= Design of a Human Being)
NINGEN NO JOKEN (1961) d/co-s Kobayashi fn Jumpei Gomikawa w Nakadai S Sho 3 parts (= The Human Condition: Part 1 No Greater Love 208min/Part 2 Road to Eternity 181min/Part 3 A Soldier's Prayer 190min)
NINJA BUGEICHO (1967) d/p/pc/co-s Oshima anim 131min (= Band of Ninja)
NINOS (1961) d Grau
NINOTCHKA (1939) d Lubitsch co-s B Wilder, Brackett c Daniels a Gibbons w Garbo, M Douglas, Lugosi 110min MGM
Ninth Circle, The = DEVETI KRUG (1960)
NIOK (1957) d/s Sechan *29min
NIPPON KONCHUKI (1963) d Imamura S 123min Nik (= The Insect Woman)
NIPPON NO OBOCHAN (1962) d Imai (= Old Women of Japan)
NIPPON NO SEISHUM (1968) d Kobayashi S 130min Toho (= Hymn to a Tired Man/Diary of a Tired Man)
NISHIGINZA EKIMAE (1958) d Imamura (= Lights of Night)
NISHIJIN NO SHIMAI (1952) d Yoshimura c Miyagawa (= The Sisters of Nishijin)
NISHIZUMI SENSHACHO-DEN (1940) d Yoshimura 123min Sho (= The Story of the Tank-Commander Nishizumi)
NITCHEVO (1925) d De Baroncelli w Vanel
NITCHEVO (1937) d De Baroncelli rm 1925 90min
NITWITS, THE (1935) d G Stevens c Cronjager w Grable 81min RKO
NIWA NO KOTORI (1922) d/s Kinugasa (= Two Little Birds)
NIWATORI WA FUTATABI NAKU (1954) d Gosho (= The Cock Crows Twice)
NJU (1924) d/s Czinner w Bergner, Jannings, Veidt 2227m
No = NEM (1965)
NAOH'S ARK (1929) d Curtiz st Zanuck co-c Mohr w M Loy, G O'Brien, Fazenda WB
NOB HILL (1945) d Hathaway c Cronjager co-a L Wheeler w Raft, J Bennett 95min Fox
NOBI (1959) d Ichikawa S 108min Dai (= Fires on the Plain)
NO BLADE OF GRASS (1970) d/p Wilde PV* 96min MGM
NOBODY LIVES FOREVER (1946) d Negulesco c Edeson w Brennan, Garfield 100min WB

NOBODY RUNS FOREVER (1968) *d* Thomas *m* Delerue *w* Plummer, Palmer, Tone *101min JAR
NOBODY'S DARLING (1943) *d* A Mann 71min Rep
NOBODY'S WIDOW (192?) *d* Crisp *c* AC Miller 6421ft Pat
NOBODY WAVED GOODBYE (1964) *d/s* Owen *co-p* Kroitor 80min NFBC
No Breaks = OH YEAH! (1929)
NOCES DE SABLE, LES (1948) *d/st André Zwobada s/cy/wv* Cocteau 50min (= *Daughter of the Sands*)
NOCES VENITIENNES, LES (1958) *d* Cavalcanti *w* De Sica S* 93min
NOCHE DE VERANO (1962) *d/co-s/st* Grau 90min
NOCH MINDERJAHRIG (1957) *d/co-s* Tressler 95min (= *Unter Achzehn*)
NOCH V SENTYABRE (1939) *d/w* Barnet 2916m (= *A Night in September*)
No Clouds in the Sky = SORA WA HARETARI (1925)
NOCTURNE (1954) *d* Alexeieff, *Georges Violet m* Chopin anim
NOCTURNE, LE (1919) *d/s* Feuillade 1230m
NOCTURNO (1934) *d* Machaty
NO DEFENCE (1929) *d* Bacon 5728ft WB
NODLANDING (1952) *d* Skouen (= *Bad Luck*)
NO DOWN PAYMENT (1957) *d* Ritt *p* Wald *s* Yordan *c* La Shelle *co-a* Wheeler *m* Harling *w* Woodward, J Hunter, Randall, Rush CS 105min Fox
NO ESCAPE (1953) *d/s* Charles Bennett *w* Ayres 76min UA
No Fight Without Money = MUSEN FUSEN (1925)
NOGENT, ELDORADO DU DIMANCHE (1929) *d/s* Carné, *Michel Sanvoisin* 600m
NOGIKU NO GOTOKI KIMI NARIKI (1955) *d/s* Kinoshita 100min Sho (= *My First Love Affair/She Was Like a Wild Chrysanthemum/She Was Like a Daisy*)
NOGI SHOGUN TO KUMA SAN (1926) *d* Mizoguchi Nik
NO GREATER GLORY (1934) *d* Borzage *s* Swerling *fn* (*The Paul Street Boys*) *Terence Molnar c* August 2108m Col
No Greater Love = NINGEN NO JOKEN (1957) Part I
No Highway (UK) = NO HIGHWAY IN THE SKY (1951)
NO HIGHWAY IN THE SKY (1951) *d* Koster *fn* (*No Highway*) *Nevil Shute w* Dietrich, J Stewart, Hawkins 98min Fox (= *No Highway*)
NOIA, LA (1963) *d/co-s* Damiani *p* Ponti *fn Albert Moravia w* B Davis, Catherine Spaak, Buchholz, I Miranda 118min (= *The Empty Canvas*)
NOISE FROM THE DEEP, A (1913) *d* Sennett *w* Normand, Arbuckle 1rl Key
NOI VIVI (1942) *d Goffredo Alessandrini w* Valli
NO LIMIT (1931) *d* Tuttle *c* Milner *w* Bow, Foster 73min Par
NO LOVE FOR JOHNNIE (1961) *d* Thomas *m* Arnold *w* Finch CS 111min JAR
NO MAN OF HER OWN (1950) *d* Leisen *c* Fapp *co-a* Dreier *m* Friedhofer *w* Stanwyck 98min Par
NO MINOR VICES (1948) *d/p* Milestone *c* Barnes *e* Parrish *m* Waxman *w* D Andrews, Palmer 96min MGM
NO MORE LADIES (1935) *d Edward H Griffith p* Thalberg *co-s* D Stewart *w* Montgomery, J Crawford, C Ruggles, Tone, Oliver 81min MGM
NO MORE ORCHIDS (1932) *d* W Lang *c* August *w* Lombard 71min Col
NO MOTHER TO GUIDE HIM (1919) *d* St Clair *Erle C Kenton s* Sennett *w* Turpin 2rs *pc* Sennett
NO MY DARLING DAUGHTER (1961) *d* Thomas *w* M Redgrave 96min JAR
NO NAME ON THE BULLET (1959) *d/co-p* J Arnold *c* Lipstein *w* A Murphy CS* 77min U
NON CANTO PIU (1943) *d/co-s* Freda 80min
NON C'E PACE TRA GLI ULIVI (1950) *d/co-st/co-s* De Santis *co-s* Lizzani *w* Vallone, Bosè 99min (= *Blood on Easter Sunday/No Peace Among the Olives*)
Non ci credo! = SUPERSTIZIONE (1948)
NON COUPABLE (1947) *d/ad* Decoin *w* M Simon 90min
Non Credo più all' amore = ANGST, DIE (1954)
NONE BUT THE BRAVE (1965) *d/p* Sinatra *ex-p* H W Koch *as-p* Daniels *c* Lipstein *w* Sinatra 105min WB
NONE BUT THE LONELY HEART (1944) *d/s* Odets *fn Richard Llewellyn c* G Barnes *m* Eisler *w* E Barrymore, Duryea, C Grant 113min RKO
NONE SHALL ESCAPE (1944) *d* De Toth *c* Garmes 85min Col
NON FACCIO LA GUERRA, FACCIO L'AMORE (1966) *d* Rossi *w* Catherine Spaak TS* (= *Don't Make War Make Love*)
NONNA SABELLA, LA (1957) *d/co-s* Risi *co-s* Festa Campanile 90min (= *Oh! Sabella*)
NO, NO NANETTE (1930) *d* Badger *c* Polito *w* Pitts 101min FN
NO, NO NANETTE (1940) *d* H Wilcox *c* Metty *w* Neagle, Mature, Pitts 96min RKO
NON SON GELOSE (1933) *d* Bragaglia
NON SONO SUPERSTIZIOSO, MA . . . (1944) *d* Bragaglia *w* De Sica
NON TI PAGO! (1942) *d* Bragaglia *w* De Filippo
NON UCCIDERE (1961) *d/co-ad* Autant-Lara *s/co-ad* Aurenche *co-ad* Bost *m* Aznavour 125min *r* Col (= *Tu Ne Tueras Point/Thou Shalt Not Kill*)
Noon = POLDEN (1931)
No Orchids For Lulu (UK) = LULU (1962)

NOOSE (1948) *d* Greville
Noose, The = PETLA (1957)
NOOSE HANGS HIGH, THE (1948) *d/p Charles Barton co-st* Taradash *w* B Abbott, Costello 77min EL
NO PARKING (1938) *d Jack Raymond st* C Reed 71min
No Peace Among the Olives = NON C'E PACE TRA GLI ULIVI (1950)
NO PLACE TO GO (1927) *d* LeRoy *c* Folsey *w* Astor 6431ft FN
NORA INU (1949) *d/co-s* Kurosawa *w* Mifune 122min
NO RANSOM (1934) *d* Newmeyer *fn Damon Runyan* 78min
NORA PRENTISS (1947) *d* Sherman *c* Howe *w* Sheridan 111min WB
NORDPOL-AHOI! (1934) *d* Morton 2237m
NO RESTING PLACE (1951) *d/co-s* Rotha 77min
NORIS (1919) *d/st* Genina
NORMETAL (1959) *d Claude Fournier* Groulx (*uc*) *e* Groulx *c* Brault
NO ROAD BACK (1956) *d Montgomery Tully w* Connery 83min
NO ROOM FOR THE GROOM (1952) *d* Sirk *w* Curtis, Laurie 82min U
NORTH BY NORTHWEST (1959) *d/p* Hitchcock *as-p* H Coleman *s* Lehman *c* Burks *co-a* Boyle *cr* Bass *m* Herrmann *w* C Grant, Saint, Mason *136min MGM
NOR THE MOON BY NIGHT (1958) *d* Annakin *92min JAR
NORTHERN PURSUIT (1943) *d* Walsh *c* Hickox *w* Flynn 94min WB
NORTH OF HUDSON BAY (1923) *d* J Ford *st/s* Furthman *w* Mix 4973ft Fox
NORTH OR NORTHWEST (1937) *d* Lye
NORTH SEA (1938) *d* Watt *p* Cavalcanti 33min GPO
NORTH STAR, THE (1943) *d* Milestone *p* Goldwyn *as-p* Menzies *st/s* Hellman *c* Howe *m* Copland *w* A Baxter, D Andrews, W Huston, Brennan, F Granger, Von Stroheim 106min *r* RKO
NORTH TO ALASKA (1960) *d/p* Hathaway *co-s* Mahin, Rackin *c* Shamroy *w* J Wayne, S Granger CS* 122min Fox
NORTH WEST FRONTIER (1959) *d* J Thompson *st* F Nugent *c* Unsworth *w* Bacall CS* 129min JAR (= *Flame over India*)
NORTHWEST MOUNTED POLICE (1940) *d/p* De Mille *co-a* Dreier *co-e* Milner *m* V Young *w* G Cooper, Carroll, Goddard, Preston, G Bancroft, Tamiroff, (Ryan) *125min Par
NORTHWEST OUTPOST (1947) *d/as-p* Dwan *2nd-d* Canutt *e* Keller *m Rudolph Frime* 91min Rep
NORTHWEST PASSAGE (1940) *d* K Vidor *m* Stothart *w* Tracy, R Young, Brennan *126min Vidor *r* MGM
Northwest Passage (1958–59) see FRONTIER RANGER (1959), FURY RIVER (1959), MISSION OF DANGER (1959
NORTHWEST RANGERS (1942) *d* J Newman *a* Gibbons *co-m* Amfitheatrof *w* Carradine 64min MGM
NO SAD SONGS FOR ME (1950) *d* Maté *p* Adler *s* H Koch *c* J Walker *w* Lindfors *w* Carey, N Wood, McIntire, Quine 89min Col
NOS ANCETRES LES EXPLORATEURS (1955) *d* Kast 19min Pat
Nose, The = NEZ, LE (1963)
NOSFERATU, EINE SYMPHONIE DES GRAUENS (1922) *d* Murnau *s* Galeen *fn* (*Dracula*) *Bram Stoker c* F Wagner 70min (1930: sound version released *Die Zwelfts Stunde - Eine Nacht des Grauens*)
No Sleep Till Dawn (UK) = BOMBES B52 (1957)
NO SOMOS DE PIEDRA (1968) *d* Summers *87min (= *We're not Made of Stone*)
NOSOTROS DOS (1954) *d/co-st/co-s* Fernandez 91min
NOSTRA GUERRA, LA (1945) *d* Lattuada *cy/n* Pietrangeli sh
NOSTRI MARITI, I (1966)
ep NEI SECOLI FEDELI *d* Risi
ep IL MARITO DI OLGA *d* Zampa *co-s* Monicelli *fst* (*Heredity*) *Maupassant w* Brialy, Tamiroff
NOSTRI SOGNI, I (1943) *d* Cottafavi *co-s* Zavattini *w* De Sica 84min *r* AA
No Sun in Venice = SAIT-ON JAMAIS? (1951)
NOT A DRUM WAS HEARD (1924) *d* Wellman *c* August 5rs Fox
NOT AS A STRANGER (1955) *d/p* Kramer *c* Planer *m* Antheil *w* Mitchum, Sinatra, De Havilland, Grahame, Bickford, B Crawford, Marvin 135min *pc* Kramer *r* UA
NOTES FOR A FILM ABOUT DONNA AND GAIL (1966) *d/co-s* Owen 16mm 48min NFBC
NOTHING BUT PLEASURE (1939) *d Jules White s* Bruckman *w* Keaton 17min Col
NOTHING BUT THE BEST (1964) *d* C Donner *s* Raphael *c* Roeg *99min
NOTHING BUT THE TRUTH (1929) *d* Schertzinger *c* Cronjager 7256ft Par
NOTHING BUT THE TRUTH (1941) *d* E Nugent *c* C Lang *co-a* Dreier *w* Hope, Goddard 90min Par
NOTHING BUT TROUBLE (1944) *d Sam Taylor co-st/co-s* Rouse *co-a* Gibbons *w* Laurel, Hardy 69min MGM
Nothing ever Happens = NUNCA PASA NADA (1963)
NOTHING SACRED (1937) *d* Wellman *p* Selznick *s* B Hecht *a* Wheeler *w* Lombard, March *75min *r* UA
Nothing Unusual = INGENTINGOVANLIGT (1957)

NO TIME FOR COMEDY (1940) *d* Keighley *p* J Warner, Wallis *co-s* JJ Epstein *c* E Haller *w* J Stewart, R Russell, C Ruggles 93min WB
NO TIME FOR FLOWERS (1952) *d* D Siegel *w* Lindfors 83min RKO
NO TIME FOR LOVE (1943) *d/p* Leisen *as-p* Kohlmar *c* C Lang *co-a* Dreier *m* V Young *w* Colbert, MacMurray, Haydn 83min Par
NO TIME FOR SERGEANTS (1958) *d/p* LeRoy *s* Mahin *c* Rosson 111min WB
No Time For Tears = PURPLE HEART DIARY (1951)
NO TIME TO BE YOUNG (1958) *d David Rich w* Vaughn 82min Col
NO TIME TO DIE (1957) *d/co-st/co-s* T Young *co-st/co-s* Maibaum *c* Moore *w* Mature CS* 103min (= *Tank Force*)
NOTITSEN I MORGENBLADET (1915) *d* Madsen
NOT OF THIS EARTH (1957) *d/p* Corman 65min AA
No Tomorrow = INGEN MORGONDAG (1957)
Not on Your Life = VERDUGO, EL (1963)
NOTORIOUS (1946) *d/p/st* Hitchcock *s* B Hecht *c* Tetzlaff *w* Ingrid Bergman, C Grant, Rains 102min RKO
NOTORIOUS AFFAIR, A (1930) *d* Bacon *c* E Haller *w* Rathbone, K Francis 6009ft FN
NOTORIOUS BUT NICE (1933) *d* Thorpe 65min
Notorious Gentleman = RAKE'S PROGRESS, THE (1945)
NOTORIOUS LANDLADY, THE (1962) *d* Quine *p* Kohlmar *co-s* Edwards *c* Arling *m* Duning *w* Novak, Lemmon, Astaire 123min Col
NOTRE DAME, CATHEDRALE DE PARIS (1957) *d/s* Franju *c* Fradetal *m* Wiener FS* 18min
NOTRE DAME DE PARIS (1931) *d* J Epstein 300m
NOTRE DAME DE PARIS (1957) *d* Delannoy *ad/di* Aurenche, J Prévert *fn Victor Hugo c* Kelber *m* Auric *w* Lollobrigida, Quinn S* 107min (= *The Hunchback of Notre Dame*)
NO TREES IN THE STREET (1958) *d/pc* J Thompson 96min
Notre Front Russe = OUR RUSSIAN FRONT (1941)
NOTRE PARIS (1961) *d* Gruel, *André Fontaine* anim
NOTRE PLANETE LA TERRE (1947) *d* Painlevé
NOTRE SANG (1955) *d* Leenhardt 400m
NOT SO DUMB (1930) *co/co-p* K Vidor *co-p* Hearst *w* Davies, E Nugent 75min *r* MGM
NOTTE, LA (1961) *d/st/co-s* Antonioni *c* Di Venanzo *w* Mastroianni, Moreau, Vitti, Wicki 122min (= *The Night*)
Notte a Venezia, Una = NACHT IN VENEDIG, EINE (1933)
NOTTE BRAVA, LA (1959) *d/co-s* Bolognini *co-s* Pasolini *m* Piccioni *w* Martinelli, Brialy 93min (= *Night Heat*)
NOTTE SU UNA MINORANZA (1964) *d* Mingozzi sh
NOTTI BIANCHE, LE (1957) *d/co-s co-s* Cecchi d'Amico *fst Dostoievski c* Rotunno *a* Chiari *m* Rota *w* Maria Schell, Mastroianni, Marais 107min (= *White Nights*)
NOTTI DI CABIRIA, LE (1957) *d/co-st/co-s* Fellini *p* De Laurentiis *additional di* Pasolini *co-c* Martelli, Tonti *dec* Gherardi *m* Rota *w* Masina 110min (= *Night of Cabiria*)
NOTTURNO (1949) *d* Sala 18min
NOT WANTED (1949) *d Elmer Clifton co-p/co-s* Lupino 91min
NOT WITH MY WIFE, YOU DON'T (1966) *d/p/co-st/co-s* Panama *c* C Lang *cr* Bass *w* Curtis, G Scott *118min WB
NOUS CONTINUONS LA FRANCE (1946) *d* Daquin sh
NOUS LES GOSSES (1941) *d* Daquin *c* Bachelet 91min Pat
NOUS NE FERONS JAMAIS DU CINEMA (1932) *d* Cavalcanti
NOUS NOUS FACHONS PAS (1966) *w* Darc
NOUS NE SOMMES PLUS DES ENFANTS (1934) *d* Genina
NOUS N'IRONS PLUS AU BOIS (1951) *d* Sautet sh
NOUS N'IRONS PLUS AU BOIS (1964) *d/w* Etaix *c* Boffety sh
NOUS SOMMES TOUS DES ASSASSINS (1952) *d/co-s* Cayette *co-st/di* Charles Spaak *c* Bourgoin 115min (= *Are We All Murderers?*)
NO UTA (1925) *d* Mizoguchi Nik (= *Song of the Native Country*)
NOUVEAUX EXPLOITS DE NICK CARTER (1909) *d/s* Jasset serial in 9 eps
NOUVEAU JOURNAL D'UNE FEMME EN BLANC (1966) *d* Autant-Lara *s* Aurenche 115min Gau
NOUVEAU TESTAMENT, LE (1936) *co-d/s/fpl/w* Guitry *co-d Alexandre Ryder c* Bachelet 85min
NOUVEAU HORIZONS (1953) *d/p/cy/c* Ichac CS* 435m Fox
NOUVEAUX MESSIEURS, LES (1929) *d/co-s* Feyder *co-s* Charles Spaak *fpl Francais De Croisset co-c* Périnal *des* Meerson *w* Préjean 135min
NOUVELLE MISSION DE JUDEX, LA (1917) *d/co-s* Feuillade 1 *Le Mystère d'une Nuit d'Été* (1350m); 2 *L'Adieu au Bonheur* (685m); 3 *L'Ensorcelée* (720m); 4 *La Chambre aux embûches* (860m); 5 *La forêt lantée* (840m) 6 *Une Lueur dans les Ténèbres* (715m); 7 *La Main Morte* (810m); 8 *Les Captives* (810m); 9 *Les Papiers du Docteur Howey*; 10 *Les Deux Destinées* (860m); 11 *Le Crime Involontaire* (820m); 12 *Châtiment* (610m)

NOVELLETTA, LA (1937) d Comencini sh 16mm
NOVEMBRE A PARIS (1956) d/c Reichenbach e Resnais
 *10min
NOVIO A LA VISTA (1953) d Berlanga, Bardem
NOVOSTI DNYA (1947–54) d Vertov 1948: ep
 8,19,23,34,39,44,50; 1949: ep 19,27,43,51,55; 1950:
 ep 7,58; 1951 ep 15,33,43,56; 1952: ep 9,15,31,43,54;
 1953: ep 18,27,35,55; 1954: ep 31,46,60 (= Daily
 News)
NOVYE POKHOZHDENIYA SHVEIKA (1943) d
 Yutkevich 1970m (= New Adventures of Schweik)
NOVYI VAVILON (1929) d/s L Trauberg, Kozintsev c
 Moskvin m Shostakovich w Gerasimov, Pudovkin
 2200m (= The New Babylon)
Now About These Women = FOR ATT INTE TALA OM
 ALLA DESSA KUINNOR (1964)
NOW AND FOREVER (1934) d Hathaway w G Cooper,
 Lawford, Temple, Tamiroff 81min Par
NO WAY OUT (1950) d/co-s J Mankiewicz p Zanuck c
 Krasner co-a Wheeler m A Newman w Widmark,
 Darnell, Poitier 106min Fox
NO WAY TO TREAT A LADY (1968) d Smight p S Siegel s
 Gay co-a Pereira w Steiger, Remick, Segal *108min
 Par
Now Don't Get Excited = NE KOFUN SHICHA IYAYO
 (1931)
NOWEGO JANKA MUZYKANTA (1960) d Lenica anim
NOWHERE TO GO (1958) d/co-s Holt p Balcon 87min
 MGM
NO WOMAN KNOWS (1921) d Browning fn (Fanny Her-
 self) Edna Fer 7rs U
NOW IS THE TIME (1951) d McLaren *3min NFBC
NOW OR NEVER (1921) w H Lloyd 3rs pc Roach r Pat
NOWSREEL (1948) d/p/s/c Wexler *35min
Now That I Was Born A Woman = ONNA TO UMARETA
 KARANYA (1934)
NOW, VOYAGER (1942) d Rapper p Wallis c Polito w
 Henreid, B Davis, Rains 117min WB
NOZ W WODZIE (1962) d/st/co-s Polanski co-s
 Skolimowski m Komeda 94min (= Knife in the
 Water)
NOZZE DI SANGUE (1940) d Goffredo Alessandrini co-s
 Cottafavi
NTH COMMANDMENT, THE (1923) d Borzage fst Fannie
 Hurst 8rs FPL
NU (1948) d/s Antonioni m Fusco 9min
NU BORJAR LIVET (1948) d Molander co-s Lindstrom
Nude Odyssey (UK) = ODISSEA NUDA (1961)
NUDE RESTAURANT (1967) d Warhol 16mm *96min
NUGGET JIM'S PARTNER (1916) d/w Borzage Tri
NUISANCE, THE (1933) d Conway c Toland 83min MGM
NUIT AGITEE, UNE (1912) d/s/w Linder Pat
NUIT DE DECEMBRE (1939) d C Bernhardt w Reggiani
 83min
NUIT DE LA REVANCHE, LA (1924) d/st/s Duvivier w
 Vanel
NUIT DES ESPIONS, LA (1959) d/s/w Hossein w Vlady
 80min Gau
NUIT DU CARREFOUR, LA (1932) d/s J Renoir assistant
 Becker w P Renoir 73min
NUIT DU CINEMA, LA (1942) d Guitry sh
NUIT ET BROUILLARD (1955) d Resnais s Cayrol c
 Cloquet, Vierny co-e Colpi m Eisler part* 31min
NUIT FANTASTIQUE, LA (1942) d L'Herbier s Jeanson w
 Presle 89min (= Fantastic Night)
NUITS DE FEU (1936) d/co-s L'Herbier fst Tolstoi co-c
 Thirard co-a Lourié
NUITS DE PORT SAID, LES (1931) co-d Kirsanov Par
NUITS DE PRINCE (1930) d L'Herbier c Burel
NUIT SUR LE MONT CHAUVE, UNE (1933) d/p Alexeieff
 m Moussorgsky anim 9min (= A Night on Bare
 Mountain)
NUIT TERRIBLE, UNE (1896) d Méliès 20m
NUKIASHI SASHIASHI (1934) d Yoshimura
NUMAZU HEIGAKKO (1939) d Imai (= Numazu Military
 Academy)
Numazu Military Academy = NUMAZU HEIGAKKO
 (1939)
NUMBERED MEN (1930) d LeRoy c Polito 65min FN
NUMBER 5 (1969) d/w Lennon, Yoko Ono 16mm *
NUMBER, PLEASE (1920) w H Lloyd 2rs pc Roach r Pat
NUMBER SEVENTEEN (1932) d/s Hitchcock 5766ft
NUMBER THIRTEEN (uf) (1921) d Hitchcock
NUMERO 121, IL (1917) d/s/w Ghione
Nun, The (US) = RELIGIEUSE, LA (1965)
NUNCA PASA NADA (1963) d/co-s Bardem m Delerue w
 Cassel 97min (= Nothing Ever Happens)
NUN'S STORY, THE (1959) d Zinnemann p Blanke c Planer
 a Trauner m Waxman w A Hepburn, Evans, Finch
 *149min WB
NUOVI ANGELI, I (1961) d/s Gregoretti 105min (= The
 New Angels)
NUOVO MAMMINA, LA (1909) d/s Guazzoni
NUPTIAE (1969) d Broughton c Brakhage 16mm* 14min
NURSE, THE (1912) d Brenon 1000ft
NURSE EDITH CAVELL (1939) d H Wilcox c F Young,
 August e Elmo Williams w Neagle, G Sanders, Oliver,
 Pitts 98min RKO
NURSERY (1898) p Paul 80ft
NURSERY RHYMES (1902) d G Smith (series)

Nursery School (UK) = LA MATERNELLE (1933)
NURSING A VIPER (1909) d Griffith 1rl Bio
NUSUMARETA KOI (1951) d/m Ichikawa w Mori Toho
 (= Stolen Love)
NUSUMARETA YOKUJO (1958) d Imamura (= The
 Stolen Desire)
NUSUME KAWAIYA (1928) d/co-s Mizoguchi Nik
NUTS IN MAY (1917) d Bobby Williamson w Laurel
Nutty, Naughty Chateau (US) = CHATEAU EN SUEDE
 (1963)
NUTTY PROFESSOR, THE (1963) d/co-s/w J Lewis co-a
 Pereira *107min pc J Lewis Par
NYARSAFTON PA SKANSKA SLATTEN (1961) d Troell
 (= New Year's Eve on the Plains of Scania/New
 Year's Eve on the Scanian Plains)
NYE VENNER (1956) d Jorgen Storm-Peterson s A
 Henning Jensen
NYOBO FUNSHITSU (1928) d/co-s Ozu Sho (= Wife Lost)
NYONIN AISHU (1937) d/s Naruse (= New Grief)

OASIS (1954) d Y Allégret co-p G Oswald fn Joseph Kessel m
 Misraki w Morgan, Brasseur CS* 100min Fox
OATH, THE (1921) d/p/s Walsh 7rs FN
Oath of Obedience = BUSHIDO ZANKOKU MONO-
 GATARI (1963)
Oath of Timur, The = KLYATVA TIMURA (1942)
Oath of Youth, The = KLYATVA MOLODYKH (1947)
OBCAN BRYCH (1958) d/co-s Vavra CS (= Citizen Bryon)
OBEDIENT FLAME, THE (1939) d McLaren 20min
OBJECTIF 500 MILLIONS (1966) d Schoendoerffer 90min
OBJECTIVE BURMA (1945) d Walsh ex-p Jack L Warner p
 Wald fn Macdougall c Howe m Waxman w Flynn
 142min WB
OBLIGIN' BUCKAROO, THE (1927) d Thorpe
OBLOMOK IMPERII (1929) d/co-s Ermler 2203m (= Frag-
 ment of an Empire)
OBORONA TSARITSYNA (1942) d/s S & G Vasiliev
 89min (= The Defence of Tsaritsyn)
OBOROYO NO ONNA (1936) d Gosho (= Woman of a
 Pale Night)
OBRALNI VLASTI (1956) d Frič
OBSESSION (1949) d Dmytryk w Newton 93min BL (= The
 Hidden Room)
OBSESSION (1954) d/co-s Delannoy fn (Silent as the Grave)
 William Irish m Misraki w Morgan, Vallone 89min
Obsessions (FRANCE) = FLESH AND FANTASY (1943)
OBSITOS (1917) d Balazs
OBYKNOVENNIYE FASHIZM (1965) d/co-s/e/n Romm
 130min (= Ordinary Fascism)
OCCUPE-TOI D'AMELIE (1912) d Emile Mantard w M
 Tourneur
OCCUPE-TOI D'AMELIE (1949) d Autant-Lara s/di
 Aurenche, Bost w Darrieux, Carette, Desailly 95min
 (= Keep an Eye on Amelia)
Occurence at Owl Creek Bridge, An = RIVERE DU HIBOU,
 LA (1961)
OCEANO (1971) d/co-s Quilici *100min
OCEAN'S 11 (1960) d/p Milestone s S Brown, Lederer c
 Daniels cr Bass w Sinatra, Martin, Lawford, A
 Dickinson, Conte, Romero, Tamiroff, MacLaine,
 Raft PV* 127min WB
OCH ALLA DESSA KVINNOR (1944) d Mattsson (= And
 All These Women)
OCHARCOAGA (1961) d Grau
OCHAZUKE NO AJI (1952) d/co-s Ozu Sho (= The
 Flavour of the Green Tea Over Rice)
Ochen Khorosho Zhivietsa = PROSTOI SLUCHAI (1932)
October = OKTYABRE (1927)
OCTOBER MAN, THE (1947) d R Baker w J Mills,
 Greenwood 88min BL
October Revolution = REVOLUTION D'OCTOBRE, LA
 (1967)
OCTOBRE A MADRID (1965) d/p/st/s/c Hanoun 16mm
 60min
Odd Affinity = SHOKKAKU (1969)
ODD MAN OUT (1947) d/co-p C Reed co-p Del Giudice
 co-s R C Sherriff c Krasker dec Furse m Alwyn w
 Mason, Newton 115min
Odd Obsessions = KAGI (1959)
ODDS AGAINST TOMORROW (1959) d/p Wise c Brun w
 Ryan, Winters, Grahame 95min r UA
ODESSA IN FIAMME (1942) d/co-s Gallone
ODETTE (1950) d H Wilcox w Neagle, Ustinov, T Howard
 123min
ODINNADTSATYI (1928) d/co-s/co-e/t Vertov 1600m (5
 parts) (= The Ele-nth)
ODISSEA NUDA (1961) d/co-s/co-st Rossi CS* 72min
 (= Nude Odyssey)
ODNA (1931) d/s L Trauberg, Kozintsev c Moskvin m
 Shostakovich w Gerasimov 2200m (= Alone)
ODNA SEMIA (1943) d Alexandrov (= One Family)
ODNAZMDI NOCH (1945) d/w Barnet 6rs (= One Night)
O DREAMLAND (1953) d L Anderson 12min
ODYSSEE DU CAPITAINE STEVE, L' (1956) d Pagliero
 (= Walk unto Paradise)
Oedipus Rex = EDIPO RE (1967)

OEIL DU MALIN, L' (1962) d/s Chabrol co-p Ponti c
 Rabier 80min (= The Third Love)
OEIL DU MONOCLE, L' (1962) d/co-s Lautner 105min
OEIL POUR OEIL (1956) d/co-s Cayatte di Bost c Matras
 w Jurgens UV* 113min UGC (= An Eye for an Eye)
O'ER HILL AND DALE (1931) d B Wright p Grierson
 17min EMB
OEUFS DE L'AUTRUCHE, LES (1957) d De La Patellière
 w Fresnay 90min (= The Ostrich has Two Eggs)
OEUVRE IMMORTELLE (1923) d Duvivier
OEUVRE SCIENTIFIQUE DE PASTEUR, L' (1947)
 d/s/co-c/cy Painlevé co-c Fradetal 970m
Of a Thousand Delights = VAGHE STELLE DELL'ORSA
 (1965)
OFF HIS TROLLEY (1924) d Cline p Sennett s Cline,
 Garnett Pat
Office Girl, The = SUNSHINE SUSIE (1931)
OFFICER O'BRIEN (1930) d Garnett c AC Miller 75min
 Pathe
OFFICE WIFE (1930) d Bacon 5362ft WB
Of Flesh and Blood = GRANDS CHEMINS, LES (1962)
OFF LIMITS (1953) d G Marshall st/s Kanter co-a Pereira c
 Marley w Hope, Rooney 89min Par
OF HUMAN BONDAGE (1934) d Cromwell p Berman fn
 Somerset Maugham m M Steiner w B Davis, L
 Howard 83min RKO
OF HUMAN BONDAGE (1946) d Goulding p Blanke rm
 1934 fn Simerset Maugham c Marley m Korngold w
 Parker, Henreid, A Smith 105min WB
OF HUMAN BONDAGE (1964) d K Hughes, Hathaway p
 James Woolf s Forbes fn Somerset Maugham c
 Morris w Novak, Laurence Harvey 99min MGM
OF HUMAN HEARTS (1938) d C Brown w J Stewart, W
 Huston, C Coburn 100min MGM
O'FLYNN, THE (1948) d Arthur Pierson p/co-s Fairbanks Jr
 c Edeson w Fairbanks Jr 94min U (= The Fighting
 O'Flynn)
OF MICE AND MEN (1940) d/p Milestone p Roach fn
 Steinbeck and fpl G Kaufman c Brodine m Copland w
 Meredith, Bickford 107min r UA
OF MEN AND DEMONS (1969) d J and F Hubley anim*
 9min
OF MEN AND MUSIC (1950) d Reis co-s Kurnitz, Paxton
 co-c F Crosby, Mohr co-e Parrish 82min Fox
OF PUPS AND PUZZLES (1940) d G Sidney 11min MGM
OF STARS AND MEN (1961) d/co-p/co-ad J Hubley co-
 p/co-ad F Hubley anim* 63min
OGGI DOMANI E DOPODOMANI (1964) p Ponti S*
 ep L'UOMO DAI CINQUE PALLONI d/co-s Ferreri w
 Mastroianni, Catherine Spaak
 ep LA MOGLIE BIONDA d/s Salce w Mastroianni, Catherine
 Spaak
 ep L'ORA DI PUNTA d De Filippo
OGON (1930) d Donskoi si (= The Fire)
OGNENNYE VERSTY (1957) d Samsonov rm STAGE-
 COACH (1939) 2318m (= Fiery Miles)
OGNI BAKU (1950 r 1958) d Heifitz, Zarkhi 2571m
 (= Flames over Baku)
Ogre of Athens, The = DRACOS (1956)
OHAYO (1959) d/co-s Ozu rm UMARETE WA MITA
 KEREDO (1932) *97min Sho (= Good Morning/Too
 Much Talk)
OH DAD, POOR DAD, MAMMA'S HUNG YOU IN THE
 CLOSET AND I'M FEELING SO SAD (1966) d
 Quine p Stark fpl Arthur Kopit c Unsworth w R
 Russell *86min Par
OH, DOCTOR! (1917) d/w Arbuckle w Keaton 2rs Par
O.HENRY'S FULL HOUSE (1952) fsts O.Henry n John
 Steinbeck 116min Fox (= Full House)
 ep THE LAST LEAF d Negulesco s Goff, Roberts c Joe
 Macdonald w A Baxter, Peters, Ratoff
 ep THE CLARION CALL d Hathaway s Breen c Ballard w
 Widmark
 ep THE GIFT OF THE MAGI d H King c Joe Macdonald co-a
 Wheeler m A Newman w Crain, F Granger
 ep THE RANSOM OF RED CHIEF d Hawks s Johnson c
 Krasner 20min
 ep THE COP AND THE ANTHEM d Koster s Trotti w
 Laughton, Monroe, D Wayne
OH, FOR A MAN (1930) p Hamilton MacFadden c Clarke
 w Jeanette Macdonald, Lugosi 78min Fox
Oh, For a Man! = WILL SUCCESS SPOIL ROCK
 HUNTER? (1957)
OH, KAY (1928) d LeRoy c Hickox f PG Wodehouse 6100ft
 FN
Oh! Les Femmes! = MAX ET LES FEMMES (1912)
OH LIFE — A WOE STORY - THE A TEST NEWS (1963)
 d Brakhage 16mm 5min (silent)
OH, MABEL BEHAVE (1921) co-d/p Sennett co-d Ford
 Sterling w Sennett, Normand 5rs
OH, MEN! OH, WOMEN! (1957) d/p/s N Johnson c C
 Clarke co-a Wheeler m Mockridge w G Rogers,
 Dailey, Niven, Rush CS* 90min Fox
OH, MR PORTER! (1937) d Marcel Varnel s Launder w
 Hay
OHM KRUGER (1941) d Steinhoff co-c FA Wagner w
 Jannings 3620m Tob
OHMS (1937) d Walsh w J Mills 87min Gau (= You're in the
 Army Now)
Oh! My Papa = FEVERWERK (1954)

201

OHNE DICH WIRD ES NACHT (1956) *d/w* Jurgens 104min
OH! QUE MAMBO! (1958) *d* John Berry *w* Sordi 82min
OHRFEIGEN (1969) *d* Thiele *w* Jurgens, Tiller *
OH, ROSALINDA! (1955) *d/p/s* M Powell, Pressburger *c* Challis *mf (Die Fledermaus) J Straus w* M Ferrer, M Redgrave, Walbrook, (J Schlesinger) CS* 101min (= *Fledermaus 55*)
Oh! Sabella (UK) = NONNA SABELLA, LA (1953)
OH SAILOR BEHAVE (1930) *d* A Mayo *w* Olsen, Johnson 70min WB
OH, WHAT A KNIGHT! (1937) *d/w* C Chase 2rs Col
OH, THOSE EYES! (1912) *d* Sennett *w* Normand ½rl Bio
OH! WHAT A LOVELY WAR (1969) *d/co-p* Attenborough *w* Bogarde, Cassel, Gielgud, Hawkins, More, Olivier, M Redgrave, V Redgrave, R Richardson, J Mills PV* 144min *r* Par
Oh, What a Night = ROUNDERS, THE (1914)
OH YEAH! (1929) *d/ad* Garnett *c* AC Miller *w* Pitts 8rs (sd) Pathe
OH, YOU BEAUTIFUL DOLL (1949) *d* Stahl *a* Wheeler *m* A Newman *94min Fox
OH, YOU WOMEN! (1919) *d/co-st/co-s* Emerson *co-st/co-s* Loos 5rs FPL
OIL AND WATER (1913) *d* Griffith *w* L Gish, L Barrymore 1rl Bio
OILFIELD, THE (1954) *d/s* Haanstra *p* Elton 17min
OIL FOR THE LAMPS OF CHINA (1935) *d* LeRoy *c* Gaudio *w* Crisp 110min WB
OISEAU DE PARADIS, L' (1962) *d/co-s/co-di* Camus *m* Jarre *95min
OISEAUX VONT MOURIR AU PEROU, LES (1968) *d/st/ad/di* Gary *c* Matras *w* Seberg, Ronet, Brasseur, Darrieux *95min (= *Birds in Peru/The Birds Come to Die in Peru*)
OJO DE LA CERRADURA, EL (1964) *d/co-s* Torre Nilsson 102min Col (= *The Eavesdropper*)
OJO KICHIZA (1926) *d* Kinugasa
OJUSAN (1930) *d* Ozu Sho (= *Young Miss*)
OJOSAN KAMPAI (1949) *d* Kinoshita *s* Shindo (= *Here's To The Girls*)
OJOS MAS LINDAS DEL MUNDO, LOS (1943) *d* Saslavsky
OKAMA (1927) *d/s* Gosho (= *Moon-faced*)
OKANDA, DEN (1913) *d/s* Stiller *fn Hugo Von Hoffmanthal* (= *Das Tremde Mädchen*)
OKASAN (1952) *d* Naruse Toho (= *Mother*)
OKAY AMERICA (1932) *d* Garnett *c* AC Miller *w* Ayres, O'Sullivan 80min U
OK END HERE (1963) *d* R Frank 30min
Okichi The Stranger = TOJIN OKICHI (1930)
OKLAHOMA (1954) *d* Fischinger anim 30seconds
OKLAHOMA! (1955) *d* Zinnemann *fmpl Rodgers, Hammerstein c* Surtees *m Rodgers pl/lyr Hammerstein w* Grahame, S Jones, Steiger TAO* 145min MGM
OKLAHOMA BADLANDS (1948) *d* Canutt 59min Rep
OKLAHOMA KID, THE (1939) *d* Bacon *c* Howe *w* Cagney, Bogart, Crisp 85min WB
OKLAHOMA WOMAN (1956) *d/p* Corman S 73min
OK Nero (UK) = OK NERONE (1951)
OK NERONE (1951) *d* Soldati 84min (= *OK Nero*)
Okoto and Sasuke = OKOTO TO SASUKE (1961)
OKOTO TO SASUKE (1961) *d/s* Kinugasa (= *Okoto and Sasuke*)
OKOUZLENA (1942) *d/s* Vavra
OKRAINA (1933) *d/co-s* Barnet 2700m (= *Patriots*)
OKTYABRE (1927) *d/s* Eisenstein, Alexandrov *c* Tissé *w* Tissé 165min (original only) 2800m (= *October; Ten Days that Shook the World*)
OKUMAN CHOJA (1954) *d/co-s* Ichikawa *w* Yamada Toho (= *A Billionaire*)
OKUNI TO GOHEI (1952) *d* Naruse
OKUSAMA SHAKUYOSHO (1936) *d* Gosho (= *A Married Lady Borrows Money*)
Ola and Julia = OLA OCH JULIA (1968)
O LA BORSA O LA VITA! (1933) *d/co-s* Bragaglia
OLA OCH JULIA (1968) *d/co-s* Halldoff (= *Ola and Julia*)
OLD ACQUAINTANCE (1943) *d* V Sherman *p* Blanke *c* Polito *m* Waxman *w* B Davis, M Hopkins 110min WB
OLD ACTOR, THE (1912) *d* Griffith *w* Pickford, (Marsh) 1rl Bio
Old and the New, The = STAROIE I NOVOIE (1929)
OLD ARMCHAIR, THE (1913) *d* Conway
OLDAS ES KOTES (1963) *d/s* Jancsó S 100min (= *Cantaba*)
OLD BONES OF THE RIVER (1939) *d Marcel Varnel w* Hay 90min
OLD CLOTHES (1925) *d* Cline *w* J Crawford 5600ft MGM
Old Czech Legends = STARE POVESTI CESKE (1953)
OLD DARK HOUSE, THE (1932) *d* Whale, Wyler (*uc*) *fn (Benighted)* Priestley *c* Edeson *w* Karloff, M Douglas, Laughton 71min U
OLD DARK HOUSE, THE (1962) *d/p* Castle *fn (Benighted)* Priestley *86/77min *r* Col
Older Brother, Younger Sister = ANI IMOTO (1953)
OLD-FASHIONED WAY, THE (1934) *d William Beaudine st* Fields (*ps* Charles Bogle) *w* Fields
OLD HEIDELBERG (1915) *d/ad* Amerson *p* Griffith *w* D Gish, Von Stroheim 5rs Tri
OLD HOMESTEAD, THE (1922) *d* Cruze 8rs FPL
OLD IRONSIDES (1928) *d/p* Cruze *supn* BP Schulberg *w* Beery, Karloff 10089ft FPL
OLD ISAACS, THE PAWNBROKER (1908) *st/w* Griffith Bio
Old Jockey, The = STARYI NAYEZHDNIK (1940, *r* 1959)
OLD MAID, THE (1939) *d* Goulding *p* Wallis *as-p* Blanke *c* Gaudio *m* M Steiner *w* B Davis, M Hopkins, Crisp 95min WB
OLD MAID AND FORTUNE TELLER (1904) *d* Porter 30ft Ed
OLD MAID HAVING HER PICTURE TAKEN, THE (1901) *d* Porter 38ft Ed
OLD MAN AND THE FLOWER, THE (1962) *d/p* Pintoff *8min *pc* Pintoff
OLD MAN AND THE SEA, THE (1958) *d* J Sturges, Zinnemann, H King *fn* Hemingway *co-c* Howe, F Crosby *m* Tiomkin *w* Tracy *86min WB
Old Man Motor Car (UK) = DEDECEK AUTOMOBIL (1956)
Old Mill, The = GAMLA KUARNEN, DEN (1962)
OLD RAID MULE, THE (1938) *d/w* Chase 2rs Col
OLD SAN FRANCISCO (1927) *d* Crosland *st* Zanuck *c* Mohr 9rs WB
Old Shatterhand = APACHES LAST BATTLE (1964)
OLD SOAK, THE (1926) *d Edward Sloman w* Hersholt, Fazenda 7445ft U
OLD SOUTH, THE (1940) *d* Zinnemann 15min MGM
Old Spanish Custom, A = INVADERS, THE (1934)
OLD WIVES FOR NEW (1918) *d* De Mille 6rs FPL
Old Women of Japan = NIPPON NO OBOCHAN (1962)
OLD YELLER (1957) *d* Stevenson *p* Disney *w* McGuire *83min
OLE DOLE DOFF (1967) *d/co-s/c/e* Troell 110min 9927ft SF (= *Who Saw Him Die?*)
OLIVER! (1968) *d* C Reed *p* John Woolf *st/lyr/m Lionel Bart c* Morris PV* 153min Col
OLIVER TWIST (1922) *d/co-ad/co-s* F Lloyd *p* Lesser *fn Charles Dickens w* Chaney 7600ft
OLIVER TWIST (1940) *d/p/ad/co-c/e/m/w* Bradley *fn Charles Dickens* 16mm 10rs
OLIVER TWIST (1948) *d/co-s* Lean *p* Neame *fn Charles Dickens c* G Green *m Bax w* Newton, Guinness 116min
Olive Trees of Justice, The = OLIVIERS DE LA JUSTICE, LES (1962)
OLSEN'S BIG MOMENT (1933) *d* St Clair *st* G Marshall *c* O'Connell 66min Fox
OLIVIERS DE LA JUSTICE, LES (1962) *d/co-s* Blue *m* Jarre 88min (= *The Olive Trees of Justice*)
OLTRE L'AMORE (1940) *d* Gallone *st Stendhal w* Valli
OLVIDADOS, LOS (1950) *d/co-s* Buñuel *co-s* Alcoriza *c* Figueroa 88min (= *The Young and the Damned*)
Olympia (1930) German version of SI L'EMPEREUR SAVAIT CA! (1930)
OLYMPIAD: FEST DER SCHONEIT (1938) *d/s* Riefenstahl *co-e* Ruttman 2722m Tob
OLYMPIAD: FEST DER VOLKER (1938) *d/s* Riefenstahl *co-e* Ruttmann 3429m Tob
OLYMPIA '52 (1952) *d/co-c* Marker 16mm sh
OLYMPIAN, THE (1970) *d/s/c/e* Markopoulos 16mm * 30min
OMAR KHAYYAM (1957) *d* Dieterle *c* Laszlo *co-a* Pereira *m* V Young *w* Wilde, Derek UV* 101min Par
Ombre Bianche Italian version of THE SAVAGE INNOCENTS (1960)
OMBRE DU PECHE, L' (1922) *d/s* Protazanov 6rs
OMBRELLAI (1952) *d* Maselli
OMBRELLONE, L' (1965) *d/co-s* Risi S* 90min
OMBRES QUI PASSENT (1923) *d Alexandre Wolcoff co-s/w* Mozhukhin
OMBYTE FORNOJER (1938) *d* Molander SF
OMICRON (1963) *d/s* Gregoretti *c* Di Palma 110min
OMNIBUS DES TOQUES OU LES ECHAPPES DE CHARENTON, L' (1901) *d* Méliès 20m
OMOKAGE (1948) *d/s Gosho* (= *Image*)
OMRINGADE HUSET, DET (1922) *d/co-s/w* Sjöström (*La Maison Amie*) fn Pierre Frondaie 1890m SF
OMRINGET (1960) *d* Skouen 82min SF (= *Surrounded*)
OMSTRIDTE JORD, DEN (1915) *d* Madsen
ON (1964, *r* 1966) *d/co-s* Sjöberg *w* B Andersson (= *The Island*)
ON A CLEAR DAY YOU CAN SEE FOREVER (1970) *d* Minnelli *p* HW Koch *s/lyr* A Lerner *co-cos* Beaton *w* Montand PV* 120min *pc* HW Koch, A Lerner
ON AGAIN – OFF AGAIN (1937) *d* Cline 68min RKO
ON A JEHO SESTRA (1931) *d* Frič, *Karel Lamac c* Heller (= *He and His Sister*)
ON AN ISLAND WITH YOU (1948) *d* Thorpe *p* Pasternak *w* Esther Williams, Lawford, Montalban, Charisse *104min MGM
ON APPROVAL (1945) *d/p/ad/w* C Brook 80min
ON ATTEND POLOCHON (1920) *d* Machin 260m
ON A VOLE LA JOCONDE (1965) *d/co-st* Deville *w* Vlady S* 95min
ON A VOLE UN HOMME (1933) *d* Ophuls *p* Pommer *co-m* Kaper 90min Fox
ONA ZA SHCHISCHCHAYET RODINU (1943) *d* Ernler 2189m (= *She Defends Her Country*)
ON BORROWED TIME (1939) *d Harold S Bucquet p* Franklin *fpl* Osborn *c* Ruttenberg *m* Waxman *w* L Barrymore 99min MGM
ONCE A GENTLEMAN (1930) *d* Cruze *w* Horton 80min
ONCE A JOLLY SWAGMAN (1948) *d/co-s* J Lee *w* Bogarde 100min
ONCE A SINNER (1950) *d* L Gilbert 80min
ONCE A THIEF (1965) *d* Nelson *c* Burks *m* Schifrin *w* Palance, Delon, Heflin PV 107min MGM
ONCE BEFORE I DIE (1967) *d/p* Derek *c* Arling *w* Derek, Andress *96min
ONCE IN A BLUE MOON (1935) *d/p/st/s* B Hecht, MacArthur *as-d/c* Garmes *m* Antheil 8rs Par
ONCE IN A LIFETIME (1932) *d Russell Mack ad* S Miller *fpl* G Kaufman, M Hart *w* Pitts, (Ladd) 75min
Once More = IMA HITOTABI NO (1947)
ONCE MORE, MY DARLING (1949) *d* Montgomery *c* Planer *w* Montgomery, Blyth 94min *r* UA
ONCE MORE WITH FEELING (1959) *d/co-p* Donen *s/fpl* Kurnitz *c* Périnal *t* Binder *a* Trauner *m Muir, Mathieson* from *Beethoven, Wagner, Brahms, Souza w* Brynner, Kendall, Ratoff *92min Col
Once There Was A War = DER VAR ENGANG EN KRIG (1966)
ONCE UPON A HONEYMOON (1942) *d/p/co-st* McCarey, *c* Barnes *w* C Grant, G Rogers 115min RKO
ONCE UPON A HORSE (1958) *d/p/st/s* Kanter *c* Arling *co-a* Golitzen 85min U
Once Upon A Thursday = AFFAIR OF MARTHA, THE (1942)
Once Upon A Time = BYL SOBIE RAZ (1957)
Once Upon A Time (UK) = VAR ENGANG, DER (1922)
Once Upon A Time In The West – C'ERA UNA VOLTA IL WEST (1969)
Once Upon A War (US) = DER VAR ENGANG EN KRIG (1966)
ON DANGEROUS GROUND (1951) *d* N Ray *p* Houseman *s* Bezzerides *m* Herrmann *w* Lupino, Ryan 82min RKO
ON DEMADE UNE BRUTE (1934) *co-s/w* Tati
One Against Seven (UK) = COUNTER-ATTACK (1945)
ONE AGAINST THE WORLD (1939) *d* Zinnemann 1rl MGM
ONE AM (1916) *d/s/w* Chaplin *co-c* Totheroh 2rs Mut
ONE AM (1968, *uf*) *d* Godard * see *One PM*
One Arabian Night (USA) = SUMURUN
One Born Every Minute (UK) = FLIM FLAM MAN, THE (1967)
O NECEM JINEM (1963) *d/s* Chytilova 90min (= *About Something Else/Something Different*)
ONE CLEAR CALL (1922) *d/p* Stahl 7rs FN
ONE CROWDED NIGHT (1940) *d* Reis 68min RKO
ONE DANGEROUS NIGHT (1943) *d* M Gordon *c* O'Connell 76min Col
ONE EXCITING NIGHT (1922) *d/s* Griffith 11rs UA
ONE DAY IN THE LIFE OF IVAN DENISOVICH (1971) *d/p Caspar Wrede fn Alexander Solzhenitsyn c* Nugent *w* Courtenay *100min
ONE-EYED JACKS (1961) *d* Brando *c* C Lang *co-a* Pereira *m* Friedhofer *w* Brando, Malden, Cook VV* 141min *pc* Brando *r* Par
One Family = ODNA SEMIA (1943)
One Find Day (UK) = CERTO GIORNO, UN (1968)
ONE FOOT IN HEAVEN (1941) *d/co-p* Rapper *p* J Warner, Wallis *w* March 108min WB
ONE FROGGY EVENING (1955) *d* C Jones anim* 7min WB
ONE GLORIOUS DAY (1922) *d* Cruze 5rs FPL
ONE GOOD TURN (1931) *d James Horne p* Roach *w* Laurel, Hardy 2rs (sd) *r* MGM
ONE HOUR BEFORE DAWN (1920) *d* Henry King 5rs Pat
ONE HOUR MARRIED (1926) *st* Roach *w* Normand Pat
One Hour of Happiness = EINE STUNDE GLUECK (1929)
ONE HOUR OF LOVE (1926) *d/s* Florey 7rs
ONE HOUR WITH YOU (1932) *co-d/p* Lubitsch *co-d* Cukor(*uc*) *s* Raphaelson *rm* MARRIAGE CIRCLE, THE (1924) *c* Milner *dec* Dreier *co-m Oscar Straus w* Chevalier, Jeanette MacDonald, C Ruggles 85min Par
ONE HUNDRED MEN AND A GIRL (1937) *d* Kuster *as-p* Pasternak *co-songs* Hollander *w* Durbin, Menjou 85min U
One Man Mutiny (UK) = COURTMARTIAL OF BILLY MITCHELL, THE (1955)
ONE MAN'S WAY (1964) *d* D Sanders *p* T Sanders *c* Laszlo *w* Murray 105min *r* UA
ONE MILE FROM HEAVEN (1937) *d* Dwan *w* Trevor 68min Fox
ONE MILLION BC (1940) *co-d/p* Roach *co-d Hal Roach Jr c* Brodine *w* Mature 80min *r* UA
ONE MINUTE TO ZERO (1952) *d* Garnett *m* V Young *w* Mitchum, Blyth 105min RKO
ONE MINUTE TO PLAY (1926) *d* S Wood 7732ft
ONE MORE RIVER (1934) *d* Whale *fpl Galsworthy* 85min U
ONE MORE SPRING (1935) *d* H King *c* J Seitz *w* J Gaynor, W Baxter, Darwell 87min Fox
ONE MORE TIME (1970) *d* J Lewis *w* Lawford 95min
ONE MORE TRAIN TO ROB (1971) *d* A McLaglen *co-a* Golitzen *w* Peppard *108min U

ONE MYSTERIOUS NIGHT (1944) *d* Boetticher *c* O'Connell *w* Malone (*as* Maloney) 62min Col
ONE NEW YORK NIGHT (1935) *d* Conway *w* Tone 71min MGM
One Night = ODNAZMDI NOCH (1945)
ONE NIGHT IN THE TROPICS (1940) *d* A Edward Sutherland *w* B Abbott, Costello, R Cummings 82min U
One Night of Fame (US) = AL DIAVOLO CON CELEBRITA (1948)
ONE NIGHT OF LOVE (1934) *d* Schertzinger *c* J Walker *m* A Newman *w* Darwell 80min Col
One Night of Passion = JONETSU NO ICHIYA (1929)
ONE NIGHT WITH YOU (1948) *d* T Young 92min
ONE OF OUR AIRCRAFT IS MISSING (1942) *d/co-p/co-s* M Powell *co-p/co-s* Pressburger *c* Neame *w* Ustinov 106min
ONE PLUS ONE (1968) *d/s* Godard *m/w* Rolling Stones *110min (= *Sympathy For The Devil* (2nd version))
1 + 1: EXPLORING THE KINSEY REPORTS (1961) *d/p/s* Oboler 115min
ONE PM (1969) *d/s/co-c/e* Pennebaker *co-c* R Leacock *w* Godard, R Leacock 16mm *90min *pc* R Leacock, Pennebaker (incorporates footage from Jean-Luc Godard's *One AM* (1968, *uf*))
ONE RAINY AFTERNOON (1936) *d* Rowland V Lee *co-st* Pressburger *c* Marley *m* A Newman *co-lyr* P Sturges 80min *pc* Pickford, Lasky *r* UA
ONE ROMANTIC NIGHT (1930) *d* Paul L Stein *fpl* (*The Swan*) Ferenc Molnar *c* Struss *w* L Gish, Dressler 101min *r* UA
One Room Tenants = WSPOLNY POKOJ (1960)
ONE RUN ELMER (1935) *d* Charles Lamont *w* Keaton 1753ft
ONE SHE LOVED, THE (1912) *d* Griffith *w* L Barrymore, Pickford 1rl Bio
ONESTA' DEL PECCATO, L' (1918) *d/co-st/s* Genina
One Summer of Happiness = HON DANSADE EN SOMMAR (1951)
ONE SUNDAY AFTERNOON (1949) *rm* STRAWBERRY BLONDE, THE (1941) *d* Walsh *p* Wald *co-c* Hickox *e* Nyby *w* Malone *90min WB
One Sunday Morning = NIEDZIELNY PORANEK (1955)
ONE THAT GOT AWAY, THE (1957) *d* R Baker 110min JAR
... ONE THIRD OF A NATION ... (1939) *d/p/co-s* Dudley Murphy *2nd d* I Lerner *w* S Sidney, Lumet 79min Par
1001 CRTEZ (1961) Vukotic (= *1001 Drawings*)
1001 Drawings = 1001 CRTEZ (1961)
ONE, TWO, THREE (1956, *uf*) *d* McLaren * NFBC
ONE, TWO, THREE (1961) *d/p/co-s* B Wilder *co-as-p/co-s* Diamond *fpl* Ferenc Molnar *c* Fapp *a* Trauner *m* Previn *w* Cagney, Buchholz PV 115min *co-pc* Mir *r* UA
1-2-3 (1970) *d* Whitney
ONE WAY PASSAGE (1932) *d* Garnett *w* K Francis, W Powell 69min WB
ONE WAY PENDULUM (1964) *d* P Yates *fpl* N F Simpson 85min
ONE WAY STREET (1950) *d* Fregonese *w* Mason, Duryea 79min U
ONE WAY TICKET (1935) *d* Biberman *p* BP Schulberg *co-s* Anthony *w* Nolan 72min Col
ONE WAY TO LOVE (1945) *d* Enright *c* Lawton 9rs Col
ONE WEEK (1920) *d/s* Keaton, Cline *w* Keaton 2 rs Metro
One Woman's Story (USA) = PASSIONATE FRIENDS, THE (1949)
ONE WOMAN TO ANOTHER (1927) *d* Tuttle 4022ft Par
On His Own Ground = NA SVOJI ZEMLJI (1948)
ON HIS WEDDING DAY (1913) *d* Sennett *w* Normand ½rl Key
ONI AZAMI (1926) *d* Kinugasa
ONIBABA (1965) *d/s* Shindo S 105min (= *The Demon/The Hole*)
ONIROS (1967) *d* Pollet
Oni Shli Na Vostok = ITALIANO, BRAVA GENTE (1964)
Only a Mother = BARA EN MOR (1949)
ONLY ANGELS HAVE WINGS (1939) *d/p/st* Hawks *s* Furthman *co-c* J Walker *co-m* Tiomkin *w* C Grant, Arthur, Barthelmess, Hayworth, Mitchell 121min Col
Only a Waiter = BARA EN KYPARE (1945)
ONLY EIGHT HOURS (1935) *d* G Seitz *w* R Taylor 67min MGM
ONLY GAME IN TOWN, THE (1968) *d* G Stevens *c* Decaë *w* E Taylor, Beatty *113min Fox
Only Son, The = HITORI MUSUKO (1936)
ONLY THE VALIANT (1951) *d* G Douglas *fn* Warren *c* Lindon *w* Peck 105min WB
ONLY THING, THE (1925) *d* Conway 5284ft MGM
ONLY TWO CAN PLAY (1961) *d/co-ex-p* Gilliat *co-ex-p* Launder *s* Forbes *w* Sellers, Attenborough 106min BL
ONLY WHEN I LARF (1968) *d* Dearden *p/fn* Len Deighton *w* Attenborough, Hemmings *103min Par
Only Women Have Trouble = KANASHIMI WA ONNA DAKENI (1958)
ONLY YESTERDAY (1933) *d* Stahl *w* Darwell, Oliver 108min U
ON MOONLIGHT BAY (1951) *d* Del Ruth *co-s* Shavelson *fst's* Booth Tarkington *c* E Haller *m* M Steiner *w* D Day *95min WB

On My Way to the Crusades, I Met a Girl Who ... = CINTURA DI CASTITA, LA (1967)
On Mount Ala-Tau = V GORAKH ALA-TAU (1944)
ONNA (1948) *d* Kinoshita (= *Woman*)
ONNA NO ISSHO (1952) *d/s* Shindo (= *A Woman's Life*)
ONNA GA KAIDAN O AGARU TOKI (1960) *d* Naruse *w* Mori, Nakadai S 111min Toho (= *When A Woman Ascends the Stairs*)
ONNA KOSO IE O MEMORE (1939) *d* Yoshimura
ONNA NO KUNSHO (1961) *d* Yoshimura *s* Shindo *w* Kyo, Mori (= *A Design for Dying*)
ONNA NO MACHI (1940) *d* Imai (= *Women's town*)
ONNA NO KAO (1949) *d* Imai Toho (= *Woman's Face*)
ONNA NO NAKA NI IRU TANIN (1966) *d* Naruse S 102min Toho (= *The Thin Line*)
ONNA NO REKISHI (1963) *d* Naruse *w* Nadakai S 120min Toho (= *A Woman's Life*)
ONNA NO SAKA (1961) *d* Yoshimura *s* Shindo S* 107min Sho (= *Women of Kyoto*)
ONNA NO SONO (1954) *d* Kinoshita (= *The Eternal Generation/The Garden of Women*)
ONNA NO ZA (1962) *d* Naruse (= *A Woman's Place*)
ONNA TO MISOSHIRU (1968) *d* Gosho (= *Woman and Bean Soup*)
ONNA TO UMARETA KARANYA (1934) *d* Gosho (= *Now That I Was Born a Woman*)
ONNA WA TAMOTO O GOYOJIN (1931) *d/s* Naruse
ONNA-YO AYAMARU NAKARE (1923) *d/s* Kinugasa
ONNA-YO KIMI NO NA O KEGASU NAKARE (1930) *d* Gosho (= *Woman, Don't Make Your Name Dirty*)
ONNENPOLI (1965) *d/p/s/c/e* Jarva *w* Pakkasvirta (= *Game Of Luck*)
ONO REVOLÉ ANGELINA, L' (1947) *d/co-s* Zampa *co-s* Cecchi D'Amico *w* Magnani, Zeffirelli 98min (= *Angelina*)
On Our Merry Way = A MIRACLE CAN HAPPEN (1948)
ON PURGE BEBE (1931) *d/ad* J Renoir *co-c* Sparkuhl *w* M Simon, Fernandel 1700m
ON SUCH A NIGHT (1937) *d* Dupont 73min Par
ON SUCH A NIGHT (1955) *d* Asquith 37min JAR
ON THE AVENUE (1937) *d* Del Ruth *c* Andriot *m* Irving Berlin *w* D Powell, Carroll, Faye 7950ft Fox
On the Banks of the Arax = POTU STORONU ARAKSA (1947)
On the Banks of the Niemen = NAD NIEMMEM (1939)
ON THE BEACH (1959) *d/p* Kramer *s* Paxton *fn* Nevil Shute *c* Rotunno *m* Gold *w* Peck, Perkins, Astaire, Gardner 133min *r* UA
ON THE BOWERY (1954) *d/e* Rogosin 65min
ON THE DOUBLE (1961) *d/co-s* Shavelson *c* Stradling *w* Kaye PV* 92min Par
On the Eve of War = KAISEN NO ZENYA (1943)
ON THE FIRING LINE (1912) *d* Ince
ON THE GO (1925) *d* Thorpe
ON THE JUMP (1918) *d/s* Walsh 6rs *r* Fox
On the Line of Fire – Film Reporters = NA LINII OGNYA – OPERATORY KINOKHRONIKI (1941)
ON THE LOOSE (1932) *d/p* Roach 2rs
ON THE LOOSE (1951) *d* Lederer *c* Stout *w* M Douglas, R Young 78min RKO
ON THE POLE (1960) *d/co-c/co-e* R Leacock, Pennebaker
ON THE RIVIERA (1951) *d* W Lang *p* S Siegel *c* Shamroy *chor* Cole *co-a* Wheeler *m* A Newman *w* Kaye, Tierney, Dalio *90min Fox
On the Red Front = NA KRASNOM FRONTYE (1920)
On the Tiger's Back (US) = A CAVALLO DELLA TIGRE (1961)
ON THE TOWN (1949) *co-d/chor* Gene Kelly *co-d* Donen *p* Freed *c* Rosson *co-a* Gibbons *fmpl st/lyr* Comden, A Green *m* L Bernstein *new lyr* Comden, A Green, Edens *'score'* Edens, *Lennie Hayton w* Gene Kelly, Sinatra, Ann Miller, Vera-Ellen *98min MGM
ON THE WATERFRONT (1954) *d* Kazan *p* S Spiegel *s/st* B Schulberg *c* B Kaufman *a* R Day *m* L Bernstein *w* Brando, Saint, Cobb, Malden, Steiger 108min *r* Col
On the Way to Spider Gate = TOCHUKEN KUMOEMON (1936)
ON THIN ICE (1925) *d* St Clair 6300ft WB
On This Earth = CHIJO (1957)
ON TO RENO (1922) *d* Cruze 6rs Pat
ON TRIAL (1928) *d* A Mayo 7269ft WB
On Trial (UK) = AFFAIRE MAURIZIUS, L' (1913)
ON VOUS PARLE (1960) *d/cy* Cayrol, *Claude Durand m* Bach 17min
ON WITH THE SHOW (1929) *d* Crosland *c* Gaudio * 12rs WB
On With The Motley = AMLETO E I SUO CLOWN (1920)
ON YOUR TOES (1927) *d* Newmeyer 5918ft U
ON YOUR TOES (1939) *d* Enright *co-s* Wald *c* Howe *w* O'Connor 94min WB
ONYXKNOPF, DER (1917) *d/p* May *s* Dupont 4rs
OOKAMI (1955) *d/s* Shindo (= *Wolves*)
OOMPAHS, THE (1951) *d* Cannon *8min Col
Open City = ROMA, CITTA APERTA (1945)
OPENING IN MOSCOW (1959) *d* Pennebaker *c* A Maysles 52min
OPENING SPEECH (1962) *d* McLaren 6min NFBC
OPERA CORDIS (1968) *d* Vutovic (part anim)* 11min

OPERA DE QUAT'SOUS, L' (1931) French version of DREIGROSCHENOPER, DIE *w* Préjean, Modot, Artaud 104min WB-NERO (= *The Threepenny Opera*)
OPERA MOUFFU, L' (1958) *d/p/st/s* Varda *c* Vierny *m* Delerue 20min
OPERA-MUSETTE (1942) *co-d/c* C Renoir *co-d/w* Rene Lefevre
OPERATION BETON (1954) *d/s/n* Godard 20min
OPERATION CROSSBOW (1964) *d* Michael Anderson *w* Courtenay, F Mills, Loren, T Howard, Henreid, Palmer, Peppard 70PV* 116min MGM
OPERATION DIPLOMAT (1953) *d/co-s* Guillermin 70min
Operation Disaster (US) = MORNING DEPARTURE (1949)
OPERATION EICHMANN (1961) *d* Springsteen *c* Biroc 93min UA
OPERATION H (c1963) *c* Hanoun
OPERATION LA FONTAINE (1954) *d* Dewever sh
OPERATION MAD BALL (1957) *d* Quine *co-s* Edwards *c* Lawton *w* Lemmon, Rooney 105min Col
Operation Négligé = TSUYOMUSHI ONNA TO YOWAMUSHI OTOKO (1968)
OPERATION PACIFIC (1951) *d/s* George Waggner *c* Giennon *m* M Steiner *w* J Wayne, Neal 108min WB
OPERATION PETTICOAT (1959) *d* Edwards *c* R Harlan *co-a* Golitzen *w* C Grant, Curtis *124min U
Operation San Gennaro (1965) = OPERAZIONE SAN GENNARO
OPERATION SECRET (1952) *d* Lewis Seiler *w* Malden, Cochran, Wilde 108min WB
OPERATOR 13 (1934) *d* Boleslavsky *c* Folsey *w* Davies, G Cooper 81min MGM
OPERATION X (1951) *d/p* Ratoff *c* Périnal *w* Robinson 79min (= *My Daughter Joy*)
OPERAZIONE PAURA (1966) *d/co-s* Bava *85min (= *Curse of the Dead*)
OPERAZIONE SAN GENNARO (1965) *d/co-st/co-s* Risi *co-s* Manfredi *c* Tonti *w* Manfredi, Toto *103min (= *Treasure of San Gennaro/Operation San Gennaro*)
OPERNINA (1936) *d* Gallone
OPFER (1918) *d/p/s* May 4rs
OPFER GANG (1944) *d/co-s* Harlan *2682m UFA
OPHELIA (1962) *d/co-s* Chabrol *c* Rabier *w* Valli 101min
OPIUMKERINGO (1943) *d* Balasz
OPIUMSDROMMEN (1914) *d/s* Madsen
OPOWIESC ATLANYCKA (1955) *d* Jakubowska (= *An Atlantic Story*)
OPPOSITE SEX, THE (1956) *d* D Miller *p* Pasternak *rm* THE WOMEN (1939) *c* Bronner *co-a* Gibbons *w* Allyson, Ann Miller, Moorehead, Sheridan CS* 117min MGM
OPRY HOUSE, THE (1929) *d* Iwerks *p* Disney anim 1rl
OPSTANDELSE, EN (1914) *d* Madsen
OPTA EMPFANGT (1935) *d* Alexeieff anim
OPTICAL POEM, AN (1938) *d* Fischinger *m* Liszt anim* 6min *r* MGM
Optimistic Tragedy = OPTIMISTICHESKAYA TRAGEDIYA (1963)
OPTIMISTICHESKAYA TRAGEDIYA (1963) *d/co-s* Samsanov 121min (= *Optimistic Tragedy*)
OPOWIESC ATLANYCKA (1955) *d* Jakubowska 2321m
OPUS I (1921) *d* Ruttmann 243m (= *Photodram*)
OPUS I (1964) *d* Herbert anim
OPUS II (1921) *d* Ruttmann 31m
OPUS III (1925) *d* Ruttmann 66m
OPUS III (1967) *d* Herbert anim 7min
OPUS IV (1925) *d* Ruttmann 70m
ORA DI ROMA, L' (1961) *d/co-s* Lizzani
ORAGE (1938) *d* M Allégret *s* Achard *m* Auric *w* Morgan, Boyer, Barrault 85min
ORAGE D'ETE (1949) *d/co-s* Jean Gehret *w* Vlady 95min
ORANGES DE JAFFA, LES (1938) *d* Alexeieff anim
Orator, The = UVODNI SLOVO PRONESE (1964)
'ORA PRO NOBIS' OR THE POOR ORPHAN'S LAST PRAYER (1902) *p* Paul 100ft
ORAZI E CURIAZI (1961) *d* T Young *w* Ladd S* 92min (= *Horatio/Duel of Champions*)
ORCHESTRA WIVES (1942) *d* A Mayo *c* Ballard *m* A Newman *w* Glenn Miller, Romero 98min Fox
Orchid for the Tiger, An = TIGRE SE PARFUME A LA DYNAMITE (1965)
OR DANS LA RUE, L' (1934) *d* C Bernhardt *s* Decoin *w* Darrieux
Order of the Daisy (UK) = COMPAGNONS DE LA MARGUERITE (1966)
ORDERS TO KILL (1958) *d* Asquith *w* L Gish, Casarès 111min BL
OR DES MERS, L' (1932) *d* J Epstein *c* Matras
ORDET (1943) *d* Molander *s/w* Lindstrom *w* Sjöström 100min SF
ORDET (1954) *d/s* Dreyer *rm* (1943) 64min (= *The Ward*)
Ordinary Fascism = OBYKNOVENNIYE FASHIZM (1965)
ORDINARY PEOPLE (1942) *d* J Lee, *JB Holmes*
ORDINATIONS (1954) *d* Agostini 31min
OR DU CRISTOBAL, L' (1939) *d* Becker(*uc*), *Jean Stelli c* Hayer *dec* Lourié *w* Préjean, Vanel, Parlo

OR DU DUC, L' (1965) *d/co-st* Baratier *w* Brasseur, Darrieux, Martinelli 88min

ORE DELL'AMORE, LE (1963) *d/co-s/w* Salce *w* Rondi, Riva 100min (= *The Hours of Love*)

OREILLE, L' (1923) *d* Cohl anim

ORE MO MOAE MO (1946) *d/s* Naruse

ORE RAIDERS, THE (1927) *d* Wyler 2rs U

ORFEU NEGRO (1958) *d/co-s/co-di* Camus *c* Bourgoin *105min (= *Black Orpheus*)

Organist of St Vita, The = VARHANIK N SUATEHO VITA (1929)

Organizer, The = COMPAGNI, I (1963)

ORGEUILLEUX, LES (1953) *d/co-s* Y Allegret *co-s/di* Aurenche *co-s* Bost *fn* (*Typhus*) *Jean Paul Sartre c* Phillips *m* Misraki *w* Philipe, Morgan 105min Col

ORIENT EXPRESS (1954) *d* Bragaglia *supn* Rossellini *w* Jurgens

ORIENT QUI VIENT, L' (1934) *d* Leenhardt, *Rene Zuber* Gau

Origin of Sex, The = SEI NO KIGEN (1967)

ORIGINAL CAST ALBUM: 'COMPANY' (1970) *d* Pennebaker *co-c* R Leacock, Pennebaker 16mm* 52min

ORIZURU OSEN (1934) *d* Mizoguchi *w* Yamada (= *Paper Cranes from Osen*)

ORLACS HANDE (1924) *d* Wiene *c* Krampf *w* Veidt (= *The Hands of Orlac*)

ORNAMENT DES VERLIEBTEN HERZENS, DAS (1919) *d* Reiniger *co-anim* Bartosch anim 92m

ORO DI NAPOLI, L' (1954) *d/co-s/w* De Sica *p* Ponti, De Laurentiis *co-s* Zavattini *w* Toto, Loren, Mangano, De Filippo (= *Gold of Naples*)

ORO DI ROMA, L' (1961) *d/co-s* Lizzani 110min

OROS (1960, *uf*) *d* Guerra

OR QUI BRULE, L' (1912) *d* Machin 515m

ORO NERO (1941) *d* Guazzoni

ORO PER I CESARI (1962) *d* De Toth, Freda *w* J Hunter, Girotti S* 66min (= *Gold for the Caesars*)

OROSZLAN UGRANI KESZÜL, AZ (1969) *d* Révész (= *Isle of the Lion*)

O'Rourke of the Royal Mounted (UK) = SASKATCHEWAN (1954)

Orphan, The = FINDLING, DER (1967)

ORPHANS OF THE STORM (1921) *d/s* Griffith *w* L Gish, D Gish 12rs *r* UA

ORPHEE (1950) *d/s* Cocteau *c* Hayer *dec* D'Eaubonne *m* Auric *w* Marais, Casarès, Doniol-Valcroze, Mocky 112min (= *Orpheus*)

ORPHELIN DE PARIS, L' (1923) *d/s* Feuillade 6eps: length unknown

ORPHELINE, L' (1921) *d/s* Feuillade *w* Clair, (Florey) 1 *Les Malheurs de Nemorin* (1500m); 2 *Orphelin* (800); 3 *Le Complot* (800m); 4 *L'Intruse* (800m); 5 *Delivrance* (800m); 6 *Le Traquenard* (800m); 7 *A L'Ombre du Clocher* (800m); 8 *La Conquete D'Un Heritage* (800m); 9 *Soirs de Paris* (800m); 10 *Chagrin D'Amour* (800m); 11 *le Revenant* (800m); 12 *Vers le Bonheur* (800m)

Orpheus = ORPHÉE (1950)

ORRECCHIO, L' (1946) *d/c* Bava sh

ORRIBILE SEGRETO DEL DOTTOR HICHCOCK, L' (1962) *d* Freda *ps* Robert Hampton S* 88min (= *Raptus – The Secret of Dr Hitchcock*)

ORSON WELLES (1966) *d* Reichenbach ORTF

O SAISONS, O CHATEAUX (1957) *d/st/s/n* Varda *22min (= *Castles Through the Ages*)

OSAKA MONOGATARI (1957) *d* Yoshimura, Mizoguchi (= *An Osaka Story*)

OSAKA NATSU NO JIN (1937) *d/s* Kinugasa *w* Yamada (= *The Summer Battle of Osaka*)

OSAKA NO ONNA (1958) *d/s* Kinugasa (= *A Woman of Osaka*)

OSAKA NO YADA (1954) *d/s* Gosho (= *An Inn At Osaka/Hotel At Osaka*)

Osaka Story, An = OSAKA MONOGATARI (1957)

OSCAR, THE (1966) *d/co-s* Rouse *ex-p* Levine *c* Ruttenberg *w* Boyd, Lawford, B Crawford, Oberon, Brennan, Cotton, Parker, Hope(*uc*) *119min

OSCAR (1967) *d/co-s* Molinaro *w* De Funes *85min Gau

OSCAR CHAMPION DE TENNIS (1932) *d/st/w* Tati

OSCAR WILDE (1960) *d* Ratoff *c* Périnal *w* R Richardson 96min

OSCUROS SUENOS DE AGOSTO (1967) *d* Picazo *w* Lindfors *105min (= *Dark Dreams of August*)

OSEN (1940) *d* Ermler, *I Menakev* 292m (= *Autumn*)

07, TAXI (1943) *d/s* Pagliero

O'SHAUGHNESSY'S BOY (1935) *d* Boleslavsky *c* Howe *w* Beery 88min MGM

OSHIKIRI SHINKON KI (1930) *d/s* Naruse (= *Record of Newly-Weds*)

OSKLENICKU VIC (1953) *d/co-s* Pojar *co-s* Brdecka anim (= *A Little Drop Too Much*)

OSMY DZIEN TYGODNIA (1957) *d/s* A Ford *w* Cybulski part *85min (= *The Eighth Day of the Week*)

OSONE-KE NO ASA (1946) *d* Kinoshita (= *A Morning with the Osone Family*)

OSOREZAN NO ONNA (1965) *d/s* Gosho S 98min Sho (= *An Innocent Witch*)

O SOY CUBA (1964) *d* Kalatozov *s Yevtushenko* (= *Ja-Kuba/I am Cuba*)

OSPEDALE DEL DELITTL, L' (1950) *d* Comencini

OSRAM (1956) *d* Alexeieff anim 1min (4 films)

O S S (1946) *d* Pichel *p/s* Maibaum *co-a* Dreier *c* Lindon *co-m* Amfitheatrof 107min Par

OSSESSIONE (1942) *d/co-s* Visconti *co-s* Pietrangeli, De Santis *fn* (*The Postman Always Rings Twice*) *James M Cain co-c* Tonti *w* Girotti 135min

Assi's Diary (UK) = OSSIS TAGEBUCH (1917)

OSSIS TAGEBUCH (1917) *d/co-s* Lubitsch 1rl (= *Ossi's Diary*)

OSTATNI ETAP (1948) *d/co-s* Jakubowska 110min (= *The Last Stage*)

OSTLER JOE (1908) *st/w* Griffith Bio

OSTRE SLEDOVANE VLAKY (1966) *d/w* Menzel *s* Menzel, *Bohumil Hrabal fn Hrabal* 92min (= *Closely Observed Trains*)

Ostrich has Two Eggs, The = OEUFS DE L'AUTRICHE, LES (1957)

OSUNLIGA MUREN, DEN (1944) *d* Molander SF

OSVENTNIK (1958) *d* Vukotic anim* 13min (= *The Revenger*)

OSVOBOZHDENIE (1940) *co-d/e* Dovzhenko *co-d* Solntzeva *co-c* Alexandrov 1720m (= *Liberation*)

OSVOBOZHDENNYI KITAI (1952) *d* Gerasimov (= *China Liberated*)

OSWEGO (1943) *d* W Van Dyke

OTELLO (1956) *d/s* Yutkevitch *fp Shakespeare m Khatchaturian w* Bondarchuk *2996m (= *Othello*)

OTETS SERGII (1918) *d* Protazanov *fst Tolstoi w* Mozhukhin 1920m (= *Father Sergius*)

OTHELLO (1952) *d/p/s/w* Welles *fpl Shakespeare co-c* Aldo *dec* Trauner 90min

Othello = OTELLO (1956)

OTHELLO (1966) *d Stuart Burge w* Olivier PV* 166min

OTHER HALF, THE (1919) *d/s* K Vidor *w* Pitts, D Butler 50min

OTHER LOVE, THE (1947) *d* De Toth *fn Erich Maria Remarque c* Milner *m* Rozsa *w* Stanwyck, Niven, Conte 95min *r* UA

OTHER MAN, THE (1916) *d/w* Arbuckle 2rs Tri

OTHER MEN'S WOMEN (1931) *d* Wellman *w* Cagney, Astor, Blondell 70min WB (= *Steel Highway*)

Other One, The = L'UNE ET L'AUTRE (1967)

Other Shore, The = CHUZHOY BEREZ (1930)

OTHER TOMORROW, THE (1930) *d* Bacon *c* Garmes 5754ft WB

Othon = YEUX NE PEUVENT PAS EN TOUT TEMPS SE FERMER, LES (1969)

OTLEY (1969) *d/co-s Dick Clement ex-p* Foreman *w* Courtenay, Schneider *91min

OTOKO GOKORO (1925) *d/s* Gosho (= *Man's Heart*)

OTOKO TO ONNA TO INU (1964) *d* Kuri anim 3min (= *Man, Woman and Dog*)

OTOME-GOKORO SANNIN SHIMAI (1935) *d/s* Naruse (= *Three Sisters With Maiden Hearts*)

OTOSHI ANA (1961) *d* Teshigahara (= *Pitfall/A Cheap Sweet and a Kid*)

OTOTO (1960) *d* Ichikawa *c* Miyagawa *w* Mori CS* 98min Dai (= *Her Brother*)

OTRA, LA (1947) *w* Del Rio

OTRO CRISTOBAL, EL (1962) *d* Gatti CS 115min

OTTO E MEZZO (1963) *d/co-st/co-s* Fellini *co-s* Rondi *c* Di Venanzo *dec* Gherardi *m* Rota *w* Mastroianni, Cardinale, Aimée 135min (= *Eight and a Half*)

Ouanzerbe, Capitale de la Magie = MAGICIENS NOIRS, LES (1949)

OUBLIE (1927) *d* Dulac (= *La Princesse Mandane*)

OU EST PASSE TOM? (1971) *d/ad/di* Giovanni *105min

OU ETES-VOUS DONC? (1969) *d/s* Groulx *

OURAGAN SUR LA MONTAGNE, L' (1922) *d/st/s* Duvivier

OUR BETTERS (1933) *d* Cukor *p* Selznick *fpl W Somerset Maugham m* M Steiner *w* Constance Bennett, Roland 78min RKO

Our Champions = NASHI CHEMPIONY (1950)

Our Country's Youth = MOLODOST NASHI STRANYI (1946)

OUR DAILY BREAD (1930) *d* Murnau 2580m Fox (= *City Girl*)

OUR DAILY BREAD (1934) *d/p* K Vidor *di* J Mankiewicz *m* A Newman 74min *r* UA

OUR DANCING DAUGHTERS (1928) *d Harry Beaumont c* Barnes *a* Gibbons *w* J Crawford 7652ft MGM

OUR GANG (1920–44) *co-d* G Douglas, Stevens, G Sidney *p* Roach (1920–38) *r* MGM

OUR GANG FOLLIES OF 1938 (1937) *d* G Douglas *p* Roach 2rs MGM

OUR HEARTS WERE YOUNG AND GAY (1944) *d Lewis Allen fn Otis Skinner and Kimbrough w* D Gish, C Ruggles 9rs Par

OUR HOSPITALITY (1923) *co-d/p* Keaton *co-d Jack Blystone co-s* Bruckman *w* Keaton, Talmadge 7rs Metro

Our Instructor = WARAREGA KYOKAN (1939)

Our Last Spring = EROICA (1960)

OUR LEADING CITIZEN (1939) *d* Santell *c* Milner *w* S Hayward 89min Par

Our Little Red Riding Hood = NASE KARKULKA (1960)

OUR MAN FLINT (1965) *d* Daniel Mann *c* Fapp *m* Goldsmith *w* J Coburn, Cobb CS* 107min Fox

OUR MAN IN HAVANA (1960) *d/p* C Reed *s/fn* Greene *c* Morris *w* Guinness, Ives, M O'Hara, Coward, R Richardson CS 111min Col

OUR MODERN MAIDENS (1929) *d* Conway *w* J Crawford, Fairbanks Jr 6976ft MGM

OUR MOTHER'S HOUSE (1967) *d/p* Clayton *m* Delerue *w* Bogarde *105min *r* MGM

OUR RELATIONS (1936) *d Harry Lachman p* Roach *c* Maté *w* Laurel, Hardy 65min *pc* Laurel *r* MGM

OUR RUSSIAN FRONT (1941) *d/s* Ivens, Milestone *m* Shostakovitch, Eisler *n* W Huston 1500m (= *Notre Front Russe*)

OURS, L' (1960) *d/s/c* Sechan *w* Blanche *90min (= *The Bear*)

OURS ET LA POUPEE, L' (1970) *d* Deville *w* Bardot * (= *The Bear and the Doll*)

OURSINS, LES (1928) *d* Painlevé

OURSINS, LES (1958) *d* Painlevé *rm* (1928) *12min

OUR TOWN (1940) *d* S Wood *p* Lesser *co-s/fpl* T Wilder *c* Glennon *des* Menzies *as-des* Horner *m* Copland *w* Holden, Mitchell 90min *r* UA

OUR VERY OWN (1949) *d* D Miller *c* Garmes *a* R Day *m* V Young *w* Blyth, F Granger, N Wood 93min *r* RKO

OUR VINES HAVE TENDER GRAPES (1945) *d* Rowland *s* Trumbo *c* Surtees *co-a* Gibbons *w* Robinson, M O'Brien, Moorehead 105min MGM

OUR WIFE (1931) *d James Horne p* Roach *w* Laurel, Hardy, Turpin 2rs (sd) *r* MGM

OUR WIFE (1941) *d* Stahl *w* M Douglas, C Coburn 94min Col

Our Wonderful Years = KAACHAN TO JUICHI-NIN NO KODOMO (1966)

OUTCAST (1937) *d* Florey *co-s* Schary *c* Maté 8rs Par

OUTCAST LADY (1934) *d/p* Leonard *fst M Arlen c* Rosher *w* Constance Bennett, H Marshall 77min MGM

OUTCAST OF THE ISLANDS (1951) *d* C Reed *fn Joseph Conrad w* T Howard, R Richardson *pc* C Reed *r* BL

OUTCASTS OF POKER FLAT, THE (1919) *d* J Ford *fsts* (*Outcasts of Poker Flat/The Luck of Roaring Camp*) *Bret Harte w* Carey 6rs U

OUTCASTS OF POKER FLAT, THE (1937) *d Christy Cabanna fst Bret Harte rm* (1919) *w* Heflin 68min RKO

OUTCASTS OF POKER FLAT, THE (1952) *d* J Newman *p* Blaustein *fst Bret Harte rm* (1919) *c* La Shelle *m* Friedhofer *w* A Baxter, M Hopkins 80min Fox

OUTER AND INNER SPACE (1965) *d* Warhol 16mm 70min

OUTLAW, THE (1940 *r* 1946) *co-d/p* H Hughes *co-d* Hawks(*uc*) *s* Furthman *c* Toland *m* V Young *w* J Russell, Mitchell, W Huston 123min RKO

Outlaws, The = PARANOMI, I (1958)

OUTLAWS OF THE ORIENT (1937) *d* Schoedsack 61min Col

OUTLAW STALLION, THE (1954) *d* Sears *64min Col (= *The White Stallion*)

Out of Darkness (UK) = SEDUTA ALLA SUA DESTRA (1968)

OUT OF THE CLOUDS (1955) *d/p* Dearden, *Michael Relph* *88min *pc* Ealing

Out of the Darkness (UK) = TEENAGE CAVEMAN (1958)

OUT OF THE FOG (1941) *d* Litvak *p* Wallis *co-s* Wald, Rossen *fpl* (*The Gentle People*) *Irwin Shaw c* Howe *w* Lupino, Garfield, Mitchell 93min WB

OUT OF THE NIGHT (1945) *d* Ulmer 85min (= *Strange Illusion*)

OUT OF THE PAST (1947) *d* J Tourneur *s/fn* (*Build my Gallows High*) Mainwaring (*ps* Homes) *c* Musuraca *w* Mitchum, K Douglas, R Fleming 97min RKO (= *Build my Gallows High*)

OUT OF TRUE (1951) *d* P Leacock 40min

Outpost in Malaya (US) = PLANTER'S WIFE, THE (1952)

OUTPOST IN MOROCCO (1949) *d* Florey *c* Andriot *w* Raft, Tamiroff 92min *r* UA

OUTRAGE, THE (1915) *d/p* Hepworth

OUTRAGE (1950) *d/p/co-s* Lupino *c* Stout 75min RKO

OUTRAGE, THE (1964) *d* Ritt *rm* RASHOMON (1950) *c* Howe *m* North *w* P Newman, Robinson, Laurence Harvey, Bloom 97min MGM

OUTRIDERS, THE (1950) *d* Rowland *co-a* Gibbons *m* Previn *w* McCrea, Novarro 93min MGM

OUTSIDER, THE (1961) *d* Delbert Mann *s* Stern *c* La Shelle *m* Rosenman *w* Curtis 108min U

Outsiders, The (UK) = BANDE A PART (1964)

OUTSIDE THE LAW (1921) *d/p/s* Browning *w* Chaney 8rs

OUTSIDE THE LAW (1930) *d/st* Browning *rm* (1921) *w* Robinson 81min U

OUTSIDE THE LAW (1956) *d* J Arnold *c* Glassberg *w* Danton 81min U

OUTWARD BOUND (1930) *d Robert Milton c* Mohr *w* L Howard, Fairbanks Jr 88min WB

OUTWEST (1918) *d/w* Arbuckle *w* Keaton 2rs Par (= *The Sheriff*)

OUT WEST WITH THE HARDYS (1938) *d* G Seitz *w* Rooney 90min MGM

OUTWITTING DAD (1913) *w* Hardy

OUVERT POUR CAUSE D'INVENTAIRE (1946) *d* Resnais *w* (Philipe) 16mm

The Overcoat = SHINEL (1959)

Overcoat, the (UK) = CAPPOTTO, IL (1952)

OVER GLAS GESPROKEN (1957) d/s/e Haanstra
Overgreppet = VIOL, LE (1967)
OVERLANDERS, THE (1946) d/s Watt p Balcon 91min
OVERLAND PACIFIC (1954) d Sears *73min r UA
OVER MY DEAD BODY (1942) d St Clair 68min Fox
Overtaxed, The = TARTASSATI, I (1959)
OVER THE FENCE (1917) w H Lloyd Pat
OVER THE HILL (1931) d H King co-s Furthman rm (1920)
    c J Seitz w March 94min Fox
OVER THE MOON (1939) d Thorton Freeland w Oberon,
    Harrison, (L Gilbert) 79min
OVER 21 (1945) d-c Vidor p/s Buchman fpl R Gordon c
    Maté w C Coburn, I Dunne 102min Col
OVERVAL, DE (1962) d/s Rotha 97/81min JAR (= The
    Silent Raid)
OVOCE RAJAKYCH STROMU JIME (1970) d/co-s
    Chytilova *98min (= We May Eat of the Fruit of the
    Trees of the Garden)
OWL AND THE PUSSY CAT THE (1953) d/co-p Halas,
    Batcheler fpm Edward Lear anim* 7min
OWL AND THE PUSSYCAT, THE (1970) d Ross p Stark
    des Adam w Segal PV* 96min pc Stark r Col
OX-BOW INCIDENT, THE (1942) d Wellman p/s Trotti c
    AC Miller co-a R Day w H Fonda, D Andrews,
    Quinn, Darwell 75min Fox (= Strange Incident)
OYAJI TO SONOKO (1929) d Gosho
OYSTER DREDGER, THE (1915) d/s Chaney 2rs
Oyster Princess, The (UK) = AUSTERNPRINZESSIN, DIE
    (1919)
OYSTERS ARE IN SEASON (1963) d Rogosin
OYUSAMA (1951) d Mizoguchi c Miyagawa Dai (= Miss
    Oyu)
OZVOBOZHDENNAYA FRANTSYA (1946) d Yutkevitch
    (= France Liberated)

PABLO CASALS (1955) d Baratier TV
PACHA, LE (1967) d/co-s Lautner co-s Audiard dec
    D'Eaubonne w Gabin *90min (= Showdown)
PACIENTKA DOCTORA HEGLA (1940) d/s Vavra
PACIFIC NORTHWEST (1944) d/co-c W Van Dyke s
    Maddow n W Huston
PACIFIC RENDEZVOUS (1942) d G Sidney co-s Kurnitz a
    Gibbons 76min MGM
PACIFIC 231 (1949) d Mitry m Honegger 10min
Pacific War, The = DAITOA SENSO (1968)
PACIFISTA, LA (1971) d/co-s Jancsó c Di Palma w Vitti
    *87min
PACK UP YOUR TROUBLES (1932) d G Marshall,
    Raymond McCarey p Roach w Laurel, Hardy, G
    Marshall 68min r MGM
PACSIRTA (1964) d Ranódy 105min (= Skylark)
PADDY (1970) d D Haller *87min
PADDY-THE-NEXT-BEST-THING (1923) d Graham J
    Cutts co-s H Wilcox w Marsh 7rs
PADENIE BERLINA (1949) d/co-s Mikhail Chiaureli m
    Shostakovich * Part 1: 2308m Part 2: 2273m (= The
    Fall of Berlin)
PADENIE DINASTI ROMANOVIKH (1927) d/s/e Shub
    2080m (= Fall of the Roman Dynasty)
Pä Detta Numera Vanliga Sätt = AKTENSKA PSBYRAN
    (1912)
PADLOCKED (1926) d/p Dwan c Howe w Fairbanks Jr
    6700ft FPL
PADRE (1912) d Pastrone, Dante Testa
PADRE DI FAMIGLIA, IL (1967) d/st/co-s N Loy w
    Caron, Manfredi *115min (= Head of the Family)
PADRI E FIGLI (1957) d/co-s Monicelli dec Gherardi w De
    Sica, Mastroianni 104min (= Like Father, Like Son)
PAESE DEL NASCITA MUSSOLINI, IL (1943) d Emmer,
    Enrico Gras, Tatiana Grauding
PAESTUM (1932) d Pogglioli sh
PAGADOR DE PROMESSAS, O (1962) d/s Duarte 97min
PAGAN, THE (1929) d WS Van Dyke w Novaro, Crisp,
    Adorée 7459ft MGM
PAGAN LOVE SONG (1950) d R Alton p Freed co-a
    Gibbons w Keel, Esther Williams * 76min MGM
PAGE MISS GLORY (1935) d LeRoy co-s D Daves c Folsey
    w Davies, D Powell, Astor 90min WB
Pages of Life = STRANITSY ZHIZN (1948)
PAID (1930) d S Wood co-ad/di MacArthur w J Crawford
    7700ft MGM (= Within the Law)
PAID IN FULL (1950) d Dieterle p Wallis co-m V Young w
    R Cummings, L Scott 105min Par (= Bitter Victory)
PAID TO LOVE (1927) d Hawks co-s S Miller c O'Connell w
    G O'Brien, W Powell 6888ft Fox
PAIN DE BARBARIE, LE (1948) d/s Leenhardt 15min
PAINEL (1951) d Barreto n Cavalcanti sh
PAINTED BOATS (1945) d Crichton p Balcon as-p
    Cornelius 63min
PAINTED LADY, THE (1912) d Griffith 1rl Bio
PAINTED POST (1928) d Eugene Forde w Mix 4952ft Fox
PAINTED VEIL, THE (1934) d Boleslavsky fn Somerset
    Maugham c Daniels m Stothart w Garbo, H Marshall,
    Hersholt 83min MGM
PAINTING THE CLOUDS WITH SUNSHINE (1951) d D
    Butler chor Prinz w V Mayo 86min WB
PAINT YOUR WAGON (1969) d Logan p/fpl A Lerner,
    Frederick Loewe ad Chayefsky c Fraker, Griggs

(2nd) additional songs Previn w Marvin, Eastwood,
    Seberg PV* 70 164min Par
PAIR OF SILK STOCKINGS, A (1918) d Walter Edwards
    w C Talmadge 5rs
PAISA (1946) d/p/co-s/co-s Rossellini co-s/co-st Fellini co-st
    Pagliero, Vasco Pratolini(uc) c Martelli 124min
    (= Paisan)
Paisan = PAISA (1946)
PAJAMA GAME, THE (1957) d/co-p Donen, G Abbot
    co-s/fpl G Abbot chor Fosse w D Day * 101min WB
PAJAMA PARTY (1964) d Weis w F Crosby a D Haller w
    Lamour 85min PV* AI
P.A.K. = ? MOTORIST, THE (1906)
Palanquin, The = DOCHU SUGOROKU KAGO (1926)
PALEFACE, THE (1921) d/s Keaton, Cline w Keaton
PALEFACE, THE (1948) d McLeod co-st/co-s Tashlin c
    Rennahan co-a Dreier m V Young w Hope, J Russell
    91min Par
PALERMO NORMANNA (1948) d Sala sh
PALIO (1932) d/co-s/co-e Blasetti
På Livets Ödesvägar (1913) d/s Stiller 1160m
PAL JOEY (1957) d G Sidney p Kohlmar co-m Dunning c
    Lipstein fn J O'Hara w Hayworth, Sinatra, Novak
    *111min Col
PALLE ALENE I VERDEN (1949) d A Henning Jenson s
    Henning Jenson 20min (= Palle alone in the World)
Palle Alone in the World = PALLE ALENE I VERDEN
    (1949)
PALM BEACH STORY, THE (1942) d/st P Sturges c Milner
    a Dreier m V Young w Colbert, McCrea, Astor, Rudy
    Vallee 90min Par
PALMIER A HUILE, LE (1963) d Rouch 16mm
PALM SPRINGS WEEKEND (1963) d Taurog c Lipstein
    *100min WB
PALMY DAYS (1931) d/p Edward Sutherland st/s Cantor c
    Toland w Cantor, Raft pc Goldwyn 9rs
Paloma, La (1944) = GROSSE FREIHEIT NR. 7
PALOOKA FROM PADUCAH (1935) d Charles Lamont w
    Keaton 2rs
PALS IN PARADISE (1926) d G Seitz 6696ft r PRC
PALS IN PERIL (1927) d Thorpe
PAL-UTCAI FIUK, A (1917) d Balasz
PAL-UTCAI FIUK (1924) d Balasz
PAL UTCAI FIUK, A (1969) d Fabri 105min (= Boys of
    Paul Street, The)
PAMET NASEHO (1963) d Nemec (compilation)
    (= Memory of our Time)
PAMIATKA Z CELULOZY (1954) d/co-s Kawalerowicz
    (= a Night of Remembrance)
PAMIETNIKI CHLOPOW (1952) d/s Munk 13min
PAMPA BARBARA (1943) d co-d Fregonese 100min
PAMPA SALVA JE (1966) d/co-s Fregonese w R Taylor
    70mm *108min BL (= Savage Pampas)
PAMYATI SERGO ORDZMONIKIDZYE (1937) d Vertov,
    Elisabeth Svilova co-s/co-e Vertov 2rs (= In Memory
    of Sergei Ordzhonikidzye)
PAN (1962) d Henning Jensen s Henning Jensen
PAN (1920) d Fejos
PAN (1961) d/p Van Den Horst 23min
Pan = KORT AR SOMMAREN (1962)
PANAMA HATTIE (1942) d McLeod p Freed a Gibbons c
    Folsey w Sothern, Dailey 79min MGM
Pan Chopali = ARE GA MINATO NO HI DA (1961)
PANDORA AND THE FLYING DUTCHMAN (1951)
    d/co-p/s Lewin co-p/d/s Lewin co-p Woolf c Cardiff
    w Rawsthorne w Gardner, Mason *123min MGM
Pandora's Box (UK) = BUCHSE DER PANDORA DIE
    (1928)
PANE, AMORE, E . . . (1955) d/co-st/co-s Risi c Rotunno w
    De Sica, Loren CS* 85min (= Scandal in Sorrento)
PANE, AMORE E FANTASIA (1953) d/co-s Comencini di
    De Sica w Lollobrigida, De Sica
PANE, AMORE E GELOSIA (1954) d/co-s Comencini di
    De Sica w Lollobrigida, De Sica
PANE E ZOLFO (1954) d Pontecorvo sh
PANENSTVI (1937) d/co-s Vavra
PANHANDLE (1948) d Lesley Selander co-p/co-s/w
    Edwards 85min AA
PANIC IN THE STREETS (1950) d Kazan p S Siegel s R
    Murphy c Joe Macdonald co-a Wheeler m A Newman
    w Widmark, P Douglas, Palance 93min Fox
PANIC IN YEAR ZERO (1962) d Milland co-ex-p Arkoff a
    D Haller w Milland 92min WB
PANIQUE (1946) d/co-s Duvivier fn Georges Simenon (Les
    Fiancailles de Mr Hire) co-s/co-di Charles Spaak c
    Hayer m Ibert w M Simon, romance 100min
PANTAPODES (1931) d Painlevé m Jaubert
PANTA RHEI (1951) d/s/c/e Haanstra
PANTHEA (1917) d/s Dwan co-p N Talmadge co-c Rosson
    w N Talmadge, Von Stroheim 7rs
PANTOMIMES (1954) d Paul Paviot w Mardeau *20min
PANZERGEWOLBE, DAS (1914) d May dec Leni 1103m
PANZERGEWOLBE, DIE (1925) d/co-s Lupu-Pick 2729m
PAPAGENO (1935) d/p Reiniger anim 11min
PAPA, MAMAN, LA BONNE ET MOI (1954) d/co-
    st/co-ad/di Le Chanois m Van Parys w De Funès
    97min
PAPA, MAMAN, MA FEMME ET MOI (1955) d/co-
    st/ad/di Le Chanois m Van Parys w De Funès
    105min

PAPARAZZI (1963) d/s/e Rozier w Bardot, Piccoli 600m
PAPA'S DELICATE CONDITION (1963) d G Marshall c
    Griggs co-a Piereira w Cook 98min Par
Peper = PAPIR (1943)
Paper Cranes from Osen = ORIZURU OSEU (1934)
Paper Doll's Whisper of Spring = KAMI-NINGYO HARU
    NO SASAYAKI (1926)
Paperhanger, The = WORK (1915)
PAPIER PROTEE, LE (1896) d Méliès 20m
PAPILLON FANTASTIQUE, LE (1909) d Méliès 80m
PAPIR (1943) d/s Henning Jensen 11min (= Paper)
PAPOUL (1929) d M Allégret
PAPPA SOKES (1947) d Mattsson w Björnstrand (= A
    Father Wanted)
PAQUEBOT LIBERTE, LE (1950) d Mitry (= Liberté)
PAQUEBOT TENACITY, LE (1934) d/co-s Duvivier c
    Hayer, Matras, Thirard e Le Chanois m Wiener w
    Prejean
PARABOLA D'ORO (1955) d/c/e De Seta 12min
PARACELSUS (1943) d Pabst w Krauss 106min
PARADE (1952) d/s C and R Eames c Eames m Sousa
    *6min (= Here They Come Down the Street)
PARADE DE CHAPEAUX (1936) d Alexeieff anim
PARADE EN SEPT NUITS (1941) d M Allégret st Achard
    w Barrault Pat
PARADE SOOLS (1932) d Alexeieff anim
PARADINE CASE, THE (1947) d Hitchcock p/s Selznick
    ad Reville, Bridie c Garmes m Waxman w Peck,
    Laughton, E Barrymore, C Coburn, Valli 110min
    RUA
PARADISE FOR BUSTER (1952, ur) w Keaton 39min
PARADISE FOR TWO (1927) d/p La Cava c Cronjager
    6187ft Par
PARADISE ISLAND (1930) d Glennon 8rs
Paradise Road = VLICKA V RAJI (1936)
PARADISO NELL'OMBRA DELLE SPADE (FIUME
    D'ITALIA DURANTE L'OCCUPAZIONE DEI
    LEGIONARI), IL (1920) s D'Annunzio
PARADISO PERDUTO, IL (1948) d/s Emmer, Enrico Gras
    10min (= Bosch)
PARADISO TERRESTRE (1940 r 1946) d/s Emmer, Enrico
    Gras, Tatiana Grauding
Paradiso Terrestre, Il = A CHACUN SON PARADIS
    (1956)
PARADIS PERDU (1938) d/co-s Gance c Matras w Presle
    88min
PARAKH (1960) d Roy
PARAMOUNT ON PARADE (1930) d Schertzinger,
    Lubitsch, Tuttle, Goulding, Edward Sutherland,
    Dorothy Arzner, Otto Brower, Victor Heerman,
    Edwin H Knopf, Rowland V Lee, Lothar Mendes co-c
    Milner w Arthur, G Bancroft Bow, C Brooke, G
    Cooper, K Francis, Chevalier, March, W Powell
    PARANOIAC (1963) d F Francis 80min JAR
PARANOMI, I (1958) p/d/s Koundouros w Hadjidakis
    90min (= The Outlaws/The Hunted)
PARAPLICKO (1957) d Pojar anim (= The Little Umbrella)
PARAPLUIE FANTASTIQUE OU DIX FEMMES SOUS
    UNE OMBRELLE, LE (1903) d Méliès 55m
PARAPLUIES DE CHERBOURG, LES (1964) d/s Demy c
    Rabier m Legrand dec Evein w Deneuve, Vernon
    *90min Fox
PARAS PATHAR (1958) d/s S Ray c Mitra m Shankar
    111min (= The Philosopher's Stone)
Paratrooper, The (US) = RED BERET, THE (1953)
PARA VESTIR SANTOS (1955) d Torre Nilsson 78min
    (= To Clothe the Saints)
PAR AVION (1957) d Breer anim 16mm 5min
PARDESI (1957) co-d/co-p/co-s Abbas co-d V M Pronin
    (= Khazdeni Za Tri Morya)
PARDESSUS DE DEMI-SAISON, LE (1917) d Feyder
    261m Gau
PARDESSUS LE MUR (1959) d/st Le Chanois *101min
PAR DIX-HUIT METRES DE FOND (1943) d/p Cousteau
    16min
PARDNERS (1956) d Taurog c Fapp w J Lewis, Martin,
    Moorehead VV* 90min Par
Par Dnu, O = A QUELQUES JOURS PRES (1968)
PARDON MY BERTH MARKS (1940) d Jules White s
    Bruckman w Keaton 17min Col
PARDONNEZ NOS OFFENSES (1956) d/s/w Hossein w
    Vlady 81min
PARDON US (1931) d James Parrott p Roach w Laurel,
    Hardy 55min r MGM (= Jailbirds)
PARENTS TERRIBLES, LES (1948) d/s/fpl Cocteau c
    Kelber co-dec Bérard m Auric w Marais 98min
PARENT TRAP, THE (1961) d/s Swift c Ballard w H Mills,
    M O'Hara, C Ruggles, Keith *124min
PARFUM DE LA DAME EN NOIR, LE (1931) d L'Herbier
PARFUM DE LA DAME EN NOIR, LE (1949) d Daquin
    fn Gaston Leroux m Wiener w Reggiani, Modot
    100min
PARIAS DE LA GLOIRE (1963) d Decoin w Rouet, Jurgens
    DS 100min
PARIGI E'SEMPRE PARIGI (1951) d/co-s Emmer w
    Alekan w Bosè, Mastroianni 110min (= Paris is
    Always Paris)
PARIGI O CARA (1962) d/co-s/st/w Caprioli c Di Palma
    *91min

PARINETA (1954) *d* Roy *fst Chatterjee*
PARI ORIGINAL, UN (1912) *d/s/w* Linder Pat
PARIS (1926) *d/s* Goulding *a* Gibbons *w* J Crawford 5580ft MGM
PARIS (1929) *d/p* Badger *c* Polito *w* Pitts part *100min FN
PARIS BEGUIN (1931) *d* Genina *w* Gabin, Fernandel
Paris Belongs to Me (UK) = PARIS NOUS APPARTIENT (1961)
PARIS BLUES (1961) *d* Ritt *c* Matras *a* Trauner *m Duke Ellington* *w* P Newman, Woodward, Poitier, *Louis Armstrong*, Reggiani 98min *pc* Brando *r* UA
PARIS BRULE-T-IL? (1966) *d* Clément *p* Graetz *s* Coppola, Vidal, Aurenche, Bost, *Brule french di* Moussy *w* Belmondo, Boyer, Caron, Cassel, Delon, K Douglas, G Ford, Montand, Perkins, Piccoli, Signoret, Trintignant, Welles, Stack, Gelin 70PV* (last scene only) 173min Par (= *Is Paris Burning?*)
PARIS CALLING (1941) *d Edwin L Marin* *c* Krasner *w* Bergner, R Scott, Rathbone, Cobb 95min U
PARIS-CINEMA (1929) *d* Mitry, *Pierre Chenal*
PARIS-DEAUVILLE (1935) *d* Delannoy *sh*
PARIS DES MANNEQUINS, LE (1962) *d* Reichenbach 12min
PARIS DES PHOTOGRAPHES, LE (1962) *d* Reichenbach 13min
PARIS DIX NEUF CENT . . . (1947) *d* Vedrès *ass-d* Renais 90min
PARIS EST LE DESERT FRANCAIS (1957) *d/pc* Leenhardt 762m
PARISETTE (1921) *d/s* Feuillade *w* Clair 1 *Manoela* (1·920m); 2 *Le Secret de Mme Stephen*; 3 *L'Affaire de Nevilly*; 4 *L'Enquête*; 5 *La Piste*; 6 *Grand-Père*; 7 *Le Faux Reverend*; 8 *Family House*; 9 *L'Impasse*; 10 *Le Triomphe de Cogolin*; 11 *La Fortune de Joaquim*; 12 *Le Secret de Costabella* eps 2–12: all 800m
Paris-Express = SOUVENIRS DE PARIS (1928)
PARIS HOLIDAY (1958) *d* g Oswald *p/st* Hope *w* Hope, Ekberg, P Sturges, Fernandel TR* 100min *r* UA
PARIS HONEYMOON (1939) *d* Tuttle *c* Struss *w* B Crosby, Horton, Tamiroff 92min Par
Parisian Cobbler = PARIZMSKII SAPOZHNIK (1928)
PARISIAN NIGHTS (1925) *d* Santell *c* E Haller *w* Karloff, Adorée 6278ft
PARISIAN SCANDAL, A (1922) *d* Conway 5rs U
PARISIENNE, LA (1957) *d Michel Boisrond* *w* Bardot, Boyer *87min
PARISIENNES, LES (1961) *ep Sophie d/co-st* M Allégret *co-st* Vadim *c* Thirard *w* Deneuve 90min (all film)
Paris Incident (US) = TROIS TELEGRAMMES (1950)
PARIS IN SPRING (1935) *d* Milestone *c* Tetzlaff *w* Lupino, Tamiroff 80min Par
Paris is Always Paris = PARIGI E' SEMPRE PARIGI (1951)
PARISISKOR (1927) *d* Molander SF
PARIS JAMAIS VU (1968) *d/s/co-c* Lamorisse *21min (= *Paris Rediscovered*)
PARIS LA BELLE (1959) *rm* (incorporating) SOUVENIRS DE PARIS (1928) *d/co-s* J Prévert *di/cy/lyr* *w* J Prévert *c* Vierny *co-e* Colpi * (the new sequences) 22½min
PARIS LA NUIT (1956) *d* Baratier, Valère 25min
PARIS MANGE SON PAIN (1958) *d/w* P Prévert *cy* J Prévert *w* Daquin, Trauner 20min
PARIS-MEDITERRANEE (1931) *d* May 7500ft (= *Into the Blue*)
PARIS NOUS APPARTIENT (1961) *d/co-s* Rivette *w* Brialy, Chabrol, Demy, Godard 140min *pc* Truffaut, Chabrol (= *Paris Belongs to Me*)
PARIS PALACE-HOTEL (1956) *d* Verneuil *c* Agostini *w* Boyer, Arnoul, Carette *99min
PARIS QUI DORT (1924) *d/s* Clair *w* Préjean 61min (= *Le Rayon Invisible/The Crazy Ray*)
Paris Rediscovered (UK) = PARIS JAMAIS VU (1968)
PARIS UNDERGROUND (1945) *d* Ratoff *f* Constance Bennett *c* Garmes *w* Constance Bennett, (A McLaglen) 97min *r* UA
PARIS VU PAR . . . (1964) 16mm *98min (= *Six in Paris*)
ep MONTPARNASSE ET LEVALLOIS *supn/s* Godard *c* A Maysles
ep ST GERMAIN-DES-PRES *d/co-s Jean Douchet*
ep LA MUETTE *d/s/w* Chabrol *c* Rabier
ep PLACE DE L'ETOILE *d/s/e* Rohmer 15min
ep RUE ST DENIS *d/s* Pollet
ep GARE DU NORD *d/s* Rouch
PARIS WHEN IT SIZZLES (1963) *d/co-p* Quine *co-p/s* Axelrod *st* Duvivier, Jeanson *a* D'Eaubonne *c* C Lang *w* A Hepburn, Curtis, Coward, Holden, (Dietrich) * 110min Par
PARIWAR (1956) *d* Roy, *Asit Sen* *p* Roy
PARIZHSKII SAPOZHNIK (1928) *d* Ermler 2065m (= *Parisian Cobbler*)
PARK ROW (1952) *d/co-p/s* Fuller *c* JL Russell *m* Dunlop 83min *r* UA
PARLOR, BEDROOM AND BATH (1931) *d Edward Sedgwick* *p/w* Keaton 8rs MGM
PARLORNA (1922) *d/s* Molander SF
PARMIGINA, LA (1963) *d/co-s* Pietrangeli *p* De Laurentis *m* Piccioni *w* Catherine Spaak, Manfredi
PARNELL (1937) *d* Stahl *a* Gibbons *c* Freund *w* Gable, M Loy, Crisp, Oliver 118min MGM
PAROHY (1947) *d Frantisek Sadek artistic adviser* Radok (= *The Cuckold*)
PAROLA CHE UCCIDE, LA (1914) *d* Genina
PAROLA DI LADRO (1956) *co-d/co-st/co-s* N Loy *w* Ferzetti
PAROLE (1936) *d Louis Friedlander* *w* Quinn 67min U
PAROLE FIXER (1940) *d* Florey *w* Quinn 68min Par
PAROVOZ NO B-1000 (1927, *uf*) *d* Kuleshov *s Sergei Tretyakov* (= *Locomotive No B-1000*)
PARRISH (1961) *d/p/s* Daves *m* M Steiner *w* Colbert, Malden *40min WB
Parsons Widow, The (UK) = PRASTANKAN (1920)
PART DE L'ENFANT, LA (1943) *d* Rouquier * sh
PART DE L'OMBRE, LA (1945) *d* Delannoy *s* Charles Spaak *c* Matras *m* Auric *w* Feuillère, Barrault
PARTIE DE CAMPAGNE, UNE (1936) *d/s* J Renoir *fn De Maupassant* *c* c Renoir, Bourgoin *m* Kosma "*assistants*" Becker, Cartier Bresson, Visconti *w* J Renoir 1232m
PARTIE D'ECARTE (1896) *d* Lumiere Bros
PARTIE DE CARTES, UNE (1896) *d/w* Méliès *rm* PARTIE D'ECARTE (1896) 20m
Parting at Dusk = UKIGUSA (1959)
Partings = ROZSTANIE (1961)
PARTIR (1931) *d* M Tourneur
PARTNER (1968) *d/co-s* Bertolucci *fn* (*The Double Dostoievsky*) TS* 90min
PARTNERS AGAIN (1926) *d/p* H King 6rs *r* UA
PARTNERS THREE (1919) *d* Niblo 5rs Par
PART-TIME WIFE (1930) *d/co-s* McCarey 6500ft Fox
PARTY, THE (1968) *d/p/st/co-s* Edwards *c* Ballard *m* Mancini *w* Sellers PV* 98min *r* UA
Party and the Guests, The (UK) = SLAVNOSTI A MOSTECH, O (1966)
PARTY GIRL (1958) *d* N Ray *p* Pasternak *s* Wells *c* Bronner *w* R Taylor, Charisse, Cobb CS* 99min *r* MGM
Party is Over, The (UK) = FIN DE FIESTA (1959)
PARTY'S OVER, THE (1963) *d* Hamilton (*uc*) *m* Barry 94min
PAR UN BEAU MATIN D'ETE (1964) *d/co-st* Deray *dec* Wakhévitch *w* Belmondo, Tamiroff 108min
PASAZERKA (1961, *uf*) *co-d/co-s* Munk FS 65min finished by *Witold Lesiewicz* (= *Passenger*)
PAS DE DEUX (1968) *d* McLaren 6min
PASEO SOBRE UNA GUERRA ANTIGUA (1949) *d/s* Bardem, Berlanga
PASHT (1965) *d* Brakhage * 16mm
PÅ SOLSIDAN (1936) *d* Molander *w* Ingrid Bergman
PASOPORTO A RIO (1948) *d Daniel Tinayre st* Saslavsky
PASQUA IN SICILIA (1955) *d/c/e* De Seta 16mm 12min (= *Easter in Sicily*)
PAS QUESTION LE SAMEDI (1964) *d Alex Joffe* *c* Bourgoin 113min
PASSAGE DU RHIN, LE (1960) *d/co-st/co-s* Cayatte *w* Aznavour 124min UFA (= *The Crossing of the Rhine*)
PASSAGE HOME (1955) *d* R Baker *c* Unsworth *w* Finch, Forbes 102min BL
PASSAGER, LE (1926) *d* De Baroncelli *w* Vanel
PASSAGER DE LA PLUIE (1969) *d* Clément *119min (= *Rider on the Rain*)
PASSAGERS DE LA GRANDE OURSE, LES (1941) *d* Grimault anim* 9min
PASSAGE TO MARSEILLE (1944) *d* Curtiz *p* Wallis *c* Howe *m* M Steiner *w* Bogart, Greenstreet, Rains, Lorre, Morgan 110min WB
PASSE DU DIABLE, LA (1957) *d* Schoendoerffer, *Jacques Dupont, S J Kessel* *c* Coutard CS* 80min *r* Fox
Passenger = PASAZERKA (1961)
Passing Fancy = DEKIGOKORO (1933)
PASSING STRANGER, THE (1954) *d John Arnold co-p/co-s* A Simmons 67min
PASSING THE BUCK (1919) *d/s/w* Semon 2rs Vit
Passion, La = VIE ET LA PASSION DE JESUS CHRIST, LA (1902)
Passion (US) = MADAME DUBARRY (1919)
PASSION (1954) *d* Dwan *p* Bogeaus *c* J Alton *w* Wilde, De Carlo, Burr *84min *r* RKO
Passion = VASEN (1962)
PASSION, EN (1970) *d/s* Ingmar Bergman *c* Nykvist *w* B Andersson, Von Sydow *100min SF (= *Passion*)
Passion = PASSION, EN (1970)
PASSIONATE ADVENTURE, THE (1924) *d Graham Cutts* *p* Balcon *co-s/dec* Hitchcock *w* V McLaglen, C Brook 8000ft
Passionate Affair (UK) = TENDRE ET VIOLENTE ELISABETH (1960)
PASSIONATE FRIENDS, THE (1922) *d* Elvey *fn HG Wells* 6300ft
PASSIONATE FRIENDS, THE (1949) *d* Lean *p* Neame *c* G Green *w* T Howard, Rains 91min (= *One Woman's Story*)
The Passionate Heart = HOROUCI SRDCE (1963)
PASSIONATE PASTIME (1957) *d/cy* Richter *w Marcel Duchamp* *n* Price 28min (= *Chesscetera*)
PASSIONATE PLUMBER, THE (1932) *d* Edward Sedgwick *w* Keaton, Roland 8rs *pc* Keaton *r* MGM (French version: *Le Plombier Amoureux*)
PASSIONATE QUEST, THE (1926) *d/p* Blackton *c* Musuraca *w* Fazenda 6671ft WB
Passionate Thief, The (UK) = RISATE DI GIOIA (1960)
Passion of a Woman Teacher = KYOREN NO ONNA SHISHO (1926)
PASSION DE JEANNE D'ARC, LA (1928) *d/s* Dreyer *c* Maté *dec* Warm *w* Falconetti, M Simon, Artaud 110min (= *The Passion of Joan of Arc/Jeanne d'Arc*)
PASSION FLOWER, THE (1921) *d/co-s* Brenon *w* K Francis, Bickford 9rs MGM
Passion of Joan of Arc, The = LA PASSION DE JEANNE D'ARC (1928)
PASSIONS – HE HAD THREE (1913) *d* Sennett *w* Arbuckle, Normand ½rl Key
Passion Without Limit = HATESHINAKI JONETSU (1949)
Passing Through = THE GOOD BAD MAN (1916)
Passions of the Sea = LOST AND FOUND ON A SOUTH SEA ISLAND (1923)
PASSPORT TO HELL, A (1932) *d* F Lloyd *c* J Seitz *w* Lukas, Crisp 75min Fox
Passport to Hell (UK) = CITTA SI DIFENDE, LA (1917)
PASSPORT TO PARADISE (1932) *d/st/s* G Seitz *c* Cronjager 67min
PASSPORT TO PIMLICO (1949) *d* Cornelius *p* Balcon *st/s* T Clarke *m* Auric 89min BL
PASSPORT TO SUEZ (1943) *d* De Toth *co-c* O'Connell 72min Col
PASSWORD IS COURAGE, THE (1902) *d/co-p/s* Stone *co-p/e Virginia Stone* *w* Bogarde 116min *pc* A and V Stone *r* MGM
PAST (1950) *d* Frič (= *The Trap*)
PASTASCIUTTA NEL DESERTO (1961) *d* Bragaglia (= *Spaghetti in the Desert*)
PASTEUR (1922) *d* Benoît-Lévy, J Epstein
PASTEUR (1935) *d/s/fpl/n* Guitry *c* Bachelet 75min
PASTOR HALL (1940) *d* R Boulting *p* J Boulting 98min
PASTORI DI ORGOSOLO (1958) *d/co-s/c/e* De Seta 98min
PAT AND MIKE (1952) *d* Cukor *s* R Gordon, Kanin *c* Daniels *co-des* Gibbons *m* Raksin *w* Tracy, K Hepburn, A Ray 95min MGM
PATATES, LES (1969) *d* Autant-Lara *ad/di* Aurenche *c* Kelber *100min
PATCH OF BLUE, A (1965) *d/s* G Green *c* Burks *m* Goldsmith *w* Poitier, Winters PV 105min *pc* Berman *r* MGM
PATENT LEATHER KID, THE (1927) *d/p* Santell *co-c* Edeson *w* Barthelmess 11955ft FN
PATER VOJTECH (1929) *d/s* Frič *c* Heller (= *Father Voitech*)
PATER VOJTECH (1936) *d* frič *rm* PATER VOJTECH (1929) (= *Father Voitech*)
PATMER PANCHALI (1955) *d/s* S Ray *c* Mitra *m* Shankar 122min (= *Song of the Road*)
PATHS OF GLORY (1957) *d/co-s* Kubrick *p* F Harris *fn* (*Path of Glory*) *H Cobb* *m* Fried *w* K Douglas, Meeker, Menjou 86min *r* UA
PATIENCE (1920) *d/dec* Leni *w* Veidt 1869m
PATIO, O (1959) *d* Rocha
PATRES DU DESORDRE (1967, *uf*) *d* Papatrakis 130min
PATRICIA ET JEAN-BAPTISTE (1966) *d/p/s/w* Lefebvre 83min
PATRIE (1945) *d* Daquin *m* Wiener 95min
PATRIOT, THE (1928) *d/e* Lubitsch *c* Glennon *dec* Dreier *w* Jannings, G Cooper 114min Par
Patriot, The (UK) = PATRIOTE, LE (1938)
PATRIOTE, LE (1938) *d* M Tourneur *w* P Renoir 97min
Patriots (US) = OKRAINA (1933)
PATROUILLE DE CHOC (1916) *d/st/s* Bernard-Aubert 90min
PAT'S BIRTHDAY (1962) *d* Breer, *Claes Oldenburg* 16mm 15min
PAT'S DAY OFF (1912) *d/p/w* Sennett ½rl Key
PATSY, THE (1928) *d* K Vidor *p* Hearst *c* J Seitz *a* Gibbons *w* Davies, Dressler 7289ft *r* MGM
PATSY, THE (1964) *d/co-s* J Lewis *co-a* Pereira *m* Raksin *w* J Lewis, Lorre, Carradine, Hopper, R Fleming, (Raft) 101min* Par
PATTERN OF SUPPLY (1957) *d Alan Hendry* *p* Haanstra *28min
PATTERNS (1956) *d Fielder Cook* *s/st* Serling *c* B Kaufman *w* Heflin 83min *r* UA
PATTES BLANCHES (1948) *d* Grémillon *co-s/di* Anouilh
PATTES DE MOUCHES (1936) *d/co-s* Grémillon *w* Brasseur 2500m
PATTO D'AMICIZIA (1951) *d* Nelli *sh*
PATTON (1970) *d* Schaffner *co-s/co-st* Coppola *m* Goldsmith *w* G Scott, Malden 70mm *173min Fox
PATTUGLIA DI PASSO SAN GIOVANNI, LA (1954) *d* Olmi *14min
PATTUGLIA SPERDUTO, LA (1954) *d/co-s* Nelli
PAUKI (1942) *d* I Trauberg, *I Zemgano* (= *The Spider*)
PAULA (1952) *d* Maté *p* Adler *co-s* Poe *c* Lawton *w* L Young 80min Col
PAUL DELVAUX OU LES FEMMES DEFENDUES (1971) *d/p* Storck 25min
PAUL GAUGIN (1957) *d* Quilici sh
PAUL SWAN (1965) *d* Warhol 16mm *70min
PAUL TOMKOWITZ, RAILWAY SWITCHMAN (1954) *d/co-s* Kroiter 10mm 16min NFBC
PAUL VALERY (1960) *d/s/pc* Leenhardt 20min

PAUME, LE (1971) d/co-ad/di Audiard co-dec D'Eaubonne (= Le Cri du Cormoran le Soir au-dessous des Jonques)
Paura, La = ANGST, DIE (1954)
PAUVRE PIERROT (1892) d Reynaud (paper)
PAVAGE MODERNE (1934) d Leenhardt 260m
PAVE DE PARIS, LE (1960) d/co-ad Decoin m Kosma 100min (= Pavements of Paris)
PAVILLON BRULE, LE (1941) d De Baroncelli w P Renoir, Marais
PAVLINKA (1952) d Zarkhi 2190m
PAW (1960) d/s A and B Henning Jensen *100min (= Paw – Boy of Two worlds)
Paw – Boy of Two Worlds = PAW (1960)
PAWNBROKER'S HEART, THE (1917) d Cline w Turpin 2rs Tri-Key
PAWNBROKER, THE (1965) d Lumet c B Kaufman w Steiger 115min
PAWNBROKER'S HEART, THE (1917) d Cline p Sennett w Turpin Tri-Key
PAWNSHOP, THE (1916) d/s Chaplin c Totheroh w Chaplin, Purviance 2rs Mut
PAX AETERNA (1916) d Madsen s Dreyer, Madsen
PAY AS YOU ENTER (1928) d Bacon c Brodine w Fazenda, M Loy 4815ft WB
PAY AS YOU EXIT (1936) d G Douglas p Roach 1rl MGM
PAY DAY (1938) d Hurwitz, Strand
PAY DAY (1922) d/s/w Chaplin c Totheroh w Purviance 2rs FN
PAYMASTER'S SON, THE (1913) d Ince
PAYMENT ON DEMAND (1951) d/co-s C Bernhardt w B Davis 90min RKO
PAY OFF, THE (1930) d/w L Sherman 78min RKO
PAY-OFF, THE (1935) d Florey 64min WB
PAY OR DIE (1966) d/p R Wilson c Ballard m Raksin w Borgnine 111min WB
PAYSAGES DU SILENCE (1947) d/p Cousteau 25min
PAYSANNE PERVERTIE, LA (1960) d Kiegel
PAYS DE COCAGNE (1971) d/idea Etaix *75min
PAYS D'OU JE VIENS, LE (1956) d/co-ad Carné co-ad/di Achard c Agostini w Arnoul
PAYS SANS BON SENS, UN (1970) d Perrault 16mm 117min
Pay the Devil = MAN IN THE SHADOW (1957)
PAZZA DI GIOIA (1940) d/st/s Bragaglia w De Sica
PBL (1968) d Breer anim 16mm * 1min
PBL 11 (1968) d Breer anim 16mm 1min
Peace Game, The (UK) = GLADIATORERNA (1968)
PEACEMAKERS, THE (1963) d A King 16mm 54min
Peace Valley = DOLINA MIRU (1956)
Peace Valley = DOLINA MIRU (1956)
"PEACE WITH HONOUR" (1902) p Hepworth 100ft
PEACOCK ALLEY (1922) d Leonard s Goulding 8rs pc Leonard Metro
PEARL OF THE ARMY (1916–17) d G Seitz w White serial in 15eps Pat
PEARL OF THE SOUTH PACIFIC (1955) d Dwan p Bogeaus c J Alton w V Mayo S* 85min r RKO
Pearls of Saint Lucia, The = TLAYUCAN (1962)
Pearls of the Crown (UK) = PERLES DE LA COURONNE, LES (1937)
Pearls of the Deep (UK) = PERLICKI NA DNE (1965)
Peasants = KRESTYANYE (1935)
PEAU D'ANE (1970) d/s Demy c Cloquet m Legrand w Deneuve, Marais, Seyrig, Presle *90min
PEAU DE PECHE (1926) d Benôit-Lévy, Marie Epstein
PEAU D'ESPION (1966) d/co-s Molinaro w E O'Brien *90min (= To Commit a Murder)
PEAU DE TORPEDO, LA (1970) d/co-s Delannoy c Sechan w Palmer *110min
PEAU DOUCE, LA (1964) d/co-s/di Truffaut co-s Richard c Coutard m Delerue w Desailly 118min co-pc Truffaut (= Silken Skin)
PECCATO CHE SIA UNA CANAGLIA (1955) d/co-s Blasetti fn Alberto Moravia co-s Cecchi D'Amico w De Sica, Loren, Mastroianni 96min (= Too Bad She's Bad)
PECCATRICE SENZA PECCATO, LA (1922) d Genina
Pêche et le Culte de la Mer = MAMY WATER (1955)
PECHEUR D'ISLANDE (1919) d/co-s Schoendoerffer c Coutard w Vanel CS* 87min
PECHEURS D'ISLANDE (1924) d De Baroncelli w Vanel
PECHEURS DU NIGER (1962) d/s Rouch 16mm
PECK'S BAD BOY (1921) d/ad S Wood 5000ft r FN
PECK'S BAD BOY (1934) d Cline p Lesser 70min Fox
PECK'S BAD BOY WITH THE CIRCUS (1938) d Cline 78min RKO
PECORA NERA, LA (1968) d/co-s Salce c Tonti w Gassman *110min (= The Black Sheep)
PECOS RIVER (1951) d Sears 55min Col
PEDRO PARAMO (1967) d/s Velo 110min
PEDRO'S DILEMMA (1912) d/p/w Sennett w Normand ½rl Key
PEDRO SOLL HANGEN (1941) d V Harlan 1868m r Tob
PEEPING TOM (1959) d/p M Powell c Heller *109min
PEER GYNT (1915) fpl Henrik Ibsen w C Ruggles
PEER GYNT (1942) d/co-ad/co-c/e/w Bradley fpl Ibsen m Grieg w Heston 16mm 85min
PEGGY (1916) co-d Ince Tri
Peggy on a Spree = PEGGY PA VIFT (1946)

PEGGY PA VIFT (1946) d Mattson w Björnstrand (= Peggy on a Spree)
PEGGY THE WILL O' THE WISP (1917) d Browning 5rs Metro
PEG OF OLD DRURY (1935) d H Wilcox c F Young w Neagle, Hawkins 75min r UA
PEG O'MY HEART (1923) d K Vidor c Barnes 8rs Metro
PEG O' MY HEART (1933) d/p Leonard c Barnes w Davies 86min MGM
PEHLA ADMI (1948) d Roy
PEKING EXPRESS (1951) d Dieterle p Wallis ad Furthman rm SHANGHAI EXPRESS (1932) c C Lang co-a Pereira m Tiomkin w Cotten 95min Par
PEMBERTON VALLEY, THE (1957) d A King 16mm 58min
Pem o Gerojach = KOMSOMOL (1932)
PENITENTES THE (1915) d Conway supn Griffith 5rs Tri
PENITENTIARY (1938) d Brahm co-s S Miller c Ballard 74min Col
PENNIES FROM HEAVEN (1936) d McLeod s Swerling w B Crosby 88min Col
PENNY PARADISE (1938) d C Reed 72min
PENNY SERENADE (1941) d/p G Stevens c J Walker w C Grant, I Dunne 125min Col
PENNY WISDOM (1937) d D Miller *10min
PENPOINT PERCUSSION (1950) d Don Peters w McLaren 7min NFBC
PENROD (1922) d/p Neilan co-c June 8037ft pc Neilan r FN
PENSIONATO, IL (1958) d Olmi 8min
PENSION GROONEN (1924) d Wiene
PENSION MIMOSAS (1935) d/co-s Feyder co-s/di Charles Spaak des Meerson w Rosay, Arletty 110min Tob
PENTE, LA (1931) d Autant-Lara
PENTEK REZI (1938) d Vajda 2200m
PENTHOUSE (1933) d WS Van Dyke s Goodrich, Hackett c Andriot, Rosson w M Loy, W Baxter 88min MGM
PENTHOUSE RHYTHM (1945) d Cline 60min U
People = WARAI-NO NINGEN (1960)
People = LYUDI (1966)
PEOPLE AGAINST O'HARA, THE (1951) d J Sturges co-a Gibbons c J Alton w Tracy 102min MGM
People in Luck = LES VEINARDS (1962)
PEOPLE LIKE MARIA (1958) d Watt 16mm 50min
People Meet = MENNESKER MØDES OG SOD MUSIK OPSTAAR I HJERTET (1968)
PEOPLE OF THE CUMBERLANDS, THE (1937) d/s Kazan x R Steiner 20min
People of Hemso = HEMSOBORNA (1955)
People of Kajzarju = SVET NA KAJZARJU (1952)
People of Young Character = WAKAI HITOTACHI (1954)
People on Wheels = LIDE NA KOLEKACH (1966)
People on Sunday = MENSCHEN AM SONNTAG (1929)
PEOPLE'S ENEMY, THE (1935) d Crane Wilber w M Douglas (C Coburn) 66min RKO
PEOPLE WILL TALK (1935) d Santell w C Ruggles 67min Par
PEOPLE WILL TALK (1951) d/s J Mankiewicz p Zanuck c Krasner co-a Wheeler m A Newman w C Grant, Crain 110min Fox
PEPE (1960) d G Sidney c Joe Macdonald w Dailey, C Coburn, B Crosby, Chevalier, Conte, Garson, Lawford, J Leigh, Lemmon, Novak, D Reed, D Reynolds, Robinson, Romero, Sinatra, S Jones, Hopper wv Garland CS* 195min Col
PEPE-LE-MOKO (1937) d/co-s Duvivier co-s/di Jeanson w Gabin, Dalio, Modot 80mm
PEPITA JIMENEZ (1945) d/co-s Fernandez w Montalban
PEPPERMINT FRAPPE (1967) d/co-s Saura w Geraldine Chaplin *94min
Perak against the S.S. = PERAK A S.S. (1946)
PERAK A SS (1946) d/s Trnka, Braecka st/a Trnka anim 385m (= Perak Against the S.S.)
PER AMORE ... PER MAGIA (1967) d/s Tessari fst (Aladdin's Lamp) * (= For Love ... For Magic)
PERCY (1971) d Thomas *103min
PERE DE MADEMOISELLE, LE (1953) co-d/co-ad L'Herbier co-d/co-ad Robert Paul Dagan w Arletty 100min
PERED OKTIABRE (1965) d Alexandrov (= Before October)
PERE GORIOT, LE (1922) d De Baroncelli fn Balzac
Père Hugo, Le = VICTOR HUGO (1951)
PERE NOEL A LES YEUX BLANCS, LE (1965) d Jean Eustache w Léaud 50min np Godard
PERE TRANQUILLE, LE (1946) d Clément c C Renoir 100min
PERFECT CLOWN, THE (1925) d Newmeyer w Semon 6rs
PERFECT CRIME, A (1921) d/p/s Dwan w Lombard (as Jane Peters) 5rs
PERFECT CRIME, THE (1928) d Glennon c Howe w C Brook 71min
PERFECT DAY (1929) d James Parrott p Roach st McCarey w Laurel, Hardy 2rs r MGM
PERFECT FRIDAY (1970) d P Hall w S Baker, Andress *94min
PERFECT FURLOUGH, THE (1958) d Edwards c Lathrop a Golitzen w Curtis, J Leigh CS* U 93min (= Strictly for Pleasure)
PERFECT GENTLEMAN, A (1927) d Bruckman 5607ft Pat
Perfect Lady, The = WOMAN, A (1915)

PERFECT SPECIMEN, THE (1937) d Curtiz p Wallis w Flynn, Blondell, Horton 99min FN
PERFECT STRANGERS (1950) d Windust p Wald fpl (Ladies and Gentlemen) B Hecht, MacArthur c Morley e Weisbart w G Rogers, Ritter 88min WB
PERFECT STRANGERS (1945) d/co-p A Korda c Périnal a V Korda w Donat, Kerr 102min MGM (= Vacation from Marriage)
PERFECT UNDERSTANDING (1933) d Cyril Gardner e T Dickinson w Swanson, Olivier 79min
PERFECT WOMAN, THE (1921) d David Kirkland p Emerson, Loos w C Talmadge 6rs FN
Perfido Ricatto = VEDI NAPOLI E POI MUORI (1951)
PERFIDY OF MARY, THE (1913) d Griffith w Marsh, Pickford 1rl Bio
PERFORMANCE (1968 r 1971) co-d/c Roeg co-d/as-p/st Donald Cammell m Jack Nitzsche song/w Mick Jagger *102min WB
PERFORMING PAINTER (1956) d Pintoff
PER GRAZIA RICEVUTA (1971) d/co-s/w Manfredi *118min
PERIL AU PARADIS (1964) d Gréville TV
PERILS OF PAULINE, THE (1914) d/s Louis Gashier, Donald Mackenzie c AC Miller w White, G Seitz series in 20eps Pat
PERILS OF PAULINE, THE (1947) d G Marshall p S Siegel co-a Dreier c Rennahan w Hutton 96min Par
PERIOD OF ADJUSTMENT (1962) d Hill fpl T Williams w J Fonda 112min PV* MGM
PERISCOPE, LE (1915) d/s Gance
PERLA, LA (1946) d/co-s Fernandez co-s/fn (Pearl) Steinbeck c Figueroa w Armendariz
PERLES DE LA COURONNE, LES (1937) co-d/s/st Guitry co-d Christian-Jacque m Jean Françaix w Guitry, Raimu, Arletty, Dalio, Barrault 101min r Tob
PERLICKI NA DNE (1965) co-s/fsts Borumil Hrabal co-c Ondricek 107min (= Pearls of the Deep)
  ep SMRT PANA BALTAZARA d/co-s Menzel (= Mr Baltazar's Death)
  ep PODVONIKI d/co-s Nemec (= The Impostor)
  ep AUTOMATU SVET d/co-s Chytilova (= The Snackbar World)
  ep DOMU RADOSTI d/co-s Schorm (= The House of Happiness)
  ep ROMANCE d/co-s Jaromil Jires
PERMUTATIONS (1968) d Whitney 16mm *8min
PERNIKOVA CHALOUPKA (1951) d Pojar a Trnka anim (= The Gingerbread Cottage)
PER QUALCHE DOLLARI IN PIU (1965) d Sergio Leone w Eastwood S* 130min (= For a Few Dollars More)
PERROQUET DU FILS HOQUET, LE (1963) d/s/di P Prévert c Vierny 90min ORTF
PERSECUTION AND ASSASSINATION OF JEAN-PAUL MARAT, AS PERFORMED BY THE INMATES OF THE ASYLUM OF CHARENTON UNDER THE DIRECTION OF THE MARQUIS DE SADE, THE (1966) d P Brook fpl P Weiss c Watkin *116min r UA
PERSIANE CHIUSE (1951) d Comencini w Girotti, Masina, Rossi-Drago 88min (= Behind Closed Shutters)
PERSIMMON'S DERBY (1896) p Paul 80ft
PERSONA (1966) d/s Ingmar Bergman c Nykvist w B Andersson, Björnstrand 81min SF
Personal Affair, A = LICHNOYE DELO (1932)
Personal Column (US) = PIEGES (1939)
PERSONAL HISTORY, ADVENTURES, EXPERIENCE, AND OBSERVATIONS OF DAVID COPPER-FIELD, THE YOUNGER, THE (1935) d Cukor p Selznick ad Walpole fn (David Copperfield) Charles Dickens spl eff's Vorkapich co-a Gibbons m Stothart w Fields, L Barrymore, Bartholomew, Rathbone, Oliver, Walpole, O'Sullivan 133min MGM (= David Copperfield)
PERSONALITY KID, THE (1934) d Crosland 67min WB
PERSONAL PROPERTY (1937) d WS Van Dyke c Daniels m Waxman w R Taylor, Harlow 9rs MGM
Person Unknown (UK) = SOLITI IGNOTI, I (1958)
PER UN PUGNO DI DOLLARI (1964) d Sergio Leone w Eastwood S* 100min (= For a Fistful of Dollars)
PERVENCHE (1921) d/s Machin, Henri Walschléger 2180m
PERVYI DEN (1958) d Ermler * (= The First Day)
PERVYI ESMELON (1956) d Kalatozov m Shostakovich *114min (= The First Echelon)
Pescados = REDES (1934)
PESCATORELLA (1946) d Risi sh
PESCHERECCI (1959) d/c/e De Seta 11min (= Fishermen)
PESN LYUBVI NEDOPETAYA (1919) d Kuleshov, Vitold Polonsky dec/w Kuleshov 5rs (= The Unfinished Love Story)
PESN O METALLYE (1928) d/s/e Heifitz, Zarkhi, M Schapiro, V Granatman 208m (= Song of Steel)
PESNYA O SCHASTYE (1934) d Donskoi, Vladimir Legoshin supn Yutkevich 2400m (= Song about Happiness)
PESNYA KATORZHANINA (1911) d/s Protazanov 380m (= The Prisoner's Song)
PEST, THE (1919) d Christy Cabanne w Normand 6rs pc Goldwyn
PEST FROM THE WEST (1939) d Del Lord s Bruckman w Keaton 17min Col

PET, THE (1916) d McCay anim
PETAL IN THE CURRENT, A (1919) d Browning 6rs U
PETE & JOHNNY (1961) d R Leacock
PETE KELLY'S BLUES (1955) d J Webb s Breen c Rosson w J Webb, J Leigh, E O'Brien, Marvin, Mansfield CS* 95min WB
Peter and Paula (GB) = CZERNY PETR (1964)
PETERBURGSKIYE TRUSHCHOBI (1915) d/s Protazanov, *Vladimir Gardin* (= *Petersburg Slums*)
PETER IBBETSON (1935) d Hathaway fn *Du Maurier* co-c C Lang e Heisler w G Cooper, Lupino 88min Par
PETERMANN IS DAGEGAN (1937) d/co-s Wisbar 2231m
PETE ROLEUM AND HIS COUSINS (1939) d/p/s Losey co-m Eisler 3-D* 20min
PETER PAN (1924) d Brenon s Goldbeck c Howe 10rs FPL
PETER PAN (1953) d Disney anim* 76min r RKO
Petersburg Slums = PETERBURGSKIYE TRUSACHOBI (1915)
Peter the First = PIOTR PERUYI (part 1: 1937; part 2: 1939)
Peter the Great = PIOTR PERVYI (part 1: 1937; part 2: 1939)
PETER VOSS, DER MILLIONENDIEB (1932) d/co-s Dupont 2852m
PET HOLEK NA KRKU (1967) d/co-s Schorm 90min (= *Five Girls Equals a Millstone Round One's Neck*)
PETISTOVKA (1949) d Frič (= *Motor Cycles*)
PETIT A PETIT (1970) d/st/c Rouch 16mm 105min
PETIT BABOUIN, LE (1932) d/e/m Grémillon co-c Maté 600m
PETIT CAFE, LE (1919) d Raymond Bernard s R Bernard, Linder w Linder Pat
PETIT CHANTECLAIR, LE (1910) d Cohl anim 154m
PETIT CHAPERON ROUGE, LE (1901) d Méliès fst *Charles Perrault* 160m (12 parts)
PETIT CHAPERON ROUGE, LE (1929) d/co-ad/co-di/e/dec Cavalcanti co-ad/co-di J Renoir m Jaubert w J Renoir, P Prévert
PETIT CLAUS ET LE GRAND CLAUS, LE (1964) d/co-s P Prévert co-s/di J Prévert fst Hans Christian *Andersen* c Vierny dec Grimault 70min ORTF
PETIT DIABLE, UN (1896) d Méliès w *Georgette Méliès* 20m
PETIT DISCOURS DE LA METHODE (1963) d Pierre *Patry* e/cy Jutra 27min
PETITE CHOCOLATIERE, LA (1932) d M Allégret w S Simon
Petite Lili, La = P'TITE LILI, LA (1929)
PETITE LISE, LA (1930) d Grémillon s/di Charles Spaak c Bachelet 102min
PETITE MARCHANDE D'ALLUMETTES, LA (1928) co-d/co-p/ad/ad J Renoir fst Hans Christian *Andersen* c Bachelet 887m
PETITES DEMOISELLES, LES (1964) d Deville sh ORTF
PETITES DU QUAI AUZ FLEURS, LES (1943) d M Allégret s Achard w Philipe, Gélin
PETITES FILLES MODELES, LES (1952, uf) co/d/s/e Rohmer co-d P Guilbaud 60min
PETIT JUMMY, LE (1930) d Benoît-Lévy
PETIT MONDE DE DON CAMILLO, LE (1952) d/co-s/co-di Duvivier fn *Giovanni Guareschi* c Hayer w Fernandel 91min (= *Il Piccolomardo di Don Camillo/Don Camillo/The Little World of Don Camillo*)
PETIT ROI, LE (1933) d/s Duvivier fn *André Lichtenberg* c Thirard e Le Chanois
PETIT SOLDAT, LE (1947) d/co-s Grimault co-s J Prévert fst Hans Christian *Andersen* anim* 11min
PETIT SOLDAT, LE (1960 r 1963) d/s Godard c Coutard w Karina, (Godard) 88min (= *The Little Soldier*)
PETIT SOLDAT QUI DEVIENT DIEU, LE (1908) d Cohl anim 110m
PETIT THEATRE DE JEAN RENOIR, LE (1971) d/s Renoir *110min ORTF
 ep 1 LE DERNIER REVEILLON
 ep 2 LA BELLE EPOQUE w Moreau
 ep 3 LA CIREUSE ELECTRIQUE
 ep 4 LE ROI D'YVETAT w Arnoul)
PETLA (1957) d/co-s Has (= *The Noose*)
PETRIFIED FOREST, THE (1936) d A Mayo co-s Daves c Polito w L Howard, B Davis, Bogart 83min WB
PETROLEUSES, LES (1971) d Christian-Jaque w Bardot, Cardinale, Presle *95min
PETRUS (1946) d/co-s M Allégret st/di Achard c Kelber m Kosma w Dalio, S Simon, Brasseur 95min
PETT AND POTT (1934) d/s/e Cavalcanti p Grierson dec/(w) Jennings 33min GPO
PETULIA (1968) d Lester c Roeg m Barry w Christie, G Scott, Cotten *105min r WB
PEU, BEAUCOUP, PASSIONNEMENT, UN (1971) d/co-s Enrico w Ronet *100min
PEU DE FEU, S.V.P., UN (1904) d Méliès 20m
PEU DE SOLEIL DANS L'EAU FROIDE, UN (1971) d/co-s Deray c Badal m Legrand *110min
PEUPLE ET SES FUSILS: LA GUERRE POPULAIRE AU LAOS, LE (1968) d Ivens, *Jean-Pierre Sergent, Marceline Loridan, Emmanuelle Castro, Suzanne Fenn, Antoine Bonfanti, Bernard Ortion, Anne Rullier* 100min
PEUR DES COUPS, LA (1932) d Autant-Lara

Peut-être qu'un jour Rome se permettra de choisir a son tour = YEUX NE PEUVENT PAS EN TOUT TEMPS SE FERMER, LES (1969)
PEYTON PLACE (1957) d Robson p Wald s J Hayes fn *Grace Metalious* c Mellor m Waxman w Turner, A Kennedy, Nolan CS* 162min Fox
PHAEDRA (1962) d/p/d/co-s Dassin m Theodorakis w Mercouri, Perkins, Vallone, Dassin 115min
PHANTASMES (1917) d L'Herbier
PHANTASY, A (1948) d McLaren 16m *7min NFBC
PHANTOM, A (1922) d Murnau p Pommer s Von Harbou co-dec Warm w Dagover 2905m Dec
Phantom Carriage, The = KORKARLEN (1958)
PHANTOM LADY (1944) d Siodmak w Tone, Cook 87min U
PHANTOM LIGHT, THE (1935) d M Powell 80min
Phantom Lovers (UK) = FANTASMI A ROMA (1961)
PHANTOM OF THE OPERA, THE (1925) d Julian fn (*Le Fantôme de l'Opera*) Gaston Leroux w Chaney 8464ft U
PHANTOM OF THE OPERA, THE (1943) d Arthur Lubin c Mohr co-a Golitzen w Rains 92min U
PHANTOM OF THE OPERA, THE (1962) d Fisher *84min JAR
PHANTOM OF THE RUE MORGUE (1954) d Del Ruth p Blanke co-s J R Webb fst (*Murder in the Rue Morgue*) Edgar Allan Poe c Marley w Malden *84min WB
PHANTOM OUTLAW, THE (1927) d Wyler 2rs U
PHANTOM RAIDERS (1940) d J Tourneur w Pidgeon 70min MGM
PHANTOM RIDERS, THE (1918) d J Ford p/w Carey 5rs U
PHANTOM TOLLBOOTH, THE (1970) d (anim) C Jones, Abe Levitow ex-p C Jones d (live action) David Monahan anim* 90min MGM
Pharaoh = FARAON (1965)
PHARMACIST, THE (1933) d Arthur Ripley p Sennett st/w Fields 20min Par
PHENIX CITY STORY, THE (1955) d Karlson cp-s Mainwaring w McIntire 100min AA
PHFFFT (1954) d Robson p Kohlmar s/fst Axelrod c C Lang w Novak, Lemmon, Holliday 91min Col
PHILADELPHIA STORY, THE (1940) d Cukor p Mankiewicz s D Stewart co-dec Gibbons m Waxman w C Grant, K Hepburn, J Stewart 112min MGM
PHILIPS-RADIO (1931) d/s/co-c/e Ivens 800m (= *Symphonie van den Arbeid/Industrial Symphony*)
Philosopher's Stone, The (UK) = PARASH PATHER (1958)
Phoenix = FUJICHO (1947)
PHONE CALL FROM A STRANGER (1952) d Negulesco p/s N Johnson m Waxman c Krasner w Winters, B Davis 96min Fox
PHONOGRAPHE, LE (1969) d/s Borowczyk *6min
PHOQUES DU RIO D'ORO, LES (1948–49) d/p Cousteau 12min (= *Les Phoques du Sahara*)
Phoques du Sahara, Les = PHOQUES DU RIO D'ORO, LES (1948–49)
Photodram = OPUS 1 (1921)
PHOTOGENIES (1925, ur) d J Epstein (destroyed)
PHOTOGRAPHER, THE (1947) d W Van Dyke co-s Maddow w Edward Weston 30min
PHOTOGRAPHIES VIVANTES (1954) d Borowczyk 20min
PHOTOGRAPHING A GHOST (1898) d G Smith
PHOTOGRAPHY AND THE CITY (1969) d/s C & R Eames c C Eames *15min
PHRENOLOGIE BURLESQUE (1901) d Méliès 30m
Piano Movers, The = HIS MUSICAL CAREER (1914)
PIANOS MECANIQUES, LES (1965) d Bardem w Mercouri, Mason *100min (= *The Uninhibited*)
PIANTO DELLE ZITELLE, IL (1958) d Baldi *10min
PIATKA Z ULICY BARSKIEJ (1954) d/co-s A Ford *115min (= *Five Boys from Borska Street*)
PICASSO (1954) d/s Emmer 1600m
PICASSO SUMMER (1967) d Robert Sallin w Finney, Brynner
PICCADILLY (1928) d Dupont s *Arnold Bennett* w Laughton 9763ft
PICCADILLY INCIDENT (1946) d H Wilcox w Neagle 103min ABC
PICCADILLY JIM (1936) d/co-p Leonard fst P G Wodehouse co-s Brackett c Ruttenberg w Montgomery 100min MGM
PICCOLI NAUFRAGHI (1938) d Flavio Calzavara co-s/e/w Freda co-c Tonti
PICCOLO (1960) d/s/a Vukotic *280m
PICCOLO CERINAIO, IL (1914) d Genina
PICCOLO MONDO ANTICO (1940) d/co-s Soldati p Ponti co-s Lattuada w Valli (= *Little Old-Fashioned World*)
Piccolo Mondo Di Don Camillo = PETIT MONDE DE DON CAMILLO, LE (1962)
PICCOLA POSTA (1955) d/co-st/co-s Steno w Sordi
PICCOLO SCERIFFO, IL (1950) d Sala sh
PICK A STAR (1937) d Edward Sedgwick p Roach c Brodine w Laurel, Hardy 8rs (sd) r MGM
PICKING PEACHES (1924) d Erle C Kenton w Langdon 2rs pc Sennett r Pat
PICKPOCKET (1959) d/s Bresson c Burel mf Jean-Baptiste Lully w Etaix 75min

PICKUP ON SOUTH STREET (1953) d/s Fuller c Joe Macdonald co-a Wheeler m Harline w Widmark, Peters, Ritter 80min
PICNIC (1956) d Logan p Kohlmar s Taradash fpl Inge c Howe m Duning w Holden, R Russell, Novak, Robertson CS* 115min Col
PICTURE OF DORIAN GRAY, THE (1945) d/ad Lewin p Berman fn Oscar Wilde co-a Gibbons m Stothart w G Sanders, Lawford, D Reed 110min MGM
Pictures of the Atom Bomb = GEMBAKO NO ZU (1951)
PICTURE SNATCHER (1933) d Bacon c Polito w Cagney 71min WB
PIECES OF DREAMS (1970) d D Haller m Legrand *99min r UA
PIED PIPER, THE (1942) d Pichel p/s N Johnson c Cronjager m A Newman w Preminger, A Baxter 86min Fox
PIED PIPER OF HAMELIN, THE (1959) d Windust w V Johnson, Rains *90min
PIED PIPER OF HAMELIN, THE (1960) d Reiniger anim 1rl
PIED QUI ETREINT, LE (1916) d/s Feyder 1800m Gau
 ep 1 LE MICRO BAFOUILLEUR SANS FIL 380m
 ep 2 LE RAYON NOIR 310m
 ep 3 LA GIROUETTE HUMAINE 500m
 ep 4 L'HOMME À FOULARD À POIS 610m)
PIE EATING CONTEST (1903) p Paul 80ft
PIEGE, LA (1969) d Baratier w *Arrabal* 50min
PIEGE POUR CENDRILLON (1965) d/co-s/fn Cayatte di/co-s Anouilh c Thirard CS 110min Gau
PIEGES, LES (1939) d Siodmak w Von Stroheim, Chevalier, P Renoir 115min (= *Snares/Personal Column*)
PIE IN THE SKY (1934) d/c R Steiner w Kazan, I Lerner
PIEL DE VERANO (1961) d/co-s Torre Nilsson S 100min (= *Summer Skin*)
PIERRE ET JEAN (1944) d/s Cayatte fst Guy de Maupassant 72min
PIERRE ET PAUL (1968) d/s Allio *93min
PIERRE OF THE PLAINS (1942) d G Seitz a Gibbons 66min MGM
PIERROT DES BOIS d/s/e/w Jutra c Brault 11min
PIERROT LE FOU (1965) d/s Godard fn (*Obsession*) Lionel White c Coutard w Belmondo, Karina, (Léaud, Fuller) TS* 110min (= *Crazy Pete*)
PIERWSZE LATA (1947) d Ivens 95min (= *The First Years*)
PIERWSZY DZIEN WOLNOSCI (1964) d A Ford S 97min (= *The First Day of Freedom*)
PIEUVRE, LA (1926) d Painlevé
Pig Across Paris (UK) = TRAVERSEE DE PARIS, LA (1956)
PIGEON THAT TOOK ROME, THE (1962) d/p/s Shavelson c Fapp w Heston 101min Par
PIGSKIN PALOOKA (1937) d G Douglas c AC Miller 11min
PIGSKIN PARADE (1936) d D Butler c AC Miller w Grable, Garland, Cook, Ladd 90min Fox (= *Harmony Parade*)
Pigsty (UK) = PORCILE (1969)
PIKOVAYA DAMA (1916) d Protazanov fst Alexander Pushkin w Mozhukhin 2300m (= *The Queen of Spades*)
Pile Driver = FATAL MALLET, THE (1914)
PILGRIM, THE (1923) d/s/w Chaplin c Totheroh w Purviance 4rs FN
PILGRIMAGE (1933) d J Ford di D Nichols w Foster, Hopper 90min Fox
Pilgrimage to the Virgin Mary = PROCESI K PANENCE (1961)
PILLARDS, LES (1965) p/d/co-s Deray * AA (= *La Route aux Diamants/That Man George!*)
PILLARS OF THE SKY (1956) d G Marshall co-a Golitzen c Lipstein w J Chandler, Malone, Marvin 95min CS* U
PILLOLE D'ERCOLE, LE (1960) co-d/co-s Salce w Manfredi, De Sica, Blanche 105min
PILLOW TALK (1959) d M Gordon co-p R Hunter c Arling co-a Golitzen w Hudson, D Day, Randall, Dalio, Ritter CS* 105min U
PILLOW TO POST (1945) d V Sherman m Hollander w Lupino, Greenstreet 92min WB
PILOTA RITORNA, UN (1942) d/co-s Rossellini co-s Antonioni, *Ugo Betti* w Girotti 87min
PILOTE DE GUERRE ... PILOTE DE LIGNE (1949) d Ciampi 610m
PILOT IS SAFE, THE (1941) d J Lee 9min Crown
PILOT NO. 5 (1943) d G Sidney, A Gibbons w V Johnson, Tone, Gene Kelly, Gardner, Lawford 70min MGM
PIMPERNEL SMITH (1941) d/p L Howard s De Grunwald w L Howard 118min (= *Mister V*)
PINK JUNGLE, THE (1968) d Daniel Mann c Metty w Garner, G Kennedy TS* 93min r U
PINK PANTHER, THE (1964) d/co-s Edwards c Lathrop m Mancini w Niven, Sellers, R Wagner, Cardinale TR* 114min r UA
PINK STRING AND SEALING WAX (1945) d Hamer 89min EL
PINKY (1949) d Kazan, J Ford(uc) p Zanuck s P Dunne, D Nichols c Joe Macdonald co-a Wheeler m A Newman w Crain, E Barrymore 96min Fox

PINNE E ARPIONI (1952) d Quilici sh
PHNOCCHIO (1940) p Disney fst *Collodi* co-m Harline *88min
PINTO (1919) d/st Schertzinger w Normand 5rs pc Goldwyn
PINTO BEN (1924) d/fpm/w W Hart 2rs
PINTURA MURAL MEXICANA (1953) d Velo
PIOTR PERVYI (Part 1) (1937) d/co-s Petrov w Cherkasov 2815m (= *Peter the First/Peter the Great*)
PIOTR PERVYI (Part 2) (1939) d Petrov, *Bartenev* co-s Petrov w Cherkasov 3423m (= *Peter the First/Peter the Great*)
PIPPA PASSES OR THE SONG OF CONSCIENCE (1909) d Griffith fpm *Robert Browning* 1rl Bio
PIRANAS, LAS (1967) d/co-s Berlanga 98min
PIRATE, THE (1948) d Minnelli p Freed s Goodrich, Hackett fpl *SN Behrman* co-a Gibbons m *Cole Porter* co-chor R Alton, Gene Kelly w Garland, Gene Kelly *102min MGM
PIRATE GOLD (1920) d/w G Seitz serial in 10 eps Pat
Pirates of Capri, The = PIRATI DI CAPRI, I (1949)
PIRATI DELLA MALESIA, I (1941) d Guazzoni
PIRATI DI CAPRI, I (1949) d Ulmer m Rota w L Hayward, Rossi-Drago 89min (= *The Pirates of Capri/The Masked Pirate*)
PIROGOV (1947) d Kozintsev co-c Moskvin m Shostakovich w Cherkasov 10rs
PIR V ZHIRMUNKA (1941) d Pudovkin, *Mikhail Doller* 2rs (= *Feast at Zhirmunka*)
PISCINE, LA (1968) d/co-s/co-di Deray m Legrand w Delon, Schneider, Ronet *100min (= *The Sinners*)
PISEN SVOBODY (1956) d Fric
PISITO, EL (1958) d Ferreri
Piste Du Nord, La = LOI DU NORD, LA (1939)
PISTOLA PER RINGO, UNA (1965) d/s Tessari *99min (= *A Pistol For Ringo*)
Pistolero = LAST CHALLENGE, THE (1967)
Pistolero of Red River, The = LAST CHALLENGE, THE (1967)
Pistol For Ringo, A = PISTOLA PER RINGO, UNA (1965)
Pistol Shot, A = COLPO DI PISTOLA, UN (1941)
PIT AND THE PENDULUM, THE (1961) d/p Corman co-ex-p Arkoff s Matheson fst *Poe* c F Crosby a D Haller w Price CS* 85min
Pitfall = OTOSHI ANA (1961)
PITFALL (1948) d De Toth c Wild w D Powell, L Scott, Burr 85min r UA
PITFALLS OF A BIG CITY (1919) d F Lloyd 5rs Fox
Piu Grande Amore, Il = FOCOLARE SPENTO, IL (1925)
PIZHON (1929) d Donskoi 3rs (= *The Fop*)
PIZZA TWEETY-PIE, A (1958) d Freleng anim* 7min WB
PIZZICATO PUSSYCAT (1955) d Freleng anim* 7min WB
P.J. (1968) d Guillermin c Griggs co-a Golitzen w Peppard, Burr TS* U 109min (= *New Face in Hell*)
PLACE FOR GOLD, A (1960) d/p B Wright *35min r BL
Place for Lovers, A (US) = AMANTI, GLI (1969)
PLACE IN THE SUN, A (1951) d/p G Stevens c Mellor co-s M Wilson fn (*An American Tragedy*) *Theodore Dreiser* co-a Dreier m Waxman w Clift, E Taylor, Burr, Winters 122min Par
PLACE TO GO, A (1963) d Dearden w Tushingham 86min BL
PLACE TO LIVE, A (1944) p/supn I Lerner 16mm 18min
PLACIDO (1961) d/co-s Berlanga 90min
PLAGUES AND PUPPY LOVE (1917) d/w Semon 1rl Vit
PLAIN CLOTHES (1925) d *Harry Edwards* co-st/co-s Capra w Langdon 2rs pc Sennett r Pat
PLAINSMAN, THE (1937) d/p De Mille co-c Milner co-a Dreier m Antheil w G Cooper, Arthur, Bickford, (Quinn) 110min Par
Plain People = PROSTYE LYUDI (1945 r 1956)
PLAISIR, LE (1952) d/co-s Ophuls fst (*Le Masque*, La Maison Tellier, Le Modele) *Guy de Maupassant* c Agostini, Matras co-dec d'Eaubonne mf *Offenbach* w Darrieux, Gabin, Brasseur, Gélin, S Simon 95min
PLANE CRAZY (1928) d Iwerks, Disney anim 1rl pc Disney r Col
Planet of Blood (UK) = TERRORE NELLO SPAZIO (1965)
PLANET OF THE APES (1968) d Schaffner s M Wilson, Serling c Shamroy m Goldsmith w Heston PV* 112min Fox
Planet of the Vampires (US) = TERRORE NELLO SPAZIO (1965)
Plan for Great Works = PLAN VELIKIKH RABOT (1930)
PLANNED CROPS (1943) d Lye
PLANTER'S WIFE, THE (1952) d Annakin c Unsworth w Colbert, Hawkins BL r JAR 91min (= *Outpost in Malaya*)
PLAN VELIKIKH RABOT (1930) d Room co-m *Rimsky-Korsakov* 1800m (= *Plan for Great Works*)
PLASTIC AGE, THE (1925) d W Ruggles w Bow, Roland 6488ft pc B P Schulberg
PLATINUM BLOND (1931) d Capra di Riskin ad Swerling c J Walker w L Young, Harlow 89min Col
PLATINUM HIGH SCHOOL (1960) d Haas w Cook, Duryea, Rooney 93min MGM
PLATONISCHE EHE (1919) d Leni p/co-s May
Play, The = IGRA (1962)
PLAY DIRTY (1968) d De Toth p Saltzman m Legrand w Caine PV* 117min r UA
Playful Robot, The = NESTASNI ROBOT (1956)
PLAYGIRL (1932) d Enright c Toland w L Young, Foster 60min WB
PLAYGIRL (1954) d Pevney w Winters 85min U
PLAYHOUSE, THE (1921) d/s Kenton, Cline w Keaton 2rs FN
PLAYING AROUND (1930) d Le Roy c Polito 66min FN
PLAYMATES (1941) d D Butler w J Barrymore 96min RKO
PLAY MISTY FOR ME (1971) d Eastwood a Golitzen, D Siegel *102min
PLAYTHING (1929) d *Castleton Knight* w Milland
Playtime (UK) = RECREATION, LA (1960)
PLAYTIME (1967) d/co-st/co-s/w Tati co-c Badal 70* 152min
Play for Passion, A = BIGAMISTO, IL (1956)
PLEASE BELIEVE ME (1950) d Taurog p Lewton co-a Gibbons w Kerr, R Walker, Lawford 81min MGM
PLEASE DON'T EAT THE DAISIES (1960) d Walters p Pasternak c Bronner w D Day, Niven, Haydn CS* 111min MGM
Please not Now = BRIDE SUR LE COU, LA (1961)
PLEASURE GARDEN, THE (1925) d Hitchcock p Balcon 6458ft
PLEASURE GARDEN, THE (1954) d/s Broughton c Lassally p/w L Anderson 38min
Pleasure Garden = LUSTGARDEN (1961)
PLEASURE OF HIS COMPANY, THE (1961) d Seaton fco-pl *Cornelia Otis Skinner* co-a Pereira c Burks m A Newman w Astaire, D Reynolds, Palmer, C Ruggles *115min pc Perlberg, Seaton r Par
PLEASURE SEEKERS, THE (1964) d Negulesco c Fapp w Keith, Lynley, Tierney CS* 107min Fox
Pleasures of the Flesh, The = ETSURAKU (1965)
PLEBEI (1915) d/s Protazanov fpl (*Miss Julie*) *Strindberg* 4rs (= *Plebeians*)
Plebeians = PLEBEI (1915)
PLEINS FEUX SUR L'ASSASSIN (1961) d Franju c Fradetal m Jarre w Brasseur, Trintignant 95min (= *Spotlight on Murder*)
PLEIN SOLEIL (1959) d/co-s Clément c Decaë m Rota w Delon, Ronet, Schneider *120min (= *Purple Noon*)
Plombier Amoureux, Le (1932) French version of THE PASSIONATE PLUMBER d Autant-Lara w Keaton. Fairbanks Jr 74min MGM
Plongée du 'Rubis', Une = SORTIE DU 'RUBIS', UNE (1950)
PLOTINA (1932) d/s Petrov 1500m (= *The Carpenter*)
PLOUGH AND THE STARS, THE (1937) d J Ford s D Nichols fpl *Sean O'Casey* c August w Stanwyck 72min RKO
PLOW GIRL, THE (1916) d Leonard 5rs Par
PLOW THAT BROKE THE PLAINS, THE (1936) d/s Lorentz c Strand, Hurwitz, R Steiner m V Thompson 28min
PLUCKED FROM BURNING (1901) d Paul 100ft
PLUMBER, THE (1924) d/s Cline p Sennett Pat
PLUNDER (1922–23) d G Seitz w White serial in 15eps Pat
PLUNDERERS, THE (1960) d/p Pevney co-ex-p J Chandler c Polito m Rosenman w J Chandler 93min WB
PLUNDER OF THE SUN (1953) d J Farrow w G Ford 81min WB
PLUNDER ROAD (1957) d Cornfield c E Haller w Cook 71min S Fox
PLUS BELLES ESCROQUERIES DU MONDE, LES (1963) FS 90min (= *The Beautiful Swindlers*)
ep LE GRAND ESCROC d/s Godard c Coutard m Legrand w Seberg 25min
ep NAPLES d/s Gregoretti
ep LA RIVIERE DE DIAMANTS d Polanski m Komeda CS 90min
ep L'HOMME QUI VENDIT LA TOUR EIFFEL d Chabrol c Rabier w Cassel, Blanche, Deneuve
PLUS BELLE FILLE DU MONDE NE PEUT DONNER QUE CE QU' ELLE A, LA (1938) d/s/di/c Kirsanov
PLUS BELLE QUE LA NATURE (1953) d Lautner sh
Plus Grand Succès de René Cresté, Le = JUDEX (1916)
PLUS HEUREUX DES HOMMES, LE (1952) d Ciampi 87min Pat
PLUS VIEUX METIER DU MONDE, LE (1967) co-a Evein *115min
ep NUITS ROMAINES d Bolognini w Martinelli
ep MADEMOISELLE MIMI d De Broca w Moreau, Brialy
ep AUJOUD'HUI d Autant-Lara
ep ANTICIPATION, OU L'AN 2000 d/s Godard m Legrand w Karina, Léaud
PLYASKA SMERTI (1916) d Protazanev w Mozhukhin 5rs (= *The Dance of Death*)
PLYMOUTH ADVENTURE (1952) d C Brown p Schary co-a Gibbons m Rozsa c Daniels w Tracy, V Johnson, Tierney *104min MGM
Poacher's God Daughter, The = PYTLAKOVA SCHOVANKA (1949)
POBEDA NA PRAVOBEREZHNOI UKRAINYE I IZGNANIE NEMETSIKH ZAKHVATCHIKOV ZA PREDELI UKRAINSKIKH SOVETSKIKH ZEMEL (1945) d Dovzhenko, Solntzeva cy/n Dovzhenko 74min (= *Victory in the Ukraine and the Explusion of the Germans from the Boundaries of the Ukrainian Soviet Earth*)
POBEDA - SAMYI SCHASTLIVYI (1938) d Pudovkin, *Mikhail Doller* 85min (= *Victory*)
POBOCNIK JEHO VYSOSTI (1933) d Fric c Heller
POCESTNE PANI PARDUBICKE (1944) d Fric (= *The Respectable ladies of Pardubricke*)
POCIAG (1959) d/co-s Kawalerowicz w Cybulski 100min (= *Night Train*)
POCKET CARTOON, THE (1941) d/p/s Halas, Batchelor, Mackendrick anim *3min
POCKETFUL OF MIRACLES (1961) d/co-p Capra co-as-p G Ford co-s Kanter rm LADY FOR A DAY (1933) fst (*Lady for a Day*) *Damon Runyon* co-a Pereira c Bronner w G Ford B Davis, Horton, Mitchell PV* 136min r UA
POD GWIAZDA FRYGIJSKA (1954) d/co-s Kawalerowicz (= *Under the Phrygian Star*)
PODRUGI (1935) d/s *L Arnshtam* supn Yutkevitch m Shostakovich 95min (= *Girl Friends*)
PODVED S RUNENSEM (1940) d Vavra
PODVIG RAZVEDCHIKA (1947) d/w Barnet 91min (= *The Scout's Exploits*)
POEDINOK (1957) d/s Petrov m *A Khatchaturian* 104min (= *The Duel*)
POEMA O MORYE (1958) d Solntseva s Dovzhenko CS* 110min (= *Poem of the Sea*)
POEMAT SYMFONICZNY "BAJKA" ST. MONIUSZKI (1952) d Munk 14min
Poem of the Sea = POEMA O MORYE (1958)
Poe's Tales of Terror = TALES OF TERROR (1962)
POET (1957) d Barnet
PO: FORZA 50.000 (1960) d Olmi S* 13min
POGEGNANIE Z DIABLEM (1957 d/co-s Jakubowska (= *Farewell to the Devil*)
POHADKA MAJE (1940) d/s Vavra
POIL DE CAROTTE (1925) d/co-s Duvivier co-s Feyder fn *Jules Renard*
POIL DE CAROTTE (1932) d/s Duvivier rm POIL DE CAROTTE (1925) co-c Thirard e Le Chanois 94min
POINT BLACK (1967) d Boorman fn (*The Hunter*) *Richard Stark* c Lathrop w Marvin, A Dickinson PV* 92min MGM
POINT DE CHUTE (1970) d/co-s Hossein co-s Desailly w Hossein *85min
POINT DU JOUR, LE (1948) d/co-s Daquin m Wiener w Desailly, Modot, Piccoli 101min
POINTE COURTE, LA (1954) d/st/s/n Varda e Colpi, Resnais 85min
POISON, LA (1951) d/s Guitry c Bachelet w Guitry, M Simon, De Funès 96min Gau
POISSON D'AVRIL (1954) d Grangier w Bourvil 102min
POJKEN I TRADET (1961) d/p/s Sucksforff c Fischer m *Mozart, Handel* S 85min San (= *The Boy in the Tree*)
POJKEN OCH DRAKEN (1961) d Widerberg, Troell c Widerberg (= *The Boy and the Kite*)
POKHOZHDENIYA OKTYABRINY (1924) d/s Trauberg, Kozintsev 980m (= *The Adventures of Oktyabrina*)
POKKERS UNGER, DE (1947) d/co-s A and B Henning Jensen 93min (= *Those Blasted Kids*)
POKLAD PTACIKO OSTRAVA (1952) d/s Zeman *76min (= *The Treasure of Birds' Island*)
POKOJ ZWYECIEZY SWIATA (1950) d/s Ivens, *Jerzy Bossak* 98min
POKOLENIE (1954) d Wajda dec A Ford w Cybulski, Polanski 85min (= *A Generation*)
POKORITELI MORYA (1959) d/c Karmen (= *Conquered Seas*)
POLAR PESTS (1958) d Avery p Lantz * 1rl U
POLDEN (1931) d/co-s Heifitz, Zarkhi 2100m (= *Noon*)
POLIBEK ZE STADIONU (1948) d/co-st Fric (= *A Kiss from the Stadium*)
Policarpo = POLILARPO, UFFICAILE DI SCRITTURA (1959)
Policarpo De' tappetti, Ufficiale di scrittura, = POLICARPO, UFFICIALE DI SCRITTURA (1959)
Policarpo Master Writer (UK) = POLICARPO, UFFICIALE DI SCRITTURA (1959)
POLICARPO, UFFICIALE DI SCRITTURA (1959) d Soldati c Rotunno *100min (= *Policarpo Policarpo de' Tapetti, Ufficiale di Scrittura/Policarpo, Master Writer*)
POLICE (1916) d/s Chaplin c Totheroh w Chaplin, W Ruggles, Purviance 2rs S&A
Police and Small Gangsters = KEISATSUKAN TO BUROYOKU-DAN (1959)
POLICEJNI HODINA (1960) d/s Vavra 95min (= *Time, Gentlemen, Please*)
POLICHE (1934) d/co-s Gance co-s Decoin
POLIKUSCHKA (1958) d Gallone fst *Tolstoi*
POLIS PAULUS PASKASMALL (1924) d/s Molander SF
POLITICAL PORTRAITS (1969) d/s/c/e Markopoulos 16mm *80min
POLITICIAN'S LOVE STORY, THE (1909) d Griffith w Sennett 1rl Bio
POLIZEIAKTE 909 (1934) d/s Wiene w V Harlan 2137m
POLLYANNA (1920) d *Paul Powell* p/w Pickford 6rs
POLLYANNA (1960) d/s Swift c R Harlan w Wyman, H Mills, Malden, Menjou, Crisp, Moorehead *134min
POLLY OF THE CIRCUS (1932) d Santell c Barnes w Davies, Gable, Milland 72min MGM
POLLY OF THE FOLLIES (1922) d/co-s Emerson co-s Loos w C Talmadge 7rs FN
POLLY REDHEAD (1917) d Conway 5rs

POLNOCNI DOBRUDRUZSTVI (1960) d Pojar, B Sramek co-s Pojar a Trnka anim* 26min (= A Midnight Incident)
POLOWANIE NA MUCHY (1969) d Wajda *108min (= Hunting Flies)
POLSKA KRONIKA FILMOWA NR 52 A–B (1959) d Munk 17min
POLUSTANOK (1963) d/co-s Barnet 71min (= Whistle Stop)
POLYORCHIA (1962) d/co-st Bernard-Aubert m Kosma 103min (= Les Moutons de Praxos/A l'aube du troisieme jour)
POMME DE TERRE (1934) d Y Allégret w J and P Prévert sh
POMODORO (1961) d Olmi *
POMPADOUR, DIE (1935) d V Harlan, Willy Schmidt-Gentner, Heinz Helbig co-s V Harlan 85min
POMSTA (1968) ep d Brdecka (= Revenge)
PONDELJAK ILI VTORAK (1966) d/co-s Mimica part *85min (= Monday or Tuesday)
PONJOLA (1923) d Crisp 7rs FN
PONTCARRAL, COLONEL D'EMPIRE (1942) d Delannoy c Matras
Pontius Pilate = PONZIO PILATO (1961)
PONY EXPRESS, THE (1925) d/p Cruze w Bancroft, Beery 9929ft FPL
PONY EXPRESS RIDER, THE (1916) d/s/w Mix 2rs Sel
PONY SOLDIER (1952) d J Newman m North co-a Wheeler w Power 82min Fox (= Macdonald of the Canadian Mounties)
PONZIO PILATO (1961) d Rapper w Rathbone, Marais CS* 106min
POOL OF LONDON (1951) d Dearden ex-p Balcon 85min
POOL SHARKS (1915) d Edwin Middleton w Fields
POOR BOOB (1919) d Crisp 5rs FPL
Poor But Handsome = POVERI MA BELLI (1956)
POOR LITTLE RICH GIRL, THE (1917) d M Tourneur w Pickford
POOR LITTLE RICH GIRL (1936) d Irving Cummings p Zanuck c J Seitz w Temple, Faye 72min Fox
POOR LITTLE RICH GIRL (1965) d Warhol 16mm 70min
POOR NUT, THE (1927) d Richard Wallace fpl J C Nugent, E Nugent w Arthur 6897ft FN
POOR OLD BILL (1931) d Monty Banks w Lawford
POOR RELATIONS (1919) d/s K Vidor w Pitts 50min
Poo-San = PU SAN (1953)
POPBOCNIC JEHO VYSOSTI (1938) d Fric c Heller (= Assistant to His Highness)
POP BUELL, HOOSIER FARMER IN LAOS (1965) d W Van Dyke 30min
POPIOL I DIAMENT (1958) d/co-s Wajda w Cybulski 104min (= Ashes and Diamonds)
POPIOLY (1966) d Wajda CS 234min (= Ashes)
Poppies = GUBIJINSO (1935)
POPPY (1936) d Heisler w Fields 75min Par
POPPY GIRL'S HUSBAND, THE (1919) d/pc W Hart supn Ince c August w W Hart 5rs
POPPY IS ALSO A FLOWER, THE (1966) d T Young st Ian Fleming c Alekan m Auric w Hayworth, T Howard, Roland, A Dickinson, Brynner, Wallach, Mastroianni, Boyd, Sharif, Hawkins, Tiller *105min (= Danger Grows Wild)
POPRIGUNYA (1955) d/s Samsonov supn Romm fst Anton Chekhov w Bondarchnk *91min (= The Gadfly/The Grasshopper)
POPULAR SIN, THE (1926) d St Clair c Garmes 5776ft FPL
PORCILE (1969) d/s Pasolini p Baldi w Léaud, Ferreri (2 parts) *100min (= Pigsty)
PORGY AND BESS (1959) d Preminger p Goldwyn fmpl George Gershwin c Shamroy chor Pan w Poitier TAO* 136min r Col
PORKALA (1956) d J Donner sh
PORK CHOP HILL (1959) d Milestone s J R Webb c Leavitt m Rosenman w Peck, Peppard 97min r UA
PORKY AND DAFFY (1938) p L Schlesinger co-anim Cannon anim 7min
PORKY'S DUCK HUNT (1937) d Avery p L Schlesinger co-anim Cannon anim 9min WB
PORKY'S PICNIC (1939) p L Schlesinger co-anim Canon 9min
PORKY'S MIDNIGHT MATINEE (1941) p L Schlesinger anim Cannon anim
PORKY'S NAUGHTY NEPHEW (1938) p L Schlesinger anim Cannon anim
PORKY THE RAIN MAKER (1936) d Avery p L Schlesinger 7min WB
PORKY THE WRESTLER (1936) d Avery p L Schlesinger co-anim C Jones 7min WB
Pornographer, The (UK) = JINRUIGAKU NYUMON (1966)
POR QUE TE ENGANA TU MARIDO? (1968) d/co-s Summers *92min (= Why Does Your Husband Deceive You?)
PORTA DEL CIELO, LA (1946) d/co-ad De Sica st/co-s Zavattini c Tonti w Girotti
PORT AFRICQUE (1956) d Maté m M Arnold *92min Col
PORTA PORTESE (1954) d Pontecorvo sh
PORT DU DESIR, LE (1954) d Greville c Alekan m Kosma w Gabin 94min

PORTE DES LILAS (1957) d/co-s Clair co-s Aurel w Brasseur 95min
PORTE DU LARGE, LA (1936) d/co-s L'Herbier co-s Charles Spaak (= Door to the Open Sea)
Porter, The = NEW JANITOR, THE (1914)
PORTES CLAQUENT, LES (1960) d Jacques Poitrenaud, Michel Sermaud w Deneuve 90min
PORTES DE LA NUIT, LES (1946) d Carné s/di Prevert f ballet (Le Rendez-vous) J Prévert, Kosma c Agostini dec Trauner m Kosma w Montand, Brasseur, Reggiani, Carette Pat
Port of Call = HAMNSTAD (1948)
PORT OF NEW YORK (1949) d Benedek w Brynner 82min r EL
PORT OF SEVEN SEAS (1938) d Whale s P Sturges fsts (Fanny and Marius) Pagnol m Waxman w Beery, O'Sullivan 81min MGM
Port of Wickedness = BARBARY COAST (1935)
Portrait, A = SHOZO (1948)
PORTRAIT DE HENRI GOETZ (1947) d Resnais 16mm sh
PORTRAIT FROM LIFE (1948) d Fisher w Zetterling 90m
PORTRAIT IN BLACK (1960) d M Gordon p R Hunter s/fpl Goff, Roberts c Metty w Turner, Quinn, Nolan *112min U
PORTRAIT OF A HARBOUR (1957) d A King 16mm 28min
PORTRAIT OF ALISON (1955) d/co-s G Green co-s K Hughes 84min
PORTRAIT OF A MOBSTER (1961) d Pevney m M Steiner c Polito 108min WB
Portrait of Asa = PORTRATT AV ASA (1965)
Portrait of a Sinner = ROUGH AND THE SMOOTH, THE (1959)
PORTRAIT OF JASON (1967) d/e S Clarke 105min
PORTRAIT OF JENNIE (1949) d Dieterle p/co-s Selznick co-s Osborn m Tiomkin c August w J Jones, Cotten, E Barrymore, A Francis, D Wayne 86min
Portrait of Maria (US) = MARIA CANDELARIA (1943)
Portraist of Women (UK) = NAISENKUVIA (1970)
PORTRAIT EINER BEWAHRUNG (1965) d Kluge sh
PORTRATT AV ASA (1965) d Troell (= Portrait of Asa)
PORUCHIK KIZHE (1934) d Alexander Feinzimmer m Prokofiev 86min (= Lieutenant Kizhe/The Tzar wants to Sleep)
POSLEDNI MUZ (1934) d Fric (= The Last Man)
POSLEDNI VYSTREL (1950) d J Weiss (= Last Shot)
POSSESSED (1931) d C Brown a Gibbons w J Crawford, Gable 72min MGM
POSSESSED (1947) d C Bernhardt p Wald m Waxman w J Crawford, Heflin 104min WB
POST HASTE (1934) d/e Jennings p Grierson
POSTMAN ALWAYS RINGS TWICE, THE (1946) d Garnett co-s Busch co-a Gibbons w Turner, Garfield 113min MGM
POSTO, IL (1961) d/st/s/e Olmi 92min (= The Job/Sound of Trumpets)
POTAMI, TO (1960) d/co-p/co-s Koundouros m Hadjidakis (= The River)
POTASH AND PERLMUTTER (1923) d Badger 8rs FN
POT-BOUILLE (1957) d/co-s/ad Duvivier co-s Joannon fn Emile Zola di Jeanson c Kelber m Wiener w Philipe, Darrieux, Aimée 115min (= The House of Lovers)
POTE TIN KYRIAKI (1959) d/p/s Dassin m Hadjidakis w Mercouri, Dassin 91min r UA (= Never on Sunday)
POT O' GOLD (1941) d G Marshall c Mohr w J Stewart, Goddard 86min r UA
POTOMOK CHINGIS KHAN (1928) d Pudovkin w Barnet, Pudovkin, (Sten) 3092m (= Storm over Asia/The Heir to Gengis Khan)
POT-POURRI (1963) d Low, Victor Jobin 7¼min NFBC
POTTED PSALM, THE (1947) d Broughton, Sidney Peterson
POTTERS, THE (1927) d Newmayer w Fields 6680ft FPL r Par
Pottery Maker = STORY OF A POTTER (1925)
POTU STORONU ARAKSA (1947) d/s Shub 54min (= On the Banks of the Arax)
POUDRE D'ESCAMPETTE, LA (1971) d/co-s De Broca m Legrand w Piccoli *110min
POUDRE DE VITESSE (1911) d Cohl anim
POULE MERVEILLEUSE, LA (1902) d/w Zecca Pat 25–75m
POULETTE GRISE, LA (1947) d McLaren 16mm *6min NFBC
POUPEE, LA (1962) d/p Baratier s/fn Jacques Audiberti c Coutard dec Allio co-m Kosma w Cybulski FS* 100min (= He, She or It)
POUR ETRE AIME (1933) d J Tourneur 75min Pat
POUR LA SUITE DU MONDE (1963) co-d Perrault co-d/co-c Brault 16mm 105min (= The Moontrap)
POUR L' ETOILE, S.V.P. (1908) d Méliès 77m
POURQUOI L'AMERIQUE (1969) d Rossif 100min
POURQUOI PARIS (1962) d/co-s De la Patelliere w Girardot, Aznavour 79min
POURQUOI VIENS-TU SI TARD (1959) d/st Decoin c Matras di Audiard m Aznavour w Morgan, Blanche 100min
Pour sauver la Hollande = DIGUE, LA (1911)
Poursuite, La = ROI SANS DIVERTISSEMENT (1963)

POUR UN AMOUR LOINTAIN (1968) d/co-s Séchan *95min
POUR UNE EDUCATION DE QUALITE (1969) d/s/cy/co-e Lamothe 6×30min
POUR UNE NUIT D'AMOUR (1921) d Protazanov n Clair (as Chomette) 5rs
POUR UN MAILLOT JEUNE (1965) d/s/c Lelouch *27min (= For a Yellow Jersey)
POUR UN SOU D'AMOUR (1932) d/e Grémillon dec D'Eaubonne 95min
POURVU QU'ON AIT L'IVRESSE (1957) d Pollet 19min
POUSSIERES, LES (1954) d/s Franju m Wiener 22min
POUSSIERE SUR LA VILLE (1965) d/co-e Lamothe co-c Brault 95min
POVERE BIMBE (1923) d Pastrone
POVERI MA BELLI (1956) d/co-st/co-s Risi co-s Festa Campanile (= Girl in a Bikini/Poor but Handsome) 103min
POVERI MILLIONARI (1958) d/co-st/co-s Risi co-s Festa Campanile 90min
POVERTY ROW (1925) d Hans Tiesler w G Cooper 2rs
POVEST O NEFTYANIKAKH KASPIYA (1953) d/c Karmen (= Story of the Caspian Oil Men)
POVEST PLAMENNYKH LET (1961) d Solntseva s Dovzhenko n Bondarchuk 70* 105min (= The Flaming Years)
POVODEN (1958) d/co-s Fric (= The Flood)
POWDER MY BACK (1928) d Del Ruth 7rs WB
POWER, THE (1968) co-d/p Pal co-d Haskin m Rozsa w De Carlo, A Ray, Pleshette PV* 109min MGM
POWER AMONG MEN (1959) d Gian Luigi Polidoro, Alexander Hammid supn/s T Dickinson wv Laurence Harvey *90min
POWER AND THE GLORY, THE (1933) d W Howard st/s P Sturges c Howe w Tracy 76min Fox
POWER AND THE LAND (1940) d Ivens co-c F Crosby cy Stephen Vincent Benet 36min Dept of Agriculture
POWER AND THE PRIZE, THE (1956) d Koster c Folsey w R Taylor, Ives, C Coburn, Astor S 98min MGM
POWER OF THE PRESS, THE (1928) d Capra c Cohn c Tetzlaff w Fairbanks Jr 6rs Col
POWER GIRL, THE (1942) d McLeod c Cortez w G Murphy 99min r UA (= Hello Beautiful)
POWERS OF 10 (1968) d/s C and R Eames c C Eames *7½min
POWERS THAT PRAY (1918) d H King Mut
POWER TRAIN (1962) d Teru Murakami p Dunning 16mm *13min
PO ZAKONU (1926) d/co-s/e Kuleshov fst (The Unexpected) Jack London 1673m (= By the Law/Dura Lex)
POZEGNANIA (1958) d/co-s Has 100min (= Farewells)
POZOR! (1959) d/s Brdecka (= Look Out!)
PRACTICALLY YOURS (1944) d Leisen st Krasna c C Lang co-a Dreier w V Young w Colbert, MacMurray, Benchley, De Carle 90min Par
PRAESIDENTEN (1919) d/s/a Dreyer
PRAESTEN I VEJLBY (1922) d/s Blom
PRAESTENS DATTER (1916) d/s Madsen
Prague Nights = PRAZSKE NOCI (1968)
PRAIRIE, THE (1948) d Wisbar fn James Fennimore Cooper 56min
PRAIRIE TRAILS (1920) d G Marshall w Mix 5rs Fox
Praise the Sea = PRIJS DE MAAR (1958)
Pram, The (UK) = BARNVAGNEN (1962)
PRAMIEN AUF DEN TOD (1950) d/co-s/fn Jurgens w Jurgens, Krauss 87min
PRASTANKAN (1920) d/s Dreyer (= The Parson's Widow)
PRASTEN (1913) d Sjöström 2045m
PRATIDWANDI (1971) d/s/m S Ray 100min (= The Adversary/Siddhartha and the City)
PRAVDA (1969) d Godard *60min
PRAWDZIWY KONIEC WIELKIEJ WOJNY (1957) d/co-s Kawalerowicz 96min (= The Real End of The Great War)
PRAZDNIK SVYATOVO YORGENA (1930) d/s Protazanov 2290m (= The Feast of St. Jorgen)
PRAZSKE NOCI (1968)
ep O OTRAVENE TRAVICCE d/s Milos Makovec st Brdecka (= The poison)
ep THE LAST GOLEM d/st/s Brdecka
ep O CHLEBOVICH STREVICCICH d/s Schorm st Brdecka (= Slipper of Bread)
PRECIEUSES RIDICULES, LES (1935) d Perret fpl Molière
Precious Seeds, The = DRAGOTSENNYE ZERNA (1948)
PRECURSORES DE LA PINTURA ARGENTINA (1957) d/s Torre Nilsson * sh
PREDATEL (1926) d Room co-dec Yutkevich 2100m (= Traitor)
PREDTUCHA (1947) d/s Vavra (= Presentiment)
PRELUDE A L'APRES-MIDI D'UN FAUNE (1938) d Rossellini fm Débussy sh
PRELUDE: DOG STAR MAN (1961) d Brakhage 16mm * si 25min
PRELUDE TO WAR (1942) d Capra m Tiomkin w W Huston 52min US War Department
PREMATURE BURIAL, THE (1962) d/p Corman fn Poe c F Crosby a D Haller w Milland PV* 82min AI
PREMIER CIGARE, LE (1896) d Reynaud

PREMIER DE CORDEE (1943) d Daquin 105min
PREMIERE NUIT, LA (1958) d/ad Franju c Schuftan c Colpi m Delerue 21min
PREMIER MAI (1958) d Saslavsky w Montand 89min
PREMIER RENDEZ-VOUS (1941) d Decoin w Darrieux, Gélin 102min
PREM PATRA (1962) d/p Roy 5000m
PREP AND PEP (1928) d D Butler 5830ft Fox
PRESAGIO, IL (1916) d/st/s Genina
PRESENTATION (1951–1961) d/s Rohmer w Godard, Karina 12min (= Charlotte et son steak)
Presentiment = PREDTUCHA (1947)
PRESENTING LILY MARS (1943) d Taurog p Pasternak c Ruttenberg a Gibbons w Garland, Heflin 104min MGM
PRESEPI, IL (1932) d Poggioli sh
PRESIDENT, LE (1961) d/co-s Verneuil co-s/di Audiard fn Georges Simenon m Jarre w Gabin 108min
President, The (UK) = PRAESIDENTEN (1919)
PRESIDENTESSA, LA (1953) d Germi 102min (= The Lady President)
PRESIDENT MCKINLEY AND ESCORT GOING TO THE CAPITOL (1901) d Porter 61ft Ed
PRESIDENT MCKINLEY'S FUNERAL CORTEGE AT BUFFALO, NEW YORK (1901) d Porter 165ft Ed
PRESIDENT MCKINLEY'S FUNERAL CORTEGE AT WASHINGTON D.C. (1901) d Porter 146ft Ed
PRESIDENT'S ANALYST, THE (1967) d/st/s Flicker ex-p H W Koch c Fraker co-a Pereira m Schifrin w J Coburn PV* 104min Par
PRESIDENT'S LADY, THE (1953) d/as-p Levin p S Siegel co-a Wheeler w Heston, Hayward 96min Fox
PRESIDENT VANISHES, THE (1935) d Wellman p Wanger w R Russell 86min Par
P . . . . RESPECTUEUSE, LA (1952) ad Astruc m Auric
PRESSENS MAGT (1913) d/s Blom
PRESSURE POINT (1962) d/co-s Cornfield c E Hallen e Kramer m Gold w Poitier 91min pc Kramer r UA
PRESTIGE (1932) d/co-s Garnett c Andriot w Menjou, M Douglas 73min RKO
PRETTY BABY (1950) d Windust p/co-s Kurnitz co-st Furthman c Marley 92min WB
PRETTY LADIES (1925) d Monta Bell w Pitts, Shearer, (M Loy), (J Crawford) 5828ft MGM
PRETTY MAIDS ALL IN A ROW (1971) d Vadim w Schifrin w Hudson, A Dickinson *95min MGM
PRETTY POLLY (1967) d G Green fst Coward m Legrand w H Mills, T Howard S* 102min JAR (= A Matter of Innocence)
PRETTY SISTER OF JOSE, THE (1915) d Dwan fn Frances Hodgson Burnett w Julian 5rs FPL
PREVIEW MURDER MYSTERY, THE (1936) d Florey c Struss co-a Dreier w C Ruggles 60min Par
PREZIL JSEM SVOU SMRT (1960) d Jasny 99min (= I Survived Certain Death)
PRICE OF A SONG, THE (1935) d M Powell
PRICE OF SILENCE, THE (1917) d/s F Lloyd 5rs Fox
PRIDE AND PREJUDICE (1940) d Leonard co-s Aldous Huxley fn Jane Austin c Freund co-a Gibbons m Stothart w Garson, Olivier, O'Sullivan, Oliver 117min MGM
Pride, Love and Suspicion (UK) = FIAMMATA, LA (1953)
PRIDE OF NEW YORK, THE (1917) d/s Walsh 5rs Fox
PRIDE OF PALOMAR, THE (1922) d Borzage 7500ft
PRIDE OF THE BOWERY (1940) d JH Lewis p Katzman 63min MON
PRIDE OF THE CLAN (1917) d M Tourneur w Pickford
PRIDE OF THE MARINES (1945) d/co-s Daves p Wald c Marley m Waxman w Garfield, Parker 119min WB
PRIDE OF THE SOUTH, THE (1913) d Ince w Borzage
PRIDE OF THE YANKEES, THE (1942) d S Wood p Goldwyn s H Mankiewikz c Maté m Harline w T Wright, G Cooper, Brennan, Duryea 127min RKO
PRIERE AUX ETOILES, LA (1941, uf) d Pagnol
Priest's Wife, The (UK) = MOGLIE DEL PRETE, LA (1971)
PRIGIONIERO DI SANTA CRUZ, IL (1940) d Bragaglia
PRIJDE KOCOUR, AZ (1963) d/co-s Jasny CS* 105min (= That Cat)
PRIJDU HNED (1942) d/co-s Vavra
PRIJS DE MAAR (1958) d/p Van den Horst 24min (= Praise the Sea)
PRIMA COMUNIONE (1950) d/co-p Blasetti st/co-s Zavattini co-s Cecchi D'Amico 81min (= His Majesty Mr. Jones/First Communion/Father's Dilemma)
PRIMA DELLA RIVOLUZIONE (1964) d/s Bertolucci 115min
PRIMA NOTTE, LA (1959) d Cavalcanti c Di Venanzo w Carol, De Sica, Cardinale
PRIMARY (1960) d R Leacock, Pennebaker, Robert Drew co-c A Maysles w J F Kennedy 16mm 26min
PRIMEIRA MISSA, A (1961) d/st/s/w Barreto 113min (= The First Mass)
PRIME MINISTER, THE (1942) d T Dickinson w Gielgud 109min WB

PRIME OF MISS JOAN BRODIE, THE (1968) d Neame fn Murial Spark c Moore *116min r Fox
PRIMITIVE LOVER, THE (1922) d Franklin w C Talmadge 6172ft pc C Talmadge r FN
PRIMITIVE MAN, OR WARS OF THE PRIMAL TRIBES (1913) d Griffith w Marsh 1rl Bio
PRIMO AMORE (1941) d Gallone
PRIMO AMORE (1958) d/co-st/co-s Camerini
PRIMROSE PATH (1940) d/p/co-s La Cava c August w G Rogers, McCrea 93min RKO
PRIMULA BIANCO, LA (1947) d Bragaglia p Ponti 96min
PRINCE AND THE PAUPER, THE (1937) d Keighley p Wallis fn Mark Twain c Polito w Flynn, Davis 117min WB
PRINCE AND THE SHOWGIRL, THE (1957) d/p Olivier s Rattigan c Cardiff des Furze w Olivier, Monroe *115min pc Monroe
Prince Bayaya = BAJAJA (1950)
PRINCE CHAP, THE (1916) d Neilan 5rs Sel
PRINCE DE HOMBOURG, LE (1924, uf) d Von Gerlach
PRINCE OF AVENUE A, THE (1920) d J Ford 5rs U
PRINCE OF FOXES (1949) d H King p S Siegel c Shamroy co-a Wheeler m A Newman w Power, Welles, Paxinou 107min Fox
PRINCE OF PLAYERS (1955) d/p P Dunne s M Hart c C Clarke co-a Wheeler m Herrmann w Bickford, Burton, Derek CS* 102min Fox
Prince Sami = PRINZ SAMI (1918)
PRINCESS AND THE PIRATE, THE (1944) d D Butler p Goldwyn co-s Shavelson c Milner w Hope, B Crosby, V Mayo, V McLaglen 94min r RKO
PRINCESS AND THE PLUMBER, THE (1930) d A Korda co-c O'Connell w O'Sullivan 6480ft Fox
PRINCESS COMES ACROSS, THE (1936) d W Howard c Tetzlaff a Dreier w Lombard, MacMurray 76min Par
PRINCESSE DE CLEVES, LA (1960) d Delannoy ad/di Cocteau c Alekan m Auric w Marais, Vlady S* 115min
PRINCESSE ELENA (1913) d/s Madsen
Princesse Mandane = OUBLIE (1927)
PRINCESSE MUETTE, LA (1960) d Blue
PRINCESS OF NEW YORK, THE (1921) d Crisp 5rs FPL
PRINCESS O'ROURKE (1943) d/s Krasna p Wallis c E Haller m Hollander w De Havilland, C Coburn, R Cummings, Wyman 94min WB
Princess Priscilla's Fortnight = THE RUNAWAY PRINCESS (1929)
PRINCESS VIRTUE (1917) d Leonard 6rs
Princess with the Golden Star, The = PRINCEZNA SE ZLATOV HVEZDOV (1959)
Princess Yang-Kwei Fei = YOKIMI (1955)
PRINCE VALIANT (1954) d Hathaway s D Nichols c Ballard co-a Wheeler m Waxman w Mason, J Leigh, R Wagner, Hayden, Crisp, V McLaglen CS* 100min Fox
PRINCE WHO WAS A THIEF, THE (1951) d Maté fst Theodore Dreiser c Glassberg w Curtis, Laurie 88min U
PRINCEZNA SE ZLATOV HVEZDOV (1959) d/co-s Fric * (= The Princess with the Golden Star)
PRINCIPLE DELL'IMPOSSIBLE, IL (1918) d/s Genina
PRINCIPESSA MISTERIOSA (1919) d Brenon
PRINTEMPS, LE (1968) d/co-s/co-ad/co-di Hanoun *90min
PRINTEMPS DE LA LIBERTE (1949, uf) d/s/di/m Grémillon
PRINTEMPS, L'AUTOMNE, ET L'AMOUR, LE (1954) d Grangier w Fernandel *77min
PRINZ KUCKUCK (1919) d/co-dec Leni w Veidt
PRINZ SAMI (1918) d/w Lubitsch 1rl (= Prince Sami)
PRISE DE POUVOIR PAR LOUIS XIV, LA (1966) d Rosselini fst Philippe Erlanger *100min ORTF
Prison = FANGELSE (1949)
PRISON (1965) d Warhol 16mm 70min
PRISONER, THE (1923) d Conway 5rs U
PRISONER, THE (1955) d Glenville w Guinness, Hawkins 94min Col
PRISONER OF MARS (1942, ur) d/s/c/e/a/co-s/w Anger 11min
PRISONER OF SHARK ISLAND, THE (1936) d J Ford p Zanuck as-p/s N Johnson c Glennon w Carey, w Baxter, Carradine, (Parrish) 95min Fox
PRISONER OF WAR (1954) d Marton co-a Gibbons w Reagan 80min MGM
PRISONER OF ZENDA, THE (1922) d/p Ingram fn Anthony Hope s J Seitz w (Novarro) 10467ft MGM
PRISONER OF ZENDA, THE (1937) d Cromwell p Selznick co-s D Stewart fn Hope a Wheeler m A Newman w Carroll, Colman, Astor, Fairbanks Jr, Niven 104min r UA
PRISONER OF ZENDA, THE (1952) d Thorpe p Berman fn Hope co-a Gibbons m A Newman w S Granger, Kerr, Mason *100min MGM
Prisoner's Song, The = PESNYA KATORZHANINA (1911)
PRISONNIERE, LA (1968) d/co-s Clouzot a Saulnier w Piccoli, Vanel *110min (= Women in Chains)
PRISON NURSE (1938) d Cruze 65min Rep
PRIVATE AFFAIRS OF BEL AMI, THE (1947) d/s Levin fn Maupassant c Metty m Milhaud w G Sanders, Carradine 112min co-pc Levin r UA

PRIVATE ANGELO (1949) co-d/co-p/s/w Ustinov co-d Michael Anderson co-p Del Giudice 106min
PRIVATE BUCKAROO (1942) d Cline w O'Connor 68min U
PRIVATE DETECTIVE 62 (1933) d Curtiz c Gaudio w W Powell 67min WB
PRIVATE HELL 36 (1954) d D Siegel co-s Lupino c Guffey m Leith Stevens w Lupino, Cochran, Malone 80min
PRIVATE IZZY MURPHY (1926) d Bacon 7600ft Vit
PRIVATE LIFE OF DON JUAN, THE (1934) d/p A Korda s Biro c Périnal des K Korda cos Messel w Fairbanks Sr, Oberon 89min r UA
PRIVATE LIFE OF HELEN OF TROY, THE (1927) d A Korda co-c Garmes, Hickox 7694ft FN
PRIVATE LIFE OF HENRY VIII, THE (1933) d/p A Korda co-s Biro c Périnal a V Korda w Laughton, Donat, Oberon 96min r UA
PRIVATE LIFE OF OLIVER VIII, THE (1934) d Lloyd French p Roach w Laurel, Hardy
PRIVATE LIFE OF SHERLOCK HOLMES, THE (1970) d/p/co-s B Wilder as-p/co-s Diamond c Challis m Rozsa PV* 125min r UA
PRIVATE LIFE OF THE GANNETS, THE (1937) d Julian Huxley co-c Grierson (uc) sh pc A Korda
PRIVATE LIVES (1931) d Franklin fpl Coward a Gibbons w Shearer, R Montgomery, Hersholt 83min MGM
PRIVATE LIVES OF ADAM AND EVE (1960) d Zugsmith, Rooney c Lathrop w Rooney, Weld *87min U
PRIVATE LIVES OF ELIZABETH AND ESSEX, THE (1939) d Curtiz p Wallis c Polito fpl (Elizabeth the Queen) Maxwell Anderson m Korngold w B Davis, Flynn, De Havilland, Crisp, Price 106min WB (= Elizabeth the Queen)
PRIVATE NAVY OF SGT. O'FARRELL, THE (1968) d/s Tashlin a Kinoshita w Hope, J Hunter, Lollobrigida *92min r UA
PRIVATE NUMBER (1936) d Del Ruth c Marley w R Taylor, L Young, Rathbone, Darnell 90min Fox
PRIVATE POTTER (1963) d Caspar Wrede w Courteney S 89min
PRIVATE PROPERTY (1960) d/co-p/s Leslie Stevens technical advisor Singer c McCord 79min
PRIVATE'S AFFAIR, A (1959) d Walsh p Weisbart c C Clarke co-a Wheeler m Mockridge CS* 92min Fox
PRIVATE'S PROGRESS (1956) d/co-s J Boulting p R Boulting anim Halas, Batchelor w Attenborough 102min BL
Private War of Harry Frigg, The = SECRET WAR OF HARRY FRIGG, THE (1968)
Private Wore Skirts, The = NEVER WAVE AT A WAC (1953)
PRIVATE WORLDS (1935) d/co-s La Cava p Wanger c Shamroy w Colbert, Boyer, J Bennett, McCrea 84min Par
PRIVIDENIE KOTOROYE NE VOZVRASHCHAYETSYA (1930) d Room fst (Le Revenant qui ne revient pas) Henri Barbusse 2330m (= The Ghost that will not Return)
PRIVILEGE (1966) d Watkins *103min U
PRIX DE BEAUTE (1930) d/co-s Genina st Pabst co-s Clair w L Brooks
Prix du Sang, Le = HACELDAME (1919)
PRIX ET PROFIT (1932) d Y Allégret sh
PRIZE, THE (1963) d Robson p Berman s Lehman c Daniels m Goldsmith w P Newman, Robinson PV* 136min MGM
PRIZEFIGHTER AND THE LADY, THE (1933) d/p WS Van Dyke w M Loy, W Huston 102min MGM
PRIZE OF ARMS, A (1961) d Cliff Owen co-st Roeg
PRIZE OF GOLD, A (1955) d Robson co-s Paxton c Moore w Widmark, Zetterling, Wolfit *85min Col
PROBATION (1932) d Thorpe w Grable 70min
PROBATION WIFE, THE (1919) d Franklin w N Talmadge 5rs pc N Talmadge
PROBLEME BERLIN (1958) d Hayer sh
PROBLEM GIRLS (1953) d Dupont c JL Russell 70min Col
PROCES, LE (1963) d/s/w Welles fn Kafka anim prologue Alexeieff (14min) w Perkins, Moreau, Tamiroff, Martinelli, Schneider, Paxinou 118min (= The Trial)
PROCES DE JEANNE D'ARC, LE (1961) d/s Bresson c Burel 65min (= The Trial of Joan of Arc)
PROCESI K PANENCE (1961) d Jasny 85min (= Pilgrimage to the Virgin Mary)
PROCESSION, THE (1959) d W Van Dyke 25min
PROCESSION OF PRIZE CATTLE (1898) p Hepworth 50ft
PROCESSO ALLA CITTA (1952) d/co-s Zampa 99min (= A Town on Trial)
PROCESSO DI VERONA, IL (1962) d Lizzani w Mangano
PROC UNESCO (1958) d Trnka (= Why UNESCO?)
PRODIGAL, THE (1955) d Thorpe p Schnee c Ruttenberg co-a Gibbons m Kaper w Turner CS* 106min MGM
PRODIGAL BRIDEGROOM, THE (1926) d Bacon, Earle Rodney w Turpin 2rs Pat
PRODIGAL DAUGHTERS (1923) d S Wood w Swanson 6216ft FPL
PROEKT INZHENERA PRAITA (1918) d/dec Kuleshov 4rs (= Engineer Prite's Project)
PROFESSIONALS, THE (1966) d/st/s R Brooks c C Hall m Jarre w Marvin, Lancaster, Palance, Ryan, Cardinale PV* 117min Col

PROFESSIONAL SOLDIER (1935) d Garnett c Maté w V McLaglen, Bartholemew 75min Fox

PROFESSOR BEAN'S REMOVAL (1913) d Sennett w Normand 1rl Key

PROFESSOR BEWARE (1938) d E Nugent p H Lloyd co-ad Bruckman s Daves c Stout w H Lloyd 87min Par

Professor de mi Sencra, El: Spanish version of AMOUR CHANTE, L' (1930)

PROFESSEUR DE PIANO, LE (1967) d Reichenbach

Professor Hannibal = HANNIBAL TANAR UR (1956)

PROFESSOR'S DAUGHTER, THE (1913) d Sennett w Normand ½rl Key

PROFETA, IL (1967) d Risi w Gassman *100min (= *Mr Kinky*)

Profound Longing of the Gods, A = KAMIGAMI NO FUKAKI YOKUBO (1968)

PROIBITO (1955) d/co-s Monicelli c Tonti dec Gherardi m Rota w Ferrer *90min

PROIBITO RUBARE (1947) d/co-s Comencini co-p Ponti 95min

PROIE DU VENT, LA (1926) d/s Clair 2nd d Préjean dec Meerson w Vanel 90min

PROIE POUR L'OMBRE, LA (1960) d/s/co-di Astruc dec Saulnier w Girardot, Gélin, Marquand FS 96min

PROJECT (1967) d/p Castle co-a Pereira *97min Par

Project M7 (US) = NET, THE (1952)

PROKLYATYE MILLIONY (1917) d/s Protazanov (2 parts) 8rs (= *Cursed Millions*)

PROKUROR (1917) d Protazanov w Mozhukhin 1750m (= *The Public Prosecutor*)

PROMESSE DE L'AUBE, LA (1970) d/s Dassin ex-p Levine fab Gary c Badal des Trauner m Delerue w Mercouri *100min (= *Promise at Dawn*)

PROMESSI SPOSI, I (1941) d/co-s Camerini m Pizzetti

PROMETEJ SA OTAKA VISEVICE (1965) d/co-s Mimica 104min (= *Prometheus from the Island of Visevica*)

Prometheus from the Island of Visevica = PROMETEJ SA OTAKA VISEVICE (1965)

PROMETHEE BANQUIER (1921) d L'Herbier

PROMETHEUS (1920) d Blom 12eps

Promise at Dawn = PROMESSE DE L'AUBE, LA

PROMISE HER ANYTHING (1965) d Arthur Hiller c Slocombe w Beatty, Caron *97min

PRONTO, CHI PARLA? (1946) d Bragaglia

PRO PATRIA (1914) d/co-s Blom

PROPHETESSE DE THEBES, LA (1908) d Méliès 140m

PROPERTY MAN, THE (1914) d/s/w Chaplin w Sennett 2rs Kay (= *Getting His Goat/The Roustabout*)

PROPRE DE L'HOMME, LE (1960) d/s Lelouch 80min

PROSCRIT, LE (1912) d/s Feuillade 1146m

PROSOPO TES MEDOUSAS, TO (1967) d/co-s Koundouros 86min (= *Face of the Medusa*)

PROSPECTOR'S DAUGHTER, THE (1911) d Ince

PROSPERITY (1932) d S Wood w Dressler, Foster 87min MGM

PROSTITUTION, DIE (1919) d/p/s R Oswald w Veidt, Krauss 2544m

PROTEA (1913) d/s Jasset c Andriot (serial)

PROSTOI SLUCHAI (1932) d Pudovkin, *Mikhail Dollar* 2633m (= *Ochen Khorosho Zhiviesta/A Simple Case/Life is Good*)

PROSTYE LYUDI (1945 r 1956) d/s L Trauberg, Kozintsev co-c Moskvin m Shostakovich 78min (= *Plain People*)

Protegé, The (UK) = PROTEGIDO, EL (1956)

PROTEGIDO, EL (1956) d/s Torre Nilsson 81min (= *The Protegé*)

PROTI VSEM (1957) d/co-s Vavra * (= *Against All*)

PROTSESS ESEROV (1922) d/s/t Vertov 900m (= *The Trial of the Social Revolutionaries*)

PROTSESS MIRONOVA (1920) d/w Vertov 1rl (= *The Trial of Mironov*)

PROTSESS O TROKH MILLIONAKH (1926) d/co-s Protazanov 1800m (= *The Trial of the Three Million*)

PROUD AND THE PROFANE, THE (1956) d/co-st/s Seaton co-a Pereira m V Young w Holden, Ritter, Kerr VV 111min pc Perlberg, Seaton r Par

PROUD FLESH (1925) d/co-p K Vidor co-p L Mayer 5770ft MGM

PROUD REBEL, THE (1958) d Curtiz fst (*Journal of Linnett Moore*) J Grant c McCord m Moross w De Havilland, Carradine, Ladd *103min

PROVINCIALE, LA (1953) d/co-s Soldati fn Alberto Moravia c Aldo w Lollobrigida, Ferzetti 92min (= *The Wayward Wife*)

PROVNINGENS STUND, I (1915) d/s/w Sjöström 850m

Provocateur, The = PROVOKATOR (1928)

PROVOKATOR (1928) d Turin 2315m (= *The Provocateur*)

PROWLER, THE (1951) d Losey p Spiegel (ps SP Eagle) s Trumbo(uc), H Butler c AC Miller des J Hubley w Heflin 92min pc Horizon, J Huston r UA

PROZESS, DER (1947) d Pabst 109min

PRSTYNEK (1945) d Fric (= *The Wedding Ring*)

PRUDENCE AND THE PILL (1968) d Neame, Fielder Cook c Moore w Kerr, Niven, Evans *92min

PRUDENCE ON BROADWAY (1919) d Borzage Tri

PRUDE'S FALL, THE (1925) d Graham Cutts co-p Balcon s/dec Hitchcock UFA

PRUFUNG, DER (1952) d/s A and A Thorndike

PRUNELLA (1918) d M Tourneur 5rs FPL

PRUSSIAN CUR, THE (1918) d/st/s Walsh 8rs Fox

PRVNI PARTA (1959) d/s Vavra fn Karel Capek CS (= *The First Rescue Party*)

PRZEBUDZENIE (1934) d A Ford (= *The Awakening*)

PRZEKLADANIEC (1968) d Wajda 36min (= *Roly Poly*)

PRZHEVALSKII (1951) d Yutkevich *115min

PSOHLAVCI (1954) d/co-s Fric *98min (= *Dog's Heads*)

PSYCHE 59 (1964) d Singer c Lassally w Neal, Jurgens 94min Col

PSYCHIATRY IN RUSSIA (1955) d/c A Maysles

PSYCHO (1960) d/p Hitchcock fn Robert Bloch c JL Russell cr Bass m Herrmann w J Leigh, Perkins, Miles, McIntire 108min Par

PSYCHODRAME, LE (1956) d Rossellini sh TV

PSYCHOPATH (1966) d F Francis 83min Par

PSYCOSISSIMO (1961) d/co-s Steno 95min

P'TITE LILI, LA (1929) d Cavalcanti m Milhaud w J Renoir 300m (= *La Petite Lili*)

P T 109 (1963) d Milestone (uc), *Leslie H Martinson* c Surtees w Robertson PV* 140min WB

PUBLIC DEB NO 1 (1940) d Ratoff w G Murphy, Cook, C Ruggles 105min Fox

PUBLIC ENEMY, THE (1931) d Wellman w Cagney, Harlow, Blondell 74min WB

Public Enemy No 1 = ENNEMI PUBLIC NO 1 (1953)

PUBLIC PIGEON NO 1 (1957) d McLeod S 80min RKO

Public Prosecutor = PROKUROR (1917)

PUBS AND BEACHES (1966) d R Williams anim

PUCCINI (1952) d Gallone c C Renoir m Puccini w Ferzetti *118min (= *His Two Loves*)

PUCE MOMENT (1948) d/s/c/e Anger *8min

PUEBLERINA (1948) d/st Fernandez c Figueroa

PUEBLITO (1962) d/co-st/co-s Fernandez 112min

PUEBLO EN ARMAS (1961) d/s Ivens

PUEBLO LEGEND, A (1912) d Griffith w Pickford, L Barrymore 1rl Bio

PUERTA CERRADA (1939) d Saslavsky 74min

PUGILATORI (1950) d Zurlini sh

Pugilist, The = KNOCKOUT, THE (1914)

PUGNI IN TASCA, I (1966) d/st/s Bellochio 105min (= *Fists in the Pocket*)

PUITS ET LE PENDULE, LE (1963) d/s Asturc fst (*The Pit and the Pendulum*) Edgar Allan Poe c Hayer w Ronet 37min ORTF

PULGA NA BALANÇA, UNA (1953) d Salce

PULL MY DAISY (1958) d R Frank, *Alfred Leslie cy/fpl (The Beat Generation)* Jack Kerouac c R Frank 30min

PULSE OF LIFE, THE (1917) d/s Ingram 5rs

Pumkin = KABOCHA (1928)

PUMKIN EATER, THE (1964) d Clayton p James Woolf s Pinter c Morris m Delerue w A Bancroft, Finch, Mason 118min r Col

PUNISHMENT PARK (1971) d/co-s/e Watkins 16mm* 90min

Punishment Room = SHOKEI NO HEYA (1956)

PUNITION, LA (1962) d/s Rouch co-c Brault 58min TV (= *Liberté*)

PUNT'A A CTYRLISTEK (1954) d/co-s J Weiss * (= *Doggy and the Four*)

PUNTO NERO, UN (1922) d Genina

Pupils of the Seventh Class = SEMIKLASSNIKI (1938)

PUPPE, DIE (1919) d/co-s Lubitsch c Sparkuhl 60min r UFA (= *The Doll*)

PUPPENMACHER VON KIANGNING, DER (1923) d Wiene w Krauss 1728m

Puppets = MARIONETKI (1934)

PUPPY LOVETIME (1926) d Cline s Sennett

PURCHASE PRICE (1932) d Wellman c Hickox w Stanwyck 70min WB

PURE BEAUTE (1948) d Alexeieff anim* 1min

PURE HELL OF ST TRINIAN'S, THE (1960) d Launder co-p/s Gilliat 94min

Pure Love = JUNJO (1930)

PURPLE HEART, THE (1944) d Milestone p Zanuck c AC Miller w D Andrews, Conte, F Granger 100min Fox

PURPLE HEART DIARY (1951) d Quine p Katzman 73min Col (= *No Time for Tears*)

PURPLE IS THE COLOR (1964) d J Webb

Purple Noon = PLEIN SOLEIL (1959)

PURPLE PLAIN, THE (1954) d Parrish c Unsworth e C Donner w Peck *100min

PURPLE STREAM, THE (1961) d C Donner 16mm* 28min

PUR-SANG (1925) d Autant-Lara

PURSUED (1947) d Walsh p Sperling s Busch c Howe m Steiner chor Prinz w T Wright, Mitchum 101min WB

Pursuit at Dawn = AKATSUKI NO TSUISEKI (1950)

PURSUIT OF HAPPINESS, THE (1962) d A King 16mm 57min

PURSUIT OF HAPPINESS, THE (1971) d/co-p Mulligan *93min Col

Pursuit of the Graf Spee = BATTLE OF THE RIVER PLATE, THE (1956)

PUSAN (1953) d/co-s Ichikawa anim Toho (= *Poo-san/Mr Poo*)

PUSHER-IN-THE-RACE (1929) d Florey fst F Scott Fitzgerald 3rs Par

PUSHKA (1934) d/s Romm fst Guy de Maupassant 1893m (= *Boule de Suif*)

PUSHOVER (1954) d Quine w Novak, Macmurray, Malone 88min Col

PUSS OCH KRAM (1967) d/s Cornell 94min (= *Hugs and kisses*)

PUTAIN RESPECTEUSE, LA (1952) d Pagliero, *Brabant*

Putting One Over = MASQUERADER, THE (1914)

PUTTING PANTS ON PHILIP (1928) d Bruckman supn McCarey p Roach w Laurel and Hardy 2rs MGM

PUTTO, IL (1963) d Mingozzi sh

PUTYOVKA V ZHIZN (1931) d/co-s Ekk 3330m (= *The Road to Life*)

PUZZLE OF A DOWNFALL CHILD (1970) d Jerry Schatzberg w Dunaway, Lindfors PV* 104min co-pc P Newman

PYAT LET BORBY I POBEDY (1923) d/s Vertov 1500m (= *Five Years of Struggle and Victory*)

PYGMALION (1938) d Asquith, L Howard p Pascal fpl GB Shaw m Honegger w L Howard 96min

PYGMALION ET GALATHEE (1898) d Méliès 20m

Pylon = THE TARNISHED ANGELS (1957)

PYRAMIDE DES SONNENGOTTES, DIE (1965) d Siodmak 100min

PYRAMIDE HUMAINE, LA (1959) d/s/co-c Rouch 16mm* 90min

Pyret Applies for a Job = PYRET SOKAR PLATS (c 1955)

PYTLAKOVA SCHOVANKA (1949) d Fric (= *The Poacher's God Daughter*)

PYRET SOKAR PLATS (c 1955) d Lingren (= *Pyret Applies for a Job*)

PYTEL BLECH (1962) d Chytilova 44min (= *A Bag of Fleas*)

Q-Bec My Love = SUCCES COMMERCIAL, UN (1970)

QUADRANTE D'ORO, IL (1920) d/s/p Ghione

QUADRATE (1934) d Fischinger anim* (= *Squares*)

Quadratonia = QUADRATONIEN (1967)

QUADRATONIEN (1967) d Lenica anim 12min (= *Quadratonia*)

QUADRILLE (1937) d/p/s/fpl/w Guitry

QUADRILLE (1951) d Rivette p Godard sh

QUAI DE GRENELLE (1950) d E Reinert w Arnoul 96min (= *Shake of Death/Danger is a Woman*)

QUAI DES BRUMES (1938) d Carné s/di Prévert c Schuftan dec Trauner m Jaubert w Gabin, Morgan, Simon, Brasseur

QUAI DES ORFEVRES (1947) d/co-s Clouzot c Thirard w Jouvet, Marquand 105min

QUALEN DER NACHT (1926) d/co-s C Bernhardt co-s/fpl Zuckmayer w Dieterle 1811m

QUALITY STREET (1926) d Franklin p/w Davies co-s/co-ad Lewin 7300ft MGM

QUALITY STREET (1937) d G Stevens p Berman fpl James Barrie w K Hepburn, Tone, Fontaine 83min RKO

QUAND LA FEMME S'EN MELE (1957) d Y Allégret st Charles Spaak m Misraki w Feuillère, Delon 90min

QUAND LA LIBERTE DU CIEL (1966) d/s Moussy TV

QUAND LE RIDEAU SE LEVE (1957) d/p/s/e Lelouch 16mm sh

QUANDO LE DONNE AVEVANO LA CODA (1970) d/co-s Festa Campanile *110min

QUAND SONNERA MIDI (1957) d Gréville w G Marshall 96min

QUAND TU LIRAS CETTE LETTRE (1952) d Melville c Alekan 104min

QUANTEZ (1957) d Keller co-a Golitzen w MacMurray, Malone CS* 80min U

47, MORTO CHE PARLA (1951) d/co-s Bragaglia w Toto

QUARANTINED RIVALS (1927) d A Mayo 5800ft

QUARRELSOME ANGLERS, THE (1898) p Hepworth 50ft

Quarry, The = LA CURÉE (1966)

QUARTERBACK, THE (1926) d Newmeyer c Cronjager 7114ft FPL r Par

QUARTET (1948) fsts Somerset Maugham 120min BL
ep THE COLONELS LADY d Annakin
ep ALIEN CORN d Harold French w Rosay, Bogarde
ep THE FACTS OF LIFE d Ralph Smart w Zetterling
ep THE KITE d Arthur Crabtree

QUARTIERI ALTI (1943) d/co-s Soldati

QUARTIER LATIN (1929) d Genina

QUARTIER SANS SOLEIL (1939 r 1945) d/s/di Kirsanov 90min

QUATERMASS AND THE PITT (1967) d R Baker 97min (= *Five Million Years to Earth*)

QUATORZE DIX HUIT (1962) d Aurel 90min r JAR

QUATORZE JUILLET (1933) d/s/di Clair c Périnal dec Meerson m Jaubert w Annabella, Modot 98min Tob

14 JUILLET, 1953 (1953) d/s Gance

QUATRE CENTS COUPS, LES (1959) d/st Truffaut ad/di Moussy c Decaë dec Evein w Leaud, Brialy(uc) CS 95min co-pc Truffaut (= *The 400 Blows*)

QUATRE CENTS FARCES DU DIABLE, LES (1906) d/s/dec Méliès (35 parts) 350m

QUATRE NUITS D'UN REVEUR (1971) d/s Bresson fst (*White Nights*) Dostoievski *87min

QUATRE TEMPS (1957) d Alexeieff anim

QUATRE VAGABONDS, LES (1931) d Lupu-Pick

QUATRE VERITES, LES (1962) 110min 4eps (= *The Three Fables of Love*)
ep EL LENADOR Y LA MUERTE *d* Berlanga *fst La Fontaine co-m* Aznavour *w* Vitti
ep LES DEUX PIGEONS *d/s* Clair *fst La Fontaine c* Thirard *w* Aznavour, Caron 26min
1989 (1964) *d* Leenhardt
QUATRE-VINGT-QUATRE PREND DES VACANCES, LE (1949) *d/co-ad* Joannon 93min
QUATTRI TRAMONTI, I (1920) *d/p/s/w* Ghione
QUATTRO GIORNATE DI NAPOLI, LE (1962) *d/co-st/co-s* N Loy *co-st/co-s* Festa Campanile 124min (= *The Four Days of Naples*)
QUATTRO MONACI, I (1962) *d* Bragalia * (= *The Four Monks*)
QUATTRO MOSCHETTIERI, I (1963) *d* Bragaglia * (= *The Four Musketeers*)
QUATTRO PASSI FRA LE NUVOLE (1942) *d/co-st/co-s* Blasetti *co-st* Zavattini *w* Blasetti 81min (= *Four Steps in the Clouds*)
QUEBEC-USA (1962) *co-d/c* Brault *co-d/e* Jutra 28min (= *L'Invasion Pacifique*)
QUEEN BEE (1955) *d/s* MacDougall *c* C Lang 95min *pc* Wald *r* Col
QUEEN CHRISTINA (1934) *d* Mamoulian *p* Wanger *c* Daniels *m* Stothart *w* Garbo, J Gilbert, Tamiroff(*uc*) 100min MGM
Queen Elizabeth (US) = REINE ELISABETH, LA (1912)
QUEEN HIGH (1930) *d* Newmayer *w* G Rogers, C Ruggles 88min Par
QUEEN IS CROWNED, THE (1953) *p Castleton-Knight cy* Fry *n* Olivier *90min
QUEEN KELLY (1928) *d/st/s/co-a* Von Stroheim *c* B Reynolds *co-a* R Day *w* Swanson 8rs *r* UA
Queen Of Babylon, The = CORTIGIANA DI BABILONIA, LA (1955)
Queen of Circus = KYOKUBADAN NO JOWO (1925)
Queen of Modern Times = GENDAI NO JOWO (1924)
QUEEN OF SHEBA MEETS THE ATOM MAN, THE (1963, *uf*) *d* Rice 16mm 70min
Queen of Sin, The = SODOM UND GOMORRHA (1922)
Queen of Spades, The = PIKOVAYA DAMA (1916)
QUEEN OF SPADES (1949) *d* T Dickinson *p* De Grunwald *co-as-p* Clayton *fst* Pushkin *c* Heller *cos* Messel *m* Auric *w* Evans, Walbrook 90min ABC
Queen of Spades, The = DAME DE PIQUE, LA (1965)
Queens, The (US) = LE FATE (1966)
QUEEN'S GUARDS, THE (1960) *d/p* M Powell CS* 110min
Queen's Secret, The = TAINA KOPOLEUY (1919)
QUEEN VICTORIA IN DUBLIN (1898) *p* Paul 120ft
QUEEN VICTORIA'S FUNERAL (1901) *p* Hepworth (3 parts) 400ft
QUEEN VICTORIA'S VISIT TO DUBLIN (1900) *p* Hepworth 125ft
QUEIMADA! (1968) *d/co-st* Pontecorvo *des* Gherardi *w* Brando *132min (= *Burn*)
QUE LA BETE MEURE (1969) *d* Chabrol *c* Rabier *110min (= *Killer!/This Man Must Die*)
QUEL BANDITO SONO IO (1949) *d/co-s* Soldati *p* Ponti *c* Bava
QUELE DO PAJEU (1969) *d/co-s* Duarte *st/co-s* Barreto 70* 115min
QUELLA PICCOLA DIFFERENZA (1969) *d/co-s* Tessari *92min (= *That Little Difference*)
QUELLA VECCHIA CANAGLIA (1934) *d* Bragaglia
QUELLE DROLE DE GOSSE (1935) *d* Joannon *m* Van Parys
Quelle Joie de Vivre (1961) = CHE GIOIA VIVERE
QUELLI DELLA MONTAGNA (1942) *d Aldo Vergano supn/co-s* Blasetti *co-s* Cottafavi
QUENTIN DURWARD (1955) *d* Thorpe *p* Berman *s* Ardrey *fn* (*The Adventures of Quentin Durward*) *Sir Walter Scott c* Challis *m* Kaper *w* R Taylor, Kendall CS* 101min MGM (= *The Adventures of Quentin Durward*)
QUE PEUT-IL AVOIR? (1912) *d/w* Linder Pat
QUESTA E LA VITA (1954)
ep LA PATENTE *d/co-s* Zampa *fst Pirandello w* Toto
ep IL VENTAGLINO *d/co-s/co-ad* Soldati *fst Pirandello*
QUEST FOR LOVE (1971) *d* Thomas *91min
QUESTI FANTASMI (1954) *d/co-s/fpl* De Filippo *co-s* Soldati
QUESTI FANTASMI (1967) *d/co-s* Castellani *p* Ponti *w* Gassman, Loren *120min (= *Three Ghosts/Ghosts – Italian Style*)
QUESTION D'ASSURANCE, UNE (1959) *d* Kast sh
QUESTIONE D'ONORE, UNA (1965) *d/co-s* Zampa *co-c* Di Palma *110min (= *A Question of Honour*)
Question of Honour, A = QUESTIONE D'ONORE, UNA (1965)
QUE VIVA MEXICO! (1931, *uf*) *d* Eisenstein, Alexandrov *c* Tisse 60000m approx (From this footage the following films were made: *Thunder over Mexico* (1933); *Eisenstein in Mexico* (1933); *Death Day* (1933); *Time in the Sun* (1939); *Eisenstein's Mexican Project* (1958)
QUI? (1970) *d* Kiegel *w* Ronet, Schneider *77min
QUI A TUE MAX? (1913) *d/w* Linder Pat (= *Max Assassiné*)
QUICK (1932) *d* Siodmak *p* Pommer *co-c* Rittau *w* Lillian Harvey (German-language version) 95min UFA (French version: *w* Brasseur)
QUICK BEFORE IT MELTS (1964) *d/co-p* Delbert Mann *c* R Harlan PV* 98min MGM
QUICKER 'N A WINK (1940) *d* G Sidney 9min MGM
QUICKER 'N LIGHTNIN' (1926) *d* Thorpe
Quick, Let's Get Married = CONFESSION, THE (1964, *ur*)
QUICKSAND (1950) *d* Pichel *c* Lindon *w* Rooney, Lorre 79min *r* UA
QUICKSANDS (1918) *d* Schertzinger 5rs *pc* Ince
QUICKSANDS (1923) *d* Conway *p/st* Hawks *co-c* Rosson *w* Hersholt 4593ft Par
QUIET AMERICAN, THE (1958) *d/p/s* J Mankiewicz *fn* Greene *c* Krasker *w* A Murphy, M Redgrave 120min *r* UA
QUI ETES VOUS, M SORGE (1960) *d/co-st* Ciampi S 128min
QUI ETES-VOUS, POLLY MAGGOO? (1966) *d/s* Klein *dec* Evein *m* Legrand *w* Noiret, Seyrig 102min (= *Who are you, Polly Maggoo?*)
Quiet Flows the Don = TIKHII DON (1958)
QUIET MAN, THE (1952) *d/co-p* J Ford *co-p* M Cooper *s* F Nugent *c* Hoch, Stout *m* V Young *w* J Wayne, M O'Hara, V McLaglen, Marsh (*uc*) *129min *r* Rep
QUIET ONE, THE (1948) *d/co-s/co-s* Meyers *di/cy* Agee 16mm 68min
Quiet Place in the Country, A = TRANQUILLO POSTO DI CAMPAGNA, UN (1968)
QUIET PLEASE! (1945) *d* Hanna, Barbera anim* 11min MGM
QUIET WEDDING (1940) *d* Asquith *s* Rattigan, De Grunwald *w* Lockwood 80min Par
QUILLER MEMORANDUM, THE (1966) *d* Michael Anderson *s* Pinter *m* Barry *w* Segal, Guinness, Von Sydow, G Sanders, Signoret PV* 103min JAR
QUINCY ADAMS SAWYER (1922) *d* Badger 8rs Metro
QUINT CITY USA (1963) *d* R Leacock 26min (= *Happy Mothers' Day, Mrs Fisher*)
QUITTER, THE (1934) *d* Thorpe 68min
QUI VEUT TUER CARLOS? (1969) *d/co-s* Christian-Jaque *w* Lawford *97min (= *Dead Run*)
QUO VADIS? (1901) *d/w* Zecca 50m Pat
QUO VADIS? (1912) *d/s/co-dec* Guazzoni 80min
QUO VADIS? (1925) *d Georg Jacoby fn Henryk Sinkiewicz c* Courant *w* Jannings, (Banky) 9rs
QUO VADIS (1951) *d* LeRoy, A Mann(*uc*) *co-s* Mahin *fn Sinkiewicz co-c* Surtees *co-a* Gibbons *m* Rozsa *w* R Taylor, Kerr, Ustinov, Loren(*uc*) *171min MGM

RABBIA, LA (1963)
*ep d/s Pasolini 50*min
ep d Giovanni Guareschi
RABBIT, RUN (1970) *d* Smight *fn John Updike c* Lathrop *94min WB
RABBIT OF SEVILLE, THE (1951) *d* C Jones anim* 7min WB
Rabbits' Moon = LUNE DES LAPINS, LA (1950)
RABBITSON CRUSOE (1956) *d* Freleng anim* 7min WB
RABBIT TRAP, THE (1958) *d* P Leacock *c* Glassberg *w* Borgnine 76min
RABINDRANATH TAGORE (1961) *d/s/n* S Ray 54min
RACCONTI D'ESTATE (1958) *d Gianni Francolini w* Mastroianni, Morgan S* 114min
RACCONTO DA UN AFFRESCO (1940) *d/s* Emmer, *Enrico Gras, Tatiana Grauding* 260m (= *Giotto*)
RACCONTO DELLA STURA, IL (1955) *d* Olmi *9min
RACCONTO DEL QUARTIERE (1949) *d* Zurlini sh
Race for Life = SI TOUS LES GARS DU MONDE (1955)
Race Symphony = RENNSYMPHONIE (1929)
RACERS, THE (1955) *d* Hathaway *p* Blaustein *c* Joe Macdonald *co-a* Wheeler *cr* Bass *m* North *w* K Douglas, Romero, Cobb, Roland CS* 112min Fox
RACE TRACK (1933) *d* Cruze *co-ad* W Lang 79min *pc* Cruze
RACHE DES BANDITEN, DIE (1919) *d* Jutzi 1061m
RACHE DER TOTEN, DIE (1917) *d/s* Roswald *w* Krauss
RACHEL AND THE STRANGER (1948) *d* Foster *w* Mitchum, Holden, L Young 93min RKO
RACHEL CADE (1961) *d* G Douglas *p* Blanke *c* Marley *m* M Steiner *w* A Dickinson, Finch *124min WB (= *The Sins of Rachel Cade*)
RACHEL, RACHEL (1968) *d/p* P Newman *s* Stern *m* Moross *w* Woodward 101min *r* WB
RACING ROMEO, A (1927) *d* S Wood *c* C Clarke 5992ft
RACK, THE (1950) *d Arnold Laven s* Stern *fpl* Serling *co-a* Gibbons *w* P Newman, Pidgeon, E O'Brien, Marvin, Corey 100min MGM
RACKET, THE (1928) *d* Milestone *p* H Hughes 7646ft Par
RACKET, THE (1951) *d* Cromwell *co-s* Burnett *w* Ryan, Mitchum, L Scott 88min RKO
RACKET BUSTERS (1938) *d* Bacon *co-st/co-s* Rossen *w* Bogart 71min WB
Radiances of a Thousand Suns, The (USA = BRULER DE MILLE SOLEILS (1965)
RADIO DYNAMICS (1942) *d* Fischinger anim si
RADIO PARADE OF 1935 (1934) *d Arthur Woods w* Hay 87min
RADUGA (1944) *d/co-s* Donskoi 96min (= *Rainbow*)
RAFALE, LA (1920) *d* De Baroncelli
RAFFAELLO SANZIO E LA FORNARINA (1907) *d Eduardo Bencivenga technical advisor* Guazzoni
RAFFLES (1930) *d* D'Arrast(*uc*) *co-s* Fitzgerald(*uc*) *co-c* Toland *e* Heisler *w* Colman, K Francis 80min *pc* Goldwyn *r* UA
RAFFICA DI COLTELLI (1965) *d/co-s* Bava CS*
RAFFLES (1940) *d* S Wood *p* Goldwyn *c* Toland *m* V Young *w* Niven, De Havilland 72min *r* UA
RAFFLES, THE AMATEUR CRACKSMAN (1905) *d* Blackton Vit
RAGA (1971) *d/p Howard Worth m/w* Shankar *96min
RAGAZZA CHE SAPEVA TROPPO, LA (1962) *d/co-s/co-c* Bava *w* Cortese 92min WB (= *The Evil Eye*)
RAGAZZA CON LA PISTOLA, LA (1967) *d* Monicelli *c* Di Palma *w* Vitti, S Baker TS* 100min *r* Par (= *The Girl with a Pistol*)
RAGAZZA CON LA VALIGIA, LA (1960) *d/co-s* Zurlini *w* Cardinale 135min (= *Girl with a Suitcase*)
RAGAZZA DEL PALIO, LA (1957) *d/co-s* Zampa *c* Rotunno *w* Gassman, Dors *84min (= *The Love Specialist*)
RAGAZZA DI BUBE, LA (1963) *d/co-s* Comencini *c* Di Venanzo *w* Cardinale 110min (= *Bebo's Girl*)
RAGAZZA DI MILLE MESI, LA (1961) *d* Steno 95min
RAGAZZA IN VETRINA, LA (1960) *d/co-ad/co-s* Emmer *co-ad* Pasolini *c* Martinelli *w* Vlady, Ventura 92min (= *Woman in the Window*)
RAGAZZE DI SAN FREDIANO (1954) *d* Zurlini
RAGAZZA E IL GENERALE, LA (1966) *d/co-st/co-s* Festa Campanile *p* Ponti *w* Steiger TC* 113min MGM (= *The Girl and the General*)
RAGAZZE DA MARITO (1952) *d/co-s/w* De Filippo
RAGAZZE DI PIAZZA DI SPAGNA, LE (1952) *d* Emmer *w* Bosè, De Filippo, Mastroianni 80min (= *Three Girls from Rome/Girls of the Piazza di Spagna*)
RAGAZZE DI SANFREDIANO, LE (1954) *d* Zurlini *c* Di Venanzo 102min
RAGAZZE D'OGGI (1955) *d/st/s* Zampa *co-p* Ponti CS* 98min
RAGAZZI DELLA MARINI (1958) *d* De Robertis *
RAGAZZI DELLA VIA PAAL, I (1935) *d* Monicelli
RAGE IN HEAVEN (1941) *d* WS Van Dyke *p* G Reinhardt *co-s Isherwood w* Ingrid Bergman, G Sanders, Montgomery 82min MGM
RAGE OF PARIS, THE (1921) *d* Conway 5rs U
RAGE OF PARIS, THE (1938) *d* Koster *w* Fairbanks Jr, Darrieux, L Hayward 75min U
RAGGEDY ROSE (1926) *st* Roach *w* Normand Pat
RAGING MOON, THE (1971) *d/s* Forbes *110min (= *Long Ago, Tomorrow*)
RAGMAN, THE (1925) *d* Cline 5800ft MGM
RAGTIME BEAR, THE (1949) *d* J Hubley *ex-p* Bosustow anim* 7min UPA *r* Col
RAICES (1955) *d/co-s* Alazraki *co-s/technical adviser* Velo 78min (= *The Roots*)
RAID, THE (1954) *d* Fregonese *s* Boehm *c* Ballard *w* Heflin, Marvin, A Bancroft *82min Fox
RAIDERS, THE (1916) *p/s/w* Mix 1rl Sel
RAIDERS, THE (1952) *d Lesley Selander w* Lindfors, Conte 80min U
RAID ON ROMMEL (1971) *d* Hathaway *co-a* Golitzen *w* Burton *99min U
RAILROADED (1947) *d* A Mann *w* Ireland 72min EL
Railroad Man, The (US) = FERROVIERE, IL (1916)
RAILROADER, THE (1964) *d Gerald Potterton w* Keaton 25min NFBC
RAILWAY COLLISION, A (1898) *d* Paul 1rl 40ft
Railway Workers, The = RALLARE (1947)
Rain = SADIE THOMPSON (1928)
Rain = REGEN (1929)
RAIN (1932) *d/p* Milestone *ad* Maxwell Anderson *fpl John Colton and Randolph fst* (*Miss Thompson*) *S Maugham w* J Crawford, W Huston 93min *r* UA
RAINBOW DANCE (1936) *d* Lye *4min GPO
RAINBOW JACKET, THE (1954) *d* Dearden *99min
RAINBOW MAN, THE (1929) *d* Newmeyer 96min *r* Par
RAINBOW OVER BROADWAY (1933) *d* Thorpe 72min
Rainbow = RADUGA (1944)
RAINBOW ROUND MY SHOULDER (1952) *d/co-s* Quine *co-s* Edwards *78min Col
RAINBOW TRAIL, THE (1918) *d/co-s* F Lloyd *fn Zane Grey* 6rs Fox
RAINBOW TRAIL, THE (1925) *d/ad Lynn Reynolds fn* (*The Desert Crucible*) *Zane Grey w* Mix 6rs Fox
RAINMAKER, THE (1926) *d* Badger 6055ft FPL
RAINMAKER, THE (1956) *d* Anthony *p* Wallis *c* C Lang *co-a* Pereira *m* North *w* Lancaster, K Hepburn, Corey VV* 122min Par
Rainmakers = HOMMES QUI FONT LA PLUIE, LES (1951)
RAIN OR SHINE (1930) *d* Capra *p* Cohn *co-s/di* Swerling *c* J Walker *w* Fazenda 90min Col
RAIN PEOPLE, THE (1969) *d* Coppola CS* 101min
RAINS CAME, THE (1939) *d* C Brown *p* Zanuck *co-s* P Dunne *c* AC Miller *m* A Newman *w* Power, M Loy, Darwell, Ouspenskaya 104min Fox

RAINS OF RANCHIPUR, THE (1955) d Negulesco c Krasner co-a Wheeler m Freidhofer w Turner, Burton, MacMurray CS* 104min Fox

RAINTREE COUNTRY (1957) d Dmytryk c Surtees w Clift, E Taylor, Marvin, Saint, Moorehead 70* 187min MGM

RAKE'S PROGRESS, THE (1945) d/co-p/co-s Gilliat co-p/co-s Launder m Alwyn w Harrison, Palmer 124min (= Notorious Gentleman)

RAKUDAI WA SHITA-KEREDO (1930) d/st Ozu Sho (= I Flunked, But . . .)

RALLARE (1947) d Mattsson co-s Lindstrom w Sjöström (= The Railway Workers)

Rally = BENSAA SUONISSA (1971)

RALLY ROUND THE FLAG, BOYS! (1958) d/p/co-s McCarey c Shamroy co-a Wheeler m Mockridge w P Newman, Woodward, Weld CS* 106min Fox

RAMONA (1910) d Griffith fn Helen Hunt Jacks w Pickford 1rl Bio

RAMONA (1916) d Crisp supn Lloyd Brown

RAMONA (1928) d Edwin Carewe w Del Rio, W Baxter 7650ft r UA

RAMONA (1936) d H King s Trotti m A Newman w L Young, Carradine, Darwell 90min Fox

RAMPAGE (1963) d Karlson, Hathaway (uc) c Lipstein m E Bernstein w Mitchum, Martinelli, Hawkins, Sabu *98min WB

RAMROD (1947) d De toth c R Harlan w Lake, McCrea, C Ruggles 94min r UA

RAMUNTCHO (1919) d De Baroncelli fn Pierre Loti

RAMUNTCHO (1958) d/co-s Schoendoerffer c Coutard *90min

RANCHO NOTORIOUS (1952) d F Lang s Taradash c Mohr w Dietrich, A Kennedy, M Ferrer *89min r RKO

Rancune, La = BESUCH, DER (1964)

RANDOM HARVEST (1942) d LeRoy p Franklin c Ruttenberg a Gibbons m Stothart w Garson, Colman, Lawford 124min MGM

RANGERS OF FORTUNE (1940) d S Wood c Sparkhul co-a Dreier w MacMurray, Roland 80min

RANG ES MOD (1918) d Balasz

RANGLE RIVER (1939) d Badger fn Zane Grey 72min

Ranks and People = CHINY I LYUDI (1929)

RANGO (1931) d/p Schoedsack 66min Par

The Ransacked Shop = V SNEDENEHO KRAMU (1933)

RANSALU (1967) d Peries 100min (= The Yellow Robe)

RANSOM (1928) d/st G Seitz p Cohn c J Walker 5484ft Col

RANSOM! (1955) d Alex Segal co-s/fpl (Fearful Decision) Maibaum c Arling co-a Gibbons w G Ford, D Reed 109min MGM

Ransom In Sardinia (UK) = SEQUESTRO DI PERSONA (1968)

RAPACE, LA (1968) d/s Giovanni w Ventura *126min (= Birds of Prey)

RAPE (1969) d Lennon, Yoko Ono 16mm *80min

Rape of a Country = BIJSTERE LAND VAN VELUWUM, HET (1948)

RAPE OF CZECHOSLOVAKIA, THE (1939) d J Weiss 19min (= Secret Allies)

RAPHAEL, OU LE DEBAUCHE (1971) d Deville w Ronet *110min

Rapid Stream, A = HONRYU (1926)

RAPT (1933) d Kirsanov w Parlo 7532ft (= La Separation des Races)

RAPTO, EL (1953) d/co-st/co-s Fernandez w Felix

Raptus – The Secret of Dr Hichcock = ORRIBILE SEGRETO DEL DOTTOR HICHCOCK, L' (1962)

RAPTURE (1965) d Guillermin w M Douglas, Lindblom CS 104min r Fox

RAQUETTEURS, LES (1958) co-d/c Brault co-d/e Groulx (= De Gais Lurons en Congrès/The Snowshoers)

RARE BREED, THE (1965) d A McLaglen c Clothier w J Stewart, M O'Hara, Keith PV* 108min U

RARIN' TO GO (1924) d Thorpe 5rs

RASHOMON (1950) d/co-s Kurosawa co-p Nagata c Miyagawa w Mifune, Mori, Kyo 88min Dai

RASKOLNIKOV (1923) d/s Wiene fn (Crime and Punishment) Dostoievski 3168m

RASP, THE (1931) d M Powell 4rs WB

RASPBERRY ROMANCE, THE (1925) d Bacon w Turpin 2rs Pat

RASPUTIN AND THE EMPRESS (1933) d Boleslavsky st/s McArthur c Daniels m Stothart w F, E and L Barrymore 135min MGM

RASSKAZI O LENINYE (1958) d Yutkevich co-c Moskvin *3147m (= Stories about Lenin)

RATAS, LA (1963) d Saslavsky 80min

RAT RACE, THE (1960) d Mulligan co-s/fpl Kanin co-s Perlberg, Seaton c Burks m E Bernstein w Curtis, D Reynolds *105min Par

The Rats = DIE RATTEN (1955)

RÄTSELHAFTE INSERAT, DAS (1916) d May, Karl Gerhardt p/s May

RATSEL VON BANGALOR, DAS (1917) co-d Alexander Antalffy co-d/dec Leni w Veidt 1350m

RATTEN, DIE (1955) d/p Siodmak fpl Gerhardt Hauptmann c Strindberg w Jurgens, Maria Schell (= The Rats)

RATTENFANGER VON HAMELN (1918) co-d/st/s/w Wegener co-d Rochus Gliese

RAUSCH (1919) d Lubitsch fpl (There are Crimes and Crimes) August Strindberg c Freund, Sparkhul (= Intoxication)

RAVEN, THE (1963) d/p Corman co-ex-p Arkoff fst Edgar Allen Poe s Matheson c F Crosby w Price, Lorre, Karloff PV* 81min

Raven's End (UK) = KVARTERET KORPEN (1963)

RAVIN SANS FOND, LE (1917) co-d Feyder Raymond Bernard s Tristan Bernard 1800m Gau

Ravishing Idiot, A (UK) = RAVISSANTE IDIOTE, UNE (1963)

RAVISSANTE IDIOTE, UNE (1963) d Molinaro m Legrand w Perkins, Bardot 108min (= A Ravishing Idiot)

RAW DEAL (1948) d A Mann co-p Menzies c J Alton w Burr, Trevor 82min

RAWHIDE (1926) d Thorpe

RAWHIDE (1951) d Hathaway st/s D Nichols c Krasner co-a Wheeler m Newman w Power, S Hayward 86min Fox

RAWHIDE YEARS, THE (1956) d Maté c Glassberg co-a Golitzen w Curtis, A Kennedy 85min U

RAW WIND IN EDEN (1958) d/co-s R Wilson co-a Golitzen w Esther Williams, J Chandler, De Filippo CS* 93min U

RAY MASTER, L'INAFFERABILE (1967) d Sala *95min

Rayon Invisible, Le = PARIS QUI DORT (1924)

RAZABITAYA VAZA (1913) d/s Protazanov 700m (= The Broken Vase)

RAZ DWA TRZY (1967) d L Anderson 20min (= The Singing Lesson)

RAZOR'S EDGE, THE (1946) d Goulding p Zanuck s Trotti fn Somerset Maugham c AC Miller co-a R Day m A Newman w Power, Tierney, A Baxter, Payne, C Webb, H Marshall 146min Fox

RAZGROM JAPONII (1945) s/e Heifitz, Zharki documentary footage shot by news cameramen (= The Defeat of Japan)

RAZZIA SUR LA CHNOUF (1954) d/co-ad Decoin w Gabin, Dalio 105min (= Chnouf)

REACH FOR GLORY (1961) d P Leacock 86min

REACH FOR THE SKY (1956) d/s L Gilbert 135min JAR

REACHING FOR THE MOON (1917) d/co-s Emerson p/w Fairbanks Sr co-s Loos c Edeson 5rs

REACHING FOR THE MOON (1931) d/co-s Goulding p Fairbanks Sr co-s Irving Berlin co-c June w Fairbanks Sr, B Crosby, Horton 90min r UA

REACHING FOR THE SUN (1941) d/p Wellman c Mellor w McCrea 90min Par

REACTIONS NUTRITIVES D'HALIOTIS: REACTIONS D'HALIOTIS, DE CLAMYS ET DE DIFFERENTS ECHINODERMES A LA PRESENCE DE CERTAINS STELLERIDES (1956) d Painlevé 16mm *

READY FOR THE PEOPLE (1964) d Kulik 54min WB

READY, WILLING AND ABLE (1937) d Enright co-s Wald c Polito w Wyman 10rs WB

REAL ADVENTURES, THE (1922) d/p K Vidor c Barnes 50min pc Vidor

Real End of the Great War, The = PRAWDZIWY KONIEC WIELKIEJ WOJNY (1957)

REAL GLORY, THE (1939) d Hathaway p Goldwyn as-p Riskin co-s Swerling c Maté m A Newman w G Cooper, Niven, B Crawford 95min r UA

REAP THE WILD WIND (1942) d/p De Mille co-s Charles Bennett co-c Milner co-a Dreier m V Young w Goddard, Milland, J Wayne, Preston, S Hayward, Hopper, Bickford *124min Par

Rear Guard = THE COMMAND (1954)

REAR WINDOW (1954) d/p Hitchcock s J Hayes c Burks co-a Pereira m Waxman w J Stewart, Grace Kelly, Corey, Burr, Ritter *112min Par

Reason and Emotion = ROZUM A CIT (1962)

REBECCA (1940) d Hitchcock p Selznick fn Daphne du Maurier c Barnes a Wheeler m Waxman w Olivier, Fontaine, G Sanders 130min r UA

REBECCA OF SUNNYBROOK FARM (1917) d Neilan w Pickford 6rs

REBECCA OF SUNNYBROOK FARM (1932) d Santell rm (1917) w Marsh 80min Fox

REBECCA OF SUNNYBROOK FARM (1938) d Dwan c AC Miller w Temple, R Scott 81min Fox

Rebel, The = AMAILUSA SHIRO TOKISADA (1962)

Rebel Flight to Cuba (UK) = ABSCHIED VON DEN WOLKEN (1959)

REBELION DE LOS COLGADOS, LA (1954) d Fernandez, Alfredo B Crevenna c Figueroa w Armendariz 90min

REBELL, DER (1932) d C Bernhardt, Luis Trenker

Rebellion = JOI-UCHI (1967)

REBELLION, DIE (1962) d/co-s Staudte fpl Brecht w Jurgens, Neff 105min

Rebellion in Japan = UTAGE (1967)

REBEL WITHOUT A CAUSE (1955) d/st N Ray p Weisbart s Stern c E Haller m Rosenman w Dean, N Wood CS* 111min WB

RE BURLONE, IL (1935) d/s Guazzoni

RECE DO GORY (1967) d/s/a/w Skolimowski

RECKLESS (1935) d V Fleming p Selznick c Folsen w Harlow, W Powell, Tone, R Russell 96min MGM

RECKLESS MOMENT, THE (1949) d Ophuls p Wagner c Guffey w Mason, J Bennett 82min Col

Reckless Romeo, A = CREAM PUFF ROMANCE, A (1916)

Reckless Years, The = WONDERFUL YEARS, THE (1958)

RECOIL (1963) d Wendkos w R Taylor, Miles 88min (TV ep edited into a feature)

RECOLLECTIONS OF BOYHOOD: AN INTERVIEW WITH JOSEPH WELCH (1954) d W Van Dyke c R Leacock 15min

Record Of A Tenement – Gentleman = NAGAYA SHINSHI ROKU (1947)

Record Of Newly-Weds = OSHIKIRI SHINKON KI (1930)

RECORDS AU GOUFFRE DE LA PIERRE-SAINT-MARTIN (pre-1952) d Tazieff 16mm

RECOURS EN GRACE (1960) d/co-s Benedek c Kelber m Jarre w Vallone, Riva, Girardot 100min

RECREATION (1914) d/s/w Chaplin ½rl Key

RECREATION I (1956–57) d Breer anim 16mm *2min

RECREATION II (1956–57) d Breer anim* 1½min

RECREATION, LA (1960) d François Moreuil fn Françoise Sagan w Seberg, Marquand 89min (= Playtime)

RE-CREATION OF BRIAN KENT, THE (1925) d S Wood p Lesser w Pitts 6878ft

RECUPERANTI, I (1969) d Olmi *94min RAI

RED, LA (1953) d/co-st/co-s Fernandez 66min

RED AND BLUE (1968) d T Richardson w V Redgrave, Fairbanks Jr 35min

Red and the White, The (UK) = CSILLAGOSOK, KATONAK (1967)

RED BADGE OF COURAGE, THE (1951) d/s J Huston 2nd d Marton p/cy G Reinhardt fn Stephen Crane c Rosson co-a Gibbons m Kaper w A Murphy 69min MGM

RED BALL EXPRESS (1952) d Boetticher p A Rosenberg s J Hayes w J Chandler, Poitier 84min U

Red Balloon, The (UK) = BALLON ROUGE, LE (1956)

Red Baron, The (UK) = VON RICHTOFEN AND BROWN (1971)

Red Beard = AKAHIGE (1965)

RED BERET, THE (1953) d T Young co-s Maibaum, F Nugent w Ladd *88min r Col (= The Paratrooper)

RED BULL, DER LETZTE APACHE (1920) d Jutzi 1264m

RED DANCE, THE (1928) d Walsh c C Clarke w Del Rio 9250ft Fox

RED DANUBE, THE (1949) d/st G Sidney co-a Gibbons m Rozsa w Pidgeon, E Barrymore, Lawford, J Leigh 119min MGM

Red Desert, The = DESERTO ROSSO (1964)

RED DICE (1926) d W Howard c Andriot 7257ft pc De Mille

RED DUST (1932) d V Fleming s Mahin c Rosson w Gable, Harlow, Crisp, Astor 83min MGM

REDEEMING SIN, THE (1925) d Blackton w Nazimova 7rs Vit

Re Dei Sette Mari, Il = SEVEN SEAS TO CALAIS (1962)

REDEMPTION (1911) d Jasset

REDEMPTION (1930) d/p Niblo w J Gilbert 6015ft MGM

RED ENSIGN (1934) d/co-s M Powell 67min

REDENZIONE (1915) d Gallone

REDES (1934) co-d Zinnemann co-d Emilio Gomez Muriel supn/c Strand 65min (= Pescados/The Wave)

RED GARTERS (1954) d G Marshall c Arling a Pereira *91min Par

RED HAIR (1928) d Badger w Bow 6331ft Par

RED-HAIRED ALIBI (1932) d Christy Cabanne w Temple 72min

RED-HEADED WOMAN (1932) d Conway as-p Lewin s Loos c Rosson w Harlow, Boyer 74min MGM

REDHEADS ON PARADE (1935) d McLeod p Lasky 78min Fox

REDHEADS PREFERRED (1926) d Thorpe

RED HEELS (1926) d Curtiz

RED, HOT AND BLUE (1949) d/co-s J Farrow st Lederer c Fapp co-a Dreier w Mature 84min Par

RED HOT RHYTHM (1929) d/co-s McCarey 6918ft Par

RED HOT RIDING HOOD (1943) d Avery anim* 7min MGM

RED HOT ROMANCE, A (1913) d Sennett w Norman ½rl Key

RED HOT ROMANCE (1922) d Fleming p Emerson, Loos 6rs

RED HOUSE, THE (1947) d/s Daves p Lesser c Glennon m Rozsa w Robinson 100min r UA

RE DI DENARI (1936) d Guazzoni

Red Inn, The = AUBERGE ROUGE, L' (1951)

RED KIMONO (1925) d W Lang w Power 7rs

RED LIGHT (1949) d/p Del Ruth c Glennon m Tiomkin w Raft, V Mayo, Burr 83min r UA

RED LILY, THE (1924) d/st Niblo c Milner w Novarro 7rs MGM

RED LINE 7000 (1966) d/p/co-s Hawks c Krasner co-a Pereira *127min r Par

Red Lips (UK) = ROSSETTO, IL (1960)

RED MARK, THE (1928) d Cruze 8rs Pat

RED MILL, THE (1927) d Arbuckle (ps William Goodrich) 7rs MGM

RED MOUNTAIN (1951) d Dieterle p Wallis c C Lang co-a Pereira w Ladd, L Scott *84min Par

RED PLANET MARS (1952) d Horner c Biroc 87min r UA

RED PONY, THE (1949) d/p Milestone st/s Steinbeck c Gaudio m Copland w M Loy, Mitchum 89min r Rep

Red Presnya = KRASNAYA PRESNYA (1926)

RED RIDING HOODWINKED (1955) *d* Freleng anim* 7min WB
RED RIVER (1948) *d/p* Hawks *ex-p* Feldman *co-s/fn* (*The Chisholm Trail*) B Chase *co-s* Schnee *c* R Harlan *m* Tiomkin *w* J Wayne, Clift, Dru, Brennan, Carey, Winters (*uc*) 125min *r* UA
RED RIVER SHORE (1953) *d* Keller 54min Rep
Red Shirts = CAMICIE ROSSE (1950)
RED SHOES, THE (1948) *d/p/s* M Powell, Pressburger *c* Cardiff *w* Walbrook *136min
RED SKIES OF MONTANA (1952) *d* J Newman *c* C Clarke *co-a* Wheeler *m* A Newman *w* Widmark, Boone, J Hunter *89min Fox
REDSKIN (1929) *d* Schertzinger *co-c* Cronjager, Rennahan part * 7643ft Par
Red Sun = SOLEIL ROUGE (1971)
RED SUNDOWN (1955) *d* J Arnold *p* Zugsmith *co-a* Golitzen *81min U
Red Tent, The = KRASNAYA PALATKA (1971)
RED WHITE AND ZERO ep THE RIDE OF THE VALKYRIE (1967, *ur*) *d* P Brook 12min
REFLECTIONS IN A GOLDEN EYE (1967) *d* J Huston *p* Stark *fn Carson McCullers* *c* Tonti *w* E Taylor, Brando, Keith PV* 109min WB
REFLECTIONS ON BLACK (1955) *d* Brakhage 16mm 12min
REFLET DE CLAUDE MERCOEUR, LE (1923) *d/s* Duvivier *fn Frederic Boulet*
REFORMER AND THE REDHEAD, THE (1950) *d/p/s* M Frank, Panama *c* June *co-a* Gibbons *m* Raksin *w* D Powell, Allyson 90min MGM
REFUGEE, THE (1918) *d/p* Hepworth 2rs
REGAIN (1937) *d/p/s/di* Pagnol *m* Honegger *w* Fernandel 122min (= *Harvest*)
REGATES DE SAN FRANCISCO, LES (1959) *d* Autant-Lara *s* Aurenche, Bost CS* 75min
REGEN (1929) *co-d/c/e* Ivens *co-d/s Mannus Franken* 300m (= *Rain*)
REGENBOGEN - 1, EIN FORMSPIEL (1927) *d* Fischinger anim
REGENERATION, THE (1915) *d/p/co-s* Walsh 6rs Fox
REGIMENT, LE (1896) *d* Méliès 20m
Regina Del Deserto, La = NEL SEGNO DI ROMA (1958)
REGINA DELLE AMAZZONI, LA (1960) *d* Sala *co-s* Tessari FS* 100min
REGINA DI NAVARRA, LA (1941) *d* Gallone
REGISTERED NURSE (1934) *d* Florey *c* Hickox 62min FN
REGLE DU JEU, LA (1939) *d/co-s* J Renoir *p* C Renoir *co-c* Bachelet *co-dec* Lourié *co-m* Kosma *fm Mozart, Monsigny, Saint-Saens, F Strauss* *w* Dalio, J Renoir, Modot, Carette 110min (= *The Rules of the Game*)
REGNE DU JOUR, LE (1966) *d* Perrault 16mm 118min
REIGEN, DER (1920) *d/p/s* R Oswald *w* Nielsen, Veidt
REIGN OF TERROR (1949) *d* A Mann *p* Wanger, Menzies *co-st/co-s* Yordan *c* F Alton *w* R Cummings, Dahl 91min
REIMEL IZEN (1931) *d/s/w* Kinugasa Sho (= *Before Dawn*)
REINCARNATION DE SERGE RENAUDIER, LA (1920) *d/s* Duvivier
REINE ELISABETH, LA (1912) *d Louis Mercanton* *w* S Bernhardt (= *Elisabeth, Reine d'Angleterre/Queen Elisabeth*)
REINE MARGOT, LA (1953) *d Jean Dreville* *s* Gance *fn Dumas* *w* Rosay, Moreau *150min (= *Woman of Evil*)
REISE NACH TILSIT, DIE (1939) *d/co-s* V Harlan *rm* SUNRISE (1927) 2540m *r* Tob
REISE UM DIE ERDE IN 80 TAGEN, DIE (1919) *d/p/s* R Oswald *fn Jules Verne* *w* Veidt 2578m
REIVERS, THE (1969) *d Mark Rydell fn* Faulkner *w* McQueen PV* 111min
REKAVA (1956) *d* Peries 100min (= *The Line of Destiny*)
REKOPIS ZNALEZIONY W SARAGOSSIE (1964) *d* Has *fn Jan Potocki m Krzysztof Penderecki* *w* Cybulski FS 124min (= *The Saragossa Manuscript*)
RELEVE LE (1938) *d* J Epstein
RELIC OF OLD JAPAN, A (1914) *d* Ince *w* Hayakawa
RELIGIEUSE, LA (1965) *d/co-s* Rivette *fn Diderot* *w* Karina, Presle *140min (= *The Nun*)
RELITTO, IL (1960) *d/s* Cacoyannis *w* Heflin, Lambetti 115min (= *The Wastrel*)
RELUCTANT DEBUTANTE, THE (1958) *d* Minnelli *p* Berman *c* Ruttenberg *dec* D'Eaubonne *w* Harrison, Kendall CS* 96min *r* MGM
RELUCTANT DRAGON, THE (1941) *d Alfred L Werker* *p* Disney *w* Benchley, Ladd *72min *r* RKO
Re.ıctant Millionaire, The = MUZ Z NEZNAMA (1939)
RELUCTANT SAINT, THE (1962) *d/p* Dmytryk *m* Rota *w* Maximilian Schell, Tamiroff, Montalban 105min
REMAINS TO BE SEEN (1953) *d* Weis *c* Planck *co-a* Gibbons *w* Allyson, V Johnson 89min MGM
REMARKABLE ANDREW, THE (1942) *d* Heisler *st/s* Trumbo *c* Sparkuhl *w* Holden 80min Par
REMARKABLE MR PENNYPACKER, THE (1959) *d* Levin *p* Brackett *c* Krasner *co-a* Wheeler *m* Harline *w* McGuire, C Webb, C Coburn S* 87min Fox
REMBRANDT (1936) *d/p* A Korda *co-c* Périnal, Krasker *a* V Korda *w* Laughton, Lawrence 88min *r* UA
REMBRANDT (1942) *d/co-s* Steinhoff *dec* Rohrig 106min
Rembrandt, Painter Of Men = REMBRANDT, SCHILDER VAN DE MENS (1956)
REMBRANDT, SCHILDER VAN DE MENS (1956) *d/s/e* Haanstra *20min (= *Rembrandt, Painter of Men*)
REMEMBER? (1939) *d/co-st/co-s* McLeod *c* Folsey *w* R Taylor, Ayres, Garson 83min MGM
REMEMBER LAST NIGHT? (1935) *d* Whale *w* R Young 81min U
REMEMBER THE DAY (1941) *d* H King *m* A Newman *w* Colbert, Payne 86min Fox
REMEMBER THE NIGHT (1940) *d/p* Leisen *st/s* P Sturges *c* Tetzlaff *co-a* Dreier *w* Stanwyck, MacMurray 86min Par
REMEMBER WHEN? (1925) *d Harry Edwards* *co-s* Bruckman *w* Langdon 2rs *pc* Sennett *r* Pat
REMERCIEMENT AU PUBLIC (1900) *d* Méliès 20m
REMODELING HER HUSBAND (1920) *d* L Gish *w* D Gish 5rs
REMONTONS LES CHAMPS-ELYSEES (1938) *d/s/w* Guitry *c* Bachelet
REMORQUES (1941) *d* Grémillon *s/di* J Prévert *ad* Cayatte, Charles Spaak *c* Thirard *a* Daquin *dec* Trauner *w* Gabin, Morgan 2500m
REMOTE CONTROL (1930) *d* St Clair 5955ft MGM
REMOUS (1933) *d* Greville
RENAISSANCE (1963) *d/s/dec* Borowczyk anim* 10min
RENAISSANCE DU HAVRE (1950) *d/cy* Camus *c* Fradetal 31min Gau
RECONTRE AVEC LE PRESIDENT HO CHI MINH (1968) *d* Ivens, *Marceline Loridan* *8min
RECONTRES (1960) *d/c* Mitry
RECONTRES (1961) *d* Agostini *w* Morgan 102min
REDEZVOUS, THE (1923) *d* Neilan 7415ft *co-pc* Goldwyn
RENDEZVOUS (1935) *d* W Howard *c* Daniels *w* W Powell, R Russell, Atwill, Romero 91min MGM
Rendezvous (UK) = DARLING, HOW COULD YOU? (1951)
RENDEZ-VOUS, LE (1961) *d/co-s* Delannoy *co-s/di* Bost, Aurenche *w* Girardot, G Sanders, Noiret 128min
RENDEZ-VOUS A BRAY (1971) *d/s* Delvaux *c* Cloquet *w* Karina *90min
Rendezvous At Midnight = RENDEZ-VOUS DE MINUIT (1961)
RENDEZ-VOUS DU DIABLE, LES (1958) *d/co-p* Tazieff *80min (= *Vulcano*)
RENDEZ-VOUS DE JUILLET (1949) *d/co-st/s* Becker *c* C Renoir *co-m* Wiener *w* Gélin, Ronet, Modot 68min Gau
RENDEZ-VOUS DE MAX, LE (1913) *d/s/w* Linder Pat
RENDEZ-VOUS DE MINUIT, LE (1962) *d/co-s* Leenhardt *c* Badal *dec* Evein *m* Auric *w* Palmer, Ronet 90min (= *Rendez-vous At Midnight*)
RENDEZVOUS WITH ANNIE (1946) *d/as-p* Dwan 89min Rep (= *Corporal Dolan AWOL*)
RENEGADES (1930) *d* V Fleming *s* Furthman *c* O'Connell *w* M Loy, Lugosi 90min Fox
RENNEN (1961) *d* Kluge, *Paul Kruntorad* (sh)
RENNFAHRER (1961) *d* Kluge (sh)
RENNFIEBER (1917) *d/p* Roswald 1614m
RENNSYMPHONIE (1929) *d/co-s* Richter 18min (= *Race Symphony*)
RENO (1939) *d* Farrow 73min RKO
RENTREE DES CLASSES, LA (1955) *d/co-s/e* Rozier 22min
REPAS DES FAUVES, LE (1964) *d* Christian-Jaque *s* Jeanson *w* Blanche 97min
Repast = MESHI (1951)
REPATEUR DE CERVELLE, LE (1910) *d* Cohl anim 100m
REP JE ULAZNICA (1959) *d/co-s* Vukotic anim* 11min (= *My Tail is My Ticket*)
REPORTAGE AU COURS DU TOURNAGE DE LADY L, FILM DE PETER USTINOV (1964) *d* P Prévert *w* Ustinov, P Newman, Piccoli, Noiret, Dalio 16mm 22min ORTF
Reportage Nr 1 = REPORTAZ NR 1 (1932)
Reportage Nr 2 = REPORTAZ NR 2 (1932)
REPORTAJE (1953) *d/co-st/co-s* Fernandez *c* Phillips *w* Felix, Del Rio
REPORTAZ NR 1 (1932) *d* Jakubowska, *Eugeniesz Cekalski, Jerzy Zarpycki* (sh) (= *Reportage Nr 1*)
REPORTAZ NR 2 (1932) *d* Jakubowska, *Eugeniesz Cekalski, Jerzy Zarpycki* (sh) (= *Reportage Nr 2*)
REPORT FROM THE ALEUTIANS (1943) *d/s* J Huston *m* Tiomkin *n* W Huston *47min US Signal Corps (= *Why We Fight* series)
REPORT MILLBROOK (1966) *d* J Mekas 16mm *11min extract from DIARIES NOTES AND SKETCHES (= *Report Millbrook*)
Report on the Party and the Guests = SLAVNOSTI A HOSTECH, O (1966)
REPOS DU GUERRIER, LE (1962) *d/co-s* Vadim *c* Thirard *w* Bardot, Hossein CS* 99min (= *Warriors Rest/Love on a Pillow*)
REPRODUCTION INTERDITE (1956) *d* Grangier 90min
REPUBLICANS - THE NEW BREED (1964) *d* R Leacock 27min
Republic of Sin (UK) = LA FIEVRE MONTE A EL PAO (1959)
REPULSION (1965) *d/co-s* Polanski *c* G Taylor *m* Komeda *w* Deneuve 104min
REQUIEM FOR A HEAVYWEIGHT (1962) *d* Nelson *p* Susskind *s/fTVpl* Serling *w* Quinn, Ronney 87min Col
REQUIESCANT (1967) *d* Lizzani *w* Pasolini *92min
RESAN BORT (1945) *d/s* Sjoberg SF (= *Journey Out*)
RESCUE, THE (1929) *d* Brenon *c* Barnes *w* Colman 7980ft *r* UA
RESCUED BY ROVER (1905) *p* Hepworth 425ft
RESCUED FROM AN EAGLE'S NEST (1907) *d* Porter *w* Griffith (*ps* A Lawrence Griffith) 1rl 8min
Reserved For Ladies = SERVICE FOR LADIES (1932)
RESISTANCE AND OHM'S LAW (1943) *d* Cukor US Signal Corps
The Respectable Ladies of Pardubicke = POCESTNE PANI PARDUBICKE (1944)
RESTAURANT (1965) *d* Warhol 16mm 35min
Restaurant Waiter, The = CHELOVEK 12 RESTORANA (1927)
REST IST SCHWEIGEN, DER (1959) *d/s* Käutner 2838m
RESTLESS BREED, THE (1957) *d* Dwan *w* A Bancroft S* 81min
RESTLESS SEX, THE (1920) *d* Leonard *w* Davies 6500ft Pat
RESTLESS SOULS (1919) *d/w* Conway 5rs Gau
RESTLESS WIVES (1923) *d* La Cava 5rs
Restless Years, The = WONDERFUL YEARS, THE (1958)
RESURRECTIO (1931) *d/st/s/co-e* Blasetti
RESURRECTION (1909) *d* Griffith *fn Leo Tolstoi* 1rl Bio
RETOUR, LE (1947) technical adviser Cartier-Bresson 3060ft Services Americains de L'Information
RETOUR A LA RAISON, LE (1923) *d/c* Man Ray 10min
RETOUR A LA TERRE (1938) *d/st/s/w* Tati
RETOUR A L'AUBE (1938) *d/ad* Decoin *fn Vicki Baum* *m* Misraki *w* Darrieux 86min
RETOUR A LA VIE (1949) *m* Misraki 120min
ep TANTE EMMA *d* Cayatte *st/s/di* Charles Spaak
ep ANTOINE *d Georges Lampin* *s* Charles Spaak
ep LE RETOUR DE JEAN *d/co-s* Clouzot *w* Jouvet
ep RENE *d Jean Dreville* *s* Charles Spaak
ep LOUIS *d Jean Dreville* *s* Charles Spaak *w* Reggiani
RETOUR A NEW YORK (1962) *d* Reichenbach *m* Legrand 12min
RETOUR DE DON CAMILLO, LE (1953) *d/co-ad/co-s/co-di* Duvivier *w* Fernandel 100min (= *Il Ritorno Di Don Camillo/The Return Of Don Camillo*)
RETOUR DE MAINIVELLE (1957) *d/s* De La Patellière *di* Audiard *w* Morgan, Gélin 93min (= *There's Always a Price Tag*)
RETREAT - HELL! (1952) *d* JH Lewis *p/st/s* Sperling 95min WB
RETROSCENA (1939) *d/co-st/co-s/co-e* Blasetti *co-s* Germi
RETTEN SEJRER (1917) *d/s* Madsen
RETURN, THE (1927) *s* Charles Bennett
Return, The = KOM TILLBACKA, DE (1962)
RETURN FROM THE ASHES (1965) *d/p* J Thompson *s* JJ Epstein *c* Challis *w* Maximilian Schell, Thulin PV 104min *pc* Mir *r* UA
Return Home = NAVRAT DOMU (1948)
RETURN OF DOCTOR X, THE (1939) *d* V Sherman *c* Hickox *w* Bogart 62min WB
Return Of Don Camillo, The (UK) = RETOUR DE DON CAMILLO, LE (1953)
RETURN OF DRAW EGAN, THE (1916) *supn* Ince *w* W Hart 5rs Tri
RETURN OF FRANK JAMES, THE (1940) *d* F Lang *p* Zanuck *as-p* Macgowan *co-c* Barnes *co-a* R Day *w* H Fonda, Tierney, Carradine *92min Fox
Return of Maxim, The = VOZVRASHCHENIE MAKSIMA (1937)
RETURN OF MONTE CRISTO, THE (1946) *d* Levin *c* Lawton *w* L Hayward 91min Col
RETURN OF OCTOBER, THE (1948) *d* JH Lewis *p* Maté *s* Panama, M Frank *w* G Ford 89min Col
RETURN OF PETER GRIMM, THE (1935) *d George Nicholls Jr* *p* Macgowan *c* Andriot *w* L Barrymore 84min RKO
Return of Ringo, The = RITORNO DI RINGO, EL (1965)
RETURN OF RUSTY, THE (1946) *d* Castle 64min Col
RETURN OF THE BAD MEN (1948) *d* Enright *w* R Scott, Ryan 90min RKO
RETURN OF THE FROG, THE (1938) *d* Elvey 76min *r* BL
RETURN OF THE GUN FIGHTER (1966) *d* Neilson *co-st* B Kennedy *w* R Taylor *96min
Return of the Prodigal Son, The = NAVRAT ZTRACENEHO SYNA (1966)
RETURN OF THE SEVEN (1966) *d* B Kennedy *m* E Bernstein *w* Brynner, Fernandez PV* 95min *r* UA
RETURN OF THE TEXAN (1952) *d* Daves *s* D Nichols *c* Ballard *co-a* Wheeler *w* Brennan, Dru 88min Fox
RETURN OF THE VIKINGS (1945) *d* Frend 54min
RETURN OF TRH, THE PRINCE AND PRINCESS OF WALES (1903) *p* Paul 120ft
Return of Vassily Bortnikov, The = VOZURASHCHENIE VASSILIA BORTNIKOVA (1953)
RETURN OF WILD BILL, THE (1940) *d* JH Lewis 60min Col
RETURN TO LIFE (1938) *co-d* Cartier-Bresson
RETURN TO PARADISE (1953) *d* Robson *fn J Michenner* *c* Hoch *w* G Cooper *88min UA

RETURN TO PEYTON PLACE (1961) d J Ferrer p Wald c C Clarke m Waxman w Lynley, J Chandler, Parker, Astor, Weld CS* 122min Fox
RETURN TO TREASURE ISLAND (1954) d Dupont *75min r UA (= Bandit Island of Karabei)
REUNION (1932) d Ivar Campbell w Newton 60min
REUNION (1936) d Taurog w Hersholt 80min Fox
Reunion = REUNION IN FRANCE (1942)
Reunion, The (UK) = RIMPATRIATA, LA (1963)
REUNION IN FRANCE (1942) d Dassin p J Mankiewicz c Planck a Gibbons m Waxman w J Wayne, J Crawford, Carradine, Gardner 104min MGM (= Reunion/Mademoiselle France)
REUNION IN RHYTHM (1937) d G Douglas p Roach 1rl MGM
REUNION IN VIENNA (1933) d/p Franklin w J Barrymore 92min MGM
REVAK, LO SCHIAVO DI CARTAGINE (1960) d Maté p Mahin, Rackin w Palance *86min (= Revak the Rebel/The Barbarians)
Revak The Rebel = REVAK, LO SCHIARO DI CARTAGINE (1960)
REVANCHE DE ROGER LA HONTE, LA (1946) d/s Cayatte di Charles Spaak c Thirard w Casarès, Desailly 90min
REVE, LE (1921) d De Baroncelli
REVE AU COIN DU FEU (1895) d Reynaud
REVE D'ARTISTE (1898) d Méliès 20m
REVE D'UN FUMEUR D'OPIUM, LE (1908) d Méliès 110m
REVE DU PARIA, LE (1902) d Méliès 40m
REVEILLE WITH BEVERLY (1943) d Charles Barton w Ann Miller Col
REVELATION, THE (1918) d/co-s George D Baker w Nazimova 7rs
Revelry = THE ROUNDERS (1914)
REVENANT (1946) d Christian-Jaque m Honegger w Jouvet 114min
REVENGE (1918) d Browning 5rs Metro
Revenge = ADAUCHI (1965)
Revenge = POMSTA (1968)
Revengeful Spirit Of Eros, The = EROGAMI NO ONRYO (1930)
REVENGE OF FRANKENSTEIN, THE (1958) d Fisher *89min r Col
REVENGE OF THE CREATURE (1955) d J Arnold 3D 81min U
Revenge Of The Vampire (UK) = MASCHERA DEL DEMONIO, LA (1960)
Revenge Of Yukinojo = YUKINOJO HENGE (1963)
Revenger, The = OSVETNIK (1958)
REVERIE POUR CLAUDE DEBUSSY (1951) d Mitry m Claude Debussy 12min
REVETEMENTS ROUTIERS (1934) d Leenhardt 1000m
REVISOR (1933) d Frič fst Nickolai Gogol (= Accountant)
REVIZOR (1952) d/s Petrov fpl N Gogol *132min
REVOLTE DES GUEUX, LA (1912) d Machin 285m
REVOLTEE, LA (1947) d/ad L'Herbier fn Pierre Sabatier c Matras 95min
REVOLT IN THE BIG HOUSE (1958) d Springsteen co-st/co-s Lourié 79min AA
REVOLT IN THE JUNGLE (1937) d Z Korda
REVOLT OF MAMIE STOVER, THE (1956) d Walsh p Adler s Boehm c Tover co-a Wheeler m Friedhofer w J Russell, Moorehead *93min Fox
Revolt of the Fisherman = VOSTANIE RYBAKOV (1935)
Revolt On The Volga (UK) = IL VENDICATORE (1958)
REVOLUTION D'OCTOBRE, LA (1967) d/co-p Rossif m Wiener 93min (= October Revolution)
REVOLUTION INDUSTRIELLE (1970) d/s/cy Lamothe *30min
REVOLUTIONNAIRE, LE (1965) d/p/s Lefebvre 74min
REVOLUTIONS BRYLLUP (1909) d Viggo Larsen w Blom
REVOLUTIONS BRYLLUP (1914) d/s Blom
REVUE MONTMARTROISE (1932) d Cavalcanti
REWARD, THE (1965) d/co-s Bourguignon p A Rosenberg c Joe Macdonald co-a Boyle m E Bernstein w Von Sydow, Roland, Fernandez CS* 91min r Fox
REWARD OF THE FAITHLESS, THE (1917) d/p/s Ingram 5rs
REZZOU, LE (1934) d Leenhardt, René Zuber
RFK – TWO DAYS (1965, uf) d Pennebaker w Robert F Kennedy 16mm 60min
RHAPSODY (1954) d C Vidor co-a Gibbons w E Taylor, Gassman *115min MGM
RHAPSODY IN BLUE (1945) d Rapper p Lasky co-s H Koch c Polito chor Prinz w C Coburn, Jolson, A Smith 139min WB
RHIN, FLEUVE INTERNATIONAL, LE (1952) d Bourguignon, André Zwobada c Fradetal (sh)
Rhinoceros, The = DIE NASHORNER (1963)
RHODES OF AFRICA (1936) d Berthold Viertel co-ad L Arliss w W Huston 94min 9rs Gau
RHYTHM (1956) d Lye 1min
RHYTHM ON THE RANGE (1936) d Taurog c Struss co-m Hollander w R Rogers, B Crosby 85min Par
RHYTHM ON THE RIVER (1940) d Schertzinger co-st B Wilder c Tetzlaff w Rathbone, B Crosby 92min Par
RHYTHMUS 21 (1921) d/c/dec Richter 250ft (= Film is Rhythm)

RHYTHMUS 23 (1923) d/dec Richter 200ft
RHYTHMUS 25 d Richter 250ft
RICCHEZZA SENZA DOMANI (1939) d/co-s Poggioli
Rice = KOME (1957)
RICE (1964) d W Van Dyke, Wheaton Galentine *26min
RICE AND OLD SHOES (1922) d St Clair 2rs
RICH AND STRANGE (1932) d Hitchcock co-s Reville 83min
RICHARD III (1955) d/p/w Olivier fpl Shakespeare c Heller des Furse m Walton w Bloom, S Baker, Gielgud, R Richardson VV* 161min r BL
RICHELIEU (1914) d/s Dwan fb E Bulwer Lytton w Chaney 6rs U
RICHELIEU, OR THE CARDINAL'S CONSPIRACY (1909) d Griffith w Ince 1rl Bio
RICHEST GIRL IN THE WORLD, THE (1934) d William A Seiter p Berman st/s Krasna c Musuraca w M Hopkins, McCrea 76min RKO
RICHEST MAN IN THE WORLD, THE (1930) d S Wood co-st/co-di E Nugent a Gibbons w Montgomery, E Nugent 87min r MGM (= Sins of the Children)
RICH MAN'S FOLLY (1931) d Cromwell fn (Dombey and Son) Charles Dickens 80min Par
RICH YOUNG AND PRETTY (1951) d Taurog p Pasternak co-a Gibbons w J Powell, Corey, Darrieux *95min MGM
RICKSHAW (1960) d A King 16mm 28min
RIDDLE GAWNE (1918) d Lambert Hillyer st W Hart c August w W Hart, Chaney 5rs Par
Ride A Reckless Mile (US) = THE GREAT DAN PATCH (1949)
RIDEAU CRAMOISI, LE (1952) d/s Astruc fn (La Première Diabolique) Barbey d'Aurevilly c Schuftan e Mitry w Aimée 45min
RIDEAUX BLANCS, LES (1966) d Franju s/di Duras c Fradetal m Delerue TV film
RIDE A VIOLENT MILE (1957) d/ex-p/st Warren S 80min Fox
RIDE BACK, THE (1957) d Allan H Miner c Biroc w Quinn 79min pc Aldrich r UA
RIDE 'EM HIGH (1927) d Thorpe
RIE E KELLY RIDE (1941) d Foster 59min Fox
RIDE LONESOME (1959) d/p Boetticher ex-p H Brown s B Kennedy c Lawton w R Scott, J Coburn CS* 73min pc Scott, H Brown r Col
Rider in Blue = RYTTARE I BLATT (1959)
RIDER OF THE LAW, THE (1919) d J Ford w Carey 5rs U
RIDERS OF THE NEW FOREST (1946) d P Leacock 60min
RIDERS OF THE PURPLE SAGE, THE (1918) d/co-s F Lloyd fn Zane Grey 7rs Fox
RIDERS OF THE PURPLE SAGE (1925) d Lynn Reynolds fn Zane Grey w Mix 6rs Fox
RIDERS OF VENGEANCE (1919) d/co-s J Ford co-s/w Carey
RIDE THE HIGH COUNTRY (1962) d Peckinpah s NB Stone c Ballard w McCrea, R Scott *94min MGM (= Guns in the Afternoon)
RIDE THE HIGH IRON (1957) d Weis w Burr 74min Col
RIDE THE PINK HORSE (1947) d Montgomery s B Hecht, Lederer, J Metty co-a Boyle w Montgomery 101min U
RIDE, VAQUERO! (1953) d J Farrow c Surtees co-a Gibbons m Kaper w R Taylor, Gardner, Keel, Quinn *90min MGM
RID I NATT (1942) d/s Molander w Dahlbeck SF
RIDIN' FOR LOVE (1926) d/st Wyler 2rs U
RIDING HIGH (1943) d G Marshall as-p Kohlmar co-c Struss co-a Dreier m V Young w Lamour, D Powell 89min Par (= Melody Inn)
RIDING HIGH (1950) d/p Capra st Hellinger s Riskin rm BROADWAY BILL (1934) c Barnes Laszlo co-des Dreier w B Crosby, Bickford, Hardy (uc) 112min Par
RIDING RIVALS (1926) d Thorpe
RIDING SHOTGUN (1954) d De Toth c Glennon w R Scott *75min WB
RIDIN' ROWDY, THE (1927) d Thorpe
RIEN N'EST IMPOSSIBLE A L'HOMME (1910) d Cohl anim
RIEN QUE LES HEURES (1926) d/p/co-s Cavalcanti 44min
RIFFLE BILL (1909) d/s Jasset (in 5 parts)
RIFF RAFF (1947) d Tetzlaff st/s Rackin 80min RKO
RIFIFI A TOKYO (1962) d Deray m Delerue w Vanel 90min MGM (= Rififi in Tokyo)
Rififi in Paris = DU RIFIFI A PANAME (1965)
Rififi in Tokyo = RIFIFI A TOKYO (1961)
Rififi (Means Trouble) (UK) = DU RIFIFI CHEZ LES HOMMES (1954)
RIGHT APPROACH, THE (1955) d D Butler c Leavitt CS 92min Fox
RIGHT CROSS (1950) d J Sturges st/s Schnee c Brodine co-a Gibbons m Raksin w Allyson, D Powell, Montalban, L Barrymore, Monroe 90min MGM
Right Man, The = MEGFELELO EMBER, A (1959)
Right of Man, The (UK) = PROPRE DE L'HOMME, LE (1960)
RIGHT OF WAY (1931) d/p F Lloyd c J Seitz w L Young 65min FN
RIGHT TO BE HAPPY, THE (1916) d Julian 5rs

RIGHT TO LIVE, THE (1935) d Keighley fn (Sacred Flame) Somerset Maugham c Hickox 75min WB
Right to Live, The = DROIT A LA VIE, LE (1916)
RIGOLETTO (1946) d Gallone m Verdi w Tito Gobbi 97min
RIKUGUN (1944) d Kinoshita (= Army)
RILEY THE COP (1928) d J Ford c C Clarke w Fazenda, Parrish (uc) 67min Fox
RIMES (1954) d Alexeieff, Georges Violet anim*
RIMPATRIATA, LA (1963) d/co-s Damiani 108min (= The Reunion)
RING, THE (1927) d/co-s Hitchcock co-s Reville 8007ft
Ring-a-Ding Rhythm (US) = IT'S TRAD, DAD! (1962)
RINGER, THE (1952) d Hamilton fn Edgar Wallace w Zetterling, Wolfit 78min r BL
RING OF BRIGHT WATER (1969) co-d/co-s Jack Couffer co-d/w Virginia McKenna p Strick fn Gavin Maxwell *107min
RING OF FEAR (1954) d/co-s J Grant w Mickey Spillane CS* 93min co-pc J Wayne r WB
RING OF FIRE (1961) d/co-p/s Stone c Clothier *91min MGM
RING OF STEEL (1942) d Kanin cy Tracy US Army Office of Emergency Management
RINGS ON HER FINGERS (1942) d Mamoulian p Sperling c Garmes w H Fonda, Tierney 86min Fox
RING-RING BOI (1964) d Kuri anim (= Ring Ring Boy)
Ring Ring Boy = RING-RING BOI (1964)
RINK, THE (1916) d/s/w Chaplin co-c Totheroh w Purviance 2rs Mut
RIO (1939) d Brahm st Negulesco c Mohr w Rathbone, Cummings, V McLaglen 75min U
RIO BRAVO (1959) d/p Hawks co-s Furthman c R Harlan m Tiomkin w J Wayne, Martin, A Dickinson, Brennan *141min r WB
RIO CONCHOS (1964) d G Douglas p Weisbart co-s/fn (Guns of Rio Conchos) Huffaker c Joe Macdonald m Goldsmith w Boone, Whitman, E O'Brien CS* 107min Fox
RIO ESCONDIDO (1947) d/st Fernandez co-c Figueroa w Felix part* 99min
RIO GRANDE (1950) d/co-p J Ford co-p M Cooper c Glennon, 2nd c Stout m V Young w J Wayne, M O'Hara, V McLaglen 105min r Rep
RIO LOBO (1970) d/p Hawks 2nd d Canutt c Clothier w Goldsmith w J Wayne *114min
RIO RITA (1942) d S Sylvan Simon p Berman w B Abbott, Costello 91min r MGM
RIOT (1968) d Kulik p Castle s Poe m Komeda *94min Par
RIOT IN CELL BLOCK II (1954) d D Siegel p Wanger c R Harlan 80min AA
Riot on Pier Six = NEW ORLEANS UNCENSORED (1955)
RIO Y LA MUERTE, EL (1954) d/co-s Buñuel co-s Alcoriza 90min
RIP AND STITCH TAILORS (1919) co-d St Clair s Sennett w Fazenda 2rs
RIPE EARTH (1938) d R Boulting p J Boulting
Ripening Seed (UK) = BLE EN HERBE, LE (1953)
RIP ROARIN' ROBERTS (1924) d Thorpe
RIPTIDE (1934) d/s Goulding c June w Shearer, Montgomery, H Marshall 90min MGM
RIP VAN WINKLE (1905) d Méliès fn Washington Irving 340m (10 parts)
RISATE DI GIOIA (1960) d/co-s Monicelli fn Alberto Moravia co-s Cecchi d'Amico w Magnani, Toto 105min (= The Passionate Thief)
RISE AND FALL OF LEGS DIAMOND, THE (1960) d Boetticher p Sperling c Ballard m Rosenman w Danton 101min r WB
RISE AND SHINE (1941) d Dwan p Hellinger s H Mankiewicz f (My Life and Hard Times) James Thurber c Cronjager co-a R Day w Darnell, G Murphy, Brennan 92min Fox
Rise Of Helga, The (UK) = SUSAN LENOZ (1931)
RISING OF THE MOON, THE (1957) d J Ford s F Nugent ep-fp Lady Gregory c Krasker n Power 81min r WB
Rising Sun Is Shining, The = ASAHI WA KAGAYAKU (1929)
RISING TIME, THE (1933) d Rotha 25min
RISE AMARO (1949) d/co-st/co-s De Santis p De Laurentiis co-st/co-s Lizzani c Martelli w Mangano, Gassman, Vallone 103min (= Bitter Rice)
RISQUES DU METIER, LES (1967) d/co-s Cayatte c Matras m/w Jacques Brel w Riva *105min Gau
RISVEGLIO DI UNA CITTA (1933) d Zampa (sh)
Rite, The = RITEN (1969)
RITEN (1969) d/s Ingmar Bergman c Nykvist w Thulin, Björnstrand 75min TV r SF (= The Rite)
RITMI DI NEW YORK (1938) d Sala (sh)
Ritorno di Don Camillo, Il = RETOUR DE DON CAMILLO, LE (1953)
RITORNO DI RINGO, IL (1965) d/co-s Tessari *96min (= The Return of Ringo)
RITRATTO DI PINA (1960) d Baldi
RITUAL IN TRANSFIGURED TIME (1946) d Deren 16mm 15min
Ritual of Love = A CHACUN SON PARADIS (1956)
RIVA DEI BRUTI, LA (1930) d Camerini fn (Dangerous Paradise) Joseph Conrad
RIVALEN DER LUFT (1934) d Wisbar 2669m UFA

RIVALITE D'AMOUR (1908) *d* Méliès 170m
RIVALITE DE MAX, LE (1913) *d/s/w* Linder Pat
RIVALS, THE (1912) *d/p/w* Sennett *w* Normand ½rl Key
Rival World, The = STRIJD ZONDER EINDEN (1954)
RIVE GAUCHE (1931) *d* A Korda
RIVER, THE (1929) *d* Borzage *w* J Gaynor 7814ft Fox
RIVER, THE (1937) *d/s* Lorentz *co-c* F Crosby, W Van Dyke 31min US Dept of Agriculture
RIVER, THE (1951) *d/co-s* J Renoir *c* C Renoir *co-dec* Lourié *2730m (= *Le Fleuve*)
River, The = POTAMI, TO (1960)
RIVERBEAT (1954) *d* G Green 70min
River Fuefuki, The = FUEFUKI-GAWA (1960)
RIVER OF NO RETURN (1954) *d* Preminger *c* La Shelle *co-a* Wheeler *chor* Cole *m* Mockridge *w* Mitchum, Monroe CS* 91min Fox
RIVER PIRATE, THE (1928) *d* W Howard *c* Andriot *w* V McLaglen 6937ft Fox
RIVER'S EDGE, THE (1957) *d* Dwan *p* Bogeaus *c* Lipstein *w* Milland, Quinn CS* 87min Fox
RIVER'S END (1930) *d* Curtiz *w* Bickford, Pitts 6624ft WB
RIVER'S END (1940) *d* Enright 69min WB
River Solo Flows = BUNGAWAN SOLO (1951)
River Without A Bridge = HASHI NO NAI KAWA (1969)
Riviera – Today's Eden, The (UK) = DU COTE DE LA COTE (1958)
Riviere du Hibou, La (1963) ep in AU COEUR DE LA VIE (1962) *d/s* Enrico *p* Ichac 26min (= *Incident at Owl Creek/An Occurrence at Owl Creek Bridge*)
RIVOLTA DEL GLADIATORI, LA (1958) *d* Cottafavi *w* G Marshall S* 102min (= *The Warrior and the Slave-Girl*)
R N 37 (1934) *d* Leenhardt 830m
Road A Year Long, The = CESTA DUGA GODINA DANA (1957)
ROAD BACK, THE (1937) *d* Whale *fn EM Remarque m* Tiomkin 102min U
ROAD HOUSE (1948) *d* Negulesco *co-a* Wheeler *co-m* Mockridge *w* Lupino, Wilde, Widmark 95min Fox
ROAD OF 100 DAYS (1952) *d* Kershner US Information Service
ROAD SHOW (1941) *d* G Douglas *p* Roach *co-s* Langdon *c* Brodine *w* Menjou 87min *r* UA
ROADS OF DESTINY (1921) *d* F Lloyd *fpl Channing Pollock* and *fst O'Henry* 5600ft *pc* Goldwyn
Road To Corinth, The = ROUTE DE CORINTHE, LA (1967)
Road To Eternity = NINGEN NO JOKEN Part 2 (1960)
Road To Frisco (UK) = THEY DRIVE BY NIGHT (1940)
ROAD TO GLORY, THE (1926) *d/st* Hawks *c* August 5600ft Fox
ROAD TO GLORY, THE (1936) *d* Hawks *p* Zanuck *co-s* Faulkner *c* Toland *w* March, W Baxter, L Barrymore, Ratoff 95min Fox
Road To God = KAMI ENO MICHI (1928)
ROAD TO HAPPINESS, THE (1926) *d* Curtiz
Road To Heaven, The = HIMLASPELET (1942)
ROAD TO HONG KONG, THE (1962) *d/co-s* Panama *p/co-s* M Frank *c* Hildyard *des* Furse *w* B Crosby, Hope, Lamont 91min *pc* Panama, M Frank *r* UA
Road To Hope, The (UK) = CAMMINO DELLA SPERANZA, IL (1950)
Road to Katmandu, The (UK) = CHEMINS DE KHATMANDOU (1969)
Road to Life, The = PUTYOVKA V ZHIZN (1931)
ROAD TO MANDALAY, THE (1926) *d/co-st* Browning *co-st* H Mankiewicz *w* Chaney 6562ft MGM
ROAD TO MOROCCO, THE (1942) *d* D Butler *c* Mellor *m* V Young *w* Hope, B Crosby, Lamour, Quinn, De Carlo 83min Par
ROAD TO RIO (1947) *d* McLeod *c* Laszlo *co-a* Dreier *w* B Crosby, Hope, Lamour 100min Par
ROAD TO ROMANCE, THE (1927) *d John S Robertson fn (Romance) Joseph Conrad* and *Ford Maddox Ford a* Gibbons, R Day *w* Novarro 6544ft MGM
Road to Salina (UK) = SUR LA ROUTE DE SALINA (1970)
ROAD TO SINGAPORE (1940) *d* Schertzinger *c* Mellor *co-a* Dreier *chor* Prinz *m* V Young *w* B Crosby, Lamour, Hope, C Coburn, Quinn 84min Par
ROAD TO UTOPIA (1946) *d Hal Walker c* Lindon *co-a* Dreier *m* Harline *w* Hope, B Crosby, Lamour, Benchley 89min Par
ROAD TO YESTERDAY, THE (1925) *d* De Mille *c* Marley *a* Leisen 9980ft
ROAD TO ZANZIBAR, THE (1941) *d* Schertzinger *c* Tetzlaff *w* B Crosby, Lamour, Hope 92min Par
ROAMIN' HOLIDAY (1937) *d* G Douglas *p* Roach 11min MGM
ROARIN' BRONCS (1926) *d* Thorpe 5rs
ROARING RIDER, THE (1926) *d* Thorpe
ROARING ROAD, THE (1919) *d* Cruze 5rs FPL
Roaring Timber = COME AND GET IT (1936)
ROARING TWENTIES, THE (1939) *d* Walsh *p* Hellinger, Wallis *st* Hellinger *co-s* Wald, Rossen *c* E Haller *w* Cagney, Bogart 106min WB
Roaring Years = ANNI RUGGENTI (1962)
ROAR OF THE DRAGON (1932) *d* W Ruggles *ex-p* Selznick *co-st* M Cooper *c* Cronjager *w* Horton, Pitts 68min RKO
ROBBERY (1967) *d/co-s* P Yates *ex-p* Levine *co-p* S Baker *c* Slocombe *w* S Baker *114min
ROBBERY UNDER ARMS (1957) *d* J Lee *w* Finch *99min JAR
ROBE, THE (1953) *d* Koster *s* P Dunne *fn Lloyd A Douglas c* Shamroy *co-a* Wheeler *m* A Newman *w* Burton, J Simmons, Mature, Boone, Marsh CS* 135min Fox
ROBERTA (1935) *d William A Seiter p* Berman *c* Cronjager *m Jerome Kern w* Astaire, G Rogers, R Scott 85min RKO
ROBERT BENCHLEY IN THE SEX LIFE OF THE POLYP (1928) *d Thomas H Chalmers s/w* Benchley 1rl
ROBERT BENCHLEY IN THE SPELLBINDER (1928) *d Thomas H Chalmers s/w* Benchley 1rl
ROBERT BENCHLEY IN THE TREASURER'S REPORT (1928) *d Thomas H Chalmers s/w* Benchley 1rl
ROBERT KOCH, DER BEKAMPFER DES TODES (1939) *d* Steinhoff *w* Jannings, Krauss 115min Tob
ROBIN AND THE SEVEN HOODS (1964) *d* G Douglas *ex-p* HW Koch *p* Sinatra *as-p/c* Daniels *w* Sinatra, Martin, B Crosby, Robinson, Rush PV* 103min WB
ROBIN HOOD (1922) *d* Dwan *p* Fairbanks Sr *st* Fairbanks Sr (*ps* Elton Thomas) *c* Edeson *cos* Leisen *m* Schertzinger *w* Fairbanks Sr, Berry, Pickford (*uc*) 10680ft *r* UA
Robin Hood and His Merrie Men (UA) = STORY OF ROBIN HOOD AND HIS MERRIE MEN, THE (1952)
ROBIN HOOD JNR (1923) *d* C Brown (*ps* Clarence Bricker) *m* Rapee 4rs
ROBIN HOODLUM (1948) *d* J Hubley *p* Bosustow *co-anim* Cannon anim* 11min Col
ROBIN HOOD OF ELDORADO, THE (1936) *d/co-s* Wellman 86min MGM
ROBINSON (1968) *d* Moorse
ROBINSON, EIN (1940) *d/co-s* Fanck 81min (= *Das Tagebuch Eines Matrosen*)
ROBINSON CRUSOE (1910) *d/s* Blom *fn Daniel Defoe*
ROBINSON CRUSOE (1952) *d/co-s* Buñuel *fn Defoe c* Phillips *85min (= *The Adventures of Robinson Crusoe*)
ROBINSON CRUSOE EN VINGT-CINQ TABLEAUX (1902) *d* Méliès *fn Defoe* 320m (25 parts)
Robinson Crusoeland = ATOLL K (1950)
ROBINSON CRUSOE ON MARS (1964) *d* Haskin *fn Defoe c* Hoch *co-a* Pereira TS* 109min Par
ROCAMBOLE (1947) *d* De Baroncelli 95min
Rocco and His Brothers = ROCCO E I SUOI TRATELLI (1960)
ROCCO E I SUOI FRATELLI (1960) *d/co-s* Visconti *co-s* Cecchi d'Amico, Festa Campanile *c* Rotunno *m* Rota *w* Delon, Girardot, Paxinou, C Cardinale 180min (= *Rocco and His Brothers*)
ROCKABYE (1932) *d* Cukor *m* M Steiner *w* Constance Bennett, McCrea, Lukas, Pidgeon 71min RKO
ROCK-A-BYE BABY (1958) *d/s* Tashlin *p/w* J Lewis *st* P Sturges *co-a* Pereira VV* 107min *r* Par
ROCK ALL NIGHT (1957) *d/p* Corman *c* F Crosby 62min AI
ROCK AROUND THE CLOCK (1956) *d* Sears *p* Katzman 77min Col
ROCKY (1948) *d* Karlson 76min Mon
ROCKY MOUNTAIN (1950) *d* Keighley *c* McCord *m* M Steiner, *w* Flynn 83min WB
RODA TORNET, DET (1914) *d/co-s* Stiller 864m
RODELKAVALIER, DER (1918) *d/w* Lubitsch 1rl (= *The Toboggan Cavalier*)
ROEI NO UTA (1938) *d* Mizoguchi (= *Song of the Camp*)
ROGER-LA-HONTE (1945) *d/s* Cayatte *di* Charles Spaak *w* Casarès 103min
ROGER TOUHY, GANGSTER (1944) *d* Florey *m* Friedhofer *w* V McLaglen, Quinn 65min Fox (= *The Last Gangster*)
ROGOPAG (1962) 125min (= *Laviamoci il cervello*)
ep ILLIBATEZZA *d/s* Rossellini
ep LE NOUVEAU MONDE *d/s* Godard *c* Rabier *m Beethoven* 20min
ep LA RICOTTA *d/st/s* Pasolini *w* Welles 40min
ep IL POLLO RUSPANTE *d/s* Gregoretti
ROGOPAG (1962)
ep ILLIBATEZZA *d/s* Rossellini 125min (= *Laviamoci il Cervello*)
Laviamoci il Cervello: reissue title of ROGOPAG (1962)
ROGUE COP (1954) *d* Rowland *c* J Seitz *a* Gibbons *w* R Taylor, J Leigh, Raft 92min MGM
ROGUES AND ROMANCE (1920) *d/p/st/s/w* G Seitz
ROGUES OF SHERWOOD FOREST (1950) *d* G Douglas *c* Lawton *w* Derek 80min Col
ROGUE SONG, THE (1930) *d/p* L Barrymore *m* Stothart, *Lehar w* Laurel, Hardy *105min MGM
ROGUES REGIMENT (1948) *d/co-st* Florey *co-m* Amfitheatrof *w* D Powell, Price 86min U
ROI DE COEUR, LE (1966) *d/p* De Broca *m* Delerue *w* Brasseur, Brialy, Presle *90min (= *King of Hearts*)
ROI DE LA MER, LE (1918) *d/s* De Baroncelli
ROI DES CHAMPS-ELYSEES, LE (1934) *d Max Nosseck w* Keaton *r* Par (= *The Champ of the Champs-Elysées*)
ROI DES PALACES, LE (1932) *d* Gallone *w* S Simon
ROI DU CIRCLE, LE (1924) *d* Linder, *EE Violet s* Linder *w* Linder, Banky
ROI DU VILLAGE, LE (1964) *d* Gruel anim 90min
ROI ET L'OISEAU, LE (1967) *d* Grimault anim
ROI SANS DIVERTISSEMENT (1963) *d Francois Leterrier c* Badal *w* Vanel S* 85min (= *La Poursuite*)
ROLLENDE RAD, DAS (1934) *d/p* Reiniger anim 1rl
Roller Skate = DANCE MOVIE (1963)
Rolling Sea = BARANDE HAV (1951)
Roly Poly = PRZEKLADANIEL (1968)
ROMA, CITTA APERTA (1945) *d/co-s* Rossellini *co-s* Fellini *w* Magnani, Pagliero 100min (= *Open City*)
ROMA CITTA LIBERA (1946) *d* Pagliero *w* Cortese, De Sica
ROMANA, LA (1954) *d/co-s* Zampa *p* Ponti, De Laurentiis *co-s/fn Alberto Moravia w* Lollobrigida 110min (= *Woman of Rome*)
Roman aus den Burgen, Ein = GEIER-WALLY, DER (1921)
ROMANCE (1930) *d* C Brown *c* Daniels *w* Garbo 76min MGM
ROMANCE (1965) *d* Po.ar anim* 14min
Romance for Trumpet = ROMANCE PRO KRIDLOVKU (1967)
ROMANCE IN FLANDERS, A (1937) *d* Elvey 74min *r* BL
ROMANCE IN THE DARK (1938) *d* Potter *c* Mellor *w* J Barrymore 80min Par
Romance of a Bathing Girl, The = THE GOOD-BYE KISS (1928)
ROMANCE OF A HORSE THIEF (1971) *d* Polonsky *w* Brynner, Wallach *101min
ROMANCE OF HAPPY VALLEY, A (1919) *d/p* Griffith 6rs *co-pc* Griffith
ROMANCE OF ROSY RIDGE, THE (1947) *d* Rowland *p* J Cummings *co-a* Dreier *w* V Johnson, Mitchell, J Leigh 105min MGM
ROMANCE OF THE REDWOODS, A (1917) *d/co-s* De Mille *fn* (*The White Silence*) *Jack London w* Pickford 7rs *r* FPL
ROMANCE OF THE REDWOODS (1939) *d* C Vidor *fn London w* Bickford 61min Col
ROMANCE OF THE SEA, A (1913) *d* Ince *w* Hayakawa
ROMANCE OF TRANSPORTATION IN CANADA, THE (1952) *d* Low, Koenig, *Robert Verrall* anim* 11min NFBC
Romance Of Yushima, The = YUSHIMA NO SHIRAUME (1955)
ROMANCE ON THE HIGH SEAS (1948) *d/co-p* Curtiz *co-s* JJ Epstein *ad* Diamond *w* D Day 99min WB (= *It's Magic*)
ROMANCE PRO KRIDLOVKU (1967) *d* Vavra 94min (= *Romance for Trumpet*)
ROMANCERA MARROQUIN (1936) *d/s* Velo
ROMANCE SENTIMENTALE (1930) *d* Alexandrov *c* Tissé
ROMAN DE MAX, LE (1912) *d/s/w* Linder Pat
ROMAN DE SOEUR LOUISE, LE (1908) *d/s* Feuillade 280m
Roman de Werther, Le (1938) = WERTHER
ROMAN D'UN JEUNE HOMME PAUVRE, LE (1935) *d/s* Gance *w* Fresnay
ROMAN D'UN TRICHEUR, LE (1936) *d/s/fn/w* Guitry 2500m
ROMAN HOLIDAY (1953) *d/p* Wyler *c* Alekan, Planer *co-a* Pereira *m* Auric *w* Peck, A Hepburn 119min Par
ROMANOFF AND JULIET (1961) *d/p/s/fpl* Ustinov *c* Krasker *dec* Trauner *w* Ustinov, Tamiroff *103min U
ROMAN S BASOU (1949) *d/s/a* Trnka *fst Anton Chekov* *400m (= *The Story of a Double Bass*)
ROMAN SCANDALS (1933) *d* Tuttle *p* Goldwyn *co-st* G Kaufman *c* Toland *e* Heisler *a* R Day *w* Cantor, Ball, Darwell 85min *r* UA
Roman Signorina = BELLA DI ROMA, LA (1955)
ROMAN SPRING OF MRS STONE, THE (1961) *d Jose Quintero p* De Rochemont *s* Lambert *fn* T Williams *w* Beatty, V Leigh, Lenya *104min WB
ROMANTICA AVVENTURA, UNA (1940) *d/co-s* Camerini *co-s* Soldati, Castellani *fn Thomas Hardy*
ROMANTIC AGE, THE (1927) *d* Florey *c* Brodine 5267ft Col
ROMANTIC AGE, THE (1948) *d* Greville *w* Zetterling 86min
ROMANTICI A VENEZIA (1947) *d/s* Emmer, *Enrico Gras* 308m (= *Romantics in Venice*)
Romantics in Venice = ROMANTICI A VENEZIA (1947)
ROMANTIKI (1941) *d/co-s* Donskoi 106min (= *Children of the Soviet Artic*)
ROMANZA, IL (1913) *d* Martoglio
ROMANZE IN MOLL (1943) *d/co-s* Käutner 2728m Tob
ROMANZO DI UN' EPOCA (1941) *d/s* Emmer, *Enrico Gras, Tatiana Grauding* 314m
ROMA ORE UNDICI (1952) *d/co-s* De Santis *p* Graetz *co-s* Zavattini, Petri *c* Martelli *w* Vallone, Bosè, Girotti
ROME ADVENTURE (1962) *d/p/s* Daves *c* Lawton *m* M Steiner *w* A Dickinson, Pleshette *119min WB (= *Lovers Must Learn*)
ROMEO AND JULIET (1916) *d J Gordon Edwards fpl Shakespeare w* Bara 7rs
ROMEO AND JULIET (1936) *d* Cukor *p* Thalberg *fpl Shakespeare c* Daniels *sp eff* Vorkopitch *co-a* Gibbons *co-cos* Messel *m* Stothart *w* L Howard,

Shearer, J Barrymore, Oliver, Rathbone 124min MGM
Romeo and Juliet (1954) = GIULETTA E ROMEO
Romeo and Juliet (UK) = GIULIETTA E ROMEO (1964)
ROMEO AND JULIET (1965) *d* Czinner *w* *Fonteyn, Nureyev* *125min
ROMEO AND JULIET (1968) *d/co-s* Zeffirelli *fpl Shakespeare* *c* De Santis *m* Rota *n* Olivier *152min Par
Romeo and Juliet in the Snow (UK) = ROMEO UND JULIA IM SCHNEE (1920)
ROMEO, JULIE A TMA (1960) *d/co-s* J Weiss 95min (= *Romeo, Juliet and Darkness/Sweet Light in a Dark Room*)
Romeo, Juliet and Darkness (UK) = ROMEO, JULIE A TAM (1960)
ROMEO UND JULIA IM SCHNEE (1920) *d/co-s* Lubitsch *c* Sparkuhl UFA (= *Romeo and Juliet in the Snow*)
Rome-Paris-Rome (US) = SIGNORI IN CARROZZA! (1951)
Rommel – Desert Fox (1951) = DESERT FOX
ROMOLA (1925) *d* H King *fn George Eliot* *w* D & L Gish, Colman 12974ft Metro
RONDA ESPANOLA (1951) *d* Vajda *
RONDE, LA (1950) *d/co-s* Ophuls *fpl* (*Der Reigen*) *Arthur Shnitzler* *c* Matras *dec* D'Eaubonne *m* *Oscar Straus* *w* Walbrook, Reggiani, Signoret, S Simon, Gélin, Barrault, Philipe, I Miranda 97min
ROSA DI GRANADA, LA (1916) *d/s* Ghione
ROSALIE (1966) *d* Borowczyk *fst* (*Rosalie Prudent*) *Guy de Maupassant* 15min
ROSALIE (1937) *d* WS Van Dyke *w* Oliver 118min MGM
ROSA PER TUTTI, UNA (1965) *d* Rossi *w* Cardinale, Manfredi, Tamiroff *109min (= *Rose For Everyone/Every Man's Woman*)
ROSE (1936) *d* Rouleau
Rose and The Gold, The = DEL ROSA .... AL AMARILLO (1963)
Rose and the Mignonette = ROSE ET LE RESEDA, LA (1945)
ROSEANNA MCCOY (1949) *d* Reis *p* Goldwyn *c* Garmes *w* F Granger, Bickford 100min RKO
ROSE BERND (1957) *d* Staudte *w* Vallone, Maria Schell 2673m
ROSE DE LA MER, LA (1946) *d* De Baroncelli
ROSE ET LANDRY (1963) *d* Roach 16mm 28min
ROSE ET LE RADIS, LE (1955) *d/m* Gruel anim
ROSE ET LE RESEDA, LA (1945) *d* Michel *fpm Louis Aragon* *m* Auric *n* Barrault 12min (= *Rose and the Mignonette*)
Rose For Everyone, A (UK) = UNA ROSA PER TUTTI (1961)
ROSE FRANCE (1918) *d* L'Herbier
ROSE-MARIE (1936) *d* WS Van Dyke *co-s* Goodrich, Hackett *c* Daniels *w* Jeanette Macdonald, Eddy, J Stewart, Niven 110min MGM
ROSE MARIE (1954) *d/p* LeRoy *co-a* Gibbons *2nd chor* Berkeley (*uc*) *m* Stothart *w* Keel, A Blyth CS* 115min MGM
ROSEMARY'S BABY (1968) *d/s* Polanski *p* Castle *fn Ira Levin* *c* Fraker *des* Sylbert *m* Komeda *w* M Farrow, Cassavetes, R Gordon Cook *134min Par
ROSEN FUR BETTINA (1956) *d* Pabst *m* *Tchaikovsky, Ravel* (= *Licht in der Finsternis/Ballerina*)
RONDE, LA (1964) *d* Vadim *s* Anouilh *rm* 1950 *c* Decaë *w* Karina, Brialy, J Fonda, Catherine Spaak *110min
Roof, The (1956) = IL TETTO
Roof Garden, The (US) = TERRAZA, LA (1963)
Rooftree = TVARBALK (1966)
ROOKIE OF THE YEAR (1955) *d* J Ford *w* Miles, J Wayne 29min TV
ROOKIES (1927) *d* S Wood *co-a* Gibbons 6640ft MGM
Room, The = HEYA (1967)
ROOM AT THE TOP (1958) *d* Clayton *co-p* James Woolf, Attenborough *c* F Francis *w* Laurence Harvey, Signoret, Wolfit 117min *r* BL
ROOM FOR ONE MORE (1952) *d* Taurog *p* Blanke *c* Burks *m* M Steiner *w* C Grant 98min WB
ROOM SERVICE (1938) *d William A Seiter* *p* Berman *w* H, G, C Marx, Ann Miller, Ball 78min RKO
Room 23 = BEDROOM BLUNDER, A (1917)
Room With Thick Walls = KABE ATSUKI HEYA (1953)
Roots, The = RAICES (1954)
ROOTS OF HEAVEN (1958) *d* J Huston *p* Zanuck *s/fn* Gary *c* Morris *m* M Arnold *w* Flynn, J Howard, Welles, Lukas, CS* 125min Fox
ROOTY TOOT TOOT (1952) *d* J Hubley *ex-p* Bosustow anim* 8min UPA *r* Col
ROPE (1948) *d/co-p* Hitchcock *w* J Stewart, F Granger *81min WB
ROPED (1919) *d* J Ford *w* Carey 6rs U
ROPE OF SAND (1949) *d* Dieterle *p* Wallis *ad* Paxton *c* C Lang *m* Waxman *w* Rains, Lorre, Lancaster, Henreid 104min Par
ROQUEVILLARD, LES (1922) *d/s* Duvivier *fn Henry Bordeaux*
ROSA BLANCA, LA (1954) *d/co-st/co-s* Fernandez *c* Figueroa
ROSEN FUR DEN STAATSANWALT (1959) *d/st* Staudte 98min

ROSENKAVALIER, DER (1925) *d/s* Wiene *fmpl Richard Strauss* 6047ft Par
ROSENKAVALIER, DER (1961) *d* Czinner *fmpl R Strauss* *192min
ROSENMONTAG (1930) *d* Steinhoff *co-dec* Rohrig 83min
Rosen Pa Tistelon = HAUSGAMARNA (1915)
Rosentopf Case, The (UK) = FALL ROSENTOPF, DER (1918)
ROSE OF CIMARRON (1952) *d* Keller *c* Struss *72min Fox
ROSE OF THE RANCHO, THE (1914) *d/s* De Mille *w* Darwell *pc* Lasky
Rose Of The Sea = UMI NO BARA (1945)
ROSE OF WASHINGTON SQUARE (1939) *d* Ratoff *p/s* N Johnson *c* Freund *w* Power, Faye, Jolson 86min Fox
Rose On His Arm, The = TAIYO TO BARA (1956)
ROSE O' THE SEA (1922) *d* Niblo *p* Mayer 7rs WB (Ass FN)
ROSE ROSSE PER ANGELICA (1966) *d/co-s* Steno *fst Alexander Dumas* CS*
ROSE ROUGE, LA (1950) *d* Pagliero *w* Arnoul
ROSE SCARLATTE (1940) *d/w* De Sica
ROSES OF PICARDY (1927) *d/co-p* Elvey *co-p* Saville 8500ft Gau
ROSE TATTOO, THE (1955) *d* Daniel Mann *p* Wallis *ad* Kanter *s/fpl* T Williams *c* Howe *co-a* Pereira *m* North *w* Lancaster, Magnani VV 117min Par
ROSIER DE MADAME HUSSON, LE (1932) *d* Bernard Deschamps *fst* *Maupassant* *w* Fernandel, Rosay 66min
ROSIER DE MADAME HUSSON, LE (1950) *d Jean Boyer* *fst* *Maupassant* *m* Misraki *w* Bourvil 84min (= *Virtuous Isidore*)
Rosina, The Foundling = ROZINA SEBRANEC (1945)
ROSITA (1923) *d* Lubitsch *fpl* (*Don Caesar de Bazan*) *Adolphe D'Ennery* *c* Rosher *w* Pickford 85min *pc* Pickford *r* UA
ROSSETTO, IL (1960) *d/co-s* Damiani *co-s* Zavattini *m* Fusco *w* Germi 95min (= *Red Lips*)
Rossignol de L'Empreur de Chine, Le (1951): French version of CISARUV SLAVIK (1949)
ROSSIYA NIKOLAYA II I LEV TOLSTOY (1928) *d/s/e* Shub 1700m (= *The Russia of Nicholas II and Lev Tolstoi*)
ROTAGG (1946) *d* Mattsson (= *Bad Eggs*)
ROTAIE (1929) *d* Camerini
ROTATION (1949) *d/s* Staudte 2375m Defa
ROTE, DIE (1962) *d* Käutner 101min (= *The Redhead*)
ROTHENBURGER, DIE (1918) *d/co-s/w* Lupu-Pick 1664m
ROTI (1942) *d/p* Mehboob
ROTMANAD (1971) *d/co-s* Halldoff *104min SF
ROTTEN TO THE CORE (1965) *d* J Boulting *p/co-s* R Boulting *c* F Young PV 88min BL
ROTTERDAM-EUROPOORT (1966) *d* Ivens *cy* Marker *n* Montand *20min
ROUE, LA (1922) *d/s* Gance *co-c* Burel, Brun *m* Honegger Pat
ROUE, LA (1956) *d* *Andre Haguet* *s* Gance *rm* 1922 S 100min (= *Wheels of Fate*)
ROUE TOURNE, LA (1942, *uf*) *d* Y Allégret
ROUGE EST MIS, LE (1956) *d/s* Grangier *w* Gabin, Mocky 115min Gau
ROUGE ET LE NOIR, LE (1954) *d* Autant-Lara *s/di* Aurenohe, Bost *fn Stendhal* *c* Kelber *w* Darrieux, Philipe *146min (= *Scarlet and Black*)
ROUGH AND THE SMOOTH, THE (1959) *d* Siodmak *fn Robin Maugham* *des* Adam *w* Tiller, Bendix, Wolfit 96min (= *Portrait of a Sinner*)
Rough Company = VIOLENT MAN, THE (1955)
ROUGH HOUSE, THE (1917) *d/w* Arbuckle *w* Keaton 2rs
ROUGHLY SPEAKING (1945) *d* Curtiz *p* Blanke *c* J Walker *e* Weisbart *m* M Steiner *w* R Russell 117min WB
ROUGHNECK, THE (1925) *d* Conway *w* G O'Brien 7619ft Fox
ROUGH RIDERS (1927) *d* V Fleming *c* Howe *w* Astor, G Bancroft 12,071ft Par
ROUGH RIDIN' (1924) *d/w* Thorpe *c* E Haller 4650ft
ROUGH SEA AT DOVER (1895) *p* Paul 80ft
ROUGHSHOD (1949) *d* Robson *s* Mainwaring (*ps* Homes), H Butler *c* Biroc *w* Grahame 88min RKO
ROUGH SHOOT (1952) *d* Parrish *p* Stross *w* McCrea 88min *r* UA (= *Shoot First*)
ROUGH TOUGHS AND ROOF TOPS (1917) *d/s/w* Semon 1rl
ROULI-ROULANT (1966) *d/co-c/e/cy* Jutra *co-c* Brault 14min
ROUNDERS, THE (1914) *d/s/w* Chaplin *w* Arbuckle 1rl Key (= *Oh, What a Night/Two of a Kind/Revelry*)
ROUNDERS, THE (1965) *d/s* B Kennedy *w* H Fonda, G Ford PV* 85min MGM
Round-up, The (UK) = SZEGENYLEGENYEK (1965)
Roustabout, The = PROPERTY MAN, THE (1914)
ROUSTABOUT (1964) *d John Rich* *p* Wallis *c* Ballard *w* Presley, Stanwyck S* 101min Par
Route aux Diamants, La = PILLARDS, LES (1965)
ROUTE DE CORINTHE, LA (1967) *d/w* Chabrol *c* Rabier *w* Seberg, Ronet, Marquand *90min (= *The Road to Corinth*)
Route des Diamants, La = PILLARDS, LES (1965)

ROUTE EST BELLE, LA (1930) *d* Florey
ROUTE IMPERIALE, LA (1935) *d* L'Herbier
ROUTE NAPOLEON, LA (1953) *d* Delannoy *m* Misraki *w* Fresnay 100min
Rover, The (UK) = AVVENTURIERO, L' (1967)
ROVESNIK VEKA (1960) *d* Samsonov *96min (= *Man of the Century*)
ROWER (1957, *uf*) *d* Polanski (= *The Bicycle*)
ROXIE HART (1942) *d* Wellman *p/s* N Johnson *c* Shamroy *m* A Newman *w* G Rogers, Menjou 75min Fox
ROYAL AFRICAN RIFLES, THE (1953) *d* *Lesley Selander* *w* L Hayward *76min AA *r* Mon
ROYAL BALLET, THE (1959) *d* Czinner *132min
ROYAL BED (1930) *d/w* L Sherman *w* Astor 75min RKO
ROYAL CAVALCADE (1935) *d* Brenon
ROYAL ENGINEER'S BALLOON, THE (1900) *p* Paul 60ft
ROYAL FAMILY OF BROADWAY, THE (1931) *d* Cukor, *Cyril Gardner* *co-s* H Mankiewicz *fn* (*The Royal Family*) G Kaufman, *Edna Ferber* *c* Folsey *e* Dmytryk *w* March 79min Par
Royal Hunt = KUNGAJAKT (1944)
ROYAL HUNT OF THE SUN (1968) *d* I Lerner *co-p/s* Yordan *fpl Peter Shaffer* *a* Lourié *w* Plummer FS* 121min JAR
ROYAL REVIEW OF SCOTTISH VOLUNTEERS, THE (1906) *p* Paul 250ft
ROYAL RIDER, THE (1929) *d* H Brown *c* McCord 6063ft FN
ROYAL SCANDAL, A (1945) *d* Preminger *supn/p* Lubitsch *co-fpl* (*Czarina*) Biro *rm* FORBIDDEN PARADISE (1924) *c* AC Miller *co-a* Wheeler *m* A Newman *w* Bankhead, C Coburn, A Baxter, Price 94min Fox (= *Czarina*)
ROYAL WEDDING (1951) *d* Donen *p* Freed *st/s* A Lerner *co-a* Gibbons *co-chor* Donen, Astaire *w* Astaire, J Powell, Lawford *93min MGM (= *Wedding Bells*)
ROYAUME DES FEES, LE (1903) *d* Méliès *fpl* (*La Biche au Bois*) *Goignard Brothers* 350m (30 parts)
ROZBIGIMI ZABAWE (1958) *d* Polanski (sh)
ROZMARING (1938) *d* Vajda 2550m
ROZMARNE LETO (1908) *d/co-s* Menzel *75min (= *Indian Summer/Capricious Summer*)
ROZINA SEBRANEL (1945) *d/co-s* Vavra (= *Rosina, The Foundling*)
ROZSTANIE (1961) *d* Has 90min (= *Partings*)
ROZTOMILY CLOVEK (1941) *d* Frič
ROZUM A CIT (1962) *d/s* Brdecka (= *Reason and Emotion*)
R P M (1970) *d/p* Kramer *w* Quinn *92min *r* Col
RUBAIYAT OF OMAR KHAYYAM, THE (1922) *d* *Ferdinando Earle* *w* Novarro
RUBE AND THE BARON, THE (1913) *d/p/w* Sennett *w* Normand ½rl Key
RUBEZAHLS HOCHZEIT (1916) *d/s/w* Wegener *cr* Reiniger
RUBY GENTRY (1952) *d/co-p* K Vidor *c* R Harlen *w* J Jones, Heston, Malden 80min *co-pc* K Vidor *r* Fox
RUDDIGORE (1967) *d* Batchelor *p* Halas, Batchelor *f* *operetta Gilbert and Sullivan* anim* 54min
RUDYARD KIPLING'S JUNGLE BOOK (1942) *d* Z Korda, De Toth (2nd) *p* A Korda *fst Kipling* *co-c* Garmes *dec* V Korda *m* Rozsa *w* Sabu *105min (= *The Jungle Book*)
RUE DE L'ESTRAPADE (1953) *d/co-s* Becker *dec* D'Eaubonne *co-m* Van Parys *w* Gélin, Vernon 95min (= *Francoise Steps Out*)
RUE DES PRAIRIES (1959) *d/co-s* De La Patellière *w* Gabin 87min
RUE DES VERTUS (1939, *uf*) *d* Carné *s/di* J Prévert *dec* Traunder *m* Jaubert
RUGGLES OF RED GAP (1923) *d/p* Cruze *rm* 1918 *w* Horton 8rs FPL
RUGGLES OF RED GAP (1935) *d* McCarey *rm* 1923 *e* Dmytryk *w* Laughton, C Ruggles, Pitts 91min Par
RUISSEAU, LE (1938) *d* Autant-Lara *w* Rosay, M Simon 100min
RUKA (1964) *d/st/a* Trnka *19min (= *The Hand*)
RULERS OF THE SEA (1939) *d/p* F Lloyd *c* Stout, Sparkuhl *co-a* Dreier *w* Fairbanks Jr, Lockwood, G Bancroft, Ladd 96min Par
Rules of the Game = LA REGLE DU JEU (1939)
RULING PASSION (1916) *d* Brenon 5rs Fox
RUMBA (1939–41) *d* McLaren 2½min
RUMBLE ON THE DOCKS (1956) *d* Sears *p* Katzman 82min Col
Rumiantsev Case, The = DELO RUMIANTSEVA (1956)
RUNAWAY BRIDE (1930) *d* Crisp *w* Astor 69min RKO
RUNAWAY GIRLS (1928) *d* Sandrich 5842ft Col
RUNAWAY PRINCESS, THE (1929) *d* Asquith 7053ft MGM (= *Princess Priscilla's Fortnight*)
RUNAWAY ROMANY (1918) *d* *George Lederer* *st/s/w* Davies
RUN FOR COVER (1955) *d* N Ray *c* Fapp *co-a* Pereira *w* Cagney, Lindfors, Derek, Hersholt, Borgnine VV* 93min Par
RUN FOR THE SUN (1956) *d/co-s* R Boulting *co-s* D Nichols *c* La Shelle *w* Widmark S* 99min *r* UA
RUN FOR YOUR MONEY, A (1949) *d* Frend *p* Balcon *c* Slocombe *w* Guinness 85min JAR
RUNNER, THE (1962) *d/s* Owen *cy WH Auden* 11min

RUNNING AWAY BACKWARDS (1964) d A King 16mm 60min (= Coming of Age In Ibiza)
RUNNING, JUMPING AND STANDING STILL FILM (1959) d/co-c/co-e/m Lester p/co-c/co-e/w Sellers 11min
RUNNING MAN, THE (1963) d/p C Reed c Krasker m Alwyn w Laurence Harvey, Remick PV* 103min Col
RUNNING TARGET (1956) d Marvin R Weinstein s/c C Hall 83min r UA (= My Brother Down There)
RUNNING WILD (1927) d La Cava w Fields 6368ft Par
RUN OF THE ARROW (1957) d/p/s Fuller c Biroc m V Young w Steiger, Meeker, Keith, Montiel, A Dickinson S* 85min RKO
RUN SILENT, RUN DEEP (1958) d Wise p H Hecht c R Harlan m Waxman w Gable, Lancaster 93min r UA
Run With The Devil (UK) = VIA MARGUTTA (1959)
RUOTA DEL VIZIO, LA (1920) d/s Genina
Rupimono = 813 (1923)
RUPTURE (1961) co-d/co-s/w Etaix co-d/co-s Jean-Claude Carrière 11min (= The Break)
RUPTURE, LA (1970) d/s Chabrol c Rabier w Cassel *124min
RURAL THIRD DEGREE A (1913) u Sennett w Normand ½rl Kev
RUSCELLO DI RIPASOTTILE, IL (1941) d Rossellini (sh)
RUSH HOUR (1941) d Asquith 6min MOI
RUSHIN' BALLET (1937) d G Douglas p Roach 972ft MGM
Russian Miracle, The (UK) = RUSSICHE WUNDER, DAS (1963)
Russian Question, The = RUSSKII VOPROS (1948)
RUSSIANS ARE COMING, THE RUSSIANS ARE COMING, THE (1966) d/p Jewison c Biroc a Boyle w Saint, Keith PV* 126min r UA
Russian Souvenir = RUSSKII SOUVENIR (1957)
Russia of Nicholas II and Lev Tolstoi, The = ROSSIYA NIKOLAYA II I LEV TOLSTOY (1928)
RUSSICHE WUNDER, DAS (1963) I d/s A and A Thorndike 110min Defa (= The Russian Miracle)
RUSSICHE WUNDER, DAS (1963) II d A and A Thorndike 105min Defa
RUSSKII SUVENIR (1960) d Alexandrev * (= The Russian Souvenir)
RUSSKII VOPROS (1948) d/s Romm fpl Constantin Simonov m Khatchaturian 90min (= The Russian Question)
RUSTLE OF SILK, THE (1923) d/p Brenon 7rs FPL
RUSTLERS, THE (1919) d J Ford 2rs U
RUSTLERS ROUNDUP, THE (1933) d Henry MacRae w Mix 60min U
RUTHLESS (1948) d Ulmer c Glennon w Greenstreet, L Hayward, Burr 105min EL
RUUSUJEN AIKA (1969) co-d/p/s/c/e Jarva co-d Titta Karakorpi 106min (= Time Of Roses)
RUY BLAS (1947) d Pierre Billon ad/di Cocteau fn Victor Hugo w Darrieux, Marais 104min
RUZENA NASKOVA (1960) d/co-s Frič
RYAN'S DAUGHTER (1970) d Lean co-2nd d Frend st/s Bolt c F Young m Jarre w Mitchum, T Howard, J Mills PV70* 206min MGM
RYNOX (1931) d M Powell 48min
RYOJU (1961) d Goshe (= Hunting Rifle)
RYTHMETIC (1956) d McLaren, Evelyn Lambert *8min NFBC
RYTTARE I BLATT (1959) d Mattsson S* 111min (= Rider in Blue)
RYSOPIS (1964) d/p/s/e/a/w Skolimowski 76min
RYURI NO KISHI (1956) d/s Shinde

SAADIA (1953) d/p/s Lewin c Challis w Wilde, M Ferrer, M Simon *76min MGM
SAAKAS GONINGUMI d Naruse
SABISHII RANBOMONO (1927) d Gosho (= The Lonely Roughneck)
SABISHIKI MURA (1924) d Kinugasa (= Lonely Village)
SABLES (1927) d Kirsanov
SABOTAGE (1936) d Hitchcock co-p Balcon s Charles Bennett, Reville fn (The Secret Agent) Joseph Conrad di Ian Hay e Frend w S Sidney 77min r JAR (= The Woman Alone)
SABOTEUR (1942) d/st Hitchcock co-p F Lloyd w R Cummings 109min U
SABOTEUR-CODE NAME MORITURI, THE (1965) d Wicki p A Rosenberg s Taradash c C Hall m Goldsmith w Brando, Brynner, T Howard CS* 115min Fox
SABOTEUR DU VAL DE LOIRE, LE (1956) d/cy Demy 26min Pat
SABRA (1934) d A Ford
SABRA (1970) d/co-s De La Patellière w Tamiroff 100min
Sabre and the Arrow (UK) = LAST OF THE COMANCHES (1952)
SABRINA (1954) d/p/co-s B Wilder co-s Lehman c C Lang co-a Pereira m Hollander w Bogart, A Hepburn, Holden, Dalio 114min Par (= Sabrina Fair)
Sabrina Fair (UK) = SABRINA (1954)
SACCO DI ROMA E CLEMENTO VII, IL (1920) d/co-s Guazzoni

SACCO IN PLYPAC (1961) d Olmi
SACHA GUITRY (1965) d De Givray TV
SACKCLOTH AND SCARLET (1925) d/p H King co-s Furthman 7rs FPL
SACRED FLAME, THE (1929) d A Mayo fn Somerset Maugham 7rs Vit
SADDLE CYCLONE, THE (1926) d Thorpe
SADDLE MATES (1928) d Thorpe 5rs
SADDLE THE WIND (1958) d Parrish s Serling c Folsey w Cassavetes, Crisp, R Taylor CS* 84min MGM
SADDLE TRAMP (1950) d Fregonese w McCrea 77min U
Sad Idiot = KANASHIKI HAKUCHI (1924)
SADIE MCKEE (1934) d C Brown w Tone, J Crawford, Tamiroff 90min MGM
SADIE THOMPSON (1928) d/s Walsh fst (Rain) Somerset Maugham co-c Barnes w L Barrymore, Swanson, Walsh 8250ft pc Swanson r UA
Sadist, The (UK) = TRAFRACKEN (1966)
SADO-NO TAMAGO (1966) d Kuri anim 10min (= The Eggs)
SAD SACK, THE (1957) d G Marshall p Wallis c Griggs co-a Pereira w J Lewis, D Wayne, Lorre VV 95min Par
Sad Song Of The Defeated = HAIZAN NO UTA WA KANASHI (1922)
Sad Story Of A Barmaid = JOKYU AISHI (1930)
SAEFANGST I NORDGRONLAND, EN d B Henning Jensen e A Henning Jensen
SAETTA, PRINCIPE PER UN GIORNO (1925) d Camerini
SAFARI (1956) d T Young co-c Moore w J Leigh, Mature CS* 92min r Col
SAFARI YA GARI (1961) d/c A and D Maysles
SAFECRACKER, THE (1957) d/w Milland S 96min r MGM
SAFEGUARDING MILITARY INFORMATION (1943) w G Rogers 16mm 1rl
SAFE IN HELL (1931) d Wellman 75min FN
SAFETY CURTAIN, THE (1918) d Franklin w N Talmadge 6rs Gau
SAFETY IN NUMBERS (1938) d St Clair c C Clarke 59min Fox
SAFETY LAST (1923) d Newmeyer w H Lloyd 87min Pat
SAFO (1964) d Alcoriza
SAGA OF ANATAHAN, THE (1953) d/p/s/c/n Von Sternberg 92min (= Anatahan)
SAGA OF HEMP BROWN, THE (1958) d Richard Carlson c Lathrop S* 80min U
Saga Of The Great Buddha = DAIBUTSU KAIGEN (1952)
SAHARA (1943) d/co-s Z Korda co-s Lawson f incident in screenplay of TRINIADSTAT (1937) c Maté m Rozsa w Bogart, Duryea, Lawford 97min
SAHARA HARE (1955) d Freleng anim* 7min WB
SAIDA A ENLEVE MANNEKEN-PISS (1913) d Machin 145m
SAIGON (1959) p/c A King
SAIKAKU ICHIDAI ONNA (1952) d Mizoguchi w Mifune 15rs (= The Life of O-Haru)
SAILOR AND THE DEVIL, THE (1967) d R Williams, Errol Le Cain 7min
SAILOR BE GOOD (1933) d Cruze 68min RKO
SAILOR BEWARE (1951) d Hal Walker p Wallis co-s Rackin w Martin, J Lewis, (Dean) 108min Par
SAILOR FROM GIBRALTAR, THE (1967) d/co-s T Richardson co-s Isherwood fn Duras c Coutard w Moreau, Welles, V Redgrave 91min r UA
SAILOR-MADE MAN, A (1921) d Newmeyer p/co-st Roach w H Lloyd c 4000ft
Sailor of the King = SINGLEHANDED (1951)
SAILORS, BEWARE! (1927) d Fred Guiol w Laurel, Hardy Pat
SAILORS DO CARE (1944) d/co-s L Gilbert
SAILOR'S HOLIDAY (1929) d Newmeyer c AC Miller 59min Pat
SAILOR'S HOLIDAY (1944) d William Berke c Guffey w Winters 60min Col
SAILOR'S LADY (1940) d Dwan w D Andrews 66min Fox
SAILOR'S LUCK (1933) d Walsh c AC Miller 64min Fox
SAILOR'S SWEETHEART, A (1927) d Bacon w Fazenda 5480ft WB
Saint and Her Fool, The = HEILIGE UND IHR NARR, DIE (1928)
ST. BENNY THE DIP (1951) d Ulmer w Bartholomew 79min
SAINT JOAN (1957) d/p Preminger s Greene fpl George Bernard Shaw c Périnal des Furse cr Bass w Seberg, Widmark, Walbrook, Gielgud, (Hemmings) 110min r UA
ST. LOUIS BLUES (1939) d Walsh w Lamour, Nolan 87min Par
SAINT LOUIS KID (1934) d Enright co-s S Miller w Cagney 67min WB
ST. MARTIN'S LANE (1938) d Tim Whelan p Pommer co-e Hamer w Laughton, V Leigh, Harrison 86min co-pc Pommer, Laughton (= Sidewalks of London)
SAINTS AND SINNERS (1949) d/p/co-s L Arliss 85min BL
SAINT STRIKES BACK, THE (1939) d J Farrow fn (Angels of Doom) Leslie Charteris w G Sanders 67min RKO
SAINT-TROPEZ BLUES (1960) d/s Moussy w Chabrol *95min

ST VALENTINE'S DAY MASSACRE, THE (1967) d/p Corman c Krasner w Segal, Meeker PV* 100min Fox
SAIT-ON JAMAIS? (1957) d/s Vadim w Thirard m MJQ w Marquand, Hossein, Arnoul CS* 90min (= When the Devil Drives/No Sun in Venice)
SAKURU ONDO (1934) d Gosho
SALAIRE DE LA PEUR, LE (1953) d/co-s Couzot c Thirard m Auric w Montand, Vanel 155min
SALAUDS VONT EN ENFER, LES (1955) d/s Hossein w Hossein, Vlady, Reggiani 91min
SALAIRE DU PECHE, LE (1956) d/co-s De La Patellière c Alekan w Darrieux, Moreau 110min
SALAVAT YULAYEV (1941) d Protazanov 2098m
SALKA VALKA (1953) d Mattsson s Lindstrom c Nykvist
SALESMAN (1969) d/c A and D Maysles 16mm 90min
SALLY AND SAINT ANNE (1952) d Maté c Classberg w Blyth, McIntyre 90min
SALLY BISHOP (1923) d Elvey 8000ft
SALLY IN OUR ALLEY (1927) d W Lang p Cohn 5892ft Col
SALLY IN OUR ALLEY (1931) d Elvey 78min
SALLY, IRENE, AND MARY (1925) d/p/s Goulding co-a Gibbons w Constance Bennett, J Crawford 5400ft MGM
SALLY, IRENE AND MARY (1938) d William A Seiter w G Lee Fox
SALLY OF THE SAWDUST (1925) d Griffith co-c Bitzer w Fields 10rs r UA
SALLY OF THE SUBWAY (1932) d/st/s/di G Seitz c Cronjager 63min
SALOME (1918) d I Gordon Edwards w Bara 8rs
SALOME (1922) d Charles Bryant fpl Oscar Wilde w Nazimova 5595ft pc Nazimova
SALOME (1953) d Dieterle p Adler c C Lang w Laughton, S Granger, Hayworth *103min Col
SALOME AND DELILAH (1963) d Warhol 16mm si 30min
SALOME, WHERE SHE DANCED (1945) d Charles Lamont p Wanger co-c Mohr w De Carlo * U
SALON DORA GREEN (1933) d Galeen 78min
SALON MEXICO (1948) d/st/s Fernandez c Figueroa 85min
Salt for Svanetia = SOL SVANETII (1950)
SALT OF THE EARTH (1953) d Biberman s M Wilson 94min
SALTO MORTALE (1931) d Dupont w Sten, Walbrook 2738m
SALTY O'ROURKE (1945) d Walsh c Sparkuhl co-a Dreier w Ladd 100min Par
SALUDOS AMIGOS (1942) p Disney 43min
SALUTE (1929) d J Ford c August w G O'Brien, (D Butler, J Wayne) 7610ft Fox
SALUTE JOHN CITIZEN d Elvey 97min
SALUTE TO FRANCE (1944) co-d/co-s J Renoir co-d Kanin co-s P Dunne, Meredith 'etc' w Meredith (all work on film uc) 20min Office of War Information
SALUT LES CUBAINS (1969) d/c Varda 29min Pat (= Hello Cubans)
SALVAGE (1921) d H King 6rs
SALVATION HUNTERS, THE (1925) d/p/s/e Von Sternberg 5930ft r UA
SALVATION NELL (1931) d/pc Cruze 84min
SALVATORE GIULIANO (1962) d Rosi co-s Cecchi D'Amico c Di Venanzo m Piccioni 107min
SALVIAMO, LA MONTAGNA MUORE (1952) d Nelli sh
SALZBURG PILGRIMAGE (1957) d Czinner CS* 28min
SAMIDARE SOSHI (1924) d Mizoguchi Nik (= May Rain and Silk Paper)
SAMMA NO AJI (1962) d/co-s Ozu *115min Sho (= An Autumn Afternoon/The Widower/The Taste of Mackerel)
SAMMY GOING SOUTH (1963) d Mackendrick w Robinson CS* 128min BL (= A Boy Ten Feet Tall)
SAMOURI, LE (1967) d/s Melville c Decaë w Delon *104min (= The Samurai)
SAMSON (1936) d M Tourneur
SAMSON (1961) d/co-s Wajda FS 105min
SAMSON AND DELILAH (1949) d/p De Mille, f Judges 13–16 c Barnes co-a Dreier m V Young w Lamarr, Mature, G Sanders *131min Par
Samson And The Seven Miracles Of The World (US) = MACISTE ALLA CORTE DEL GRAN KHAN (1961)
SAMSON UND DALILA (1923) d Curtiz UFA
SAMURAI (1965) d Kuri anim 7min
Samurai, The (UK) = SAMOURAI, LE (1967)
SAN ANTONIO (1945) d D Butler, Walsh (uc) co-st/co-s Burnett c Glennon m M Steiner chor Prinz w Flynn, A Smith 108min WB
SANBYAKU ROKUJUGO-YA (1948) d Ichikawa 2 parts (= 365 Nights)
SANCTUARY (1961) d T Richardson s Poe fns (Sanctuary and Requiem For a Nun) Faulkner m North w Remick, Montand CS 90min Fox
SAND! (1919) d/s Lambert Hillyer c August w/pc W Hart
SAN DEMETRIO, LONDON (1943) d/co-s Frend p Balcon as-p/co-s Hamer co-c Slocombe 105min
SANDERS OF THE RIVER (1935) d Z Korda fn E Wallace co-s Biro co-c Périnal e Crichton dec V Korda w Paul Robeson 96min
SANDESAYA (1960) d Peries 120min (= The Message)

SAND PEBBLES, THE (1966) d/p Wise c Joe Macdonald m Goldsmith w McQueen, Attenborough PV* 155min pc Wise, McQueen r Fox

SANDPIPER, THE (1965) d Minnelli s Trumbo, M Wilson c Krasner w Saint, E Taylor, Burton PV* 117min MGM

SANDS OF DEE, THE (1911) d Griffith fpm Charles Kingsley w Pickford, Marsh 1rl Bio

Sandra (US) = VAGHE STELLE DELL'ORSA (1965)

SANDS OF IWO-JIMA (1949) d Dwan co-s J Grant m V Young w J Wayne 108min Rep

SANDS OF THE KALAHARI (1965) d/co-p/s Endfield ex-p Levine co-p/w S Baker PV* 119min Par

SAN FRANCESCO, IL POVERELLO D'ASSISI (1911) d/s Guazzoni w Ghione

SAN FRANCISCO (1936) d/co-p WS Van Dyke co-p Emerson s Loos co-di Von Stroheim co-songs Freed, Kaper a Gibbons w Tracy, Gable, Jeanette Macdonald 115min MGM

SAN FRANCISCO (1945) d W Van Dyke e Meyers

SAN FRANCISCO STORY, THE (1952) d Parrish c J Seitz m Friedhofer w McCrea, De Carlo 80min WB

SANG A LA TETE, LE (1956) d Grangier fn (Le Fils Cardinand) Georges Simenon w Gabin 83min

SANGAREE (1953) d Edward Ludwig co-c Lindon co-a Pereira 3D* 94min Par

SANG DES BETES, LE (1949) d/s Franju cy Painlevé c Fradetal m Kosma

SANG D'UN POETE, LE (1930) d/s/e/n Cocteau p Vicomte de Noailles c Périnal dec D'Eaubonne m Auric 55min (= The Blood of a Poet)

SANGE FRIA, A (1940) d Daniel Tinayre p/st Saslavsky

SAN GENNARO (1947) d/s Emmer, Enrico Gras

SANGEN OM DEN ELDRODA BLOMMAN (1919) d/co-s Stiller co-s Molander 2084m (= Dans les Remous/ Song of the Scarlet Flower)

SANGEN OM DEN ELDRODA BLOMMAN (1956) d Molander s Lindström w Kulle, Jacobsson, Bjork S* 102min SF

SANG ET LUMIERE (1953) d Rouquier co-di Audiard w Gélin *99min

SANJURO (1962) d/co-s Kurosawa w Mifune, Nakadai S 96min pc Kurosawa r Toho

SANJU-SANGENDO TOSHIYA MONOGATAR (1945) d Naruse

SAN MICHELE AVEVA UN GALLO (1971) d/s P and V Taviani fst Tolstoi 90min RAI

SAN MINIATO, LUGLIO 1944 (1954) d P and V Taviani co-s Orsini sh

SAN QUENTIN (1937) d Bacon co-s S Miller c Hickox w Bogart, Sheridan 70min WB

SAN QUENTIN (1946) d G Douglas w Burr 66min RKO

SANS FAMILLE (1934) d M Allégret

SANS FAMILLE (1958) d Michel w Brasseur *100min

Sanshiro at Ginza = GINZA SANSHIRO (1950)

Sansho The Bailiff = SANSHO DAYU (1954)

SANSHO DAYU (1954) d Mizoguchi c Miyagawa 119min Dai (= Sansho The Bailiff)

SANS LAISSER D'ADRESSE (1950) d/co-ad/di Le Chanois m Kosma w Carette 90min

SANS LENDEMAIN (1939) d/co-s Ophuls c Schuftan dec Lourié w Feuillère 82min

SANTA (1943) d Foster w Montalban 94min

SANTA CLAUS (1898) d G Smith 74ft

SANTA FE (1951) d Pichel p H Brown c Lawton w R Scott, Pichel *89min Col

SANTA FE TRAIL (1940) d Curtiz p J Warner, Wallis c Polito w Flynn, De Havilland, Reagan, Heflin 110min WB

SANTA NOTTE (1947) d/c Bava sh

SANT HANDER INTE HAR (1950) d Ingmar Bergman c Fischer w Kjellin 68min SF (= High Tension/This Can't Happen Here)

SANTIAGO (1956) d G Douglas co-s/fn Rackin c J Seitz w Ladd, Nolan *73min WB (= The Gun Runner)

SANTO GUERREIRO CONTRA DRAGAO DA MALDADE, O (1969) d/co-p/s/a Rocha *95min (= Antonio Das Mortes)

SANTUARIO (1952) d Barreto p Cavalcanti sh

SAO PAULO EN FESTA (1954, uf) d Barreto sh

SAP, THE (1929) d A Mayo w Horton 7363ft WB

SAPHEAD, THE (1920) d Winchell Smith w Keaton 5rs Metro

SAPPHIRE (1959) d Dearden *92min JAR

SAPPHO (1934) d/s Perret fn Alphonse Daudet

SAPS AT SEA (1940) d G Douglas p Roach co-st/co-s Langdon w Laurel, Hardy, Turpin 57min r UA

SARABAND FOR DEAD LOVERS (1948) d Dearden, Michael Relph co-s Mackendrick s Slocombe m Rawsthorne w Rosay, S Granger, Greenwood *

SARACEN BLADE, THE (1954) d Castle p Katzman w Montalban *77min Col

Saragossa Manuscript, The = REKOPIS ZNALEZIONY W SARAGOSSIE (1964)

SARA LAR SIG FOLKVETT (1937) d Molander SF

SARAH LAWRENCE (1940) d W Van Dyke 15min

SARATOGA (1937) d Conway as-p Emerson co-st/co-s Loos c June a Gibbons w Gable, Harlow, L Barrymore, Pidgeon 92min MGM

SARATOGA TRUNK (1946) d S Wood p Wallis c E Haller m M Steiner w G Cooper, Ingrid Bergman, Flora Robson 135min WB

SARVTID (1941) d/s/c/e Sucksdorff 9min SF

SASKATCHEWAN (1954) d Walsh p A Rosenberg c J Seitz w Ladd, Winters *87min U (= O'Rourke of the Royal Mounted)

SASOM I EN SPEGEL (1961) d/s Ingmar Bergman c Nykvist m Bach w H Andersson, Von Sydow, Björnstrand 91min SF (= Through a Glass Darkly)

SATANA LIKUYUSHCHII (1917) d/s Protazanov w Mozhukhin 3683m (= Satan Triumphant)

SATANAS (1920) d Murnau supn/e Wiene c Freund w Veidt

SATAN BUG, THE (1964) d/p J Sturges co-s Clavell c Surtees m Goldsmith w D Andrews, A Francis PV* 114min r UA

SATAN EN PRISON (1907) d Mèliés 98m

SATAN MET A LADY (1936) d Dieterle fn Hammett c Edeson w B Davis 71min WB

SATAN NEVER SLEEPS (1962) d/p/co-s McCarey c Morris w Holden, C Webb CS* 127min Fox

Satan Triumphant = SATANA LIKUYUSHCHII (1917)

SATASHI GA KOWARERU TOKI (1967) d Imai (= When the Cookie Crumbles)

SA TETE (1929) d/st/s J Epstein

SATIN WOMAN, THE (1927) d/st/s W Lang c June 7000ft

SATSUEIJI ROMANSU-RENAI ANNAI (1932) d Gosho (= A Studio romance)

SATSUJINKYO SHIDAI (1966) d/p/c/dec Kuri anim* 10min (= Au Fou!)

SATSUJINSHA NO KAO (1950) d Kinugasa (= The Face Of A Murderer)

SATURDAY AFTERNOON (1926) d Harry Edwards w Langdon 3rs pc Sennett r Pat

SATURDAY ISLAND (1951) d Heisler w Darnell *102min (= Island of Desire)

SATURDAY NIGHT (1922) d De Mille c Struss 9rs FPL

SATURDAY NIGHT AND SUNDAY MORNING (1960) d Reisz p Saltzman, T Richardson s/fn Alan Sillitoe c F Francis e Holt w Finney 89min BL

SATURDAY NIGHT KID, THE (1929) d A Edward Sutherland co-st G Abbott t J Mankiewicz w Bow, Arthur, Oliver, Harlow 6015ft Par

SATURDAY'S CHILDREN (1929) d La Cava ppl Maxwell Anderson c J Seitz 6742ft FN

SATURDAY'S CHILDREN (1940) d V Sherman p J Warner, H Wallis as-p Blanke co-s JJ Epstein fpl Maxwell Anderson c Howe w Garfield, Rains 101min WB

SATURDAY'S HERO (1951) d D Miller s Buchman c Garmes w D Reed, Derek, A Ray (as Da Re) 111min Col

Saturday Train, the = TRENO DEL SABATO, IL (1963)

SATURNIN OU LE BON ALLUMEUR (1921) d/s Feuillade w Clair, Florey 800m

Satyricon = FELLINI SATYRICON (1969)

SAUDADE (1936) d/s Velo 2rs

Saumon Atlantique, Le = A PROPOS D'UNE RIVIERE (1955)

Saucepan Journey, The = KASTRULLRESAN (1950)

SAUSALITO (1967) d Warhol 16mm *30min (segment of Four Stars)

SAUVETAGE EN RIVIERE (1896) d Méliès 40m (2 parts)

SAVAGE, THE (1926) d Newmeyer c Folsey 6275ft FN

SAVAGE, THE (1952) d G Marshall s Boehm c J Seitz co-a Pereira w Heston *95min Par

SAVAGE EYE, THE (1959) d/p/s/e Strick, Maddow, Meyers tech adviser I Lermer co-c Wexler m Rosenman 66min

SAVAGE FRONTIER (1953) d Keller 57min Rep

SAVAGE INNOCENTS, THE (1960) d/s N Ray co-c Tonti w Quinn, O'Toole(uc) TR* 110min r JAR/Par (Italian version: Ombre Bianche)

Savage Pampas = PAMPA SALVAJE (1966)

Savage Princess = AAN (1952)

SAVED BY THE BELLE (1939) d/w C Chase 2 rs Col

SAVING MABEL'S DAD (1913) d Sennett w Normand ½rl Key

SAVINGS OF BILL BLEWITT, THE (1937) d Watt p Cavalcanti 25min GPO

SAWDUST (1923) d Conway 4940ft U

Sawdust and Tinsel = GYCKLARNAS AFTON (1953)

SAWMILL, THE (1921) d/s Semon, Taurog w Semon, Hardy 2rs Vit

SAY IT AGAIN (1926) d La Cava c Cronjager 7443ft FPL

SAY IT IN FRENCH (1938) d/p Stone c Milner song Carmichael w Milland 70min Par

SAY IT WITH SABLES (1928) d/co-st Capra p Cohn c J Walker 7rs Col

SAY IT WITH SONGS (1929) d Bacon co-st Zanuck c Garmes w Jolson 10rs WB

SAYONARA (1957) d Logan p Goetz s Osborn c Garmes m Waxman chor Prinz w Brando, Garner, Montalban 147min WB

SAYONARA KONNICHIWA (1959) d Ichikawa w Kyo S* Dai (= Goodbye, Good Day)

SAY ONE FOR ME (1959) d/p/co-s(uc) Tashlin co-a Wheeler w B Crosby, D Reynolds, R Wagner CS* 119min pc B Crosby r Fox

SBAGLIO DI ESSERE VIVO, LO (1945) d Bragaglia w De Sica, I Miranda

SBANDATI, GLI (1955) d/co-st/co-s Maselli c Di Venanzo m Fusco w Bosè, I Miranda, Mocky 90min

SBARCO DI ANZIO, LO (1968) d Dmytryk p De Laurentiis c Rotunno w Mitchum, A Kennedy, Ryan PV* 117min r Col (= The Battle for Anzio/Anzio)

SCALDINO, LO (1919) d/s Genina fpl Luigi Pirandello

SCALP HUNTERS, THE (1968) d Pollack m E Bernstein w Lancaster, Winters PV* 103min r UA

SCAMPOLO (1928) d Genina

SCANDAL (1917) d Charles Giblyn w C Talmadge 6rs

SCANDAL AT SCOURIE (1953) d Negulesco co-a Gibbons w Garson, Pidgeon, Moorehead *90min MGM

SCANDALE, LE (1936) d L'Herbier

SCANDALE, LE (1966) d Chabrol c Rabier w Perkins, Ronet TS* 105min r U (= The Champagne Murders)

SCANDAL IN PARIS, A (1946) d Sirk m Eisler 100min r UA

Scandal In Sorrento (UK) = PANE, AMORE, E . . . (1955)

SCANDAL SHEET (1931) d Cromwell w K Francis, G Bancroft 77min Par

SCANDAL SHEET (1952) d Karlson co-s Poe fn (Dark Page) Fuller c Guffey w B Crawford, D Reed, Derek 82min Col (= Dark Page)

SCAPEGOAT, THE (1959) d/s Hamer p Balcon ad Vidal fn Daphne du Maurier m Kaper w Guinness, B Davis 92min MGM

SCAPOLO, LO (1955) d/st/co-s Pietrangeli c Di Venanzo w Sordi 105min (= Alberto il Conquistatore)

SCARAMOUCHE (1923) d/p Ingram s Goldbeck fn Rafael Sabatini c J Seitz w Novarro, J Tourneur 10rs MGM

SCARAMOUCHE (1952) d G Sidney fn Sabatini co-a Gibbons m V Young w S Granger, J Leigh, M Ferrer, Parker *115min MGM

SCARECROW, THE (1920) d/s Keaton, Cline w Keaton 2rs Metro

SCARED STIFF (1953) d G Marshall p Wallis c Laszlo co-a Pereira w Marvin, J Lewis, L Scott, C Miranda, B Crosby(uc), Hope(uc), Malone 108min Par

SCARF, THE (1951) d/s Dupont c Planer w Emlyn Williams 93min r UA

Scarface = SCARFACE, SHAME OF THE NATION (1932)

SCARFACE MOB, THE (1959) d Karlson fn 'The Untouchables' Elliot Ness, Oscar Fraley w Stack 104min WB

SCARFACE, SHAME OF THE NATION (1932) d/co-p Hawks co-p H Hughes st B Hecht ad/di S Miller, Mahin, Burnett c Garmes, O'Connell w Muni, Karloff, Raft 90min r UA

Scarlet and Black (UK) = ROUGE ET LE NOIR, LE (1954)

SCARLET COAT, THE (1955) d J Sturges co-a Gibbons w Wilde, G Sanders, A Francis CS* 101min MGM

SCARLET DAWN (1932) d Dieterle c E Haller w Fairbanks Jr 58min WB

SCARLET DAYS (1919) d/p Griffith co-c Bitzer w Barthelmess 7rs

SCARLET DROP, THE (1918) d/st Ford c B Reynolds w Carey 5rs U

SCARLET EMPRESS, THE (1934) d Von Sternberg f diary Catherine the Great c Glennon co-dec Dreier m Tchaikovsky, Mendelssohn w Dietrich, (Darwell) 13rs Par

SCARLET HOUR, THE (1956) d/p Curtiz co-st/co-s Tashlin c Lindon co-a Pereira m Leith Stevens VV 95min Par

SCARLET LETTER, THE (1926) d Sjöström fn Nathaniel Hawthorne w L Gish 88min MGM

SCARLET PAGES (1930) d Enright 65min WB

SCARLET PIMPERNEL, THE (1935) d Harold Young p A Korda fst Baroness Orczy co-s Biro w L Howard, Oberon

Scarlet Pimpernel, The = ELUSIVE PIMPERNEL, THE (1950)

SCARLET SHADOW, THE (1919) d Leonard 6000ft U

SCARLET STREET (1945) d/p F Lang ex-p Wanger s D Nichols fn/fpl (La Chienne) Georges de la Fouchardière, Mouézy-Eon c Krasner a Golitzen w Robinson, J Bennett, Duryea 102min r U

SCARLET THREAD (1951) d L Gilbert w Laurence Harvey 81min

Scarlet Woman, The = FEMME ECARLATE (1969)

SCARS OF DRACULA, THE (1970) d R Baker *96min

SCARY TIME, A (1960) d/co-s/c S Clarke 16min

Scattered Clouds = MIDARE-GUMO (1967)

SCAVENGERS, THE (1959) d Cromwell 78min

SCEICCO BIANCO, LO (1952) d/co-st/co-s/dec Fellini co-st Antonioni m Rota w Sordi, Masina 85min (= The White Sheik)

SCELERATS, LES (1950) d/s/w Hossein dec Evein, Saulnier, Morgan 95min

SCENE OF THE CRIME (1949) d Rowland s Schnee co-a Gibbons m Previn w V Johnson, McIntire, Dahl 94min MGM

SCENES DE LA VIE CRUELLE (1912-14) d René Leprince p Zecca (series) Pat

SCENES DE LA VIE DE CAFE (1962) d Reichenbach

SCENES FROM COUNTRY LIFE (1917) d Blackton fsts Paula Blackton (6 films: The Collie Market; Diary of a Puppy; The Fairy Godfather; The Little Strategist; Satin and Calico; A Spring Idyll) Vit

SCENES FROM UNDER CHILDHOOD (1967-70) d Brakhage (4 sections, 2-4 si) 16mm *143min

410

Scent of Incense, The = KOGE (1964)
SCENT OF MYSTERY (1960) *d* Cardiff *w* Lukas TR70* Smell-O-Vision 125min
SCHAATSENRIJDEN (1929) *d/s/c/e* Ivens 200m
SCHACHNOVELLE (1960) *d/co-s* G Oswald *fst* Stefan Zweig *w* Bloom, Jurgens 104min (= *Three Moves to Freedom*)
SCHATTEN WERDEN LANGER, DIE (1962) *d/co-s* Vajda 90min (= *Girls in the Shadows*)
SCHATZ, DER (1923) *d/s* Pabst *co-dec* Rohrig *w* Krauss 69min
SCHATZ DER AZTEKEN, DER (1964) *d* Siodmak 102min
SCHEMA D'UNE IDENTIFICATION (1946) *d* Resnais *w* Philipe 16mm si sh
SCHERBEN (1921) *d* Lupu-Pick *s* C Mayer, Lupu-Pick *w* Krauss 1356m
SCHERZO (1932) *d/s/c* Cortez sh
SCHERZO (1939) *d* McLaren anim* 2¼min
SCHIAVE ESISTONO ANCORA, LE (1963) *d* Quilici, Robert Malenotti *co-c* Tonti *90min (= *Slave Trade In The World Today*)
SCHICKSAL AUS ZWEITER HAND (1949) *d/s* Staudte 105min
SCHIFF DER VERLORENE MENSCHEN, DAS (1929) *d/s* M Tourneur *w* Modot, Dietrich 2659m
SCHIFF IN NOT (1936) *d* Ruttmann 385m
SCHINDERHANNES (1928) *d/co-s* Bernhardt *fpl* Zuckmayer *c* Krampf *dec* Richter 2703m
SCHINDERHANNES, DER (1958) *d* Käutner *fpl* Zuckmayer *w* Jurgens, Maximilian Schell 115min
SCHLOSS, DAS (1969) *d/s* Rudolf Noelte *p/w* Maximilian Schell *fn* Kafka *90min
SCHLOSS VÖGELOD (1921) *d* Murnau *p* Pommer *s* Mayer *c* Wagner, Laszlo *a* Warm Dec (= *The Haunted Castle*)
SCHLUSSAKKORD (1936) *d/co-s* Sirk *w* Dagover 101min
School = SZKOLA (1958)
SCHOOL AT RINCON SANTO (1963) *d* Blue
School for Cats = KOCICI SKOLA (1963)
SCHOOL FOR HUSBANDS (1937) *d* Marton *w* Harrison 72min *r* JAR
SCHOOL FOR SCANDAL (1930) *d* Elvey 77min
School for Scandal = SHKOLA ZLOSLOVIYA (1952)
SCHOOL FOR SECRETS (1946) *d/s/co-p* Ustinov *co-p* Del Giudice *c* Hildyard *m* Rawsthorne *w* Attenborough, R Richardson 108min
SCHOOL FOR SCOUNDRELS (1960) *d* Hamer *fns* (*Gamesmanship*; *Oneupmanship*; *Lifemanship*) Stephen Potter 94min WB
SCHOOL HOUSE SCANDAL, A (1919) *d* Cline 2rs Fox
School Of Freedom = JIYU GAKKU (1951)
School, The Beginning of Life = SKOLA ZAKLAD ZIVOTA (1938)
SCHOT IS TE BOORD, HET (1952) *d/p* Van Den Horst 18min (= *Shoot the Nets*)
SCHPOUNTZ, LE (1938) *d/p/st/s* Pagnol *w* Fernandel
SCHRAFFT'S COMMERCIAL (1969) *d* Warhol *1min
SCHUETZ MACHINE (1967) *d/s* C and R Eames *c* C Eames *7¼min
SCHUHPALAST PINKUS (1916) *d/w* Lubitsch 85min (= *Schuh-Salon Pinkus/Shoestore Pinkus*)
Schuh-Salon Pinkus = SCHUPALAST PINKUS (1916)
SCHULD DER LAVINIA MORLAND, DIE (1920) *d/p/co-s* May *co-dec* Leni 2662m
SCHULFREUND, DER (1960) *d/p* Siodmak 98min (= *Mein Schulfreund*)
SCHUT, DER (1964) *d* Siodmak 120min
SCHWABEN MADLE (1919) *d* Lubitsch 3rs (= *The Schwab Maiden/The Girl From Swabia*)
The Schwab Maiden (UK) SCHWABEN MADLE (1919)
SCHWARZE CHAUFFEUR, DER (1917) *d/p/s* May 5 rs
SCHWARZE FRACHT (1956, *uf*) *d* Riefenstahl * (= *Black Cargo*)
SCHWARZE MORITZ (1916) *d/w* Lubitsch 1rl (= *Black Moritz*)
SCHWARZER KIES (1961) *d* Käutner 319m UFA
SCHWEIGEN IM WALDE, DAS (1929) *d/w* Dieterle *p* Pasternak 2408m (= *The Silence of the Forest*)
SCIENCE AGAINST CANCER (1948) *d* Low
SCIPIO L'AFRICANO (1937) *d* Gallone *m* Pizzette *w* I Miranda
SCIUSCIA (1946) *d/co-s* de Sica *st/co-s* Zavattini 90min (= *Shoeshine*)
SCOFFER, THE (1921) *d/p* Dwan 7rs *r* FN
SCONOSCIUTO DI SAN MARINO, LO (1948) *d* Cottafavi, M Waszinsky *w* Magnani, De Sica
SCOPERTA DELL' AFRICA (c.1966) *d* Quilici RAI
SCORPIO LETTERS, THE (1966) *d/p* Thorpe *c* Fredericks *97min MGM
SCORPIO RISING (1964) *d/s/c/e* Anger 16mm *31min
SCOTLAND YARD (1930) *d* W Howard *w* J Bennett, Crisp 65min Fox
SCOTLAND YARD (1941) *d* Foster 67min Fox
SCOTT OF THE ANTARCTIC (1948) *d* Frend *p* Balcon *s* Ivor Montagu *co-c* Cardiff, Unsworth *co-e* Holt(*uc*) *m* Vaughan Williams *w* J Mills *111min
SCOUNDREL, THE (1935) *d/p/st/s* B Hecht, MacArthur *as-d/c* Garmes *m* Antheil *w* Coward 76min Par
Scout's Exploits, The = PODVIG RAZVEDCHIKA (1947)
Scowls Of Paris = GRIMACI PARIZHI (1924)

SCRAM (1932) *d* Raymond McCarey *p* Roach *w* Laurel, Hardy 2rs (sd) *r* MGM
SCRAMBLED EGGS (1939) *d* Avery (*ps* Lovy) *p* Lantz anim* 1rl U
SCRAPPER, THE (1917) *d/s/w* J Ford *c* B Reynolds 2rs U
SCRATCH MY BACK (1920) *d* Sidney Olcott *w* W Rogers 6rs
SCREAMING MIMI (1958) *d* G Oswald *p* H Brown *c* Guffey *w* Ekberg, G Lee 79min Col
SCREEN SNAPSHOTS (1922–23) *co-p* Cohn *co-s* Jack Cohn series of 26 Pat
SCREEN TEST 1 (1965) *d* Warhol *s* Ronald Tavel 16mm 70min
SCREEN TEST 2 (1965) *d* Warhol *s* Ronald Tavel 16mm 70min
SCREWBALL SQUIRREL (1944) *d* Avery anim* 7min MGM
SCREWY TRUANT, THE (1945) *d* Avery anim* 7min MGM
SCROOGE (1935) *d* Henry Edwards *supn/e* Brahm 67min
SCROOGE (1970) *d* Neame *fst* (*A Christmas Carol*) Dickens *c* Morris *w* Finney, Guinness, Evans PV* 118min
SCUOLA DEI TIMIDI, LA (1942) *d* Bragaglia
SCUOLA D'EROI (1913) *d/s* Guazzoni
SCUOLA ELEMENTARE (1954) *d/st/co-s* Lattuada *co-s* Charles Spaak
SCUSI, FACCIAMO L'AMORE? (1968) *d/co-s* Caprioli *w* Feuillère TC* 95min (= *Listen, Let's Make Love*)
SCUSI, LEI E'FAVOREVOLE O CONTRARIO? (1967) *d* Sordi *w* Sordi, Ekberg, B Andersson, Mangano, Masina
SEA CHASE, THE (1955) *d/p* J Farrow *c* Clothier *w* J Wayne, Turner CS* 117min WB
SEA DEVILS (1953) *d* Walsh *s* B Chase *fn* (*Les Travailleurs de la Mer*) Victor Hugo *w* De Carlo, Hudson, Forbes *90min RKO
SEA FURY (1958) *d/co-s* Endfield *w* V McLaglen 97min JAR
SEA GOD, THE (1930) *d/s* G Abbott *c* Stout 90min Par
Sea Gull, The = WOMAN OF THE SEA, A (1926)
SEA GULL, THE (1968) *d/p* Lumet *fpl* Chekhov *w* V Redgrave, Mason, Signoret 141min *pc* Lumet *r* WB
SEAGULLS OVER SORRENTO (1954) *d/co-s* R Boulting *p* J Boulting *c* G Taylor *chor* Gene Kelly *w* Gene Kelly 92min MGM (= *Crest Of The Wave*)
SEA HAWK, THE (1924) *d* F Lloyd 12rs FN
SEA HAWK, THE (1940) *d* Curtiz *p* J Warner, Wallis *as-p* Blanke *s* H Koch, S Miller *c* Polito *co-sp eff* Haskin *m* Korngold *w* Flynn, Rains, Crisp, Roland 127min WB
SEA HORSES (1926) *d/p* Dwan *c* Howe *w* W Powell, G Bancroft 6565ft FPL
SEA ISLAND (1948) *d* James Algar *p* Disney *27min *r* RKO
SEAL OF SILENCE, THE (1913) *d* Ince
Seamstress, The = SVADLENKA (1936)
SEANCE ON A WET AFTERNOON (1964) *d/co-p/s* Forbes *co-p/w* Attenborough *m* Barry 111min JAR
SEA NIMPHS, THE (1914) *d* Arbuckle *p* Sennett *w* Arbuckle, Normand 2rs Key
Sea Of Fireworks = UNI NO HANABI (1951)
SEA OF GRASS, THE (1946) *d* Kazan *p* Berman *co-a* Gibbons *m* Stothart *w* Tracy, K Hepburn, M Douglas, R Walker, Carey 131min MGM
SEA OF SAND (1958) *d* G Green *w* Attenborough 97min JAR
SEA PIRATE, THE (1967) *d* Rowland *83min *r* Par
SEARCH, THE (1948) *d* Zinnemann *w* Clift, Corey 105min MGM
SEARCHERS, THE (1956) *d* J Ford *co-p* M Cooper *s* F Nugent *c* Hoch *m* M Steiner *w* J Wayne, J Hunter, Miles, N Wood, (Marsh) VV* 119min *r* WB
SEARCH FOR BEAUTY (1934) *d* Erle C Kenton *w* Lupino, Sheridan (as Clara Lou Sheridan) 78min Par
SEARCH FOR BRIDEY MURPHY, THE (1956) *d/s* Noel Langley *w* L Hayward, T Wright VV 84min Par
SEARCH FOR OIL, THE (1953) *d/s* Haanstra *p* Elton 39min
SEARCHING EYE, THE (1963) *d* Bass
Searching Heart, The (UK) = COEUR D'AMOUR EPRIS (1952)
Searching The Hearts Of Students = CESTA DO HUBIN STUDAKOVY DUSE (1939)
SEARCHING WIND, THE (1946) *d* Dieterle *p* Wallis *s/fpl* Hellman *c* Garmes *m* V Young *w* R Young, S Sidney 108min Par
SEARCH INTO DARKNESS (1962) *d* William Jersey *p* W Van Dyke *19min
SEAS BENEATH (1931) *d* J Ford *s* D Nichols *c* August *w* G O'Brien 99min Fox
SEA SHALL NOT HAVE THEM, THE (1954) *d/co-s* L Gilbert *w* M Redgrave, Bogarde 92min
Seashell And The Clergyman, The (UK) = COQUILLE ET LE CLERGYMAN, LA (1926)
Season For Love, The (UK) = MORTE-SAISON DES AMOURS, LA (1961)
Seasons Of Our Love = STAGIONI DEL NOSTRA AMORE, LE (1966)
SEA SQUAW, THE (1925) *d* Harry Edwards *w* Langdon 2rs *pc* Sennett *r* Pat
Sea Vultures = HAVSGAMARNA (1915)

Sea Wall, The = DIGA SUL PACIFICO, LA (1958)
SEA WOLF, THE (1930) *d* Santell *fn* Jack London 87min Fox
SEA WOLF, THE (1941) *d* Curtiz *p* J Warner, Wallis *as-p* Blanke *s* Rossen *fn* Jack London *c* Polito *m* Korngold *w* Robinson, Lupino, Garfield 100min WB
SEBASTIAN (1967) *d* David Greene *co-p* M Powell *m* Goldsmith *w* Bogarde, Palmer, Gielgud PV* 100min
Second Breath, The (UK) = DEUXIEME SOUFFLE, LE (1965)
SECOND CHANCE (1953) *d* Maté *co-s* Boehm *w* Mitchum, Darnell, Palance 3D* 82min RKO
SECOND CHORUS (1941) *d* Potter *c* Sparkuhl *w* Astaire, Goddard, Meredith 83min Par
SECOND FIDDLE (1957) *d* Elvey 73min *r* BL
SECOND FLOOR MYSTERY (1930) *d* Del Ruth *w* L Young 58min WB
SECOND GREATEST SEX, THE (1955) *d* G Marshall *w* Crain CS* 87min U
SECOND-HAND LOVE (1923) *d* Wellman 5rs Fox
SECOND HONEYMOON (1937) *d* W Lang *p* Zanuck *w* L Young, Power, Trevor 79min Fox
SECOND HUNDRED YEARS, THE (1927) *d* Fred Guiol *p* Roach *w* Laurel, Hardy
Second Lawyer = DRUHA SMENA (1940)
SECONDS (1966) *d* Frankenheimer *c* Howe *cr* Bass *m* Goldsmith *w* Hudson 106min
SECOND TIME AROUND, THE (1961) *d* V Sherman *w* D Reynolds, Ritter CS* 99min Fox
SECOND WIFE (1930) *d* Russell Mack *co-s* Glennon 67min RKO
Second Wind (US) = DEUXIEME SOUFFLE, LE (1965)
SECRET, THE (1955) *d/s* Endfield *80min
SECRET AGENT (1936) *d* Hitchcock *co-p* Balcon *s* Charles Bennett, Reville *fst* (*Ashenden*) Somerset Maugham *di* Ian Hay *e* Frend *w* Carroll, Gielgud, Carroll, Palmer, R Young, M Redgrave 83min Gau
SECRET AGENT OF JAPAN (1942) *d* Pichel *c* Andriot 72min Fox
Secret aLLies = RAPE OF CZECHOSLOVAKIA (1939)
SECRET BEYOND THE DOOR (1948) *d/p* F Lang *ex-p* Wanger *c* Cortez *m* Rozsa *w* J Bennett, M Redgrave 98min *r* U
SECRET BRIDE, THE (1934) *d* Dieterle *w* Stanwyck 76min WB
SECRET CEREMONY (1968) *d* Losey *m* Richard Rodney Bennett *des* R Macdonald *w* E Taylor, M Farrow, Mitchum *109min *r* JAR
SECRET DE SŒUR ANGELE, LE (1955) *d/st/ad/co-di* Joannon *a* D'Eaubonne *w* Vallone 97min
SECRET DU LONESTAR, LE (1920) *d* De Baroncelli
SECRET DE MAXERLING, LE (1949) *d/co-s* Delannoy *w* Marais 90min
Secret Four, The (UK) = KANSAS CITY CONFIDENTIAL (1953)
SECRET FURY, THE (1950) *d* M Ferrer *w* Colbert, Ryan 86min RKO
SECRET GARDEN, THE (1949) *d* F Wilcox *p* C Brown *s* Ardray *c* June *co-a* Gibbons *m* Kaper *w* M O'Brien, H Marshall, Lancaster part *92min MGM
SECRET HEART, THE (1946) *d* Leonard *c* Folsey *a* Gibbons *w* Colbert, Pidgeon, Allyson, L Barrymore 97min MGM
Secret Interlude (UK) = VIEW FROM POMPEY'S HEAD, THE (1955)
SECRET INVASION, THE (1964) *d* Corman *c* Arling *m* Friedhofer *w* S Granger, Vallone, Rooney PV* 95min *r* UA (= *Dubious Patroits*)
SECRET LIFE OF AN AMERICAN WIFE, THE (1968) *d/p/s* Axelrod *c* Shamroy *m* Billy May *w* Matthau 92min *r* Fox
SECRET LIFE OF WALTER MITTY, THE (1947) *d* McLeod *p* Goldwyn *fst* James Thurber *c* Garmes *m* Rakson *w* Kaye, V Mayo, Karloff 105min RKO
SECRET LIVES (1938) *d* Greville
SECRET MAN, THE (1917) *d* J Ford *c* B Reynolds *w* Carey 5rs U
Secret Mission = SEKRETNAYA MISSIYA (1950)
Secret Of Abee X = GEHEIMNIS DES ABEE X, DAS (1927)
Secret Of A Wife = TSUMA NO HIMITSU (1924)
SECRET OF CONVICT LAKE, THE (1951) *d* M Gordon *co-a* Wheeler *w* G Ford, Tierney, E Barrymore 83min Fox
SECRET OF MY SUCCESS, THE (1965) *d/s* Stone *e* Virginia Stone *w* S Jones *pc* A and V Stone PV* 112min MGM
SECRET OF SANTA VITTORIA, THE (1969) *d/p* Kramer *co-s* Maddow *c* Rotunno *m* Gold *w* Quinn, Magnani, Kruger, Cortese PV* 140min *r* UA
Secret of Stamboul, The = SPY IN WHITE, THE (1936)
SECRET OF THE AIR, THE (1914) *d* Brenon
SECRET OF THE CHATEAU (1934) *d* Thorpe 67min U
SECRET OF THE INCAS (1954) *d* Jerry Hopper *c* Lindon *w* R Young, Heston 101min Par
Secret of the Sahara = STEEL LADY, THE (1953)
Secret of the Three Sword Points, The = SEGRETO DELLE TRE PUNTE, IL (1952)
SECRET PEOPLE (1952) *d/co-s* T Dickinson *p* Balcon *w* A Hepburn, Cortese, Reggiani 96min

SECRET PARTNER, THE (1961) d Dearden w S Granger 91min MGM
SECRET PLACE, THE (1956) d C Donner 98min JAR
SECRETS (1924) d Borzage c Gandie w N Talmadge 8363ft FN
SECRETS (1933) d Borzage c June m A Newman w Pickford, L Howard 10min r UA
Secrets (UK) = HEIMLICHKEITEN (1968)
SECRETS D'ALCOVE (1954) m Van Parys 96min (= *The Bed/Il Letto*)
 ep LE BILLET DE LOGEMENT d/co-s/co-ad/co-di Decoin w Moreau
 ep LE LIT DE LA POMPADOUR d Delannoy w Carol
SECRETS OF A CO-ED (1943) d JH Lewis 67min (= *Silent Witness*)
SECRETS OF AN ACTRESS, THE (1938) d Keighley c Hickox w K Francis 71min WB
SECRETS OF A SECRETARY (1931) d/co-s G Abbott st Brackett c Folsey w Colbert, H Marshall 71min Par
SECRETS OF CHINATOWN (1934) d Newmeyer 63min
SECRETS OF THE LONE WOLF (1941) d Dmytryk 7rs Col
SECRETS OF THE UNDERGROUND (1942) d William Morgan st/co-s Mainwaring (ps Homes) 71min
Secrets of Women = KVINNORS VANTAN (1952)
SECRETS OF WU SIN (1933) d/e Thorpe 65min
SECRET WAR OF HARRY FRIGG, THE (1968) d Smight c Metty co-a Golitzen w P Newman TS* 110min r U (= *The Private War of Harry Frigg*)
SECRET WAYS, THE (1961) d Karlson, Widmark (uc) p/w Widmark fn Alistair Maclean 112min U
SECUESTRADOR, EL (1958) d/co-s Torre Nilsson 75min (= *The Kidnapper*)
SEDDOK, SON OF SATAN (1963) d/p Bava 87min (= *Atom Age Vampire*)
SEDMI KONT (1966) d Vukotic, *Joseph Medved* S* 88min (= *The Seventh Continent*)
SEDMIKRASKY (1966) d/co-st/co-s Chytilova co-st Juracek part *76min (= *Daisies*)
SEDOTTA E ABBANDONATA (1963) d/co-st/co-s Germi 123min
SEDOVCHY (1940) d/c Karmen (= *The Sedovites*)
Sedovites, The = SEDOVCHY (1940)
Seduced and Abandoned (UK) = SEDOTTA E ABBAN-DONATA (1963)
Seducer - Man Of Straw, The (UK) = UOMO DI PAGLIA, L' (1957)
Seduction of the South (UK) = BRIGANTI ITALIANI, I (1961)
SEDUTTORE, IL (1914) d/co-s Rossi w Sordi
SEE AMERICA THIRST (1930) d William James Craft c AC Miller w Langdon sd 6256ft U
SEED (1931) d Stahl w B Davis, Pitts 97min U
SEEDS OF WISDOM (1946) d D Miller
SEE MORE, PRIVATE HARGROVE (1944) d W Ruggles s Kurnitz c Lawton a Gibbons w D Reed, R Walker 101min MGM
SEE HOW THEY RUN (1955) d/co-s L Arliss 84min BL
SEEING STARS (1938) d R Boulting p J Boulting
SEELEN KAUFER, DER (1919) d Lupu-Pick
SEELISCHE KONSTRUKTIONEN (c 1929) d Fischinger 7min (= *Spiritual Constructions*)
SEE MY LAWYER (1945) d Cline fco-pl Maibaum w Olsen, Johnson, Roman 6249ft U
See Know Evil (US) = BLIND TERROR (1971)
SEESCHLACHT, DIE (1917) d R Oswald w Jannings, Krauss, Veidt
See You At Mao = BRITISH SOUNDS (1968)
See You In Hell, Darling = AMERICAN DREAM, AN (1966)
SEGNO DI VENERE, IL (1955) d Risi co-st/co-s Zavattini, Comencini w Loren, De Sica, Sordi, Vallone 98min (= *Sign of Venus*)
SEGODNYA (1924) d/s Vertov anim 195m (= *Today*)
SEGODNYA (1930) d/co-s/e Shub 73min (= *Today*)
SEGRETO DEL CASTELLO DI MONROE, IL (1914) d Genina
SEGRETO DELLE TRE PUNTE, IL (1952) d Bragaglia w Girotti (= *The Secret of the Three Sword Points*)
SEHNSUCHT (1920) d Murnau w Veidt *1765m (=*Longing*)
SEHNSUCHT 202 (1932) d Max Neufeld co-s Pressburger w Rainer 85min
SEI DONNE PER L'ASSASSINO (1964) d/co-s Bava *90min r AA (= *Blood and Black Lace*)
SEIFEN BLASEN (1929) d Dudow sh
SEIGER, DER (1923) d Ruttmann 60m
SEINE A RECONTRE PARIS, LA (1957) d/s Ivens cy J Prévert n/w Reggiani 31min
SEI MOGLIE DI BARBABLU, LE (1950) d Bragaglia w Toto 85min
SEIN BESTER FREUND (1918) d/p May 4rs
SEINE FRAU DIE UNBEKANNTE (1923) d/s Christensen w Dagover 2232m Dec (= *His Mysterious Adventure*)
SEINE MAJESTAT DAS BETTLEKIND (1920) d A Korda
SEIN GROSSER BLUFF (1927) d Harry Piel s Galeen w Dietrich 2948m
SEI NO KIGEN (1967) d/s Shindo 100min Sho (= *The Origin of Sex/Libido*)
SEIN SCHWIERIGSTER FALL (1915) d/p/co-s May 4rs
SE IO FOSSI ONESTO (1942) d/co-s Bragaglia co-s/w De Sica

Sei per otto, quarantotto = TUTTA LA CITTA CANTA (1945)
SEISHUN (1925) d/s Gosho (= *Youth*)
SEISHUN KAIDAN (1955) d Ichikawa Nik (= *Ghost Story of Youth*)
SEISHUN NO YUME IMA IZUKO (1932) d Ozu Sho (= *Where Are The Dreams Of Youth?*)
SEISHUN NO YUMEJI (1922) d/s Mizoguchi (= *Dreams Of Youth*)
SEISHUN ZANKOKU MONOGATARI (1960) d/s Oshima *96min Sho (= *Naked Youth, a Story of Cruelty*)
SEISHUN ZENIGATA HEIJI (1953) d/co-s Ichikawa Toho (= *Youth of Heiji Zenigata*)
SEKISHUN-CHO (1959) d Kinoshita
SEKRETNAYA MISSIYA (1950) d Romm m Khatcha-turian 104min (= *Secret Mission*)
SEL DE LA TERRE, LE (1950) d Rouquier c Fradetal sh
SELFISH YATES (1918) d W Hart supn Ince c August w W Hart 5rs pc W Hart
SELF MADE LADY (1932) d/p George King w L Hayward
SELSKAYA UCHITELNITSA (1947) d Donskoi 105min (= *Varvara/The Village Teacher*)
SELSKII VRACH (1952) d Gerasimov 116min (= *The Country Doctor*)
SELTSAMEN ABENTEUER DES HERRN FRIDOLIN B., DIE (1948) d/s Staudte 86min Defa
SEME DELL'UOMO, IL (1969) d/co-s Ferreri w Girardot *101min
SEMERO SMELYKH (1936) d Gerasimov co-s Yutkevich 92min (= *The Bold Seven*)
Semia Tarassa = NEPOKORENNIYE (1945)
SEMIKLASSNIKI (1938) d Protazanov, G Levkoyev 82min (= *Pupils of the Seventh Class*)
SEMINOLE (1953) d Boetticher c Metty co-a Golitzen w Hudson, Quinn, Marvin *86min U
Senator, Der = JAHRE VERGEHEN, DIE (1945)
SENATOR WAS INDISCREET, THE (1948) d G Kaufman p N Johnson s MacArthur c Mellor m Amfitheatrof w W Powell, (M Loy) 81min U
SENBAZURU (1953) d Yoshimura s Shindo fn Yasunari Kawabata c Miyagawa w Mori (= *Thousand Cranes*)
SEND ME NO FLOWERS (1964) d Jewison p Keller s JJ Epstein c Fapp co-a Golitzer w Hudson, D Day, Randall *100min U
Sendung des Yoghi, Die: Part I of INDISCHE GRABMAL, DAS (1921)
SENILITA (1962) d Bolognini m Piccioni w Cardinale 110min
SENKA NO HATE (1950) d Yoshimura (= *End Of War Diasasters*)
SEN NOCI SVATOJANSKE (1959) d/p/co-s/cy/a Trnka co-s Brdecka fpl Shakespeare S* 77min (= *A Mid-summer Night's Dream*)
SENORITA (1927) d Badger 6634ft Par
SENSATION HUNTERS (1933) d C Vidor c Hickox 66min Mon
Sensations = SENSATIONS OF 1945 (1944)
SENSATIONS OF 1945 (1944) d/p Stone co-c Marley 85min pc Stone r UA (= *Sensations*)
SENS DE LA MORT, LE (1922) d/s Protazanov w Clair (as Chomette) 1700m
SENSELESS (1962) d Rice f idea J Mekas 16mm 28min [includes footage from THE DANCING MASTER (1961), uf)]
SENSITIVA, LA (1970) d Mingozzi
SENSO (1954) d/co-s Visconti co-s Cecchi d'Amico fst Camillo Boito c Aldo, Krasker m Bruckner, Verdi w Valli, F Granger, Girotti, Marquand *115min (= *The Wanton Countess*)
SENTENCE, LA (1959) d Valère s Moussy c Decaë dec Evein, Saulnier w Vlady, Hossein Pat
SENTIMENTAL JOURNEY (c 1943) d P Brook fn Lawrence Stearne
SENTIMENTAL JOURNEY (1946) d W Lang c Brodine co-a Wheeler w Payne, M O'Hara, Bendix 94min Fox
SENZA COLPA (1915) d Gallone
SENZA PIETA (1948) d/co-s Lattuada p Ponti co-st/co-s Fellini c Tonti dec Gherardi m Rota 91min (= *Without Pity*)
SENZA SAPERE NIENTE DI LEI (1969) d/co-s Comencini *95min
SENZA VELI (1952) d/co-s Gallone *95min
Separate Beds = WHEELER DEALERS, THE (1963)
SEPARATE TABLES (1958) d Delbert Mann p H Hecht co-s/fpl Rattigan co-s Gray c C Lang m Raksin w Niven, Kerr, Lancaster, Hayworth 99min r UA
Séparation des races, La = RAPT (1933)
SEPPUKU (1963) d Kobayashi w Nakadai S 135min Sho (= *Harakiri*)
SEPT CHATEAUX DU DIABLE, LES (1901) d/w Zecca 50m Pat
SEPTEMBER AFFAIR (1951) d Dieterle p Wallis c C Lang m V Young w Fontaine, Cotten, Rosay 104min Par
September Nights = ZARIJOVE NOCI (1956)
SEPTEMBER STORM (1960) d Haskin w Dru CS 99min Fox
SEPT FOIS FEMME (1967) d De Sica ex-p Levine s Zavattini c Matras dec Evein w MacLaine, Caine, Gassmann, Sellers, Ekberg, Martinelli, Noiret *99min (= *Woman Times 7*)

SEPTIEME JURE, LE (1961) d Lautner w Blanche 96min
SEPTIMA PAGINA (1950) d Vajda
SEPT PECHES CAPITAUX, LES (1900) d Méliès 60m
SEPT PECHES CAPITAUX, LES (1951) 150min
 ep L'AVARICE ET LA COLERE d/co-s/w De Filippo w Rossi-Drago
 ep L'ORGEUIL d Autant-Lara s/di Aurenche, Bost w Morgan, Rosay
 ep L'ENVIE d/co-s Ros ellini fst (*La Chatte*) Colette 20min
 ep LA LUXURE d Y Allégret s Bost, Aurenche dec Trauner w Romance, Ronet
 ep LA HUITIEME PECHE d Georges Lacombe w Philipe
 ep d Carlo-Rim
 ep d Jean Dreville
SEPT PECHES CAPITAUX, LES (1961) S 110min Pat
 ep L'ENVIE d Molinaro m Legrand
 ep LA GOURMANDISE d De Broca m Legrand
 ep LA LUXURE d/st/s/di Demy f idea Roger Peyrefitte c Decaë dec Evein m Legrand w Trintignant, Desailly, Presle
 ep L'ORGEUIL d/s Vadim c Decaë w Vlady
 ep LA PARESSE d/s Godard c Decaë m Legrand w Costantine
 ep L'AVARICE d Chabrol c Rabier dec Evein w Cassel, Brialy
 ep d Sylvain Dhomme
SEPT PECHES CAPITAUX, LES (1961) ep ORGEUIL, L' d/s Vadim c Decaë w Vlady * pc Franco-Londres
SEPT PECHES CAPITAUX, LES (1961) ep PARESSE, LA d/s Godard c Decaë m Legrand w Constantine FS (= *The Seven Capital Sins*)
SEQUESTRATI DI ALTONA, I (1963) d De Sica p Ponti fpl (*Les Sequestres d'Altona*) Sartre co-ad Zavattini m Shostakovich w Loren, Maximilian Schell, March, R Wagner 113min Fox (= *The Condemned of Altona*)
SEQUESTRO DE PERSONA (1968) d/co-s Mingozzi *110min (= *Ransom in Sardinia*)
SERAGLIO, THE (1958) d Reiniger m Mozart anim* 1rl
SERDTSYE BETSYA VNOV (1956) d Room 93min (= *A New Heart*)
SERDTSYE MATERI (1967) d/p Donskoi S 100min (= *Heart of a Mother/Sons and Mothers*)
SEREDTSYE SOLOMONA (1932) d Gerasimov, M Kressin s Gerasimov 1700m (= *The Heart of Solomon*)
SEREBRISTAYA PYL (1953) d Room c Tissé 102min (= *Silver Dust*)
SERENADE (1921) d Walsh 7rs FN
SERENADE (1927) d d'Arrast w Menjou 5209ft Par
SERENADE, THE (1935) d Lamont w Keaton
SERENADE (1956) d A Mann p Blanke co-s Goff, Roberts c Marley w Lanza, Fontaine, Price, Montiel *120min WB
SERENADE AUX NUAGES (1945) d/co-s Cayatte 103min
SERENATA DA UN SOLDO (1932) d Zurlini sh
SERENAL (1959) d McLaren 16mm *5min NFBC
SERENITY (1954–61, uf) d/s/c/e Markopoulos *90min
SERGEANT DEADHEAD, THE ASTRONUT (1965) d Taurog co-p Arkoff c F Crosby w Romero, Keaton PV* 89min AI
SERGEANT MADDEN (1939) d Von Sternberg c J Seitz co-a Gibbons w Beery 82min MGM
SERGEANT RUTLEDGE (1960) d J Ford co-p/co-s Gold-beck c Clothier w J Hunter, Marsh *111min r WB
SERGEANT RYKER (1967) d Kulik w Marvin, Miles, Nolan *85min U (= *The Court Martial of Sgt Ryker/The Case Against Paul Ryker*)
SERGEANTS 3 (1961) d J Sturges ex-p HW Koch p Sinatra st/s Burnett c Hoch w Sinatra, Martin, Lawford PV* 112min r UA
SERGEANT YORK (1941) d Hawks p Lasky, Wallis co-s H Koch, J Huston c Polito, Edeson m M Steiner w G Cooper, Brennan 134min WB
SERGO ORDZHONIKIDZYE (1937) d Vertov, *Elizabeth Svilova* 5rs
SERIOUS CHARGE (1959) d T Young c Périnal co-songs Lionel Bart w Quayle 99min
SERPENT, THE (1917) d/p/s Walsh 6rs Fox
SERPENT OF THE NILE (1953) d Castle p Katzman w R Fleming, Burr *80min Col
SERTANEJO, O (1924) d Barreto sh
SERUM DU DOCTEUR NORMET, LE (1925) d Painlevé
SERVANT, THE (1963) d/co-p Losey s Pinter c Slocombe des R Macdonald w Bogarde, (Pinter) 115min
SERVANT IN THE HOUSE, THE (1920) d Conway w J Gilbert 9rs
SERVANTS' ENTRANCE (1934) d F Lloyd s Raphaelson c Mohr w Ayres, J Gaynor 88min Fox
SERVICE DELUXE (1938) d Rowland V Lee co-st Caspary w Price, C Ruggles, Constance Bennett 85min U
SERVICE FOR LADIES (1927) d D'Arrast (ps H D'abbadie) c Rosson w Menjou 6190ft Par
SERVICE FOR LADIES (1932) d/p A Korda w L Howard, (Oberon) 93min (= *Reserved For Ladies*)
SESTO CONTINENTO (1954) d/co-c/w Quilici *95min (= *Blue Continent/Sixth Continent*)
SESTRA ANGELIKA (1932) d Frič (= *Sister Angelica*)
SETENTA VECES SIETE (1962) d/co-s Torre Nilsson 89min (= *The Female/Seventy Times Seven*)
SET FREE (1918) d Browning 5rs

SETTE CANNE, UN VESTITO (1950) d/s Antonioni 10min
SETTE CONTRO LA MORTE (1964) d/p Ulmer (= The Cavern)
SETTE PECCATI CAPITALI, I = SEPT PECHES CAPITAUX, LES (1951)
SETTE SPADE DEL VENDICATORE, LE (1962) d/co-s Freda rm DON CESARE DI BAZAN (1942) S* 84min (= Sette Spade per il re/The Seventh Sword)
Sette Spade per il re = SETTE SPADE DEL VENDICATORE, LE (1962)
SET-UP, THE (1949) d Wise c Krasner w Ryan 72min RKO
SEUL OU AVEC DES AUTRES (1962) d Arcand, Héroux, Venne technical adviser Brault e Groulx 65min
SEVE DE LA TERRE (1955) d Alexeieff anim* 2min (= The Earth's Sap)
SEVEN ANGRY MEN (1955) d Warren w J Hunter 90min r UA
SEVEN BRIDES FOR SEVEN BROTHERS (1954) d Donen p J Cummings co-s Goodrich, Hackett c Folsey co-a Gibbons chor Kidd w Keel, J Powell S* 102min MGM
Seven Capital Sins, The (US) = SEPT PECHES CAPITAUX, LES (1962)
SEVEN CHANCES (1925) d/p Keaton co-s Bruckman w Keaton, Arthur 6rs
SEVEN DAYS ASHORE (1944) d John H Auer c Metty w Dumont, Malone (as Maloney), (V Mayo) 74min RKO
SEVEN DAYS IN MAY (1964) d Frankenheimer s Serling w Lancaster, K Douglas, March, Gardner, E O'Brien 118min Par
SEVEN DAYS LEAVE (1942) d/p Tim Whelan e Wise chor Walters w Mature, Ball 87min RKO
Seven Days . . . Seven Nights = MODERATO CANTABILE (1960)
SEVEN DAYS TO NOON (1950) d J Boulting p/co-s R Boulting 94min BL
Seven Deadly Sins (UK) = SEPT PECHES CAPITAUX, LES (1951)
SE VENDE UN PALACIO (1943) d Vajda
711 OCEAN DRIVE (1950) d J Newman c Planer w E O'Brien, Dru 102min Col
7 FACES OF DR. LAO, THE (1964) d/p Pal c Bronner m Harline w Randall *99min MGM
SEVEN FOOTPRINTS TO SATAN (1929) d Christensen c Polito 60min FN
SEVEN HILLS OF ROME, THE (1958) d Rowland w Lanza TR* 107min MGM
SEVEN KEYS (1962) d Jackson 57min
SEVEN KEYS TO BALDPATE (1925) d Newmeyer 6648ft FPL r Par
SEVEN LITTLE FOYS, THE (1955) d/co-s Shavelson co-a Pereira w Hope VV* 95min Par
SEVEN MEN FROM NOW (1956) d Boetticher co-p A McLaglen st/s Kennedy c Clothier w R Scott, Marvin *78min pc J Wayne r WB
SEVEN MILES FROM ALCATRAZ (1942) d Dmytryk 62min RKO
Seven Samurai, The = SHICHININ NO SAMURAI (1954)
SEVEN SEAS TO CALAIS (1962) d Maté CS* 101min (= Il Re dei sette mari)
SEVEN SINNERS (1925) d/co-st/co-ad Milestone co-st/co-ad Zanuck w C Brook 6600ft WB
SEVEN SINNERS (1940) d Garnett p Pasternak c Maté w Dietrich, J Wayne, B Crawford 87min U
SEVEN SWEETHEARTS (1942) d Borzage p Pasternak c Folsey m Waxman w Heflin 98min MGM
"1776", OR, THE HESSIAN RENEGADES (1909) d Griffith w Pickford 1rl Bio
Seventeen Years Old = SJUTTON AR (1957)
7TH CAVALRY (1956) d JH Lewis p H Brown as-p R Scott c Rennahan w R Scott *75min Col
Seventh Continent, The = SEDMI KONTINENT (1966)
SEVENTH CROSS, THE (1944) d Zinneman p Berman c Freund co-a Gibbons w Tracy, Moorehead 110min MGM
SEVENTH DAWN, THE (1963) d L Gilbert c F Young w Holden 123min r UA
SEVENTH DAY, THE (1922) d H King 6rs
SEVENTH HEAVEN (1927) d Borzage co-m Rapee w J Gaynor, D Butler 8500ft Fox
SEVENTH HEAVEN (1937) d H King w S Simon, J Stewart, Hersholt 102min Fox
SEVEN THIEVES (1960) d Hathaway p/s Boehm c Leavitt co-a Wheeler w Robinson, Wallach, Steiger CS* 100min pc Boehm
Seventh Seal, The = SJUNDE INSEGLET, DET (1956)
SEVENTH SIN, THE (1957) d Neame, Minnelli (uc) fn (The Painted Veil) Somerset Maugham c June w Parker, G Sanders CS* 93min MGM
Seventh Sword, The (US) = SETTE SPADE DEL VENDICATORE, LE (1962)
SEVEN THUNDERS (1957) d Fregonese w Boyd, (J Scheslinger) 100min JAR
SEVENTH VEIL, THE (1945) d Compton Bennett w Mason 94min BL
SEVENTH VICTIM, THE (1943) d Robson p Lewton c Musuraca 71min RKO
SEVEN TILL FIVE (1934–35) d McLaren 16mm 10min
70 (1971) d Breer anim* 16mm 7min

SEVENTY DEADLY PILLS (1964) d/s Jackson 55min
Seventy Times Seven (UK) = SETENTA VECES CIETE (1962)
SEVEN WAVES AWAY (1956) d/s Richard Sale m Arthur Bliss w Power, Zetterling, Nolan 95min co-pc Power
SEVEN WAYS FROM SUNDOWN (1960) d Keller st/s Huffaker co-a Golitzen w A Murphy, McIntyre *87min U
7 WOMEN (1966) d J Ford c La Shelle m E Bernstein w A Bancroft PV* 87min r MGM
SEVEN WONDERS OF THE WORLD (1956) d Garnett, Tetzlaff, Marton, Mantz, Thompson Cinerama* 120min
SEVEN YEARS BAD LUCK (1921) d/p/s/w Linder 5rs
SEVEN YEAR ITCH, THE (1955) d/co-p/co-s B Wilder co-p Feldman co-s/fpl Axelrod c Krasner co-a Wheeler m A Newman cr Bass w Monroe, Ewell, (C Jones) CS* 105min r Fox
SEVILLANA, LA (1930) d Novarro
SEX (1920) d Niblo 5400ft
Sex = ANDY WARHOL'S WOMEN (1971)
SEX AND THE SINGLE GIRL (1964) d Quine co-s Joseph Heller c C Lang w Curtis, N Wood, H Fonda, M Ferrer *114min pc Quine r WB
Sex Can Be Difficult (US) = AMORE DIFFICILE, L' (1962)
SEXE FAIBLE, LE (1934) d Siodmak w Brasseur
SEX HYGIENE (1941) d J Ford p Zanuck c Barnes 30min
Sex In Chains = GESCHLECHT IN FESSELN (1928)
Sex In The Afternoon (UK) = ALTA INFIDELTA (1964)
SEX KITTENS GO TO COLLEGE (1960) d/p/st Zugsmith w Weld, Carradine 94min AA
Sex Quartet (UK) = FATE, LE (1966)
SEXUAL MEDITATIONS No. 1: MOTEL (1970) d Brakhage *8mm 12min
SFIDA, LA (1958) d co-st/co-s Rosi co-st/co-s Cecchi D'Amico c Di Venanzo 95min
SFINGA SORRIDE PRIMA DI MORIRE STOP – LONDRA, LA (1964) d/s Tessari
SHACKLES OF GOLD (1922) d Brenon 7rs Fox
Shadow, The = CIEN (1956)
Shadow Army (US) = ARMEE DES OMBRES, L' (1969)
SHADOWED (1946) d J Sturges Col
SHADOW IN THE SKY (1951) d Wilcox s Maddow c Folsey m Kaper w Meeker 78min MGM
SHADOW LAUGHS, THE (1933) d/s Arthur Hoerl w (Romero) 67min
SHADOW OF A DOUBT (1943) d Hitchcock co-s T Wilder, Reville m Tiomkin w Cotten, T Wright 108min U
SHADOW OF DOUBT (1935) d G Seitz c C Clarke 73min MGM
Shadow of the Guillotine (UK) = MARIE ANTOINETTE (1913)
SHADOW OF THE PAST, THE (1913) d Ince 3rs
SHADOW OF THE THIN MAN (1941) d WS Van Dyke st/co-s Kurnitz f characters Hammett c Daniels w W Powell, M Loy, D Reed, Antony 97min MGM
SHADOW ON THE MOUNTAIN (1931) d Elton p Grierson 15min
SHADOW ON THE WALL (1949) d Jackson c June m Previn w Sothern 84min
SHADOWS (1961) d Cassavetes co-p Papatakis m C Mingus 87min
Shadows In Sunlight = MAHIRU NO ANKOKU (1956)
Shadow Of Glory (US) = SOMBRAS DE GLORIA (1930)
SHADOWS OF PARIS (1924) d/p Brenon 6549ft
SHADOWS OF THE PAST (1928) d W Lang 5100ft
Shadows Over Yoshiwara = JUJIRO (1928)
SHAGAI, SOVIET! (1926) d/co-s/t/e Vertov 1650m (= Stride, Soviet!)
SHAKEDOWN, THE (1928) d Wyler w J Huston, (Wyler) 73min U
SHAKEDOWN (1950) d Pevney c Glassberg 80min U
SHAKE HANDS WITH THE DEVIL (1959) d/p Michael Anderson s Goff, Roberts w Cagney, R Harris, Murray, M Redgrave 111min r UA
SHAKESPEARE'S TRAGEDY, KING LEAR (1909) d Blackton fpl (King Lear) Shakespeare
SHAKESPEARE WALLAH (1965) d/co-s Ivory c Mitra m S Ray 125min
SHAKHMATNAYA GORYACHKA (1925) d Pudovkin, Nikolai Shpikovsky w Barnet, Protazanov 400m (= Chess Fever)
SHAKHTORY (1934 r 1937) d Yutkevich 2996m (= Miners)
SHAKIEST GUN IN THE WEST, THE (1968) d Alan Rafkin co-st Tashlin S* 100min U
SHAKALAKO (1968) d Dmytryk c Moore w Connery, Bardot, Boyd, Hawkins FS* 113min
SHALL WE DANCE (1937) d Sandrich w Astaire, Rogers, Horton 106min RKO
SHALOM (1969) d De la Patellière w Tamiroff
Shame, The = SKAMMEN (1968)
Shameless Old Lady, The = VIEILLE DAME INDIGNE, LA (1964)
SHAMROCK HANDICAP, THE (1926) d J Ford w J Gaynor 5685ft Fox
SHANE (1953) d/p G Stevens c Griggs co-a Pereira m V Young w Ladd, Heflin, Arthur, Palance, Cook *118min Par
SHANGHAI COBRA, THE (1945) d Karlson 64min Mon

SHANGHAIED (1915) d/s Chaplin c Totheroh w Chaplin, W Ruggles, Purviance 2rs S & A
SHANGHAIED LOVE (1931) d G Seitz c Tetzlaff w Beery 75min Col
SHANGHAIED LOVERS (1924) d Del Ruth w Langdon 2rs pc Sennett r Pat
SHANGHAI GESTURE, THE (1941) d/co-s Von Sternberg co-s Furthman w Tierney, W Huston, Mature, Ouspenskaya, (Dalio) 105min r UA
SHANGHAI STORY, THE (1954) d/p F Lloyd co-s S Miller w Roman, E O'Brien 90min Rep
SHANGHAI NO TSUKI (1941) d Naruse (= The Moon Over Shanghai)
Shark = CAINE (1968)
SHARK MONROE (1918) d/pc W Hart c August w W Hart 5rs
Shark Reef (UK) = SHE-GODS OF SHARK REEF (1957)
SHCHEDROYE LETO (1951) d Barnet 87min (= Bountiful Summer)
SHCHORS (1939) co-d/s Dovzhenko co-d Solntzeva 140min
SHE (1911) w Cruze
SHE (1935) d Pichel, Lansing C Holden p M Cooper fn Rider Haggard additional di D Nichols w R Scott, (Anthony) 11rs RKO
SHE (1965) d Robert Day fn Rider Haggard w Andress S* 106min MGM
She and Her = ASSOLUTO NATURALE, L' (1969)
SHEBA (1919) d/p Hepworth w Colman 5rs
SHE COULDN'T SAY NO (1930) d Bacon 7rs WB
SHE COULDN'T SAY NO (1954) d Bacon rm 1930 c Wild w Mitchum, J Simmons 88min RKO
SHE COULDN'T TAKE IT (1935) d Garnett p BP Schulberg c Shamroy w Raft, J Bennett, Nolan 89min Col
She Defends Her Country = ONA ZA SHCHSHAYET RODINU (1943)
SHE DONE HIM WRONG (1933) d L Sherman fpl (Diamond Lil) West c C Lang dance d H Hecht w West, C Grant, Roland 66min Par
Sheep Has Five Legs, The = MOUTON A CINQ PATTES, LE (1954)
SHEEPMAN, THE (1958) d G Marshall st/co-s J Grant c Bronner w G Ford, McLaine *85min MGM
SHE-GODS OF SHARK REEF (1957) d Corman c F Crosby w Montiel *62min
SHE GOES TO WAR (1929) d/p H King co-c Gaudio 9500ft r UA
SHE GOT WHAT SHE WANTED (1930) d/co-p Cruze 81min
SHE HAD TO EAT (1937) d St Clair 74min Fox
SHE HAD TO SAY YES (1933) d Berkeley, George Amy w L Young 62min FN
SHE HAD TO SAY YES (1953) d Bacon w Mitchum, J Simmons 89min Rko (= Beautiful But Dangerous)
She Has Lived Her Destiny = KANOJO TO UNMEI (1924)
SHEIK STEPS OUT, THE (1937) d Pichel w Novarro 67min Rep
SHE LEARNED ABOUT SAILORS (1934) d G Marshall w Ayres, Faye 78min Fox
SHE LOVED A FIREMAN (1938) d J Farrow c O'Connell w Sheridan 57min WB
SHE LOVED A SAILOR (1916) d Victor Heerman p Sennett s Del Ruth 2rs Tri-Key
SHE LOVES ME NOT (1934) d E Nugent c C Lang chor Prinz w B Crosby, Hopkins 83min Par
SHE MARRIED HER BOSS (1935) d La Cava s Buchman c Shamroy w Colbert, M Douglas Col
SHENANDOAH (1965) d A McLaglen c Clothier co-a Golitzen w J Stewart, G Kennedy *105min U
SHEEPLORD OF THE HILLS, THE (1941) d Hathaway co-c C Lang co-a Dreier w J Wayne, Corey *98min Par
She Played With Fire (US) = FORTUNE IS A WOMAN (1956)
Sheriff, The = OUT WEST (1917)
SHERIFF OF CIMARRON (1945) d Canutt 6rs Rep
SHERIFF OF FRACTURED JAW, THE (1958) d Walsh c Heller w Mansfield CS* 110min Fox
SHERIFF'S BLUNDER, THE (1916) d/s/w Mix 2rs Sel
SHERLOCK HOLMES (1909) d/s/w Madsen fsts Conan Doyle
SHERLOCK HOLMES (1922) d Albert Parker fsts Conan Doyle w J Barrymore, W Powell, Hopper 8200ft
SHERLOCK HOLMES (1932) d W Howard fsts Conan Doyle c Barnes w C Brook 65min Fox
SHERLOCK HOLMES (1963) d Fisher
SHERLOCK JR (1924) d/p/w Keaton co-s Bruckman 5rs Metro
SHERMAN SAID IT (1933) d C Chase (as Parrott) p Roach w C Chase 2rs MGM
SHE'S A SOLDIER, TOO (1944) d Castle w Winters 67min Col
SHE'S BACK ON BROADWAY (1953) d G Douglas p Blanke w V Mayo, Cochran *95min WB
SHE'S NO LADY (1937) d C Vidor 63min Par
SHE'S OIL MINE (1941) d Jules White w Keaton 17min Col
SHESTAYA CHAST MIRA (1926) d/co-s/t/e Vertov 1767m (6 parts) (= A Sixth of the World)
She Was Like a Daisy = NOGIKU NO GOTOKI KIMI NARIKI (1955)
She-Wolf, The (US) = LUPA, LA (1953)

413

She-Wolves, The = LOUVES, LES (1957)
SHE WORE A YELLOW RIBBON (1949) d/co-p J Ford co-p M Cooper co-s F Nugent c Hoch w J Wayne, Dru, V McLaglen, G O'Brien *103min r RKO
SHIBAIDO (1944) d Naruse (= Theatre)
SHICHIMENCHO NO YUKUE (1924) d Mizoguchi Nik (= Turkeys in a Row)
SHICHININ NO SAMURAI (1954) d/co-s Kurosawa w Mifune 200min Toho (= The Seven Samurai/The Magnificent Seven)
SHIELD FOR MURDER (1954) d HW Koch, E O'Brien p Schenk w E O'Brien, C Jones 80min r UA
SHIIKU (1961) d Oshima fn Kensaburo Ohe 105min (= The Catch)
SHIKAMO KARERA WA YUKU (1931) d Mizoguchi Nik (= And Yet They Go On)
SHIMA NO RATAI JIKEN (1931) d/s Gosho (= Island of Naked Scandal)
SHIMPU-REN (1933) d/s Mizoguchi
SHINDO (1936) d/s Gosho (2 parts) (= The New Road)
SHINEL (1926) d L Traubert s Yuri Tinyanov fsts (The Cloak and Nevski Prospect) N V Gogol co-c Moskvin w Gerasimov 1921m (= The Cloak)
SHINEL (1959) d Batalov fpl NV Gogol 75min (= The Overcoat)
SHINE ON HARVEST MOON (1944) d D Butler c Edeson chor Prinz w Sheridan 112min WB
SHIN HEIKE MONOGATARI (1955) d Mizoguchi c Miyagawa *113min Dai (= New Tales of the Taira Clan)
SHINING HOUR, THE (1938) d Borzage p J Mankiewicz co-s Ogden Nash c Folsey m Waxman w J Crawford, M Douglas, R Young 75min MGM
Shining Sun Becomes Clouded = TERU HI KUMORU HI (1926)
SHINING VICTORY (1941) d Rapper p J Warner, Wallis co-s H Koch c Howe w Crisp 80min WB
SHIN JOSEIKAN (1928) d Gosho (= A New Kind Of Woman)
SHINJUKU DOROBO NIKKI (1968) d/co-s/e Oshima part *94min pc Oshima (= Diary of a Shinjuku Thief)
SHINJU YOIMACHIGUSA (1925) d Kinugasa
SHIN ONOGA TSUMI (1926) d Mizoguchi Nik (= My Fault Continued)
SHINSETSU (1942) d Gosho (= New Show)
SHIP AHOY (1919) d/s/w C Chase (as Parrott)
SHIP CAFE (1935) d Florey c Sparkuhl 65min Par
SHIP COMES IN, A (1928) d W Howard c Andriot Pat
SHIPMATES (1931) d/p Harry Pollard co-ad/co-di Daves w Montgomery 73min MGM
SHIPMATES FOREVER (1935) d Borzage s Daves c Polito w D Powell 109min FN
SHIP OF FOOLS (1965) d/p Kramer c Laszlo m Gold w V Leigh, J Ferrer, Signoret, Marvin, Werner, Segal, Kjellin 149min Col
Ships Attacking Forts = KORABLI SHTURMUYUT BASTIONY (1953)
SHIPS WITH WINGS (1941) d/co-s Sergei Nolbandov p Balcon e Hamer 89min r UA
SHIP THAT DIED OF SHAME, THE (1955) d/co-p/s Dearden co-p Balcon w Attenborough 91min
Ship To India, A = SKEPP TILL INDIALAND (1947)
SHIPYARD (1934) d/s Rotha 24min GB
SHIRAGIKU WA NAGEKU (1925) d Mizoguchi
SHIRASAGI (1959) d/s Kinugasa S* 102min Dai (= The Snowy Heron/The White Heron)
SHIRAYURI WA NAGEKU (1925) d Mizoguchi fn John Galsworthy Nik (= Lament of a White Lady)
SHIROGANE SHINJU (1956) d/s Shindo
SHIROI GAKE (1961) d Imai S 122min (= The Cliff)
SHIROI KIBA (1960) d Gosho (= White Fangs)
SHIROI YAJU (1959) d Naruse (= White Beast)
SHITO NO DENSETSU (1963) d Kinoshita (= A Legend Or Was It?)
SHITTO (1949) d Yoshimura (= Jealousy)
Shivers In Summer = FRENESIA DELL'ESTATE (1963)
SHIZUKANARU KETTO (1949) d/co-s Kurosawa w Mifune 95min Dai (= Quiet Duel)
SHKOLA ZLOSLOVIYA (1952) d Room 161w (= School for Scandal)
SHLI SOLDATY (1958) d/s L Trauberg w Bondarchuk 86min (= Soldiers Were Marching)
SHOCK CORRIDOR (1963) d/p/s/fn Fuller c Cortez co-a Lourie 101min r AA
Shocking = TUE MANI SUL MIO CORPO, LE (1970)
SHOCKING MISS PILGRIM, THE (1946) d/s Seaton p Perlberg c Shamroy m George and Ira Gershwin w Grable 85min Fox
SHOCKPROOF (1949) d Sirk co-s Fuller c Lawton w Wilde 29min Col
SHOCK TREATMENT (1964) d D Sanders p A Rosenberg s Boehm c Leavitt m Goldsmith w Bacall 94min Fox
Shock Troops (US) = HOMME DE TROP, UN (1966)
Shock Troops (UK) = HOMME QUI MENT, L' (1969)
SHOE BLACK, THE (1895) p Paul
SHOES, THE (1961) d/p Pintoff 35min
Shoeshine = SCIUSCIA (1946)
SHOES OF THE FISHERMAN, THE (1968) d Michael Anderson c Garmes m North w Quinn, Olivier, Werner, De Sica, Gielgud, I Miranda PV*

SHOES THAT DANCED, THE (1919) d Borzage Tri
Shoestore Pinkus (UK) = SCHUHPALAST PINKUS (1916)
SHOHIN-SHUSOKU (1924) d/s Kinugasa
SHOHIN-SHUTO (1924) d/s Kinugasa
SHOJO NO SHI (1927) d/s Gosho (= Death Of A Maiden)
SHOJO NYUYO (1930) d Gosho (= The Girl Nyuyo)
SHOJO-YO SAYONARA (1933) d Gosho (= Goodbye, My Girl)
SHOKEI NO MEYA (1956) d Ichikawa Dai (= Punishment Room)
SHOKKAKU (1969) d/s Shindo S 105min Toho (= Odd Affinity)
SHONEN (1969) d/pc Oshima part *97min (= Boy)
SHONEN-KI (1951) d Kinoshita (= Youth)
Shoot First (US) = ROUGH SHOOT (1952)
SHOOTING OF DAN MCGOO, THE (1945) d Avery *8min MGM
SHOOTING STARS (1927) co-d/s/e Asquith co-d A Brambe 116min
SHOOT OUT (1971) d Hathaway co-a Golitzen w Peck *94min
Shoot The Nets = SCHOT IS TE BOORD, HET (1952)
Shoot The Pianist (UK) = TIREZ SUR LA PIANISTE (1960)
Shoot The Piano Player (US) = TIREZ SUR LE PIANISTE (1960)
SHOP AROUND THE CORNER, THE (1940) d/p Lubitsch s Raphaelson fpl Nikolaus Laszlo c Daniels a Gibbons w J Stewart 98min MGM
SHOPWORN ANGEL, THE (1938) d Potter p J Mankiewicz c Ruttenberg co-e Vorkapich w J Stewart, Pidgeon 9rs MGM
SHORE ACRES (1920) d Ingram 6rs Metro
SHORI NO HI MADE (1945) d Naruse (= Victory In The Sun)
SHORT AND SUITE (1959) d McLaren, Evelyn Lambert *5min NFBC
SHORT CUT TO HELL (1957) d Cagney rm THIS GUN FOR HIRE (1942) 87min Par
SHOTGUNS THAT KICK (1914) d/w Arbuckle p Sennett 1rl Key
SHOT IN THE DARK, A (1964) d/p/co-s Edwards fpl Kurnitz adapted fpl Achard c Challis m Mancini w Sellers, G Sanders, Forbes PV* 101min r UA
Shot In The Heart, A = BALLE AU COEUR, UNE (1965)
SHOULD A HUSBAND FORGIVE? (1919) d/st/s Walsh 7rs Fox
SHOULDER ARMS (1918) d/s Chaplin c Totheroh w Chaplin, Purviance 3rs FN
SHOULD MARRIED MEN GO HOME (1928) d James Parrott p Roach supn/st McCarey w Laurel, Hardy (2rs) r MGM
SHOW, THE (1927) d Browning w J Gilbert 6309ft MGM
SHOW BIZ BUGS (1957) d Freleng anim* 7min WB
SHOW BOAT (1936) d Whale fn Edna Ferber fmpl Oscar Hammerstein II, Jerome Kern chor Prinz w I Dunne 110min U
SHOW BOAT (1951) d G Sidney p Freed s Mahin fmpl Oscar Hammerstein II, Jerome Kern co-a Gibbons chor R Alton w Gardner, Keel, J Brown, Moorehead, Champion *107min MGM
Showdown (UK) = PACHA, LE (1967)
SHOW GIRL IN HOLLYWOOD (1930) d LeRoy c Polito 80min FN
SHOWMAN (1963) d/c A and D Maysles w Levine 52min
Show Must Go On = THREE MAXIMS, THE (1936)
SHOW-OFF, THE (1926) d St Clair c Garmes w L Brooks 3rs FPL
SHOW OF SHOWS, THE (1929) d John G Adolfi supn Zanuck w M Loy, Turpin, Fairbanks Jr, J Barrymore, Barthelmess, Fazenda, L Young, Sothern (as Harriet Lake) *11692ft WB
SHOW PEOPLE (1928) d/co-p K Vidor co-p Hearst, Davies w Davies, Fairbanks Sr 7453ft r MGM
SHOW THEM NO MERCY (1935) d G Marshall c Glennon w Romero 76min Fox
SHOZO (1948) d Konoshita s Kurosawa (= A Portrait)
SHRI 420 (1955) d/p/w Raj Kapoor s Abbas
SHRIKE, THE (1955) d J Ferrer p A Rosenberg c Daniels cr Bass w J Ferrer, Allyson 88min U
SHUBUN (1950) d/co-s Kurosawa w Mifune 122min Sho (= Scandal)
SHUKUJO TO HIGE (1931) d Ozu Sho (= The Lady and Her Favorites)
SHUKUJO WA NANI O WASURETAKA (1937) d/co-s Ozu Sho (= What Did The Lady Forget?)
SHUKUZU (1953) d/s Shindo w Yoshimura w Yamada (= Epitome/Geisha-Girl Ginko)
SHUNSETSU (1950) d Yoshimura (= Spring Snow)
SHURAJO HIBUN (1952) d/s Kinugasa (2parts)
SHUU (1956) d Naruse (= Sudden Rain)
SIAMO DONNE (1953) 102min (= We, the Women)
ep ANNA MAGNANI d/co-s Visconti co-s Zavattini, Cecchi d'Amico w Magnani 18min
ep ISA MIRANDA d/co-s Zampa st Zavattini w I Miranda
ep INGRID BERGMAN d Rossellini co-s Zavattini w Ingrid Bergman 20min
ep ALIDA VALLI d Gianni Francolini w Valli
Siberian Lady Macbeth, The = SIBIRSKA LEDI MAGBET (1962)

Siberians, The = SIBIRYAKI (1940)
SIBIRSKA LEDI MAGBET (1962) d Wajda CS 95min (= The Siberian Lady Macbeth/Lady Macbeth of Siberia)
SIBIRYAKI (1940) d Kuleshov 10rs (= The Siberians)
SICARIO, IL (1961) d/co-s Damiani co-s Zavattini w Germi S 100min
Sicilian Clan, The = CLAN DES SICILIENS, LE (1969)
SICK ABED (1920) d S Wood fpl Ethel Watts Mumford 5rs
Siddhartha and the City = PRATIDWANDI (1971)
SIDE SHOW (1931) d Del Ruth co-s Enright 7rs 68min WB
SIDE SHOW OF LIFE, THE (1924) d/p Brenon co-s Goldbeck c Howe 8rs FPL
SIDE STREET (1929) d/co-s St Clair co-c Musuraca 78min RKO
SIDE STREET (1949) d A Mann c Ruttenberg w F Granger 83min MGM
Sidewalks of London (US) = ST. MARTIN'S LANE (1938)
SIDEWALKS OF NEW YORK (1931) d Jules White, Zion Myers p/w Keaton 8rs MGM
SIE (1954) d/p/s Thiele w Tiller 95min
SIEBEN VOM RHEIM (1954) d/s A and A Thorndike 62min
SIEG DES GLAUBENS (1933) d Riefenstahl
SIEGE AT RED RIVER, THE (1954) d Maté co-s Boehm c Cronjager co-a Wheeler w V Johnson, Dru *81min Fox
SIEGE OF PINCHGUT, THE (1959) d/co-s Watt p Balcon w A Ray 104min ABC
SIEGFRIED part 1 of DIE NIGELUNGEN (1924)
SIEGFRIEDS TOD (1933) sound version of SIEGFRIED (1924) 82min UFA
SIEMPRE TUYA (1951) d/co-st/co-s Fernandez c Figueroa
SIE NANNTEN IHN GRINGO (1966) d Rowland CS* 93min (= Man Called Gringo/La Ley del Forestero)
SIERO DELLA VERITA, IL (1949) d Risi sh
SIERRA (1950) d Alfred E Green c Metty w Ives, A Murphy 82min U
Sierra de Tervel = ESPOIR, L' (1939 r 1945)
SIE UND DIE DREI (1922) d Dupont 2500m
SIGNAL (1918) d Aleksandr Arkatov co-c Tissé 600m
SIGNAL TOWER, THE (1924) d C Brown c B Reynolds w Beery 7rs U
SIGNE ARSENE LUPIN (1959) d Ives Robert s Rappeneau w Ives Robert, Valli 110min
SIGNE DU LION, LE (1959) d/s Rohmer c Hayer w Godard 100min pc Chabrol
SIGN OF FOUR, THE (1923) d/s Elvey fsts Conan Doyle 6500ft
SIGN OF THE CROSS, THE (1932) d/p De Mille co-s Buchman c Struss a Leisen Chor Prinz w March, Laughton, Colbert, Carradine 107min Par (reissued in 1944 with prologue by D Nichols)
SIGN OF THE PAGAN (1954) d Sirk c Metty co-a Golitzen w J Chandler, Palance CS* 92min U
SIGN OF THE RAM, THE (1948) d J Sturges s Charles Bennett c Guffey 86min r Col
Sign Of Venus (UK) = SEGNO DI VENERE, IL (1955)
SIGN OF ZORRO, THE (1960) d/co-s Foster 91min (edited from TV series)
SIGN ON THE DOOR, THE (1921) d/co-s Brenon w N Talmadge 7rs
SIGNORA DELLE CAMELIE, LA (1947) d Gallone
SIGNORA DI BEIRUT, LA (1965, uf) d Vajda
SIGNORA DI TUTTI, LA (1934) d/co-s Orphuls e Poggioli m Amfitheatrof w I Miranda
SIGNORA PARADISO (1934) d/s Guazzoni
SIGNORA SENZA CAMELIE, LA (1953) d/st/co-s Antonioni co-s Cecchi d'Amico, Maselli m Fusco w Bosè 105min
SIGNOR BRUSCHINO, IL (1968) d Sala
SIGNORI E SIGNORE (1966) d/co-s Germi 116min (= The Birds, The Bees, and The Italians)
SIGNORI IN CARROZZA! (1951) d/co-s Zampa 102min (= Rome–Paris–Rome)
SIGNORINA CICLONE, LA (1916) d/co-s Genina
SIGNORINETTE (1942) d/co-s/e Zampa
SIGNOR MAX, IL (1937) d/co-s Comencini co-s Soldati w De Sica
SIGRIE, LE (1969) d/s Rouch, Germaine Dieterlen 16mm
SI J'AVAIS QUATRE DROMEDAIRES (1966) d/s/c/e Marker 73min
SI J'ETAIS ROI (1910) d Méliès
SI JOLIE PETITE PLAGE, UNE (1948) d Y Allégret c Alekan w Philipe, Carette 88min (= Such a Pretty Little Beach)
SIKKIM, TERRE SECRETE (1956) d Bourguignon * (= Le Langage du Sourire)
SI L'EMPEREUR SAVAIT CA! (1930) d Feyder fpl (Olympia) Ferenc Molnar c Daniels dec Gibbons w Rosay 2372m MGM (= Olympia/His Glorious Night)
SILENCE (1926) d Julian c Marley 7518ft PRC
SILENCE, LE (1920) d/s Delluc
Silence, The = TYSTNADEN (1963)
Silence and Cry (UK) = CSEND ES KIALTAS (1968)
SILENCE DE LA MER, LE (1948) d/s/co-e Melville c/co-e Decaë 86min pc Melville
SILENCE EST D'OR, LE (1947) d/co-p/s/di Clair co-c Thirard m Van Parys w Chevalier, Modot 100min RKO

Silence of the Forest, The = SCHWEIGEN IM WALDE, DAS (1929)
Silence of the Heart, The = GOLU HADAWATHA (1968)
SILENCERS, THE (1966) *d* Karlson *c* Guffey *m* E Bernstein *w* Martin, Malden, Charisse *104min Col
Silent Barricade, The = MEMA BARIKADA (1949)
SILENT BATTLE, THE (1916) *d* Conway 5rs
SILENT JOURNEY (1955) *d* J Mekas
SILENT LIE, THE (1917) *d* Walsh 5rs Fox
SILENT MAN, THE (1917) *d/w* W Hart *c* August 5rs *pc* Ince
SILENT MASTER, THE (1917) *d/s* Perret *c* Andriot
SILENT PARTNER, THE (1917) *d* Neilan *st* Goulding 5rs
SILENT PARTNER, THE (1927) *d* Wyler 2rs U
Silent Raid, The = OVERVAL, DE (1962)
SILENT SHELBY (1922) *d/w* Borzage
SILENT SOUND SENSE STARS SUBOTNICK AND SENDER (1962) *d* Brakhage 16mm 2min
SILENT STRANGER, THE (1924) *d Albert Rogell p* H Brown *st* Heisler 5040ft Mon
SILENT VILLAGE, THE (1943) *d/p/s* Jennings 36min Crown
SILENT WATCHER, THE (1924) *d* F Lloyd *c* Brodine 8rs FN
Silent Witness = SECRETS OF A CO-ED (1943)
Silent World, The = MONDE DU SILENCE, LE (1956)
SILHOUETTE DES TEUFELS, DIE (1917) *d/p* May 4rs
SILHOUETTES (1925–29) *d* Fischinger anim
Silken Skin (US) = PEAU DOUCE, LA (1964)
SILKEN SPIDER, THE (1916) *d/w* Borzage Tri
SILK EXPRESS (1933) *d* Enright *c* Gaudio 61min WB
SILK HOSIERY (1920) *d* Niblo *p* Ince 4900ft FPL
SILK STOCKINGS (1927) *d* W Ruggles *c* B Reynolds 6166ft U
SILK STOCKINGS (1957) *d* Mamoulian *p* Freed *st* (*Ninotchka*) *Melchior Lengyel fco-pl* G Kaufman *c* Bronner *m Cole Porter,* André Previn *w* Astaire, Charisse, Lorre CS* 117min MGM
SILK STOCKING SAL (1924) *d* Browning 5300ft
SILURAMENTO DELL'OCEANA, IL (1917) *d/st/s* Genina
SILVER BULLET, THE (1942) *d* JH Lewis 56min U
SILVER CHALICE, THE (1955) *d* Saville *m* Waxman *w* V Mayo, Palance, P Newman, N Wood CS 193min WB
SILVER CITY (1951) *d* Haskin *c* Rennahan *co-a* Pereira *w* E O'Brien, De Carlo *90min Par (= *High Vermilion*)
SILVER CORN, THE (1933) *d* Cromwell *w* I Dunne. McCrea 75min RKO
Silver Dust = SEREBRISTAYA PYL (1953)
SILVER HORDE, THE (1920) *d* F Lloyd 6000ft Goldwyn
SILVER LINING, THE (1932) *d/p* Crosland *w* O'Sullivan 75min *r* UA (= *Thirty Days*)
SILVER LODE (1954) *d* Dwan *p* Bogeaus *c* J Alton *w* Payne, Duryea, L Scott *80min RKO
SILVER QUEEN (1942) *d* Bacon *c* R Harlan 81min *r* UA
SILVER RIVER (1948) *d* Walsh *c* Hickox *m* M Steiner *w* Flynn, Sheridan, Mitchell 110min WB
SILVER WINGS (1922) *d Edwin Carewe,* J Ford *co-c* Ruttenberg 8271ft Fox
SIMAO, O CAOLHO (1952) *d/p* Cavalcanti
Simfoniya Donbass = ENTUZIAZM (1930)
SIMILITUDES DE LONGEURS ET DES VITESSES (1937) *d* Painlevé
SIMON BOLIVAR (1969) *d* Blasetti *w* Maximilian Schell *
SIMON DEL DESIERTO (1965) *d/s* Buñuel *c* Figueroa 42min (= *Simon of the Desert*)
Simon of the Desert = SIMON DEL DESIERTO (1965)
Simon the Swiss = VOYOU, LE (1970)
Simple Case, A = PROSTOI SLUCHAI (1932)
SIMPLE CHARITY (1910) *d* Griffith *w* Pickford 1rl Bio
SIMPLE HISTOIRE, UNE (1957) *d/p/s/c* Hanoun *m Vivaldi, Cimarosa* 16mm *6mm
SIN (1915) *d/s* Brenon 5rs Fox
Sin = GREKA (1916)
Sin, The = HAKAI (1962)
Sincere Heart = MAGAKORO (1953)
SINCERELY YOURS (1955) *d* G Douglas *p* Blanke *c* Clothier *w* Malone, Dru *115min WB
Sincerity = MAGOKORO (1939)
SINCE YOU WENT AWAY (1944) *d* Cromwell *p/s* Selznick *c* Cortez, Garmes *a* Pereira *m* M Steiner *chor* Walters *w* Cotten, J Jones, Colbert, Temple, L Barrymore, R Walker, Moorehead, Nazimova, (Roman), (R Fleming) 172min *r* UA
SIN FLOOD, THE (1921) *d* F Lloyd 5rs *pc* Goldwyn
SINFUL DAVEY (1969) *d* J Huston *ex-p* W Mirisch *s* JR Webb *co-c* F Young PV* 95min Mir *r* UA
SINGAPORE (1947) *d* Brahm *st/co-s* S Miller *w* Gardner, MacMurray 79min U
SINGAPORE WOMAN (1941) *d* Negulesco *c* McCord *w* A Smith 64min WB
SINGE EN HIVER, UN (1962) *d* Verneuil *di* Audiard *w* Belmondo, Gabin 102min (= *It's Hot in Hell*)
SINGER JIM McKEE (1924) *d Clifford S Smith p/pc/st/w* W Hart 7rs
SINGER NOT THE SONG, THE (1961) *d* R Baker *w* Bogarde, J Mills CS 132min JAR
Singer's Paradise = WONDERFUL LIFE (1964)
SINGING BLACKSMITH, THE (1938) *d* Ulmer 110min
SINGING FOOL, THE (1928) *d* Bacon *c* Haskin *w* Jolson 9552ft WB
SINGING KID, THE (1936) *d* Keighley *c* Barnes *w* Jolson, Horton 85min FN
Singing Lesson, The = RAZ DWA TRZY (1967)
SINGING MARINE, THE (1937) *d* Enright *st/s* Daves *w* D Powell, Wyman, Darwell 12rs WB
SINGING NUN, THE (1965) *d* Koster *c* Krasner *w* Montalban, D Reynolds, Moorehead, Garson
SINGING OUTLAW (1937) *d* JH Lewis 56min U
SINGIN' IN THE RAIN (1952) *co-d/co-chor* Gene Kelly, Donen *p* Freed *s* Comden, A Green *c* Rosson *co-a* Gibbons *co-m* Edens *w* Gene Kelly, D Reynolds, O'Connor, Charisse *102min MGM
SINGLE HANDED (1951) *d* R Boulting *p* J Boulting *fn* (*Brown on Resolution*) *CS Forester c* G Taylor *w* J Hunter, (J Schlesinger) 84min Fox (= *Able Seaman Brown/Brown On Resolution/Sailor of the King*)
SINGLE STANDARD, THE (1929) *d John S Robertson a* Gibbons *w* Garbo. McCrea) 6574ft MGM
SING ME A LOVE SONG (1936) *d* Enright *co-s* Wald *w* Pitts, Sheridan 79min WB
SINGOALLA (1949) *d* Christian-Jaque *w* Lindfors 77min (= *Mask and the Sword*)
SING WHILE YOU'RE ABLE (1937) *d* Neilan 70min
Sing Young People = UTAE WAKODOTACHI (1963)
SING YOUR WAY HOME (1945) *d* A Mann 72min RKO
SING YOU SINNERS (1938) *d/p* W Ruggles *c* Struss *co-a* Dreier *song* Carmichael *w* B Crosby, MacMurray, O'Connor 88min Par
SINHALESE DANCE, A (1950) *d* Peries 16mm 8min
SINISTER MAN, THE (1961) *d* C Donner *fn Edgar Wallace* 60min
SINK THE BISMARCK (1960) *d* L Gilbert *c* Challis 97min Fox
SINKING OF THE LUSITANIA, THE (1918) *d* McCay anim
SINLESS SINNER, A (1919) *d* Brenon
SIN MONGOLII (1936) *d* I Trauberg, *R Suslovich* 89min (= *Son of Mongolia*)
Sinners, The = PISCINE, LA (1968)
SINNER'S HOLIDAY (1930) *d John G Adolfi w* Blondell, Cagney 60min WB
SINNERS IN HEAVEN (1924) *d/p* Crosland 7rs FPL
SINNERS IN PARADISE (1938) *d* Whale 64min U
SIN OF HAROLD DIDDLEBOCK, THE (1946) *d/p/st/s* P Sturges *w* H Lloyd 77min *r* UA (= *Mad Wednesday*)
SIN OF JESUS (1961) *d* R Frank *fst Isaac Babel* 40min
SIN OF MADELON CLAUDET, THE (1931) *d Edward Selwyn di* MacArthur *w* H Hayes, Hersholt, R Young
SIN OF MARTHA QUEED, THE (1921) *d/p/s* Dwan *c* Gaudio 6rs
SINS OF HER PARENT (1916) *d/s* F Lloyd 5rs Fox
Sins of Lola Montes = LOLA MONTES (1955)
SINS OF MAN (1936) *d* Ratoff, *Otto Brower p* Zanuck *as-p* Macgowan *w* Hersholt 77min Fox
Sins of Rachel Cade, The = RACHEL CADE (1961)
Sins of Rome (US) = SPARTACO (1952)
SINS OF ST. ANTHONY, THE (1920) *d* Cruze FPL
Sins of the Children = RICHEST MAN IN THE WORLD, THE (1930)
SIN'S PAY DAY (1932) *d* G Seitz *c* Cronjager 61min
SIN TOWN (1942) *d* Enright *w* Constance Bennett, B Crawford 75min U
SIN UNIFORME (1948) *d* Vajda 82min
SI PARIS NOUS ETAIT CONTE (1956) *d/s* Guitry *c* Agostini *m Jean Françaix w* Guitry, Arnoul, Darrieux, Marais, Morgan, Philipe, Carette, (*Maurice Utrillo*), De Funes *130min
Sir Arne's Treasure = HERR ARNE'S PENGAR (1919)
SIREN, THE (1927) *d* Jaslom *p* Cohn *c* June 5996ft Col
SIRENE DU MISSISSIPPI, LA (1969) *d/ad/di* Truffaut *w* Deneuve, Belmondo FS* 125min *co-pc* Truffaut (= *Mississippi Mermaid*)
SIREN OF ATLANTIS (1948) *d Gregg R Tallas, Arthur Ripley* (*uc*), Sirk (*uc*), Brahm (*uc*) *c* Struss *w* Montez 75min *r* UA (= *Atlantis, The Lost Continent*)
SIREN OF BAGDAD (1953) *d* Quine *p* Katzman *w* Henreid *72min Col
SIREN OF IMPULSE, A (1912) *d* Griffith *w* Marsh 1rl Bio
SIREN'S SONG, THE (1919) *d J Gordon Edwards w* Bara 5rs
SIRIUS REMEMBERED (1959) *d* Brakhage 16mm* si 12min
SIRKUS FANDANGO (1954) *d* Skouen (= *Circus Fandango*)
SIROCCO (1951) *d* C Bernhardt *c* Guffey *w* Bogart, Cobb 85min Col
Sirocco d'hiver = SIROKKO (1969)
SIROKKO (1969) *d/co-s* Jancso *w* Vlady S* 80min (= *Sirocco d'hiver/Winter Wind*)
SIS HOPKINS (1919) *d* Badger *w* Normand 5rs *pc* Goldwyn
SISKA (1962) *d* Kjellin *co-s* Sjöman *co-c* Fischer *w* H Andersson SF
SISSI (1932) *d* Reiniger anim 1rl
SISSIGNORA (1942) *d/co-s* Poggioli *p* Ponti *co-s* Lattuada
SISTA PARET UT (1956) *d/co-s* Sjöberg *st/co-s* Ingmar Bergman *w* Dahlbeck, B Andersson, H Andersson, Kulle SF (= *Last Pair Out*)
SISTA STEGEN, DE (1960) *d* Cromwell *c* Nykvist *w* Dahlbeck 98min (= *A Matter of Morals*)
Sister Angelica = SESTRA ANGELIKA (1932)
SISTER KENNY (1946) *d/p/st/co-s* D Nichols *co-s Mary McCarthy c* Barnes *w* R Russell 116min RKO
SISTERS (1911) *co-d* Ince *w* Pickford
SISTERS, THE (1938) *d* Litvak *p* Wallis *w* B Davis, Flynn, (S Hayward) 95min WB
Sisters of Gion = GION NO SHIMAI (1936)
Sisters of Nishijin, The = NISHIJIN NO SHIMAI (1952)
SI TOUS LES GARS DU MONDE . . . (1955) *d/co-s* Christian-Jaque *co-s* Clouzot *c* Thirard *w* Trintignant 110min (= *Race For Life*)
SIT TIGHT (1931) *d* Bacon 9rs WB
SITTING PRETTY (1948) *d* W Lang *c* Brodine *co-a* Wheeler *w* M O'Hara, C Webb, R Young 84min Fox
SITUATION HOPELESS–BUT NOT SERIOUS (1965) *d/p* G Reinhardt *s Sylvia Reinhardt fn* (*The Hiding Place*) *Robert Shaw w* Redford 98min Par
SIUZHET DLYA NEBOLSHOVO RASSKAZA (1968) *d* Yutkevich *w* Vlady 70* 90min (= *Lika, le Grand Amour de Tchekhov/Lika, Tchekhov's Love*)
SIVA L'INVISIBLE (1904) *d* Méliès 25m
SI VERSAILLES M'ETAIT CONTE (1954) *d/s* Guitry *m Jean Françaix w* Guitry, Barrault, Bourvil, Colbert, Gélin, Marais, Philipe, *Edith Piaf,* Presle, Vanel, Welles, Bardot, Desailly, Rossif *160min
SIX BEST CELLARS, THE (1920) *d* Crisp 5rs FPL
SIX BLACK HORSES (1962) *d* Keller *s* B Kennedy *co-a* Golitzen *w* A Murphy, Duryea *80min U
SIX BRIDGES TO CROSS (1955) *d* Pevney *p* A Rosenberg *c* Daniels *song* Mancini *w* Curtis 96min U
SIX CENT MILLE FRANCS PAR MOIS (1933) *d* Joannon
SIX CENTS MILLIONS AVEC VOUS (1958) *d/s* Ivens *300m
SIX CYLINDER LOVE (1917) *d/s/w* Mix 2rs Fox
6 DAY BIKE RIDER (1934) *d* Bacon 69min WB
SIX ET DEMI-ONZE (1927) *d/p* J Epstein *c* Périnal, J Epstein (= *Un Kodak*)
SIX FEET FOUR (1919) *d* H King 6rs
SIX HOURS TO LIVE (1932) *d* Dieterle *c* J Seitz *w* W Baxter 80min Fox
SIXIEME FACE DU PENTAGONE, LA (1968) *d/s/co-c* Marker *co-c* Reichenbach 16mm 28min
Six in Paris (UK) = PARIS VU PAR . . . (1964)
6 JUIN A L'AUBE, LE (1945) *d/s/cy/m* Grémillon 58min
SIX OF A KIND (1934) *d* McCarey *w* C Ruggles, Fields 62min Par
Sixth Continent (US) = SESTO CONTINENTO (1954)
6.30 COLLECTION (1936) *d* Watt, B Wright *p* Grierson 16min GPO
Sixth of the World, A = SHESTAYA CHAST MIRA (1926)
6000 ENEMIES (1939) *d* G Setiz *c* J Seitz *w* Pidgeon 60min MGM
633 SQUADRON (1963) *d Walter E Grauman s* Clavell, H Koch *w* Robertson PV* 101min *r* UA
SIXTY GLORIOUS YEARS (1938) *d* H Wilcox *c* F Young *w* Neagle, Walbrook *95min
69 (1968) *d* Breer anim* 16mm 6min
SIXTY-NINE (1969) *d/pc/s/w* J Donner S* 90min
66 (1966) *d* Breer anim 16mm 6min
SJAELETYVEN (1915) *d* Madsen
SJOVE AAR, DE (1959) *d* Kjaerulff-Schmidt
SJUNDE INSEGLET, DET (1957) *d/s* Ingmar Bergman *c* Fischer *w* Björnstrand, Von Sydow, B Andersson, Lindblom 95min SF
SJUTTON AR (1957) *d/co-s* Kjellin (= *Seventeen Years Old*)
SKAEBNENATTEN (1926) *d/s* Madsen
SKAL VI LEGE SKJUL (1969) *d/co-s Tom Hedegard co-s* Kjaerulff-Schmidt *75min (= *Let's Play Hide and Seek*)
SKAMMEN (1968) *d/s* Ingmar Bergman *c* Nykvist *w* Von Sydow, Björnstrand, Lindstom, Sjöman 103min SF (= *The Shame*)
SKANDAL UM EVA (1930) *d* Pabst *c* F Wagner 95min Nero
SKARLATINA (1924) *d* Ermler 1230m
SKEDADDLE GOLD (1927) *d* Thorpe
SKELETON DANCE, THE (1930) *p* Disney anim 1rl *r* Col
SKELETON FROLIC (1937) *d* Iwerks anim* 1rl *r* Col
SKEPP SOM MOTAS (1915) *d* Sjöström 950m
SKEPP TILL INDIALAND (1947) *d/s* Ingmar Bergman *c* Strindberg 102min (= *The Land of Desire/A Ship to India*)
Sketch of Madame Tuki = YUKI FUJIN EZU (1950)
SKIDOO (1968) *d/p* Preminger *c* Shamroy *w* G Marx, Romero, Raft, Rooney, Meredith PV* 98min
SKID ROW (1956) *d* A King 16mm 38min
SKILSMISSENS BORN (1939) *d/s* Christensen (= *The Children of Divorce*)
SKIN DEEP (1929) *d* Enright 7rs WB
Skin Deep = UNE ET L'AUTRE, L' (1967)
SKIN GAME, THE (1931) *d/s* Hitchcock *ad/di* Reville *fpl John Galsworthy* 85min
SKIN GAME, THE (1971) *d* G Douglas, *Paul Bogart p* Keller *w* Garner *102min
SKIPPER SURPRISED HIS WIFE, THE (1950) *d* E Nugent *c* Lipstein *co-a* Gibbons *m* Kaper *w* R Walker 85min MGM
SKIPPY (1931) *d* Taurog *s* McLeod, J Mankiewicz *c* Struss 85min Par

SKIRT SHY (1921, *ur*) *d* Cruze
SKI TROOP ATTACK (1960) *d/p/w* Corman 62min
SKLAVENKONIGIN, DIE (1924) *d* Curtis (= *Moon of Israel*)
Skogsdotterns Hemlighet = KARLEK STARKARE AN HAT (1913)
Skola Zaklad Zivota (1938) *d* Frič (= *School, the Beginning of Life*)
SKOMARARE BLIV VID DIN LAST (1915) *d/s* Sjöström 913m
SKOTTET (1914) *d* Stiller 947m
SKOVENS BORN (1917) *d/s* Madsen
SKRIVANCI NA NITICH (1969) *d* Menzel *fst Bohumil Hrabal* (= *Larks on a Thread*)
SKUGGOR OVER SNON (1945) *d/s/c/e* Sucksdorff 11min SF
SKULL, THE (1965) *d* F Francis 83min Par
SKY BIKE, THE (1967) *d/s* Frend *62min
SKY FULL OF MOON (1952) *d/s* Foster *p* Franklin *c* June *co-a* Gibbons 73min MGM
Sky is Clear, The = SORA WA HARETARI (1925)
SKYLARK (1941) *d/p* Sandrich *fn/fpl* Raphaelson *c* C Lang *co-a* Dreier *w* Milland, Colbert 94min Par
Skylark = PACSIRTA (1964)
SKY MURDER (1940) *d* G Seitz *c* Lawton *w* Pigeon 72min MGM
SKY PILOT, THE (1921) *d/co-p* K Vidor *c* O'Connell *w* D Butler 77min *r* FN
Sky Pirate, A = SKY PIRATE, THE (1914)
SKY PIRATE, THE (1921) *d/w* Arbuckle 1rl Key (= *A Sky Pirate*)
SKY RANGER, THE (1921) *d/w* G Seitz serial in 15eps Par
SKY RANGER, THE (1928) *d* H Brown 2rs
SKYROCKET, THE (1926) *d* Neilan 7350ft
SKYSCRAPER, THE (1958) *d* W Van Dyke, S Clarke *co-c* Pennebaker *e* S Clark part* 15min
SKYSCRAPER SYMPHONY (1927–8) *d/st* Florey *s/co-c/e* Vorkapich *co-c* Toland sh
SKY SPIDER (1931) *d* Thorpe 69min
SKY'S THE LIMIT, THE (1943) *d* Edward H Griffith *c* Metty *chor* Astaire *m* Harline *w* Lawford, Astaire, Ryan 89min RKO
SKYWAYMAN, THE (1928) *d* H Brown 2rs
SKY WEST AND CROOKED (1965) *d/p/w* J Mills *w* H Mills *102min
SLALOM (1965) *d* Salce *w* Gassman 97min
SLANDER (1956) *d* Rowland *w* V Johnson, Blyth, Cochran 81min MGM
SLANT AR EN SLANT, INTE SANT, EN (*c* 1955) *d* Lindgren (= *A Coin is a Coin*)
SLAP HAPPY LION (1947) *d* Avery *p* Quimby anim* 7min MGM
Slasher, The (US) = COSH BOY (1952)
SLATTERY'S HURRICANE (1949) *d* De Toth *p* Perlberg *st/co-s Herman Wouk co-s* R Murphy *c* C Clarke *co-a* Wheeler *w* Widmark, Darnell, Lake 83min Fox
SLAVA (1958) *d* Pojar *co-s* Brdecka anim* 15min (= *Fame*)
SLAVA SOVETSKIM GEROINYAM (1938) *d/s* Vertov, *Elisabeth Svilova* 1rl (= *To the Glory of Soviet Heroines*)
Slave, The = FIGLIO DI SPARTACUS, IL (1962)
SLAVES (1969) *d/co-s* Biberman *c* Brun *w* Boyd *110min WB
SLAVE SHIP (1937) *d* Garnett *p* Zanuck *as-p* N Johnson *ad* Faulkner *co-a* Trotti *m* A Newman *w* Beery, Rooney, G Saunders, W Baxter, Darwell 8315ft Fox
SLAVES OF BABYLON (1953) *d* Castle *p* Katzman *w* Conte *81min Col
Slave Trade in the World Today, The = SCHIAVE ESISTONO ANCORA, LE (1963)
SLAVNOSTI A HOSTECH, O (1966) *d/co-s/w* Nemec *w* Schorm 71min (= *The Party and the Guests/Report on the Party and the Guests*)
SLEEP (1963) *d* Warhol 16mm si 360min
Sleeping Beauty, The = SPYASHAYA KRASAVITSA (1930)
SLEEPING BEAUTY, THE (1954) *d* Reiniger *fst Brothers Grimm* anim 10min
SLEEPING BEAUTY (1958) *p* Disney *fst Charles Perrault sp eff* Iwerks *co-anim* C Jones *m* (*Sleeping Beauty*) *Tchaikovsky* 70mm* 75min
SLEEPING CAR (1933) *d* Litvak Gau
Sleeping Car Murders, The = COMPARTIMENT TUEURS (1965)
SLEEPING TIGER, THE (1954) *d/p* Losey (*ps* Victor Hanbury) *co-s* Foreman (*ps* Derek Frye) *des* R MacDonald *m* M Arnold *w* Bogarde, A Smith 98min
SLEEP, MY LOVE (1948) *d* Sirk *co-s* St Clair *w* R Cummings, Colbert 97min *r* UA
SLENDER THREAD, THE (1965) *d* Pollack *s* Silliphant *c* Griggs *co-a* Pereira *w* A Bancroft, Poitier 98min Par
SLEPAYA (1930) *d* Kalatozov (= *Blind*)
SLEUTHS AT THE FLORAL PARADE, THE (1913) *d/p/w* Sennett *w* Normand
SLEUTH'S LAST STAND, THE (1913) *d/p/w* Sennett 1rl Key
Slice of Life (UK) = TEMPI NOSTRI (1954)
SLIGHT CASE OF LARCENY, A (1953) *d* Weis *st* Poe *c* June *co-a* Gibbons *w* Rooney 71min MGM

SLIGHT CASE OF MURDER (1938) *d* Bacon *p* Wallis *c* Hickox *w* Robinson 85min WB
SLIGHTLY DANGEROUS (1943) *d* W Ruggles *p* Berman *co-s* Lederer *c* Rosson *a* Gibbons *m* Kaper *w* Turner, R Walker, Brennan 94min MGM
SLIGHTLY FRENCH (1949) *d* Sirk *c* Lawton *m* Duning *w* Lamour 81min Col
SLIGHTLY HONORABLE (1940) *d/p* Garnett *a* Golitzen *w* B Crawford 83min *r* UA
SLIGHTLY MARRIED (1932) *d* Thorpe 65min
SLIGHTLY SCARLET (1956) *d* Dwan *p* Bogeaus *fst* (*Love's Lovely Counterfeit*) *James M Cain c* J Alton *w* R Fleming, Payne S* 99min RKO
SLIGHTLY TERRIFIC (1944) *d* Cline 61min U
SLIGHTLY USED (1927) *d* A Mayo *c* Mohr 6300ft WB
SLIM (1937) *d* Enright *p* Wallis *c* Hickox *w* H Fonda, Wyman 9rs WB
SLIM PRINCESS, THE (1920) *d* Schertzinger *w* Normand 6rs *pc* Goldwyn
SLIPPING WIVES (1927) *d* Fred Guiol *w* Laurel, Hardy Pat
SLOT I ET SLOT, ET (1954) *co-d/s* Dreyer 16mm (= *Krogen og kronenborg/Castle within a Castle*)
SLOWCE M (1963) *d* Brdecka (= *The Letter M*)
SLUCHAI V VULKANYE (1941) *d* Kuleshov, *Alexandra Khoklova, Eugene Schneider, Vladimir Shneiderov* 7rs (= *Incident in a Volcano*)
Slug in the Heater, A (US) = BALLE DANS LE CANON, UNE (1958)
Slump is over, The = CRISE EST FINIE, LA (1934)
SMALL BACK ROOM, THE (1948) *d/p/s* M Powell, Pressburger *fn Nigel Balchin c* Challis *w* Hawkins, Forbes 106min BL (= *Hour of Glory*)
SMALLEST SHOW ON EARTH, THE (1957) *d* Dearden *c* Slocombe *w* Sellers 81min BL
Small Space = CHIISANA KUKAN (1964)
SMALL TOWN GIRL (1936) *d* Wellman *co-s* Machin, Goodrich, Hackett *a* Gibbons *co-m* Stothart *w* J Granger, J Stewart, R Taylor 90min MGM
SMALL TOWN GIRL (1953) *d* Leslie Kardos *p* Pasternak *c* Ruttenberg *co-a* Gibbons *m* Previn *w* F Granger, Ann Miller, J Powell *93min MGM
SMALL TOWN IDOL, A (1921) *d* Erle C Kenton *p/st/s* Sennett *w* Turpin 7rs *r* FN
SMALL VOICE, THE (1947) *d* Fergus McDonnell *w* Keel 83min
SMALL WORLD OF SAMMY LEE, THE (1963) *d/p/s* K Hughes 107min BL
SMART ALEC (1951) *d* Guillermin 58min
SMART SET (1928) *d* Conway 6476ft MGM
SMART WOMAN (1931) *d* La Cava *c* Musuraca *w* Astor, Horton 68min RKO
SMART WORK (1931) *d* Arbuckle (*ps* William Goodrich) 1rl
SMARTY (1934) *d* Florey *c* Barnes *w* Blondell, Horton 64min WB
SMASHING TIME (1967) *d* D Davis, *co-p* Ponti *w* Tushingham *96min *r* Par
SMASH-UP (1947) *d* Heisler *p* Wanger *s* Lawson *c* Cortez *a* Golitzen *m* Amfitheatrof *w* S Hayward 103min U (= *The Story of a Woman*)
SMIC, SMAC, SMOC (1971) *d/s/di/c* Lelouch *100min
Smile of Our Earth = DAICHI WA HOHOEMU (1925)
SMILE PLEASE (1924) *d* Hampton Del Ruth *w* Langdon 2rs *pc* Sennett *r* Pat
Smiles of a Summer Night = SOMMARNATTENS LEENDE (1955)
Smiling Character, A = HOHOEMU HINSEI (1930)
SMILING LIEUTENENT, THE (1931) *d/co-s* Lubitsch *co-s* Raphaelson *c* Folsey *dec* Dreier *w* Chevalier, Colbert, M Hopkins, C Ruggles 82min Par
SMILING THROUGH (1922) *d/co-s* Franklin
SMILIN' THROUGH (1932) *d* Franklin *co-di* D Stewart *c* Garmes *w* Shearer, L Howard, March 97min MGM
SMILIN' THROUGH (1941) *d* Borzage *p* Saville *co-s* D Stewart *w* Jeanette Macdonald *100min MGM
SMITH (1917) *d/p* Elvey *fpl* S Maugham 3440ft
SMITH'S BABY (1926) *d* Cline *s* Sennett
SMITHSONIAN INSTITUTION, THE (1965) *d/s* C and R Eames *c* C Eames *m* E Bernstein 36min
SMITHSONIAN NEWSREEL, THE (1965) *d/s* C and R Eames *c* C Eames 20min
SMITH'S VACATION (1926) *d/co-s* Cline *p* Sennett Pat
SMOG (1962) *d/co-st/co-s* Rossi *co-s* Festa Campanile *w* Girardot 100min MGM
SMOKED HUSBAND, A (1908) *d* Griffith 144m Bio
SMOKE JUMPERS (1953) *d* J Newman 16mm * 11min
SMOKY (1946) *d* Louis King *c* C Clarke *co-a* Wheeler *w* MacMurray, A Baxter, Ives 87min Fox
SMOKY CANYON (1951) *d* Sears 55min Col
SMOULDERING FIRES (1924) *d* C Brown 8rs U
Smugglarens Dotter = HAVSGAMARNA (1915)
Smuggler's Ball, The (UK) = BANQUET DES FRAUDERS (1952)
SMULTRONSTALLET (1957) *d/s* Ingmar Bergman *c* Fischer *w* Sjöström, B Andersson, Thulin, Björnstrand, Von Sydow, Lindblom 95min SF (= *Wild Strawberries*)
Snake of Death (UK) = QUAI DES GRENELLE (1950)
SNAKE PIT, THE (1948) *d/co-p* Litvak *co-a* Wheeler *m* A Newman *w* De Havilland, Marsh 108min Fox

SNAKE WOMAN, THE (1960) *d* Furie 68min *r* UA
Snares (UK) = PIEGES (1939)
SNIPER, THE (1952) *d* Dmytryk *c* Guffey *m* Antheil *w* Menjou 87min *pc* Kramer *r* Col
SNOB, THE (1921) *d* S Wood 4015ft
SNOBS, LES (1961) *d/s* Mocky *m* Kosma *w* Blanche 90min
SNOOKUMS (1912–14) *d* Cohl, *George MacManus* anim series
SNORKEL, THE (1917) *d* G Green 90min Col
SNOWBALL (1960) *d* Jackson 69min JAR
SNOWBALL AND HIS PAL (1912) *d/w* Conway
SNOWED UNDER (1936) *d* Enright 63min WB
Snow Flurry = KAZAHANA (1959)
Snowshoers, The = RAQUETTEURS, LES (1958)
SNOWS OF KILIMANJARO, THE (1952) *d* H King *p* Zanuck *fst* Hemingway *c* Shamroy *co-a* Wheeler *m* Herrmann *w* Peck, S Hayward, Gardner, Dalio, Neff *117min Fox
SNOW WHITE AND ROSE RED (1953) *d* Reiniger *fst Brothers Grimm* anim 10min
SNOWTIME (1938) *d* Iwerks anim* 7min *r* Col
SNOW WHITE AND THE SEVEN DWARFS (1937) *p* Disney *fst Brothers Grimm* *co-m* Harline *83min *r* RKO
Snow White and the Three Clowns (UK) = SNOW WHITE AND THE THREE STOOGES (1961)
SNOW WHITE AND THE THREE STOOGES (1961) *d* W Lang *c* Shamroy CS* 107min Fox (= *Snow White and the Three Clowns*)
Snowy Heron, The = SHIRASAGI (1959)
SNUFF SMITH, YARD BIRD (1942) *d* Cline 67min Mon
SOAK THE RICH (1936) *d/p/st/s* B Hecht, MacArthur *c* Shamroy 86min Par
SO ALONE (1958) *d* J Ford *c* Hoch, Lassally *m* M Arnold 8min
SOAP OPERA (1964) *d* Warhol 16mm si 70min (= *The Lester Persky Story*)
SOAPSUDS LADY, THE (1925) *d* Cline *p* Sennett Pat
SO BIG (1925) *d* Charles Brabin *c* McCord *w* Beery, Hersholt 8562ft FN
SO BIG (1932) *d* Wellman *c* Hickox *w* Stanwyck, B Davis 90min WB
SO BIG (1953) *d* Wise *p* Blanke *c* Fredricks *w* Wyman, Hayden 101min WB
SOBRE MADRID (1960) *d* Grau
SOCIAL BUCCANEER, THE (1916) *d* Conway 5rs
SOCIAL CELEBRITY, A (1926) *d/p* St Clair *c* Garmes *w* L Brooks 6rs FPL
SOCIAL REGISTER (1934) *d* Neilan *fpl* Loos, Emerson 72min Col
SOCIETA' OVESTTICINO-DINAMO (1955) *d* Olmi *30min
SOCIETY DOCTOR (1935) *d* G Seitz *w* R Taylor 64min MGM
SOCIETY SCANDAL, A (1924) *d/p* Dwan *c* Rosson *w* Swanson 6857ft FPL
SOCIETY SECRETS (1921) *d* McCarey 4795ft U
SOCIETY SMUGGLERS (1939) *d* May 65min U
So Close to Life = NARA LIVET (1957)
SOCRATE (1970) *d/p/co-s/e* Rossellini *120min
SO DARK THE NIGHT (1946) *d* JH Lewis *c* Guffey *co-m* Freidhofer 70min Col
SODA WATER COWBOY, A (1926) *d* Thorpe
SO DEAR TO MY HEART (1948) *d* Harold Schuster *p* Disney *c* Hoch *w* Ives, Carey 82min RKO
SODOM AND GOMORRAH (1962) *d* Aldrich, *Sergio Leone s* H Butler *des* Adam *m* Rozsa *w* S Baker, Aimée, S Granger *153min *r* JAR
SODOM UND GOMORRAH (1922) *d/co-s* Curtiz UFA (= *The Queen of Sin*)
SO ENDS OUR NIGHT (1941) *d* Cromwell *co-p* Lewin *fn* (*Flotsam*) *Erich Maria Remarque c* Daniels *des* Menzies *w* March, G Ford, Von Stroheim, Sten 117min UA
SOEURS ENNEMIES, LES (1917) *d* Dulac
SOFA COMPACT (1954) *d/s* C and R Eames *c* C Eames *11min
SOFT CUSHIONS (1927) *d* Cline 6rs Par
SOFU TESHIGAHARA (1957) *d* Teshigahara *w* Sofu Teshigahara
SOGNU DI UN GIORNO, IL (1916) *d/st* Genina
SOGNI NEL CASSETTO, I (1957) *d/st* Castellani *w* Baldi 90min
OSGNO DI BUTTERFLY, IL (1939) *d* Gallone *m* Puccini *w* Gobbi
SOGNO DI UNA NOTTE DI MEZZA SBORNIA, IL (1959) *d/w* De Filippo 90min
SOGNO DI ZA LA VIE, IL (1923) *d/p/s/w* Ghione
SOGNO DI ZORRO, IL (1951) *d* Soldati *w* Gassman, Loren 93min
SOHO (1933) *d* Naruse (= *Careless*)
SOHO (1943) *d/p/s/c* K Hughes
SOIGNE TON GAUCHE (1936) *d/c* Clément *s/di/w* Tati sh
SOIR DE RAPLE, UN (1932) *d* Gallone *s* Decoin, Clouzot *m* Van Parys 94min
SOIR .... UN TRAIN, UN (1968) *d/s/co-song* Delvaux *c* Cloquet *w* Montand, Aimée *90min
SOIS BELLE ET TAIS-TOI (1958) *d/co-st/co-s* M Allégret *co-s* Vadim *c* Thirard *m* Wiener *w* Delon, Belmondo
SOLD (1915) *d* Porter FP

SOLDATESSE, LE (1965) d Zurlini w Karina 136min
SOLDATI IN CITTA (1952) d Zurlini sh
SOLDIER BLUE (1970) d Nelson ex-p Levine PV* 112min
SOLDIER IN THE RAIN (1963) d Nelson p/s Edwards c
Lathrop m Mancini w McQueen, Weld 88min AA
SOLDIER OF FORTUNE (1955) d Dmytryk p Alder c
Tover co-a Wheeler w Grable, S Hayward, Sten CS*
96min Fox
Soldier of Victory = ZOL NIERZ ZWYCIESTWA (1953)
Soldier on Duty = CAPORALE DI GIORNATA (1958)
Soldiers, The = CARABINIERS, LES (1963)
SOLDIER'S COURTSHIP, THE (1896) p Paul 40ft
SOLDIER'S HONOR, THE (1913) d Ince
SOLDIERS IN WHITE (1941) d B Reeves Eason w Parker
*20min WB
SOLDIERS OF FORTUNE (1919) d Dwan c Polito w Beery
7rs
Soldier's Pay, A (UK) = SOLDIER'S PLAYTHING, A
(1930)
SOLDIER'S PLAYTHING, A (1930) d Curtiz w Langdon,
Hersholt 58min (= A Soldier's Pay)
Soldier's Prayer, A = NINGEN NO JOKEN Part 3 (1961)
SOLDIERS THREE (1951) d Garnett p Berman fn Kipling c
Mellor co-a Gibbons w S Granger, Pidgeon£ Niven,
Newton 87min MGM
Soldiers Were Marching = SHLI SOLDATY (1958)
Sold into Egypt = GUISEPPE VENDUTO DAI FRATELLI
(1960)
SOLE (1929) d/co-s/e Blasetti
SOLE CHE MUOVE, IL (1964) d Mingozzi sh
SOLEIL DES VOYOUS, LE (1967) d Delannoy w Gabin,
Stack S* 100min (= The Action Man)
SOLEIL NOIR (1966) d De La Patellière w Gélin S* 100min
(= Black Sun/Dark Sunlight)
SOLEIL ROUGE (1971) d T Young c Alekan m Jarre w
Andress, Mifune, Delon *115min (= Red Sun)
SOLE NEGLI OCCHI, IL (1953) d/co-st/s Pietrangeli co-s
Cecchi d'Amico w Ferzetti 94min
SOLE SORGE ANCORA, IL (1947) d Aldo Vergano co-s
De Santis (= The Sun Rises Again)
SOLID GOLD CADILLAC, THE (1956) d Quine p
Kohlmer fco-pl G Kaufman c C Lang m Mockridge w
Holliday, P Douglas 99min Col
SOLILOQUY (1951) d Peries 16min 12min
SOLIMANE IL CONQUISTARE (1961) d Mimica, Mario
Tota co-s Mimica S* 91min (= Suleiman the Con-
queror)
SOLITARE MAN (1933) d Conway w H Marshall 69min
MGM
SOLITI IGNOTI, I (1958) d/co-s Monicelli co-s Cecchi
d'Amico c Di Venanzo w Gassman, Cardinale
Mastroianni, Toto 105min (= Person Unknown)
SO LITTLE TIME (1951) d Compton Bennett w Maria
Schell 88min
SOLITUDE (1961) d Borowczyk, Lenica anim
SOLO (1969) d/co-s/w Mocky *90min
SOLO CONTRO ROMA (1962) d Freda, N Vicario S*
94min (= Vengence of the Gladiators/The Fall of
Rome)
SOLOMON AND SHEBA (1959) d/ex-p K Vidor c F Young
co-a R Day w Brynner, Lollobrigida, G Sanders S*
141min r UA
SO LONG AT THE FAIR (1950) d T Fisher, Anthony
Darnborough w J Simmons, Bogarde 86min
SL LONG LETTY (1929) d Bacon 5878ft WB
SOLO PER TE (1938) d Gallone
SOLO PER TE, LUCIA (1952) d Rossi
SOL OVER DANIMARK (1936) d/s Madsen
SOLSTIK (1953) d A and B Henning Jensen
SOL SVANETII (1930) d/s Kalatozov 1500m (= Salt for
Svanetia)
SOLUTIONS FRANCAISES (1939) d Painlevé m Jaubert
SOLUTIONS FRANCAISES (1947) d Painlevé rm 1939 m
Jaubert
SOMBRAS DE GLORIA (1930) d Stone 100min
(= Shadows of Glory)
SOMBRERO (1953) d/s Foster c June co-a Gibbons w
Montalban, De Carlo, Charisse *103min MGM
SOMEBODY UP THERE LIKES ME (1956) d Wise s
Lehman c Ruttenberg co-a Gibbons m Kaper w P
Newman, McQueen 113min MGM
SOME CAME RUNNING (1958) d Minnelli p S Siegel fn
James Jones c Daniels m E Bernstein w Sinatra,
Martin, MacLaine, A Kennedy CS* 136min r MGM
SOME DAY (1935) d M Powell w Lockwood 68min
SOME KIND OF A NUT (1969) d/s Kanin p W Mirisch
co-c Guffey w D Van Dyke, A Dickinson *89min r
UA
SOME LIARS (1919) d H King 5rs
Some Like It Cold = A NOI PIACE FREDDO (1960)
SOME LIKE IT HOT (1959) d/p/co-s B Wilder co-as-p/co-s
Diamond c C Lang w Monroe, Curtis, Lemmon, Raft
121min co-pc Mir r UA
SO MUCH FOR SO LITTLE (1949) d C Jones, Freleng
anim* 11min WB
Some Nerve = GENTLEMEN OF NERVE (1914)
Some of Us May Die = JOURNEY, THE (1958)
SOMEONE AT THE DOOR (1936) d Brenon 75min
SOMEONE TO REMEMBER (1943) d Siodmak w Lawford
80min

SOME PEOPLE (1962) d C Donner w Hemmings *93min
SOMETHING ALWAYS HAPPENS (1934) d M Powell
69min
SOMETHING BIG (1971) d/p A McLaglen w Martin, Keith
*107min
Something Different (UK) = O NICEM JINEM (1963)
SOMETHING FOR THE BIRDS (1952) d Wise co-s
Diamond c La Shelle co-a Wheeler w Neal, Mature
81min Fox
SOMETHING FOR THE BOYS (1944) d Lewis Seiler c
Miranda w Holliday 87min Fox
SOMETHING IN THE WIND (1947) d Pichel co-s Kurnitz
c Krasner w Durbin, O'Connor 89min U
SOMETHING MONEY CAN'T BUY (1952) d/co-s Jackson
m Rota 83min JAR
SOMETHING OF VALUE (1957) d/s R Brooks p Berman c
R Harlan m Rozsa w Hudson, Poitier 113min r
MGM
SOMETHING'S GOT TO GIVE (1962, uf) d Cukor co-p A
Rosenberg co-s Kanter w Monroe, Martin, Charisse
Fox [re-made as MOVE OVER DARLING (1963)]
SOMETHING SIMPLE (1934) d C Chase (as Parrott),
Walter Weems p Roach w C Chase 2rs MGM
SOMETHING TO LIVE FOR (1952) d/p G Stevens c
Barnes co-a Pereira m N Young w Fontaine, T
Wright, Milland 89min Par
SOMETHING TO SHOUT ABOUT (1943) d/p Ratoff c
Planer w Charisse (ps Lily Norwood) 89min Col
SOMETHING TO SING ABOUT (1937) d/st/m Schert-
zinger w Cagney 92min
SOMETHING TO THINK ABOUT (1920) d De Mille co-c
Struss w Swanson 7rs FPL
SOMETHING WILD (1961) d/co-s Garfein n R Day cr Bass
m Copland w C Baker, Meeker 112min r UA
SOMETIMES A GREAT NOTION (1971) d P Newman,
Richard Colla(uc) s Gay fn Ken Kesey m Mancini w
P Newman, H Fonda, Remick *114min U
Somewhere Beneath the Wild Sky = KONO HIROI SORA
NO DOKOKANI (1954)
SOMEWHERE I'LL FIND YOU (1942) d W Ruggles p
Berman c Rosson a Gibbons w Gable, Turner, V
Johnson 108min MGM
Somewhere in France (US) = FOREMAN WENT TO
FRANCE, THE (1942)
SOMEWHERE IN THE NIGHT (1946) d/co-s J Man-
kiewicz c Brodine w Conte, Nolan 110min Fox
SOMMAREN MED MONIKA (1952) d/co-s Ingmar
Bergman c Fischer w H Andersson 97min SF
(= Monika/Summer with Monika)
SOMMARLEK (1950) d/co-st/s Ingmar Bergman c Fischer
w Kjellin 96min SF (= Illicit Interlude/Sumer Inter-
lude)
SOMMARNATTENS LEENDE (1955) d/s Ingmar Berg-
man c Fischer w Dahlbeck, Jacobsson, H Andersson,
Björnstrand, Kulle, B Andersson 110min SF
SOMMAR OCH SYNDARE (1960) d Mattsson *84min
(= Summer and Sinners)
SOMMARSAGA, EN (1912) d Sjöström (= A Summer's
Tale)
SOMMARSAGA, EN (1941) d/s/c/e Sucksdorff 13min SF
SOMMERKRIG (1965) d Kjaerulff-Schmidt 28min
(= Summer War)
SOMMERTAG (1960) d Troell (= A Summer Day)
SOM NATT OCH DAG (1969) d/s Cornell *113min San
(= Like Night and Day)
SO MUCH FOR SO LITTLE (1949) d C Jones, Freleng
anim* 11min WB
SONAD SKULD (1914) d/co-s Sjöström 988m
SONATAS (1959) d Bardem co-c Figueroa *95min
SONATE A KREUTZER, LA (1956) d/s/e/w Rohmer p
Godard n Briarly 16mm 50min
SON COMES HOME, A (1936) d Dupont c Mellor 75min
Par
SONDAG I SEPTEMBER, EN (1963) d/s J Donner w H
Andersson 115min (= A Sunday in September)
SON-DAUGHTER, THE (1932) d C Brown w Novarro, H
Hayes 79min MGM
SONDEURS D'ABIMES (1943) d/co-c Ichac 22min
SONG AND DANCE MAN, THE (1926) d Brenon c Howe
6997ft FPL
SONG AND DANCE MAN (1936) d Dwan w Trevor;
Dumont 72min Fox
SONG FOR TOMORROW (1948) d Fisher 62min r JAR
Song of a Flower Basket = HANAKOGO NO UTA (1937)
Song of a Lantern = UTA ANDON (1943)
SONG OF BERNADETTE, THE (1943) d H King p Perl-
berg s Seaton c AC Miller m A Newman w J Jones,
Bickford, Price, Cobb, Dalio, Darnell 156min Fox
SONG OF CEYLON, THE (1943) d/s/c B Wright p
Grierson 40min GPO
Song of Happiness = PESNYA O SCHASTYE (1934)
SONG OF LIFE, THE (1922) d/p Stahl 7rs FN
SONG OF LOVE, THE (1924) d Borzage w N Talmadge 8rs
FN
SONG OF LOVE (1947) d/p C Brown co-a Gibbons w
Henreid, R Walker, K Hepburn 119min MGM
SONG OF NORWAY (1970) d/co-p/s Stone, 2nd d Canutt w
Robinson *138min

SONG OF PARIS (1952) d Guillermin w Vernon 80min
SONG OF RUSSIA (1943) d Ratoff p Pasternak c Stradling
a Gibbons m Stothart fm Tchaikovsky w R Taylor,
Benchley 107min MGM
SONG OF SONGS, THE (1933) d/p Mamoulian c Milner a
Dreier co-song Hollander w Dietrich 83min Par
Song of Steel = PESN O METALLYE (1928)
SONG OF SURRENDER (1949) d Leisen p/s Maibaum c
Fapp co-a Dreier m V Young w Rains 93min Par
Song of the Camp = ROEI NO UTA (1938)
SONG OF THE FLAME (1930) d Crosland c Garmes 72min
FN
SONG OF THE ISLANDS (1942) d W Lang w Grable,
Mature, Mitchell *74min Fox
Song of the Mountain Pass = TOGE NO UTA (1923)
Song of the Native Country = NO UTA (1925)
SONG OF THE OPEN ROAD (1944) d S Sylvan Simon w
Fields, J Powell 93min r UA
Song of the Prairie = ARIE PRERIE (1949)
Song of the Road (UK) = PATHER PANCHALI (1955)
Song of the Scarlet Flower = SANGEN OM DEN
ELDRODA BLOMMAN (1919)
SONG OF THE SHIRT, THE (1908) d Griffith fpm Thomas
Hood 180min Bio
SONG OF THE SOUTH (1946) p Disney fs Uncle Remus s
Toland co-m Amfitheatrof *94min
SONG OF THE WEST (1930) d Enright c Garmes 78min
WB
Song of Victory = HINYO KU (1945)
SONG O' MY HEART (1930) d Borzage w O'Sullivan 85min
Fox
SONGS (1964-70) d Brakhage w Mekas 8mm * 420min
(31 films including FIFTEEN SONG TRAITS
(47min), TWENTY-THIRD PSALM BRANCH
(100min))
SONG TO REMEMBER, A (1944) d C Vidor s Buchman
co-c Gaudio m Rozsa w Muni, Oberon, Wilde
*113min Col
SONG WITHOUT END (1960) d C Vidor, Cukor(uc) p
Goetz c Howe w Bogarde, Page CS* 141min Col
SONNENSTRAHL (1933) d/co-st Fejos w Annabella 80min
SONNY (1922) d H King w Barthelmess 7rs
SONNY BOY (1929) d A Mayo c B Reynolds w Horton,
Jolson 6048ft WB
SON OF ALI BABA (1952) d Kurt Neumann w Curtis,
Laurie *75min U
SON OF A SAILOR (1933) d Bacon 73min WB
SON OF CAPTAIN BLOOD (1964) d Tulio Demicheli p H
Brown *88min Par
SON OF DRACULA (1943) d Siodmak 80min U
SON OF FLUBBER (1963) d Stevenson w MacMurray
*100min pc Disney
SON OF FURY (1941) d Cromwell p Zanuck s P Dunne m A
Newman w Power, G Sanders, Carradine, Tierney
98min Fox
SON OF HIS FATHER, A (1925) d Fleming 6925ft FPL
SON OF INDIA (1931) d Feyder c Rosson w Novarro
1237ft MGM
SON OF KONG (1933) d Schoedsack 68min RKO
SON OF MONTE CRISTO, THE (1940) d/p Rowland V
Lee w L Hayward, J Bennett, G Saunders 102min r
UA
SON OF PALEFACE (1952) d/co-s Tashlin c Wild a Pereira
w Hope, J Russell, R Rogers *95min r Par
SON OF SINBAD (1955) d Tetzlaff w Price S* 88min RKO
SON OF THE GODS (1930) d/p F Lloyd c E Haller w
Barthelmess, Constance Bennett 72min FN
Son of Mongolia = SIN MONGOLII (1936)
SON OF THE SHEIK, THE (1926) d/p George Fitzmaurice
c Barnes a Menzies w Valentino, Banky 6685ft r UA
SONO YO NO TSUMA (1930) d Ozu sh (= That Night's
Wife)
SONO YO WA WASURENAI (1962) d Yoshimura (= A
Night to Remember/Hiroshima Heartache)
SONG AND LOVERS (1960) d Cardiff p Wald s T Clarke,
Lambert fn DH Lawrence c F Francis w T Howard
CS* 100min Fox
Sons and Mothers (US) = SERDTSYE MATERI (1967)
SONS OF ADVENTURE (1948) d Canutt 60min Rep
SONS OF KATIE ELDER, THE (1965) d Hathaway p
Wallis c Ballard co-a Pereira m E Bernstein w J
Wayne, Martin, G Kennedy PV* 122min Par
SONS OF LIBERTY (1939) d Curtiz *20min WB
Sons of Satan (UK) = BASTARDI, I (1968)
SONS OF THE DESERT (1933) d William A Seiter p Roach
w Laurel, Hardy, C Chase 7rs (sd) r MGM (= Sons
of the Legion/Fraternally Yours/Convention City)
Sons of the Legion = SONS OF THE DESERT (1933)
SONS OF THE SEA (1939) d Elvey *82min
Sons of Thunder = ARRIVANO I TITANI (1962)
SONS O' GUNS (1936) d Bacon s Wald, JJ Epstein c Polito
80min WB
SON TORNATA PER TE (1953) d Comencini 85min
(= Heidi)
SOPHOMORE, THE (1929) d McCarey co-p J Kennedy w
Ayres 6516ft Pat
SOPRALUOGHI IN PALESTINA PER 'IL VANGELO
SECONDO MATTEO' (1964) d/cy/co-n Pasolini
50min
SOPRAVVISTO, IL (1916) d Genina

SO PROUDLY WE HAIL (1943) d/p Sandrich c C Lang co-a Dreier w Colbert, Goddard, Lake, De Carlo 126min Par

SORA WA HARETARI (1925) d Gosho (= No Clouds in the Sky/The Sky is Clear)

SORCELLERIE CULINAIRE (1904) d Méliès 80m

Sorcerer, The = YOSO (1963)

Sorcerer, The (UK) = SORTILEGES (1944)

SORCERERS, THE (1968) d/s Michael Reeves w Karloff *85min

SORCIERE, LA (1955) d Michel w Vlady, Ronet 97min

SORCIERES DE SALUM, LES (1957) d/w Rouleau fpl Arthur Miller c C Renoir m Auric w Montand, Signoret

Sordid Affair, A (UK) = MALEDETTO IMBROGLIO, UN (1959)

SO RED THE ROSE (1935) d K Vidor c Milner w R Scott, R Cummings 82min Par

SORELLE MATERASSI, LE (1943) d Poggioli 98min

SOROCHINSHAYA YAMARKA (1939) d/s Ekk fpl N Gogol *97min (= Sorochinsky Fair)

Sorochinsky Fair = SOROCHINSKAYA YAMARKA (1939)

SOROK PERVYI (1927) d Protazanov 1800m (= The Forty-First/The Isle of Death)

SOROK PERVYI (1956) d Chukhrai rm 1927 *2536m (= The Forty-First)

SOROK SERDETS (1931) d/e Kuleshov 5rs (= Forty Hearts)

SORORITY GIRL (1958) d/p Corman 60min AI (= The Bad One)

SORORITY HOUSE (1939) d J Farrow s Trumbo c Musuraca w Lake (ps Constance Keane) 64min RKO

SORPASSO, IL (1962) d Risi w Gassman, Trintignant, Catherine Spaak 105min (= Easy Life)

SORREL AND SON (1927) d/s Brenon c Howe 9000ft r UA

SORRIDA PREGO (1944) d Zurlini sh

Sorrowing Mother, The = MATER DOLOROSA (1917)

SORROWS (1969) d/s/c/e Markopoulos 16mm * 6min

SORROWS OF SATAN, THE (1926) d Griffith w Menjou 9rs FPL

SORRY, WRONG NUMBER (1948) d/co-p Litvak co-p Wallis c Polito co-a Dreier m Waxman w Stanwyck, Lancaster, Corey 90min Par

SORTE KANSLER, DEN (1912) d/s Blom

SORTIE DU 'RUBIS', UNE (1950) d/p Cousteau 292m (= Une Plongée du 'Rubis')

SORTILEGES (1944) d Christian-Jaque 103min

SOS EISBERG (1933) d Garnett, Fanck co-s Fanck w Marton, Riefenstahl 70min

So Sind die Menwchen = ABSCHIED (1930)

SOS (1928) d Gallone

SOSHUN (1956) d/co-s Ozu 144min Sho (= Early Spring)

SOS ICEBERG (1933) d Garnett, Fanck e Harbou w Riefenstahl 70min U

SOS KINDTAND (1943) d/s A and B Henning Jensen 7min (= SOS Molars)

SOS Molars = SOS KINDTAND (1943)

SOS NORONHA (1956) d/co-s Rouquier c Decaë w Marais *100min

SOS PACIFIC (1959) d G Green w Constantine 91min JAR

SOS RADIO SERVICE (1936) d Cavalcanti

SOS Submarine = UOMINI SAL FONDO (1941)

SO'S YOUR OLD MAN (1926) d La Cava w Fields 6347ft FPL

SOTAREN (1966) d Grede sh (= The Chimney Sweep)

SO THAT MEN ARE FREE (1962) d W Van Dyke 30min

SO THIS IS COLLEGE (1929) d S Wood co-s Daves a Gibbons w E Nugent, Montgomery 9143ft MGM

SO THIS IS AFRICA (1933) d Cline 60min Col

SO THIS IS LONDON (1939) d Thornton Freeland w G Saunders, S Granger 85min

SO THIS IS LOVE (1928) d Capra p Cohn w June 6 rs Col

SO THIS IS LOVE (1953) d G Douglas p Blanke c Burks co-m M Steiner w Grayson *100min WB (= The Grace Moore Story)

SO THIS IS NEW YORK (1948) d R Fleischer p Kramer co-s Foreman m Tiomkin r UA

SO THIS IS HARRIS! (1933) d/co-st Sandrich 3 rs sd RKO

SO THIS IS PARIS (1926) d Lubitsch w M Loy 60min WB

SO THIS IS PARIS (1954) d Quine a Golitzen, Lourié w Curtis *96min U

SOTTO IL SEGNO DELLO SCORPIONE (1968) d/st/s P and V Taviani w Bosè *91min

SOTTO IL SOLE DI ROMA (1948) d/co-st/co-s Castellani m Rota w Sordi

SOUFFLE AU COEUR, LE (1971) d/s Malle w Gélin *100min

SOUL HERDER, THE (1917) d J Ford c B Reynolds w Carey, Hersholt 3rs U

SOUL MATES (1926) d Conway 6073ft MGM

SOUL OF BROADWAY, THE (1915) d/s Brenon 6rs Fox

SOULS AT SEA (1937) d Hathaway co-s C Lang co-a Dreier w G Cooper, Raft, Carey, R Cummings, Ladd 92min Par

SOUL TO SOUL (1971) d/s/e D Sanders *96min

SOUND AND THE FURY, THE (1959) d Ritt p Wald co-s Ravetch fn Faulkner c C Clarke co-a Wheeler m North w Brynner, Woodward, Rosay CS* 115min Fox

SOUND BARRIER, THE (1952) d/p Lean st/s Rattigan c Hildyard a V Korda m M Arnold w R Richardson 118min r BL (= Breaking the Sound Barrier)

Sounds from the Mountains = YAMA NO OTO (1954)

Sounding Wave = TONENDE WELLE (1928)

SOUND OFF (1952) d Quine s Quine, Edwards w Rooney *83min Col

SOUND OF FURY, THE (1950) d Endfield 92min r UA

SOUND OF MUSIC, THE (1965) d/p Wise s Lehman fmpl Rodgers, Hammerstein c McCord w J Andrews, Plummer, Parker, Haydn TAO* 174min Fox

Sound of Trumpets (US) = POSTO, IL (1961)

SOUPE AUX POULETS, LA (1963) d Agostini w Brasseur 90min

SOUPIRANT, LE (1963) d/co-s/w Etaix *85min (= The Suitor)

Source de Beauté, La = FIORITURES (1915)

SOURIANTE MADAME BEUDET (1923) d/s Dulac

SOURIRE, LE (1960) d Bourguignon m Delerue *22min

Sourire aux Lèvres = BONJOUR SOURIRE (1955)

SOURIS LA SEMAINE PROCHAINE, UNE (1967) d Herbert anim

SOUS LE CIEL DE PARIS COULE LA SEINE (1951) d/s/co-ad Duvivier c Hayer cy Jeanson m Wiener 98min (= Under the Paris Sky)

SOUS LES TOITS DE PARIS (1930) d/s/di Clair co-c Périnal des Meerson co-m M Van Parys w Préjean, Modot, Gréville 95min Tob

SOUS LES YEUX D'OCCIDENT (1936) d M Allégret fn (Under Western Eyes) Joseph Conrad dec Lourié w P Renoir, Barrault, Fresnay, M Simon

SOUTHERNER, THE (1945) d/s J Renoir ad H Butler c Andriot a Lourié w Z Scott 95min MGM (= L'Homme du Sud)

SOUTHERN PRIDE (1917) d H King 4140ft Mut

SOUTHERN YANKEE, A (1948) d Edward Sedgwick st Frank, Panama gagman Keaton c June co-a Gibbons 90min MGM

SOUTH OF ALGIERS (1953) d J Lee w Heflin *95min ABC (= The Golden Mask)

SOUTH OF SANTA FE (1932) d Glennon 60min

SOUTH OF ST LOUIS (1949) d Enright p Sperling co-st/co-s JR Webb c Freund m M Steiner w McCrea, A Smith, Malone *83min r WB

SOUTH OF TAHITI (1941) d George Waggner w Montez, B Crawford 75min U

SOUTH PACIFIC (1958) d Logan p Adler s Osborn fmpl Logan, Rodgers, Hammerstein c Shamroy co-a Wheeler chor Prinz w M Gaynor TAO* 171min r Fox

SOUTH RIDING (1938) d/p Saville w R Richardson 85min r UA

SOUTH SEA ROSE (1929) d Dwan c Rosson w Bickford 67min Fox

Southwest to Sonora (UK) = APPALOOSA (1965)

South Wind (2 parts) = MINAMI NO KAZE (1942)

SOUVENIR D'ITALIE (1957) d/co-s Pietrangeli c Tonti w Ferzetti, Sordi, De Sica, Girotti *95min r JAR (= It Happened in Rome)

SOUVENIRS DE PARIS (1928) d/st/e/w P Prévert, Marcel Duhamel co-c Man Ray w J Prévert sh (= Paris Express) see also PARIS LA BELLE (1959)

SOUVENIRS PERDUS (1949) d Christian-Jaque c Matras m Kosma w Feuillère, Montand, Philipe, Brasseur 105min (= Lost Property)

Soviet Art = SOVETSKOI ISKUSSTVO (1944)

SOVETSKIE IGRUSHKI (1924) d/s Vertov anim 349m (= Soviet Toys)

SOVETSKOI ISKUSSTVO (1944) d Vertov, Elisabeth Svilova (= Soviet Art)

Soviet Toys = SOVETSKIE IGRUSHKI (1924)

SOVVERSIVI (1967) d/s P and V Taviani m Fusco 105min

SO WELL REMEMBERED (1947) d Dmytryk s Paxton c F Young m Eisler w J Mills, T Howard 114min RKO/JAR

SOWING THE WIND (1916) p Hepworth 5rs

SOWING THE WIND (1921) d/s Stahl 9rs FN

SOY MEXICO (1968) d/c Reichenbach S* 90min

SO YOU WON'T SQUAWK (1941) d Del Lord w Keaton 16min Col

SOY PURO MEXICANO (1942) d/st/s Fernandez w Armendariz

SPACE (1965) d Warhol 16mm 70min

SPACE CHILDREN, THE (1958) d J Arnold c Laszlo co-a Pereira 69min Par

SPACEREK STAROMIEJSKI (1958) d/s Munk *20min (= A Walk in the Old City of Warsaw)

SPACEWAYS (1913) d Fisher 76min

SPADA E LA CROCE, LA (1958) d Bragaglia CS* 110min (= The Sword and the Cross)

Spaghetti in the Desert = PASTASCIUTTA NEL DESERTO (1961)

Spain = ISPANIYA (1939)

SPALICEK (1947) d/st/s/e/a Trnka anim Pojar part anim* 75min (= The Czech Year)

SPANIARD, THE (1925) d/p Walsh c Milner 6635ft

SPANISH ABC (1938) d T Dickinson 40min

SPANISH AFFAIR (1957) d D Siegel c Leavitt co-a Pereira m Amfitheatrof VV* 93min r Par

SPANISH DANCER, THE (1923) d Brenon c Howe w Beery, Negri 9rs FPL

SPANISH DILEMMA, A (1912) d/w Sennett w Normand ½rl Bio

SPANISH EARTH (1937) d/s/co-c Ivens cy/n Hemingway co-m V Thompson 57min

SPANISH GARDENER, THE (1956) d P Leacock fn AJ Cronin c Challis w Bogarde *97min

SPANISH GIPSY, THE (1911) d Griffith 1rl Bio

SPANISH MAIN, THE (1945) d Borzage co-s H Mankiewicz c Barnes m Eisler w M O'Hara, Henried *100min RKO

SPANKING BREEZES (1926) d Cline s Sennett

Spare Man (US) = ALBERT, RN (1953)

SPARE TIME (1939) d/s Jennings p Cavalcanti 15rs GPO

Spark = HIBANA (1922)

Spark = HIBANA (1956)

SPARTACO (1952) d/co-s Freda w Girotti 120min (= Spartacus the Gladiator/Sins of Rome)

SPARTACUS (1960) d Kubrick, A Mann(uc) 2nd d/co-e I Lerner ex-p K Douglas s Trumbo fn Howard Fast co-c Metty des Golitzen cr Bass m North w K Douglas, Olivier, J Simmons, Ustinov, Curtis 70TR* 196min U

Spartacus the Gladiator (UK) = SPARTACO (1952)

SPARTAKIADA (1956) d Frič * (= The Spartakiade)

The Spartakiade = SPARTAKIADA (1956)

SPATNE NAMALOVANA SLEPICE (1963) d/s Brdecka (= The Grotesque Chicken)

SPAWN OF THE NORTH (1938) d Hathaway p Lewis co-s Furthman c C Lang w H Fonda, Raft, Lamour, J Barrymore, Tamiroff 130min Par

SPEAK EASILY (1931) d Edward Sedgwick w Keaton, Hopper 8rs MGM

SPEAKING FROM AMERICA (1939) d Jennings p Cavalcanti GPO

SPECIAL AGENT (1935) d Keighley c Hickox w B Davis, Pichel 78min WB

SPECIAL DELIVERY (1927) d Arbuckle (ps William Goodrich) w Cantor 6rs Par

Special Delivery (US) = VOM HIMMEL GEFALLEN (1955)

SPECTER OF THE ROSE (1946) d/p/st/s B Hecht as-p/c Garmes 90min Rep (= Spectre of the Rose)

Spectre of the Rose (UK) = SPECTER OF THE ROSE (1946)

SPECTRE VERT, LE (1930) d Feyder fst B Hecht c Daniels des Gibbons MGM (= The Unholy Night)

SPECTRO, LO (1962) d Freda (ps Robert Hampton) S* 93min (= The Ghost)

SPEECH BY BONAR LAW (1910) Used Hepworth's Vivaphone process

SPEECH BY F E SMITH (1910) Used Hepworth's Vivaphone process

SPEED (1922–23) d G Seitz serial in 15eps Pat

SPEED KINGS, THE (1913) d Sennett w Normand, Arbuckle 1rl Key

SPEED QUEEN, THE (1913) d Sennett w Normand 1rl Key

SPEEDWAY (1968) d Taurog c Ruttenberg w Presley PV* 94min MGM

SPEEDY (1928) d Ted Wilde w H Lloyd 7690ft pc H Lloyd Par/FPL

SPEEDY GONZALES (1955) d Freleng anim* 7min WB

SPEEDY SMITH (1927) d Bruckman 5005ft

SPEEDY SPURS (1926) d Thorpe

SPEJBL NA STOPE (1956) d/anim Pojar (= Spejbl on the Trail)

Spejbl on the Trail = SPEJBL NA STOPE (1956)

SPELLBOUND (1945) d Hitchcock p Selznick s B Hecht c Barnes m Rozsa dream sequence Dali w Ingrid Bergman, Peck, R Fleming 111min r UA

SPENCER'S MOUNTAIN (1963) d/p Daves c Lawton m M Steiner w H Fonda, M O'Hara, Crisp PV* 119min WB

SPENDERS, THE (1921) d Conway

SPENDTHRIFT (1936) d/co-s Walsh p Wagner c Shamroy w H Fonda 70min Par

SPERDUTA DI ALLAH, LA (1928) d/co-s Guazzoni

SPERDUTI NEL BUIO (1914) d Martoglio 2000m

SPETTACOLO DI PUPI, UNO (1953) d Maselli

SPHERES (1969) d McLaren m Bach 16mm* 7min

SPHYNX (1918) d Balasz

SPIAGGIA, LA (1953) d/co-st/s Lattuada co-s Charles Spaak m Piccioni w Carol, Vallone *102min (= The Beach)

Spider, The = PAUKI (1942)

SPIDER, THE (1931) d Menzies, Kenneth McKenna c Howe 59min Fox

SPIDER AND THE FLY, THE (1949) d Hamer c Unsworth e Holt 95min

SPIDER AND THE ROSE, THE (1923) d John McDermott w Fazenda 6800ft

Spider's Strategy, The = STRATEGIA DEL RAGNO (1970)

SPIEGEL VAN HOLLANDE (1950) d/s/c/e Haanstra 10min (= Mirror of Holland)

Spiel der Wellen = TONENDE WELLE (1928)

SPIELER, THE (1928) d/co-s Garnett c AC Miller 56min Pat

SPIEL MIT DEM FEUER, DAS (1921) d Wiene, George Kroll co-dec Rohrig 2134m

SPIEZENG VON PARIS, DER (1925) d Curtiz
Spies = SPIONE (1928)
Spie Vengone dal Semifreddo, Le = DR GOLDFOOT AND THE GIRL BOMBS (1966)
SPINA DORSALE DEL DIAVOLO, LA (1971) d B Kennedy st/s Huffaker c Tonti des Chiari m Piccioni w J Huston, Montalban PV* 99min co-pc De Laurentiis (= The Deserter)
SPINNEN, DIE: Part 1 DER GOLDENE SEE (1919) d/s F Lang p Pommer co-a Warm w Dagover 1900m Dec
SPINNEN, DIE: Part 2 DAS BRILLANTEN SCHIFF (1920) d/s F Lang p Pommer co-a Warm w Dagover 2219m Dec
Spin of a Coin (UK) = GEORGE RAFT STORY, THE (1961)
SPINOUT (1966) d Taurog p Pasternak co-st/co-s Flicker c Fapp w Presley PV* 93min MGM (= California Holiday)
SPIONE (1928) d/co-p/co-s F Lang co-p Pommer co-s Von Harbou c FA Wagner w Lupu-Pick 4364m (= Spies)
SPIRAL ROAD, THE (1962) d Mulligan co-s Mahin c R Harlan m Goldsmith w Hudson *145min U
SPIRALS (c1925) d Fischinger anim
SPIRAL STAIRCASE, THE (1945) d Siodmak p Schary c Musuraca w McGuire, E Barrymore, R Fleming 83min RKO
SPIRITISTEN (1914) d/co-s Madsen
SPIRIT IS WILLING, THE (1967) d/p Castle co-a Pereira w Miles *100min Par
SPIRIT OF ST LOUIS, THE (1957) d B Wilder s B Wilder, Mayes fab Charles A Lindbergh ad Lederer c Burks, Marley aerial montage c Eames m Waxman w J Stewart CS* 135min r WB
Spirit of the People (UK) = ABE LINCOLN IN ILLINOIS (1940)
Spirit of the Pond, The = MA NO IKE (1923)
SPIRIT OF YOUTH, THE (1929) d W Lang 6216ft
Spiritual Constructions = SEELISCHE KONSTRUK-TIONEN (c1929)
SPITE MARRIAGE (1929) d Edward Sedgwick w Keaton (sd) 7rs MGM (= Buster se Marie)
SPITFIRE (1934) d Cromwell c Cronjager w K Hepburn, R Young 88min RKO
Spitting Image, The = ALS TWEE DRUPPELS WATER (1963)
SPLADATESSE (1964) m Piccioni
SPLENDID HAZARD, A (1920) d/p Dwan 6rs
SPLENDID ROAD, THE (1925) d F Lloyd c Brodine 7646ft FN
SPLENDOR (1935) d E Nugent p Goldwyn c Toland m A Newman w M Hopkins, McCrea, Niven 77min r UA
SPLENDORIE E MISERIE DI MADAME ROYALE (1970) d/co-st/s Caprioli w Ronet
SPLENDOR IN THE GRASS (1961) d/p Kazan st/s Inge c B Kaufman des Sylbert set dec Callahan w N Wood, Beatty *124min r WB
SPLIT SECOND (1953) d/p D Powell c Musuraca w A Smith 85min RKO
SPOILERS, THE (1942) d Enright p F Lloyd c Krasner w Dietrich, R Scott, J Wayne, Carey, Barthelmess 87min U
SPOOK SPEAKS, THE (1940) d Jules White co-s Bruckman w Keaton 18min Col
SPOOK SPORT (1939–41) d McLaren, Mary Ellen Bute m (La Danse Macabre) Saint Saëns *8min
SPOOKY HOOKY (1937) d G Douglas p Roach 1rl MGM
SPORT ET PARAPLUIE (1947) d Michel sh
SPORTING CHANCE (1919) d H King 5rs
Sporting Fame = NASHI CHEMPIONY (1950)
SPORTING GOODS (1928) d St Clair c Cronjager 5831ft Par
Sporting Honour = SPORTIVNAYA CHEST (1951)
SPORTING LIFE (1918) d/p M Tourneur 7rs
SPORTING LIFE (1925) rm 1918 d M Tourneur w M Loy 7rs U
SPORTING VENUS (1925) d Neilan a Gibbons w Colman 5938ft MGM
SPORTIVNAYA CHEST (1951) d Petrov *107min (= Sporting Honour)
Sportivnaya Slava = NASHI CHEMPIONY (1950)
SPORT MINORE (1951) d Maselli
SPORT OF KINGS, THE (1930) d/p/s Saville 96min
SPORTSMAN, THE (1920) d Semon, Taurog w Semon 2rs Vit
SPOSA BELLA, LA (1960) d/s N Johnson c Rotunno w Bogarde, Gardner, Cotten 105min r MGM (= The Angel Wore Red)
SPOSA DELLA MORTE, LA (1915) d Ghione
SPOTKANIA W MRAKU (1960) d/co-s Jakubowska (= Encounters in the Dark)
SPOTLIGHT SCANDALS (1943) d William Beaudine co-p Katzman w Langdon 79min Mon
SPREE! (1967) d Leisen w Mansfield 80min
Spring = VESNA (1947)
Spring Awakening = HARU NO MEZAME (1947)
Spring Banquet, A = HARU KORO NO HANA NO EN (1958)
Spring Comes with the Ladies = HARU WA GOFUJIN KARA (1932)

Spring Dreams = HARU NO YUME (1960)
Spring in Southern Islands = NANTO NO HARU (1925)
Spring of Life = LIVETS VAR (1957)
Spring Snow = SHUNSETSU (1950)
SPRINGFIELD RIFLE (1952) d De Toth co-s Warren m M Steiner w G Cooper, Chaney *93min WB
SPRING HANDICAP (1937) d Brenon 6317ft
SPRING IN PARK LANE (1948) d H Wilcox w Neagle 90min r BL
Spring in the Meadows of Dalby = VAR I DALBY HAGE (1962)
SPRING OFFENSIVE (1940) d Jennings p Cavalcanti 20min GPO (= An Unrecorded Victory)
SPRING PARADE (1940) d Koster p Pasternak w Durbin, Cummings 89min U
SPRINGTIME FOR HENRY (1934) d/co-s Tuttle p Lasky c J Seitz 73min Fox
Springtime in Italy (UK) = E PRIMAVERA (1940)
SPRING TONIC (1935) d Bruckman fco-pl (Man Eating Tiger) B Hecht c O'Connell w Ayres, Pitts, Trevor 58min Fox
Sprung ins Glück = GESCHICHTE EINER KLEINER PARISERIN, DIE (1927)
SPUDS (1927) d/s/w Semon Pat
SPUK IM HAUSE DES PROFESSORS, DER (1914) d May 1058m
SPYASHCHAYA KRASAVITSA (1930) d S and G Vasiliev s Alexandrov (= The Sleeping Beauty)
SPY IN BLACK, THE (1939) d M Powell s Pressburger m Rozsa w Veidt 82min r Col (= U-Boat 29)
SPY IN WHITE, THE (1936) d Marton fn (The Eunuch of Stamboul) Denis Wheatley, George A Hill w Mason 59min (= The Secret of Stamboul)
Spy in Your Eye = BERLINO APPUNTAMENTO PER LE SPIE (1965)
Spy Isn't Dead Yet, The = KANCHO IMADA SHISEZU (1942)
SPY OF NAPOLEAN (1936) d Elvey c Courant w Barthel-mess 101min
SPY RING, THE (1938) d JH Lewis w Wyman 56min U (= International Spy)
SPY WHO CAME IN FROM THE COLD, THE (1965) d/p Ritt fn John Le Carré c Morris w Burton, Bloom, Werner 112min
SQUADRONE BIANCO (1936) d/co-s Genina 99min
SQUADRON 992 (1939) d Watt p Cavalcanti GPO
SQUALL, THE (1929) d A Korda c J Seitz w M Loy, L Young, Pitts 9456ft FN
Squarcia = LUNGA STRADA AZZURA, LA (1957)
SQUARE DEAL SANDERSON (1919) d Lambert Hillyer c August w W Hart 5rs pc W Hart
Squarehead, The = MABEL'S MARRIED LIFE (1914)
Square of Violence (UK) = NASILJE NA TRGU (1961)
SQUARE RING, THE (1953) d/p Dearden, Michael Relph w Kendall 83min
Squares = QUADRATE (1934)
SQUARE SHOOTER, THE (1927) d Wyler 2rs U
SQUAW MAN, THE (1914) d De Mille, Oscar Apfel s De Mille pc Lasky
SQUAW MAN, THE (1918) d De Mille rm 1914 6rs FPL
SQUAW MAN, THE (1931) d/p De Mille rm 1914 c Rosson co-a Leisen m Stothart w W Baxter, Bickford 106min MGM
SQUEAKER, THE (1937) d W Howard p A Korda fn Edgar Wallace c Périnal w Newton 77min r UA (= Murder on Diamond Row)
SREDNI VASHTAR (1942) d Bradley fst Saki 20min
SRPNOVA NEDELE (1960) d Vavra * (= August Sunday)
SSAKI (1962) d/co-s Polanski m Komeda 10min
S S Ionian = HER LAST TRIP (1939)
STAALKONGENS VILJE (1913) d Madsen
STABLEMATES (1938) d S Wood co-s Mainbaum c J Seitz w Beery, Rooney 89min
STACHKA (1924) d Eisenstein co-s Eisenstein, Alexandrov c Tissé w Alexandrov 1969m (= Strike)
STAD (1958) d Troell
STADION (1958) d Stanislaw Jedryka technical adviser Borowczyk *21min
STADT DER VERHEISSUNG (1935) d Ruttmann
STADT IN SICHT (1923) d/s Galeen 1776m
STAGECOACH (1939) d/p J Ford ex-p Wanger s D Nichols c Glennon w J Wayne, Trevor, Carradine, Mitchell, G Bancroft, Canutt 97min r UA
STAGECOACH (1966) d G Douglas rm 1939 c Clothier m Goldsmith w B Crosby, R Cummings, Heflin CS* 114min Fox
STAGE DOOR (1937) d La Cava p Berman fpl Edna Ferber, G Kaufman w K Hepburn, G Rogers, Menjou, Ball, Ann Miller 92min RKO
STAGE DOOR CANTEEN (1943) d Borzage p Lesser c Wild des Horner w Roman, Bankhead, Darwell, H Hayes, Hersholt, H Marx, E Nugent, K Hepburn, Lawrence, Oberon, Weissmuller, Muni, Raft, G Lee 132min r UA
STAGE FRIGHT (1950) d/p Hitchcock ad Reville additonal di Bridie w Dietrich, Wyman 110min r WB
STAGE HAND, THE (1920) d/s Semon, Taurog w Semon 2rs Vit
STAGE ROMANCE, A (1922) d Brenan fpl (Kean, ou Désordre et Génie) A Dumas 7rs Fox

STAGE RUSTLER, THE (1908) d Wallace McCutcheon w Griffith
STAGE STRUCK (1925) d/p Dwan w Swanson 6691ft FPL
STAGE STRUCK (1936) d Berkeley c Haskin w D Powell, Wyman 10rs WB
STAGE STRUCK (1958) d Lumet co-c Planer m North w H Fonda, Plummer, H Marshall, Greenwood S 95min RKO
STAGIONI DEL NOSTRO AMORE, LE (1966) d Vancini c Di Palma w Aimée 105min (= Seasons of Our Love)
Stahl = ARBEIT MACHT GLUCKLICH (1933)
STAINED GLASS AT FAIRFORD, THE (1956) d/p Wright n Donat, Betjeman *
Stain on His Conscience, A = MRJLA NA SAVJESTI (1968)
STAIRCASE (1969) d/p Donen s/fpl Charles Dyer c Challis cr Binder w Burton, Harrison PV* 98min pc Donen r Fox
Stairway to Heaven = MATTER OF LIFE AND DEATH, A (1946)
STAKE OUT ON DOPE STREET (1958) d/co-s Kershner c Wexler (ps Mark Jeffrey) 83min WB
STALAG 17 (1953) d/p/co-s B Wilder c Laszlo co-a Pereira m Waxman w Holden, Preminger 121min Par
STALINGRADSKAYA BITVA (1949) d Petrov Part 1: 2691m; Part 2: 2560m (= Battle of Stalingrad)
STALINGRADSKAYA BITVA (1970) d Chukhrai (= Battle of Stalingrad)
STALKING MOON, THE (1969) d Mulligan ad Mayes c C Lang w Peck, Saint PV* 109min WB
STAMBOUL QUEST (1934) d S Wood s H Mankiewicz c Howe w M Loy 88min MGM
STAMMEN LEVER AN (1937) d Fejos 280m SF
STAMPEDE (1949) d Lesley Selander co-p/co-s Edwards 78min AA
Stampeded (UK) = BIG LAND, THE (1957)
Stamp Fantasia = KITTE-NO GENSO (1959)
STAND AND DELIVER (1928) d/p Crisp 5423ft Pat
STAND BY FOR ACTION (1942) d/co-p Leonard co-s H Mankiewicz cr Rosher a Gibbons w R Taylor, Laughton, Brennan, Quine 109min
STAND-IN (1937) d Garnett p Wanger c C Clarke w L Howard, Blondell, Bogart 10rs r UA
STAND UP AND CHEER (1934) d Hamilton MacFadden w Temple 80min Fox
STAND UP AND FIGHT (1939) d WS Van Dyke p LeRoy w Beery, R Taylor, Bickford 105min MGM
STANLEY AND LIVINGSTONE (1939) d H King as-p MacGowan co-s P Dunne c Barnes w Tracy, Brennan, C Coburn 101min Fox
STAR! (1968) d Wise c Laszlo chor Kidd w J Andrews TAO* 174min pc Wise r Fox
STAR, THE (1953) d Heisler c Laszlo w B Davis, Hayden, N Wood 89min Fox
STAR BOARDER, THE (1914) d Sennett w Chaplin 1rl Key (= Hash House Hero)
STAR DUST (1940) d W Lang p Zanuck c Marley w Darnell, Payne 85min Fox
STARE POVESTI CESKE (1953) d/co-s/a Trnka co-s Brdecka *83min (= Old Czech Legends)
STARFISH, THE (1950) d Schlesinger, Alan Cooke 38min
Star for a Night = BLACK SHEEP (1935)
STAR IN THE DUST (1955) d Haas p Zugsmith co-a Golitzen *80min U
STAR IN THE NIGHT (1945) d D Siegel 20min WB
STAR IS BORN, A (1937) d/co-st Wellman p Selznick a Wheeler m M Steiner w J Gaynor, March, Menjou, Turner 111min r UA
STAR IS BORN, A (1954) d Cukor s M Hart rm 1937 c Leavitt colour consultant Hoyningen-Huene w Garland, Bickford CS* 182min r WB
STARKASTE, DEN (1929) d/st Sjoberg SF (= The Strong-est)
STARKER ALS DIE NACHT (1954) d Dudow 117min Defa
STARK MAD (1929) d Bacon 7rs WB
STARLIFT (1951) d Del Ruth c McCord w D Day, V Mayo, Roman, Cagney, G Cooper, Parsons, R Scott, Wyman 103min WB
STAR MAKER, THE (1939) d Del Ruth c Struss w B Crosby 94min Par
Star Named Wormwood, A = HUEZDA ZVANA PELYNEK (1964)
STAR OF BETHLEHEM, THE (1956) d Reiniger anim* 18min
Star of Married Couples = MEOTO BOSHI (1926)
STAROIE I NOVOIE (1929) d/s Eisenstein, Alexandrov c Tissé 2469m (= Generalnaya Linnia/The Old and the New/The General Line)
STAR REPORTER, THE (1932) d M Powell 44min
Stars = CSILLAGOSOK (1950)
STARS AND STRIPES (1939–41) d McLaren *3min
STARS IN MY CROWN (1950) d J Tourneur w McCrea 89min MGM
STARS IN YOUR EYES (1956) d Elvey S* 96min r BL
STARS LOOK DOWN, THE (1939) d C Reed fn AJ Cronin w M Redgrave, Lockwood, Emlyn Williams 105min
STARS OVER BROADWAY (1935) d Keighley s Wald, JJ Epstein c Barnes co-chor Berkeley 89min WB

STAR SPANGLED RHYTHM (1942) *d* G Marshall *co-s* G Kaufman, M Frank, Panama *co-a* Dreier *w* B Crosby, Milland, Hope, Lake, MacMurray, Lamour, D Powell, Ladd, Tone, Goddard, Bendix, S Hayward, P Sturges, De Mille, Preston 99min Par
STAR WITNESS, THE (1931) *d* Wellman *w* W Huston 68min WB
STARYI NAYEZHDNIK (1940 *r* 1959) *d* Barnet (= *The Old Jockey*)
STASS ET COMPAGNIE (1916) *d/s* Gance
STASTNOV CESTU (1943) *d/s* Vavra
State Department Store = UNIVERMAG (1922)
STATE FAIR (1933) *d* H King *c* Mohr *w* J Gaynor, Ayres, Foster, W Rogers 80min Fox
STATE FAIR (1945) *d* W Lang *co-c* Shamroy *co-a* Wheeler *co-m* A Newman *w* D Andrews, Crain 100min Fox
STATE FAIR (1945) *d* W Lang *p* Perlberg *fmpl Rogers, Hammerstein c* Shamroy *co-a* Wheeler *co-m* A Newman *w* D Andrews, Crain 100min Fox
STATE FAIR (1962) *d* J Ferrer *p* Brackett *s* Breen *c* Mellor *m R Rogers w* Ewell, Faye CS* 118min Fox
STATE OF THE UNION (1948) *d/co-p* Capra *c* Folsey *a* Gibbons *m* V Young *w* Tracy, K Hepburn, V Johnson, Menjou 122min *r* MGM
STATE SECRET (1950) *d/co-p/s* Gilliat *co-p* Launder *c* Krasker *m* Alwyn *w* Fairbanks Jr, Hawkins 104min BL
STATE STREET SADIE (1928) *d* A Mayo 9rs WB
STATIC IN THE ATTIC (1939) *d/w* C Chase 2rs Col
STATION 6 – SAHARA (1964) *d* Holt *co-s* Forbes *w* C Baker 101min *r* BL (= *Endstation 13 Sahara*)
STATIONS WEST (1948) *d Sidney Lanfield c* Wild *w* D Powell, Moorehead, Ives 92min RKO
STATION 307 (1955) *d* Malle sh
STATUES MEURENT AUSSI, LES (1950–53, *ur*) *d/s/cy* Resnais, Marker *c* Cloquet *e* Resnais 30min
STAY AWAY JOE (1968) *d* Tewkesbury *w* Presley, Meredith PV* 101min MGM
STAZIONE, LA (1952) *d* Zurlini sh
STAZIONE TERMINI (1953) *d/co-p* De Sica *co-p* De Laurentiis *co-s* Zavattini *co-s/di Capote c* Aldo *w* J Jones, Clift 85min (= *Indiscretion of an American Wife*)
STEADY COMPANY (1932) *d Edward Ludwig w* Foster, Pitts 70min U
Steady Now = HONEN ZO (1953)
STEAMBOAT BILL JR (1928) *d Charles 'Chuck' Reisner w* Keaton 7rs *r* UA
STEAMBOAT ROUND THE BEND (1935) *d* J Ford *s* D Nichols, Trotti *w* W Rogers 80min Fox
STEAMBOAT WILLIE (1928) *d* Iwerks anim 1rl *pc* Disney
Steel = ACCIAIO (1932)
STEEL (1970) *d* Peries 20min
STEEL HELMET, THE (1950) *d/co-p/s* Fuller 84min
Steel Highway = OTHER MENS' WOMEN (1931)
STEEL LADY, THE (1953) *d* Dupont *c* F Crosby *m* A Newman 84min *r* UA (= *Secret of the Sahara/-Treasure of Kalifa*)
STEEL TOWN (1943) *d* W Van Dyke
Steel Town, The = ZOCELEMI (1950)
STEEL TRAP, THE (1952) *d/st/s* Stone *c* Laszlo *m* Tiomkin *w* Cotten, T Wright 85min Fox
STEFANIE IN RIO (1960) *d* C Bernhardt 89min
STELLA (1955) *d/s* Cacoyannis *m* Hadjidakis *w* Mercouri 94min
STELLA DALLAS (1926) *d* H King *p* Goldwyn *c* Edeson *w* Coleman, Hersholt 1000ft *r* UA
STELLA DALLAS (1937) *d* K Vidor *p* Goldwyn *c* Maté *a* R Day *m* A Newman *w* Stanwyck 104min *r* UA
STELLA MARIS (1918) *d* Neilan *w* Pickford 6rs
STEMNING I APRIL (1947) *d/s* A and B Henning Jensen
Stepchild = NASANU NAKA (1932)
STEP DOWN TO TERROR (1958) *d* Keller *c* Metty *a* Golitzen 75min U
STEPHEN STEPS OUT (1923) *d Joseph Henabery w* Fairbanks Jr 5652ft FDL *r* Par
STEP ON IT (1922) *d* Conway 5rs U
STEPPA, LA (1962) *d/co-s* Lattuada *fn Anton Chekov w* Vlady, Vanel *110min (= *The Steppe*)
Steppe, The (UK) = STEPPA, LA (1962)
STEPPING OUT (1919) *d* Niblo *p* Ince 5096ft FPL
STEPS OF AGE, THE (1951) *d/s* Maddow 16mm 25min
STERNE UBER COLOMBO (1953) *d* V Harlan 100min
STERN VON BETHLEHEM, DER (1921) *d* Reiniger anim 1rl
STERN VON DAMASKUS, DER (1919) *d* Curtiz
Stern Young Man, The = STROGI YUNOSHA (1936)
STIGMATE, LE (1924) *d* Feuillade, *Maurice Champreux s* Feuillade (1: *Le Mort Vivant*; 2: *Les Deux Mères*; 3: *L'Évasion*; 4: *Nocturnes*; 5: *La Mère Prodigue*; 6: *La Main*)
STILLA FLIRT, EN (1939) *d* Molander SF
STIMULANTIA (1967) 108min 8 eps SF
ep NEGRESSEN I SKAPET *d/s* Sjoman
ep DANIEL *d/c* Ingmar Bergman
ep HAN-HON *d/s* J Donner *c* Fischer *w* H Andersson
ep SMYCKET *d/s* Molander *fst* Maupassant *c* Fischer *w* Ingrid Bergman, Bjornstrand
STINGAREE (1934) *d* Wellman *w* I Dunne 76min RKO
STING OF THE LASH, THE (1921) *d* H King

STOCKS (1898) *p* Paul 80ft
STO GAVARIT MOC? (1924) *d/s* Room 760m (= *What Says MOC?*)
Stolen Airship, The = VKRADENA VZDUCHOLOD (1966)
STOLEN ASSIGNMENT (1955) *d* Fisher 62min BL
STOLEN BRIDE, THE (1927) *d* A Korda 7179ft FN
Stolen Desire, The = NUSUMARETA YOKUJO (1958)
STOLEN DRINK, THE (1899) *p* Hepworth 50ft
STOLEN FACE (1952) *d* Fisher *w* Henreid, L Scott 71min
Stolen Frontier, The = ULUOPENA HRANICE (1947)
STOLEN GLORY (1912) *d/p/w* Sennett *w* Normand ½rl Key
STOLEN HARMONY (1935) *d Alfred Werker w* Nolan, Raft 74min Par
Stolen Heart, The = GESTOKLENE HERZ, DAS (1934)
STOLEN HEAVEN (1931) *d/s* G Abbott *c* Folsey 73min Par
STOLEN HEAVEN (1938) *d/p* Stone *c* Mellor *co-a* Dreier *chor* Prinz 80min Par
STOLEN HOLIDAY (1937) *d* Curtiz *p* Wallis *c* Hickox *w* Rains, K Francis 80min WB
STOLEN KISSES (1929) *d* Enright *c* B Reynolds 7rs WB
Stolen Kisses = BAISERS VOLES (1968)
STOLEN LIFE (1939) *d* Czinner *w* Bergner, M Redgrave, Michael Anderson 91min
STOLEN LIFE, A (1946) *d* C Bernhardt *c* Polito, E Haller *m* M Steiner *w* B Davis, G Ford, C Ruggles 107min WB
Stolen Love = NUSUMARETA KUI (1917)
STOLEN MAGIC (1915) *d/p/w* Sennett *w* Normand 2rs Tri
STOLEN PURSE, THE (1913) *d/p/w* Sennett ½rl Key
STOLEN RANCH, THE (1926) *d* Wyler 5rs U
STOLEN SWEETS (1934) *d* Thorpe 75min
STOOL PIGEON, THE (1915) *d* Chaney 2rs
STOPOVER TOKYO (1957) *d/s* Breen *c* C Clarke *co-a* Wheeler *w* R Wagner, E O'Brien S* 100min Fox
Stop the Old Fox = KAGERO EZU (1959)
STOP TRAIN 349 (1964) *d Rolf Haedrich w* J Ferrer 95min AA
STOP, YOU'RE KILLING ME (1952) *d* Del Ruth *fco-pl Damon Runyon c* McCord *w* Trevor, B Crawford, Dumont *86min WB
STORA AVENTYRET, DET (1953) *d/p/s/c/e/w* Sucksdorff 73min San (= *The Great Adventure*)
STORE HJERTE, DET (1924) *d/s* Blom
STORE MAGT, DEN (1924) *d/s* Blom
STORIA D'AMORE, UNA (1942) *d/co-st/co-s* Camerini
STORIA DEL TREDICI (1917) *d* Gallone
STORIA DI PINTURICCHIO, UNA (1938) *d* Sala sh
Storia di una mummia, La = KALIDDA (1918)
STORIA DI UN ELEFANTE (1954) *d* Quilici sh
STORIA DI UN PECCATO, LA (1917) *d* Gallone
STORIA MODERNA: L'APE REGINA, UNA (1963) *d/co-s* Ferreri *co-s* Festa Campanile *w* Vlady 95min (= *The Conjugal Bed*)
STORIE DI GIOVANI (1967) *d* Olmi RAI
Stories about Lenin = RASSKAZI O LENINYE (1958)
STORK BITES MAN (1947) *d* Enfield 66min *r* UA
STORM, THE (1930) *d* Wyler *w* J Huston 80min U
Storm, The = VIHAR (1952)
STORM AT DAYBREAK (1933) *d* Boleslavsky *c* Folsey *w* K Francis, W Huston, Tamiroff 68min MGM
STORM CENTRE (1956) *d/co-st/co-s* Taradash *p* Blaustein *c* Guffey *cr* Bass *m* Duning *w* B Davis, Keith 87min *r* Col
STORMFAGELN (1914) *d* Stiller 1322m
STORM FEAR (1956) *d/p* Wilde *c* La Shelle *m* E Bernstein *w* Wilde, Duryea 88min *r* UA
STORM IN A TEACUP (1937) *d/p* Saville *ad* Bridie *fpl* (*Sturm in Wasserglas*) *Bruno Frank w* Harrison, V Leigh 87min
Storm of Passion (US) = STURME DER LEIDENSCHAFT (1932)
STORM OF STRANGERS (1969) *d/s* Maddow 16mm 26min
Storm over Asia = POTOMOK CHINGIS KHAN (1928)
STORM OVER THE NILE (1955) *d* Z Korda, T Young *p* Z Korda *co-ad/di* Biro *w* Laurence Harvey CS* 113min Col
STORM OVER TIBET (1951) *d* Marton *co-p* Benedek *m* Honegger 87min Col
STORM OVER TJURO (1953) *d/s* Mattsson
Storm over Tjuro = STORM OVER TJURO (1953)
STORM WARNING (1951) *d* Heisler *p* Wald *co-st/co-s* R Brooks *m* Amfitheatrof *w* G Rogers, Reagan, D Day, Cochran 93min WB
STORMY WEATHER (1943) *d* Stone *c* Shamroy 77min Fox
STORSTE I VERDEN, DET (1919) *d/s* Madsen
STORSTE KAERLIGHED, DEN (1914) *d* Blom
STORSTROMSBROEN (1950) *d/s* Dreyer 11min
Story from Chikamatsu = CHIKAMATSU MONOGATARI (1954)
STORY IN THE ROCKS (1959) *d Han Van Gelder p* Haanstra *17min
STORY OF A POTTER (1925) *d/s/e* Flaherty 14min (= *Pottery Maker*)
Story from Echigo = ECHIGO TSUTSUISHI OYASHIRAZU (1964)
Story of Barbara = HISTORIEN OM BARBARA (1967)
Story of a Beloved Wife, The = AISAI MONOGATARI (1951)
Story of a Double Bass, The = ROMAN S BASOU (1949)

Story of a School = YAMABIKO GEKKO (1952)
Story of a Woman, The = SMASH-UP (1947)
STORY OF DR CARVER, THE (1938) *d* Zinnemann 10min MGM
STORY OF DR EHRLICH'S MAGIC BULLET, THE (1940) *d* Dieterle *p* Wallis *co-s* J Huston *di* Rapper *c* Howe *w* Robinson, R Gordon, Crisp, Ouspenskaya WB (= *Dr Ehrlich's Magic Bullet*)
STORY OF DR WASSELL, THE (1944) *d/p* De Mille *co-s* Charles Bennett *co-c* Milner *co-a* Dreier *m* V Young *w* G Cooper, De Carlo *137min Par
STORY OF ESTHER COSTELLO, THE (1957) *d* D Miller *p* James and John Woolf *ex-p* Clayton *c* Krasker *m* Auric *w* J Crawford, Quinn 103min Col
Story of Floating Weeds, A = UKIGUSA MONOGATARI (1934)
STORY OF G I JOE, THE (1945) *d* Wellman *c* Metty *w* Meredith, Mitchum 109min *r* UA (= *War Correspondent*)
STORY OF GILBERT AND SULLIVAN, THE (1953) *d/co-p/co-s* Gilliat *co-p* Launder *c* Challis *w* Finch 109min BL
STORY OF ISRAEL: THUS SPAKE THEODOR HERZL (1967) *d/s* Cavalcanti 52min
Story of Kinuyo = KINUYO MONOGATARI (1930)
STORY OF LOUIS PASTEUR, THE (1935) *d* Dieterle *p* Wallis *c* Gaudio *w* Muni, Tamiroff 85min WB
STORY OF MANKIND, THE (1957) *d/p/co-s Irwin Allen c* Musuraca *w* Carradine, C Coburn, Colman, Horton, Lamarr, Lorre, H, G, C Marx, V Mayo, Moorehead, Price, Romero *100min WB
STORY OF OMOCO, THE (1946) *d/p* B Wright 9min
Story of Pure Love = JUN-AI MONOGATARI (1957)
STORY OF ROBIN HOOD, THE (1952) *d* Annakin *c* Green *2nd c* Unsworth *w* Finch *84min *pc* Disney *r* RKO (= *The Story of Robin Hood and His Merrie Men/Robin Hood and His Merrie Men*)
Story of Robin Hood and His Merrie Men, The = STORY OF ROBIN HOOD, THE (1952)
STORY OF RUTH, THE (1960) *d* Koster *c* Arling *m* Waxman *w* Lindfors CS* 132min Fox
Story of Spring, The = ALLEGORIA DI PRIMAVERA (1949)
Story of Tank Commander Nishizumi, The = NISHIZUMI SENSHACHO-DEN (1940)
Story of the Caspian Oil Men = POVEST O NEFTYANIKAKH KASPIYA (1953)
Story of the Count of Monte Cristo, The (UK) = COMTE DE MONTE CRISTO, LE (1961)
Story of the Last Chrysanthemums, The = ZAMGIKU MONOGATARI (1939)
STORY OF THE MOTOR CAR ENGINE, THE (1959) *d* R Williams, *Erwin Broner* anim* 9min
STORY OF THREE LOVES, THE (1953) *p* Franklin *121min MGM
ep MADEMOISELLE *d* Minnelli *co-c* Rosson *a* Gibbons *m* Rozsa *w* E Barrymore, Caron, F Granger
ep THE JEALOUS LOVER *d* G Reinhardt *co-a* Gibbons *co-c* Rosson *w* Mason
ep EQUILIBRIUM *d* G Reinhardt *w* K Douglas
STORY OF VERNON AND IRENE CASTLE, THE (1939) *d* Potter *w* Astaire, G Rogers, Oliver 93min RKO
STORY OF WILL ROGERS, THE (1952) *d* Curtiz *m* V Young *109min WB
STORY OF WOOL, THE (1940) *d* P Leacock 20min
STORY ON PAGE ONE, THE (1959) *d/s* Odets *p* Wald *c* Howe *co-a* Wheeler *m* E Bernstein *w* Hayworth CS 123min *r* Fox
STRACCIAROLI (1951) *d* Maselli sh
STRADA, LA (1954) *d/co-st/co-s* Fellini *p* Ponti, De Laurentiis *c* Martelli *m* Rota *w* Masina, Quinn 94min
STRADE DI NAPOLI (1946) *d* Risi sh
STRADA PER FORT ALAMO, LA (1964) *d* Bava
Straightforward Boy, A = TOKKAN KOZO (1929)
STRAIGHT FROM THE SHOULDER (1936) *d* Heisler 65min Par
STRAIGHT, PLACE AND SHOW (1938) *d* D Butler 66min Fox (= *They're Off*)
STRAIGHT ROAD, THE (1914) *d* Dwan 4rs FP
STRAIGHT SHOOTIN' (1927) *d* Wyler 5rs U
STRAIGHT SHOOTING (1917) *d* J Ford *w* Carey 5rs U
STRAIT JACKET (1963) *d/p* Castle *c* Arling *w* J Crawford, G Kennedy 93min Col
STRANITSY ZHIZN (1948) *d* Barnet, *A Macheret* 71min (= *Pages of Life*)
STRANGLING THREADS (1923) *d/p* Hepworth *rm* THE COBWEB (1917) 6600ft
STRANA RODNAYA (1946) *e(uc)/cy* Dovzhenko
STRANDED (1935) *d* Borzhage *s* Daves *c* Hickox *w* K Francis 76min FN/WB
STRANDHUGG (1949) *d/s/c/e* Sucksdorff 15min SF
STRANGE AFFAIR OF UNCLE HARRY, THE (1945) *d* Siodmak *co-p* Feldman *w* G Saunders 82min U (= *Uncle Harry/The Zero Murder Case*)
STRANGE BEDFELLOWS (1965) *d/p/co-st/co-s* M Frank *co-st* Panama *co-a* Golitzen *w* Hudson, Lollobrigida *99min *r* JAR
STRANGE CARGO (1940) *d* Borzage *p* J Mankiewicz *a* Gibbons *m* Waxman *w* Gable, J Crawford, Lorre, Lukas 113min MGM

Strange Deception (US) = CRISTO PROBITO, IL (1950)

STRANGE DOOR, THE (1951) *d* Pevney *fst R L Stevenson c* Glassberg *w* Laughton, Karloff 81min U

STRANGE HOLIDAY (1945) *d/st/s* Oboler *c* Surtees *w* Rains 52min (= *Day After Tomorrow*)

Strange Illusion = OUT OF THE NIGHT (1945)

STRANGE IMPERSONATION (1946) *d* A Mann 68min Rep

Strange Incident = OX-BOW INCIDENT, THE (1942)

STRANGE INTERLUDE (1932) *d/p* Leonard *fpl Eugene O'Neill c* Garmes *w* Gable, O'Sullivan, Shearer, R Young 78min MGM (= *Strange Interval*)

Strange Interval (UK) = STRANGE INTERLUDE (1932)

STRANGE INTRUDER (1956) *d* Rapper *c* E Haller *w* Lupino 82min AA

STRANGE JUSTICE (1932) *d* Schertzinger *w* Foster, Pichel 72min RKO

STRANGE LADY IN TOWN (1955) *d/p* LeRoy *c* Rosson *m* Tiomkin *w* Garson, D Andrews CS* 112min WB

STRANGE LOVE OF MARTHA IVERS, THE (1946) *d* Milestone *p* Wallis *s* Rossen *c* Milner *m* Rozsa *w* Stanwyck, Heflin, K Douglas, L Scott 116min

STRANGE LOVE OF MOLLY LOUVAIN, THE (1932) *d* Curtiz 72min FN

Strange Obsession, The = STREGA IN AMORE, LA (1966)

STRANGE ONE, THE (1957) *d* Garfein *p* Spiegel *c* Guffey *m* K Hopkins *w* Peppard 100min *r* Col (= *End as a Man*)

STRANGE PEOPLE (1933) *d* Thorpe 64min

STRANGER, THE (1946) *d/co-s/w* Welles *co-p(uc)/co-s(uc)* J Huston *co-p* Spiegel (*ps* SP Eagle) *c* Metty *m* Kaper *w* Robinson, L Young 95min *r* RKO

Stranger, The (UK) = INTRUDER, THE (1961)

Stranger, The = STRANIERO, LO (1967)

STRANGER CAME HOME, THE (1954) *d* Fisher *w* Goddard 80min (= *The Unholy Tour*)

Stranger in Between = HUNTED (1952)

STRANGER IN MY ARMS, A (1958) *d* Käutner *p* R Hunter *c* Daniels *co-a* Golitzen *w* Allyson, Astor, Chandler, C Coburn S* 88min U

STRANGER IN TOWN, A (1943) *d* Rowland *a* Gibbons *m* Amfitheatrof 67min MGM

STRANGER ON HORSEBACK (1955) *d* J Touneur *c* Rennahan *w* McCrea, Carradine, McIntire *66min *r* UA

STRANGER ON THE PROWL (1952) *d* Losey (*ps* Andrea Forzano) *s* Barzman (*ps* Andrea Forzano) *c* Alekan *w* Muni 100min *r* UA (= *Encounter/Imbarco a Mezzanotte*)

STRANGERS ALL (1935) *d* C Vidor 70min RKO

STRANGER'S BANQUET (1922) *d/p* Neilan 6842ft

Stranger's Hand, The (UK) = MANO DELLO STRANIERO, LA (1953)

Strangers in the House (UK) = INCONNUS DANS LA MAISON, LES (1942)

STRANGERS IN THE NIGHT (1944) *d* A Mann 56min Rep

STRANGERS OF THE NIGHT (1923) *d/co-p* Wiblo *co-p* Mayer 8rs MGM

STRANGERS ON A TRAIN (1951) *d/p* Hitchcock *co-s* R Chandler *fn Patricia Highsmith c* Burks *m* Tiomkin *w* F Granger, R Walker, Roman 101min WB

STRANGER'S RETURN, THE (1933) *d/p* K Vidor *c* Daniels *w* L Barrymore, M Hopkins, Tone 88min MGM

STRANGERS WHEN WE MEET (1960) *d/co-p* Quine *s/fn* E Hunter *c* C Lang *m* Duning *w* K Douglas, Rush, Novak, Matthau S* 117min Col

STRANGER WORE A GUN, THE (1953) *d* De Toth *p* H Brown *w* R Scott, Trevor, Marvin, Borgnine TC* 80min Col

STRANGE VICTORY (1948) *d/e* Hurwitz

STRANGE WIVES (1934) *d* Thorpe *w* Romero 75min U

STRANGE WOMAN, THE (1946) *d* Ulmer *c* Andriot *w* Lamarr, G Saunders, L Hayward 101min *r* UA

Strangler, The (US) = EAST OF PICCADILLY (1939)

STRANGLER, THE (1963) *d* Topper *co-a* Pereira 89min AA

STRANGLER OF THE SWAMP (1945) *d/co-st/s* Wisbar *rm* FAHRMANN MARIA 1936 60min

STRANGLERS OF BOMBAY, THE (1959) *d* Fisher S 80min

STRANIERO, LO (1967) *d/co-s* Visconti *p* De Laurentiis *co-s* Cecchi d'Amico *fn* (*L'Etranger*) *Albert Camus co-c* Rotunno *m* Piccioni *w* Mastroianni, Karina *104min (= *The Stranger*)

STRATEGIA DEL RAGNO (1970) *d/co-s* Bertolucci *fst* (*Theme of the Traitor and the Hero*) *JL Borges w* Valli *110min (= *The Spider's Strategy*)

STRATEGIC AIR COMMAND (1935) *d* A Mann *c* Daniels *co-a* Pereira *m* V Young *w* J Stewart, Allyson VV* 114min Par

STRATEGY OF TERROR (1969) *d* Smight *w* Rush *90min U

STRATTON STORY, THE (1949) *d* S Wood *p* J Cummings *co-s* Wells *c* Rosson *a* Gibbons *w* J Stewart, Allyson, Moorehead 106min MGM

Strauss' Great Waltz = WALTZES FROM VIENNA (1933)

STRAVINSKY (1965) *d* Kroitor, Koenig *c/e* Koenig *m/w Iqor Stravinsky* 16mm 49min

STRAWBERRY BLONDE, THE (1941) *d* Walsh *p* J Warner, Wallis *co-s* JJ Epstein *rm* ONE SUNDAY AFTERNOON (1933) *c* Howe *w* Cagney, Hayworth, De Havilland 99min WB

STRAW DOGS (1971) *d/co-s* Peckinpah *118min

STRAZIANI MA DI BACI SAZIAMI (1968) *d/co-st/co-s* Risi *w* Manfredi *104min (= *Torture Me But Kill Me With Kisses*)

STREAK OF LUCK, A (1926) *d* Thorpe

STREAMLINED SWING (1938) *d/w* Keaton 1rl MGM

STREET ANGEL (1928) *d* Borzage *w* J Gaynor 9221ft Fox

STREETCAR NAMED DESIRE, A (1951) *d* Kazan *p* Feldman *s/fpl* T Williams *a* R Day *e* Wiesbart *m* North *w* V Leigh, Brando, Malden 122min *r* WB

STREET OF CHANCE (1930) *d* Cromwell *c* C Lang *w* W Powell, Arthur, K Francis, Cromwell 76min Par

STREET OF FORGOTTEN MEN, THE (1925) *d* Brenon *c* Rosson *w* L Brooks 6366ft FPL

Street of Shame = AKASEN CHITAI (1956)

STREET OF SIN (1928) *d* Stiller, Von Sternberg *c* Glennon *w* Jannings 6382ft

STREET SCENE (1931) *d* K Vidor *p* Goldwyn *s/fpl Elmer Rice c* Barnes *a* R Day *m* A Newman *w* S Sidney *r* UA

Street Sketches = GAIJO NO SUKECHI (1925)

Streets of Sorrow = post-synchronised version of FREUDLOSE GASSE, DIE (1925) *r* 1937 in USA

STREET WITH NO NAME, THE (1948) *d* Keighley *c* Joe Macdonald *co-a* Wheeler *w* Widmark, Nolan, Pevney 91min Fox

STREGA IN AMORE, LA (1966) *d* Damiani *fn* (*Aura*) *Carlos Fuentes* 103min (= *The Witch in Love/The Strange Obsession*)

STREGHE, LE (1966) *m* Piccioni *w* Mangano *100min *pc* De Laurentiis (= *The Witches*)

ep LA STREGA BRUCIATA *d* Visconti *co-s* Zavattini *c* Rotunno *w* Girardot, Girotti (= *The Witch Burned Alive*)

ep SENSO CIVICO *d* Bolognini *w* Sordi (= *Civic Sense*)

ep LA TERRA VISTA DELLA LUNA *d/s* Pasolini *w* Toto (= *The Earth as Seen from the Moon*)

ep LA SICILIANA *d/co-s* Rossi (= *The Girl from Sicily*)

ep UNA SERA COME LE ALTRE *d* De Sica *co-s* Zavattini *w* Eastwood (= *A Night Like Any Other*)

STREJKEN (1913) *d/co-s/w* Sjöström 1070m (= *Arbetoven*)

Strength of Love = AI WA CHIKARA DA (1930)

STRESSES ES TRES, TRES (1968) *d/co-s* Saura 100min

STRIATIONS (1970) *d* McLaren

STRICTLY DISHONORABLE (1931) *d* Stahl *st* P Sturges *co-c* Freund *w* Lukas 94min U

STRICTLY DISHONORABLE (1951) *d/p/s* M Frank, Panama *fpl* P Sturges *c* June *a* Gibbons, Peters *w* J Leigh 86min MGM

STRICTLY DYNAMITE (1934) *d* E Nugent *a* Cronjager *w* Foster 71min RKO

Strictly for Pleasure = PERFECT FURLOUGH, THE (1958)

Stride, Soviet! = SHAGAI, SOVET! (1926)

STRIDEN GAR VIDARE (1941) *d* Molander *w* Sjöström, Kjellin 100min

STRJD ZONDER EINDEN (1954) *d/s/e* Haanstra *25min

Strike = STACHKA (1924)

STRIKE ME PINK (1936) *d* Taurog, R Alton *p* Goldwyn *co-c* Toland *m* A Newman 99min *r* UA

Strikers, The (US) = COMPAGNI, I (1963)

STRIKE UP THE BAND (1940) *d* Berkeley *p* Freed *c* June *co-m* Edens, Freed, *Gershwin w* Garland, Rooney 121min MGM

STRIPPER, THE (1963) *d* Schaffner *p* Wald *fpl* (*A Loss of Roses*) Inge *c* Fredricks *m* Goldsmith *w* Woodward, Trevor, Lynley, G Lee CS 95min Fox

STRIPTEASE (1957) *d* Borowczyk, Lenica anim 1min

Striptease Lady = LADY OF BURLESQUE (1943)

STROGI YUNOSHNA (1936) *d* Room (= *The Stern Young Man*)

STROM, DER (1942) *d* Rittau 89min

STROMBOLI (*pre* 1952) *d* Tazieff 16mm

Stromboli = STROMBOLI, TERRA DI DIO (1949)

STROMBOLI, TERRA DI DIO (1949) *d/co-p/st/co-s* Rossellini *co-p/w* Ingrid Bergman *c* Martelli 107min *r* RKO (= *Stromboli*)

STRONG BOX (1929) *d* J Ford *c* August *w* V McLaglen, Ryan 63min Fox

STRONGER PASSION, THE (1922) *d* Brenon

STRONGEST, THE (1920) *d/s* Walsh *w* Adorée 5rs Fox

Strongest, The = STARKASTE, DEN (1929)

STRONG MAN, THE (1926) *d* Capra *p/w* Langdon 6882ft FN

STRONG REVENGE, A (1913) *d/p/w* Sennett *w* Normand ½rl Key

Strong Woman, Weak Man = TSUYOMUSHI ONNA TO YOWAMUSHI OTOKO (1968)

STROP (1962) *d* Chytilova *w* Menzel 40min (= *Ceiling*)

STRUGGLE, THE (1931) *d* Griffith *co-st* Loos, Emerson *c* Ruttenberg 77min *r* UA

Struggle in Italy = LOTTE IN ITALIA (1969)

Stud, The = ETALON L' (1969)

STUDENT PRINCE IN OLD HEIDELBERG, THE (1928) *d* Lubitsch *a* Gibbons, R Day *e* Marton *w* Novarro, Shearer, Hersholt 9400ft MGM

STUDENT PRINCE, THE (1954) *d* Thorpe *p* Pasternak *co-a* Gibbons *w* Blyth *wv* Lanza CS* 106min MGM

STUDENT VON PRAG, DER (1913) *d Stella Rye w* Wegener

STUDENT VON PRAG, DER (1926) *d/co-s* Galeen *co-c* Krampf *dec* Warm *w* Veidt, Krauss 3173m

STUDENT VON PRAG, DER (1935) *d Arthur Robison dec* Warm *w* Walbrook 87min

STUDIE I (1952) *d* P Weiss

STUDIE II (1953) *d* P Weiss 7min (= *Hallucinationer/Hallucinations*)

STUDIE III (1953) *d* P Weiss

STUDIE IV (1954) *d* P Weiss (= *Frigorelse*)

STUDIE V (1955) *d* P Weiss (= *Vaxelspel*)

STUDIEN NR 1–4 (1921–27) *d* Fischinger anim

STUDIE NR 5 (1928–9) *d* Fischinger anim

STUDIE NR 6 (1929) *d* Fischinger anim 2min

STUDIE NR 7 (1929) *d* Fischinger anim 3min

STUDIE NR 8 (1930) *d* Fischinger *m* Dukas anim 3min

STUDIE NR 9 (1931) *d* Fischinger *m Brahms* anim 4min

STUDIE NR 10 (1931) *d* Fischinger *m Verdi* anim 4min

STUDIEN NR 11–12 (1932–36) *d* Fischinger anim 8min

STUDIO MURDER MYSTERY, THE (1929) *d* Tuttle *c* Milner *w* March 6070ft Par

Studio of Dr Faustus, The = ATEL EINTERIOR (1956)

Studio Romance, A = SATSUEIJI, ROMANSU-RENAI ANNAI (1932)

STUDS LONIGAN (1960) *d* Lerner *p/s* Yordan *co-c* Wexler *m* Goldsmith 95min *r* UA

STUFFIE (1940) *d* Zinnemann sh MGM

STUNDE DER VERSUCHUNG, DIE (1936) *d* Wegener 74min UFA

STUNDE GLUCK, EINE (1930) *d/w* Dieterle (= *One Hour of Happiness*)

STURME DER LEIDENSCHAFT (1932) *d* Siodmak *p* Pommer *co-m* Hollander *w* Jannings, Sten 101min UFA (= *Storm of Passion/Tempest*)

STURME UBER DEM MONTBLANC (1930) *d/s* Franck *w* Riefenstahl 108min

STURM UBER LA SARRAZ (1929) *d* Richter, Eisenstein, *Ivor Montagu s* Richter *c* Tissé *w* Richter, Eisenstein, Ruttmann, Balasz, Moussinac (= *Kampf des Unabhangigen Gegen den Kommerziellen Film*)

STURSTROEMBROEN (1950) *d/s* Dreyer 196m

STUTTGART (1935) *d* Ruttmann 15min

STUTZEN DER GESELLSCHAFT (1935) *d* Sirk 84min

SUBARASHIKI NICHIYOBI (1947) *d/co-s* Kurosawa 108min Toho

SUBIDA AL CIELO (1951) *d* Buñuel *c* Philips 85min

SUBMARINE (1928) *d* Capra *c* J Walker 9rs Col

SUBMARINE COMMAND (1951) *d* J Farrow *c* Lindon *co-a* Pereira *w* Holden, Bendix 87min Par

SUBMARINE D-I (1937) *d* Bacon 99min WB

SUBMARINE PATROL (1938) *d* J Ford *p* Zanuck *c* AC Miller *w* G Bancroft, Carradine 95min Fox

SUBMARINE PIRATE, A (1915) *d Charles Avery, Syd Chaplin w* W Ruggles 4rs Tri-Key

Submarine Zone (UK) = ESCAPE TO GLORY (1940)

Substitute = SUROGAT (1961)

SUBTERRANEANS, THE (1960) *d* Macdougall *p* Freed *fn J Kerouac c* Ruttenberg *m* Previn *w* Peppard, Caron CS* 89min MGM

SUBWAY EXPRESS (1931) *d* Newmeyer *c* J Walker 68min Col

SUCCESS AT ANY PRICE (1934) *d F Walter Roben co-s/fpl* (*Success Story*) Lawson *w* Fairbanks Jr 75min RKO

SUCCES COMMERCIAL, UN *d/s/pc* Iefebvre 83min (= *Q-Bec My Love*)

SUCCES DE LA PRESTIDIGITATION, LE (1912) *d/s/w* Linder Pat (= *Max Escamoteur*)

Such a Pretty Little Beach (UK) = SI JOLIE PETITE PLAGE, UNE (1948)

SUCH GOOD FRIENDS (1971) *d/p* Preminger *100min

SUCHKIND 312 (1956) *d* Machaty 100min

Such Men are Dangerous = THE RACERS (1955)

SUDAN (1945) *d John Rawlins w* Montez * 76min U

SUDBA CHELOVEKA (1959) *d/w* Bondarchuk *fn Mikhail Sholokhov* 92min (= *Destiny of a Man*)

SUD CHESTI (1948) *d* Room 100min (= *The Tribunal of Honour*)

SUDDEN DANGER (1955) *d* Cornfield 85min *r* UA

SUDDEN FEAR (1952) *d* D Miller *c* C Lang *m* E Bernstein *w* J Crawford, Palance, Grahame 110min RKO

SUDDENLY IT'S SPRING (1947) *d* Leisen *c* Fapp *m* V Young *w* Goddard, MacMurray 87min Par

SUDDENLY LAST SUMMER (1959) *d* J Mankiewicz *p* Spiegel *s* Vidal, T Williams *fpl* T Williams *c* Hildyard *w* E Taylor, Cliff K Hepburn 114min Col

Sudden Rain = SHUU (1956)

SUEZ (1938) *d* Dwan *p* Zanuck *co-s* P Dunne *c* Marley *w* Power, L Young, Annabella 104min Fox

Suffragetten, Den = MODERNA SUFFRAGETTEN, DEN (1913)

Sugar = SUKKER (1942)

Sugar and Spice (1915) = ZUCKER UND ZIMT

SUGAR DADDIES (1927) *d Fred Guiol p* Roach *w* Laurel, Hardy 2rs *r* MGM

SUGATA SANSHIRO (1943) *d/s/co-e* Kurosawa 80min Toho (= *Judo Saga*)

SUICIDE (1965) *d* Warhol 16mm *70min
SUICIDE CLUB, THE (1914) *d/p* Elvey *fn* R L Stevenson
SUITOR, THE (1920) *d/s* Semon, Taurog *w* Semon 2rs Vit
Suicide Troops of the Watch Tower = BORO NO KESSHITAI (1942)
Suitor, The = SOUPIRANT, LE (1963)
SUJATA (1959) *d/p* Roy 150min
SUKI NAREBA KOSO (1928) *d/s* Gosho (= *If You Like It*)
SUKKER (1942) *d/s* B Henning Jensen 7min (= *Sugar*)
Suleiman the Conqueror = SOLIMANE IL CONQUISTARE (1961)
SULFATARA (1955) *d/c/e* De Seta
SULLA VIA DI DAMASCO (1947) *co-d/co-s/n* Emmer *co-d/co-s* Enrico Gras
Sulle Rame di Verdi = LOUGHI VERDIANI (1948)
SULLIVANS, THE (1944) *d* Bacon *m* Mockridge *w* A Baxter, Mitchell 112min Fox
SULLIVAN'S TRAVELS (1941) *d/s/st* P Sturges *c* J Seitz *w* McCrea, Lake 91min Par
SULT (1966) *d/co-s* Carlsen *m* Komeda *w* Lindblom 110min *pc* Carlsen (= *Hunger*)
SULTANS, LES (1966) *d/co-s* Delannoy *c* Thirard *w* Lollobrigida, Noiret *95min
SUMKA DIPKURERA (1927) *d/ad/w* Dovzhenko 1647m (= *The Diplomatic Pouch*)
Summer and Sinners = SOMMAR OCH SYNDARE (1960)
SUMMER AND SMOKE (1961) *d* Glenville *p* Wallis *co-s* Poe *fpl* T Williams *c* C Lang *m* E Bernstein *w* Page, Lawrence Harvey PV* 118min Par
SUMMER BACHELORS (1926) *d/p* Dwan *c* Ruttenberg 6727ft Fox
Summer Battle of Osaka, The = OSAKA NATSU NO JIN (1937)
Summer Clouds, The = IWASHIGUMO (1958)
Summer Clouds = BOLOND APRILIS (1957)
Summer Day, A = SOMMERTAG (1960)
SUMMER GIRLS, THE (1918) *d* Cline *w* Fazenda 2rs Sennett
SUMMER HOLIDAY (1962) *d* P Yates *chor* Ross S* 109min
SUMMER HOLIDAY (1947) *d* Mamoulian *p* Freed *co-s* Goodrich, Hackett *fpl* (*Ah Wilderness*) Eugene O'Neill *co-a* Gibbons *chor* Walters *w* Rooney, W Huston, Moorehead, A Francis *92min MGM
Summer Interlude = SOMMARLEK (1950)
SUMMER LOVE (1957) *d* Haas 85min
SUMMER MADNESS (1955) *d/co-s* Lean *c* Hildyard *dec* V Korda *co-cr* R MacDonald *w* K Hepburn, I Miranda 100min *r* BL
SUMMER MAGIC (1962) *d* Neilson *w* H Mills, Mcguire *109min *pc* Disney
Summer Manoeuvres = GRANDES MANOEVRES, LES (1955)
Summer Night is Sweet, The = LJUVLIG AR SOMMARNATTEN (1961)
SUMMER OF '42 (1971) *d* Mulligan *c* Surtees *m* Legrand *102min WB
SUMMER PLACE, A (1960) *d/p/s* Davis *m* M Steiner *w* McGuire, A Kennedy *130min WB
Summer Skin (UK) = PIEL DE VERANO (1961)
SUMMER STOCK (1950) *d* Walters *p* Pasternak *co-s* Wells *c* Planer *co-a* Gibbons *chor* Gene Kelly *w* Gene Kelly, Garland *109min MGM (= *If You Feel Like Singing*)
SUMMER STORM (1944) *d/co-s* Sirk *fst* (*The Duel*) A Chekov *c* Stout *w* Darnell, G Sanders, Horton 106min *r* UA
Summer Tale, A = SOMMARSAGA (1912)
Summertime (US) = SUMMER MADNESS (1955)
Summer War = SOMMERKRIG (1965)
Summer With Monika = SOMMAREN MED MOMIKA (1952)
SUMMER WORLD, A (1961, *uf*) *d* Schaffner
SUMURUN (1920) *d* Lubitsch *f* (*Arabian Nights*) *c* Sparkuhl *w* Lubitsch, Negri, Wegener 90min (= *One Arabian Night*)
SUN, THE (1903) *p* Paul 60ft (= *The Midnight Sun at Scaro*)
Sun, The = NICHIRIN (1925)
SUN ALSO RISES, THE (1957) *d* H King *p* Zanuck *fn* Hemingway *co-a* Wheeler *m* Friedhofer *w* Gardner, Power, M Ferrer, Flynn, Ratoff, Dalio CS* 129min Fox
SUNA NO ONNA (1964) *d* Teshigahara 127min (= *Woman of the Dunes*)
SUN COMES UP, THE (1948) *d* Thorpe *c* June *m* Previn *w* Jeanette Macdonald, Nolan *93min MGM
SUNDAY, BLOODY SUNDAY (1971) *d* Schlesinger *w* Finch *110min *r* UA
SUNDAY BY THE SEA (1953) *d/s* A Simmons *c* Lassally 13min
SUNDAY DINNER FOR A SOLDIER (1944) *d* Bacon *c* Joe MacDonald *co-a* Wheeler *m* A Newman *w* A Baxter, Darwell 87min Fox
Sunday in August = DOMENICA D'AGOSTO (1950)
SUNDAY IN NEW YORK *d* Tewkesbury *s* Krasna *w* Robertson, J Fonda *105min MGM
Sunday in September, A = SONDAG I SEPTEMBER, EN (1963)

SUNDAY PUNCH (1942) *d* D Miller *a* Gibbons *w* Dailey, Gardner 76min MGM
Sunday Romance, A = BAKARUHABAN (1956)
Sundays and Cybele = CYBELE OU LES DIMANCHES DE VILLE D'AVRAY (1962)
SUNDE DER HELGA ARNDT, DIE (1916) *d/p/co-s* May 4rs
SUNDOWN (1941) *d* Hathaway *p* Wanger *c* C Lang *a* Golitzen *m* Rozsa *w* Tierney, G Sanders, Carey 90min *r* UA
SUNDOWNERS, THE (1960) *d* Zinnemann *c* Hildyard *m* Tiomkin *w* Kerr, Mitchum, Ustinov, Preston 133min WB
Sunflower = I GIRASOLI (1970)
SUNKEN ROCKS (1919) *d/p* Hepworth 5rs
SUNKEN SILVER (1925) *d/p* G Seitz serial in 10eps Pat
SUNNY (1941) *d/p* H Wilcox *c* Metty *m* Elmo Williams *m* Jerome Kern *w* Neagle, Horton 98min RKO
SUNNYSIDE (1919) *d/s/w* Chaplin *c* Totheroh *w* Purviance 3rs FN
SUNNY SIDE OF THE STREET (1951) *d* Quine *71min Col
SUNNYSIDE UP (1926) *d* Crisp *c* Marley 5994ft
SUNNY SIDE UP (1929) *d/s* D Butler *w* J Gaynor 11131ft Fox
SUNRISE (1927) *d* Murnau *s* C Mayer *co-c* Struss *co-a* Ulmer *w* J Gaynor, G O'Brien 117min Fox
Sun Rises Again, The = SOLE SORGE ANCORA, IL (1947)
The Sun's Burial = TAIYO NO HAICABA (1960)
SUNSET BEACH ON LONG ISLAND (1967) *d* Warhol 16mm *30min (= *Segment of Four Stars*)
SUNSET BOULEVARD (1950) *d/co-s* B Wilder *p/co-s* Brackett *c* J Seitz *co-a* Dreier *m* Waxman *w* Swanson, Holden, Von Stroheim, J Webb, (De Mille, Hopper, Keaton) 111min Par
SUNSET PASS (1933) *d* Hathaway *fn* Zane Gray *rm* 1929 *c* Stout *w* R Scott, Carey 64min Par
SUNSHINE (1916) *d* Cline *p* Sennett *w* Swanson Tri-Key
SUN SHINES BRIGHT, THE (1953) *d/co-p* J Ford *co-p* M Cooper *c* Stout *m* V Young *w* Darwell 90min Rep
SUNSHINE SUSIE (1931) *d* Saville 87min (= *Office Girl, The*)
SUN UP (1925) *d/p/s/ad* Goulding 5819ft MGM
SUO DESTINO, IL (1938) *d/co-s* Guazzoni
SUOLA ROMANA, LA (1960) *d* Maselli
SUOR LETIZIA (1956) *d/co-s* Camerini *co-s* Zavattini *c* Di Venanzo *w* Magnani, Rossi-Drago 89min (= *Last Temptation*)
SUPERDIABOLICI, I (1965) *d/co-s* Steno *
SUPERSTITION (1922) *d* Dwan 5rs
SUPERSTIZIONE *d/s* Antonioni *m* Fusco 9min (= *Non ci credo!*)
SUPPORT YOUR LOCAL GUNFIGHTER (1971) *d/ex-p* B Kennedy *s* J Grant *w* Garner, Pleshette, Blondell *92min *pc* B Kennedy, Garner *r* UA
SUPPORT YOUR LOCAL SHERIFF! (1969) *d* B Kennedy *w* Garner, Brennan *93min *r* UA
SURE FIRE (1921) *d* J Ford 5rs U
SURF AND SEAWEED (1931) *d/c* R Steiner 11min
SURFING MOVIE (1968) *d* Warhol * 16mm
SUR LA ROUTE DE SALINA (1970) *d/co-s* Lautner *a* D'Eaubonne *w* Hayworth *95min (= *Road to Salina*)
SUR LE PONT D'AVIGNON (1956) *d/s* Franju *c* Fradetal *m* Jarre FS *11min
SURMENES, LES (1958) *d* Daniol-Valcroze *s* Truffaut *w* Brialy 21min
SUROGAT (1961) *d/a* Vukotic anim* 274m (= *Ersatz/ Substitute*)
SURPRISE PACKAGE (1960) *d/p* Donen *c* Challis *s* Kurnitz *fn* Art Buchwald *w* Brynner, Coward, M Gaynor 99min Col
SURRENDER (1927) *d* Edward Sloman *w* Mozhukhin 8249ft U
SURRENDER (1931) *d* W Howard *fn* (*Axelle*) Pierre Benoit *c* Howe *w* B Baxter 69min Fox
SURRENDER (1950) *d/as-p* Dwan *p* Yates *co-s/st* J Grant *w* Brennan, Darwell 90min Rep
Surrounded = OMRINGET (1960)
SURVIVAL! (1968) *d/co-p* Dassin *s/co-p* Irwin Shaw *70min
Surviving Shinsengumi, The = IKONOKOTTA SHINSENGUMI (1932)
SUSANA (1951) *d* Bunuel 82min (= *Demonio y Carne*)
SUSAN AND GOD (1940) *d* Cukor *s* Loos *dec* Gibbons *m* Stothart *w* J Crawford, March, Hayworth, Dailey 115min MGM (= *The Gay Mrs Trexal*)
SUSAN LENOX (1931) *d/p* Leonard *c* Daniels *w* Garbo, Gable, Hersholt 8rs MGM (= *The Rise of Helga*)
SUSANNA TUTTA PANNA (1957) *d* Steno *p* Ponti *w* Manfredi
SUSAN SLADE (1961) *d/p/s* Daves *c* Ballard *m* M Steiner *w* McGuire, Nolan *116min WB
SUSAN SLEPT HERE (1954) *d/co-s(uc)* Tashlin *c* Musuraca *m* Harline *w* D Powell, D Reynolds, A Francis, Benny (*uc*) *98min RKO
SUSAN STARR (1962) *d* Hope Ryden *co-p* R Leacock 57min
SUSPECT, THE (1945) *d* Siodmak *w* Laughton 85min U
SUSPECT (1960) *d/co-p* R Boulting *co-p* J Boulting 81min BL

SUSPENSE (1946) *d* Tuttle *st/s* Yordan *c* Struss *w* (Winters) *100min Mon
SUSPICION (1918) *d* Stahl
SUSPICION (1941) *d* Hitchcock *co-s* Raphaelson, Reville *m* Waxman *w* C Grant, Fontaine 99min RKO
SUSPICIOUS WIVES (1922) *d* Stahl
SUSSIE (1945) *d* Mattson *w* Björnstrand
SUSUME DOKURITSUKI (1943) *d* Kinugasa (= *Forward Flag of Independence*)
SUTTER'S GOLD (1936) *d* Cruze *w* Carey 94min U
SUVUROV (1941) *d* Pudovkin, *Mikhail Doller* *w* Cherkasov 108min
SUZANNA (1923) *d* Richard Jones *supn* Sennett *w* Normand 8rs
SUZANNE (1932) *co-d/w* Rouleau *co-d* Joannon
SUZANNE ET LES BRIGANDS (1948) *d* Ciampi 76min
SVADLENKA (1936) *d* Frič (= *The Seamstress*)
SVANGER PA SLOTTET, DET (1959) *d* Kjellin *co-s* Ekman *c* Fischer *w* Björnstrand CS* 97min (= *Swinging at the Castle*)
SVARTA HORISONTER (1936) *d* Fejos SF (*Danstavlingen i esira* 285m/*Skonhetssalongen i djungeln* 278m/ *Verldens mest anvandbara trad* 280m/*Vera faders gravar* 289m/*Havets djavul* 280m/*Djungeldansen* 300m)
SVARTA MASKERNA, DE (1912) *d/co-s* Stiller *w* Sjöström 1080m
SVARTA PALMKRONOR (1967) *d/s* Lindgren *c* Fischer *w* Von Sydow, B Andersson *143min San (= *The Black Palm Trees*)
SVARTA ROSOR (1932) *d* Molander SF
SVD (1927) *d* L Trauberg, Kozintsev *c* Moskvin *w* Gerasimov 2100m (= *The Club of the Big Deed*)
Svegliati e uccidi = LUTRING (1966)
SVEJK V CIVILU (1927) *d* Machaty
SVENGALI (1931) *d* A Mayo *w* J Barrymore, Crisp 81min WB
SVETLO PRONIKA TMOU (1931) *d/s* Vavra
SVETLYI PUT (1940) *d* Alexandrov 78min (= *The Bright Path/Tanya*)
SVET NA KAJZARJU (1952) *d* Stiglic (= *People of Kajzarju*)
SVET PATRI NAM (1937) *d/co-st/co-s* Frič *c* Heller (= *The World Belongs to Them*)
SVITATO, LO (1956) *d/co-s* Lizzani
S VYLOUCENIM VEREJNOSTI (1933) *d* Frič (= *Closed Books*)
SWAIN (1950) *d/s/c/e/w* Markopoulos *fst* (*Fanshawe*) *Nathaniel Hawthorne* *m* Villa Lobos 16mm *24min
SWAMP WATER (1941) *d* J Renoir *p* Pichel *s* D Nichols *c* Marley *w* Brennan, W Huston, A Baxter, D Andrews, Carradine 93min Fox
SWAMP WOMEN (1956) *d* Corman *67min
SWAN, THE (1956) *d* C Vidor *p* Schafy *fn* Ferenc Molnar *c* Surtees, Ruttenberg *a* Gibbons *m* Kaper *w* Grace Kelly, Guinness, Moorehead CS* 112min MGM
SWANEE RIVER (1939) *d* Sidney Lanfield *p* Zanuck *c* Glennon *w* Jolson 84min Fox
SWEDEN (1960) *d* W Van Dyke 60min
SWEDENHEILMS (1935) *d* Molander *w* Ingrid Bergman SF
SWEEPINGS (1933) *d* Cromwell *c* Cronjager *w* L Barrymore 80min RKO
SWEET ADELINE (1935) *d* LeRoy *p* Wallis *st/m* Jerome Kern, Oscar Hammerstein II *c* Polito *w* I Dunne 81min WB
SWEET AND LOW DOWN (1944) *d* A Mayo *c* Ballard *w* Darnell 76min Fox
Sweet and Sour (UK) = DRAGEES AU POIVRE (1963)
SWEET AND THE BITTER, THE (1962) *d/p/s* Clavell
SWEET AND TWENTY (1909) *d* Griffith *w* Pickford 1rl Bio
SWEET BIRD OF YOUTH (1962) *d/s* R Brooks *p* Berman *fpl* T Williams *c* Krasner *w* P Newman, Page CS* 120min *r* MGM
SWEET CHARITY (1969) *d/chor* Fosse *fpl* Simon, Coleman, Fields *fs* (*Le Notti di Cabiria*) Fellini, Pinelli, Flaiano *c* Surtees *co-a* Golitzen *w* MacLaine, Montalban PV70* 149min U
SWEETHEART DAYS (1921) *d* St Clair *s* Sennett 2rs Sen
SWEETHEART OF THE CAMPUS (1941) *d* Dmytryk 67min Col
SWEETHEARTS (1938) *d* WS Van Dyke *co-e* Vorkapich *w* Jeanette Macdonald 120min MGM
SWEETHEARTS AND WIVES (1930) *d* Badger *c* J Seitz *w* C Brook 78min FN
SWEETHEARTS ON PARADE (1930) *d* Neilan 65min Col
SWEETHEARTS ON PARADE (1953) *d/as-p* Dwan *90min Rep
SWEET HUNTERS (1969) *d/co-s/lyr* Guerra *mf* Carl Orff, Tadeusz Penderecki Tadeusz Baird *w* Hayden *100min
SWEET LAVENDER (1915) *d/p/c* Hepworth 5000ft
Sweet Light in a Dark Room (US) = ROMEO, JULIE A TMA (1959)
SWEET MAMA (1930) *d* Cline 7rs FN
SWEET PICKLE, A (1925) *d/s* Cline *p* Sennett Pat
SWEET ROSIE O'GRADY (1943) *d* Irving Cummings *m* A Newman *w* Grable 74min
SWEET SMELL OF SUCCESS (1957) *d* Mackendrick *ex-p* H Hecht *co-s/fst* Lehman *co-s* Odets *c* Howe *m* E Bernstein *w* Lancaster, Curtis 96min *r* UA

SWEET TORONTO (1971) d Pennebaker co-p/co-c R Leacock, Pennebaker w Bo Diddley, Jerry Lee Lewis, Chuck Berry, Little Richard, Lennon, Yoko Ono, Eric Clapton, Klaus Voorman super 16mm *140min

SWELL GUY (1946) d Tuttle p Hellinger s R Brooks c Gaudio w Blyth 87min U

SWIMMER, THE (1968) d/co-p Perry, Pollack(uc) w Lancaster *95min r Col

Swindle, The = BIDONE, IL (1955)

SWINGER, THE (1966) d/p G Sidney c Biroc *81min Par

SWING HIGH, SWING LOW (1937) d Leisen c Tetzlaff co-a Dreier w Lombard, MacMurray, Lamour, Quinn 96min Par

Swinging at the Castle = SVANGER PA SLOTTET, DET (1959)

SWINGING THE LAMBETH WALK (1939) d Lye

SWINGIN' ON A RAINBOW (1945) d William Beaudine w Langdon 72min Rep

SWING IT, PROFESSOR (1937) d Neilson 58min

SWING OUT THE BLUES (1944) d St Clair 69min Col

SWING PARADE OF 1946 (1946) d Karlson 73min Mon

SWING SHIFT CINDERELLA (1945) d Avery *8min MGM

SWING SHIFT MAISIE (1943) d McLeod MGM (= The Girl in Overalls)

SWING TIME (1936) d G Stevens p Berman m Jerome Kern w G Rogers, Astaire 105min RKO

SWINGTIME JOHNNY (1944) d Cline s Bruckman 60min U

SWING YOUR LADY (1937) d Enright p Wallis c Edeson w Bogart, Reagan, Fazenda 72min WB

SWISS FAMILY ROBINSON (1960) d Annakin m Alwyn w J Mills, McGuire PV* 126min

SWISS MISS (1938) d John G Blystone p Roach co-st Negulesco c Brodine w Laurel, Hardy 72min

Switchboard Operator = LJUBAVNI SLUCAJ, TRAGEDIJA SLUZBENICE P.T.T. (1967)

Sword and Dice = KARD ES KOCKA (1959)

Sword and the Cross, The = SPADA E LA CROCE, LA (1958)

SWORD AND THE FLUTE, THE (1951) d Ivory co-m Shankar 16mm *24min

Sword and the Sumo Ring, A = IPPON GATANA DOHYOIRI (1934)

SWORD IN THE STONE, THE (1963) p Disney fn TH White *80min

SWORD OF D'ARTAGNAN, THE (1951) d Boetticher 50min

Sword of Lancelot = LANCELOT AND GUINEVERE (1962)

Sword of Penitence = ZANGE NO YAIBA (1927)

SWORD OF SHERWOOD FOREST (1960) d Fisher S* 80min r Col

SWORDSMAN, THE (1947) d JH Lewis m Friedhofer *81min Col

Swords of Blood = CARTOUCHE (1961)

Symphony of the Donbass = ENTUZIAZM (1930)

SYLVESTER (1924) d Lupu-Pick 1529m UFA

SYLVIA (1965) d G Douglas s Boehm c Ruttenberg co-a Pereira m Raksin w E O'Brien, Lawford, Sothern, C Baker, Dru, A Ray, Lindfors 115min Par

SYLVIA SCARLETT (1936) d Cukor p Berman fn Compton MacKenzie c August w K Hepburn, C Grant 90min RKO

SYLVIE DESTIN (1965) d/s Kirsanov

SYLVIE ET LE FANTOME (1945) d Autant-Lara s/di Aurenche c Agostini w Tati, Carette, Desailly 90min

Sympathy for the Devil = ONE PLUS ONE (1969)

SYMPHONIE DIAGONALE (1924) d Eggeling

SYMPHONIE FANTASTIQUE, LA (1942) d Christian-Jaque w Barrault, Jules Berry 89min

SYMPHONIE MECANIQUE (1955) d Mitry m Pierre Boulez PV 3 screens 12½min

SYMPHONIE NR 3 IN ES-DUR, OPUS 55 'EROICA' VON LUDWIG VAN BEETHOVEN (1967) d Colpi m Beethoven w Rafael Kubelik and Berlin Philharmonic Orchestra *38min (=Beethoven 3rd Symphony - Eroica)

SYMPHONIE PASTORALE, LA (1946) d/co-ad Delannoy co-ad/co-di Aurenche fn André Gide co-di Bost c Thirard m Auric w Morgan, Desailly 105min

SYMPHONIE POUR UN MASSACRE (1963) d/co-st/co-s Deray c C Renoir w Vanel 110min (= The Corrupt)

Symphonie van den arbeid = PHILIPS-RADIO (1931)

SYMPHONY IN SLANG (1951) d Avery p Quimby *7min MGM

SYMPHONY OF SIX MILLION (1932) d La Cava w I Dunne, Rathbone 85min RKO (= Melody of Life)

Symphony of the Tropics = FAJA LOBBI (1960)

SYNANON (1965) d/p Quine w Conte, E O'Brien 107min pc Quine r Col (= Get off my Back)

SYNCOPATION (1942) d/p Dieterle co-s Yordan m Leith Stevens e J Sturges w Menjou, G Bancroft 88min RKO

SYNCOPATION (1929) d Glennon 85min RKO

SYND (1928) d Molander fpl (Brott och Brott) August Strindberg SF

SYNDENS DATTER (1915) d/s Blom

SYSKONBADD 1782 (1966) d/s Sjö man fpl ('Tis Pity She's a Whore) John Ford w B Andersson, Björnstrand, Kulle, Lindstrom 96min San (= My Sister, My Love)

SYSTEME DE LAW, LE (1965) d De Givray TV

SZAKADEK (1955) d Ranódy (= Discord)

SZEGENYLEGENYEK (1965) d Jancso S 94min (= The Round-Up)

SZENZACIO (1922) d Fejos

SZENZACIO! (1936) d Vajda, Istvan Szekely 80min

SZERELEM HAROM EJSZAKAJA, EGY (1967) d Révész S* 110min (= Three Nights of Love)

SZKOLA (1958) d/s/c Borowczyk anim* 9min (= School)

SZTUKA MLODYCH (1949) d/s Munk 20min

SZYFRY (1966) d Has m Krzysztof Penderecki w Cybulski 80min (= The Code)

TABIYAKUSHA (1940) d/s Naruse (= An Itinerant Actor)

TABLAO A LA LUNA (1962) d Saslavsky

TABLE AUX CREVES, LA (1951) d/co-s Verneuil fn Marcel Aymé w Fernendel 92min (= The Village Feud)

TABU (1931) co-d/co-s/pc Murnau co-d/st/co-s/co-c Flaherty co-c F Crosby m Reisenfeld 90min

TACCHINO PREPOTENTE, IL (1939) d Rossellini c Bava sh

TAENK PAA ET TAL (1968) d/s Kjaerulff-Schmidt w B Andersson *98min (= Think of a Number)

TAG DER FREIHEIT – UNSERE WEHRMACHT (1935) d Reifenstahl

TAGEBUCH DES DR. HART, DAS (1916) d Leni 3rs

TAGEBUCH EINER VERLORENEN, DAS (1918) d/p/s R Oswald w Veidt, Krauss 1934m

TAGEBUCH EINER VERLORENEN, DAS (1929) d Pabst w L Brooks 130min

Tagebuch eines Matrosen, Das = ROBINSON, EIN (1940)

TAIHEIYO HITORIBOTCHI (1963) d Ichikawa w Mori CS* 104min r Nik (= Alone on the Pacific/My Enemy the Sea)

Tailor from Torzhka, The = ZAKROISHCHIK IZ TORZHKA (1925)

TAILOR MADE MAN, A (1931) d S Wood w Hopper 77min

TAIL SPIN (1939) d Del Ruth p H Brown w Faye, Constance Bennett, Wyman 84min Fox

TAINA KOROLEVY (1919) d/s Protazanov fn Eleanor Glyn (Three Weeks) w Mozhukhin 1800m (= The Queen's Secret)

TAIYO NO HAKABA (1960) d/co-s Oshima *87min Sho

TAIYO TO BARA (1956) d Kinoshita (= The Rose on his Arm)

TAJEMSTVI KRVE (1953) d/co-s Frič *104min (= The Mystery of Blood)

TAJINKÓ MÚRA (1940) d Imai (= Village of Tajinko)

TAKARA NO YAMA (1929) d/st Ozu sh (= The Treasure Mountain)

TAKE A GIANT STEP (1959) d P Leacock co-s JJ Epstein c Arling 100min

TAKE A LETTER, DARLING (1942) d Leisen as-p Kohlmar co-a Dreier w R Russell, MacMurray 93min Par

TAKE CARE OF MY LITTLE GIRL (1951) d Negulesco co-s JJ Epstein co-a Wheeler m A Newman w M Gaynor, Crain, J Hunter, Peters *93min Fox

TAKE HER SHE'S MINE (1963) d/p Koster s N Johnson c Ballard m Goldsmith w J Stewart CS *98min Fox

Take it all = A TOUT PRENDRE (1963)

TAKEKURABE (1955) d Gosho w Yamada (= Growing Up/Daughters of Yoshiwara)

TAKE ME HOME (1928) d Neilan t H Mankiewicz 5614ft FPL

TAKE ME OUT TO THE BALL GAME (1949) d Berkeley p Freed co-s Wells st/chor Gene Kelly, Donen c Folsey co-a Gibbons lyr Comden, A Green, Edens w Sinatra, Gene Kelly, F Williams, Garrett w *93min MGM

TAKE ME TO TOWN (1953) d Sirk co-p R Hunter c Metty a Golitzen w Sheridan, Hayden *81min U

TAKE MY LIFE (1947) d Neame c G Green 79min

TAKE THE HIGH GROUND (1953) d R Brooks p Schary c J Alton m Tiomkin w Widmark, Malden *101min MGM

TAKE YOUR MEDECINE (1930) d Cline p Sennett 11min

TAKING A CHANCE (1928) d McLeod 4840ft Fox

TAKING OFF (1971) d/co-s Forman c Ondricek *92min r U

TAKINO SHIRAITO (1933) co-d Mizoguchi (= White Threads of the Cascades)

TAKOVA LASKA (1959) d/co-s J Weiss m Beethoven 80min (= Appassionata)

Talent Competition (UK) = KONKURS (1963)

TALE OF FIVE CITIES, A (1952) 99min
ep WIRD EUROPE WIEDER LACHEN d Staudte (uc)

Tale of Genji, A = GENJI MONOGATARI (1951)

TALE OF THE FOOTHILLS, A (1912) d Ince

TALE OF TWO CITIES, A (1917) d/ad F Lloyd fn Charles Dickens w (Dumont) 7rs Fox

TALE OF TWO CITIES, A (1935) d Conway 2nd d Lewton, J Tourneur fn Dickens p Selznick m Stothart w Rathbone, Colman, Oliver 120min MGM

TALE OF TWO CITIES, A (1958) d Thomas s T Clarke fn Dickens w Bogarde 117min JAR

TALE OF TWO WORLDS, A (1921) d F Lloyd c Brodine 5500ft MGM

Tales by Capek = CAPKOVY POVIDKY (1947)

Tales from a Country by the Sea = KAIKOKUKI (1928)

TALES OF HOFFMAN, THE (1951) d/p/s M Powell, Pressburger f opera Offenbach c Challis *127min r BL

TALES OF MANHATTAN (1942) d/st/co-s Duvivier co-p Spiegel (ps SP Eagle) co-st/co-s B Hecht, D Stewart, Trotti c J Walker co-des R Day w Hayworth, Boyer, Mitchell, G Rogers, H Fonda, Laughton, G Sanders, Robinson, Marsh, Romero 120min Fox (section with Fields, Dumont ur)

TALES OF TERROR (1962) d/p Corman co-ex-p Arkoff s Matheson c F Crosby a D Haller w Price, Rathbone, Lorre PV* (= Poe's Tales of Terror)

Tales of the Floating Reeds = UKIGUSA (1919)

TALK ABOUT A STRANGER (1952) d Bradley c J Alton co-a Gibbons w G Murphy 65min MGM

TALK OF HOLLYWOOD, THE (1930) d/p Sandrich

TALK OF THE DEVIL (1936) d/st C Reed

TALK OF THE TOWN, THE (1942) d/p G Stevens s Shaw, Buchman, c Tetzlaff m Hollander w C Grant, Arthur, Colman, Ingram 117min Col

TALL HEADLINES (1952) d T Young p Stross w Zetterling

TALL MEN, THE (1955) d Walsh s Boehm, F Nugent co-a Wheeler m V Young w Gable, J Russell, Ryan CS* 121min Fox

TALL STORY (1960) d/p Logan s JJ Epstein co-m Previn w Perkins, J Fonda 91min WB

TALL T, THE (1957) d Boetticher p H Brown s B Kennedy c Lawton w R Scott, O'Sullivan *78min pc Scott, H Brown r Col

TALL TALES (1941) d W Van Dyke m Ives, Josh White 10min

TALL TARGET, THE (1951) d A Mann co-st Mainwaring (ps Homes) co-s Losey w D Powell, Menjou 78min MGM

TALL TEXAN, THE (1952) d/e Elmo Williams w Cobb 82min

TAMAHINE (1963) d P Leacock w Hawkins CS* 95min

TAMANGO (1957) d/co-s John Berry c Séchan w Jurgens CS* 98min

TAMBORA (1938) d Fejos 41min SF

Tambour des Dogons, Le = TAMBOURS DE PIERRE (1964)

TAMBOURS DE PIERRE (1964) d Rouch 16mm (= Le Tambour des Dogons/Eléments pour une etude de rhythme)

T'AMERO SEMPRE (1932) d/st Camerini

T'AMERO SEMPRE (1943) d/co-st Camerini rm 1932 w Valli, Jules Berry

TAMING OF THE SHREW (1908) d Griffith fpl William Shakespeare 340m Bio

TAMING OF THE SHREW, THE (1929) d/ad Sam Taylor fpl Shakespeare c Struss co-a Menzies pc/w Pickford, Fairbanks Jr 68min r UA

TAMING OF THE SHREW, THE (1967) d/co-s Zeffirelli p Burton, E Taylor, Zeffirelli co-s Cecchi d'Amico fpl Shakespeare co-c Morris m Rota w Burton, E Taylor PV* 122min Col

TAMING OF THE SNOOD, THE (1940) d Jules White co-s Bruckman w Keaton 19min Col

TAMING THE MEKONG (1965) d W Van Dyke 30min

TAMMY AND THE BACHELOR (1957) d Pevney p R Hunter c Arling w D Reynolds, Brennan CS* 89min U

TAMMY AND THE DOCTOR (1963) d Keller p R Hunter co-a Golitzen c Metty *88min U

TAMMY, TELL ME TRUE (1968) d Keller p R Hunter co-a Golitzen *97min U

TAM, TAM MAYUMBA (1954) d GG Napolitano 2nd d Quilici w Vanel *100min

TANGANIYIKA (1954) d De Toth w Roman, Heflin *81min U

TANGIER (1946) d George Waggner w Montez, Sabu 76min U

TANGLED AFFAIR, A (1913) d Sennett w Normand ½rl Key

TANGLEWOOD STORY, THE (1950) c B Kaufman 16mm 20min US State Dept

TANGO TANGLES (1914) d Sennett w Chaplin, Arbuckle 1rl Key (= Charlie's Recreation/Music Hall)

TANIN NO KAO (1965) d/p Teshigahara w Kyo, Nakadai 124min (= The Face of Another)

Tank Force (US) = NO TIME TO DIE (1957)

TANNED LEGS (1929) d Neilan 6377ft RKO

TANOSHIKIKANA JINSEI (1944) d/s Naruse

TANSY (1921) d/p Hepworth 5610ft

TANT D'AMOUR PERDU (1958) d/co-st/co-ad Joannon w Fresnay, Ferzetti 90min Gau

TANTE ESTHER (1956) d Dewever sh

TANTE ZITA (1967 d Enrico *105min (= Aunt Zita/Zita)

TANT GRON, TANT BRUN OCH TANT GREDELIN (1946) d/s Lindstrom (= Aunt Green, Aunt Brown and Aunt Lilac)

TANT QU'ON A LA SANTE (1965) d/co-s/w Etaix 78min (= As Long as You're Healthy)

Tanya = SVETLYĬ PUT (1940)

TANZ AUF DEM VULKAN (1938) d/co-st/co-s Steinhoff 86min r Tob

TANZER MEINE FRAU, DER (1925) d/co-s A Korda dec Leni 2207m

Tanz geht weiter, Der: German version of THOSE WHO DANCE (1930) d/w Dieterle c Hickox 65min WB

TAP ROOTS (1948) d G Marshall p Wanger c Hoch, Lindon w Heflin, S Hayward, Karloff 109min U

TAQDEER (1943) d/p Mehboob 11min (= Fate)

TARAHUMARA (1965) d/s Alcoriza 135min (= Always Further On)

TARAKANOVA (1928) d R Bernard w Artaud

TARANTA, LA (1962) d Mingozzi sh

TARANTULA (1955) d/co-st J Arnold co-a Golitzen 80min U

TARAS BULBA (1962) d J Thompson p H Hecht c Joe MacDonald m Waxman w Curtis, Brynner PV* 124min r UA

TARAS SHEVCHENKO (1951) d/s Igor Savchenko w Bondarchuk *114min

TARAWA (c 1945) p Sperling

TARAWA BEACHHEAD (1958) d Wendkos w Danton 76min Col

TARDE DE DOMINGO, UNA (1956) d/co-s/e Saura 30min

TARDE DE TOROS (1955) d Vajda *86min

TARES (1918) d/p/c Hepworth 2rs

TARGET FOR TONIGHT (1941) d/s Watt 50min Crown

TARGETS (1968) d/p/co-st/s/w Peter Bogdanovich ex-p Corman w Karloff *90min

TARIS (1931) d/s/e Vigo c B Kaufman (= La Natation/La Natation, par Jean Taris, Champion de France/Taris, Roi de l'eau/Jean Taris, Champion de Natation)

Taris, Roi de l'eau = TARIS (1931)

TARNISHED (1950) d Keller 60min Rep

TARNISHED ANGELS, THE (1957) d Sirk p Zugsmith fn (Pylon) Faulkner c Glassberg w Hudson, Stack, Malone CS 91min U (= Pylon)

TARNISHED LADY (1931) d Cukor s/fst (New York Lady) D Stewart w Bankhead, C Brook 65min Par

TARNISHED REPUTATIONS (1920) d/s Perret Pat

TARS AND STRIPES (1935) d Charles Lamont w Keaton 20min

Tartari, I = TARTARS, THE (1960)

TARTARIN DE TARASCON (1934) d Raymond Bernard fn Alphonse Daudet w Raimu

TARTARIN DE TARASCON (1962) d/co-s Blanche fn Daudet w Blanche 105min

TARTARS, THE (1960) d Thorpe w Welles, Mature *83min r MGM (= I Tartari)

TARTASSATI, I (1959) d Steno w Toto, De Funès 105min (= The Overtaxed)

TARTUFF (1925) d Murnau p Pommer s C Mayer fpl Molière c Freund co-dec Röhrig w Jannings, Krauss, Dagover 5908ft UFA

TARZAN AND HIS MATE (1934) d/a Gibbons co-c C Clarke fst Edgar Rice Burroughs w Weissmuller, O'Sullivan 105min MGM

TARZAN AND JANE REGAINED SORT OF (1963) d Warhol part * 16mm si 120min

TARZAN AND THE AMAZONS (1945) d Kurt Neumann p Lesser c Stout w Weissmuller, Ouspenskaya 76min RKO

TARZAN AND THE HUNTRESS (1947) d Kurt Neumann p Lesser c Stout w Weissmuller 72min RKO

Tarzan and the Jungle Queen (UK) = TARZAN'S PERIL (1951)

TARZAN AND THE LEOPARD WOMAN (1946) d Kurt Neumann p Lesser c Struss w Weissmuller 72min RKO

TARZAN AND THE MERMAIDS (1948) d Florey p Lesser co-c Figueroa m Tiomkin w Weissmuller 68min RKO

TARZAN ESCAPES (1936) d Thorpe co-s J Farrow w Weissmuller, O'Sullivan 95min MGM

TARZAN FINDS A SON! (1939) d Thorpe w Weissmuller, O'Sullivan 90min MGM

TARZAN GOES TO INDIA (1962) d/co-s Guillermin CS* 87min r MGM

TARZAN'S DESERT MYSTERY (1943) d William Thiele p Lesser c R Harlan, Wild w Weissmuller 70min RKO

TARZAN'S GREATEST ADVENTURE (1959) d/co-s Guillermin w Connery * 84min r Par

TARZAN'S NEW YORK ADVENTURE (1942) d Thorpe a Gibbons w Weissmuller, O'Sullivan, C Bickford 71min MGM

TARZAN'S PERIL (1951) d Haskin p Lesser c Struss 79min RKO (= Tarzan and the Jungle Queen)

TARZAN'S SAVAGE FURY (1952) d Endfield p Lesser c Struss 80min RKO

TARZAN'S SECRET TREASURE (1941) d Thorpe w Weissmuller, O'Sullivan MGM

TARZAN THE APE MAN (1932) d WS Van Dyke c Rosson w O'Sullivan, Weissmuller 99min MGM

TARZAN, THE APE MAN (1959) d J Newman rm 1932 *82min MGM

TARZAN TRIUMPHS (1943) d William Thiele p Lesser c Wild w Weissmuller 75min RKO

TASK FORCE (1949) d/s Davis p Wald co-c Burks m Waxman w G Cooper, Brennan part *116min WB

TASSELS IN THE AIR (1938) d/w C Chase 2rs Col

TASTE OF FEAR (1961) d Holt c Slocombe 82min

TASTE OF HONEY, A (1961) d/p/co-s T Richardson co-s/fpl Shelagh Delaney c Lassally w Tushingham 100min BL

Taste of Mackerel, The = SAMMA NO AJI (1962)

TAT DER GRAFIN WORMS, DIE (1916) d May, Karl Gerhardt p/s May 5rs (= Ein Einsam Grab)

TATHAPIL (1950) d Roy

TATIANA (1923) d Litvak w Petrov (= Hearts and Dollars)

TATOUE, LE (1968) d De La Patellière w Gabin, De Funès S* 95min

TATTERED DRESS, THE (1957) d J Arnold p Zugsmith co-a Golitzen w J Chandler, Crain CS 92min U

TAUSEND AUGEN DES DR MABUSE, DIE (1961) d/p/co-s F Lang 103min (= The Thousand Eyes of the Mabuse)

TAVASZI ZAPOR (1932) d/co-s Fejos co-c Marley w Annabella (= Marie Legende Hongroise) 1857m

TAVOLA DEI POVERI, LA (1932) d/co-s/co-e Blasetti co-s Soldati

TAXI (1932) d Del Ruth w Cagney, L Young, Raft 70min WB

TAXI (1953) d Ratoff rm SANS LAISSER D'ADRESSE (1950) co-a Wheeler c Krasner w Dailey, Page 77min Fox

TAXI DI NOTTE (1950) d/p Gallone 98min (= Bambino)

TAXI POUR TOBRUK (1961) d/co-s De la Patellière co-s Audiard w Aznavour, Ventura S 132min (= Taxi to Tobruk)

TAXI 13 (1928) d Neilan e Berman 5760ft

Taxi to Tobruk (UK) = TAXI POUR TOBRUK, UN (1961)

TAYLOR MEAD'S ASS (1964) d Warhol 16mm si 70min

TAZA, SON OF COCHISE (1954) d Sirk p R Hunter c Metty w Hudson, J Chandler, Rush 3-D* 79min U

TCHAIKOVSKY (1970) d Igor Talankin ex-p Tiomkin fm Tchaikovsky wv Laurence Harvey 70mm 105min

TEA AND SYMPATHY (1956) d Minnelli p Berman c J Alton w Kerr CS* 122min MGM

Teacher, The = UCHITEL (1939)

TEACHER'S PET (1958) d Seaton co-a Pereira w Gable, D Day VV 120min pc Perlberg, Seaton r Par

TEA FOR THREE (1927) d/p Leonard 5273ft MGM

TEA FOR TWO (1950) d D Butler w D Day 98min WB

TEAHOUSE OF THE AUGUST MOON, THE (1956) d Daniel Mann p J Cummings c J Alton w Brando, G Ford, Kyo CS* 123min MGM

TEARING DOWN THE SPANISH FLAG (1898) d Blackton

TEARIN' INTO TROUBLE (1927) d Thorpe

TEARIN' LOOSE (1925) d Thorpe w Arthur 4900ft

TEAR THAT BURNED, THE (1914) d John G O'Brien w L Gish 2rs

TEBYE FRONT (1943) co-d/s Vertov co-d Elizabeth Svilova 6rs (= Kazakhstan Frontu/To the Front/To the Kazakhstan Front)

TECHNIQUES MINIERES (1970) d/s/cy Lamothe *

Teddy Bear, The (US) = BAMSE (1968)

TEDDY BY KOURIL (1919) d/co-s/w Machaty

TEE FOR TWO (1925) d/s Cline p Sennett Pat

TEENAGE CAVEMAN (1958) d/p Corman c F Crosby 64min (= Out of the Darkness)

TEENAGE CRIME WAVE (1955) d Sears 77min Col

TEENAGE DOLL (1957) d/p Corman c F Crosby 68min AA

TEENAGE REBEL (1956) d/song Goulding p/co-s C Brackett c Joe Macdonald co-a L Wheeler co-m Harline w G Rogers CS 94min Fox

TEEN KANYA (1961) d/s/m S Ray 171min (= Three Daughters/Two Daughters)

TEKKA BUGYO (1954) d/s Kinugasa

TELEFTEO PSEMMA, TO (1957) d/s/co-e Cacoyannis c Lassally m Hadjidakis 104min (= A Matter of Dignity)

TELEPHONE GIRL (1924) co-d St Clair co-s Zanuck 12eps × 2rs

TELEPHONE GIRL, THE (1927) d Brenon 5455ft Par

Telephone Ring in the Evening, A = DENWA WA YUGATA NI NARU (1959)

TELEVISION SPY (1939) d Dmytryk w Quinn 58min Par

TELL 'EM NOTHING (1926) d McCarey Pat

TELL ENGLAND (1931) d Asquith 7850ft (= Battle of Gallipoli)

TELLING THE WORLD (1928) d S Wood c Daniels a Gibbons 80min MGM

Tell It Like It Is (US) = ÇA IRA (1964)

TELL IT TO SWEENEY (1927) d/p La Cava 6006ft Par

TELL IT TO THE JUDGE (1949) d Foster p Adler c J Walker w R Russell, R Cummings 87min Col

TELL ME IN THE SUNLIGHT (1967) d/p/c/w Cochran *82min

TELL ME LIES (1968) d/ad P Brook w Scofield 116min

TELL ME THAT YOU LOVE ME, JUNIE MOON (1970) d/p Preminger c B Kaufman a Wheeler co-cr-c Cortez *113min

Tell Me Tonight (UK) = LIED EINER NACHT, DAS (1932)

TELL-TALE HEART, THE (1941) d Dassin fst Edgar Allan Poe 2rs MGM

TELLTALE LIGHT, THE (1913) d Sennett w Normand, Arbuckle 1rl Key

TELL THEM WILLIE BOY IS HERE (1969) d/s Polonsky c C Hall co-a Golitzen w Redford S* 98min U

TEMOIN DE MINUIT, LE (1953) d Kirsanov 80min

TEMPELDANSERINDENS ELSKOV (1914) d Madsen

TEMPERAMENTAL HUSBAND, A (1912) d Sennett w Normand ¼rl Key

TEMPERAMENTAL WIFE, A (1919) d David Kirkland supn/s/fpl (Information Please) Emerson, Loos w C Talmadge

TEMPEST (1927) d Sam Taylor dec Menzies m Riesenfeld w J Barrymore 9300ft r UA

Tempest (UK) = STURME DER LEIDENSCHAFT (1932)

Tempest (UK) = TEMPESTA, LA (1958)

TEMPESTA, LA (1958) d Lattuada 2nd d Antonioni p De Laurentiis fn (The Revolution of Pugacio) Alexander Pushkin c Tonti dec Chiari m Piccioni w Mangano, Meflin, Lindfors, Gassmann, Moorehead *121min (= Tempest)

TEMPESTAIRE, LE (1947) d J Epstein 20min

TEMPESTA SU CEYLON (1963) d G Oswald w Rossi-Drago, Ronet S* 83min

Tempesta su Parigi: 2nd part of MISERABILI, I (1947)

TEMPETE DANS UNE CHAMBRE A COUCHER, UNE (1901) d/w Zecca 50m Pat

TEMPETE SUR L'ASIE (1938) d R Oswald w Veidt

TEMPI DURI PER I VAMPIRI (1959) d/co-st/co-s Steno *98min

TEMPI NOSTRI (1954) d/co-s Blasetti d/co-s Cecchi d'Amico, Alberto Moravia w De Sica, Mastroianni, De Filippo, Montand, M Simon, Caprioli, Loren, Toto, Sordi 110min (= Slice of Life)

TEMPLE OF THE SWINGING DOLL (1960) d Wendkos m Raksin w Lindfors 48min TV (edited for theatrical release)

TEMPO DI ROMA (1963) d De la Patellière w Arletty, Aznavour 92min

TEMPORARY WIDOW, THE (1930) d Gustav Ucicky w Olivier, Lillian Harvey 7364ft UFA

TEMPO SI E FERMATO, IL (1959) d/s Olmi 20min (= Time Stood Still)

TEMPS DES CERISES, LE (1938) d Le Chanois

TEMPS DU GHETTO, LE (1961) d Rossif m Jarre 80min

TEMPS PERDU, LE (1964) d Brault 30min TV

Temptation = YUWAKU (1948fi

TEMPTATION (1915) d/s De Mille pc Lasky

TEMPTATION (1946) d Pichel w Oberon, Lukas 99min U

TEMPTRESS, THE (1926) d Stiller, Niblo fn Vicente Blasco Ibanez c Gaudio w Garbo, L Barrymore 8500ft MGM

Ten Black Women = KUROI JUNIN NO ONNA (1961)

TEN CENTS A DANCE (1931) d L Barrymore p Cohn st/di Swerling c E Haller w Stanwyck 80min Col

TEN COMMANDMENTS, THE (1923) d De Mille co-c Glennon, Rennahan, Marley, Stout co-a Leisen m Reisenfeld w M Loy part * 14rs FPL

TEN COMMANDMENTS, THE (1956) d/p De Mille co-c Griggs, Marley co-a Pereira co-chor Prinz m E Bernstein w Heston, A Baxter, De Carlo, Derek, Carradine, Brynner, Robinson, Price VV* 222min Par

Ten Days That Shook the World = OKTYABRE (1927)

TENDERLOIN (1928) d Curtiz c Mohr 7782ft WB

TENDER COMRADE (1943) d Dmytryk st/s Trumbo m Harline w G Rogers, Ryan, Darwell 102min RKO

TENDERFOOT, THE (1932) d Enright c Toland w G Rogers 70min WB

TENDERFOOT COURAGE (1927) d Wyler 2rs U

TENDER GAME (1958) d/co-s J Hubley co-s/e F Hubley co-anim Cannon anim 5min

TENDER-HEARTED BOY, THE (1913) d Griffith s/w L Barrymore Bio

TENDER IS THE NIGHT (1962) d H King fn Fitzgerald c Shamroy m Herrmann w J Jones, Fontaine, Lukas, Ewell CS* 146min Fox

TENDER TRAP, THE (1955) d Walters s JJ Epstein w Sinatra, D Reynolds, D Wayne CS* 101min MGM

10 DOLLARS RAISE (1935) d G Marshall w Horton 70min Fox

TENDRE ET VIOLENTE ELISABETH (1960) d/co-ad Decoin fn/di Henri Troyat m Van Parys w Marquand 105min (= Passionate Affair)

TENDRE ENNEMIE, LA (1936) d/co-s Ophuls c Schuftan 69min

TENDRON D'ACHILLE, LE (1933) d Christian-Jaque

TENERIFFE (1932) d Y Allégret sh

TEN GENTLEMEN FROM WEST POINT (1942) d Hathaway p Perlberg s Maibaum ad Seaton c Shamroy co-a Day w M O'Hara, Edwards 102min Fox

TENGOKU TO JIGOKU (1963) d/pc/co-s Kurosawa fn (King's Ransom) E Hunter (ps Ed McBain) w Mifune, Nakadai S 143min r Toho (= Heaven and Hell/High and Low)

TENGOKU NI MUSUBE KOI (1933) d Gosho (= Heaven Linked with Love)

TENICHIBO TO IGANOSUKE (1926) d Linugasa

TENICHIBO TO IGANOSUKE (1933) d/s Kinugasa

Ten Little Niggers (UK) = AND THEN THERE WERE NONE (1945)

10, MAMMETA E TU (1958) d Bragaglia (= Me, Mother and You)

TENNESSEE CHAMP (1954) d F Wilcox co-a Gibbons c Folsey w Winters *70min MGM

TENNESSEE JOHNSON (1942) d Dieterle c Rosson a Gibbons m Stothart w L Barrymore 103min MGM

TENNESSEE'S PARTNER (1955) d/co-s Dwan p Borgeaus fst Bret Harte c J Alton w Payne, R Fleming, Reagan, (A Dickinson) S* 87min r RKO

TEN NORTH FREDERICK (1958) d/s P Dunne p Brackett fn John O'Hara co-a Wheeler m Harline w G Cooper CS 102min Fox

Tenor, Inc., The (UK) = G.M.B.H. TENOR, DER (1916)

TENORI PER FORZA (1948) d/co-p/co-s/e(uc)/wv Freda w Manfredi, Salce 1rl

10 RILLINGTON PLACE (1971) d R Fleischer w Attenborough *111min Col

TEN SECONDS TO HELL (1959) d/co-s Aldrich c Laszlo a Adam w Palance, J Chandler, Carol 89min r UA

TENSION (1949) d John Berry m Previn w Charisse 91min MGM

TENSION AT TABLE ROCK (1956) d Warren c Biroc m Tiomkin w Malone, A Dickinson *93min RKO

TEN TALL MEN (1951) d/co-st Goldbeck p H Hecht as-p Aldrich w Lancaster, Roland *97min r Col

TENTATION DE SAINT-ANTOINE, LA (1898) d Méliès 20m

TENTATIVO SENTIMENTALE, UN (1963) d/s/co-ad Festa Campanile, Massimo Franciosa m Piccioni w Ferzetti 91min

TENTH AVENUE ANGEL (1948) d Rowland c Surtees w M O'Brien, G Murphy 74min MGM

10.30 P.M. SUMMER (1966) d/p/co-s Dassin co-p Litvak co-s/fn Duras w Mercouri, Finch, Schneider *85min

TEN THOUSAND BEDROOMS (1957) d Thorpe p Pasternak c Bronner w Martin, Henreid CS* 113min

Tenth Victim, The (UK) = DECIMA VITTIMA, LA (1965)

TEN YEAR PLAN, THE (1945) d/co-s L Gilbert 17min

TEODORA, IMPERATRICE DI BISANZIO (1953) d/co-s/co-di/co-ad Freda *124min (= Theodora, Slave Empress)

TEOREMA (1968) d/s/fn Pasolini w Stamp, Mangano, Girotti *98min (= Theorem)

TE QUIERO PARA MI (1944) d Vajda w Montiel

TERESA (1951) d Zinnemann co-st/s Stern w Meeker, Steiger

TERESA RAQUIN (1915) d Martoglio

TERESA VENERDI (1941) d/co-s/w De Sica co-s Zavattini (uc) w Magnani

TEREZA BRZKOVA (1961) d/co-st Frič

TERJE VIGEN (1916) d/w Sjöström s Molander fpm Henrik Ibsen 1170m

TERMINUS (1960) d J Schlesinger 30min

Terminus Love (UK) = ENDSTATION LIEBE (1957)

TERM OF TRIAL (1962) d/s Glenville p James Woolf c Morris w Olivier, Stamp, Signoret 130min

Terrace, The (US) = TERRAZA, LA (1963)

TERRACO AUGUSTA (1933) d/s Velo, Fernando Mantilla 2rs

TERRA DEL MELODRAMMA, LA (1947) d/s Emmer, Enrico Gras

TERRA EM TRANSE (1967) d/s/co-p Rocha 105min

TERRA INCOGNITA (1959) d/c Borowczyk f pinscreen Alexeieff anim *2¼min

TERRAIN VAGUE (1960) d/co-s Carné c C Renoir co-m Legrand

TERRA MADRE (1931) d/co-s/co-e Blasetti

TERRA PROMESSA (1913) d Baldassarre Negroni w Ghione

TERRA SENZA DONNE (1929) d Gallone (= Das Land Ohne Frauen)

TERRA TREMA, LA (1947) d/s Visconti c Aldo 160min

TERRAZA, LA (1963) d/co-s Torre Nilsson 88min (= The Roof Garden/The Terrace)

TERRE DE FEU (1938) d/co-p L'Herbier co-p Michel

Terre sans pain = HURDES, LAS (1932)

TERREUR DES BATIGNOLLES, LA (1936) d Clouzot

TERREUR, LE (1924) d Edward José w White

TERRIBLE BEAUTY, A (1960) d Garnett p Stross w Mitchum, R Harris 90min r UA (= The Night Fighter)

TERRIBLE RAILWAY ACCIDENT, THE (1896) p Paul

TERRIBLY TALENTED (1948) d Alexander Hammid p W Van Dyke c B Kaufman

TERROR, THE (1920) d/s Jacques Jaccard st/w Mix 5rs Fox

TERROR, THE (1928) d Del Ruth w Fazenda, Horton 7654ft 9rs WB

TERROR, THE (1963) d/p Corman as-p Coppola w Karloff * 81min

TERRORE NELLO SPAZIO (1965) d Bava S* 86min (= Planet of Blood/Planet of the Vampires)

TERROR IN A TEXAS TOWN (1958) d JH Lewis c Rennahan w Hayden 80min r UA

TERROR ISLAND (1920) d Cruze 7rs FPL

TERRORISTA, IL (1963) d/co-st/co-s De Bosio co-p Olmi m Piccioni 105min

TERROR ON A TRAIN (1953) d Tetzlaff c F Young w G Ford 72min MGM (= Time Bomb)

TERROR TRAIL (1933) d Armand Schaefer w Mix 62min U

TERU HI KUMORU HI (1926) d Kinugasa (= Shining Sun Becomes Clouded)

TERZA LICEO (1954) d/co-s Emmer c Bava (= High School)

TESHA (1928) d/p/st/s Saville 7805ft

TESS OF THE D'URBERVILLES (1924) d Neilan fn Thomas Hardy 8rs MGM

TESS OF THE STORM COUNTRY (1914) d Porter w Pickford

TESS OF THE STORM COUNTRY (1922) d John S Robertson w 1914 w Hersholt, Pickford 10rs

TESS OF THE STORM COUNTRY (1932) d Santell rm 1922 co Mohr w C Rugglets, J Gaynor 80min Fox

TESTAMENT DES MR MABUSE, DAS (1932) d/p/co-s F Lang co-s Von Harbou co-c F Wagner Nero (= The Last Will of Dr Mabuse)

TESTAMENT D'ORPHEE, LE (1960) d/s Cocteau m Auric, Martial Solal, Gluck, Bach, Wagner w Cocteau, Casarès, Brynner, Léaud, Gélin, Marais, Aznavour, Bosè, Picasso 83min

TESTAMENT DU DOCTEUR CORDELIER, LE (1961) d/p/s J Renoir m Kosma w Barrault, Modot 100min (= Experiment in Evil)

TESTAMENTETS HEMMELIGHED (1914)

TESTAMENTO DEL VIRREY, EL (1944) d Vajda

Testament of Orpheus, The = TESTAMENT D'ORPHEE, LE (1960)

TESTIMONE, IL (1946) d/st/co-s Germi supn/co-s Blasetti co-s Zavattini c Tonti 92min

TEST PILOT (1938) d V Fleming c June Waxman co-e Vorkapich w Gable, M Loy, Tracy, L Barrymore 118min MGM

TETE CONTRE LES MURS, LA (1958) d Franju s Mocky fn Hervé Bazin c Schuftan m Jarre w Mocky, Brasseur, Aimée, Aznavour 98min (= The Keepers)

TETE DE TURC (1936) d/co-s Becker (= Le Bourreau/Une Tête qui rapporte)

TETE D'UN HOMME, LA (1933) d/co-s Duvivier fn Georges Simenon c Thirard

TETE LA PREMIERE, LA (1965) d Sautet CS

Tete qui rapporte, The = TETE DE TURC (1935)

TETES DE FEMMES, FEMMES DE TETE (1916) d Feyder w Rosay 842m Gau

TETICKA (1941) d/co-s Frič (= Auntie's Fantasies)

TETNO POLSKIEGO MANCHESTERU (1928) d A ford sh

TETTES ISMERETLEN, A (1957) d Ranódy 94min (= Danse Macabre)

TETTO, IL (1956) d De Sica s Zavattini 95min (= The Roof)

TEUFELS GENERAL, DES (1955) d/co-s Käutner fpl Zuckmayer w Jurgens 3291m

TEXAN, THE (1930) d Cromwell c Milner w G Cooper 72min Par

TEXAS (1941) d G Marshall w Holden, G Ford, Trevor, G Bancroft 93min Col

TEXAS ACROSS THE RIVER (1966) d M Gordon p Keller c Metty w Martin, Delon * 101min U

TEXAS, BROOKLYN, AND HEAVEN (1948) d Castle c Mellor w A Murphy 76min r UA (= The Girl from Texas)

TEXAS CARNIVAL (1951) d Walters co-st Wells co-a Gibbons w Esther Williams, Ann Miller, Keel *77min MGM

TEXAS RANGERS, THE (1935) d/p/co-st K Vidor c Cronjager co-a Dreier w MacMurray, Nolan 95min Par

TEXAS RANGERS, THE (1951) d Karlson *68min Col

TEXAS STAGECOACH (1940) d JH Lewis 59min Col

TEXTILES AND ORNAMENTAL ARTS OF INDIA (1955) d/s C and R Eames c C Eames *11½min

TEZKY ZIVOT DOBRODRUHA (1941) d Frič (= Adventure is a Hard Life)

THANKS A MILLION (1935) d Del Ruth p Zanuck s N Johnson c Marley w D Powell 87min Fox

THANK YOU (1925) d J Ford w G O'Brien 7rs Fox

THANK YOU, MR MOTO (1937) d/co-s Foster w Lorre, Carradine 67min Fox

THANK YOUR LUCKY STARS (1943) d D Butler p Hellinger co-s Panama, M Panama chor Prinz w Bogart, Cantor, B Davis, Flynn, Garfield, Horton, De Havilland, Lupino, Sheridan, A Smith 127min WB

THAN, LE PECHEUR (1957) d Schoendoerffer c Coutard sh

THANOS & DESPINA (1968) d Papatakis 96min

THAT BRENNAN GIRL (1946) d/p Santell 95min Rep

That Cat = PRIJDE KOCOUR, AZ (1965)

THAT CERTAIN AGE (1938) d Edward Ludwig p Pasternak w Durbin, M Douglas 95min U

THAT CERTAIN FEELING (1956) d/p/co-s M Frank, Panama co-s Diamond co-a Pereira c Griggs w Hope, Saint, G Sanders VV* 103min Par

THAT CERTAIN THING (1928) d Capra p Cohn c J Walker 7rs Col

THAT CERTAIN WOMAN (1937) d/s Goulding c E Haller m M Steiner w H Fonda, B Davis (10rs) WB

THAT DANGEROUS AGE (1950) d Ratoff 72min

That Fine Day = TISTEGA LEPEGA DNE (1963)

THAT ETERNAL PING-PONG (1902) p Hepworth 100ft

THAT FORSYTE WOMAN (1949) d Compton Bennett fn (The Forsyte Saga) John Galsworthy co-a Gibbons m Kaper w Flynn, Garson, Pidgeon, R Young, J Leigh 113min MGM (= The Forsyte Saga)

THAT FUNNY FEELING (1965) d Thorpe p Keller w O'Connor *93min U

THAT GANG OF MINE (1940) d JH Lewis p Katzman 62min Mon

THAT GIRL OF BURKE'S (1916) d/w Borzage Tri

THAT GOSH-DARN MORTGAGE (1926) d/s Cline p Sennett Pat

THAT HAMILTON WOMAN (1941) d/p A Korda c Maté m Rozsa w Olivier, V Leigh 125min r UA (= Lady Hamilton)

THAT I MAY LIVE (1937) d Dwan 70min Fox

That Jane from Maine = IT HAPPENED TO JANE (1959)

That Joyous Eve = MAKKERS STAAKT UW WILD GERAAS (1960)

THAT KIND OF WOMAN (1959) d Lumet co-p Ponti c B Kaufman co-a Pereira m Amfitheatrof w Loren, G Sanders VV 94min Par

THAT LADY (1955) d T Young c Krasker w De Havilland, Scofield, Lee, Roland, Rosay CS* 100min r Fox

THAT LADY IN ERMINE (1948) co-d/p Lubitsch co-d Preminger(uc) s Raphaelson c Shamroy co-a Wheeler co-m Hollander w Grable, Fairbanks Jr, Romero *89min Fox

THAT LITTLE BAND OF GOLD (1915) d/w Arbuckle p Sennett w Normand 2rs Key

That Little Difference = QUELLA PICCOLA DIFFERENZA (1969)

That Man from Rio = HOMME DE RIO, L' (1963)

That Man George! (US) = PILLARDS, LES (1955)

THAT MAN'S HERE AGAIN (1937) d Lewis King co-s Trumbo 59min WB

THAT MIDNIGHT KISS (1949) d Taurog p Pasternak c Surtees co-a Gibbons w E Barrymore, Lanza *96min MGM

THAT MINSTREL MAN (1914) d/w Arbuckle 2rs Key

THAT MODEL FROM PARIS (1926) d Louis J Gasnier, Florey 6200ft

THAT MOTHERS MIGHT LIVE (1938) d Zinnemann 1rl MGM

THAT NIGHT (1917) d Cline s Sennett

THAT NIGHT IN LONDON (1932) d Rowland V Lee w Donat 78min

THAT NIGHT IN RIO (1941) d Irving Cummings co-s Seaton co-c Shamroy w C Miranda, Montez, Faye *90min Fox

That Night's Wife = SONO YO NO TSUMA (1930)

That Others May Live = ULICA GRANICZNA (1948)

THAT RAGTIME BAND (1913) d Sennett w Normand 1rl Key

THAT'S MY DADDY (1927) d Newmeyer 6073ft U

THAT'S MY MAN (1947) d Borzage c Gaudio 104min Rep

THAT'S MY WIFE (1929) d Lloyd French p Roach supn/st McCarey w Laurel, Hardy 2rs r MGM

That Splendid November = BELLISSIMA NOVEMBRE, UN (1971)

THAT'S RIGHT YOU'RE WRONG (1939) d D Butler w Menjou, Horton 94min RKO

THAT'S THE WAY IT IS (1970) d D Sanders c Ballard w Presley PV* 108min

That They May Live (UK) = J'ACCUSE (1937)

THAT TOUCH OF MINK (1962) d Delbert Mann c Metty w C Grant, D Day PV* 99min U

THAT UNCERTAIN FEELING (1941) d/p Lubitsch s D Stewart c Barnes a Golitzen w Oberon, M Douglas, Meredith 82min r UA

THAT WOMAN OPPOSITE (1957) d Compton Bennett 83min BL

THAUMATOPOEA (1960) d Enrico *22min

Thaw = LEDOLOM (1931)

Theatre = SHIBAIDO (1944)

THEATRE DE MONSIEUR ET MADAME KABAL, LE (1967) d/st/s/dec Borowczyk anim* 80min

THEATRE NATIONAL POPULAIRE, LE (1956) d/s Franju c Fradetal m Jarre w Casarès 28min

THEIR BIG MOMENT (1934) d Cruze w Pitts 68min RKO

THEIR FIRST DIVORCE CASE (1911) d/w Sennett ½rl Bio

THEIR FIRST KIDNAPPING CASE (1912) d/w Sennett ½rl Bio

THEIR FIRST MISTAKE (1932) d G Marshall p Roach w Laurel, Hardy 21min r MGM

THEIR FIRST MISUNDERSTANDING (1911) co-d Ince w Pickford

Their First Trip to Tokyo = TOKYO MONOGATARI (1913)

THEIR FIRST VACATION (1922) d St Clair 2rs

Their Legacy = KATEI NO JIJYO (1962)

THEIR PURPLE MOMENT (1928) d James Parrott p Roach supn McCarey w Laurel, Hardy (2rs) r MGM

Their Secret Affair (UK) = TOP SECRET AFFAIR (1957)

THELEMA ABBEY (1955) d/s/e Anger 10min TV

Thelma Jordan = FILE ON THELMA JORDAN (1949)

THEM (1955) d G Douglas c Hickox m Kaper *94min WB

THEMA AMORE (1961) d Kluge sh

THEME ET VARIATIONS (1928) d Dulac sh

THEM THAR HILLS (1934) d Charles Rogers p Roach w Laurel, Hardy (2rs) r MGM

THEN AND NOW (1948, ur) d T Dickinson p Pressburger fn Somerset Maugham w G Sanders

THEODORA GOES WILD (1936) d Boleslavsky s Buchman c J Walker w I Dunne, M Douglas, Mitchell 95min Col

Theodora, Slave Empress (US) = TEODORA, IMPERATRICE DI BISANZIO (1953)

THEODOR PISTEK (1958) d/co-s Frič

Theorem (UK) = TEOREMA (1968)
There Came Two Men = DET KOM TVA MAN (1958)
THERE GOES KELLY (1945) *d* Karlson 61min Mon
THERE GOES MY HEART (1938) *d* McLeod *p* Roach *c* Brodine *w* March 84min *r* UA
THERE HE GOES (1925) *d Harry Edwards w* Langdon 2rs *pc* Sennett *r* Pat
THERE IS ANOTHER SUN (1950) *d* L Gilbert *w* Laurence Harvey 95min (= *Wall of Death*)
THERE IS A SEASON (1953) *d* W Van Dyke 20min
There Lived an Old Man and an Old Woman = ZHILI-BYLI STARIK SO STARUKHOI (1964)
THERE'S A GIRL IN MY SOUP (1970) *d* R Boulting *p* Frankovich, J Boulting *w* Sellers *94min
There's Always a Price Tag (UK) = RETOUR DE MANIVELLE (1957)
THERE'S ALWAYS TOMORROW (1956) *d* Sirk *p* R Hunter *c* Metty *w* Stanwyck, J Bennett, MacMurray, Darwell 86min U
THERESE (1916) *d/co-s* Sjöström
Therèse = THERESE DESQUEYROUX (1962)
THERESE DESQUEYROUX (1962) *d/co-s* Franju *fn/di Francois Mauriac c* Matras *m* Jarre *w* Riva, Noiret 109min (= *Therèse*)
THERESE ETIENNE (1957) *d/co-s* De la Patellière *w* Arnoul CS 90min
THERESE RAQUIN (1928) *d/s* Feyder *fn Emile Zola* (= *Du sollst nicht ehe brechen*)-
THERESE RAQUIN (1953) *d/co-s* Carne *co-s/di* Charles Spaak *fn Zola w* Signoret, Vallone
THERE'S MAGIC IN MUSIC (1938) *d* Stone 80min (= *Magic in Music*)
THERE'S NO BUSINESS LIKE SHOW BUSINESS (1954) *d* W Lang *p* S Siegel *st* Trotti *co-a* Wheeler *c* Shamroy *chor* R Alton *w* O'Connor, Merman, Monroe, Dailey, M Gaynor CS* 117min Fox
THERE'S ONE BORN EVERY MINUTE (1942) *d Harold Young w* E Taylor 60min U
THERE WAS A CROOKED MAN (1970) *d/p* J Mankiewicz *w* K Douglas, H Fonda, Meredith PV* 126min WB
There Was a Father = CHICHI ARIKI (1942)
These are the Damned (US) = DAMNED, THE (1962)
THESE DANGEROUS YEARS (1957) *d* H Wilcox *p/w* Neagle 92min
THESE THOUSAND HILLS (1958) *d* R Fleischer *p* Weisbart *c* C Clarke *co-a* Wheeler *m* Harline *w* Remick, Murray *95min Fox
THESE THREE (1936) *d* Wyler *p* Goldwyn *s/fpl* (*The Children c Hour*) Hellman *c* Toland *a* R Day *m* A Newman *w* M Hopkins, McCrea, Oberon, Brennan 93min *r* UA
THESE WILDER YEARS (1956) *d* Rowland *c* Folsey *co-a* Gibbons *w* Cagney, Stanwyck, Pidgeon 91min MGM
THEY ALL COME OUT (1939) *d* J Tourneur 70min MGM
THEY ALL KISSED THE BRIDE (1942) *d Alexander Hall c* J Walker *w* J Crawford, M Douglas 85min Col
THEY CALL ME MISTER TIBBS (1970) *d* G Douglas *co-s* JR Webb *w* Poitier *108min Mir
THEY CAME FROM BEYOND SPACE (1966) *d* F Francis *85min
THEY CAME TO A CITY (1944) *d/co-s* Dearden *fpl* Priestley 87min
THEY CAME TO BLOW UP AMERICA (1943) *d Edward Ludwig c* Andriot *m* Friedhofer *w* G Sanders, Sten 73min Fox
THEY CAME TO CORDURA (1959) *d/co-s* Rossen *p* Goetz *c* Guffey *w* G Cooper, Hayworth, Heflin, Conte CS* 123min Col
They Caught The Ferry (US) = NAAEDE FAERGEN, DE (1948)
THEY DARE NOT LOVE (1941) *d* Whale *st* J Grant *co-s* Charles Bennett *c* Planer *w* Lukas 76min Col
THEY DIED WITH THEIR BOOTS ON (1941) *d* Walsh *p* Walsh *c* Glennon *m* M Steiner *w* Flynn, De Havilland, A Kennedy, Quinn, Greenstreet 140min WB
THEY DRIVE BY NIGHT (1940) *d* Walsh *p* Wallis *as-p* Hellinger *co-s* Wald *c* Edeson *co-sp/eff* Haskin *w* Raft, Sheridan, Lupino, Bogart 95min WB (= *Road to Frisco*)
THEY FLEW ALONE (1942) *d/p* H Wilcox *m* Alwyn *w* Neagle, Newton 104min (= *Wings and the Woman*)
THEY GAVE HIM A GUN (1937) *d* WS Van Dyke *co-s* Maibaum *c* Rosson *w* Tracy, Tone 94min MGM
THEY GO BOOM (1929) *d James Parrott p* Roach *st* McCarey *w* Laurel, Hardy (2rs) *r* MGM
THEY GOT ME COVERED (1942) *d* D Butler *p* Goldwyn *s* Kurnitz *m* Harline *w* Hope, Lamour, Preminger 94min RKO
THEY HAD TO SEE PARIS (1929) *d* Borzage *w* W Rogers 8620ft Fox
THEY KNEW WHAT THEY WANTED (1940) *d* Kanin *p* Pommer *s* Ardrey *m* A Newman *e* J Sturges *w* Lombard, Laughton, Carey, Ewell, Malden 96min RKO
THEY LEARNED ABOUT WOMEN (1930) *d* Conway, S Wood 72min MGM
THEY LIVE AGAIN (1938) *d* Zinnemann 1rl MGM
THEY LIVE BY NIGHT (1948) *d/ad* N Ray *p* Houseman *ex-p* Schary *s* Schnee *m* Harline *w* F Granger 95min RKO (= *The Twisted Road/Your Red Wagon*)
THEY MADE ME A CRIMINAL (1939) *d* Berkeley *p* Wallis *c* Howe *m* M Steiner *w* Rains, Sheridan, Garfield 92min WB
THEY MADE ME A FUGITIVE (1947) *d* Cavalcanti *c* Heller *w* T Howard 104min (= *I Became a Criminal*)
THEY MET IN BOMBAY (1941) *d* C Brown *co-s* Loos *c* Daniels *a* Gibbons *m* Stothart *w* Gable, R Russell, Lorre 86min MGM
THEY NEVER COME BACK (1932) *d* Newmeyer 62min
THEY'RE A WEIRD MOB (1966) *d/p* M Powell *112min
They're Off (UK) = STRAIGHT, PLACE AND SHOW (1937)
THEY RODE WEST (1954) *d* Karlson *co-s* F Nugent *c* Lawton *w* D Reed *84min Col
THEY SERVE ABROAD (1942) *d* R Boulting *p* J Boulting
THEY SHALL HAVE MUSIC (1939) *d* A Mayo *p* Goldwyn *co-s* Lawson *c* Toland *w* McCrea 101min *r* UA (= *Melody of Youth*)
THEY SHOOT HORSES, DON'T THEY? (1969) *d* Pollack *co-s* Poe *c* Lathrop *des* Horner *w* J Fonda PV* 120min *r* Fox
They Staked Their Lives = MED LIVET SOM INSATS (1939)
They Went to Vostok = ITALIANO, BRAVA GENTE (1964)
THEY WERE EXPENDABLE (1945) *d/p* J Ford *c* August *m* Stothart *w* Montgomery, J Wayne, D Reed 136min MGM
THEY WERE NOT DIVIDED (1950) *d/p/s* T Young 102min
THEY WHO DARE (1954) *d* Milestone *w* Bogarde, Tamiroff * 107min
THEY WON'T BELIEVE ME (1947) *d* Pichel *c* Wild *co-a* Boyle *e* Elmo Williams *w* R Young, S Hayward 95min RKO
THEY WON'T FORGET (1937) *d* LeRoy *co-s* Rossen *c* Edeson *w* Rains, Turner, Cook 96min WB
THEY WOULD ELOPE (1909) *d* Griffith *w* Pickford 1rl Bio
THICKER THAN WATER (1935) *d James Horne p* Roach *w* Laurel, Hardy (2rs) *r* MGM
THIEF, THE (1952) *d/co-s* rouse *c* Leavitt *w* Milland 85min U
THIEF OF BAGDAD, THE (1924) *d* Walsh *p/w* Fairbanks Sr *st* Fairbanks Sr (*ps* Elton Thomas) *c* Edeson *co-dec* Menzies 14rs
THIEF OF BAGDAD, THE (1940) *d* M Powell, *Tim Whelan, Ludwig Berger 2nd d* De Toth *p* A Korda *as-p* Menzies *st* Biro *c* Périnal *dec* V Korda *co-cos* Messel *m* Rozsa *e* Crichton *w* Veidt, Sabu *106min *r* UA
Thief of Bagdad, The = LADRO DI BAGDAD, IL (1960)
Thief of Venice, The = LADRO DI VENEZIA, IL (1951)
THIEVES FALL OUT (1941) *d* Enright *c* Hickox *w* Quinn 72min WB
THIEVES' GOLD (1918) *d* J Ford *w* Carey 5rs U
THIEVES' HIGHWAY (1949) *d* Dassin *c* Brodine *co-a* Wheeler *w* Cobb, Conte, Cortese, Pevney 94min Fox
THIGH LINE LYRE TRIANGULAR (1961) *d* Brakhage 16mm *5min
THING, THE (1951) *d Christian Nyby p* Hawks *s* Lederer *c* R Harlan *m* Tiomkin 87min (= *The Thing From Another World*)
Thing from Another World, The = THING, THE (1951)
THINGS ARE LOOKING UP (1934) *d Albert De Courville w* (V Leigh) 77min
THINGS TO COME (1936) *d/a* Menzies *p* A Korda *fn HG Wells c* Périnal *dec* V Korda *cos* Leger *m Arthur Bliss w* R Richardson, Massey, G Sanders 113min
THINK (1964–65) *d/s* C and R Eames *c* C Eames *m* E Bernstein *13½min (Single screen version: *View from the People Wall*)
THINK FAST, MR MOTO (1937) *d/co-s* Foster *w* Lorre 66min Fox
Think of A Number = TAENK PAA ET TAL (1968)
Thin Line, The = ONNA NO NAKA NI IRU TANIN (1966)
THIN MAN, THE (1934) *d* WS Van Dyke *s* Goodrich, Hackett *fn* Hammett *c* Howe *w* O'Sullivan, M Loy, Romero, W Powell 93min MGM
THIN MAN GOES HOME, THE (1944) *d* Thorpe *co-st/s* Riskin *co-st* Kurnitz *f characters* Hammett *c* Freund *co-a* Gibbons *w* W Powell, M Loy 10rs MGM
THIN RED LINE, THE (1964) *d* Marton *fn James Jones m* M Arnold CS 99min AA
THIRD DAY, THE (1965) *d/p* Smight *c* Surtees *w* Peppard, H Marshall PV* 119min WB
THIRD DEGREE, THE (1926) *d* Curtiz *c* Mohr 8rs WB
THIRD FINGER, LEFT HAND (1940) *d* Leonard *c* Folsey *w* M Loy, M Douglas 96min MGM
Third Lover, The = OEIL DU MALIN, L' (1961)
THIRD MAN, THE (1949) *d* C Reed *s/fn* Greene *c* Krasker *zither m Karas w* Welles, Cotten, T Howard, Valli 93min *pc* Selznick, A Korda *r* BL
THIRD SECRET, THE (1964) *d* Crichton *c* Slocombe *w* Hawkins, Attenborough CS 103min Fox
Third Sex, The = DRITTE GESCHLECHT, DAS (1957)
THIRD VOICE, THE (1959) *d/co-p/s* Cronfield *c* E Haller *w* E O'Brien CS 79min *r* Fox
Thirst = TORST (1949)
Thirteen, The = TRINADISAT (1937)
THIRTEEN FRIGHTENED GIRLS (1963) *d/p* Castle *89min Col (= *The Candy Web*)
THIRTEEN GHOSTS (1960) *d/p* Castle *c* Biroc *88min Col
13 HOURS BY AIR (1936) *d* Leiser *w* MacMurray, Bennett, Pitts 80min Par
13 MOST BEAUTIFUL BOYS (1965) *d* Warhol 16mm si 40min
13 MOST BEAUTIFUL WOMEN (1965) *d* Warhol 16mm si 40min
13 REVIR (1946) *d* Frič (= *Beat 13*)
13 RUE MADELEINE (1947) *d* Hathaway *p* De Rochemont *c* Brodine *m* A Newman *w* Cagney, Conte, Annabella, Malden 95min Fox
THIRTEENTH CHAIR, THE (1919) *d/s* Perret Pat
THIRTEENTH CHAIR, THE (1929) *d* Browning *w* Lugosi 73min MGM
THIRTEENTH CHAIR, THE (1937) *d* G Seitz *c* Clarke *a* Gibbons 66min MGM
Thirteenth Chamber, The = TRINACTA KOMANTA (1968)
13th LETTER, THE (1951) *d/p* Preminger *s* H Koch *c* La Shelle *co-a* Wheeler *m* North *w* Darnell, Boyer, Rosay 85min Fox
13 WEST STREET (1961) *d* P Leacock *fn* (*The Tiger Among Us*) *Leigh Brackett c* Lawton *w* Ladd, Steiger 78min
THIRTY (1959) *d/p/w* J Webb 96min WB (= *Deadline Midnight*)
THIRTY A WEEK (1918) *d Harry Beaumont w* Bankhead 5rs
35 BOULEVARD GENERAL KOENIG (1971) *d/s/c/e* Markopoulos 16mm *
30-FOOT BRIDE OF CANDY ROCK, THE (1959) *d Sidney Miller w* Costello S 75min Col
THIRTY DAYS (1922) *d* Cruze 5rs FPL
Thirty Days = SILVER LINING, THE (1932)
THIRTY-NINE STEPS, THE (1935) *d* Hitchcock *p* Balcon *fn John Buchan ad* Charles Bennett, Reville *di Ian Hay w* Donat, Carroll 87min Gau
THIRTY-NINE STEPS, THE (1959) *d* Thomas *fn John Buchan* *93min JAR
THIRTY SECONDS OVER TOKYO (1944) *d* LeRoy *s* Trumbo *c* Surtees, Rosson *co-a* Gibbons *m* Stothart *w* Tracy, V Johnson, R Walker, Mitchum, (Edwards) 138min MGM
36 HOURS (1964) *d/s* Seaton *p* Perlberg *c* Lathrop *w* Garner, Saint PV 115min MGM
33,333 (1924) *d/s* Molander SF
Thirty Times Your Money = HEJA ROLAND (1966)
30 YEARS OF EXPERIMENT (1951) compilation including ten Richter films, Eggeling's DIAGONAL SYMPHONY, Ruttman's OPUS IV and an extract from DREAMS THAT MONEY CAN BUY ep LA SEMAINE DE LA BONTE part* 58min
THIS ABOVE ALL (1942) *d* Litvak *p* Zanuck *fn Eric Knight c* AC Miller *co-a* R Day *m* A Newman *w* Power, Fontaine, Mitchell 110min Fox
This Can't Happen Here = SANT HANDER INTE HAR (1950)
THIS CHARMING COUPLE (1949) *d* W Van Dyke
THIS COULD BE THE NIGHT (1957) *d* Wise *p* Pasternak *c* R Harlan *w* J Simmons, P Douglas Pitts, CS 103min MGM
This Crazy Urge = VOGLIA MATTA, LA (1967)
THIS DAY AND AGE (1933) *d/p* De Mille *c* Marley *co-a* Dreier *dec* Leisen *w* Bickford 86min Par
THIS EARTH IS MINE (1959) *d* H King *c* Hoch, Metty *m* Friedhofer *w* J Simmons, Hudson Rains, McGuire CS* 123min U
THIS GUN FOR HIRE (1942) *d* Tuttle *co-s* Burnett *fn* Greene *c* J Seitz *w* Lake, Preston, Ladd, De Carlo 80min Par
THIS HAPPY BREED (1944) *d* Lean *c* Neame *w* J Mills, Newton *111min *r* BL
THIS HAPPY FEELING (1958) *d/s* Edwards *p* R Hunter *c* Arling *co-a* Golitzen *w* D Reynolds, Jurgens, Astor, A Smith CS* 92min U
THIS HERO STUFF (1919) *d* H King 5rs
THIS IS CINERAMA (1953) *d* Schoedsack(*uc*), *Ruth Rose co-p* M Cooper *co-supn* (*European sequence*) Todd *120min
This is England extended version of HEART OF BRITAIN, THE (1941)
THIS IS IT (1971) *d* Broughton 10min
THIS IS KOREA! (1951) *d* J Ford *50min US Navy-Rep
THIS ISLAND EARTH (1955) *d* J Newman *co-a* Golitzen 87min
This Is My Affair = I CAN GET IT FOR YOU WHOLESALE (1951)
THIS IS MY LOVE (1954) *d* Heisler *c* June *w* Darnell, Duryea 81min RKO
THIS IS THE ARMY (1943) *d* Curtiz *p* J Warne, Wallis *c* Glennon, Polito *m/w Irving Berlin w* G Murphy *121min WB
THIS IS THE LIFE (1917) *d* Walsh 5rs Fox
THIS IS THE LIFE (1935) *d* Neilan *co-s* Trotti 63min Fox
THIS IS THE NIGHT (1932) *d* Tuttle *c* Milner *w* C Ruggles, C Grant 78min Par
THIS LAND IS MINE (1943) *d/co-p/co-s* Renoir *co-p/co-s/di* Nichols *dec* Lourié *w* Laughton, G Sanders, M O'Hara 104min RKO

THIS LOVE OF OURS (1945) d Dieterle fpl Luigi Pirandello c Ballard w Oberon, Rains 90min U
THIS MAN IS MINE (1934) d Cromwell w I Dunne 76min RKO
This Man Must Die = QUE LA BETE MEURE (1969)
This Man Reuter = DESPATCH FROM REUTERS, A (1939)
THIS MAN'S NAVY (1945) d Wellman st/s B Chase co-a Gibbons w Beery 100min MGM
THIS MODERN AGE (1931) d Nicholas Grinde w J Crawford 76min MGM
THIS PROPERTY IS CONDEMNED (1966) d Pollack p Houseman co-s Coppola fpl T Williams c Howe co-a Pereira w N Wood, Redford *110min Par
THIS RECKLESS AGE (1932) d/co-a Tuttle s/di J Mankiewicz w C Ruggles 80min Par
THIS SIDE OF HEAVEN (1934) d W Howard c Rosson w L Barrymore 76min MGM
This Special Friendship = AMITIES PARTICULIERES, LES (1964)
THIS SPORTING LIFE (1963) d Anderson p Reisz s/fn David Storey m Roberto Gerhard w R Harris 134min r JAR
THIS TIME FOR KEEPS (1947) d Thorpe p Pasternak c Freund w Esther Williams *104min MGM
THIS WAS JAPAN (1945) d/p B Wright 12min
THIS WAY PLEASE (1937) d Florey co-a Dreier w Grable 8rs Par
This Way, That Way = ANO TE KONO TE (1952)
THIS WOMAN IS MINE (1941) d/p F Lloyd co-s S Miller w Brennan 92min U
THIS WONDERFUL WORLD (1957) d Grierson TV
THOMAS CROWN AFFAIR, THE (1968) d/p Jewison c Wexler m Boyle m Legrand a Dunaway, McQueen PV* 102min Mir co-pc McQueen r UA
Thomas Gordeyev = FOMA GORDEYEV (1959)
THOMAS GRAALS BASTA BARN (1918) d/co-s Stiller co-s Molander w Sjöström
THOMAS GRAALS BASTA FILM (1917) d Stiller s Molander w Sjöström 1794m
THOMAS GRAALS MYNDLING (1922) d/s Molander w Sjöström SF
THOMAS L'IMPOSTEUR (1965) d/co-s Franju co-s/co-di/fn Cocteau c Fradetal m Auric w Riva 93min (= Thomas, the Imposter)
Thomas, the Imposter = THOMAS L'IMPOSTEUR (1965)
THOROUGHBRED, THE (1930) d Thorpe 57min
THOROUGHBREDS DON'T CRY (1937) d Alfred E Green co-m/co-lyr Freed w Garland, Rooney 80min MGM
THOROUGHLY MODERN MILLIE (1967) d Hill p R Hunter c Metty co-a Golitzen m E Bernstein w J Andrews, Lillie *138min U
THORVALDSEN (1949) d/s Dreyer 10min
THOSE ATHLETIC GIRLS (1918) d Cline p/st Sennett w Fazenda 2rs Key
Those Blasted Kids = POKKERS UNGER, DE (1947)
THOSE COUNTRY KIDS (1914) d/w Arbuckle w Normand 1rl Key
THOSE DARING YOUNG MEN IN THEIR JAUNTY JALOPIES (1968) d/p/co-s Annakin w Bourvil, Curtis, Darc, Hawkins PV* 125min r Par (= Monte Carlo or Bust)
THOSE HAPPY DAYS (1914) d/w Arbuckle 1rl Key
THOSE HIGH GREY WALLS (1939) d C Vidor 81min Col
THOSE LOVE PANGS (1914) d/s/w Chaplin 1rl Key
THOSE MAGNIFICENT MEN IN THEIR FLYING MACHINES OR HOW I FLEW FROM LONDON TO PARIS IN 25 HOURS AND 11 MINUTES (1965) d/co-s Annakin c Challis w Sordi, Cassel TAO* 152min Fox
THOSE WE LOVE (1932) d Florey co-s G Abbott c Edeson w Astor 76min
THOSE WERE THE DAYS (1934) d Thomas Bentley w Hay 80min
THOSE WHO DANCE (1930) d William Beaudine (German version: Tanz geht weiter, Der)
THOSE WITHOUT SIN (1917) d-general De Mille p Neilan 5rs
Thousand and One Nights With Toho, A = TOHO SEN-ICHIYA (1947)
Thousand Cranes = SENBAZURU (1953)
Thousand Eyes of Dr Mabuse, The = TAUSEND AUGEN DES DR MABUSE, DIE (1961)
THOUSANDS CHEER (1943) d G Sidney p Pasternak c Folsey a Gibbons co-m Stothart co-songs Edens w Gene Kelly, Astor, L Barrymore, D Reed, M O'Brien, Allyson, Rooney, Garland, Sothern, Ball 126min MGM
Thou Shalt Honour Thy Wife = DU SKAL AERE DIN HUSTRU (1925)
Thou Shalt Not Kill = NON UCCIDERE (1961)
THREAD OF DESTINY (1910) d Griffith w Pickford 1rl Bio
Threatening Sky, The = CIEL, LA TERRE, LE (1966)
THREE AGES, THE (1923) co-d/p Keaton co-d Cline co-s Bruckman w Keaton, Beery, Hardy
THREE BAD MEN (1926) d/co-s J Ford w G O'Brien 8000ft Fox
THREE BLIND MICE (1945) d Dunning 16mm 5min

THREE BRAVE MEN (1957) d/s P Dunne c C Clarke co-a Wheeler w Milland, Borgnine CS 88min Fox
THREE CABALLEROS, THE (1944) p Disney c Rennahan *70min r RKO
THREE CAME HOME (1950) d Negulesco p/s N Johnson c Krasner co-a Wheeler m L Newman w Colbert 106min Fox
THREE CHEERS FOR THE IRISH (1940) d Bacon p Wallis co-s Wald w Mitchell 99min WB
THREE COINS IN THE FOUNTAIN (1954) d Negulesco p S Siegel c Krasner co-a Wheeler m V Young w C Webb, McGuire, Peters CS* 102min Fox
THREE COMRADES (1938) d Borzage p J Mankiewicz co-s Fitzgerald, Mankiewicz fn Erich Maria Remarque c Ruttenberg a Gibbons co-e Vorkapich m Waxman w R Taylor, Tone, R Young 98min MGM
THREE-CORNERED HAT, THE (1935) d D'Arrast
THREE CORNERED MOON (1933) d E Nugent p BP Schulberg c Shamroy w Colbert 77min Par
THREE DARING DAUGHTERS (1948) d F Wilcox p Pasternak c June w Jeanette Macdonald, J Powell *115min MGM (= The Birds and the Bees)
Three Daughters = TEEN KANYA (1961)
Three Eggs In A Glass = TRI VEJCE DO SKLA (1937)
Three Encounters = TRI VSTRECHI (1948)
Three Fables of Love, The: 3eps of QUATRE VERITES, LES (1962) without ep EL LENADOR Y LA MUERTE
THREE FACES EAST (1926) d Julian c Marley w C Brook 7419ft PRC
THREE FACES EAST (1930) d Del Ruth w Von Stroheim, Constance Bennett, Holden 71min WB
Three Faces of a Woman = TRE VOLTI, I (1964)
THREE FACES OF EVE, THE (1957) d/s N Johnson c Cortez co-a Wheeler w Woodward, Cobb, D Wayne CS 91min Fox
Three Fat Men, The = TRI TOLSTYAKA (1966)
THREE FILMS: BLUE WHITE, BLOOD'S TONE, VEIN (1965) d Brakhage 16mm * si 10min
Three Forbidden Stories = TRE STORIE PROIBITE (1952)
THREE FOR THE SHOW (1955) d Potter fst (Too Many Husbands) Somerset Maugham c Arling m Duning w Grable, Lemmon, Champion CS* 93min Col
Three Generations of Danjuro = DANJURO SANDAI (1944)
Three Girls from Rome = RAGAZZE DI PIAZZA DI SPAGNA, LE (1952)
THREE GODFATHERS (1936) d Boleslavsky p J Mankiewicz c Ruttenberg w Brennan 82min MGM
THREE GODFATHERS (1948) d/co-p J Ford co-p M Cooper co-s F Nugent rm MARKED MEN (1919) c Hoch w J Wayne, Armendariz, Darwell (Marsh) *106min r MGM
THREE GUYS NAMED MIKE (1951) d Walters co-a Gibbons m Kaper w Wyman, V Johnson, Keel 90min MGM
THREE HEARTS FOR JULIA (1943) d Thorpe c Folsey a Gibbons m Stothart w M Douglas, Sothern 89min MGM
Three Heroines = TRI GEROINI (1938)
365 DAYS IN HOLLYWOOD (1934) d G Marshall w Faye 74min Fox
365 Nights = ZANBYAKU ROKUJUGO-YA (1948)
300 SPARTANS, THE (1962) d/co-p Mate c Unsworth m Hadjidakis CS* 114min Fox
300 Years Ago = TRISTA LET TOMU (1956)
THREE HUSBANDS (1950) d Reis p Goldsmith c Planer w Darwell, Emlyn Williams 78min r UA
THREE INSTALLATIONS (1952) d/n L Anderson c Lassally 28min
THREE IN THE ATTIC (1968) d/p R Wilson co-ex-p Arkoff *91min
3 INTO 2 WON'T GO (1969) d P Hall c Lassally w Steiger, Bloom *94min
THREE JUMPS AHEAD (1923) d/s J Ford w Mix 4854ft Fox
THREE LITTLE GIRLS IN BLUE (1946) d Bruce Humberstone m A Newman w Vera-Ellen 90min Fox
THREE LITTLE PUPS THE (1954) d Avery anim* 7min MGM
THREE LITTLE WORDS (1950) d Thorpe p J Cummings st/s Wells co-a Gibbons w Astaire, Vera-Ellen, Dahl, D Reynolds *102min MGM
Three Loves = MITTSU NO AI (1954)
THREE LOVES HAS NANCY (1938) d Thorpe p Krasna c Daniels w J Gaynor, Montgomery, Tone 69min MGM
THREE MAXIMS, THE (1936) d/p H Wilcox w Neagle 86min (= The Show Must Go On)
THREE MEN AND A GIRL (1919) d Neilan 5rs Par
Three Men and a Girl = KENTUCKY MOONSHINE (1938)
THREE MEN IN A BOAT (1956) d Annakin p Woolf Bros w Laurence Harvey CS* 95min r BL
THREE MEN ON A HORSE (1936) d LeRoy co-st G Abbott c Polito w Blondell 88min FN
Three Meshchanskaya Street = TRETYA MESHCHANSKAYA (1927)
THREE MOUNTED MEN (1918) d J Ford w Carey 6rs U
Three Moves to Freedom = SCHACHNOVELLE (1960)

THREE MUSKETEERS, THE (1921) d Niblo p Fairbanks Sr fn Dumas Père c Edeson w Edeson w Fairbanks Sr, Menjou 11700ft UA
THREE MUSKETEERS, THE (1939) d Dwan p Zanuck fn Dumas c Marley w Carradine 73min Fox
THREE MUSKETEERS, THE (1948) d G Sidney s Ardrey fn Dumas co-a Gibbons m Stothart w Turner, Gene Kelly, Allyson, Heflin, Lansbury, Price *125min MGM
THREE MUST-GET-THERES, THE (1922) d/pc/s/w Linder 4900ft UA
Three Nights of Love = SZERELEM HAROM EJSZAKAJA, EGY (1967)
THREE O'CLOCK IN THE MORNING (1923) d Thorpe 2rs
THREE ON A COUCH (1966) d/p/w J Lewis w J Leigh *109min Col
THREE ON A LIMB (1936) d Charles Lamont w Keaton 2rs
THREE ON A MATCH (1932) d LeRoy c Polito w B Davis, Bogart, Blondell 64min FN
THREE PASSIONS, THE (1929) d/p/ad Ingram 7576ft r UA
Threepenny Opera, The = DREIGROSCHENOPER, DIE (1931)
Threepenny Opera, The = DREIGROSCHENOPER, DIE (1963)
Three Pirates, The = TRE CORSARI, I (1952)
Three Resurrected Drunkards = KAETTEKITA YOPPARAI (1968)
THREE RING CIRCUS (1954) d Pevney p Wallis co-a Pereira w Martin, J Lewis, Dru VV* 103min Par
THREE-RING MARRIAGE (1928) d Neilan e Heisler 5800ft FN
THREE'S A CROWD (1927) d/w Langdon 5668ft pc Langdon r FN
THREE SAILORS AND A GIRL (1953) d Del Ruth fpl G Kaufman w J Powell, (Lancaster) *95min WB
THREE SECRETS (1950) d Wise p Sperling co-st/co-s Rackin c Hickox w Parker, Roman, Neal 98min WB
Three Sisters = TRI SESTRY (1964)
THREE SISTERS (1970) d Olivier, John Sichel fpl Chekhov c Unsworth m Walton w Olivier *157min
Three Sisters With Maiden Hearts = OTOME-GOKORO SANNIN SHIMAI (1935)
THREE SMART BOYS (1937) d G Douglas p Roach 10½min
THREE SMART GIRLS (1936) d Koster as-p Pasternak w Durbin, Milland 84min U
THREE SMART GIRLS GROW UP (1939) d Koster p Pasternak w Durbin 90min U
Three Songs of Lenin = TRI PESNI O LENINYE (1934)
Three Stars = HAROM CSILLAG (1960)
Three Strange Loves = TORST (1949)
THREE STRANGERS (1946) d Negulesco st/s J Huston, H Koch c Edeson w Greenstreet, Lorre 92min WB
THREE STRIPES IN THE SUN (1955) d/s R Murphy c Guffey m Duning w A Ray 93min Col (= The Gentle Sergeant)
3.10 TO YUMA (1957) d Daves c Lawton m Duning w G Ford, Heflin 92min Col
Three Times a Woman = FEMMINE TRE VOLTE (1957)
Three Telegrams = TROIS TELEGRAMMES (1950)
THREE VIOLENT PEOPLE (1957) d Maté s J Grant c Griggs co-a Pereira w Heston, A Baxter, Roland VV* 100min Par
3 Wax Men = WACHSFIGURENKABINETT, DAS (1929)
THREE WEEKENDS (1928) d Badger c Rosson w Bow 5962ft Par
THREE WEEKS (1924) d Crossland 8rs MGM
THREE WEEKS IN PARIS (1926) d Del Ruth ad Zanuck 6rs WB
THREE WISE FOOLS (1923) d/co-s K Vidor w Pitts 70min pc Goldwyn
THREE WISE GUYS, THE (1936) d G Seitz st Damon Runyan a Gibbons w R Young 73min MGM
THREE WISHES, THE (1954) d Reiniger fst Brothers Grimm anim 1rl
THREE WOMEN (1924) d/co-st Lubitsch 75min WB
Three Women Around Yoshinaka = YOSHINAKA O MEGURU SANNIN NO ONNA (1956)
THREE WORD BRAND (1921) d/s Lambert Hillyer c August w W Hart 7rs pc W Hart
3 YUGOSLAVIAN PORTRAITS (1961) d A King 16mm 29min
THRILL HUNTER, THE (1933) d G Seitz c Tetzlaff 60min Col
THRILLING (1965) ep L'AUTOSTRADA DEL SOLE d Lizzani p De Laurentiis co-s Chiari w Manfredi, Sordi
THRILL OF A ROMANCE (1945) d Thorpe p Pasternak w V Johnson, ESther Williams *11rs MGM
THRILL OF IT ALL, THE (1963) d Jewison p R Hunter c Metty co-a Golitzen w D Day, Garner, Pitts *108min U
THRILL OF YOUTH, THE (1932) d Thorpe 62min
Throne of Blood = KUMONOSU-JO (1957)
Through a Glass Darkly = SASOM I EN SPEGEL (1961)
THROUGH A LENS BRIGHTLY: MARK TURBYFILL (1966) d/s/c/e Markopoulos 16mm *15min
THRU DIFFERENT EYES (1929) d/p John Blystone w W Baxter, S Sidney 5166ft Fox

427

THUMBELINA (1955) d Reiniger anim 1rl
Thunder Across The Pacific = WILD BLUE YONDER, THE (1951)
THUNDER AFLOAT (1939) d G Seitz c J Seitz a Gibbons w Beery, Tone 94min MGM
THUNDERBALL (1965) d T Young co-p Saltzman co-s Maibaum c Moore des Adam m Barry w Connery PV* 125min r UA
THUNDER BELOW (1932) d Richard Wallace co-s Buchman c C Lang w Bankhead, Bickford, Lukas 67min Par
THUNDER BAY (1953) d A Mann p A Rosenberg st/co-s J Hayes c Daniels co-a Golitzen w J Stewart, Dru, Duryea, Roland CS* 103min U
THUNDER BIRDS (1942) d Wellman p/s Trotti co-a R Day w Tierney, Lawford *78min Fox
THUNDERBOLT (1929) d Von Sternberg co-st/co-s Furthman di H Mankiewicz dec Dreier w G Bancroft 95min Par (si version: t J Mankiewicz)
THUNDERBOLT (1947) d Wyler, J Sturges w J Stewart 44min Mon
THUNDERHOOF (1948) d Karlson 77min Col
THUNDERING CARAVANS (1952) d Keller 54min Rep
THUNDERING HERD, THE (1925) d W Howard fn Zane Grey c Andriot 7187ft Par-FPL
THUNDERING HERD, THE (1933) d Hathaway rm (1925) c B Reynolds w R Scott, Carey 57min Par
THUNDERING ROMANCE (1925) d Thorpe w Arthur 4750ft
THUNDER IN THE EAST (1953) d C Vidor s Swerling c Garmes m Friedhofer w Boyer, Kerr, Ladd 98min Par
THUNDER IN THE SUN (1958) d/co-s Rouse ad Stern c Cortez m Mockridge w S Hayward, J Chandler *81min Par
THUNDER OF DRUMS, A (1961) d J Newman w Boone, P Douglas CS* 97min MGM
THUNDER ON THE HILL (1951) d Sirk c Daniels w Colbert, Blyth 84min U
Thunder Over Hawaii = NAKED PARADISE (1956)
THUNDER OVER MEXICO (1933) p Lesser m Reisenfeld 7rs [see QUE VIVA MEXICO (1931)]
THUNDER OVER THE PLAINS (1953) d De Toth p Weisbart c Glennon w R Scott, Cook *83min WB
THUNDER RIDERS (1927) d Wyler 4363ft U
THUNDER ROAD (1958) d Arthur Ripley st/w Mitchum 92min r UA
THUNDER ROCK (1942) d R Boulting p J Boulting fpl Ardrey w M Redgrave, Mason, Palmer 110min r MGM
Thunderstorm = GROZA (1934)
THUNDERSTORM (1955) d Guillermin s Mainwaring m Misraki 88min BL
Thursday = GIOVEDI, IL (1962)
THURSDAY'S CHILDREN (1953) d/s Guy Brenton, L Anderson c Lassally wv Burton 20min
Thus Another Day = KYO MO MATA KAKUTE ARINAN (1959)
THX 1138 (1971) d/st/co-s/e George Lucas ex-p Coppola m Schifrin *95min
THY NAME IS WOMAN (1924) d Niblo c Milner w Novarro 9rs
TIBERONEROS (1962) d Alcoriza (= *Morte Espreita no mar, A*)
TIBET PROIBITO (1949) d/e Maselli
TIC, UN (1908) d/s Feuillade
Ticket to Paradise = BILJET TILL PARADISET (1962)
TICKET TO TOMAHAWK, A (1950) d/co-st/co-s Richard Sale co-a Wheeler w Brennan, Dailey, A Baxter, Monroe 90min Fox
TICKLE ME (1965) d Taurog c Griggs w Presley PV* 90min AA
TICKLISH AFFAIR, A (1963) d G Sidney p Pasternak c Krasner w S Jones PV* 89min MGM
TICK... TICK... TICK (1969) d/co-p Nelson c Griggs w G Kennedy, March PV* 97min MGM
TI CONOSCO, MASCHERINA! (1943) d/st/s/w De Filippo
TIDE OF EMPIRE (1929) d Dwan w Adorée 6552ft MGM
TIDES OF BARNEGAT, THE (1917) d Neilan 5rs
TIDES OF PASSION (1925) d Blackton w Marsh 7rs Vit
TIEFLAND (1922) d A E Licho co-s (uc) V Harlan, Pabst 1700m
TIEFLAND (1954) d/p/s/c/w Riefenstahl 99min
TIENS, VOUS ETES A POITIERS (1916) d Feyder 618m Gau
TIERRA CALIENTE (1954) d/s Velo 2rs
TIERRA DEL FUEGO SE APAGA, LA (1955) d/co-s Fernandez c Figueroa 80min
TIERRA DE LOS ALVARGONZALEZ, LA (1969) d Picazo
TIFUSARI (1963) d/s Mimica anim* 14½min (= *Typhoid*)
Tiger and the Pussycat, The = TIGRE, IL (1967)
TIGER BAY (1959) d J Thompson w Buchholz, J and H Mills 105min JAR
TIGER BY THE TAIL (1955) d John Gilling s Goldbeck 82min r UA (= *Cross Up*)
TIGER HUNT IN ASSAM (1958) d W Van Dyke *60min
Tiger in the Sky = McCONNELL STORY, THE (1955)
TIGER IN THE SMOKE (1956) d R Baker c Unsworth 94min JAR

Tiger Likes Fresh Meat, The = TIGRE AIME LA CHAIR FRAICHE, LE (1964)
TIGER MAN, THE (1918) d/pc/w W Hart c August 5rs
TIGER MORSE (1966) d Warhol 16mm *20min (segment of *Four Stars*)
Tiger of Bengal (UK): 95min version DER TIGER VON ESCHNAPUR and DAS INDISCHE GRABMAL (1959)
TIGER ROSE (1923) d/p Franklin co-st De Belasco ad Goulding 5727ft WB
TIGER SHARK (1932) d Hawks c Gaudio w Robinson 80min FN
TIGER VON ESCHNAPUR, DER (1959) d/co-s F Lang fn Von Harbou rm DAS INDISCHE GRABMAL Part 1 (1921) *97min
Tight Little Island = WHISKY GALORE (1948)
TIGHT SPOT (1955) d Karlson c Guffey w G Rogers, Robinson, Keith 97min Col
TIGRA, LA (1954) d Torre Nilsson 85min
TIGRE, IL (1967) d/co-st Risi ex-p Levine w Gassmann, Parker *105min (= *The Tiger and the Pussycat*)
TIGRE AIME LA CHAIR FRAICHE, LE (1964) d Chabrol c Rabier 100min Gau (= *The Tiger Likes Fresh Meat*)
TIGRE REALE (1916) d Pastrone fst Verga
TIGRE SE PARFUME A LA DYNAMITE, LE (1965) d/w Chabrol c Rabier *110min co-pc De Laurentiis (= *An Orchid For The Tiger*)
TIH MINH (1918) d/s Feuillade 1: *Le Philtre d'oubli* (1125m); 2: *Drames dans la nuit* (725m); 3: *Les mystères de la Villa Circe* (880m); 4: *L'Homme dans la malle* (750m); 5: *Chez les fous* (645m); 6: *Oiseaux de nuit* (760m); 7: *L'Evocation* (650m); 8: *Sous le voile* (715m); 9: *La Branche de salut* (720m); 10: *Mercredi* (870m); 11: Le Document 29; 12: *Justice* (780m)
TIGRESS, THE (1927) d G Seitz p Cohn c J Walker 5357ft Col
TI HO SPOSATO PER ALLEGRIA (1967) d/co-s Salce c Di Palma w Vitti *
TIJERA D'ORO, LA (1958) d Alazraki
TIKHII DON (1958) d/s Gerasimov fn Mikhail Sholokov (2 parts) *117min (= *Quiet Flows The Don*)
Tiko and the Shark = TI-KOYO E IL SUO PESCECANE (1962)
TI-KOYO E IL SUO PESCECANE (1962) d/co-s Quilici *100min (= *Tiko and the Shark*)
TILL GLADJE (1949) d/s Ingmar Bergman c Fischer mf Mozart, Mendelssohn, Smetana, Beethoven w Sjöström 95min (= *To Joy*)
TILL I COME BACK TO YOU (1918) d De Mille 6rs FPL
TILLIE AND GUS (1933) d Francis Martin c B Reynolds w Fields 58min Par
TILLIE'S PUNCTURED ROMANCE (1915) d Sennett w Dressler, Chaplin, Normand, C Chase 6rs Key
TILLIE'S PUNCTURED ROMANCE (1928) d/p Edward Sutherland w Fields, Fazenda 5733ft r Par
TILL OSTERLAND (1925) d Molander w Veidt SF
TILL THE CLOUDS ROLL BY (1946) d Richard Whorf p Freed ad Wells co-c Folsey s Gibbons w Allyson, Garland, Champion, Heflin, V Johnson, Sinatra, R Walker, Esther Williams, Charisse *120min MGM
TILL THE END OF TIME (1946) d Dmytryk p Schary fn (*They Dream of Home*) Busch w Wild m Harline w Mitchum, McGuire 105min RKO
TILL WE MEET AGAIN (1944) d Borzage c Sparkuhl w Milland 63min Par
'TIL WE MEET AGAIN (1936) d Florey c Milner w H Marshall 72min Par
'TIL WE MEET AGAIN (1940) d Goulding p J Warner, Wallis c Gaudio w Oberon, Astor 99min WB
TIMBUKTU (1958) d J Tourneur w Mature, De Carlo 81min r UA
TIME AND TERRAIN (1947) d Low *10min NFBC
TIME AND THE TOUCH, THE (1962) d/co-s Alazraki (ps Carlos J Arconti) 110min
Time Bomb = TERROR ON A TRAIN (1953)
Time for Action = TIP ON A DEAD JOCKEY (1957)
TIME FOR DYING, A (1969) d/s Boetticher p/w A Murphy c Ballard *90min r U
TIME FOR KILLING, A (1968) d Karlson, Corman p H Brown w G Ford PV* 88min Col (= *The Long Ride Home*)
TIME, GENTLEMEN, PLEASE (1952) d L Gilbert 79min
Time, Gentlemen, Please = POLICEJNI HODINA (1960)
Time In The Sun (1940) p/co-e Marie Seton 56min [see QUE VIVA MEXICO (1931)]
TIME LIMIT (1957) d Malden co-p Malden co-p Widmark w Widmark, Basehart 96min r UA
Time Lost and Time Remembered = I WAS HAPPY HERE (1965)
Timely Mediator = TOKI NO UJIGAMI (1932)
TIME MACHINE, THE (1960) d/p Pál fn HG Welles 103min MGM
Time of Indifference = INDIFFERENTI, GLI (1963)
Time of Reckoning = FUSHIN NO TOKI (1968)
TIME OF YOUR LIFE, THE (1948) d Potter p William Cagney fpl William Saroyan c Howe w Cagney, Bendix, B Crawford 109min r UA
Time of Roses = RUUSUJEN AIKA (1969)

TIME OUT FOR ROMANCE (1937) d St Clair w Trevor 72min Fox
TIME OUT OF MIND (1947) d/p Siodmak 88min U
TIME OUT OF WAR, A (1954) d/co-p/co-s D Sanders co-p/co-s/c T Sanders 23min
TIMESLIP (1953) d/s K Hughes 93min
Times of Joy and Sorrow = YOROKUBI MO KANASHIMI MO IKUTOSHITSUKI (1957)
TIMES SQUARE LADY (1935) d G Seitz w R Taylor 69min MGM
Time Stood Still = TEMPO SE'FERMATO, IL (1959)
TIME, THE COMEDIAN (1925) d Leonard 5rs MGM
TIME, THE PLACE AND THE GIRL, THE (1946) d D Butler chor Prinz 105min WB
TIME TO LOVE AND A TIME TO DIE, A (1958) d Sirk c Metty co-a Golitzen m Rozsa CS* 133min U
TIME WITHOUT PITY (1957) d Losey co-p A Simmons s Barzman fpl (*Someone Waiting*) Emlyn Williams c F Francis des consultant R MacDonald w M Redgrave 88min
TIMID YOUNG MAN, THE (1936) d Sennett w Keaton 1786ft co-pc Sennett
TIMMERFABRIEK (1930) d/s/co-c/co-e Ivens 300m
Timothy Leary's Wedding = YOU'RE NOBODY TILL SOMEBODY LOVES YOU (1969)
TINGLER, THE (1959) d/p Castle w Price 80min Col
TIN GODS (1926) d/p Dwan w Adorée 8568ft FPL
TIN PAN ALLEY (1940) d W Lang as-p Macgowan c Shamroy m A Newman w Grable, Payne, Cook 94min Fox
TINSEL TREE (1942, ur) d/s/c/e Anger 3min
TIN STAR, THE (1957) d A Mann p Perlberg, Seaton s D Nichols c Groggs a Pereira m E Bernstein w H Fonda, Perkins VV 93min Par
TINTED VENUS (1921) d/p Hepworth 5000ft
TIP ON A DEAD JOCKEY (1957) d Thorpe s Lederer fst Shaw c Folsey w R Taylor, Malone CS 98min MGM (= *Time For Action*)
TIP TOES (1927) d H Wilcox w D Gish, W Rogers 7rs Par-FPL
TIRE-AU-FLANC (1928) d/co-ad J Renoir c Bachelet w M Simon
TIRE-AU-FLANC (1933) d Ferdenand Rivers s Cavalcanti w S Simon
TIRE AU FLANC 62 (1961) d/co-s De Givray co-s Truffaut c Coutard FS 87min pc Truffaut
TIREZ SUR LE PIANISTE (1960) d/co-ad/co-di Truffaut co-ad/co-di Moussy fn (*Down There*) David Goodis c Coutard w Aznavour CS 80min (= *Shoot the Pianist/Shoot the Piano Player*)
TISTEGA LEPEGA DNE (1963) d Stiglic (= *That Fine Day*)
TITANIC (1953) d Negulesco p/co-st/co-s C Brackett co-s Breen c Joe MacDonald co-a Wheeler w Stanwyck, R Wagner, Ritter, C Webb 98min Fox
Titan – the Story of Michelangelo = MICHELANGELO, DAS LEBEN EINES TITANEN (1940)
TITFIELD THUNDERBOLT, THE (1953) d Crichton 2nd d Holt st/s T Clarke c Slocombe e Holt m Auric *84min
TIT FOR TAT (1935) d Charles Rogers p Roach w Laurel, Hardy 2rs
TITO IN DEUTSCHLAND (1965) d/s A and A Thorndike
TIVOLIGARDEN SPILLER (1954) d/s A and B Henning Jensen
Tjuvskytten = KARLEK STARKARE AN HAT (1913)
TLAYUCAN (1962) d/s Alcoriza 93min (= *The Pearls of Saint Lucia*)
T-MEN (1947) d/co-s (uc) A Mann c J Alton 91min
TO (1964) d Kjaerulff-Schmidt 89min (= *Two People*)
TOA (1949) d/st/fpl/w Guitry 85min
TOBACCO ROAD (1941) d J Ford p Zanuck s N Johnson fn Erskine Caldwell c AC Miller co-a R Day w Tierney, D Andrews 84min Fox
To Be a Crook = FILLE ET DES FUSIL, UNE (1964)
TO BE A MAN (1963) d I Lerner w Heflin 99min (= *Cry of Battle*)
TO BE OR NOT TO BE (1942) d/co-p/co-st Lubitsch c Maté dec V Korda w Lombard, Benny, Stack 99min r UA
TOBIAS BUNTSCHUM (1926) d/s/w Madsen fpl Gerhart Hauptman
TOBIE EST UN ANGE (1941, ur) d Y Allégret c Alekan
TOBOGGAN (1935) d/s/di Decoin
Toboggan Cavalier, The = RODELKAVALIER, DER (1918)
TOBY AND THE TALL CORN (1955) d R Leacock p W Van Dyke 30min
TO CATCH A THIEF (1955) d/p Hitchcock s J Hayes c Burks co-a Pereira w C Grant, Grace Kelly, Vanel *107min Par
TOCCATA (1967) d/p Van den Horst 30min
TOCCATA FOR TOY TRAINS (1957) d/s C and R Eames c C Eames m E Bernstein *14min
TOCHER (1937) d Reiniger m Benjamin Britten anim 1rl GPO
TOCHTER DES SAMURAI, DIE (1937) d/co-p/s Fanck 120min (= *Die Liebe der Mitsu*)
TOCHUKEN KUMOEMON (1936) d/s Naruse (= *On the Way to Spider Gate*)
To Clothe the Saints = PARA VESTIR SANTOS (1955)

To Commit a Murder = PEAU D'ESPION (1966)
Toda Brother and His Sisters, The = TODA-KE NO KYODAI (1941)
TODA-KE NO KYODAI (1941) d/co-s Ozu Sho (= *The Toda Brother and His Sisters*)
Today = SEGODNYA (1924)
Today = SEGODNYA (1930)
Today For The Last Time = DNES NAPOSLED (1958)
TODAY WE LIVE (1933) d/p Hawks di/fst (*Turnabout*) Faulkner w J Crawford, G Cooper, R Young, Tone 113min MGM
TODAY WE LIVE (1937) d Grierson, *Ralph Bond* p Rotha 23min
To Die In Madrid = MOURIR A MADRID (1963)
To Dig a Pit = CAVAR UN FOSO (1966)
TO EACH HIS OWN (1946) d Leisen p/st/co-s C Brackett c Fapp co-a Dreier m V Young w De Havilland 122min Par
To Each His Own = A CIASCUNO IL SUO (1966)
TO, E MORTA LA NONNA! (1964) d/co-s Monicelli *
TOGE NO UTA (1923) d/s Mizoguchi Nik
TOGETHER AGAIN (1944) d C Vidor co-st Biberman c J Walker w I Dunne, Boyer, C Coburn 93min Col
TO HAVE AND HAVE NOT (1945) d/p Hawks s Furthman, Faulkner fn Hemingway c Hickox songs Carmichael w Bogart, Brennan, Bacall, Carmichael, Dalio 100min WB
TO HEAR YOUR BANJO PLAY (1941) d W Van Dyke co-c R Leacock e I Lerner m Pete Seeger 20min
TO HELL AND BACK (1955) d Jesse Hibbs p A Rosenberg fab/w A Murphy CS* 106min U
TOHOKU NO ZUNMUTACHI (1957) d Ichikawa S Toho (= *The Men of Tohoku*)
TOHO SENICHI-YA (1947) co-d Ichikawa
TOI KUMO (1955) d Kinoshita (= *Distant Clouds*)
TOI . . . LE VENIN (1958) d/s/w Hossein w Vlady 92min
TOJIN OKICHI (1930) d Mizoguchi Nik (= *Okichi the Stranger*)
TOJIN OKICHI (1931) d Kinugasa
To Joy = TILL GLADJE (1949)
TOKAI KOKYOGAKU (1929) d Mizoguchi Nik (= *Metropolitan Symphony*)
TO KILL A MOCKINGBIRD (1962) d Mulligan fn Harper Lee c Harlan co-a Golitzen m E Bernstein w Peck 129min U
TOKI NO UJIGAMI (1932) d Mizoguchi Nik (= *Timely Mediator*)
TOKKAN KOZO (1929) d/co-st Ozu Sho (= *A Straightforward Boy*)
TOKYO BOSHOKU (1957) d/co-s Ozu w Yamada Sho (= *Twilight In Tokyo*)
Tokyo is a Nice Place = TOKYO YOI TOKO (1935)
TOKYO JOE (1949) d Heisler c Lawton w Bogart 88min Col
TOKYO KOSHIN-KYOKU (1929) d Mizoguchi Nik (= *Tokyo March*)
Tokyo March = TOKYO KOSHIN-KYOKU (1929)
TOKYO MONOGATARI (1953) d/co-s Ozu w Mori 140min Sho (= *Tokyo Story*)
TOKYO NO GASSHO (1931) d/co-s Ozu Sho (= *Chorus of Tokyo*)
TOKYO NO ONNA (1933) d Ozu Sho (= *Woman of Tokyo*)
TOKYO NO YADO (1935) d Ozu Sho (= *Inn In Tokyo, An*)
Tokyo Olympiad = TOKYO ORINPIKKU (1965)
TOKYO ORINPIKKU (1965) d/c/co-s Ichikawa co-c supn Miyagawa CS* 130min r Toho (= *Tokyo Olympiad*)
TOKYO SENSO SENGO HIWA (1971) d/co-s Oshima 94min (= *He Died After the War*)
Tokyo Story = TOKYO MONOGATARI (1953)
TOKYO YOI TOKO (1935, uf) d/s Ozu Sho (= *Tokyo is a Nice Place*)
TOL'ABLE DAVID (1921) d H King s Goulding w Barthelmess 7rs FN
TOL'ABLE DAVID (1930) d John Blystone p Cohn w Carradine (as Peter Richmond) 65min Col
TOLLE HEIRAT VON LALO, DIE (1919) d/co-s Lupu-Pick 1584m
TOLL GATE, THE (1920) d/co-sy Lambert Hillyer p/co-st/w W Hart c August 6rs co-pc W Hart
TOLL OF THE SEA, THE (1922) d Chester M Franklin p Kalmus * 5rs
To Love = ATT ALSKA (1964)
To Love Again = AI FUTATABI (1971)
TOM AND JERRY MIX (1917) d/s/w Mix 2rs Fox
TO MARY – WITH LOVE (1936) d Cromwell as-p Macgowan w M Loy, W Baxter, Trevor 87min Fox
TOMB OF LIGEIA, THE (1964) d/p Corman fst Poe w Price S* 82min (= *Ligeia*)
TOMBOY BESSIE (1912) d Sennett, Normand ½rl Bio
TOM BROWN OF CULVER (1932) d Wyler w (Power) (8rs) U
TOM BROWN'S SCHOOLDAYS (1940) d Stevenson fn Arthur Hughes c Musuraca w Bartholemew 86min RKO
TOM BROWN'S SCHOOLDAYS (1951) d Gordon Parry fn Thomas Hughes w Newton 96min
TOM, DICK, AND HARRY (1941) d Kanin e J Sturges w G Rogers, G Murphy, Meredith 86min RKO
TOM JONES (1963) d/p T Richardson s Osborne fn Henry Fielding c Lassally w Finney, Evans, Greenwood *128min r UA
TOMMI (1931) d/s Protasanov 1730m

TOMORROW AT SEVEN (1933) d Enright 62min RKO
TOMORROW IS FOREVER (1945) d Pichel m M Steiner w Welles, Colbert, N Wood 105min RKO
Tomorrow's Dancers = ASHITA NO ODORIKO (1939)
TOMORROW WE LIVE (1942) d Ulmer 66min
TOM SAWYER (1930) d Cromwell c C Lang w Darwell 85min Par
TOM THUMB (1958) d/p Pal w Sellers *98min MGM
TONARI NO YANE NO SHITA (1931) d Naruse
TONARI-NO YARO (1965) d Kuri anim (= *The Man Next Door*)
TONENDE WELLE (1928) d Ruttmann (= *Spiel der Wellen/Sounding Wave*)
To New Shores = ZU NEUEN UFERN (1937)
TO NEZNATE HADIMRSKU (1931) d Frič, *Karel Lamac* c Heller (= *Hadimrsku Doesn't Know*)
TONI (1935) d/co-ad J Renoir co-c C Renoir 95min
TONIGHT AND EVERY NIGHT (1945) d/p Saville c Maté w Hayworth, Winters 92min Col
TONIGHT OR NEVER (1931) d LeRoy c Toland m A Newman w Swanson, M Douglas, Karloff 80min r UA
Tonight or Never = CE SOIR OU JAMAIS (1960)
TONIGHT WE RAID CALAIS (1943) d Brahm c Ballard co-a R Day w Cobb 70min Fox
TONIGHT WE SING (1953) d Leisen co-s Kurnitz c Shamroy co-a Wheeler w D Wayne *109min Fox
TONIO KROGER (1964) d Thiele fst Thomas Mann w Brialy, Tiller 93min
TONITE LET'S ALL MAKE LOVE IN LONDON (1967) d/c/e Peter Whitehead w V Redgrave, Caine, Christie *72min
TONNELIER, LE (1942) d/s Rouquier sh
TONNERRE, LE (1921) d/s Delluc fn Mark Twain (= *Evangeline et le Tonnerre*)
TONNERRE DE DIEU, LE (1965) d/co-s De la Patellière w Gabin, Palmer S 91min (= *God's Thunder*)
TON OMBRE EST LA MIENNE (1961) d Michel
TONTONS FLINGUEURS, LES (1963) d/co-s Lautner w Blanche, Ventura 92min
TONY ROME (1967) d G Douglas p A Rosenberg c Biroc w Sinatra, Conte PV* 109min Fox
Too Bad She's Bad = PECCATO CHE SIA UNA CANAGLIA (1955)
TOO HOT TO HANDLE (1938) d Conway co-s Mahin c Rosson w Gable, M Loy, Pidgeon 105min MGM
TOO HOT TO HANDLE (1960) d T Young c Heller w Mansfield *100min
TOO LATE BLUES (1962) d/p/co-s Cassavetes c Lindon m Raksin 100min Par
TOO LATE FOR TEARS (1949) d Haskin c Mellor w L Scott, Duryea, A Kennedy 99min r UA
TOO LATE THE HERO (1970) d/p/co-st/co-s Aldrich c Biroc w Caine, Robertson, H Fonda 70* 144min pc Aldrich
TOO MANY CROOKS (1927) d Newmeyer w G Bancroft 5399ft FPL r Par
TOO MANY GIRLS (1940) d/p G Abbott fpl Richard Gogers, Lorenz Hart w V Johnson, Ann Miller 85min RKO
TOO MANY HUSBANDS (1940) d/p W Ruggles fpl S Maugham c J Walker m Hollander w M Douglas, MacMurray, Arthur 84min Col
TOO MANY HIGHBALLS (1933) d Bruckman 2rs Par
TOO MANY KISSES (1925) d Paul Sloane c Rosson w W Powell, H Marx 5759ft FPL r Par
TOO MANY MILLIONS (1918) d Cruze rs r FPL
TOO MANY TOO SOON (1961) d Peries 20min
Too Many Women = GOD'S GIFT TO WOMEN (1931)
TOO MUCH JOHNSON (1919) d Crisp 5rs FPL
Too Much Talk = OHAYO (1959)
TOO MUCH, TOO SOON (1958) d/co-s Napoleon p Blanke co-c Musuraca m Gold w Flynn, Malone, Danton 121min WB
Too Soon To Die = LUTRING (1966)
TOO YOUNG TO KISS (1951) d Leonard s Goodrich, Hackett c Ruttenberg co-a Gibbons w Allyson, V Johnson 91min MGM
TOO YOUNG TO MARRY (1931) d LeRoy c Hickox w L Young 67min WB (= *Broken Dishes*)
TO PARIS WITH LOVE (1955) d Hamer w Guinness *78min r JAR
TOPAZ (1969) d/p Hitchcock c Hildyard m Jarre w Piccoli, Noiret *125min U
TOPAZE (1933) d Lewis Gasnier fpl Pagnol
TOPAZE (1933) d D'Arrast ex-p Selznick as-p Macgowan fpl Pagnol c Andriot m M Steiner w J Barrymore, M Loy, Jouvet, Feuillère 78min RKO
TOPAZE (1936) d/st/s Pagnol
TOPAZE (1951) d/p/st/s Pagnol rm (1933) w Fernandel 135min
TOP HAT (1935) d Sandrich p Berman songs Irving Berlin w Astaire, G Rogers, Horton, Ball 105min RKO
TOPI GRIGI, I (1918) d/s/w Ghione (8 parts)
TOPKAPI (1964) d/p Dassin c Alekan m Hadjidakis w Mercouri, Ustinov, Maximilian Schell, Tamiroff *120min r UA
TO PLEASE A LADY (1950) d/p C Brown c Rosson co-a Gibbons w Gable, Stanwyck, Menjou 91min MGM (= *Indianapolis*)

TOPO GIGIO E I SEI LADRI (1967) Ichikawa anim* 90min (= *Topo Gigio: la guerra del missile/Toppo Jijo no Botan Senso*)
Topo Gigio: la guerra del missile = TOPO GIGIO E I SEI LADRI (1967)
TOP O' THE MORNING (1949) d D Miller c Lindon co-a Dreier w B Crosby, Blyth 100min Par
TOPPER (1937) d McLeod p Roach c Brodine song Carmichael w Constance Bennett, C Grant, (Carmichael) 97min MGM
TOPPER RETURNS (1941) d Del Ruth p Roach co-s G Douglas c Brodine w Blondell 85min r UA
TOPPER TAKES A TRIP (1939) d McLeod p Roach c Brodine co-m Friedhofer w Constance Bennett 85min r UA
Toppo Jijo no Botan Senso = TOPO GIGIO E I SEI LADRI (1967)
TOP SPEED (1930) d LeRoy c Hickox 80min FN
TOP SECRET AFFAIR (1957) d Potter ex-p Sperling c Cortez w K Douglas, Hayward 107min WB (= *Their Secret Affair*)
TOPS (1969) d/s C and R Eames c C Eames *7¼min
Tora-no-o = TORA NO O O FUMU OTOKOTACHI! (1945)
TORA NO O O FUMU OTOKOTACHI (1945) d/s Kurosawa w Mori 58min Toho (= *Tora-no-o*)
TORA! TORA! TORA! (1970) d R Fleischer, *Toshio Masuda, Kinji Fukasaku* p Elmo Williams co-a R Day m Goldsmith w Cotten PV* 144min Fox
TORCH, THE (1950) d Fernandez as-p Goddard co-st Alazraki s/di John Steinbeck fn ENAMORADA (1948) w Goddard, Armendariz, Roland 78min (= *The Bandit General*)
TORCH SONG (1953) d/chor Walters co-s J Hayes co-a Gibbons w J Crawford (Walters) *90min MGM
TORCHES HUMAINES DE JUSTINIEN, LES (1908) d Méliès 50m
TORERO! (1955) d/co-s Velo 80min
TORINO NEI CENTI'ANNI (1961) d Rossellini s Orsini 45min RAI
Torment = HETS (1944)
TORMENT (1949) d/co-p/s Guillermin 78min
Tormented Flame = JOEN (1959)
TORMENTO GENTILE (1916) d/w Ghione
TORNA A SORRENTO (1946) d Bragaglia
TORNADO, THE (1917) d/s/w J Ford 2rs U
TORN CURTAIN (1966) d/p Hitchcock w P Newman, J Andrews *128min U
Torpedo Bay (UK) = FINCHE DURA LA TEMPESTA (1962)
TORPEDO RUN (1953) d Pevney c Folsey w G Ford, Borgnine CS* 98min MGM
TORPEDO SQUADRON (1942) d J Ford 8mm* 8min
Torrent, The = IBANEZ' TORRENT (1926)
TORRID ZONE (1940) d Keighley p J Warner, Wallis as-p Hellinger co-s Wald c Howe w Cagney, Sheridan 88min WB
TORST (1949) d Ingmar Bergman c Fischer w Ekman 88min SF (= *Thirst/Three Strange Loves*)
TORTILLA FLAT (1942) d V Fleming co-s Mahin fn John Steinbeck c Freund a Gibbons m Waxman w Tracy, Lamarr, Garfield, Tamiroff 105min MGM
TORTURE GARDEN (1967) d F Francis w Palance, Meredith 93min Col
Torture Me But Kill me With Kisses = STRAZIAMI, MA DI BACI SAZIAMI (1968)
TO SAVE HER SOUL (1909) d Griffith w Pickford 1rl Bio
TOSCA (1908, ur) w S Bernhardt
TOSCA, LA (1940) d/s J Renoir, Visconti, *Karl Koch* m Puccini w M Simon, Girotti 91min
TOSCA (1956) d/p Gallone c Rotunno m Puccini CS* 112min
TOSCANINI: HYMN OF THE NATIONS (1944) d Alexander Hackenschmeid m Verdi 28min pc I Lerner r Par
TO SEE OR NOT TO SEE (1969) d Pojar co-p Koenig anim* 15min NFBC
TOSEI TAMATEBAKO (1925) d Gosho (= *A Casket For Living*)
TOSEN FRAN STORMYRTORPET (1917) d/co-s Sjöström 1749m
TO SIR WITH LOVE (1966) d/p/s Clavell w Poitier *105min Col
To Skin A Spy = AVEC LA PEAU DES AUTRES (1966)
TOTAL WAR IN BEITAIN (1946) d Rotha 21min
TOTENSCHIFF, DAS (1959) d/co-s Tressler fn B Traven w Buchholz 90min
Totet nicht mehr = MISERICORDIA (1919)
To The Front = TEBYE FRONT (1943)
To the Glory of Soviet Heroines = SLAVA SOVETSKIM GEROYNIAM (1938)
To The Kazakhstan Front = TEBYE FRONT (1943)
TO THE LADIES (1923) d/p Cruze fpl G Kaufman, *Marc Connelly* w Horton 6rs FPL
TO THE LAST MAN (1923) d V Fleming c Howe 7rs FPL
TO THE LAST MAN (1933) d Hathaway fn Zane Grey c B Reynolds w R Scott 61min Par
TO THE PUBLIC DANGER (1948) d Fisher 44min
TO THE SHORES OF IWO JIMA (1945) p Sperling *20min US Navy & Marine Corps

TO THE VICTOR (1948) d Daves p Wald s R Brooks c Burks w Lindfors, Malone 100min WB

TOTO (1933) d J Tourneur p Pat

TOTO A COLORI (1952) co-d/st/s Steno co-d Monicelli p Ponti, De Laurentiis w Toto *100min (= Toto In Colour)

TOTO CERCA CASA (1948) d Steno, Monicelli p Ponti 78min (= Toto Wants a Home)

TOTO CERCA MOGLIE (1950) d Bragaglia w Toto

TOTO CONTRO I QUATTRO (1963) d Steno w Toto

TOTO DIABOLICUS (1962) d Steno w Toto

TOTO E CAROLINA (1954) d/co-s Monicelli w Toto

TOTO E I RE DI ROMA (1951) d Steno, Monicelli co-s Risi w Toti, Sordi

TOTO E LE DONNE (1952) d Steno, Monicelli w Toto

TOTO, EVA E IL PENNELLO PROIBITO (1959) d/st Steno w Toto, De Funès 90min

Toto in Colour = TOTO A COLORI (1952)

TOTO LE MOKO (1949) d Bragaglia w Toto

TOTON (1919) d Borzage Tri

TOTO NELLA LUNA (1959) d/co-st/co-s Steno w Toto 90min

TOTO, PEPPINO E LA ... MALA FEMMINA (1956) d Camillo Mastrocinque w Toto, Manfredi 90min

Toto Wants a Home = TOTO CERCA CASA (1948)

TOTSUGA HI (1956) d Yoshimura (= Date for Marriage)

Totte et sa chance = GESCHICHTE EINER KLEINER PARISERIN, DIE (1927)

TOUCHDOWN (1931) d McLeod 8rs Par

TOUCHEZ-PAS AU GRISBI (1954) d/co-s Becker dec D'Eaubonne m Wiener w Gabin, Moreau, Ventura 85min (= Honour among Thieves)

TOUCH OF EVIL (1958) d/s/w Welles p Zugsmith c Metty co-a Golitzen m Mancini w Heston, J Leigh, Tamiroff, Dietrich, (Cotten) 93min U

TOUCH OF LARCENY, A (1959) d Hamilton w Miles, G Sanders, Mason 91min r Par

TOUCH OF THE CHILD, THE (1918) d/p/ad Hepworth 4800ft

Tough Guy of 1900 = GUAPO DEL 1900, UN (1960)

TOUHA (1958) d/co-s Jasny 102min (= Desire)

TOUR, LA (1928) d Clair co-c Périnal

TOUR AU LARGE (1926) d/s/m/e Grémillon a Daquin 1600m

TOURBILLON DE PARIS, LE (1928) d Duvivier w Dagover

TOUR DE CHANT (1932) d/s Cavalcanti

TOUR DE CHANT, LE (1934) d/s Cavalcanti

TOUR DE LONDRES ET LES DERNIERS MOMENTS D'ANNE DE BOLEYN, LA (1905) d Méliès 135m (5 parts)

TOUR DE NESLE, LA (1954) d/s Gance fn Dumas w Brasseur *120min

TOURISTE ENCORE (1963) d Malle sh

TOURNAMENT (1968) d Ichikawa

TOURNOI, LE (1929) d/ad J Renoir

TOUS LES ENFANTS DU MONDE (1964) d Michel sh

TOUS LES GARÇONS S'APPELLENT PATRICK (1957) d Godard s Rohmer w Brialy 21min (= Charlotte et Veronique)

TOUS PEUVENT ME TUER (1957) d/co-s Decoin w Aimée, Brialy, Rossi-Drago FS 102min (= Anyone Can Kill Me)

TCUT ÇA NE VAUT PAS L'AMOUR (1931) d J Tourneur w Gabin 87min Pat

TOUT LA MEMOIRE DU MONDE (1956) d/e Resnais c Cloquet m Jarre 22min

TOUTE SA VIE (1930) d Cavalcanti Par (= A Cancao do berco)

TOUT L'OR DU MONDE (1961) d/co-s/co-di Clair m Van Parys w Bourvil, Noiret 100min

TOUT PETIT FAUST, LE (1910) d Cohl anim 125m

TOUT POUR L'AMOUR (1933) d May

TOVARICH (1937) d Litvak p Wallis c C Lang m M Steiner w Boyer, Colbert, Rathbone 98min WB

TOVARNYI No. 717 (1931) d N Lebadev s Petrov, B Schwartz 1740m (= Train No. 717)

TOWARD THE UNKNOWN (1956) d/p LeRoy c Rosson w Holden, Nolan, Garner *115min WB (= Brink of Hell)

TOWED IN A HOLE (1933) d G Marshall p Roach w Laurel, Hardy 19min r MGM

TOWER HOUSE (1955) d Brakhage, Joseph Cornell c Brakhage si* 10min

TOWER OF LIES, THE (1925) d Sjöström w Chaney, Shearer 6500ft MGM

Tower of Lilies = HIME-YURI NO TO (1953)

TOWER OF LONDON (1962) d Corman w Price 79min r UA

TOWN, THE (1943) d Von Sternberg p P Dunne 12min

TOWN CALLED BASTARD, A (1971) d Parrish FS* 97min (= A Town Called Hell)

Town Called Hell, A = TOWN CALLED BASTARD, A (1971)

TOWN LIKE ALICE, A (1956) d/s J Lee fn Nevil Shute c Unsworth w Finch 117min JAR

Town of Anger = IKARI NO MACHI (1950)

Town of Fire = JOEN NO CHIMATA (1922)

Town of Love and Hope, A = AI TO KIBO NO MACHI (1959)

Town on Trial, A = PROCESSO ALLA CITTA (1952)

TOWN ON TRIAL (1957) d Guillermin co-s Hughes w J Mills, C Coburn 96min r Col

Town People = MACHI NO HITOBITO (1926)

TOWN WITHOUT PITY (1961) d/p G Reinhardt m Tiomkin w K Douglas 105min r UA

TOYS IN THE ATTIC (1963) d Hill p W Mirisch s Poe fpl Hellman c Biroc m Duning w Martin, Page, Tierney PV* 90min r AA

TOY WIFE, THE (1938) d Thorpe p M Cooper a Gibbons w Rainer, M Douglas, R Young 95min MGM

Trachoma = TRAKOM (1964)

TRACKED BY POLICE (1927) d Enright 6rs WB

TRACKING THE SLEEPING DEATH (1938) d Zinnemann 10min MGM

TRACK OF THE CAT (1954) d Wellman c Clothier w Mitchum, T Wright CS* 102min WB

TRADER HORN (1931) d WS Van Dyke w Carey 123min MGM

TRADE TATTOO (1937) d Lye *5min GPO

TRADE WINDS (1938) d/st Garnett p Wanger c Maté m A Newman w March, J Bennett, Sothern, Mitchell 90min r UA

TRADGARDSMASTAREN (1917) d/w Sjöström s Stiller 950m (= Falkst Alarm/Varlden's Grymhet)

TRADIMENTO, IL (1951) d/co-s Freda st/co-s Monicelli w Gassmann 85min

TRAFIC (1971) d/s/w Tati *100min

Traffic in Souls = CARGAISONS BLANCHES (1937)

TRAFRACKEN (1966) d/s Lindgren w Björnstrand 90min (= The Sadist/The Coffin)

Tragedie de Lourdes, La = CREDO (1924)

TRAGEDIE IMPERIALE, LA (1938) d L'Herbier dec Lourié m Milhaud 101min

TRAGICA NOTTE (1941) d/co-s Soldati

Tragic Pursuit, The = CACCIA TRAGICA (1947)

TRAGODIE DER LIEBE (1923) d/p May dec Leni w Jannings, Dietrich 4 parts: 1939m/1790m/1719m/-1964m

TRAGODIE EINER EHE (1926) d Elvey 2351m UFA

TRAGODIE IM HAUSE HABSBURG (1924) d/p A Korda s Biro 3057m

TRAIDORES DE SAN ANGEL, LOS (1967) d/co-s Torre Nilsson *90min (= Traitors of San Angel)

TRAILING THE COUNTERFEIT (1911) d/w Sennett ½rl Bio

TRAIL OF '98, THE (1929) d/p C Brown c J Seitz w Del Rio, Carey, J Tourneur, (Costello) 11000ft MGM

TRAIL OF THE LONESOME PINE, THE (1916) d/s De Mille pc Lasky

TRAIL OF THE LONESOME PINE, THE (1936) d Hathaway p Wanger w H Fonda, MacMurray, S Sidney 102min Par

TRAIL OF THE VIGILANTES (1940) d Dwan co-c Krasner w Tone, B Crawford 75min U

TRAIL STREET (1947) d Enright w R Scott, Ryan 84min RKO

TRAIN, THE (1965) d Frankenheimer m Jarre w Lancaster, Moreau, M Simon, Scofield 113min r UA

TRAIN DE LA VICTOIRE, LE (1964) d Ivens

TRAIN D'ENFER (1965) d Grangier w Marais *92min

TRAIN DE PLAISIR (1935) d Joannon

TRAIN DU LABRADOR, LE (1967) d/s/cy Lamothe

TRAINING FOR HUSBANDS (1920) d Cline 2rs Fox

Train No. 717 = TOVARNYI NO. 717 (1931)

TRAIN OF EVENTS (1949) d Dearden, Crichton, Sidney Cole w Finch 89min Ealing

Train of the Central Executive, The = AGITPOEZHD VTSIKA (1921)

TRAIN SANS YEUX, LE (1928) d/e Cavalcanti st Delluc

Traitor = PREDATEL (1926)

TRAITOR'S GATE (1964) d F Francis 80min BL/Col

Traitors of San Angel = TRAIDORES DE SAN ANGEL (1967)

TRAKOM (1964) co-d Troell (= Trachoma)

Tramel s'en fiche = MYSTERE DE LA TOUR EIFFEL, LE (1927)

TRAMENTO (1913) d Baldessarre Negroni w Ghione

TRAMP, THE (1915) d/s Chaplin c Totteroh w Chaplin, Purviance 2rs S & A

TRAMP AND TURPENTINE BOTTLE (1902) p Paul 60ft (= Greediness Punished)

TRAMP, TRAMP, TRAMP (1926) d Harry Edwards co-st Capra w Langdon, J Crawford 5831ft pc Langdon r FN

TRANQUILLO POSTO IN CAMPAGNA, UN (1968) d/co-st/co-s Petri w V Redgrave *106min (= A Quiet Place in the Country)

TRANSATLANTIC (1931) d W Howard c Howe w M Loy, Montgomery 78min Fox

Transatlantic Tunnel = TUNNEL, THE (1935)

TRANS-EUROP EXPRESS (1966) d/s/w Robbe-Grillet w Trintignant 92min

TRANSFIGURATIONS, LES (1909) d Cohl anim 122m

TRANSGRESSION (1931) d Brenon w K Francis 72min RKO

TRANSIT (1966, uf) d Wicki co-s/fpl Max Frisch

TRANSMISSIONS HYDRAULIQUES, LES (1955) d Leenhardt 33min

Transport of Fire = TRANSPORT OGNYA (1929)

TRANSPORT OGNYA (1929) d Alexander Ivanov s Zarkhi, Heifitz 2106m (= Transport of Fire)

TRAP, THE (1958) d/co-p/co-s Panama co-p M Frank c Fapp co-a Pereira w Widmark, Cobb *84min Par (= The Baited Trap)

Trap, The = PAST (1950)

TRAPEZE (1956) d C Reed s R Webb c Krasker m M Arnold w Lancaster, Curtis, Lollobrigida CS* 106min

Trap for Cinderella, A = PIEGE POUR CENDRILLON (1965)

TRAPIANTO, I (1969) d Steno *100min

TRAPPED (1949) d R Fleischer 79min r EL

Trapped in Tangiers = AGGUATO A TANGIERI (1957)

TRAQUE, LE (1950) d Tuttle w Signoret 91min (= Gunman in the Streets)

TRASH (1970) d Paul Morrisey p Warhol *103min

TRATTA DELLE BIANCHE, LA (1952) d Comencini co-p Ponti, De Laurentiis co-s Pietrangeli w Gassmann, Loren, Rossi-Drago 96min (= Girls Marked Danger-/White Slave Trade)

TRAUMENDE MUND, DER (1932) d/co-s Czinner co-s Mayer fm Beethoven, Wagner w Bergner 2541m Pat

TRAUMEREI (1944) d/co-s Harald Brown 110min Ufa

TRAUM VON LIESCHEN MULLER (1961) d Käutner

TRAVELING BOY (1950) d/s C and R Eames c C Eames *

TRAVELING EXECUTIONER, THE (1970) d/p Smight c Lathrop m Goldsmith *94min MGM

TRAVELING SALESLADY (1935) d Enright c Barnes w Blondell 64min WB

TRAVERSEE DE PARIS, LA (1956) d Autant-Lara s/di Aurenche, Bost fn Marcel Aymé w Gabin, Bourvil, De Funès 85min (= Pig Across Paris)

TRAVERSEUR D'ATLANTIQUE, LE (1936) d Joannon

TRAVIATA, LA (1949) d Gallone m Verdi 82min (= The Lost One)

TRAVIATA '53 (1953) d Cottafavi m Fusco w De Filippo 99min r

T.R. BASKIN (1971) d Ross *89min

TRE AQUILOTTI, I (1942) co-d Rossellini w Sordi

TREASON (1933) d G Seitz 61min Col

TREASURE GIRL (1930) d Boleslavsky sh Pat

TREASURE ISLAND (1920) d/p M Tourneur fn RL Stevenson w Chaney 6rs

TREASURE ISLAND (1934) d V Fleming s Mahin fn Stevenson co-c June, Rosson m Stothart w Beery, L Barrymore 103min MGM

TREASURE ISLAND (c1938) d Bradley sh

TREASURE ISLAND (1950) d Haskin fn Stevenson c F Young w Newton *96min pc Disney r RKO

Treasure Mountain, The = TAKURA NO YAMA (1929)

Treasure of Birds' Island, The = POKLAD PTACIKO OSTRAVA (1952)

Treasure of Kalifa = STEEL LADY, THE (1953)

TREASURE OF LOST CANYON, THE (1951) d Tetzlaff fn (The Treasure of Franchard) RL Stevenson c Metty w W Powell 81½min U

Treasure of San Gennaro = OPERAZIONE SAN GENNARO (1965)

TREASURE OF THE GOLDEN CONDOR (1953) d/s Daves c Cronjager co-a Wheeler w Wilde *93min Fox

TREASURE OF THE SIERRA MADRE, THE (1948) d/co-s J Huston p Blanke co-s Rossen (uc) fn B Traven c McCord m M Steiner w Bogart, W Huston, (J Huston) 126min WB

Treatise on Japanese Bawdy Song, A = NIHON SHUNKA-KO (1967)

TRE CORSARI, I (1952) d Soldati fn Emilio Salgari 77min pc Ponti, De Laurentiis (= The Three Pirates)

TREE GROWS IN BROOKLYN, A (1945) d Kazan c Shamroy a Wheeler m A Newman w McGuire, Blondell, Nolan, (Marsh) 128min Fox

TRE FILI FINO A MILANO (1958) d Olmi *18min

Treichville = MOI, UN NOIR (1958)

TREIZE JOURS EN FRANCE (1968) d Lelouch, Reichenbach 115min r (= Challenge in the Snow)

TRELAWNEY OF THE WELLS (1916) d/p Hepworth fpl Sir Arthur Pinero 4875ft

TRE MENO DUE (1920) d Genina co-st Camerini

TRENO DEL SABATO, IL (1963) d/co-s Sala w Rossi-Drago 110min r (= The Saturday Train)

TRE NOTTI D'AMORE (1964) TS*
ep LA VEDOVA d/co-s Castellani co-s Gherardi w Catherine Spaak
ep LA MOGLIE BAMBINA d Rossi m Fusco w Catherine Spaak

TRENTE ANS OU LA VIE D'UN JOUEUR (1903) d Zecca Pat

TRENT'S LAST CASE (1920) d C Brook

TRENT'S LAST CASE (1929) d Hawks fn E C Bentley c Rosson w Crisp 96min Fox

TRENT'S LAST CASE (1952) d/p H Wilcox w Welles, Lockwood 90min r BL

TRESA (1915) d/s/w Ghione

TRES CAUTOS (1949) d Berlanga

TRE SENTIMENTALI, I (1920) d/s Genina

TRES ESPEJOS (1947) d Vajda

TRESOR DE CANTENAC, LE (1950) d/s/w Guitry 95min

TRESORS DE SATAN, LES (1902) d Méliès 50m

TRESPASSER, THE (1929) d/p/s Goulding co-c Toland, Barnes w Swanson, Holden 91min r UA
TRE STORIE PROIBITE (1952) d/co-st/co-s Genina c Aldo w Rossi-Drago, Ferzetti 115min (= Three Forbidden Stories)
33.333 (1924) d/s Molander SF
TRETYA MESHCHANSKAYA (1927) co-d/co-s Room co-d/co-dec Yutkevitch 2025m (= Three Meshchanskaya Street/Bed and Sofa)
TRE VOLTI DELLA PAURA, I (1963) d/co-s Bava fsts Chekhov, Snyder, Tolstoi w Karloff *95min (= Black Sabbath)
TRE VOLTI, I (1964) d Bolognini p De Laurentiis c Martelli, Di Palma m Piccioni w Sordi, R Harris S* 120min (PREFAZIONE d Antonioni w De Laurentiis)
TRIAGE, LE (1940) d Clément sh
TRIAL (1955) d Robson c Surtees co-a Gibbons m Amfitheatrof w G Ford, McGuire, A Kennedy 105min MGM
Trial, The = PROCES, LE (1963)
Trial of Joan of Arc, The = PROCES DE JEANNE D'ARC, LE (1961)
TRIAL OF MARY DUGAN, THE (1941) d McLeod c Folsey w R Young 90min MGM
Trial of Mironov, The = PROTSESS MIRONOVA (1920)
Trial of the Social Revolutionaries, The = PROTSESS ESEROV (1922)
Trial of the Three Million, The = PROTSESS O TROKH MILLIONAKH (1926)
TRIAL OF VIVIENNE WARE, THE (1932) d W Howard w J Bennett, Pitts 60min Fox
TRIALS OF OSCAR WILDE, THE (1960) d/s K Hughes des Adam w Finch, Mason 70* 123min
TRIANGOLO GIALLO, IL (1917) d/s Ghione (4 parts)
TRIA TULA, LA (1964) d/co-s Picazo
TRIBULATIONS D'UN CHINOIS EN CHINE, LES (1965) d De Broca fn Jules Verne c Séchan m Delerue w Belmondo, Andress *110min AA (= Up To His Ears/Up To Here)
Tribunal of Honour, The = SUD CHESTI (1945)
TRIBUTE TO A BAD MAN (1956) d Wise pc Surtees co-a Gibbons m Rozsa w Cagney CS* 95min MGM
TRICETJEDNA VE STINU (1964) d/co-st J Weiss 90min (= Ninety on the Shade)
TRICHEURS, LES (1958) d Carné c C Renoir w Belmondo (= Youthful Sinners)
Tricky Girl = KARAKURI MUSUME (1927)
TRIFLING WOMEN (1922) d/p/st Ingram c J Seitz w Novarro 8000ft MGM
TRI GEROINI (1938) d/s/e Vertov, Elisabeth Svilova 1rl (= Three Heroines)
TRIGULLIO MINORE (1947) d Risi sh
TRILBY (1917) d M Tourneur 2nd d C Brown fn G Du Maurier
TRILOGY (1969) d/p Perry co-s Truman Capote co-c Brun w Page 100min r AA eps MIRIAM/AMONG THE PATHS TO EDEN/A CHRISTMAS MEMORY Truman Capote's Trilogy)
TRIMMED IN SCARLET (1923) d Conway 4765ft U
TRINACTA KOMANTA (1968) d Vavra (= The Thirteenth Chamber)
TRINADTSAT (1937) d/co-s Romm 86min (= The Thirteen)
TRIO (1950) eps MR KNOWALL and THE VERGER d Annakin st/co-s W Somerset Maugham co-c Unsworth 91min BL r JAR
TRIO (1967) d/st Mingozzi pc Baldi 105min
TRIP, THE (1967) d/p Corman *85min AI
TRIPES AU SOLEIL, LES (1958) d/co-st Bernard-Aubert 105min
TRI PESNI O LENINYE (1934) d/s/e Vertov 67min (= Three Songs of Lenin)
TRIPLE CROSS (1966) d T Young c Alekan w Plummer, Brynner, Schneider, T Howard *140min
TRIPLE TROUBLE (1918) Compilation including parts of WORK (1915), POLICE (1916), and LIFE (1915, uf); also footage shot (1918) co-d/co-s/w Chaplin w Purviance, W Ruggles 2rs S & A
Trip on the Ice, A = AUF EIS GEFUHRT (1915)
Trip Through The Columbia Exposition, A = TRIP AROUND THE PAN-AMERICAN EXPOSITION, A (1901)
TRIP AROIUND THE PAN-AMERICAN EXPOSITION, A (1901) d Porter 261ft Ed (= A Trip Through the Columbia Exposition)
TRIP TO PARIS, A (1938) d St Clair 63min Fox
TRI SESTRY (1964) d/s Samsonov fpl Anton Chekhov S 112min (= Three Sisters)
TRISTA LET TOMU (1956) d Petrov *107min (= 300 Years Ago)
TRISTANA (1970) d/co-s/ad Bunuel w Deneuve *105min
TRISTI AMORI (1943) d Gallone
TRI TOLSTYAKA (1966) d Batalov, Josif Shapiro co-s/w Batalov (= The Three Fat Men)
TRIUMPH (1924) d/p De Mille c Glennon w Pitts 8288ft FPL r Par
TRIUMPH DES WILLENS (1936) d Riefenstahl 120min (= Triumph of the Will)
Triumph of the Will = TRIUMPH DES WILLENS (1936)

TRI VEJCE DO SKLA (1937) d Frič (= Three Eggs in a Glass)
TRI VSTRECHI (1948) d Pudovkin, Yutkevitch, Alexander Ptushko *93min (= Three Encounters)
TROFEI D'AFRICA (1954) d Quilici sh
TROG (1971) d F Francis w J Crawford *93min
317 SECTION, LA (1965) d/fn Schoendoerffer c Coutard 94min
TROIS CHAMBRES A MANHATTAN (1965) d/co-s Carné fn Georges Simenon c Schuftan w Girardot, Ronet, Ferzetti
TROIS ENFANTS DANS LE DESORDRE (1966) d/co-s Joannon w Bourvil S* 95min Gau
TROIS FEMMES, TROIS AMES (1951) d Michel fn Maupassant 104min (ep ZORA c Alekan/ep CORA-LIE/ep MOUCHE)
TROIS FONT LA PAIRE, LES (1957) co-d/s Guitry co-d Clément Duhour c Agostini w Simon, Carette 75min Gau
TROIS HOMMES EN CORSE (1949) d Decaë
TROIS JOURS A VIVRE (1956) d/s Grangier w Moreau 85min
TROIS MOUSQUETAIRES, LES (1953) d André Hunebelle s Audiard fn Alexandre Dumas w Bourvil *120min
TROIS-SIX-NEUF (1937) d/w Rouleau
TROIS TELEGRAMMES (1950) d/co-ad/di Decoin c Hayer m Kosma 83min (= Three Telegrams/Paris Incident)
TROJAN WOMEN, THE (1971) d/co-p/s Cacoyannis fpl Euripides m Theodorakis w K Hepburn, V Redgrave
TROLD KAN TAEMMES (1914) d/s Madsen
TRONE DE FRANCE, LE (1936) d Alexeieff anim
TRONO E LA SEGGIOLA, IL (1918) d Genina
TROOPER HOOK (1957) d/co-s Warren w Stanwyck, McCrea 81min r UA
TROPIC OF CANCER (1969) d/p/co-s Strick fn Henry Miller co-e Meyers *88min Par
Troppa Bella = AMANTE SEGRETA, L' (1941)
TROTS (1952) d Molander s Sjöman w H Andersson, Dahlbeck, Kulle 95min SF
TROUBLE INDEMNITY (1950) d J Hubley anim* 6min UPA r Col
TROU, LE (1960) d/co-s/co-di Becker co-s/co-di/fn Giovanni co-s Aurel c Cloquet w (Catherine Spaak) 115min (= The Hole)
Troubadour, The = TROVATORE, IL (1950)
TROUBLE ALONG THE WAY (1953) d Curtiz c Stout w J Wayne, D Reed, C Coburn 110min WB
TROUBLE BREWING (1924) d/s Semon, James Davis w Semon 2rs Vit
TROUBLED WATERS (1936) d Albert Parker w Mason
Troubled Waters = NIGORIE (1953)
TROUBLE IN MOROCCO (1937) d Schoedsack 60min Col
TROUBLE IN PARADISE (1932) d/p Lubitsch s Raphaelson c Milner dec Dreier w M Hopkins, K Francis, H Marshall, C Ruggles, Horton 80min Par
TROUBLEMAKER, THE (1964) co-st/co-s/w Flicker 81min
Trouble Makers = HIGH TENSION (1936)
Troubles = MAKING A LIVING (1914)
TROUBLE SHOOTER, THE (1924) d Conway w Mix 6rs Fox
Troubleshooter = MAN WITH A GUN (1955)
Troubles of a Tired Traveller, The = UNDRESSING EXTRAORDINARY (1901)
TROUBLESOME COLLAR, THE (1903) p Paul 90ft
TROUBLE WITH ANGELS, THE (1966) d Lupino c Lindon m Goldsmith w R Russell, H Mills 112min Col
TROUBLE WITH GIRLS, THE (1969) d Tewkesbury w Presley, Carradine, Price *97min r MGM
TROUBLE WITH HARRY, THE (1955) d/p Hitchcock s J Hayes fn Jack Trevor Story c Burks co-a Pereira m Herrmann w MacLaine *99min Par
TROUBLE WITH WIVES, THE (1925) d St Clair 6400ft FPL
TROU NORMAND, LE (1952) d Jean Boyer w Bardot, Bourvil 100min
TROUVAILLE DE BUCHU, LA (1916) d/s Feyder w Rosay 141m Gau
TROVATORE, IL (1950) d/co-s Gallone m Verdi 104min (= The Troubadour)
TRUE BLUE (1918) d/st/s F Lloyd 6rs Fox
TRUE CONFESSION (1937) d W Ruggles p Lewin c Tetzlaff m Hollander w Lombard, MacMurray, J Barrymore 84min Par
True Friends = VERNYE DRUZYA (1954)
TRUE GLORY, THE (1945) d C Reed, Kanin co-s Ustinov m Alwyn 84min r Col
TRUE GRIT (1969) d Hathaway p Wallis c Ballard m E Bernstein w J Wayne *128min Par
TRUE HEART SUSIE (1919) d/p Griffith w L Gish 6rs
TRUE STORY OF JESSE JAMES, THE (1957) d N Ray rm THE JAMES BROTHERS (1939) c Joe MacDonald co-a Wheeler c Harline w R Wagner, J Hunter, Moorehead, Carradine CS* 92min Fox (= The James Brothers)
TRUE STORY OF LILLI MARLENE, THE (1944) d/s/w Jennings 30min Crown
TRUET LYKKE (1914) c Blom

TRUE TO LIFE (1943) d G Marshall co-st Barzman c C Lang co-a Dreier m V Young co-songs Carmichael w Tone, D Powell, De Carlo 94min Par
TRUE TO THE NAVY (1930) d Tuttle di H Mankiewicz c Milner w Bow, March 71min Par
TRULLI DI ALBEROBELLO, I (1943) d Chiari
TRUMAN CAPOTE (1966) d/c A and D Maysles 29min TV
Truman Capote's Trilogy = TRILOGY (1969)
TRUMPIN' TROUBLE (1926) d Thorpe
TRUNK CONVEYOR (1954) d/n L Anderson 38min
TRUNK CRIME (1939) d R Boulting p J Boulting 50min pc R and J Boulting
TRUST, THE (1915) d/w Chaney 1rl
TRUT (1944) d/s/c/e Sucksdorff 19min SF
TRUTH ABOUT COMMUNISM, THE (1963) n Reagan sh
Truth About Our Marriage = VERITE SUR LE BEBE DONGE, LA (1951)
TRUTH ABOUT SPRING, THE (1965) d Thorpe w J Mills, H Mills *102min r U
Truth Cannot Be Hidden, The = HUSZ EURE EGYMASTOL (1962)
Tsar Wants To Sleep, The = PORUCHIK KIZHE (1934)
TSENA CHELOVEKA (1928) d Danskoi, Mikhail Averbach 1900m (= Man's Value)
TSUKIGATA HANPEITA (1925) d Kinugasa
TSUKIGATA HANPEITA (1956) d/s Kinugasa (2 parts)
TSUKI NO WATARIDORI (1951) d/s Kinugasa (= Migratory Birds Under the Moon)
TSUMA (1953) d Naruse Toho (= A Wife)
TSUMA NO HIMITSU (1924) d Kinugasa (= Secret of A Wife)
TSUMA NO KOKORO (1956) d Naruse w Mifune (= Wife's Heart)
TSUMA TOSHITE ONNA TOSHITE (1961) d Naruse (= As a Wife, as a Woman)
TSUMA YO BARA NO YONI (1935) d/s Naruse (= Wife, Be Like a Rose)
Tsuruhachi and Tsurujiro = TSURUHACHI TSURUJIRO (1938)
TSURUHACHI TSURUJIRO (1938) d/s Naruse w Yamada (= Tsuruhachi and Tsurujiro)
TSUYOMUSHI ONNA TO YOWAMUSHI OTOKO (1968) d Shindo S 97min Sho (= Operation Negligé/ Strong Woman, Weak Man)
TSVET NAD ROSSIEI (1947, ur) d Yutkevitch s/fpl Nicholai Pogodin (= Light Over Russia)
TUDOR ROSE (1936) d/s Stevenson p Balcon e Fisher w J MIlls 78min (= Lady Jane Grey)
TUE MANI SUL MIO CORPO, LE (1970) d Rondi *95min (= Shocking)
TU ES DANSE ET VERTIGE (1967) d Coutard sh
TU ES PIERRE (1958) d Agostini CS* 90min
TUGBOAT ANNIE (1933) d LeRoy c Toland w Dressler, Beery, O'Sullivan, R Young 87min MGM
TUGBOAT GRANNY (1956) d Freleng anim* 7min WB
TU IMAGINES ROBINSON (1968) d Pollet *
TULIPE NOIRE, LA (1963) d/co-s Christian-Jaque fn Dumas c Decaë w Delon, Tamiroff 70* 115min
TULSA (1949) d Heisler p Wanger co-s F Nugent c Hoch w S Hayward, Preston, Armendariz 90min EL
TU M'AS SAUVE LA VIE (1950) d/s/fpl/w Guitry w Fernandel 89min
TUMBLEWEEDS (1925) d King Baggott c August w W Hart 7rs pc W Hart
Tu i e tueras point = NON UCCIDERE (1961)
Tuning His Ivories = LAUGHING GAS (1914)
TUNES OF GLORY (1960) d Neame w Guinness, J Mills *107min r UA
TUNNEL SOUS LA MANCHE OU LE CAUCHEMAR FRANCO-ANGLAIS, LE (1907) d Méliès 330m (30 parts)
TUNISIAN VICTORY (1943) d R Boulting (uc), Capra co-m Alwyn (uc), Tiomkin co-n W Huston (uc) 76min British and US Service Film Units
TUNNEL, DER (1933) d C Bernhardt c Krampf w Gabin (= Le Tunnel)
Tunnel, Le: French version of TUNNEL, DER (1933)
TUNNEL, THE (1935) d Elvey w W Huston, G Arliss 94min (= Transatlantic Tunnel)
TUNNEL OF LOVE, THE (1958) d Gene Kelly c Bronner w D Day, Widmark CS* 98min MGM
Tunnel 28 = ESCAPE FROM EAST BERLIN (1962)
TURBINA (1941) d/s Vavra
TURBINE D'ODIO (1941) d Gallone
Turkeys in a Row = SHICHIMENCHO NO YUKUE (1924)
TURKSIB (1929) d/st/co-s Turin 1666m
TURNABOUT (1940) d/p Roach c Brodine w Menjou, M Astor 83min r UA
TURNING POINT, THE (1952) d Dieterle c Lindon co-a Pereira w Holden, E O'Brien, A Smith 85min Par
TURN IN THE ROAD, THE (1918) d/s K Vidor 50min
TURN THE KEY SOFTLY (1953) d/co-s J Lee c Unsworth 81min JAR
TURN TO THE RIGHT (1922) d Ingram co-s Mathis c J Seitz 6rs MGM
TUSALAVA (1928) d Lye 9min
TUTTA LA CITTA CANTA (1945) d/co-s/e Freda co-s Fellini 87min (= Sei Per Otto, Quarantotto)
TUTTA LA VITA IN VENTIQUATTRO ORE (1944) d Bragaglia

431

TUTTI A CASA (1960) d/co-s Comencini p De Laurentiis w Sordi, Reggiani 115min (= *Everybody Go Home*)

TUTTI INAMORATI (1959) d Giuseppe Orlandini supn/co-s Rossi co-s Festa Campanile w Mastroianni 105min (= *Everybody in Love*)

TUTTLES OF TAHITI, THE (1942) d C Vidor p Lesser c Musuraca w Laughton 91min RKO

TUTTO PER LA DONNA (1940) d/co-st/co-s Soldati

TVA MANNISKOR (1945) d/co-s/co-e Dreyer c Fischer

TVARBALK (1966) d/s/e J Donner w H Anderson 90min (= *Rooftree*)

Tvillingsystrarna = LANDSHOVDINGENS DOTTRAR (1915)

TWEET AND SOUR (1956) d Freleng anim* 7min WB

TWEETIE PIE (1947) d Freleng anim WB

TWEETY'S CIRCUS (1955) d Freleng anim* 7min WB

TWEET ZOO (1957) d Freleng anim* 7min WB

TWELVE ANGRY MEN (1957) d Lumet co-p/s/fpl Rose co-p H Fonda c B Kaufman m K Hopkins w H Fonda, Cobb 95min r UA

Twelve Chapters About Women = JOSEI NI KANSURU JUNISHO (1954)

Twelve Hours To Live = E PIU FACILE CHE UN CAMELLO ... (1950)

12 MILES OUT (1927) d Conway w J Gilbert, J Crawford 7400ft Metro

Twelve Millions = ALLEMAN (1964)

TWELVE O'CLOCK HIGH (1949) d H King p Zanuck c Shamroy co-a Wheeler m A Newman w Peck 132min Fox

TWELVE-TEN (1919) d/p Brenon

TWELVE TO THE MOON (1960) d Bradley c J Alton 74min Col

TWENTIETH CENTURY (1934) d/p Hawks s/fpl MacArthur, B Hecht c August w J Barrymore, Lombard 91min Col

25th Hour, The = VINGT-CINQUIEME HEURE, LA (1966)

24 DOLLAR ISLAND, THE (1926, uf) d/s/e Flaharty 20min

Twenty-Four Eyes = NIJUSHI NO HITOMI (1954)

Twenty-Four Hours of a Secret Life = CHIKAGAI NIJUYOJIKAN (1947)

24 HOURS OF A WOMAN'S LIFE (1952) d Saville w Oberon *75min r AA (= *Affair in Monte Carlo*)

Twenty Hours = HUSZ ORA (1964)

Twenty Million Dollar Mystery, The = ZUDORA (1914-15)

TWENTY MILLION SWEETHEARTS (1934) d Enright co-si Wald c Hickox w D Powell, G Rogers 89min WB

TWENTY MINUTES OF LOVE (1914) d Sennett w Chaplin 1rl Key (= *He Loved Her So/Cops and Watchers*)

20 MULE TEAM (1940) d Thorpe co-s Maibaum w Beery, A Baxter 84min MGM

21-87 (1963) d Arthur Lipsett p Low

21 MILES (1942) d Watt 8min

TWENTY PLUS TWO (1961) d J Newman w Crain, Moorehead 102min AA (= *It Started In Tokyo*)

20 POUNDS A TON (1955) d L Anderson 5min

20,000 LEAGUES UNDER THE SEA (1954) d R Fleischer p Disney fn Jules Verne co-c Planer sp eff Iwerks e Elmo Williams w Mason, K Douglas, Lukas, Lorre CS* 126min

TWENTY THOUSAND YEARS IN SING SING (1932) d Curtiz w Tracy, B Davis 81min FN

23½ HOURS LEAVE (1919) d H King p Ince fst Mary Roberts Rinehart 5rs FPL

23 PACES TO BAKER STREET (1956) d Hathaway c Krasner co-a Wheeler m Harline w Miles, V Johnson CS* 103min Fox

Twenty Two Misfortunes = DVADTSAT DVA NES-CHASTYA (1930)

Twenty Years of Soviet Cinema = KINO ZA DVADTSAT LET (1940)

TWICE A MAN (1963) d/s/c/e Markopoulos 16mm* 60min

Twice on a Certain Night = ARU YO FUTATABI (1956)

TWICE TWO (1933) d James Parrott p Roach w Laurel, Hardy 12min r MGM

TWICE UPON A TIME (1953) d Pressburger w Hawkins 75min

TWILIGHT FOR THE GODS (1958) d Pevney c Glassberg w Hudson, Charisse, A Kennedy *120min U

Twilight in Tokyo = TOKYO BOSHOKU (1957)

TWIN HUSBANDS (1922) d St Clair 2rs

TWIN PAWNS, THE (1920) d/s Perret fn (*Woman in White*) Wilkie Collins Pat

TWIN'S TEA PARTY (1898) p Paul 1rl (= *Children At Table*)

TWIN TRIGGERS (1926) d Thorpe

TWIRLIGIG (1952) d McLaren anim 3min

TWISTED NERVE (1968) d/co-s R Boulting m Herrmann w H Mills *118min pc J and R Boulting r BL

Twisted Road, The = THEY LIVE BY NIGHT (1948)

TWISTED TRIGGERS (1926) d Thorpe w Arthur 4470ft

Twist of Fate = BEAUTIFUL STRANGER, THE (1954)

Two Acres Of Land = DO BIGHA ZAMIN (1953)

TWO AGAINST THE WORLD (1932) d A Mayo 81min WB

TWO AGAINST THE WORLD (1936) d William McGann c Hickox w Bogart 64min WB

TWO ALONE (1934) d E Nugent c Andriot w Pitts 75min RKO

Two American Audiences = GODARD ON GODARD (1969)

TWO AND TWO MAKE SIX (1961) d F Francis 89min BL

TWO ARABIAN KNIGHTS (1927) d Milestone co-p H Hughes c August, Gaudio w Karloff 7450ft r AA

Two Are Guilty = GLAIVE ET LA BALANCE, LE (1962)

TWO BAGATELLES (1952) d McLaren 16mm anim* 2min NFBC

2 BAROQUE CHURCHES IN GERMANY (1955) d/s C and R Eames c C Eames *10½min

Two-buldi-two = DVA-BULDI-DVA (1929)

TWO COCKNEYS IN A CANOE (1899) p Hepworth 50ft

Two Colonels, The = DUE COLONELLI (1962)

TWO CROWDED HOURS (1931) d M Powell 3999ft Fox

Two Daughters (US) = TEEN KANYA (1968)

TWO DAUGHTERS OF EVE (1912) w L Gish

TWO DOWN AND ONE TO GO (1945) d Capra US Army

TWO-FACED WOMAN (1941) d Cukor p G Reinhardt c Ruttenberg co-dec Gibbons m Kaper chor R Alton w Garbo, M Douglas, Constance Bennett, R Gordon 94min MGM

TWO FACES OF DR JEKYLL, THE (1960) d Fisher S* 88min r Col (= *House of Fright*)

TWO FATHERS (1944) d/s Asquith 13min WB

TWO FISTED (1935) d Cruze w Tamiroff 60min Par

TWO-FISTED RANGERS (1939) d JH Lewis 62min Col

TWO-FISTER, THE (1926) d Wyler 2rs U

TWO FLAGS WEST (1950) d Wise st/co-s F Nugent c Shamroy co-a Wheeler m A Newman w Cotten, Darnell, J Chandler, Wilde 92min Fox

TWO FLAMING YOUTHS (1927) d John Waters co-t H Mankiewicz w Fields 5319ft Par

TWO FOOLS IN A CANOE (1898) p Hepworth 50ft

TWO FOR THE ROAD (1967) d/p Donen c Challis m Mancini w A Hepburn, Finney PV* 112min pc Donen r Fox

TWO FOR THE SEESAW (1962) d Wise p W Mirisch c McCord m Previn w Mitchum, MacLaine PV 120min r UA

TWO FOR TONIGHT (1935) d Tuttle c Struss w J Bennett, B Crosby 61min Par

Two Frosts, the = DVA MRAZICI (1954)

TWO GIRLS AND A SAILOR (1944) d Thorpe p Pasternak c Surtees a Gibbons w V Johnson, Allyson, Gardner 124min MGM

Two Grilled Fish = FUTATSU-NO YAKIZAKANA (1968)

TWO GUYS FROM MILWAUKEE (1946) d D Butler co-st/co-s Diamond c Edeson m Hollander w (Bogart) 90min WB

TWO GUYS FROM TEXAS (1948) d D Butler co-s Diamond co-c Edeson chor Prinz w Malone 84min WB (= *Two Texas Knights*)

Two Half times In Hell = KET FELIDO A POKOLBAN (1961)

TWO-HEADED SPY, THE (1959) d De Toth w Hawkins 93min Col

TWO HEARTS IN WALTZ TIME (1934) d Gallone 79min

2 IN A TAXI (1941) d Florey 7rs Col

Two in the Shadow = MIDARE-GUMO (1967)

TWO KINDS OF WOMEN (1932) d William C De Mille c Struss w M Hopkins 75min Par

TWO LEFT FEET (1963) d/p R Baker 93min BL

Two Little Birds = NIWA NO KOTORI (1922)

TWO LOVERS (1928) d/p Niblo p S Goldwyn w R Colman, Lukas, Banky 8136ft r UA

TWO LOVERS (1961) d Walters p Blaustein s Maddow c Ruttenberg m Kaper w MacLaine, Laurence Harvey, Hawkins CS* 100min MGM

TWO MEMORIES (1909) d Griffith 1rl Bio

Two Men and a Wardrobe = EWAG LUDZIE Z SZASA (1959)

TWO MEN OF THE DESERT (1913) d Griffith w Carey, Crisp, Marsh 1rl Bio

TWO MOUSEKETEERS, THE (1951) d Hanna, Barbera p Quimby anim* 7min MGM

TWO MRS CARROLLS, THE (1947) d Peter Godfrey p Hellinger c Marley w Bogart, Stanwyck, A Smith 99min WB

TWO MULES FOR SISTER SARA (1970) d D Siegel fst Boetticher w MacLaine, Eastwood PV* 116min

TWONKY, THE (1953) d/p/s Oboler c Biroc w Conreid 72min r UA

TWO O'CLOCK COURAGE (1945) d A Mann 66min RKO

TWO O'CLOCK IN THE MORNING (1928) d Stone

Two of a Kind = ROUNDERS, THE (1914)

TWO OF A KIND (1951) d Levin fn (*Lefty Farrell*) J Grant c Guffey w E O'Brien, L Scott 75min Col

TWO OLD BOYS AT THE MUSIC HALL (1900) d G Smith

TWO ON THE TILES (1951) d Guillermin 72min

TWO ORPHANS, THE (1915) d/s Brenon 7rs Fox

Two Orphans, The = DUE ORFANELLE, LE (1942)

Two or Three Things I Know About Her = DEUX OU TROIS CHOSES QUE JE SAIS D'ELLE (1966)

Twopenny Magic = ZWEIGROSCHENZAUBER (1929)

Two Pennyworth of Hope = DUE SOLDI DI SPERANZA (1951)

Two People = TO (1964)

Two People = TVA MANNISKOR (1945)

TWO RODE TOGETHER (1961) d J Ford s F Nugent c Lawton m Duning w J Stewart, Widmark, S Jones, McIntire *109min Col

Two Sauries = NIHIKO-NO SAMA (1959)

TWO SECONDS (1932) d LeRoy c Polito w Robinson 68min FN

TWO SMART PEOPLE (1946) d Dassin c Freund co-a Gibbons w Ball, Cook, Nolan 93min MGM

Two Stone Lanterns = FUTATSU DORO (1933)

TWO TARS (1928) d James Parrott p Roach supn/st McCarey w Laurel, Hardy (3rs) r MGM

Two Texas Knights = TWO GUYS FROM TEXAS (1948)

TO THE ENDS OF THE EARTH (1948) d Stevenson p Buchman c Guffey w D Powell 109min Col

TWO TICKETS TO BROADWAY (1951) d Charles V Kern p H Hughes c Cronjager, Wild w J Leigh, Ann Miller *106min RKO

2001: A SPACE ODYSSEY (1968) d/p/co-s Kubrick co-s/fst (*The Sentinel*) A C Clarke c Unsworth co-m R & J Strauss Cinerama PV* 139min MGM

2000 WOMEN (1944) d/co-s Launder co-s Gilliat 97min JAR

2 Times 2 are Sometimes 5 = KETSZER KETTO NEHA OT (1954)

Two Vikings, The = HAR KOMMER BARSARKARNA (1965)

TWO VIRGINS (1969) d Lennon, Yoko Ono *19min

TWO WEEKS (1920) d Franklin w C Talmadge 4000ft WB

TWO WEEKS IN ANOTHER TOWN (1962) d Minnelli p Houseman s Schnee fn Shaw c Krasner m Raksin w K Douglas, Robinson, Charisse, Trevor CS* 107min MGM

Two Weeks in September = A COEUR JOIE (1967)

TWO WEEKS TO LIVE (1943) d St Clair 76min

TWO WEEKS WITH LOVE (1950) d Rowland p J Cummings co-a Gibbons w J Powell, Montalban, D Reynolds 92min MGM

Two Women = CIOCIARA, LA (1961)

TWO WORLDS (1930) d/p Dupont 9914ft

TWO YANKS IN TRINIDAD (1942) d Ratoff 84min Col

TWO YEARS BEFORE THE MAST (1946) d J Farrow p/co-s S Miller fn RH Dana jr c Laszlo m V Young w Ladd, Bendix 98min Par

TYOMIEHEN PAIVAKIRJA (1967) d/p/co-s/c/e Jarva 90min (= *A Worker's Diary*)

Typhoid = TIFUSARI (1963)

TYPHON SUR NAGASAKI (1957) d Ciampi c Alekan w Marais, Darrieux *

TYPHOON, THE (1914) co-d Ince w Borzage 1200m

TYRANNISKE FASTMANNEN, DEN (1912) d/s/w Stiller 664m

TYSTNADEN (1963) d/s Ingmar Bergman c Nykvist mf JS Bach w Thulin, Lindblom 95min SF (= *The Silence*)

UBERGANG UBER DEN EBRO, DER (c1964) d Gatti TV

UBIISTVO NA ULITSYE DANTE (1956) d/co-s Romm *105min (= *Murder on Dante Street*)

UBIITSI VYKHODYAT NA DOROGU (1942) d Pudovkin, Yuri Tarich co-s Pudovkin fpl Brecht 7rs (= *Murderers are at Large*)

U-Boat 29 = SPY IN BLACK, THE (1939)

U-Boat 55 (UK) = HAIE UND KLEINE FISCHE (1957)

U-BOOTE WESTWARTS (1941) d Rittau 100min UFA

U-BU (1951) d Quilici sh

UCCELLACCI E UCCELLINI (1966) d/s Pasolini w Toto 86min (= *The Hawks and the Sparrows*)

UCHITEL (1939) d/s Gerasimov 106min (= *The Teacher*)

UDAYER PATHE (1942) d Roy

UDVARI LEVEGO (1949) d Balasz

UGETSU MONOGATARI (1953) d/co-s Mizoguchi p Nagata c Miyagawa w Mori, Kyo 96min Dai

UGLY AMERICAN, THE (1963) d/p George England s Stern co-a Golitzen w Brando *120min U

UJRAELOK (1920) d Fejos

UKHABY ZHIZNI (1928) d/co-s Room 2080m (= *Hard Life*)

UKHOD VELIKOVO STARTSA (1912) d Protazanov 800m (= *Departure of a Grand Old Man*)

UKIFUNE (1957) d/s Kinugasa (= *Floating Vessel*)

UKIGUMO (1955) d Naruse w Mori 124min Toho (= *Floating Clouds*)

UKIGUSA (1959) d/co-s Ozu rm UKIGUSA MONO-GATARI (1934) c Miyagawa w Kyo *119min Dai (= *Floating Weeds/Parting at Dusk*)

UKIGUSA MONOGATARI (1934) d Ozu Sho (= *A Story of Floating Weeds*)

UKIYO BURO (1929) d/s Gosho (= *The Bath Harem*)

UKJENT MANN (1952) d/s Henning Jensen

ULICA GRANICZNA (1948) d/co-s A Ford 116min (= *Border Street/That Others May Live*)

ULICKA V RAJI (1936) d Fric c Heller (= *Paradise Road*)

ULISSE (1955) d/co-s Camerini co-s B Hecht, Shaw p Ponti, De Laurentiis co-c Rosson, Tonti w Mangano, K Douglas, Quinn *104min (= *Ulysses*)

ULTIMA AVVENTURA, L' (1931) d/co-s Camerini

ULTIMA CARTA, L' (1913) d Baldessarre Negroni w Ghione
ULTIMA IMPRESA, L' (1917) d/s/w Ghione
ULTIMA LIVREA, L' (1920) d/p/s/w Ghione
ULTIMA NEMICA, L' (1937) d Barbaro
ULTIMATUM (1938) d Wiene, Siodmak (uc) w Von Stroheim, Parlo
ULTIMI GIORNI DI POMPEI, GLI (1926) d Gallone fn Bulwer Lytton (= The Last Days of Pompeii)
ULTIMI GIORNI DI POMPEII, GLI (1959) d Mario Bonnard co-s Tessari w Reeves S* 105min (= The Last Days of Pompeii)
ULTIMISSIME DELLA NOTTE (1923) d/p/s/w Ghione
ULTIMO AMORE (1946) d Luigi Chiarini co-s Rondi
ULTIMO LORD, L' (1926) d/pc/s Genina
ULTIMO PARADISO, L' (1956) d/st/co-s Quilici S* 95min (= The Last Paradise)
ULTIMO TRAVESTIMENTO, L' (1916) d Genina
ULUOPENA HRANICE (1947) d/co-s J Weiss (= The Stolen Frontier)
ULYSSE OU LES MAUVAISES RENCONTRES (1948) d Astruc w Gélin 16mm sh
Ulysses (UK) = ULISSE (1955)
ULYSSES (1967) d/p/co-s Strick fn James Joyce 140min
UMARETE WA MITA KEREDO (1932) d/st Ozu 89min Sho (= I Was Born, But . . .)
UMBERTO D (1952) d/co-p/co-ad De Sica st/co-s Zavattini c Aldo 80min
UMI NO BARA (1945) d Kinugasa (= Rose of the Sea)
UMI NO HANABI (1951) d Kinoshita (= Sea of Fireworks)
UMI NO YARODOMO (1957) d/s Shindo (= Harbour Rats)
UNACCUSTOMED AS WE ARE (1929) d Lewis Foster p Roach st McCarey w Laurel, Hardy (2rs) r MGM
UNAFRAID, THE (1915) d/s De Mille pc Lasky
UNBEKANNTE, DIE (1936) d/co-s Wisbar w Jurgens 2537m
UNBEKANNTE MORGEN, DAS (1923) d/p/s A Korda w Krauss * 2280m
UNBEZAHMBARE LENI PEICKERT, DIE (1969) d Kluge
UNCENSORED (1942) d Asquith co-s Rattigan w Glenville 167min BL
UNCERTAIN GLORY (1944) d Walsh co-st May c Hickox w Flynn, Lukas 102min WB
UNCERTAIN LADY (1934) d Freund w Horton 66min U
UNCHANGING SEA, THE (1910) d Griffith fst Charles Kingsley 1rl Bio
UNCHARTED CHANNELS (1920) d H King 5rs
UNCHARTED WATERS (1933) d Anstey p Grierson
UNCLE, THE (1964) d/co-s D Davis 87min BL
Uncle Harry = STRANGE AFFAIR OF UNCLE HARRY, THE (1945)
UNCLE JAKE (1933) d Cline s Sennett 2rs Par
UNCLE TOM'S CABIN (1903) d Porter 507ft Ed
UNCLE VANYA (1958) co-d/co-p/w Tone co-d John Goetz fpl Anton Chekhov
Unconquered = NEPOKORENNIYE (1945)
UNCONQUERED (1947) d/p De Mille co-s Charles Bennett c Rennahan co-a Dreier m V Young w G Cooper, Goddard, Karloff 147min Par
UND DAS IST DIE HAUPTSACHE (1931) d/p May 2413m
UNDEAD, THE (1957) d/p Corman
UNDEFEATED (1969) d A McLaglen c Clothier w J Wayne, Hudson PV* 118min Fox
UNDEN FREADRELAND (1914) d/s Madsen
UNDER AGE (1941) d Dmytryk 60min Col
UNDER A TEXAS MOON (1930) d Curtiz w M Loy 82min WB
UNDER CAPRICORN (1949) d/co-p Hitchcock s Bridie c Cardiff cost Furse w Ingrid Bergman, Cotten *116min WB
UNDERCOVER (1943) d Sergei Nolbandov w (S Baker) 88min
UNDERCOVER GIRL (1950) d Pevney w A Smith 83min U
UNDERCOVER MAN (1949) d JH Lewis p Rossen s Boehm c Guffey w G Ford 85min Col
UNDER COVER OF NIGHT (1937) d G Seitz c C Clarke 72min MGM
Undercover Rogue (US) = WHITE VOICES (1963)
UNDER CRIMSON SKIES (1920) d Ingram 6rs U
Undercurrent = YORU NO KAWA (1956)
UNDERCURRENT (1946) d Minnelli p Berman c Freund co-a Gibbons m Stothart w K Hepburn, R Taylor, Mitchum 116min MGM
UNDER EIGHTEEN (1932) d A Mayo w Foster 77min WB
UNDER FALSK FLAGG (1935) d Molander SF
UNDERGROUND (1928) d Asquith 7982ft
UNDERGROUND (1941) d V Sherman p J Warner, Wallis c Hickox 95min WB
UNDER MINDERNES TRAE (1913) d Madsen st Blom
UNDER MONTANA SKIES (1930) d Thorpe 58min
UNDER MY SKIN (1950) d Negulesco fst (My Old Man) Hemingway co-a Wheeler m Amfitheatrof w Garfield, Presle 86min Fox
UNDER ONE ROOF (1949) d L Gilbert UN Film Board
UNDER PRESSURE (1935) d Walsh co-st/co-s B Chase c Mohr w V McLaglen 72min Fox
Under Silk Garments = ITSWARERU SEISO (1951)

UNDER SKAEBNENS HJUL (1913) d Madsen
UNDERSTANDING HEART, THE (1927) d Conway 7rs MGM
UNDER THE BLACK EAGLE (1928) d WS Van Dyke 5901ft MGM
UNDER THE DAISIES (1913) d Van Dyke Brooke w N Talmadge 2rs Vit
UNDER THE GREENWOOD TREE (1929) d Harry Lachman ad Launder fn Thomas Hardy t Gilliat 8386ft
UNDER THE GUN (1950) d Tetzlaff w Conte 84min U
UNDER THE LASH (1921) d S Wood w Swanson 5675ft FPL r Par
Under the Paris Sky (UK) = SOUS LE CIEL DE PARIS COULE LA SEINE (1950)
Under the Phrygian Star = POD GWIAZDA FRYGIJSKA (1954)
UNDER THE RED ROSE (1924) d Crosland 10rs
UNDER THE RED ROSE (1937) d Sjöström co-s Bjro c Périnal, Howe w Veidt, Annabella 81min
UNDER THE TONTO RIM (1933) d Hathaway fn Zane Gray c Stout 63min Par
UNDER THE TOP (1918) d Crisp s Emerson, Loos 5rs FPL
UNDER THE YUM YUM TREE (1963) d/co-s Swift c Biroc w Lemmon, Lynley *110min Col
UNDERTOW (1949) d Castle c Glassberg w Hudson 70min U
UNDER TWO FLAGS (1916) p J Gordon Edwards fn Ouida w Bara 6rs Fox
UNDER TWO FLAGS (1922) d/ad Browning fn Ouida 8rs
UNDER TWO FLAGS (1936) d F Lloyd p Zanuck fn Ouida w Colman, Colbert, v McLaglen, R Russell 103min Fox
Underverket = MIRAKLET (1913)
UNDERWATER (1954) d J Sturges c Wild w J Russell, Roland 99min RKO
UNDERWATER WARRIOR (1958) d Marton c Biroc w Dailey CS 90min MGM
UNDERWORLD (1927) d Von Sternberg st B Hecht ad Furthman c Glennon dec Dreier w C Brook, G Bancroft, Semon 7453ft Par
UNDERWORLD STORY, THE (1950) d Endfield c Cortez w H Marshall 79min r UA (= The Whipped)
UNDER YOUR HAT (1940) d Elvey 79min r BL
UNDER YOUR SPELL (1936) d Preminger w Ratoff 62min Fox
UN, DEUX, TROIS, QUATRE! (1960) d T Young c Alekan co-dec Wakhévitch cy Chevalier w Charisse *140min 4 parts (= Black Tights)
UNDRESSING EXTRAORDINARY (1901) p Paul 200ft (= The Troubles of a Tired Traveller)
UNDYING MONSTER, THE (1942) d Brahm c Ballard co-a R Day co-m Raksin 60min Fox
UNE ET L'AUTRE, L' (1967) d/s Allio c Badal w Noiret *81min (= The Other One/Skin Deep)
Unexpected (UK) = IMPREVISTO, L' (1961)
UNEXPECTED UNCLE (1941) d Peter Godfrey p Garnett co-s Daves w C Coburn 67min RKO
UNFAITHFUL (1931) d Cromwell c C Lang w Lukas 70min Par
UNFAITHFUL, THE (1947) d V Sherman p Wald c E Haller m M Steiner w Ayres, Sheridan 109min WB
Unfaithful = UTRO (1966)
UNFAITHFULLY YOURS (1948) d/p/s P Sturges c Milner co-a Wheeler m A Newman w Harrison, Darnell 105min Fox
Unfaithfuls, The = INFEDELI, LE (1952)
UNFINISHED BUSINESS (1941) d/p La Cava m Waxman w I Dunne, R Montgomery 96min U
UNFINISHED DANCE, THE (1947) d Koster p Pasternak c Surtees co-a Gibbons m Stothart w M O'Brien, Charisse 101min MGM
Unfinished Love Song, The = PESN LYUBVI NE-DOPETAIA (1919)
Unfinished Story = NEOKONCHENNAYA POVEST (1955)
UNFINISHED SYMPHONY (1934) co-d/ad Asquith 91min
Unforeseeable Novelties = IMPREVISIBLE NOUVEAUTES (1961)
UNFORGIVEN, THE (1960) d J Huston, 2nd d Fernandez s Maddow c Planner m Tiomkin w Lancaster, A Hepburn, Bickford, L Gish, A Murphy CS* 121min r UA
UNGDOMSAVENTYR, EN (1921) d/s Molander SF
UNGKARLSPAPPAN (1939) d Molander SF
UNGLASSED WINDOWS CAST A TERRIBLE RE-FLECTION (1953) d Brakhage 16mm si 35min
UNGUARDED HOUR, THE (1936) d S Wood w L Young, Tone 90min MGM
UNGUARDED MOMENT, THE (1956) d Keller co-st R Russell c Daniels co-a Golitzen w Esther Williams *95min U
UNGUARDED WOMEN (1924) d Crosland 6rs FPL
UNHEILBRINGENDE PERLE, DIE (1913) d/s May 3rs
UNHEIMLICHE GAST, DER (1922) d Duvivier
UNHEIMLICHE GESCHICHTEN (1919) d/p/s R Oswald fsts Poe and RL Stevenson w Veidt
UNHEIMLICHE GESCHICHTEN (1932) d R Oswald rm 1919 w Wegener 89min (= The Living Dead)
Unholy Desire (US) = AKAI SATSUI (1964)

UNHOLY NIGHT, THE (1929) d L Barrymore fst B Hecht w Karloff 2878m MGM
UNHOLY PARTNERS (1941) d LeRoy c Barnes a Gibbons w Robinson, Dalio 94min MGM
UNHOLY THREE, THE (1925) d Browning w Chaney 6848ft MGM
UNHOLY THREE, THE (1930) d Conway ad/di E Nugent, JC Nugent w Chaney, E Nugent 75min MGM
Unholy Tour, The (US) = STRANGER CAME HOME (1954)
UNHOLY WIFE, THE (1957) d J Farrow c Ballard m Amfitheatrof w Steiger * 95min RKO
Uninhibited, the (US) = PIANOS MECANIQUES, LES (1965)
UNINVITED, THE (1944) d Lewis Allen p C Brackett c C Lang co-a Dreier m V Young w Milland 98min Par
UNION PACIFIC (1939) d/p De Mille c Milner co-a Dreier chor Prinz co-m Antheil w Stanwyck, McCrea, Tamiroff, Preston, Quinn 135min Par
UNION STATION (1950) d Maté s Boehm co-a Dreier c Fapp w Holden 80min Par
UNIVERMAG (1922) d Vertov 600m (= State Department Store)
UNIVERSE (1960) co-d/co-dec Low co-d/s Kroitor co-c Koenig 28min NFBC
UNKNOWN, THE (1927) d/st Browning w Chaney, J Crawford 5517ft MGM
UNKNOWN LOVE, THE (1919) d Perret Pat
UNKNOWN MAN, THE (1951) d Thorpe c Mellor co-a Gibbons w Pidgeon 86min MGM
UNKNOWN TERROR (1957) d Warren c Biroc S 77min Fox
UNKNOWN TREASURES (1926) d A Mayo 6rs
UNNATURAL HISTORY CARTOONS (1926–27) d Lantz, Clyde Geronimi, Dave Hand anim series pc Bray
UNNEPI VACSORA (1956) d Revesz 98min (= Gala Dinner)
UNPAINTED WOMAN, THE (1919) d Browning fn Sinclair Lewis 6rs U
Unreconciled = NICHT VERSOEHNT (1965)
Unrecorded Victory, An = SPRING OFFENSIVE (1940)
Unscrupulous Ones, The = CAFAJESTES, OS (1962)
UNSEEN, THE (1945) d Lewis Allen p Houseman co-s R Chandler c J Seitz co-a Dreier w McCrea, H Marshall 81min Par
UNSEEN ENEMY, AN (1912) d Griffith w L Gish, Carey 1rl Bio
UNSER TAGLICH BROT (1940) d/co-s Dudow m Eisler 104min Defa
UNSINKABLE MOLLY BROWN, THE (1964) d Walters as-p Edens c Fapp w D Reynolds PV* 128min MGM
UNSTERBLICHE GELIEBTE (1956) d V Harlan 106min
UNSTERBLICHE HERZ, DAS (1939) d/co-s V Harlan 107min Tob
UNSUSPECTED, THE (1947) d Curtiz w Rains, Constance Bennett 103min WB
UNTAMED (1930) d Conway w J Crawford, Montgomery 7911ft MGM
UNTAMED (1955) d H King co-a Wheeler m Waxman w Power, S Hayward, Moorehead CS* 111min Fox
UNTAMED FRONTIER (1952) d Fregonese w Cotten, Winters * 75min U
UNTAMED LADY, THE (1926) d Tuttle w Swanson 6132ft FPL r Par
Untamed Woman = ARAKURE (1957)
UNTAMED YOUTH (1957) d HW Koch 80min WB
UNTEL PERE ET FILS (1940) d/co-s Duvivier p Graetz co-s/di Achard, Charles Spaak m Wiener w Raimu, Jouvet, Morgan wv Boyer 115min (= Heart of a Nation)
Unter Achzehn = NOCH MINDERJAHRIG (1957)
UNTER AUSSCHLOSS DER OFFENTLICHKEIT (1937) d Wegener 96min
UNTER DEN BRUCKEN (1945) d/co-s Käutner w Neff (as Knef) 91min UFA
UNTERNEHMEN TEITPNENSCHWERT (1958) d A and A Thorndike Defa
UNTER JUDEN (1923) d Christensen
UNTIL I DIE (1940) d B Hecht
Until Our Next Meeting = MATA AU HIMADE (1950)
Until the Day We Meet Again = MATA AU HI MADE (1932)
Until the Day We Meet Again = MATA AU HIMADE (1950)
UNTIL THEY SAIL (1957) d Wise m Raksin c Ruttenberg w J Simmons, Fontaine, P Newman, Laurie CS 95min MGM
UNTITLED FILM (1959) d Rice
UNTITLED SHORT (1949) d Rivette 16mm 20min
Unusual Case, An = CHASTNYI SLUCHAI (1934)
Unvanquished (UK) = APARAJITO (1957)
UNWELCOME MRS HATCH, THE (1914) d Dwan 4rs FPL
UNWILLING HERO, AN (1921) d/p Badger 5rs pc Goldwyn
U OLUJI (1952) d Mimica w Lattuada (= In the Storm)
UOMINI, CHE MASCALZONI!, GLI (1932) d/co-st/co-s Camerini co-s Soldati w De Sica

UOMINI CONTRO (1970) d/co-p/co-s Rosi m Piccioni * 105min

UOMINI DI MARMO (1954) d Pontecorvo

UOMINI E CIELI (1943) d/st/s/m De Robertis c Bava

UOMINI E I TORI, GLI (1959) d Mingozzi sh

UOMINI E LUPI (1956) d/co-st De Santis co-st/co-s Petri w Mangano, Montand, Armendariz CS* 105min

UOMINI IN PUI (1955) d Nicolo Ferrari p Antonioni sh

UOMINI-OMBRA (1955) d/s De Robertis

UOMINI SUL FONDO (1941) d/p/st/co-s/co-m De Robertis co-s Rossellini 70min (= SOS Submarine)

UOMO A META, UN (1966) d/p/st/co-s De Seta 95min (= Almost a Man)

UOMO DA BRUCIARE, UN (1962) d/s Orsini, P and V Taviani 93min (= A Man for Burning)

UOMO DAI PALLONCINI, L' (1968) d/co-s Ferreri p Ponti c Tonti w Mastroianni, Catherine Spaak S* (complete version of OGGI DOMANI E DOPO DOMANI ep L'UOMO DAI CINQUE PALLONI)

UOMO DELLA CROCE, L' (1943) d/co-s Rossellini 88min

UOMO DI PAGLIA, L' (1957) d/co-s Germi 87min (= The Seducer – Man of Straw/A Sordid Affair)

UOMO, LA BESTIA E LA VIRTU, L' (1953) d/co-s Steno fpl Pirandello w Welles, Toto * (= Man, Beast and Virtue)

U OZERA (1970) d/s Gerasimov S 155min (= By the Lake)

UP FROM THE BEACH (1965) d Parrish w Robertson, R Crawford CS 99min Fox

UP IN ARMS (1944) d E Nugent p Goldwyn c Rennahan w Kaye, D Andrews, Cook, Dumont, (V Mayo) *105min r RKO

UP IN MABEL'S ROOM (1944) d Dwan c Lawton 76min r UA

UPON THIS ROCK (1970) d/s Harry Rosky c Tonti w Welles, Evans, Bogarde, R Richardson *90min

UPPBROTT (1948) d/s/e Sucksdorff 10min SF

Upper Hand, The = DU RIFIFI A PANAME (1965)

UP PERISCOPE (1958) d G Douglas w Garner, E O'Brien S* 111min WB

UPPERWORLD (1934) d Del Ruth B Hecht c Gaudio w Astor, G Rogers, Rooney 72min WB

UP, RIGHT AND WRONG (1947) d Dunning, Low

UP ROMANCE ROAD (1918) d H King 5rs

Upside Down = HUMAN FLY, THE (1896)

UPSTREAM (1927) d J Ford c C Clarke 5510ft Fox

UPSTREAM (1931) d Elton 18min

UP THE DOWN STAIRCASE (1967) d Mulligan *124min WB

UP THE RIVER (1930) d/co-s(uc) J Ford c August w Tracy, Bogart, (Parrish) 92min Fox

UPTIGHT! (1968) d/co-s Dassin rm THE INFORMER (1935) c B Kaufman des Trauner *104min Par

Up to Here (US) = TRIBULATIONS D'UN CHINOIS EN CHINE, LES (1965)

Up to His Ears = TRIBULATIONS D'UN CHINOIS EN CHINE, LES (1965)

UPTOWN NEW YORK (1932) d Schertzinger c Brodine 80min

U.P. TRAIL, THE (1921) d Conway 6000ft

Up Your Legs Forever = LEGS (1970)

URAL (1918) d Kuleshov c Tissé

URANIUM BOOM (1956) d Castle p Katzman 67min Col

URASHIMA TARO NI KOEI (1946) d Naruse (= The Descendants of Taro Urashima)

URBANISME AFRICAIN (1962) d/s Rouch 16mm

URILANY SZOBAT KEVES (1937) d Balasz

URLAUB AUF SYLT (1957) d/s A and A Thorndike

URLO, L' (1970) d/s Brass *100min

Ursus in the Valley of the Lions = URSUS NELLA VALLE DEI LEONI (1961)

URSUS NELLA VALLE DEI LEONI (1961) d Bragaglia CS* 92min (= Ursus in the Valley of the Lions)

URUWASHIKI SAIGETZU (1955) d Kobayashi (= Beautiful Days)

URTAIN, EL REY DE LA SELVA HUMANA (1970) d Summers *100min (= Urtain, His Family, His Friends)

Urtain, His Family, His Friends = URTAIN, EL REY DE LA SELVA HUMANA (1970)

USA, EN VRAC (1956) d/p/s/c Lelouch 16mm * sh

U SAMOVO SINEVO MORYA (1936) d Barnet, S Mardanov 72min (= By the Bluest of Seas)

USO (1963) (= When Women Lie/Lies)
ep d Linugasa s Shindo
ep d Yoshimura

UTA ANDON (1943) d Naruse w Yamada (= Song of a Lantern)

UTA ANDON (1960) d/s Kinugasa (= The Lantern)

UTAE WAKODOTACHI (1963) d Kinoshita (= Sing Young People)

UTAGE (1967) d Gosho S 99min Sho (= Rebellion in Japan)

UTAH BLAINE (1957) d Sears p Katzman 75min Col

UTAH KID, THE (1930) d Thorpe w Karloff 6rs

Utamaro and His Five Women = UTAMARO O MEGURU GONIN NO ONNA (1940)

UTAMARO O MEGURU GONIN NO ONNA (1946) d Mizoguchi Sho (= Utamaro and His Five Women)

UTAZAS A KOPONYAM KORUL (1970) d/s Revesz *84min (= Journey Round My Skull)

Utopia = ATOLL K (1950)

UTOSZEZOH (1967) d Fabri 129min (= Late Season)

UTRO (1966) d A Henning Jensen w Bjork 95min (= Unfaithful)

UTRO INDII (1959) d/c Karmen (= Indian Morning)

UTVANDRARNA (1970 r 1971) d/co-s/c/e Troell w Von Sydow CS* 191min SF

UVODNI SLOVO PRONESE (1964) d Pojar anim* 11min (= The Orator/A Few Words of Introduction)

UWAKI WA KISHA NI NOTTE (1931) d/s Naruse (= Fickleness Gets on the Train)

UWASA NO MUSUME (1935) d Naruse (= The Girl in the Rumour)

UWASA NO ONNA (1954) d Mizoguchi c Miyagawa Dai (= The Woman in the Rumour)

Vacances de Max, Les = MAX PART EN VACANCES (1913)

VACANCES DE M. HULOT, LES (1951) d/co-st/co-s/w Tati 96min (= Monsieur Hulot's Holiday)

VACANCES DU DIABLE, LES (1931) d Cavalcanti

VACANCES EN ENFER (1960) d Jean Kerchbron c Fradetal 81min

VACANCES PORTUGAISES, LES (1963) d Kast c Coutard m Delerue w Deneuve, Daniol-Valcroze, Gélin 97min

VACANZA, LA (1971) d/st/co-s/e Brass w V Redgrave *100min

VACANZE A ISCHIA (1957) d/co-s Camerini co-s Festa Campanile, De Seta(uc) c Martelli w De Sica S*

VACANZE COL CANGSTER (1952) d/co-st/co-s Risi w Girotti 90min (= Vacation with a Gangster)

Vacation from Marriage (US) = PERFECT STRANGERS (1945)

Vacation with a Gangster (UK) = VACANZE COL GANGSTER (1952)

VACHE ET LE PRISONNIEUR, LA (1959) d Verneuil s Jeanson w Fernandel 119min

VAD SKA VI GORA UN DA (1958) d P Weiss (= What shall we do now?)

VAGABOND, THE (1916) d/s Chaplin co-c Totheroh w Chaplin, Purviance, Bacon 2rs Mut

Vagabond, The = AWARA (1951)

VAGABOND KING, THE (1930) d/p Ludwig Berger ad/di H Mankiewicz w Jeanette MacDonald 104min Par

VAGABOND KING, THE (1956) d Curtiz c Burks co-a Pereira VV* 88min Par

VAGABOND, LOVER, THE (1929) d Neilan w Dressler 6217ft RKO

VAGABOND TRAIL, THE (1924) d Wellman c August 5rs Fox

VAGHE STELLE DELL'ORSA (1965) d/co-s Visconti co-s Cecchi d'Amico m César Franck w Cardinale 100min (= Of a Thousand Delights/Sandra)

VALENTIN DOBROTIVY (1942) d/co-s Frič

VALERII CHKALOV (1941) d Kalatozov 2783m (= Wings of Victory)

VALERIE (1959) d G Oswald c Laszlo w Ekberg, Hayden 84min r UA

VALIANT, THE (1929) d W Howard co-c Andriot w Muni 61min Fox

VALIANT, THE (1962) d R Baker w J Mills 90min r UA

VALIANT IS THE WORD FOR CARRIE (1936) d/p W Ruggles w Carey 110min Par

VALIGIA DEI SOGNI, LA (1954) d Comencini

VALLE DE LOS CAIDOS, EL (1965) d Marton c Hildyard *26min pc Bronston

Valley Between Love and Death, The = AI TO SHI NO TANIMA (1954)

Valley of Eagles = VALLEY OF THE EAGLES (1951)

VALLEY OF HUNTED MEN, THE (1928) d Thorpe 4520ft r Pat

VALLEY OF SILENT MEN, THE (1922) d Borzage 7rs

VALLEY OF THE DOLLS (1967) d Robson p Weisbart fn Jacqueline Suzann m Previn c Daniels w S Hayward PV* 122min Fox

VALLEY OF THE EAGLES (1951) d/p/s T Young 86min (= Valley of Eagles)

VALLEY OF THE GIANTS, THE (1919) d Cruze 5rs FPL

VALLEY OF THE GIANTS, THE (1938) d Keighley co-s S Miller c Polito m M Steiner w Trevor *79min WB

VALLEY OF THE MOON, THE (1914) d Hobart Bosworth fn Jack London w Conway 7rs

VALLEY OF THE SUN (1942) d G Marshall c Wild w Ball 84min RKO

VALLEY TOWN (1940) d/co-s W Van Dyke co-s Maddow e I Lerner 27min

VALSE BRILLANTE DE CHOPIN (1936) d Ophuls c Planer mf Chopin

VALSE DE PARIS, LA (1950) d/st/s/di Achard c Matras cos Christian Dior w Fresnay 92min

VALSE ROYALE (1935 fi d Grémillon co-dec Röhrig 95min

VAMPING VENUS (1928) d Cline w Fazenda 6021ft FN

VAMPIRE, LE (1945) d/c Painlevé 9min

VAMPIRE DE DUSSELDORF, LE (1964) d/s/w Hossein p Ponti

VAMPIRE LOVERS, THE (1970) d R Baker fst (Carmilla) Sheridan Le Fanu *91min

VAMPIRES, LES (1915–16) d/s Feuillade 1915 1: La Tete Coupee; 2: La Bague qui tue; 3: Le Cryptogramme Rouge/1916 4: Le Spectre; 5; 6: Les Yeux qui fascinent; 7: Satanas; 8: Le Maître de la foudre; 9: L'Homme des poisons (1252m); 10: Les Noces Sanglantes (1410m)

VAMPIRI, I (1956) d/co-s Freda c Bava CS 85min (= Lust of the Vampire)

VAMP TILL READY (1936) d C Chase (as Parrott), Harold Law p Roach w C Chase 2rs MGM

VAMPRYEN ELLER EN KVINNAS SLAV (1912) d/s Stiller w Sjöström

VAMPYR, OU L'ETRANGE AVENTURE DE ALLAN GRAY (1932) d/co-p/co-s Dreyer c Maté dec Warm 70min

VANDET PA LANDET (1946) d/co-s Dreyer sh

VANESSA (1935) d W Howard p Selznick c June m Stothart w H Hayes, Montgomery 74min MGM

Vangelo 70 original title of AMORE E RABBIA (1967 r 1969)

VANGELO SECONDO MATTEO, IL (1964) d Pasolini m Bach, Mozart, Prokofiev, Webern, Bacalov 140min (= The Gospel According to St Matthew)

VANISHED (1971) d Kulik w Widmark, Parker 240min TV

VAN GOCH (1948) d/e Resnais 20min

VANINA (1922) d Von Gerlach s C Mayer w Wegener 1550m

VANINA VANINI (1961) d/co-s Rossellini fn (Chroniques Italiennes and other works) Stendhal w Carol *125min (= The Betrayer)

VANISHING AMERICAN, THE (1925) d G Seitz fn Zane Grey 9916ft FPL r Par

VANISHING PRAIRIE, THE (1954) p Disney sp eff Iwerks *71min

VANISHING VIRGINIAN, THE (1941) d Borzage c Lawton 97min MGM

VANISHING WEST, THE (1928) d Thorpe serial in 10eps

VANITY (1927) d/p Crisp c AC Miller 5923ft Pat

VANITY FAIR (1911) d Blackton Vit

VANITY STREET (1932) d Nicholas Grinde c August w Bickford 68min Col

VANQUISHED, THE (1953) d Edward Ludwig c Lindon co-a Pereira w Payne *84min Par

VANSKELIGT VALG, ET (1913) d/s Madsen

VAR ENGANG, DER (1922) d/co-s Dreyer

VARGTIMMEN (1968) d/s Ingmar Bergman c Nykvist w Von Sydow, Thulin 89min SF (= Hour of the Wolf)

VARHANIK N SVATEHO VITA (1929) d/co-s Frič (= The Organist of St Vita)

VARIATIONS (1941–43) d/c Whitney, James Whitney 16mm series

VARIAZONI SINFONICHE (1949) d/c Bava sh

VAR I DALBY HAGE (1962) d Troell (= Spring in the Meadows of Dalby)

VARIETE (1925) d/s Dupont p Pommer c Freund w Jannings 2844m UFA (= Vaudeville/Variety)

VARIETIES (1971) d/s Bardem c Matras *95min

Variety (US) = VARIETE (1925)

VARIETY GIRL (1947) d G Marshall co-st/co-s Tashlin co-c Lindon co-a Dreier w B Crosby, Hope, G Cooper, Milland, Ladd, Stanwyck, Goddard, Lamour, Lake, Holden, L Scott, Lancaster, Hayden, Preston, Bendix, De Mille, Leisen, G Marshall 83min Par

Variety Lights (UK) = LUCI DEL VARIETA (1950)

VAR I MAJ, DET (1914) d/s Sjöström

Varldens Grymhet = TRADGARDSMASTAREN (1912)

VARSITY (1928) d Tuttle c Stout 70min Par

VARSITY SHOW (1937) d Keighley co-s Wald c Barnes, Polito w D Powell 107min WB

VARUJ! (1947) d/co-s Frič (= The Warning)

Varvara = SELSKAYA UCHITYELNITSA (1947)

VASEN (1962) d/st/s/a Trnka *20min (= Passion)

VASENS HEMMELIGHED (1913) d/s Blom

VASHA ZNAKOMAYA (1927) d/co-s/e Kuleshov dec Alexander Rodchenko 1800m (= Zhurnalistka/The Journalist/Your Acquaintance)

VASYA REFORMATOR (1926) d F Lokatinsky, Dovzhenko, Iosif Rona s Dovzhenki 1603m (= Vasya the Reformer)

Vasya the Reformer = VASYA REFORMATOR (1926)

VATERS LETZTER WILLE, DES (1917) d/p May 4rs

Väter und Söhne: German version of MARKURELLS I WADKOPING (1930)

Vaudeville (UK) = VARIETE (1925)

VAUTOUR DE LA SIERRA, LE (1909) d/s Jasset

VAXDOCKAN (1962) d Mattson 94min (= The Doll)

Vaxelspel = STUDIE V (1955)

V BOLSHOM GORODYE (1927) d/s Donskoi, Mikhail Averbach (= In the Big City)

V DNI OKTYABRYA (1958) d/co-s Vasiliev * 12rs (= In the October Days)

VECCHIA GUARDIA (1934) d/co-s/co-e Blasetti c Martelli

VED FAENGSLETS PORT (1910) d Blom w Nielsen

VEDI NAPOLI E POI MUORI (1951) d Freda songs Freda, Toto 82min (= Perfido Ricatto)

VEDOVA, LA (1955) d/ad Milestone w Tamiroff 90min (= The Widow)

VEDOVO, IL (1959) d/co-st/co-s Risi w Sordi 90min

VEG ZUM NACHBARN (1963) d Vukotic anim (= The Way to the Neighbour)

VEILLEES D'ARMES (1935) d L'Herbier w Annabella, P Renoir 98min

VEINARDS, LES (1962) 94min (= People in Luck)
ep LA VEDETTE d/s De Broca w De Funès, Blanche, Darc

VELBOUD UCHEM JEHLY (1936) d/co-s Vavra

VEL D'HIV (1959) co-d Rossif cy Audiard m Jarre 14min Col

VELIKAYA OTECHESTVENNAYA (1965) d/c Karmen 129min (= The Great Patriotic War)

VELIKAYA SILA (1950) d/s Ermler 105min (= Great Strength)

VELIKII GRAZHDANIN (1938–39) d/co-s Ermler m Shostakovich Part 1 (1938) 117min / Part 2 (1939) 133min (= A Great Citizen)

VELIKII PERELOM (1946) d Ermler 107min (= The Great Turning Point)

VELIKII PUT (1927) d/s/e Shub 2350m (= The Great Road)

VELIKII UTESHITEL (1933) d/s/dec/e Kuleshov fst O. Henry 2693m (= The Great Consoler)

VELIKII VOIN ALBANII SKANDERBEG (1954) d Yutkevich *120min (= The Great Warrior Skander-beg)

VELIKI STRAH (1958) d Vukotic anim* 12min (= The Great Fear)

VELVET FINGERS (1920–21) d/s/w G Seitz Pat serial in 15 eps

VELVET UNDERGROUND AND NICO, THE (1966) d Warhol 16mm 70min

VEM DOMER? (1921) d/co-s Sjöström SF

VENNA D'ORO, LA (1955) d/co-s Bolognini co-s De Santis w Girotti

VENDANGES, LES (1922) d J Epstein

VENDANGES (1929) d/p/s/e Rouquier sh

VENDEMIAIRE (1918) d/s Feuillade (prologue and 3 parts: La Vigne/La Cuvé/Le Vin Nouveau) 3030m

VENDETTA (1942) d J Newman m Amfitheatrof 11min MGM

VENDETTA (1946 r 1950) d M Ferrer (uc: H Hughes, P Sturges, Heisler, Ophuls) p H Hughes s Burnett, P Sturges fn (Colomba) Prosper Merimée co-c Planer 84min RKO

Vendetta della signora, La = BESUCH, DER (1964)

VENDETTA DI AQUILA NERA, LA (1951) d/co-s Freda f Pushkin 82min

VENDETTA DI ERCOLE, LA (1960) d Cottafavi w B Crawford S* 88min (= Goliath and the Dragon)

VENDICATORE, IL (1959) d/w Dieterle S* 110min (= Revolt on the Volga/Dubrowsky)

VENERE IMPERIALE (1958 r 1962) d Castellani(uc), Delannoy w Lollobrigida, Boyd, Ferzetti, Girotti, Presle S* 140min

VENEZIA, CITTA MODERNA (1958) d Olmi S* 15min

VENEZIA, LA LUNA, E TU (1958) d/co-s Risi co-s Festa-Campanile w Manfredi, Sordi *90min (= Venice, the Moon and You)

VENEZIANISCHE NACHT, EINE (1913) d M Reinhardt 1222m

VENGA A PRENDERE IL CAFFE DA NOI (1970) d/co-s Lattuada *98min

VENGANZA, LA (1958) d/s Bardem w Vallone *96min (= Vengeance)

VENGEANCE (1930) d A Mayo c B Reynolds 6283ft

Vengeance = VENGANZA, LA (1958)

VENGEANCE (1962) d F Francis 83min BL

VENGEANCE DE BOUDDHA OU LA FONTAINE SACREE, LA (1901) d Méliès 30m

VENGEANCE DU DOMESTIQUE, LA (1912) d/s/w Linder Pat

Vengeance of the 47 Ronin, The = CHUSHINGURA (1932)

Vengeance of the Gladiators (UK) = SOLO CONTRO ROMA (1962)

VENGEANCE VALLEY (1951) d Thorpe c Folsey co-a Gibbons w Lancaster, R Walker, Dru *82min MGM

VENGERKAK (1917) d Balasz

VENICE: THEME AND VARIATIONS (1957) d/p/c Ivory 16mm * 28min

Venice, The Moon and You (UK) = VENEZIA, LA LUNA, E TU (1958)

VENT D'EST (1969) d/co-s Godard w Rocha *90min (= East Wind)

VENTOTTE TONNELLATE (1953) d Zurlini sh

VENT SE LEVE, LE (1958) d/co-st Ciampi c Thirard w Jurgens 90min

VENUS (1929) p Louis Mercanton w C Talmadge 8rs r UA

VENUS AVEUGLE, LA (1940) d/s Gance c Burel, Alekan w Romance 100min

VENUS DE L'OR, LE (1938) d/co-s Delannoy

VENUS DU COLLEGE, LA (1932) d Duvivier

VENUS ET SES AMANTS (1951) cy Cocteau

Venus Imperiale = VENERE IMPERIALE (1958 r 1962)

VENUS OF VENICE (1927) d Neilan c Barnes w C Talmadge, Hopper 6324ft r FN

VENUS VICTRIX (1917) d Dulac

VERA CRUZ (1954) d Aldrich st B Chase co-s JR Webb c Laszlo m Freidhofer w Lancaster, G Cooper, Romero, Borgnine, Montiel S* 92min r UA

Vera the Lawyer = ADVOKATKA VERA (1937)

VERBOTEN (1958) d/p/s Fuller c Biroc co-m Beethoven, Wagner 87min

VERDENS UNDERGANG (1916) d/s Blom

VERDICT, THE (1946) d D Siegel c E Haller m Hollander w Greenstreet, Lorre 86min WB

VERDUGO, EL (1963) d/co-s Berlanga w Manfredi 110min (= The Executioner/Not on Your Life)

VEREDA DA SALVAÇAO (1965) d/p/s Duarte 100min

VERGINE MODERNE, LA (1954) d/w Pagliero

VERGINE PER IL PRINCIPE, UNA (1965) d/co-s Festa Campanile w Gassmann S* 107min (= A Maiden for the Prince/A Virgin for the Prince)

VERGINI DI ROMA, LE (1960) d Bragaglia, Cottafavi(uc) *90min (= Amazons of Rome/The Virgins of Rome/-Warrior Women)

VERGISS MEIN NICHT (1935) d Genina

VERITAS VINCIT (1919) d/p/co-st May do-dec Leni 3448m (3 parts)

VERITE, LA (1960) d/co-s Clouzot c Thirard w Bardot, Vanel 124min

VERITE SUR LE BEBE DONGE, LA (1951) d Decoin fn Georges Simenon w Darrieux, Gabin 89min (= Truth About Our Marriage)

VERKAUFTE BRAUT, DIE (1932) d/co-s Ophuls f opera (The Bartered Bride) Smetana 76min (= The Bartered Bride)

VERLIEBTE FIRMA, DIE (1931) d/co-s Ophuls 72min

VERLORENE, DIE (1951) d/co-s/w Lorre 90min

VERLORENE PARADIES, DAS (1923) d Ruttmann

VERLORENE SCHATTEN, DER (1921) co-d/w Wegener co-d Rochus Gliese

VERLORENE SCHUH, DER (1922) d/co-s Ludwig Berger c Krampf 2349m

VERNOST MATERI (1967) d/p Donskoi S 90min (part 2) (= A Mother's Devotion)

VERNYE DRUZYA (1954) d Kalatozov *102min (= True Friends)

VERONIQUE ET SON CANCRE (1958) d/s/e Rohmer 20min

VERRAT AN DEUTSCHLAND (1954) d/co-s V Harlan 109min

VERSAILLES (1966) d/s Lamorisse c Alekan *19min

VERSCHLEIERTE BILD VON GROSS KLEINDORF (1913) d May 2rs

VERSCHWORUNG ZU GENUA, DIE (1921) d/co-dec Leni 2500m

VERSO LA VITA (1948) d Risi sh

VERTIGE, LE (1927) d L'Herbier

VERTIGO (1958) d/p Hitchcock as-p Coleman fn (D'Entre Les morts) Pierre Boileau and Thomas Narcejac c Burks co-a Pereira m Herrmann cr Bass w J Stewart, Novak *128min Par

VERUNTERSUCHUNG (1931) d Siodmak p Pommer 93min UFA

VERWEHTE SPUREN (1938) d/co-s V Harlan co-s Von Harbou 82min r Tob

VERWIRRUNG DER LIEBE (1959) d/s Dudow 107min Defa

VERY EYE OF NIGHT (1959) d Deren 15min

Very Handy Man, A (UK) = LIOLA (1963)

VERY HONOURABLE GUY, A (1934) d Bacon 62min WB

VERY IMPORTANT PERSON (1961) d Annakin 98min r JAR

Very Private Affair, A (UK) = VIE PRIVEE (1961)

VERY SPECIAL FAVOUR, A (1965) d M Gordon co-a Golitzen w Hudson, Caron, Boyer *104min U

VERY THOUGHT OF YOU, THE (1944) d/co-s Daves p Wald c Glennon m Waxman w Parker 99min WB

VESELAYA KANAREIKA (1929) d/e Kuleshov w Pudov-kin 6rs (= The Gay Canary)

VESELY CIRKUS (1951) d/co-s/a Trnka *12½min (= The Happy Circus)

VESNA (1947) d Alexandrov w Cherkasov (= Spring)

VESSEL OF WRATH (1938) d Pommer c Hamer w Laughton, Newton 95min co-pc Pommer, Laughton (= The Beachcomber)

VESTERHAVSDRENGE (1950) d/s A and B Henning Jensen (= Boys from the West Coast)

VESTIRE GLI IGNUDI (1954) d Pagliero co-s Charles Spaak w Rossi-Drago, Ferzetti

VESYOYLE REBYATA (1934) d/s Alexandrov (= The Jolly Fellows/Moscow Laughs/Jazz Comedy) 82min

VETEMENTS SIGRAND, LES (1937) d Alexeieff anim

VETER S VOSTOKA (1941) d Room 88min (= Wind from the East)

VETER V LITSO (1930) d Heifitz, Zarkhi 2208m (= Facing the Wind)

VETTA (1956) d J Donner sh

VEUVE EN OR, UNE (1969) d/s Audiard dec D'Eaubonne *87min

VEUVE JOYEUSE, LA (1912) d Emile Chautard w M Tourneur

VEUVES DE QUINZE ANS, LES (1964) d Rouch 25min

VENEZIA, LA GONDOLA (1951) d Sala sh

V FOR VICTORY (1941–43) d McLaren m Souza *2min NFBC

V GORAKH ALA-TAU (1944) d Vertov, Elisabeth Svilova 2rs (= On Mount Ala-Tau)

V GORODYE S (1966) d/s Heifitz fst (Ionycg) Anton Chekhov 105min (= In the Town of S)

V GORAKH YUGOSLAVII (1946) d Room c Tissé 86min (= In the Mountains of Yugoslavia)

V I (1944) p Jennings 10min

VIACCIA, LA (1961) d Bolognini co-s Festa Campanile m Piccioni w Belmondo, Cardinale, Germi 106min (= The Love Makers)

VIA CRUCIS (1918) d Blom s Dreyer

VIA DEI CESSATI SPIRITI (1959) d Baldi

VIA DEI PIOPPONI (1961) d Mingozzi sh

VIA DEL PETROLIO, LA (1966) d/s/cy Bertolucci 16mm RAI (Part 1 Le Origini 48min/Part 2 Il Viaggio 40min/Part 3 Attraverso l'Europa 45min)

VIA EMILIA KM 147 (1949) d Lizzani sh

VIA FAST FREIGHT (1921 ur) d Cruze

VIAGGIO AL SUD (1949) d Lizzani sh

VIAGGIO IN ITALIA (1953) d/co-s Rossellini w Ingrid Bergman, G Sanders 75min (= The Lonely woman)

VIALE DELLA SPERANZA (1953) d/p/co-st/co-s Risi co-s De Santis c Bava w Mastroianni

VIA MARGUTTA (1959) d/st/co-s Camerini m Piccioni 108min (= Run with the Devil)

Vice and Virtue (UK) = VICE ET LA VERTUE, LE (1962)

VICE ET LA VERTU, LE (1962) d/co-s Vadim fn (Justine) De Sade w Hossein, Deneuve, Girardot CS* 100min Gau (= Vice and Virtue)

VICE SQUAD, THE (1931) d Cromwell c C Lang w K Francis, Lukas 80min Par

VICE VERSA (1947) d/st/s/co-p Ustinov co-p Del Giudice c Hildyard 111min

VICHINGO VENUTO DAL SUD, IL (1971) d/co-s Steno *101min

VICIOUS YEARS, THE (1950) d Florey 79min (= The Gangsters We Made)

VICKI (1953) d Horner c Krasner co-a Wheeler w Crain, Peters 85min Fox

VICTIM (1961) d Dearden c Heller w Bogarde 100min JAR

VICTIMAS DEL PECADO (1950) d/co-st/co-s Fernandez c Figueroa

VICTIMES DE L'ALCOOLISME, LES (1902) d/w Zecca 75min Pat

VICTIM OF CIRCUMSTANCES, A (1911) d Sennett w Normand ½rl Bio

VICTIM OF MISFORTUNE, A (1905) p Paul 250ft

VICTOIRE SUR L'ANNAPURNA (1953) d/p/e/co-n Ichac 16mm *52min (= Conquest of Annapurna)

VICTOR HUGO (1951) co-d/s Leenhardt co-d Yvonne Gerber 33min (= Le Père Hugo)

VICTORIA THE GREAT (1937) d H Wilcox c F Young co-e Elmo Williams w Neagle, Walbrook, Henreid 112min

VICTORS, THE (1963) d/p/s Foreman c Challis cr Bass w Peppard, Wallach, Ronet, Moreau, Schneider, Mercouri, Finney, Kjellin PV 175min Col

VICTORY (1919) d/p M Tourneur fn Joseph Conrad w Beery, Chaney 2rs

VICTORY (1940) d Cromwell w March 78min Par

Victory = POBEDA-SAMYI SCHASTLIVYI (1938)

Victory in the Sun = SHORI NO HI MADE (1945)

Victory in the Ukraine and the Expulsion of the Germans from the Boundaries of the Ukrainian Soviet Earth = POBEDA NA PRAVOBEREZHNOI UKRAINYE I IZGNANIE NEMETSIKH ZAKHVATCHIKOV ZA PREDELI UKRAINSKIKH SOVETSKIKH ZEMEL (1945)

VICTORY LANE (1968) d A Mekas

VICTORY THROUGH AIR POWER (1943) d Potter anim p Disney c Rennahan *65min

VIDALITA (1949) d Saslavsky

VIE, UNE (1958) d/co-s Astruc fn Guy de Maupassant c C Renoir w Maria Schell, Marquand *86min

VIE A DEUX, LA (1958) d Clement Duhour s Guitry w Brasseur, Feuillère de Funès, Palmer, Marais, Philipe, Darrieux, Fernandel, Duhour 102min

VIE A L'ENVERS, LA (1964) d/s Jessua 92min (= Life Upside Down)

VIE A REBOURS, LA (1907) d Cohl anim

VIE COMMENCE DEMAIN, LA (1950) d Vedrès m Milhaud 87min

VIE CONJUGALE, LA (1963) d/co-st/co-s Cayatte CS 112min (ep 1 Jean-Marc / ep 2 Françoise)

VIE DE CHATEAU, LA (1965) d/co-s Rappeneau co-s Cavalier cr Borowczk m Legrand w Brasseur, Deneuve, Noiret 93min (= Chateau Life)

VIE DE BOHEME, LA (1941) d L'Herbier fn Henri Murger

VIE DES AUTRES, LA (1955) d Dewever sh

VIE DU CHRIST, LA (1906) d Alice Guy, Jasset

VIE D'UN FLEUVE, LA (1933) d Lods m Jaubert

VIE D'UN HOMME, LA (1938) d Le Chanois

VIE D'UN HONNETE HOMME, LA (1952) d/s/lyr Guitry c Bachelet w M Simon, De Funès

VIE DU VIDE, LA (1952) d Baratier

VIE EST A NOUS, LA (1936) d/co-d/co-s J Renoir, Le Chanois, Becker, Cartier-Bresson co-c Renoir, Bourgoin w Modot 13min French Communist Party

VIE ET LA PASSION DE JESUS CHRIST, LA (1902) d Zecca, Lucien Nonguet w Zecca 350m 18 parts Pat (= La Passion)

VIEIL AGE (1961) d Jaques Giraldeau e Groulx 28min NFBC

VIEILLE DAME INDIGNE, LA (1964) d/s Allio fst Brecht 88min (= The Shameless Old Lady)

VIEILLES DAMES DE L'HOSPICE, LES (1917) d Feyder s Tristan Bernard 523m Gau

VIEJECITO, EL (1959) d Summers sh

VIE, L'AMOUR, LA MORT, LA (1969) d/co-s Lelouch *115min (= Life, Love, Death)

VIE MIRACULEUSE DE THERESE MARTIN, LA (1929) d/s Duvivier co-c Thirard dec Christian-Jaque

VIENNESE NIGHTS (1930) d Crosland co-st/co-s Oscar Hammerstein II w Hersholt, Pidgeon 107min WB

VIE PARISIENNE, LA (1936) d Siodmak fpl Offenbach

VIE PERDUE, UNE (1933) d/w Rouleau

VIE PRIVEE (1962) d/co-s Malle co-s Rappeneau c Decaë dec Evein w Bardot, Mastroianni – 113min r MGM (= A Very Private Affair)

VIEREN MAAR (1954) d Van Den Horst 20min (= Lekko)

VIERGE DU RHIN, LA (1953) d Grangier w Gabin 82min

VIERGES, LES (1968) d/co-s Mocky c Shuftan w Aznavour, Blanche 89min (= The Virgins)

VIER UM DIE FRAU (1920) d/co-s F Lang co-s Von Harbou Dec

VIE SANS JOIE, UNE (1924) d Albert Dieudonné p/s J Renoir co-c Bachelet 1800m (= Catherine)

VIE TELLE QU'ELLE EST, LA (1911–13) d/s Feuillade 1911 Le Chef-lieu de canton (548m); En grève (260m); Le mariage de l'aînée (370m); La Poison (357m); Le Roi Lear au village (360m); La Souris Blanche (313m); Tant que vous serez heureux (440m); La Tare (900m); Le Trust-les batailles de l'argent (600m); Les Vipères (360m) 1912 L'Accident (495m); Les Braves Gens (770m); Le Nain (421m); Le Pont sur l'abime (544m) 1913 S'affranchir (1074m)

VIETNAM (1954) d/c Karmen

VIET-NAM! (1965) d Ivens 40min

VIETNAM, VIETNAM (1968–71, ur) d J Ford c 60min

VIEUX CHALAND, LE (1932) d J Epstein 300m

VIEUX DE LA VIEILLE, LES (1960) d/co-s Grangier w Gabin, Fresnay

VIEW FROM POMPEY'S HEAD, THE (1955) d/p/s P Dunne c Joe Macdonald co-a Wheeler m E Bernstein CS* 97min Fox Secret Interlude

View from the Bridge, A = VU DU PONT (1962)

View from the People Wall: single screen version of THINK (1964–65)

VIGILE, IL (1960) d/co-s Zampa w Sordi, De Sica 100min (= The Cop)

VIGILIA DI MEZZA ESTATE, LA (1959) d Baldi

VIGIL IN THE NIGHT (1940) d/p Stevens fn A J Cronin m A Newman w Lombard 96min RKO

VICHAR (1952) d Fabri (= The Storm)

VIHREA LESKI (1968) d Jaako Pakkasvirta p Jarva

VIKHRI VRAZHDEBNYE (1956) d Kalatozov 126min (= The Hostile Wind)

VIKINGS, THE (1958) d R Fleischer 2nd d Elmo Williams, Canutt c P K Douglas, Bresler c Cardiff e Elmo Williams w K Douglas, Curtis, Borgnine, J Leigh TR* 114min r UA

Viking Women (UK) – VIKING WOMEN VERSUS THE SEA SERPENT (1957)

VIKING WOMEN VERSUS THE SEA SERPENT (1951) d/p Corman 63min

VILDFAGLER (1954) d/co-s Sjöberg SF 100min (= Wild Birds)

VILLA DEI MOSTRI, LA (1950) d/s Antonioni m Fusco 10min

VILLA DESTIN (1921) d L'Herbier

VILLAGE BLACKSMITH, THE (1922) d J Ford fmp Longfellow w D Butler 8rs Fox

Village Bride, The = MURA NO HANAYOME (1927)

Village Feud, The = TABLE AUX CREVES, LA (1951)

VILLAGE HERO, THE (1911) d/w Sennett ½rl Bio

VILLAGE MAGIQUE, LE (1954) d/st/di Le Chanois co-s De Seta (uc) m Kosma w Bose *95min

Village Mill, The = GROMADA (1952)

Village of Tajinko = TAJINKO MURA (1940)

VILLAGE SCANDAL, THE (1915) d/w Arbuckle p Sennett 2rs Tri

VILLAGE TALE (1935) d Cromwell c Musuraca w R Scott 80min RKO

Village Teacher, The = SELSKAYA UCHITELNITSA (1947)

VILLAIN STILL PURSUED HER, THE (1940) d Cline c Ballard w Keaton 65min RKO

VILLANELLE DES BERCEAUX, LA (1932) d J Epstein 300m

VILLA RIDES (1968) d Kulik co-s Peckinpah c Hildyard m Jarre w Brynner, Mitchum PV* 123min Par

VILLA SANTO-SOSPIR, LA (1952) d/p/s/c/w Cocteau * 16mm

VILLES-LUMIERE (1919) d Paul de Roubaix, Enrico *21min

VILLE PAS COMME LES AUTRES, UNE (1956) d/p/s/c Lelouch

VINDEN FRAN VASTER (1942) d Sucksdorff 18min SF

VINDEN OCH FLODEN (1951) d/s/c/e Sucksdorff 10min SF

VINDICTA (1923) d/s Feuillade 1: La Terre qui tremble- (1550m); 2: L'Intrus (1200m); 3: L'Emmuré (1200m); 4: Le Mariage de blanche Césarin (1200m); 5: Soir Nuptial (1000m)

VIND ROSE, DIE (1956) supn/prologue Ivens, Cavalcanti
ep d Jorge Amado
ep d Wu Kuo Yin, Mus Chin Min
ep d Yannik Bellon w Montand, Signoret
ep GIOVANNA d Pontecorvo
ep d/s Gerasimov

VINGARNA (1966) d/s Stiller

VINGT-CINQUIEME HEURE, LA (1966) d/co-s Verneuil p Ponti m Delerue w Quinn, Dalio, M Redgrave, Reggiani FS* 133min (= The 25th Hour)

VINGT DEUX, RUE DE LA VICTOIRE (1966) d/s Moussy TV

VINGT MILLE LIEVES SUR LA TERRE (1960) d/s Pagliero

VINGT/ QUATRE HEURES D'AMANTS (1964) d/s/c Lelouch 20min

VINGT QUATRE HEURES DE LA VIE D'UN CLOWN (1946) d/p/s Melville sh

VINGT QUATRE HEURES EN TRENTES MINUTES (1928) d Lods

VINTI, I (1953) d/co-s Antonioni co-s Cecchi d'Amico, Rosi m Fusco w Mocky 110min (= Youth and Perversion)

VINYL (1965) d Warhol s Ronald Tavel 16mm 70min

VIOL, LE (1967) d/st/s/di Doniol-Valcroze w B Andersson 90min San (= Overgreppet)

Violence = BORYOKU (1952)

Violence at Noon = HAKUCHO NO TORIMA (1966)

VIOLENT IS THE WORD FOR CURLY (1938) d/w C Chase 2rs Col

VIOLENT MEN, THE (1955) d Maté c Guffey m M Steiner w G Ford, Stanwyck, Robinson, Keith CS* 96min Col (= Rough Company)

VIOLENT PLAYGROUND (1958) d Dearden 108min JAR

VIOLENT ROAD (1958) d HW Koch w Keith 86min WB (= Hell's Highway)

VIOLENT SATURDAY (1955) d R Fleischer p Adler s Boehm c C Clarke co-a Wheeler m Freidhofer w Mature, Borgnine, Martin, S Sidney CS* 91min Fox

VIOLENZA, LA (1965) d Mingozzi sh

VIOLETTE NEI CAPELLI (1942) d/s Bragaglia

VIOLINIST, THE (1960) d/p Pintoff *8min

VIOLIN MAKER, THE (1915) d/w Chaney 1rl

VIOLINMAKER OF CREMONA, THE (1909) d Griffith w Pickford 1rl Bio

V.I.P.'S THE (1963) d Asquith p De Grunwald st/s Rattigan c Hildyard w E Taylor, Burton, Welles, Martinelli PV* 119min MGM

Virgin for the Prince, A (UK) = VERGINE PER IL PRINCIPE, UNA (1965)

Virgin from Oyuki = MARIA NO OYUKI (1935)

VIRGINIA (1941) d/p/co-st Edward H Griffith m V Young w Carroll, Hayden, MacMurray *110min Par

VIRGINIA CITY (1940) d Curtiz p J Warner, Wallis co-s H Koch c Polito m M Steiner w Flynn, M Hopkins, R Scott, Bogart 121min WB

VIRGINIAN, THE (1914) d De Mille pc Lasky

VIRGINIAN, THE (1929) d V Fleming fn Owen Wister w G Cooper, W Huston 8717ft Par

VIRGIN ISLAND (1958) d Jackson c F Francis w Cassavetes * 94min BL

VIRGIN OF STAMBOUL, THE (1920) d/co-s Browning 7rs

VIRGIN QUEEN, THE (1955) d Koster p Brackett co-a Wheeler m Waxman c C Clarke w B Davis, H Marshall CS* 92min Fox

Virgins, The (UK) = VIERGES, LES (1963)

Virgins of Rome, The = VERGINI DI ROMA, LE (1960)

VIRGIN SOLDIERS, THE (1969) d John Dexter ex-p Foreman *96min

Virgin Spring, The = JUNGFRUKALLAN (1959)

VIRIDIANA (1961) d/co-s Buñuel m Handel 90min

Virtuous Isidore = ROSIER DE MADAME HUSSON, LE (1950)

VIRTUOUS SIN, THE (1930) d Louis Gasnier, Cukor w W Huston, K Francis, Veidt 80min Par (= Cast Iron)

VIRTUOUS THIEF, THE (1919) d Niblo 4rs FPL

VIRTUOUS VAMP, THE (1919) d David Kirkland p Emerson, Loos w C Talmadge 5rs

VISAGES DE FRANCE (1936) d Kirsanov

VISAGES D'ENFANTS (1925) d Feyder, Rosay s/dec Feyder co-c Burel 2500m

VISAGES DE PARIS (1955) d/c Reichenbach cy Doniol-Valcroze m Legrand *18min

Visit, The = BESUCH, DER (1964)

VISITA, LA (1963) d/co-st/co-s Pietrangeli 115min Fox

VISITE, UNE (1954) d Truffaut c Rivette e Resnais 16mm

VISITE A CESAR DOMELA (1947) d Resnais 16mm sh

VISITE A FELIX LABISSE (1947) d Resnais 16mm sh

VISITE A HANS HARTUNG (1947) d Resnais 16mm sh

VISITE A LUCIEN COUTAUD (1947) d Resnais 16mm sh

Visite à Max Ernst = JOURNEE NATURELLE (1947)

VISITE A OSCAR DOMINGUEZ (1947) d Resnais 16mm sh

VISITEURS DU SOIR, LES (1942) d Carné co-s/co-di J Prevert dec/co-st Trauner, Wakhévitch co-m Kosma w Arletty, Jules Berry 120min (= The Devils' Envoys)

VISIT TO A SMALL PLANET (1960) d Taurog p Wallis fpl Vidal c Griggs w J Lewis 85min Par

VI SOM GAR KOKSVAGEN (1933) d/s Molander SF

VISPA TERESA, LA (1939) d Rossellini c Bava sh

VISSI D'ARTE, VISSI D'AMORE (1952) d Gallone c C Renoir m Puccini w Ferzetti

VITA AGRA, LA (1964) d Lizzani m Piccioni 110min

Vita Avventurosa di Milady, La = BOIA DI LILLA, LA (1952)

VITA DA CANI (1950) d Steno, Monicelli p Ponti c Bava w Lollobrigida 108min (= It's a Dog Life)

VITA DIFFICILE, UNA (1961) d Risi w Sordi 115min pc De Laurentiis (= A Difficult Life)

VITA E BELLA, LA (1944) d/s Bragaglia w Magnani

VITA FRUN (1962) d Mattsson w Bjork (= Lady in White)

VITA SEMPLICE, LA (1945) d/st/s De Robertis

VITA VIOLENTA, UN (1962) d/co-s Rondi, Paolo Heusch fn Pasolini 100min

VITELLONI, I (1953) d/co-st/co-s Fellini co-c Martelli des Chiari m Rota w Sordi 103min (= The Loafers/The Young and the Passionate)

VITTEL (1926) d Autant-Lara sh

VITTNESBORD OM HENNE (1961) d J Donner c Fischer sh

VIVACIOUS LADY (1938) d/p G Stevens w J Stewart, G Rogers, C Coburn 90min RKO

VIVA CISCO KID (1940) d Foster c C Clarke co-a R Day w Romero 70min Fox

VIVA LAS VEGAS (1964) d/co-p G Sidney co-p J Cummings c Biroc w Presley PV* 86min MGM (= Love in Las Vegas)

VIVA L'ITALIA (1960) d/co-s Rossellini * 138min

VIVA MARIA! (1965) d/co-s Malle c Decaë dec Evein w Bardot, Moreau PV* 120min

VIVAN LOS NOVIOS! (1970) d Berlanga *85min

VIVA VILLA! (1934) d Conway, Hawks(uc) p Selznick s B Hecht s Howe, C Clarke w Beery 115min MGM

VIVA ZAPATA! (1952) d Kazan p Zanuck s John Steinbeck c Joe Macdonald co-a Wheeler m North w Brando, Peters, Quinn 113min Fox

VIVE HENRI IV … VIVE L'AMOUR! (1961) d Autant-Lara co-s Aurenche co-s/di Jeanson w De Sica, Mercouri, Brasseur, Darrieux S* 118min r Gau

VIVE LA VIE (1937) d J Epstein

VIVE LE SABOTAGE (1907) d/s Feuillade

VIVERE IN PACE (1946) d/co-st/co-s Zampa p Ponti co-s Cecchi d'Amico m Rota 89min

VIVI O PREFERIBILMENTE MORTI (1969) d/co-s Tessari *92min

VIVRE LA NUIT (1968) d/ad Camus *90min

Vivre Libre = THIS LAND IS MINE (1943)

VIVRE POUR VIVRE (1967) d/co-s Lelouch w Montand, Girardot *130min

VIVRE SA VIE (1962) d/s Godard c Coutard m Legrand w Karina, Brice Parain 85min (= It's my Life/My Life to Live)

Vixen, The (UK) = LUPA, LA (1953)

VIZA NA ZLOTO (1958) d Stiglic 102min (= The False Passport)

VIZIVAROSI NYAR (1965) d Fabri TV (= A Hard Summer)

V KITAI (1941) d/c Karmen (= In China)

VKRADENA VZDUCHOLOD (1966) d/s Zeman * 80min (= The Stolen Airship)

VLADIMIR AND ROSA (1971) d Godard, J P Gorin 16mm *106min

VLADIMIR ILYICH LENIN (1948) d Romm, V Belyaev m Khatchaturian 10rs

VLAST VITA (1945) d Vavra

VLCI JAMA (1957) d/co-s J Weiss 95min (= Wolf Trap)

V LYUDYAKH (1939) d Donskoi fab Maxim Gorky 90min (= My Apprenticeship)

VOCATION IRRESISTIBLE, UNE (1934) d Delannoy sh

VOGLIA DA MORIRE, UNA (1965) d/s Tessari w Girardot, Vallone 100min

VOCE DEL SILENZIO, LA (1952) d/co-s Pabst w Gélin, Marais (= The House of Silence)

VOCE DI PAGANINI, LA (1947) d/co-s De Robertis

VOCI BIANCHE, LE (1963) d/co-s Festa Campanile, Massimo Franciosa w Aimée CS* 100min (= White Voices/Undercover Rogue)

VOGLIA MATTA, LA (1962) d/co-s/w Salce w Catherine Spaak S 105min (= This Crazy Urge/Crazy Desire)

VOGLIO TRADIRE MIO MARITO (1925) d Camerini

VOICE FROM THE MINARET (1923) d F Lloyd w N Talmadge 7rs FN

VOICE IN THE DARK, A (1920) d F Lloyd 4315ft pc Goldwyn

VOICE IN THE MIRROR (1958) d Keller c Daniels co-a Golitzen w Matthau CS 102min U

Voice in the Night, The (US) = FREEDOM RADIO (1940)

VOICE OF BRITAIN, THE (1936) d Stuart Legg p Grierson w Jennings 56min GPO

VOICE OF BUGLE ANN, THE (1936) d Thorpe c E Haller w L Barrymore, O'Sullivan 70min MGM

VOICE OF THE TURTLE, THE (1947) d Rapper c Polito m M Steiner w Reagan, Parker 103min WB

VOICE OF THE WATER, THE (1966) d/s Haanstra *92min

VOICE OF THE WHISTLER (1945) d/co-s Castle 61min Col

VOICE OF THE WORLD (1932) d Elton 3rs

VOICI LE TEMPS DES ASSASSINS (1956) d/co-s/co-di/co-ad Duvivier c Thirard m Wiener w Gabin 113min (= Murder à la carte)

VOIE LACTEE, LA (1968) d/co-s Buñuel w Seyrig *102min (= The Milky Way)
VO IMYA RODINY (1943) d/s Pudovkin, Dmitri Vasiliev w Pudovkin 90min (= In the Name of the Fatherland)
VO IMYA ZHIZNI (1947) d/co-s Heifitz, Zarkhi w Charkasov 101min (= In the Name of Life)
VOINA I MIR (1915) d Protazanov, Vladimir Gardin fn Tolstoi Part 1: 1800m Part 2: 1200m (= War and Peace)
VOINA I MIR (1964–67) d/co-s/w Bondarchuk fn Tolstoi 70* 507min Part 1 Andrei Bolkonsky (1964) / Part 2 Natasha Rostova (1966) / Part 3 Borodino, 1812 (1967) / Part 4 Pierre Bezukhov (1967) (= War and Peace)
VOIOS KERDOJEL (1918) d Balasz
VOIR MIAMI (1962) d/e Groulx
VOISIN-VOISINE (1911) d/s/w Linder Pat
VOITURES D'EAU, LES (1969) d/st Perrault 110min
VOLCAN INTERDIT, LE (1965) d/p Tazieff cy Marker *80min (= The Forbidden Volcano)
VOLCANO (1926) d W Howard c Andriot 5462ft Par-FPL
Volcano (UK) = VULCANO (1950)
Volcano = RENDEZ-VOUS DU DIABLE, LES (1958)
VOLCA NOL (1955) d Stiglic m Prokofiev (= The Living Nightmare)
Volchayevsk Days = VOLOCHAYEVSKIE DNI (1938)
VOLEUR, LE (1933) d M Tourneur
VOLEUR, LE (1967) d/co-s Malle c Decäe w Belmondo *120min r UA
VOLEUR DE FEMMES, LE (1936) d/s Gance 86min
VOLEUR DE PARATONNERRE, LE (1945) d/s Grimault st Aurenche m Wiener anim* 10min
VOLEUR DE TIBIDABO, LE (1964) d/w Ronet w Karina 112min
VOLGA BOATMAN, THE (1926) d De Mille c Marley a Leisen m Reisenfeld 10660ft
VOLGA-VOLGA (1938) d/s Alexandrov 90min
VOLKSFIEND, EIN (1937) d/co-s Steinhoff fpl Henrik Ibsen 102min
VOLKSKRANKHEIT KREBS (1940) d/co-s Ruttmann (= Jeder Achte)
VOLPONE (1939–41) d M Tourneur fpl Ben Jonson w Jouvet 100min
VOLNITSA (1955) d G Roshal s L Trauberg *106min
VOLNYI VETER (1961) d L Trauberg, A tontichkin (= Free Wind)
VOLOCHAYEVSKIE DNI (1938) d/s S and G Vasiliev m Shostakovitch 112min (= Volochayevsk Days)
VOLTAIRE (1933) d John G Adolfi c Gaudio w G Arliss 72min WB
VOLTI DELL'AMORE, I (1923) d Gallone
VOLUNTEER, THE (1943) d/p/s M Powell, Pressburger w R Richardson 40min
VOM BLITZ ZUM FERNSEHBILD (1936) d Richter 8rs
VOM HIMMEL GEFALLEN (1955) d Brahm c Brun w Cotten 86min (= Special Delivery)
VON RICHTOFEN AND BROWN (1971) d/p Corman m Friedhofer *97min r UA (= The Red Baron)
VON RYAN'S EXPRESS (1965) d Robson co-s Mayes c Daniels m Goldsmith w Sinatra, T Howard *117min Fox
VORGLUTEN DES BALKANBRANDES (1912) d/s May 3rs
VORMITTAGSSPUK (1928) d/dec Richter m Hindermith w Milhaud, Hindermith, Richter 450ft (= Ghosts Before Breakfast)
VOR UNS LIEGT DAS LEBEN (1948) d/co-s Rittau 93min (= Die Fünf vom Titan)
VORUNTERSUCHUNG (1931) d Siodmak p Pommer 93min UFA (= Auteur d'une enquete)
VOSTANIE RYBAKOV (1935) d Piscator (= Revolt of the Fisherman)
VOUS N'AVEZ RIEN A DECLARER? (1936) d Joannon, Y Allégret di Anoulih, Aurenche w Brasseur
VOUS VERREZ LA SEMAINE PROCHAINE (1929) d/s/e Cavalcanti w J Renoir
VOYAGE A BIARRITZ, LE (1962) d Grangier w Fernandel, Arletty 92min
VOYAGE AU CONGO (1927) d M Allégret p Andre Gide
VOYAGE DANS LA LUNE, LE (1902) d/p/s/dec/cos/w Méliès 285m 30parts
VOYAGE DANS LE CIEL (1936) d Painlevé
VOYAGE DE BADABOU, LE (1955) d/m Gruel anim
VOYAGE DE LA FAMILLE BOURRICHON, LE (1913) d Méliès fst Eugene Labiche 405m
VOYAGE DU PERE, LE (1966) d De la Patellière w Fernandel, Palmer S* 90min
VOYAGE EN ALGERIE (1950) d Vierny
VOYAGE EN BALLON, LE (1960) d Lamorisse S* 85min
VOYAGE IMAGINAIRE, LE (1925) d/s Clair w Préjean 80min
VOYAGE OF THE 'ARCTIC' OR HOW CAPTAIN KETTLE DISCOVERED THE NORTH POLE (1903) p Paul 600ft
VOYAGE SANS ESPOIR (1944) d Christian-Jaque w Marais
VOYAGES DE GULLIVER (1902) d Méliès fn Jonathon Swift 80m
VOYAGES DE NOCES (1933) d May

VOYAGES DE NOCES EN ESPAGNE (1912) d/s/w Linder Pat
VOYAGE-SURPRISE (1946) d/st/co-ad/co-s/w P Prévert co-ad/di/lyr J Prévert c Bourgoin m Kosma co-dec Trauner w Carol, P Prévert 85min Pat
VOYAGEUR, LE (1956) d Gruel fpm Apollinaire anim 10min
VOYAGEUR DE LA TOUSSAINT, LE (1942) d Daquin fn Georges Simenon w Desailly, Jules Berry, Reggiani 102min
VOYAGEUR SANS BAGAGES, LE (1943) d/co-ad/di/fpl Anoulih co-ad Aurenche c Matras m François Poulenc w Fresnay, P Renoir
VOYANTE, LA (1923 uf) w S Bernhardt
VOYOU, LE (1970) d/co-s/c Lelouch w Trintignant, Doniol-Valcroze *120min (= Simon the Swiss)
VOZVRASHCHENIE MAKSIMA (1937) d/co-s L Trauberg, Kozintsev c Moskvin m Shostakovich 112min (= The Return of Maxim)
VOZVRASHCHENIE VASILIYA BORTNIKOVA (1953) d Pudovkin *92min (= The Return of Vassily Bortnikov)
VRAI JEU, LE (1931) d Leenhardt
V RAIONYE VYSOTY A (1941) d/s Vertov, Elisabeth Svilova (= Height A)
VRAZDA PO CESKU (1967) d/co-s J Weiss 87min (= Murder Czech Style)
VREDENS DAG (1943) d/co-s Dreyer 105min (= Day of Wrath/Dies Irae)
VSE PRO LASKA (1930) d/co-s Frič (= All for Love)
VSEROSSIISKII STAROSTA KALININ (1920) d/s/c/e Vertov (= Kalinin, Starost of Russia)
VSICHNI DOBRI RODACI (1968) d Jasny (= All Good Citizens)
VSKRYTIE MOSHCHEI SERGIYA RADONEZHSKOVO (1920) d/s/co-c Vertov 2rs (= The Exhumation of the Remains of Sergei Radonezhkovo)
V SNEDENEHO KRAMU (1933) d Frič (= The Ransacked Shop)
VSTANOU NOVI BOJOVNICI (1950) d J Weiss 100min (= New Heroes Will Arise)
VSTRECHA NA ELBE (1949) d Alexandrev c Tissé m Shostakovich 110min (= Meeting on the Elbe)
VSTRECHNYI (1932) d/co-s Yutkevich, Ermler m Shostakovich 3170m (= Counterplan)
VU DU PONT (1962) d Lumet p Graetz co-s Aurenche fpl Arthur Miller c Kelber dec Saulnier w Vallone 114min r Par (= A View from the Bridge)
VULCANO (1950) d/p Dieterle a Chiari w Magnani 108min (= Volcano)
VULTURES OF THE SEA (1928) d Thorpe serial in 10 eps
Vyborg Side, The = VYBORGSKAYA STORONA (1939)
VYBORGSKAYA STORONA (1939) d/s L Trauberg, Kozintsev co-c Moskvin m Shostakovich 120min (= The Vyborg Side)
VYNALEZ ZKAZY (1958) d/s Zeman 83min (= An Invention for Destruction)
VYSOTA (1957) d Zarkhi (= The Heights)
VZDUCHOLOD A LASKA (1947) d Brdecka (= The Zeppelin and Love)
VZTEKLY ZENICH (1919) d Karel Lamac co-s Machaty c Heller w Machaty

WABASH AVENUE (1950) d Kaster p Perlberg co-st/co-s Lederer c Arling a Wheeler w Mature, Grable 92min Fox
WACHSFIGUREN KABINETT, DAS (1924) d/dec Leni s Galeen w Dieterle, Veidt, Jannings, Krauss 2147m UFA
WACKIEST SHIP IN THE ARMY, THE (1960) d/s R Murphy c Lawton m Duning w Lemmon CS* 99min Col
WACO (1966) d Springsteen co-a Pereira w J Russell, Keel, Corey TS* 85min Par
WAGA AI (1960) d Gosho S* 96min Sho (= When A Woman Loves)
WAGA KOISESHI OTOME (1946) d Kinoshita (= The Girl I Loved)
WAGA KOI WA MOENU (1948) d Mizoguchi s Shindo Sho (= Flame of My Love)
WAGA SEISHUN NI KUINASHI (1946) d/co-s Kurosawa 110min Toho
WAGA SHOGAI NO KAGAYAKERU HI (1948) d Yoshimura (= The Day Our Lives Shine)
WAGES FOR WIVES (1925) d Borzage 6650ft Fox
WAGES OF VIRTUE (1924) d/p Dwan w Swanson 7093ft FPL
WAGONMASTER (1950) d/co-p J Ford co-p M Cooper co-s F Nugent c Glennon 2nd c Stout w Dru, Darwell 86min r RKO
WAGON SHOW, THE (1927) d H Brown 6208ft FN
WAGON ROLLS AT NIGHT, THE (1941) d Enright p J Warner, Wallis c Hickox w Bogart, S Sidney 84min WB
WAGON TRACKS (1919) d Lambert Hillyer c August w W Hart 5rs pc W Hart

WÄHLE DAS LEBEN (1963) d/co-p/s Leiser 100min (= Choose Life)
WAIKIKI WEDDING (1937) d Tuttle c Struss chor Prinz m V Young w B Crosby, Quinn (10rs) Par
Waiter, The = CAUGHT IN A CABARET (1914)
WAITERS' BALL, THE (1916) d/w Arbuckle 2rs
WAITER'S PICNIC, THE (1913) d Sennett w Arbuckle, Normand 1rl Key
Waiting Women = KVINNORS VÄNTAN (1952)
WAIT TILL THE SUN SHINES, NELLIE (1952) d H King c Shamroy co-a Wheeler m A Newman w D Wayne, Peters *108min Fox
WAIT UNTIL DARK (1967) d T Young p M Ferrer c C Lang m Mancini w A Hepburn *108min WB
WAKADO NO YUME (1928) d/s Ozu Sho (= Dreams of Youth)
WAKAI HITO (1952) d/co-s Ichikawa Toho (= Young Generation)
WAKAI HITOTACHI (1954) d Yoshimura (= People of Young Character)
WAKAKIHI (1929) d/co-s Ozu Sho (= Days of Youth)
WAKAKI HI NO CHUJI (1925) d Kinugasa
WAKAKI HI NO KANGEKI (1931) d Gosho (= Memories of Young Days)
WAKARE-GUMO (1951) d/s Gosho (= Dispersing Clouds/Drifting Clouds)
WAKEFIELD EXPRESS (1952) d L Anderson c Lassally 33min
WAKE ISLAND (1942) d J Farrow co-st/co-s Burnett c Sparkuhl co-a Dreier w Preston, Bendix 78min Par
WAKE ME WHEN IT'S OVER (1960) d/p LeRoy s Breen c Shamroy co-a Wheeler m Mockridge CS* 126min Fox
WAKE UP AND DREAM (1946) d Bacon co-a Wheeler w Payne 98min Fox
Wake Up and Kill = LUTRING (1966)
WAKING UP THE TOWN (1925) d/co-st Cruze co-c Edeson w Shearer 5800ft pc Pickford r UA
WAKODO NO YUME (1928) d Ozu
WALKABOUT (1971) d/co-c Roeg m Barry *100min r Fox
WALK A CROOKED MILE (1948) d G Douglas w Burr 91min Col
Walk Cheerfully = HOGARAKA NI AYUME (1930)
WALK DON'T RUN (1966) d Walters p S Siegel w C Grant PV* 117min Col
WALK EAST ON BEACON (1952) d Alfred Werker p De Rochemont f article (The Crime of the Century) J Edgar Hoover c Brun w G Murphy 98min r Col
WALKING BACK (1928) d Julian 5035ft r Pat
WALKING DEAD, THE (1936) d Curtiz c Mohr w Karloff 66min WB
WALKING DOWN BROADWAY (1933, ur) co-d/co-s/di Von Stroheim(uc) co-d Walsh(uc) c Howe w Pitts Fox (= Hello, Sister)
WALKING DOWN BROADWAY (1938) d Foster w Trevor 59min Fox
WALKING HILLS, THE (1949) d J Sturges c Lawton w R Scott, A Kennedy 78min Col
WALKING MY BABY BACK HOME (1953) d Bacon c Glassberg w O'Connor, J Leigh 95min U
Walking to Heaven = GYALOG A MENNYORSZAGBA (1959)
Walk in the Night, The (UK) = GANG IN DIE NACHT, DER (1921)
Walk in the Old City of Warsaw, A = SPACEREK STAROMIEJSKI (1958)
WALK IN THE SPRING RAIN, A (1970) d G Green p/s Silliphant c E Lang m E Bernstein w Quinn, Ingrid Bergman PV* 98min Col
WALK IN THE SUN, A (1945) d/p Milestone s Rossen fn H Brown c R Harlan w D Andrews, Conte 111min Fox
Walk into Paradise = ODYSSEE DU CAPITAINE STEVE, L' (1956)
WALK LIKE A DRAGON (1960) d/p/co-st/co-s Clavell co-st/co-s Mainwaring c Griggs co-a Pereira 95min Par
WALK ON THE WILD SIDE (1962) d Dmytryk p Feldman c Joe Macdonald cr Bass m E Bernstein w Laurence Harvey, J Fonda, A Baxter, Stanwyck 114min Col
WALKOVER (1965) d/s/e/w Skolimowski 78min
WALK SOFTLY, STRANGER (1950) d Stevenson c Wild w Valli, Cotten 81min RKO
WALK WITH LOVE AND DEATH, A (1969) d/co-p J Huston m Delerue w J Huston *90min r Fox
Wall of Death (US) = THERE IS ANOTHER SUN (1950)
WALL OF NOISE (1963) d R Wilson c Ballard w Pleshette, Meeker 112min WB
WALLOP, THE (1921) d J Ford w Carey 5rs U
WALLOPING WALLACE (1924) d Thorpe 4830ft
WALLS OF JERICHO, THE (1948) d Stahl p/s Trotti c AC Miller co-a Wheeler m Mockridge w Wilde, Darnell, K Douglas, A Baxter 106min Fox
Waltz At Noon = MAHIRU NO ENBUKYOKU (1949)
WALTZES FROM VIENNA (1933) d Hitchcock co-s Reville m Johann Strauss Elder and Younger 80min JAR (= Strauss' Great Waltz)
WALTZ OF THE TOREADORS (1962) d Guillermin fpl Anoulih w Sellers *102min JAR
WALZERKRIEG (1933) d Ludwig Berger co-dec Rohrig 93min UFA

437

WANDERER, THE (1913) *d* Griffith 1rl Bio
WANDERER, THE (1926) *d/p* Walsh *c* Milner *w* Beery 8173ft FPL
WANDERING JEW, THE (1923) *d* Elvey 8300ft
WANDERING JEW, THE (1933) *d* Elvey *m* Reisenfeld *w* Veidt 108min
WANDERNDE BILD, DAS (1920) *d/co-s* F Lang *co-s* Von Harbou
WANING SEX, THE (1926) *d* Leonard *w* Shearer MGM
WANTERS, THE (1923) *d/p* Stahl *w* Shearer(*uc*) 7rs FN
Wanton Countess, The = SENSO (1954)
WARAI-NO NINGEN (1960) *d* Kuri anim (= *People*)
WAR AND PEACE (1956) *d/co-s* K Vidor *2nd d* Soldati *p* De Lautentiis, Ponti *co-s* Camerini, Shaw(*uc*) Aurenche(*uc*), Bost(*uc*) *c* Cardiff, Tonti *a* Chari *m* Rota *w* A Hepburn, M Ferrer, H Fonda, Gassmann, Ekberg, J Mills VV* 208min Par
War and Peace = VOINA I MIR (1915)
War and Peace (US and UK) 2 part (357min) version of VOINA I MIR (1964–65)
WARAREGA KYOKAN (1939) *d* Imai (= *Our Instructor*)
WAR BRIDES (1916) *d/p* Brenon *w* Barthelmess, Nazimova 8rs
WAR COMES TO AMERICA (1945) *d/co-s* Litvak *m* Tiomkin *n* W Huston 60min US Army Pictorial Service
War Correspondent = THE STORY OF GI JOE (1945)
WARDROBE, THE (1959) *d/p* Dunning *2min
WARE CASE, THE (1939) *d* Stevenson *p* Balcon *w* C Brook 72min *r* Fox
WAR GAME, THE (1963) *d* Zetterling 15min
WAR GAME, THE (1965) *d/s* Watkins 50min BBC
War-Gods of the Deep (US) = CITY IN THE SEA (1965)
WAR HUNT (1961) *d/co-p* D Sanders *co-p* T Sanders *c* McCord *w* Pollack, Redford 81min *r* UA
WARLOCK (1959) *d/p* Dmytryk *s* Arthur *a* MacDonald *co-a* L Wheeler *m* Harline *w* Widmark, H Fonda, Quinn, Malone CS* 121min Fox
War Lord (1937 = WEST OF SHANGHAI
WAR LORD, THE (1965) *d* Schaffner *fpl* Leslie Stevens *c* Metty *co-a* Golitzen *w* Heston, Boone PV* 123min U
WAR LOVER, THE (1962) *d* P Leacock *s* H Koch *fn* John Hersey *w* McQueen, R Wagner 105min
WARM CORNER, A (1930) *d/p/s* Saville
Warm Current = DANRYU (1939)
WARMING UP (1928) *d* Newmeyer *c* Cronjager *w* Arthur 6509ft Par FPL
WARNING, THE (1927) *d/s* G Seitz *p* Cohn *c* June 5791ft Col
Warning, The = VARUJ! (1947)
WARNING SHOT (1967) *d/p* Kulik *c* Biroc *co-a* Pereira *m* Goldsmith *w* Parker, G Sanders, L Gish, Pidgeon *100min Par
WAR OF THE SATELLITES (1958) *d/p/w* Corman *c* F Crosby *a* D Haller 66min AA
WAR OF THE WORLDS, THE (1953) *d* Haskin *p* Pal *fn* HG Wells *c* Barnes *a* Pereira *85min Par
War on the Plains = ACROSS THE PLAINS (1911)
WARPATH (1951) *d* Haskin *c* Rennahan *w* E O'Brien 95min Par
WARRENDALE (1966) *d/p* A King 16mm 100min
WARRENS OF VIRGINIA, THE (1915) *d* De Mille *pc* Lasky
Warrior and the Slave Girl, The (UK) = RIVOLTA DEI GLADIATORI, LA (1958)
Warriors, The (US) = DARK AVENGER (1955)
WARRIOR'S HUSBAND, THE (1933) *d/co-s* W Lang *c* Mohr 72min Fox
Warrior's Rest (UK) = REPOS DU GUERRIER, LE (1962)
Warrior Women = VERGINI DI ROMA, LE (1960)
WARUI YATSU HODO YOKU NEMURU (1960) *d/co-p/co-s* Kurosawa *w* Mifune, Mori S 151min *pc* Kurosawa *r* Toho (= *The Bad Sleep Well*)
WARUM SIND SIE GEGEN UNS? (1958) *d/s* Wicki 65min
WAR WAGON, THE (1967) *d* B Kennedy *s/fn* (*Badman*) Huffaker *c* Clothier *m* Tiomkin *w* J Wayne, K Douglas, Keel PV* 101min *pc* J Wayne *r* U
WASEI KENKA TOMODACHI (1929) *d* Ozu Sho (= *Fighting Friends*)
WASHINGTON MERRY-GO-ROUND (1932) *d* Cruze *st* Maxwell Anderson *s* Swerling *co-c* Tetzlaff 78min Col (= *Invisible Power*)
WASP WOMAN, THE (1959) *d/p* Corman *a* D Haller 73min
Wastrel, the = RELITTO, IL (1960)
WATASHI NO SUBETE O (1954) *d/co-s* Ichikawa Toho (= *All of Myself*)
WATASHI WA NISAI (1962) *d* Ichikawa S* 88min Dai (= *Being Two Isn't Easy*)
WATCH ON THE RHINE (1943) *d* Shumlin *p* Wallis *s* Hammett *fpl* Hellman *co-c* Mohr *m* M Steiner *w* B Davis, Lukas 114min WB
Watch the Birdie = ZAOSTRIT PROSIM (1956)
WATERFRONT (1950) *d* Michael Anderson *w* Newton, Burton 80min JAR
WATER GIPSIES, THE (1931) *d* Elvey 78min
WATERLOO (1970) *d/co-s* Bondarchuk *p* De Laurentiis *m* Rota *w* Steiger, Plummer, Welles, Hawkins PV* 132min Col

WATERLOO BRIDGE (1931) *d* Whale *c* Edeson *w* B Davies 81min U
WATERLOO BRIDGE (1940) *d* LeRoy *p* Franklin *c* Ruttenberg *a* Gibbons *m* Stothart *w* V Leigh, r Taylor, Ouspenskaya 105min MGM
WATERLOO ROAD (1944) *d/s* Gilliatt *w* S Granger, J Mills 76min JAR
WATER NYMPH, THE (1912) *d* Sennett *w* Normand ½rl Key
WATERS OF TIME (1951) *d/p/s* B Wright *m* Rawsthorne 37min
WATERTIGHT (1943) *d/s* Cavalcanti *p* Balcon
WATUSI (1958) *d* Kurt Neumann *s* Clavell *fn* H Rider Haggard *85min MGM
Wave, The = REDES (1934)
WAVE, A WAC, AND A MARINE, A (1944) *d* Karlson 70min Mon
WAVES AND SPRAY (1898) *d* G Smith
WAX EXPERIMENTS (1920–24) *d* Fischinger anim
Waxworks (UK) = WACHSFIGUREN KABINETT (1924)
WAY AHEAD, THE (1944) *d* C Reed *co-st/co-s* Eric Ambler *co-s* Ustinov *w* Niven, Ustinov, T Howard 115min *r* EL
WAY DOWN EAST (1920) *d/p* Griffith *co-c* Bitzer *w* L Gish, L Sherman, Barthelmess, (Shearer) 13rs *pc* Griffith *r* UA
WAY DOWN EAST (1935) *d* H King *rm* 1920 *w* H Fonda 80min Fox
WAY FOR A SAILOR (1930) *d* S Wood *co-s/di* MacArthur *w* Beery, J Gilbert 83min
WAY IN THE WILDERNESS, A (1940) *d* Zinnemann 1rl MGM
WAY OF A GAUCHO (1952) *d* J Tourneur *p/s* P Dunne *co-a* Wheeler *co-m* A Newman *w* Tierney *91min Fox
WAY OF ALL FLESH, THE (1927) *d* V Fleming *co-st* Biro *st/s* Furthman *fn* Samuel Butler *c* Milner *w* Jannings 8486ft Par
WAY OF ALL MEN, THE (1930) *d/p* F Lloyd *w* Fairbanks Jr, Beery 69min FN (German Version: DIE MASKE FÄLLT *d* Dieterle)
WAY OF A MAN, THE (1923–24) *d/s* G Seitz Pat serial in 10eps
WAY OF A WOMAN, THE (1919) *d* Leonard 5rs Sel
WAY OF LOST SOULS, THE (1930) *d* Czinner
WAY OF MAN, THE (1909) *d* Griffith *w* Pickford 1rl Bio
WAY OF PEACE, THE (1947) *d/s* Tashlin *n* Ayres 16mm 18min
WAY OF THE REDMAN, THE (1914) *p/s/w* Mix 1000ft Sel
WAY OF THE STRONG, THE (1928) *d* Capra *p* Cohn *c* Reynolds 6rs Col
Way of the Wicked (UK) = CE CORPS TANT DESIRE (1958)
WAY OF THE WORLD, THE (1910) *d* Griffith 1rl Bio
WAY OUT (1967) *d/p* Yeaworth *102min
WAY OUT WEST (1930) *d* Niblo 8rs MGM
WAY OUT WEST (1937) *d* James Horne *p* Roach *w* Laurel, Hardy 65min *pc* Laurel *r* MGM
WAY TO SHADOW GARDEN, THE (1955) *d* Brakhage 16mm 10min
Way to the Neighbour, The = VEG ZUM NACHBARN (1963)
WAY TO THE STARS, THE (1945) *d* Asquith *st/co-s* Rattigan *co-s* De Grunwald, *Captain R Sherman* *w* M Redgrave, J Mills, T Howard 109min *r* UA (= *Johnny in the Clouds*)
WAYWARD BUS, THE (1957) *d* Victor Vicas *p* Brackett *fn* John Steinbeck *c* C Clarke *co-a* Wheeler *m* Harline *w* Mansfield CS 89min
Wayward Wife (UK) = PROVINCIALE, LA (1952)
WAY ... WAY OUT (1966) *d* G Douglas *c* Clothier *m* Schifrin *w* J Lewis, Ekberg, Keith CS* 101min Fox
WAY WEST, THE (1967) *d* A McLaglen *p* H Hecht *co-s* Maddow *c* Clothier *m* Kaper *w* K Douglas, Mitchum, Widmark PV* 122min *r* UA
WEAK AND THE WICKED, THE (1953) *d/co-s* J Thompson *c* G Taylor 88min *r* ABC
WEAKER SEX, THE (1948) *d* R Baker 84min
We are all Demons! = KLABAUTERMANDEN (1969)
We are Building = WIJ BOUWEN (1930)
We are Living = DIKKOI IKITERU (1950)
WE ARE NOT ALONE (1939) *d* Goulding *exp* Wallis *as-p* Blanke *c* Gaudio *w* Muni 112min WB
WE ARE THE LAMBETH BOYS (1959) *d* Reisz *c* Lassally 52min
WEARY RIVER (1929) *d* F Lloyd *c* E Haller *w* Barthelmess, Holden 8000ft FN
WEATHER WIZARDS (1938) *d* Zinnemann 1rl MGM
WEB, THE (1947) *d* M Gordon *st* Kurnitz *c* Glassberg *w* Bendix, Price, E O'Brien 87min U
WEB OF EVIDENCE (1959) *d* Cardiff *fn* (*Beyond This Place*) AJ Cronin *w* Miles, v Johnson, Emlyn Williams 90min *r* AA (= *Beyond this Place*)
Web of Passion = A DOUBLE TOUR (1959)
WE CAN'T HAVE EVERYTHING (1918) *d* De Mille 6rs FPL
Wedding Bells (UK) = ROYAL WEDDING (1950)
WEDDING BELLS OUT OF TUNE (1921) *d* St Clair *p/s* Sennett *w* Fazenda 2rs
Wedding Breakfast (UK) = CATERED AFFAIR, A (1956)

WEDDING MARCH, THE (1928) *d/co-s* Von Stroheim *c* B Reynolds, Mohr *a/co-s* Von Stroheim, R Day *w* Von Stroheim, Pitts Part I: *c* 11rs Part II (*r* as THE HONEYMOON): *c* 7rs FPL
Wedding March = KEKKON KOSHIN-KYOKU (1957)
WEDDING NIGHT, THE (1935) *d* K Vidor *p* Goldwyn *c* Toland *e* Heisler *a* R Day *m* A Newman *w* G Cooper, Sten, Brennan 82min *pc* goldwyn *r* UA
WEDDING REHEARSAL (1932) *d/p* A Korda *fpl* Biro *w* Oberon 84min
Wedding Ring, The = PRSTYNEK (1945)
WEDDINGS AND BABIES (1958) *d/p/s* Engel *w* Lindfors 81min
We Die Alone (UK) = NI LIV (1957)
WE DIVE AT DAWN (1943) *d* Asquith *w* J Mills 98min
WEDLOCK HOUSE: AN INTERCOURSE (1959) *d* Brakhage 16mm si 11min
Weekend = WOCHENENDE (1928)
WEEKEND (1962) *d* Kjaerulff-Schmidt 85min
WEEKEND (1968) *d/s* Godard *c* Coutard *co-m* Mozart *w* Darc, Léaud *105min
WEEKEND AT THE WALDORF (1945) *d/co-p* Leonard *fn* Vicki Baum *rm* GRAND HOTEL (1932) *co-a* Gibbons *w* G Rogers, Turner, Pidgeon, V Johnson, Benchley 130min MGM
WEEKEND A ZUYDCOOTE (1964) *d* Verneuil *c* Decaë *w* Belmondo & Catherine Spaak FS* 119min (= *Weekend in Dunkirk*)
WEEKEND EN MER (1962) *d* Reichenbach
WEEKEND FOR THREE (1941) *d* Reis *p* Garnett *st* B Schulberg *c* Metty *w* Conreid, Pitts, Horton 65min RKO
Weekend in Dunkirk = WEEKEND A ZUYDCOOTE (1964)
WEEKEND IN HAVANA (1941) *d* W Lang *w* Faye, C Miranda, Payne, Romero 80min Fox
WEEKEND IN PARIS (1961) *d* C Donner 16mm * sh
Weekend Italian Style (UK) = OMBRELLONE, L' (1965)
WEEK ENDS ONLY (1932) *d* Crosland *c* Mohr *w* J Bennett 65min Fox
WEEKEND WITH FATHER (1951) *d* Sirk *co-a* Boyle *w* Heflin, Neal 83min U
Weeping blue Sky = AOZORA NI NAKU (1931)
Weeping for a Bandit = LLANTO POR UN BANDIDO (1964)
WEE WILLIE WINKIE (1937) *d* J Ford *p* Zanuck *fst* Rudyard Kipling *c* AC Miller *m* A Newman *w* Temple, V McLaglen, Romero 99min Fox
WEE SANDY (1962) *d* Reiniger anim 1rl
We Expect Victory There = MY ZHDOM VAS S POBEDOI (1941)
WE FAW DOWN (1928) *d* McCarey *p* Roach *w* Laurel, Hardy 2rs MGM (= *We Slip Up*)
WEGE DES SCHROCKENS (1921) *d* Curtiz 4397ft
WEG NACH OBEN, DER (1950) *d* Andrew Thorndike 83min Defa
Weg Nach Shanghai, Der = MOSKAU-SHANGHAI (1936)
WEIB DES PHARAO, DAS (1922) *d* Lubitsch *co-c* Sparkuhl *w* Jannings, Wegener 6rs UFA (= *The Loves of Pharaoh*)
WEIBSTEUFEL, DER (1966) *d/co-s* Tressler 92min (= *A Devil of a Woman*)
WEIR-FALCON SAGA, THE (1969) *d* Brakhage 16mm * si 29min
WEISSE HOLLE VON PIZ PALU, DIE (1929) *d/cos* Fanck *co-d* Pabst *w* Riefenstahl 3330m
WEISSE PFAU, DER (1920) *d/co-s* Dupont *co-s/coa* Leni 1780m
WEISSE RAUSCH, DER (1931) *d/s* Fanck *w* Riefenstahl 2565m
WEISSE SCHATTEN (1951) *d/co-s* Kautner 83min
WEISSE SKLAVIN, DIE (1927) *d* Genina *w* Vanel
WELCOME DANGER (1929) *d/co-s* Bruckman *w* H Lloyd 10657ft *pc* H Lloyd *r* Par
WELCOME HOME (1925) *d/p* Cruze *fpl* Kaufman, *Edna Ferber* 5909ft FPL
Welcome, Mr Marshall = BIENVENIDO MR MARSHALL (1952)
WELCOME STRANGER (1947) *d* E Nugent *co-a* Dreier *w* B Crosby 107min Par
WELCOME TO BRITAIN (1943) *d* Asquith, Meredith *w* Meredith, Hope 60min
WELCOME TO HARD TIMES (1967) *d/s* B Kennedy *w* H Fonda, A Ray, Cook *105min MGM (= *Killer on a Horse*)
WELFARE OF THE WORKERS (1940) *d* Jennings GPO
WE LIVE AGAIN (1934) *d/p* Mamoulian *co-s* P Sturges *fn* (*Resurrection*) Tolstoi *c* Toland *m* A Newman *w* Sten, March 84min *pc* Goldwyn
WE LIVE IN TWO WORLDS (1937) *d* Cavalcanti *p* Grierson *s* Priestley *m* Jaubert 15min
WELL, THE (1951) *co-d/co-s* Ropuse *co-d* Leo Popkin *c* Laszlo 85min *r* UA
WELL GROOMED BRIDE, THE (1946) *d* Sidney Lanfield *p* Kohlmar *c* J Seitz *co-a* Dreier *w* De Havilland, Milland 75min Par
WELLS FARGO (1937) *d/p* F Lloyd *c* Sparkuhl *co-a* Dreier *m* V Young *w* McCrea, R Cummings, Nolan 115min Par

Well, Young Man? = HOGY ALLUNK, FIATALEMBER? (1963)

WELSH SINGER, A (1915) *d/w* Henry Edwards *w* Evans

WELTSPIEGEL, DIE (1918) *d/co-s* Lupu-Pick 6rs

WELTSPIEGEL (1923) *d* Lupu-Pick

WELTSTRASSE SEE (1938) *d* Ruttmann 14½min (= *Hamburg*)

We May Eat of the Fruit of the Trees of the Garden = OVOCE RAJSKYCH STROMU JIME (1970)

WENN DIE MUSIK NICHT WAR (1935) *d* Gallone *m* Liszt 95min (= *Liszt Rhapsody*)

WENN VIER DASSELBE TUN (1917) *d/cos* Lubitsch *w* Jannings 1rl (= *When Four do the Same*)

WENT THE DAY WELL? (1942) *d* Cavalcanti *p* Balcon *fst* Greene 92min *r* UA

We of the Urals = MY S URALA (1944)

WE'RE ALL GAMBLERS (1927) *d/p* Cruze *c* Glennon 5935ft Par

WE'RE IN THE MONEY (1935) *d* Enright *w* Blondell 65min WB

WE'RE NO ANGELS (1955) *d* Curtiz *s* Macdougall *c* Griggs *co-a* Pereira *m* Hollander *w* Bogart, A Ray, Ustinov, J Bennett, Rathbone VV* 106min Par

WE'RE NOT DRESSING (1934) *d* Taurog *c* C Lang *e* Heisler *w* B Crosby, Lombard, Milland 63min Par

We're Not Made of Stone = NO SOMOS DE PIEDRA (1968)

WE'RE NOT MARRIED (1952) *d* Goulding *p/s* N Johnson *co-a* Wheeler *m* Mockridge *w* G Rogers, Monroe, Darwell, P Douglas, M Gaynor, D Wayne 85min Fox

WEREWOLF, THE (1956) *d* Sears *p* Katzman *c* Lindon 83min Col

WERFT ZUM GRAUEN HECHT, DIE (1935) *d/co-s* Wisbar 100min

WERTHER (1939) *d/co-s* Ophuls *fn* (*Die Leiden des jungen Werthers*) *Johann Wolfgang von Goethe c* Schuftan *co-dec* Lourié *m* Paul Dessau *mf* Bach, Mozart, Schubert, Beethoven 85min (= *Le Roman de Werther*)

WE SAIL AT MIDNIGHT (1943) *d* J Ford *cy* Odets 20min

We Slip Up = WE FAW DOWN (1928)

WESTBOUND (1959) *d* Boetticher *p* Blanke *c* Marley *w* R Scott, V Mayo* 96min WB

WESTERN APPROACHES (1944) *d/s* Jackson *c* Cardiff *83min BL

WESTERN BLOOD (1918) *d/ad* Lynn F Reynolds *st/w* Mix 5rs Fox

WESTERNER, THE (1940) *d* Wyler *p* Goldwyn *s* Swerling, Busch *c* Toland *w* G Cooper, Brennan, D Andrews 100min *r* UA

WESTERN MASQUERADE, A (1916) *p/s/w* Mix 1rl Sel

WESTERN UNION (1941) *d* F Lang *as-p* H Brown *fn* Zane Grey *co-c* Cronjager *co-a* R Day *w* R Young, R Scott, Carradine *93min Fox

WESTFRONT 1918 – VIER VON INFANTERIE (1930) *d* Pabst 96min Nero

WESTINGHOUSE ABC (1965) *d/s* C & R Eames *c* C Eames *m* E Bernstein *

West Of Montana = MAIL ORDER BRIDE (1963)

WEST OF SHANGHAI (1937) *d* J Farrow *c* O'Connell *w* Karloff 7rs WB (= *War Lord*)

WEST OF ZANZIBAR (1928) *d* Browning *w* Chaney, W Baxter 6150ft MGM

WEST OF ZANZIBAR (1954) *d/st* Watt *m* Rawsthorne *94min JAR

WEST POINT STORY, THE (1950) *d* Del Ruth *w* Cagney, V Mayo, D Day 107min WB

WEST POINT WIDOW (1941) *d* Siodmak *p* S Siegel *c* Sparkuhl *co-a* Dreier 63min Par

WEST SIDE STORY (1961) *co-d/p* Wise *co-d/chor* Robbins *s* Lehman *c* Fapp *cr* Bass *m* L Bernstein *w* N Wood PV70* 155min *r* UA

WESTWARD THE WOMEN (1951) *d* Wellman *p* Schary *st* Capra *s* Schnee *c* Mellor *co-a* Gibbons *w* R Taylor, McGuire 118min MGM

We, the Women = SIAMO DONNE (1953)

WET PARADE, THE (1932) *d* V Fleming *ad* Mahin *fn* Sinclair *w* W Huston, M Loy, R Young 120min MGM

WE WERE DANCING (1942) *d/co-p* Leonard *fpl* (*Tonight at 8.30*) Coward *a* Gibbons *m* Kaper *w* Shearer, M Douglas, Gardner 94min MGM

WE WERE STRANGERS (1949) *d/co-s* J Huston *p* Spiegel (*ps* SP Eagle) *c* Metty *m* Antheil *w* Garfield, J Jones, Armendariz, Roland, Novarro, (J Huston) 106min *pc* J Huston, Spiegel *r* Col

We, Women = SIAMO DONNE (1953)

WHALING IN THE PACIFIC (c1950) *d* Flynn *sh*

WHARF ANGEL, THE (1934) *d* Menzies, *George Somnes c* Milner *w* V McLaglen 63min Par

WHAT A CARVE UP! (1961) *d* Jackson 88min

WHAT AM I BID? (1919) *d* Leonard 6rs U

What a Night! = MICSODA EJSZAKA (1958)

WHAT A WAY TO GO (1964) *d* J Thompson *s/lyr* Comden, a Green *c* Shamroy *w* MacLaine, P Newman, Mitchum, Martin, Gene Kelly, R Cummings, D Van Dyke, Dumont CS* 111min Fox

WHAT A WIDOW (1930) *d/p* Dwan *exp* J Kennedy *c* Barnes *w* Swanson 90min *r* UA

WHAT A WOMAN (1943) *d* Irving Cummings *w* R Russell, (Winters) 94min Col

What Did The Lady Forget? = SHUKUJO WA NANI O WASURETAKA (1937)

WHAT DID YOU DO IN THE WAR, DADDY? (1966) *d/p/co-st* Edwards *c* Lathrop *m* Mancini *w* J Coburn, A Ray PV* 115min Mir *r* UA

What Do You Think? = ANATA WA NANI O KANGAETE IRU KA? (1967)

WHATEVER HAPPENED TO AUNT ALICE? (1969) *d* Lee H Katzin *c* Biroc *w* R Gordon, Page *101min *pc* Aldrich

WHAT EVER HAPPENED TO BABY JANE? (1962) *d/p* Aldrich *c* E Häller *w* B Davis, J Crawford 133min *pc* Aldrich *r* WB

WHAT EVERY WOMAN KNOWS (1934) *d* La Cava *as-p* Lewin *fpl* Sir JM Barrie *m* Stothart *w* Crisp, H Hayes 92min MGM

WHAT EVERY WOMAN LEARNS (1919) *d* Niblo *m* Stothart 9rs

WHAT EVERY WOMAN WANTS (1954) *d* Elvey 90min

WHAT HAPPENED TO JONES (1920) *d* Cruze 5rs FPL

WHAT HAPPENED TO ROSA (1920) *d* Schertzinger *w* Normand 5rs *pc* Goldwyn

What Lola Wants (UK) = DAMN YANKEES (1959)

WHAT LOVE WILL DO (1921) *d* W Howard *p* Fox 4252ft Fox

WHAT NEXT, CORPORAL HARGROVE? (1945) *d* Thorpe *st/s* Kurnitz *w* R Walker 95min MGM

WHAT! NO BEER? (1933) *d* Edward Sedgwick *w* Keaton 7rs MGM

WHAT PRICE GLORY? (1926) *d* Walsh *fco-pl* Maxwell Anderson *w* Del Rio, V McLaglen 12rs Fox

WHAT PRICE GLORY? (1952) *d* J Ford *p* S Siegel *co-fpl* Maxwell Anderson *rm* 1926 *c* Joe Macdonald *co-a* Wheeler *m* A Newman *w* Cagney, Dailey, R Wagner *111min Fox

WHAT PRICE HOLLYWOOD? (1932) *d* Cukor *p* Selznick *m* M Steiner *w* Constance Bennett, L Sherman, Ratoff 87min RKO

What says M.O.C.? = STO GOVORIT MOC? (1924)

WHAT'S BREWIN' BRUIN? (1947) *d c* Jones anim* 7min WB

WHAT'S COOKIN'? (1942) *d* Cline 69min U

What shall we do now? = VAD SKA VI GORA UN DA (1958)

What's Happening = YEAH YEAH YEAH NEW YORK MEETS THE BEATLES (1964)

WHAT'S HIS NAME (1914) *d* De Mille *pc* Lasky

What's in it for Harry? = HOW TO MAKE IT (1968, *ur*)

WHAT'S NEW, PUSSYCAT? (1965) *d* C Donner *co-p* Feldman *c* Badal *cr* R Williams *w* Sellers, O'Toole, Schneider, Andress *108min *r* UA

WHAT'S OPERA DOC? (1957) *d* C Jones anim* 7min WB

WHAT'S SO BAD ABOUT FEELING GOOD? (1968) *d/p/co-st/co-s* Seaton *co-st/co-s* Pirosh *co-a* Golitzen *w* Peppard *94min *r* U

WHAT'S YOUR HURRY? (1920) *d* S Wood 5rs

WHAT THE DAISY SAID (1910) *d* Griffith *w* Pickford 1rl Bio

WHAT WIVES WANT (1923) *d* Conway 5rs U

WHEELER DEALERS, THE (1963) *d* Arthur Hiller *c* C Lang *w* Remick, Garner PV* 105min (= *Separate Beds*)

WHEEL OF CHANCE (1928) *d* Santell *c* E Haller *w* Barthelmess, Franklin 6813ft FN

WHEEL OF LIFE, THE (1929) *d/song* Schertzinger *ad* J Farrow *c* Cronjager 58min Par

Wheels of Fate (UK) = ROUE, LA (1956)

WHEN A MAN LOVES (1926) *d* Crosland *c* Haskin *w* J Barrymore 10049ft WB

WHEN A MAN RIDES ALONE (1918) *d* H King

WHEN A MAN'S A MAN (1924) *d* Cline

WHEN A MAN'S A MAN (1935) *d* Cline *p* Lesser *w* G O'Brien 70min BL

WHEN A MAN'S A PRINCE (1926) *d* Cline *s* Sennett *w* Turpin 1rl

WHEN A MAN SEES RED (1917) *d/s* F Lloyd 7rs Fox

When Angels Don't Fly = SUOR LETIZIA (1956)

When a Woman Ascends the Stairs = ONNA GA KAIDAN O AGARU TOKI (1960)

When a Woman Loves = WAGA AI (1960)

When Darkness Falls = NAR MORKRET FALLER (1960)

WHEN DOCTORS DISAGREE (1919) *d* Schertzinger *w* Normand 5rs *pc* Goldwyn

WHEN DO WE EAT? (1918) *d* Niblo *p* Ince 5rs FPL

WHEN DREAMS COME TRUE (1913) *d* Sennett *w* Normand, Arbuckle 1rl Key

When Four Do the Same (UK) = WENN VIER DASSELBE TUN (1917)

WHEN HUSBANDS FLIRT (1926) *d* Wellman 5505ft Col

WHEN IN ROME (1952) *d/p* C Brown *co-s* Schnee *c* Daniels *co-a* Gibbons *w* V Johnson, P Douglas 78min MGM

When I Was Dead = ALS ICH TOT WAR (1916)

WHEN KNIGHTS WERE BOLD (1908) *d* Wallace McCutcheon *w* Griffith Bio

WHEN KNIGHTS WERE BOLD (1916) *d/p* Elvey 4rs

WHEN LADIES MEET (1941) *d/co-p* Leonard *co-s* Loos *a* Gibbons *m* Kaper *w* J Crawford, R Taylor, Garson, H Marshall 108min MGM

WHEN LEE SURRENDERS (1912) *d* Ince *w* Borzage

When Love Comes to the Village = NAR KARLEKEN KOM TILL BYN (1950)

WHEN LOVE IS BLIND (1919) *d* Cline *p/s* Sennett *w* Turpin 2rs

WHEN LOVE TOOK WINGS (1915) *d/w* Arbuckle *p* Sennett 1rl Key

WHEN MAGOO FLEW (1954) *p* Bosustow CS* 1rl UPA *r* Col

WHEN MEN BETRAY (1918) *d* Ivan Abramson *w* Bankhead

WHEN MY BABY SMILES AT ME (1948) *d* W Lang *s* Trotti *co-a* Wheeler *m* A Newman *w* Grable, Dailey *98min Fox

WHEN STRANGERS MARRY (1933) *d* Badger 68min Col

WHEN STRANGERS MARRY (1944) *d* Castle *co-s* Yordan *m* Tiomkin *w* Mitchum, R Fleming 67min Mon

WHEN SUMMER COMES (1922) *d* Del Ruth *w* Turpin 2rs FN

WHEN THE CAT'S AWAY (1929) *d* Iwerks *p* Disney anim 1rl

WHEN THE CLOUDS ROLL BY (1919) *d* V Fleming, *Ted Reed p/co-st/co-s/w* Fairbanks Sr 6rs

When the Cookie Crumbles = SATASHI GA KOWARERU TOKI (1967)

WHEN THE DALTONS RODE (1940) *d* G Marshall *c* Mohr *w* R Scott, K Francis, G Bancroft, B Crawford 80min U

When the Devil Drives (UK) = SAIT-ON JAMAIS? (1957)

When the Door Opened = ESCAPE (1940)

WHEN THE LIGHTS GO ON AGAIN (1944) *d* W Howard 75min PRC

WHEN THE PIE WAS OPENED (1939) *d* Lye 10min

When Thief Meets Thief = JUMP FOR GLORY (1937)

WHEN TOMORROW COMES (1939) *d/p* Stahl *w* I Dunne, Boyer 90min U

WHEN WE WERE 21 (1920) *d* H King 5rs Pat

WHEN WILLIE COMES MARCHING HOME (1950) *d* J Ford *p* Kohlmar *co-a* Wheeler *m* A Newman *w* Dailey, (Marsh) 82min Fox

When Women Lie = USO (1963)

When Words Fail (US) = DONDE MUEREN ZAS PALABRAS (1946)

WHEN WORLDS COLLIDE (1951) *d* Maté *p* Pal *s* Boehm *c* J Seitz *co-a* Pereira *m* Leith Stevens *w* Rush *81min Par

When You Can't Believe Anyone = FUSHIN NO TOKI (1968)

WHEN YOU'RE IN LOVE (1937) *d/s* Riskin *as-p* Everett Riskin *c* J Walker *w* C Grant, L Brooks, Mitchell 11rs Col

When You're Married = MABEL'S MARRIED LIFE (1954)

WHERE ANGELS GO, TROUBLE FOLLOWS (1968) *d* Neilson *c* Leavitt *a* Wheeler *m* Schifrin *w* R Russell, R Taylor, V Johnson *95min Col

Where Are the Dreams of Youth? = SEISHUN NO YUME IMA IZUKO (1932)

Where Chimneys Are Seen = ENTOTSU NO MIERU BASHO (1953)

WHERE DANGER LIVES (1950) *d* J Farrow *c* Musuraca *w* Mitchum, Rains, O'Sullivan 84min RKO

WHERE DO WE GO FROM HERE (1945) *d* Ratoff *p* Perlberg *c* Shamroy *co-a* Wheeler *co-m/co-lyr* Weill *w* MacMurray, Quinn, Preminger *77min Fox

WHERE EAGLES DARE (1969) *d* Brian G Hutton *w* Burton, Eastwood, Marvin PV70* 155min MGM

WHERE EAST IS EAST (1929) *d/st* Browning *w* Chaney 70min MGM

Where is My Treasure? WO IST MEIN SCHATZ? (1916)

WHERE IS THIS LADY? (1933) *d* Vajda, *W Victor Hanbury* 77min BL

WHERE IT'S AT (1969) *d/s* Kanin *c* Guffey 106min *r* UA

WHERE LOVE HAS GONE (1964) *d* Dmytryk *p* Levine *s* J Hayes *fn* Harold Robbins *c* Joe Macdonald *co-a* Pereira *w* S Hayward, B Davis S* 114min Par

Where Mountains Float = HVOR BJERGENE SEJLER (1955)

WHERE NO VULTURES FLY (1951) *d/st* Watt *p* Balcon *c* Unsworth *m* Rawsthorne *107min JAR (= *Ivory Hunter*)

WHERE'S CHARLEY? (1952) *d* D Butler *chor* Kidd 97min WB

WHERE'S JACK? (1968) *d* Clavell *p* S Baker *m* E Bernstein *w* S Baker *119min *r* Par

WHERE'S THAT FIRE (1939) *d* Marcel Varnel *w* Hay 74min Fox

WHERE THE BOYS ARE (1960) *d* Levin *p* Pasternak *s* Wells *c* Bronner *m* V Young CS* 99min MGM

Where the Hot Wind Blows = LOI, LA (1958)

WHERE THE PAVEMENT ENDS (1923) *d/p/ad* Ingram *fn* John Russell *c* J Seitz *w* Novarro 7rs MGM

Where There's a Will (US) = GOOD MORNING, BOYS (1937)

Where the River Bends = BEND OF THE RIVER (1952)

WHERE THE SIDEWALK ENDS (1950) *d/p* Preminger *s* B Hecht *c* La Shelle *co-a* Wheeler *m* Mockridge *w* D Andrews, Tierney, Malden 95min Fox

Where the Truth Lies = MALEFICES (1962)

WHERE THE WEST BEGINS (1919) *d* H King 5rs

WHEREVER SHE GOES (1953) *d/s* M Gordon 80min

WHERE WERE YOU WHEN THE LIGHTS WENT OUT? (1968) *d Hy Averback w* D Day PV* 90min MGM
WHERE WILL THEY GO? (1958) *d* A King 16mm 28min
WHICH WAY TO THE FRONT? (1970) *d/p/w* Jerry Lewis *96min WB (= *Ja, Ja, mein General! but which way to the front?*)
WHICH WOMAN (1918) *d* Browning 5rs (= *Quelle Femme!*)
WHILE AMERICA SLEEPS (1939) *d* Zinnemann 20min MGM
WHILE PARIS SLEEPS (1932) *d* Dwan *w* V McLaglen 66min Fox
WHILE THE CITY SLEEPS (1928) *d* Conway *w* Chaney 7448ft MGM
WHILE THE CITY SLEEPS (1956) *d* F Lang *c* Laszlo *w* D Andrews, R Fleming, Mitchell, Price, Lupino, G Sanders, (Marsh) 100min RKO
WHILE THE PATIENT SLEPT (1935) *d* Enright *p* H Brown *c* Edeson 67min WB
WHILE THE SUN SHINES (1947) *d* Asquith *co-s/p* De Grunwald *co-s/fpl* Rattigan *c* Hildyard 61min Pat
WHIP, THE (1917) *d* M Tourneur
WHIP HAND, THE (1951) *d/a* Menzies *c* Musuraca *w* Burr 82min RKO
Whipped, The = UNDERWORLD STORY, THE (1950)
WHIPSAW (1935) *d* S Wood *st* J Grant *c* Howe *w* M Loy, Tracy 9rs MGM
WHIRLPOOL (1949) *d/p* Preminger *co-s* B Hecht *c* AC Miller *co-a* Wheeler *m* Raksin *w* Tierney, J Ferrer, Bickford, Conte 97min Fox
WHISKY GALORE (1949) *d* Mackendrick *p* Balcon *co-s/fn Compton Mackenzie w* Greenwood 82min
WHISPERERS, THE (1967) *d/s* Forbes *m* Barry *w* Evans 106min *r* UA
WHISPERING CHORUS, THE (1918) *d* De Mille FPL
WHISTLE AT EATON FALLS, THE (1951) *d* Siodmak *p* De Rochemong *c* Brun *w* D Gish, Borgnine, A Francis 96min Col
WHISTLE DOWN THE WIND (1961) *d* Forbes *p* Attenborough *m* M Arnold *w* H Mills 99min JAR
Whistle in My Heart, A = KOTAN NO KUCHIBUE (1959)
WHISTLER, THE (1944) *d* Castle 60min Col
Whistle Stop = POLUSTANOK (1963)
WHISTLING IN THE DARK (1933) *d/s* E Nugent *c* Brodine 78min MGM
WHITE ANGEL, THE (1936) *d* Dieterle *p* Blanke *c* Gaudio *w* K Francis 75min FN
WHITE BANNERS (1938) *d* Goulding *p* Wallis *as-p* Blanke *m* M Steiner *w* Rains 88min WB
White Beast = SHIROI YAJU (1950)
WHITE BUS, THE (1966) *d* L Anderson *s Shelagh Delaney c* Ondricek part *46min *r* UA
WHITE CAPS, THE (1905) *d* Porter 320ft Ed
WHITE CARGO (1942) *d* Thorpe *p* Saville *a* Gibbons *m* Kaper *w* Lamarr, Pidgeon 9rs MGM
WHITE CHRISTMAS (1954) *d* Curtiz s Krasna, Panama, M Frank *c* Griggs *co-a* Pereira *chor* R Alton *w* B Crosby, Kaye, Vera-Ellen VV* 120min Par
WHITE CIRCLE, THE (1920) *d/p* M Tourneur *s* Furthman, J Gilbert *fst* (*The Pavillion on the Links*) *RL Stevenson* 5rs
WHITE CLIFFS OF DOVER, THE (1944) *d* C Brown *p* Franklin *c* Folsey *a* Gibbons *m* Stothart *w* I Dunne, V Johnson, Lawford 126min MGM
WHITE COCKATOO, THE (1935) *d* Crosland *c* Gaudio 73min WB
WHITE CORRIDORS (1957) *d/co-s* Jackson 102min Gau
WHITE DOVE, THE (1920) *d* H King 5rs
White Eagle, The = BELYI OREL (1928)
WHITE FANG (1936) *d* D Butler *fn Jack London c* AC Miller *w* Darwell 74min Fox
White Fangs = SHIROI KIBA (1960)
WHITE FLANNELS (1927) *d* Bacon 5900ft WB
WHITE FLOOD (1940) *co-d* Meyers
WHITE GOLD (1927) *d* W Howard *co-ad* Garnett *co-t* J Farrow *c* Andriot *w* G Bancroft 6108ft *pc* De Mille
WHITE HANDS (1922) *d/s Lambert Hillyer w* G O'Brien 5654ft
WHITE HEAT (1949) *d* Walsh *co-s* Goff, Roberts *c* Hickox *m* M Steiner *w* Cagney, V Mayo, E O'Brien, Cochran 114min WB
WHITE HEATHER, THE (1919) *d* M Tourneur *w* J Gilbert 6rs
White Heron, The = SHIRASAGI (1959)
White Line, The (US) = CUORI SENZA FRONTIERE (1950)
White Nights = NOTTI BIANCHE, LE (1957)
WHITE OAK (1921) *d Lambert Hillyer st/w* W Hart *c* August 7rs *pc* W Hart
WHITE PEBBLES (1927) *d* Thorpe 4485ft
WHITE RAVEN, THE (1917) *d/ad George D Baker w* E Barrymore 6rs
WHITE ROSE, THE (1923) *d* Griffith *w* Marsh 10rs *r* UA
WHITE ROSES (1910) *d* Griffith *w* Pickford 1rl Bio
WHITE SAVAGE (1943) *d* Arthur Lubin s Brooks *w* Montez, Sabu part *75min Mon
WHITE SHADOW, THE (1923) *d/co-s Graham Cutts p* Balcon *e/dec* Hitchcock *w* C Brook 4047ft
WHITE SHADOWS IN THE SOUTH SEAS (1928) *d* WS Van Dyke *co-st* Flaherty 90min MGM
White Sheik, The = SCEICCO BIANCO, LO (1952)
WHITE SISTER, THE (1924) *d* H King *w* L Gish, Colman 12rs
WHITE SISTER, THE (1933) *d* V Fleming *s* D Stewart *c* Daniels *m* Stothart *w* H Hayes, Gable 110min MGM
White Slave Trade (UK) = TRATTA DELLE BIANCHE, LA (1952)
White Slide, The = BILA SPONA (1960)
White Stallion, The = OUTLAW STALLION, THE (1954)
White Stallion, The = CRIN BLANC, LE CHEVAL SAUVAGE (1956)
White Threads of the Cascades = TAKINO SHIRAITO (1933)
WHITE TIGER, THE (1923) *d/s* Browning 7rs U
WHITE TOWER, THE (1950) *d* Tetzlaff *c* Rennahan *w* G Ford, Valli, Rains 98min RKO
WHITE UNICORN, THE (1948) *d Bernard Knowles w* Greenwood, Lockwood
White Voices (UK) = VOCI BIANCHE, LE (1963)
White Warrior, The = AGI MURAD, IL DIAVOLO BIANCO (1958)
WHITEWASH AND MILLER (1898) *p* Paul
WHITE WITCH DOCTOR (1953) *d* Hathaway *s* Goff, Roberts *c* Shamroy *co-a* Wheeler *m* Herrmann *w* S Hayward, Mitchum *96min Fox
WHITE ZOMBIE (1932) *d Victor Halperin w* Lugosi 73min *r* UA
Whither Germany? (US) = KUHLE WAMPE (1932)
Who are you, Polly Maggoo? (UK) = QUI ETES VOUS, POLLY MAGGOO? (1966)
WHO DONE IT? (1955) *d* Dearden 82min
WHO HAS BEEN ROCKING MY DREAMBOAT? (1941, *ur*) *d/s/c/e* Anger 7min
WHO IS JAMES JONES? (1967) *d/ex-p* A King 16mm * (ep in series *The Creative Person*)
WHO IS THE MAN? (1924) *d Walter Summers w* Gielgud
WHO KILLED MARY WHATS'ER NAME? (1971) *d* Pintoff *90min
Whole Family Works, The = HATARAKU IKKA (1939)
WHOLE TOWN'S TALKING, THE (1935) *d* J Ford *s* Swerling *fst* Burnett *di* Riskin *c* August *w* Robinson, Arthur, (Parrish) 95min Col
WHOLE TRUTH, THE (1958) *d* Guillermin *p* Clayton *w* S Granger, D Reed, G Sanders 85min Col
WHOM THE GODS DESTROY (1915) *d* Brenon
WHOM THE GODS DESTROY (1916) *d/co-p/ad* Blackton 5rs Vit
WHOM THE GODS DESTROY (1934) *d* W Lang *s* Buchman *w* R Young, Tamiroff 75min Col
WHOM THE GODS WOULD DESTROY (19191) *d* Borzage FN
WHOOPEE (1930) *d Thornton Freeland p* Goldwyn *c* Garmes, Rennahan, Toland *w* Cantor, (Grable) 94min *r* UA
WHO PAYS (1916) *d* H King Pat serial in 8 eps
WHO'S AFRAID OF VIRGINIA WOOLF? (1966) *d* M Nichols *p/s* Lehman *fpl Edward Albee c* Wexler *m* North *w* Burton, E Taylor, Segal 132min WB
Who Saw Him Die? = OLE DOLE DOFF (1967)
WHO'S BEEN SLEEPING IN MY BED? (1963) *d* Daniel Mann *c* Ruttenberg *co-a* Pereira *m* Duning *w* Martin, Conte PV* 103min Par
WHOSE LITTLE WIFE ARE YOU (1918) *d* Cline *p/s* Sennett *w* Turpin 2rs
WHO'S GOT THE ACTION? (1962) *d* Daniel Mann *c* Ruttenberg *w* Martin, Turner, Matthau PV* 93min Par
WHO'S MINDING THE STORE (1963) *d/co-s* Tashlin *co-a* Pereira *w* J Lewis, Moorehead *90min Par
WHO'S YOUR LADY FRIEND? (1937) *d* C Reed 73min
WHO WAS THAT LADY? (1960) *d* G Sidney *p/s* Krasna *m* Previn *w* Curtis, Martin, J Leigh 115min Col
WHO WRITES TO SWITZERLAND (1937) *d/s* Cavalcanti
WHY BRING THAT UP? (1929) *d/co-s* G Abbott 7779ft Par
WHY CHANGE YOUR WIFE (1920) *d* De Mille *w* Swanson 7rs FPL
Why Does Your Husband Deceive You? = POR QUE TE ENGANA TU MARIDO? (1968)
WHY GIRLS LOVE SAILORS (1927) *d Fred Guiol w* Laurel, Hardy Pat
WHY HE GAVE UP (1911) *d* Sennett *w* Normand ½rl Bio
WHY MAN CREATES (1968) *d/p/co-s* Bass 16mm* 25min
WHY MEN LEAVE HOME (1924) *d/p* Stahl 8rs FN
WHY MUST I DIE? (1960) *d* Del Ruth 86min
WHY SMITH LEFT HOME (1919) *d* Crisp 8rs FPL
Why UNESCO? = PROC UNESCO (1958)
WHY WE FIGHT (c1945) *co-d* Litvak, Capra series in 12 parts
WHY WORK? (1923) *d* Newmeyer *w* H Lloyd Pat
WICHITA (1955) *d* J Tourneur *p* W Mirisch *c* Lipstein *w* McCrea, Miles CS* 81min AA
WICKED (1931) *d* Dwan *c* Marley *w* V McLaglen 55min Fox
WICKED AS THEY COME (1956) *d/co-s* K Hughes *m* Arnold *w* Dahl, H Marshall 94min *r* Col
WICKED DARLING, THE (1919) *d* Browning *w* Chaney 6rs
WICKED LADY, THE (1945) *d/s* L Arliss *e* Fisher *w* Mason, Lockwood 104min EL
WICKED WOMAN (1953) *d/co-s* Rouse 77min U
WIDEBOY (1952) *d/s* K Hughes 67min
WIDE OPEN (1930) *d* A Mayo *w* Fazenda, Horton 6386ft WB
Widow, the = VEDOVA, LA (1955)
Widower, The = SAMMA NO AJI (1962)
WIDOW IN SCARLET (1932) *d* G Seitz *c* Cronjager 64min
Wie er in die Welt kam = GOLEM, DER (1920)
WIE ICH DETEKTIV WURDE (1916) *d/p/s* May 4rs
WIE LEBT DER BERLINER ARBEITER (1930, *uf*) *d* Dudow
Wife, A = TSUMA (1953)
Wife, Be Like A rose = TSUMA YO BARA NO YONI (1935)
WIFE, DOCTOR AND NURSE (1937) *d* W Lang *co-s* Trotti *c* Cronjager *w* L Young, W Baxter, Cook 85min Fox
WIFE, HUSBAND AND FRIEND (1939) *d* Ratoff *as-p/s* N Johnson *w* W Baxter, Romero, L Young 80min Fox
Wife Lost = NYOBO FUNSHITSU (1928)
WIFE OF GENERAL LING, THE (1937) *d* Vajda 72min
WIFE OF MONTE CRISTO, THE (1946) *d/co-s* Ulmer 79min PRC (= *Monte Cristo – Masked Avenger*)
WIFE OF THE CENTAUR (1924) *d* K Vidor *p* L Mayer *w* J Gilbert 7rs 81min
WIFE SAVERS (1928) *d Ralph Cedar p* Cruze *as-p* BP Schulberg *w* Beery, Pitts 5434ft Par
Wife's Heart = TSUMA NO KOKORO (1956)
WIFE VS SECRETARY (1936) *d* C Brown *co-s* Krasna, Mahin *c* June *co-m* Stothart *w* M Loy, Gable, Harlow, J Stewart 88min MGM
WIFE WANTED (1946) *d* Karlson *co-p/w* K Francis 73min Mon
Wigwam, De = BRANDENDE STRAAL (1911)
WIJ BOUWEN (1930) *d/s/c/e* Ivens 1800m (= *We are Building*) in 4 parts: Part 1 *Nieuwe Architektur* 300m / Part 2 *Heien* 600m / Part 3 *Caisson Bouw Rotterdam*, 300m / Part 4 *Zuid Limburg – Spoorwegboum in Limbourg* 600m
WILD AND THE WILLING, THE (1962) *d* Thomas 112min JAR
WILD AND WONDERFUL (1963) *d* Michael Anderson *p* H Hecht *co-a* Golitzen *w* Curtis *87min U
WILD AND WOOLLY (1917) *d* Emerson *p/w* Fairbanks Sr *s* Loos *c* Edeson 5rs
WILD ANGELS, THE (1966) *d/p* Corman PV* 93min AI
Wild Beasts = DRAVCI (1948)
WILD BILL HICKOK (1923) *d Clifford S Smith p/pc/st/w* W Hart 7rs
WILD BILL HICKOK RIDES (1941) *d* Enright *c* McCord *w* Constance Bennett 81min WB
Wild Birds = VILDFÖGLER (1954)
WILD BLUE YONDER, THE (1951) *d* Dwan *p* H Yates *m* V Young *w* Corey, Brennan 98min Rep (= *Thunder Across the Pacific/Bombs over Japan*)
WILD BOYS OF THE ROAD (1933) *d* Wellman 77min FN
WILD BUNCH, THE (1969) *d/co-s* Peckinpah *c* Ballard *w* Holden, E O'Brien, Borgnine, Ryan, Fernandez PV70* 145min
WILDCAT, THE (1953) *d/s* Haanstra *p* Elton 33min
Wildcat, The = BERGKATZE, DIE (1921)
Wild Child = ENFANT SAUVAGE, L' (1970)
WILD COMPANY (1930) *d* McCarey *c* O'Connell *w* Lugosi 7000ft Fox
WILD FLOWER (1914) *d/co-s* Dwan 4rs FPL
WILD GEESE CALLING (1941) *d* Brahm, H Brown *c* Ballard *m* A Newman *w* H Fonda, J Bennett 77min Fox
WILD GIRL (1932) *d* Walsh *fst* (*Salomy Jane's Kiss*) *Bret Harte c* Brodine *w* J Bennett, Pichel 78min Fox
WILD GOLD (1934) *d* G Marshall *st* D Nichols, Trotti *w* Trevor 75min Fox
WILD GOOSE CHASE, THE (1915) *d/co-s* De Mille *co-s/fpl William De Mille pc* Lasky
WILD GOOSE CHASER, THE (1924) *d* Bacon *st* Capra *w* Turpin 2rs Par
WILD HARE, A (1940) *d* Avery *p* L Schlesinger *1rl WB
WILD HARVEST (1947) *d* Garnett *c* J Seitz *co-a* Dreier *m* Freidhofer *w* Ladd, Lamour, Preston, Nolan 93min Par
Wild Heart, The = GONE TO EARTH (1950)
WILD HEATHER (1921) *d/p* Hepworth 5000ft
WILD HERITAGE (1958) *d* Haas *c* Lathrop *co-a* Golitzen, Boyle *w* O'Sullivan CS* 78min U
WILD HORSE (1931) *d* Thorpe, *Sidney Algier* 77min
WILD HORSE MESA (1925) *d* G Seitz *c* Glennon *w* Fairbanks Jr 7164ft FPL *r* Par
WILD HORSE MESA (1932) *d* Hathaway *fn Zane Grey rm* 1925 *w* R Scott 58min Par
WILD IN THE COUNTRY (1961) *d* P Dunne *p* Wald *s* Odets *c* Mellor *m* K Hopkins *w* Presley, Weld CS* 114min *r* Fox
WILD IS THE WIND (1957) *d* Cukor *p* Wallis *c* C Lang, Griggs *co-a* Pereira *m* Tiomkin *w* Mangnani, Quinn VV 114min *r* Par
Wild Love = INAMORATI, GLI (1955)
WILD 90 (1968) *d/co-p* Mailer *c* Pennebaker *w* Mailer, Pennebaker 16mm 90min
WILD NORTH, THE (1952) *d* Marton *c* Surtees *co-a* Gibbons *m* Kaper *w* S Granger, Corey, Charisse *97min MGM

WILD OATS LANE (1926) d/pc Neilan 6900ft
WILD ONE, THE (1953) d Benedek s Paxton c Mohr m Leith Stevens w Brando, Marvin 79min pc Kramer r Col
WILD ORANGES (1922) d/co-s K Vidor co-s Mathis 7rs 66m pc Goldwyn
WILD ORCHIDS (1929) d Franklin c Daniels w Garbo 9499ft MGM
WILD PARTY, THE (1956) d Horner c Leavitt w Quinn 81min r UA
WILD RACERS, THE (1968) d D Haller *79min r AI
WILD RIVER (1960) d/p Kazan s Osborn co-a Wheeler m K Hopkins w Clift, Remick CS* 110min r Fox
WILD ROVERS (1971) d/co-p/s Edwards c Lathrop m Goldsmith w Holden, Malden PV70* 132min
WILD SEED (1965) d Brian G Hutton c C Hall 99min U
WILD STALLION (1926) d A McLaglen, LD Collins p W Mirisch *70min Mon
Wild Strawberries = SMULTRONSTALLET (1957)
WILD WOMEN (1918) d J Ford p/w Carey 5rs U
WILFUL PEGGY (1910) d Griffith w Pickford 1rl Bio
WILHELM PIEK – DAS LEBEN UNSERES PRASIDEN-TEN (1951) d/s Andrew Thorndike 79min
WILL ANY GENTLEMAN? (1953) d Michael Anderson *84min ABC
WILLARD (1971) d Daniel Mann m North w Borgnine *95min pc B Crosby
WILLIAM FOX MOVIETONE FOLLIES OF 1929 (1929) d/st D Butler 14rs Fox
WILLIE THE KID (1952) d Cannon m Gold *7min pc UPA r Col
Will of the Wisp (UK) = FEU FOLLET, LE (1963)
Willows of Ginza (US) = GINZA NO YANAGI (1932)
WILL SUCCESS SPOIL ROCK HUNTER? (1957) d/p/st/s Tashlin fpl Axelrod c Joe Macdonald co-a Wheeler m Mockridge w Mansfield, Randall, Blondell, (G Marx) CS* 95min Fox (= Oh, For a Man!)
WILLY TOBLER UND DER UNTERGANG DER 6 FLOTTE (1971) d Kluge
WILSON (1944) d H King p Zanuck st/s Trotti fco-pl (In Time to Come) Houseman c Shamroy m A Newman w Mitchell, C Coburn, Price, Dalio *154min Fox
WINCHESTER '73 (1950) d A Mann p A Rosenberg co-s B Chase c Daniels w J Stewart, Winters, Duryea, McIntire, Hudson, Curtis 86min U
WIND, THE (1928) d Sjöström fn Dorothy Scarborough co-dec Gibbons w L Gish 6400ft MGM
WIND ACROSS THE EVERGLADES (1958) d N Ray s B Schulberg c Brun w Plummer, Ives, G Lee *93min r WB
WINDBAG THE SAILOR (1936) d William Beaudine w Hay 85min
Windfall in Athens = KYRIAKATIKO XYPNIMA (1953)
WINDFLOWERS (1967) d/m A Mekas 16mm 64min
WINDJAMMER (1958) co-d/p De Rochemont co-d Bill Colleran co-c Brun *127min
WINDMILL IN BARBADOS (1933) d B Wright p Grierson EMB
Window, The = MADO (1965)
WINDOW CLEANER (1932) d Asquith
Wind from the East = VETER S VOSTOKA (1941)
WINDOM'S WAY (1958) d Neame c Challis w Finch *108min JAR
WINDOW, THE (1949) d Tetzlaff w A Kennedy, Roman 73min RKO
WINDOW CLEANER, THE (1932) d Asquith
WINDOW WATER BABY MOVING (1959) d Brakhage 16mm * si 12min
WINDS OF CHANGE (1925) d F Lloyd c Brodine w V McLaglen 9753ft pc F Lloyd r FN
WINDS OF FOGO, THE (1970) d Low *20min NFBC
WINDY DAY (1968) d J and F Hubley anim* 9min
WINE OF YOUTH (1924) d K Vidor p L Mayer 1920m
WINE, WOMEN AND SONG (1932) d Brenon 70min
WING AND A PRAYER (1944) d Hathaway co-a L Wheeler m Friedhofer w D Andrews, Bickford 97min Fox
WINGED VICTORY (1944) d Cukor p Zanuck s/fpl M Hart co-a Wheeler w Crain, E O'Brien, Cobb, Holliday, Malden, Ritt 130min Fox
WINGS (1929) d Wellman co-c Harlan w Bow, G Cooper, Hopper 12267ft Par
Wings and the Woman = THEY FLEW ALONE (1942)
WINGS FOR THE EAGLE (1942) d Bacon w Sheridan 84min WB
WINGS OF ADVENTURE (1930) d Thorpe 6rs
WINGS OF DANGER (1952) d Fisher w Kendall 73min
WINGS OF EAGLES, THE (1957) d J Ford p Schnee w J Wayne, M O'Hara, Dailey, Marsh *110min MGM
WINGS OF THE HAWK (1953) d Boetticher p A Rosen-berg w Heflin 3-D* 80min U
WINGS OF THE MORNING (1937) d Harold D Shuster co-c Cardiff w Annabella, H Fonda *86min Fox
WINGS OF THE NAVY (1939) d Bacon w Payne, De Havilland 89min WB
Wings of Victory = VALERII CHKALOV (1941)
WINGS OVER AFRICA (1936) d Vajda 63min
WINGS OVER HONOLULU (1937) d Potter w Milland 77min U

WINNER TAKE ALL (1932) d Del Ruth w Cagney 68min WB
WINNING (1969) d James Goldstone w P Newman, Wood-ward, R Wagner PV* 123min U
WINNING OF BARBARA WORTH, THE (1926) d H King p Goldwyn fn Harold Bell Wright w Colman, Banky, G Cooper 9rs r UA
WINNING OF WONEGA, THE (1912) d Ince
WINNING TEAM, THE (1952) d Lewis Seiler c Hickox w D Day, Reagan 98min WB
WINNING TICKET, THE (1935) d/co-p Charles F Riesner co-2nd d J Tourneur co-p J Cummings co-st Seaton c C Clarke w Tamiroff 70min MGM
WINSLOW BOY, THE (1948) d Asquith co-s/p De Grunwald co-s/fpl Rattigan c F Young cos m Messe Alwyn w Donat 117min BL
Winter Light = NATTVARDSGASTERNA (1962)
WINTER MEETING (1948) d Windust p Blanke c E Haller w B Davis 104min WB
WINTERSET (1936) d Santell p Berman fpl Maxwell Ander-son c Marley w Meredith, Ball, Carradine 78min RKO
WINTERTIME (1943) d Brahm c Joe Macdonald, C Clarke co-m A Newman w Wilde, Romero 82min Fox
Winter Wind = SIROKKO (1969)
WIN THAT GIRL (1927) d D Butler 5310ft Fox
WIPING SOMETHING OFF THE SLATE (1900) p Hep-worth 75ft anim
WIR MACHEN MUSIK (1942) d/s Käutner 95min
WISE GIRLS (1929) d E Mason Hopper ad/fpl (Kempy) JC Nugent, E Nugent c Daniels w E Nugent 8818ft MGM
WISE GUY, THE (1926) d/pc F Lloyd s Furthman c Brodine 7775ft FN
Wise Guys, The (US) = GRANDES GUEULES, LES (1965)
WISE KID (1922) d Browning 5rs U
WISHING RING, THE (1914) d M Tourneur 5rs
Witchcraft through the Ages = HAXAN (1921)
Witches, The (US) = STREGHE, LE (1966)
WITCHING HOUR, THE (1934) d Hathaway c B Reynolds 69min Par
Witch in Love, The = STREGA IN AMORE, LA (1966)
WITCH'S CRADLE, THE (1944, uf) d Deren
WITH A SONG IN MY HEART (1952) d W Lang p/st/s Trotti c Shamroy co-a Wheeler w S Hayward, D Wayne, Ritter, R Wagner *117min Fox
With Bated Breath (UK) = COL CUORE IN GOLA (1967)
WITHIN THE LAW (1923) d F Lloyd c Brodine w N Talmadge 9rs FN
Within the Law = PAID (1930)
WITHIN THE LAW (1939) d Machaty co-s Lederer c Lawton 65min MGM
WITH LEE IN VIRGINIA (1912) d Ince
WITH LOVE AND HISSES (1927) d Fred Guiol w Laurel, Hardy Pat
Without Dowry = BEZPRIDANNITSA (1937)
WITHOUT HONOR (1949) d Pichel s Poe c Lindon m M Steiner w Tone, Moorehead 69min r UA
Without Pity (UK) = SENZA PIETA (1948)
WITHOUT RESERVATIONS (1946) d LeRoy p Lasky c Krasner c J Wayne, Colbert, Parsons, (C Grant) 107min RKO
Without Warning = INVISIBLE MENACE, THE (1938)
WITH SIX YOU GET EGGROLL (1968) d Howard Morris w D Day, Keith PV* 95min
WITNESSES, THE (1967) d Rossif m Jarre n Lindfors 82min
WITNESS FOR THE PROSECUTION (1957) d/co-s B Wilder co-s Kurnitz fpl/fn Agatha Christie c R Harlan a Trauner w Power, Dietrich, Laughton 116min r UA
WITNESS TO MURDER (1954) d Rowland c J Alton w Stanwyck, G Sanders 83min UA
WIVES NEVER KNOW (1936) d E Nugent w Menjou, C Ruggles 75min Par
WIVES OF MEN (1918) d/st/s Stahl 7rs
WIVES UNDER SUSPICION (1938) d Whale rm THE KISS BEFORE THE MIRROR (1935) 75min U
WIZARD OF OZ, THE (1925) d/w Semon 7rs
WIZARD OF OZ, THE (1939) d V Fleming p LeRoy fn Frank L Baum c Rosson co-a Gibbons w Garland 101min MGM
WM MCKINLEY RECEIVING TELEGRAM AN-NOUNCING HIS ELECTION (1896) d Dickson, Bitzer
WOCHENENDE (1928) d Ruttmann (= Weekend)
WOGEN DES SCHICKSALS (1918) d/p/s May 4rs
WO IST MEIN SCHATZ? (1916) d/w Lubitsch 1rl (= Where is my Treasure?)
WOLF HUNTERS, THE (1949) d Boetticher 70min Mon
WOLF OF WALL STREET, THE (1929) d Rowland V Lee c Milner w G Bancroft, Lucas 76min Par
Wolfpack (UK) = HALBSTARKEN, DIE (1956)
WOLF'S CLOTHING (1927) d Del Ruth s Zanuck 6400ft WB
WOLF'S CLOTHING (1936) d Marton
WOLF SONG (1929) d V Fleming w G Cooper 5992ft Par
Wolf Trap (UK) = VLCI JAMA (1957)
Wolo Czarwienko = BALLET PRIMADONNAN (1916)
WOLVES (1930) d Albert De Courville w D Gish
Wolves = OOKAMI (1955)

WOLVES OF THE RAIL (1918) d/w W Hart supn Ince c August 5rs pc W Hart
Woman = AURAT (1939)
Woman = ONNA (1948)
WOMAN (1918) d/p M Tourneur 7rs
WOMAN, A (1915) d/s Chaplin c Totheroh w Chaplin, Purviance 2rs S & A (= A Perfect Lady/Charlie and the Perfect Lady)
Woman Alone, The (US) = SABOTAGE (1936)
Woman and Bean Soup = ONNA TO MISOSHIRU (1968)
WOMAN AND THE LAW (1918) d/s Walsh 7rs Fox
Woman at the Helm = ASSZONY A TELEPEN (1962)
WOMAN BARBER (1898) d G Smith
WOMAN CHASES MAN (1937) d John Blystone p Goldwyn co-s Anthony c Toland m A Newman w Crain, M Hopkins, McCrea, B Crawford 71min r UA
WOMAN DISPUTED, THE (1928) d/p H King co-d Sam Taylor m Riesenfeld w N Talmadge, Roland 9rs r UA
Woman, Don't Make Your Name Dirty = ONNA-YO KIMI NO NA O KEGASU NAKARE (1930)
WOMAN FROM MONTE CARLO, THE (1932) d Curtiz c E Haller w W Huston, Dagover 65min FN
WOMAN FROM MOSCOW, THE (1928) d Ludwig Berger s/t J Farrow c Milner w Negri, Lukas 6938ft Par
WOMAN GOD FORGOT, THE (1917) d De Mille 6rs r FPL
WOMANHANDLED (1925) d La Cava c Cronjager FPL
WOMAN HATER (1948) d T Young w S Granger, Feuillère 105min
WOMAN HE MARRIED, THE (1922) d Niblo 7rs
WOMAN HUNGRY (1930) d Badger co-c Polito 59min FN
Woman Hunt (UK) = AU ROYAUME DES CIEUX (1949)
WOMAN I LOVE, THE (1937) d Litvak rm L'EQUIPAGE (1935) co-m Honegger w M Hopkins, L Hayward, Muni 83min RKO
WOMAN IN A DRESSING GOWN (1957) d/co-p J Thompson c G Taylor 94min ABC
Woman in black = DAMEN I SVART (1958)
Woman in Chains (UK) = PRISONNIERE, LA (1968)
WOMAN IN HIDING (1949) d M Gordon fst JR Webb c Daniels w Lupino 92min U
WOMAN IN HIS HOUSE, THE (1920) d Stahl 7rs FN
WOMAN IN HIS LIFE, THE (1933) d G Seitz c June 75min MGM
Woman in July, A = STRIPPER, THE (1963)
WOMAN IN QUESTION, THE (1950) d Asquith 88min BL (= Five Angles on Murder)
WOMAN IN RED, THE (1935) d Florey c Polito w Stanwyck 68min FN
WOMAN IN ROOM 13, THE (1920) d F Lloyd 5000ft Goldwyn
WOMAN IN ROOM 13, THE (1932) d H King c J Seitz w M Loy 67min Fox
WOMAN IN THE HALL, THE (1947) d/co-s J Lee w J Simmons 93min
Woman in the Rumour = UWASA NO ONNA (1954)
WOMAN IN THE SUITCASE (1920) d Niblo 5000ft FPL
WOMAN IN THE WINDOW, THE (1944) d F Lang p/s N Johnson c Krasner w Robinson, J Bennett, Duryea 99min r RKO
Woman in the Window (UK) = RAGAZZA IN VETRINA, LA (1960)
WOMAN IN WHITE, THE (1929) d H Wilcox fn Wilkie Collins 6702ft
Woman in White = KVINNA I VITT (1949)
Woman in White, A (UK) = JOURNAL D'UNE FEMME EN BLANC, LE (1965)
Woman is a Flower = FEMME FLEUR, LA (1965)
Woman Like Satan, A (UK) = FEMME ET LA PANTIN, LA (1959)
WOMAN OBSESSED (1959) d Hathaway p/s Boehm c Mellor co-a Wheeler m Friedhofer w S Hayward, Boyd CS* 102min Fox
WOMAN OF AFFAIRS, A (1928) d C Brown c Daniels w Garbo, J Gilbert, Fairbanks Jr 8319ft MGM
Woman of a Pale Night = OBOROYO NO ONNA (1936)
WOMAN OF BRONZE, THE (1923) d K Vidor c O'Connell 1650ft
Woman of Darkness = YNGSJOMORDET (1966)
WOMAN OF EXPERIENCE, A (1931) d H Brown s/di/fpl (The Registered Woman) J Farrow c Mohr w Pitts 73min RKO
Woman of Evil (UK) = REINE MARGOT, LA (1953)
Woman of Musashino = MUSASHINO FUJIN (1951)
Woman of Osaka = NANIWA ONNA (1940)
Woman of Osaka, A = OSAKA NO ONNA (1958)
WOMAN OF PARIS, A (1923) d/p/s Chaplin co-c Totheroh w Chaplin, Menjou, Purviance 8rs r UA
Woman of Pleasure = KANRAKU NO ONNA (1925)
Woman of Rome (UK) = ROMANA, LA (1954)
WOMAN OF STRAW (1963) d Dearden s Heller w Lollo-brigida, Connery, R Richardson *117min r UA
Woman of Summer = STRIPPER, THE (1963)
Woman of the Dunes = SUNA NO ONNA (1964)
Woman of the River (UK) = DONNA DEL FIUME, LA (1954)
WOMAN OF THE SEA, A (1926, ur) d/s Von Sternberg p Chaplin w Purviance (= The Sea Gull)
Woman of the Snow, The (UK) = KAIDAN ep YUKI-ONNA (1964)

WOMAN OF THE WORLD, A (1925) d St Clair c Glennon w Negri 6353ft FPL r Par
WOMAN OF THE YEAR, THE (1942) d G Stevens p J Mankiewicz c Ruttenberg w Waxman w K Hepburn, Tracy, Bendix 112min MGM
Woman of Tokyo = TOKYO NO ONNA (1933)
WOMAN ON THE BEACH, THE (1947) d/co-s J Renoir m Eisler w J Bennett, Ryan, Bickford 71min RKO (= *La Femme sur la plage*)
WOMAN ON THE RUN (1950) d/co-s Foster c Mohr w Sheridan 77min U
WOMAN ON TRIAL, THE (1927) d/p Stiller as-p BP Schulberg c Glennon w Negri 5960ft Par
WOMAN PURSUED (1931) d Boleslavsky 75min RKO
WOMAN REBELS, A (1936) d Sandrich w K Hepburn, A Marshall, Crisp, Heflin 88min RKO
WOMAN'S ANGLE, THE (1952) d/co-s L Arliss 87min ABC
WOMAN'S DEVOTION, A (1956) d/w Henreid w Meeker 88min Rep
WOMAN'S FACE, A (1941) d Cukor p Saville co-s D Stewart dec Gibbons m Kaper w J Crawford, M Douglas, Veidt 106min MGM
Woman's Face = ONNA NO KAO (1949)
WOMAN'S FOOL, A (1918) d J Ford c B Reynolds w Carey 5rs U
Woman's Heresy, A = JASHUMON NO ONNA (1924)
Woman's Life, A = ONNA NO ISSHO (1952)
Woman's Life, A = ONNA NO REKISHI (1963)
Woman's Place, A = ONNA NO ZA (1962)
WOMAN'S PLACE (1921) d V Fleming p Emerson, Loos 6rs
WOMAN'S SECRET, A (1949) d N Ray p/s H Mankiewicz ex-p Schary m Holland w M O'Hara, M Douglas, Grahame 85min RKO
Woman's Testament, A = JOKYO (1960)
WOMAN'S VENGEANCE, A (1948) d/p Z Korda s Aldous Huxley a Lourié m Rozsa w Boyer, Blyth 96min U
WOMAN'S WORLD (1954) d Negulesco p Brackett c Joe Macdonald a Wheeler w C Webb, Allyson, Bacall, MacMurray, Wilde, Heflin CS* 94min Fox
WOMAN THEY ALMOST LYNCHED, THE (1953) d Dwan 90min Rep
Woman Times 7 (US) ' SEPT FOIS FEMME (1967)
WOMAN TO WOMAN (1924) d/co-s Graham Cutts co-p Balcon, Saville co-s/dec Hitchcock e Reville w C Brook 7455ft
WOMAN TO WOMAN (1929) d/co-p Saville rm 1924 8039ft
WOMAN TRAP (1929) d Wellman 6168ft Par
WOMAN UNDER OATH, A (1919) d Stahl
WOMAN, WAKE UP (1922) d/p K Vidor c Barnes 72min
WOMAN WANTED (1935) d G Seitz c C Clarke w O'Sullivan, McCrea 70min MGM
Woman Who Did, The = FRAU MIT DEM SCHLECHTEN RUF, DIE (1925)
Woman Who Touched the Legs, The = ASHI NI SAWATTA ONNA (1952)
Woman with a Dagger = ZHENSHCHINA Z KINZHALOM (1916)
WOMAN-WISE (1937) d Dwan 70min Fox
WOMAN WITH 4 FACES, THE (1923) d Brenon c Howe FPL
WOMAN WITH NO NAME, THE (1950) d/co-s Vajda c Heller 84min
Woman Without a Face = KVINNA UTAN ANSIKTE (1947)
WOMEN, THE (1939) d Cukor co-s Loos, Fitzgerald(uc) co-c Ruttenberg co-dec Gibbons w Shearer, J Crawford, R Russell, Goddard, Fontaine, Hopper part *132min MGM
Women are Strong = JOSEI WAT SUYOSHI (1924)
WOMEN AT WAR (1943) d Negulesco *20min WB/US Army
WOMEN EVERYWHERE (1930) d A Korda p Fox co-s/co-di Biro co-st Z Korda 84min Fox
WOMEN IN LOVE (1970) d K Russell fn DH Lawrence m Delerue *130min r UA
WOMEN IN THE WIND (1939) d J Farrow c Hickox w K Francis 65min WB
WOMEN LOVE DIAMONDS (1927) d/p/st Goulding 6373ft MGM
WOMEN MEN FORGET (1920) d Stahl 6000ft
WOMEN MEN MARRY (1931) d Charles Hutchison c Shamroy w R Scott 76min
WOMEN OF ALL NATIONS (1931) d Walsh c Andriot w V McLaglen, Bogart, Lugosi 72min Fox
Women of Kyoto = ONNA NO SAKA (1961)
Women of the Ginza = GINZA NO ONNA (1955)
Women of the Night = YORU NO ONNA TACHI (1948)
Women of the World = DONNA DEL MONDO, LA (1962)
Women on the Firing Line = HIJOSEN NO ONNA (1933)
Women's Town = ONNA NO MACHI (1940)
Women's Victory = JOSEI NO SHORI (1946)
WOMEN THEY TALK ABOUT (1928) d Bacon 5229ft WB
WOMEN WITHOUT NAMES (1940) d Florey c C Lang co-a Dreier 62min Par
WOMEN WON'T TELL (1933) d Thorpe w Darwell 67min
WONDER BAR (1934) d Bacon c Polito w Jolson, K Francis, Del Rio, D Powell, Darwell 81min WB

WONDERFUL COUNTRY, THE (1959) d Parrish ex-p Mitchum s Ardrey co-c F Crosby a Horner m North w Mitchum, Armendariz *98min r UA
WONDERFUL LIFE (1964) d Furie S* 113min WB (= *Singer's Paradise*)
WONDERFUL THING, THE (1922) d/co-s Brenon 7rs FN
WONDERFUL THINGS (1958) d H Wilcox 84min
WONDERFUL WORLD OF THE BROTHERS GRIMM, THE (1962) d Levin, Pal p Pal m Harline w Bloom, Laurence Harvey Cinerama* 129min MGM
WONDERFUL YEARS, THE (1958) d Käutner p R Hunter c Laszlo co-a Golitsen w T Wright CS* 84min U (= *The Reckless Years/The Restless Years*)
WONDER MAN (1945fi d Bruce Humberstone p Goldwyn co-s Shavelson co-c Milner w Kaye, Vera-Ellen, V Mayo *98min r RKO
WONDER OF WOMEN (1929) d C Brown 8796ft MGM
WONDER RING, THE (1955) d Brakhage 16mm * si 4min
Wonders of Aladdin = MERAVIGLIE DI ALADINO, LE (1961)
WONDERWALL (1968) d Joseph Massot m Harrison *92min
WON IN A CLOSET (1914) w Normand 1rl Key
Wooden Head = MOKUSEKI (1940)
WOODEN HORSE, THE (1950) d/co-s J Lee w Forbes, Finch 100min r BL
Wooden Soldiers = BABES IN TOYLAND (1934)
Word, The = ORDET (1954)
WORDS AND MUSIC (1948) d Taurog p Freed co-a Gibbons chor R Alton w Allyson, Garland, Gene Kelly, Rooney, Sothern, Charisse, J Leigh, Quine, Vera-Ellen 119min MGM
WORDS FOR BATTLE (1941) d/s Jennings cy Olivier 8min Crown
WORK (1915) d/s Chaplin c Totheroh w Chaplin, Purviance 2rs S & A (= *The Paperhanger*)
WORKERS AND JOBS (1935) d/p Elton 15min
Worker's Diary, A = TYOMEHEN PAIVAKIRJA (1967)
WORKING AND PLAYING TO HEALTH (1953) d W Van Dyke
WORK IS A 4-LETTER WORD (1968) d P Hall fpl Henry Livings *93min r JAR
WORK PARTY (1942) d Lye
World and his Wife, The (UK) = STATE OF THE UNION (1948)
WORLD AND ITS WOMAN, THE (1919) d F Lloyd a Gibbons 7rs pc Goldwyn
World Belongs to Them, The = SVET PATRI NAM (1937)
WORLD AND THE FLESH, THE (1932) d Cromwell c Struss w G Bancroft, M Hopkins 75min Par
WORLD CHANGES, THE (1933) d LeRoy p Wallis c Gaudio w Muni, Astor, (Quine) 90min FN
World Down Here = JIN KYO (1924)
WORLD FOR RANSOM (1954) d/co-p Aldrich c Biroc w Duryea 82min r AA
WORLD IN HIS ARMS, THE (1952) d Walsh p A Rosenberg s B Chase c Metty co-a Golitzen w Peck, Blyth, Quinn, McIntire, Forbes *104min U
WORLD IS RICH, THE (1948) d/e Rotha 36min Col
World Melody = MELODIE DER WELT, DIE (1929)
WORLD MOVES ON, THE (1934) d J Ford co-m M Steiner, G Gershwin w Carroll, Tone 90min Fox
World of Apu, The = APUR SANSAR (1919)
WORLD OF DONG KINGMAN, THE (1953) d/p/c Howe 16mm sh
WORLD OF HENRY ORIENT, THE (1964) d Hill co-s N Johnson co-c B Kaufman m E Bernstein w Sellers PV* 106min r UA
World of Paul Delvaux, The = MONDE DE PAUL DELVAUX, LE (1946)
WORLD OF PLENTY (1943) p Rotha 46min
World of Strangers, A = DILEMMA (1962)
WORLD OF SUZIE WONG, THE (1960) d Quine p Stark fpl Osborn c Unsworth m Duning w Holden *123min Par
WORLD PREMIERE (1941) d Tetzlaff p S Siegel c Fapp w J Barrymore 70min Par
WORLD'S HEAVYWEIGHT CHAMPIONSHIP CONTEST BETWEEN JACK DEMPSEY AND GEORGES CARPENTIER, THE (1921) 5rs pc Quimby
WORLD, THE FLESH AND THE DEVIL, THE (1958) d/s Macdonald m Rozsa w M Ferrer CS 95min MGM
WORLD WAS HIS JURY, THE (1958) d Sears p Katzman w O'Brien 82min Col
WORLD WITHOUT END (1953) d/s B Wright, Rotha m Elisabeth Lutyens 60min (= *Je suis un homme*)
World without Sun = MONDE SANS SOLEIL, LE (1964)
WOULD-BE SHRINER, THE (1912) d/w Sennett ½rl Bio
WOUNDED BIRD, THE (1956) d Pintoff
WOW (1969) d/s/co-e Jutra part *95min
W PLAN, THE (1930) d/p/s Saville c F Young w Carroll 104min
Wrath of Dionysus, The = GNEV DIONISA (1914)
WRATH OF THE GODS, THE (1914) co-d Ince w Borzage
WRECKING CREW, THE (1968) d Karlson c Leavitt w Martin *104min Col
WRECK OF THE MARY DEARE, THE (1959) d Michael Anderson p Blaustein fn Hammond Innes c Ruttenberg, F Young m Duning w G Cooper, Heston, M

Redgrave, Emlyn Williams, R Harris CS* 105min r MGM
Wrested from the Sea = ZEE ONTRUKT, DER (1949)
Wrestler and the Clown, The = BORETS I KLOUN (1957)
WRITTEN ON THE WIND (1956) d Sirk p Zugsmith c Metty co-a Golitzen w Hudson, Bacall, Stack, Malone *98min U
WR - MISTERIJE OGANIZMA (1971) d/s Makaveyev *80min (= *WR - Mysteries of the Organism*)
WR - Mysteries of the Organism = WR - MISTERIJE ORGANIZMA (1971)
WRONG AGAIN (1929) d/f McCarey w Laurel, Hardy 2rs r MGM
WRONG BOX, THE (1966) d/p Forbes fn RL Stevenson and Lloyd Osbourne m Barry w J Mills, R Richardson, Caine, Sellers *110min r Col
WRONG MAN, THE (1957) d/p Hitchcock as-p H Coleman co-s/fst (True Story of Christopher Emmanuel Balestrero) Maxwell Anderson c Burks m Herrmann w H Fonda, Miles 105min WB
WRONG ROAD, THE (1937) d Cruze 7rs Rep
WRONG WAY OUT, THE (1938) d Machaty 2rs MGM
WSPOLNY POKOJ (1960) d/s Has 90min (= *One Room Tenants*)
WSZYSTKO NA SPRZEDAZ (1968) d/s Wajda *105min (= *Everything for Sale*)
WUNDERBARER SOMMER, EIN (1958) d Tressler
WUNDER DES MALACHIAS, DAS (1961) d/co-s Wicki 126min (= *Malachias*)
WUNDER DES SCHNEESCHUHS, DAS (1920) co-d/co-s/co-c/w Fanck co-d/co-s Dr Tauern 1822m
WUNDER DES SCHNEESCHUHS, DAS Teil 2: EINE FUCHSJAGD AUF SKIERN DURCHS ENGADIN (1922) d/s/co-c Fanck 2466m
WUSA (1970) d S Rosenberg co-p P Newman w P Newman, Woodward, Perkins, Laurence Harvey PV* 114min r Par
WUTHERING HEIGHTS (1939) d Wyler p Goldwyn s Ben Hecht, MacArthur fn Emily Bronte c Toland m A Newman w Oberon, Olivier, Niven, Crisp 103min r UA
WYOMING (1928) d/st WS Van Dyke 4435ft
WYOMING (1940) d Thorpe co-s H Butler w Beery 89min MGM
WYOMING RENEGADE (1955) d Sears *73min Col
WYSCIG POKOJU WARSZAWA–BERLINA–PRAGA (1952) d Ivens 44min

X-15 PILOT (1961) co-d Robert Andrew co-d/c R Leacock
X-PARONI (1964) co-d Jarva, Jaakko Pakkasvirta, Spede Pasaseu co-d/p/s/c/e/ Jarva (= *Baron X*)
X-THE MAN WITH THE X-RAY EYES (1963) d/p Corman co-ex-p Arkoff c F Crosby a D Haller w Milland 80min AI (= *The Man with the X-Ray Eyes*)

YABU NO NAKA NO KURONEKO (1968) d/s Shindo S 108min Toho (= *Kuroneko/Black Cat*)
YABURE-DAIKO (1949) d Kinoshita w Mori (= *The Broken Drum*)
YAGODKA LYUBVI (1926) d/s Dovzhenko 802m (= *Love's Berries*)
YAGUA (1941) d Fejos SF
YAHUDI (1958) d Roy
YAKOV SVERDLOV (1940) d/co-s Yutkevich 125min
YAMABIKO GEKKO (1952) d Imai (= *Echo School/Story of a School*)
YAMA NO OTO (1954) d Naruse Toho (= *Sounds from the Mountains/The Echo*)
YAMATA (1919) d A Korda
YANGTSE INCIDENT (1957) d Michael Anderson p Wilcox w Tamiroff 113min BL
YANK AT ETON, A (1942) d Taurog c Freund a Gibbons w Rooney, Bartholemew, Lawford 88min MGM
YANK AT OXFORD, A (1938) d Conway p Balcon co-st Gilliat c Rosson e Frend w R Taylor, L Barrymore, O'Sullivan, V Leigh MGM
YANKEE (1966) d Brass *95min
YANKEE CLIPPER, THE (1927) d Julian 7920ft PRC
YANKEE DOODLE DANDY (1943) d Curtiz p J Warner, Wallis co-s JJ Epstein c Howe chor Prinz co-e D Siegel w Cagney, W Huston 126min WB
YANKEE DOODLE MOUSE, THE (1943) d Hanna, Barbera p Quimby anim* 8min MGM
Yankee in King Arthur's Court, A = CONNECTICUTT YANKEE IN KING ARTHUR'S COURT, A (1949)
YANKEE NO! (1960) d R Leacock co-d A Maysles
YANKEE PASHA (1954) d Pevney w R Fleming, J Chandler, Cobb 84min U
YANK IN LONDON, A (1945) d H Wilcox w Neagle
YANK IN THE RAF, A (1941) d H King p Zanuck m A Newman w Power, Grable 98min Fox

YANK ON THE BURMA ROAD, A (1942) *d* G Seitz *co-st/co-s* H Butler 65min MGM
Yank in Rome, A = AMERICANO IN VACANZA, UN (1945)
YEAH YEAH YEAH NEW YORK MEETS THE BEATLES (1964) *d/c* A and D Maysles *w* The Beatles TV (= *What's Happening*)
Year 1919, The = GOD DEVYATNADISATII (1938)
YEARLING, THE (1946) *d* C Brown *p* Franklin *s* Osborn *co-c* Arling *c* Gibbons *m* Stothart *w* Peck, Wyman *134min MGM
Yearning = AKOGARE (1935)
Yearning = MIDARERU (1964)
YEARS BETWEEN, THE (1946) *d* Compton Bennett *w* M Redgrave 100min BL
YEARS OF CHANGE (1950) *d* W Van Dyke *c* R Leacock
YEHUDI MENUHIN – CHEMIN DE LUMIÈRE (1971) *d* Reichenbach, *Bernard Gavoty w Yehudi Menuhin*, Shankar *85min
YELLOW BALLOON, THE (1952) *d/s* J Thompson 80min
YELLOW CAESAR, THE (1941) *d* Cavalcanti *e* Crichton 24min
YELLOW CANARY, THE (1943) *d* H Wilcox *w* Neagle 98min
YELLOW CANARY, THE (1963) *d* Kulik *s* Serling *c* F Crosby *m* K Hopkins CS* 93min Fox
Yellow Car, The = GULA BILEN, DEN (1963)
Yellow Crow = KIIROI KARASU (1957)
YELLOW FLAME, THE (1913) *d* Ince 840m
YELLOW JACK (1938) *d* G Seitz *co-e* Vorkapich *w* Montgomery 83min MGM
YELLOW LILY, THE (1928) *d* A Korda *s* Biro *c* Garmes *w* C Brook 7187ft FN
Yellow Passport, The (UK) = YELLOW TICKET, THE (1931)
Yellow Robe, The = RANSALU (1967)
YELLOW ROLLS ROYCE, THE (1964) *d* Asquith *p* De Grunwald *st/s* Rattigan *c* Hildyard *w* Harrison, Moreau, Ingrid Bergman, McLaine, G Scott, Sharif, Delon, I Miranda PV* 122min MGM
YELLOW SANDS (1938) *d* Brenon *w* Newton 69min
YELLOW SKY (1948) *d* Wellman *p/s* Trotti *fst* Burnett *c* Joe Macdonald *m* A Newman *w* Peck, Widmark, A Baxter 97min Fox
YELLOWSTONE KELLY (1959) *d* G Douglas *s* B Kennedy *c* Guthrie *w* Danton *91min WB
YELLOW SUBMARINE, THE (1968) *d* Dunning *songs/m* Lennon, McCartney anim* 87min *r* UA
YELLOW TICKET, THE (1931) *d* Walsh *s/co-di* Furthman *c* Howe *w* L Barrymore, Olivier, Karloff 88min Fox (= *The Yellow Passport*)
Yenendi = HOMMES QUI FONT LA PLUIE, LES (1951)
YE-RAI-SHANG (1951) *d/co-s* Ichikawa Toho (= *Nightshade Flower*)
YERMA (1962, *uf*) *d/s* Cavalcanti
Yes = IGEN (1964)
Yes he has been with me = DET AR HOS MIG HAN HAR VARIT (1963)
YES, MY DARLING DAUGHTER (1939) *d* Keighley *p* J Warner, Wallis *w* C Ruggles 86min WB
YES OR NO (1920) *d* Roy William Neill *c* E Haller
Yesterday Girl (UK) = ABSCHIED VON GESTERN (1966)
YEATERDAY IS OVER YOUR SHOULDER (1940) *d* T Dickinson sh
Yesterday, Today and Tomorrow = IERI, OGGI, DOMANI (1963)
YEUX CERNES, LES (1964) *d/s/w* Hossein 100min
YEUX DE L'AMOUR, LES (1960) *d* De la Patellière *w* Darrieux, Brialy 105min
YEUX NE PEUVENT PAS EN TOUT TEMPS SE FERMER OU PEUT-ETRE QU'UN JOUR ROME SE PERMETTRA DE CHOISIR A SON TOUR, LES (1970) *d/s* Straub, *Danièle Huillet fpl* (*Othon*) *Pierre Corneille e* Straub 87min (= *Othon*)
YEUX SANS VISAGE, LES (1959) *d/co-ad* Franju *co-a* Sautet *c* Shuftan *m* Jaare *w* Brasseur, Valli 90min (= *Eyes without a Face/The Horror Chamber of Dr Faustus*)
YEVO PRIZYU (1925) *d* Protazanov 1700m (= *His Call/Broken Chains*)
YEVO ZOVUT SUKHE-BATOR (1942) *d/co-s* Heifitz, Zarkhi *w* Cherkasov 106min (= *His Name is Sukhe-Bator*)
YIELD TO THE NIGHT (1956) *d* J Thompson *c* G Taylor 99min (= *Blonde Sinner*)
YNGSJOMORDET (1966) *d* Mattsson *s* Dahlbeck *w* Lindblom, Lindstrom 120min SF (= *Woman of Darkness*)
YOAKE MAE (1953) *d* Yoshimura *s* Shindo (= *Before Dawn*)
YOGOTO NO YUME (1933) *d/s* Naruse (= *Everynight Dreams*)
YOIDORE TENSHI (1948) *d/co-s* Kurosawa *w* Mifune 98min Toho (= *Drunken Angel*)
YOJIMBO (1961) *d/p/co-s* Kurosawa *c* Miyagawa *w* Mifune, Yamada, Nakadai S 110min *r* Toho
Yokel, The = BOOB, THE (1926)
YOKIHI (1955) *d* Mizoguchi *w* Kyo, Mori *102min Dai (= *Princess Yang-Kwei Fei*)
YOKI NO URAMACHI (1939) *d* Yoshimura (= *Lively Alley*)

YOKU (1958) *d* Gosho (= *Avarice*)
YOKUBO (1953) *d* Yoshimura *s* Shindo *c* Miyagawa (= *Desires*)
YOLANDA AND THE THIEF (1945) *d* Minnelli *p* Freed *co-a* Gibbons *w* Astaire *107min MGM
YONJU-HASSAI NO TEIKO (1956) *d* Yoshimura
YOROKUBI MO KANASHIMI MO IKUTOSHITSUKI (1957) *d* Kinoshita (= *The Lighthouse/Times of Joy and Sorrow*)
YORU (1923) *d/s* Mizoguchi Nik (= *Night*)
YORU HIRAKU (1931) *d/s* Gosho
YORU NO CHO (1957) *d* Yoshimura *c* Miyagawa *w* Kyo (= *Night Butterflies*)
YORU NO KAWA (1956) *d* Yoshimura *c* Miyagawa (= *Night River/Undercurrent*)
YORU NO MENEKO (1928) *d* Gosho
YORU NO NAGARE (1960) *d* Naruse, *Yuzo Kawashima w* Yamada S* 110min Toho (= *Flowing Night/The Lovelorn Geisha*)
YORU NO ONNA TACHI (1948) *d* Mizoguchi Sho (= *Women of the Night*)
YORU NO SUGAO (1958) *d* Yoshimura *s* Shindo *w* Kyo S* 121min Dai (= *The Naked Face of Night/The Ladder of Success*)
YORU NO TSUZUMI (1958) *d* Imai *s* Shindo *w* Mori 95min Sho (= *Night Drum/The Adulteress*)
YOSHINAKA O MEGURU SANNIN NO ONNA (1956) *d/s* Kinugasa (= *Three Women Around Yoshinaka*)
YOSHIWARA (1937) *d/co-s* Ophuls *c* Shuftan *m* Paul Dessau 88min
YOSO (1963) *d/s* Kinugasa (= *The Sorcerer*)
Yotsuya Ghost Story, The = YOTSUYA KAIDAN (1949)
YOTSUYA KAIDAN (1949) *d* Kinoshita 2 parts (= *The Yotsuya Ghost Story/Illusion of Blood*)
YOTTSU NO KOI NO MONOGATARI (1947) (= *Four Love Stories/Circus of Love*)
  ep d Naruse
  ep d Kinugasa
YOU AND ME (1938) *d/p* F Lang *st* Krasna *c* C Lang *co-a* Dreier *co-m* Weill *w* S Sidney, Raft, R Cummings, Carey 90min Par
YOU BELONG TO ME (1941) *d/p* W Ruggles *st* Trumbo *c* J Walker *m* Hollander *w* Stanwyck, H Fonda, Buchanan 94min Col
YOU CAME ALONG (1945) *d* J Farrow *p* Wallis *c* Heller *w* R Cummings, L Scott, Roman 103min Par
YOU CAN'T BELIEVE EVERYTHING (1918) *d* Conway *w* Swanson
YOU CAN'T CHEAT AN HONEST MAN (1939) *d* G Marshall *st* Fields (*ps* Charles Bogle) *c* Krasner *w* Fields 76min U
YOU CAN'T GET AWAY WITH MURDER (1939) *d* Lewis Seiler *c* Polito *w* Bogart 79min WB
YOU CAN'T HAVE EVERYTHING (1937) *d* Taurog *p* Zanuck *st* Ratoff *c* Andriot *w* Faye 99min Fox
YOU CAN'T RUN AWAY FROM IT (1956) *d/p* D Powell *co-s* Riskin *rm* IT HAPPENED ONE NIGHT (1934) *c* Lawton *w* Lemmon, Bickford, Allyson CS* 95min Col
You Can't Sleep Here (UK) = I WAS A MALE WAR BRIDE (1949)
YOU CAN'T TAKE IT WITH YOU (1938) *d/p* Capra *s* Riskin *fpl* G Kaufman, M Hart *c* J Walker *m* Tiomkin *w* Arthur, L Barrymore, J Stewart, Ann Miller 126min Col
You Don't Need Pyjamas at Rosie's = FIRST TIME, THE (1968)
YOU FOR ME (1952) *d* Weis *co-a* Gibbons *w* Lawford 71min MGM
YOU GOTTA STAY HAPPY (1948) *d* Potter *c* Metty *m* Amfitheatrof *w* Fontaine, J Stewart 100min U
YOU'LL FIND OUT (1940) *d/p/co-st* D Butler *w* Lorre, Karloff, Lugosi 96min RKO
YOU LUCKY PEOPLE (1955) *d* Elvey S 79min
YOU NEVER KNOW WOMEN (1926) *d* Wellman *w* C Brook, Shearer 6064ft FPL
YOUNG AMERICA (1932) *d* Borzage *w* Tracy 70min Fox
Young and Eager (UK) = CLAUDELLE INGLISH (1961)
YOUNG AND INNOCENT (1937) *d* Hitchcock *co-s* Charles Bennett, Reville *fn* Josephine Tey 84min JAR (= *The Girl was Young*)
Young and the Damned, The = OLVIDADOS, LOS (1950)
Young and the Passionate, The (UK) = VITELLONI, I (1953)
YOUNG AND WILLING (1942) *d/p* Edward H Griffith *co-a* Dreier *w* Holden, S Hayward 84min *r* UA
Young Aphrodites = MIKRES AFRODITES (1963)
YOUNG APRIL (1926) *d* Crisp *c* Marley 6858ft
YOUNG AS YOU FEEL (1931) *d* Borzage *w* W Rogers 73min Fox
YOUNG AS YOU FEEL (1940) *d* St Clair *c* C Clarke 59min Fox
YOUNG AT HEART (1955) *d* G Douglas *p* Blanke *co-s* JJ Epstein *c* McCord *w* D Day, Sinatra, E Barrymore, Malone *117min WB
YOUNG BESS (1953) *d* G Sidney *p* Franklin *co-a* Gibbons *m* Rozsa *w* J Simmons, S Granger, Kerr, Laughton *112min MGM
YOUNG BILLY YOUNG (1969) *d/s* B Kennedy *w* Mitchum, A Dickinson *89min *r* UA

YOUNGBLOOD HAWKE (1964) *d/s* Daves *c* Lawton *m* M Steiner *w* Astor, Pleshette, Page 137min WB
YOUNG CAPTIVES, THE (1959) *d* Kershner *co-a* Pereira 61min Par
YOUNG CASSIDY (1965) *d* Cardiff, J Ford *fab* (*Mirror in My House*) Sean O'Casey *w* Rod Taylor, Christie, M Redgrave, Evans *110min *r* MGM
Young Chopin, The = MLODOSC SZOPIN (1952)
YOUNG DR KILDARE (1938) *d* Harold S Bucquet *co-s* Goldbeck *c* J Seitz *w* Ayres, L Barrymore 81min MGM
YOUNG DOCTORS, THE (1961) *d* Karlson *m* E Bernstein *w* March, Segal *n* Reagan 100min *r* UA
YOUNG DONOVAN'S KID (1931) *d* Niblo *c* Cronjager *w* Karloff 9rs
YOUNG EAGLES (1930) *d* Wellman *c* Stout *w* Arthur, Lukas 70min Par
Young Generation = WAKAI HITO (1952)
YOUNGER GENERATION, THE (1929) *d* Capra *p* Cohn *c* Tetzlaff *w* Hersholt 8rs Col
Young Guard, The = MOLODAYA GVARDIYA (1948)
Young Have No Morals, The (UK) = DRAGUEURS, LES (1959)
Young Husbands (UK) = GIOVANI MARITI (1958)
YOUNG IDEAS (1943) *d* Dassin *a* Gibbons *w* Gardner, H Marshall 77min MGM
YOUNG IN HEART, THE (1938) *d* Richard Wallace *p* Selznick *ad* Charles Bennett *s* Osborn *c* Shamroy *m* Waxman *w* Goddard, Fairbanks Jr, J Gaynor 90min *r* UA
Young Invaders, The = DARBY'S RANGERS (1957)
YOUNG LAND, THE (1957) *d* Tetzlaff *co-c* Hoch *m* Tiomkin 89min
YOUNG LIONS, THE (1958) *d* Dmytryk *fn* Shaw *c* Joe Macdonald *co-a* Wheeler *m* Friedhofer *w* Brando, Clift, Martin, Rush, Maximilian Schell CS 167min Fox
YOUNG LOVERS, THE (1954) *d* Asquith 95min BL (= *Chance Meeting*)
YOUNG MAN OF MANHATTAN (1930) *d* Monta Bell *w* G Rogers, C Ruggles, Colbert 75min Par
Young Man of Music (UK) = YOUNG MAN WITH A HORN (1950)
YOUNG MAN'S FANCY (1920) *d* St Clair *s* Sennett 2rs
YOUNG MAN WITH A HORN (1950) *d* Curtiz *co-s* Foreman *c* McCord *w* K Douglas, Bacall, D Day, Carmichael 112min WB (= *Young Man of Music*)
YOUNG MAN WITH IDEAS (1952) *d* Leisen *c* Ruttenberg *co-a* Gibbons *w* G Ford, Roman 85min MGM
Young Miss = OJOSAN (1930)
YOUNG MR LINCOLN (1939) *d* J Ford *p* Macgowan *ex-p* Zanuck *s* Trotti *c* Glennon *co-a* R Day *m* A Newman *w* H Fonda 101min *r* Fox
YOUNG MR PITT, THE (1942) *d* C Reed *s* Gilliat, Launder *c* F Young *w* Donat, J Mills 118min *r* Fox
YOUNG NOWHERES (1929) *d/p* F Lloyd *c* E Haller *w* Barthelmess 7850ft
YOUNG ONE, THE (1960) *d/co-s* Bunuel *co-s* H Butler (*ps* HB Addis) *c* Figueroa 95min (= *Island of Shame/La Joven*)
YOUNG ONES, THE (1961) *d* Furie *c* Slocombe *chor* Ross *108min WB
Young Ones, The = JOVENES, LOS (1961)
YOUNG PEOPLE (1940) *d* Dwan *p* H Brown *c* Cronjager *co-a* R Day *w* Temple 78min Fox
YOUNG PHILADELPHIANS, THE (1959) *d* V Sherman *w* P Newman, Rush, Keith, Vaughn 136min WB
YOUNG RACERS, THE (1963) *d/p/w* Corman *c* F Crosby *87min AI
Young Rebel, The = AVVENTURE E GLI AMORI DI MIGUEL CERVANTES, LE (1967)
YOUNG SAVAGES, THE (1961) *d* Frankenheimer *ex-p* H Hecht *fn* (*A Matter of Conviction*) E Hunter *c* Lindon *w* Lancaster, Winters 100min *r* UA
Young Scarface (US) = BRIGHTON ROCK (1947)
YOUNG STRANGER, THE (1957) *d* Frankenheimer *m* Rosenman 84min U
YOUNG TOM EDISON (1940) *d* Taurog *co-st/co-s* Schary, H Butler *a* Gibbons *w* Rooney, G Bancroft 82min MGM
YOUNG VETERANS, THE (1941) *d* Crichton *p* Cavalcanti 23min
Young Virgin = HAKOIRI MUSUME (1935)
Young Wolves, The = JEUNES LOUPS, LES (1968)
YOU ONLY LIVE ONCE (1937) *d* F Lang *p* Wanger *c* Shamroy *m* A Newman *w* S Sidney, H Fonda 86min *r* UA
YOU ONLY LIVE TWICE (1967) *d* L Gilbert *co-p* Saltzman *fn* Ian Fleming *c* F Young *des* Adam *m* Barry *w* Connery PV* 116min *r* UA
Your Acquaintance = VASHA ZNAKOMAYA (1927)
YOU'RE A BIG BOY NOW (1967) *d/s* Coppola *w* Page 96min WB
YOU'RE A SWEETHEART (1937) *d* D Butler *w* Faye, G Murphy 96min U
YOU'RE DARN TOOTIN' (1928) *d* Edgar Kennedy *p* Roach *supn* McCarey *w* Laurel, Hardy 2rs *r* MGM (= *The Music Blasters*)
YOU'RE FIRED (1919) *d* Cruze *fst* (*The Halberdier*) O Henry 5rs FPL

You're in the Army now = O.H.M.S. (1937)
YOU'RE IN THE NAVY NOW (1951) *d* Hathaway *p* Kohlmar *st/s* R Murphy *c* Joe Macdonald *co-a* Wheeler *w* G Cooper, Marvin, J Webb 93min Fox
You're Lying = NI LJUGER (1970)
YOU'RE MY EVERYTHING (1949) *d* W Lang *p/co-s* Trotti *c* Arling *co-a* Wheeler *m* A Newman *w* Dailey, A Baxter, Keaton *94min
YOU'RE NOBODY TILL SOMEBODY LOVES YOU (1969) *d* Pennebaker *p* R Leacock, Pennebaker 15min (= *Timothy Leary's Wedding*)
YOU'RE NOT SO TOUGH (1940) *d* May 71min U
YOU'RE ONLY YOUNG ONCE (1938) *d* G Seitz *w* Rooney 78min MGM
YOU'RE TELLING ME (1934) *d* Erle C Kenton *w* Fields 67min Par
YOUR LAST ACT (1941) *d* Zinnemann 11min MGM
YOUR MONEY OR YOUR WIFE (1959) *d* A Simmons 91min JAR
Your Red Wagon = THEY LIVE BY NIGHT (1948)
YOURS, MINE AND OURS (1968) *d/co-s* Shavelson *w* Ball, H Fonda, V Johnson 111min *pc* Ball *r* UA
YOU SAID A HATFUL! (1934) *d* C Chase (*as* Parrott) *p* Roach *w* C Chase 2rs MGM
YOU SAID A MOUTHFUL (1932) *d* Bacon *w* G Rogers 71min WB
Youth = SEISHUN (1925)
Youth = SHONEN-KI (1951)
Youth and Perversion = VINTI, I (1952)
Youthful Sinners = TRICHEURS, LES (1958)
YOUTH GETS A BREAK (1941) *d/s* Losey *co-c* W Van Dyke 20min
Youth of Heiji Zenigata = SEISHUN ZENIGATA HEIJI (1953)
Youth of Maxim, The = YUNOST MAKSIMA (1935)
YOUTH OF POLAND, THE (1957) *d/c* A and D Maysles
YOUTH ON TRIAL (1945) *d* Boetticher 59min Col
YOUTH RUNS WILD (1944) *d* Robson *p* Lewton 67min RKO
Youth Speaks = KOMSOMOL (1932)
YOUTH TAKES A FLING (1938) *d* A Mayo *p* Pasternak *w* McCrea 77min U
YOU WERE MEANT FOR ME (1948) *d* Bacon *p* Kohlmar *c* Milner *co-a* Wheeler *w* Dailey, Crain 92min Fox
You Who Are About to Enter = I SOM HAR INTRADEN (1945)
YO VAI PAIVA (1962) *d/p/s/c/e* Jarva, Jaakko Pakkasvirta * (= *Night or Day*)
YOYO (1965) *d/co-s/w* Etaix 97min
YUBILEI (1944) *d/s* petrov 40min (= *Jubilee*)
YUKI FUJIN EZU (1950) *d* Mizoguchi (= *Sketch of Madame Yuki*)
YUKIKO (1955) *d* Imai
YUKINOJO HENGE (1963) *d* Ichikawa S* 113min Dai (= *The Revenge of Yukinojo/An Actor's Revenge*)
Yukinojo's Disguise = YUKINOJO HENGE (parts 1 and 2 1935, part 3 1936)
YUKINOJO HENGE (1935) *d/co-s* Kinugasa (parts 1 and 2) (= *Yukinojo's Revenge/Yukinojo's Disguise*)
YUKINOJO HENGE (1936) *d/co-s* Kinugasa (part 3) (= *Yukinojo's Revenge/ Yukinojo's Disguise*)
YUKINOJO HENGE (1963) *d* Ichikawa S* 113min Dai (= *The Revenge of Yukinojo/An Actor's Revenge*)
Yukinojo's Disguise = YUKINOJO HENGE (1935–36)
Yukinojo's Revenge = YUKINOJO HENGE (1935–36)
YUKI NO YO NO KETTO (1954) *d/s* Kinugasa (= *The Duel of a Snowy Night*)
YUKONERS, THE (1956) *d* A King 16mm 28min
YUNBOGI NO NIKKI (1965) *d/p/s/c* Oshima 30min (= *The Diary of Yunbogi*)
YUNOST MAKSIMA (1935) *d/s* L Trauberg, Kozintsev *c* Moskvin *m* Shostakovich 97min (= *The Youth of Maxim*)
YUSHIMA NO SHIRAUME (1955) *d/s* Kinugasa (= *The Romance of Yushima*)
YUWAKA (1948) *d* Yoshimura (= *Temptation*)
YUYAKE-KUMO (1956) *d* Kinoshita (= *Clouds at Twilight/Farewell to Dreams*)
YVETTE (1928) *d/s/e* Cavalcanti *fn* Guy de Maupassant

Z (1968) *d/co-ad* Costa-Gavras *fn* Vassili Vassilikos *c* Coutard *m* Theodorakis *w* Montand, Trintignant *125min
ZAAK MP, DE (1960) *d* Haanstra (= *The MP Case*)

ZABRISKIE POINT (1970) *d/co-s* Antonioni *p* Ponti *co-m* Pink Floyd, Rolling Stones, Grateful Dead, John Fahey PV* 110min MGM
ZACARANI DVORAC U DUDINCIMA (1951) *d* Vikotic anim (= *The Enchanted Castle at Dudinci*)
ZACHAROVANAYA DESNA (1965) *d* Solntseva *s* Dovzhenko *81min (= *The Enchanted Desna*)
ZACZELO SIE W HISZPANII (1950) *d/e* Munk 30min
ZAGOVOR OBRECHYONNIKH (1950) *d* Kalatozov *103min (= *Conspiracy of the Doomed*)
Zakonye Bolshoi Zemli = ALITET UKHODIT V GORI (1949)
ZAKROISHCHIK IZ TORZHKA (1925) *d* Protazanov 1700m (= *The Tailor from Torzhka*)
ZA LA MORT CONTRE ZA LA MORT (1921) *d/p/s/w* Ghione
ZA LA MORT ET ZA LA VIE (1924) *d/p/s/w* Ghione
Za la Mort e Za la Vie = BANDA DELLE CIFRE, LA (1915)
ZANGE NO YAIBA (1927) *d/st* Ozu Sho (= *Sword of Penitence*)
ZANGIKU MONOGATARI (1939) *d* Mizoguchi Sho (= *The Story of the Last Chrysanthemums*)
ZAOSTRIT PROSIM (1956) *d/co-s* Frič (= *Watch the Birdie*)
ZARAK (1956) *d* T Young *2nd d* Canutt *s* Mainbaum *co-c* Moore *w* Mature, Ekberg CS* 94min *r* Col
ZARIJOVE NOCI (1956) *d/co-s* Jasny (= *September Nights*)
ZASADIL DEDEK REPU (1945) *d/st/a* Trnka *anim* Pojar anim* 9min (= *Grandpa Planted a Beet*)
ZAVADA NENI NA VASEM PRIJIMACI (1961) *d/s* Brdecka
ZA VITRINOI UNIVERMAGA (1956) *d* Samsonov *130min (= *Behind the Shop Windows*)
ZAZA (1923) *d/p* Dwan *c* Rosson *w* Swanson 7076ft FPL
ZAZA (1939) *d* Cukor *p* Lewin *c* C Lang *e* Dmytryk *w* Colbert, H Marshall 81min Par
ZAZA (1942) *d/co-s* Catellani *m* Rota *w* I Miranda
ZAZIE DANS LA METRO (1960) *d* Malle *s* Malle, Rappeneau *fn* Queneau *dec* Evein *technical adviser* Klein *w* Noiret, Carioli *88min
ZBABELEC (1961) *d/co-s* J Weiss 113min (= *The Coward*)
ZDRAVSTVUI MOSKVA (1946) *d* Yutkevich 101min (= *Greetings, Moscow*)
ZDRAVSTVUITYE DETI! (1962) *d* Donskoi 88min (= *Hello, Children*)
ZEE ONTRUKT, DER (1949) *d* Van den Horst (= *Wrested from the Sea*)
ZEHN MINUTEN MOZART (1930) *d* Reiniger *m* Mozart anim 1rl
ZEMLYA (1930) *d/s* Dovzhenko 1740m (= *Earth*)
ZEMNA (1951) *d* Kinoshita (= *The Good Fairy*)
ZENOBIA (1939) *d* G Douglas *p* Roach *c* Struss *w* Hardy, Langdon 71min *r* UA (= *Elephants Never Forget*)
Zeppelin and Love, The = VZDUCHOLOD A LASKA (1947)
ZERO DE CONDUITE (1933) *d/s/di* Vigo *c* B Kaufman *m* Jaubert *w* Storck 47min
ZERO IN THE UNIVERSE (1965) *d/co-s/e/w* Moorse 85min
Zero Murder Case, The = STRANGE AFFAIR OF UNCLE HARRY, THE (1945)
ZERO NO HAKKEN (1963) *d* Kuri anim (= *The Discovery of Zero*)
ZE SOBOTY NA NEDELI (1931) *d/co-s* Machaty (= *From Saturday to Sunday*)
ZEZOWATE SZCZESCIE (1959) *d* Munk 120min (= *Bad Luck/Cross-Eyed Fortune*)
ZHENSHCHINA S KINZHALOM (1918) *d* Protazanov *w* Mozkukhin 1650m (= *Woman with a Dagger*)
ZHENSHCHINA ZAKHOCHET – CHORTA OBMORO-CHIT (1914) *d* Protazanov 630m (= *The Lady Knows a Little of it – from the Devil*)
ZHILI-BYLI STARIK SO STARUKHOI (1964) *p* Chukhrai 14rs (2 parts) (= *There Lived an Old Man and an Old Woman*)
ZHIVOI LENIN (1948) *d/e* Romm, *Maria Slavinskaya* 25min (= *Lenin Lives*)
ZHIVOI TRUP (1929) *d* Fyodor Otsep *w* Pudovkin, Barnet 2233m (= *The Living corpse*)
ZHIZN V TSITADELI (1947) *d* Herbert Rappaport *s* L Trauberg 90min (= *Life in the Citadel*)
ZHUKOVSKY (1950) *d* Pudovkin, *Dmitri Vasiliev* *90min
ZHUMORESKI (1924) *d/s* Vertov anim 60m (= *Humoresque*)

ZHURNALIST (1967) *d/s/w* Gerasimov 205min (2 parts) (= *The Journalist*)
Zhurnalistka = VASHA ZNAKOMAYA (1927)
ZIA SMEMORATA, LA (1941) *d/co-s* Vajda
ZIEGFELD FOLLIES (1946) *d* Minnelli *p/co-lyr* Freed *co-c* Folsey *co-a* Gibbons *chor* R Alton *co-lyr/co-m* Edens *w* Astaire, Ball, Garland, Esther Williams, Gene Kelly, W Powell, Charisse, V Johnson *100min MGM
ZIEGFELD GIRL (1941) *d* Leonard *p* Berman *c* June *chor* Berkeley *m* Stothart *w* J Stewart, Garland, Lamarr, Turner, Horton, Dailey 131min MGM
ZIGOMAR (1910) *d/s* Jasset *co-c* Andriot
ZIGOMAR CONTRE NICK CARTER (1912) *d/s* Jasset *c* Andriot serial
ZIGOMAR PEAU D'ANGVILLE (1912) *d/s* Jasset *co-c* Andriot serial
ZIGOMAR, ROI DES VOLEURS (1911) *d/s* Jasset *c* Andriot serial
ZIJEME V PRAZE (1934) *d/s* Vavra
ZIPP, THE DODGER (1914) *d/w* Arbuckle Key 1rl
ZIRKUSBLUT (1916) *d/p/s* R Oswald *w* Krauss 1645m
Zita = TANTE ZITA (1967)
ZIVOT JE PES (1933) *d/co-st/co-s* Frič (= *Dog's Life*)
ZLATA RENATA (1965) *d* Vavra (= *The Golden Queening*)
ZLATE KAPRADI (1963) *d/s* J Weiss CS 125min (= *Golden Bracken*)
ZLATE RYBCE, O (1951) *d/s/a* Trnka *anim* 15½min (= *The Golden Fish*)
ZLATE GORY (1931) *d/co-s* Yutkevich *m* Shostakovich 131min (= *Golden Mountains*)
ZLOCIN V DIVCI SKOLE (1965) *co-d* Ladislav Rychman. Ivo Novak 111min 3 eps (= *Crime at the Girl's School*) title ep *d* Menzel 39min
ZLOTO (1962) *d* Has *s* 90min (= *Gold*)
ZLY CHLOPIEC (1950) *d* Wajda *Anton Chekov* 5½min
ZOCELEMI (1950) *d* Frič (= *The Steel Town*)
ZOGU SUGATA SANSHIRO (1945) *d/s* Kurosawa 83min Toho
ZOLNIERZ ZWYCIESTWA (1953) *d/s* Jakubowska (= *Soldier of Victory*)
ZOLOTOI MED (1928) *co-d* Petrov *co-d/s* N Beresnev 1739m (= *Golden Honey*)
ZOMBIES ON BROADWAY (1945) *d* G Douglas *w* Lugosi 68min RKO
ZONA PERICULOSA (1951) *d* Maselli
ZONE DE LA MORT, LA (1916) *d/s* Gance *c* Burel
ZONE MOMENT (1956) *d* Brakhage 16mm* si 3min
ZOO (1962) *d* Haanstra 10min
Zoo, The (US) = CHIRIAKHANA (1967)
ZO O KUTTA RENCHU (1947) *d* Yoshimura (= *The Fellows Who Ate the Elephant*)
ZORBA THE GREEK (1965) *d/p/s* Cacoyannis *fn* Nikos Kazantzakis *c* Lassally *m* Theodorakis *w* Quinn 141min Fox
ZOTZ! (1962) *d/p* Castle *w* Dumont 85min Col
ZOU-ZOU (1934) *d* M Allégret
ZOYA (1944) *d/co-s* Lev Arnshtam *m* Shostakovich *w* Batalov 95min
ZUCKER UND ZIMT (1915) *co-d/co-s/w* Lubitsch 2rs (= *Sugar and Spice*)
ZUDORA (1914–15) *d* William D Taylor *w* Cruze series in 9eps (= *The Twenty Million Dollar Mystery*)
ZUIDERZEE (1930) *d/s/co-c/e* Ivens 1500m
ZULU (1964) *d/co-p/co-s* Enfield *co-p/w* S Baker *m* Barry *w* Hawkins, Caine, Jacobsson TR* 135min Par
ZUM PARADIES DER DAMEN (1922) *d/co-s/w* Lupu-Pick *fn* (*Au Bonheur des Dames*) *Emile Zola co-c* Sparkuhl 3008m
ZU NEUEN UFERN (1937) *d/co-s* Sirk *w* Jurgens 106min (= *To New Shores*)
ZURCHER VERLOBUNG, DIE (1957) *d/co-s* Käutner *w* Wicki 106min
ZUR CHRONIK VON GRIESHUUS (1925) *d* Von Gerlach *s* Von Harbou *co-dec* Rohrig, Poelzig 2966m UFA
ZUZU THE BAND LEADER (1913) *d* Sennett *w* Normand 2rs Key
ZVENIGORA (1928) *d* Duvzhenko 1799m
ZVIRATKA A PETROVSTI (1946) *d/st/a* Trnka *anim* Pojar anim* 8½min (= *The Animals and the Brigands*)
ZWEI GROSCHENZAUBER (1929) *d* Richter (= *Two-penny Magic*)
Zwolfte Stunde, Die (1930) sound version of NOSFERATU, EINE SYMPHONIE DES GRAUENS (1922) (= *Eine Nacht des Grauens*)